A London
Bibliography of the
Social Sciences

BRITISH LIBRARY OF POLITICAL AND ECONOMIC SCIENCE

A London Bibliography of the Social Sciences

Ninth Supplement

1974

VOLUME XXXII

MANSELL LONDON 1975

*This Bibliography has been computer typeset from
the machine-readable subject catalogue of the
British Library of Political and Economic Science by*
Mansell Information/Publishing Limited
3 Bloomsbury Place, London WC1A 2QA

ISBN 0 7201 0524 2
Library of Congress Card Number 31-9970

Printed and bound in Great Britain at
The Scolar Press Limited, Ilkley, Yorkshire

© 1975 *The British Library of Political and Economic Science*

Preface

The present supplement to *A London Bibliography of the Social Sciences* is to some extent experimental, being the first to be produced by combining computer sorting of subject headings with computer typesetting. Inevitably, therefore, it contains a number of mechanical imperfections, which there has not been time to eliminate; for example, lines or even whole entries out of their true order, and some reversals of upper and lower case letters. For these we apologise to users of the Bibliography in the hope that they will not find many.

With a few exceptions all cross references and references to related headings are again omitted. Readers are, as a guide, referred to the 'List of subject headings used in the Bibliography arranged under topics', which is to be found at the end of the volume. This list also includes under the section *Geography, history and topography*, a list of individual countries and places used as main headings. A list of the subject sub-divisions used with geographical names is included at the beginning of the index.

D. A. Clarke *October* 1975

Contents

VOLUMES I-XXXII

VOLUMES I-IV *Original Compilation*

Holdings up to 1929 of the
British Library of Political and Economic Science
Edward Fry Library of International Law
Goldsmith's Library of Economic Literature,
  University of London
National Institute of Industrial Psychology
Royal Anthropological Institute
Royal Institute of International Affairs
Royal Statistical Society

Special collections in the libraries of
The Reform Club (*political and historical pamphlets*)
University College, London (*the Hume, Ricardo and other economic and political collections*)
The University of London (*works on economics and related subjects*)

VOLUME V *First Supplement*

Additions from 1929 to 1931 to the collections included in Volumes I–IV

VOLUME VI *Second Supplement*

Additions from 1931 to 1936 to the
British Library of Political and Economic Science
Edward Fry Library of International Law
Goldsmith's Library of Economic Literature

VOLUMES VII-IX *Third Supplement*

Additions from 1936 to 1950, other than works in the Russian language, to the
British Library of Political and Economic Science
Edward Fry Library of International Law

VOLUMES X-XI *Fourth Supplement*

Additions from 1950 to 1955 in all languages, and also from 1936 to 1950 in Russian, to the
British Library of Political and Economic Science
Edward Fry Library of International Law

VOLUMES XII-XIV *Fifth Supplement*

Additions from 1955 to 1962 to the
British Library of Political and Economic Science
Edward Fry Library of International Law

VOLUMES XV-XXI *Sixth Supplement*

Additions from 1962 to 1968 to the
British Library of Political and Economic Science
Edward Fry Library of International Law
Volume XXI contains indexes to Volumes XV–XXI

VOLUMES XXII-XXVIII *Seventh Supplement*

Additions from 1969 to 1972 to the
British Library of Political and Economic Science
Edward Fry Library of International Law
Volume XXVIII contains an index to
Volumes XXII–XXVIII

VOLUMES XXIX-XXXI *Eighth Supplement*

Additions from 1972 to 1973 to the
British Library of Political and Economic Science
Edward Fry Library of International Law
Volume XXXI contains an index to
Volumes XXIX–XXXI

VOLUME XXXII *Ninth Supplement*

Additions during 1974 to the
British Library of Political and Economic Science
Edward Fry Library of International Law
with index

PERIODICALS LISTS

An alphabetical list of the periodicals in the British Library of Political and Economic Science in 1929 is given in Volume IV; supplementary lists up to 1936 are given in Volumes V and VI, after which they have been discontinued.

AUTHOR INDEX

Author indexes are given in Volumes IV (for Volumes I–III), V, and VI, but not in later volumes.
Volumes I–XIV were published by the
British Library of Political and Economic Science,
Houghton Street, London WC2

A London Bibliography of the Social Sciences

AACHEN

— Politics and government.

PLUM (GUENTER) Gesellschaftsstruktur und politisches Bewusstsein in einer katholischen Region, 1928-1933: Untersuchung am Beispiel des Regierungsbezirks Aachen. Stuttgart, 1972. pp. 319. *bibliog. (Institut für Zeitgeschichte. Studien zur Zeitgeschichte)*

— Social history.

PLUM (GUENTER) Gesellschaftsstruktur und politisches Bewusstsein in einer katholischen Region, 1928-1933: Untersuchung am Beispiel des Regierungsbezirks Aachen. Stuttgart, 1972. pp. 319. *bibliog. (Institut für Zeitgeschichte. Studien zur Zeitgeschichte)*

ABBREVIATIONS.

PUGH (ERIC) Second dictionary of acronyms and abbreviations: more abbreviations in management, technology and information science. London, 1974. pp. 410.

ABBREVIATIONS, PORTUGUESE.

JOINT PUBLICATIONS RESEARCH SERVICE. Abbreviations in the Latin American press. New York, 1972. pp. 172.

ABBREVIATIONS, SPANISH.

JOINT PUBLICATIONS RESEARCH SERVICE. Abbreviations in the Latin American press. New York, 1972. pp. 172.

ABBREVIATIONS, YUGOSLAV.

ZIDAR (JOSIP) compiler. Rečnik jugoslovenskih skraćenica; A dictionary of Yugoslav abbreviations, etc. Beograd, 1971. pp. 349. *In Serbo-Croat, English, French, German, Spanish and Russian.*

ABDEL AZIZ AL SAUD, King of Saudi Arabia.

See SAUD I, King of Saudi Arabia.

ABERDEEN

— Social history.

MACLAREN (A. ALLAN) Religion and social class: the disruption years in Aberdeen. London, 1974. pp. 268.

ABIDJAN

— Social conditions.

GIBBAL (JEAN MARIE) Citadins et paysans dans la ville africaine: l'exemple d'Abidjan. Grenoble, 1974. pp. 403.

ABOLITIONISTS.

QUARLES (BENJAMIN) Allies for freedom: blacks and John Brown. New York, 1974. pp. 244. *bibliog.*

ABORTION.

CARETTONI (TULLIA) and GATTO (SIMONE) L'aborto: problemi e leggi. [Palermo, 1973]. pp. 216.

LEE (LUKE TSUNG-CHOU) Brief survey of abortion laws of five largest countries. Medford, Mass., 1973. pp. 8. *(Tufts University. Fletcher School of Law and Diplomacy. Law and Population Monograph Series. No.14) (Reprinted from Population Report, Series F, No.1)*

LEE (LUKE TSUNG-CHOU) International status of abortion legalization. Medford, Mass., 1973. pp. 338-364. *(Tufts University. Fletcher School of Law and Diplomacy. Law and Population Monograph Series. No.16) (Reprinted from The abortion experience, Howard J. Osofsky and Joy D. Osofsky, editors).*

SCOTT (MICHAEL JAMES) Abortion: the facts. London, 1973. pp. 62.

SIMMS (MADELEINE) Report on non-medical abortion counselling. London, 1973. pp. 32. *bibliog.*

COHEN (MARSHALL) and others, eds. The rights and wrongs of abortion: a Philosophy and Public Affairs reader. Princeton, N.J., 1974. pp. 127.

KOHL (MARVIN) The morality of killing: sanctity of life, abortion and euthanasia. London, 1974. pp. 112. *bibliog.*

— Canada.

PELRINE (ELEANOR WRIGHT) Abortion in Canada. Toronto, 1971. pp. 133. *bibliog.*

CANADA. Statistics Canada. Therapeutic abortions. a., 1972 (1st issue)- Ottawa. *In English and French.*

— Europe, Eastern.

DAVID (HENRY PHILIP) Family planning and abortion in the socialist countries of central and eastern Europe: a compendium of observations and readings. New York, [1970]. pp. 306. *bibliogs.*

— India.

CHANDRASEKHAR (SRIPATI) Abortion in a crowded world: the problem of abortion with special reference to India. London, 1974. pp. 184. *bibliog. (Seattle. University of Washington. John Danz Lectures. 1971)*

— Italy.

FRONTORI (LAURA) and POGLIANA (LUISA) Doppia faccia: società, maternità, aborto. Milano, 1973. pp. 147.

— South Africa.

SOUTH AFRICA. Commission of Inquiry into the Abortion and Sterilization Bill. 1974. Report (R.P.68/1974). in SOUTH AFRICA. Parliament. House of Assembly. Votes and proceedings; (with Printed annexures).

— Sweden.

SWEDEN. Justitiedepartementet. Abortkommittén. 1971. Rätten till abort. Stockholm, 1971. 1 vol. (various pagings). *(Sweden. Statens Offentliga Utredningar. 1971. 58) With English summary.*

— United Kingdom.

CHURCH OF ENGLAND. National Assembly. Board for Social Responsibility. Abortion: an ethical discussion; [report of a committee; I.T. Ramsey, chairman]. London, 1965 repr. 1973. pp. 70.

— — Scotland.

HOROBIN (GORDON) ed. Experience with abortion: a case study of north-east Scotland. London, 1973. pp. 379.

— United States.

PILPEL (HARRIET F.) Brief survey of U.S. population law: address delivered at the International Advisory Committee on Population and Law, 1971. Medford, Mass., [1971]. pp. 11. *(Tufts University. Fletcher School of Law and Diplomacy. Law and Population Monograph Series. No.2)*

TIETZE (CHRISTOPHER) Two years' experience with a liberal abortion law: its impact on fertility trends in New York City. New York, 1973. pp. 6. *(Reprinted from Family Planning Perspectives, vol. 5).*

WALBERT (DAVID F.) and BUTLER (JOHN DOUGLAS) eds. Abortion, society and the law. Cleveland, Ohio, 1973. pp. 395.

ABSE (LEO).

ABSE (LEO) Private member. London, 1973. pp. 296. *bibliog.*

ABTEITAL.

See GADER VALLEY.

ABUSE OF ADMINISTRATIVE POWER

— United Kingdom.

WHEARE (Sir KENNETH CLINTON) Maladministration and its remedies. London, 1973. pp. 172. *(Hamlyn Lectures. 25th Series)*

ACADEMIC ACHIEVEMENT.

WANKOWSKI (J.A.) Temperament, motivation and academic achievement: studies of success and failure of a random sample of students in one university. Birmingham, [1972?]. 2 vols. (in 1). *bibliog. (Birmingham. University. Educational Survey)*

OGBU (JOHN U.) The next generation: an ethnography of education in an urban neighborhood. New York, 1974. pp. 275. *bibliog.*

ACCIDENT LAW

— New Zealand.

NEW ZEALAND. General Assembly. House of Representatives. Select Committee on Compensation for Personal Injury. 1970. Report...; G.F. Gair, chairman. Wellington, 1970. pp. 84.

CAMPBELL (IAN B.) The Accident Compensation Act 1972. Wellington, 1973. fo. 36. *(Victoria University of Wellington. Industrial Relations Centre. Occasional Papers in Industrial Relations. No. 7)*

ACCIDENTS.

WORLD HEALTH ORGANIZATION. Public Health Papers. Geneva, 1959 in progress.

MALIK (LYNDA P.) Sociology of accidents. Villanova, [1970]. pp. 224. *bibliog.*

— Prevention.

MELINEK (S.J.) A method of evaluating human life for economic purposes. Borehamwood, Fire Research Station, 1972. pp. 16. *(Fire Research Notes. No. 950)*

ACCION NACIONAL (MEXICO).

MABRY (DONALD J.) Mexico's Accion Nacional: a Catholic alternative to revolution. Syracuse, N.Y., 1973. pp. 269. *bibliog.*

ACCOUNTING.

PATON (WILLIAM ANDREW) the Elder. Accounting theory: with special reference to the corporate enterprise; [reprint of the book first published in 1922]. Lawrence, 1973. pp. 508.

SCOTT (D.R.) The cultural significance of accounts, [reprint of work first issued in 1931]. Lawrence, Ka., 1973. pp. 316.

FIVE monographs on business income; [reprint of the work originally published in New York, 1950]. Lawrence, Kansas, 1973. pp. 271. *(American Institute of Certified Public Accountants. Study Group on Business Income. Pamphlets. 3)*

SPACEK (LEONARD) A search for fairness in financial reporting to the public: selected addresses... 1956-(1973). Chicago, [1969-73]. 2 vols. *bibliog.*

HOPWOOD (ANTHONY G.) An accounting system and managerial behaviour. Farnborough, Hants, [1973]. pp. 237. *bibliog.*

McLEAN (ALASDAIR THOMAS) ed. Business and accounting in Europe. Farnborough, Hants, [1973]. pp. 269. *bibliogs.*

VICTORIA UNIVERSITY OF WELLINGTON. Department of Accountancy. Annual Seminar on Advanced Accountancy, 21st, 1973. Management accounting in a changing environment. Wellington, 1973. 1 vol. (various pagings).

BIRD (PETER) The interpretation of published accounts. 2nd ed. London, H.M.S.O., 1974. pp. 30. *(Civil Service College [U.K.]. Occasional Papers. No. 14)*

ACCOUNTING (Cont.)

DEWHURST (R.F.J.) An investigation of the possibility of using regression analysis to evaluate in money terms the routine outputs of the accounts department of a business organisation. Coventry, 1974. pp. 21, xxiii. *bibliog.* (*University of Warwick. Centre for Industrial Economic and Business Research. [Warwick Research in Industrial and Business Studies]. No. 48*)

EDEY (HAROLD CECIL) and YAMEY (BASIL SELIG) eds. Debits, credits, finance and profits: [papers presented to William Baxter on his retirement from the chair of accounting at the London School of Economics]. London, 1974. pp. 163. *bibliog.*

GAMBLING (TREVOR) Societal accounting. London, 1974. pp. 230. *bibliog.*

LEWIS (RALPH F.) Planning and control for profit;... UK and Commonwealth edition. London, 1974. pp. 208. *bibliog.*

— **Dictionaries and encyclopaedias.**

LEXIKON der Wirtschaft: Rechnungsführung und Statistik; (Herausgeber: Arno Donda). Berlin, [1974]. pp. 527.

ACCOUNTING AS A PROFESSION.

U.K. Civil Service Commission. 1971. Accountants in government service. rev. ed. [London], 1971. pp. 20.

BINDENGA (ANDREAS JACOBUS) Het vrije beroep van accountant: enige uitgangspunten voor wijzigingen in de organisatie van het openbaar accountantsberoep als gevolg van ontwikkelingen in dat beroep. Alphen aan den Rijn, 1973. pp. 503. *bibliog. With an English summary.*

ACCULTURATION.

OLIVEIRA (ROBERTO CARDOSO DE) O Indio e o mundo dos brancos: uma interpretação sociologica da situação dos Tukuna. São Paulo, 1972. pp. 139. *bibliog.*

WEAVER (SALLY M.) Medicine and politics among the Grand River Iroquois: a study of the non-conservatives. Ottawa, National Museums of Canada, 1972. pp. 182. *bibliog.* (*National Museum of Man [Canada]. Publications in Ethnology. No. 4) With French summary.*

NEAL (FRANK R.) Modal personality and sociocultural variation: cultural relativism and existential paralysis; with an empirical comparison of Italians and Mexican-Americans. Helsinki, 1974. pp. 62. *bibliog.* (*Helsinki. Yliopisto. Research Group for Comparative Sociology. Research Reports. No. 5.)*

ACHIEVEMENT MOTIVATION.

CHAPMAN (MARIAN) and HILL (RUSSELL A.) eds. Achievement motivation: an analysis of the literature. Philadelphia, [1971]. pp. 250. *bibliog.*

WANKOWSKI (J.A.) Temperament, motivation and academic achievement: studies of success and failure of a random sample of students in one university. Birmingham, [1972?]. 2 vols. (in 1). *bibliog.* (*Birmingham. University. Educational Survey)*

DE VOS (GEORGE A.) Socialization for achievement: essays on the cultural psychology of the Japanese...; with contributions by Hiroshi Wagatsuma [and others]. Berkeley, [1973]. pp. 597. *bibliog.*

ACRONYMS.

PUGH (ERIC) Second dictionary of acronyms and abbreviations: more abbreviations in management, technology and information science. London, 1974. pp. 410.

ACT (PHILOSOPHY).

NORDENFELT (LENNART) Explanation of human actions. Uppsala, 1974. pp. 134. *bibliog.* (*Uppsala. Universitet. Filosofiska Föreningen, and Filosofiska Institutionen. Filosofiska Studier. No.20)*

ACTUARIAL SCIENCE.

BENJAMIN (BERNARD) and COX (PETER R.) The actuary's role in financial management. London, H.M.S.O., 1973. pp. 34. *bibliog.*

ADAMS (Sir GRANTLEY HERBERT).

HOYOS (F.A.) Grantley Adams and the social revolution: the story of the movement that changed the pattern of West Indian society. London, 1974. pp. 280. *bibliog.*

ADAT LAW

— **Malaya.**

HOOKER (M.B.) Adat laws in modern Malaya: land tenure, traditional government and religion. Kuala Lumpur, 1972. pp. 294. *bibliog.*

ADEMOLA (Sir ADETOKUNBO).

COKER (FOLARIN) The Rt. Honourable Sir Adetokunbo Ademola...: a biography. rev. ed. Lagos, 1972. pp. 92.

ADEN.

U.K. Central Office of Information. Reference Division. 1966. Aden and South Arabia. London, 1966. pp. 39. *bibliog.*

ADENAUER (KONRAD).

WAGNER (WOLFGANG) Die Bundespräsidentenwahl, 1959: (Adenauer-Studien, II; herausgegeben von Rudolf Morsey und Konrad Repgen). Mainz, [1972]. pp. 99. *bibliog.* (*Katholische Akademie in Bayern. Kommission für Zeitgeschichte. Veröffentlichungen. Reihe B: Forschungen. Band 13)*

ADJUSTMENT (PSYCHOLOGY).

MÄÄTTÄNEN (MATTI) The relation between psychological and social factors affecting maladjustment. Helsinki, 1972. pp. 49. (*Finland. Suomen Virallinen Tilasto. Finlands Officiella Statistik. 32. Sosiaalisia Erikoistutkimuksia. 28)*

ADLER (MAX)

— **Bibliography.**

SCHROTH (HANS) and EXENBERGER (HERBERT) compilers. Max Adler, 1873-1937: eine Bibliographie. Wien, [1973]. pp. 63. (*Ludwig-Boltzmann-Institut für Geschichte der Arbeiterbewegung. Schriftenreihe. 2)*

ADMINISTRATION.

RATIONALISIERUNG der öffentlichen Verwaltung; ([by] Hans Künzi [and others]). Bern, [1971]. pp. 50. (*Zürich. Universität. Institut für Betriebswirtschaftliche Forschung. Schriftenreihe. Band 3)*

ADMINISTRATIV utvikling i forvaltningen: mål og virkemidler: foredrag ved Nordisk Konferanse, Oslo, 31. mai-2. juni 1972; utgitt av Statens Rasjonaliseringsdirektorat, Norge [and others]. Oslo, 1972. pp. 106. *bibliog.*

ILCHMAN (WARREN FREDERICK) Administering alternatives and alternatives in administration: some preliminary observations. Vienna, [1972]. pp. 16. (*Wiener Institut für Entwicklungsfragen. Occasional Papers. 72/3)*

YIN (ROBERT K.) Some remarks on evaluating administrative decentralization. [Santa Monica], 1972. pp. 7. (*Rand Corporation. [Papers]. 4844)*

LARIS CASILLAS (JORGE) Sobre la ciencia administrativa. [Toluca], Direccion General de Hacienda del Estado de Mexico, 1973. pp. 165. *bibliog.* (*Coleccion Estudios Administrativos. 1)*

MEYER (POUL) Systemic aspects of public administration. Copenhagen, 1973. pp. 183.

PUSIĆ (EUGEN) Administration and development: choice within limits. Vienna, [1973]. pp. 23. (*Wiener Institut für Entwicklungsfragen. Occasional Papers. 73/3)*

ROHLFING (GERD) Der Entscheidungsprozess in der öffentlichen Verwaltung aus betriebswirtschaftlicher Sicht. Göttingen, 1973. pp. 217. *bibliog.*

SCHAFFER (BENJAMIN BERNARD) The administrative factor: papers in organization, politics and development. London, 1973. pp. 329.

SKJEI (STEPHEN S.) Information for collective action: a microanalytic view of plural decision-making. Lexington, [1973]. pp. 188.

SZAMEL (LAJOS) Legal problems of socialist public administrative management. Budapest, 1973. pp. 233.

WAMSLEY (GARY L.) and ZALD (MAYER NATHAN) The political economy of public organizations: a critique and approach to the study of public administration. Lexington, [1973]. pp. 110.

ZENTNER (HENRY) Prelude to administrative theory: essays in social structure and social process. Calgary, [1973]. pp. 205.

— **Bibliography.**

GRASHAM (W.E.) and JULIEN (GERMAIN) compilers. Bibliography: Canadian public administration; Administration publique canadienne: bibliographie. Toronto, [1972]. pp. 261. *Preface and table of contents in English and French.*

U.K. Overseas Development Administration. Library. 1973. Public administration: a select bibliography. 3rd ed. [London], 1973. pp. 120.

— **Study and teaching.**

NORWAY. Utvalget for Forvaltningsutdanning. 1972. Forvaltningsutdanning: utredning 2 fra Utvalget, etc. Oslo, 1972. pp. 36. (*Norway. Norges Offentlige Utredninger. 1972.7)*

NETHERLANDS. Studiecomissie Coördinatie Wetenschappelijk Onderwijs - Hoger Economisch en Administratief Onderwijs. 1973. Rapport. 's-Gravenhage, 1973. pp. 37.

SCHAFFER (BENJAMIN BERNARD) ed. Administrative training and development: a comparative study of East Africa, Zambia, Pakistan, and India. New York, 1974. pp. 445. *bibliog.*

— **Underdeveloped areas.**

See UNDERDEVELOPED AREAS — Administration.

ADMINISTRATIVE ACTS

— **Italy.**

CUGURRA (GIORGIO) L'attività di alta amministrazione. Padova, 1973. pp. 398. (*Rome. Università. Istituto di Diritto Pubblico. Pubblicazioni. Serie 3. vol. 23)*

ADMINISTRATIVE AGENCIES

— **United Kingdom.**

RYLE (GEORGE) Forest service: the first forty-five years of the Forestry Commission of Great Britain. Newton Abbot, [1969]. pp. 340.

GIDDINGS (P.J.) Marketing boards and ministers: a study of agricultural marketing boards as political and administrative instruments. Farnborough, [1974]. pp. 247.

— **United States.**

KOSTIN (P.V.) FBR - portret vo ves' rost. Moskva, 1970. pp. 230.

HIRSCH (RICHARD) and TRENTO (JOSEPH JOHN) The National Aeronautics and Space Administration. New York, 1973. pp. 245. *bibliog.*

MICHAEL (JAMES R.) ed. Working on the system: a comprehensive manual for citizen access to federal agencies. New York, [1974]. pp. 950.

ADMINISTRATIVE AND POLITICAL DIVISIONS

— **Australia.**

AUSTRALIA. Parliament. House of Representatives. Select Committee on the Naming of Electoral Divisions. 1969. Report. in AUSTRALIA. Parliament. Parliamentary papers, 1969, vol.6.

— — **Western Australia.**

WESTERN AUSTRALIA. Local Government Assessment Committee. 1968. Reports on aspects of local government in Western Australia; [G.F. Mathea, chairman]. Perth, 1968. pp. 86, 6 maps.

— **Ghana.**

ASSOCIATED CONSULTANTS. A guide to your constituency. Accra, [196-?]. pp. 315.

— **Russia — Estonia.**

RIANZHIN (VALENTIN ANATOL'EVICH) Problemy territorial'noi organizatsii Sovetskogo gosudarstva: na materialakh Estonskoi SSR. Leningrad, 1973. pp. 80.

— — **Tatar Republic.**

GEOGRAFICHESKAIA kharakteristika administrativnykh raionov Tatarskoi ASSR. Kazan', 1972. pp. 252. *bibliog.*

— **Sri Lanka.**

LEITAN (GENEVIEVE RITA TRESSIBELLE) Local government and administration in Ceylon; [Ph.D. (London) thesis]. 1973. fo. 319. *bibliog. Typescript: unpublished. This thesis is the property of London University and may not be removed from the Library.*

— **Switzerland — Zürich (Canton).**

ZUERICH (CANTON). Statistisches Amt. 1967. Siedlungen und Gemeinden des Kantons Zürich. Ausgabe 1966. Zürich, 1967. pp. 260. *(Statistische Mitteilungen. 3. Folge. Heft 59)*

— **United Kingdom.**

U.K. Local Government Boundary Commission for England. 1972. Names for non-metropolitan districts. London, 1972. pp. (2). *(Circulars. 72/1)*

U.K. Local Government Boundary Commission for England. Reports. No. 5. London, 1973. pp. 4.

U.K. Local Government Boundary Commission for England. Reports. No. 6. London, 1973. pp. 10.

U.K. Local Government Boundary Commission for England. 1973. Constitution of parishes by reference to existing urban district and borough boundaries. London, 1973. pp. (3). *(Circulars. 73/1)*

U.K. Local Government Boundary Commission for England. 1973. Initial review of electoral arrangements. London, 1973. pp. (4). *(Circulars. 73/2)*

LONDON. University. London School of Economics and Political Science. Department of Geography. Urban change in Britain, 1961-1971...: working reports. London, 1974 in progress.

— — **Ireland, Northern.**

IRELAND, NORTHERN. [Ministry of Development]. 1972. [Local government boundaries maps]: final district electoral areas, 1972 [and General map]. [Belfast, 1972]. 27 maps.

— **United States.**

BARONE (MICHAEL) and others. The almanac of American politics: the senators, the representatives, their records, states and districts, 1974. 2nd ed. London, 1974. pp. 1240.

ADMINISTRATIVE COURTS

— **France.**

MOUSNIER (ROYLAND) and others. Le Conseil du Roi de Louis XII à la Révolution. Paris, 1970. pp. 378. *(Paris. Université. Faculté des Lettres et Sciences Humains. Publications. Série Recherches. Tome 56)*

— **United Kingdom.**

WRAITH (RONALD EDWARD) and HUTCHESSON (PETER G.) Administrative tribunals. London, 1973. pp. 376. *bibliog.*

FARMER (JAMES A.) Tribunals and government. London, [1974]. pp. 250.

LISTER (RUTH) Justice for the claimant: a study of supplementary benefit appeal tribunals. London, 1974. pp. 67. *(Child Poverty Action Group. Poverty Research Series. 4)*

ADMINISTRATIVE DISCRETION

— **United States.**

KADISH (MORTIMER R.) and KADISH (SANFORD H.) Discretion to disobey: a study of lawful departures from legal rules. Stanford, 1973. pp. 241.

ADMINISTRATIVE LAW

— **Bulgaria.**

ANGELOV (ANGEL S.) and others. Uchebnik po administrativno pravo na Narodna Republika Bŭlgariia: obshta chast. Sofiia, 1967. pp. 519. *bibliog.*

— **France.**

BAYLE (GABRIEL) L'enrichissement sans cause en droit administratif. Paris, 1973. pp. 227. *bibliog.*

GILLI (JEAN PAUL) ed. La continuité des services publics: études. [Paris, 1973]. pp. 207.

— **Hungary.**

SZAMEL (LAJOS) Legal problems of socialist public administrative management. Budapest, 1973. pp. 233.

— **Poland.**

STUDIA z zakresu prawa administracyjnego; ku czci Prof. dra Mariana Zimmermanna. Poznań, 1973. pp. 167. *(Poznań. Poznańskie Towarzystwo Przyjaciół Nauk. Wydział Historii i Nauk Społecznych. Komisja Nauk Społecznych. Prace. t.16, z.2)*

— **Russia.**

KORENEV (ALEKSEI PETROVICH) Kodifikatsiia sovetskogo administrativnogo prava: teoreticheskie problemy. Moskva, 1970. pp. 134.

CHECHOT (DMITRII MIKHAILOVICH) Administrativnaia iustitsiia: teoreticheskie problemy. Leningrad, 1973. pp. 134.

— **Spain.**

GOMEZ ANTON (FRANCISCO) La Ley Regimen Juridico de la Administracion del Estado. Madrid, 1959. pp. 192. *bibliog. (Spain. Presidencia. Secretaria General Tecnica. Estudios Administrativos. 1)*

— **United Kingdom.**

DE SMITH (STANLEY ALEXANDER) Constitutional and administrative law. 2nd ed. Harmondsworth, 1973. pp. 750.

GRIFFITH (JOHN ANEURIN GREY) and STREET (HARRY) Principles of administrative law. 5th ed. London, 1973. pp. 331. *bibliog.*

PHILLIPS (OWEN HOOD) Leading cases in constitutional and administrative law. 4th ed. London, 1973. pp. 395.

ADMINISTRATIVE PROCEDURE.

INTERNATIONAL CONGRESS OF ADMINISTRATIVE SCIENCES, 14TH, 1968. La protection des citoyens dans les procédures administratives, à l'exclusion des recours juridictionnels: version définitive du rapport général; par Bertil Wennergren. Bruxelles, 1969. pp. 59.

— **Russia.**

DODIN (EVGENII VASIL'EVICH) Dokazatel'stva v administrativnom protsesse. Moskva, 1973. pp. 192.

— **United Kingdom.**

GANZ (G.) Administrative procedures. London, 1974. pp. 118.

ADMINISTRATIVE REMEDIES.

INTERNATIONAL CONGRESS OF ADMINISTRATIVE SCIENCES, 14TH, 1968. La protection des citoyens dans les procédures administratives, à l'exclusion des recours juridictionnels: version définitive du rapport général; par Bertil Wennergren. Bruxelles, 1969. pp. 59.

— **India.**

INDIA. Administrative Reforms Commission. Study Team on Redress of Citizens' Grievances. 1970. Report...1966. [Delhi, 1970]. pp. 17.

— **Russia.**

BONNER (ALEKSANDR TIMOFEEVICH) and KVITKIN (VLADIMIR TROFIMOVICH) Sudebnyi kontrol' v oblasti gosudarstvennogo upravleniia: uchebnoe posobie. Moskva, 1973. pp. 111.

— **United Kingdom.**

WHEARE (Sir KENNETH CLINTON) Maladministration and its remedies. London, 1973. pp. 172. *(Hamlyn Lectures. 25th Series)*

ADMINISTRATIVE RESPONSIBILITY

— **Russia.**

LYSOV (MIKHAIL DANILOVICH) Otvetstvennost' dolzhnostnykh lits po sovetskomu ugolovnomu pravu. Kazan', 1972. pp. 176.

ADOLESCENCE.

PHILLIPS (A.S.) Adolescence in Jamaica. Kingston, Jam., [1973]. pp. 148. *bibliog.*

COLEMAN (JOHN C.) Relationships in adolescence. London, 1974. pp. 214. *bibliog.*

ADOPTION

— **America, Latin.**

CURSO REGIONAL INTERAMERICANO SOBRE COLOCACION FAMILIAR, ADOPCION, Y LIBERTAD VIGILADA, MONTEVIDEO, 1970. I curso regional..., Montevideo, Octubre 5 al 25 de 1970. Montevideo, Inter-American Children's Institute, 1972. pp. 313. *bibliog.*

— **Denmark.**

DENMARK. Adoptionsudvalg. 1971. Aendring af adoptionsloven: betaenkning I fra Justitsministeriets adoptionsudvalg. [Copenhagen], 1971. pp. 96. *(Denmark. Betaenkninger. Nr.624)*

— **France.**

FRANCE. Direction de la Documentation. La Documentation Française. Notes et Etudes Documentaires. No. 3,064. Le régime de l'adoption en France: loi du 1er mars 1963 et décret du 10 mai 1963. Paris, 1964. pp. 14.

— **United Kingdom.**

ROWE (JANE) and LAMBERT (LYDIA) Children who wait: a study of children needing substitute families. London, 1973. pp. 195. *bibliog.*

ADVERTISING.

KELLY (M.P.) and COWLING (KEITH) Advertising, market structure and price-cost margins. Coventry, [1973]. fo.20. *bibliog. (University of Warwick. Centre for Industrial Economic and Business Research. [Warwick Research in Industrial and Business Studies]. No. 37)*

REEKIE (W. DUNCAN) Advertising: its place in political and managerial economics. London, 1974. pp. 163.

— **Canada.**

ELKIN (FREDERICK) Rebels and colleagues: advertising and social change in French Canada. Montreal, 1973. pp. 227.

ADVERTISING (Cont.)

— Europe, Eastern.

HANSON (PHILIP) Advertising and socialism: the nature and extent of consumer advertising in the Soviet Union, Poland, Hungary and Yugoslavia. London, 1974. pp. 171. *bibliog.*

— France.

DIVIER (PIERRE FRANÇOIS) Le mensonge en publicité: sa répression et sa prévention en France. [Paris, 1972]. pp. 246.

ADVERTISING, NEWSPAPER

— United Kingdom.

TIMES LITERARY SUPPLEMENT, THE. Advertising in the T.L.S... 1902-1972. London, [1972]. 1 pamphlet (unpaged).

AERIAL PHOTOGRAPHY IN AGRICULTURE.

CANADA. Program Planning Office for Resource Satellites and Remote Airborne Sensing. Working Group on Agriculture and Geography. 1971. Resource satellites and remote airborne sensing for Canada. Report no.2. Agriculture and Geography; [C.V. Parker, chairman]. Ottawa, 1971. pp. 23. *With French summary.*

AERIAL PHOTOGRAPHY IN FORESTRY.

CANADA. Program Planning Office for Resource Satellites and Remote Airborne Sensing. Working Group on Forestry and Wildlands. 1971. Resource satellites and remote airborne sensing for Canada. Report no.5. Forestry and wildlands; [L. Sayn-Wittgenstein, chairman]. Ottawa, 1971. pp. 17. *With French summary.*

AERIAL PHOTOGRAPHY IN GEOLOGY.

CANADA. Program Planning Office for Resource Satellites and Remote Airborne Sensing. Working Group on Agriculture and Geography. 1971. Resource satellites and remote airborne sensing for Canada. Report no.2. Agriculture and Geography; [C.V. Parker, chairman]. Ottawa, 1971. pp. 23. *With French summary.*

CANADA. Program Planning Office for Resource Satellites and Remote Airborne Sensing. Working Group on Geology. 1971. Resource satellites and remote airborne sensing for Canada. Report no.6. Geology; [Alan F. Gregory, chairman]. Ottawa, 1971. pp. 26. *With French summary.*

AERIAL PHOTOGRAPHY IN GLACIOLOGY.

CANADA. Program Planning Office for Resource Satellites and Remote Airborne Sensing. Working Group on Ice Reconnaissance and Glaciology. 1971. Resource satellites and remote airborne sensing for Canada. Report no.7. Ice reconnaissance and glaciology; [D.C. Archibald, chairman]. Ottawa, 1971. pp. 37. *With French summary.*

AERIAL PHOTOGRAPHY IN HYDROLOGY.

CANADA. Program Planning Office for Resource Satellites and Remote Airborne Sensing. Working Group on Water Resources. 1971. Resource satellites and remote airborne sensing for Canada. Report no.8. Water resources; [R.K. Lane, chairman]. Ottawa, 1971. pp. 25. *bibliog. With French summary.*

AERONAUTICS

— Germany, Eastern — Laws and regulations.

KNEIFEL (JOHN L.) L'aviation civile en République Démocratique Allemande: une étude de l'évolution de l'aviation civile et du droit aerien de la R.D.A. depuis 1949 et ses rapports juridiques et économiques avec les compagnies aériennes des états du COMECON et d'autres pays. Berlin, 1972. pp. 377. *bibliog. With English summary.*

— United States.

HIRSCH (RICHARD) and TRENTO (JOSEPH JOHN) The National Aeronautics and Space Administration. New York, 1973. pp. 245. *bibliog.*

AERONAUTICS, COMMERCIAL.

ELLISON (A.P.) and STAFFORD (E.M.) The dynamics of the civil aviation industry. Farnborough, Hants, [1974]. pp. 348. *bibliog.*

MARX (JUERG) Die regionalpolitische Rolle des regionalen Luftverkehrs. Zürich, 1974. pp. 231. *bibliog.*

— Freight.

SMITH (PETER S.) Air freight: operations, marketing and economics. London, 1974. pp. 434. *bibliog.*

— Canada.

KESTEN (H.J.) A case study of decision-making within the Canadian Transport Commission: the application of Northwest Territorial Airways. Toronto, 1974. fo. 67. *bibliog. (Toronto. University, and York University (Toronto). Joint Program in Transportation. Transportation Papers. No.2)*

— France.

ELEMENTS pour un schéma directeur de l'équipement aéronautique; [prepared by a working group; Henri Mazen, chairman]. Paris, 1972. pp. 156. *bibliog. (France. Délégation à l'Aménagement du Territoire et à l'Action Régionale. Travaux et Recherches de Prospective. 25)*

SCHEMA général d'aménagement de la France: schéma directeur de l'équipement aéronautique; [report of a working group]. [Paris], 1973. pp. 87. *(France. Délégation à l'Aménagement du Territoire et à l'Action Régionale. Travaux et Recherches de Prospective. 35) Chart in end pocket.*

— Germany, Eastern.

KNEIFEL (JOHN L.) L'aviation civile en République Démocratique Allemande: une étude de l'évolution de l'aviation civile et du droit aerien de la R.D.A. depuis 1949 et ses rapports juridiques et économiques avec les compagnies aériennes des états du COMECON et d'autres pays. Berlin, 1972. pp. 377. *bibliog. With English summary.*

— Sweden — Freight.

STRINNHOLM (JAN) Varutransporter med flyg: flygfraktstudier med empirisk belysning af flygfrakt i Sveriges utrikeshandel samt flygfrakt över Arlanda. Uppsala, 1974. pp. 306. *bibliog. (Uppsala. Universitet. Kulturgeografiska Institutionen. Geografiska Regionstudier. Nr. 11) With English summary.*

— United Kingdom.

U.K. Parliament. House of Lords. Committee on the Civil Aviation Bill. Official report. d., Jl 19-21 1971 (1st-3rd sittings). London. *Photocopies.*

AIR TRANSPORT AND TRAVEL INDUSTRY TRAINING BOARD [U.K.]. Report and statement of accounts. a., 1972/3- Staines. *Formerly included in the file of British Parliamentary Papers.*

MANPOWER IN AIR TRANSPORT AND TRAVEL: a report from the Air Transport and Travel Industry Training Board. a., 1972/1975 [3rd]- Staines. *Each issue covers 3 yrs.*

AIR TRANSPORT AND TRAVEL INDUSTRY TRAINING BOARD [U.K.]. Manpower in air transport, 1972 to 1975. [Staines, 1972]. pp. 11.

— — Scotland.

U.K. Civil Aviation Authority. 1974. Air transport in the Scottish highlands and islands. London, 1974. pp. (121).

— — Wales.

WELSH COUNCIL. Civil aviation in Wales. [Cardiff?], 1974. pp. 8.

— United States — Freight.

SCHNEIDER (LEWIS MICHAEL) The future of the U.S. domestic air freight industry: an analysis of management strategies. Boston, [Mass.], 1973. pp. 217. *bibliog.*

AERONAUTICS AND STATE

— Canada.

KESTEN (H.J.) A case study of decision-making within the Canadian Transport Commission: the application of Northwest Territorial Airways. Toronto, 1974. fo. 67. *bibliog. (Toronto. University, and York University (Toronto). Joint Program in Transportation. Transportation Papers. No.2)*

AEROPLANE INDUSTRY AND TRADE

— United Kingdom.

BRISTOL INTERNATIONAL SOCIALISTS. Boom, or bust?: the crisis in the aircraft industry. Bristol, [197-]. pp. 42.

MACCRINDLE (ROBERT ALEXANDER) and GODFREY (PETER) Rolls-Royce Limited: investigation under Section 165(a) (i) of the Companies Act 1948; report. London, H.M.S.O., 1973. 1 vol. (various pagings).

HARTLEY (KEITH) A market for aircraft: a critique and a proposal for radical reconstruction of British government procurement policy. London, 1974. pp. 72. *bibliog. (Institute of Economic Affairs. Hobart Papers. 57)*

AEROPLANE INDUSTRY WORKERS

— United Kingdom.

BRISTOL INTERNATIONAL SOCIALISTS. Boom, or bust?: the crisis in the aircraft industry. Bristol, [197-]. pp. 42.

AEROPLANES

— Noise.

AUSTRALIA. Parliament. House of Representatives. Select Committee on Aircraft Noise. 1969. Report... (being a report that the Committee have been unable to complete their inquiry). in AUSTRALIA. Parliament. Parliamentary papers, 1969, vol.6.

GAUTRIN (JEAN FRANÇOIS) The economics of aircraft noise: an essay with British data; [Ph.D.(London) thesis]. 1972. fo. 249. *bibliog. Typescript: unpublished. This thesis is the property of London University and may not be removed from the Library.*

AEROSPACE INDUSTRIES

— France.

FRANCE. Direction de la Documentation. La Documentation Française. Notes et Etudes Documentaires. No. 3,764. L'industrie aéronautique et spatiale française; [by] J. Noetinger. Paris, 1971. pp. 32.

AESTHETICS.

SMITH (ARTHUR) Writer on heuristics. Four uses of heuristics; [models for project design and large idea-systems]. Rochdale, [1973]. pp. 207. *bibliog.*

AFGHANISTAN

— Economic policy.

ETIENNE (GILBERT) L'Afghanistan ou les aléas de la coopération. Paris, 1972. pp. 296. *bibliog. (Paris. Université. Institut d'Etude du Développement Economique et Social. Collection Tiers Monde)*

— Politics and government.

BHANEJA (BALWANT) Afghanistan: political modernization of a mountain-kingdom. New Delhi, 1973. pp. 87. *bibliog.*

AFRICA

— Bibliography.

GEERAERTS (PIERRE) La Bibliothèque Africaine: quatre-vingt-cinq ans d'activité bibliographique africaine. Bruxelles, Bibliothèque Africaine, 1972. pp. 90.

AHMADU BELLO UNIVERSITY. Kashim Ibrahim Library. Catalogue of Africana; compiled by Adakole Ochai. [Zaria], 1974. pp. 196.

— Biography.

DICKIE (JOHN) and RAKE (ALAN) Who's who in Africa: the political, military and business leaders of Africa. London, [1973]. pp. 602.

— Capitals.

BEST (ALAN C.G.) and YOUNG (BRUCE S.) Focus on Africa: capitals for the homelands. Stellenbosch, 1972. pp. 1043-1055. *(From Journal for Geography, vol. 3, no. 10, April, 1972)* Xerox copy.

— Census.

FRANCE. Institut National de la Statistique et des Etudes Economiques. 1970. Situation des recensements et des enquêtes démographiques dans les états africains et malgache au 1er janvier 1970. Paris, 1970. pp. 63.

— Commerce.

DIA BONDO (THEOPHILE LUKUSA) and PORTER (RICHARD C.) A constant-market-share look at African exports in the 1960s. Ann Arbor, 1973. pp. 24. *bibliog. (Michigan University. Center for Research on Economic Development. Discussion Papers. No.28)*

PEARSON (SCOTT R.) and COWNIE (JOHN) Commodity exports and African economic development. Lexington, Mass., [1974]. pp. 285.

— — Philippine Islands.

PHILIPPINE ISLANDS. Department of Commerce and Industry. Research and Information Division. 1965. Philippine trade with the African countries; editor, Socorro B. Ramos. rev. ed. Manila, 1965. pp. 32.

— Description and travel.

MORAVIA (ALBERTO) pseud. [i.e. Alberto PINCHERLE] Which tribe do you belong to?;...translated from the Italian by Angus Davidson. London, 1974. pp. 218.

— Discovery and exploration.

CORDEIRO DE SOUSA (LUCIANO BAPTISTA) compiler. Viagens explorações e conquistas dos Portuguezes: colecção de documentos. Lisboa, 1881. 6 pts. (in 1 vol.). *(Portugal. Memorias do Ultramar)*

— Economic conditions.

AFRICAN PERFORMANCE: biennial review and appraisal of performance in Africa in implementing the goals and objectives of the Second United Nations Development Decade. bien., [1971/1972](1st)- Addis Ababa.

NGOUDI (NGOM) La réussite de l'intégration économique en Afrique. Paris, [1971]. pp. 141. *bibliog.*

UNITED STATES. Agency for International Development. Office of Statistics and Reports. 1971. A.I.D. economic data book: Africa. Washington, 1971. Microfiche [6 cards]

PEARSON (SCOTT R.) and COWNIE (JOHN) Commodity exports and African economic development. Lexington, Mass., [1974]. pp. 285.

— Economic integration.

BROWNLIE (IAN) ed. Basic documents on African affairs. Oxford, 1971. pp. 556. *bibliog.*

NGOUDI (NGOM) La réussite de l'intégration économique en Afrique. Paris, [1971]. pp. 141. *bibliog.*

— Economic policy.

U.K. Colonial Office. Summer Conference on African Administration. [Papers, reports, etc.]. a., 1947-1960 (1st-11th sessions); ceased pbln. Cambridge. *Not held 1950, 1952, 1955. (African [Publications]).*

BROWNLIE (IAN) ed. Basic documents on African affairs. Oxford, 1971. pp. 556. *bibliog.*

URBANIZATION, national development, and regional planning in Africa: [papers of an interdisciplinary panel presented as part of the African Studies Association's fifteenth annual meeting, 1972]; (edited by Salah El-Shakhs [and] Robert Obudho). New York, 1974. pp. 227. *bibliog.*

— Foreign relations.

BROWNLIE (IAN) ed. Basic documents on African affairs. Oxford, 1971. pp. 556. *bibliog.*

JENSEN (PETER FØGE) Soviet research on Africa, with special reference to international relations. Uppsala, 1973. pp. 68. *bibliogs. (Nordiska Afrikainstitutet. Research Reports. No. 19)*

COLSTON RESEARCH SOCIETY. Symposium, 25th, 1973. Foreign relations of African states; edited by K. Ingham; proceedings of the. London, 1974. pp. 344. *bibliog. (Colston Research Society and Bristol. University. Colston Papers. vol.25)*

MAHGOUB (MOHAMED AHMED) Democracy on trial: reflections on Arab and African politics. London, 1974. pp. 318.

See also EUROPEAN ECONOMIC COMMUNITY — Africa.

— — China.

OGUNSANWO (CORNELIUS ALABA ABIODUN ADEBOYEJO) China's policy in Africa, 1958-71. London, 1974. pp. 310. *bibliog. (London. University. London School of Economics and Political Science. Centre for International Studies. International Studies)*

— — United Kingdom.

UZOIGWE (GODFREY N.) Britain and the conquest of Africa: the age of Salisbury. Ann Arbor, [1974]. pp. 403. *bibliog.*

— History.

FREEMAN-GRENVILLE (G.S.P.) Chronology of African history. Oxford, 1973. pp. 312.

— — Sources.

BROWNLIE (IAN) ed. Basic documents on African affairs. Oxford, 1971. pp. 556. *bibliog.*

— Industries.

COLLOQUE INTERNATIONAL SUR LE DEVELOPPEMENT INDUSTRIEL AFRICAIN, DAKAR, 1972. Colloque international sur le développement industriel africain; ...organisé conjointement par le gouvernement de la République du Sénégal et le Centre Européen pour le Développement Industriel et la Mise en valeur de l'Outre- Mer; [proceedings]. Dakar, [1973]. pp. 349. *in French and English.*

— Nationalism.

MAZRUI (ALI A.) Towards a pax Africana: a study of ideology and ambition. Chicago, 1967. pp. 287.

PAN-AFRICAN SEMINAR ON THE JUCHE IDEA OF COMRADE KIM IL SUNG, FREETOWN, 1972. Documents and deliberations of the seminar. Beirut, [1973]. pp. 184.

MPHAHLELE (EZEKIEL) The African image. rev. ed. London, 1974. pp. 316. *bibliog.*

— Politics and government.

U.K. Colonial Office. Summer Conference on African Administration. [Papers, reports, etc.]. a., 1947-1960 (1st-11th sessions); ceased pbln. Cambridge. *Not held 1950, 1952, 1955. (African [Publications]).*

BROWNLIE (IAN) ed. Basic documents on African affairs. Oxford, 1971. pp. 556. *bibliog.*

JALLOH (ABDUL A.) Political integration in French-speaking Africa. Berkeley, [1973]. pp. 208. *bibliog. (California University. Institute of International Studies. Research Series. No.20)*

NYERERE (JULIUS KAMBARAGE) Freedom and development; Uhuru na maendeleo: a selection from writings and speeches, 1968-1973. Dar es Salaam, 1973. pp. 400.

AFRICA and international organization; [including papers given at a symposium held in 1970 under the auspices of the Center for African Studies, St. John's University, New York]; edited by Yassin El-Ayouty [and] Hugh C. Brooks. The Hague, 1974. pp. 250.

HATCH (JOHN CHARLES) Africa emergent: Africa's problems since independence. London, 1974. pp. 233. *bibliog.*

MAHGOUB (MOHAMED AHMED) Democracy on trial: reflections on Arab and African politics. London, 1974. pp. 318.

— — Bibliography.

SHAW (ROBERT B.) and SKLAR (RICHARD L.) compilers. A bibliography for the study of African politics. Los Angeles, 1973. pp. 206. *(California University. African Studies Center. Occasional Papers. No. 9)*

— Population.

FRANCE. Institut National de la Statistique et des Etudes Economiques. 1970. Situation des recensements et des enquêtes démographiques dans les états africains et malgache au 1er janvier 1970. Paris, 1970. pp. 63.

— — Bibliography.

FRANCE. Institut National de la Statistique et des Etudes Economiques. Département de la Coopération. 1972. Bibliographie démographique 1945-1970. Paris, 1972. pp. 83.

— Presidents.

SELASSIE (BEREKET H.) The executive in African governments. London, 1974. pp. 288.

— Race question.

MPHAHLELE (EZEKIEL) The African image. rev. ed. London, 1974. pp. 316. *bibliog.*

— Relations (general) with China.

DEICH (TAT'IANA LAZAREVNA) Maoizm - ugroza Afrike. Moskva, 1972. pp. 168.

— Relations (general) with Europe.

ZAGHI (CARLO) L'Africa nella coscienza europea e l'imperialismo italiano. Napoli, [1973]. pp. 576.

— Relations (general) with Russia.

GORBATOV (OLEG MARKOVICH) and CHERKASSKII (LEONID IAKOVLEVICH) Sotrudnichestvo SSSR so stranami Arabskogo Vostoka i Afriki. Moskva, 1973. pp. 342. *bibliog.*

— Relations (general) with Spain.

SAEZ DE GOVANTES (LUIS) El africanismo español. Madrid, 1971. pp. 233.

— Social conditions.

AFRICAN PERFORMANCE: biennial review and appraisal of performance in Africa in implementing the goals and objectives of the Second United Nations Development Decade. bien., [1971/1972](1st)- Addis Ababa.

AFRICA (Cont.)

MPHAHLELE (EZEKIEL) The African image. rev. ed. London, 1974. pp. 316. *bibliog.*

— Social life and customs.

MORAVIA (ALBERTO) pseud. [i.e. Alberto PINCHERLE] Which tribe do you belong to?;...translated from the Italian by Angus Davidson. London, 1974. pp. 218.

— Statistics.

BONDESTAM (LARS) Some notes on African statistics: collection, reliability and interpretation. Uppsala, 1973. pp. 55,ix. *(Nordiska Afrikainstitutet. Research Reports. No. 18)*

AFRICA, CENTRAL

— Industries.

ISMAÏL (TOUFIK) L'industrie dans l'économie de l'Afrique centrale: Sénégal, Côte d'Ivoire, Cameroun, Congo (Kinshasa). Louvain, 1970. pp. 249. *bibliog.* *(Louvain. Université. Faculté des Sciences Economiques, Sociales et Politiques. [Publications]. Nouvelle Série. No.85)*

FRANCE. Direction de la Documentation. La Documentation Française. Notes et Etudes Documentaires No. 3,830. L'industrialisation des états de l'Union douanière et économique de l'Afrique centrale (U.D.E.A.C.); [by] Attilio Gaudio. Paris, 1971. pp. 43. *bibliog.*

AFRICA, EAST

— Economic conditions.

DUALISM and rural development in East Africa: [report of a seminar held by the Danish Institute for Development Research, 1973; edited by Roger Leys]. Copenhagen, 1973. pp. 209.

MORGAN (WILLIAM THOMAS WILSON) East Africa. London, 1973. pp. 410. *bibliogs.*

— Economic integration.

NIXSON (F.I.) Economic integration and industrial location: an East African case study. London, [1973]. pp. 181. *bibliog.*

— Industries.

NIXSON (F.I.) Economic integration and industrial location: an East African case study. London, [1973]. pp. 181. *bibliog.*

— Intellectual life.

MAZRUI (ALI A.) Cultural engineering and nation building in East Africa. Evanston, Ill., 1972. pp. 301.

— Nationalism.

MAZRUI (ALI A.) Cultural engineering and nation building in East Africa. Evanston, Ill., 1972. pp. 301.

— Politics and government.

HORRUT (CLAUDE) Les décolonisations Est-africaines. Paris, [1971]. pp. 231. *bibliog.* *(Bordeaux. Université. Centre d'Etude d'Afrique Noire. Bibliothèque. Série Afrique Noire. 2)*

MAZRUI (ALI A.) Cultural engineering and nation building in East Africa. Evanston, Ill., 1972. pp. 301.

STRAYER (ROBERT W.) and others. Protest movements in colonial East Africa: aspects of early African response to European rule. Syracuse, 1973. pp. 96. *(Syracuse University. Maxwell Graduate School of Citizenship and Public Affairs. Program of Eastern African Studies. Eastern African Studies. 12)*

— Rural conditions.

DUALISM and rural development in East Africa: [report of a seminar held by the Danish Institute for Development Research, 1973; edited by Roger Leys]. Copenhagen, 1973. pp. 209.

— Social conditions.

MAZRUI (ALI A.) Cultural engineering and nation building in East Africa. Evanston, Ill., 1972. pp. 301.

— Social life and customs.

SHORTER (AYLWARD) East African societies. London, 1974. pp. 155. *bibliog.*

AFRICA, NORTH

— Foreign relations — Europe.

EUROPE and the Maghreb: a series of papers by C. Gasteyger [and others]. Paris, [1972]. pp. 72. *(Atlantic Institute. Atlantic Papers. 1972.1)*

— History.

RUMEU DE ARMAS (ANTONIO) España en el Africa atlantica. Madrid, 1956-57. 2 vols. (in 1).

VILAR RAMIREZ (JUAN BAUTISTA) España en Argelia, Tunez, Ifni y Sahara, durante el siglo XIX. Madrid, 1970. pp. 174. *bibliog.*

— Politics and government.

ELITES, pouvoir et légitimité au Maghreb; par M. Teitler [and others]. Paris, 1973. pp. 237. *(Centre National de la Recherche Scientifique. Centre de Recherches et d'Etudes sur les Sociétés Méditerranéennes. Collection)*

La FORMATION des élites politiques maghrébines; [by] Lhachmi Berrady [and others]. Paris, [1973]. pp. 246.

ZARTMAN (IRA WILLIAM) ed. Man, state and society in the contemporary Maghrib. New York, 1973. pp. 531. *bibliog.*

— Social conditions.

ZARTMAN (IRA WILLIAM) ed. Man, state and society in the contemporary Maghrib. New York, 1973. pp. 531. *bibliog.*

AFRICA, SUBSAHARAN.

LAND-locked countries of Africa: [papers of a seminar organized by the Scandinavian Institute of African Studies in Oslo, September 1972]; edited by Zdenek Cervenka. Uppsala, 1973. pp. 369. *bibliog.*

— Description and travel.

CAMPBELL (ALEXANDER) Journalist. The heart of Africa. London, 1954. pp. 479.

WOLFERS (MICHAEL) Black man's burden revisited. London, [1974]. pp. 152.

— Economic conditions.

SMITH (PRUDENCE) ed. Africa in transition: some BBC talks on changing conditions in the Union and the Rhodesias. London, [1958]. pp. 179. *bibliog.*

— Economic policy.

NDEGWA (PHILIP) Requirements of more rapid growth in "black Africa" during the next decade;... paper written for the Columbia University Development Conference... 1970. n.p., [1970]. fo. 29.

MAZRUI (ALI A.) and PATEL (HASU H.) eds. Africa in world affairs: the next thirty years. New York, [1973]. pp. 265.

— Foreign economic relations.

STALLINGS (BARBARA) Economic dependency in Africa and Latin America. Beverly Hills, [1972]. pp. 60. *bibliog.*

— Foreign relations.

BARRATT (JOHN) Southern Africa: intra-regional and international relations; [paper read to a conference in September 1972]. Johannesburg, 1973. pp. 24,vi.

MAZRUI (ALI A.) and PATEL (HASU H.) eds. Africa in world affairs: the next thirty years. New York, [1973]. pp. 265.

— — Russia.

STEVENS (CHRISTOPHER ANTHONY) Relations between the U.S.S.R. and Africa between 1953 and 1972, with special reference to Ghana, Guinea, Kenya, Mali, Nigeria, Somalia and Tanzania; [Ph.D. (london) thesis]. [1973]. 1 vol. (various foliation). Typescript: unpublished. *This thesis is the property of London University and may not be removed from the Library.*

— History.

CORNEVIN (ROBERT) and CORNEVIN (MARIANNE) L'Afrique noire de 1919 à nos jours. [Paris], 1973. pp. 251. *bibliog.*

WEINSTEIN (WARREN) and GROTPETER (JOHN J.) The pattern of African decolonization: a new interpretation. Syracuse, 1973. pp. 123. *(Syracuse University. Maxwell Graduate School of Citizenship and Public Affairs. Program of Eastern African Studies. Eastern African Studies. 10)*

COQUERY-VIDROVITCH (CATHERINE) and MONIOT (HENRI) L'Afrique noire de 1800 à nos jours. Paris, 1974. pp. 462. *bibliog.*

PERSPECTIVES nouvelles sur le passé de l'Afrique noire et de Madagascar: mélanges offerts à Hubert Deschamps. Paris, 1974. pp. 315. *bibliog.* *(Paris. Université de Paris I (Panthéon-Sorbonne). Publications. Série Etudes. tome 7)* In French or English.

— Kings and rulers — Succession.

COMAROFF (JOHN LIONEL) Competition for office and political processes among the Barolong boo Ratshidi of the South Africa-Botswana borderland; [Ph.D.(London) thesis]. 1973. fo. 521. *bibliog.* Typescript: unpublished. *This thesis is the property of London University and may not be removed from the library.*

— Nationalism.

SHAMUYARIRA (NATHAN M.) ed. Essays on the liberation of southern Africa. Dar es Salaam, 1971. pp. 95. *(Dar es Salaam. University. Studies in Political Science. No. 3)*

— — Bibliography.

ANSARI (S.) compiler. Liberation struggle in southern Africa: a bibliography of source material. Gurgaon, Haryana, 1972. pp. 118.

— Politics and government.

CAMPBELL (ALEXANDER) Journalist. The heart of Africa. London, 1954. pp. 479.

GUTTERIDGE (WILLIAM F.) The coming confrontation in Southern Africa. London, 1971. pp. 19. *(Institute for the Study of Conflict. Conflict Studies. No. 15)*

SHAMUYARIRA (NATHAN M.) ed. Essays on the liberation of southern Africa. Dar es Salaam, 1971. pp. 95. *(Dar es Salaam. University. Studies in Political Science. No. 3)*

CARTER (GWENDOLEN MARGARET) Black initiatives for change in southern Africa. [Edinburgh, 1973]. pp. 18. *(Edinburgh. University. Centre of African Studies. Melville J. Herskovits Memorial Lectures. 11th)*

HAKES (JAY E.) Weak parliaments and military coups in Africa: a study in regime instability. Beverly Hills, [197?]. pp. 37. *bibliog.*

MAZRUI (ALI A.) and PATEL (HASU H.) eds. Africa in world affairs: the next thirty years. New York, [1973]. pp. 265.

UN-OAU CONFERENCE ON SOUTHERN AFRICA, OSLO, 1973. The UN-OAU Conference on Southern Africa, Oslo, 9-14 April 1973...; edited by Olav Stokke and Carl Widstrand. Uppsala, 1973. 2 vols. (in 1).

— Population.

MAZRUI (ALI A.) and PATEL (HASU H.) eds. Africa in world affairs: the next thirty years. New York, [1973]. pp. 265.

WOLF (BERNARD) Anti-contraception laws in sub-Saharan francophone Africa: sources and ramifications. Medford, Mass., 1973. pp. 40. *(Tufts University. Fletcher School of Law and Diplomacy. Law and Population Monograph Series. No.15)*

— Race question.

SMITH (PRUDENCE) ed. Africa in transition: some BBC talks on changing conditions in the Union and the Rhodesias. London, [1958]. pp. 179. *bibliog.*

GUTTERIDGE (WILLIAM F.) The coming confrontation in Southern Africa. London, 1971. pp. 19. *(Institute for the Study of Conflict. Conflict Studies. No. 15)*

CARTER (GWENDOLEN MARGARET) Black initiatives for change in southern Africa. [Edinburgh, 1973]. pp. 18. *(Edinburgh. University. Centre of African Studies. Melville J. Herskovits Memorial Lectures. 11th)*

— Relations (general) with Europe.

GOOD (KENNETH) Western domination in Africa. Syracuse, N.Y., 1972. pp. 71. *(Syracuse University. Maxwell Graduate School of Citizenship and Public Affairs. Program of Eastern African Studies. Eastern African Studies. No. 7)*

— Relations (general) with the United States.

GOOD (KENNETH) Western domination in Africa. Syracuse, N.Y., 1972. pp. 71. *(Syracuse University. Maxwell Graduate School of Citizenship and Public Affairs. Program of Eastern African Studies. Eastern African Studies. No. 7)*

— Religion.

SHORTER (AYLWARD) African culture and the Christian church: an introduction to social and pastoral anthropology. London, 1973. pp. 229. *bibliog.*

— Social conditions.

SMITH (PRUDENCE) ed. Africa in transition: some BBC talks on changing conditions in the Union and the Rhodesias. London, [1958]. pp. 179. *bibliog.*

SHORTER (AYLWARD) African culture and the Christian church: an introduction to social and pastoral anthropology. London, 1973. pp. 229. *bibliog.*

LITTLE (KENNETH LINDSAY) Urbanization as a social process: an essay on movement and change in contemporary Africa. London, 1974. pp. 153. *bibliog.*

WOLFERS (MICHAEL) Black man's burden revisited. London, [1974]. pp. 152.

— Statistics, Vital.

SOURCES et analyse des données démographiques: application à l'Afrique d'expression française et à Madagascar; [by] Institut National d'Etudes Démographiques [and others]. [Paris], 1973 in progress.

AFRICA, WEST

— Commerce — United Kingdom.

DAVIES (P.N.) The trade makers: Elder Dempster in West Africa, 1852-1972. London, 1973. pp. 526. *bibliog.*

— Description and travel.

HARRISON-CHURCH (RONALD JAMES) Some geographical aspects of West African development. [rev. ed]. [Athens, Ohio, 1970]. fo. 29. *(Ohio University. Center for International Studies. Papers in International Studies. Africa Series. No. 10)*

HARRISON-CHURCH (RONALD JAMES) West Africa: a study of the environment and of man's use of it;... with a chapter on soils and soil management [by] P.R. Moss. 7th ed. London, 1974. pp. 526. *bibliog.*

— Economic conditions.

HARRISON-CHURCH (RONALD JAMES) Some geographical aspects of West African development. [rev. ed]. [Athens, Ohio, 1970]. fo. 29. *(Ohio University. Center for International Studies. Papers in International Studies. Africa Series. No. 10)*

AMIN (SAMIR) Neo-colonialism in West Africa; translated from the French by Francis McDonagh. Harmondsworth, 1973. pp. 298. *bibliog.*

MALDANT (BORIS) and HAUBERT (MAXIME) Croissance et conjoncture dans l'Ouest africain. Paris, 1973. pp. 350. *(Paris. Université. Institut d'Etude du Développement Economique et Social. Etudes Tiers Monde)*

HARRISON-CHURCH (RONALD JAMES) West Africa: a study of the environment and of man's use of it;... with a chapter on soils and soil management [by] P.R. Moss. 7th ed. London, 1974. pp. 526. *bibliog.*

— Industries.

ISMAÏL (TOUFIK) L'industrie dans l'économie de l'Afrique centrale: Sénégal, Côte d'Ivoire, Cameroun, Congo (Kinshasa). Louvain, 1970. pp. 249. *bibliog.* *(Louvain. Université. Faculté des Sciences Economiques, Sociales et Politiques. [Publications]. Nouvelle Série. No.85)*

— Population.

INTERNATIONAL AFRICAN SEMINAR. 11th Seminar, Dakar, 1972. Modern migrations in western Africa: studies presented and discussed at the...seminar...; edited with an introduction by Samir Amin. London, 1974. pp. 426. *Text in French and English with a summary in the other language.*

— Rural conditions — Bibliography.

[ASIEDU (E.S.) compiler.] Social and rural development: West Africa (general): [a bibliography]. [1972]. fo.8. *Xerographic copy.*

— Social conditions.

HARRISON-CHURCH (RONALD JAMES) West Africa: a study of the environment and of man's use of it;... with a chapter on soils and soil management [by] P.R. Moss. 7th ed. London, 1974. pp. 526. *bibliog.*

— — Bibliography.

[ASIEDU (E.S.) compiler.] Social and rural development: West Africa (general): [a bibliography]. [1972]. fo.8. *Xerographic copy.*

AFRICAN LANGUAGES.

ITALY. Ministero degli Affari Esteri. Comitato per la Documentazione dell'Opera dell'Italia in Africa. L'Italia in Africa. Serie Scientifico-Culturale. Il contributo italiano alla conoscenza delle lingue parlate in Africa, dal cinquecento al primo sessantennio del secolo XX; testo di Antonio Enrico Leva. Roma, 1969. pp. 294. *bibliog.*

AFRICAN LITERATURE.

MUTISO (G.C.M.) Socio-political thought in African literature: weusi?. London, 1974. pp. 182. *bibliog.*

AFRICAN METHODIST EPISCOPAL CHURCH.

GEORGE (CAROL V.R.) Segregated sabbaths: Richard Allen and the emergence of independent black churches, 1760-1840. New York, 1973. pp. 205. *bibliog.*

AFRICAN NATIONAL COUNCIL.

AFRICAN NATIONAL COUNCIL. No future without us: the story of the African National Council in Zimbabwe (Southern Rhodesia). London, [1973?]. pp. 48.

AFRICAN STUDIES.

FORD (NICK AARON) Black studies: threat or challenge. Port Washington, N.Y., 1973. pp. 217. *bibliog.*

— Russia.

JENSEN (PETER FØGE) Soviet research on Africa, with special reference to international relations. Uppsala, 1973. pp. 68. *bibliogs. (Nordiska Afrikainstitutet. Research Reports. No. 19)*

AFRICANS IN LITERATURE.

MPHAHLELE (EZEKIEL) The African image. rev. ed. London, 1974. pp. 316. *bibliog.*

AFRO—ASIAN PEOPLE'S SOLIDARITY MOVEMENT.

DOLIDZE (DMITRII IUSUPOVICH) Problemy edinstva antiimperialisticheskoi bor'by: istoriia dvizheniia afro-aziatskoi solidarnosti 1954-1972 gg. Moskva, 1973. pp. 120.

AGE (PSYCHOLOGY).

BENGTSON (VERN L.) The social psychology of aging. Indianapolis, [1973]. pp. 55. *bibliog.*

AGE AND EMPLOYMENT.

INTERNATIONAL LABOUR ORGANISATION. Advisory Committee on Salaried Employees and Professional Workers. 7th Session. Reports. 3. Problems and opportunities of employment and re-employment of older workers in commerce and offices: (third item on the agenda). Geneva, 1974. pp. 43.

— Netherlands.

FUNCTIONAL age of industrial workers: a transversal survey of ageing capacities and a method for assessing functional age; ([report of a research project carried out at the] Netherlands Institute for Preventive Medicine TNO); edited by Johan Maurits Dirken. Groningen, 1972. pp. 251. *bibliogs.*

— Sweden.

ARBETSKRAV och arbetsförmåga hos äldre: en sammanställning med special hänsyn till åldrandets betydelse; [by] Sven Forssman [and others]. Stockholm, 1969. pp. 92. *bibliog. (Arbetsmedicinske Institutet. Rapporter. Nr. 14)*

AGGREGATES.

WILSON (ROBERT) Economist. On the theory of aggregation. Stanford, 1973. fo. 16. *(Stanford University. Institute for Mathematical Studies in the Social Sciences. Technical Reports. [New Reports] . No. 89)*

AGGREGATES (BUILDING MATERIALS).

U.K. Advisory Committee on Aggregates. 1973. Preliminary report: aggregates: the issues; [R.B. Verney, chairman]. [London], 1973. 1 pamphlet (various pagings).

U.K. Department of the Environment. Statistics Construction Division. 1973. Production of aggregates in Great Britain: sand and gravel 1971 and 1972; crushed rock, 1972; a publication of the government statistical service. [London, 1973]. pp. 20.

A SURVEY of the locations, disposal and prospective uses of the major industrial by-products and waste materials; [by] W. Gutt [and others]. Garston, [1974]. pp. 82,1 map. *(Building Research Establishment [U.K.]. Current Papers. 74/19)*

AGGRESSION (INTERNATIONAL LAW).

ZOUREK (JAROSLAV) L'interdiction de l'emploi de la force en droit international. Leiden, 1974. pp. 128. *bibliog. (Institut Henry Dunant. "Teneat Lex Gladium". No. 3)*

AGGRESSIVENESS (PSYCHOLOGY).

INTERNATIONAL INSTITUTE FOR PEACE. Symposium, 1971. Aggressionstrieb und Krieg;...herausgegeben von Walter Hollitscher; (aus dem Englischen übersetzt von Rudolf Hermstein). Stuttgart, [1973]. pp. 164.

FROMM (ERICH) The anatomy of human destructiveness. London, 1974. pp. 521. *bibliog.*

AGING.

BENGTSON (VERN L.) The social psychology of aging. Indianapolis, [1973]. pp. 55. *bibliog.*

GUSTAVUS ADOLPHUS COLLEGE. Nobel Conference, 8th, 1972. The end of life: a discussion at the... conference...; edited by John D. Roslansky. Amsterdam, 1973. pp. 83. *bibliogs.*

AGING (Cont.)

AMERICAN ACADEMY OF POLITICAL AND SOCIAL SCIENCE. Annals. vol. 415. Political consequences of aging; special editor of this volume Frederick R. Eisele. Philadelphia, 1974. pp. 301. *bibliog.*

AGNEW (SPIRO THEODORE).

COHEN (RICHARD M.) and WITCOVER (JULES) A heartbeat away: the investigation and resignation of Vice President Spiro T. Agnew. New York, 1974. pp. 373.

AGRARIAN REFORM.

See LAND REFORM.

AGRICULTURAL ADMINISTRATION

— **Italy.**

CALANDRA (PIERO) L'amministrazione dell'agricoltura: profili storici. Bologna, [1972]. pp. 84. *(Istituto Nazionale di Economia Agraria and Istituto per la Scienza dell'Amministrazione Pubblica. Agricoltura e Regioni. 5)*

Il TRASFERIMENTO dell'agricoltura alle Regioni: tavola rotonda sul decreto delegato di trasferimento delle funzioni amministrative dello Stato in materia di agricoltura e foreste; con Feliciano Benvenuti [and others]. Bologna, [1972]. pp. 131. *(Istituto Nazionale di Economia Agraria and Istituto per la Scienza dell'Amministrazione Pubblica. Agricoltura e Regioni. 4)*

— **Venezuela.**

VENEZUELA. Ministerio de Agricultura y Cria. Division de Organizacion y Metodos. 1969. Organizacion y administracion del sector agropecuario de Venezuela. Caracas, 1969. pp. 827.

AGRICULTURAL ASSISTANCE, DANISH

— **India — Mysore.**

FOLKE (STEEN) and others. An evaluation of the Danish Mysore project: an Indo-Danish agricultural-educational scheme. Copenhagen, Mellemfolkeligt Samvirke, 1969. pp. 255. *bibliog.*

AGRICULTURAL ASSISTANCE, SWEDISH

— **Ethiopia.**

STÅHL (MICHAEL) Contradictions in agricultural development: a study of three minimum package projects in southern Ethiopia. Uppsala, 1973. pp. 65. *bibliog. (Nordiska Afrikainstitutet. Research Reports. No. 14)*

AGRICULTURAL COLONIES

— **Ecuador.**

ECUADOR. Junta Nacional de Planificacion y Coordinacion Economica. 1964. Plan general de desarrollo economico y social (version preliminar). Tomo 2. El aprovechamiento de la tierra y el mar. Libro sexto. Reforma a la estructura de tenencia de la tierra y expansion de la frontera agricole. Capitulo 2. Colonizacion. Quito, [1964?]. pp. 399.

— **India.**

FARMER (BERTRAM HUGHES) Agricultural colonization in India since independence. London, 1974. pp. 372.

— **Israel.**

TAMSMA (R.) De moshav ovdiem: invloeden op de sociale geografie van Israel's coöperatieve kleine-boerendorpen zonder loonarbeid. Assen, [1973?]. pp. 454. *With English summary. Maps in end-pocket.*

AGRICULTURAL CREDIT

— **Italy.**

TABASSO (LUIGI) Credito agrario e regioni. Bologna, [1973]. pp. 83. *(Istituto Nazionale di Economia Agraria and Istituto per la Scienza dell'Amministrazione Pubblica. Agricoltura e Regioni. 9)*

— **Nepal.**

NEPAL RASTRA BANK. Research Department. 1972. Agricultural credit survey, Nepal. Kathmandu, 1972. 4 vols. (in 2).

— **Russia.**

SEMENOV (VIKTOR NIKOLAEVICH) Finansy i kredit v sovkhozakh: ekonomicheskii eksperiment v sovkhozakh, perevedennykh na polnyi khoziaistvennyi raschet. Moskva, 1969. pp. 175.

SEMENOV (VIKTOR NIKOLAEVICH) Rol' finansov i kredita v razvitii sel'skogo khoziaistva: metodologicheskie i prakticheskie voprosy mekhanizma vozdeistviia finansovo-kreditnykh otnoshenii na razvitie sel'skogo khoziaistva. Moskva, 1973. pp. 287.

— **Underdeveloped areas.**

See UNDERDEVELOPED AREAS — Agricultural credit.

— **United Kingdom.**

WILSON (JOHN STUART GLADSTONE) Availability of capital and credit to United Kingdom agriculture. London, H.M.S.O., 1973. pp. 255.

— **United States.**

NELSON (AARON GUSTAVE) and others. Agricultural finance. 6th ed. Ames, 1973. pp. 413. *bibliogs.*

AGRICULTURAL EDUCATION.

UNITED NATIONS EDUCATIONAL, SCIENTIFIC AND CULTURAL ORGANIZATION. 1964. Education and agricultural development. Paris, 1964. pp. 62. *bibliog. (Freedom From Hunger Campaign. Basic Studies. No.15)*

— **Belgium.**

SERGEANT (L.) L'enseignement agricole de plein exercice en Belgique. Bruxelles, 1972. pp. 82,8. *bibliog. (Belgium. Institut Economique Agricole. Cahiers. No. 145)*

— **France.**

FRANCE. Service de l'Enseignement Technique et de la Formation Professionnelle Agricoles. 1971. L'enseignement technique et la formation professionnelle agricoles. [Paris, 1971]. pp. 86. *(Ministère de l'Agriculture. Bulletin d'Information. Numéro Spécial)*

— **United Kingdom.**

AGRICULTURAL, HORTICULTURAL AND FORESTRY INDUSTRY TRAINING BOARD [U.K.]. Annual report and accounts. a., 1972/3- Beckenham. *Formerly included in the file of British Parliamentary Papers.*

AGRICULTURAL EXTENSION WORK

— **Ghana.**

DUMOR (E.) and AMONOO (E.) The focus and concentrate programme in the Somanya district: evaluation of an extension programme. Cape Coast, Ghana, 1973. pp. 60,xiv. *University of Cape Coast. Centre for Development Studies. Research Report Series. Papers. No.14)*

— **Italy.**

BENEDICTIS (MICHELE DE) Natura e contenuti dell'assistenza tecnica in relazione ai piani zonali. [Portici, 1970?]. pp. 8. *(Naples. Università. Centro di Specializzazione e Ricerche Economico-Agrarie per il Mezzogiorno. Estratti. n. 83) (Estratto dal quaderno Il Nostro Mezzogiorno, 1970)*

AGRICULTURAL GEOGRAPHY.

FERRO (GAETANO) Aspetti della geografia agraria: la ricomposizione fondiaria come strumento di pianificazione territoriale. Varese, [1966]. pp. 54. *Bound with VALLEGA (ADALBERTO) La media valle di Blenio.*

CLOUT (HUGH D.) Rural geography: an introductory survey. Oxford, 1972. pp. 204. *bibliogs.*

TARRANT (JOHN R.) Agricultural geography. Newton Abbot, [1974]. pp. 279.

— **Switzerland.**

VALLEGA (ADALBERTO) La media valle di Blenio: un'area di ricomposizione fondiaria. Varese, [1966]. pp. 79. *Bound with FERRO (GAETANO) Aspetti della geografia agraria.*

AGRICULTURAL INNOVATIONS.

PALMER (INGRID) Science and agricultural production. (UNRISD Reports. No.72.8). Geneva, United Nations Research Institute for Social Development, 1972. pp. 100. *(Studies on the Green Revolution. No.4)*

FOOD, population and employment: the impact of the green revolution: [papers from a workshop sponsored by Cornell University Program on Science, Technology and Society]; edited by Thomas T. Poleman and Donald K. Freebairn. New York, 1973. pp. 272.

— **Russia.**

SAGACH (MIKHAIL FEDOROVICH) Tekhnicheskii progress v sel'skom khoziaistve; pod redaktsiei... I.I. Martynenko. Kiev, 1973. pp. 230. *bibliog.*

AGRICULTURAL LABOURERS.

ONE WORLD ONLY, 1972. Social aspects in the participation of rural and agricultural manpower in development: an international forum under the auspices of the Friedrich-Ebert-Stiftung, Manila, 1972; (editor: Klaus Pretzer). Rizal, [1972]. pp. 279. *(Friedrich-Ebert-Stiftung. [Asian Labour Institute]. Reports. 7)*

SAVY (ROBERT) Social security in agriculture and rural areas. Geneva, International Labour Office, 1972. pp. 268. *bibliog. (Studies and Reports. New Series. No. 78)*

INTERNATIONAL LABOUR CONFERENCE. 59th Session. Reports. 6. Organisations of rural workers and their role in economic and social development: sixth item on the agenda. Geneva, 1973-74. 2 pts.

— **Mathematical models.**

GAUDE (JACQUES) Emploi agricole et migrations dans une économie dualiste. Genève, 1972. pp. 224. *(International Labour Office. Travaux et Recherches)*

— **Africa, Subsaharan.**

CLEAVE (JOHN H.) African farmers: labor use in the development of smallholder agriculture. New York, 1974. pp. 253. *bibliog.*

— **Australia.**

STEVENS (FRANK S.) Aborigines in the Northern Territory cattle industry. Canberra, 1974. pp. 226. *bibliog. (Academy of the Social Sciences in Australia. Aborigines in Australian Society. 11)*

— **Belgium.**

TAMBUYZER (C.) L'évolution régionale de l'agriculture en tant que secteur d'emploi. Bruxelles, 1973. pp. 47. *(Belgium. Institut Economique Agricole. Cahiers. No. 157)*

— **France.**

JEGOUZO (GUENHAEL) L'exode agricole: étude socio-économique. [Paris], 1972. pp. 36. *bibliog. (France. Direction de la Documentation. La Documentation Française. Notes et Etudes Documentaires. No. 3928)*

VINCIENNE (MONIQUE) Du village à la ville: le système de mobilité des agriculteurs. Paris, [1972]. pp. 358. *bibliog. (Paris. École Pratique des Hautes Études. Section des Sciences Economiques et Sociales. Recherches Coopératives. 7)*

— **Guatemala.**

SNEE (CAROLE A.) Current types of peasant-agricultural worker coalitions and their historical development in Guatemala. Cuernavaca, 1969. pp. 129. *bibliog. (Centro Intercultural de Documentacion. Cidoc Cuadernos. No. 31)*

AGRICULTURE.

— India — Gujarat.

BREMAN (JAN) Patronage and exploitation: changing agrarian relations in South Gujarat, India. Berkeley, [1974]. pp. 287. *bibliog.*

— — Punjab.

AGGARWAL (PARTAP C.) The green revolution and rural labour: a study of Ludhiana. New Delhi, [1973]. pp. 148. *bibliog.*

— Italy.

PRETI (LUIGI) Le lotte agrarie nella valle padana. Torino, 1955 repr. 1973. pp. 481.

BARBADORO (IDOMENEO) Storia del sindacalismo italiano dalla nascita al fascismo. Firenze, 1973. 2 vols. (in 1).

— Netherlands.

KLAVER (IMKE) Herinneringen van een friese landarbeider: enkele opgetekende zaken uit het jongste verleden tot 1925: inkele oanteikene dingen út de jonge tiid oan 1925; ingeleid door Ger Harmsen. Nijmegen, [1974]. pp. 245. *Parallel Frisian and Dutch texts.*

— Norway.

NORWAY. Budsjettnemnda for Jordbruket. 1970. Innstilling om prognose over arbeidsforbruket i jordbruket fram til 1980. [Oslo, 1970]. fo. 57.

ARBEIDSTID i jordbruket: utredning om revisjon av arbeidstidsbestemmelsene i lov av 19. desember 1958 om arbeidsvilkår i jordbruket; fra et utvalg oppnevnt... av 21. november 1968. Oslo, 1972. pp. 28. *(Norway. Norges Offentlige Utredninger. 1972.3)*

— Russia.

SHUMILOV (MIKHAIL NIKOLAEVICH) Oktiabr'skaia sotsialisticheskaia revoliutsiia i istoricheskie sud'by batrachestva. Moskva, 1967. pp. 231.

BULOCHNIKOVA (LIDIIA ANDREEVNA) Tekhnicheskii progress i ispol'zovanie rabochei sily v sel'skom khoziaistve. Moskva, 1973. pp. 135.

KARNAUKHOVA (EVFRAZIIA STEPANOVNA) Uchet zatrat obshchestvennogo truda: voprosy metodologii i opyt issledovaniia trudoemkosti proizvodstva sel'skokhoziaistvennykh produktov. Moskva, 1973. pp. 328.

— — Moldavian Republic.

KODITSA (N.) Ekonomicheskie problemy ispol'zovaniia trudovykh resursov v sel'skom khoziaistve Moldavii. Kishinev, 1973. pp. 183.

— — Ukraine.

VYBRYK (VIL' IVANOVYCH) Kvalifikovana robocha syla v kolhospakh: pytannia vidtvorennia. Kyïv, 1972. pp. 151.

KHYZHNIAK (VASYL' PETROVYCH) Komunistychne vykhovannia trudivnykiv sela: z dosvidu ideino- vykhovnoï roboty partiinykh orhanizatsii Ukraïny na seli v 1959-1970 rr. Kyïv, 1973. pp. 153. *bibliog.*

— South Africa.

AINSLIE (ROSALYNDE) Masters and serfs: farm labour in South Africa. London, 1973. pp. 55.

— Spain — Statistics.

SPAIN. Instituto Nacional de Estadistica. 1966. Primer censo agrario de España, octubre de 1962: el factor humano en las explotaciones agrarias. Madrid, 1966. pp. 196.

— Switzerland.

SWITZERLAND. Office Fédéral des Assurances Sociales. 1970. Allocations familiales aux travailleurs agricoles et aux petits paysans: recueil des dispositions en vigueur des barêmes et du commentaire au 1er janvier 1970. [Bern, 1970]. pp. 64.

— United Kingdom.

DUNBABIN (J.P.D.) Rural discontent in nineteenth-century Britain. London, 1974. pp. 320.

OXFORDSHIRE RECORD SOCIETY. [Oxfordshire Records Series]. vol. 48. Agricultural trade unionism in Oxfordshire, 1872-81; edited by Pamela Horn. [Oxford], 1974. pp. 144.

— — Scotland.

SMITH (J.H.) Historian. Joe Duncan: the Scottish farm servants and British agriculture. [Edinburgh, 1973]. pp. 254.

— United States.

PEREZ (JOSÉ G.) Viva la huelga'. the struggle of the farm workers. New York, [1973]. pp. 15.

STEIN (WALTER J.) California and the dust bowl migration. Westport, Conn., [1973]. pp. 302. *bibliog.*

AGRICULTURAL LAWS AND LEGISLATION

— France.

BASTID-BURDEAU (GENEVIEVE) La genèse de l'initiative législative: un cas: l'agriculture, 1958-1968. Paris, 1973. pp. 107. *bibliog. (Paris. Université de Paris II. Travaux et Recherches. Série Science Politique. 3)*

AGRICULTURAL MACHINERY

— Information services.

UNITED NATIONS INDUSTRIAL DEVELOPMENT ORGANIZATION. Guides to Information Sources. No. 8. Information sources on the agricultural implements and machinery industry. (UNIDO/LIB/SER.D/8). New York, United Nations, 1973. pp. 108. *bibliog.*

— Japan.

PAUER (ERICH) Technik, Wirtschaft, Gesellschaft: der Einfluss wirtschaftlicher und gesellschaftlicher Veränderungen auf die Entwicklung der landwirtschaftlichen Geräte in der vorindustriellen Epoche Japans ab dem 17.Jahrhundert. Wien, 1973. pp. 285. *bibliog. (Vienna. Universität. Institut für Japanologie. Beiträge zur Japanologie. Band 10) With English summary.*

AGRICULTURAL PRICE SUPPORTS

— Switzerland.

AUSGLEICHSZAHLUNGEN an die schweizerische Landwirtschaft: Bericht der vom EVD eingesetzten vorbereitenden Expertenkommission; [H. Popp, chairman]. Bern, 1973. pp. 197.

AGRICULTURAL PRICES

— Belgium.

BELGIUM. Institut Economique Agricole. Cahiers. Bruxelles, 1962 in progress.

BELGIUM. Institut Economique Agricole. Notes. Bruxelles, 1964 in progress.

AGRICULTURAL SOCIETIES

— France.

FRANCE. Direction de la Documentation. La Documentation Française. Notes et Etudes Documentaires. No. 3,780. Les formes nouvelles du commerce de détail en République fédérale d'Allemagne: "shopping centers", supermarchés, succursalisme; [by] Jean-Roger Schneider. Paris, 1971. pp. 14.

FRANCE. Direction de la Documentation. La Documentation Française. Notes et Etudes Documentaires. Nos, 3,785-3, 786. Les chambres d'agriculture; [by] François Houillier. Paris, 1971. pp. 71.

— Reunion Island.

PINARD (D.) La S.E.G.A.: Société d'Etudes et de Gestion pour l'Agriculture. [St. Denis], 1971. fo. 15. *(Réunion. [Secrétariat Général pour les Affaires Economiques. Documentation et Etudes]. Bulletin de Conjoncture. Supplément. No. 10)*

FAVAREL (G.) La S.A.F.E.R.: Société d'Aménagement Foncier et d'Etablissement Rural de la Réunion. [St. Denis], 1972. fo. 18. *(Réunion. [Secrétariat Général pour les Affaires Economiques. Documentation et Etudes]. Bulletin de Conjoncture. Supplément. No. 11)*

— Switzerland.

JAGGI (E.) Agricultural co-operatives and associations in Switzerland;... translated from the German by J.A.E. Morley. [London, 1974]. pp. 71. *(Horace Plunkett Foundation. Occasional Papers. No.40)*

AGRICULTURAL WAGES

— Netherlands — Statistics.

NETHERLANDS. Centraal Bureau voor de Statistiek. 1971. Statistiek der lonen in de landbouw 1964/65-1969/70. 's- Gravenhage, 1971. pp. 106.

— Russia.

VOLKOV (VLADIMIR FEDOROVICH) and MALAKHOV (ALEKSANDR KIRILLOVICH) Zarabotnaia plata i premirovanie rabotnikov sovkhozov. Moskva, 1967. pp. 183.

GARIPOV (KADIM NABIEVICH) Analiz ispol'zovaniia sredstv na oplatu truda v kolkhozakh i sovkhozakh. Moskva, 1973. pp. 144.

VORONTSOV (ALEKSEI PAVLOVICH) Proizvoditel'nost' truda i zarabotnaia plata v sovkhozakh. Moskva, 1973. pp. 231.

AGRICULTURE.

BERESFORD (TRISTRAM) Limits of efficiency: notes for a definition of efficiency in farming. Belfast, [1968]. pp. 15. *bibliog. (Belfast. Queen's University. George Scott Robertson Memorial Lectures. No. 18)*

KEMPER (MAX) Marxismus und Landwirtschaft; [reprint of work originally published in 1929]. Stuttgart, [1973]. pp. 117. *bibliog.*

KROPOTKIN (PETR ALEKSEEVICH) Prince. Fields, factories and workshops tomorrow; edited, introduced and with additional material by Colin Ward. London, 1974. pp. 205.

NATIONAL PLANNING ASSOCIATION. Reports. No.136. Feast or famine: the uncertain world of food and agriculture and its policy implications for the United States; by Willard W. Cochrane. Washington, [1974]. pp. 19.

— Economic aspects.

BELGIUM. Institut Economique Agricole. Cahiers. Bruxelles, 1962 in progress.

FOOD AND AGRICULTURE ORGANIZATION. Agriculture Planning Studies. Rome, 1963 in progress.

BELGIUM. Institut Economique Agricole. Notes. Bruxelles, 1964 in progress.

ITALY. Ministero degli Affari Esteri. Comitato per la Documentazione dell'Opera dell'Italia in Africa. L'Italia in Africa. Serie Economica-Agraria. Vol.1. L'avvaloramento e la colonizzazione. Tomo 1. L'opera di avvaloramento agricolo e zootecnico; testo di Armando Maugini. Roma, 1969. pp. 148. *bibliog.*

OSSERVATORIO DI ECONOMIA AGRARIA PER L'EUROPA. Indagine sulla politica agraria di struttura. Roma, 1970. pp. 443. *(Italy. Direzione Generale della Bonifica e della Colonizzazione. Studi e Ricerche sulla Bonifica e sullo Sviluppo)*

GOFFAUX (MARIE HENRIETTE) Problèmes d'actualité au Royaume-Uni en matière d'économie agricole. [Paris], Ministère de l'Agriculture, 1972. 2 vols. (in 1).

AGRICULTURE (Cont.)

GRIFFIN (KEITH) The green revolution: an economic analysis. (UNRISD Reports. No. 72.6). Geneva, United Nations Research Institute for Social Development, 1972. pp. 153. *(Studies on the Green Revolution. No.3)*

QUADEN (GUY) Parité pour l'agriculture et disparités entre agriculteurs: essai critique sur la politique des revenus agricoles. Liège, 1973. pp. 236. *bibliog. (Liège. Université. Faculté de Droit. Collection Scientifique. 35)*

— — Mathematical models.

RECHERCHES D'ECONOMIE ET DE SOCIOLOGIE RURALES; [pd. by] Institut National de la Recherche Agronomique [France]. irreg., 1967-1971 (nos.1-4); ceased pbln. Paris. *With summaries in English.*

THIRSK (WAYNE R.) Ease of factor substitution in agriculture. Houston, 1972. pp. 24. *(Rice University. Program of Development Studies. Papers. No. 34)*

ERICSON (OLLE) and others. Ekonomisk jord- och skogsbruksplan: modellstudier. Stockholm, 1973. 2 parts(in 1). *bibliog. (Jordbrukets Utredningsinstitut. Meddelanden. 1973. Nr. 2) With English summary.*

— History.

FLORES (XAVIER-ANDRÉ) Agricultural organisations and economic and social development in rural areas. Geneva, International Labour Office, 1971. pp. 586. *bibliog. (Studies and Reports. nEW sERIES. nO. 77)*

— Productivity — Mathematical models.

WARR (PETER) A subjective equilibrium theory of share tenancy. Cambridge, Mass., 1972. pp. 26. *bibliog. (Harvard University. Center for International Affairs. Economic Development Reports. No. 222)*

NATH (S.K.) Seasonal variation in agricultural activity and estimating the marginal product of labour. Coventry, 1973. pp. 30. *bibliog. (University of Warwick. Department of Economics. Warwick Economic Research Papers. No. 32)*

THIRSK (WAYNE R.) A note on Z goods, marketed surplus and the labor intensity of small farm agriculture. Houston, 1973. pp. 22. *(Rice University. Program of Development Studies. Papers. 40)*

— Statistics.

ORGANISATION FOR ECONOMIC CO-OPERATION AND DEVELOPMENT. Directorate for Agriculture. 1969. Statistiques agricoles; Agricultural statistics; 1955-1968. Paris, 1969. pp. 209. *In English and French.*

BLAKESLEE (LEROY L.) and others. World food production, demand, and trade. Ames, Iowa, 1973. pp. 417.

— Africa, East.

MORGAN (WILLIAM THOMAS WILSON) East Africa. London, 1973. pp. 410. *bibliogs.*

— Africa, North.

DUMONT (RENÉ) Notes sur les implications sociales de la révolution verte dans quelques pays d'Afrique; [edited by] Antonio Barreto. (UNRISD Reports. No.71.5) (UNRISD/71/C.92). Geneva, United Nations Research Institute for Social Development, 1971. pp. 166. *([Studies on the Green Revolution. No.1])*

— Africa, West.

DUMONT (RENÉ) Notes sur les implications sociales de la révolution verte dans quelques pays d'Afrique; [edited by] Antonio Barreto. (UNRISD Reports. No.71.5) (UNRISD/71/C.92). Geneva, United Nations Research Institute for Social Development, 1971. pp. 166. *([Studies on the Green Revolution. No.1])*

CONFERENCE ON FACTORS OF AGRICULTURAL GROWTH IN WEST AFRICA, LEGON, 1971. Factors of agricultural growth in West Africa; proceedings of an international conference;... edited by I.M. Ofori. Legon, 1973. pp. 291.

— Algeria.

DUPRAT (GERARD) Révolution et autogestion rurale en Algérie. Paris, 1973. pp. 486. *bibliog. (Fondation Nationale des Sciences Politiques. Cahiers. 189)*

— America, Latin.

INTER-AMERICAN COMMITTEE FOR AGRICULTURAL DEVELOPMENT. 1973. Agrarian structure in Latin America: a resume of the CIDA land tenure studies...; edited by Solon Barraclough...with Juan Carlos Collarte. Lexington, Mass., [1973]. pp. 351.

— — History.

INTERNATIONAL CONFERENCE OF ECONOMIC HISTORY, 4TH, BLOOMINGTON, 1968. Tierras nuevas: expansion territorial y ocupacion del suelo en America, siglos XVI-XIX; (ponencias presentadas al IV Congreso...); [edited by Alvaro Jara]. Mexico, 1969. pp. 138. *(Mexico City. Colegio de Mexico. Centro de Estudios Historicos. Nueva Serie. 7)*

— — Terminology.

SANTOS DE MORAIS (CLODOMIR) Diccionario de reforma agraria: latinoamerica. San Jośe, 1973. pp. 552. *bibliog.*

— Angola — History.

GUERRA (GUILHERME) Subsidios para o estudo da evolução historica da agricultura angolana. [Luanda, 1964]. pp. 38. *bibliog. Separata da revista Agronomia Angolana, n.°17, 1963.*

— Antigua.

REPORT on the sugar industry and agriculture of Antigua; [C.J.M. Bennett, chairman]. London, Ministry of Overseas Development, 1966. fo.105. *bibliog.*

— Argentine Republic — Tierra del Fuego — Statistics.

TIERRA DEL FUEGO [ARGENTINE REPUBLIC]. Direccion General de Estadistica y Census. 1966. Censo territorial de 1966: (poblacion, vivienda, agropecuario); decreto no. 323/65. [Ushuaia?, 1966?]. pp. 141.

— Asia.

SHAND (R.T.) ed, Technical change in Asian agriculture. Canberra, 1973. pp. 319. *bibliog.*

— — Bibliography.

COMMONWEALTH BUREAU OF AGRICULTURAL ECONOMICS. Annotated Bibliographies. Series C. [Oxford], 1973 in progress.

— — Productivity.

SYMPOSIUM ON CHANGES IN FOOD HABITS IN RELATION TO INCREASE OF PRODUCTIVITY, MANILA, 1972. Changes in food habits in relation to increase of productivity: report of the symposium held in Manila, August 22-28, 1972. [Tokyo], Asian Productivity Organization, 1973. pp. 370.

— Australia.

AUSTRALIA. Bureau of Agricultural Economics. 1971. Rural industry in Australia. Canberra, 1971. pp. 95.

DAVIDSON (B.R.) The northern myth: a study of the physical and economic limits to agricultural and pastoral development in tropical Australia. 3rd ed. Carlton, Va., 1972. pp. 298.

SHILTON (PETER) Urban influences on the agricultural areas of the central coast with particular reference to part-time farming. Armidale, N.S.W., 1973. pp. 192. *bibliog. (University of New England, Armidale. Department of Geography. Research Series in Applied Geography. No. 35)*

— Austria.

VIENNA. Kammer für Arbeiter und Angestellte. Wirtschaftswissenschaftliche Abteilung, und Wirtschaftspolitische Abteilung. Die Landwirtschaft in der Industriegesellschaft: eine Studie. Wien, [1969]. pp. 118. *(Schriftenreihe)*

— Bangladesh.

THOMAS (JOHN W.) Writer on Agriculture. Agricultural production, equity and rural organization in East Pakistan: preliminary draft for presentation to the Pakistan Rural Development Workshop, Michigan State University, July, 1971. [East Lansing, 1971?]. pp. 41.

— Belgium.

BELGIUM. Institut Economique Agricole. Cahiers. Bruxelles, 1962 in progress.

BELGIUM. Institut Economique Agricole. Notes. Bruxelles, 1964 in progress.

AGRICULTURE BELGE, L': aperçu succinct (formerly Aperçu succinct de l'agriculture belge); ([pd. by] Institut Economique Agricole, Ministère de l'Agriculture [Belgium]). a., 1969- Bruxelles. *(Notes de l'Institut Economique Agricole)*

— — Accounting.

RESULTATS provisoires des comptabilités agricoles pour l'exercice comptable 1971-1972, par W. Vertriest [and others]. Bruxelles, 1972. fo. 20. *(Belgium. Institut Economique Agricole. Notes. No. 31)*

— Borneo.

NORTH BORNEO. 1960. The development of the Keningau Plain. [Jesselton], 1960. pp. 7, 1 map. *(Legislative Council. Papers. 1960. No.6)*

— Brazil.

MARGOLIS (MAXINE L.) The moving frontier: social and economic change in a southern Brazilian community. Gainesville, 1973. pp. 275. *bibliog. (Florida University. School of Inter-American Studies. Latin American Monographs. 2nd Series. No. 11)*

PAIVA (RUY MILLER) and others. Brazil's agricultural sector: economic behavior, problems and possibilities; [prepared for the 15th International Conference of Agricultural Economists]. São Paulo, 1973. pp. 451.

— — Statistics.

FUNDAÇÃO GETULIO VARGAS. Centro de Estudos Agricolas. Salarios, preços de terras e serviços no meio rural, 1966 e 1967. [Rio de Janeiro, 1968]. pp. 48.

-Pernambuco.

ROSA E SILVA (JOSE MARCELINO DA) Subsidios para o estudo do problema agrario em Pernambuco. 1. A estrutura fundiaria por municipios e por zonas ecologicas e suas relações com o valor da produção agricola e o numero de habitantes. Recife, CODEPE, 1963. pp. 21, (74).

— — São Paulo.

SÃO PAULO (STATE). Instituto de Economia Agricola. 1973. Modernization of agriculture in the state of São Paulo. São Paulo, 1973. pp. 316.

— Canada — Prince Edward Island.

BRADLEY (L.F.) and BEAULIEU (ANDREE) Social and geographical aspects of agricultural land use in Prince Edward Island: a case study of the O'Leary area. Ottawa, 1973. pp. 32. *bibliog. (Canada. Lands Directorate. Geographical Papers. No. 54)*

— — Quebec.

MORRISSETTE (HUGUES) Les conditions du développement agricole au Québec. Québec, 1972. pp. 173. *bibliog. (Quebec. Université Laval. Département de Géographie. Travaux. 2)*

— China — History.

ENGELBORGHS-BERTELS (MARTHE) La Chine rurale: des villages aux communes populaires. Bruxelles,[1974]. pp. 195. *bibliog.*

— Colombia — Statistics.

COLOMBIA. Departamento Administrativo Nacional de Estadistica. Censo Agropecuario, 1970-71. Censo agropecuario, 1970-1971: datos preliminares. Bogota, 1971. 2 pts. (in 1 vol.).

AGRICULTURE (Cont.)

— — Antioquia.

ANTIOQUIA. Secretaria de Agricultura. 1970. Bases generales para el desarrollo de actividades agropecuarias en el Magdalena Medio. Medellin, 1970. fo. 144.

ANTIOQUIA. Secretaria de Agricultura. 1970. Bases para el desarrollo de actividades agropecuarias en el Bajo Cauca. Medellin, 1970. fo. 151.

— Costa Rica — Statistics.

COSTA RICA. Direccion General de Estadistica y Censos. Censo Agropecuario, 1973. Censos nacionales de 1973: agropecuario. [San Jose, 1973 in progress].

— Cyprus.

CYPRUS. Ministry of Agriculture and Natural Resources. 1970. Recent trends of agricultural production and productivity in Cyprus; by Rogiros Chr. Michaelides. Nicosia, 1970. pp. 13.

— Czechoslovakia.

IVANIČKA (KOLOMAN) ed. Problems of development of rural space economy: Problemy vyvoja ekonomiky ruralnej krajiny. Bratislava, 1971. pp. 231. *bibliogs.* *(Univerzita Komenskeho Bratislava. Acta Geographica Universitatis Comenianae. Economico-Geographica. Nr. 10)*

— Denmark.

DENMARK. Landøkonomiske Driftsbureau. 1972. Specialiserede driftsformer. København, 1972. pp. 88. *(Undersøgelser. 29)*

— — Productivity.

HANSEN (JENS) Produktivitetsudviklingen ved produktion af forskellige landbrugsprodukter. København, 1973. p. 54. *(Denmark. Landøkonomiske Driftsbureau. Memoranda. 5)*

— Ecuador — Statistics.

ECUADOR. Division de Estadistica y Censos. 1969. Encuesta agropecuaria nacional, 1968. Quito, 1969. pp. 87.

— Ethiopia.

WORLD LAND USE SURVEY. Occasional Papers. No. 11. Welenkomi: a socio-economic and nutritional survey of a rural community in the Central Highlands of Ethiopia; by Mesfin Wolde-Mariam [and others]. Berkhamsted, 1971. pp. 67. Map in end pocket.

— Europe.

ROESSING (RALF BERND) Die agrarpolitischen Konzeptionen der Schweiz, Grossbritanniens, der EWG und der USA. Bern, 1972. pp. 291. *bibliog.*

— — History.

CHERUBINI (GIOVANNI) Agricoltura e società rurale nel medioevo. Firenze, [1972]. pp. 124. *bibliog.*

ABEL (WILHELM) Massenarmut und Hungerkrisen im vorindustriellen Europa: Versuch einer Synopsis. Hamburg, 1974. pp. 427.

— European Economic Community countries.

FAURE (EDGAR) Exposé...[au] Congrès de la F.N.S.E.A.; Toulouse, le 23 février 1968. Paris, 1968. pp. 74. *(France. Ministère de l'Agriculture. Bulletin d'Information. Numéro Spécial)*

POELMANS (JACQUELINE) and LECOMTE (JACQUES) L'agriculture européenne et les pays tiers. Bruxelles, 1972. pp. 180. *bibliog. (Brussels. Université Libre. Institut d'Etudes Européennes. Thèses et Travaux Economiques. 7)*

EUROPEAN COMMUNITIES. Commission. Situation de l'agriculture dans la Communauté élargie. a., 1973 [1st]- Bruxelles.

CHIAROMONTE (GERARDO) and others. Agricoltura, Mercato comune e regioni. *Roma, 1973. pp. 136.*

CLERC (FRANÇOIS) Ingénieur agronome. Le Marché commun agricole. 5th ed. Paris, 1973. pp. 128. *bibliog.*

EUROPEAN COMMUNITIES. Commission. 1973. Improvement of the common agricultural policy: Commission communication to the Council, 5 November 1973. [Brussels], 1973. pp. 23. *(Bulletin of the European Communities. Supplements. [1973/17]).*

FENNELL (ROSEMARY) The common agricultural policy: a synthesis of opinion. Wye, 1973. pp. 106. *bibliog. (London. University. Wye College. Centre for European Agricultural Studies. Reports. No. 1)*

JOSLING (TIMOTHY EDWARD) The common agricultural policy; (transcript of... lecture held on 31 January 1972). [London], Civil Service College, [1973?]. fo. 20. *(Lectures on the European Community. Series A. No. 4)*

LE ROY (PIERRE) of the Institut d'Etudes Politiques de Paris. L'avenir du Marché commun agricole. [Paris], 1973. pp. 188. *bibliog.*

STEFANO (FRANCESCO DE) Nixon-round e agricoltura comunitaria. [Portici, 1973]. pp. 51-55. *(Naples Università. Centro di Specializzazione e Ricerche Economico-Agrarie per il Mezzogiorno. Estratti. n. 123) (Estratto da Politica Agraria, anno xx,n.3)*

THIEDE (GUENTHER) La produzione agricola nella CEE: localizzazione regionale e tendenze evolutive. Bologna, [1973]. pp. 129. *(Istituto Nazionale di Economia Agraria and Istituto per la Scienza dell'Amministrazione Pubblica. Agricoltura e Regioni.8)*

FRANCE. Direction de la Documentation. La Documentation Française. Notes et Etudes Documentaires. Nos. 4,061-4, 062-4,063. L'Europe agricole et l'élargissement du Marché Commun; par Marc Konczaty et Daniel Merten. [Paris], 1974. pp. 107. *bibliog.*

— — Bibliography.

COMMONWEALTH BUREAU OF AGRICULTURAL ECONOMICS. EEC agricultural policy. Pt. 3. International trade; compiled by Jean Kestner. [Oxford], 1973. pp. 23. *(Annotated Bibliographies. No.16) Compiled from World Agricultural Economics and Rural Sociology Abstracts.*

NEVILLE-ROLFE (EDMUND) Food and agriculture in the Common Market: political and economic aspects; a selective reading list of publications in the Six member countries of the European Economic Community between 1967 and 1972, with a commentary. Oxford, 1973. pp. 157.

— Finland — Statistics.

FINLAND. Suomen Virallinen Tilasto. Finlands Officiella Statistik. 3. Maatalous. 66. Yleinen maatalouslaskenta 1969 etc. Helsinki, 1970-1971. 3 vols. (in 1)

— France.

RECHERCHES D'ECONOMIE ET DE SOCIOLOGIE RURALES; [pd. by] Institut National de la Recherche Agronomique [France]. irreg., 1967-1971 (nos.1-4); ceased pbln. Paris. *With summaries in English.*

FRANCE. Ministère de l'Agriculture. Direction Départementale de l'Agriculture du Doubs. 1971. Contribution à l'étude du schéma directeur d'aménagement et d'urbanisme de Besançon. Besançon, 1971. pp. 108.

FRANCE. Direction de la Documentation. La Documentation Française. Notes et Etudes Documentaires. No. 4,033. La conférence annuelle agricole. [Paris], 1973. pp. 33. *bibliog.*

PICCHI (ANTONIO) Le regioni e l'agricoltura in Francia. Bologna, [1973]. pp. 82. *(Istituto Nazionale di Economia Agraria and Istituto per la Scienza dell'amministrazione Pubblica. Agricoltura e Regioni. 10)*

QUELLE agriculture pour la France?: crise agraire et solutions démocratiques; ([by] Ferand Clavaud [and others]) . Paris, [1974]. pp. 221.

— — History.

ASSOCIATION FRANÇAISE DES HISTORIENS ECONOMISTES. Congrès National, 1er, 1969. Les fluctuations du produit de la dîme: conjoncture décimale et domaniale de la fin du moyen âge au XVIIIe siècle; communications et travaux rassemblés et présentés par Joseph Goy et Emmanuel Le Roy Ladurie. Paris, 1972. pp. 397. *(Paris. Ecole Pratique des Hautes Etudes. Section des Sciences Economiques et Sociales. Centre de Recherches Historiques. Cahiers des Etudes Rurales.3)*

HOUEE (PAUL) Les étapes du développement rural. Paris, [1972]. 2 vols.

LE ROY LADURIE (EMMANUEL) Le territoire de l'historien. [Paris, 1973]. pp. 544.

POSTEL-VINAY (GILLES) La rente foncière dans le capitalisme agricole: analyse de la voie "classique" du développement du capitalisme dans l'agriculture à partir de l'exemple du soissonnais. Paris, 1974. pp. 286. *bibliog.*

— — Statistics.

FRANCE. Ministère de l'Agriculture et du Développement Rural. Service Central des Enquêtes et Etudes Statistiques. 1972. Recensement général de l'agriculture, 1970-1971: résultats France entière. Paris, 1972. 7 vols. (in 2).

— Germany.

GERMANY (BUNDESREPUBLIK). Bundesministerium für Ernährung, Landwirtschaft und Forsten. Ertragslage des Garten- und Weinbaues. a., 1973- Bonn.

FORSCHUNGSGESELLSCHAFT FÜR AGRARPOLITIK UND AGRARSOZIOLOGIE. Forschungsstelle. Strukturwandel und Strukturpolitik: Beiträge zur agrarischen und regionalen Entwicklung in der Bundesrepublik Deutschland; ... (Heinrich Niehaus ...zum 75.Geburtstag...zugeeignet). Bonn, 1973. pp. 271. *bibliogs.*

OTZEN (HANS) Der Agrarexport der Bundesrepublik Deutschland. Hamburg, 1974. pp. 115. *bibliog.*

— — History.

MEITZEN (AUGUST) Georg Hanssen als Agrar-Historiker. [Tübingen, 1881]. pp. 47. *(Separatabzug aus der Zeitschrift für die gesamte Staatswissenschaft)*

KLEIN (ERNST) Geschichte der deutschen Landwirtschaft im Industriezeitalter. Wiesbaden, 1973. pp. 192. *bibliog.*

— — Mathematical models.

STRUFF (RICHARD) Dimensionen der wirtschaftsräumlichen Entwicklung: Abgrenzung von Gebietstypen zur regionalen und sektoralen Einkommensanalyse in der Bundesrepublik Deutschland. Bonn, 1973. pp. 279. *bibliog. (Forschungsgesellschaft für Agrarpolitik und Agrarsoziologie. [Publications]. 218)*

— — Statistics.

DENNUKAT (GERHARD) and HASSKAMP (HEINRICH) Census of agriculture, 1971. Stuttgart, 1972. pp. 12. *(Germany (Bundesrepublik). Statistisches Bundesamt. Studies on Statistics. No. 26)*

— Ghana.

THORNTON (D.S.) and others. Agriculture in south-east Ghana;...report[s] of the Reading/Legon Joint Research Project in Village Development, south-east Ghana. [Reading], 1973. 2 vols. (in 1). *bibliogs. (Reading. University. Department of Agricultural Economics and Management. Development Studies. Nos. 12 and 13)*

— Hungary.

FISCHER (LEWIS ANTHONY) and UREN (PHILIP ERNEST) The new Hungarian agriculture. Montreal, 1973. pp. 138. *bibliog.*

AGRICULTURE (Cont.)

— India.

INDIA. Department of Agriculture. Expert Committee on Assessment and Evaluation of the Intensive Agricultural District Programme. 1969-71. Modernising Indian agriculture: (fourth) report on the intensive agricultural district programme, 1960-68. [New Delhi, 1969-71]. 2 vols.(in 1).

DASGUPTA (AJIT K.) Agriculture and economic development in India. New Delhi, [1973]. pp. 117.

SHARMA (PREM S.) Agricultural regionalisation of India. Delhi, 1973. pp. 190. *bibliog.*

BHARADWAJ (KRISHNA) Production conditions in Indian agriculture: a study based on farm management surveys. Cambridge, 1974. pp. 128. *bibliog. (Cambridge. University. Department of Applied Economics. Occasional Papers. 33)*

— — Accounting.

MAJUMDAR (A.G.) Distribution of agricultural income arising from crop production in India 1960-61 and 1970-71. New Delhi, [1973]. pp. 108. *(Economic and Scientific Research Foundation. Monographs. 4)*

— — Productivity — Mathematical models.

EVENSON (ROBERT EUGENE) Labor in the Indian agriculture sector. [New Haven], 1972. pp. 53. *bibliog.*

— — Statistics.

INDIAN AGRICULTURE IN BRIEF; [pd. by] Directorate of Economics and Statistics, Ministry of Agriculture [India].irreg., Ja 1970 (10th ed.)- New Delhi.

— — Andhra Pradesh.

NARAYANA (D.L.) and others. Studies in the economics of farm management in Cuddapah district (Andhra Pradesh): report[s] for the year[s] 1967-68, 1968-69. [Delhi, Controller of Publications, 1973]. 2 vols. (in 1).

— — Kerala.

PILLAI (VELU PILLAI RAMAN) and PANIKAR (PUTHENVEETIL GOVINDA KESAVA) Studies in the economics of farm management in Kerala: report for year 1964-65. [Delhi, Manager of Publications, 1972]. pp. 448.

— — Madhya Pradesh.

PATEL (M.L.) Agro-economic survey of tribal Mandla. Delhi, 1969. pp. 135.

AZARIAH (H.S.) and ATHAVALE (M.C.) Studies in economics of farm management in Raipur (Madhya Pradesh): combined report for the years 1962-63 to 1964-65. Delhi, Manager of Publications], 1972 [or rather 1973]. pp. 95.

— — Madras.

RAJU (A.) and SUBRAMANIAN (R.) Village production plan in the Athoor Panchayat Union, Madurai district, Madras: a study. Gandhigram, 1964. pp. 37.

— — Mysore.

FOLKE (STEEN) and others. An evaluation of the Danish Mysore project: an Indo- Danish agricultural-educational scheme. Copenhagen, Mellemfolkeligt Samvirke, 1969. pp. 255. *bibliog.*

REGIONAL FARM MANAGEMENT RESEARCH CENTRE [BANGALORE]. Studies in the economics of farm management: Bangalore district (Mysore): report[s] for the year[s] 1960-61 [and] 1961-62. [Delhi, Manager of Publications, 1972]. 2 pts.

— — Orissa.

MISRA (B.) Studies in the economics of farm management in Cuttack district (Orissa): report[s] for the year[s] 1967-68, 1968-69, 1969-70. [Delhi, Controller of Publications, 1973]. 3 vols. (in 1).

— — Punjab.

AGGARWAL (PARTAP C.) The green revolution and rural labour: a study of Ludhiana. New Delhi, [1973]. pp. 148. *bibliog.*

KAHLON (A.S.) and others. Studies in economics of farm management, Ferozepur district (Punjab): report[s] for the year[s] 1967-68, 1968-69, 1969-70. [Delhi, Controller of Publications, 1973]. 3 vols. (in 2).

— — Uttar Pradesh.

LAVANIA (GAURI SHANKER) Studies in the economics of farm management in Deoria district (Uttar Pradesh): report[s] for the year[s] 1966-67, 1967-68, 1968-69. [Delhi, Controller of Publications, 1973]. 3 vols. (in 2).

SINGH (ROSHAN) and SINGH (RANBIR) Studies in economics of farm management in Uttar Pradesh (Muzaffarnagar District): report for the year 1966-67. [Delhi, Manager of Publications, 1972]. pp. 548.

— — — Taxation.

DWIVEDI (D.N.) Problems and prospects of agricultural taxation in Uttar Pradesh.New Delhi, 1973. pp. 228.

— Ireland (Republic).

IRISH FARMERS' ASSOCIATION. People and the land. Dublin, 1972. pp. 143.

— Israel — Statistics.

ISRAEL. Central Bureau of Statistics. Census of Agriculture, 1971. Census of agriculture, 1971. Jerusalem, 1972 in progress. *In English and Hebrew.*

— Italy.

COTTONE (ELVIRA) ed. Riorganizzazione capitalistica e lotta di classe nelle campagne. Roma, [1972]. pp. 126.

MARCIANI (GIOVANNI ENRICO) Andamenti e linee evolutive delle produzioni agricole, 1951-1981. Milano, 1972. pp. 485. *(Associazione per lo Sviluppo dell'Industria nel Mezzogiorno. Centro per gli Studi sullo Sviluppo Economico. Collana di Monografie)*

BOLAFFI (GUIDO) and VAROTTI (ADRIANO) Agricoltura capitalistica e classi sociali in Italia, 1948-1970. Bari, [1973]. pp. 323. *bibliog.*

CHIAROMONTE (GERARDO) Agricoltura, sviluppo economico, democrazia: la politica agraria e contadina dei comunisti, 1965-1972. Bari, [1973]. pp. 370.

CHIAROMONTE (GERARDO) and others. Agricoltura, Mercato comune e regioni. **Roma, 1973. pp. 136.**

CONTINI (BRUNO) and PACI (MASSIMO) Difesa del suolo e sviluppo dell'agricoltura: un'analisi di sistemi applicata al Polesine. Bologna, [1973]. pp. 343. *bibliog.*

— — History.

PRETI (LUIGI) Le lotte agrarie nella valle padana. Torino, 1955 repr. 1973. pp. 481.

— — Statistics.

ITALY. Instituto Centrale di Statistica. Censimento Generale dell'Agricoltura, 1970. 2 censimento generale dell'agricoltura, 25 ottobre 1970. Roma, 1971 in progress.

— — Lombardy — History.

ASPETTI di vita agricola lombarda, secoli XVI-XIX. Milano, 1973. pp. 307. *(Milan. Università Cattolica del Sacro Cuore. Istituto di Storia Economica e Sociale. Contributi. vol. 1)*

— — Piedmont — History.

ROTELLI (CLAUDIO) Una campagna medievale: storia agraria del Piemonte fra il 1250 e il 1450. Torino, [1973]. pp. 378.

— Ivory Coast.

ANCEY (G.) Exploitations agricoles en pays Diamala - Djimini: aspects de la vie rurale. [Abidjan], 1969. pp. 177. *(France. Office de la Recherche Scientifique et Technique Outre-Mer. Sciences Humaines. Vol. 2. No. 6)*

— Jamaica.

YALLAHS VALLEY LAND AUTHORITY. Yallahs Valley Land Authority, 1951-1966: 15th anniversary brochure. [Kingston?, 1966?]. pp. 52.

— Japan — History.

PAUER (ERICH) Technik, Wirtschaft, Gesellschaft: der Einfluss wirtschaftlicher und gesellschaftlicher Veränderungen auf die Entwicklung der landwirtschaftlichen Geräte in der vorindustriellen Epoche Japans ab dem 17.Jahrhundert. Wien, 1973. pp. 285. *bibliog. (Vienna. Universität. Institut für Japanologie. Beiträge zur Japanologie. Band 10) With English summary.*

— Jordan — Statistics.

AGRICULTURAL SAMPLE SURVEY IN THE GHORS; ([pd. by] Department of Statistics... Jordan). a., 1972, 1973. Amman. *In English and Arabic.*

— Kenya.

FORDHAM (PAUL) Rural development in the Kenya highlands: a report of geographical field work carried out during August 1971. Nottingham, [1973]. pp. 122. *(Nottingham. University. Department of Geography. Geographical Field Group. Regional Studies. No.17)*

ODERO-OGWEL (LAWI) and CLAYTON (ERIC S.) A regional programming approach to agricultural sector analysis: an application to Kenya agriculture. Ashford, Kent, 1973. pp. 88. *(London. University. Wye College. School of Rural Economics and Related Studies. Agrarian Development Studies. Reports. No. 5)*

— Libya — Tripolitania — Statistics.

TRIPOLITANIA. Nazirate of Agriculture and Forests. Statistics Division. 1960. Agricultural statistics estimates for Tripolitania, 1950-1959. [Tripoli], 1960. fo.7,8. *In English and Arabic.*

— Madagascar.

ROUVEYRAN (JEAN CLAUDE) La logique des agricultures de transition: l'exemple des sociétés paysannes malgaches. [Tananarive], 1972. pp. 277. *bibliog.*

— Malawi — Statistics.

MALAWI. National Statistical Office. 1970. National sample survey of agriculture, 1968/69 (customary land in rural areas only). [Zomba], 1970. pp. 172,13.

— Netherlands.

NETHERLANDS. Ministerie van Landbouw en Visserij. Foreign Information Service. 1968. Agriculture in the Netherlands. The Hague, 1968. pp. 87. *Map in end-pocket.*

BERKEL (TH. L. VAN) Midden-Maasland: Sociaal-economische schets van een ruilverkavelingsgebied in de omgeving van Oss. [Den Haag], Landbouw-Economisch Instituut, 1970. pp. 122. *Map in end-pocket.*

— — History.

BAARS (C.) De geschiedenis van de landbouw in de Beijerlanden. Wageningen, 1973. pp. 234. *bibliog. (Centrum voor Landbouwpublikaties en Landbouwdocumentatie. Verslagen van Landbouwkundige Onderzoekingen. 801) With English summary.*

BOERENGROEP WAGENINGEN. Agri-business of binnenlandse kolonie II: (sociaal-ekonomische positie van de boer; landbouw en milieu). Wageningen, [1974]. pp. 133.

BOERENGROEP WAGENINGEN. Over boeren, bazen en banken: de maatschappelijke positie van de boer in historisch perspektief. Wageningen, [1974]. pp. 77.

DE VRIES (JAN) The Dutch rural economy in the golden age, 1500-1700. New Haven, Conn., 1974. pp. 316. *bibliog.*

— — Statistics.

NETHERLANDS. Centraal Bureau voor de Statistiek. 1972. Landbouwtelling 1970. 's-Gravenhage, 1972. 2 vols. (in 1). *With English summary.*

AGRICULTURE (Cont.)

— Nigeria.

NIGERIAN ECONOMIC SOCIETY. Annual Conference, 1972. Rural development in Nigeria: proceedings, etc. Ibadan, [1973]. pp. 300.

OKURUME (GODWIN E.) Foreign trade and the subsistence sector in Nigeria: the impact of agricultural exports on domestic food supplies in a peasant economy. New York, 1973. pp. 136. *bibliog.*

— Norway.

NORWAY. Budsjettnemnda for Jordbruket. 1970. Innstilling om prognose over arbeidsforbruket i jordbruket fram til 1980. [Oslo, 1970]. fo. 57.

NORWAY. Statistiske Centralbyrå. 1973. Driftsformer i jordbruket. Oslo, 1973. pp. 94. *(Statistiske Analyser. 7) With English summary.*

— — History.

NORDGÅRD (ASBJØRN) Jordbruk i kontraksjon og spesialisering: en studie...i 125 kommuner på Østlandet, 1929-1959. Oslo, [1972]. pp. 232. *bibliog. With summary and table of contents in English.*

— Peru.

STEIN (WILLIAM W.) Changing Vicos agriculture. Buffalo, N.Y., 1972. fo. 69,iv. *(New York State University. Council on International Studies. Special Studies. No. 15)*

— Portugal.

PORTUGAL. Secretaria de Estado da Agricultura. 1960-64. A agricultura e o II plano de fomento: ciclo de conferências [1959-1963]. vols. 1-2, 4-5. [Lisbon], 1960-64. 4 vols. (in 2).

— Roumania.

CONSTANTINESCU (OLGA) Critica teoriei "România ţară eminamente agricolă". Bucureşti, 1973. pp. 323. *bibliog. (Academia de Ştiinţe Sociale şi Politice a Republicii Socialiste România. Institutul de Cercetări Economice. Bibliotheca Oeconomica. 26). With English, French and Russian tables of contents.*

— Russia.

L-N (DM.) pseud. Kul'turnaia pomoshch' derevne. Moskva, 1917. pp. 30.

LAPKES (IAKOV BENTSIANOVICH) Intensifikatsiia sel'skogo khoziaistva i sistemy zemledeliia. Moskva, 1964. pp. 239.

SEL'SKOE khoziaistvo SSSR: tsifry i fakty. Moskva, 1972. pp. 155.

AHRARNA polityka KPRS na suchasnomu etapi. Kyïv, 1973. pp. 190.

BARBASHIN (ANATOLII IVANOVICH) Ekonomicheskoe obosnovanie i organizatsionnye formy spetsializatsii sel'skogo khoziaistva. Moskva, 1973. pp. 199.

BELOV (MIKHAIL IVANOVICH) Mezhotraslevye balansy sel'skogo khoziaistva soiuznoi respubliki. Moskva, 1973. pp. 127.

PERSHIN (PAVEL NIKOLAEVICH) Narysy ahrarnykh problem budivnytstva sotsializmu. Kyïv, 1973. pp. 339.

ROGACHEV (SERGEI VLADIMIROVICH) Ekonomicheskie zakony i razvitie sel'skogo khoziaistva. Moskva, 1973. pp. 231.

— — Accounting.

KOSTIUK (POLIKARP ALEKSANDROVICH) Bukhgalterskii uchet v sel'skokhoziaistvennykh predpriatiiakh. 2nd ed. Minsk, 1973. pp. 256.

— — History.

GUROV (PETR IAKOVLEVICH) and GONCHAROV (ALEKSANDR DMITRIEVICH) Leninskaia agrarnaia politika. Moskva, 1973. pp. 190.

NIL'VE (ANNA IL'INICHNA) Bor'ba V.I. Lenina s revizionizmom v agrarnom voprose i ee mezhdunarodnoe znachenie; pod redaktsiei E.L. Boginoi. Moskva, 1973. pp. 147.

PUTSKOVA (ZOIA STEPANOVNA) Deiatel'nost' partiinykh organizatsii avtonomnykh respublik Srednego Povolzh'ia po razvitiiu material'no-tekhnicheskoi bazy sel'skogo khoziaistva v poslevoennyi period. Kazan', 1973. pp. 152.

SCHEIBERT (PETER) Die russische Agrarreform von 1861: ihre Probleme und der Stand ihrer Erforschung. Köln, 1973. pp. 195. *bibliog.*

— — Mathematical models.

ONISHCHENKO (ALEKSEI MOISEEVICH) Spetsializatsiia sel'sko-khoziaistvennogo proizvodstva: metodologicheskie problemy optimizatsii. Kiev, 1973. pp. 292.

— — Productivity.

KARNAUKHOVA (EVFRAZIIA STEPANOVNA) Uchet zatrat obshchestvennogo truda: voprosy metodologii i opyt issledovaniia trudoemkosti proizvodstva sel'skokhoziaistvennykh produktov. Moskva, 1973. pp. 328.

PANKOVA (KLARA IVANOVNA) Voprosy intensifikatsii i ekonomicheskogo stimulirovaniia proizvodstva v sovkhozakh. Moskva, 1973. pp. 126.

VORONTSOV (ALEKSEI PAVLOVICH) Proizvoditel'nost' truda i zarabotnaia plata v sovkhozakh. Moskva, 1973. pp. 231.

MASHENKOV (VLADIMIR FEDOROVICH) Proizvoditel'nost' truda v sel'skom khoziaistve. Moskva, 1974. pp. 223.

— — Statistics.

PESTRZHETSKII (D.I.) Okolo zemli; iz kursa lektsii sel'sko-khoziaistvennoi statistiki, chitannogo v 1921/2 gg. v Politekhnikume v Viunsdorfe bliz Berlina (Y.M.C.A.). Berlin, 1922. pp. 135.

— — Armenia.

ARUTIUNIAN (LUSANDR MKRTICHEVICH) Sotsial'no-ekonomicheskie izmeneniia v derevne Armianskoi SSR. Erevan, 1973. pp. 303.

— — Latvia — Mathematical models.

AKADEMIIA NAUK LATVIISKOI SSR. Institut Ekonomiki. Matematicheskie Metody v Ekonomike. vyp.11. Voprosy sozdaniia avtomatizirovannykh sistem planirovaniia v sel'skom khoziaistve. Riga, 1973. pp. 115.

— — Lithuania.

KEZYS (ALEKSANDRAS) Agriculture in Lithuania. Vilnius, 1973. pp. 92.

— — Russia (RSFSR).

RUSSIA (RSFSR). Gosudarstvennyi Planovyi Komitet. 1973. Metodicheskie ukazaniia po planirovaniiu sel'skogo khoziaistva RSFSR. Moskva, 1973. pp. 375.

— — Ukraine — History.

TELYCHUK (PAVLO PETROVYCH) Ekonomichni osnovy ahrarnoï revoliutsiï na Ukraïni. Kyïv, 1973. pp. 189.

— — — Productivity.

LUSHCH (HANNA IVANIVNA) Intensyfikatsiia kolhospnoho vyrobnytstva: pytannia vymiru ta analizu. Kyïv, 1972. pp. 144. *With Russian summary and table of contents.*

HORODNII (VOLODYMYR VASYL'OVYCH) Hosprozrakhunok i material'ne stymuliuvannia u kolhospakh. Kyïv, 1973. pp. 112.

— Senegal.

ROCH (JEAN) Eléments d'analyse du système agricole en milieu wolof mouride: l'exemple de Darou Rahmane II. [Dakar], Office de la Recherche Scientifique et Technique Outre-Mer, Centre de Dakar-Hann, 1968. fo. 56. *bibliog.*

— South Africa.

BOARD (CHRISTOPHER) A sample survey to assess the effect on Bantu agriculture of the rehabilitation programme. Johannesburg, 1964. pp. 229-235. *(From South African Journal of Science, vol. 60, no.8)*

— — Natal.

GREYLING (JACOB JOHANNES CAROLUS) and DAVIES (RONALD JOHN) Indian agricultural holdings on the Natal North Coast. Report 1. Land-subdivision, land-ownership and land-occupation. Natal, Town and Regional Planning Commission, 1970. 3 vols. *bibliog. Vol. 3 is Atlas.*

— Sweden.

SWEDEN. Jordbruksdepartementet. Utredningen om Stöd till Jordbruket i Norra Sverige. 1970. Jordbruket i norra Sverige. Stockholm, 1970. pp. 123. *(Sweden. Statens Offentliga Utredningar. 1970.72)*

ERICSON (OLLE) and others. Ekonomisk jord- och skogsbruksplan: modellstudier. Stockholm, 1973. 2 parts(in 1). *bibliog. (Jordbrukets Utredningsinstitut. Meddelanden. 1973. Nr. 2) With English summary.*

— — Taxation.

SWEDEN. Finansdepartementet. Jordbruksbeskattningskommittén. 1971. Jordbruksbeskattningen. Stockholm, 1971. pp. 203. *(Sweden. Statens Offentliga Utredningar. 1971. 78)*

— — Skaraborg — History.

HERLITZ (LARS) Jordegendom och ränta: omfördelningen av jordbrukets merprodukt i Skaraborgs län under frihetstiden. Lund, 1974. pp. 387. *bibliog. (Göteborgs Universitet. Ekonomisk-Historiska Institutionen. Meddelanden. 31) With English summary.*

— Switzerland.

SOZIALDEMOKRATISCHE PARTEI DER SCHWEIZ. Ein Wort an die schweiz. Landwirtschaft: zu den Nationalratswahlen im Oktober 1919. n.p., [1919]. 1 pamphlet (unpaged).

— Tanzania.

CONYERS (D.) Agro-economic zones of Tanzania. [Dar es Salaam], 1973. pp. 85. *(Dar es Salaam. University. Bureau of Resource Assessment and Land Use Planning. Research Papers. No. 25)*

— Tropics.

HASWELL (MARGARET ROSARY) Tropical farming economics. London, 1973. pp. 174. *bibliog.*

— Uganda — Buganda.

RICHARDS (AUDREY ISABEL) and others, eds. Subsistence to commercial farming in present-day Buganda: an economic and anthropological study. Cambridge, 1973. pp. 336. *bibliog.*

— Underdeveloped areas.

See UNDERDEVELOPED AREAS — Agriculture.

— United Kingdom.

ECONOMIC change and agriculture: [papers presented at a conference, "Agriculture '67", organized by the Agricultural Adjustment Unit, University of Newcastle upon Tyne]; edited by J. Ashton and S.J. Rogers. Edinburgh, 1967. pp. 360.

NORTHERN ECONOMIC PLANNING COUNCIL. Challenge of the changing north: agriculture, horticulture, forestry and fishing. [Newcastle], 1967. pp. 71. *Xerox copy.*

AGRICULTURE (Cont.)

DAVEY (BRIAN HUMPHREY) Agriculture in the United Kingdom: current developments and future directions. Newcastle upon Tyne, 1972. pp. 37. *bibliog.* (*Newcastle-upon-Tyne. University. Department of Agricultural Economics. Agricultural Adjustment Unit. Bulletins. No. 17*)

GOFFAUX (MARIE HENRIETTE) Problèmes d'actualité au Royaume-Uni en matière d'économie agricole. [Paris], Ministère de l'Agriculture, 1972. 2 vols. (in 1).

AGRICULTURAL DEVELOPMENT AND ADVISORY SERVICE [U.K.]. Agriculture in the urban fringe: a survey of the Slough/Hillingdon area. [London], 1973. pp. 24. (*Technical Reports. 30*)

ECONOMIC DEVELOPMENT COMMITTEE FOR THE AGRICULTURAL INDUSTRY. Common Market Sub-Committee. Problem Areas Working Group. UK farming and the Common Market: hills and uplands; a report. London, National Economic Development Office, 1973. pp. 39.

— — **Accounting.**

U.K. Ministry of Agriculture, Fisheries and Food. Agricultural Land Service. Technical Reports. 25. An enquiry into the expenses of agricultural land ownership, England and Wales, 1967-68. [London], 1970. pp. 29.

LONDON. University. Wye College. School of Rural Economics and Related Studies. Farm business statistics for South East England: supplement for 1974. [Ashford, 1974]. pp. 52.

READING. University. Department of Agricultural Economics and Management. Farm business data. Reading, 1974. pp. 47.

— — **History.**

HAVINDEN (MICHAEL ASHLEY) ed. Husbandry and marketing in the South-West, 1500-1800. Exeter, 1973. pp. 74. (*Exeter. University. Department of Economic History. Exeter Papers in Economic History. No. 8*)

PERRY (P.J.) British farming in the great depression, 1870-1914: an historical geography. Newton Abbot, [1974]. pp. 208. *bibliog.*

RAVENSDALE (J.R.) Liable to floods: village landscape on the edge of the fens, AD 450-1850. London, 1974. pp. 206. *bibliog.*

— — **Hampshire.**

SOUTH HAMPSHIRE PLAN ADVISORY COMMITTEE. Study Reports. Group A. Rural Conservation. No. 1. Agriculture and horticulture. [Winchester, 1970]. pp. 34,x.

— — **Lincolnshire — History.**

BECKWITH (IAN STANLEY) The history of fields and farms in Gainsborough. [Gainsborough, 1973]. pp. 51.

— — **Ireland, Northern.**

YOUNG (JAMES ALEXANDER) Agricultural progress and future trends in Northern Ireland. [Belfast, 1972]. pp. 36. (*Belfast. Queen's University. George Scott Robertson Memorial Lectures. No. 22*)

— — **Taxation.**

IRELAND, NORTHERN. Ministry of Agriculture. 1973. Value added tax and the farmer: booklet of instructions on VAT. Belfast, 1973. pp. 6.

— — **Scotland — Accounting.**

EDINBURGH. Edinburgh School of Agriculture. Economics Department. Bulletins. [New Series]. No. 7. Profitability of farming in south-east Scotland, 1971-72. Edinburgh, 1973. pp. 70.

— **United States.**

ROESSING (RALF BERND) Die agrarpolitischen Konzeptionen der Schweiz, Grossbritanniens, der EWG und der USA. Bern, 1972. pp. 291. *bibliog.*

NATIONAL PLANNING ASSOCIATION. Reports. No.136. Feast or famine: the uncertain world of food and agriculture and its policy implications for the United States; by Willard W. Cochrane. Washington, [1974]. pp. 19.

— — **New Jersey — History.**

SCHMIDT (HUBERT G.) Agriculture in New Jersey: a three-hundred-year history. New Brunswick, [1973]. pp. 335. *bibliog.*

— **Uruguay — Statistics.**

INTER-AMERICAN INSTITUTE OF AGRICULTURAL SCIENCES. 1968. Curso de capacitacion en elaboracion de projectos de subdivision de tierras (1968-69): parte práctica; projecto de desarrollo y ampliación de la Colonia Tomas Berreta, Depto. de Río Negro, Uruguay; presentación resumida. Montevideo, [1968?]. fo. 227.

— **Venezuela.**

VENEZUELA. Ministerio de Agricultura y Cria. Direccion de Planificacion Agropecuaria. 1960. Atlas agricola de Venezuela. [Caracas, 1960]. unpaged.

— — **Statistics.**

VENEZUELA. Direccion General de Estadistica. Censo Agropecuario, 1971. Censo 71: IV censo agropecuario. Caracas, 1973 in progress.

— **West Indies.**

WEST INDIAN AGRICULTURAL ECONOMICS CONFERENCE, 4TH, CAVE HILL, BARBADOS, 1969. Proceedings of the...conference held at the University of the West Indies, etc. St. Augustine, Trinidad, [1969?]. pp. 135. *bibliogs.*

— **Yugoslavia — Statistics.**

YUGOSLAVIA. Savezni Zavod za Statistiku. Studije, Analize i Prikazi. 60. Statistički prikaz razvoja poljoprivrede, 1950-1971; Statistical Review of Agricultural Development, 1950-1971. Beograd, 1973. pp. 105. *With brief English summary.*

AGRICULTURE, COOPERATIVE

— **Communist countries.**

STARODUBROVSKAIA (VERA NIKOLAEVNA) Kooperativnaia sobstvennost' v sel'skom khoziaistve sotsialisticheskikh stran. Moskva, 1970. pp. 352.

— **European Economic Community countries.**

FRANCE. Direction de la Documentation. La Documentation Française. Notes et Etudes Documentaires. Nos. 4,003-4, 004. L'agriculture de groupe dans le cadre de la Communauté Economique Européenne. [Paris], 1973. pp. 67.

— **France.**

Les GROUPEMENTS fonciers agricoles. [Paris, 1971]. pp. 104. (*France. Ministère de l'Agriculture. Bulletin d'Information. Numéro Spécial*)

FRANCE. Ministère de l'Agriculture. 1972. L'organisation économique des agriculteurs. [Paris], 1972. pp. 55.

— **Germany.**

FINK (EBERHARD) Die Agrarkommune: Wirtschaftsprogramm für Landbau, Forst, Fischerei und die Landindustrie, etc. Berlin, [1920]. pp. 30.

— **Hungary — Law and legislation.**

DOMÉ (MÁRIA GY.) Legal aspects of the associations of agricultural cooperatives;...(translated by József Decsényi). Budapest, 1973. pp. 135.

— **India — Gujarat.**

CHOUDHARY (K.M.) and others. An assessment of cooperative farming societies in Gujarat and Rajasthan: a few case studies. Vallabh Vidyanagar, 1972. pp. 377.

— — **Rajasthan.**

CHOUDHARY (K.M.) and others. An assessment of cooperative farming societies in Gujarat and Rajasthan: a few case studies. Vallabh Vidyanagar, 1972. pp. 377.

— **Israel.**

TAMSMA (R.) De moshav ovdiem: invloeden op de sociale geografie van Israel's coöperatieve kleine-boerendorpen zonder loonarbeid. Assen, [1973?]. pp. 454. *With English summary. Maps in end-pocket.*

ABARBANEL (JAY S.) The co-operative farmer and the welfare state: economic change in an Israeli moshav. Manchester, [1974]. pp. 236. *bibliog.*

— **Italy.**

MUSENGA (RADISLAO) Attività nel campo degli impianti cooperativi per la trasformazione dei prodotti agricoli. Roma, Cassa per Opere Straordinarie di Pubblico Interesse nell'Italie Meridionale, 1966. pp. 78.

— **Korea.**

KIM (IL-SUNG) On the victory of socialist agricultural co-operativization and the future development of agriculture in our country: report to the National Congress of Agricultural Co-operatives, January 5, 1959. Pyongyang, 1972. pp. 72.

— **Netherlands — Accounting.**

WIND (D.) De toepassing van de ledenrekening als financieringsvorm bij enkele sectoren van agrarische coöperaties. Wageningen, 1970. pp. 138. *bibliog.*

— **Peru.**

KRESSIN (JAN) and SPIEGEL (ERICH) Agrarreform und Produktionsgenossenschaften in Peru. Berlin, 1973. pp. 86. (*Berlin. Freie Universität. Lateinamerika-Institut. Materialien zur Lehre und Forschung. Nr. 1*) *With summaries in various languages.*

— **Russia.**

RYTIKOV (ALEKSANDR NIKOLAEVICH) Pervaia bol'shevistskaia vesna. Samara, 1930. pp. 47.

OBUKHOVSKII (VLADIMIR MIKHAILOVICH) Ispol'zovanie proizvodstvennykh fondov v kolkhozakh i sovkhozakh. Moskva, 1973. pp. 240.

BADIR'IAN (GRIGORII GALUSTOVICH) Ökonomik der Landwirtschaft der UdSSR;...herausgegeben von C. Howitz; (auszugsweise Übersetzung [from the Russian]: Josef Bothe [and others]). Berlin, 1974. pp. 272.

IGNATOVSKII (PAVEL ARTEM'EVICH) Die Bauernschaft und die Wirtschaftspolitik der Partei auf dem Lande; (Übersetzer [from the Russian]: Hans Bär). Berlin, 1974. pp. 299.

— — **Finance.**

BELOUSENKO (GRIGORII FEDOROVICH) Finansovoe khoziaistvo kolkhoza. Moskva, 1973. pp. 200.

SEMENOV (VIKTOR NIKOLAEVICH) Rol' finansov i kredita v razvitii sel'skogo khoziaistva: metodologicheskie i prakticheskie voprosy mekhanizma vozdeistviia finansovo-kreditnykh otnoshenii na razvitie sel'skogo khoziaistva. Moskva, 1973. pp. 287.

— — **Moldavian Republic.**

POBEDA kolkhoznogo stroia v Mordovskoi ASSR: sbornik dokumentov i materialov. Saransk, 1970. pp. 493.

SEBESTOIMOST', rentabel'nost, pribyl': na primere kolkhozov i sovkhozov Moldavii. Kishinev, 1973. pp. 155.

— — **Russia (RSFSR).**

NEKRASOV (KLAVDII VASIL'EVICH) Bor'ba Kommunisticheskoi partii za pobedu kolkhoznogo stroia v Severnom krae, 1929-1937 gg. Vologda, 1973. pp. 174. *bibliog.*

— — Ukraine.

PTUSHCHENKO (VOLODYMYR OLEKSANDROVYCH) Mizhkolhospna i derzhavno-kolhospna kooperatsiia na Ukraïni. L'viv, 1969. pp. 241.

DZYKOVYCH (VIRA IAKOVLIVNA) and UL'IANOV (MYKHAILO HRYHOROVYCH) Formuvannia i vykorystannia osnovnykh vyrobnychykh fondiv kolhospiv Ukraïny. Kyïv, 1973. pp. 127. *With Russian summary.*

— Switzerland.

JAGGI (E.) Agricultural co-operatives and associations in Switzerland;... translated from the German by J.A.E. Morley. [London, 1974]. pp. 71. *(Horace Plunkett Foundation. Occasional Papers. No.40)*

— Thailand.

THAILAND. Department of Land Cooperatives. 1962. Land cooperatives in Thailand. [Bangkok], 1962. fo. 13.

— United Kingdom.

BAILEY (D.G.) and GIBBONS (E.T.) Agricultural co-operative activities and case histories of co-operatives. Newcastle upon Tyne, 1970. pp. 31. *bibliog. (Newcastle-upon-Tyne. University. Department of Agricultural Economics. Agricultural Adjustment Unit. Technical Papers. 9)*

AGRICULTURAL CO-OPERATION AND MARKETING SERVICES LIMITED. Annual report. a., 1972/3(1st)- London.

AGRICULTURE AND STATE.

OSSERVATORIO DI ECONOMIA AGRARIA PER L'EUROPA. Indagine sulla politica agraria di struttura. Roma, 1970. pp. 443. *(Italy. Direzione Generale della Bonifica e della Colonizzazione. Studi e Ricerche sulla Bonifica e sullo Sviluppo)*

FLORES (XAVIER-ANDRÉ) Agricultural organisations and economic and social development in rural areas. Geneva, International Labour Office, 1971. pp. 586. *bibliog. (Studies and Reports. nEW sERIES. nO. 77)*

BISHAY (FAHMI K.) Models for spatial agricultural development planning. Rotterdam, 1974. pp. 172. *bibliog. (Erasmus Universiteit Rotterdam. Centre for Development Planning. Studies in Development and Planning. vol. 3)*

— Africa, East.

ITALY. Ministero degli Affari Esteri. Comitato per la Documentazione dell'Opera dell'Italia in Africa. L'Italia in Africa. Serie Economico-Agraria. Vol.1. L'avvaloramento e la colonizzazione. Tomo 2. L'opera di avvaloramento agricolo e zootecnico in Eritrea, in Somalia e in Etiopia; testi di L.M. Bologna [and others]. Roma, 1970. pp. 453. *bibliog.*

— Canada.

CROWN (ROBERT W.) and HEADY (EARL OREL) Policy integration in Canadian agriculture. Ames, 1972. pp. 238.

— Chile.

CHILE: reforma agraria y gobierno popular; [by] Solon Barraclough [and others]. Buenos Aires, [1973]. pp. 247.

— China.

BROADBENT (K.P.) ed. Centrally planned agriculture: China and USSR: a compilation of review articles and annotated bibliography. [Oxford], Commonwealth Bureau of Agricultural Economics, 1972. pp. 42. *bibliogs. (Review Publications. No.2)*

— Colombia — Antioquia.

ANTIOQUIA. Secretaria de Agricultura. 1967. Consejo Departamental de Desarrollo Rural: organismos que lo integran. Medellin, 1967. fo. 96. *(Publicacion Especial. 80)*

— Cyprus.

CYPRUS. Department of Agriculture, 1960. Contributions towards a development plan for Cyprus agriculture; ([by] D. Christodoulou). Nicosia, 1960. pp. 20.

— European Economic Community countries.

CONDORELLI (LUIGI) and STROZZI (GEROLAMO) L'agricoltura fra Comunità Economica Europea, stato e regioni. Bologna, [1973]. pp. 51. *(Istituto Nazionale di Economia Agraria and Istituto per la Scienza dell'Amministrazione Pubblica. Agricoltura e Regioni. 7)*

GERMANY (BUNDESREPUBLIK). Bundesministerium für Ernährung, Landwirtschaft und Forsten. Wissenschaftlicher Beirat. 1973. Zur Reform der Agrarpolitik der EWG: Gutachten des... Beirats...abgeschlossen am 29. Juni 1973. Hiltrup bei Münster, 1973. 1 vol. (various pagings). *(Landwirtschaft-Angewandte Wissenschaft. Heft 166)*

— Germany.

CASSESE (SABINO) and PESCE (UGO) eds. L'agricoltura in uno stato regionale: il caso tedesco. Bologna, [1972]. pp. 94. *(Istituto Nazionale di Economia Agraria and Istituto per la Scienza dell'Amministrazione Pubblica. Agricoltura e Regioni.6)*

— Hungary.

FISCHER (LEWIS ANTHONY) and UREN (PHILIP ERNEST) The new Hungarian agriculture. Montreal, 1973. pp. 138. *bibliog.*

— India.

INDIA. Department of Agriculture. Expert Committee on Assessment and Evaluation of the Intensive Agricultural District Programme. 1969-71. Modernising Indian agriculture: (fourth) report on the intensive agricultural district programme, 1960-68. [New Delhi, 1969-71]. 2 vols.(in 1).

SINGH (S.P.) Centre-state relations in agricultural development. Delhi, [1973]. pp. 377. *bibliog.*

HUNTER (GUY) and BOTTRALL (ANTHONY) eds. Serving the small farmer: policy choices in Indian agricultural development. London, 1974. pp. 250.

— Libya.

ITALY. Ministero degli Affari Esteri. Comitato per la Documentazione dell'Opera dell'Italia in Africa. L'Italia in Africa. Serie Economico-Agraria. Vol. 1. L'avvaloramento e la colonizzazione. Tomo 3. L'opera di avvaloramento agricolo e zootecnico della Tripolitania e della Cirenaica; testi di P. Ballico e G. Palloni. Roma, 1971. pp. 405. *bibliog.*

— Nepal.

NEPAL. Land Reform Department. Planning, Analysis and Publicity Division. 1973. Evaluation of land reform in Nepal; based on the work of M. A. Zaman. Kathmandu, 1973. pp. 124. *bibliog.*

— Puerto Rico.

BAGUE RAMIREZ (JAIME) Movimientos de reforma agraria en Puerto Rico (1510-1961). [San Juan, Departamento de Agricultura, 1968]. pp. 313. *bibliog. Issued as Revista de Agricultura de Puerto Rico, vol. 55, 1968, nos. 1-2.*

— Russia.

BROADBENT (K.P.) ed. Centrally planned agriculture: China and USSR: a compilation of review articles and annotated bibliography. [Oxford], Commonwealth Bureau of Agricultural Economics, 1972. pp. 42. *bibliogs. (Review Publications. No.2)*

— Solomon Islands.

BRITISH SOLOMON ISLANDS PROTECTORATE. 1964. Agricultural and fisheries policy. Honiara, 1964. pp. (iii), 52. *(White Papers. B.S.I.P. 6)*

— United Kingdom.

WINNIFRITH (Sir ALFRED JOHN DIGBY) The Ministry of Agriculture, Fisheries and Food. London, 1962. pp. 271. *(Royal Institute of Public Administration. New Whitehall Series. No. 11)*

U.K. Ministry of Agriculture, Fisheries and Food. 1971. At the farmer's service: a handy reference to various services available to farmers in England and Wales, 1971-72. [London, 1971]. pp. 107.

BURDENS and benefits of farm-support policies; by T.E. Josling [and others]. London, 1972. pp. 85. *(Trade Policy Research Centre. Agricultural Trade Papers. No. 1)*

— United States.

JOHNSON (DAVID GALE) Farm commodity programs: an opportunity for change. Washington, D.C., 1973. pp. 114. *(American Enterprise Institute for Public Policy Research. Evaluative Studies. 7)*

AGRICULTURE AS A PROFESSION.

U.K. Ministry of Agriculture, Fisheries and Food. 1969. A career in the National Agricultural Advisory Service. [London, 1969]. pp. 20.

AGRICULTURISTS

— Russia.

TIURINA (ALEKSANDRA PETROVNA) Formirovanie kadrov spetsialistov i organizatorov kolkhoznogo proizvodstva, 1946-1958 gg. Moskva, 1973. pp. 311.

AIMS OF INDUSTRY.

AIMS OF INDUSTRY. Your company and free enterprise, 1974. London, [1973]. pp. 20.

IVENS (MICHAEL WILLIAM) Blackshirts under the bed. London, [1974]. pp. 4.

AIR

— Pollution.

WORLD HEALTH ORGANIZATION. Expert Committee on Urban Air Pollution with Particular Reference to Motor Vehicles. 1969. Urban air pollution with particular reference to motor vehicles: report, etc. Geneva, 1969. pp. 53. *(Technical Report Series. No. 410)*

CANADA. Program Planning Office for Resource Satellites and Remote Airborne Sensing. Working Group on Atmospheric Constituents. 1971. Resource satellites and remote airborne sensing for Canada. Report no.3. Atmospheric constituents; [S.O. Winthrop, chairman]. Ottawa, 1971. pp. 32. *bibliogs. With French summary.*

— — Laws and regulations — United Kingdom.

GARNER (JOHN FRANCIS) and CROW (R.K.) Clean air: law and practice. 3rd ed. London, 1969. pp. 506.

U.K. [Department of the Environment]. 1973. Air pollution legislation in Great Britain. [London, 1973]. fo. 8.

— — Australia.

AUSTRALIA. Parliament. Senate. Select Committee on Air Pollution. 1969-70. Report; (with Minutes of evidence) in AUSTRALIA. Parliament. Parliamentary papers, 1969, vol.5.

— — Canada.

CANADA. Air Pollution Control Directorate. Clean Air Act: annual report. a., 1972/3 [1st]- Ottawa. *In English and French.*

— — France.

FRANCE. Service de l'Environnement Industriel. 1973. La pollution de l'air en France: résultats de mesures. [Paris], 1973. pp. 90. *(Environnement. 17)*

AIR (Cont.)

— — United Kingdom.

CLEAN AIR COUNCIL [U.K.]. Information about industrial emissions to the atmosphere; report by a working party of the...Council, under the chairmanship of P.G. Sharp. London, H.M.S.O., 1973. pp. 35.

U.K. Central Office of Information. 1973. Towards cleaner air: a review of Britain's achievements;... prepared... for the Department of the Environment and the British Overseas Trade Board. London, 1973. pp. 31.

— — United States.

CARLIN (ALAN P.) and KOCHER (GEORGE E.) Environmental problems: their causes, cures, and evolution, using southern California smog as an example. Santa Monica, 1971. pp. 107. *(Rand Corporation. [Rand Reports]. 640)*

LOS ANGELES (COUNTY). Air Pollution Control District. Profile of air pollution control. Los Angeles, 1971. pp. 84.

SCHACHTER (ESTHER RODITTI) Enforcing air pollution controls: case study of New York City. New York, 1974. pp. 104.

AIR LINES

— Bolivia.

ORELLANA VARGAS (IGNACIO) El L[oyd] A[ereo] B[oliviano] y sus 45 años de vigencia: realidad de la aviacion comercial boliviana. Cochabamba, 1970. pp. 73.

— France.

FRANCE. Direction de la Documentation. La Documentation Française. Notes et Etudes Documentaires. Nos. 3,849-3, 850. Air France: entreprise nationale de transports aériens; [by] D.X. Heutey. Paris, 1971. pp. 94.

DROUOT (GUY) and BONNAUD (JACQUES) Deux entreprises publiques devant leur avenir: Air-France et SNCF. Paris, 1973. pp. 240. *bibliog. (Université d'Aix-Marseille. Faculté de Droit et de Science Politique. Travaux et Mémoires. No. 18)*

— United Kingdom.

BRITISH AIRWAYS BOARD. Annual report and accounts. a., 1972/3 [1st]- [London].

LANSBURY (RUSSELL DUNCAN) Management services in a British airline: a study of occupational specialisation; [Ph.D. (London) thesis]. 1973. fo. 529. *bibliog. Typescript: unpublished. This thesis is the property of London University and may not be removed from the Library.*

NICOLSON (DAVID LANCASTER) The management of change in British Airways. London, [1974]. pp. 8..

— — Employees.

COMMISSION ON INDUSTRIAL RELATIONS [U.K.]. Pan American World Airways Incorporated. London, H.M.S.O., 1973. pp. 21. *(Reports. No. 55)*

AIR RAID PRECAUTIONS.

STRACHEY (JOHN ST.LOE) Post D: some experiences of an air raid warden. London, 1941. pp. 135.

AIR—SHIPS.

COUGHLIN (S.) An appraisal of the rigid airship in the UK freight market. Cranfield, 1973. pp. 102. *bibliog. (Cranfield Institute of Technology. Centre for Transport Studies. Reports. 3)*

AIR TRAFFIC CONTROL

— Norway — Mathematical models.

NILSSEN (BJARNE) Data generation program specifications Oslo area. [Oslo], Institute of Transport Economy, 1972. fo. 82.

— United States.

COST comparisons of advanced air traffic management systems: prepared for the U.S. Department of Transportation; [by] D. J. Dreyfuss [and others]. Santa Monica, 1973. pp. 154. *bibliog. (Rand Corporation. [Rand Reports]. 1319)*

SOME user benefits achievable from an advanced air traffic management system; prepared for the U.S. Department of Transportation, [by] T.F. Kirkwood [and others]. Santa Monica, 1973. pp. 145. *bibliog. (Rand Corporation. [Rand Reports]. 1320)*

AIR WARFARE.

SALLAGAR (F.M.) Operation "STRANGLE" (Italy, Spring 1944): a case study of tactical air interdiction. Santa Monica, 1972. pp. 95. *bibliog. (Rand Corporation. [Rand Reports]. 851)*

AIRPORT NOISE.

NOISE ADVISORY COUNCIL [U.K.]. Aircraft noise: review of aircraft departure routeing policy; report by a working group of the Council; [Eric Epson, chairman]. London, H.M. S.O., 1974. pp. 29, 1 map.

AIRPORTS

— United Kingdom.

HEATHROW AIRPORT, LONDON, CONSULTATIVE COMMITTEE. Report. a., 1972/3 [1st public report]- London.

U.K. Commission on the Third London Airport. 1972. Papers and proceedings: microfilm supplement; [Eustace Roskill, chairman]. London, 1972. Microfilm : 10 reels.

U.K. Department of Trade and Industry. 1972. Passengers in Wales, West, Midlands, North East and Northern Ireland: origin and destination survey, 7 June-4 October 1971. London, 1972. pp. 55.

MAPLIN DEVELOPMENT AUTHORITY [U.K.]. Report and accounts. a., 1973/4 [1st]. London.

DOGANIS (RIGAS SOTIRIS) and THOMPSON (G.F.) The economics of British airports: report of an investigation... [by the] Transport Studies Group... Polytechnic of Central London. London, 1973. pp. 236.

McKIE (DAVID) A sadly mismanaged affair: a political history of the third London airport. London, 1973. pp. 256.

U.K. Department of the Environment. 1973. Local government reorganisation: transfer of property: airports.London, 1973. fo. 5.

U.K. Department of the Environment. 1973. The Maplin project: designation area for the new town: a consultation document. London, 1973. pp. 18, 5 maps.

U.K. Department of the Environment. 1973. The Maplin project: surface access corridor: a consultation document. [London], 1973. pp. 14, 2 maps.

LESSONS of Maplin: is the machinery for governmental decision- making at fault?; [by] Christopher Foster [and others]. London, 1974. pp. 58. *(Institute of Economic Affairs. Occasional Papers. 40)*

— United States.

JAMAICA BAT ENVIRONMENTAL STUDY GROUP. Jamaica Bay and Kennedy Airport: a multidisciplinary environmental study. Washington, 1971. 2 vols. (in 1).

AKANS (AFRICAN PEOPLE).

OPPONG (CHRISTINE) Marriage among a matrilineal elite: a family study of Ghanaian senior civil servants. London, 1974. pp. 187. *bibliog.*

ALABAMA

— Economic conditions.

BARNEY (WILLIAM L.) The secessionist impulse: Alabama and Mississippi in 1860. Princeton, [1974]. pp. 371. *bibliog.*

— Politics and government.

BARNEY (WILLIAM L.) The secessionist impulse: Alabama and Mississippi in 1860. Princeton, [1974]. pp. 371. *bibliog.*

ALASKA

— Economic conditions.

RICH (PAMELA E.) and TUSSING (ARLON R.) The national park system in Alaska: an economic impact study. [Fairbanks], 1973. pp. 88. *(University of Alaska. Institute of Social, Economic and Government Research. ISEGR Reports. No. 35)*

— Economic policy.

RICH (PAMELA E.) and TUSSING (ARLON R.) The national park system in Alaska: an economic impact study. [Fairbanks], 1973. pp. 88. *(University of Alaska. Institute of Social, Economic and Government Research. ISEGR Reports. No. 35)*

— History.

NASKE (CLAUS M.) An interpretative history of Alaskan statehood. Anchorage, 1973. pp. 192. *bibliog.*

— Politics and government.

NASKE (CLAUS M.) An interpretative history of Alaskan statehood. Anchorage, 1973. pp. 192. *bibliog.*

ALBANIA

— Nationalism.

HASKAJ (ZIHNI) ed. Mendimi politik e shoqëror i Rilindjes kombetare shqiptare: përmbledhje artikujsh nga shtypi. v.1. 1879-19o8. Tiranë, 1971. pp. 512.

ALBIZU CAMPOS (PEDRO).

RIBES TOVAR (FEDERICO) Albizu Campose: Puerto Rican revolutionary. New York, [1971]. pp. 252. *bibliog.*

ALCOHOL

— Physiological effects.

FORT (JOEL) Alcohol: our biggest drug problem. New York, [1973]. pp. 180. *bibliog.*

ALCOHOLICS

— Norway.

ALKOHOLISTOMSORGEN: utbygging, administrasjon og finansiering: utredning fra et utvalg oppnevnt av Sosialdepartementet den 6. mai 1970. Oslo, 1972. pp. 67. *(Norway. Norges Offentlige Utredninger. 1972. 17)*

— South Africa.

SELECTED papers on alcoholism. [Pretoria], 1970. pp. 61. *bibliog. (South Africa. Department of Social Welfare and Pensions. [Research Division]. Research and Information. Publication 1970/No. 4)*

— United Kingdom.

BURTON (MARY) pseud. An alcoholic in the family. London, 1974. pp. 175.

— United States.

BAHR (HOWARD M.) Skid row: an introduction to disaffiliaton. New York, 1973. pp. 335.

ALCOHOLISM

— Treatment.

WORLD HEALTH ORGANIZATION. Expert Committee on Mental Health. 1967. Services for the prevention and treatment of dependence on alcohol and other drugs: fourteenth report of the...Committee, etc. Geneva, 1967. pp. 45. *(Technical Report Series. No. 363)*

SELECTED papers on alcoholism. [Pretoria], 1970. pp. 61. *bibliog. (South Africa. Department of Social Welfare and Pensions. [Research Division]. Research and Information. Publication 1970/No. 4)*

— United States.

FORT (JOEL) Alcohol: our biggest drug problem. New York, [1973]. pp. 180. *bibliog.*

ALGERIA

— Constitutional law.

BELKHERROUBI (ABDELMADJID) La naissance et la reconnaissance de la République algérienne. Bruxelles, 1972. pp. 176. *bibliog.*

— Economic policy.

CHALIAND (GERARD) and MINCES (JULIETTE) L'Algérie indépendante: bilan d'une révolution nationale. Paris, 1972. pp. 175. *bibliog.*

— History — 1945— .

THEIS (LAURENT) and RATTE (PHILIPPE) La guerre d'Algérie; ou, Le temps des méprises; avec le témoignage de quinze personnalités. Tours, [1974]. pp. 303.

— Politics and government.

DUPRAT (GERARD) Révolution et autogestion rurale en Algérie. Paris, 1973. pp. 486. *bibliog. (Fondation Nationale des Sciences Politiques. Cahiers. 189)*

— Rural conditions.

DUPRAT (GERARD) Révolution et autogestion rurale en Algérie. Paris, 1973. pp. 486. *bibliog. (Fondation Nationale des Sciences Politiques. Cahiers. 189)*

— Social conditions.

BOURDIEU (PIERRE) Sociologie de l'Algérie. 5th ed. Paris, 1974. pp. 128. *bibliog.*

— Statistics.

ALGERIA. Ministère de l'Information et de la Culture. Direction de la Documentation et des Publications. 1973. L'Algérie en chiffres (1962-1972). Alger, [1973?]. pp. 174.

ALGERIANS IN FRANCE.

SALAH (ALI) La communauté algérienne: étude sur l'immigration algérienne dans le Département du Nord, 1945-1972. Lille, [1973]. pp. 213. *bibliog.*

BENDIFALLAH (SMAIL) L'immigration algérienne et le droit français. Paris, 1974. pp. 311.

MICHEL (ANDRÉE) The modernization of North African families in the Paris area. The Hague, [1974]. pp. 387. *bibliog.* With appendices in French.

ALGORITHMS.

HO (JAMES K.) and MANNE (ALAN S.) Nested decomposition for dynamic models. Stanford, 1973. 1 vol. (various pagings). *bibliog. (Stanford University. Institute for Mathematical Studies in the Social Sciences. Technical Reports. [New Series]. No. 96)*

HANSEN (TERJE) On the approximation of Nash equilibrium points in an N-person noncooperative game. [Philadelphia], 1974. pp. 15. *bibliog. (Reprinted from Society for Industrial and Applied Mathematics Journal on Applied Mathematics, vol. 26, no. 3, May 1974)*

ALIEN LABOUR

— Austria.

OESTERREICHISCHES KOMITEE FÜR SOZIALARBEIT. Österreichische Konferenz für Sozialarbeit, 3., 1971. Gastarbeiter in Österreich. Wien, [1972]. pp. 84. *(Schriften zur Sozialarbeit. Heft 10)*

ARBEITSKREIS FÜR ÖKONOMISCHE UND SOZIOLOGISCHE STUDIEN. Gastarbeiter: wirtschaftliche und soziale Herausforderung. Wien, [1973]. pp. 167. *bibliog.*

— Belgium.

MARTENS (ALBERT) 25 jaar Wegwerparbeiders: het Belgisch immigratiebeleid na 1945. Leuven, 1973. pp. 322. *bibliog. (Katholieke Universiteit te Leuven. Sociologisch Onderzoeksinstituut. Afdeling Arbeids- en Industriële Sociologie. Rapport 1973/2)*

— Denmark.

HJARNØ (JAN) Fremmedarbejdere: en etnologisk undersøgelse af arbejdskraftseksportens virkninger i Tyrkiet. København, Nationalmuseet, 1971. pp. 76.

— Europe.

PAINE (SUZANNE) Exporting workers: the Turkish case. London, 1974. pp. 227. *bibliog. (Cambridge. University. Department of Applied Economics. Occasional Papers. 41)*

— European Economic Community countries.

COUNCIL OF EUROPE. Standing Committee on the European Convention on Establishment (Individuals). Periodical report. irreg., 1971(1st)- Strasbourg.

— France.

HOMMES ET MIGRATIONS. Etudes. No. 118. Le VIe plan et les travailleurs étrangers. Paris, 1971. pp. 83. *bibliog.*

FRANCE. Ministère des Affaires Sociales. Service des Etudes et Prévisions. Division de la Statistique et des Etudes. 1973. Résultats d'une enquête sur la main-d'oeuvre étrangère effectuée en juillet 1971. Paris, 1973. fo. 19.

GARNIER (RAYMOND) L'affaire de Trouhans. Paris, [1973]. pp. 153.

MINCES (JULIETTE) Les travailleurs étrangers en France: enquête. Paris, [1973]. pp. 476. *bibliog.*

PINOT (FRANÇOISE) Les travailleurs immigrés dans la lutte de classes. Paris, 1973. pp. 93.

VALABREGUE (CATHERINE) L'homme déraciné: le livre noir des travailleurs étrangers. [Paris], 1973. pp. 205.

COLLECTIF D'ALPHABETISATION and GROUPE D'INFORMATION ET DE SOUTIEN DES TRAVAILLEURS IMMIGRES. Le petit livre juridique des travailleurs immigrés: conditions de séjour et de travail. Paris, 1974. pp. 97. *bibliog.*

— Germany.

WARUM brauchen wir Gastarbeiter?; (Mitarbeiter: Lutz v. Rosenstiel [and others]). 2nd ed. Rosenheim, 1971. pp. 32.

BORRIS (MARIA) Ausländische Arbeiter in einer Grosstadt: eine empirische Untersuchung am Beispiel Frankfurt. Frankfurt am Main, [1973]. pp. 318. *bibliog.*

GERMANY (BUNDESREPUBLIK). Bundesanstalt für Arbeit. 1973. Repräsentativuntersuchung '72 über die Beschäftigung ausländischer Arbeitnehmer im Bundesgebiet und ihre Familien- und Wohnverhältnisse. Nürnberg, 1973. pp. 178.

UHLIG (OTTO) Die ungeliebten Gäste: ausländische Arbeitnehmer in Deutschland. München, [1974]. pp. 199.

— — Bibliography.

GERMANY (BUNDESREPUBLIK). Deutscher Bundestag. Wissenschaftliche Dienste. 1973. Ausländische Arbeitnehmer in der Bundesrepublik Deutschland: Auswahlbibliographie. Bonn, 1973. pp. 60. *(Bibliographien. 34)*

— Netherlands.

BRAAM (S.) Suriname en de Surinamers als maatschappelijke vreemdelingen in Nederland. Den Haag, [1973]. pp. 128.

HALBERTSMA (HERRE A.) Arbeiders te gast. Utrecht, [1973]. pp. 126. *bibliog.*

— Switzerland.

HAGEN (ECKEHART) Arbeitsmotive von Gastarbeitern: Ergebnisse einer Befragung schweizerischer und italienischer Arbeitskräfte in der Schweiz. Bern, [1973]. pp. 319. *bibliog. (Hochschule St.Gallen für Wirtschafts- und Sozialwissenschaften. Schriftenreihe Betriebswirtschaft. Band 2)*

HOFFMANN-NOWOTNY (HANS JOACHIM) Soziologie des Fremdarbeiterproblems: eine theoretische und empirische Analyse am Beispiel der Schweiz. Stuttgart, 1973. pp. 377. *bibliog.* With summaries in various languages.

LAMBELET (JOHN C.) and SCHILTKNECHT (KURT) On the importance of an elastic supply of foreign labor and capital: simulation results for the Swiss economy. Zürich, [1973]. pp. 77. *bibliog. (Zürich. Eidgenössische Technische Hochschule. Institut für Wirtschaftsforschung. Untersuchungen. Neue Folge. Band 8)*

— United Kingdom.

SLATTER (STUART ST.P.) and others. The employment of non-English speaking workers: what industry must do. [London], Community Relations Commission, 1974. pp. 32.

ALIENATION (SOCIAL PSYCHOLOGY).

JOSEPHSON (ERIC) and JOSEPHSON (MARY) eds. Man alone: alienation in modern society. New York, 1962 repr. 1970. pp. 592. *bibliog.*

JOHNSON (FRANK) ed. Alienation: concept, term and meanings. New York, [1973]. pp. 402. *bibliogs.*

POGOSIAN (VIL ANDRANIKOVICH) Problema otchuzhdeniia v "Fenomenologii dukha" Gegelia. Erevan, 1973. pp. 129.

ALIENS

— Switzerland.

HUGENTOBLER (EUGEN) Ausländerpolitik heute: dritte Überfremdungsinitiative, der falsche Weg. [Zürich, 1974]. pp. 16. *(Wirtschaftsförderung: Gesellschaft zur Förderung der Schweizerischen Wirtschaft. Stimmen zur Staats- und Wirtschaftspolitik. 56)*

— — Bern (Canton).

BERN (CANTON). Statistisches Bureau. 1970. Überfremdungsinitiative 1970: Resultate im Kanton Bern, etc.Bern, 1970. fo. 21, 47. *(Beiträge zur Statistik des Kantons Bern. Politische Statistik. Reihe F. Heft 1)* In French and German.

ALINSKY (SAUL DAVID).

BAILEY (ROBERT) Radicals in urban politics: the Alinsky approach. Chicago, 1974. pp. 187. *bibliog.*

ALLEN (RICHARD).

GEORGE (CAROL V.R.) Segregated sabbaths: Richard Allen and the emergence of independent black churches, 1760-1840. New York, 1973. pp. 205. *bibliog.*

ALLENDE (SALVADOR).

ALLENDE (SALVADOR) La revolucion chilena. Buenos Aires, [1973]. pp. 209.

CASTRO RUZ (FIDEL) and ALLENDE BUSSI (BEATRIZ) Homenaje a Salvador Allende; (discursos pronunciados por... Beatriz Allende Bussi...y por...Fidel Castro, el día 28 de septiembre de 1973 en el acto conmemorativo del XIII aniversario de la creacion de los Comites de Defensa de la Revolucion). La Habana, 1973. pp. 105.

GARCES (JOAN E.) El estado y los problemas tacticos en el gobierno de Allende. Buenos Aires, 1973 repr. 1974. pp. 309.

LAFOURCADE (ENRIQUE) Salvador Allende. Barcelona, [1973]. pp. 215.

RUIZ-ESQUIDE JARA (MARIANO) El socialismo traicionado. Santiago de Chile, 1973. pp. 191.

ALLENDE (SALVADORE) (Cont.)

CERDA (CARLOS) Génocide au Chili; (suivi de Hommage à Salvador Allende, de Fidel Castro). Paris, 1974. pp. 134.

CORDOBA CLAURE (TED) Chile no. Buenos Aires, 1974. pp. 222.

VARAS (FLORENCIA) and VERGARA (JOSE MANUEL) Operacion Chile. Buenos Aires, [1974]. pp. 260.

ALLIANCE FOR PROGRESS.

OBERTO G. (LUIS ENRIQUE) and CASAS GONZALEZ (ANTONIO) Venezuela y el C[omite] I[nteramericano de la] A[lianza para el] P[rogreso]. [Caracas], Oficina Central de Coordinacion y Planificacion, [1973 or rather 1974]. pp. 137.

ALMSHOUSES AND WORKHOUSES

— **United Kingdom.**

LONGMATE (NORMAN) The workhouse. London, 1974. pp. 320. *bibliog.*

ALSACE

— **History — 1940—1945, German occupation.**

KETTENACKER (LOTHAR) Nationalsozialistische Volkstumspolitik im Elsass. Stuttgart, 1973. pp. 389. *bibliog. (Institut für Zeitgeschichte. Studien zur Zeitgeschichte)*

ALTENA

— **Politics and government.**

PESCHKE (KLAUS) Die Bedeutung der liberalen Parteien und der Sozialdemokratie für das politische Leben im Wahlkreis Altena-Iserlohn von der Reichsgründung 1871 bis zum Jahre 1890. [Altena, 1973]. pp. 150. *bibliog. (Verein Freunde der Burg Altena. Altenaer Beiträge. Neue Folge. Band 8)*

ALTHUSSER (LOUIS).

GLUCKSMANN (MIRIAM ANNE) Structuralist analysis in contemporary social thought: a comparison of the theories of Claude Lévi-Strauss and Louis Althusser. London, 1974. pp. 197. *bibliog.*

ALUMINIUM INDUSTRY AND TRADE.

ORGANISATION FOR ECONOMIC CO-OPERATION AND DEVELOPMENT. Industry Committee. 1973. Problems and prospects of the primary aluminium industry. Paris, 1973. pp. 80, 29.

AMAZON VALLEY

— **Economic policy.**

BRAZIL. Superintendência do Desenvolvimento da Amazônia. Sudam em revista. m., 1971 (ano 2); ceased pbln. Belem.

— **Social conditions.**

TRIBES of the Amazon basin in Brazil 1972; report for the Aborigines Protection Society by Edwin Brooks [and others]. London, 1973. pp. 201.

— **Social policy.**

BRAZIL. Superintendência do Desenvolvimento da Amazônia. Sudam em revista. m., 1971 (ano 2); ceased pbln. Belem.

AMBEDKAR (BHIMARAO RAMJI).

AMBEDKAR MEMORIAL COMMITTEE. Souvenir released... on the eve of installation of the portrait of Dr. Baba Saheb B.R. Ambedkar in the London School of Economics. London, 1972. pp. 84.

AMENDMENTS (PARLIAMENTARY PRACTICE).

BROUILLET (ALAIN) Le droit d'amendement dans la constitution de la Ve République: étude pratique de son utilisation pour l'élaboration de la loi d'orientation foncière. Paris, 1973. pp. 159. *bibliog. (Paris. Université de Paris I (Panthéon- Sorbonne). Publications. Série Science Politique. 3)*

AMENDOLA (GIOVANNI).

CAPONE (ALFREDO) Etica e politica in Giovanni Amendola, 1908-1915: lezioni di storia delle dottrine politiche tenute nell'anno accademico 1972-73. Roma, [1973]. pp. 230.

AMERICA

— **Foreign economic relations.**

CONFERENCE ON TRADE POLICIES IN THE AMERICAS, SOUTHERN METHODIST UNIVERSITY, 1972. Trade and investment policies in the Americas; edited by Stephen E. Guisinger. Dallas, [1973]. pp. 101.

— **Population.**

INTER-AMERICAN BAR ASSOCIATION. Human Rights Committee. Population and the role of law in the Americas: proceedings of a seminar. Medford, Mass., 1974. pp. 62. *(Tufts University. Fletcher School of Law and Diplomacy. Law and Population Monograph Series. No.18)*

— **Race question.**

HOETINK (HARRY) Slavery and race relations in the Americas: comparative notes on their nature and nexus. New York, 1973. pp. 232. *bibliog.*

AMERICA, LATIN

— **Commerce — Statistics.**

ANUARIO ESTADISTICO CENTROAMERICANO DE COMERCIO EXTERIOR; [pd. by Seccion de Estadistica, Secretaria Permanente del Tratado General de Integracion Economica Centroamericana]. a., 1971- Guatemala.

— **Commercial policy.**

ASOCIACION LATINOAMERICANA DE LIBRE COMERCIO. 1972. Recopilacion de normas sobre valoracion aduanera de las mercaderias en los paises de la ALALC. [Montevideo], 1972. 1 vol. (various pagings).

SIDERI (S.) Analysis and overall evaluation of Latin American trade policies. The Hague, 1973. pp. 21. *(Hague. Institute of Social Studies. Occasional Papers. No. 42)*

— **Constitutional history.**

GARCIA LAGUARDIA (JORGE MARIO) Origenes de la democracia constitucional en Centroamerica. San Jose, C.R., 1971. pp. 351. *bibliog.*

— **Economic conditions.**

CALELLO (HUGO) Ideologia y neocolonialismo. Caracas, 1969. pp. 159.

UNITED STATES. Agency for International Development. Office of Statistics and Reports. 1971. A.I.D. economic data book: Latin America. Washington, 1971. Microfiche [5 cards].

BEAUJEU-GARNIER (JACQUELINE) L'économie de l'Amérique latine. 7th ed. Paris, 1973. pp. 128.

INTER-AMERICAN COMMITTEE FOR AGRICULTURAL DEVELOPMENT. 1973. Agrarian structure in Latin America: a resume of the CIDA land tenure studies...; edited by Solon Barraclough...with Juan Carlos Collarte. Lexington, Mass., [1973]. pp. 351.

— — **Mathematical models.**

CANTARELLI (DAVIDE) Struttura produttiva, ritardo tecnologico ed esportazioni dell'America Latina: un'analisi econometrica interregionale. [Verona, 1974]. pp. 169. *bibliog.* Extracted from *Annali, Serie 1, vol. 5*, published by the University of Padua.

— **Economic history.**

JARA (ALVARO) Problemas y metodos de la historia economica hispanoamericana. [Caracas, 1969]. pp. 93. *(Caracas. Universidad Central de Venezuela. Facultad de Humanidades y Educacion. Escuela de Historia. Publicaciones. Serie Varia. vol. 8)*

MAURO (FREDERIC) Desproduits et des hommes: essais historiques latino-américains, XVIe-XXe siècles. Paris, [1972]. pp. 174. *(Paris. Ecole Pratique des Hautes Etudes. Section des Sciences Economiques et Sociales. Centre de Recherches Historiques. Civilisations et Sociétés. 34)*

MACLEOD (MURDO J.) Spanish central America: a socioeconomic history, 1520-1720. Berkeley, [1973]. pp. 554. *bibliog.*

— **Economic integration.**

La REPUBLICA Dominicana frente a la integracion economica; ([by] Clara de Ravelo [and others]); seminario auspiciado por la Universidad Catolica Madre y Maestra y celebrado el 15 y el 16 de julio del 1967 en el Hotel Montaña, Jarabacoa. Santiago de los Caballeros, D.R., 1967. pp. 185. *(Santiago (Dominican Republic). Universidad Catolica Madre y Maestra. Coleccion Estudios)*

ECUADOR. Ministerio de Industrias y Comercio. Direccion de Integracion. 1969. Documentos basicos de la integracion subregional. Quito, 1969. pp. 133. *(Boletines. No. 67)*

FORO NACIONAL SOBRE VENEZUELA Y LA INTEGRACION LATINOAMERICANA, CARACAS, 1971. Informe final. Caracas, Oficina Central de Coordinacion y Planificacion, [1972]. pp. 293.

KAPLAN (MARCOS) Aspectos politicos de la planificacion en America Latina. Montevideo, [1972]. pp. 219.

SECRETARIA PERMANENTE DEL TRATADO GENERAL DE INTEGRACION ECONOMICA CENTROAMERICANA. 1973-74. El desarrollo integrado de Centroamerica en la presente década: bases propuestas para el perfeccionamiento y la reestructuración del Mercado Común Centroamericano. Buenos Aires, Instituto para la Integración de América Latina, 1973-74. 11 vols. (in 5).

INSTITUTO CENTROAMERICANO DE ADMINISTRACION PUBLICA. Documentos sobre aspectos institucionales de la integracion centroamericana. San José, 1973. 1 vol. (various pagings).

— **Economic policy.**

SOCIO-ECONOMIC PROGRESS IN LATIN AMERICA: annual report; ([pd. by] Inter-American Development Bank). a., 1971 [1st]- Washington.

KAPLAN (MARCOS) Aspectos politicos de la planificacion en America Latina. Caracas, [Comision de Administracion Publica], 1971. pp. 50. *(Cuadernos para la Reforma Administrativa. 3)*

KAPLAN (MARCOS) Aspectos politicos de la planificacion en America Latina. Montevideo, [1972]. pp. 219.

VASENA (ADALBERT KRIEGER) and PAZOS (JAVIER) Latin America: time to regain. Paris, 1972. pp. 248. *Second draft prepared for the Atlantic Institute.*

THURBER (CLARENCE E.) and GRAHAM (LAWRENCE S.) eds. Development administration in Latin America. Durham, N.C., 1973. pp. 453. *(American Society for Public Administration. Comparative Administration Group. Comparative Administration Group Series)*

VASENA (ADALBERT KRIEGER) and PAZOS (JAVIER) Latin America: a broader world role. London, 1973. pp. 207.

BEYOND Cuba: Latin America takes charge of its future: [based on a conference organised by the Rand Corporation in Warrenton, Virginia, 1972]; edited by Luigi R. Einaudi. New York, [1974]. pp. 248. *bibliog.*

— **Foreign economic relations.**

PLAZA (GALO) Latin America in transition: its relations with the industrialized world. Paris, [1971]. pp. 40. *(Atlantic Institute. Atlantic Papers. 1971.1)*

KAPLAN (MARCOS) Aspectos politicos de la planificacion en America Latina. Montevideo, [1972]. pp. 219.

STALLINGS (BARBARA) Economic dependency in Africa and Latin America. Beverly Hills, [1972]. pp. 60. *bibliog.*

VASENA (ADALBERT KRIEGER) and PAZOS (JAVIER) Latin America: time to regain. Paris, 1972. pp. 248. *Second draft prepared for the Atlantic Institute.*

VASENA (ADALBERT KRIEGER) and PAZOS (JAVIER) Latin America: a broader world role. London, 1973. pp. 207.

— — **United States.**

IANNI (OCTAVIO) Imperialismo y cultura de la violencia en America Latina; traduccion de Claudio Colombiani y Jose Thiago Cintra. Mexico, 1970. pp. 126.

CONFERENCE ON TRADE POLICIES IN THE AMERICAS, SOUTHERN METHODIST UNIVERSITY, 1972. Trade and investment policies in the Americas; edited by Stephen E. Guisinger. Dallas, [1973]. pp. 101.

— **Foreign relations.**

OZANAM (DIDIER) Les sources de l'histoire de l'Amérique Latine: guide du chercheur dans les archives françaises. 1. Les affaires étrangères. [Paris], 1963. pp. 109. *(Paris. Université. Institut des Hautes Etudes de l'Amérique Latine. Cahiers. No. 4)*

BEYOND Cuba: Latin America takes charge of its future: [based on a conference organised by the Rand Corporation in Warrenton, Virginia, 1972]; edited by Luigi R. Einaudi. New York, [1974]. pp. 248. *bibliog.*

— — **Paraguay.**

SALUM-FLECHA (ANTONIO) Historia diplomatica del Paraguay de 1869 a 1938. Asuncion, 1972. pp. 215. *bibliog.*

— — **United States.**

GUILLEN (ABRAHAM) Desafio al Pentagono: la guerrilla latinoamericana. Montevideo, [1969]. pp. 183.

SCHILLING (PAULO R.) El imperio Rockefeller: America Latina documentos; [and] La estrategia norteamericana en America Latina: de la doctrina Monroe al informe Rockefeller; ensayo; [translated from the English by Rosario Lorente]. Montevideo, [1970]. pp. 129.

GUARESTI (JUAN JOSE) the Younger. La guerra de las comunidades: el federalismo argentino. Buenos Aires, 1970. pp. 272. *bibliog.*

— **History.**

CAMACHO (GEORGE) Latin America: a short history. London, 1973. pp. 298. *bibliog.*

COLLIER (SIMON D.W.) From Cortes to Castro: an introduction to the history of Latin America, 1492-1973. London, 1974. pp. 429.

— — **Historiography.**

ORTEGA Y MEDINA (JUAN A.) Historiografía sovietica iberoamericanista, 1945-1960. Mexico, 1961. pp. 195. *(Mexico City. Universidad Nacional Autonoma de Mexico. Facultad de Filosofia y Letras. Seminario de Historiografía Mexicana Moderna)*

— — **Sources.**

OZANAM (DIDIER) Les sources de l'histoire de l'Amérique Latine: guide du chercheur dans les archives françaises. 1. Les affaires étrangères. [Paris], 1963. pp. 109. *(Paris. Université. Institut des Hautes Etudes de l'Amérique Latine. Cahiers. No. 4)*

— — **To 1600.**

HANKE (LEWIS ULYSSES) Bartolome de las Casas: pensador politico, historiador, antropologo; [version española de Antonio Fernandez Travieso]. Buenos Aires, [1968]. pp. 125. *bibliog.*

— — **1806—1830, Wars of Independence.**

El MOVIMIENTO emancipador de Hispanoamerica: actas y ponencias ([of the] Mesa Redonda de la Comision de Historia del Instituto Panamericano de Geografía e Historia). Caracas, Academia Nacional de la Historia, 1961. 3 vols. *(Organization of American States. Pan American Institute of Geography and History. Commission on History. Mesa Redonda. tomos 1-3)*

— **Intellectual life.**

CARPENTIER (ALEJO) Literatura y conciencia politico en America Latina. Madrid, [1969]. pp. 143.

— **Languages.**

ESCOBAR (ALBERTO) Lenguaje y discriminacion social en America Latina. Lima, 1972. pp. 201.

— **Politics and government.**

PIÑEIRO (ARMANDO ALONSO) Paredon de America. Buenos Aires, [1962]. pp. 125.

NUN (JOSE) Latin America: the hegemonic crisis and the military coup. Berkeley, [1969]. pp. 73. *bibliog.* *(California University. Institute of International Studies. Politics of Modernization Series. No. 7)*

SALAMANCA ZAMORANO (HUMBERTO) Bolivia y la quiebra de los mitos latinoamericanos. La Paz, 1969. pp. 110. *bibliog.*

STATISTICAL ABSTRACT OF LATIN AMERICA. Supplement Series. 2. Latin American political statistics; [edited by] Kenneth Ruddle and Philip Gillette. Los Angeles, 1972. pp. 121.

HALPERIN DONGHI (TULIO) The aftermath of revolution in Latin America;... translated from the Spanish by Josephine de Bunsen. New York, 1973. pp. 149. *bibliog.*

INSTITUTO CENTROAMERICANO DE ADMINISTRACION PUBLICA. Documentos sobre aspectos institucionales de la integracion centroamericana. San José, 1973. 1 vol. (various pagings).

KERN (ROBERT) ed. The caciques: oligarchical politics and the system of caciquismo in the Luso-Hispanic world. Albuquerque, [1973]. pp. 202.

O'DONNELL (GUILLERMO A.) Modernization and bureaucratic-authoritarianism: studies in South American politics. Berkeley, [1973]. pp. 219. *bibliog.* *(California University. Institute of International Studies. Politics of Modernization Series. No. 9)*

THURBER (CLARENCE E.) and GRAHAM (LAWRENCE S.) eds. Development administration in Latin America. Durham, N.C., 1973. pp. 453. *(American Society for Public Administration. Comparative Administration Group. Comparative Administration Group Series)*

ADIE (ROBERT F.) and POITRAS (GUY E.) Latin America: the politics of immobility. Englewood Cliffs, [1974]. pp. 278. *bibliogs.*

BEYOND Cuba: Latin America takes charge of its future: [based on a conference organised by the Rand Corporation in Warrenton, Virginia, 1972]; edited by Luigi R. Einaudi. New York, [1974]. pp. 248. *bibliog.*

HODGES (DONALD CLARK) The Latin American revolution: politics and strategy from apro-marxism to guevarism. New York, 1974. pp. 287. *bibliog.*

PIKE (FREDRICK BRAUN) and STRITCH (THOMAS) eds. The new corporation: social-political structures in the Iberian world. Notre Dame, [1974]. pp. 218. *(Notre Dame. University. Committee on International Relations. International Studies)*

— **Population.**

CONSEJO LATINOAMERICANO DE CIENCIAS SOCIALES. Comision de Poblacion y Desarrollo. Grupo de Trabajo sobre Migraciones Internas. Migracion y desarrollo. Buenos Aires, 1972 in progress. *(Consejo Latinoamericano de Ciencias Sociales. Serie Poblacion. Informe de Investigacion) Library has vols. 1 and 2.*

STATISTICAL ABSTRACT OF LATIN AMERICA. Supplement Series. 4. Urbanization in 19th century Latin America: statistics and sources; [by] Richard E. Boyer and Keith A. Davies. Los Angeles, 1973. pp. 82. *bibliogs.*

SANCHEZ-ALBORNOZ (NICOLAS) The population of Latin America: a history;...translated by W.A.R. Richardson. Berkeley, [1974]. pp. 299. *bibliog.*

— **Race question.**

SOLAUN (MAURICIO) and KRONUS (SIDNEY) Discrimination without violence: miscegenation and racial conflict in Latin America. New York, [1973]. pp. 240. *bibliog.*

— **Relations (general) with Eastern Germany.**

GERMANY (DEUTSCHE DEMOKRATISCHE REPUBLIK). Staatsrat. Abteilung Presse und Information. 1969. Tagebuch einer Freundschaftsreise: Bericht über die Reise einer Delegation der Volkskammer der DDR nach Kolumbien, Ekuador und Chile vom 3.-30. Juli 1968. Berlin, 1969. pp. 64.

— **Relations (general) with France.**

FRANCE. Direction de la Documentation. La Documentation Française. Notes et Etudes Documentaires. Nos. 3,083-3, 084. L'Amérique Latine et la France; [by] Olivier Rostand. Paris, 1964. 2 pts. *bibliog.*

— **Social conditions.**

CALELLO (HUGO) Ideologia y neocolonialismo. Caracas, 1969. pp. 159.

GARCIA (ANTONIO) Estructura social y desarrollo latinoamericanos. Santiago de Chile, Instituto de Capacitacion e Investigacion en Reforma Agraria, 1969. pp. 134.

DAVIS (STANLEY M.) and GOODMAN (LOUIS WOLF) eds. Workers and managers in Latin America. Lexington, Mass., [1972]. pp. 308.

— **Social History.**

MACLEOD (MURDO J.) Spanish central America: a socioeconomic history, 1520-1720. Berkeley, [1973]. pp. 554. *bibliog.*

— **Social policy.**

SOCIO-ECONOMIC PROGRESS IN LATIN AMERICA: annual report; ([pd. by] Inter-American Development Bank). a., 1971 [1st]- Washington.

KAPLAN (MARCOS) Aspectos politicos de la planificacion en America Latina. Caracas, [Comision de Administracion Publica], 1971. pp. 50.*(Cuadernos para la Reforma Administrativa. 3)*

— **Statistics.**

STATISTICAL ABSTRACT OF LATIN AMERICA. Supplement Series. 2. Latin American political statistics; [edited by] Kenneth Ruddle and Philip Gillette. Los Angeles, 1972. pp. 121.

AMERICA, NORTH

— **Description and travel.**

WHITE (CHARLES LANGDON) and others. Regional geography of Anglo-America. 4th ed. Englewood Cliffs, [1974]. pp. 617. *bibliogs.*

— **Discovery and exploration.**

MORISON (SAMUEL ELIOT) The European discovery of America: the northern voyages, A.D. 500-1600. New York, 1971. pp. 712. *bibliogs.*

AMERICA, NORTH (Cont.)

QUINN (DAVID BEERS) England and the discovery of America, 1481-1620, etc. London, 1974. pp. 497, xviii. *bibliog.*

— **Emigration and immigration.**

KERO (REINO) Migration from Finland to North America in the years between the United States Civil War and the First World War. Turku, 1974. pp. 260. *bibliog.* (*Åbo. Turun Yliopisto. Julkaisuja. Sarja B. Osa 130*)

PRICE (CHARLES ARCHIBALD) The great white walls are built: restrictive immigration to North America and Australasia, 1836-1888. Canberra, 1974. pp. 323. *bibliog.*

AMERICAN LOYALISTS.

NORTON (MARY BETH) The British-Americans: the loyalist exiles in England 1774- 1789. London, 1974. pp. 333. *bibliog. First published in the United States in 1972.*

AMERICAN PERIODICALS.

LITVAK (ISAIAH ALLAN) and MAULE (CHRISTOPHER JOHN) Cultural sovereignty: the Time and Reader's Digest case in Canada. New York, 19£4. pp. 140.

AMERY (JULIAN).

AMERY (JULIAN) Approach march: a venture in autobiography.

AMHARAS.

HOBEN (ALLAN) Land tenure among the Amhara of Ethiopia: the dynamics of cognatic descent. Chicago, 1973. pp. 273. *bibliog.* (*Haile Sellassie I University. Institute of Ethiopian Studies and Faculty of Law. Monographs in Ethiopian Land Tenure. vol. 4*)

AMIN (IDI).

MARTIN (DAVID) Journalist. General Amin. London, 1974. pp. 254.

AMSTERDAM

— **Population.**

AMSTERDAM. Bureau van Statistiek. Statistische Mededelingen. No. 187. De bevolking van de 19e-eeuwse gordel in Amsterdam. Amsterdam, 1973. pp. 86.

— **Social history.**

BURKE (PETER) Historian. Venice and Amsterdam: a study of seventeenth-century élites. London, 1974. pp. 154. *bibliog.*

ANALYSIS (PHILOSOPHY).

CORNFORTH (MAURICE CAMPBELL) Marxism and the linguistic philosophy. 2nd ed. London, 1967 repr. 1971. pp. 384.

MILLER (LIBUSE LUKAS) Knowing, doing, and surviving: cognition in evolution. New York, [1973]. pp. 343. *bibliog.*

ANARCHISM AND ANARCHISTS.

MATHILDELLA (ALESSIR) ed. Aussprüche und Auszüge über Anarchismus. Berlin, 1909. pp. 16, iv. *bibliog.*

BOOKCHIN (MURRAY) Post-scarcity anarchism. Berkeley, Calif., [1971]. pp. 288.

BARTSCH (GUENTER) Der internationale Anarchismus 1862-1972. Hannover, Niedersächsische Landeszentrale für Politische Bildung, 1972. pp. 67.

BAKUNIN (MIKHAIL ALEKSANDROVICH) Selected writings; edited and introduced by Arthur Lehning; translations from the French by Steven Cox; translations from the Russian by Olive Stevens. London, 1973. pp. 288. *bibliog.*

EUROPE EN FORMATION, L'. No. 163-164. Anarchisme et fédéralisme; [by] Alexandre Marc [and others]. Paris, 1973. pp. 170. London, 1973. pp. 456.

WITTKOP (JUSTUS F.) Unter der schwarzen Fahne: Aktionen und Gestalten des Anarchismus. Frankfurt am Main, [1973]. pp. 270. *bibliog.*

GRAHAM (MARCUS) ed. Man! : an anthology of anarchist ideas, essays, poetry and commentaries. London, [1974]. pp. 638.

— **Bibliography.**

BETTINI (LEONARDO) Bibliografia dell'anarchismo. Firenze, 1972 in progress.

— **Dictionaries and encyclopaedias.**

ENCICLOPEDIA anarquista: edicion castellana. Mexico, 1972 in progress. *Originally published in French under the direction of Sebastien Faure.*

— **Brazil.**

DULLES (JOHN W.F.) Anarchists and communists in Brazil, 1900-1935. Austin, [1973]. pp. 603. *bibliog.*

— **France.**

GRAVE (JEAN) Quarante ans de propagande anarchiste; présenté et annoté par Mireille Delfau. [Paris, 1973]. pp. 605 *bibliog.*

— **Germany.**

HORCHEM (HANS JOSEF) West Germany's Red Army anarchists. London, 1974. pp. 13. (*Institute for the Study of Conflict. Conflict Studies. No. 46*)

— **Italy.**

ATTENTATO al Diana: (processo agli anarchici nell'assise di Milano, 9 maggio-1 giugno 1922). Roma, 1973. pp. 213.

SANTARELLI (ENZO) Il socialismo anarchico in Italia. 2nd ed. Milano, 1973. pp. 232.

I MORTI: (gli anarchici del 1899); [originally published in Ancona, 1899]. Pistoia, [1974]. pp. 32.

— **Russia.**

KANEV (SERAFIM NIKOLAEVICH) Oktiabr'skaia revoliutsiia i krakh anarkhizma: bor'ba partii bol'shevikov protiv anarkhizma 1917-1922 gg. Moskva, 1974. pp. 415, [xv].

— **United Kingdom.**

VEYSEY (LAURENCE R.) The communal experience: anarchist and mystical counter-cultures in America. New York, [1973]. pp. 495.

— **United States.**

KEBABIAN (JOHN S.) compiler. The Haymarket affair and the trial of the Chicago anarchists, 1886: original manuscripts, letters, articles and printed material of the anarchists and of the state prosecutor, Julius S. Grinnell; Grinnell's own collection, etc. New York, 1970. pp. 51. (*Kraus (Hans P.). Rare Books. Monograph Series. vol. 4.*

ANATOMY, HUMAN

— **History.**

BECK (FELIX) Anatomy: phoenix or fraud?; an inaugural lecture delivered in the University of Leicester, 6 December 1973. Leicester, 1974. pp. 13.

ANDAHUAYLAS (PROVINCE)

— **Social conditions.**

PERU. Direccion de Comunidades Campesinas. 1971. Datos basicos e inventario del patrimonio comunal de las comunidades de la provincia de Andahuaylas. [Lima, 1971]. pp. 59. (*Zac-Andahuaylas. No.2*)

ANDALUSIA

— **Social conditions.**

LUQUE BAENA (ENRIQUE) Estudio antropologico social de un pueblo del sur. Madrid, [1974]. pp. 251. *bibliog.*

ANDEAN GROUP.

KUCZYNSKI (MICHAEL) and HUELIN (DAVID) The Andean Group: two papers on trade liberalization and industrial planning and on the treatment of foreign capital under the Agreement of Cartagena, first given at the...Institute of Latin American Studies, April 1973. London, 1973. pp. 32.

ANDHRA PRADESH

— **Economic conditions.**

ANDHRA PRADESH. Planning Department. Review of progress: annual plan (formerly Third five-year plan: review of progress). a., 1961/2, 1965/6, 1966/7. Hyderabad.

ANDHRA PRADESH. Planning and Co-operation Department. Annual plan (formerly Third five-year plan: annual plan). a., 1964/5, 1965/6, 1967/8, 1968/9, 1972/3. Hyderabad.

— **Economic policy.**

ANDHRA PRADESH. Planning and Co-operation Department. 1972. Fourth five-year plan, Andhra Pradesh, 1969-70 to 1973-74; outline and programmes. [Hyderabad, 1972]. pp. 286.

— **Social conditions.**

ANDHRA PRADESH. Planning and Co-operation Department. Annual plan (formerly Third five-year plan: annual plan). a., 1964/5, 1965/6, 1967/8, 1968/9, 1972/3. Hyderabad.

— **Social policy.**

ANDHRA PRADESH. Planning and Co-operation Department. 1972. Fourth five-year plan, Andhra Pradesh, 1969-70 to 1973-74; outline and programmes. [Hyderabad, 1972]. pp. 286.

ANGERS

— **Growth.**

FRANCE. Direction de la Documentation. La Documentation Française. Notes et Etudes Documentaires. Nos. 4,065-4, 066-4,067. Les villes françaises: Angers et son agglomération; par Jacques Jeanneau. [Paris], 1974. pp. 79. *bibliog.*

ANGLESEY

— **Economic conditions.**

SADLER (PETER G.) and others. Regional income multipliers: the Anglesey study. [Bangor], 1973. pp. 109. (*Wales. University. University College of North Wales. Bangor Occasional Papers in Economics. No.1*)

— **Economic policy.**

DEVELOPMENT PLANNING PARTNERSHIP. Anglesey county structure plan: report of survey and discussion of alternatives; ([and] written statement); prepared on behalf of the County. Llangefni, 1974. 2 vols. (in 1).

— **Social policy.**

DEVELOPMENT PLANNING PARTNERSHIP. Anglesey county structure plan: report of survey and discussion of alternatives; ([and] written statement); prepared on behalf of the County. Llangefni, 1974. 2 vols. (in 1).

ANGOLA.

ABSHIRE (DAVID M.) and SAMUELS (MICHAEL A.) eds. Portuguese Africa: a handbook. New York, 1969. pp. 480.

— **Description and travel.**

HUIBREGTSE (P.K.) Angola, the real story; translated by Nicolette Buhr. Den Haag, [1973?]. pp. 244.

— **Economic conditions.**

ANGOLA. Secretaria Provincial de Planeamento, Integração Economica, Fazenda e Contabilidade. 1971. Conjuntura economica de Angola: exposição feita em 24 de abril de 1970, ao Conselho Legislativo de Angola, pelo Secretario Provincial de Planeamento, Integração Economica, Fazenda e Contabilidade. [Luanda, 1970 or rather 1971]. pp. 30.

BOAVIDA (AMERICO) Angola: five centuries of Portuguese exploitation. Richmond, B.C., 1972. pp. 124.

HUIBREGTSE (P.K.) Angola, the real story; translated by Nicolette Buhr. Den Haag, [1973?]. pp. 244.

— **Economic history.**

ANGOLA. Secretaria Provincial de Economia. 1970. Economia de Angola: evolução e perspectivas 1962-1969; palavras escritas na abertura do primeiro dos quatro volumes do relatorio da Secretaria Provincial de Economia; anexos estatisticos: Angola em numeros, 1962-1969; Angola na economia da Africa intertropical. [Luanda, 1970]. pp. 158.

— **Economic policy.**

ANGOLA. Secretaria Provincial de Economia. 1970. Economia de Angola: evolução e perspectivas 1962-1969; palavras escritas na abertura do primeiro dos quatro volumes do relatorio da Secretaria Provincial de Economia; anexos estatisticos: Angola em numeros, 1962-1969; Angola na economia da Africa intertropical. [Luanda, 1970]. pp. 158.

ANGOLA. Secretaria Provincial de Planeamento, Integração Economica, Fazenda e Contabilidade. 1971. Conjuntura economica de Angola: exposição feita em 24 de abril de 1970, ao Conselho Legislativo de Angola, pelo Secretario Provincial de Planeamento, Integração Economica, Fazenda e Contabilidade. [Luanda, 1970 or rather 1971]. pp. 30.

WORLD COUNCIL OF CHURCHES. Programme to Combat Racism. Cunene Dam scheme and the struggle for the liberation of southern Africa. Geneva, 1971. pp. 45.

— **History.**

GONZAGA (NORBERTO) Historia de Angola, 1482-1963. [Luanda, Centro de Informação e Turismo, 1966?]. pp. 380. *bibliog.*

— **Nationalism.**

BARNETT (DONALD L.) and HARVEY (ROY) The revolution in Angola: M[ovimento] P[opulár de] L[ibertação de] A[ngola], life histories and documents. Indianapolis, [1972]. pp. 312.

BOAVIDA (AMERICO) Angola: five centuries of Portuguese exploitation. Richmond, B.C., 1972. pp. 124.

COMMITTEE FOR FREEDOM IN MOZAMBIQUE, ANGOLA AND GUINE, and AFRICA RESEARCH GROUP. War on three fronts: the fight against Portuguese colonialism. London, [1972?]. pp. (44).

NETO (ANTONIO AGOSTINHO) Messages to companions in the struggle; [speeches]. Richmond, B.C., 1972. pp. 30.

— **Politics and government.**

ANGOLA. Commissão de Provincia da União Nacional. 1966. Angola: 40 anos de Revolução nacional. [Luanda, 1966]. pp. 186.

HUIBREGTSE (P.K.) Angola, the real story; translated by Nicolette Buhr. Den Haag, [1973?]. pp. 244.

— **Social conditions.**

HEIMER (FRANZ WILHELM) ed. Social change in Angola; with contributions by G.J. Bender [and others]. München, [1973]. pp. 279. (*Arnold-Bergstraesser-Institut für Kulturwissenschaftliche Forschung. Materialien zu Entwicklung und Politik. 4*) Map in end pocket.

HUIBREGTSE (P.K.) Angola, the real story; translated by Nicolette Buhr. Den Haag, [1973?]. pp. 244.

ANNUNZIO (GABRIELE D').

CASTRIS (ARCANGELO LEONE DE) Il decadentismo italiano: Svevo, Pirandello, D'Annunzio. Bari, [1974]. pp. 262.

ANSCHLUSS MOVEMENT, 1918—1938.

SUVAL (STANLEY) The Anschluss question in the Weimar era: a study of nationalism in Germany and Austria, 1918-1932. Baltimore, [1974]. pp. 240. *bibliog.*

ANTARCTIC REGIONS.

FRANCE. Direction de la Documentation. La Documentation Française. Notes et Etudes Documentaires. No. 4,005. Les terres australes et antarctiques françaises. [Paris], 1973. pp. 42. *bibliog.*

NEW ZEALAND GEOGRAPHY CONFERENCE, 7TH, HAMILTON, 1972. Proceedings...; edited by Evelyn Stokes. [Christchurch], 1973. pp. 298. *bibliogs.* (*New Zealand Geographical Society. Conference Series. No. 7*)

ANTHROPOGEOGRAPHY.

CLAVAL (PAUL) Principes de géographie sociale. Paris, [1973]. pp. 351.

INTERNATIONAL GEOGRAPHICAL UNION. Commission on Applied Geography. International Meeting, 4th, 1971. Géographie et perspectives à long terme: Geography and long term prospects;...editor, Michel Phlipponneau, etc. Sablé, [1973]. pp. 467. *In French or English.*

INTERNATIONAL GEOGRAPHICAL UNION. Commission on Applied Geography. International Meeting, 5th, Waterloo, Ontario, 1972. Applied geography and the human environment: proceedings of the...meeting...; edited by Richard E. Preston. Waterloo, Ont., [1973]. pp. 397. (*University of Waterloo [Ontario]. Department of Geography. Publication Series. No. 2*)

JOHNSTON (R.J.) Spatial structures: introducing the study of spatial systems in human geography. London, 1973. pp. 137. *bibliog.*

SUNDERLAND (ERIC) Elements of human and social geography: some anthropological perspectives. Oxford, 1973. pp. 107. *bibliog.*

— **Chad.**

CABOT (JEAN) and BOUQUET (CHRISTIAN) Le Tchad. Paris, 1973. pp. 128. *bibliog.*

— **India — Rajasthan.**

SHARMA (R.C.) Settlement geography of the Indian desert. New Delhi, 1972. pp. 199. *bibliog.*

— **Italy.**

COLE (JOHN W.) and WOLF (ERIC ROBERT) The hidden frontier: ecology and ethnicity in an Alpine valley. New York, [1974]. pp. 348. *bibliog.*

— **Puerto Rico.**

PICO (RAFAEL) The geography of Puerto Rico. Chicago, 1974. pp. 439. *bibliog.*

— **United Kingdom.**

CLOUT (HUGH D.) Rural geography: an introductory survey. Oxford, 1972. pp. 204. *bibliogs.*

ANTHROPOLOGISTS.

HATCH (ELVIN) Theories of man and culture. New York, [1973]. pp. 384. *bibliog.*

ANTHROPOLOGISTS, BRITISH.

HENSON (HILARY) British social anthropologists and language: a history of separate development. Oxford, 1974. pp. 147. *bibliog.*

ANTHROPOLOGY.

LOCAL-level politics: social and cultural perspectives; edited by Marc J. Swartz; [result of a conference sponsored by the Wenner-Gren Foundation for Anthropological Research, held at Burg Wartenstein, July, 1966]. Chicago, 1968. pp. viii, 437. *bibliogs.*

GRENDI (EDOARDO) ed. L'antropologia economica: [readings]. Torino, [1972]. pp. 299. *bibliog.*

ASAD (TALAL) ed. Anthropology and the colonial encounter. London, [1973]. pp. 286. *bibliog.*

CONFERENCE ON ANTHROPOLOGY AND MENTAL HEALTH, STANFORD, 1971. Cultural illness and health: essays in human adaptation; edited by Laura Nader and Thomas W. Maretzki. Washington, [1973]. pp. 145. *bibliogs.* (*American Anthropological Association. Anthropological Studies. No. 9*)

CRUMP (STEPHEN THOMAS) Man and his kind. London, 1973. pp. 154. *bibliog.*

DAVY (GEORGES) L'homme, le fait social et le fait politique: [collection of articles and other writings originally published 1919-1969]. Paris, [1973]. pp. 324. (*Paris. Ecole Pratique des Hautes Etudes. Section des Sciences Economiques et Sociales. Textes de Sciences Sociales. 9*)

DELFENDAHL (BERNHARD) Le clair et l'obscur: critique de l'anthropologie savante; défense de l'anthropologie amateur. Paris, [1973]. pp. 222.

HATCH (ELVIN) Theories of man and culture. New York, [1973]. pp. 384. *bibliog.*

LEVI-STRAUSS (CLAUDE) Anthropologie structurale deux. [Paris, 1973]. pp. 450.

DAVIS (JOHN HORSLEY RUSSELL) ed. Choice and change: essays in honour of Lucy Mair. London, 1974. pp. 259. *bibliog.* (*London. University. London School of Economics and Political Science. Monographs on Social Anthropology. No.50*)

SCHNEIDER (HAROLD KENNETH) Economic man: the anthropology of economics. New York, [1974]. pp. 278. *bibliog.*

— **Methodology.**

EPSTEIN (ARNOLD LEONARD) ed. The craft of social anthropology. London, 1967. pp. xx, 276. *bibliog.*

— **Study and teaching — Hong Kong.**

ANTHROPOLOGY and sociology in Hong Kong: field projects and problems of overseas scholars: proceedings of a symposium, February 8-9, 1969; compiled by Marjorie Topley. Hong Kong, 1969. pp. 143. *bibliog.*

ANTICLERICALISM

— **Germany.**

WENDEL (HERMANN MAX CARL LUDWIG) Sozialdemokratie und antikirchliche Propaganda: ein erweiterter Vortrag. Leipzig, 1907. pp. 31.

ANTICOMMUNIST MOVEMENTS

— **Russia.**

NATSIONAL'NO-TRUDOVOI SOIUZ NOVOGO POKOLENIIA. Programmye polozheniia i Ustav, etc. Belgrad, 1938. pp. 52.

BURD-VOSKHODOV (ALEKSANDR PAVLOVICH) Moskva dalekaia.... Moscow, the wide.... Moscou, la lointanie [sic]... [New York?, 1950]. pp. 219. *Added title page has subtitle: The immortals [sic] Russian's [sic] "liberators".*

HOLMSTON (A.) Izbrannye stat'i i rechi. Buenos Aires, 1953. pp. 224,13.

— — **White Russia.**

BAZHKO (ALES' TSIMAFEEVYCH) Tatal'nae bankrutstva. Minsk, 1973. pp. 119.

ANTINAZI MOVEMENT.

ANTINAZI MOVEMENT.

DORTMUND. Informations- und Presseamt. Dortmund, Karfreitag 1945: die Massenerschiessungen in der Bittermark und im Romberg-Park. Dortmund, [1971]. pp. 30.

BILLSTEIN (AUREL) ed. Der eine fällt, die anderen rücken nach...: Dokumente des Widerstandes und der Verfolgung in Krefeld, 1933-1945; zusammengestellt im Auftrag der Vereinigung der Verfolgten des Naziregimes, etc. Frankfurt/Main, [1973]. pp. 343. *bibliog.*

BLUDAU (KUNO) Gestapo, geheim'.: Widerstand und Verfolgung in Duisburg, 1933-1945. Bonn-Bad Godesberg, [1973]. pp. 324. *bibliog.* (*Friedrich-Ebert-Stiftung. Forschungsinstitut. Schriftenreihe. Band 98*)

BLUMENBERG-LAMPE (CHRISTINE) Das wirtschaftspolitische Programm der "Freiburger Kreise": Entwurf einer freiheitlich-sozialen Nachkriegswirtschaft; Nationalökonomen gegen den Nationalsozialismus. Berlin, [1973]. pp. 180. *bibliog.*

DOKUMENTATIONSARCHIV DES ÖSTERREICHISCHEN WIDERSTANDES. Festschrift: 10 Jahre Dokumentationsarchiv des österreichischen Widerstandes. Wien, [1973]. pp. 28.

KRETZSCHMAR (ERNST) ed. Widerstandskampf Görlitzer Antifaschisten, 1933-1945: Erinnerungen, Dokumente, Kurzbiographien; ([compiled for the] Kreiskommission zur Erforschung der Geschichte der örtlichen Arbeiterbewegung bei der SED-Kreisleitung Görlitz). Görlitz, 1973. pp. 101.

ROEDER (WERNER) Die deutschen Exilgruppen in Grossbritannien, 1940-1945: ein Beitrag zur Geschichte des Widerstandes gegen den Nationalsozialismus. 2nd ed. Bonn-Bad Godesberg, [1973]. pp. 322. *bibliog.* (*Friedrich-Ebert-Stiftung. Forschungsinstitut. Schriftenreihe. Band 58*)

SALM (FRITZ) Im Schatten des Henkers: vom Arbeitswiderstand in Mannheim gegen faschistische Diktatur und Krieg. Frankfurt/Main, [1973]. pp. 301.

DOHNANYI (KLAUS VON) Alone with one's conscience: the 30th anniversary of the 20 July. [Mainz, 1974]. pp. 14.

KUCKHOFF (GRETA) Vom Rosenkranz zur Roten Kapelle: ein Lebensbericht. Frankfurt am Main, 1974. pp. 434.

MAMMACH (KLAUS) Die deutsche antifaschistische Widerstandsbewegung, 1933-1939. Berlin, 1974. pp. 304.

WERNER (GERHART) Aufmachen! Gestapo!: ÜBER DEN Widerstand in Wuppertal, 1933- 1945; mit Beiträgen von Karl Ibach [and others]. Wuppertal, 1974. pp. 62.

— Bibliography.

HISTORIOGRAPHIE der Deutschen Demokratischen Republik über den deutschen antifaschistischen Widerstandskampf in den Jahren 1933 bis 1945: Überblick über Veröffentlichungen...1960 bis 1965; zusammengestellt...von Karl Heinz Biernat [and others]. Berlin, 1965. pp. 67.

ANTIOQUIA

— Economic policy.

ANTIOQUIA. Departamento Administrativo de Planeacion. 1967. Quinto plan cuatrienal 1968-1971; sector publico departamental. Medellin, 1967. pp. 306.

— Social policy.

ANTIOQUIA. Departamento Administrativo de Planeacion. 1967. Quinto plan cuatrienal 1968-1971; sector publico departamental. Medellin, 1967. pp. 306.

ANTIPATHIES AND PREJUDICES.

MARTIN (JAMES GILBERT) and FRANKLIN (CLYDE W.) Minority group relations. Columbus, Ohio, [1973]. pp. 338.

ANTISEMITISM.

CODREANU (CORNELIU ZELEA) La Garde de Fer: pour les légionnaires; [with appendix of letters and documents]. Paris, 1938; Grenoble, 1972. pp. 470.

POLIAKOV (LEON) The history of anti-semitism;... translated from the French by Richard Howard. London, 1974 in progress.

— Germany.

VON MALTITZ (HORST) The evolution of Hitler's Germany: the ideology, the personality, the moment. New York, [1973]. pp. 479. *bibliog.*

— Italy.

NOLA (ALFONSO M. DI) and others. Antisemitismo in Italia, 1962-1972. Firenze, [1973]. pp. 260.

— Russia.

LEGAGNEUX (ROBERT) Defendant. Soviet anti-semitism: the Paris trial; edited and with an introduction by Emanuel Litvinoff. London, 1974. pp. 120.

ANTWERP.

FRANCE. Direction de la Documentation. La Documentation Française. Notes et Etudes Documentaires. No. 3,846. Le port d'Anvers; [by] Pierre Barbusse. Paris, 1971. pp. 30.

— Economic history.

ASAERT (G.) De Antwerpse scheepvaart in de XVe eeuw, 1394-1480: bijdrage tot de ekonomische geschiedenis van de stad Antwerpen. Brussel, 1973. pp. 505. *bibliog.* (*Academie voor Wetenschappen, Letteren en Schone Kunsten van België. Verhandelingen. Klasse der Letteren. Jaargang 35. nr. 72*) With English summary.

APARTMENT HOUSES

— United Kingdom.

U.K. Ministry of Housing and Local Government. Sociological Research Station. 1964. Families living at high density. [London, 1964]. fo. 87.

HAMMERSMITH. Department of the Borough Architect and Director of Borough Development. Living in a council flat: a survey of attitudes on five estates; (prepared... by Janet Thomson). London, 1974. pp. 68,fo.14.

SUTCLIFFE (ANTHONY) ed. Multi-storey living: the British working-class experience. New York, 1974. pp. 249.

APEL (HANS).

APEL (HANS) Bonn, den ...: Tagebuch eine Bundestagsabgeordneten. Köln, [1972]. pp. 180.

APHASIA.

WHITAKER (HARRY A.) On the representation of language in the human brain: problems in the neurology of language and the linguistic analysis of aphasia. Edmonton, [1971]. pp. 224. *bibliog.*

BLUMSTEIN (SHEILA E.) A phonological investigation of aphasic speech. The Hague, 1973. pp. 117. *bibliog.*

GOODGLASS (HAROLD) and BLUMSTEIN (SHEILA) eds. Psycholinguistics and aphasia. Baltimore, [1973]. pp. 346. *bibliogs.*

SCHUELL (HILDRED) Aphasia theory and therapy: selected lectures and papers of Hildred Schuell; edited with an introductory chapter by Luther F. Sies. Baltimore, [1974]. pp. 300. *bibliogs.*

APPALACHIAN MOUNTAINS

— Economic policy.

APPALACHIAN REGIONAL COMMISSION. State and regional development plans in Appalachia, 1968. Washington, 1968. pp. 237.

— Social policy.

APPALACHIAN REGIONAL COMMISSION. State and regional development plans in Appalachia, 1968. Washington, 1968. pp. 237.

APPANAGE.

LEGUAI (ANDRE) Les ducs de Bourbon pendant la crise monarchique du XVe siècle: contribution à l'étude des apanages. Dijon, [1962]. pp. 219. *bibliog.*

APPELLATE PROCEDURE

— Poland.

MIELCAREK (EUGENIUSZ) Wnioski rewizji cywilnej. Warszawa, 1973. pp. 203. *bibliog.* With German summary.

APPRENTICES

— France.

[DUFRENE ( )] La misère des apprentifs imprimeurs, appliquée par le détail à chaque fonction de ce pénible état; vers burlesques; [reprint of work originally published 1710; issued by E. Morin] . Paris, 1900. pp. 14.

— Philippine Islands.

PHILIPPINE ISLANDS. Office of Apprenticeship. Annual report. a., 1969/70- Manila.

— United Kingdom.

VENABLES (ETHEL) Apprentices out of their time: a follow-up study. London, 1974. pp. 199. *bibliog.*

APULIA

— History.

COLARIZI (SIMONA) Dopoguerra e fascismo in Puglia, 1919-1926. Bari, 1971. pp. 454. (*Rome. Università. Istituto di Storia Moderna. Ricerca su "Partito, Stato e Società Civile nell'Italia Fascista 1922-1945". 1*)

AQUATIC SPORTS FACILITIES

— United Kingdom.

INLAND WATERWAYS AMENITY ADVISORY COUNCIL [U.K.]. Remainder waterways: a report to the Secretary of State for the Environment containing the recommendations of the Advisory Council in respect of proposals received between 1968 and 1971 for the addition of certain of the 'remainder' waterways to the cruising waterway system. [London], 1971. pp. 60.

INLAND WATERWAYS AMENITY ADVISORY COUNCIL [U.K.]. Waterway facilities: a report to the Secretary of State for the Environment on the leisure potential of the inland waterway system. [London], 1972. pp. 24.

TANNER (MICHAEL FRANCIS) Water Resources and recreation. London, Sports Council, 973. pp. 88. *bibliog.* (*Studies. 3*)

— — Wales.

SPORTS COUNCIL FOR WALES. A strategy for water recreation. Cardiff, [1974?]. pp. 117. *bibliog.*

ARAB COUNTRIES

— Defences.

TAHTINEN (DALE R.) The Arab-Israeli military balance today. Washington, [1973]. pp. 37. (*American Enterprise Institute for Public Policy Research. Foreign Affairs Studies. 9*)

TAHTINEN (DALE R.) The Arab-Israeli military balance since October 1973. Washington, [1974]. pp. 43. (*American Enterprise Institute for Public Policy Research. Foreign Affairs Studies. 11*)

— Economic conditions.

GUINE (ANTOINE) ed. Etude sur les états du Golfe Arabe. [Damascus, 1973]. fo. 117.

— **Economic policy.**

STEPHENS (ROBERT) The Arabs' new frontier. London, 1973. pp. 256.

— **Foreign opinion.**

HATEM (MOHAMED ABDEL KADER) Information and the Arab cause. London, 1974. pp. 320.

— **Foreign relations.**

MAHGOUB (MOHAMED AHMED) Democracy on trial: reflections on Arab and African politics. London, 1974. pp. 318.

— — **Israel.**

LADEIKIN (VLADIMIR PETROVICH) Istochnik opasnogo krizisa: rol' sionizma v razzhiganii konflikta na Blizhnem Vostoke. Moskva, 1973. pp. 296.

— — **Russia.**

SMOLANSKY (OLES M.) The Soviet Union and the Arab East under Khrushchev. Lewisburg, [1974]. pp. 326. bibliog. (Columbia University. Middle East Institute. Modern Middle East Series. vol. 6)

— **Nationalism.**

ABU-GHAZALEH (ADNAN MOHAMMED) Arab cultural nationalism in Palestine during the British mandate. Beirut, 1973. pp. 114. bibliog. (Institute for Palestine Studies. Monograph Series. No. 34)

HATEM (MOHAMED ABDEL KADER) Information and the Arab cause. London, 1974. pp. 320.

— **Politics and government.**

MALONE (JOSEPH J.) The Arab lands of western Asia. Englewood Cliffs, [1973]. pp. 269. bibliog.

— **Relations (general) with Russia.**

GORBATOV (OLEG MARKOVICH) and CHERKASSKII (LEONID IAKOVLEVICH) Sotrudnichestvo SSSR so stranami Arabskogo Vostoka i Afriki. Moskva, 1973. pp. 342. bibliog.

ARABIA, SAUDI.

See SAUDI ARABIA.

ARABIC LITERATURE.

ABU-GHAZALEH (ADNAN MOHAMMED) Arab cultural nationalism in Palestine during the British mandate. Beirut, 1973. pp. 114. bibliog. (Institute for Palestine Studies. Monograph Series. No. 34)

ARABS IN ISRAEL.

CARRE (OLIVIER) L'idéologie palestinienne de résistance: analyse de textes, 1964-1970. Paris, 1972. pp. 164. (Fondation Nationale des Sciences Politiques. Travaux et Recherches de Science Politique. 20)

FERGUSON (PAMELA) The Palestine problem. London, 1973. pp. 158. bibliog.

TERROR in Palestine. London, [1973?]. 1 pamphlet (unpaged).

ARABS IN PALESTINE.

ABU-GHAZALEH (ADNAN MOHAMMED) Arab cultural nationalism in Palestine during the British mandate. Beirut, 1973. pp. 114. bibliog. (Institute for Palestine Studies. Monograph Series. No. 34)

ARAUCANIAN INDIANS

— **Religion and mythology.**

DOWLING DESMADRYL (JORGE) Religion, chamanismo y mitologia mapuches. Santiago de Chile, [1971]. pp. 149. bibliog.

ARBITRATION, INDUSTRIAL.

BLEGVAD (BRITT MARI PERSSON) and others. Arbitration as a means of solving conflicts; (in cooperation with Kirsten Gamst-Nielsen). København, 1973. pp. 191. bibliog.

RANDOLPH (LILLIAN L.) Third-party settlement of disputes in theory and practice. New York, 1973. pp. 335. bibliog.

— **Colombia.**

RUEDA ROSERO (ULPIANO) Los conflictos de trabajo: la huelga; el arbitramento. Bogota, 1969. pp. 92. bibliog.

— **Norway.**

INNSTILLING om voldgiftsordning for statstjenestemenn som ikke har streikerett; avgitt av en komité oppnevnt av Lønn-og Prisdepartementet 30. november 1970. Orkanger, 1971. pp. 11.

— **United States.**

NATIONAL ACADEMY OF ARBITRATORS, ANNUAL MEETING, 25TH, 1972. Labor arbitration at the quarter-century mark: proceedings...; edited by Barbara D. Dennis and Gerald G. Somers. Washington, D.C., [1973]. pp. 466.

PRASOW (PAUL) The arbitrator's role. Los Angeles, 1974. pp. 8. (California University. Institute of Industrial Relations. Reprints. No. 240)

ARBITRATION, INTERNATIONAL.

AMERICAN ARBITRATION ASSOCIATION. New strategies for peacefull resolution of international business disputes New York, 1971. pp. 252

RANDOLPH (LILLIAN L.) Third-party settlement of disputes in theory and practice. New York, 1973. pp. 335. bibliog.

ARBITRATION AND AWARD

— **Communist countries.**

PFAFF (DIETER) and others. Die Aussenhandelsschiedsgerichtbarkeit der sozialistischen Länder im Handel mit der Bundesrepublik Deutschland unter Berücksichtigung des internationalen Privatrechts. Heidelberg, [1973]. pp. 887.

— **Denmark.**

BLEGVAD (BRITT MARI PERSSON) and others. Arbitration as a means of solving conflicts; (in cooperation with Kirsten Gamst-Nielsen). København, 1973. pp. 191. bibliog.

— **Russia.**

DOBROVOL'SKII (ARKADII ALEKSANDROVICH) ed. Arbitrazhnyi protsess v SSSR. Moskva, 1973. pp. 224.

KALLISTRATOVA (RIMMA FEDOROVNA) Gosudarstvennyi arbitrazh: problemy sovershenstvovaniia organizatsii i deiatel'nosti. Moskva, 1973. pp. 206.

— — **Costs.**

FAL'KOVICH (MARK SAMUILOVICH) and VINOKUR (SAMUIL ISAAKOVICH) Gosudarstvennaia poshlina v organakh gosarbitrazha. Moskva, 1973. pp. 63.

— **Sweden.**

BLEGVAD (BRITT MARI PERSSON) and others. Arbitration as a means of solving conflicts; (in cooperation with Kirsten Gamst-Nielsen). København, 1973. pp. 191. bibliog.

— **United Kingdom.**

PARRIS (JOHN) The law and practice of arbitration. London, 1974. pp. 145.

ARBOLEYA MARTINEZ (MAXIMILIANO).

BENAVIDES (DOMINGO) El fracaso social del catolicismo español: Arboleya-Martinez, 1870-1951. Barcelona, 1973. pp. 832. bibliog.

ARCHAEOLOGY.

U.K. Ordnance Survey. 1973. Field archaeology in Great Britain. 5th ed. Southampton, 1973. pp. 184. bibliog.

ARCHAEOLOGY, INDUSTRIAL

— **United Kingdom.**

ATKINSON (FRANK) The industrial archaeology of north-east England: the counties of Northumberland and Durham and the Cleveland district of Yorkshire. Newton Abbot, [1974]. 2 vols. bibliog.

ARCHITECTURE

— **Germany.**

TAYLOR (ROBERT R.) The word in stone: the role of architecture in the National Socialist ideology. Berkeley, [1974]. pp. 298. bibliog.

ARCHITECTURE AS A PROFESSION.

U.K. Civil Service Commission. 1970. Architects in government service. London, 1970. pp. 28.

ARCHIVES

— **Belgium.**

CENTRE INTERUNIVERSITAIRE D'HISTOIRE CONTEMPORAINE. Cahiers. 1. Louvain, 1957. pp. 53.

— **Rhodesia.**

NATIONAL ARCHIVES OF RHODESIA. Report of the Director of National Archives. a., 1972- Salisbury.

— **United Kingdom.**

U.K. Public Record Office, Lists and Indexes. Supplementary Series. No. 11. List of Board of Trade records to 1913. New York, Kraus Reprint Corporation, 1964. pp. 266.

U.K. Public Record Office. Lists and Indexes. Supplementary Series. No. 12. List of Treasury records, 1838-1938. New York, Kraus Reprint Corporation, 1970. pp. 359.

IRELAND, NORTHERN. Public Record Office. 1973- . Eighteenth century Irish official papers in Great Britain: private collections. Belfast, 1973 in progress. :

COBB (HENRY STEPHEN) Sources for economic history amongst the parliamentary records in the House of Lords Record Office. [London, 1973]. pp. 16. (U.K. Parliament. House of Lords. Record Office. Memoranda. No. 50)

U.K. Department of the Environment. 1973. Local Government Act 1972: local authority records. London, 1973. fo. 9.

U.K. Parliament. House of Lords. Record Office. Memoranda. No. 1. Select list of classes of records in the House of Lords Record Office; compiled by Maurice F. Bond. 9th ed. [London, 1973]. pp. 12.

HAZLEHURST (CAMERON) and WOODLAND (CHRISTINE) compilers. A guide to the papers of British Cabinet ministers 1900-1951. London, 1974. pp. 174. (Royal Historical Society. Guides and Handbooks. Supplementary Series. No. 1)

ARCISZEWSKI (FRANCISZEK ADAM).

ARCISZEWSKI (FRANCISZEK ADAM) Patrząc krytycznie, etc. London, 1972. pp. 310.

ARCTIC REGIONS.

OLENICOFF (S.M.) Territorial waters in the Arctic: the Soviet position. Santa Monica, 1972. pp. 52. bibliog. (Rand Corporation. [Rand Reports]. 907)

ARCTIC REGIONS (Cont.)

— Economic conditions.

SYMPOSIUM FOR ANTHROPOLOGICAL RESEARCH IN THE NORTH, LULEÅ AND TROMSØ, 1969. Circumpolar problems: habitat, economy, and social relations in the Arctic: [arranged by the Nordic Council for Anthropological Research]; edited by Gösta Berg. Oxford, 1973. pp. 194. *bibliogs.* (*Wenner-Gren Center Foundation for Scientific Research. International Symposium Series. vol.21*)

— International status.

PHARAND (DONAT) The law of the sea of the Arctic, with special reference to Canada. Ottawa, 1973. pp. 367. *bibliog.* (*Ottawa. Université. Faculté de Droit. Collection des Travaux. Monographies Juridiques. No. 7*)

— Social conditions.

SYMPOSIUM FOR ANTHROPOLOGICAL RESEARCH IN THE NORTH, LULEÅ AND TROMSØ, 1969. Circumpolar problems: habitat, economy, and social relations in the Arctic: [arranged by the Nordic Council for Anthropological Research]; edited by Gösta Berg. Oxford, 1973. pp. 194. *bibliogs.* (*Wenner-Gren Center Foundation for Scientific Research. International Symposium Series. vol.21*)

AREA STUDIES.

INTERNATIONAL studies: present status and future prospects: [proceedings of a conference]..., editor, Fred W. Riggs. Philadelphia, 1971. pp. 271. (*American Academy of Political and Social Science. Monographs.* [No.] 12)

GEOGRAPHERS abroad: essays on the problems and prospects of research in foreign areas [presented at a conference held at the University of Chicago, 1972; edited by] Marvin W. Mikesell. Chicago, 1973. pp. 296. *Chicago. University. Department of Geography. Research Papers. No. 152*)

ARGENLIEU (THIERRY D').

See THIERRY D'ARGENLIEU (GEORGES LOUIS MARIE).

ARGENTINE REPUBLIC

— Appropriations and expenditures.

ARGENTINE REPUBLIC. Ministerio de Cultura y Educacion. Subsecretaria Economia Financiera. 1971. Presente y futuro de la obra social. [Buenos Aires, 1971]. pp. 101.

— Army — History.

AUZA (NESTOR TOMAS) El ejercito en la epoca de la Confederacion, 1852-1861. Buenos Aires, 1971. pp. 263. (*Circulo Militar. Coleccion: Historico-Militar. vol.633-634*)

— Census.

ARGENTINE REPUBLIC. Census, 1970. Censo nacional de poblacion, familias y viviendas, 1970: resultados obtenidos por muestra: total del pais. [Buenos Aires, 1973?]. pp. 56.

ARGENTINE REPUBLIC. Census, 1970. Censo nacional de poblacion, familias y viviendas, 1970: resultados provisionales: localidades con 1000 y mas habitantes: todo el pais. [Buenos Aires, 1973]. pp. 55.

— Commerce.

ARGENTINE REPUBLIC. Secretaria de Estado de Comercio Exterior. 1970. Exportaciones argentinas clasificadas segun grado de elaboracion y tradicionalidad, años 1966/69. [Buenos Aires, 1970?]. fo.52.

— — Statistics.

ARGENTINE REPUBLIC. Instituto Nacional de Estadistica y Censos. Intercambio comercial. m., Ja 1973- Buenos Aires.

— Economic conditions.

SAMPAY (ARTURO ENRIQUE) Ideas para la revolucion de nuestro tiempo en la Argentina. Buenos Aires, 1968 repr. 1969. pp. 156.

DIAMAND (MARCELO) Doctrinas economicas, desarrollo e independencia: economia para las estructuras productivas desequilibradas; caso argentino. Buenos Aires, 1973. pp. 464.

— — Maps.

QUARGNOLO (JORGE) Atlas del potencial argentino; ([with statistical appendix]: Potencial economico argentino). Buenos Aires, 1972. pp. 159, 32.

— Economic history.

ROQUE GONDRA (LUIS) Historia economica de la Republica Argentina. Buenos Aires, [1943]. pp. 488. *bibliog.*

ROSA (JOSE MARIA) Analisis historico de la dependencia argentina. Buenos Aires, 1973. pp. 94.

— Economic policy.

Los PLANES de estabilizacion en la Argentina; [by] Aldo Ferrer [and others]. Buenos Aires, [1969]. pp. 132.

LEBEDINSKY (MAURICIO) Argentina: bases economicas de la politica; metodologia general y aplicada. Buenos Aires, [1970]. pp. 174.

ARGENTINE REPUBLIC. Poder Ejecutivo Nacional. 1973. Plan trienal para la reconstruccion y la liberacion nacional, 1974- 1977. [Buenos Aires], 1973. pp. 369.

DIAMAND (MARCELO) Doctrinas economicas, desarrollo e independencia: economia para las estructuras productivas desequilibradas; caso argentino. Buenos Aires, 1973. pp. 464.

LASCANO (MARCELO RAMON) Crisis de la politica economica argentina. Buenos Aires, [1973]. pp. 288.

PERON (JUAN DOMINGO) Juan Peron en la Argentina, 1973: sus discursos, sus dialogos, sus conferencias; plan trienal 1974-77. [Buenos Aires, 1974]. pp. 395.

— — Bibliography.

ARGENTINE REPUBLIC. Consejo Federal de Inversiones. Biblioteca. 1972. Desarrollo economico y planificacion en la Republica Argentina: seleccion bibliografica, 1930-1972; [compiled by] Alfredo Estevez [and others]. Buenos Aires, 1972. pp. 394. (*Consejo Federal de Inversiones. Serie Tecnica. No. 13*)

— Foreign economic relations — Belgium.

BELGIUM. Office Belge du Commerce Extérieur. 1970. La mission économique belge en Argentine, juin 1970: rapport. Bruxelles, 1970. pp. 37. (*Informations du Commerce Extérieur. Suppléments. Série C. No. 5*)

— Foreign population.

NATALE (OSCAR A.) and CABELLO (PLACIDO) Algunos aspectos cuantitativos de la poblacion extranjera originaria de paises limitrofes. Buenos Aires, 1973. pp. 66. (*Argentine Republic. Consejo Federal de Inversiones. Serie Tecnica. No. 19*)

— History.

MERCHENSKY (MARCOS) Las corrientes ideologicas en la historia argentina. Buenos Aires, [1961]. pp. 315.

PONCE (ANIBAL) El viento en el mundo: examen de la España actual en el centenario de Fourier. Buenos Aires, 1963. pp. 188.

BUSANICHE (JOSE LUIS) Estanislao Lopez y el federalismo del litoral. Buenos Aires, [1969]. pp. 174.

— — Sources.

PINO MONTES DE OCA (O. DEL) ed. La revolucion del 90: Leandro N. Alem, Aristobulo del Valle, etc. Buenos Aires, [1955]. pp. 157.

ROSAS (JUAN MANUEL DE) defendant. Juicio criminal a Don Juan Manuel de Rosas; [documents compiled, with notes, by Vicente Zito Lema]. Buenos Aires, [1969]. pp. 111.

— — 1817—1860.

COMISION CENTRAL DE HOMENAJE A ANGEL VICENTE PEÑALOZA. Angel Vicente Peñaloza; [by Pedro Santos Martinez and others]. Buenos Aires, 1969. pp. 301.

— — 1910—1943.

SCHILLIZZI MORENO (HORACIO A.) Argentina contemporanea: fraude y entrega, 1930-1943. Buenos Aires, 1973. 2 vols. (in 1). *bibliog.*

— — 1943— .

LUNA (FELIX) Argentina de Peron a Lanusse, 1943-1973. Buenos Aires, 1973. pp. 230.

— Industries.

LAVALLE (FRANCISCO JOSE) Fomento de la pequeña y mediana industria en el interior del pais. Buenos Aires, 1968. pp. 93. *bibliog.*

— Politics and government.

MERCHENSKY (MARCOS) Las corrientes ideologicas en la historia argentina. Buenos Aires, [1961]. pp. 315.

SAMPAY (ARTURO ENRIQUE) Ideas para la revolucion de nuestro tiempo en la Argentina. Buenos Aires, 1968 repr. 1969. pp. 156.

CARDOSO (FERNANDO HENRIQUE) Ideologias de la burguesia industrial en sociedades dependientes: Argentina y Brasil. Mexico, 1969 repr. 1972. pp. 239. *bibliog.*

SOLOMONOFF (JORGE N.) Ideologias del movimiento obrero y conflicto social: de la organizacion nacional hasta la Prima Guerra Mundial. Buenos Aires, [1971]. pp. 314. *bibliog.*

SCENNA (MIGUEL ANGEL) F.O.R.J.A.: una aventura argentina; de Yrigoyen a Peron. Buenos Aires, [1972]. 2 vols. (in 1).

BOTANA (NATALIO R.) and others. El regimen militar, 1966-1973. Buenos Aires, 1973. pp. 522.

CERESOLE (NORBERTO) and MASTRORILLI (CARLOS P.) Peronismo: teoria e historia del socialismo nacional. Buenos Aires, [1973]. pp. 432.

LUNA (FELIX) Argentina de Peron a Lanusse, 1943-1973. Buenos Aires, 1973. pp. 230.

JOHNSON (KENNETH F.) Peronism: the final gamble. London, 1974. pp. 18. (*Institute for the Study of Conflict. Conflict Studies. No. 42*)

— Population.

CICOUREL (AARON VICTOR) Theory and method in a study of Argentine fertility. New York, [1974]. pp. 212. *bibliog.*

— Rural conditions.

VICAT (BLANCA ELENA) Tres familias en un obraje del norte argentino. Buenos Aires, 1972. pp. 326.

— Social policy.

ARGENTINE REPUBLIC. Ministerio de Cultura y Educacion. Subsecretaria Economia Financiera. 1971. Presente y futuro de la obra social. [Buenos Aires, 1971]. pp. 101.

ARGENTINE REPUBLIC. Poder Ejecutivo Nacional. 1973. Plan trienal para la reconstruccion y la liberacion nacional, 1974- 1977. [Buenos Aires], 1973. pp. 369.

PERON (JUAN DOMINGO) Juan Peron en la Argentina, 1973: sus discursos, sus dialogos, sus conferencias; plan trienal 1974-77. [Buenos Aires, 1974]. pp. 395.

— Statistics, Vital.

ARGENTINE REPUBLIC. Departamento de Atencion Medica. 1969. Mortalidad en la Republica Argentina: tasas especificas y ajustadas por edad y sexo y otros indicadores derivados de las estadisticas de mortalidad, 1959-1961. [Buenos Aires], 1969. pp. 79. *(Publicaciones. No.4)*

ARGENTINE REPUBLIC. Departamento de Atencion Medica. 1969. Mortalidad por causa, edad y sexo en la Republica Argentina, 1959-1961. [Buenos Aires, 1969]. pp. 197.

ARGENTINE REPUBLIC. Departamento de Atencion Medica. 1970. Mortalidad en la Republica Argentina: tasas especificas y ajustadas por edad y sexo y otros indicadores derivados de las estadisticas de mortalidad, 1962-1965: comparacion trienio 1959- 1961 con cuatrienio 1962-1965. [Buenos Aires], 1970. pp. 95. *(Publicaciones. No.5)*

ARIZONA

— Economic conditions.

KELSO (MAURICE M.) and others. Water supplies and economic growth in an arid environment: an Arizona case study. Tucson, [1973]. pp. 327. *bibliog.*

ARKHANGEL'SK (OBLAST')

— Politics and government.

PLAMENNOE slovo bortsov revoliutsii: listovki arkhangel'skikh bol'shevikov, 1903-1917. Arkhangel'sk, 1972. pp. 99.

ARMAMENTS.

INSTITUT ROYAL DES RELATIONS INTERNATIONALES. Les aspects économiques du réarmement; par un groupe d'étude de l'Institut, etc. [Brussels], 1951. pp. 236.

— Mathematical models.

LUTERBACHER (URS) Dimensions historiques de modèles dynamiques de conflit: application aux processus de course aux armements, 1900-1965. Leiden, 1974. pp. 175. *bibliog. (Geneva. Graduate Institute of International Studies. Collection de Relations Internationales. 2)*

ARMED FORCES.

INTERNATIONAL INSTITUTE FOR STRATEGIC STUDIES. Adelphi Papers. No. 103. Force in modern societies: the military profession; [papers given at the 15th annual conference, Travemünde, 1973]. London, 1973. pp. 45.

— History — Bibliography.

HIGHAM (ROBIN) ed. Official histories: essays and bibliographies from around the world. Manhattan, Ka., 1970. pp. 644. *(Kansas State University of Agriculture and Applied Science. Library. Bibliography Series. No.8)*

— Political activity.

INTERNATIONAL INSTITUTE FOR STRATEGIC STUDIES. Adelphi Papers. No. 102. Force in modern societies: its place in international politics; [papers given at the 15th annual conference, Travemünde, 1973]. London, 1973. pp. 26.

— Underdeveloped areas.

See UNDERDEVELOPED AREAS — Armed Forces.

ARMENIA

— Rural conditions.

ARUTIUNIAN (LUSANDR MKRTICHEVICH) Sotsial'no-ekonomicheskie izmeneniia v derevne Armianskoi SSR. Erevan, 1973. pp. 303.

ARMENIAN QUESTION.

TORIGUIAN (SHAVARSH) The Armenian question and international law. Beirut, 1973. pp. 330. *bibliog.*

ARMENIANS IN TURKEY.

KERR (STANLEY ELPHINSTONE) The lions of Marash: personal experiences with American Near East Relief, 1919-1922. Albany, N.Y., 1973. pp. 318. *bibliog.*

ARMIES

— Officers.

TEITLER (GERKE) De wording van het professionele officierskorps: een sociologisch- historische analyse. Rotterdam, 1974. pp. 309. *bibliog. With an English summary.*

ARNAL (MOSEN JESUS).

ARNAL (MOSEN JESUS) Por que fui secretario de Durruti: narracion. Tarrega, [1972]. pp. 266.

ARRAS

— Politics and government.

BOBROWSKI (EDOUARD) Aux urnes, citoyens...: [municipal elections, Arras, 1971]. Paris, [1973]. pp. 259.

ART.

PSYCHOLOGIE comparative et art: hommage à I. Meyerson. [Paris], 1972. pp. 306.

— Philosophy.

LIFSHITS (MIKHAIL ALEKSANDROVICH) The philosophy of art of Karl Marx;...translated from the russian by Ralph N. Winn; [reprint of translation first published in 1938]. London, 1973. pp. 118.

WOLLHEIM (RICHARD ARTHUR) On art and the mind: essays and lectures. London, 1973. pp. 340.

— Psychology.

WOLLHEIM (RICHARD ARTHUR) On art and the mind: essays and lectures. London, 1973. pp. 340.

ART, PRIMITIVE.

FORGE (ANTHONY) ed. Primitive art and society. London, 1973. pp. 286. *bibliogs.*

ART AND SOCIETY.

FORGE (ANTHONY) ed. Primitive art and society. London, 1973. pp. 286. *bibliogs.*

ELME (PATRICK D') Peinture et politique. [Paris, 1974]. pp. 150.

FRASER (JOHN) b. 1928. Violence in the arts. London, 1974. pp. 192.

ART AND STATE

— Russia.

JAMES (CARADOG VAUGHAN) Soviet socialist realism: origins and theory. London, 1973. pp. 146. *bibliog.*

— United States.

McKINZIE (RICHARD D.) The New Deal for artists. Princeton, [1973]. pp. 203. *bibliog.*

ART INDUSTRIES AND TRADE

— United Kingdom.

U.K. Treasury. 1973. Private owners and public collections; note. [London], 1973. fo. 8.

ART OBJECTS.

MEYER (KARL ERNEST) The plundered past. London, 1974. pp. 353.

ARTHRITIS.

OFFICE OF HEALTH ECONOMICS. [Studies in Current Health Problems]. No. 45. Rheumatism and arthritis in Britain. London, [1973]. pp. 44. *bibliog.*

ARTIFICIAL INSEMINATION, HUMAN.

CIBA FOUNDATION. Symposia. New Series. 17. Law and ethics of A[rtificial I[nsemination by] D[onor] and embryo transfer. Amsterdam, 1973. pp. 110. *bibliogs.*

ARTIFICIAL INTELLIGENCE.

ARBIB (MICHAEL A.) The metaphorical brain: an introduction to cybernetics as artificial intelligence and brain theory. New York, [1972]. pp. 243. *bibliog.*

ARTIFICIAL intelligence: a paper symposium; [by Sir James Lighthill and others]. London, Science Research Council, 1973. pp. 45.

ARTISANS

— Ecuador.

ECUADOR. Secretaria General de Planeacion Economica. 1968. Evaluacion del programa de desarrollo artesanal; [by] Danilo Bassi Zambelli. Quito, 1968. pp. 117. *(Documentos. No.01-14)*

ECUADOR. Secretaria General de Planeacion Economica. 1969. Programa de artesania y pequeñas industrias, 1969-1973; version preliminar para discusion; [by Danilo Bassi-Zambelli and Gustavo Chambers M.]. Quito, 1969. pp. 252. *(Documentos. No. 02-14)*

— Germany — Hesse.

HESSE. Statistisches Landesamt. Beiträge zur Statistik Hessens. Neue Folge. Nr. 57. Handwerkszählung 1968. Wiesbaden, 1973. pp. 243.

ARTS

— China.

ASIAN PEOPLES' ANTI-COMMUNIST LEAGUE. Pamphlets. No.172. Chiang Ching - Mao Tse-Tung's wife. [Taipei], 1973. pp. 44.

— Germany.

BRENNER (HILDEGARD) ed. Ende einer bürgerlichen Kunst-Institution: die politische Formierung der Preussischen Akademie der Künste ab 1933; (eine Dokumentation). Stuttgart, [1972]. pp. 174. *(Vierteljahrshefte für Zeitgeschichte. Schriftenreihe. Nr. 24)*

— United Kingdom.

U.K. Central Office of Information. Reference Division. Reference Pamphlets. 114. The promotion of the arts in Britain. London, 1973. pp. 33. *bibliog.*

ARTS AND COMMUNISM.

See COMMUNISM AND THE ARTS.

ARTSYBASHEV (MIKHAIL PETROVICH).

ARTSYBASHEV (MIKHAIL PETROVICH) Cheremukha: zapiski pisatelia. t.2. Varshava, 1927. pp. 179. *Articles originally published in "Za svobodu". Vol.1 entitled Zapiski pisatelia.*

ARYANS.

POLIAKOV (LEON) The Aryan myth: a history of racist and nationalist ideas in Europe; translated [from the French] by Edmund Howard. London, 1974. pp. 388. *(Brighton. University of Sussex. Columbus Centre. Studies in the Dynamics of Persecution and Extermination)*

ASIA

— Commerce.

UNITED NATIONS. Economic Commission for Asia and the Far East. Development Programming Techniques Series. Bangkok, 1960 in progress.

— — Europe.

STEENSGAARD (NIELS) Carracks, caravans and companies: the structural crisis in the European-Asian trade in the early 17th century. [Copenhagen, 1973]. pp. 448. *bibliog. (Scandinavian Institute of Asian Studies. Monograph Series. No. 17)*

ASIA (Cont.)

— — European Economic Community countries.

GHAI (DHARAM P.) The enlargement of the E.E.C. and the Asian Commonwealth countries. London, Commonwealth Secretariat, 1973. pp. 57. (*Commonwealth Economic Papers. No.2*)

— — Pacific, The.

PACIFIC TRADE AND DEVELOPMENT CONFERENCE, 5TH, TOKYO, 1973. Structural adjustments in Asian-Pacific trade: papers and proceedings...; edited by Kiyoshi Kojima. Tokyo, 1973. 2 vols. (in 1). (*Japan Economic Research Center. Center Papers. No.21*) Paged continuously.

— — United Kingdom.

GHAI (DHARAM P.) The enlargement of the E.E.C. and the Asian Commonwealth countries. London, Commonwealth Secretariat, 1973. pp. 57. (*Commonwealth Economic Papers. No.2*)

— Economic policy.

UNITED NATIONS. Economic Commission for Asia and the Far East. Development Programming Techniques Series. Bangkok, 1960 in progress.

INTERREGIONAL SEMINAR ON DEVELOPMENT PLANNING, 5TH, BANGKOK, 1969. Development prospects and planning for the coming decade (with special reference to Asia); report of the...Seminar [held in]...Bangkok, Thailand 15-26 September 1969. (ST/TAO/SER. C/133). New York, United Nations, 1971. pp. 178.

ONE WORLD ONLY, BANGKOK, 1971. Social aspects of economic development planning in Asia, (editor: Erwin Kristoffersen). Bangkok, [1972?]. pp. 321. (*Friedrich-Ebert-Stiftung. Asian Labour Institute. Reports. 5*)

— Foreign economic relations — United Kingdom.

FABIAN SOCIETY. Fabian Tracts. [No.] 420. Labour in Asia: a new chapter?; editor, Colin Jackson. London, 1973. pp. 52.

— Foreign relations — Australia.

SERONG (FRANCIS PHILLIP) An Australian view of revolutionary war. London, 1971. pp. 16. (*Institute for the Study of Conflict. Conflict Studies. No. 16*)

— — Russia.

McLANE (CHARLES B.) Soviet-Asian relations. vol. 2 of his Soviet-Third World relations. New York, 1973.

— — United Kingdom.

FABIAN SOCIETY. Fabian Tracts. [No.] 420. Labour in Asia: a new chapter?; editor, Colin Jackson. London, 1973. pp. 52.

— — United States.

KIM (IL-SUNG) Let us completely frustrate U.S. imperialist aggression and intervention in Asia: speech... welcoming Samdech Norodom Sihanouk, head of state of Cambodia... April 16, 1973. Pyongyang, 1973. pp. 20.

WILCOX (WAYNE AYRES) The emergence of Bangladesh: problems and opportunities for a redefined American policy in South Asia. Washington, 1973. pp. 79. (*American Enterprise Institute for Public Policy Research. Foreign Affairs Studies. 7*)

— Industries.

ONE WORLD ONLY, TOKYO, 1969. Industrialization and technological change in Asia: its implication for the Asian labour movement; (editor: Dieter Bielenstein). Tokyo, [1970?]. pp. 163. (*Friedrich-Ebert-Stiftung. Asian Labour Institute. Reports. 3*)

— Politics and government.

DORÉ (FRANCIS) Les régimes politiques en Asie. Paris, [1973]. pp. 492. *bibliog.*

POPULATION, politics, and the future of southern Asia; [papers presented at a conference convened by the Southern Asian Institute of Columbia University, 1971]; edited by W. Howard Wriggins and James F. Guyot. New York, 1973. pp. 402.

RAHUL (RAM) Politics of central Asia. London, 1974. pp. 185. *bibliog.*

— Population.

POPULATION, politics, and the future of southern Asia; [papers presented at a conference convened by the Southern Asian Institute of Columbia University, 1971]; edited by W. Howard Wriggins and James F. Guyot. New York, 1973. pp. 402.

— Relations (general) with Russia.

BULGANIN (NIKOLAI ALEKSANDROVICH) and KHRUSHCHEV (NIKITA SERGEEVICH) N.A. Bulganin and N.S. Khrushchov: full texts of speeches and statements in India, Burma and Afghanistan. London, Soviet News, 1955. pp. 47.

— Rural conditions.

RURAL settlements in monsoon Asia: proceedings of I[nternational] G[eographical] U[nion] symposia at Varanasi and Tokyo [in 1971, organized by the IGU Commission on Rural Settlements in Monsoon Asia]; edited by R.L. Singh. Varanasi, 1972. pp. 510.

— Social policy.

UNITED NATIONS. Economic Commission for Asia and the Far East. Development Programming Techniques Series. Bangkok, 1960 in progress.

ONE WORLD ONLY, BANGKOK, 1971. Social aspects of economic development planning in Asia, (editor: Erwin Kristoffersen). Bangkok, [1972?]. pp. 321. (*Friedrich-Ebert-Stiftung. Asian Labour Institute. Reports. 5*)

ASIA, SOUTHEAST

— Commercial policy.

SEMINAR ON EXCHANGE RATES AS A PROBLEM OF THE SOUTHEAST ASIA REGION.SINGAPORE, 1972. Exchange rate policy in Southeast Asia. Lexington, [1973]. pp. 105.

— Economic conditions.

GHOSH (A.P.) Development planning in south-east Asia: an input-output approach;... in collaboration with D. Chakravarti and H. Sarkar.Rotterdam. 1974. pp. 118. *bibliog.*

— Economic policy.

DEVELOPMENT in Southeast Asia: issues and dilemmas; papers presented at an academic conference held in conjunction with the Inaugural Conference of the [Southeast Asian Social Science] Association...1971, Hong Kong; edited by S.S. Hsueh. [Hong Kong?, 1972]. pp. 186.

FRANCE. Direction de la Documentation. La Documentation Française. Notes et Etudes Documentaires. Nos. 3,951-3, 952. Les perspectives économiques de l'Asie du Sud-Est, 1970- 1990. [Paris], 1973. pp. 87.

NEW directions in the international relations of southeast Asia: economic relations; papers presented at a conference organized by the Institute of Southeast Asian Studies; edited by Lee Soo Ann. Singapore, 1973. pp. 133. *bibliog.*

GHOSH (A.P.) Development planning in south-east Asia: an input-output approach;... in collaboration with D. Chakravarti and H. Sarkar.Rotterdam. 1974. pp. 118. *bibliog.*

— — Mathematical models.

PAAUW (DOUGLAS S.) and FEI (JOHN C.H.) The transition in open dualistic economies: theory and Southeast Asian experience. New Haven, 1973. pp. 306. (*Yale University. Economic Growth Center. Publications*)

— Foreign economic relations — Japan.

NEW directions in the international relations of southeast Asia: economic relations; papers presented at a conference organized by the Institute of Southeast Asian Studies; edited by Lee Soo Ann. Singapore, 1973. pp. 133. *bibliog.*

— Foreign relations.

CROZIER (BRIAN) A conflict-free South-East Asia?. London, 1972. pp. 22. (*Institute for the Study of Conflict. Conflict Studies. No. 22*)

BHANEJA (BALWANT) The politics of triangles: the alignment patterns in South Asia, 1961-71. Delhi, [1973]. pp. 192. *bibliog.*

NEW directions in the international relations of southeast Asia: the great powers and southeast Asia; papers presented at a conference organized by the Institute of Southeast Asian Studies; edited by Lau Teik Soon. Singapore, 1973. pp. 205.

CONFLICT and stability in Southeast Asia; [papers of a seminar held in the Institute of International Relations, University of British Columbia in 1972]; edited by Mark W. Zacher and R. Stephen Milne. Garden City, N.Y., 1974. pp. 489.

— — China.

FITZGERALD (CHARLES PATRICK) China and Southeast Asia since 1945. London, 1973. pp. 110. *bibliog.*

— — United States.

INDOCHINA handbook 1972: an 'Indochina' special. London, [1972?]. pp. 48. *Articles on the Vietnam conflict previously appearing in the magazine Indo-China.*

— History.

VON DER MEHDEN (FRED R.) South-East Asia 1930-1970: the legacy of colonialism and nationalism. London, [1974]. pp. 144.

— Industries.

UNITED NATIONS EDUCATIONAL, SCIENTIFIC AND CULTURAL ORGANIZATION. Research Centre on Social and Economic Development in Southern Asia. 1959. Unesco Research Centre on the Social Implications of Industrialization in Southern Asia: organization and objectives. Calcutta, [1959]. pp. 17.

— Nationalism.

NATIONALISM, revolution and evolution in South-East Asia: (papers...read at a colloquium held at the University of Hull... 1968); [edited by] Michael Leifer. Zug, [1970]. pp. 175. (*Hull. University. Centre for South-East Asian Studies. Monographs on South-East Asia. No.2*)

— Politics and government.

NATIONALISM, revolution and evolution in South-East Asia: (papers...read at a colloquium held at the University of Hull... 1968); [edited by] Michael Leifer. Zug, [1970]. pp. 175. (*Hull. University. Centre for South-East Asian Studies. Monographs on South-East Asia. No.2*)

CROZIER (BRIAN) A conflict-free South-East Asia?. London, 1972. pp. 22. (*Institute for the Study of Conflict. Conflict Studies. No. 22*)

MODERNIZATION in South-East Asia: [based on a conference held in Singapore, 1971 under the auspices of the Institute of Southeast Asian Studies]; edited by Hans-Dieter Evers. Singapore, 1973. pp. 249. *bibliog.*

— Social conditions.

UNITED NATIONS EDUCATIONAL, SCIENTIFIC AND CULTURAL ORGANIZATION. Research Centre on Social and Economic Development in Southern Asia. 1959. Unesco Research Centre on the Social Implications of Industrialization in Southern Asia: organization and objectives. Calcutta, [1959]. pp. 17.

MODERNIZATION in South-East Asia: [based on a conference held in Singapore, 1971 under the auspices of the Institute of Southeast Asian Studies]; edited by Hans-Dieter Evers. Singapore, 1973. pp. 249. *bibliog.*

VON DER MEHDEN (FRED R.) South-East Asia 1930-1970: the legacy of colonialism and nationalism. London, [1974]. pp. 144.

— Social policy.

DEVELOPMENT in Southeast Asia: issues and dilemmas; papers presented at an academic conference held in conjunction with the Inaugural Conference of the [Southeast Asian Social Science] Association...1971, Hong Kong; edited by S.S. Hsueh. [Hong Kong?, 1972]. pp. 186.

ASIATICS IN THE UNITED KINGDOM.

OXFORD (ALEC) Implications of youth work in Asian community: report of a conference organised by the National Association of Indian Youth,...Birmingham...1973. [Leicester], 1973. pp. 49. *(Youth Service Information Centre. Occasional Papers. 7)*

ASSASSINATION.

RAPOPORT (DAVID C.) Assassination and terrorism; [expanded version of a series of talks broadcast by the Canadian Broadcasting Corporation]. Toronto, [1971]. pp. 88 .

— France.

PLUME (CHRISTIAN) and DEMARET (PIERRE) Target De Gaulle: the thirty-one attempts to assassinate the general;... translated from the French by Richard Barry. London, 1974. pp. 294.

— Spain.

BORRAS BETRIU (RAFAEL) and others, eds. El dia en que mataron a Carrero Blanco. Barcelona, 1974. pp. 412.

— United Kingdom — Ireland, Northern.

DILLON (MARTIN) and LEHANE (DENIS CHARLES) Political murder in Northern Ireland. Harmondsworth, 1973. pp. 318.

ASSESSMENT

— United Kingdom.

CITIZENS' RIGHTS OFFICE. [A practical guide for ratepayers appealing against the rating assessment imposed upon housing]. London, [1973]. fo. 36.

ASSIMILATION (SOCIOLOGY).

MARTENS (ALBERT) 25 jaar Wegwerparbeiders: het Belgisch immigratiebeleid na 1945. Leuven, 1973. pp. 322. *bibliog. (Katholieke Universiteit te Leuven. Sociologisch Onderzoeksinstituut. Afdeling Arbeids- en Industriële Sociologie. Rapport 1973/2)*

RICHARDSON (ALAN) Psychologist. British immigrants and Australia: a psycho-social inquiry. Canberra, 1974. pp. 209. *bibliog. (Academy of the Social Sciences in Australia. Immigrants in Australia. 4)*

ASSOCIATIONS, INSTITUTIONS, ETC.

— Austria.

DOKUMENTATIONSARCHIV DES ÖSTERREICHISCHEN WIDERSTANDES. Festschrift: 10 Jahre Dokumentationsarchiv des österreichischen Widerstandes. Wien, [1973]. pp. 28.

— Germany.

DEUTSCHER FREMDENVERKEHRSVERBAND. 1902-1972, Deutscher Fremdenverkehrsverband, DFV; (verantwortlich für den Inhalt: Ernst Bernhauer). Bonn, [1972]. pp. 144.

— Russia.

ODOM (WILLIAM E.) The Soviet volunteers: modernization and bureaucracy in a public mass organization. Princeton, [1973]. pp. 360. *bibliog.*

ASTRINGENTS.

VINOGRADOV (BORIS NIKOLAEVICH) Syr'evaia baza promyshlennosti viazhushchikh veshchestv SSSR. Moskva, 1971. pp. 321. *bibliog.*

ASTRONAUTICS IN EARTH SCIENCES.

CANADA. Program Planning Office for Resource Satellites and Remote Airborne Sensing. Working Group on Satellite and Ground Station Engineering. 1971. Resource satellites and remote airborne sensing for Canada. Report no.9. Satellite and ground station engineering; [R.E. Barrington, chairman]. Ottawa, 1971. pp. 37. *With French summary.*

ATHEISM.

KOZHURIN (IAKOV IAKOVLEVICH) Iz istorii bor'by za nauchnyi ateizm: A. Bebel' i G.V. Plekhanov. Leningrad, 1972. pp. 84.

ATEIZM, religiia, sovremennost'. Leningrad, 1973. pp. 226.

PROKOSHINA (EKATERINA SERGEEVNA) Ocherk svobodomysliia i ateizma v Belorussii v XIX v. Minsk, 1973. pp. 226.

SEGIZBAEV (ORAZ AMANGALIEVICH) Traditsii svobodomysliia i ateizma v dukhovnoi kul'ture kazakhskogo naroda. Alma-Ata, 1973. pp. 168.

VORONTSOV (GEORGII VASIL'EVICH) Leninskaia programma ateisticheskogo vospitaniia v deistvii, 1917-1937 gg. Leningrad, 1973. pp. 176.

— Dictionaries and encyclopaedias.

MARECHAL (PIERRE SYLVAIN) Dictionnaire des athées anciens et modernes;... troisième édition, augmentée des suppléments de J. Lalande, de plusieurs articles inédits, et d'une notice nouvelle sur Maréchal et ses ouvrages; par J.B.L. Germond. Paris, 1853. 1 vol. (various pagings).

ATLANTA

— Race question.

HUTCHESON (JOHN D.) Racial attitudes in Atlanta. Atlanta, 1973. pp. 82. *(Emory University. Center for Research in Social Change. Publications. Series B. Report No.2)*

ATLANTIC, THE

— Foreign relations — Japan.

JAPAN and the Atlantic world: [papers of a conference organized by the Atlantic Institute in 1972; edited by Curt Gasteyger]. Farnborough, Hants, [1972]. pp. 88. *(Atlantic Institute. Atlantic Papers. 1972.3)*

ATLANTIC COMMUNITY.

IVANOVA (INESSA MIKHAILOVNA) Kontseptsiia "atlanticheskogo soobshchestva" vo vneshnei politike SShA. Moskva, 1973. pp. 279.

JOSHUA (WYNFRED) Nuclear weapons and the Atlantic Alliance. New York, [1973]. pp. 60. *bibliog. (National Strategy Information Center. Strategy Papers. No. 18)*

CATLIN (Sir GEORGE EDWARD GORDON) Kissinger's Atlantic charter. Gerrards Cross, 1974. pp. 144.

HADLEY (GUY) Transatlantic partnership and problems. Tunbridge Wells, 1974. pp. 83. *bibliog.*

ATLASES.

ROSNER (CHARLES) ed. The world of De La Rue: the Old World and the New; presented on the occasion of the one hundred and fiftieth anniversary of the house of De la Rue, 1813-1963. [London, 1963]. 1 vol. (unpaged).

The PENGUIN world atlas; (geographic editor, Peter Hall); prepared by the Cartographic Department of the Clarendon Press. Harmondsworth, 1974. pp. 253.

ATOMIC BOMB

— Testing.

TOULAT (JEAN) Objectif Mururoa avec Bollarddière. Paris, [1974]. pp. 275.

ATOMIC ENERGY.

U.K. Central Office of Information. Reference Division. 1955. The Commonwealth and nuclear development. London, 1955. pp. 52. *bibliog.*

SWEDEN. Industridepartementet. 1970. Svensk atomenergipolitik: (motiv och riktlinjer för statens insatser på atomenergiområdet 1947-1970). [Stockholm]. 1970. pp. 215.

INGLIS (DAVID RITTENHOUSE) Nuclear energy: its physics and its social challenge. Reading, Mass., [1973]. pp. 395. *bibliog.*

— Economic aspects.

THIRIET (LUCIEN) and LIEVRE (PAUL) Facteurs et incertitudes de la rentabilité du recours à l'énergie nucléaire dans le dessalement des eaux. Gif-sur-Yvette, 1969. pp. 30. *bibliog. (France. Commissariat à l'Energie Atomique. Etudes Economiques) In English and French.*

ATOMIC ENERGY INDUSTRIES.

NUCLEAR ENERGY AGENCY. Activity report. a., [Jl 1971/D 1972](1st)- Paris.

— Europe.

ALBONETTI (ACHILLE) Europe and nuclear energy. Paris, [1972]. pp. 80. *(Atlantic Institute. Atlantic Papers. 1972.2)*

— France.

FRANCE. Direction de la Documentation. La Documentation Française. Notes et Etudes Documentaires. Nos. 3,945-3, 946. Le Commissariat à l'Energie Atomique face à l'avenir, par François Goure. [Paris], 1972. pp. 56. *bibliog.*

— Sweden.

SWEDEN. Industridepartementet. 1970. Svensk atomenergipolitik: (motiv och riktlinjer för statens insatser på atomenergiområdet 1947-1970). [Stockholm]. 1970. pp. 215.

ATOMIC ENERGY RESEARCH

— France.

FRANCE. Commissariat à l'Energie Atomique. 1968. Grenoble Nuclear Research Center. [Grenoble, 1968]. pp. 58.

FRANCE. Commissariat à l'Energie Atomique. 1968. The Fontenay aux-Roses Research Center. [Paris? 1968?]. pp. 47.

FRANCE. Commissariat à l'Energie Atomique. 1969. Saclay Nuclear Research Center and the National Institute of Nuclear Sciences and Technologies. [Paris?, 1969?]. pp. 88.

ATOMIC POWER

— International control.

WILLRICH (MASON) ed. International safeguards and nuclear industry;...[by] Henry D. Smyth [and others, members of the American Society of International Law's Panel on Nuclear Energy and World Order]. Baltimore, [1973]. pp. 307.

ATOMIC POWER—PLANTS

— Environmental aspects.

COCHRAN (THOMAS B.) The liquid metal fast breeder reactor: an environmental and economic critique. Baltimore, [1974]. pp. 271.

— Location.

THIRIET (LUCIEN) Tailles et localisations optimales des usines de retraitement des combustibles nucléaires, etc. Gif-sur-Yvette, 1967. pp. (iii), 60bis. *bibliog. (France. Commissariat à l'Energie Atomique. Etudes Economiques) In English and French.*

ATOMIC POWER—PLANTS (Cont.)

THIRIET (LUCIEN) and DELEDICQ (ANDRE) Application de la sous-optimalité en programmation dynamique à la localisation et la cadence optimales de construction des équipements. Gif-sur-Yvette, 1968. pp. 32. *bibliog. (France. Commissariat à l'Energie Atomique. Etudes Economiques) In English and French.*

ATOMIC WEAPONS.

NELIN (IURII GRIGOR'EVICH) Atom i NATO. Moskva, 1970. pp. 131.

WILLIAMS (SHELTON L.) Nuclear nonproliferation in international politics: the Japanese case. Denver, 1971-1972. pp. 74. *(Denver. University. Social Science Foundation and Graduate School of International Studies. Monograph Series in World Affairs. vol.9. no.3)*

LUTTWAK (EDWARD) The strategic balance 1972. New York, 1972. pp. 132. *(Georgetown University. Center for Strategic and International Studies. Washington Papers. vol.[1]/3)*

SECURITY, order, and the bomb: nuclear weapons in the politics and defence planning of non-nuclear weapon states; [papers presented at a conference organized by the Norwegian Institute of International Affairs in 1971]; edited by Johan Jórgen Holst. Oslo, [1972]. pp. 208. *bibliog.*

INTERNATIONAL INSTITUTE FOR STRATEGIC STUDIES. Adelphi Papers. No. 96. The Alliance and Europe: part 1: crisis stability in Europe and theatre nuclear weapons; by Wolfgang Heisenberg. London, 1973. pp. 35.

INTERNATIONAL INSTITUTE FOR STRATEGIC STUDIES. Adelphi Papers. No.99. Nuclear weapons and Chinese policy; by Harry Gelber. Kondon, 1973. pp. 37.

JOSHUA (WYNFRED) Nuclear weapons and the Atlantic Alliance. New York, [1973]. pp. 60. *bibliog. (National Strategy Information Center. Strategy Papers. No. 18)*

JOSHUA (WYNFRED) and HAHN (WALTER F.) Nuclear politics: America, France and Britain. Beverly Hills, [1973]. pp. 84. *bibliog. (Georgetown University. Center for Strategic and International Studies. Washington Papers. vol. 1/9)*

MOULTON (HARLAND B.) From superiority to parity: the United States and the strategic arms race, 1961-1971. Westport, Conn., [1973]. pp. 333. *bibliog.*

STOCKHOLM INTERNATIONAL PEACE RESEARCH INSTITUTE. Nuclear proliferation problems. Cambridge, Mass., [1974]. pp. 312.

— Testing.

FRANCE. Comité Interministériel pour l'Information. 1973. Livre blanc sur les expériences nucléaires. [Paris, 1973]. pp. 116.

— — Congresses.

CONFERENCE ON THE DISCONTINUANCE OF NUCLEAR WEAPONS TESTS, GENEVA,1958- . Official records: verbatim records, no.1, 31 October 1958 no.340, 9 September 1961, [and] checklist of documents issued between October 31, 1958, and March 20, 1961. Geneva, 1958-61. Microfilm: 6 reels.

ATOMIC WEAPONS AND DISARMAMENT.

GOLDBLAT (JOZEF) and RATHJENS (GEORGE W.) Strategic arms limitation. London, 1972. 2 pts. *(Stockholm International Peace Research Institute. Research Reports. Nos. 5 and 6)*

WOLFE (THOMAS W.) Soviet attitudes toward MBFR and the USSR's military presence in Europe. [Santa Monica], 1972. pp. 17. *(Rand Corporation. [Papers]. 4819)*

BULL (HEDLEY) The Moscow agreements and strategic arms limitation. Canberra, 1973. pp. 50. *(Australian National University. Strategic and Defence Studies Centre. Canberra Papers on Strategy and Defence. No. 15)*

CHICAGO. University. Center for Policy Study. Arms Control and Foreign Policy Seminar. SALT: problems and prospects: (papers prepared for the... Seminar); edited by Morton A. Kaplan. Morristown, [1973]. pp. 251.

FURET (MARIE FRANÇOISE) Le désarmement nucléaire. Paris, [1973]. pp. 303. *bibliog. (Revue Générale de Droit International Public. Publications. Nouvelle Série. No.19)*

INTERNATIONAL ARMS CONTROL SYMPOSIUM, 5TH, PHILADELPHIA, 1971. SALT: implications for arms control in the 1970s; William R. Kintner and Robert L. Pfaltzgraff, editors. Pittsburgh, [1973]. pp. 447.

QUESTER (GEORGE H.) The politics of nuclear proliferation. Baltimore, [1973]. pp. 249.

SCIENTIFIC AMERICAN. Arms control: (readings from Scientific American); with introductions by Herbert F. York. San Francisco, [1973]. pp. 427. *bibliogs.*

LEGAULT (ALBERT) and LINDSEY (GEORGE) The dynamics of the nuclear balance. Ithaca, 1974. pp. 273.

SMITH (DAN) of the Campaign for Nuclear Disarmament. After the Indian bomb. London, [1974]. pp. 12.

WILLRICH (MASON) and RHINELANDER (JOHN B.) eds. SALT: the Moscow agreements and beyond. New York, [1974]. pp. 361. *bibliog.*

— Congresses.

CONFERENCE ON THE DISCONTINUANCE OF NUCLEAR WEAPONS TESTS, GENEVA,1958- . Official records: verbatim records, no.1, 31 October 1958 no.340, 9 September 1961, [and] checklist of documents issued between October 31, 1958, and March 20, 1961. Geneva, 1958-61. Microfilm: 6 reels.

ATROCITIES

— Burundi.

LEMARCHAND (RENE) and MARTIN (DAVID) Journalist. Selective genocide in Burundi. London, 1974. pp. 36. *bibliog. (Minority Rights Group. Reports. No. 20)*

— Cyprus.

The DRAMA of Cyprus: ten tales of horror; [with photocopiesof seven further statements and two newspaper cuttings]. Nicosia, 1974. pp. 12, (12).

— Mozambique.

INTERNATIONAL DEFENCE AND AID FUND [FOR SOUTHERN AFRICA]. Special Reports. No. 2. Terror in Tete: a documentary report of Portuguese atrocities in Tete district, Mozambique, 1971-1972. London, 1973. pp. 48.

ATTENTION.

KAHNEMAN (DANIEL) Attention and effort. Englewood Cliffs, [1973]. pp. 246. *bibliog.*

ATTITUDE (PSYCHOLOGY).

ROKEACH (MILTON) Beliefs, attitudes and values: a theory of organization and change.San Francisco, 1968 repr. 1972. pp. 214. *bibliog.*

LEMON (NIGEL) Attitudes and their measurement. London, 1973. pp. 294. *bibliog.*

TRANSGAARD (HENNING) The cognitive component of attitudes and beliefs: structure and empirical methods: a review of some conceptualizations and of some empirical methods for discovering and assigning structure. København, 1973. pp. 89. *(Socialforskningsinstituttet. Studier. Nr. 27)*

WIGGINS (LEE M.) Panel analysis: latent probability models for attitude and behavior processes. Amsterdam, 1973. pp. 255. *bibliog.*

ATTITUDE CHANGE.

HIMMELFARB (SAMUEL) and EAGLY (ALICE HENDRICKSON) eds. Readings in attitude change. New York, [1974]. pp. 655. *bibliog.*

AUCKLAND

— Civic improvement.

AUCKLAND. Town Planning Division. Central area proposals: a series of planning proposals for the future development of the central area of Auckland. Auckland, [1971]. pp. 128.

AUCKLAND. Town Planning Division. Central area survey: data collected for the preparation of a plan for the future development of the central area of Auckland. Auckland, [1971]. pp. 100.

— Economic history.

STONE (R.C.J.) Makers of fortune: a colonial business community and its fall. Auckland, N.Z., 1973. pp. 240. *bibliog.*

AUDIO—VISUAL LIBRARY SERVICE.

CONFERENCE ON MULTI-MEDIA RESOURCE ORGANIZATION IN HIGHER EDUCATION, HULL, 1970. A challenge for librarians?: a report on the joint NCET/ASLIB Audio Visual Group Conference...[by] Richard Fothergill. London, 1971. pp. 76. *(National Council for Educational Technology. Working Papers. 4)*

AUDITING.

AMERICAN ENTERPRISE INSTITUTE FOR PUBLIC POLICY RESEARCH. Legislative Analyses. 93rd Congress. No. 12. The Federal Reserve audit bill. Washington, 1973. pp. 13.

AUGSPURG (ANITA).

HEYMANN (LIDA GUSTAVA) and AUGSPURG (ANITA) Erlebtes-Erschautes: deutsche Frauen kämpfen für Freiheit, Recht und Frieden 1850-1940; herausgegeben von Margrit Twellmann. Meisenheim am Glan, 1972. pp. 311. *bibliog.*

AUSTRALASIA

— Emigration and immigration.

PRICE (CHARLES ARCHIBALD) The great white walls are built: restrictive immigration to North America and Australasia, 1836-1888. Canberra, 1974. pp. 323. *bibliog.*

— Population — Bibliography.

WARE (HELEN) ed. Fertility and family formation: Australasian bibliography and essays 1972. Canberra, 1973. pp. 269, A 80. *(Australian National University. Research School of Social Sciences. Department of Demography. Australian Family Project)*

AUSTRALIA.

FINANCIAL TIMES. Australia in the seventies: a survey...; edited by Michael Southern. Harmondsworth, 1973. pp. 229. *bibliog.*

— Commercial policy.

LLOYD (PETER JOHN) Non-tariff distortions of Australian trade. Canberra, 1973. pp. 243. *bibliog.*

— Constitution.

AUSTRALIA. Parliament. Joint Committee on Constitutional Review. 1959. Report. in AUSTRALIA. Parliament. Parliamentary papers. 1959- 60. vol.3.

— Constitutional law.

HOWARD (COLIN) Australian federal constitutional law. 2nd ed. Melbourne, 1972. pp. 535.

— Defences.

SERONG (FRANCIS PHILLIP) An Australian view of revolutionary war. London. 1971. pp. 16. *(Institute for the Study of Conflict. Conflict Studies. No. 16)*

AUSTRALIA. Department of Defence. 1973. Australian defence: report on the reorganisation of the defence group of departments; [by Sir Arthur Tange]; (with Statement by the Deputy Prime Minister and Minister for Defence). Canberra, 1973. 1 vol. (various pagings).

— **Economic conditions.**

AUSTRALIA. Australian News and Information Bureau, [Canberra]. 1970. Australia: (an economic and investment reference). [new ed.]. [Canberra, 1970]. pp. 112. *bibliog.*

— **Economic history.**

GOODWIN (CRAUFURD D.W.) The image of Australia: British perception of the Australian economy from the eighteenth to the twentieth century. Durham, N.C., 1974. pp. 255. *(Duke University. Commonwealth-Studies Center. Publications. No. 42)*

— **Economic policy.**

DAVIDSON (B.R.) The northern myth: a study of the physical and economic limits to agricultural and pastoral development in tropical Australia. 3rd ed. Carlton, Va., 1972. pp. 298.

— **Emigration and immigration.**

RICHARDSON (ALAN) Psychologist. British immigrants and Australia: a psycho-social inquiry. Canberra, 1974. pp. 209. *bibliog. (Academy of the Social Sciences in Australia. Immigrants in Australia. 4)*

— **Executive departments.**

AUSTRALIA. Department of Defence. 1973. Australian defence: report on the reorganisation of the defence group of departments; [by Sir Arthur Tange]; (with Statement by the Deputy Prime Minister and Minister for Defence). Canberra, 1973. 1 vol. (various pagings).

— **Foreign opinion.**

GOODWIN (CRAUFURD D.W.) The image of Australia: British perception of the Australian economy from the eighteenth to the twentieth century. Durham, N.C., 1974. pp. 255. *(Duke University. Commonwealth-Studies Center. Publications. No. 42)*

— **Foreign relations.**

CAMILLERI (JOSEPH ANTHONY) and TEICHMANN (MAX) Security and survival: the new era in international relations. South Yarra, Victoria, 1973. pp. 226. *bibliog.*

— — Asia.

SERONG (FRANCIS PHILLIP) An Australian view of revolutionary war. London, 1971. pp. 16. *(Institute for the Study of Conflict. Conflict Studies. No. 16)*

— — **East (Near East).**

AUSTRALIA. Parliament. Joint Committee on Foreign Affairs. 1969. Report... on the Middle East situation. in AUSTRALIA. Parliament. Parliamentary papers, 1969, vol.6.

— **Full employment policies.**

AUSTRALIA. Department of Labour and National Service. 1970. An analysis of full employment in Australia. Melbourne, 1970. pp. 48. *(Labour Market Studies. No.2)*

— **Industries.**

AUSTRALIA. Commonwealth Bureau of Census and Statistics. 1972. Australian national accounts: input-output tables, 1962-63; prepared... by J.P. O'Neill. Canberra, [1972]. pp. 205. *Chart in end pocket.*

— — Directories.

AUSTRALIA. Department of Trade and Industry. Office of Secondary Industry. 1966. Directory of overseas investment in Australian manufacturing industry, 1966. Canberra, [1966]. pp. 159.

AUSTRALIA. Department of Trade and Industry. Office of Secondary Industry. 1971. Directory of overseas investment in Australian manufacturing industry, 1971. Canberra, [1971]. pp. 205.

— **Native races.**

WORLD COUNCIL OF CHURCHES. Programme to Combat Racism. More facts and figures: aboriginal issues; racism in Australia. Geneva, 1971. pp. 37. *bibliog.*

— **Parliament.**

AUSTRALIA. Parliament. Joint Select Committee on the New and Permanent Parliament House. 1969. Report on the alternative sites of Capital Hill and the Camp Hill area for the new and permanent Parliament House. in AUSTRALIA. Parliament. Parliamentary papers, 1969, vol.6.

— — Elections.

BUTLER (DAVID HENRY EDGEWORTH) The Canberra model: essays on Australian government. London, 1974. pp. 146.

— — **House of Representatives.**

HUGHES (COLIN ANFIELD) and GRAHAM (BRUCE DESMOND) Voting for the Australian House of Representatives, 1901-1964. Canberra, 1974. pp. 544,xii. *Supplement to the same authors' A handbook of Australian government and politics 1890-1964, to which it also contains Corrigenda.*

— **Relations (general) with Canada.**

AUSTRALIA. Parliamentary Mission to Canada. 1970. Official report of the... Mission... [1969]. in AUSTRALIA. Parliament. Parliamentary papers, 1969, vol.5.

— **Social conditions.**

REID (ELIZABETH) and ALTMAN (DENNIS) Equality: the new issues; [2 lectures originally delivered at the 1973 Fabian Winter Lecture Series Equality under Labor]. Melbourne, [1973?]. pp. 16. *(Victorian Fabian Society. Victorian Fabian Pamphlets. [No]. 28)*

AUSTRALIAN ABORIGINES.

BURRIDGE (KENELM O.L.) Encountering aborigines: a case study: anthropology and the Australian aboriginal. New York, [1973]. pp. 260. *bibliog.*

CRANSTONE (BRYAN ALLAN LEFEVRE) The Australian aborigines; (prepared by the Ethnography Department [of the British Museum]). London, 1973. pp. 47. *bibliog.*

STEVENS (FRANK S.) Aborigines in the Northern Territory cattle industry. Canberra, 1974. pp. 226. *bibliog. (Academy of the Social Sciences in Australia. Aborigines in Australian Society. 11)*

AUSTRIA.

AUSTRIA. Bundespressedienst. 1961. Austria: facts and figures. 4th ed. Vienna, 1961. pp. 108.

— **Boundaries.**

WITZIG (DANIEL) Die Vorarlberger Frage: die Vorarlberger Anschlussbewegung an die Schweiz,...1918-1922. Basel, 1974. pp. 527. *bibliog.*

— **Commercial treaties — Italy.**

SCHOBER (ERNST GEORG) Das regionale Handelsabkommen Trentino-Südtirol, Nordtirol-Vorarlberg. Innsbruck, 1971. pp. 127. *bibliog.*

— **Constitution.**

SCHWARZ (WALTER) Arbeitsrecht und Verfassung: Antrittsvorlesung, gehalten am 26. November 1970 an der Universität Graz. Wien, [1972]. pp. 45. *bibliog. (Vienna. Kammer für Arbeiter und Angestellte. Schriftenreihe)*

— **Economic conditions.**

NEMSCHAK (FRANZ) Österreichs Wirtschaft an der Jahreswende 1971/72: Rückschau und Ausblick. Wien, 1972. pp. 20. *(Österreichisches Institut für Wirtschaftsforschung. Vorträge und Aufsätze. Nr. 31)*

— **Economic policy.**

SUPPANZ (HANNES) and ROBINSON (DEREK) Prices and incomes policy: the Austrian experience. Paris, Organisation for Economic Co-operation and Development, 1972. pp. 72.

HOLLERER (SIEGFRIED) Verstaatlichung und Wirtschaftsplanung in Österreich, 1946- 1949. Wien, 1974. pp. 258. *bibliog. (Vienna. Hochschule für Welthandel. Dissertationen. 15)*

— **Foreign economic relations — United Kingdom.**

HELLEINER (KARL F.) Free trade and frustration: Anglo-Austrian negotiations 1860-70. Toronto, [1973]. pp. 152. *bibliog.*

— **Foreign relations.**

DUMBA (CONSTANTIN THEODOR) Dreibund- und Entente-Politik in der Alten und Neuen Welt. Zürich, [1931]. pp. 482.

See also EUROPEAN ECONOMIC COMMUNITY — Austria.

— — Italy.

SIEGLER (HEINRICH) Die österreichisch-italienische Einigung über die Regelung des Südtirolkonflikts. Bonn, [1970]. pp. 35.

— — Switzerland.

WITZIG (DANIEL) Die Vorarlberger Frage: die Vorarlberger Anschlussbewegung an die Schweiz,...1918-1922. Basel, 1974. pp. 527. *bibliog.*

— **History — 1918—1938.**

OESTERREICH 1927 bis 1938: Protokoll des Symposiums in Wien, 23. bis 28. Oktober 1972. Wien, 1973. pp. 276. *(Theodor-Körner-Stiftungsfonds, and Leopold-Kunschak- Preis. Wissenschaftliche Kommission zur Erforschung der Österreichischen Geschichte der Jahre 1927 bis 1938. Veröffentlichungen. Band 1)*

WITZIG (DANIEL) Die Vorarlberger Frage: die Vorarlberger Anschlussbewegung an die Schweiz,...1918-1922. Basel, 1974. pp. 527. *bibliog.*

— — **1934, Socialist Uprising.**

REISBERG (ARNOLD) Februar 1934: Hintergründe und Folgen. Wien, [1974]. pp. 254.

— — 1938—1945.

POLTAVSKII (MOISEI ANATOL'EVICH) Diplomatiia imperializma i malye strany Evropy, 1938-1945 gg. Moskva, 1973. pp. 303.

— **Industries.**

AUSTRIA. Statistisches Zentralamt. Industriestatistik. a., (in 2 pts.)- 1971[3.Jg.]- Wien.

— **Intellectual life.**

McGRATH (WILLIAM J.) Dionysian art and populist politics in Austria. New Haven, 1974. pp. 269. *bibliog.*

— **Militia.**

NUSSER (HORST G.W.) Konservative Wehrverbände in Bayern, Preussen und Österreich, 1918-1933; mit einer Biographie von Forstrat Georg Escherich, 1870-1941. München, [1973]. 2 vols.

— **Nationalrat.**

ALT (THEODOR RUDOLF) Hundert Jahre im Dienste der Österreichischen Volksvertretung. Wien, Österreichische Staatsdruckerei, 1948. pp. 204.

— — Elections.

FABER (PETER) Die Nationalratswahlen 1970 in den Wiener Tageszeitungen: eine inhaltsanalytische Untersuchung. Wien, 1973. pp. 255. *bibliog. (Vienna. Universität. Institut für Publizistik. Schriftenreihe. Band 3)*

— **Politics and government.**

MIGSCH (ERWIN) Sozialprogramme und Wirklichkeit: (Analyse und Vergleich der für Österreich wesentlichen Ideologien). Wien, [1962]. pp. 62. *(Österreichischer Gewerkschaftsbund. Aktuelle Probleme unserer Zeit)*

AUSTRIA (Cont.)

FISCHER (ERNST) of the Austrian Communist Party. Das Ende einer Illusion: Erinnerungen, 1945-1955. Wien, [1973]. pp. 400.

VODOPIVEC (ALEXANDER) Die Quadratur des Kreisky: Österreich zwischen parlamentarischer Demokratie und Gewerkschaftsstaat. Wien, [1973]. pp. 368.

HAUTMANN (HANS) and KROPF (RUDOLF) Die österreichische Arbeiterbewegung vom Vormärz bis 1945: sozialökonomische Ursprünge ihrer Ideologie und Politik. Wien, [1974]. pp. 214. *bibliog.* (*Ludwig-Boltzmann-Institut für Geschichte der Arbeiterbewegung. Schriftenreihe. 4*)

McGRATH (WILLIAM J.) Dionysian art and populist politics in Austria. New Haven, 1974. pp. 269. *bibliog.*

— **Population.**

AUSTRIA. Statistisches Zentralamt. 1972. Wohnungswechsel: Ergebnisse des Mikrozensus. Wien, 1972. pp. 86. (*Beiträge zur Österreichischen Statistik. Heft 288*)

HELCZMANOVSKI (HEIMOLD) ed. Beiträge zur Bevölkerungs- und Sozialgeschichte Österreichs, nebst einem Überblick über die Entwicklung der Bevölkerungs- und Sozialstatistik; im Auftrag des Österreichischen Statistischen Zentralamtes. Wien, 1973. pp. 448.

— **Social policy.**

STAININGER (OTTO) ed. Ferdinand Hanusch, 1866-1923: ein Leben für den sozialen Aufstieg; herausgegeben ... im Auftrag der Österreichischen Gesellschaft für Kulturpolitik. Wien, [1973]. pp. 109. (*Ludwig-Boltzmann-Institut für Geschichte der Arbeiterbewegung. Schriftenreihe. 3*)

SOZIALISTISCHE PARTEI ÖSTERREICHS. Humankonferenz, 3., 1973. Humanpolitik im modernen Österreich: 3. Humankonferenz...27. September 1973. [Vienna], 1974. pp. 72.

— **Statistics — Bibliography.**

ARNBERGER (ERIK) compiler. Österreichisches statistisches Quellenmaterial und Veröffentlichungen, die Statistik enthalten 1945-1956; zusammengestellt im Österreichischen Statistische n Zentralamt. [Vienna, 1957?]. pp. 36. (*Sonderdruck aus: Berichte zur deutschen Landeskunde, Band 19, Heft 1*)

AUSTRIA—HUNGARY

— **History.**

PAULEY (BRUCE F.) The Habsburg legacy, 1867-1939. New York, [1972]. pp. 189. *bibliog.*

— **Nationalism.**

CURTICĂPEANU (V.) Le mouvement culturel pour le parachèvement de l'état national roumain, 1918. Bucarest, 1973. pp. 264. (*Academia Republicii Socialiste România. Secţia de Ştiinţe Istorice, Filozofice şi Economico-Juridice. Bibliotheca Historica Romaniae. Monographies. 12*)

AUSTRIAN LITERATURE

— **History and criticism.**

WILLIAMS (CEDRIC ELLIS) The broken eagle: the politics of Austrian literature from empire to Anschluss. London, 1974. pp. 281. *bibliog.*

AUSTRIAN WIT AND HUMOUR.

BROER (WOLFGANG) Wort als Waffe: politischer Witz und politische Satire in der Republik Österreich, 1918-1927; Versuch einer Darstellung und Auswertung. Wien, 1973. 2 vols. *bibliogs.* (*Vienna. Universität. Dissertationen. 100*)

AUSTRIANS IN ITALY.

TOEPFER (LORE) Die Abwanderung deutschsprachiger Bevölkerung aus Südtirol nach 1955. Innsbruck, 1973. pp. 135. *bibliog.*

AUTHORITARIANISM.

McKINNEY (DAVID W.) The authoritarian personality studies: an inquiry into the failure of social science research to produce demonstrable knowledge. The Hague, 1973. pp. 304. *bibliogs.*

AUTHORITY.

BOSSLE (LOTHAR) Der Autoritäts- und Machtanspruch des Politikers und Staatsmannes. Hannover, 1973. pp. 51. (*Niedersaechsische Landeszentrale für Politische Bildung. Schriftenreihe. Das Autoritätsproblem. 3*)

KEIZEROV (NIKOLAI MIRONOVICH) Vlast' i avtoritet: kritika burzhuaznykh teorii. Moskva, 1973. pp. 264.

ACTON (HARRY BURROWS) The idea of a spiritual power. London, 1974. pp. 31. (*London. University. London School of Economics and Political Science. Auguste Comte Memorial Trust Lectures. 10*)

FONDAZIONE GIOACCHINO VOLPE. Incontro Romano, 1°, 1973. Autorità e libertà: [papers]. Roma, [1974]. pp. 282.

MILGRAM (STANLEY) Obedience to authority: an experimental view. London, 1974. pp. 224. *bibliog.*

AUTHORS, DUTCH.

ZWAN (A. VAN DER) De sociale positie van de auteur in Nederland: verslag van een verkennend onderzoek. 's-Gravenhage, Staatsuitgeverij, 1972. pp. 43. *bibliog.*

AUTHORS, GERMAN.

RADDATZ (FRITZ J.) Erfolg oder Wirkung: Schicksale politischer Publizisten in Deutschland. München, [1972]. pp. 137. *bibliog.*

SCHWENGER (HANNES) Schriftsteller und Gewerkschaft: Ideologie, Überbau, Organisation. Darmstadt, 1974. pp. 220. *bibliog.*

AUTHORSHIP.

ORAGE (ALFRED RICHARD) Readers and writers, 1917-1921. New York, 1922. pp. 181.

AUTISM.

WING (LORNA) Children apart: autistic children and their families. rev. ed. London, 1973. pp. 24.

AUTOGRAPHS

— **Collections.**

SOTHEBY AND COMPANY. Bibliotheca Phillippica, medieval manuscripts, new series, eighth part: catalogue of manuscripts on vellum, paper and papyrus of the 4th to the 17th century from the celebrated collection formed by Sir Thomas Phillips, 1792-1872, etc. London, [1973]. pp. 127.

SOTHEBY AND COMPANY. Bibliotheca Phillippica, new series, twelfth part: catalogue of English manuscripts, autograph letters and charters from the celebrated collection formed by Sir Thomas Phillipps, Bt., 1792-1872, etc. London, [1974]. pp. 154.

AUTOMATION

— **Social aspects.**

INTERNATIONAL LABOUR CONFERENCE. 57th Session. Reports. 6. Labour and social implications of automation and other technological developments: sixth item on the agenda. Geneva, 1972. pp. 75.

STONEMAN (P.S.) The effect of computerisation on the demand for labour in the U.K. Coventry, [1974]. pp. 18. (*University of Warwick. Department of Economics. Warwick Economic Research Papers. No. 47*)

— **Russia.**

SILANT'EVA (NINA ALEKSANDROVNA) Ekonomicheskie problemy avtomatizatsii protsessov upravleniia proizvodstvom. Moskva, 1972. pp. 192. *bibliog.*

AUTOMOBILE DRIVERS

— **Psychology.**

QUENAULT (S.W.) and PARKER (P.M.) Driver behaviour: newly qualified drivers. Crowthorne, 1973. pp. 15. (*U.K. Transport and Road Research Laboratory. Reports. LR 567*)

AUTOMOBILE INDUSTRY AND TRADE

— **Canada — Mathematical models.**

WILTON (D.A.) An econometric evaluation of the effects of the Canada-United States automobile agreement on the Canadian automotive manufacturing industry. Kingston, Ontario, [1971?]. fo.24. *bibliog.* (*Kingston, Ontario. Queen's University. Institute for Economic Research. Discussion Papers. No. 42*)

— **Europe.**

HU (Y.S.) The impact of U.S. investment in Europe: a case study of the automotive and computer industries. New York, 1973. pp. 291.

— **France.**

FRANCE. Direction de la Documentation. La Documentation Française. Notes et Etudes Documentaires. No. 3,811. L'industrie automobile en France. Paris, 1971. pp. 34.

— **Germany.**

RAISCH (MANFRED) Die Konzentration in der deutschen Automobilindustrie: betriebswirtschaftliche Bestimmungsfaktoren und Auswirkungen. Berlin, [1973]. pp. 150. *bibliog.*

DAUTEL (PETER) Konzentration und Wettbewerb in der Herstellung und im Vertrieb von Lastkraftwagen in der Bundesrepublik Deutschland.Berlin, [1974]. pp. 226. *bibliog.*

— **Italy.**

LIBERTINI (LUCIO) La FIAT negli anni sessanta. Roma, [1973]. pp. 292. *bibliog.*

VITIELLO (ANTONIO) Come nasce l'industria subalterna: il caso Alfasud a Napoli 1966-1972. Napoli, [1973]. pp. 99.

GUIDI (GIANFRANCO) and others. FIAT: struttura aziendale e organizzazione dello sfruttamento. Milano, [1974]. pp. 255.

— **Japan.**

DUNCAN (WILLIAM CHANDLER) U.S.-Japan automobile diplomacy: a study in economic confrontation. Cambridge, Mass., [1973]. pp. 202. *bibliog.*

— **Russia.**

VLASOV (BORIS VLADIMIROVICH) and others, eds. Ekonomika avtomobil'noi i traktornoi promyshlennosti. Moskva, 1973. pp. 318.

— **United Kingdom.**

NATIONAL CONFERENCE ON WORKERS' CONTROL AND INDUSTRIAL DEMOCRACY, 7TH, SHEFFIELD, 1969. Democracy in the motor industry; edited by Ken Coates, with contributions by Ernest Mandel [and others]. Nottingham, 1969 repr. 1970. pp. 58.

WISDOM (T.H.) 50 years of progress: the history of the Automotive Products Organisation over the past 50 years. [Leamington Spa, 1970]. pp. 48.

NATIONAL ECONOMIC DEVELOPMENT OFFICE. Industrial review to 1977: motors; (with supplementary note on the oil supply/price problem). London, 1973 [-74]. pp. 81; (6).

CUBBIN (JOHN S.) Quality change and pricing behaviour in the U.K. car industry, 1956-68. Coventry, [1973]. pp. 28. *bibliog.* (*University of Warwick. Centre for Industrial Economic and Business Research. [Warwick Research in Industrial and Business Studies]. No.38*)

— **United States.**

NADER (RALPH) Unsafe at any speed; the designed-in dangers of the American automobile. 2nd ed. New York, 1973. pp. 367.

ROTHSCHILD (EMMA) Paradise lost: the decline of the auto-industrial age. London, 1974. pp. 264. *bibliog.*

AUTOMOBILE INDUSTRY WORKERS

— **United Kingdom.**

FISHWICK (F.) and HARLING (C.J.) Shiftworking in the motor industry; a study carried out at the Cranfield School of Management...for the Economic Development Committee for the Motor Manufacturing Industry: detailed study and assessment. London, National Economic Development Office, 1974. pp. 177. *bibliog.*

FISHWICK (F.) and HARLING (C.J.) Shiftworking in the motor industry; a study carried out at the Cranfield School of Management...for the Economic Development Committee for the Motor Manufacturing Industry: summary report and conclusions. London, National Economic Development Office, 1974. pp. 37.

— **United States — Ohio.**

KRUCHKO (JOHN G.) The birth of a union local: the history of U[nited] A[utomobile] W[orkers] Local 674, Norwood, Ohio, 1933 to 1940. Ithaca, N.Y., 1972. pp. 74.

AUTOMOBILE OWNERSHIP.

MOGRIDGE (MARTIN J.H.) Car ownership forecasting in London. [London], 1973. pp. 33. (*London. Greater London Council. Department of Planning and Transportation. Research Memoranda. 386*)

FAIRHURST (M.H.) The influence of public transport on car ownership in London. [London], London Transport Executive, 1974. pp. 22. (*Economic and Operational Research Office. Operational Research Reports. 203*)

AUTOMOBILE PARKING

— **Germany.**

DEUTSCHES INSTITUT FÜR WIRTSCHAFTSFORSCHUNG. Sonderhefte. [Neue Folge]. Nr.100. Makroökonomische Entscheidungskriterien für den Aufbau alternativ grosser Park-and-Ride-Systeme..., dargestellt am Beispiel Hamburgs; ([by] Joachim Niklas). Berlin, 1974. pp. 61.

— **United Kingdom.**

OXFORD. University. University travel and parking survey; [carried out jointly with the City Council]. Oxford, 1972. pp. 178.

AUTOMOBILE PURCHASING.

NATIONAL CITIZENS' ADVICE BUREAUX COUNCIL. Buying a secondhand car: do's and don'ts. London, 1973. pp. 16.

AUTOMOBILE THIEVES

— **Finland.**

VIRTANEN (KATRIINA) Vaikuttiko lainmuutos? Tutkimus vuoden 1964 lainmuutoksen vaikutuksesta autonanastusrikollisuuteen; [English summary: An analysis of the effect of the 1964 law amendment designed to provide more effective measures against car thieves in Finland]. Helsinki, 1970. fo. 108. (*Kriminologinen Tutkimuslaitos. Sarja M. 5*)

AUTOMOBILES.

INSTITUTO NACIONAL DEL TRANSPORTE [COLOMBIA]. Estudio de necesidades de vehiculos para 1971. Bogota, 1970. pp. 80.

SWEDEN. Handelsdepartementet. Konsumentutredningen. 1971. Bilen och konsumenten. Stockholm, 1971. pp. 136. *bibliog.* (*Sweden. Statens Offentliga Utredningar. 1971.86*)

— **Prices.**

CUBBIN (JOHN S.) Quality change and pricing behaviour in the U.K. car industry, 1956-68. Coventry, [1973]. pp. 28. *bibliog.* (*University of Warwick. Centre for Industrial Economic and Business Research. [Warwick Research in Industrial and Business Studies]. No.38*)

— **Safety measures.**

NADER (RALPH) Unsafe at any speed; the designed-in dangers of the American automobile. 2nd ed. New York, 1973. pp. 367.

— **Social aspects.**

— — **Belgium.**

L'AUTOMOBILE dans la société; ([by] A. Godart [and others]). Bruxelles, 1972. pp. 196. (*Brussels. Université Libre. Institut de Sociologie. Sociologie de l'Automobile*)

— — **United Kingdom**

TOWNROE (P.M.) ed. Social and political consequences of the motor car. Newton Abbot, [1974]. pp. 189. *bibliog.*

— **Speed.**

FREEMAN FOX AND ASSOCIATES. Speed/flow relationships on suburban main roads; a report on a study carried out for the Road Research Laboratory. London, 1972. pp. 25.

— **Statistics — Colombia.**

INSTITUTO NACIONAL DEL TRANSPORTE [COLOMBIA]. Estudio de necesidades de vehiculos para 1971. Bogota, 1970. pp. 80.

— — **Norway.**

ØSTMOE (KNUT) and UTVIK (KNUT) Personbilutviklingen frem mot 1990; utviklingen i bestand, opphugging og nyregistreringer. [Oslo], Transportøkonomisk Institutt, 1972. pp. 50,10.

— — **Sweden.**

JACOBSSON (LARS) Car forecast for Sweden, 1972-1985. Stockholm, 1973. pp. 120. *bibliog.* (*Stockholm. Konjunkturinstitutet. Occasional Papers. 8*)

— — **United Kingdom.**

MOGRIDGE (MARTIN J.H.) Car ownership forecasting in London. [London], 1973. pp. 33. (*London. Greater London Council. Department of Planning and Transportation. Research Memoranda. 386.*)

AVALOV (ZURAB DAVIDOVICH).

AVALOV (ZURAB DAVIDOVICH) Nezavisimost' Gruzii v mezhdunarodnoi politike, 1918-1921 g.g.: vospominaniia, ocherki. Paris, 1924. pp. 319.

AWOLOWO (OBAFEMI).

AKINSANYA (OLU) A mini biography of Chief Obafemi Awolowo. Lagos, 1972. pp. 28.

AZAÑA Y DIAZ (MANUEL).

AGUADO (EMILIANO) Don Manuel Azaña Diaz. Barcelona, 1972. pp. 399.

AZERBAIJAN

— **Biography.**

AZERBAIJAN. Verkhovnyi Sovet. 1968. Deputaty Verkhovnogo Soveta Azerbaidzhanskoi SSR: sed'moi sozyv. Baku, 1968. pp. 400. *In Azerbaijani and Russian.*

— **Constitutional history.**

ISTORIIA gosudarstva i prava Azerbaidzhanskoi SSR, 1920-1934 gg. Baku, 1973. pp. 552.

— **Economic history.**

SUMBATZADE (ALI SUMBATOVICH) Sotsial'no-ekonomicheskie predposylki pobedy Sovetskoi vlasti v Azerbaidzhane. Moskva, 1972. pp. 254.

AZORES

— **Industries.**

PORTUGAL. Instituto Nacional de Estatistica. 1966. Inquerito industrial..., 1.º semestre de 1964; Enquête industrielle..., 1er semestre 1964: 1. Arquipelago da Madeira, distrito do Funchal. 2. Arquipelago dos Açores. [Lisbon, 1966]. 2 pts.

BADEN—WUERTTEMBERG

— **Economic conditions.**

WIRTSCHAFTLICHE Probleme des Landes Baden Württemberg: [papers of a conference held in 1973]; herausgegeben von Alfred E. Ott. Tübingen, 1974. pp. 193. (*Tübingen. Institut für Angewandte Wirtschaftsforschung. Schriftenreihe. Band 23*) 3 graphs in end pocket.

— **Economic policy.**

KREUTER (HANSHEINZ) Industrielle Standortaffinität und regionalpolitische Standortlenkung, dargestellt am Beispiel Boden-Württembergs. Berlin, [1974]. pp. 426. *bibliog. With summaries in English and French.*

BAECK (LEO).

REICHMANN (EVA G.) Grösse und Verhängnis deutsch-jüdischer Existenz: Zeugnisse einer tragischen Begegnung; [selected essays and lectures, 1930-1971]; mit einem Geleitwort von Helmut Gollwitzer. Heidelberg, 1974. pp. 295. *bibliog.*

BAESCHLIN (HEINRICH THEOPHIL).

VEREIN FÜR WIRTSCHAFTSHISTORISCHE STUDIEN. Schweizer Pioniere der Wirtschaft und Technik. 27. Zwei Schaffhauser Pioniere: Friedrich Peyer im Hof, 1817- 1900; Heinrich Theophil Bäschlin, 1845-1887. Zürich, 1973. pp. 107. *bibliog.*

BAGUIO CITY

— **Markets.**

DAVIS (WILLIAM G.) Social relations in a Philippine market: self-interest and subjectivity. Berkeley, [1973]. pp. 315. *bibliog.*

BAHAMAS

— **Census.**

BAHAMAS. Census, 1970. Commonwealth of the Bahama Islands: report of the 1970 census of population. Nassau, 1972. pp. 481,5.

— **Statistics.**

BAHAMAS. Department of Statistics. Statistical abstract. a., 1970- Nassau.

BAHIA

— **History.**

MATTOSO (KATIA M. DE QUEIROS) Presença francesa no movimento democratico baiano de 1789. Salvador, [Brazil], 1969. pp. 163. *bibliog.*

BAHIMA (AFRICAN PEOPLE).

ELAM (YITZCHAK) The social and sexual roles of Hima women: a study of nomadic cattle breeders in Nyabushozi county, Ankole, Uganda. Manchester, [1973]. pp. 243. *bibliog.*

BAKU

— **Civic improvement.**

AKHMEDOV (ALI ISLAMOVICH) and VEZIROV (SHAMSADDIN AGMADOVICH) Gorod i transport. Baku, 1973. pp. 116.

BAKUNIN (MIKHAIL ALEKSANDROVICH).

ARVON (HENRI) Bakounine: absolu et révolution. Paris, 1972. pp. 130. *bibliog.*

BAKUNIN (MIKHAIL ALEKSANDROVICH (Cont.)

UCHENYE ZAPISKI KAFEDR OBSHCHESTVENNYKH NAUK VUZOV G.LENINGRADA. Filosofiia. vyp. 13. Filosofskie i sotsiologicheskie issledovaniia. Leningrad, 1972. pp. 238.

CONFINO (MICHAEL) ed. Daughter of a revolutionary: Natalie Herzen and the Bakunin- Nechayev circle;...translated by Hilary Sternberg and Lydia Bott. London, 1974. pp. 416.

DUCLOS (JACQUES) Bakounine et Marx: ombre et lumière; en annexe: La confession de Bakounine à Nicholas 1er; traduit du russe, etc.[Paris, 1974]. pp. 479.

BALANCE OF PAYMENTS.

CAIRNCROSS (Sir ALEXANDER KIRKLAND) Control of long-term international capital movements. Washington, [1973]. pp. 104. bibliog. (Brookings Institution. Brookings Staff Papers)

GRAY (HENRY PETER) An aggregate theory of international payments adjustment. London, 1974. pp. 213.

— Barbados.

BARBADOS. Statistical Service. Balance of payments. bien., 1964/1966 (no.1)- [Bridgetown].

— East (Near East).

ASHTOR (ELIYAHU) Les métaux précieux et la balance des payements du Proche- Orient à la basse époque. Paris, 1971. pp. 125. bibliog. (Paris. Ecole Pratiquè des Hautes Etudes. Section des Sciences Economiquès et Sociales. Centre de Recherches Historiques. Monnaie, Prix, Conjoncture. 10)

— Finland.

FINLAND. Tilastokeskus. 1971. Suomen maksutase vuosina 1969 ja 1970, etc. Helsinki, 1971. pp. 4. (Tilastotiedotus. KT. 1971.3)

— Germany — Mathematical models.

BARTOLOMEI (J.A.) Balance des paiements et politique monétaire: l'expérience allemande entre 1958 et 1968. Louvain, 1972. pp. 107. bibliog. (Louvain. Université. Faculté des Sciences Economiques, Sociales et Politiques. [Publications]. Nouvelle Série. No. 96)

— Ivory Coast.

BALANCE DES PAIEMENTS DE LA REPUBLIQUE DE COTE D'IVOIRE; ([pd. by] Comité de la Balance des Paiements, Ministère de l'Economie et des Finances [Ivory Coast]). a., 1970- [Abidjan].

— Swaziland.

SWAZILAND. Central Statistical Office. Balance of payments. a., 1969-70/1970-71 [1st]- Mbabane.

— Underdeveloped areas.

See UNDERDEVELOPED AREAS — Balance of payments.

— United Kingdom.

ASH (J.C.K.) How well does the National Institute forecast the balance of payments?. [Reading], 1973. fo. 33. bibliog. (Reading. University. Department of Economics. Discussion Papers in Economics. Series A. No. 51)

— United States.

INTERNATIONAL ECONOMIC POLICY ASSOCIATION. The United States balance of payments: from crisis to controversy. Washington, D.C., [1972]. pp. 109.

SLIGHTON (ROBERT L.) and others. The effect of untied development loans on the U.S. balance of payments. Santa Monica, 1972. pp. 92. (Rand Corporation. Rand Reports. R.973)

MIKESELL (RAYMOND FRECH) and FURTH (J. HERBERT) Foreign dollar balances and the international role of the dollar. New York, 1974. pp. 125. (National Bureau of Economic Research. Studies in International Economic Relations. No. 7)

BALANCE OF POWER.

LUTTWAK (EDWARD) The strategic balance 1972. New York, 1972. pp. 132. (Georgetown University. Center for Strategic and International Studies. Washington Papers. vol.[1]/3)

BUCHAN (ALASTAIR) Change without war: the shifting structures of world power. London, 1974. pp. 112. (British Broadcasting Corporation. Reith Lectures. 1973)

BUCHAN (ALASTAIR) The end of the postwar era: a new balance of world power. London, [1974]. pp. 347.

BALDWIN (STANLEY) 1st Earl Baldwin.

HYDE (HARFORD MONTGOMERY) Baldwin: the unexpected prime minister. London, 1973. pp. 616. bibliog.

BALKAN STATES

— Nationalism.

KARPAT (KEMAL H.) An inquiry into the social foundations of nationalism in the Ottoman state: from social estates to classes, from millets to nations. Princeton, N.J., 1973. pp. 116. (Princeton University. Center of International Studies. Research Monographs. No.39)

BALMACEDA (JOSE MANUEL).

RAMIREZ NECOCHEA (HERNAN) Balmaceda y la contrarrevolucion de 1891. 3rd ed. Santiago de Chile, 1972. pp. 268. bibliog.

BLAKEMORE (HAROLD) British nitrates and Chilean politics, 1886-1896: Balmaceda and North. London, 1974. pp. 260. (London. University. Institute of Latin American Studies. Monographs. 4)

BALTIC, THE

— Commerce.

SOOM (ARNOLD) Der baltische Getreidehandel im 17. Jahrhundert. Stockholm, 1961. pp. 350. bibliog. (Vitterhets Historie och Antikvitets Akademien. Handlingar. Historiska Serien. 8)

BALTIC STATES

— Economic conditions.

CONFERENCE ON BALTIC STUDIES, 3RD, TORONTO, 1972. Problems of mininations: Baltic perspectives; [papers presented at the conference]; editors: Arvids Ziedonis [and others]. San José, Ca., 1973. pp. 214.

— Economic history.

CZOLLEK (ROSWITHA) Faschismus und Okkupation: wirtschaftspolitische Zielsetzung und Praxis des faschistischen deutschen Besatzungsregimes in den baltischen Sowjetrepubliken während des zweiten Weltkrieges. Berlin, 1974. pp. 224. bibliog. (Akademie der Wissenschaften der DDR. Zentralinstitut für Geschichte. Schriften. Band 39)

— History.

MYLLYNIEMI (SEPPO) Die Neuordnung der baltischen Länder 1941-1944: zum nationalsozialistischen Inhalt der deutschen Besatzungspolitik. Helsinki, 1973. pp. 308. bibliog. (Suomen Historiallinen Seura. Historiallisia Tutkimuksia. 90)

RAUCH (GEORG VON) The Baltic states: the years of independence: Estonia, Latvia, Lithuania, 1917-1940;... translated from the German by Gerald Onn. London, [1974]. pp. 265. bibliog.

VENNER (DOMINIQUE) Baltikum: dans le Reich de la défaite, le combat des Corps- francs, 1918-1923. Paris [1974]. pp. 366. bibliog.

— — Historiography.

LATVIISKII GOSUDARSTVENNYI UNIVERSITET. Uchenye Zapiski. t.185. Germaniia i Pribaltika. 2. Riga, 1973. pp. 99.

— Politics and government.

CONFERENCE ON BALTIC STUDIES, 3RD, TORONTO, 1972. Problems of mininations: Baltic perspectives; [papers presented at the conference]; editors: Arvids Ziedonis [and others]. San José, Ca., 1973. pp. 214.

— Social conditions.

CONFERENCE ON BALTIC STUDIES, 3RD, TORONTO, 1972. Problems of mininations: Baltic perspectives; [papers presented at the conference]; editors: Arvids Ziedonis [and others]. San José, Ca., 1973. pp. 214.

BANAT

— History.

SUCIU (I.D.) Revoluția de la 1848-1849 in Banat. [București], 1968. pp. 249. bibliog.

BANCO DE PORTUGAL.

SOARES (L. RIBEIRO) Money in Portugal: a short history; [translated by Matilde Paes Parente and Maria Aguiar]. [Lisbon], 1971. pp. 86.

BANCROFT (HUBERT HOWE).

CLARK (HARRY) A venture in history: the production, publication and sale of the Works of Hubert Howe Bancroft. Berkeley, 1973. pp. 177. (California University. Publications. Librarianship. 19)

BANDA (HASTINGS KAMAZU).

SHORT (PHILIP) Banda. London, 1974. pp. 357. bibliog.

BANDAMA RIVER

— Barrage.

IVORY COAST. Bureau National d'Etudes Techniques de Développement. 1970. Barrage du Bandama: recensement foncier. [Abidjan?, 1970?]. pp. [75].

BANGALORE

— Industries.

HUMAN problems of industry in Bangalore; ([by] Thelma Dawson [and others]); edited by M.M. Thomas [and] H.F.J. Daniel. Bangalore, 1965. pp. 65.

BANGLADESH

— Description and travel.

SHCHEDROV (IVAN MIKHAILOVICH) Bangladesh: utro novoi zhizni; iz bloknotov korrespondenta. Moskva, 1973. pp. 128.

— Economic conditions.

DUTT (KALYAN) and others. Bangladesh economy: an analytical study. New Delhi, 1973. pp. 267.

ROBINSON (EDWARD AUSTIN GOSSAGE) Economic prospects of Bangladesh. London, [1973]. pp. 59.

— Economic policy.

ROBINSON (EDWARD AUSTIN GOSSAGE) Economic prospects of Bangladesh. London, [1973]. pp. 59.

INTERNATIONAL ECONOMIC ASSOCIATION. Conference, [1973?], Dacca. The economic development of Bangladesh within a socialist framework: proceedings of a conference...; edited by E.A.G. Robinson and Keith Griffin. London, 1974. pp. 330.

— Foreign opinion.

QUADERI (FAZLUL QUADER) ed. Bangladesh genocide and world press: [articles from press and radio]. 2nd ed. Dacca, 1972. pp. 455.

BANKS AND BANKING.

— Nationalism.

CHANDRAKAR (K.) Bangla Desh: a case for solidarity with the liberation struggle. Manchester, 1971. pp. 14.

QUADERI (FAZLUL QUADER) ed. Bangladesh genocide and world press: [articles from press and radio]. 2nd ed. Dacca, 1972. pp. 455.

BHATTACHARJEE (G.P.) Renaissance and freedom movement in Bangladesh. Calcutta, 1973. pp. 361. *bibliog.*

LEVY (BERNARD HENRI) Bangla Desh: nationalisme dans la révolution. Paris, 1973. pp. 322. *bibliog.*

MALEK (ABDUL) From East Pakistan to Bangladesh: a history of exploitation and repression. Manchester, 1973. pp. 38.

— Politics and government.

BANGLA DESH ASSOCIATION LANCASHIRE AND ADJOINING COUNTIES. The birth of a nation: Bangla Desh and its background. n.p. [197-]. pp. 20.

BHATTACHARJEE (G.P.) Renaissance and freedom movement in Bangladesh. Calcutta, 1973. pp. 361. *bibliog.*

BRASS (PAUL R.) and FRANDA (MARCUS F.) eds. Radical politics in south Asia. Cambridge, Mass., [1973]. pp. 449. *(Massachusetts Institute of Technology. Center for International Studies. Studies in Communism, Revisionism and Revolution. 19)*

MALEK (ABDUL) From East Pakistan to Bangladesh: a history of exploitation and repression. Manchester, 1973. pp. 38.

WILCOX (WAYNE AYRES) The emergence of Bangladesh: problems and opportunities for a redefined American policy in South Asia. Washington, 1973. pp. 79. *(American Enterprise Institute for Public Policy Research. Foreign Affairs Studies. 7)*

— Rural conditions.

THOMAS (JOHN W.) Writer on Agriculture. Agricultural production, equity and rural organization in East Pakistan: preliminary draft for presentation to the Pakistan Rural Development Workshop, Michigan State University, July, 1971. [East Lansing, 1971?]. pp. 41.

BANK EMPLOYEES

— Norway.

NORWAY. Likelønnsrådet. 1971. Kvinner i bankvirksomhet: en undersøkelse av lønn, stilling og utdanning: 9. melding om lønnsspørsmÅl. Oslo, 1971. pp. 27.

BANK EXAMINATION

— United Kingdom.

INSTITUTE OF BANKERS. Wilde Committee. The Institute of Bankers educational policy review. Part 1. The Institute's future role as a qualifying association: a report. London, 1973. pp. 47.

BANK FOR INTERNATIONAL SETTLEMENTS.

FRANCE. Direction de la Documentation. La Documentation Française. Notes et Etudes Documentaires. Nos. 3,953-3, 954. La Banque des Règlements Internationaux, par Robert Pierot. [Paris], 1973. pp. 73.

BANK OF CANADA.

ACHESON (A.L. KEITH) and CHANT (JOHN F.) Bureaucratic theory and the choice of central bank goals: the case of the Bank of Canada. [Ottawa, 1972]. fo. 40. *bibliog. (Carleton University. Carleton Economic Papers)*

BANK OF ENGLAND.

STOCKDALE (Sir EDMUND) The Bank of England in 1934. n.p., [1967]. pp. 316.

BANK OF JAPAN.

BANK OF JAPAN. Economic Research Department. The Bank of Japan: its organization and monetary policies. [Tokyo], 1973. pp. 50.

BANKING AS A PROFESSION.

INSTITUTE OF BANKERS. Wilde Committee. The Institute of Bankers educational policy review. Part 1. The Institute's future role as a qualifying association: a report. London, 1973. pp. 47.

BANKING LAW

— Denmark.

DENMARK. Arbejdsgruppen vedr. Revision af Bank- og Sparekasseloven. 1971. Beretning afgivet til Handelsministeren. [Copenhagen], 1971. pp. 136.

— Europe, Eastern.

MEZNERICS (IVÁN) Law of banking in East-West trade. Leiden, 1973. pp. 427.

— European Economic Community countries.

Le SECRET bancaire dans la C.E.E. et en Suisse: rapport national du Colloque organisé par le Centre d'Economie Bancaire internationale et le Centre Universitaire d'Etudes des Communautés européennes...octobre 1971. Paris, 1973. pp. 207. *(Paris. Université de Paris I (Panthéon-Sorbonne) Publications. Série Droit Privé. 1)*

— Switzerland.

Le SECRET bancaire dans la C.E.E. et en Suisse: rapport national du Colloque organisé par le Centre d'Economie Bancaire internationale et le Centre Universitaire d'Etudes des Communautés européennes...octobre 1971. Paris, 1973. pp. 207. *(Paris. Université de Paris I (Panthéon-Sorbonne) Publications. Série Droit Privé. 1)*

— United Kingdom.

PERRY (F.E.) Law and practice relating to banking. 2nd ed. Harmondsworth, 1972. pp. 431.

CHORLEY (ROBERT SAMUEL THEODORE) 1st Baron Chorley. Law of banking;...assisted by J. Milnes Holden. 6th ed. London, 1974. pp. 425.

HOLDEN (JAMES MILNES) The law and practice of banking. London, 1971-74. 2 vols. *Vol. 1 is of the second edition. Vol. 2 is of the fifth edition.*

BANKRUPTCY

— Denmark.

DENMARK. Konkurslovsudvalget. 1971. Konkurs og tvangsakkord: betaenkning 2 afgivet af det af Justitsministeriet den 29. januar 1958 nedsatte udvalg. København, 1971. pp. 407. *(Denmark. Betaenkninger. Nr. 606)*

— France.

PELLERIN (PIERRE) Barrister-at-Law. The French law of bankruptcy and winding up of limited companies: the conflict of laws arising therefrom. London, 1907. pp. 117.

— Ireland (Republic).

EIRE. Bankruptcy Law Committee. 1973. Report on the law and practice concerning bankruptcy and the administration of insolvent estates of deceased persons; [F.G.O. Budd, chairman]. Dublin, [1973]. pp. 593. *bibliog.*

— United Kingdom — Scotland.

SCOTLAND. Working Party on Insolvency, Bankruptcy and Liquidation. 1971. Insolvency, bankruptcy and liquidation in Scotland; [Lord Kilbrandon, chairman]. Edinburgh, 1971. pp. 151. *(Scotland. Scottish Law Commission. Memoranda. No.16)*

BANKS AND BANKING.

INTERNATIONAL BANKING SUMMER SCHOOL. 25th School, 1972. The world banking challenge: lectures and proceedings, etc. Washington, [1972]. pp. 158.

STANFORD (JON D.) Money, banking and economic activity. Sydney, [1973]. pp. 130. *bibliogs.*

MARSHALL (ROBERT HERMAN) and SWANSON (RODNEY B.) The monetary process: essentials of money and banking. Boston, [Mass., 1974]. pp. 484. *bibliogs.*

— — Africa, Subsaharan.

MENSAH (AYAOVI) Untersuchungen zur Bankenstruktur ausgewählter Länder Afrikas: eine Studie aus afrikanischer Sicht. Göttingen, 1973. pp. 530. *bibliog.*

— Argentine Republic.

CARBONELL TUR (ANTONIO) La estabilidad monetaria y la banca comercial en la Republica Argentina: periodo 1935-1969. Buenos Aires, [1970 repr.] 1971. pp. 302. *bibliog.*

— Australia — Statistics.

BUTLIN (SYDNEY JAMES) and others. Australian banking and monetary statistics, 1817-1945. Sydney, 1971. pp. 562. *(Reserve Bank of Australia. Occasional Papers. No. 4A)*

WHITE (R.C.) Australian banking and monetary statistics, 1945-1970. Sydney, 1973. pp. 681. *(Reserve Bank of Australia. Occasional Papers. No. 4B)*

— Canada.

BAUM (DANIEL JAY) The banks of Canada in the Commonwealth Caribbean: economic nationalism and multinational enterprises of a medium power. New York, 1974. pp. 158.

— Caribbean area.

BAUM (DANIEL JAY) The banks of Canada in the Commonwealth Caribbean: economic nationalism and multinational enterprises of a medium power. New York, 1974. pp. 158.

— Denmark.

HOLST (SVEND) Naestved Diskontobank 1871-1971: utraditionel byhistorie;... i anledning af... 100 aars jubilaeum, etc. Naestved, 1971. pp. 63.

— Europe — Periodicals.

PEMBERTON (JOHN E.) compiler. European materials in British university libraries: a bibliography and union catalogue;...with A survey by William E. Paterson. London, 1973. pp. 42.

— European Economic Community countries.

HUTTON (ROBIN) and WILD (SIDNEY) Banking in Europe: the challenge of Britain's entry into the E.E.C. London, [1973]. pp. 30. *(Institute of Bankers. Ernest Sykes Memorial Lectures. 1973)*

— France.

FRANCE. French Embassy, London. Service de Presse et d'Information. 1971. The French banking system. London, [1971]. pp. 23.

FRANCE. Délégation à l'Aménagement du Territoire et à l'Aménagement du Territoire et à l'Action Régionale. 1972. La décentralisation du tertiaire: les banques et les assurances: documents. [Paris, 1972]. pp. 57.

BOUVIER (JEAN) Un siècle de banque française. [Paris, 1973]. pp. 285.

NETTER (MARCEL) Les institutions monétaires en France. 3rd ed. Paris, 1973. pp. 128.

HINCKER (FRANÇOIS) Expériences bancaires sous l'Ancien Régime. [Paris], 1974. pp. 96. *bibliog.*

— Gabon.

FREDIANI (LORENZO) The banking system of Gabon and the Central Bank of Equatorial Africa and Cameroon. Milan, 1974. pp. 343.

BANKS AND BANKING (Cont.)

— Germany.

POHL (MANFRED) Die Geschichte der Saarländischen Kreditbank Aktiengesellschaft. Saarbrücken, 1972. pp. 146. *bibliog. (Kommission für Saarländische Landesgeschichte und Volksforschung. Veröffentlichungen. 5)*

POHL (MANFRED) Wiederaufbau: Kunst und Technik der Finanzierung, 1947-1953; die ersten Jahre der Kreditanstalt für Wiederaufbau. Frankfurt/Main, [1973]. pp. 240. *bibliog.*

SAUER (SAROLF) Wettbewerbsposition und Wettbewerbspolitik der Filialgrossbanken in der BRD. Wien, 1974. pp. 112. *bibliog. (Österreichische Bankwissenschaftliche Gesellschaft. Schriftenreihe. Heft 47)*

— India.

SHRIVASTAVA (N.N.) Evolution of the techniques of monetary management in India. Bombay, [1972]. pp. 415. *bibliog.*

SEMINAR ON THE REFORM OF THE INDIAN BANKING SYSTEM, MADRAS, 1972. Reform of the Indian banking system; proceedings of a seminar...; edited by S.L.N. Simha. Madras, 1973. pp. 400.

— Italy.

BALLETTA (FRANCESCO) Il Banco di Napoli e le rimesse degli emigrati, 1914-1925. Napoli, 1972. pp. 211. *bibliog. (Institut International d'Histoire de la Banque. Gens d'Affaires, Banques, Monnaies, Finances. 2)*

VITALE (ELIGIO) La riforma degli istituti di emissione e gli 'scandali bancari' in Italia, 1892-1896. Roma, Archivio Storico, 1972. 3 vols. (in 2).

— Japan.

INDUSTRIAL BANK OF JAPAN. [Annual report]. a., 1973- Tokyo.

BANK OF JAPAN. Economic Research Department. Money and banking in Japan;... translated by S. Nishimura; edited by L.S. Pressnell. London, 1973. pp. 456.

— Lesotho.

ONADO (MARCO) and PORTERI (ANTONIO) The banking system and the formation of savings in Lesotho. Milan, 1974. pp. 139. *(Cassa di Risparmio delle Provincie Lombarde. The Credit Markets of Africa. 9)*

— Malaysia.

LEE (SHENG-YI) The monetary and banking development of Malaysia and Singapore. Singapore, [1974]. pp. 404. *bibliog.*

— Netherlands.

BUIST (MARTEN GERBERTUS) At spes non fracta: Hope and Co. 1770-1815, merchant bankers and diplomats at work; [translated by Derek S. Jordan]. Den Haag, 1974. pp. 716. *bibliog.*

— Singapore.

LEE (SHENG-YI) The monetary and banking development of Malaysia and Singapore. Singapore, [1974]. pp. 404. *bibliog.*

— Switzerland.

TROXLER (WERNER P.) Johann Rudolf Forcart-Weiss Söhne: ein Beitrag zur Unternehmergeschichte. Bern, 1973. pp. 128. *bibliog. (Zürich. Universität. Historisches Seminar. Geist und Werk der Zeiten. No. 36)*

RUEHL (FRANK) Zur Nachfrage der Schweizer Banken nach Liquiditätsreserven, 1959-1970. Zürich, [1974]. pp. 226. *bibliog.* With English summary.

— Syria.

OFFICE ARABE DE PRESSE ET DE DOCUMENTATION. Serie "Etudes". 150. La nouvelle politique monétaire et bancaire en Syrie. Damas, [1973?]. fo. 42.

— United Kingdom.

CHALMERS (ERIC B.) The money world: a guide to money and banking in the age of inflation. London, 1974. pp. 211.

— United Kingdom — Scotland.

FLEMING (JAMES SIMPSON) Scottish banking: a historical sketch. 3rd ed. Edinburgh, 1877. pp. 65.

— United States.

RITTER (LAWRENCE S.) ed. Money and economic activity: readings in money and banking. 3rd ed. New York, [1967]. pp. 450.

WILLIAMS (HAROLD R.) and WOUDENBERG (HENRY W.) Money, banking, and monetary theory: problems and concepts... a study guide to accompany Chandler, The economics of money and banking, 6th ed. 2nd ed. New York, [1973]. pp. 324.

— — Iowa.

ERICKSON (ERLING A.) Banking in frontier Iowa, 1836-1865. Ames, Iowa, 1971. pp. 183. *bibliog.*

BANKS AND BANKING, CENTRAL.

DE KOCK (MICHIEL HENDRIK) Central banking. 4th ed. London, 1974. pp. 325.

— Argentine Republic.

BANCO CENTRAL DE LA REPUBLICA ARGENTINA. La creacion del Banco Central y la experiencia monetaria argentina entre los años 1935-1943. [Buenos Aires, 1972]. 2 vols. *Appendices in end pocket.*

— Canada.

ACHESON (A.L. KEITH) and CHANT (JOHN F.) Bureaucratic theory and the choice of central bank goals: the case of the Bank of Canada. [Ottawa, 1972]. fo. 40. *bibliog. (Carleton University. Carleton Economic Papers)*

— India.

BHATTACHARYYA (P.C.) Central banking in a developing economy. Bombay, 1971. pp. 283.

— Scandinavia.

RUEHL (HARALD) Das währungspolitische Instrumentarium der nordischen Zentralbanken. Bern, 1972. pp. 250, xxxviii. *bibliog.*

— Sri Lanka.

KARUNATILAKE (HALWALAGE NEVILLE SEPALA) Central banking and monetary policy in Sri Lanka. Colombo, 1973. pp. 209.

BANKS AND BANKING, INTERNATIONAL.

ARNOULT (ERIK) and LEMAIRE (JEAN PAUL) Euro-émissions: nouvelles perspectives bancaires internationales.[Paris, 1972]. pp. 230. *bibliog.*

DYSON (RICHARD GEORGE) New patterns in British banking overseas: the presidential address...[to] the Institute of Bankers. London, 1973. pp. 16.

LEES (FRANCIS A.) International banking and finance. London, 1974. pp. 419.

STEUBER (URSEL) Internationale Banken: Auslandsaktivitäten von Banken *bibliog.* bedeutender Industrieländer. Hamburg, 1974. pp. 204. *bibliog. (Hamburg. Hamburgisches Welt-Wirtschafts-Archiv. Studien zur Aussenwirtschaft und Entwicklungspolitik)*

BANQUE CENTRALE DES ETATS DE L'AFRIQUE EQUATORIALE ET DU CAMEROUN.

FREDIANI (LORENZO) The banking system of Gabon and the Central Bank of Equatorial Africa and Cameroon. Milan, 1974. pp. 343.

BANQUE DE FRANCE.

BRUNET (PATRICE) L'organisation de la Banque de France. Paris, 1973. pp. 119. *bibliog. (Paris. Université de Paris II. Travaux et Recherches. Série Science Administrative. 4)*

BANQUE DU ZAIRE.

BANQUE DU ZAIRE. Rapport annuel. a., 1971/2- Kinshasa.

BANTUS.

RETIEF (G.M.) Die bantoe in die stad: misdaad. Pretoria, [1968]. pp. 28. *bibliog.*

DAVIS (R. HUNT) Bantu education and the education of Africans in South Africa. Athens, Ohio, [1972]. fo. 53. *(Ohio University. Center for International Studies. Papers in International Studies. Africa Series. No.14)*

HAMMOND-TOOKE (W.D.) ed. The Bantu-speaking peoples of Southern Africa. 2nd ed. London, 1974. pp. 525. *bibliog.*

BAPTISTS

— Russia.

BOURDEAUX (MICHAEL) Faith on trial in Russia. London, 1971. pp. 192. *bibliog.*

— United States.

DAVIS (LAWRENCE B.) Immigrants, Baptists and the protestant mind in America. Urbana, [1973]. pp. 230. *bibliog.*

BARBADOS

— Commerce.

BARBADOS. Statistical Service. Monthly statistics of overseas trade. m., Jl 1973 (no.1)- , with gap (nos. 2,3). St. Michael.

— Politics and government.

HOYOS (F.A.) Grantley Adams and the social revolution: the story of the movement that changed the pattern of West Indian society. London, 1974. pp. 280. *bibliog.*

BARCELONA

— Economic history.

DURAN I SANPERE (AGUSTI) Barcelona i la seva historia: la societat i l'organitzacio del treball. Barcelona, 1973. pp. 698.

— Growth.

MATAS PERICE (ALFRED) Al sud-oest del riu Besos: deu anys de la vida d'un barri barceloni. Barcelona, 1970. pp. 204.

— Poor.

MATAS PERICE (ALFRED) Al sud-oest del riu Besos: deu anys de la vida d'un barri barceloni. Barcelona, 1970. pp. 204.

— Social history.

BATLLE GALLART (CARMEN) La crisis social y economica de Barcelona a mediados del siglo XV. Barcelona, 1973. 2 vols. (in 1). *(Anuario de Estudios Medievales. Anejos. 3)*

BARING (EVELYN) 1st Earl of Cromer.

DUNDAS (LAWRENCE JOHN LUMLEY) 2nd Marquess of Zetland. Lord Cromer: being the authorized life of Evelyn Baring, first Earl of Cromer. London, 1932. pp. 366.

BARMEN.

See WUPPERTAL.

BARNARD (CHESTER IRVING).

WOLF (WILLIAM B.) Conversations with Chester I. Barnard. New York, 1973. pp. 58. *(Cornell University. New York State School of Industrial and Labor Relations. ILR Paperbacks. No. 12)*

BAROLONG BOO RATSHIDI.

COMAROFF (JOHN LIONEL) Competition for office and political processes among the Barolong boo Ratshidi of the South Africa-Botswana borderland; [Ph. D.(London) thesis]. 1973. fo. 521. *bibliog. Typescript: unpublished. This thesis is the property of London University and may not be removed from the library.*

BARRY (TOM).

BARRY (TOM) Guerilla days in Ireland. Tralee, 1962 repr. 1971. pp. 207. *First published in 1949.*

BARTHOU (LOUIS).

BOUSQUET-MELOU (JEAN) Louis Barthou et la circonscription d'Oloron, 1889-1914. Paris, [1972]. pp. 268. *bibliog. (Bordeaux. Université. Institut d'Etudes Politiques. Centre d'Etude et de Recherche sur la Vie Locale. Série Vie Locale. 3)*

BASEL (CITY)

— Social history.

WULLSCHLEGER (EUGEN) Aus der Geschichte der Arbeiterbewegung in Basel: Vortrag, gehalten in den Volksbildungskursen des Arbeiterbundes. Basel, 1912. pp. 32.

BASEL—LAND (CANTON)

— Population.

LEIMGRUBER (WALTER) Studien zur Dynamik und zum Strukturwandel der Bevölkerung im südlichen Umland von Basel. Basel, 1972. pp. 199. *bibliog. (Geographisch-Ethnologische Gesellschaft. Basler Beiträge zur Geographie. Heft 15) With summaries in various languages.*

BASEL—STADT (CANTON)

— Surveys.

BACHMANN (EMIL) Die Basler Stadtvermessung. rev. ed. Basel, Justizdepartement, 1969. pp. 96.

BÄSCHLIN.

See BAESCHLIN.

BASQUE PROVINCES

— Nationalism.

SALABERRI (KEPA) El proceso de Euskadi en Burgos: el sumarisimo 31/69. Paris, 1971. pp. 319.

KERMAN ORTIZ DE ZARATE (RICARDO) El problema revolucionario vasco. Buenos Aires, [1972]. pp. 204. *bibliog.*

ARENILLAS (JOSE MARIA) The Basque country: the national question and the socialist revolution;...[English translation of an essay first published in Barcelona in 1937]. Leeds, [1973]. pp. 27. *(Independent Labour Party. Square One Pamphlets)*

BATETELA (AFRICAN TRIBE).

STORME (MARCEL) La mutinerie militaire au Kasai en 1895: introduction. Bruxelles, 1970. pp. 162. *bibliog. (Académie Royale des Sciences d'Outre-Mer. Classe des Sciences Morales et Politiques. [Meémoires in -8!. Nouvelle Série. [Tome] 38. [Fasc.] 4)*

BATSWANA.

See TSWANA (BANTU TRIBE).

BATTLE

— Civic improvement.

EAST SUSSEX. County Council. Battle town plan and town centre map: proposals, 1972-1981 [and] technical appendix. [Lewes], 1972. 2 vols. (in 1).

BAUER (OTTO).

LESER (NORBERT) Zwischen Reformismus und Bolschewismus: der Austromarxismus als Theorie und Praxis. Wien, [1968]. pp. 600.

BAUSSART (ELIE).

NEUVILLE (JEAN) Adieu à la démocratie chrétienne?: Elie Baussart et le mouvement ouvrier...introduction biographique de Jean Quériat, etc. Bruxelles, [1973]. pp. 158.

BAVARIA

— Economic conditions.

FRANCE. Direction de la Documentation. La Documentation Française. Notes et Etudes Documentaires. Nos. 3,805-3, 806-3,807. Les économies des Länder de la République Fédérale d'Allemagne: l'économie de la Bavière; [by] Daniel Kanmacher. Paris, 1971. pp. 119. *bibliog.*

— Economic history.

SCHMIDT (JOCHEN) Bayern und das Zollparlament: Politik und Wirtschaft in den letzten Jahren vor der Reichsgründung, 1866/67-1870: zur Strukturanalyse Bayerns im Industriezeitalter. München, 1973. pp. 442. *bibliog. (Munich. Stadtarchiv. Neue Schriftenreihe. Band 64)*

— Foreign relations — Prussia.

SCHMIDT (JOCHEN) Bayern und das Zollparlament: Politik und Wirtschaft in den letzten Jahren vor der Reichsgründung, 1866/67-1870: zur Strukturanalyse Bayerns im Industriezeitalter. München, 1973. pp. 442. *bibliog. (Munich. Stadtarchiv. Neue Schriftenreihe. Band 64)*

— Industries.

BAVARIA. Statistisches Landesamt. 1967. Die Industrie in Bayern von 1950 bis 1965. [München, 1967]. pp. [212]. *(Bavaria. Beiträge zur Statistik Bayerns. Heft 280)*

— Landtag — Elections.

FINK (WILLIBALD) Die NPD bei der Bayerischen Landtagswahl, 1966: eine ökologische Wahlstudie. München, [1969]. pp. 110. *bibliog. (Hanns-Seidel-Stiftung. Berichte und Studien. Band 2)*

— Politics and government.

THRAENHARDT (DIETRICH) Wahlen und politische Strukturen in Bayern, 1848-1953: historisch-soziologische Untersuchungen zum Entstehen und zur Neuerrichtung eines Parteiensystems. Düsseldorf, 1973. pp. 360. *bibliog. (Germany (Bundesrepublik). Kommission für Geschichte des Parlamentarismus und der Politischen Parteien. Beiträge zur Geschichte des Parlamentarismus und der Politischen Parteien. Band 51)*

— Statistics.

BAVARIA. Statistisches Landesamt. 1973. Daten zur Gebietsreform. [München, 1973]. pp. 85.

BAYAKA.

ROOSENS (EUGEEN) De Yaka van Kwaango; (socio-culturele verandering in Midden- Afrika; een gevalstudie). Antwerpen, [1971]. pp. 372. *bibliog.*

BAZILI (NIKOLAI ALEKSANDROVICH).

BAZILI (NIKOLAI ALEKSANDROVICH) Nicolas de Basily, diplomat of Imperial Russia, 1903-1917: memoirs. Stanford, [1973]. pp. 201. *(Stanford University. Hoover Institution on War, Revolution and Peace. Hoover Institution Publications. 125)*

BEARINGS (MACHINERY)

— Trade and manufacture — Russia.

PERVYI podshipnikovyi: istoriia Pervogo gosudarstvennogo podshipnikovogo zavoda, 1932-1972. Moskva, 1973. pp. 302. *bibliog.*

BEBEL (AUGUST).

KOZHURIN (IAKOV IAKOVLEVICH) Iz istorii bor'by za nauchnyi ateizm: A. Bebel' i G.V. Plekhanov. Leningrad, 1972. pp. 84.

BECCARIA BONESANA (CESARE) Marchese.

MAESTRO (MARCELLO T.) Cesare Beccaria and the origins of penal reform. Philadelphia, 1973. pp. 179. *bibliog.*

BECKER (CARL LOTUS).

BECKER (CARL LOTUS) "What is the good of history?": selected letters... 1900-1945; edited... by Michael Kammen. Ithaca, N.Y., 1973. pp. 372. *bibliog.*

BECKERATH (ERWIN VON).

BLUMENBERG-LAMPE (CHRISTINE) Das wirtschaftspolitische Programm der "Freiburger Kreise": Entwurf einer freiheitlich-sozialen Nachkriegswirtschaft; Nationalökonomen gegen den Nationalsozialismus. Berlin, [1973]. pp. 180. *bibliog.*

BEDFORDSHIRE

— Population.

BEDFORDSHIRE. County Council. County review: population aspect report. Bedford, 1972. fo. 90.

BEECHER (CATHERINE ESTHER).

SKLAR (KATHRYN KISH) Catherine Beecher: a study in American domesticity. New Haven, Conn., 1973. pp. 356. *bibliog.*

BEEF.

BAKER (TERENCE J.) and others. A study of the Irish cattle and beef industries. Dublin, 1973. pp. 141. *(Economic and Social Research Institute. Papers. No.72)*

MORRIS (S.T.) and NIXON (B.R.) Semi-intensive beef: a case study based on an experiment at Dartington Cattle Breeding Centre, 1967-1972. Exeter, 1973. pp. 48.

BEETS AND BEET SUGAR

— Denmark.

DENMARK. Landøkonomiske Driftsbureau. 1974. Roedyrkning. København, 1974. pp. 16. *(Meddelelse. Nr. 15)*

BEGGING

— India — Bombay(State).

MOORTHY (M.V.) Beggar problem in Greater Bombay: a research study... undertaken under the auspices of the Indian Conference of Social Work, etc. Bombay, 1959. pp. 111,7.

— Nigeria.

CONFERENCE ON THE REHABILITATION OF BEGGARS IN NIGERIA, UNIVERSITY OF IBADAN, 1972. The rehabilitation of beggars in Nigeria: proceedings of a national conference; compiled and edited by Francis Olu. Okediji [and others]. [Ibadan, 1972]. pp. 74.

BEIJERLAND

— Economic history.

BAARS (C.) De geschiedenis van de landbouw in de Beijerlanden. Wageningen, 1973. pp. 234. *bibliog. (Centrum voor Landbouwpublikaties en Landbouwdocumentatie. Verslagen van Landbouwkundige Onderzoekingen. 801) With English summary.*

BELFAST

— Civic improvement.

IRELAND, NORTHERN. Ministry of Development. 1973. Belfast urban area plan: statement by the Ministry. Belfast, [1973]. pp. 15.

BELGIAN NEWSPAPERS.

PAEPE (JEAN LUC DE) "La Réforme", organe de la démocratie libérale, 1884-1907. Leuven, 1972. pp. 179. *bibliog*. (*Centre Interuniversitaire d'Histoire Contemporaine. Cahiers. 64*)

BENS (ELS DE) De Belgische dagbladpers onder Duitse censuur, 1940-1944. Antwerpen, [1973]. pp. 564. *bibliog*.

BELGIUM

— Census.

BELGIUM. Census, 1970. Recensement de la population, 31 décembre 1970. Bruxelles, 1973 in progress.

— Commerce — Portugal.

STOLS (EDDY) De Spaanse Brabanders of de handelsbetrekkingen der Zuidelijke Nederlanden met de Iberische wereld, 1598-1648. Brussel, 1971. 2 vols. *bibliog*. (*Vlaamse Academie voor Wetenschappen, Letteren en Schone Kunsten van Belgie. Klasse der Letteren. Verhandelingen. Nr. 70*)

— — Spain.

STOLS (EDDY) De Spaanse Brabanders of de handelsbetrekkingen der Zuidelijke Nederlanden met de Iberische wereld, 1598-1648. Brussel, 1971. 2 vols. *bibliog*. (*Vlaamse Academie voor Wetenschappen, Letteren en Schone Kunsten van Belgie. Klasse der Letteren. Verhandelingen. Nr. 70*)

— Constitution.

STEXHE (PAUL DE) La revision de la constitution belge, 1968-1971. Namur, 1972. pp. 502. (*Namur. Facultés Universitaires Notre-Dame de la Paix. Faculté de Droit. Travaux. n.8*)

WIGNY (PIERRE) La troisième revision de la constitution. Bruxelles, 1972. pp. 449.

— Economic history.

MOUREAUX (PHILIPPE) Les préoccupations statistiques du gouvernement des Pays-Bas autrichiens et le dénombrement des industries dressé en 1764. Bruxelles, 1971. pp. 535. *bibliog*. (*Brussels. Université Libre. Faculté de Philosophie et Lettres. [Travaux]. Tome 48*)

— Economic policy.

WAUWE (LUDO VAN) België - Europa: unitaire of regionale ekonomie?. Antwerp, 1973. pp. 168. *bibliog*.

— Emigration and immigration.

MARTENS (ALBERT) 25 jaar Wegwerparbeiders: het Belgisch immigratiebeleid na 1945. Leuven, 1973. pp. 322. *bibliog*. (*Katholieke Universiteit te Leuven. Sociologisch Onderzoeksinstituut. Afdeling Arbeids- en Industriële Sociologie. Rapport 1973/2*)

— Executive departments.

INSTITUT BELGE D'INFORMATION ET DE DOCUMENTATION. Ce qu'il faut savoir...du Ministère de la Justice. Bruxelles, [1971]. fo. 38.

INSTITUT BELGE D'INFORMATION ET DE DOCUMENTATION. Ce qu'il faut savoir...du Ministère des Communications, Postes, Télégraphes et Téléphones. Bruxelles, [1971]. fo. 36.

— Foreign economic relations.

WAUWE (LUDO VAN) België - Europa: unitaire of regionale ekonomie?. Antwerp, 1973. pp. 168. *bibliog*.

— — Argentine Republic.

BELGIUM. Office Belge du Commerce Extérieur. 1970. La mission économique belge en Argentine, juin 1970: rapport. Bruxelles, 1970. pp. 37. (*Informations du Commerce Extérieur. Suppléments. Série C. No. 5*)

— — China.

KURGAN-VAN HENTENRYK (GINETTE) Léopold II et les groupes financiers belges en Chine: la politique royale et ses prolongements, 1895-1914. Bruxelles, [1972]. pp. 969. *bibliog*. (*Académie Royale de Belgique. Classe des Lettres et des Sciences Morales et Politiques. Mémoires. Collection in-8°. 2e série. Tome 61. Fasc. 2*)

— — Indonesia.

BELGIUM. Office Belge du Commerce Extérieur. 1970. La mission économique belge en Indonesie, janvier 1970: rapport. Bruxelles, 1970. pp. 44. (*Informations du Commerce Extérieur. Suppléments. Série C. No. 2*)

— Foreign population.

BRAECKMAN (COLETTE) Les étrangers en Belgique. Bruxelles, [1973]. pp. 324. *bibliog*.

— Foreign relations.

VANLANGENHOVE (FERNAND) La Belgique et ses garants, l'été 1940: contribution à l'histoire de la politique extérieure de la Belgique pendant la Seconde Guerre mondiale. Bruxelles, 1972. pp. 228. *bibliog*. (*Académie Royale de Belgique. Classe des Lettres et des Sciences Morales et Politiques. Mémoires. Collection in-8°. 2ème Série. Tome 61, fasc. 3*)

— — Europe.

TAMSE (C.A.) Nederland en België in Europa, 1859-1871: de zelfstandigheidspolitiek van twee kleine staten. Den Haag, 1973. pp. 371. *bibliog*.

— History — 1940—1945, German occupation.

SELLESLAGH (FRANS) ed. L'emploi de la main d'oeuvre belge sous l'occupation, 1940. Bruxelles, 1970. pp. 127. (*Centre de Recherches et d'Etudes Historiques de la seconde Guerre Mondiale [Belgium]. Documents. 1*)

JONGHE (ALBERT DE) Hitler en het politieke lot van België, 1940-1944: de vestiging van een zivilverwaltung in België en Noord- Frankrijk. Antwerpen, 1972 in progress. *bibliog*.

CHARLES (JEAN LEON) and DASNOY (PHILIPPE) Les dossiers secrets de la police allemande en Belgique: la Geheime Feldpolizei en Belgique et dans le Nord de la France. Brussels, 1972-73. 2 vols.

— Languages.

COPPIETERS (FRANZ) The community problem in Belgium. Brussels, Belgian Information and Documentation Institute, 1971. fo. 40.

BECQUET (CHARLES FRANÇOIS) Le différend wallo-flamand. [Nalinnes-lez-Charleroi], 1972 in progress. *bibliog*. (*Institut Jules Destrée pour la Défense et l'Illustration de la Wallonie. Etudes et Documents*)

VERDOODT (ALBERT) compiler. Les problèmes des groupes linguistiques en Belgique: [a bibliography]. Louvain, [1973]. fo. 235. *bibliog*. (*Louvain. Université. Institut de Linguistique. Cours et Documents. 1*)

— Occupations.

PONTANUS (FERNAND) La population active en Belgique: 1910-1961 et tendances récentes; un demi-siècle d'évolution. Bruxelles, 1974. pp. 243. *bibliog*. (*Brussels. Université Libre. Institut de Sociologie. Groupe d'Etude de la Population Active. Etudes Démographiques*)

— Politics and government.

COPPIETERS (FRANZ) The community problem in Belgium. Brussels, Belgian Information and Documentation Institute, 1971. fo. 40.

JONGHE (ALBERT DE) Hitler en het politieke lot van België, 1940-1944: de vestiging van een zivilverwaltung in België en Noord- Frankrijk. Antwerpen, 1972 in progress. *bibliog*.

COLLARD (LEO) Front des progressistes et crise de la démocratie. [Nivelles, 1972]. pp. 156.

WITTE (ELS) Politieke machtsstrijd in en om de voornaamste Belgische steden, 1830-1848. [Brussels], 1973. 2 vols. (in 1). *bibliog*. (*Pro Civitate. Collection Histoire. Série in-8°. No. 37*) With English and French summaries.

— Population.

PONTANUS (FERNAND) La population active en Belgique: 1910-1961 et tendances récentes; un demi-siècle d'évolution. Bruxelles, 1974. pp. 243. *bibliog*. (*Brussels. Université Libre. Institut de Sociologie. Groupe d'Etude de la Population Active. Etudes Démographiques*)

— Religion.

VOYE (LILIANE) Sociologie du geste religieux: de l'analyse de la pratique dominicale en Belgique à une interprétation théorique. Bruxelles, [1973]. pp. 314. *bibliog*.

— Rural conditions.

HIERNAUX (J. PIERRE) Culture et maîtrise du devenir en milieu rural: quelques aspects d'une analyse culturelle réalisée au niveau des habitants de la vallée de l'Aisne. Bruxelles, 1972. pp. 94. (*Belgium. Direction Générale des Arts et des Lettres. Documentation et Enquêtes. No. 7*)

— Social policy.

BELGIUM. Ministère de la Culture Française. 1968. Plan quinquennal de politique culturelle. Livres 2,3,4(fasc.1),6,7. [Bruxelles, 1968]. 5 parts (in). Other parts out of print.

DELEECK (HERMAN) Opstellen over inkomensverdeling sociale zekerheid en sociaal beleid.Antwerp, 1972. pp. 247.

— Statistics.

MOUREAUX (PHILIPPE) Les préoccupations statistiques du gouvernement des Pays-Bas autrichiens et le dénombrement des industries dressé en 1764. Bruxelles, 1971. pp. 535. *bibliog*. (*Brussels. Université Libre. Faculté de Philosophie et Lettres. [Travaux]. Tome 48*)

BELGIUM. Institut National de Statistique. 1974. Développement de la statistique en 1972 et 1973 et perspectives pour 1974. Bruxelles, [1974?]. pp. 23.

— Statistics, Medical.

KLEIN-BEAUPAIN (THERESE) and LEFEVERE (GUSTAAF) Les indicateurs sociaux de santé. Bruxelles, [1974]. pp. 223. (*Brussels. Université Libre. Institut de Sociologie. Etudes d'Economie Sociale*)

BELIEF AND DOUBT.

SCHEIBE (KARL E.) Beliefs and values. New York, [1970]. pp. 159. *bibliog*.

NEEDHAM (RODNEY) Belief, language and experience. Oxford, [1972]. pp. 269. *bibliog*.

BELO HORIZONTE

— Poor.

MINAS GERAIS. Departamento de Habitação Popular. 1966. Levantamento da população favelada de Belo Horizonte: dados preliminares. Belo Horizonte, 1966. pp. 68.

BEMBA (AFRICAN TRIBE).

ROBERTS (ANDREW D.) A history of the Bemba: political growth and change in north- eastern Zambia before 1900. London, 1973. pp. 420. *bibliog*.

BENADIR

— History — Sources.

ITALY. Ministero degli Affari Esteri. Comitato per la Documentazione dell'Opera dell'Italia in Africa. L'Italia in Africa. Serie Storica. Vol. 2. Oceano Indiano. Tomo 2. Documenti relativi a Zanzibar e al Benadir, 1884-1891; a cura di Carlo Giglio. Roma, 1967. pp. 397.

BENEDICTINES IN THE UNITED KINGDOM.

STANBROOK ABBEY. An exhibit of productions from Stanbrook Abbey Press, 1876- 1966: 22 April - May 1968. London, [1968]. pp. 8.

BENELUX

— Industries.

FRANCE. Direction de la Documentation. La Documentation Française. Notes et Etudes Documentaires. No. 3,896. Fusions et concentrations d'entreprises au Benelux, par H.W. de Jong. [Paris], 1972. pp. 46. bibliog.

BENGAL

— Economic history.

MODERN Bengal: a socio-economic survey; [proceedings of a seminar held at the Institute of Historical Studies, Calcutta] in September 1971; edited by S.P. Sen. Calcutta, 1973. pp. 97.

— Famines.

VENKATARAMANI (M.S.) Bengal famine of 1943: the American response. Delhi, [1973]. pp. 137.

— Nationalism.

SARKAR (SUMIT) The Swadeshi movement in Bengal, 1903-1908. New Delhi, 1973. pp. 552. bibliog.

GORDON (LEONARD A.) Bengal: the nationalist movement, 1876-1940. New York, 1974. pp. 407. bibliog. (Columbia University. Southern Asian Institute. Southern Asian Institute Series)

— Politics and government.

SARKAR (SUMIT) The Swadeshi movement in Bengal, 1903-1908. New Delhi, 1973. pp. 552. bibliog.

GORDON (LEONARD A.) Bengal: the nationalist movement, 1876-1940. New York, 1974. pp. 407. bibliog. (Columbia University. Southern Asian Institute. Southern Asian Institute Series)

— Social history.

MODERN Bengal: a socio-economic survey; [proceedings of a seminar held at the Institute of Historical Studies, Calcutta] in September 1971; edited by S.P. Sen. Calcutta, 1973. pp. 97.

BENGAL, WEST

— Economic conditions.

CHAUDHURI (M.R.) The industrial landscape of West Bengal: an economic- geographic appraisal. Calcutta, [1971]. pp. 205. bibliog.

— Industries.

CHAUDHURI (M.R.) The industrial landscape of West Bengal: an economic- geographic appraisal. Calcutta, [1971]. pp. 205. bibliog.

— Statistics.

WEST BENGAL. Bureau of Applied Economics and Statistics. Statistical handbook. a., 1963- Calcutta.

WEST BENGAL. Bureau of Applied Economics and Statistics. 1969. Statistical atlas of West Bengal, 1967. [Calcutta], 1969. pp. 63.

BEN—GURION (DAVID).

AVI-HAI (AVRAHAM) Ben Gurion, state-builder: principles and pragmatism, 1948-1963. New York, [1974]. pp. 354. bibliog.

BENJAMIN (WALTER).

GUENTHER (HENNING) Walter Benjamin und der humane Marxismus: (zwischen Marxismus und Theologie). Olten, [1974]. pp. 188.

BENN (ANTHONY NEIL WEDGWOOD).

YORICK, pseud. The ugly face of Mr. Wedgwood Benn. London, [1974]. pp. 8.

BENNETT (JOHN COLEMAN).

GRENHOLM (CARL HENRIC) Christian social ethics in a revolutionary age: an analysis of the social ethics of John C. Bennett, Heinz-Dietrich Wendland and Richard Shaull. Uppsala, 1973. pp. 351. bibliog.

BENTHAM (JEREMY).

JAMES (M.H.) ed. Bentham and legal theory. [Belfast, 1973]. pp. 154. (Reprinted from Northern Ireland Legal Quarterly, 1973)

PAREKH (BHIKHUBHAI CHHOTALAL) ed. Jeremy Bentham: ten critical essays. London, 1974. pp. 204. bibliog.

BENTINCK (Lord WILLIAM CAVENDISH).

ROSSELLI (JOHN) Lord William Bentinck: the making of a liberal imperialist, 1774-1839. Berkeley, [1974]. pp. 384.

BENZENE

— Physiological effect.

INTERNATIONAL LABOUR CONFERENCE. 56th Session. Reports. 6. Sixth item on the agenda: protection against hazards arising from benzene. Geneva, 1971. 2 pts.

BERGER (VICTOR L).

MILLER (SALLY M.) Victor Berger and the promise of constructive socialism. 1910-1920. Westport, Conn., 1973. pp. 275. bibliog.

BERKELEY (GEORGE) Bishop of Cloyne.

BENNETT (JONATHAN) Locke, Berkeley, Hume: central themes. Oxford, 1971. pp. 361. bibliog.

TIPTON (I.C.) Berkeley: the philosophy of immaterialism. London, 1974. pp. 397. bibliog.

BERLIN

— Economic history.

CZADA (PETER) Die Berliner Elektroindustrie in der Weimarer Zeit: eine regionalstatistisch-wirtschaftshistorische Untersuchung. Berlin, 1969. pp. 367. bibliog. (Berlin. Freie Universität. Friedrich-Meinecke- Institut. Historische Kommission zu Berlin. Einzelveröffentlichungen. Band 4)

— History — 1945— , Allied occupation.

PROWE (DIETHELM) Weltstadt in Krisen, 1949-1958. Berlin, 1973. pp. 359. bibliog. (Berlin. Freie Universität. Friedrich-Meinecke- Institut. Historische Kommission zu Berlin. Veröffentlichungen. Band 42)

— Politics and government.

RASCHKE (JOACHIM) Innerparteiliche Opposition: die Linke in der Berliner SPD. Hamburg, 1974. pp. 437.

— Riot, June, 1953.

GERMANY (BUNDESREPUBLIK). Bundesministerium für Gesamtdeutsche Fragen. 1968. It happened in June 1953: facts and dates. Bonn, 1968. pp. 58.

BERLIN QUESTION (1945—).

MAHNCKE (DIETER) Berlin im geteilten Deutschland. München, 1973. pp. 325. bibliog. (Deutsche Gesellschaft für Auswärtige Politik. Forschungsinstitut. Schriften. Band 34)

PROWE (DIETHELM) Weltstadt in Krisen, 1949-1958. Berlin, 1973. pp. 359. bibliog. (Berlin. Freie Universität. Friedrich-Meinecke- Institut. Historische Kommission zu Berlin. Veröffentlichungen. Band 42)

BARK (DENNIS L.) Agreement on Berlin: a study of the 1970-72 quadripartite negotiations. Washington, D.C., 1974. pp. 131. (American Enterprise Institute for Public Policy Research and Stanford University. Hoover Institution on War, Revolution and Peace. AEI-Hoover Policy Studies. 10)

BERN (CANTON)

— Appropriations and expenditures.

BERN (CANTON). Statisches Bureau. 1971. Die Ausgaben der bernischen Gemeinden 1968, etc. Bern, 1971. pp. 52, [fo. 18]. (Beiträge zur Statistik des Kantons Bern. Finanzstatistik. Reihe B. Heft 7) In French and German.

— Economic conditions.

BERN (CANTON). Statistisches Bureau. 1971. Wachstum der Steuerkraft im Kanton Bern 1950-1968, etc. Bern, 1971. fo. 104, 37. (Beiträge zur Statistik des Kantons Bern. Finanzstatistik. Reihe B. Heft 4) Folding map in end pocket. In French and German.

— Economic history.

GERBER (FRITZ) Wandel im ländlichen Leben: eine sozialökonomische und sozialpsychologische Untersuchung in fünf Gemeinden des Oberemmentals. Bern, 1974. pp. 362. bibliog.

— Economic policy.

RYTZ (HANS RUDOLF) Geistliche des alten Bern zwischen Merkantilismus und Physiokratie: ein Beitrag zur Schweizer Sozialgeschichte des 18. Jahrhunderts. Basel, 1971. pp. 229. bibliog.

BODMER (WALTER) Die Wirtschaftspolitik Berns und Freiburgs im 17. und 18. Jahrhundert. [Bern, 1973]. pp. 108. (Historischer Verein des Kantons Bern. Archiv. Band 57)

— Politics and government.

AEMMER (ROBERT WALTER) Die Sozialdemokratie im Kanton Bern, 1890-1914. Zürich, 1973. pp. 302. bibliog.

— Population.

BERN (CANTON). Statistisches Bureau. 1971. Wachstum der Bevölkerung im Kanton Bern, 1870-1970, etc. Bern, 1971. pp. 85. (Beiträge zur Statistik des Kantons Bern. Bevölkerungsstatistik. Reihe A. Heft 4) In French and German.

BERN (CANTON). Statistisches Bureau. 1973. Bevölkerungsbewegung im Kanton Bern 1950-1970, etc. Bern, 1973. pp. 111. (Beiträge zur Statistik des Kantons Bern. Bevölkerungsstatistik. Reihe A. Heft 6) In French and German.

— Social history.

GERBER (FRITZ) Wandel im ländlichen Leben: eine sozialökonomische und sozialpsychologische Untersuchung in fünf Gemeinden des Oberemmentals. Bern, 1974. pp. 362. bibliog.

— Statistics, Vital.

BERN (CANTON). Statistisches Bureau. 1970. Ehe, Geburt und Tod im Kanton Bern, etc. Bern, 1970. fo. 55. (Bern (Canton). Statistisches Bureau. Beiträge zur Statistik des Kantons Bern. Bevölkerungsstatistik. Reihe A. Heft 3) In German and French.

BERNHEIM (EMILE).

LACROSSE (JACQUES) and BIE (PIERRE DE) Emile Bernheim: histoire d'un grand magasin. Bruxelles, [1972]. pp. 255.

BESANÇON.

FRANCE. Direction de la Documentation. La Documentation Française. Notes et Etudes Documentaires. Nos. 3,712-3, 713. Les villes françaises : Besançon; [by] Geneviève Charles. Paris, 1970. pp. 56. *bibliog*.

BESSARABIA

— Annexation to Russia.

KOPANSKII (IAKOV MIKHAILOVICH) Internatsional'nye traditsii bor'by za vossoedinenie Bessarabii s Sovetskoi Rodinoi, 1918-1940 gg. Kishinev, 1973. pp. 110.

BETEL NUTS.

WEST BENGAL. State Statistical Bureau. 1967. Report on the sample survey of arecanut in West Bengal: third round, 1964-65. Alipore. 1967. fo. 50.

BETHMANN—HOLLWEG (THEOBALD VON).

GUTSCHE (WILLIBALD) Aufstieg und Fall eines kaiserlichen Reichskanzlers: Theobald von Bethmann Hollweg, 1856-1921; ein politisches Lebensbild. Berlin, 1973. pp. 268. *bibliog*.

BEVERAGES.

FOOD, DRINK AND TOBACCO INDUSTRY TRAINING BOARD [U.K.]. Annual report and accounts. a., 1972/3- Croydon. *Formerly included in the file of British Parliamentary Papers*.

BEXLEY

— Civic improvement.

BEXLEY. Borough Council. Planning for the people of Bexley: a guide to town planning in the borough, 1971. London, [1971]. pp. 31.

BHARATIYA JANA SANGH.

BHARATIYA JANA SANGH. Party documents, (1951-1972). New Delhi, 1973 in progress.

BHILS.

AURORA (GURDIP SINGH) Tribe-caste-class encounters: some aspects of folk-urban relations in Alirajpur Tehsil. Hyderabad, [1972]. pp. 293. *bibliog*.

BHUTTO (ZULFIKAR ALI).

MUKERJEE (DILIP) Zulfiqar Ali Bhutto: quest for power. Delhi, [1972]. pp. 240.

BIBLE, NEW TESTAMENT

— Legends.

HALBWACHS (MAURICE) La topographie légendaire des Evangiles en Terre Sainte: étude de mémoire collective. 2nd ed. Paris, 1971. pp. 173. *bibliog*.

BIBLIOGRAPHICAL SERVICES.

THOMAS (PAULINE ANN) Bibliographic information in library systems. London, [1973]. pp. 52. *bibliog*. (*Association of Special Libraries and Information Bureaux. Aslib Occasional Publications. No. 13*)

BIBLIOGRAPHY

— Early printed books — 16th century.

CLARKE (DEREK ASHDOWN) and HEANEY (HOWELL J.) compilers. A selective check list of bibliographical scholarship for 1970. [Charlottesville, Va., 1972]. pp. 228-36. (*A reprint from Studies in Bibliography, Volume twenty-five, 1972*)

CLARKE (DEREK ASHDOWN) and HEANEY (HOWELL J.) compilers. A selective check list of bibliographical scholarship for 1971. [Charlottesville, Va., 1973]. pp. 271-290. (*A reprint from Studies in Bibliography, volume twenty-six, 1973*)

— Rare books.

CLARKE (DEREK ASHDOWN) and HEANEY (HOWELL J.) compilers. A selective check list of bibliographical scholarship for 1970. [Charlottesville, Va., 1972]. pp. 228-36. (*A reprint from Studies in Bibliography, Volume twenty-five, 1972*)

CLARKE (DEREK ASHDOWN) and HEANEY (HOWELL J.) compilers. A selective check list of bibliographical scholarship for 1971. [Charlottesville, Va., 1973]. pp. 271-290. (*A reprint from Studies in Bibliography, volume twenty-six, 1973*)

BIBLIOGRAPHY, NATIONAL

— Hungarian.

MAGYAR KÖZGAZDASÁGI ÉS STATISZTIKAI IRODALOM BIBLIOGRÁFIA: Hungarian bibliography of economics and statistics; ([pd. by] Központi Statisztikai Hivatal Könyvtár és Dokumentációs Szolgálat [and] MTA Közgazdaságtudományi Intézetének Könyvtára). a., 1968[v.8]- Budapest. *In Hungarian, Russian and English*.

— Jamaican.

WILLIAMS (ROSALIE I.) compiler. Jamaican national bibliography: 1964-1970 cumulation. Kingston, 1973. pp. 322.

— Taiwanese.

NATIONAL CENTRAL LIBRARY, [TAIPEI]. Selected bibliography of the Republic of China. Taipei, 1957. pp. 59.

BIELLA

— Economic history.

FERRARIS (PINO) Sviluppo industriale e lotta di classe nel Biellese. Torino, [1972]. pp. 189.

BIG BUSINESS

— Denmark.

TEGLERS (HANS EDVARD) Penge og positioner: rapport om det private Danmark. København, 1973. pp. 206.

— Europe.

VERNON (RAYMOND) ed. Big business and the state: changing relations in western Europe. London, 1974. pp. 310.

— European Economic Community countries.

ROWLEY (ANTHONY) ed. The barons of European industry. London, 1974. pp. 160.

— Germany.

RAISCH (MANFRED) Die Konzentration in der deutschen Automobilindustrie: betriebswirtschaftliche Bestimmungsfaktoren und Auswirkungen. Berlin, [1973]. pp. 150. *bibliog*.

— Pakistan.

WHITE (LAWRENCE J.) Industrial concentration and economic power in Pakistan. Princeton, [1974]. pp. 212. *bibliog*.

— Sweden.

SWEDEN. Statens Pris-och Kartellnämnd. 1971. Storföretag och koncentrationstendenser: (koncentrationstendenser inom svensk industri under 1960-talet) 1963-1967 (-1970). [Lund, 1971]. pp. 160.

— United States.

DEMARIS (OVID) Dirty business: the corporate-political money-power game. New York, [1974]. pp. 442.

MANSFIELD (EDWIN) ed. Monopoly power and economic performance: the problem of industrial concentration. 3rd ed. New York, [1974]. pp. 228. *bibliog*.

BIHAR

— Economic conditions.

HAJRA (S.) Bihar and Punjab: a study in regional economic disparity. New Delhi, [1973]. pp. 122.

SINHA (SACHCHIDANANDA) The internal colony: a study in regional exploitation. New Delhi, 1973. pp. 159.

— Rural conditions.

JANNUZI (FRANK TOMASSON) Agrarian crisis in India: the case of Bihar. Austin, [1974]. pp. 233. *bibliog*.

BILINGUALISM.

LEOPOLD (WERNER F.) Speech development of a bilingual child: a linguist's record; [reprint of volumes originally published 1939-49]. New York, 1970. 4 vols. *bibliogs*. (*Northwestern University. Studies in the Humanities. Nos. 6,11,18,19*)

KESSLER (CAROLYN) The acquisition of syntax in bilingual children. Washington, [1971]. pp. 109. *bibliog*.

HEATH (SHIRLEY BRICE) Telling tongues: language policy in Mexico: colony to nation. New York, [1972]. pp. 300. *bibliog*.

ERVIN-TRIPP (SUSAN M.) Language acquisition and communicative choice: essays...; selected and introduced by Anwar S. Dil. Stanford, 1973. pp. 383. *bibliog*. (*Linguistic Research Group of Pakistan. Language Science and National Development*)

BILLS OF LADING.

DEUTSCHER VEREIN FÜR INTERNATIONALES SEERECHT. Schriften. Reihe A: Berichte und Vorträge. Heft 16. Die Revision der Haager Regeln: Vortrag von Rolf Herber gehalten... am 7 März 1974. Hamburg, 1974. pp. 18.

— United Kingdom.

SCRUTTON (Sir THOMAS EDWARD) Charterparties and bills of lading; eighteenth edition by Sir Alan Abraham Mocatta [and others]. London, 1974. pp. 624.

BINANDELI (PAPUAN PEOPLE).

See OROKAIVAS.

BIOLOGICAL CHEMISTRY.

ESSMAN (WALTER B.) and NAKAJIMA (SHINSHU) eds. Current biochemical approaches to learning and memory. Flushing, N.Y., [1973]. pp. 205. *bibliogs*.

BIOLOGICAL WARFARE.

MINDERHOUT (LEO VAN) and others. Biologiese en chemiese oorlogvoering: met een onderzoek naar de aktiviteiten van het Medisch Biologisch Laboratorium van RVO- TNO te Rijswijk. Nijmegen, 1972. pp. 61.

BIRMINGHAM

— Civic improvement.

LLEWELYN-DAVIES WEEKS [AND PARTNERS]. Inner area study: Birmingham: progress report. [London], Department of the Environment, [1974]. pp. 18.

LLEWELYN-DAVIES WEEKS [AND PARTNERS]. Inner area study: Birmingham: project report. [London], Department of the Environment, [1974]. pp. 77.

— History.

HENNOCK (E.P.) Fit and proper persons : ideal and reality in nineteenth-century urban government. Montreal, 1973. pp. 395. *bibliog*.

SUTCLIFFE (ANTHONY) and SMITH (ROGER) Birmingham 1939-1970; (History of Birmingham, vol. 3). London, 1974. pp. 514. *Published for Birmingham City Council*.

— Social conditions.

LLEWELYN-DAVIES WEEKS [AND PARTNERS]. Inner area study: Birmingham: progress report. [London], Department of the Environment, [1974]. pp. 18.

LLEWELYN-DAVIES WEEKS [AND PARTNERS]. Inner area study: Birmingham: project report. [London], Department of the Environment, [1974]. pp. 77.

SPENCER (DAVID) of the Centre for Urban and Regional Studies, Birmingham, and LLOYD (JOHN) Sociologist. A childs eye view of Small Heath, Birmingham: perception studies for environmental education;...with a technical appendix by Brian Goodey. Birmingham, 1974. 1 vol. (various pagings). *bibliog.* (*Birmingham. University. Centre for Urban and Regional Studies. Research Memoranda. No.34*)

— Transit systems.

WEST MIDLANDS PASSENGER TRANSPORT EXECUTIVE. A passenger transport development plan for the West Midlands. n.p., [1973?]. pp. 88.

BIRTH CONTROL.

UNITED NATIONS. Department of Economic and Social Affairs. Population Studies. New York, 1948 in progress.

POPULATION CONFERENCE, 4TH, PARIS, 1971. An assessment of family planning programmes: summary proceedings of the fourth annual population conference of the Development Centre, Paris, 20-22nd October, 1971. Paris, Organisation for Economic Co-operation and Development, 1972. pp. 193.

BOGUE (DONALD JOSEPH) and others. An empirical model for demographic evaluation of the impact of contraception and marital status on birth rates with computerized applications to the setting of targets and quotas for family planning programs. Chicago, 1973. pp. 155. (*Chicago. University. Community and Family Study Center. R.F.P.I. Family Planning Evaluation Manuals. No. 6*)

ROGERS (EVERETT MITCHELL) Communication strategies for family planning. New York, [1973]. pp. 451. *bibliog.*

SUITTERS (BERYL) Be brave and angry: chronicles of the International Planned Parenthood Federation. London, 1973. pp. 424.

UTZINGER (ROLF PETER) Bevölkerungspolitik, Kontrazeption, Geburtenkontrollprogramme. Zürich, 1973. pp. 294. *bibliog.*

CIBA FOUNDATION. Symposia. Human rights in health: Ciba Foundation symposium 23 (new series); [proceedings; edited by Katherine Elliott and Julie Knight]. Amsterdam, 1974. pp. 304. *bibliogs.*

— Bibliography.

POPULATION, POPULATION AND FAMILY EDUCATION AND FAMILY PLANNING: accessions list; [pd.by] Population Education Clearing House Section of the Unesco Regional Office for Education in Asia. q.(approx.), current issues only kept. Bangkok.

— Law and legislation.

LEE (LUKE TSUNG-CHOU) Law, human rights and population: a strategy for action; background paper for the U.N. Second Asian Population Conference...1972. Medford, Mass., [1972]. pp. [17]. (*Tufts University. Fletcher School of Law and Population Monograph Series. No.6*) (Reprinted from the Virginia Journal of International Law, vol.12, no.3)

INTERNATIONAL ADVISORY COMMITTEE ON POPULATION AND LAW. Annual Meetings, 2nd, 1972. Human rights and population from the perspectives of law, policy and organization: proceedings. Medford, Mass., 1973. pp. 101. (*Tufts University. Fletcher School of Law and Diplomacy. Law and Population Book Series. No. 5*)

LEE (LUKE TSUNG-CHOU) Brief survey of abortion laws of five largest countries. Medford, Mass., 1973. pp. 8. (*Tufts University. Fletcher School of Law and Diplomacy. Law and Population Monograph Series. No.14*) (Reprinted from Population Report, Series F, No.1)

LEE (LUKE TSUNG-CHOU) International status of abortion legalization. Medford, Mass., 1973. pp. 338-364. (*Tufts University. Fletcher School of Law and Diplomacy. Law and Population Monograph Series. No.16*) (Reprinted from The abortion experience, Howard J. Osofsky and Joy D. Osofsky, editors).

STEPAN (JAN) and KELLOGG (EDMUND H.) The world's laws on voluntary sterilization for family planning purposes. Medford, Mass., [1973]. pp. 69. (*Tufts University. Fletcher School of Law and Diplomacy. Law and Population Monograph Series. No.8*)

COHEN (MORRIS L.) Law and population classification plan. Medford, Mass., [1974]. pp. 13. (*Tufts University. Fletcher School of Law and Diplomacy. Law and Population Monograph Series. No.5*)

— — Africa, Subsaharan.

WOLF (BERNARD) Anti-contraception laws in sub-Saharan francophone Africa: sources and ramifications. Medford, Mass., 1973. pp. 40. (*Tufts University. Fletcher School of Law and Diplomacy. Law and Population Monograph Series. No.15*)

— — America.

INTER-AMERICAN BAR ASSOCIATION. Human Rights Committee. Population and the role of law in the Americas: proceedings of a seminar. Medford, Mass., 1974. pp. 62. (*Tufts University. Fletcher School of Law and Diplomacy. Law and Population Monograph Series. No.18*)

— — Europe, Eastern.

MAGGS (PETER B.) Law and population growth in Eastern Europe. Medford, Mass., [1972]. pp. 30. (*Tufts University. Fletcher School of Law and Diplomacy. Law and Population Monograph Series. No.3*)

— — France.

DOUBLET (JACQUES) and VILLEDARY (HUBERT DE) Law and population growth in France. Medford, Mass., 1973. pp. 87. (*Tufts University. Fletcher School of Law and Diplomacy. Law and Population Monograph Series. No.12*)

— — Indonesia.

INDONESIAN PLANNED PARENTHOOD ASSOCIATION. Committee on Legal Aspects. Legal aspects of family planning in Indonesia. Medford, Mass., [1972]. pp. 48. (*Tufts University. Fletcher School of Law and Diplomacy. Law and Population Monograph Series. No.4*)

— — Jamaica.

ROSEN (ROBERT C.) Law and population growth in Jamaica. Medford, Mass., 1973. pp. 44. (*Tufts University. Fletcher School of Law and Diplomacy. Law and Population Monograph Series. No.10*)

— — Singapore.

HALL (PETER) Law and population growth in Singapore. Medford, Mass., 1973. pp. 57. (*Tufts University. Fletcher School of Law and Diplomacy. Law and Population Monograph Series. No.9*)

— — United Kingdom.

KLOSS (DIANA M.) and RAISBECK (BERTRAM L.) Law and population growth in the United Kingdom. Medford, Mass., 1973. pp. 47. (*Tufts University. Fletcher School of Law and Diplomacy. Law and Population Monograph Series. No.11*)

— — United States.

PILPEL (HARRIET F.) Brief survey of U.S. population law: address delivered at the International Advisory Committee on Population and Law, 1971. Medford, Mass., [1971]. pp. 11. (*Tufts University. Fletcher School of Law and Diplomacy. Law and Population Monograph Series. No.2*)

— America, Latin.

STYCOS (JOSEPH MAYONE) Clinics, contraception, and communication: evaluation studies of family planning programs in four Latin American countries. New York, [1973]. pp. 207.

— China.

TIEN (H. YUAN) China's population struggle: demographic decisions of the People's Republic, 1949-1969. Columbus, [1973]. pp. 405. *bibliog.*

— Ecuador.

ECUADOR. Division de Estadistica y Censos. 1967. Encuesta de fecundidad, levantada en las principales ciudades y en algunas parroquias rurales del pais. Quito, 1967.. pp. 255,6.

— Europe, Eastern.

DAVID (HENRY PHILIP) Family planning and abortion in the socialist countries of central and eastern Europe: a compendium of observations and readings. New York, [1970]. pp. 306. *bibliogs.*

— India.

SIMMONS (GEORGE B.) The Indian investment in family planning. New York, [1971]. pp. 213. *bibliog.* (*Population Council. Occasional Papers*)

FAMILY PLANNING ASSOCIATION OF INDIA. Report. a., 1972/3- Bombay.

HARRIMAN (EDWARD CLEMENTS) Indian population policy and the family planning programme; [Ph.D.(London) thesis]. 1973. fo. 286. *bibliog.* Typescript: unpublished. This thesis is the property of London University and may not be removed from the Library.

MANDELBAUM (DAVID GOODMAN) Human fertility in India: social components and policy perspectives. Berkeley, [1974]. pp. 132. *bibliog.*

— Jamaica.

STYCOS (JOSEPH MAYONE) and BACK (KURT WOLFGANG) Prospects for fertility reduction: the Jamaica Family Life Project of the Conservation Foundation; a preliminary report. New York, 1957. fo. 113.

— Kenya.

BONDESTAM (LARS) Population growth control in Kenya. Uppsala, 1972. fo. 48,5,2. *bibliog.* (*Nordiska Afrikainstitutet. Research Reports. No. 12*)

— Nigeria.

ACSADI (GYÖRGY T.) and others. Surveys of fertility, family, and family planning in Nigeria. Ile-Ife, Nigeria, 1972. 1 vol. (various pagings). (*Ife. University. Institute of Population and Manpower Studies. Publications. No. 2*)

— Pakistan.

PAKISTAN. [Population Planning Council]. Progress report of Pakistan Population Planning Programme: statistical summary.m., Ja 1973- [Islamabad].

— Sweden.

SWEDEN. Socialdepartementet. 1970. Family planning and the status of women in Sweden: report... to the United Nations. Stockholm, 1970. fo. 63. (*Stencil. 1970. 3*)

— Underdeveloped areas.

See UNDERDEVELOPED AREAS — Birth control.

— United Kingdom.

MORRIS (GEORGE MICHAEL) Overpopulation: everyone's baby. London, 1973. pp. 192. *bibliog.*

BIRTH CONTROL (Cont.)

CRAFTS (N.F.R.) and IRELAND (NORMAN J.) Family limitation and the English demographic revolution: a simulation approach. Coventry, 1974. pp. 42. *(University of Warwick. Department of Economics. Warwick Economic Research Papers. No.43)*

— **United States.**

TOWARD the end of growth: population in America; [papers originating in a conference held in Buck Hill Fall, Pennsylvania in 1972; by] Charles F. Westoff and others. Englewood Cliffs, N.J., [1973]. pp. 177. *bibliogs.*

BISMARCK—SCHOENHAUSEN (OTTO EDUARD LEOPOLD VON) Prince.

HALLMANN (HANS) ed. Revision des Bismarckbildes: die Diskussion der deutschen Fachhistoriker, 1945-1955. Darmstadt, 1972. pp. 493.

STEHLIN (STEWART A.) Bismarck and the Guelph problem 1866-1890: a study in particularist opposition to national unity. The Hague, 1973. pp. 253. *bibliog.*

WALLER (BRUCE) Bismarck at the crossroads: the reorientation of German foreign policy after the Congress of Berlin, 1878-1880. London, 1974. pp. 273. *bibliog.*

BISSELL (CLAUDE T.)

BISSELL (CLAUDE T.) Halfway up Parnassus: a personal account of the University of Toronto, 1932-1971. Toronto, [1974]. pp. 197.

BLACK PANTHER PARTY.

COMMISSION OF INQUIRY INTO THE BLACK PANTHERS AND THE POLICE. Search and destroy; a report by the Commission...; Roy Wilkins and Ramsey Clark, chairmen. New York, [1973]. pp. 284.

BLACK POWER.

FISH (JOHN HALL) Black power/white control: the struggle of the Woodlawn Organization in Chicago. Princeton, [1973]. pp. 356. *bibliog. (Center for the Scientific Study of Religion. Studies in Religion and Sociology)*

THOMAS (TONY) ed. Black liberation and socialism. New York, 1974. pp. 207.

BLEDINGTON

— **History.**

ASHBY (MABEL K.) The changing English village: a history of Bledington, Gloucestershire, in its setting, 1066-1914. Kineton, 1974. pp. 425.

BLENIO VALLEY.

VALLEGA (ADALBERTO) La media valle di Blenio: un'area di ricomposizione fondiaria. Varese, [1966]. pp. 79. *Bound with* FERRO (GAETANO) Aspetti della geografia agraria.

BLIND

— **United States.**

ORGANIZATION FOR SOCIAL AND TECHNICAL INNOVATION. Blindness and services to the blind in the United States: a report to the Subcommittee on Rehabilitation, National Institute of Neurological Diseases and Blindness, originally presented, June 1968. Cambridge, Mass., [1971]. pp. 212. *bibliogs.*

BLOCKADE.

CHAYES (ABRAM) The Cuban missile crisis. London, 1974. pp. 157. *(American Society of International Law. International Crises and the Role of Law)*

BLOOD

— **Transfusion.**

The ECONOMICS of charity: essays on the comparative economics and ethics of giving and selling, with applications to blood;... [by] Armen A. Alchian [and others]. London, 1973. pp. 197. *(Institute of Economic Affairs. Readings. 12)*

BLUE WHALE.

SPENCE (A. MICHAEL) Blue whales and applied control theory. Stanford, 1973. pp. 52. *bibliog. (Stanford University. Institute for Mathematical Studies in the Social Sciences. Technical Reports. [New Series]. No. 108)*

BLUM (LEON).

LOGUE (WILLIAM) Léon Blum: the formative years, 1872-1914. Dekalb, Ill., [1973]. pp. 344. *bibliog.*

BODIN (JEAN).

FOURNOL (ETIENNE MAURICE) Bodin: prédécesseur de Montesquieu; étude sur quelques théories politiques de la République et de l'Esprit des lois; [originally published 1896]. New York, 1972. pp. 176.

INTERNATIONALE BODIN TAGUNG IN MÜNCHEN, 1970. Verhandlungen ...; herausgegeben von Horst Denzer. München, [1973]. pp. 547. *bibliog. (Munich. Universität. Geschwister-Scholl- Institut für Politische Wissenschaft. Münchener Studien zur Politik. 18. Band) In various languages.*

KING (PRESTON THEODORE) The ideology of order: a comparative analysis of Jean Bodin and Thomas Hobbes. London, 1974. pp. 352. *bibliog.*

BODRUM.

MANSUR (FATMA) Bodrum: a town in the Aegean. Leiden, 1972. pp. 264. *pp. 249-264 misplaced before pp. 241-8.*

BOEHM—BAWERK (EUGEN VON).

HENNINGS (K.H.) Böhm-Bawerk on the rate of interest: a reinterpretation. [Reading], 1973. fo. 25. *bibliog. (Reading. University. Department of Economics. Discussion Papers in Economics. No. 47)*

BOEHNY (FERDINAND).

BOEHNY (FERDINAND) Die sozialistische Jugendbewegung des Ersten Weltkrieges als politischer Faktor. ?bASEL[, 1964] . PP. 14. (sONDERDRUCK AUS DEM oEFFENTLICHEN dIENST, jAHRGANG 1964, nRN.45 BIS 49)

BOGOTA

— **Civic improvement.**

BOGOTA. Departamento Administrativo de Planeacion Distrital. Renovacion urbana de Sans Façon. Bogota, [1969]. pp. 146. *bibliog. (Estudios e Informes de Una Ciudad en Marcha, 1967-1969. Tomo 2)*

— **Population.**

OLIVARES M. (JUAN) Proyecciones de la poblacion del Distrito Especial de Bogota, 1965-1985. Bogota, 1970. pp. 91.

BOGS, FENS AND MARSHES

— **United Kingdom.**

RAVENSDALE (J.R.) Liable to floods: village landscape on the edge of the fens, AD 450-1850. London, 1974. pp. 206. *bibliog.*

BÖHNY.

See BOEHNY.

BOLIVAR (SIMON).

SEIS ensayos sobre el ideario del Libertador. [Caracas, 1972]. pp. 314. *(Premio Oscar Garcia Uslar. 1962-1972)*

BOLIVIA

— **Biography.**

MONTENEGRO R. (EDMUNDO) Diccionario biografico de personalidades en Bolivia: año 1968. La Paz, 1968. pp. 152.

— **Census.**

BOLIVIA. Census, 1900. Censo general de la poblacion de la republica de Bolivia, segun el empadronamiento de 1o de septiembre de 1900. [La Paz, 1902-04] repr. 1973. 2 vols.

— **Commercial policy.**

WILKIE (JAMES W.) Bolivian foreign trade: historical problems and MNR revolutionary policy, 1952-1964. Buffalo, N.Y., 1971. fo. 46. *bibliog. (New York State University. Council on International Studies. Special Studies. No.6)*

— **Description and travel.**

VIEDMA Y NARVAEZ (FRANCISCO DE) Descripcion geografica y estadistica de la provincia de Santa Cruz de la Sierra; [prepared from the editions of 1836 and 1889]. 3rd ed. Cochabamba, 1969. pp. 296.

— **Economic history — Sources.**

CAMDEN SOCIETY . [Publications]. 4th Series. vol. 13. Camden miscellany. vol. 25. London, 1974. pp. 278.

— **Foreign relations — Chile.**

SOTOMAYOR (CARLOS MARTINEZ) Relaciones entre Chile y Bolivia. [Santiago], 1963. pp. 30. *(Chile. Ministerio de Relaciones Exteriores, Discurso y Documentos. 1)*

— — **United Kingdom.**

QUEREJAZU CALVO (ROBERTO) Bolivia y los ingleses, 1825-1948. La Paz, 1973. pp. 402. *bibliog.*

— **Politics and government.**

SALAMANCA ZAMORANO (HUMBERTO) Bolivia y la quiebra de los mitos latinoamericanos. La Paz, 1969. pp. 110. *bibliog.*

BAPTISTA GUMUCIO (MARIANO) Paginas para la revolucion. La Paz, 1970. pp. 157.

GALLARDO LOZADA (JORGE) De Torres a Banzer: diez meses de emergencia en Bolivia. Buenos Aires, 1972. pp. 499.

BOLLARDIERE (JACQUES MARIE ROCH ANDRE PARIS DE).

TOULAT (JEAN) Objectif Mururoa avec Bollarddière. Paris, [1974]. pp. 275.

BOLOGNA

— **Politics and government.**

ONOFRI (NAZARIO SAURO) I giornali bolognesi nel ventennio fascista. [Bologna, 1972]. pp. 295.

BOLOGNA (PROVINCE)

— **Economic conditions.**

I COMPRENSORI nella provincia de Bologna: studi, documenti, statistiche e bibliografia; [by a study group]. Bologna, 1968. pp. 236. *bibliog. (Bologna (Province). Collana di Studi e Monografie)*

— **Economic policy.**

I COMPRENSORI nella provincia de Bologna: studi, documenti, statistiche e bibliografia; [by a study group]. Bologna, 1968. pp. 236. *bibliog. (Bologna (Province). Collana di Studi e Monografie)*

BOMBAY (CITY)

— **Social conditions.**

MOORTHY (M.V.) Beggar problem in Greater Bombay: a research study... undertaken under the auspices of the Indian Conference of Social Work, etc. Bombay, 1959. pp. 111,7.

BOMBAY (PRESIDENCY)

— Politics and government.

JOHNSON (GORDON) Provincial politics and Indian nationalism: Bombay and the Indian National Congress, 1880 to 1915. Cambridge, 1973. pp. 207. *bibliog*. (Cambridge. University. Centre of South Asian Studies. *Cambridge South Asian Studies. 14*)

BOMBAY (STATE)

— Industries.

KAPADIA (K.M.) and PILLAI (S. DEVADAS) Industrialization and rural society: a study of Atul-Bulsar region. Bombay, 1972. pp. 260.

— Rural conditions.

KAPADIA (K.M.) and PILLAI (S. DEVADAS) Industrialization and rural society: a study of Atul-Bulsar region. Bombay, 1972. pp. 260.

BOMBING, AERIAL.

JONES (NEVILLE) The origins of strategic bombing: a study of the development of British air strategic thought and practice up to 1918. London, 1973. pp. 240. *bibliog*.

BONHOEFFER (DIETRICH).

BOSANQUET (MARY) The life and death of Dietrich Bonhoeffer. London, 1968 repr. 1969. pp. 287.

BONUS SYSTEM

— Russia.

VOLKOV (VLADIMIR FEDOROVICH) and MALAKHOV (ALEKSANDR KIRILLOVICH) Zarabotnaia plata i premirovanie rabotnikov sovkhozov. Moskva, 1967. pp. 183.

BOOK CLUBS

— United Kingdom.

WILLIAMS (Sir HAROLD HERBERT) Book clubs and printing societies of Great Britain and Ireland. London, 1929. pp. 127.

BOOK INDUSTRIES AND TRADE.

HITCHCOCK (FREDERICK HILLS) ed. The building of a book: a series of practical articles written by experts in the various departments of book making and distributing. 2nd ed. New York, 1929. pp. 315.

UNITED NATIONS EDUCATIONAL, SCIENTIFIC AND CULTURAL ORGANIZATION. Department of Mass Communication. Reports and Papers on Mass Communication. Paris, 1953 in progress.

— Asia.

UNITED NATIONS EDUCATIONAL, SCIENTIFIC AND CULTURAL ORGANIZATION. Regional seminar on Promotion and Distribution of Reading Materials, Madras, 1959. Final report. Karachi, 1960. pp. 11.

UNITED NATIONS EDUCATIONAL, SCIENTIFIC AND CULTURAL ORGANIZATION. Regional Seminar on Professional Cooperation in the Book-World, Colombo, 1961. Final report. Karachi, 1962. pp. 16.

SANKARANARAYANAN (N.) ed. Book distribution and promotion problems in South Asia. Madras, [1964?]. pp. 278.

— Cuba — Exhibitions.

HAVANA. Biblioteca Nacional Jose Marti. Movimiento editorial en Cuba, 1959-1960: exposicion de libros, folletos y revistas. La Habana, 1961. pp. 44.

— Germany.

WARD (ALBERT) Book production, fiction, and the German reading public, 1740-1800. Oxford, 1974. pp. 214. *bibliog*.

— — Exhibitions.

STIFTUNG BUCHKUNST. 20 Jahre Buchkunst: Ergebnisse der Wettbewerbe, 1951 bis 1970, Bundesrepublik Deutschland. Frankfurt am Main, [1971?]. pp. 103.

— Italy.

FRANCE. Direction de la Documentation. La Documentation Française. Notes et Etudes Documentaires. No. 3,735. Le livre en Italie; [by] Yves Fumel. Paris, 1970. pp. 29. *bibliog*.

— Underdeveloped areas.

See UNDERDEVELOPED AREAS — Book industries and trade.

— United Kingdom.

JOSEPH (MICHAEL) The commercial side of literature. London, [1925]. pp. 254.

PLANT (MARJORIE) The English book trade: an economic history of the making and sale of books. 3rd ed. London, 1974. pp. 520.

BOOKKEEPING.

SOVERSHENSTVOVANIE bukhgalterskogo ucheta i ekonomicheskogo analiza. Kishinev, 1973. pp. 124.

BOOKS.

DO books matter? [proceedings of a seminar organized jointly by the Working Party on Library and Book Trade Relations and the National Book League, in London in 1972];... edited by Brian Baumfield. Leeds, 1973. pp. 86.

— Conservation and restoration.

WORKING PARTY ON THE CONSERVATION OF LIBRARY MATERIALS. The care of books and documents. London, 1972. pp. 23. *bibliog*. (Library Association. Research Publications. No. 10)

— History — Bibliography.

ABHB: annual bibliography of the history of the printed book and libraries; edited by Hendrik D.L. Vervliet. The Hague, 1973.(vol.1).

— — Russia.

LUPPOV (SERGEI PAVLOVICH) Kniga v Rossii v pervoi chetverti XVIII veka. Leningrad, 1973. pp. 374. *Continuation of the author's Kniga v Rossii v XVII veke.*

— Statistics.

UNIVERSITY OF BATH. Library. Design of Information Systems in the Social Sciences. Working Papers. No. 7. Size and growth of monograph literature, with particular reference to the social sciences. Bath, 1974. 1 vol. (various pagings).

BOOKS AND READING.

WARD (ALBERT) Book production, fiction, and the German reading public, 1740-1800. Oxford, 1974. pp. 214. *bibliog*.

BOOKS AND READING FOR CHILDREN.

CANDEL (FRANCISCO) Inmigrantes y trabajadores. Barcelona, [1972]. pp. 239.

BOOKSELLERS AND BOOKSELLING

— Australia.

BRODSKY (ISADORE) Sydney's phantom book shops. Sydney, 1973. pp. 144. *bibliog*.

— Austria.

PRACHNER (GEORG) Buchhandlung. 40 Jahre Buchhandlung... 1785 gegründet und trägt seit 1. August 1931 den Namen Georg Prachner. [Vienna, 1971]. pp. viii.

— Germany.

REINICKE (HANS) Tobias Loeffler: ein Kapitel zur Geschichte Mannheims in der Zeit Karl Theodors. Mannheim, 1966. pp. 40. *bibliog*.

BENDER (A.) Buchhandlung. Vom Werden der Bender'schen Buchhandlung 1775-1817-1967. Mannheim, [1967]. pp. 27.

— New Zealand.

BOOKSELLERS ASSOCIATION OF NEW ZEALAND. Bookselling in New Zealand, 1971. Wellington, [imprint, 1972]. pp. 27.

— United Kingdom.

PUBLISHERS' ASSOCIATION. Book distribution: a handbook for booksellers and publishers on the ordering and distribution of books in the United Kingdom; home trade only. 2nd ed. London, 1972. pp. 46.

JOY (THOMAS) The bookselling business. London, 1974. pp. 246.

BOOT (JESSE) 1st Baron Trent.

CHAPMAN (STANLEY D.) Jesse Boot of Boots the chemists: a study in business history. London, 1974. pp. 221.

BOOTH FAMILY.

U.K. [National Register of Archives]. 1973. Report on the correspondence of Charles Booth (1840-1916), Mary Catherine Booth (1847-1939) and other members of the Booth and Macaulay families; (a handlist of the personal correspondence... in the University of London Library; compiled by T.D. Rogers and H.M. Young). London, 1973. fo. 317.

BOOTS AND SHOES

— Trade and Manufacture — Belgium.

DESCHEPPER (VICTOR) Dix années d'industrie de la chaussure en Belgique: une étude statistique. [Bruxelles, imprint, 1961?]. pp. 106. *(Institut Economique et Social des Classes Moyennes [Belgium]. Cahiers) In French and Flemish.*

— — United Kingdom.

FOOTWEAR, LEATHER AND FUR SKIN INDUSTRY TRAINING BOARD [U.K.]. Report and statement of accounts. a., 1972/3- Sutton Coldfield. *Formerly included in the file of British Parliamentary Papers.*

BOPHUTHATSWANA

— Politics and government.

SOUTH AFRICA. Report of the Controller and Auditor-General on the... accounts... of the Bophuthatswana Government and on the accounts of the lower authorities in Bophuthatswana. a., 1972/3 [1st]- Pretoria. *Included in the file of SOUTH AFRICA. Parliament. House of Assembly. Votes and proceedings; (with Printed annexures).*

BORDEAUX

— Growth

FRANCE. Délégation à l'Aménagement du Territoire et à l'Action Régionale. 1973. Schéma général d'aménagement de la France: Bordeaux: ville océane, métropole régionale. [Paris], 1973. pp. 142. *bibliog. (Travaux et Recherches de Prospective. 40) Map in end pocket*

— Politics and government.

LAGROYE (JACQUES) Société et politique: J. Chaban-Delmas à Bordeaux. [Paris, 1973]. pp. 345. *bibliog. (Bordeaux. Université. Institut d'Etudes Politiques. Centre d'Etude et de Recherche sur la Vie Locale. Série Vie Locale. 4)*

BORDER PATROLS

— Russia.

POGRANICHNYE voiska SSSR, 1929-1938: sbornik dokumentov i materialov. Moskva, 1972. pp. 775.

BORNEO

— Economic policy.

NORTH BORNEO. 1959. Development plan, 1959-1964. Jesselton, 1959. pp. (6). *(Legislative Council. Papers. 1959. No. 31)*

NORTH BORNEO. 1960. Development plan, 1959-1964. Jesselton, 1960. fo. (2). *(Legislative Council. Papers. 1960. No.43)*

— Social policy.

NORTH BORNEO. 1959. Development plan, 1959-1964. Jesselton, 1959. pp. (6). *(Legislative Council. Papers. 1959. No. 31)*

NORTH BORNEO. 1960. Development plan, 1959-1964. Jesselton, 1960. fo. (2). *(Legislative Council. Papers. 1960. No.43)*

BOSTON, MASSACHUSETTS

— Social conditions.

FRIED (MARC) The world of the urban working class. Cambridge, Mass., 1973. pp. 410. *bibliog.*

BOTSWANA

— Census.

BOTSWANA. Census, 1971. Report on the population census, 1971. Gaborone, 1972. 1 vol. (various pagings), 3 maps.

— Economic policy.

BOTSWANA. Ministry of Finance and Development Planning. 1973. National development plan 1973-78. Gaborone, [1973]. 2 pts. (in 1 vol.). *Map in end pocket.*

— History.

SILLERY (ANTHONY) Botswana: a short political history. London, 1974. pp. 219. *bibliog.*

— Politics and government.

SILLERY (ANTHONY) Botswana: a short political history. London, 1974. pp. 219. *bibliog.*

— Social policy.

BOTSWANA. Ministry of Finance and Development Planning. 1973. National development plan 1973-78. Gaborone, [1973]. 2 pts. (in 1 vol.). *Map in end pocket.*

BOUNDARIES (ESTATES)

— Australia — Northern Territory.

AUSTRALIA. Department of the Interior. 1969. Northern Territory (Administration) Act: Boundaries Ordinance 1968 together with statement of reasons for withholding assent to the Ordinance. in AUSTRALIA. Parliament. Parliamentary papers, 1969, vol.10.

BOUNTIES

— France.

FRANCE. Direction de la Documentation. La Documentation Française. Notes et Etudes Documentaires. Nos. 3,996-3, 997-3,998. La Caisse des dépots et consignations. [Paris], 1973. pp. 100. *bibliog.*

BOURBON FAMILY.

LEGUAI (ANDRE) Les ducs de Bourbon pendant la crise monarchique du XVe siècle: contribution à l'étude des apanages. Dijon, [1962]. pp. 219. *bibliog.*

BOWLAND FOREST.

PORTER (JOHN) Ph.D. The reclamation and settlement of Bowland, with special reference to the period 1500-1650; [Ph.D.(London) thesis]. 1973[or rather 1974]. fo. 267. *Typescript: unpublished. This thesis is the property of London University and may not be removed from the library.*

BOYS

— Societies and clubs.

GOODWIN (Sir REGINALD) A matter of faith. London, [1973]. pp. 20. *(National Association of Boys' Clubs. Basil Henriques Memorial Lectures. 1973)*

HARRISON (FREDERICK MADDISON WILLIAM) Reginald Anthony Colmer Symes: one of Scunthorpe's greatest citizens, 1877-1933. [Wollaton, Notts., 1973]. pp. 46.

PARKER (HOWARD J.) View from the boys: a sociology of downtown adolescents. Newton Abbot, [1974]. pp. 237.

BRABANT (DUCHY)

— Economic history — Sources.

VERLINDEN (CHARLES) and others, eds. Dokumenten voor de geschiedenis van prijzen en lonen in Vlaanderen en Brabant...(XIVe-XIXe eeuw). Brugge, 1959 in progress. *bibliogs.* (Ghent. Université. Faculté de Philosophie et Lettres. Recueil de Travaux. Fascicules 125, etc.)

BRACKEN (BRENDAN).

BOYLE (ANDREW) Poor, dear Brendan: the quest for Brendan Bracken. London, 1974. pp. 377. *bibliog.*

BRAHMANS.

VEEN (KLAAS W. VAN DER) I give thee my daughter: a study of marriage and hierarchy among the Anavil Brahmans of South Gujarat; [translated by Nanette Jockin]. Assen, 1972. pp. 297. *bibliog.*

BRAIN.

ARBIB (MICHAEL A.) The metaphorical brain: an introduction to cybernetics as artificial intelligence and brain theory. New York, [1972]. pp. 243. *bibliog.*

ECCLES (Sir JOHN CAREW) The understanding of the brain. New York, [1973]. pp. 238. *bibliog. (Indiana University. Patten Foundation. Lectures. 1972)*

SOMMERHOFF (GERD) Logic of the living brain. London, [1974]. pp. 413. *bibliog.*

BRAIN DRAIN.

LUFT (HAROLD) Determinants of the flow of physicians to the United States. Santa Monica, 1970. pp. 118. *bibliog. (Rand Corporation. [Papers]. 4538)*

BRAIN RESEARCH.

WOLTHUIS (OTTO) and SUTHERLAND (STUART) Problems and prospects of fundamental research in multi-disciplinary fields: brain and behaviour. Paris, Organisation for Economic Co-operation and Development, 1972. pp. 62. *(Science Policy Studies)*

BRANDT (WILLY).

KERN (ERICH) pseud. [i.e. Erich Knud KERNMAYR] Willy Brandt: Schein und Wirklichkeit: eine Dokumentation. Rosenheim, 1973. pp. 118.

STEWART-SMITH (DUDLEY GEOFFREY) ed. Brandt and the destruction of NATO: [a collection of articles, two of which were previously published in Osteuropa, and Orbis].Richmond, Surrey, 1973. pp. 101.

KUPER (ERNST) Frieden durch Konfrontation und Kooperation: die Einstellung von Gerhard Schröder und Willi [sic] Brandt zur Entspannungspolitik. Stuttgart, 1974. pp. 534. *bibliog. (Hamburg. Hansische Universität. Seminar für Sozialwissenschaften. Sozialwissenschaftliche Studien. Heft 14)*

PRITTIE (TERENCE CORNELIUS FARMER) Willy Brandt: portrait of a statesman. London, [1974]. pp. 350. *bibliog.*

BRASILIA

— Bibliography.

BRAZIL. Congresso. Câmara dos Deputados. Centro de Documentação e Informação. 1972. Brasilia. Brasilia, 1972. pp. 1078. *(Bibliografias. 3)*

— Civic improvement.

EPSTEIN (DAVID G.) Brasilia, plan and reality: a study of planned and spontaneous urban development. Berkeley, Cal., [1973]. pp. 206. *bibliog.*

BRASS INDUSTRY AND TRADE

— United Kingdom.

PILLER (NORMAN) Instead of the butler's apron. Luton, 1974. pp. 433.

BRAZIL.

BRAZIL. Ministerio das Relações Exteriores. Departamento de Administração .Grupo de Trabalho para a Elaboração do Livro 'Brasil'. 1970. Brasil, [1969]. [Brasilia, 1970?]. pp. 1261. *Map in end pocket.*

— Census.

BRAZIL. Census, 1970. (VIII recenseamento geral, 1970): censo demografico: Brasil. Rio de Janeiro, [1973]. pp. 272.

— Commerce.

QUEIROZ (JOSE MARIA VILAR DE) Brasil: exportação e importação; Brazil: export and import, etc. Rio de Janeiro, [1973?]. pp. 307. *In Portuguese, English and French.*

HIERSEMENZEL (UWE LUDWIG) Die Rolle der Exporte in der wirtschaftlichen Entwicklung Brasiliens. Göttingen, [1974]. pp. 121. *bibliog. (Göttingen. Universität. Ibero-Amerika- Institut für Wirtschaftsforschung. Arbeitsberichte. Heft 14)*

— Economic conditions.

BRASIL: realidade e desenvolvimento. 2nd ed. São Paolo, 1973. pp. 558.

MARGOLIS (MAXINE L.) The moving frontier: social and economic change in a southern Brazilian community. Gainesville, 1973. pp. 275. *bibliog. (Florida University. School of Inter-American Studies. Latin American Monographs. 2nd Series. No. 11)*

— Economic history.

HIERSEMENZEL (UWE LUDWIG) Die Rolle der Exporte in der wirtschaftlichen Entwicklung Brasiliens. Göttingen, [1974]. pp. 121. *bibliog. (Göttingen. Universität. Ibero-Amerika- Institut für Wirtschaftsforschung. Arbeitsberichte. Heft 14)*

— Economic policy.

BRAZIL. Grupo de Trabalho para o Desenvolvimento do Nordeste. 1967. Uma politica de desenvolvimento econômico para o nordeste. 2nd ed. Recife, 1967. pp. 92.

BRAZIL. Superintendência do Desenvolvimento do Nordeste. Assessoria Tecnica. Relatorio anual. a., 1970- Recife.

IANNI (OCTAVIO) Estado e planejamento econômico no Brasil, 1930-1970. Rio de Janeiro, 1971. pp. 316.

BRASIL: realidade e desenvolvimento. 2nd ed. São Paolo, 1973. pp. 558.

STEPAN (ALFRED C.) ed. Authoritarian Brazil: origins, policies, and future. New Haven, 1973. pp. 265.

WOGART (JAN PETER) Stabilisierungs- und Wachstumspolitik in Brasilien: die Bekämpfung der Inflation nach 1964. Stuttgart, [1974]. pp. 129. *bibliog. (Institut für Iberoamerika-Kunde. Schriftenreihe. Band 23) With summaries in English and Portuguese.*

— Foreign relations.

SCHOOYANS (MICHEL) Destin du Brésil: la technocratie militaire et son idéologie.[Gembloux, 1973]. pp. 230.

— Foreign relations — Portugal.

MAXWELL (KENNETH R.) Conflicts and conspiracies: Brazil and Portugal 1750-1808. Cambridge, 1973. pp. 289. *bibliog.*

— — United States.

McCANN (FRANK D.) The Brazilian-American alliance, 1937-1945. Princeton, [1973]. pp. 527. *bibliog.*

— History.

MAURO (FREDERIC) Histoire du Brésil. Paris, 1973. pp. 127. *bibliog.*

POPPINO (ROLLIE E.) Brazil: the land and people. 2nd ed. New York, 1973. pp. 385. *bibliog.*

— — To 1821.

MAXWELL (KENNETH R.) Conflicts and conspiracies: Brazil and Portugal 1750-1808. Cambridge, 1973. pp. 289. *bibliog.*

— — 1889— .

CARONE (EDGARD) Revoluçoes do Brasil contemporâneo, 1922/1938. São Paulo, 1965. pp. 174. *bibliog.*

— Politics and government.

SCHILLING (PAULO R.) Hélder Câmara; (traduccion del portugues por Aide Castagno). Montevideo, [1969]. pp. 111. *Contains extracts from the speeches and writings of Camara.*

CARDOSO (FERNANDO HENRIQUE) Ideologias de la burguesia industrial en sociedades dependientes: Argentina y Brasil. Mexico, 1969 repr. 1972. pp. 239. *bibliog.*

AMES (BARRY) Rhetoric and reality in a militarized regime: Brazil since 1964. Beverly Hills, [1973]. pp. 55. *bibliog.*

BRASIL: realidade e desenvolvimento. 2nd ed. São Paolo, 1973. pp. 558.

MEDICI (EMILIO GARRASTAZU) A verdadeira paz. 2nd ed. [Brasilia], 1973. pp. 205.

SCHOOYANS (MICHEL) Destin du Brésil: la technocratie militaire et son idéologie. [Gembloux, 1973]. pp. 230.

SCHWARTZ (STUART B.) Sovereignty and society in colonial Brazil: the high court of Bahia and its judges, 1609-1751. Berkeley, Cal., [1973]. pp. 438. *bibliog.*

STEPAN (ALFRED C.) ed. Authoritarian Brazil: origins, policies, and future. New Haven, 1973. pp. 265.

BOURNE (RICHARD) Getulio Vargas of Brazil, 1883-1954: sphinx of the pampas. London, 1974. pp. 236. *bibliog.*

EVANS (ROBERT DERVEL) Brazil: the road back from terrorism. London, [1974]. pp. 20. *bibliog. (Institute for the Study of Conflict. Conflict Studies. No. 47)*

— Population.

CARVALHO (JOSÉ ALBERTO MAGNO DE) Analysis of regional trends in fertility, mortality and migration in Brazil, 1940-1970; [Ph.D. (London) thesis]. 1973. fo. 202. *bibliog. Typescript: unpublished. This thesis is the property of London University and may not be removed from the Library.*

HUGON (PAUL) Demografia brasileira: ensaio de demoeconomia brasileira. São Paulo, 1973. pp. 342.

— Race question.

MONK (ABRAHAM) Black and white race relations in Brazil. Buffalo, N.Y., 1971. fo. 56. *bibliog. (New York State University. Council on International Studies. Special Studies. No. 4)*

FERNANDES (FLORESTAN) O negro no mundo dos brancos. São Paulo, 1972. pp. 285.

SKIDMORE (THOMAS E.) Black into white: race and nationality in Brazilian thought. New York, 1974. pp. 299. *bibliog.*

— Rural conditions.

ALENCAR ARARIPE (J.C.) Do sonho de Brasilia a realidade do Nordeste. Fortaleza, 1960. pp. 109.

FUNDAÇÃO GETULIO VARGAS. Centro de Estudos Agricolas. Orçamentos familiares rurais; [Estado do Espirito Santo, Minas Gerais, Ceara, Pernambuco, Estado de São Paulo , Estado de Santa Catarina, Rio Grande do Sul; by Sylvio Wanick Ribeiro and others]. [Rio de Janeiro], 1969-71. 7 vols(in 2).

CANA e reforma agraria; [by] Gilberto Freyre [and others]. [2nd ed.] Recife, Instituto Joaquim Nabuco de Pesquisas Sociais, 1970. pp. 372.

— Social conditions.

MARGOLIS (MAXINE L.) The moving frontier: social and economic change in a southern Brazilian community. Gainesville, 1973. pp. 275. *bibliog. (Florida University. School of Inter-American Studies. Latin American Monographs. 2nd Series. No. 11)*

POPPINO (ROLLIE E.) Brazil: the land and people. 2nd ed. New York, 1973. pp. 385. *bibliog.*

— Social history.

SCHWARTZ (STUART B.) Sovereignty and society in colonial Brazil: the high court of Bahia and its judges, 1609-1751. Berkeley, Cal., [1973]. pp. 438. *bibliog.*

— Social policy.

BRAZIL. Superintendência do Desenvolvimento do Nordeste. Assessoria Tecnica. Relatorio anual. a., 1970- Recife.

BREACH OF THE PEACE

— Russia.

DAN'SHIN (IVAN NIKOLAEVICH) Ugolovno-pravovaia okhrana obshchestvennogo poriadka. Moskva, 1973. pp. 200.

BREEDER REACTORS.

COCHRAN (THOMAS B.) The liquid metal fast breeder reactor: an environmental and economic critique. Baltimore, [1974]. pp. 271.

BREMEN

— Constitutional history.

BIEBUSCH (WERNER) Revolution und Staatsstreich: Verfassungskämpfe in Bremen von 1848 bis 1854. Bremen, 1973. pp. 391. *bibliog. (Bremen. Staatsarchiv. Veröffentlichungen. Band 40)*

— History.

GELBERG (BIRGIT) Auswanderung nach Übersee: soziale Probleme der Auswandererbeförderung in Hamburg und Bremen von der Mitte des 19. Jahrhunderts bis zum Ersten Weltkrieg. Hamburg, 1973. pp. 67. *bibliog. (Verein für Hamburgische Geschichte. Beiträge zur Geschichte Hamburgs. Band 10)*

BRENTWOOD

— Civic improvement.

ESSEX. Town Design Group. Land use/transportation study: Brentwood. [Chelmsford], 1967. fo. 32.

BRESCIA (PROVINCE)

— History.

CHIARINI (ROBERTO) Politica e società nella Brescia zanardelliana: le elezioni politiche a suffragio ristretto, 1876-1880. Milano, 1973. pp. 341. *(Pavia. Università. Instituto di Storia Moderna e Contemporanea. Collana. 5)*

BREST

— Growth.

FRANCE. Direction de la Documentation. La Documentation Française. Notes et Etudes Documentaires. Nos. 4,073-4, 074-4,075. Les villes françaises: Brest; par Jean Bienfait. [Paris], 1974. pp. 128. *bibliog.*

BRETT (REGINALD BALIOL) 2nd Viscount Esher.

FRASER (PETER) Winner of Prince Consort Prize, 1954. Lord Esher: a political biography. London, [1973]. pp. 496. *bibliog.*

BREWIN (ELIZABETH).

See PEPPERELL (ELIZABETH).

BREWING INDUSTRIES

— Germany.

GLOSSNER (JOSEF) Die Konzentrationsbewegung im deutschen Braugewerbe. [Neumarkt i.d. Opf., 1968]. pp. 88. *bibliog.*

BREZHNEV (LEONID IL'ICH).

DORNBERG (JOHN) Brezhnev: the masks of power. London, 1974. pp. 317. *bibliog.*

BRIAND (ARISTIDE).

SIEBERT (FERDINAND) Aristide Briand, 1862-1932: ein Staatsmann zwischen Frankreich und Europa. Erlenbach-Zürich, [1973]. pp. 704. *bibliog.*

BRICK TRADE

— Austria.

NOZICKA (KLAUS) Die österreichische Ziegelindustrie. Wien, 1971. pp. 90. *bibliog. (Vienna. Hochschule für Welthandel. Geographisches Institut. Wiener Geographische Schriften. 35) With English summary.*

BRIDE PRICE.

GOODY (JOHN RANKINE) and TAMBIAH (S.J.) Bridewealth and dowry. Cambridge, 1973. pp. 169. *bibliog.*

BRIDGES

— United Kingdom.

U.K. Committee on Steel Box Girder Bridges. 1973. Inquiry into the basis of design and method of erection of steel box-girder bridges; report...: abridged version; [A.W. Merrison,chairman]. London, 1973. pp. 33.

— United Kingdom — Scotland.

SCOTTISH COUNCIL (DEVELOPMENT AND INDUSTRY). By bridge to Skye. Inverness, 1969. pp. 15.

BRIGANDS AND ROBBERS

— Brazil.

MACHADO (CHRISTINA MATTA) As taticas de guerra dos cangaceiros. Rio de Janeiro, 1969. pp. 223. *bibliog.*

OLIVEIRA (AGLAE LIMA DE) Lampião, cangaço e nordeste. 2nd ed. Rio de Janeiro, [1970]. pp. 440. *bibliog.*

BRISTOL

— Civic improvement.

BRUTON (MICHAEL J.) An introduction to factor analysis and its application in planning. Oxford, 1971. pp. 123. (Oxford Polytechnic. Department of Town Planning. Oxford Working Papers in Planning Education and Research. 8)

BRISTOL. City Planning Department. The Cribbs Causeway out-of-town shopping (centre) enquiry, January-May 1972; a report of the proceedings. Bristol, 1972. pp. 212. Maps at end.

— Docks.

CASSON CONDER AND PARTNERS. Bristol city docks: redevelopment study [prepared for Bristol City Council]. London, 1972. pp. 34.

— Economic history.

LARGE (DAVID) and WHITFIELD (ROBERT) The Bristol Trades Council, 1873-1973. Bristol, 1973. pp. 35. bibliog. (Historical Association. Bristol Branch. Local History Pamphlets. No. 32)

— Riots.

THOMAS (SUSAN) The Bristol riots. Bristol, 1974. pp. 28. bibliog. (Historical Association. Bristol Branch. Local History Pamphlets. No. 34)

BRITISH BROADCASTING CORPORATION.

CURRAN (Sir CHARLES J.) A maturing democracy: the role of broadcasting; a speech...to the National Liberal Club, London, 14 March 1973. London, [1973]. pp. 23. Includes French text of same speech given in substance to the Anglo-French Colloquy on Communications, 7 April 1973.

BRITISH COLUMBIA

— Commerce.

SHEARER (RONALD A.) and others. Trade liberalization and a regional economy: studies of the impact of free trade on British Columbia. Toronto, [1971]. pp. 203. (Private Planning Association of Canada. Canada in the Atlantic Economy. 11)

— Economic conditions.

SHEARER (RONALD A.) and others. Trade liberalization and a regional economy: studies of the impact of free trade on British Columbia. Toronto, [1971]. pp. 203. (Private Planning Association of Canada. Canada in the Atlantic Economy. 11)

— Population.

PEOPLES of the living land: geography of cultural diversity in British Columbia: [prepared in connection with a symposium on Cultural discord in the modern world, organized by the Department of Geography, Simon Fraser University, as part of the 22nd International Geographical Congress, Montreal, 1972]; edited by Julian V. Minghi. Vancouver, [1972]. pp. 242. (Canadian Association of Geographers. British Columbia Division. Occasional Papers. No. 15)

BRITISH COUNCIL OF CHURCHES.

PAYNE (ERNEST ALEXANDER) Thirty years of the British Council of Churches, 1942-1972. London [1972]. pp. 60.

BRITISH IN AUSTRALIA.

RICHARDSON (ALAN) Psychologist. British immigrants and Australia: a psycho-social inquiry. Canberra, 1974. pp. 209. bibliog. (Academy of the Social Sciences in Australia. Immigrants in Australia. 4)

BRITISH IN INDIA.

MUDFORD (PETER) Birds of a different plumage: a study of British-Indian relations from Akbar to Curzon. London, 1974. pp. 314. bibliog.

BRITISH IN THE WEST INDIES.

BRIDENBAUGH (CARL) and BRIDENBAUGH (ROBERTA) No peace beyond the line: the English in the Caribbean, 1624- 1690. New York, 1972. pp. 440. (Beginnings of the American People. 2)

BRITISH MUSEUM.

MILLER (EDWARD J.) That noble cabinet: a history of the British Museum. London, 1973. pp. 400. bibliog.

BRITISH SOUTH AFRICA COMPANY.

NORTHERN RHODESIA. 1964. The British South Africa Company's claims to mineral royalties in Northern Rhodesia. Lusaka, 1964. pp. 33.

BRITISH VIRGIN ISLANDS

— Economic policy.

KLUMB (HENRY) Firm and ROBBINS (STANTON) AND COMPANY. Development and land use in program for the British Virgin Islands; report prepared... in consultation with Herbert Croucher. [Tortola, Administrator's Office, 1960]. fo. 46.

BRITISH VIRGIN ISLANDS. Development Advisory Committee. 1966. Report... relating to the period 1966-1971: [M.S. Staveley, chairman]. Tortola, 1966. pp. 65.

— Social policy.

BRITISH VIRGIN ISLANDS. Development Advisory Committee. 1966. Report... relating to the period 1966-1971: [M.S. Staveley, chairman]. Tortola, 1966. pp. 65.

BRITTANY

— Nationalism.

CAERLÉON (RONAN) Les Bretons le dos au mur: le F[ront de] L[ibération de la] B[retagne] devant la Cour de Sûreté de l'état. Paris, [1973]. pp. 221.

BROCKDORFF—RANTZAU (ULRICH EDUARD FERDINAND ALEXANDER VON) Graf.

WENGST (UDO) Graf Brockdorff-Rantzau und die aussenpolitischen Anfänge der Weimarer Republik. Bern, 1973. pp. 163. bibliog.

BROEKMEYER (MARIUS).

MARIUS Broekmeyer tussen wetenschap en demagogie: hoe een welbekende slavist op weg naar een betere wereld het spoor bijster raakte. Amsterdam, 1974. pp. 48.

BROWN (GEORGE) Communist.

JENKINS (MICK) George Brown: portrait of a communist leader. Manchester, [197-?]. pp. 30.

BROWN (JOHN) American abolitionist.

QUARLES (BENJAMIN) Allies for freedom: blacks and John Brown. New York, 1974. pp. 244. bibliog.

BRUNSWICK

— Social conditions.

HEIDEMANN (CLAUS) and STAPF (KURT HERMANN) Die Hausfrau in ihrer städtischen Umwelt: eine empirische Studie zur urbanen Ökologie am Beispiel Braunschweigs. Braunschweig, 1969. pp. 156. bibliog. (Technische Universität Braunschweig. Institut für Stadtbauwesen. Veröffentlichungen. Heft 4)

BRUSSELS

— Growth.

VANDERMOTTEN (CHRISTIAN) Le marché des terrains à bâtir dans la région bruxelloise, 1912-1968. Bruxelles, 1971. pp. 257. bibliog.

— Libraries.

GEERAERTS (PIERRE) La Bibliothèque Africaine: quatre-vingt-cinq ans d'activité bibliographique africaine. Bruxelles, Bibliothèque Africaine, 1972. pp. 90.

— Social conditions.

DELRUELLE-VOSSWINKEL (NICOLE) and ROGGEMANS (MARIE LAURE) La grande ville: rapports sociaux et attractivité du centre-ville; enquêtes menées dans une commune centrale et des communes périphériques de l'agglomération bruxelloise. Bruxelles, [1974]. pp. 176, 4. (Brussels. Université Libre. Centre de Sociologie Générale et de Méthodologie. L'Agglomération Bruxelloise. 3)

— Water supply.

VIRE (LILIANE) La distribution publique d'eau à Bruxelles, 1830-1870. [Brussels], 1973. pp. 238. bibliog. (Pro Civitate. Collection Histoire. Série in-8°. No. 33)

BUCKERIDGE (NICHOLAS).

BUCKERIDGE (NICHOLAS) Journal and letter book of Nicholas Buckeridge, 1651-1654; edited by John R. Jenson. Minneapolis, [1973]. pp. 104.

BUDAPEST.

FRANCE. Direction de la Documentation. La Documentation Française. Notes et Etudes Documentaires. Nos. 3,886-3, 887. Les grandes villes du monde: Budapest; [par Laszlo Fodor et Joseph Schultz]. [Paris], 1972. pp. 76. bibliog.

— History.

BARDY (ROLAND) 1919: la commune de Budapest. Paris, [1973]. pp. 244. bibliog.

BUDENNYI (SEMEN MIKHAILOVICH).

BUDENNYI (SEMEN MIKHAILOVICH) Proidennyi put'. Moskva, 1958-73. 3 vols.

BUDGET.

HANSMEYER (KARL HEINRICH) and RUERUP (BERT) Staatswirtschaftliche Planungsinstrumente. Tübingen, [1973]. pp. 88. bibliogs.

CAIDEN (NAOMI JOY) and WILDAVSKY (AARON BERNARD) Planning and budgeting in poor countries. New York, [1974]. pp. 369. bibliog.

— Austria.

DANNEBERG (ROBERT) Ein Blick in den Bundeshaushalt. Wien, 1929. pp. 24.

— Canada.

GILLESPIE (W. IRWIN) The Federal budget as plan, 1968-1972. [Toronto], 1973. pp. 64-84. (Offprint from Canadian Tax Journal, vol. XXI, no. 1)

GOW (DONALD) The progress of budgetary reform in the government of Canada. Ottawa, 1973. pp. 60. (Canada. Economic Council. Special Studies. No. 17)

— — Quebec.

QUEBEC (PROVINCE). Department of Finance. Budget Speech. a., 1974/5- Quebec.

— Denmark.

DENMARK. Budgetdepartementet. Budget redegørelse. a., 1972- København.

— France.

REUNION. Trésorerie Général. 1972. Exécution du budget de l'état dans le département: dépenses, recettes, F.I.D.O.M., 1967-1971. [St. Denis], 1972. pp. 45. (Réunion. [Secretariat Général pour les Affaires Economiques. Documentation et Etudes]. Bulletin de Conjoncture. Supplément. No.12)

FRANCE. Direction de la Documentation. La Documentation Française. Notes et Etudes Documentaires. Nos. 3,965-3, 966. Les techniques de préparation et de contrôle du budget de l'état, par Pierre Lequéret. [Paris], 1973. pp. 67.

— Guyana.

GUYANA. Ministry of Finance. 1963. Budget speech...delivered by the Minister of Finance...in the Legislative Assembly of British Guiana, December 31, 1962. Georgetown, [1963]. pp. 16. (*Guyana. Legislative Assembly. Sessional Papers. 1962. No.8*)

GUYANA. Ministry of Finance. 1964. 1964 budget speech delivered by the Minister of Finance... December 31, 1963. Georgetown, [1964]. pp. 35. (*Guyana. Legislative Assembly. Sessional Papers. 1963. No.4*)

— India.

GUPTA (BAIJ NATH) Indian federal finance and budgetary policy. Allahabad, 1970. pp. 467. *bibliog.*

— Korea.

KOREA (REPUBLIC). Economic Planning Board. Overall resources budget. a., 1971 (terminal year of the second Five-Year Economic Development Plan)- Seoul.

— Mexico — Mexico (State).

MEXICO (STATE). Statutes, etc. 1972. Ley organica del presupuesto de egresos del Estado de Mexico. Toluca, Dirreccion General de Hacienda del Estado de Mexico, [1972]. pp. 73. (*Coleccion Documentos. 3*)

— Nepal.

BEYER (JOHN C.) Budget innovations in developing countries: the experience of Nepal. New York, 1973. pp. 185. *bibliog.*

— Pakistan.

PAKISTAN. Ministry of Finance. 1972. Fiscal policy in Pakistan: a historical perspective. [Islamabad, 1972]. 2 vols. (in 1).

— Poland.

OKULICZ (TADEUSZ) Prawo bud'zetowe: zbiór podstawowych przepisów z objaśnieniami; stan prawny na dzień 1 sierpnia 1973 r. Warszawa, 1973. pp. 316.

— Russia — Georgia.

OKROSTSVARIDZE (IVAN EFREMOVICH) Biudzhetnaia sistema i biudzhetnye prava Gruzinskoi SSR, 1921- 1972 gg. Tbilisi, 1973. pp. 177.

— South Africa.

SOUTH AFRICA. Ministry of Finance. 1965. Budget speeches, 1965-'66: speeches delivered in the House of Assembly by... the Minister of Finance and the... Minister of Transport on the 24th and 3rd March, 1965, respectively, etc. Cape Town, [1965]. pp. 26.

— Sri Lanka.

SRI LANKA. Ministry of Finance. Budget speech. a., 1974- Colombo.

— Switzerland.

WEILENMANN (JAKOB) Der Einfluss des Bundeshaushalts auf den schweizerischen Konjunkturverlauf: eine empirische Untersuchung des Zeitraums 1950-1970. Bern, 1974. pp. 192. *bibliog.*

— United Kingdom.

JACKSON (PETER McLEOD) and McGILVRAY (JAMES WILLIAM) The impact of tax changes on income distribution: the 1973 budget. London, 1973. pp. 23. (*Institute for Fiscal Studies. Publications. No. 8*)

— United States.

LEE (ROBERT D.) and JOHNSON (RONALD W.) Public budgeting systems. Baltimore, [1973] repr. 1974. pp. 356. *bibliog.*

NISKANEN (WILLIAM A.) Structural reform of the federal budget process. Washington, D.C., 1973. pp. 60. (*American Enterprise Institute for Public Policy Research. Domestic Affairs Studies. 12*)

PUBLIC claims on U.S. output: federal budget options in the last half of the seventies; [by] David J. Ott [and others]. Washington, D.C., 1973. pp. 218. (*American Enterprise Institute for Public Policy Research. Domestic Affairs Studies. 18*)

WEIDENBAUM (MURRAY L.) and others. Matching needs and resources: reforming the federal budget. Washington, D.C.,1973. pp. 114. (*American Enterprise Institute for Public Policy Research. Domestic Affairs Studies. 11*)

BUDGET IN BUSINESS.

ATKINS (DEREK R.) The hybridisation of administered price and administered budget controls. Coventry, 1973. pp. 22. *bibliog.* (*University of Warwick. Centre for Industrial Economic and Business Research. [Warwick Research in Industrial and Business Studies]. No.41*)

BUENOS AIRES (PROVINCE)

— Economic policy.

BUENOS AIRES (PROVINCE). Asesoria Provincial de Desarrollo. 1970. Planificacion del desarrollo en la provincia de Buenos Aires, 1966-1970. [Buenos Aires], 1970. 4 vols.(in 1). (*Folletos. No. 20*)

— Social policy.

BUENOS AIRES (PROVINCE). Asesoria Provincial de Desarrollo. 1970. Planificacion del desarrollo en la provincia de Buenos Aires, 1966-1970. [Buenos Aires], 1970. 4 vols.(in 1). (*Folletos. No. 20*)

BUILDING

— Repair and reconstruction.

U.K. Committee on Building Maintenance. 1972. Building maintenance; the report of the Committee. London, 1972. pp. 65. (*U.K. Department of the Environment. R and D Bulletins*)

— Italy.

TREVISO (PROVINCE). Ufficio Studi. Alcuni aspetti dell'andamento dell'attività edilizia in provincia di Treviso dal 1955 al 1964. Treviso, 1969. fo. 32,(54).

— Jamaica — Statistics.

JAMAICA. Department of Statistics. Economic Indicators Section. 1969. Building activity in Jamaica, 1966-68; [prepared by J.C. McMillan]. [Kingston, 1969]. pp. 50.

JAMAICA. Department of Statistics. 1974. Building activity in Jamaica, 1965-1972. [Kingston, 1974]. pp. 59.

— Zambia.

ZAMBIA. Ministry of Power, Transport and Works. Buildings Branch. Report. a., 1965/6, 1968- Lusaka.

BUILDING AND LOAN ASSOCIATIONS

— United Kingdom.

CLARK (H. GORDON) Building society amalgamations: unions and transfers of engagements. 2nd ed. London, 1973. pp. 47. (*Building Societies Institute. Building Society Administration. No.4.*)

GOSDEN (PETER HENRY JOHN HEATHER) Self-help: voluntary associations in the 19th century. London, 1973. pp. 295. *bibliog.*

REVELL (JACK) U.K. building societies. Bangor, 1973. pp. 29. (*Wales. University. University College of North Wales. Economic Research Papers. FIN 5*)

GHOSH (DEBAPRIYA) The economics of building societies. Farnborough, Hants., [1974]. pp. 132. *bibliog.*

GREER (RUPERT L.) Building societies?. London, 1974. pp. 27. (*Fabian Society. Research Series. [No.] 319*)

BUILDING MATERIALS.

SZCZELKUN (STEFAN A.) Survival scrapbook 1: shelter. Brighton, [1972]. 1 vol. (unpaged). *bibliogs.*

— Information services.

UNITED NATIONS INDUSTRIAL DEVELOPMENT ORGANIZATION. Guides to Information Sources. No. 9. Information sources on building boards from wood and other fibrous materials (UNIDO/LIB/SER.D/9). New York, United Nations, 1974. pp. 82. *bibliog.*

BUILDING MATERIALS INDUSTRY

— Russia — Uzbekistan.

IUSUPOVA (NAILIA MINIAKHMETOVNA) Razvitie promyshlennosti stroitel'nykh materialov Uzbekistana. Tashkent, 1973. pp. 150.

BUILDINGS

— Repair and reconstruction.

U.K. Committee on Building Maintenance. 1969. Building maintenance; the interim report of a Committee appointed by the Minister of Public Building and Works. London, 1969. pp. 23. (*U.K. Ministry of Public Building and Works. R and D Bulletins*)

BUILDINGS, PREFABRICATED.

See INDUSTRIALIZED BUILDING.

BUKHARA (OBLAST')

— Economic history.

EKONOMIKA i kul'tura Bukharskoi oblasti posle Velikogo Oktiabria. Bukhara, 1968. pp. 270. (*Bukharskii Gosudarstvennyi Pedagogicheskii Institut. Uchenye Zapiski. vyp.15*)

BUKHARIN (NIKOLAI IVANOVICH).

COHEN (STEPHEN F.) Bukharin and the Bolshevik revolution: a political biography, 1888-1938. New York, 1973. pp. 498,xvii. *bibliog.*

BUKOVINA

— Rural conditions.

KRAVETS' (MYKOLA MYKOLAIOVYCH) Selianstvo Skhidnoï Halychyny i Pivnichnoï Bukovyny u druhii polovyni XIX st. L'viv, 1964. pp. 239.

BUKOVSKII (VLADIMIR KONSTANTINOVICH).

BUKOVSKII (VLADIMIR KONSTANTINOVICH) Stories and statements, selected...by Comité international pour la défense des droits de l'homme. Paris, [1971?]. 1 pamphlet (unpaged).

BULB INDUSTRY

— Belgium.

MENEVE (I.) Inleidende studie over de afzet van begonia's en gloxinia's. [Gent, 1963]. fo. 88. (*Belgium. Station d'Economie Rurale de l'Etat. Communications. 57*)

BULGARIA

— Constitution.

SPASOV (BORIS) La Bulgarie (traduit en français par Stantcho Djoumaliev).Paris, [1973]. pp. 400.

— Economic conditions.

MATEEV (EVGENI) Balans na narodnoto stopanstvo. 3rd ed. Sofiia, 1972. pp. 327.

— Foreign relations — Germany, Eastern.

A CONTRIBUTION to peace and security in Europe: treaties between the German Democratic Republic [and Hungary, and between the GDR and Bulgaria]. Dresden, [1967?]. pp. 96. *Mainly speeches and statements, together with texts of the treaties.*

BULGARIA (Cont.)

— Relations (general) with Russia.

OKTIABR' i bolgarskie internatsionalisty. Moskva, 1973. pp. 334. *bibliog.*

BULGARIANS IN THE UKRAINE.

DIKHAN (MIKHAIL DMITRIEVICH) Bolhary-politemihranty u sotsialistychnomu budivnytstvi na Ukraïni v 1924-1929 rr.

BUNKE (HAYDEE TAMARA).

TANIA: la guerrillera inolvidable. Havana, 1970. pp. 359. Kyiv, 1973. pp. 159.

BURDEN OF PROOF

— United Kingdom.

WOLCHOVER (DAVID) Affixing guilt: problems in the criminal burden of proof; ten summary trials. London, 1973. pp. 15. *Privately printed.*

BUREAUCRACY.

TESCONI (CHARLES A.) and MORRIS (VAN CLEVE) The anti-man culture: bureautechnocracy and the schools. Urbana, Ill., [1972]. pp. 232. *bibliog.*

JACOBY (HENRY) The bureaucratization of the world;... translated from the German by Eveline L. Kanes. Berkeley, Calif., [1973]. pp. 241. *bibliog.*

KATZ (ELIHU) and DANET (BRENDA) eds. Bureaucracy and the public: a reader in official-client relations. New York, [1973]. pp. 534. *bibliog.*

MANDEL (ERNEST) On bureaucracy: a Marxist analysis. London, [1973]. pp. 40. *(International Marxist Group. Red Pamphlets. No.5)*

NISKANEN (WILLIAM A.) Bureaucracy: servant or master?; lessons from America; with commentaries by Douglas Houghton [and others]. London, 1973. pp. 103. *(Institute of Economic Affairs. Hobart Paperbacks. 5)*

CLEAVES (PETER S.) Bureaucratic politics and administration in Chile. Berkeley, Calif., [1974]. pp. 352. *bibliog.*

COLEMAN (JAMES SAMUEL) Power and the structure of society. New York, [1974]. pp. 112. *bibliog. (Pennsylvania University. Fels Center of Government. Fels Lectures on Public Policy Analysis)*

BURGENLAND

— Commerce.

ZIRKOVITS (ERNST) Burgenlands Handel einst und jetzt: die Entwicklung der Interessenvertretung der burgenländischen Handelskammer ... von 1850 bis 1973. Wien, [1973]. pp. 119. *bibliog.*

— Population.

KOVÁCS (TIBOR) Das südliche Burgenland in den Volkszählungen der Jahre 1857 und 1869. Eisenstadt, 1972. pp. 210. *(Burgenländische Forschungen. Heft 63)*

BURGUNDY

— Commerce — United Kingdom.

MUNRO (JOHN H.A.) Wool, cloth, and gold: the struggle for bullion in Anglo-Burgundian trade, 1340-1478. Brussels, 1972. pp. 241. *bibliog.*

— Economic history.

MUNRO (JOHN H.A.) Wool, cloth, and gold: the struggle for bullion in Anglo-Burgundian trade, 1340-1478. Brussels, 1972. pp. 241. *bibliog.*

— History.

VAUGHAN (RICHARD) Professor of Medieval History, University of Hull. Philip the Good: the apogee of Burgundy. London, 1970. pp. 456. *bibliog.*

— Population.

MILLOT (BENOÎT) Capital humain et migrations interrégionales. Dijon, [1971]. fo. 196. *bibliog.*

BURKE (EDMUND).

BEVAN (RUTH A.) Marx and Burke: a revisionist view. La Salle, [1973]. pp. 197. *bibliog.*

O'GORMAN (FRANK) Edmund Burke: his political philosophy. London, 1973. pp. 153. *bibliog.*

BURMA.

FRANCE. Direction de la Documentation. La Documentation Française. Notes et Etudes Documentaires. No. 3,005. L'Union Birmane. Paris, 1963. pp. 28. *bibliog.*

— Bibliography.

TRAGER (FRANK N.) compiler. Burma: a selected and annotated bibliography. New Haven, 1973. pp. 356.

— Economic history.

ADAS (MICHAEL) The Burma delta: economic development and social change on an Asian rice frontier, 1852-1941. Madison, Wisc., 1974. pp. 256. *bibliog.*

— Foreign relations — China.

PETTMAN (RALPH) China in Burma's foreign policy. Canberra, 1973. pp. 56. *(Australian National University. Contemporary China Centre. Contemporary China Papers. No. 7)*

— History.

MYA SEIN, Daw. The administration of Burma: (Sir Charles Crosthwaite and the consolidation of Burma); [reprint of the first edition of 1938] with an introduction by Josef Silverstein. Kuala Lumpur, 1973. pp. 186. *bibliog.*

— — Historiography.

SARKISYANZ (EMANUEL) Peacocks, pagodas and Professor Hall: a critique of the persisting use of historiography as an apology for British empire-building in Burma. Athens, [1972]. fo.57. *(Ohio University. Center for International Studies. Papers in International Studies. Southeast Asia Series. No.24)*

— Nationalism.

YOON (WON Z.) Japan's scheme for the liberation of Burma: the role of the Minami Kikan and the "thirty comrades". Athens, Oh., 1973. fo. 54. *bibliog. (Ohio University. Center for International Studies. Papers in International Studies. Southeast Asia Series. No. 27)*

— Relations (military) with Japan.

YOON (WON Z.) Japan's scheme for the liberation of Burma: the role of the Minami Kikan and the "thirty comrades". Athens, Oh., 1973. fo. 54. *bibliog. (Ohio University. Center for International Studies. Papers in International Studies. Southeast Asia Series. No. 27)*

— Social history.

ADAS (MICHAEL) The Burma delta: economic development and social change on an Asian rice frontier, 1852-1941. Madison, Wisc., 1974. pp. 256. *bibliog.*

BURNEY (HENRY).

HALL (DANIEL GEORGE EDWARD) Henry Burney: a political biography. London, 1974. pp. 330. *bibliog.*

BURUNDI

— Politics and government.

LEMARCHAND (RENE) and MARTIN (DAVID) Journalist. Selective genocide in Burundi. London, 1974. pp. 36. *bibliog. (Minority Rights Group. Reports. No. 20)*

BURYAT REPUBLIC

— History — 1917—1921, Revolution.

KHAPTAEV (PAVEL TABINAEVICH) Buriatiia v gody grazhdanskoi voiny. Ulan-Ude, 1967. pp. 264. *bibliog.*

— Social conditions.

IZ opyta konkretno-sotsiologicheskikh issledovanii. Ulan-Ude, 1968. pp. 162. *(Buriatskii Institut Obshchestvennykh Nauk. Trudy. vyp.11)*

BUSINESS.

FIVE monographs on business income; [reprint of the work originally published in New York, 1950] . Lawrence, Kansas, 1973. pp. 271. *(American Institute of Certified Public Accountants. Study Group on Business Income. Pamphlets. 3)*

DEKKER (JOHN) Business and television. London, [1973]. pp. 8. *(Foundation for Business Responsibilities. Seminar Papers.)*

— Directories.

EUROPEAN directory of economic and corporate planning, 1973-74. Epping, 1973. pp. 442.

— International Cooperation.

RAAD VOOR HET MIDDEN- EN KLEINBEDRIJF. Werkgroep Europese N.V. Rapport inzake europese rechtsvormen en hun betekenis voor het midden- en kleinbedrijf: (Europese rechtsvormen). 's-Gravenhage, 1969. pp. 60. *(Raad voor het Midden- en Kleinbedrijf. [Publikaties]. 1969, no. 1) With summaries in English, French, and German.*

ADVIES inzake de Europese Groepering van economisch belang (EGEB): [report of a working party]; (Europese rechtsvormen 2). 's-Gravenhage, 1972. pp. 62. *(Raad voor het Midden- en Kleinbedrijf. [Publikaties]. 1972, no. 1)*

BUSINESS AND POLITICS

GREEN (ROBERT T.) Political instability as a determinant of U.S. foreign investment. Austin, 1972. pp. 122. *bibliog. (Texas University. Bureau of Business Research. Studies in Marketing. No.17)*

— Germany.

MERSON (ALLAN LESLIE) Nazis and monopoly capital: new evidence reviewed;...(paper originally read in the history course of the Communist University in 1972). London, 1973. pp. 19. *(Communist Party of Great Britain. History Group. Our History. No.57)*

— India.

KOCHANEK (STANLEY A.) Business and politics in India. Berkeley, [1974]. pp. 382. *bibliog.*

— United States.

ERSHKOWITZ (HERBERT) The attitude of business toward American foreign policy, 1900-1916. University Park, Penn., [1967]. pp. 77. *bibliog. (Pennsylvania State University. Penn State Studies. No. 21)*

MICHELMAN (IRVING S.) The crisis meeters: business response to social crises. Clifton, N.J., 1973. pp. 418.

DEMARIS (OVID) Dirty business: the corporate-political money-power game. New York, [1974]. pp. 442.

— Zaire.

VANDERLINDEN (JACQUES) Contribution à l'étude de la crise congolaise de 1960: notes au sujet de quelques documents inédits relatifs aux réactions du secteur privé. Bruxelles, 1972. pp. 93. *bibliog. (Académie Royale des Sciences d'Outre-Mer. Classe des Sciences Morales et Politiques. [Mémoires in-80 Nouvelle Série. [Tome] 42. [fasc.] 1)*

BUSINESS CYCLES.

KLEIN (PHILIP A.) and GORDON (RICHARD L.) The steel industry and U.S. business cycles. University Park, Penn., [1971]. pp. 108. *(Pennsylvania State University. Penn State Studies. No.33)*

SANT (MORGAN EUGENE CYRIL) The geography of business cycles: a case study of economic fluctuations in East Anglia, 1951-68; [based on the thesis of the same title]. [London, 1973]. pp. 64. *(London. University. London School of Economics and Political Science. Department of Geography. Geographical Papers. No. 5)*

WATERMAN (ANTHONY M.C.) The measurement of economic fluctuations in Canada, January 1947 to December 1969;... prepared for the Prices and Incomes Commission. Ottawa, Information Canada, 1973. pp. 135.

WEILENMANN (JAKOB) Der Einfluss des Bundeshaushalts auf den schweizerischen Konjunkturverlauf: eine empirische Untersuchung des Zeitraums 1950-1970. Bern, 1974. pp. 192. *bibliog.*

— **Mathematical models.**

LAMBRINIDES (MATTHEW J.) A spectral and cross-spectral analysis of the long swing hypothesis. Coventry, 1973. pp. 61. *bibliog. (University of Warwick. Department of Economics. Warwick Economic Research Papers. No. 35)*

BUSINESS EDUCATION

— **Denmark.**

[DENMARK. Undervisningsministeriet. 1969]. Commercial education in Denmark. [Copenhagen], 1969. fo. 16.

BUSINESS ETHICS.

ACTON (HARRY BURROWS) The ethics of capitalism. London, [1972]. pp. 9. *(Foundation for Business Responsibilities. Seminar Papers)*

IDEMITSU (SAZO) Be a true Japanese. [Tokyo, 1973]. pp. 174.

ADAIR (JOHN) Management and morality: the problems and opportunities of social capitalism. Newton Abbot, [1974]. pp. 189.

DUNSTAN (GORDON REGINALD) A moralist in the city. London, 1974. pp. 8. *(Foundation for Business Responsibilities. Sir George Earle Memorial Lectures. 1974)*

BUSINESS LAW

— **European Economic Community countries.**

RAAD VOOR HET MIDDEN- EN KLEINBEDRIJF. Werkgroep Europese N.V. Rapport inzake europese rechtsvormen en hun betekenis voor het midden- en kleinbedrijf: (Europese rechtsvormen). 's-Gravenhage, 1969. pp. 60. *(Raad voor het Midden- en Kleinbedrijf. [Publikaties]. 1969, no. 1)* With summaries in English, French, and German.

ADVIES inzake de Europese Groepering van economisch belang (EGEB): [report of a working party]; (Europese rechtsvormen 2). 's-Gravenhage, 1972. pp. 62. *(Raad voor het Midden- en Kleinbedrijf. [Publikaties]. 1972, no. 1)*

PARKLAND RESEARCH EUROPE. Guide to national practices in western Europe: a guide to commercial business and legal practices and attitudes in the continental EEC countries and Switzerland; [edited by Victor Selwyn]; research directed by Parkland Research Europe SA. London, [1973]. pp. 223.

BUSINESS LIBRARIES.

BURKETT (JACK) Industrial and related library and information services in the United Kingdom. 3rd ed. London, 1972. pp. 263. *bibliog.*

BUSINESSMEN.

— **America, Latin.**

CARDOSO (FERNANDO HENRIQUE) Ideologias de la burguesia industrial en sociedades dependientes: Argentina y Brasil. Mexico, 1969 repr. 1972. pp. 239. *bibliog.*

— **Europe.**

ROWLEY (ANTHONY) ed. The barons of European industry. London, 1974. pp. 160.

— **European Economic Community countries.**

ROWLEY (ANTHONY) ed. The barons of European industry. London, 1974. pp. 160.

— **Venezuela.**

GURUCEAGA (JUAN DE) ed. Geografia economica de Venezuela. [Caracas, 1959]. pp. 283.

BUTTER.

KUHL (ESTHER ELISABETH) Der schweizerische Buttermarkt unter besonderer Berücksichtigung der Konkurrenzprodukte, Speiseöle, Speisefette und Margarine. Zürich, 1974. pp. 181. *bibliog.*

BYZANTINE EMPIRE

— **History.**

ANGOLD (MICHAEL) A Byzantine government in exile: government and society under the Laskarids of Nicaea, 1204-1261. London, 1974. pp. 332. *bibliog.*

CAB AND OMNIBUS SERVICE

— **France.**

CAUSSE (BERNARD) Les fiacres de Paris aux XVIIe et XVIIIe siècles. Paris, 1972. pp. 88. *bibliog. (Paris. Université de Paris II. Travaux et Recherches. Série Sciences Historiques. 3)*

CABINET MINISTERS

— **Spain.**

BORRAS BETRIU (RAFAEL) and others, eds. El dia en que mataron a Carrero Blanco. Barcelona, 1974. pp. 412.

— **United Kingdom.**

HAZLEHURST (CAMERON) and WOODLAND (CHRISTINE) compilers. A guide to the papers of British Cabinet ministers 1900-1951. London, 1974. pp. 174. *(Royal Historical Society. Guides and Handbooks. Supplementary Series. No. 1)*

HEADEY (BRUCE W.) British cabinet ministers: the roles of politicians in executive office. London, 1974. pp. 316. *bibliog.*

CABINET SYSTEM

SWAAN (ABRAM DE) Coalition theories and cabinet formations: a study of formal theories of coalition formation applied to nine European parliaments after 1918. Amsterdam, 1973. pp. 347. *bibliog.*

— **Australia.**

BUTLER (DAVID HENRY EDGEWORTH) The Canberra model: essays on Australian government. London, 1974. pp. 146.

— **United Kingdom.**

COOKE (A.B.) and VINCENT (JOHN RUSSELL) The governing passion: cabinet government and party politics in Britain 1885-86. Brighton, 1974. pp. 516.

CADIZ

— **Economic history.**

EVERAERT (JOHN G.) De internationale en koloniale handel der Vlaamse firma's te Cadiz, 1670-1700. Brugge, 1973. pp. 975. *bibliog. (Ghent. Université. Faculte de Philosophie et Lettres. Recueil de Travaux. Fascicule 154).* Summary in French.

CAFIERO (CARLO).

DAMIANI (FRANCO) Carlo Cafiero nella storia del primo socialismo italiano. Milano, [1974]. pp. 221. *bibliog.*

CAIRNES (JOHN ELLIOTT).

BORDO (MICHAEL DAVID) The monetary theory and policy of John E. Cairnes. [Ottawa, 1973]. fo. 33. ii. *bibliog. (Carleton University. Carleton Economic Papers)*

CALABRIA

— **History.**

GUARASCI (ANTONIO) Politica e società in Calabria dal Risorgimento alla Repubblica. Chiaravalle, 1973 in progress.

MASCIA (ROBERTO) Ferdinando II e la crisi socio-economica della Calabria nel 1848. Napoli, [1973]. pp. 145.

CALCUTTA

— **Transit systems.**

INDIA. Metropolitan Transport Team. 1969. Report on mass transportation system in Calcutta. [New Delhi], 1969. pp. 72.

CALIFORNIA

— **Emigration and immigration.**

STEIN (WALTER J.) California and the dust bowl migration. Westport, Conn., [1973]. pp. 302. *bibliog.*

— **Government publications.**

CALIFORNIA STATE PUBLICATIONS: annual listing; compiled by California State Library. m., with annual cumulation, 1972 (v.26)- Sacramento. *Annual cumulation only kept permanently.*

— **Politics and government.**

WILLIAMS (R. HAL) The Democratic Party and California politics, 1880-1896. Stanford, 1973. pp. 290. *bibliog.*

CALVINISM.

SCHILLING (HEINZ) Niederländische Exulanten im 16. Jahrhundert: ihre Stellung im Sozialgefüge und im religiosen Leben deutscher und englischer Städte. Gütersloh, [1972]. pp. 200. *bibliog. (Verein für Reformationsgeschichte. Schriften. Nr.187)*

CAMARA (HELDER) Archbishop of Olinda and Recife.

SCHILLING (PAULO R.) Hélder Câmara; (traduccion del portugues por Aide Castagno). Montevideo, [1969]. pp. 111. *Contains extracts from the speeches and writings of Camara.*

CAMBODIA

— **Foreign relations.**

SIMON (SHELDON W.) War and politics in Cambodia: a communications analysis. Durham, N.C., 1974. pp. 178. *bibliog.*

— **Politics and government.**

SIMON (SHELDON W.) War and politics in Cambodia: a communications analysis. Durham, N.C., 1974. pp. 178. *bibliog.*

— **Population.**

MIGOZZI (JACQUES) Cambodge: faits et problèmes de population. Paris, 1973. pp. 303. *bibliog. (Paris. Ecole Pratique des Hautes Etudes. Section des Sciences Economiques et Sociales. Centre de Documentation et de Recherches sur l'Asie du Sud-Est et le Monde Insulindien. Atlas Ethno-Linguistique. 2ème série. Monographies)*

CAMBRIDGE

— **Transit systems.**

HILL (MORRIS) Planning for multiple objectives: an approach to the evalution of transportation plans. Philadelphia, [1973]. pp. 273. *bibliog. (Regional Science Research Institute. Monograph Series. No.5)*

CAMBRIDGESHIRE

CAMBRIDGESHIRE

— **Economic history.**

HART (CYRIL EDWIN) The hidation of Cambridgeshire. [Leicester], 1974. pp. 67. *bibliog. (Leicester. University. Department of English Local History. Occasional Papers. 2nd Series. No.6)*

SPUFFORD (MARGARET) Contrasting communities: English villagers in the sixteenth and seventeenth centuries. London, 1974. pp. 374.

— **Social history.**

SPUFFORD (MARGARET) Contrasting communities: English villagers in the sixteenth and seventeenth centuries. London, 1974. pp. 374.

CAMDEN.

PYKETT (ANDREW NICHOLAS) The sense of place and the perceived environment : a theory, and its application in the London borough of Camden; [Ph.D. (London) thesis]. [1974]. fo. 299. *bibliog. Typescript: unpublished. This thesis is the property of London University and may not be removed from the library.*

— **Civic improvement.**

CAMDEN. Department of Planning and Communications. Camden scene 1971: a planning survey. [London, Borough of Camden, 1971]. pp. 86. *bibliog.*

CAMEROONS

— **Economic history.**

MANDENG (PATRICE) Auswirkungen der deutschen Kolonialherrschaft in Kamerun: die Arbeitskräftebeschaffung in den Südbezirken Kameruns... 1884-1914. Hamburg, [1973]. pp. 204. *bibliog. (Vereinigung von Afrikanisten in Deutschland. Schriften. Band 4)*

CAMEROUN.

FRANCE. Direction de la Documentation. La Documentation Française. Notes et Etudes Documentaires. No. 2,756. Le Cameroun sous tutelle britannique à l'heure du plébiscite. Paris, 1961. pp. 13. *bibliog.*

— **Commerce.**

LENTHE-EBOA (CHARLES) Der Beitrag des Aussenhandels für das wirtschaftliche Wachstum der Republik Kamerun. [Mannheim, 1971?]. pp. 307. *bibliog.*

— **Economic conditions.**

FRANCE. Direction de la Documentation. La Documentation Française. Notes et Etudes Documentaires. No. 2,946. Organisation économique et sociale de l'Etat fédéré du Cameroun occidental (République fédérale du Cameroun). Paris, 1962. pp. 31. *bibliog.*

EWUSI (KODWO) West African economies: some basic economic problems. Legon, 1971. fo.89. *(Ghana University. Institute of Statistical, Social and Economic Research. Technical Publication Series. No.25)*

IMBERT (JEAN) Le Cameroun. Paris, 1973. pp. 127. *bibliog.*

— **Economic policy.**

NDONGKO (WILFRED A.) Regional economic planning in Cameroon. Uppsala, 1974. pp. 21. *(Nordiska Afrikainstitutet. Research Reports. No.21)*

— **History.**

IMBERT (JEAN) Le Cameroun. Paris, 1973. pp. 127. *bibliog.*

— **Politics and government.**

IMBERT (JEAN) Le Cameroun. Paris, 1973. pp. 127. *bibliog.*

— **Social conditions.**

FRANCE. Direction de la Documentation. La Documentation Française. Notes et Etudes Documentaires. No. 2,946. Organisation économique et sociale de l'Etat fédéré du Cameroun occidental (République fédérale du Cameroun). Paris, 1962. pp. 31. *bibliog.*

IMBERT (JEAN) Le Cameroun. Paris, 1973. pp. 127. *bibliog.*

— **Statistics, Vital.**

PODLEWSKI (ANDRE M.) Un essai d'observation permanente des faits d'état civil dans l'Adamaoua: recherche méthodologique sur la collecte des données démographiques dans les pays dépourvus de données permanentes. Paris, Office de la Recherche Scientifique et Technique Outre-Mer, 1970. pp. 150. *(Travaux et Documents. No.5) With English summary.*

CAMPAIGN FUNDS.

KRAEHE (RAINER) Le financement des partis politiques: contribution à l'étude du statut constitutionnel des partis politiques. Paris, [1973]. pp. 126. *bibliog. (Rouen. Université. Publications. 18)*

OWENS (JOHN ROBERT) Trends in campaign spending in California, 1958-1970: tests of factors influencing costs. Princeton, 1973. pp. 84. *(Citizens' Research Foundation. Studies. No. 22)*

SCHLETH (UWE) Parteifinanzen: eine Studie über Kosten und Finanzierung der Parteientätigkeit, etc. Meisenheim am Glan, 1973. pp. 542. *bibliog.*

CAMPBELL (ALEXANDER).

CAMPBELL (ALEXANDER) Journalist. The heart of Africa. London, 1954. pp. 479.

CAMPOS (PEDRO ALBIZU).

See ALBIZU CAMPOS (PEDRO).

CANADA

— **Boundaries.**

PHARAND (DONAT) The law of the sea of the Arctic, with special reference to Canada. Ottawa, 1973. pp. 367. *bibliog. (Ottawa. Université. Faculté de Droit. Collection des Travaux. Monographies Juridiques. No. 7)*

— **Census.**

WARGON (SYLVIA T.) Definitions of family and household in population statistics, with special reference to the Canadian population statistics. Ottawa, 1971. fo. 13. *bibliog. (Canada. Statistics Canada. Census Division. Working Papers (Demographic and Socio-economic Series). No. 9)*

CANADA. Census, 1971. Advance bulletin[s]: [series AE: economic characteristics] . [Ottawa], 1974 in progress. *In English and French.*

CANADA. Census, 1971. Census tract bulletin[s]: series B: population and housing characteristics by census tracts. [Ottawa], 1974 in progress. In English and French. :

— **Commerce.**

CANADA. Statistics Canada. Exports: merchandise trade. a., 1970/1972[1st]- Ottawa. *In English and French.*

CANADA. Statistics Canada. Imports: merchandise trade. a., 1970/1972[1st]- Ottawa. *In English and French.*

EXPORT DEVELOPMENT CORPORATION [CANADA]. Annual report. a., 1973- Ottawa. *In English and French.*

— **Commercial policy.**

EARL (JOHN F.) The Atlantic Provinces: protection and free trade. [Fredericton], 1973. 1 vol. (various pagings).

— **Constitution.**

CREIGHTON (DONALD GRANT) Towards the discovery of Canada: selected essays. Toronto, [1972]. pp. 315.

— **Constitutional law.**

LASKIN (BORA) Canadian constitutional law: cases, text and notes on distribution of legislative power; fourth edition [by] Albert S. Abel. Toronto, 1973. pp. 980.

— **Economic conditions.**

MURPHY (RAE) and STAROWICZ (MARK) eds. Corporate Canada: 14 probes into the workings of a branch-plant economy; a Last Post special; [selected articles]. Toronto, 1972. pp. 156.

OFFICER (LAWRENCE H.) and SMITH (LAWRENCE B.) eds. Issues in Canadian economics. Toronto, [1974]. pp. 418.

— — **Mathematical models.**

The STRUCTURE OF RDX2: [by] John F. Helliwell [and others]. [Ottawa], 1971. 2 vols. (in 1). *bibliog. (Bank of Canada. Staff Research Studies. No. 7)*

McCRACKEN (M.C.) An overview of CANDIDE [Canadian Disaggregated Interdepartmental Econometric] model 1.0. Ottawa, Information Canada, 1973. pp. 335. *(CANDIDE Project Papers. No. 1)*

— **Economic history.**

CREIGHTON (DONALD GRANT) Towards the discovery of Canada: selected essays. Toronto, [1972]. pp. 315.

NEILL (ROBIN) National policy and regional development: a footnote to the Deutsch report on Maritime Union. [Ottawa, 1972]. fo.21. *(Carleton University. Carleton Economic Papers)*

WATERMAN (ANTHONY M.C.) The measurement of economic fluctuations in Canada, January 1947 to December 1969;... prepared for the Prices and Incomes Commission. Ottawa, Information Canada, 1973. pp. 135.

— **Economic policy.**

CANADIAN LABOUR CONGRESS. Memorandum to the government of Canada...March 5, 1973. Ottawa, 1973. pp. 62.

EARL (JOHN F.) The Atlantic Provinces: protection and free trade. [Fredericton], 1973. 1 vol. (various pagings).

GILLESPIE (W. IRWIN) The Federal budget as plan, 1968-1972. [Toronto], 1973. pp. 64-84. *(Offprint from Canadian Tax Journal, vol. XXI, no. 1)*

PHILLIPS (PAUL ARTHUR) and SELDON (JAMES) Macroeconomics and the Canadian economy. Toronto, [1973]. pp. 180.

OFFICER (LAWRENCE H.) and SMITH (LAWRENCE B.) eds. Issues in Canadian economics. Toronto, [1974]. pp. 418.

— **Emigration and immigration.**

LAVOIE (YOLANDE) L'émigration des Canadiens aux États-Unis avant 1930: mesure de phénomène. Montréal, 1972. pp. 89. *bibliog.*

— **Foreign economic relations.**

ENGLISH (HARRY EDWARD) and others. Canada in a wider economic community. Toronto, [1972]. pp. 151. *(Private Planning Association of Canada. Canada in the Atlantic Economy. 13)*

— — **United States.**

MURPHY (RAE) and STAROWICZ (MARK) eds. Corporate Canada: 14 probes into the workings of a branch-plant economy; a Last Post special; [selected articles]. Toronto, 1972. pp. 156.

PENTLAND (CHARLES CORRIE) The Canadian dilemma. Farnborough, Hants, [1973]. pp. 56. *(Atlantic Institute. Atlantic Papers. 1973.2)*

— — **West Indies.**

WEST INDIES, UNIVERSITY OF THE. West Indies-Canada economic relations; selected papers prepared by the university...in connection with the Canada- Commonwealth Caribbean conference, July 1966. [Mona], 1967. pp. 137.

— **Foreign relations.**

SOWARD (FREDERIC HUBERT) The Department of External Affairs and Canadian autonomy, 1899-1939. Ottawa, 1972. pp. 22. *bibliog. (Canadian Historical Association. Historical Booklets. No.7)*

STANKIEWICZ (WLADYSLAW JOZEF) Canada-U.S. relations and Canadian foreign policy. West Chesterfield, 1973. pp. 47.

PEARSON (LESTER BOWLES) Memoirs 1948-1957: the international years;...edited by John A. Munro and Alex I. Inglis. London, 1974. pp. 344.

See also EUROPEAN ECONOMIC COMMUNITY — Canada.

— — **United States.**

STANKIEWICZ (WLADYSLAW JOZEF) Canada-U.S. relations and Canadian foreign policy. West Chesterfield, 1973. pp. 47.

LOGAN (R.M.) Canada, the United States and the third Law of the Sea Conference. [Montreal, 1974]. pp. 117. *bibliog.*

— — **Vietnam.**

CULHANE (CLAIRE) Why is Canada in Vietnam?: the truth about our foreign aid. Toronto, 1972. pp. 126.

— **Historical geography.**

HARRIS (R. COLE) and WARKENTIN (JOHN) Canada before confederation: a study in historical geography,... cartographer, Miklos Pinther. New York, 1974. pp. 338. *bibliogs.*

— **History — Historiography.**

CREIGHTON (DONALD GRANT) Towards the discovery of Canada: selected essays. Toronto, [1972]. pp. 315.

— — **Sources.**

PAGE (ROBERT J.D.) Imperialism and Canada, 1895-1903. Toronto, [1972]. pp. 117. *bibliog.*

— — **1791—1841.**

PAQUET (GILLES) and WALLOT (JEAN PIERRE) Patronage et pouvoir dans le Bas-Canada, 1794-1812: un essai d'économie historique. Montréal, 1973. pp. 185. *bibliog.*

— — **1867— .**

BROWN (ROBERT CRAIG) and COOK (RAMSAY) Canada 1896-1921: a nation transformed. Toronto, [1974]. pp. 412.

— **Industries.**

GEORGE (ROY E.) A leader and a laggard: manufacturing industry in Nova Scotia, Quebec and Ontario. Toronto, [1970]. pp. 220. *(Social Science Research Council of Canada. Atlantic Provinces Studies. 2)*

CANADA. Statistics Canada. Manufacturing and Primary Industries Division. 1973. Growth patterns in manufacturing employment by counties and census divisions; La croissance de l'emploi dans les industries manufacturières, par comtés et par divisions de recensement; 1961-1970. Ottawa, 1973. pp. 134. *bibliog. In English and French.*

PORTER (ALLAN A.) Productivity, costs and prices: an examination of trends in selected manufacturing industries. Ottawa, 1973. pp. 366. *(Canada. Department of Labour. Economics and Research Branch. Occasional Papers. No. 7)*

— — **Mathematical models.**

LORANGER (JEAN GUY) Elasticité de substitution et rendements dans l'industrie manufacturière canadienne...; communication présentée au VIIIe congrès annuel de l'Association canadienne d'Economique, Université de Toronto, les 3, 4, 5 juin 1974. Montréal, [1974]. fo. 45. *bibliog. (Montreal. Université. Département des Sciences Economiques. Cahiers. No. 7408)*

— **Languages.**

DARNELL (REGNA) ed. Linguistic diversity in Canadian society. Edmonton, [1971]. pp. 307. *bibliogs.*

— **Maps, Topographic.**

CANADA. Program Planning Office for Resource Satellites and Remote Airborne Sensing. Working Group on Cartography and Photogrammetry. 1971. Resource satellites and remote airborne sensing for Canada. Report no.4. Cartography and Photogrammetry; [R.E. Moore, chairman]. Ottawa, 1971. pp. 8. *With French summary.*

— **Nationalism.**

NELLES (VIV) and ROTSTEIN (ABRAHAM) eds. Nationalism or local control: responses to George Woodcock; [first published in the October 1972 issue of The Canadian Forum]. Toronto, 1973. pp. 95.

— **Parliament.**

CANADA. Privy Council Office. 1973. Members of parliament and conflict of interest; Les membres du parlement et les conflits d'intérêts. Ottawa, 1973. pp. 69,74. *In English and French.*

KORNBERG (ALLAN) and others. Legislatures and societal change: the case of Canada. Beverly Hills, [1973]. pp. 64. *bibliog.*

— **Politics and government.**

BEDER (E.A.) The missing political party. Toronto, [1972]. pp. 110.

The CANADIAN voter's guidebook; edited by Jim McDonald and Jack MacDonald. Toronto, [1972]. pp. 247.

WESTELL (ANTHONY) Paradox: Trudeau as prime minister. Scarsborough, Ontario, [1972]. pp. 262.

ZINK (LUBOR J.) Trudeaucracy. Toronto, [1972]. pp. 150.

CANADIAN LABOUR CONGRESS. Memorandum to the government of Canada...March 5, 1973. Ottawa, 1973. pp. 62.

NELLES (VIV) and ROTSTEIN (ABRAHAM) eds. Nationalism or local control: responses to George Woodcock; [first published in the October 1972 issue of The Canadian Forum]. Toronto, 1973. pp. 95.

PEARSON (LESTER BOWLES) Memoirs 1948-1957: the international years;...edited by John A. Munro and Alex I. Inglis. London, 1974. pp. 344.

PRESTHUS (ROBERT V.) Elites in the policy process. London, 1974. pp. 525.

SCHWARTZ (MILDRED A.) Politics and territory: the sociology of regional persistence in Canada. . Montreal, 1974. pp. 344.

— — **Bibliography.**

GRASHAM (W.E.) and JULIEN (GERMAIN) compilers. Bibliography: Canadian public administration; Administration publique canadienne: bibliographie. Toronto, [1972]. pp. 261. *Preface and table of contents in English and French.*

— **Population.**

JACKSON (J.E. WINSTON) and POUSHINSKY (NICHOLAS J.) Migration to northern mining communities: structural and social- psychological dimensions. Winnipeg, 1971. pp. 158. *bibliog. (Manitoba University. Center for Settlement Studies. Series 2: Research Reports No. 8)*

MARSDEN (LORNA R.) Population probe: (Canada). [Toronto, 1972]. pp. 179. *bibliog.*

TRUDEL (MARCEL) La population du Canada en 1663. Montréal, [1973]. pp. 368. *bibliog.*

— **Relations (general) with Australia.**

AUSTRALIA. Parliamentary Mission to Canada. 1970. Official report of the... Mission... [1969]. in AUSTRALIA. Parliament. Parliamentary papers, 1969, vol.5.

— **Relations (general) with the United States.**

LITVAK (ISAIAH ALLAN) and MAULE (CHRISTOPHER JOHN) Cultural sovereignty: the Time and Reader's Digest case in Canada. New York, 1974. pp. 140.

— **Social conditions.**

PROTEST, violence and social change; [edited by] Richard P. Bowles [and others]. Scarborough, Ont., [1972]. pp. 209. *bibliog.*

ELKIN (FREDERICK) Rebels and colleagues: advertising and social change in French Canada. Montreal, 1973. pp. 227.

KORNBERG (ALLAN) and others. Legislatures and societal change: the case of Canada. Beverly Hills, [1973]. pp. 64. *bibliog.*

CANADIAN NATIONAL RAILWAYS.

CANADA. Statistics Canada. Canadian National Railways and Canadian Pacific Limited. a., 1968/1972 (1st)- Ottawa. *In English and French.*

CANADIAN PACIFIC LIMITED.

CANADA. Statistics Canada. Canadian National Railways and Canadian Pacific Limited. a., 1968/1972 (1st)- Ottawa. *In English and French.*

CANADIAN PERIODICALS.

LITVAK (ISAIAH ALLAN) and MAULE (CHRISTOPHER JOHN) Cultural sovereignty: the Time and Reader's Digest case in Canada. New York, 1974. pp. 140.

CANALS

— **Canada.**

HEISLER (JOHN P.) The canals of Canada. Ottawa, National Historic Sites Service, 1973. pp. 182. *bibliog. (Canadian Historic Sites: Occasional Papers in Archaeology and History. No.8)*

— **United Kingdom.**

INLAND WATERWAYS AMENITY ADVISORY COUNCIL [U.K.]. Remainder waterways: a report to the Secretary of State for the Environment containing the recommendations of the Advisory Council in respect of proposals received between 1968 and 1971 for the addition of certain of the 'remainder' waterways to the cruising waterway system. [London], 1971. pp. 60.

INLAND WATERWAYS AMENITY ADVISORY COUNCIL [U.K.]. Waterway facilities: a report to the Secretary of State for the Environment on the leisure potential of the inland waterway system. [London]. 1972. pp. 24.

WARD (J.R.) The finance of canal building in eighteenth-century England. London, 1974. pp. 224. *bibliog.*

CANALS, INTEROCEANIC.

UNITED STATES. Atlantic-Pacific Interoceanic Canal Study Commission. 1971. Interoceanic canal studies, 1970; [Robert B. Anderson, chairman]. [Washington, 1971]. 1 vol. (various pagings).

CANBERRA

— Slaughter houses.

AUSTRALIA. Parliament. Senate. Select Committee on the Canberra Abattoir. 1969. Report; (with Minutes of evidence). in AUSTRALIA. Parliament. Parliamentary papers; 1969, vol.6.

CANCER.

INTERNATIONAL LABOUR CONFERENCE. 58th Session. Reports. 7. Control and prevention of occupational cancer: seventh item on the agenda. Geneva, 1972-73. 2 pts.

INTERNATIONAL LABOUR CONFERENCE. 59th Session. Reports. 5. Control and prevention of occupational hazards caused by carcinogenic substances and agents; fifth item on the agenda. Geneva, 1973-74. 2 pts.

— United Kingdom.

HILL (GERRY BERNARD) and others. Cancer incidence in Great Britain 1963-1966. London, 1972. pp. 61. *(U.K. Office of Population Censuses and Surveys. Studies on Medical and Population Subjects. No. 24)*

— — Scotland.

HOWITT (LEWIS FINNIGAN) Cancer registration: cases registered 1965-67; five uear survival rates cases registered 1959-61. [Edinburgh], Scottish Home and Health Department, 1973. pp. 60. *(Scottish Health Service Studies. no.26)*

— Yugoslavia — Slovenia.

YUGOSLAVIA. Savezni Zavod za Statistiku. Studije, Analize i Prikazi. 66. Stope preživljenja raka; Cancer survival rates; [by Nevena Stojkov and Nebojša Marić]. Beograd, 1974. pp. 59. *With English summary.*

CANNING (GEORGE).

HINDE (WENDY) George Canning. London, 1973. pp. 519.

CANNING AND PRESERVING

— Industry and trade — Russia — Moldavian Republic.

URSUL (M.M.) Konservnaia promyshlennost' Moldavskoi SSR: puti razvitiia i razmeshcheniia konservnoi promyshlennosti i ee syr'evoi bazy; pod redaktsiei...M.M. Radula. Kishinev, 1962. pp. 183. *bibliog.*

CANTEMIR (DIMITRIE).

See DIMITRIE CANTEMIR, Prince of Moldavia.

CANTERBURY

— Church history.

MAGEN (BEATE) Die Wallonengemeinde in Canterbury von ihrer Gründung bis zum Jahre 1635. Bern, 1973. pp. 287. *bibliog.*

CANVASSING.

TASMANIA. Consumers Protection Council. 1972. Report on sales methods of two firms marketing encyclopaedias, July 1972. in TASMANIA. Parliament. Journals and Printed Papers. 1972, no. 36.

CAPE OF GOOD HOPE

— Population.

CAPE OF GOOD HOPE. Provincial Administration. Regional Planning Section. 1968. Greater Cape Town region: a report. [Cape Town, 1968]. fo.53. *(Planning Reports. No.2)*

CAPE TOWN

— Population.

CAPE OF GOOD HOPE. Provincial Administration. Regional Planning Section. 1968. Greater Cape Town region: a report. [Cape Town, 1968]. fo.53. *(Planning Reports. No.2)*

CAPE VERDE ISLANDS

— History.

TENREIRO (FRANCISCO) Cabo Verde e S. Tomé e Principe: esquema de uma evolução conjunta. Praia, Imprensa Nacional, 1956. pp. 16. *Separata do Boletim de Propaganda e Informação Cabo Verde.*

CAPITAL.

ORGANISATION FOR ECONOMIC CO-OPERATION AND DEVELOPMENT. Committee for Invisible Transactions. Country Capital- Market Series. [Paris], 1969 in progress.

HIRSHLEIFER (JACK) Investment, interest and capital. Englewood Cliffs, [1970]. pp. 320. *bibliogs.*

CAPITAL MARKET SYMPOSIUM, NEW YORK, 1970. Financial development and economic growth: the economic consequences of underdeveloped capital markets; Arnold W. Sametz, editor. New York, 1972. pp. 257.

KUZNETS (SIMON SMITH) Population, capital, and growth: selected essays. London, 1974. pp. 342.

ROBBINS (HORACE H.) Fictive capital and fictive profit: the welfare-military state; a political economy based on economic fictions. New York, [1974]. pp. 417.

— Mathematical models.

MANNE (ALAN S.) On the efficiency price of capital in a dual economy. Stanford, 1973. fo. 32. *(Stanford University. Institute for Mathematical Studies in the Social Sciences. Technical Reports. [New Series]. No. 81)*

KLUNDERT (TH. VAN DE) and SCHAIK (A. VAN) On shift and share of durable capital. Tilburg, 1974. pp. 17. *bibliog. (Tilburg. Katholieke Hogeschool. Tilburg Institute of Economics. Research Memoranda. EIT 46)*

LORANGER (JEAN GUY) Estimation d'un modele dynamique d'equilibre non concurrentiel de la demande de capital. Montreal, 1974. fo. 41. *bibliog. (Montréal. Université. Département des Sciences Economiques. Cahiers. no. 7405)*

— Communist countries.

NOTKIN (ALEKSANDR IL'ICH) ed. Sotsialisticheskoe nakoplenie: voprosy teorii i planirovaniia. Moskva, 1973. pp. 414.

— European Economic Community countries.

BOLLMANN (ULRICH) Zehn Jahre Eurokapitalmarkt: Entwicklung, Struktur und Formen. Bern, 1973. pp. 183. *bibliog.*

— Russia.

OVCHARENKO (GEORGII ALEKSEEVICH) and PANKRATOV (FEDOR LEONT'EVICH) Pereotsenka osnovnykh fondov. Moskva, 1971. pp. 160.

OBUKHOVSKII (VLADIMIR MIKHAILOVICH) Ispol'zovanie proizvodstvennykh fondov v kolkhozakh i sovkhozakh. Moskva, 1973. pp. 240.

PERLAMUTROV (VILEN LEONIDOVICH) Problemy ispol'zovaniia oborotnykh sredstv v promyshlennosti. Moskva, 1973. pp. 213.

— — Mathematical models.

BUNICH (PAVEL GRIGOR'EVICH) and others. Ekonomiko-matematicheskie metody upravleniia oborotnymi sredstvami. Moskva, 1973. pp. 240.

— — Ukraine.

DZYKOVYCH (VIRA IAKOVLIVNA) and UL'IANOV (MYKHAILO HRYHOROVYCH) Formuvannia i vykorystannia osnovnykh vyrobnychykh fondiv kolhospiv Ukraïny. Kyïv, 1973. pp. 127. *With Russian summary.*

— Yugoslavia.

TURČIĆ (IVAN) Regionalni aspekt efikasnosti društvene privrede Jugoslavije. Zagreb, 1973. pp. 106. *With English summary.*

CAPITAL BUDGET

JUNNELIUS (CHRISTIAN) Investeringsprocessens utformning vid olika organisationsstrukturtyper: The capital budgeting process and organisational structures. Helsingfors, 1974. pp. 315. *bibliog. (Svenska Handelshögskolan. Ekonomi och Samhälle. Nr. 22) In Swedish, with English summary.*

— Mathematical models.

CHATEAU (JEAN PIERRE) Vers une programmation des politiques financières conflictuelles du budget de capital de la firme multinationale. Montréal, 1974. fo. 42. *bibliog. (Montréal. Universitité. Département des Sciences Economiques. Cahiers. No. 7406)*

CAPITAL FORMATION.

See SAVING AND INVESTMENT.

CAPITAL GAINS TAX

— United Kingdom.

SANDFORD (CEDRIC T.) Taxing inheritance and capital gains: towards a comprehensive system of capital taxation. London, 1965. pp. 69. *bibliog. (Institute of Economic Affairs. Hobart Papers. 32)*

CAPITAL INVESTMENTS.

JORGENSON (DALE W.) The theory of investment behavior. Berkeley, 1965. fo. 43. *(California University. Institute of Business and Economic Research. Committee on Econometrics and Mathematical Economics. Working Papers. No. 69)*

ORGANISATION FOR ECONOMIC CO-OPERATION AND DEVELOPMENT. Committee for Invisible Transactions. Country Capital- Market Series. [Paris], 1969 in progress.

CASSON (MARK C.) A confusion in the neo-neo-classical theory of investment. [Reading], 1973. fo. 15. *bibliog. (Reading. University. Department of Economics. Discussion Papers in Economics. Series A. no. 50)*

MERRETT (ANTHONY JOHN WATKIN) and SYKES (ALLEN) The finance and analysis of capital projects. 2nd ed. London, 1973. pp. 573. *bibliogs.*

— Communist countries.

BELOVIgC (ALEXANDER) Planirovanie i finansirovanie kapital'nykh vlozhenii v stranakh- chlenakh SEV. Moskva, 1973. pp. 71. *bibliog.*

— Fiji Islands.

FIJI. Bureau of Statistics. 1971. A survey of private sector capital investment expenditure in Fiji in 1969. [Suva], 1971. pp. 41.

— Poland.

POLAND. Główny Urząd Statystyczny. Rocznik statystyczny inwestycji i środków trwałych. a., 1973 [2nd]- Warszawa. *(Statystyka Polski.[2nd series])*

— Russia — Uzbekistan.

EFFEKTIVNOST' kapital'nykh vlozhenii v promyshlennost' Uzbekskoi SSR. Tashkent, 1969. pp. 180.

— — White Russia.

PROBLEMY formirovaniia i ispol'zovaniia fonda razvitiia proizvodstva. Minsk, 1973. pp. 248.

— **United Kingdom.**

NATIONAL ECONOMIC DEVELOPMENT OFFICE. Process Plant Working Party. Process industries investment forecasts: the eighth report by the...Working Party. London, 1973. pp. 51.

NATIONAL ECONOMIC DEVELOPMENT OFFICE. Process Plant Working Party. Process industries investment forecasts: the ninth report by the...Working Party. London, 1974. pp. 50.

— — **Mathematical models.**

BOATWRIGHT (B.D.) and EATON (J.R.) The estimation of investment functions for U.K. manufacturing industry. London, 1971. fo. 24. bibliog. (London Graduate School of Business Studies. Econometric Forecasting Unit. [Discussion Papers?])

CAPITAL LEVY

— **Ireland (Republic).**

EIRE. Department of Finance. 1974. Capital taxation; laid by the Minister for Finance before each House of the Oireachtas, 28 February, 1974. Dublin, [1974]. pp. 66.

CAPITAL PUNISHMENT

— **Canada.**

ANDERSON (FRANK W.) A concise history of capital punishment in Canada. Calgary, [1973]. pp. 80. bibliog.

— **United States.**

BOWERS (WILLIAM J.) Executions in America. Lexington, Mass., [1974]. pp. 489. bibliog.

CAPITALISM.

GRAF (GEORG ENGELBERT) Was muss der Arbeiter vom Kapitalismus una Sozialismus wissen?: Leitsätze. 3rd ed. Elberfeld, [1923]. pp. 16.

GRAF (GEORG ENGELBERT) Vom Kapitalismus zum Sozialismus: Leitsätze, Geschichtszahlen, Bücherverzeichnis. Berlin, [1931]. pp. 54. bibliog.

DOBB (MAURICE HERBERT) Political economy and capitalism: some essays in economic tradition. rev. ed. London, 1940 repr. 1972. pp. 357.

SILBERSTEIN (ENRIQUE) Los asaltantes de caminos. Buenos Aires, [1969]. pp. 120.

INTERNATIONALISM. Pamphlets. No.1. Dollar crisis or crisis of capitalism?. New York, [1971?]. pp. 13.

WINDHOFF (BERND) Darstellung und Kritik der Konvergenztheorie: gibt es eine Annäherung der sozialistischen und kapitalistischen Wirtschaftssysteme?. Bern, 1971. pp. 224. bibliog.

ACTON (HARRY BURROWS) The ethics of capitalism. London, [1972]. pp. 9. (Foundation for Business Responsibilities. Seminar Papers)

BARNSBY (GEORGE) Dictatorship of the bourgeoisie: social control in the nineteenth- century Black Country. London, 1972. 1 vol. (unpaged). bibliog. (Communist Party of Great Britain. Historians' Group. Our History. No.55)

JANCO (MANUEL) and FURJOT (DANIEL) Informatique et capitalisme. Paris, 1972. pp. 272. bibliog.

AKTUAL'NYE ekonomicheskie problemy sovremennogo kapitalizma. Moskva, 1973. pp. 230.

BOCCARA (PAUL) Etudes sur le capitalisme monopoliste d'état, sa crise et son issue. Paris, [1973]. pp. 451.

BRANDES (VOLKHARD) Die Krise des Imperialismus: Grenzen der kapitalistischen Expansion und der Wiederaufbau der Arbeiterbewegung. Frankfurt am Main, [1973]. pp. 106.

FORMAN (JAMES D.) Capitalism: economic individualism to today's welfare state. New York, 1973. pp. 134. bibliog.

GUERIN (DANIEL) Fascism and big business; (translated from the French). New York, 1973. pp. 318.

KASVIO (ANTTI) Den statsmonopolistiska kapitalismen i Finland: (STAMOKAP); material för ett forskningsprojekt; oversat fra finsk af Christer Karjalainen. [Grenå, 1973]. pp. 64. (Scandinavian Summer University. Skriftserie. Nr.1)

KORSCH (KARL) and others. Zusammenbruchstheorie des Kapitalismus oder revolutionäres Subjekt: [new edition of essays, originally published in 1933 and 1934, inspired by Henryk Grossmann's Das Akkumulations- und Zusammenbruchsgesetz des kapitalistischen Systems]. Berlin, [1973]. pp. 126. bibliog.

LEFEBVRE (HENRI) La survie du capitalisme: la re-production des rapports de production. Paris, [1973]. pp. 275.

MAGEE (BRYAN EDGAR) and others. The new capitalism; [transcript of a discussion with] Peter Walker [and] Bill McCarthy;...transmitted: 26 April 1973. [London, 1973]. fo.35. (Thames Television. Something to Say)

MEISNER (JOACHIM) Kapitalizm a socjalizm: współzawodniczące systemy ekonomiczne. Warszawa, 1973. pp. 166. bibliog.

MOTYLEV (VENIAMIN VOL'FOVICH) Mirovoe kapitalisticheskoe khoziaistvo: tendentsii razvitiia i protivorechiia. Moskva, 1973. pp. 166. (Akademiia Nauk SSSR. Ekonomicheskaia Seriia)

QUIN (CLAUDE) and HERZOG (PHILIPPE) Ce que coûte le capitalisme à la France. Paris, [1973]. pp. 187.

TIUL'PANOV (SERGEI IVANOVICH) and SHEINIS (VIKTOR LEONIDOVICH) Aktual'nye problemy politicheskoi ekonomii sovremennogo kapitalizma. Leningrad, 1973. pp. 282.

TORKANOVSKII (VIKTOR SEMENOVICH) Novye iavleniia v razvitii monopolisticheskogo kapitala. Leningrad, 1973. pp. 196.

VERCELLI (ALESSANDRO) Teoria della struttura economica capitalistica: il metodo di Marx e i fondamenti della critica all'economia politica. Torino. 1973. pp. 262. bibliogs. (Fondazione Luigi Einaudi. Studi. 15)

WALLERSTEIN (IMMANUEL) The modern world-system. New York, [1974 in progress]. bibliogs.

DALTON (GEORGE) Economic systems and society: capitalism, communism and the third world. Harmondsworth, 1974. pp. 250. bibliog.

ENGELHARDT (KLAUS) and HEISE (KARL HEINZ) Militär-Industrie-Komplex im staatsmonopolistischen Herrschaftssystem. Berlin, 1974. pp. 304.

FABRA (PAUL) L'anti-capitalisme: essai de réhabilitation de l'économie politique. Paris, [1974]. pp. 432.

JALEE (PIERRE) L'exploitation capitaliste: initiation au marxisme. Paris, 1974. pp. 137.

KUCZYNSKI (JUERGEN) Warum sind wir gegen den Kapitalismus?. rev. ed. Berlin, 1974. pp. 47.

RIDLEY (NICHOLAS) The new capitalism. London. 1974. pp. 8. (Foundation for Business Responsibilities. Seminar Papers)

RODINSIN (MAXIME) Islam and capitalism; translated by Brian Pearce. London, 1974. pp. 308.

RODINSON (MAXIME) Islam and capitalism; translated by Brian Pearce. London, 1974. pp. 308.

SILK (LEONARD SOLOMON) and others. Capitalism: the moving target. New York, [1974]. pp. 159.

VANIN (VADIM IVANOVICH) Gosudarstvennyi kapitalizm v KNR. Moskva, 1974. pp. 326. bibliog.

CAPITALISTS AND FINANCIERS

— **New Zealand.**

STONE (R.C.J.) Makers of fortune: a colonial business community and its fall. Auckland, N.Z., 1973. pp. 240. bibliog.

— **United States.**

DEBOUZY (MARIANNE) Le capitalisme "sauvage" aux États-Unis, 1860-1900. Paris, [1972]. pp. 238. bibliog.

WHEELER (GEORGE) Pierpont Morgan and friends: the anatomy of a myth. Englewood Cliffs, [1973]. pp. 338. bibliog.

CARABOBO

— **Population.**

VENEZUELA. Direccion General de Estadistica. Division de Muestreo. 1973. Investigacion conjunta: encuesta regional de hogares por muestreo, Estado Carabobo, agosto 1968...:empleo, desempleo y analfabetismo. Caracas, 1973. pp. 242.

CARACAS

— **Politics and government.**

BREWER-CARIAS (ALLAN RANDOLPH) Problemas institucionales del area metropolitana de Caracas y del desarrollo regional y urbano. Caracas, Comision de Administracion Publica, 1971. fo. 60.

CARDIGANSHIRE

— **Politics and government.**

MADGWICK (PETER JAMES) and others. The politics of rural Wales: a study of Cardiganshire. London, 1973. pp. 272. bibliog.

— **Social conditions.**

MADGWICK (PETER JAMES) and others. The politics of rural Wales: a study of Cardiganshire. London, 1973. pp. 272. bibliog.

CARDIJN (JOSEPH).

VERHOEVEN (JOSEPH) Joseph Cardijn, prophète de notre temps. 3rd ed. Bruxelles, [1972]. pp. 202.

CARDINALS

— **United Kingdom.**

WILKIE (WILLIAM E.) The cardinal protectors of England: Rome and the Tudors before the reformation. London. 1974. pp. 262. bibliog.

CARGO HANDLING.

INTERNATIONAL LABOUR CONFERENCE. 58th Session. Reports. 5. Social repercussions of new methods of cargo handling (docks): fifth item on the agenda. Geneva, 1972-73. 2 pts.

INTERNATIONAL LABOUR CONFERENCE. 57th Session. Reports. 5. Social repercussions of new methods of cargo handling (docks): fifth item on the agenda. Geneva, 1972. 2 pts.

CARGO PREFERENCE.

HENELL (OLOF) Flag discrimination: purposes, motives and economic consequences. Helsingfors, 1956. pp. 55. bibliog. (Svenska Handelshögskolan. Ekonomi och Samhälle. Nr.3)

CARIBBEAN AREA

— **Economic conditions.**

McDONALD (VINCENT R.) The Caribbean economies: perspectives on social, political and economic conditions. New York, [1972]. pp. 196.

IMPERIALISMO y clases sociales en el Caribe; ([by Mercedes Acosta [and others]). Buenos Aires, [1973]. pp. 235.

CARIBBEAN AREA (Cont.)

POWELL (DAVID) Problems of economic development in the Caribbean;... compiled from a study by Irene Hawkins. London, 1973. pp. 74. *(British-North American Committee. Publications. 13)*

— **Economic policy.**

POWELL (DAVID) Problems of economic development in the Caribbean;... compiled from a study by Irene Hawkins. London, 1973. pp. 74. *(British-North American Committee. Publications. 13)*

— **Foreign economic relations — United States.**

IMPERIALISMO y clases sociales en el Caribe; ([by Mercedes Acosta [and others]). Buenos Aires, [1973]. pp. 235.

— **Foreign relations.**

See also EUROPEAN ECONOMIC COMMUNITY — Caribbean Area.

— **History.**

BRIDENBAUGH (CARL) and BRIDENBAUGH (ROBERTA) No peace beyond the line: the English in the Caribbean, 1624- 1690. New York, 1972. pp. 440. *(Beginnings of the American People. 2)*

— **Nationalism.**

BAUM (DANIEL JAY) The banks of Canada in the Commonwealth Caribbean: economic nationalism and multinational enterprises of a medium power. New York, 1974. pp. 158.

— **Politics and government.**

McDONALD (VINCENT R.) The Caribbean economies: perspectives on social, political and economic conditions. New York, [1972]. pp. 196.

— **Social conditions.**

McDONALD (VINCENT R.) The Caribbean economies: perspectives on social, political and economic conditions. New York, [1972]. pp. 196.

CARICATURES AND CARTOONS

— **United Kingdom.**

CUMMINGS (MICHAEL) These uproarious years: a pictorial post-war history; by Cummings of the Daily Express. London, 1954. pp. 89.

— **United States.**

FITZGERALD (RICHARD) Art and politics: cartoonists of the 'Masses' and 'Liberator'. Westport, Conn., 1973. pp. 254. *bibliog.*

CARLISTS.

CENTRO DE ESTUDIOS HISTORICOS Y POLITICOS "GENERAL ZUMALACARREGUI" Que es el Carlismo?...por Francisco Elias de Tejada y Spinola [and others]. Madrid, 1971. pp. 206.

CARRERO BLANCO (LUIS).

BORRAS BETRIU (RAFAEL) and others, eds. El dia en que mataron a Carrero Blanco. Barcelona, 1974. pp. 412.

CARROTS.

HINTON (WILFRED LYNN) The economics of carrot production and marketing in Britain...: a commodity study. Cambridge, 1971. pp. 53. *bibliog. (Agricultural Enterprise Studies in England and Wales. Economic Reports. No.6)*

CARTAGENA, COLOMBIA

— **Race question.**

SOLAUN (MAURICIO) and KRONUS (SIDNEY) Discrimination without violence: miscegenation and racial conflict in Latin America. New York, [1973]. pp. 240. *bibliog.*

CARTOONISTS

— **United States.**

FITZGERALD (RICHARD) Art and politics: cartoonists of the 'Masses' and 'Liberator'. Westport, Conn., 1973. pp. 254. *bibliog.*

CASABLANCA.

FRANCE. Direction de la Documentation. La Documentation Française. Notes et Etudes Documentaires. Nos. 3,797-3, 798. Les grandes villes d'Afrique et de Madagascar: Casablanca; [by] Daniel Noin. Paris, 1971. pp. 73. *bibliog.*

CASAS (BARTOLOME DE LAS) Bishop of Chiapa.

HANKE (LEWIS ULYSSES) Bartolome de las Casas: pensador politico, historiador, antropologo; [version española de Antonio Fernandez Travieso]. Buenos Aires, [1968]. pp. 125. *bibliog.*

CASSEL

— **Economic history.**

LASCH (MANFRED) Untersuchungen über Bevölkerung und Wirtschaft der Landgrafschaft Hessen-Kassel und der Stadt Kassel...bis zum Tode Landgraf Karls, 1730. Kassel, 1969. pp. 392. *bibliog. (Zeitschrift des Vereins für Hessische Geschichte und Landeskunde. Beihefte. Heft 9)*

— **Population.**

LASCH (MANFRED) Untersuchungen über Bevölkerung und Wirtschaft der Landgrafschaft Hessen-Kassel und der Stadt Kassel...bis zum Tode Landgraf Karls, 1730. Kassel, 1969. pp. 392. *bibliog. (Zeitschrift des Vereins für Hessische Geschichte und Landeskunde. Beihefte. Heft 9)*

CASTE

— **India.**

BECK (BRENDA E.F.) Peasant society in Konku: a study of right and left subcastes in south India. Vancouver, [1972]. pp. 334. *bibliog.*

AHMAD (IMTIAZ) ed. Caste and social stratification among the Muslims. Delhi, 1973. pp. 256. *bibliog.*

LAKSHMANNA (CHINTAMANI) Caste dynamics in village India. Bombay, [1973]. pp. 144. *bibliog.*

CASTRO RUZ (FIDEL).

SUCHLICKI (JAIME) ed. Cuba, Castro, and revolution. Coral Gables, [1972]. pp. 250.

GONZALEZ (EDWARD) Cuba under Castro: the limits of charisma. Boston, [1974]. pp. 241.

CATALOGUES, BOOKSELLERS

— **United Kingdom.**

MARLBOROUGH RARE BOOKS LIMITED. Catalogues. 47. Some recent acquisitions including woodcut books of the 15th and 16th centuries, fine sets of engravings, colour plate books, modern illustrated books, etc. London, [1962]. 1 vol. (unpaged).

SOTHEBY AND COMPANY. The Willis King III Library: the first portion: catalogue of valuable printed books of the 15th to 20th century, the property of a gentleman. London, [1971]. 1 vol. (unpaged).

SOTHEBY AND COMPANY. Bibliotheca Phillippica, new series, tenth part: catalogue of books printed in England and of English books printed abroad before 1641...from the celebrated collection formed by Sir Thomas Phillipps, Bt., 1792-1872, etc. London, [1973-74]. 3 pts. (in 1vol.).

SOTHEBY AND COMPANY. Bibliotheca Phillippica, medieval manuscripts, new series, eighth part: catalogue of manuscripts on vellum, paper and papyrus of the 4th to the 17th century from the celebrated collection formed by Sir Thomas Phillips, 1792-1872, etc. London, [1973]. pp. 127.

SOTHEBY AND COMPANY. The celebrated library of Harrison D. Horblit Esq., removed from Ridgefield, Connecticut:...early science, navigation and travel, including Americana, with a few medical books. London, [1974 in progress].

SOTHEBY AND COMPANY. Bibliotheca Phillippica, new series...part 9: catalogue of oriental manuscripts, Indian and Persian miniatures (from the celebrated collection formed by Sir Thomas Phillipps, Bt., 1792-1872, etc). London, [1974]. pp. 126.

SOTHEBY AND COMPANY. Bibliotheca Phillippica, new series, twelfth part: catalogue of English manuscripts, autograph letters and charters from the celebrated collection formed by Sir Thomas Phillipps, Bt., 1792-1872, etc. London, [1974]. pp. 154.

CATALOGUES, LIBRARY.

MANCHESTER. Public Libraries. Reference Library subject catalogue. Section 655. Printing. Part 1. General works, history of printing; edited by G.E. Haslam. Manchester. 1961. 1 vol. (unpaged)

COLLISON (ROBERT LEWIS WRIGHT) Published library catalogues: an introduction to their contents and use. London, 1973. pp. 184. *bibliog.*

AHMADU BELLO UNIVERSITY. Kashim Ibrahim Library. Catalogue of Africana; compiled by Adakole Ochai. [Zaria], 1974. pp. 196.

CATALOGUING.

WORKING GROUP ON THE INTERNATIONAL STANDARD BIBLIOGRAPHIC DESCRIPTION. International Standard Bibliographic Description (for single volume and multi-volume monographic publications) recommended by the...group...set up at the International Meeting of Cataloguing Experts, Copenhagen, 1969; [chairman A.J. Wells]. London, 1971. pp. 30.

CATALONIA

— **Economic history — Sources.**

OLLE ROMEU (JOSEP M.) ed. El moviment obrer a Catalunya, 1840-1843: textos i documents. Barcelona, [1973]. pp. 428. *bibliog. In Catalan or Spanish.*

— **History.**

SEMPRUN-MAURA (CARLOS) Révolution et contre-révolution en Catalogne, 1936-1937. Tours, [1974]. pp. 307.

— **Nationalism.**

ROSSINYOL (JAUME) Le problème national catalan. Paris, [1974]. pp. 710. *bibliog.*

— **Politics and government.**

MOLAS (ISIDRE) Lliga catalana: un estudi d'estasiologia. Barcelona, 1972 repr. 1973. 2 vols. *bibliog.*

AINAUD DE LASARTE (JOSEP MARIA) and JARDI I CASANY (ENRIC) Prat de la Riba: home de govern. Barcelona, [1973]. pp. 320. *bibliog.*

— **Population.**

CANDEL (FRANCISCO) Inmigrantes y trabajadores. Barcelona, [1972]. pp. 239.

CATAMARCA (PROVINCE)

— **Economic policy.**

CATAMARCA (PROVINCE). Equipo Tecnico Interministerial. 1968. Plan de desarrollo: accion inmediata, 1968-1971. Catamarca, 1968. pp. various.

— **Social policy.**

CATAMARCA (PROVINCE). Equipo Tecnico Interministerial. 1968. Plan de desarrollo: accion inmediata, 1968-1971. Catamarca, 1968. pp. various.

CATERERS AND CATERING

— Canada.

CANADA. Statistics Canada. Accommodation, food and recreational services: employment, earnings and hours of work. irreg., 1972- Ottawa. *In English and French.*

— United Kingdom.

HOTEL AND CATERING INDUSTRY TRAINING BOARD [U.K.]. Report and statement of accounts. a., 1972/3- Wembley. *Formerly included in the file of British Parliamentary Papers.*

CATHOLIC ACTION

— Spain.

A[CCION] C[ATOLICA] O[BRERA] La evangelizacion de los pobres. Barcelona, 1964. pp. 101. *bibliog.*

BENAVIDES (DOMINGO) El fracaso social del catolicismo español: Arboleya-Martinez, 1870-1951. Barcelona, 1973. pp. 832. *bibliog.*

CATHOLIC CHURCH

— Doctrinal and controversial works.

SACHERI (CARLOS A.) La iglesia clandestina. Buenos Aires, 1970. pp. 182.

— Relations (diplomatic) — Treaties.

CATHOLIC CHURCH. Treaties. 1929-1954. Patti Lateranensi, convenzioni e accordi successivi fra il Vaticano e l'Italia fino al 31 dicembre (1954). [Vatican City], 1955-72. 2 vols.(in 1).

— Relations (diplomatic) with Italy.

GARZIA (ITALO) Il negoziato diplomatico per i Patti Lateranensi. Milano, 1974. pp. 127. *(Politico, Il. Quaderni. n.13) With English summary.*

— Relations (diplomatic) with the United Kingdom.

WILKIE (WILLIAM E.) The cardinal protectors of England: Rome and the Tudors before the reformation. London, 1974. pp. 262. *bibliog.*

CATHOLIC CHURCH IN BRAZIL.

BRUNEAU (THOMAS C.) The political transformation of the Brazilian Catholic church. London, 1974. pp. 270. *bibliog. (McGill University. Centre for Developing-Area Studies. Perspectives on Development. 2)*

CATHOLIC CHURCH IN GERMANY.

PLUM (GUENTER) Gesellschaftsstruktur und politisches Bewusstsein in einer katholischen Region, 1928-1933: Untersuchung am Beispiel des Regierungsbezirks Aachen. Stuttgart, 1972. pp. 319. *bibliog. (Institut für Zeitgeschichte. Studien zur Zeitgeschichte.)*

CATHOLIC CHURCH IN IRELAND.

GANNON (JACK) Catholic political culture and the constitution of Ireland. Belfast, 1972. pp. 82. *First issued 1971.*

MILLER (DAVID WILLIAM) Church, state and nation in Ireland 1898-1921. Dublin, 1973. pp. 579. *bibliog.*

CATHOLIC CHURCH IN LATIN AMERICA.

FLORIDI (ULISSE ALESSIO) and STIEFBOLD (ANNETTE E.) The uncertain alliance: the Catholic Church and labor in Latin America. Miami, 1973. pp. 108. *(Miami (Florida). University. Center for Advanced International Studies. Monographs in International Affairs)*

CATHOLIC CHURCH IN MOZAMBIQUE.

HASTINGS (ADRIAN) Wiriyamu. London, 1974. pp. 158.

CATHOLIC CHURCH IN POLAND.

KOŚCIÓŁ KATOLICKI NA ZIEMIACH POLSKI W CZASIE II WOJNY ŚWIATOWEJ: materiały i studia; [pd. by] Akademia Teologii Katolickiej. irreg., 1973 (zeszyt 1)- Warszawa.

CATHOLIC CHURCH IN SWITZERLAND

— Societies.

ALTERMATT (URS) Der Weg der Schweizer Katholiken ins Ghetto: die Entstehungsgeschichte der nationalen Volksorganisationen im Schweizer Katholizismus, 1848-1919. Zürich, [1972]. pp. 468. *bibliog.*

CATHOLIC CHURCH IN THE ARGENTINE REPUBLIC.

MAYOL (ALEJANDRO) and others. Los catolicos posconciliares en la Argentina, 1963-1969. Buenos Aires, 1970. pp. 414.

CATHOLICS IN ITALY.

GHERARDI (GABRIELE) I cattolici cercano un partito. Bologna, [1967]. pp. 188.

BEDESCHI (LORENZO) ed. La terza pagina de Il Popolo, 1923-1925; cattolici democratici e clerico-fascisti. Roma, 1973. pp. 463.

MALGERI (FRANCESCO) I cattolici dall'unità al fascismo: momenti e figure. Chiaravalle, [1973]. pp. 316.

CATHOLICS IN MEXICO.

MABRY (DONALD J.) Mexico's Accion Nacional: a Catholic alternative to revolution. Syracuse, N.Y., 1973. pp. 269. *bibliog.*

CATHOLICS IN SICILY.

RENDA (FRANCESCO) Socialisti e cattolici in Sicilia, 1900-1904: le lotte agrarie. Caltanissetta, [1972]. pp. 463.

CATHOLICS IN SPAIN.

CHRISTIAN (WILLIAM A.) Person and God in a Spanish valley. New York, [1972]. pp. 215. *bibliog.*

CATHOLICS IN SWITZERLAND.

ALTERMATT (URS) Der Weg der Schweizer Katholiken ins Ghetto: die Entstehungsgeschichte der nationalen Volksorganisationen im Schweizer Katholizismus, 1848-1919. Zürich, [1972]. pp. 468. *bibliog.*

CATHOLICS IN THE UNITED KINGDOM.

MILLER (JOHN) Fellow of Gonville and Caius College, Cambridge. Popery and politics in England, 1660-1668. Cambridge, 1973. pp. 288. *bibliog.*

CATHOLICS IN THE UNITED STATES.

ABRAMSON (HAROLD J.) Ethnic diversity in Catholic America. New York, [1973]. pp. 207. *bibliog.*

STEINBERG (STEPHEN) The academic melting pot: Catholics and Jews in American higher education;... a report prepared for the Carnegie Commission on Higher Education. New York, [1974]. pp. 183. *bibliog.*

CATTLE

— Ireland (Republic).

BAKER (TERENCE J.) and others. A study of the Irish cattle and beef industries. Dublin, 1973. pp. 141. *(Economic and Social Research Institute. Papers. No.72)*

CATTLE TRADE

— Australia.

STEVENS (FRANK S.) Aborigines in the Northern Territory cattle industry. Canberra, 1974. pp. 226. *bibliog. (Academy of the Social Sciences in Australia. Aborigines in Australian Society. 11)*

CAUCASUS

— Economic conditions.

ZAKAVKAZSKII ekonomicheskii raion. Moskva, 1973. pp. 245. *bibliog. (Akademiia Nauk SSSR. Sovet po Izucheniiu Proizvoditel'nykh Sil. Razvitie i Razmeshchenie Proizvoditel'nykh Sil SSSR)*

— History.

PETRICIOLI (MARTA) L'occupazione italiana del Caucaso: "un ingrato servizio" da rendere a Londra. Milano, 1972. pp. 93. *(Politico, Il. Quaderni. n.10) With English summary.*

— Politics and government.

DOLUNTS (GURGEN KARAPETOVICH) Kirov na Severnom Kavkaze. Moskva, 1973. pp. 192.

DZHIBLADZE (D.) Bol'sheviki Zakavkaz'ia v bor'be s trotskistsko- zinov'evskim blokom. Tbilisi, 1973. pp. 69.

LEZHAVA (ANTON POLIKARPOVICH) Iz istorii revoliutsionnogo sodruzhestva narodov Gruzii i Severnogo Kavkaza, 1905-1921 gg. Tbilisi, 1973. pp. 95.

SHIGABUDINOV (MAGOMED SHIGABUDINOVICH) Rabochee dvizhenie na Severnom Kavkaze v gody reaktsii, 1907- 1910 gg. Makhachkala, 1973. pp. 143.

VATEISHVILI (DZHUANSHER LEVANOVICH) Russkaia obshchestvennaia mysl' i pechat' na Kavkaze v pervoi treti XIX veka. Moskva, 1973. pp. 460. *With English summary.*

CAUSATION.

BENNETT (JONATHAN) Locke, Berkeley, Hume: central themes. Oxford, 1971. pp. 361. *bibliog.*

CECIL FAMILY.

CECIL (Lord EDWARD CHRISTIAN DAVID GASCOYNE) The Cecils of Hatfield House. London, 1973. pp. 320. *bibliog.*

CELESTITE.

See STRONTIUM ORES.

CEMENT INDUSTRIES

— Russia.

VINOGRADOV (BORIS NIKOLAEVICH) Syr'evaia baza promyshlennosti viazhushchikh veshchestv SSSR. Moskva, 1971. pp. 321. *bibliog.*

— — Soviet Far East.

KAMBULOV (VALENTIN ALEKSANDROVICH) 60 let slavnogo sluzheniia Rodine: sbornik materialov po istorii Spasskogo tsementnogo zavoda. Vladivostok, 1967. pp. 54. *bibliog.*

CENSORSHIP.

TRIBE (DAVID) Questions of censorship. London, 1973. pp. 368. *bibliog.*

— Germany.

ATZROTT (OTTO) Sozialdemokratische Druckschriften und Vereine, (verboten auf Grund des Reichsgesetzes gegen die gemeingefährlichen Bestrebungen der Sozialdemokratie vom 21.Oktober 1878... Neudruck der Ausgabe Berlin, 1886; [with] Nachtrag, 1888). Glashütten im Taunus, 1971. 1 vol.(various pagings).

— South Africa.

SOUTH AFRICA. Parliament. House of Assembly. Select Committee on the Publications and Entertainments Amendment Bill. 1973. Report (with Proceedings and Minutes of evidence); [J.T. Kruger, chairman] (S.C. 7 - 1973). in SOUTH AFRICA. Parliament. House of Assembly. Select Committee reports.

CENSORSHIP (Cont.)

SOUTH AFRICA. Commission of Inquiry into the Publications and Entertainments Amendment Bill. 1974. Report (R.P. 17/1974). in SOUTH AFRICA. Parliament. House of Assembly. Votes and proceedings; (with Printed annexures).

— United Kingdom.

RUSSELL (NORMAN) Censorship. London, [1972]. pp. 16.

CENSUS.

UNITED NATIONS. Department of Economic and Social Affairs. Population Studies. New York, 1948 in progress.

CENTRAL AFRICAN REPUBLIC.

FRANCE. Direction de la Documentation. La Documentation Française. Notes et Etudes Documentaires. Nos. 3,833-3, 834. La République Centrafricaine; [by] Pierre Kalck. Paris, 1971. pp. 82. *bibliog.*

— Rural conditions.

GOSSELIN (G.) Le changement social et les institutions du développement dans une population réfugiée;... avec une introduction par Raymond Apthorpe. (UNRISD Reports. No.70.17) (UNRISD/70/C.61). Genève, Institut de Recherche des Nations Unies pour le Développement Social, 1970. pp. 112. *bibliog.*

CENTRAL AMERICAN COMMON MARKET.

CASTRILLO ZELEDON (MARIO) El regimen de libre comercio en Centroamerica. San Jose, C.R., 1970. pp. 335.

FRANCE. Direction de la Documentation. La Documentation Française. Notes et Etudes Documentaires. No. 3,767. Genèse et évolution du marché commun centraméricain; [by] Raymond Prats. Paris, 1971. pp. 48.

CENTRAL BUSINESS DISTRICTS

— Spain.

SPAIN. Direccion General de Comercio Interior. 1972. Los futuros centros comerciales en España y su situacion actual en el extranjero. Madrid, 1972. pp. 175. *(Coleccion Estudios.* [5]*)*

CENTRAL PLACES.

ONESTA (P.A.) and DU TOIT (M.) A note on central place theory and its possible use in regional planning in South Africa. [Stellenbosch, 1971]. pp. 893-895. *(From Journal for Geography (Stellenbosch), 1971) Xerographic copy.*

STABLER (JACK C.) and WILLIAMS (PETER R.) The dynamics of a system of central places. Reading, 1973. pp. 32. *bibliog. (Reading. University. Department of Geography. Reading Geographical Papers. No.22)*

ONE-DIMENSIONAL central place theory; [by] Michael F. Dacey [and others]. Evanston, Ill., 1974. pp. 125. *bibliog. (Northwestern University. Studies in Geography. No.21)*

— Finland.

KYTÖMÄKI (JORMA) Patterns of consumer travel behaviour in southwestern Finland. Helsinki, 1973. pp. 112. *bibliog. (Suomen Maantieteellinen Seura. Fennia. 124)*

— Nigeria.

MABOGUNJE (AKIN L.) Growth poles and growth centres in the regional development of Nigeria. (UNRISD Reports. No. 71.3) (UNRISD/71/C.78). Geneva, United Nations Research Institute for Social Development, 1971. pp. 85. *bibliog.*

— United Kingdom.

LONDON. University. London School of Economics and Political Science. Department of Geography. Urban change in Britain, 1961-1971...: working reports. London, 1974 in progress.

CENTRE PARTIES

— Belgium.

NEUVILLE (JEAN) Adieu à la démocratie chrétienne?: Elie Baussart et le mouvement ouvrier...introduction biographique de Jean Quériat, etc. Bruxelles, [1973]. pp. 158.

— Chile.

RUIZ-ESQUIDE JARA (MARIANO) El socialismo traicionado. Santiago de Chile, 1973. pp. 191.

— France.

BOUDET (ROLAND) Le combat centriste. Paris, [1973]. pp. 151.

— Germany.

GRUENTHAL (GUENTHER) Reichsschulgesetz und Zentrumspartei in der Weimarer Republik. Düsseldorf, [1968]. pp. 324. *bibliog. (Germany(Bundesrepublik). Kommission für Geschichte des Parlamentarismus und der Politischen Parteien. Beiträge zur Geschichte des Parlamentarismus und der Politischen Parteien. Band 39)*

BISCHOFF (DETLEF) Franz Josef Strauss, die CSU und die Uussenpolitik: Konzeption und Realität am Beispiel der Grossen Koalition. Meisenheim am Glan ,1973. pp. 346. *bibliog.*

RICHTER (JOERG) 1941- , ed. Klassenkampf von oben?; oder, Angstmacher von rechts: Dokumente und Analysen eines gescheiterten Wahlkampfes. Reinbek bei Hamburg, 1973. pp. 206.

SOZIALDEMOKRATISCHE PARTEI DEUTSCHLANDS. Vorstand. Dokumentation über die Werbekampagnen der CDU/CSU und der CDU/CSU-Hilfsorganisationen im Bundestagswahlkampf 1972. Bonn, 1973. pp. 228. *Diagram in end pocket.*

VEEN (HANS JOACHIM) Die CDU/CSU-Opposition im parlamentarischen Entscheidungsprozess: zur Strategie und zum Einfluss ... in der Gesetzgebungsarbeit des 6.Deutschen Bundestages, 1969-1972. München, 1973. pp. 119. *bibliog.*

KOCH (HANS GERHARD) and BAMBERG (HANS DIETER) CDU/CSU: verhinderte Staatspartei. Starnberg, [1974]. pp. 239.

SCHMIDT (STEPHAN) ed. Schwarze Politik aus Bayern: ein Lesebuch zur CSU; herausgegeben...in Zusammenarbeit mit dem Presseausschuss Demokratische Initiative. Darmstadt, [1974]. pp. 156.

— Italy.

CAPUA (GIOVANNI DI) Le carte democristiane. Roma, 1972. pp. 351.

PALLOTTA (GINO) Il qualunquismo e l'avventura di Guglielmo Giannini. Milano, [1972]. pp. 182.

BEDESCHI (LORENZO) ed. La terza pagina de Il Popolo, 1923-1925; cattolici democratici e clerico-fascisti. Roma, 1973. pp. 463.

MALGERI (FRANCESCO) I cattolici dall'unità al fascismo: momenti e figure. Chiaravalle, [1973]. pp. 316.

— Spain.

ALZAGA VILLAAMIL (OSCAR) La primera democracia cristiana en España. Barcelona, 1973. pp. 355.

— Switzerland.

ALTERMATT (URS) Der Weg der Schweizer Katholiken ins Ghetto: die Entstehungsgeschichte der nationalen Volksorganisationen im Schweizer Katholizismus, 1848-1919. Zürich, [1972]. pp. 468. *bibliog.*

CERAMIC INDUSTRIES

— United Kingdom.

CERAMICS, GLASS AND MINERAL PRODUCTS INDUSTRY TRAINING BOARD [U.K.]. Report and statement of accounts. a., 1972/3- Harrow. *Formerly included in the file of British Parliamentary Papers.*

CEREBRAL PALSIED CHILDREN

— Bibliography.

PILLING (DORIA) compiler. The child with cerebral palsy: social emotional and educational adjustment; an annotated bibliography. Slough, 1973. pp. 61.

CERVIX UTERI

— Cancer.

WAKEFIELD (JOHN) ed. Seek wisely to prevent: studies of attitudes and action in a cervical cytology programme. London, H.M.S.O., 1972. pp. 193. *bibliog.*

CHABAN—DELMAS (JACQUES).

LAGROYE (JACQUES) Société et politique: J. Chaban-Delmas à Bordeaux. [Paris, 1973]. pp. 345. *bibliog. (Bordeaux. Université. Institut d'Etudes Politiques. Centre d'Etude et de Recherche sur la Vie Locale. Série Vie Locale. 4)*

ROUANET (PIERRE) Le cas Chaban. Paris, [1974]. pp. 367.

CHAD

— Economic conditions.

CABOT (JEAN) and BOUQUET (CHRISTIAN) Le Tchad. Paris, 1973. pp. 128. *bibliog.*

CHAMBERS OF COMMERCE

— Austria.

ZIRKOVITS (ERNST) Burgenlands Handel einst und jetzt: die Entwicklung der Interessenvertretung der burgenländischen Handelskammer ... von 1850 bis 1973. Wien, [1973]. pp. 119. *bibliog.*

CHAMULA INDIANS.

See TZOTZIL INDIANS.

CHANCE.

ALDANOV (MARK ALEKSANDROVICH) pseud. [i.e. LANDAU (MARK ALEKSANDROVICH)] Ul'mskaia noch': filosofiia sluchaia. N'iu-Iork, 1953. pp. 349.

HARDY (ALISTER CLAVERING) and others. The challenge of chance: experiments and speculations. London, 1973. pp. 280.

CHANNEL TUNNEL.

CHANNEL TUNNEL OPPOSITION ASSOCIATION. The Channel Tunnel project: an independent appraisal. Folkestone, 1973. pp. 7.

EUROPEAN FERRIES LTD. The Channel Tunnel project: an objective appraisal. London, 1973. pp. 14.

CHANNEL TUNNEL OPPOSITION ASSOCIATION. The White Paper on the Channel Tunnel: a reply by the... Association. Folkestone, [1974]. pp. 16.

U.K. British Railways Board. 1974. Channel tunnel: London-tunnel new rail link: a document for consultation. [London], 1974. pp. 23.

CHARENTE

— Economic conditions.

FRANCE. Direction de la Documentation. La Documentation Française. Notes et Etudes Documentaires. Nos. 3,731-3, 732-3,733. Les économies régionales: l'économie de la région Poitou-Charentes. Paris, 1970. pp. 120. *bibliog.*

— Industries.

PINARD (JACQUES) Les industries du Poitou et des Charentes: étude de l'industrialisation d'un milieu rural et de ses villes. Poitiers, 1972. pp. 516. *bibliog. Maps in end pocket.*

CHARITIES

— United Kingdom.

ANGLO-AMERICAN CONFERENCE ON THE ROLE OF PHILANTHROPY IN THE 1970S, DITCHLEY PARK, 1972. Philanthropy in the 70s: an Anglo-American discussion...; edited by John J. Corson and Harry V. Hodson. New York, [1973]. pp. 116.

HEYWOOD (JAMES FRANK) and QUILLAM (MARY) Fund raising by charities; [prepared for the National Council of Social Service]. London, [1973]. pp. 64.

— — Directories.

NATIONAL COUNCIL OF SOCIAL SERVICE. Charities Aid Fund. Directory of grant-making trusts. [3rd ed.] Tonbridge, [1973]. pp. 920.

— United States.

ANGLO-AMERICAN CONFERENCE ON THE ROLE OF PHILANTHROPY IN THE 1970S, DITCHLEY PARK, 1972. Philanthropy in the 70s: an Anglo-American discussion...; edited by John J. Corson and Harry V. Hodson. New York, [1973]. pp. 116.

TRATTNER (WALTER I.) From poor law to welfare state: a history of social welfare in America. New York, [1974]. pp. 276. *bibliogs.*

CHARITY.

The ECONOMICS of charity: essays on the comparative economics and ethics of giving and selling, with applications to blood;... [by] Armen A. Alchian [and others]. London, 1973. pp. 197. *(Institute of Economic Affairs. Readings. 12)*

CHARITY ORGANIZATION.

HEYWOOD (JAMES FRANK) and QUILLAM (MARY) Fund raising by charities; [prepared for the National Council of Social Service]. London, [1973]. pp. 64.

SLADEN (CHRISTOPHER) Getting across: a publicity primer for voluntary organisations. London, [1973]. pp. 62. *bibliogs.*

CHARTER PARTIES.

KURZ (CHARLES) Oil tanker chartering: an economic and historical analysis. Philadelphia, Pa., [1969?]. fo. 102. *bibliog.*

— United Kingdom.

SCRUTTON (Sir THOMAS EDWARD) Charterparties and bills of lading; eighteenth edition by Sir Alan Abraham Mocatta [and others]. London, 1974. pp. 624.

CHARTERS

— Catalogues.

SOTHEBY AND COMPANY. Bibliotheca Phillippica, medieval manuscripts, new series, eighth part: catalogue of manuscripts on vellum, paper and papyrus of the 4th to the 17th century from the celebrated collection formed by Sir Thomas Phillips, 1792-1872, etc. London, [1973]. pp. 127.

SOTHEBY AND COMPANY. Bibliotheca Phillippica, new series, twelfth part: catalogue of English manuscripts, autograph letters and charters from the celebrated collection formed by Sir Thomas Phillipps, Bt., 1792-1872, etc. London, [1974]. pp. 154.

CHARTISM.

GAMMAGE (ROBERT GEORGE) History of the Chartist movement, 1837-1854;...second edition, 1894, with an introduction by John Saville; and Gammage's pamphlet: The social oppression of the working classes, its causes and cure. New York, 1969. pp. 465.

CHATHAM ISLANDS

— Economic conditions.

NEW ZEALAND. Department of Industries and Commerce. 1972. Economic survey of the Chatham Islands. [Wellington], 1972. pp. 274. *bibliog.*

CHECHEN INGUSH REPUBLIC

— History.

OCHERKI istorii Checheno-Ingushskoi ASSR s drevneishikh vremen do nashikh dnei. Groznyi, 1967-72. 2 vols. *bibliog.*

CHELMSFORD

— Population.

ESSEX. County Planning Department. Chelmsford study: population in Chelmsford. Chelmsford, Essex County Council, [1972]. pp. 106.

CHELYABINSK (OBLAST')

— Statistics.

CHELYABINSK (OBLAST'). Statisticheskoe Upravlenie. Narodnoe khoziaistvo Cheliabinskoi oblasti: statisticheskii sbornik. Cheliabinsk, 1971. pp. 478. *Cover has title: Cheliabinskaia oblast' v tsifrakh.*

CHEMICAL INDUSTRIES

— Belgium.

ANDRE-FELIX (ANNETTE) Les débuts de l'industrie chimique dans les Pays-Bas autrichiens. Bruxelles, 1971. pp. 148. *bibliog.*

— Guatemala.

GUATEMALA. Comision Nacional del Salario. 1966. Estudio economico para la determinacion del salario minimo en la industria de substancias y productos quimicos. Guatemala, 1966. pp. 68.

— Poland.

LIENING (ERNST) Entwicklungstendenzen in der Chemiewirtschaft des Ostblocks. Teil III. Polen. Berlin, 1967. pp. 140. *bibliog. (Berlin. Freie Universität. Osteuropa-Institut. Berichte: Wirtschaftswissenschaftliche Folge. Nr.24)*

— Russia.

BREKHOV (KONSTANTIN IVANOVICH) Khimicheskoe i neftianoe mashinostroenie v vos'moi piatiletke. Moskva, 1971. pp. 56.

— United Kingdom.

CHEMICAL AND ALLIED PRODUCTS INDUSTRY TRAINING BOARD [U.K.]. Report and statement of accounts. a., 1972/3- Staines. *Formerly included in the file of British Parliamentary Papers.*

ECONOMIC DEVELOPMENT COMMITTEE FOR CHEMICALS. Industrial review to 1977: chemicals. London, National Economic Development Office, 1973. pp. 37.

CHEMICAL WARFARE.

MINDERHOUT (LEO VAN) and others. Biologiese en chemiese oorlogvoering: met een onderzoek naar de aktiviteiten van het Medisch Biologisch Laboratorium van RVO- TNO te Rijswijk. Nijmegen, 1972. pp. 61.

CHEMICAL WORKERS

— Austria.

FRANTA (KARL) and HORAK (KURT) 70 Jahre Gewerkschaft der Chemiearbeiter: unser Weg. Wien, [1972]. pp. 95. *bibliog.*

— European Economic Community countries.

ECONOMIC DEVELOPMENT COMMITTEE FOR CHEMICALS. Chemicals manpower in Europe: report of a comparative study of industrial relations and manpower productivity in the UK, France, Germany and Holland. London, National Economic Development Office, 1973. pp. 67.

— Norway.

SLEMMESTAD ARBEIDERFORENING. 22. mars 1896-1971: 75 år. [Slemmestad, 1971]. pp. 23.

— United Kingdom.

CHEMICAL AND ALLIED PRODUCTS INDUSTRY TRAINING BOARD [U.K.]. Working Party on the Training Implications of Productivity Agreements. The training implications of manpower productivity agreements; [C. Denard, chairman]. [Staines], 1970. pp. 13. *bibliog. (Information Papers. No. 4)*

CHEMICAL AND ALLIED PRODUCTS INDUSTRY TRAINING BOARD [U.K.]. Report and statement of accounts. a., 1972/3- Staines. *Formerly included in the file of British Parliamentary Papers.*

COMMISSION ON INDUSTRIAL RELATIONS [U.K.]. Recognition of white-collar unions in engineering and chemicals. London, H.M.S.O., 1973. pp. 75. *(Studies. 3)*

ECONOMIC DEVELOPMENT COMMITTEE FOR CHEMICALS. Chemicals manpower in Europe: report of a comparative study of industrial relations and manpower productivity in the UK, France, Germany and Holland. London, National Economic Development Office, 1973. pp. 67.

CHEMICALS

— Manufacture and Industry — Safety measures.

INTERNATIONAL LABOUR CONFERENCE. 56th Session. Reports. 6. Sixth item on the agenda: protection against hazards arising from benzene. Geneva, 1971. 2 pts.

— Transportation.

INTER-GOVERNMENTAL MARITIME CONSULTATIVE ORGANIZATION. 1972. Code for the construction and equipment of ships carrying dangerous chemicals in bulk. London, [1972]. pp. 41.

CHEMIN DE FER DU NORD.

CARON (FRANÇOIS) Histoire de l'exploitation d'un grand réseau: la Compagnie du Chemin der Fer du Nord, 1846-1937. Paris, 1973. pp. 619. *bibliog. (Paris. Ecole Pratique des Hautes Etudes. Section des Sciences Economiques et Sociales. Centre de Recherches Historiques. Industrie et Artisanat. 7)*

CHEPSTOW

— Politics and government.

BIRBECK (THOMAS T.) and DAVIES (S.C.) The history of Chepstow Rural District Council. Chepstow, 1974. pp. 60.

CHESHIRE

— History.

MORRILL (J.S.) Cheshire 1630-1660: county government and society during the English revolution. London, 1974. pp. 357. *bibliog.*

— Transit systems.

SOUTH EAST LANCASHIRE AND NORTH EAST CHESHIRE PASSENGER TRANSPORT EXECUTIVE. Public transport plan for the future. [Manchester], 1973. pp. 107.

CHEST

CHEST

— Diseases.

SCOTLAND. Scottish Health Services Council. Standing Medical Advisory Committee. 1973. The future of the chest services in Scotland; report by a sub- committee; [J.W. Crofton, chairman]. Edinburgh, 1973. pp. 70.

CHIANG (CHING).

ASIAN PEOPLES' ANTI-COMMUNIST LEAGUE. Pamphlets. No.172. Chiang Ching - Mao Tse-Tung's wife. [Taipei], 1973. pp. 44.

CHICAGO

— Civic improvement.

CONDIT (CARL WILBUR) Chicago, 1930-70: building, planning and urban technology. Chicago, 1974. pp. 351. bibliog.

— Haymarket Square Riot, 1886.

KEBABIAN (JOHN S.) compiler. The Haymarket affair and the trial of the Chicago anarchists, 1886: original manuscripts, letters, articles and printed material of the anarchists and of the state prosecutor, Julius S. Grinnell; Grinnell's own collection, etc. New York, 1970. pp. 51. (Kraus (Hans P.). Rare Books. Monograph Series. vol. 4.

— Police.

COMMISSION OF INQUIRY INTO THE BLACK PANTHERS AND THE POLICE. Search and destroy; a report by the Commission...; Roy Wilkins and Ramsey Clark, chairmen. New York, [1973]. pp. 284.

— Race question.

FISH (JOHN HALL) Black power/white control: the struggle of the Woodlawn Organization in Chicago. Princeton, [1973]. pp. 356. bibliog. (Center for the Scientific Study of Religion. Studies in Religion and Society)

CHICHERIN (GEORGII VASIL'EVICH).

GOROKHOV (IVAN MATVEEVICH) and others. G.V. Chicherin - diplomat leninskoi shkoly; pod obshchei redaktsiei i so vstupitel'noi stat'ei A.A. Gromyko. 2nd ed. Moskva, 1973. pp. 222.

CHICHESTER (ARTHUR) Baron Chichester of Belfast.

HEALY (TIMOTHY MICHAEL) The great fraud of Ulster; [reprint of the 1917 edition, with a new] foreword by Dennis Kennedy. Tralee, 1971. pp. 154. bibliog.

CHILD PSYCHIATRY.

HARRISON (SAUL I.) and McDERMOTT (JOHN F.) eds. Childhood psychopathology: an anthology of basic readings. New York, [1972]. pp. 903. bibliog.

BARKER (PHILIP) Care can prevent: child care or child psychiatry?. London, 1973. pp. 80. bibliog. (National Children's Home and Orphanage. Convocation Lectures. 1973)

DOCKAR-DRYSDALE (BARBARA E.) Consultation in child care: collected papers, etc. London, 1973. pp. 140.

WATSON (LUKE S.) Child behavior modification: a manual for teachers, nurses, and parents. New York, [1973]. pp. 147. bibliog.

CHILD STUDY.

SJØLUND (ARNE) The effect of daycare institutions on children's development: an analysis of international research. København, Danish National Institute of Social Research, 1971. fo. 69. bibliog. Summary of 'Børnehavens og vuggestuens betydning for barnets udvikling', published as Socialforskningsinstituttets Publikationer 38.

HARRISON (SAUL I.) and McDERMOTT (JOHN F.) eds. Childhood psychopathology: an anthology of basic readings. New York, [1972]. pp. 903. bibliog.

BRANDT-EMLER (LINDA JANE) A study of the development of skill in multiple-classification by children; [Ph.D. (London) thesis]. 1973. fo. 155. bibliog. Typescript: unpublished. This thesis is the property of London University and may not be removed from the Library.

SJØLUND (ARNE) Daycare institutions and children's development;... translated from the Danish by W. Glyn Jones. Farnborough, [1973]. pp. 308. bibliog.

WOLFF (SULAMMITH) Children under stress. rev. ed. Harmondsworth, 1973 repr. 1974. pp. 283. bibliog.

BROPHY (JERE E.) and GOOD (THOMAS L.) Teacher-student relationships: causes and consequences. New York, [1974]. pp. 400. bibliog.

BRYANT (PETER) Perception and understanding in young children: an experimental approach. London, [1974]. pp. 195. bibliog.

RICHARDS (MARTIN PAUL MEREDITH) ed. The integration of a child into a social world. London, 1974. pp. 316. bibliogs.

ROHWER (WILLIAM D.) and others. Understanding intellectual development: three approaches to theory and practice. Hinsdale, Ill., [1974]. pp. 429. bibliog.

SPENCER (DAVID) of the Centre for Urban and Regional Studies, Birmingham, and LLOYD (JOHN) Sociologist. A childs eye view of Small Heath, Birmingham: perception studies for environmental education;...with a technical appendix by Brian Goodey. Birmingham, 1974. 1 vol. (various pagings). bibliog. (Birmingham. University. Centre for Urban and Regional Studies. Research Memoranda. No.34)

CHILD WELFARE.

GOLDSTEIN (JOSEPH) and others. Beyond the best interests of the child. New York, [1973]. pp. 170.

— Study and teaching — United Kingdom.

CENTRAL TRAINING COUNCIL IN CHILD CARE [U.K.]. staff development and in-service study. Paper 2. Unqualified entrants and trainee social workers. [London, 1970]. pp. 16.

CENTRAL TRAINING COUNCIL IN CHILD CARE [U.K.]. Study Group on Fieldwork Training. 1st report. [London], 1970. pp. 24.

CENTRAL TRAINING COUNCIL IN CHILD CARE [U.K.]. Study Group on Fieldwork Training. The structure of courses: some implications for the patterns of fieldwork training. [London], 1970. pp. 24. (Discussion Papers. No. 1)

CENTRAL TRAINING COUNCIL IN CHILD CARE [U.K.]. Study Group on Fieldwork Training. Community placements: some experiments in social work education. [London], 1970. pp. 36. (Discussion Papers. No. 4)

CENTRAL TRAINING COUNCIL IN CHILD CARE [U.K.]. Study Group on Fieldwork Training. Playgroups: the development of dual purpose groups in social work education. [London], 1970. fo. 12. (Discussion Papers. No. 3)

CENTRAL TRAINING COUNCIL IN CHILD CARE [U.K.]. Study Group on Fieldwork Training. The residential placement in the training of social workers. [London], 1970. fo. 24. (Discussion Papers. No. 2)

CENTRAL TRAINING COUNCIL IN CHILD CARE [U.K.]. Study Group on Fieldwork Training. Working with groups: the development of experience in group work as a basic part of social work education. [London], 1970. pp. 32. (Discussion Papers. No. 5)

STUDY GROUP ON PLACEMENTS IN RESIDENTIAL ESTABLISHMENTS [U.K.]. Practical work placements in residential child care establishments as a resource in social work education; report; [K.M. Griffiths, chairman]. [London], Central Training Council in Child Care, 1971. pp. 28.

WORKING PARTY ON CRITERIA FOR SELECTION FOR QUALIFYING RESIDENTIAL CHILD CARE COURSES [U.K.]. Criteria for selection for qualifying residential child care courses; report; [Barbara Chumbley, chairman]. [London], Central Training Council in Child Care, 1972. pp. 40. bibliog.

— America, Latin.

CURSO REGIONAL INTERAMERICANO SOBRE COLOCACION FAMILIAR, ADOPCION, Y LIBERTAD VIGILADA, MONTEVIDEO, 1970. I curso regional..., Montevideo, Octubre 5 al 25 de 1970. Montevideo, Inter-American Children's Institute, 1972. pp. 313. bibliog.

REUNION SUDAMERICANA DE BIENESTAR DEL MENOR, 2ND, BUENOS AIRES, 1970. (Segunda) Reunion..., Buenos Aires, Republica Argentina, 19-23 de Octubre de 1970. Montevideo, Instituto Interamericano del Niño, 1972. fo. 99.

— France.

POUR une réforme de l'Aide Sociale à l'Enfance: texte du rapport Dupont-Fauville et documents. Paris, [1973]. pp. 262.

— Jamaica.

BRODBER (ERNA) Abandonment of children in Jamaica. [Mona], 1974. pp. 104. bibliog. (West Indies, University of the. Institute of Social and Economic Research. Law and Society in the Caribbean. No. 3)

— Netherlands.

STEMPELS (A.) Beschermd door anderen: kinderen in recht en mensenmaatschappij. Amsterdam. 1971. pp. 143. bibliog.

NETHERLANDS. Directie Kinderbescherming. 1972. Verslag over de jaren 1964 tot en met 1968. 's-Gravenhage, 1972. pp. 197.

— United Kingdom.

CLEGG (Sir ALEC) and MEGSON (BARBARA) Children in distress. 2nd ed. Harmondsworth, 1973. pp. 176.

HOWELLS (JOHN GWILYM) Remember Maria. London, [1974]. pp. 117. bibliog.

RENVOIZE (JEAN) Children in danger: the causes and prevention of baby battering. London, 1974. pp. 193. bibliog.

— — Isle of Man.

ISLE OF MAN. Board of Education. Annual report of the work of the...Board... in the exercise of their functions under the Children and Young Persons Acts, 1966 to 1971. a., 1972/3 (20th)- Douglas.

— United States.

KADUSHIN (ALFRED) Child welfare services. 2nd ed. New York, [1974]. pp. 753. bibliogs.

CHILDREN

— Care and hygiene.

CENTRAL UNION FOR CHILD WELFARE IN FINLAND. Publications. No. 26. Health service for children in Finland. [Helsinki, 1957]. pp. 39.

LANDELIJKE WERKGROEP ANTI-AUTORITAIRE EN SOCIALISTIESE OPVOEDING. Techniques Kollektief. Anti-autoritaire en socialistiese opvoeding. Nijmegen, 1970. pp. 112. bibliog.

SJØLUND (ARNE) Daycare institutions and children's development;... translated from the Danish by W. Glyn Jones. Farnborough, [1973]. pp. 308. bibliog.

— — Korea.

KIM (IL-SUNG) On the work of the Women's Union. Pyongyang, 1971. pp. 67.

— — United Kingdom.

The SCHOOL years in Newcastle upon Tyne, 1952-62: being a further contribution to the study of a thousand families; by F.J.W. Miller [and others]. London, 1974. pp. 362. *bibliog.*

— — Scotland.

SCOTLAND. Joint Working Party on the Integration of Medical Work. Sub-Group on the Child Health Service. 1973. Towards an integrated child health service;...report; [Sir John Brotherston, chairman]. Edinburgh, 1973. pp. 103.

— Employment.

INTERNATIONAL LABOUR CONFERENCE. 58th Session. Reports. 4. Minimum age for admission to employment: fourth item on the agenda. Geneva, 1972-73. 2 pts.

INTERNATIONAL LABOUR CONFERENCE. 57th Session. Reports. 4. Minimum age for admission to employment: fourth item on the agenda. Geneva, 1972. 2 pts.

IMPROVING the lot of the chimney sweeps: one book and nine pamphlets, 1785-1840. New York, 1972. 1 vol.(various pagings). *Facsimile reprints.*

KITTERINGHAM (JENNIE) Country girls in 19th century England. Oxford, [1973]. pp. 75. *(History Workshop. Pamphlets. No. 11)*

LONDON. Greater London Council. Inner London Education Authority. Employment of children: by-laws made by the Inner London Education Authority on 9 September 1968, etc.; [and] street trading: by-laws made by the Inner London Education Authority on 12 July 1972, etc. [London, 1973]. pp. 3.

— — — Indexes.

IRISH UNIVERSITY PRESS. Index to British parliamentary papers on children's employment. Dublin, [1973]. pp. 443.

— Growth.

NEW ZEALAND. Family Health Branch. 1971. Physical development of New Zealand school children, 1969; a survey. Wellington, 1971. pp. 119. *(Department of Health. Special Report Series. 38)*

— Institutional care — United Kingdom.

CENTRAL TRAINING COUNCIL IN CHILD CARE [U.K.]. Study Group on Fieldwork Training. The residential placement in the training of social workers. [London], 1970. fo. 24. *(Discussion Papers. No. 2)*

STUDY GROUP ON PLACEMENTS IN RESIDENTIAL ESTABLISHMENTS [U.K.]. Practical work placements in residential child care establishments as a resource in social work education; report; [K.M. Griffiths, chairman]. [London], Central Training Council in Child Care, 1971. pp. 28.

WORKING PARTY ON THE STAFF DEVELOPMENT NEEDS OF RESIDENTIAL CHILD CARE STAFF WITHOUT PROFESSIONAL TRAINING [U.K.]. Draft report on progress of Working Party up to August 1971 for submission to the Central Council for Education and Training in Social Work; [J.R. Howells, chairman]. [London], Central Training Council in Child Care, [1971]. 1 pamphlet (various pagings).

MIDDLEMORE HOMES COMMITTEE. One hundred years of child care: (the story of Middlemore Homes, 1872-1972). [Birmingham, 1972]. pp. 43.

WORKING PARTY ON CRITERIA FOR SELECTION FOR QUALIFYING RESIDENTIAL CHILD CARE COURSES [U.K.]. Criteria for selection for qualifying residential child care courses; report; [Barbara Chumbley, chairman]. [London], Central Training Council in Child Care, 1972. pp. 40. *bibliog.*

— Language.

LEOPOLD (WERNER F.) Speech development of a bilingual child: a linguist's record; [reprint of volumes originally published 1939-49]. New York, 1970. 4 vols. *bibliogs. (Northwestern University. Studies in the Humanities. Nos. 6,11,18,19)*

KESSLER (CAROLYN) The acquisition of syntax in bilingual children. Washington, [1971]. pp. 109. *bibliog.*

BLOOM (LOIS) One word at a time: the use of single word utterances before syntax. The Hague, 1973. pp. 262.

BROWN (ROGER W.) A first language: the early stages. London, 1973. pp. 437. *bibliog.*

ERVIN-TRIPP (SUSAN M.) Language acquisition and communicative choice: essays...; selected and introduced by Anwar S. Dil. Stanford, 1973. pp. 383. *bibliog. (Linguistic Research Group of Pakistan. Language Science and National Development)*

SCHAERLAEKENS (A.M.) The two-word sentence in child language development: a study based on evidence provided by Dutch-speaking triplets. The Hague, 1973. pp. 198. *bibliog.*

— Law.

GOLDSTEIN (JOSEPH) and others. Beyond the best interests of the child. New York, [1973]. pp. 170.

— — Germany, Eastern.

GERMANY (DEUTSCHE DEMOKRATISCHE REPUBLIK). Statutes, etc. 1973. Youth in the socialist State: law on the participation of young people in the organization of an advanced socialist society...: youth law of the GDR, draft. Berlin, [1973]. pp. 64.

— — Netherlands.

STEMPELS (A.) Beschermd door anderen: kinderen in recht en mensenmaatschappij. Amsterdam. 1971. pp. 143. *bibliog.*

NETHERLANDS. Directie Kinderbescherming. 1972. Verslag over de jaren 1964 tot en met 1968. 's-Gravenhage, 1972. pp. 197.

— — Venezuela.

VENEZUELA. Despacho del Ministro de Estado para la Juventud, la Ciencia y la Cultura. 1973. Primer informe sobre la juventud venezolana. [Tomo 1] . Documento de trabajo. Recopilacion de normas vigentes relativas al menor. Caracas, 1973. fo. 97.

VENEZUELA. Despacho del Ministro de Estado para la Juventud, la Ciencia y la Cultura. 1973. Primer informe sobre la juventud venezalana. [Tomo 1] . Documento de trabajo. Recopilacion de normas vigentes relativas al menor. Caracas, 1973. fo. 97.

— Management — Study and teaching.

GRANT (BEATRICE) Sketches of intellectual education, and hints on domestic economy, addressed to inexperienced mothers: with an appendix containing an essay on the instruction of the poor. Inverness, 1812. 2 vols. *Privately printed.*

— Nutrition.

U.K. Department of Health and Social Security. Reports on Health and Social Subjects. No.6. First report by the Sub-Committee on Nutritional Surveillance; [Sir Frank Young, chairman]. London, 1973. pp. 25. *bibliog.*

CHILDREN (INTERNATIONAL LAW).

GORODETSKAIA (IRINA KONSTANTINOVNA) Mezhdunarodnaia zashchita prav i interesov detei. Moskva, 1973. pp. 112.

CHILDREN AND POLITICS.

GARCIA (F. CHRIS) Political socialization of Chicano children: a comparative study with Anglos in California schools. New York, 1973. pp. 255. *bibliog.*

COLES (ROBERT) Children and political authority. Cape Town, 1974. pp. 34. *(Cape Town. University. T.B. Davie Memorial Lectures. 15)*

CHILDREN IN COLOMBIA.

CONFERENCIA NACIONAL SOBRE FAMILIA, INFANCIA Y JUVENTUD, 1a, BOGOTA, 1970. Prima conferencia nacional sobre familia, infancia y juventud; celebrada en Bogota del 2 al 7 de marzo de 1970, con el patrocinio del...UNICEF. Bogota, 1970. pp. 576.

CHILDREN IN FINLAND.

CENTRAL UNION FOR CHILD WELFARE IN FINLAND. Publications. No. 26. Health service for children in Finland. [Helsinki, 1957]. pp. 39.

CHILDREN IN HONG KONG.

WILSON (RICHARD W.) The moral state: a study of the political socialization of Chinese and American children. New York, [1974]. pp. 290. *bibliog.*

CHILDREN IN TAIWAN.

WILSON (RICHARD W.) The moral state: a study of the political socialization of Chinese and American children. New York, [1974]. pp. 290. *bibliog.*

CHILDREN IN THE UNITED KINGDOM.

LOCKE (MICHAEL) and CONSTABLE (MOIRA) The kids don't notice; [a Shelter report on the effects of bad housing conditions on children]. London, 1973. pp. 23.

— Bibliography.

PARFIT (JESSIE) and others. Spotlight on sources of information about children. London, [1974]. pp. 30. *(National Children's Bureau. Spotlight. 4)*

CHILDREN IN THE UNITED STATES.

ESPENSHADE (THOMAS J.) The cost of children in urban United States. Berkeley, [1973]. pp. 94. *bibliog. (California University. Institute of International Studies. Population Monograph Series. No. 14)*

ELDER (GLEN H.) Children of the great depression: social change in life experience.Chicago, 1974. pp. 400. *bibliog.*

WILSON (RICHARD W.) The moral state: a study of the political socialization of Chinese and American children. New York, [1974]. pp. 290. *bibliog.*

CHILDREN OF DIVORCED PARENTS.

ZUERICH (CANTON). Jugendamt. 1967. Probleme mit Kindern aus geschiedener Ehe. [Zürich, 1967]. pp. 72.

CHILDREN OF IMMIGRANTS

— Education — United Kingdom.

U.K. National Committee for Commonwealth Immigrants. Education Panel. 1966. Problems of language for immigrants: the choice of languages in the curriculum in English schools. [London, 1966 repr. 1970]. pp. 5.

BRITISH COUNCIL OF CHURCHES. Education Department. Religious education in a multi-religious society; report on a consultation in the West Riding of Yorkshire organised in collaboration with the Community Relations Commission. [London], Community Relations Commission, [1969]. pp. 6.

COMMUNITY RELATIONS COMMISSION. The background to the educational difficulties of some West Indian children in Britain. [London, 1971]. pp. 4.

HAWKINS (ERIC) ed. A time for growing: a handbook for organisers of summer projects. London, Community Relations Commission, [1971]. pp. 74. *bibliog.*

The MULTI-racial school: a professional perspective; edited by Julia McNeal and Margaret Rogers. Harmondsworth, 1971. pp. 154. *bibliogs.*

ARROWSMITH (PAT) The colour of six schools. London, 1972. pp. 132. *Not available for consultation.*

COMMUNITY RELATIONS COMMISSION. Educational needs of children from minority groups. London, 1974. pp. 19.

CHILDREN OF IMMIGRANTS (Cont.)

TAYLOR (FRANCINE) Race, school and community: (a survey of research and literature on education in multi-racial Britain). Windsor, 1974. pp. 200. *bibliog.*

— Germany.

CANDEL (FRANCISCO) Inmigrantes y trabajadores. Barcelona, [1972]. pp. 239.

CHILDREN OF MILITARY PERSONNEL

— United States.

YOHALEM (ALICE M.) Desegregation and career goals: children of Air Force families. New York, 1974. pp. 140. *(Columbia University. Graduate School of Business. Conservation of Human Resources Studies)*

CHILDREN'S PERIODICALS, BELGIAN.

PLUVINAGE-PATERNOSTRE (ANNE) L'adolescent et sa presse: analyse de contenu des publications destinées aux jeunes. Bruxelles, [1971]. pp. 112. *bibliog. (Brussels. Université Libre. Collège de la Diffusion Culturelle. Cahiers d'Etude de Sociologie Culturelle. 2)*

CHILDREN'S PERIODICALS, FRENCH.

PLUVINAGE-PATERNOSTRE (ANNE) L'adolescent et sa presse: analyse de contenu des publications destinées aux jeunes. Bruxelles, [1971]. pp. 112. *bibliog. (Brussels. Université Libre. Collège de la Diffusion Culturelle. Cahiers d'Etude de Sociologie Culturelle. 2)*

CHILE.

CHILE: a critical study; [by] Pablo Baraona Urzua [and others]. Santiago, 1972. pp. 324.

— Armed forces.

POLLONI ROLDAN (ALBERTO) Las fuerzas armadas de Chile en la vida nacional. Santiago de Chile, 1972. pp. 483. *bibliog.*

— Economic conditions.

GALDAMES G. (JUAN) and AUDA J. (JAIME) Chile: un pais andino del Pacifico Sur. Santiago de Chile, [1972]. pp. 176.

RAMOS (SERGIO) Chile: una economia de transicion?. Santiago de Chile, [1972]. pp. 262. *(Santiago de Chile. Universidad de Chile. Centro de Estudios Socioeconomicos. Cuadernos. 15)*

CHILE. Oficina de Planificacion Nacional. 1973. Balances economicos de Chile, 1960-1970. Santiago, 1973. pp. 258. *(Serie 4. No.2. Balances Economicos)*

ECKAUS (RICHARD S.) and ROSENSTEIN-RODAN (PAUL N.) eds. Analysis of development problems: studies of the Chilean economy. Amsterdam, 1973. pp. 430. *bibliog.*

— Economic history.

RAMIREZ NECOCHEA (HERNAN) Balmaceda y la contrarrevolucion de 1891. 3rd ed. Santiago de Chile, 1972. pp. 268. *bibliog.*

— Economic policy.

PICO CAÑAS (GERMAN) Realizaciones y planes. [Santiago], 1950. pp. 30.

CHILE. Oficina de Planificacion Nacional. 1971. Plan de reconstruccion, 1971-1973, de las provincias de Coquimbo, Agoncagua, Santiago, Valparaiso y O'Higgins, afectadas por el sismo del 8 de julio de 1971. Santiago de Chile, 1971. pp. 256. *(Serie 5. No.3. Publicaciones Especiales)*

EDWARDS (THOMAS L.) Economic development and reform in Chile: progress under Frei, 1964-1970. East Lansing, Mich., 1972. fo. 54. *bibliog. (Michigan State University. Latin American Studies Center. Monograph Series. No. 8)*

RAMOS (SERGIO) Chile: una economia de transicion?. Santiago de Chile, [1972]. pp. 262. *(Santiago de Chile. Universidad de Chile. Centro de Estudios Socioeconomicos. Cuadernos. 15)*

ECKAUS (RICHARD S.) and ROSENSTEIN-RODAN (PAUL N.) eds. Analysis of development problems: studies of the Chilean economy. Amsterdam, 1973. pp. 430. *bibliog.*

— Executive departments.

CLEAVES (PETER S.) Bureaucratic politics and administration in Chile. Berkeley, Calif., [1974]. pp. 352. *bibliog.*

— Foreign relations — Bolivia.

SOTOMAYOR (CARLOS MARTINEZ) Relaciones entre Chile y Bolivia. [Santiago], 1963. pp. 30. *(Chile. Ministerio de Relaciones Exteriores, Discurso y Documentos. 1)*

— — United States.

URIBE (ARMANDO) Le livre noir de l'intervention américaine au Chili. Paris, [1974]. pp. 224.

— History.

RIVAS VICUÑA (MANUEL) Historia politica y parlamentaria de Chile. I. Las administraciones de 1891 a 1910. II. La administracion de Ramon Barros Luco (1910-1915). III. La administracion de Juan Luis Sanfuentes (1915-1920); ordenada segun diversos manuscritos del autor, con varios apendices relativos a dicha "historia", a los sucesos de 1920 a 1934 y documentos concernientes a Rivas Vicuña. Santiago de Chile, Ediciones de Biblioteca Nacional, 1964. 3 vols.

— History — 1891, Revolution.

RAMIREZ NECOCHEA (HERNAN) Balmaceda y la contrarrevolucion de 1891. 3rd ed. Santiago de Chile, 1972. pp. 268. *bibliog.*

— Politics and government.

RIVAS VICUÑA (MANUEL) Historia politica y parlamentaria de Chile. I. Las administraciones de 1891 a 1910. II. La administracion de Ramon Barros Luco (1910-1915). III. La administracion de Juan Luis Sanfuentes (1915-1920); ordenada segun diversos manuscritos del autor, con varios apendices relativos a dicha "historia", a los sucesos de 1920 a 1934 y documentos concernientes a Rivas Vicuña. Santiago de Chile, Ediciones de Biblioteca Nacional, 1964. 3 vols.

INTERNATIONAL TELEPHONE AND TELEGRAPH CORPORATION. Subversion in Chile: a case study in U.S. corporate intrigue in the Third World; [memoranda of the Corporation with an introduction by a group representing the Bertrand Russell Peace Foundation and others]. Nottingham, 1972. pp. 114. *(Spokesman, The. Spokesman Books)*

ALLENDE (SALVADOR) La revolucion chilena. Buenos Aires, [1973]. pp. 209.

ALLENDE (SALVADOR) Su pensamiento politico. Santiago de Chile, 1973. pp. 430.

CASTRO RUZ (FIDEL) and ALLENDE BUSSI (BEATRIZ) Homenaje a Salvador Allende; (discursos pronunciados por... Beatriz Allende Bussi...y por...Fidel Castro, el dia 28 de septiembre de 1973 en el acto conmemorativo del XIII aniversario de la creacion de los Comites de Defensa de la Revolucion. La Habana, 1973. pp. 105.

CHILE. Secretaria General de Gobierno. 1973. Libro Blanco del cambio de gobierno en Chile, 11 de septiembre de 1973. 2nd ed. Santiago, 1973. pp. 264.

The COUP in Chile: firsthand report and assessment; by Hugo Blanco and other revolutionaries who escaped. New York, 1973. pp. 23. *(Reprinted from Intercontinental Press, October 8 and 22, 1973)*

FOLEY (GERRY) and MIAH (MALIK) Tragedy in Chile: lessons of the revolutionary upsurge and its defeat; [shortened versions of articles appearing originally in Intercontinental Press and Young Socialist]. New York, [1973]. pp. 23.

GARCES (JOAN E.) El estado y los problemas tacticos en el gobierno de Allende. Buenos Aires, 1973 repr. 1974. pp. 309.

MOSS (ROBERT) Chile's marxist experiment. Newton Abbot, [1973]. pp. 225. *bibliog.*

MOSS (ROBERT) The Santiago model: 1 : revolution within democracy?. London, 1973. pp. 16. *(Institute for the Study of Conflict. Conflict Studies. No. 31)*

MOSS (ROBERT) The Santiago model: 2 : polarisation of politics. London, 1973. pp. 12. *(Institute for the Study of Conflict. Conflict Studies. No. 32)*

PANORAMA DDR. The GDR's fervent solidarity with the courageous Chilean people. Berlin, [1973]. pp. 15.

La TRAGEDIA chilena: testimonios. Buenos Aires, [1973]. pp. 385.

BLAKEMORE (HAROLD) British nitrates and Chilean politics, 1886-1896: Balmaceda and North. London, 1974. pp. 260. *(London. University. Institute of Latin American Studies. Monographs. 4)*

CERDA (CARLOS) Génocide au Chili; (suivi de Hommage à Salvador Allende, de Fidel Castro). Paris, 1974. pp. 134.

CHICAGO COMMISSION OF INQUIRY INTO THE STATUS OF HUMAN RIGHTS IN CHILE. Report of the Chicago Commission...: Santiago, Chile, February 16-23, 1974. Chicago, [1974]. 1 vol. (various pagings).

CHILE: una tragedia americana. Buenos Aires, 1974. pp. 259.

CORDOBA CLAURE (TED) Chile no. Buenos Aires, 1974. pp. 222.

DISASTER in Chile: Allende's strategy and why it failed; [articles taken mainly from 1970-1973 issues of Intercontinental Press]; edited...by Les Evans. New York, 1974. pp. 271.

LEFTWICH (ADRIAN) ed. South Africa: economic growth and political change; with comparative studies of Chile, Sri Lanka and Malaysia. London, 1974. pp. 357.

NAJMAN (MAURICE) ed. Le Chili est proche: révolution et contre-révolution dans le Chili de l'Unité populaire: textes. Paris, 1974. pp. 310.

RAPTIS (MICHEL) Revolution and counter-revolution in Chile: a dossier on workers' participation in the revolutionary process; translated by John Simmonds. London, [1974]. pp. 174.

SELSER (GREGORIO) Una empresa multinacional: la ITT en los Estados Unidos y en Chile. Buenos Aires, 1974. pp. 257.

VARAS (FLORENCIA) and VERGARA (JOSE MANUEL) Operacion Chile. Buenos Aires, [1974]. pp. 260.

WHITEHEAD (LAURENCE) The lesson of Chile. London, 1974. pp. 40. *(Fabian Society. Research Series. [No.] 317)*

— Population.

GALDAMES G. (JUAN) and AUDA J. (JAIME) Chile: un pais andino del Pacifico Sur. Santiago de Chile, [1972]. pp. 176.

— Presidents — Election.

NUÑEZ (CARLOS) Chile: la ultima opcion electoral ?. Santiago de Chile, 1970. pp. 116.

FRANCIS (MICHAEL J.) The Allende victory: an analysis of the 1970 Chilean presidential election. Tucson, [1973]. pp. 76. *(Arizona University. Institute of Government Research. Comparative Government Studies. No. 4)*

— Relations (general) with Eastern Germany.

PANORAMA DDR. The GDR's fervent solidarity with the courageous Chilean people. Berlin, [1973]. pp. 15.

— Social policy.

CHILE. Oficina de Planificacion Nacional. 1971. Plan de reconstruccion, 1971-1973, de las provincias de Coquimbo, Agoncagua, Santiago, Valparaiso y O'Higgins, afectadas por el sismo del 8 de julio de 1971. Santiago de Chile, 1971. pp. 256. *(Serie 5. No.3. Publicaciones Especiales)*

CHIMNEY SWEEPS.

IMPROVING the lot of the chimney sweeps: one book and nine pamphlets, 1785-1840. New York, 1972. 1 vol.(various pagings). *Facsimile reprints.*

CHINA

— Armed forces.

WHITSON (WILLIAM W.) Chinese military and political leaders and the distribution of power in China, 1956-1971; a report prepared for Defense Advanced Research Projects Agency and Department of State. Santa Monica, 1973. pp. 474. *(Rand Corporation. [Rand Reports]. 1091)*

— — Political activity.

KAU (YING-MAO) The People's Liberation Army and China's nation-building. White Plains, N.Y., [1973]. pp. 407. *bibliog.*

— Army.

KAU (YING-MAO) The People's Liberation Army and China's nation-building. White Plains, N.Y., [1973]. pp. 407. *bibliog.*

CORR (GERARD H.) The Chinese red army: campaigns and politics since 1949. Reading, 1974. pp. 176. *bibliog.*

— Boundaries.

MOSELEY (GEORGE V.H.) The consolidation of the south China frontier. Berkeley, Calif., 1973. pp. 192. *bibliog.*

— — India.

LAMB (ALASTAIR) The Sino-Indian border in Ladakh. Canberra, 1973. pp. 113.

— Commerce.

KUNZE (BERND) Die Wirtschaftsbeziehungen zwischen der Volksrepublik China und den westlichen Industriestaaten: ([report for] CEPES, Europäische Vereinigung für Wirtschaftliche und Soziale Entwicklung). [Bonn, 1973]. pp. 181. *bibliog.*

WHITSON (WILLIAM W.) ed. Doing business with China: American trade opportunities in the 1970s. New York, 1974. pp. 587.

— — Portugal.

MOURA (CARLOS FRANCISCO) Macau e o comercio portuguȗes com a China e o Japão nos seculos XVI e XVII: as viagens da China e do Japão; a nau do trato; as galeotas. Macau, Imprensa Nacional, 1973. pp. 35. *bibliog. Separata dos no. 1 do vol. vii do Boletim do Instituto Luis de Camões.*

— — United Kingdom — Scotland.

SCOTTISH HISTORY SOCIETY. [Publications] 4th series. vol. 10. William Melrose in China, 1845-1855: the letters of a Scottish tea merchant; edited by Hoh-cheung Mui and Lorna H. Mui. Edinburgh, 1973. pp. 301. *6 papers in end pocket.*

— — United States.

NEILAN (EDWARD) and SMITH (CHARLES R.) The future of the China market: prospects for Sino-American trade. Washington, 1974. pp. 94. *bibliog. (American Enterprise Institute for Public Policy Research and Stanford University. Hoover Institution on War, Revolution and Peace. AEI-Hoover Policy Studies. 11)*

WHITSON (WILLIAM W.) ed. Doing business with China: American trade opportunities in the 1970s. New York, 1974. pp. 587.

— Constitution.

KITAISKAIA Narodnaia Respublika: ekonomika, gosudarstvo i pravo, kul'tura. Moskva, 1970. pp. 227.

— Defences.

INTERNATIONAL INSTITUTE FOR STRATEGIC STUDIES. Adelphi Papers. No.99. Nuclear weapons and Chinese policy; by Harry Gelber. Kondon, 1973. pp. 37.

— Description and travel.

PRIMAKOV (VITALII MARKOVICH) Zapiski volontera: grazhdanskaia voina v Kitae; (otvetstvennyi redaktor L.P. Deliusin, vstupitel'naia stat'ia i primechaniia R.A. Mirovitskoi). Moskva, 1967. pp. 215. *First published 1930.*

— Economic conditions.

KITAISKAIA Narodnaia Respublika: ekonomika, gosudarstvo i pravo, kul'tura. Moskva, 1970. pp. 227.

AXILROD (ERIC) The political economy of the Chinese revolution. Kowloon, Hong Kong, [1972]. pp. 541. *bibliog.*

KUITENBROUWER (JOOST B.W.) Growth and equality in India and China: a historical comparative analysis. The Hague, 1973. pp. 42. *(Hague. Institute of Social Studies. Occasional Papers. No. 38)*

SCHRAM (STUART R.) ed. Authority, participation and cultural change in China; essays by a European study group. Cambridge, 1973. pp. 350. *(London. University. School of Oriental and African Studies. Contemporary China Institute. Publications)*

SWAMY (SUBRAMANIAN) Economic growth in China and India, 1952-1970: a comparative appraisal. Chicago, 1973. pp. 84.

VANIN (VADIM IVANOVICH) Gosudarstvennyi kapitalizm v KNR. Moskva, 1974. pp. 326. *bibliog.*

— Economic policy.

FRANCE. Direction de la Documentation. La Documentation Française. Notes et Etudes Documentaires. Nos. 3,066-3, 067. La planification économique des communes populaires chinoises: documents. Paris, 1964. 2 pts.

AXILROD (ERIC) The political economy of the Chinese revolution. Kowloon, Hong Kong, [1972]. pp. 541. *bibliog.*

KUITENBROUWER (JOOST B.W.) Growth and equality in India and China: processes, policies and theory formation. The Hague, 1973. pp. 61. *(Hague. Institute of Social Studies. Occasional Papers. No. 39)*

ROBINSON (JOAN) Economic management, China, 1972. London, 1973. pp. 37. *(Anglo-Chinese Educational Institute. Modern China Series. No. 4)*

— Foreign economic relations — Belgium.

KURGAN-VAN HENTENRYK (GINETTE) Léopold II et les groupes financiers belges en Chine: la politique royale et ses prolongements, 1895-1914. Bruxelles, [1972]. pp. 969. *bibliog. (Académie Royale de Belgique. Classe des Lettres et des Sciences Morales et Politiques. Mémoires. Collection in-8º. 2e série. Tome 61. Fasc. 2)*

— Foreign relations.

HANSEN (JOSEPH) Marxist, and LUND (CAROLINE) Nixon's Moscow and Peking summits: their meaning for Vietnam. New York, [1972]. pp. 31.

TATU (MICHEL) Le triangle Washington-Moscou-Pékin et les deux Europe(s). [Paris, 1972]. pp. 149.

ADIE (WILLIAM ANDREW CHARLES) Chinese foreign policy. Johannesburg, 1973. pp. 20.

CHINA and the world community; [papers of a conference sponsored by the Australian Institute of International Affairs, Melbourne, 1972] edited by Ian Wilson. Sydney, 1973. pp. 304.

GRIFFITH (WILLIAM E.) Peking, Moscow, and beyond: the Sino-Soviet-American triangle. Washington, D.C., 1973. pp. 71. *(Georgetown University. Center for Strategic and International Studies. Washington Papers. vol.[1]/6)*

INTERNATIONAL INSTITUTE FOR STRATEGIC STUDIES. Adelphi Papers. No.99. Nuclear weapons and Chinese policy; by Harry Gelber. Kondon, 1973. pp. 37.

MOSELEY (GEORGE V.H.) The consolidation of the south China frontier. Berkeley, Calif., 1973. pp. 192. *bibliog.*

THORNTON (RICHARD C.) China, the struggle for power 1917-1972. Bloomington, [1973]. pp. 403.

DAVIES (JOHN PATON) Dragon by the tail: American, British, Japanese and Russian encounters with China and one another. London, 1974. pp. 448.

GITTINGS (JOHN) The world and China, 1922-1972. London, 1974. pp. 303. *bibliog.*

— — Africa.

OGUNSANWO (CORNELIUS ALABA ABIODUN ADEBOYEJO) China's policy in Africa, 1958-71. London, 1974. pp. 310. *bibliog. (London. University. London School of Economics and Political Science. Centre for International Studies. International Studies)*

— — Asia, Southeast.

FITZGERALD (CHARLES PATRICK) China and Southeast Asia since 1945. London, 1973. pp. 110. *bibliog.*

— — Burma.

PETTMAN (RALPH) China in Burma's foreign policy. Canberra, 1973. pp. 56. *(Australian National University. Contemporary China Centre. Contemporary China Papers. No. 7)*

— — Cuba.

CHENG (YING-HSIANG) Idylle sino-cubaine, brouille sino-soviétique. Paris, 1973. pp. 311. *(Fondation Nationale des Sciences Politiques. Travaux et Recherches de Science Politique. 24)*

— — East (Near East).

MA'OZ (MOSHE) Soviet and Chinese relations with the Palestinian guerrilla organizations. Jerusalem, 1974. pp. 35. *bibliog. (Hebrew University. Leonard Davis Institute for International Relations. Jerusalem Papers on Peace Problems. No. 4)*

— — France.

FRANCE. Direction de la Documentation. La Documentation Française. Notes et Etudes Documentaires. Nos.4014-4015. Les relations franco-chinoises, 1945-1973. [Paris], 1973. pp. 57. *bibliog.*

— — India.

HU (CHI-HSI) Pékin et le mouvement communiste indien. Paris, 1972. pp. 153. *(Fondation Nationale des Sciences Politiques. Travaux et Recherches de Science Politique. 22)*

KAPUR (HARISH) The embattled tringele: Moscow, Peking, New Delhi. New York, 1973. pp. 175. *bibliog.*

RAM (MOHAN) Politics of Sino-Indian confrontation. Delhi, 1973. pp. 241. *bibliog.*

— — Japan.

BAMBA (NOBUYA) Japanese diplomacy in a dilemma: new light on Japan's China policy, 1924-1929. Vancouver, 1972. pp. 440. *bibliog.*

KATO (SHUICHI) The Japan-China phenomenon: conflict or compatibility; ... translated from the Japanese by David Chibbett. London, 1974. pp. 103.

— — Russia.

GEL'BRAS (VILIA GDALIVICH) Kitai: krizis prodolzhaetsia. Moskva, 1973. pp. 223.

CHINA (Cont.)

KAPUR (HARISH) The embattled tringele: Moscow, Peking, New Delhi. New York, 1973. pp. 175. *bibliog.*

SULZBERGER (CYRUS LEO) The coldest war: Russia's game in China. New York, [1974]. pp. 113.

— — United States.

HUNT (MICHAEL H.) Frontier defense and the open door: Manchuria in Chinese-American relations, 1895-1911. New Haven, 1973. pp. 281. *bibliog.*

SERGEICHUK (S.) SShA i Kitai. 2nd ed. Moskva, 1973. pp. 238. *1st ed. has subtitle: politika SShA v otnoshenii Kitaia, 1948-1968.*

HSIAO (GENE T.) ed. Sino-American détente and its policy implications. New York, 1974. pp. 319.

— — Vietnam.

WELCOME the signing of the Paris agreement on Viet Nam. Peking, 1973. pp. 37.

— History.

KITAI: obshchestvo i gosudarstvo; sbornik statei. Moskva, 1973 pp. 357. *bibliog.*

— — 1900 .

DES FORGES (ROGER V.) Hsi-Liang and the Chinese national revolution. New Haven, 1973. pp. 274. *bibliog.*

RONNING (CHESTER) A memoir of China in revolution: from the Boxer rebellion to the People's Republic. New York, [1974]. pp. 306.

— — 1912—1949, REPUBLIC.

FRIEDMAN (EDWARD) Backward toward revolution: the Chinese Revolutionary Party. Berkeley, [1974]. pp. 237. *(Michigan University. Center for Chinese Studies. Michigan Studies on China)*

— — 1912—1937.

PRIMAKOV (VITALII MARKOVICH) Zapiski volontera: grazhdanskaia voina v Kitae; (otvetstvennyi redaktor L.P. Deliusin, vstupitel'naia stat'ia i primechaniia R.A. Mirovitskoi). Moskva, 1967. pp. 215. *First published 1930.*

VIDNYE sovetskie kommunisty - uchastniki kitaiskoi revoliutsii. Moskva, 1970. pp. 111.

— — 1945— .

ARAY (SIWITT) Les cent fleurs: Chine, 1956-1957. [Paris, 1973]. pp. 187. *bibliog.*

— Industries.

MUROMTSEVA (ZOIA ANDREEVNA) Problemy industrializatsii Kitaiskoi Narodnoi Respubliki. Moskva, 1971. pp. 142. *bibliog.*

— Intellectual life.

KITAISKAIA Narodnaia Respublika: ekonomika, gosudarstvo i pravo, kul'tura. Moskva, 1970. pp. 227.

— Maps.

HSIEH (CHIAO-MIN) Atlas of China;... edited by Christopher L. Salter. New York, [1973]. pp. 282. *bibliog.*

— Nationalism.

KAU (YING-MAO) The People's Liberation Army and China's nation-building. White Plains, N.Y., [1973]. pp. 407. *bibliog.*

— Politics and government.

BEHIND China's "great cultural revolution"; by Peng Shu-tse [and others]. New York, 1967 repr. 1970. pp. 63.

GRAY (JACK) and CAVENDISH (PATRICK) Chinese communism in crisis: Maoism and the cultural revolution. London, Pall Mall Press, 1968 repr. 1970. pp. viii, 279.

AXILROD (ERIC) The political economy of the Chinese revolution. Kowloon, Hong Kong, [1972]. pp. 541. *bibliog.*

HUANG (PHILIP C.) Liang Ch'i-ch'ao and modern Chinese liberalism. Seattle, [1972]. pp. 231. *bibliog. (Washington State University. Institute for Comparative and Foreign Area Studies. Publications on Asia. No.22)*

MAOISM unmasked: collection of Soviet press articles; (compiled by V.F. Feoktistov). Moscow, 1972. pp. 246.

BETTELHEIM (CHARLES) Révolution culturelle et organisation industrielle en Chine. Paris, 1973. pp. 153.

COLLIER (JOHN) Maoist and COLLIER (ELSIE) China's socialist revolution. London, 1973. pp. 270.

DES FORGES (ROGER V.) Hsi-Liang and the Chinese national revolution. New Haven, 1973. pp. 274. *bibliog.*

GEL'BRAS (VILIA GDALIVICH) Kitai: krizis prodolzhaetsia. Moskva, 1973. pp. 223.

IDEOLOGY and politics in contemporary China: [selected papers of a conference held in Santa Fe, 1971]; edited by Chalmers Johnson. Seattle, [1973]. pp. 388. *(American Council of Learned Societies and Social Science Research Council. Joint Committee on Contemporary China. Subcommittee on Chinese Government and Politics. Studies in Chinese Government and Politics. 4)*

KAROL (K.S.) pseud. [i.e. Karol KEWES] La deuxième révolution chinoise. Paris, [1973]. pp. 563.

LÖTVEIT (TRYGVE) Chinese communism 1931-1934: experience in civil government. Lund, 1973. pp. 290. *bibliog. (Scandinavian Institute of Asian Studies. Monograph Series. No. 16)*

THORNTON (RICHARD C.) China, the struggle for power 1917-1972. Bloomington, [1973]. pp. 403.

WHITSON (WILLIAM W.) Chinese military and political leaders and the distribution of power in China. 1956-1971; a report prepared for Defense Advanced Research Projects Agency and Department of State. Santa Monica, 1973. pp. 474. *(Rand Corporation. [Rand Reports]. 1091)*

ZHELOKHOVTSEV (ALEKSEI NIKOLAEVICH) "Kul'turnaia revoliutsiia" s blizkogo rasstoianiia: zapiski ochevidtsa. Moskva, 1973. pp. 262. *A revised version of the account first published in Novyi mir, 1968.*

MACFARQUHAR (RODERICK L.) The origins of the cultural revolution. London, 1974 in progress. *bibliog.*

BARNETT (ARTHUR DOAK) Uncertain passage: China's transition to the post-Mao era. Washington, D.C., [1974]. pp. 387.

FRIEDMAN (EDWARD) Backward toward revolution: the Chinese Revolutionary Party. Berkeley, [1974]. pp. 237. *(Michigan University. Center for Chinese Studies. Michigan Studies on China)*

MAO (TSE-TUNG) Mao Tse-tung unrehearsed: talks and letters, 1956-1971; edited and introduced by Stuart Schram; translated by John Chinnery and Tieyun. Harmondsworth, [1974]. pp. 352.

— Population.

LIU (NANMING I) Contribution à l'étude de la population chinoise. Genève, [1935]. pp. 252. *bibliog. (Bibliothèque Sino-Internationale. Publications. No.3)*

TIEN (H. YUAN) China's population struggle: demographic decisions of the People's Republic, 1949-1969. Columbus, [1973]. pp. 405. *bibliog.*

— Relations (general) with Africa.

DEICH (TAT'IANA LAZAREVNA) Maoizm - ugroza Afrike. Moskva, 1972. pp. 168.

— Relations (general) with Japan.

KATO (SHUICHI) The Japan-China phenomenon: conflict or compatibility; ... translated from the Japanese by David Chibbett. London, 1974. pp. 103.

— Relations (general) with Russia.

VLADIMIROV (OLEG EVGEN'EVICH) and RIAZANTSEV (VLADIMIR IVANOVICH) Stranitsy politicheskoi biografii Mao Tsze-duna. 2nd ed. Moskva, 1973. pp. 112.

— Relations (general) with the United States — Bibliography.

McCUTCHEON (JAMES M.) compiler. China and America: a bibliography of interactions, foreign and domestic. Honolulu, [1972]. pp. 75. *(Hawaii University. East-West Bibliographic Series. 1)*

— Rural conditions.

WHYTE (ROBERT ORR) Rural nutrition in China. Hong Kong, 1972. pp. 54. *bibliog.*

ENGELBORGHS-BERTELS (MARTHE) La Chine rurale: des villages aux communes populaires. Bruxelles,[1974]. pp. 195. *bibliog.*

— Social conditions.

HUANG (JOE C.) Heroes and villains in communist China: the contemporary Chinese novel as a reflection of life. London, [1973]. pp. 345. *bibliog.*

KUITENBROUWER (JOOST B.W.) Growth and equality in India and China: a historical comparative analysis. The Hague, 1973. pp. 42. *(Hague. Institute of Social Studies. Occasional Papers. No. 38)*

SCHRAM (STUART R.) ed. Authority, participation and cultural change in China; essays by a European study group. Cambridge, 1973. pp. 350. *(London. University. School of Oriental and African Studies. Contemporary China Institute. Publications)*

DAVIES (JOHN PATON) Dragon by the tail: American, British, Japanese and Russian encounters with China and one another. London, 1974. pp. 448.

— Social history.

ENGELBORGHS-BERTELS (MARTHE) La Chine rurale: des villages aux communes populaires. Bruxelles,[1974]. pp. 195. *bibliog.*

— Social life and customs.

HSÜ-BALZER (EILEEN) and others. China day by day. New Haven, 1974. pp. 111.

— Social policy.

ASCHER (ISAAC) China's social policy. London, 1972. pp. 59. *(Anglo-Chinese Educational Institute. Modern China Series. No. 3)*

KUITENBROUWER (JOOST B.W.) Growth and equality in India and China: processes, policies and theory formation. The Hague, 1973. pp. 61. *(Hague. Institute of Social Studies. Occasional Papers. No. 39)*

CHINESE IN AUSTRALASIA.

PRICE (CHARLES ARCHIBALD) The great white walls are built: restrictive immigration to North America and Australasia, 1836-1888. Canberra, 1974. pp. 323. *bibliog.*

CHINESE IN NORTH AMERICA.

PRICE (CHARLES ARCHIBALD) The great white walls are built: restrictive immigration to North America and Australasia, 1836-1888. Canberra, 1974. pp. 323. *bibliog.*

CHINESE IN THE UNITED STATES

— Bibliography.

McCUTCHEON (JAMES M.) compiler. China and America: a bibliography of interactions, foreign and domestic. Honolulu, [1972]. pp. 75. *(Hawaii University. East-West Bibliographic Series. 1)*

CHINESE LANGUAGE

— Dictionaries — English.

DOOLIN DENNIS J.) and RIDLEY (CHARLES PRICE) A Chinese-English dictionary of communist Chinese terminology. Stanford, [1973]. pp. 569. *(Stanford University. Hoover Institution on War, Revolution and Peace. Hoover Institution Publications. 124)*

CHINESE LITERATURE.

HUANG (JOE C.) Heroes and villains in communist China: the contemporary Chinese novel as a reflection of life. London, [1973]. pp. 345. *bibliog.*

CHINESE REVOLUTIONARY PARTY.

FRIEDMAN (EDWARD) Backward toward revolution: the Chinese Revolutionary Party. Berkeley, [1974]. pp. 237. *(Michigan University. Center for Chinese Studies. Michigan Studies on China)*

CHOICE (PSYCHOLOGY).

SEN (AMARTYA KUMAR) Behaviour and the concept of preference: (an inaugural lecture). London, [1973]. pp. 23.

CHOICE OF TRANSPORTATION

MANHEIM (MARVIN L.) and others. Search and choice in transport systems planning: summary report. Cambridge, Mass., 1968. pp. 342. *(Massachusetts Institute of Technology. Transportation Systems Division. Search and Choice in Transport Systems Planning. vol. 1)*

— Mathematical models.

WEDDEPOHL (H.N.) An application of game theory to a problem of choice between private and public transport. Tilburg, 1973. pp. 24. *bibliog. (Tilburg. Katholieke Hogeschool. Tilburg Institute of Economics. Research Memoranda. EIT 43)*

WATSON (PETER L.) The value of time: behavioral models of modal choice. Lexington, Mass., [1974]. pp. 170. *bibliog.*

CHOLERA.

SERAO (MATILDE) Il ventre di Napoli; [reprint of work originally published in 1905] con introduzione di Gianni Infusino. [Naples, 1973]. pp. 125.

CHRISTIAN ETHICS

— Comparative studies.

GRENHOLM (CARL HENRIC) Christian social ethics in a revolutionary age: an analysis of the social ethics of John C. Bennett, Heinz-Dietrich Wendland and Richard Shaull. Uppsala, 1973. pp. 351. *bibliog.*

CHRISTIAN SCIENCE

— United States.

GOTTSCHALK (STEPHEN) The emergence of Christian Science in American religious life. Berkeley, Ca., [1973]. pp. 305.

CHRISTIANITY.

GUINNESS (OS) The dust of death:... a critique of the establishment and the counter culture, and a proposal for a third way. London, 1973. pp. 416.

— Dictionaries and encyclopaedias.

CROSS (FRANK LESLIE) and LIVINGSTONE (ELIZABETH A.) eds. The Oxford dictionary of the Christian Church. 2nd ed. London, 1974. pp. 1518. *bibliogs.*

CHRISTIANITY AND ECONOMICS.

RYTZ (HANS RUDOLF) Geistliche des alten Bern zwischen Merkantilismus und Physiokratie: ein Beitrag zur Schweizer Sozialgeschichte des 18. Jahrhunderts. Basel, 1971. pp. 229. *bibliog.*

CROWLEY (J.E.) This Sheba, self: the conceptualization of economic life in eighteenth-century America. Baltimore, [1974]. pp. 161. *(Johns Hopkins University. Studies in Historical and Political Science. Series 92. No.2)*

CHRISTIANITY AND INTERNATIONAL AFFAIRS.

CAMARA (HELDER) Archbishop of Olinda and Recife. Structures of injustice: [speeches delivered during a visit to Germany and England in June 1972]. London, [1972?]. pp. 42.

CHRISTIANITY AND OTHER RELIGIONS.

HOLMES (ANN) Church, property and people: a study of the attitudes of churches to their property in three multi-racial, multi-faith areas: Bradford, Derby and Lambeth. London, 1973. pp. 57.

CHRISTIANITY AND POLITICS.

BOEHTLINGK (ARTHUR) Die römische Gefahr und die Reichstagswahl: eine politische Ansprache, Lörrach, 26.April 1903. Lörrach, 1903. pp. 27.

GHERARDI (GABRIELE) I cattolici cercano un partito. Bologna, [1967]. pp. 188.

TORRES RESTREPO (CAMILO) Obras escogidas. Montevideo, [1968]. pp. 256.

GIAMPICCOLI (FRANCO) Chiesa e tabù politico. Torino, 1971. pp. 87.

HOUTART (FRANÇOIS) and ROUSSEAU (ANDRE) L'église et les mouvements révolutionnaires: Vietnam, Amérique Latine, colonies portugaises. Bruxelles, [1972]. pp. 173. *bibliog.*

TORRES RESTREPO (CAMILO) Revolutionary writings; [edited with] introduction by Maurice Zeitlin; [amplified and revised version of the 1969 edition, published by Herder and Herder]. rev. ed. New York, 1972. pp. 371.

ÅBO. Akademi. Acta Academiae Aboensis. Humaniora. 45. 2. Religion och politik: studier i finländsk politisk idéevärld och politisk miljö vid 1900-talets början; av Heimer Lindström. Åbo, 1973. pp. 224. *bibliog.*

OLIVIER (BERNARD) Développement ou libération?: pour une théologie qui prend parti. Bruxelles, [1973]. pp. 181. *bibliog.*

POWELL (JOHN ENOCH) No easy answers. London, 1973 repr. 1974. pp. 135.

RICHARDSON (Sir ALAN) The political Christ. London, 1973. pp. 118.

GHEERBRANT (ALAIN) The rebel church in Latin America; translated by Rosemary Sheed. Harmondsworth, 1974. pp. 357.

CHRISTIANITY IN AFRICA.

SHORTER (AYLWARD) African culture and the Christian church: an introduction to social and pastoral anthropology. London, 1973. pp. 229. *bibliog.*

CHRISTIANS IN CHINA.

PATTERSON (GEORGE NEILSON) Christianity in communist China. Waco, Tex., [1969]. pp. 174.

CHRISTIANS IN IRELAND.

NEW ULSTER MOVEMENT. Publications. [No. 9]. Tribalism or Christianity in Ireland?. Belfast, [1973?]. 1 pamphlet (unpaged).

CHROMIUM ORES

— Rhodesia.

AMERICAN ASSOCIATION FOR THE UNITED NATIONS. Student and Young Adult Division. Rhodesian chrome. New York, 1973. pp. 96.

CHUBAR (VLAS IAKOVYCH).

CHUBAR (VLAS IAKOVYCH) Vybrani statti i promovy. Kyïv, 1972. pp. 628.

CHURCH AND ECONOMICS.

SMITH (GEORGE L.) Religion and trade in New Netherland: Dutch origins and American development. Ithaca, 1973. pp. 266. *bibliog.*

— Catholic Church.

PESCH (HEINRICH) Neubau der Gesellschaft. Freiburg im Breisgau, 1919. pp. 24. *(Stimmen der Zeit. Flugschriften. 1. Heft)*

HAURAND (PETER WILHELM) Das nationalökonomische System von Heinrich Pesch, S.J.; in seinen Grundzügen dargestellt. M. Gladbach, 1922. pp. 104. *bibliog.*

CHURCH AND LABOUR

ARBEITSKONFLIKTE und Arbeitskampf: Auswirkungen und Berechtigungen von Arbeitskonflikten; [papers of an international conference sponsored by the International Humanum Foundation]. Köln, [1973]. pp. 168. *(International Humanum Foundation. Gesellschaft, Kirche, Wirtschaft. Band 6)*

— America, Latin.

FLORIDI (ULISSE ALESSIO) and STIEFBOLD (ANNETTE E.) The uncertain alliance: the Catholic Church and labor in Latin America. Miami, 1973. pp. 108. *(Miami (Florida). University. Center for Advanced International Studies. Monographs in International Affairs)*

CHURCH AND RACE PROBLEMS

— South Africa.

SOUTH AFRICAN COUNCIL OF CHURCHES and CHRISTIAN INSTITUTE OF SOUTHERN AFRICA. Study Project on Christianity in Apartheid Society. Church Commission. Apartheid and the church;... report of the Church Commission...; (general editor Peter Randall). Johannesburg, 1972. pp. 92. *(Study Project on Christianity in Apartheid Society. Publications. No. 8)*

— United Kingdom.

HOLMES (ANN) Church, property and people: a study of the attitudes of churches to their property in three multi-racial, multi-faith areas: Bradford, Derby and Lambeth. London, 1973. pp. 57.

CHURCH AND SOCIAL PROBLEMS.

CAMARA (HELDER) Archbishop of Olinda and Recife. Structures of injustice: [speeches delivered during a visit to Germany and England in June 1972]. London, [1972?]. pp. 42.

POWELL (JOHN ENOCH) No easy answers. London, 1973 repr. 1974. pp. 135.

BIGO (PIERRE) L'eglise et la révolution du tiers monde. Paris, 1974. pp. 284.

— Catholic church.

PASTORE (GIULIO) La giustizia sociale e le zone sottosviluppate: conferenza al Convegno dell'UCID sulla "Mater et Magistra", Milano 18-11- 1961. Roma, [1962?]. pp. 26.

SEMAINE SOCIALE WALLONNE. 53me Semaine. Idéologies et action militante; ([by] P. Delooz [and others]). Bruxelles, [1972]. pp. 225.

McCORMACK (ARTHUR) The population explosion: a Christian concern. New York, 1973. pp. 78.

CHURCH AND SOCIAL PROBLEMS (Cont.)

— America, Latin — Catholic Church.

TORRES RESTREPO (CAMILO) Obras escogidas. Montevideo, [1968]. pp. 256.

IGLESIA latinoamericana: protesta o profecia?;... direccion, recopilacion e introduccion de cada documento, Juan Jose Rossi, etc. Avellaneda, 1969. pp. 462.

TORRES RESTREPO (CAMILO) Revolutionary writings; [edited with] introduction by Maurice Zeitlin; [amplified and revised version of the 1969 edition, published by Herder and Herder]. rev. ed. New York, 1972. pp. 371.

GHEERBRANT (ALAIN) The rebel church in Latin America; translated by Rosemary Sheed. Harmondsworth, 1974. pp. 357.

— Argentine Republic — Catholic Church.

POLEMICA en la iglesia: documentos de obispos argentinos y sacerdotes para el Tercer Mundo, 1969-1970. [Buenos Aires], 1970. pp. 125.

— Brazil — Catholic Church.

BRUNEAU (THOMAS C.) The political transformation of the Brazilian Catholic church. London, 1974. pp. 270. bibliog. (McGill University. Centre for Developing-Area Studies. Perspectives on Development. 2)

— Caribbean area.

McCORMACK (MICHAEL) Liberation or development: the role of the church in the new Caribbean. Bridgetown, [1971]. pp. 24. (Caribbean Ecumenical Consultation for Development. Study Papers. No. 5)

— Denmark.

DENMARK. Kirkeministeriet. Strukturkommission. 1971. Betaenkning om folkekirken i det moderne samfund. København, 1971. 2 vols. (Denmark. Betaenkninger. Nr. 610)

— Italy — Catholic Church.

TRAMONTIN (SILVIO) Carità o giustizia?: idee ed esperienze dei cattolici sociali italiani dell'800. [Turin, 1973]. pp. 157. bibliog.

— South Africa.

The ROLE of the church in socio-economic development in Southern Africa: a consultation held in Umpumulo (Natal); organized by Missiological Institute, Umpumulo [and] the Christian Academy in Southern Africa. [Umpumulo?, 1971?]. pp. 191.

— United Kingdom.

SHEPPARD (DAVID STUART) Bishop of Woolwich. Built as a city: God and the urban world today. London, 1974. pp. 380.

— United States — Catholic Church.

MILLER (WILLIAM D.) A harsh and dreadful love: Dorothy Day and the Catholic Worker movement. London, [1973]. pp. 370. bibliog.

CHURCH AND STATE

ZIEGLER (ADOLF WILHELM) Religion, Kirche und Staat in Geschichte und Gegenwart: (ein Handbuch). München, 1969-74. 3 vols. bibliogs.

— Catholic Church.

SACHERI (CARLOS A.) La iglesia clandestina. Buenos Aires, 1970. pp. 182.

SMALLEY (BERYL) The Becket conflict and the schools: a study of intellectuals in politics. Oxford, 1973. pp. 258.

RUFFINI (FRANCESCO) Relazioni tra Stato e Chiesa: lineamenti storici e sistematici; a cura di F. Margiotta Broglio. Bologna, [1974]. pp. 313. (Florence. Università degli Studi di Firenze. Seminario di Storia delle Istituzioni Religiose e Relazioni fra Stato e Chiesa. Religione e Società. 1)

CHURCH AND STATE IN BRAZIL.

BRUNEAU (THOMAS C.) The political transformation of the Brazilian Catholic church. London, 1974. pp. 270. bibliog. (McGill University. Centre for Developing-Area Studies. Perspectives on Development. 2)

CHURCH AND STATE IN COMMUNIST COUNTRIES.

BARBERINI (GIOVANNI) Stati socialisti e confessioni religiose. Milano, 1973. pp. 537. (Perugia. Università. Istituto di Diritto Pubblico. Pubblicazioni. 3)

CHURCH AND STATE IN FRANCE.

LAPERRIERE (GUY) La "Séparation" à Lyon, 1904-1908: étude d'opinion publique. Lyon, 1973. pp. 220. bibliog. (Centre d'Histoire du Catholicisme. Collection. No. 9)

LARKIN (MAURICE) Church and state after the Dreyfus affair: the separation issue in France. London, 1974. pp. 294. bibliog.

CHURCH AND STATE IN IRELAND.

MILLER (DAVID WILLIAM) Church, state and nation in Ireland 1898-1921. Dublin, 1973. pp. 579. bibliog.

CHURCH AND STATE IN ITALY.

RUFFINI (FRANCESCO) Relazioni tra Stato e Chiesa: lineamenti storici e sistematici; a cura di F. Margiotta Broglio. Bologna, [1974]. pp. 313. (Florence. Università degli Studi di Firenze. Seminario di Storia delle Istituzioni Religiose e Relazioni fra Stato e Chiesa. Religione e Società. 1)

TREXLER (RICHARD C.) The spiritual power: republican Florence under interdict. Leiden, 1974. pp. 208. bibliog.

CHURCH AND STATE IN LATIN AMERICA.

IGLESIA latinoamericana: protesta o profecia?;... direccion, recopilacion e introduccion de cada documento, Juan Jose Rossi, etc. Avellaneda, 1969. pp. 462.

CHURCH AND STATE IN MALTA.

SMITH (HARRISON) Mussolini and Strickland. Malta, 1974. pp. 42. (Reprinted from Scientia, vol. 36, 1973)

CHURCH AND STATE IN MEXICO.

QUIRK (ROBERT EMMETT) The Mexican revolution and the Catholic Church 1910-1929. Bloomington, Ind., [1973]. pp. 276.

BAILEY (DAVID C.) Viva Cristo Rey!: the Cristero rebellion and the church- state conflict in Mexico. Austin, [1974]. pp. 346. bibliog.

CHURCH AND STATE IN RUSSIA.

KAHLE (WILHELM) Geschichte der evangelisch-lutherischen Gemeinden in der Sovetunion, 1917-1938. Leiden, 1974. pp. 625. bibliog.

SIMON (GERHARD) Church, state and opposition in the U.S.S.R.; translated by Kathleen Matchett, etc. London, [1974]. pp. 248. bibliog.

CHURCH AND STATE IN SARDINIA.

CORRIAS CORONA (MARIA) Stato e chiesa nelle valutazioni dei politici sardi, 1848-1853. Milano, [1972]. pp. 202. (Cagliari. Università. Seminario di Scienze Politiche. Quaderni. Serie dell' Istituto di Filosofia Politica e Giuridica)

CHURCH AND STATE IN THE ARGENTINE REPUBLIC.

MAYOL (ALEJANDRO) and others. Los catolicos posconciliares en la Argentina, 1963-1969. Buenos Aires, 1970. pp. 414.

CHURCH AND STATE IN THE UNITED KINGDOM.

SMALLEY (BERYL) The Becket conflict and the schools: a study of intellectuals in politics. Oxford, 1973. pp. 258.

CHURCH AND STATE IN TONGA.

LATUKEFU (SIONE) Church and state in Tonga: the Wesleyan Methodist missionaries and political development, 1822-1875. Canberra, 1974. pp. 302. bibliog.

CHURCH AND STATE IN ZAIRE.

CENTRE DE RECHERCHE ET D'INFORMATION SOCIO-POLITIQUES. Etudes Africaines du CRISP. Les relations entre l'église et l'état au Zaire. Bruxelles, 1972. fo. 72.

CHURCH AND UNDERDEVELOPED AREAS.

HUERNI (BETTINA S.) Der Beitrag des Ökumenischen Rates der Kirchen zur Entwicklungshilfe. Bern, [1973]. pp. 360. bibliog. With English summary.

CHURCH HISTORY.

BROOKE (CHRISTOPHER NUGENT LAWRENCE) Medieval church and society: collected essays. London, 1971. pp. 256.

CHURCH PROPERTY

— United Kingdom.

HOLMES (ANN) Church, property and people: a study of the attitudes of churches to their property in three multi-racial, multi-faith areas: Bradford, Derby and Lambeth. London, 1973. pp. 57.

CHURCH SCHOOLS

— Australia.

ALBINSKI (HENRY STEPHEN) The Australian Labor Party and the aid to parochial schools controversy. University Park, Penn., 1966. pp. 55. (Pennsylvania State University. Penn State Studies. No. 19)

KNIGHT (PATRICIA) The case against church schools. London, [1974]. pp. 17.

CHURCHILL (Sir WINSTON LEONARD SPENCER).

BOADLE (DONALD GRAEME) Winston Churchill and the German question in British foreign policy, 1918-1922. The Hague, 1973. pp. 193. bibliog.

KAVANAGH (DENNIS A.) Crisis, charisma and British political leadership: Winston Churchill as the outsider. London, [1974]. pp. 42. bibliog.

PELLING (HENRY MATHISON) Winston Churchill. London, 1974. pp. 724. bibliog.

CHUVASH REPUBLIC

— Bibliography.

KAGAN (A.S.) and others, compilers. Chuvashskaia ASSR: ukazatel' literatury. Cheboksary, 1969. pp. 143.

CINEMAS

— Statistics.

SOUTH AFRICA. Bureau of Statistics. 1969. Census of cinemas, café-bioscopes and drive-in theatres, 1964-65. Pretoria, [1969]. pp. 31. (Reports. No. 04-51-01) In English and Afrikaans.

SOUTH AFRICA. Bureau of Statistics. 1973. Census of cinemas, café-bioscopes and drive-in theatres, 1969-70. Pretoria, [1973]. pp. 42. (Reports. No. 04-51-02) In English and Afrikaans.

— Guatemala — Employees.

GUATEMALA. Comision Nacional del Salario. 1966. Monografia para la determinacion del salario minimo en la industria de teatros y cines. Guatemala, 1966. pp. 51.

CISKEIAN TERRITORIAL AUTHORITY
— Politics and government.

CISKEI. Legislative Assembly. Debates. sess., 1973 (2nd Assembly, 1st session)- King William's Town. *In English or Afrikaans.*

CITATION INDEXES.

UNIVERSITY OF BATH. Library. Design of Information Systems in the Social Sciences. Working Papers. No. 5. Citation patterns in the social sciences: results of pilot citation study and selection of source journals for main citation study. [Bath], 1972. 1 vol. (various pagings).

CITIES AND TOWNS.

LEFEBVRE (HENRI) Espace et politique: le droit à la ville. 2. Paris, [1972]. pp. 175.

BARNETT (J. ROSS) and MERCER (JOHN) Urban political analysis and new directions in political geography. Iowa City, 1973. fo. 21. *bibliog. (Iowa University. Department of Geography. Discussion Paper Series. No. 22)*

CASTELLS (MANUEL) Luttes urbaines et pouvoir politique. Paris, 1973. pp. 135.

DAVIS (KINGSLEY) Cities and mortality; [reprint of a paper delivered at the International Population Conference, Liege, 1973]. Berkeley, Ca., [1973]. pp. 22. *(California University. Institute of International Studies. Population Reprint Series. No. 433) With French summary.*

FALUDI (ANDREAS K.F.) Planning theory. Oxford, 1973. pp. 306. *bibliogs.*

GERMANI (GINO) ed. Modernization, urbanization and the urban crisis. Boston, [1973]. pp. 275.

STONE (PETER ALBERT) The structure, size and costs of urban settlements. Cambridge, 1973. pp. 280. *bibliog. (National Institute of Economic and Social Research. Economic and Social Studies. 28)*

The UNKNOWN urban realm: methodology and results of a content analysis of the papers presented at the congress Citizen and city in the year 2000; by Ulrich Neveling [and others]. The Hague, 1973. pp. 188. *(European Cultural Foundation. Plan Europe 2000. Project 3. vol. 2)*

HICKS (URSULA KATHLEEN) The large city: a world problem. London, 1974. pp. 270.

POLSKA AKADEMIA NAUK. Instytut Geografii. Geographia Polonica. 28. [Papers on physical and economic geography]. Warszawa, 1974. pp. 144. *bibliogs.*

URBAN ethnicity: [papers presented at the annual conference of the Association of Social Anthropologists of the Commonwealth, held in London in 1971]; edited by Abner Cohen. London, 1974. pp. 391. *bibliogs. (Association of Social Anthropologists of the Commonwealth. A.S.A. Monographs. 12)*

— Growth.

HOYT (HOMER) According to Hoyt: 53 years of Homer Hoyt: articles on law, real estate cycle, economic base, sector theory, shopping centers, urban growth, 1916-1969. [2nd ed.] [Washington, 1970?]. pp. 855. *bibliog.*

UNITED NATIONS. Department of Economic and Social Affairs. Population Studies. No.44. Growth of the world's urban and rural population, 1920-2000. (ST/SOA/SER.A/44) New York, 1969. pp. 124.

URBANIZATSIIA, nauchno-tekhnicheskaia revoliutsiia i rabochii klass: nekotorye voprosy teorii, kritika burzhuaznykh kontseptsii; Urbanization, scientific and technological revolution, and working class: theory - some aspects, bourgeois conceptions: critical survey. Moskva, 1972. pp. 268. *With English table of contents.*

BUSSEY (ELLEN M.) The flight from rural poverty: how nations cope. Lexington, Mass., [1973]. pp. 132.

CALOIA (ANGELO) Forme e dimensioni urbane nel processo di crescita economica. Milano, 1973. pp. 232.

PRED (ALLAN R.) and TÖRNQVIST (GUNNAR) Systems of cities and information flows: two essays. Lund, 1973. pp. 121. *bibliogs. (Lund. Universitet. Geografiska Institution. Lund Studies in Geography. Series B. Human Geography. No. 38)*

RICHARDSON (HARRY W.) The economics of urban size. Farnborough, Hants., [1973]. pp. 243. *bibliog.*

ROBSON (BRIAN T.) Urban growth: an approach. London, 1973. pp. 268. *bibliog.*

JOHNSON (JAMES HENRY) ed. Suburban growth: geographical processes at the edge of the western city. London, [1974]. pp. 257. *bibliogs.*

— — Mathematical models.

CONSTABLE DEREK) Urban growth processes: a critical assessment of the Forrester model. Reading, 1973. pp. 49. *bibliog. (Reading. University. Department of Geography. Reading Geographical Papers. No. 2)*

— Information storage and retrieval systems.

See INFORMATION STORAGE AND RETRIEVAL SYSTEMS — Cities and towns.

— Planning.

HOYT (HOMER) According to Hoyt: 53 years of Homer Hoyt: articles on law, real estate cycle, economic base, sector theory, shopping centers, urban growth, 1916-1969. [2nd ed.] [Washington, 1970?]. pp. 855. *bibliog.*

BRUTON (MICHAEL J.) An introduction to factor analysis and its application in planning. Oxford, 1971. pp. 123. *(Oxford Polytechnic. Department of Town Planning. Oxford Working Papers in Planning Education and Research. 8)*

SWEDEN. Statens Råd för Byggnadsforskning. 1971. Urban and regional research in Sweden; etc. Stockholm, 1971. pp. 145. *(Sweden. Statens Institut för Byggnadsforskning. Documents. 1971. 4) In English, French and Russian.*

BREWER (GARRY D.) Accommodating increased demands for public participation in urban renewal decisionmaking. [Santa Monica], 1972. pp. 5. *(Rand Corporation. [Papers]. 4868)*

FAIR (T.J.D.) The metropolitan imperative: inaugural lecture...delivered 27 October 1971 [at the University of Witwatersrand]. Johannesburg, 1972. pp. 24. *bibliog.*

KOLL (MICHAEL) ed. African urban development: four political approaches; by Treufried Grau [and others]. Düsseldorf, [1972]. pp. 215. *(Arnold-Bergstraesser-Institut für Kulturwissenschaftliche Forschung. Materialien. Band 31)*

EDINBURGH. University. Department of Urban Design and Regional Planning. Planning Research Unit. Threshold analysis manual; prepared...for the Scottish Development Department. Edinburgh, H.M.S.O., 1973. pp. 201. *bibliog.*

GRUEN (VICTOR) Centers for the urban environment: survival of the cities. New York, [1973]. pp. 266.

KOZŁOWSKI (JERZY) Analiza progowa za granicą: próba oceny i rozwinięcia. Warszawa, 1973. pp. 123. *bibliog. (Polska Akademia Nauk. Komitet Przestrzennego Zagospodarowania Kraju. Studia. t. 42) With Russian and English summaries.*

MANN (ROY) Rivers in the city. New York, 1973. pp. 256.

BRUTON (MICHAEL J.) ed. The spirit and purpose of planning. London, 1974. pp. 233.

RATCLIFFE (JOHN) An introduction to town and country planning. London, 1974. pp. 378. *bibliogs.*

ROBERTS (MARGARET) Town planner. An introduction to town planning techniques. London, 1974. pp. 406. *bibliog.*

SIMMIE (JAMES MARTIN) Citizens in conflict: the sociology of town planning. London, 1974. pp. 235.

UNITED NATIONS. Centre for Housing, Building and Planning. 1974. Human settlements: the environmental challenge; a compendium of United Nations papers prepared for the Stockholm Conference on the Human Environment 1972. London, 1974. pp. 209.

— — Bibliography.

SWEDEN. Statens Institut för Byggnadsforskning. 1969. Social aspects of housing and urban development: a bibliography; compiled and published in agreement with the United Nations Centre for Housing, Building and Planning; Department of Economic and Social Affairs, New York. Stockholm, 1969. pp. 173. *(Documents. 1969.3)*

U.K. Department of the Environment. Library. 1971. Participation in planning. [London, 1971]. fo. 7. *(Bibliographies. No. 151)*

U.K. Department of the Environment. Library. 1973. New towns. [London], 1973. 1 vol. (various pagings). *(Bibliography Series. No. 65)*

— — Mathematical models.

HOUSE (PETER W.) The urban environmental system: modeling for research, policy- making and education. Beverly Hills, [1973]. pp. 316. *bibliog.*

REIF (BENJAMIN) Models in urban and regional planning. Aylesbury, 1973. pp. 246. *bibliog.*

PATTERNS of urban change: the New Haven experience; [by] David Birch [and others]. Lexington, [1974]. pp. 161. *bibliogs.*

WILSON (ALAN GEOFFREY) Urban and regional models in geography and planning. London, [1974]. pp. 418. *bibliogs.*

— — Research.

SWEDEN. Statens Råd för Byggnadsforskning. 1971. Urban and regional research in Sweden; etc. Stockholm, 1971. pp. 145. *(Sweden. Statens Institut för Byggnadsforskning. Documents. 1971. 4) In English, French and Russian.*

FORBES (JEAN) ed. Studies in social science and planning. Edinburgh, 1974. pp. 321. *bibliogs.*

— — Study and teaching.

CUDDY (MICHAEL) Perspectives in the design and evaluation of educational projects. [Oxford], 1973. pp. 46. *(Oxford Polytechnic. Department of Town Planning. Oxford Working Papers in Planning Education and Research. 16)*

— — — Europe.

BERNSTEIN (BEVERLY) A survey of European programmes: education for urbanization in developing countries. [New York, 1972?]. pp. 114. *bibliog. (Ford Foundation. International Urbanization Survey. Working Papers. 288)*

— Africa — Planning.

URBANIZATION, national development, and regional planning in Africa: [papers of an interdisciplinary panel presented as part of the African Studies Association's fifteenth annual meeting, 1972]; (edited by Salah El-Shakhs [and] Robert Obudho). New York, 1974. pp. 227. *bibliog.*

— Africa, Subsaharan — Growth.

ROSSER (COLIN) Urbanization in tropical Africa: a demographic introduction. [New York, 1972?]. pp. 74. *(Ford Foundation. International Urbanization Survey. Working Papers. 272)*

LITTLE (KENNETH LINDSAY) Urbanization as a social process: an essay on movement and change in contemporary Africa. London, 1974. pp. 153. *bibliog.*

— — Planning.

KOLL (MICHAEL) ed. African urban development: four political approaches; by Treufried Grau [and others]. Düsseldorf, [1972]. pp. 215. *(Arnold-Bergstraesser-Institut für Kulturwissenschaftliche Forschung. Materialien. Band 31)*

CITIES AND TOWNS (Cont.)

— America, Latin.

CINQ aspects de sociétés latino-américaines; [by Carlos M. Rama and others]. Paris, [1965]. pp. 151. (Paris. Université. Institut des Hautes Etudes de l'Amérique Latine. Cahiers. No. 7)

LATIN American urban research; [series editors] Francine F. Rabinovitz and Felicity M. Trueblood. Beverly Hills, [1971 in progress]. bibliogs.

— — Growth.

VILLES et régions en Amerique latine. Paris, 1970. pp. 120. (Paris. Université. Institut des Hautes Etudes de l'Amérique Latine. Laboratoire Associé 3. Recherche Coopérative sur Programme 147. Cahiers No. 1)

MORSE (RICHARD McGEE) ed. The urban development of Latin America, 1750-1920: [based on a graduate seminar on Latin American urban history at Stanford University 1971]. Stanford, 1971. pp. 129. bibliogs.

STATISTICAL ABSTRACT OF LATIN AMERICA. Supplement Series. 4. Urbanization in 19th century Latin America: statistics and sources; [by] Richard E. Boyer and Keith A. Davies. Los Angeles, 1973. pp. 82. bibliogs.

— — Statistics.

STATISTICAL ABSTRACT OF LATIN AMERICA. Supplement Series. 4. Urbanization in 19th century Latin America: statistics and sources; [by] Richard E. Boyer and Keith A. Davies. Los Angeles, 1973. pp. 82. bibliogs.

— Asia — Growth.

POPULATION, politics, and the future of southern Asia; [papers presented at a conference convened by the Southern Asian Institute of Columbia University, 1971]; edited by W. Howard Wriggins and James F. Guyot. New York, 1973. pp. 402.

— Australia — Growth.

BURNLEY (I.H.) ed. Urbanization in Australia: the post-war experience. Cambridge, 1974. pp. 248.

— Belgium — Planning.

BILLET (M.) and VALVEKENS-HAVEN (S.) Samenlevingsopbouw: critische situatieschets in Nederland en Vlaanderen; onder leiding van F. van Mechelen. Leuven, 1972. pp. 260. bibliog. (Katholieke Universiteit te Leuven. Sociologisch Onderzoeksinstituut. Studiegroep voor Kultuurbevordering. [Publications]. 14)

— Brazil — Growth.

GARDNER (JAMES A.) Urbanization in Brazil. [New York, 1972?]. pp. 198. (Ford Foundation. International Urbanization Survey. Working Papers. 280)

— — Planning.

GARDNER (JAMES A.) Urbanization in Brazil. [New York, 1972?]. pp. 198. (Ford Foundation. International Urbanization Survey. Working Papers. 280)

— Canada.

CANADA. Ministry of State for Urban Affairs. Annual report. a., 1972/3 (2nd)- Ottawa.

POWELL (ALAN) ed. The city: attacking modern myths; edited...for the University League for Social Reform. Toronto, [1972]. pp. 263.

— — Growth.

URBAN futures for central Canada: perspectives on forecasting urban growth and form; edited by Larry S. Bourne [and others]. Toronto, [1974]. pp. 368. bibliogs.

— — Planning.

RESEARCH GROUP FOR EUROPEAN MIGRATION PROBLEMS. Publications. 18. Immigrant integration and urban renewal in Toronto; by Brigitte Neumann [and others]. The Hague, 1973. pp. 101. bibliog.

SCHWILGIN (F.A.) Town planning guidelines. Ottawa, Information Canada, 1973. pp. 168. bibliog.

— Chile — Planning.

ROBIN (JOHN P.) and TERZO (FREDERICK C.) Urbanization in Chile. [New York, 1972?]. pp. 57. (Ford Foundation. International Urbanization Survey. Working Papers. 284)

— Colombia — Planning.

ROBIN (JOHN P.) and TERZO (FREDERICK C.) Urbanization in Colombia. [New York, 1972?]. pp. 100. (Ford Foundation. International Urbanization Survey. Working Papers. 281)

HEALEY (PATSY) Urban planning under conditions of rapid urban growth: a case study approach; [Ph.D. (London) thesis]. 1973. fo. 406. bibliog. Typescript: unpublished. This thesis is the property of London University and may not be removed from the Library.

— Cuba — Planning.

ACOSTA (MARUJA) and HARDOY (JORGE) Urban reform in revolutionary Cuba;... translated by Mal Bochner. New Haven, Conn., [1973]. pp. 111. bibliog. (Yale University. Antilles Research Program. Occasional Papers.1)

— Europe.

UNITED NATIONS. Department of Economic and Social Affairs. European Social Development Programme. Reports . New York, 1967 in progress.

— Europe, Eastern — Planning.

STVÁN (JAROMÍR) Physical, socio-economic and environmental planning in countries of Eastern Europe: their interaction at the city and city sub-area levels. Stockholm, 1973. pp. 80. (Sweden. Statens Institut för Byggnadsforskning. Documents. 1973.4)

— France.

CHARRE (J.G.) and COYAUD (L.M.) Les villes françaises: étude des villes et agglomérations de plus de 5,000 habitants. [Paris, 1969 in progress].

GILLIE (F.B.) Comparative comments on small towns in Ireland, Norway and France. The Hague, 1973. pp. 109. (Hague. Institute of Social Studies. Occasional Papers. No. 28)

INSTITUT DE DEVELOPPEMENT DES RECHERCHES APPLIQUEES EN SCIENCES SOCIALES. Schéma général d'aménagement de la France. Paris, 1973. pp. 176. bibliog. (France. Délégation à l'Aménagement du Territoire et à l'Action Régionale. Travaux et Recherches de Prospective. 43)

JEANSON (FRANCIS) L'action culturelle dans la cité. Paris, [1973]. pp. 253.

— — Growth.

L'ANALYSE interdisciplinaire de la croissance urbaine: ([proceedings of a symposium held at the] Centre interdisciplinaire d'Etudes urbaines de l'Université de Toulouse [in 1971]). Paris, 1972. pp. 387. (Centre National de la Recherche Scientifique. Colloques Nationaux. No. 931)

PRETECEILLE (EDMOND) La production des grands ensembles. Paris, [1973]. pp. 170. bibliog.

— — Planning.

L'INFORMATION, l'éducation et la participation des citoyens dans le processus de développement urbain, sous la direction de P. Bolle. [Paris], Ministère de l'Equipement et du Logement, 1968. pp. 244.

BIAREZ (SYLVIE) Une politique d'urbanisme: les Z[ones à] U[rbaniser par] P[riorité]. [Grenoble, 1973]. pp. 297. bibliog.

BROUILLET (ALAIN) Le droit d'amendement dans la constitution de la Ve République: étude pratique de son utilisation pour l'élaboration de la loi d'orientation foncière. Paris, 1973. pp. 159. bibliog. (Paris. Université de Paris I (Panthéon- Sorbonne). Publications. Série Science Politique. 3)

— Germany.

PEHNT (WOLFGANG) ed. Die Stadt in der Bundesrepublik Deutschland: Lebensbedingungen, Aufgaben, Planung. Stuttgart, [1974]. pp. 506. bibliog.

— Goa, Daman and Diu — Statistics.

GOA, DAMAN AND DIU. Bureau of Economics, Statistics and Evaluation. Statistics of municipal towns and cities. a., 1970-71/1971-2[1st]- Panaji.

— India.

MOOKHERJEE (DEBNATH) and MORRILL (RICHARD L.) Urbanization in a developing economy: Indian perspectives and patterns. Beverly Hills, [1973]. pp. 75. bibliog.

BHARDWAJ (R.K.) Urban development in India. Delhi, 1974. pp. 456. bibliog.

— — Planning.

INDIA. Working Group on Housing and Urban Development in the Third Five Year Plan. 1960. Report. [Delhi], 1960. pp. 241.

ROSSER (COLIN) Urbanization in India. [New York, 1972?]. pp. 106. (Ford Foundation. International Urbanization Survey. Working Papers. 278)

RAHEJA (BHAGWAN DASS) Urban India and public policy. Bombay, [1973]. pp. 323. bibliog.

— Ireland (Republic).

GILLIE (F.B.) Comparative comments on small towns in Ireland, Norway and France. The Hague, 1973. pp. 109. (Hague. Institute of Social Studies. Occasional Papers. No. 28)

— Ivory Coast.

COHEN (MICHAEL A.) Urban policy and political conflict in Africa: a study of the Ivory Coast. Chicago, [1974]. pp. 262. bibliog.

— Jamaica — Growth.

TROWBRIDGE (JAMES W.) Urbanization in Jamaica. [New York, 1972?]. pp. 30. bibliog. (Ford Foundation. International Urbanization Survey. Working Papers. 279)

— — Planning.

TROWBRIDGE (JAMES W.) Urbanization in Jamaica. [New York, 1972?]. pp. 30. bibliog. (Ford Foundation. International Urbanization Survey. Working Papers. 279)

— Japan — Growth.

WHITE (JAMES W.) Political implications of cityward migration: Japan as an exploratory test case. Beverly Hills, [1973]. pp. 59. bibliog.

— Kenya — Growth.

LAURENTI (LUIGI) and GERHART (JOHN) Urbanization in Kenya: urbanization trends and prospects; by Luigi Laurenti; Rural development and urban growth; by John Gerhart. [New York, 1972?]. pp. 45,19. bibliog. (Ford Foundation. International Urbanization Survey. Working Papers. 274)

— Mexico — Planning.

MERINO MAÑON (JOSE) La fiscalidad del suelo y el desarrollo urbano. Toluca, Direccion General de Hacienda del Estado de Mexico, 1972. pp. 110. (Coleccion Estudios Fiscales. 4)

— Morocco — Planning.

JOHNSON (KATHERINE MARSHALL) Urbanization in Morocco. [New York, 1972?]. pp. 135. (Ford Foundation. International Urbanization Survey. Working Papers. 276)

CITIES AND TOWNS (Cont.)

— Netherlands — Planning.

NEDERLANDS INSTITUUT VOOR RUIMTELIJKE ORDENING EN VOLKSHUISVESTING and VERENIGING VAN NEDERLANDSE GEMEENTEN. Werkgroep. Projectontwikkeling: een analyse van verschillende aspecten van de samenwerking tussen gemeente en projectonwikkelingsmaatschappij; rapport, etc. Alphen aan den Rijn, 1971. pp. 84. (*Nederlands Instituut voor Ruimtelijke Ordening en Volkshuisvesting. Publikaties. Nr. 78*)

BILLET (M.) and VALVEKENS-HAVEN (S.) Samenlevingsopbouw: critische situatieschets in Nederland en Vlaanderen; onder leiding van F. van Mechelen. Leuven, 1972. pp. 260. *bibliog. (Katholieke Universiteit te Leuven. Sociologisch Onderzoeksinstituut. Studiegroep voor Kultuurbevordering. [Publications]. 14)*

NETHERLANDS. Commissie ter Bestudering van de Financiële Consequenties van Sanering en Stadsreconstructies. 1972. Stadsvernieuwing: eerste rapport van de Commissie. 's-Gravenhage, 1972. pp. 136.

— Nigeria.

LLOYD (PETER CUTT) Power and independence: urban Africans' perception of social inequality. London, 1974. pp. 248. *bibliog.*

GREEN (LESLIE) and MILONE (VINCENT) Urbanization in Nigeria: a planning commentary. [New York, 1972?]. pp. 44. *(Ford Foundation. International Urbanization Survey. Working Papers. 273)*

— Norway.

GILLIE (F.B.) Comparative comments on small towns in Ireland, Norway and France. The Hague, 1973. pp. 109. *(Hague. Institute of Social Studies. Occasional Papers. No. 28)*

JOHNSEN (YNGVAR) Survey of Norwegian planning legislation and organization. [Oslo, Kommunal- og arbeidsdepartementet, 1970]. pp. 34.

— Peru.

PERU. Direccion de Comunidades Campesinas. 1971. Datos basicos e inventario del patrimonio comunal de las comunidades de la provincia de Andahuaylas. [Lima, 1971]. pp. 59. *(Zac-Andahuaylas. No.2)*

ROBIN (JOHN P.) and TERZO (FREDERICK C.) Urbanization in Peru. [New York, 1972?]. pp. 64. *(Ford Foundation. International Urbanization Survey. Working Papers. 283)*

— Poland — Growth.

POLSKA AKADEMIA NAUK. Instytut Geografii. Geographia Polonica. 27. (Contemporary urbanization processes: proceedings of the first Polish-Soviet Geographical Seminar, Szymbark, Poland. May-June, 1971). Warszawa, 1973. pp. 189, and map. *bibliogs.*

— Puerto Rico — Planning.

PUERTO RICO. Puerto Rico Planning Board. 1970. Politica sobre uso de terrenos: informe para discusion. [San Juan?], 1970. pp. 94. *2 charts in end pocket.*

— Rhodesia — Planning.

RHODESIA. Town Planning Department. Annual report of the Chief Town Planning Officer. a., 1973- Salisbury.

— Russia.

HARRIS (CHAUNCY DENNISON) Cities of the Soviet Union: studies in their functions, size, density, and growth. Chicago, [1970]. pp. 484. *bibliog. (Association of American Geographers. Monograph Series. 5)*

SEMIN (SERGEI IVANOVICH) Preodolenie sotsial'no-ekonomicheskikh razlichii mezhdu gorodom i derevnei. Moskva, 1973. pp. 159.

TRUFANOV (IVAN PAVLOVICH) Problemy byta gorodskogo naseleniia SSSR; otv. redaktor...V.A. Ezhov. Leningrad, 1973. pp. 144.

— — Growth.

POLSKA AKADEMIA NAUK. Instytut Geografii. Geographia Polonica. 27. (Contemporary urbanization processes: proceedings of the first Polish-Soviet Geographical Seminar, Szymbark, Poland. May-June, 1971). Warszawa, 1973. pp. 189, and map. *bibliogs.*

— — Planning.

KRUGLIAKOV (IULII GDAL'EVICH) Kompleksnaia rekonstruktsiia zhilykh kvartalov staroi zastroiki: opyt Leningrada. Leningrad, 1971. pp. 89.

KRAVCHUK (IAKOV TERENT'EVICH) Formirovanie novykh gorodov. Moskva, 1973. pp. 112.

MASHINSKII (L.O.) Gorod i priroda: gorodskie zelenye nasazhdeniia. Moskva, 1973. pp. 228. *bibliog.*

PASHCHENKO (N.E.) and SEGEDINOV (A.A.) Ekonomika gradostroitel'stva: na moskovskom opyte. Moskva, 1973. pp. 264.

— — Kazakstan — Planning.

GRADOSTROITEL'STVO Kazakhstana. Alma-Ata, 1973. pp. 78,[ci].

— — Soviet North — Planning.

NAZAROVA (LARISA GRIGOR'EVNA) and POLUEKTOV (VLADIMIR EVGEN'EVICH) Opyt proektirovaniia i stroitel'stva gorodov Krainego Severa: na primere Noril'ska. Moskva, 1973. pp. 176. *bibliog.*

— Singapore — Planning.

YEUNG (YUE-MAN) National development policy and urban transformation in Singapore: a study of public housing and the marketing system. Chicago, 1973. pp. 204. *bibliog. (Chicago. University. Department of Geography. Research Papers. No. 149)*

— South Africa.

DAVIES (R.J.) and YOUNG (BRUCE .S.) Manufacturing in South African cities. [Cape Town, 1970]. pp. 595-605, 608-620. *(From Journal for Geography, vol. 3, no. 6, April 1970) Xerographic copy.*

DAVIES (R.J.) and YOUNG (BRUCE S.) Manufacturing and size of place in the South African urban system. [Cape Town, 1970]. pp. 699-713. *(From Journal for Geography, vol. 3, no. 7, Sept. 1970) Xerographic copy. Bound with their Manufacturing in South African cities.*

DAVIES (R.J.) and YOUNG (BRUCE S.) Manufacturing in South African cities. [Cape Town, 1970]. pp. 595-605, 608-620. *(From Journal for Geography, vol. 3, no. 6, April 1970) Xerographic copy.*

PAUW (BERTHOLD ADOLF) The second generation: a study of the family among urbanized Bantu in East London. 2nd ed. Cape Town, 1973. pp. 241. *(Rhodes University. Institute of Social and Economic Research. Xhosa in Town. 3)*

— — Planning.

FAIR (T.J.D.) The metropolitan imperative: inaugural lecture...delivered 27 October 1971 [at the University of Witwatersrand]. Johannesburg, 1972. pp. 24. *bibliog.*

SOUTH AFRICA. Parliament. House of Assembly. Select Committee on Urban Development. 1973. Report (with Proceedings and Minutes of evidence); [W.A. Cruywagen, chairman] (S.C. 6 - 1973). in SOUTH AFRICA. Parliament. House of Assembly. Select Committee reports.

— Sweden — Planning.

FRANCE. Direction de la Documentation. La Documentation Française. Notes et Etudes Documentaires. Nos. 3,756-3, 757. L'urbanisme en Suède. Paris, 1971. pp. 94.

— Thailand.

ROMM (JEFF) Urbanization in Thailand. [New York, 1972?]. pp. 161. *bibliog. (Ford Foundation. International Urbanization Survey. Working Papers. 285)*

— Turkey — Growth.

WEIKER (WALTER F.) Decentralizing government in modernizing nations: growth center potential of Turkish provincial cities. Beverley Hills, Calif., [1972]. pp. 72. *bibliog.*

— — Planning.

KELES (RUSEN Y.) Urbanization in Turkey. [New York, 1972?]. pp. 170. *bibliog. (Ford Foundation. International Urbanization Survey. Working Papers. 277)*

— Uganda.

JACOBSON (DAVID) Anthropologist. Itinerant townsmen: friendship and social order in urban Uganda.Menlo Park, Calif. [1973]. pp. 150. *bibliog.*

— Underdeveloped areas

See UNDERDEVELOPED AREAS — Cities and towns.

— United Kingdom.

LINDSAY (WALTON) and others. New towns: a comparative atlas; [prepared within the New Towns Study]. Cambridge, 1972. pp. 24 and folder of maps. *(Cambridge. University. School of Architecture. Land Use and Built Form Studies. Working Papers. 62)*

STAFFORDSHIRE. Education Department. Local History Source Books. No. 12. State of large towns in north Staffordshire; [sources]. [Stafford, 1972]. fo. 34.

EVERITT (ALAN MILNER) ed. Perspectives in English urban history. London, 1973. pp. 271. *bibliog.*

MORE help for the cities; [by] Sydney Chapman [and others]. London, 1974. pp. 16. *(Conservative Political Centre. [Publications]. No.555)*

— — Bibliography.

VEAL (A.J.) New communities in the United Kingdom: a classified bibliography. Birmingham, 1973. pp. 99. *(Birmingham. University. Centre for Urban and Regional Studies. Research Memoranda. No. 21)*

— — Growth.

CLAWSON (MARION) and HALL (PETER GEOFFREY) Planning and urban growth: an Anglo-American comparison. Baltimore, [1973]. pp. 300.

CORDEY-HAYES (MARTYN) and GLEAVE (D.) Migration movements and the differential growth of city regions in England and Wales:...paper presented at the European Regional Science Association Congress in Vienna, August 1973. London, 1973. pp. 38. *bibliog. (Centre for Environmental Studies. Research Papers. 1)*

ROBSON (BRIAN T.) Urban growth: an approach. London, 1973. pp. 268. *bibliog.*

— — Planning.

MORRISON (RACHEL) Town and country planning. London, 1949. pp. 16. *bibliog. (Current Affairs. No. 76)*

SOUTH HAMPSHIRE PLAN ADVISORY COMMITTEE. Study Reports. Group C. Urban Form. No. 1. Urban form. Winchester, 1969. pp. 23,ii. *bibliog.*

SOUTH HAMPSHIRE PLAN ADVISORY COMMITTEE. Study Reports. Group C. Urban Form. No. 2. The built environment. Winchester, 1969. pp. 26,iii.

U.K. Statutes, etc. 1971. ch. 78. Town and Country Planning Act. Town and Country Planning Act, 1971: tables of comparison, showing 1. The mode in which earlier enactments are dealt with by the Act. 2. The sections of the Act and corresponding provisions in earlier Acts. London, 1972. pp. 52.

CLAWSON (MARION) and HALL (PETER GEOFFREY) Planning and urban growth: an Anglo-American comparison. Baltimore, [1973]. pp. 300.

HOLLIDAY (JOHN) ed. City centre redevelopment: a study of the British city centre planning and case studies of five English city centres. London, 1973. pp. 244. *bibliog.*

CITIES AND TOWNS (Cont.)

LICHFIELD (NATHANIEL) AND ASSOCIATES and INBUCON/AIC MANAGEMENT CONSULTANTS LIMITED. The Oldham study: environmental planning and management. London, H.M.S.O., 1973. pp. 59. *bibliog.*

McLOUGHLIN (JOHN BRIAN) Control and urban planning. London, 1973. pp. 287. *bibliog.*

TARN (JOHN NELSON) Five per cent philanthropy: an account of housing in urban areas between 1840 and 1914. Cambridge, 1973. pp. 211. *bibliog.*

U.K. Department of the Environment. 1973. The Maplin project: designation area for the new town: a consultation document. London, 1973. pp. 18, 5 maps.

U.K. Department of the Environment. 1973. New towns;...produced...on the occasion of the United Nations Seminar on New Towns, June, 1973. London, 1973. pp. 156. *bibliog. In English, French and Spanish.*

U.K. Department of the Environment. 1973. Public participation in general improvement areas. London, 1973. pp. 50. (*Area Improvement Notes. 8*)

U.K. Department of the Environment. 1973. Structure plans: the examination in public. [London, 1973]. pp. 13.

URWICK, ORR AND PARTNERS and ASHWORTH (GRAHAM) The Rotherham study. London, H.M.S.O., 1973. 2 pts.

BRUTON (MICHAEL J.) ed. The spirit and purpose of planning. London, 1974. pp. 233.

CHERRY (GORDON E.) The evolution of British town planning: a history of town planning in the United Kingdom during the 20th century and of the Royal Town Planning Institute, 1914-74..Leighton Buzzard, 1974. pp. 275.

DOBRY (GEORGE) Review of the development control system: interim report; presented to the Secretary of State for the Environment and the Secretary of State for Wales. London, H.M.S.O., 1974. pp. 102.

FRIEND (JOHN K.) and others. Public planning: the inter-corporate dimension. London, 1974. pp. 534. *bibliog.*

HORROCKS (MERYL) Social development work in the new communities. Birmingham, 1974. pp. 65. *bibliog.* (*Birmingham. University. Centre for Urban and Regional Studies. Occasional Papers. No. 27*)

NORTHAMPTON DEVELOPMENT CORPORATION. Background to new towns. [Northampton], 1974. fo. 67.

— — — Bibliography.

U.K. Department of the Environment. Library. 1971. Development control: strengths and weaknesses. [London, 1971?]. pp. 5. (*Bibliographs. No. 154*)

U.K. Department of the Environment. Library. 1971. Structure and local planning. [London, 1971]. fo.5. (Bibliographies. No.152)

U.K. Department of the Environment. Library. 1973. New towns. [London], 1973. 1 vol. (various pagings). (*Bibliography Series. No. 65*)

— — Wales — Planning.

WELSH COUNCIL. Mid Wales: the growth town programme. [Cardiff?], 1973. fo. 41,1map.

— United States.

DOWNS (ANTHONY) Urban problems and prospects. Chicago, [1970] repr. 1971. pp. 293.

EISINGER (PETER K.) The conditions of protest behavior in American cities; [revised version of paper prepared for a seminar panel at the 1971 meeting of the American Political Science Association at Chicago]. Madison, 1972. fo.49. (*Wisconsin University, Madison. Institute for Research on Poverty. Discussion Papers*)

ABERBACH (JOEL D.) and WALKER (JACK L.) Race in the city: political trust and public policy in the new urban system. Boston, [Mass., 1973]. pp. 293.

FUSFELD (DANIEL ROLAND) The basic economics of the urban racial crisis. New York, [1973]. pp. 122. *bibliog.*

LYNCH (HOLLIS R.) The black urban condition: a documentary history, 1866-1971. New York, [1973]. pp. 469. *bibliog.*

PROPERTY taxes, housing and the cities; [by] George E. Peterson [and others]. Lexington, [1973]. pp. 203.

BISH (ROBERT L.) and KIRK (ROBERT J.) Economic principles and urban problems. Englewood Cliffs, [1974]. pp. 199.

HAVLICK (SPENSER W.) The urban organism: the city's natural resources from an environmental perspective. New York, [1974]. pp. 515. *bibliog.*

LAND use, urban form and environmental quality: [report of a study conducted at the University of Chicago for the Office of Research and Development of the U.S. Environmental Protection Agency]; [by] Brian J.L. Berry [and others]. Chicago, 1974. pp. 440. *bibliog.* (*Chicago. University. Department of Geography. Research Papers. No. 155*)

ROSSI (PETER HENRY) and others. The roots of urban discontent: public policy, municipal institutions and the ghetto. New York, [1974]. pp. 499.

— — Growth.

BERRY (BRIAN JOE LOBLEY) Growth centers in the American urban system. Cambridge, Mass., [1973]. 2 vols. *bibliog.*

CLAWSON (MARION) and HALL (PETER GEOFFREY) Planning and urban growth: an Anglo-American comparison. Baltimore, [1973]. pp. 300.

COOK (ANN) and others, eds. City life, 1865-1900: views of urban America. New York, 1973. pp. 292.

McKELVEY (BLAKE) American urbanization: a comparative history. Glenview, Ill., [1973]. pp. 166. *bibliogs.*

PRED (ALLAN R.) Urban growth and the circulation of information: the United States system of cities, 1790-1840. Cambridge, Mass., 1973. pp. 348.

— — Planning.

BOULDING (KENNETH EWART) and others, eds. Transfers on an urbanized economy: theories and effects of the grants economy. Belmont, Calif., [1973]. pp. 376.

CLAWSON (MARION) and HALL (PETER GEOFFREY) Planning and urban growth: an Anglo-American comparison. Baltimore, [1973]. pp. 300.

HOUSE (PETER W.) The urban environmental system: modeling for research, policy- making and education. Beverly Hills, [1973]. pp. 316. *bibliog.*

LINOWES (R. ROBERT) and ALLENSWORTH (DON TRUDEAU) The politics of land use: planning, zoning, and the private developer. New York, 1973. pp. 166.

STEVENS (JOSEPH L.) Impact of federal legislation and programs on private land in urban and metropolitan development. New York, 1973. pp. 238. *bibliog.*

MEYERS (EDWARD M.) and MUSIAL (JOHN J.) Urban incentive tax credits: a self-correcting strategy to rebuild central cities. New York, [1974]. pp. 140.

NEEDLEMAN (MARTIN L.) and NEEDLEMAN (CAROLYN EMERSON) Guerrillas in the bureaucracy: the community planning experiment in the United States. New York, [1974]. pp. 368. *bibliog.*

SCHUSSHEIM (MORTON J.) The modest commitment to cities. Lexington, Mass., [1974]. pp. 232.

WASHNIS (GEORGE J.) Community development strategies: case studies of major model cities. New York, 1974. pp. 415.

— Upper Volta.

SKINNER (ELLIOTT PERCIVAL) African urban life: the transformation of Ouagadougou. Princeton, [1974]. pp. 487. *bibliog.*

— Venezuela — Planning.

ROBIN (JOHN P.) and TERZO (FREDERICK C.) Urbanization in Venezuela. [New York, 1972?]. pp. 51. (*Ford Foundation. International Urbanization Survey. Working Papers. 282*)

ACEDO MENDOZA (CARLOS) Reforma urbana. [Caracas], Fundacion para el Desarrollo de la Comunidad y Fomento Municipal, [1973?]. 1 vol. (various pagings).

HEALEY (PATSY) Urban planning under conditions of rapid urban growth: a case study approach; [Ph.D. (London) thesis]. 1973. fo. 406. *bibliog. Typescript: unpublished. This thesis is the property of London University and may not be removed from the Library.*

— Zambia — Planning.

SIMMANCE (ALAN J.F.) Urbanization in Zambia. [New York, 1972]. pp. 52. (*Ford Foundation . International Urbanization Survey. Working Papers. 275*)

CITIZEN PARTICIPATION.

See POLITICAL PARTICIPATION.

CITY NOISE.

ROBINSON (D.W.) An outline guide to criteria for the limitation of urban noise. London, H.M.S.O., 1970. pp. 43. (*Aeronautical Research Council [U.K.]. Current Papers. No. 1112*)

CITY PLANNERS

WYATT (RAYMOND G.) Is planning a profession?. Oxford, 1973. pp. 33. *bibliog.* (*Oxford Polytechnic. Department of Town Planning. Oxford Working Papers in Planning Education and Research. 18*)

CITY TRAFFIC.

FRANCE. Ministère de l'Intérieur. 1972. Directives sur l'amélioration de la circulation des transports collectifs de surface dans les villes. [Paris], 1972. pp. 50, [23].

— Italy.

FANO (PIETRO L.) and PONTI (MARCO) Il traffico urbano in Italia. Milano, [1972]. pp. 199. *bibliog.* (*Istituto per gli Studi sullo Sviluppo Economico e il Progresso Tecnico. Collana Isvet. n.21*)

— United Kingdom.

WEBSTER (F.V.) and OLDFIELD (R.H.) A theoretical study of bus and car travel in central London. Crowthorne, 1972. pp. 22. (*U.K. Transport and Road Research Laboratory. Reports. LR 451*)

URBAN freight distribution: studies of operations in shopping streets at Newbury and Camberley; by A.W. Christie [and others]. Crowthorne, 1973. pp. 81. (*U.K. Transport and Road Research Laboratory. Reports. LR 603*)

CIVICS, AMERICAN.

HENNESSY (BERNARD CHARLES) Political internships: theory, practice, evaluation. University Park, Penn., [1970] repr. 1972. pp. 129. (*Pennsylvania State University. Penn State Studies. No. 28*)

CIVICS, NORTHERN IRISH.

RUSSELL (JAMES LYON) Some aspects of the civic education of secondary schoolboys in Northern Ireland. [Belfast], Northern Ireland Community Relations Commission, 1972. fo. 34. (*Research Papers*)

CIVIL ENGINEERING

— United Kingdom.

TILBURY GROUP. The Tilbury Group. [London], 1960. pp. 41.

CIVIL ENGINEERS

— France.

THOENIG (JEAN CLAUDE) L'ère des technocrates: le cas des Ponts et Chaussées. Paris, 1973. pp. 281.

CIVIL LAW

— Austria.

AUSTRIA. Statutes, etc. 1811-1966. The General civil code of Austria; translated from the German edition of August 1, 1966 with the assistance of the 1866 translation by Joseph von Winiwarter; revised... and annotated by Paul L. Baeck. New York, 1972. pp. 293.

— France.

FRANCE. Statutes, etc. 1790-1973. Code civil: (dernière édition officielle du 30 août 1816; redigeé avec le concours de Pierre André Moreau). 73rd ed. Paris, 1973. pp. 1262.

— Russia.

CHEREPAKHIN (BORIS BORISOVICH) ed. Voprosy grazhdanskogo prava i protsessa. Leningrad, 1969. pp. 199.

KRASAVCHIKOV (OKTIABR' ALEKSEEVICH) ed. Sovetskoe grazhdanskoe pravo. 2nd ed. Moskva, 1972-3. 2 vols.

DAVYDOV (VLADIMIR IVANOVICH) Problemy kodifikatsii grazhdanskogo zakonodatel'stva. Kishinev, 1973. pp. 207.

KUNIK (IAKOV ABRAMOVICH) ed. Sovetskoe grazhdanskoe pravo. Moskva, 1973. pp. 512. *bibliog.*

— — Kazakstan.

SOVETSKOE grazhdanskoe pravo Kazakhskoi SSR: uchebnoe posobie. vyp.2. Alma-Ata, 1969. pp. 179.

— — Lithuania.

LITHUANIA. Statutes, etc. 1972. Grazhdanskii kodeks Litovskoi Sovetskoi Sotsialisticheskoi Respubliki: ofitsial'nyi tekst s izmeneniiami i dopolneniiami na 1 dekabria 1972 g. i s prilozheniem postateino-sistematizirovannykh materialov. Vil'nius, 1973. pp. 623.

CIVIL PROCEDURE.

INTERNATIONAL ASSOCIATION OF LEGAL SCIENCE. Conference, 1971. Fundamental guarantees of the parties in civil litigation: studies in national, international and comparative law; (proceedings of the Conference);...edited by Mauro Cappelletti and Denis Tallon. Milano, 1973. pp. 821. *(Florence. Università degli Studi di Firenze. Istituto di Diritto Comparato. Studi di Diritto Comparato. 5) In English or French.*

— Czechoslovakia.

OBČANSKÝ soudní řád: komentář. díl 1. Praha, 1970. pp. 711.

— Poland.

WENGEREK (EDMUND) Postępowanie zabezpieczające i egzekucyjne: komentarz do części drugiej kodeksu postępowania cywilnego; egzekucję z nieruchomości i ze statków morskich /art. 921-1022/ opracował Mieczysław Tyczka. Warszawa, 1972. pp. 787. *bibliog.*

— Russia.

TRUBNIKOV (PETR IAKOVLEVICH) Nadzornoe proizvodstvo po grazhdanskim delam. Moskva, 1967. pp. 144.

CHEREPAKHIN (BORIS BORISOVICH) ed. Voprosy grazhdanskogo prava i protsessa. Leningrad, 1969. pp. 199.

— — Ukraine.

KONONENKO (I.P.) ed. Tsyvil'nyi protsesual'nyi kodeks Ukraïns'koï RSR: naukovo-praktychnyi komentar. Kyïv, 1973. pp. 496.

— United Kingdom.

JUSTICE (BRITISH SECTION OF THE INTERNATIONAL COMMISSION OF JURISTS) Going to law: a critique of English civil procedure; chairman of committee, Sir John Foster. London, 1974. pp. 68. *bibliog.*

CIVIL RIGHTS.

INTERNATIONAL LABOUR CONFERENCE. 54th Session. Reports. 7. Seventh item on the agenda: trade union rights and their relation to civil liberties. Geneva, 1969. pp. 70.

INTERNATIONAL ADVISORY COMMITTEE ON POPULATION AND LAW. Annual Meetings, 2nd, 1972. Human rights and population from the perspectives of law, policy and organization: proceedings. Medford, Mass., 1973. pp. 101. *(Tufts University. Fletcher School of Law and Diplomacy. Law and Population Book Series. No. 5)*

SHAFER (RAYMOND P.) Government control of individual behavior: its right and its proper role; ([with] The American Public Health Association awards for excellence). [Washington, 1973]. pp. 35. *(American Public Health Association. Matthew B. Rosenhaus Lectures. 1st, 1973)*

COLEMAN (JAMES SAMUEL) Power and the structure of society. New York, [1974]. pp. 112. *bibliog. (Pennsylvania University. Fels Center of Government. Fels Lectures on Public Policy Analysis)*

LAMONT (CORLISS) Voice in the wilderness: collected essays of fifty years. Buffalo, N.Y., [1974]. pp. 327.

— Chile.

CHICAGO COMMISSION OF INQUIRY INTO THE STATUS OF HUMAN RIGHTS IN CHILE. Report of the Chicago Commission...: Santiago, Chile, February 16-23, 1974. Chicago, [1974]. 1 vol. (various pagings).

— Communist countries.

HAUSER (MAX) Menschenrechte im Sowjetsystem. Bern, 1973. pp. 268. *bibliog.*

— France.

RIVERO (JEAN) Les libertés publiques. Paris, 1973 in progress.

LEVINE (MICHAEL) Affaires non classées: enquêtes et dossiers de la Ligue des Droits de l'Homme. [Paris, 1973]. pp. 392.

— Germany, Eastern.

GRAEFRATH (BERNHARD) Die wirtschaftlichen, sozialen und kulturellen Menschenrechte in der Deutschen Demokratischen Republik. Berlin, 1970. pp. 93. *(DDR-Komitee für Menschenrechte. Schriften)*

POPPE (EBERHARD) Working people and their rights: GDR gives full scope to human rights; [translated from the German]. Berlin, 1973. pp. 60.

— Ireland (Republic).

IRISH ASSOCIATION OF CIVIL LIBERTY. Your rights as an Irish citizen. Dublin, 1972. pp. 43.

— Israel.

GERIES (SABRI) Democratic freedoms in Israel;...translated by Meric Dobson. Beirut, 1972. pp. 109. *(Institute for Palestine Studies. Monograph Series. No. 30)*

SHAHAK (ISRAEL) Civil rights in Israel today. London, [1972?]. pp. 14.

SHAHAK (ISRAEL) Israeli League for Human and Civil Rights: the Shahak papers; compiled and edited by Adnan Amad. Beirut, [1973]. pp. 262.

— Puerto Rico.

PUERTO RICO. Civil Rights Commission. 1973. Informes...Tomo 1. Informe 01 hasta el informe 012 [años 1959-1968]. Orford, 1973. pp. 858. *bibliog.*

— Russia.

HAUSER (MAX) Menschenrechte im Sowjetsystem. Bern, 1973. pp. 268. *bibliog.*

KUTSOVA (ELEONORA FEDOROVNA) Garantii prav lichnosti v sovetskom ugolovnom protsesse: predmet, tsel', soderzhanie. Moskva, 1973. pp. 199.

SHEEHY (ANN) The Crimean Tatars, Volga Germans and Meskhetians: Soviet treatment of some national minorities. new ed. London, 1973. pp. 36. *bibliog. (Minority Rights Group. Reports. No. 6)*

SAKHAROV (ANDREI DMITRIEVICH) Sakharov speaks;...edited and with a foreword by Harrison E. Salisbury. London, 1974. pp. 245.

— Sweden.

DANELIUS (HANS) Human rights in Sweden; (translation: Roger Tanner). 2nd ed. Stockholm, [1973]. pp. 61.

— United Kingdom.

FUNDAMENTAL rights: a volume of essays to commemorate the 50th anniversary of the founding of the Law School in Exeter, 1923- 1973; edited by J.W. Bridge [and others]. London, 1973. pp. 324.

HAZELL (ROBERT) Conspiracy and civil liberties: a memorandum submitted to the Law Commission by the Cobden Trust and the National Council for Civil Liberties. London, 1974. pp. 128. *(Social Administration Research Trust. Occasional Papers on Social Administration. No. 55)*

— — Ireland, Northern.

FARRELL (MIKE) The struggle in the north. 2nd ed. London, 1972. pp. 37.

HADDEN (TOM) and HILLYARD (PADDY) Justice in Northern Ireland: a study in social confidence. London, [1973]. pp. 74.

ARTHUR (PAUL) The People's Democracy, 1968-1973. Belfast, 1974. pp. 159. *bibliog.*

— United States.

RAINWATER (LEE) and YANCEY (WILLIAM L.) The Moynihan Report and the politics of controversy:... including the full text of The negro family: the case for national action; by Daniel Patrick Moynihan. Cambridge, Mass., [1967] repr. 1969. pp. 493. *(Trans-action-Social Science and Modern Society. Social Science and Public Policy Reports)*

EQUAL opportunity in the United States: a symposium on civil rights; co-sponsored by the Lyndon Baines Johnson Library and the University of Texas at Austin, [1972]; edited by Robert C. Rooney. Austin, 1973. pp. 175.

KONVITZ (MILTON RIDVAS) ed. Bill of Rights reader: leading constitutional cases. 5th ed. Ithaca, 1973. pp. 747. *(Cornell University. Cornell Studies in Civil Liberty)*

— Vietnam.

The MONTAGNARDS of South Vietnam. London, 1974. pp. 28. *bibliog. (Minority Rights Group. Reports. No. 18)*

CIVIL RIGHTS (INTERNATIONAL LAW).

LEE (LUKE TSUNG-CHOU) Law, human rights and population: a strategy for action; background paper for the U.N. Second Asian Population Conference...1972. Medford, Mass., [1972]. pp. [17]. *(Tufts University. Fletcher School of Law and Diplomacy. Law and Population Monograph Series. No.6) (Reprinted from the Virginia Journal of International Law, vol.12, no.3)*

HALLER-ZIMMERMANN (MARGARETA) Die UNO- Menschenrechtskonventionen und die rechtliche Stellung der Frau in der Schweiz. Zürich, [1973]. pp. 197. *bibliog. (Zuerich. Universität. Rechts- und Staatswissenschaftliche Fakultät. Zuercher Beiträge zur Rechtswissenschaft. [Neue Folge]. Heft 431)*

HUMANITARIAN intervention and the United Nations: [proceedings of a conference held in Charlottesville, Va. in 1972]; edited by Richard B. Lillich. Charlottesville, Va., 1973. pp. 240. *bibliog. (Virginia University. School of Law. Virginia Legal Studies)*

MALLISON (W.T.) and MALLISON (S.V.) An international law appraisal of the juridical characteristics of the resistance of the people of Palestine: the struggle for human rights. Beirut, 1973. pp. 38. *(Palestine Research Center. Palestine Essays. No. 31)*

CIVIL SERVICE

CIVIL SERVICE

JACOBSEN (BERTIL) and ANDERSEN (BENT ROLD) Den departementale planlaegningsvirksomhed. [Copenhagen?, Arbejdsministeriet], 1970. pp. 48. *bibliog.*

— Burma.

MYA SEIN, Daw. The administration of Burma: (Sir Charles Crosthwaite and the consolidation of Burma); [reprint of the first edition of 1938] with an introduction by Josef Silverstein. Kuala Lumpur, 1973. pp. 186. *bibliog.*

— France.

BAECQUE (FRANCIS DE) L'administration centrale de la France. Paris, [1973]. pp. 398. *bibliog.*

— Germany.

GERMANY (BUNDESREPUBLIK). Deutscher Bundestag. Wissenschaftliche Dienste. 1973. Reform des öffentlichen Dienstrechts: Vorschläge aus dem Bericht der Studienkommission. Bonn, 1973. pp. 33. *(Materialien. 34)*

JOHNSON (NEVIL) Government in the Federal Republic of Germany: the executive at work. Oxford, 1973. pp. 218. *bibliog.*

KOENIG (PIERRE) La fonction publique en Allemagne fédérale. [Paris, 1973]. pp. 96. *bibliog.*

— Ghana.

PEASAH (JOSEPH AWUA) The evolution of the Ghana civil service, 1945-1960: a study in bureaucracy, politics, and anti-colonial nationalism; [Ph.D. (London) thesis]. 1973. fo. 310. *bibliog. Typescript: unpublished. This thesis is the property of London University and may not be removed from the Library.*

— Kenya.

KENYA. Public Service Structure and Remuneration Commission. 1971. Report...1970-71; chairman: D.N. Ndegwa. [Nairobi], 1971. pp. 397. *3 charts in end pocket.*

— Nigeria.

REFORM of the Nigerian public service: report of a conference held at the Institute of Administration, Ahmadu Bello University, Zaria, October 1971; (editor, Mahmud Tukur). [Zaria, imprint], [1972?]. pp. 340.

— Russia.

LESAGE (MICHEL) La fonction publique en Union soviétique. [Paris, 1973]. pp. 96. *bibliog.*

— Spain.

LALINDE ABADIA (JESUS) Los medios personales de gestion del poder publico en la historia española. Madrid, Instituto de Estudios Administrativos, 1970 [or rather 1971]. pp. 221. *bibliog. (Estudios de Historia de la Administracion)*

— Switzerland.

RATIONALISIERUNG der öffentlichen Verwaltung; ([by] Hans Künzi [and others]). Bern, [1971]. pp. 50. *(Zürich. Universität. Institut für Betriebswirtschaftliche Forschung. Schriftenreihe. Band 3)*

CIVIL SERVICE — Underdeveloped Areas.

See UNDERDEVELOPED AREAS — Civil Service.

— United Kingdom.

U.K. Civil Service Department. Account of central civil service training. a., 1970/71, 1971/2 [1st, 2nd]; ceased pbln. London.

U.K. Civil Service Commission. 1971. The work of government departments. [London], 1971. pp. 64.

RIDLEY (NICHOLAS) Industry and the civil service. London, [1973]. pp. 13.

— — Yearbooks.

CIVIL SERVICE YEAR BOOK, THE; ([pd. by] Civil Service Department [U.K.]). a., 1974 [1st]- London.

— Venezuela.

BREWER-CARIAS (ALLAN RANDOLPH) Reforma administrativa y desarrollo economico y social en Venezuela. Caracas, [Comision de Administracion Publica], 1970. pp. 30.*(Cuadernos para la Reforma Administrativa. 2) Reprinted from the International Review of Administrative Sciences, 1970.*

BREWER-CARIAS (ALLAN RANDOLPH) El estatuto del funcionario publico en la Ley de Carrera Administrativa. Caracas, Comision de Administracion Publica, 1971. pp. 253.

CIVIL SERVICE PENSIONS

— United Kingdom.

U.K. Government Actuary's Department. 1973. National Health Service Act, 1946: report by the Government Actuary on the National Health Service superannuation scheme, 1962-1969. London, 1973. pp. 19.

CIVIL SUPREMACY OVER THE MILITARY

— Germany, Eastern.

HERSPRING (DALE ROY) East German civil-military relations: the impact of technology, 1949-72. New York, 1973. pp. 216. *bibliog.*

CIVIL WAR.

BOND (JAMES EDWARD) The rules of riot: internal conflict and the law of war. Princeton, [1974]. pp. 280. *bibliog.*

CIVILIAN DEFENCE.

KALSHOVEN (FRITS) and RÖLING (BERNARD VICTOR ALOYSIUS) De positie van de niet-bezette burgerbevolking in een gewapend conflict, in het bijzonder met het oog op de massaal werkende strijdmiddelen, NBC-wapens: praeadviezen. [Deventer], 1970. pp. 78. *(Nederlandse Vereniging voor Internationaal Recht. Mededelingen. No. 61)*

CIVILIZATION.

MUMFORD (LEWIS) Interpretations and forecasts, 1922-1972: studies in literature, history, biography, technics, and contemporary society. [London, 1974]. pp. 522. *First published in New York in 1973.*

— Bibliography.

UNITED NATIONS EDUCATIONAL, SCIENTIFIC AND CULTURAL ORGANIZATION. 1973. Bibliography of publications issued by Unesco or under its auspices: the first twenty-five years, 1946 to 1971. Paris, 1973. pp. 385. *In English and French.*

— Philosophy.

MILLER (LIBUSE LUKAS) Knowing, doing, and surviving: cognition in evolution. New York, [1973]. pp. 343. *bibliog.*

CIVILIZATION, MODERN.

EISENSTADT (SHMUEL N.) Modernization: protest and change. Jerusalem, [1966]. pp. 166.

LEARNED (S.S.) An America to love: viewpoints per an immigrant's son. Fontana, Calif., [1972]. pp. 206.

INDUSTRIEGEWERKSCHAFT METALL FÜR DIE BUNDESREPUBLIK DEUTSCHLAND. Internationale Arbeitstagung, 4., 1972. Aufgabe Zukunft: Qualität des Lebens; Beiträge... 11. bis 14. April 1972 in Oberhausen...; Redaktion: Günter Friedrichs. Frankfurt am Main, 1973-74. 10 vols. *With summaries in English and French.*

GUINNESS (OS) The dust of death:... a critique of the establishment and the counter culture, and a proposal for a third way. London, 1973. pp. 416.

ILLICH (IVAN D.) Tools for conviviality. London, 1973. pp. 110.

MAGEE (BRYAN EDGAR) and others. Prospects for mankind; [transcript of a discussion with] Herman Kahn and Robert Jungk;...transmitted 31 May 1973. [London, 1973]. fo. 37. *(Thames Television. Something to Say)*

PAWLEY (MARTIN) The private future: causes and consequences of community collapse in the West. London, [1973]. pp. 208.

ADORNO (THEODOR WIESENGRUND) Minima moralia: reflections from damaged life; translated from the German by E.F.N. Jephcott. London, 1974. pp. 251.

HEILBRONER (ROBERT LOUIS) An inquiry into the human prospect. New York, [1974]. pp. 150.

KOESTLER (ARTHUR) The heel of Achilles: essays, 1968-1973. London, 1974. pp. 254.

MULLER (HERBERT JOSEPH) Uses of the future. Bloomington, Ind., [1974]. pp. 264.

QUELLE crise?; quelle société?; [by] R. Aron [and others]. Grenoble, [1974]. pp. 185.

SOLZHENITSYN (ALEKSANDR ISAEVICH) Letter to Soviet leaders; translated by Hilary Sternberg [from an unpublished letter written in 1973]. London, 1974. pp. 59.

THRING (MEREDITH W.) Machines - masters or slaves of man?. Stevenage, Herts, [1974]. pp. 115.

CIVILIZATION, OCCIDENTAL.

HOGG (QUINTIN McGAREL) Baron Hailsham. The acceptable face of western civilisation. London, 1973. pp. 22. (Conservative Political Centre. [Publications]. No. 535]

MARTIN (DAVID ALFRED) Tracts against the times. Guildford, 1973. pp. 186.

CLARKE (SAMUEL).

FERGUSON (JAMES P.) The philosophy of Dr. Samuel Clarke and its critics. New York, [1974]. pp. 292. *bibliog.*

CLARKSON (STEPHEN).

CLARKSON (STEPHEN) City lib: parties and reform. Toronto, 1972. pp. 227.

CLASSIFICATION

— Books.

GROLIER (ERIC DE) A study of general categories applicable to classification and coding in documentation;... translated from the French... (revised by Anthony Thompson). Paris, 1962. pp. 248.

— — Law.

COHEN (MORRIS L.) Law and population classification plan. Medford, Mass., [1974]. pp. 13. *(Tufts University. Fletcher School of Law and Diplomacy. Law and Population Monograph Series. No.5)*

CLAUSEWITZ (CARL VON).

WALLACH (JEHUDA L.) Das Dogma der Vernichtungsschlacht: die Lehren von Clausewitz und Schlieffen und ihre Wirkungen in zwei Weltkriegen; (aus dem Englischen von Hans Jürgen Baron von Koskull). Frankfurt am Main, 1967. pp. 475. *bibliog.*

CLAUSTHAL—ZELLERFELD

— Politics and government.

PLESSE (SIGURD) Die nationalsozialistische Machtergreifung im Oberharz: Clausthal-Zellerfeld, 1929-1933. Clausthal-Zellerfeld, 1970. pp. 95.

CLAY INDUSTRIES

— United Kingdom.

ROLT (LIONEL THOMAS CASWELL) The potters' field: a history of the South Devon ball clay industry. Newton Abbot, [1974]. pp. 159. *bibliog.*

CLAYTON (GEOFFREY HARE) Archbishop of Cape Town.

PATON (ALAN) Apartheid and the archbishop: the life and times of Geoffrey Clayton, Archbishop of Cape Town. London, 1974. pp. 311.

CLEMENCEAU (GEORGES EUGÈNE BENJAMIN).

WATSON (DAVID ROBIN) Georges Clemenceau: a political biography. London, 1974. pp. 463. *bibliog.*

CLERGY

— **Spain.**

DOMINGUEZ ORTIZ (ANTONIO) Las clases privilegiadas en la España del Antiguo Regimen Madrid, [1973]. pp. 464. *bibliog.*

— **United States.**

HALL (DOUGLAS T.) and SCHNEIDER (BENJAMIN) Organizational climates and careers: the work lives of priests. New York, 1973. pp. 291. *bibliog.*

CLERKS.

INTERNATIONAL LABOUR ORGANISATION. Advisory Committee on Salaried Employees and Professional Workers. 7th Session. Reports. 2. Conditions of work and life of employees in commerce and offices: (second item on the agenda). Geneva, 1974. pp. 81.

— **United Kingdom.**

BAIN (GEORGE SAYERS) The growth of white-collar unionism. Oxford, 1970. pp. 233. *bibliog.*

BAIN (GEORGE SAYERS) and others. Social stratification and trade unionism: a critique. London, 1973. pp. 174. *bibliog. (Warwick Studies in Industrial Relations)*

COMMISSION ON INDUSTRIAL RELATIONS [U.K.]. Recognition of white-collar unions in engineering and chemicals. London, H.M.S.O., 1973. pp. 75. *(Studies. 3)*

HILTON (RICHARD NOEL) Office employment and the demand for retail services in central London; [Ph. D. (London) thesis]. [1973]. fo. 278. *Typescript: unpublished. This thesis is the property of London University and may not be removed from the library.*

— **United States.**

NATIONAL INDUSTRIAL CONFERENCE BOARD. Conference Board Reports. Studies in Personnel Policy. No.220. White-collar unionization; by Edward R. Curtin. New York, [1970]. pp. 70.

CLIMATOLOGY.

CLIMATIC resources and economic activity: a symposium [held under the auspices of the Geography Department, University College of Wales, Aberystwyth, 1972]; edited by James A. Taylor...contributors, J.A. Taylor [and others]. Newton Abbot, [1974]. pp. 264. *bibliogs.*

CLIVE (ROBERT) Baron Clive.

BENCE-JONES (MARK) Clive of India. London, 1974. pp. 377. *bibliog.*

CLOCK AND WATCHMAKING

— **Switzerland.**

SCHULZ (DIETER) Staatliche Eingriffe bei strukturellen Branchenkrisen und ihre Vereinbarkeit mit der Marktwirtschaft, dargestellt am Beispiel des Schweizer Uhrenstatuts. [Freiburg im Breisgau, imprint, 1973?]. pp. 171. *bibliog.*

CLOTHING TRADE

— **European Economic Community countries.**

ECONOMIC DEVELOPMENT COMMITTEE FOR THE CLOTHING INDUSTRY. European Study Group. Employment practices in EEC clothing industries; (with Appendices). London, National Economic Development Office, 1974. 2 pts.

— **Germany.**

SALMON (KURT) ASSOCIATES. European Division. The 11 billion Mark market: a study of the market for ladies' outerwear in West Germany; prepared... on behalf of the Economic Development Committee for the Clothing Industry. London, National Economic Development Office, 1972. pp. 124.

— **United Kingdom.**

CLOTHING AND ALLIED PRODUCTS INDUSTRY TRAINING BOARD [U.K.]. Report and statement of accounts. a., 1972/3- Leeds. *Formerly included in the file of British Parliamentary Papers.*

SALMON (KURT) ASSOCIATES. European Division. The 11 billion Mark market: a study of the market for ladies' outerwear in West Germany; prepared... on behalf of the Economic Development Committee for the Clothing Industry. London, National Economic Development Office, 1972. pp. 124.

ECONOMIC DEVELOPMENT COMMITTEE FOR THE CLOTHING INDUSTRY. The anatomy of purchasing clothing machinery: a study of the attitudes of clothing manufacturers towards the purchase of technologically advanced equipment. London, National Economic Development Office, 1974. pp. 52.

STATISTICAL DIGEST OF THE UK CLOTHING INDUSTRY; ([pd. by] Economic Development Committee for the Clothing Industry, National Economic Development Office [U.K.]). irreg. F 1974 (1st ed., 2nd impression)- London.

— **United States.**

WRONG (ELAINE GALE) The negro in the apparel industry. Philadelphia, [1974]. pp. 170. *(Pennsylvania University. Wharton School of Finance and Commerce. Industrial Research Unit. Racial Policies of American Industry. Report No. 31)*

CLOTHING WORKERS

— **European Economic Community countries.**

ECONOMIC DEVELOPMENT COMMITTEE FOR THE CLOTHING INDUSTRY. European Study Group. Employment practices in EEC clothing industries; (with Appendices). London, National Economic Development Office, 1974. 2 pts.

— **United States.**

HASKEL (HARRY) A leader of the garment workers: the biography of Isidore Nagler. New York, 1950. pp. 351. *bibliog.*

CLUSTER ANALYSIS.

EVERITT (BRIAN) Cluster analysis. London, 1974. pp. 122. *bibliog. (U.K. Social Science Research Council. Reviews of Current Research. ll)*

COAL

— **Argentine Republic.**

ARGENTINE REPUBLIC. Consejo Federal de Inversiones. 1963. Programa de desarrollo de la cuenca de Rio Turbio, en función del desarrollo de la explotación del carbón. Tomo 1. Estudio preliminar. [Buenos Aires], 1963. 1 vol. (various pagings).

— **European Economic Community countries.**

COMITE D'ETUDE DES PRODUCTEURS DE CHARBON D'EUROPE OCCIDENTALE. Energy in Europe: the importance of coal; a report. [London, National Coal Board], 1974. pp. 48.

— **Germany — Transportation.**

SCHULTZE-RHONHOF (FRIEDRICH CARL) Die Verkehrsströme der Kohle im Raum der Bundesrepublik Deutschland zwischen 1913 und 1957: eine wirtschaftsgeographische Untersuchung. Bad Godesberg, Bundesanstalt für Landeskunde und Raumforschung, 1964. pp. 86, 12 maps, 2 folding maps in end pocket. *bibliog. (Zentralausschuss für Landeskunde and Germany (Bundesrepublik). Institut für Landeskunde. Forschungen zur Deutschen Landeskunde. Band 146)*

— **United Kingdom.**

U.K. National Coal Board. Report and accounts; (with Statistical tables). a., 1972/3 (27th)- London. *Formerly included in the file of British Parliamentary Papers.*

U.K. National Coal Board. 1972. 25 years, 1947/72: black diamonds silver anniversary. [London, 1972]. pp. 45.

U.K. National Coal Board. 1972. 25 years, 1947/72: coal and science; the second of a series of articles to mark the 25th anniversary of the creation of the National Coal Board. London, 1972. pp. (7).

JACKSON (MICHAEL P.) The price of coal. London, 1974. pp. 217. *bibliog.*

ROBINSON (COLIN) The energy 'crisis' and British coal: the economics of the fuel market in the 1970s and beyond. London, 1974. pp. 61. *bibliog. (Institute of Economic Affairs. Hobart Papers. 59)*

— — **Transportation.**

FINCH (ROGER) Coals from Newcastle: the story of the north east coal trade in the days of sail. Lavenham, 1973. pp. 208. *bibliog.*

COAL MINERS

— **Germany.**

TEUBER (HEINRICH) Für die Sozialisierung des Ruhrbergbaus: [new ed. of series of articles originally published in 1926]; herausgegeben von Hellmut G. Haasis und Erhard Lucas. Frankfurt, [1973]. pp. 131.

— **United Kingdom.**

DAVISON (JACK) Northumberland miners, 1919-1939. Newcastle upon Tyne, 1973. pp. 289. *bibliog.*

DOUGLASS (DAVID) Pit talk in County Durham: a glossary of miners' talk together with the memories of wardley colliery, pit songs and piliking. ?oXFORD], 1973?. PP. 78. *(hISTORY wORKSHOP. pAMPHLETS. nO. 10.)*

JONES (ALAN) and THOMPSON (RON) After the miners' strike, what next? London, [1973?]. pp. 50.

U.K. National Coal Board. Press Office. 1973. The Coal Board's offer to mineworkers: what it means in the paypacket. [London, 1973]. fo. 3.

— **United States.**

KRAMER (LEO), INC. The health-impaired miner under black lung legislation: prepared [for the Manpower Administration of the U.S. Department of Labor]; edited by Ewan Clague. New York, 1973. pp. 130.

COAL MINES AND MINING

— **Environmental aspects.**

— — **United Kingdom**

U.K. National Coal Board. 1972. 25 years, 1947/72: coal and the environment; the first of a series of studies to mark the 25th anniversary of the creation of the National Coal Board. [London, 1972]. pp. (7).

— **European Economic Community countries.**

EUROPEAN COMMUNITIES. Commission. Cahiers de Reconversion Industrielle. Bruxelles, 1963 in progress.

COAL MINES AND MINING (Cont.)

— France.

FRANCE. Houillères du Bassin d'Aquitaine Rapport de gestion.a., 1960-1968 (15e-23e exercices); ceased pbln. Albi.

FRANCE. Houillères du Bassin de Blanzy. Rapport de gestion. a., 1960-1968; ceased pbln. n.p.

FRANCE. Houillères du Bassin des Cévennes. Rapport de gestion. a., 1960-1968 (15e-23e exercices); ceased pbln. Alès.

GILLET (MARCEL) Les charbonnages du nord de la France aux XIXe siècle. Paris, [1973]. pp. 527. *bibliog.* (*Paris. École Pratique des Hautes Études. Section des Sciences Économiques et Sociales. Industrie et Artisanat. 8*)

— Germany.

RIEDEL (MATTHIAS) Eisen und Kohle für das Dritte Reich: Paul Pleigers Stellung in der NS-Wirtschaft. Göttingen, [1973]. pp. 375. *bibliog.*

— India — Government ownership.

KUMARAMANGALAM (SURENDRA MOHAN) Coal industry in India: nationalisation and tasks ahead. New Delhi, 1973. pp. 79.

— Russia — Kazakstan.

BAISHEV (SAKTAGAN BAISHEVICH) and TRUKHIN (P.M.) eds. Ugol'naia promyshlennost' Kazakhstana za 50 let: tekhniko- ekonomicheskii spravochnik. Alma-Ata, 1968. pp. 402.

— — Ukraine.

ZIMOGLIADOV (FELIKS ROMANOVICH) Kommunisticheskaia partiia Sovetskogo Soiuza vo glave trudovoi aktivnosti mass, 1928-1941 gg.: iz opyta raboty partiinykh organizatsii Donbassa. Moskva, 1973. pp. 160.

— United Kingdom.

DOUGLASS (DAVID) Pit talk in County Durham: a glossary of miners' talk together with the memories of Wardley colliery, pit songs and piliking. [Oxford?, 1973]. pp. 78. (*History Workshop. Pamphlets. No.10*)

EZRA (Sir DEREK JOSEPH) Address... to the annual conference of the National Union of Mineworkers at Inverness, 4 July, 1973. [London, National Coal Board, 1973]. pp. 12.

GRANT (PHILIP ANDREW) The coalmines of Durham city. Durham, 1973. pp. 21. *bibliog.* (*Durham. University. Department of Geography. Occasional Publications (New Series). No. 2*)

U.K. National Coal Board. 1974. Plan for coal: the National Coal Board's proposals for long-term investment in the mining industry. [London, 1974]. fo. 8.

— — Government ownership.

COATES (KEN) ed. Democracy in the mines; some documents of the controversy on mines nationalisation up to the time of the Sankey Commission. Nottingham, 1974. pp. 131.

— United States — Government ownership.

JOHNSEN (JULIA EMILY) compiler. Government regulation of the coal industry; supplementary to handbook, Government ownership of coal mines. New York, 1926. pp. 144. *bibliog.*

COALITION GOVERNMENTS.

BROWNE (ERIC C.) Coalition theories: a logical and empirical critique. Beverly Hills, [1973]. pp. 94. *bibliog.*

SWAAN (ABRAM DE) Coalition theories and cabinet formations: a study of formal theories of coalition formation applied to nine European parliaments after 1918. Amsterdam, 1973. pp. 347. *bibliog.*

FACH (WOLFGANG) Koalition und Opposition in spieltheoretischer Sicht: ein Beitrag zur Analyse und Kritik der neuen politischen Ökonomie. Berlin, [1974]. pp. 200. *bibliog.*

— Germany.

BISCHOFF (DETLEF) Franz Josef Strauss, die CSU und die Uussenpolitik: Konzeption und Realität am Beispiel der Grossen Koalition. Meisenheim am Glan ,1973. pp. 346. *bibliog.*

MAURER (ILSE) Reichsfinanzen und Grosse Koalition: zur Geschichte des Reichskabinetts Müller, 1928-1930. Bern, 1973. pp. 269. *bibliog.*

— United Kingdom.

U.K. Parliament. House of Commons. Library. Research Division. Background Papers. No. 38. Coalition governments in Britain in the twentieth century. [London, 1974]. pp. 11.

COAST CHANGES.

MITCHELL (JAMES K.) Community response to coastal erosion: individual and collective adjustments to hazard on the Atlantic shore. Chicago, 1974. pp. 209. *bibliog.* (*Chicago. University. Department of Geography. Research Papers. No.156*)

COASTS

— Recreational use.

LINDSEY. County Council. The Lindsey coast: a policy for holiday development. [Lincoln], 1973. pp. 21.

— France.

PERSPECTIVES pour l'aménagement: le littoral français: rapport de première phase; [report of a working group]. [Paris, Délégation à l'Aménagement du Territoire et à l'Action Régionale], 1972. pp. 37.

PERSPECTIVES pour l'aménagement: littoral français: rapport au gouvernement; [report of a working group]. [Paris, 1974]. pp. 268.

— Ireland (Republic).

BRADY, SHIPMAN AND MARTIN and HYDE (NIALL) National coastline study. Dublin, 1972 in progress.

— United Kingdom.

LINDSEY. County Council. The Lindsey coast: a policy for holiday development. [Lincoln], 1973. pp. 21.

COASTWISE SHIPPING

— Germany.

ROEHLK (FRAUKE) Schiffahrt und Handel zwischen Hamburg und den Niederlanden in der zweiten Hälfte des 18. und zu Beginn des 19. Jahrhunderts.Wiesbaden, 1973. 2 vols. (in 1). *bibliog.* (*Vierteljahrschrift für Sozial- und Wirtschaftsgeschichte. Beihefte. Nr.60*) Table in end pocket

— Netherlands.

ROEHLK (FRAUKE) Schiffahrt und Handel zwischen Hamburg und den Niederlanden in der zweiten Hälfte des 18. und zu Beginn des 19. Jahrhunderts.Wiesbaden, 1973. 2 vols. (in 1). *bibliog.* (*Vierteljahrschrift für Sozial- und Wirtschaftsgeschichte. Beihefte. Nr.60*) Table in end pocket.

— Norway.

FOSS (BJØRN) Rutefartens økonomi. [Oslo], Transportøkonomisk Institutt, 1967. pp. 171. *With English summary.*

NORWAY. Statistiske Centralbyrå. 1972. Godstransport på kysten: skip i innenlandsk rutefart 1969, etc. Oslo, 1972. pp. 71. (*Norges Offisielle Statistikk. Rekke A. 519*) *In English and Norwegian.*

NORWAY. Statistiske Centralbyrå. 1972. Godstransport på kysten: leie- og egentransport med skip 25-500 br. tonn 1970, etc. Oslo, 1972. pp. 91. (*Norges Offisielle Statistikk. Rekke A. 516*) *In English and Norwegian.*

— United Kingdom.

FINCH (ROGER) Coals from Newcastle: the story of the north east coal trade in the days of sail. Lavenham, 1973. pp. 208. *bibliog.*

COCONUT.

WEST BENGAL. State Statistical Bureau. 1967. Report on the sample survey of coconut in West Bengal: third round, 1964-65. Alipore, 1967. fo. 50.

COCONUT OIL.

LABYS (WALTER C.) Dynamic commodity models: specification, estimation, and simulation. Lexington, [1973]. pp. 350. *bibliog.*

CODREANU (CORNELIU ZELEA).

CODREANU (CORNELIU ZELEA) La Garde de Fer: pour les légionnaires; [with appendix of letters and documents]. Paris, 1938; Grenoble, 1972. pp. 470.

COFFEE

— Kenya.

COFFEE BOARD OF KENYA. Annual report, balance sheet and accounts. a., 1970/71- Nairobi.

COFFEE TRADE.

NORTH LONDON HASLEMERE GROUP. Coffee: the rules of neo-colonialism; a study of international coffee trade and the International Coffee Agreement. London, 1972. pp. 24.

— Sierra Leone.

SIERRA LEONE. Beoku-Betts Commission of Inquiry on the Special Coffee Deal of the Sierra Leone Produce Marketing Board. 1968. Report; [R.W. Beoku-Betts, chairman]. [Freetown, 1967 [or rather 1968]. pp. 25.

COGNITION.

BERRY (J.W.) and DASEN (P.R.) eds. Culture and cognition: readings in cross-cultural psychology. London, 1974. pp. 487. *bibliog.*

BRUNER (JEROME SEYMOUR) Beyond the information given: studies in the psychology of knowing; selected, edited and introduced by Jeremy M. Anglin. London, 1974. pp. 502. *bibliog.*

COLE (MICHAEL) and SCRIBNER (SYLVIA) Culture and thought: a psychological introduction. New York, [1974]. pp. 227. *bibliogs.*

COINAGE

— Ireland (Republic).

IRISH DECIMAL MONTHLY; pd. by the Irish Decimal Currency Board [Eire]. m., My 1969 - Oc 1970 (nos.1-17), with gap (Ap 1970, no.12). Dublin.

COKE INDUSTRY.

PROBLEMS and prospects in the coking industry in the OECD countries. Paris, Organisation for Economic Co-operation and Development, 1972. pp. 84.

— European Economic Community countries.

MIDDENDORF (HEINZ WERNER) Untersuchungen über die Struktur und die Wirtschaftlichkeit der Koksversorgung der eisenschaffenden Industrie der Europäischen Gemeinschaft. Düsseldorf, 1971. 1 vol.(various pagings). (*Wirtschaftsvereinigung Eisen- und Stahlindustrie. Schriftenreihe zu Betriebswirtschaftlichen Fragen. Heft 5*)

COLBERT FAMILY.

BOURGEON (JEAN LOUIS) Les Colbert avant Colbert: destin d'une famille marchande. Paris, 1973. pp. 271. (*Paris. Université de Paris IV (Paris-Sorbonne). Publications. Nouvelle Série Recherches. 6*)

COLE (GEORGE DOUGLAS HOWARD).

CARPENTER (L.P.) G.D.H. Cole: an intellectual biography. Cambridge, 1973. pp. 271. *bibliog.* (*Conference on British Studies. Biographical Series*)

COLLECTIVE BARGAINING.

HUTT (WILLIAM HAROLD) The strike-threat system: the economic consequences of collective bargaining. New Rochelle, N. Y., [1973]. pp. 294.

KELLER (BERNDT) Theorien der Kollektivverhandlungen: ein Beitrag zur Problematik der Arbeitsökonomik. Berlin, [1974]. pp. 237. *bibliog.*

— Mathematical models.

ATHERTON (WALLACE N.) Theory of union bargaining goals. Princeton, N.J., [1973]. pp. 168.

— Canada.

ALBRIGHT (W. PAUL) Collective bargaining: a Canadian simulation. Toronto, [1973]. pp. 92.

CANADA. Department of Labour. Collective Bargaining Division. Research bulletin: collective agreement data. irreg., current issues only kept. Ottawa.

— Europe.

INSTITUTE OF PERSONNEL MANAGEMENT. Information Department. Collective bargaining in Western Europe; [coordinated by J.R.Appleyard; prepared by J. Goss and M. Goodman]. London, 1973. pp. 119. *bibliog.* (*Institute of Personnel Management. Information Reports. New Series. 13*)

— India.

TANDON (B.K.) Collective bargaining and the Indian scene. Delhi, 1972. pp. 472.

— United Kingdom.

COMMISSION ON INDUSTRIAL RELATIONS [U.K.]. Con-Mech (Engineers) Limited. London, H.M.S.O., 1973. pp. 8. (*Reports. No. 53*)

COMMISSION ON INDUSTRIAL RELATIONS [U.K.]. Edinburgh Corporation Transport Department. London, H.M.S.O., 1973. pp. 13. (*Reports. No. 56*)

COMMISSION ON INDUSTRIAL RELATIONS [U.K.]. General Accident Fire and Life Assurance Corporation Limited: second report. London, H.M.S.O., 1973. pp. 47. (*Reports. No. 52*) *First report issued as British Parliamentary Paper, Cmnd. 4247, session 1969/70.*

COMMISSION ON INDUSTRIAL RELATIONS [U.K.]. Pan American World Airways Incorporated. London, H.M.S.O., 1973. pp. 21. (*Reports. No. 55*)

TRADES UNION CONGRESS. General Council. Economic policy and collective bargaining in 1973: (report to a special Trades Union Congress). London, 1973. pp. 46.

TRADES UNION CONGRESS. General Council. Collective bargaining and the social contract. London, [1974]. pp. 11.

— United States.

NEW YORK (CITY). Office of Collective Bargaining. Annual report. a., 1968, 1970/71- New York.

BUNKER (CHARLES S.) Collective bargaining: non-profit sector. Columbus, Ohio, [1973]. pp. 271. *bibliogs.*

CARR (ROBERT KENNETH) and VAN EYCK (DANIEL K.) Collective bargaining comes to the campus. Washington, D.C., [1973]. pp. 314. *bibliog.*

SPERO (STERLING DENHARD) and CAPOZZOLA (JOHN M.) The urban community and its unionised bureaucracies: pressure politics in local government labor relations. New York, [1973]. pp. 361. *bibliog.*

LIEB (ROBERT C.) Labor in the transportation industries. New York, 1974. pp. 125. *bibliog.*

SCHOEN (STERLING H.) and HILGERT (RAYMOND L.) Cases in collective bargaining and industrial relations: a decisional approach. rev. ed. Homewood, Ill., 1974. pp. 360. *bibliogs.*

— — Bibliography.

PEZDEK (ROBERT V.) compiler. Public employment: bibliography. Ithaca, 1973. pp. 185. (*Cornell University. New York State School of Industrial and Labor Relations. Bibliography Series. No. 11*)

— — New York(State).

JENSEN (VERNON H.) Strife on the waterfront: the port of New York since 1945. Ithaca, 1974. pp. 478. *bibliog.*

COLLECTIVE LABOUR AGREEMENTS.

WEISBERGER (JUNE) Examples of language and interpretation in public sector collective bargaining agreements: a guide for public officials and other interested parties. Ithaca, 1974. pp. 115. (*Cornell University. New York State School of Industrial and Labor Relations. Institute of Public Employment. Monographs. No.3*)

— Argentine Republic.

ARGENTINE REPUBLIC. Direccion Nacional de Recursos Humanos. Division de Estadisticas Sociales. 1971. Convenciones colectivas de trabajo: analisis de las actualizaciones de convenios colectivos y de empresa, 1967, 1968, 1969 y 1970; indice de los salarios basicos de convenios. Buenos Aires, 1971. pp. 120.

— Italy.

BORDINI (M.) and others. Contratti '72 e crisi economica: ricerca effettuata dalla ISRIL Co-operativa. 2nd ed. Roma, 1972. pp. 170.

— Spain.

SPAIN. Ministerio de Trabajo. Departamento de Documantacion, Publicaciones y Bibliotecas. 1958. Convenios colectivos sindicales. Madrid, 1958. pp. 100.

— Sweden.

KOMMUNISTISK TIDSKRIFT. Skriftserie. 1971. Nr.3. De antifackliga klasslagarna. Stockholm, 1971. pp. 124. *bibliog.*

— United Kingdom.

CHEMICAL AND ALLIED PRODUCTS INDUSTRY TRAINING BOARD [U.K.]. Working Party on the Training Implications of Productivity Agreements. The training implications of manpower productivity agreements; [C. Denard, chairman]. [Staines], 1970. pp. 13. *bibliog.* (*Information Papers. No. 4*)

COLLECTIVISM.

BLUHM (WILLIAM THEODORE) Ideologies and attitudes: modern political culture. Englewood Cliffs, [1974]. pp. 385. *bibliogs.*

COLLEGE TEACHERS.

See TEACHERS.

COLLINS (MICHAEL).

RYAN (DESMOND) Michael Collins and the invisible army; [a novel]. Tralee, 1968 repr. 1971. pp. 164. *First published in 1932 as The invisible army.*

COLLISIONS AT SEA

— Prevention.

INTERNATIONAL CONFERENCE ON SAFETY OF LIFE AT SEA, 1960. Final act of the Conference with Annexes including the text of the adopted Convention; (with Supplement). London, Inter-Governmental Maritime Consultative Organization, [1970]. 2 parts. *In English and French.*

INTERNATIONAL CONFERENCE ON REVISION OF THE INTERNATIONAL REGULATIONS FOR PREVENTING COLLISIONS AT SEA, 1972. Final act of the Conference with attachments including the text of the adopted Convention. London, Inter-Governmental Maritime Consultative Organization, [1973]. pp. 128. *In English and French.*

COLOGNE

— Commerce.

THIERFELDER (HILDEGARD) Köln und die Hanse. Köln, 1970. pp. 25. (*Cologne. Universität. Forschungsinstitut für Sozial- und Wirtschaftsgeschichte. Kölner Vorträge zur Sozial- und Wirtschaftsgeschichte. Heft 7*)

COLOMBIA

— Congreso — Rules and practice.

COLOMBIA. Congreso. Camara de Representantes. Secretaria General. 1969. Reglamento general de la Camara de Representantes y constitucion politica de Colombia; edicion de 1969. Bogota, 1969. pp. 327.

— Constitution.

COLOMBIA. Congreso. Camara de Representantes. Secretaria General. 1969. Reglamento general de la Camara de Representantes y constitucion politica de Colombia; edicion de 1969. Bogota, 1969. pp. 327.

SACHICA APONTE (LUIS CARLOS) Constitucionalismo colombiano. 3rd ed. Bogota, 1972. pp. 532. *bibliog.*

— Constitutional law.

ZAFRA ROLDAN (GUSTAVO) El derecho a la constitucion. Bogotá, 1974. pp. 329. *bibliog.*

— Economic conditions.

POSADA (FRANCISCO) Colombia: violencia y subdesarrollo. [Bogota, 1969]. pp. 168.

COLOMBIA. Departamento Nacional de Planeacion. 1972. Guidelines for a new strategy; [introduction to the development plan presented to Congress on December 2, 1971]. Bogota, 1972. pp. 159.

— — Bibliography.

BOZZI ANDERSON (DIANA) compiler. Bibliografia comentada sobre economia colombiana, 1963-1970. Bogota, 1971. pp. 230. (*Universidad de los Andes [Bogota]. Centro de Estudios sobre Desarrollo Economico. Biblioteca*)

— Economic history.

POSADA (FRANCISCO) Colombia: violencia y subdesarrollo. [Bogota, 1969]. pp. 168.

— Economic policy.

COLOMBIA. Ministerio de Desarrollo Economico. Memoria. a., 1970- [Bogota].

COLOMBIA. Departamento Nacional de Planeacion. 1970. Plan de desarrollo economico y social, 1970-1973. Volumen general en dos tomos ([and] Anexo[s] I-[VI]. Bogota], 1970. 8 vols. (in 7).

COLOMBIA. Departamento Nacional de Planeacion. 1972. Guidelines for a new strategy; [introduction to the development plan presented to Congress on December 2, 1971]. Bogota, 1972. pp. 159.

— — Mathematical models.

THIRSK (WAYNE R.) Income distribution, efficiency and the experience of Colombian farm mechanization. Houston, 1972. pp. 54. (*Rice University. Program of Development Studies. Papers. No. 33*)

— Industries.

COLOMBIA. Departamento Administrativo Nacional de Estadistica. Industria manufacturera nacional. a., 1966- [Bogota].

— Politics and government.

POSADA (FRANCISCO) Colombia: violencia y subdesarrollo. [Bogota, 1969]. pp. 168.

COLOMBIA. (Cont.)

TAYLOR (PHILIP BATES) Thoughts on comparative effectiveness: leadership and the democratic left in Colombia and Venezuela. Buffalo, N.Y., 1971. fo. 42,xvi. *(New York State University. Council on International Studies. Special Studies. No. 2)*

— Presidents — Election.

CAMPOS (JUDITH TALBOT) and McCAMANT (JOHN F.) Cleavage shift in Colombia: analysis of the 1970 elections. Beverly Hills, Calif., [1972]. pp. 82. *bibliog.*

— Social policy.

COLOMBIA. Departamento Nacional de Planeacion. 1970. Plan de desarrollo economico y social, 1970-1973. Volumen general en dos tomos ([and] Anexo[s] I-[VI]. [Bogota], 1970. 8 vols. (in 7).

COLOMBO

— Economic history.

DHARMASENA (KARUNASINGHE) The development of the port of Colombo, 1860-1939; [Ph.D. (London) thesis]. 1973 [or rather, 1974]. fo. 265. *bibliog. Typescript: unpublished. This thesis is the property of London University and may not be removed from the Library.*

— Harbour.

DHARMASENA (KARUNASINGHE) The development of the port of Colombo, 1860-1939; [Ph.D. (London) thesis]. 1973 [or rather, 1974]. fo. 265. *bibliog. Typescript: unpublished. This thesis is the property of London University and may not be removed from the Library.*

COLONIES.

FRANCE. Direction de la Documentation. La Documentation Française. Notes et Etudes Documentaires. No. 3,734. L'O.N.U. et la décolonisation; [by] Patrick Daillier. Paris, 1970. pp. 48.

COLONIES IN AFRICA.

WEINSTEIN (WARREN) and GROTPETER (JOHN J.) The pattern of African decolonization: a new interpretation. Syracuse, 1973. pp. 123. *(Syracuse University. Maxwell Graduate School of Citizenship and Public Affairs. Program of Eastern African Studies. Eastern African Studies. 10)*

COLOURED PEOPLE (SOUTH AFRICA).

SOUTH AFRICA. Department of Information. 1962. A future for the coloured people. Pretoria, 1962. pp. 11. *(Digest of South African Affairs. Fact Papers. No.101).*

VENTER (J.D.) and GOOSEN (D.S.) The drinking pattern of the Coloureds in the Transvaal and the Orange Free State. [Pretoria], 1966. pp. 97. *bibliog. (South Africa. National Bureau of Educational and Social Research. Research Series. No. 20)*

PHILLIPS (BRUCE D.) The coloured population of the Port Elizabeth/Uitenhage region: a socio-economic study. Port Elizabeth, 1971. pp. 97. *(University of Port Elizabeth. Institute for Planning Research. Research Reports. No.7) With Afrikaans summary.*

O'TOOLE (JAMES) Watts and Woodstock: identity and culture in the United States and South Africa. New York, [1973]. pp. 154. *bibliog.*

— Education.

SOUTH AFRICA. Bureau of Statistics. 1973. Education: schools for Coloured and Asians, 1970. Pretoria, 1973. pp. 83. *(Reports. No.21-03-04) In English and Afrikaans.*

Columbia.

COLUMBIA, MARYLAND.

BROOKS (RICHARD OLIVER) New towns and communal values: a case study of Columbia, Maryland. New York, 1974. pp. 229. *bibliog.*

COLUMBIA RIVER.

WILSON (JAMES WOOD) People in the way: the numan aspects of the Columbia River project. Toronto, [1973]. pp. 200. *bibliog.*

COLWELL (MARIA).

HOWELLS (JOHN GWILYM) Remember Maria. London, [1974]. pp. 117. *bibliog.*

COMECON.

See COUNCIL FOR MUTUAL ECONOMIC ASSISTANCE.

COMMERCE.

RICHARDSON (J. DAVID) Constant-market-shares analysis of export growth. Ann Arbor, 1970. fo. 129. *bibliog. (Michigan University. Research Seminar in International Economics. Seminar Discussion Papers. No. 16)*

HENDERSON (J.V.) Trade and factor mobility with increasing returns to scale. Kingston, 1971. fo. 37. *bibliog. (Kingston, Ontario. Queen's University. Institute for Economic Research. Discussion Papers. No. 62)*

BASILE (ANTOINE) Commerce extérieur et développement de la petite nation: essai sur les contraintes de l'exiguité économique. Beyrouth, 1972. pp. 396. *bibliog.*

DENTON (GEOFFREY) and O'CLEIREACAIN (SEAMUS) Subsidy issues in international commerce. London, 1972. pp. 59. *(Trade Policy Research Centre. Thames Essays No. 5)*

ORGANISATION FOR ECONOMIC CO-OPERATION AND DEVELOPMENT. High Level Group on Trade and Related Problems. 1972. Policy perspectives for international trade and economic relations: report...to the Secretary-General of OECD. Paris, 1972. pp. 168.

CAMBRIDGE. University. Overseas Studies Committee. [Summer Conference, 1972]. Trade strategies for development; papers of the ninth Cambridge conference on development problems, September 1972...; edited by Paul Streeten. London, 1973. pp. 375.

CHACHOLIADES (MILTIADES) The pure theory of international trade. Chicago, [1973]. pp. 451. *bibliogs.*

HUGHES (HELEN) ed. Prospects for partnership: industrialization and trade policies in the 1970s; a seminar held at the International Bank for Reconstruction and Development, October 5 and 6, 1972. Baltimore, 1973. pp. 289.

MAINWARING (L.) A neo-Ricardian analysis of international trade. [Reading], 1973. fo. 12,ii. *(Reading. University. Department of Economics. Discussion Papers in Economics. No. 54)*

SIRC (LJUBO) Outline of international trade: commodity flows and division of production between countries. London, [1973]. pp. 156. *bibliog.*

EVANS (DOUGLAS) The politics of trade: the evolution of the superbloc. London, 1974. pp. 128.

HINDLEY (BRIAN V.) Theory of international trade. London, [1971]. pp. 171. *bibliog. (London. University. London School of Economics and Political Science. LSE Handbooks in Economic Analysis)*

The INTERNATIONAL division of labour: problems and perspectives; [proceedings of an] international symposium [in Kiel, 1973] organized by Institut für Weltwirtschaft [and] Gesellschaft für Wirtschafts- und Sozialwissenschaften (Verein für Socialpolitik); edited by Herbert Giersch. Tübingen, 1974. pp. 556.

ROBINSON (JOAN) Reflections on the theory of international trade: lectures given in the University of Manchester. Manchester, [1974]. pp. 18.

SCAMMELL (WILLIAM McCONNELL) International trade and payments. London, 1974. pp. 607. *bibliog.*

VEREIN FÜR SOZIALPOLITIK. Schriften. Neue Folge. Band 78. Probleme der weltwirtschaftlichen Arbeitsteilung: (Verhandlungen auf der Arbeitstagung...und des Instituts für Weltwirtschaft in Kiel vom 12.-15. Juli 1973; herausgegeben von Herbert Giersch und Heinz-Dieter Haas). Berlin, [1974]. pp. 651.

— History — Sources.

GOITEIN (SOLOMON DOB FRITZ) compiler. Letters of medieval Jewish traders; translated from the Arabic with introductions and notes by S.D. Goitein. Princeton, [1973]. pp. 359.

— Mathematical models.

TURNOVSKY (STEPHEN J.) Technological and price uncertainty in a Ricardian model of international trade. Canberra, 1972. fo. 30. *bibliog. (Australian National University. Research School of Social Sciences. Department of Economics. Working Papers in Economics and Econometrics. No. 12)*

FINDLAY (RONALD E.) International trade and development theory. New York, 1973. pp. 230. *bibliog.*

— Underdeveloped Areas.

See UNDERDEVELOPED AREAS — Commerce.

COMMERCIAL ASSOCIATIONS

— Mexico.

SHAFER (ROBERT JONES) Mexican business organizations: history and analysis. Syracuse, N. Y., 1973. pp. 397. *bibliog.*

— United Kingdom.

COMMISSION OF INQUIRY INTO INDUSTRIAL AND COMMERCIAL REPRESENTATION. Report. London, 1972. pp. 127.

COMMERCIAL CRIMES

— United States.

DEMARIS (OVID) Dirty business: the corporate-political money-power game. New York, [1974]. pp. 442.

COMMERCIAL FINANCE COMPANIES

— France.

FRANCE. Direction de la Documentation. La Documentation Française. Notes et Etudes Documentaires. Nos. 3,967-3, 968. Le Crédit Foncier de France. [Paris], 1973. pp. 60.

COMMERCIAL LAW

— Denmark.

KOBBERNAGEL (JAN) Erhvervsretten i grundtraek. 8th ed. København, 1974. pp. 375. *bibliog. (Copenhagen. Handelshøjskolen. Skriftraekke G. 1)*

— Germany.

CONGRES INTERNATIONAL DE DROIT COMPARE, 1974. 9e Congrès. Deutsche handels- und wirtschaftsrechtliche Landesberichte zum IX. Internationalen Kongress für Rechtsvergleichung, Sektion III ; Herausgeber Ernst von Caemmerer. Stuttgart, 1974. pp. 129. *(Zeitschrift für das gesamte Handelsrecht und Wirtschaftsrecht. Beihefte. Abhandlungen aus dem gesamten Bürgerlichen Recht, Handelsrecht und Wirtschaftsrecht. 46. Heft) With summaries in various languages.*

— Russia.

KUNIK (IAKOV ABRAMOVICH) ed. Regulirovanie gosudarstvennoi torgovli v SSSR. 2nd ed. Moskva, 1973. pp. 303.

— United States.

AMERICAN LAW INSTITUTE and NATIONAL CONFERENCE OF COMMISSIONERS ON UNIFORM STATE LAWS. Uniform commercial code: 1972 official text, with comments, etc. Philadelphia, [1972 repr. 1973]. pp. 816.

COMMERCIAL LEASES

— **Belgium.**

GUSTOT (ANDRE) Les baux commerciaux: commentaire et jurisprudence. 3rd ed. Bruxelles, Institut Economique et Social des Classes Moyennes, 1972. pp. 139. *bibliog.*

COMMERCIAL POLICY.

NEGOZIATI commerciali internazionali: conflitto o cooperazione?; International trade negotiations: conflict or co-operation?; [proceedings of a seminar held in Milan, 1973, under the auspices of the Ente Autonomo Fiera Internazionale Milano]. Milano, 1973. pp. 237.

UNITED NATIONS. Conference on Trade and Development, 3rd, Santiago de Chile, 1972. Proceedings of the... conference..., third session, Santiago de Chile, 13 April to 21 May 1972. (TD/180). New York, 1973. 6 vols. (in 3)

COMMERCIAL PRODUCTS.

COMMODITY TRADE AND PRICE TRENDS (formerly Commodity price trends); ([pd. by] International Bank for Reconstruction and Development [and] International Development Association). a., 1970, 1971, 1973- [Washington]. *In English, French and Spanish.*

UNITED NATIONS. Conference on Trade and Development, 3rd, Santiago de Chile, 1972. Proceedings of the... conference..., third session, Santiago de Chile, 13 April to 21 May 1972. (TD/180). New York, 1973. 6 vols. (in 3)

PRAVOTOROV (GEORGII BORISOVICH) Stoimostnye kategorii i sposob proizvodstva: problemy teorii i metodologii. Moskva, 1974. pp. 303.

— **Classification.**

NETHERLANDS ANTILLES. Dienst Economische Zaken en Welvaartszorg. Afdeling Statistiek. 1955-57. De in-, uit- en doorvoerstatistiek: toelichting en codelijsten. [Willemstad], 1955-57. 2 pts.

UNITED NATIONS. Statistical Office. Statistical Papers. Series M. No. 43. Rev.1. Classification of commodities by industrial origin: links between the Standard International Trade Classification. (ST/STAT/SER.M/ 43/Rev.1) New York, 1971. pp. 145.

CANADA. Statistics Canada. 1972- . Standard commodity classification manual. 3rd ed. Ottawa, 1972 in progress.

ASOCIACION LATINOAMERICANA DE LIBRE COMERCIO. 1972. Recopilacion de normas sobre valoracion aduanera de las mercaderias en los paises de la ALALC. [Montevideo], 1972. 1 vol. (various pagings).

CANADA. Customs and Excise Division. 1973. Canadian international trade classification numeric index. Ottawa, 1973. 1 vol. (loose-leaf).

[SCANDINAVIA]. Nordisk Statistisk Skriftserie. 28. Gemensam nordisk näringsstatistik varuförteckning, etc. Stockholm, 1974. 1 vol. (unpaged)

— **Mathematical models.**

LABYS (WALTER C.) Dynamic commodity models: specification, estimation, and simulation. Lexington, [1973]. pp. 350. *bibliog.*

— **Africa.**

PEARSON (SCOTT R.) and COWNIE (JOHN) Commodity exports and African economic development. Lexington, Mass., [1974]. pp. 285.

COMMERCIAL VEHICLES.

U.K. Department of the Environment. Directorate of Statistics. 1972. The transport of goods by road, 1970-1972. [London], 1972. fo.20,4.

URBAN freight distribution: studies of operations in shopping streets at Newbury and Camberley; by A.W. Christie [and others]. Crowthorne, 1973. pp. 81. *(U.K. Transport and Road Research Laboratory. Reports. LR 603)*

COMMISSIONS OF INQUIRY.
See GOVERNMENTAL INVESTIGATIONS.

COMMITTEES.

U.K. Civil Service Department. 1971. Committee procedure. [London, 1971]. pp. 18.

CLAESSON (GÖRAN C-O.) Statens Ostyriga Utredande: betänkande om kommittéväsendet. Stockholm, 1972. pp. 211. *(Studieförbundet Näringsliv och Samhälle. Studier och Debatt. 1972. Nr.3)*

COMMODITY EXCHANGES

— **United Kingdom.**

GRANGER (CLIVE W.J.) ed. Trading in commodities: an Investors' Chronicle guide. Cambridge, 1974. pp. 116. *bibliog.*

COMMONWEALTH DEVELOPMENT CORPORATION.

PARTNERS IN DEVELOPMENT: finance plus management; ([pd. by] Commonwealth Development Corporation). a., 1973- London.

COMMUNES (CHINA).

FRANCE. Direction de la Documentation. La Documentation Française. Notes et Etudes Documentaires. Nos. 3,066-3, 067. La planification économique des communes populaires chinoises: documents. Paris, 1964. 2 pts.

COMMUNICATION.

UNITED NATIONS EDUCATIONAL, SCIENTIFIC AND CULTURAL ORGANIZATION. Department of Mass Communication. Reports and Papers on Mass Communication. Paris, 1953 in progress.

VOPROSY teorii i praktiki massovykh sredstv propagandy. vyp.4. Moskva, 1971. pp. 415.

LERBINGER (OTTO) Designs for persuasive communication. Englewood Cliffs, [1972]. pp. 283.

COTTERET (JEAN MARIE) Gouvernants et gouvernés: la communication politique. [Paris], 1973. pp. 178. *bibliog.*

Det KOMMUNIKATIONSBEVIDSTE salg; [by] Otto Ottesen, red., Johan Arndt [and others]. København, 1973. pp. 91. *(Copenhagen. Handelshøjskolen. Skriftraekke F. 45)*

MUELLER (CLAUS) The politics of communication : a study in the political sociology of language, socialization, and legitimation. New York, 1973. pp. 226. *bibliog.*

SCHRAMM (WILBUR LANG) Men, messages, and media: a look at human communication. New York, [1973]. pp. 341.

INTERNATIONAL CONFERENCE ON COMMUNICATIONS, 1ST, TOKYO, 1972. Communication: linking today's business and tomorrow's world: [proceedings of the conference] organized by Research Institute of Telecommunications and Economics and Japan Management Association. Tokyo, [1974]. pp. 145.

SERVAN-SCHREIBER (JEAN LOUIS) The power to inform: media, the information business;... translated...with the cooperation of Paris Research Associates. New York, [1974]. pp. 297.

— **Social aspects.**

COMMUNICATIONS technology and social policy: understanding the new "cultural revolution": [based on papers discussed at a symposium held at the Annenberg School of Communications, University of Pennsylvania, 1972]; edited by George Gerbner [and others]. New York, [1973]. pp. 573. *bibliogs.*

— **Underdeveloped areas.**

See also UNDERDEVELOPED AREAS
— Communication.

— — **United States.**

MANDELBAUM (SEYMOUR J.) Community and communications. New York, [1972]. pp. 153.

— **United States.**

PRED (ALLAN R.) Urban growth and the circulation of information: the United States system of cities, 1790-1840. Cambridge, Mass., 1973. pp. 348.

COMMUNICATION AND TRAFFIC

— **Belgium.**

INSTITUT BELGE D'INFORMATION ET DE DOCUMENTATION. Ce qu'il faut savoir...du Ministère des Communications, Postes, Télégraphes et Téléphones. Bruxelles, [1971]. fo. 36.

— **Germany.**

GERMANY (BUNDESREPUBLIK). Statistisches Bundesamt. Ausgaben der öffentlichen Haushalte für das Verkehrs- und Nachrichtenwesen. a., 1971- Wiesbaden. *(Finanzen und Steuern. Reihe 5. Sonderbeiträge zur Finanzstatistik).*

— **Portugal.**

PORTUGAL. Presidência do Conselho. 1953. 25 anos de administração publica: Ministerio das Comunicações. Lisboa, 1953. pp. 67.

COMMUNICATION IN THE SOCIAL SCIENCES.

HAGE (JERALD) Communication and organizational control: cybernetics in health and welfare settings. New York, [1974]. pp. 273. *bibliog.*

COMMUNICATIONS RESEARCH.

CURRENT BRITISH RESEARCH ON MASS MEDIA AND MASS COMMUNICATION: register of ongoing and recently completed unpublished research. a., My 1974 [1st issue]- Leicester.

HALLORAN (JAMES D.) Mass media and society: the challenge of research: an inaugural lecture delivered in the University of Leicester, 25 October 1973. Leicester, 1974. pp. 30. *bibliog.*

COMMUNISM.

PUJA (FRIGYES) Edinstvo i diskussiia v mezhdunarodnom kommunisticheskom dvizhenii; perevod s vengerskogo. Moskva, 1970. pp. 160.

BIEŃKOWSKI (WŁADYSŁAW) Drogi wyjścia. Paryṡ, 1971. pp. 85.

BRINKMANN (HEINRICH) Stalin, Theoretiker der Bürokratie: eine Streitschrift gegen den offenen Stalinismus und gegen die verlegenen Entstalinisierer. 's Gravenhage, 1971 repr.1972. pp. 167. *bibliog.*

KOMMUNISTISCHER STUDENTENBUND GÖTTINGEN. Die Differenzen zwischen Lenin und Rosa Luxemburg im Kampf gegen Revisionismus und Opportunismus in der Sozialdemokratie. 2nd ed. Göttingen, 1971. pp. 59.

PANNEKOEK (ANTON) Partij, raden, revolutie: samengesteld en van aantekeningen voorzien door Jaap Kloosterman. Amsterdam, 1972. pp. 238. *bibliog.*

ROZVYTOK naukovoho komunizmu v suchasnykh umovakh. Kyïv, 1972. pp. 203.

BOR'BA kommunistov protiv ideologii trotskizma. Moskva, 1973. pp. 222.

NAUCHNO-tekhnicheskaia revoliutsiia i sotsializm. Moskva, 1973. pp. 366.

EL'MEEV (VASILII IAKOVLEVICH) and KAZAKOV (ANATOLII PAVLOVICH) eds. Kommunizm i sotsial'nyi progress. Leningrad, 1973. pp. 326.

COMMUNISM. (Cont.)

FELICE (FRANCO DE) Fascismo, democrazia, fronte popolare: il movimento comunista alla svolta del VII Congresso dell'Internazionale. Bari, [1973]. pp. 569.

FRANK (PIERRE) La Quatrième Internationale: contribution à l'histoire du mouvement trotskyste. [2nd ed.]. Paris, 1973. pp. 180. *bibliog.*

HUNDT (MARTIN) Wie das "Manifest" entstand. Berlin, 1973. pp. 139.

MARXISTISCHE AUFBAUORGANISATION. Die Krise der kommunistischen Parteien: Probleme der gegenwärtigen Revisionismuskritik. München, 1973. pp. 309. *bibliog.*

NECHIPURENKO (VASILII IGNAT'EVICH) V.I. Lenin o zashchite sotsialisticheskogo Otechestva: printsipy internatsionalizma i zashchita Otechestva. Moskva, 1973. pp. 223. *bibliog.*

PROTOPOPOV (ANATOLII SERGEEVICH) SSSR i mezhdunarodnyi rabochii klass v bor'be za mir. Moskva, 1973. pp. 212. *bibliog.*

RABOCHII klass - glavnaia revoliutsionnaia sila. Moskva, 1973. pp. 400.

RAZVITOE sotsialisticheskoe obshchestvo: sushchnost'', kriterii zrelosti, kritika revizionistskikh kontseptsii. Moskva, 1973. pp. 422.

REICH (WILHELM) What is class consciousness?; [originally published in German in 1934 under the pseudonym of Ernst Parell]. 2nd ed. [London], 1973. pp. 76.

SHALIN (MIKHAIL ALEKSEEVICH) Antikommunizm i ideologicheskaia bor'ba na sovremennom etape. Kazan', 1973. pp. 242.

SUSLOV (MIKHAIL ANDREEVICH) Marksizm-leninizm - internatsional'noe uchenie rabochego klassa. Moskva, 1973. pp. 263. *Collected articles and speeches.*

SWORAKOWSKI (WITOLD S.) ed. World communism: a handbook, 1918-1965. Stanford, 1973. pp. 576. *bibliogs. (Stanford University. Hoover Institution on War, Revolution and Peace. Hoover Institution Publications. 108)*

The TRANSITIONAL program for socialist revolution; [programme by Leon Trotsky adopted at the Founding Conference of the Fourth International in 1938; with discussions with Trotsky and] introductory essays by Joseph Hansen and George Novack. New York, 1973. pp. 223.

UCHENYE ZAPISKI KAFEDR OBSHCHESTVENNYKH NAUK VUZOV LENINGRADA. Problemy Nauchnogo Kommunizma. vyp.7. Metodologicheskie problemy teorii nauchnogo kommunizma; pod redaktsiei... A.K. Belykh. Leningrad, 1973. pp. 175.

UL'IANOVSKII (ROSTISLAV ALEKSANDROVICH) Der Sozialismus und die befreiten Länder; (aus dem Russischen übersetzt von einem Übersetzerkollektiv). Berlin, 1973. pp. 452.

ZAGLADIN (V.V.) and RYZHENKO (F.D.) eds. Sovremennoe revoliutsionnoe dvizhenie i natsionalizm. Moskva, 1973. pp. 320.

ARZAMASTSEV (ALEKSANDR MIKHAILOVICH) Kazarmennyi "kommunizm": kriticheskii ocherk. Moskva, 1974. pp. 168.

DALTON (GEORGE) Economic systems and society: capitalism, communism and the third world. Harmondsworth, 1974. pp. 250. *bibliog.*

HONECKER (ERICH) Die Rolle der Arbeiterklasse und ihrer Partei in der sozialistischen Gesellschaft: [collected articles and speeches, 1971-73]. Berlin, 1974. pp. 389.

KORSCH (KARL) Politische Texte; herausgegeben und eingeleitet von Erich Gerlach und Jürgen Seifert. Frankfurt am Main, [1974]. pp. 400.

KREISKY (BRUNO) Aspekte des demokratischen Sozialismus: Aufsätze, Reden, Interviews; mit einem Vorwort von Ossip K. Flechtheim. München, [1974]. pp. 200. *bibliog.*

LEONHARD (WOLFGANG) Three faces of marxism; the political concepts of Soviet ideology, maoism, and humanist marxism; (translated by Ewald Osers). New York, [1974]. pp. 497. *bibliog.*

MERKEL (RENATE) Marx und Engels über Sozialismus und Kommunismus: zur Herausbildung der Auffassung...in der Entstehungsperiode des wissenschaftlichen Kommunismus, 1842-1846. Berlin, 1974. pp. 311.

NEUBERT (HARALD) Der antiimperialistische Kampf und die Politik der friedlichen Koexistenz: zur Strategie der kommunistischen Weltbewegung in der Auseinandersetzung zwischen Sozialismus und Imperialismus. Berlin,1974. pp. 80.

SHITOV (NIKOLAI FEDOROVICH) V.I. Lenin i proletarskii internatsionalizm, 1917-1924 gg. Moskva, 1974. pp. 359.

THAELMANN (ERNST) Geschichte und Politik: Artikel und Reden, 1925 bis 1933. Frankfurt am Main, 1974. pp. 238.

ZETKIN (CLARA) Zur Theorie und Taktik der kommunistischen Bewegung; (herausgegeben von Katja Haferkorn und Heinz Karl). Leipzig, 1974. pp. 511.

— **History.**

GRANDJONC (JACQUES) Marx et les communistes allemands à Paris, 1844: contribution à l'étude de la naissance du marxisme. Paris, 1974. pp. 264. *bibliog.*

— **Africa.**

PAN-AFRICAN SEMINAR ON THE JUCHE IDEA OF COMRADE KIM IL SUNG, FREETOWN, 1972. Documents and deliberations of the seminar. Beirut, [1973]. pp. 184.

— **America, Latin.**

PIÑEIRO (ARMANDO ALONSO) Paredon de America. Buenos Aires, [1962]. pp. 125.

HERMAN (DONALD L.) ed. The communist tide in Latin America: a selected treatment. Austin, [1973]. pp.214. *(Reprinted from the Texas Quarterly, vol. 15 no.1, 1972)*

HODGES (DONALD CLARK) The Latin American revolution: politics and strategy from apro-marxism to guevarism. New York, 1974. pp. 287. *bibliog.*

— **Asia.**

TROTSKII (LEV DAVYDOVICH) Perspectives and tasks in the East; (speech on the third anniversary of the Communist University for Toilers of the East, April 21, 1924); translated from the Russian by R. Chappell. London, 1973. pp. 15.

— **Bessarabia.**

KOPANSKII (IAKOV MIKHAILOVICH) Internatsional'nye traditsii bor'by za vossoedinenie Bessarabii s Sovetskoi Rodinoi, 1918-1940 gg. Kishinev, 1973. pp. 110.

— **Brazil.**

MARIGHELA (CARLOS) La guerra revolucionaria. Mexico, 1970. pp. 101. *bibliog.*

DULLES (JOHN W.F.) Anarchists and communists in Brazil, 1900-1935. Austin, [1973]. pp. 603. *bibliog.*

— **China.**

BEHIND China's "great cultural revolution"; by Peng Shu- tse [and others]. New York, 1967 repr. 1970. pp. 63.

GEL'BRAS (VILIA GDALIVICH) Mao's pseudo-socialism. Moscow, [1967?]. pp. 156.

GRAY (JACK) and CAVENDISH (PATRICK) Chinese communism in crisis: Maoism and the cultural revolution. London, Pall Mall Press, 1968 repr. 1970. pp. viii, 279.

MAOISM unmasked: collection of Soviet press articles; (compiled by V.F. Feoktistov). Moscow, 1972. pp. 246.

ASIAN PEOPLES' ANTI-COMMUNIST LEAGUE. Pamphlets. No.172. Chiang Ching - Mao Tse-Tung's wife. [Taipei], 1973. pp. 44.

BETTELHEIM (CHARLES) Révolution culturelle et organisation industrielle en Chine. Paris, 1973. pp. 153.

COLLIER (JOHN) Maoist and COLLIER (ELSIE) China's socialist revolution. London, 1973. pp. 270.

GEL'BRAS (VILIA GDALIVICH) Kitai: krizis prodolzhaetsia. Moskva, 1973. pp. 223.

HOUN (FRANKLIN WILLINGTON) A short history of Chinese communism. [2nd ed.] Englewood Cliffs,]1973]. pp. 278.

IDEOLOGY and politics in contemporary China: [selected papers of a conference held in Santa Fe, 1971]; edited by Chalmers Johnson. Seattle, [1973]. pp. 388. *(American Council of Learned Societies and Social Science Research Council. Joint Committee on Contemporary China. Subcommittee on Chinese Government and Politics. Studies in Chinese Government and Politics. 4)*

KAROL (K.S.) pseud. [i.e. Karol KEWES] La deuxième révolution chinoise. Paris, [1973]. pp. 563.

KIM (ILPYONG J.) The politics of Chinese communism: Kiangsi under the Soviets. Berkeley, [1973]. pp. 232. *bibliog.*

LÖTVEIT (TRYGVE) Chinese communism 1931-1934: experience in civil government. Lund, 1973. pp. 290. *bibliog. (Scandinavian Institute of Asian Studies. Monograph Series. No. 16)*

SHIH (PING) Life of workers under Chinese Communist persecution. [Taiwan], 1973. pp. 80. *(Asian Peoples' Anti-Communist League. Pamphlets. No. 174)*

THOMSON (GEORGE DERWENT) Capitalism and after: the rise and fall of commodity production. London, [1973]. pp. 148. *bibliog.*

THORNTON (RICHARD C.) China, the struggle for power 1917-1972. Bloomington, [1973]. pp. 403.

THREE major struggles on China's philosophical front, 1949-64. Peking, 1973. pp. 66.

ZHELOKHOVTSEV (ALEKSEI NIKOLAEVICH) "Kul'turnaia revoliutsiia" s blizkogo rasstoianiia: zapiski ochevidtsa. Moskva, 1973. pp. 262. *A revised version of the account first published in Novyi mir, 1968.*

MACFARQUHAR (RODERICK L.) The origins of the cultural revolution. London, 1974 in progress. *bibliog.*

ARZAMASTSEV (ALEKSANDR MIKHAILOVICH) Kazarmennyi "kommunizm": kriticheskii ocherk. Moskva, 1974. pp. 168.

LEONHARD (WOLFGANG) Three faces of marxism; the political concepts of Soviet ideology, maoism, and humanist marxism; (translated by Ewald Osers). New York, [1974]. pp. 497. *bibliog.*

MAO (TSE-TUNG) Mao Tse-tung unrehearsed: talks and letters, 1956-1971; edited and introduced by Stuart Schram; translated by John Chinnery and Tieyun. Harmondsworth, [1974]. pp. 352.

— — **Terminology.**

DOOLIN DENNIS J.) and RIDLEY (CHARLES PRICE) A Chinese-English dictionary of communist Chinese terminology. Stanford, [1973]. pp. 569. *(Stanford University. Hoover Institution on War, Revolution and Peace. Hoover Institution Publications. 124)*

— **Czechoslovakia.**

SOVREMENNYI pravyi revizionizm: kriticheskii analiz. Moskva, 1973. pp. 615.

— **Europe, Eastern.**

KING (ROBERT R.) Minorities under Communism: nationalities as a source of tension among Balkan communist states. Cambridge, Mass., 1973. pp. 326. *bibliog.*

COMMUNISM. (Cont.)

— France.

KRIEGEL (ANNIE) Communismes au miroir français: temps, cultures et sociétés en France devant le communisme. [Paris, 1974]. pp. 253.

— Germany.

BRINKMANN (HEINRICH) Stalin, Theoretiker der Bürokratie: eine Streitschrift gegen den offenen Stalinismus und gegen die verlegenen Entstalinisierer. 's Gravenhage, 1971 repr.1972. pp. 167. *bibliog.*

KOMMUNISTISCHER BUND WESTDEUTSCHLAND. Gründungskonferenz, 1973. Ergebnisse der Gründungskonferenz: (Gründungserklärung, Programm, Statut, Resolutionen). [Mannheim, 1973]. pp. 61.

MARXISTISCHE AUFBAUORGANISATION. Die Krise der kommunistischen Parteien: Probleme der gegenwärtigen Revisionismuskritik. München, 1973. pp. 309. *bibliog.*

KORSCH (KARL) Politische Texte; herausgegeben und eingeleitet von Erich Gerlach und Jürgen Seifert. Frankfurt am Main, [1974]. pp. 400.

— — Bavaria.

RETZLAW (KARL) Spartakus: Aufstieg und Niedergang; Erinnerungen eines Parteiarbeiters. 2nd ed. Frankfurt, 1972. pp. 511.

— Germany, Eastern.

EINFUEHRUNG in die politische Ökonomie des Sozialismus; (Autoren: Willy Becker [and others]). Berlin, 1974. pp. 503.

HONECKER (ERICH) Die Rolle der Arbeiterklasse und ihrer Partei in der sozialistischen Gesellschaft: [collected articles and speeches, 1971-73]. Berlin, 1974. pp. 389.

NEUMANN (PHILIPP) Writer on communism. Zurück zum Profit: zur Entwicklung des Revisionismus in der DDR. Berlin, 1974. pp. 288.

— Hungary.

A MAGYAR forradalmi munkásmozgalom története. kötet 1,2. 2nd ed. Budapest, 1970. pp. 563.

SHAWCROSS (WILLIAM) Crime and compromise: Janos Kadar and the politics of Hungary since revolution. London, [1974]. pp. 311.

— India.

CHATTOPADHYAY (GAUTAM) Communism and Bengal's freedom movement. New Delhi, 1970 in progress.

HU (CHI-HSI) Pékin et le mouvement communiste indien. Paris, 1972. pp. 153. (*Fondation Nationale des Sciences Politiques. Travaux et Recherches de Science Politique. 22*)

SUNDARAYYA (P.) Telangana people's struggle and its lessons. Calcutta, 1972. pp. 592.

— Indonesia.

PALMIER (LESLIE HUGH) Communists in Indonesia. London, [1973]. pp. 302. *bibliog.*

— Italy.

LISI (ARCANGELO) Storia del movimento operaio di Locorotondo, dai miei ricordi. Locorotondo, [197-?]. pp. 63.

PARTITO COMUNISTA INTERNAZIONALE. Storia della sinistra comunista, (1912-1920). Milan, 1972-73. 2 vols. *Vol. 1 originally published 1964 and reprinted 1973.*

VETTORI (GIUSEPPE) ed. La sinistra extraparlamentare in Italia: storia, documenti, analisi politica. Roma, 1973. pp. 377. *bibliog.*

MACCIOCCHI (MARIA ANTONIETTA) Per Gramsci. Bologna, [1974]. pp. 427. *bibliog.*

MACCIOCCHI (MARIA ANTONIETTA) Pour Gramsci. Paris, [1974]. pp. 429. *bibliog.*

— Mongolia.

SHIRENDYB (BAZARYN) Izbrannye proizvedeniia; (perevedeno s mongol'skogo avtorom). Moskva, 1973. pp. 339.

SHIRENDYB (BAZARYN) V.I. Lenin i mongol'skii narod. Moskva, 1970. pp. 60.

— Netherlands.

GROOT (PAUL DE) De dertiger jaren 1930-(1939): herinneringen en overdenkingen. Amsterdam, 1965-67. 2 vols.

LIAGRE BÖHL (HERMAN DE) Herman Gorter: zijn politieke aktiviteiten van 1909 tot 1920 in de opkomende kommunistische beweging in Nederland. Nijmegen, 1973. pp. 317. *bibliog.*

— Nigeria.

WATERMAN (PETER) Communist theory in the Nigerian trade union movement. The Hague, 1973. pp. 26. (*Hague. Institute of Social Studies. Occasional Papers. No.41*)

— Roumania.

GEORGESCU (TITU) Progress and revolution in the tradition of the Romanian people, 1848-1971. Bucharest, 1971. pp. 132.

— Russia.

NOL'DE (BORIS) Baron. Lenins Räte-Republik: ein Beitrag zur Geschichte der politischen und wirtschaftlichen Entwicklung im neuen Russland; aus dem Französischen übersetzt von R. Paderstein. Berlin, 1920. pp. 44.

POPOV (GEORGII) Stremiashchimsia v Rossiiu...; zhizn' v Sovetskoi respublike, s 31 original'nymi fotografiiami. Berlin, 1924. pp. 232.

ARTSYBASHEV (MIKHAIL PETROVICH) Cheremukha: zapiski pisatelia. t.2. Varshava, 1927. pp. 179. *Articles originally published in "Za svobodu". Vol.1 entitled Zapiski pisatelia.*

PIATNITSKII (OSIP ARONOVICH) pseud. [i.e. Iosif Aronovich TARSHIS] Memoirs of a Bolshevik; [reprint of the work first published in London, 1933]. Westport, Conn., 1973. pp. 224.

SABIK-VOGULOV ( ) V pobezhdennoi Germanii. n.p., 1947. pp. 78.

SHUMILOV (MIKHAIL NIKOLAEVICH) Oktiabr'skaia sotsialisticheskaia revoliutsiia i istoricheskie sud'by batrachestva. Moskva, 1967. pp. 231.

ISTORIIA natsional'no-gosudarstvennogo stroitel'stva v SSSR: natsional'no-gosudarstvennoe stroitel'stvo v SSSR v period sotsializma i stroitel'stva kommunizma, 1937-1967 gg. Moskva, 1970. pp. 276.

SAVASTIUK (ANTON IVANOVICH) V. I. Lenin o pobede sotsializma v SSSR; pod redaktsiei ... K.P. Buslova. Minsk, 1970. pp. 222. *bibliog.*

EKONOMICHESKIE i sotsial'no-politicheskie problemy kommunisticheskogo stroitel'stva v SSSR: materialy nauchnoi konferentsii Instituta marksizma-leninizma pri TsK KPSS, Akademii obshchestvennykh nauk pri TsK KPSS, Vysshei partiinoi shkoly pri TsK KPSS, sektsii obshchestvennykh nauk AN SSSR na temu: "XXIV s"ezd KPSS i razvitie marksistko-leninskoi teorii", 29 sentiabria 1 oktiabria 1971 g. Moskva, 1972. pp. 351.

AGEEV (VALENTIN MIKHAILOVICH) Metodologicheskie i teoreticheskie problemy osnovnogo ekonomicheskogo zakona sotsializma. Moskva, 1973. pp. 208.

FEDOSEEV (PETR NIKOLAEVICH) Kommunismus und Philosophie; (übersetzt [from the Russian] von Leon Nebenzahl). Berlin, 1973. pp. 594.

GIMPEL'SON (EFIM GILEVICH) "Voennyi kommunizm": politika, praktika, ideologiia. Moskva, 1973. pp. 296.

INTERNATSIONAL'NE i natsional'ne v sotsialistychnomu suspil'stvi. Kyïv, 1973. pp. 243.

KAS'IANENKO (VASILII IGNAT'EVICH) Problemy sozdaniia material'no-tekhnicheskoi bazy kommunizma: istoriograficheskii ocherk. Moskva, 1973. pp. 182.

KUMANEV (VIKTOR ALEKSANDROVICH) Revoliutsiia i prosveshchenie mass. Moskva, 1973. pp. 335. *bibliog.*

LIEBMAN (MARCEL) Le léninisme sous Lénine. Paris, [1973]. 2 vols.

METODICHESKOE posobie po nauchnomu kommunizmu; dlia shkol osnov marksizma-leninizma. 2nd ed. Moskva, 1973. pp. 319.

PIVTSAIKIN (GEORGII IVANOVICH) Obshchestvennye otnosheniia razvitogo sotsializma. Minsk, 1973. pp. 261.

PREOBRAZHENSKII (EVGENII ALEKSEEVICH) From New Economic Policy to socialism: a glance into the future of Russia and Europe; (translated from the Russian, 1962, by Brian Pearce). London, 1973. pp. 116.

SIUSIUKALOV (BORIS IVANOVICH) Sotsialisticheskoe obshchestvo: problemy dialektiki razvitiia. Moskva, 1973. pp. 278.

SOVETSKOE gosudarstvo - god pervyi. Moskva, 1973. pp. 263.

STEKLOV (IURII MIKHAILOVICH) Izbrannoe. Moskva, 1973. pp. 262. *bibliog.*

TIKHOMIROV (IURII ALEKSANDROVICH) Pouvoir et administration dans la société socialiste. Paris, 1973. pp. 193.

VARLAMOV (KONSTANTIN IVANOVICH) Leninskaia kontseptsiia sotsialisticheskogo upravleniia: genezis, stanovlenie. Moskva, 1973. pp. 398.

KORSCH (KARL) Politische Texte; herausgegeben und eingeleitet von Erich Gerlach und Jürgen Seifert. Frankfurt am Main, [1974]. pp. 400.

LEONHARD (WOLFGANG) Three faces of marxism; the political concepts of Soviet ideology, maoism, and humanist marxism; (translated by Ewald Osers). New York, [1974]. pp. 497. *bibliog.*

MARCUSE (HERBERT) Die Gesellschaftslehre des sowjetischen Marxismus; (Übersetzung [from the English]: Alfred Schmidt). Darmstadt, 1974. pp. 256.

PASHKOV (ANATOLII IGNAT'EVICH) Ökonomische Probleme des Sozialismus; Übersetzung aus dem Russischen ([by] Cay-Harro Dahl [and others]). Berlin, 1974. pp. 470.

— — Azerbaijan.

SUMBATZADE (ALI SUMBATOVICH) Sotsial'no-ekonomicheskie predposylki pobedy Sovetskoi vlasti v Azerbaidzhane. Moskva, 1972. pp. 254.

— — Estonia.

KÜNG (ANDRES) Estland zum Beispiel: nationale Minderheit und Supermacht; Übersetzung aus dem Schwedischen von Karl Leonhard). Stuttgart, [1973]. pp. 192. *bibliog.*

— — Georgia.

50 let Sovetskoi Gruzii i Kompartii Gruzii: materialy i dokumenty. [Tbilisi, 1971]. pp. 238.

— — Latvia.

KAPENIECE (ILGA) The year of change; (translated from the Latvian by J. Vejš). Riga, 1973. pp. 80. *bibliog.*

— — Tajikistan.

SADYKOV (MARUF SADYKOVICH) Istoricheskii opyt KPSS po stroitel'stvu sotsializma v Tadzhikistane, 1917-1959 gg. Dushanbe, 1967. pp. 434. *bibliog.*

— — Turkmenistan.

AKMURADOV (KURBANMUKHAMED) Izmenenie sotsial'noi struktury obshchestva v period perekhoda ot sotsializma k kommunizmu; otvetstvennyi redaktor... G.O. Muradova. Ashkhabad, 1972. pp. 216.

COMMUNISM. (Cont.)

— — Ukraine.

CHUBAR (VLAS IAKOVYCH) Vybrani statti i promovy. Kyïv, 1972. pp. 628.

— — Ukraine, Western.

OLEKSIUK (MYROSLAV MYRONOVYCH) Prohresyvna presa Zakhidnoï Ukraïny v borot'bi na zakhyst SRSR, 20-30-ti roky. Kyïv, 1973. pp. 228.

— — Uzbekistan.

EKONOMIKA i kul'tura Bukharskoi oblasti posle Velikogo Oktiabria. Bukhara, 1968. pp. 270. *(Bukharskii Gosudarstvennyi Pedagogicheskii Institut. Uchenye Zapiski. vyp.15)*

— Spain.

CARRILLO (SANTIAGO) Problemas del socialismo. Paris, [1969]. pp. 127.

— Switzerland.

Die KOMMUNISTEN in der Schweiz nach den bei Weitling vorgefundenen Papieren: wörtlicher Abdruck des Kommissionalberichtes an die Hohe Regierung des Standes Zürich; ([by] Johann Caspar Bluntschli);...als Anhang, Sebastian Seiler: Der Schriftsteller Wilhelm Weitling und der Kommunistenlärm in Zürich; eine Verteidigungsschrift...; [reprint of the original editions of 1843]. Glashütten im Taunus, 1973. pp. 130,26.

ULMER (HANS) Wollen wir den Klassenkampf?. St. Gallen, [1973]. pp. 63. *bibliog. (Landesverband Freier Schweizer Arbeiter. Soziale Schriftenreihe. Heft 52)*

— Taiwan.

TWENTY-sixth anniversary of the "February 28" uprising of the people of Taiwan province. Peking, 1973. pp. 23.

— Underdeveloped Areas.

See UNDERDEVELOPED AREAS — Communism.

— United Kingdom.

GROVES (REGINALD) The Balham group: how British Trotskyism began. London, 1974. pp. 111.

TRORY (ERNIE) Between the wars: recollections of a communist organiser. Brighton, 1974. pp. 159.

— Yugoslavia.

HRONOLOGIJA radničkog pokreta u Srbiji. knj.2. Od 1919. do 1941. godine. Beograd, 1969. pp. 397. *In Cyrillic.*

HAGEMANN (MICHAEL) and KLEMENČIČ (ALEKKA) Die sozialistische Marktwirtschaft Jugoslawiens. Stuttgart, 1974. pp. 303. *bibliog.*

COMMUNISM AND CHRISTIANITY

SEMAINE DE LA PENSEE MARXISTE, 1972. Chrétiens et communistes...;avec la participation de J. Arnault [and others]. Paris, [1973]. pp. 268.

— Catholic Church — America, Latin.

GHEERBRANT (ALAIN) The rebel church in Latin America; translated by Rosemary Sheed. Harmondsworth 1974. pp. 357.

— China.

PATTERSON (GEORGE NEILSON) Christianity in communist China. Waco, Tex., [1969]. pp. 174.

COMMUNISM AND EDUCATION.

LEVITAS (MAURICE) Marxist perspectives in the sociology of education. London, 1974. pp. 208. *bibliog.*

COMMUNISM AND ISLAM.

MASSELL (GREGORY J.) The surrogate proletariat: Moslem women and revolutionary strategies in Soviet Central Asia, 1919-1929. Princeton, [1974]. pp. 448. *bibliog.*

COMMUNISM AND LITERATURE.

KUNITSYN (GEORGII IVANOVICH) Politika i literatura. Moskva, 1973. pp. 592.

COMMUNISM AND RELIGION.

RELIGIIA v planakh antikommunizma. Moskva, 1970. pp. 222.

BOURDEAUX (MICHAEL) Faith on trial in Russia. London, 1971. pp. 192. *bibliog.*

FRANCE. Direction de la Documentation. La Documentation Française. Notes et Etudes Documentaires. Nos. 3,790-3, 791. Les problèmes religieux en Europe orientale, 1945-1970; [by] Thomas Schreiber [and others]. Paris, 1971. pp. 78. *bibliog.*

KOSTIUKOV (IVAN VASIL'EVICH) Bluzhdaiushchie dushi: razdum'ia o vere i zhizni. Moskva, 1971. pp. 136.

ATEIZM, religiia, sovremennost'. Leningrad, 1973. pp. 226.

BARBERINI (GIOVANNI) Stati socialisti e confessioni religiose. Milano, 1973. pp. 537. *(Perugia. Università. Istituto di Diritto Pubblico. Pubblicazioni. 3)*

VORONTSOV (GEORGII VASIL'EVICH) Leninskaia programma ateisticheskogo vospitaniia v deistvii, 1917-1937 gg. Leningrad, 1973. pp. 176.

PORTELLI (HUGUES) Gramsci et la question religieuse. Paris, [1974]. pp. 321. *bibliog.*

COMMUNISM AND THE ARTS.

KIM (IL-SUNG) On creating revolutionary literature and art: speech to workers in the field of literature and art, November 7, 1964. Pyongyang, 1972. pp. 22.

ISKUSSTVO i ideologiia. Moskva, 1973. pp. 503.

COMMUNISM AND ZIONISM.

DUA (GERSZON) Belyi terror v Palestine; predislovie M. Litvakova; perevel s evreiskogo M. Zel'manov. Moskva, 1926. pp. 40.

IVANOV (IURII SERGEEVICH) Ostorozhno: sionizm! Ocherki po ideologii, organizatsii i praktike sionizma. 2nd ed. Moskva, 1971. pp. 206.

BRODSKII (ROMAN MIKHAILOVICH) Sionizm i ioho klasova sut'. Kyïv, 1973. pp. 96.

COMMUNISM IN EDUCATION.

GOMEZ PEREZ (RAFAEL) Universidad: problema politico. Pamplona, 1971. pp. 139. *bibliog.*

COMMUNIST COUNTRIES.

JOUET (MICHEL) Le socialisme se porte bien. Paris, [1974]. pp. 128.

— Commerce.

GERMANY (BUNDESREPUBLIK). Statistisches Bundesamt. Aussenhandel der Ostblockländer. irreg., 1970/1972- Wiesbaden. *(Aussenhandel. Reihe 7: Sonderbeiträge.)*

TYVONCHUK (IVAN OPANASOVYCH) Zovnishnia torhivlia ta efektyvnist' sotsialistychnoho vidtvorennia: pytannia teoriï. L'viv, 1973. pp. 182.

— — United Kingdom — Mathematical models.

LOBBAN (P.W.M.) A model for forecasting U.K. exports to the Sino-Soviet bloc. London, 1971. fo. 25. *(London Graduate School of Business Studies. Econometric Forecasting Unit. Discussion Papers. No. 23)*

— Economic conditions.

LASKI (KAZIMIERZ) The rate of growth and the rate of interest in the socialist economy.New York, 1972. pp. 238. *(Oesterreichisches Institut für Wirtschaftsforschung. Studien über Wirtschafts- und Systemvergleiche. Band 4) With German and Russian summaries.*

MEISNER (JOACHIM) Kapitalizm a socjalizm: współzawodniczące systemy ekonomiczne. Warszawa, 1973. pp. 166. *bibliog.*

CAMPBELL (ROBERT WELLINGTON) Soviet-type economies: performance and evolution. rev ed. London, 1974. pp. 259. *bibliog.*

— — Statistics.

STATISTIKA stran-chlenov SEV. Moskva, 1973. pp. 269.

— — Study and teaching.

TSAGA (VIKTORIIA FRANTSEVNA) Ekonomicheskaia teoriia antikommunizma v tupike. Leningrad, 1973. pp. 254.

— Economic integration.

MIKUL'SKII (KONSTANTIN IVANOVICH) Problemy effektivnosti sotsialisticheskoi ekonomiki: iz opyta khoziaistvennogo stroitel'stva v stranakh SEV. Moskva, 1972. pp. 283.

WEISS (GERHARD) Der objektive Charakter der sozialistischen ökonomischen Integration: das Komplexprogramm ... der Mitgliedsländer des RGW. Berlin, 1972. pp. 58.

XXIV s''ezd KPSS i aktual'nye problemy politicheskoi ekonomii. Moskva, 1973. pp. 239.

AL'TSHULER (ARKADII BORISOVICH) Sotrudnichestvo sotsialisticheskikh gosudarstv: raschety, kredity, pravo. Moskva, 1973. pp. 175.

BONDARENKO (EVGENIIA LAVRENT'EVNA) Vyravnivanie ekonomicheskikh urovnei stran-chlenov SEV. Moskva, 1973. pp. 80.

CHUKANOV (OLIMP ALEKSEEVICH) and others, eds. Nauchno-tekhnicheskii progress i sotrudnichestvo stran SEV. Moskva, 1973. pp. 207.

GUZEK (MARIAN) Ekonomicheskaia integratsiia stran sotsializma; [sokrashchennyi perevod s pol'skogo]. Moskva, 1973. pp. 135.

KOZLOV (IGOR' DMITRIEVICH) and SHMAKOVA (ELENA KONSTANTINOVNA) Sotrudnichestvo stran-chlenov SEV v energetike. Moskva, 1973. pp. 141.

SHAGALOV (GRIGORII LAZAREVICH) Problemy optimal'nogo planirovaniia vneshneekonomicheskikh sviazei: voprosy teorii i metodologii. Moskva, 1973. pp. 295.

SHIRIAEV (IURII SEMENOVICH) Ekonomicheskii mekhanizm sotsialisticheskoi integratsii: ocherk teorii. Moskva, 1973. pp. 198.

SUPRUN (VOLODYMYR OLEKSIIOVYCH) Pitannia mizhnarodnoï sotsialistychnoï spetsializatsiï vyrobnytstva. Kyïv, 1973. pp. 167. *With Russian summary.*

TYVONCHUK (IVAN OPANASOVYCH) Zovnishnia torhivlia ta efektyvnist' sotsialistychnoho vidtvorennia: pytannia teoriï. L'viv, 1973. pp. 182.

USENKO (EVGENII TROFIMOVICH) ed. Mezhvedomstvennye sviazi v usloviiakh sotsialisticheskoi ekonomicheskoi integratsii: pravovoi aspekt. Moskva, 1973. pp. 175.

KORMNOV (IURII FILIPPOVICH) Spezialisierung und Kooperation der Produktion der RGW- Länder; (Übersetzer [from the Russian]: Cay-Harro Dahl). Berlin, [1974]. pp. 272.

STEPANENKO (STANISLAV IVANOVICH) Sovershenstvovanie nauchno-tekhnicheskogo sotrudnichestva stran SEV.Moskva, 1974. pp. 261.

See also COUNCIL FOR MUTUAL ECONOMIC ASSISTANCE.

— Economic policy.

WINDHOFF (BERND) Darstellung und Kritik der Konvergenztheorie: gibt es eine Annäherung der sozialistischen und kapitalistischen Wirtschaftssysteme?. Bern, 1971. pp. 224. *bibliog.*

INTENSIFIKATSIIA proizvodstva v evropeiskikh stranakh SEV: faktory ekonomicheskogo rosta. Moskva, 1972. pp. 224.

MIKUL'SKII (KONSTANTIN IVANOVICH) Problemy effektivnosti sotsialisticheskoi ekonomiki: iz opyta khoziaistvennogo stroitel'stva v stranakh SEV. Moskva, 1972. pp. 283.

LEWANDOWSKI (JĘDRZEJ) ed. System funkcjonowania gospodarki socjalistycznej, etc. Warszawa, 1973. pp. 378. *With English and Russian summaries.*

MARCZEWSKI (JEAN) Crise de la planification socialiste?. Paris, 1973. pp. 298.

BAHRII (PETRO ILARIONOVYCH) Dynamik und Struktur der gesellschaftlichen Produktion im Sozialismus: methodische und analytische Probleme; (in die deutsche Sprache übertragen von Dieter Graf). Berlin, 1974. pp. 380.

CAMPBELL (ROBERT WELLINGTON) Soviet-type economies: performance and evolution. rev ed. London, 1974. pp. 259. *bibliog.*

WILCZYNSKI (JOZEF) Technology in Comecon: acceleration of technological progress through economic planning and the market. London, 1974. pp. 379.

— — **Mathematical models.**

NOTKIN (ALEKSANDR IL'ICH) ed. Sotsialisticheskoe nakoplenie: voprosy teorii i planirovaniia. Moskva, 1973. pp. 414.

— **Foreign relations.**

KIM (IL-SUNG) Let us intensify the anti-imperialist, anti-U.S. struggle. Pyongyang, 1968. pp. 10. *(Reprinted from Tricontinental, August 12, 1967)*

DIPLOMATIIA sotsializma; predislovie A.A. Gromyko. Moskva, 1973. pp. 318.

— — **Europe.**

TOWARDS a peaceful Europe: a study of the opportunities which détente provides for further improving East-West relations: written by a group sponsored by Friends Peace and International Relations Committee. London, 1973. pp. 38.

— **Manufactures.**

STROGOVA (ALLA IVANOVNA) Proizvodstvo predmetov narodnogo potrebleniia v stranakh-chlenakh SEV. Moskva, 1973. pp. 125.

— **Relations (general) with the Ukraine.**

VKLAD Ukraïns'koï RSR u naukovo-kul'turne spivrobitnytstvo Radians'koho Soiuza z ievropeis'kymy sotsialistychnymy kraïnamy. Kyïv, 1970. pp. 198.

COMMUNIST EDUCATION
— **Russia.**

AKADEMIIA OBSHCHESTVENNYKH NAUK. Kafedra Teorii i Metodov Ideologicheskoi Raboty. Voprosy teorii i metodov ideologicheskoi raboty. vyp.1. Moskva, 1972. pp. 454.

PARTIIA i sotsialisticheskaia kul'tura: XXIV s''ezd KPSS i problemy dukhovnoi kul'tury sotsializma. Moskva, 1972. pp. 287.

MOSTOVOI (STEPAN NIKOLAEVICH) Leninskie printsipy ideinovospitatel'noi raboty. Moskva, 1972. pp. 311.

KUMANEV (VIKTOR ALEKSANDROVICH) Revoliutsiia i prosveshchenie mass. Moskva, 1973. pp. 335. *bibliog.*

— — **Ukraine.**

NIKITINA (ELENA IVANOVNA) and PRESS (TAMARA NATANOVNA) Rabochee obshchezhitie: opyt vospitatel'noi raboty. Moskva, 1971. pp. 111.

KHYZHNIAK (VASYL' PETROVYCH) Komunistychne vykhovannia trudivnykiv sela: z dosvidu ideino- vykhovnoï roboty partiinykh orhanizatsii Ukraïny na seli v 1959-1970 rr. Kyïv, 1973. pp. 153. *bibliog.*

COMMUNIST ETHICS.

ZHURAVKOV (MIKHAIL GAVRILOVICH) Sotsializm i moral': nekotorye cherty i osobennosti formirovaniia morali sovetskogo obshchestva. Moskva, 1974. pp. 263.

COMMUNIST PARTIES.

FEJTÖ (FRANÇOIS) Dictionnaire des partis communistes et des mouvements révolutionnaires, précédé d'un essai sur la crise actuelle de l'internationalisme marxiste. [Paris, 1971]. pp. 235. *bibliog.*

BERLINGUER (ENRICO) and MARCHAIS (GEORGES) Democrazia e sicurezza in Europa: (la politica del PCF e del PCI verso la Comunità europea e l'unità delle masse lavoratrici, etc.). Roma, [1973]. pp. 76.

CERRETI (GIULIO) Con Togliatti e Thorez: quarant'anni di lotte politiche. Milano, 1973. pp. 387.

RABOCHII klass i ego partiia v sovremennom sotsialisticheskom obshchestve: [polnye teksty vystuplenii i otvetov na voprosy uchastnikov konferentsii, 21-23 maia, 1973 g., v Varshave]. Praga, 1973. pp. 271.

BIRCHALL (IAN H.) Workers against the monolith: the communist parties since 1943. London, 1974. pp. 256. *bibliog.*

COMMUNIST PARTY
— **Canada.**

COMMUNIST PARTY OF CANADA. The road to socialism in Canada: the program of the Communist party of Canada. Toronto, 1972. pp. 70.

— **China.**

ASIAN PEOPLES' ANTI-COMMUNIST LEAGUE. Pamphlets. No. 168. Mao's purge of senior military cadre. Taipei, 1972. pp. 151.

MAO (TSE-TUNG) Report to the second plenary session of the seventh Central Committee of the Communist Party of China. 3rd ed. Peking, 1973. pp. 24.

VLADIMIROV (OLEG EVGEN'EVICH) and RIAZANTSEV (VLADIMIR IVANOVICH) Stranitsy politicheskoi biografii Mao Tsze-duna. 2nd ed. Moskva, 1973. pp. 112.

— **Czechoslovakia.**

KUHN (HEINRICH) Zeittafel zur Geschichte der Kommunistischen Partei der Tschechoslowakei: von den Anfängen der Arbeiterbewegung bis zur Gegenwart. München, 1973. pp. 135. *(Sudetendeutsches Archiv. Veröffentlichungen. 7)*

— **France.**

MARTY (ANDRE) Le Parti communiste français né et forgé dans la lutte contre la guerre. Paris, [1972]. pp. 23.

AIMS OF INDUSTRY. The Extreme Left in Europe. 1. Organisation and financing of the French Communist Party. London, [1974]. pp. 14.

LE BRAZ (YVES) Les rejetés: l'affaire Marty-Tillon; pour une histoire différente du PCF. Paris, [1974]. pp. 281. *bibliog.*

TIERSKY (RONALD) French communism, 1920-1972. New York, 1974. pp. 425. *bibliog.*

— **Germany.**

THAELMANN (ERNST) Der revolutionäre Ausweg und die KPD: Rede auf der Plenartagung des Zentralkomitees der Kommunistischen Partei Deutschlands am 19. Februar 1932 in Berlin; [originally published in 1932]. Frankfurt, 1971. pp. 96. *Facsimile reprint.*

SCHNEIDER (JOHANNES) Kommunistische Untergrundarbeit in der Bundesrepublik Deutschland. München, [1961]. pp. 49.

RETZLAW (KARL) Spartakus: Aufstieg und Niedergang; Erinnerungen eines Parteiarbeiters. 2nd ed. Frankfurt, 1972. pp. 511.

GRUPPE ARBEITERPOLITIK. Der Faschismus in Deutschland: Analysen der KPD-Opposition aus den Jahren 1928-1933: [selected articles from the periodical "Gegen den Strom", mainly by August Thalheimer]. Frankfurt am Main, [1973]. pp. 220. *bibliog.*

HEMJE-OLTMANNS (DIRK) Arbeiterbewegung und Einheitsfront: zur Diskussion der Einheitsfronttaktik in der KPD, 1920/21. Westberlin, 1973. pp. 139. *bibliog.*

MARXISTISCHE AUFBAUORGANISATION. Die Krise der kommunistischen Parteien: Probleme der gegenwärtigen Revisionismuskritik. München, 1973. pp. 309. *bibliog.*

REIMANN (MAX) Entscheidungen 1945-1956. Frankfurt am Main, 1973. pp. 227.

ECKERT (RAINER) and SEIDERER (AXEL) Sozialdemokratie und Jungsozialisten: Politik, Programm und Gesellschaftstheorie; eine marxistische Kritik. Frankfurt/Main, 1974. pp. 194.

FICHTER (TILMAN) Kampf um Bosch: ... die Betriebspolitik der KPD nach 1945, am Beispiel der Firma Robert Bosch GmbH; [and] Eugen Eberle: Sieben Jahre offensiver Kampf gegen das Kapital. Berlin, [1974]. pp. 191. *bibliog.*

MAMMACH (KLAUS) Die deutsche antifaschistische Widerstandsbewegung, 1933-1939. Berlin, 1974. pp. 304.

THAELMANN (ERNST) Geschichte und Politik: Artikel und Reden, 1925 bis 1933. Frankfurt am Main, 1974. pp. 238.

— — **Congresses.**

KOMMUNISTISCHE PARTEI DEUTSCHLANDS. Parteikonferenz, Draveil, 1939. Die Berner Konferenz der KPD, 30 . Januar-1.Februar 1939; [held at Draveil near Juvisy, south of Paris, called Berner Konferenz for security reasons]; herausgegeben und eingeleitet von Klaus Mammach. Berlin, 1974. pp. 152.

— — **Party work.**

WALTER (GERD) Theoretischer Anspruch und politische Praxis der DKP: eine Analyse am Beispiel der Betriebsarbeit. Meisenheim am Glan, 1973. pp. 135. *bibliog.*

— **Germany, Eastern.**

MATTHESS (ERICH) and NAUMANN (HEINZ) Demokratische Bodenreform und antifaschistisch-demokratische Justizentwicklung im Kreis Plauen, 1945-1946, etc. Plauen, 1969. pp. 79. *(Vogtländisches Kreismuseum Plauen. Museumsreihe. Heft 35)*

MORAW (FRANK) Die Parole der "Einheit" und die Sozialdemokratie: zur parteiorganisatorischen und gesellschaftspolitischen Orientierung der SPD ... 1933-1948. Bonn-Bad Godesberg, [1973]. pp. 262. *bibliog. (Friedrich-Ebert-Stiftung. Forschungsinstitut. Schriftenreihe. Band 94)*

HONECKER (ERICH) Die Rolle der Arbeiterklasse und ihrer Partei in der sozialistischen Gesellschaft: [collected articles and speeches, 1971-73]. Berlin, 1974. pp. 389.

— — **Party work.**

SOZIALISTISCHE EINHEITSPARTEI DEUTSCHLANDS. Zentralkomitee. Abteilung Propaganda. Aufgaben und Erfahrungen der Partei- und Massenpropaganda nach dem VIII. Parteitag der SED. Berlin, 1972. pp. 108. *(Der Parteiarbeiter)*

— **Hungary.**

KHAINAS (VASYL' VASYL'OVYCH) Borot'ba Komunistychnoï partiï Uhorshchyny za iedynyi robitnychyi i narodnyi front, proty fashyzmu i viiny, 1933-1939. L'viv, 1969. pp. 210.

COMMUNIST PARTY. (Cont.)

— Indonesia.

CAYRAC-BLANCHARD (FRANÇOISE) Le Parti communiste indonesien. Paris, 1973. pp. 217. *bibliog.* (*Fondation Nationale des Sciences Politiques . Travaux et Recherches de Science Politique. 26*)

MORTIMER (REX) Indonesian communism under Sukarno: ideology and politics, 1959- 1965. Ithaca, 1974. pp. 464. *bibliog.*

— Italy.

DETTI (TOMMASO) Serrati e la formazione del Partito comunista italiano: storia della frazione terzinternazionalista, 1921-1924. Roma, 1972. pp. 547.

MASSOLA (UMBERTO) Memorie, 1939-1941. Roma, 1972. pp. 167.

CHIAROMONTE (GERARDO) Agricoltura, sviluppo economico, democrazia: la politica agraria e contadina dei comunisti, 1965-1972. Bari, [1973]. pp. 370.

CHIAROMONTE (GERARDO) and others. Agricoltura, Mercato comune e regioni. *Roma, 1973. pp. 136.*
AGRICULTURE : Italy. 1973.

FLORES (MARCELLO) Fronte Popolare e democrazia progressiva: la politica del PCI dal 1935 al 1946. Roma, [1973]. pp. 157.

GALANTE (SEVERINO) La politica del PCI e il Patto Atlantico: "Rinascita" 1946-'49. Padova, [1973]. pp. 257. (*Padua. Università. Istituto di Scienze Storiche, and Centro di Studi e Documentazioni per la Storia Contemporanea e le Relazioni Internazionali. Collana. 1*)

LONGO (LUIGI) I centri dirigenti del PCI nella Resistenza. Roma, 1973. pp. 515.

RAVERA (CAMILLA) Diario di trent'anni, 1913-1943. Roma, 1973. pp. 698.

TROCCHI (FRANCESCO) Angelo Tasca e l'"Ordine Nuovo": la formazione del Partito Comunista Italiano. Milano, [1973]. pp. 191. *bibliog.*

VACCA (GIUSEPPE) ed. P[artito] C[omunista] I[taliano], Mezzogiorno e intellettuali dalle alleanze all'organizzazione. Bari, [1973]. pp. 478.

AMENDOLA (GIORGIO) Lettere a Milano: ricordi e documenti, 1939-1945. Roma, 1974. pp. 763. *bibliog.*

I COMUNISTI a Torino, 1919-1972: lezioni e testimonianze: (le relazioni e le testimonianze di un corso...organizzato dall'Unione culturale torinese...marzo-aprile 1973); prefazione di Gian Carlo Pajetta. Roma, 1974. pp. 338.

— Norway.

GILBERG (TROND) The Soviet Communist party and Scandinavian communism: the Norwegian case. Oslo, [1973]. pp. 271. *bibliog.*

— Palestine.

HEN-TOV (JACOB) The Communist International, the Palestine Communist Party, and the political unrest in Palestine in 1929;...paper submitted to the conference on "The Middle East in revolution"...April 1970. n.p., [1970?]. pp. 33.

— Poland.

WYGODZKI (STANISŁAW) Zatrzymany do wyjaśnienia. Pary'z, 1968. pp. 205.

POLSKA ZJEDNOCZONA PARTIA ROBOTNICZA. Komitet Centralny. Report...on the period between the 5th and 6th congresses. Warsaw, 1971. pp. 47.

— Russia.

TESLIN (E.) Ein merkwürdiges Dokument...; den denkenden und fühlenden Arbeitern gewidmet; [discussion of a controversy within the Communist Party in the U.S.S.R., 1921]. [Zürich, 1922]. pp. 14.

PIATNITSKII (OSIP ARONOVICH) pseud. [i.e. Iosif Aronovich TARSHIS] Memoirs of a Bolshevik; [reprint of the work first published in London, 1933]. Westport, Conn., 1973. pp. 224.

OCHERKI istorii Kuibyshevskoi organizatsii KPSS. Kuibyshev, 1967. pp. 642.

SADYKOV (MARUF SADYKOVICH) Istoricheskii opyt KPSS po stroitel'stvu sotsializma v Tadzhikistane, 1917-1959 gg. Dushanbe, 1967. pp. 434. *bibliog.*

GONCHAROV (ALEKSANDR DMITRIEVICH) Pod"em kul'tury sela -delo partiinoe. Moskva, 1970. pp. 120.

OCHERKI istorii Krasnoiarskoi partiinoi organizatsii. t.2. Krasnoiarsk, 1970. pp. 390.

SBYTOV (VLADIMIR FILIPPOVICH) KPSS - boevoi avangard stroitelei kommunizma. Moskva, 1970. pp. 168.

KIRSTEIN (TATJANA) Die Konsultation von "Aussenstehenden" durch den Partei- und Staatsapparat sowie den Obersten Sowjet der UdSSR als stabilisierender Faktor des sowjetischen Herrschaftssystems. Berlin, 1972. pp. 131. *bibliog.* (*Berlin. Freie Universität. Osteuropa-Institut. Philosophische und Soziologische Veröffentlichungen. Band 11*)

KOMMUNISTICHESKAIA PARTIIA SOVETSKOGO SOIUZA. O partiinoi i sovetskoi pechati, radioveshchanii i televidenii: sbornik dokumentov i materialov. Moskva, 1972. pp. 635.

VOPROSY ekonomicheskoi politiki KPSS na sovremennom etape: dlia sistemy partiinoi ucheby i ekonomicheskogo obrazovaniia. 2nd ed. Moskva, 1972. pp. 407.

AHRARNA polityka KPRS na suchasnomu etapi. Kyïv, 1973. pp. 190.

BARKER (ENNO) Die Rolle der Parteiorgane in der sowjetischen Wirtschaftslenkung, 1957-1965: zum Verhältnis von Partei und Staat in der Periode der Chruščevschen Wirtschaftsreformen. Berlin, 1973. pp. 252. *bibliog.* (*Berlin. Freie Universität. Osteuropa-Institut. Philosophische und Soziologische Veröffentlichungen. Band 12*)

BREZHNEV (LEONID IL'ICH) O vneshnei politike KPSS i Sovetskogo gosudarstva: rechi i stat'i. Moskva, 1973. pp. 599.

GEROICHESKII put' KPSS: k 70-letiiu II s"ezda partii! Moskva, 1973. pp. 231.

GILBERG (TROND) The Soviet Communist party and Scandinavian communism: the Norwegian case. Oslo, [1973]. pp. 271. *bibliog.*

ISTORIIA Kommunisticheskoi partii Sovetskogo Soiuza. 4th ed. Moskva, 1973. pp. 752.

IUDIN (IVAN NIKOLAEVICH) Sotsial'naia baza rosta KPSS. Moskva, 1973. pp. 295.

KOMMUNISTICHESKAIA PARTIIA SOVETSKOGO SOIUZA. Ustav Kommunisticheskoi partii Sovetskogo Soiuza: utverzhden XXII s"ezdom, chastichnye izmeneniia vneseny XXIII i XXIV s"ezdami KPSS. Moskva, 1973. pp. 62.

LEKTSII po istorii KPSS. vyp.2. 3rd ed. Moskva, 1973. pp. 477.

LIPITSKII (SEMEN VASIL'EVICH) Voennaia deiatel'nost' Tsk RKP/b/, 1917-1920. Moskva, 1973. pp. 317.

NEKRASOV (KLAVDII VASIL'EVICH) Bor'ba Kommunisticheskoi partii za pobedu kolkhoznogo stroia v Severnom krae, 1929-1937 gg. Vologda, 1973. pp. 174. *bibliog.*

PARTIIA i rabochii klass v usloviiakh stroitel'stva kommunizma. Moskva, 1973. pp. 303.

PARTIIA v bor'be za sotsializm i kommunizm. Leningrad, 1973. pp. 182.

RÉVÉSZ (LÁSZLÓ) Kommentar zum Statut der KPdSU: eine Untersuchung von Parteitheorie und -praxis in der Sowjetunion und in den osteuropäischen Volksdemokratien im Licht des Statuts der Kommunistischen Partei der Sowjetunion. Bern, [1973]. pp. 890. *bibliog.*

SAVKO (ALEKSANDR PAVLOVICH) Partiinoe rukovodstvo Sovetami v period stroitel'stva kommunizma.Moskva, 1973. pp. 187.

UCHENYE ZAPISKI KAFEDR OBSHCHESTVENNYKH NAUK VUZOV LENINGRADA. Istoriia KPSS. vyp.13. KPSS - organizator bratskoi druzhby narodov SSSR. Leningrad, 1973. pp. 154.

VOPROSY ekonomicheskoi politiki KPSS na sovremennom etape: dlia sistemy partiinoi ucheby i ekonomicheskogo obrazovaniia. 3rd ed. Moskva, 1973. pp. 350.

VOPROSY istorii partii v trudakh V.I. Lenina. Moskva, 1973. pp. 316.

ZIMOGLIADOV (FELIKS ROMANOVICH) Kommunisticheskaia partiia Sovetskogo Soiuza vo glave trudovoi aktivnosti mass, 1928-1941 gg.: iz opyta raboty partiinykh organizatsii Donbassa. Moskva, 1973. pp. 160.

HABERL (OTHMAR NIKOLA) Die Emanzipation der KP Jugoslawiens von der Kontrolle der Komintern/KPdSU, 1941-1945. München, 1974. pp. 86. *bibliog.* (*Munich. Südost-Institut München. Untersuchungen zur Gegenwartskunde Südosteuropas. 8*)

IGNATOVSKII (PAVEL ARTEM'EVICH) Die Bauernschaft und die Wirtschaftspolitik der Partei auf dem Lande; (Übersetzer [from the Russian]: Hans Bär). Berlin, 1974. pp. 299.

See also **SOCIAL DEMOCRATIC PARTY (RUSSIA).**

— — Congresses.

XXIV s"ezd KPSS i voprosy teorii gosudarstva i prava. Moskva, 1972. pp. 399.

PARTIIA i sotsialisticheskaia kul'tura: XXIV s"ezd KPSS i problemy dukhovnoi kul'tury sotsializma. Moskva, 1972. pp. 287.

UCHENYE ZAPISKI KAFEDR OBSHCHESTVENNYKH NAUK VUZOV G.LENINGRADA. Filosofiia. vyp. 13. Filosofskie i sotsiologicheskie issledovaniia. Leningrad, 1972. pp. 238.

UCHENYE ZAPISKI KAFEDR OBSHCHESTVENNYKH NAUK VUZOV LENINGRADA. Problemy Nauchnogo Kommunizma. vyp. 6. XXIV s"ezd KPSS i aktual'nye problemy nauchnogo kommunizma. Leningrad, 1972. pp. 160.

XXIV s"ezd KPSS i aktual'nye problemy politicheskoi ekonomii. Moskva, 1973. pp. 239.

KERIMOV (DZHANGIR ALI-ABASOVICH) ed. XXIV s"ezd KPSS ob ukreplenii Sovetskogo gosudarstva i razvitii sotsialisticheskoi demokratii. Moskva, 1973. pp. 276.

— — Party work.

UCHENYE ZAPISKI KAFEDR OBSHCHESTVENNYKH NAUK VUZOV LENINGRADA. Istoriia KPSS. vyp.12. Leninskim kursom. Leningrad, 1972. pp. 184.

ANDRUKHOV (NIKOLAI ROMANOVICH) Partiinoe stroitel'stvo posle Oktiabria, 1917-1924 gg. Moskva, 1973. pp. 216.

KOMMUNISTICHESKAIA PARTIIA SOVETSKOGO SOIUZA. Voprosy organizatsionno-partiinoi raboty KPSS: sbornik dokumentov. Moskva, 1973. pp. 301.

NEKOTORYE voprosy organizatsionno-partiinoi raboty. Moskva, 1973. pp. 334.

SPRAVOCHNIK propagandista. [vyp.6]. Moskva, 1973. pp. 271.

— — Programme.

McNEAL (ROBERT HATCH) compiler. Guide to the decisions of the Communist Party of the Soviet Union 1917-1967: Ukazatel' reshenii Kommunisticheskoi partii Sovetskogo Soiuza 1917-1967. Toronto, [1972]. pp. 329. *In Russian and English.*

— — Caucasus.

DZHIBLADZE (D.) Bol'sheviki Zakavkaz'ia v bor'be s trotskistsko- zinov'evskim blokom. Tbilisi, 1973. pp. 69.

— — Kazakstan.

GOLIKOVA (Z.A.) and others. Kompartiia Kazakhstana za 50 let, 1921-1971 gg.: rost i regulirovanie sostava partiinoi organizatsii respubliki. Alma-Ata, 1972. pp. 343. *Colophon gives title as: Kommunisticheskaia partiia Kazakhstana, etc.*

— — Moldavian Republic.

KOMPARTIIA Moldavii v gody sotsialisticheskogo i kommunisticheskogo stroitel'stva. Kishinev, 1973. pp. 91.

— — Ukraine.

SHEVCHUK (VASYL' PETROVYCH) Na vyrishal'nomu napriami: Komunistychna partiia Ukraïny v borot'bi za naukovo-tekhnichnyi prohres u vazhkii promyslovosti, 1959-1965 rr. Kyïv, 1970. pp. 230.

KOMUNISTYCHNA partiia - orhanizator zdiisnennia lenins'koï natsional'noï polityky na Ukraïni. Kyïv, 1972. pp. 323.

NARYSY istoriï Vinnyts'koï oblasnoï partiinoï orhanizatsiï. Odesa, 1972. pp. 328.

KONOVALOV (MYKHAILO ANDRIIOVYCH) Vyrishal'na syla sotsialistychnoï rekonstruktsiï: diial'nist' KP Ukraïny po pidhotovtsi ta vykhovanniu industrial'no-tekhnichnykh kadriv, 1928-1937 rr. Kyïv, 1973. pp. 229.

PANIOTOV (IVAN ILLICH) Komunistychna partiia Ukraïny v borot'bi za rozvytok narodnoï osvity, 1931-1941 rr. Kharkiv, 1973. pp. 186. *bibliog.*

— — — Party work.

KHYZHNIAK (VASYL' PETROVYCH) Komunistychne vykhovannia trudivnykiv sela: z dosvidu ideino- vykhovnoï roboty partiinykh orhanizatsii Ukraïny na seli v 1959-1970 rr. Kyïv, 1973. pp. 153. *bibliog.*

— — White Russia.

KOMMUNISTICHESKAIA partiia Belorussii v rezoliutsiiakh i resheniiakh s'ezdov i plenumov TsK, 1918-1970. Minsk, 1973 in progress.

GERASIMENKO (GEORGII GEORGIEVICH) Deiatel'nost' Kompartii Belorussii po vovlecheniiu trudiashchikhsia mass v upravlenie gosudarstvom, 1925-1937. Minsk, 1973. pp. 230.

NIKONOVICH (BORIS FEOFILOVICH) KPB v bor'be za osushchestvlenie leninskikh printsipov narodnogo kontrolia. Minsk, 1973. pp. 208.

— — White Russia, Western.

OREKHVO (N.S.) and STASHKEVICH (N.S.) compilers. Gody ispytanii i muzhestva; sbornik sostavili i literaturno obrabotali vospominaniia ... N.S. Orekhvo, etc. Minsk, 1973. pp. 415.

— Spain.

HERMET (GUY) The communists in Spain: study of an underground political movement;... translated from the French by S. Seago and H. Fox. Farnborough, Hants, [1974]. pp. 238. *bibliog.*

— Sweden.

HIRDMAN (YVONNE) Sveriges kommunistiska parti, 1939-1945. Stockholm, 1974. pp. 311. *bibliog. With English summary.*

KOKK (ENN) V[änster]P[artiet] K[ommunisterna] och S[veriges] K[ommunistiska] P[arti]: de grälande tvillingpartierna; mål, organisation, arbetsmetoder. [Stockholm, 1974]. pp. 130.

— Switzerland.

PARTEI DER ARBEIT DER SCHWEIZ. Was will die Partei der Arbeit der Schweiz?: (Thesen zur Politik..., angenommen an der Landeskonferenz der Partei vom 12./13. Juni 1971 in Lausanne). [Zürich, 1971]. pp. 54. *(Sonderdruck aus dem Vorwärts)*

— United States.

LUND (CAROLINE) The Czechoslovak frame-up trials and the U.S. Communist Party; with Jiri Pelikan's appeal to Angela Davis and statements by the Australian, Dutch and Italian CPs. New York, 1973. pp. 15.

— Vietnam.

ROUSSET (PIERRE) Le Parti communiste vietnamien: contribution à l'étude du mouvement communiste au Vietnam. Paris, 1973. pp. 142. *(Fourth International. French section, and others. Livres Rouges)*

— Yugoslavia.

HABERL (OTHMAR NIKOLA) Die Emanzipation der KP Jugoslawiens von der Kontrolle der Komintern/KPdSU, 1941-1945. München, 1974. pp. 86. *bibliog. (Munich. Südost-Institut München. Untersuchungen zur Gegenwartskunde Südosteuropas. 8)*

COMMUNIST PARTY PURGES.

LEVYTSKY (BORIS) ed. The Stalinist terror in the thirties: documentation from the Soviet press. Stanford, [1974]. pp. 521. *bibliog. (Stanford University. Hoover Institution on War, Revolution and Peace. Hoover Institution Publications. 126)*

COMMUNIST REVISIONISM.

JUST (STEPHANE) Révisionnisme liquidateur contre trotskysme: défense du trotskysme, 2. Paris, [1971]. pp. 337.

HRZAL (LADISLAV) Die Auseinandersetzung mit dem Revisionismus und dem Antikommunismus während der krisenhaften Entwicklung in der ČSSR 1968/69. Frankfurt/Main, 1973. pp. 47.

NIL'VE (ANNA IL'INICHNA) Bor'ba V.I. Lenina s revizionizmom v agrarnom voprose i ee mezhdunarodnoe znachenie; pod redaktsiei E.L. Boginoi. Moskva, 1973. pp. 147.

SOVREMENNYI pravyi revizionizm: kriticheskii analiz. Moskva, 1973. pp. 615.

FARIS (RALPH M.) Revisionist Marxism: the opposition within. Amsterdam, 1974. pp. 90.

COMMUNIST STATE.

CHIRKIN (VENIAMIN EVGEN'EVICH) Formy sotsialisticheskogo gosudarstva. Moskva, 1973. pp. 270.

KOPEICHIKOV (VLADIMIR VLADIMIROVICH) Mekhanizm gosudarstva v sovetskoi federatsii. Moskva, 1973. pp. 200.

SOVETSKOE gosudarstvo - god pervyi. Moskva, 1973. pp. 263.

TIKHOMIROV (IURII ALEKSANDROVICH) Pouvoir et administration dans la société socialiste. Paris, 1973. pp. 193.

EREMIN (IURII ELEAZAROVICH) Klassy i demokratiia. Moskva, 1974. pp. 206.

COMMUNIST STRATEGY.

INSTITUTE FOR THE STUDY OF CONFLICT. The peacetime strategy of the Soviet Union. London, [1973]. pp. 83. *(Institute for the Study of Conflict. Special Reports)*

TÁBORSKÝ (EDUARD) Communist penetration of the third world. New York, [1973]. pp. 500. *bibliog.*

HODGES (DONALD CLARK) The Latin American revolution: politics and strategy from apro-marxism to guevarism. New York, 1974. pp. 287. *bibliog.*

COMMUNISTIC SETTLEMENTS

— France.

COLIN (HELENE) and PARADELLE (MICHEL) Les jeunes et le mouvement communautaire: approche sociopsychanalytique. Bruxelles, 1974. pp. 192.

— Germany.

LINSE (ULRICH) Die Kommune der deutschen Jugendbewegung: ein Versuch zur Überwindung des Klassenkampfes...; die "kommunistische Siedlung Blankenburg " bei Donauwörth, 1919/20. München, 1973. pp. 185. *bibliog. (Zeitschrift für Bayerische Landesgeschichte. Beihefte. Reihe B. 5)*

— Israel.

COHEN (REUVEN) The kibbutz settlement: principles and processes; (translated from Hebrew by Harry Statman). [Tel-Aviv], 1972. pp. 362.

— United Kingdom.

GORMAN (CLEM) Making communes: (survey/manual: coming together, locating, buying/converting, relationships, food). London, [1971]. pp. 136. *bibliog.*

RIGBY (ANDREW) Alternative realities: a study of communes and their members. London, 1974. pp. 341. *bibliog.*

RIGBY (ANDREW) Communes in Britain. London, 1974. pp. 157.

— United States.

ROBERT OWEN BICENTENNIAL CONFERENCE, NEW HARMONY, INDIANA, 1971. Robert Owen's American legacy: proceedings...; edited by Donald E. Pitzer; [sponsored by the Department of History, Indiana State University, Evansville, and by Harmonie Associates, New Harmony, Indiana]. Indianapolis, 1972. pp. 88.

FELLMAN (MICHAEL) The unbounded frame: freedom and community in nineteenth century American utopianism. Westport, Conn., 1973. pp. 203. *bibliog.*

VEYSEY (LAURENCE R.) The communal experience: anarchist and mystical counter-cultures in America. New York, [1973]. pp. 495.

SPECK (ROSS V.) and others. The new families: youth, communes, and the politics of drugs. London, 1974. pp. 190. *First published in New York in 1972.*

COMMUNISTS.

LAZITCH (BRANKO) and DRAŠKOVIĆ (MILORAD M.) Biographical dictionary of the Comintern. Stanford, 1973. pp. 458. *(Stanford University. Hoover Institution on War, Revolution and Peace. Hoover Institution Publications. 121)*

COMMUNISTS, FRENCH.

FRANCOTTE (ROBERT) Une vie de militant communiste. Paris, [1973]. pp. 317.

COMMUNISTS, GERMAN.

INSTITUT FÜR MARXISMUS-LENINISMUS (BERLIN). Geschichte der deutschen Arbeiterbewegung: biographisches Lexikon; Redaktionskommission: R.Grau [and others]. Berlin, 1970. pp. 528.

SCHAUL (DORA) ed. Résistance: Erinnerungen deutscher Antifaschisten; [by] Otto Niebergall [and others]. Frankfurt/ Main, 1973. pp. 477.

COMMUNITY.

NISBET (ROBERT ALEXANDER) The social philosophers: community and conflict in western thought.London, 1974. pp. 466.

PLANT (RAYMOND) Community and ideology: an essay in applied social philosophy. London, 1974. pp. 94. *bibliog.*

COMMUNITY AND COLLEGE.

NASH (GEORGE) The university and the city: eight cases of involvement;... with chapters by Dan Waldorf [and] Robert E. Price; a report prepared for the Carnegie Commission on Higher Education. New York, [1973]. pp. 151. bibliogs.

COMMUNITY AND SCHOOL.

McDILL (EDWARD L.) and RIGSBY (LEO C.) Structure and process in secondary schools: the academic impact of educational climates. Baltimore, [1973]. pp. 201. bibliog.

LITWAK (EUGENE) and MEYER (HENRY JOSEPH) School, family and neighborhood: the theory and practice of school-community relations. New York, 1974. pp. 300.

COMMUNITY ANTENNA TELEVISION

— Law and legislation — United States.

BABE (ROBERT E.) Public and private regulation of cable television. Ottawa, 1973. pp. 70. (Carleton University. Carleton Economic Papers)

The ROLE of analysis in regulatory decisionmaking: the case of cable television: [based on a panel discussion at the 1972 annual meeting of the Western Economic Association]; Rolla Edward Park, editor. Lexington, [1973]. pp. 109. bibliog.

— United States.

ASPEN WORKSHOP CONFERENCE ON THE CABLE AND CONTINUING EDUCATION, 1973. Aspen notebook: cable and continuing education: ([edited by] Richard Adler [and] Walter S. Baer). New York, 1973. pp. 193. bibliog.

POOL (ITHIEL DE SOLA) ed. Talking back: citizen feedback and cable technology. Cambridge, Mass., [1973]. pp. 325.

COMMUNITY CENTRES

— Singapore.

SEAH CHEE MEOW. Community centres in Singapore: their political involvement. Singapore, 1973. pp. 142. bibliog.

COMMUNITY DEVELOPMENT.

UNITED NATIONS. Department of Economic and Social Affairs. 1971. Popular participation in development: emerging trends in community development. (ST/SOA/106). New York, 1971. pp. 273. bibliogs.

NETHERLANDS. Directorate of Regional and Community Development. 1972. Community development: an open offer to community: a short survey of goals, instruments and forms of community development. The Hague, [1972]. pp. 27.

PUSIĆ (EUGEN) Participation and the multidimensional development of complexity. Vienna, [1972]. pp. 30. (Wiener Institut für Entwicklungsfragen. Occasional Papers. 72/2)

KUITENBROUWER (JOOST B.W.) Continuity and discontinuity in community development theory. The Hague, 1973. pp. 10. (Hague. Institute of Social Studies. Occasional Papers. No.30)

PUSIĆ (EUGEN) Administration and development: choice within limits. Vienna, [1973]. pp. 23. (Wiener Institut für Entwicklungsfragen. Occasional Papers. 73/3)

— Study and teaching — United States.

WARGANEGARA (ZULKIFLI) Report on community development program training sponsored by A[gency for] I[nternational] D[evelopment], February- September 1969. [Djakarta, Direktorat Djenderal Pembangunan Masjarakat Desa], 1969. fo. 99.

— Argentine Republic.

ARGENTINE REPUBLIC. Ministerio de Bienestar Social. Subsecretaria de Promocion y Asistencia Social. 1971. Informe nacional sobre desarrollo de comunidades. [Buenos Aires?], 1971. 1 vol. (unpaged).

— Europe.

UNITED NATIONS. Department of Economic and Social Affairs. European Social Development Programme. Reports . New York, 1967 in progress.

— Indonesia.

WARGANEGARA (ZULKIFLI) Report on community development program training sponsored by A[gency for] I[nternational] D[evelopment], February- September 1969. [Djakarta, Direktorat Djenderal Pembangunan Masjarakat Desa], 1969. fo. 99.

— Mexico.

GARCIA RUIZ (RAMON) Educacion, cambios y desarrollo de la comunidad. Mexico, 1970. pp. 183. bibliog.

— Norway.

MARGINAL regions: essays on social planning: [papers from a seminar held in Swansea in 1972]; edited by Maurice Broady. London, [1973]. pp. 120. bibliog.

— Rhodesia.

PASSMORE (GLORIA C.) Theoretical aspects of local government and community action in the African rural areas of Rhodesia. Salisbury, 1971.pp. 95. (University of Rhodesia. Department of Political Science. Monographs in Political Science. No. 3)

— Tanzania.

CEDILLO (VALENTIN G.) Rural development through Ujamaa: a Tanzania case report. Vienna, [1973]. pp. 55,(25). bibliog. (Wiener Institut für Entwicklungsfragen. Occasional Papers. 73/11)

— Underdeveloped areas.

See UNDERDEVELOPED AREAS — Community Developement.

— United Kingdom.

MARGINAL regions: essays on social planning: [papers from a seminar held in Swansea in 1972]; edited by Maurice Broady. London, [1973]. pp. 120. bibliog.

MAYO (MARJORIE) Community development and urban deprivation. London, [1974]. pp. 35.

— — Ireland, Northern.

NORTHERN IRELAND COMMUNITY RELATIONS COMMISSION. Annual report. a., [D 1969/D 1970] (1st)- Belfast.

COMMUNITY HEALTH SERVICES

— United States — New York.

HYMAN (HERBERT HARVEY) ed. The politics of health care: nine case studies of innovative planning in New York City. New York, 1973. pp. 205. bibliogs.

COMMUNITY LIFE.

A BOOK of visions: a directory of alternative society projects 1973; thanks to the 300 or so people who entered the Alternative Society Ideas-pool, January to April 1973. London, 1973. pp. 221.

COMMUNITY MENTAL HEALTH SERVICES

— United States.

GOLDENBERG (I. IRA) ed. The helping professions in the world of action. Lexington, [1973]. pp. 273. bibliogs.

HECK (EDWARD T.) and others. A guide to mental health services. [Pittsburgh, 1973]. pp. 139.

— — New York (City).

KAPLAN (SEYMOUR R.) and ROMAN (MELVIN) The organization and delivery of mental health services in the ghetto: the Lincoln Hospital experience. New York, 1973. pp. 315.

COMMUNITY ORGANIZATION.

BILLET (M.) and VALVEKENS-HAVEN (S.) Samenlevingsopbouw: critische situatieschets in Nederland en Vlaanderen; onder leiding van F. van Mechelen. Leuven, 1972. pp. 260. bibliog. (Katholieke Universiteit te Leuven. Sociologisch Onderzoeksinstituut. Studiegroep voor Kultuurbevordering. [Publications]. 14)

UNITED NATIONS. Commission on the Status of Women. 1972. Participation of women in community development; report of the Secretary-General. (E/CN.6/514/Rev.1) New York, 1972. pp. 68.

BRAGER (GEORGE A.) and SPECHT (HARRY) Community organizing. New York, [1973]. pp. 363.

CLARK (TERRY NICHOLS) Community power and policy outputs: a review of urban research. Beverly Hills, [1973]. pp. 98.

FISH (JOHN HALL) Black power/white control: the struggle of the Woodlawn Organization in Chicago. Princeton, [1973]. pp. 356. bibliog. (Center for the Scientific Study of Religion. Studies in Religion and Society)

BROOKS (RICHARD OLIVER) New towns and communal values: a case study of Columbia, Maryland. New York, 1974. pp. 229. bibliog.

GREIFER (JULIAN L.) ed. Community action for social change : a casebook of current projects. New York, 1974. pp. 290. bibliog.

HORROCKS (MERYL) Social development work in the new communities. Birmingham, 1974. pp. 65. bibliog. (Birmingham. University. Centre for Urban and Regional Studies. Occasional Papers. No. 27)

WARREN (ROLAND LESLIE) and others. The structure of urban reform: community decision organizations in stability and change. Lexington, Mass., [1974]. pp. 220.

WASHNIS (GEORGE J.) Community development strategies: case studies of major model cities. New York, 1974. pp. 415.

COMMUNITY POWER.

AIKEN (MICHAEL) and MOTT (PAUL E.) eds. The structure of community power. New York, [1970]. pp. 540. bibliog.

CLARK (TERRY NICHOLS) Community power and policy outputs: a review of urban research. Beverly Hills, [1973]. pp. 98.

NEIGHBOURHOOD control in the 1970s: politics, administration and citizen participation; [background papers for a conference sponsored by the Center for Governmental Studies in Washington, D.C., held May 1970, Boulder, Colo.; edited by] George Frederickson. New York, [1973]. pp. 290.

YATES (DOUGLAS) Neighborhood democracy: the politics and impacts of decentralization. Lexington, Mass., [1973]. pp. 202. bibliog.

BAILEY (ROBERT) Radicals in urban politics: the Alinsky approach. Chicago, 1974. pp. 187. bibliog.

COMMUNITY WELFARE COUNCILS

— United Kingdom — Scotland.

ROWE (ANDREW J.B.) Community councils. Edinburgh, [1973]. pp. 24. bibliog. (Scottish Council of Social Service. Occasional Papers)

COMMUTING

— Belgium.

ZAKALNYCKYJ (WLADYMYR) Attitude des migrants journaliers à l'égard de l'emploi en région. Bruxelles, 1973. pp. 185. bibliog.

— Germany — North Rhine—Westphalia.

NORTH RHINE-WESTPHALEN. Statistisches Landesamt. Beiträge zur Statistik des Landes Nordrhein-Westfalen. Sonderreihe Volkszählung 1970. Heft 11a. Die Pendelwanderer in Nordrhein-Westfalen am 27.Mai 1970: Regierungsbezirk Düsseldorf, Köln, Aachen: Ergebnisse der Volkszählung 1970. Düsseldorf, 1973. pp. 266.

NORTH RHINE-WESTPHALIA. Statistisches Landesamt. Beiträge zur Statistik des Landes Nordrhein-Westfalen. Sonderreihe Volkszählung 1970. Heft 11b. Die Pendelwanderer in Nordrhein-Westfalen am 27. Mai 1970: Regierungsbezirk Münster, Detmold, Arnsberg: Ergebnisse der Volkszählung 1970. Düsseldorf, 1973. pp. 315.

NORTH RHINE-WESTPHALIA. Statistisches Landesamt. Beiträge zur Statistik des Landes Nordrhein-Westfalen. Sonderreihe Volkszählung 1970. Heft 12a. Verkehrsmittel und Zeitaufwand der Pendelwanderer in Nordrhein-Westfalen am 27. Mai 1970: Landes- und Kreisergebnisse. Düsseldorf, 1974. pp. 351.

— Italy.

TREVISO (PROVINCE). Ufficio Studi. Indagine sui movimenti pendolari dei lavoratori dell'industria in provincia di Treviso. Treviso, 1970-71. 2 vols. (in 1). Lacking map no.18 and table no.17.

— Norway.

REIERSEN (JAN EINAR) Utpendlingen fra Sotra til Bergenshalvøya før Sotrabua. [Bergen, 1973]. pp. 143. bibliog. (Forskningsprosjektet Bergen Sentrum. Rapportar. Nr. 10)

— South Africa.

YOUNG (BRUCE S.) Journey to work patterns and labour sheds in the Durban region. [Johannesburg?], 1973. pp. 238-246. (From South African Geographer, vol. 4, no. 3) Xerographic copy.

— United Kingdom.

SARICKS (CHRISTOPHER LEE) Commuter choice and station catchment areas in metropolitan rail transport, with special reference to the London region; [M. Phil. (London) thesis]. 1973. fo. 154. bibliog. Typescript: unpublished. This thesis is the property of London University and may not be removed from the Library.

COMPAGNONNAGES.

BERNARD (JEAN) Le compagnonnage: rencontre de la jeunesse et de la tradition. Paris, [1972]. pp. 620.

COMPENSATION (LAW)

— Norway.

NORWAY. Erstatningslovkomitéen. 1971. Innstilling...Komitéen til i nordisk samarbeid å utrede spørsmålet om ny lovgivning om erstatning for tap i fremtidig ervery og for tap av forsørger. Bergen, 1971. pp. 68.

— United Kingdom.

ENCYCLOPEDIA of the law of compulsory purchase and compensation; general editor Harold J.J. Brown. London, 1960-74. 2 vols. Loose-leaf.

COMPETITION.

CARTELL (JEAN) and COSSE (PIERRE YVES) La concurrence capitaliste. Paris, [1973]. pp. 189.

KIRZNER (ISRAEL MAYER) Competition and entrepreneurship. Chicago, 1973. pp. 246.

SACKS (STEPHEN R.) Entry of new competitors in Yugoslav market socialism. Berkeley, [1973]. pp. 141. bibliog. (California University. Institute of International Studies. Research Series. No. 19)

SAUER (SAROLF) Wettbewerbsposition und Wettbewerbspolitik der Filialgrossbanken in der BRD. Wien, 1974. pp. 112. bibliog. (Österreichische Bankwissenschaftliche Gesellschaft. Schriftenreihe. Heft 47)

COMPETITION, INTERNATIONAL.

MUELLER-HILLEBRAND (VEIT) Das Vordringen der japanischen Konkurrenz auf den Weltmärkten im Vergleich zum deutschen Export. Nürnberg, 1972. pp. 337, xxii. (Erlangen. Universität. Institut für Exportforschung. Berichte)

COMPUTER INDUSTRY

— Canada.

CANADA. Statistics Canada. Computer service industry. a., 1972 (1st)- Ottawa. In English and French.

FORSYTH (GEORGE R.) and OWEN (BRIAN) The Canadian computer supply industry study. Ottawa, 1973. pp. 124,124. (Canada. Computer/Communications Task Force. Background Papers. 1) In English and French.

— Europe.

HU (Y.S.) The impact of U.S. investment in Europe: a case study of the automotive and computer industries. New York, 1973. pp. 291.

COMPUTER SIMULATION.

COMPUTER simulation in human population studies; [proceedings of a conference held at Pennsylvania State University, 1972, sponsored by the Social Science Research Council]; edited by Bennett Dyke [and] Jean Walters MacCluer. New York, 1973. pp. 518. bibliog.

COMPUTER STORAGE DEVICES.

SHETLER (A.C.) and GLASEMEN (S.) Computer memory management at Rand. Santa Monica, 1971. pp. 104. (Rand Corporation. [Papers]. 4585)

COMPUTERS.

LUKASHEVICH (SERGEI IVANOVICH) Opredelenie ekonomicheskoi effektivnosti primeneniia EVM. Minsk, 1970. pp. 87.

SHORTER (EDWARD) The historian and the computer: a practical guide. Englewood Cliffs, N.J., [1971]. pp. 149.

STATISTIKA i elektronno-vychislitel'naia tekhnika v ekonomike: sbornik statei. vyp.5. Moskva, 1972. pp. 311. bibliog.

U.K. Department of Trade and Industry. Computers, Systems and Electronics Division. 1972. Computer installations: accommodation and fire precautions. rev. ed. London, 1972. pp. 33.

WARE (WILLIS H.) The ultimate computer. [Santa Monica], 1972. pp. 23. (Rand Corporation. [Papers]. 4825)

BODINGTON (STEPHEN) Computers and socialism. Nottingham, 1973. pp. 245. bibliog.

DOUGLAS (ALEXANDER SHAFTO) Computers and society: (an inaugural lecture). [London, 1973]. pp. 12. bibliog.

PENNEY (G.) ed. Computers in the social sciences: a studyguide. Manchester, [1973]. pp. 48. bibliog.

STATISTIKA i elektronno-vychislitel'naia tekhnika v ekonomike: sbornik statei. vyp.6. Moskva, 1973. pp. 225. bibliog.

U.K. Social Science Research Council. Panel on Computing and the Social Sciences. 1973. Computing and the social sciences: a report to the SSRC. London, [1973]. fo. 26.

BRIER (ALAN) and ROBINSON (IAN) Lecturer in Sociology, Brunel University. Computers and the social sciences. London, 1974. pp. 285. bibliogs.

DOW (R.) Computers and management today and tomorrow: a 1970's reassessment. [Berkhamsted, 1974]. pp. 14. (Ashridge Management College. Papers in Management Studies)

CONCENTRATION CAMPS

FISHER (LAWRENCE VICTOR) A study of the factors influencing the diffusion of innovation with special reference to the application of the computer in process control; [Ph.D.(London) thesis]. 1973 [or rather 1974]. fo. 194. bibliog. Typescript: unpublished. This thesis is the property of London University and may not be removed from the Library.

— Research.

STONEMAN (PAUL S.) The choice of technique: the example of computerisation. Coventry, [1974]. pp. 24. (University of Warwick. Department of Economics. Warwick Economic Research Papers. No. 46)

The ROLE of the computer in economic and social research in Latin America: [selected papers of a conference held in Cuernavaca, Mexico, sponsored by the National Bureau of Economic Research and others]; edited by Nancy D. Ruggles. New York, 1974. pp. 399.

DI FORINO (A. CARACCIOLO) and others. Problems and prospects of fundamental research in multi-disciplinary fields: computer science. Paris, Organisation for Economic Co-operation and Development, 1972. pp. 51. (Science Policy Studies)

— Social aspects.

BUTLER (DAVID) information scientist. Should we build systems to fit people or people to fit systems?. London, [1973]. pp. 7. (Foundation for Business Responsibilities. Discussion Papers)

GOTLIEB (C.C.) and BORODIN (ALLAN) Social issues in computing. New York, [1973]. pp. 284. bibliogs.

SCOTLAND. Consultative Committee on the Curriculum. Computers and the Schools Committee. 1972. Computers and the schools; final report; [B.T. Bellis, chairman]. Edinburgh, 1972. pp. 21. (Scottish Education Department. Curriculum Papers. 11)

COMTE (ISIDORE AUGUSTE MARIE FRANÇOIS XAVIER).

COMTE (ISIDORE AUGUSTE MARIE FRANÇOIS XAVIER) Confessions and testament of Auguste Comte: and his correspondence with Clotilde de Vaux; edited by Albert Crompton; (translated by several members of the Church of Humanity, Liverpool). Liverpool, 1910. pp. 547.

ACTON (HARRY BURROWS) The idea of a spiritual power. London, 1974. pp. 31. (London. University. London School of Economics and Political Science. Auguste Comte Memorial Trust Lectures. 10)

COMTE (ISIDORE AUGUSTE MARIE FRANÇOIS XAVIER) The crisis of industrial civilization: the early essays...; introduced by Ronald Fletcher. London, 1974. pp. 251. bibliog.

CONCENTRATION CAMPS

— Canada.

LAFLAMME (JEAN) Les camps de detention au Quebec durant la première guerre mondiale. Montréal, 1973. fo. 51.

— Germany.

ALS sozialdemokratischer Arbeiter im Konzentrationslager Papenburg. Moskau, 1935. pp. 74.

BILLIG (JOSEPH) Les camps de concentration dans l'économie du Reich hitlérien. Paris, 1973. pp. 346. bibliog.

— Indonesia.

SALIM (I.F.M.) Vijftien jaar Boven-Digoel: concentratiekamp in Nieuw- Guinea: bakermat van de Indonesische onafhankelijkheid. Amsterdam, [1973]. pp. 436. bibliog.

— Russia.

SOLZHENITSYN (ALEKSANDR ISAEVICH) Arkhipelag GULag, 1918-1956: opyt khudozhestvennogo issledovaniia. Paris, 1973 in progress.

CONCEPTION
— Prevention.

INTERNATIONAL PLANNED PARENTHOOD FEDERATION. Central Medical Committee. Systemic contraception; edited ... by R.L. Kleinman. London, 1973. pp. 82. *bibliog.*

See also STERILIZATION (BIRTH CONTROL).

CONCESSIONS
— Russia — Caucasus.

DZHIBLADZE (D.N.) Kontsessionnye predpriiatiia v Zakavkaz'e, 1926-1929 gg. Tbilisi, 1973. pp. 62.

CONCORDAT OF 1929 (ITALY).

GARZIA (ITALO) Il negoziato diplomatico per i Patti Lateranensi. Milano, 1974. pp. 127. *(Politico, Il. Quaderni. n.13) With English summary.*

CONCORDAT OF 1933 (GERMANY).

VOLK (LUDWIG) Das Reichskonkordat vom 20. Juli 1933: von den Ansätzen in der Weimarer Republik bis zur Ratifizierung am 10. September 1933. Mainz, [1972]. pp. 266. *bibliog. (Katholische Akademie in Bayern. Kommission für Zeitgeschichte. Veröffentlichungen. Reihe B: Forschungen. Band 5)*

CONCORDE (JET TRANSPORTS).

COMMITTEE FOR ENVIRONMENTAL CONSERVATION. Some effects of supersonic flight. London, 1972. pp. 63. *bibliogs.*

WILSON (ANDREW) Journalist. The Concorde fiasco. Harmondsworth, 1973. pp. 157.

CONDUCT OF LIFE.

The MESSAGE of man: a book of ethical scriptures, gathered from many sources and arranged. London, 1894 repr. 1895. pp. 323.

FACIUS (JOHANNES) and others. The little white book;...(translated and adapted from the Danish). Bromley, Kent, 1971. pp. 73.

HANSEN (SØREN) AND JENSEN (JESPER) The little red school-book;...translated from Danish by Berit Thornberry. London, 1971. pp. 208. *Unexpurgated edition.*

HANSEN (SØREN) and JENSEN (JESPER) The little red school-book;...translated from Danish by Berit Thornberry. rev. ed. London, 1971. pp. 208. *Expurgated edition.*

CONFEDERATION OF STATES.

SOCIETY FOR MIDDLE EAST CONFEDERATION. Confederation in the Middle East: various proposals [by Hugh Schoenfield and others]. Haifa, 1973. pp. 24.

CONFIDENTIAL COMMUNICATIONS
— Banking.

Le SECRET bancaire dans la C.E.E. et en Suisse: rapport national du Colloque organisé par le Centre d'Economie Bancaire internationale et le Centre Universitaire d'Etudes des Communautés européennes...octobre 1971. Paris, 1973. pp. 207. *(Paris. Université de Paris I (Panthéon-Sorbonne) Publications. Série Droit Privé. 1)*

CONFLICT (PSYCHOLOGY).

BONDURANT (JOAN VALERIE) ed. Conflict: violence and nonviolence. Chicago, 1971. pp. 206.

DEUTSCH (MORTON) The resolution of conflict: constructive and destructive processes. New Haven, 1973. pp. 420. *bibliog. (Yale University. Carl Hovland Memorial Lectures)*

CONFLICT OF GENERATIONS.

HEER (FRIEDRICH) Challenge of youth; (translated from the German by Geoffrey Skelton). London, [1974]. pp. 224.

CONFLICT OF INTERESTS (PUBLIC OFFICE)
— Canada.

CANADA. Privy Council Office. 1973. Members of parliament and conflict of interest; Les membres du parlement et les conflits d'intérêts. Ottawa, 1973. pp. 69,74. *In English and French.*

CONFUCIUS AND CONFUCIANISM.

KELEN (BETTY) Confucius: in life and legend. London, 1974. pp. 160. *bibliog.*

CONGO (BRAZZAVILLE)
— Economic conditions.

VENNETIER (PIERRE) Pointe-Noire et la façade maritime du Congo-Brazzaville. Paris, Office de la Recherche Scientifique et Technique Outre-Mer, 1968. pp. 458. *bibliog. (Mémoires O.R.S.T.O.M. 26)*

— History.

MASSAGA (WOUNGLY) La révolution au Congo: contribution à l'étude des problèmes politiques d'Afrique centrale. Paris, 1974. pp. 182.

— Politics and government.

GAUZE (RENE) The politics of Congo-Brazzaville;... translation, editing, and supplement by Virginia Thompson and Richard Adloff. Stanford, [1973]. pp. 283. *bibliog. (Stanford University. Hoover Institution on War, Revolution and Peace. Hoover Institution Publications. 129)*

MASSAGA (WOUNGLY) La révolution au Congo: contribution à l'étude des problèmes politiques d'Afrique centrale. Paris, 1974. pp. 182.

— Social conditions.

VENNETIER (PIERRE) Pointe-Noire et la façade maritime du Congo-Brazzaville. Paris, Office de la Recherche Scientifique et Technique Outre-Mer, 1968. pp. 458. *bibliog. (Mémoires O.R.S.T.O.M. 26)*

CONNALLY (JOHN BOWDEN).

CRAWFORD (ANN FEARS) and KEEVER (JACK) John B. Connally: portrait in power. Austin, Texas, 1973. pp. 460. *bibliog.*

ASHMAN (CHARLES R.) Connally: the adventures of big bad John. New York, 1974. pp. 305.

CONSENT (LAW)
— Poland.

LEWASZKIEWICZ-PETRYKOWSKA (BIRUTA) Wady oświadczenia woli w polskim prawie cywilnym. Warszawa, 1973. pp. 212. *bibliog. With French summary.*

CONSERVATION OF NATURAL RESOURCES
— Pacific, The.

SYMPOSIUM ON NATURE CONSERVATION IN THE PACIFIC, CANBERRA, 1971. Nature conservation in the Pacific: proceedings of the symposium... of the Twelfth Pacific Science Congress... 1971; (editors A.B. Costin and R.H. Groves). Canberra, 1973. pp. 337. *bibliogs.*

— Russia.

PRYDE (PHILIP R.) Conservation in the Soviet Union. Cambridge, 1972. pp. 301. *bibliog.*

— — Ukraine.

SHEMSHUCHENKO (IURII SERHIIOVYCH) and POHORILKO (VIKTOR FEDOROVYCH) Administratyvno-pravova okhorona pryrody Ukraïns''koï RSR. Kyïv, 1973. pp. 128. *With brief Russian summary.*

— Sweden.

SWEDEN. Inrikesdepartementet. 1973. Planning Sweden: regional development planning and management of land and water resources. Stockholm, 1973. pp. 142.

— United States.

RICHARDSON (ELMO R.) Dams, parks and politics: resource development and preservation in the Truman-Eisenhower era. [Lexington, Ky., 1973]. pp. 247.

HAVLICK (SPENSER W.) The urban organism: the city's natural resources from an environmental perspective. New York, [1974]. pp. 515. *bibliog.*

— Zambia.

ZAMBIA. Natural Resources Advisory Board. Annual report. a., 1972(1st)- Lusaka.

CONSERVATISM.

BARROW (JOHN PENROSE) The noble lie and the politics of reaction; [an] inaugural lecture... at University of London King's College June 5th 1972. [London, 1972]. pp. 19.

MARRIS (PETER) Loss and change. London, 1974. pp. 178. *bibliog. (Institute of Community Studies. Reports)*

CONSERVATISM IN FRANCE.

ANDERSON (MALCOLM) Conservative politics in France. London, 1974. pp. 381. *bibliog.*

CONSERVATISM IN GERMANY.

MOHLER (ARMIN FRIEDRICH ADOLF) Die Konservative Revolution in Deutschland, 1918-1932: ein Handbuch. 2nd ed. Darmstadt, 1972. pp. 554. *bibliog. Classified subject bibliography on pp. 171-505.*

CONSERVATISM IN THE UNITED KINGDOM.

JESSOP (ROBERT DOUGLAS) Traditionalism, conservatism and British political culture. London, 1974. pp. 287. *bibliog.*

CONSERVATIVE PARTY (UNITED KINGDOM).

FIELD (FRANK) 1942- . One nation: the Conservatives' record since June 1970. London, 1974. pp. 12. *(Child Poverty Action Group. Poverty Pamphlets. 12)*

GHOSH (S.C.) Decision-making and power in the British Conservative Party: a study of the Indian problem 1929-1934. Calcutta, 1972. pp. 235. *bibliog.*

BERRINGTON (HUGH) Backbench opinion in the House of Commons, 1945-55. Oxford, 1973. pp. 265.

LILLEY (PETER) and others. Alternative manifesto; [by members of the Bow Group]. London, [1973]. pp. 24.

U.K. Historical Manuscripts Commission. 1973. Report on the records of the Rushcliffe Conservative Association, 19th-20th century; reproduced for Nottinghamshire Record Office. London, 1973. fo. (2).

U.K. Historical Manuscripts Commission. 1973. Report on the records of the South Nottingham Conservative Association, 20th century; reproduced for Nottinghamshire Record Office. London, 1973. single sheet.

U.K. Historical Manuscripts Commission. 1973. Report on the records of the West Bridgford Conservative Association, 20th century; reproduced for Nottinghamshire Record Office. London, 1973. single sheet.

BRUCE-GARDYNE (JOCK) Whatever happened to the quiet revolution?: the story of a brave experiment in government. London, 1974. pp. 176.

CONSERVATIVE AND UNIONIST PARTY. The campaign guide, 1974; [edited by Anthony Greenland]. London, 1974. pp. 721.

CONSERVATIVE AND UNIONIST PARTY. Firm action for a fair Britain: the Conservative manifesto, 1974. London, 1974. pp. 32.

CONSERVATIVE AND UNIONIST PARTY. Putting Britain first: a national policy from the Conservatives. London, [1974]. pp. 31.

CONSERVATIVE POLITICAL CENTRE. [Publications]. 542. CPC: the vote catchers. London, 1974. 1 pamphlet (unpaged). *bibliog.*

COUNTER INFORMATION SERVICES. The unacceptable face: special report on the Conservative government, 1970/74. London, [1974]. pp. 15.

FABIAN SOCIETY. Fabian Tracts. [No.] 432. One nation? : housing and conservative policy. London, 1974. pp. 43.

GAMBLE (ANDREW) The Conservative nation. London, 1974. pp. 300. *bibliog.*

GORBIK (VIACHESLAV ALEKSANDROVICH) Antirabochaia politika pravitel'stva konservatorov i polozhenie trudiashchikhsia v poslevoennoi Anglii. Kiev, 1974. pp. 111.

LINDSAY (T.F.) and HARRINGTON (MICHAEL) Journalist. The Conservative party, 1918-1970. London, 1974. pp. 271. *bibliog.*

MORE help for the cities; [by] Sydney Chapman [and others]. London, 1974. pp. 16. *(Conservative Political Centre. [Publications]. No.555)*

SOUTHGATE (DONALD GEORGE) ed. The Conservative leadership, 1832-1932. London, 1974. pp. 277. *bibliog.*

CONSOLIDATION AND MERGER OF CORPORATIONS

— Australia.

STANDING COMMITTEE OF STATE AND COMMONWEALTH ATTORNEYS-GENERAL [AUSTRALIA]. Company Law Advisory Committee. Second interim report. in AUSTRALIA. Parliament. Parliamentary papers, 1969. vol.1.

— Europe — Bibliography.

U.K. Department of Trade and Industry. Library Services. Economics Division. 1974. Monopolies and mergers in Great Britain and Europe: recent information. London, 1974. fo. 5. *(Bibliographical Series. No. 74/1)*

— European Economic Community countries.

EUROPEAN COMMUNITIES. Commission. 1973. Draft convention on the international merger of sociétés anonymes [and] report on the draft convention, etc. [Brussels], 1973. pp. 123. *(Bulletin of the European Communities. Supplements. [1973/13])*

— France.

GUYON (YVES) and COQUEREAU (GEORGES) Le groupement d'intérêt économique: régime juridique et fiscal. 2nd ed. Paris, 1973. pp. 411. *bibliog.*

— Japan.

FRANCE. Direction de la Documentation. La Documentation Française. Notes et Etudes Documentaires. No. 3,724. Fusions et concentrations au Japon: les grandes entreprises; [by] Marie-Agnès Blanchon. Paris, 1970. pp. 43. *bibliog.*

— Norway.

FUSJONER: [reprints of] 9 artikler i Bedriftsøkonomen, 1972. Bergen, 1973. pp. 45.

— United Kingdom.

PANEL ON TAKE-OVERS AND MERGERS. The City code on take-overs and mergers; (amended June 1974). London, 1974. pp. 50. *With Supplement.*

— — Bibliography.

U.K. Department of Trade and Industry. Library Services. Economics Division. 1974. Monopolies and mergers in Great Britain and Europe: recent information. London, 1974. fo. 5. *(Bibliographical Series. No. 74/1)*

— United States.

UNITED STATES. Federal Trade Commission. Bureau of Economics. 1972. Conglomerate merger performance: an empirical analysis of nine corporations; [by Stanley E. Boyle and Philip W. Jaynes]. Washington, 1972. pp. 203.

MARKHAM (JESSE WILLIAM) Conglomerate enterprise and public policy. Boston, 1973. pp. 218. *bibliog.*

WINSLOW (JOHN F.) Conglomerates unlimited: the failure of regulation. Bloomington, Ind., [1973]. pp. 296.

CONSOLIDATION OF LAND HOLDINGS.

DEUTSCHER GEODÄTENTAG, 48., FREIBURG, 1963. Aufgaben der Flurbereinigung bei der Neuordnung des ländlichen Raumes: Vorträge, etc. Stuttgart, 1964. pp. 58. *bibliog. (Schriftenreihe für Flurbereinigung. Heft 38)*

FERRO (GAETANO) Aspetti della geografia agraria: la ricomposizione fondiaria come strumento di pianificazione territoriale. Varese, [1966]. pp. 54. *Bound with VALLEGA (ADALBERTO) La media valle di Blenio.*

— Argentine Republic.

CARRERA (RODOLFO RICARDO) Regimen juridico aplicable a los minifundios de la provincia de La Rioja; informe final. Buenos Aires, 1973. pp. 131. *bibliog. (Argentine Republic. Consejo Federal de Inversiones. Serie Tecnica. No. 23)*

— Switzerland.

VALLEGA (ADALBERTO) La media valle di Blenio: un'area di ricomposizione fondiaria. Varese, [1966]. pp. 79. *Bound with FERRO (GAETANO) Aspetti della geografia agraria.*

CONSPIRACY

— United Kingdom.

HAZELL (ROBERT) Conspiracy and civil liberties: a memorandum submitted to the Law Commission by the Cobden Trust and the National Council for Civil Liberties. London, 1974. pp. 128. *(Social Administration Research Trust. Occasional Papers on Social Administration. No. 55)*

ROBERTSON (GEOFF) Whose conspiracy?. [London, 1974]. pp. 53.

CONSTANCE

— Economic history.

KRUEMMER (HEINZ) Die Wirtschafts- und Sozialstruktur von Konstanz in der Zeit von 1806 bis 1850. Sigmaringen, 1973. pp. 162. *bibliog. (Constance. Stadtarchiv. Konstanzer Geschichts- und Rechtsquellen. Band 19)*

— Social history.

KRUEMMER (HEINZ) Die Wirtschafts- und Sozialstruktur von Konstanz in der Zeit von 1806 bis 1850. Sigmaringen, 1973. pp. 162. *bibliog. (Constance. Stadtarchiv. Konstanzer Geschichts- und Rechtsquellen. Band 19)*

CONSTANT DE REBECQUE (HENRI BENJAMIN DE).

RUDLER (GUSTAVE) Benjamin Constant député de la Sarthe, 1819-1822: conférence faite à la Salle des Concerts Du Mans, le 16 juin 1912; inauguration du monument Benjamin Constant, 14 juillet 1913. Le Mans, 1913. pp. 64.

CONSTITUTIONAL COURTS

— Italy.

SORRENTINO (FEDERICO) Corte costituzionale e Corte di giustizia delle Comunità europee. Milano, 1970-73. 2 vols. (in 1). *(Genoa. Università. Facoltà di Giurisprudenza. Annali. Collana. 27, 34)*

CONSTITUTIONAL LAW.

DUVERGER (MAURICE) Institutions politiques et droit constitutionnel. 13th ed. Paris, [1973 in progress].

CONSTITUTIONS.

FRIEDRICH (CARL JOACHIM) Limited government: a comparison. Englewood Cliffs, [1974]. pp. 139. *bibliog.*

CONSTITUTIONS, STATE

— United States.

STURM (ALBERT LEE) Modernizing state constitutions, 1966-1972: [report prepared for the Council of State Governments]. Lexington, Kentucky, 1973. pp. 50.

CONSTRUCTION INDUSTRY.

HILLEBRANDT (PATRICIA MARGUERITE) Economic theory and the construction industry. London, 1974. pp. 233. *bibliog.*

— Belgium.

VERSICHELEN (MARTHE) Verlaten beroepen?: oorzaken en achtergronden van het aanhoudend tekort aan arbeidskrachten in de bouwnijverheid. Gent, [1970?]. pp. 231. *bibliog. With summary in French.*

Le SECTEUR de la construction face aux besoins de logements: [journée d'étude, Bruxelles, 2 mars 1972]. [Bruxelles], Institut National du Logement, 1973. pp. 48.

— — Statistics.

BELGIUM. Institut National de Statistique. Statistiques de la construction et du logement. a., 1974(no.5)- Bruxelles.

— Canada.

HAYTHORNE (GEORGE VICKERS) Construction and inflation;... prepared for the Prices and Incomes Commission. Ottawa, Information Canada, 1973. pp. 181.

— — Mathematical models.

WASLANDER (H.E.L.) CANDIDE [Canadian Disaggregated Interdepartmental Econometric] model 1.0: residential construction. Ottawa, Information Canada, 1973. pp. 27. *(CANDIDE Project Papers. No. 3)*

— — Statistics.

CANADA. Statistics Canada. Non-residential building contracting industry. a. 1971 (1st)- Ottawa. *In English and French.*

— Ecuador — Statistics.

ECUADOR. Division de Estadistica y Censos. 1969. Primer censo de construccion, 1966. Quito, [1969?]. pp. 87.

— France.

FRANCE. Ministère de l'Equipement et du Logement. 1971. Tendances et politiques actuelles dans le domaine de l'habitation, de la construction et de la planification:monographie nationale de la France. Neuilly-sur-Seine, 1971. pp. 61.

— Germany.

DEUTSCHES INSTITUT FÜR WIRTSCHAFTSFORSCHUNG. Sonderhefte. [Neue Folge]. Nr. 97. Zeitreihen für das Bauvolumen in der Bundesrepublik Deutschland für die Jahre 1960 bis 1971: Ergebnisse einer Neuberechnung; ([by] Wolfgang Kirner und Gerda Noack).Berlin, 1973. pp. 77. *With English summary.*

— — Bavaria.

BAVARIA. Statistisches Landesamt. 1967. Die bayerische Bauwirtschaft: das Bauhauptgewerbe von 1950 bis 1966. [München, 1967]. pp. [140]. *(Bavaria. Beiträge zur Statistik Bayerns. Heft 278)*

— Guatemala.

GUATEMALA. Comision Nacional del Salario. 1966. Estudio económico para la determinacion del salario minimo en la industria de la construccion. Guatemala, 1966. pp. 84.

CONSTRUCTION INDUSTRY. (Cont.)

— **Italy.**

INDOVINA (FRANCESCO) ed. Lo sprecò edilizio. Padova, 1972 repr. 1973. pp. 334.

CACCIARI (PAOLO) and POTENZA (STEFANIA) Il ciclo edilizio: riforma della casa e sviluppo capitalistico in Italia negli anni '60. Roma, 1973. pp. 214.

— **Jamaica — Statistics.**

JAMAICA. Department of Statistics. Economic Indicators Section. 1969. Building activity in Jamaica, 1966-68; [prepared by J.C. McMillan]. [Kingston, 1969]. pp. 50.

JAMAICA. Department of Statistics. 1974. Building activity in Jamaica, 1965-1972. [Kingston, 1974]. pp. 59.

— **Netherlands.**

NEDERLANDS INSTITUUT VOOR RUIMTELIJKE ORDENING EN VOLKSHUISVESTING and VERENIGING VAN NEDERLANDSE GEMEENTEN. Werkgroep. Projectontwikkeling: een analyse van verschillende aspecten van de samenwerking tussen gemeente en projectonwikkelingsmaatschappij; rapport, etc. Alphen aan den Rijn, 1971. pp. 84. (*Nederlands Instituut voor Ruimtelijke Ordening en Volkshuisvesting. Publikaties. Nr. 78*)

— **Russia — Finance.**

FINANSOVO-kreditnye problemy ekonomicheskoi reformy v stroitel'stve. Moskva, 1973. pp. 191.

KIRILLOV (NIKOLAI NIKOLAEVICH) and LAPIDUS (MIKHAIL KHLOVENOVICH) Finansirovanie i kreditovanie stroitel'stva v novykh usloviiakh khoziaistvovaniia. Moskva, 1973. pp. 121.

— **Sweden.**

SJÖSTRAND (SVEN ERIK) Företagsorganisation: en taxonomisk ansats, med en typisering av 38 svenska byggnadsföretag. Stockholm, [1973]. pp. 456. *bibliog. With English summary.*

— **Switzerland — Ticino.**

TICINO (CANTON). Ufficio delle Ricerche Economiche. 1972. Studio previsionale sulla capacita' produttiva del settore edile nel cantone Ticino, dal 1972 al 1980. Bellinzona, 1972. fo. 73. *bibliog.* (*Quaderni. 7*) *With summaries in French and German.*

— **Underdeveloped areas.**

See UNDERDEVELOPED AREAS — Construction industry.

— **United Kingdom.**

CONSTRUCTION INDUSTRY TRAINING BOARD [U.K.]. Report and statement of accounts. a., 1972/3- London. *Formerly included in the file of British Parliamentary Papers.*

BAYLEY (L. GORDON) Building: teamwork or conflict?. London, 1973. pp. 117.

LOCKE (BRIAN) Resources innovation and investment (in the construction industry); [a paper delivered] at the Royal Society, London, 1973 with comment papers by S.P. Christie [and others]. Boreham Wood, [1973]. 1 vol. (various pagings). *bibliog.*

ECONOMIC DEVELOPMENT COMMITTEE FOR BUILDING. Regional construction forecasts to 1977. London, National Economic Development Office, 1974. 4 pts. (in 1 vol.)

HILLEBRANDT (PATRICIA MARGUERITE) Economic theory and the construction industry. London, 1974. pp. 233. *bibliog.*

— **United States.**

GREBLER (LEO) Large scale housing and real estate firms: analysis of a new business enterprise. New York, 1973. pp. 182. (*California University. Graduate School of Management. Housing, Real Estate and Urban Land Studies Program Series*)

CONSTRUCTION WORKERS

— **Germany, Eastern.**

VOIGT (DIETER) Montagearbeiter in der DDR: eine empirische Untersuchung über Industrie-Bauarbeiter in den volkseigenen Grossbetrieben. Darmstadt, [1973]. pp. 266. *bibliog.*

— **United Kingdom.**

UNION OF CONSTRUCTION, ALLIED TRADES AND TECHNICIANS. National Delegate Conference. Report of proceedings. bien., 1972(1st)- London.

ECONOMIC DEVELOPMENT COMMITTEE FOR BUILDING. Earnings in the building industry: a survey of operatives' earnings and hours in May 1973. [London, National Economic Development Office, 1974]. pp. 30.

— **United States.**

DUBINSKY (IRWIN) Reform in trade union discrimination in the construction industry: operation dig and its legacy. New York, 1973. pp. 311. *bibliog.*

CONSULAR LAW.

AHMAD (MOHAMMED ALI) L'institution consulaire et le droit international: étude de la Convention de Vienne du 24 avril 1963 sur les relations consulaires et la pratique des Etats dans ce domaine. Paris, 1973. pp. 311. *bibliog.*

CONSUMER CREDIT

— **Mexico.**

BANCO DE MEXICO. Oficina Tecnica de la Direccion. Estudios Monetarios y Crediticios de Caracter Especial. El credito al consumo en Monterrey, N.L., 1967; [edited by Consuelo Meyer L.]. Mexico, 1972-73. 5 vols.

— **United States.**

HENDRICKS (GARY) and others. Consumer durables and installment debt: a study of American households. Ann Arbor, 1973. pp. 231.

CONSUMER EDUCATION.

SWEDEN. Handelsdepartementet. Konsumentutredningen. 1971. Konsumentpolitik: riktlinjer och organisation; [with English summary]: consumer policy: principles and organization. Stockholm, 1971. pp. 276. (*Sweden. Statens Offentliga Utredningar. 1971.37*)

THORELLI (HANS B.) and THORELLI (SARAH V.) Consumer information handbook: Europe and North America. New York, 1974. pp. 525. *bibliog.*

CONSUMER PROTECTION

— **America, North.**

THORELLI (HANS B.) and THORELLI (SARAH V.) Consumer information handbook: Europe and North America. New York, 1974. pp. 525. *bibliog.*

— **Canada.**

CANADA. Department of Consumer and Corporate Affairs. 1973- . [Notes for addresses, etc. by the Hon. Herb Gray]. [Ottawa], 1973 in progress.

— **Europe.**

THORELLI (HANS B.) and THORELLI (SARAH V.) Consumer information handbook: Europe and North America. New York, 1974. pp. 525. *bibliog.*

— **France.**

GAUSSEL (ALAIN) Un panier de mensonges. Paris, [1973]. pp. 189.

— **Sweden.**

SWEDEN. Handelsdepartementet. Konsumentutredningen. 1971. Konsumentpolitik: riktlinjer och organisation; [with English summary]: consumer policy: principles and organization. Stockholm, 1971. pp. 276. (*Sweden. Statens Offentliga Utredningar. 1971.37*)

KING (DONALD BARNETT) Consumer protection experiments in Sweden. South Hackensack, N.J., 1974. pp. 116.

— **United Kingdom.**

U.K. Central Office of Information. Reference Division. 1973. Developments in consumer protection. London, 1973. pp. 7.

HOBSON (JOHN WALLER) The freedom of the market place. London, 1974. pp. 6.

CONSUMERS.

HENAULT (GEORGES MAURICE) Le comportement du consommateur: une approche multidisciplinaire. Montréal, 1973. pp. 179. *bibliog.*

NEIRYNCK (JACQUES) and HILGERS (WALTER) Le consommateur piégé: le dossier noir de la consommation. Bruxelles, [1973]. pp. 288.

SEN (AMARTYA KUMAR) Behaviour and the concept of preference: (an inaugural lecture). London, [1973]. pp. 23.

WARD (SCOTT) and ROBERTSON (THOMAS S.) eds. Consumer behavior: theoretical sources. Englewood Cliffs, [1973]. pp. 576. *bibliogs.*

ZALTMAN (GERALD) and others. Metatheory and consumer research. New York, [1973]. pp. 226. *bibliog.*

SIMMONS (PETER J.) Choice and demand. London, 1974. pp. 120. *bibliog.*

— **Finland.**

KYTÖMÄKI (JORMA) Patterns of consumer travel behaviour in southwestern Finland. Helsinki, 1973. pp. 112. *bibliog.* (*Suomen Maantieteellinen Seura. Fennia. 124*)

— **United Kingdom.**

DAVIES (ROSSER LLEWELYN) Patterns and profiles of consumer behaviour. Newcastle upon Tyne, 1973. pp. 87. *bibliog.* (*Newcastle-upon-Tyne. University. Department of Geography. Research Series. No. 10*)

HOLLIMAN (JONATHAN) Consumers' guide to the protection of the environment. 2nd ed. London, 1974. pp. 257. *bibliogs.*

— — **Mathematical models.**

DORRINGTON (J.C.) and RENTON (G.A.) A study of the effects of direct taxation on consumers' expenditure;... paper prepared for the conference on Modelling of the U.K. Economy... 3-6 July 1972. London, [1972?]. fo. 46. *bibliog.* (*London Graduate School of Business Studies. Econometric Forecasting Unit. Discussion Papers. No. 25*)

— **United States.**

CONFERENCE ON CONSUMER INCENTIVES IN HEALTH CARE USES, WASHINGTON, 1973. Consumer incentives for health care: [papers of the conference held by the Public Services Laboratory]; edited by Selma J. Mushkin. New York, 1974. pp. 431. *bibliogs.*

CONSUMPTION (ECONOMICS).

PRESVELOU (CLIO) Sociologie de la consommation familiale. Bruxelles, [1968]. pp. 319. *bibliog.*

ORGANISATION FOR ECONOMIC CO-OPERATION AND DEVELOPMENT. Economic Policy Committee. Working Party No. 2. 1972. Expenditure trends in OECD countries 1960-1980. Paris, 1972. pp. 131.

ASSOCIATION FRANÇAISE DE SCIENCE ECONOMIQUE. Journées d'études des 24 et 25 septembre 1970, Faculté de Droit, Paris: (consommations collectives). Paris, 1973. pp. 166. (*Cahiers. No.1*)

WARD (SCOTT) and ROBERTSON (THOMAS S.) eds. Consumer behavior: theoretical sources. Englewood Cliffs, [1973]. pp. 576. *bibliogs.*

FALTIN (GUENTER) Dauerhafte Konsumgüter und "Permanent Income" - Hypothese: zur Operationalisierung von Einkommenserwartungen. Berlin, [1974]. pp. 117. *bibliog.*

— Mathematical models.

BURAČAS (ANTANAS) Gipotezy i modeli lichnykh potrebitel'skikh raskhodov v usloviiakh razvitogo kapitalizma. Vil'nius, 1969. pp. 405, lxxix. bibliog. With English summary.

DIEWERT (W.E.) Harberger's welfare indicator and revealed preference theory. Stanford, 1973. fo. 24. bibliog. (Stanford University. Institute for Mathematical Studies in the Social Sciences. Technical Reports. [New Series]. No. 104)

METODE de previzionare a fondului de consum și a elementelor sale componente. București, 1973. pp. 412. bibliog. (Academia de Științe Sociale și Politice a Republicii Socialiste România. Institutul de Cercetări Economice. Bibliotheca Oeconomica. 25). With English, Russian, French and German tables of contents.

WILLIG (ROBERT) Consumer's surplus: a rigorous cookbook. Stanford, 1973. pp. 55. bibliog. (Stanford University. Institute for Mathematical Studies in the Social Sciences. Technical reports. [New Series]. No. 98)

ZWEIFEL (PETER) Empirische Untersuchungen zur Konsumnachfrage in der Schweiz. Zürich, 1974. pp. 184. bibliog.

— Brazil.

FUNDAÇÃO GETULIO VARGAS. Centro de Estudos Agricolas. As estruturas de consumo e os orçamentos familiares. [Rio de] Janeiro, 1968. fo. 30.

FUNDAÇÃO GETULIO VARGAS. Centro de Estudos Agricolas. Orçamentos familiares rurais; [Estado do Espirito Santo, Minas Gerais, Ceara; Pernambuco, Estado de São Paulo, Estado de Santa Catarina, Rio Grande do Sul; by Sylvio Wanick Ribeiro and others]. [Rio de Janeiro], 1969-71. 7 vols(in 2).

— Canada — Mathematical models.

SCHWEITZER (THOMAS T.) and SIEDULE (TOM) CANDIDE [Canadian Disaggregated Interdepartmental Econometric] model 1.0: savings and consumption. Ottawa, Information Canada, 1973. pp. 71. (CANDIDE Project Papers. No. 2)

— France.

FRANCE. Institut National de la Statistique et des Etudes Economiques. Collections de l'I.N.S.E.E. SÉRIE M. Ménages. Paris, 1970 in progress.

— India.

GUPTA (DEVENDRA B.) Consumption patterns in India: a study of inter-regional variations. Bombay, [1973]. pp. 156. bibliog.

— Pakistan.

SOLIGO (RONALD) Factor intensity of consumption patterns, income distribution and employment growth in West Pakistan (a report to A.I.D.). [New Haven], 1972. pp. 29. bibliog. Typescript.

— Russia.

KOMAROV (VASILII EFIMOVICH) and CHERNIAVSKII (URIEL' GEORGIEVICH) Dokhody i potreblenie naseleniia SSSR. Moskva, 1973. pp. 239.

MIZHENSKAIA (EL'VINA FEDOROVNA) Lichnye potrebnosti pri sotsializme. Moskva, 1973. pp. 152.

STOLIAROV (IVAN IGNAT'EVICH) Rol' lichnogo potrebleniia v sotsialisticheskom vosproizvodstve. Gor'kii, 1973. pp. 192.

UCHENYE ZAPISKI KAFEDR OBSHCHESTVENNYKH NAUK VUZOV LENINGRADA. Politicheskaia Ekonomiia. vyp. 14. Raspredelitel'nye otnosheniia sotsializma i ikh razvitie na sovremennom etape. Leningrad, 1973. pp. 208.

LEVIN (BORIS MIKHAILOVICH) Sotsial'no-ekonomicheskie potrebnosti: zakonomernosti formirovaniia i razvitiia. Moskva, 1974. pp. 316.

SHUTOV (IGOR' NIKOLAEVICH) Die individuelle Konsumtion im Sozialismus; (Übersetzer [from the Russian]: Ingrid Stolte). Berlin, 1974. pp. 248.

SHVYRKOV (VLADISLAV VASIL'EVICH) and SHVYRKOVA (TAMARA SERGEEVNA) Modelirovanie vnutrigodichnykh kolebanii sprosa. Moskva, 1973. pp. 175. bibliog.

— Switzerland — Mathematical models.

ZWEIFEL (PETER) Empirische Untersuchungen zur Konsumnachfrage in der Schweiz. Zürich, 1974. pp. 184. bibliog.

— United States.

HENDRICKS (GARY) and others. Consumer durables and installment debt: a study of American households. Ann Arbor, 1973. pp. 231.

CONTEMPT OF COURT

— United Kingdom.

SUNDAY TIMES. The thalidomide children and the law: a report. London, 1973. pp. 156.

CONTENT ANALYSIS (COMMUNICATION).

FABER (PETER) Die Nationalratswahlen 1970 in den Wiener Tageszeitungen: eine inhaltsanalytische Untersuchung. Wien, 1973. pp. 255. bibliog. (Vienna. Universität. Institut für Publizistik. Schriftenreihe. Band 3)

CONTINENTAL SHELF.

INTERREGIONAL SEMINAR ON THE DEVELOPMENT OF THE MINERAL RESOURCES OF THE CONTINENTAL SHELF, PORT-OF-SPAIN, 1971. Interregional seminar...[held at] Port-of-Spain, Trinidad and Tobago, 5-16 April, 1971: technical papers, (ST/TAO/SER. C/138). New York, United Nations, 1972. pp. 172. In English and French.

CONTRACEPTIVES.

BOGUE (DONALD JOSEPH) and NELSON (JAMES) Writer on Population. The fertility components and contraceptive history techniques for measuring contraceptive use-effectiveness. Chicago, 1971. pp. 75. (Chicago. University. Community and Family Study Center. R.F.F.P.I. Family Planning Evaluation Manuals. No. 5)

See also ORAL CONTRACEPTIVES.

CONTRACTS

— Russia.

BABALIAN (LEV ARMENAKOVICH) Dogovor kak osnovanie vozniknoveniia obiazatel'stva mezhdu gosudarstvennymi organizatsiiami. Erevan, 1973. pp. 206.

CONTRACTS (INTERNATIONAL LAW).

PAZARCI (HÜSEYIN) Responsabilité internationale des états en matière contractuelle. Ankara, 1973. pp. 144. bibliog. (Ankara. Universitesi. Siyasal Bilgiler Fakültesi. Yayinlari. 350)

CONTROL THEORY.

SPENCE (A. MICHAEL) Blue whales and applied control theory. Stanford, 1973. pp. 52. bibliog. (Stanford University. Institute for Mathematical Studies in the Social Sciences. Technical Reports. [New Series]. No. 108)

CONVERTIBILITY (MONEY).

MAYER (HELMUT W.) The anatomy of official exchange-rate intervention systems. Princeton, N.J., 1974. pp. 34. (Princeton University. Department of Economics and Sociology. International Finance Section. Essays in International Finance. No. 104)

CONVEYANCING

— United Kingdom.

FARRAND (JULIAN THOMAS) Contract and conveyance. 2nd ed. London, 1973. pp. 488.

WILKINSON (H.W.) The standard conditions of sale of land: a commentary on the Law Society and National Conditions of Sale. 2nd ed. London, 1974. pp. 217.

CONVICT LABOUR

— Russia.

BUSHUEV (IVAN AFANAS'EVICH) Novoe v ispravitel'no-trudovom zakonodatel'stve. Moskva, 1970. pp. 127.

— Russia — Russia (RSFSR).

BLINOV (VLADIMIR MIKHAILOVICH) ed. Kommentarii k ispravitel'no-trudovomu kodeksu RSFSR. Moskva, 1973. pp. 279.

COOK (THOMAS).

SWINGLEHURST (EDMUND) The romantic journey: the story of Thomas Cook and Victorian travel. London, 1974. pp. 208. bibliog.

COOLS (ANDRÉ).

LEPERE-BRAHIMI (CHRISTIANE) André Cools de la contestation à la gestion progressiste. Bruxelles, [1972]. pp. 105.

COOPERATION.

REINAGL (LEOPOLD) Sozialisierung durch die Selbstversorger-Genossenschaft. [Vienna, 1920]. pp. 16.

MUELLER (HANS) of Zürich. Von der liberalen zur sozialen Genossenschaftstheorie: ein Beitrag zur Geschichte der genossenschaftlichen Ideenbewegung. Jena, 1924. pp. 38.

COOPERATIVE INFORMATION. Supplements. No. 2. Cooperative chronology. Geneva, International Labour Office, 1973. pp. 307,xiii.

KAPLAN DE DRIMER (ALICIA) and DRIMER (BERNARDO) Las cooperativas: fundamentos, historia, doctrina. Buenos Aires, 1973. pp. 622. bibliog.

— Bibliography.

COOPERATIVE INFORMATION. Supplements. No. 1. Geneva, International Labour Office, 1973. pp. 390. bibliog.

— Austria.

SAUER (MANFRED) 100 Jahre O sterreichischer Genossenschaftsverband, (1872- 1972). [Vienna, 1972]. pp. 61.

— Europe.

UNITED NATIONS. Department of Economic and Social Affairs. European Social Development Programme. Reports. New York, 1967 in progress.

— Germany.

NEUBOHN (HEINZ JOACHIM) Entwicklungstendenzen im westdeutschen Genossenschaftswesen. Stuttgart, 1972. pp. 58. bibliog. (Deutscher Sparkassen- und Giroverband. Sparkassenhefte. Nr. 47)

— Israel.

MALKOSH (NOAH) Cooperation in Israel. Tel Aviv, [1961?]. pp. 90. (General Federation of Labour in Israel. Histadrut Pocket Books. No. 2)

— Liberia.

SEIBEL (HANS DIETER) and MASSING (ANDREAS) Traditional organizations and economic development: studies of indigenous cooperatives in Liberia. New York, 1974. pp. 263. bibliog.

— Norway.

OVESEN (LIV) Consumers' co-operation in Norway. [Oslo, 1972]. pp. 30.

COOPERATION. (Cont.)

— Russia.

KABANOV (VLADIMIR VASIL'EVICH) Oktiabr'skaia revoliutsiia i kooperatsiia, 1917 g. - mart 1919 g. Moskva, 1973. pp. 296.

— Senegal.

LAVILLE (PIERRE) Associations rurales et socialisme contractuel en Afrique occidentale: étude de cas; le Sénégal. [Paris, 1972]. pp. 371. bibliog.

— Spain.

PEREZ BARO (ALBERT) Historia de la cooperacion catalana. Barcelona, 1974. pp. 243.

— Tanzania.

CEDILLO (VALENTIN G.) Rural development through Ujamaa: a Tanzania case report. Vienna, [1973]. pp. 55,(25). bibliog. (Wiener Institut für Entwicklungsfragen. Occasional Papers. 73/11)

— United Kingdom.

BAXTER (ROBERT) Lecturer in Politics. Co-operative democracy in industry. London, 1973. pp. 15. (Co-operative Party. Discussion Pamphlets)

CO-OPERATIVE UNION. (Women in the co-operative movement): report of study group on the situation and role of women in the co-operative movement. Manchester, [1973?]. pp. 8.

GOSDEN (PETER HENRY JOHN HEATHER) Self-help: voluntary associations in the 19th century. London, 1973. pp. 295. bibliog.

BACKSTROM (PHILIP N.) Christian Socialism and co-operation in Victorian England: Edward Vansittart Neale and the co-operative movement. London, 1974. pp. 238. bibliog.

— — Bibliography.

SMETHURST (JOHN B.) A bibliography of co-operative societies' histories. Manchester, [1974?]. pp. 122.

— United States.

KNAPP (JOSEPH GRANT) The advance of American cooperative enterprise, 1920-1945. Danville, [1973]. pp. 646.

COOPERATIVE MARKETING OF FARM PRODUCE

— Germany.

SCHEUTEN (ROLF) Stellung und Bedeutung der Winzergenossenschaften in der Bundesrepublik Deutschland. Köln, [1972]. pp. 356. bibliog. (Institut für Mittelstandsforschung. Schriften zur Mittelstandsforschung. Band 46)

COOPERATIVE SOCIETIES

— Germany — Finance.

HOMANN (JOERG) Ansätze zur Lösung der Finanzierungsproblematik der Genossenschaften. Hamburg, 1973. pp. 201. bibliog.

— Netherlands.

NETHERLANDS. Commissie Sociaal-Economische Politiek en Arbeids-vraagstukken. 1969. Rapport inzake het midden- en kleinbedrijf en samenwerkingsvormen. 's-Gravenhage, 1969. pp. 85. (Raad voor het Midden- en Kleinbedrijf. [Publikaties]. 1969, no. 3)

— Poland.

BRZEZIŃSKI (JACEK) and WILKOSZEWSKA (DANUTA) Spółdzielcze ośrodki "Praktyczna Pani" jako społeczno- gospodarcza instytucja 'zycia miejskiego. Warszawa, 1973. pp. 63. bibliog. (Spółdzielczy Instytut Badawczy. Seria Studiów Socjologicznych Samorządowych. Nr.4)

— Russia — Finance.

KAZANTSEVA (EKATERINA MIKHAILOVNA) and LITVINOV (IVAN KUZ'MICH) Finansovyi plan kooperativnykh organizatsii. Moskva, 1973. pp. 96.

— Switzerland.

AUSGEWAEHLTE Aufsätze über die Genossenschaftsbewegung der schweizerischen Konsumenten; [edited by Hans Handschin]. [Basel, 1937]. pp. 159. (Verband Schweizerischer Konsumvereine. Genossenschaftliche Volksbibliothek. Nr. 39)

— United Kingdom.

PETCH (ARTHUR W.) Co-operative employees and superannuation funds. Manchester, [imprint], 1928. pp. 63.

PETCH (ARTHUR W.) Co-operative employees and superannuation funds. rev. ed. [Manchester], 1930. pp. 92.

BAILEY (D.G.) and GIBBONS (E.T.) Agricultural co-operative activities and case histories of co- operatives. Newcastle upon Tyne, 1970. pp. 31. bibliog. (Newcastle-upon-Tyne. University. Department of Agricultural Economics. Agricultural Adjustment Unit. Technical Papers. 9)

COPPER INDUSTRY AND TRADE

— America, Latin.

INGRAM (GEORGE M.) Expropriation of U.S. property in South America: nationalization of oil and copper companies in Peru, Bolivia, and Chile. New York, 1974. pp. 392. bibliog.

COPPER MINES AND MINING

— Spain.

AVERY (DAVID) Not on Queen Victoria's birthday: the story of the Rio Tinto mines. London, 1974. pp. 464. bibliog.

— United Kingdom — Cornwall.

NOALL (CYRIL) The St. Just mining district. Truro, 1973. pp. 179.

— Zaire.

KATZENELLENBOGEN (S.E.) Railways and the copper mines of Katanga. Oxford, 1973. pp. 165. bibliog.

COPRA.

NEW HEBRIDES. Condominium Bureau of Statistics. Statistical bulletin: Principal exports: tonnages by port and country [and]: Copra: stocked and received for export at Vila and Santo. m., F 1974- Vila. In English and French.

COPYRIGHT

— Canada.

CANADA. Bureau of Intellectual Property. Annual report. a., 1972/3 [1st]- Hull, Canada. In English and French.

— United Kingdom.

CAVENDISH (J.M.) A handbook of copyright in British publishing practice. London, 1974. pp. 210. bibliog.

COUNCIL FOR EDUCATIONAL TECHNOLOGY FOR THE UNITED KINGDOM. Evidence to the Committee to consider the law on copyright and designs. London, [1974]. pp. 16.

— United States.

NIMMER (MELVILLE B.) The United States copyright law and the Berne Convention: the implications of the prospective revision of each. Geneva, 1966. pp. 94.

COPYRIGHT, INTERNATIONAL.

NIMMER (MELVILLE B.) The United States copyright law and the Berne Convention: the implications of the prospective revision of each. Geneva, 1966. pp. 94.

CORNISHMEN IN THE UNITED STATES.

ROWE (WILLIAM JOHN) The hard-rock men: Cornish immigrants and the North American mining frontier. Liverpool, 1974. pp. 322. bibliog.

CORNWALL.

THOMAS (CHARLES) b. 1928. The importance of being Cornish;...an inaugural lecture delivered in the University of Exeter on 8 March 1973. Exeter, 1973. pp. 21.

CORONARY HEART DISEASE.

MILLER (DONALD F.) Pervasive politics: a study of the Indian district. Melbourne, 1972. pp. 226. (Melbourne. University. Department of Political Science. Melbourne Politics Monographs)

CORPORAL PUNISHMENT.

KNEALE (ANGELA) Against birching: judicial corporal punishment in the Isle of Man. London, [1973]. pp. 98.

CORPORATE STATE.

PIKE (FREDRICK BRAUN) and STRITCH (THOMAS) eds. The new corporation: social-political structures in the Iberian world. Notre Dame, [1974]. pp. 218. (Notre Dame. University. Committee on International Relations. International Studies)

CORPORATION LAW

— Denmark.

DENMARK. Firmalovudvalg. 1971. Betaenkning. [Copenhagen], 1971. pp. 105. (Denmark. Betaenkninger. Nr.613)

— European Economic Community countries.

FRANCE. Direction de la Documentation. La Documentation Française. Notes et Etudes Documentaires. No. 3,719. Le projet de société commerciale européenne; Paul Turot. .Paris, 1970. pp. 46. bibliog.

BRITISH ACCOUNTING AND FINANCE ASSOCIATION. Annual Conference, 3rd, 1972. British financial strategy and company law reform for the E.E.C. [Sheffield?, 1972]. pp. 69.

EUROPEAN COMMUNITIES. Commission. 1972. Proposal for a fifth directive on the structure of sociétés anonymes. Brussels, 1972. pp. 68. (Bulletin of the European Communities. Supplements. [1972/10])

EUROPEAN COMMUNITIES. Commission. 1972. Company law: EEC fifth directive; a CBI English translation. London, 1973. pp. 198.

SCHMITTHOFF (CLIVE MACMILLAN) ed. The harmonisation of European company law. London, 1973. pp. 243. (United Kingdom National Committee of Comparative Law. United Kingdom Comparative Law Series. vol. 1)

DAVIN (LOUIS E.) and DETIENNE (J.) Mutations contemporaines; l'université, la C.E.E. et le droit des sociétés. Bruxelles, 1974. pp. 101. (Liège. Université. Séminaire Interdisciplinaire de Science Economique des Professeurs Harsin et Davin. Documents et Travaux. No. 9)

MACH (OLIVIER) L'entreprise et les groupes de sociétés en droit européen de la concurrence. Genève, 1974. pp. 278. bibliog.

SCHMITTHOFF (CLIVE MACMILLAN) ed. European company law texts, including the proposed Regulation on Merger Control, etc. London, 1974. pp. 322. (British Institute of International and Comparative Law. Studies in International and Comparative Law. No.7)

— France.

FRANCE. Statutes, etc. 1857-1971. Code des sociétés; (rédigé avec le concours de Pierre André Moreau). Paris, 1971. pp. 1014.

CORPORATIONS.

FRANCE. Groupe Prospective Juridique Appliquée. 1972. Préparation du VIe Plan... droit et financement des entreprises: rapport du Groupe Prospective Juridique Appliquée; [Michel Vasseur, chairman]. Paris, 1971 or rather 1972. pp. 209.

— Netherlands.

CHESTER (M.G.) and VOGELAAR (F.O.W.) English/Dutch company law: a review for lawyers and businessmen in the light of EEC requirements. London, [1974]. pp. 104.

— United Kingdom.

ALLAN (DAVID R.) Socialising the company. London, 1974. pp. 48. (Young Fabian Group. Young Fabian Pamphlets. 37)

CHESTER (M.G.) and VOGELAAR (F.O.W.) English/Dutch company law: a review for lawyers and businessmen in the light of EEC requirements. London, [1974]. pp. 104.

— United States.

HENN (HARRY G.) Handbook of the law of corporations and other business enterprises. 2nd ed. St. Paul, Minn., 1970. pp. 956.

CORPORATIONS.

TIMES 1000, THE: leading companies in Britain and overseas. a., 1971/2- London.

COLEMAN (JAMES SAMUEL) Power and the structure of society. New York, [1974]. pp. 112. bibliog. (Pennsylvania University. Fels Center of Government. Fels Lectures on Public Policy Analysis)

MARRIS (ROBIN) ed. The corporate society: [papers with editorial commentaries]. London, 1974. pp. 403. bibliogs. (Harvard University. Harvard University Program on Technology and Society. Harvard Studies in Technology and Society)

— Accounting.

INSTITUTE OF COST AND MANAGEMENT ACCOUNTANTS and SOCIETY FOR LONG RANGE PLANNING. Corporate planning and the role of the management accountant;... edited by Philip Sadler and Alan Robson. [London, 1972?]. pp. 125. bibliog.

— Finance.

HOFMANN (SABINE) Zum Einfluss der Selbstfinanzierung auf das wirtschaftliche Wachstum. Berlin, 1971. pp. 146, xxvi. bibliog.

BEN-ZION (URI) The cost of capital and the demand for money by firms. Minneapolis, 1973. fo. 11. bibliog. (Minnesota University. Center for Economic Research. Discussion Papers. No. 27)

LISTER (R.J.) ed. Studies in optimal financing: [readings]. London, 1973. pp. 201. bibliogs.

— Taxation.

HEERDEN (KOENRAAD VAN DER) Dubbele belasting heffing van uitgedeelde winsten van besloten en open vennootschappen. Deventer, [1973]. pp. 210. bibliog. With English summary.

ORGANISATION FOR ECONOMIC CO-OPERATION AND DEVELOPMENT. Fiscal Committee. 1973. Company tax systems in OECD member countries. Paris, 1973. pp. 140. bibliog.

— Canada.

MURPHY (RAE) and STAROWICZ (MARK) eds. Corporate Canada: 14 probes into the workings of a branch-plant economy; a Last Post special; [selected articles]. Toronto, 1972. pp. 156.

— — Finance.

CANADIAN TAX FOUNDATION. Corporate Management Tax Conference, 1974. Tax aspects of corporate financing: [papers of the conference, edited by Martina Vandermeer]. [Toronto, 1974]. pp. 174.

— — Taxation.

CANADIAN TAX FOUNDATION. Corporate Management Tax Conference, 1973. 1. Tax treatment of executive compensation: 2. use of corporations by executives and professionals. [Toronto, 1973]. pp. 114.

CANADIAN TAX FOUNDATION. Corporate Management Tax Conference, 1974. Tax aspects of corporate financing: [papers of the conference, edited by Martina Vandermeer]. [Toronto, 1974]. pp. 174.

— European Economic Community countries.

GUILDSTREAM RESEARCH SERVICES. Britain and the Common Market. London, 1973. 4 vols. (in 1).

— — Accounting.

MORRIS (R.C.) Corporate reporting standards and practices in Europe: a critical commentary on the E.E.C.'s draft fourth directive on published company accounts with reference to the institutional and accounting backgrounds of member countries. Bristol, 1973. pp. 107. bibliog. (Institute of Chartered Accountants in England and Wales. Research Committee. Occasional Papers. No. 2)

— — Finance.

BRITISH ACCOUNTING AND FINANCE ASSOCIATION. Annual Conference, 3rd, 1972. British financial strategy and company law reform for the E.E.C. [Sheffield?, 1972]. pp. 69.

— Finland — Finance.

JUNNELIUS (CHRISTIAN) Investeringsprocessens utformning vid olika organisationsstrukturtyper: The capital budgeting process and organisational structures. Helsingfors, 1974. pp. 315. bibliog. (Svenska Handelshögskolan. Ekonomi och Samhälle. Nr. 22) In Swedish, with English summary.

— — Taxation.

MEYER (HENRIK) Kvantitativ analys av skattereformeffekter: konstruktion av lineära programmeringsmodeller med tillämpning på finländska handelsföretag; Quantitative analysis of effects of tax reforms: building of linear programming models, etc.. Helsingfors, 1971. pp. 220. bibliog. (Svenska Handelshögskolan. Ekonomi och Samhälle. Nr. 19) With English summary.

— France — Finance.

FRANCE. Groupe Prospective Juridique Appliquée. 1972. Préparation du VIe Plan... droit et financement des entreprises: rapport du Groupe Prospective Juridique Appliquée; [Michel Vasseur, chairman]. Paris, 1971 or rather 1972. pp. 209.

— Germany — Taxation.

FLAEMIG (CHRISTIAN) Die Auswirkungen der Steuerreform auf die Kapitalgesellschaften in der Bundesrepublik Deutschland. Baden-Baden, [1974]. pp. 157. bibliog.

— — Hesse — Taxation.

HESSE. Statistisches Landesamt. Beiträge zur Statistik Hessens. Neue Folge. Nr.60. Die veranlagten Einkommen 1968: Ergebnisse der Einkommensteuerstatistik und der Körperschaftsteuerstatistik 1968. Wiesbaden, 1974. pp. [170].

— Ireland (Republic) — Taxation.

EIRE. Department of Finance. 1974. Company taxation in Ireland: proposals for corporation tax; laid by the Minister for Finance before each House of the Oireachtas, March, 1974. Dublin, [1974]. pp. 76.

— Netherlands — Taxation.

BARTEL (JOHANNES CORNELIS KASPER WILLEM) Inkomstenbelastingaspecten van de opbrengst van aandelen. Deventer, [1973]. pp. 276. bibliog. With English summary.

— Switzerland — Accounting.

BRUNNER (JEAN PIERRE) Die Publizität der schweizerischen Aktiengesellschaften, insbesondere das Postulat der Bilanzklarheit, etc. Zürich, 1973. pp. 203,11,30. bibliog.

— United Kingdom.

TIMES 1000, THE: leading companies in Britain and overseas. a., 1971/2- London.

ALLAN (DAVID R.) Socialising the company. London, 1974. pp. 48. (Young Fabian Group. Young Fabian Pamphlets. 37)

The BRITISH public company: its role, responsibilities and accountability; (based on a series of papers given at a two-day B[ritish] I[nstitute of] M[anagement] conference held in November 1973). London, [1974]. pp. 60. (British Institute of Management. Occasional Papers. New Series. OPN.12)

— — Accounting.

COMPANY FINANCIAL RESULTS; (prepared by the National Economic Development Office on behalf of the E[conomic] D[evelopment] C[ommittee] for Mechanical Engineering). a., 1968-9/1972-3(5th)- London.

ECONOMIC DEVELOPMENT COMMITTEE FOR THE MECHANICAL ENGINEERING INDUSTRY Company financial results, 1967/68-1971/72. [London, National Economic Developement Office, 1973] pp. 96

ECONOMIC DEVELOPMENT COMMITTEE FOR THE MECHANICAL ENGINEERING INDUSTRY. Inflation and company accounts in mechanical engineering. London, National Economic Development Office, 1973. pp. 56.

— — Finance.

MACCRINDLE (ROBERT ALEXANDER) and GODFREY (PETER) Rolls-Royce Limited: investigation under Section 165(a) (i) of the Companies Act 1948; report. London, H.M.S.O., 1973. 1 vol. (various pagings).

STABLE (RONDLE OWEN CHARLES) and LEACH (Sir RONALD GEORGE) Report on the affairs of Maxwell Scientific International (Distribution Services) Limited, Robert Maxwell and Co. Limited and final report on the affairs of Pergamon Press Limited: investigation under section 165(b) of the Companies Act 1948. London, H.M.S.O., 1973. pp. 351-664,(15).

ECONOMIC DEVELOPMENT COMMITTEE FOR MACHINE TOOLS. A financial study of British machine tool companies; [by Peat, Marwick, Mitchell and Company]. London, National Economic Development Office, 1974. pp. 129.

— — — Mathematical models.

LOBBAN (P.W.M.) The corporate sector: progress report [on research at the London Business School on a quarterly econometric model of the U.K.]. London, [1972?]. 1 vol. (various foliations)

— — Taxation.

CLARK (LAURENCE HENRY) Corporation tax - the imputation system: an introduction to the taxation of companies under the Finance Act 1972. [London], 1972. pp. 66. (Institute of Chartered Accountants in England and Wales. General Educational Trust. Publications)

— United States.

JACOBY (NEIL HERMAN) Corporate power and social responsibility: a blueprint for the future. New York, [1973]. pp. 282. (Columbia University. Graduate School of Business. Studies of the Modern Corporation)

KEATING (WILLIAM DENNIS) Emerging patterns of corporate entry into housing. Berkeley, 1973. pp. 152. bibliog. (California University. Center for Real Estate and Urban Economics. Special Reports. 8)

VOTAW (DOW) and SETHI (S. PRAKASH) The corporate dilemma: traditional values versus contemporary problems. Englewood Cliffs, [1973]. pp. 243.

NEEDHAM (JAMES J.) The threat to corporate growth. [Philadelphia], 1974. pp. 60.

CORPORATIONS. (Cont.)

BITTKER (BORIS I.) and EUSTICE (JAMES S.) Federal income taxation of corporations and shareholders: (with Supplement). 2nd ed. Branford, Conn., [1966]. pp. 774.

CORPORATIONS, AMERICAN.

HORST (THOMAS) At home abroad: a study of the domestic and foreign operations of the American food-processing industry. Cambridge, Mass., [1974]. pp. 145. *bibliog.*

— America, Latin.

INGRAM (GEORGE M.) Expropriation of U.S. property in South America: nationalization of oil and copper companies in Peru, Bolivia, and Chile. New York, 1974. pp. 392. *bibliog.*

— Canada.

LEVITT (KARI) Silent surrender: the American economic empire in Canada. New York, 1971. pp. 185.

REID (TIMOTHY ESCOTT HERRIOT) ed. Foreign ownership: villain or scapegoat?. Toronto, [1972]. pp. 96. *bibliog.*

— — Quebec.

DRACHE (DANIEL) ed. Quebec: only the beginning: the manifestoes of the Common Front; [translations of manifestoes of various labour organizations]. Toronto, 1972. pp. 272.

— Chile.

INTERNATIONAL TELEPHONE AND TELEGRAPH CORPORATION. Subversion in Chile: a case study in U.S. corporate intrigue in the Third World; [memoranda of the Corporation with an introduction by a group representing the Bertrand Russell Peace Foundation and others]. Nottingham, 1972. pp. 114. *(Spokesman, The. Spokesman Books)*

SELSER (GREGORIO) Una empresa multinacional: la ITT en los Estados Unidos y en Chile. Buenos Aires, 1974. pp. 257.

— Europe.

HELLMANN (RAINER) Puissance et limites des multinationales; traduit de l'allemand par Willy de Schepper. [Tours, 1974]. pp. 232. *bibliog.*

— United Kingdom.

ECONOMISTS ADVISORY GROUP. United States industry in Britain: an EAG business research study written by John H. Dunning. London, [1974?]. fo. 105.

CORPORATIONS, BRITISH.

AIMS OF INDUSTRY. When it doesn't pay to be British!. London, [1974]. pp. 9.

— Chile.

BLAKEMORE (HAROLD) British nitrates and Chilean politics, 1886-1896: Balmaceda and North. London, 1974. pp. 260. *(London. University. Institute of Latin American Studies. Monographs. 4)*

CORPORATIONS, FOREIGN

— Canada.

REID (TIMOTHY ESCOTT HERRIOT) ed. Foreign ownership: villain or scapegoat?. Toronto, [1972]. pp. 96. *bibliog.*

SAFARIAN (ALBERT EDWARD) Foreign ownership of Canadian industry. 2nd ed. Toronto, [1973]. pp. 346. *bibliog.*

— United Kingdom.

AIMS OF INDUSTRY. When it doesn't pay to be British!. London, [1974]. pp. 9.

— — Taxation.

STROBEL (JUERGEN) Die ertragsteuerliche Behandlung ausländischer Niederlassungen in Grossbritannien unter besonderer Berücksichtigung des deutsch-englischen Doppelbesteuerungsabkommens. Erlangen, 1973. pp. 169. *bibliog.*

CORPORATIONS, NON—PROFIT

— Canada.

CUMMING (PETER A.) Proposals for a new not-for-profit corporations law for Canada. [Ottawa, 1974]. 2 vols. (in 1).

CORPORATIONS, PUBLIC.

TURVEY (RALPH) ed. Public enterprise: selected readings. Harmondsworth, 1968. pp. 396. *bibliog.*

— European Economic Community countries.

EUROPEAN CENTRE FOR PUBLIC ENTERPRISES. The evolution of the public enterprises in the community of the Nine; [by] A. Bizaguet [and others]. Brussels, 1973. pp. 317.

— France.

GODCHOT (JACQUES E.) Les sociétés d'économie mixte et l'aménagement du territoire. Paris, 1958. pp. 223. *bibliog.*

DROUOT (GUY) and BONNAUD (JACQUES) Deux entreprises publiques devant leur avenir: Air-France et SNCF. Paris, 1973. pp. 240. *bibliog.* *(Université d'Aix-Marseille II. Faculté de Droit et de Science Politique. Travaux et Mémoires. No. 18)*

— — Finance.

LOUIT (CHRISTIAN) Les finances des entreprises publiques. Paris, 1974. pp. 397. *bibliog.*

— India.

INDIA. Committee on Plan Projects. Management Group. 1965. The Shipping Corporation of India: a study of planning and control. Vol. 1. [New Delhi, 1965]. 1 vol. (various pagings). *bibliog.* *Vol.2 not required by Library.*

MATHUR (BIRENDRA PRASAD) Public enterprises in perspective: aspects of financial administration and control in India. Bombay, 1973. pp. 225.

— United Kingdom.

TURVEY (RALPH) Economic analysis and public enterprises;... with a contribution by Herbert Christie. London, 1971. pp. 150.

ROY (DONALD) State holding companies. London, 1974. pp. 30. *(Young Fabian Group. Young Fabian Pamphlets. 40)*

U.K. Parliament. House of Commons. Library. Research Division. Background Papers. No.36. Statistics on nationalised industries. [London], 1974. pp. 25.

— — Accounting.

REED (P.W.) The economics of public enterprise. London, 1973. pp. 236.

CORRESPONDENCE SCHOOLS AND COURSES.

[DENMARK. Undervisningsministeriet. 1968]. Correspondence education in Denmark: its background, history and present status. [Copenhagen], 1968. fo. 13.

PERRATON (HILARY DAVID) Broadcasting and correspondence. Cambridge, [1973]. pp. 42. *bibliog.* *(National Extension College. Reports. Series 2. No. 2)*

CORRUPTION (IN POLITICS)

— America, Latin.

KERN (ROBERT) ed. The caciques: oligarchical politics and the system of caciquismo in the Luso-Hispanic world. Albuquerque, [1973]. pp. 202.

— Ghana.

GHANA. 1968. White Paper on the report of the Commission of Enquiry into the functions, operations and administration of the Workers Brigade. [Accra], 1968. pp. 11. *(W[hite] P[apers]. 1968. No. 8) Bound with the Report.*

— Sierra Leone.

SIERRA LEONE. Beoku-Betts Commission of Inquiry on the Special Coffee Deal of the Sierra Leone Produce Marketing Board. 1968. Report; [R.W. Beoku-Betts, chairman]. [Freetown, 1967 [or rather 1968]. pp. 25.

SIERRA LEONE. Percy Davies Commission of Inquiry into the Activities of the Freetown City Council from 1st January, 1964 to 23rd March, 1967. 1969. Report...; and the government statement thereon; [Percy R. Davies, chairman]. [Freetown, 1969]. pp. 114.

— Spain.

KERN (ROBERT) ed. The caciques: oligarchical politics and the system of caciquismo in the Luso-Hispanic world. Albuquerque, [1973]. pp. 202.

— Uganda.

UGANDA. Commission of Enquiry into Allegations made by the late Daudi Ocheng on the 4th February, 1966. 1971. Evidence and findings of the Commission; [Sir Clement Nageon de L'Estang, chairman]. Kampala, 1971. pp. 874.

— United States.

COHEN (RICHARD M.) and WITCOVER (JULES) A heartbeat away: the investigation and resignation of Vice President Spiro T. Agnew. New York, 1974. pp. 373.

See also WATERGATE AFFAIR, 1972—

CORSICA

— Economic conditions.

FRANCE. Mission Interministérielle pour l'Aménagement et l'Equipement de la Corse. 1972. Schéma général d'aménagement de la France: schéma d'aménagement de la Corse. [Paris], 1972. pp. 95. *(France. Délégation à l'Aménagement du Territoire et à l'Action Régionale. Travaux et Recherches de Prospective. 32)*

— Economic policy.

FRANCE. Mission Interministérielle pour l'Aménagement et l'Equipement de la Corse. 1972. Schéma général d'aménagement de la France: schéma d'aménagement de la Corse. [Paris], 1972. pp. 95. *(France. Délégation à l'Aménagement du Territoire et à l'Action Régionale. Travaux et Recherches de Prospective. 32)*

COST.

THIRLBY (GEORGE F.) After cost and choice. [1973]. fo. 11. *Mimeographed copy of typescript.*

— Mathematical models.

KNUDSEN (NIELS CHR.) Production and cost models of a multi-product firm: a mathematical programming approach. Odense, 1973. pp. 300. *bibliog.* *(Odense Universitet. Studies in History and Social Sciences. vol.13)*

COST ACCOUNTING.

ASHTON (DAVID) Solutions to the reciprocal service cost allocation problem. Coventry, 1973. pp. 32. *bibliog.* *(University of Warwick. Centre for Industrial Economic and Business Research. [Warwick Research in Industrial and Business Studies]. No. 42)*

COST AND STANDARD OF LIVING.

JACK (JANE) The standard of living. 2. Canoe or Cadillac?. London, 1950. pp. 16. *bibliog.* *(Current Affairs. No. 114)*

MACRAE (DONALD GUNN) The standard of living. 3. The good old days?. London, 1950. pp. 15. *bibliog.* *(Current Affairs. No. 115)*

PRESVELOU (CLIO) Sociologie de la consommation familiale. Bruxelles, [1968]. pp. 319. *bibliog.*

UNITED NATIONS. Statistical Office. Statistical Papers. Series M. No. 14. Rev.1. Retail price comparisons for international salary determination. (ST/STAT/SER.M/14/Rev.1) New York, 1971. pp. 171.

FRICKE (DIETER) Einkommen und Anspruchsniveau. Opladen, 1972. pp. 76. *bibliog. (North Rhine-Westphalia. Forschungsberichte des Landes Nordrhein-Westfalen. Nr.2213)*

KAUSEL (ANTON) Internationaler Preis- und Lohnvergleich für Wien und 21 Weltstädte. Wien, 1973. pp. 39. *(Arbeitsgemeinschaft für Lebensniveauvergleiche. Was Heisst Gut Leben? 4)* With English summary.

— **MATHEMATICAL MODELS.**

BURAČAS (ANTANAS) Gipotezy i modeli lichnykh potrebitel'skikh raskhodov v usloviiakh razvitogo kapitalizma. Vil'nius, 1969. pp. 405, lxxix. *bibliog.* With English summary.

— **Belgium.**

EVERAET (HUBERT) Le niveau de vie des agriculteurs: enquête sociale sur les facteurs qui influencent le revenu et l'équipement ménager. Bruxelles, 1972. fo. 50. *(Belgium. Institut Economique Agricole. Cahiers. No. 150)*

— **Denmark.**

BERTELSEN (OLE) and USSING (JYTTE) Familiestørrelse og livsstil, etc. København, 1974. pp. 104. *bibliog. (Socialforskningsinstituttet. Publikationer. 60)*

— **Finland.**

FINLAND. Tilastokeskus. 1973- . Hushållsbudgetundersökningen 1966. Helsinki, 1973 in progress. *(Tilastollisia Tiedonantoja. 51)*

— **France.**

FRANCE. Institut National de la Statistique et des Etudes Economiques. Collections de l'I.N.S.E.E. SÉRIE M. Ménages . Paris, 1970 in progress.

FRANCE. Institut National de la Statistique et des Etudes Economiques. Collections de l'I.N.S.E.E. Série. R. Régions . Paris, 1970 in progress.

FRANCE. Comité de Liaison entre l'I[nstitut] N[ational de la] S[tatistique et des] E[tudes] E[conomiques], les Administrations Economiques et les Organisations Professionnelles, Syndicales et Sociales. 1970. Eléments du niveau de vie. Paris, 1970. pp. 98.

— **French Guiana.**

FRANCE. Institut National de la Statistique et des Etudes Economiques. 1969. Une enquête sur les consommations des ménages dans le département de la Guyane 1968. Paris, [1969?]. pp. 21.

— **Germany.**

BOSCH (HEINZ DIETER) Zur Vermögenssituation der privaten Haushalte in der Bundesrepublik Deutschland. Berlin, [1971-73]. 2 vols.(in 1). *bibliog. (Bonn. Universität. Institut für das Spar-, Giro- und Kreditwesen. Untersuchungen über das Spar-, Giro- und Kreditwesen. Band 60)*

RICHARZ (IRMINTRAUT) Herrschaftliche Haushalte in vorindustrieller Zeit im Weserraum. Berlin, [1971]. pp. 236. *bibliog.*

FRICKE (DIETER) Einkommen und Anspruchsniveau. Opladen, 1972. pp. 76. *bibliog. (North Rhine-Westphalia. Forschungsberichte des Landes Nordrhein-Westfalen. Nr.2213)*

KUNZ (DIETRICH) and EULER (MANFRED) Possibilities and limits of continuous family budget surveys. Stuttgart, 1972. pp. 11. *(Germany (Bundesrepublik). Statistisches Bundesamt. Studies on Statistics. No. 27)*

GERMANY (BUNDESREPUBLIK). Statistisches Bundesamt. 1973. Einnahmen und Ausgaben privater Haushalte 1969. Stuttgart, 1973. pp. 194. *(Preise, Löhne, Wirtschaftsrechnungen. Reihe 18. Einkommens- und Verbrauchsstichproben. 4)*

— **Greece.**

GREECE. Ethnike Statistike Hyperesia. 1972. Household expenditure survey carried out in the urban areas of Greece during the years 1962/63 up to 1968/69. Athens, 1972. pp. 148. *([Publications]. S. Levels of living, etc. 5)* In Greek and English.

— **Iraq.**

IRAQ. Central Bureau of Statistics. Section of Research and Publicity. 1962. The household budget enquiry in the city of Baghdad and its environs. Baghdad, 1962. pp. (ii),25(28). In English and Arabic.

— **Korea.**

ANNUAL REPORT ON THE FAMILY INCOME AND EXPENDITURE SURVEY; [pd. by] Bureau of Statistics, Economic Planning Board, Republic of Korea. a., 1972- Seoul.

— **Netherlands.**

NETHERLANDS. Centraal Bureau voor de Statistiek. 1972. Het nationaal budgetonderzoek 1963/65: een analyse van de uitkomsten. 's-Gravenhage, 1972. pp. 97. *(Statistische en Econometrische Onderzoekingen. 12)* With English summary.

— **Netherlands Antilles.**

NETHERLANDS ANTILLES. Bureau voor de Statistiek. 1970. De verlegging van het basisjaar van het prijsindexcijfer van de kosten van het levensonderhoud. Curacao, 1970. fo. 6.

— **New Caledonia.**

FRANCE. Institut National de la Statistique et des Etudes Economiques. 1972. Les budgets familiaux en Nouvelle-Calédonie 1969. Paris, [1972?]. 2 vols. (in 1)

— **Nigeria.**

NIGERIA. Federal Office of Statistics. 1967. Report on enquiries into the income and expenditure patterns of lower and middle income households at Oshogbo/Ife/Ilesha: 1963/64. Lagos, [1967]. pp. 79. *(Urban Consumer Surveys in Nigeria. 1967/2)*

NIGERIA. Federal Office of Statistics. 1967. Report on enquiries into the income and expenditure patterns of lower and middle income households at Ondo/Akure/Owo, 1964/65. Lagos, [1967]. pp. 80. *(Urban Consumer Surveys in Nigeria. 1967/3)*

NIGERIA. Federal Office of Statistics. 1967. Report on enquiries into the income and expenditure patterns of lower and middle income households at Onitsha, 1963/64. Lagos, [1967]. pp. 82. *(Urban Consumer Surveys in Nigeria. 1967/1)*

NIGERIA. Agricultural Statistics Unit. 1973. Rural consumption enquiry: non-food items, Western Region, 1965-1966. Lagos, [1973]. pp. 8. *(Rural Economic Surveys of Nigeria. 1973/7)*

— **Norway.**

INNSTILLING om barnefamilienes økonomi; fra et utvalg oppnevnt ved Kronprinsregentens resolusjon av 10. mai 1968. Otta, 1971. pp. 248.

— **Reunion Island.**

FRANCE. Institut National de la Statistique et des Etudes Economiques. 1967. Enquête sur les dépenses des ménages à la Réunion en 1966: milieu rural. Paris, [1967]. pp. 66.

— **Russia.**

MAIER (VLADIMIR FEDOROVICH) Dokhody naseleniia i rost blagosostoianiia naroda. Moskva, 1968. pp. 220.

FROMENT-MEURICE (GABRIELLE) La vie soviétique. 2nd ed. Paris, 1973. pp. 127.

— **Sierra Leone.**

SIERRA LEONE. Central Statistics Office. 1971. Household survey of the Northern Province, urban areas, March, 1968-December 1969: final report: household expenditure and income and economic characteristics. Freetown, [1971]. pp. 104.

— **South Africa.**

POTGIETER (J.F.) The poverty datum line in two cities and three towns in the Eastern province/border area. [Port Elizabeth], 1972. pp. 36. *bibliog. (University of Port Elizabeth. Institute for Planning Research. Research Reports. No.11)*

PILLAY (P. NESEN) Poverty datum line study among Africans in Durban. Durban, 1973. pp. 34. *(Natal. University. Department of Economics. Occasional Papers. No. 3)*

POTGIETER (J.F.) The poverty datum line in the major urban centres of the Republic. Port Elizabeth, 1973. pp. 63. *bibliog. (University of Port Elizabeth. Institute for Planning Research. Research Reports. No.12)*

— **Thailand.**

THAILAND. National Economic and Social Development Board. 1973. The third national economic and social development plan, 1972-1976. Bangkok, [1973]. pp. 285,67.

— **United Kingdom.**

ASH (J.C.K.) Quarterly forecasting at the N[ational] I[nstitute of] E[conomic and] S[ocial] R[esearch]: personal income and expenditure. [Reading], 1973. fo. 23. *bibliog. (Reading. University. Department of Economics. Discussion Papers in Economics. No.40)*

— **United States.**

ESPENSHADE (THOMAS J.) The cost of children in urban United States. Berkeley, [1973]. pp. 94. *bibliog. (California University. Institute of International Studies. Population Monograph Series. No. 14)*

— **Venezuela.**

BANCO CENTRAL DE VENEZUELA. Estudio sobre presupuestos familiares e indices de costo de vida para el area Puerto La Cruz-Barcelona. Caracas, 1971. pp. 126.

COST EFFECTIVENESS.

BENEFIT-COST AND POLICY ANALYSIS : an Aldine annual on forecasting, decision-making, and evaluation. a., 1972- Chicago.

BARRELL (DAVID) Cost benefit analysis in transportation planning. [Oxford], 1972. pp. 89. *bibliog. (Oxford Polytechnic. Department of Town Planning. Oxford Working Papers in Planning Education and Research. 10)*

CHURCHILL (ANTHONY) and others. Road user charges in Central America. [Washington], International Bank for Reconstruction and Development, [1972]. pp. 176. *bibliog. (World Bank Staff Occasional Papers. No. 15)*

MELINEK (S.J.) A method of evaluating human life for economic purposes. Borehamwood, Fire Research Station, 1972. pp. 16. *(Fire Research Notes. No. 950)*

GEORGI (HANSPETER) Cost-benefit and public investment in transport: a survey. London, 1973. pp. 204.

HARRISON (A.J.) and MACKIE (P.J.) The comparability of cost benefit and financial rates of return;... [with] an annex by A. Peaker. London, H.M.S.O., 1973. pp. 17. *bibliog. (Government Economic Service Occasional Papers. 5)*

KOZŁOWSKI (JERZY) Analiza progowa za granicą: próba oceny i rozwinięcia. Warszawa, 1973. pp. 123. *bibliog. (Polska Akademia Nauk. Komitet Przestrzennego Zagospodarowania Kraju. Studia. t. 42)* With Russian and English summaries.

NASH (CHRISTOPHER A.) and others. An evaluation of cost-benefit analysis criteria. [Southampton], 1973. fo.25. *bibliog. (Southampton. University. Discussion Papers in Economics and Econometrics. No. 7311)*

COST EFFECTIVENESS. (Cont.)

SHELDON (NANCY W.) and BRANDWEIN (ROBERT) The economic and social impact of investments in public transit. Lexington, Mass., [1973]. pp. 170. bibliog.

STANLEY (JOHN K.) A cardinal utility framework for project evaluation. [Southampton], 1973. fo.34. bibliog. (Southampton. University. Discussion Papers in Economics and Econometrics. No. 7305)

TURČIĆ (IVAN) Regionalni aspekt efikasnosti društvene privrede Jugoslavije. Zagreb, 1973. pp. 106. With English summary.

VIRENQUE (P.H.) and others. Haveninvesteringen op de linker-Scheldeoever: welvaart en kosten-batenanalyse. Antwerp, [1973]. pp. 115. bibliog. With English summary.

CAMPBELL (RITA RICARDO) Food safety regulation: a study of the use and limitations of cost-benefit analysis. Washington, D.C., 1974. pp. 59. bibliog. (American Enterprise Institute for Public Policy Research and Stanford University. Hoover Institution on War, Revolution and Peace. AEI-Hoover [Policy] Studies. 12)

HARRISON (ANTHONY J.) The economics of transport appraisal. London, 1974. pp. 293. bibliog.

LITTLE (IAN MALCOLM DAVID) and MIRRLEES (JAMES A.) Project appraisal and planning for developing countries. London, 1974. pp. 388. bibliog.

COSTS (LAW)

— Ireland (Republic).

EIRE. Committee on Court Practice and Procedure. 1972. Seventeenth interim report:... court fees. Dublin, [1972]. pp. 24.

— Tanzania.

McCOMB (THOMAS) Guide to civil procedure and the assessment of court fees payable in civil suits, execution proceedings, civil appeals, criminal private prosecutions, criminal appeals and court brokers' duties and fees; ...assisted by J.A. Vakil. Dar es Salaam, 1935. pp. 153.

COSTS, INDUSTRIAL.

COWLING (KEITH) and WATERSON (MICHAEL) Price-cost margins and market structure. Coventry, 1974. pp. 22. bibliog. (University of Warwick. Department of Economics. Warwick Economic Research Papers. No. 44)

— Canada.

PORTER (ALLAN A.) Productivity, costs and prices: an examination of trends in selected manufacturing industries. Ottawa, 1973. pp. 366. (Canada. Department of Labour. Economics and Research Branch. Occasional Papers. No. 7)

— United States.

HUETTNER (DAVID) Plant size, technological change, and investment requirements: a dynamic framework for the long-run average cost curve. New York, 1974. pp. 183. bibliog.

CÔTE D'AZUR

— Description and travel.

RICHARD (RENE) and BARTOLI (CAMILLE) La Côte d'Azur assassinée?. Paris, [1971]. pp. 137.

COTENTIN.

— Social history.

GOUBERVILLE (GILLES DE) Un sire de Gouberville: gentilhomme campagnard au Cotentin de 1553 à 1562; publié par Abbé A. Tollemer; précédé d'une introduction par E. Le Roy Ladurie. 2nd ed. Paris, 1873 repr. 1972. pp. 841. (Maison des Sciences de l'Homme. Rééditions. 10) Material from the Journal arranged by subject with comment by Abbé Tollemer.

COTTAGE INDUSTRIES

— Norway.

INNSTILLING om Samisk husflid som stottenaering; fra en komité oppnevnt ved kongelig resolusjon av 13. juni 1969. Orkanger, 1970. pp. 32.

COTTON GROWING AND MANUFACTURE

— United Kingdom.

TURNER (HERBERT ARTHUR) Trade union growth, structure and policy: a comparative study of the cotton unions in England. Toronto, 1962. pp. 413.

COTTON AND ALLIED TEXTILES INDUSTRY TRAINING BOARD [U.K.]. Report and statement of accounts. a., 1972/3- Manchester. Formerly included in the file of British Parliamentary Papers.

REACH (ANGUS BETHUNE) Manchester and the textile districts in 1849; edited by C. Aspin. Helmshore, 1972. pp. 122.

COTTON TRADE

— Japan.

HAUSER (WILLIAM B.) Economic institutional change in Tokugawa Japan: Osaka and Kinai cotton trade. London, 1974. pp. 239. bibliog.

COUNCIL FOR MUTUAL ECONOMIC ASSISTANCE.

COUNCIL FOR MUTUAL ECONOMIC ASSISTANCE. 1968. Charter of the Council for Mutual Economic Assistance. Moscow, 1968. pp. 15.

COUNCIL FOR MUTUAL ECONOMIC ASSISTANCE. 1971. Comprehensive programme for the further extension and improvement of co-operation and the development of socialist economic integration by the CMEA member-countries. Moscow, 1971. pp. 99.

BRABANT (JOZEF M.P.) Bilateralism and structural bilateralism in intra-C[ouncil for] M[utual] E[conomic] A[ssistance] trade. Rotterdam, 1973. pp. 290. bibliog.

KOHLMEY (GUNTHER) Vergesellschaftung und Integration im Sozialismus. Berlin, 1973. pp. 229. (Akademie der Wissenschaften der DDR. Zentralinstitut für Wirtschaftswissenschaften. Schriften. Nr. 8)

LAVIGNE (MARIE) Le programme du Comecon et l'intégration socialiste. Paris, 1973. pp. 389. bibliog.

The MARKET of socialist economic integration: [selected papers of an international conference held in Budapest in 1970]; edited by T. Kiss. Budapest, 1973. pp. 234.

MEZHDUNARODNAIA sotsialisticheskaia valiuta stran-chlenov SEV. Moskva, 1973. pp. 96.

PROFT (GERHARD) and others. Planung in der sozialistischen ökonomischen Integration. Berlin, 1973. pp. 170. bibliog.

SODRUZHESTVO sotsialisticheskoe: SEV; itogi i perspektiv. Moskva, 1973. pp. 272,[xv].

STELZL (DIETHARD) Die internationalen Banken des Rats für gegenseitige Wirtschaftshilfe. München, [1973]. pp. 191. bibliog. (Osteuropa-Institut, München. Gegenwartsfragen der Ost-Wirtschaft. Band 7)

BRABANT (JOZEF M.P. VAN) Essays on planning, trade and integration in Eastern Europe. Rotterdam, 1974. pp. 310.

COUNCIL FOR MUTUAL ECONOMIC ASSISTANCE. 1974. Collected reports on various activities of bodies of the C.M.E.A. in 1973. Moscow, 1974. pp. 250.

COUNCIL FOR MUTUAL ECONOMIC ASSISTANCE. 1974. Sbornik informatsii o deiatel'nosti organov SEV v 1973g. Moskva, 1974. pp. 211.

HEWETT (EDWARD A.) Foreign trade prices in the Council for Mutual Economic Assistance. London, 1974. pp. 196. (National Association for Soviet and East European Studies. Soviet and East European Studies)

INTERNATIONALE sozialistische Währung der Mitgliedsländer des RGW: Übersetzung ([by] Peter Freide [and] Gerhard Huber) aus dem Russischen. Berlin, 1974. pp. 83.

JAHN (WOLFGANG) of the University of Halle, and others. Sozialistische Integration zum Wohle unserer Völker: ein Übersichts- und Informationsmaterial. Berlin, 1974. pp. 158.

Die SOZIALISTISCHE ökonomische Integration: ihre Leitung, Planung und Stimulierung; (Autorenkollektiv: Gerhard Fröhlich [and others]). Berlin, 1974. pp. 141.

STEFFENS (ROLF) Integrationsprobleme im Rat für Gegenseitige Wirtschaftshilfe, RGW: Lösungsansätze bis zum Komplexprogramm des RGW. Hamburg, 1974. pp. 295. bibliog. (Hamburg. Hamburgisches Welt-Wirtschafts-Archiv. Veröffentlichungen)

WILCZYNSKI (JOZEF) Technology in Comecon: acceleration of technological progress through economic planning and the market. London, 1974. pp. 379.

COUNCIL OF EUROPE.

WEBER (JUERGEN) Der Europarat und Osteuropa: Entwicklung, Probleme und Möglichkeiten der Osteuropapolitik der Strassburger Organisation. Bonn, [1972]. pp. 400. bibliog.

PRICE (N.H.) and others. On-line searching of Council of Europe conventions and agreements: a study in bilingual document retrieval. Harwell, 1974. pp. 13. (U.K. Atomic Energy Authority. [Research Group. Reports.] AERE-R7673)

COUNSELLING.

TRUAX (CHARLES B.) and CARKHUFF (ROBERT R.) Toward effective counseling and psychotherapy: training and practice. Chicago, 1967 repr. 1973. pp. 416. bibliog.

CARKHUFF (ROBERT R.) Helping and human relations: a primer for lay and professional helpers. New York, [1969]. 2 vols. bibliogs.

CLARK (TED) and JAFFE (DENNIS T.) Toward a radical therapy: alternate services for personal and social change. New York, [1973]. pp. 287. bibliog.

NEWSOM (AUDREY) and others. Student counselling in practice. London, [1973]. pp. 196. bibliog.

SIMMS (MADELEINE) Report on non-medical abortion counselling. London, 1973. pp. 32. bibliog.

ETHICAL standards in counselling: papers presented by a working party to the Standing Conference for the Advancement of Counselling; edited by H.J. Blackham. London, [1974]. pp. 69.

COUNTERREVOLUTIONS

— Chile.

RAMIREZ NECOCHEA (HERNAN) Balmaceda y la contrarrevolucion de 1891. 3rd ed. Santiago de Chile, 1972. pp. 268. bibliog.

— Europe.

MAYER (ARNO J.) Dynamics of counterrevolution in Europe, 1870-1956: an analytic framework. New York, 1971. pp. 173. bibliog.

COUNTRY HOMES

— United Kingdom.

MAHON (DAVID) No place in the country: a report on second homes in England and Wales; edited by Moira Constable. London, 1973. fo. 21.

— — Wales.

CAERNARVONSHIRE. County Planning Department. Second homes. [Caernarvon, 1973?]. pp. 94.

MERIONETH. County Planning Office. Merioneth structure plan: (subject report no. 17): second homes. Dolgellau, [1973]. pp. 54.

COUPS D'ETAT.

NUN (JOSE) Latin America: the hegemonic crisis and the military coup. Berkeley, [1969]. pp. 73. *bibliog.* (*California University. Institute of International Studies. Politics of Modernization Series. No. 7*)

THOMPSON (WILLIAM R.) The grievances of military coup-makers. Beverly Hills, [1973]. pp. 73. *bibliog.*

COURT OF JUSTICE OF THE EUROPEAN COMMUNITIES.

WALL (EDWARD HAROLD) The Court of Justice of the European Communities: jurisdiction and procedure. London, 1966. pp. 322.

EUROPEAN COMMUNITIES. Court of Justice. 1967. Recueil de textes: organisation, compétences et procédure de la Cour. 2nd ed. Luxembourg, 1967. pp. 351.

LEPPÄ (SEPPO) Voiko rikostilastoon luottaa. Helsinki, 1973. fo. 69. *bibliog.* (*Kriminologinen Tutkimuslaitos. Sarja M. 32*) *With English summary.*

SORRENTINO (FEDERICO) Corte costituzionale e Corte di giustizia delle Comunità europee. Milano, 1970-73. 2 vols. (in 1). (*Genoa. Università. Facoltà di Giurisprudenza. Annali. Collana. 27, 34*)

COURTET (VICTOR).

BOISSEL (JEAN) Victor Courtet, 1813-1867: premier théoricien de la hiérarchie des races; contribution à l'histoire de la philosophie politique du romantisme. Paris, 1972. pp. 226. (*Montpellier. Université. Faculté des Lettres et Sciences Humaines. Publications. 36.*)

COURTS

— Australia.

NEUMANN (EDDY) The High Court of Australia: a collective portrait 1903-1972. 2nd ed. Sydney, 1973. fo. 131. *bibliog.* (*Sydney. University. Department of Government and Public Administration. Occasional Monographs. No.6*)

— Brazil.

SCHWARTZ (STUART B.) Sovereignty and society in colonial Brazil: the high court of Bahia and its judges, 1609-1751. Berkeley, Cal., [1973]. pp. 438. *bibliog.*

— Germany, Eastern.

REILAND (WERNER) Die gesellschaftlichen Gerichte der DDR. Tübingen, 1971. pp. 240. *bibliog.* (*Munich institut für Ostrecht. Studien. Band 23*)

— Ireland (Republic) — Officials and employees.

EIRE. Committee on Court Practice and Procedure. 1972. Sixteenth interim report...: the jurisdiction of the Master of the High Court. Dublin, [1972]. pp. 23.

— Pakistan.

MANNAN (M.A.) The superior courts of Pakistan: the development of their powers and jurisdiction. Lahore, 1973. pp. 488. *bibliog.*

— Russia.

FILIPPOV (EVGENII IVANOVICH) Kommentarii k Polozheniiu o tovarishcheskikh sudakh. Moskva, 1972. pp. 135.

BOKHAN (VLADIMIR FEDOROVICH) Formirovanie ubezhdenii suda. Minsk, 1973. pp. 159.

— — Latvia.

KOMMENTARII k polozheniiu o tovarishcheskikh sudakh Latviiskoi SSR. 3rd ed. Riga, 1973. pp. 268.

— United Kingdom.

FABIAN SOCIETY. Fabian Tracts. [No.] 427. Tribunals: a social court?; [by] Julian Fulbrook [and others]; Society of Labour Lawyers report. London, 1973. pp. 16.

MORRISON (FRED L.) Courts and the political process in England. Beverly Hills, [1973]. pp. 224.

U.K. Law Commission. Working Papers. No. 53. Family law: matrimonial proceedings in magistrates' courts. London, 1973. pp. 121.

— United States.

HISTORY of the Supreme Court of the United States; (general editor: Paul A. Freund). New York, [1971 in progress].

MURPHY (WALTER F.) and others. Public evaluations of constitutional courts: alternative explanations. Beverly Hills, [1973]. pp. 63. *bibliog.*

ABRAHAM (HENRY JULIAN) Justices and presidents: a political history of appointments to the Supreme Court. New York, 1974. pp. 310. *bibliog.*

— — Bibliography.

TOMPKINS (DOROTHY LOUISE CAMPBELL) compiler. Court organization and administration: a bibliography. Berkeley, 1973. pp. 200.

COUVIN

— Population.

BERTRAND (FRANÇOIS) La population de la châtellenie de Couvin aux XVIIe et XVIIIe siècles. Presgaux, 1972. pp. 127. *bibliog.*

COVENTRY

— Social conditions.

COVENTRY. Social Services Department. Helping people in need: (a manual of advice on welfare benefits in Coventry). a., My 1973 (2nd ed.)- Coventry.

— Transit systems.

CITY OF COVENTRY TRANSPORTATION STUDY GROUP. The report of the study group on the second and final phase of the Coventry transportation study. Coventry, 1972-73. 5 vols. (in 2). *bibliogs.* Includes The technical report, parts 1 and 2; The final analysis, parts 1 and 2; and The final analysis: the results.

CREATIVE THINKING (EDUCATION).

VALK (M.A.) The development of creativity in social work student training; based on material for a talk given to the Association of Tutors to Certificate in Social Work and Residential Social Work Courses. [London, Central Council for Education and Training in Social Work, 1972?]. pp. 20.

CREDIT

— Belgium.

VANES (F.R.) and VERHEIRSTRAETEN (A.) De geldkapitaalmarkt. 2nd ed, Leuven, 1972 in progress. *bibliog.*

— Canada — Nova Scotia.

SEARS (JOHN T.) Institutional financing of small business in Nova Scotia. Toronto, [1972]. pp. 248. *bibliog.* (*Social Science Research Council of Canada. Atlantic Provinces Studies. 3*)

— France.

KARLIN (MICHEL) Le sens et la portée du contrôle du crédit, en France, depuis 1945: essai d'introduction du facteur politique, à partir de l'analyse technique. [Paris, 1973]. pp. 308. *bibliog. With summaries in various languages.*

— Germany.

IRMLER (HEINRICH) Möglichkeiten und Grenzen der Kreditpolitik. Tübingen, 1971. pp. 21. (*Walter Eucken Institut. Vorträge und Aufsätze. 33*)

— Italy.

PARRILLO (FRANCESCO) Politica creditizia e stabilizzazione economica. Roma, 1974. pp. 134. (*Estratto dalla rivista Credito Popolare, NN. 3-4, 1974*)

— Malaysia.

MOKHZANI BIN ABDUL RAHIM. Credit in a Malay peasant economy; [Ph.D.(London) thesis]. 1973. fo. 472. *bibliog. Typescript: unpublished. This thesis is the property of London University and may not be removed from the Library.*

— Pakistan.

FAROOQ (DANIAL M.) Inflation, money and credit in Pakistan. Islamabad, United States Agency for International Development, 1973. 1 pamphlet (various pagings).

— Russia.

GLEBOV (ANATOLII EFIMOVICH) and IANCHENKO (STEPAN EFIMOVICH) Rol' kredita v razvitii sotsialisticheskikh form khoziaistva. Minsk, 1972. pp. 151.

KIRILLOV (NIKOLAI NIKOLAEVICH) and LAPIDUS (MIKHAIL KHLOVENOVICH) Finansirovanie i kreditovanie stroitel'stva v novykh usloviiakh khoziaistvovaniia. Moskva, 1973. pp. 121.

LITUNOVSKAIA (MARIIA KSENOFONTOVNA) Finansovo-kreditnye istochniki nauchno-tekhnicheskogo progressa. Moskva, 1973. pp. 159.

POPADIUK (KIRILL NIKITICH) Finansy i kredit v raspredelenii natsional'nogo dokhoda. Moskva, 1973. pp. 176.

SHUMOV (NIKOLAI SERGEEVICH) Finansirovanie i kreditovanie promyshlennosti. 2nd ed. Moskva, 1973. pp. 288.

— Spain.

SPAIN. Instituto de Credito Oficial. Memoria del credito oficial. a., 1971 [1st issue]- Madrid. *Supersedes in part* SPAIN. Instituto de Credito a Medio y Largo Plaza. Memoria; [with] Anexo estadistico.

— Sweden.

EFFECTS of credit policy: Swedish survey evidence, 1969-1971. Stockholm, 1973. pp. 211. (*Stockholm. Konjunkturinstitut. Occasional Papers. 7*)

CREOLE DIALECTS

— Jamaica.

BAILEY (BERYL LOFTMAN) Jamaican creole syntax: a transformational approach. Cambridge, 1966. pp. 164. *bibliog.*

CRIME AND CRIMINALS.

MAGEE (BRYAN EDGAR) and others. Crime or disease?; [transcript of a discussion with] Antony Flew [and] Baroness Wootton of Abinger;...transmitted 7 June 1973. [London, 1973]. fo. 32. (*Thames Television. Something to Say*)

PRINS (HERSCHEL A.) Criminal behaviour: an introduction to its study and treatment. London, 1973. pp. 245. *bibliog.*

— Europe.

HOLLE (ROLF) Die Kriminalität in der Bundesrepublik Deutschland im Vergleich zu Österreich, Frankreich, den Niederlanden, Dänemark, Schweden, England u. Wales und Italien, 1955- 1964. Wiesbaden, 1968. pp. 92. (*Germany (Bundesrepublik). Bundeskriminalamt. Schriftenreihe. 1968.2*)

— Finland.

LEPPÄ (SEPPO) Voiko rikostilastoon luottaa. Helsinki, 1973. fo. 69. *bibliog.* (*Kriminologinen Tutkimuslaitos. Sarja M. 32*) *With English summary.*

— South Africa.

PRETORIUS (J.L.) 'N ekologiese ontleding van Blanke misdaad in Johannesburg. [Pretoria, 1966]. pp. 86. *bibliog.* (*South Africa. National Bureau of Educational and Social Research. Research Series. No. 36*)

CRIME AND CRIMINALS. (Cont.)

PRETORIUS (J.L.) 'N ontleding van die Suid-Afrikaanse misaadstatistiek. [Pretoria, 1967]. fo. 67. *(South Africa. National Bureau of Educational and Social Research. Research Series. No. 53)*

— **Uganda.**

CLINARD (MARSHALL BARRON) and ABBOTT (DANIEL J.) Crime in developing countries: a comparative perspective. New York, [1973]. pp. 319.

— **Underdeveloped areas.**

See UNDERDEVELOPED AREAS — Crime and criminals.

— **United Kingdom.**

PRINS (HERSCHEL A.) Criminal behaviour: an introduction to its study and treatment. London, 1973. pp. 245. *bibliog.*

— **United States.**

The ECONOMICS of crime and punishment: a conference sponsored by American Enterprise Institute for Public Policy Research [and Virginia Polytechnic Institute and State University, Center for Study of Public Choice; edited by Simon Rottenberg]. Washington, [1973]. pp. 232.

RECKLESS (WALTER CADE) The crime problem. 5th ed. New York, [1973]. pp. 718.

BECKER (GARY S.) and LANDES (WILLIAM M.) eds. Essays in the economics of crime and punishment. New York, 1974. pp. 268. *(National Bureau of Economic Research. Human Behavior and Social Institutions. 3)*

PYLE (GERALD F.) and others. The spatial dynamics of crime. Chicago, 1974. pp. 221. *bibliog.* *(Chicago. University. Department of Geography. Research Papers. No.159)*

CRIME PREVENTION

— **Canada.**

EVANS (ROBERT) Developing policies for public security and criminal justice. Ottawa, 1973. pp. 115. *(Canada. Economic Council. Special Studies. No. 23)*

— **United Kingdom.**

CARTER (R.L.) Theft in the market: an economic analysis of costs and incentives in improving prevention by government and private police and reducing loss by insurance. London, 1974. pp. 96. *bibliog.* *(Institute of Economic Affairs. Hobart Papers. 60)*

CRIMEA

— **History — Sources.**

KRYM v period Velikoi Otechestvennoi voiny 1941-1945: sbornik dokumentov i materialov. Simferopol', 1973. pp. 488.

— — **1917—1921, Revolution — Personal narratives.**

MAKAROV (PAVEL VASIL'EVICH) Ad"iutant Generala Mai-Maevskogo: iz vospominanii nachal'nika otriada krasnykh partizanov v Krymu, etc. Leningrad, [1925?]. pp. 197.

CRIMEAN WAR, 1853—1856.

LEVIN (SHNEER MENDELEVICH) Ocherki po istorii russkoi obshchestvennoi mysli, vtoraia polovina XIX - nachalo XX veka: [glavy iz dvukh nezavershennykh rukopisei, Raznochinskii period russkogo osvoboditel'nogo dvizheniia v osveshchenii dorevoliutsionnoi istoriografii i Krymskaia voina i russkoe obshchestvo; otv. redaktor S.N. Valk]. Leningrad, 1974. pp. 442.

CRIMES ABOARD AIRCRAFT.

SHUBBER (SAMI) Jurisdiction over crimes on board aircraft. The Hague, 1973. pp. 369. *bibliog.*

CRIMINAL ANTHROPOLOGY.

PRETORIUS (J.L.) 'N ekologiese ontleding van Blanke misdaad in Johannesburg. [Pretoria, 1966]. pp. 86. *bibliog.* *(South Africa. National Bureau of Educational and Social Research. Research Series. No. 36)*

CRIMINAL INVESTIGATION

— **Russia.**

LUZGIN (IGOR' MIKHAILOVICH) Metodologicheskie problemy rassledovaniia. Moskva, 1973. pp. 215.

TSVETKOV (PAVEL PETROVICH) Issledovanie lichnosti obviniaemogo: na predvaritel'nom sledstvii i v sude pervoi instantsii. Leningrad, 1973. pp. 149.

CRIMINAL JURISDICTION.

BASSIOUNI (M. CHERIF) International extradition and world public order. Leyden, 1974. pp. 630.

CRIMINAL JUSTICE, ADMINISTRATION OF

— **Canada.**

CANADA. Department of the Solicitor General. 1973. The criminal in Canadian society: a perspective on corrections. Ottawa, 1973. pp. 46, 49. *bibliog.* In English and French.

EVANS (ROBERT) Developing policies for public security and criminal justice. Ottawa, 1973. pp. 115. *(Canada. Economic Council. Special Studies. No. 23)*

— **Italy.**

PELLEGRINI (EDGARDO) Gli ermellini da guardia: (magistratura e repressione in Italia, 1968-1973). Roma, [1973]. pp. 159.

GIUSTIZIA penale e riforma carceraria in Italia: atti del seminario organizzato dal Centro di Studi e Iniziative ... Roma, 1973; [by] Gianfilippo Benedetti [and others]. Roma, 1974. pp. 382. *(Centro di Studi e Iniziative per la Riforma dello Stato. Quaderni. 1)*

— **Sweden.**

SWEDEN. Justitiedepartementet. Kommittén för Anstaltsbehandling inom Kriminalvården. 1971. Kriminalvård i anstalt. Stockholm, 1971. pp. 354. *bibliog.* *(Sweden. Statens Offentliga Utredningar. 1971.74)* With English summary.

— **United States.**

BALBUS (ISAAC D.) The dialectics of legal repression: black rebels before the American criminal courts. New York, [1973]. pp. 269.

COLE (GEORGE F.) Politics and the administration of justice. Beverly Hills, [1973]. pp. 234.

CRIMINAL LAW

— **Australia.**

LAW COUNCIL OF AUSTRALIA. Draft criminal code for the Australian territories; submitted to the Attorney-General... together with commentary by the Council's Co-ordinating Committee. in AUSTRALIA. Parliament. Parliamentary papers, 1969, vol.10.

— **Europe — History and criticism.**

IMMINK (P.W.A.) La liberté et la peine: étude sur la transformation de la liberté et sur le développement du droit pénal public en Occident avant le XIIe siècle; éditée d'après le manuscrit et les notes de lauteur par P. Sarolea. Assen, 1973. pp. 289.

— **France.**

SAINT-JOURS (YVES) Le droit pénal de la sécurité sociale. Paris, 1973. pp. 137. *bibliog.* *(Paris. Université de Paris II. Travaux et Recherches. Série Sciences Criminelles. 1)*

— **Germany.**

WORM (MANFRED) SPD und Strafrechtsreform: (die Stellung der Sozialdemokratischen Partei Deutschlands zur Strafrechtsreform, etc.). München, [1968]. pp. 159. *bibliog.* *(Politische Studien. Beihefte. 8)*

— **Poland.**

PROBLEMY nowego prawa karnego: materiály konferencji naukowej zorganizowanej przez Komitet Nauk Prawnych Polskiej Akademii Nauk w dniach 4-6 maja 1970 roku w Warszawie. Wrocław, 1973. pp. 236.

— **Russia.**

KURS sovetskogo ugolovnogo prava. Leningrad, 1968-73. 3 vols.

SOVETSKOE ugolovnoe pravo: chast' obshchaia. Moskva, 1972. pp. 583. *bibliog.*

DAN'SHIN (IVAN NIKOLAEVICH) Ugolovno-pravovaia okhrana obshchestvennogo poriadka. Moskva, 1973. pp. 200.

IVANOV (VALENTIN NIKOLAEVICH) Ugolovnoe zakonodatel'stvo Soiuza SSR i soiuznykh respublik: edinstvo i osobennosti. Moskva, 1973. pp. 208.

KUZNETSOVA (NINEL' FEDOROVNA) and MIKHAILOVSKAIA (INGA BORISOVNA) eds. Effektivnost' primeneniia ugolovnogo zakona. Moskva, 1973. pp. 208.

LENINSKIE idei v nauke ugolovnogo prava: sbornik statei. Leningrad, 1973. pp. 100.

RUSSIA (USSR). Statutes, etc. 1959-71. Sbornik postanovlenii Plenuma i opredelenii kollegii Verkhovnogo Suda SSSR po ugolovnym delam, 1959-1971 gg.; pod redaktsiei... G.Z. Anashkina. Moskva, 1973. pp. 412.

VLADIMIROV (VLADIMIR ALEKSANDROVICH) ed. Sovetskoe ugolovnoe pravo: posobie dlia narodnykh zasedatelei. Moskva, 1973. pp. 215.

— — **Kazakstan.**

KAZAKSTAN. Statutes, etc. 1971. Ugolovnyi kodeks Kazakhskoi SSR: ofitsial'nyi tekst s izmeneniiami i dopolneniiami na 1 noiabria 1971 goda. Alma-Ata, 1972. pp. 250.

— — **Latvia.**

LATVIISKII GOSUDARSTVENNYI UNIVERSITET. Uchenye Zapiski. t.188. Sovershenstvovanie ugolovnogo i ugolovno-protsessual'nogo zakonodatel'stva. Riga, 1973. pp. 185.

— — **Ukraine.**

UKRAINE. Statutes, etc. 1972. Ugolovnyi kodeks Ukrainskoi SSR: ofitsial'nyi tekst s izmeneniiami i dopolneniiami na 1 aprelia 1972 goda i postateinymi materialami. Kiev, 1972. pp. 277.

— — **White Russia.**

GORELIK (IOSIF ISAAKOVICH) and TISHKEVICH (IVAN STANISLAVOVICH) eds. Ugolovnoe pravo BSSR: chast' obshchaia. Minsk, 1973. pp. 365. *bibliog.*

— **United Kingdom.**

ARCHBOLD (JOHN FREDERICK) Pleading, evidence and practice in criminal cases; thirty-eighth edition by T.R. Fitzwalter Butler and Stephen Mitchell; (with supplement). London, 1973. pp. 1663.

ELLIOTT (DEREK WILLIAM) and WOOD (JOHN CROSSLEY) A casebook on criminal law. 3rd ed. London, 1974. pp. 558.

CRIMINAL LIABILITY

— **Poland.**

PRUSAK (FELIKS) Pociągnięcie podejrzanego do odpowiedzialności w procesie karnym. Warszawa, 1973. pp. 295. *bibliog.* With Russian and German summaries.

CULTURAL PROPERTY, PROTECTION OF.

— United Kingdom.

GRIEW (EDWARD JAMES) Dishonesty and the jury: an inaugural lecture delivered in the University of Leicester, 6 November 1973. Leicester, 1974. pp. 24.

CRIMINAL PROCEDURE

— Poland.

KLIMEK (JÓZEF) Udział związków zawodowych w procesie karnym. Warszawa, 1973. pp. 159.

WALTOŚ (STANISŁAW) Postępowania szczególne w procesie karnym: postępowania kodeksowe. Warszawa, 1973. pp. 362. *bibliog. With French and Russian summaries.*

— Russia.

KUTSOVA (ELEONORA FEDOROVNA) Garantii prav lichnosti v sovetskom ugolovnom protsesse: predmet, tsel', soderzhanie. Moskva, 1973. pp. 199.

— — Latvia.

LATVIISKII GOSUDARSTVENNYI UNIVERSITET. Uchenye Zapiski. t.188. Sovershenstvovanie ugolovnogo i ugolovno-protsessual'nogo zakonodatel'stva. Riga, 1973. pp. 185.

— — Russia (RSFSR).

RUSSIA (R.S.F.S.R.). Statutes, etc. 1972. Ugolovno-protsessual'nyi kodeks RSFSR: ofitsial'nyi tekst s izmeneniiami na 10 dekabria 1972 g. s prilozheniem postateino- sistematizirovannykh materialov. Moskva, 1973. pp. 246.

— — White Russia.

ZDANOVICH (A.A.) ed. Kommentarii k Ugolovno-protsessual'nomu kodeksu Belorusskoi SSR. 3rd ed. Minsk, 1973. pp. 504.

— United Kingdom.

ARCHBOLD (JOHN FREDERICK) Pleading, evidence and practice in criminal cases; thirty-eighth edition by T.R. Fitzwalter Butler and Stephen Mitchell; (with supplement). London, 1973. pp. 1663.

CRIMINAL REGISTERS

— United States.

MILLER (HERBERT S.) The closed door: the effect of a criminal record on employment with state and local public agencies. Washington, 1972. pp. 252. *Prepared at Georgetown University for the Manpower Administration, U.S. Department of Labor.*

CRIMINAL STATISTICS

— Australia — New South Wales.

NEW SOUTH WALES. Bureau of Crime Statistics and Research. Petty sessions. a., 1972 [1st]- Sydney. *(Statistical Reports)*

— Canada.

CANADA. Statistics Canada. Crime and traffic enforcement statistics. a., 1972/1973 [1st issue]- Ottawa. *In English and French.*

— Finland.

ANTTILA (INKERI) and JAAKKOLA (RISTO) Unrecorded criminality in Finland. Helsinki, 1966. pp. 36. *bibliog. (Kriminologinen Tutkimuslaitos. Sarja A. 2)*

CRISPI (FRANCESCO).

MORI (RENATO) La politica estera di Francesco Crispi, 1887-1891. Roma, 1973. pp. 286.

CROATIA

— Economic conditions.

OMRCANIN (IVO) Economic wealth of Croatia. Philadelphia, [1973]. pp. 165. *bibliog.*

— — Mathematical models.

PRILOG izradi projekcije dugoročnog razvoja društvenog sektora privrede SR Hrvatske: modelski pristup. Zagreb, 1974. pp. 101.

— History.

GAZI (STEPHEN) A history of Croatia. New York, [1973]. pp. 368. *bibliog.*

— Politics and government.

MAČEK (VLADKO) Vodja govori: ličnost, izjave, govori i politički rad vodje Hrvata, Dra. Vladka Mačka; sabrao i uredio Mirko Glojnarić. Zagreb, 1936. pp. 349.

CROP YIELDS.

BARRETO (ANTONIO) ed. A study of the social and economic implications of the large scale introduction of high-yielding varieties of foodgrain: a selection of readings; an Institute staff study. (UNRISD Reports. No.71.6) (UNRISD/72/C.3). Geneva, United Nations Research Institute for Social Development, 1971. pp. 173. *([Studies on the Green Revolution. No.2])*

DUMONT (RENÉ) Notes sur les implications sociales de la révolution verte dans quelques pays d'Afrique; [edited by] Antonio Barreto. (UNRISD Reports. No.71.5) (UNRISD/71/C.92). Geneva, United Nations Research Institute for Social Development, 1971. pp. 166. *([Studies on the Green Revolution. No.1])*

EUROPEAN COMMUNITIES. Statistical Office. EEC crop reports: review of the harvest year and prospects, etc. a., 1972(no.1)- [Luxembourg].

PALMER (INGRID) Food and the new agricultural technology. (UNRISD Reports. No.72.9). Geneva, United Nations Research Institute for Social Development, 1972. pp. 85. *(Studies on the Green Revolution. No.5)*

PALMER (INGRID) Science and agricultural production. (UNRISD Reports. No.72.8). Geneva, United Nations Research Institute for Social Development, 1972. pp. 100. *(Studies on the Green Revolution. No.4)*

CROSTHWAITE (Sir CHARLES HAUKES TOD).

MYA SEIN, Daw. The administration of Burma: (Sir Charles Crosthwaite and the consolidation of Burma); [reprint of the first edition of 1938] with an introduction by Josef Silverstein. Kuala Lumpur, 1973. pp. 186. *bibliog.*

CROWN LANDS

— Sweden.

KULLBERG (ANDERS) Johan Gabriel Stenbock och reduktionen: godspolitik och ekonomiförvaltning, 1675-1705. Stockholm, [1973]. pp. 174. *bibliog. (Uppsala. Universitet. Historiska Institutionen. Studia Historica Upsaliensia. 51) With German summary.*

CRUELTY TO CHILDREN

— New Zealand.

FERGUSSON (DAVID M.) and others. Child abuse in New Zealand: a report on a nationwide survey of the physical ill-treatment of children in New Zealand. Wellington, Government Printer, 1972. pp. 342. *bibliog.*

— United Kingdom.

U.K. [Department of Health and Social Security]. 1972. The "battered baby" syndrome: an analysis of reports submitted by medical officers of health and children's officers. [London, 1972]. fo. 10.

CRUSADES.

PRAWER (JOSHUA) The world of the crusaders. London, [1972]. pp. 160.

CUBA

— Bibliography.

HAVANA. Biblioteca Nacional Jose Marti. Movimiento editorial en Cuba, 1959-1960: exposicion de libros, folletos y revistas. La Habana, 1961. pp. 44.

— Commerce.

CUBA. Ministerio de Comercio del Gobierno Revolucionario. Direccion de la Opinion Publica. Boletin oficial. m., My 1960- F 1961 ([ano.1, no.] 1/2- ano 2, no.2). La Habana.

— Economic policy.

DUMONT (RENÉ) Is Cuba socialist?...translated by Stanley Hochman. London, 1974. pp. 159.

— Foreign relations.

SUCHLICKI (JAIME) ed. Cuba, Castro, and revolution. Coral Gables, [1972]. pp. 250.

— — China.

CHENG (YING-HSIANG) Idylle sino-cubaine, brouille sino-soviétique. Paris, 1973. pp. 311. *(Fondation Nationale des Sciences Politiques. Travaux et Recherches de Science Politique. 24)*

— — Russia.

TORRES RAMIREZ (BLANCA) Las relaciones cubano-sovieticas, 1959-1968. Mexico, 1971. pp. 142. *bibliog. (Mexico City. Colegio de Mexico. Jornadas. 71)*

CROZIER (BRIAN) Soviet pressures in the Caribbean: the satellisation of Cuba. London, 1973. pp. 20. *(Institute for the Study of Conflict. Conflict Studies. No. 35)*

— — United States.

GELLMAN (IRWIN F.) Roosevelt and Batista: good neighbor diplomacy in Cuba, 1933- 1945. Albuquerque, [1973]. pp. 303. *bibliog.*

— Industries.

CUBA. Ministerio de Comercio del Gobierno Revolucionario. Direccion de la Opinion Publica. Boletin oficial. m., My 1960- F 1961 ([ano.1, no.] 1/2- ano 2, no.2). La Habana.

— Politics and government.

SUCHLICKI (JAIME) ed. Cuba, Castro, and revolution. Coral Gables, [1972]. pp. 250.

CASTRO RUZ (FIDEL) Today we are an entire people conquering new heights. (speech... on the occasion of the 20th anniversary of the attack on the Moncada Garrison). [Havana?], 1973. pp. 58.

DUMONT (RENÉ) Is Cuba socialist?...translated by Stanley Hochman. London, 1974. pp. 159.

GONZALEZ (EDWARD) Cuba under Castro: the limits of charisma. Boston, [1974]. pp. 241.

— Race question.

MARTINEZ-ALIER (VERENA) Marriage, class and colour in nineteenth century Cuba: a study of racial attitudes and sexual values in a slave society. London, 1974. pp. 202. *bibliog.*

— Social conditions.

SUCHLICKI (JAIME) ed. Cuba, Castro, and revolution. Coral Gables, [1972]. pp. 250.

— Statistics.

STATISTICAL ABSTRACT OF LATIN AMERICA. [Supplement Series. 1]. Cuba 1968; [edited by] C. Paul Roberts [and] Mukhtar Hamour. Los Angeles. 1970. pp. 210.

CULTURAL PROPERTY, PROTECTION OF.

MEYER (KARL ERNEST) The plundered past. London, 1974. pp. 353.

— United Kingdom.

U.K. Treasury. 1973. Private owners and public collections; note. [London], 1973. fo. 8.

CULTURAL RELATIONS.

CULTURAL RELATIONS.
UNITED NATIONS EDUCATIONAL, SCIENTIFIC AND CULTURAL ORGANIZATION. Department of Mass Communication. Reports and Papers on Mass Communication. Paris, 1953 in progress.

CULTURE.
UNITED NATIONS EDUCATIONAL, SCIENTIFIC AND CULTURAL ORGANIZATION. Studies and Documents on Cultural Policies . Paris, 1969 in progress.

JEANSON (FRANCIS) L'action culturelle dans la cité. Paris, [1973]. pp. 253.

LEVINE (ROBERT ALAN) Culture, behaviour and personality. London, 1973. pp. 319. *bibliog.*

THEODÓRAKIS (MIKES) Culture et dimensions politiques; traduit du grec par Jean Criticos et Pierre Comberousse. [Paris, 1973]. pp. 362.

COLE (MICHAEL) and SCRIBNER (SYLVIA) Culture and thought: a psychological introduction. New York, [1974]. pp. 227. *bibliogs.*

CUNENE RIVER
— Regulation.
WORLD COUNCIL OF CHURCHES. Programme to Combat Racism. Cunene Dam scheme and the struggle for the liberation of southern Africa. Geneva, 1971. pp. 45.

CURTIS (DOUGLAS).
CURTIS (DOUGLAS) Dartmoor to Cambridge: the autobiography of a prison graduate. London, [1973]. pp. 191.

CURVES.
FRIEDMAN (ANDREW) Choosing among S-shaped curves for diffusion processes. Coventry, 1974. pp. 33. *(University of Warwick. Centre for Industrial Economic and Business Research. [Warwick Research in Industrial and Business Studies]. No. 45)*

CUTLERY
— United Kingdom.
TRADES UNIONS COMMISSION. The Sheffield outrages: report presented to the Trades Unions Commissioners in 1867: with an introduction by Sidney Pollard. Bath, 1971. pp. 452. *(Documents of Social History) Reprint of 1867 publication. Original also available in British Parliamentary Papers, 1867, vol. xxxii.*

CYBERNETICS.
ARBIB (MICHAEL A.) The metaphorical brain: an introduction to cybernetics as artificial intelligence and brain theory. New York, [1972]. pp. 243. *bibliog.*

PRAVOVAIA kibernetika. [sb.2]. Moskva, 1973. pp. 248.

— Research — Russia.
CASSEL (SIMON) Soviet cybernetics research: a preliminary study of organizations and personalities. Santa Monica, 1971. pp. 201. *bibliog. (Rand Corporation. Rand Reports. 909)*

CYCLING
— United Kingdom.
MITCHELL (C.G.B.) Pedestrian and cycle journeys in English urban areas. Crowthorne, 1973. pp. 41. *(U.K. Transport and Road Research Laboratory. Reports. LR 497)*

CYPRUS
— Constitution.
BLITTERSDORFF (WINRICH VON) Freiherr. Pluralismus der Bevölkerungsgruppen in der Verfassungsstruktur Südafrikas und Zyperns. Hamburg, 1972. pp. 135. *bibliog. (Hamburg. Institut für Auswärtige Politik. Darstellungen zur Auswärtigen Politik. Band 13)*

— Economic conditions.
CYPRUS. 1954. Cyprus ten-year development plan: progress report for the year 1953. [Nicosia, 1954]. fo. (13).

CYPRUS. 1956. Cyprus ten-year development plan: progress report for the year 1955. [Nicosia, 1956]. fo. 14.

— History.
ORR (Sir CHARLES WILLIAM JAMES) Cyprus under British rule; [reprint of work first published in 1918]. London, 1972. pp. 192.

EHRLICH (THOMAS) Cyprus, 1958-1967. London, 1974. pp. 164. *(American Society of International Law. International Crises and the Role of Law)*

KOUMOULIDES (JOHN T.A.) Cyprus and the war of Greek independence, 1821-1829. rev. ed. London, 1974. pp. 117. *bibliog.*

— Nationalism.
CROUZET (FRANÇOIS) Le conflit de Chypre, 1946-1959. Bruxelles, 1973. 2 vols.(in 1). *bibliog. (Carnegie Endowment for International Peace. European Centre. Case Studies of International Conflicts. 4)*

— Politics and government.
ORR (Sir CHARLES WILLIAM JAMES) Cyprus under British rule; [reprint of work first published in 1918]. London, 1972. pp. 192.

LOIZOS (PETER) Social organizations and political change in a Cypriot village; [Ph.D. (London) thesis]. 1972. 1 vol. (various foliations). BIBLIOG. tYPESCRIPT: UNPUBLISHED. tHIS THESIS IS THE PROPERTY OF lONDON uNIVERSITY AND MAY NOT BE REMOVED FROM THE lIBRARY.

MACKENZIE (KENNETH) Cyprus; the ideological crucible. London, 1972. pp. 15. *(Institute for the Study of Conflict. Conflict Studies. No. 26)*

XYDIS (STEPHEN G.) Cyprus: reluctant republic. The Hague, 1973. pp. 553. *bibliog.*

COMMITTEE FOR PEACE IN CYPRUS. This is not just an island: the facts on the Turkish intervention in Cyprus. Istanbul, 1974. pp. 22.

VANEZIS (P.N.) Makarios: pragmatism v. idealism. London, 1974. pp. 203. *bibliog.*

— Population.
BLITTERSDORFF (WINRICH VON) Freiherr. Pluralismus der Bevölkerungsgruppen in der Verfassungsstruktur Südafrikas und Zyperns. Hamburg, 1972. pp. 135. *bibliog. (Hamburg. Institut für Auswärtige Politik. Darstellungen zur Auswärtigen Politik. Band 13)*

— Social conditions.
CYPRUS. 1954. Cyprus ten-year development plan: progress report for the year 1953. [Nicosia, 1954]. fo. (13).

CYPRUS. 1956. Cyprus ten-year development plan: progress report for the year 1955. [Nicosia, 1956]. fo. 14.

CZECHOSLOVAKIA.
— Civilization.
BITTNER (KONRAD) Deutsche und Tschechen: eine Erwiderung [to criticisms of the author's work entitled Deutsche und Tschechen: zur Geistesgeschichte des böhmischen Raumes]. Brünn, [1938]. pp. 20.

MUEHLBERGER (JOSEF) Zwei Völker in Böhmen: Beitrag zu einer nationalen, historischen und geistesgeschichtlichen Strukturanalyse. München, 1973. pp. 302. *bibliog.*

— Economic conditions.
NĚKTERÉ problémy vývoje československého národního hospodářství po druhé světové válce: Some problems of the development of the Czechoslovak national economy after the Second World War. [Prague], 1965. pp. 307. *In French or English.*

SEKERA (JIŘÍ) The economy; (translated from the Czech by Marian Vilbrová). Prague, 1966. pp. 77.

IVANIČKA (KOLOMAN) ed. Problems of development of rural space economy: Problemy vyvoja ekonomiky ruralnej krajiny. Bratislava, 1971. pp. 231. *bibliogs. (Univerzita Komenskeho Bratislava. Acta Geographica Universitatis Comenianae. Economico-Geographica. Nr. 10)*

KU kritike nemarxistickych ekonomićych názorov: zbornik VŠE. Bratislava, 1973. pp. 186.

— Economic history.
TEICHOVA (ALICE) An economic background to Munich: international business and Czechoslovakia, 1918-1938. London, 1974. pp. 422. *bibliog. (National Association for Soviet and East European Studies. Soviet and East European Studies)*

— Economic policy.
SEKERA (JIŘÍ) The economy; (translated from the Czech by Marian Vilbrová). Prague, 1966. pp. 77.

ILO INTER-REGIONAL SEMINAR ON PROGRAMMES AND POLICIES FOR SMALL-SCALE INDUSTRY WITHIN THE FRAMEWORK OF OVER-ALL ECONOMIC DEVELOPMENT PLANNING, PRAGUE, 1966. Report on...seminar...held in Prague,...19 September-7 October 1966. (ILO/TAP/INT/R.14) Geneva, 1968. pp. ii, 191.

— Foreign relations — Russia.
DOKUMENTY i materialy po istorii sovetsko-chekhoslovatskikh otnoshenii . Moskva, 1973 in progress.

— History.
MUEHLBERGER (JOSEF) Zwei Völker in Böhmen: Beitrag zu einer nationalen, historischen und geistesgeschichtlichen Strukturanalyse. München, 1973. pp. 302. *bibliog.*

MASARYK (THOMAS GARRIGUE) The meaning of Czech history;... [selected extracts from books, articles, etc.] edited... by René Wellek; translated by Peter Kussi. Chapel Hill, N.C., [1974]. pp. 169.

— — Chronology.
KUHN (HEINRICH) Zeittafel zur Geschichte der Kommunistischen Partei der Tschechoslowakei: von den Anfängen der Arbeiterbewegung bis zur Gegenwart. München, 1973. pp. 135. *(Sudetendeutsches Archiv. Veröffentlichungen. 7)*

— — To 1526.
BITTNER (KONRAD) Deutsche und Tschechen: eine Erwiderung [to criticisms of the author's work entitled Deutsche und Tschechen: zur Geistesgeschichte des böhmischen Raumes]. Brünn, [1938]. pp. 20.

— — 1968— , Intervention.
BERGMANN (PHILIP) pseud. Self-determination: the case of Czechoslovakia, 1968-1969. Bellinzona, 1972. pp. 159. *bibliog.*

DOKUMENTAČNÍ KOMISE K 231 V EXILU. Zpráva Dokumentační komise K 231; k vydání připravili Otakar Rambousek a... Ladislav Gruber. [Toronto, 1973]. pp. 189.

— Industries.
ILO INTER-REGIONAL SEMINAR ON PROGRAMMES AND POLICIES FOR SMALL-SCALE INDUSTRY WITHIN THE FRAMEWORK OF OVER-ALL ECONOMIC DEVELOPMENT PLANNING, PRAGUE, 1966. Report on...seminar...held in Prague,...19 September-7 October 1966. (ILO/TAP/INT/R.14) Geneva, 1968. pp. ii, 191.

— Nationalism.
SERTSOVA (ANISIIA PETROVNA) Sotsializm i razvitie natsii: ob opyte SSSR i ChSSR. Moskva, 1973. pp. 304.

— Politics and government.

DEAN (ROBERT W.) Nationalism and political change in eastern Europe: the Slovak question and the Czechoslovak reform movement. Denver, [1973]. pp. 67. *(Denver. University. Social Science Foundation and Graduate School of International Studies. Monograph Series in World Affairs. vol. 10, No. 1)*

SOVREMENNYI pravyi revizionizm: kriticheskii analiz. Moskva, 1973. pp. 615.

— Statistics.

CZECHOSLOVAKIA. Federální Statistický Úřad. 1970. C''isla pro každého, 1970/71. Praha, 1970. pp. 414.

DAHOMEY

— Economic history.

ELWERT (GEORG) Wirtschaft und Herrschaft von 'Dâxome', Dahomey, im 18. Jahrhundert, etc. München, 1973. pp. 206. *bibliog.*

— Social history.

ELWERT (GEORG) Wirtschaft und Herrschaft von 'Dâxome', Dahomey, im 18. Jahrhundert, etc. München, 1973. pp. 206. *bibliog.*

DAIRYING

— Kenya.

IVANIČKA (KOLOMAN) ed. Problems of development of rural space economy: Problemy vyvoja ekonomiky ruralnej krajiny. Bratislava, 1971. pp. 231. *bibliogs. (Univerzita Komenskeho Bratislava. Acta Geographica Universitatis Comenianae. Economico-Geographica. Nr. 10)*

— United Kingdom.

LUXTON (H.W.B.) Summer milk production: a study in south west England. Exeter, 1974. pp. 109. *(Exeter. University. Agricultural Economics Unit. Reports. No. 191)*

— — Scotland.

SCOTLAND. Scottish Milk Marketing Board. Marketing Services Department. 1969. Milk production '69: a comment on the results of the 1969 Scottish dairy farm census. [Paisley, 1969]. pp. 78.

DAMAGES

— Russia.

SMIRNOV (VIKTOR TIMOFEEVICH) Obiazatel'stva, voznikaiushchie iz prichineniia vreda: metodicheskie ukazaniia po spetskursu dlia studentov zaochnogo otdeleniia. Leningrad, 1973. pp. 72. *bibliog.*

— United Kingdom.

MUNKMAN (JOHN HENRY) Damages for personal injuries and death. 5th ed. London, 1973. pp. 292.

DANGEROUS GOODS

— Transportation.

OFFICE CENTRAL DES TRANSPORTS INTERNATIONAUX PAR CHEMINS DE FER. International convention concerning the carriage of goods by rail (CIM): annex I. International regulations concerning the carriage of dangerous goods by rail (RID); [with Amendments]. 5th ed. London, H.M.S.O., 1973 in progress.

DANUBE VALLEY

— Economic policy.

FRANCE. Direction de la Documentation. La Documentation Française. Notes et Etudes Documentaires. No. 3,217. Le complexe économique du Bas-Danube: documents. Paris, 1965. pp. 24.

DANZIG.

See GDAŃSK.

DARTMOUTH COLLEGE

— History.

STITES (FRANCES N.) Private interest and public gain: the Dartmouth College case, 1819. Amherst, [1972]. pp. 176. *bibliog.*

DATA LIBRARIES.

INTERNATIONAL EXPERT MEETING ON DATA BANKS FOR DEVELOPMENT, SAINT-MAXIMIN, 1971. Data banks for development: (proceedings of the...meeting... Saint-Maximin, France, May 24-28, 1971; held under the aegis of United Nations Industrial Development Organization) [and others]. Marseille, Observatoire Economique Méditerranéen, [1971]. pp. 266.

INTERNATIONAL OSLO SYMPOSIUM ON DATA BANKS AND SOCIETY, 1ST, 1971. The first International Oslo Symposium on Data Banks and Society: the proceedings, etc. Oslo, 1972. pp. 150. *(Institutt for Privatrett. Avdeling for EDB-spørsmål. Publikasjoner. Nr. 2)*

DAVENPORT (NICHOLAS).

DAVENPORT (NICHOLAS E.H.) Memoirs of a city radical. London, [1974]. pp. 258.

DAVIES (JOHN PATON).

DAVIES (JOHN PATON) Dragon by the tail: American, British, Japanese and Russian encounters with China and one another. London, 1974. pp. 448.

DAVIS (JOHN WILLIAM).

HARBAUGH (WILLIAM HENRY) Lawyer's lawyer: the life of John W. Davis. New York, 1973. pp. 648.

DAVIS (WILLIAM MORRIS).

CHORLEY (RICHARD JOHN) and others. The history of the study of landforms; or, The development of geomorphology. London, 1964 in progress. *bibliogs.*

DAVITT (MICHAEL).

KUNINA (VALERIIA EMMANUILOVNA) Maikl Devitt - syn irlandskogo naroda, 1846-1906: stranitsy zhizni i bor'by. Moskva, 1973. pp. 160.

DAWES (HENRY LAURENS).

OTIS (DELOS SACKET) The Dawes Act and the allotment of Indian lands;...edited... by Francis Paul Prucha. Norman, Okla., [1973]. pp. 197.

DAY (DOROTHY).

MILLER (WILLIAM D.) A harsh and dreadful love: Dorothy Day and the Catholic Worker movement. London, [1973]. pp. 370. *bibliog.*

DAY NURSERIES.

LANDELIJKE WERKGROEP ANTI-AUTORITAIRE EN SOCIALISTIESE OPVOEDING. Technies Kollektief. Anti-autoritaire en socialistiese opvoeding. Nijmegen, 1970. pp. 112. *bibliog.*

SJØLUND (ARNE) The effect of daycare institutions on children's development: an analysis of international research. København, Danish National Institute of Social Research, 1971. fo. 69. *bibliog. Summary of 'Børnehavens og vuggestuens betydning for barnets udvikling', published as Socialforskningsinstituttets Publikation 38.*

SJØLUND (ARNE) Daycare institutions and children's development;... translated from the Danish by W. Glyn Jones. Farnborough, [1973]. pp. 308. *bibliog.*

— France.

FRANCE. Comité du Travail Féminin. 1973. Rapport sur les équipements d'accueil de la petite enfance. [Paris], 1973. pp. 47, [32].

— United Kingdom.

BRITISH HUMANIST ASSOCIATION. Women's Liberation Project Group. Survey of local authority day nurseries and nursery schools/classes in the 32 London boroughs; carried out by Pat Knight. London, [1972?]. fo. 14.

GREENWICH. [Department of Social Services]. Programme Planning Section. Day care and play for under-5's in Greenwich: (key issue report). [London], 1972. fo. 62.

— United States.

YOUNG (DENNIS R.) and NELSON (RICHARD R.) Public policy for day care of young children: organization, finance and planning. Lexington, Mass., [1973]. pp. 115.

DEAF

— Research — United Kingdom.

U.K. Department of Health and Social Security. Reports on Health and Social Subjects. No.4. Deafness: report of a departmental enquiry into the promotion of research; [by] Annette Rawson. London, 1973. pp. 49. *bibliog.*

DEATH.

GUSTAVUS ADOLPHUS COLLEGE. Nobel Conference, 8th, 1972. The end of life: a discussion at the... conference...; edited by John D. Roslansky. Amsterdam, 1973. pp. 83. *bibliogs.*

— Causes.

SWEDEN. Statistiska Centralbyrån. 1971. Dödlighet och dödsorsaker med regional fördelning, 1964-1967; Mortality and causes of death by regions, 1964-1967. Stockholm, 1971. pp. 79. *(Sveriges Officiella Statistik) With summary and table headings etc. in English.*

DEBTS, PUBLIC

— Uruguay.

URUGUAY. Statutes, etc. 1959-60. Unificacion y consolidacion de la deuda publica nacional interna: (ley de 31 de diciembre de 1959 [and] decretos del 27 de enero de 1960). Montevideo, 1960. pp. 22.

DECADENCE IN LITERATURE.

CASTRIS (ARCANGELO LEONE DE) Il decadentismo italiano: Svevo, Pirandello, D'Annunzio. Bari, [1974]. pp. 262.

DECENTRALIZATION IN GOVERNMENT.

MENARD (LUC ALEXANDRE) Administrations centrales et aménagement du territoire: (rapport au gouvernement). [Paris, 1973]. pp. 79.

— France.

BASDEVANT-GAUDEMET (BRIGITTE) La Commission de décentralisation de 1870: contribution à l'étude de la décentralisation en France au XIXe siècle. Paris, 1973. pp. 162. *bibliog. (Paris. Université de Paris II. Travaux et Recherches. Série Sciences Historiques. 5)*

MENARD (LUC ALEXANDRE) Administrations centrales et aménagement du territoire: (rapport au gouvernement). [Paris, 1973]. pp. 79.

RIDLEY (FREDERICK FERNAND) The French prefectoral system: an example of integrated administrative decentralisation. London, 1973. pp. 42. *(U.K. Commission on the Constitution, 1969. Research Papers. 4)*

FRANCE. Direction de la Documentation. La Documentation Française. Notes et Etudes Documentaires. No. 4,064. La réforme régionale: loi du 5 juillet 1972; par Pierre Abrial. Paris, 1974. pp. 57.

— Germany.

JOHNSON (NEVIL) Federalism and decentralisation in the Federal Republic of Germany. London, 1973. pp. 63. *(U.K. Commission on the Constitution, 1969. Research Papers. 1)*

DECENTRALIZATION IN GOVERNMENT. (Cont.)

— Italy.

Il TRASFERIMENTO dell'agricoltura alle Regioni: tavola rotonda sul decreto delegato di trasferimento delle funzioni amministrative dello Stato in materia di agricoltura e foreste; con Feliciano Benvenuti [and others]. Bologna, [1972]. pp. 131. *(Istituto Nazionale di Economia Agraria and Istituto per la Scienza dell'Amministrazione Pubblica. Agricoltura e Regioni. 4)*

— Turkey.

WEIKER (WALTER F.) Decentralizing government in modernizing nations: growth center potential of Turkish provincial cities. Beverley Hills, Calif., [1972]. pp. 72. *bibliog.*

— Underdeveloped areas.

See UNDERDEVELOPED AREAS — Decentralization in government.

— United Kingdom — Scotland.

SCOTTISH COUNCIL (DEVELOPMENT AND INDUSTRY). International Forum, 1st, Aviemore, 1970. The influence of centralisation on the future; [proceedings]. Edinburgh, 1970. pp. 123.

— United States.

NEIGHBOURHOOD control in the 1970s: politics, administration and citizen participation; [background papers for a conference sponsored by the Center for Governmental Studies in Washington, D.C., held May 1970, Boulder, Colo.; edited by] George Frederickson. New York, [1973]. pp. 290.

The NEW federation: possibilities and problems in restructuring American government: a conference of the Woodrow Wilson International Center for Scholars; [editor, Joseph Foote]. Washington, [1973]. pp. 55.

YATES (DOUGLAS) Neighborhood democracy: the politics and impacts of decentralization. Lexington, Mass., [1973]. pp. 202. *bibliog.*

— Yugoslavia.

WILBANKS (THOMAS J.) Environmental management with areally decentralized government;... a report of the Syracuse University Environmental Policy Project. Ljubljana, 1973. 1 vol.(various foliations).

DECIMAL SYSTEM.

IRISH DECIMAL MONTHLY; pd. by the Irish Decimal Currency Board [Eire]. m., My 1969 - Oc 1970 (nos.1-17), with gap (Ap 1970, no.12). Dublin.

— Australia.

AUSTRALIA. Decimal Currency Committee. 1960. Report; [Walter Scott, chairman]. in AUSTRALIA. Parliament. Parliamentary papers, 1960-61, vol.4.

DECISION—MAKING.

DAM (CORNELIS VAN) Belissen in onzekerheid. Leiden, 1973. pp. 198. *bibliog. With an English summary.*

LEONARDZ (BJÖRN) To stop or not to stop: some elementary optimal stopping problems with economic interpretations. Stockholm, [1973]. pp. 178. *bibliog.*

PETTIGREW (ANDREW M.) The politics of organizational decision-making. London, 1973. pp. 302. *bibliog.*

ROHLFING (GERD) Der Entscheidungsprozess in der öffentlichen Verwaltung aus betriebswirtschaftlicher Sicht. Göttingen, 1973. pp. 217. *bibliog.*

The ROLE of analysis in regulatory decisionmaking: the case of cable television: [based on a panel discussion at the 1972 annual meeting of the Western Economic Association]; Rolla Edward Park, editor. Lexington, [1973]. pp. 109. *bibliog.*

SFEZ (LUCIEN) Critique de la décision. Paris, 1973. pp. 368. *bibliog. (Fondation Nationale des Sciences Politiques. Cahiers. 190)*

SKJEI (STEPHEN S.) Information for collective action: a microanalytic view of plural decision-making. Lexington, [1973]. pp. 188.

VROOM (VICTOR HAROLD) and YETTON (PHILIP W.) Leadership and decision-making. Pittsburgh, [1973]. pp. 233. *bibliog.*

CURWEN (PETER J.) Managerial economics. London, 1974. pp. 245. *bibliogs.*

HALL (ANTHONY S.) and ALGIE (JIMMY) A management game for social services. London, [1974]. pp. 55.

KESTEN (H.J.) A case study of decision-making within the Canadian Transport Commission: the application of Northwest Territorial Airways. Toronto, 1974. fo. 67. *bibliog. (Toronto. University, and York University (Toronto). Joint Program in Transportation. Transportation Papers. No.2)*

LESSONS of Maplin: is the machinery for governmental decision- making at fault?; [by] Christopher Foster [and others]. London, 1974. pp. 58. *(Institute of Economic Affairs. Occasional Papers. 40)*

SEMIN (GÜN REFIK) Risk-taking in group decision making; [Ph. D. (London) thesis]. 1973[or rather 1974]. fo . 282. *bibliog. Typescript: unpublished. This thesis is the property of London University and may not be removed from the Library.*

TOYNE (PETER) Organisation, location and behaviour: decision-making in economic geography. London, 1974. pp. 285. *bibliog.*

— Mathematical models.

FISHBURN (PETER C.) Mathematics of decision theory. The Hague, [1972]. pp. 104. *bibliog.*

DEE, RIVER.

BINNIE AND PARTNERS and MAUNSELL (G.) AND PARTNERS. Dee estuary scheme phase IIa: [report] (and Supplementary report). [London], H.M.S.O., 1971[-74]. 3 vols. *bibliog.*

DEFENCE (CRIMINAL PROCEDURE)

— Germany.

SAARBRUECKEN. Universität. Annales Universitatis Saraviensis. Rechts- und Wirtschaftswissenschaftliche Abteilung. Band 73. Der Verteidiger: ein Organ der Rechtspflege;...von Wolfgang Knapp. Köln, 1974. pp. 163. *bibliog.*

— Russia.

AVRAKH (IAKOV SOLOMONOVICH) Psikhologicheskie problemy zashchity po ugolovnym delam. Kazan', 1972. pp. 106.

DEFENCE CONTRACTS

— Germany.

KEMPE (MARTIN) SPD und Bundeswehr: Studien zum militärisch-industriellen Komplex. Köln, [1973]. pp. 278.

DEFENCES, NATIONAL.

GEWELDLOZE actie en sociale verdediging; [by] F. Bekkers [and others]. Rotterdam, 1971. pp. 153. *(Mens en Maatschappif. Boekafleveringen. 1971)*

BOSERUP (ANDERS) and MACK (ANDREW) War without weapons: non-violence in national defence. London, 1974. pp. 194. *bibliog.*

DEFICIT FINANCING

— India.

RAKSHIT (GANGADHAR) Role of deficit financing in the context of Indian planning. Calcutta, 1973. pp. 171. *bibliog.*

DEGREES, ACADEMIC

— Australia.

AUSTRALIA. Committee of Inquiry into Awards in Colleges of Advanced Education. 1969. Report. in AUSTRALIA. Parliament. Parliamentary papers, 1969, vol.2.

— United Kingdom.

PRIESTLEY (BARBARA) compiler. British qualifications...: a comprehensive guide to educational, technical, professional and academic qualifications in Britain. 5th ed. London, 1974. pp. 986.

DEGRELLE (LEON).

DANNAU (WIM) Face à face avec le rexisme. Strombeek-Bever, [1971]. pp. 158.

DANNAU (WIM) Ainsi parla Léon Degrelle;...interviews au magnétophone et conversations avec...Léon Degrelle...recueillies par Wim Dannau de 1965 à 1972, les commentaires de l'auteur, etc. [Strombeek, 1973]. 3 vols.

DELBOS (YVON).

DREIFORT (JOHN E.) Yvon Delbos at the Quai d'Orsay: French foreign policy during the Popular Front, 1936-1938. Lawrence, [1973]. pp. 273. *bibliog.*

DELFT

— Civic improvement.

NATIONALE WONINGRAAD [NETHERLANDS]. Renovatie-onderzoek Delft: rapporteurs: H. Priemus [and] L.van Duyvendijk. 's-Gravenhage, Staatsuitgeverij, 1971. 2 vols. (in 1)

DELINQUENT GIRLS

— United States.

GIALLOMBARDO (ROSE) The social world of imprisoned girls: a comparative study of institutions for juvenile delinquents. New York, [1974]. pp. 317.

DELINQUENT WOMEN

— Italy.

DE FILIPPIS TRUCCO (ANNA MARIA) Criminalità femminile: analisi secondaria su alcuni aspetti del fenomeno. Roma, 1972. pp. 91. *bibliog. (Italy. Direzione Generale per gli Istituti di Prevenzione e di Pena. Ufficio Studi e Ricerche. Quaderni. 4)*

— United Kingdom.

RADICAL ALTERNATIVES TO PRISON. Holloway Campaign Group. Alternatives to Holloway. London, [1972]. pp. 71.

DELINQUENTS

— Italy.

SALIERNO (GIULIO) Il sottoproletariato in Italia: per un approccio politico e metodologico al problema dell'alleanza tra classe operaia e "Lumpenproletariat". Roma, [1972]. pp. 139. *bibliog.*

DE MEDINA (Sir SOLOMON).

See MEDINA (Sir SOLOMON DE).

DEMOCRACY.

HAMBURGER (GERD) Das kleine gelbe Schülerbuch. Graz, [1971]. pp. 160.

CAPITANT (RENE) Démocratie et participation politique dans les institutions françaises de 1875 à nos jours. Paris, [1972]. pp. 185.

FEDELE (MARCELLO) Teoria e critica della liberaldemocrazia: testi e documenti per un'interpretazione alternativa. Bari, [1972]. pp. 418. *bibliog.*

GULIEV (VLADIMIR EVGEN'EVICH) Demokratie und Imperialismus: Ideologien, politische Realitäten; (Übersetzung [from the Russian]: Gertrud Lehmann). Berlin, 1972. pp. 267.

DAHL (ROBERT ALAN) and TUFTE (EDWARD R.) Size and democracy. Stanford, 1973. pp. 148.

HAYEK (FRIEDRICH AUGUST) Economic freedom and representative government; fourth Wincott Memorial Lecture...1973. London, 1973. pp. 22. *(Institute of Economic Affairs. Occasional Papers. 39)*

KARSCH (FRIEDERUN CHRISTA) Demokratie und Gewaltenteilung: zur Problematik der Verfassungsinterpretation in der BRD. Köln, [1973]. pp. 125. *bibliog. (Zeitschrift Demokratie und Recht. Beihefte. 3)*

PURCELL (EDWARD A.) The crisis of democratic theory: scientific naturalism and the problem of value. Lexington, [1973]. pp. 331. *bibliog.*

DUVERGER (MAURICE) Modern democracies: economic power versus political power...; translated by Charles L. Markmann. Hinsdale, Ill., 1974. pp. 198.

EREMIN (IURII ELEAZAROVICH) Klassy i demokratiia. Moskva, 1974. pp. 206.

HILL (DILYS M.) Democratic theory and local government. London, 1974. pp. 243.

HOLDEN (BARRY) The nature of democracy. London, 1974. pp. 240.

DEMOCRATIC PARTY (UNITED STATES).

POTTER (DAVID MORRIS) The south and the concurrent majority; edited by Don E. Fehrenbacher and Carl N. Degler. Baton Rouge, [1972]. pp. 89. *(Louisiana State University. Walter Lynwood Fleming Lectures in Southern History. 1968)*

BUENKER (JOHN D.) Urban liberalism and progressive reform. New York, [1973]. pp. 299. *bibliog.*

WILLIAMS (R. HAL) The Democratic Party and California politics, 1880-1896. Stanford, 1973. pp. 290. *bibliog.*

CADDY (DOUGLAS) The hundred million dollar payoff. New Rochelle, N.Y., [1974]. pp. 448.

GARSON (ROBERT ANTHONY) The Democratic Party and the politics of sectionalism, 1941-1948. Baton Rouge, [1974]. pp. 353. *bibliog.*

YARNELL (ALLEN) Democrats and progressives: the 1948 presidential election as a test of postwar liberalism. Berkeley, 1974. pp. 155. *bibliog.*

DEMOCRATISCHE SOCIALISTEN '70.

SCHEPS (J.H.) Kink in de kabel: scheuring en polarisatie P[artij] v[an] d[e] A[rbeid]-D[emocratische S[ocialisten] '70. Apeldoorn, [1972]. pp. 96.

DEMOGRAPHY.

WARGON (SYLVIA T.) Definitions of family and household in population statistics, with special reference to the Canadian population statistics. Ottawa, 1971. fo. 13. *bibliog. (Canada. Statistics Canada. Census Division. Working Papers (Demographic and Socio-economic Series). No. 9)*

— Bibliography.

PALLI (H.) and PULLAT (R.) compilers. Eesti ajaloolise demograafia bibliograafia; (Bibliografiia po istoricheskoi demografii Estonii; Estonian historical demography bibliography). Tallinn, 1969. pp. 132. *In Estonian, Russian and English.*

— History — Netherlands.

KERSSEBOOM (WILLEM) Essais d'arithmétique politique: contenant trois traités sur la population de la province de Hollande et Frise occidentale, la durée de survie des veuves, la durée des mariages, la relation entre la population et le nombre de naissances, le nombre de couples, etc.;...[and] Kersseboom et son oeuvre: la table de mortalité; par M. van Haaften. [Paris], Institut National d'Etudes Démographiques, 1970. pp. 171. *bibliog.*

— Mathematical models.

BOGUE (DONALD JOSEPH) and others. An empirical model for demographic evaluation of the impact of contraception and marital status on birth rates with computerized applications to the setting of targets and quotas for family planning programs. Chicago, 1973. pp. 155. *(Chicago. University. Community and Family Study Center. R.F.F.P.I. Family Planning Evaluation Manuals. No. 6)*

— Methodology.

UNITED NATIONS. Department of Economic and Social Affairs. Population Studies. New York, 1948 in progress.

BOGUE (DONALD JOSEPH) Demographic techniques of fertility analysis. Chicago, 1971. pp. 116. *(Chicago. University. Community and Family Study Center. R.F.F.P.I. Family Planning Evaluation Manuals. No. 2)*

PRESSAT (ROLAND) L'analyse démographique: concepts, méthodes, résultats. 3rd ed. Paris, 1973. pp. 321.

SOM (RANJAN KUMAR) Recall lapse in demographic enquiries. Bombay, [1973]. pp. 212. *bibliog.*

PRESSAT (ROLAND) A workbook in demography;... translated by E. Grebenik. London, 1974. pp. 292.

VAN DE WALLE (ETIENNE) The female population of France in the 19th century: a reconstruction of 82 départements. Princeton, [1974]. pp. 483. *bibliog.*

DEMONSTRATIONS

— Canada.

PROTEST, violence and social change; [edited by] Richard P. Bowles [and others]. Scarborough, Ont., [1972]. pp. 209. *bibliog.*

— Pacific, The.

TOULAT (JEAN) Objectif Mururoa avec Bollarddière. Paris, [1974]. pp. 275.

DENAZIFICATION.

BUNGENSTAB (KARL ERNST) Umerziehung zur Demokratie?: Re-education-Politik im Bildungswesen der US-Zone, 1945-1949. d Düsseldorf, [1970]. pp. 250. *bibliog. With English summary.*

DENMARK

— Biography.

HVIDT (KRISTIAN) and NEMETH (CSABA) eds. Folketinget håndbog 1973; (efter valget 4. December: biografier, partiprogrammer, valgstatistik m.m.). København, 1974. pp. 408.

— Commerce — Europe.

BRIXTOFTE (PETER) Konsekvenserne for Danmark af handelsaftalerne mellem EF og Finland, Island, Portugal, Schweiz, Sverige og Østrig. [Copenhagen], 1973. pp. 216.

— Defences.

HAAGERUP (NIELS JØRGEN) Dansk sikkerheds politik og det nye Europa. Copenhagen, Forsvarets Oplysnings- og Velfaerdstjeneste, 1972. pp. 52.

— Economic conditions.

DENMARK. Danmarks Statistik. 1973. Input-output tabeller for Danmark 1966. København, 1973. 2 vols. (in 1). *(Statistiske Undersøgelser. Nr. 30) 8 tables in end pocket. With English summary.*

— — Mathematical models.

HANSEN (JØRGEN) Economist, and PALDAM (MARTIN) SMEC: en kvartalsmodel af den danske økonomi; (med et bidrag af Jørgen Rosted). København, Statens Trykningskontor, 1973. pp. 326. *bibliog.*

— Economic policy.

DENMARK. 1973. PP II: perspektivplan-redegørelse 1972-1987; [with supplements]. København, 1973 in progress. Library has main report and supplements 1,3-5.

ILLERIS (SVEN) and PEDERSEN (POUL OVE) eds. Regionaludvikling i Danmark: en artikelsamling om anvendelsen af regionalanalytiske metoder på danske forhold. [Copenhagen], 1973. pp. 261. *bibliogs.*

— Executive departments.

DENMARK. Udvalg vedrørende Organisationen af Ministeriet for Grønlands Budget- og Regnskabsvaesen. 1972. Betaenkning vedrørende Grønlandsadministrationens budget- og regnskabsvaesen, etc. København, 1972. pp. 128. *(Denmark. Betaenkninger. Nr. 646)*

DENMARK. Udvalget vedrørende Statsskatteadministrationen. 1972. Betaenkning vedr orende statsskatteadministrationen. København, 1972. pp. 131. *(Denmark. Betaenkninger. Nr. 651)*

— Folketinget.

HVIDT (KRISTIAN) and NEMETH (CSABA) eds. Folketinget håndbog 1973; (efter valget 4. December: biografier, partiprogrammer, valgstatistik m.m.). København, 1974. pp. 408.

— Foreign relations

See also EUROPEAN ECONOMIC COMMUNITY — Denmark.

— Norway.

BLOM (IDA) Kampen om Eirik Raudes land: pressgruppepolitikk i grønlandsspørsmålet, 1921-1931. Oslo, 1973. pp. 439. *bibliog.*

— Industries.

DENMARK. Danmarks Statistik. Industristatistik: Industrial statistics. a., 1971- København.

TEGLERS (HANS EDVARD) Penge og positioner: rapport om det private Danmark. København, 1973. pp. 206.

— Social policy.

SOCIALPOLITISK FORENING. Sommermøde, 48., 1972. Social planlaegning: beslutning og gennemførelse; 3 foredrag... [by Per Holmberg, and others]. København, 1973. pp. 86. *(Småskrifter. Nr. 44)*

— Statistics, Vital.

DENMARK. Statistiske Departement. 1868. Tabeller over vielser, fødsler og dødsfald i Kongeriget Danmark i aarene 1860 til 1864: inledning til tabellerne. Kjøbenhavn, 1868. pp. 24. *(Statistisk Tabelvaerk. Raekke 3. Bind 12)*

DENTAL CARE

— United States.

FELDSTEIN (PAUL J.) Financing dental care: an economic analysis. Lexington, [1973]. pp. 259. *bibliog.*

DENTAL ECONOMICS.

FELDSTEIN (PAUL J.) Financing dental care: an economic analysis. Lexington, [1973]. pp. 259. *bibliog.*

DENTISTRY

— Bibliography.

RICHARDS (N. DAVID) and COHEN (LOIS K.) compilers. Social sciences and dentistry: a critical bibliography; [compiled for the Commission on Dental Practice of the International Dental Federation]. [Brussels, 1971?]. pp. 381. *bibliogs.*

DEPARTMENT STORES

— Belgium.

LACROSSE (JACQUES) and BIE (PIERRE DE) Emile Bernheim: histoire d'un grand magasin. Bruxelles, [1972]. pp. 255.

DEPRESSION, MENTAL.

ANTHONY (HELEN SYLVIA) Depression, psychopathic personality and attempted suicide in a borstal sample; (a Home Office Research Unit report). London, 1973. pp. 43. *bibliog.* (*U.K. Home Office. Home Office Research Studies. 19*)

DESERTION AND NON—SUPPORT

— Ireland (Republic).

EIRE. Committee on Court Practice and Procedure. 1974. Nineteenth interim report...: desertion and maintenance. Dublin, [1974]. pp. 20.

O'HIGGINS (KATHLEEN) Marital desertion: an exploratory study. Dublin, 1974. pp. 183. *bibliog.* (*Economic and Social Research Institute. Broadsheets. No. 9*)

DESERTS

— India.

SHARMA (R.C.) Settlement geography of the Indian desert. New Delhi, 1972. pp. 199. *bibliog.*

DESIGN, INDUSTRIAL.

CROSS (NIGEL) and others, eds. Man-made futures: readings in society, technology and design. London, 1974. pp. 365.

PAPANEK (VICTOR) Design for the real world: human ecology and social change. St. Albans, 1974. pp. 318. *bibliog.*

DESIGN PROTECTION

— Canada.

CANADA. Bureau of Intellectual Property. Annual report. a., 1972/3 [1st]- Hull, Canada. *In English and French.*

— United Kingdom.

WHITE (THOMAS ANTHONY BLANCO) Patents for inventions and the protection of industrial designs. 4th ed. London, 1974. pp. 749.

DETERRENCE (STRATEGY).

AMERICAN arms and a changing Europe: dilemmas of deterrence and disarmament; [by] Warner R. Schilling [and others]. New York, 1973. pp. 218.

DETROIT

— Social history.

KATZMAN (DAVID M.) Before the ghetto: black Detroit in the nineteenth century. Urbana, Ill., [1973]. pp. 254. *bibliog.*

DEUTSCHE BUNDESBANK.

GREULICH (GEORG) Dritte deutsche Inflation und Notenbankpolitik: eine Analyse seit 1948. 2nd ed. Weinheim/Bergstrasse, 1973. pp. 237. *bibliog.*

DEUTSCHE DEMOKRATISCHE PARTEI.

OPITZ (REINHARD) Der deutsche Sozialliberalismus, 1917-1933. Köln, [1973]. pp. 310. *bibliog.*

PORTNER (ERNST) Die Verfassungspolitik der Liberalen, 1919: ein Beitrag zur Deutung der Weimarer Reichsverfassung. Bonn, 1973. pp. 278. *bibliog.*

STEPHAN (WERNER) Aufstieg und Verfall des Linksliberalismus, 1918-1933: Geschichte der Deutschen Demokratischen Partei. Göttingen, [1973]. pp. 520. *bibliog.*

DEUTSCHE VOLKSPARTEI.

PORTNER (ERNST) Die Verfassungspolitik der Liberalen, 1919: ein Beitrag zur Deutung der Weimarer Reichsverfassung. Bonn, 1973. pp. 278. *bibliog.*

DE VALERA (EAMON).

FITZGIBBON (CONSTANTINE) The life and times of Eamon de Valera. Dublin, [1973]. pp. 150.

DEVELOPMENT BANKS.

BACHEM (HANS ERICH) New aspects of development banking with particular reference to the promotion of small and medium-sized industries. New Delhi, 1973. pp. 25. (*Industrial Finance Corporation of India. Silver Jubilee Memorial Lectures. 1973*)

HEHL (HAUKE) Okonomische Entwicklungsfunktionen nationaler Entwicklungsbanken: dargestellt am Beispiel der Indischen Union. Berlin, [1973]. pp. 209. *bibliog.* With summaries in various languages.

LOGANATHAN (CHELLIAH) Development savings banks and the third world: a tool for the diffusion of economic power. New York, 1973. pp. 180.

— India.

HEHL (HAUKE) Okonomische Entwicklungsfunktionen nationaler Entwicklungsbanken: dargestellt am Beispiel der Indischen Union. Berlin, [1973]. pp. 209. *bibliog.* With summaries in various languages.

DEVELOPMENT CREDIT CORPORATIONS

— Colombia.

PAETZ (HANS JUERGEN) Regionale Entwicklungsgesellschaften in Kolumbien. Göttingen, [1970]. pp. 133. *bibliog.* (*Göttingen. Universität. Ibero-Amerika- Institut für Wirtschaftsforschung. Arbeitsberichte. Heft 8*)

DEVIANT BEHAVIOUR.

DOUGLAS (JACK D.) ed. Research on deviance. New York, [1972]. pp. 268.

FILSTEAD (WILLIAM J.) ed. An introduction to deviance: readings in the process of making deviants. Chicago, [1972]. pp. 255.

BAHR (HOWARD M.) and CAPLOW (THEODORE) Old men drunk and sober. New York, 1973. pp. 407. *bibliog.*

MILGRAM (STANLEY) and SHOTLAND (R. LANCE) Television and antisocial behavior: field experiments. New York, 1973. pp. 183.

TAYLOR (IAN) Criminologist, and TAYLOR (LAURIE) eds. Politics and deviance: [papers selected from the proceedings of the National Deviancy Conference]. Harmondsworth, 1973. pp. 208.

COHEN (ALBERT KIRCIDEL) The elasticity of evil: changes in the social definition of deviance; [based on the Alix Mitchell Memorial Lecture given in Oxford on 1 December 1972]. Oxford, [1974]. pp. 39. (*Oxford. University. Penal Research Unit. Occasional Papers. No. 7*)

OPP (KARL DIETER) Abweichendes Verhalten und Gesellschaftsstruktur. Darmstadt, [1974]. pp. 302.

SELBY (HENRY ANDERSON) Zapotec deviance: the convergence of folk and modern sociology. Austin, [Texas, 1974]. pp. 166. *bibliog.*

WALKER (NIGEL) Explaining misbehaviour: an inaugural lecture. London, 1974. pp. 23. *bibliog.*

— Bibliography.

NATIONAL DEVIANCY CONFERENCE. The sociology of deviance: a bibliography. n.p., 1973. pp. 81.

DEVONSHIRE

— Industries.

ROLT (LIONEL THOMAS CASWELL) The potters' field: a history of the South Devon ball clay industry. Newton Abbot, [1974]. pp. 159. *bibliog.*

DEWEY (JOHN).

HOOK (SIDNEY) Education and the taming of power. La Salle, Ill., 1973. pp. 310.

DHOFAR

— Nationalism.

GULF COMMITTEE. Dhofar: Britain's colonial war in the Gulf; a collection of documents and articles. London, 1972. pp. 72.

DIAGNOSIS, RADIOSCOPIC.

U.K. Department of Health and Social Security. 1972. Work measurement in radio-diagnostic departments. London, 1972. pp. 42. (*Management Services (NHS) [Reports]. 5*)

DIALECTIC.

PRA (MARIO DAL) La dialettica in Marx, dagli scritti giovanili all'Introduzione alla critica dell'economia politica. 2nd ed. Bari, 1972. pp. 327.

ADORNO (THEODOR WIESENGRUND) Negative dialectics;...translated by E.B. Ashton. London, 1973. pp. 416.

STIEHLER (GOTTFRIED) ed. Veränderung und Entwicklung: Studien zur vormarxistischen Dialektik. Berlin, 1974. pp. 310.

DIALYSIS.

FOX (RENEE CLAIRE) and SWAZEY (JUDITH P.) The courage to fail: a social view of organ transplants and dialysis. Chicago, 1974. pp. 395. *bibliog.*

DIAMONDS.

SOUTH AFRICA. Commission of Inquiry into the Diamond Industry of the Republic of South Africa and the Territory of South- West Africa. 1973. Report (R.P.85/1973). in SOUTH AFRICA. Parliament. House of Assembly. Votes and proceedings; (with Printed annexures).

DIDEROT (DENIS).

STRUGNELL (ANTONY) Diderot's politics: a study of the evolution of Diderot's political thought after the Encyclopédie. The Hague, 1973, pp. 251. *bibliog.*

DIET

— Africa, Subsaharan.

MAY (JACQUES M.) The ecology of malnutrition in the French speaking countries of West Africa and Madagascar, etc. New York, 1968. pp. 433. *bibliogs.* (*Studies in Medical Geography. vol. 8*)

MAY (JACQUES M.) and McLELLAN (DONNA L.) The ecology of malnutrition in seven countries of southern Africa and in Portuese Guinea: the Republic of South Africa, South West Africa etc. New York, 1971. pp. 432. *bibliogs.* (*American Geographical Society. Studies in Medical Geography. vol.10*)

— China.

WHYTE (ROBERT ORR) Rural nutrition in China. Hong Kong, 1972. pp. 54. *bibliog.*

— Madagascar.

MAY (JACQUES M.) The ecology of malnutrition in the French speaking countries of West Africa and Madagascar, etc. New York, 1968. pp. 433. *bibliogs.* (*Studies in Medical Geography. vol. 8*)

— United States.

HILLIARD (SAM BOWERS) Hog meat and hoecake: food supply in the Old South, 1840-1860. Carbondale, Ill., [1972]. pp. 296.

DIETZGEN (JOSEPH).

DIETZGEN (JOSEPH) Pièces pour un dossier: L'essence du travail intellectuel; Ecrits philosophiques annotés par Lénine; [edited by] Jean Pierre Osier. Paris, 1973. pp. 249.

DIFFUSION OF INNOVATIONS.

L'ACQUISITION des techniques par les pays non-initiateurs: ([papers presented at a conference organized by the] Centre National de la Recherche Scientifique [and] International Cooperation in History of Technology Committee [held at Pont-à-Mousson in 1970]). Paris, 1973. pp. 624. *(Centre National de la Recherche Scientifique. Colloques Internationaux. No. 538) Papers in English and French, with a summary in the alternative language.*

ZALTMAN (GERALD) and others. Innovations and organizations. New York, [1973]. pp. 212. *bibliog.*

FISHER (LAWRENCE VICTOR) A study of the factors influencing the diffusion of innovation with special reference to the application of the computer in process control; [Ph.D.(London) thesis]. 1973 [or rather 1974]. fo. 194. *bibliog. Typescript: unpublished. This thesis is the property of London University and may not be removed from the Library.*

NABSETH (LARS) and RAY (GEORGE F.) eds. The diffusion of new industrial processes: an international study.London, 1974. pp. 324. *bibliog. (National Institute of Economic and Social Research. Economic and Social Studies. 29)*

DIGITAL COMPUTER SIMULATION.

COMPUTER simulation techniques: [by] Thomas H. Naylor [and others]. New York, [1966]. pp. 352. *bibliogs.*

DILAPIDATIONS.

WEST (WILLIAM ALEXANDER) The law of dilapidations, with some hints on practice. 7th ed. London, 1974. pp. 360.

DIPLOMACY.

ALBRECHT-CARRIÉ (RENÉ) A diplomatic history of Europe since the Congress of Vienna. rev. ed. New York, [1973]. pp. 764. *bibliog.*

SYMCOX (GEOFFREY) ed. War, diplomacy and imperialism, 1618-1763: [selected documents]. London, 1974. pp. 338. *bibliog.*

DIPLOMATIC DOCUMENTS.

UNITED STATES. Department of State. Bureau of Public Affairs. Historical Office. 1968. Public availability of diplomatic archives. [Washington], 1968. pp. 25.

DIPLOMATIC NEGOTIATIONS IN INTERNATIONAL DISPUTES.

YIN (CHING-YAO) Negotiations in an era of negotiation. [Taipei], 1973. pp. 69. *(Asian Peoples' Anti-Communist League. Pamphlets. No. 171)*

DIPLOMATS, BRITISH

— Correspondence, reminiscences, etc.

GORE-BOOTH (PAUL HENRY) Baron Gore-Booth. With great truth and respect. London, 1974. pp. 440.

DIPLOMATS, FRENCH

— Correspondence, reminiscences, etc.

MASSIGLI (RENE) La Turquie devant la guerre: mission à Ankara. [Paris, 1964]. pp. 511.

DIPLOMATS, RUSSIAN

— Correspondence, reminiscences, etc.

MATVEEV (ANDREI ARTAMONOVICH) Russkii diplomat vo Frantsii: zapiski Andreia Matveeva; publikatsiia podgotovlena I.S. Sharkovoi, pod redaktsiei A.D. Liublinskoi. Leningrad, 1972. pp. 296.

DIPLOMATS, SWEDISH

— Correspondence, reminiscences, etc.

HÄGGLÖF (GUNNAR) Fredens vägar, 1945-1950. Stockholm, [1973]. pp. 213.

DIRECTORS OF CORPORATIONS

— United States.

NATIONAL INDUSTRIAL CONFERENCE BOARD. Conference Board Reports. No. 547. The board of directors: new challenges; new directions; [report of a conference held by the Board in 1971]. New York, [1972]. pp. 73.

— Venezuela.

GURUCEAGA (JUAN DE) ed. Geografia economica de Venezuela. [Caracas, 1959]. pp. 283.

DISABILITY EVALUATION.

SAINSBURY (SALLY) Measuring disability. London, 1973. pp. 125. *bibliog. (Social Administration Research Trust. Occasional Papers on Social Administration. No. 54)*

DISARMAMENT.

INTERNATIONAL FEDERATION OF LEAGUE OF NATIONS SOCIETIES. Disarmament: notes for speakers, based on the general resolution adopted by the International Federation...at its 15th plenary Congress, Budapest, 27th May, 1931, etc. Brussels, [1932?]. fo. 49.

U.K. Central Office of Information. Reference Division. 1956. The disarmament question. London, 1956. pp. 54.

INTERNATIONAL SUMMER SCHOOL ON DISARMAMENT AND ARMS CONTROL, 1ST , FRASCATI, 1966. Proceedings of the first course; ([edited by] Edoardo Amaldi and Carlo Schaerf). Frascati, [1967?]. pp. 491.

AMERICAN arms and a changing Europe: dilemmas of deterrence and disarmament; [by] Warner R. Schilling [and others]. New York, 1973. pp. 218.

CLEMENS (WALTER CARL) The superpowers and arms control: from cold war to interdependence.Lexington, Mass., [1973]. pp. 180. *bibliog.*

DOUGHERTY (JAMES E.) How to think about arms control and disarmament. New York, [1973]. pp. 200. *bibliog. (National Strategy Information Center. Strategy Papers. No. 17)*

RANGER (ROBERT JOHN) Arms control concepts and proposals within a changing political context 1958-1972; [Ph.D.(London) thesis]. [1973]. 1 vol. (various foliations). *bibliog. Typescript: unpublished. This thesis is the property of London University and may not be removed from the Library.*

HAFTENDORN (HELGA) Abrüstungs- und Entspannungspolitik zwischen Sicherheitsbefriedigung und Friedenssicherung: zur Aussenpolitik der BRD, 1955-1973. Düsseldorf, [1974]. pp. 536. *bibliog.*

STOCKHOLM INTERNATIONAL PEACE RESEARCH INSTITUTE. Force reductions in Europe; (prepared by Olga Suković [and others]). Stockholm, [1974]. pp. 105. *(SIPRI Monographs)*

— Economic aspects — United States.

The ECONOMIC consequences of reduced military spending; Bernard Udis, editor. Lexington, Mass., [1973]. pp. 395.

DISASTER RELIEF.

An INTERNATIONAL disaster relief force: report of the conference held by the Church of England Board for Social Responsibility, 17th November 1972. London, 1973. pp. 24.

— Bangladesh.

CHEN (LINCOLN C.) ed. Disaster in Bangladesh. New York, 1973. pp. 290. *bibliogs.*

— United States.

KUNREUTHER (HOWARD) Recovery from natural disasters: insurance or federal aid?. Washington, 1973. pp. 71. *bibliog. (American Enterprise Institute for Public Policy Research. Evaluative Studies. 12)*

DISASTERS.

BARKUN (MICHAEL) Disaster and the millennium. New Haven, 1974. pp. 246. *bibliog.*

DISCOVERIES (IN GEOGRAPHY)

— European.

MORISON (SAMUEL ELIOT) The European discovery of America: the northern voyages, A.D. 500-1600. New York, 1971. pp. 712. *bibliogs.*

DISCRIMINATION

— United Kingdom.

GLENNERSTER (HOWARD) and HATCH (STEPHEN) eds. Positive discrimination and inequality;... [by] Jack Barnes [and others]. London, 1974. pp. 40. *(Fabian Society. Research Series. [No]. 314)*

DISCRIMINATION IN EMPLOYMENT

— Ireland (Republic).

GEARY (ROBERT CHARLES) and Ó MUIRCHEARTAIGH (F.S.) Equalization of opportunity in Ireland: statistical aspects. Dublin, 1974. pp. 122. *(Economic and Social Research Institute. Broadsheets. 10)*

— United Kingdom — Ireland, Northern.

IRELAND, NORTHERN. Working Party on Discrimination in the Private Sector of Employment. 1973. Report and recommendations...; chairman: William van Straubenzee. Belfast, 1973. pp. 46.

— United States.

KORDA (MICHAEL) Male chauvinism: how it works. London, 1974. pp. 235. *bibliog. First published in New York in 1972.*

DUBINSKY (IRWIN) Reform in trade union discrimination in the construction industry: operation dig and its legacy. New York, 1973. pp. 311. *bibliog.*

LYLE (JEROLYN R.) and ROSS (JANE L.) Women in industry: employment patterns of women in corporate America. Lexington, [1973]. pp. 164. *bibliog.*

McCALL (JOHN JOSEPH) Income, mobility, racial discrimination, and economic growth. Lexington, [1973]. pp. 212. *bibliog.*

MADDEN (JANICE FANNING) The economics of sex discrimination. Lexington, Mass., [1973]. pp. 140. *bibliog.*

PRINCETON UNIVERSITY CONFERENCE ON DISCRIMINATION IN LABOR MARKETS, 1971. Discrimination in labor markets; edited by Orley Ashenfelter and Albert Rees. Princeton, N.J., [1973]. pp. 181.

TURGEON (LYNN) The economics of discrimination. Budapest, 1973. pp. 32. *bibliog. (Magyar Tudományos Akadémia. Afro-Azsiai Kutató Központ. Studies on Developing Countries. No. 62)*

POLLAK (LOUIS H.) Discrimination in employment: the American response; (lecture...delivered...at the annual conference of the Race Relations Board at Nottingham in 1973). London, [1974]. pp. 29.

DISSENTERS.

LEECH (KENNETH) Youthquake: the growth of a counter-culture through two decades. London, 1973. pp. 246.

— Africa, East.

STRAYER (ROBERT W.) and others. Protest movements in colonial East Africa: aspects of early African response to European rule. Syracuse, 1973. pp. 96. *(Syracuse University. Maxwell Graduate School of Citizenship and Public Affairs. Program of Eastern African Studies. Eastern African Studies. 12)*

— Russia.

SAKHAROV (ANDREI DMITRIEVICH) Sakharov speaks;...edited and with a foreword by Harrison E. Salisbury. London, 1974. pp. 245.

SAUNDERS (GEORGE) ed. Samizdat: voices of the Soviet opposition. New York, 1974. pp. 464.

— United Kingdom.

RIGBY (ANDREW) Alternative realities: a study of communes and their members. London, 1974. pp. 341. *bibliog.*

— United States.

EISINGER (PETER K.) The conditions of protest behavior in American cities; [revised version of paper prepared for a seminar panel at the 1971 meeting of the American Political Science Association at Chicago]. Madison, 1972. fo.49. *(Wisconsin University, Madison. Institute for Research on Poverty. Discussion Papers)*

CONTAGIOUS conflict: the impact of American dissent on European life: [papers of a study conference held by the European Association for American Studies in Geneva in 1972]; edited by A.N.J Den Hollander. Leiden, 1973. pp. 263.

DISSERTATIONS, ACADEMIC

— United Kingdom — Bibliography.

BRITISH SOCIOLOGICAL ASSOCIATION. Register of postgraduate theses, 1974; (compiled by Carl Riddell). [London], 1974. pp. 63.

DISTRIBUTION (PROBABILITY THEORY).

BJØRNSTAD (JAN F.) A multiple test procedure for a series of binomial distributions with non-decreasing probabilities. [Oslo], 1973. fo. 9. *(Oslo. Universitet. Socialøkonomiske Institutt. Memoranda)*

DURBIN (JAMES) Distribution theory for tests based on the sample distribution function. Philadelphia, [1973]. pp. 64. *bibliog. (Conference Board of the Mathematical Sciences. Regional Conference Series in Applied Mathematics. No. 9)*

MOORS (J.J.A.) On the absolute moments of a normally distributed random variable. Tilburg, 1973. pp. 17. *bibliog. (Tilburg. Katholieke Hogeschool. Tilburg Institute of Economics. Research Memoranda. EIT 39)*

DISTRIBUTIVE EDUCATION.

DISTRIBUTIVE INDUSTRY TRAINING BOARD [U.K.]. Report and statement of accounts. a., 1972/3- Manchester. *Formerly included in the file of British Parliamentary Papers.*

DISTRICT OF COLUMBIA

— Politics and government.

SMITH (SAM) Captive capital: colonial life in modern Washington. Bloomington, [1974]. pp. 303. *bibliog.*

DIVERSIFICATION IN INDUSTRY

— Mathematical models.

KELLY (M.P.) The determinants of diversification: a simple profit-maximization model. Coventry, 1974. pp. 15, iv. *bibliog. (University of Warwick. Centre for Industrial Economic and Business Research. [Warwick Research in Industrial and Business Studies]. No. 49)*

— Zambia.

YOUNG (ALISTAIR) Industrial diversification in Zambia. New York, 1973. pp. 328. *bibliog.*

DIVIDENDS

— Mathematical models.

CHATEAU (JEAN PIERRE) Politique de distribution des profits des sociétés: une approche économétrique. Montréal, 1972. fo. 79. *bibliog. (Montréal. Université. Département des Sciences Economiques. Cahiers. No. 7212)*

— Canada.

CHATEAU (JEAN PIERRE) La politique de distribution de dividendes des sociétés, une étude microéconométrique. Montreal, 1974. fo. 42. *bibliog. (McGill University. Faculty of Management. Discussion Papers. No. 7401)*

DIVISION OF LABOUR.

COUNCIL FOR MUTUAL ECONOMIC ASSISTANCE. 1962. Basic principles of international socialist division of labour. Moscow, 1962. pp. 31.

LOON (P.J. VAN) Division of labour. Bergen op Zoom, [1972]. pp. 52.

GORZ (ANDRÉ) compiler. Critique de la division du travail: textes de Karl Marx [and others]. Paris, [1973]. pp. 299.

The INTERNATIONAL division of labour: problems and perspectives; [proceedings of an] international symposium [in Kiel, 1973] organized by Institut für Weltwirtschaft [and] Gesellschaft für Wirtschafts- und Sozialwissenschaften (Verein für Socialpolitik); edited by Herbert Giersch. Tübingen, 1974. pp. 556.

KROPOTKIN (PETR ALEKSEEVICH) Prince. Fields, factories and workshops tomorrow; edited, introduced and with additional material by Colin Ward. London, 1974. pp. 205.

VEREIN FÜR SOZIALPOLITIK. Schriften. Neue Folge. Band 78. Probleme der weltwirtschaftlichen Arbeitsteilung: (Verhandlungen auf der Arbeitstagung...des Instituts für Weltwirtschaft in Kiel vom 12.-15. Juli 1973; herausgegeben von Herbert Giersch und Heinz-Dieter Haas. Berlin, [1974]. pp. 651.

DIVORCE

— France.

Le DIVORCE et les Français. I. Enquête d'opinion; [by] Anne Boigeol [and others]. [Paris], 1974. pp. 194. *(France. Institut National d'Etudes Démographiques. Travaux et Documents. Cahiers. No. 69)*

— Italy.

BONETTI (ALBERTO) and MONDUCCI (MARIO) 12 maggio '74: fine dell'ipoteca clericale; cronaca di un referendum. Manduria, 1974. pp. 133. *bibliog.*

COLETTI (ALESSANDRO) Il divorzio in Italia: storia di una battaglia civile e democratica. [2nd ed.] Roma, 1974. pp. 204.

LENOCI (VITO VITTORIO) Divorzio: Parlamento e cittadini; relazione e dibattito sulla legge;... con i saggi di Miriam Mafai e Ruggero Orfei. Milano, [1974]. pp. 224.

— Netherlands.

NETHERLANDS. Centraal Bureau voor de Statistiek. 1970. Huwelijks- en hertrouwtafels voor Nederland, afgeleid uit waarnemingen over de perioden 1948-1949, 1950-1955, 1956-1960 en 1961-1965: aanhangsel: huwelijksontbindingskansen sedert 1948. 's- Gravenhage, 1970. pp. 69.

— United Kingdom.

LATEY (WILLIAM) The law and practice in divorce and matrimonial causes; fifteenth edition [by] W. Latey [and others]. London, 1973. pp. 2114.

DIVORCEES.

NETHERLANDS. Interdepartementale Werkgroep Onvolledige Gezinnen. 1972. Rapport betreffende de financiële positie van de gescheiden vrouwen en haar gezinnen. 's-Gravenhage, 1972. pp. 32.

DNEPROPETROVSK

— Lodging houses.

NIKITINA (ELENA IVANOVNA) and PRESS (TAMARA NATANOVNA) Rabochee obshchezhitie: opyt vospitatel'noi raboty. Moskva, 1971. pp. 111.

DOCK WORKERS.

INTERNATIONAL LABOUR CONFERENCE. 58th Session. Reports. 5. Social repercussions of new methods of cargo handling (docks): fifth item on the agenda. Geneva, 1972-73. 2 pts.

INTERNATIONAL LABOUR CONFERENCE. 57th Session. Reports. 5. Social repercussions of new methods of cargo handling (docks): fifth item on the agenda. Geneva, 1972. 2 pts.

— Sierra Leone.

SIERRA LEONE. Board of Inquiry into the Docks Dispute. 1967. Report...; by G.S. Panda. Freetown, [1967]. pp. 11,xiv.

— United Kingdom.

TOPHAM (ANTHONY) ed. Democracy on the docks. Nottingham, 1970. pp. 87.

BROWN (RAYMOND) M.Sc. (Econ.) Waterfront organisation in Hull 1870-1900. Hull, 1972. pp. 103. *(Hull. University. Occasional Papers in Economic and Social History. No. 5)*

HILL (STEPHEN RODERICK) A comparative occupational analysis of dock foremen and dock workers in the Port of London; [Ph.D.(London) thesis]. 1973. 1 vol.(various foliations). *Typescript: unpublished. This thesis is the property of London University and may not be removed from the Library.*

JOINT SPECIAL COMMITTEE ON THE PORTS INDUSTRY [U.K.]. Final report; [Lord Aldington and J.L. Jones, joint chairman]. London, [1974]. pp. 16.

TAPLIN (E.L.) Liverpool dockers and seamen, 1870-1890. Hull, 1974. pp. 96. *bibliog. (Hull. University. Occasional Papers in Economic and Social History. No. 6)*

— United States.

PILCHER (WILLIAM W.) The Portland longshoremen: a dispersed urban community. New York, [1972]. pp. 128. *bibliog.*

JENSEN (VERNON H.) Strife on the waterfront: the port of New York since 1945. Ithaca, 1974. pp. 478. *bibliog.*

RUBIN (LESTER) The negro in the longshore industry. Philadelphia, [1974]. pp. 164. *(Pennsylvania University. Wharton School of Finance and Commerce. Industrial Research Unit. Racial Policies of American Industry. Report No. 29)*

DOCUMENTATION.

GROLIER (ERIC DE) A study of general categories applicable to classification and coding in documentation;... translated from the French... (revised by Anthony Thompson). Paris, 1962. pp. 248.

INTERNATIONAL SYMPOSIUM ON THE DOCUMENTATION OF THE UNITED NATIONS AND OTHER INTERGOVERNMENTAL ORGANIZATIONS, GENEVA, 1972. Sources, organization, utilization of international documentation: proceedings of the...Symposium...Geneva, 21-23 August 1972; organized by United Nations Institute for Training and Research [and others]. The Hague, International Federation for Documentation, 1974. pp. 586.

DOG RACING

— United Kingdom.

NATIONAL GREYHOUND RACING SOCIETY OF GREAT BRITAIN. Memorandum: observations and comments by the...Society on the destructive effect of the 10% tax on greyhound racing totalisators and why this discriminatory taxation should be withdrawn or reduced. [1952?]. fo. 12, 14 sheets of cuttings. *Typescript and newspaper cuttings: unpublished.*

DOLLAR.

INTERNATIONALISM. Pamphlets. No.1. Dollar crisis or crisis of capitalism?. New York, [1971?]. pp. 13.

GROVE (DAVID L.) A proposed solution for the dollar overhang problem. Tübingen, 1972. pp. 14. *(Kiel. Universität. institut für Weltwirtschaft. Kieler Vorträge. Neue Folge. 74)*

MIKESELL (RAYMOND FRECH) and FURTH (J. HERBERT) Foreign dollar balances and the international role of the dollar. New York, 1974. pp. 125. *(National Bureau of Economic Research. Studies in International Economic Relations. No. 7)*

DOMESTIC ECONOMY

— Switzerland.

ZUERICH (CANTON). Statistisches Amt. 1967. Haushaltführung und hauswirtschaftliche Ausbildung der Zürcher Frauen: Ergebnisse einer Frauenbefragung im Kanton Zürich. Zürich, 1967. pp. 63. *(Statistische Mitteilungen. 3. Folge. Heft 60)*

— United States.

SKLAR (KATHRYN KISH) Catherine Beecher: a study in American domesticity. New Haven, Conn., 1973. pp. 356. *bibliog.*

DOMESTIC EDUCATION

— Switzerland.

ZUERICH (CANTON). Statistisches Amt. 1967. Haushaltführung und hauswirtschaftliche Ausbildung der Zürcher Frauen: Ergebnisse einer Frauenbefragung im Kanton Zürich. Zürich, 1967. pp. 63. *(Statistische Mitteilungen. 3. Folge. Heft 60)*

DOMESTIC RELATIONS

— Australia.

FINLAY (H.A.) and BISSETT-JOHNSON (A.) Family law in Australia. Melbourne, 1972. pp. 638.

— Cameroun.

MELONE (STANISLAS) La parenté et la terre dans la stratégie du développement: l'expérience camerounaise; étude critique. Paris, 1972. pp. 201. *bibliog.*

— Italy.

RUSSO (ENNIO) ed. Studi sulla riforma del diritto di famiglia: ricerca a cura dell'Istituto di diritto privato dell'Università di Messina. [Milan], 1973. pp. 668.

— Netherlands.

NETHERLANDS. Statutes, etc. 1969. Nieuw burgerlijk wetboek. Boek 1. Personen- en familierecht. 's-Gravenhage, 1969. pp. 117.

— Poland.

POLAND. Statutes, etc. 1964. Kodeks rodzinny i opiekuńczy. Warszawa, 1973. pp. 52.

— Roumania.

CADERE (VICTOR G.) L'économie planifiée et la famille en droit socialiste roumain. Paris, 1972. pp. 207. *bibliogs. (Paris. Université de Paris II. Travaux et Recherches. Série Droit Comparé. 1)*

— Russia.

RUSSIA (R.S.F.S.R.). Statutes, etc. 1918. The first code of laws of the Russian Socialistic Federal Soviet Republic (dealing with acts relating to civil conditions and relationships, to marriage, family and guardianship);... edited by the People's Commissariat of Justice. Petrograd, 1919. pp. 48.

DZYBA (R.A.) Ravnopravie suprugov - osnovnoi printsip sovetskogo semeinogo prava. Kazan', 1972. pp. 84.

RUSSIA (U.S.S.R.) Statutes, etc. 1968. Fundamentals of legislation of the USSR and the Union Republics on marriage and the family; Fundamentals of land legislation of the USSR and the Union Republics. Moscow, 1972. pp. 77.

— — Ukraine.

SEREDA (ANATOLII DANYLOVYCH) Sim'ia i zakon. Kyïv, 1973. pp. 132.

— United Kingdom.

GRANT (HUBERT BRIAN) Family law; second edition by Jennifer Levin. London, 1973. pp. 172.

LATEY (WILLIAM) The law and practice in divorce and matrimonial causes; fifteenth edition [by] W. Latey [and others]. London, 1973. pp. 2114.

CRETNEY (STEPHEN MICHAEL) Principles of family law. London, 1974. pp. 382.

DOMINICA

— Industries.

WILLIAMS (RANDOLPH LAMBERT) Industrial development of Dominica. [Mona], 1971. pp. 100. *bibliog.*

DOMINICAN REPUBLIC

— Economic conditions.

ALVARO BOBADILLA (PEDRO) Aspectos de la industria y la economia dominicanas en la decada del 60. Santo Domingo, 1970. pp. 518.

— Economic policy.

La REPUBLICA Dominicana frente a la integracion economica; ([by] Clara de Ravelo [and others]); seminario auspiciado por la Universidad Catolica Madre y Maestra y celebrado el 15 y el 16 de julio de 1967 en el Hotel Montaña, Jarabacoa. Santiago de los Caballeros, D.R., 1967. pp. 185. *(Santiago (Dominican Republic). Universidad Catolica Madre y Maestra. Coleccion Estudios)*

— Emigration and immigration.

CORTEN (ANDRE) La migration des travailleurs haitiens vers les centrales sucrières dominicaines. n.p., [1970]. pp. 713-731. *Xerox copy.*

— Executive Departments.

DOMINICAN REPUBLIC. Oficina Nacional de Administracion y Personal. 1972. Manual de organizacion del gobierno. Santo Domingo, 1972. 1 vol. (various pagings). *(Publicaciones. No.35)*

— Foreign relations.

JIMENES GRULLON (J.I.) La Republica Dominicana: una ficcion; analisis de la evolucion historica y de la presencia actual del coloniaje y el colonialismo en Santo Domingo. Merida, Venezuela, 1965. pp. 267.

— History.

JIMENES GRULLON (J.I.) La Republica Dominicana: una ficcion; analisis de la evolucion historica y de la presencia actual del coloniaje y el colonialismo en Santo Domingo. Merida, Venezuela, 1965. pp. 267.

— Intellectual life.

JIMENES GRULLON (J.I.) La Republica Dominicana: una ficcion; analisis de la evolucion historica y de la presencia actual del coloniaje y el colonialismo en Santo Domingo. Merida, Venezuela, 1965. pp. 267.

— Politics and government.

WALKER (MALCOLM TRAFFORD) Politics and the power structure: a rural community in the Dominican Republic. New York, [1972]. pp. 177. *bibliog.*

— Rural conditions.

WALKER (MALCOLM TRAFFORD) Politics and the power structure: a rural community in the Dominican Republic. New York, [1972]. pp. 177. *bibliog.*

DONETS BASIN

— Economic history.

ZIMOGLIADOV (FELIKS ROMANOVICH) Kommunisticheskaia partiia Sovetskogo Soiuza vo glave trudovoi aktivnosti mass, 1928-1941 gg.: iz opyta raboty partiinykh organizatsii Donbassa. Moskva, 1973. pp. 160.

DORR (THOMAS WILSON).

GETTLEMAN (MARVIN E.) The Dorr rebellion: a study in American radicalism, 1833-1849. New York, [1973]. pp. 257. *bibliog.*

DORR REBELLION, 1842.

GETTLEMAN (MARVIN E.) The Dorr rebellion: a study in American radicalism, 1833-1849. New York, [1973]. pp. 257. *bibliog.*

DORTMUND

— Massacre.

DORTMUND. Informations- und Presseamt. Dortmund, Karfreitag 1945: die Massenerschiessungen in der Bittermark und im Romberg-Park. Dortmund, [1971]. pp. 30.

DOWRY

— Africa.

GOODY (JOHN RANKINE) and TAMBIAH (S.J.) Bridewealth and dowry. Cambridge, 1973. pp. 169. *bibliog.*

— Asia.

GOODY (JOHN RANKINE) and TAMBIAH (S.J.) Bridewealth and dowry. Cambridge, 1973. pp. 169. *bibliog.*

DRAGOMANOV (MIKHAIL PETROVICH).

ARNAUDOV (MIKHAIL) Mikhail Dragomanov: zhivot, idei, znachenie za bŭlgarskiia folklor; rech, dŭrzhana na 30 oktomvrii 1932 g., po sluchai na osveshtavane pametnika na Dragomanov v Sofiia; Michel Dragomanov: sa vie, ses idées, ses travaux sur le folklore bulgare. Sofiia, 1933. pp. 33. *(Sofia. Universitet. Istoriko-Filologicheskii Fakultet. Godishnik. kn.29,5)*

DRAINAGE.

GREGORY (KENNETH JOHN) and WALLING (D.E.) Drainage basin form and process: a geomorphological approach. London, 1973. pp. 456. *bibliog.*

— United Kingdom — Ireland, Northern.

HUTTON (J.B.E.) Report of a public inquiry into the proposed River Main drainage scheme. Belfast, H.M.S.O., 1972. pp. 49, 1 map.

DREAMS.

LEE (SIDNEY GILMORE McKENZIE) and MAYES (ANDREW R.) eds. Dreams and dreaming: selected readings. Harmondsworth, 1973. pp. 508. *bibliogs.*

DRINKING AND ROAD ACCIDENTS

DRINKING AND ROAD ACCIDENTS

— Australia.

AUSTRALIA. Parliament. Joint Committee on the Australian Capital Territory. 1969. Report on whether breath analysing equipment should be introduced into the Australian Capital Territory to assist in detecting and preventing persons driving motor vehicles while their ability to do so is impaired by the consumption of alcohol. in AUSTRALIA. Parliament. Parliamentary papers, 1969, vol.6.

— United States.

TRAVELERS INSURANCE COMPANY. Voices in Society. Death by ounces. Hartford, Conn., 1972. pp. 20.

DRINKING WATER

— Netherlands.

NETHERLANDS. Rijksinstituut voor Drinkwatervoorziening. 1969. De toekomstige drinkwatervoorziening van Nederland. 's-Gravenhage, 1969. pp. 109.

DROITWICH

— Civic improvement.

FRIEND (JOHN K.) and others. Public planning: the inter-corporate dimension. London, 1974. pp. 534. bibliog.

DROUGHTS

— Africa.

SYMPOSIUM ON DROUGHT IN AFRICA, LONDON, 1973. Drought in Africa; (report of the...symposium); edited by David Dalby and R.J. Harrison Church. London, [1973?]. pp. 124. bibliogs.

— Africa, West.

SHEETS (HAL) and MORRIS (ROGER) Disaster in the desert: failures of international relief in the West African drought. Washington, [1974]. pp. 167. (Carnegie Endowment for International Peace. Humanitarian Policy Studies Program. Special Reports)

— Brazil.

BRAZIL. Superintendência do Desenvolvimento do Nordeste. 1973. Plano de ação contra as calamidades publicas de seca e enchentes. [Recife], 1973. pp. 135. Map in end pocket.

DRUG TRADE (PHARMACEUTICAL).

ROBSON (JOHN) Author of 'Take a pill'. 'Take a pill': the drug industry, private or public?. London, 1972. pp. 50.

LOUIS (CHARLES) Les médicaments et l'industrie pharmaceutique. Bruxelles, [1973]. pp. 226. bibliog.

— United Kingdom.

SMEETON (A.E.) The story of Evans Medical, 1809-1959; published to commemorate the 150th anniversary of the foundation of the company. Liverpool, [1959]. 1 vol. (unpaged).

CHAPMAN (STANLEY D.) Jesse Boot of Boots the chemists: a study in business history. London, 1974. pp. 221.

DRUGS.

MITCHELL (ALEXANDER ROSS KERR) Drugs: the parents' dilemma;... with additional sections by Kenneth Myers [and] Terence Jones. 4th ed. London, 1972. pp. 158. bibliog.

UTREDNING om legemiddelkontrollens fremtidige organisasjon; fra et utvalg oppnevnt av Sosialdepartementet 18. februar 1971. Oslo, 1972. pp. 27. (Norway. Norges Offentlige Utredninger. 1972. 28)

HONIGFELD (GILBERT) and HOWARD (ALFREDA) Psychiatric drugs: a desk reference. New York, 1973. pp. 227. bibliog.

LOUIS (CHARLES) Les médicaments et l'industrie pharmaceutique. Bruxelles, [1973]. pp. 226. bibliog.

DUE PROCESS OF LAW.

INTERNATIONAL ASSOCIATION OF LEGAL SCIENCE. Conference, Florence, 1971. Fundamental guarantees of the parties in civil litigation: studies in national, international and comparative law; (proceedings of the Conference);...edited by Mauro Cappelletti and Denis Tallon. Milano, 1973. pp. 821. (Florence. Università degli Studi di Firenze. Istituto di Diritto Comparato. Studi di Diritto Comparato. 5) In English or French.

DUISBURG

— History.

BLUDAU (KUNO) Gestapo, geheim'.: Widerstand und Verfolgung in Duisburg, 1933-1945. Bonn-Bad Godesberg, [1973]. pp. 324. bibliog. (Friedrich-Ebert-Stiftung. Forschungsinstitut. Schriftenreihe. Band 98)

DUKHOBORS.

PORAKISHVILI (Z.I.) Dukhobory v Gruzii. Tbilisi, 1970. pp. 148.

DULLES (JOHN FOSTER).

HOOPES (TOWNSEND) The devil and John Foster Dulles. Boston, [Mass., 1973]. pp. 562. bibliog.

DUMBA (CONSTANTIN THEODOR).

DUMBA (CONSTANTIN THEODOR) Dreibund- und Entente-Politik in der Alten und Neuen Welt. Zürich, [1931]. pp. 482.

DUMONT (LOUIS).

DELFENDAHL (BERNHARD) Le clair et l'obscur: critique de l'anthropologie savante; défense de l'anthropologie amateur. Paris, [1973]. pp. 222.

DUNCAN (JOSEPH F.).

SMITH (J.H.) Historian. Joe Duncan: the Scottish farm servants and British agriculture. [Edinburgh, 1973]. pp. 254.

DUPLESSIS (MAURICE).

RUMILLY (ROBERT) Maurice Duplessis et son temps. Montreal, [1973]. 2 vols.

DUPUY (BENOÎT MARIE).

MOUREAUX (PHILIPPE) Les préoccupations statistiques du gouvernement des Pays-Bas autrichiens et le dénombrement des industries dressé en 1764. Bruxelles, 1971. pp. 535. bibliog. (Brussels. Université Libre. Faculté de Philosophie et Lettres. [Travaux]. Tome 48)

DURABLE GOODS, CONSUMER.

FALTIN (GUENTER) Dauerhafte Konsumgüter und "Permanent Income" - Hypothese: zur Operationalisierung von Einkommenserwartungen. Berlin, [1974]. pp. 117. bibliog.

DURBAN

— Poor.

PILLAY (P. NESEN) Poverty datum line study among Africans in Durban. Durban, 1973. pp. 34. (Natal. University. Department of Economics. Occasional Papers. No. 3)

DURHAM (COUNTY)

— Industries.

McCORD (NORMAN) and ROWE (D.T.) Northumberland and Durham: industry in the nineteenth century. Newcastle upon Tyne, 1971. pp. 80.

— Social conditions.

MOORE (ROBERT) Pit-men, preachers and politics: the effects of Methodism in a Durham mining community. London, 1974. pp. 292. bibliog.

— Social history.

JAMES (MERVYN) Family, lineage and civil society: a study of society, politics and mentality in the Durham region, 1500-1640. Oxford, 1974. pp. 233. bibliog.

DURKHEIM (EMILE).

DAVY (GEORGES) L'homme, le fait social et le fait politique: [collection of articles and other writings originally published 1919-1969]. Paris, [1973]. pp. 324. (Paris. Ecole Pratique des Hautes Etudes. Section des Sciences Economiques et Sociales. Textes de Sciences Sociales. 9)

DURKHEIM (EMILE) On morality and society: selected writings; edited...by Robert N. Bellah. Chicago, 1973. pp. 244. bibliog.

DUSHANBE.

MAMADNAZAROV (KHUDONAZAR) Nastoiashchee i budushchee Dushanbe. Dushanbe, 1972. pp. 103.

DUST

— Prevention.

CONFERENCE ON TECHNICAL MEASURES OF DUST PREVENTION AND SUPPRESSION IN MINES, LUXEMBURG, 1972. Proceedings of the Conference...Luxemburg, 11-13th October 1972. Luxemburg, European Communities, 1973. pp. 693,xxxiv.

DUTCH GUIANA

— Population.

LAMUR (H.E.) The demographic evolution of Surinam 1920-1970: a socio- demographic analysis; translated by Dirk H. van der Elst. The Hague, 1973. pp. 207. bibliog. (Instituut voor Taal-, Land- en Volkenkunde. Verhandelingen. [Deel] 65) With Dutch summary.

DUTCH WEST INDIA COMPANY.

SMITH (GEORGE L.) Religion and trade in New Netherland: Dutch origins and American development. Ithaca, 1973. pp. 266. bibliog.

DWELLINGS.

SZCZELKUN (STEFAN A.) Survival scrapbook 1: shelter. Brighton, [1972]. 1 vol. (unpaged). bibliogs.

— Australia.

MELBOURNE AND METROPOLITAN BOARD OF WORKS. Technical Advisory Committee. Residential planning standards;... report. [Melbourne], 1970. fo. 46.

— United Kingdom — Maintenance and repair.

DUNCAN (T.L.C.) and CURRY (JANET) Housing improvement policies in England and Wales. Birmingham, 1973. pp. 213,fo. 6. bibliog. (Birmingham. University. Centre for Urban and Regional Studies. Research Memoranda. No. 28)

U.K. Department of the Environment. 1973. Public participation in general improvement areas. London, 1973. pp. 50. (Area Improvement Notes. 8)

— Yugoslavia.

JURKOVIĆ (PERO) Financiranje stambene izgradnje u Jugoslaviji. Zagreb, 1973. pp. 151. bibliog.

DYE INDUSTRY

— Germany.

HOECHST in England, 1901-1914: zur Geschichte des Werkes Ellesmere Port der Meister Lucius Brüning Limited. [Frankfurt am Main], 1971. pp. 104. (Farbwerke Hoechst. Dokumente aus Hoechster Archiven. 45)

— United Kingdom.

HOECHST in England, 1901-1914: zur Geschichte des Werkes Ellesmere Port der Meister Lucius Brüning Limited. [Frankfurt am Main], 1971. pp. 104. (Farbwerke Hoechst. Dokumente aus Hoechster Archiven. 45)

DYNAMIC PROGRAMMING.

THIRIET (LUCIEN) and DELEDICQ (ANDRE) Application de la sous-optimalité en programmation dynamique à la localisation et la cadence optimales de construction des équipements. Gif-sur-Yvette, 1968. pp. 32. *bibliog.* (*France. Commissariat à l'Energie Atomique. Etudes Economiques*) *In English and French.*

EARTH

— Bibliography.

WINTON (HARRY NATHANIEL MCQUILLIAN) ed. Man and the environment: a bibliography of selected publications of the United Nations system, 1946-1971. New York, 1972. pp. 305.

EARTH SCIENCE RESEARCH

— United Kingdom.

U.K. Natural Environment Research Council. 1972. The observations of the... Council on 'A framework for government research and development' (Cmnd.4814); submission to the Secretary of State for Education and Science. [London], 1972. 1 pamphlet (various pagings).

EARTH STATIONS (SATELLITE TELECOMMUNICATION)

— Canada.

CANADA. Program Planning Office for Resource Satellites and Remote Airborne Sensing. Working Group on Satellite and Ground Station Engineering. 1971. Resource satellites and remote airborne sensing for Canada. Report no.9. Satellite and ground station engineering; [R.E. Barrington, chairman]. Ottawa, 1971. pp. 37. *With French summary.*

EAST (FAR EAST)

— Commerce.

HYDE (FRANCIS EDWIN) Far Eastern trade, 1860-1914. London, 1973. pp. 229.

EAST (NEAR EAST)

See also ORIENTAL STUDIES.

— Economic conditions.

MIDDLE EAST RECORD; (pd. by Shiloah Center for Middle Eastern and African Studies, Tel Aviv University). Jerusalem, 1968 (vol.4).

U.K. Central Office of Information. Reference Division. 1956. Britain and Middle East development. London, 1956. pp. 38.

— Foreign relations.

U.K. Central Office of Information. Reference Division. 1956. The security of the Middle East. London, 1956. pp. 22,xiii.

MIDDLE EAST RECORD; (pd. by Shiloah Center for Middle Eastern and African Studies, Tel Aviv University). Jerusalem, 1968 (vol.4). **east (near east) -- pOLITICS AND GOVERNMENT. 1968.**

BURRELL (R.M.) and COTTRELL (ALVIN J.) Iran, the Arabian peninsula, and the Indian ocean. New York, [1972]. pp. 46. *bibliog.* (*National Strategy Information Center. Strategy Papers. No. 14*)

ISSAWI (CHARLES PHILIP) Oil, the Middle East and the world. New York, 1972. pp. 86. *bibliog.* (*Georgetown University. Center for Strategic and International Studies. Washington Papers. 4*)

SHWADRAN (BENJAMIN) The Middle East, oil and the great powers. 3rd ed. New York, 1973. pp. 630. *bibliog.* (*Tel Aviv. University. Shiloah Center for Middle Eastern and African Studies. Monograph Series*)

ALLEN (Sir RICHARD HUGH SEDLEY) Imperialism and nationalism in the fertile crescent: sources and prospects of the Arab-Israeli conflict. New York, 1974. pp. 686. *bibliog.*

— — Australia.

AUSTRALIA. Parliament. Joint Committee on Foreign Affairs. 1969. Report... on the Middle East situation. in AUSTRALIA. Parliament. Parliamentary papers, 1969, vol.6.

— — China.

MA'OZ (MOSHE) Soviet and Chinese relations with the Palestinian guerrilla organizations. Jerusalem, 1974. pp. 35. *bibliog.* (*Hebrew University. Leonard Davis Institute for International Relations. Jerusalem Papers on Peace Problems. No. 4*)

— — Europe.

SACHAR (HOWARD MORLEY) Europe leaves the Middle East, 1936-1954. London, 1974. pp. 687,xxxviii. *bibliog.*

— — Russia.

LANDIS (LINCOLN) Politics and oil: Moscow in the Middle East. New York, 1973. pp. 201. *bibliog.*

INSTITUTE FOR THE STUDY OF CONFLICT. Study Group. Soviet objectives in the Middle East. London, 1974. pp. 27. (*Institute for the Study of Conflict. Special Reports*)

KOHLER (FOY D.) and others. The Soviet Union and the October 1973 Middle East War: the implications for detente. Miami, [1974]. pp. 131. (*Miami (Florida). University. Center for Advanced International Studies. Monographs in International Affairs*)

MA'OZ (MOSHE) Soviet and Chinese relations with the Palestinian guerrilla organizations. Jerusalem, 1974. pp. 35. *bibliog.* (*Hebrew University, Leonard Davis Institute for International Relations. Jerusalem Papers on Peace Problems. No. 4*)

The SOVIET Union and the Middle East: the post-World War II era; [papers presented at a conference organized by the Center for Russian and East European Studies at Stanford University, 1969]; edited by Ivo J. Lederer and Wayne S. Vucinich. Stanford, [1974]. pp. 302. (*Stanford University. Hoover Institution on War, Revolution and Peace. Hoover Institution Publications. 133*).

— — United Kingdom.

NUTTING (Sir ANTHONY) Britain and Palestine: a legacy of deceit. London, [1972?]. pp. 15.

MANGOLD (PETER) The role of force in British policy towards the Middle East, 1957-1966. [Ph.D. (London) thesis]. 1973. fo. 307. *bibliog. Typescript: unpublished. This thesis is the property of London University and may not be removed from the Library.*

— — United States.

The MIDDLE East: quest for an American policy; [papers of a conference held in 1970 at the 47th session of the Institute of World Affairs, sponsored by the University of Southern California]; edited by Willard A. Beling. Albany, N.Y., 1973. pp. 347.

— History.

LANDAU (JACOB M.) Middle eastern themes: papers in history and politics. London, 1973. pp. 309. *bibliog.*

ALLEN (Sir RICHARD HUGH SEDLEY) Imperialism and nationalism in the fertile crescent: sources and prospects of the Arab-Israeli conflict. New York, 1974. pp. 686. *bibliog.*

— Industries.

BARTHEL (GUENTER) Industrialization in the Arab countries of the Middle East: problems and trends. Berlin, 1972. pp. 248. *bibliog.*

— Nationalism.

KARPAT (KEMAL H.) An inquiry into the social foundations of nationalism in the Ottoman state: from social estates to classes, from millets to nations. Princeton, N.J., 1973. pp. 116. (*Princeton University. Center of International Studies. Research Monographs. No.39*)

ALLEN (Sir RICHARD HUGH SEDLEY) Imperialism and nationalism in the fertile crescent: sources and prospects of the Arab-Israeli conflict. New York, 1974. pp. 686. *bibliog.*

— Politics and government.

BENOIST-MECHIN (JACQUES) Le roi Saud; ou, L'Orient à l'heure des relèves. Paris, [1960]. pp. 575.

INTERNATIONAL DOCUMENTS ON PALESTINE; [pd. by] Institute for Palestine Studies [and] the University of Kuwait. a., 1968 [2nd]- Beirut.

LANDAU (JACOB M.) Middle eastern themes: papers in history and politics. London, 1973. pp. 309. *bibliog.*

The MIDDLE East: quest for an American policy; [papers of a conference held in 1970 at the 47th session of the Institute of World Affairs, sponsored by the University of Southern California]; edited by Willard A. Beling. Albany, N.Y., 1973. pp. 347.

— Relations (general) with Russia.

CHERNIKOV (IHOR FEDIROVYCH) Druzhnia pidtrymka i spivrobitnytstvo Ukraïns'ka RSR u vidnosynakh Radians'koho Soiuzu z kraïnamy Blyz'koho i Seredn'oho Skhodu, 1922-1939. Kyïv, 1973. pp. 122. *With Russian summary and table of contents.*

— Yearbooks.

MIDDLE EAST ANNUAL REVIEW. a., 1974 [1st]- Saffron Walden.

EAST INDIA COMPANY.

BUCKERIDGE (NICHOLAS) Journal and letter book of Nicholas Buckeridge, 1651-1654; edited by John R. Jenson. Minneapolis, [1973]. pp. 104.

EAST INDIANS IN AFRICA.

CHATTOPADHYAYA (HARAPRASAD) Indians in Africa: a socio-economic study. Calcutta, 1970. pp. 464. *bibliog.*

BHATIA (PREM) Indian ordeal in Africa. Delhi, [1973]. pp. 152.

EAST INDIANS IN GUYANA.

RAUF (MOHAMMAD A.) Indian village in Guyana: a study of cultural change and ethnic identity. Leiden, 1974. pp. 120. *bibliog.*

EAST INDIANS IN NATAL.

LÖTTER (JOHANN MORGENDALL) and DE VOS (H.V.N.) Die drinkpatroon van die Indiërs in Natal. [Pretoria], 1966. pp. 70. *bibliog.* (*South Africa. National Bureau of Educational and Social Research. Research Series. No 35*)

GREYLING (JACOB JOHANNES CAROLUS) and DAVIES (RONALD JOHN) Indian agricultural holdings on the Natal North Coast. Report 1. Land-subdivision, land-ownership and land-occupation. Natal, Town and Regional Planning Commission, 1970. 3 vols. *bibliog. Vol. 3 is Atlas.*

EAST INDIANS IN SOUTH AFRICA.

SOUTH AFRICA. Bureau of Statistics. 1973. Education: schools for Coloured and Asians, 1970. Pretoria, 1973. pp. 83. (*Reports. No.21-03-04*) *In English and Afrikaans.*

EAST INDIANS IN THE BRITISH EMPIRE.

TINKER (HUGH) A new system of slavery: the export of Indian labour overseas, 1830-1920. London, 1974. pp. 432. *bibliog.*

EAST INDIANS IN THE UNITED KINGDOM.

TILBE (DOUGLAS) The Ugandan Asian crisis. London, 1972. pp. 19. (*British Council of Churches. Community and Race Relations Unit. CRRU Booklets*)

MAMDANI (MAHMOOD) From citizen to refugee: Uganda Asians come to Britain. London, 1973. pp. 127.

EAST INDIANS IN THE UNITED KINGDOM (Cont.)

HUMPHRY (DEREK) and WARD (MICHAEL) Passports and politics. Harmondsworth, 1974. pp. 187.

EAST INDIANS IN TRINIDAD.

LA GUERRE (JOHN GAFFAR) ed. Calcutta to Caroni: the East Indians of Trinidad. [St. Andrews, Jamaica], 1974. pp. 111. *bibliog.*

EAST INDIANS IN UGANDA.

JOINT COUNCIL FOR THE WELFARE OF IMMIGRANTS. The unemployed, homeless and destitute: a report on the situation of British Asians in Uganda. Southall, 1970. fo. 14. *Typescript.*

TILBE (DOUGLAS) The Ugandan Asian crisis. London, 1972. pp. 19. *(British Council of Churches. Community and Race Relations Unit. CRRU Booklets)*

MAMDANI (MAHMOOD) From citizen to refugee: Uganda Asians come to Britain. London, 1973. pp. 127.

HUMPHRY (DEREK) and WARD (MICHAEL) Passports and politics. Harmondsworth, 1974. pp. 187.

EAST LONDON

— Social conditions.

PAUW (BERTHOLD ADOLF) The second generation: a study of the family among urbanized Bantu in East London. 2nd ed. Cape Town, 1973. pp. 241. *(Rhodes University. Institute of Social and Economic Research. Xhosa in Town. 3)*

EAST—WEST TRADE (1945—).

BOLZ (KLAUS) and KUNZE (BERND) Wirtschaftsbeziehungen zwischen Ost und West: Handel und Kooperation; ([report for] CEPES, Europäische Vereinigung für Wirtschaftliche und Soziale Entwicklung). [Bonn, 1973]. pp. 137, xxxiii. *bibliog.*

KUNZE (BERND) Die Wirtschaftsbeziehungen zwischen der Volksrepublik China und den westlichen Industriestaaten: ([report for] CEPES, Europäische Vereinigung für Wirtschaftliche und Soziale Entwicklung). [Bonn, 1973]. pp. 181. *bibliog.*

MEZNERICS (IVÁN) Law of banking in East-West trade. Leiden, 1973. pp. 427.

MASNATA (ALBERT) East-West economic co-operation: problems and solutions;... translated from the French by John Cuthbert-Brown. Farnborough, Hants., [1974]. pp. 144.

MOEGLICHKEITEN und Grenzen einer Verbesserung des Ost-West-Handels und der Ost-West-Kooperation: Symposium aus Anlass des 80.Geburtstages von...Fritz Baade; herausgegeben von Herbert Giersch. Tübingen, 1974. pp. 143.

EASTERN QUESTION (FAR EAST).

MEZHDUNARODNYE otnosheniia na Dal'nem Vostoke. Moskva, 1973 in progress.

EASTERN QUESTION (NEAR EAST).

DELEGATION DE RUSSIE, D'UKRAINE ET DE GEORGIE À LA CONFERENCE DE LAUSANNE. Mémorandum relatif au problème d'Orient, [prepared by] G. Tchitcherine [and] C. Rekovski. Lausanne, 1922. pp. 10.

CHIKHACHEV (PETR ALEKSANDROVICH) Velikie derzhavy i Vostochnyi vopros. Moskva, 1970. pp. 224. *Selection of papaers first published between 1854 and 1861.*

SHUKLA (RAM LAKHAN) Britain, India and the Turkish Empire, 1853-1882. New Delhi, [1973]. pp. 262. *bibliog.*

ECOLOGICAL RESEARCH

— United Kingdom.

U.K. Natural Environment Research Council. 1972. The observations of the... Council on 'A framework for government research and development' (Cmnd.4814); submission to the Secretary of State for Education and Science. [London], 1972. 1 pamphlet (various pagings).

ECOLOGY.

BOUGHEY (ARTHUR S.) Ecology of populations. 2nd ed. New York, [1973]. pp. 182. *bibliogs.*

CALDER (NIGEL) ed. Nature in the round: a guide to environmental science. London, [1973]. pp. 294. *bibliogs.*

OWEN (DENIS FRANK) What is ecology?. London, 1974. pp. 188. *bibliog.*

— Mathematical models.

PAQUETTE (NEIL) and FRANKLAND (PHILLIP) A discussion of decision making under conditions of environmental uncertainty. Iowa City, 1973. fo. 22. *bibliog. (Iowa University. Department of Geography. Discussion Paper Series. No. 21)*

— Study and teaching.

CONSERVATION TRUST. Education for our future. Walton-on-Thames, 1973. pp. 20. *bibliog.*

— Africa.

POLLOCK (NORMAN CHARLES) Animals, environment and man in Africa. Farnborough, Hants., [1974]. pp. 159.

— United Kingdom.

LINDSEY. County Council. Countryside recreation: the ecological implications:...lowland Britain with particular reference to the countryside of Lindsey; [compiled by R.J. Lloyd]. [Lincoln], 1970. pp. 125.

— United States.

GARVEY (GERALD) Energy, ecology, economy:...a project of the Center of International Studies, Princeton University. Princeton, 1972; London, 1974. pp. 235.

ECONOMIC ASSISTANCE.

GUTH (WILFRIED) Entwicklungspolitik in der Krise. Tübingen, 1972. pp. 31. *(Kiel. Universität. Institut für Weltwirtschaft. Kieler Vorträge. Neue Folge. 72)*

HASLEMERE DECLARATION GROUP. The Haslemere declaration: a radical analysis of the relationships between the rich world and the poor world. 6th ed. London, 1972. pp. 28. *bibliog.*

WITTKOPF (EUGENE R.) Western bilateral aid allocations: a comparative study of recipient state attributes and aid received. Beverly Hills, Calif., [1972]. pp. 62. *bibliog.*

BENDAVID (AVROM) Developed and underdeveloped: a radical view of constructive relationships. The Hague, 1973. pp. 10. *(Hague. Institute of Social Studies. Occasional Papers. No. 43)*

BUDHOO (DAVISON L.) The integrated theory of development assistance: an initial statement. [Mona], 1973. pp. 79. *bibliog.*

CALLIES (HANS ULRICH) Der Einfluss von Entwicklungshilfeleistungen auf den Konjunkturverlauf und die Beschäftigung im Geberland, unter besonderer Berücksichtigung der BRD. Tübingen, [1973]. pp. 295. *bibliog. (Bochum. Ruhr-Universität. Institut für Entwicklungsforschung und Entwicklungspolitik. Bochumer Schriften zur Entwicklungsforschung und Entwicklungspolitik. Band 15)*

HUERNI (BETTINA S.) Der Beitrag des Ökumenischen Rates der Kirchen zur Entwicklungshilfe. Bern, [1973]. pp. 360. *bibliog. With English summary.*

MAGEE (BRYAN EDGAR) and others. Foreign aid - necessary? useful? damaging?; [transcript of a discussion with] P.T. Bauer [and] R. Prentice;... transmitted: 21 June 1973. [London, 1973]. fo.29. *(Thames Television. Something to Say).*

MICHALOPOULOS (CONSTANTINE) Payments arrangements for less developed countries: the role of foreign assistance. Princeton, [1973]. pp. 25. *bibliog. (Princeton University. Department of Economics and Sociology. International Finance Section. Essays in International Finance. No.102)*

POUR un nouvel équilibre mondial Nord-Sud: (rapport tripartite; Amérique du Nord, Communauté européenne, Japon). Lausanne, 1973. pp. 52. *(Lausanne Université. Centre de Recherches Européennes.Publications. 4. L'Europe et les Pays Tiers)*

RADETZKI (MARIAN) Aid and development: a handbook for small donors. New York, 1973. pp. 323. *bibliog.*

WHITE (JOHN) 1933- . The politics of foreign aid. London, 1974. pp. 316. *bibliog.*

— Dictionaries and encyclopaedias.

U.K. Overseas Development Administration. Information Department. 1971. ABC of development assistance: a glossary of some terms and institutions. London, 1971. pp. 83.

ECONOMIC ASSISTANCE, AMERICAN.

LAUDICINA (PAUL A.) World poverty and development: a survey of American opinion. Washington, D.C., 1973. pp. 126. *bibliog. (Overseas Development Council. Monographs. No. 8)*

OVERSEAS DEVELOPMENT COUNCIL. The United States and the developing world: agenda for action, 1973; Robert E. Hunter, project director. Washington, 1973. pp. 162.

HOWE (JAMES W.) and others. The U.S. and the developing world: agenda for action 1974; [by] James W. Howe and the staff of the Overseas Development Council. New York, 1974. pp. 211.

WEISSMAN (STEVE) and others. The Trojan horse: a radical look at foreign aid;...[with] members of Pacific Studies Center and the North American Congress on Latin America. San Francisco, [1974]. pp. 249.

ECONOMIC ASSISTANCE, BRITISH.

U.K. Advisory Committee on Protein. 1974. British aid and the relief of malnutrition; report; [Sir Joseph Hutchinson, chairman]. [London], 1974. pp. 30. *bibliog.*

— Bibliography.

U.K. Overseas Development Administration. Library. 1971. Select bibliography on British aid to developing countries. 3rd ed. [London], 1971. pp. 23.

U.K. Overseas Development Administration. Library. 1974. British aid: a select bibliography. 4th ed. [London], 1974. pp. 18.

ECONOMIC ASSISTANCE, DANISH.

DANISH INTERNATIONAL DEVELOPMENT AGENCY. Report on Denmark's participation in international development cooperation 1968-71. [Copenhagen], 1971. pp. 211.

ECONOMIC ASSISTANCE, DOMESTIC

— France.

FRANCE. Direction de la Documentation. La Documentation Française. Notes et Etudes Documentaires. Nos. 3,996-3, 997-3,998. La Caisse des dépôts et consignations. [Paris], 1973. pp. 100. *bibliog.*

— United States.

BRECHER (CHARLES) The impact of Federal antipoverty policies. New York, 1973. pp. 126. *bibliog. (Columbia University. Graduate School of Business. Conservation of Human Resources Project. Conservation of Human Resources Studies)*

DUGAN (DENNIS J.) and LEAHY (WILLIAM HARRALL) eds. Perspectives on poverty. New York, 1973. pp. 198. *bibliogs.*

KURTZ (DONALD V.) The politics of a poverty habitat. Cambridge, Massachussetts, [1973]. pp. 243. *bibliog.*

STEVENS (JOSEPH L.) Impact of federal legislation and programs on private land in urban and metropolitan development. New York, 1973. pp. 238. *bibliog.*

NEUBECK (KENNETH J.) Corporate response to urban crisis. Lexington, Mass, [1974]. pp. 166. bibliog.

ECONOMIC ASSISTANCE, DUTCH.

NETHERLANDS. Nationale Raad van Advies inzake Hulpverlening aan Minder Ontwikkelde Landen. 1969. Advies algemene samenstelling hulpprogramma 1970, mei 1969, no.28. [s'Gravenhage], 1969. pp. 19.

NEDERLANDSE INVESTERINGSBANK VOOR ONTWIKKELINGSLANDEN. Annual report. a., 1973- The Hague. *In English.*

ECONOMIC ASSISTANCE, EUROPEAN.

EUROPEAN COMMUNITIES. Commission. 1972. Memorandum...on a Community policy on development cooperation: programme for initial actions; 2 February 1972. [Brussels], 1972. pp. 23. *(Bulletin of the European Communities. Supplements. [1972/2])*

DURIEUX (JEAN) The European Community and the developing world; transcript of... lecture held on 20 March 1972). [London], Civil Service College, [1973?]. fo. 21. *(Lectures on the European Community. Series A. No. 11)*

JONES (DAVID) of the Overseas Development Institute. Europe's chosen few: policy and practice of the EEC aid programme. London, [1973]. pp. 100.

— Africa, Subsaharan.

EUROPEAN COMMUNITIES. Directorate-General for Development and Cooperation. 1974. European Development Fund. Brussels, 1974. pp. 112.

ECONOMIC ASSISTANCE, GERMAN.

CALLIES (HANS ULRICH) Der Einfluss von Entwicklungshilfeleistungen auf den Konjunkturverlauf und die Beschäftigung im Geberland, unter besonderer Berücksichtigung der BRD. Tübingen, [1973]. pp. 295. bibliog. *(Bochum. Ruhr-Universität. Institut für Entwicklungsforschung und Entwicklungspolitik. Bochumer Schriften zur Entwicklungsforschung und Entwicklungspolitik. Band 15)*

ECONOMIC ASSISTANCE, NORWEGIAN.

NORWAY. Direktoratet for Utviklingshjelp. 1970. Norway's aid to the developing countries: survey 1969. Oslo, [1970]. pp. 70.

NORWAY. Direktoratet for Utviklingshjelp. 1972. Norges utviklingshjelp: prinsipper og retningslinjer. [Oslo]. 1972. pp. 79.

NORWAY. Statistiske Centralbyrå. 1972. Attitudes to Norwegian development assistance, 1972. Oslo, 1972. pp. 78.

NORWAY'S ASSISTANCE TO DEVELOPING COUNTRIES; (pd. by) Norwegian Agency for International Development. a., 1973- Oslo.

NORWAY. Direktoratet for Utviklingshjelp. 1973. On the main topics of Norway's co-operation with the developing countries. [Oslo], 1973. pp. 82.

ECONOMIC ASSISTANCE, SWEDISH

— Africa, East.

RADETZKI (MARIAN) Aid and development: a handbook for small donors. New York, 1973. pp. 323. bibliog.

ECONOMIC ASSISTANCE IN AFGHANISTAN.

ETIENNE (GILBERT) L'Afghanistan ou les aléas de la coopération. Paris, 1972. pp. 296. bibliog. *(Paris. Université. Institut d'Etude du Développement Economique et Social. Collection Tiers Monde)*

ECONOMIC ASSISTANCE IN THE BRITISH EMPIRE.

PARTNERS IN DEVELOPMENT: finance plus management; ([pd. by] Commonwealth Development Corporation). a., 1973- London.

ECONOMIC ASSISTANCE IN TUNISIA.

WOLFSON (MARGARET) Aid management in developing countries: a case study: the implementation of three aid projects in Tunisia. Paris, Organisation for Economic Co-operation and Development, 1972. pp. 49. *(Development Centre. Technical Papers)*

ECONOMIC CONDITIONS.

SAVASTIUK (ANTON IVANOVICH) V. I. Lenin o pobede sotsializma v SSSR; pod redaktsiei ... K.P. Buslova. Minsk, 1970. pp. 222. bibliog.

AKTUAL'NYE ekonomicheskie problemy sovremennogo kapitalizma. Moskva, 1973. pp. 230.

MOTYLEV (VENIAMIN VOL'FOVICH) Mirovoe kapitalisticheskoe khoziaistvo: tendentsii razvitiia i protivorechiia. Moskva, 1973. pp. 166. *(Akademiia Nauk SSSR. Ekonomicheskaia Seriia)*

SOREVNOVANIE dvukh sistem: ekonomika i trudiashchiesia. Moskva, 1973. pp. 400. *With brief English summaries and table of contents.*

— Bibliography.

ORGANISATION FOR ECONOMIC COOPERATION AND DEVELOPMENT. Library. Special Annotated Bibliographies. [Paris], 1964 in progress.

— Underdeveloped areas.

See UNDERDEVELOPED AREAS — Economic conditions.

ECONOMIC DEVELOPMENT.

PASTORE (GIULIO) La giustizia sociale e le zone sottosviluppate: conferenza al Convegno dell'UCID sulla "Mater et Magistra", Milano 18-11- 1961. Roma, [1962?]. pp. 26.

RUSSO (GIUSEPPE) Progresso tecnologico e sviluppo economico. San Donato Milanese, [1967?]. pp. 103. *(Scuola Enrico Mattei di Studi Superiori sugli Idrocarburi. La scuola in azione. 8)*

HAGEN (EVERETT EINAR) The economics of development. Homewood, Irwin, 1968 repr. 1973. pp. xviii, 536. bibliog. *(Irwin Series in Economics)*

INTERREGIONAL SEMINAR ON LONG-TERM ECONOMIC PROJECTIONS, 1ST, ELSINORE, 1966. Sectorial aspects of projections for the world economy; first interregional seminar...[held at] Elsinore, Denmark 14-27 August 1966. (ST/TAO/SER.C/105). New York, United Nations, 1969. 3 vols.(in 1).

SCHIAVO-CAMPO (SALVATORE) and SINGER (HANS WOLFGANG) Perspectives of economic development. Boston, [1970]. pp. 351.

UNITED NATIONS. Department of Economic and Social Affairs. 1970. Selected experiences in regional development. (ST/SOA/101). New York, 1970. pp. 146.

HOFMANN (SABINE) Zum Einfluss der Selbstfinanzierung auf das wirtschaftliche Wachstum. Berlin, 1971. pp. 146, xxvi. bibliog.

INTERREGIONAL SEMINAR ON DEVELOPMENT PLANNING, 5TH, BANGKOK, 1969. Development prospects and planning for the coming decade (with special reference to Asia); report of the...Seminar [held in]...Bangkok, Thailand 15-26 September 1969. (ST/TAO/SER. C/133). New York, United Nations, 1971. pp. 178.

BAECK (LOUIS) Groei en onkruid in de welvaartsstaat. Antwerpen, [1972]. pp. 194. bibliogs.

BERGER (PETER L.) On the concept of alternatives in development. Vienna, [1972]. pp. 19. *(Wiener Institut für Entwicklungsfragen. Occasional Papers. 72/1)*

CAPITAL MARKET SYMPOSIUM, NEW YORK, 1970. Financial development and economic growth: the economic consequences of underdeveloped capital markets; Arnold W. Sametz, editor. New York, 1972. pp. 257.

EPSTEIN (TRUDE SCARLETT) and PENNY (DAVID H.) eds. Opportunity and response: case studies in economic development. London, [1972]. pp. 268. bibliog.

FIRESTONE (OTTO JOHN) ed. Economic growth reassessed. Ottawa, 1972. pp. 248. *(Ottawa. Université. Cahiers des Sciences Sociales. No. 7)*

FRANCOME (COLIN) The poverty of growth. [Thornton Heath, Surrey, imprint], 1972. pp. 23.

INTENSIFIKATSIIA proizvodstva v evropeiskikh stranakh SEV: faktory ekonomicheskogo rosta. Moskva, 1972. pp. 224.

LASKI (KAZIMIERZ) The rate of growth and the rate of interest in the socialist economy.New York, 1972. pp. 238. *(Oesterreichisches Institut für Wirtschaftsforschung. Studien über Wirtschafts- und Systemvergleiche. Band 4) With German and Russian summaries.*

LATTES (ROBERT) Pour une autre croissance. Paris, [1972]. pp. 157.

ONE WORLD ONLY, 1972. Social aspects in the participation of rural and agricultural manpower in development: an international forum under the auspices of the Friedrich-Ebert-Stiftung, Manila, 1972; (editor: Klaus Pretzer). Rizal, [1972]. pp. 279. *(Friedrich-Ebert-Stiftung. [Asian Labour Institute]. Reports. 7)*

ZAREMBKA (PAUL) Toward a theory of economic development. San Francisco, 1972. pp. 249. bibliog.

DUALISM and rural development in East Africa: [report of a seminar held by the Danish Institute for Development Research, 1973; edited by Roger Leys]. Copenhagen, 1973. pp. 209.

BARBERA (HENRY) Rich nations and poor in peace and war: continuity and change in the development hierarchy of seventy nations from 1913 through 1952. Lexington, Mass., [1973]. pp. 213. bibliog.

BENOT (YVES) Qu'est-ce que le développement?. Paris, 1973. pp. 185. bibliog.

BOS (HENDRICUS CORNELIS) and others, eds. Economic structure and development: essays in honour of Jan Tinbergen. Amsterdam, 1973. pp. 283.

BUTTLER (FRIEDRICH) Entwicklungspole und räumliches Wirtschaftswachstum: Untersuchungen zur Identifikation und Inzidenz von Entwicklungspolen; das spanische Beispiel, 1964-1971. Tübingen, 1973. pp. 376. bibliog.

CAMBRIDGE. University. Overseas Studies Committee. [Summer Conference, 1972]. Trade strategies for development; papers of the ninth Cambridge conference on development problems, September 1972...; edited by Paul Streeten. London, 1973. pp. 375.

CHODAK (SZYMON) Societal development: five approaches with conclusions from comparative analysis. New York, 1973. pp. 357. bibliog.

CHOWDHURY (P.N.) Economics of research and development. New Delhi, 1973. pp. 163. bibliog.

DALY (HERMAN E.) ed. Toward a steady-state economy. San Francisco, [1973]. pp. 332. bibliogs.

DATTA (AMLAN) Perspectives of economic development. London, [1973]. pp. 246.

DUALISM and rural development in East Africa: [report of a seminar held by the Danish Institute for Development Research,1973; edited by Roger Leys]. Copenhagen, 1973. pp. 209.

FÖLDI (TAMÁS) ed. Economic development and planning: selected studies; ([by members of the] Institute of Economics, Hungarian Academy of Sciences; translated by Gy. Hajdu and J. Racz). Budapest, 1973. pp. 160.

GRANDAMY (RENE) La Physiocratie: théorie générale du développement économique. Paris, [1973]. pp. 148.

ECONOMIC DEVELOPMENT. (Contd.)

HEHL (HAUKE) Okonomische Entwicklungsfunktionen nationaler Entwicklungsbanken: dargestellt am Beispiel der Indischen Union. Berlin, [1973]. pp. 209. *bibliog. With summaries in various languages.*

HEINTZ (PETER) The future of development. Bern, [1973]. pp. 152.

KUCZYNSKI (JUERGEN) Das Gleichgewicht der Null: zu den Theorien des Null- Wachstums. Frankfurt/Main, 1973. pp. 76.

KUITENBROUWER (JOOST B.W.) On the practice and theory of affluence and poverty: some reflections. The Hague, 1973. pp. 26. *(Hague. Institute of Social Studies. Occasional Papers. No. 33)*

MASSE (PIERRE) La crise du développement. [Paris, 1973]. pp. 183.

MEDVEDEV (VLADIMIR AFINOGENOVICH) Sotsialisticheskoe vosproizvodstvo i strukturnye sdvigi v ekonomike. Moskva, 1973. pp. 183.

MISHRA (R.S.) Economics of development, with special reference to India. Bombay, [1973]. pp. 337.

NUSSBAUM (HEINRICH VON) ed. Die Zukunft des Wachstums: kritische Antworten zum "Bericht des Club of Rome". Düsseldorf, [1973]. pp. 351. *bibliog.*

PRATS (YVES) Décentralisation et développement. [Paris, 1973]. pp. 262. *bibliog. (Institut International d'Administration Publique. Bibliothèque. 2)*

RICH (WILLIAM) Smaller families through social and economic progress. Washington, 1973. pp. 73. *bibliog. (Overseas Development Council. Monographs. No. 7)*

SABATTINI (GIANFRANCO) Saggi di politica economica. Cagliari, [1973]. pp. 183. *bibliog.*

SHANKS (MICHAEL) The quest for growth. London, 1973. pp. 64. *bibliog.*

SOKOLINSKII (ZALMAN VENIAMINOVICH) Teorii nakopleniia. Moskva, 1973. pp. 150.

TEUNE (HENRY) and MLINAR (ZRAVKO) The concept of development: theory and policy. Vienna, [1973]. fo.6. *(Wiener Institut für Entwicklungsfragen. Occasional Papers. 73/6)*

USHER (DAN) The measurement of economic growth. Kingston, Ont., 1973. 1 vol. (various pagings). *(Kingston, Ontario. Queen's University. Institute for Economic Research. Discussion Papers. No.131)*

WHEAT (LEONARD F.) Regional growth and industrial location: an empirical viewpoint. Lexington, [1973]. pp. 223.

WILLIAMS (BABATUNDE A.) Alternatives in development: political science and policy analysis. Vienna, [1973]. pp. 27. *(Wiener Institut für Entwicklungsfragen. Occasional Papers. 73/2)*

BAIROCH (PAUL) Révolution industrielle et sous-développement. 4th ed. Paris, 1974. pp. 381. *bibliog. (Paris. Ecole Pratique des Hautes Etudes. Section des Sciences Economiques et Sociales. Le Savoir Historique. 9)*

BECKERMAN (WILFRED) In defence of economic growth. London, 1974. pp. 287. *Some of the contents originally appeared in Minerva and the Oxford Economic Papers.*

CHONA (M.C.) Towards a humanist strategy of development. Vienna, 1974. pp. 30. *(Wiener Institut für Entwicklungsfragen. Occasional Papers. 74/1)*

The ECONOMIC growth controversy; [proceedings of a symposium held at Lehigh University in October 1972 under the auspices of the Center for Social Research and the Department of Economics]; edited by Andrew Weintraub [and others]. London, [1974]. pp. 229.

HUMAN ecology and world development: proceedings of a symposium organised jointly by the Commonwealth Human Ecology Council and the Huddersfield Polytechnic, held in Huddersfield...in April 1973; edited by Anthony Vann and Paul Rogers. London, [1974]. pp. 180.

KADT (EMANUEL J. DE) and WILLIAMS (GAVIN) eds. Sociology and development. London, 1974. pp. 374. *bibliogs. (British Sociological Association. Explorations in Sociology. 4)*

KUZNETS (SIMON SMITH) Population, capital, and growth: selected essays. London, 1974. pp. 342.

LAOT (LAURENT) La croissance économique en question: le socialisme nécessaire?. Paris, [1974]. pp. 199.

LAUTERBACH (ALBERT T.) Psychological challenges to modernization. Amsterdam, 1974. pp. 190.

MAILLET (PIERRE) La croissance économique. 4th ed. Paris, 1974. pp. 128. *bibliog.*

ONYEMELUKWE (CLEMENT CHUKWUKADIBIA) Economic underdevelopment: an inside view. London, 1974. pp. 123.

PASINETTI (LUIGI L.) Growth and income distribution: essays in economic theory. London, 1974. pp. 151.

PITCHFORD (JOHN DAVID) Population in economic growth. Amsterdam, 1974. pp. 280. *bibliogs.*

SELLEKAERTS (WILLY) ed. Economic development and planning: essays in honour of Jan Tinbergen. London, 1974. pp. 266. *bibliog.*

THIRLWALL (ANTHONY PHILIP) Inflation, saving and growth in developing economies. London, 1974. pp. 256.

VEDOVATO (GIUSEPPE) Etudes sur les problèmes du développement. Florence, 1974. pp. 229. *(Rivista di Studi Politici Internazionali. Biblioteca)*

VEREIN FÜR SOZIALPOLITIK. Schriften. Neue Folge. Band 77. Beiträge zur Beurteilung von Entwicklungsstrategien; von Reinhard Blum [and others]; herausgegeben von Hermann Priebe. Berlin, [1974]. pp. 150.

WACHSTUM bis zur Katastrophe?: Pro und Contra zum Weltmodell; ([by] Dennis L. Meadows [and others]); herausgegeben von Horst E. Richter; [based on the proceedings of two meetings in Frankfurt in October, 1973]. Stuttgart, [1974]. pp. 132.

— **Bibliography.**

DARCHAMBEAU (VALERE) compiler. Les théories et techniques du développement: Theories and techniques of development. Bruxelles, 1973. pp. 375. *(International Centre for African Social and Economic Documentation. Bibliographical Enquiries. No.2) Introduction in English and French.*

— **Mathematical models.**

BURMEISTER (EDWIN) and DOBELL (A. RODNEY) Mathematical theories of economic growth. London, [1970]. pp. 444.

DEGREVE (DANIEL) D'une analyse historique de la Révolution industrielle à un diagnostic du sous-développement. [Liège, 1971?]. pp. 109. *bibliog. (Liege. Université. Seminaire Interdisciplinaire de Science Economique des Professeurs Harsin et Davin. Bibliothèque. No.5) (Extrait revu de Cultures et Développement)*

BROCK (WILLIAM A.) Some results on the uniqueness of steady states in a "Leontief- neoclassical" model of optimal growth with many goods. Canberra, 1972. fo. 38. *bibliog. (Australian National University. Research School of Social Sciences. Department of Economics. Working Papers in Economics and Econometrics. No. 11)*

SOLIGO (RONALD) and LAND (JAMES W.) Models of development incorporating distribution aspects. Houston, 1972. pp. 27. *(Rice University. Program of Development Studies. Papers. No. 22)*

FINDLAY (RONALD E.) International trade and development theory. New York, 1973. pp. 230. *bibliog.*

FORRESTER (NATHAN B.) The life cycle of economic development. Cambridge, Mass., 1973. pp. 194.

HOEL (MICHAEL) The development of the capital return in neoclassical growth theory. Oslo, 1973. fo. 38. *bibliog. (Oslo. Universitet. Socialøkonomiske Institutt. Memoranda)*

INTERNATIONAL ECONOMIC ASSOCIATION. Conference, [1970], Jerusalem. Models of economic growth: proceedings...; edited by James A. Mirrlees and N.H. Stern. New York, 1973. pp. 372. *bibliogs.*

LOGAN (J.) Optimal planning near the end of a finite programme. Canberra, 1973. pp. 28. *bibliog. (Australian National University. Research School of Social Sciences. Department of Economics. Working Papers in Economics and Econometrics. No.15)*

MANAFIKHI (MOHAMAD FARIZ) Econometric models for economic growth, with application to the Syrian economy;...a Master of Science thesis [Cairo], etc. 1973. fo. 178, 5. *With Arabic summary.*

PAAUW (DOUGLAS S.) and FEI (JOHN C.H.) The transition in open dualistic economies: theory and Southeast Asian experience. New Haven, 1973. pp. 306. *(Yale University. Economic Growth Center. Publications)*

— **Social aspects.**

GOULET (DENIS) The cruel choice: a new concept in the theory of development. New York, 1971. pp. 362.

RAO (M.S.A.) Tradition, rationality, and change: essays in sociology of economic development and social change. Bombay, 1972. pp. 182. *bibliog.*

— **Terminology.**

ORGANISATION FOR ECONOMIC CO-OPERATION AND DEVELOPMENT. Development Centre. 1972. Macrothesaurus: a basic list of economic and social development terms. Paris, 1972. pp. 457.

ECONOMIC FORECASTING.

UNITED NATIONS. Economic Commission for Asia and the Far East. Development Programming Techniques Series.. Bangkok, 1960 in progress.

UNITED STATES. Office of Regional Development Planning. 1967. Guide to economic projections and forecasts. [Washington, 1967 repr. 1968]. pp. 113. *bibliog.*

INTERREGIONAL SEMINAR ON LONG-TERM ECONOMIC PROJECTIONS, 1ST, ELSINORE, 1966. Sectorial aspects of projections for the world economy; first interregional seminar...[held at] Elsinore, Denmark 14-27 August 1966. (ST/TAO/SER.C/105). New York, United Nations, 1969. 3 vols.(in 1).

ASH (J.C.K.) Quarterly forecasting at the N[ational] I[nstitute of] E[conomic and] S[ocial] R[esearch]: gross domestic product. [Reading], 1972. pp. 42. *bibliog. (Reading. University. Department of Economics. Discussion Papers in Economics. No.38)*

ASH (J.C.K.) How well does the National Institute forecast the balance of payments?. [Reading], 1973. fo. 33. *bibliog. (Reading. University. Department of Economics. Discussion Papers in Economics. Series A. No. 51)*

ASH (J.C.K.) Quarterly forecasting at the N[ational] I[nstitute of] E[conomic and] S[ocial] R[esearch]: gross fixed investment. [Reading], 1973. fo.13. *bibliog. (Reading. University. Department of Economics. Discussion Papers in Economics. No.45)*

ASH (J.C.K.) Quarterly forecasting at the N[ational] I[nstitute of] E[conomic and] S[ocial] R[esearch]: personal income and expenditure. [Reading], 1973. fo. 23. *bibliog. (Reading. University. Department of Economics. Discussion Papers in Economics. No.40)*

ASH (J.C.K.) and SMYTH (D.J.) Who forecasts the British economy best?: an assessment of half- yearly forecasts of gross domestic product published by the Treasury, NIESR, OECD, The Sunday Times and The Sunday Telegraph. [Reading], 1973. fo. 25. *bibliog. (Reading. University. Department of Economics. Discussion Papers in Economics. Series A. No. 52)*

ASSESSING the future and policy planning: [based on a conference held at the National Bureau of Standards, Gaithersburg, Maryland in 1970]; editors, Walter A. Hahn and Kenneth F. Gordon. New York, [1973]. pp. 344.

— Mathematical models.

LOBBAN (P.W.M.) A model for forecasting U.K. exports to the Sino-Soviet bloc. London, 1971. fo. 25. (*London Graduate School of Business Studies. Econometric Forecasting Unit. Discussion Papers. No. 23*)

LOBBAN (P.W.M.) The corporate sector: progress report [on research at the London Business School on a quarterly econometric model of the U.K.]. London, [1972?]. 1 vol. (various foliations)

ANCHISHKIN (ALEKSANDR IVANOVICH) Prognozirovanie rosta sotsialisticheskoi ekonomiki. Moskva, 1973. pp. 294.

ASH (J.C.K.) and SMYTH (D.J.) Forecasting the United Kingdom economy. Farnborough, Hants, [1973]. pp. 267.

BRISCOE (GEOFFREY) and HIRST (M.) A further appreciation of demand forecasting models: some methods based on survey information. Coventry, 1973. pp. 55,vii,d. bibliog. (*University of Warwick. Centre for Industrial Economic and Business Research. [Warwick Research in Industrial and Business Studies]. No. 43*)

INTERREGIONAL SEMINAR ON LONG-TERM PROJECTIONS, 2ND, DAKAR, 1971. Long-term projections for development planning: problems and experience: report on the...seminar...[held at] Dakar, Senegal, 16-27 August 1971. (ST/TAO/SER. C/142). New York, United Nations, 1973. pp. 31.

MERKIES (ARNOLDUS HUBERTUS QUIRINUS MARIA) Selection of models by forecasting intervals. Dordrecht, [1973]. pp. 136. *bibliog.*

The MEDIUM term: models of the British economy; edited by G.D.N. Worswick and F.T. Blackaby for the National Institute of Economic and Social Research and the Social Science Research Council; [papers prepared for the conference held in London on 10 and 11 April, 1973]. London, 1974. pp. 246. *bibliogs.*

ECONOMIC HISTORY.

FISCHER (WOLFRAM) Wirtschaft und Gesellschaft im Zeitalter der Industrialisierung: Aufsätze, Studien, Vorträge. Göttingen, 1972. pp. 547.

STEWART (MICHAEL JAMES) Keynes and after. 2nd ed. Harmondsworth, 1972 repr. 1973. pp. 317. *bibliog.*

BARBERA (HENRY) Rich nations and poor in peace and war: continuity and change in the development hierarchy of seventy nations from 1913 through 1952. Lexington, Mass., [1973]. pp. 213. *bibliog.*

CAIN (LOUIS P.) and USELDING (PAUL J.) eds. Business enterprise and economic change: essays in honor of Harold F. Williamson. Kent, Ohio, [1973]. pp. 323. *bibliogs.*

COLEMAN (DONALD CUTHBERT) What has happened to economic history?: an inaugural lecture. Cambridge, [1973]. pp. 32.

RUSIŃSKI (WŁADYSŁAW) Zarys historii gospodarczej powszechnej: czasy nowo'zytne i najnowsze, 1500-1949. 2nd ed. Warszawa, 1973. pp. 729. *bibliog. With Russian and English tables of contents.*

WALLERSTEIN (IMMANUEL) The modern world-system. New York, [1974 in progress]. *bibliogs.*

VILJOEN (STEPHANUS PETRUS DU TOIT) Economic systems in world history. London, 1974. pp. 313. *bibliog.*

— Mathematical models.

DEGREVE (DANIEL) D'une analyse historique de la Révolution industrielle à un diagnostic du sous-développement. [Liège, 1971?]. pp. 109. *bibliog. (Liège. Université. Seminaire Interdisciplinaire de Science Economique des Professeurs Harsin et Davin. Bibliothèque. No.5) (Extrait revu de Cultures et Développement)*

— Methodology.

FLOUD (RODERICK) ed. Essays in quantitative economic history. Oxford, 1974. pp. 250. *bibliog.*

ECONOMIC INDICATORS

— Thailand.

THAILAND. National Economic Development Board. Economic Studies Division. 1971. Economic progress of Thailand: selected indicators. [Bangkok, 1971]. fo. 67.

ECONOMIC LEGISLATION

— Austria.

UHL (HARALD) Handwerk und Zünfte in Eferding: Materialien zum grundherrschaftlichen Zunfttypus. Wien, 1973. pp. 159. bibliog. (*Oesterreichische Akademie der Wissenschaften. Philosophisch-Historische Klasse. Kommission für die Savigny-Stiftung. Fontes Rerum Austriacarum. 3.Abteilung. Fontes Iuris. 3.Band*)

— Germany.

CONGRES INTERNATIONAL DE DROIT COMPARE, 1974. 9e Congrès. Deutsche handels- und wirtschaftsrechtliche Landesberichte zum IX. Internationalen Kongress für Rechtsvergleichung, Sektion III ; Herausgeber Ernst von Caemmerer. Stuttgart, 1974. pp. 129. (*Zeitschrift für das gesamte Handelsrecht und Wirtschaftsrecht. Beihefte. Abhandlungen aus dem gesamten Bürgerlichen Recht, Handelsrecht und Wirtschaftsrecht. 46. Heft) With summaries in various languages.*

SCHMIDT (WERNER) Dipl.-Kfm., Dipl.-Vw., Dr. Der Wandel der Unternehmerfunktionen in der Bundesrepublik Deutschland unter dem Einfluss der Konzertierten Aktion. Berlin, [1974]. pp. 138. *bibliog.*

— Roumania.

CADERE (VICTOR G.) L'économie planifiée et la famille en droit socialiste roumain. Paris, 1972. pp. 207. *bibliogs. (Paris. Université de Paris II. Travaux et Recherches. Série Droit Comparé. 1)*

— Venezuela.

VENEZUELA. Statutes, etc. 1949-73. La planificacion en Venezuela: normas legales y reglamentarias. Caracas, 1973. pp. 298, 1 map.

ECONOMIC POLICY.

POLISH-EGYPTIAN SEMINAR, 2nd SESSION, WARSAW, 1970. Long-range and regional planning: papers delivered at the. Warszawa, 1971. pp. 259. (*Instytut Gospodarki Krajow Rozwijajacych Sie. Prace i Materialy. No. 5*)

TUCHTFELDT (EGON) Zielprobleme in der modernen Wirtschaftspolitik. Tübingen, 1971. pp. 50. (*Walter Eucken Institut. Vorträge und Aufsätze. 34*)

GEMEINWIRTSCHAFT im Wandel der Gesellschaft: Festschrift für Hans Ritschl zu seinem 75.Geburtstag am 19.Dezember 1972; herausgegeben von Gisbert Rittig und Heinz-Dietrich Ortlieb. Berlin, 1972. pp. 235. *bibliog.*

WEST (E.G.) 'Pure' versus 'operational' economics in regional policy. [Ottawa, 1972]. fo. 60. (*Carleton University. Carleton Economic Papers*)

SUCHESTOW (MARCEL) Econognosis: a revised economic knowledge. New York, 1973 in progress.

BEGEER (WILLEM) and others, eds. Economie dezer dagen: (opstellen aangeboden aan prof. drs. H.W. Lambers ter gelegenheid van zijn 25-jarig hoogleraarschap aan de Nederlandse Economische Hogeschool). Rotterdam, 1973. pp. 345. *bibliog.*

DAHL (HELMER) Challenge of the future: responsibilities of state and free enterprise. [London, 1973]. pp. 22. (*Aims of Industry. The Future of Capitalism*)

EMANUEL (A.) Issues of regional policies: a report. Paris, Organisation for Economic Co-operation and Development, 1973. pp. 274.

ECONOMIC POLICY.

FÖLDI (TAMÁS) ed. Economic development and planning: selected studies; ([by members of the] Institute of Economics, Hungarian Academy of Sciences; translated by Gy. Hajdu and J. Racz). Budapest, 1973. pp. 160.

HAYEK (FRIEDRICH AUGUST) Economic freedom and representative government; fourth Wincott Memorial Lecture...1973. London, 1973. pp. 22. (*Institute of Economic Affairs. Occasional Papers. 39*)

INTERREGIONAL SEMINAR ON DEVELOPMENT PLANNING, 6TH, QUITO, 1971. Regional planning: report of the...seminar... [held at] Quito, Ecuador, 20 September-1 October 1971. (ST/TAO/SER. C/143). New York, United Nations, 1973. pp. 52.

MENDES-FRANCE (PIERRE) and ARDANT (GABRIEL) Economist. Science économique et lucidité politique. [Paris, 1973]. pp. 381.

NATIONAL INDUSTRIAL CONFERENCE BOARD. Annual Financial Conference, 8th. Major economic issues of the 1970s: [papers of one session]; edited by Michael E. Levy. New York, [1973]. pp. 46.

SAINT-GEOURS (JEAN) and others. La politique économique des principaux pays indusriels de l'occident. 2nd ed. Paris, 1973. pp. 583. *bibliog.*

ŠIK (OTA) Argumente für den dritten Weg. Hamburg, 1973. pp. 213.

SOZIALWISSENSCHAFTEN im Dienste der Wirtschaftspolitik: Wilhelm Bickel zum 70.Geburtstag; herausgegeben von Heinz Haller [and others]. Tübingen, [1973]. pp. 415. *bibliog. In German or English.*

ULRICH (FRANZ HEINRICH) Strukturänderungen in der Wirtschaft. Tübingen, 1973. pp. 15. (*Kiel. Universität. Institut für Weltwirtschaft. Kieler Vorträge. Neue Folge. 75*)

VEREIN FÜR SOZIALPOLITIK. Schriften. Neue Folge. Band 74. Macht und ökonomisches Gesetz: (Verhandlungen auf der Jubiläumstagung in Bonn...1972, aus Anlass des Eisenacher Kongresses von 1872; herausgegeben von Hans K. Schneider und Christian Watrin). Berlin, [1973]. 2 vols.

WALTERS (ALAN A.) The politicisation of economic decisions. London, [1973]. pp. 8. (*Aims of Industry. The Future of Capitalism*)

PAPANDREOU (ANDREAS GEORGE) and ZOHAR (URI) Project selection for national plans. New York, 1974 in progress. *bibliog.*

BALOGH (THOMAS) Baron Balogh. The economics of poverty. 2nd ed. London, 1974. pp. 291.

COOPER (RICHARD N.) Economic mobility and national economic policy. Stockholm, [1974]. pp. 64. (*Wicksell Lecture Society. Wicksell Lectures. 1973*)

NISHIYAMA (CHIAKI) and ALLEN (GEORGE CYRIL) The price of prosperity: lessons from Japan. London, 1974. pp. 66. bibliog. (*Institute of Economic Affairs. Hobart Papers. 58*)

ROBBINS (HORACE H.) Fictive capital and fictive profit: the welfare-military state; a political economy based on economic fictions. New York, [1974]. pp. 417.

SAMUELS (WARREN J.) Pareto on policy. Amsterdam, 1974. pp. 232. *bibliog.*

SELLEKAERTS (WILLY) ed. Economic development and planning: essays in honour of Jan Tinbergen. London, 1974. pp. 266. *bibliog.*

ŠIK (OTA) Für eine Wirtschaft ohne Dogma: [collection of three articles and four interviews]. München, [1974]. pp. 209. *bibliog.*

VEREIN FÜR SOZIALPOLITIK. Schriften. Neue Folge. Band 76. Struktur- und stabilitätspolitische Probleme in alternativen Wirtschaftssystemen; von Jiri Kosta [and others]; herausgegeben von Christian Watrin. Berlin, [1974]. pp. 161. *bibliogs.*

— Bibliography.

ORGANISATION FOR ECONOMIC COOPERATION AND DEVELOPMENT. Library. Special Annotated Bibliographies. [Paris], 1964 in progress.

ECONOMIC POLICY. (Cont.)

— Mathematical models.

MODELES de planification décentralisée: typologie critique et voies de recherches; ([by] Bernard Boucon [and others]).Grenoble, 1973. pp. 239. *bibliogs.*

GØRTZ (ERIK) Measures of the effects of economic policy. [Odense], 1973. pp. 75. *bibliog. (Odense Universitet. Studies in History and Social Sciences. vol.9)*

MANNE (ALAN S.) Multi-sector models for development planning: a survey. Stanford, 1973. pp. 51. *bibliog. (Stanford University. Institute for Mathematical Studies in the Social Sciences. Technical Reports. [New Series]. No. 91)*

— Underdeveloped areas.

See UNDERDEVELOPED AREAS — Economic policy.

ECONOMIC RESEARCH.

SURVEYS of applied economics; [commissioned by] the Royal Economic Society [and] the Social Science Research Council. London, 1973 in progress. bibliogs.

— America, Latin.

The ROLE of the computer in economic and social research in Latin America: [selected papers of a conference held in Cuernavaca, Mexico, sponsored by the National Bureau of Economic Research and others]; edited by Nancy D. Ruggles. New York, 1974. pp. 399.

— United Kingdom.

PRAGER (THEODOR) Tendenzen und Schwerpunkte der britischen Wirtschaftsforschung: Veröffentlichung des Bundesministeriums für Wissenschaft und Forschung. Wien, 1974. pp. 106. *bibliogs.*

ECONOMIC STABILIZATION.

FISCAL policy and demand management: Fiskalpolitik und Globalsteuerung:... Symposium 1972 ([held at the] Institut für Weltwirtschaft an der Universität Kiel]; edited by Herbert Giersch. Tübingen, 1973. pp. 262. *In English or German.*

ECONOMIC SURVEYS.

SOCIAL AND COMMUNITY PLANNING RESEARCH. Survey research and privacy: report of a working party. London, [1973]. fo. 61. *bibliog.*

— India.

SEMINAR ON DATA COLLECTION TECHNIQUES IN THE NATIONAL SAMPLE SURVEY, CALCUTTA, 1969. Proceedings...; edited by M.N. Murthy. [New Delhi, 1971]. pp. 318. *bibliogs.*

ECONOMIC ZONING

— Russia.

PAVLENKO (VIKTOR FEDOROVICH) Territorial'noe i otraslevoe planirovanie: territorial'noe planirovanie v usloviiakh otraslevogo upravleniia khoziaistvom. Moskva, 1971. pp. 103.

ISPOL'ZOVANIE mezhotraslevykh rezervov ekonomicheskogo raiona. Leningrad, 1973. pp. 192.

IUSUPOV (VITALII ANDREEVICH) Sochetanie otraslevogo i territorial'nogo upravleniia promyshlennost'iu SSSR. Kazan', 1973. pp. 127.

NOVOE v geografii proizvoditel'nykh sil SSSR. Moskva, 1973. pp. 142.

TEORETICHESKIE voprosy ekonomicheskoi geografii. Leningrad, 1973. pp. 160.

— — Mathematical models.

GRANBERG (ALEKSANDR GRIGOR'EVICH) Optimizatsiia territorial'nykh proportsii narodnogo khoziaistva. Moskva, 1973. pp. 248. *bibliog.*

SATUNOVSKII (LEON MIKHAILOVICH) Mezhotraslevye modeli territorial'nogo planirovaniia. Vil'nius, 1973. pp. 142.

— — Ukraine.

UKRAINSKAIA SSR: ekonomicheskie raiony. Moskva, 1972. pp. 315. *bibliog. (Akademiia Nauk SSSR. Sovet po Izucheniiu Proizvoditel'nykh Sil. Razvitie i Razmeshchenie Proizvoditel'nykh Sil SSSR)*

— Tanzania.

CONYERS (D.) Agro-economic zones of Tanzania. [Dar es Salaam], 1973. pp. 85. *(Dar es Salaam. University. Bureau of Resource Assessment and Land Use Planning. Research Papers. No. 25)*

— United Kingdom.

LONDON. University. London School of Economics and Political Science. Department of Geography. Urban change in Britain, 1961-1971...: working reports. London, 1974 in progress.

— United States.

HANSEN (NILES M.) The future of nonmetropolitan America: studies in the reversal of rural and small town population decline. Lexington, mass [1973]. pp. 187.

SAMPLE (C. JAMES) Patterns of regional economic change: a quantitative analysis of U.S. regional growth and development. Cambridge, Mass., [1974]. pp. 296. *bibliog.*

ECONOMICS.

FRAZER (WILLIAM JOHNSON) Crisis in economic theory: a study of monetary policy, analysis, and economic goals. Gainesville, Fla., 1973. pp. 526. *bibliog.*

FABRA (PAUL) L'anti-capitalisme: essai de réhabilitation de l'économie politique. Paris, [1974]. pp. 432.

MYRDAL (GUNNAR) Against the stream: critical essays on economics. London, 1974. pp. 336.

— Bibliography.

MAGYAR KÖZGAZDASÁGI ÉS STATISZTIKAI IRODALOM BIBLIOGRÁFIA: Hungarian bibliography of economics and statistics; ([pd. by] Központi Statisztikai Hivatal Könyvtár és Dokumentációs Szolgálat [and] MTA Közgazdaságtudományi Intézetének Könyvtára). a., 1968[v.8]- Budapest. *In Hungarian, Russian and English.*

BIBLIOGRAPHY [of works by] Harry G. Johnson. [London, 1973]. 1 vol. (various foliations). *Typescript.*

— Dictionaries and encyclopaedias.

LEXIKON der Wirtschaft: Industrie; (Herausgeber: Hans Borchert). Berlin, 1970. pp. 904.

EKONOMICHESKAIA entsiklopediia: politicheskaia ekonomiia. Moskva, 1972 in progress.

LEXIKON der Wirtschaft: Preise; (Herausgeber und Redaktionskollektiv: Kurt Ambrée [and others]). Berlin, 1973. pp. 276.

LEXIKON der Wirtschaft: Rechnungsführung und Statistik; (Herausgeber: Arno Donda). Berlin, [1974]. pp. 527.

— History.

DOBB (MAURICE HERBERT) Political economy and capitalism: some essays in economic tradition. rev. ed. London, 1940 repr. 1972. pp. 357.

GERSCH (ALEXANDER) On the theory of exchange value. Würzburg, afterwards Barcelona, [imprint, 1969-72]. 2 vols.

SENF (BERND) Wirtschaftliche Rationalität, gesellschaftliche Irrationalität: die "Verdrängung" gesellschaftlicher Aspekte durch die bürgerliche Ökonomie. Berlin, 1972. pp. 254, xii. *bibliog.*

DALY (HERMAN E.) ed. Toward a steady-state economy. San Francisco, [1973]. pp. 332. *bibliogs.*

VECA (SALVATORE) Marx e la critica dell'economia politica. Milano, 1973. pp. 244. *bibliog.*

ANIKIN (ANDREI VLADIMIROVICH) Ökonomen aus drei Jahrhunderten: das Leben und Wirken der Ökonomen vor Marx und Engels; Übersetzung aus dem Russischen ([by] Günter Wermusch). Berlin, 1974. pp. 388.

DMITRIEV (VLADIMIR K.) Economic essays on value, competition and utility; translated [from the Russian edition of 1904] by D. Fry and edited...by D.M. Nuti. London, 1974. pp. 231. *bibliog.*

EAGLY (ROBERT V.) The structure of classical economic theory. New York, 1974. pp. 142.

WEILLER (JEAN) and DUPUIGRENET-DESROUSSILLES (GUY) Les cadres sociaux de la pensée économique. Paris, 1974. pp. 264.

— — Austria.

DITTRICH (ERHARD) Die deutschen und österreichischen Kameralisten. Darmstadt, 1974. pp. 160. *bibliog.*

— — Germany.

DITTRICH (ERHARD) Die deutschen und österreichischen Kameralisten. Darmstadt, 1974. pp. 160. *bibliog.*

— — Russia.

GRIGOR'IAN (GRIGORII SEMENOVICH) and ABALKIN (LEONID IVANOVICH) eds. Nekotorye voprosy razvitiia sovetskoi ekonomicheskoi nauki za 50 let Sovetskoi vlasti. Moskva, 1969. pp. 128. *(Moscow. Moskovskii Institut Narodnogo Khoziaistva. Nauchnye Trudy. vyp. 71)*

— — Switzerland.

RYTZ (HANS RUDOLF) Geistliche des alten Bern zwischen Merkantilismus und Physiokratie: ein Beitrag zur Schweizer Sozialgeschichte des 18. Jahrhunderts. Basel, 1971. pp. 229. *bibliog.*

— Information storage and retrieval systems.

See INFORMATION STORAGE AND RETRIEVAL SYSTEMS — Economics.

— Methodology.

SUCHESTOW (MARCEL) Econognosis: a revised economic knowledge. New York, 1973 in progress.

— Periodicals — Bibliography.

BRATISLAVA. Ústredná Ekonomická Knižnica. Séria: Ekonomické Bibliografie. úpis ekonomických časopisov. 2.č. Socialistické krajiny;... List of economic periodicals. 2nd vol. Socialist countries, etc. Bratislava, 1973. pp. 334.

ÚSTREDNÁ EKONOMICKÁ KNIŽNICA. Séria: Ekonomické Bibliografie. Súpis ekonomických časopisov. 2.č. Socialistické krajiny;... List of economic periodicals. 2nd vol. Socialist countries, etc. Bratislava, 1973. pp. 334.

— Philosophy.

GAMERBERG KIZER (GRACIELA) Observaciones sobre la influencia de la ideologia en la ciencia economica. Caracas, [1969]. pp. 63. *bibliog.*

JOHNSON (GLENN L.) and ZERBY (LEWIS K.) What economists do about values: case studies of their answers to questions they don't dare ask. East Lansing, Mich., [1973]. pp. 253. *bibliog.*

LATOUCHE (SERGE) Epistémologie et économie: essai sur une anthropologie sociale freudo-marxiste. Paris, [1973]. pp. 583.

PESTIEAU (JOSEPH) Essai contre le défaitisme politique: imagination politique et intelligence économique. Montréal, 1973. pp. 255. *bibliog.*

— Psychological aspects.

MINKES (ARON LEONARD) Business and a behavioural tradition: (an inaugural lecture delivered in the University of Birmingham on 21 November 1972).Birmingham, 1973. pp. 20. *bibliog.*

ECONOMICS.

REYNAUD (PIERRE LOUIS) Précis de psychologie économique. [Paris], 1974. pp. 268. *bibliog.*

— Societies.

RYTZ (HANS RUDOLF) Geistliche des alten Bern zwischen Merkantilismus und Physiokratie: ein Beitrag zur Schweizer Sozialgeschichte des 18. Jahrhunderts. Basel, 1971. pp. 229. *bibliog.*

RUIZ Y GONZALEZ DE LINARES (ERNESTO) Las Sociedades Economicas de los Amigos del Pais. Burgos, 1972. pp. 71. *bibliog.* (*Consejo Superior de Investigaciones Cientificas. Institucion Fernan Gonzalez. Publicaciones*)

INSTITUTE OF ECONOMIC AFFAIRS. Progress report, 1974. London, 1974. pp. 12.

— Study and teaching — France.

LHOMME (JEAN) Pour une sociologie de la connaissance économique. Paris, [1974]. pp. 279.

— — Germany.

SCHIRMER (KURT PETER) Die neueren Bestrebungen zu einer Reform des volkswirtschaftlichen Studiums in der Bundesrepublik Deutschland. Göttingen, 1973. 1 vol.(various pagings). *bibliog.*

— — Hungary.

25 éves a marxista közgazdászképzés. Budapest, 1973. pp. 286.

— — Netherlands.

NETHERLANDS. Studiecomissie Coördinatie Wetenschappelijk Onderwijs - Hoger Economisch en Administratief Onderwijs. 1973. Rapport. 's-Gravenhage, 1973. pp. 37.

— Terminology.

FRANCE. Centre d'Etude des Revenus et des Coûts. 1971. Les Français et le vocabulaire économique: résultats et leçons d'une enquête. Paris, 1971. pp. 82. (*Documents. No. 9*)

GALLAIS-HAMONNO (JANINE) The language of macroeconomics: manuel d'anglais économique: la macroéconomie. Paris, 1971. pp. 290.

— 1876— .

GERTSEN (ALEKSANDR IVANOVICH) Byloe i dumy: pervoe polnoe izdanie. Berlin, 1921. 5 vols.

DOBB (MAURICE HERBERT) Political economy and capitalism: some essays in economic tradition. rev. ed. London, 1940 repr. 1972. pp. 357.

COLE (GEORGE DOUGLAS HOWARD) Socialist economics. London, 1950. pp. 158.

AL'TER (LEV BENITSIANOVICH) Izbrannye proizvedeniia. Moskva, 1971 in progress.

CARSON (RICHARD L.) and PAQUET (GILLES) Elements for a theory of systemic change. [Ottawa, 1971]. fo. 40, xi. (*Carleton University. Carleton Economic Papers*)

GALLAIS-HAMONNO (JANINE) The language of macroeconomics: manuel d'anglais économique: la macroéconomie. Paris, 1971. pp. 290.

GOBBATO (ONORIO) Livello dell'occupazione estabilità monetaria: implicazioni per la politica economica. Milano, 1971. pp. 91. *bibliog.* (*Rome. Università. Istituto di Politica Economica e Finanziaria. Pubblicazioni.* [13])

MUELLER (MAX GERHARD) ed. Readings in macroeconomics. 2nd ed. London, [1971]. pp. 475.

OSTROVITIANOV (KONSTANTIN VASIL'EVICH) Izbrannye proizvedeniia v dvukh tomakh. Moskva, 1972-73. 2 vols. *bibliog.*

CROUCH (ROBERT L.) Macroeconomics. New York, [1972]. pp. 425. *bibliogs.*

ECONOMIC freedom, stability and growth: [seminars given at Western Michigan University under the sponsorship of the Department of Economics, Winter semester, 1971]. [Kalamazoo, 1972]. pp. 80. (*Western Michigan University. College of Business. Business Research and Service Institute. Current Issues in Business and Economics. No.1*)

GEMEINWIRTSCHAFT im Wandel der Gesellschaft: Festschrift für Hans Ritschl zu seinem 75.Geburtstag am 19.Dezember 1972; herausgegeben von Gisbert Rittig und Heinz-Dietrich Ortlieb. Berlin, 1972. pp. 235. *bibliog.*

HANSON (JOHN LLOYD) Economic aspects of industry and commerce. 4th ed. London, 1972. pp. 363. *bibliog.*

STEWART (MICHAEL JAMES) Keynes and after. 2nd ed. Harmondsworth, 1972 repr. 1973. pp. 317. *bibliog.*

LANGE (OSKAR) Dzieła. Warszawa, 1973 in progress.

SUCHESTOW (MARCEL) Econognosis: a revised economic knowledge. New York, 1973 in progress.

SURVEYS of applied economics; [commissioned by] the Royal Economic Society [and] the Social Science Research Council. London, 1973 in progress. *bibliogs.*

ALLINGHAM (MICHAEL) Equilibrium and disequilibrium: a quantitative analysis of economic interaction. Cambridge, Mass., [1973]. pp. 160. *bibliog.*

BEGEER (WILLEM) and others, eds. Economie dezer dagen: (opstellen aangeboden aan prof. drs. H.W. Lambers ter gelegenheid van zijn 25-jarig hoogleraarschap aan de Nederlandse Economische Hogeschool). Rotterdam, 1973. pp. 345. *bibliog.*

BOS (HENDRICUS CORNELIS) and others, eds. Economic structure and development: essays in honour of Jan Tinbergen. Amsterdam, 1973. pp. 283.

CARTER (CHARLES FREDERICK) born 1919. The science of wealth: an elementary textbook of economics. 3rd ed. London, 1973. pp. 213.

CASSEL (DIETER) Grundbegriffe der Makroökonomik: eine Einführung in die Kreislaufanalyse und volkswirtschaftliche Gesamtrechnung für Lehrende. [Hannover], 1973. pp. 104. (*Niedersaechsische Landeszentrale für Politische Bildung. Schriftenreihe. Für die Hand des Lehrers. Heft 13*)

DONALDSON (PETER) Economics of the real world. London, 1973. pp. 244.

KREGEL (J.A.) The reconstruction of political economy: an introduction to post- Keynesian economics. London, 1973. pp. 218.

KRUBER (KLAUS PETER) Grundlagen der Mikroökonomik: eine Einführung in die Markttheorie und Wettbewerbspolitik für Lehrende. Hannover, 1973. pp. 99. (*Niedersaechsische Landeszentrale für Politische Bildung. Schriftenreihe. Für die Hand des Lehrers. Heft 14*)

KUCZYNSKI (JUERGEN) Das Gleichgewicht der Null: zu den Theorien des Null- Wachstums. Frankfurt/Main, 1973. pp. 76.

LEVI (ARRIGO) Journey among the economists;...translated by Muriel Grindrod. London, 1973. pp. 282. *bibliog.*

LOMBARDINI (SIRO) ed. Teoria dell'impresa e struttura economica: (testi di E.M. Chamberlin) [and others]. Bologna, [1973]. pp. 384. *bibliog.*

NEVIN (EDWARD THOMAS) An introduction to micro-economics. London, 1973. pp. 361.

NORTH (DOUGLASS CECIL) and MILLER (ROGER LEROY) The economics of public issues. 2nd ed. New York, [1973]. pp. 184.

PHILLIPS (PAUL ARTHUR) and SELDON (JAMES) Macroeconomics and the Canadian economy. Toronto, [1973]. pp. 180.

SCHACHTER (GUSTAV) and DALE (EDWIN L.) The economist looks at society. Lexington, Mass., [1973]. pp. 373. *bibliogs.*

TSAGOLOV (NIKOLAI ALEKSANDROVICH) ed. O sisteme kategorii i zakonov politicheskoi ekonomii. Moskva, 1973. pp. 271.

VEBLEN (THORSTEIN) Essays, reviews and reports: previously uncollected writings; edited and with an introduction, New light on Veblen, by Joseph Dorfman. Clifton, N.J., 1973. pp. 690.

VEREIN FÜR SOZIALPOLITIK. Schriften. Neue Folge. Band 74. Macht und ökonomisches Gesetz: (Verhandlungen auf der Jubiläumstagung in Bonn...1972, aus Anlass des Eisenacher Kongresses von 1872; herausgegeben von Hans K. Schneider und Christian Watrin). Berlin, [1973]. 2 vols.

WAGNER (LESLIE) and BALTAZZIS (NIKOS) eds. Readings in applied microeconomics. Oxford, 1973. pp. 435. *bibliogs.*

WEINTRAUB (SIDNEY) b. 1914, and others. Keynes and the monetarists and other essays: [lectures delivered at the Graduate School of Business Administration of the University of Puerto Rico, 1970-71]. New Brunswick, [1973]. pp. 227.

ZAHN (PETER) Economist. Die Phillips-Relation für Deutschland: eine lohn- und inflationstheoretische Untersuchung. Berlin, 1973. pp. 259. *bibliog.*

BILAS (RICHARD A.) and ALESSIO (FRANK J.) The essentials of macroeconomic analysis. Dallas, 1974. pp. 345. *bibliog.*

BLAUG (MARK) The Cambridge revolution: success or failure?: a critical analysis of Cambridge theories of value and distribution. London, 1974. pp. 102. *bibliog.* (*Institute of Economic Affairs. Hobart Paperbacks. 6*)

BOTTA (FRANCO) ed. Il dibattito su Sraffa: [a collection of readings]. Bari, [1974]. pp. 273.

CROSSER (PAUL K.) Prolegomena to all future metaeconomics: formation and deformation of economic thought. St. Louis, [1974]. pp. 197.

DMITRIEV (VLADIMIR K.) Economic essays on value, competition and utility; translated [from the Russian edition of 1904] by D. Fry and edited...by D.M. Nuti. London, 1974. pp. 231. *bibliog.*

DUNNING (JOHN HARRY) ed. Economic analysis and the multinational enterprise. London, 1974. pp. 405. *bibliog.*

HEESTERMAN (A.R.G.) Macro-economic market regulation. London, 1974. pp. 256. *bibliog.*

KRAUSS (MELVYN B.) and JOHNSON (HARRY GORDON) General equilibrium analysis: a micro-economic text. London, 1974. pp. 342.

MINC (BRONISLAW) L'économie politique du socialisme...; traduit du polonais par Anna Posner. 2nd ed. , Paris, 1974. pp. 550.

MUELLER (KLAUS O.W.) Neokeynesianismus: kritische Untersuchung einer modernen staatsmonopolkapitalistischen Wirtschaftslehre. 2nd ed. Westberlin, 1974. pp. 260.

PASINETTI (LUIGI L.) Growth and income distribution: essays in economic theory. London, 1974. pp. 151.

PERLMAN (MORRIS) Macroeconomics. London, [1974]. pp. 160. *bibliog.* (*London. University. London School of Economics and Political Science. LSE Handbooks in Economic Analysis*)

PISSARIDES (CHRISTOFORUS ANTONIU) Individual behaviour in markets with imperfect information; [Ph. D. (London) thesis]. [1974S].fo. 240,16. *bibliog.* With reprint of article in end pocket. Typescript: unpublished. This thesis is the property of London University and may not be removed from the Library.

PLANT (Sir ARNOLD) Selected economic essays and addresses. London, 1974. pp. 248. *bibliog.*

RUYS (P.H.M.) Public goods and decentralization: the duality approach in the theory of value. Tilburg, 1974. pp. 236. *bibliog.* (*Tilburg. Katholieke Hogeschool. Tilburg Institute of Economics. Tilburg Studies on Economics. 10*)

ECONOMICS. (Cont.)

SHACKLE (GEORGE LENNOX SHARMAN) Keynesian kaleidics: the evolution of a general political economy. Edinburgh, [1974]. pp. 92.

ECONOMICS, COMPARATIVE.

DEGREVE (DANIEL) D'une analyse historique de la Révolution industrielle à un diagnostic du sous-développement. [Liège, 1971?]. pp. 109. bibliog. (Liege. Université. Seminaire Interdisciplinaire de Science Economique des Professeurs Harsin et Davin. Bibliothèque. No.5) (Extrait revu de Cultures et Développement)

WINDHOFF (BERND) Darstellung und Kritik der Konvergenztheorie: gibt es eine Annäherung der sozialistischen und kapitalistischen Wirtschaftssysteme?. Bern, 1971. pp. 224. bibliog.

CARSON (RICHARD L.) Comparitive economic systems. New York, [1973]. pp.717. bibliogs.

LOUCKS (WILLIAM NEGELE) and WHITNEY (WILLIAM G.) Comparative economic systems. 9th ed. New York, [1973]. pp. 411. bibliogs.

MEISNER (JOACHIM) Kapitalizm a socjalizm: współzawodniczące systemy ekonomiczne. Warszawa, 1973. pp. 166. bibliog.

NAUCHNO-tekhnicheskaia revoliutsiia i sotsializm. Moskva, 1973. pp. 366.

PRYOR (FREDERIC L.) Property and industrial organization in communist and capitalist nations. Bloomington, [1973]. pp. 513. bibliog. (Indiana University. International Development Research Center. Studies in Development. No.7)

TSAGA (VIKTORIIA FRANTSEVNA) Ekonomicheskaia teoriia antikommunizma v tupike. Leningrad, 1973. pp. 254.

DALTON (GEORGE) Economic systems and society: capitalism, communism and the third world. Harmondsworth, 1974. pp. 250. bibliog.

GROSSMAN (GREGORY) Economic systems. 2nd ed. Englewood Cliffs, N.J., [1974]. pp. 195. bibliog.

MACHEL (SAMORA MOISES) Mozambique: sowing the seeds of revolution. [London, 1974]. pp. 68.

PICKERSGILL (GARY M.) and PICKERSGILL (JOYCE E.) Contemporary economic systems: a comparative view. Englewood Cliffs, [1974]. pp. 356. bibliogs.

VEREIN FÜR SOZIALPOLITIK. Schriften. Neue Folge. Band 76. Struktur- und stabilitätspolitische Probleme in alternativen Wirtschaftssystemen; von Jiří Kosta [and others]; herausgegeben von Christian Watrin. Berlin, [1974]. pp. 161. bibliogs.

VILJOEN (STEPHANUS PETRUS DU TOIT) Economic systems in world history. London, 1974. pp. 313. bibliog.

ECONOMICS, MATHEMATICAL.

UNITED NATIONS. Economic Commission for Asia and the Far East. Development Programming Techniques Series.. Bangkok, 1960 in progress.

GREEN (H.A. JOHN) Aggregation in economic analysis: an introductory survey. Princeton, N.J., 1964. pp. 129. bibliog.

BURMEISTER (EDWIN) and DOBELL (A. RODNEY) Mathematical theories of economic growth. London, [1970]. pp. 444.

BRONSARD (CAMILLE) Dualité microéconomique et théorie du second best. Louvain, 1971. pp. 174. bibliog. (Louvain. Université. Faculté des Sciences Economiques, Sociales et Politiques. [Publications]. Nouvelle Série. No. 88)

THEIL (HENRI) Principles of econometrics. New York, [1971]. pp. 736. bibliog.

FOURASTIE (JACQUELINE) Essai sur la mesure des quantités économiques. Paris, 1972. pp. 200. bibliog. (Paris. Ecole Pratique des Hautes. Etudes. Section des Sciences Economiques et Sociales. Centre d'Etudes Economiques. Etudes et Mémoires. 68)

GAUDE (JACQUES) Emploi agricole et migrations dans une économie dualiste. Genève, 1972. pp. 224. (International Labour Office. Travaux et Recherches)

MAJUMDAR (MUKUL) and MANNE (ALAN S.) Leontief trajectory optimization. Stanford, 1972. fo. 28. bibliog. (Stanford University. Institute for Mathematical Studies in the Social Sciences. Technical Reports. [New Series]. No. 78)

PONSARD (CLAUDE) ed. Graphes de transfert et analyse économique...; [by] A.L. Dumay [and others]. Paris, 1972. pp. 252.bibliogs.(Revue d'Economie Politique. Numéros Spéciaux)

STATISTIKA i elektronno-vychislitel'naia tekhnika v ekonomike: sbornik statei. vyp.5. Moskva, 1972. pp. 311. bibliog.

AHMAVAARA (YRJÖ) Cybernetic Lectures on Marxist economics. Tampere, 1973. 2 vols. (in 1). (Tampere. Yliopisto Tutkimuslaitos. Tutkimuksia. B21)

ALLINGHAM (MICHAEL) Equilibrium and disequilibrium: a quantitative analysis of economic interaction. Cambridge, Mass., [1973]. pp. 160. bibliog.

ARROW (KENNETH JOSEPH) Stability independent of adjustment speed. Stanford, 1973. fo. 32. bibliog. (Stanford University. Institute for Mathematical Studies in the Social Sciences. Technical Reports. [New Series]. No. 95)

CONTINI (BRUNO) Introduzione alla econometria. Bologna, [1973]. pp. 314. bibliog.

ELLMAN (MICHAEL JOHN) Planning problems in the USSR: the contribution of mathematical economics to their solution, 1960-1971. Cambridge, 1973. pp. 222. bibliog. (Cambridge. University. Department of Applied Economics. Monographs. 24)

GILES (D.E.A.) Essays on econometric topics: from theory to practice. Wellington, 1973. pp. 81. bibliog. (Reserve Bank of New Zealand. Research Papers. No.10)

GOLOVACH (ANATOLII VARFOLOMEEVICH) and others. Kriterii matematicheskoi statistiki v ekonomicheskikh issledovaniiakh. Moskva, 1973. pp. 136. bibliog.

GREEN (JERRY R.) and SHESHINSKI (EYTAN) Competitive inefficiencies in the presence of constrained transactions. Stanford, 1973. fo. 33. bibliog. (Stanford University. Institute for Mathematical Studies in the Social Sciences. Technical Reports. [New Series]. No. 105)

GRUBBSTRÖM (ROBERT W.) Economic decisions in space and time: theoretical and experimental inquiries into the cause of economic motion. [Linköping, 1973]. pp. 379. bibliog.

HART (P.E.) Moment distributions in economics: an exposition. [Reading], [1973]. fo. 13. bibliog. (Reading. University. Department of Economics. Discussion Papers in Economics. Series A. No.56)

KOUTSOGIANNES (A.) Theory of econometrics: an introductory exposition of econometric methods. London, 1973. pp. 601. bibliog.

KUSKA (EDWARD ARTHUR) Maxima, minima and comparative statics: a textbook for economists. London, [1973]. pp. 263. (London. University. London School of Economics and Political Science. LSE Handbooks in Economic Analysis)

LAU (LAWRENCE J.) Applications of duality theory: a comment. Stanford, 1973. pp. 39. bibliog. (Stanford University. Institute for Mathematical Studies in the Social Sciences. Technical Reports. [New Series] No. 99)

LEONARDZ (BJÖRN) To stop or not to stop: some elementary optimal stopping problems with economic interpretations. Stockholm, [1973]. pp. 178. bibliog.

LUND (PHILIP J.) and MINER (D.A.) The nature of the error term in distributed lag models. [Reading], 1973. pp. 22. bibliog. (Reading. University. Department of Economics. Discussion Papers in Economics. No. 46)

LUR'E (ALEKSANDR L'VOVICH) Ekonomicheskii analiz modelei planirovaniia sotsialisticheskogo khoziaistva. Moskva, 1973. pp. 435. bibliog. Contains O matematicheskikh metodakh reshenii zadach na optimum pri planirovanii sotsialisticheskogo khoziaistva and some other papers.

MANNE (ALAN S.) On the efficiency price of capital in a dual economy. Stanford, 1973. fo. 32. (Stanford University. Institute for Mathematical Studies in the Social Sciences. Technical Reports. [New Series]. No. 81)

MORISHIMA (MICHIO) Short lectures on Leon Walras. Siena, 1973. pp. 72. (Offprint from Economic Notes, vol.2, no.2) With French and German summaries.

NEVIN (EDWARD THOMAS) An introduction to micro-economics. London, 1973. pp. 361.

NICOLA (PIERCARLO) Equilibrio generale e crescita economica. Bologna, [1973]. pp. 167. bibliog.

QUINCEY (ROGER W.) and NEAL (FRANK) Using mathemathics in economics. London, 1973. pp. 249.

ROWLEY (JOHN CHRISTOPHER ROBIN) Econometric estimation. London, [1973]. pp. 234. bibliogs. (London. University. London School of Economics and Political Science. LSE Handbooks in Economic Analysis)

SCARF (HERBERT E.) The computation of economic equilibria. New Haven, 1973. pp. 249. bibliog. (Yale University. Department of Economics. Cowles Foundation for Research in Economics. Monographs. 24)

SCHMALENSEE (RICHARD) Applied microeconomics: problems in estimation, forecasting and decision-making. San Francisco, [1973]. pp. 118. bibliogs.

SIMS (CHRISTOPHER A.) Distributed lags. Minneapolis, 1973. 1 vol. (various foliations). bibliog. (Minnesota University. Center for Economic Research. Discussion Papers. No. 28)

SMITH (V. KERRY) Monte Carlo methods: their role for econometrics. Lexington, Mass., [1973]. pp. 153. bibliog.

STATISTIKA i elektronno-vychislitel'naia tekhnika v ekonomike: sbornik statei. vyp.6. Moskva, 1973. pp. 225. bibliog.

USHER (DAN) The measurement of economic growth. Kingston, Ont., 1973. 1 vol. (various pagings). (Kingston, Ontario. Queen's University. Institute for Economic Research. Discussion Papers. No.131)

VAL'TUKH (KONSTANTIN KURTOVICH) ed. Problemy narodnokhoziaistvennogo optimuma. Novosibirsk, 1973. pp. 384.

WEDDEPOHL (H.N.) Dual sets and dual correspondences and their application to equilibrium theory. Tilburg, 1973. pp. 46. bibliog. (Tilburg. Katholieke Hogeschool. Tilburg Institute of Economics. Research Memoranda. EIT 38)

WILSON (ROBERT) Economist. On the theory of aggregation. Stanford, 1973. fo. 16. (Stanford University. Institute for Mathematical Studies in the Social Sciences. Technical Reports. [New Reports] . No. 89)

CUDDY (J.D.A.) Quantitative methods in economics: an introduction to statistical inference estimation and modelling. Rotterdam, 1974. pp. 180. bibliog.

DMITRIEV (VLADIMIR K.) Economic essays on value, competition and utility; translated [from the Russian edition of 1904] by D. Fry and edited...by D.M. Nuti. London, 1974. pp. 231. bibliog.

FRIEDMAN (ANDREW) Choosing among S-shaped curves for diffusion processes. Coventry, 1974. pp. 33. (University of Warwick. Centre for Industrial Economic and Business Research. [Warwick Research in Industrial and Business Studies]. No. 45)

PETERS (P.J.L.M.) Interrelated macro-economic systems. Tilburg, 1974. pp. 170. *bibliog.* *(Tilburg. Katholieke Hogeschool. Tilburg Institute of Economics. Tilburg Studies on Economics. 9)*

WEINTRAUB (E.ROY) General equilibrium theory. London, 1974. pp. 64. *bibliog.*

WYNN (R.F.) and HOLDEN (K.) An introduction to applied econometric analysis. London, 1974. pp. 245. bibliogs.

ECONOMICS, PRIMITIVE.

GRENDI (EDOARDO) ed. L'antropologia economica: [readings]. Torino, [1972]. pp. 299. *bibliog.*

SCHNEIDER (HAROLD KENNETH) Economic man: the anthropology of economics. New York, [1974]. pp. 278. *bibliog.*

— **Terminology.**

GASTELLU (JEAN MARC) Lexique de termes Sérer ÀCONTENU économique en usage à Ngohe. [Dakar, Office de la Recherche Scientifique et Technique Outre-Mer], 1968. fo. 34.

ECONOMIES OF SCALE.

ALESCH (DANIEL J.) and DOUGHARTY (L.A.) Economies-of-scale analysis in state and local government...: a report prepared for Council on Intergovernmental Relations, State of California. Santa Monica, 1971. pp. 56. *bibliog. (Rand Corporation. [Rand Reports]. 748)*

WHITE (NORMAN ARTHUR) The economics of scale in the international petroleum industry; [Ph.D.(London) thesis]. 1973. 1 vol. (various foliations). *bibliog. Typescript: unpublished. This thesis is the property of London University and may not be removed from the Library.*

ECONOMISTS.

LEVI (ARRIGO) Journey among the economists;...translated by Muriel Grindrod. London, 1973. pp. 282. *bibliog.*

ANIKIN (ANDREI VLADIMIROVICH) Ökonomen aus drei Jahrhunderten: das Leben und Wirken der Ökonomen vor Marx und Engels; Übersetzung aus dem Russischen ([by] Günter Wermusch). Berlin, 1974. pp. 388.

ECONOMISTS, ARGENTINIAN.

SUAREZ (FRANCISCO) Los economistas argentinos: el proceso de institucionalizacion de nuevas profesiones. Buenos Aires, [1973]. pp. 174. *bibliog.*

ECONOMISTS, AUSTRIAN.

DITTRICH (ERHARD) Die deutschen und österreichischen Kameralisten. Darmstadt, 1974. pp. 160. *bibliog.*

ECONOMISTS, GERMAN.

DITTRICH (ERHARD) Die deutschen und österreichischen Kameralisten. Darmstadt, 1974. pp. 160. *bibliog.*

ECONOMISTS, RUSSIAN.

JEFFRIES (IAN) The Stalinist economic system as a model for underdeveloped countries: the development of Soviet thought since 1953; [Ph.D.(London) thesis]. [1974]. fo. 301. *bibliog. Typescript: unpublished. This thesis is the property of London University and may not be removed from the Library.*

ECONOMISTS, SPANISH.

TRIAS FARGAS (RAMON) and PUIG BASTARD (PEDRO) Las condiciones de trabajo de los economistas españoles: el empleo y la remuneracion de los Licenciados en Ciencias Economicas. Barcelona, 1972. pp. 291.

ECUADOR

— **Boundaries — Peru.**

CHIRINOS SOTO (ENRIQUE) Peru y Ecuador. Lima, 1968. pp. 55.

— **Commerce — Latin American Free Trade Association countries.**

ECUADOR. Ministerio de Industrias y Comercio. Direccion de Integracion. 1969. Intercambio comercial del Ecuador con los paises miembros de la ALALC, 1962-1967. Quito, 1969. pp. 139. *(Boletines. No. 65)*

— **Economic conditions.**

ROBALINO GONZAGA (CESAR RAUL) El desarrollo economico del Ecuador: la ineficiencia de la economia, la evolucion de la economia, la estrategia de desarrollo. Quito, Junta Nacional de Planificacion y Coordinacion, [1970?]. pp. 460.

— **Economic policy.**

ECUADOR. Junta Nacional de Planificacion y Coordinacion Economica. 1964. Plan general de desarrollo economico y social (version preliminar). Tomo 1. Fines y medios de una politica de desarrollo. Libro segundo. La transformacion: sus objectivos y medios (and Reforma tributaria). Quito, [1964]. 2 pts. (in 1 vol.)

ECUADOR. Junta Nacional de Planificacion y Coordinacion Economica. 1965. Jornadas industriales. [Quito], 1965. pp. 197.

LINNEMANN (HANS) Regiones económicas del Ecuador: su integración y desarrollo; estudio preliminar; preparado para el gobierno del Ecuador. [Quito, 1965]. pp. 100.

ECUADOR. Junta Nacional de Planificacion y Coordinacion Economica. 1966. Politica planificada para el desarrollo: resumen del plan general de desarrollo economico y social del Ecuador. Quito, 1966. pp. 129.

ROBALINO GONZAGA (CESAR RAUL) El desarrollo economico del Ecuador: la ineficiencia de la economia, la evolucion de la economia, la estrategia de desarrollo. Quito, Junta Nacional de Planificacion y Coordinacion, [1970?]. pp. 460.

ECUADOR. [Junta Nacional de Planificacion y Coordinacion Económica]. 1972. Plan integral de transformacion y desarrollo, 1973-77; resumen general. [Quito, 1972]. pp. 417.

— **Industries.**

ECUADOR. Junta Nacional de Planificacion y Coordinacion Economica. 1965. Jornadas industriales. [Quito], 1965. pp. 197.

— **Manufactures.**

ECUADOR. Instituto Nacional de Estadistica. Encuesta de manufactura y mineria. a., 1968, 1969, 1971- Quito.

— **Social policy.**

ECUADOR. Junta Nacional de Planificacion y Coordinacion Economica. 1964. Plan general de desarrollo economico y social (version preliminar). Tomo 1. Fines y medios de una politica de desarrollo. Libro segundo. La transformacion: sus objectivos y medios (and Reforma tributaria). Quito, [1964]. 2 pts. (in 1 vol.)

ECUADOR. Junta Nacional de Planificacion y Coordinacion Economica. 1966. Politica planificada para el desarrollo: resumen del plan general de desarrollo economico y social del Ecuador. Quito, 1966. pp. 129.

ECUADOR. [Junta Nacional de Planificacion y Coordinacion Economica]. 1972. Plan integral de transformacion y desarrollo, 1973-77; resumen general. [Quito, 1972]. pp. 417.

— **Statistics, Vital.**

ECUADOR. Division de Estadistica y Censos. 1967. Encuesta de fecundidad, levantada en las principales ciudades y en algunas parroquias rurales del pais. Quito, 1967.. pp. 255,6.

EDINBURGH

— **Officials and employees.**

COMMISSION ON INDUSTRIAL RELATIONS [U.K.]. Edinburgh Corporation Transport Department. London, H.M.S.O., 1973. pp. 13. *(Reports. No. 56)*

EDUCATION.

UNITED NATIONS EDUCATIONAL, SCIENTIFIC AND CULTURAL ORGANIZATION. Department of Mass Communication. Reports and Papers on Mass Communication. Paris, 1953 in progress.

UNITED NATIONS EDUCATIONAL, SCIENTIFIC AND CULTURAL ORGANIZATION. Educational Studies and Documents. New Series . Paris, 1971 in progress.

HOLT (JOHN CALDWELL) What do I do on Monday?. London, 1971. pp. 318. *bibliog.*

EDUCATION for cultural pluralism; papers from a conference held in London, December 15-17, 1970 under the auspices of the Cultural Department, World Jewish Congress...; edited by E.M. Eppel. London, 1972. pp. 133.

POIGNANT (RAYMOND) Education in the industrialised countries. The Hague, 1973. pp. 324. *(European Cultural Foundation. Plan Europe 2000. Project 1. vol.5)*

HUSÉN (TORSTEN) The learning society. London, 1974. pp. 268. *bibliog.*

— **Aims and objectives.**

BLANSHARD (BRAND) The uses of a liberal education: and other talks to students;... [speeches and essays] edited by Eugene Freeman. London, 1974. pp. 415. *First published in the United States in 1973.*

— **Economic aspects.**

SHEEHAN (JOHN) The economics of education. London, 1973. pp. 140. *bibliog.*

WEST (E.G.) The economics of compulsory education. [Ottawa, 1973]. fo. 47. *(Carleton University. Carleton Economic Papers)*

— **Experimental methods.**

CENTRE FOR EDUCATIONAL RESEARCH AND INNOVATION. Case Studies of Educational Innovation. Paris, 1973. 4 vols. (in 2).

— **Finance.**

INTERNATIONAL INSTITUTE FOR EDUCATIONAL PLANNING. Fundamentals of Educational Planning . Paris, Unesco, 1970 in progress.

— **Philosophy.**

CURLE (ADAM) Education for liberation. London, 1973. pp. 144. *bibliog.*

HOOK (SIDNEY) Education and the taming of power. La Salle, Ill., 1973. pp. 310.

PETERS (RICHARD STANLEY) Psychology and ethical development: a collection of articles on psychological theories, ethical development and human understanding. London, 1974. pp. 480.

— **Productivity.**

HEIM (JOHN) and PERL (LEWIS) The educational production function: implications for educational manpower policy. Ithaca, 1974. pp. 38. *bibliog. (Cornell University. New York State School of Industrial and Labor Relations. Institute of Public Employment. Monographs. No.4)*

— **Statistics.**

JALLADE (JEAN-PIERRE) and others. Occupational and educational structures of the labour force and levels of economic development. Paris, Organisation for Economic Co-operation and Development, 1970-71. 2 vols.

EDUCATION. (Cont.)

— Angola — History.

SANTOS (FRANCISCO MARTINS DOS) Historia do ensino em Angola. [Luanda], Serviços de Educação, 1970. pp. 361.

— Argentine Republic.

CIRIGLIANO (GUSTAVO F.J.) Educacion y politica: el paradojal sistema de la educacion argentina. Buenos Aires, 1969. pp. 152.

— — History.

TEDESCO (JUAN CARLOS) Educacion y sociedad en la Argentina, 1880-1900. Buenos Aires, 1970. pp. 226. bibliog.

— Australia — South Australia.

SOUTH AUSTRALIA. Committee of Enquiry into Education in South Australia. 1971. Education in South Australia: report of the Committee... 1969-1970; [Peter Henry Karmel, Chairman]. Adelaide, 1971. pp. 649.

— Belgium.

BELGIUM. Ministère de la Culture Française. 1971. Culture et communauté: politique de l'éducation permanente. [Brussels, 1971]. pp. 150.

— — History.

VROEDE (MAURITS DE) Van schoolmeester tot onderwijzer: de opleiding van de leerkrachten in België en Luxembourg, van het eind van de 18 de eeuw tot omstreeks 1842. Leuven, 1970. pp. 563. bibliog. (Katholieke Universiteit te Leuven. Werken op het Gebied van het Geschiedenis en de Filologie. 5de Reeks. Deel 7)

— Botswana.

STYRELSEN FÖR INTERNATIONELL UTVECKLING [SWEDEN]. Education and training in Botswana: a survey by a mission from the Swedish International Development Authority. [Stockholm?], 1972. pp. 95.

VAN RENSBURG (PATRICK) Report from Swaneng Hill: education and employment in an African country. Stockholm, 1974. pp. 235.

— Canada — Classification.

ORGANISATION FOR ECONOMIC CO-OPERATION AND DEVELOPMENT. Directorate for Scientific Affairs. 1973. Canada; Greece; Yugoslavia. Paris, 1973. pp. 78. bibliogs. (Classification of Educational Systems in OECD Member Countries)

— — Finance.

CANADA. Statistics Canada. Financial statistics - elementary and secondary education. annual, 1970 (1st)- Ottawa. In English and French.

— China.

WANG (SING-TAI) Changes in Chinese communist education. [Taipei], 1972. pp. 112. (Asian Peoples' Anti-Communist League. Pamphlets. No. 167)

EDUCATION in China; [by] Peter Mauger [and others]. London, 1974. pp. 81. bibliog. (Anglo-Chinese Educational Institute. Modern China Series. No.5)

— — History.

CHEN (THEODORE HSI-EN) The Maoist educational revolution. New York, 1974. pp. 295.

— Colombia.

REUNION DE ESTUDIO SOBRE LA TRANSFORMACION EDUCATIVA DEL PAIS, BOGOTA, 1968. Reunion de Estudio... Bogota, 8 y 9 de Agosto de 1968. [Bogota, Ministerio de Educacion Nacional, 1968]. fo. 77.

— Europe.

SAUVY (ALFRED) and others. Access to education: new possibilities. The Hague, 1973. pp. 157. (European Cultural Foundation. Plan Europe 2000. Project 1, vol. 3)

— European Economic Community countries.

EUROPEAN COMMUNITIES. Commission. 1973. For a Community policy on education. [Brussels], 1973. pp. 61. (Bulletin of the European Communities. Supplements. [1973/10])

— Germany.

KNIRIM (CHRISTA) Erziehungsleitbilder in Stadt- und Landfamilien der Bundesrepublik Deutschland. Bonn, 1974. pp. 248. bibliog. (Forschungsgesellschaft für Agrarpolitik und Agrarsoziologie. [Publications]. 223)

BUNGENSTAB (KARL ERNST) Umerziehung zur Demokratie?: Re-education-Politik im Bildungswesen der US-Zone, 1945-1949. d Düsseldorf, [1970]. pp. 250. bibliog. With English summary.

BUNGENSTAB (KARL ERNST) Umerziehung zur Demokratie?: Re-education-Politik im Bildungswesen der US-Zone, 1945- 1949. Düsseldorf, [1970]. pp. 250. bibliog. With English summary.

— — Statistics.

BILDUNG IM ZAHLENSPIEGEL; ([pd. by] Bundesministerium für Bildung und Wissenschaft [and] Statistisches Bundesamt). a., 1974 [1st]- Bonn [and] Wiesbaden.

— Germany, Eastern.

DIFFICULT years bear fruit: the birth and development of the German Democratic Republic. [rev. ed.] Dresden, [1974]. pp. 144.

— Greece — Classification.

ORGANISATION FOR ECONOMIC CO-OPERATION AND DEVELOPMENT. Directorate for Scientific Affairs. 1973. Canada; Greece; Yugoslavia. Paris, 1973. pp. 78. bibliogs. (Classification of Educational Systems in OECD Member Countries)

— Guatemala.

SEXTON (JAMES D.) Education and innovation in a Guatemalan community: San Juan la Laguna. Los Angeles, 1972. pp. 72. bibliog. (California University. Latin American Center. Latin American Studies. vol. 19)

— India — History.

BASU (APARNA) The growth of education and political development in India, 1898- 1920. Delhi, 1974. pp. 258. bibliog.

— Iran.

FURTER (PIERRE) Possibilities and limitations of functional literacy: the Iranian experiment. Paris, United Nations Educational, Scientific and Cultural Organization, 1973. pp. 59. bibliog. (Educational Studies and Documents. New Series. No. 9)

— Italy.

CAVALLINI (GRAZIANO) ed. Socializzare la scuola: ricerca interdisciplinare per un modello di scuola alternativa; di Angelo Beretta [and others]. Bologna, [1973]. pp. 252. bibliog. (Associazione per la Ricerca Sperimentale sui Problemi dei Giovani. Studi e Ricerche IARD. 4)

— History.

BARBAGLI (MARZIO) Disoccupazione intellettuale e sistema scolastico in Italia, 1859- 1973. Bologna, [1974]. pp. 481.

— Jamaica.

FONER (NANCY) Status and power in rural Jamaica: a study of educational and political change. New York, [1973]. pp. 172. bibliog.

— Korea.

KIM (IL-SUNG) Talk to delegation of Japan National Socialist Mayors Association, May 14, 1972. Pyongyang, 1972. pp. 26.

— Lesotho.

WILLIAMS (JOHN COX) Lesotho: three manpower problems: education, health, population growth. Pretoria, 1971. pp. 70. (Africa Institute. Communications. No. 16)

— Luxembourg — History.

LUXEMBOURG. Ministère de l'Education Nationale. 1974. L'education nationale au Luxembourg: cartes et graphiques 1960- 1971. Luxembourg, 1974. 49 sheets, transparency.

VROEDE (MAURITS DE) Van schoolmeester tot onderwijzer: de opleiding van de leerkrachten in België en Luxembourg, van het eind van de 18 de eeuw tot omstreeks 1842. Leuven, 1970. pp. 563. bibliog. (Katholieke Universiteit te Leuven. Werken op het Gebied van het Geschiedenis en de Filologie. 5de Reeks. Deel 7)

— Malaysia — Statistics.

EDUCATIONAL STATISTICS OF MALAYSIA; [pd.by] the Ministry of Education, Malaysia. a., 1938/1967 [1st], 1968 [2nd]- Kuala Lumpur.

— Netherlands.

NETHERLANDS. Ministerie van Onderwijs en Wetenschappen. 1970. Nieuwe lijnen voor het onderwijs van morgen. [Den Haag, 1970?]. pp. 40.

— Netherlands Antilles.

NETHERLANDS. Kabinet voor Surinaamse en Nederlands- Antilliaanse Zaken. 1972. Het onderwijs in de Nederlandse Antillen. [The Hague?, 1972?]. pp. 33.

— New Zealand.

McLAREN (IAN A.) Education in a small democracy: New Zealand. London, 1974. pp. 172. bibliog.

— Nicaragua.

CASTILLA URBINA (MIGUEL DE) Educacion para la modernizacion en Nicaragua. Buenos Aires, 1972. pp. 162.

— Nigeria.

NIGERIA. 1961. Educational development, 1961-70. Lagos, 1961. pp. 10. (Sessional Papers. 1961. No. 3)

— — History.

FAFUNWA (A. BABS) History of education in Nigeria. London, 1974. pp. 264. bibliog.

— Norway — Statistics.

NORWAY. Statistiske Centralbyrå. Utdanningsstatistikk (formerly Undervisningsstatistikk): avsluttet utdanning: Educational statistics: education finished. a., 1st half 1971[1st]; 1971/2[2nd]- Oslo.

— Poland — History.

SUCHODOLSKI (BOGDAN) Komisja Edukacji Narodowej na tle roli oświaty w dziejowym rozwoju Polski. Warszawa, 1972. pp. 276.

— Roumania.

FRANCE. Direction de la Documentation. La Documentation Française. Notes et Etudes Documentaires. No. 3,875. L'enseignement en Roumanie; [par Paul Poudade]. [Paris], 1972. pp. 24. bibliog.

— Russia — Bibliography.

PEDAGOGICHESKAIA bibliografiia, 1931-1935. Moskva, 1970. pp. 863.

— — History.

IZ istorii sovetskoi kul'tury. Moskva, 1972. pp. 167.

KUMANEV (VIKTOR ALEKSANDROVICH) Revoliutsiia i prosveshchenie mass. Moskva, 1973. pp. 335. bibliog.

SINEL (ALLEN) The classroom and the chancellery: state educational reform in Russia under Count Dmitry Tolstoi. Cambridge, Mass., 1973. pp. 335. *bibliog. (Harvard University. Russian Research Center. Studies. 72)*

— — Ukraine — History.

PANIOTOV (IVAN ILLICH) Komunistychna partiia Ukraïny v borot'bi za rozvytok narodnoï osvity, 1931-1941 rr. Kharkiv, 1973. pp. 186. *bibliog.*

— South Africa.

SOUTH AFRICA. Department of Information. 1969. Stepping into the future: education for South Africa's developing nations. [Pretoria, 1969?]. pp. 40.

SOUTH AFRICA. Department of Information. 1969. Education for success. [Pretoria, 1969?]. pp. 40.

— — Transkeian Territories.

TRANSKEI. Department of Education. Report. a., 1965, 1968- Umtata.

— Sweden.

SWEDEN. Prognosinstitut. 1972. Trender och prognoser: befolkning, utbildning och arbetsmarknad, etc. Stockholm, 1972. pp. 179. *(Information i Prognosfrågor. 1972.10)*

SWEDEN. Census, 1970. Folk- och bostadsräkningen 1970: resultat från evalveringsstudierna avseende sysselsättning och utbildning, etc. Stockholm, 1974. pp. 84. *(Sweden. Statistiska Centralbyrån. Statistiska Meddelanden. Be/1974/3)*

— Underdeveloped areas.

See UNDERDEVELOPED AREAS — Education.

— United Kingdom.

NATIONAL UNION OF TEACHERS. Into the 70's: a policy for a new education act. London, [1969]. pp. 40.

The CASE for academic freedom and democracy: [by] John Griffith [and others]. London, [1972]. pp. 15.

BOYD (DAVID) Elites and their education. Windsor, 1973. pp. 159. *bibliog.*

BOYSON (RHODES) Battle lines for education. London, 1973. pp. 18. *(Conservative Political Centre. [Publications]. No. 538)*

FOWLER (GERALD) and others, eds. Decision-making in British education. London, 1973. pp. 486.

PETERSON (ALEXANDER DUNCAN CAMPBELL) Liberal education for all. London, [1973]. pp. 18. *(Liberal Party. Strategy 2,000. 1st Series. No. 2)*

YOUR local education; [by] John Pratt [and others]. Harmondsworth, 1973. pp. 256. *bibliog.*

HEAD (DAVID) ed. Free way to learning: educational alternatives in action. Harmondsworth, 1974. pp. 167.

KOGAN (MAURICE) and PACKWOOD (TIM) Advisory councils and committees in education. London, 1974. pp. 100. *bibliog.*

LOCKE (MICHAEL) Power and politics in the school system: a guidebook. London, 1974. pp. 184. *bibliog.*

ST. JOHN-STEVAS (NORMAN ANTHONY FRANCIS) Standards and freedom. London, 1974. pp. 13. *(Conservative Political Centre. [Publications]. No. 557)*

— — Economic aspects.

BYRNE (EILEEN M.) Planning and educational inequality: a study of the rationale of resource-allocation. Windsor, 1974. pp. 386. *bibliog.*

— — Experimental methods.

GARNETT (EMMELINE) Area resource centre: an experiment. London, 1972. pp. 116.

— — History.

STEPHENS (W.B.) Regional variations in education during the industrial revolution 1780-1870: the task of the local historian. Leeds, 1973. pp. 35. *(Leeds. University. Museum of the History of Education. Educational Administration and History: Monographs. No.1.)*

SIMON (BRIAN) The politics of educational reform, 1920-1940. London, 1974. pp. 400. *bibliog.*

SYLVESTER (DAVID WILLIAM) Robert Lowe and education. Cambridge, 1974. pp. 240. *bibliog.*

WARDLE (DAVID) The rise of the schooled society: the history of formal schooling in England. London, 1974. pp. 182. *bibliog.*

— — Hertfordshire — History.

HURT (JOHN S.) Bringing literacy to rural England: the Hertfordshire example. London, 1972. pp. 33.

— — — Finance.

LONDON. Greater London Council. Inner London Education Authority. Capital and revenue estimates. a., 1974/5- London.

— — Scotland.

McKECHIN (WILLIAM J.) Education after reorganisation: trad or progressive?. Paisley, 1973. pp. 77. *(Paisley College of Technology. Local Government Research Unit. Occasional Papers. 4)*

— — Wales.

MERIONETH. County Planning Office. Merioneth structure plan: (subject report no. 5): education. Dolgellau, [1973]. pp. 39.

— United States.

GOODMAN (PAUL) b. 1911. Compulsory miseducation: [revised edition first published in the United States in 1964]. Harmondsworth, 1971 repr. 1973. pp. 127.

TESCONI (CHARLES A.) and MORRIS (VAN CLEVE) The anti-man culture: bureautechnocracy and the schools. Urbana, Ill., [1972]. pp. 232. *bibliog.*

BREMBECK (COLE SPEICHER) and HILL (WALKER H.) eds. Cultural challenges to education: the influence of cultural factors in school learning. Lexington, Mass., [1973]. pp. 160.

SIEBER (SAM D.) and WILDER (DAVID E.) eds. The school in society: studies in the sociology of education. New York, [1973]. pp. 440. *bibliogs.*

CORWIN (RONALD G.) Education in crisis: a sociological analysis of schools and universities in transition. New York, [1974]. pp. 380.

SORKIN (ALAN L.) Education, unemployment, and economic growth. Lexington, Mass., [1974]. pp. 186.

— — Economic aspects.

BENSON (CHARLES SCOTT) The economics of public education. 2nd ed. Boston, [1968]. pp. 368. *bibliog.*

BOLINO (AUGUST C.) Career education: contributions to economic growth. New York, 1973. pp. 234. *bibliog.*

MINCER (JACOB) Schooling, experience and earnings. New York, 1974. pp. 152. *bibliog. (National Bureau of Economic Research. Human Behavior and Social Institutions. 2)*

— — Finance.

BUTZ (WILLIAM P.) and JORDAN (PAUL L.) Population growth and resource requirements for U.S. education: prepared for the Commission on Population Growth and the American Future. Santa Monica, 1972. pp. 87.

ALEXANDER (KERN) and JORDAN (K. FORBIS) eds. Constitutional reform of school finance. Lexington, Mass., [1973]. pp. 228.

EDUCATION, ELEMENTARY.

LEVIN (BETSY) and others. The high cost of education in cities: an analysis of the purchasing power of the educational dollar. Washington, D.C., [1973]. pp. 96.

PIELE (PHILIP K.) and HALL (JOHN STUART) Budgets, bonds and ballots: voting behavior in school financial elections. Lexington, [1973]. pp. 216. *bibliog.*

— — History.

GOOD (HARRY GEHMAN) and TELLER (JAMES DAVID) A history of American education. 3rd ed. New York, [1973]. pp. 570. *bibliogs.*

— — California — Finance.

BARRO (STEPHEN M.) Alternatives in California school of finance. Santa Monica, 1971. pp. 106. *(Rand Corporation. [Rand Reports]. 663)*

— Yugoslavia — Classification.

ORGANISATION FOR ECONOMIC CO-OPERATION AND DEVELOPMENT. Directorate for Scientific Affairs. 1973. Canada; Greece; Yugoslavia. Paris, 1973. pp. 78. *bibliogs. (Classification of Educational Systems in OECD Member Countries)*

— Zambia.

HAY (HOPE) Northern Rhodesia learns to read. London, 1947. pp. 29.

EDUCATION, COMPARATIVE.

BAUER (GUENTHER) Vergleichende Studie über die Reife- und Abschlussprüfungen an den allgemeinbildenden höheren Schulen der Länder Österreich, Bundesrepublik Deutschland, Schweiz und England; [herausgegeben im Auftrage des Bundesministeriums für Unterricht]. Wien, [1969]. pp. 143. *bibliog. (Beiträge zur pädagogischen Psychologie. Heft 275- 283)*

BEREDAY (GEORGE ZYGMUNT FIJALKOWSKI) Universities for all. San Francisco, 1973. pp. 158. *bibliog.*

KNIRIM (CHRISTA) Erziehungsleitbilder in Stadt- und Landfamilien der Bundesrepublik Deutschland. Bonn, 1974. pp. 248. *bibliog. (Forschungsgesellschaft für Agrarpolitik und Agrarsoziologie. [Publications]. 223)*

EDUCATION, ELEMENTARY.

MARGOLIN (EDYTHE) Sociocultural elements in early childhood education. New York, [1974]. pp. 400. *bibliogs.*

— Netherlands.

NETHERLANDS. Ministerie van Onderwijs en Wetenschappen. 1970. Voorontwerp van een wet op het basisonderwijs, 1. 's-Gravenhage, 1970. pp. 55.

— United Kingdom.

EDUCATION in the middle years; the first report from the Schools Council Middle Years of Schooling Project, Department of Educational Research, University of Lancaster; [by] E.H. Badcock [and others]. London, 1972. pp. 112. *(U.K. Department of Education and Science. Schools Council. Working Papers. 42)*

MYERS (DONALD A.) and MYERS (LILIAN) eds. Open education re-examined. Lexington, Mass., [1973]. pp. 139. *bibliog.*

OGILVIE (ERIC) Gifted children in primary schools:...the report of the Schools Council enquiry into the teaching of gifted children of primary age, 1970-71. London, 1973. pp. 279. *bibliog. (U.K. Department of Education and Science. Schools Council. Research Studies)*

SUTHERLAND (GILLIAN) Policy-making in elementary education, 1870-1895. Oxford, 1973. pp. 391. *bibliog.*

— — Scotland — Curricula.

SCOTLAND. Scottish Education Department. 1973. Primary education in Scotland: mathematics. Edinburgh, 1973. pp. 48. *(Curriculum Papers. 13)*

EDUCATION, ELEMENTARY. (Cont.)

— United States.

MYERS (DONALD A.) and MYERS (LILIAN) eds. Open education re-examined. Lexington, Mass., [1973]. pp. 139. *bibliog.*

EDUCATION, HIGHER.

NITSCH (WOLFGANG) and WELLER (WALTER) Social science research on higher education and universities...; under the direction of Dietrich Goldschmidt. The Hague, 1970 in progress. *bibliog. (International Committee for Social Science Information and Documentation. Confluence. vols. 9, etc.)*

EXPERIENTIAL techniques in higher education; a report of a workshop held at the University of Surrey 13-15 April 1973; written by Dave Bond...[and others]. [Guildford], 1973. pp. 38.

FURTH (DOROTEA) ed. Short-cycle higher education: a search for identity. Paris. Organisation for Economic Co-operation and Development, 1973. pp. 414. *bibliog.*

[INTERNATIONAL CONFERENCE ON HIGHER EDUCATION, 2ND, LANCASTER, 1972]. The implications of mass higher education; papers. Amsterdam, 1973. pp. 274. *bibliogs. (Higher Education, vol. 2, no. 2 (special issue))*

POST-secondary education in a technological society: [based on the Nuffield Canadian Seminar held at Cap-Rouge in June 1971]; edited by...T.H. McLeod. Montreal, 1973. pp. 247. *In English and French.*

WEST (E.G.) Efficiency versus equity in higher education. [Ottawa, 1973]. fo. 47. *(Carleton University. Carleton Economic Papers)*

— Bibliography.

NITSCH (WOLFGANG) and WELLER (WALTER) Social science research on higher education and universities...; under the direction of Dietrich Goldschmidt. The Hague, 1970 in progress. *bibliog. (International Committee for Social Science Information and Documentation. Confluence. vols. 9, etc.)*

ALTBACH (PHILIP G.) and NYSTROM (BRADLEY) compilers. Higher education in developing countries: a select bibliography. Cambridge, Mass., 1970. pp. 113. *(Harvard University. Center for International Affairs. Occasional Papers in International Affairs. No. 24)*

— Asia, Southeast.

YIP (YAT HOONG) ed. Development of higher education in Southeast Asia: problems and issues. Singapore, 1973. pp. 226.

— Canada.

CROWLEY (RONALD W.) Towards free post-secondary education?. Kingston, 1971. fo. 24. *(Kingston, Ontario. Queen's University. Institute for Economic Research. Discussion Papers. No. 58)*

HARVEY (EDWARD) Educational systems and the labour market. Don Mills, Ont., [1974]. pp. 223.

— Europe.

EMBLING (JOHN FRANCIS) A fresh look at higher education: European implications of the Carnegie Commission reports. Amsterdam, 1974. pp. 263. *bibliog.*

— European Economic Community countries.

SOLOMON (RHONA RACHEL) and SMITH (ALEXANDER MAIR) Higher education in the European Economic Community. Manchester, 1973. pp. 30. *bibliog.*

— Germany.

KERN (BAERBEL) Einflüsse sozioökonomischer Faktoren auf die Ausbildungsentscheidungen von Abiturienten in vier ausgewählten Regionen Niedersachsens: ein Beitrag zur Bildungsmobilität. Göttingen, 1973. 1 vol.(various pagings).

— Hawaiian Islands.

PSACHAROPOULOS (GEORGE) Enrollment projections for higher education in the State of Hawaii, 1969-1980. Honolulu, 1969. pp. 158.

— Mexico.

SEMINARIO NACIONAL POR LA REFORMA Y DEMOCRATIZACION DE LA ENSEÑANZA, 1º. Por la reforma y democratizacion de la enseñanza: documentos del primer seminario nacional; ([sponsored by] Central Nacional de Estudiantes Democraticos). Mexico, 1969. pp. 127.

— Netherlands.

NETHERLANDS. Centraal Planbureau. 1972. Kwantitatieve en financiële effecten van de herstructurering van het wetenschappelijk onderwijs. 's-Gravenhage, 1972. pp. 24. *(Monografiën. No. 13)*

— Russia.

REMENNIKOV (BENIAMIN MATVEEVICH) Vysshaia shkola v sisteme vosproizvodstva rabochei sily v SSSR. Moskva, 1973. pp. 168.

— Underdeveloped areas.

See UNDERDEVELOPED AREAS — Education, Higher.

— United Kingdom.

BEARD (RUTH M.) and others. Objectives in higher education. 2nd ed. London, 1974. pp. 147. *bibliog. (Society for Research into Higher Education. Working Party on Teaching Methods. Publications. 1)*

MURGATROYD (STEPHEN J.) and THOMAS (STEPHEN) M.A. Education beyond school. London, 1974. pp. 16. *(Young Fabian Group. Young Fabian Pamphlets. 39)*

SOCIETY FOR RESEARCH INTO HIGHER EDUCATION. Annual Conference, 9th, 1973. Research into higher education, 1973; papers presented at the... conference...; edited by Colin Flood Page and Jill Gibson.London, 1974. pp. 94. *bibliogs.*

— United States.

EMERGING patterns in American higher education: [including papers from the annual meeting of the American Council on Education, San Francisco, 1964]; edited by Logan Wilson. Washington, [1965] repr. 1966. pp. 292.

CARNEGIE COMMISSION ON HIGHER EDUCATION. Reform on campus: changing students, changing academic programs; a report and recommendations. New York, 1972. pp. 137. *bibliog.*

CARNEGIE COMMISSION ON HIGHER EDUCATION. Governance of higher education: six priority problems: a report and recommendations, etc. New York, 1973. pp. 249.

CARNEGIE COMMISSION ON HIGHER EDUCATION. Higher education: who pays?: who benefits?: who should pay?: a report and recommendations, etc. New York, 1973. pp. 190. *bibliog.*

CARNEGIE COMMISSION ON HIGHER EDUCATION. Opportunities for women in higher education: their current participation, prospects for the future, and recommendations for action: a report and recommendations by the...Commission. New York, 1973. pp. 282. *bibliog.*

CARNEGIE COMMISSION ON HIGHER EDUCATION. Priorities for action: final report...; with technical notes and appendixes. New York, [1973]. pp. 243. *bibliogs.*

CARNEGIE COMMISSION ON HIGHER EDUCATION. The purposes and the performance of higher education in the United States: approaching the year 2000. New York, 1973. pp. 107. *bibliog.*

CARNEGIE COMMISSION ON HIGHER EDUCATION. Toward a learning society: alternative channels to life, work and service; a report and recommendations by the... Commission, etc. New York, 1973. pp. 112. *bibliog.*

LADD (EVERETT CARLL) and LIPSET (SEYMOUR MARTIN) Professors, unions and American higher education;... prepared for the Carnegie Commission on Higher Education. Berkeley, Calif., [1973]. pp. 124. *bibliog.*

BLANSHARD (BRAND) The uses of a liberal education: and other talks to students;... [speeches and essays] edited by Eugene Freeman. London, 1974. pp. 415. *First published in the United States in 1973.*

FOGEL (WALTER A.) and MITCHELL (DANIEL J.B.) Higher education decision making and the labor market. Los Angeles, 1974. pp. 49. *bibliog. (California University. Institute of Industrial Relations. Reprints. No. 239)*

SOCIETY FOR RESEARCH INTO HIGHER EDUCATION. Annual Conference, 9th, 1973. Research into higher education, 1973; papers presented at the... conference...; edited by Colin Flood Page and Jill Gibson.London, 1974. pp. 94. *bibliogs.*

STEINBERG (STEPHEN) The academic melting pot: Catholics and Jews in American higher education;... a report prepared for the Carnegie Commission on Higher Education. New York, [1974]. pp. 183. *bibliog.*

TOURAINE (ALAIN) The academic system in American society;... third of a series of essays sponsored by the Carnegie Commission on Higher Education. New York, [1974]. pp. 319. *bibliog.*

— — Economic aspects.

McMAHON (WALTER W.) Investment in higher education. Lexington, Mass., [1974]. pp. 200. *bibliog.*

— — Finance.

HARTMAN (ROBERT W.) Financing the opportunity to enter the "educated labor market". Washington, 1974. pp. 24. *bibliog. (Brookings Institution. Reprints. 285)*

HARTMAN (ROBERT W.) The rationale for federal support for higher education. Washington, 1974. pp. 21. *bibliog. (Brookings Institution. Reprints. 283)*

— — Pennsylvania.

SACK (SAUL) History of higher education in Pennsylvania. Harrisburg, Pennsylvania Historical and Museum Commission, 1963. 2 vols. *bibliog.*

EDUCATION, HUMANISTIC.

ZAMBIA. Ministry of Development Planning and National Guidance. Annual report. a., 1971(1st)- Lusaka.

BLANSHARD (BRAND) The uses of a liberal education: and other talks to students;... [speeches and essays] edited by Eugene Freeman. London, 1974. pp. 415. *First published in the United States in 1973.*

EDUCATION, PRESCHOOL.

MARGOLIN (EDYTHE) Sociocultural elements in early childhood education. New York, [1974]. pp. 400. *bibliogs.*

— United Kingdom.

BLACKSTONE (TESSA ANN VOSPER) Education and day care for young children in need: the American experience. London, [1973]. pp. 72. *bibliog. (Centre for Studies in Social Policy. Doughty Street Papers. No.1)*

DENBY (MAEVE) Pre-school: the cycle of opportunity?. London, [1973]. pp. 22. *bibliog.*

NATIONAL UNION OF TEACHERS. Working Party on Educational Provision for the Pre-school Child. The provision of pre-school education in England and Wales: a report. London, [1973]. pp. 20.

— — Scotland.

WATT (JOYCE S.) and others. Project four: (an experiment in educational and social action);...edited by D.A. Walker. Dundee, [1973]. pp. 79.

— United States.

BEREITER (CARL EDWARD) and ENGELMANN (SIEGFRIED) Teaching disadvantaged children in the preschool. Englewood Cliffs, N.J., [1966]. pp. 312.

BLACKSTONE (TESSA ANN VOSPER) Education and day care for young children in need: the American experience. London, [1973]. pp. 72. *bibliog. (Centre for Studies in Social Policy. Doughty Street Papers. No.1)*

EDUCATION, SECONDARY.

HEARNDEN (ARTHUR) Paths to university: preparation, assessment, selection. London, 1973. pp. 165. *bibliog. (U.K. Department of Education and Science. Schools Council. Research Studies)*

— Europe.

KING (EDMUND JAMES) and others. Post-compulsory education: a new analysis in western Europe. London, [1974]. pp. 483.

— United Kingdom.

EDUCATION in the middle years; the first report from the Schools Council Middle Years of Schooling Project, Department of Educational Research, University of Lancaster; [by] E.H. Badcock [and others]. London, 1972. pp. 112. *(U.K. Department of Education and Science. Schools Council. Working Papers. 42)*

BUCKS STEP. Our schools at the crossroads: the story of Buckinghamshire's search for a secondary education policy. Chesham, Bucks., [1973]. pp. 56.

BULLIVANT (ANTHONY) Schools for all our children - comprehensives. Billericay, [1973]. pp. 24. *bibliog. (Home and School Council of Great Britain. Working Papers)*

RUBINSTEIN (DAVID) and SIMON (BRIAN) The evolution of the comprehensive school, 1926-1972. 2nd ed. London, 1973. pp. 136. *bibliog.*

SARAN (RENE) Policy-making in secondary education: a case study. Oxford, 1973. pp. 282.

AINSWORTH (MARJORIE E.) and BATTEN (ERIC J.) The effects of environmental factors on secondary educational attainment in Manchester: a Plowden follow-up. London, 1974. pp. 212. *bibliog. (U.K. Department of Education and Science. Schools Council. Research Studies)*

— — Curricula.

TAYLOR (PHILIP HAMPSON) and others. The English sixth form: a case study in curriculum research. London, 1974. pp. 186. *bibliog.*

— — Economic aspects.

BARBER (C. RENATE) Cost effectiveness of education. Oxford, [1967]. pp. 12,2. *(Oxford Polytechnic. Social Science Research Unit. Occasional Papers. 1)*

— — London.

LONDON. Greater London Council. Inner London Education Authority. Transfer Section. Transfer at eleven: a review for the future: a report... presented to the Schools Sub-Committee of the Education Committee on 31 January 1974 suggesting that the gradual reorganization of secondary schools raises the question of whether the reasons for the Authority's transfer arrangements are still valid and setting out possible alternatives as a basis for the widest public discussion. [London, 1974]. pp. 16.

— — Scotland.

MILLAR (HUGH) and WHITE (DAVID) Depute Rector of the Auchenharvie Academy. Comprehensive education - has it changed anything?: a study of secondary schools in Ayrshire. Saltcoats, Ayrshire, [1973]. pp. 28.

— — Curricula.

SCOTLAND. Consultative Committee on the Curriculum. Computers and the Schools Committee. 1972. Computers and the schools; final report; [B.T. Bellis, chairman]. Edinburgh, 1972. pp. 21. *(Scottish Education Department. Curriculum Papers. 11)*

SCOTLAND. Scottish Education Department. 1972. Technical education in secondary schools; [D.G. Robertson, chairman of the Working Party]. Edinburgh, 1972. pp. 43. *(Curriculum Papers. 10)*

— United States.

McDILL (EDWARD L.) and RIGSBY (LEO C.) Structure and process in secondary schools: the academic impact of educational climates. Baltimore, [1973]. pp. 201. *bibliog.*

EDUCATION, URBAN

For works on education in particular cities see EDUCATION — [country] — [city].

— United Kingdom.

PARKINSON (MICHAEL) Politics of urban education; research report...into the formation of education policy in an urban setting. [Liverpool, 1972?]. pp. 57.

— United States.

HUMMEL (RAYMOND C.) and NAGLE (JOHN M.) Urban education in America: problems and prospects. New York, 1973. pp. 298.

LA NOUE (GEORGE R.) and SMITH (BRUCE L.R.) The politics of school decentralization. Lexington, Mass., [1973]. pp. 284.

RIST (RAY C.) The urban school: a factory for failure; a study of education in American society. Cambridge, Mass., [1973]. pp. 265. *bibliog.*

EDUCATION AND STATE.

UNITED NATIONS EDUCATIONAL, SCIENTIFIC AND CULTURAL ORGANIZATION. Educational Studies and Documents. New Series. Paris, 1971 in progress.

CONFERENCE ON POLICIES FOR EDUCATIONAL GROWTH, PARIS, 1970. Conference...[held in] Paris, 3rd-5th June, 1970; general report; educational policies for the 1970's. Paris, Organisation for Economic Co-operation and Developement, 1971. pp. 157.

— Australia.

ALBINSKI (HENRY STEPHEN) The Australian Labor Party and the aid to parochial schools controversy. University Park, Penn., 1966. pp. 55. *(Pennsylvania State University. Penn State Studies. No. 19)*

— Germany.

GRUENTHAL (GUENTHER) Reichsschulgesetz und Zentrumspartei in der Weimarer Republik. Düsseldorf, [1968]. pp. 324. *bibliog. (Germany(Bundesrepublik). Kommission für Geschichte des Parlamentarismus und der Politischen Parteien. Beiträge zur Geschichte des Parlamentarismus und der Politischen Parteien. Band 39)*

— Pakistan.

PAKISTAN. Department of Films and Publications. 1972. Education for the masses: the new policy. Karachi, 1972]. pp. 45.

— Portugal.

PORTUGAL. Presidência do Conselho. 1954. 25 anos de administração publica: Ministerio da Educação Nacional. Lisboa, 1954. pp. 211.

— South Africa.

DAVIS (R. HUNT) Bantu education and the education of Africans in South Africa. Athens, Ohio, [1972]. fo. 53. *(Ohio University. Center for International Studies. Papers in International Studies. Africa Series. No.14)*

— United Kingdom.

FOWLER (GERALD) and others, eds. Decision-making in British education. London, 1973. pp. 486.

SUTHERLAND (GILLIAN) Policy-making in elementary education, 1870-1895. Oxford, 1973. pp. 391. *bibliog.*

EDUCATION OF ADULTS.

INTERNATIONAL LABOUR CONFERENCE. 58th Session. Reports. 6. Paid educational leave: sixth item on the agenda. Geneva, 1972-73. 2 pts.

INTERNATIONAL LABOUR CONFERENCE. 59th Session. Reports. 4. Paid educational leave: fourth item on the agenda. Geneva, 1973-74. 2 pts.

— Denmark.

[DENMARK. Undervisningsministeriet. 1970]. The organization, administration and financing of adult education. [Copenhagen], 1970. fo. 10.

— France.

MEIGNANT (ALAIN) L'intervention sociopédagogique dans les organisations industrielles: contribution à la recherche et à l'action dans le domaine de l'éducation des adultes en milieu industriel, à propos de deux expériences. Paris, [1972]. pp. 227. *bibliog.*

— India.

KAKKAR (N.K.) Workers' education in India. New Delhi, 1973. pp. 404. *bibliog.*

— Norway.

NORWAY. Voksenopplaeringsrådet. 1972. Structure and organization of adult education in Norway. Oslo, 1972. pp. 102.

— Tanzania.

HALL (BUDD L.) Wakati wa Furaha: an evaluation of a radio study group campaign. Uppsala, 1973. pp. 47. *(Nordiska Afrikainstitutet. Research Reports. No. 13)*

— United Kingdom.

COATES (KEN) and SILBURN (RICHARD) Adult education and social research: a case paper. Nottingham, 1968. pp. 22. *bibliog. (Nottingham. University. Department of Adult Education. Occasional Papers in Social Research. No.2)*

RUDDOCK (RALPH) Sociological perspectives on adult education. Manchester, [1972]. pp. 64. *(Manchester. University. Department of Adult Education. Manchester Monographs. 2)*

WORKING PARTY ON YOUTH AND ADULT SERVICES IN INNER LONDON. Report: (a chance to choose); [the Earl of Longford, chairman]. London, Inner London Education Authority, [1972]. pp. 97.

LEGGE (CHARLES DEREK) compiler. Register of research in progress in adult education, 1973: a list of ongoing research in the United Kingdom concerned with the education of adults: compiled...on behalf of the Standing Conference on University Teaching and Research in the Education of Adults (SCUTREA). [Manchester, 1973]. pp. 107.

— — Bibliography.

STYLER (WILLIAM EDWARD) compiler. A bibliographical guide to adult education in rural areas 1918-1972.Hull, 1973. pp. 50.

— United States.

ASPEN WORKSHOP CONFERENCE ON THE CABLE AND CONTINUING EDUCATION, 1973. Aspen notebook: cable and continuing education: ([edited by] Richard Adler [and] Walter S. Baer). New York, 1973. pp. 193. *bibliog.*

CARNEGIE COMMISSION ON HIGHER EDUCATION. Toward a learning society: alternative channels to life, work and service; a report and recommendations by the... Commission, etc. New York, 1973. pp. 112. *bibliog.*

HESBURGH (THEODORE M.) and others. Patterns for lifelong learning. San Francisco, 1973. pp. 135. *bibliog.*

EDUCATION OF CHILDREN.

EDUCATION OF CHILDREN.

GRANT (BEATRICE) Sketches of intellectual education, and hints on domestic economy, addressed to inexperienced mothers: with an appendix containing an essay on the instruction of the poor. Inverness, 1812. 2 vols. *Privately printed.*

HOLT (JOHN CALDWELL) How children learn; [first published in the United States in 1967]. Harmondsworth, 1970 repr. 1973. pp. 173.

EDUCATION OF PRISONERS.

TITOV (NIKOLAI IVANOVICH) and ASATRIAN (GAGIK ZAVENOVICH) Vospitatel'noe vozdeistvie ugolovnogo nakazaniia. Erevan, 1973. pp. 103.

EDUCATION OF WOMEN.

MICHAELS (RUTH) New opportunities for women: a survey of mature women students. Hatfield, 1973. pp. 36. *(Hatfield Polytechnic. Occasional Papers. No.1)*

— France.

FRANCE. Comité du Travail Féminin. 1972. Formation professionnelle: rapport de la Commission. [Paris], 1972. fo. 51.

— United States.

CARNEGIE COMMISSION ON HIGHER EDUCATION. Opportunities for women in higher education: their current participation, prospects for the future, and recommendations for action: a report and recommendations by the...Commission. New York, 1973. pp. 282. *bibliog.*

SKLAR (KATHRYN KISH) Catherine Beecher: a study in American domesticity. New Haven, Conn., 1973. pp. 356. *bibliog.*

WOMEN in higher education: [including papers presented at the 55th Annual Meeting of the American Council on Education]; edited by W. Todd Furniss [and] Patricia Albjerg Graham. Washington, D.C., [1974]. pp. 336.

EDUCATIONAL ACCOUNTABILITY.

MEHRENS (WILLIAM A.) and LEHMANN (IRVIN J.) Measurement and evaluation in education and psychology. New York, [1973]. pp. 718. *bibliogs.*

EDUCATIONAL ANTHROPOLOGY.

BREMBECK (COLE SPEICHER) and HILL (WALKER H.) eds. Cultural challenges to education: the influence of cultural factors in school learning. Lexington, Mass., [1973]. pp. 160.

OGBU (JOHN U.) The next generation: an ethnography of education in an urban neighborhood. New York, 1974. pp. 275. *bibliog.*

EDUCATIONAL ASSISTANCE.

INTERNATIONAL INSTITUTE FOR EDUCATIONAL PLANNING. Fundamentals of Educational Planning . Paris, Unesco, 1970 in progress.

EDUCATIONAL ASSISTANCE, AUSTRALIAN

— Asia, Southeast.

HODGKIN (MARY C.) The innovators: the role of foreign trained persons in Southeast Asia. Sydney, 1972. pp. 118. *bibliog.*

EDUCATIONAL BROADCASTING.

For related headings see RADIO IN EDUCATION ; TELEVISION IN EDUCATION.

EDUCATIONAL EQUALIZATION.

BOUDON (RAYMOND) L'inégalité des chances: la mobilité sociale dans les sociétés industrielles. Paris, [1973]. pp. 237. *bibliog.*

BOUDON (RAYMOND) Education, opportunity, and social inequality: changing prospects in western society. New York, [1974]. pp. 220. *bibliog.*

— United States.

HOGAN (JOHN C.) The schools, the courts and the public interest. Lexington, Mass., [1974]. pp. 262. *bibliog.*

EDUCATIONAL INNOVATIONS.

CENTRE FOR EDUCATIONAL RESEARCH AND INNOVATION. Case Studies of Educational Innovation. Paris, 1973. 4 vols. (in 2).

— Africa.

INNOVATIONS dans l'enseignement en Afrique: orientations et administration; (documents présentés lors d'un colloque... Addis-Abéba...1971); rédigé par J.A. Ponsioen. La Haye, [1973]. pp. 312.

— Asia, Southeast.

HODGKIN (MARY C.) The innovators: the role of foreign trained persons in Southeast Asia. Sydney, 1972. pp. 118. *bibliog.*

— Tanzania.

LEMA (A.A.) National attitude and educational innovation: a case study of change of attitude of the Tanzanian society towards education for self-reliance. Vienna, [1973]. pp. 34. *(Wiener Institut für Entwicklungsfragen. Occasional Papers. 73/8)*

EDUCATIONAL LAW AND LEGISLATION

— Germany.

GRUENTHAL (GUENTHER) Reichsschulgesetz und Zentrumspartei in der Weimarer Republik. Düsseldorf, [1968]. pp. 324. *bibliog. (Germany(Bundesrepublik). Kommission für Geschichte des Parlamentarismus und der Politischen Parteien. Beiträge zur Geschichte des Parlamentarismus und der Politischen Parteien. Band 39)*

— United States.

HOGAN (JOHN C.) The schools, the courts and the public interest. Lexington, Mass., [1974]. pp. 262. *bibliog.*

EDUCATIONAL PLANNING.

INTERNATIONAL INSTITUTE FOR EDUCATIONAL PLANNING. Fundamentals of Educational Planning . Paris, Unesco, 1970 in progress.

UNITED NATIONS EDUCATIONAL, SCIENTIFIC AND CULTURAL ORGANIZATION. Educational Studies and Documents. New Series . Paris, 1971 in progress.

CONFERENCE ON POLICIES FOR EDUCATIONAL GROWTH, PARIS, 1970. Conference...[held in] Paris, 3rd-5th June, 1970; general report; educational policies for the 1970's. Paris, Organisation for Economic Co-operation and Developement, 1971. pp. 157.

MIKLOS (E.) and others. Perspectives on educational planning. [Edmonton, Human Resources Research Council, 1972]. pp. 175. *bibliogs.*

LONG-RANGE policy planning in education. Paris, Organisation for Economic Cooperation Developement, 1973. pp. 391.

— European Economic Community countries.

EUROPEAN COMMUNITIES. Commission. 1973. For a Community policy on education. [Brussels], 1973. pp. 61. *(Bulletin of the European Communities. Supplements. [1973/10])*

— Germany.

ORGANISATION FOR ECONOMIC CO-OPERATION AND DEVELOPMENT. Reviews of National Policies for Education. Germany. Paris, 1972. pp. 150.

EDUCATIONAL PSYCHOLOGY.

KEEVES (JOHN P.) Educational environment and student achievement: a multivariate study of the contributions of the home, the school and the peer group to change in mathematics and science performance during the first year at secondary school. Stockholm, [1972]. pp. 311. *bibliog. (Stockholms Universitet. Acta Universitatis Stockholmiensis. Stockholm Studies in Educational Psychology. 20)*

MORRISON (ARNOLD) and McINTYRE (DONALD) Teachers and teaching. 2nd ed. Harmondsworth, 1973. pp. 246. *bibliog.*

EDUCATIONAL RESEARCH.

NITSCH (WOLFGANG) and WELLER (WALTER) Social science research on higher education and universities...; under the direction of Dietrich Goldschmidt. The Hague, 1970 in progress. *bibliog. (International Committee for Social Science Information and Documentation. Confluence. vols. 9, etc.)*

CENTRE FOR EDUCATIONAL RESEARCH AND INNOVATION. Case Studies of Educational Innovation. Paris, 1973. 4 vols. (in 2).

CENTRE FOR EDUCATIONAL RESEARCH AND INNOVATION. Case Studies of Educational Innovation . Paris, 1973. 4 vols.(in 2).

— Bibliography.

NITSCH (WOLFGANG) and WELLER (WALTER) Social science research on higher education and universities...; under the direction of Dietrich Goldschmidt. The Hague, 1970 in progress. *bibliog. (International Committee for Social Science Information and Documentation. Confluence. vols. 9, etc.)*

— United Kingdom.

LEGGE (CHARLES DEREK) compiler. Register of research in progress in adult education, 1973: a list of ongoing research in the United Kingdom concerned with the education of adults: compiled...on behalf of the Standing Conference on University Teaching and Research in the Education of Adults (SCUTREA). [Manchester, 1973]. pp. 107.

WARD (ARTHUR VERNON) Resources for educational research and development. Windsor, Berks., 1973. pp. 131. *bibliog.*

TAYLOR (PHILIP HAMPSON) and others. The English sixth form: a case study in curriculum research. London, 1974. pp. 186. *bibliog.*

EDUCATIONAL SOCIOLOGY.

BARBAGLI (MARZIO) and DEI (MARCELLO) Le vestali della classe media: ricerca sociologica sugli insegnanti. Bologna, 1969 repr. 1972. pp. 378. *(Istituto "Carlo Cattaneo". Studi e Ricerche. 1)*

INTERNATIONAL INSTITUTE FOR EDUCATIONAL PLANNING. Fundamentals of Educational Planning . Paris, Unesco, 1970 in progress.

OPEN UNIVERSITY. Faculty of Educational Studies. School and Society Course Team. School and society: a sociological reader. London, 1971. pp. 240. *bibliogs.*

MIDWINTER (ERIC CLARE) ed. Projections: an educational priority area at work. London, [1972]. pp. 111.

RUDDOCK (RALPH) Sociological perspectives on adult education. Manchester, [1972]. pp. 64. *(Manchester. University. Department of Adult Education. Manchester Monographs. 2)*

BOUDON (RAYMOND) L'inégalité des chances: la mobilité sociale dans les sociétés industrielles. Paris, [1973]. pp. 237. *bibliog.*

ORTLIEB (HEINZ DIETRICH) ed. Destruktive Zeitzünder: asoziale Tendenzen in unserer Bildungsreform; ... mit weiteren Beiträgen von Max Liedtke [and others]. Hamburg, 1973. pp. 54. *(Hamburg, Hamburgisches Welt-Wirtschafts-Archiv. Veröffentlichungen)*

PERSPECTIVES on inequality: a reassessment of the effect of family and schooling in America. Cambridge, Mass., [1973]. pp. 128. *(Harvard Educational Review. Reprint Series. No. 8)*

POUNDS (RALPH LINNAEUS) and BRYNER (JAMES R.) The school in American society. 3rd ed. New York, [1973]. pp. 618. *bibliog.*

SAUVY (ALFRED) and others. Access to education: new possibilities. The Hague, 1973. pp. 157. *(European Cultural Foundation. Plan Europe 2000. Project 1, vol. 3)*

SIEBER (SAM D.) and WILDER (DAVID E.) eds. The school in society: studies in the sociology of education. New York, [1973]. pp. 440. *bibliogs.*

SUGARMAN (BARRY) The school and moral development. London, 1973. pp. 285. *bibliogs.*

AINSWORTH (MARJORIE E.) and BATTEN (ERIC J.) The effects of environmental factors on secondary educational attainment in Manchester: a Plowden follow-up. London, 1974. pp. 212. *bibliog.* *(U.K. Department of Education and Science. Schools Council. Research Studies)*

BANKS (OLIVE LUCY) Sociology and education: some reflections on the sociologist's role; an inaugural lecture delivered in the University of Leicester, 5 February 1974. Leicester, 1974. pp. 24.

BOUDON (RAYMOND) Education, opportunity, and social inequality: changing prospects in western society. New York, [1974]. pp. 220. *bibliog.*

CORWIN (RONALD G.) Education in crisis: a sociological analysis of schools and universities in transition. New York, [1974]. pp. 380.

EGGLESTON (S. JOHN) ed. Contemporary research in the sociology of education: (a selection of contemporary research papers together with some of the formative writings of the recent past). [London, 1974]. pp. 388. *bibliogs.*

EMMERIJ (LOUIS) Can the school build a new social order?. Amsterdam, 1974. pp. 220. *bibliog.*

LEVITAS (MAURICE) Marxist perspectives in the sociology of education. London, 1974. pp. 208. *bibliog.*

MARGOLIN (EDYTHE) Sociocultural elements in early childhood education. New York, [1974]. pp. 400. *bibliogs.*

OGBU (JOHN U.) The next generation: an ethnography of education in an urban neighborhood. New York, 1974. pp. 275. *bibliog.*

The TEACHER in a changing society; edited by John D. Turner [and] J. Rushton. Manchester, [1974]. pp. 98. *bibliog.*

EDUCATIONAL STATISTICS.

POPHAM (W. JAMES) and SIROTNIK (KENNETH A.) Educational statistics: use and interpretation. 2nd ed. New York, [1973]. pp. 413. *bibliogs.*

EDUCATIONAL TESTS AND MEASUREMENTS.

MEHRENS (WILLIAM A.) and LEHMANN (IRVIN J.) Measurement and evaluation in education and psychology. New York, [1973]. pp. 718. *bibliogs.*

MOORE (BRYAN McASKIE) and others Data collection. Bletchley, 1973. pp. 148. *bibliogs.* *(Open University. Educational Studies: a third level course: methods of educational enquiry. Block 3)*

EFERDING

— Gilds.

UHL (HARALD) Handwerk und Zünfte in Eferding: Materialien zum grundherrschaftlichen Zunfttypus. Wien, 1973. pp. 159. *bibliog.* *(Oesterreichische Akademie der Wissenschaften. Philosophisch-Historische Klasse. Kommission für die Savigny-Stiftung. Fontes Rerum Austriacarum. 3.Abteilung. Fontes Iuris. 3.Band)*

EFFICIENCY, INDUSTRIAL.

U.K. National Board for Prices and Incomes. NBPI Guides. 4. Efficiency and productivity. London, [1969]. pp. 13. *bibliog.*

FEODORITOV (VOLODAR IAKOVLEVICH) Problemy povysheniia ekonomicheskoi effektivnosti proizvodstva. Leningrad, 1970. pp. 192. *bibliog.*

LIBERMAN (EVSEI GRIGOR'EVICH) Ekonomicheskie metody povysheniia effektivnosti obshchestvennogo proizvodstva. Moskva, 1970. pp. 175.

CHERNIAVSKII (VASILII OSIPOVICH) Effektivnost' proizvodstva i optimal'nost' planirovaniia. Moskva, 1973. pp. 191.

FEDORENKO (NIKOLAI PROKOF'EVICH) and BUNICH (PAVEL GRIGOR'EVICH) eds. Mekhanizm ekonomicheskogo stimulirovaniia pri sotsializme: opyt i problemy. Moskva, 1973. pp. 255.

MALYSHEV (PAVEL ALEKSEEVICH) and SHILIN (IVAN GRIGOR'EVICH) Kriterii effektivnosti sotsialisticheskogo vosproizvodstva: sotsial'no-ekonomicheskii aspekt. Moskva, 1973. pp. 382.

OKTIABR'SKII (PAVEL IAKOVLEVICH) Sushchnost' i kriterii ekonomicheskoi effektivnosti obshchestvennogo proizvodstva. Leningrad, 1973. pp. 54. *bibliog.*

SELEZNEV (ALEKSANDR ZAKHAROVICH) Stimulirovanie effektivnosti proizvodstva i pribyl'. Moskva, 1973. pp. 159.

VYBORNOV (VALENTIN IVANOVICH) and MAVRISHCHEV (VIKTOR SEMENOVICH) Ekonomicheskaia effektivnost' promyshlennogo proizvodstva: metody izmereniia i puti povysheniia. Minsk, 1973. pp. 247. *bibliog.*

GORBUNOV (EDUARD PETROVICH) Struktura i effektivnost' obshchestvennogo proizvodstva. Moskva, 1974. pp. 199.

EGG TRADE

— European Economic Community countries.

ECONOMIC DEVELOPMENT COMMITTEE FOR THE AGRICULTURAL INDUSTRY. Common Market Sub-Committee. UK farming and the Common Market: eggs; a report. London, National Economic Development Office, 1973. pp. 42.

— United Kingdom.

ECONOMIC DEVELOPMENT COMMITTEE FOR THE AGRICULTURAL INDUSTRY. Common Market Sub-Committee. UK farming and the Common Market: eggs; a report. London, National Economic Development Office, 1973. pp. 42.

EGOISM.

LE DANTEC (FELIX) L'égoïsme: seule base de toute société; étude des déformations résultant de la vie en commun. Paris, 1912. pp. 327.

EGYPT

— History — 1956, Intervention.

BOWIE (ROBERT RICHARDSON) Suez 1956. London, 1974. pp. 148. *(American Society of International Law. International Crises and the Role of Law)*

— Population.

OMRAN (ABDEL RAHIM) ed. Egypt: population problems and prospects. Chapel Hill, 1973. pp. 448. *bibliog.*

— Public works.

INTERNATIONAL LABOUR OFFICE. Development Programme: Technical Assistance Sector. [United Arab Republic] R.11. Report to the government of the United Arab Republic on the development of labour-intensive methods in public works. (ILO/AP/UAR/R.11). Geneva, 1971. pp. 66.

— Religion.

GILSENAN (MICHAEL) Saint and Sufi in modern Egypt: an essay in the sociology of religion. Oxford, 1973. pp. 248. *bibliog.*

— Rural conditions.

FAKHOURI (HANI) Kafr El-Elow: an Egyptian village in transition. New York, 1972. pp. 134. *bibliog.*

EIGHT HOUR MOVEMENT.

BAUER (STEPHAN) Der Weg zum Achtstundentag. Zürich, 1919. pp. 31.

EIRIK RAUDES LAND.

BLOM (IDA) Kampen om Eirik Raudes land: pressgruppepolitikk i grønlandsspørsmålet, 1921-1931. Oslo, 1973. pp. 439. *bibliog.*

EL BIERZO, SPAIN

— Economic conditions.

MANTERO Y GARCIA-LORENZANA (MARIA DEL CARMEN) Analisis economico de la region de El Bierzo. Leon, 1972. pp. 286. *bibliog.*

ELDER DEMPSTER LINES.

DAVIES (P.N.) The trade makers: Elder Dempster in West Africa, 1852-1972. London, 1973. pp. 526. *bibliog.*

ELECTION LAW

— Canada — Quebec.

BERNARD (ANDRE) and LAFORTE (DENIS) La législation électorale au Québec, 1790-1967. Montréal, 1969. pp. 197. *bibliog.*

— Germany.

BREDTHAUER (RUEDIGER) Das Wahlsystem als Objekt von Politik und Wissenschaft: die Wahlsystemdiskussion in der BRD 1967/68, etc. Meisenheim am Glan, 1973. pp. 173. *bibliog.*

MISCH (AXEL) Das Wahlsystem zwischen Theorie and Taktik: zur Frage von Mehrheitswahl und Verhältniswahl in der Programmatik der Sozialdemokratie bis 1933. Berlin, [1974]. pp. 290. *bibliog.*

— Netherlands.

NETHERLANDS. Ministerie van Binnenlandse Zaken. Naar een nieuwe grondwet? Documentatiereeks. Deel 3. Adviezen van politieke en maatschappelijke organen over vernieuwing van grondwet en kieswet (juni 1968-juli 1969); onder redactie van H.Th.J.F. van Maarseveen met medewerking van J.L. Bouwens. 's-Gravenhage, 1969. pp. 198.

— Tasmania.

TASMANIA. Parliament. Standing Committee on Subordinate Legislation. 1972. Report on Local Government (Electoral) Regulations 1964 (S.R. 1964 No. 22); [L.H. Carins, chairman]. in TASMANIA. Parliament. Journals and Printed Papers. 1972, no. 2.

ELECTIONS.

MACKIE (THOMAS T.) and ROSE (RICHARD) The international almanac of electoral history. London, 1974. pp. 434. *bibliogs.*

— America, Latin.

STATISTICAL ABSTRACT OF LATIN AMERICA. Supplement Series. 2. Latin American political statistics; [edited by] Kenneth Ruddle and Philip Gillette. Los Angeles, 1972. pp. 121.

— Argentine Republic.

CANTON (DARIO) Elecciones y partidos politicos en la Argentina: historia, interpretacion y balance, 1910-1966. Buenos Aires, 1973. pp. 277.

ELECTIONS (Cont.)

— Canada — Toronto.

CLARKSON (STEPHEN) City lib: parties and reform. Toronto, 1972. pp. 227.

— Colombia.

SEPULVEDA NIÑO (SATURNINO) Las elites colombianas en crisis: de partidos policlasistas a partidos monoclasistas. [Bogota], 1970. pp. 196. *bibliog.*

— France.

HOUDAYER (RAYMOND) Les élections et l'esprit public dans le département de la Sarthe de 1789 au 18 brumaire an VIII; d'après les documents des Archives Nationales. Le Mans, 1911. pp. 72.

BOBROWSKI (EDOUARD) Aux urnes, citoyens...: [municipal elections, Arras, 1971]. Paris, [1973]. pp. 259.

DUIGOU (DANIEL) Guide des élections; (avec la collaboration de Jean- François Thoraval). Paris, [1973]. pp. 243.

— Germany.

JUETTNER (ALFRED) Wahl und wählen: Bedeutung, Funktion und Technik der Wahl im parlamentarisch-demokratischen Staat. München, [1964]. pp. 88. *(Bavaria. Landeszentrale für Heimatdienst. Arbeitshefte. 11)*

LAVIES (RALF RAINER) Nichtwählen als Kategorie des Wahlverhaltens: empirische Untersuchung zur Wahlenthaltung in historischer, politischer und statistischer Sicht. Düsseldorf, [1973]. pp. 194. *bibliog. (Germany (Bundesrepublik Deutschland). Kommission für Geschichte des Parlamentarismus und der Politischen Parteien. Beiträge zur Geschichte des Parlamentarismus und der Politischen Parteien. Band 48)*

GERMANY (BUNDESREPUBLIK). Deutscher Bundestag. Wissenschaftliche Dienste. 1974. Materialien zu den Landtags- und Kommunalwahlen im Jahre 1974.Bonn, 1974. pp. 60. *(Materialien. 36)*

— — Baden—Württemberg.

WAHLKAMPF als Ritual?: Studien zur Bundestagswahl von 1969 im Wahlkreis Heidelberg-Mannheim/Land; ([by] Rüdiger Andel [and others; edited by] Peter Haungs). Meisenheim am Glan, 1974. pp. 336.

— — Bavaria.

THRAENHARDT (DIETRICH) Wahlen und politische Strukturen in Bayern, 1848-1953: historisch-soziologische Untersuchungen zum Entstehen und zur Neuerrichtung eines Parteiensystems. Düsseldorf, 1973. pp. 360. *bibliog. (Germany (Bundesrepublik). Kommission für Geschichte des Parlamentarismus und der Politischen Parteien. Beiträge zur Geschichte des Parlamentarismus und der Politischen Parteien. Band 51)*

— — North Rhine—Westphalia.

KUEHR (HERBERT) Parteien und Wahlen im Stadt- und Landkreis Essen in der Zeit der Weimarer Republik, etc. Düsseldorf, [1973]. pp. 309. *bibliog. (Germany (Bundesrepublik). Kommission für Geschichte des Parlamentarismus und der Politischen Parteien. Beiträge zur Geschichte des Parlamentarismus und der Politischen Parteien. Band 49)*

PESCHKE (KLAUS) Die Bedeutung der liberalen Parteien und der Sozialdemokratie für das politische Leben im Wahlkreis Altena-Iserlohn von der Reichsgründung 1871 bis zum Jahre 1890. [Altena, 1973]. pp. 150. *bibliog. (Verein Freunde der Burg Altena. Altenaer Beiträge. Neue Folge. Band 8)*

— — Saarland.

SAARBRUECKEN. Universität. Annales Universitatis Saraviensis. Rechts- und Wirtschaftswissenschaftliche Abteilung. Band 71. Faktoren der Wahlentscheidung: eine wahlsoziologische Analyse am Beispiel der saarländischen Landtagswahl 1970... ; von Jürgen W. Falter. Köln, 1973. pp. 256. *bibliog.*

— India.

INDIA. Ministry of Information and Broadcasting. Directorate of Advertising and Visual Publicity. 1967. Fourth general elections: an analysis. [New Delhi, 1967]. pp. 297. *2 maps in end pocket.*

INDIA. Election Commission. 1973. Report on the fifth general elections in India, 1971-72: narrative and reflective part. [Delhi, 1973]. pp. 245.

— — Bengal, West.

ASSOCIATION OF INDIAN COMMUNISTS OF GREAT BRITAIN. On fascist terror in West Bengal; [published on behalf of the Association of Indian Communists of Great Britain]. Coventry, 1972. pp. 11.

— — Rajasthan.

BHAMBHRI (CHANDRA PRAKASH) and VERMA (P.S.) The urban voter: municipal elections in Rajasthan: an empirical study. Delhi, 1973. pp. 222.

VARMA (SHANTI PRASAD) and NARAIN (IQBAL) Voting behaviour in a changing society: a case study of the fourth general election in Rajasthan. Delhi, 1973. pp. 385.

— Israel.

ARIAN (ALAN) ed. The elections in Israel, 1969. Jerusalem, 1972. pp. 311.

— Italy.

GHINI (CELSO) Le elezioni in Italia, 1946-1968. Milano, 1968. pp. 372.

ULLRICH (HARTMUT) Le elezioni del 1913 a Roma: i liberali fra massoneria e Vaticano. Milano, 1972. pp. 119. *(Nuova Rivista Storica. Biblioteca. N. 32)*

— Japan.

FRANCE. Direction de la Documentation. La Documentation Française. Notes et Etudes Documentaires. No. 2,661. L'évolution électorale du Japon depuis la dernière guerre (1945-1959); (texte établi par la Maison franco-japonaise de Tokio, sur la base des études publiées par Hirotatsu Fujiwara et avec la collaboration de cet auteur). Paris, 1960. pp. 46.

— Mexico.

MICHAELS (ALBERT L.) The Mexican election of 1940. Buffalo, N.Y., 1971. fo. 53. *(New York State University. Council on International Studies. Special Studies. No. 5)*

— Norway.

NORWAY. Lokalforvaltningsutvalget. 1972. Valg av fylkesting. Oslo, 1972. pp. 120. *(Norway. Norges Offentlige Utredninger. 1972.13)*

— Papua New Guinea.

EPSTEIN (ARNOLD LEONARD) and others, eds. The politics of dependence: Papua New Guinea 1968. Canberra, 1971. pp. 398. *bibliog.*

— Philippine Islands.

PHILIPPINE ISLANDS. Commission on Elections. 1967. Report... to the President... and the Congress on the manner the elections were held on November 9, 1965. Manila, 1967. pp. 315.

PHILIPPINE ISLANDS. Commission on Elections. 1971. Report...to the President of the Philippines and the Congress on the manner the election for delegates to the Constitutional Convention was held on November 10,1970. Manila, 1971. pp. 441.

PHILIPPINE ISLANDS. Commission on Elections. 1973. Report...to the President of the Philippines and the Congress on the manner the election was held on November 8, 1971. Manila, 1973. pp. 802.

— Senegal.

SENEGAL. Statutes, etc. 1852-1957. Elections municipales: recueil des textes applicables au 15 octobre 1956; (with Rectifications, etc.). Saint-Louis, [1957]. pp. 98.

— Sierra Leone.

SIERRA LEONE. Dove-Edwin Commission of Inquiry into the Conduct of the 1967 General Elections in Sierra Leone. 1967. Report...; and the government statement thereon; [G.F.Dove- Edwin, chairman]. [Freetown, 1967]. pp. 26.

— Sweden.

SWEDEN. Civildepartementet. Kommunalvalskommittén. 1971. Kommunala val. Stockholm, 1971. pp. 109. *(Sweden. Statens Offentliga Utredningar. 1971.4)*

SWEDEN. Statistiska Centralbyrån. 1974. Allmänna valen 1973, etc. Stockholm, 1974. 2 pts. (in 1 vol.). *(Sveriges Officiella Statistik)*

— United States.

POTTER (DAVID MORRIS) The south and the concurrent majority; edited by Don E. Fehrenbacher and Carl N. Degler. Baton Rouge, [1972]. pp. 89. *(Louisiana State University. Walter Lynwood Fleming Lectures in Southern History. 1968)*

HAWLEY (WILLIS D.) Nonpartisan elections and the case for party politics. New York, [1973]. pp. 202. *bibliog.*

SILBEY (JOEL HENRY) ed. Political ideology and voting behavior in the age of Jackson. Englewood Cliffs, [1973]. pp. 189. *bibliog.*

— — Campaign funds.

CADDY (DOUGLAS) The hundred million dollar payoff. New Rochelle, N.Y., [1974]. pp. 448.

NICHOLS (DAVID) Financing elections: the politics of an American ruling class. New York, 1974. pp. 191.

— — Maryland.

EVITTS (WILLIAM J.) A matter of allegiances: Maryland from 1850 to 1861. Baltimore, [1974]. pp. 212. *bibliog. (Johns Hopkins University. Studies in Historical and Political Science. Series 92. [No.] 1)*

— Venezuela.

VENEZUELA. Consejo Supremo Electoral. Division de Registro Electoral y Estadistica. 1964. Resultado de las votaciones efectuadas el 1o. de Diciembre de 1963. [Caracas: 1964?]. 1 vol. (unpaged).

VENEZUELA. Consejo Supremo Electoral. 1970. Datos estadisticos de las votaciones de 1968. Caracas, 1970. pp. 203. *(Serie Estadistica. 2)*

VENEZUELA. Consejo Supremo Electoral. 1970. Votacion obtenida por partidos a nivel de municipios y parroquias (en 1968). Caracas, 1970. 1 vol. (unpaged). *(Serie Estadistica. No. 3)*

ELECTRIC ENGINEERING

— United Kingdom.

NATIONAL ECONOMIC DEVELOPMENT OFFICE. Industrial review to 1977: electrical engineering. London, 1974. pp. 35.

ELECTRIC INDUSTRIES

— Germany.

CZADA (PETER) Die Berliner Elektroindustrie in der Weimarer Zeit: eine regionalstatistisch-wirtschaftshistorische Untersuchung. Berlin, 1969. pp. 367. *bibliog. (Berlin. Freie Universität. Friedrich-Meinecke- Institut. Historische Kommission zu Berlin. Einzelveröffentlichungen. Band 4)*

— Russia — Soviet Central Asia.

SAVRANCHUK (PETR TERENT'EVICH) and SHELUKHIN (KONSTANTIN IVANOVICH) Razvitie elektrotekhnicheskoi promyshlennosti v respublikakh Srednei Azii. Frunze, 1966. pp. 35.

ELECTRIC POWER PLANTS

— Environmental aspects.

SCOTT (DAVID LOGAN) Pollution in the electric power industry: its control and costs. Lexington, Mass., [1973]. pp. 104. *bibliog.*

— United States.

BALL (R.H.) and others. California's electricity quandary, 2: planning for power plant siting; prepared for the California State Assembly. Santa Monica, 1972. pp. 98. *bibliog. (Rand Corporation. [Rand Reports]. 1115)*

ELECTRICITY IN TRANSPORTATION.

POLE (NICHOLAS) Oil and the future of personal mobility. Cambridge, 1973. pp. 64.

ELECTRICITY SUPPLY

— Australia — Canberra.

HAWKINS (ROBERT G.) The retail electricity market: a study of the residential and commercial sectors in New South Wales and the Australian Capital Territory. Canberra, 1974. fo.40. *bibliog. (Australian National University. Research School of Social Sciences. Department of Economics. Working Papers in Economics and Econometrics. No. 21)*

— — New South Wales

HAWKINS (ROBERT G.) The retail electricity market: a study of the residential and commercial sectors in New South Wales and the Australian Capital Territory. Canberra, 1974. fo.40. *bibliog. (Australian National University. Research School of Social Sciences. Department of Economics. Working Papers in Economics and Econometrics. No. 21)*

— Austria — Statistics.

AUSTRIA. Bundesministerium für Verkehr. Sektion Elektrizitätswirtschaft. 1971-73. Bestandsstatistik der Unternehmen und Kraftwerke in Österreich, Stichtag: 1 Jänner 1969. [Vienna, 1971-73]. 2 vols.(in 1). *(Bundesstatistik der Österreichischen Elektrizitätswirtschaft)*

— Belgium.

BELGIUM. Administration de l'Energie. 1973. Organisation du secteur de l'énergie électrique en Belgique.Bruxelles, 1973. pp. 29, 33. *In French and Flemish.*

— British Virgin Islands.

BRITISH VIRGIN ISLANDS. Electricity Board. Report for the year. a., 1972- Tortola.

— Ecuador.

ECUADOR. Junta Nacional de Planificacion y Coordinacion Economica. 1964. Plan general de desarrollo economico y social; version preliminar. Tomo 4. Las obras y servicios publicos economicos. Libro segundo. Energia: [programa de electrificacion]. Quito, [1964?]. pp. 208, 12 maps.

— France.

FRANCE. Electricité de France. Résultats techniques d'exploitation. a., 1973- Paris.

— Norway.

VOGT (JOHAN) Elektrisitetslandet Norge: fra norsk vassdrags- og elektrisitetsvesens historie. Oslo, 1971. pp. 216.

— Russia.

ELEKTROENERGETICHESKAIA baza ekonomicheskikh raionov SSSR. Moskva, 1974. pp. 229. *bibliog.*

— — Mathematical models.

METODY otsenki razvitiia elektroenergetiki. Moskva, 1973. pp. 155.

— — Azerbaijan.

ABDULSALIMZADE (G.IA.) Osushchestvlenie leninskogo plana elektrifikatsii v Azerbaidzhane. Baku, 1968. pp. 192.

— — Kazakstan.

PETRUSHIN (NIKOLAI IVANOVICH) Elektrifikatsiia i proizvoditel'nye sily Kazakhstana. Alma-Ata, 1973. pp. 207.

— — Siberia.

ALEKSEEV (VENIAMIN VASIL'EVICH) Elektrifikatsiia Sibiri: istoricheskoe issledovanie; The electrification of Siberia; a historical essey [sic]. Novosibirsk, 1973 in progress.

— — Ukraine.

VASYLEVS'KYI (HEORHII ARKADIIOVYCH) Elektroenerhetyka Karpat. Uzhhorod, 1970. pp. 134.

— South Africa — Statistics.

SOUTH AFRICA. Bureau of Statistics. Census of electricity, gas and steam. bien., 1963/4- Pretoria. *In English and Afrikaans.*

— Sweden — Rates.

SWEDEN. Statens Vattenfallsverk. 1973. Swedish State Power Board high-voltage tariffs as from 1973: into the era of nuclear power. London, Electricity Council, Overseas Activities Translation Service, 1973. fo. 31.

— United Kingdom.

ELECTRICITY SUPPLY INDUSTRY TRAINING BOARD [U.K.]. Report and statement of accounts. a., 1972/3, 1973/4; ceased pbln. London. *Formerly included in the file of British Parliamentary Papers.*

LONDON ELECTRICITY BOARD. Annual report and accounts. a., 1972/3- London. *Formerly included in the file of British Parliamentary Papers.*

YORKSHIRE ELECTRICITY BOARD. Annual report and accounts, together with the report of the Yorkshire Electricity Consultative Council. a., 1972/3- Leeds. *Formerly included in the file of British Parliamentary Papers.*

U.K. Department of Energy. Electricity: report of the Secretary of State for Energy. a., 1973/4- London. *Formerly included in the file of British Parliamentary Papers.*

— United States.

LEUCHTENBURG (WILLIAM EDWARD) Flood control politics: the Connecticut River Valley problem 1927-1950; [reprint of work first published in 1953]. New York, 1972. pp. 339. *bibliog.*

FUNIGIELLO (PHILIP J.) Toward a national power policy: the New Deal and the electric utility industry, 1933-1941. Pittsburgh, [1973]. pp. 296. *bibliog.*

— — Government ownership.

JOHNSEN (JULIA EMILY) compiler. Government ownership of electric utilities. New York, 1936. pp. 329. *bibliog.*

— — California.

DOCTOR (R.D.) and others. California's electricity quandary, 3: slowing the growth rate; prepared for the California State Assembly. Santa Monica, 1972. pp. 141. *bibliog. (Rand Corporation. [Rand Reports]. 1116)*

MOOZ (WILLIAM E.) and MOW (C.C) California's electricity quandary, 1: estimating future demand; prepared for the Resources Agency of California. Santa Monica, 1972. pp. 60. *bibliog. (Rand Corporation. [Rand Reports]. 1084)*

— Venezuela — Statistics.

VENEZUELA. Direccion General de Estadistica. Estadisticas industriales: energia electrica. a., 1971- Caracas.

— Zaire.

KALENGA (MALU WA) Les solutions possibles du probleme du deficit energetique de la region du Shaba en Republique du Zaire. Kinshasa, 1972. pp. 124.

ELECTRONIC DATA PROCESSING.

RICHARDSON (M.) and CUNNINGHAM (A.D.) Vetting of industrial survey questionnaires by computer. Eastcote, Business Statistics Office, 1971. pp. 19.

GYENES (L.) 50-point traffic census: the automatic processing of hourly flows. Crowthorne, 1973. pp. 11. *(U.K. Transport and Road Research Laboratory. Reports. LR 558)*

SUNDGREN (BO) An infological approach to data bases. Stockholm, 1973. pp. 478. *bibliog. (Sweden. Statistiska Centralbyřan. Urval. No. 7)*

TAPPER (COLIN) Computers and the law. London, [1973]. pp. 314. *bibliog.*

INTEGRATED municipal information systems: the use of the computer in local government; [by] Kenneth L. Kraemer [and others]. New York, 1974. pp. 105. *bibliog.*

— Banks and banking.

FLANNERY (MARK J.) and JAFFEE (DWIGHT M.) The economic implications of an electronic monetary transfer system. Lexington, Mass., [1973]. pp. 209. *bibliog.*

— Law.

AITKEN (WILLIAM) of the Edinburgh Regional Computing Centre, and others. Computers for lawyers: a report presented to the Scottish Legal Computer Research Trust, etc. [Edinburgh], 1972. pp. 159. *bibliog.*

ELECTRONIC INDUSTRIES

— France.

FRANCE. Direction de la Documentation. La Documentation Française. Notes et Etudes Documentaires. No. 3,042. L'industrie électronique française; [by] René Prévost. Paris, 1963. pp. 30.

— United Kingdom.

ECONOMIC DEVELOPMENT COMMITTEE FOR ELECTRONICS. Industrial review to 1977: electronics: background report. London, National Economic Development Office, 1973. fo. 94.

ECONOMIC DEVELOPMENT COMMITTEE FOR ELECTRONICS. Industrial review to 1977: electronics: summary report and recommendations. London, National Economic Development Office, 1973. pp. 31.

ELITE.

SEPULVEDA NIÑO (SATURNINO) Las elites colombianas en crisis: de partidos policlasistas a partidos monoclasistas. [Bogota], 1970. pp. 196. *bibliog.*

DELRUELLE-VOSSWINKEL (NICOLE) Les notables en Belgique: analyse des résultats d'une enquête. Bruxelles, [1972]. pp. 321. *(Brussels. Université Libre. Centre de Sociologie Générale et de Méthodologie. [Collection])*

BOYD (DAVID) Elites and their education. Windsor, 1973. pp. 159. *bibliog.*

CAVALLI (LUCIANO) ed. Classe dirigente e sviluppo regionale: ricerca sulla classe dirigente toscana di Gianfranco Bettin [and others]. Bologna, [1973]. pp. 196.

DHIRAVEGIN (LIKHIT) Political attitudes of the bureaucratic elite and modernization in Thailand. Bangkok, 1973. pp. 94. *bibliog.*

ELITES, pouvoir et légitimité au Maghreb; par M. Teitler [and others]. Paris, 1973. pp. 237. *(Centre National de la Recherche Scientifique. Centre de Recherches et d'Etudes sur les Sociétés Méditerranéennes. Collection)*

ELIZUR (YUVAL) and SALPETER (ELIAHU) Who rules Israel?. New York, [1973]. pp. 342.

ELITE. (Cont.)

La FORMATION des élites politiques maghrébines; [by] Lhachmi Berrady [and others]. Paris, [1973]. pp. 246.

FRANK (ROBERT SHELBY) Linguistic analysis of political elites: a theory of verbal kinesics. Beverly Hills, [1973]. pp. 59. *bibliog.*

GRUNER (ERICH) Politische Führungsgruppen im Bundesstaat. Bern, [1973]. pp. 104. *(Allgemeine Geschichtsforschende Gesellschaft der Schweiz. Monographien zur Schweizer Geschichte. Band 7)*

JACOBSON (DAVID) Anthropologist. Itinerant townsmen: friendship and social order in urban Uganda. Menlo Park, Calif., [1973]. pp. 150. *bibliog.*

STOLLBERG (GUNNAR) Die soziale Stellung der intellektuellen Oberschicht im England des 12. Jahrhunderts. LÜBECK 1973. pp. 184. *bibliog.*

STRUVE (WALTER) Elites against democracy: leadership ideals in bourgeois political thought in Germany, 1890-1933. Princeton, [1973]. pp. 486. *bibliog.*

WHITSON (WILLIAM W.) Chinese military and political leaders and the distribution of power in China, 1956-1971; a report prepared for Defense Advanced Research Projects Agency and Department of State. Santa Monica, 1973. pp. 474. *(Rand Corporation. [Rand Reports]. 1091)*

BAYLIS (THOMAS A.) The technical intelligentsia and the East German elite: legitimacy and social change in mature communism. Berkeley, [1974]. pp. 314. *bibliog.*

BURKE (PETER) Historian. Venice and Amsterdam: a study of seventeenth-century élites. London, 1974. pp. 154. *bibliog.*

DOLBEARE (KENNETH M.) Political change in the United States: a framework for analysis. New York, [1974]. pp. 246. *bibliog.*

HERADSTVEIT (DANIEL) Arab and Israeli elite perceptions. Oslo, [1974]. pp. 148.

PRESTHUS (ROBERT V.) Elites in the policy process. London, 1974. pp. 525.

STANWORTH (PHILIP) and GIDDENS (ANTHONY) eds. Elites and power in British society. London, 1974. pp. 261.

SULEIMAN (EZRA N.) Politics, power, and bureaucracy in France: the administrative elite. Princeton, [1974]. pp. 440. *bibliog.*

ELIZABETH I, Queen of England.

JOHNSON (PAUL) Elizabeth I: a study in power and intellect. London, [1974]. pp. 511. *bibliog.*

ELY

— Civic improvement.

[CAMBRIDGESHIRE AND ISLE OF ELY. County Planning Department]. The heart of Ely: a study of the town centre; a report for public discussion. [Cambridge], 1971. pp. 26.

EMIGRANT REMITTANCES

— Italy.

BALLETTA (FRANCESCO) Il Banco di Napoli e le rimesse degli emigrati, 1914-1925. Napoli, 1972. pp. 211. *bibliog. (Institut International d'Histoire de la Banque. Gens d'Affaires, Banques, Monnaies, Finances. 2)*

EMIGRATION AND IMMIGRATION.

ZWINGMANN (CHARLES A.) and PFISTER-AMMENDE (MARIA) eds. Uprooting and after.... Berlin, 1973. pp. 361. *bibliog.*

EMIGRATION AND IMMIGRATION LAW

— France.

BENDIFALLAH (SMAIL) L'immigration algérienne et le droit français. Paris, 1974. pp. 311.

— Germany.

STANGE (SIEGFRIED) Die aufenthaltsrechtliche Stellung der Fremden in der Bundesrepublik Deutschland unter besonderer Berücksichtigung von Ehe und Familie. Bern, 1973. pp. 138. *bibliog.*

— Russia.

INSTITUTE OF JEWISH AFFAIRS. Background Papers. No. 24. The Soviet "diploma tax". [London], 1972. pp. 15.

EMILIA—ROMAGNA.

REGIONE EMILIA-ROMAGNA, LA: organo dell'Unione Regionale della Provincie Emiliane. bi-m., 1969-1971 (anni 15-17), with gap (Ja/F 1971: anno 17, no.1). Bologna.

— Commerce — Statistics.

EMILIA-ROMAGNA. Servizi Statistici. 1973. Struttura e tendenze dell'industria e del commercio in Emilia-Romagna: censimenti 1951, 1961, 1971; a cura di Franco Tassinari. Bologna, 1973. pp. 504. *(Note e documentazioni. Serie 1.4)*

— History.

MOVIMENTO operaio e fascismo nell'Emilia-Romagna, 1919-1923; ([by] Luciano Casali [and others]). Roma, 1973. pp. 363.

— Industries — Statistics.

EMILIA-ROMAGNA. Servizi Statistici. 1973. Struttura e tendenze dell'industria e del commercio in Emilia-Romagna: censimenti 1951, 1961, 1971; a cura di Franco Tassinari. Bologna, 1973. pp. 504. *(Note e documentazioni. Serie 1.4)*

EMINENT DOMAIN

— America, Latin.

GALEANO (LUIS ARMANDO) La expropiacion forzosa en las leyes agrarias integrales sudamericanas. [Madrid, 1970]. pp. 164. *bibliog.*

INGRAM (GEORGE M.) Expropriation of U.S. property in South America: nationalization of oil and copper companies in Peru, Bolivia, and Chile. New York, 1974. pp. 392. *bibliog.*

— United Kingdom.

ENCYCLOPEDIA of the law of compulsory purchase and compensation; general editor Harold J.J. Brown. London, 1960-74. 2 vols. *Loose-leaf.*

EMME VALLEY

— Economic conditions.

BERN (CANTON). Statistisches Bureau. 1972. Die Region Oberes Emmental: Grundlagen für Regionalpolitik und Regionalplanung. Bern, 1972. pp. 154. *(Beiträge zur Statistik des Kantons Bern. Regionalanalyse. Reihe G. Heft 2)*

GERBER (FRITZ) Wandel im ländlichen Leben: eine sozialökonomische und sozialpsychologische Untersuchung in fünf Gemeinden des Oberemmentals. Bern, 1974. pp. 362. *bibliog.*

EMOTIONS.

EKMAN (PAUL) and others. Emotion in the human face: guidelines for research and an integration of findings. New York, [1972]. pp. 191. *bibliog.*

STRONGMAN (K.T.) The psychology of emotion. London, [1973]. pp. 235. *bibliog.*

EMPLOYEE MORALE.

Les ATTITUDES des travailleurs et des employeurs à l'égard de l'emploi. [Paris, 1973]. pp. 166. *bibliog. (France. Centre d'Etudes de l'Emploi. Cahiers. 2) With summaries in English and German.*

EMPLOYEE OWNERSHIP.

COPEMAN (GEORGE HENRY) Employee share participation in nationalized and other enterprises. London, [1974]. pp. 18. *bibliog.*

— Denmark.

DANSK ARBEJDSGIVERFORENING. Konsekvenserne af økonomisk demokrati. 2nd ed. [Copenhagen, 1973]. pp. 43.

DENMARK. Arbejdsministeriet. 1973. Bills aiming at economic democracy; [with] annex: The possible development of the Employees' Fund and the investment of its resources. [Copenhagen?], 1973. fo. 7, 5.

EMPLOYEES, DISMISSAL OF

— Hungary.

GARANCSY (GABRIELLA) Labour law relation and its termination in Hungarian law. Budapest, 1973. pp. 117.

— Russia.

NIKITINSKII (VASILII IVANOVICH) and PANIUGIN (VALENTIN EVGEN'EVICH) Dela ob uvol'nenii rabochikh i sluzhashchikh. Moskva, 1973. pp. 88. *(Vsesoiuznyi Nauchno-Issledovatel'skii Institut Sovetskogo Zakonodatel'stva. Bibliotechka Sud'i i Narodnogo Zasedatelia)*

— Sweden.

GONÄS (LENA) Företagsnedläggning och arbetsmarknadspolitik: en studie av sysselsättningskriserna vid Oskarshamns Varv. Uppsala, 1974. pp. 240. *bibliog. (Uppsala. Universitet. Kulturgeografiska Institutionen. Geografiska Regionstudier. Nr. 10) With English summary.*

— United Kingdom.

TRADES UNION CONGRESS. Job security: a guide for negotiators. London, 1973 [or rather 1974]. pp. 8.

EMPLOYEES, RATING OF.

STAFF appraisal; [by] G.A. Randell [and others]. London, 1972 repr. 1973. pp. 79. *bibliog.*

U.K. Department of Employment. 1972. Department of Employment staff: annual reports: notes for the guidance of reporting and countersigning officers on the completion of annual reports. [London, 1972]. pp. 24. *(Circulars. 16/18)*

STAFF appraisal; [by] G.A. Randell [and others]. rev.ed. London, 1974. pp. 147. *bibliog. (Institute of Personnel Management. Management Paperbacks)*

EMPLOYEES, RELOCATION OF

— United Kingdom.

TRADES UNION CONGRESS. Job security: a guide for negotiators. London, 1973 [or rather 1974]. pp. 8.

EMPLOYEES, TRAINING OF.

INTERNATIONAL LABOUR CONFERENCE. 55th Session. Reports. 6. Sixth item on the agenda: vocational training of seafarers. Geneva, 1970. pp. 41.

CASSON (MARK C.) Training labour and management: an extension of the theory of production. [Reading], 1973. fo. 18. *bibliog. (Reading. University. Department of Economics. Discussion Papers in Economics. No. 48)*

GRAHAM (DAVID RALPH) and LUFT (KATHLEEN) The role of business in the economic redevelopment of the rural community. Austin, Tex., 1973. pp. 114. *bibliog. (Texas University. Bureau of Business Research. Research Monographs. No. 36)*

— Switzerland.

UNTEREGGER (MEINRAD) The rate of return on training in Switzerland: an empiricial [sic] investigation of essentially blue-collar, male-dominated occupations covering 20 Swiss cities and towns for the period 1946-1970. [Zürich, imprint], 1972. pp. 130. *bibliog.*

EMPLOYEES' REPRESENTATION IN MANAGEMENT.

— United Kingdom.

CENTRAL TRAINING COUNCIL IN CHILD CARE [U.K.]. staff development and in-service study. Paper 2. Unqualified entrants and trainee social workers. [London, 1970]. pp. 16.

CHEMICAL AND ALLIED PRODUCTS INDUSTRY TRAINING BOARD [U.K.]. Working Party on the Training Implications of Productivity Agreements. The training implications of manpower productivity agreements; [C. Denard, chairman]. [Staines], 1970. pp. 13. bibliog. *(Information Papers. No. 4)*

COUNCIL FOR TRAINING IN SOCIAL WORK [U.K.]. Graduate trainees in the health and welfare services. London, 1970. pp. (7). *(Discussion Papers. No.3)*

U.K. Working Party on Selection for Training. 1970. Report; [S. Thorley, chairman]. [London, 1970]. 1 vol. (various pagings). *bibliogs.*

CENTRAL TRAINING COUNCIL IN CHILD CARE [U.K.]. Staff development and in-service study. Paper 3. Continuing needs for professional development. [London, 1971]. pp. 15.

WORKING PARTY ON THE STAFF DEVELOPMENT NEEDS OF RESIDENTIAL CHILD CARE STAFF WITHOUT PROFESSIONAL TRAINING [U.K.]. Draft report on progress of Working Party up to August 1971 for submission to the Central Council for Education and Training in Social Work; [J.R. Howells, chairman]. [London], Central Training Council in Child Care, [1971]. 1 pamphlet (various pagings).

AGRICULTURAL, HORTICULTURAL AND FORESTRY INDUSTRY TRAINING BOARD [U.K.]. Annual report and accounts. a., 1972/3- Beckenham. *Formerly included in the file of British Parliamentary Papers.*

AIR TRANSPORT AND TRAVEL INDUSTRY TRAINING BOARD [U.K.]. Report and statement of accounts. a., 1972/3- Staines. *Formerly included in the file of British Parliamentary Papers.*

CARPET INDUSTRY TRAINING BOARD [U.K.]. Report and statement of accounts. a., 1972/3- Wilmslow, Cheshire. *Formerly included in the file of British Parliamentary Papers.*

CERAMICS, GLASS AND MINERAL PRODUCTS INDUSTRY TRAINING BOARD [U.K.]. Report and statement of accounts. a., 1972/3- Harrow. *Formerly included in the file of British Parliamentary Papers.*

CHEMICAL AND ALLIED PRODUCTS INDUSTRY TRAINING BOARD [U.K.]. Report and statement of accounts. a., 1972/3- Staines. *Formerly included in the file of British Parliamentary Papers.*

CLOTHING AND ALLIED PRODUCTS INDUSTRY TRAINING BOARD [U.K.]. Report and statement of accounts. a., 1972/3- Leeds. *Formerly included in the file of British Parliamentary Papers.*

CONSTRUCTION INDUSTRY TRAINING BOARD [U.K.]. Report and statement of accounts. a., 1972/3- London. *Formerly included in the file of British Parliamentary Papers.*

COTTON AND ALLIED TEXTILES INDUSTRY TRAINING BOARD [U.K.]. Report and statement of accounts. a., 1972/3- Manchester. *Formerly included in the file of British Parliamentary Papers.*

DISTRIBUTIVE INDUSTRY TRAINING BOARD [U.K.]. Report and statement of accounts. a., 1972/3- Manchester. *Formerly included in the file of British Parliamentary Papers.*

ELECTRICITY SUPPLY INDUSTRY TRAINING BOARD [U.K.]. Report and statement of accounts. a., 1972/3, 1973/4; ceased pbln. London. *Formerly included in the file of British Parliamentary Papers.*

ENGINEERING INDUSTRY TRAINING BOARD [U.K.]. Report and accounts. a., 1972/3- London. *Formerly included in the file of British Parliamentary Papers.*

FOOD, DRINK AND TOBACCO INDUSTRY TRAINING BOARD [U.K.]. Annual report and accounts. a., 1972/3- Croydon. *Formerly included in the file of British Parliamentary Papers.*

FOOTWEAR, LEATHER AND FUR SKIN INDUSTRY TRAINING BOARD [U.K.]. Report and statement of accounts. a., 1972/3- Sutton Coldfield. *Formerly included in the file of British Parliamentary Papers.*

FURNITURE AND TIMBER INDUSTRY TRAINING BOARD [U.K.]. Report and statement of accounts. a., 1972/3- High Wycombe. *Formerly included in the file of British Parliamentary Papers.*

GAS INDUSTRY TRAINING BOARD [U.K.]. Report and statement of accounts. a., 1972/3, 1973/4; ceased pbln. London. *Formerly included in the file of British Parliamentary Papers.*

HOTEL AND CATERING INDUSTRY TRAINING BOARD [U.K.]. Report and statement of accounts. a., 1972/3- Wembley. *Formerly included in the file of British Parliamentary Papers.*

IRON AND STEEL INDUSTRY TRAINING BOARD [U.K.]. Annual report. a., 1972/3- London. *Formerly included in the file of British Parliamentary Papers.*

MAN-MADE FIBRES PRODUCING INDUSTRY TRAINING BOARD [U.K.]. Report and statement of accounts. a., 1972/3- London. *Formerly included in the file of British Parliamentary Papers.*

PRINTING AND PUBLISHING INDUSTRY TRAINING BOARD [U.K.]. Report and statement of accounts. a., 1972/3- London. *Formerly included in the file of British Parliamentary Papers.*

ROAD TRANSPORT INDUSTRY TRAINING BOARD [U.K.]. Report and statement of accounts. a., 1972/3- Wembley. *Formerly included in the file of British Parliamentary Papers.*

RUBBER AND PLASTICS PROCESSING INDUSTRY TRAINING BOARD [U.K.]. Report and statement of accounts. a., 1972/3- Brentford. *Formerly included in the file of British Parliamentary Papers.*

SHIPBUILDING INDUSTRY TRAINING BOARD [U.K.]. Report and statement of accounts. a., 1972/3- South Harrow. *Formerly included in the file of British Parliamentary Papers.*

WOOL, JUTE AND FLAX INDUSTRY TRAINING BOARD [U.K.]. Report and statement of accounts. a., 1972/3- Bradford. *Formerly included in the file of British Parliamentary Papers.*

KNITTING, LACE AND NET INDUSTRY TRAINING BOARD [U.K.]. Report and statement of accounts. a., 1973/4- Nottingham. *To 1971/2 included in the file of British Parliamentary Papers*

CENTRAL COUNCIL FOR EDUCATION AND TRAINING IN SOCIAL WORK [U.K.]. Social work: creating opportunities for staff development. London, 1973. pp. 8. *(Papers. 1)*

CENTRAL COUNCIL FOR EDUCATION AND TRAINING IN SOCIAL WORK [U.K.]. Social work: in service study scheme for residential staff. London, 1973. pp. 22. *(Papers. 2)*

— — Costs.

KNITTING, LACE AND NET INDUSTRY TRAINING BOARD [U.K.]. Cost of operative training: a guide to working out the cost of operative training in your firm. [Nottingham, 1972]. pp. 16.

— — Yearbooks.

PERSONNEL AND TRAINING MANAGEMENT YEARBOOK [AND DIRECTORY]. a., 1974 [2nd]- London. Supersedes INDUSTRIAL TRAINING YEARBOOK.

— United States.

KOBRAK (PETER) Private assumption of public responsibilities: the role of American business in urban manpower programs. New York, 1973. pp. 257. *bibliog.*

EMPLOYEES' MAGAZINES, HANDBOOKS, ETC.

MARKS (WINIFRED ROSE) Preparing an employee handbook. London, 1972. pp. 53.

EMPLOYEES' REPRESENTATION IN MANAGEMENT.

NORWAY. Departementet for Sociale Saker. Arbeiderkommisjonen av 1918. 1922. Innstilling...angående lov om sjømenns medvirkning i driftsledelsen. Kristiania, 1922. pp. 46.

INTERNATIONAL LABOUR CONFERENCE. 54th Session. Reports. 8. Eighth item on the agenda: protection and facilities afforded to workers' representatives in the undertaking. Geneva, 1969-70. 2 pts.

NATIONAL CONFERENCE ON WORKERS' CONTROL AND INDUSTRIAL DEMOCRACY, 7TH, SHEFFIELD, 1969. Democracy in the motor industry; edited by Ken Coates, with contributions by Ernest Mandel [and others]. Nottingham, 1969 repr. 1970. pp. 58.

TOPHAM (ANTHONY) ed. Democracy on the docks. Nottingham, 1970. pp. 87.

INNSTILLING om demokrati i bedriftslivet: fra et utvalg oppnevnt ved kongelig resolusjon av 5. januar 1968. [Oslo?], 1971. pp. 76.

INSTITUTE OF PERSONNEL MANAGEMENT. Workers' participation in Western Europe; [prepared by J.R. Appleyard with the cooperation of J.A.G. Coates]. London, 1971. pp. 103. bibliog. *(Information Reports. New Series. 10)*

JOENS (LILY) Mitbestimmung: Rückschritt nach links?; zum Regierungsentwurf Betriebsverfassung. Bonn, [1971]. pp. 28. *(Christlich-Demokratische Union Deutschlands. Wirtschaftsrat. Information. 5)*

KLEY (GISBERT) Funktionsgerechte Mitbestimmung: Partnerschaft der Zukunft. Bonn, [1971]. pp. 23. *(Christlich-Demokratische Union Deutschlands. Wirtschaftsrat. Information. 3)*

ALEXANDER (K.C.) Participative management: the Indian experience. New Delhi, [1972]. pp. 132. *bibliog.*

ASPLUND (CHRISTER) Some aspects of workers' participation: a survey prepared for the ICFTU. Brussels, 1972. pp. 72. *bibliog.*

INSTITUT FÜR MARXISTISCHE STUDIEN UND FORSCHUNGEN. Mitbestimmung und Gewerkschaften, 1945 bis 1949: Dokumente und Materialien. Frankfurt/Main, 1972. pp. 128. *(Neudrucke zur Sozialistischen Theorie und Gewerkschaftspraxis. Band 1)*

LATTMANN (CHARLES) Das norwegische Modell der selbstgesteuerten Arbeitsgruppe: ein Beitrag zur Verwirklichung der Mitbestimmung am Arbeitsplatz. Bern, [1972]. pp. 60. bibliog. *(Hochschule St. Gallen für Wirtschafts- und Sozialwissenschaften. Institut für Betriebswirtschaft. Betriebswirtschaftliche Mitteilungen. 56)*

A RESEARCH into consultative management at Long Lartin Prison; by P. Shapland [and others]. [London], 1972. pp. 122. bibliog. *(U.K. Prison Department. Office of the Chief Psychologist. CP Reports. Series 1. No. 2)*

BAXTER (ROBERT) Lecturer in Politics. Co-operative democracy in industry. London, 1973. pp. 15. *(Co-operative Party. Discussion Pamphlets)*

BOW GROUP. Industrial Democracy Research Group. Employee participation in British companies: an examination of all levels of employee participation in industry; [John Goss, convener]. London, 1973. pp. 44. *(Bow Group Reports)*

DAEUBLER (WOLFGANG) Das Grundrecht auf Mitbestimmung und seine Realisierung durch tarifvertragliche Begründung von Beteiligungsrechten. Frankfurt am Main, [1973] repr. 1974. pp. 569. *bibliog.*

GORDON-BROWN (IAN) and others. Works councils, employee directors, supervisory boards: a guide to the debate. London, 1973. pp. 32. *(Industrial Participation Association. Study Papers. No. 2)*

EMPLOYEES' REPRESENTATION IN MANAGEMENT. (Cont.)

GOSS (JOHN M.) Industrial relations and employee participation in management in Norway. Brighton, [1973]. fo. 36. *bibliog. (Brighton. University of Sussex. Centre for Contemporary European Studies. Research Papers. No. 5)*

GOSS (JOHN M.) Industrial relations and moves towards industrial democracy in Ireland. Brighton, [1973]. fo.30. *bibliog. (Brighton. University of Sussex. Centre for Contemporary European Studies. Research Papers. No. 4)*

INDUSTRIAL PARTICIPATION ASSOCIATION. Employee directors and supervisory boards. London, [1973]. pp. 16.

MACBEATH (INNIS) The European approach to worker-management relationships. London, 1973. pp. 86.

PARTICIPATION in management: industrial democracy in three West European countries: report of a conference by the Industrial Relations Research Associations of Belgium, Germany and the Netherlands, November 1972; edited by W. Albeda. Rotterdam, 1973. pp. 103. *(Netherlands Industrial Relations Research Association. Publications. vol. 1)*

NETHERLANDS. Werkgroep-Hartog. 1973. Tweede rapport...: de subsidiëring van het wonen: van object- naar subjectsubsidiëring. 's-Gravenhage, 1973. pp. 73.

RUEEGG (HANS) Mitbestimmung: Motive und Konsequenzen. [Zürich, 1973]. pp. 14. *(Wirtschaftsförderung: Gesellschaft zur Förderung der Schweizerischen Wirtschaft. Stimmen zur Staats- und Wirtschaftspolitik. 54) (Sonderdruck aus Schweizer Monatshefte, Heft 12, März 1973)*

TRADES UNION CONGRESS. General Council. Industrial democracy: interim report. London, 1973. pp. 46.

WILSON (HAROLD) Democracy in industry: a speech delivered at the N.W. Regional Conference of the Labour Party, 17 March 1973. London, [1973]. pp. 16. *(Labour Party. Edinburgh Series of Policy Speeches. No. 3)*

FABIAN SOCIETY. Fabian Tracts. [No.] 430. Towards a worker managed economy; [by] Jeremy Bray [and] Nicholas Falk. London, 1974. pp. 28. *bibliog.*

FABIAN SOCIETY. Fabian Tracts. [No]. 431. Working power: policies for industrial democracy; [produced by the Fabian working party on industrial democracy]; editor Giles Radice. London, 1974. pp. 21.

FULDA (JOHANNES F.) Gedanken zur "Mitbestimmungs"-Frage: eine Zwischenbilanz. [Zürich, 1974]. pp. 11. *(Wirtschaftsförderung: Gesellschaft zur Förderung der Schweizerischen Wirtschaft. Stimmen zur Staats- und Wirtschaftspolitik. 57) (Sonderdruck aus Schweizer Monatshefte, Heft 5, August 1974)*

GARCIA (MARIA DE LOURDES A. COSTA LEITE) Os conselhos de empresa na Europa. Lisboa, 1974. pp. 75. *bibliog. Portugal. Direcção de Serviços do Trabalho. Estudos Laborais. 4) With abstracts in English, French and German.*

GUEST (DAVID) and FATCHETT (DEREK J.) Worker participation: individual control and performance. London, 1974. pp. 252. *bibliog.*

HEINTZELER (WOLFGANG) The co-determination problem in Western Germany. London, [1974]. pp. 19.

HORNER (JOHN) b. 1911. Studies in industrial democracy. London, 1974. pp. 256. *bibliog.*

JENKINS (DAVID) Job power: blue and white collar democracy. London, 1974. pp. 375. *bibliog.*

KOERNER (MANFRED) Mitbestimmung der Arbeitnehmer als Instrument gesamtwirtschaftlicher Einkommenspolitik. Göttingen, [1974]. pp. 171. *bibliog. (Hamburg. Hansische Universität. Institut für Europäische Wirtschaftspolitik. Wirtschaftspolitische Studien. 33) With summaries in English and French.*

LEVINSON (CHARLES) ed. Industry's democratic revolution. London, 1974. pp. 350.

SOCIAL POLICY RESEARCH LIMITED and WOOD (JOHN CROSSLEY) Worker participation in Britain; a business study. London, [1974]. pp. 144.

EMPLOYERS' ASSOCIATIONS

— Italy.

La POLITICA del padronato italiano dalla ricostruzione all'"autunno caldo"; [by] Ada Collidà [and others]. Bari, [1972]. pp. 206.

— United Kingdom — Ireland, Northern — Directories.

IRELAND, NORTHERN. Ministry of Health and Social Services. Industrial Relations Division. 1972. Directory of principal organisations of employers and workpeople in Northern Ireland. 16th ed. Belfast, 1972. pp. 39.

EMPLOYMENT (ECONOMIC THEORY).

GORDON (DAVID M.) Theories of poverty and under-employment: orthodox, radical, and dual labor market perspectives. Lexington, [1972]. pp. 177. *bibliog.*

CISEK (GUENTER) Internationale Personalorganisation. Berlin, [1974]. pp. 143. *bibliog.*

EMPLOYMENT AGENCIES

— United States.

HASENFELD (YEHESKEL) Manpower placement: service delivery for the hard-to-employ. Ann Arbor, 1973. pp. 95. *bibliog. (Michigan University, and Wayne State University. Institute of Labor and Industrial Relations. Policy Papers in Human Resources and Industrial Relations. 21)*

EMPLOYMENT FORECASTING

— Germany.

HECHELTJEN (PETER) Bevölkerungsentwicklung und Erwerbstätigkeit: ein Beitrag zur Simulation sozioökonomischer Systeme, mit Prognosen für die Bundesrepublik Deutschland. Opladen, [1974]. pp. 319. *bibliog.*

— United Kingdom.

SHIPBUILDING INDUSTRY TRAINING BOARD [U.K.]. Manpower Forecasting Panel. Notes for guidance on the technique of manpower planning in the shipbuilding industry. South Harrow, [1973]. pp. 23. *bibliog. (Shipbuilding Industry Training Board [U.K.]. Information Papers. No. 2)*

EMPLOYMENT MANAGEMENT.

URWICK (LYNDALL) and BRECH (EDWARD FRANZ LEOPOLD) The human factor in management, 1795-1943: two articles from the series "The pioneers of scientific management", etc. London, 1944. pp. 40.

INTERNATIONAL LABOUR ORGANISATION. Labour-Management Relations Series. Geneva, 1957 in progress.

U.K. Working Party on Selection for Training. 1970. Report; [S. Thorley, chairman]. [London, 1970]. 1 vol. (various pagings). *bibliogs.*

U.K. Department of Employment. Industrial Relations Division. Central Information Service. 1973- . Some organisations in the management and personnel field. rev. ed. London, 1973 in progress. 1 vol. (various pagings). *(Information Papers. [New Series] No. 6)*

Les ATTITUDES des travailleurs et des employeurs à l'égard de l'emploi. [Paris, 1973]. pp. 166. *bibliog. (France. Centre d'Etudes de l'Emploi. Cahiers. 2) With summaries in English and German.*

ALLEGRO (JACQUES TOBIAS) Socio-technische organisatieontwikkeling. Leiden, 1973. pp. 268. *bibliog. With English summary.*

BARBER (DAVID) Basic personnel procedures: guidance on setting up a personnel department. London, 1973. pp. 52. *bibliog.*

GARRETT (JOHN) Management Consultant. Policies towards people. London, [1973]. pp. 6. *(Foundation for Business Responsibilities. Sir Frederic Hooper Essay Award. 1973)*

NASH (ALLAN N.) and MINER (JOHN BURNHAM) eds. Personnel and labor relations: an evolutionary approach. New York, [1973]. pp. 498. *bibliogs.*

SHAFRITZ (JAY M.) Position classification: a behavioral analysis for the public service. New York, 1973. pp. 133. *bibliog.*

SILLS (PATRICK A.) The behavioural sciences: techniques of application. London, 1973. pp. 45. *bibliogs.*

FOX (ALAN) Man mismanagement. London, 1974. pp. 179. *bibliogs.*

SLATTER (STUART ST. P.) and others. The employment of non-English speaking workers: what industry must do. [London], Community Relations Commission, 1974. pp. 32.

EMPLOYMENT STABILIZATION

— United States.

JOHNSEN (JULIA EMILY) compiler. Stability of employment. New York, 1931. pp. 206. *bibliog.*

ENCOMIENDAS (SPANISH AMERICA).

ZAVALA (SILVIO ARTURO) La encomienda indiana. 2nd ed. Mexico, 1973. pp. 1043. *bibliog.*

ENCYCLOPAEDIAS AND DICTIONARIES.

ENCYCLOPAEDIA BRITANNICA. The new Encyclopaedia Britannica. 15th ed. Chicago, [1974]. 30 vols. *bibliogs. Comprises:- Propaedia (1 vol.) Micro-paedia (10 vols.) Macropaedia (19 vols.)*

ENDOGAMY AND EXOGAMY.

WESTERMARCK (EDWARD) Recent theories of exogamy. [1933?]. fo. 175-216. *Typescript, with the author's manuscript corrections, of an article published in Sociological Review, vol.26, no.1, Jan. 1934.*

ENDOWMENTS.

WHITAKER (BENJAMIN CHARLES GEORGE) The foundations: an anatomy of philanthropy and society. London, 1974. pp. 256. *bibliog.*

ENGELS (FRIEDRICH).

McLEISH (JOHN) The theory of social change: four views considered. London, Routledge and Kegan Paul, 1969 repr. 1972. pp. xiii, 95. *bibliog. (International Library of Sociology and Social Reconstruction)*

NIKONENKO (STANISLAV STEPANOVICH) and RIABOV (FELIKS GRIGOR'EVICH) Velikii soratnik Marksa. Moskva, 1970. pp. 96.

TARATUTA (EVGENIIA ALEKSANDROVNA) Russkii drug Engel'sa. Moskva, 1970. pp. 143.

FRIEDRICH Engels, Mitbegründer des wissenschaftlichen Sozialismus: Protokoll der internationalen wissenschaftlichen Konferenz... Berlin, 12-13 November 1970; (Redaktion: Waldtraut Opitz [and others, for the] Institut für Marxismus-Leninismus beim ZK der SED). Berlin, 1971. pp. 450.

KURUMA (SAMEZO) ed. Marx-Lexikon zur politischen Ökonomie. Glashütten im Taunus, 1973. 3 vols. *bibliogs.*

MALYI (IL'IA GRIGOR'EVICH) Voprosy statistiki v trudakh Fridrikha Engel'sa. Moskva, 1973. pp. 140.

MARCUS (STEVEN) Engels, Manchester, and the working class. New York, [1974]. pp. 271. *bibliog.*

MERKEL (RENATE) Marx und Engels über Sozialismus und Kommunismus: zur Herausbildung der Auffassung...in der Entstehungsperiode des wissenschaftlichen Kommunismus, 1842-1846. Berlin, 1974. pp. 311.

SETTEMBRINI (DOMENICO) Due ipotesi per il socialismo in Marx ed Engels. Bari, 1974. pp. 317.

— Bibliography.

LEVIN (LEV ABRAMOVICH) compiler. K. Marks, F. Engel's, V.I. Lenin: ukazatel' bibliograficheskikh rabot, 1961-1972. Moskva, 1973. pp. 288.

ENGINEERING

— Study and teaching — United Kingdom.

GLYNN (ERICA) and others. The relevance of school learning experience to performance in industry; report on a feasibility study carried out by the Centre for Science Education in co-operation with Engineering Industry Training Board, November 1970 to June 1971. [Watford, Engineering Industry Training Board], 1971. fo. 43.

ENGINEERING INDUSTRY TRAINING BOARD [U.K.]. Report and accounts. a., 1972/3- London. *Formerly included in the file of British Parliamentary Papers.*

— India.

MAJUMDAR (A.G.) The Indian engineering industry: trends and prospects. New Delhi, 1972. pp. 162.

— United Kingdom.

ENGINEERING EMPLOYERS' FEDERATION. Research Department. The engineering industry in an inflationary environment. [London], 1972. fo. 69.

SENKER (PETER) and HUGGETT (CHARLOTTE) Technology and manpower in the UK engineering industry: an interim report 1973; a report on a study by the Science Policy Research Unit, University of Sussex. Watford, Engineering Industry Training Board, 1973. pp. 44. *(Occasional Papers. No.3)*

ENGINEERING AS A PROFESSION.

U.K. Civil Service Commission. 1969. Engineers in government service. rev. ed. London, 1969. pp. 54.

ENGINEERS

— United Kingdom.

COMMISSION ON INDUSTRIAL RELATIONS [U.K.]. Con-Mech (Engineers) Limited. London, H.M.S.O., 1973. pp. 8. *(Reports. No. 53)*

COMMISSION ON INDUSTRIAL RELATIONS [U.K.]. G. Clancey Limited. London, H.M.S.O., 1973. pp. 25. *(Reports. No. 54)*

COMMISSION ON INDUSTRIAL RELATIONS [U.K.]. Recognition of white-collar unions in engineering and chemicals. London, H.M.S.O., 1973. pp. 75. *(Studies. 3)*

INDUSTRIAL RESEARCH AND INFORMATION SERVICES. A.U.E.W.(E.) postal ballots. London, 1973. pp. 32.

— United States.

CAIN (GLEN GEORGE) and others. Labor market analysis of engineers and technical workers. Baltimore, [1973]. pp. 88. *bibliog.*

ENGLISH LANGUAGE

— Dialects.

WRIGHT (PETER) The language of British industry. London, 1974. pp. 206. *bibliog.*

— Grammar.

MUIR (JAMES) b.1932. A modern approach to English grammar: an introduction to systemic grammar. London, 1972. pp. 149. *bibliog.*

CRESSWELL (M.J.) Logics and languages. London, 1973. pp. 273. *bibliog.*

BARON (DENNIS E.) Case grammar and diachronic English syntax. The Hague, 1974. pp. 132. *bibliog.*

— Slang.

WRIGHT (PETER) The language of British industry. London, 1974. pp. 206. *bibliog.*

— — Dictionaries.

LANDY (EUGENE E.) The underground dictionary. London, 1972. pp. 206.

— Study and teaching.

SLATTER (STUART ST. P.) and others. The employment of non-English speaking workers: what industry must do. [London], Community Relations Commission, 1974. pp. 32.

— Syntax.

KESSLER (CAROLYN) The acquisition of syntax in bilingual children. Washington, [1971]. pp. 109. *bibliog.*

BARON (DENNIS E.) Case grammar and diachronic English syntax. The Hague, 1974. pp. 132. *bibliog.*

POSTAL (PAUL MARTIN) On raising: one rule of English grammar and its theoretical implications. Cambridge, Mass., [1974]. pp. 447. *bibliog.*

— Usage.

SOUTHEASTERN CONFERENCE ON LINGUISTICS, 8TH, GEORGETOWN UNIVERSITY, 1972. New ways of analyzing variation in English: [proceedings of combined meetings of the Southeastern Conference and the first Annual Colloquium on New Ways of Analyzing Variation in English]; Charles-James N. Bailey [and] Roger W. Shuy, editors.. Washington, [1973]. pp. 373. *bibliogs.*

TRUDGILL (PETER) The social differentiation of English in Norwich. Cambridge, 1974. pp. 211. *bibliog.*

ENGLISH LANGUAGE IN THE UNITED STATES.

DILLARD (JOEY LEE) Black English: its history and usage in the United States. New York, [1972]. pp. 361. *bibliog.*

LABOV (WILLIAM) Language in the inner city: studies in the black English vernacular. Philadelphia, [1972]. pp. 412. *bibliog.*

ENGLISH LITERATURE

— History and criticism.

KUCZYNSKI (JUERGEN) Gestalten und Werke. (Band 2). Soziologische Studien zur englischsprachigen und französischen Literatur. Berlin, 1971. pp. 499.

ROGERS (PAT) The Augustan vision. London, [1974]. pp. 318. *bibliog.*

— Periodicals.

EDDY (SPENCER L.) The founding of the Cornhill Magazine. Muncie, Indiana, 1970. pp. 49. *(Ball State University. Ball State Monographs. No. 19)*

ENGLISH NEWSPAPERS.

U.K. National Register of Archives. 1973. Labour Party archives: Daily Citizen, 1912-15. London, 1973. fo.2.

ENGLISH PERIODICALS.

EDDY (SPENCER L.) The founding of the Cornhill Magazine. Muncie, Indiana, 1970. pp. 49. *(Ball State University. Ball State Monographs. No. 19)*

ROLPH (C.H.) pseud. [i.e. Cecil Rolph HEWITT] Kingsley: the life, letters and diaries of Kingsley Martin. London, 1973. pp. 413.

KUCZYNSKI (JUERGEN) Die vertauschte Eule der Minerva: der Wissenschaftler in der kapitalistischen Gesellschaft. Berlin, 1974. pp. 80.

ENLIGHTENMENT.

GORDON (LEV S.) Studien zur plebejisch-demokratischen Tradition in der französischen Aufklärung; (aus dem Russischen übersetzt von Wolfgang Techtmeier). Berlin, 1972. pp. 371. *bibliog.*

GUSDORF (GEORGES) L'avènement des sciences humaines au siècle des lumières. Paris, 1973. pp. 589.

ENTLEBUCH

— Economic history.

BUCHER (SILVIO) Bevölkerung und Wirtschaft des Amtes Entlebuch im 18. Jahrhundert: eine Regionalstudie...der Schweiz im Ancien Régime. Luzern, [1974]. pp. 280. *bibliog. (Lucerne (Canton). Staatsarchiv. Luzerner Historische Veröffentlichungen. Band 1) With summaries in English and French.*

— Population.

BUCHER (SILVIO) Bevölkerung und Wirtschaft des Amtes Entlebuch im 18. Jahrhundert: eine Regionalstudie...der Schweiz im Ancien Régime. Luzern, [1974]. pp. 280. *bibliog. (Lucerne (Canton). Staatsarchiv. Luzerner Historische Veröffentlichungen. Band 1) With summaries in English and French.*

ENTRE RIOS

— Economic conditions — Statistics.

ARGENTINE REPUBLIC. Consejo Federal de Inversiones. 1963. Analisis economico de la provincia de Entre Rios. [Tomo] 2. Apendice estadistico. [Buenos Aires, 1963]. 1 vol. (unpaged). *(Analisis Macroeconomicos de las Provincia Argentinas. Vol.2)*

ENTREPRENEUR.

DEROSSI (FLAVIA ZACCONE) The Mexican entrepreneur. Paris, Organisation for Economic Co-operation and Development, 1971. pp. 428. *bibliog. (Development Centre. Studies)*

FOGARTY (MICHAEL PATRICK) Irish entrepreneurs speak for themselves. Dublin, 1973. pp. 141. *(Economic and Social Research Institute. Broadsheets. No.8)*

KIRZNER (ISRAEL MAYER) Competition and entrepreneurship. Chicago, 1973. pp. 246.

LYNN (RICHARD) ed. The entrepreneur: eight case studies. London, 1974. pp. 175.

PAYNE (PETER LESTER) British entrepreneurship in the 19th century. London, 1974. pp. 80. *bibliog. (Economic History Society. Studies in Economic History)*

YAMAMURA (KOZO) A study of Samurai income and entrepreneurship: quantitative analyses of economic and social aspects of the Samurai in Tokugawa and Meiji Japan. Cambridge, Mass., 1974. pp. 243. *bibliog. (Harvard University. East Asian Research Center. Harvard East Asian Series. No.76)*

ENVIRONMENT.

See subdivision Environmental aspects under special subjects; and headings beginning with the word ENVIRONMENTAL.

ENVIRONMENT, HUMAN.

See HUMAN ECOLOGY.

ENVIRONMENTAL ENGINEERING.

RICH (LINVIL GENE) Environmental systems engineering. New York, [1973]. pp. 448.

ENVIRONMENTAL HEALTH.

Het MILIEU van onze samenleving: (teksten...uitgesproken op 9 mei 1970 te Leiden tijdens een interdisciplinaire bijeenkomst; [by] V. Westhoff [and others]. Bussum, 1970. pp. 128. *bibliogs. (Annalen van het Thijmgenootschap. Jaargang 58, aflevering 2)*

SINCLAIR (THOMAS CRAIG) and others. Innovation and human risk; the evaluation of human life and safety in relation to technical change;...[a project of the] Science Policy Research Unit, University of Sussex. London, [1972]. pp. 36. *bibliog.*

ENVIRONMENTAL LAW.

BARROS (JAMES) and JOHNSTON (DOUGLAS M.) The international law of pollution. New York, [1974]. pp. 476. *bibliogs. In English or French.*

ENVIRONMENTAL LAW. (Cont.)

— Japan.

TOKYO. Metropolitan Government. Ordinances, local laws, etc. The Tokyo metropolitan environmental pollution control ordinance and its enforcement regulation. Tokyo, 1971. pp. 84.

— Switzerland.

BUEHLER (THEODOR) Der Natur- und Heimatschutz nach schweizerischen Rechten. Zürich, [1973]. pp. 117. *bibliog.*

— United Kingdom.

BIGHAM (DEREK ALASTAIR) The law and administration relating to protection of the environment.London, 1973. pp. 359.

— United States.

ANDERSON (FREDERICK R.) NEPA in the courts: a legal analysis of the National Environmental Policy Act. Washington, D.C., [1973]. pp. 324.

ENVIRONMENTAL POLICY.

BECKERMAN (WILFRED) Naturwissenschafter, Wirtschaftswissenschafter und Umweltkatastrophe: (gekürzte deutsche Fassung des in englischer Sprache ... gehaltenen Vortrags). Tübingen, 1972. pp. 31. *(Kiel. Universität. Institut für Weltwirtschaft. Kieler Vorträge. Neue Folge. 73)*

The ECONOMICS of environmental quality; [by] James C. Hite [and others]. Washington, [1972]. pp. 113. *(American Enterprise Institute for Public Policy Research. Domestic Affairs Studies. 5)*

INTERNATIONAL YOUTH FEDERATION FOR ENVIRONMENTAL STUDIES AND CONSERVATION. Youth and environment 1971: some reports and action proposals from [three conferences held in 1971];...edited by David Withrington [and others]. Amsterdam, 1972. pp. 150.

BORRIE (WILFRED DAVID) Population, environment, and society. Auckland, [1973], pp. 106. *(Auckland. University. Sir Douglas Robb Lectures. 1972)*

CALDER (NIGEL) ed. Nature in the round: a guide to environmental science. London, [1973]. pp. 294. *bibliogs.*

DAHL (HELMER) Challenge of the future: responsibilities of state and free enterprise. [London, 1973]. pp. 22. *(Aims of Industry. The Future of Capitalism).*

NORTH ATLANTIC TREATY ORGANIZATION. Committee on the Challenge of Modern Society. 1973. Environment and regional planning: a pilot study, etc. [Brussels?, 1973?]. 1 vol. (various pagings). *(Environmental Studies. No. 17)*

SIEBERT (HORST) Das produzierte Chaos: Okonomie und Umwelt. Stuttgart, [1973]. pp. 184.

UNITED NATIONS. Conference on the Human Environment, Stockholm, 1972. [Basic documents contributed by the United Nations, other international organizations and the participating countries]. Various places, 1973. 403 pts. *Guide to the microfiche edition of the conference bibliography shelved at Z 2(U.N.). Microfilm: 7 reels, 16mm.*

UNITED NATIONS. Conference on the Human Environment, Stockholm, 1972. Report of the United Nations Conference...[held at] Stockholm, 5-16 June 1972. (A/CONF.48/14/Rev.1). New York, 1973. pp. 77.

UTTON (ALBERT E.) and HENNING (DANIEL H.) eds. Environmental policy: concepts and international implications. New York, 1973. pp. 266. *(Reprinted from Natural Resources Journal, vol.11, 1971 no.3 and vol. 12, 1972 no.2)*

WALTER (INGO) Environmental management and the international economic order. New York, [1973]. pp. 85. *(New York (City). University. Center for International Studies. Policy Papers. vol. 5, no. 3)*

LAULAN (YVES) Le Tiers Monde et la crise de l'environnement. [Paris], 1974. pp. 144. *bibliog.*

MANenvironment - a better fit?: is there a role for the social scientist?; [edited] by Dennis Donnelly; a conference under the auspices of the Occupational Section of the British Psychological Society...Oxford...1973. Birmingham, 1974. pp. 104,2. *(Birmingham. University. Centre for Urban and Regional Studies. Research Memoranda. No.26)*

SHINN (ROBERT A.) The international politics of marine pollution control. New York, 1974. pp. 200. *bibliog.*

UNITED NATIONS. Centre for Housing, Building and Planning. 1974. Human settlements: the environmental challenge; a compendium of United Nations papers prepared for the Stockholm Conference on the Human Environment 1972. London, 1974. pp. 209.

— Bibliography.

GOODEY (BRIAN) and others. The last environmental perception checklist. Birmingham, 1973. pp. 233. *(Birmingham. University. Centre for Urban and Regional Studies. Research Memoranda. No. 22)*

UNITED NATIONS. Conference on the Human Environment, Stockholm, 1972. A guide to the microfiche edition of the conference bibliography. Ann Arbor, Xerox University Microfilms, 1973. fo. 27.

— America, Latin.

DEAN (WARREN) Confronting the environmental crisis in Latin America; a prod to action. New York, 1973. pp. 16. *(New York (City). University. Ibero-American Language and Area Center. Occasional Papers. No. 2)*

— Canada — Saskatchewan.

SASKATCHEWAN. Department of the Environment. Annual report. a., 1972/3 (1st)- Regina.

— European Economic Community countries.

EUROPEAN COMMUNITIES. Commission. 1972. Communication from the Commission to the Council on a European Communities' programme concerning the environment; submitted on 24 March 1972. Brussels, 1972. pp. 69. *(Bulletin of the European Communities. Supplements. [1972/5])*

COMMITTEE FOR ENVIRONMENTAL CONSERVATION. Transport, the environment and the European Economic Community.London, [1973]. pp. 8.

EUROPEAN COMMUNITIES. Commission. 1973. Programme of environmental action of the European Communities; ...forwarded by the Commission to the Council on 17 April 1973.[Brussels], 1973. pp. 67. *(Bulletin of the European Communities. Supplements. [1973/3])*

ANALYSE socio-économique de l'environnement : problèmes de méthode; documents présentés au symposium tenu à Saint- Nizier, Grenoble, 1972. Paris, [1973]. pp. 248. *(Maison des Sciences de l'Homme. Environnement et Sciences Sociales. 3)*

SOCIETE D'ETUDE ET DE RELATIONS PUBLIQUES. L'environnement en Basse-Seine: [étude... réalisée pour... la Mission d'Etude Basse-Seine]. Paris, [1973?]. fo. 72

— Germany.

SCHACKMANN (HEINRICH) Umwelt und Wirtschaft im Ruhrgebiet. Düsseldorf, [1972]. pp. 24. *(Volks- und Betriebswirtschaftliche Vereinigung im Rheinisch-Westfälischen Industriegebiet. Schriften. Sonderveröffentlichungen. 14)*

LAEMMEL (PETER) Umweltschutz in Ballungsräumen, dargestellt am Beispiel des Hamburger Raumes. Göttingen, [1974]. pp. 300. *bibliog. (Hamburg. Hansische Universität. Institut für Europäische Wirtschaftspolitik. Wirtschaftspolitische Studien. 32)*

— — Bavaria.

BAVARIA. Staatsministerium für Landesentwicklung und Umweltfragen. 1972. Umweltbericht. [Munich], 1972. pp. 96.

— Italy.

CONFEDERAZIONE GENERALE DELL'INDUSTRIA ITALIANA. Servizio Studi e Rilevazioni. Collana di Studi e Documentazione. 31.Prime indicazioni sugli interventi dell'industria privata a difesa dell'ambiente; (a cura di Francesco Galli and others).Roma, 1973. pp. 216.

— Netherlands.

LEK (BRAM VAN DER) Het milieuboekje: over produktie, vervuiling en actie. Amsterdam, 1972. pp. 109. *bibliog.*

MILIEU AKTIECENTRUM NEDERLAND. De mens moet blijven. [Rotterdam, 1973]. pp. 57.

— Norway.

NORWAY. Utenriksdepartementet. 1972. Norway's national report to the United Nations Conference on the Human Environment. [Oslo, 1972?]. pp. 55.

SMITH (DOUGLAS V.) Technology, ecosystems, and planning: thoughts on contradictions in industrial Norway and a procedure for planning. Oslo, 1972. fo. 100.

— South Africa.

CLARKE (JAMES) Journalist. Our fragile land: South Africa's environmental crisis. Johannesburg, [1974]. pp. 134.

SWEDEN. Finansdepartementet. Långtidsutredningen. 1971. [Svensk ekonomi fram till 1977]; 1970 års lÅngtidsutredning. Bilaga. 8. Miljövården i Sverige under 70-talet. Stockholm, 1971. pp. 56. *(Sweden. Statens Offentliga Utredningar. 1971. 12)*

— United Kingdom.

CIVIC TRUST FOR THE NORTH WEST. Environmental quality: a measuring system; a report prepared... for the Environment[al] Health and Protection Administration, City of Liverpool. [Manchester], 1971. fo. 36.

LIBERAL PARTY CONFERENCE ON THE ENVIRONMENT, LONDON, 1970. The pollution of our environment: papers. [London, 1971]. pp. 92. *bibliog.*

COMMISSION ON MINING AND THE ENVIRONMENT. Report of the commission...; [S. Zuckerman, chairman]; ([and] The exploration , evaluation and mining of non-ferrous metallic ores:... supplement to chapter 4). London, 1972. pp. 92. Map and supplement to chapter 4 in end pocket.

CONFERENCE ON TOURISM AND THE ENVIRONMENT, LONDON, 1971. Tourism and the environment; papers presented at [the] Conference. London, British Tourist Authority, [1972]. pp. 58.

HOUSE (JOHN WILLIAM) ed. The UK space: resources, environment and the future. London, [1973]. pp. 371.

YORKSHIRE AND HUMBERSIDE ECONOMIC PLANNING COUNCIL. Yorkshire and Humberside environmental progress report, 1966-1973.[Leeds?, 1973]. pp. 76, 1 map. *bibliog.*

BROOKS (PETER F.) Problems of the environment: an introduction. London, 1974. pp. 223. *bibliogs.*

McKNIGHT (ALLAN D.) and others, eds. Environmental pollution control: technical, economic and legal aspects. London, 1974. pp. 324. *bibliogs.*

U.K. Department of the Environment. 1974. Progress sustained: changes in the British environmental scene; report to the second session of the governing council of the United Nations environment programme. [London, 1974]. pp. 38. *bibliog.*

— United States.

CARLIN (ALAN P.) and KOCHER (GEORGE E.) Environmental problems: their causes, cures, and evolution, using southern California smog as an example. Santa Monica, 1971. pp. 107. *(Rand Corporation. [Rand Reports]. 640)*

GARVEY (GERALD) Energy, ecology, economy:...a project of the Center of International Studies, Princeton University. Princeton, 1972; London, 1974. pp. 235.

BERKMAN (RICHARD LYLE) and VISCUSI (W. KIP) Damming the West: (Ralph Nader's study group report on the Bureau of Reclamation). New York, 1973. pp. 272.

BRENNER (MICHAEL J.) The political economy of America's environmental dilemma. Lexington, [1973]. pp. 177.

HAEFELE (EDWIN T.) Representative government and environmental management. Baltimore, [1973]. pp. 188.

LAPP (RALPH EUGENE) The logarithmic century. Englewood Cliffs, [1973]. pp. 263.

ROSENBAUM (WALTER A.) The politics of environmental concern. New York, 1973. pp. 298.

The AMERICAN environment: [papers from a seminar held at the Institute of United States Studies in the University of London]; edited by W.R. Mead. London, 1974. pp. 69. *(London. University. Institute of United States Studies. Monographs. 1)*

The ECONOMICS of environmental improvement; [by] Donald T. Savage [and others]. Boston, [Mass., 1974]. pp. 210.

GROWTH policy: population, environment and beyond; [by] Kan Chen [and others]. Ann Arbor, [1974]. pp. 237. *bibliog.*

SMITH (GRAHAME J.) and others. Our ecological crisis: its biological, economic, and political dimensions. New York, [1974]. pp. 198. *bibliogs.*

— — New Mexico.

VAN DRESSER (PETER) Development on a human scale. New York, 1973. pp. 116.

ENVIRONMENTAL POLICY RESEARCH.

WORLD HEALTH ORGANIZATION. Technical Report Series. No. 406. Research into environmental pollution: report of five WHO scientific groups. Geneva, 1968. pp. 83.

ENVIRONMENTAL PROTECTION.

BAUMOL (WILLIAM JACK) Environmental protection, international spillovers and trade. Stockholm, [1971]. pp. 59. *(Wicksell Lecture Society. Wicksell Lectures. 1971)*

POLLUTION abatement: (record of a seminar held at the University of East Anglia in October 1971); edited by K.M. Clayton and R.C. Chilver. Newton Abbot, [1973]. pp. 203.

HOLLIMAN (JONATHAN) Consumers' guide to the protection of the environment. 2nd ed. London, 1974. pp. 257. *bibliogs.*

— France.

FRANCE. Ministère de la Protection de la Nature et de l'Environnement. 1972. 2 années d'environnement. [Paris, 1972]. pp. 41.

— Germany, Eastern.

GERECKE (LOTHAR) How do we protect our environment? information, facts and data from the GDR. Berlin, 1974. pp. 63.

— Sweden.

SWEDEN. Jordbruksdepartementet. 1970. Environment protection - an expanding task for society. [Stockholm, 1970]. pp. 32.

— United Kingdom.

ALDOUS (TONY) Battle for the environment. [London], 1972. pp. 288. *bibliog.*

KIMBER (RICHARD) and RICHARDSON (JEREMY JOHN) eds. Campaigning for the environment. London, 1974. pp. 228. *bibliog.*

— United States.

SCOTT (JOHN C.) of the University of Michigan, and others. Toward environmental understanding: an evaluation of the 1972 Youth Conservation Corps; a report prepared for the U.S. Forest Service...and the U.S. Department of the Interior. Ann Arbor, Mich., 1973. pp. 319.

LAND use, urban form and environmental quality: [report of a study conducted at the University of Chicago for the Office of Research and Development of the U.S. Environmental Protection Agency]; [by] Brian J.L. Berry [and others]. Chicago, 1974. pp. 440. *bibliog. (Chicago. University. Department of Geography. Research Papers. No. 155)*

— Yugoslavia.

WILBANKS (THOMAS J.) Environmental management with areally decentralized government;... a report of the Syracuse University Environmental Policy Project. Ljubljana, 1973. 1 vol.(various foliations).

EPIDEMIOLOGY.

SUSSER (MERVYN WILFRED) Causal thinking in the health sciences: concepts and strategies of epidemiology. New York, 1973. pp. 181.

SYMPOSIUM ON PSYCHIATRIC EPIDEMIOLOGY, 2ND, MANNHEIM, 1972. Roots of evaluation: the epidemiological basis for planning psychiatric services: proceedings...; edited by J.K. Wing and H. Häfner. London, 1973. pp. 360. *bibliogs.*

SYDENSTRICKER (EDGAR) The challenge of facts: selected public health papers...; edited by Richard V. Kasius. New York, 1974. pp. 386. *bibliog.*

EQUAL PAY FOR EQUAL WORK

— Netherlands.

REBELSE meiden blijven strijden . Den Haag, 1974 in progress.

— United Kingdom.

TRADES UNION CONGRESS. Conference of Affiliated Unions to discuss the Implementation of Equal Pay, 1973. Report. London, 1973. pp. 63.

MEPHAM (G.J.) Equal opportunity and equal pay: a review of objectives, problems and progress. London, 1974. pp. 209. *bibliog.*

EQUALITY.

FALLERS (LLOYD A.) Inequality: social stratification reconsidered. Chicago, 1973. pp. 330. *bibliog.*

KUITENBROUWER (JOOST B.W.) On the practice and theory of affluence and poverty: some reflections. The Hague, 1973. pp. 26. *(Hague. Institute of Social Studies. Occasional Papers. No. 33)*

LABOUR RESEARCH DEPARTMENT. The 2 nations: inequality in Britain today. London, 1973. pp. 28.

PERSPECTIVES on inequality: a reassessment of the effect of family and schooling in America. Cambridge, Mass., [1973]. pp. 128. *(Harvard Educational Review. Reprint Series. No. 8)*

REISSMAN (LEONARD) Inequality in American society: social stratification. Glenview, Ill., [1973]. pp. 137.

SHOSTAK (ARTHUR B.) and others. Privilege in America: an end to inequality?. Englewood Cliffs, N.J., [1973]. pp. 150. *bibliog.*

FIELD (FRANK) 1942- . Unequal Britain: a report on the cycle of inequality. London, 1974. pp. 64. *bibliog.*

GLENNERSTER (HOWARD) and HATCH (STEPHEN) eds. Positive discrimination and inequality;... [by] Jack Barnes [and others]. London, 1974. pp. 40. *(Fabian Society. Research Series. [No]. 314)*

POLANYI (GEORGE) and WOOD (JOHN B.) How much inequality?: an inquiry into the evidence. London, 1974. pp. 85. *(Institute of Economic Affairs. Research Monographs. 31)*

WEDDERBURN (DOROTHY) ed. Poverty, inequality and class structure. London, 1974. pp. 247.

EQUATIONS.

ATTFIELD (C.L.F.) Least squares and maximum likelihood estimation of non-linear (in parameters) models. [Norwich], 1973. pp. 23. *bibliog. (University of East Anglia. Economics Discussion Papers. No. 18)*

EQUATIONS, SIMULTANEOUS.

LARGE sparse sets of linear equations: proceedings of the Oxford conference of the Institute of Mathematics and its Applications held in April, 1970; edited by J.K. Reid. London, 1971. pp. 284.

BYRON (RAYMOND PETER) Testing structural specification using the unrestricted reduced form. Canberra, 1973. pp. 25. *bibliog. (Australian National University. Research School of Social Sciences. Department of Economics. Working Papers in Economics and Econometrics. No. 14)*

EQUITY

— United Kingdom.

KEETON (GEORGE WILLIAMS) and SHERIDAN (LIONEL ASTOR) A case-book on equity and trusts. 2nd ed. London, 1974. pp. 369.

SAMUELS (ROGER) Equity and succession. London, 1974. pp. 218.

ERITREA

— Nationalism.

ABIR (MORDECHAI) The contentious Horn of Africa. London, 1972. pp. 19. *(Institute for the Study of Conflict. Conflict Studies. No. 24)*

— Politics and government.

ABIR (MORDECHAI) The contentious Horn of Africa. London, 1972. pp. 19. *(Institute for the Study of Conflict. Conflict Studies. No. 24)*

EROSION, SOIL.

See SOIL EROSION.

ERZBERGER (MATTHIAS).

MOELLER (ALEX) Reichsfinanzminister Matthias Erzberger und sein Reformwerk. Bonn, 1971. pp. 68. *bibliog. (Blickpunkt Finanzen. Heft 7)*

ESCALATOR CLAUSE

— United Kingdom.

FRIEDMAN (MILTON) Monetary correction: a proposal for escalator clauses to reduce the costs of ending inflation. London, 1974. pp. 54. *bibliog. (Institute of Economic Affairs. Occasional Papers. 41)*

ESCHERICH (GEORG).

NUSSER (HORST G.W.) Konservative Wehrverbände in Bayern, Preussen und Österreich, 1918-1933; mit einer Biographie von Forstrat Georg Escherich, 1870-1941. München, [1973]. 2 vols.

ESKIMOS.

ALLIANCE in Eskimo society; [papers presented at a symposium held during the meeting of the American Anthropological Association, New York, 1971]; edited by Lee Guemple. Seattle, [1972]. pp. 131. *bibliog. (American Ethnological Society. Annual Spring Meeting, 1971. Proceedings. Supplement)*

— Canada.

PETITOT (EMILE) The Amerindians of the Canadian northwest in the 19th century, as seen by Emile Petitot...; edited by Donat Savoie. Ottawa, 1971. 2 vols. (in 1). *bibliog. (Canada. Northern Science Research Group. MDRP [Reports]. 9-10)*

ESPIONAGE, RUSSIAN
— Germany.

KUCKHOFF (GRETA) Vom Rosenkranz zur Roten Kapelle: ein Lebensbericht. Frankfurt am Main, 1974. pp. 434.

— United Kingdom.

COURTNEY (ANTHONY TOSSWILL) The enemies within. London, [1974?]. pp. 16.

ESSEN
— Politics and government.

KUEHR (HERBERT) Parteien und Wahlen im Stadt- und Landkreis Essen in der Zeit der Weimarer Republik, etc. Düsseldorf, [1973]. pp. 309. bibliog. (Germany (Bundesrepublik Deutschland). Kommission für Geschichte des Parlamentarismus und der Politischen Parteien. Beiträge zur Geschichte des Parlamentarismus und der Politischen Parteien. Band 49)

ESSEX
— Economic history.

BOOKER (JOHN) B.A. Essex and the industrial revolution. Chelmsford, 1974. pp. 244. (Essex. Records Committee. Essex Record Office Publications. No.66)

ESSONNE (DEPARTMENT).
— Economic conditions.

FRANCE. Direction de la Documentation. La Documentation Française. Notes et Etudes Documentaires. Nos. 3,774-3, 775. Les nouveaux départements de la région parisienne: le département de l'Essonne; [by] la Direction de la Coordination et de l'Action Economique de la Préfecture de l'Essonne. Paris, 1971. pp. 80.

— Social conditions.

FRANCE. Direction de la Documentation. La Documentation Française. Notes et Etudes Documentaires. Nos. 3,774-3, 775. Les nouveaux départements de la région parisienne: le département de l'Essonne; [by] la Direction de la Coordination et de l'Action Economique de la Préfecture de l'Essonne. Paris, 1971. pp. 80.

ESTATE PLANNING
— United Kingdom.

STANLEY (OLIVER) ed. The creation and protection of capital. London, 1974. pp. 285.

ESTATES (SOCIAL ORDERS)
— Turkey.

KARPAT (KEMAL H.) An inquiry into the social foundations of nationalism in the Ottoman state: from social estates to classes, from millets to nations. Princeton, N.J., 1973. pp. 116. (Princeton University. Center of International Studies. Research Monographs. No.39)

ESTONIA.

KÜNG (ANDRES) Estland zum Beispiel: nationale Minderheit und Supermacht; Übersetzung aus dem Schwedischen von Karl Leonhard). Stuttgart, [1973]. pp. 192. bibliog.

— Industries.

VEIMER (ARNOL'D TYNUVICH) Razvitie promyshlennosti Estonskoi SSR za semiletie, 1959-1965 gg. Moskva, 1967. pp. 247.

— Population — Bibliography.

PALLI (H.) and PULLAT (R.) compilers. Eesti ajaloolise demograafia bibliograafia; (Bibliografiia po istoricheskoi demografii Estonii; Estonian historical demography bibliography). Tallinn, 1969. pp. 132. In Estonian, Russian and English.

ETHICAL RELATIVISM.

ADORNO (THEODOR WIESENGRUND) Minima moralia: reflections from damaged life; translated from the German by E.F.N. Jephcott. London, 1974. pp. 251.

ETHICS.

GUENDLING (JOHN E.) Value systems: the moral and eudaemonic components. Chicago, [1973]. pp. 151.

SMITH (ARTHUR) Writer on heuristics. Four uses of heuristics; [models for project design and large idea-systems]. Rochdale, [1973]. pp. 207. bibliog.

NEW studies in ethics; [edited by W.D. Hudson]. London, 1974. 2 vols. bibliogs.

PETERS (RICHARD STANLEY) Psychology and ethical development: a collection of articles on psychological theories, ethical development and human understanding. London, 1974. pp. 480.

ETHIOPIA
— History — Sources.

ITALY. Ministero degli Affari Esteri. Comitato per la Documentazione dell'Opera dell'Italia in Africa. L'Italia in Africa. Serie Storica. Vol. 1. Etiopia, Mar Rosso. Tomi 6-7. Documenti, 1887- 1888, 1888-1889; a cura di Carlo Giglio. Roma, 1972. 2 vols.

— Politics and government.

ABIR (MORDECHAI) The contentious Horn of Africa. London, 1972. pp. 19. (Institute for the Study of Conflict. Conflict Studies. No. 24)

CRUMMEY (DONALD) Priests and politicians: protestant and catholic missions in orthodox Ethiopia 1830-1868. Oxford, 1972. pp. 176. bibliog.

— Religion.

CRUMMEY (DONALD) Priests and politicians: protestant and catholic missions in orthodox Ethiopia 1830-1868. Oxford, 1972. pp. 176. bibliog.

— Rural conditions.

WORLD LAND USE SURVEY. Occasional Papers. No. 11. Welenkomi: a socio-economic and nutritional survey of a rural community in the Central Highlands of Ethiopia; by Mesfin Wolde-Mariam [and others]. Berkhamsted, 1971. pp. 67. Map in end pocket.

— Social life and customs.

TURTON (DAVID ANTHONY) The social organisation of the Mursi: a pastoral tribe of the lower Omo valley, south west Ethiopia; [Ph.D. (London) thesis]. 1973. fo. 425. bibliog. Typescript: unpublished. This thesis is the property of London University and may not be removed from the Library.

ETHNOLOGY.

URBAN ethnicity: [papers presented at the annual conference of the Association of Social Anthropologists of the Commonwealth, held in London in 1971]; edited by Abner Cohen. London, 1974. pp. 391. bibliogs. (Association of Social Anthropologists of the Commonwealth. A.S.A. Monographs. 12)

See also names of peoples and tribes.

— Afghanistan.

JONES (SCHUYLER) Men of influence in Nuristan: a study of social control and dispute settlement in Waigal Valley, Afghanistan. London, 1974. pp. 299. bibliog.

— Africa.

TESSLER (MARK A.) and others. Tradition and identity in changing Africa. New York, [1973]. pp. 363. bibliog.

— Africa, East.

ITALY. Ministero degli Affari Esteri. Comitato per la Documentazione dell'Opera dell'Italia in Africa. L'Italia in Africa. Serie ScientificoCulturale. Studi italiani di etnologia e folklore dell'Africa Orientale, Eritrea, Etiopia, Somalia; testo di Ester Panetta. Roma, 1973 in progress.

— Africa, Subsaharan.

La NOTION de personne en Afrique noire; [papers of a conference held in] Paris, 11-17 octobre 1971. Paris, 1973. pp. 596. bibiogs. (Centre National de la Recherche Scientifique. Colloques Internationaux. No. 544) In French and English.

MAIR (LUCY PHILIP) African societies. London, 1974. pp. 251. bibliog.

— Canada.

PETITOT (EMILE) The Amerindians of the Canadian northwest in the 19th century, as seen by Emile Petitot...; edited by Donat Savoie. Ottawa, 1971. 2 vols. (in 1). bibliog. (Canada. Northern Science Research Group. MDRP [Reports]. 9-10)

— — Bibliography.

GREGOROVICH (ANDREW) Canadian ethnic groups bibliography: a selected bibliography of ethno-cultural groups in Canada and the province of Ontario. Toronto, Department of the Provincial Secretary and Citizenship of Ontario, 1972. pp. 208.

— — British Columbia.

NORRIS (JOHN M.) Strangers entertained: a history of the ethnic groups of British Columbia. [Vancouver], British Columbia Centennial '71 Committee, 1971. pp. 254.

— Egypt — Nubia.

FERNEA (ROBERT ALAN) Nubians in Egypt: peaceful people; notes on Nubian architecture and architectural drawings by Horst Jaritz; (photographs by Georg Gerster). Austin, Texas, [1973]. pp. 146. bibliog.

— Ethiopia.

LEVINE (DONALD N.) Greater Ethiopia: the evolution of a multiethnic society. Chicago, 1974. pp. 229. bibliog.

— Europe.

OCHERKI obshchei etnografii: zarubezhnaia Evropa. Moskva, 1966. pp. 476. bibliog.

— India.

FRANCE. Direction de la Documentation. La Documentation Française. Notes et Etudes Documentaires. Nos. 3,714-3, 715-3,716. Les provinces et les ethnies de l'Inde; [by] R. Breton. Paris, 1970. pp. 111. bibliog.

PRASAD (SAILESHWAR) Where the three tribes meet: a study in tribal interaction. Allahabad, 1974. pp. 232. bibliog.

— Papua New Guinea.

BERNDT (RONALD MURRAY) and LAWRENCE (PETER) eds. Politics in New Guinea: traditional and in the context of change; some anthropological perspectives. Washington, 1973. pp. 430. bibliogs.

— Solomon Islands.

ROSS (HAROLD M.) Baegu: social and ecological organization in Malaita, Solomon Islands. Urbana, Ill., [1973]. pp. 334. bibliog. (Illinios University. Illinois Studies in Anthropology. No. 8)

ETHNOPSYCHOLOGY.

BERRY (J.W.) and DASEN (P.R.) eds. Culture and cognition: readings in cross-cultural psychology. London, 1974. pp. 487. bibliog.

BEUCHELT (ENO) Ideengeschichte der Völkerpsychologie. Meisenheim am Glan, 1974. pp. 574. bibliog.

NEAL (FRANK R.) Modal personality and sociocultural variation: cultural relativism and existential paralysis; with an empirical comparison of Italians and Mexican-Americans. Helsinki, 1974. pp. 62. bibliog. (Helsinki. Yliopisto. Research Group for Comparative Sociology. Research Reports. No. 5)

EUROBOND MARKET.

PARK (YOON S.) The Euro-bond market: function and structure. New York, 1974. pp. 177. bibliog.

EURODOLLAR MARKET.

ARNOULT (ERIK) and LEMAIRE (JEAN PAUL) Euro-émissions: nouvelles perspectives bancaires internationales.[Paris, 1972]. pp. 230. bibliog.

PUMPLUEN (JUERGEN) Das Eurodollar System: eine Analyse der Komponenten und herrschenden Hypothesen. Berlin, 1972. pp. 208. bibliog.

BELL (GEOFFREY) The Euro-dollar market and the international financial system. London, 1973. pp. 125. bibliog.

BOLLMANN (ULRICH) Zehn Jahre Eurokapitalmarkt: Entwicklung, Struktur und Formen. Bern, 1973. pp. 183. bibliog.

A DEBATE on the Eurodollar market; [papers and speeches of 1971 and 1972 by Guido Carli and others]. [Rome, 1973]. pp. 189. (Ente per Gli Studi Monetari, Bancari e Finanziari Luigi Einaudi. Quaderni di Richerche. Num. 11)

FREEDMAN (CHARLES) A model of the Eurodollar market. Minneapolis, 1973. fo. 47. bibliog. (Minnesota University. Center for Economic Research. Discussion Papers. No. 25)

KEINATH (KARL) Geldschöpfung auf dem Euro-Dollarmarkt. Tübingen, 1973. pp. 129. bibliog. With summaries in various languages.

EUROPE

— Boundaries.

McNEILL (WILLIAM HARDY) Europe's steppe frontier 1500-1800. Chicago, 1964. pp. 252. bibliog.

— Civilization.

DIVERGING parallels: a comparison of American and European thought and action; [papers of study conferences of the European Association for American Studies held in Rome in 1967 and in Brussels in 1970]; edited by A.N.J. den Hollander. Leiden, 1971. pp. 222.

VANSITTART (PETER) Worlds and underworlds: Anglo-European history through the centuries. London, 1974. pp. 316. bibliog.

— — American influences.

CONTAGIOUS conflict: the impact of American dissent on European life: [papers of a study conference held by the European Association for American Studies in Geneva in 1972]; edited by A.N.J Den Hollander. Leiden, 1973. pp. 263.

— Colonies.

MIEGE (JEAN LOUIS) Expansion européenne et décolonisation de 1870 à nos jours. Paris, 1973. pp. 414. bibliog.

— Commerce.

McLEAN (ALASDAIR THOMAS) ed. Business and accounting in Europe. Farnborough, Hants, [1973]. pp. 269. bibliogs.

— — Asia.

STEENSGAARD (NIELS) Carracks, caravans and companies: the structural crisis in the European-Asian trade in the early 17th century. [Copenhagen, 1973]. pp. 448. bibliog. (Scandinavian Institute of Asian Studies. Monograph Series. No. 17)

— — Denmark.

BRIXTOFTE (PETER) Konsekvenserne for Danmark af handelsaftalerne mellem EF og Finland, Island, Portugal, Schweiz, Sverige og Østrig. [Copenhagen], 1973. pp. 216.

— Defences.

EUROPEAN security and the Soviet problem: report of a study group of the Institute for the Study of Conflict, London, July-November 1971; rapporteur, Brian Crozier; participants, Max Beloff [and others]. [London], 1972. pp. 64. (Institute for the Study of Conflict. Special Reports)

HAAGERUP (NIELS JØRGEN) Dansk sikkerheds politik og det nye Europa. Copenhagen, Forsvarets Oplysnings- og Velfaerdstjeneste, 1972. pp. 52.

AMERICAN arms and a changing Europe: dilemmas of deterrence and disarmament; [by] Warner R. Schilling [and others]. New York, 1973. pp. 218.

ERA of negotiations: European security and force reductions; [by] Wolfgang Klaiber [and others]. Lexington, Mass., [1973]. pp. 192.

INTERNATIONAL INSTITUTE FOR STRATEGIC STUDIES. Adelphi Papers. No. 96. The Alliance and Europe: part 1: crisis stability in Europe and theatre nuclear weapons: by Wolfgang Heisenberg. London, 1973. pp. 35.

INTERNATIONAL INSTITUTE FOR STRATEGIC STUDIES. Adelphi Papers. No. 98. The Alliance and Europe: part 2: defence with fewer men; by Kenneth Hunt. London, 1973. pp. 42.

The DEFENCE of western Europe; papers presented at [a residential seminar at] the National Defence College, Latimer, in September 1972; edited by John C. Garnett. London, 1974. pp. 134.

LAWRENCE (RICHARD D.) and RECORD (JEFFREY) U.S. force structure in NATO: an alternative: a staff paper. Washington, [1974]. pp. 136. (Brookings Institution. Studies in Defense Policy)

STOCKHOLM INTERNATIONAL PEACE RESEARCH INSTITUTE. Force reductions in Europe; (prepared by Olga Šuković [and others]). Stockholm, [1974]. pp. 105. (SIPRI Monographs)

WALL (PATRICK) Europe's back door: the Soviet maritime threat. London, [1974]. pp. 22.

WILLIAMS (GEOFFREY LEE) and WILLIAMS (ALAN LEE) Crisis in European defence: the next ten years. London, 1974. pp. 334.

— Description and travel.

MONKHOUSE (FRANCIS JOHN) A regional geography of western Europe. 4th ed. London, 1974. pp. 704. bibliog.

— Directories.

EUROPEAN directory of economic and corporate planning, 1973-74. Epping, 1973. pp. 442.

— Economic conditions.

MONKHOUSE (FRANCIS JOHN) A regional geography of western Europe. 4th ed. London, 1974. pp. 704. bibliog.

— Economic history.

LOMBARD (MAURICE) Espaces et réseaux du haut moyen âge. Paris, [1972]. pp. 231. bibliog. (Paris. Ecole Pratique des Hautes Etudes. Section des Sciences Economiques et Sociales. Le Savoir Historique. 2)

DUBY (GEORGES) Guerriers et paysans, VII-XIIe siècle: premier essor de l'économie européenne. [Paris, 1973]. pp. 308. bibliog.

MILWARD (ALAN S.) and SAUL (S.B.) The economic development of continental Europe, 1780-1870. London, 1973. pp. 548. bibliogs.

SHANKS (MICHAEL) The quest for growth. London, 1973. pp. 64. bibliog.

WALLERSTEIN (IMMANUEL) The modern world-system. New York, [1974 in progress]. bibliogs.

ABEL (WILHELM) Massenarmut und Hungerkrisen im vorindustriellen Europa: Versuch einer Synopsis. Hamburg, 1974. pp. 427.

DUBY (GEORGES) The early growth of the European economy: warriors and peasants from the seventh to the twelfth century;... translated by Howard B. Clarke. London, [1974]. pp. 292. bibliog.

EARLE (PETER) ed. Essays in European economic history 1500-1800. Oxford, 1974. pp. 273.

GESELLSCHAFT FÜR SOZIAL- UND WIRTSCHAFTSGESCHICHTE. 4. Arbeitstagung, 1971. Wirtschaftspolitik und Arbeitsmarkt: Bericht...in Wien am 14. und 15. April 1971;...herausgegeben von Hermann Kellenbenz. Wien, 1974. pp. 328. (Vienna. Universität. Institut für Wirtschafts- und Sozialgeschichte. Sozial- und Wirtschaftshistorische Studien)

POLLARD (SIDNEY) European economic integration, 1815-1970. London, [1974]. pp. 180. bibliog.

— Economic integration.

SUPTHUT (CHRISTIAN ROBERT) Der Einfluss der europäischen Wirtschaftsintegration auf die Papierindustrie der BRD unter besonderer Berücksichtigung des Aussenhandels. Berlin, 1972. pp. 199. bibliog.

CURZON (VICTORIA) The essentials of economic integration: lessons of EFTA experience. London, 1974. pp. 319. bibliog.

FREYMOND (JEAN) Le IIIe Reich et la réorganisation économique de l'Europe, 1940-1942: origines et projets. Leiden, 1974. pp. 302. bibliog. (Geneva. Graduate Institute of International Studies. Collection de Relations Internationales.3)

HARRISON (REGINALD J.) Europe in question: theories of regional international integration.London, 1974. pp. 256.

POLLARD (SIDNEY) European economic integration, 1815-1970. London, [1974]. pp. 180. bibliog.

— Emigration and immigration.

KAYSER (BERNARD) Cyclically-determined homeward flows of migrant workers and the effects of emigration. Paris, Organisation for Economic Co-operation and Development, 1972. pp. 56. bibliog.

— Famines.

ABEL (WILHELM) Massenarmut und Hungerkrisen im vorindustriellen Europa: Versuch einer Synopsis. Hamburg, 1974. pp. 427.

— Foreign economic relations — Germany.

FREYMOND (JEAN) Le IIIe Reich et la réorganisation économique de l'Europe, 1940-1942: origines et projets. Leiden, 1974. pp. 302. bibliog. (Geneva. Graduate Institute of International Studies. Collection de Relations Internationales.3)

— — United States.

HIERONYMI (OTTO) Economic discrimination against the United States in Western Europe, 1945-1958: dollar shortage and the rise of regionalism. Genève, 1973. pp. 232. bibliog.

SCIENCE policy and business: the changing relation of Europe and the United States:...David W. Ewing, editor. Boston, 1973. pp. 110. (Harvard University. Graduate School of Business Administration. John Diebold Lectures. 1971)

— Foreign relations.

TATU (MICHEL) Le triangle Washington-Moscou-Pékin et les deux Europe(s). [Paris, 1972]. pp. 149.

BERLINGUER (ENRICO) and MARCHAIS (GEORGES) Democrazia e sicurezza in Europa: (la politica del PCF e del PCI verso la Comunità europea e l'unità delle masse lavoratrici, etc.). Roma, [1973]. pp. 76.

HASSNER (PIERRE) Europe in the age of negotiation. Beverly Hills, [1973]. pp. 82. bibliog. (Georgetown University. Center for Strategic and International Studies. Washington Papers. vol. 1/8)

EUROPE. (Cont.)

MORGAN (ROGER P.) High politics, low politics: toward a foreign policy for Western Europe. Beverly Hills, [1973]. pp. 65. bibliog. (Georgetown University. Center for Strategic and International Studies. Washington Papers. vol. 1/11)

POLTAVSKII (MOISEI ANATOL'EVICH) Diplomatiia imperializma i malye strany Evropy, 1938-1945 gg. Moskva, 1973. pp. 303.

The DEFENCE of western Europe; papers presented at [a residential seminar at] the National Defence College, Latimer, in September 1972; edited by John C. Garnett. London, 1974. pp. 134.

ZORGBIBE (CHARLES) L'insécurité européenne. Paris, 1974. pp. 127. bibliog.

— — Congresses.

HUOPANIEMI (JUKKA) Parliaments and European rapprochement: [report on] the conference of the Inter-Parliamentary Union on European Co-operation and Security, Helsinki, January 1973. Leiden, 1973. pp. 138.

— — Africa, North.

EUROPE and the Maghreb: a series of papers by C. Gasteyger [and others]. Paris, [1972]. pp. 72. (Atlantic Institute. Atlantic Papers. 1972.1)

— — Belgium.

TAMSE (C.A.) Nederland en België in Europa, 1859-1871: de zelfstandigheidspolitiek van twee kleine staten. Den Haag, 1973. pp. 371. bibliog.

— — Communist countries.

TOWARDS a peaceful Europe: a study of the opportunities which détente provides for further improving East-West relations: written by a group sponsored by Friends Peace and International Relations Committee. London, 1973. pp. 38.

— — East (Near East).

SACHAR (HOWARD MORLEY) Europe leaves the Middle East, 1936-1954. London, 1974. pp. 687,xxxviii. bibliog.

— — Europe Eastern.

GRIBANOV (M.) Security for Europe: prospects for an all-European conference. Moscow, 1972. pp. 100.

— — Netherlands.

TAMSE (C.A.) Nederland en België in Europa, 1859-1871: de zelfstandigheidspolitiek van twee kleine staten. Den Haag, 1973. pp. 371. bibliog.

— — United States.

GASTEYGER (CURT) Europe and America at the crossroads. Paris, [1972]. pp. 50. (Atlantic Institute. Atlantic Papers. 1971.4)

BUCHAN (ALASTAIR) Europe and America: from alliance to coalition. Farnborough, Hants, [1973]. pp. 48. (Atlantic Institute. Atlantic Papers. 1973.4)

TUTHILL (JOHN W.) The decisive years ahead. Farnborough, Hants, [1973]. pp. 77. (Atlantic Institute. Atlantic Papers. 1972.4)

— Government publications.

PEMBERTON (JOHN E.) compiler. European materials in British university libraries: a bibliography and union catalogue;...with A survey by William E. Paterson. London, 1973. pp. 42.

— Historical geography.

POUNDS (NORMAN JOHN GREVILLE) An historical geography of Europe, 450 B.C.-A.D. 1330. Cambridge, 1973. pp. 475.

— History.

RUEHLE (OTTO) Die Revolutionen Europas: [reprint of work originally published in 1927]. Wiesbaden, 1973. 3 vols. bibliogs.

— History — Sources.

GERTSEN (ALEKSANDR IVANOVICH) Byloe i dumy: pervoe polnoe izdanie. Berlin, 1921. 5 vols.

SYMCOX (GEOFFREY) ed. War, diplomacy and imperialism, 1618-1763: [selected documents]. London, 1974. pp. 338. bibliog.

— — 476—1492.

MUNDY (JOHN HINE) Europe in the high middle ages, 1150-1309. London, 1973. pp. 611. bibliogs.

— — 1492—1648.

SHENNAN (J.H.) The origins of the modern European state, 1450-1725. London, 1974. pp. 135.

— — 1789— .

ALBRECHT-CARRIÉ (RENÉ) A diplomatic history of Europe since the Congress of Vienna. rev. ed. New York, [1973]. pp. 764. bibliog.

HARVIE (CHRISTOPHER) War and society in the nineteenth century: prepared...for the [War and Society] Course Team. Bletchley, 1973. pp. 208. bibliogs. (Open University. Arts: a third level course: war and society. Block IV, units 10-13)

— — 1789—1815.

OPEN UNIVERSITY. War and Society Course Team. The revolutionary and Napoleonic period; [course material prepared by Clive Emsley and Ian Donnachie]. Bletchley, 1973. pp. 168. bibliog. (Open University. Arts: a third level course: war and society. Block III, units 6-9)

— — 1848—1871.

HEERS (MARIE LOUISE) Du printemps des peuples à l'affrontement des nations, 1848-1914.Paris, 1974. pp. 255. bibliog.

— — 1848—1849.

MARX (KARL) and ENGELS (FRIEDRICH) Articles from the Neue Rheinische Zeitung, 1848-49. Moscow, 1972. pp. 303.

STEARNS (PETER N.) 1848: the revolutionary tide in Europe. New York, [1974]. pp. 278. bibliog.

— — 1871—1918.

HEERS (MARIE LOUISE) Du printemps des peuples à l'affrontement des nations, 1848-1914.Paris, 1974. pp. 255. bibliog.

— History, Military.

BEELER (JOHN HERBERT) Warfare in feudal Europe, 730-1200. Ithaca, N.Y., 1971. pp. 272. bibliog.

— Intellectual life.

GERTSEN (ALEKSANDR IVANOVICH) Byloe i dumy: pervoe polnoe izdanie. Berlin, 1921. 5 vols.

DIVERGING parallels: a comparison of American and European thought and action; [papers of study conferences of the European Association for American Studies held in Rome in 1967 and in Brussels in 1970]; edited by A.N.J. den Hollander. Leiden, 1971. pp. 222.

— Languages — Bibliography.

PRICE (GLANVILLE) compiler. The present position of minority languages in Western Europe: a selective bibliography. Cardiff, 1969. pp. 81.

— Nationalism.

SALVI (SERGIO) Le nazioni proibite: guida a dieci colonie "interne" dell'Europa occidentale. Firenze, [1973]. pp. 623. bibliog.

POLIAKOV (LEON) The Aryan myth: a history of racist and nationalist ideas in Europe; translated [from the French] by Edmund Howard. London, 1974. pp. 388. (Brighton. University of Sussex. Columbus Centre. Studies in the Dynamics of Persecution and Extermination)

— Periodicals.

PEMBERTON (JOHN E.) compiler. European materials in British university libraries: a bibliography and union catalogue;...with A survey by William E. Paterson. London, 1973. pp. 42.

— Politics and government.

SWEDEN. Justitiedepartementet. Grundlagberedningen. 1970. Riksdagsgrupperna: Regeringsbildningen: studier utförda på uppdrag, etc. Stockholm, 1970. pp. 152. bibliogs. (Sweden. Statens Offentliga Utredningar. 1970.16)

MARX (KARL) and ENGELS (FRIEDRICH) Articles from the Neue Rheinische Zeitung, 1848-49. Moscow, 1972. pp. 303.

FRANCE. French Embassy, London. Service de Presse et d'Information. 1973. The European Summit Conference, Paris, 19-21 October 1972.London, [1973]. pp. 34.

— Population.

UNITED NATIONS. Department of Economic and Social Affairs. European Social Development Programme. Reports . New York, 1967 in progress.

— Relations (general) with Africa.

ZAGHI (CARLO) L'Africa nella coscienza europea e l'imperialismo italiano. Napoli, [1973]. pp. 576.

— Relations (general) with Africa, Subsaharan.

GOOD (KENNETH) Western domination in Africa. Syracuse, N.Y., 1972. pp. 71. (Syracuse University. Maxwell Graduate School of Citizenship and Public Affairs. Program of Eastern African Studies. Eastern African Studies. No. 7)

— Relations (general) with Sweden.

SWEDEN in Europe, 1971; [by Kurt Samuelson and others]. [Stockholm], Royal Ministry for Foreign Affairs, 1971. pp. 94.

— Relations (general) with Switzerland.

SWITZERLAND. Département Politique Fédéral. 1970. La Suisse et l'Europe. Berne, 1970. pp. 43.

— Relations (general) with the United States.

CONTAGIOUS conflict: the impact of American dissent on European life: [papers of a study conference held by the European Association for American Studies in Geneva in 1972]; edited by A.N.J Den Hollander. Leiden, 1973. pp. 263.

— Social history.

CHERUBINI (GIOVANNI) Agricoltura e società rurale nel medioevo. Firenze, [1972]. pp. 124. bibliog.

— Social policy.

UNITED NATIONS. Department of Economic and Social Affairs. European Social Development Programme. Reports . New York, 1967 in progress.

EUROPE, EASTERN

— Commerce.

MARER (PAUL) Postwar pricing and price patterns in socialist foreign trade, 1946- 1971. [Bloomington], [1972]. pp. 99. bibliog. (Indiana University. International Development Research Center. IDRC Reports. 1)

BRABANT (JOZEF M.P.) Bilateralism and structural bilateralism in intra-C[ouncil for] M[utual] E[conomic] A[ssistance] trade. Rotterdam, 1973. pp. 290. bibliog.

McMILLAN (C.H.) The bilateral character of Soviet and Eastern European foreign trade. [Ottawa], 1973. fo. 38. bibliog. (Carleton University. Carleton Economic Papers)

— — India.

CHISHTI (SUMITRA) India's trade with east Europe. New Delhi, [1973?]. pp. 118.

— **Commercial policy.**

BRABANT (JOZEF M.P. VAN) Essays on planning, trade and integration in Eastern Europe. Rotterdam, 1974. pp. 310.

— **Economic conditions.**

FRANCE. Direction de la Documentation. La Documentation Française. Notes et Etudes Documentaires. Nos. 3,978-3, 979-3,980-3,981. L'Europe de l'Est en 1972; [par Thomas Schreiber]. [Paris], 1973. pp. 171. *bibliog.*

BLANC (ANDRE) L'Europe socialiste. Paris, 1974. pp. 263.

— **Economic history.**

BEREND (IVAN T.) and RÁNKI (GYÖRGY) Economic development in east-central Europe in the 19th and 20th centuries. New York, 1974. pp. 402. *bibliog.*

— **Economic integration.**

FRANCE. Direction de la Documentation. La Documentation Française. Notes et Etudes Documentaires. No. 3,217. Le complexe économique du Bas-Danube: documents. Paris, 1965. pp. 24.

— **Economic policy.**

CENTRO STUDI E RICERCHE SUI PROBLEMI ECONOMICO-SOCIALI. Seminario Internazionale, 5o, 1969. Piano e moneta nelle economie dell'Est: [proceedings]. Milano, [1972]. pp. 213. *(Est, L'. Quaderni. 1)*

HOEHMANN (HANS HERMANN) and others, eds. Die Wirtschaftsordnungen Osteuropas im Wandel: Ergebnisse und Probleme der Wirtschaftsreformen. Freiburg im Breisgau, 1972. 2 vols. *bibliog.*

FEIWEL (GEORGE R.) Essays on planning in Eastern Europe. Napoli, 1973. pp. 91. *(Istituto di Studi per lo Sviluppo Economico. Quaderni d'Istituto. 2)*

— — **Bibliography.**

GERMANY (BUNDESREPUBLIK). Deutscher Bundestag. Wissenschaftliche Dienste. 1973. Experimente sozialistische Marktwirtschaft: jugoslawisches, tschechoslowakisches und ungarisches Modell: Auswahlbibliographie mit Annotationen. Bonn, 1973. pp. 80. *(Bibliographien. 35)*

— **Foreign relations — Europe.**

GRIBANOV (M.) Security for Europe: prospects for an all-European conference. Moscow, 1972. pp. 100.

See also EUROPEAN ECONOMIC COMMUNITY — Europe, Eastern.

— — **Germany.**

STEWART-SMITH (DUDLEY GEOFFREY) ed. Brandt and the destruction of NATO: [a collection of articles, two of which were previously published in Osteuropa, and Orbis].Richmond, Surrey, 1973. pp. 101.

KUPER (ERNST) Frieden durch Konfrontation und Kooperation: die Einstellung von Gerhard Schröder und Willi [sic] Brandt zur Entspannungspolitik. Stuttgart, 1974. pp. 534. *bibliog. (Hamburg. Hansische Universität. Seminar für Sozialwissenschaften. Sozialwissenschaftliche Studien. Heft 14)*

— — **Russia.**

GAWENDA (J.A.B.) The Soviet domination of Eastern Europe in the light of international law. Richmond, 1974. pp. 220. *bibliog.*

— **History.**

McNEILL (WILLIAM HARDY) Europe's steppe frontier 1500-1800. Chicago, 1964. pp. 252. *bibliog.*

PAULEY (BRUCE F.) The Habsburg legacy, 1867-1939. New York, [1972]. pp. 189. *bibliog.*

— **Nationalism.**

KING (ROBERT R.) Minorities under Communism: nationalities as a source of tension among Balkan communist states. Cambridge, Mass., 1973. pp. 326. *bibliog.*

— **Politics and government.**

FRANCE. Direction de la Documentation. La Documentation Française. Notes et Etudes Documentaires. Nos. 3,978-3, 979-3,980-3,981. L'Europe de l'Est en 1972; [par Thomas Schreiber]. [Paris], 1973. pp. 171. *bibliog.*

— **Population.**

MAGGS (PETER B.) Law and population growth in Eastern Europe. Medford, Mass., [1972]. pp. 30. *(Tufts University. Fletcher School of Law and Diplomacy. Law and Population Monograph Series. No.3)*

— **Relations (general) with the United Kingdom.**

SPEAIGHT (RICHARD) Cultural interchange with East Europe. Brighton, [1971]. pp. 105. *(Brighton. University of Sussex. Centre for Contemporary European Studies. Research Papers. No. 2)*

— **Religion.**

FRANCE. Direction de la Documentation. La Documentation Française. Notes et Etudes Documentaires. Nos. 3,790-3, 791. Les problèmes religieux en Europe orientale, 1945-1970; [by] Thomas Schreiber [and others]. Paris, 1971. pp. 78. *bibliog.*

BEESON (TREVOR) Discretion and valour: religious conditions in Russia and Eastern Europe; [report of a working party appointed by the British Council of Churches]. [London], 1974. pp. 348. *bibliog.*

EUROPEAN ATOMIC ENERGY COMMUNITY.

BERNARD (NADINE) and others. Le Comité économique et social [de la Communauté économique européenne et de la Communauté européenne de l'énergie atomique]. Bruxelles, 1972. pp. 277. *bibliog. (Brussels. Université Libre. Institut d'Etudes Européennes. Thèses et Travaux Politiques)*

EUROPEAN COAL AND STEEL COMMUNITY.

EUROPEAN COAL AND STEEL COMMUNITY. Auditor's report for the year. a., 1972[1st]- Luxembourg.

EUROPEAN COMMUNITIES.

EUROPEAN COMMUNITIES. 1965. Traité instituant un conseil unique et une commission unique des communautés européennes et documents annexes, etc. [Brussels, 1965]. pp. 73.

EUROPEAN COMMUNITIES. 1966- . [Speeches, addresses, etc. by Presidents, Vice Presidents and members of the Commission]. [Luxembourg], 1966 in progress.

LINDBERG (LEON N.) and SCHEINGOLD (STUART A.) Europe's would-be policy: patterns of change in the European Community. Englewood Cliffs, [1970]. pp. 314.

EUROPEAN COMMUNITIES. Press and Information [Service], Brussels Office. 1971- . European Community: the facts. Brussels, 1971 in progress.

EUROPEAN COMMUNITIES. 1952-72. Official Journal of the European Communities: special (English) edition, 1952-72; [secondary legislation of the European Communities]; (with Supplements; Corrigenda to instruments; Texts of Acts previously omitted; Subject index and numerical list). Luxembourg, 1972-73. 34 parts (in 9 vols.). *The Subject index and numerical list was prepared by the Department of Trade and Industry Library Services and published by HMSO.*

BROAD (ROGER) and JARRETT (ROBERT JOHN) Community Europe today; [revised edition of Community Europe: a short guide to the Common Market]. London, [1972]. pp. 255.

EUROPEAN COMMUNITIES.

MORGAN (ROGER) West European politics since 1945: the shaping of the European Community. London, 1972. pp. 243. *bibliog.*

PAULUS (DANIEL) La création du Comité permanent de l'emploi des Communautés européennes. Bruxelles, 1972. pp. 129. *(Brussels. Université Libre. Institut d'Etudes Européennes. Travaux)*

SPINELLI (ALTIERO) The European adventure; tasks for the enlarged community. London, 1972. pp. 194.

WATERKAMP (RAINER) Das Europa der Neun. Hannover, Niedersächsische Landeszentrale für Politische Bildung, 1972. pp. 167.

DEVELOPMENTS IN THE EUROPEAN COMMUNITIES: report (presented to the members of the Dáil and Seanad [Eire]). s-a., N 1973 (2nd)- Dublin.

DEVELOPMENTS IN THE EUROPEAN COMMUNITIES: report (presented to the members of the Dáil and Seanad [Eire]). s-a., N 1973 (2nd)- Dublin.

DAILY Telegraph guide to the Common Market; edited by Walter Farr. rev. ed. London, 1973. pp. 224.

BARBER (JAMES P.) and REED (BRUCE) eds. European Community: vision and reality;...assisted by Richard Gibbs and Robert Masterton. London, [1973]. pp. 434. *bibliog.*

DAHRENDORF (RALF) Plädoyer für die Europäische Union. München, [1973]. pp. 242.

DAHRENDORF (RALF) Towards a European science policy. Southampton, 1973. pp. 19. *(Southampton. University. Fawley Foundation. Lectures. 19)*

EUROPEAN COMMUNITIES. 1973. Treaties establishing the European Communities: treaties amending the treaties; documents concerning the accession. Luxembourg, 1973. pp. 1502.

MOWAT (ROBERT CASE) Creating the European Community. London, 1973. pp. 235. *bibliog.*

SHONFIELD (ANDREW) Europe: journey to an unknown destination; an expanded version of the BBC Reith Lectures 1972. London, 1973. pp. 96. *(British Broadcasting Corporation. Reith Lectures. 1972)*

SOAMES (Sir CHRISTOPHER) and others. Three views of Europe.. London, 1973. pp. 46. *(Conservative Political Centre. [publications]. No. 536)*

CONSTANTINESCO (VLAD) Compétences et pouvoirs dans les Communautés Européennes: contribution à l'étude de la nature juridique des Communautés. Paris, [1974]. pp. 492. *bibliog.*

PARTINGTON (LENA) compiler. The European Communities: a guide to the literature and an indication of sources of information. [London], 1974. pp. 101. *(U.K. Department of the Environment. Library. Information Series)*

EUROPEAN COMMUNITIES. [Press and Information Service, London Office]. Press releases. irreg., current issues only kept. London.

— **Germany.**

DEUTSCHE GESELLSCHAFT FUR AUSWARTIGE POLITIK. Forschungsinstitut. Regionale Verflechtung der Bundesrepublik Deutschland: empirische Analysen und theoretische Probleme. München, 1973. pp. 311. *(Schriften. Band 33)*

— **Greenland.**

DENMARK. Udenrigsministeriet. Markedssekretariat. 1972. Grønland og EF. [Copenhagen?, 1972]. 1 vol (unpaged). *Parallel texts in Danish and Greenlandic.*

— **Ireland (Republic).**

DEVELOPMENTS IN THE EUROPEAN COMMUNITIES: report (presented to the members of the Dáil and Seanad [Eire]). s-a., N 1973 (2nd)- Dublin.

EUROPEAN COMMUNITIES. (Cont.)

— Switzerland.

SWITZERLAND. Conseil Fédéral. 1971. L'évolution de l'intégration européenne et la position de la Suisse, du 11 août 1971. [Berne, 1971]. pp. 134.

— United Kingdom.

BARBER (JAMES P.) and REED (BRUCE) eds. European Community: vision and reality;...assisted by Richard Gibbs and Robert Masterton. London, [1973]. pp. 434. *bibliog.*

KAHN-FREUND (OTTO) European Community law and the British legal system; (transcript of... lecture held on 7 February 1972). [London], Civil Service College, [1973?]. fo. (31). *(Lectures on the European Community. Series A. No.5)*

SOAMES (Sir CHRISTOPHER) and others. Three views of Europe.. London, 1973. pp. 46. *(Conservative Political Centre. [publications]. No. 536]*

EUROPEAN CONVENTION ON ESTABLISHMENT (INDIVIDUALS).

COUNCIL OF EUROPE. Standing Committee on the European Convention on Establishment (Individuals). Periodical report. irreg., 1971(1st)- Strasbourg.

EUROPEAN CONVENTION ON HUMAN RIGHTS.

CASTBERG (FREDE) The European Convention on Human Rights; edited by Torkel Opsahl and Thomas Ouchterlony. Leiden. 1974. pp. 198. *bibliog.*

EUROPEAN COOPERATION.

COUNCIL OF EUROPE. European Treaties Series. Strasbourg, 1949 in progress.

SWITZERLAND. Conseil Fédéral. 1971. L'évolution de l'intégration européenne et la position de la Suisse, du 11 août 1971. [Berne, 1971]. pp. 134.

— Congresses.

HUOPANIEMI (JUKKA) Parliaments and European rapprochement: [report on] the conference of the Inter-Parliamentary Union on European Co- operation and Security, Helsinki, January 1973. Leiden, 1973. pp. 138.

EUROPEAN ECONOMIC COMMUNITY.

HALLSTEIN (WALTER) Der unvollendete Bundesstaat: europäische Erfahrungen und Erkenntnisse. Düsseldorf, 1969. pp. 283.

I COMUNISTI italiani e l'Europa: atti del Convegno promosso dal Cespe e dai gruppi parlamentari del Pci, Roma, 23-25 novembre 1971. Roma, 1971. pp. 359. *(Politica ed Economia. Quaderni. 3)*

MEYNAUD (JEAN) and SIDJANSKI (DUSAN) Les groupes de pression dans la Communauté européenne, 1958- 1968: structure et action des organisations professionnelles. Bruxelles, 1971. pp. 728. *(Brussels. Université Libre. Institut d'Etudes Européennes. Thèses et Travaux Politiques)*

BAMFIELD (J.A.N.) A consumer's guide to the Common Market. Loughborough, [1972]. pp. 52. *(Co-operative Union. Education Department. Topic for Today. No.3)*

BERNARD (NADINE) and others. Le Comité économique et social [de la Communauté économique européenne et de la Communauté européenne de l'énergie atomique]. Bruxelles, 1972. pp. 277. *bibliog. (Brussels. Université Libre. Institut d'Etudes Européennes. Thèses et Travaux Politiques)*

EUROPEAN COMMUNITIES. Commission. 1972. The enlarged Community: outcome of the negotiations with the applicant states. Brussels, 1972. pp. 69. *(Bulletin of the European Communities. Supplements. [1972/1])*

HALLSTEIN (WALTER) Europe in the making;... translated by Charles Roetter. London, 1972. pp. 343.

BAILEY (RICHARD) The European Community in the world. London, 1973. pp. 200. *bibliog.*

CHARNLEY (ALAN H.) The EEC: a study in applied economics. London, [1973]. pp. 337. *bibliogs.*

CONDORELLI (LUIGI) and STROZZI (GEROLAMO) L'agricoltura fra Comunità Economica Europea, stato e regioni. Bologna, [1973]. pp. 51. *(Istituto Nazionale di Economia Agraria and Istituto per la Scienza dell'Amministrazione Pubblica. Agricoltura e Regioni. 7)*

DEUTSCHES INSTITUT FÜR WIRTSCHAFTSFORSCHUNG. Sonderhefte. [Neue Folge]. Nr. 96. Wirtschaftspolitische Prioritätsunterschiede in der EG als Hindernisse für die Errichtung der Wirtschafts- und Währungsunion und Instrumente zu ihrer Überwindung; ([by] Fritz Franzmeyer und Bernhard Seidel). Berlin, 1973. pp. 162. *With English summary.*

The EUROPEAN community and the outsiders: [selected papers of a conference sponsored by the History Department of Waterloo Lutheran University in 1971; edited by] Peter Stingelin. Don Mills, Ont., [1973]. pp. 168.

GOODWIN (GEOFFREY LAWRENCE) The search for European unity: the place of the EEC; (transcript of... lecture held on 10 January 1972). [London], Civil Service College, [1973?. FO.19. *(LECTURES ON THE eUROPEAN cOMMUNITY. sERIES a. nO.1)*

GRAHL-MADSEN (ATLE) Européisk Felleskap. Bergen, 1973. pp. 55. *(Norges Handelshøyskole. Saertrykk-Serie. Nr.99) (Saertrykk av Bedriftsøkonomen, Nr.3,4,6 og 7/1972)*

GRAHL-MADSEN (ATLE) Handelsavtalene mellom EF og seks EFTA-stater. Bergen, 1973. pp. 116. *(Norges Handelshøyskole. Saertrykk-Serie. Nr.102) (Saertrykk av Bedriftsøkonomen, Nr.10/1972)*

HALLSTEIN (WALTER) Die Europäische Gemeinschaft; [fourth version of the work originally published in German as Der unvollendete Bundesstaat]. Düsseldorf, 1973. pp. 421.

JAUMONT (BERNARD) and others. Le Marché commun contre l'Europe. Paris, [1973]. pp. 192.

LECTURES ON THE EUROPEAN COMMUNITY. Series A. No. 12. The prospects?; (transcript of the panel discussion held on 27 March 1972). [London], Civil Service College, [1973?]. fo. 27.

MAYNE (RICHARD) The institutions of the EEC: their political development; (transcript of... lecture held on 17 January 1972). [London], Civil Service College, [1973?]. fo. 28. *(Lectures on the European Community. Series A. No.2)*

NOEL (EMILE) The present state of the Community; (with Appendix); (transcript of... lecture held on 24 January 1972). [London], Civil Service College, [1973?]. 2 pts. *(Lectures on the European Community. Series A. No.3)*

PRYCE (ROY) The politics of the European community. London, 1973. pp. 209. *bibliog. (Brighthton. University of Sussex. Centre for Contemporary European Studies. European Community Studies)*

MANSHOLT (SICCO LEENDERT) La crise: conversations avec Janine Delaunay. [Paris, 1974]. pp. 251.

— Africa.

PATTISON (KATHERINE JEAN) The European Economic Community and the developing countries: a political analysis with particular reference to association under Part IV of the Rome Treaty; [Ph.D. (London) thesis]. 1973. fo. 379. *bibliog. Typescript: unpublished. This thesis is the property of London University and may not be removed from the Library.*

— Austria.

BEIRAT FÜR WIRTSCHAFTS- UND SOZIALFRAGEN. [Publikationen. 23]. Die Verträge mit den Europäischen Gemeinschaften. Wien, 1972. pp. 124.

— Belgium.

WAUWE (LUDO VAN) België - Europa: unitaire of regionale ekonomie?. Antwerp, 1973. pp. 168. *bibliog.*

— Canada.

CANADA. Parliament. Senate. Standing Committee on Foreign Affairs. 1973. Canadian relations with the European Community; report; Les relations du Canada avec la Communauté européenne; rapport. Ottawa, 1973. pp. 52,52. *In English and French.*

PENTLAND (CHARLES CORRIE) The Canadian dilemma. Farnborough, Hants, [1973]. pp. 56. *(Atlantic Institute. Atlantic Papers. 1973.2)*

— Caribbean Area.

BILLERBECK (KLAUS) The negotiations on association between the Commonwealth Caribbean and the European community: problems and approaches for solution. Berlin, 1973. pp. 70. *(Deutsches Institut für Entwicklungspolitik. Occasional Papers. 16)*

— Denmark.

DANMARKS KOMMUNISTISKE PARTI. EEC, Faellesmarkedet, hvad er det?: (nej til monopolernes Faellesmarked;... redigeret af et udvalg ved Knud Jespersen) . 2nd ed. [Copenhagen, 1972]. pp. 32.

BRIXTOFTE (PETER) Konsekvenserne for Danmark af handelsaftalerne mellem EF og Finland, Island, Portugal, Schweiz, Sverige og Østrig. [Copenhagen], 1973. pp. 216.

JENSEN (KAARE TOFTKAER) Denmark's EEC representatives. Copenhagen, Ministry of Foreign Affairs, Press and Cultural Relations Department, [1973]. fo. 7.

— Europe, Eastern.

RANSOM (CHARLES) The European Community and Eastern Europe. London, 1973. pp. 112. *bibliog. (Brighton. University of Sussex. Centre for Contemporary European Studies. European Community Studies)*

— Germany.

SUPTHUT (CHRISTIAN ROBERT) Der Einfluss der europäischen Wirtschaftsintegration auf die Papierindustrie der BRD unter besonderer Berücksichtigung des Aussenhandels. Berlin, 1972. pp. 199. *bibliog.*

— Germany, Eastern.

SCHARPE (PETER) Europäische Wirtschaftsgemeinschaft und Deutsche Demokratische Republik: die Entwicklung ihrer Rechtsbeziehungen seit 1958 unter besonderer Berücksichtigung des innerdeutschen Handels. Tübingen, 1973. pp. 194. *bibliog. (Tübingen. Universität. Rechts- und Wirtschaftswissenschaftliche Fakultät. Rechtswissenschaftliche Abteilung. Juristische Studien. Band 50)*

— Ireland (Republic).

COUGHLAN (ANTHONY) The alternatives to membership. Dublin, 1972. pp. 20. *(Common Market Study Group. Ireland and the Common Market. 4)*

COUGHLAN (ANTHONY) Why Ireland should not join'. 2nd ed. Dublin, 1972. pp. 32. *(Common Market Study Group. Ireland and the Common Market. [8?])*

NEVIN (EDWARD THOMAS) and MOYNAGH (JAMES) Bishop of Calabar. Yes or no!: the economic and political implications. Dublin, 1972. pp. 16. *(Common Market Study Group. Ireland and the Common Market. 5)*

O'CONNELL (EMMETT) The consequences of monetary union and its effects on peripheral regions. Dublin, 1972. pp. 31. *(Common Market Study Group. Ireland and the Common Market. 6)*

O'RAIFEARTAIGH (T. F.) Ireland and the E.E.C.: the cultural aspects; [expanded version of a speech given to a symposium on the E.E.C. in Dublin in 1972]. Dublin, [1972?]. 1 pamphlet (unpaged).

O' SNODAIGH (PÁDRAIG) A second Act of Union?. Dublin, 1972. pp. 16. *(Common Market Study Group. Ireland and the Common Market. 7)*

— New Zealand.

NEW ZEALAND. 1971. New Zealand and the European Economic Community. Wellington, 1971. pp. 28.

EUROPEAN ECONOMIC COMMUNITY COUNTRIES.

— Norway.

NORWAY. Utenriksdepartementet. 1967. Om Norges forhold til de europeiske fellesskap. [Oslo?, 1967]. pp. 106. *(Norway. Stortinget. Stortingsmeldinger. 1966-67. Nr.86)*

NORWAY. Utenriksdepartementet. 1972. Om Norges tilslutning til De Europeiske Fellesskap. [Oslo?, 1972]. 1 vol., various pagings. *(Norway. Stortinget. Stortingsmeldinger. 1971-72, Nr. 50)*

GRAHL-MADSEN (ATLE) Avtaleverket om frihandel mellom Norge og EF. Bergen, 1973. pp. 252-61. *(Norges Handelshøyskole. Saertrykk-Serie. Nr. 104) (Saertrykk av Bedriftsøkonomen, Nr.5/1973)*

— Scandinavia.

DREYER (H. PETER) Scandinavia faces Europe. Farnborough, Hants, [1973]. pp. 77. *(Atlantic Institute. Atlantic Papers. 1973.1)*

— Spain.

ACUERDO entre España y la Comunidad Economica Europea. [Bilbao, 1970]. pp. 157.

POU SERRADELL (VICTOR) España y la Europa Comunitaria. [Pamplona], 1973. pp. 335. *bibliog.*

— Sweden.

SWEDEN. Handelsdepartementet. 1972. Sveriges avtal med EEC och CECA. Stockholm, 1972. pp. 184. *(EEC Information)*

— Switzerland.

LIPPUNER (HANS) Die Bundesfinanzen und die EWG-Steuerharmonisierung, unter besonderer Berücksichtigung der Umsatzsteuer. Bern, 1970. pp. 148. *bibliog.*

BOSSHARD (RUDOLF) Schweizerische Privatwirtschaft und europäische Integration;... Vortrag gehalten... 1971 in St. Gallen. [Zürich, 1971]. pp. 16. *(Wirtschaftsförderung: Gesellschaft zur Förderung der Schweizerischen Wirtschaft. Stimmen zur Staats- und Wirtschaftspolitik. 50)*

WINTERBERGER (GERHARD) Die Schweiz und die EWG: Bestandesaufnahme und Würdigung. [Zürich, 1972]. pp. 9. *(Wirtschaftsförderung: Gesellschaft zur Förderung der Schweizerischen Wirtschaft. Stimmen zur Staats- und Wirtschaftspolitik. 53) (Sonderdruck aus Schweizer Monatshefte, Heft 6, September 1972)*

— United Kingdom.

BRITISH TOURIST AUTHORITY. Britain and the Common Market: an assessment of the possible effects on tourism to the UK if Britain joins. [London], 1971. pp. 8.

NORTH LONDON HASLEMERE GROUP. Sugar today, jam tomorrow?: a study of the sell-out over Commonwealth sugar in the Common Market negotiations. London, [1971]. pp. (11).

BURDENS and benefits of farm-support policies; by T.E. Josling [and others]. London, 1972. pp. 85. *(Trade Policy Research Centre. Agricultural Trade Papers. No. 1)*

FRANCE. Direction de la Documentation. La Documentation Française. Notes et Etudes Documentaires. Nos. 3,882-3, 883. L'adhésion de la Grande-Bretagne aux Communautés Européennes, [par Françoise de la Serre]. [Paris], 1972. 2 parts.

NORTH WEST ECONOMIC PLANNING COUNCIL. Implications for the North West of UK entry to the EEC. Manchester, 1972. fo. 13.

FUKUDA (HARUKO) Britain in Europe: impact on the third world. London, 1973. pp. 194.

GUILDSTREAM RESEARCH SERVICES. Britain and the Common Market. London, 1973. 4 vols. (in 1).

THELEN (KLAUS) Die Vereinbarkeit des Vertrages zur Gründung der Europäischen Wirtschaftsgemeinschaft mit der britischen Verfassung. Köln, [1973]. pp. 283. *bibliog. (Cologne. Universität. Institut für das Recht der Europäischen Gemeinschaften. Kölner Schriften zum Europarecht. Band 21)*

BRITAIN in the Common Market: a new business opportunity: [record of a conference held jointly by the London Graduate School of Business Studies and the Manchester Business School at Peterlee, March 1973]; edited by M.E. Beesley and D.C. Hague. London, 1974. pp. 298.

RIPPON (AUBREY GEOFFREY FREDERICK) Our future in Europe: the case for staying in the European Community. London, 1974. pp. 24. *(Conservative Political Centre. [Publications]. No. 560)*

— United States.

BRAND (ROBERT A.) Relations between the European Community and the United States; (transcript of... lecture held on 21 February 1972). [London], Civil Service College, [1973?]. fo. (20). *(Lectures on the European Community. Series A. No.7)*

EUROPEAN ECONOMIC COMMUNITY ASSOCIATED COUNTRIES.

VAZQUEZ LABOURDETTE (ALEJANDRO) La asociacion con la comunidad economica europea. Sevilla, 1970. pp. 244. *bibliog. (Seville. Universidad. Publicaciones. Serie Derecho. No.8)*

MATHEWS (ALAN) The E.E.C. and the third world: an analysis of the Yaunde agreements. London, 1971. pp. 25. *(Europe-Africa Research Project. Europe/Africa Pamphlets. 20)*

EWG-Zollpräferenzen und Welthandelsstruktur: die Auswirkungen der Assoziierungs- und Präferenzabkommen auf die Struktur des Welthandels; [by] Karl Fasbender [and others]; Projektleitung, Dietrich Kebschull. Hamburg, 1973. pp. 296. *bibliog. (Hamburg. Hamburgisches Welt-Wirtschafts-Archiv. Studien zur Aussenwirtschaft und Entwicklungspolitik)* With English summary.

JONES (DAVID) of the Overseas Development Institute. Europe's chosen few: policy and practice of the EEC aid programme. London, [1973]. pp. 100.

PATTISON (KATHERINE JEAN) The European Economic Community and the developing countries: a political analysis with particular reference to association under Part IV of the Rome Treaty; [Ph.D. (London) thesis]. 1973. fo. 379. *bibliog. Typescript: unpublished. This thesis is the property of London University and may not be removed from the Library.*

— Commerce.

EUROPEAN COMMUNITIES. Commission. 1973. (Renewal and enlargement of the association with the AASM and certain Commonwealth developing countries): memorandum...to the Council on 9 April 1973. [Brussels], 1973. pp. 38. *(Bulletin of the European Communities. Supplements. [1973/1]*

EUROPEAN COMMUNITIES. Directorate-General for Development and Cooperation. 1974. European Development Fund. Brussels, 1974. pp. 112.

— Economic policy.

EUROPEAN COMMUNITIES. Commission. 1973. (Renewal and enlargement of the association with the AASM and certain Commonwealth developing countries): memorandum...to the Council on 9 April 1973. [Brussels], 1973. pp. 38. *(Bulletin of the European Communities. Supplements. [1973/1]*

EUROPEAN COMMUNITIES. Directorate-General for Development and Cooperation. 1974. European Development Fund. Brussels, 1974. pp. 112.

— Statistics.

EUROPEAN COMMUNITIES. Statistical Office. Associés: annuaire statistique des A.O.M. [Associés d'Outre-Mer]. a., 1970. Luxembourg.

EUROPEAN ECONOMIC COMMUNITY COUNTRIES.

EUROPEAN COMMUNITIES. Commission. 1973. (Attainment of the economic and monetary union): communication... to the Council on 30 April 1973. [Brussels], 1973. pp. 19. *(Bulletin of the European Communities. Supplements. [1973/5])*

— Commerce.

EUROPEAN FREE TRADE ASSOCIATION. 1972. The trade effects of EFTA and the EEC 1959-1967. Geneva, 1972. pp. 168.

PARKLAND RESEARCH EUROPE. Guide to national practices in western Europe: a guide to commercial business and legal practices and attitudes in the continental EEC countries and Switzerland; [edited by Victor Selwyn]; research directed by Parkland Research Europe SA . London, [1973]. pp. 223.

ROBERTSON (DAVID H.) The enlarged European Community in the international trading system. [Reading], 1973. pp. 29. *(Reading. University. Department of Economics. Discussion Papers in Economics. No. 39)*

KREININ (MORDECHAI ELIHAU) Trade relations of the EEC: an empirical investigation. New York, 1974. pp. 126.

TABER (GEORGE M.) Patterns and prospects of Common Market trade. London, 1974. pp. 192.

— — Bibliography.

COMMONWEALTH BUREAU OF AGRICULTURAL ECONOMICS. EEC agricultural policy. Pt. 3. International trade; compiled by Jean Kestner. [Oxford], 1973. pp. 23. *(Annotated Bibliographies. No.16) Compiled from World Agricultural Economics and Rural Sociology Abstracts.*

— — Asia.

GHAI (DHARAM P.) The enlargement of the E.E.C. and the Asian Commonwealth countries. London, Commonwealth Secretariat, 1973. pp. 57. *(Commonwealth Economic Papers. No.2)*

— — South Africa.

SOUTH AFRICA. Planning Advisory Council. Subsidiary Committee for the Optimum Utilization of Mineral Resources in the Republic of South Africa and in South West Africa, 1970. The mineral trade between South Africa and the European Economic Community; a report. Pretoria, 1970. pp. 132. *bibliog.*

— Commercial policy.

EWG-Zollpräferenzen und Welthandelsstruktur: die Auswirkungen der Assoziierungs- und Präferenzabkommen auf die Struktur des Welthandels; [by] Karl Fasbender [and others]; Projektleitung, Dietrich Kebschull. Hamburg, 1973. pp. 296. *bibliog. (Hamburg. Hamburgisches Welt-Wirtschafts-Archiv. Studien zur Aussenwirtschaft und Entwicklungspolitik)* With English summary.

EUROPEAN COMMUNITIES. Commission. 1973. Development of an overall approach to trade in view of the coming multilateral negotiations in GATT: memorandum... to the Council forwarded on 9 April and amended on 22 May 1973. [Brussels], 1973. pp. 12. *(Bulletin of the European Communities. Supplements. [1973/2])*

EUROPEAN COMMUNITIES. Commission. 1973. (Towards the establishment of a European industrial base): memorandum... on the technological and industrial policy programme... presented to the Council on 7 May 1973. [Brussels], 1973. pp. 23. *(Bulletin of the European Communities. Supplements. [1973/7]*

KREININ (MORDECHAI ELIHAU) Trade relations of the EEC: an empirical investigation. New York, 1974. pp. 126.

— Commercial treaties.

BRIXTOFTE (PETER) Konsekvenserne for Danmark af handelsaftalerne mellem EF og Finland, Island, Portugal, Schweiz, Sverige og Østrig. [Copenhagen], 1973. pp. 216.

— Economic conditions.

GUILDSTREAM RESEARCH SERVICES. Britain and the Common Market. London, 1973. 4 vols. (in 1).

— Economic policy.

EUROPEAN COMMUNITIES. Commission. Cahiers de Reconversion Industrielle . Bruxelles, 1963 in progress.

ECONOMIC COMMUNITY COUNTRIES. (Cont.)

La POLITIQUE régionale du Marché Commun: ([papers presented at a round table at the] Centre d'Etudes Européennes, Université Catholique de Louvain [in 1969]). Bruxelles, 1971. pp. 218.

DEUTSCHES INSTITUT FÜR WIRTSCHAFTSFORSCHUNG. Sonderhefte. [Neue Folge]. Nr. 96. Wirtschaftspolitische Prioritätsunterschiede in der EG als Hindernisse für die Errichtung der Wirtschafts- und Währungsunion und Instrumente zu ihrer Überwindung; ([by] Fritz Franzmeyer und Bernhard Seidel). Berlin, 1973. pp. 162. *With English summary.*

EUROPEAN COMMUNITIES. Commission. 1973. Report on the regional problems in the enlarged community. Brussels, 1973. pp. 289.

EUROPEAN COMMUNITIES. Commission. 1973. Report on the regional problems in the enlarged Community; presented to the Council on 4 May. [Brussels], 1973. pp. 14. *(Bulletin of the European Communities. Supplements. [1973/8])*

LIND (HAROLD) Regional policy in Britain and the Six; (transcript of ... lecture held on 13 March 1972). [London], Civil Service College, [1973?]. fo. 28. *(Lectures on the European Community. Series A. No. 10)*

ARNAUD-AMELLER (PAULE) Europe: vers une politique conjoncturelle commune. Paris, 1974. pp. 126. *bibliog. (Fondation Nationale des Sciences Politiques. Travaux et Recherches de Sciences Economiques)*

— Foreign economic relations.

EUROPEAN COMMUNITIES. Commission. 1972. Memorandum...on a Community policy on development cooperation: programme for initial actions; 2 February 1972. [Brussels], 1972. pp. 23. *(Bulletin of the European Communities. Supplements. [1972/2])*

DURIEUX (JEAN) The European Community and the developing world; (transcript of... lecture held on 20 March 1972). [London], Civil Service College, [1973?]. fo. 21. *(Lectures on the European Community. Series A. No. 11)*

FUKUDA (HARUKO) Britain in Europe: impact on the third world. London, 1973. pp. 194.

PATTISON (KATHERINE JEAN) The European Economic Community and the developing countries: a political analysis with particular reference to association under Part IV of the Rome Treaty; [Ph.D. (London) thesis]. 1973. fo. 379. *bibliog. Typescript: unpublished. This thesis is the property of London University and may not be removed from the Library.*

— — Africa, Subsaharan.

EUROPEAN COMMUNITIES. Commission. 1973. (Renewal and enlargement of the association with the AASM and certain Commonwealth developing countries): memorandum...to the Council on 9 April 1973. [Brussels], 1973. pp. 38. *(Bulletin of the European Communities. Supplements. [1973/1])*

— Industries.

EUROPEAN COMMUNITIES. Commission. Cahiers de Reconversion Industrielle. Bruxelles, 1963 in progress.

EUROPEAN COMMUNITIES. Commission. 1973. (Towards the establishment of a European industrial base): memorandum... on the technological and industrial policy programme... presented to the Council on 7 May 1973. [Brussels], 1973. pp. 23. *(Bulletin of the European Communities. Supplements. [1973/7])*

GUILDSTREAM RESEARCH SERVICES. Britain and the Common Market. London, 1973. 4 vols. (in 1).

MALTZAHN (DIETRICH) Industrial policy in an enlarged Community; (transcript of... lecture held on 28 February 1972). [London], Civil Service College, [1973?]. fo. 19. *(Lectures on the European Community. Series A. No.8)*

TOULEMON (ROBERT) and FLORY (JEAN) Une politique industrielle pour l'Europe. [Paris], 1974. pp. 272.

— Social policy.

EUROPEAN COMMUNITIES. Commission. 1973. Guidelines for a social action programme; presented... to the Council on 19 April 1973. [Brussels], 1973. pp. 13. *(Bulletin of the European Communities. Supplements. [1973/4])*

— Statistics.

EUROPEAN COMMUNITIES. Statistical Office. General Statistics. Série Spéciale: Tableaux Entrées-Sorties, 1965 . [Luxembourg], [1970-73].

EUROPEAN FEDERATION.

HALLSTEIN (WALTER) Der unvollendete Bundesstaat: europäische Erfahrungen und Erkenntnisse. Düsseldorf, 1969. pp. 283.

CHARLTON (SUE ELLEN M.) The French left and European integration. Denver, Col., [1972]. pp. 111. *bibliog. (Denver. University. Social Science Foundation and Graduate School of International Studies. Monograph Series in World Affairs. vol.9, no.4)*

HALLSTEIN (WALTER) Europe in the making;... translated by Charles Roetter. London, 1972. pp. 343.

MASCLET (JEAN CLAUDE) ed. L'Europe politique. [Paris, 1972]. pp. 96. *bibliog.*

PATERSON (WILLIAM EDGAR) The German Social Democratic Party and European integration, 1949-57: a case-study of opposition in foreign affairs; [Ph.D (London) thesis]. 1972. fo. 239. *bibliog. Typescript: unpublished. This thesis is the property of London University and may not be removed from the Library.*

GOODWIN (GEOFFREY LAWRENCE) The search for European unity: the place of the EEC; (transcript of... lecture held on 10 January 1972). [London], Civil Service College, [1973?. FO.19. *(lECTURES ON THE eUROPEAN cOMMUNITY. sERIES a. nO.1)*

La GREFFE européenne; ([by] Henri Rieben [and others]). Lausanne, 1973. pp. 133. *(Lausanne. Université. Centre de Recherches Européennes. Publications)*

La VOCATION européenne d'Otto de Hapsbourg-Lorraine; ([by] Marcel Regamey [and others]). Lausanne, 1973. pp. 183. *bibliog. (Lausanne. Université. Centre de Recherches Européennes. Publications. 1. Histoire, Précurseurs et Promoteurs de l'Union de l'Europe)*

Le FEDERALISME et Alexandre Marc. Lausanne, 1974. pp. 235. *bibliog. (Lausanne. Université. Centre de Recherches Européennes. Publications. 1. Histoire, Précurseurs et Promoteurs de l'Union de l'Europe)*

FONTAINE (PASCAL) Le Comité d'Action pour les Etats-Unis d'Europe de Jean Monnet. Lausanne, 1974. pp. 242. *bibliog. (Lausanne. Université. Centre de Recherches Européennes. Publications. 2. Le Processus d'Union de l'Europe)*

HARRISON (REGINALD J.) Europe in question: theories of regional international integration.London, 1974. pp. 256.

PATERSON (WILLIAM EDGAR) The SPD and European integration. Farnborough, [1974]. pp. 177. *bibliog.*

EUROPEAN FREE TRADE ASSOCIATION.

EUROPEAN FREE TRADE ASSOCIATION. 1966. EFTA: European Free Trade Association... a single market of 100,000,000 people. [Geneva, 1966?]. pp. 24.

EUROPEAN FREE TRADE ASSOCIATION. 1973. The European Free Trade Association: Austria, Finland, Iceland, Norway, Portugal, Sweden, Switzerland and Liechtenstein. Geneva, 1973. pp. 13.

GRAHL-MADSEN (ATLE) Handelsavtalene mellom EF og seks EFTA-stater. Bergen, 1973. pp. 116. *(Norges Handelshøyskole. Saertrykk-Serie. Nr.102) (Saertrykk av Bedriftsøkonomen, Nr.10/1972)*

SZOKOLÓCZY-SYLLABA (ADRIENNE) EFTA: restrictive business practices. Bern, 1973. pp. 270. *bibliog. (Institut für Europäisches und Internationales Wirtschafts- und Sozialrecht and Centre d'Etudes Juridiques Européennes. Schweizerische Beiträge zum Europarecht. Band 13)*

CURZON (VICTORIA) The essentials of economic integration: lessons of EFTA experience. London, 1974. pp. 319. *bibliog.*

EUROPEAN FREE TRADE ASSOCIATION COUNTRIES

— Commerce.

EUROPEAN FREE TRADE ASSOCIATION. 1972. The trade effects of EFTA and the EEC 1959-1967. Geneva, 1972. pp. 168.

— — Germany.

DEUTSCHE HANDELSKAMMER IN OESTERREICH, WIEN, and others. Die Entwicklung der deutschen Marktanteile im Einfuhr der neutralen EFTA-Länder Oesterreich, Schweden, Schweiz im Zeitraum 1960 bis 1968. [Zurich, imprint, 1969]. pp. 71.

— — Philippine Islands.

PHILIPPINE ISLANDS. Department of Commerce and Industry. Research and Information Division. 1965. Philippine trade with the EFTA countries; editor Socorro B. Ramos. Manila, 1965. pp. 45.

— Economic policy.

EUROPEAN FREE TRADE ASSOCIATION. Economic Development Committee. 1968. Regional policy in EFTA: an examination of the growth centre idea; [report of a Working Party, P.B.M. James, chairman].Edinburgh, 1968. pp. 232. *bibliog. (Glasgow. University. Department of Economic and Social Research. Social and Economic Studies. Occasional Papers. No. 10)*

— Industries.

EUROPEAN FREE TRADE ASSOCIATION. Economic Development Committee Working Party. 1971. Regional policy in EFTA: industrial mobility; an examination of industrial mobility in the context of regional policies in EFTA countries. Geneva, 1971. pp. 160.

EUROPEAN FUND.

EUROPEAN COMMUNITIES. Commission. 1973. (Monetary organization of the Community): report... to the Council on the adjustment of short-term monetary support arrangements and the conditions for progressive pooling of reserves: presented...on 28 June 1973. [Brussels], 1973. pp. 17. *bibliog. (Bulletin of the European Communities. Supplements. [1973/12])*

EUROPEAN INVESTMENT BANK.

FRANCE. Direction de la Documentation. La Documentation Française. Notes et Etudes Documentaires. Nos. 4,022-4, 023. La Banque Européenne d'Investissement, par Marc Becker. [Paris], 1973. pp. 61. *bibliog.*

EUROPEAN NEWSPAPERS

— Bibliography — Union lists.

PEMBERTON (JOHN E.) compiler. European materials in British university libraries: a bibliography and union catalogue;...with A survey by William E. Paterson. London, 1973. pp. 42.

EUROPEAN PARLIAMENT.

WORKING PARTY EXAMINING THE PROBLEM OF THE ENLARGEMENT OF THE POWERS OF THE EUROPEAN PARLIAMENT. 1972. Report of the Working Party...: report Vedel. Brussels, European Communities, 1972. pp. 89. *(Bulletin of the European Communities. Supplements. [1972/4])*

EUROPEAN COMMUNITIES. Commission. 1973. Strengthening of the budgetary powers of the European Parliament: project... presented to the Council on 8 June 1973. [Brussels], 1973. pp. 15. *(Bulletin of the European Communities. Supplements. [1973/9])*

Il PARLAMENTO europeo e il problema della sua elezione a suffragio universale: seminario di studi promosso dal Centro Studi sulle Comunità Europee dell'Università di Pavia, 30 ottobre 1971. Milano, 1973. pp. 71. *(Politico, Il. Quaderni. n.11)* With English summaries.

SOAMES (Sir CHRISTOPHER) and others. Three views of Europe.. London, 1973. pp. 46. *(Conservative Political Centre. [publications]. No. 536)*

EUROPEAN PERIODICALS

— Bibliography — Union lists.

PEMBERTON (JOHN E.) compiler. European materials in British university libraries: a bibliography and union catalogue;...with A survey by William E. Paterson. London, 1973. pp. 42.

EUROPEAN RESETTLEMENT FUND.

TRYFONAS (CHRISTOS) Le Fonds de Réétablissement du Conseil de l'Europe: contribution à la théorie des organes subsidiaires des organisations internationales. Paris, 1974. pp. 575. *bibliog. (Revue Générale de Droit International Public. Publications. Nouvelle Série. No. 21)*

EUROPEAN STUDIES.

REGISTER OF COURSES IN EUROPEAN STUDIES IN BRITISH UNIVERSITIES AND POLYTECHNICS; pd. by University Association for Contemporary European Studies. irreg., 1973/4- London.

EUROPEAN WAR, 1914—1918.

SHERMER (DAVID) World War I; edited by S.L. Mayer. London, 1973. pp. 256.

MARWICK (ARTHUR J.B.) War and social change in the twentieth century: a comparative study of Britain, France, Germany, Russia and the United States. London, 1974. pp. 258. *bibliog.*

— Aerial operations.

JONES (NEVILLE) The origins of strategic bombing: a study of the development of British air strategic thought and practice up to 1918. London, 1973. pp. 240. *bibliog.*

— Blockades.

FARRAR (MARJORIE MILBANK) Conflict and compromise: the strategy, politics and diplomacy of the French blockade, 1914-1918. The Hague, 1974. pp. 216. *bibliog.*

— Campaigns.

WALLACH (JEHUDA L.) Das Dogma der Vernichtungsschlacht: die Lehren von Clausewitz und Schlieffen und ihre Wirkungen in zwei Weltkriegen; (aus dem Englischen von Hans Jürgen Baron von Koskull). Frankfurt am Main, 1967. pp. 475. *bibliog.*

— Campaigns
— — Eastern.

ISTRATI (EVGENIIA NIKOLAEVNA) Demokraticheskoe dvizhenie za mir na Rumynskom fronte v 1917 godu; pod redaktsiei... A.S. Esaulenko. Kishinev, 1973. pp. 148. *bibliog.*

— — Western.

PEDRONCINI (GUY) Pétain: général en chef, 1917-1918. Paris, 1974. pp. 463. *bibliog. (Paris. Université de Paris I (Panthéon- Sorbonne). Publications. Nouvelle Série. Recherches. 8)*

— Causes.

BOUDIN (LOUIS BOUDIANOFF) Socialism and war: [reprint of the work originally published in 1916]; with a new introduction...by James Weinstein. New York, 1972. pp. 267.

KANN (ROBERT ADOLF) Kaiser Franz Joseph und der Ausbruch des Weltkrieges: eine Betrachtung über den Quellenwert der Aufzeichnungen von Dr. Heinrich Kanner. Wien, 1971. pp. 24. *(Österreichische Akademie der Wissenschaften. Philosophisch-Historische Klasse. Sitzungsberichte. 274. Band. 3. Abhandlung)*

BERGHAHN (VOLKER R.) Rüstung und Machtpolitik: zur Anatomie des "Kalten Krieges" vor 1914. Düsseldorf, [1973]. pp. 94.

HOELZLE (ERWIN) Der Geheimnisverrat und der Kriegsausbruch 1914. Göttingen, 1973. pp. 39. *(Ranke-Gesellschaft. Historisch-Politische Hefte. Heft 23)*

— Diplomatic history.

THEODOULOU (CHRISTOS A.) Greece and the Entente, August 1, 1914-September 25, 1916. Thessaloniki, 1971. pp. 379. *bibliog. (Hidryma Meleton Chersonesou Tou Haimou. [Publications]. 129)*

KOBLIK (STEVEN) Sweden: the neutral victor: Sweden and the Western powers, 1917-1918: a study of Anglo-American-Swedish relations. Stockholm, [1972]. pp. 233. *bibliog. (Lund. Universitet. Historiska Institutionen. Lund Studies in International History. No. 3)*

MENGER (MANFRED) Die Finnlandpolitik des deutschen Imperialismus, 1917-1918. Berlin, 1974. pp. 242. *bibliog. (Akademie der Wissenschaften der DDR. Zentralinstitut für Geschichte. Schriften. Band 38)*

— Economic aspects — Russia.

SIDOROV (ARKADII LAVROVICH) Ekonomicheskoe polozhenie Rossii v gody pervoi mirovoi voiny. Moskva, 1973. pp. 655.

— Historiography.

KANN (ROBERT ADOLF) Kaiser Franz Joseph und der Ausbruch des Weltkrieges: eine Betrachtung über den Quellenwert der Aufzeichnungen von Dr. Heinrich Kanner. Wien, 1971. pp. 24. *(Österreichische Akademie der Wissenschaften. Philosophisch-Historische Klasse. Sitzungsberichte. 274. Band. 3. Abhandlung)*

— Influence and results.

ANGELL (NORMAN) pseud. [i.e. Sir Ralph Norman Angell LANE] The fruits of victory: a sequel to "The great illusion"; [reprint of the work originally published in 1921, including the introduction to the American edition]; with a new introduction... by S.J. Stearns. New York, 1972. pp. 338.

WINTER (J.M.) Socialism and the challenge of war: ideas and politics in Britain, 1912-18. London, 1974. pp. 310. *bibliog.*

— Jews.

OPPENHEIMER (FRANZ) Die Judenstatistik des preussischen Kriegsministeriums. München, 1922. pp. 48.

— Peace.

MANTOUX (ETIENNE) La paix calomniée; ou, Les conséquences économiques de M. Keynes. [Paris, 1946]. pp. 333.

ISTRATI (EVGENIIA NIKOLAEVNA) Demokraticheskoe dvizhenie za mir na Rumynskom fronte v 1917 godu; pod redaktsiei... A.S. Esaulenko. Kishinev, 1973. pp. 148. *bibliog.*

— Reparations.

KRUEGER (PETER) Deutschland und die Reparationen 1918/19: die Genesis des Reparationsproblems in Deutschland zwischen Waffenstillstand und Versailler Friedensschluss. Stuttgart, [1973]. pp. 224. *bibliog. (Vierteljahrshefte für Zeitgeschichte. Schriftenreihe. Nr.25)*

— Treaties.

GRABSKI (WŁADYSŁAW) Wspomnienia ze Spa; wstęp i przypisy opracował Stanisław Kirkor. Londyn, 1973. pp. 54.

— War work.

NATIONAL UNION OF TEACHERS. National Union of Teachers war record, 1914-1919: a short account of duty and work accomplished during the war. London, 1920. pp. 207.

— Belgium.

WILS (LODE) Flamenpolitik en aktivisme: Vlaanderen tegenover België in de eerste wereldoorlog. Leuven, [1974]. pp. 272. *bibliog.*

— Finland.

MENGER (MANFRED) Die Finnlandpolitik des deutschen Imperialismus, 1917-1918. Berlin, 1974. pp. 242. *bibliog. (Akademie der Wissenschaften der DDR. Zentralinstitut für Geschichte. Schriften. Band 38)*

— France.

CASTEX (HENRI) Les comités secrets: 1917, la paix refusée, un million de morts inutiles. [Paris, 1972]. pp. 239. *bibliog.*

FARRAR (MARJORIE MILBANK) Conflict and compromise: the strategy, politics and diplomacy of the French blockade, 1914-1918. The Hague, 1974. pp. 216. *bibliog.*

— Germany.

DEUTSCHLAND in der Weltpolitik des 19. und 20.Jahrhunderts: (Fritz Fischer zum 65.Geburtstag; [edited by] Imanuel Geiss [and] Bernd Jürgen Wendt). Düsseldorf, [1973]. pp. 594. *bibliog. In various languages.*

KOCKA (JUERGEN) Klassengesellschaft im Krieg: deutsche Sozialgeschichte, 1914- 1918. Göttingen, 1973. pp. 230. *bibliog.*

— Greece.

SMITH (MICHAEL LLEWELLYN) Ionian vision: Greece in Asia Minor, 1919-1922. London, 1973. pp. 401. *bibliog.*

— Italy.

ITALY. Camera dei Deputati. Segretariato Generale. Archivio Storico. 1967. Comitati segreti sulla condotta della guerra, giugno - dicembre 1917. [Roma, 1967]. pp. 249.

— Russia — Latvia.

GERMANIS (ULDIS) Oberst Vacietis und die lettischen Schützen im Weltkreig und in der Oktoberrevolution. Stockholm, 1974. pp. 336. *bibliog. (Stockholms Universitet. Acta Universitatis Stockholmiensis. Stockholm Studies in History. 20)* With English summary.

— Switzerland.

BOEHNY (FERDINAND) Die sozialistische Jugendbewegung des Ersten Weltkrieges als politischer Faktor. ?bASEL[, 1964] . PP. 14. (sONDERDRUCK AUS DEM oEFFENTLICHEN dIENST, jAHRGANG 1964, nRN.45 BIS 49)

SCHOCH (JUERG) Die Oberstenaffäre: eine innenpolitische Krise, 1915/1916. Bern, 1972. pp. 169. *bibliog.*

— United Kingdom.

WINTER (J.M.) Socialism and the challenge of war: ideas and politics in Britain, 1912-18. London, 1974. pp. 310. *bibliog.*

— United States.

DEVLIN (PATRICK ARTHUR) Baron Devlin. Too proud to fight: Woodrow Wilson's neutrality. London, 1974. pp. 731. *bibliog.*

EUROPEANS IN NIGERIA.

ISICHEI (ELIZABETH ALLO) The Ibo people and the Europeans: the genesis of a relationship - to 1906. London, 1973. pp. 207. *bibliog.*

EUTHANASIA.

KOHL (MARVIN) The morality of killing: sanctity of life, abortion and euthanasia. London, 1974. pp. 112. *bibliog.*

WILSHAW (CHARLES) The right to die: a rational approach to voluntary euthanasia. London, [1974]. pp. 23.

EUZKADI TA ASKATASUNA.

SALABERRI (KEPA) El proceso de Euskadi en Burgos: el sumarisimo 31/69. Paris, 1971. pp. 319.

EVALUATION RESEARCH (SOCIAL ACTION PROGRAMMES)

— United States.

SOCIAL experiments and social program evaluation; [proceedings of a symposium sponsored by the Washington Operations Research Council held at the National Bureau of Standards, May 1972]; edited by James G. Abert and Murray Kamrass. Cambridge, Mass., [1974]. pp. 199.

EVIDENCE (LAW)

— Russia.

MUKHIN (IVAN IOSIFOVICH) Ob"ektivnaia istina i nekotorye voprosy otsenki sudebnykh dokazatel'stv pri osushchestvlenii pravosudiia. Leningrad, 1971. pp. 184.

DODIN (EVGENII VASIL'EVICH) Dokazatel'stva v administrativnom protsesse. Moskva, 1973. pp. 192.

EVIDENCE, CRIMINAL

— Russia.

BOKHAN (VLADIMIR FEDOROVICH) Formirovanie ubezhdenii suda. Minsk, 1973. pp. 159.

TEORIIA dokazatel'stv v sovetskom ugolovnom protsesse. 2nd ed. Moskva, 1973. pp. 735.

— United Kingdom.

STURGE (HAROLD FRANCIS RALPH) and RESTON (CLIFFORD A.) The main rules of evidence in criminal cases. Chichester, 1972. pp. 20.

ARCHBOLD (JOHN FREDERICK) Pleading, evidence and practice in criminal cases; thirty-eighth edition by T.R. Fitzwalter Butler and Stephen Mitchell; (with supplement). London, 1973. pp. 1663.

EXAMINATIONS.

BAUER (GUENTHER) Vergleichende Studie über die Reife- und Abschlussprüfungen an den allgemeinbildenden höheren Schulen der Länder Österreich, Bundesrepublik Deutschland, Schweiz und England; (herausgegeben im Auftrage des Bundesministeriums für Unterricht). Wien, [1969]. pp. 143. *bibliog.* (*Beiträge zur pädagogischen Psychologie. Heft 275- 283*)

— United Kingdom.

MILLER (C.M.L.) and PARLETT (MALCOLM) Up to the mark: a study of the examination game. London, 1974. pp. 128. *bibliog.* (*Society for Research into Higher Education. [Research into Higher Education] Monographs. 21*)

— — Ireland, Northern.

IRELAND, NORTHERN. General Certificate of Education Committee. 1969. Report... 1965-1969: [F.A. Vick, chairman]. Belfast, 1969. pp. 41.

— — Scotland.

SCOTTISH COUNCIL FOR RESEARCH IN EDUCATION. International Examination Inquiry. The prognostic value of university entrance examinations in Scotland. London, 1934. pp. 126.

EXCAVATIONS (ARCHAEOLOGY)

— South Africa.

CALIFORNIA UNIVERSITY. Anthropological Records. vol. 28. Montagu Cave in prehistory: a descriptive analysis; by Charles M. Keller. Berkeley, 1973. pp. 98, (30), 53 plates. *bibliog.*

EXCHANGE.

GERSCH (ALEXANDER) On the theory of exchange value. Würzburg, afterwards Barcelona, [imprint, 1969-72]. 2 vols.

EXECUTIONS (LAW)

— Ireland (Republic).

EIRE. Committee on Court Practice and Procedure. 1972. Eighteenth interim report...: execution of money judgments orders and decrees. Dublin, [1972]. pp. 26.

EXECUTIONS AND EXECUTIONERS

— United States.

BOWERS (WILLIAM J.) Executions in America. Lexington, Mass., [1974]. pp. 489. *bibliog.*

EXECUTIVE ADVISORY BODIES

— Sweden.

CLAESSON (GÖRAN C-O.) Statens Ostyriga Utredande: betänkande om kommittéväsendet. Stockholm, 1972. pp. 211. (*Studieförbundet Näringsliv och Samhälle. Studier och Debatt. 1972. Nr.3*)

— United Kingdom.

KOGAN (MAURICE) and PACKWOOD (TIM) Advisory councils and committees in education. London, 1974. pp. 100. *bibliog.*

EXECUTIVE POWER

— Africa.

SELASSIE (BEREKET H.) The executive in African governments. London, 1974. pp. 288.

— United States.

ANDERSON (DONALD F.) William Howard Taft: a conservative's conception of the presidency. Ithaca, 1973. pp. 355. *bibliog.*

SCHLESINGER (ARTHUR MEIER) the Younger. The imperial presidency. Boston, 1973. pp. 505.

EXECUTIVES

— Salaries, pensions, etc.

MANAGEMENT CENTRE EUROPE. Executive Compensation Service. Executive remuneration: the United Kingdom: annual report. Brussels, 1973 (9th).

NIGERIA. National Manpower Board. Manpower Studies. No. 12. The remuneration of management in the private sector, 1972. Lagos, 1973. pp. 15.

— Taxation — Canada.

CANADIAN TAX FOUNDATION. Corporate Management Tax Conference, 1973. 1. Tax treatment of executive compensation: 2. use of corporations by executives and professionals. [Toronto, 1973]. pp. 114.

— America, Latin.

DAVIS (STANLEY M.) and GOODMAN (LOUIS WOLF) eds. Workers and managers in Latin America. Lexington, Mass., [1972]. pp. 308.

— France.

DOUBLET (JACQUES) and PASSELECQ (OLIVIER) Les cadres. Paris, 1973. pp. 128. *bibliog.*

— India.

HAJRA (S.) and RAMAKRISHNAN (P.) Managerial manpower in Indian industry, 1969-80. New Delhi, 1971. pp. 48. (*Economic and Scientific Research Foundation. Monographs. 2*)

— United Kingdom.

MARSH (ARTHUR) Managers and shop stewards: shop floor revolution?. London, 1973. pp. 174.

JERVIS (FRANK ROBERT JOSEPH) Bosses in British business: managers and management from the industrial revolution to the present day. London, 1974. pp. 184. *bibliog.*

EXECUTIVES, TRAINING OF.

SINGER (EDWIN J.) Effective management coaching. London, 1974. pp. 191. *bibliog.*

EXISTENTIALISM.

ADORNO (THEODOR WIESENGRUND) Negative dialectics;...translated by E.B. Ashton. London, 1973. pp. 416.

EXPENDITURES, PUBLIC.

ORGANISATION FOR ECONOMIC CO-OPERATION AND DEVELOPMENT. Economic Policy Committee. Working Party No. 2. 1972. Expenditure trends in OECD countries 1960-1980. Paris, 1972. pp. 131.

EXPLORERS, PORTUGUESE.

CORDEIRO DE SOUSA (LUCIANO BAPTISTA) compiler. Viagens explorações e conquistas dos Portuguezes: collecção de documentos. Lisboa, 1881. 6 pts. (in 1 vol.). (*Portugal. Memorias do Ultramar*)

EXPORT CREDIT

— Belgium.

BELGIUM. Office National du Ducroire. 1972. L'Office National du Ducroire 1972. Bruxelles, 1972. pp. 29.

— Canada.

EXPORT DEVELOPMENT CORPORATION [CANADA]. Annual report. a., 1973- Ottawa. *In English and French.*

— European Economic Community countries.

GLOTZBACH (MICHAEL) Die staatliche Ausfuhrkreditversicherung in Frankreich und Deutschland: eine rechtsvergleichende Darstellung unter Berücksichtigung der Harmonisierungsbestrebungen im Gemeinsamen Markt. Berlin, [1973]. pp. 167. *bibliog.* (*Mainz. Universität. Institut für Internationales Recht des Spar-, Giro- und Kreditwesens. Untersuchungen über das Spar-, Giro- und Kreditwesen. Abteilung B: Rechtswissenschaft. Band 3*)

— United Kingdom — Examinations, questions, etc.

SYLVESTER-EVANS (G.) Finance of foreign trade: examination questions answered. London, 1973. pp. 123.

EXPORT MARKETING

— Study and teaching.

LISTON (DAVID J.) Education and training for overseas trade. London, British Overseas Trade Board, 1973. pp. 61. *bibliog.*

EXSERVICEMEN

— Employment — United Kingdom.

U.K. Ministry of Defence. 1973. Report of the other ranks resettlement survey, 1972 (second survey). [London, 1973]. pp. 35.

— **United States.**

LEVITAN (SAR A.) and CLEARY (KAREN A.) Old wars remain unfinished: the veteran benefits system. Baltimore, [1973]. pp. 190.

EXTERNALITIES (ECONOMICS).

MEADE (JAMES EDWARD) The theory of economic externalities: the control of environmental pollution and similar social costs. Leiden, 1973. pp. 92. *(Geneva. Graduate Institute of International Studies. International Economics Series. 2)*

PAGE (TALBOT) Economics of involuntary transfers: a unified approach to pollution and congestion externalities. Berlin, 1973. pp. 159. *bibliog.*

STAAF (ROBERT J.) and TANNIAN (FRANCIS X.) eds. Externalities: theoretical dimensions of political economy. New York, [1974]. pp. 354. *bibliogs.*

EXTRADITION.

BASSIOUNI (M. CHERIF) International extradition and world public order. Leyden, 1974. pp. 630.

EXTRAORDINARY REMEDIES

— **Russia.**

CHECHOT (DMITRII MIKHAILOVICH) Neiskovye proizvodstva. Moskva, 1973. pp. 166.

FACTOR ANALYSIS.

BRUTON (MICHAEL J.) An introduction to factor analysis and its application in planning. Oxford, 1971. pp. 123. *(Oxford Polytechnic. Department of Town Planning. Oxford Working Papers in Planning Education and Research. 8)*

FACTORIES

— **United States.**

ZIMILES (MARTHA) and ZIMILES (MURRAY) Early American mills. New York, [1973]. pp. 290. *bibliog.*

FACTORY AND TRADE WASTE.

CONFEDERAZIONE GENERALE DELL'INDUSTRIA ITALIANA. Servizio Studi e Rilevazioni. Collana di Studi e Documentazione. 31. Prime indicazioni sugli interventi dell'industria privata a difesa dell'ambiente; (a cura di Francesco Galli and others). Roma, 1973. pp. 216.

FACTORY INSPECTION

— **Burma.**

INTERNATIONAL LABOUR OFFICE. Development Programme: Technical Assistance Sector. [Burma] R.35. Report to the government of the Union of Burma on industrial hygiene and occupational health. (ILO/TAP/Burma/R35). Geneva, 1971. pp. 18.

FAIRS.

HUYNEN (J.M.H) Trends in trade fairs...: history, environment, marketing, motivation. Valkenburg, [1973]. pp. 372. *bibliog. With summaries in English and Dutch.*

FAISAL I, King of Iraq.

ALDANOV (MARK ALEKSANDROVICH) pseud. [i.e. LANDAU (MARK ALEKSANDROVICH)] Iunost' Pavla Stroganova i drugie kharakteristiki. Belgrad, [1935?]. pp. 188.

FAMILY.

Les RÔLES familiaux dans les civilisations différentes: études sur la famille; [report of a seminar on family roles organized by two study groups of the Institut de Sociologie of the Université Libre of Brussels]. Bruxelles, [1971]. pp. 125.

WARGON (SYLVIA T.) Definitions of family and household in population statistics, with special reference to the Canadian population statistics. Ottawa, 1971. fo. 13. *bibliog. (Canada. Statistics Canada. Census Division. Working Papers (Demographic and Socio-economic Series). No. 9)*

FARBER (BERNARD) Family and kinship in modern society. Glenview, Ill., [1973]. pp. 179. *bibliog.*

NYE (FRANCIS IVAN) and BERARDO (FELIX M.) The family: its structure and interaction. New York, [1973]. pp. 658.

RODGERS (ROY H.) Family interaction and transaction: the developmental approach. Englewood Cliffs, [1973]. pp. 273. *bibliogs.*

— **Canada — Nova Scotia.**

TREMBLAY (MARC ADELARD) and LAPLANTE (MARC) Famille et parenté en Acadie: évolution des structures et des relations familiales et parentales à l'Anse-des-Lavallée. Ottawa, National Museums of Canada, 1971. pp. 174. *bibliog. (National Museum of Man [Canada]. Publications in Ethnology. No. 3) With English summary.*

— **Colombia.**

CONFERENCIA NACIONAL SOBRE FAMILIA, INFANCIA Y JUVENTUD, la, BOGOTA, 1970. Prima conferencia nacional sobre familia, infancia y juventud; celebrada en Bogota del 2 al 7 de marzo de 1970, con el patrocinio del...UNICEF. Bogota, 1970. pp. 576.

— **France.**

FRICKE (ELSE) Familienpolitik in Frankreich: Darstellung und sozioökonomische Analyse. Berlin, 1972. pp. 437. *bibliog.*

MICHEL (ANDRÉE) The modernization of North African families in the Paris area. The Hague, [1974]. pp. 387. *bibliog. With appendices in French.*

— **Germany.**

TOMAN (WALTER) and PREISER (SIEGFRIED) Familienkonstellationen und ihre Störungen: ihre Wirkungen auf die Person, ihre sozialen Beziehungen und die nachfolgende Generation. Stuttgart, 1973. pp. 83. *bibliog.*

KNIRIM (CHRISTA) and others. Familienstrukturen in Stadt und Land: eine Untersuchung der Rollenbeziehungen zwischen den Ehegatten, den Eltern und Kindern und den Generationen. Bonn, 1974. pp. 203. *bibliog. (Forschungsgesellschaft für Agrarpolitik und Agrarsoziologie. [Publications]. 222)*

KRUELL (MARIANNE) Geschlechtsrollenleitbilder in Stadt- und Landfamilien der Bundesrepublik Deutschland. Bonn, 1974. pp. 284. *bibliog. (Forschungsgesellschaft für Agrarpolitik und Agrarsoziologie. [Publications]. 224)*

— **Ghana.**

OPPONG (CHRISTINE) Marriage among a matrilineal elite: a family study of Ghanaian senior civil servants. London, 1974. pp. 187. *bibliog.*

— **India.**

SHAH (A.M.) The household dimension of the family in India: a field study in a Gujarat village and a review of other studies. New Delhi, [1973]. pp. 281. *bibliog.*

CHEKKI (DANESH A.) Modernization and kin network. Leiden, 1974. pp. 184. *bibliog.*

— **Martinique.**

DUBREUIL (GUY) La famille martiniquaise: analyse et dynamique. [Montréal, 1974]. pp. 103-129. *bibliog. (Extrait de la revue Anthropologica, vol. 7, no. 1, 1965) With English summary.*

— **Norway.**

INNSTILLING om barnefamiliens okonomi; fra et utvalg oppnevnt ved Kronprinsregentens resolusjon av 10. mai 1968. Otta, 1971. pp. 248.

— **Puerto Rico.**

NERLOVE (MARC) and SCHULTZ (T. PAUL) Love and life between the censuses: a model of family decision making in Puerto Rico, 1950-1960. Santa Monica, 1970. pp. 105. *bibliog. (Rand Corporation. [Research Memoranda]. 6322)*

FAMILY ALLOWANCES.

— **South Africa.**

PAUW (BERTHOLD ADOLF) The second generation: a study of the family among urbanized Bantu in East London. 2nd ed. Cape Town, 1973. pp. 241. *(Rhodes University. Institute of Social and Economic Research. Xhosa in Town. 3)*

SOUTH AFRICA. Census, 1970. Population census, 1970: families: geographical distribution. [Pretoria, 1974 in progress]. *(Bureau of Statistics. Reports. No. 02-03-01) In English and Afrikaans.*

— **Switzerland.**

HELD (THOMAS) and LEVY (RENE) Die Stellung der Frau in Familie und Gesellschaft: eine soziologische Analyse am Beispiel der Schweiz. Frauenfeld, [1974]. pp. 378. *bibliog. (Schweizerische Gesellschaft für Soziologie. Reihe Soziologie in der Schweiz. 1) With summaries in French and English.*

— **Tunisia.**

CAMILLERI (CARMEL) Jeunesse, famille et développement: essai sur le changement socio-culturel dans un pays du tiers-monde, Tunisie. Paris, 1973. pp. 506. *(Centre National de la Recherche Scientifique. Centre de Recherches et d'Etudes sur les Sociétés Méditerranéennes. Collection)*

— **United Kingdom.**

HOLMAN (ROBERT) ed. Socially deprived families in Britain; (reprinted with supplement). London, 1970. repr. 1973. pp. 235, 28.

U.K. Social Survey. [Reports. New Series.] 466. Families and their needs, with particular reference to one-parent families; by Audrey Hunt [and others];...an enquiry carried out in 1970...on behalf of the Department of Health and Social Security. London, 1973. 2 vols.

— **United States.**

GEISMAR (LUDWIG L.) 555 families: a social-psychological study of young families in transition. New Brunswick, N.J., [1973]. pp. 267.

PERSPECTIVES on inequality: a reassessment of the effect of family and schooling in America. Cambridge, Mass., [1973]. pp. 128. *(Harvard Educational Review. Reprint Series. No. 8)*

SCHNEIDER (DAVID MURRAY) and SMITH (RAYMOND T.) Class differences and sex roles in American kinship and family structure. Englewood Cliffs, [1973]. pp. 132. *bibliog.*

YORBURG (BETTY) The changing family. New York, 1973. pp. 230.

NIEMI (RICHARD G.) How family members perceive each other: political and social attitudes in two generations. New Haven, 1974. pp. 214. *bibliog.*

FAMILY, RURAL.

See RURAL FAMILIES.

FAMILY, SINGLE PARENT.

See SINGLE PARENT FAMILY.

FAMILY ALLOWANCES.

SWITZERLAND. Département Fédéral de l'Intérieur. 1967. Die Familienzulagenordnungen der EWG-Staaten, Grossbritanniens, Oesterreichs und der Schweiz; Bericht des Eidgenössischen Departementes des Innern für die 9. Tagung europäischer Minister für Familienfragen, Genf 1967. [Bern?, 1967?]. pp. 115.

— **Argentine Republic.**

ARGENTINE REPUBLIC. Direccion Nacional de Recursos Humanos. Departamento Socio-Economico. 1971. Asignaciones familiares en la Republica Argentina: su evolucion. [Buenos Aires, 1971]. pp. 103. *bibliog. (Informes Socioeconomicos. Cuadernos de Investigaciones. No.7)*

FAMILY ALLOWANCES. (Cont.)

— Belgium.

BELGIUM. Office National d'Allocations Familiales pour Travailleurs Salariés. 1973. Etude socio-démographique des familles attributaires, des enfants bénéficaires du régime des allocations familiales pour travailleurs salariés en 1971: annexe 1 au rapport sur l'exercice 1971. Bruxelles, 1973. pp. 132.

— Brazil.

MONTEIRO DA SILVA (CORSINDIO) Salario-familia: beneficio a funcionario em razão de seu dependente. [Brasilia], Departamento Administrativo do Pessoa Civil, 1968. pp. 178.

— Denmark.

DENMARK. Socialministeriet. 1970. Børnetilskud [og] bidragsforskud. [Copenhagen?, 1970?]. pp. 14.

DENMARK. Statutes, etc. 1969-71. The Family Allowances and other Family Benefits Act, 1969,as amended. [Copenhagen, 1971?]. fo. 10.

— Switzerland.

SWITZERLAND. Office Fédéral des Assurances Sociales. 1970. Allocations familiales aux travailleurs agricoles et aux petits paysans: recueil des dispositions en vigueur des barèmes et du commentaire au 1er janvier 1970. [Bern, 1970]. pp. 64.

— United Kingdom.

U.K. Statutes, etc. 1946- . The law relating to family allowances and national insurance: the statutes, regulations and orders as now in force, annotated and indexed;... compiled by J. St.L. Brockman; revised and edited by P.C. Nilsson; (with Supplements). [rev. ed.] London, 1973 in progress. 2 vols. (loose-leaf).

MARSDEN (DENNIS) Mothers alone: poverty and the fatherless family. rev. ed. Harmondsworth, 1973. pp. 412.

— Uruguay.

CARDOZO (RAMON) and FOLADORI (WALTER) Regimen de asignaciones familiares del Uruguay. Montevideo, 1970. pp. 781.

FAMILY FARMS

— Finland.

TORVELA (MATIAS) and MÄKI (SEPPO) Perheviljelmän koko rationaalisessa maataloustuotannossa viljelmämalleihin perustuva tutkimus, etc. Helsinki, 1974. pp. 79. (Maatalouden Taloudellisen Tutkimuslaitos. Julkaisuja. 30)

FAMILY SIZE.

RICH (WILLIAM) Smaller families through social and economic progress. Washington, 1973. pp. 73. bibliog. (Overseas Development Council. Monographs. No. 7)

YAUKEY (DAVID) Marriage reduction and fertility. Lexington, [1973]. pp. 115.

BERTELSEN (OLE) and USSING (JYTTE) Familiestørrelse og livsstil, etc. København, 1974. pp. 104. bibliog. (Socialforskningsinstituttet. Publikationer. 60)

FAMILY SOCIAL WORK

— France.

GEMAEHLING (GENEVIEVE) and others. Service social et familles socialement handicapées. [Paris], Caisse Nationale des Allocations Familiales, [1970]. pp. 251. bibliog. (Etudes. [12])

— Netherlands.

NETHERLANDS. Werkgroep Gezinsbenadering. 1971. Rapport. 's- Gravenhage, 1971. pp. 114.

— United Kingdom.

FRIMHURST: (an experience of freedom; une expérience de la liberté). Pierrelaye, [1973]. 1 vol. (various pagings). (Igloos: le 4e monde. Nos. 77-79) In French and English.

FAMILY therapy in social work;...papers [presented at a conference held by the Family Welfare Association in London in 1973]; edited by Walter H. Finn. [London, 1974]. pp. 54.

FAMINES.

AYKROYD (WALLACE RUDDELL) The conquest of famine. London, 1974. pp. 216.

FARM INCOME

— European Economic Community countries.

QUADEN (GUY) Parité pour l'agriculture et disparités entre agriculteurs: essai critique sur la politique des revenus agricoles. Liège, 1973. pp. 236. bibliog. (Liège. Université. Faculté de Droit. Collection Scientifique. 35)

— Finland.

IHAMUOTILA (RISTO) Viljelijöiden työtulojen taso kirjanpitotiloilla 1956-1965: Summary: Labour income level of farmers on Finnish book-keeping farms in 1956-1965. Helsinki, 1968. pp. 172. bibliog. (Maatalouden Taloudellisen Tutkimuslaitos. Julkaisuja. No. 10)

— Norway.

NORWAY. Statistiske Centralbyrå. 1971. Bøndenes formue, gjeld og inntekt 1968, etc. Oslo, 1971. pp. 81. (Norges Offisielle Statistikk. Rekke A. 384) With English summary.

— United Kingdom — Wales.

WALES. University. University College of Wales. Department of Agricultural Economics. Farm incomes in Wales, 1971-72: financial results for 345 identical farms. Aberystwyth, [1973?]. pp. 52.

FARM MANAGEMENT.

PILLAI (VELU PILLAI RAMAN) and PANIKAR (PUTHENVEETIL GOVINDA KESAVA) Studies in the economics of farm management in Kerala: report for year 1964-65. [Delhi, Manager of Publications, 1972]. pp. 448.

REGIONAL FARM MANAGEMENT RESEARCH CENTRE [BANGALORE]. Studies in the economics of farm management: Bangalore district (Mysore): report[s] for the year[s] 1960-61 [and] 1961-62. [Delhi, Manager of Publications, 1972]. 2 pts.

SINGH (ROSHAN) and SINGH (RANBIR) Studies in economics of farm management in Uttar Pradesh (Muzaffarnagar District): report for the year 1966-67. [Delhi, Manager of Publications, 1972]. pp. 548.

AZARIAH (H.S.) and ATHAVALE (M.C.) Studies in economics of farm management in Raipur (Madhya Pradesh): combined report for the years 1962-63 to 1964-65. Delhi, Manager of Publications], 1972 [or rather 1973]. pp. 95.

KAHLO (A.S.) and others. Studies in economics of farm management, Ferozepur district (Punjab): report[s] for the year[s] 1967-68, 1968-69, 1969-70. [Delhi, Controller of Publications, 1973]. 3 vols. (in 2).

LAVANIA (GAURI SHANKER) Studies in the economics of farm management in Deoria district (Uttar Pradesh): report[s] for the year[s] 1966-67, 1967-68, 1968-69. [Delhi, Controller of Publications, 1973]. 3 vols. (in 2).

MISRA (B.) Studies in the economics of farm management in Cuttack district (Orissa): report[s] for the year[s] 1967-68, 1968-69, 1969-70. [Delhi, Controller of Publications, 1973]. 3 vols. (in 1).

NARAYANA (D.L.) and others. Studies in the economics of farm management in Cuddapah district (Andhra Pradesh): report[s] for the year[s] 1967-68, 1968-69. [Delhi, Controller of Publications, 1973]. 2 vols. (in 1).

FARM MECHANIZATION

— Colombia.

THIRSK (WAYNE R.) Income distribution, efficiency and the experience of Colombian farm mechanization. Houston, 1972. pp. 54. (Rice University. Program of Development Studies. Papers. No. 33)

— Denmark.

DENMARK. Landøkonomiske Driftsbureau. 1972. Mekaniseringsomkostninger. København, 1972. pp. 20. (Meddelelse. Nr. 11)

— Pakistan.

GOTSCH (CARL H.) Tractor mechanization and rural development in Pakistan. Cambridge, Mass., 1972. pp. 65. (Harvard University. Center for International Affairs. Development Research Group. Economic Development Reports. No. 227)

— Reunion Island.

RIVIERE (CLAUDE) French overseas civil servant. La Régie de Mécanoculture. [St. Denis], 1971. fo. 29. (Réunion. [Secrétariat Général pour les Affaires Economiques. Documentation et Etudes]. Bulletin de Conjoncture. Supplément. No. 10)

— Russia.

SINIUKOV (MIKHAIL IVANOVICH) Effektivnost' ispol'zovaniia tekhniki v sel'skom khoziaistve. Moskva, 1970. pp. 184.

FARM PRODUCE

— Belgium — Marketing.

BELGIUM. Institut Economique Agricole. Cahiers. Bruxelles, 1962 in progress.

BELGIUM. Institut Economique Agricole. Notes. Bruxelles, 1964 in progress.

— Brazil.

FUNDAÇÃO GETULIO VARGAS. Centro de Estudos Agricolas. Orçamentos familiares rurais; [Estado do Espirito Santo, Minas Gerais, Ceara, Pernambuco, Estado de São Paulo , Estado de Santa Catarina, Rio Grande do Sul; by Sylvio Wanick Ribeiro and others]. [Rio de Janeiro], 1969-71. 7 vols(in 2).

— Canada — Marketing.

MARKETING BOARD SEMINAR, WINNIPEG, 1972. Market regulation in Canadian agriculture: papers presented at the...Seminar...sponsored by the Department of Agricultural Economics and Farm Management...University of Manitoba, etc.Winnipeg, 1972. pp. 180. (Manitoba University. Department of Agricultural Economics and Farm Management. Occasional Series. No. 3)

— European Economic Community countries.

ELLIS (FRANK) and others. Farmers and foreigners: impact of the Common Agricultural Policy on the associates and associables. London, [1973]. pp. 86.

— Malawi — Marketing.

MALAWI. Agro-Economic Survey. 1974. Agro-economic survey: report no. 13: institutional demand of agricultural produce in Zomba and Lilongwe; prepared by J. Lavrijsen. Lilongwe, 1974. fo. 73.

— Sierra Leone — Marketing.

SIERRA LEONE. Beoku-Betts Commission of Inquiry into the Sierra Leone Produce Marketing Board. 1968. Report...with particular reference to the sale of palm oil, rice and coffee haulers, nut-cracking machine and the industrialisation programme undertaken by the Board during the period January, 1961 to March, 1967; [R.W. Beoku-Betts, chairman]. [Freetown, 1968]. pp. 120.

— United Kingdom — Marketing.

AGRICULTURAL CO-OPERATION AND MARKETING SERVICES LIMITED. Annual report. a., 1972/3(1st)- London.

HAVINDEN (MICHAEL ASHLEY) ed. Husbandry and marketing in the South-West, 1500-1800. Exeter, 1973. pp. 74. (Exeter. University. Department of Economic History. Exeter Papers in Economic History. No. 8)

GIDDINGS (P.J.) Marketing boards and ministers: a study of agricultural marketing boards as political and administrative instruments. Farnborough, [1974]. pp. 247.

— Venezuela.

VENEZUELA. Ministerio de Agricultura y Cria. Direccion de Planificacion Sectorial. Division de Estadistica. 1969. Directorio de instalaciones para productos agropecuarios. Caracas, 1968 [or rather 1969]. pp. 202.

FARMERS

— Africa, Subsaharan.

CLEAVE (JOHN H.) African farmers: labor use in the development of smallholder agriculture. New York, 1974. pp. 253. bibliog.

— Belgium.

EVERAET (HUBERT) Le niveau de vie des agriculteurs: enquête sociale sur les facteurs qui influencent le revenu et l'équipement ménager. Bruxelles, 1972. fo. 50. (Belgium. Institut Economique Agricole. Cahiers. No. 150)

— France.

FRANCE. Ministère de l'Agriculture. Statistique Agricole Supplément. Série Etudes. No.73. Projections pour 1975 de la population agricole familiale; [étude...réalisée par S. Tonani]. [Paris], 1971. pp. 97.

— Netherlands.

BOERENGROEP WAGENINGEN. Agri-business of binnenlandse kolonie II: (sociaal-ekonomische positie van de boer; landbouw en milieu). Wageningen, [1974]. pp. 133.

BOERENGROEP WAGENINGEN. Over boeren, bazen en banken: de maatschappelijke positie van de boer in historisch perspektief. Wageningen, [1974]. pp. 77.

— Norway.

NORWAY. Statistiske Centralbyrå. 1971. Bøndenes formue, gjeld og inntekt 1968, etc. Oslo, 1971. pp. 81. (Norges Offisielle Statistikk. Rekke A. 384) With English summary.

— Switzerland.

SWITZERLAND. Office Fédéral des Assurances Sociales. 1970. Allocations familiales aux travailleurs agricoles et aux petits paysans: recueil des dispositions en vigueur des barèmes et du commentaire au 1er janvier 1970. [Bern, 1970]. pp. 64.

— Uganda.

HUTTON (CAROLINE) Reluctant farmers?: a study of unemployment and planned rural development in Uganda. Nairobi, 1973. pp. 331. bibliog. (Makerere Institute of Social Research. East African Studies. No.33)

— — Buganda.

RICHARDS (AUDREY ISABEL) and others, eds. Subsistence to commercial farming in present-day Buganda: an economic and anthropological study. Cambridge, 1973. pp. 336. bibliog.

— United States.

HUNT (ROBERT LEE) A history of farmer movements in the Southwest, 1873-1925. [College Station, Tex., 1935]. pp. 192.

FARMS

— Valuation.

CLARK (COLIN) The value of agricultural land. Oxford, 1973. pp. 117.

— Belgium.

TAMBUYZER (C.) L'avenir de l'exploitation agricole belge. Bruxelles, 1972. fo. 21. (Belgium. Institut Economique Agricole. Notes. No. 30)

TAMBUYZER (C.) L'évolution régionale de l'agriculture en tant que secteur d'emploi. Bruxelles, 1973. pp. 47. (Belgium. Institut Economique Agricole. Cahiers. No. 157)

— Botswana.

BOTSWANA. Central Statistics Office. Freehold farm survey. a., 1970/71- Gaborone.

— Denmark.

JØRGENSEN (AAGE) and JØRGENSEN (NIELS C.) Nogre faktorers indvirkning p° a ejendomspriserne i landbruget. København, 1971. pp. 70. (Denmark. Landøkonomiske Driftsbureau. Memoranda. 3) With English summary.

— India.

KHUSRO (ALI M.) The economics of land reform and farm size in India. Madras, 1973. pp. 162. bibliog. (Delhi. Institute of Economic Growth. Studies in Economic Growth. No. 14)

— Malawi.

MALAWI. National Statistical Office. 1970. National sample survey of agriculture, 1968/69 (customary land in rural areas only). [Zomba], 1970. pp. 172,13.

— Norway.

NORWAY. Statistiske Centralbyrå. 1972. Alder og yrkeskombinasjonar i jordbruket og korleis desse faktorane verkar inn på drifta av bruka, etc. Oslo, 1972. pp. 63. (Statistiske Analyser. 5)

— Thailand.

GRIMBLE (R.J.) The central highlands of Thailand: a study of farming systems. [London, Overseas Development Administration, 1973]. pp. 73.

— United Kingdom.

ECONOMIC DEVELOPMENT COMMITTEE FOR THE AGRICULTURAL INDUSTRY. Common Market Sub-Committee. Problem Areas Working Group. UK farming and the Common Market: hills and uplands; a report. London, National Economic Development Office, 1973. pp. 39.

ECONOMIC DEVELOPMENT COMMITTEE FOR THE AGRICULTURAL INDUSTRY. Productivity Steering Group. Farm productivity; a report on factors affecting productivity at the farm level; [Edmund Bacon, chairman]. London, H.M.S.O., 1973. pp. 15.

— United Kingdom — Wales.

DENBIGHSHIRE. County Planning Officer. Tourism and Recreation Research Reports. 4. Farms and tourism in upland Denbighshire; Colin A.J. Jacobs, County Planning Officer. [Ruthin], 1973. pp. 52. bibliog.

FARMS, COLLECTIVE

See also AGRICULTURE, COOPERATIVE.

— Russia.

SIMUSH (PETR IOSIFOVICH) Sotsial'no-ekonomicheskie problemy razvitiia kolkhozov. Moskva, 1973. pp. 119.

— — Law and legislation.

KALANDADZE (AVKSENTII MELITONOVICH) Vnutrikolkhoznye pravootnosheniia v SSSR. Leningrad, 1974. pp. 112.

— — Ukraine.

LUSHCH (HANNA IVANIVNA) Intensyfikatsiia kolhospnoho vyrobnytstva: pytannia vymiru ta analizu. Kyïv, 1972. pp. 144. With Russian summary and table of contents.

VYBRYK (VIL' IVANOVYCH) Kvalifikovana robocha syla v kolhospakh: pytannia vidtvorennia. Kyïv, 1972. pp. 151.

HORODNII (VOLODYMYR VASYL'OVYCH) Hosprozrakhunok i material'ne stymuliuvannia u kolhospakh. Kyïv, 1973. pp. 112.

FARMS, FAMILY.

See FAMILY FARMS.

FARMS, SIZE OF

— Denmark.

DENMARK. Landøkonomiske Driftsbureau. 1973. Bedriftsudvidelse. København, 1973. pp. 81. (Undersøgelser. 30) With English summary.

— Finland.

TORVELA (MATIAS) and MÄKI (SEPPO) Perheviljelmän koko rationaalisessa maataloustuotannossa viljelmämalleihin perustuva tutkimus, etc. Helsinki, 1974. pp. 79. (Maatalouden Taloudellisen Tutkimuslaitos. Julkaisuja. 30)

FASCISM.

CARSTEN (FRANCIS LUDWIG) The rise of fascism. London, Batsford, 1967. pp. 256. bibliog.

GALKIN (ALEKSANDR ABRAMOVICH) Sotsiologiia neofashizma. Moskva, 1971. pp. 198. bibliog.

GREGOR (A.JAMES) The fascist persuasion in radical politics. Princeton, [1974]. pp. 472. bibliog.

POULANTZAS (NICOS) Fascism and dictatorship: the Third International and the problem of fascism; translated from the French by Judith White. London, 1974. pp. 366.

SCHULZ (GERHARD) Faschismus, Nationalsozialismus: Versionen und theoretische Kontroversen, 1922-1972. Frankfurt/M, [1974]. pp. 222. bibliog.

— Belgium.

DANNAU (WIM) Face à face avec le rexisme. Strombeek-Bever, [1971]. pp. 158.

DANNAU (WIM) Ainsi parla Léon Degrelle;...interviews au magnétophone et conversations avec...Léon Degrelle...recueillies par Wim Dannau de 1965 à 1972, les commentaires de l'auteur, etc. [Strombeek, 1973]. 3 vols.

— France.

DIOUDONNAT (PIERRE MARIE) Je suis partout, 1930-1944: les maurrassiens devant la tentation fasciste. Paris, [1973]. pp. 471.

MACHEFER (PHILIPPE) Ligues et fascismes en France, 1919-1939. [Paris], 1974. pp. 96. bibliog.

— Germany.

ROSSAINT (JOSEPH C.) Die aktuelle politische Lage in der Bundesrepublik Deutschland und die neonazistische Gefahr: Rede gehalten auf dem Kongress der V[ereinigungen der] V[erfolgten des] N[aziregimes in der Bundesrepublik Deutschland]... 1971. Wien, 1971. pp. 23.

VEREINIGUNG DER VERFOLGTEN DES NAZIREGIMES. Kongress, 1973. Antifaschismus heute: gemeinsamer Kampf und Demokratisierung aller Gesellschaftsbereiche; Bericht über den Bundeskongress...in Hannover. Frankfurt am Main, 1973. pp. 192.

— Hungary.

KHAINAS (VASYL' VASYL'OVYCH) Borot'ba Komunistychnoï partiï Uhorshchyny za iedynyi robitnychyi i narodnyi front, proty fashyzmu i viiny, 1933-1939. L'viv, 1969. pp. 210.

FASCISM. (Cont.)

— Italy.

CAVANDOLI (ROLANDO) Le origini del fascismo a Reggio Emilia. Roma, [1972]. pp. 271. *bibliog.*

UNIONE REGIONALE DELLE PROVINCE TOSCANE. Contro ogni ritorno: dal fascismo alla costituzione repubblicana. [Florence, 1972]. pp. 135.

LAURA (ERNESTO G.) Immagine del fascismo: come nacque, come conquistò l'Italia, chi lo aiutò, come finì, attraverso fotografie e documenti originali. Milano, [1973 in progress].

AMENDOLA (GIORGIO) Fascismo e Mezzogiorno. Roma, [1973]. pp. 210.

BOCCA (GIORGIO) L'Italia fascista. Milano, 1973. pp. 141. *bibliog.*

CORSI (HUBERT) Le origini del fascismo nel Grossetano, 1919-1922. Roma, [1973]. pp. 199.

Il FASCISMO e le autonomie locali [papers given at a seminar in 1972]; a cura di Sandro Fontana. Bologna, [1973]. pp. 435.

GALLO (MAX) Mussolini's Italy: twenty years of the fascist era;... translated by Charles Lam Markmann. New York, [1973]. pp. 452. *bibliog.*

GRAMSCI (ANTONIO) Sul fascismo; a cura di Enzo Santarelli. Roma, 1973. pp. 451.

GUERIN (DANIEL) Fascism and big business; (translated from the French). New York, 1973. pp. 318.

LYTTELTON (ADRIAN) ed. Italian fascisms from Pareto to Gentile;... translated from the Italian... by Douglas Parmée. London, 1973. pp. 318. *bibliog.*

MAURANO (SILVIO) Ricordi di un giornalista fascista. Milano, [1973]. pp. 361.

MOVIMENTO operaio e fascismo nell'Emilia-Romagna, 1919-1923; ([by] Luciano Casali [and others]). Roma, 1973. pp. 363.

Il REGIME contro la Destra: [debates in the Italian Parliament concerning the prosecution of Giorgio Almirante]. Milano, [1973]. pp. 344.

SALVEMINI (GAETANO) The origins of fascism in Italy: [based on a lecture course at Harvard and written in 1942]; edited... by Roberto Vivarelli. New York, [1973]. pp. 445. *bibliog.*

SANTARELLI (ENZO) ed. Il fascismo: testimonianze e giudizi storici;...testi antologici da A. Tasca [and others]. Messina, 1973. pp. 159. *bibliog.*

SEMINARIO DI STORIA CONTEMPORANEA, 8°, 1972. Fascismo e società italiana; [papers] a cura di Guido Quazza. Torino, [1973]. pp. 253.

SILVA (UMBERTO) Ideologia e arte del fascismo. Milano, [1973]. pp. 158.

ZEPPI (STELIO) Il pensiero politico dell'idealismo italiano e il nazionalfascismo. Firenze, 1973. pp. 303.

ARALDI (VINICIO) Camicie nere a Montecitorio: storia parlamentare dell'avvento del fascismo. Milano, 1974. pp. 371. *bibliog.*

ROSSINI (GIUSEPPE) De Gasperi e il fascismo. Roma, 1974. pp. 303.

SARTI (ROLAND) ed. The ax within: Italian fascism in action. New York, 1974. pp. 278. *bibliog.*

UVA (BRUNO) La nascita dello stato corporativo e sindacale fascista. Assisi, [1974]. pp. 302.

— Roumania.

CODREANU (CORNELIU ZELEA) La Garde de Fer: pour les légionnaires; [with appendix of letters and documents]. Paris, 1938; Grenoble, 1972. pp. 470.

— San Marino.

CARLOTTI (ANNA LISA) Storia del partito fascista sammarinese. Milano, [1973]. pp. 260. *bibliog.*

— Spain.

[CARRERO BLANCO (LUIS)] Comentarios de un español; las tribulaciones de Don Prudencio; diplomacia subterranea; ([by] "Juan de la Cosa" [pseud.]). Madrid, 1973. pp. 339.

NIN DE CARDONA (JOSE MARIA) Jose Antonio: la posibilidad politica truncada. Madrid, 1973. pp. 251. *bibliog.*

— United States.

DIAMOND (SANDER A.) The Nazi movement in the United States, 1924-1941. Ithaca, 1974. pp. 380. *bibliog.*

FASHION.

MODA: za i protiv. Moskva, 1973. pp. 287.

FATHER SEPARATED CHILDREN.

HOPKINSON (ANNE) Families without fathers. London, 1973. pp. 32. *bibliog.*

MARSDEN (DENNIS) Mothers alone: poverty and the fatherless family. rev. ed. Harmondsworth, 1973. pp. 412.

FATHERS.

STONE (ROBERT C.) and SCHLAMP (FREDRIC T.) Welfare and working fathers: low-income family life styles. Lexington, Mass., [1971]. pp. 284. *bibliog.*

FEAR.

GRAY (JEFFREY A.) The psychology of fear and stress. London, [1971]. pp. 256. *bibliog.*

FECUNDITY.

UNITED NATIONS. Department of Economic and Social Affairs. Population Studies. New York, 1948 in progress.

ECUADOR. Division de Estadistica y Censos. 1967. Encuesta de fecundidad, levantada en las principales ciudades y en algunas parroquias rurales del pais. Quito, 1967.. pp. 255,6.

BERN (CANTON). Statistisches Bureau. 1968. Bevölkerungsanalyse im Kanton Bern: relative Fruchtbarkeit, 1958-1963. Bern, 1968. fo. 15. *(Sonderhefte. 14)*

SWEDEN. Statistiska Centralbyrån. 1969. Fertility for birth cohorts of Swedish women, 1870-1940. Stockholm, 1969. fo. 39. *(Statistiska Meddelanden. Be/1969/9) With Swedish summary.*

BOGUE (DONALD JOSEPH) Demographic techniques of fertility analysis. Chicago, 1971. pp. 116. *(Chicago. University. Community and Family Study Center. R.F.F.P.I. Family Planning Evaluation Manuals. No. 2)*

ACSADI (GYÖRGY T.) and others. Surveys of fertility, family, and family planning in Nigeria. Ile-Ife, Nigeria, 1972. 1 vol. (various pagings). *(Ife. University. Institute of Population and Manpower Studies. Publications. No. 2)*

LERIDON (HENRI) Natalité, saisons et conjoncture économique. Paris, 1973. pp. 147. *bibliog. (France. Institut National d'Etudes Démographiques. Travaux et Documents. Cahiers. No. 66)*

MAURER (KENNETH) and others. Marriage, fertility, and labor force participation of Thai women: an econometric study;... a report prepared for Agency for International Development. Santa Monica, 1973. pp. 54. *bibliog. (Rand Corporation. [Rand Reports]. 829)*

NORMAN (K.) and GILJE (E.K.) Analytic graduation of age specific fertility rates in the London boroughs. [London], 1973. pp. 118. *bibliog. (London. Greater London Council. Department of Planning and Transportation. Research Memoranda. 423)*

SCHULTZ (T. PAUL) Economic factors affecting population growth: a preliminary survey of economic analyses of fertility. Minneapolis, 1973. fo. 27. *bibliog. (Minnesota University. Center for Economic Research. Discussion Papers. No. 29)*

TIETZE (CHRISTOPHER) Two years' experience with a liberal abortion law: its impact on fertility trends in New York City. New York, 1973. pp. 6. *(Reprinted from Family Planning Perspectives, vol. 5)*

YAUKEY (DAVID) Marriage reduction and fertility. Lexington, [1973]. pp. 115.

CICOUREL (AARON VICTOR) Theory and method in a study of Argentine fertility. New York, [1974]. pp. 212. *bibliog.*

KNODEL (JOHN E.) The decline of fertility in Germany, 1871-1939. Princeton, N.J., [1974]. pp. 306. *bibliog.*

MANDELBAUM (DAVID GOODMAN) Human fertility in India: social components and policy perspectives. Berkeley, [1974]. pp. 132. *bibliog.*

VAN DE WALLE (ETIENNE) The female population of France in the 19th century: a reconstruction of 82 départements. Princeton, [1974]. pp. 483. *bibliog.*

— Bibliography.

WARE (HELEN) ed. Fertility and family formation: Australasian bibliography and essays 1972. Canberra, 1973. pp. 269, A 80. *(Australian National University. Research School of Social Sciences. Department of Demography. Australian Family Project)*

— Mathematical models.

GILJE (EIVIND) Analytic graduation of age-specific fertility rates. Oslo, 1972. pp. [46]. *(Norway, Statistiske Centralbyrå. Artikler. Nr. 51)*

DAS GUPTA (PRITHWIS) A stochastic model of human reproduction. Berkeley, Calif, [1973]. pp. 129. *bibliog. (California University. Institute of International Studies. Population Monograph Series. No. 11)*

LERIDON (HENRI) Aspects biométriques de la fécondité humaine. [Paris], 1973. pp. 184. *bibliog. (France. Institut National d'Etudes Démographiques. Travaux et Documents. Cahiers. No.65)*

FEDERAL GOVERNMENT.

Le FEDERALISME et le développement des ordres juridiques: Federalism and development of legal systems; travaux du colloque de Moscou, septembre 1970, [sponsored by the International Association of Legal Science]. Bruxelles, 1971. pp. 227. *In English or French.*

EUROPE EN FORMATION, L'. No. 163-164. Anarchisme et fédéralisme; [by] Alexandre Marc [and others]. Paris, 1973. pp. 170.

— Australia.

AUSTRALIA. Northern Territory. Legislative Council. Select Committee... appointed to Inquire into Necessity or Otherwise for Constitutional Reform in the Northern Territory. 1958. Report; [R.J. Withnall, chairman]. Canberra, [1958]. pp. 20.

HOWARD (COLIN) Australian federal constitutional law. 2nd ed. Melbourne, 1972. pp. 535.

RICHARDSON (J.E.) Patterns of Australian federalism. Canberra, 1973. pp. 142. *(Australian National University. Centre for Research on Federal Financial Relations. Research Monographs. No.1)*

VILE (MAURICE JOHN CRAWLEY) Federalism in the United States, Canada and Australia. London, 1973. pp. 46. *(U.K. Commission on the Constitution, 1969. Research Papers. 2)*

— Canada.

SMILEY (DONALD V.) Canada in question: federalism in the seventies. Toronto, [1972]. pp. 190.

VILE (MAURICE JOHN CRAWLEY) Federalism in the United States, Canada and Australia. London, 1973. pp. 46. *(U.K. Commission on the Constitution, 1969. Research Papers. 2)*

PREVOST (JEAN PIERRE) La crise du fédéralisme canadien. [Paris, 1972]. pp. 96. *bibliog.*

— **Germany.**

THOMPSON (D.M.) The constitutional and financial relationship between Bund and Laender in the Federal German Republic. London, H.M. Treasury, 1972. 1 vol. (unpaged).

JOHNSON (NEVIL) Federalism and decentralisation in the Federal Republic of Germany. London, 1973. pp. 63. *(U.K. Commission on the Constitution, 1969. Research Papers. 1)*

JOHNSON (NEVIL) Government in the Federal Republic of Germany: the executive at work. Oxford, 1973. pp. 218. *bibliog.*

SCHMIDT (JOCHEN) Bayern und das Zollparlament: Politik und Wirtschaft in den letzten Jahren vor der Reichsgründung, 1866/67-1870: zur Strukturanalyse Bayerns im Industriezeitalter. München, 1973. pp. 442. *bibliog. (Munich. Stadtarchiv. Neue Schriftenreihe. Band 64)*

STORBECK (ANNA CHRISTINE) Die Regierungen des Bundes und der Länder seit 1945: Ergänzungsband, 1969 bis 1973; bearbeitet von Jürgen Jekewitz. München, [1973]. pp. 281.

LAUFER (HEINZ) and WIRTH (JUTTA) Die Landesvertretungen in der Bundesrepublik Deutschland. München, [1974]. pp. 292. *bibliog.*

— **India.**

SINHA (SACHCHIDANANDA) The internal colony: a study in regional exploitation. New Delhi, 1973. pp. 159.

— **Malaysia.**

MILNE (ROBERT STEVEN) and RATNAM (K.J.) Malaysia: new states in a new nation; political development of Sarawak and Sabah in Malaysia. London, 1974. pp. 501. *bibliog.*

— **Russia.**

KOPEICHIKOV (VLADIMIR VLADIMIROVICH) Mekhanizm gosudarstva v sovetskoi federatsii. Moskva, 1973. pp. 200.

TSAMERIAN (IVAN PETROVICH) Teoreticheskie problemy obrazovaniia i razvitiia Sovetskogo mnogonatsional'nogo gosudarstva. Moskva, 1973. pp. 295.

— **United States.**

The NEW federation: possibilities and problems in restructuring American government: a conference of the Woodrow Wilson International Center for Scholars; [editor, Joseph Foote]. Washington, [1973]. pp. 55.

VILE (MAURICE JOHN CRAWLEY) Federalism in the United States, Canada and Australia. London, 1973. pp. 46. *(U.K. Commission on the Constitution, 1969. Research Papers. 2)*

DERTHICK (MARTHA) Between state and nation; regional organizations of the United States. Washington, [1974]. pp. 242.

FEDERAL RESERVE BANKS.

AMERICAN ENTERPRISE INSTITUTE FOR PUBLIC POLICY RESEARCH. Legislative Analyses. 93rd Congress. No. 12. The Federal Reserve audit bill. Washington, 1973. pp. 13.

FEEDS

— **United Kingdom.**

U.K. Parliament. House of Commons. Library. Research Division. Background Papers. No. 34. Animal feeding stuffs; [by Priscilla Baines]. [London, 1973]. fo. 13. *bibliog.*

FELTRINELLI (GIANGIACOMO).

ERAMO (LUCE D') Cruciverba politico: come funziona in Italia la strategia della diversione; (topografia politico-economica dei più noti quotidiani italiani esaminati all'epoca dell' affare Feltrinelli). Firenze, [1974]. pp. 341.

FENDELS

— **Economic history.**

SINT (FRANZ) Fendels: die Wiedergenesung eines sterbenden Oberinntaler Bergdorfes. Innsbruck, 1973. pp. 57. *bibliog.*

FENIANS.

O'DONOVAN ROSSA (DIARMUID) Rossa's recollections, 1838-1898; [reprint of the first edition, New York 1898]; introduction by Sean O Luing and a new index. Shannon, [1972]. pp. 410. *bibliog.*

FERDINAND II, King of the Two Sicilies.

MASCIA (ROBERTO) Ferdinando II e la crisi socio-economica della Calabria nel 1848. Napoli, [1973]. pp. 145.

FERENBALM

— **History.**

ANDEREGG (JEAN PIERRE) Ferenbalm: Struktur und Entwicklung einer Landgemeinde. Bern, 1973. pp. 211. *bibliog.*

FERREIRA DA SILVA (VIRGOLINO) known as Lampião.

MACHADO (CHRISTINA MATTA) As taticas de guerra dos cangaceiros. Rio de Janeiro, 1969. pp. 223. *bibliog.*

OLIVEIRA (AGLAE LIMA DE) Lampião, cangaço e nordeste. 2nd ed. Rio de Janeiro, [1970]. pp. 440. *bibliog.*

FERTILIZER INDUSTRY.

UNITED NATIONS. Economic Commission for Asia and the Far East. Mineral Resources Development Series. New York, 1952 in progress.

— **Underdeveloped areas.**

See UNDERDEVELOPED AREAS — Fertilizer industry.

FERTILIZERS AND MANURES.

FOOD AND AGRICULTURE ORGANIZATION. 1970. Fertilizers and their use: a pocket guide for extension officers. 2nd ed. Rome, 1970. pp. 54. *bibliog.*

FEUDALISM.

GANSHOF (FRANÇOIS LOUIS) Feudalism; translated by Philip Grierson. 3rd ed. London, 1964 repr. 1971. pp. 170. *bibliog.*

— **Europe.**

BEELER (JOHN HERBERT) Warfare in feudal Europe, 730-1200. Ithaca, N.Y., 1971. pp. 272. *bibliog.*

DUBY (GEORGES) Guerriers et paysans, VII-XIIe siècle: premier essor de l'économie européenne. [Paris, 1973]. pp. 308. *bibliog.*

DUBY (GEORGES) The early growth of the European economy: warriors and peasants from the seventh to the twelfth century;... translated by Howard B. Clarke. London, [1974]. pp. 292. *bibliog.*

— **France.**

LEWIS (ARCHIBALD ROSS) Knights and samurai: feudalism in northern France and Japan. London, 1974. pp. 101. *bibliog.*

— **Japan.**

LEWIS (ARCHIBALD ROSS) Knights and samurai: feudalism in northern France and Japan. London, 1974. pp. 101. *bibliog.*

— **Palestine.**

RILEY-SMITH (JONATHAN) The feudal nobility and the Kingdom of Jerusalem, 1174-1277. London, 1973. pp. 351. *bibliog.*

FINANCE.

— **United Kingdom.**

BROWN (REGINALD ALLEN) Origins of English feudalism; [with documents]. London, 1973. pp. 164.

FFRENCH—BEYTAGH (GONVILLE AUBIE) Dean of Johannesburg.

The STATE v. the Dean of Johannesburg; prepared for the S.A. Institute of Race Relations by a member of the legal profession. Johannesburg, [1972]. pp. 43.

FIBRES, SYNTHETIC.

MAN-MADE FIBRES PRODUCING INDUSTRY TRAINING BOARD [U.K.]. Report and statement of accounts. a., 1972/3- London. *Formerly included in the file of British Parliamentary Papers.*

FIJI ISLANDS

— **Statistics.**

ANNUAL STATISTICAL ABSTRACT, FIJI; [pd. by] Bureau of Statistics [Fiji]. a., 1969(1st)- Suva.

FINANCE.

BURNS (JOSEPH M.) The saving-investment process in a theory of finance: a dissertation, etc. Chicago, 1967. fo. 121. *bibliog.*

HENRION (ROBERT) Institutions et opérations financières. 4th ed. [Brussels, 1972]. 2 vols. (in 1).

BARTLETT (RANDALL) Economic foundations of political power. New York, [1973]. pp. 206. *bibliog.*

BENJAMIN (BERNARD) and COX (PETER R.) The actuary's role in financial management. London, H.M.S.O., 1973. pp. 34. *bibliog.*

FISCAL policy and demand management: Fiskalpolitik und Globalsteuerung:... Symposium 1972 ([held at the] Institut für Weltwirtschaft an der Universität Kiel); edited by Herbert Giersch. Tübingen, 1973. pp. 262. *In English or German.*

HANSMEYER (KARL HEINRICH) and RUERUP (BERT) Staatswirtschaftliche Planungsinstrumente. Tübingen, [1973]. pp. 88. *bibliogs.*

HOUGHTON (R.W.) ed. Public finance : selected readings. 2nd ed. Harmondsworth, 1973. pp. 543. *bibliog.*

SOZIALWISSENSCHAFTEN im Dienste der Wirtschaftspolitik: Wilhelm Bickel zum 70.Geburtstag; herausgegeben von Heinz Haller [and others]. Tübingen, [1973]. pp. 415. *bibliog. In German or English.*

UNITED NATIONS. Conference on Trade and Development, 3rd, Santiago de Chile, 1972. Proceedings of the... conference..., third session, Santiago de Chile, 13 April to 21 May 1972. (TD/180). New York, 1973. 6 vols. (in 3)

EDEY (HAROLD CECIL) and YAMEY (BASIL SELIG) eds. Debits, credits, finance and profits: [papers presented to William Baxter on his retirement from the chair of accounting at the London School of Economics]. London, 1974. pp. 163. *bibliog.*

— **Bibliography.**

ORGANISATION FOR ECONOMIC COOPERATION AND DEVELOPMENT. Library. Special Annotated Bibliographies. [Paris], 1964 in progress.

BREALEY (RICHARD A.) and PYLE (C.) compilers. A bibliography of finance and investment. London, 1973. pp. 361.

— **Barbados — Statistics.**

BARBADOS. Statistical Service. Financial statistics. irreg. 1959/1968 (no.1), 1962/1972 (no.3)- Bridgetown.

FINANCE. (Cont.)

— Belgium.

BELGIUM. Ministère des Finances. 1971. Finances 1968-1971. [Brussels?, 1971]. pp. 27.

HENRION (ROBERT) Institutions et opérations financières. 4th ed. [Brussels, 1972]. 2 vols. (in 1).

BELGIUM. Ministère des Finances. Service d'Etudes et de Documentation. 1974. Les finances de l'état en 1974. [Brussels, 1974]. pp. 108.

— Canada.

ROBINSON (ALBERT J.) and CUTT (JAMES) eds. Public finance in Canada: selected readings. 2nd ed. Toronto, [1973]. pp. 389.

STRICK (J.C.) Canadian public finance. Toronto, [1973]. pp. 184.

— — Accounting.

CANADA. Department of Supply and Services. Annual report. a., 1969/70 (1st)- Ottawa. *In English and French.*

— Communist countries.

BUTAKOV (DANIIL DMITRIEVICH) Finansovye problemy khoziaistvennykh reform v stranakh-chlenakh SEV.Moskva, 1973. pp. 224.

SEVAST'IANOV (ALEKSANDR ALEKSANDROVICH) Finansy v sisteme proizvodstvennykh otnoshenii razvitogo sotsializma.Moskva, 1973. pp. 160.

— European Economic Community countries.

EUROPEAN COMMUNITIES. Commission. 1973. (Attainment of the economic and monetary union): communication... to the Council on 30 April 1973. [Brussels], 1973. pp. 19. *(Bulletin of the European Communities. Supplements. [1973/5])*

EUROPEAN COMMUNITIES. Commision. 1973. (Monetary organization of the Community): report... to the Council on the adjustment of short—term monetary support arrangements and the conditions for progressive pooling of reserves: presented...on 28 June 1973. [Brussels], 1973. pp 17. *bibliog. (Bulletin of the European Communities. Supplements. [1973/12])*

ITALY. Ragioneria Generale dello Stato. 1972. Comparazione dei bilanci statali nei sei paesi della C.E.E. Roma, 1972. pp. 341.

— Finland — Accounting.

FINLAND. Suomen Tilastollinen Päätoimisto. 1968. Kansantalouden tilinpito; Nationalbokföring; National accounting 1964-1968, I-II. Helsinki, 1968. pp. 58. *(Tilastotiedotus. 1968. No. Kt 1968:3) Tables in Finnish,Swedish and English.*

— France.

MALLETT (MARC GEORGE) La politique financière des Jacobins. Paris, 1913. pp. 449. *bibliog.*

FRANCE. Intergroupe Financement de l'Industrie. 1971. Préparation du VIe Plan... rapport de l'Intergroupe. Paris, 1971. 2 vols.

— Germany.

GRESSER (KLAUS) Probleme der mehrjährigen öffentlichen Finanzplanung. Berlin, [1974]. pp. 255. *bibliog.*

— — Hamburg.

WENNER (HANS JOACHIM) Handelskonjunkturen und Rentenmarkt am Beispiel der Stadt Hamburg um die Mitte des 14. Jahrhunderts. Hamburg, 1972. pp. 129. *bibliog. (Verein für Hamburgische Geschichte. Beiträge zur Geschichte Hamburgs. Band 9)*

— Ghana.

COX-GEORGE (NOAH ARTHUR WILLIAM) Studies in finance and development: the Gold Coast (Ghana) experience, 1914-1950. London, 1973. pp. 217. *bibliog.*

— Greenland — Accounting.

DENMARK. Udvalg vedrørende Organisationen af Ministeriet for Grønlands Budget- og Regnskabsvaesen. 1972. Betaenkning vedrørende Grønlandsadministrationens budget- og regnskabsvaesen, etc. København, 1972. pp. 128. *(Denmark. Betaenkninger. Nr. 646)*

— India.

GUPTA (BAIJ NATH) Indian federal finance and budgetary policy. Allahabad, 1970. pp. 467. *bibliog.*

BHATTACHARYYA (SABYASACHI) Financial foundations of the British Raj: men and ideas in the post-Mutiny period of reconstruction of Indian public finance, 1858-1872. Simla, 1971. pp. 355. *bibliog.*

SHRIVASTAVA (N.N.) Evolution of the techniques of monetary management in India. Bombay, [1972]. pp. 415. *bibliog.*

— Italy.

EINAUDI (LUIGI) and MENICHELLA (DONATO) Fine dell'autarchia e miracolo economico, 1946-1959. Roma, [1973?]. pp. 551. *(Reprinted from Banca d'Italia, Assemblea generale ordinaria dei partecipanti, Relazioni del governatore)*

— — Accounting.

ITALY. Camera dei Deputati. Commissioni Permanenti. V. Bilancio. 1972. Problemi della spesa e della contabilità pubblica: indagine conoscitiva. [Rome], 1972. pp. 780. *(Italy. Servizio Commissioni Parlamentari. Indagini Conoscitive e Documentazioni Legislative. 14)*

— Malaysia.

SNODGRASS (DONALD R.) The fiscal system as an income redistributor in West Malaysia. Cambridge, Mass., [1972?]. pp. 43. *(Harvard University. Center for International Affairs. Economic Development Reports. No. 224)*

— — Kedah — Accounting.

FEDERATION OF MALAYSIA. [Audit Department]. Report of the Auditor-General: State of Kedah. a., 1971- Kuala Lumpur. *In Malay and English.*

— — Sarawak — Accounting.

FEDERATION OF MALAYSIA. [Audit Department]. Report of the Auditor General: State of Sarawak. a., 1969 [1st]- Kuala Lumpur. *In Malay and English.*

— — Selangor — Accounting.

FEDERATION OF MALAYSIA. [Audit Department]. Report of the Auditor-General: State of Selangor. a., 1971- Kuala Lumpur. *In Malay and English.*

— Mexico.

PICHARDO PAGAZA (IGNACIO) Ensayos sobre politica fiscal de Mexico. Toluca, Direccion General de Hacienda del Estado de Mexico, 1972. pp. 312. *(Coleccion Estudios Fiscales. 3)*

— Morocco.

GUILLEN (PIERRE) Les emprunts marocains, 1902-1904. [Paris, 1972?]. pp. 173. *bibliog. (Paris. Université de Paris I (Panthéon Sorbonne). Publications. Série Internationale. 1)*

— New Zealand.

DEANE (RODERICK S.) and others. Financial asset behaviour and government financing transactions in New Zealand. Wellington, 1973. pp. 71. *bibliogs. (Reserve Bank of New Zealand. Research Papers. No.11)*

— Norway.

NORWAY. Finans- og Tolldepartementet. 1968. Om gjennomføringen av nasjonalbudsjettet 1968. [Oslo, 1968]. pp. 87. *(Norway. Stortinget. Stortingsmeldinger. 1967-68. Nr. 70)*

NORWAY. Statistiske Centralbyrå. 1973. De offentlige sektorers finanser 1968-1970; Public sector finances 1968-1970. Oslo, 1973. pp. 55. *(Norges Offisielle Statistikk. Rekke A.555) In English and Norwegian.*

— Pakistan.

PAKISTAN. Ministry of Finance. 1972. Fiscal policy in Pakistan: a historical perspective. [Islamabad, 1972]. 2 vols. (in 1).

— Poland — Law.

OKULICZ (TADEUSZ) Prawo bud'zetowe: zbiór podstawowych przepisów z objaśnieniami; stan prawny na dzień i sierpnia 1973 r. Warszawa, 1973. pp. 316.

— Russia.

TSENTRAL'NYI ARKHIV RSFSR. Russkie finansy i evropeiskaia birzha v 1904-1906 gg.; pod redaktsiei i s predisloviem E.A. Preobrazhenskogo, etc. Moskva, 1926. pp. 400. *Xerographic reprint.*

BROMBERG (GELLA L'VOVNA) and others. Ekonomicheskaia rabota finansovoi sluzhby predpriiatiia; pod redaktsiei... A.M. Birmana. Moskva, 1970. pp. 103.

LUSHIN (STANISLAV IVANOVICH) Edinstvo material'nykh i finansovykh proportsii v narodnom khoziaistve; pod obshchei redaktsiei... A.G. Aganbegiana. Moskva, 1970. pp. 208.

BUDAVEI (VSEVOLOD IUR'EVICH) and SITARIAN (STEPAN ARAMAISOVICH) eds. Finansy i nauchno-tekhnicheskii progress. Moskva, 1973. pp. 239.

FINANSY i effektivnost' proizvodstvennykh fondov; avtorskii kollektiv pod rukovodstvom V.K. Senchagova. Moskva, 1973. pp. 176.

ISAEV (BORIS LEONIDOVICH) Balansy mezhotraslevykh finansovykh sviazei. Moskva, 1973. pp. 278. *bibliog.*

KNIAZEV (GRIGORII IVANOVICH) Finansovyi plan predpriiatiia i kontrol' za ego ispolneniem; pod redaktsiei V.N. Maslennikova. Moskva, 1973. pp. 143.

KURCHENKO (LARISA FEDOROVNA) Balansovyi metod v finansovom planirovanii. Moskva, 1973. pp. 112.

LITUNOVSKAIA (MARIIA KSENOFONTOVNA) Finansovo-kreditnye istochniki nauchno-tekhnicheskogo progressa. Moskva, 1973. pp. 159.

POPADIUK (KIRILL NIKITICH) Finansy i kredit v raspredelenii natsional'nogo dokhoda. Moskva, 1973. pp. 176.

SHERMENEV (MIKHAIL KUZ'MICH) Finansovye rezervy v rasshirennom vosproizvodstve. Moskva, 1973. pp. 207.

SHUMOV (NIKOLAI SERGEEVICH) Finansirovanie i kreditovanie promyshlennosti. 2nd ed. Moskva, 1973. pp. 288.

SYCHEV (N.G.) ed. Finansy predpriiatii i otraslei narodnogo khoziaistva. 2nd ed. Moskva, 1973. pp. 470.

VOZNESENSKII (ERNEST ALEKSANDROVICH) Finansovyi kontrol' v SSSR. Moskva, 1973. pp. 134.

ZVEREV (ARSENII GRIGOR'EVICH) Zapiski ministra. Moskva, 1973. pp. 270.

— — Ukraine.

PAVLENKO (GRIGORII GRIGOR'EVICH) and others. Gosbank i razvitie narodnogo khoziaistva Ukrainy. Kiev, 1974. pp. 183.

— Saint—Pierre and Miquelon — Accounting.

SAINT-PIERRE AND MIQUELON. Service Local. Compte définitif des recettes et des dépenses. a., 1971- Saint-Pierre.

— South Africa — Accounting.

SOUTH AFRICA. Report of the Controller and Auditor-General on the... accounts... of the Bophuthatswana Government and on the accounts of the lower authorities in Bophuthatswana. a., 1972/3 [1st]- Pretoria. *Included in the file of SOUTH AFRICA. Parliament. House of Assembly. Votes and proceedings; (with Printed annexures).*

SOUTH AFRICA. Report of the Controller and Auditor-General on the accounts of the kwaZulu Government and of the lower authorities in the area. a., 1972/3- Pretoria. *Included in the file of SOUTH AFRICA. Parliament. House of Assembly. Votes and proceedings; (with Printed annexures).*

SOUTH AFRICA. Report of the Controller and Auditor-General on the accounts of the Gazankulu Government and of the accounts of lower authorities in the area. a., 1972/3 [1st]- Pretoria. *Included in the file of SOUTH AFRICA. Parliament. House of Assembly. Votes and proceedings; (with Printed annexures).*

— — Port Elizabeth.

BOTHA (D.J.J.) Urban taxation and land use: report of a one-man commission appointed by the City Council of Port Elizabeth. [Port Elizabeth, 1970]. pp. 192.

— Spain.

SPAIN. Direccion General de Politica Financiere. Memoria estadistica. a., 1971 [ist issue]- Madrid.

— — Law.

USERA (GABRIEL DE) Legislacion de hacienda española; autorizada...y declarada de utilidad general por orden ministerial de 1 de marzo de 1946. 5th ed. Madrid, [1952]. pp. 488. *(Biblioteca de Ciencias Economicas)*

— Sri Lanka — Accounting.

STATE ACCOUNTS OF THE REPUBLIC OF SRI LANKA. a., [Oc 1971]/D 1972[1st]- Colombo.

— Sweden.

SWEDEN. Finansdepartementet. Långtidsutredningen. 1971. [Svensk ekonomi fram till 1977]; 1970 års långtidsutredning. Bilaga. 4. Finansiella tillväxtaspekter 1960-1975; utarbetad...av Willem van der Hoeven. Stockholm, 1971. pp. 65. *(Sweden. Statens Offentliga Utredningar. 1971. 7)*

— Switzerland.

BODMER (GUIDO) Die bernischen Infrastruktur-Subventionen: Versuch eines interkantonalen Vergleiches. Bern, 1969. fo.84,(78). bibliog. *(Bern (Canton). Statistisches Bureau. Sonderhefte. 18)*

LIPPUNER (HANS) Die Bundesfinanzen und die EWG-Steuerharmonisierung, unter besonderer Berücksichtigung der Umsatzsteuer. Bern, 1970. pp. 148. bibliog.

SWITZERLAND. Administration Fédérale des Finances. Subventions fédérales. a., 1973[1st]- Berne. *File includes 1972 as a reprint from "La Vie économique" pd. by Bureau Fédéral de Statistique.*

— — Basel—Stadt (Canton).

BASEL-STADT (CANTON). Regierungsrat. 1970. Finanz- und Investitionsplan 1970-1974. 2. Bericht zum Stand der Finanzplanung im Kanton Basel-Stadt. [Basel, 1970]. pp. 102.

— — Bern (Canton).

BODMER (GUIDO) Die bernischen Infrastruktur-Subventionen: Versuch eines interkantonalen Vergleiches. Bern, 1969. fo.84,(78). bibliog. *(Bern (Canton). Statistisches Bureau. Sonderhefte. 18)*

— — Zürich (Canton).

ZUERICH (CANTON). Statistisches Amt. 1971. Zürcher Staatsfinanzen 1945-1967. Zürich, 1971. pp. 196. bibliog. *(Statistische Mitteilungen. 3. Folge. Heft 73)*

— Underdeveloped areas.

UNDERDEVELOPED AREAS
— Finance.
— United Kingdom.

U.K. Public Record Office. Lists and Indexes. Supplementary Series. No. 12. List of Treasury records, 1838-1938. New York, Kraus Reprint Corporation, 1970. pp. 359.

HOUGHTON (R.W.) ed. Public finance : selected readings. 2nd ed. Harmondsworth, 1973. pp. 543. bibliog.

KING (DAVID N.) Financial and economic aspects of regionalism and separatism. London, 1973. pp. 99. *(U.K. Commission on the Constitution, 1969. Research Papers. 10)*

— — Accounting.

PITBLADO (Sir DAVID) Public accountability; (transcript of... lecture held on 3 April 1973). [London], Civil Service College, [1973]. fo. 30. *(Lectures on the Control of Public Expenditure. No. 5)*

— — Leicester.

P.A. MANAGEMENT CONSULTANTS LTD. Economic Studies Division. An evaluation of future social services expenditure on behalf of the city of Leicester. [London, 1974]. pp. 157.

— — Wales.

REVELL (JACK) and TOMKINS (CYRIL R.) Personal wealth and finance in Wales. [Cardiff?], Welsh Council, 1974. pp. 71.

— United States.

HYMAN (DAVID N.) The economics of governmental activity. New York, [1973]. pp. 333.

TAX FOUNDATION. Research Publications. New Series. No. 28. The financial outlook for state and local government to 1980. New York, [1973]. pp. 116.

WHEELER (GEORGE) Pierpont Morgan and friends: the anatomy of a myth. Englewood Cliffs, [1973]. pp. 338. bibliog.

The ECONOMICS of public finance: essays by Alan S. Blinder [and others]. Washington, D.C., [1974]. pp. 435. bibliog. *(Brookings Institution. National Committee on Government Finance. Studies of Government Finance)*

SCHRIFTGIESSER (KARL) The Commission on Money and Credit: an adventure in policy- making. Englewood Cliffs, [1974]. pp. 165. bibliog.

— — Accounting.

TENNER (IRVING) and LYNN (EDWARD S.) Municipal and governmental accounting. 4th ed. Englewood Cliffs, [1960]. pp. 592. bibliog.

— Yugoslavia.

DIMITRIJEVIC (DIMITRIJE) and MACESICH (GEORGE) Money and finance in contemporary Yugoslavia. New York, 1973. pp. 261. bibliog.

— Zaire.

BANQUE DU ZAIRE. Rapport annuel. a., 1971/2- Kinshasa.

FINANCIAL INSTITUTIONS.

HENRION (ROBERT) Institutions et opérations financières. 4th ed. [Brussels, 1972]. 2 vols. (in 1).

REVELL (JACK) Financial centres, financial institutions and economic change. Bangor, [1973]. pp. 20. bibliog. *(Wales. University. University College of North Wales. Economic Research Papers. FIN 4)*

— Belgium.

HENRION (ROBERT) Institutions et opérations financières. 4th ed. [Brussels, 1972]. 2 vols. (in 1).

— India.

INDIA. Administrative Reforms Commission. 1970. Report on treasuries. [Delhi, 1970]. pp. 36.

INDIA. Administrative Reforms Commission. Task Force on Treasuries. 1970. Report, [1968]. [Delhi, 1970]. pp. 7.

BHATT (V.V.) Structure of financial institutions. Bombay, [1972]. pp. 198.

— Italy.

ITALY. Ragioneria Generale dello Stato. 1969. La Ragioneria Generale dello Stato: centenario, 1869-1969. Roma, 1969. pp. 196.

— Norway.

EIDE (LEIF) The Norwegian monetary and credit system. Oslo, 1973. pp. 62. *(Norges Bank. Skriftserie. No.1)*

— Portugal.

PORTUGAL. Presidência do Conselho. 1953. 25 anos de administração publica: Ministerio das Finanças. Lisboa, 1953. pp. 75.

FINES (PENALTIES)
— Finland.

MÄKINEN (TUIJA) Lükennesakot varallisuuteen kohdistuvana rangaistuksena, etc. Helsinki, 1974. fo. 33. *(Kriminologinen Tutkimuslaitos. Sarja M. 35) With English summary.*

— Ireland (Republic).

EIRE. Committee on Court Practice and Procedure. 1971. Fifteenth interim report...: on the spot fines. Dublin, [1971]. pp. 11.

FINLAND.

NICKELS (SYLVIE) and others. Finland: an introduction. 2nd ed. London, 1973. pp. 377. bibliog.

— Census.

FINLAND. Census, 1970. Censuses of population, housing and buildings in Finland 31 December 1970. English summary of preliminary tables. Helsinki, 1972. fo. 22. *(Finland. Tilastokeskus. Tilastotiedotus. VL. 1972. 17)*

— Commerce.

SUKSELAINEN (TUOMAS) Finnish export performance in 1961-1972: a constant-market-shares approach. Helsinki, 1974. pp. 74.

— Defences.

FINLAND. Parlamentariska Försvarskommittén. 1971. Betänkande. Helsingfors, 1971. pp. 53. *(Finland. Kommittébetänkande. 1971. A 18)*

— Economic conditions.

HUSTICH (ILMARI) Finlands skärgård: en ekonomisk-geografisk översikt. Helsingford, 1964. pp. 154. bibliog. *(Svenska Handelshögskolan. Ekonomi och Samhälle. Nr. 10)*

— — Statistics.

FINLAND. Suomen Virallinen Tilasto. Finlands Officiella Statistik. 35.2. Lükeyrityslaskenta 1964, etc. Helsinki, 1971 in progress. Tables in Finnish, Swedish and English.

— Economic history.

SCHYBERGSON (PER) Hantverk och fabriker.... Finlands konsumtionsvaruindustri, 1815- 1870. Helsingfors, 1973-74. 3 vols. (in 1). bibliog. *(Societas Scientiarum Fennica. Bidrag till Kännedom av Finlands Natur och Folk. H.114, 116,117)*

FINLAND. (Cont.)

— Economic policy.

FINLAND. Kuntien Taloussunnittelukomitea. 1970. Betänkande av Kommittén för Kommunernas Ekonomiska Planering; [Jussi Linnamo, chairman]. Helsingfors, 1970. fo. 180. (Finland. Komiteanmietinnöt. 1970. B 84)

FINLAND. Taloudellinen Suunnittelukeskus. 1973. Growth prospects for the Finnish economy up to 1980. Helsinki, 1972 [or rather 1973]. pp. 183.

KASVIO (ANTTI) Den statsmonopolistiska kapitalismen i Finland: (STAMOKAP); material för ett forskningsprojekt; oversat fra finsk af Christer Karjalainen. [Grenå, 1973]. pp. 64. (Scandinavian Summer University. Skriftserie. Nr.1)

— Emigration and immigration.

KERO (REINO) Migration from Finland to North America in the years between the United States Civil War and the First World War. Turku, 1974. pp. 260. bibliog. (Åbo. Turun Yliopisto. Julkaisuja. Sarja B. Osa 130)

— Foreign relations.

FRANCE. Direction de la Documentation. La Documentation Française. Notes et Etudes Documentaires. Nos. 3,837-3, 838. La politique extérieure de la Finlande; [by] Alain Bézard. Paris, 1971. pp. 68. bibliog.

YEARBOOK OF FINNISH FOREIGN POLICY; [pd. by] the Finnish Institute of International Affairs. a., 1973[1st]- Helsinki.

— — Germany.

MENGER (MANFRED) Die Finnlandpolitik des deutschen Imperialismus, 1917-1918. Berlin, 1974. pp. 242. bibliog. (Akademie der Wissenschaften der DDR. Zentralinstitut für Geschichte. Schriften. Band 38)

— — Russia.

VAYRYNEN (RAIMO) Conflicts in Finnish-Soviet relations: three comparative case studies. Tampere, 1972. pp. 270. (Tampere. Yliopisto. Acta Universitatis Tamperensis. Ser. A. vol. 47)

— Government publications.

FINLAND. Valtion Painatuskeskuksen. Luettelo. irreg., 1973- Helsinki.

— Industries.

SCHYBERGSON (PER) Hantverk och fabriker...: Finlands konsumtionsvaruindustri, 1815- 1870. Helsingfors, 1973-74. 3 vols. (in 1). bibliog. (Societas Scientiarum Fennica. Bidrag till Kännedom av Finlands Natur och Folk. H.114, 116,117)

— Politics and government.

ÅBO. Akademi. Acta Academiae Aboensis. Humaniora. 45. 2. Religion och politik: studier i finländsk politisk idéevärld och politisk miljö vid 1900-talets början; av Heimer Lindström. Åbo, 1973. pp. 224. bibliog.

— Population, Rural.

STONE (KIRK H.) Northern Finland's post-war colonizing and emigration: a geographical analysis of rural demographic counter-currents. The Hague, 1973. pp. 94.

TAURIAINEN (JUHANI) and KOIVULA (SAMULI) The conditions in and problems of rural depopulation areas. Helsinki, 1973. pp. 162, 12. bibliog. (Finland. Suomen Virallinen Tilasto. Finlands Officiella Statistik. 32. Sosiaalisia Erikoistutkimuksia. 33)

— Social conditions.

HARANNE (MARKKU) and ALLARDT (ERIK) Attitudes toward modernity and modernization: an appraisal of an empirical study. Helsinki, 1974. pp. 109. (Helsinki, Yliopisto. Research Group for Comparative Sociology. Research Reports. No.6)

— Social policy.

FINLAND. Taloudellinen Suunnittelukeskus. 1973. Quality of life: social goals and measurement: summary of a study of social indicators made by a Division of the Economic Council of Finland. Helsinki, 1973. fo. 68.

FINNMARK

— Economic policy.

BJØRNLAND (DAG) Finnmark fylke: perspektiver for naeringsliv, sysselsetting og folkemengde. [Oslo], Transportøkonomisk Institutt, [1972]. pp. 63.

FIREMEN.

WORKING PARTY TO REVIEW HIGHER TRAINING IN THE FIRE SERVICE [U.K.]. Reports; [R.F.D. Shuffrey, chairman]. [London], 1973. fo 52.

FIRMS.

SYMPOSIUM ON INDUSTRIAL ECONOMICS, UNIVERSITY OF WARWICK, 1972. Market structure and corporate behaviour: theory and empirical analysis of the firm; edited by Keith Cowling. London, 1972. pp. 200. bibliog.

CASSON (MARK C.) Dynamic production functions and the theory of the firm. [Reading], [1973]. fo. 35. bibliog. (Reading. University. Department of Economics. Discussion Papers in Economics. No. 41)

EKERN (STEINAR) On the theory of the firm in incomplete markets; a dissertation submitted to... Stanford University, etc. [Stanford], 1973. fo. 141. bibliog.

HAWKINS (C.J.) Theory of the firm. London, 1973. pp. 96. bibliog.

LAING (GORDON JAMES) Limits to growth in business organisations: simulation experiments in communications and in the use of capital; [Ph.D. (London) thesis]. [1973]. fo. 471. bibliog. Typescript: unpublished. This thesis is the property of London University and may not be removed from the Library.

LOMBARDINI (SIRO) ed. Teoria dell'impresa e struttura economica: (testi di E.M. Chamberlin) [and others]. Bologna, [1973]. pp. 384. bibliog.

CURWEN (PETER J.) Managerial economics. London, 1974. pp. 245. bibliogs.

— History — Germany.

HOECHST in England, 1901-1914: zur Geschichte des Werkes Ellesmere Port der Meister Lucius Brüning Limited. [Frankfurt am Main], 1971. pp. 104. (Farbwerke Hoechst. Dokumente aus Hoechster Archiven. 45)

SCHAPER (CHRISTA) Die Hirschvogel von Nürnberg und ihr Handelshaus. Nürnberg, 1973. pp. 351. bibliog. (Nuremberg. Verein für Geschichte der Stadt Nürnberg. Nürnberger Forschungen. 18. Band)

FICHTER (TILMAN) Kampf um Bosch: ... die Betriebspolitik der KPD nach 1945, am Beispiel der Firma Robert Bosch GmbH; [and] Eugen Eberle: Sieben Jahre offensiver Kampf gegen das Kapital. Berlin, [1974]. pp. 191. bibliog.

— — Japan.

ROBERTS (JOHN G.) Mitsui: three centuries of Japanese business. New York, 1973. pp. 564. bibliog.

— — Malaysia.

BOUSTEADS; [history of the company]. [London, 1963]. pp. 40.

— — Russia.

EFREMTSEV (GRIGORII PETROVICH) Istoriia Kolomenskogo zavoda: ocherk istorii Kolomenskogo teplovozostroitel'nogo zavoda imeni V.V. Kuibysheva za 110 let, 1863-1973. Moskva, 1973. pp. 351. bibliog.

ISTORIIA Tul'skogo oruzheinogo zavoda, 1712-1972, etc. Moskva, 1973. pp. 494. bibliog.

PERVYI podshipnikovyi: istoriia Pervogo gosudarstvennogo podshipnikovogo zavoda, 1932-1972. Moskva, 1973. pp. 302. bibliog.

— — — Russia (RSFSR).

SUDAREV (MIKHAIL SERGEEVICH) Stranitsy istorii: 175 let Mullovskoi sukonnoi fabriki. Ul'ianovsk, 1963. pp. 150. bibliog.

VOLOKHOV (VALENTIN PETROVICH) Brianskii ordena Trudovogo Krasnogo Znameni mashinostroitel'nyi zavod: ocherk revoliutsionnykh i trudovykh traditsii kollektiva. Tula, 1966. pp. 230.

GOD rozhdeniia 1943-i: istoricheskii ocherk o Bereznikovskom ordena Trudovogo Krasnogo Znameni titano-magnievom kombinate. Perm', 1968. pp. 259.

ETAPY bol'shogo puti: k 75-letiiu lokomotivnogo depo Kurgan. Kurgan, 1971. pp. 31.

— — — Soviet Far East.

KAMBULOV (VALENTIN ALEKSANDROVICH) 60 let slavnogo sluzheniia Rodine: sbornik materialov po istorii Spasskogo tsementnogo zavoda. Vladivostok, 1967. pp. 54. bibliog.

— — — White Russia.

BORODULIN (MARK MOISEEVICH) and others. Rovesnik veka. Minsk, 1969. pp. 102.

— — Sweden.

ALTHIN (TORSTEN) Vattenbyggnadsbyrån, 1897-1947: historik. Stockholm, 1947. pp. 182. bibliog.

— — Switzerland.

RUTZ (MARIANNE) Die Walzmühle in Frauenfeld: ein Kapitel aus der Geschichte der Industrialisierung der Schweiz. [Zürich, imprint, 1973]. pp. 198. bibliog.

TROXLER (WERNER P.) Johann Rudolf Forcart-Weiss Söhne: ein Beitrag zur Unternehmergeschichte. Bern, 1973. pp. 128. bibliog. (Zürich. Universität. Historisches Seminar. Geist und Werk der Zeiten. No. 36)

VEREIN FÜR WIRTSCHAFTSHISTORISCHE STUDIEN. Schweizer Pioniere der Wirtschaft und Technik. 27. Zwei Schaffhauser Pioniere: Friedrich Peyer im Hof, 1817- 1900; Heinrich Theophil Bäschlin, 1845-1887. Zürich, 1973. pp. 107. bibliog.

— — United Kingdom.

CENTRAL MINING AND INVESTMENT CORPORATION. Fiftieth anniversary. London, [1955?]. 1 vol. (unpaged).

GARBUTT (JOHN L.) Manbré and Garton Limited, 1855-1955: a hundred years of progress. [London, 1955]. pp. 51.

RUBBER REGENERATING COMPANY. The Rubber Regenerating Company Limited, Manchester, England: 1909-1959. Manchester, [1959]. pp. 38.

SMEETON (A.E.) The story of Evans Medical, 1809-1959; published to commemorate the 150th anniversary of the foundation of the company. Liverpool, [1959]. 1 vol. (unpaged).

TILBURY GROUP. The Tilbury Group. [London], 1960. pp. 41.

BOUSTEADS; [history of the company]. [London, 1963]. pp. 40.

LITTLE (BRYAN) (Capper Pass): the first hundred and fifty years. London, [1963]. pp. 33. bibliog.

ROSNER (CHARLES) ed. The world of De La Rue: the Old World and the New; presented on the occasion of the one hundred and fiftieth anniversary of the house of De la Rue, 1813-1963. [London, 1963]. 1 vol. (unpaged).

SLOUGH ESTATES LIMITED. Slough Estates Limited, 1920-1970. [Slough, 1970]. pp. 36.

WISDOM (T.H.) 50 years of progress: the history of the Automotive Products Organisation over the past 50 years. [Leamington Spa, 1970]. pp. 48.

HOECHST in England, 1901-1914: zur Geschichte des Werkes Ellesmere Port der Meister Lucius Brüning Limited. [Frankfurt am Main], 1971. pp. 104. *(Farbwerke Hoechst. Dokumente aus Hoechster Archiven. 45)*

JACKSON (GORDON) Grimsby and the Haven Company, 1796-1846. Grimsby, [1971]. pp. 102.

FOLEY (JOHN) The food makers: a history of General Foods Ltd. Banbury, 1972. pp. 65.

HAMPSON (CYRIL GARFORTH) 150th anniversary history of Robert Fletcher and Son Ltd. Manchester, [1973]. pp. 69.

REES (GORONWY) St. Michael: a history of Marks and Spencer. rev. ed. London, 1973. pp. 284.

SETH-SMITH (MICHAEL) Two hundred years of Richard Johnson and Nephew. Manchester, 1973. pp. 292. *bibliog.*

WARNER (OLIVER) Chatto and Windus: a brief account of the firm's origin, history and development. London, 1973. pp. 33.

CHAPMAN (STANLEY D.) Jesse Boot of Boots the chemists: a study in business history. London, 1974. pp. 221.

JERVIS (FRANK ROBERT JOSEPH) Bosses in British business: managers and management from the industrial revolution to the present day. London, 1974. pp. 184. *bibliog.*

MUTTON (NORMAN) The Foster family: a study of a Midland industrial dynasty 1786-1899; [Ph. D. (London) thesis]. [1974]. fo. 352. *bibliog. Typescript: unpublished. Offprints of three articles bound in at end. This thesis is the property of London University and may not be removed from the Library.*

PAFFORD (ELIZABETH R.) and PAFFORD (JOHN HENRY PYLE) Employer and employed: Ford, Ayrton and Co. Ltd., silk spinners, with worker participation... 1870-1970. Edington, 1974. pp. 77. *bibliog. (Pasold Research Fund. Pasold Occasional Papers. vol. 2)*

PILLER (NORMAN) Instead of the butler's apron. Luton, 1974. pp. 433.

SWINGLEHURST (EDMUND) The romantic journey: the story of Thomas Cook and Victorian travel. London, 1974. pp. 208. *bibliog.*

— **Mathematical models.**

DAVIS (E.G.) A dynamic model of the regulated firm with a price adjustment mechanism. [Ottawa, 1973]. fo. 15,8. *bibliog. (Carleton University. Carleton Economic Papers)*

KNUDSEN (NIELS CHR.) Production and cost models of a multi-product firm: a mathematical programming approach. Odense, 1973. pp. 300. *bibliog. (Odense Universitet. Studies in History and Social Sciences. vol.13)*

— **France.**

FRANCE. Institut National de la Statistique et des Etudes Economiques. Collections de l'I.N.S.E.E. Série E. Entreprises. . Paris, 1969 in progress.

— **Russia.**

ERMOLIN (MIKHAIL VASIL'EVICH) Predpriiatie v sisteme ekonomicheskikh otnoshenii sotsializma: mesto i rol' predpriiatiia v razvitii sotsialisticheskoi ekonomiki. Leningrad, 1973. pp. 136.

FISCHER (ERNST).

FISCHER (ERNST) of the Austrian Communist Party. Das Ende einer Illusion: Erinnerungen, 1945-1955. Wien, [1973]. pp. 400.

FISCHER (ERNST) of the Austrian Communist Party. An opposing man; translated [from the German] by Peter and Betty Ross. London, 1974. pp. 418.

FISCHER (JOHN ARBUTHNOT) 1st Baron Fischer.

MACKAY (RUDDOCK FINLAY) Fischer of Kilverstone. Oxford, 1973. pp. 539. *bibliog.*

FISH TRADE

— **United Kingdom.**

TEMPLETON (J.) Going metric in the fish industry. [Aberdeen], Torry Research Station, [1969]. pp. 8. *(Torry Advisory Notes. No.40)*

FISHERIES

— **Atlantic.**

INTERNATIONAL COMMISSION FOR THE NORTHWEST ATLANTIC FISHERIES. Annual proceedings (formerly Annual report). a., 1951/2 (2nd)- Dartmouth, N.S., etc.

INTERNATIONAL COMMISSION FOR THE NORTHWEST ATLANTIC FISHERIES. Statistical bulletin. a., 1953(v.3)- Dartmouth, N.S. (formerly Halifax, N.S.).

NORTH-EAST ATLANTIC FISHERIES COMMISSION. Report of the meeting. a., My 1968 (6th)- London.

— **Australia.**

NEWTON (RICHARD L.) The north coast fishing industry; report prepared for the Clarence and Richmond-Tweed Regional Devopment Committees by the Department of Geography. University of New England, Armidale. Armidale, 1968[repr. 1973]. pp. 115,xxxii. *bibliog. (University of New England, Armidale. Department of Geography. Research Series in Applied Geography. No. 36) Lacks Appendix 1.*

— **Canada.**

JOHNSTONE (KEN) The vanishing harvest: the Canadian fishing crisis. Montreal, [1972]. pp. 87.

— — **Newfoundland.**

FARSTAD (NELVIN) Fisheries developement in Newfoundland: aspects of developement, location and infrastructure. Bergen, 1972. pp. 125. *bibliog.*

— **India — Kerala.**

ASARI (T.R. THANKAPPAN) The impact of the Indo-Norwegian project on the growth and development of Indian fisheries; submitted to the FAO International Conference on Investment in Fisheries, held in Rome 18th-24th September 1969. [Oslo? Norwegian Agency for International Development, 1969?]. pp. 11.

— **Indian Ocean.**

INDO-PACIFIC FISHERIES COUNCIL. Proceedings. Section 1. bien., 1962 (10th session)- Bangkok. *For 1968 (13th session) file includes only Summary report. Draft report is kept until superseded by the Proceedings.*

— **Japan.**

FRANCE. Direction de la Documentation. La Documentation Française. Notes et Etudes Documentaires. Nos. 3,778-3, 779. Les activités maritimes du Japon; [by] Albert Boyer. Paris, 1971. pp. 52.

— — **Statistics.**

FISHERIES STATISTICS OF JAPAN; [pd. by] Statistics and Information Department, Ministry of Agriculture and Forestry, ... Japan. a., 1971- Tokyo.

— **Norway — Finance.**

INNSTILLING om offentlig finansiering av fiske og fiskeforedling; fra et utvalg oppnevnt av Fiskeridepartementet 26. mars 1969. Otta, 1970. pp. 34.

— — **Statistics.**

NORWAY. Statistiske Centralbyrå. 1973- . Fiskeritellingen, 1. oktober 1971. Oslo, 1973 in progress. *(Norway. Norges Offisielle Statistikk. Rekke A. 559 etc.) With English summary.*

— **Pacific Ocean.**

INTERNATIONAL NORTH PACIFIC FISHERIES COMMISSION. Annual report. a., 1955 [2nd]- Vancouver.

INDO-PACIFIC FISHERIES COUNCIL. Proceedings. Section 1. bien., 1962 (10th session)- Bangkok. *For 1968 (13th session) file includes only Summary report. Draft report is kept until superseded by the Proceedings.*

— **Russia.**

ZHURAVKOV (VALERII ONUFRIEVICH) and ZINGER (IL'IA SAMOILOVICH) Novye metody planirovaniia i upravleniia rybnoi promyshlennost'iu. Moskva, 1967. pp. 133. *bibliog.*

EFFEKTIVNOST' ispol'zovaniia osnovnykh fondov rybnoi promyshlennosti. Moskva, 1970. pp. 160. *bibliog.*

STUDENETSKII (SERGEI ALEKSANDROVICH) Organizatsiia i material'no-tekhnicheskaia baza promyshlennogo rybolovstva SSSR. Moskva, 1973. pp. 336. *bibliog.*

— **Solomon Islands.**

BRITISH SOLOMON ISLANDS PROTECTORATE. 1964. Agricultural and fisheries policy. Honiara, 1964. pp. (iii), 52. *(White Papers. B.S.I.P. 6)*

— **Sweden.**

SWEDEN. Statistiska Centralbyrån. 1967. Fiske 1964 och 1965: redovisning för ost- och sydkustlänen samt Hallands län, etc. Stockholm, 1967. pp. 54. *(Statistiska Meddelanden. J/1967/26)*

— — **Finance.**

SWEDEN. Jordbruksdepartementet. Fiskprisutredningen. 1969. Finansieringen av investeringar i fisket. [Stockholm?], 1969. fo. 86. *(Sweden. Jo[rdbruksdepartementet]. [Stencil]. 1969. 8)*

— **United Kingdom.**

WINNIFRITH (Sir ALFRED JOHN DIGBY) The Ministry of Agriculture, Fisheries and Food. London, 1962. pp. 271. *(Royal Institute of Public Administration. New Whitehall Series. No. 11)*

NORTHERN ECONOMIC PLANNING COUNCIL. Challenge of the changing north: agriculture, horticulture, forestry and fishing. [Newcastle], 1967. pp. 71. *Xerox copy.*

FRANCE. Direction de la Documentation. La Documentation Française. Notes et Etudes Documentaires. No. 3,727. Les activités maritimes du Royaume-Uni de Grande-Bretagne et d'Irlande du Nord . Paris, 1970. pp. 47.

— **United States — Alaska.**

TUSSING (ARLON R.) and others, eds. Alaska fisheries policy: economics,resources and management. Fairbanks, 1972. pp. 470. *bibliogs. (University of Alaska. Institute of Social, Economic and Government Research. ISEGR Reports. No.33)*

FISHERMEN

— **Canada — Newfoundland.**

FARIS (JAMES C.) Cat Harbour: a Newfoundland fishing settlement. [St. John's, 1972]. pp. 184. *(St. John's. Memorial University of Newfoundland. Institute of Social and Economic Research. Newfoundland Social and Economic Studies. No. 3)*

— **Norway.**

NORWAY. Statistiske Centralbyrå. 1973- . Fiskeritellingen, 1. oktober 1971. Oslo, 1973 in progress. *(Norway. Norges Offisielle Statistikk. Rekke A. 559 etc.) With English summary.*

FISHING BOATS.

INTER-GOVERNMENTAL MARITIME CONSULTATIVE ORGANIZATION. 1969. Recommendation on intact stability of fishing vessels. London, [1969]. pp. 24.

FLANDERS

FLANDERS
— Commerce.

EVERAERT (JOHN G.) De internationale en koloniale handel der Vlaamse firma's te Cadiz, 1670-1700. Brugge, 1973. pp. 975. bibliog. (Ghent. Université. Faculte de Philosophie et Lettres. Recueil de Travaux. Fascicule 154). Summary in French.

— Economic history.

NICHOLAS (DAVID) Town and countryside: social, economic and political tensions in fourteenth-century Flanders. Brugge, 1971. pp. 374. bibliog. (Ghent. Université. Faculté de Philosophie et Lettres. Recueil de Travaux. Fascicule 152)

— — Sources.

VERLINDEN (CHARLES) and others, eds. Dokumenten voor de geschiedenis van prijzen en lonen in Vlaanderen en Brabant...(XIVe-XIXe eeuw). Brugge, 1959 in progress. bibliogs. (Ghent. Université. Faculté de Philosophie et Lettres. Recueil de Travaux. Fascicules 125, etc.)

— Social history.

NICHOLAS (DAVID) Town and countryside: social, economic and political tensions in fourteenth-century Flanders. Brugge, 1971. pp. 374. bibliog. (Ghent. Université. Faculté de Philosophie et Lettres. Recueil de Travaux. Fascicule 152)

FLAX INDUSTRY
— United Kingdom.

WOOL, JUTE AND FLAX INDUSTRY TRAINING BOARD [U.K.]. Report and statement of accounts. a., 1972/3- Bradford. *Formerly included in the file of British Parliamentary Papers.*

FLEMISH MOVEMENT.

BOCK (EUGEEN DE) Ondergang en herstel; of, Het begin van de "Vlaamse beweging". Antwerp, 1970. pp. 292. bibliog.

LAMBERTY (MAX) De Vlaamse opstanding. Leuven, [1971-73]. 2 vols.

BECQUET (CHARLES FRANÇOIS) Le différend wallo-flamand. [Nalinnes-lez-Charleroi], 1972 in progress. bibliog. (Institut Jules Destrée pour la Défense et l'Illustration de la Wallonie. Etudes et Documents)

WILS (LODE) Flamenpolitik en aktivisme: Vlaanderen tegenover België in de eerste wereldoorlog. Leuven, [1974]. pp. 272. bibliog.

FLETCHER (JOHN WILLIAM).

FLETCHER (JOHN WILLIAM) A menace to society: my 35 years in prison - for stealing... 40[pounds]. London, 1972. pp. 142.

FLIGHT CREWS
— United Kingdom.

U.K. Committee on Flight Time Limitations. 1973. Report...; chairman: Douglas Bader. London, 1973. pp. 65.

FLINTSHIRE
— Economic policy.

FLINTSHIRE. County Planning Department. Flintshire countryside report. Mold, Flintshire, 1972. pp. 50.

FLOOD CONTROL
— Brazil.

BRAZIL. Superintendência do Desenvolvimento do Nordeste. 1973. Plano de ação contra as calamidades publicas de seca e enchentes. [Recife], 1973. pp. 135. *Map in end pocket.*

— Italy.

CONTINI (BRUNO) and PACI (MASSIMO) Difesa del suolo e sviluppo dell'agricoltura: un'analisi di sistemi applicata al Polesine. Bologna, [1973]. pp. 343. bibliog.

— United States.

LEUCHTENBURG (WILLIAM EDWARD) Flood control politics: the Connecticut River Valley problem 1927-1950; [reprint of work first published in 1953]. New York, 1972. pp. 339. bibliog.

FLOODS.

UNITED NATIONS. Economic Commission for Asia and the Far East. Water Resources Series. Nos. 23 onwards . New York, 1963 in progress.

FLORENCE
— Religion.

TREXLER (RICHARD C.) The spiritual power: republican Florence under interdict. Leiden, 1974. pp. 208. bibliog.

FLOUR MILLS
— Switzerland.

RUTZ (MARIANNE) Die Walzmühle in Frauenfeld: ein Kapitel aus der Geschichte der Industrialisierung der Schweiz. [Zürich, imprint, 1973]. pp. 198. bibliog.

FLOW OF FUNDS
— Finland — Accounting.

FINLAND. Tilastokeskus. Rahoitustilinpito: (Flow-of-funds accounts). a., 1970/1971 [2nd]- Helsinki. *In Finnish, with notes in Swedish and English. (Tilastotiedotus)*

FOLK LORE
— Africa, East.

ITALY. Ministero degli Affari Esteri. Comitato per la Documentazione dell'Opera dell'Italia in Africa. L'Italia in Africa. Serie ScientificoCulturale. Studi italiani di etnologia e folklore dell'Africa Orientale, Eritrea, Etiopia, Somalia; testo di Ester Panetta. Roma, 1973 in progress.

— Bulgaria.

ARNAUDOV (MIKHAIL) Mikhail Dragomanov: zhivot, idei, znachenie za bŭlgarskiia folklor; rech, dŭrzhana na 30 oktomvrii 1932 g., po sluchai na osveshtavane pametnika na Dragomanov v Sofiia; Michel Dragomanov: sa vie, ses idées, ses travaux sur le folklore bulgare. Sofiia, 1933. pp. 33. (Sofia. Universitet. Istoriko-Filologicheskii Fakultet. Godishnik. kn.29,5)

— France.

BELMONT (NICOLE) Mythes et croyances dans l'ancienne France. [Paris, 1973]. pp. 187. bibliog.

— Russia — Soviet North.

FOL'KLOR i etnografiia Russkogo Severa. Leningrad, 1973. pp. 280.

FOLK SONGS, BRITISH.

DOUGLASS (DAVID) Pit talk in County Durham: a glossary of miners' talk together with the memories of Wardley colliery, pit songs and piliking. [Oxford?, 1973]. pp. 78. (History Workshop. Pamphlets. No.10)

ELBOURNE (ROGER PHILLIP) Industrialization and popular culture: a case study of Lancashire handloom weavers, 1780-1840; [M. Phil. (London) thesis]. [1974]. fo. 243. bibliog. *Typscript: unpublished. This thesis is the property of London University and may not be removed from the library.*

FOOD.

SZCZELKUN (STEFAN A.) Survival scrapbook 2: food. Brighton, [1972]. 1 vol. (unpaged). bibliogs.

FOOD, FROZEN.

FRANCE. Direction de la Documentation. La Documentation Française. Notes et Etudes Documentaires. No. 3,240. Les produits surgelés en Europe occidentale. Paris, 1965. pp. 27. bibliog.

FOOD ADDITIVES.

CAMPBELL (RITA RICARDO) Food safety regulation: a study of the use and limitations of cost-benefit analysis. Washington, D.C., 1974. pp. 59. bibliog. (American Enterprise Institute for Public Policy Research and Stanford University. Hoover Institution on War, Revolution and Peace. AEI-Hoover [Policy] Studies. 12)

FOOD AND AGRICULTURE ORGANIZATION
— Bibliography.

FAO BOOKS IN PRINT; [pd. by] Food and Agriculture Organization of the United Nations. a., current issue only kept. [Rome].

FOOD CONSUMPTION
— Africa, Subsaharan.

PARIS. Université. Institut d'Etude du Développement Economique et Social. Groupe de Recherche 'Santé et Nutrition dans le Processus du Développement'. L'approvisionnement des villes dans les états africains et malgache: horizon 1985. Paris, Secrétariat d'Etat aux Affaires Etrangères, 1973. pp. 318. bibliog.

— Africa, West.

LEWICKI (TADEUSZ) West African food in the middle ages, according to Arabic sources;... with the assistance of Marion Johnson. London, 1974. pp. 262. bibliog.

— France.

FRANCE. Institut National de la Statistique et des Etudes Economiques. Collections de l'I.N.S.E.E. SÉRIE M. Ménages . Paris, 1970 in progress.

— Hawaiian Islands.

JAMISON (JOHN A.) Consumer food costs: a comparative study of Honolulu and the San Francisco Bay area. Stanford, Ca., 1968. pp. 102. bibliog.

— Nigeria.

NIGERIA. Agricultural Statistics Unit. 1973. Rural consumption enquiry: food items, 1963/64 and 1965/66. Lagos, 1972 [or rather 1973]. pp. 36. (Rural Economic Surveys of Nigeria. 1973/6)

— Sweden.

HOLMSTRÖM (SVEN J.R.) and SJÖHOLM (BENGT) Livsmedlens andel i våra utgifter. 3rd ed. Stockholm, 1973. pp. 54. (Jordbrukets Utredningsinstitut. Meddelanden. 1973. Nr. 4) *With English summary.*

— United States — California.

JAMISON (JOHN A.) Consumer food costs: a comparative study of Honolulu and the San Francisco Bay area. Stanford, Ca., 1968. pp. 102. bibliog.

FOOD CONTAMINATION.

WELLFORD (HARRISON) Sowing the wind: (a report from Ralph Nader's Center for Study of Responsive Law on Food Safety and the Chemical Harvest). New York, 1973. pp. 384.

YOUNG (JOHNATHAN C.) Suspected food poisoning in Consett, County Durham. Durham, 1974. pp. 21. bibliog. (Durham. University. Department of Geography. Occasional Publications (New Series). No. 3)

FOOD HABITS.

SYMPOSIUM ON CHANGES IN FOOD HABITS IN RELATION TO INCREASE OF PRODUCTIVITY, MANILA, 1972. Changes in food habits in relation to increase of productivity: report of the symposium held in Manila, August 22-28, 1972. [Tokyo], Asian Productivity Organization, 1973. pp. 370.

FOOD INDUSTRY AND TRADE

— France.

PARIS. Chambre de Commerce et d'Industrie. Centre d'Observation Economique. Distribution des commerces alimentaires dans la région parisienne.[Paris, 1962]. pp. 55. *bibliog. Maps in end pocket.*

FRANCE. Ministère de l'Agriculture. Industries agricoles et alimentaires: enquête annuelle d'entreprise (formerly Etude sur la structure des entreprises agricoles et alimentaires). a., 1968- Paris. *Not pd.* 1969. *(Statistique agricole. Supplément. Série Etudes)*

— Germany.

MOELLER (UWE) Die Stellung der Nahrungs- und Genussmittelindustrie im Prozess der Industrialisierung. Bern, 1973. pp. 315. *bibliog.*

— Russia — Moldavian Republic — Mathematical models.

OPTIMAL'NOE planirovanie razvitiia otraslei i predpriiatii. Kishinev, 1973. pp. 120.

— Sierra Leone.

SIERRA LEONE. Beoku-Betts Commission of Inquiry into the Sierra Leone Produce Marketing Board. 1968. Report...with particular reference to the sale of palm oil, rice and coffee haulers, nut-cracking machine and the industrialisation programme undertaken by the Board during the period January, 1961 to March, 1967; [R.W. Beoku-Betts, chairman]. [Freetown, 1968]. pp. 120.

— United Kingdom.

FOOD, DRINK AND TOBACCO INDUSTRY TRAINING BOARD [U.K.]. Annual report and accounts. a., 1972/3- Croydon. *Formerly included in the file of British Parliamentary Papers.*

FOLEY (JOHN) The food makers: a history of General Foods Ltd. Banbury, 1972. pp. 65.

— United States.

WELLFORD (HARRISON) Sowing the wind: (a report from Ralph Nader's Center for Study of Responsive Law on Food Safety and the Chemical Harvest). New York, 1973. pp. 384.

HORST (THOMAS) At home abroad: a study of the domestic and foreign operations of the American food-processing industry. Cambridge, Mass., [1974]. pp. 145. *bibliog.*

FOOD POISONING.

YOUNG (JOHNATHAN C.) Suspected food poisoning in Consett, County Durham. Durham, 1974. pp. 21. *bibliog. (Durham. University. Department of Geography. Occasional Publications (New Series). No. 3)*

FOOD PRESERVATIVES.

U.K. Food Additives and Contaminants Committee. 1972. Report on the review of the Preservatives in Food Regulations, 1962. London, 1972. pp. 89. *bibliogs.*

FOOD PRICES

— Brazil.

BRAZIL. Departamento de Estatisticas Industrias, Comerciais e de Serviços. 1969. Inquerito nacional de preços: gêneros alimenticios; comercio varejista das capitais, 1967 a (agosto de 1969). [Rio de Janeiro, 1969]. 4 vols.

— Canada.

CANADA. Food Prices Review Board. Quarterly report. q., S 1973[1st]- Ottawa.

— Hawaiian Islands.

JAMISON (JOHN A.) Consumer food costs: a comparative study of Honolulu and the San Francisco Bay area. Stanford, Ca., 1968. pp. 102. *bibliog.*

— Tasmania.

TASMANIA. Consummers Protection Council. 1972. Report on food and grocery prices in Tasmania. in TASMANIA. Parliament. Journals and Printed Papers. 1972, no. 14.

— United States.

SEXTON (DONALD E.) Groceries in the ghetto. Lexington, Mass., [1973]. pp. 141. *bibliog.*

— — California.

JAMISON (JOHN A.) Consumer food costs: a comparative study of Honolulu and the San Francisco Bay area. Stanford, Ca., 1968. pp. 102. *bibliog.*

FOOD RELIEF.

AYKROYD (WALLACE RUDDELL) The conquest of famine. London, 1974. pp. 216.

FOOD SUPPLY.

BARRETO (ANTONIO) ed. A study of the social and economic implications of the large scale introduction of high-yielding varieties of foodgrain: a selection of readings; an Institute staff study. (UNRISD Reports. No.71.6) (UNRISD/72/C.3). Geneva, United Nations Research Institute for Social Development, 1971. pp. 173. *([Studies on the Green Revolution. No.2])*

SZCZELKUN (STEFAN A.) Survival scrapbook 2: food. Brighton, [1972]. 1 vol. (unpaged). *bibliogs.*

BLAKESLEE (LEROY L.) and others. World food production, demand, and trade. Ames, Iowa, 1973. pp. 417.

BORGSTROM (GEORG) Focal points: a global food strategy. New York, 1973. pp. 320. *bibliog.*

FOOD, population and employment: the impact of the green revolution: [papers from a workshop sponsored by Cornell University Program on Science, Technology and Society]; edited by Thomas T. Poleman and Donald K. Freebairn. New York, 1973. pp. 272.

JOSLING (TIMOTHY EDWARD) An international grain reserve policy. [Washington, D.C.], 1973. pp. 17. *(British-North American Committee. Publications. 11)*

AYKROYD (WALLACE RUDDELL) The conquest of famine. London, 1974. pp. 216.

CIBA FOUNDATION. Symposia. Human rights in health: Ciba Foundation symposium 23 (new series); [proceedings; edited by Katherine Elliott and Julie Knight]. Amsterdam, 1974. pp. 304. *bibliogs.*

NATIONAL PLANNING ASSOCIATION. Reports. No.136. Feast or famine: the uncertain world of food and agriculture and its policy implications for the United States; by Willard W. Cochrane. Washington, [1974]. pp. 19.

— Statistics.

ORGANISATION FOR ECONOMIC CO-OPERATION AND DEVELOPMENT. Directorate for Agriculture. 1969. Statistiques agricoles; Agricultural statistics; 1955-1968. Paris, 1969. pp. 209. *In English and French.*

— Africa, Subsaharan.

MAY (JACQUES M.) The ecology of malnutrition in the French speaking countries of West Africa and Madagascar, etc. New York, 1968. pp. 433. *bibliogs. (Studies in Medical Geography. vol. 8)*

MAY (JACQUES M.) and McLELLAN (DONNA L.) The ecology of malnutrition in seven countries of southern Africa and in Portuese Guinea: the Republic of South Africa, South West Africa etc. New York, 1971. pp. 432. *bibliogs. (American Geographical Society. Studies in Medical Geography. vol.10)*

PARIS. Université. Institut d'Etude du Développement Economique et Social. Groupe de Recherche 'Santé et Nutrition dans le Processus du Développement'. L'approvisionnement des villes dans les états africains et malgache: horizon 1985. Paris, Secrétariat d'Etat aux Affaires Etrangères, 1973. pp. 318. *bibliog.*

— China.

NAUMOV (IVAN NIKOLAEVICH) Prodovol'stvennaia problema v Kitae. Moskva, 1973. pp. 247. *bibliog.*

— India.

DAS (RAM) Planning India's food and nutrition. Lucknow, 1972. pp. 174. *bibliog.*

— Madagascar.

MAY (JACQUES M.) The ecology of malnutrition in the French speaking countries of West Africa and Madagascar, etc. New York, 1968. pp. 433. *bibliogs. (Studies in Medical Geography. vol. 8)*

— Nigeria.

OKURUME (GODWIN E.) Foreign trade and the subsistence sector in Nigeria: the impact of agricultural exports on domestic food supplies in a peasant economy. New York, 1973. pp. 136. *bibliog.*

— United Kingdom.

WINNIFRITH (Sir ALFRED JOHN DIGBY) The Ministry of Agriculture, Fisheries and Food. London, 1962. pp. 271. *(Royal Institute of Public Administration. New Whitehall Series. No. 11)*

U.K. National Register of Archives. 1971. [Labour Party archives: list of the records of the Consumers' Council; compiled by R.A. Storey and T.W.M. Jaine]. [London], 1971. fo. 55.

— United States.

HILLIARD (SAM BOWERS) Hog meat and hoecake: food supply in the Old South, 1840-1860. Carbondale, Ill., [1972]. pp. 296.

FORD (GERALD RUDOLPH) President of the United States.

VESTAL (BUD) Jerry Ford, up close: an investigative biography. New York, [1974]. pp. 214.

FORECASTING.

NEWBOLD (PAUL) Forecasting methods. London, H.M.S.O., 1973. pp. 34. *(Civil Service College [U.K.]. Occasional Papers. No. 18)*

WYROBISZ (STANISŁAW) Polska czterdziestomilionowa: wybrane przesłanki i elementy prognozy. Warszawa, 1973. pp. 217.

— Mathematical models.

U.K. Department of the Environment. 1973. Using predictive models for structure plans. London, 1973. pp. 72. *bibliogs.*

FOREIGN EXCHANGE.

Le CHANGE à terme: technique, théorie, politique; table ronde réunie à Paris les 17-19 avril 1972; édition préparée par Paul Coulbois. Paris, 1972. pp. 205. *In English or French.*

LUTZ (FRIEDRICH AUGUST) Das Problem der internationalen Währungsordnung. Erlenbach-Zürich, [1972]. pp. 29. *(Schweizerisches Institut für Auslandforschung. Schriftenreihe zu Aktuellen Problemen aus Politik und Wirtschaft. 6)*

WALLICH (HENRY CHRISTOPHER) and others. The monetary crisis of 1971: the lessons to be learned. Washington, D.C., 1972. pp. 79. *(Per Jacobsson Foundation. [Lectures]. 1972)*

WASSERMAN (MAX JUDD) and others. International money management. [New York, 1972]. pp. 232. *bibliog.*

CLARKE (STEPHEN V.O.) The reconstruction of the international monetary system: the attempts of 1922 and 1933. Princeton, 1973. pp. 44. *bibliog. (Princeton University. Department of Economics and Sociology. International Finance Section. Princeton Studies in International Finance. No.33)*

FISCHER (JOSEF A.) Zur Theorie der optimalen Währungsräume. [Erlangen, imprint, 1973?]. pp. 201,xxiii. *bibliog.*

FOREIGN EXCHANGE. (Cont.)

GRASSMAN (SVEN) Exchange reserves and the financial structure of foreign trade. Farnborough, Hants, [1973]. pp. 198. *bibliog.*

FELLNER (WILLIAM) Controlled floating and the confused issue of money illusion. Washington, 1973 repr. 1974. pp. 3-31. *(American Enterprise Institute for Public Policy Research. Reprints. No.22). (Reprinted from Banca Nazionale del Lavoro Quarterly Review, No.106, 1973)*

MAKIN (JOHN H.) Capital flows and exchange-rate flexibility in the post-Bretton Woods era. Princeton, 1974. pp. 25. *bibliog. (Princeton University. Department of Economics and Sociology. International Finance Section. Essays in International Finance. No. 103)*

MAYER (HELMUT W.) The anatomy of official exchange-rate intervention systems. Princeton, N.J., 1974. pp. 34. *(Princeton University. Department of Economics and Sociology. International Finance Section. Essays in International Finance. No. 104)*

WOOD (G.E.) M.A. Domestic macro policy under different exchange rate regimes. Coventry, 1974. pp. 15. *bibliog. (University of Warwick. Department of Economics. Warwick Economic Research Papers. No. 45)*

— Law — Canada.

SHEPHERD (SIDNEY ALBERT) Foreign exchange and foreign trade in Canada: an outline. 4th ed. Toronto, [1973]. pp. 336.

— Asia, Southeast.

SEMINAR ON EXCHANGE RATES AS A PROBLEM OF THE SOUTHEAST ASIA REGION, SINGAPORE, 1972. Exchange rate policy in Southeast Asia. Lexington, [1973]. pp. 105.

— Canada.

CANADA. Foreign Exchange Control Board. Annual report to Minister of Finance. a., 1948, 1949. Ottawa.

— Communist countries.

AL'TSHULER (ARKADII BORISOVICH) Sotrudnichestvo sotsialisticheskikh gosudarstv: raschety, kredity, pravo. Moskva, 1973. pp. 175.

MEZHDUNARODNAIA sotsialisticheskaia valiuta stran-chlenov SEV. Moskva, 1973. pp. 96.

INTERNATIONALE sozialistische Währung der Mitgliedsländer des RGW: Übersetzung ([by] Peter Freide [and] Gerhard Huber) aus dem Russischen. Berlin, 1974. pp. 83.

— European Economic Community countries.

CONFERENCE ON THE IMPLICATIONS OF EUROPEAN MONETARY INTEGRATION FOR THE UNITED STATES, BROOKINGS INSTITUTION, 1972. European monetary unification and its meaning for the United States; (Lawrence B. Krause and Walter S. Salant, editors). Washington, D.C., [1973]. pp. 322.

— Germany.

BOECK (KLAUS) and GEHRMANN (DIETER) Die DM als internationale Reservewährung: Bedeutung, Ursachen und Probleme. Hamburg, 1974. pp. 75. *(Hamburg. Hamburgisches Welt-Wirtschafts-Archiv. Studien zur Aussenwirtschaft und Entwicklungspolitik)*

— Sri Lanka.

INTERNATIONAL BANK FOR RECONSTRUCTION AND DEVELOPMENT. 1968. The problem of foreign exchange and long-term growth of Ceylon; [report submitted for meeting of Aid Ceylon Group, Paris, 1968; Manfred G. Blobel, chief of mission]. [Colombo, Ministry of Planning and Economic Affairs, 1968] . pp. 68.

— Sweden.

GRASSMAN (SVEN) Exchange reserves and the financial structure of foreign trade. Farnborough, Hants, [1973]. pp. 198. *bibliog.*

— Switzerland.

COLOMBO (GIOVANNI ANTONIO) Politique conjoncturelle en économie ouverte : les limites extérieures de la politique monétaire suisse. Berne, 1973. pp. 193. *bibliog.*

FOREIGN TRADE PROMOTION

— Germany, Eastern.

AUSSENWIRTSCHAFTLICHE Tätigkeit in Produktions- und Aussenhandelsbetrieben: Grundlagen, Erfahrungen, Probleme; ([by] Walter Kupferschmidt [and others]); ... unter Leitung von Christa Luft. Berlin, [1974]. pp. 192. *bibliog.*

FOREIGN TRADE REGULATION.

HEYDEN (ALBRECHT VON DER) Das Exportkartell: eine Untersuchung zu den Grundlagen der Beurteilungskriterien für Exportkartelle im deutschen und englischen Recht der Wettbewerbsbeschränkungen und im Vertrag über die Gründung der EWG. Bern, 1972. pp. 298. *bibliog.*

GOLT (SIDNEY) The GATT negotiations, 1973-75: a guide to the issues. London, 1974. pp. 82. *(British-North American Committee. Publications. 14)*

— United States.

METZGER (STANLEY D.) Lowering nontariff barriers: U.S. law, practice, and negotiating objectives. Washington, [1974]. pp. 249.

FOREMEN

— United Kingdom.

HILL (STEPHEN RODERICK) A comparative occupational analysis of dock foremen and dock workers in the Port of London; [Ph.D.(London) thesis]. 1973. 1 vol.(various foliations). *Typescript: unpublished. This thesis is the property of London University and may not be removed from the Library.*

FOREST INVENTORIES.

See FOREST SURVEYS.

FOREST PRODUCTS

— Malawi.

MALAWI. Agro-Economic Survey. 1974. Agro-economic survey: 12th report: rural consumers of forest produce survey; prepared by T.W. Bieze. Lilongwe, 1974. fo. 9.

FOREST REPRODUCTION

— Tasmania.

TASMANIA. Parliament. Legislative Council. Select Committee on Forest Regeneration. 1972. Forest regeneration; report... with minutes of proceedings; [J.H. Dixon, chairman]. in TASMANIA. Parliament. Journals and Printed Papers. 1972, no. 70.

FOREST SURVEYS.

— Belize.

JOHNSON (MARTIN STEPHEN) and CHAFFEY (D.R.) A forest inventory of part of the Mountain Pine Ridge, Belize...; with a contribution by C.J. Birchall. Tolworth, 1973. pp. 117. *bibliog. (U.K. Overseas Development Administration. Land Resources Division. Land Resource Studies. No. 13) 2 maps in end pocket.*

— Fiji Islands.

BERRY (M.J.) and HOWARD (W.J.) Fiji forest inventory. Tolworth, 1973. 3 vols. *bibliog. (U.K. Overseas Development Administration. Land Resources Division. Land Resource Studies. No. 12) Map in end pocket.*

FORESTERS

— Finland.

HEIKINEIMO (LAURI) and RISTIMAKI (TOINI) Suomen metsätyövoima, maaseudun työvoiman tutkimus 1961: Forest labour force in Finland, Finnish rural labour force study, 1961, summary. Helsinki, 1965. pp. 90. *(Finland. Työvoimatutkimustoimisto. Työvoimatutkimuksia. 2)*

— Norway.

NORWAY. Statistiske Centralbyrå. Norges Offisielle Statistikk. Rekke 3. 228. Socialstatistik. 1. Arbeids- og lónningsforhold ved skovdrift og tómmerflódning, etc. Kristiania, 1895. pp. 128. *With French summary.*

FORESTRY SOCIETIES

— Canada.

FENSOM (K.G.) Expanding forestry horizons : a history of the Canadian Institute of Forestry, Institut Forestier du Canada, 1908- 1969. [Montreal, 1972]. pp. 547.

FORESTS AND FORESTRY

— Colombia.

COLOMBIA. Ministerio de Agricultura. 1968. Plan cuatrienal de desarrollo forestal, 1968-1971; preparado por Ricardo Lombo T. [and others], etc. Bogota, 1968. pp. 103. *(Serie Planeamiento. No. 13)*

— Finland — Accounting.

KUNNAS (KEIKKI J.) Forestry in national accounts: report of IUFRO working group 1, section 31. Helsinki, Metsäntutkimuslaitos, 1971. pp. 19. *(Folia Forestalia. 121)*

— Finland — Taxation.

VARJO (UUNO) Uber die Produktivität der Acker- und Waldböden Finnlands. Helsinki, 1972. pp. 50. *bibliog. (Suomen Maantieteellinen Seura. Fennia. 113) With English summary.*

— Nigeria.

NIGERIA (WESTERN STATE). Forestry Advisory Commission. Annual report. a., Oc 1968/Mr 1971 (1st)- Ibadan.

— Sweden.

ERICSON (OLLE) and others. Ekonomisk jord- och skogsbruksplan: modellstudier. Stockholm, 1973. 2 parts(in 1). *bibliog. (Jordbrukets Utredningsinstitut. Meddelanden. 1973. Nr. 2) With English summary.*

— United Kingdom.

NORTHERN ECONOMIC PLANNING COUNCIL. Challenge of the changing north: agriculture, horticulture, forestry and fishing. [Newcastle], 1967. pp. 71. *Xerox copy.*

RYLE (GEORGE) Forest service: the first forty-five years of the Forestry Commission of Great Britain. Newton Abbot, [1969]. pp. 340.

SOUTH HAMPSHIRE PLAN ADVISORY COMMITTEE. Study Reports. Group A. Rural Conservation. No. 2. Forestry. Winchester, 1969. pp. 23.

AGRICULTURAL, HORTICULTURAL AND FORESTRY INDUSTRY TRAINING BOARD [U.K.]. Annual report and accounts. a., 1972/3- Beckenham. *Formerly included in the file of British Parliamentary Papers.*

— United States.

PINKETT (HAROLD T.) Gifford Pinchot: private and public forester. Urbana, [1970]. pp. 167. *bibliog.*

CARROLL (CHARLES F.) The timber economy of Puritan New England. Providence, [1973]. pp. 221.

FORMOSA.

See TAIWAN.

FORTRAN (COMPUTER PROGRAM LANGUAGE).

LAND (AILSA HORTON) and POWELL (S.) Fortran codes for mathematical programming: linear, quadratic and discrete. London, [1973]. pp. 249. *bibliog.*

FOS

— Harbour.

FRANCE. Direction de la Documentation. La Documentation Française. Notes et Etudes Documentaires. No. 3,769. Fos, europort du sud; [by] les Services du Port autonome de Marseille. Paris, 1971. pp. 38.

FOSTER FAMILY.

MUTTON (NORMAN) The Foster family: a study of a Midland industrial dynasty 1786-1899; [Ph. D. (London) thesis]. [1974]. fo. 352. *bibliog. Typescript: unpublished. Offprints of three articles bound in at end. This thesis is the property of London University and may not be removed from the Library.*

FOSTER HOME CARE.

GOLDSTEIN (JOSEPH) and others. Beyond the best interests of the child. New York, [1973]. pp. 170.

— Denmark.

GRØNHØJ (BODIL) and PRUZAN (VITA) Idealer og praksis: om anbringelse af børn i familiepleje; etc. København, 1974. pp. 245. *bibliog. (Socialforskningsinstituttet. Publikationer. 63) With English summary.*

— Sweden.

SAMBERGS (ÅKE) Familjevård i landsbygdsmiljö. Stockholm, 1973. pp. 64. *bibliog. (Jordbrukets Utredningsinstitut. Meddelanden. 1973. Nr. 5) With English summary.*

— United Kingdom.

HOWELLS (JOHN GWILYM) Remember Maria. London, [1974]. pp. 117. *bibliog.*

FOUNDLINGS

— France.

ROQUET (HENRY) Les enfants abandonnés dans le Haut-Maine aux XVIe, XVIIe et XVIIIe siècles. Le Mans, 1922. pp. 46.

FOUNDRYMEN

— United Kingdom.

FOUNDRY INDUSTRY TRAINING COMMITTEE [U.K.]. Statistical review. a., 1967/8 [1st]- London.

ENGINEERING INDUSTRY TRAINING BOARD [U.K.]. Report and accounts. a., 1972/3- London. *Formerly included in the file of British Parliamentary Papers.*

FOUNDRY INDUSTRY TRAINING COMMITTEE [U.K.]. Annual report. a., 1973/4- London.

COMMISSION ON INDUSTRIAL RELATIONS [U.K.]. G. Clancey Limited. London, H.M.S.O., 1973. pp. 25. *(Reports. No. 54)*

FOURIER (FRANÇOIS CHARLES MARIE).

PONCE (ANIBAL) El viento en el mundo: examen de la España actual en el centenario de Fourier. Buenos Aires, 1963. pp. 188.

FRANCE

— Appropriations and expenditures.

BERNARD (YVES) The French control of public expenditure and its integration within the national economic policy; (transcript of... lecture held on 16 April 1973). [London], Civil Service College, [1973]. fo. 20. *(Lectures on the Control of Public Expenditure. No. 6)*

— Armed forces — Political activity.

PORCH (DOUGLAS) Army and revolution: France 1815-1848. London, 1974. pp. 182. *bibliog.*

— Army — History.

PORCH (DOUGLAS) Army and revolution: France 1815-1848. London, 1974. pp. 182. *bibliog.*

— Census.

FRANCE. Census, 1954. [Recensement de 1954]: villes et agglomérations urbaines: répartition de la population par catégories de communes ou d'agglomérations. Paris, 1955. pp. 115.

FRANCE. Census, 1962. Recensement de 1962: villes et agglomérations urbaines. Paris, 1964. pp. 215.

FRANCE. Census, 1968. Recensement de 1968: tableaux statistiques de population légale, communes de plus de 2000 habitants. Paris, 1968. pp. 100.

FRANCE. Census, 1968. Recensement de 1968: population légale et statistiques communales complémentaires; évolutions démographiques 1962- 1968 et 1954-1962. Paris, 1969. 95 pts. (in 5) *Pt.20, Corsica, not published.*

FRANCE. Census, 1968. Recensement général de la population de 1968: résultats des sondages au 1/20 et au 1/4: structure de la population totale, sexe, âge, état matrimonial, nationalité, catégorie de population, etc. [Paris], 1972. pp. 205.

FRANCE. Census, 1962. Recensement général de la population de 1962: résultats du sondage au 1/20 et de l'exploitation exhaustive pour la France entière: migrations 1954-1962. Paris, 1973. pp. 355.

— Climate.

LE ROY LADURIE (EMMANUEL) Le territoire de l'historien. [Paris, 1973]. pp. 544.

— Colonies.

SARTRE (JEAN PAUL) Situations. [Paris, 1947, repr. 1973, in progress].

AGERON (CHARLES ROBERT) ed. L'anticolonialisme en France de 1871 à 1914; [documents]. [Paris, 1973]. pp. 96. *bibliog.*

GUERIN (DANIEL) Ci-gît le colonialisme: Algérie, Inde...; témoignage militant. Paris, [1973]. pp. 505.

La QUESTION coloniale et la section française de la IVe Internationale. Paris, 1973. pp. 82.

— — Administration.

SENEGAL. Statutes, etc. 1946-52. Décret du 25 octobre 1946 portant création d'assemblées représentatives territoriales en Afrique Occidentale Française; loi no.52-130 du 6 février 1952 relative à la formation des assemblées...d'Afrique Occidentale Française, d'Afrique Equatoriale Française, etc. Saint-Louis, 1957. pp. 39.

— — Economic conditions.

FRANCE. Secrétariat Général pour l'Administration des Départements d'Outre-Mer. Service des Affaires Economiques et des Investissements. 1973. Perspectives de l'économie des DOM. [Paris], 1973. pp. 62.

FRANCE. Secrétariat Général pour l'Administration des Départements d'Outre-Mer. Service des Affaires Economiques et des Investissements. 1974. Bilan 1973 de l'économie des DOM. [Paris], 1974. pp. 89.

— — Economic policy.

FRANCE. Secrétariat Général pour l'Administration des Départements d'Outre-Mer. Service des Affaires Economiques et des Investissements. 1973. Perspectives de l'économie des DOM. [Paris], 1973. pp. 62.

— — Officials and employees.

FRANCE. Institut National de la Statistique et des Etudes Economiques. 1972. Recensement des agents de l'etat et des collectivités locales des départements d'outre-mer, 1er mars 1967. Paris, [1972?]. fo. 35.

— — Population.

FRANCE. Institut National de la Statistique et des Etudes Economiques. 1973. Statistique du mouvement de la population dans les départements d'outre-mer: Martinique, Guadeloupe, Guyane, Réunion, année 1965 à 1970. Paris, 1973. pp. 187.

FRANCE. Secrétariat Général pour l'Administration des Départements d'Outre-Mer. Service des Affaires Economiques et des Investissements. 1973. Perspectives de l'économie des DOM. [Paris], 1973. pp. 62.

— — Social policy.

FRANCE. Secrétariat d'Etat Chargé des Départements et Territoires d'Outre - Mer. 1973. Politique sociale dans les Départements d'Outre - Mer: la solidarité nationale et son bilan. [Paris, 1973?]. pp. 68.

— — Statistics, Vital.

FRANCE. Institut National de la Statistique et des Etudes Economiques. 1973. Statistique du mouvement de la population dans les départements d'outre-mer: Martinique, Guadeloupe, Guyane, Réunion, année 1965 à 1970. Paris, 1973. pp. 187.

— Commerce.

FRANCE. Institut National de la Statistique et des Etudes Economiques. Collections de l'I.N.S.E.E. Série E. Entreprises. . Paris, 1969 in progress.

DELEAGE (JEAN) and CASMECASSE ( ) La fonction commerciale dans l'industrie. [Paris?], Ministère du Développement Industriel et Scientifique, 1971. fo.78.

TARRADE (JEAN) Le commerce colonial de la France à la fin de l'Ancien régime: l'évolution du régime de "l'Exclusif" de 1763 à 1789. Paris, 1972. 2 vols. *bibliog. (Poitiers. Université. Faculté des Lettres et Sciences Humaines. Publications. 12)*

— Commercial treaties — Switzerland.

BRAND (URS) Die schweizerisch-französischen Unterhandlungen über einen Handelsvertrag und der Abschluss des Vertragswerkes von 1864, etc. Bern, 1968. pp. 321. *bibliog.*

— Constitution.

AMBLER (JOHN STEWARD) and SCHEINMAN (LAWRENCE) The government and politics of France. Boston, [1971]. pp. 257. *bibliog.*

BROUILLET (ALAIN) Le droit d'amendement dans la constitution de la Ve République: étude pratique de son utilisation pour l'élaboration de la loi d'orientation foncière. Paris, 1973. pp. 159. *bibliog. (Paris. Université de Paris I (Panthéon- Sorbonne). Publications. Série Science Politique. 3)*

MOLLET (GUY) Quinze ans après... 1958-1973: (la constitution de 1958). Paris, [1973]. pp. 168.

DEBRE (JEAN LOUIS) Les idées constitutionnelles du Général de Gaulle. Paris, 1974. pp. 461.

— Constitutional history.

TROPER (MICHEL) La séparation des pouvoirs et l'histoire constitutionnelle française. Paris, 1973. pp. 251. *bibliog.*

— Constitutional law.

MALLARD (HENRI VICTOR) Le droit constitutionnel: (dossiers de droit constitutionnel: documents, exercises, solutions). Paris, 1973. 2 vols. (in 1). *bibliog.*

— Description and travel.

MATVEEV (ANDREI ARTAMONOVICH) Russkii diplomat vo Frantsii: zapiski Andreia Matveeva; publikatsiia podgotovlena I.S. Sharkovoi, pod redaktsiei A.D. Liublinskoi. Leningrad, 1972. pp. 296.

— Economic conditions.

CAHIERS FRANÇAIS D'INFORMATION. [Paris], 1945-48. 12 parts.

FRANCE. (Cont.)

FRANCE. Direction de la Documentation. La Documentation Française. Notes et Etudes Documentaires. Nos. 3,868-3, 869-3,870-3,871. Les économies régionales: l'économie de la région Centre. Paris, 1972. pp. 163. *bibliog.*

FRANCE. Ministère de l'Economie et des Finances. Direction des Relations Economiques Extérieures. 1972. L'ouverture sur l'extérieur de l'économie française 1962-1971. [Paris? 1972?]. 1 pamphlet (unpaged).

CAZES (GEORGES) and REYNAUD (ALAIN) Les mutations récentes de l'économie française: de la croissance à l'aménagement. Paris, 1973. pp. 217. *bibliog.*

COFFEY (PETER) Economist. The social economy of France. London, 1973. pp. 133.

L'ENVOL de la France: portrait de la France dans les années 80: [report of a project carried out in the Hudson Institute]; directeur du projet: Edmund Stillman. [Paris, 1973]. pp. 188.

FRANCE and its future, 1973-1985; [report of a project carried out in the Hudson Institute]; project leader, Edmund Stillman. Croton-on-Hudson, 1973. pp. 133.

GEOGRAPHIE économique et ferroviaire des pays de la C.E.E. et de la Suisse. Fascicule 6. France, géographie économique et ferroviaire, etc. [Paris. S.N.C.F., 1973]. pp. 335, 48.

GEORGE (PIERRE) France: a geographical study;... translated by I.B. Thompson. London, 1973. pp. 228. *bibliog.*

— — Maps.

ORGANISATION D'ETUDES D'AMENAGEMENT DE L'AIRE METROPOLITAINE DE NANTES-SAINT-NAZAIRE. Introduction à la connaissance de l'espace régional: [maps]. [Nantes, 1970]. 42 maps (in 1 vol.).

— Economic history.

MEUVRET (JEAN) Etudes d'histoire économique: recueil d'articles. Paris, 1971. pp. 344. *bibliog. (Annales: économies, sociétés, civilisations. Cahiers. 32)*

CONJONCTURE économique, structures sociales: hommage à Ernest Labrousse; [edited by Fernand Braudel and others]. Paris, 1974. pp. 547. *bibliog. (Paris. Ecole Pratique des Hautes Etudes. Section des Sciences Economiques et Sociales. Civilisations et Sociétés. 47)*

— Economic policy.

CAHIERS FRANÇAIS D'INFORMATION. [Paris], 1945-48. 12 parts.

FRANCE. Institut National de la Statistique et des Etudes Economiques. Collections de l'I.N.S.E.E. Série C. Comptes et Planification. Paris, 1969 in progress.

FRANCE. Institut National de la Statistique et des Etudes Economiques. Collections de l'I.N.S.E.E. Série R. Régions. Paris, 1970 in progress.

FRANCE. Comité Interministériel pour l'Information. 1972. Vous en 1975: comment le VIe Plan peut changer vos conditions de vie. [Paris, 1972]. pp. 58.

FRANCE. Commissariat Général du Plan. 1972. 1985: la France face au choc du futur. [Paris, 1972]. pp. 220. *(Plan et prospectives. 8)*

FRANCE. Groupe de Prospective Technologique. 1972. Technologie et aménagement du territoire: premières réflexions. Paris, 1972. pp. 211. *(France. Délégation à l'Aménagement du Territoire et à l'Action Régionale. Travaux et Recherches de Prospective. 33)*

OMNIUM TECHNIQUE D'AMENAGEMENT. Schéma général d'aménagement de la France: une image de la France en l'an 2000; documents, méthode de travail. Paris, 1972. pp. 334. *(France. Délégation à l'Aménagement du Territoire et à l'Action Régionale. Travaux et Recherches de Prospective. 30)*

BERNARD (YVES) The French control of public expenditure and its integration within the national economic policy; (transcript of... lecture held on 16 April 1973). [London], Civil Service College, [1973]. fo. 20. *(Lectures on the Control of Public Expenditure. No. 6)*

FRANCE. Direction de la Documentation. La Documentation Française. Notes et Etudes Documentaires. Nos. 3,959-3, 960. Les programmes finalisés dans le VIe Plan, [par Bernard Lion]. [Paris], 1973. pp. 57.

FRANCE. Direction de la Documentation. La Documentation Française. Notes et Etudes Documentaires. Nos. 3,991-3, 992. Fonctions collectives et planification. [Paris], 1973. pp. 71.

FRANCE. Direction de la Documentation. La Documentation Française. Notes et Etudes Documentaires. Nos. 4,037-4, 038. Le contenu des fonctions collectives. Paris, 1973. pp. 47.

OPPENHEIM (JEAN PIERRE) La C.F.D.T. et la planification. Paris, [1973]. pp. 323. *bibliog.*

QUIN (CLAUDE) and HERZOG (PHILIPPE) Ce que coûte le capitalisme à la France. Paris, [1973]. pp. 187.

— Etats Généraux.

HAYDEN (J. MICHAEL) France and the Estates General of 1614. London, 1974. pp. 334. *bibliog.*

— Executive departments.

DURAND-BARTHEZ (PASCAL) Histoire des structures du Ministère de la Justice, 1789-1945. Paris, 1973. pp. 91. *bibliog. (Paris. Université de Paris II. Travaux et Recherches. Série Science Administrative. 5)*

THOENIG (JEAN CLAUDE) L'ère des technocrates: le cas des Ponts et Chaussées. Paris, 1973. pp. 281.

SULEIMAN (EZRA N.) Politics, power, and bureaucracy in France: the administrative elite. Princeton, [1974]. pp. 440. *bibliog.*

— Foreign economic relations — Russia.

GIRAULT (RENE) Emprunts russes et investissements français en Russie 1887-1914: recherches sur l'investissement international. Paris, 1973. pp. 624. *bibliog. (Paris. Université de Paris I (Panthéon-Sorbonne). Publications. Nouvelle Série. Recherches. 3)*

— Foreign population.

VALABREGUE (CATHERINE) L'homme déraciné: le livre noir des travailleurs étrangers. [Paris], 1973. pp. 205.

— Foreign relations.

FRANCE. Direction de la Documentation. La Documentation Française. Notes et Etudes Documentaires. No. 3,728. La France et l'O.N.U.; [by] Aleth Manin. Paris, 1970. pp. 32.

DREIFORT (JOHN E.) Yvon Delbos at the Quai d'Orsay: French foreign policy during the Popular Front, 1936-1938. Lawrence, [1973]. pp. 273. *bibliog.*

MORSE (EDWARD L.) Foreign policy and interdependence in Gaullist France. Princeton, [1973]. pp. 332.

PONDAVEN (PHILIPPE) La Parlement et la politique extérieure sous la IVe République. Paris, 1973. pp. 135. *bibliog. (Paris. Université de Paris II. Travaux et Recherches. Série Science Politique. 2)*

WOOD (ROBERT S.) France in the world community: decolonization, peacekeeping, and the United Nations. Leiden, 1973. pp. 226. *bibliog. (John F. Kennedy Institute. Center for International Studies. Publications. Nr.8)*

See also UNITED NATIONS — France.

— — China.

FRANCE. Direction de la Documentation. La Documentation Française. Notes et Etudes Documentaires. Nos.4014-4015. Les relations franco-chinoises, 1945-1973. [Paris], 1973. pp. 57. *bibliog.*

— — Israel.

CROSBIE (SYLVIA KOWITT) A tacit alliance: France and Israel from Suez to the six day war. Princeton, [1974]. pp. 277. *bibliog. (Columbia University. Middle East Institute. Modern Middle East Series. [No.] 7)*

— — Switzerland.

BRAND (URS) Die schweizerisch-französischen Unterhandlungen über einen Handelsvertrag und der Abschluss des Vertragswerkes von 1864, etc. Bern, 1968. pp. 321. *bibliog.*

— — Taiwan.

FRANCE. Direction de la Documentation. La Documentation Française. Notes et Etudes Documentaires. Nos.4014-4015. Les relations franco-chinoises, 1945-1973. [Paris], 1973. pp. 57. *bibliog.*

— — Turkey.

MASSIGLI (RENE) La Turquie devant la guerre: mission à Ankara. [Paris, 1964]. pp. 511.

— — United Kingdom.

BULLEN (ROGER JOHN) Palmerston, Guizot and the collapse of the Entente Cordiale. London, 1974. pp. 352. *bibliog.*

— Government publications.

FRANCE. Commission de Coordination de la Documentation Administrative. 1973. Répertoire des publications périodiques et de série de l'administration française. Paris, 1973. pp. 368.

— History.

ZELDIN (THEODORE) France, 1848-1945. Oxford, 1973 in progress.

JACKSON (JOHN HAMPDEN) ed. A short history of France from early times to 1972; by Herbert Butterfield [and others]. 2nd ed. London, 1974. pp. 246.

— — Historiography.

LE ROY LADURIE (EMMANUEL) Le territoire de l'historien. [Paris, 1973]. pp. 544.

— — To 1515, Mediaeval period.

DUBY (GEORGES) Hommes et structures du moyen âge: recueil d'articles. Paris, [1973]. pp. 424. *(Paris. Ecole Pratique des Hautes Etudes. Section des Sciences Economiques et Sociales. Le Savoir Historique. 1)* :

— — 1328—1589, House of Valois.

LEGUAI (ANDRE) Les ducs de Bourbon pendant la crise monarchique du XVe siècle: contribution à l'étude des apanages. Dijon, [1962]. pp. 219. *bibliog.*

— — 1789—1799, Revolution.

GREULICH (HERMAN) Vor hundert Jahren und heute: die Revolution des Bürgertums und der Befreiungskampf der arbeitenden Klasse; Vortrag, gehalten an der Märzfeier 1895 in Bern. 2nd ed. Zürich, 1912. pp. 31.

GOTTSCHALK (LOUIS REICHENTHAL) and MADDOX (MARGARET) Lafayette in the French revolution: from the October days through the Federation. Chicago, 1973. pp. 586.

KENNEDY (MICHAEL L.) The Jacobin Club of Marseilles, 1790-1794. Ithaca, 1973. pp. 245. *bibliog.*

SOBOUL (ALBERT) Mouvement populaire et gouvernement révolutionnaire en l'an II, 1793-1794. [Paris, 1973]. pp. 510. *bibliog.*

— — — Causes and character

SCHMITT (EBERHARD) ed. Die Französische Revolution: Anlässe und langfristige Ursachen; [selection of previously published articles and extracts from books]. Darmstadt, 1973. pp. 533. *bibliog. In various languages.*

— — — Documents, etc., sources.

GOUBERT (PIERRE) and DENIS (MICHEL) eds. 1789: les Français ont la parole; cahiers de doléances des Etats généraux...; suivis d'un glossaire pratique de la langue de quatre-vingt-neuf. [Paris, 1964 repr. 1970]. pp. 268. *bibliog.*

FRANCE. (Cont.)

HARDMAN (JOHN) ed. French revolution documents. vol.2. 1792-95. Oxford, 1973. pp. 441.

WALZER (MICHAEL) ed. Regicide and revolution: speeches at the trial of Louis XVI;...translated by Marian Rothstein. London, 1974. pp. 219.

— — — Finance, confiscations, etc.

MALLETT (MARC GEORGE) La politique financière des Jacobins. Paris, 1913. pp. 449. *bibliog.*

— — — Influence.

MATTOSO (KATIA M. DE QUEIROS) Presença francesa no movimento democratico baiano de 1789. Salvador, [Brazil], 1969. pp. 163. *bibliog.*

KOVALENKO (LEONID ANTONOVYCH) Velyka frantsuz'ka burzhuazna revoliutsiia i hromads'ko-politychni rukhy na Ukraïni v kintsi XVIII st. Kyïv, 1973. pp. 167.

— — — 1830, July Revolution.

RADER (DANIEL L.) The journalists and the July Revolution in France: the role of the political press in the overthrow of the Bourbon restoration, 1827-1830. The Hague, 1973. pp. 283. *bibliog.*

— — 1852—1870, Second Empire.

GERARD (ALICE) ed. Le Second Empire, innovation et réaction. [Paris], 1973. pp. 96. *bibliog.*

— — 1940—1945, German Occupation.

BETEILLE (PIERRE) and RIMBAUD (CHRISTIANE) Le procès de Riom. [Paris, 1973]. pp. 284. *bibliog.*

MAURIAC (CLAUDE) The other de Gaulle: (diaries 1944-1954); translated by Moura Budberg and Gordon Latta. London, 1973. pp. 378.

— — 1945— .

MAURIAC (CLAUDE) The other de Gaulle: (diaries 1944-1954); translated by Moura Budberg and Gordon Latta. London, 1973. pp. 378.

— History, military.

MYSYROWICZ (LADISLAS) Autopsie d'une défaite: origines de l'effondrement militaire français de 1940. Lausanne, [1973]. pp. 385. *bibliog.*

— Industries.

FRANCE. Institut National de la Statistique et des Etudes Economiques. Collections de l'I.N.S.E.E. Série E. Entreprises. . Paris, 1969 in progress.

FRANCE. Institut National de la Statistique et des Etudes Economiques. 1969. Les établissements de 1000 salariés et plus en France en 1968, d'après le fichier des entreprises et des établissements de l'I.N.S.E.E. Paris, 1969. pp. 232.

FRANCE. Ministère du Développement Industriel et Scientifique. Service Central de la Statistique et des Informations Industrielles. Statistiques industrielles par régions et par activités. a., 1970[1st]- Paris.

DELEAGE (JEAN) and CASMECASSE ( ) La fonction commerciale dans l'industrie. [Paris?], Ministère du Développement Industriel et Scientifique, 1971. fo.78.

FRANCE. Intergroupe Financement de l'Industrie. 1971. Préparation du VIe Plan... rapport de l'Intergroupe. Paris, 1971. 2 vols.

— Intellectual life.

GORDON (LEV S.) Studien zur plebejisch-demokratischen Tradition in der französischen Aufklärung; (aus dem Russischen übersetzt von Wolfgang Techtmeier. Berlin, 1972. pp. 371. *bibliog.*

FLANNER (JANET) Paris was yesterday, 1925-1939;... edited by Irving Drutman. London, 1973. pp. 232.

ABRAMSKY (CHIMEN) ed. Essays in honour of E.H. Carr; edited by C. Abramsky assisted by Beryl J. Williams. London, 1974. pp. 387. *bibliog.*

— Military policy.

JOSHUA (WYNFRED) and HAHN (WALTER F.) Nuclear politics: America, France and Britain. Beverly Hills, [1973]. pp. 84. *bibliog.* (*Georgetown University. Center for Strategic and International Studies. Washington Papers. vol. 1/9*)

— Navy — History.

FAIVRE (JEAN PAUL) Le Contre-Amiral Hamelin et la Marine française. Paris, [1962]. pp. 195. *bibliog.*

— Officials and employees.

FRANCE. Institut National de la Statistique et des Etudes Economiques. 1968. Recensement des agents de l'état et des collectivités locales du 1er octobre 1962: résultats détaillés exploitation des bulletins individuels. [Paris, 1968. pp. 169.

MOUSNIER (ROYLAND) and others. Le Conseil du Roi de Louis XII à la Révolution. Paris, 1970. pp. 378. (*Paris. Université. Faculté des Lettres et Sciences Humains. Publications. Série Recherches. Tome 56*)

FRANCE. Direction Générale de l'Administration et de la Fonction Publique. 1972. Les fonctionnaires de l'état. Paris, 1971 (or rather 1972). pp. 179.

SULEIMAN (EZRA N.) Politics, power, and bureaucracy in France: the administrative elite. Princeton, [1974]. pp. 440. *bibliog.*

— Parliament.

AVRIL (PIERRE) Les Français et leur parlement. [Paris, 1972]. pp. 147.

PONDAVEN (PHILIPPE) La Parlement et la politique extérieure sous la IVe République. Paris, 1973. pp. 135. *bibliog.* (*Paris. Université de Paris II. Travaux et Recherches. Série Science Politique. 2*)

— — Elections.

CHARLOT (JEAN) Quand la gauche peut gagner: les élections législatives des 4- 11 mars 1973. Paris, [1973]. pp. 217,(191).

— Politics and Government.

MOUSNIER (ROYLAND) and others. Le Conseil du Roi de Louis XII à la Révolution. Paris, 1970. pp. 378. (*Paris. Université. Faculté des Lettres et Sciences Humains. Publications. Série Recherches. Tome 56*)

ANDERSON (MALCOLM) Conservative politics in France. London, 1974. pp. 381. *bibliog.*

— — Bibliography.

WYLIE (LAURENCE WILLIAM) and others. France: the events of May-June 1968; a critical bibliography. [Cambridge, Mass., 1973]. pp. 118.

— — 1328—1589.

AUTRAND (FRANÇOISE) Pouvoir et société en France, XIVe-XVe siècles. [Paris, 1974]. pp. 96. *bibliog.*

— — 1589—1789.

HAYDEN (J. MICHAEL) France and the Estates General of 1614. London, 1974. pp. 334. *bibliog.*

— — 1789—1900.

BROUGHAM (HENRY PETER) 1st Baron Brougham and Vaux. La crise en France; ou, Examen approfondi de la situation morale et politique de ce pays; renaissance d'un parti qu'on avait cru mort; ses probabilit´s de succès;... traduit de l'anglais par Varfuge. Bruxelles, 1839. pp. 58.

WIECLAWIK (LUCIENNE DE) Alphonse Rabbe dans la mêlée politique et littéraire de la Restauration. Paris, 1963. pp. 598. *bibliogs.*

PORCH (DOUGLAS) Army and revolution: France 1815-1848. London, 1974. pp. 182. *bibliog.*

— — 1870—1940.

BONNEFOUS (EDOUARD) Histoire politique de la Troisième République. tome 5. La République en danger: des ligues au Front populaire, 1930- 1936. 2nd ed. Paris, 1973. pp. 482. *bibliog.*

FLANNER (JANET) Paris was yesterday, 1925-1939;... edited by Irving Drutman. London, 1973. pp. 232.

MYSYROWICZ (LADISLAS) Autopsie d'une défaite: origines de l'effondrement militaire français de 1940. Lausanne, [1973]. pp. 385. *bibliog.*

LOCKE (ROBERT R.) French legitimists and the politics of moral order in the early Third Republic. Princeton, [1974]. pp. 321. *bibliog.*

PFEIFFER (PETER) Das 'Grand Ministère' Léon Gambettas, 10. November 1881-26. Januar 1882: ein Beitrag zur Parlamentsgeschichte der Dritten Republik. [Karlsruhe, imprint, 1974?]. pp. 202. *bibliog.*

— — 1900— .

RIOUX (JEAN PIERRE) Revolutionnaires du Front populaire: choix de documents, 1935- 1938. [Paris, 1973]. pp. 444. *bibliog.*

KRIEGEL (ANNIE) Communismes au miroir français: temps, cultures et sociétés en France devant le communisme. [Paris, 1974]. pp. 253.

POPELIN (CLAUDE) Arènes politiques. [Paris, 1974]. pp. 243.

SULEIMAN (EZRA N.) Politics, power, and bureaucracy in France: the administrative elite. Princeton, [1974]. pp. 440. *bibliog.*

— — 1940—1945.

CAHIERS FRANÇAIS, LES (formerly Les Documents, previously Documents d'information); [pd. by] Comité Français de la Libération Nationale, Commissariat à l'Information). m. (formerly s-m.), Oc 1 1941 - My 1944 (nos.[3]-55). Londres.

— — 1945— .

ROSSEL (ANDRE) Editor of Journaux du temps passé, ed. Mai 68: (images, affiches, etc.);...réalisé sur une maquette de François Doat. [Paris], 1968. 8 pts.

FRANCE. Direction de la Documentation. La Documentation Française. Notes et Etudes Documentaires. Nos. 3,722-3, 723. Chronologie des événements de mai-juin 1968. Paris, 1970. pp. 98.

AMBLER (JOHN STEWARD) and SCHEINMAN (LAWRENCE) The government and politics of France. Boston, [1971]. pp. 257. *bibliog.*

CHARLTON (SUE ELLEN M.) The French left and European integration. Denver, Col., [1972]. pp. 111. *bibliog.* (*Denver. University. Social Science Foundation and Graduate School of International Studies. Monograph Series in World Affairs. vol.9, no.4*)

SERVAN-SCHREIBER (JEAN JACQUES) Appel à la réforme: six mois de campagne, mai à novembre 1971. [Paris, 1972]. pp. 190.

AUBIER (JEAN MARIE) La république du général. [Paris, 1973]. pp. 285.

CROZIER (MICHEL) The stalled society. New York, 1973. pp. 177.

FOHLEN (CLAUDE) ed. Mai 1968: révolution ou psychodrame?. [Paris, 1973]. pp. 95. *bibliog.*

HOYLES (ANDRÉE) Imagination in power: the occupation of factories in France in 1968. Nottingham, 1973. pp. 72.

MARCHAIS (GEORGES) Le défi démocratique. Paris, [1973]. pp. 249.

MILHAUD (JEAN) Mon ami l'état. [Paris], 1973. pp. 143.

NOËL (LÉON) L'avenir du Gaullisme: le sort des institutions de la Ve République. [Paris, 1973]. pp. 111.

FRANCE. (Cont.)

— Population.

FRANCE. Institut National de la Statistique et des Etudes Economiques. Collections de l'I.N.S.E.E. Série D. Démographie et Emploi . Paris, 1969 in progress.

OBSERVATOIRE ECONOMIQUE MEDITERRANEEN. Population 1968 Midi Méditerranéen: démographie. Marseille, [1969]. pp. 20.

FRANCE. Institut National de la Statistique et des Etudes Economiques. Collections de l'I.N.S.E.E. Série. R. Régions . Paris, 1970 in progress.

ATELIER CENTRAL D'ETUDES D'AMENAGEMENT RURAL. Aménagement rural: les sources d'information statistique et documentaire. Paris, 1971. pp. 303. *bibliog.*

MILLOT (BENOÎT) Capital humain et migrations interrégionales. Dijon, [1971]. fo. 196. *bibliog.*

DOUBLET (JACQUES) and VILLEDARY (HUBERT DE) Law and population growth in France. Medford, Mass., 1973. pp. 87. (*Tufts University. Fletcher School of Law and Diplomacy. Law and Population Monograph Series. No.12*)

FRANCE. Institut National de la Statistique et des Etudes Economiques. Direction Régionale de Lille. 1973. Région Nord 1962-1972: population, emploi, établissements, données comparées suivant les arrondissements. [Lille, 1973]. pp. 96.

LE ROY LADURIE (EMMANUEL) Le territoire de l'historien. [Paris, 1973]. pp. 544.

NOIN (DANIEL) Géographie démographique de la France. Paris, [1973]. pp. 158. *bibliog.* (*Rouen. Université. Publications. Série Littéraire. 19*)

TUGAULT (YVES) La mesure de la mobilité: cinq études sur les migrations internes. [Paris], 1973. pp. 226. *bibliog.* (*France. Institut National d'Etudes Démographiques. Travaux et Documents. Cahiers. No.67*)

VAN DE WALLE (ETIENNE) The female population of France in the 19th century: a reconstruction of 82 départements. Princeton, [1974]. pp. 483. *bibliog.*

— Population, Rural.

MASLOWSKI (JACQUELINE) and PAILLAT (PAUL) Conditions de vie et besoins des personnes agées en France. III. Les ruraux agés non agricoles. [Paris], 1973. pp. 246. (*France. Institut National d'Etudes Démographiques. Travaux et Documents. Cahiers. No. 68*)

— Presidents.

DUVERGER (MAURICE) La monarchie républicaine. Paris, [1974]. pp. 284.

— Relations (general) with Latin America.

FRANCE. Direction de la Documentation. La Documentation Française. Notes et Etudes Documentaires. Nos. 3,083-3, 084. L'Amérique Latine et la France; [by] Olivier Rostand. Paris, 1964. 2 pts. *bibliog.*

— Relations (general) with Poland.

FRANCE. Direction de la Documentation. La Documentation Française. Notes et Etudes Documentaires. No. 3,922. Les relations franco-polonaises, 1945-1972, par Jadwiga Castagné. [Paris], 1972. pp. 48. *bibliog.*

— Relations (general) with Russia.

FRANCE. Direction de la Documentation. La Documentation Française. Notes et Etudes Documentaires. No. 3,746. Visite officielle de M. Georges Pompidou, Président de la République, en U.R.S.S., 6-13 octobre 1970. Paris, 1970. pp. 29.

ORLIK (OL'GA VASIL'EVNA) Peredovaia Rossiia i revoliutsionnaia Frantsiia, I polovina XIX v. Moskva, 1973. pp. 299.

— Relations (general) with Yugoslavia.

FRANCE. Direction de la Documentation. La Documentation Française. Notes et Etudes Documentaires. No. 3,773. Les relations franco-yougoslaves, 1945-1970; [by] Paul Yankovitch. Paris, 1971. pp. 29.

— Rural conditions.

ATELIER CENTRAL D'ETUDES D'AMENAGEMENT RURAL. Aménagement rural: les sources d'information statistique et documentaire. Paris, 1971. pp. 303. *bibliog.*

FRANCE. Ministère de l'Agriculture. Direction Départementale de l'Agriculture du Doubs. 1971. Contribution à l'étude du schéma directeur d'aménagement et d'urbanisme de Besançon. Besançon, 1971. pp. 108.

HOUEE (PAUL) Les étapes du développement rural. Paris, [1972]. 2 vols.

— Social conditions.

COFFEY (PETER) Economist. The social economy of France. London, 1973. pp. 133.

CROZIER (MICHEL) The stalled society. New York, 1973. pp. 177.

PETONNET (COLETTE) Those people: the subculture of a housing project;...translated from the French by Rita Smidt. Westport, Conn., [1973]. pp. 293. *bibliog.*

— Social history.

BELMONT (NICOLE) Mythes et croyances dans l'ancienne France. [Paris, 1973]. pp. 187. *bibliog.*

CONJONCTURE économique, structures sociales: hommage à Ernest Labrousse; [edited by Fernand Braudel and others]. Paris, 1974. pp. 547. *bibliog.* (Paris. Ecole Pratique des Hautes Etudes. Section des Sciences Economiques et Sociales. Civilisations et Sociétés. 47)

— Social life and customs.

FLANNER (JANET) Paris was yesterday, 1925-1939;... edited by Irving Drutman. London, 1973. pp. 232.

— Social policy.

CAHIERS FRANÇAIS D'INFORMATION. [Paris], 1945-48. 12 parts.

FRANCE. Comité Interministériel pour l'Information. 1972. Vous en 1975: comment le VIe Plan peut changer vos conditions de vie. [Paris, 1972]. pp. 58.

FRANCE. Commissariat Général du Plan. 1972. 1985: la France face au choc du futur. [Paris, 1972]. pp. 220. (*Plan et prospectives. 8*)

FRICKE (ELSE) Familienpolitik in Frankreich: Darstellung und sozioökonomische Analyse. Berlin, 1972. pp. 437. *bibliog.*

OMNIUM TECHNIQUE D'AMENAGEMENT. Schéma général d'aménagement de la France: une image de la France en l'an 2000; documents, méthode de travail. Paris, 1972. pp. 334. (*France. Délégation à l'Aménagement du Territoire et à l'Action Régionale. Travaux et Recherches de Prospective. 30*)

FRANCE. Direction de la Documentation. La Documentation Française. Notes et Etudes Documentaires. Nos. 3,959-3, 960. Les programmes finalisés dans le VIe Plan, [par Bernard Lion]. [Paris], 1973. pp. 57.

FRANCE. Direction de la Documentation. La Documentation Française. Notes et Etudes Documentaires. Nos. 3,991-3, 992. Fonctions collectives et planification. [Paris], 1973. pp. 71.

FRANCE. Direction de la Documentation. La Documentation Française. Notes et Etudes Documentaires. Nos. 4,037-4, 038. Le contenu des fonctions collectives. Paris, 1973. pp. 47.

THEVENET (AMEDEE) L'aide sociale en France. Paris, 1973. pp. 128. *bibliog.*

— Statistics, vital.

VALLIN (JACQUES) La mortalité par génération en France, depuis 1899. [Paris], 1973. pp. 483. *bibliog.* (*France. Institut National d'Etudes Démographiques. Travaux et Documents. Cahiers. No. 63*)

FRANCHISES (RETAIL TRADE).

RAAD VOOR HET MIDDEN- EN KLEINBEDRIJF. Franchising. 's-Gravenhage, 1973. pp. 48. ([*Publikaties*]. *1973, no. 3*)

FRANCIS JOSEPH I, Emperor of Austria.

KANN (ROBERT ADOLF) Kaiser Franz Joseph und der Ausbruch des Weltkrieges: eine Betrachtung über den Quellenwert der Aufzeichnungen von Dr. Heinrich Kanner. Wien, 1971. pp. 24. (*Österreichische Akademie der Wissenschaften. Philosophisch-Historische Klasse. Sitzungsberichte. 274. Band. 3. Abhandlung*)

FRANKFURT—AM—MAIN

— Industries.

MAY (HEINZ DIETER) Junge Industrialisierungstendenzen im Untermaingebiet unter besonderer Berücksichtigung der Betriebsverlagerungen aus Frankfurt am Main. Frankfurt am Main, 1968. pp. 157. *bibliog.* (*Frankfurt am Main. Universität. Geographisches Institut. Rhein-Mainische Forschungen. Heft 65*)

— Social conditions.

BORRIS (MARIA) Ausländische Arbeiter in einer Grosstadt: eine empirische Untersuchung am Beispiel Frankfurt. Frankfurt am Main, [1973]. pp. 318. *bibliog.*

— Street cleaning.

FRANKFURT AM MAIN. Stadtreinigungsamt. 100 Jahre Stadtreinigung Frankfurt am Main, 1872-1972. Frankfurt am Main, [1972]. pp. 68.

FRANKFURT—AM—MAIN UNIVERSITY

— Institute of Social Research.

JAY (MARTIN) The dialectical imagination: a history of the Frankfurt School and the Institute of Social Research, 1923-1950. London, 1973. pp. 382. *bibliog.*

FRANKLIN (HENRY).

FRANKLIN (HENRY) The flag-wagger. London, 1974. pp. 204.

FRAUD

— Germany.

SAARBRUECKEN. Universität. Annales Universitatis Saraviensis. Rechts- und Wirtschaftswissenschaftliche Abteilung. Band 72. Die Abgrenzung des Betrugs von Diebstahl und Unterschlagung;...von Leonhard E. Backmann. Saarbrücken, 1974. pp. 183. *bibliog.*

— United Kingdom.

BOWER (GEORGE SPENCER) and TURNER (Sir ALEXANDER KINGCOME) The law of actionable misrepresentation, stated in the form of a code, followed by a commentary and appendices...; third edition by A.K. Turner. London, 1974. pp. 488.

FREE CHURCH OF SCOTLAND.

MACLAREN (A. ALLAN) Religion and social class: the disruption years in Aberdeen. London, 1974. pp. 268.

FREE PARTY (TURKEY).

WEIKER (WALTER F.) Political tutelage and democracy in Turkey: the Free Party and its aftermath. Leiden, 1973. pp. 317. *bibliog.*

FREE PORTS AND ZONES

— Syria.

OFFICE ARABE DE PRESSE ET DE DOCUMENTATION. Les zones franches en Syrie: étude économique, statistique et législative. Damas, [1972]. fo. 84.

FREE THOUGHT.

PROKOSHINA (EKATERINA SERGEEVNA) Ocherk svobodomysliia i ateizma v Belorussii v XIX v. Minsk, 1973. pp. 226.

SEGIZBAEV (ORAZ AMANGALIEVICH) Traditsii svobodomysliia i ateizma v dukhovnoi kul'ture kazakhskogo naroda. Alma-Ata, 1973. pp. 168.

FREE WILL AND DETERMINISM.

WICKLUND (ROBERT A.) Freedom and reactance. Potomac, Md., 1974. pp. 205. *bibliog.*

FREEDOM OF MOVEMENT.

CONFERENCE OF JURISTS ON RIGHT TO FREEDOM OF MOVEMENT, 1968. International Year of Human Rights: report and conclusions of the Conference of Jurists...[(sponsored by the International Commission of Jurists [and others]). Bangalore, [1968?]. pp. 134.

FREEMASONS

— Russia.

SVITKOV (N.) Masonstvo v russkoi emigratsii, k 1 ianvaria 1932 g.: sostavlennoe na osnovanii mas. dokumentov. Parizh, 1932. pp. 32.

POKROVSKII (ALEKSANDR) Russkie masony v emigratsii. Parizh, 1941. pp. 16.

FREETOWN

— Politics and government.

SIERRA LEONE. Percy Davies Commission of Inquiry into the Activities of the Freetown City Council from 1st January, 1964 to 23rd March, 1967. 1969. Report...; and the government statement thereon; [Percy R. Davies, chairman]. [Freetown, 1969]. pp. 114.

FREGE (GOTTLOB).

DUMMETT (MICHAEL ANTHONY EARDLEY) Frege: philosophy of language. London, 1973. pp. 698. *bibliog.*

FREIBURG (CANTON)

— Economic policy.

BODMER (WALTER) Die Wirtschaftspolitik Berns und Freiburgs im 17. und 18. Jahrhundert. [Bern, 1973]. pp. 108. (*Historischer Verein des Kantons Bern. Archiv. Band 57*)

FREIBURG IM BREISGAU UNIVERSITY.

KREUTZBERGER (WOLFGANG) Studenten und Politik, 1918-1933: der Fall Freiburg im Breisgau. Göttingen, 1972. pp. 239. *bibliog.*

BLUMENBERG-LAMPE (CHRISTINE) Das wirtschaftspolitische Programm der "Freiburger Kreise": Entwurf einer freiheitlich-sozialen Nachkriegswirtschaft; Nationalökonomen gegen den Nationalsozialismus. Berlin, [1973]. pp. 180. *bibliog.*

FREIE DEMOKRATISCHE PARTEI.

FREIE DEMOKRATISCHE PARTEI. Parteitag, 1971. Freiburger Thesen der F.D.P. zur Gesellschaftspolitik. Bonn, [1971?]. pp. 87.

FREIE DEMOKRATISCHE PARTEI. Bundesvorstand. Zeugnisse liberaler Politik: 25 Jahre F.D.P., 1948-1973; [collection of speeches and articles]. Bonn, 1973. pp. 288.

FREIGHT AND FREIGHTAGE

— Netherlands — Mathematical models.

HOPPE (HELMUT R.) and NOORTMAN (H.J.) Aktuelle Probleme der Seehafen- und Regionalpolitik. Göttingen, 1972. pp. 36. (*Münster in Westfalen. Westfälische Wilhelms- Universität. Institut für Verkehrswissenschaft. Vorträge und Studien. Heft 13*)

— Norway.

NORWAY. Statistiske Centralbyrå. 1972. Godstransport på kysten: skip i innenlandsk rutefart 1969, etc. Oslo, 1972. pp. 71. (*Norges Offisielle Statistikk. Rekke A. 519*) In English and Norwegian.

NORWAY. Statistiske Centralbyrå. 1972. Godstransport på kysten: leie- og egentransport med skip 25-500 br. tonn 1970, etc. Oslo, 1972. pp. 91. (*Norges Offisielle Statistikk. Rekke A. 516*) In English and Norwegian.

— United Kingdom.

BONWIT (RALF) Writer on Transport. In place of congestion: some observations on the transport of freight. Loughborough, 1973. fo. 113.

COUGHLIN (S.) An appraisal of the rigid airship in the UK freight market. Cranfield, 1973. pp. 102. *bibliog.* (*Cranfield Institute of Technology. Centre for Transport Studies. Reports. 3*)

FREIGHTERS.

INTER-GOVERNMENTAL MARITIME CONSULTATIVE ORGANIZATION. 1969. Recommendation on intact stability for passenger and cargo ships under 100 metres in length. London, [1969]. pp. 18.

FRENCH CANADIANS.

TREMBLAY (MARC ADELARD) and LAPLANTE (MARC) Famille et parenté en Acadie: évolution des structures et des relations familiales et parentales à l'Anse-des-Lavallée. Ottawa, National Museums of Canada, 1971. pp. 174. *bibliog.* (*National Museum of Man [Canada]. Publications in Ethnology. No. 3*) With English summary.

ELKIN (FREDERICK) Rebels and colleagues: advertising and social change in French Canada. Montreal, 1973. pp. 227.

RIOUX (MARCEL) Les Québécois. [Paris, 1974]. pp. 189. *bibliog.*

FRENCH FICTION.

GODENNE (RENE) La nouvelle française. Paris, 1974. pp. 176. *bibliog.*

FRENCH IN FOREIGN COUNTRIES.

FRANCE. Direction de la Documentation. La Documentation Française. Notes et Etudes Documentaires. No. 3,975. Les Français établis à l'étranger par Léonce Clement. [Paris], 1973. pp. 45.

FRENCH LITERATURE

— History and criticism.

KUCZYNSKI (JUERGEN) Gestalten und Werke. (Band 2). Soziologische Studien zur englischsprachigen und französischen Literatur. Berlin, 1971. pp. 499.

GODENNE (RENE) La nouvelle française. Paris, 1974. pp. 176. *bibliog.*

FRENCH NEWSPAPERS.

BRUNOIS (RICHARD) Le Figaro face aux problèmes de la presse quotidienne. Paris, 1973. pp. 222.

HIRTZ (COLETTE) L'Est Républicain, 1889-1914: naissance et développement d'un grand quotidien régional. Grenoble, 1973. pp. 176. *bibliog.*

FRENCH PERIODICALS.

DIOUDONNAT (PIERRE MARIE) Je suis partout, 1930-1944: les maurrassiens devant la tentation fasciste. Paris, [1973]. pp. 471.

FRANCE. Commission de Coordination de la Documentation Administrative. 1973. Répertoire des publications périodiques et de série de l'administration française. Paris, 1973. pp. 368.

CHAPIER (HENRY) Quinze ans de "Combat". Paris, [1974]. pp. 119.

FRENCH POLYNESIA

— Statistics.

FRENCH POLYNESIA. Service du Plan. Section Statistique. Annuaire statistique. a., 1972- Papeete.

FRENCH WEST INDIES

— Politics and government.

SABLE (VICTOR) Les Antilles sans complexes: une expérience de décolonisation. Paris, 1972. pp. 309.

FREUD (SIGMUND).

McLEISH (JOHN) The theory of social change: four views considered. London, Routledge and Kegan Paul, 1969 repr. 1972. pp. xiii, 95. *bibliog.* (*International Library of Sociology and Social Reconstruction*)

FOUGEYROLLAS (PIERRE) Marx, Freud et la révolution totale. Paris, [1972]. pp. 642.

EYSENCK (HANS JÜRGEN) and WILSON (GLENN D.) eds. The experimental study of Freudian theories. London, 1973. pp. 405. *bibliogs.*

FRIENDLY SOCIETIES

— Australia.

AUSTRALIA. Department of Social Security. Annual report on the operations of the registered medical and hospital benefits organizations. a., 1970/71 (1st)- Canberra.

— Canada.

WORKERS BENEVOLENT ASSOCIATION OF CANADA. Friends in need: the W.B.A. story; a Canadian epic in fraternalism; (editorial board: Anthony Bilecki [and others]). Winnipeg, 1972. pp. 398.

— Italy.

PAPA (EMILIO RAFFAELE) Origini delle società operaie: libertà di associazione e organizzazioni operaie di mutuo soccorso in Piemonte, 1848-1861. Milano, [1967]. pp. 368.

— Senegal.

LAVILLE (PIERRE) Associations rurales et socialisme contractuel en Afrique occidentale: étude de cas; le Sénégal. [Paris, 1972]. pp. 371. *bibliog.*

— United Kingdom.

LIVERPOOL CANNED GOODS PERMANENT BENEFIT SOCIETY. Rules. Liverpool, 1901. pp. 16.

GOSDEN (PETER HENRY JOHN HEATHER) Self-help: voluntary associations in the 19th century. London, 1973. pp. 295. *bibliog.*

FRIENDS, SOCIETY OF

— United States.

COMFORT (WILLIAM WISTAR) The Quakers: a brief account of their influence on Pennsylvania. [rev. ed.] Gettysburg, 1948 [repr. with revisions 1963?]. pp. 65. *bibliog.* (*Pennsylvania History Studies. No. 2*)

FRIENDS, SOCIETY OF, AND WORLD POLITICS.

ORR (E.W.) The Quakers in peace and war, 1920 to 1967. Eastbourne, 1974. pp. 203.

FRIENDSHIP.

DUCK (STEVEN W.) Personal relationships and personal constructs: a study of friendship formation. London, [1973]. pp. 170. *bibliog.*

FRIESLAND

— Economic history.

FABER (J.A.) Drie eeuwen Friesland: economische en sociale ontwikkelingen van 1500 tot 1800. Wageningen, 1972. 2 vols.(in 1). *bibliog. (Wageningen. Landbouwhogeschool. Afdeling Agrarische Geschiedenis. Bijdragen. 17) With English summary.*

FRIULI—VENEZIA GIULIA

— Economic conditions.

CENTRO DI STUDI E PIANI ECONOMICI. Tavola economica della regione Friuli-Venezia Giulia, anno 1965. Roma, 1970. pp. 97.

FRONDIZI (ARTURO).

BARRERA (MARIO) Information and ideology: a case study of Arturo Frondizi. Beverly Hills, [1973]. pp. 48. *bibliog.*

FRONT DE LIBERATION DU QUEBEC.

REGUSH (NICHOLAS M.) Pierre Vallières: the revolutionary process in Quebec. New York, 1973. pp. 211. *bibliog.*

FRONTIER AND PIONEER LIFE

— Canada.

LEVERIDGE (ANNA MARIA) Your loving Anna: letters from the Ontario frontier; [edited by] Louis Tivy. Toronto, [1972]. pp. 120.

— United States.

WINTHER (OSCAR OSBURN) The transportation frontier: trans-Mississippi West, 1865-1890.New York, [1964]. pp. 224. *bibliog.*

PORTER (KENNETH WIGGINS) The negro on the American frontier. New York, 1971. pp. 529.

HOLLON (WILLIAM EUGENE) Frontier violence: another look. New York, 1974. pp. 279. *bibliog.*

— — Pennsylvania.

WOLF (GEORGE D.) The Fair Play settlers of the West Branch Valley, 1769- 1784: a study of frontier ethnography. Harrisburg, Pennsylvania Historical and Museum Commission, 1969. pp. 122. *bibliog.*

FRONTIER WORKERS.

BAUVIR (LOUIS) Les travailleurs frontaliers des régions wallonnes: synthèse historique, juridique et statistique, analyse d'une enquête socio-économique. Liège, 1967. pp. 302. *(Revue du Travail. Janvier-Février, 1968. Annexe) Folding map in end pocket.*

DEMARET (JEAN MARIE) Les travailleurs frontaliers occupés dans le département du Nord. [Lille], Echelon Régional de l'Emploi, 1972. fo. 36.

Il FENOMENO dei frontalieri in Lombardia: atti del Convegno di Como del 23-24 giugno 1971. [Varese, 1972]. pp. 442.

FROTHINGHAM (JELENA LOZANIĆ—).

See LOZANIĆ-FROTHINGHAM (JELENA).

FRUIT CULTURE

— Belgium.

JANSSENS (J.) Bedrijfsuitkomsten van enige belgische fruitteeltbedrijven: boekjaar 1961-1962. [Gent, 1963?]. fo. 17. *(Belgium. Station d'Economie Rurale de l'Etat. Communications. 54)*

JANSSENS (J.) Bedrijfsuitkomsten van enige belgische fruitteeltbedrijven: boekjaar 1962-1963. [Gent, 1964?]. fo. 21. *(Belgium. Station d'Economie Rurale de l'Etat. Communications. 58)*

JANSSENS (J.) Bedrijfsuitkomsten betreffende 34 fruitteeltbedrijven: boekjaar 1963-1964. [Gent, 1965?]. fo. 64. *(Belgium. Station d'Economie Rurale de l'Etat. Communications. 61) With summary in French.*

FUERZA DE ORIENTACION RADICAL DE LA JOVEN ARGENTINA.

SCENNA (MIGUEL ANGEL) F.O.R.J.A.: una aventura argentina; de Yrigoyen a Peron. Buenos Aires, [1972]. 2 vols. (in 1).

FUNCTIONS, TRANSCENDENTAL.

CHRISTENSEN (LAURITS R.) and others. Transcendental logarithmic utility functions. Stanford, 1973. pp. 48. *bibliog. (Stanford University. Institute for Mathematical Studies in the Social Sciences. Technical Reports. [New Series]. No. 94)*

FUND RAISING.

HEYWOOD (JAMES FRANK) and QUILLAM (MARY) Fund raising by charities; [prepared for the National Council of Social Service]. London, [1973]. pp. 64.

FUR TRADE

— United Kingdom.

FOOTWEAR, LEATHER AND FUR SKIN INDUSTRY TRAINING BOARD [U.K.]. Report and statement of accounts. a., 1972/3- Sutton Coldfield. *Formerly included in the file of British Parliamentary Papers.*

FURNITURE INDUSTRY AND TRADE

— United Kingdom.

FURNITURE AND TIMBER INDUSTRY TRAINING BOARD [U.K.]. Report and statement of accounts. a., 1972/3- High Wycombe. *Formerly included in the file of British Parliamentary Papers.*

GABON

— Economic conditions.

EWUSI (KODWO) West African economies: some basic economic problems. Legon, 1971. fo.89. *(Ghana University. Institute of Statistical, Social and Economic Research. Technical Publication Series. No.25)*

FRANCE. Direction de l'Aide au Développement des Etats Francophones d'Afrique au Sud du Sahara et de la République Malgache. Secteur Information Economique et Conjoncture. 1973. Gabon 1970-1971: dossier d'information économique. Paris, 1973. pp. 24,fo. 39.

GADER VALLEY.

ROTHER-HOHENSTEIN (BAERBEL) Bevölkerung und Wirtschaft im Gadertal, Dolomiten. Frankfurt/Main, 1973. pp. 205. *bibliog. (Frankfurt am Main. Universität. Seminar für Wirtschaftsgeographie. Frankfurter Wirtschafts- und Sozialgeographische Schriften. Heft 14)*

GAINSBOROUGH

— Economic history.

BECKWITH (IAN STANLEY) The history of fields and farms in Gainsborough. [Gainsborough, 1973]. pp. 51.

GALICIA (EASTERN EUROPE)

— Rural conditions.

KRAVETS' (MYKOLA MYKOLAIOVYCH) Selianstvo Skhidnoï Halychyny i Pivnichnoï Bukovyny u druhii polovyni XIX st. L'viv, 1964. pp. 239.

GALICIA (SPAIN)

— Economic policy.

MEILAN (JOSE LUIS) España 71: el territorio, protagonista del desarrollo. Madrid, 1971. pp. 219.

— Social history.

RODRIGUEZ VILAMOR (JOSE) La rebelion de los campesinos gallegos. Algorta, Spain, 1970. pp. 77. *bibliog.*

GALLICANISM.

MARTIMORT (AIME GEORGES) Le gallicanisme. Paris, 1973. pp. 128. *bibliog.*

GAMBETTA (LEON MICHEL).

PFEIFFER (PETER) Das 'Grand Ministère' Léon Gambettas, 10. November 1881-26. Januar 1882: ein Beitrag zur Parlamentsgeschichte der Dritten Republik. [Karlsruhe, imprint, 1974?]. pp. 202. *bibliog.*

GAMBIA

— Census.

GAMBIA. Census, 1973. Population census, 1973: provisional report. [Banjul], 1973. fo. 25.

— History.

QUINN (CHARLOTTE A.) Mandingo kingdoms of the Senegambia: traditionalism, Islam, and European expansion. London, 1972. pp. 211. *bibliog.*

GAMBLING

— United Kingdom.

U.K. Parliament. House of Lords. Committee on the Gaming Bill. Official report. d.(approx,), Jl 1-18 1968 (1st 7th sittings). London. *Photocopies.*

— United States.

WEINSTEIN (DAVID) and DEITCH (LILLIAN) The impact of legalized gambling: the socioeconomic consequences of lotteries and off-track betting. New York, 1974. pp. 208. *bibliog.*

GAMES

— New Zealand.

SUTTON-SMITH (BRIAN) The folkgames of children. Austin, 1972. pp. 559. *bibliog. (American Folklore Society. Bibliographical and Special Series. vol. 24)*

— United States.

SUTTON-SMITH (BRIAN) The folkgames of children. Austin, 1972. pp. 559. *bibliog. (American Folklore Society. Bibliographical and Special Series. vol. 24)*

GAMES, THEORY OF.

SHUBIK (MARTIN) and BREWER (GARRY D.) Models, simulations and games: a survey;...a report prepared for Advanced Research Projects Agency. Santa Monica, 1972. pp. 160. *(Rand Corporation. [Rand Reports]. 1060)*

FARARO (THOMAS J.) Mathematical sociology: an introduction to fundamentals. New York, [1973]. pp. 802. *bibliog.*

MUNIER (BERTRAND) Jeux et marchés. Paris, 1973. pp. 172. *bibliogs.*

TEDESCHI (JAMES T.) and others. Conflict, power and games: the experimental study of interpersonal relations. Chicago, 1973. pp. 270. *bibliog.*

FACH (WOLFGANG) Koalition und Opposition in spieltheoretischer Sicht: ein Beitrag zur Analyse und Kritik der neuen politischen Ökonomie. Berlin, [1974]. pp. 200. *bibliog.*

HANSEN (TERJE) On the approximation of Nash equilibrium points in an N-person noncooperative game. [Philadelphia], 1974. pp. 15. *bibliog. (Reprinted from Society for Industrial and Applied Mathematics Journal on Applied Mathematics, vol. 26, no. 3, May 1974)*

— Bibliography.

SHUBIK (MARTIN) and others. The literature of gaming, simulation and model-building: index and critical abstracts;...a report prepared for Advanced Research Projects Agency. Santa Monica, 1972. pp. 121. (Rand Corporation. [Rand Reports]. 620)

GANDHI (INDIRA).

BHATIA (KRISHAN) Indira: a biography of Prime Minister Gandhi. London, 1974. pp. 290. bibliog.

GANDHI (MOHANDAS KARAMCHAND).

KRIPALANI (J.B.) Gandhi, his life and thought. New Delhi, 1970 repr. 1971. pp. 508. bibliog. (Builders of Modern India)

GANGULI (BIRENDRANATH) Gandhi's social philosophy: perspective and relevance. New York, [1973]. pp. 453.

HUTCHINS (FRANCIS G.) India's revolution: Gandhi and the Quit India movement. Cambridge, Mass., 1973. pp. 326. bibliog.

IYER (RAGHAVAN NARASIMHAN) The moral and political thought of Mahatma Gandhi. New York, 1973. pp. 449. bibliog.

KOESTLER (ARTHUR) The heel of Achilles: essays, 1968-1973. London, 1974. pp. 254.

NANDA (B.R.) Gokhale, Gandhi and the Nehrus: studies in Indian nationalism. London, 1974. pp. 203.

GARIBALDI (GIUSEPPE).

VENTURI (ALFREDO) Garibaldi in Parlamento...: le esperienze di un eroe istintivo alle prese con il meccanismo delle istituzioni. Milano, [1973]. pp. 195.

RIDLEY (JASPER) Garibaldi. London, 1974. pp. 718. bibliog.

GAS, NATURAL.

TIRATSOO (E.N.) Natural gas: a study. 2nd ed. Beaconsfield, [1972]. pp. 400.

MEDICI (MARIO) The natural gas industry: a review of world resources and industrial applications. London, 1974. pp. 356. bibliogs.

— America, North.

WAVERMAN (LEONARD) Natural gas and national policy: a linear programming model of North American natural gas flows. Toronto, [1973]. pp. 122. bibliog.

— Asia.

UNITED NATIONS. Economic Commission for Asia and the Far East. Mineral Resources Development Series . New York, 1952 in progress.

— Australasia.

UNITED NATIONS. Economic Commission for Asia and the Far East. Mineral Resources Development Series . New York, 1952 in progress.

— United Kingdom.

U.K. Department of Trade and Industry. Offshore Supplies Office. 1973. Offshore supplies interest relief grants: a guide for industry. London, 1973. pp. 14.

U.K. Interdepartmental Working Party on Education and Training for Offshore Development. 1973. Education and training for offshore development; report; [B.A. Smith, chairman]. London, Department of Employment, Training Division, [1973]. 1 vol. (various pagings).

GAS INDUSTRY

— Belgium.

BELGIUM. Administration de l'Energie 1972. Organisation du secteur du gaz en Belgique. Bruxelles, 1972. fo. 33,35. In French and Flemish.

— South Africa — Statistics.

SOUTH AFRICA. Bureau of Statistics. Census of electricity, gas and steam. bien., 1963/4- Pretoria. In English and Afrikaans.

— United Kingdom.

BRITISH GAS CORPORATION. Annual report and accounts. a., 1972/3 (1st)- London. Formerly included in the file of British Parliamentary Papers.

GAS INDUSTRY TRAINING BOARD [U.K.]. Report and statement of accounts. a., 1972/3, 1973/4; ceased pbln. London. Formerly included in the file of British Parliamentary Papers.

GASPERI (ALCIDE DE).

ROSSINI (GIUSEPPE) De Gasperi e il fascismo. Roma, 1974. pp. 303.

GATESHEAD

— History.

MANDERS (FRANCIS WILLIAM DAVID) A history of Gateshead. Gateshead, Corporation, 1973. pp. 368.

GAUCHOS.

RODRIGUEZ MOLAS (RICARDO) Historia social del gaucho. Buenos Aires, 1968. pp. 603.

GAULLE (CHARLES DE).

MOLCHANOV (NIKOLAI NIKOLAEVICH) General de Goll'. Moskva, 1972. pp. 496.

AUBIER (JEAN MARIE) La république du général. [Paris, 1973]. pp. 285.

CROZIER (BRIAN) De Gaulle. London, 1973. 2 vols. bibliog.

MAURIAC (CLAUDE) The other de Gaulle: (diaries 1944-1954); translated by Moura Budberg and Gordon Latta. London, 1973. pp. 378.

POUGET (JEAN) Un certain capitaine de Gaulle. [Paris, 1973]. pp. 285.

DEBRE (JEAN LOUIS) Les idées constitutionnelles du Général de Gaulle. Paris, 1974. pp. 461.

GEORGES (ALFRED) pseud. Charles de Gaulle et la guerre d'Indochine. Paris,[1974]. pp. 189.

PISANI (EDGARD) Le Général indivis. Paris, [1974]. pp. 252.

PLUME (CHRISTIAN) and DEMARET (PIERRE) Target De Gaulle: the thirty-one attempts to assassinate the general;... translated from the French by Richard Barry. London, 1974. pp. 294.

GAY LIBERATION MOVEMENT.

HUMPHREYS (LAUD) Out of the closets: the sociology of homosexual liberation. Englewood Cliffs, [1972]. pp. 176.

GAZA STRIP.

TESSIER (ARLETTE) Gaza. Beirut, [1971]. pp. 36. (Palestine Research Center. Palestine Essays. No. 27)

GAZANKULU

— Politics and government.

SOUTH AFRICA. Report of the Controller and Auditor-General on the accounts of the Gazankulu Government and of the accounts of lower authorities in the area. a., 1972/3 [1st]- Pretoria. Included in the file of SOUTH AFRICA. Parliament. House of Assembly. Votes and proceedings; (with Printed annexures).

GDAŃSK

— Commerce.

STARK (WALTER) Lübeck und Danzig in der zweiten Hälfte des 15. Jahrhunderts: Untersuchungen zum Verhältnis der wendischen und preussischen Hansestädte, etc. Weimar, 1973. pp. 275. bibliog. (Historiker-Gesellschaft der Deutschen Demokratischen Republik. Hansische Arbeitsgemeinschaft. Abhandlungen zur Handels- und Sozialgeschichte. Band 11)

— Harbour.

STĘPNIAK (HENRYK) Rada Portu i Dróg Wodnych w Wolnym Mieście Gdańsku.Gdańsk, 1971. pp. 235. bibliog. (Gdańsk. Gdańskie Towarzystwo Naukowe. Wydział I Nauk Społecznych i Humanistycznych. Seria Monografii. Nr.43) With English and Russian summaries.

— History.

LEVINE (HERBERT S.) Hitler's free city: a history of the Nazi party in Danzig, 1925-39. Chicago, 1973. pp. 223. bibliog.

— Politics and government.

LEVINE (HERBERT S.) Hitler's free city: a history of the Nazi party in Danzig, 1925-39. Chicago, 1973. pp. 223. bibliog.

GENERAL AGREEMENT ON TARIFFS AND TRADE.

JAEGELER (FRANZ JUERGEN) Kooperation oder Konfrontation: GATT-Runde 1973. Hamburg, 1974. pp. 168. bibliog. (Hamburg. Hamburgisches Welt-Wirtschafts-Archiv. Studien zur Aussenwirtschaft und Entwicklungspolitik)

GENERAL STRIKE, UNITED KINGDOM, 1926.

MORRIS (MARGARET) The British general strike, 1926. London, 1973. pp. 40. bibliog. (Historical Association. General Series. G.82)

GENERATIVE GRAMMAR.

BRAME (MICHAEL K.) ed. Contributions to generative phonology. Austin, [1972]. pp. 327. bibliogs.

JACKENDOFF (RAY S.) Semantic interpretation in generative grammar. Cambridge, Mass., [1972]. pp. 400. bibliog.

BACH (EMMON) Syntactic theory. New York, [1974]. pp. 298. bibliog.

FODOR (JERRY ALAN) and others. The psychology of language: an introduction to psycholinguistics and generative grammar. New York, [1974]. pp. 537. bibliog.

GENEROSITY.

RUSHTEN (JOHN PHILIPPE) Social learning and cognitive development: alternative approaches to an understanding of generosity in 7 to 11 year olds: (Ph.D. [London] thesis). 1973. fo. 210. bibliog. Typescript: unpublished. This thesis is the propery ofLondon University and may not be removed from the Library

GENETIC PSYCHOLOGY.

DENENBERG (VICTOR H.) ed. Readings in the development of behavior. Stamford, Conn., [1972]. pp. 483. bibliogs.

The NATURE and nurture of behavior: developmental psychobiology: (readings from Scientific American); with introductions by William T. Greenough. San Francisco, [1973]. pp. 143. bibliogs.

GENETIC RESEARCH.

NETHERLANDS. Geneeskundige Raad. 1967. Het anthropogenetisch onderzoek in Nederland. [The Hague?, 1967?]. pp. 38. (Rapporten. 2)

GENETICS.

WORLD HEALTH ORGANIZATION. Scientific Group on Research on Human Population Genetics. 1968. Research on human population genetics: report, etc. Geneva, 1968. pp. 32. *(Technical Report Series. No. 387)*

ADVANCES in human genetics and their impact on society: proceedings of a symposium of the American Association for the Advancement of Science, held at Chicago...; editor, Daniel Bergsma [and others]. White Plains, N.Y., 1972. pp. 118. *(National Foundation-March of Dimes. Birth Defects: Original Article Series, vol. 8, no. 4)*

BAER (ADELA S.) ed. Heredity and society: readings in social genetics. New York, [1973]. pp. 382. *bibliogs.*

MERTENS (THOMAS ROBERT) and ROBINSON (SANDRA K.) eds. Human genetics and social problems: a book of readings. New York, [1973]. pp. 212. *bibliogs.*

GENEVA (CITY)

SONDEREGGER (FRITZ) Geneva as a center of international organizations. Zurich, [1973]. pp. 15.

— Economic history.

BERGIER (JEAN FRANÇOIS) Genève et l'économie européenne de la renaissance. Paris, 1963. pp. 519. *bibliog. (Paris. Ecole Pratique des Hautes Etudes. Section des Sciences Economiques et Sociales. Centre de Recherches Historiques. Affaires et Gens d'Affaires. 29)*

— Fairs.

BERGIER (JEAN FRANÇOIS) Genève et l'économie européenne de la renaissance. Paris, 1963. pp. 519. *bibliog. (Paris. Ecole Pratique des Hautes Etudes. Section des Sciences Economiques et Sociales. Centre de Recherches Historiques. Affaires et Gens d'Affaires. 29)*

GENEVA CONVENTIONS.

TOMAN (JIŘÍ) Index of the Geneva Conventions for the protection of war victims of 12 August 1949. Leiden, 1973. pp. 194. *(Institut Henry Dunant. Collection Scientifique. vol. 3)*

GENGIS KHAN, Great Khan of the Moguls.

See JENGHIS KHAN, Great Khan of the Moguls.

GENOCIDE.

TORIGUIAN (SHAVARSH) The Armenian question and international law. Beirut, 1973. pp. 330. *bibliog.*

GENTILE (GIOVANNI).

CICALESE (MARIALUISA) La formazione del pensiero politico di Giovanni Gentile, 1896- 1919. Milano, [1972]. pp. 238. *(Genoa. Università. Centro di Ricerca del C.N.R. Studi sul Pensiero Filosofico e Religioso dei Secoli XIX e XX. 22)*

GEOGRAPHICAL RESEARCH.

GEOGRAPHERS abroad: essays on the problems and prospects of research in foreign areas [presented at a conference held at the University of Chicago, 1972; edited by] Marvin W. Mikesell. Chicago, 1973.pp. 296. Chicago. University. Department of Geography. Research Papers. No. 152)

GEOGRAPHY.

ABLER (RONALD) and others. Spatial organization: the geographer's view of the world. London, [1972]. pp. 587. *bibliogs.*

NEW ZEALAND GEOGRAPHY CONFERENCE, 7TH, HAMILTON, 1972. Proceedings...; edited by Evelyn Stokes. [Christchurch], 1973. pp. 298. *bibliogs. (New Zealand Geographical Society. Conference Series. No. 7)*

— Computer programs.

BAKER (LAURIE) A selection of geographical computer programs. London, 1973 [or rather 1974]. pp. 118. *bibliog. (London. University. London School of Economics and Political Science. Department of Geography. Geographical Papers. No. 6)*

— Statistical methods.

McGREGOR (JOHN R.) A delimitation of Indiana manufacturing regions;...Numerical analysis: a different approach to analysis of geographical data; [by] Howard W. Dennis [and others]; Agricultural productivity of prairie, forest, and prairie-forest transition soils in Illinois; [by] Paul W. Mausel. Terre Haute, Ind., 1973. pp. 67. *(Indiana State University. Department of Geography and Geology. Professional Papers. No. 4)*

HAMMOND (ROBERT) and McCULLAGH (PATRICK S.) Quantitative techniques in geography: an introduction. Oxford, 1974. pp. 318. *bibliog.*

— Study and teaching.

NEW ZEALAND GEOGRAPHY CONFERENCE, 7TH, HAMILTON, 1972. Proceedings...; edited by Evelyn Stokes. [Christchurch], 1973. pp. 298. *bibliogs. (New Zealand Geographical Society. Conference Series. No. 7)*

— Terminology.

VILA (MARCO AURELIO) Vocabulario geografico de Venezuela. [Caracas], Corporacion Venezolana de Fomento, [1971]. pp. 400.

GEOGRAPHY, ECONOMIC.

ESTALL (ROBERT CHARLES) and BUCHANAN (ROBERT OGILVIE) Industrial activity and economic geography: a study of the forces behind the geographical location of productive activity in manufacturing industry. 3rd ed. London, 1973. pp. 252.

TEORETICHESKIE voprosy ekonomicheskoi geografii. Leningrad, 1973. pp. 160.

HODDER (BRAMWELL WILLIAM) and LEE (ROGER) Economic geography. London, 1974. pp. 207. *bibliog.*

HOYLE (BRIAN STEWART) ed. Spatial aspects of development. London, [1974]. pp. 372. *bibliogs.*

POLSKA AKADEMIA NAUK. Instytut Geografii. Geographia Polonica. 28. [Papers on physical and economic geography]. Warszawa, 1974. pp. 144. *bibliogs.*

TOYNE (PETER) Organisation, location and behaviour: decision-making in economic geography. London, 1974. pp. 285. *bibliog.*

GEOGRAPHY, MATHEMATICAL.

INTERNATIONAL GEOGRAPHICAL UNION. Commission on Quantitative Methods. Meeting, 1972. Proceedings...; edited by Maurice Yeates. Montreal, 1974. pp. 182. *bibliogs.*

GEOGRAPHY, POLITICAL.

SOJA (EDWARD W.) The political organization of space. Washington, 1971. pp. 54. *bibliog. (Association of American Geographers. Commission on College Geography. Resource Papers. No.8)*

BARNETT (J. ROSS) and MERCER (JOHN) Urban political analysis and new directions in political geography. Iowa City, 1973. fo. 21. *bibliog. (Iowa University. Department of Geography. Discussion Paper Series. No. 22)*

COHEN (SAUL BERNARD) Geography and politics in a world divided. 2nd ed. New York, 1973. pp. 334. *bibliog.*

GEOLOGY

— Australia — Northern Territory.

AUSTRALIA. Department of the Interior. Bulletins of the Northern Territory of Australia. No.14. Geological report on the country between Pine Creek and Tanami; [by H.I. Jensen]. [Melbourne], 1915. fo. 22.

— Nigeria.

KOWAL (JAN M.) and KNABE (DANUTA T.) An agroclimatological atlas of the northern states of Nigeria; with explanatoprry notes. Samaru-Zaria, [1972]. pp. 111, 17 maps.

— South Africa.

SOUTH AFRICA. Geological Survey. Bulletins. No.42. The geology of Durban and environs; by L.C. King and R.M. Maud. Pretoria, 1964. pp. 54. *bibliog. Map in end pocket. With summary in Afrikaans.*

— United Kingdom.

U.K. Geological Survey. Memoirs. [Sheet Memoirs. New Series]. 322, 323. Geology of the country around Boscastle and Holsworthy: explanation of the inland areas of one-inch geological sheet 322 and 1:50 000 geological sheet 323, new series; by M.C. McKeown [and others]. London, 1973. pp. 148. *bibliog.*

— — Ireland, Northern.

WILSON (H.E.) Regional geology of Northern Ireland. Belfast, H.M.S.O., 1972. pp. 113. *bibliog.*

GEORGE IV, King of Great Britain and Ireland.

HIBBERT (CHRISTOPHER) George IV: regent and king, 1811-1830. London, 1973. pp. 430. *bibliog.*

GEORGE (DAVID LLOYD) 1st Earl Lloyd George.

MORGAN (KENNETH OWEN) Lloyd George. London, [1974]. pp. 224. *bibliog.*

GEORGIA

— Foreign relations.

AVALOV (ZURAB DAVIDOVICH) Nezavisimost' Gruzii v mezhdunarodnoi politike, 1918-1921 g.g.: vospominaniia, ocherki. Paris, 1924. pp. 319.

— History.

GEORGIA (RUSSIA). 1921. Mémoire sur l'invasion de la Géorgie par les armées de la Russie des Soviets. Paris, 1921. pp. 8.

GEORGIA (RUSSIA). 1921. A tous les partis socialistes et organisations ouvrières. [Paris, 1921]. pp. 4.

— Politics and government.

50 let Sovetskoi Gruzii i Kompartii Gruzii: materialy i dokumenty. [Tbilisi, 1971]. pp. 238.

— Religion.

PORAKISHVILI (Z.I.) Dukhobory v Gruzii. Tbilisi, 1970. pp. 148.

GEORGIA (UNITED STATES)

— Economic conditions.

FOCUS on the future of Georgia, 1970-1985; edited by William H. Schabacker, Russell S. Clark, Homer C. Cooper; papers prepared for use by the Advisory Commission on Educational Goals of the State Board of Education. Atlanta, Georgia Department of Education, 1970. pp. 537.

— Economic policy.

COASTAL PLAINS REGIONAL COMMISSION. Economic development plan. Washington, the Commission, 1971. pp. 111.

COASTAL PLAINS REGIONAL COMMISSION [UNITED STATES]. Regional plan in brief. [Washington, the Commission], 1973. pp. 20.

— Politics and government.

FOCUS on the future of Georgia, 1970-1985; edited by William H. Schabacker, Russell S. Clark, Homer C. Cooper; papers prepared for use by the Advisory Commission on Educational Goals of the State Board of Education. Atlanta, Georgia Department of Education, 1970. pp. 537.

— Social conditions.

FOCUS on the future of Georgia, 1970-1985; edited by William H. Schabacker, Russell S. Clark, Homer C. Cooper; papers prepared for use by the Advisory Commission on Educational Goals of the State Board of Education. Atlanta, Georgia Department of Education, 1970. pp. 537.

GEOTHERMAL RESOURCES

— United States.

AMERICAN NUCLEAR SOCIETY. Annual Meeting, Las Vegas, 1972. Special Session on Geothermal Energy. Geothermal energy: resources, production, stimulation; edited by Paul Kruger and Carel Otte. Stanford, [1973]. pp. 360. *bibliogs.*

— — Bibliography.

TOMPKINS (DOROTHY LOUISE CAMPBELL) compiler. Power from the earth: geothermal energy. Berkeley, 1972. pp. 34. *(California University. Institute of Governmental Studies. Public Policy Bibliographies. 3)*

GERLACH (HELLMUT VON).

GERLACH (HELLMUT VON) Ein Demokrat kommentiert Weimar: die Berichte...an die Carnegie-Friedensstiftung in New York, 1922-1930; herausgegeben...von Karl Holl und Adolf Wild. Bremen, [1973]. pp. 268. *bibliog.*

GERMAN DRAMA.

STEINER (GERHARD) Jakobinerschauspiel und Jakobinertheater. Stuttgart, [1973]. pp. 336. *bibliog.*

GERMAN LANGUAGE

— Dictionaries.

AGRICOLA (ERHARD) and others, eds. Wörter und Wendungen: Wörterbuch zum deutschen Sprachgebrauch; (Autoren: Christiane Agricola [and others]). 6th ed. Leipzig, 1973. pp. 818.

GOERNER (HERBERT) and KEMPCKE (GUENTER) eds. Synonymwörterbuch: sinnverwandte Ausdrücke der deutschen Sprache; (Autoren: Marie-Elizabeth Fritze [and others]).Leipzig, 1973. pp. 643.

— — English.

LANGENSCHEIDT'S encyclopaedic dictionary of the English and German languages, based on the original work by E. Muret and D. Sanders. part 2. German-English: completely revised 1974; edited by Otto Springer. London, 1974 in progress. *Library has vol. 1: A-K.*

— Grammar.

KAUFMANN (GERHARD) Grammarian. Grammatik der deutschen Grundwortarten: Systeme morphologisch-syntaktischer Merkmale als Grundlage zur Datenverarbeitung. München, [1967]. pp. 116. *bibliog. (Goethe-Institut. Arbeitsstelle für Wissenschaftliche Didaktik. Schriften. Band 1)*

— Idioms, corrections, errors.

AGRICOLA (ERHARD) and others, eds. Wörter und Wendungen: Wörterbuch zum deutschen Sprachgebrauch; (Autoren: Christiane Agricola [and others]). 6th ed. Leipzig, 1973. pp. 818.

— Middle High German.

TRIER (JOST) Der deutsche Wortschatz im Sinnbezirk des Verstandes von den Anfängen bis zum Beginn des 13. Jahrhunderts; [reprint of the first edition of 1931]. Heidelberg, 1973. pp. 347.

— Old High German.

TRIER (JOST) Der deutsche Wortschatz im Sinnbezirk des Verstandes von den Anfängen bis zum Beginn des 13. Jahrhunderts; [reprint of the first edition of 1931]. Heidelberg, 1973. pp. 347.

— Synonyms and antonyms.

GOERNER (HERBERT) and KEMPCKE (GUENTER) eds. Synonymwörterbuch: sinnverwandte Ausdrücke der deutschen Sprache; (Autoren: Marie-Elizabeth Fritze [and others]).Leipzig, 1973. pp. 643.

— Syntax.

ESAU (HELMUT) Nominalization and complementation in modern German. Amsterdam, 1973. pp. 314.

— Vocabulary.

TRIER (JOST) Der deutsche Wortschatz im Sinnbezirk des Verstandes von den Anfängen bis zum Beginn des 13. Jahrhunderts; [reprint of the first edition of 1931]. Heidelberg, 1973. pp. 347.

GERMAN NEWSPAPERS.

Der FALL Küchenhoff; oder, Agitation mit falschem Etikett: wie politische Gegnerschaft zu "Bild" wissenschaftlich verbrämt werden sollte; (herausgegeben von der Axel Springer Verlag AG, Abteilung Information). Berlin, 1972. pp. 113.

ROEDER (ELMAR) Der konservative Journalist Ernst Zander und die politischen Kämpfe seines "Volksboten". München, 1972. pp. 339. *bibliog. (Munich. Stadtarchiv. Neue Schriftenreihe. Band 58)*

GERMAN PERIODICALS.

STREITHOFEN (HEINRICH B.) SPD und katholische Kirche: eine Untersuchung über das Kirchenbild des Vorwärts. Stuttgart, [1974]. pp. 87. *(Institut für Gesellschaftswissenschaften Walberberg. Walberberger Gespräche)*

— Bibliography.

SPALL (PETER VAN) compiler. Ubersicht deutschsprachiger Periodika der unabhängigen sozialistischen Linken. Offenbach, 1973. pp. 40.

GERMAN REUNIFICATION QUESTION (1949—).

BUCZYLOWSKI (ULRICH) Kurt Schumacher und die deutsche Frage: Sicherheitspolitik und strategische Offensivkonzeption vom August 1950 bis September 1951. Stuttgart-Degerloch, 1973. pp. 228. *bibliog.*

FREIE DEMOKRATISCHE PARTEI. F.D.P. zum Grundvertrag: Beiträge und Dokumentation. Bonn, 1973. pp. 40.

GERMANY (BUNDESREPUBLIK). Bundesministerium für Innerdeutsche Beziehungen. 1973. Die Entwicklung der Beziehungen zwischen der Bundesrepublik Deutschland und der Deutschen Demokratischen Republik: Bericht und Dokumentation. [Bonn], 1973. pp. 154.

LUDZ (PETER CHRISTIAN) Two Germanys in one world. Farnborough, [1973]. pp. 64. *(Atlantic Institute. Atlantic Papers. 1973. 3)*

MATTFELD (ANTJE) Modelle einer Normalisierung zwischen den beiden deutschen Staaten: eine rechtliche Betrachtung. Düsseldorf, [1973]. pp. 198. *bibliog.*

RUESS (GISELA) Anatomie einer politischen Verwaltung: das Bundesministerium für gesamtdeutsche Fragen; innerdeutsche Beziehungen, 1949- 1970. München, [1973]. pp. 205. *bibliog. (Munich. Universität. Geschwister-Scholl-Institut für Politische Wissenschaft. Münchener Studien zur Politik. 23.Band)*

SCHWEIGLER (GEBHARD) Nationalbewusstsein in der BRD und der DDR. Düsseldorf, [1973]. pp. 235. *bibliog.*

JAENECKE (HEINRICH) 30 Jahre und ein Tag: die Geschichte der deutschen Teilung.Düsseldorf, 1974. pp. 400. *bibliog.*

PORTISCH (HUGO) Die deutsche Konfrontation: Gegenwart und Zukunft der beiden deutschen Staaten. Wien, [1974]. pp. 351. *bibliog.*

GERMANS.

THOSE Germans...and how we see them; with a preface by George Mikes: articles selected and introduced by Rolf Breitenstein: published on behalf of the Embassy of the Federal Republic of Germany. London, 1973. pp. 159.

GERMANS IN BRAZIL.

DELHAES-GUENTHER (DIETRICH VON) Industrialisierung in Südbrasilien: die deutsche Einwanderung und die Anfänge der Industrialisierung in Rio Grande do Sul. Köln, 1973. pp. 346. *bibliog. With summaries in various languages.*

GERMANS IN CZECHOSLOVAKIA.

BITTNER (KONRAD) Deutsche und Tschechen: eine Erwiderung [to criticisms of the author's work entitled Deutsche und Tschechen: zur Geistesgeschichte des böhmischen Raumes]. Brünn, [1938]. pp. 20.

MUEHLBERGER (JOSEF) Zwei Völker in Böhmen: Beitrag zu einer nationalen, historischen und geistesgeschichtlichen Strukturanalyse. München, 1973. pp. 302. *bibliog.*

BACHSTEIN (MARTIN K.) Wenzel Jaksch und die sudetendeutsche Sozialdemokratie. München, 1974. pp. 306. *bibliog. (Ludwigshafen. Collegium Carolinum. Veröffentlichungen. Band 29)*

GERMANS IN FRANCE.

SCHAUL (DORA) ed. Résistance: Erinnerungen deutscher Antifaschisten; by] Otto Niebergall [and others]. Frankfurt/Main, 1973. pp. 477.

GRANDJONC (JACQUES) Marx et les communistes allemands à Paris, 1844: contribution à l'étude de la naissance du marxisme. Paris, 1974. pp. 264. *bibliog.*

GERMANS IN ITALY.

COLE (JOHN W.) and WOLF (ERIC ROBERT) The hidden frontier: ecology and ethnicity in an Alpine valley. New York, [1974]. pp. 348. *bibliog.*

GERMANS IN POLAND.

MEISSLER (WOLFGANG) Kirche unter dem Kreuz: Beiträge und Erinnerungen über 17 Jahre "hinter Oder und Neisse". Leer (Ostfriesland), [1971]. pp. 40. *bibliog.*

KREKELER (NORBERT) Revisionsanspruch und geheime Ostpolitik der Weimarer Republik: die Subventionierung der deutschen Minderheit in Polen. Stuttgart, [1973]. pp. 158. *bibliog. (Vierteljahrshefte für Zeitgeschichte. Schriftenreihe. Nr.27)*

GERMANS IN RUSSIA.

SHEEHY (ANN) The Crimean Tatars, Volga Germans and Meskhetians: Soviet treatment of some national minorities. new ed. London, 1973. pp. 36. *bibliog. (Minority Rights Group. Reports. No. 6)*

GERMANS IN THE BALTIC STATES.

LATVIISKII GOSUDARSTVENNYI UNIVERSITET. Uchenye Zapiski. t.185. Germaniia i Pribaltika. 2. Riga, 1973. pp. 99.

GERMANS IN THE UNITED KINGDOM.

RICHARDSON (DAVID) The Shotley Bridge swordmakers: their strange history. Newcastle upon Tyne, [1973]. pp. 66. *bibliog.*

GERMANS IN THE UNITED STATES.

DIAMOND (SANDER A.) The Nazi movement in the United States, 1924-1941. Ithaca, 1974. pp. 380. *bibliog.*

GERMANY

— **Air force.**

GALLAND (A.) and others. The Luftwaffe at war, 1939-1945;...English version edited by David Mondey. Chicago, 1973. pp. 247.

— **Appropriations and expenditures.**

GERMANY (BUNDESREPUBLIK). Statistisches Bundesamt. 1973. Ausgaben der öffentlichen Haushalte für soziale Sicherung 1970. Stuttgart, 1973. pp. 116. *(Finanzen und Steuern. Reihe 5. Sonderbeiträge zur Finanzstatistik)*

— **Armed forces.**

KEMPE (MARTIN) SPD und Bundeswehr: Studien zum militärisch-industriellen Komplex. Köln, [1973]. pp. 278.

— **Bibliography.**

PICHT (ROBERT) compiler. Kommentierte Bibliographie: Deutschland nach 1945. Bonn-Bad Godesberg, [1973?]. pp. 259. *(Deutscher Akademischer Austauschdienst. Deutschlandstudien. 1)*

— **Biography.**

INSTITUT FÜR MARXISMUS-LENINISMUS (BERLIN). Geschichte der deutschen Arbeiterbewegung: biographisches Lexikon; Redaktionskommission: R.Grau [and others]. Berlin, 1970. pp. 528.

— **Boundaries.**

MROHS (EDMUND) and HUEKELS (J.M.) Die Grenze: Trennung oder Begegnung: eine Untersuchung über die Bedeutung der Grenze und der Grenzverwischung im deutsch-niederländischen Grenzraum Achterhoek and Borken/Bocholt. 's-Gravenhage, Staatsuitgeverij, 1970. 2 pts. *In German and Dutch, with summaries in English and French.*

— **Bundestag.**

THAYSEN (UWE) Parlamentsreform in Theorie und Praxis:...eine empirische Analyse der Parlamentsreform im 5. Deutschen Bundestag. Opladen, 1972. pp. 324. *bibliog.*

VEEN (HANS JOACHIM) Die CDU/CSU-Opposition im parlamentarischen Entscheidungsprozess: zur Strategie und zum Einfluss ... in der Gesetzgebungsarbeit des 6.Deutschen Bundestages, 1969-1972. München, 1973. pp. 119. *bibliog.*

LIESEGANG (HELMUTH C.F.) ed. Parlamentsreform in der Bundesrepublik Deutschland: Dokumente zur Reform von Aufgabe und Arbeit des Parlaments, etc. Berlin, 1974. pp. 162. *bibliog.*

— — **Committees.**

GERMANY (BUNDESREPUBLIK). Deutscher Bundestag. Wissenschaftliche Dienste. 1973. Die Ausschüsse des Deutschen Bundestages, 1. - 7. Wahlperiode: systematisches Verzeichnis nach Wahlperioden und alphabetisches Gesamtverzeichnis, Stand 1. Juni 1973. Bonn, 1973. pp. 159. *(Materialien. 33)*

— — **Elections.**

BERTSCH (HERBERT) Wer sitzt im Bonner Bundestag?: eine dokumentarische Analyse der Bundestagswahlen, 1961. Berlin, [1961 repr. 1962]. pp. 127.

MUENSTER IN WESTFALEN. Westfälische Wilhems-Universität. Institut für Politikwissenschaft. Wahl '72: Parteien, Programme, Wahlverfahren, Wähler; ([by] Wichard Woyke [and others]). Opladen, 1972. pp. 126.

DIALOG: Magazin für Politik, Wirtschaft und Kultur. Wahlkampf '72: Fakten und Zahlen. Bonn, 1973. pp. 203.

HESSE. Statistisches Landesamt. Beiträge zur Statistik Hessens. Neue Folge. Nr. 53. Die Wahl zum siebten Deutschen Bundestag in Hessen am 19. November 1972. Wiesbaden, 1973. pp. 137.

KALTEFLEITER (WERNER) Zwischen Konsens und Krise: eine Analyse der Bundestagswahl, 1972. Köln, 1973. pp. 209. *bibliog. (Verfassung und Verfassungswirklichkeit. Band 7. Jahrbuch 1973, Teil 1)*

RICHTER (JOERG) 1941- , ed. Klassenkampf von oben?; oder, Angstmacher von rechts: Dokumente und Analysen eines gescheiterten Wahlkampfes. Reinbek bei Hamburg, 1973. pp. 206.

SOZIALDEMOKRATISCHE PARTEI DEUTSCHLANDS. Vorstand. Dokumentation über die Werbekampagnen der CDU/CSU und der CDU/CSU-Hilfsorganisationen im Bundestagswahlkampf 1972. Bonn, 1973. pp. 228. *Diagram in end pocket.*

WAHLKAMPF als Ritual?: Studien zur Bundestagswahl von 1969 im Wahlkreis Heidelberg-Mannheim/Land; ([by] Rüdiger Andel [and others]; edited by Peter Haungs). Meisenheim am Glan, 1974. pp. 336.

WAHLKAMPF und Parteiorganisation: eine Regionalstudie zum Bundestagswahlkampf, 1969; ([by] Klaus von Beyme [and others]). *Tübingen, 1974. pp. 314.*

— **Civilization.**

KATER (MICHAEL H.) Das "Ahnenerbe" der SS, 1935-1945: ein Beitrag zur Kulturpolitik des Dritten Reiches. Stuttgart, 1974. pp. 523. *bibliog. (Institut für Zeitgeschichte. Studien zur Zeitgeschichte)*

— **Commerce.**

GERMANY (BUNDESREPUBLIK). Statistisches Bundesamt. Aussenhandel mit den Entwicklungsländern: Spezialhandel. a., 1972- Wiesbaden. *(Aussenhandel. Reihe 7. Sonderbeiträge)*

MUELLER-HILLEBRAND (VEIT) Das Vordringen der japanischen Konkurrenz auf den Weltmärkten im Vergleich zum deutschen Export. Nürnberg, 1972. pp. 337, xxii. *(Erlangen. Universität. Institut für Exportforschung. Berichte)*

OTZEN (HANS) Der Agrarexport der Bundesrepublik Deutschland. Hamburg, 1974. pp. 115. *bibliog.*

— — **European Free Trade Association countries.**

DEUTSCHE HANDELSKAMMER IN OESTERREICH, WIEN, and others. Die Entwicklung der deutschen Marktanteile im Rahmen der Einfuhr der neutralen EFTA-Länder Oesterreich, Schweden, Schweiz im Zeitraum 1960 bis 1968. [Zurich, imprint, 1969]. pp. 71.

— — **Germany, Eastern.**

SCHARPE (PETER) Europäische Wirtschaftsgemeinschaft und Deutsche Demokratische Republik: die Entwicklung ihrer Rechtsbeziehungen seit 1958 unter besonderer Berücksichtigung des innerdeutschen Handels. Tübingen, 1973. pp. 194. *bibliog. (Tübingen. Universität. Rechts- und Wirtschaftswissenschaftliche Fakultät. Rechtswissenschaftliche Abteilung. Juristische Studien. Band 50)*

— — **Netherlands.**

ROEHLK (FRAUKE) Schiffahrt und Handel zwischen Hamburg und den Niederlanden in der zweiten Hälfte des 18. und zu Beginn des 19. Jahrhunderts.Wiesbaden, 1973. 2 vols. (in 1). *bibliog. (Vierteljahrschrift für Sozial- und Wirtschaftsgeschichte. Beihefte. Nr.60) Table in end pocket.*

— — **Sweden.**

FRITZ (MARTIN) German steel and Swedish iron ore, 1939-1945. Göteborg, 1974. pp. 137. *bibliog. (Göteborgs Universitet. Ekonomisk-Historiska Institutionen. Meddelanden. 29)*

— **Commercial policy.**

PROTEKTION und Branchenstruktur der westdeutschen Wirtschaft; ([by] Juergen B. Donges [and others]). Tübingen, 1973. pp. 393. *bibliog. (Kiel. Universität. Institut für Weltwirtschaft. Kieler Studien. 123)*

— **Constitution.**

KROEGER (KLAUS) Widerstandsrecht und demokratische Verfassung. Tübingen, 1971. pp. 23.

GERIGK (ALFRED) Der Staat, mit dem wir leben. Freiburg im Breisgau, [1972]. pp. 334. *bibliog.*

GERMANY (BUNDESREPUBLIK). Deutscher Bundestag. Wissenschaftliche Dienste. 1973. Die Änderungen des Grundgesetzes, Nr.1 bis 31, mit Übersichtstabelle nach Artikeln, Änderungsgesetzen und kurzen Inhaltsangaben: Stand 27.Febr. 1973. Bonn, 1973. pp. 127. *(Materialien. 31)*

KARSCH (FRIEDERUN CHRISTA) Demokratie und Gewaltenteilung: zur Problematik der Verfassungsinterpretation in der BRD. Köln, [1973]. pp. 125. *bibliog. (Zeitschrift Demokratie und Recht. Beihefte. 3)*

LIESEGANG (HELMUTH C.F.) ed. Parlamentsreform in der Bundesrepublik Deutschland: Dokumente zur Reform von Aufgabe und Arbeit des Parlaments, etc. Berlin, 1974. pp. 162. *bibliog.*

— — **Bibliography.**

GERMANY (BUNDESREPUBLIK). Deutscher Bundestag. Wissenschaftliche Dienste. 1974. Verfassungsreform: zur Revision des Grundgesetzes für die Bundesrepublik Deutschland vom 23.Mai 1949: Auswahlbibliographie mit Annotationen. Bonn, 1974. pp. 43. *(Bibliographien. 36)*

— **Constitutional history.**

PORTNER (ERNST) Die Verfassungspolitik der Liberalen, 1919: ein Beitrag zur Deutung der Weimarer Reichsverfassung. Bonn, 1973. pp. 278. *bibliog.*

STEHLIN (STEWART A.) Bismarck and the Guelph problem 1866-1890: a study in particularist opposition to national unity. The Hague, 1973. pp. 253. *bibliog.*

STORBECK (ANNA CHRISTINE) Die Regierungen des Bundes und der Länder seit 1945: Ergänzungsband, 1969 bis 1973; bearbeitet von Jürgen Jekewitz. München, [1973]. pp. 281.

NICLAUSS (KARLHEINZ) Demokratiegründung in Westdeutschland: die Entstehung der Bundesrepublik, 1945-1949. München, [1974]. pp. 285. *bibliog.*

— **Constitutional law.**

BERNSTEIN (HERBERT) and ZWEIGERT (KONRAD) Die Rehabilitierung einer aufgelösten politischen Partei: verfassungsrechtliche und prozessuale Betrachtungen. Tübingen, 1972. pp. 34.

ZEITLER (ADOLF FRANZ) Streikrecht und grundgesetz. [Ausburg, imprint, 1973]. pp. 170. *bibliog.*

LEISNER (WALTER) Zur Abgrenzung von gesetzlicher und privater Krankenversicherung: eine verfassungsrechtliche Untersuchung. Köln, 1974. pp. 57. *(Verband der Privaten Krankenversicherung. Dokumentationen. 3)*

— **Defences.**

BERGHAHN (VOLKER R.) Rüstung und Machtpolitik: zur Anatomie des "Kalten Krieges" vor 1914. Düsseldorf, [1973]. pp. 94.

ENGELHARDT (KLAUS) and HEISE (KARL HEINZ) Militär-Industrie-Komplex im staatsmonopolistischen Herrschaftssystem. Berlin, 1974. pp. 304.

HAFTENDORN (HELGA) Abrüstungs- und Entspannungspolitik zwischen Sicherheitsbefriedigung und Friedenssicherung: zur Aussenpolitik der BRD, 1955-1973. Düsseldorf, [1974]. pp. 536. *bibliog.*

— **Economic conditions.**

Das BRUTTOINLANDSPRODUKT der kreisfreien Städte und Landkreise 1961, 1968 und 1970. [Stuttgart]. Gemeinschaftsveröffentlichung der Statistischen Landesämter, 1973. pp. 163, 3 maps. *(Volkswirtschaftliche Gesamtrechnungen der Länder. Heft 4)*

BURTENSHAW (DAVID) Economic geography of West Germany. London, 1974. pp. 247. *bibliog.*

GERMANY. (Cont.)

— — Mathematical models.

STAEGLIN (REINER) and WESSELS (HANS) Input-Output-Rechnung für die Bundesrepublik Deutschland, 1954, 1958, 1962, 1966. Berlin, 1973. pp. 169. *(Deutsches Institut für Wirtschaftsforschung. DIW-Beiträge zur Strukturforschung. Heft 27) With summaries in English and French.*

— Economic history.

NEELSEN (KARL) Wirtschaftsgeschichte der BRD: ein Grundriss. Berlin, 1971. pp. 318.

FISCHER (WOLFRAM) Wirtschaft und Gesellschaft im Zeitalter der Industrialisierung: Aufsätze, Studien, Vorträge. Göttingen, 1972. pp. 547.

BILLIG (JOSEPH) Les camps de concentration dans l'économie du Reich hitlérien. Paris, 1973. pp. 346. *bibliog.*

GUERIN (DANIEL) Fascism and big business; (translated from the French). New York, 1973. pp. 318.

HENNING (FRIEDRICH WILHELM) Die Industrialisierung in Deutschland 1800 bis 1914. Paderborn, [1973]. pp. 304. *bibliog.*

MAURER (ILSE) Reichsfinanzen und Grosse Koalition: zur Geschichte des Reichskabinetts Müller, 1928-1930. Bern, 1973. pp. 269. *bibliog.*

HENNING (FRIEDRICH WILHELM) Das industrialisierte Deutschland, 1914 bis 1972. Paderborn, [1974]. pp. 292. *bibliog.*

— — Historiography.

HENNIG (EIKE) Thesen zur deutschen Sozial- und Wirtschaftsgeschichte, 1933 bis 1938. Frankfurt am Main, 1973. pp. 264. *bibliog.*

— — Mathematical models.

ZAHN (PETER) Economist. Die Phillips-Relation für Deutschland: eine lohn- und inflationstheoretische Untersuchung. Berlin, 1973. pp. 259. *bibliog.*

— Economic policy.

VARGA (JENŐ) Der deutsche Imperialismus: die historischen Wurzeln seiner Besonderheiten; ([reprint of work originally published in 1946 by the] sowjetische Militärverwaltung in Deutschland). Berlin, 1970. pp. 45.

DUEREN (ALBRECHT) Anpassungsprobleme strukturschwacher Branchen und Regionen in der Bundesrepublik. Tübingen, 1972. pp. 25. *(Kiel. Universität. Institut fe ür Weltwirtschaft. Kieler Vorträge. Neue Folge. 71)*

FRIEDRICH (OTTO ANDREAS) and BARZEL (RAINER) Soziale Marktwirtschaft: Grundlage der Freiheit. Bonn, [1972]. pp. 19. *(Christlich-Demokratische Union Deutschlands. Wirtschaftsrat. Information. 6)*

ARNDT (ERICH) Währungsstabilität und Lohnpolitik: über die wirtschaftlichen und sozialen Folgen von Inflationen. Tübingen, 1973. pp. 60. *With summaries in various languages.*

BLAICH (FRITZ) Kartell- und Monopolpolitik im kaiserlichen Deutschland: das Problem der Marktmacht im deutschen Reichstag zwischen 1879 und 1914. Düsseldorf, [1973]. pp. 329. *bibliog. (Germany (Bundesrepublik). Kommission für Geschichte des Parlamentarismus und der Politischen Parteien. Beiträge zur Geschichte des Parlamentarismus und der Politischen Parteien. Band 50)*

BLUMENBERG-LAMPE (CHRISTINE) Das wirtschaftspolitische Programm der "Freiburger Kreise": Entwurf einer freiheitlich-sozialen Nachkriegswirtschaft; Nationalökonomen gegen den Nationalsozialismus. Berlin, [1973]. pp. 180. *bibliog.*

CALLIES (HANS ULRICH) Der Einfluss von Entwicklungshilfeleistungen auf den Konjunkturverlauf und die Beschäftigung im Geberland, unter besonderer Berücksichtigung der BRD. Tübingen, [1973]. pp. 295. *bibliog. (Bochum. Ruhr-Universität. Institut für Entwicklungsforschung und Entwicklungspolitik. Bochumer Schriften zur Entwicklungsforschung und Entwicklungspolitik. Band 15)*

TUCHTFELDT (EGON) ed. Soziale Marktwirtschaft im Wandel. Freiburg im Breisgau, 1973. pp. 256.

PROLETARIAT in der BRD: Reproduktion, Organisation, Aktion; ([by] Martin Anders [and others]). Berlin, 1974. pp. 633.

MUELLER (KLAUS O.W.) Neokeynesianismus: kritische Untersuchung einer modernen staatsmonopolkapitalistischen Wirtschaftslehre. 2nd ed. Westberlin, 1974. pp. 260.

SCHMIDT (WERNER) Dipl.-Kfm., Dipl.-Vw., Dr. Der Wandel der Unternehmerfunktionen in der Bundesrepublik Deutschland unter dem Einfluss der Konzertierten Aktion. Berlin, [1974]. pp. 138. *bibliog.*

STRUFF (RICHARD) Dimensionen der wirtschaftsräumlichen Entwicklung: Abgrenzung von Gebietstypen zur regionalen und sektoralen Einkommensanalyse in der Bundesrepublik Deutschland. Bonn, 1973. pp. 279. *bibliog. (Forschungsgesellschaft für Agrarpolitik und Agrarsoziologie. [Publications]. 218)*

— Emigration and immigration.

GELBERG (BIRGIT) Auswanderung nach Übersee: soziale Probleme der Auswandererbeförderung in Hamburg und Bremen von der Mitte des 19. Jahrhunderts bis zum Ersten Weltkrieg. Hamburg, 1973. pp. 67. *bibliog. (Verein für Hamburgische Geschichte. Beiträge zur Geschichte Hamburgs. Band 10)*

MARSCHALCK (PETER) Deutsche Überseewanderung im 19. Jahrhundert: ein Beitrag zur soziologischen Theorie der Bevölkerung. Stuttgart, [1973]. pp. 128. *bibliog. (Arbeitskreis für Moderne Sozialgeschichte. Industrielle Welt. Band 14)*

— Executive departments.

HUETTNER (KARL) Das Statistische Bundesamt. Bonn, [1972]. pp. 215.

RUESS (GISELA) Anatomie einer politischen Verwaltung: das Bundesministerium für gesamtdeutsche Fragen; innerdeutsche Beziehungen, 1949- 1970. München, [1973]. pp. 205. *bibliog. (Munich. Universität. Geschwister-Scholl- Institut für Politische Wissenschaft. Münchener Studien zur Politik. 23.Band)*

— Foreign economic relations.

CHODOROWSKI (JERZY) Niemiecka doktryna gospodarki wielkiego obszaru: Grossraumwirtschaft, 1800-1945. Wrocław, 1972. pp. 423. *bibliog. With Russian, English and German summaries.*

— — Europe.

FREYMOND (JEAN) Le IIIe Reich et la réorganisation économique de l'Europe, 1940-1942: origines et projets. Leiden, 1974. pp. 302. *bibliog. (Geneva. Graduate Institute of International Studies. Collection de Relations Internationales.3)*

— India.

DAGLI (VADILAL) ed. India and Germany: a survey of economic relations. Bombay, 1970. pp. 232. *bibliog. (Commerce. Commerce Economic Studies. 6)*

— Foreign opinion.

KRUEGER (ARND) Die Olympischen Spiele 1936 und die Weltmeinung: ihre aussenpolitische Bedeutung, unter besonderer Berücksichtigung der USA. Berlin, [1972]. pp. 255. *bibliog.*

— Foreign relations.

KRAUSE (FRITZ) Writer on politics. Antimilitaristische Opposition in der BRD, 1949-55. Frankfurt am Main, [1971]. pp. 185.

SCHMID (CARLO) Gesammelte Werke in Einzelausgaben. Bern, 1973 in progress. *bibliogs.*

BISCHOFF (DETLEF) Franz Josef Strauss, die CSU und die Uussenpolitik: Konzeption und Realität am Beispiel der Grossen Koalition. Meisenheim am Glan ,1973. pp. 346. bibliog.

BRANDT (WILLY) Reden und Interviews, Herbst 1971 bis Frühjahr 1973. Hamburg, 1973. pp. 365.

BRAUNMUEHL (CLAUDIA VON) Kalter Krieg und friedliche Koexistenz: die Aussenpolitik der SPD in der Grossen Koalition. Frankfurt am Main, 1973. pp. 161.

DEUTSCHLAND in der Weltpolitik des 19. und 20.Jahrhunderts: (Fritz Fischer zum 65.Geburtstag; [edited by] Imanuel Geiss [and] Bernd Jürgen Wendt). Düsseldorf, [1973]. pp. 594. *bibliog. In various languages.*

GERLACH (HELLMUT VON) Ein Demokrat kommentiert Weimar: die Berichte...an die Carnegie-Friedensstiftung in New York, 1922-1930; herausgegeben...von Karl Holl und Adolf Wild. Bremen, [1973]. pp. 268. *bibliog.*

HILDEBRAND (KLAUS) The foreign policy of the Third Reich;... translated [from the German] by Anthony Fothergill. London, 1973. pp. 209. *bibliog.*

LUDZ (PETER CHRISTIAN) Two Germanys in one world. Farnborough, [1973]. pp. 64. *(Atlantic Institute. Atlantic Papers. 1973. 3)*

POST (GAINES) The civil-military fabric of Weimar foreign policy. Princeton, [1973]. pp. 398. *bibliog.*

ROTH (REINHOLD) Parteiensystem und Aussenpolitik: zur Bedeutung des Parteiensystems für den aussenpolitischen Entscheidungsprozess in der BRD. Meisenheim am Glan, 1973. pp. 159. *bibliog.*

WOLLSTEIN (GUENTER) Vom Weimarer Revisionismus zu Hitler: das Deutsche Reich und die Grossmächte in der Anfangsphase der nationalsozialistischen Herrschaft in Deutschland. Bonn, [1973]. pp. 325. *bibliog.*

HAFTENDORN (HELGA) Abrüstungs- und Entspannungspolitik zwischen Sicherheitsbefriedigung und Friedenssicherung: zur Aussenpolitik der BRD, 1955-1973. Düsseldorf, [1974]. pp. 536. *bibliog.*

WALLER (BRUCE) Bismarck at the crossroads: the reorientation of German foreign policy after the Congress of Berlin, 1878-1880. London, 1974. pp. 273. *bibliog.*

See also EUROPEAN ECONOMIC COMMUNITY — Germany; UNITED NATIONS — Germany.

— — Treaties.

GERMANY (BUNDESREPUBLIK). Treaties. 1972. Treaty between the German Democratic Republic and the Federal Republic of Germany on questions relating to traffic. Dresden, [1972]. pp. 29.

FREIE DEMOKRATISCHE PARTEI. F.D.P. zum Grundvertrag: Beiträge und Dokumentation. Bonn, 1973. pp. 40.

GELBERG (LUDWIK) Układ PRL-NRF z 7 grudnia 1970 r.: analiza prawna. Wrocław, 1974. pp. 124. *bibliog. With Russian, English and German tables of contents.*

— — Europe, Eastern.

STEWART-SMITH (DUDLEY GEOFFREY) ed. Brandt and the destruction of NATO: [a collection of articles, two of which were previously published in Osteuropa, and Orbis].Richmond, Surrey, 1973. pp. 101.

KUPER (ERNST) Frieden durch Konfrontation und Kooperation: die Einstellung von Gerhard Schröder und Willi [sic] Brandt zur Entspannungspolitik. Stuttgart, 1974. pp. 534. *bibliog. (Hamburg. Hansische Universität. Seminar für Sozialwissenschaften. Sozialwissenschaftliche Studien. Heft 14)*

— — Finland.

MENGER (MANFRED) Die Finnlandpolitik des deutschen Imperialismus, 1917-1918. Berlin, 1974. pp. 242. *bibliog. (Akademie der Wissenschaften der DDR. Zentralinstitut für Geschichte. Schriften. Band 38)*

GERMANY. (Cont.)

— — Germany, Eastern.

GERMANY (BUNDESREPUBLIK). Bundesministerium für Innerdeutsche Beziehungen. 1973. Die Entwicklung der Beziehungen zwischen der Bundesrepublik Deutschland und der Deutschen Demokratischen Republik: Bericht und Dokumentation. [Bonn], 1973. pp. 154.

— — Poland.

RACHOCKI (JANUSZ) ed. Polska - NRF: przesłanki i proces normalizacji stosunków, etc. Poznań, 1972. pp. 435. (Poznań. Instytut Zachodni. Studia Niemcoznawcze. Nr. 21)

KELLERMANN (VOLKMAR) Brücken nach Polen: die deutsch-polnischen Beziehungen und die Weltmächte 1939-1973. Stuttgart, [1973]. pp. 227. bibliog.

KREKELER (NORBERT) Revisionsanspruch und geheime Ostpolitik der Weimarer Republik: die Subventionierung der deutschen Minderheit in Polen. Stuttgart, [1973]. pp. 158. bibliog. (Vierteljahrshefte für Zeitgeschichte. Schriftenreihe. Nr. 27)

— — Spain.

PROCTOR (RAYMOND) Agonia de un neutral: las relaciones hispanoalemanas durante la segunda guerra mundial y la Division Azul. [Madrid, 1972]. pp. 354. bibliog.

ABENDROTH (HANS HENNING) Hitler in der spanischen Arena: die deutsch-spanischen Beziehungen...1936-1939. Paderborn, [1973]. pp. 411. bibliog.

— — Switzerland.

BOURGEOIS (DANIEL) Le troisième Reich et la Suisse, 1933-41. Neuchatel, [1974]. pp. 463. bibliog.

— — United Kingdom.

GILBERT (MARTIN) and GOTT (RICHARD) The appeasers. [2nd ed.] London, 1967. pp. 444. bibliog.

BOADLE (DONALD GRAEME) Winston Churchill and the German question in British foreign policy, 1918-1922. The Hague, 1973. pp. 193. bibliog.

— History — Historiography.

HALLMANN (HANS) ed. Revision des Bismarckbildes: die Diskussion der deutschen Fachhistoriker, 1945-1955. Darmstadt, 1972. pp. 493.

— — Sources.

GERMANY. Reichskanzlei. 1921-1922. Die Kabinette Wirth I und II: 10. Mai 1921 bis 26. Oktober 1921, 26. Oktober 1921 bis 22. November 1922; bearbeitet von Ingrid Schulze-Bidlingmaier. Boppard am Rhein, 1973. 2 vols. (Akten der Reichskanzlei, Weimarer Republik)

MEYER (HENRY CORD) ed. Germany from empire to ruin, 1913-1945. London, 1973. pp. 359. bibliog.

VEREINIGUNG DER DEUTSCHEN PARLAMENTSDIREKTOREN. Parlamentspraxis in der Weimarer Republik: die Tagungsberichte der Vereinigung der deutschen Parlamentsdirektoren, 1925 bis 1933; bearbeitet von Martin Schumacher. Düsseldorf, [1974]. pp. 272. bibliog. (Germany (Bundesrepublik). Quellen zur Geschichte des Parlamentarismus und der Politischen Parteien. 3. Reihe. Band 2)

— — 843—1273.

HAMPE (KARL) Germany under the Salian and Hohenstaufen emperors; translated (from the twelfth German edition) with an introduction by Ralph Bennett. Oxford, 1973. pp. 315.

— — 1517—1871.

BENECKE (G.) Society and politics in Germany, 1500-1750. London, 1974. pp. 436. bibliog.

— — 1789—1900.

DEUTSCHLAND in der Weltpolitik des 19. und 20. Jahrhunderts: (Fritz Fischer zum 65. Geburtstag; [edited by] Imanuel Geiss [and] Bernd Jürgen Wendt). Düsseldorf, [1973]. pp. 594. bibliog. In various languages.

— — 1848—1849, Revolution.

BIEBUSCH (WERNER) Revolution und Staatsstreich: Verfassungskämpfe in Bremen von 1848 bis 1854. Bremen, 1973. pp. 391. bibliog. (Bremen. Staatsarchiv. Veröffentlichungen. Band 40)

— — 1871— .

UPHEAVAL and continuity: a century of German history: [including lectures delivered at the London School of Economics and University College, London, 1971-2]; edited by E.J. Feuchtwanger. London, [1973]. pp. 192. bibliog.

— — 1900— .

DEUTSCHLAND in der Weltpolitik des 19. und 20. Jahrhunderts: (Fritz Fischer zum 65. Geburtstag; [edited by] Imanuel Geiss [and] Bernd Jürgen Wendt). Düsseldorf, [1973]. pp. 594. bibliog. In various languages.

MEYER (HENRY CORD) ed. Germany from empire to ruin, 1913-1945. London, 1973. pp. 359. bibliog.

— — 1918—1933.

MAURER (ILSE) Reichsfinanzen und Grosse Koalition: zur Geschichte des Reichskabinetts Müller, 1928-1930. Bern, 1973. pp. 269. bibliog.

— — 1918—1929, Allied Occupation.

RENIER (HENRI) Die Wahrheit über die Ruhrbesetzung. Berlin, 1923. pp. 40. RUHR -- Politics and government. 1923.

— — 1918—1919, Revolution.

RETZLAW (KARL) Spartakus: Aufstieg und Niedergang; Erinnerungen eines Parteiarbeiters. 2nd ed. Frankfurt, 1972. pp. 511.

TEUBER (HEINRICH) Für die Sozialisierung des Ruhrbergbaus: [new ed. of series of articles originally published in 1926]; herausgegeben von Hellmut G. Haasis und Erhard Lucas. Frankfurt, [1973]. pp. 131.

— — 1920, Kapp Putsch.

LUCAS (ERHARD) Märzrevolution 1920: der bewaffnete Arbeiteraufstand im Ruhrgebiet in seiner inneren Struktur und in seinem Verhältnis zu den Klassenkämpfen in den verschiedenen Regionen des Reiches. Frankfurt am Main, [1973]. pp. 251. bibliog.

TEUBER (HEINRICH) Für die Sozialisierung des Ruhrbergbaus: [new ed. of series of articles originally published in 1926]; herausgegeben von Hellmut G. Haasis und Erhard Lucas. Frankfurt, [1973]. pp. 131.

ELIASBERG (GEORGE) Der Ruhrkrieg von 1920; mit einer Einführung von Richard Löwenthal. Bonn-Bad Godesberg, [1974]. pp. 304. bibliog. (Friedrich-Ebert-Stiftung. Forschungsinstitut. Schriftenreihe. Band 100)

— — 1933—1945.

EMMERSON (JAMES THOMAS) The German reoccupation of the Rhineland: a study in multilateral diplomacy, March 1935 to October 1936; [Ph.D. (London) thesis]. [1974]. fo. 383. bibliog. Typescript: unpublished. This thesis is the property of London University and may not be removed from the Library.

— — 1944—1955, Allied occupation.

LATOUR (CONRAD F.) and VOGELSANG (THILO) Okkupation und Wiederaufbau: die Tätigkeit der Militärregierung in der amerikanischen Besatzungszone Deutschlands, 1944-1947. Stuttgart, 1973. pp. 227. bibliog. (Institut für Zeitgeschichte. Studien zur Zeitgeschichte)

— — 1945— .

LOEWENTHAL (RICHARD) and SCHWARZ (HANS PETER) eds. Die zweite Republik: 25 Jahre Bundesrepublik Deutschland; eine Bilanz; ([by] Hans-Peter Schwarz [and others]). Stuttgart, [1974]. pp. 970. bibliog.

— History, Military.

FISCHER (KURT) Historian. Deutsche Truppen und Entente-Intervention in Südrussland 1918-19. Boppard am Rhein, 1973. pp. 160. bibliog. (Militärgeschichtliches Forschungsamt. Militärgeschichtliche Studien. 16)

— Industries.

STAEGLIN (REINER) Input-Output-Rechnung; Aufstellung von Input-Output- Tabellen; konzeptionelle und empirisch-statistische Probleme. Berlin, 1968. pp. 104. bibliog. (Deutsches Institut für Wirtschaftsforschung. Beiträge zur Strukturforschung. Heft 4)

PROTEKTION und Branchenstruktur der westdeutschen Wirtschaft; ([by] Juergen B. Donges [and others]). Tübingen, 1973. pp. 393. bibliog. (Kiel. Universität. Institut für Weltwirtschaft. Kieler Studien. 123)

VOGL (FRANK) German business after the economic miracle. London, 1973. pp. 264.

— — Statistics.

BECKERMANN (THEO) Das Handwerk im Wachstum der Wirtschaft: eine statistische Analyse. Berlin, [1974]. pp. 141. (Rheinisch-Westfälisches Institut für Wirtschaftsforschung, Essen. Schriftenreihe. Neue Folge. 34)

— Kings and rulers.

HAMPE (KARL) Germany under the Salian and Hohenstaufen emperors; translated (from the twelfth German edition) with an introduction by Ralph Bennett. Oxford, 1973. pp. 315.

— Military policy.

POST (GAINES) The civil-military fabric of Weimar foreign policy. Princeton, [1973]. pp. 398. bibliog.

— Militia.

NUSSER (HORST G.W.) Konservative Wehrverbände in Bayern, Preussen und Österreich, 1918-1933; mit einer Biographie von Forstrat Georg Escherich, 1870-1941. München, [1973]. 2 vols.

— Moral conditions.

BLEUEL (HANS PETER) Strength through joy: sex and society in Nazi Germany; edited... by Heinrich Fraenkel: translated from the German by J. Maxwell Brownjohn. London, 1973. pp. 272.

— Nationalism.

MOHLER (ARMIN FRIEDRICH ADOLF) Die Konservative Revolution in Deutschland, 1918-1932: ein Handbuch. 2nd ed. Darmstadt, 1972. pp. 554. bibliog. Classified subject bibliography on pp. 171-505.

— Navy — History.

BOEHM (EKKEHARD) Überseehandel und Flottenbau: hanseatische Kaufmannschaft und deutsche Seerüstung, 1879-1902. Düsseldorf, [1972]. pp. 417. bibliog. (Hamburg. Hansische Universität. Studien zur Modernen Geschichte. Band 8)

DUELFFER (JOST) Weimar, Hitler und die Marine: Reichspolitik und Flottenbau, 1920-1939. Düsseldorf, [1973]. pp. 615. bibliog.

HERWIG (HOLGER H.) The German naval officer corps: a social and political history, 1890-1918. Oxford, 1973. pp. 298. bibliog.

— — Officers.

HERWIG (HOLGER H.) The German naval officer corps: a social and political history, 1890-1918. Oxford, 1973. pp. 298. bibliog.

— **Officials and employees.**

GERMANY (BUNDESREPUBLIK). Deutscher Bundestag. Wissenschaftliche Dienste. 1973. Die Beamteten und die Parlamentarischen Staatssekretäre im Bund, 1949-1973. Bonn, 1973. pp. 23. *(Materialien. 30)*

— **Politics and government — Bibliography.**

GERMANY (BUNDESREPUBLIK). Deutscher Bundestag. Wissenschaftliche Dienste. 1972. Planung in Politik und Verwaltung in der Bundesrepublik Deutschland. Bonn, 1972. pp. 96. *(Bibliographien. 30)*

MOHLER (ARMIN FRIEDRICH ADOLF) Die Konservative Revolution in Deutschland, 1918-1932: ein Handbuch. 2nd ed. Darmstadt, 1972. pp. 554. *bibliog. Classified subject bibliography on pp. 171-505.*

— — **1517—1871.**

BENECKE (G.) Society and politics in Germany, 1500-1750. London, 1974. pp. 436. *bibliog.*

— — **1871—1918.**

BOEHTLINGK (ARTHUR) Die römische Gefahr und die Reichstagswahl: eine politische Ansprache, Lörrach, 26.April 1903. Lörrach, 1903. pp. 27.

GELLATELY (ROBERT JOHN) The politics of economic despair: shopkeepers and German politics, 1890-1914. London, [1974]. pp. 317. *bibliog.*

MOMMSEN (WOLFGANG JUSTIN) Max Weber und die deutsche Politik, 1890-1920. 2nd ed. Tübingen, 1974. pp. 586. *bibliog.*

— — **1918—1945.**

MOHLER (ARMIN FRIEDRICH ADOLF) Die Konservative Revolution in Deutschland, 1918-1932: ein Handbuch. 2nd ed. Darmstadt, 1972. pp. 554. *bibliog. Classified subject bibliography on pp. 171-505.*

GERLACH (HELLMUT VON) Ein Demokrat kommentiert Weimar: die Berichte...an die Carnegie-Friedensstiftung in New York, 1922-1930; herausgegeben...von Karl Holl und Adolf Wild. Bremen, [1973]. pp. 268. *bibliog.*

REICH (WILHELM) What is class consciousness?; [originally published in German in 1934 under the pseudonym of Ernst Parell]. 2nd ed. [London], 1973. pp. 76.

SOHN-RETHEL (ALFRED) Ökonomie und Klassenstruktur des deutschen Faschismus: Aufzeichnungen und Analysen; herausgegeben von Johannes Agnoli [and others]. Frankfurt am Main, 1973. pp. 210.

VON MALTITZ (HORST) The evolution of Hitler's Germany: the ideology, the personality, the moment. New York, [1973]. pp. 479. *bibliog.*

— — **1945— .**

FUER die Aktionseinheit der deutschen Arbeiterklasse, 1945- 1964; (Redaktionskollegium: Günter Benser [and others, for the] Institut für Marxismus-Leninismus beim ZK der SED). Berlin, 1965. pp. 443.

CHRISTLICH-DEMOKRATISCHE UNION DEUTSCHLANDS. Bundesgeschäftsstelle. Sozialdemokratische Legenden und die deutsche Wirklichkeit. Bonn, [1969]. pp. 30.

KRAUSE (FRITZ) Writer on politics. Antimilitaristische Opposition in der BRD, 1949-55. Frankfurt am Main, [1971]. pp. 185.

MANN (GOLO) Radikalisierung und Mitte: zwei Vorträge. Stuttgart, [1971]. pp. 48.

ROSSAINT (JOSEPH C.) Die aktuelle politische Lage in der Bundesrepublik Deutschland und die neonazistische Gefahr: Rede gehalten auf dem Kongress der V[ereinigungen der] V[erfolgten des] N[aziregimes in der Bundesrepublik Deutschland]... 1971. Wien, 1971. pp. 23.

GERIGK (ALFRED) Der Staat, mit dem wir leben. Freiburg im Breisgau, [1972]. pp. 334. *bibliog.*

SCHMID (CARLO) Gesammelte Werke in Einzelausgaben. Bern, 1973 in progress. *bibliogs.*

BRANDT (WILLY) Reden und Interviews, Herbst 1971 bis Frühjahr 1973. Hamburg, 1973. pp. 365.

HORCHEM (HANS JOSEF) West Germany: "the Long March through the institutions". London, 1973. pp. 20. *(Institute for the Study of Conflict. Conflict Studies. No. 33)*

JAEGGI (URS) Kapital und Arbeit in der Bundesrepublik: Elemente einer gesamtgesellschaftlichen Analyse. Frankfurt am Main, 1973. pp. 406. *bibliog.*

JOHNSON (NEVIL) Government in the Federal Republic of Germany: the executive at work. Oxford, 1973. pp. 218. *bibliog.*

REIMANN (MAX) Entscheidungen 1945-1956. Frankfurt am Main, 1973. pp. 227.

ROEDER (KARL HEINZ) and others. Widersprüche und Tendenzen im Herrschaftssystem der BRD: zu Problemen imperialistischer Herrschaftskonzeptionen und praktiken. Berlin, 1973. pp. 111.

STORBECK (ANNA CHRISTINE) Die Regierungen des Bundes und der Länder seit 1945: Ergänzungsband, 1969 bis 1973; bearbeitet von Jürgen Jekewitz. München, [1973]. pp. 281.

VEREINIGUNG DER VERFOLGTEN DES NAZIREGIMES. Kongress, 1973. Antifaschismus heute: gemeinsamer Kampf und Demokratisierung aller Gesellschaftsbereiche; Bericht über den Bundeskongress...in Hannover. Frankfurt am Main, 1973. pp. 192.

LIESEGANG (HELMUTH C.F.) ed. Parlamentsreform in der Bundesrepublik Deutschland: Dokumente zur Reform von Aufgabe und Arbeit des Parlaments, etc. Berlin, 1974. pp. 162. *bibliog.*

LOEWENTHAL (RICHARD) and SCHWARZ (HANS PETER) eds. Die zweite Republik: 25 Jahre Bundesrepublik Deutschland; eine Bilanz; ([by] Hans-Peter Schwarz [and others]).Stuttgart, [1974]. pp. 970. *bibliog.*

NICLAUSS (KARLHEINZ) Demokratiegründung in Westdeutschland: die Entstehung der Bundesrepublik, 1945-1949. München, [1974]. pp. 285. *bibliog.*

PORTISCH (HUGO) Die deutsche Konfrontation: Gegenwart und Zukunft der beiden deutschen Staaten. Wien, [1974]. pp. 351. *bibliog.*

— **Population.**

WIETING (ROLF G.) and HUEBSCHLE (JOERG) Struktur und Motive der Wanderungsbewegungen in der Bundesrepublik, unter besonderer Berücksichtigung der kleinräumigen Mobilität: Untersuchung der PROGNOS AG im Auftrag des Bundesministers des Innern. Basel, 1968. 1 vol. (various pagings).

GERMANY (BUNDESREPUBLIK). Statistisches Bundesamt. 1973. Wohnbevölkerung in den Postleiteinheiten und in ausgewählten administrativen Gebietseinheiten am 27.5.1970: Ergebnis der Volkszählung 1970. Stuttgart, 1973. pp. 99. *(Systematische Verzeichnisse)*

GRUENDEL (JOHANNES) ed. Sterbendes Volk?: Fakten, Ursachen, Konsequenzen des Geburtenrückganges in der Bundesrepublik;...mit Beiträgen von Hans-Ulrich Gallwas [and others; based on a conference held in 1972]. Düsseldorf, 1973. pp. 151. *(Katholische Akademie in Bayern. Schriften. Band 68)*

KNODEL (JOHN E.) The decline of fertility in Germany, 1871-1939. Princeton, N.J., [1974]. pp. 306. *bibliog.*

— **Presidents — Election.**

WAGNER (WOLFGANG) Die Bundespräsidentenwahl, 1959: (Adenauer-Studien, II; herausgegeben von Rudolf Morsey und Konrad Repgen). Mainz, [1972]. pp. 99. *bibliog. (Katholische Akademie in Bayern. Kommission für Zeitgeschichte. Veröffentlichungen. Reihe B: Forschungen. Band 13)*

GERMANY, EASTERN.

— **Relations (general) with Russia.**

VISHNIAKOV-VISHNEVETSKII (KONSTANTIN ANATOL'EVICH) V.I. Lenin i revoliutsionnye sviazi rossiiskogo i germanskogo proletariata, 1903-1910 gg. Leningrad, 1974. pp. 220.

— **Social conditions.**

JAEGGI (URS) Kapital und Arbeit in der Bundesrepublik: Elemente einer gesamtgesellschaftlichen Analyse. Frankfurt am Main, 1973. pp. 406. *bibliog.*

— **Social history.**

FISCHER (WOLFRAM) Wirtschaft und Gesellschaft im Zeitalter der Industrialisierung: Aufsätze, Studien, Vorträge. Göttingen, 1972. pp. 547.

ENGELSING (ROLF) Zur Sozialgeschichte deutscher Mittel- und Unterschichten. Göttingen, 1973. pp. 314.

KOCKA (JUERGEN) Klassengesellschaft im Krieg: deutsche Sozialgeschichte, 1914- 1918. Göttingen, 1973. pp. 230. *bibliog.*

— — **Historiography.**

HENNIG (EIKE) Thesen zur deutschen Sozial- und Wirtschaftsgeschichte, 1933 bis 1938. Frankfurt am Main, 1973. pp. 264. *bibliog.*

— **Social policy.**

METZE (INGOLF) Soziale Sicherung und Einkommensverteilung: eine empirische Untersuchung über die Wirkungen ... auf die verfügbaren Einkommen der privaten Haushalte. Berlin, [1974]. pp. 170.

— **Statistics.**

HUETTNER (KARL) Das Statistische Bundesamt. Bonn, [1972]. pp. 215.

NIMMERGUT (JOERG) Deutschland in Zahlen: Ausgabe 1974; (Daten, Fakten, Trends). München, [1973]. pp. 176. *bibliog.*

GERMANY, EASTERN.

PANORAMA DDR. 100 questions, 100 answers: GDR; (translated by Intertext Berlin). Berlin, [1974]. pp. 144.

— **Armed forces — Political activity.**

HERSPRING (DALE ROY) East German civil-military relations: the impact of technology, 1949-72. New York, 1973. pp. 216. *bibliog.*

— **Army.**

HERSPRING (DALE ROY) East German civil-military relations: the impact of technology, 1949-72. New York, 1973. pp. 216. *bibliog.*

— **Biography.**

BUCH (GUENTHER) Namen und Daten: Biographien wichtiger Personen der DDR. Berlin, [1973]. pp. 332.

— **Commerce.**

ILLGEN (KONRAD) Geographie und territoriale Organisation des Binnenhandels: eine Einführung. Gotha, [1970]. pp. 191. *bibliog.*

— — **Germany.**

SCHARPE (PETER) Europäische Wirtschaftsgemeinschaft und Deutsche Demokratische Republik: die Entwicklung ihrer Rechtsbeziehungen seit 1958 unter besonderer Berücksichtigung des innerdeutschen Handels. Tübingen, 1973. pp. 194. *bibliog. (Tübingen. Universität. Rechts- und Wirtschaftswissenschaftliche Fakultät. Rechtswissenschaftliche Abteilung. Juristische Studien. Band 50)*

— **Commercial policy.**

GROTE (GERHARD) ed. Planung der Aussenwirtschaft in der DDR;...(Autoren: Klaus Apel [and others]). Berlin, 1973. pp. 160.

GERMANY EASTERN. (Cont.)

AUSSENWIRTSCHAFTLICHE Tätigkeit in Produktions- und Aussenhandelsbetrieben: Grundlagen, Erfahrungen, Probleme; ([by] Walter Kupferschmidt [and others]); ... unter Leitung von Christa Luft. Berlin, [1974]. pp. 192. *bibliog.*

— Constitution.

GERIGK (ALFRED) Der Staat, mit dem wir leben. Freiburg im Breisgau, [1972]. pp. 334. *bibliog.*

CHARVIN (ROBERT) La République démocratique allemande (R.D.A.). Paris, [1973]. pp. 389.

— Economic conditions.

ARNOLD (KARL HEINZ) The national economy under socialist conditions: objectives and results in the GDR. Berlin, 1974. pp. 62.

— Economic policy.

DAMUS (RENATE) Entscheidungsstrukturen und Funktionsprobleme in der DDR-Wirtschaft. Frankfurt am Main, 1973. pp. 232.

Die MATERIALWIRTSCHAFT der Deutschen Demokratischen Republik; [by an] Autorenkollektiv unter Leitung von Carl-Jürgen Strauss. 3rd ed. Berlin, 1973. pp. 570. *bibliog.*

KECK (ALFRED) Leistung, Wachstum, Wohlstand: unser Nationaleinkommen, Quelle des gesellschaftlichen Reichtums. Berlin, 1973. pp. 152.

DEUTSCHES INSTITUT FÜR WIRTSCHAFTSFORSCHUNG. Sonderhefte. [Neue Folge]. Nr. 98. System und Entwicklung der DDR-Wirtschaft; von Peter Mitzscherling [and others]. Berlin, 1974. pp. 298.

DIFFICULT years bear fruit: the birth and development of the German Democratic Republic. [rev. ed.] Dresden, [1974]. pp. 144.

POLITISCHE Ökonomie und Wirtschaftsleitung; (Autorenkollektiv: R. Beloussow [and others]). Berlin, 1974. pp. 354.

— Foreign economic relations.

GROTE (GERHARD) ed. Planung der Aussenwirtschaft in der DDR;...(Autoren: Klaus Apel [and others]). Berlin, 1973. pp. 160.

— Foreign relations.

LUDZ (PETER CHRISTIAN) Two Germanys in one world. Farnborough, [1973]. pp. 64. (*Atlantic Institute. Atlantic Papers. 1973. 3*)

AUSSENPOLITIK der DDR: für Sozialismus und Frieden; ([by] Gerhard Hahn [and others]). Berlin, 1974. pp. 302.

SCHWABE (ERNST OTTO) We want to live in peace: but how?: the G[erman] D[emocratic] R[epublic] presents its views. Berlin, 1974. pp. 63.

See also EUROPEAN ECONOMIC COMMUNITY — Germany, Eastern.

— — Treaties.

GERMANY (BUNDESREPUBLIK). Treaties. 1972. Treaty between the German Democratic Republic and the Federal Republic of Germany on questions relating to traffic. Dresden, [1972]. pp. 29.

FREIE DEMOKRATISCHE PARTEI. F.D.P. zum Grundvertrag: Beiträge und Dokumentation. Bonn, 1973. pp. 40.

— — Bulgaria.

A CONTRIBUTION to peace and security in Europe: treaties between the German Democratic Republic [and Hungary, and between the GDR and Bulgaria]. Dresden, [1967?]. pp. 96. *Mainly speeches and statements, together with texts of the treaties.*

— — Germany.

GERMANY (BUNDESREPUBLIK). Bundesministerium für Innerdeutsche Beziehungen. 1973. Die Entwicklung der Beziehungen zwischen der Bundesrepublik Deutschland und der Deutschen Demokratischen Republik: Bericht und Dokumentation. [Bonn], 1973. pp. 154.

— — Hungary.

A CONTRIBUTION to peace and security in Europe: treaties between the German Democratic Republic [and Hungary, and between the GDR and Bulgaria]. Dresden, [1967?]. pp. 96. *Mainly speeches and statements, together with texts of the treaties.*

— Industries.

Die MATERIALWIRTSCHAFT der Deutschen Demokratischen Republik; [by an] Autorenkollektiv unter Leitung von Carl-Jürgen Strauss. 3rd ed. Berlin, 1973. pp. 570. *bibliog.*

— Politics and government.

FUER die Aktionseinheit der deutschen Arbeiterklasse, 1945-1964; (Redaktionskollegium: Günter Benser [and others, for the] Institut für Marxismus-Leninismus beim ZK der SED). Berlin, 1965. pp. 443.

CHARVIN (ROBERT) La République démocratique allemande (R.D.A.). Paris, [1973]. pp. 389.

GERMAN Democratic Republic: state and society. 2nd ed. Dresden, 1973. pp. 64.

BAYLIS (THOMAS A.) The technical intelligentsia and the East German elite: legitimacy and social change in mature communism. Berkeley, [1974]. pp. 314. *bibliog.*

DIFFICULT years bear fruit: the birth and development of the German Democratic Republic. [rev. ed.] Dresden, [1974]. pp. 144.

PORTISCH (HUGO) Die deutsche Konfrontation: Gegenwart und Zukunft der beiden deutschen Staaten. Wien, [1974]. pp. 351. *bibliog.*

— Relations (general) with Chile.

PANORAMA DDR. The GDR's fervent solidarity with the courageous Chilean people. Berlin, [1973]. pp. 15.

— Relations (general) with Germany.

FUER die Aktionseinheit der deutschen Arbeiterklasse, 1945-1964; (Redaktionskollegium: Günter Benser [and others, for the] Institut für Marxismus-Leninismus beim ZK der SED). Berlin, 1965. pp. 443.

— Relations (general) with Latin America.

GERMANY (DEUTSCHE DEMOKRATISCHE REPUBLIK). Staatsrat. Abteilung Presse und Information. 1969. Tagebuch einer Freundschaftsreise: Bericht über die Reise einer Delegation der Volkskammer der DDR nach Kolumbien, Ekuador und Chile vom 3.-30. Juli 1968. Berlin, 1969. pp. 64.

— Social conditions.

GERMAN Democratic Republic: state and society. 2nd ed. Dresden, 1973. pp. 64.

— Social policy.

SOZIALISTISCHE EINHEITSPARTEI DEUTSCHLANDS. Zentralkomitee. 1972,6. Tagung. Sixth session of the Central Committee of the Socialist Unity Party of Germany, Berlin, 6 and 7 July, 1972. Berlin, 1972. pp. 70. (*Sozialistische Einheitspartei Deutschlands. Information Service. [Publications]. 1972.2*)

POPPE (EBERHARD) Working people and their rights: GDR gives full scope to human rights; [translated from the German]. Berlin, 1973. pp. 60.

— Volkskammer — Biography.

GERMANY (DEUTSCHE DEMOKRATISCHE REPUBLIK). Volkskammer. Präsidium. 1972. Die Volkskammer der Deutschen Demokratischen Republik. 6. Wahlperiode. Berlin, 1972. pp. 855, 2 maps in end pocket.

GERTSEN (ALEKSANDR IVANOVICH).

GERTSEN (ALEKSANDR IVANOVICH) Byloe i dumy: pervoe polnoe izdanie. Berlin, 1921. 5 vols.

AUTOUR d'Alexandre Herzen: (révolutionnaires et exilés du XIXe siècle); documents inédits publiés par Marc Vuilleumier [and others]. Genève, 1973. pp. 347. (*Geneva. Université. Faculté des Lettres. Section d'Histoire. Etudes et Documents. 8*)

ŚLIWOWSKA (WIKTORIA) and ŚLIWOWSKI (RENÉ) Aleksander Hercen. Warszawa, 1973. pp. 670. *bibliog.*

UCHENYE ZAPISKI KAFEDR OBSHCHESTVENNYKH NAUK VUZOV LENINGRADA. Filosofiia. vyp.14. Filosofskie i sotsiologicheskie issledovaniia. Leningrad, 1973. pp. 212.

GERTSEN (NATALIIA ALEKSANDROVNA).

CONFINO (MICHAEL) ed. Daughter of a revolutionary: Natalie Herzen and the Bakunin-Nechayev circle;...translated by Hilary Sternberg and Lydia Bott. London, 1974. pp. 416.

GHANA.

U.K. Central Office of Information. Reference Division. 1956. The making of Ghana. London, 1956. pp. 46.

— Commerce.

REYNOLDS (EDWARD) Historian. Trade and economic change on the Gold Coast, 1807-1874. Harlow, 1974. pp. 207. *bibliog.*

— Economic conditions.

EWUSI (KODWO) West African economies: some basic economic problems. Legon, 1971. fo.89. (*Ghana University. Institute of Statistical, Social and Economic Research. Technical Publication Series. No.25*)

— — Mathematical models.

BRECHER (RICHARD A.) Summary of The labor-and-land surplus economy (Ghana). [New Haven], 1972. pp. 19. *bibliog.*

— Economic history.

COX-GEORGE (NOAH ARTHUR WILLIAM) Studies in finance and development: the Gold Coast (Ghana) experience, 1914-1950. London, 1973. pp. 217. *bibliog.*

REYNOLDS (EDWARD) Historian. Trade and economic change on the Gold Coast, 1807-1874. Harlow, 1974. pp. 207. *bibliog.*

— Economic policy.

FOOD AND AGRICULTURE ORGANIZATION. 1963. Final report on survey of the Lower Volta river flood plain. Rome, 1963. 5 vols. Microfilm: 1 reel.

EWUSI (KODWO) Economic development planning in Ghana. New York, [1973]. pp. 85. *bibliog.*

— History.

AGBODEKA (FRANCIS) Ghana in the twentieth century. Accra, 1972. pp. 152. *bibliog.*

— Officials and employees.

OPPONG (CHRISTINE) Marriage among a matrilineal elite: a family study of Ghanaian senior civil servants. London, 1974. pp. 187. *bibliog.*

— Politics and government.

DANQUAH (JOSEPH BOAKYE) Historic speeches and writings on Ghana; compiled by H.K. Akyeampong. Accra, [1966?]. pp. 180.

DUNN (JOHN) and ROBERTSON (A.F.) Dependence and opportunity: political change in Ahafo. London, 1973. pp. 400.

ARMAH (KWESI) Ghana: Nkrumah's legacy. London, 1974. pp. 185. *bibliog.*

— Statistics.

GHANA. Central Bureau of Statistics. Statistical year book. a., 1965/6 [5th]- Accra.

GIANNINI (GUGLIELMO).

PALLOTTA (GINO) Il qualunquismo e l'avventura di Guglielmo Giannini. Milano, [1972]. pp. 182.

GIBRALTAR

— History.

HILLS (GEORGE) Rock of contention: a history of Gibraltar. London, 1974. pp. 510. bibliog.

GIFTED CHILDREN.

HITCHFIELD (E.M.) In search of promise: a long-term, national study of able children and their families. London, 1973. pp. 219. bibliog. (National Children's Bureau. Studies in Child Development)

— Education — United Kingdom.

OGILVIE (ERIC) Gifted children in primary schools:...the report of the Schools Council enquiry into the teaching of gifted children of primary age, 1970-71. London, 1973. pp. 279. bibliog. (U.K. Department of Education and Science. Schools Council. Research Studies)

GIFTS

— Taxation — United Kingdom.

SANDFORD (CEDRIC T.) and others. An accessions tax: a study of the desirability and feasibility of replacing the United Kingdom estate duty by a cumulative tax on recipients of gifts and inheritances. London, 1973. pp. 220. (Institute for Fiscal Studies. Publications. No. 7)

GILYAKS.

BOIKO (VLADIMIR IVANOVICH) Opyt sotsiologicheskogo issledovaniia problem razvitiia narodov Nizhnego Amura; otvetstvennyi redaktor...A.P. Okladnikov. Novosibirsk, 1973. pp. 211.

GIOLITTI (GIOVANNI).

COLAPIETRA (RAFFAELE) ed. Giovanni Giolitti: biografia politica e interpretazioni storiografiche; testi antologici da G. Giolitti [and others]. Messina, 1973. pp. 179.

GIPSIES

— Norway.

INNSTILLING om arbeidet blant norske sigøynere: fra et utvalg oppnevnt av Sosialdepartementet i oktober 1969. Bergen, 1970. pp. 21.

— United Kingdom.

GYPSY COUNCIL. We shall not be moved;... campaign handbook. London, [1973]. fo. (13).

— — Scotland.

SIMSON (WALTER) A history of the gipsies; with specimens of the gipsy language;...edited with...a disquisition on the past, present and future of gipsydom by James Simson. London, 1865. pp. 575.

GIRAUD (HENRY).

GIRAUD (HENRY) Mon été chez LIP. Paris, [1974]. pp. 173.

GIRLS.

KITTERINGHAM (JENNIE) Country girls in 19th century England. Oxford, [1973]. pp. 75. (History Workshop. Pamphlets. No. 11)

GLACIAL EPOCH.

ANDREWS (JOHN THOMAS) ed. Glacial isostasy. Stroudsburg, Pa., [1974]. pp. 491. bibliogs.

GLACIERS

— Iceland.

POLSKA AKADEMIA NAUK. Instytut Geografii. Geographia Polonica. 26. Scientific results of the Polish Geographical Expedition to Vatnajökull, Iceland, 1968: a collection of reports by the research groups; edited by Rajmund Galon. Warszawa, 1973. pp. 311, and maps. bibliogs.

GLASS INDUSTRY AND TRADE

— United Kingdom.

CERAMICS, GLASS AND MINERAL PRODUCTS INDUSTRY TRAINING BOARD [U.K.]. Report and statement of accounts. a., 1972/3- Harrow. Formerly included in the file of British Parliamentary Papers.

GLENROTHES.

GLENROTHES DEVELOPMENT CORPORATION. Department of Architecture, Planning and Quantity Surveying. Glenrothes New Town... : master plan; report. [Glenrothes], 1970. pp. 121.

GLENROTHES DEVELOPMENT CORPORATION. Department of Architecture, Planning and Quantity Surveying. Social survey, 1971: report on results of social and economic survey carried out in August 1971. Glenrothes, 1972. fo.68.

GOA, DAMAN AND DIU

— Statistics, Vital.

GOA, DAMAN AND DIU. Office of the Chief Registrar of Births and Deaths. Annual report on registration of births and deaths. a., 1971- Panaji, Goa.

GOAL (PSYCHOLOGY).

MASSARIK (FRED) Goal setting as codetermined by institutional and class factors. Los Angeles, 1969. pp. 279-294. bibliog. (California University. Institute of Industrial Relations. Reprints. No.196) (Reprinted from The course of human life, 1968)

GOD.

DULUMAN (EVGRAF KALEN'EVICH) Ideia boga: issledovatel'skii i polemicheskii ocherk. Moskva, 1970. pp. 176.

GODOY Y ALVAREZ DE FABIA (MANUEL DE) Duque de Alcudia.

YOUNG (RAYMOND ARTHUR) La influencia de Godoy en el desarrollo de los Estados Unidos de America, a costa de Nueva España. Mexico, 1968. pp. 146.

GODWIN (MARY).

TOMALIN (CLAIRE) The life and death of Mary Wollstonecraft. London, [1974]. pp. 316. bibliog.

GOEBBELS (JOSEPH).

SCHAUMBURG-LIPPE (FRIEDRICH CHRISTIAN ZU) Prinz. Dr. G[oebbels]: ein Porträt des Propagandaministers. 3rd ed. Wiesbaden, 1972. pp. 288.

GOERLITZ

— History.

KRETZSCHMAR (ERNST) ed. Widerstandskampf Görlitzer Antifaschisten, 1933-1945: Erinnerungen, Dokumente, Kurzbiographien; ([compiled for the] Kreiskommission zur Erforschung der Geschichte der örtlichen Arbeiterbewegung bei der SED-Kreisleitung Görlitz). Görlitz, 1973. pp. 101.

GOETTINGEN UNIVERSITY.

NUERNBERGER (RICHARD) Die Lehre von der Politik an der Universität Göttingen während der französischen Revolution. Göttingen, [1971]. pp. 29. (Göttingen. Akademie der Wissenschaften. Nachrichten. Philologisch-Historische Klasse. Jahrgang 1971, Nr. 2)

GOKHALE (GOPAL KRISHNA).

NANDA (B.R.) Gokhale, Gandhi and the Nehrus: studies in Indian nationalism. London, 1974. pp. 203.

GOLD.

GREEN (TIMOTHY) The world of gold today. London, 1973. pp. 287. bibliog.

GOLDS.

BOIKO (VLADIMIR IVANOVICH) Opyt sotsiologicheskogo issledovaniia problem razvitiia narodov Nizhnego Amura; otvetstvennyi redaktor...A.P. Okladnikov. Novosibirsk, 1973. pp. 211.

GOMPERS (SAMUEL).

KAUFMAN (STUART BRUCE) Samuel Gompers and the origins of the American Federation of Labor, 1848-1896. Westport, Conn., 1973. pp. 274. bibliog.

GORE—BOOTH (PAUL HENRY) Baron Gore—Booth.

GORE-BOOTH (PAUL HENRY) Baron Gore-Booth. With great truth and respect. London, 1974. pp. 440.

GOR'KII (MAKSIM) pseud.

PROZHOGIN (VASILII ELIZAROVICH) Problematika truda v tvorchestve M. Gor'kogo i sovremennost'. Kiev, 1974. pp. 271.

GOR'KII (OBLAST')

— Statistics.

GOR'KII (OBLAST'). Statisticheskoe Upravlenie. Narodnoe khoziaistvo Gor'kovskoi oblasti za piatiletku, 1966- 1970 gg.: statisticheskii sbornik. Gor'kii, 1971. pp. 211.

GOROKANS.

FINNEY (BEN R.) Big-men and business: entrepreneurship and economic growth in the New Guinea highlands. Honolulu, [1973]. pp. 206. bibliog.

GORTER (HERMAN).

ROLAND-HOLST (HENRIETTE) Herman Gorter; [reprint of work first published in 1933]. Amsterdam, 1973. pp. 160.

LIAGRE BÖHL (HERMAN DE) Herman Gorter: zijn politieke aktiviteiten van 1909 tot 1920 in de opkomende kommunistische beweging in Nederland. Nijmegen, 1973. pp. 317. bibliog.

GOSCHEN (GEORGE JOACHIM) 1st Viscount Goschen.

SPINNER (THOMAS J.) George Joachim Goschen: the transformation of a Victorian liberal. Cambridge, 1973. pp. 263. bibliog. (Conference on British Studies. Biographical Series)

GOSUDARSTVENNYI BANK SSSR.

PAVLENKO (GRIGORII GRIGOR'EVICH) and others. Gosbank i razvitie narodnogo khoziaistva Ukrainy. Kiev, 1974. pp. 183.

GOUBERVILLE (GILLES DE).

GOUBERVILLE (GILLES DE) Un sire de Gouberville: gentilhomme campagnard au Cotentin de 1553 à 1562; publié par Abbé A. Tollemer; précédé d'une introduction par E. Le Roy Ladurie. 2nd ed. Paris, 1873 repr. 1972. pp. 841. (Maison des Sciences de l'Homme. Rééditions. 10) Material from the Journal arranged by subject with comment by Abbé Tollemer.

GOUGH (RICHARD).

HEY (DAVID G.) An English rural community: Myddle under the Tudors and Stuarts. Leicester, 1974. pp. 260. bibliog.

GOVERNMENT, COMPARATIVE.

GROTH (ALEXANDER J.) Comparative politics: a distributive approach. New York, [1971]. pp. 289.

GOVERNMENT, COMPARATIVE. (Cont.)

BILL (JAMES ALBAN) and HARDGRAVE (ROBERT L.) Comparative politics: the quest for theory. Columbus, [1973]. pp. 261. *bibliog.*

BLONDEL (JEAN) 1929- . Comparative legislatures. Englewood Cliffs, N.J., [1973]. pp. 173. *bibliog.*

CRICK (BERNARD ROWLAND) Basic forms of government: a sketch and a model. London, 1973. pp. 96. *bibliog.*

BURLING (ROBBINS) The passage of power: studies in political succession. New York, [1974]. pp. 322. *bibliog.*

DUVERGER (MAURICE) Modern democracies: economic power versus political power...; translated by Charles L. Markmann. Hinsdale, Ill., 1974. pp. 198.

FRIEDRICH (CARL JOACHIM) Limited government: a comparison. Englewood Cliffs, [1974]. pp. 139. *bibliog.*

SELASSIE (BEREKET H.) The executive in African governments. London, 1974. pp. 288.

TAI (HUNG-CHAO) Land reform and politics: a comparative analysis. Berkeley, [1974]. pp. 565.

GOVERNMENT, RESISTANCE TO.

KROEGER (KLAUS) Widerstandsrecht und demokratische Verfassung. Tübingen, 1971. pp. 23.

KADISH (MORTIMER R.) and KADISH (SANFORD H.) Discretion to disobey: a study of lawful departures from legal rules. Stanford, 1973. pp. 241.

MOTHE (DANIEL) Le métier de militant. Paris, [1973]. pp. 187.

USEEM (MICHAEL) Conscription, protest, and social conflict: the life and death of a draft resistance movement. New York, [1973]. pp. 329. *bibliog.*

GOVERNMENT AND THE PRESS

— Norway.

INNSTILLING om Statens lånekasse for aviser; fra et utvalg oppnevnt...av 17. oktober 1969. Orkanger, 1971. pp. 65.

— United States.

SIGAL (LEON V.) Reporters and officials: the organization and politics of newsmaking. Lexington, Mass., [1973]. pp. 221. *bibliog.*

GOVERNMENT BUSINESS ENTERPRISES

— European Economic Community countries.

CENTRE EUROPEEN DE L'ENTREPRISE PUBLIQUE. Congrès, 5e, 1971. L'entreprise publique élement dynamique de la politique industrielle. [Brussels, 1972]. pp. 242.

— France.

FRANCE. Institut National de la Statistique et des Etudes Economiques. Collections de l'I.N.S.E.E. Série E. Entreprises. . Paris, 1969 in progress.

— India.

NIGAM (RAJ KUMAR) ed. Management of public sector in India. Bombay, 1971. pp. 333. *Articles from the journal Lok Udyog.*

GOVERNMENT INFORMATION

— Netherlands.

HAAK (C.P.M.VAN DER) Bekendmaken en bekend raken: evaluatie van de eerste vijf jaar overheidsvoorlichting over de Algemene Bijstandswet, 1962-1967, etc. 's-Gravenhage, Staatsuitgeverij, 1972. pp. 279. *bibliog. With English summary.*

GOVERNMENT LENDING

— Australia.

GILBERT (R.S.) The Australian Loan Council in federal fiscal adjustments, 1890-1965. Canberra, 1973. pp. 337. *bibliog.*

— Taiwan.

BANK OF COMMUNICATIONS [TAIWAN]. Annual report. a., 1962-1968, 1970- Taipei.

— United Kingdom — Ireland, Northern.

NORTHERN IRELAND FINANCE CORPORATION. Accounts... together with the Report of the Comptroller and Auditor-General thereon. a., 1972/3- Belfast.

— United States.

LARKINS (DAN) $300 billion in loans: an introduction to Federal credit programs. Washington, D.C., 1972. pp. 69. *(American Enterprise Institute for Public Policy Research. Domestic Affairs Studies. 6)*

GOVERNMENT LIABILITY

— France.

BRECHON-MOULENES (CHRISTINE) Les régimes législatifs de responsabilité publique. Paris, 1974. pp. 559. *bibliog.*

GOVERNMENT OWNERSHIP.

GOSUDARSTVENNAIA sobstvennost' i antimonopolisticheskaia bor'ba v stranakh razvitogo kapitalizma. Moskva, 1973. pp. 391. *bibliog.*

— Austria.

HOLLERER (SIEGFRIED) Verstaatlichung und Wirtschaftsplanung in Österreich, 1946- 1949. Wien, 1974. pp. 258. *bibliog. (Vienna. Hochschule für Welthandel. Dissertationen. 15)*

— France.

DUBOIS (PIERRE) Mort de l'état-patron. Paris, [1974]. pp. 303.

— Germany.

HEINEMANN (BRUNO) Ziele und Gefahren der Sozialisierung. Berlin, 1919. pp. 23.

NEURATH (OTTO) Vollsozialisierung und Arbeiterorganisation: Vortrag, gehalten in der Reichenberger Turnhalle am 28.Juni 1920. Reichenberg, [1920]. pp. 24.

NEURATH (OTTO) Vollsozialisierung: von der nächsten und übernächsten Zukunft. Jena, 1920. pp. 47. *bibliog.*

INSTITUT FÜR MARXISTISCHE STUDIEN UND FORSCHUNGEN. Gewerkschaften und Nationalisierung in der BRD: (Dokumente und Materialien). Frankfurt/Main, 1973. pp. 144. *(Neudrucke zur Sozialistischen Theorie und Gewerkschaftspraxis. Band 5)*

— United Kingdom.

TOPHAM (ANTHONY) ed. Democracy on the docks. Nottingham, 1970. pp. 87.

AIMS OF INDUSTRY. To fight together or hang separately: against "the most corporatist document". [London, 1973]. pp. 4.

KELF-COHEN (REUBEN) British nationalisation, 1945-1973. London, 1973. pp. 288. *bibliog.*

LABOUR PARTY. Study Group on the Public Sector. The National Enterprise Board: Labour's State holding company; report of a Labour Party Study Group. London, [1973]. pp. 24. *(Labour Party. Opposition Green Papers)*

AIMS OF INDUSTRY. The importance of being earnest: the case for Mr. Benn. London, [1974]. pp. 5.

AIMS OF INDUSTRY. The industries that Labour wants to nationalize. London, 1974. 8 pts. (in 1 vol.).

BROADWAY (FRANK) National Jenkins Products Limited (a subsidiary of National Enterprise Board); progress report to 1980. London, [1974]. pp. 12.

N.O.P. MARKET RESEARCH. Social Research Unit. Electors' preferences between working for private or nationalized industry; a report prepared for Aims of Industry... (synopsis by Aims of Industry). London, [1974]. pp. 2.

ROY (DONALD) State holding companies. London, 1974. pp. 30. *(Young Fabian Group. Young Fabian Pamphlets. 40)*

GOVERNMENT PUBLICATIONS.

CHILDS (JAMES BENNETT) Government publications: documents. Washington, 1973. pp. 140. *bibliogs. (Reprinted from Encyclopedia of library and information science, vol.10)*

— Bibliography.

HIGHAM (ROBIN) ed. Official histories: essays and bibliographies from around the world. Manhattan, Ka., 1970. pp. 644. *(Kansas State University of Agriculture and Applied Science. Library. Bibliography Series. No.8)*

GOVERNMENT PUBLICITY

— Sweden.

ELDER (NEIL COLBERT MCAULEY) Regionalism and the publicity principle in Sweden. London, 1973. pp. 31. *(U.K. Commission on the Constitution, 1969. Research Papers. 3)*

— Switzerland.

NEF (MAX) Ausbau der Information aus dem Bundeshaus: Schlussbericht; erstattet von Max Nef, über seine Tätigkeit als Berater des Bundesrates für Presse- und Informationsfragen in der Zeit vom 1.Januar 1966-29.Februar 1968. [Bern?, 1968]. pp. 60.

GOVERNMENT PURCHASING

— Canada.

CANADA. Department of Supply and Services. Annual report. a., 1969/70 (1st)- Ottawa. *In English and French.*

STEGEMANN (KLAUS F.) and ACHESON (A.L. KEITH) Canadian government purchasing policy. [Ottawa, 1971]. fo. 79. *(Carleton University. Carleton Economic Papers)*

— European Free Trade Association countries.

EUROPEAN FREE TRADE ASSOCIATION. 1971. Public procurement in EFTA; list of public agencies and enterprises responsible for major public procurement in the European Free Trade Area. Geneva, 1971. pp. 54.

— Norway.

STATENS innkjop: utredning om statens innkjop fra et utvalg oppnevnt av Lønns- og prisdepartementet... av 5. desember 1969. Oslo, 1972. pp. 134. *(Norway. Norges Offentlige Utredninger. 1972.19)*

— Zambia.

ZAMBIA. Government Stores Department. Annual report. a., 1970/1972- Lusaka.

GOVERNMENT SPENDING POLICY

— United States.

GOVERNMENT spending and land values: public money and private gain: (proceedings of a symposium sponsored by the Committee on Taxation, Resources and Economic Development...at the University of Wisconsin, Madison, 1971); edited by C. Lowell Harriss. Madison, 1973. pp. 239. *(Committee on Taxation, Resources and Economic Development. Publications. 6)*

HYMAN (DAVID N.) The economics of governmental activity. New York, [1973]. pp. 333.

GOVERNMENTAL INVESTIGATIONS

— Sweden.

CLAESSON (GÖRAN C-O.) Statens Ostyriga Utredande: betänkande om kommittéväsendet. Stockholm, 1972. pp. 211. (Studieförbundet Näringsliv och Samhälle. Studier och Debatt. 1972. Nr.3)

— United Kingdom.

DASH (SAMUEL) Justice denied: a challenge to Lord Widgery's report on "Bloody Sunday". New York, [1972]. pp. 48.

— United States.

POPPER (FRANK) The President's commissions. New York, 1970. pp. 73.

SCHRIFTGIESSER (KARL) The Commission on Money and Credit: an adventure in policy-making. Englewood Cliffs, [1974]. pp. 165. bibliog.

— — Bibliography.

TOLLEFSON (ALAN M.) and CHANG (HENRY C.) compilers. A bibliography of presidential commissions, committees, councils, panels and task forces, 1961-1972. Minneapolis, 1973. pp. 30.

GRABSKI (WŁADYSŁAW).

GRABSKI (WŁADYSŁAW) Wspomnienia ze Spa; wstęp i przypisy opracował Stanisław Kirkor. Londyn, 1973. pp. 54.

GRADUATES

— France.

VRAIN (PHILIPPE) Les débouchés professionnels des étudiants: lettres, droit, sciences économiques, etc. [Paris, 1973]. pp. 145. (France. Centre d'Etudes de l'Emploi. Cahiers. 3) With summaries in English and German.

— Italy.

BARBAGLI (MARZIO) Disoccupazione intellettuale e sistema scolastico in Italia, 1859- 1973. Bologna, [1974]. pp. 481.

— Nigeria.

UNIVERSITY GRADUATE EMPLOYMENT: a sample survey of employment experience amongst Nigerian men and women graduating in [the year]; ([pd. by) National Manpower Board, Federal Ministry of Economic Development and Reconstruction, Nigeria. a., 1973 (v.1)- Lagos. (Manpower Studies).

— South Africa.

WESSELS (DINA M.) The employment potential of graduate housewives in the P[retoria-] W[itwatersrand-] V[ereeniging] region. Pretoria, South African Human Sciences Research Council, 1972 in progress. bibliog.

— United Kingdom.

COUNCIL FOR TRAINING IN SOCIAL WORK [U.K.]. Graduate trainees in the health and welfare services. London, 1970. pp. (7). (Discussion Papers. No.3)

U.K. Civil Service Commission. 1970. Careers for graduates: posts in government service, 1971. [London, 1970]. pp. 109. bibliog.

MARSH (ALAN) Postgraduate students' assessment of their social science training: a survey of the attitudes of SSRC-supported students towards their postgraduate training. London, Social Science Research Council Survey Unit, 1972. pp. 104. (Occasional Papers in Survey Research.2)

McLONE (R.R.) The training of mathematicians: a research report. London, Social Science Research Council, [1973]. pp. 94.bibliog.

GRADUATE opportunities, 1975; ([with] GRID '75: GO's recruiters index and directory). London, [1974]. pp. 824. GRID '75 in end pocket.

— United States.

FREEMAN (RICHARD BARRY) The market for college-trained manpower: a study in the economics of career choice. Cambridge, Mass., 1971. pp. 264.

EDUCATIONAL TESTING SERVICE. Graduate and professional school opportunities for minority students...1973-74. 5th ed. Princeton, N.J., [1973]. pp. 211.

HARTMAN (ROBERT W.) Financing the opportunity to enter the "educated labor market". Washington, 1974. pp. 24. bibliog. (Brookings Institution. Reprints. 285)

GRAIN

— France.

ALTMANN (CECILE) Structure de la production céréalière en France. Paris, Institut National de la Recherche Agronomique, Département d'Economie et de Sociologie Rurales, 1970 in progress. (Série Travaux de Recherche. No. 1)

FRANCE. Direction de la Documentation. La Documentation Française. Notes et Etudes Documentaires. Nos. 3,901-3, 902. Les productions végétales en France: les céréales. [Paris], 1972. pp. 72.

— India.

KHUSRO (ALI M.) Buffer stocks and storage of foodgrains in India. Bombay, [1973]. pp. 144.

— Sweden.

SJÖHOLM (BENGT) En studie av spannmålsarealerna, 1971. Stockholm, 1973. pp. 34. (Jordbrukets Utredningsinstitut. Meddelanden. 1973. Nr. 3) With English summary.

— United Kingdom.

CRACKNELL (BASIL EDWARD) Minimum import prices and levies: the case for a change in the U. K. system; (addendum to the Britton report, Cereals in the United Kingdom). [London, Home-Grown Cereals Authority], 1969. pp. 55. Bound with author's Past and future cereals production in the U.K.

HOME-GROWN CEREALS AUTHORITY. Annual report and accounts. a., 1970/71(6th)- London. Formerly included in the file of British Parliamentary Papers.

CRACKNELL (BASIL EDWARD) Past and future cereals production in the U.K.: a regional analysis; (a supplement to the Britton report, Cereals in the United Kingdom). [London, Home-Grown Cereals Authority], 1970. pp. 74. Bound with author's Minimum import prices and levies.

NIAB CROP CONFERENCE, 12TH, [CAMBRIDGE?], 1972. U.K. cereal production after entering the Common Market. Cambridge, [1972]. pp. 83.

GRAIN TRADE.

JOSLING (TIMOTHY EDWARD) An international grain reserve policy. [Washington, D.C.], 1973. pp. 17. (British-North American Committee. Publications. 11)

— Baltic, The.

SOOM (ARNOLD) Der baltische Getreidehandel im 17. Jahrhundert. Stockholm, 1961. pp. 350. bibliog. (Vitterhets Historie och Antikvitets Akademien. Handlingar. Historiska Serien. 8)

— European Economic Community countries.

STURGESS (I.M.) Price and marketing prospects for UK cereal growers within the EEC; a study sponsored by the Home-Grown Cereals Authority; prepared...under the direction of J. Ashton. London, 1973. pp. 155. bibliog.

— India.

MOORE (JOHN R.) and others. Indian foodgrain marketing. New Delhi, 1973. pp. 188. bibliog.

— Sweden.

SOOM (ARNOLD) Der baltische Getreidehandel im 17. Jahrhundert. Stockholm, 1961. pp. 350. bibliog. (Vitterhets Historie och Antikvitets Akademien. Handlingar. Historiska Serien. 8)

— United Kingdom.

STURGESS (I.M.) Price and marketing prospects for UK cereal growers within the EEC; a study sponsored by the Home-Grown Cereals Authority; prepared...under the direction of J. Ashton. London, 1973. pp. 155. bibliog.

BLACK (MICHAEL) Grain futures in practice; [produced by Market and Planning Services Ltd. for Commodity Analysis Limited]. London, 1974. pp. 35. bibliog.

GRAMMAR, COMPARATIVE AND GENERAL.

LEWIS (M. BLANCHE) Sentence analysis in modern Malay...: with examples drawn from two plays by Za'ba. Cambridge, 1969. pp. 345.

BOTHA (RUDOLF P.) and WINCKLER (WALTER K.) The justification of linguistic hypotheses: a study of nondemonstrative inference in transformational grammar. The Hague, 1973. pp. 350. bibliog.

STANFORD WORKSHOP ON GRAMMAR AND SEMANTICS, 1970. Approaches to natural language: proceedings...; edited by K.J. J. Hintikka [and others]. Dordrecht, [1973]. pp. 526. bibliog.

— Mathematical models.

WALL (ROBERT) Introduction to mathematical linguistics. Englewood Cliffs, N.J., [1972]. pp. 337. bibliog.

— Phonology.

BRAME (MICHAEL K.) ed. Contributions to generative phonology. Austin, [1972]. pp. 327. bibliogs.

KISSEBERTH (CHARLES W.) ed. Studies in generative phonology;... [papers from the Department of Linguistics, University of Illinois]. Edmonton, [1973]. pp. 195. bibliogs.

URBANA CONFERENCE ON PHONOLOGY, 1971. Issues in phonological theory: proceedings...; edited by Michael J. Kenstowicz and Charles W. Kisseberth. The Hague, 1973. pp. 176. bibliogs.

— Syntax.

SYNTAX AND SEMANTICS; ed. by John P. Kimball. a., 1972-1973 (v.1-2). New York.

BARTSCH (RENATE) and VENNEMANN (THEO) Semantic structures: a study in the relation between semantics and syntax. Frankfurt/Main, [1972] repr. 1973. pp. 186. bibliogs.

CHICAGO LINGUISTIC SOCIETY. Regional Meeting, 9th, 1973. Comparative Syntax Festival. You take the high node and I'll take the low node: papers from the Comparative Syntax Festival: the Differences between main and subordinate clauses;... a paravolume to Papers from the ninth Regional Meeting; edited by Claudia Corum [and others]. Chicago, [1973]. pp. 422. bibliogs.

FILLENBAUM (SAMUEL) Syntactic factors in memory. tHE hAGUE, 1973. PP. 98. BIBLIOG.

GRAMSCI (ANTONIO).

BONOMI (GIORGIO) Partito e rivoluzione in Gramsci. Milano, 1973. pp. 167.

ROMANO (FEDERICO) ed. Gramsci e il liberalismo antiliberale. Roma, 1973. pp. 127. bibliog.

MACCIOCCHI (MARIA ANTONIETTA) Per Gramsci. Bologna, [1974]. pp. 427. bibliog.

GRAMSCI (ANTONIO). (Cont.)

MACCIOCCHI (MARIA ANTONIETTA) Pour Gramsci. Paris, [1974]. pp. 429. *bibliog.*

PORTELLI (HUGUES) Gramsci et la question religieuse. Paris, [1974]. pp. 321. *bibliog.*

GRANADA (PROVINCE)
— Economic history.

CALERO AMOR (ANTONIO MARIA) Historia del movimiento obrero en Granada, 1909-1923. Madrid, 1973. pp. 374. *bibliog.*

GRANT (CLARA ELLEN).

GRANT (CLARA ELLEN) From 'me' to 'we': forty years on Bow Common. London, [c.1940]. pp. 197.

GRANT (JOHN DOUGLAS).

GRANT (JOHN DOUGLAS) Member of Parliament. London, 1974. pp. 190.

GRANT (ULYSSES SIMPSON) President of the United States.

MANTELL (MARTIN E.) Johnson, Grant, and the politics of reconstruction. New York, 1973. pp. 209. *bibliog.*

GRANTS—IN—AID.

DAWSON (DIANE) Revenue and equalization in Australia, Canada, West Germany and the U.S.A. London, 1973. pp. 92. *(U.K. Commission on the Constitution, 1969. Research Papers. 9)*

MATHEWS (RUSSELL LLOYD) ed. Fiscal equalisation in a federal system. Canberra, 1974. pp. 142. *bibliog. (Australian National University. Centre for Research on Federal Financial Relations. Research Monographs. No.4)*

— Mathematical models.

VARDY (DAVID ALLAN) Regional public goods, spillovers and optimizing federal subsidies. Kingston, Ontario, [1971]. fo. 77. *(Kingston, Ontario. Queen's University. Institute for Economic Research. Discussion Papers. No. 43)*

— European Economic Community countries.

FRANCE. Direction de la Documentation. La Documentation Française. Notes et Etudes Documentaires. No. 3,917. Les aides à l'expansion industrielle régionale dans les pays du Marché commun, par Philippe de Castelbajac. [Paris], 1972. pp. 39.

— Ireland (Republic).

EIRE. Dáil Éireann. Committee of Public Accounts. 1972. Interim and final reports (Order of Dáil of 1 December 1970); [Patrick Hogan, chairman]. Dublin, 1972. pp. 407. *In English and Irish.*

— United Kingdom.

U.K. Department of the Environment. 1973. Local government finance in England and Wales: consultation paper. London, 1973. fo. 6.

— United States.

BOULDING (KENNETH EWART) and others, eds. Transfers on an urbanized economy: theories and effects of the grants economy. Belmont, Calif., [1973]. pp. 376.

LEVITAN (SAR A.) ed. The federal social dollar in its own back yard. Washington, [1973]. pp. 283.

GRAPH THEORY.

PONSARD (CLAUDE) ed. Graphes de transfert et analyse économique...; [by] A.L. Dumay [and others]. Paris, 1972. pp. 252. *bibliogs. (Revue d'Economie Politique. Numéros Spéciaux)*

DOERFLER (WILLIBALD) and MUEHLBACHER (JOERG) Graphentheorie für Informatiker. Berlin, 1973. pp. 140. *bibliog.*

GRAUBUENDEN
— Constitutional history.

BARBER (BENJAMIN R.) The death of communal liberty: a history of freedom in a Swiss mountain canton. Princeton, [1974]. pp. 302. *bibliog.*

— History.

BARBER (BENJAMIN R.) The death of communal liberty: a history of freedom in a Swiss mountain canton. Princeton, [1974]. pp. 302. *bibliog.*

GRAVE (JEAN).

GRAVE (JEAN) Quarante ans de propagande anarchiste; présenté et annoté par Mireille Delfau. [Paris, 1973]. pp. 605 *bibliog.*

GRAVEL
— United Kingdom.

ALLENDER (RONALD) and HOLLYER (STUART EDWIN) The sand and gravel resources of the area south and west of Woodbridge, Suffolk: description of 1 : 25 000 resource sheet TM 24. London, 1972. pp. 128. *bibliog. (U.K. Institute of Geological Sciences. Reports. No. 72/9) (Assessments of British Sand and Gravel Resources. No. 3) Map in end pocket.*

HAGGARD (HUMPHREY JAMES EDGCOMBE) The sand and gravel resources of the country around Witham, Essex: description of 1 : 25 000 resource sheet TL 81. London, 1972. pp. 90. *bibliog. (U.K. Institute of Geological Sciences. Reports. No. 72/6) (Assessments of British Sand and Gravel Resources. No. 2) Map in end pocket.*

AMBROSE (J.D.) The sand and gravel resources of the country around Layer Breton and Tolleshunt D'Arcy, Essex: description of 1 : 25 000 resource sheet TL 91 and part of TL 90. London, 1973. pp. 34. *bibliog. (U.K. Institute of Geological Sciences. Reports. No. 73/8) (Assessments of British Sand and Gravel Resources. No. 7) Map in end pocket.*

AMBROSE (J.D.) The sand and gravel resources of the country around Maldon, Essex: description of 1 : 25 000 resource sheet TL 80. London, 1973. pp. 60. *bibliog. (U.K. Institute of Geological Sciences. Reports. No. 73/1) (Assessments of British Sand and Gravel Resources. No.4) Map in end pocket.*

EATON (C.H.) The sand and gravel resources of the country around Terling, Essex: description of 1 : 25 000 resource sheet TL 71. London, 1973. pp. 120. *bibliog. (U.K. Institute of Geological Sciences. Reports. No. 73/5) (Assessments of British Sand and Gravel Resources. No.6) Map in end pocket.*

NICKLESS (E.F.P.) The sand and gravel resources of the country around Hethersett, Norfolk: description of 1: 25 000 sheet TG 10. London, 1973. pp. 80. *bibliog. (U.K. Institute of Geological Sciences. Reports. No. 73/4) (Assessments of British Sand and Gravel Resources. No.5) Map in end pocket.*

GREAT LAKES
— Economic policy.

UPPER GREAT LAKES REGIONAL COMMISSION [UNITED STATES]. Annual report. a., Ja 1972 [covering 1970/71]- Washington.

UPPER GREAT LAKES REGIONAL COMMISSION [UNITED STATES]. Regional economic development plan and five-year program (final draft). [Washington], 1970. pp. 119. *bibliog.*

GREAT POWERS.

EVANS (DOUGLAS) The politics of trade: the evolution of the superbloc. London, 1974. pp. 128.

GREECE
— Economic conditions.

COMMERCIAL BANK OF GREECE, and others. Investment guide to Greece.. 3rd ed. Athens, 1973. pp. 142.

— Economic policy.

GIANNITSIS (ANASTASIOS) Private Auslandskapitalien im Industrialisierungsprozess Griechenlands, 1953 bis 1970. Berlin, 1974. pp. 292. *bibliog.*

— Foreign relations.

THEODOULOU (CHRISTOS A.) Greece and the Entente, August 1, 1914-September 25, 1916. Thessaloniki, 1971. pp. 379. *bibliog. (Hidryma Meleton Chersonesou Tou Haimou. [Publications]. 129)*

— History — 1821—1829, War of Independence.

The STRUGGLE for Greek independence: essays to mark the 150th anniversary of the Greek War of Independence: [based on a seminar organised by the School of Slavonic and East European Studies and King's College, University of London in 1971]; edited by Richard Clogg. London, 1973. pp. 259.

KOUMOULIDES (JOHN T.A.) Cyprus and the war of Greek independence, 1821-1829. rev. ed. London, 1974. pp. 117. *bibliog.*

— — 1917— .

KOUSOULAS (DIMITRIOS GEORGE) Modern Greece: profile of a nation. New York, [1974]. pp. 300. *bibliog.*

— — 1917—1944.

SMITH (MICHAEL LLEWELLYN) Ionian vision: Greece in Asia Minor, 1919-1922. London, 1973. pp. 401. *bibliog.*

— Industries.

KINTIS (ANDREAS A.) The demand for labour in Greek manufacturing: an econometric analysis. Athens, 1973. pp. 179. *bibliog. (Center of Planning and Economic Research, [Athens]. Research Monograph Series. 20)*

— Politics and government.

THEODÓRAKIS (MIKES) Culture et dimensions politiques; traduit du grec par Jean Criticos et Pierre Comberousse. [Paris, 1973]. pp. 362.

NIKOLINAKOS (MARIOS) Widerstand und Opposition in Griechenland: vom Militärputsch 1967 zur neuen Demokratie. Darmstadt, [1974]. pp. 330. *bibliog.*

GREECE, ANCIENT
— Economic history.

FINLEY (MOSES I.) ed. Problèmes de la terre en Grèce ancienne: recueil de travaux.Paris, 1973. pp. 330. *(Paris. Ecole Pratique des Hautes Etudes. Section des Sciences Economiques et Sociales. Centre de Recherches Historiques. Civilisations et Sociétés. 33). In various languages.*

— Politics and government.

RYDER (TIMOTHY THOMAS BENNETT) Koine eirene: general peace and local independence in ancient Greece. London, 1965. pp. 184. *bibliog.*

— Social history.

FINLEY (MOSES I.) Studies in ancient society. London, 1974. pp. 324.

GREEKS IN TURKEY.

SMITH (MICHAEL LLEWELLYN) Ionian vision: Greece in Asia Minor, 1919-1922. London, 1973. pp. 401. *bibliog.*

GREEN BELTS
— France.

FRANCE. Comité Interministériel d'Action pour la Nature et l'Environnement. 1973. Protection et aménagement des espaces verts: rapport du Comité...du 20 juillet 1972 et principaux règlements. Paris, 1973. pp. 233. *(Environnement. 11)*

— United Kingdom.

HILLINGDON. Planning Department. Open land and the green belt: a background paper and interim policy. Hillingdon, 1973. pp. 127.

GREENLAND
— History.

BLOM (IDA) Kampen om Eirik Raudes land: pressgruppepolitikk i grønlandsspørsmålet, 1921-1931. Oslo, 1973. pp. 439. bibliog.

GRENADA
— Economic conditions.

U.K. Central Office of Information. Reference Division. Reference Pamphlets. 115. Grenada. London, 1974. pp. 31.

— Social conditions.

U.K. Central Office of Information. Reference Division. Reference Pamphlets. 115. Grenada. London, 1974. pp. 31.

GRENOBLE UNIVERSITY.

CLAUSTRE (HENRI) Vivre dans l'université. Grenoble, [1973]. pp. 271.

GRIFFITH (ARTHUR).

DAVIS (RICHARD P.) Arthur Griffith and non-violent Sinn Fein. Dublin, 1974. pp. 232. bibliog.

GRIGIONI.

See GRAUBUENDEN.

GRIMSBY
— Docks.

JACKSON (GORDON) Grimsby and the Haven Company, 1796-1846. Grimsby, [1971]. pp. 102.

— Transit systems.

SCOTT, WILSON, KIRKPATRICK AND PARTNERS. Grimsby transportation study: final report ([prepared for] Grimsby County Borough Council). London, 1972. pp. 118. Map in end pocket.

GRIPENSTEDT (JOHAN AUGUST).

GASSLANDER (OLLE) J.A. Gripenstedt: statsman och företagare. [Lund], [1949]. pp. 463. bibliog.

GRISONS.

See GRAUBUENDEN.

GROCERY TRADE
— United States.

SEXTON (DONALD E.) Groceries in the ghetto. Lexington, Mass., [1973]. pp. 141. bibliog.

GROENMAN (SJOERD).

PERPETUUM mobile: thema's en toepassingen in de sociologie van Groenman; redactie J.E. Ellemers [and others]. Assen, 1974. pp. 208. bibliog.

GROOT (PAUL DE).

GROOT (PAUL DE) De dertiger jaren 1930-(1939): herinneringen en overdenkingen. Amsterdam, 1965-67. 2 vols.

GROS (JOSE).

GROS (JOSE) Abriendo camino: relatos de un guerrillero comunista; prologo de Dolores Ibarruri. [Paris, 1972]. pp. 270.

GROSS DOMESTIC PRODUCT
— Argentine Republic — Mendoza (Province).

MENDOZA (PROVINCE). Direccion de Estadisticas e Investigaciones Economicas. 1972. Producto bruto interno 1961/69. [Mendoza, 1972?]. fo. 30. (Mendoza (Province). Direccion de Estadisticas e Investigaciones Economicas. Estudios Especiales. No.83)

MENDOZA (PROVINCE). Direccion de Estadisticas e Investigaciones Economicas. 1972. Producto bruto interno 1970/1971. [Mendoza, 1972?]. fo.38. (Mendoza (Province). Direccion de Estadisticas e Investigaciones Economicas. Estudios Especiales. No.85)

— France.

FRANCE. Centre d'Etude des Revenus et des Coûts. 1969. Prix, coûts et revenus en France de 1949 à 1968. Paris, 1969. pp. 62. (Documents. No. 2)

— Hong Kong.

HONG KONG. Census and Statistics Department. Estimates of gross domestic product. a., 1966/1971 [1st issue]- Hong Kong.

— South Africa.

SOUTH AFRICA. Bureau of Statistics. Gross geographic product by magisterial district. irreg., 1968[1st]- Pretoria.

— United Kingdom.

ASH (J.C.K.) Quarterly forecasting at the N[ational] I[nstitute of] E[conomic and] S[ocial] R[esearch]: gross domestic product. [Reading], 1972. pp. 42. bibliog. (Reading. University. Department of Economics. Discussion Papers in Economics. No.38)

ASH (J.C.K.) and SMYTH (D.J.) Who forecasts the British economy best?: an assessment of half- yearly forecasts of gross domestic product published by the Treasury, NIESR, OECD, The Sunday Times and The Sunday Telegraph. [Reading], 1973. fo. 25. bibliog. (Reading. University. Department of Economics. Discussion Papers in Economics. Series A. No. 52)

— Yugoslavia.

YUGOSLAVIA. Savezni Zavod za Statistiku. Studije, Analize i Prikazi. 61. Privredni bilansi Jugoslavije, 1966-1971; Economic balances of Yugoslavia, 1966-1971. Beograd, 1973. pp. 257. With English summary.

GROSS NATIONAL PRODUCT
— Communist countries.

BAHRII (PETRO ILARIONOVYCH) Dynamik und Struktur der gesellschaftlichen Produktion im Sozialismus: methodische und analytische Probleme; (in die deutsche Sprache übertragen von Dieter Graf). Berlin, 1974. pp. 380.

— Russia.

OKTIABR'SKII (PAVEL IAKOVLEVICH) Sushchnost' i kriterii ekonomicheskoi effektivnosti obshchestvennogo proizvodstva. Leningrad, 1973. pp. 54. bibliog.

GORBUNOV (EDUARD PETROVICH) Struktura i effektivnost' obshchestvennogo proizvodstva. Moskva, 1974. pp. 199.

— — Kirghizia.

TEMPY i proportsii rasshirennogo vosproizvodstva v Kirgizii. Frunze, 1973. pp. 61.

— Thailand.

GOULD (JOSEPH S.) Estimates of gross national product and net national income of Thailand 1938/39, 1946, 1947 and 1948. [Bangkok], 1950. fo. 5.

GROSSETO (PROVINCE)
— Politics and government.

CORSI (HUBERT) Le origini del fascismo nel Grossetano, 1919-1922. Roma, [1973]. pp. 199.

GROUPS, THEORY OF.

HALLINAN (MAUREEN T.) The structure of positive sentiment. Amsterdam, 1974. pp. 115. bibliog.

GUADELOUPE
— Population.

FRANCE. Institut National de la Statistique et des Etudes Economiques. 1972. Tendances démographiques dans les départements insulaires d'outre-mer: Martinique, Guadeloupe et Réunion. Paris, [1972?]. pp. 261.

GUARANTEED ANNUAL INCOME.

NUFFIELD CANADIAN SEMINAR, SAINTE-ADELE, QUEBEC, 1972. Le revenu annuel garanti: une approche intégrée: documents de travail et rapports du Séminaire...tenu...sous les auspices du Conseil canadien de Développement social. Ottawa, 1973. pp. 351.

— Canada.

NUFFIELD CANADIAN SEMINAR, SAINTE-ADELE, QUEBEC, 1972. Le revenu annuel garanti: une approche intégrée: documents de travail et rapports du Séminaire...tenu...sous les auspices du Conseil canadien de Développement social. Ottawa, 1973. pp. 351.

GUATEMALA.

FRANCE. Direction de la Documentation. La Documentation Française. Notes et Etudes Documentaires. No. 3,127. Le Guatemala. Paris, 1964. pp. 27. bibliog.

— Politics and government.

JOHNSON (KENNETH F.) Guatemala: from terrorism to terror. London, 1972. pp. 19. (Institute for the Study of Conflict. Conflict Studies. No. 23)

— Statistics, Vital.

GUATEMALA. Direccion General de Estadistica. Departamento de Estudios Especiales y Estadisticas Continuas. 1967. Tablas de vida, Republica de Guatemala, 1964; preparadas... por J. Antonio Barrera Tunchez... bajo la direccion y supervision [de] Luis Eduardo Contreras R. Guatemala, [1967]. pp. 67.

GUERRILLA WARFARE.

INSTITUT MARKSIZMA-LENINIZMA. La guerra partigiana vista dai classici del marxismo-leninismo; [edited by B. Ponomarev]. Mosca, [1945]; Milano, [1971?]. pp. 119.

GUILLEN (ABRAHAM) Desafio al Pentagono: la guerrilla latinoamericana. Montevideo, [1969]. pp. 183.

GRUNDY (KENNETH W.) Guerrilla struggle in Africa: an analysis and preview. New York, 1971. pp. 204.

LIBERTI (EGIDIO) ed. Tecniche della guerra partigiana nel Risorgimento: testi di autori mazziniani. [Firenze, 1972]. pp. 651. (Centro per la Storia della Tecnica in Italia. Pubblicazioni. Sezione 1. Vol.3)

JOHNSON (CHALMERS) Autopsy on people's war. Berkeley, Calif., [1973]. pp. 118.

FAIRBAIRN (GEOFFREY) Revolutionary guerrilla warfare: the countryside version. Harmondsworth, 1974. pp. 400.

GUERRILLAS

TANIA: la guerrillera inolvidable. Havana, 1970. pp. 359.

— Africa, Subsaharan.

GRUNDY (KENNETH W.) Guerrilla struggle in Africa: an analysis and preview. New York, 1971. pp. 204.

— Africa, Subsaharan — Bibliography.

ANSARI (S.) compiler. Liberation struggle in southern Africa: a bibliography of source material. Gurgaon, Haryana, 1972. pp. 118.

GUERRILLAS. (Cont.)

— America, Latin.

PIÑEIRO (ARMANDO ALONSO) Paredon de America. Buenos Aires, [1962]. pp. 125.

GOTT (RICHARD) Rural guerrillas in Latin America. rev. ed. Harmondsworth, 1973. pp. 637. *bibliog.*

— Angola.

BARNETT (DONALD L.) and HARVEY (ROY) The revolution in Angola: M[ovimento] P[opulár de] L[ibertação de] A[ngola], life histories and documents. Indianapolis, [1972]. pp. 312.

NETO (ANTONIO AGOSTINHO) Messages to companions in the struggle; [speeches]. Richmond, B.C., 1972. pp. 30.

BRUCE (NEIL) Portugal's African wars. London, 1973. pp. 22. (*Institute for the Study of Conflict. Conflict Studies. No. 34*)

PINTO (RUI DE) The making of a middle cadre: the story of Rui de Pinto; taped and edited by Don Barnett. Richmond, B.C., [1973]. pp. 107. (*Liberation Support Movement. Information Center. Life Histories from the Revolution. Angola, MPLA.1*)

— Baltic States.

VENNER (DOMINIQUE) Baltikum: dans le Reich de la défaite, le combat des Corps- francs, 1918-1923. Paris [1974]. pp. 366. *bibliog.*

— Bolivia.

DEBRAY (REGIS) La guérilla du Che. Paris, [1974]. pp. 188.

— Brazil.

CARLOS Marighella; [a brief biography with extracts from his writings]. [Havana, 1970]. pp. 101.

MARIGHELA (CARLOS) La guerra revolucionaria. Mexico, 1970. pp. 101. *bibliog.*

— Colombia.

ROJAS (ROBINSON) Colombia: surge el primer Vietnam en America Latina; (reportaje a la guerra revolucionaria del pueblo en Colombia). [Santiago de Chile?], 1970. pp. 64.

— East (Near East).

INSTITUTE FOR THE STUDY OF CONFLICT. Research Department. Since Jordan: the Palestinian fedayeen. London, 1973. pp. 18. *bibliog.* (*Institute for the Study of Conflict. Conflict Studies. No. 38*)

MA'OZ (MOSHE) Soviet and Chinese relations with the Palestinian guerrilla organizations. Jerusalem, 1974. pp. 35. *bibliog.* (*Hebrew University. Leonard Davis Institute for International Relations. Jerusalem Papers on Peace Problems. No. 4*)

— Germany.

VENNER (DOMINIQUE) Baltikum: dans le Reich de la défaite, le combat des Corps- francs, 1918-1923. Paris [1974]. pp. 366. *bibliog.*

— Guatemala.

FUENTES MOHR (ALBERTO) Secuestro y prision: dos caras de la violencia en Guatemala. San Jose, 1971. pp. 213.

JOHNSON (KENNETH F.) Guatemala: from terrorism to terror. London, 1972. pp. 19. (*Institute for the Study of Conflict. Conflict Studies. No. 23*)

— Mozambique.

BRUCE (NEIL) Portugal's African wars. London, 1973. pp. 22. (*Institute for the Study of Conflict. Conflict Studies. No. 34*)

— Peru.

BLANCO GALDOS (HUGO) El camino de nuestra revolucion. Lima, 1964. pp. 64.

— Portuguese Guinea.

BRUCE (NEIL) Portugal's African wars. London, 1973. pp. 22. (*Institute for the Study of Conflict. Conflict Studies. No 34*)

— South Africa.

TUROK (BEN) Strategic problems in South Africa's liberation struggle: a critical analysis. Richmond, B.C., 1974. pp. 66.

— Spain.

GROS (JOSE) Abriendo camino: relatos de un guerrillero comunista; prologo de Dolores Ibarruri. [Paris, 1972]. pp. 270.

TELLEZ (ANTONIO) La guerrilla urbana en España: Sabate. Paris, [1972]. pp. 213.

TELLEZ (ANTONIO) Sabate: guerrilla extraordinary; ... translated by Stuart Christie. London, 1974. pp. 183.

— United Kingdom.

STOKE NEWINGTON 8 DEFENCE GROUP. If you want peace, prepare for war. London, [1972]. pp. 32.

— Ireland.

BARRY (TOM) Guerilla days in Ireland. Tralee, 1962 repr. 1971. pp. 207. *First published in 1949.*

— Uruguay.

MAYANS (ERNESTO) ed. Tupamaros: antologia documental. Cuernavaca, 1971. 1 vol. (various pagings). (*Centro Intercultural de Documentacion. Cidoc Cuadernos. No.60*)

MOSS (ROBERT) Uruguay: terrorism versus democracy. London, 1971. pp. 10. (*Institute for the Study of Conflict. Conflict Studies. No. 14*)

COSTA (OMAR) ed. Los tupamaros. 2nd ed. Mexico, 1972. pp. 346.

JACKSON (Sir GEOFFREY HOLT SEYMOUR) People's prison. London, 1973. pp. 222.

LABROUSSE (ALAIN) The Tupamaros: urban guerrillas in Uruguay, translated by Dinah Livingstone. Harmondsworth, 1973. pp. 168.

PORZECANSKI (ARTURO C.) Uruguay's Tupamaros: the urban guerrilla. New York, 1973. pp. 80. *bibliog.*

— Venezuela.

VALSALICE (LUIGI) Guerriglia e politica: l'esempio del Venezuela, 1962-1969. Firenze, [1973]. pp. 264. *bibliog.* (*Centro di Ricerche per l'America Latina. Documentazione Latino-Americana.1*)

GUERRILLAS (INTERNATIONAL LAW).

BOND (JAMES EDWARD) The rules of riot: internal conflict and the law of war. Princeton, [1974]. pp. 280. *bibliog.*

GUEVARA (ERNESTO).

DEBRAY (REGIS) La guérilla du Che. Paris, [1974]. pp. 188.

GUJARAT

— Economic policy.

GUJARAT. General Administration Department (Planning). 1972. Perspective plan of Gujarat, 1974-1984. Baroda, 1972. 3 vols.

— Rural conditions.

BREMAN (JAN) Patronage and exploitation: changing agrarian relations in South Gujarat, India. Berkeley, [1974]. pp. 287. *bibliog.*

— Social life and customs.

VEEN (KLAAS W. VAN DER) I give thee my daughter: a study of marriage and hierarchy among the Anavil Brahmans of South Gujarat; [translated by Nanette Jockin]. Assen, 1972. pp. 297. *bibliog.*

— Social policy.

GUJARAT. General Administration Department (Planning). 1972. Perspective plan of Gujarat, 1974-1984. Baroda, 1972. 3 vols.

GURVICH (GEORGII DAVYDOVICH).

BALANDIER (GEORGES) Gurvitch. [Paris], 1972. pp. 120. *bibliog.*

GUYANA

— Appropriations and expenditures.

ODLE (MAURICE A.) An analysis of public expenditure in a small, open and underdeveloped country: a case study of Guyana; [Ph.D. (London) thesis]. 1973. fo. 319. *bibliog. Typescript: unpublished. This thesis is the property of London University and may not be removed from the Library.*

— Boundaries — Venezuela.

ROUT (LESLIE B.) Which way out?: a study of the Guyana-Venezuela boundary dispute. East Lansing, [1971]. fo. 130. *bibliog.* (*Michigan State University. Latin American Studies Center. Monograph Series. No.4*)

— Foreign relations.

TROTMAN (DONALD A.B.) Guyana and the world...: commentaries on national and international affairs,1968-1973. [Georgetown], [1973?]. pp. 100.

HABERMAS (JUERGEN).

JAEGER (WOLFGANG) Offentlichkeit und Parlamentarismus: eine Kritik an Jürgen Habermas. Stuttgart, [1973]. pp. 107.

WILLMS (BERNARD) Kritik und Politik: Jürgen Habermas; oder, Das politische Defizit der "Kritischen Theorie". Frankfurt am Main, 1973. pp. 207.

HÄGGLÖF (GUNNAR).

HÄGGLÖF (GUNNAR) Fredens vägar, 1945-1950. Stockholm, [1973]. pp. 213.

HAGUE

— International Court of Justice.

HIDAYATULLAH (MOHAMMAD) The South-West Africa case. Bombay, [1967]. pp. 144.

ELIAN (GEORGE) The International Court of Justice. Leiden, 1971. pp. 150.

FRANCE. Direction de la Documentation. La Documentation Française. Notes et Etudes Documentaires. Nos. 3,890-3, 891. La jurisprudence de la Cour Internationale de Justice de 1946 à 1971. par Raymond Goy. [Paris]. 1972. pp. 76. *bibliog.*

HAITI

— Civilization.

CULTURE et développement en Haiti: symposium Haiti organisé sous les auspices du Département d'Anthropologie de l'Université de Montréal et du Centre d'Etudes Haitiennes, 6-9 mai 1970; [edited by Emerson Douyon]. [Ottawa, 1972]. pp. 237.

— Economic policy.

CULTURE et développement en Haiti: symposium Haiti organisé sous les auspices du Département d'Anthropologie de l'Université de Montréal et du Centre d'Etudes Haitiennes, 6-9 mai 1970; [edited by Emerson Douyon]. [Ottawa, 1972]. pp. 237.

— **Emigration and immigration.**

CORTEN (ANDRE) La migration des travailleurs haitiens vers les centrales sucrières dominicaines. n.p., [1970]. pp. 713-731. *Xerox copy.*

— **History.**

OTT (THOMAS O.) The Haitian revolution, 1789-1804. Knoxville, [1973]. pp. 232. *bibliog.*

HAITIANS IN THE DOMINICAN REPUBLIC.

CORTEN (ANDRE) La migration des travailleurs haitiens vers les centrales sucrières dominicaines. n.p., [1970]. pp. 713-731. *Xerox copy.*

HALFWAY HOUSES

— **Canada.**

CANADA. Task Force on Community-based Residential Centres. 1973. Report; [W.R. Outerbridge, chairman]. Ottawa, 1973. pp. 85, 92. *bibliog. In English and French.*

HALL (DANIEL GEORGE EDWARD).

SARKISYANZ (EMANUEL) Peacocks, pagodas and Professor Hall: a critique of the persisting use of historiography as an apology for British empire- building in Burma. Athens, [1972]. fo.57. *(Ohio University. Center for International Studies. Papers in International Studies. Southeast Asia Series. No.24)*

HALLIER (JEAN EDERN).

HALLIER (JEAN EDERN) La cause des peuples. Paris, [1972]. pp. 251.

HALLUCINOGENIC DRUGS.

HARNER (MICHAEL J.) ed. Hallucinogens and shamanism. New York, 1973. pp. 200. *bibliogs.*

WELLS (BRIAN) Psychedelic drugs: psychological, medical and social issues. Harmondsworth, 1973. pp. 250. *bibliog.*

HAMBURG

— **Commerce.**

BOEHM (EKKEHARD) Überseehandel und Flottenbau: hanseatische Kaufmannschaft und deutsche Seerüstung, 1879-1902. Düsseldorf, [1972]. pp. 417. *bibliog. (Hamburg. Hansische Universität. Studien zur Modernen Geschichte. Band 8)*

ROEHLK (FRAUKE) Schiffahrt und Handel zwischen Hamburg und den Niederlanden in der zweiten Hälfte des 18. und zu Beginn des 19. Jahrhunderts. Wiesbaden, 1973. 2 vols. (in 1). *bibliog. (Vierteljahrschrift für Sozial- und Wirtschaftsgeschichte. Beihefte. Nr.60) Table in end pocket.*

— **Economic history.**

WENNER (HANS JOACHIM) Handelskonjunkturen und Rentenmarkt am Beispiel der Stadt Hamburg um die Mitte des 14. Jahrhunderts. Hamburg, 1972. pp. 129. *bibliog. (Verein für Hamburgische Geschichte. Beiträge zur Geschichte Hamburgs. Band 9)*

— **Floods.**

RAMPE (JOHANNES) Flutkatastrophe 1962: wirtschaftliche Hilfsmassnahmen; Abschlussbericht, etc. Hamburg, [1970]. pp. 46. *(Hamburg. Behörde für Wirtschaft und Verkehr. Schriftenreihe. Heft 8)*

— **History.**

GELBERG (BIRGIT) Auswanderung nach Übersee: soziale Probleme der Auswandererbeförderung in Hamburg und Bremen von der Mitte des 19. Jahrhunderts bis zum Ersten Weltkrieg. Hamburg, 1973. pp. 67. *bibliog. (Verein für Hamburgische Geschichte. Beiträge zur Geschichte Hamburgs. Band 10)*

— **Social history.**

KROHN (HELGA) Die Juden in Hamburg: die politische, soziale und kulturelle Entwicklung einer jüdischen Grosstadtgemeinde nach der Emanzipation, 1848-1918. Hamburg, 1974. pp. 247. *bibliog.*

HAMELIN (JACQUES FELIX EMMANUEL).

FAIVRE (JEAN PAUL) Le Contre-Amiral Hamelin et la Marine française. Paris, [1962]. pp. 195. *bibliog.*

HAMILTON (ANNE) Duchess of Hamilton.

MARSHALL (ROSALIND K.) Ph. D. The days of Duchess Anne: life in the household of the Duchess of Hamilton, 1656-1716. London, 1973. pp. 256. *bibliog.*

HAMPSHIRE

— **Economic history — Sources.**

HAMPSHIRE ARCHIVISTS' GROUP. Publications. No.2. Transport in Hampshire and the Isle of Wight: a guide to the records. [Portsmouth], 1973. pp. 126.

— **Economic policy.**

SOUTH HAMPSHIRE PLAN ADVISORY COMMITTEE. Study Reports. Group G. Trends and Changes in Society. No.1. Technological change. Winchester, 1970. pp. 31. *bibliog.*

— **Industries.**

SOUTH HAMPSHIRE PLAN ADVISORY COMMITTEE. Study Reports. Group D. People, Activities and Housing. No.2. Employment. Winchester, [1967]. pp. 67.

— **Population.**

SOUTH HAMPSHIRE PLAN ADVISORY COMMITTEE. Study Reports. Group D. People, Activities and Housing. No.1. Population. Winchester, [1967?]. pp. 60.

— **Social conditions.**

SOUTH HAMPSHIRE PLAN ADVISORY COMMITTEE. Study Reports. Group D. People, Activities and Housing. No.6. Social and community life. Winchester, 1970. pp. 28, vi.

SOUTH HAMPSHIRE PLAN ADVISORY COMMITTEE. Study Reports. Group G. Trends and Changes in Society. No. 2. Social change; by D. McQuail [and others]. [Winchester, 1970?]. pp. 36.

— **Social policy.**

SOUTH HAMPSHIRE PLAN ADVISORY COMMITTEE. Study Reports. Group G. Trends and Changes in Society. No.1. Technological change. Winchester, 1970. pp. 31. *bibliog.*

SOUTH HAMPSHIRE PLAN ADVISORY COMMITTEE. Study Reports. Group G. Trends and Changes in Society. No. 2. Social change; by D. McQuail [and others]. [Winchester, 1970?]. pp. 36.

HAMPSTEAD

— **History.**

THOMPSON (FRANCIS MICHAEL LONGSTRETH) Hampstead: building a borough, 1650-1964. London, 1974. pp. 459.

HANDICAPPED

— **Employment — United Kingdom.**

DESPITE disability: career achievement by handicapped people. Reading, 1974. pp. 136.

— **France.**

LENOIR (RENE) Les exclus: un français sur dix. 2nd ed. Paris, [1974]. pp. 172.

— **Norway.**

NORWAY. Sosialdepartementet. 1970. Lov om sosial omsorg av 5. juni 1964: rundskriv nr. 13: Om kommunenes oppgaver i omsorgen for funksjonshemmede. Oslo, [1970]. pp. 23.

— **Sweden.**

SWEDEN. Socialdepartementet. Handikapputredningen. 1970. Bättre socialtjänst för handikappade: förslag... om bättre färdmöjligheter för handikappade och bättre samordning i handikappfrågor. Stockholm, 1970. pp. 73. *(Sweden. Statens Offentliga Utredningar. 1970. 64) With English summary.*

— **United Kingdom.**

HILLINGDON. [Social Services Department]. Meals services/handicapped persons survey: report on a sample survey to estimate the demand for meals services in Hillingdon and to estimate the number of impaired and handicapped persons in the borough. [London], 1972. 1 vol.(various pagings).

KENSINGTON AND CHELSEA. Social Services Department. Survey of handicapped and impaired persons and persons aged 75 or over and living alone in the...Borough...; research...by Judith Buckle and Philip Baldwin. London, 1972. pp. 103.

NEWCASTLE-UPON-TYNE. Social Services Department. Report on the survey of chronically sick and disabled people resident in Newcastle upon Tyne, 1972. Newcastle-upon-Tyne, [1972]. 2 vols. (in 1) *Included in vol.1, Summary and conclusions, and in vol. 2, Notes on report, etc.*

STUDIES in disability in Exeter and Edinburgh; by C.P. Lowther [and others]. Exeter, 1973. pp. 38. *(Exeter. University. Institute of Biometry and Community Medicine. Publications. No. 1)*

— **United States.**

CULL (JOHN G.) and HARDY (RICHARD E.) Understanding disability for social and rehabilitation services. Springfield, Ill., [1973]. pp. 205. *bibliogs.*

HANDICAPPED CHILDREN

— **Bibliography.**

PILLING (DORIA) compiler. The child with spina bifida: social, emotional and educational adjustment; an annotated bibliography. Slough, 1973, pp. 46.

— **Education — Denmark.**

DENMARK. Undervisningsministeriet. International Relations Division. 1971. Developments towards a coherent system of education for the handicapped. [Copenhagen, 1971]. pp. 16.

JØRGENSEN (I. SKOV) Special education in Denmark: summary of school legislation concerning special education in the Scandinavian countries. [Copenhagen, Ministry of Education], 1971. fo. 14.

— — **Netherlands.**

MÄKEL (N.W.) Educational care of the handicapped child. The Hague, Ministry of Education and Science, 1969. pp. 46.

— — **South Africa.**

SOUTH AFRICA. Interdepartmental Committee of Inquiry into Educational Facilities for Educable White Children who suffer from Chronic Illnesses. 1973. Report..., 1967 (R.P. 80/1973). in SOUTH AFRICA. Parliament. House of Assembly. Votes and proceedings; (with Printed annexures).

— **Sweden.**

OLOW (INGEMAR) Rörelsehindrade barn och ungdomar: deras behandling och vård. [Stockholm, 1971]. pp. 56. *bibliog. (Sweden. Skolöverstyrelsen. Kompendier. 6)*

— **United Kingdom.**

PARFIT (JESSIE) Spotlight on physical and mental assessment;...[with supplements]. London, [1971] in progress. *(National Children's Bureau. Spotlight. 1)*

PARFIT (JESSIE) Spotlight on services for the young handicapped child. London, [1972]. pp. 162. *(National Children's Bureau. Spotlights. 3)*

HANDICAPPED CHILDREN. (Cont.)

— — Bibliography.

PILLING (DORIA) compiler. The handicapped child: research review. vol.3. Mental handicap:the severely subnormal; the educationally subnormal. London, 1973. pp. 651. *bibliog. (National Children's Bureau. Studies in Child Development)*

— United States.

SERVICES for handicapped youth: a program overview; prepared for the Department of Health, Education, and Welfare [by] James S. Kakalik [and others]. Santa Monica, 1973. pp. 341. *bibliog. (Rand Corporation. [Rand Reports]. 1220)*

HANDICRAFT

— Macao.

AMARO (ANA MARIA) Alguns aspectos do artesanato em Macau. Macau, Centro de Informação e Turismo, [1973?]. pp. 49.

— United Kingdom.

COUNCIL FOR SMALL INDUSTRIES IN RURAL AREAS. Report. bien., Ap 1970/Mr 1972 [2nd]- London.

HANOVER

— Nationalism.

STEHLIN (STEWART A.) Bismarck and the Guelph problem 1866-1890: a study in particularist opposition to national unity. The Hague, 1973. pp. 253. *bibliog.*

HANSA TOWNS.

SPADING (KLAUS) Holland und die Hanse im 15. Jahrhundert: zur Problematik des Übergangs vom Feudalismus zum Kapitalismus. Weimar, 1973. pp. 189. *bibliog. (Historiker-Gesellschaft der Deutschen Demokratischen Republik. Hansische Arbeitsgemeinschaft. Abhandlungen zur Handels- und Sozialgeschichte. Band 12)*

HANSEATIC LEAGUE.

THIERFELDER (HILDEGARD) Köln und die Hanse. Köln, 1970. pp. 25. *(Cologne. Universität. Forschungsinstitut für Sozial- und Wirtschaftsgeschichte. Kölner Vorträge zur Sozial- und Wirtschaftsgeschichte. Heft 7)*

HANSSEN (GEORG).

MEITZEN (AUGUST) Georg Hanssen als Agrar-Historiker. [Tübingen, 1881]. pp. 47. *(Separatabzug aus der Zeitschrift für die gesammte Staatswissenschaft)*

HANUSCH (FERDINAND).

STAININGER (OTTO) ed. Ferdinand Hanusch, 1866-1923: ein Leben für den sozialen Aufstieg; herausgegeben ... im Auftrag der Österreichischen Gesellschaft für Kulturpolitik. Wien, [1973]. pp. 109. *(Ludwig-Boltzmann-Institut für Geschichte der Arbeiterbewegung. Schriftenreihe. 3)*

HARBOURS.

HOPPE (HELMUT R.) and NOORTMAN (H.J.) Aktuelle Probleme der Seehafen- und Regionalpolitik. Göttingen, 1972. pp. 36. *(Münster in Westfalen. Westfälische Wilhelms- Universität. Institut für Verkehrswissenschaft. Vorträge und Studien. Heft 13)*

WANHILL (S.R.C.) Optimum size seaport - a further analysis. Bangor, 1974. pp. 6. *(Wales. University. University College of North Wales. Economic Research Papers. REG. 10)*

— Safety measures.

SOCIETY OF CONSERVATIVE LAWYERS. Safety in British ports: report of an investigation into the present position and some recommendations by a committee of the Society of Conservative Lawyers. London, 1974. pp. 28. *(Conservative Political Centre. [Publications]. No. 549)*

— Costa Rica.

TRANSPORTATION CONSULTANTS, INC. Republic of Costa Rica: report on port and railway study; prepared with the assistance of United Nations. Special Fund; executing agency: International Bank for Reconstruction and Development. [Washington, 1964]. 1 vol. (various pagings). *bibliog.* Microfilm: 1 reel.

— Netherlands.

BELD (C.A. VAN DEN) and MIDDELHOEK (A.J.) Evaluation of seaport projects. The Hague, Central Planning Bureau, 1971. pp. 25. *(Occasional Papers. 1971/No.3)*

VIRENQUE (P.H.) and others. Haveninvesteringen op de linker-Scheldeoever: welvaart en kosten-batenanalyse. Antwerp, [1973]. pp. 115. *bibliog.* With English summary.

— United Kingdom.

ANNUAL DIGEST OF PORT STATISTICS (formerly Digest of port statistics); [pd. by] National Ports Council. a., 1966 [1st]- London. *From 1973 in 2 pts.*

NATIONAL PORTS COUNCIL. Annual report and accounts. a., 1972[9th]- London.

ADAMS (GEORGE) Organisation of the British port transport industry. London, National Ports Council, 1973. pp. 262. *bibliogs.*

SOCIETY OF CONSERVATIVE LAWYERS. Safety in British ports: report of an investigation into the present position and some recommendations by a committee of the Society of Conservative Lawyers. London, 1974. pp. 28. *(Conservative Political Centre. [Publications]. No. 549)*

— — Port charges.

WEBSTER (PERCY JOHN KINNERSLEY) A charges structure for the ports of the United Kingdom; [Ph. D. (London) thesis]. 1973. fo. 143. *bibliog.* Typescript: unpublished. *This thesis is the property of London University and may not be removed from the Library.*

— — Wales.

WELSH COUNCIL. The Welsh ports. [Cardiff?], 1973. fo.46,5maps.

— United States.

FEREJOHN (JOHN A.) Pork barrel politics: rivers and harbors legislation, 1947-1968. Stanford, 1974. pp. 288. *bibliog.*

HARDIE (JAMES KEIR).

U.K. National Register of Archives. 1973. Labour Party archives: miscellaneous accessions: Keir Hardie Memorial Committee: J.Keir Hardie MSS. London, 1973. single sheet.

HASSELMANN (WILHELM).

BERS (GUENTER) Wilhelm Hasselmann, 1844-1916: sozialrevolutionärer Agitator und Abgeordneter des Deutschen Reichstages. Köln, 1973. pp. 171. *bibliog.*

HAUSAS.

RAYNAUT (CLAUDE) Structures normatives et relations électives: étude d'une communauté villageoise haoussa. Paris, [1973]. pp. 314. *bibliog.*

HAUSHOFER (ALBRECHT).

LAACK-MICHEL (URSULA) Albrecht Haushofer und der Nationalsozialismus: ein Beitrag zur Zeitgeschichte. Stuttgart, [1974]. pp. 407. *bibliog.*

HAUTE—LOIRE

— Economic history.

MERLEY (JEAN) L'industrie en Haute-Loire de la fin de la Monarchie de Juillet aux débuts de la Troisième République. Lyon, [1972]. pp. 450. *bibliog.*

HAWAIIAN ISLANDS

— Population.

RENAUD (BERTRAND M.) Population dynamics in Hawaii. Honolulu, 1973. pp. 143. *bibliog.*

HAY (JOHN) 2nd Earl of Tweeddale.

U.K. Parliament. House of Lords. Record Office. Memoranda. No. 47. Letters of the second Earl of Tweeddale, 1672 to 1692; a list compiled by D.J. Johnson. [London, 1972]. pp. 6.

HEALTH ATTITUDES.

HERZLICH (CLAUDINE) Health and illness: a social psychological analysis;... translated by Douglas Graham. London, 1973. pp. 159. *bibliog. (European Association of Experimental Social Psychology. European Monographs in Social Psychology. 5)*

HEALTH EDUCATION.

WORLD HEALTH ORGANIZATION. Expert Committee on Planning and Evaluation of Health Education Services. 1969. Planning and evaluation of health education services; report, etc.Geneva, 1969. pp. 32. *(Technical Report Series. No. 409)*

UNITED NATIONS EDUCATIONAL, SCIENTIFIC AND CULTURAL ORGANIZATION. Educational Studies and Documents. New Series. Paris, 1971 in progress..

HEALTH OFFICERS

— United Kingdom.

CLARK (JUNE) A family visitor: a descriptive analysis of health visiting in Berkshire. London, [1973]. pp. 124. *bibliog.*

HOBBS (PATRICIA) Aptitude or environment?: a study of the group teaching activities of health visitors. London, [1973]. pp. 164. *bibliog.*

HEERHUGOWAARD

— Politics and government.

FRIESWIJK (JOHAN) Gemeentepolitiek en opbouwwerk: een verkenning van de problematiek aan de hand van de gebeurtenissen rond het opbouwwerk in Heerhugowaard. Deventer, 1973. pp. 77. *(Nederlands Instituut voor Maatschappelijke Opbouw. Nimocahiers. 13)*

HEGEL (GEORG WILHELM FRIEDRICH).

ADORNO (THEODOR WIESENGRUND) Negative dialectics;...translated by E.B. Ashton. London, 1973. pp. 416.

POGOSIAN (VIL ANDRANIKOVICH) Problema otchuzhdeniia v "Fenomenologii dukha" Gegelia. Erevan, 1973. pp. 129.

ROSEN (STANLEY) G.W.F. Hegel: an introduction to the science of wisdom. New Haven, 1974. pp. 302. *bibliog.*

HEIDEGGER (MARTIN).

ADORNO (THEODOR WIESENGRUND) Negative dialectics;...translated by E.B. Ashton. London, 1973. pp. 416.

GOLDMANN (LUCIEN) Lukacs et Heidegger; fragments posthumes établis et présentés par Youssef Ishaghpour. [Paris, 1973]. pp. 177.

HEIDELBERG

— Politics and government.

WAHLKAMPF als Ritual?: Studien zur Bundestagswahl von 1969 im Wahlkreis Heidelberg-Mannheim/Land; ([by] Rüdiger Andel [and others; edited by] Peter Haungs). Meisenheim am Glan, 1974. pp. 336.

HEINEMANN (GUSTAV WALTER).

BRAUN (JOACHIM) Journalist. Der unbequeme Präsident: [Gustav Heinemann]. Karlsruhe, [1972]. pp. 230.

HELSINKI

— Industries — Statistics.

HELSINKI. Kaupungin Tilastotoimisto. Vuoden 1964 liikeyrityslaskenta Helsingissä: 1964 års företagsräkning i Helsingfors; ([by] Elisabeth Elfvengren). Helsinki, 1971. pp. 111. (*Helsingin Kaupungin Tilasto. 7 : 7. Erikoistutkimukset*) In Finnish and Swedish, with English summary.

— Social conditions.

SWEETSER (FRANK L.) Metropolitan and regional social ecology of Helsinki. Helsinki, 1973. pp. 165. bibliog. (*Societas Scientiarum Fennica. Commentationes Scientiarum Socialium. 5*)

HENRY IV, King of England.

KIRBY (JOHN LAVAN) Henry IV of England. London, 1970. pp. 280. bibliog.

HENRY VII, King of England.

CHRIMES (STANLEY BERTRAM) Henry VII. London, 1972. pp. 373. bibliog.

HERALDRY

— United Kingdom.

SMITH (CHRISTOPHER J.) The civic heraldry of Warwickshire: an account of the armorial bearings of local authorities in Warwickshire prior to the local government reforms of 1974. [Coventry, 1973]. pp. 63. (*Historical Association. Coventry Branch. Coventry and Warwickshire History Pamphlets. No. 9*)

HEREN (LOUIS).

HEREN (LOUIS) Growing up poor in London. London, 1973. pp. 208.

HEROIN.

WALDORF (DAN) Careers in dope. Englewood Cliffs, N.J., [1973]. pp. 186. bibliog.

HERZEN (ALEXANDER)

See GERTSEN (ALEKSANDR IVANOVICH).

HERZL (THEODOR).

STEWART (DESMOND) Theodor Herzl: artist and politician. London, 1974. pp. 395. bibliog.

HESS (RUDOLF).

SCHWARZWAELLER (WULF) "Der Stellvertreter des Führers": Rudolf Hess, der Mann in Spandau. Wien, [1974]. pp. 304. bibliog.

HESSE

— Economic history.

LASCH (MANFRED) Untersuchungen über Bevölkerung und Wirtschaft der Landgrafschaft Hessen-Kassel und der Stadt Kassel...bis zum Tode Landgraf Karls, 1730. Kassel, 1969. pp. 392. bibliog. (*Zeitschrift des Vereins für Hessische Geschichte und Landeskunde. Beihefte. Heft 9*)

— Industries.

HESSE. Statistisches Landesamt. Beiträge zur Statistik Hessens. Neue Folge. Nr.49. Industriezensus 1967. Wiesbaden, 1973. pp. 125.

HESSE. Statistisches Landesamt. Beiträge zur Statistik Hessens. Neue Folge. Nr. 57. Handwerkszählung 1968. Wiesbaden, 1973. pp. 243.

— Officials and employees.

HESSE. Statistisches Landesamt. Beiträge zur Statistik Hessens. Neue Folge. Nr.59. Das Personal des Landes, der Gemeinden und Gemeindeverbände am 2.10.1972: Ergebnisse der Personalstandstatistik. Wiesbaden, 1973. 1 vol.(various pagings).

— Population.

LASCH (MANFRED) Untersuchungen über Bevölkerung und Wirtschaft der Landgrafschaft Hessen-Kassel und der Stadt Kassel...bis zum Tode Landgraf Karls, 1730. Kassel, 1969. pp. 392. bibliog. (*Zeitschrift des Vereins für Hessische Geschichte und Landeskunde. Beihefte. Heft 9*)

HEUSS (THEODOR).

HESS (JUERGEN C.) Theodor Heuss vor 1933: ein Beitrag zur Geschichte des demokratischen Denkens in Deutschland. Stuttgart, [1973]. pp. 230. bibliog.

HEYMANN (LIDA GUSTAVA).

HEYMANN (LIDA GUSTAVA) and AUGSPURG (ANITA) Erlebtes-Erschautes: deutsche Frauen kämpfen für Freiheit, Recht und Frieden 1850-1940; herausgegeben von Margrit Twellmann. Meisenheim am Glan, 1972. pp. 311. bibliog.

HEYWORTH (LAWRENCE).

PLAYNE (MARY ELIZABETH) compiler. 1896: a happy New Year to my sisters; [letters and papers concerning the Potter family and Lawrence Heyworth]. [Stroud, imprint, 1896]. pp. 34.

HIDAGE.

HART (CYRIL EDWIN) The hidation of Cambridgeshire. [Leicester], 1974. pp. 67. bibliog. (*Leicester. University. Department of English Local History. Occasional Papers. 2nd Series. No.6*)

HIGHER EDUCATION AND STATE

— United States.

WHITEHEAD (JOHN S.) The separation of college and state: Columbia, Dartmouth, Harvard, and Yale, 1776-1876. New Haven, 1973. pp. 262. bibliog. (*Yale University. Yale Historical Publications. Miscellany. 97*)

HIJACKING OF AIRCRAFT.

CLYNE (PETER) An anatomy of skyjacking. London, [1973]. pp. 200.

EMANUELLI (CLAUDE) Les moyens de prévention et de sanction en cas d'action illicite contre l'aviation civile internationale. Paris, [1974]. pp. 159. bibliog.

HILL FARMING

— Switzerland.

GERBER (FRITZ) Wandel im ländlichen Leben: eine sozialökonomische und sozialpsychologische Untersuchung in fünf Gemeinden des Oberemmentals. Bern, 1974. pp. 362. bibliog.

HILLINGDON

— Population.

HILLINGDON. Borough Council. The population of Hillingdon: a descriptive analysis of the demographic and social characteristics of the population of Hillingdon. London, 1972. fo. 54. bibliog.

HIP JOINT

— Dislocation.

La LUXATION congénitale de la hanche; [by] Jean Sutter [and others]. [Paris], 1972. pp. 242. (*France. Institut National d'Etudes Démographiques. Travaux et Documents. Cahiers. No. 62*)

HIPPIES

— United States.

LEGMAN (GERSHON) The fake revolt. New York, 1967. pp. 60.

HISTORY

SPECK (ROSS V.) and others. The new families: youth, communes, and the politics of drugs. London, 1974. pp. 190. *First published in New York in 1972.*

HIRSCHVOGEL FAMILY.

SCHAPER (CHRISTA) Die Hirschvogel von Nürnberg und ihr Handelshaus. Nürnberg, 1973. pp. 351. bibliog. (*Nuremberg. Verein für Geschichte der Stadt Nürnberg. Nürnberger Forschungen. 18. Band*)

HISTORIANS, AMERICAN.

SIRACUSA (JOSEPH M.) New Left diplomatic histories and historians: the American revisionists. Port Washington, N.Y., 1973. pp. 138. bibliog.

HISTORIANS, POLISH

— Bibliography.

SKWIROWSKA (STEFANIA) compiler. Bibliographie des travaux des historiens polonais en langues étrangères [sic] parus dans les années 1945-1968; Bibliografia prac historyków polskich w językach obcych za lata 1945-1968. Wrocław, 1971. pp. 91.

HISTORICAL LIBRARIES

— Directories.

INTERNATIONAL ASSOCIATION OF LABOUR HISTORY INSTITUTIONS. Directory. [London?, 1974]. 1 vol. (looseleaf).

HISTORICAL SOCIETIES

— United Kingdom.

WILLIAMS (Sir HAROLD HERBERT) Book clubs and printing societies of Great Britain and Ireland. London, 1929. pp. 127.

HISTORIOGRAPHY.

BROOKE (CHRISTOPHER NUGENT LAWRENCE) Medieval church and society: collected essays. London, 1971. pp. 256.

BENSON (LEE) Toward the scientific study of history: selected essays. Philadelphia, [1972]. pp. 352.

L'HISTORIEN entre l'ethnologue et le futurologue: actes du séminaire international sous les auspices de l'Association Internationale pour la Liberté de la Culture [and others], Venise, 2-8 avril 1971. Paris, [1972]. pp. 296. (*Paris. Ecole Pratique des Hautes Etudes. Section des Sciences Economiques et Sociales. Le Savoir Historique. 4*)

HISTORY

— Bibliography.

SKWIROWSKA (STEFANIA) compiler. Bibliographie des travaux des historiens polonais en langues étrangères [sic] parus dans les années 1945-1968; Bibliografia prac historyków polskich w językach obcych za lata 1945-1968. Wrocław, 1971. pp. 91.

— Methodology.

BENSON (LEE) Toward the scientific study of history: selected essays. Philadelphia, [1972]. pp. 352.

IVANOV (VLADIMIR VASIL'EVICH) Sootnoshenie istorii i sovremennosti kak metodologicheskaia problema: ocherki po marksistsko-leninskoĭ metodologii istoricheskogo issledovaniia. Moskva, 1973. pp. 288. bibliog.

MELANGES en l'honneur de Fernand Braudel. Toulouse, [1973]. 2 vols. bibliog. *In various languages.*

CONJONCTURE économique, structures sociales: hommage à Ernest Labrousse; [edited by Fernand Braudel and others]. Paris, 1974. pp. 547. bibliog. (Paris. Ecole Pratique des Hautes Etudes. Section des Sciences Economiques et Sociales. Civilisations et Sociétés. 47)

— Philosophy.

BENSON (LEE) Toward the scientific study of history: selected essays. Philadelphia, [1972]. pp. 352.

HISTORY. (Cont.)

PRINTSIP istorizma v poznanii sotsial'nykh iavlenii. Moskva, 1972. pp. 291.

MAGEE (BRYAN EDGAR) and others. The role of history; [transcript of a discussion with] J.H. Plumb [and] Veronica Wedgwood;...transmitted: 26 July 1973. [London, 1973]. fo. 36. *(Thames Television. Something to Say)*

MAY (ERNEST RICHARD) "Lessons" of the past: the use and misuse of history in American foreign policy. New York, 1973. pp. 220. *bibliog.*

POTTER (DAVID MORRIS) History and American society: essays...; edited by Don E. Fehrenbacher. New York, 1973. pp. 422.

MUMFORD (LEWIS) Interpretations and forecasts, 1922-1972: studies in literature, history, biography, technics, and contemporary society. [London, 1974]. pp. 522. *First published in New York in 1973.*

— **Statistical methods.**

SHORTER (EDWARD) The historian and the computer: a practical guide. Englewood Cliffs, N.J., [1971]. pp. 149.

FLOUD (RODERICK) An introduction to quantitative methods for historians. Princeton, 1973. pp. 220. *bibliog.*

— **Study and teaching — Germany.**

MANN (GOLO) Radikalisierung und Mitte: zwei Vorträge. Stuttgart, [1971]. pp. 48.

— **Study and teaching — Germany, Eastern.**

LUECKE (PETER R.) Die neueste Zeit, 1917-1963, in den Geschichtsbüchern der sowjetzonalen Schule. Bonn, Bundesministerium für Gesamtdeutsche Fragen, 1967. pp. 101.

HISTORY, LOCAL

— **Methodology.**

IREDALE (DAVID) Local history research and writing: a manual for local history writers. Leeds, [1974]. pp. 225. *bibliog.*

HISTORY, MODERN

— **Bibliography.**

WALES. University. University College of Wales. Library. The Ifor B. Powell pamphlet collection in the Library of University College, Cardiff: a checklist. Cardiff, 1972. pp. 35.

— **20th century.**

JALEE (PIERRE) L'exploitation eveil du Tiers Monde, 1914-1973. [Paris, 1974]. pp. 272. *bibliog.*

VIDALENC (JEAN) Des grands impérialismes à l'éveil du Tiers Monde, 1914- 1973. [Paris, 1974]. pp. 272. *bibliog.*

— — **Yearbooks.**

UNIVERSALIA: les événements, les hommes, les problèmes en [ ]. a., 1974 (en 1973) [1st issue]- Paris. *Supplements ENCYCLOPAEDIA universalis.*

HISTORY, UNIVERSAL.

ROSNER (CHARLES) ed. The world of De La Rue: the Old World and the New; presented on the occasion of the one hundred and fiftieth anniversary of the house of De la Rue, 1813-1963. [London, 1963]. 1 vol. (unpaged).

SHIH (CHUN) On studying some world history. Peking, 1973. pp. 59.

HITLER (ADOLF).

FEST (JOACHIM C.) Hitler: eine Biographie. Frankfurt/M, [1973]. pp. 1190. *bibliog.*

KERN (ERICH) pseud. [i.e. Erich Knud KERNMAYR] Adolf Hitler und der Krieg: der Feldherr. Preuss. Oldendorf (Westf), 1973. pp. 462. *bibliog.*

VON MALTITZ (HORST) The evolution of Hitler's Germany: the ideology, the personality, the moment. New York, [1973]. pp. 479. *bibliog.*

FEST (JOACHIM C.) Hitler; translated from the German by Richard and Clara Winston. London, [1974]. pp. 844. *bibliog.*

MASER (WERNER VIKTOR) Adolf Hitler: Mein Kampf; der Fahrplan eines Welteroberers: Geschichte, Auszüge, Kommentare. Esslingen, [1974]. pp. 454. *bibliog.*

HIVES (FRANK).

HIVES (FRANK) Ju-ju and justice in Nigeria; told by Frank Hives and written down by Gascoigne Lumley. Harmondsworth, 1940. pp. 192. *First published in 1930.*

HOBBES (THOMAS).

NEUENDORFF (HARTMUT) Der Begriff des Interesses: eine Studie zu den Gesellschaftstheorien von Hobbes, Smith und Marx. Frankfurt am Main, 1973. pp. 163. *bibliog.*

KING (PRESTON THEODORE) The ideology of order: a comparative analysis of Jean Bodin and Thomas Hobbes. London, 1974. pp. 352. *bibliog.*

HOBBS (MAY).

HOBBS (MAY) Born to struggle. London, 1974. pp. 164.

HOCKING (WILLIAM ERNEST).

THIGPEN (ROBERT BYRON) Liberty and community: the political philosophy of William Ernest Hocking. The Hague, 1972. pp. 121. *bibliog.*

HOF (JOHANN FRIEDRICH PEYER IM).

See PEYER IM HOF (JOHANN FRIEDRICH).

HOFFA (JAMES RIDDLE).

HUTCHINSON (JOHN) of the Institute for Industrial Relations, California University. Hoffa. Los Angeles, 1969. pp. 9. *bibliog. (California University. Institute of Industrial Relations. Reprints. No. 206) Reprinted from California Management Review, vol. 11, No. 4, 1969.*

HOHOFF (WILHELM).

DIETZ (EDUARD) Wilhelm Hohoff und der Bund katholischer Sozialisten. Karlsruhe-Rüppurr, [1928]. pp. 19. *(Bund der Religiösen Sozialisten Deutschlands. Schriften der Religiösen Sozialisten. Nr. 6)*

HOLIDAYS.

INTERNATIONAL LABOUR CONFERENCE. 54th Session. Reports. 4. Fourth item on the agenda: holidays with pay. Geneva, 1969-70. 2 pts.

FRANCE. Direction de la Documentation. La Documentation Française. Notes et Etudes Documentaires. Nos. 3,915-3, 916. L'étalement des vacances: Belgique, Grande-Bretagne, Italie, Pays-Bas, R.F.A., Suède. [Paris], 1972. pp. 90. *bibliog.*

— **European Economic Community countries.**

BARRY (ANTHONY) Holidays and hours of work in the European Community. London, 1974. pp. 74. *bibliog.*

— **Norway.**

NORWAY. Statistiske Centralbyrå. 1970. Ferieundersøkelsen 1968, etc. Oslo, 1970. pp. 50. *(Norges Offisielle Statistikk. Rekke A. 348)*

— **United Kingdom.**

LAVERY (P). Patterns of holidaymaking in the Northern region. Newcastle-upon-Tyne, 1971. pp. 57. *bibliog. (Newcastle-upon-Tyne. University. Department of Geography. Research Series. No.9)*

BRITISH TOURIST AUTHORITY. Research Department. The British on holiday: a summary of regular surveys on the taking of holidays of four nights or more by British adults, 1951- 1972. London, 1973. pp. 15.

LABOUR RESEARCH DEPARTMENT. Hours and holidays. London, 1974. pp. 16.

HOLLAND—AMERICA LINE.

SCHAAP (DICK) A bridge to the seven seas: (a hundred years of the Holland America line); [translated by Dick Schaap]. London, 1973. pp. 120.

HOLY ROMAN EMPIRE

— **History.**

BENECKE (G.) Society and politics in Germany, 1500-1750. London, 1974. pp. 436. *bibliog.*

HOME AND SCHOOL.

ANDERSEN (BENT BØGH) and HANSEN (ERIK JØRGEN) Foraeldre og skole: resultater fra en postspørgeskemaundersøgelse blandt foraeldre til elever på 8. klassetrin: rapport nr. 3 fra ungdomsforløbsundersøgelsen. København, 1972. pp. 106. *(Socialforskningsinstitutt. Studier. Nr. 25)*

LITWAK (EUGENE) and MEYER (HENRY JOSEPH) School, family and neighborhood: the theory and practice of school-community relations. New York, 1974. pp. 300.

— **Bibliography.**

SHARROCK (ANNE) compiler. Home and school: a select annotated bibliography. Windsor, 1971. pp. 31.

HOME HELPS.

U.K. Social Work Service. 1973. Review of the home help service in England, February-July, 1972. [London], 1973. fo. 39,iii.

HOME LABOUR

— **Italy.**

Il LAVORO a domicilio in Lombardia: atti del Convegno di Milano del 10 luglio 1972. [Milano], Giunta Regionale Lombardia, Assessorato al Lavoro e Movimenti Demografici, [1972]. pp. 379.

HOME OWNERSHIP.

OIJEN (ANTONIUS LAMBERTUS VAN) Woningfinanciering en rente bezien van het standpunt van de gezinshuishouding. [Rotterdam, 1973]. pp. 283. *bibliog. With English summary.*

STANLEY (JOHN) Shared purchase: a new route to home-ownership. London, 1974. pp. 24. *(Conservative Political Centre. [Publications]. No. 545)*

HOME RULE

— **Ireland.**

DAUNT (WILLIAM JOSEPH O'NEILL) Ireland and her agitators. Dublin, 1845. pp. 376.

IRELAND, NORTHERN. Public Record Office. 1962. Ulster and Home Rule, 1885-1914: a display of documents shewing the Ulster Covenant against the contemporary historical background. Belfast, [1962]. pp. 11.

BUCKLAND (PATRICK) Irish unionism, 1885-1922. London, 1973. pp. 48. *bibliog. (Historical Association. General Series. G.81)*

— **Scotland.**

KING (DAVID N.) Financial and economic aspects of regionalism and separatism. London, 1973. pp. 99. *(U.K. Commission on the Constitution, 1969. Research Papers. 10)*

— **Wales.**

KING (DAVID N.) Financial and economic aspects of regionalism and separatism. London, 1973. pp. 99. *(U.K. Commission on the Constitution, 1969. Research Papers. 10)*

HOMELESSNESS.

See HOUSING.

HOMICIDE

— Finland.

PYRRÖ (LEENA) Henkirikokset Suomessa vuosina 1969-1972, etc. Helsinki, 1973. fo. 36. *(Kriminologinen Tutkimuslaitos. Sarja M. 23) With English summary.*

HOMOEOPATHY.

KAUFMAN (MARTIN) Homeopathy in America: the rise and fall of a medical heresy. Baltimore, [1971]. pp. 205. *bibliog.*

HOMOSEXUALITY.

GAY INFORMATION. Gay Liberation Pamphlets. No. 1. Psychiatry and the homosexual: a brief analysis of oppression. London, [1973]. pp. 32.

WEINBERG (MARTIN S.) and WILLIAMS (COLIN J.) Male homosexuals: their problems and adaptations. New York, 1974. pp. 316.

— Australia.

REID (ELIZABETH) and ALTMAN (DENNIS) Equality: the new issues; [2 lectures originally delivered at the 1973 Fabian Winter Lecture Series Equality under Labor]. Melbourne, [1973?]. pp. 16. *(Victorian Fabian Society. Victorian Fabian Pamphlets. [No]. 28)*

— United States.

BARNETT (WALTER) Sexual freedom and the constitution: an inquiry into the constitutionality of repressive sex laws. Albuquerque, [1973]. pp. 333.

HONDURAS

— Foreign relations — Salvador.

CARIAS (MARCO VIRGILIO) and SLUTZKY (DANIEL) eds. La guerra inutil: analisis socio-economico del conflicto entre Honduras y El Salvador. San Jose, C.R., 1971. pp. 338.

— Population.

HONDURAS. Direccion General de Estadistica y Censos. 1971-72. Boletin informativo de la encuesta demografica nacional de Honduras (EDENH); edition in English. San Jose, 1971-72. 4 pts. (in 1 vol.).

— Statistics.

HONDURAS. Consejo Superior de Planificacion Economica. 1966. Compendio estadistico, 1966. Tegucigalpa, 1966. pp. 335.

HONESTY.

GRIEW (EDWARD JAMES) Dishonesty and the jury: an inaugural lecture delivered in the University of Leicester, 6 November 1973. Leicester, 1974. pp. 24.

HONG KONG

— Commerce.

HONG KONG. Department of Commerce and Industry. Annual statistical review. a., 1972/3 [1st]- Hong Kong.

— Economic conditions.

GEIGER (THEODORE) Tales of two city-states: the development progress of Hong Kong and Singapore. Washington, D.C., [1973]. pp. 233. *bibliog. (National Planning Association. Studies in Development Progress. No. 3)*

— Economic policy.

RABUSHKA (ALVIN) The changing face of Hong Kong: new departures in public policy. Washington, D.C., 1973. pp. 79. *(American Enterprise Institute for Public Policy Research and Stanford University. Hoover Institution on War, Revolution and Peace. AEI-Hoover Policy Studies. 6)*

— History.

ENDACOTT (GEORGE BEER) A history of Hong Kong. 2nd ed. Hong Kong, 1973. pp. 337. *bibliog.*

— Industries.

HONG KONG. Department of Commerce and Industry. Annual statistical review. a., 1972/3 [1st]- Hong Kong.

— Markets.

TSE (FU YUEN) Street trading in modern Hong Kong; [Ph.D. (London) thesis]. 1974. fo. 376. *bibliog. Typescript: unpublished. This thesis is the property of London University and may not be removed from the Library.*

— Politics and government.

GEIGER (THEODORE) Tales of two city-states: the development progress of Hong Kong and Singapore. Washington, D.C., [1973]. pp. 233. *bibliog. (National Planning Association. Studies in Development Progress. No. 3)*

HOPE FAMILY.

BUIST (MARTEN GERBERTUS) At spes non fracta: Hope and Co. 1770-1815, merchant bankers and diplomats at work; [translated by Derek S. Jordan]. Den Haag, 1974. pp. 716. *bibliog.*

HOPS.

U.K. Hops Marketing Board. Chairman's speech [at the] annual general meeting of registered hop producers. a., 1961- London.

HORMUZ

— History.

STEENSGAARD (NIELS) Carracks, caravans and companies: the structural crisis in the European-Asian trade in the early 17th century. [Copenhagen, 1973]. pp. 448. *bibliog. (Scandinavian Institute of Asian Studies. Monograph Series. No. 17)*

HORTICULTURE

— Germany.

GERMANY (BUNDESREPUBLIK). Bundesministerium für Ernährung, Landwirtschaft und Forsten. Ertragslage des Garten- und Weinbaues. a., 1973- Bonn.

— United Kingdom.

NORTHERN ECONOMIC PLANNING COUNCIL. Challenge of the changing north: agriculture, horticulture, forestry and fishing. [Newcastle], 1967. pp. 71. *Xerox copy.*

HINTON (WILFRED LYNN) Outlook for horticulture...: a study in agricultural policy and adjustment with particular reference to Britain and the Common Market. Cambridge, 1968. pp. 59. *bibliogs. (Cambridge. University. School of Agriculture. Farm Economics Branch. Occasional Papers. No. 12)*

SOUTH HAMPSHIRE PLAN ADVISORY COMMITTEE. Study Reports. Group A. Rural Conservation. No. 1. Agriculture and horticulture. [Winchester, 1970]. pp. 34,x.

AGRICULTURAL, HORTICULTURAL AND FORESTRY INDUSTRY TRAINING BOARD [U.K.]. Annual report and accounts. a., 1972/3- Beckenham. *Formerly included in the file of British Parliamentary Papers.*

HOSPITAL CARE

— Germany.

BRANDECKER (KARL) Zur Reform des Krankenhauswesens: das Interesse des Krankenhauses am Selbstzahler bisher und in Zukunft; Probleme, Analysen. Köln, 1974. pp. 64. *bibliog. (Verband der Privaten Krankenversicherung. Dokumentationen. 2)*

HOSPITALS

— Administration.

GREENFIELD (HARRY I.) Hospital efficiency and public policy. New York, 1973. pp. 80.

GREEN (STEPHEN) The hospital: an organizational analysis. Glasgow, [1974]. pp. 121. *bibliog.*

HAGE (JERALD) Communication and organizational control: cybernetics in health and welfare settings. New York, [1974]. pp. 273. *bibliog.*

— Canada.

HORNE (J.M.) and others. Medical education in Canadian teaching hospitals: a statistical cost analysis. Ottawa, 1970 [or rather 1971]. fo. 74. *bibliog. (Carleton University. Carleton Economic Papers)*

— Denmark.

LANGTIDSBEHANDLING på sygehuse: betaenkning I afgivet af det af Sundhedsstyrelsen den 3. marts 1969 nedsatte udvalg, etc. København, 1970. pp. 79. *bibliog.*

— New Zealand.

NEW ZEALAND. Department of Health. National Health Statistics Centre. Health statistics report: Hospital management data. a., 1972/3[1st]- Wellington.

NEW ZEALAND. Department of Health. National Health Statistics Centre. 1973. Census of public, private and maternity hospital patients, and old people's homes, 1971. Wellington, 1973. pp. 58. *(Department of Health. Special Report Series. No. 41)*

— Norway.

INNSTILLING om normer for sykehjem: fra en komité oppnevnt av Sosialdepartementet 17. april 1969. Orkanger, 1970. pp. 47.

— Switzerland — Staff.

BASEL-STADT (CANTON). Arbeitsgruppe Personalplanung für die Spitäler. 1970-1972. Zwischenbericht[e] 1-[3]. [Basle?], 1970-1972. 3 vols.

— — Bern

BERN (CANTON). Statistisches Bureau. 1973. Eine Produktionsfunktion für Bezirksspitäler, etc. Bern, 1973. fo.15, 15[3]. *(Beiträge zur Statistik des Kantons Bern. Produktionsstatistik. Reihe C. Heft 2) In French and German.*

— — Valais.

VALAIS (CANTON). Département de la Santé Publique. 1970. Spital- und sozialmedizinische Planung: Übersicht. [Sion?], 1970. pp. 50.

— United Kingdom.

U.K. Committee on Hospital Complaints Procedure. 1973. Report; [Sir Michael Davies, chairman]. London, 1973. pp. 163. *bibliog.*

— — Administration.

JOINT WORKING PARTY ON THE ORGANISATION OF MEDICAL WORK IN HOSPITALS [U.K.]. Second report; [Sir George Godber, chairman]. London, H.M.S.O., 1972. pp. 43. *bibliog.*

JOINT WORKING PARTY ON THE ORGANISATION OF MEDICAL WORK IN HOSPITALS [U.K.]. Third report; [Sir George Godber, chairman]. London, H.M.S.O., 1974. pp. 39.

— — Cost of operation.

OLOWOKURE (THEOPHILUS OLATUNJI) The comparability of hospital costs between units and over time; [Ph.D.(London) thesis]. 1973. fo. 424. *bibliog. Typescript: unpublished. This thesis is the property of London University and may not be removed from the Library.*

HOSPITALS. (Cont.)

— — Food Service.

EGON RONAY ORGANISATION. A survey of hospital catering. London, 1972. fo. 20.

— — Ireland, Northern.

IRELAND, NORTHERN. Ministry of Health and Local Government. 1963. Summary of the hospital building programme of the Northern Ireland Hospitals Authority, March 1963. Belfast, 1963. pp. 24.

— — Wales — Location.

WELSH COUNCIL. Hospital location and accessibility in Wales. [Cardiff?], 1973. fo. 44.

— United States.

SOMERS (ANNE RAMSAY) The hospital in the evolving health care system. San Francisco, 1972. pp. 21. *(Mount Zion Hospital and Medical Center. Mark Berke Memorial Lectures. 1972)*

— — Staff.

ARCHIBALD (K.A.) The supply of professional nurses and their recruitment and retention by hospitals. New York, 1971. pp. 95. *bibliogs. (Rand Corporation. [Rand Reports]. 836)*

HOSPITALS, GYNAECOLOGIC AND OBSTETRIC.

FAIRFIELD (JOSEPHINE LETITIA DENNY) Maternity work in L.C.C. hospitals, 1931-1936. London, 1938. pp. 21. *(From Proceedings of the Royal Society of Medicine, vol. XXXI, 1938)*

MATERNITY services: integration of maternity work; [report of a joint sub-committee of the Standing Nursing and Midwifery Advisory Committee and the Standing Medical Advisory Committee of the Scottish Health Services Council; R.A. Tennent, chairman]. Edinburgh, H.M.S.O., 1973. pp. 56.

HOTELS, TAVERNS, ETC.

— Canada — Employees.

CANADA. Statistics Canada. Accommodation, food and recreational services: employment, earnings and hours of work. irreg., 1972- Ottawa. *In English and French.*

— Cyprus — Employees.

ILO INTER-REGIONAL MEETING OF EXPERTS IN VOCATIONAL TRAINING FOR THE HOTEL AND TOURIST INDUSTRY, NICOSIA, 1969. Report on meeting... [held in] Nicosia, Cyprus, 24 November-6 December 1969. (ILO/TAP/INT/R.20).. Geneva, 1970. pp. 81.

— United Kingdom

SANDLES (ARTHUR) Prospects for the small hotelier...: a summary of the Hotel and Catering EDC's report Hotel prospects to 1980. London, H.M.S.O., 1973. pp. 43.

— — Employees.

HOTEL AND CATERING INDUSTRY TRAINING BOARD [U.K.]. Report and statement of accounts. a., 1972/3- Wembley. *Formerly included in the file of British Parliamentary Papers.*

HOURS OF LABOUR.

EVANS (ARCHIBALD A.) Flexibility in working life: opportunities for individual choice. Paris, Organisation for Economic Co-operation and Development, 1973. pp. 110. *bibliog.*

PEARSON (JOHN WARD) The 8-day week. New York, [1973]. pp. 161. *bibliog.*

U.K. Department of Employment. Industrial Relations Division. Central Information Service. 1973. Flexible working hours; (with Appendices 1-5). London, 1973. 6 pts. *bibliog. (Wallet Series. No. 7)*

— Canada.

CANADA. Statistics Canada. Accommodation, food and recreational services: employment, earnings and hours of work. irreg., 1972- Ottawa. *In English and French.*

— European Economic Community countries.

EUROPEAN COMMUNITIES. Statistical Office. Social Statistics. Luxembourg, 1960 in progress.

BARRY (ANTHONY) Holidays and hours of work in the European Community. London, 1974. pp. 74. *bibliog.*

— Norway.

INNSTILLING om virkninger av arbeidstidsforkortelsen i 1968 fra 45 til 42½ time pr. uke; fra et utvalg oppnevnt av Kommunal- og Arbeidsdepartementet, etc. Orkanger, 1971. pp. 42.

ARBEIDSTID i jordbruket: utredning om revisjon av arbeidstidsbestemmelsene i lov av 19. desember 1958 om arbeidsvilkår i jordbruket; fra et utvalg oppnevnt... av 21. november 1968. Oslo, 1972. pp. 28. *(Norway. Norges Offentlige Utredninger. 1972.3)*

— Russia.

SILIN (IL'IA L'VOVICH) Kommentarii k Polozheniiu o rabochem vremeni i vremeni otdykha rabotnikov zheleznodorozhnogo transporta. Moskva, 1973. pp. 159.

— Switzerland.

GREULICH (HERMAN) Ein Kampf um die Menschwerdung: gegen die Verlängerung der Arbeitszeit, Art. 41 des Fabriksgesetzes. Aarau, [1922]. pp. 48.

— United Kingdom.

BAUM (STEPHEN J.) and YOUNG (W. McEWAN) A practical guide to flexible working hours. London, 1973. pp. 186.

U.K. Committee on Flight Time Limitations. 1973. Report...; chairman: Douglas Bader. London, 1973. pp. 65.

LABOUR RESEARCH DEPARTMENT. Hours and holidays. London, 1974. pp. 16.

SUMMERS (DEREK) Flexible working hours: a case study. London, 1974. pp. 77.

— United States — New York.

NEW YORK (STATE). Department of Labor. Division of Research and Statistics. 1973. Employment statistics. Vol. 10. Civilian work force, New York State, major areas and counties, 1966-1970; employees in nonagricultural establishments, by industry..., by month, 1966-1970...[and] annual averages, 1966-1970; earnings and hours in nonagricultural establishments..., 1966-1970. Albany, 1973. pp. 214.

HOUSE BUYING.

HOUSEOWNERS' ASSOCIATION. Buying a house in: Hampstead, Highgate, Muswell Hill, Crouch End, Archway, Golders Green, Camden Town, Kentish Town, Tufnell Park. London, [1972]. pp. 37.

NATIONAL ASSOCIATION OF CITIZENS' ADVICE BUREAUX. Buying a house or flat: do's and don'ts. rev.ed. London, 1973. pp. 23.

ADAMS (ROBIN) and JACOBS (ANTHONY) Help for the first-time house buyer. London, [1974]. pp. 16. *(Liberal Publication Department. Liberal Focus. No. 6)*

STANLEY (JOHN) Shared purchase: a new route to home-ownership. London, 1974. pp. 24. *(Conservative Political Centre. [Publications]. No. 545)*

HOUSE PRICES.

See REAL PROPERTY — Prices.

HOUSEHOLD APPLIANCES.

VILLENEUVE (ANDRE) Comportements de gestion d'un compte chèque postal: [and] Evolution de l'équipement des ménages jusqu'au début de 1970. [Paris], 1970. pp. 83. *(France. Institut National de la Statistique et des Etudes Economiques. Collections de l'INSEE. Série M. Ménages. 4) With summaries in English and Spanish.*

LIFSHEY (EARL) The housewares story: (a history of the American housewares industry). Chicago, 1973. pp. 384.

HOUSES.

See DWELLINGS.

HOUSING.

EVANS (ALAN W.) The economics of residential location. London, 1973. pp. 281. *bibliog.*

KARN (VALERIE A.) Housing standards and costs: a comparison of British standards and costs with those in the U.S.A., Canada, and Europe. Birmingham, 1973. pp. 71. *(Birmingham. University. Centre for Urban and Regional Studies. Occasional Papers. No. 25)*

— Bibliography.

SWEDEN. Statens Institut för Byggnadsforskning. 1969. Social aspects of housing and urban development: a bibliography; compiled and published in agreement with the United Nations Centre for Housing, Building and Planning; Department of Economic and Social Affairs, New York. Stockholm, 1969. pp. 173. *(Documents. 1969.3)*

— Finance.

KARN (VALERIE A.) Housing standards and costs: a comparison of British standards and costs with those in the U.S.A., Canada, and Europe. Birmingham, 1973. pp. 71. *(Birmingham. University. Centre for Urban and Regional Studies. Occasional Papers. No. 25)*

— Statistics.

COMPENDIUM OF HOUSING STATISTICS; ([pd. by] Statistical Office, Department of Economic and Social Affairs, United Nations. a., 1971 (1st issue)- New York. *In English and French.*

— Argentine Republic.

SINDICATO DE LUZ Y FUERZA. Grupo de Trabajo Estadistico. Encuesta sobre necesidad de vivienda. [Buenos Aires, 1967?]. fo. 154.

— — Statistics.

ARGENTINE REPUBLIC. Census, 1970. Censo nacional de poblacion, familias y viviendas, 1970: resultados provisionales: localidades con 1000 y mas habitantes: todo el pais. [Buenos Aires, 1973]. pp. 55.

— — Tierra del Fuego — Statistics.

TIERRA DEL FUEGO [ARGENTINE REPUBLIC]. Direccion General de Estadistica y Census. 1966. Censo territorial de 1966: (poblacion, vivienda, agropecuario); decreto no. 323/65. [Ushuaia?, 1966?]. pp. 141.

— Asia.

ONE WORLD ONLY, 1973. Prospects and feasibilities of low-cost housing activities in Asia: an international forum under the auspices of the Friedrich Ebert Stiftung; (editor: Dieter Bielenstein).[Tokyo, 1973?]. pp. 314. *(Friedrich-Ebert-Stiftung. Asian Labour Institute. Reports. 8.)*

— Australia — Melbourne.

MELBOURNE AND METROPOLITAN BOARD OF WORKS. Technical Advisory Committee. Residential planning standards;... report. [Melbourne], 1970. fo. 46.

— Belgium.

Le SECTEUR de la construction face aux besoins de logements: [journée d'étude, Bruxelles, 2 mars 1972]. [Bruxelles], Institut National du Logement, 1973. pp. 48.

HOUSING.

— — Statistics.

BELGIUM. Institut National de Statistique. Statistiques de la construction et du logement. a., 1974(no.5)- Bruxelles.

— Brazil — Brasilia.

EPSTEIN (DAVID G.) Brasilia, plan and reality: a study of planned and spontaneous urban development. Berkeley, Cal., [1973]. pp. 206. *bibliog.*

— Canada — Mathematical models.

WASLANDER (H.E.L.) CANDIDE [Canadian Disaggregated Interdepartmental Econometric] model 1.0: residential construction. Ottawa, Information Canada, 1973. pp. 27. *(CANDIDE Project Papers. No. 3)*

— — Statistics.

CANADA. Census, 1971. Census tract bulletin[s]: series B: population and housing characteristics by census tracts. [Ottawa], 1974 in progress. In English and French. :

— — Montreal.

AMES (Sir HERBERT BROWN) The city below the hill: (a sociological study of a portion of the city of Montreal, Canada [first published in 1897]); with an introduction by P.F.W. Rutherford. Toronto, [1972]. pp. 116.

— — Quebec (Province).

DIVAY (GERARD) and GODBOUT (JACQUES) Une politique de logement au Québec?. Montreal, 1973. pp. 265. *(Québec. Université Laval. Centre de Recherches Urbaines et Régionales. Cahiers. No. 5)*

— — Toronto.

DENNIS (MICHAEL) and FISH (SUSAN A.) Programs in search of a policy: low income housing in Canada. Toronto, 1972. pp. 392.

— Colombia.

COLOMBIA. Departamento Nacional de Planeacion. 1970. El sector vivienda: descripcion, desarrollo y bases de politica. Bogota, 1970. fo. 119.

— Denmark.

DENMARK. Økonomiske Råd. Formandskabet. 1970. Boligmarkedet og boligbyggeriet: problemer og perspektiver. København, 1970. pp. 153.

MARTINI (STEN) Nyere forsradsmiljøer: en undersøgelse af beboere og boligmiljøer i 6 nyere boligområder i forstaederne til København og Odense, etc. København, 1974. pp. 346. *bibliog. (Socialforskningsinstituttet. Publikationer. 61) With English summary.*

— Finland — Finance.

LUJANEN (M.) and SEPPOVAARA (J.) Financing of housing in Finland; prepared for the Economic Commission for Europe Committee on Housing, Building and Planning. [Helsinki], National Housing Board, 1971. pp. 27.

— Finland — Statistics.

FINLAND. Census, 1970. Censuses of population, housing and buildings in Finland 31 December 1970. English summary of preliminary tables. Helsinki, 1972. fo. 22. *(Finland. Tilastokeskus. Tilastotiedotus. VL. 1972. 17)*

— France.

OBSERVATOIRE ECONOMIQUE MEDITERRANEEN. Population 1968 Midi Méditerranéen: logements. Marseille, [1969]. pp. 22.

FRANCE. Ministère de l'Equipement et du Logement. 1971. Tendances et politiques actuelles dans le domaine de l'habitation,de la construction et de la planification: monographie nationale de la France. Neuilly-sur-Seine, 1971. pp. 61.

— — Finance.

FRANCE. Direction de la Documentation . La Documentation Française. Notes et Etudes Documentaires. Nos. 3,704-3, 705. Le financement du logement en France; [by] Mireille Cabane avec la collaboration de la Direction de la Construction du Ministère de l'Equipement et du Logement. Paris, 1970. pp. 66. *bibliog.*

TOPALOV (CHRISTIAN) Les promoteurs immobiliers: contribution à l'analyse de la production capitaliste du logement en France. Paris, [1974]. pp. 413. *bibliog.*

— Germany.

CHRISTIANSEN (URSULA) Obdachlos weil arm: gesellschaftliche Reaktionen auf die Armut.Giessen, 1973. pp. 209. *bibliog.*

— Greece — Statistics.

GREECE. Ethnike Statistike Hyperesia. 1973. Prosorina synoptika apotelesmata tes genikes apographes katoikion, 14 es Martiou 1971. [Athens], 1973. pp. 40.

— Hong Kong.

PRYOR (E.G.) Housing in Hong Kong. Hong Kong, 1973. pp. 46. *bibliog.*

— India.

INDIA. Working Group on Housing and Urban Development in the Third Five Year Plan. 1960. Report. [Delhi], 1960. pp. 241.

HOUSING MINISTERS' CONFERENCE, 6th, BHUBANESWAR, 1961. Proceedings. [Delhi], Ministry of Works, Housing and Supply, [1962] . pp. 272.

INDIA. Working Group on Housing and Urban and Rural Planning for the Fourth Five-Year Plan. 1965-66. Report; (with Supplement: reports of the five sub-groups). [Delhi], 1965 [or rather 1965-66]. 2 pts.

— Italy.

INDOVINA (FRANCESCO) ed. Lo spreco edilizio. Padova, 1972 repr. 1973. pp. 334.

CACCIARI (PAOLO) and POTENZA (STEFANIA) Il ciclo edilizio: riforma della casa e sviluppo capitalistico in Italia negli anni '60. Roma, 1973. pp. 214.

DAOLIO (ANDREINA) ed. Le lotte per la casa in Italia: Milano, Torino, Roma, Napoli. Milano, 1974. pp. 282.

— — Milan.

CERASI (MAURICE) and FERRARESI (GIORGIO) La residenza operaia a Milano. Roma, 1974. pp. 367.

— — Treviso.

TREVISO (PROVINCE). L'azione dei comuni nel settore dell'edilizia residenziale: atti del convegno, 19 dicembre 1970. Treviso, [1971?]. pp. 138.

— Jamaica.

— — Statistics.

JAMAICA. Department of Statistics. Economic Indicators Section. 1969. Building activity in Jamaica, 1966-68; [prepared by J.C. McMillan]. [Kingston, 1969]. pp. 50.

JAMAICA. Department of Statistics. Continuous Social and Demographic Survey Unit. 1970. A survey of housing conditions in Delacree Pen, January, 1969; (prepared by Dexter L. Rose). [Kingston], 1970. pp. 66.

JAMAICA. Department of Statistics. 1974. Building activity in Jamaica, 1965-1972. [Kingston, 1974]. pp. 59.

— Japan — Statistics.

JAPAN. Census of Housing, 1968. 1968 housing survey of Japan. Vols. 1-2. [Tokyo, 1970]. 5 pts.(in 3 vols.) *In English and Japanese.*

— Netherlands.

PRIEMUS (HUGO) and REVET (W.) Het oude-woningbezit van een middelgrote stad. 's-Gravenhage, 1970. pp. 136. *(Research-Instituut voor de Woningbouw. Woningbouwstudies. 5)*

NETHERLANDS. Ministerie van Volkshuisvesting en Ruimtelijke Ordening. 1972. Nota volkshuisvesting: nota…aan de Tweede Kamer der Staten-Generaal van 19 april 1972. 's-Gravenhage, 1972. pp. 159.

ENGBERTS (G.E.) Woningmarkt- en woningbehoeft-onderzoek: de wederzijdse relatie tussen beleid en onderzoek. Deventer, 1973. pp. 79.

NETHERLANDS. Ministerie van Volkshuisvesting en Ruimtelijke Ordening. 1973. De woningbouw in de jaren 1974 tot en met 1977. 's-Gravenhage, 1973. pp. 17.

NETHERLANDS. Raad voor de Volkshuisvesting. 1973. Advies inzake de nota volkshuisvesting. 's-Gravenhage, 1973. pp. 31.

WONINGMARKT en overheid; inleidingen gehouden tijdens de leergang…van de Stichting Postdoctoraal Onderwijs in het Bouwen op 8 en 9 juni 1972 te Delft, etc. 's-Gravenhage, Staatsuitgeverij, 1973. pp. 153. *bibliog.*

— — Finance.

NETHERLANDS. Werkgroep-Hartog. 1973. Tweede rapport…: de subsidiëring van het wonen: van object- naar subjectsubsidiëring. 's-Gravenhage, 1973. pp. 73.

OIJEN (ANTONIUS LAMBERTUS VAN) Woningfinanciering en rente bezien van het standpunt van de gezinshuishouding. [Rotterdam, 1973]. pp. 283. *bibliog. With English summary.*

— Poland.

BALL (MICHAEL) and HARLOE (MICHAEL) Housing policy in a socialist country: the case of Poland. London, 1974. pp. 58. *(Centre for Environmental Studies. Research Papers. 8)*

— Puerto Rico.

PUERTO RICO. Urban Renewal and Housing Administration. Planning Office. 1971. Industrialized housing systems for Puerto Rico: a survey of construction methods for programs of social interest. [San Juan, 1971]. pp. 75. *bibliog.*

PUERTO RICO. Urban Renewal and Housing Administration. Planning Office. 1972. Experimental program of industrialized housing : second phase report. [San Juan], 1972. fo. 85. *bibliog.*

PUERTO RICO. Urban Renewal and Housing Administration. Planning Office. 1973. Experimental program of industrialized housing: (first part: one family dwelling: model H-743). [San Juan, 1973]. fo. 39.

SAFA (HELEN ICKEN) The urban poor of Puerto Rico: a study in development and inequality. New York, [1974]. pp. 116. *bibliog.*

— Russia — Law.

LANDKOF (SAMUIL NAUMOVICH) and others. Zhilishchnoe i zhilishchno-stroitel'noe zakonodatel'stvo. 3rd ed. Kiev, 1967. pp. 272.

SURKOV (VIKTOR VASYL'OVYCH) and BUTKO (IHOR PYLYPOVYCH) Obmin zhylykh prymishchen'. 2nd ed. Kyiv, 1969. pp. 128.

RUSSIA (USSR). Statutes, etc. 1928-1972. Zakonodatel'stvo o zhilishchno-kommunal'nom khoziaistve. Moskva, 1972-3. 2 vols.

POTIUKOV (ALEKSANDR GEORGIEVICH) Zhilishchnoe pravo: uchebno-metodicheskoe posobie dlia studentov zaochnogo obucheniia. Leningrad, 1973. pp. 95. *bibliog.*

HOUSING. (Cont.)

— Sicily.

INDAGINI bio-demografiche sulla popolazione siciliana; ([by] Carmelo Pennino [and others]). Palermo [1969]. pp. 209. *(Palermo. Università. Istituto di Scienze Demografiche. Collana di Studi Demografici. 3) With summaries in English and French.*

— Sierra Leone — Statistics.

SIERRA LEONE. Central Statistics Office. 1967. Household survey of the Western Province, November, 1966- January, 1968: household characteristics and housing conditions. Freetown, [1967]. pp. 39.

— South Africa — Johannesburg.

JOHANNESBURG. City Engineer's Department. Forward Planning Branch. Greater Johannesburg area: population report. Johannesburg, 1970. fo. 70.

— Sweden.

JONSSON (LINNEA) Hushåll och utrymmesstandard år 1960. Lund, 1968. pp. 194. *bibliog. (Sweden. Statistiska Centralbyrån. Monografiserie i Anslutning, till Folk- och Bostadsräkningen i Sverige 1960. 4) With English summary.*

— Thailand — Statistics.

THAILAND. Census, 1970. 1970 population and housing census: whole kingdom. [Bangkok], 1973. pp. 158.

THAILAND. Census, 1970. 1970 population and housing census: [regional series]. [Bangkok], 1973. 4 pts. (in 1 vol.).

— United Kingdom.

SOUTH HAMPSHIRE PLAN ADVISORY COMMITTEE. Study Reports. Group D. People, Activities and Housing. No.4. Housing. Winchester, [1970?]. pp. 31, xviii.

VOLUNTARY HOUSING ANNUAL CONFERENCE, UNIVERSITY OF NOTTINGHAM, 1970. Voluntary housing into the seventies; [held] under the auspices of the Catholic Housing Aid Society. London, [1971]. fo. 126.

STANDING CONFERENCE ON LONDON AND SOUTH EAST REGIONAL PLANNING. Land availability for residential development; report by the technical panel on a recent publication by the Shankland Cox Partnership for the Housing Research Foundation. [London], 1972. pp. 5.

FABIAN SOCIETY. Fabian Tracts. [No.] 421. Rented housing and social ownership; [by] Malcolm Wicks. London, 1973. pp. 24.

LANSLEY (STEWART) and FIEGEHEN (GUY) Housing allowances and inequality. London, 1973. pp. 24. *(Young Fabian Group. Young Fabian Pamphlets. 36)*

LOCKE (MICHAEL) and CONSTABLE (MOIRA) The kids don't notice; [a Shelter report on the effects of bad housing conditions on children]. London, 1973. pp. 23.

MAHON (DAVID) No place in the country: a report on second homes in England and Wales; edited by Moira Constable. London, 1973. fo. 21.

NATIONAL AND LOCAL GOVERNMENT OFFICERS ASSOCIATION. Housing Working Party. Housing: the way ahead; report. [London, 1973]. pp. 79.

PERRY (JANE) The fair housing experiment: community relations councils and the housing of minority groups. London, 1973. pp. 53.

TARN (JOHN NELSON) Five per cent philanthropy: an account of housing in urban areas between 1840 and 1914. Cambridge, 1973. pp. 211. *bibliog.*

WILSON (DES) Minority report: a diary of protest 1970-73. London, 1973. pp. 168.

BERRY (FRED) Housing: the great British failure. London, 1974. pp. 281.

FABIAN SOCIETY. Fabian Tracts. [No.] 432. One nation? : housing and conservative policy. London, 1974. pp. 43.

FIELD (FRANK) 1942- . Housing and poverty. London, [1974]. pp. 10.

GAULDIE (ENID) Cruel habitations: a history of working-class housing, 1780-1918. London, 1974. pp. 363. *bibliog.*

HOLMES (CHRIS) Housing strategy in stress areas. London, [1974]. pp. 17.

JOHNSON (JAMES HENRY) and others. Housing and the migration of labour in England and Wales. Farnborough, Hants, [1974]. pp. 299. *bibliog.*

NATIONAL BUILDING AGENCY. Housing associations: a review of recent trends. London, 1974. pp. 23.

SHELTER. Housing: plan for action. London, 1974. fo. 10.

WALLERSTEIN (IMMANUEL) The modern world-system. New York, [1974 in progress]. *bibliogs.*

— — Finance.

PARKER (ROY ALFRED) The housing Finance Bill and council tenants. London, 1972. pp. 13. *(Child Poverty Action Group. Poverty Pamphlets. 9)*

MANDELKER (DANIEL ROBERT) Housing subsidies in the United States and England. Indianapolis, [1973]. pp. 246. *bibliog.*

— — Law.

WEST (WILLIAM ALEXANDER) The law of housing; third edition by Keith Davies. London, 1974. pp. 316. *bibliog.*

— — Statistics.

U.K. Census, 1971. Census, 1971: England and Wales: housing. London, 1974. 4 pts. (in 1 vol.).

U.K. Census, 1971. Census, 1971: Great Britain: housing summary tables. London, 1974. pp. 43.

— — Birmingham.

PARSONS (HELEN K.) Recent private development in older areas of Birmingham: a study of the characteristics of the owner-occupiers, the type of accommodation they bought and their criteria for selection: together with site histories and attitudes of local builders. Birmingham, 1973. fo. 47,pp. 12. *(Birmingham. University. Centre for Urban and Regional Studies. Research Memoranda. No. 19)*

— — Coventry.

COVENTRY council houses: the new slums; a report prepared by Wood End, Willenhall, Hillfields and other corporation tenants in Coventry in association with Coventry Community Workshop [and others]. London, [1973]. pp. 44.

— — Liverpool.

SHELTER NEIGHBOURHOOD ACTION PROJECT. Another chance for cities: SNAP 69/72. Liverpool, 1972. pp. 225.

CURRY (JANET) The Liverpool improved houses study: an introductory study of the organisation, procedures and policy of a charitable housing association; its relationship with local authorities; and its function within the housing system. Birmingham, 1973. fo. 52,viii. *(Birmingham. University. Centre for Urban and Regional Studies. Research Memoranda. No. 24)*

WEINBERGER (BARBARA) Liverpool estates survey: a study of tenants' attitudes to their accommodation and neighbourhood in four selected council estate areas.Birmingham, 1973. pp. 83. *(Birmingham. University. Centre for Urban and Regional Studies. Research Memoranda. No. 25)*

— — London.

BARCLAY (RENE T.) The St. Pancras Housing Association in Camden: what it is and why; a history 1924 to 1972. [London], 1972. pp. 20.

ISLINGTON POVERTY ACTION GROUP. Working Papers. 1. Homeless in Islington. [London?, 1972?]. fo. 34. *Xerox copy.*

LONDON. Greater London Council. Thamesmead annual report. a., 1973/4- London.

JACKSON (ALAN ARTHUR) Semi-detached London: suburban development, life and transport, 1900-39. London, 1973. pp. 381. *bibliog.*

LEE (TREVOR ROSS) Concentration and dispersal: a study of West Indian residential patterns in London, 1961-1971; [Ph.D. (London) thesis]. 1973. fo. 351. *bibliog. Typescript: unpublished. This thesis is the property of London University and may not be removed from the Library.*

PAHL (RAYMOND EDWARD) London: what next? the case for a Joint Inner London Rehabilitation Organisation; [a] lecture. London, 1973. pp. 30.

HARLOE (MICHAEL) and others. The organization of housing: public and private enterprise in London. London, [1974]. pp. 190.

SOCIAL AND COMMUNITY PLANNING RESEARCH and PROJECT PLANNING ASSOCIATES [U.K.]. Housing in Westminster in 1972. London, Westminster City Council, [1974?]. pp. 163. *(Westminster. Department of Architecture and Planning. Westminster Development Plan Publications. Research Reports. R2)*

— — York.

CHILD POVERTY ACTION GROUP. York Branch. Housing Study Group. Housing : an issue in York. [York], 1973. pp. 57. *bibliog.*

— — Yorkshire.

MURIE (ALAN) Household movement and housing choice: a study based on the West Yorkshire Movers Survey, 1969. Birmingham, 1974. pp. 131. *(Birmingham. University. Centre for Urban and Regional Studies. Occasional Papers. No. 28)*

— — Ireland, Northern.

NORTHERN IRELAND HOUSING EXECUTIVE. Accounts...; together with the report of the Comptroller and Auditor-General thereon. a., 1971/2 [1st]- Belfast. *Included in the file of IRELAND, NORTHERN. Northern Ireland Assembly. Assembly papers.*

— — Scotland.

WATSON (C.J.) Household movement in west central Scotland: a study of housing chains and filtering. Birmingham, 1973. 1 vol. (various pagings). *(Birmingham. University. Centre for Urban and Regional Studies. Occasional Papers. No. 26)*

— — — Edinburgh.

SHELTER HOUSING AID CENTRE, [EDINBURGH]. Progress report 1973: 2000 and on. Edinburgh, 1973. pp. 15.

— — — Glasgow.

SHELTER HOUSING AID CENTRE, [GLASGOW]. Report. Glasgow, [1973]. 1 vol. (unpaged).

— — Wales.

CAERNARVONSHIRE. County Planning Department. Second homes. [Caernarvon, 1973?]. pp. 94.

MERIONETH. County Planning Office. Merioneth structure plan: (subject report no. 17): second homes.Dolgellau, [1973]. pp. 54.

MERIONETH. County Planning Office. Merioneth structure plan: (subject report no. 3): housing. Dolgellau, [1973]. pp. 38.

U.K. Welsh Office. 1973. Land availability for housing, etc. Cardiff, 1973. pp. 6. *(Circulars. 241/73)*

WELSH COUNCIL. Housing in Wales. [Cardiff?], 1974. pp. 85.

— **United States.**

ABRAMS (EDWIN D.) and BLACKMAN (EDWARD B.) Managing low and moderate income housing. New York, 1973. pp. 166.

BABCOCK (RICHARD F.) and BOSSELMAN (FRED P.) Exclusionary zoning: land use regulation and housing in the 1970s. New York, 1973. pp. 210.

GREBLER (LEO) Large scale housing and real estate firms: analysis of a new business enterprise. New York, 1973. pp. 182. *(California University. Graduate School of Management. Housing, Real Estate and Urban Land Studies Program Series)*

HOUSING development and municipal costs; [by] George Sternlieb [and others]. New Brunswick, N.J., [1973]. pp. 378. *bibliog.*

KEATING (WILLIAM DENNIS) Emerging patterns of corporate entry into housing. Berkeley, 1973. pp. 152. *bibliog. (California University. Center for Real Estate and Urban Economics. Special Reports. 8)*

LINOWES (R. ROBERT) and ALLENSWORTH (DON TRUDEAU) The politics of land use: planning, zoning, and the private developer. New York, 1973. pp. 166.

MUTH (RICHARD F.) Public housing: an economic evaluation. Washington, 1973. pp. 61. *(American Enterprise Institute for Public Policy Research. Evaluative Studies. 5)*

PROPERTY taxes, housing and the cities; [by] George E. Peterson [and others]. Lexington, [1973]. pp. 203.

WELFELD (IRVING H.) America's housing problem: an approach to its solution. Washington, D.C., 1973. pp. 75. *(American Enterprise Institute for Public Policy Research. Evaluative Studies. 10)*

SCHUSSHEIM (MORTON J.) The modest commitment to cities. Lexington, Mass., [1974]. pp. 232.

STERNLIEB (GEORGE S.) and PAULUS (VIRGINIA) eds. Housing, 1971-1972: an AMS anthology. New York, [1974]. pp. 498.

— — **Bibliography.**

PAULUS (VIRGINIA) ed. Housing: a bibliography, 1960-1972. New York, [1974]. pp. 339.

— — **Finance.**

COMMITTEE FOR ECONOMIC DEVELOPMENT. Research and Policy Committee. Statements on National Policy. Financing the nation's housing needs. New York, 1973. pp. 69.

DOWNS (ANTHONY) Federal housing subsidies: how are they working?. Lexington, Mass., [1973]. pp. 141. *bibliog.*

MANDELKER (DANIEL ROBERT) Housing subsidies in the United States and England. Indianapolis, [1973]. pp. 246. *bibliog.*

WEHNER (HARRISON G.) Sections 235 and 236: an economic evaluation of H[ousing and] U[rban] D[evelopment Act]'s principal housing subsidy programs. Washington, D.C., 1973. pp. 46. *(American Enterprise Institute for Public Policy Research. Evaluative Studies. 8)*

— — **Law.**

STEVENS (JOSEPH L.) Impact of federal legislation and programs on private land in urban and metropolitan development. New York, 1973. pp. 238. *bibliog.*

— — **Des Moines.**

ERMUTH (FREDERICK) Residential satisfaction and urban environmental preferences. Downsview, Ont., 1974. pp. 193. *bibliog. (York University (Toronto). Department of Geography. Geographical Monographs. No. 3)*

— — **Georgia.**

HOUSING GOAL REPORT OF GEORGIA; prepared by Bureau of State Planning and Community Affairs [Georgia, United States].a., 1971 (2nd)- n.p.

— — **New York (City).**

DESALVO (JOSEPH S.) An economic analysis of New York City's Mitchell-Lama housing program. New York, 1971. pp. 97. *bibliog. (Rand Corporation. [Rand Reports]. 610)*

WOODFILL (BARBARA M.) New York city's Mitchell-Lama program: middle-income housing?. New York, 1971. pp. 100. *(Rand Corporation. [Rand Reports]. 786)*

LOWRY (IRA S.) and others. Welfare housing in New York City. New York, 1972. pp. 265. *(Rand Corporation. [Rand Reports]. 1164)*

CHUNG (HYUNG C.) The economics of residential rehabilitation: social life of housing in Harlem. New York, 1973. pp. 224. *bibliog.*

STERNLIEB (GEORGE S.) and INDIK (BERNARD P.) The ecology of welfare: housing and the welfare crisis in New York city. New Brunswick, N.J., [1973]. pp. 292.

— — **Newark, New Jersey.**

STERNLIEB (GEORGE S.) and BURCHELL (ROBERT WILLIAM) Residential abandonment: the tenement landlord revisited. New Brunswick, 1973. pp. 444. *bibliog.*

HOUSING, COOPERATIVE

— **India.**

INDIA. Working Group on Housing Co-operatives. 1964. Report. [Delhi], 1964. pp. 56.

— **United Kingdom.**

WARD (COLIN) Tenants take over. London, 1974. pp. 176. *bibliog.*

— — **Directories.**

HOUSING CORPORATION. Directory of housing society schemes: England, Scotland and Wales (excluding the south east of England). London, 1973. pp. 65.

HOUSING, PUBLIC

See PUBLIC HOUSING.

HOUSING MANAGEMENT.

ABRAMS (EDWIN D.) and BLACKMAN (EDWARD B.) Managing low and moderate income housing. New York, 1973. pp. 166.

HOUSING, RURAL

— **Egypt.**

FATHY (HASSAN) Architecture for the poor: an experiment in rural Egypt. Chicago, 1973. pp. 233.

HOWELL (GEORGE).

BISHOPSGATE INSTITUTE. George Howell collection: index to the correspondence, 1864-1910.London, 1973. pp. (12).

HOXTON

— **Social conditions.**

HOBBS (MAY) Born to struggle. London, 1974. pp. 164.

HRVATSKA SELJAČKA STRANKA.

MAČEK (VLADKO) Vodja govori: ličnost, izjave, govori i politički rad vodje Hrvata, Dra. Vladka Mačka; sabrao i uredio Mirko Glojnarić. Zagreb, 1936. pp. 349.

HSI—LIANG.

DES FORGES (ROGER V.) Hsi-Liang and the Chinese national revolution. New Haven, 1973. pp. 274. *bibliog.*

HUGENBERG (ALFRED).

GURATZSCH (DANKWART) Macht durch Organisation: die Grundlegung des Hugenbergschen Presseimperiums. Düsseldorf, [1974]. pp. 486. *bibliog. (Hamburg. Hansische Universität. Studien zur Modernen Geschichte. Band 7)*

HULL

— **Economic policy.**

McKINSEY AND COMPANY, INC. Stimulating economic development: city and county of Kingston upon Hull; [report to the Reorganization Committee]. [New York], 1971. 1 vol. (various pagings).

HUMAN BEHAVIOUR.

WOLTHUIS (OTTO) and SUTHERLAND (STUART) Problems and prospects of fundamental research in multi-disciplinary fields: brain and behaviour. Paris, Organisation for Economic Co-operation and Development, 1972. pp. 62. *(Science Policy Studies)*

WIGGINS (LEE M.) Panel analysis: latent probability models for attitude and behavior processes. Amsterdam, 1973. pp. 255. *bibliog.*

POWERS (WILLIAM T.) Behavior: the control of perception. London, 1974. pp. 296. *bibliogs.*

ROSS (HELEN E.) Behaviour and perception in strange environments. London, 1974. pp. 171.

HUMAN CAPITAL.

INTERNATIONAL INSTITUTE FOR EDUCATIONAL PLANNING. Fundamentals of Educational Planning . Paris, Unesco, 1970 in progress.

INTERNATIONAL LABOUR CONFERENCE. 59th Session. Reports. 8. Human resources development: vocational guidance and vocational training; eighth item on the agenda. Geneva, 1973-74. 2 pts.

— **Communist countries.**

NIEDUSZYŃSKI (MIECZYSŁAW) Analiza nakładów na usługi socjalne w krajach RWPG. Warszawa, 1973. pp. 303. *bibliog. With Russian and English summaries.*

— **France.**

MILLOT (BENOÎT) Capital humain et migrations interrégionales. Dijon, [1971]. fo. 196. *bibliog.*

— **Russia.**

POLOZOV (VLADIMIR ROMANOVICH) and KOMAROV (GEORGII FILIPPOVICH) Problemy planomernogo formirovaniia i ispol'zovaniia promyshlennykh rabochikh: opyt sotsial'no-ekonomicheskogo issledovaniia v g. Leningrade. Leningrad, 1968. pp. 124.

PROBLEMY ispol'zovaniia rabochei sily v usloviiakh nauchno- tekhnicheskoi revoliutsii. Moskva, 1973. pp. 263.

REMENNIKOV (BENIAMIN MATVEEVICH) Vysshaia shkola v sisteme vosproizvodstva rabochei sily v SSSR. Moskva, 1973. pp. 168.

SOTSIAL'NO-ekonomicheskie problemy ispol'zovaniia rabochei sily. Moskva, 1973. pp. 208.

— — **Kazakstan.**

PROBLEMY truda i narodnaseleniia v Kazakhstane. Alma-Ata, 1973. pp. 174.

— — **Moldavian Republic.**

FORMIROVANIE trudovykh resursov i razvitie sfery uslug. Kishinev, 1972. pp. 272.

— — **Tatar Republic.**

NUGAEV (RASHID ALIMZHANOVICH) Sotsial'no-ekonomicheskie problemy zaniatosti i ispol'zovaniia rabochei sily: na primere Tatarskoi ASSR. Kazan', 1972. pp. 121.

HUMAN CAPITAL. (Cont.)

— **United States.**

McMAHON (WALTER W.) Investment in higher education. Lexington, Mass., [1974]. pp. 200. *bibliog.*

— **Yugoslavia.**

THOMAS (HENDRIK) Personal income distribution in Yugoslavia: a human capital approach to the analysis of personal income differences in the industry of a labor-managed market economy. [Ithaca, N.Y.,] 1973. fo.266. bibliog.

HUMAN ECOLOGY.

SPROUT (HAROLD HANCE) and SPROUT (MARGARET TUTTLE) The ecological perspective on human affairs: with special reference to international politics. Princeton, 1965. pp. 234.

HEIDEMANN (CLAUS) and STAPF (KURT HERMANN) Die Hausfrau in ihrer städtischen Umwelt: eine empirische Studie zur urbanen Ökologie am Beispiel Braunschweigs. Braunschweig, 1969. pp. 156. *bibliog.* (*Technische Universität Braunschweig. Institut für Stadtbauwesen. Veröffentlichungen. Heft 4*)

Het MILIEU van onze samenleving: (teksten...uitgesproken op 9 mei 1970 te Leiden tijdens een interdisciplinaire bijeenkomst); [by] V. Westhoff [and others]. Bussum, 1970. pp. 128. *bibliogs.* (*Annalen van het Thijmgenootschap. Jaargang 58, aflevering 2*)

BOUGHEY (ARTHUR S.) ed. Readings in man, the environment and human ecology. New York, [1973]. pp. 595. *bibliogs.*

FULLER (RICHARD BUCKMINSTER) Earth, Inc; [a collection of recent writings]. New York, 1973. pp. 180.

HUMAN ecology and world development: proceedings of a symposium organised jointly by the Commonwealth Human Ecology Council and the Huddersfield Polytechnic, held in Huddersfield...in April 1973; edited by Anthony Vann and Paul Rogers. London, [1974]. pp. 180.

PAPANEK (VICTOR) Design for the real world: human ecology and social change. St. Albans, 1974. pp. 318. *bibliog.*

PYKETT (ANDREW NICHOLAS) The sense of place and the perceived environment : a theory, and its application in the London borough of Camden; [Ph.D. (London) thesis]. [1974]. fo. 299. *bibliog. Typescript: unpublished. This thesis is the property of London University and may not be removed from the library.*

SMITH (GRAHAME J.) and others. Our ecological crisis: its biological, economic, and political dimensions. New York, [1974]. pp. 198. *bibliogs.*

— **Bibliography.**

GOODEY (BRIAN) and others. The last environmental perception checklist. Birmingham, 1973. pp. 233. (*Birmingham. University. Centre for Urban and Regional Studies. Research Memoranda. No. 22*)

— **Directories.**

CIVIC TRUST. Environmental directory: national and regional organisations of interest to those concerned with amenity and the environment. London, 1974. 1 pamphlet (unpaged).

— **Study and teaching.**

SCOTT (JOHN C.) of the University of Michigan, and others. Toward environmental understanding: an evaluation of the 1972 Youth Conservation Corps; a report prepared for the U.S. Forest Service...and the U.S. Department of the Interior. Ann Arbor, Mich., 1973. pp. 319.

TEACHING and environment: international colloquy, Aix-en- Provence, October 16-21, 1972. Paris, 1973. pp. 48. (*Environnement. 9*)

SPENCER (DAVID) of the Centre for Urban and Regional Studies, Birmingham, and LLOYD (JOHN) Sociologist. A childs eye view of Small Heath, Birmingham: perception studies for environmental education;...with a technical appendix by Brian Goodey. Birmingham, 1974. 1 vol. (various pagings). *bibliog.* (*Birmingham. University. Centre for Urban and Regional Studies. Research Memoranda. No.34*)

HUMAN ENGINEERING.

BELL (CLIFFORD R.) Men at work. London, 1974. pp. 119. *bibliogs.*

HUMAN INFORMATION PROCESSING.

GARNER (WENDELL R.) The processing of information and structure. Potomac, Md., 1974. pp. 203. *bibliogs.* (*Michigan University. Paul M. Fitts Memorial Lectures. 1973*)

HUMANISM

— **20th century.**

ANDERSON (WALT) Politics and the new humanism. Pacific Palisades, Calif., [1973]. pp. 149.

LAMONT (CORLISS) Voice in the wilderness: collected essays of fifty years. Buffalo, N.Y., [1974]. pp. 327.

HUMANISTIC ETHICS.

The MESSAGE of man: a book of ethical scriptures, gathered from many sources and arranged. London, 1894 repr. 1895. pp. 323.

HUMANITIES.

GUSDORF (GEORGES) L'avènement des sciences humaines au siècle des lumières. Paris, 1973. pp. 589.

HUMBERSIDE

— **Politics and government.**

HUMBERSIDE. County Council. Minutes. irreg., My 1974- Kingston-upon-Hull.

HUME (DAVID).

BENNETT (JONATHAN) Locke, Berkeley, Hume: central themes. Oxford, 1971. pp. 361. *bibliog.*

HUNDRED YEARS' WAR, 1339—1453.

BARNIE (JOHN) War in medieval society: social values and the Hundred Years War, 1337-99. London, [1974]. pp. 204. *bibliog.*

HUNGARY

— **Bibliography.**

BAKO (ELEMER) Guide to Hungarian studies. Stanford, [1973]. 2 vols. (*Stanford University. Hoover Institution on War, Revolution and Peace. Bibliographical Series. 52*)

— **Economic conditions.**

ERSHOV (E.B.) ed. Mezhotraslevye issledovaniia v Vengrii. Moskva, 1973. pp. 264.

— — **Bibliography.**

MAGYAR KÖZGAZDASÁGI ÉS STATISZTIKAI IRODALOM BIBLIOGRÁFIA: Hungarian bibliography of economics and statistics; ([pd. by] Központi Statisztikai Hivatal Könyvtár és Dokumentációs Szolgálat [and] MTA Közgazdaságtudományi Intézetének Könyvtára). a., 1968[v.8]- Budapest. *In Hungarian, Russian and English.*

— — **Statistics.**

HUNGARY. Központi Statisztikai Hivatal. Report of the Hungarian Statistical Office on the economic development and plan-fulfilment. a., 1973- Budapest.

— **Economic history.**

BEREND (IVAN T.) and RANKI (GYORGY) Hungary: a century of economic development. Newton Abbot, 1974. pp. 263. *bibliog.*

— **Economic policy.**

CSIKÓS-NAGY (BÉLA) Fünf Jahre nach der ungarischen Wirtschaftsreform. Tübingen, 1973. pp. 21. (*Kiel. Universität. Institut für Weltwirtschaft. Kieler Vorträge. Neue Folge. 77*)

KÁDÁR (JÁNOS) For a socialist Hungary: speeches, articles, interviews, 1968- 1972; (translated by Gyula Gulyas and Karoly Ravasz). [Budapest, 1974]. pp. 404.

— **Foreign relations — Germany, Eastern.**

A CONTRIBUTION to peace and security in Europe: treaties between the German Democratic Republic [and Hungary, and between the GDR and Bulgaria]. Dresden, [1967?]. pp. 96. *Mainly speeches and statements, together with texts of the treaties.*

— — **Russia.**

RUSSIA (U.S.S.R.). Ministerstvo Inostrannykh Del. 1974. Sovetsko-vengerskie otnosheniia, 1948-1970 gg.: dokumenty i materialy. Moskva, 1974. pp. 726.

— **History — 1683—1848.**

ANDICS (ERZSÉBET) Metternich und die Frage Ungarns; (aus dem Ungarischen übersetzt von Zoltán Jókai). Budapest, 1973. pp. 514.

— **History — 1918—1945.**

LEHAR (ANTONO) eRINNERUNGEN: gEGENREVOLUTION UND rESTAURATIONSVERSUCHE IN uNGARN, 1918-1921; HERAUSGEGEBEN VON pETER bROUCEK. wIEN, 1973. PP. 280.

— — **1918—1919, Revolution.**

TÁRSADALOM és nemzet a Magyar Tanácsköztársaságban: Az Eötvös Loránd Tudományegyetem Tudományos Ülésszaka a Magyar Tanácsköztársaság kikiáltásának 50. évfordulója alkalmából, 1969. március 14. Budapest, 1970. pp. 182.

BARDY (ROLAND) 1919: la commune de Budapest. Paris, [1973]. pp. 244. *bibliog.*

— **Országgyűlés — Elections.**

TOTH (ADALBERT) Parteien und Reichstagswahlen in Ungarn, 1848-1892. München, 1973. pp. 383. *bibliog.* (*Munich. Südost-Institut München. Südosteuropäische Arbeiten. 70*)

— **Parliament.**

See HUNGARY — Országgyűlés.

— **Politics and government.**

KHAINAS (VASYL' VASYL'OVYCH) Borot'ba Komunistychnoï partiï Uhorshchyny za iedynyi robitnychyi i narodnyi front, proty fashyzmu i viiny, 1933-1939. L'viv, 1969. pp. 210.

SHAWCROSS (WILLIAM) Crime and compromise: Janos Kadar and the politics of Hungary since revolution. London, [1974]. pp. 311.

— **Social policy.**

KÁDÁR (JÁNOS) For a socialist Hungary: speeches, articles, interviews, 1968- 1972; (translated by Gyula Gulyas and Karoly Ravasz). [Budapest, 1974]. pp. 404.

— **Statistics — Bibliography.**

MAGYAR KÖZGAZDASÁGI ÉS STATISZTIKAI IRODALOM BIBLIOGRÁFIA: Hungarian bibliography of economics and statistics; ([pd. by] Központi Statisztikai Hivatal Könyvtár és Dokumentációs Szolgálat [and] MTA Közgazdaságtudományi Intézetének Könyvtára). a., 1968[v.8]- Budapest. *In Hungarian, Russian and English.*

HUNTING

— **Africa.**

POLLOCK (NORMAN CHARLES) Animals, environment and man in Africa. Farnborough, Hants., [1974]. pp. 159.

HUSBAND AND WIFE

— United Kingdom.

PUGH (LESLIE M.) Matrimonial proceedings before magistrates; third edition by L. M. Pugh and J.B. Horsman. London, 1974. pp. 658.

HYDERABAD (CITY)

— Growth.

ALAM (SHAH MANZOOR) and KHAN (WAHEEDUDDIN) Metropolitan Hyderabad and its region: a strategy for development. New York, [1972]. pp. 315.

HYDERABAD (STATE)

— Politics and government.

SUNDARAYYA (P.) Telangana people's struggle and its lessons. Calcutta, 1972. pp. 592.

HYDRAULIC ENGINEERING

— Sweden.

ALTHIN (TORSTEN) Vattenbyggnadsbyrån, 1897-1947: historik. Stockholm, 1947. pp. 182. *bibliog.*

HYDROLOGY.

UNITED NATIONS. Economic Commission for Asia and the Far East. Water Resources Series. Nos. 23 onwards . New York, 1963 in progress.

DOMENICO (PATRICK A.) Concepts and models in groundwater hydrology. New York, [1972]. pp. 405. *bibliogs.*

HYGIENE, PUBLIC.

WORLD HEALTH ORGANIZATION. Technical Report Series. Geneva, 1950 in progress.

WORLD HEALTH ORGANIZATION. Public Health Papers.. Geneva, 1959 in progress.

HILLEBOE (HERMAN ERTRESVAAG) and others. Approaches to national health planning;...with a chapter by I.D. Bogatryev and M.P. Rojtman. Geneva, World Health Organization, 1972. pp. 108. *(Public Health Papers. No.46)*

REINKE (WILLIAM A.) ed. Health planning: qualitative aspects and quantitative techniques. Baltimore, 1972. pp. 350. *bibliogs. (Johns Hopkins University. School of Hygiene and Public Health. Department of International Health. Johns Hopkins Monographs in International Health)*

CIBA FOUNDATION. Symposia. Human rights in health: Ciba Foundation symposium 23 (new series); [proceedings; edited by Katherine Elliott and Julie Knight]. Amsterdam, 1974. pp. 304. *bibliogs.*

— Bangladesh.

CHEN (LINCOLN C.) ed. Disaster in Bangladesh. New York, 1973. pp. 290. *bibliogs.*

— Belgium.

BELGIUM. Ministère de la Santé Publique et de la Famille. Service d'Etudes Générales. Activité du Ministère, etc. a., 1972- Bruxelles.

— France.

FRANCE. Ministère de la Santé Publique et de la Sécurité Sociale. Direction de l'Administration Générale, du Personnel et du Budget. Division de la Documentation Générale, des Publications et de la Bibliothèque. 1971. La protection sanitaire et sociale en France. [Paris, 1971]. pp. 191.

FRANCE. Direction de la Documentation. La Documentation Française. Notes et Etudes Documentaires, No. 4,051. La lutte contre l'insalubrité, par Jacques Baschwitz. [Paris], 1974. pp. 30.

— Germany.

GERMANY (BUNDESREPUBLIK). Statistisches Bundesamt. Ausgaben der öffentlichen Haushalte für Gesundheit, Sport und Erholung. 1964/1969[1st]; a., 1970- Wiesbaden. *1964/1969 as Aufwendungen von Bund, Ländern und Gemeinden (Gv.) für Gesundheitspflege und Sport. (Finanzen und Steuern. Reihe 5. Sonderbeiträge zur Finanzstatistik).*

— Macao.

MACAO. Health and Welfare Department. 1968. Macau and its public health. [Macao], 1968. pp. 23.

— Malta.

VITAL STATISTICS AND STATISTICAL INFORMATION ON THE INCIDENCE AND MORTALITY OF DISEASE IN THE MALTESE ISLANDS; [pd. by Department of Health] Malta. a., 1972- Valletta.

— Netherlands.

NETHERLANDS. Ministerie van Volksgezondheid en Milieuhygiëne. 1971. Vijftig jaar Verslagen en mededelingen 's-Gravenhage, 1971. pp. 209. *(Verslagen en Mededelingen [betreffende de] Volksgezondheid. 1971. 1)*

AKTIEGROEP MEDICIJNEN NIJMEGEN. Gezondheidszorg in Nederland: beschouwingen over arbeids- en bedrijfsgeneeskunde...; onder redaktie van Frans Huysmans [and others]. Nijmegen, 1973. pp. 386.

— Portugal.

PORTUGAL. Presidência do Conselho. 1953. 25 anos de administração publica: Ministerio do Interior. Lisboa, 1953. pp. 67.

— Portugal — Colonies.

PORTUGAL. Statutes, etc. 1969. Regulamento dos serviços de Saúde e assistência do ultramar; decreto N.o 49073 de 21 de junho de 1969 (rectificado). Lisboa, 1969. pp. 115.

— Russia.

KHROMOV (BORIS MIKHAILOVICH) and SVESHNIKOV (ANATOLII VLADIMIROVICH) Zdravookhranenie Leningrada: kratkii istoricheskii ocherk. Leningrad, 1969. pp. 207. *bibliog.*

POTULOV (BORIS MIKHAILOVICH) Leninskaia zabota o zdorov'e trudiashchikhsia. Moskva, 1970. pp. 135.

POPOV (G.A.). Principles of health planning in the USSR. Geneva, World Health Organization, 1971. pp. 172. *(Public Health Papers. No. 43)*

— — Georgia.

SHASHIKASHVILI (NAVRESTAN R.) Etapy razvitiia zdravookhraneniia v Gruzii. Tbilisi, 1973. pp. 197.

— — Ruthenia — Bibliography.

CHUMARINA (Z.M.) and NASEKOVS'KA (H.S.) compilers. Rozvytok okhorony zdorov''ia na Zakarpatti za roky Radians'koï vlady, 1946-1966 rr.: bibliohrafichnyi pokazhchyk.Uzhhorod, 1967. pp. 70.

— — Soviet North.

MURMANSK (OBLAST'). Otdel Zdravookhraneniia. Zdravookhranenie i zdorov'e naseleniia Murmanskoi oblasti. Murmansk, 1968. pp. 169. *bibliog.*

— Scandinavia.

TROEDSSON (STEN) Sjukvårdsorganisationen i de nordiska länderna. [Stockholm], 1970. pp. 48. *(Sjukvårdens och Socialvårdens Planerings- och Rationaliseringsinstitut. Rapporter. 1970.8.) Tables in English and Swedish.*

— Switzerland — Valais.

VALAIS (CANTON). Département de la Santé Publique. 1970. Spital- und sozialmedizinische Planung: Übersicht. [Sion?], 1970. pp. 50.

— Underdeveloped areas.

— See UNDERDEVELOPED AREAS — Public health.

— United Kingdom.

BROCKINGTON (COLIN FRASER) The health of the community: principles of public health for practitioners and students. 3rd ed. London, 1965. pp. 356. *bibliog.*

BUCKINGHAMSHIRE. [Department of Health and Welfare]. Health of the community: (annual reports of the County Medical Officer of Health and Principal School Medical Officer). a., 1972- Aylesbury.

U.K. Department of Health and Social Security. Annual report on departmental research and development. a., 1973 [1st]- London.

The SCHOOL years in Newcastle upon Tyne, 1952-62: being a further contribution to the study of a thousand families; by F.J.W. Miller [and others]. London, 1974. pp. 362. *bibliog.*

— — Scotland.

— United States.

SYDENSTRICKER (EDGAR) The challenge of facts: selected public health papers...; edited by Richard V. Kasius. New York, 1974. pp. 386. *bibliog.*

— — New York (City).

ACTON (JAN PAUL) and others. Population health surveys for 1964, 1965 and 1966, (1968, 1969- 70): codebook and marginals; prepared for... the Office of Economic Opportunity [and others]. Santa Monica, 1973. 3 vols. (in 1). *(Rand Corporation. [Rand Reports]. 1096, 1161-62)*

HYPOTHESIS.

BOTHA (RUDOLF P.) and WINCKLER (WALTER K.) The justification of linguistic hypotheses: a study of nondemonstrative inference in transformational grammar. The Hague, 1973. pp. 350. *bibliog.*

IATSUNSKII (VIKTOR KORNEL'EVICH).

IATSUNSKII (VIKTOR KORNEL'EVICH) Sotsial'no-ekonomicheskaia istoriia Rossii XVIII-XIX vv.: izbrannye trudy. Moskva, 1973. pp. 302.

IBADAN

— Civic improvement.

KOLL (MICHAEL) ed. African urban development: four political approaches; by Treufried Grau [and others]. Düsseldorf, [1972]. pp. 215. *(Arnold-Bergstraesser-Institut für Kulturwissenschaftliche Forschung. Materialien. Band 31)*

IBADAN UNIVERSITY.

NIGERIA. 1971. Comments of the federal military government on the report of the Commission of Inquiry into the disturbances on the campus of the University of Ibadan. Lagos, 1971. pp. 17.

IBOS.

ISICHEI (ELIZABETH ALLO) The Ibo people and the Europeans: the genesis of a relationship - to 1906. London, 1973. pp. 207. *bibliog.*

NSUGBE (PHILIP O.) Ohaffia: a matrilineal Ibo people. Oxford, 1974. pp. 136. *bibliog.*

ICE

— Canada.

CANADA. Program Planning Office for Resource Satellites and Remote Airborne Sensing. Working Group on Ice Reconnaissance and Glaciology. 1971. Resource satellites and remote airborne sensing for Canada. Report no.7. Ice reconnaissance and glaciology; [D.C. Archibald, chairman]. Ottawa, 1971. pp. 37. *With French summary.*

ICELAND

ICELAND
— Emigration and immigration.

NORDISK HISTORIKERMØDE, 1971. Emigrationen fra Norden indtil I. Verdenskrig: rapporter til... i København, 1971, 9-12 august; [edited by Kristian Hvidt]. [Copenhagen, 1971]. pp. 168. *bibliogs. In various Scandinavian languages.*

IDEALISM.

RESCHER (NICHOLAS) Conceptual idealism. Oxford, 1973. pp. 204.

ZEPPI (STELIO) Il pensiero politico dell'idealismo italiano e il nazionalfascismo. Firenze, 1973. pp. 303.

IDEMITSU (SAZO).

IDEMITSU (SAZO) Be a true Japanese. [Tokyo, 1973]. pp. 174.

IDENTIFICATION (PSYCHOLOGY).

WINCH (ROBERT FRANCIS) and GORDON (MARGARET T.) Familial structure and function as influence. Lexington, Mass., [1974]. pp. 274. *bibliog.*

IDEOLOGY.

Les IDEOLOGIES dans le monde actuel; [by] Michel Amiot [and others]. Paris, [1971]. pp. 232. *bibliogs. (Nice. Université. Centre d'Etudes de la Civilisation Contemporaine. Collection)*

ASHFORD (DOUGLAS ELLIOTT) Ideology and participation. Beverly Hills, [1972]. pp. 300. *bibliog.*

FAYE (JEAN PIERRE) Langages totalitaires. Paris, [1972]. pp. 771.

SEMAINE SOCIALE WALLONNE. 53me Semaine. Idéologies et action militante; ([by] P. Delooz [and others]). Bruxelles, [1972]. pp. 225.

TESCONI (CHARLES A.) and MORRIS (VAN CLEVE) The anti-man culture: bureautechnocracy and the schools. Urbana, Ill., [1972]. pp. 232. *bibliog.*

BROWN (L.B.) Ideology. Harmondsworth, 1973. pp. 208. *bibliog.*

HIKEL (GERALD KENT) Beyond the polls: political ideology and its correlates. Lexington, Mass., [1973]. pp. 150. *bibliog.*

BAGLIONI (GUIDO) L'ideologia della borghesia industriale nell' Italia liberale. Torino, [1974]. pp. 565.

BLUHM (WILLIAM THEODORE) Ideologies and attitudes: modern political culture. Englewood Cliffs, [1974]. pp. 385. *bibliogs.*

DRUCKER (HENRY MATTHEW) The political uses of ideology. London, 1974. pp. 170. *bibliog.*

PLANT (RAYMOND) Community and ideology: an essay in applied social philosophy. London, 1974. pp. 94. *bibliog.*

IK.

TURNBULL (COLIN MACMILLAN) The mountain people. London, 1973. pp. 309.

ILLE ET VILAINE (DEPARTMENT)
— Economic conditions.

FRANCE. Direction de la Documentation. La Documentation Française. Notes et Etudes Documentaires. Nos. 4,070-4, 071-4,072. Les départements français. 35. Ille-et-Vilaine, Bretagne; (monographie... rédigée par Bernard Larvaron). Paris, 1974. pp. 114.

— Politics and government.

FRANCE. Direction de la Documentation. La Documentation Française. Notes et Etudes Documentaires. Nos. 4,070-4, 071-4,072. Les départements français. 35. Ille-et-Vilaine, Bretagne; (monographie... rédigée par Bernard Larvaron). Paris, 1974. pp. 114.

ILLEGITIMACY.

TURNER (J. NEVILLE) Improving the lot of children born outside marriage: a comparison of three recent reforms: England, New Zealand and West Germany. London, [1973]. pp. 69.

— United Kingdom.

DEWAR (DIANA) Orphans of the living: a study of bastardy. London, 1968. pp. 208.

ILLINOIS
— Constitution.

BURMAN (IAN D.) Lobbying at the Illinois Constitutional Convention. Urbana, Ill., [1973]. pp. 119. *(Illinois University. Institute of Government and Public Affairs. Studies in Illinois Constitution Making)*

— Government publications.

PUBLICATIONS OF THE STATE OF ILLINOIS; issued by...Secretary of State and State Librarian. s-a. (formerly a.), 1970- Springfield, Illinois.

ILLITERACY.

UNITED NATIONS EDUCATIONAL, SCIENTIFIC AND CULTURAL ORGANIZATION. Educational Studies and Documents. New Series. Paris, 1971 in progress.

— Ethiopia.

SJÖSTRÖM (ROLF) and SJÖSTRÖM (MARGARETA) YDLC: a literacy campaign in Ethiopia; an introductory study and a plan for further research. Uppsala, 1973. pp. 72. *bibliog. (Nordiska Afrikainstitutet. Research Reports. No. 20)*

— Iran.

FURTER (PIERRE) Possibilities and limitations of functional literacy: the Iranian experiment. Paris, United Nations Educational, Scientific and Cultural Organization, 1973. pp. 59. *bibliog. (Educational Studies and Documents. New Series. No. 9)*

— Underdeveloped areas.

See UNDERDEVELOPED AREAS — Illiteracy.

— Zambia.

HAY (HOPE) Northern Rhodesia learns to read. London, 1947. pp. 29.

ILLUSTRATED BOOKS.

MARLBOROUGH RARE BOOKS LIMITED. Catalogues. 47. Some recent acquisitions including woodcut books of the 15th and 16th centuries, fine sets of engravings, colour plate books, modern illustrated books, etc. London, [1962]. 1 vol. (unpaged).

IM HOF (JOHANN FRIEDRICH PEYER).

See PEYER IM HOF (JOHANN FRIEDRICH).

IMPEACHMENTS
— United Kingdom.

TITE (COLIN G.C.) Impeachment and parliamentary judicature in early Stuart England. London, 1974. pp. 249. *bibliog.*

IMPERIAL PREFERENCE.

CAPIE (FORREST HUNTER) Ottawa: an aspect of imperial commercial policy. Coventry, 1974. pp. 46. *(University of Warwick. Department of Economics. Warwick Economic Research Papers. No. 41)*

IMPERIALISM.

VARGA (JENŐ) Der deutsche Imperialismus: die historischen Wurzeln seiner Besonderheiten; ([reprint of work originally published in 1946 by the] sowjetische Militärverwaltung in Deutschland). Berlin, 1970. pp. 45.

KIM (IL-SUNG) Let us intensify the anti-imperialist, anti-U.S. struggle. Pyongyang, 1968. pp. 10. *(Reprinted from Tricontinental, August 12, 1967)*

BERTRAND RUSSELL CENTENARY SYMPOSIUM ON SPHERES OF INFLUENCE IN THE AGE OF IMPERIALISM, LINZ, 1972. Spheres of influence in the age of imperialism; papers submitted to the Bertrand Russell Centenary Symposium...;[by] Noam Chomsky [and others]. Nottingham, 1972. pp. 144.

GULIEV (VLADIMIR EVGEN'EVICH) Demokratie und Imperialismus: Ideologien, politische Realitäten; (Übersetzung [from the Russian]: Gertrud Lehmann). Berlin, 1972. pp. 267.

HALL (GUS) Imperialism today: an evaluation of major issues and events of our time. New York, 1972. pp. 382.

PAGE (ROBERT J.D.) Imperialism and Canada, 1895-1903. Toronto, [1972]. pp. 117. *bibliog.*

ASAD (TALAL) ed. Anthropology and the colonial encounter. London, [1973]. pp. 286. *bibliog.*

BENOT (YVES) Qu'est-ce que le développement?. Paris, 1973. pp. 185. *bibliog.*

BERTRAND RUSSELL CENTENARY SYMPOSIUM ON SPHERES OF INFLUENCE IN THE AGE OF IMPERIALISM, LINZ, 1972. Spheres of influence and the third world; papers submitted to the Bertrand Russell Centenary Symposium...;[by] Vladimi Dedijer [and others]. Nottingham, 1973. pp. 123.

BRANDES (VOLKHARD) Die Krise des Imperialismus: Grenzen der kapitalistischen Expansion und der Wiederaufbau der Arbeiterbewegung. Frankfurt am Main, [1973]. pp. 106.

GULIEV (VLADIMIR EVGEN'EVICH) Sovremennoe imperialisticheskoe gosudarstvo: voprosy teorii. Moskva, 1973. pp. 207.

SHALIN (MIKHAIL ALEKSEEVICH) Antikommunizm i ideologicheskaia bor'ba na sovremennom etape. Kazan', 1973. pp. 242.

WEISSKOPF (THOMAS E.) Sources of American imperialism: a contribution to the debate between orthodox and radical theorists. Ann Arbor, 1973. pp. 46. *bibliog. (Michigan University. Center for Research on Economic Development. Discussion Papers. No. 32)*

YOUNG (MARILYN BLATT) ed. American expansionism: the critical issues. Boston, [Mass., 1973]. pp. 184. *bibliog.*

ZAGHI (CARLO) L'Africa nella coscienza europea e l'imperialismo italiano. Napoli, [1973]. pp. 576.

COHEN (BENJAMIN J.) The question of imperialism: the political economy of dominance and dependence. London, 1974. pp. 280. *bibliog.*

KUENTZEL (ULRICH) Der nordamerikanische Imperialismus: zur Geschichte der US-Kapitalausfuhr. Darmstadt, 1974. pp. 253. *bibliog.*

SYMCOX (GEOFFREY) ed. War, diplomacy and imperialism, 1618-1763: [selected documents]. London, 1974. pp. 338. *bibliog.*

IMPORT QUOTAS
— New Zealand.

NATIONAL DEVELOPMENT COUNCIL [NEW ZEALAND]. Committee on Industrial Policy. Report on industrial protection in New Zealand: review of recommendation 209A. [Wellington, Government Printer], 1972. pp. 47.

— United States.

MINTZ (ILSE) U.S. import quotas: costs and consequences. Washington, [1973]. pp. 85. *(American Enterprise Institute for Public Policy Research. Domestic Affairs Studies. 10)*

INCENTIVES IN INDUSTRY.

SHEPEL' (VIKTOR MAKSIMOVICH) Stimulirovanie truda: psikhologicheskii aspekt. Moskva, 1969. pp. 88. *bibliog.*

INCOME.

FEDORENKO (NIKOLAI PROKOF'EVICH) and BUNICH (PAVEL GRIGOR'EVICH) eds. Mekhanizm ekonomicheskogo stimulirovaniia pri sotsializme: opyt i problemy. Moskva, 1973. pp. 255.

LAW (P.J.) On a proposal by Liberman for enterprise incentive funds. Coventry, 1973. pp. 25. *bibliog. (University of Warwick. Department of Economics. Warwick Economic Research Papers. No. 34)*

MIROSHNIKOV (PETR SEMENOVICH) and others. Material'noe stimulirovanie nauchno-tekhnicheskogo progressa. Kiev, 1973. pp. 159. *bibliog.*

VAKHLAMOV (IVAN ALEKSEEVICH) and SEDLOV (PAVEL ALEKSEEVICH) Material'noe pooshchrenie v oblasti nauchno-tekhnicheskogo progressa: pravovye voprosy. Moskva, 1973. pp. 175.

INCLOSURES.

PORTER (JOHN) Ph.D. The reclamation and settlement of Bowland, with special reference to the period 1500-1650; [Ph.D.(London) thesis]. 1973[or rather 1974]. fo. 267. *Typescript: unpublished. This thesis is the property of London University and may not be removed from the library.*

INCOME.

FIVE monographs on business income; [reprint of the work originally published in New York, 1950] . Lawrence, Kansas, 1973. pp. 271. *(American Institute of Certified Public Accountants. Study Group on Business Income. Pamphlets. 3)*

CHAMPERNOWNE (DAVID GAWEN) The distribution of income between persons. Cambridge, 1973. pp. 287.

SADLER (PETER G.) and others. Regional income multipliers: the Anglesey study. [Bangor], 1973. pp. 109. *(Wales. University. University College of North Wales. Bangor Occasional Papers in Economics. No.1)*

CONFERENCE ON THE POLITICAL ECONOMY OF INCOME DISTRIBUTION, WASHINGTON, D.C., 1973. Redistribution through public choice; [papers of the conference; edited by] Harold M. Hochman and George E. Peterson. New York, 1974. pp. 341.

— Mathematical models.

MOGRIDGE (MARTIN J.H.) A systems theory of personal income distribution. London, 1972. pp. 83. *bibliog. (Centre for Environmental Studies. Working Papers. 35)*

SOLIGO (RONALD) and LAND (JAMES W.) Models of development incorporating distribution aspects. Houston, 1972. pp. 27. *(Rice University. Program of Development Studies. Papers. No. 22)*

CREEDY (JOHN) Aggregation and the income distribution. [Reading], 1973. fo. 16. *bibliog. (Reading. University. Department of Economics. Discussion Papers in Economics. Series A. No. 55)*

CREEDY (JOHN) The dynamics of income change. [Reading], 1973. 1 pamphlet (various foliations). *bibliog. (Reading. University. Department of Economics. Discussion Papers in Economics. No. 53)*

HOEL (MICHAEL) The optimal capital income - from the wage earners' point of view. [Oslo], 1973. fo. 15. *bibliog. (Oslo. Universitet. Socialøkonomiske Institutt. Memoranda)*

PITCHFORD (JOHN DAVID) and TURNOVSKY (STEPHEN J.) Some effects of taxes on inflation and income distribution. Canberra, 1974. pp. 40. *(Australian National University. Research School of Social Sciences. Department of Economics. Working Papers in Economics and Econometrics. No.20)*

ZERWAS (ARNOLD) Simulationsexperimente zur Einkommens- und Vermögensverteilung.Berlin, [1974]. pp. 149. *bibliog.*

— Australia.

HENDERSON (RONALD FRANK) Income inflation in Australia. Adelaide, 1972. pp. 12. *(Adelaide. University. Joseph Fisher Lectures in Commerce. 1971)*

— Belgium.

DELEECK (HERMAN) Opstellen over inkomensverdeling sociale zekerheid en sociaal beleid.Antwerp, 1972. pp. 247.

— Canada.

CANADA. Statistics Canada. Income estimates for counties and census divisions. a., 1966/1969[1st]- Ottawa. *In English and French.*

CANADA. Statistics Canada. Family incomes: census families. a., 1971[3rd]- Ottawa. *In English and French.*

DODGE (DAVID A.) and SARGENT (JOHN H.) Towards a new tax-transfer system in Canada: an analysis of the changes proposed in the white papers on income security, unemployment insurance and taxation. Kingston, 1971. fo. 45. *(Kingston, Ontario. Queen's University. Institute for Economic Research. Discussion Papers. No.49)*

CANADA. Statistics Canada. Consumer Income and Expenditure Division. 1973. Incomes of unemployed individuals and their families; Revenus des chomeurs et de leur famille; 1971. Ottawa, 1973. pp. 90. *In English and French.*

CANADA. Census, 1971. Advance bulletin[s]: [series AE: economic characteristics] . [Ottawa], 1974 in progress. *In English and French.*

— Colombia.

THIRSK (WAYNE R.) Income distribution, efficiency and the experience of Colombian farm mechanization. Houston, 1972. pp. 54. *(Rice University. Program of Development Studies. Papers. No. 33)*

— Finland.

UUSITALO (HANNU) On the distribution of income in Scandinavia. Helsinki, 1973. pp. 72. *(Helsinki. Yliopisto. Research Group for Comparative Sociology. Research Reports. No. 2)*

— France.

FRANCE. Centre d'Etude des Revenus et des Coûts. 1969. Prix, coûts et revenus en France de 1949 à 1968. Paris, 1969. pp. 62. *(Documents. No. 2)*

— Germany.

METZE (INGOLF) Soziale Sicherung und Einkommensverteilung: eine empirische Untersuchung über die Wirkungen ... auf die verfügbaren Einkommen der privaten Haushalte. Berlin, [1974]. pp. 170.

— — Mathematical models.

STRUFF (RICHARD) Dimensionen der wirtschaftsräumlichen Entwicklung: Abgrenzung von Gebietstypen zur regionalen und sektoralen Einkommensanalyse in der Bundesrepublik Deutschland. Bonn, 1973. pp. 279. *bibliog. (Forschungsgesellschaft für Agrarpolitik und Agrarsoziologie. [Publications]. 218)*

— India.

INDIA. Labour Bureau. 1971. Report on survey as to how workers support themselves during retrenchment, lay-off, closure and strikes and collection of data regarding indebtedness. [Delhi, 1971]. pp. 236.

— Japan.

YAMAMURA (KOZO) A study of Samurai income and entrepreneurship: quantitative analyses of economic and social aspects of the Samurai in Tokugawa and Meiji Japan. Cambridge, Mass., 1974. pp. 243. *bibliog. (Harvard University. East Asian Research Center. Harvard East Asian Series. No.76)*

— Korea.

ANNUAL REPORT ON THE FAMILY INCOME AND EXPENDITURE SURVEY; [pd. by] Bureau of Statistics, Economic Planning Board, Republic of Korea. a., 1972- Seoul.

— Malaysia.

LIM (LIN LEAN) Some aspects of income differentials in West Malaysia. Kuala Lumpur, 1971. pp. 141. *bibliog. (University of Malaya. Faculty of Economics and Administration. Monograph Series on Malaysian Economic Affairs. 2)*

SNODGRASS (DONALD R.) The fiscal system as an income redistributor in West Malaysia. Cambridge, Mass., [1972?]. pp. 43. *(Harvard University. Center for International Affairs. Economic Development Reports. No. 224)*

— Netherlands.

VERENIGING VOOR DE STAATHUISHOUDKUNDE. Praeadviezen. 1973. Inkomensnivellering: verkenning van feiten, wenselijkheden, mogelijkheden en gevolgen: preadviezen van G.R. Mustert [and others]. 's-Gravenhage, 1973. pp. 178.

MUSTERT (G.R.) The development of the income distribution in the Netherlands after the second world war: a Markovian approach. Tilburg, 1974. pp. 20,9,5. *(Tilburg. Katholieke Hogeschool. Tilburg Institute of Economics. Research Memoranda. EIT 47)*

— Nigeria.

NIGERIA. Federal Office of Statistics. 1967. Report on enquiries into the income and expenditure patterns of lower and middle income households at Onitsha, 1963/64. Lagos, [1967]. pp. 82. *(Urban Consumer Surveys in Nigeria. 1967/1)*

NIGERIA. Federal Office of Statistics. 1967. Report on enquiries into the income and expenditure patterns of lower and middle income households at Ondo/Akure/Owo, 1964/65. Lagos, [1967]. pp. 80. *(Urban Consumer Surveys in Nigeria. 1967/3)*

NIGERIA. Federal Office of Statistics. 1967. Report on enquiries into the income and expenditure patterns of lower and middle income households at Oshogbo/Ife/Ilesha: 1963/64. Lagos, [1967]. pp. 79. *(Urban Consumer Surveys in Nigeria. 1967/2)*

— Norway.

NORWAY. Tekniske Beregningsutvalg for Inntektsoppgjóorene. 1968 Innstilling, etc. Oslo, 1968. pp. 62.

NORWAY. Statistiske Centralbyrå. 1972. Den personlige inntektsfordeling 1958, 1962 og 1967, etc. Oslo, 1972. pp. 61. *(Statistiske Analyser. 3)*

NORWAY. Statistiske Centralbyrå. 1972. Lavinntektsundersøkelsen 1967; Survey of low income groups 1967.Oslo, 1972. pp. 44. *(Statistiske Analyser. 4)*

NORWAY. Statistiske Centralbyrå. 1973. Inntektsstatistikk 1970: personlige inntekstakere og husholdninger; Income statistics 1970: personal income earners and households. Oslo, 1973. pp. 113. *(Norges Offisielle Statistikk. Rekke A. 543) In English and Norwegian.*

NORWAY. Statistiske Centralbyra. 1973. Statistikk over lavinntektsgrupper 1970; Statistics on low income groups 1970. Oslo, 1973. pp. 129. *(Norges Offisielle Statistikk. Rekke A. 556) In English and Norwegian.*

— Pakistan.

KHAN (TAUFIQ M.) ed. Studies on national income and its distribution. Karachi, [1970]. pp. 191. *(Pakistan Institute of Development Economics. Readings in Development Economics. No.5)*

SOLIGO (RONALD) Factor intensity of consumption patterns, income distribution and employment growth in West Pakistan (a report to A.I.D.). [New Haven], 1972. pp. 29. *bibliog. Typescript.*

— Panama.

McLURE (CHARLES E.) The distribution of income and tax incidence in Panama, 1969. Houston, Tex., 1972. pp. 39. *(Rice University. Program of Development Studies. Papers. No.36)*

INCOME. (Cont.)

— Russia.

MAIER (VLADIMIR FEDOROVICH) Dokhody naseleniia i rost blagosostoianiia naroda. Moskva, 1968. pp. 220.

KOMAROV (VASILII EFIMOVICH) and CHERNIAVSKII (URIEL' GEORGIEVICH) Dokhody i potreblenie naseleniia SSSR. Moskva, 1973. pp. 239.

KOVALEVSKII (G.T.) and LUTOKHINA (E.A.) eds. Formy chistogo dokhoda pri sotsializme. Minsk, 1973. pp. 342.

POPADIUK (KIRILL NIKITICH) Finansy i kredit v raspredelenii natsional'nogo dokhoda. Moskva, 1973. pp. 176.

— Scandinavia.

UUSITALO (HANNU) On the distribution of income in Scandinavia. Helsinki, 1973. pp. 72. (*Helsinki. Yliopisto. Research Group for Comparative Sociology. Research Reports. No. 2*)

PÖNTINEN (SEPPO) and UUSITALO (HANNU) Household incomes in the Scandinavian countries. Helsinki, 1974. pp. 107. (*Helsinki. Yliopisto. Research Group for Comparative Sociology. Research Reports. No. 3*)

— Spain.

BUTTLER (FRIEDRICH) Einkommensredistributive und raumstrukturelle Regionalpolitik im Rahmen der spanischen Entwicklungspläne. Göttingen, [1969]. pp. 83. *bibliog. (Göttingen. Universität. Ibero-Amerika- Institut für Wirtschaftsforschung. Arbeitsberichte. Heft 5)*

— Sri Lanka.

DUTTA (AMITA) International migration, trade, and real income: a case study of Ceylon, 1920-38. Calcutta, 1973. pp. 171. *bibliog.*

— Sweden.

SWEDEN. Inrikesdepartementet. Låginkomstutredningen. 1970. Svenska folkets inkomster: betänkande...del 1. Stockholm, 1970. pp. 309. *bibliog.* (*Sweden. Statens Offentliga Utredningar. 1970.34*)

— Thailand.

THAILAND. National Economic and Social Development Board. 1973. The third national economic and social development plan, 1972-1976. Bangkok, [1973]. pp. 285,67.

— Turkey.

KRZYZANIAK (MARIAN) and ÖZMUCUR (SÜLEYMAN) The distribution of income and the short-run burden of taxes in Turkey, 1968. Houston, 1972. pp. 38. *bibliog.* (*Rice University. Program of Development Studies. Papers. No. 28*)

— United Kingdom.

CLEGG (HUGH ARMSTRONG) How to run an incomes policy and why we made such a mess of the last one. London, 1971. pp. 88.

WILLIS (KENNETH G.) Models of population and income: economic planning in rural areas. Newcastle upon Tyne, 1971. pp. 65. (*Newcastle-upon-Tyne. University. Department of Agricultural Economics. Agricultural Adjustment Unit. Research Monographs. No. 1*)

ASH (J.C.K.) Quarterly forecasting at the N[ational] I[nstitute of] E[conomic and] S[ocial] R[esearch]: personal income and expenditure. [Reading], 1973. fo. 23. *bibliog.* (*Reading. University. Department of Economics. Discussion Papers in Economics. No.40*)

BURDZHALOV (FELIKS EDUARDOVICH) Gosudarstvenno-monopolisticheskaia politika dokhodov: kontseptsiia i praktika; po materialam Velikobritanii. Moskva, 1973. pp. 240.

FIELD (FRANK) 1942- . An incomes policy for poor families: a memorandum to the Chancellor of the Exchequer. London, 1973. pp. 12. (*Child Poverty Action Group. Poverty Pamphlets. 14*)

JACKSON (PETER McLEOD) and McGILVRAY (JAMES WILLIAM) The impact of tax changes on income distribution: the 1973 budget. London, 1973. pp. 23. (*Institute for Fiscal Studies. Publications. No. 8*)

CORINA (JOHN) and MEYRICK (A.J.) Incomes policy in crisis: an overview 1973-4. Oxford, [1974]. fo. 51.

POLANYI (GEORGE) and WOOD (JOHN B.) How much inequality?: an inquiry into the evidence. London, 1974. pp. 85. (*Institute of Economic Affairs. Research Monographs. 31*)

— United States.

GREENBERG (DAVID H.) and KOSTERS (MARVIN) Income guarantees and the working poor: the effect of income maintenance programs on the hours of work of male family heads. Santa Monico, 1970. pp. 134. (*Rand Corporation.* [*Rand Reports*]. *579*)

SMITH (WARREN LOUNSBURY) and TEIGEN (RONALD L.) eds. Readings in money, national income and stabilization policy. rev. ed. Homewood, Illinois, 1970 repr. 1971. pp. 647.

GREENBERG (DAVID H.) Income guarantees and the working poor in New York City: the effect of income maintenance programs on the hours of work of male family heads. New York, 1971. pp. 103. (*Rand Corporation.* [*Rand Reports*]. *658*)

BOULDING (KENNETH EWART) and others, eds. Transfers in an urbanized economy: theories and effects of the grants economy. Belmont, Calif., [1973]. pp. 376.

McCALL (JOHN JOSEPH) Income, mobility, racial discrimination, and economic growth. Lexington, [1973]. pp. 212. *bibliog.*

TAUSSIG (MICHAEL K.) Alternative measures of the distribution of economic welfare. Princeton, 1973. pp. 89. (*Princeton University. Department of Economics and Sociology. Industrial Relations Section. Research Report Series. No. 116*)

CONFERENCE ON THE POLITICAL ECONOMY OF INCOME DISTRIBUTION, WASHINGTON, D.C., 1973. Redistribution through public choice; [papers of the conference; edited by] Harold M. Hochman and George E. Peterson. New York, 1974. pp. 341.

MINCER (JACOB) Schooling, experience and earnings. New York, 1974. pp. 152. *bibliog.* (*National Bureau of Economic Research. Human Behavior and Social Institutions. 2*)

— — New York.

SCHAFFER (RICHARD LANCE) Income flows in urban poverty areas: a comparison of the community income accounts of Bedford-Stuyvesant and Borough Park. Lexington, [1973]. pp. 110. *bibliog.*

— Yugoslavia.

THOMAS (HENDRIK) Personal income distribution in Yugoslavia: a human capital approach to the analysis of personal income differences in the industry of a labor-managed market economy. [Ithaca, N.Y.,] 1973. fo.266. bibliog.

INCOME TAX

— Mathematical models.

SHESHINSKI (EYTAN) An example of income tax schedules which are optimal for the maxi- min criterion. Stanford, 1972. fo. 15. *bibliog.* (*Stanford University. Institute for Mathematical Studies in the Social Sciences. Technical Reports.* [*New Series*]. *No. 74*)

— Australia — Law.

RYAN (K.W.) Manual of the law of income tax in Australia. 3rd ed. Sydney, 1972. pp. 285.

— Belgium — Colonies.

BELGIUM. Ministère des Colonies. 1919. Guide à l'usage du personnel chargé de l'application des dispositions du décret du 17 juillet 1914 sur l'impôt indigène. [Brussels?, 1919?]. pp. 116.

— Canada.

BONZANIGO (ROCCO) Canadian taxation of business and investment income of non-residents.Bern, 1973. pp. 97. *bibliog.*

STITT (H.J.) and BAKER (S.R.) International taxation and Canadian tax reform. Don Mills, Ont., [1972]. pp. 120.

— Denmark.

DENMARK. Statens Ligningsdirektorat. 1973. Indkomst- og formueskat. København, 1973. pp. 266. (*Meddelelser. 1*)

— — Law

HEMMINGSEN (KJELD) Skatteretten: introduktion til skattesystemet indtoegter og udgifter. København, 1974. pp. 129. (*Copenhagen. Handelshøjskolen. Skriftraekke G.11*)

— Germany.

GERMANY (BUNDESREPUBLIK). Statistisches Bundesamt. Einkommen- und Körperschaftsteuer. trien., 1968- Wiesbaden. (*Finanzen und Steuern. Reihe 6.1*)

GERMANY (BUNDESREPUBLIK). Statistisches Bundesamt. Lohnsteuer. trien., 1968- Wiesbaden. (*Finanzen und Steuern. Reihe 6. 2*)

— — Hesse.

HESSE. Statistisches Landesamt. Beiträge zur Statistik Hessens. Neue Folge. Nr. 47. Der Bruttolohn und seine Besteuerung 1968: Ergebnisse der Lohnsteuerstatistik 1968. Wiesbaden, 1972. pp. 49.

HESSE. Statistisches Landesamt. Beiträge zur Statistik Hessens. Neue Folge. Nr.60. Die veranlagten Einkommen 1968: Ergebnisse der Einkommensteuerstatistik und der Körperschaftsteuerstatistik 1968. Wiesbaden, 1974. pp. [170].

— Jamaica.

TIRADO (IRMA G.) La elasticidad-ingreso de la contribucion sobre ingresos en Puerto Rico y Jamaica, 1955-1963. Rio Piedras, P.R., 1967. pp. 142. *bibliog.* (*Puerto Rico University. Institute of Caribbean Studies. Special Studies. No.4*)

— Netherlands.

NETHERLANDS. Centraal Planbureau. 1972. De druk van de inkomstenbelasting in de komende jaren: gevolgen voor diverse inkomensniveaus van alternatieve tariefaanpassingen van de imkomstenbelasting, 1971-1976. 's-Gravenhage, 1972. pp. 54. (*Monografieën. 14*)

BARTEL (JOHANNES CORNELIS KASPER WILLEM) Inkomstenbelastingaspecten van de opbrengst van aandelen. Deventer, [1973]. pp. 276. *bibliog. With English summary.*

— Puerto Rico.

TIRADO (IRMA G.) La elasticidad-ingreso de la contribucion sobre ingresos en Puerto Rico y Jamaica, 1955-1963. Rio Piedras, P.R., 1967. pp. 142. *bibliog.* (*Puerto Rico University. Institute of Caribbean Studies. Special Studies. No.4*)

— Sweden — Mathematical models.

JAKOBSSON (ULF) and NORMANN (Goran) Inkomstbeskattningen i den ekonomiska politiken: en kvantitativ analys av systemet för personlig inkomstbeskattning, 1952-1971. Stockholm, [1974]. pp. 280. *bibliog. With summary and table of contents in English.*

— United Kingdom.

ATKINSON (A.B.) The tax credit scheme and the redistribution of income. London, 1973. pp. 89. *bibliog.* (*Institute for Fiscal Studies. Publications. No. 9.*)

— — Foreign income.

SUMPTION (ANTHONY) Taxation of overseas income. London, 1973. pp. 187.

— — Law.

SUMPTION (ANTHONY) Taxation of overseas income. London, 1973. pp. 187.

— — Mathematical models.

DORRINGTON (J.C.) A structural approach to estimating the built-in flexibility of U.K.taxes on personal income. London, [1972?]. fo. 24. bibliog. (London Graduate School of Business Studies. Econometric Forecasting Unit. Discussion Papers. No. 28)

— United States.

BITTKER (BORIS I.) and EUSTICE (JAMES S.) Federal income taxation of corporations and shareholders: (with Supplement). 2nd ed. Branford, Conn., [1966]. pp. 774.

— Zambia.

ZAMBIA. Central Statistical Office. Income-tax statistics. irreg., 1969- Lusaka.

INCUNABULA

— Bibliography.

CLARKE (DEREK ASHDOWN) and HEANEY (HOWELL J.) compilers. A selective check list of bibliographical scholarship for 1970. [Charlottesville, Va., 1972]. pp. 228-36. (A reprint from Studies in Bibliography, Volume twenty-five, 1972)

CLARKE (DEREK ASHDOWN) and HEANEY (HOWELL J.) compilers. A selective check list of bibliographical scholarship for 1971. [Charlottesville, Va., 1973]. pp. 271-290. (A reprint from Studies in Bibliography, volume twenty-six, 1973)

INDENTURED SERVANTS.

TINKER (HUGH) A new system of slavery: the export of Indian labour overseas, 1830-1920. London, 1974. pp. 432. bibliog.

INDEPENDENT REGULATORY COMMISSIONS

— France.

LEBRETON (JEAN PIERRE) and ROBINET (ANDRE PAUL) La Commission centrale des Marchés: politiquè économique et réforme administrative. Paris, 1973. pp. 98. bibliog. (Paris. Université de Paris II. Travaux et Recherches. Série Science Administrative. 6)

INDEX NUMBERS (ECONOMICS).

DENMARK. Danmarks Statistik. 1971. Indeksberegninger i Danmarks Statistik. København, 1971. pp. 73.

STATISTIKA stran-chlenov SEV. Moskva, 1973. pp. 269.

NOVOZHILOVA (ELENA MIKHAILOVNA) Indeksnyi metod analiza v torgovle. Moskva, 1974. pp. 128.

INDIA

— Appropriations and expenditures.

MATHEW (T.) Economic objectives and tax-expenditure policies of India 1950- 1970. New Delhi, 1974. pp. 56. (Economic and Scientific Research Foundation. Monographs. 5)

— Army.

MASON (PHILIP) A matter of honour: an account of the Indian army, its officers and men. London, 1974. pp. 580. bibliog.

— Biography.

INDIA. Parliament. Lok Sabha. Secretariat. 1967. Parliament of India: fourth Lok Sabha; Who's who, 1967. New Delhi, 1967. pp. 680.

HARYANA. Vidhan Sabha. Secretariat. 1972. Who's who, 1972. Chandigarh, 1972. pp. 355.

— Boundaries — China.

LAMB (ALASTAIR) The Sino-Indian border in Ladakh. Canberra, 1973. pp. 113.

— Commerce.

DAGLI (VADILAL) ed. India's foreign trade. Bombay, 1973. pp. 452. bibliog. (Commerce. Commerce Economic Studies. 9)

— Commerce — Europe, Eastern.

CHISHTI (SUMITRA) India's trade with east Europe. New Delhi, [1973?]. pp. 118.

— Constitution.

INDIA. Constitution. 1973. The constitution of India as modified up to the 1st January 1973. [New Delhi, 1973]. pp. 307.

— Constitutional history.

GUPTA (D.C.) Indian National Movement and constitutional development. 2nd ed. Delhi, 1973. pp. 615. bibliog.

SINGH (BHAWANI) Council of States in India: a structural and functional profile. Meerut, [1973]. pp. 360. bibliog.

MOORE (ROBIN JAMES) The crisis of Indian unity, 1917-1940. Oxford, 1974. pp. 334. bibliog.

— Economic conditions.

INTERNATIONAL MONETARY FUND. 1954. Economic development with stability: a report to the government of India...; by E.M. Bernstein [and others]. [New Delhi], Ministry of Finance, [1954]. pp. 84.

CHAKRAVERTI (A.K.) Structure of the Indian economy. Calcutta, 1968. pp. 330. bibliog.

SUNDRAM (J.D.) Rural industrial development. Bombay, 1970. pp. 181.

BHATTACHARYA (DEBESH) The role of technological progress in Indian economic development. Calcutta, 1972. pp. 276. bibliog.

BHATT (V.V.) Two decades of development: the Indian experiment. Bombay, 1973. pp. 111. bibliog.

KUITENBROUWER (JOOST B.W.) Growth and equality in India and China: a historical comparative analysis. The Hague, 1973. pp. 42. (Hague. Institute of Social Studies. Occasional Papers. No. 38)

MEHTA (BALRAJ) Crisis of Indian economy. New Delhi, 1973. pp. 194.

ROY (AJIT) Economics and politics of garibi hatao. Calcutta, 1973. pp. 144,iv.

SAU (RANJIT KUMAR) Indian economic growth: constraints and prospects. Calcutta, [1973]. pp. 116. bibliog.

SWAMY (SUBRAMANIAN) Economic growth in China and India, 1952-1970: a comparative appraisal. Chicago, 1973. pp. 84.

— — Statistics.

DATA base of Indian economy: review and reappraisal; [papers of a series of seminars organized by the Indian Econometric Society]; editor C.R. Rao. Calcutta, 1972 in progress.

— Economic policy.

INDIA. Committee on Plan Projects. Development Administration Unit. 1966. Role and function of panchayati raj institutions in planning and development. [New Delhi], 1966. pp. 73, 3. bibliog.

NARAYAN (B.K.) Southern states through plans: a regional analysis. Delhi, 1970. pp. 168.

SUNDRAM (J.D.) Rural industrial development. Bombay, 1970. pp. 181.

BHATTACHARYYA (KHAGENDRANATH) Planning: economics and economy; the Indian context. Calcutta, 1971. pp. 215.

BHULESHKAR (ASHOK V.) ed. Towards socialist transformation of Indian economy. Bombay, 1972. pp. 422.

SUBBIAH (B.V.) The world population crisis: a case study of India. Allahabad, 1972. pp. 156.

BHAGWATI (JAGDISH NATWARLAL) India in the international economy: a policy framework for a progressive society. Hyderabad, [1973]. pp. 35. (Institute of Public Enterprise. Lal Bahadur Shastri Memorial Lectures. 1973)

BHATT (V.V.) Two decades of development: the Indian experiment. Bombay, 1973. pp. 111. bibliog.

CHAND (MAHESH) and LOHKAR (R.N.) Aspects of economic theory, liquidity, growth and policy in India. Allahabad, 1973. pp. 262.

CHOWDHURY (P.N.) Economics of research and development. New Delhi, 1973. pp. 163. bibliog.

DASGUPTA (AJIT K.) Agriculture and economic development in India. New Delhi, [1973]. pp. 117.

DELHI. Institute of Economic Growth. Inflation and India's economic crisis; by V.K.R.V. Rao [and others]. Delhi, [1973]. pp. 71.

HEHL (HAUKE) Okonomische Entwicklungsfunktionen nationaler Entwicklungsbanken: dargestellt am Beispiel der Indischen Union. Berlin, [1973]. pp. 209. bibliog. With summaries in various languages.

KUITENBROUWER (JOOST B.W.) Growth and equality in India and China: processes, policies and theory formation. The Hague, 1973. pp. 61. (Hague. Institute of Social Studies. Occasional Papers. No 39)

MEHTA (BALRAJ) Crisis of Indian economy. New Delhi, 1973. pp. 194.

MISHRA (R.S.) Economics of development, with special reference to India. Bombay, [1973]. pp. 337.

RAKSHIT (GANGADHAR) Role of deficit financing in the context of Indian planning. Calcutta, 1973. pp. 171. bibliog.

ROY (AJIT) Economics and politics of garibi hatao. Calcutta, 1973. pp. 144,iv.

SAU (RANJIT KUMAR) Indian economic growth: constraints and prospects. Calcutta, [1973]. pp. 116. bibliog.

VAKIL (CHANDULAL NAGINDAS) ed. Industrial development of India: policy and problems; Kamalnayan Bajaj commemoration volume). New Delhi, 1973. pp. 491.

WADHVA (CHARAN D.) ed. Some problems of India's economic policy: selected readings on planning, agriculture and foreign aid. Bombay, 1973. pp. 496.

AURORA (GROVER) and others. India's fifth five-year plan...: the shape of things to come, with... current comments and criticism from press, public and parliamentarians. Delhi, 1974. pp. 143.

BEHARI (BEPIN) Economic growth and technological change in India. Delhi, [1974]. pp. 274. bibliog.

LAKSHMANAN (M.S.) Economic development in India. Delhi, 1974. pp. 214.

MATHEW (T.) Economic objectives and tax-expenditure policies of India 1950- 1970. New Delhi, 1974. pp. 56. (Economic and Scientific Research Foundation. Monographs. 5)

— — Mathematical models.

GAIHA (RAGHAV) and VASHISHTHA (PREM) An input-output analysis of key sectors in the Indian economy. Delhi, [1972]. fo. 24.

INDIA. (Cont.)

— Executive departments.

INDIA. Administrative Reforms Commission. Study Team on Scientific Departments. 1970. Report. [Delhi], 1970. pp. 130.

INDIA. Central Statistical Organisation. 1971. Statistical system in India, 1970. [Delhi, 1971]. pp. 74. *bibliog.*

— Famines.

See also BENGAL — Famines.

— Foreign economic relations.

BHAGWATI (JAGDISH NATWARLAL) India in the international economy: a policy framework for a progressive society. Hyderabad, [1973]. pp. 35. *(Institute of Public Enterprise. Lal Bahadur Shastri Memorial Lectures. 1973)*

— — Germany.

DAGLI (VADILAL) ed. India and Germany: a survey of economic relations. Bombay, 1970. pp. 232. *bibliog. (Commerce. Commerce Economic Studies. 6)*

— — Nepal.

RAWAT (POORAN CHAND) Indo-Nepal economic relations. Delhi, 1974. pp. 287.

— Foreign relations.

GANGAL (S.C.) India and the Commonwealth. Agra, 1970. pp. 152. *bibliog.*

KULKARNI (VENKATESH BALKRISHNA) Is India a big power?. Delhi, 1972. pp. 167.

MENON (KUMARA PADMANABHA SIVASANKARA) The Indo-Soviet treaty: setting and sequel. 2nd ed. Delhi, 1972. pp. 156.

CHAWLA (VIJAY) India and the super powers. Jaipur, 1973. pp. 148. *bibliog.*

SHUKLA (RAM LAKHAN) Britain, India and the Turkish Empire, 1853-1882. New Delhi, [1973]. pp. 262. *bibliog.*

BURKE (SAMUEL MARTIN) Mainsprings of Indian and Pakistani foreign policies. Minneapolis, [1974]. pp. 308. *bibliog.*

— — China.

HU (CHI-HSI) Pékin et le mouvement communiste indien. Paris, 1972. pp. 153. *(Fondation Nationale des Sciences Politiques. Travaux et Recherches de Science Politique. 22)*

KAPUR (HARISH) The embattled triangle: Moscow, Peking, New Delhi. New York, 1973. pp. 175. *bibliog.*

RAM (MOHAN) Politics of Sino-Indian confrontation. Delhi, 1973. pp. 241. *bibliog.*

— — Iran.

ISLAM (RIAZUL) Indo-Persian relations: a study of the political and diplomatic relations between the Mughul empire and Iran. Teheran, [1970]. pp. 287. *bibliog. (Iranian Culture Foundation. Sources of the History and Geography of Iran. No.32)*

— — Russia.

KAPUR (HARISH) The embattled tringele: Moscow, Peking, New Delhi. New York, 1973. pp. 175. *bibliog.*

RAY (HEMEN) Indo-Soviet relations, 1955-1971. Bombay, 1973. pp. 302.

— — Sikkim.

RAO (P.R.) India and Sikkim, 1814-1970. New Delhi, 1972. pp. 227. *bibliog.*

— — United Kingdom.

CHAMBERLAIN (M.E.) Britain and India: the interaction of two peoples. Newton Abbot, 1974. pp. 272. *bibliog.*

— — United States.

AZIZ (QUTUBUDDIN) Mission to Washington: an expose of India's intrigues in the United States of America in 1971 to dismember Pakistan. Karachi, 1973. pp. 234.

VENKATARAMANI (M.S.) Bengal famine of 1943: the American response. Delhi, [1973]. pp. 137.

— Full employment policies.

INDIA. Committee on Unemployment. 1972. Interim report…on some short-term measures for employment. [Delhi], 1972. pp. 58.

— Government publications — Bibliography.

INDIA. Parliament. Lok Sabha. Secretariat. 1958. List of publications (periodical or ad hoc) issued by various ministries of the government of India. 3rd ed. [New Delhi, 1958]. pp. 282.

INDIA. Ministry of Labour and Employment. Library. Bibliographical Series. 14. Catalogue of publications of the Ministry of Labour and Employment. New Delhi, [1962]. pp. 57.

— — Union lists.

MACDONALD (TERESA) Union catalogue of the serial publications of the Indian government, 1858-1947, held in libraries in Britain. London, 1973. pp. 154.

— History — 1765—1947, British occupation.

CHOUDHARY (SUKHBIR) Indian people fight for national liberation: non-cooperation, Khilafat and revivalist movements, 1920-22. New Delhi, 1972. pp. 456. *bibliog.*

MUDFORD (PETER) Birds of a different plumage: a study of British-Indian relations from Akbar to Curzon. London, 1974. pp. 314. *bibliog.*

— Industries.

ALAGH (YOGINDER K.) Regional aspects of Indian industrialization. Bombay, 1972. pp. 79. *(Bombay (City). University. Economics Series. No. 21)*

NANDI (KESAB LAL) Growth in selected Indian industries: some facets of industrial planning in a growing democracy. Calcutta, 1972. pp. 147. *bibliog.*

KUTHIALA (S.K.) From tradition to modernity. New Delhi, 1973. pp. 227. *bibliog.*

NATIONAL COUNCIL OF APPLIED ECONOMIC RESEARCH. Sanctioned capacities in non-engineering industries. New Delhi, 1973. pp. 1058.

VAKIL (CHANDULAL NAGINDAS) ed. Industrial development of India: policy and problems; Kamalnayan Bajaj commemoration volume). New Delhi, 1973. pp. 491.

— Languages.

ALL INDIA LANGUAGE CONFERENCE, CALCUTTA, 1958. Modern India rejects Hindi; report of the…conference. [Calcutta, 1958?]. pp. 150.

— Nationalism.

CHOUDHARY (SUKHBIR) Indian people fight for national liberation: non-cooperation, Khilafat and revivalist movements, 1920-22. New Delhi, 1972. pp. 456. *bibliog.*

GUPTA (D.C.) Indian National Movement and constitutional development. 2nd ed. Delhi, 1973. pp. 615. *bibliog.*

HUTCHINS (FRANCIS G.) India's revolution: Gandhi and the Quit India movement. Cambridge, Mass., 1973. pp. 326. *bibliog.*

JOHNSON (GORDON) Provincial politics and Indian nationalism: Bombay and the Indian National Congress, 1880 to 1915. Cambridge, 1973. pp. 207. *bibliog. (Cambridge. University. Centre of South Asian Studies. Cambridge South Asian Studies. 14)*

ZAIDI (A. MOIN) The way out to freedom: an inquiry into the Quit India Movement conducted by participants. New Delhi, 1973. pp. 254.

BASU (APARNA) The growth of education and political development in India, 1898- 1920. Delhi, 1974. pp. 258. *bibliog.*

MOORE (ROBIN JAMES) The crisis of Indian unity, 1917-1940. Oxford, 1974. pp. 334. *bibliog.*

NANDA (B.R.) Gokhale, Gandhi and the Nehrus: studies in Indian nationalism. London, 1974. pp. 203.

— Officials and employees — Salaries, allowances, etc.

INDIA. Central Pay Commission. 1973. Report of the third Central Pay Commission; [Reghubar Dayal, chairman]. [Delhi]. 1973. 4 vols. (in 1).

— Parliament — Committees.

PARLIAMENTARY committees in India: [based on the proceedingsof a seminar organized by the Institute of Constitutional and Parliamentary Studies];… editor Subhash C. Kashyap. New Delhi, [1973]. pp. 143. *bibliog.*

— — Elections.

ROY (RAMASHRAY) The uncertain verdict: a study of the 1969 elections in four Indian states. New Delhi, 1973. pp. 288.

— — Rules and practice.

SINGH (BHAWANI) Council of States in India: a structural and functional profile. Meerut, [1973]. pp. 360. *bibliog.*

— Politics and government.

APPADORAI (ANGADIPURAM) Documents on political thought in modern India. Bombay, 1973 in progress.

— — 1765—1947.

GHOSH (S.C.) Decision-making and power in the British Conservative Party: a study of the Indian problem 1929-1934. Calcutta, 1972. pp. 235. *bibliog.*

— — 1919—1947.

HUTCHINS (FRANCIS G.) India's revolution: Gandhi and the Quit India movement. Cambridge, Mass., 1973. pp. 326. *bibliog.*

ZAIDI (A. MOIN) The way out to freedom: an inquiry into the Quit India Movement conducted by participants. New Delhi, 1973. pp. 254.

MOORE (ROBIN JAMES) The crisis of Indian unity, 1917-1940. Oxford, 1974. pp. 334. *bibliog.*

— — 1947— .

GIRI (V.V.) President speaks: a compilation of the speeches made by President V.V. Giri from May, 1969 to March, 1970; [edited] by Nagendra Singh. Delhi, [1972?]. pp. 208.

KULKARNI (VENKATESH BALKRISHNA) Is India a big power?. Delhi, 1972. pp. 167.

BRASS (PAUL R.) and FRANDA (MARCUS F.) eds. Radical politics in south Asia. Cambridge, Mass., [1973]. pp. 449. *(Massachusetts Institute of Technology. Center for International Studies. Studies in Communism, Revisionism and Revolution. 19)*

RAHEJA (BHAGWAN DASS) Urban India and public policy. Bombay, [1973]. pp. 323. *bibliog.*

KHARE (BRIJ B.) India: political attitudes and social change. New Delhi, [1974]. pp. 264. *bibliog.*

— Population.

BHATTACHARYA (DURGAPRASAD) A guide to the population estimates of Eastern India 1811-1830. Calcutta, 1972. pp. 56.

SUBBIAH (B.V.) The world population crisis: a case study of India. Allahabad, 1972. pp. 156.

AGARWALA (SHRIMAN NARAYAN) India's population problems. rev. ed. Bombay, 1973. pp. 193.

HARRIMAN (EDWARD CLEMENTS) Indian population policy and the family planning programme; [Ph.D.(London) thesis]. 1973. fo. 286. bibliog. Typescript: unpublished. This thesis is the property of London University and may not be removed from the Library.

MANDELBAUM (DAVID GOODMAN) Human fertility in India: social components and policy perspectives. Berkeley, [1974]. pp. 132. bibliog.

— Relations (general) with the United Kingdom.

MUDFORD (PETER) Birds of a different plumage: a study of British-Indian relations from Akbar to Curzon. London, 1974. pp. 314. bibliog.

— Religion.

TEJASANANDA (SWAMI) The Ramakrishna movement: its ideal and activities. 3rd ed. Howrah, 1964. pp. 53.

POCOCK (DAVID FRANCIS) Mind, body and wealth: a study of belief and practice in an Indian village. Oxford, [1973]. pp. 187.

— Rural conditions.

SUNDRAM (J.D.) Rural industrial development. Bombay, 1970. pp. 181.

MULAY (SUMATI) and RAY (G.L.) Towards modernization: a study of peasantry in rural Delhi. Delhi, 1973. pp. 159. bibliog.

GUPTA (GIRI RAJ) Marriage, religion and society: pattern of change in an Indian village. Delhi, [1974]. pp. 187. bibliog.

KESSINGER (TOM G.) Vilyatpur 1848-1968: social and economic change in a north Indian village. Berkeley, [1974]. pp. 227.

— Social conditions.

GANGULI (BIRENDRANATH) Gandhi's social philosophy: perspective and relevance. New York, [1973]. pp. 453.

KUITENBROUWER (JOOST B.W.) Growth and equality in India and China: a historical comparative analysis. The Hague, 1973. pp. 42. (Hague. Institute of Social Studies. Occasional Papers. No. 38)

KUTHIALA (S.K.) From tradition to modernity. New Delhi, 1973. pp. 227. bibliog.

ROY (AJIT) Economics and politics of garibi hatao. Calcutta, 1973. pp. 144,iv.

DUBE (SHYAM CHARAN) Contemporary India and its modernization. Delhi, [1974]. pp. 145.

KHARE (BRIJ B.) India: political attitudes and social change. New Delhi, [1974]. pp. 264. bibliog.

— Social history.

RAGHUVANSHI (V.P.S.) Indian society in the eighteenth century. New Delhi, [1969]. pp. 374. bibliog.

— Social policy.

INDIA. Committee on Plan Projects. Development Administration Unit. 1966. Role and function of panchayati raj institutions in planning and development. [New Delhi], 1966. pp. 73, 3. bibliog.

SUBBIAH (B.V.) The world population crisis: a case study of India. Allahabad, 1972. pp. 156.

DUBEY (S.N.) Administration of social welfare programmes in India. Bombay, [1973]. pp. 214. bibliogs. (Tata Institute of Social Sciences. Tata Institute of Social Sciences Series. No.27)

KUITENBROUWER (JOOST B.W.) Growth and equality in India and China: processes, policies and theory formation. The Hague, 1973. pp. 61. (Hague. Institute of Social Studies. Occasional Papers. No. 39)

ROY (AJIT) Economics and politics of garibi hatao. Calcutta, 1973. pp. 144,iv.

DUBE (SHYAM CHARAN) Contemporary India and its modernization. Delhi, [1974]. pp. 145.

— Statistics.

INDIA. Central Statistical Organisation. 1971. Statistical system in India, 1970. [Delhi, 1971]. pp. 74. bibliog.

INDIA—PAKISTAN CONFLICT, 1971.

MISRA (KASHI PRASAD) The role of the United Nations in the Indo-Pakistani conflict, 1971. Delhi, [1973]. pp. 197.

INDIAN NATIONAL CONGRESS.

ZAIDI (A. MOIN) ed. The great upheaval 1969-1972: the case of the Indian National Congress in ferment based on documents emanating from official sources. Delhi, 1972. pp. 607.

JOHNSON (GORDON) Provincial politics and Indian nationalism: Bombay and the Indian National Congress, 1880 to 1915. Cambridge, 1973. pp. 207. bibliog. (Cambridge. University. Centre of South Asian Studies. Cambridge South Asian Studies. 14)

KAUSHIK (HARISH P.) The Indian National Congress in England, 1885-1920. Delhi, [1973]. pp. 155, xlviii. bibliog.

INDIAN OCEAN REGION.

BURRELL (R.M.) and COTTRELL (ALVIN J.) Iran, the Arabian peninsula, and the Indian ocean. New York, [1972]. pp. 46. bibliog. (National Strategy Information Center. Strategy Papers. No. 14)

LABROUSSE (HENRI) Le Golfe et le Canal: la réouverture du canal de Suez et la paix internationale. [Paris], 1973. pp. 164. bibliog.

INDIANA

— Industries.

McGREGOR (JOHN R.) A delimitation of Indiana manufacturing regions;...Numerical analysis: a different approach to analysis of geographical data; [by] Howard W. Dennis [and others]; Agricultural productivity of prairie, forest, and prairie-forest transition soils in Illinois; [by] Paul W. Mausel. Terre Haute, Ind., 1973. pp. 67. (Indiana State University. Department of Geography and Geology. Professional Papers. No. 4)

INDIANS OF CENTRAL AMERICA

— Guatemala.

COMMUNITY culture and national change: [essays by] Richard N.Adams [and others]; (Margaret A.L. Harrison, Robert Wauchope, editors). New Orleans, 1972. pp. 275. bibliogs. (Tulane University of Louisiana. Middle American Research Institute. Publications. No.24)

INDIANS OF MEXICO.

HEATH (SHIRLEY BRICE) Telling tongues: language policy in Mexico: colony to nation. New York, [1972]. pp. 300. bibliog.

INDIANS OF NORTH AMERICA.

DE LA GARZA (RUDOLPH O.) and others, eds. Chicanos and native Americans: the territorial minorities; [including papers presented at the Workshop on Southwest Ethnic Groups: Sociopolitical Environment and Education, El Paso, 1972]. Englewood Cliffs, N. J., [1973]. pp. 205.

McNICKLE (D'ARCY) Native American tribalism: Indian survivals and renewals. New York, 1973. pp. 190.

— Economic conditions.

GILBREATH (KENT) Red capitalism: an analysis of the Navajo economy. Norman, Okla., [1973]. pp. 157. bibliog.

INDONESIA.

— Government relations.

NOVACK (GEORGE) Genocide against the Indians: its role in the rise of U.S. capitalism. New York, 1970. pp. 31.

PRUCHA (FRANCIS PAUL) ed. Americanizing the American Indians: writings by the "Friends of the Indian", 1880-1900. Cambridge, Mass., 1973. pp. 358. bibliog.

— History.

PORTER (KENNETH WIGGINS) The negro on the American frontier. New York, 1971. pp. 529.

— Land tenure.

OTIS (DELOS SACKET) The Dawes Act and the allotment of Indian lands;...edited... by Francis Paul Prucha. Norman, Okla., [1973]. pp. 197.

— Legal status, laws, etc.

PRICE (MONROE E.) Law and the American Indian: readings, notes and cases. Indianapolis, [1973]. pp. 807. bibliog.

— Urban residence.

DOSMAN (EDGAR J.) Indians: the urban dilemma. Toronto, [1972]. pp. 192.

— Canada.

WILSON (JAMES) b. 1948. Canada's Indians. London, 1974. pp. 32. bibliog. (Minority Rights Group. Reports. No. 21)

— — North West Territories.

PETITOT (EMILE) The Amerindians of the Canadian northwest in the 19th century, as seen by Emile Petitot...; edited by Donat Savoie. Ottawa, 1971. 2 vols. (in 1). bibliog. (Canada. Northern Science Research Group. MDRP [Reports]. 9-10)

— — Saskatchewan.

DOSMAN (EDGAR J.) Indians: the urban dilemma. Toronto, [1972]. pp. 192.

— Virginia.

CRAVEN (WESLEY FRANK) White, red, and black: the seventeenth-century Virginian. Charlottesville, 1971. pp. 114. (Virginia University. Richard Lectures. 1970)

INDIANS OF SOUTH AMERICA

— Bolivia.

REINAGA (FAUSTO) Tesis india. [La Paz, 1971]. pp. 188.

— Brazil.

COWELL (ADRIAN) The tribe that hides from man. London, 1973. pp. 251.

TRIBES of the Amazon basin in Brazil 1972; report for the Aborigines Protection Society by Edwin Brooks [and others]. London, 1973. pp. 201.

— Peru.

DAVIES (THOMAS M.) Indian integration in Peru: a half century of experience, 1900- 1948. Lincoln, Neb., [1974]. pp. 204. bibliog.

INDIVIDUALISM.

SHAFER (RAYMOND P.) Government control of individual behavior: its right and its proper role; ([with] The American Public Health Association awards for excellence). [Washington, 1973]. pp. 35. (American Public Health Association. Matthew B. Rosenhaus Lectures. 1st, 1973)

INDONESIA.

NEILL (WILFRED T.) Twentieth-century Indonesia. New York, 1973. pp. 413. bibliog.

INDONESIA. (Cont.)

— Census.

BHATTA (J.N.) The future census, October 1961, of Indonesia. Djakarta, [1961]. pp. 2,18. *bibliog*. *(Indonesia. Departemen Angkatan Darat. Direktorat Topografifi Dinas Geografifi Publications. 10)*

— Constitution.

INDONESIA. Department of Information. 1968. Towards a sound democratic mechanism. [Djakarta, 1968]. fo. (115).

— Economic conditions.

FRANCE. Direction de la Documentation. La Documentation Française. Notes et Etudes Documentaires. Nos. 3,808-3, 809. L'économie indonésienne: structures et conjoncture; [by] Bernard Dorléans. Paris, 1971. pp. 85. *bibliog*.

— Economic policy.

INDONESIA. Department of Information. 1968. Towards a sound democratic mechanism. [Djakarta, 1968]. fo. (115).

INDONESIA. Department of Information. 1969. Indonesia develops five year development plan 1969/'70-1973/'74: [digest]. [Djakarta, 1969]. fo. 34.

The BASIC patterns of the national general program and the five-year development program: a supplement of the statement of the Acting President before the Working Committee of the MPRS (Congress) on February 29, 1968. [Djakarta, 1970]. fo. 15.

SOEMARDJAN (SELO) Imbalances in development: the Indonesian experience. Athens, [1972]. fo. 21. *(Ohio University. Center for International Studies. Papers in International Studies. Southeast Asia Series. No. 25)*

— Foreign economic relations — Belgium.

BELGIUM. Office Belge du Commerce Extérieur. 1970. La mission économique belge en Indonesie, janvier 1970: rapport. Bruxelles, 1970. pp. 44. *(Informations du Commerce Extérieur. Suppléments. Série C. No. 2)*

— Foreign relations.

ANAK AGUNG GDE AGUNG (IDE) Twenty years Indonesian foreign policy, 1945-1965. The Hague, [1973]. pp. 640. *bibliog*.

INTERNATIONAL INSTITUTE FOR STRATEGIC STUDIES. Adelphi Papers. No. 104. Indonesia's future and South-East Asia; by Peter Polomka. London, 1974. pp. 40.

— Industries.

DONGES (JUERGEN B.) and others. Industrial development policies for Indonesia. Tübingen; 1974. pp. 178. *bibliog*. *(Kiel. Universität. Institut für Weltwirtschaft. Kieler Studien. 126)*

— Parliament — Elections.

HULL INTERNATIONAL COLLOQUIUM ON SOUTH-EAST ASIA, 2ND, 1971. Indonesia after the 1971 elections: [papers presented at the Colloquium]; edited by Oey Hong Lee. London, 1974. pp. 116. *(Hull. University. Centre for South-East Asian Studies. Monographs on South-East Asia. No.5)*

— Politics and government.

INDONESIA. Department of Information. 1968. Towards a sound democratic mechanism. [Djakarta, 1968]. fo. (115).

KAHANE (REUVEN) The problem of political legitimacy in an antagonistic society: the Indonesian case. Beverly Hills, [1973]. pp. 51. *bibliog*.

BRACKMAN (ARNOLD C.) Indonesia: the critical years 1976-78. London, 1974. pp. 16. *(Institute for the Study of Conflict. Conflict Studies. No. 49)*

INTERNATIONAL INSTITUTE FOR STRATEGIC STUDIES. Adelphi Papers. No. 104. Indonesia's future and South-East Asia; by Peter Polomka. London, 1974. pp. 40.

MORTIMER (REX) Indonesian communism under Sukarno: ideology and politics, 1959-1965. Ithaca, 1974. pp. 464. *bibliog*.

— Social policy.

INDONESIA. Department of Information. 1968. Towards a sound democratic mechanism. [Djakarta, 1968]. fo. (115).

INDONESIA. Department of Information. 1969. Indonesia develops five year development plan 1969/'70-1973/'74: [digest]. [Djakarta, 1969]. fo. 34.

The BASIC patterns of the national general program and the five-year development program: a supplement of the statement of the Acting President before the Working Committee of the MPRS (Congress) on February 29, 1968. [Djakarta, 1970]. fo. 15.

SOEMARDJAN (SELO) Imbalances in development: the Indonesian experience. Athens, [1972]. fo. 21. *(Ohio University. Center for International Studies. Papers in International Studies. Southeast Asia Series. No. 25)*

INDO — PAKISTAN CONFLICT.

See INDIA — PAKISTAN CONFLICT.

INDUS WATERS TREATY, 1960.

GULHATI (NIRANJAN D.) Indus waters treaty: an exercise in international mediation. Bombay, 1973. pp. 472.

INDUSTRIAL ACCIDENTS.

KINNERSLY (PATRICK) The hazards of work: how to fight them. London, 1973. pp. 394.

— New Zealand.

NEW ZEALAND. Department of Statistics. Industrial injuries. a., 1968/1969 [1st]- Wellington.

— United Kingdom.

FABIAN SOCIETY. Fabian Tracts. [No.] 428. Industrial injuries: a new approach; [by] E.A. Webb:... the evidence of the Post Office Engineering Union to the Royal Commission on Civil Liability and Compensation for Personal Injury. London, 1974. pp. 24.

INDUSTRIAL CAPACITY

— United States.

HUETTNER (DAVID) Plant size, technological change, and investment requirements: a dynamic framework for the long-run average cost curve. New York, 1974. pp. 183. *bibliog*.

INDUSTRIAL DISTRICTS.

EUROPEAN FREE TRADE ASSOCIATION. 1970. Regional policy in EFTA: industrial estates. Geneva, 1970. pp. 80.

— European Free Trade Association countries.

EUROPEAN FREE TRADE ASSOCIATION. 1970. Regional policy in EFTA: industrial estates. Geneva, 1970. pp. 80.

— United Kingdom.

SLOUGH ESTATES LIMITED. Slough Estates Limited, 1920-1970. [Slough, 1970]. pp. 36.

INDUSTRIAL EQUIPMENT

— Poland.

KUBIAK (ANDRZEJ F.) Regionalne zró'znicowanie wyposa'zenia zakładów przemysłowych we własne urządzenia infrastrukturalne. Warszawa, 1974. pp. 130. *bibliog*. *(Polska Akademia Nauk. Komitet Przestrzennego Zagospodarowania Kraju. Studia. 44)* With Russian and English summaries.

— Underdeveloped areas

See UNDERDEVELOPED AREAS — Industrial equipment.

INDUSTRIAL HYGIENE.

SINCLAIR (THOMAS CRAIG) and others. Innovation and human risk; the evaluation of human life and safety in relation to technical change;...[a project of the] Science Policy Research Unit, University of Sussex. London, [1972]. pp. 36. *bibliog*.

— Sweden.

BOLINDER (ERIK) and OHLSTRÖM (BO) Stress på svenska arbetsplatser: en enkätundersökning bland LO-medlemmarna rörande psykiska påfrestningar i arbetsmiljön. [Stockholm, 1971]. pp. 123. *bibliog*.

The HUMAN work environment: Swedish experiences, trends, and future problems: a contribution to the United Nations conference on the human environment; [prepared by a working party] . [Stockholm], Royal Ministry for Foreign Affairs, [1972]. pp. 68.

— United Kingdom — Law and legislation.

U.K. Department of Employment. 1973. Proposals for a safety and health at work bill. [London], 1973. pp. 36.

INDUSTRIAL LAWS AND LEGISLATION.

EUROPEAN COMMUNITIES. Commission. 1973. Multinational undertakings and Community regulations: communication...to the Council, presented on 8 November 1973. [Brussels], 1973. pp. 32. *(Bulletin of the European Communities. Supplements. [1973/15])*

— Australia.

GLASBEEK (HARRY JACQUES) and EGGLESTON (E.M.) Cases and materials on industrial law in Australia. Sydney, 1973. pp. 590.

— Russia.

PRAVOVYE problemy rukovodstva i upravleniia otrasl'iu promyshlennosti v SSSR. Moskva, 1973. pp. 542.

— — Kazakstan.

KAZAKSTAN. Iuridicheskaia Komissiia. 1969. Khoziaistvennaia reforma i prava predpriiatii: sbornik reshenii pravitel'stva SSSR i pravitel'stva Kazakhskoi SSR, a takzhe ukazanii vedomstvennykh organov o khoziaistvennoi reforme; pod redaktsiei...T. Urazalieva. Alma-Ata, 1969. pp. 382.

UPRAVLENIE promyshlennost'iu Kazakhskoi SSR: gosudarstvenno-pravovye problemy. Alma-Ata, 1972. pp. 298.

— United Kingdom.

CRONIN (J.B.) and GRIME (R.P.) Introduction to industrial law. London, 1974. pp. 212.

INDUSTRIAL LOAN ASSOCIATIONS

— United Kingdom.

FINANCE FOR INDUSTRY LIMITED. Report and accounts. a., 1973/4 (1st)- London.

INDUSTRIAL MANAGEMENT

— Africa, Subsaharan.

ONYEMELUKWE (CLEMENT CHUKWUKADIBIA) Men and management in contemporary Africa. London, 1973. pp. 189.

— **America, Latin.**

DAVIS (STANLEY M.) and GOODMAN (LOUIS WOLF) eds. Workers and managers in Latin America. Lexington, Mass., [1972]. pp. 308.

— **India.**

HAJRA (S.) and RAMAKRISHNAN (P.) Managerial manpower in Indian industry, 1969-80. New Delhi, 1971. pp. 48. *(Economic and Scientific Research Foundation. Monographs. 2)*

— **Netherlands.**

VERENIGING VOOR DE STAATHUISHOUDKUNDE. Prae-adviezen. 1971. De industriële sector structuurpolitiek:... preadviezen van A. Heertje, A.E. Pannenborg [and] A.A.T. van Rhijn. 's-Gravenhage, 1971. pp. 95.

— **Russia.**

SILANT'EVA (NINA ALEKSANDROVNA) Ekonomicheskie problemy avtomatizatsii protsessov upravleniia proizvodstvom. Moskva, 1972. pp. 192. *bibliog.*

BACHURIN (ALEKSANDR VASIL'EVICH) Planovo-ekonomicheskie metody upravleniia. Moskva, 1973. pp. 455.

KNIAZEV (GRIGORII IVANOVICH) Finansovyi plan predpriiatiia i kontrol' za ego ispolneniem; pod redaktsiei V.N. Maslennikova. Moskva, 1973. pp. 143.

POPOV (GAVRIIL KHARITONOVICH) ed. Funktsii i struktura organov upravleniia, ikh sovershenstvovanie. Moskva, 1973. pp. 255.

— — **Kazakstan.**

UPRAVLENIE promyshlennost'iu Kazakhskoi SSR: gosudarstvenno- pravovye problemy. Alma-Ata, 1972. pp. 298.

— — **Latvia.**

ROZHDESTVENSKII (O.) Komandiry proizvodstva: o stile raboty i avtoritete rukovoditelia. Riga, 1971. pp. 75.

— **Sweden.**

VALDELIN (JAN) Produktutveckling och marknadsföring: en undersökning av produktutvecklingsprocesser i svenska företag. Stockholm, 1974. pp. 249. *bibliog. With English summary.*

— **United Kingdom.**

U.K. Department of Employment. Industrial Relations Division. Central Information Service. 1973- . Some organisations in the management and personnel field. rev. ed. London, 1973 in progress. 1 vol. (various pagings). *(Information Papers. [New Series]. No. 6)*

CHANNON (DEREK F.) Strategy and structure of management in private and state industry. London, 1974. pp. 10.

— **Yugoslavia.**

GORUPIĆ (DRAGO) The enterprise and the development of Yugoslav economic system: articles. Zagreb, 1974. pp. 159. *One article in French.* JAPAN -- Industries. 1972.

INDUSTRIAL ORGANIZATION.

INTERNATIONAL LABOUR ORGANISATION. Labour-Management Relations Series. Geneva, 1957 in progress.

NEEDHAM (DOUGLAS) Economic analysis and industrial structure. New York, [1969]. pp. 176. *bibliogs.*

ALLEGRO (JACQUES TOBIAS) Socio-technische organisatieontwikkeling. Leiden, 1973. pp. 268. *bibliog. With English summary.*

JARDILLIER (PIERRE) L'organisation humaine du travail. Paris, 1973. pp. 125. *bibliog.*

PRYOR (FREDERIC L.) Property and industrial organization in communist and capitalist nations. Bloomington, [1973]. pp. 513. *bibliog. (Indiana University. International Development Research Center. Studies in Development. No.7)*

SCIENZA e organizzazione del lavoro: [proceedings of two meetings held by the Istituto Gramsci, 1972]. Roma, 1973. pp. 191. *bibliog.*

JENKINS (DAVID) Job power: blue and white collar democracy. London, 1974. pp. 375. *bibliog.*

KROPOTKIN (PETR ALEKSEEVICH) Prince. Fields, factories and workshops tomorrow; edited, introduced and with additional material by Colin Ward. London, 1974. pp. 205.

— **China.**

BETTELHEIM (CHARLES) Révolution culturelle et organisation industrielle en Chine. Paris, 1973. pp. 153.

— **Germany.**

HEINTZELER (WOLFGANG) The co-determination problem in Western Germany. London, [1974]. pp. 19.

— **Germany, Eastern.**

DAMUS (RENATE) Entscheidungsstrukturen und Funktionsprobleme in der DDR- Wirtschaft. Frankfurt am Main, 1973. pp. 232.

GROSSKOPF (ERHARD) and HELLER (RONALD) Sozialistischer Betriebsvergleich: ein Mittel zur Intensivierung der Produktion. Berlin, 1973. pp. 178. *bibliog.*

— **Japan.**

ORGANISATION FOR ECONOMIC CO-OPERATION AND DEVELOPMENT. Industry Committee. 1972 The industrial policy of Japan. Paris, 1972. pp. 195.

— **Netherlands.**

VERENIGING VOOR DE STAATHUISHOUDKUNDE. Prae-adviezen. 1971. De industriële sector structuurpolitiek:... preadviezen van A. Heertje, A.E. Pannenborg [and] A.A.T. van Rhijn. 's-Gravenhage, 1971. pp. 95.

— **Pakistan.**

WHITE (LAWRENCE J.) Industrial concentration and economic power in Pakistan. Princeton, [1974]. pp. 212. *bibliog.*

— **Roumania.**

NICOLESCU (OVIDIU) Perfecţionarea organizării conducerii întreprinderii: variabile organizaţionale, analize, tehnici şi metode. Bucureşti, 1973. pp. 287. *bibliog. (Academia de Ştiinţe Sociale şi Politice a Republicii Socialiste România. Institutul de Cercetări Economice. 27) With Russian, French and English tables of contents.*

— **Russia.**

BROMBERG (GELLA L'VOVNA) and others. Ekonomicheskaia rabota finansovoi sluzhby predpriiatiia; pod redaktsiei... A.M. Birmana. Moskva, 1970. pp. 103.

DUMACHEV (ANATOLII PANTELEEVICH) Khozraschetnye ob"edineniia v promyshlennosti. Leningrad, 1972. pp. 195.

SHOKHIN (ANATOLII ALEKSANDROVICH) Pravovoe polozhenie promyshlennykh ob"edinenii v SSSR. Kazan', 1972. pp. 114.

AVDAKOV (IURII KONSTANTINOVICH) and BORODIN (VLADIMIR VASIL'EVICH) Proizvodstvennye ob"edineniia i ikh rol' v organizatsii upravleniia sovetskoi promyshlennost'iu, 1917-1932 gg. Moskva, 1973. pp. 240.

IUSUPOV (VITALII ANDREEVICH) Sochetanie otraslevogo i territorial'nogo upravleniia promyshlennost'iu SSSR. Kazan', 1973. pp. 127.

ALLAKHVERDIAN (DERENIK AKOPOVICH) and SLASTENKO (EVGENII NAUMOVICH) Metodologicheskie osnovy formirovaniia ob"edinenii v promyshlennosti. Moskva, 1974. pp. 168. *bibliog.*

DUNAEV (ERNEST PAVLOVICH) Ob"edineniia predpriiatii kak forma obobshchestvleniia proizvodstva. Moskva, 1974. pp. 251.

— — **Mathematical models.**

SHCHUKIN (VIKTOR NIKOLAEVICH) Optimizatsiia proizvodstvennoi struktury otrasli i promyshlennogo predpriiatiia; otvetstvennyi redaktor...L.A. Kozlov. Novosibirsk, 1973. pp. 108. *bibliog.*

— **Sweden.**

SJÖSTRAND (SVEN ERIK) Företagsorganisation: en taxonomisk ansats, med en typisering av 38 svenska byggnadsföretag. Stockholm, [1973]. pp. 456. *bibliog. With English summary.*

BERG (CURT) Samrådssystemet: en klinisk undersökning i ett växande företag. Stockholm, 1974. pp. 257. *bibliog. With English summary.*

— — **Research.**

DALBORG (HANS) Research and development: organization and location. Stockholm, 1974. pp. 152. *bibliog.*

— **United Kingdom.**

GEORGE (KENNETH DESMOND) Industrial organization: competition, growth and structural change in Britain. 2nd ed. London, 1974. pp. 225.

INDUSTRIAL PROCUREMENT

— **United Kingdom.**

ECONOMIC DEVELOPMENT COMMITTEE FOR THE CLOTHING INDUSTRY. The anatomy of purchasing clothing machinery: a study of the attitudes of clothing manufacturers towards the purchase of technologically advanced equipment. London, National Economic Development Office, 1974. pp. 52.

INDUSTRIAL PROJECT MANAGEMENT

— **Mathematical models.**

BEALL (RICHARD BURNAP) Properties of a systems model with applications to project management; [Ph.D. (London) thesis]. 1973. 1 vol. (various foliations). *Typescript: unpublished. This thesis is the property of London University and may not be removed from the Library.*

INDUSTRIAL PROMOTION.

ALHAIQUE (CLAUDIO) Creation of an industrial promotion service. Paris, Organisation for Economic Co-operation and Development, 1972. pp. 67. *(Problems of Development)*

— **Thailand.**

THAILAND. Statutes, etc. 1960. Promotion of Industrial Investment Act, B.E. 2503. [Bangkok, 1960]. fo. 7.

INDUSTRIAL RELATIONS.

URWICK (LYNDALL) and BRECH (EDWARD FRANZ LEOPOLD) The human factor in management, 1795-1943: two articles from the series "The pioneers of scientific management", etc. London, 1944. pp. 40.

INTERNATIONAL LABOUR ORGANISATION. Labour-Management Relations Series. Geneva, 1957 in progress.

CENTO SEMINAR ON INDUSTRIAL RELATIONS, TEHRAN, 1972. CENTO seminar... [held] February 12-17, 1972 [in] Tehran, Iran. [Ankara], Central Treaty Organization, 1972. pp. 182.

INDUSTRIAL RELATIONS. (Cont.)

ARBEITSKONFLIKTE und Arbeitskampf: Auswirkungen und Berechtigungen von Arbeitskonflikten; [papers of an international conference sponsored by the International Humanum Foundation]. Köln, [1973]. pp. 168. *(International Humanum Foundation. Gesellschaft, Kirche, Wirtschaft. Band 6)*

NASH (ALLAN N.) and MINER (JOHN BURNHAM) eds. Personnel and labor relations: an evolutionary approach. New York, [1973]. pp. 498. *bibliogs.*

The SOCIAL responsibility of business and labour: critique of a conference at Ditchley Park, 2-5 November 1973; by B.J.A. Hargreaves, conference rapporteur. Enstone, Oxfordshire, [1973]. pp. 37. *(Ditchley Foundation. Ditchley Papers. No.47)*

TEULINGS (AD) ed. Onderneming en vakbeweging: ontwikkelingstendenties in de arbeidsverhoudingen. Rotterdam, 1973. pp. 171. *(Mens en Maatschappij. Boekafleveringen. 1973)*

FOX (ALAN) Beyond contract: work, power and trust relations. London, 1974. pp. 408. *bibliog.*

FOX (ALAN) Man mismanagement. London, 1974. pp. 179. *bibliogs.*

— Research.

INTERNATIONAL LABOUR OFFICE. 1973. Structure and functions of research and training institutes in the field of labour relations: labour institutes, industrial relations centres and similar bodies. Geneva, 1973. pp. 169. *In English and French.*

— — Directories.

INTERNATIONAL LABOUR OFFICE. 1973. Directory of labour relations institutes. Geneva, 1973. pp. 248.

— Study and teaching.

INTERNATIONAL LABOUR OFFICE. 1973. Structure and functions of research and training institutes in the field of labour relations: labour institutes, industrial relations centres and similar bodies. Geneva, 1973. pp. 169. *In English and French.*

INTERNATIONAL LABOUR OFFICE. 1973. Directory of labour relations institutes. Geneva, 1973. pp. 248.

— Africa, Subsaharan.

ONYEMELUKWE (CLEMENT CHUKWUKADIBIA) Men and management in contemporary Africa. London, 1973. pp. 189.

— Canada.

WOODS (HARRY DOUGLAS) and others. Labour policy in Canada; ... volume 1 of Labour policy and labour economics in Canada. 2nd ed. Toronto, [1973]. pp. 377.

CANADA. Labour Relations Board. Decisions, information. Mr 1974 (v.1, no.1)- Ottawa. *In English and French.*

— Europe.

MALLES (PAUL) The institutions of industrial relations in Continental Europe. Ottawa, Information Canada, 1973. pp. 214.

MACBEATH (INNIS) The European approach to worker-management relationships. London, 1973. pp. 86.

— European Economic Community countries.

ECONOMIC DEVELOPMENT COMMITTEE FOR CHEMICALS. Chemicals manpower in Europe: report of a comparative study of industrial relations and manpower productivity in the UK, France, Germany and Holland. London, National Economic Development Office, 1973. pp. 67.

— India.

ALEXANDER (K.C.) Participative management: the Indian experience. New Delhi, [1972]. pp. 132. *bibliog.*

AGARWAL (R.D.) ed. Dynamics of labour relations in India: a book of readings. New Delhi, 1973 repr. 1974. pp. 296.

GHOSH (P.) and NATH (SANTOSH) Labour relations in India. New Delhi, 1973. pp. 429. *bibliog.*

NAIR (K. RAMACHANDRAN) Industrial relations in Kerala. New Delhi, 1973. pp. 437. *bibliog.*

— — Mysore.

HUMAN problems of industry in Bangalore; ([by] Thelma Dawson [and others]); edited by M.M. Thomas [and] H.F.J. Daniel. Bangalore, 1965. pp. 65.

— Ireland (Republic).

GOSS (JOHN M.) Industrial relations and moves towards industrial democracy in Ireland. Brighton, [1973]. fo.30. *bibliog.* (Brighton. University of Sussex. Centre for Contemporary European Studies. Research Papers. No. 4)

— Japan.

DORE (RONALD PHILIP) British factory, Japanese factory: the origins of national diversity in industrial relations. London, 1973. pp. 432.

OKOCHI (KAZUO) and others, eds. Workers and employers in Japan: the Japanese employment relations system. Princeton, 1974. pp. 538.

— Netherlands.

BINNEVELD (JOHANNES MARTINUS WOUTER) De stakingen in de Rotterdamse metaalindustrie in 1965: een sociologische analyse van de ontwikkelingen binnen een systeem van industriële verhoudingen. Groningen, 1974. pp. 111. *bibliog. With English summary.*

JONG (JOHAN DE) Een aantal recente ontwikkelingen in het Nederlandse systeem van arbeidsverhoudingen. Rotterdam, 1974. pp. 169. *bibliog.*

— New Zealand.

MILNE (G.S.) Industrial relations in the shipping industry: the role of government. Wellington, 1973. pp. 115. *bibliog. (Victoria University of Wellington. Industrial Relations Centre. Student Research Papers in Industrial Relations. No. 1)*

— Norway.

LATTMANN (CHARLES) Das norwegische Modell der selbstgesteuerten Arbeitsgruppe: ein Beitrag zur Verwirklichung der Mitbestimmung am Arbeitsplatz. Bern, [1972]. pp. 60. *bibliog. (Hochschule St. Gallen für Wirtschafts- und Sozialwissenschaften. Institut für Betriebswirtschaft. Betriebswirtschaftliche Mitteilungen. 56)*

GOSS (JOHN M.) Industrial relations and employee participation in management in Norway. Brighton, [1973]. fo. 36. *bibliog.* (Brighton. University of Sussex. Centre for Contemporary European Studies. Research Papers. No. 5)

— Russia.

SMOLIARCHUK (VASILII IVANOVICH) Prava profsoiuzov v regulirovanii trudovykh otnoshenii rabochikh i sluzhashchikh. Moskva, 1973. pp. 175.

— Sweden.

SMITH (GÖRAN) Parterna på arbetsmarknaden. 11th ed. Stockholm, [1972]. pp. 136.

— United Kingdom.

HAWKINS (KEVIN) Conflict and change: aspects of industrial relations. London, [1972]. pp. 257. *bibliog.*

BAYLEY (L. GORDON) Building: teamwork or conflict?. London, 1973. pp. 117.

COMMISSION ON INDUSTRIAL RELATIONS [U.K.]. G. Clancey Limited. London, H.M.SO., 1973. pp. 25. *(Reports. No. 54)*

DORE (RONALD PHILIP) British factory, Japanese factory: the origins of national diversity in industrial relations. London, 1973. pp. 432.

ECONOMIC DEVELOPMENT COMMITTEE FOR CHEMICALS. Chemicals manpower in Europe: report of a comparative study of industrial relations and manpower productivity in the UK, France, Germany and Holland. London, National Economic Development Office, 1973. pp. 67.

MARSH (ARTHUR) Managers and shop stewards: shop floor revolution?. London, 1973. pp. 174.

SYKES (ANDREW JAMES MACINTYRE) Myths of industrial relations...; issued by the Working Together Campaign. London, [1973?]. pp. 10.

BAGWELL (PHILIP SIDNEY) Industrial relations. [Dublin, 1974]. pp. 166. *bibliog. (Government and Society in Nineteenth-Century Britain: Commentaries on British Parliamentary Papers)*

DOWNING (JOHN DEREK HALL) Some aspects of the presentation of industrial relations and race relations in some major British news media; [Ph. D. (London) thesis]. [1974]. fo. 287. *Typescript: unpublished. This thesis is the property of London University and may not be removed from the Library.*

FRANCE. Direction de la Documentation. La Documentation Française. Notes et Etudes Documentaires. Nos. 4,053-4, 054-4,055. Les nouvelles relations industrielles en Grande-Bretagne, par Georges Ph. Koukoules. [Paris], 1974. pp. 76. *bibliog.*

U.K. Social Survey. [Reports. New Series.] 472. Workplace industrial relations, 1972; an enquiry carried out on behalf of the Department of Employment; [by] Stanley Parker. London, 1974. pp. 100, 46.

— United States.

KLEINGARTNER (ARCHIE) and LLOYD (KENNETH) Labor-management relations in the performing arts: the case of Los Angeles. Los Angeles, 1973. pp. 5. *(California University. Institute of Industrial Relations. Reprints. No. 233) (Reprinted from California Management Review, Vol. 15, No. 2, winter 1972)*

SOMERS (GERALD GEORGE) ed. The next twenty-five years of industrial relations; [twenty-fifth anniversary publication of the Industrial Relations Research Association]. Madison, [1973]. pp. 207.

SCHOEN (STERLING H.) and HILGERT (RAYMOND L.) Cases in collective bargaining and industrial relations: a decisional approach. rev. ed. Homewood, Ill., 1974. pp. 360. *bibliogs.*

INDUSTRIAL SAFETY

— Burma.

INTERNATIONAL LABOUR OFFICE. Development Programme: Technical Assistance Sector. [Burma] R.35. Report to the government of the Union of Burma on industrial hygiene and occupational health. (ILO/TAP/Burma/R35). Geneva, 1971. pp. 18.

— European Economic Community countries.

EUROPEAN COMMUNITIES. Statistical Office. Social Statistics. Luxembourg, 1960 in progress.

— United Kingdom — Law and legislation.

U.K. Department of Employment. 1973. Proposals for a safety and health at work bill. [London], 1973. pp. 36.

INDUSTRIAL SOCIOLOGY.

MEIGNANT (ALAIN) L'intervention sociopédagogique dans les organisations industrielles: contribution à la recherche et à l'action dans le domaine de l'éducation des adultes en milieu industriel, à propos de deux expériences. Paris, [1972]. pp. 227. *bibliog.*

SOTSIAL'NI problemy vyrobnychoho kolektyvu: z dosvidu sotsiolohichnykh doslidzhen'. Kyïv, 1972. pp. 159.

La BELGIQUE face aux investissements étrangers: une approche sociologique; ([by] Marc Beckers [and others])... sous la direction de Pierre de Bie. Leuven, 1973. pp. 269.

PODMARKOV (VALENTIN GEORGIEVICH) Vvedenie v promyshlennuiu sotsiologiiu: sotsial'nye problemy sotsialisticheskogo promyshlennogo proizvodstva. Moskva, 1973. pp. 318. *bibliog.*

WORK in America; report of a special task force to the Secretary of Health, Education, and Welfare; prepared under the auspices of the W.E. Upjohn Institute for Employment Research; [James O'Toole, chairman]. Cambridge, Mass., 1973. pp. 262. *bibliog.*

DYAR (DAMIEN A.) and GILES (W. JOHN) Improving skills in working with people: interaction analysis. London, H.M.S.O., 1974. pp. 39. *bibliog. (Training Information Papers.7)*

FUERSTENBERG (FRIEDRICH) ed. Industriesoziologie, II: die Entwicklung der Arbeits- und Betriebssoziologie seit dem Zweiten Weltkrieg. Darmstadt, [1974]. pp. 320. *bibliog.*

INDUSTRIAL STATISTICS.

UNITED NATIONS. Statistical Office. Statistical Papers. Series M. No. 54. Recommendations for the 1973 world programme of industrial statistics. (ST/STAT/SER.M/54) New York, 1971-72. 3 pts.(in 1 vol.). *bibliog.*

INDUSTRIAL SURVEYS.

RICHARDSON (M.) and CUNNINGHAM (A.D.) Vetting of industrial survey questionnaires by computer. Eastcote, Business Statistics Office, 1971. pp. 19.

INDUSTRIALIZATION.

UNITED NATIONS. Economic Commission for Asia and the Far East. Development Programming Techniques Series. Bangkok, 1960 in progress.

HUGHES (HELEN) ed. Prospects for partnership: industrialization and trade policies in the 1970s; a seminar held at the International Bank for Reconstruction and Development, October 5 and 6, 1972. Baltimore, 1973. pp. 289.

INDUSTRIALIZED BUILDING

— Europe.

LAPLANTE (D.G.) and others. Report of the Technical Mission on the Use of Prefabricated Steel Components in Industrialized Building in Europe, June 4-June 23, 1967; prepared... in cooperation with the members of the Mission. [Ottawa], Department of Industry, Materials Branch, 1968. pp. 86. *bibliog.*

— Puerto Rico.

PUERTO RICO. Urban Renewal and Housing Administration. Planning Office. 1971. Industrialized housing systems for Puerto Rico: a survey of construction methods for programs of social interest. [San Juan, 1971]. pp. 75. *bibliog.*

PUERTO RICO. Urban Renewal and Housing Administration. Planning Office. 1972. Experimental program of industrialized housing : second phase report. [San Juan], 1972. fo. 85. *bibliog.*

PUERTO RICO. Urban Renewal and Housing Administration. Planning Office. 1973. Experimental program of industrialized housing: (first part) one family dwelling: model H-743]. [San Juan, 1973]. fo. 39.

INDUSTRIES, LOCATION OF.

EUROPEAN COMMUNITIES. Commission. Cahiers de Reconversion Industrielle . Bruxelles, 1963 in progress.

MAY (HEINZ DIETER) Junge Industrialisierungstendenzen im Untermaingebiet unter besonderer Berücksichtigung der Betriebsverlagerungen aus Frankfurt am Main. Frankfurt am Main, 1968. pp. 157. *bibliog. (Frankfurt am Main. Universität. Geographisches Institut. Rhein-Mainische Forschungen. Heft 65)*

DAVIES (R.J.) and YOUNG (BRUCE S.) Manufacturing and size of place in the South African urban system. [Cape Town, 1970]. pp. 699-713. *(From Journal for Geography, vol. 3, no. 7, Sept. 1970) Xerographic copy. Bound with their Manufacturing in South African cities.*

DAVIES (R.J.) and YOUNG (BRUCE S.) Manufacturing in South African cities. [Cape Town, 1970]. pp. 595-605, 608-620. *(From Journal for Geography, vol. 3, no. 6, April 1970) Xerographic copy.*

EUROPEAN FREE TRADE ASSOCIATION. Economic Development Committee Working Party. 1971. Regional policy in EFTA: industrial mobility; an examination of industrial mobility in the context of regional policies in EFTA countries. Geneva, 1971. pp. 160.

HALMEKOSKI (MATTI) Metsäteollisuuslaitoksen sijaintipaikan valintaan vaikuttavista tekijöistä metsätalouden liiketieteen kannalta. Helsinki, 1971. fo. 75. *(Finland. Valtakunnansuunnittelutoimisto. Julkaisusarja B. 14) With English summary.*

WESTELIUS (ORVAR) The individual's pattern of travel in an urban area. Stockholm, 1972. pp. 202. *bibliog. (Sweden. Statens Institut for Byggnadsforskning. Documents. 1972. D2) With Swedish summary.*

CHISHOLM (MICHAEL) and OEPPEN (JIM) The changing pattern of employment: regional specialisation and industrial localisation in Britain. London, 1973. pp. 127. *bibliog.*

ESTALL (ROBERT CHARLES) and BUCHANAN (ROBERT OGILVIE) Industrial activity and economic geography: a study of the forces behind the geographical location of productive activity in manufacturing industry. 3rd ed. London, 1973. pp. 252.

GRAHAM (DAVID RALPH) and LUFT (KATHLEEN) The role of business in the economic redevelopment of the rural community. Austin, Tex., 1973. pp. 114. *bibliog. (Texas University. Bureau of Business Research. Research Monographs. No. 36)*

HANSEN (NILES M.) The future of nonmetropolitan America: studies in the reversal of rural and small town population decline. Lexington, mass [1973]. pp. 187.

NIXSON (F.I.) Economic integration and industrial location: an East African case study. London, [1973]. pp. 181. *bibliog.*

NOVOE v geografii proizvoditel'nykh sil SSSR. Moskva, 1973. pp. 142.

THOMSON (CHARLES W.) The industrial selection scheme: a study of conflicting objectives in urban and regional planning. London, 1973. pp. 46. *bibliog. (Centre for Environmental Studies. Working Papers. 81)*

WHEAT (LEONARD F.) Regional growth and industrial location: an empirical viewpoint. Lexington, [1973]. pp. 223.

YOUNG (BRUCE S.) Journey to work patterns and labour sheds in the Durban region. [Johannesburg?], 1973. pp. 238-246. *(From South African Geographer, vol. 4, no. 3) Xerographic copy.*

ABT (ROBERT) Agglomerationseffekte in der schweizerischen Industrie. [Zürich, 1974?]. pp. 69. *bibliog.*

BACK (ROLF) and others. Industrial location patterns: a multidimensional analysis of relationships between firms and regions;... translated from the Swedish by Nancy Adler. Stockholm, [1974]. fo.239.

KREUTER (HANSHEINZ) Industrielle Standortaffinität und regionalpolitische Standortlenkung, dargestellt am Beispiel Baden-Württembergs.Berlin, [1974]. pp. 426. *bibliog. With summaries in English and French.*

MASSEY (DOREEN B.) Towards a critique of industrial location theory. London, 1974. pp. 27. *bibliog. (Centre for Environmental Studies. Research Papers. 5)*

WOLTER (FRANK) Strukturelle Anpassungsprobleme der westdeutschen Stahlindustrie: zur Standortfrage der Stahlindustrie in hochindustrialisierten Ländern. Tübingen, 1974. pp. 182. *bibliog. (Kiel. Universität. Institut für Weltwirtschaft. Kieler Studien. 127)*

— Mathematical models.

HARRIS (CURTIS C.) The urban economies, 1985: a multiregional multi-industry forecasting model. Lexington, Mass., [1973]. pp. 230.

— Research.

DALBORG (HANS) Research and development: organization and location. Stockholm, 1974. pp. 152. *bibliog.*

INDUSTRIES, SIZE OF.

FRANCE. Direction de la Documentation. La Documentation Française. Notes et Etudes Documentaires. No. 3,896. Fusions et concentrations d'entreprises au Benelux, par H.W. de Jong. [Paris], 1972. pp. 46. *bibliog.*

HJALMARSSON (LENNART) The size of distribution of firms derived from an optimal process of capacity expansion. [Oslo], 1972. pp. 37. *bibliog. (Oslo. Universitet. Sosialøkonomiske Institutt. Memoranda)*

INDUSTRY

— Classification.

UNITED NATIONS. Statistical Office. Statistical Papers. Series M. No. 43. Rev.1. Classification of commodities by industrial origin: links between the Standard International Trade Classification. (ST/STAT/SER.M/ 43/Rev.1) New York, 1971. pp. 145.

— Dictionaries and encyclopaedias.

LEXIKON der Wirtschaft: Industrie; (Herausgeber: Hans Borchert). Berlin, 1970. pp. 904.

— History.

PARKER (WILLIAM N.) Technique, spirit and form in the growth of modern industry. York, [1973]. pp. 15. *(York. University. Sir Ellis Hunter Memorial Lectures. 6)*

BAIROCH (PAUL) Révolution industrielle et sous-développement. 4th ed. Paris, 1974. pp. 381. *bibliog. (Paris. Ecole Pratique des Hautes Etudes. Section des Sciences Economiques et Sociales. Le Savoir Historique. 9)*

— Social aspects.

DIERKES (MEINOLF) and BAUER (RAYMOND AUGUSTINE) eds. Corporate social accounting. New York, 1973. pp. 413.

The SOCIAL responsibility of business and labour: critique of a conference at Ditchley Park, 2-5 November 1973; by B.J.A. Hargreaves, conference rapporteur. Enstone, Oxfordshire, [1973]. pp. 37. *(Ditchley Foundation. Ditchley Papers. No.47)*

VOTAW (DOW) and SETHI (S. PRAKASH) The corporate dilemma: traditional values versus contemporary problems. Englewood Cliffs, [1973]. pp. 243.

KEMPNER (THOMAS) and others. Business and society: tradition and change. London, 1974. pp. 288.

LONDON GRADUATE SCHOOL OF BUSINESS STUDIES. Stockton Lectures. 1973. Productivity and amenity: achieving a social balance; edited by Michael Beesley. London, 1974. pp. 135.

MARRIS (ROBIN) ed. The corporate society: [papers with editorial commentaries]. London, 1974. pp. 403. *bibliogs. (Harvard University. Harvard University Program on Technology and Society. Harvard Studies in Technology and Society)*

— — United Kingdom.

JONES (T.KEN) The human face of change: social responsibility and rationalization at British Steel. London, 1974. pp. 69. *bibliog. (Institute of Personnel Management. Handbooks)*

RIDLEY (NICHOLAS) The new capitalism. London, 1974. pp. 8. *(Foundation for Business Responsibilities. The Company and its Responsibilities)*

— — United States.

JACOBY (NEIL HERMAN) Corporate power and social responsibility: a blueprint for the future. New York, [1973]. pp. 282. *(Columbia University. Graduate School of Business. Studies of the Modern Corporation)*

INDUSTRY. (Cont.)

KOBRAK (PETER) Private assumption of public responsibilities: the role of American business in urban manpower programs. New York, 1973. pp. 257. *bibliog.*

NEUBECK (KENNETH J.) Corporate response to urban crisis. Lexington, Mass, [1974]. pp. 166. *bibliog.*

INDUSTRY AND EDUCATION.

GLYNN (ERICA) and others. The relevance of school learning experience to performance in industry; report on a feasibility study carried out by the Centre for Science Education in co-operation with Engineering Industry Training Board, November 1970 to June 1971. [Watford, Engineering Industry Training Board], 1971. fo. 43.

INTERGOVERNMENTAL CONFERENCE ON THE UTILISATION OF HIGHLY QUALIFIED PERSONNEL, 2ND, VENICE, 1971. The utilisation of highly qualified personnel: [report on] Venice Conference 15th-27th October 1971. Paris, Organisation for Economic Co-operation and Development, 1973. pp. 427. *The 1st Conference was entitled and catalogued POLICY CONFERENCE ON HIGHLY QUALIFIED MANPOWER, PARIS, 1966.*

McLONE (R.R.) The training of mathematicians: a research report. London, Social Science Research Council, [1973]. pp. 94.*bibliog.*

FALLON (PETER ROBERT) The productive roles of workers with different levels of education: an international cross-sectional study; [Ph.D. (London) thesis]. 1974. fo. 248. *bibliog. Typescript: unpublished. This thesis is the property of London University and may not be removed from the library.*

INDUSTRY AND STATE.

NORTH (DOUGLASS CECIL) and MILLER (ROGER LEROY) The economics of public issues. 2nd ed. New York, [1973]. pp. 184.

SCHULZ (DIETER) Staatliche Eingriffe bei strukturellen Branchenkrisen und ihre Vereinbarkeit mit der Marktwirtschaft, dargestellt am Beispiel des Schweizer Uhrenstatuts. [Freiburg im Breisgau, imprint, 1973?]. pp. 171. *bibliog.*

WORKSHOP IN INTERNATIONAL BUSINESS-GOVERNMENT AFFAIRS, NEW YORK, 1972. International business-government affairs: toward an era of accommodation; edited by John Fayerweather. Cambridge, Mass., [1973]. pp. 131.

— Mathematical models.

BAILEY (ELIZABETH E.) Economic theory of regulatory constraint. Lexington, [1973]. pp. 200. *bibliog.*

— Argentine Republic.

MARILUZ URQUIJO (JOSE M.) Estado e industria, 1810-1862. Buenos Aires, 1969. pp. 194.

— Europe.

VERNON (RAYMOND) ed. Big business and the state: changing relations in western Europe. London, 1974. pp. 310.

— European Economic Community countries.

FRANCE. Direction de la Documentation. La Documentation Française. Notes et Etudes Documentaires. No. 3,917. Les aides à l'expansion industrielle régionale dans les pays du Marché commun, par Philippe de Castelbajac. [Paris], 1972. pp. 39.

— France.

ADMINISTRATION et secteur privé: colloque d'Aix-en-Provence, 1er et 2 juin 1972 organisé par le Centre de Recherches Administratives...et l'Association des Licenciés en Droit d'Aix-Marseille. Paris, 1973. pp. 186.

— Germany.

GURATZSCH (DANKWART) Macht durch Organisation: die Grundlegung des Hugenbergschen Presseimperiums. Düsseldorf, [1974]. pp. 486. *bibliog. (Hamburg. Hansische Universität. Studien zur Modernen Geschichte. Band 7)*

— India.

ERDMAN (HOWARD L.) Politics and economic development in India: the Gujarat State Fertilizers Company as a joint sector enterprise. Delhi, 1973. pp. 148. *bibliog.*

— Underdeveloped areas.

See UNDERDEVELOPED AREAS — Industry and state.

— United Kingdom.

NIESING (HARTMUT) Die Gewerbeparks (industrial estates) als Mittel der staatlichen regionalen Industrialisierungspolitik, dargestellt am Beispiel Grossbritanniens. Berlin, [1970]. pp. 193. *bibliog.*

U.K. Central Office of Information. Reference Division. 1971. Industry in Britain: organisation and production. rev. ed. London, 1971. pp. 19. *bibliog.*

AIMS OF INDUSTRY. Economic Arguments. How not to give industry confidence. London, [1972]. 1 pamphlet (unpaged).

RIDLEY (NICHOLAS) Industry and the civil service. London, [1973]. pp. 13.

AIMS OF INDUSTRY. The vanishing evidence: industry's aid to government. London, [1974]. pp. 6.

AIMS OF INDUSTRY. When it doesn't pay to be British!. London, [1974]. pp. 9.

KNIGHT (ARTHUR) Private enterprise and public intervention: the Courtaulds experience. London, 1974. pp. 223.

TRADES UNION CONGRESS The TUC's initiatives: a record of the TUC's efforts to get Britain back to full-time working. London, 1974. pp. 15.

— United States.

BREYER (STEPHEN G.) and MACAVOY (PAUL WEBSTER) Energy regulation by the Federal Power Commission. Washington, [1974]. pp. 163. *(Brookings Institution. Studies in the Regulation of Economic Activity)*

DEMARIS (OVID) Dirty business: the corporate-political money-power game. New York, [1974]. pp. 442.

— Zambia.

YOUNG (ALISTAIR) Industrial diversification in Zambia. New York, 1973. pp. 328. *bibliog.*

INFANTS

— Diseases.

The SCHOOL years in Newcastle upon Tyne, 1952-62: being a further contribution to the study of a thousand families; by F.J.W. Miller [and others]. London, 1974. pp. 362. *bibliog.*

INFLATION (FINANCE).

PRACHOWNY (MARTIN F.J.) The inflationary process in open economies. Kingston, 1971. fo. 19. *bibliog. (Kingston, Ontario. Queen's University. Institute for Economic Research. Discussion Papers. No. 52)*

BORCHARDT (KNUT) Strukturwirkungen des Inflationsprozesses. Berlin, [1972]. pp. 22. *(Ifo-Institut für Wirtschaftsforschung. Sonderschriften. Nr. 38)*

FOSTER (EDWARD MERVYN) Costs and benefits of inflation. Minneapolis, 1972. pp. 30. *bibliog. (Federal Reserve Bank of Minneapolis. Studies in Monetary Economics. 1)*

ARNDT (ERICH) Währungsstabilität und Lohnpolitik: über die wirtschaftlichen und sozialen Folgen von Inflationen. Tübingen, 1973. pp. 60. *With summaries in various languages.*

BALL (ROBERT JAMES) Inflation and the theory of money. 2nd ed. London, 1973. pp. 313.

CHANT (JOHN F.) The costs of alternative approaches to the adjustment of inflationary expectations. [Ottawa], 1973. fo. 39. *bibliog. (Carlton University. Carlton Economic Papers)*

CHANT (JOHN F.) Transactions costs and losses from inflation. [Ottawa], 1973. fo. 25. *bibliog. (Carleton University. Carleton Economic Papers)*

EARL (PAUL H.) Inflation and the structure of industrial prices. Lexington, [1973]. pp. 257. *bibliog.*

EMMINGER (OTMAR) and others. L'inflation et le système monétaire international. Bâle, 1973. pp. 85. *(Per Jacobsson Foundation. [Lectures]. 1973)*

EMMINGER (OTMAR) and others. Inflation and the international monetary system. Basle, 1973. pp. 78. *(Per Jacobsson Foundation. [Lectures]. 1973)*

FISCAL policy and demand management: Fiskalpolitik und Globalsteuerung:... Symposium 1972 ([held at the] Institut für Weltwirtschaft an der Universität Kiel); edited by Herbert Giersch. Tübingen, 1973. pp. 262. *In English or German.*

FLAMANT (MAURICE) L'inflation. 2nd ed. Paris, 1973. pp. 128. *bibliog.*

GONZALEZ PAZ (JOSE) Evolucion de los presios e inflacion. Salamanca, 1973. pp. 190.

KERSCHAGL (RICHARD) Die Inflation. Wien, 1973. pp. 179.

MAGEE (BRYAN EDGAR) and others. The new inflation: [transcript of a discussion with] Aubrey Jones [and] Alan Walters;...transmitted: 2 August 1973. [London, 1973]. fo. 31. *(Thames Television. Something to Say)*

RIVOIRE (JEAN) L'inflation. Paris, [1973]. pp. 173.

BEAUVOIS (ROLAND) and others. L'inflation; conférence. Bruxelles, 1974. pp. 75. *(Société Royale d'Economie Politique de Belgique. [Publications]. No. 375)*

COWLING (KEITH) and WATERSON (MICHAEL) Price-cost margins and market structure. Coventry, 1974. pp. 22. *bibliog. (University of Warwick. Department of Economics. Warwick Economic Research Papers. No. 44)*

GEIGER (HELMUT) Herausforderungen für Stabilität und Fortschritt: [collection of lectures, 1970-1974]. Stuttgart, [1974]. pp. 211.

TAYLOR (JIM) Unemployment and wage inflation: with special reference to Britain and the U.S.A. Harlow, 1974. pp. 120. *bibliog.*

THIRLWALL (ANTHONY PHILIP) Inflation, saving and growth in developing economies. London, 1974. pp. 256.

WALTERS (ALAN A.) Money and inflation. London, [1974]. pp. 13.

— Mathematical models.

LAIDLER (DAVID E.W.) and PURDY (DAVID) eds. Inflation and labour markets. Manchester, [1974]. pp. 258. *bibliogs.*

MILLER (ROGER LEROY) and WILLIAMS (RABURN M.) Unemployment and inflation: the new economics of the wage-price spiral. St. Paul, [Minn.], 1974. pp. 110. *bibliogs.*

PEEL (D.A.) and BRISCOE (GEOFFREY) Another look at the role of excess demand variables in determining money wage inflation. Coventry, 1974. pp. 32. *bibliog. (University of Warwick. Centre for Industrial, Economic and Business Research. [Warwick Research in Industrial and Business Studies]. No.53)*

PITCHFORD (JOHN DAVID) and TURNOVSKY (STEPHEN J.) Some effects of taxes on inflation and income distribution. Canberra, 1974. fo. 40. *bibliog. (Australian National University. Research School of Social Sciences. Department of Economics. Working Papers in Economics and Econometrics. No.20)*

— **Argentine Republic.**

PABLO (JUAN CARLOS DE) Politica antiinflacionaria en la Argentina, 1967-1970. Buenos Aires, [1972]. pp. 135. *bibliog.*

— **Australia.**

HENDERSON (RONALD FRANK) Income inflation in Australia. Adelaide, 1972. pp. 12. *(Adelaide. University. Joseph Fisher Lectures in Commerce. 1971)*

— **Brazil.**

WOGART (JAN PETER) Stabilisierungs- und Wachstumspolitik in Brasilien: die Bekämpfung der Inflation nach 1964. Stuttgart, [1974]. pp. 129. *bibliog. (Institut für Iberoamerika-Kunde. Schriftenreihe. Band 23)* With summaries in English and Portuguese.

— **Canada.**

HAYTHORNE (GEORGE VICKERS) Construction and inflation;... prepared for the Prices and Incomes Commission. Ottawa, Information Canada, 1973. pp. 181.

— — **Mathematical models.**

McCOLLUM (J.F.) Inflation and interest rates in Canada; a study prepared for the Prices and Incomes Commission. Ottawa, Information Canada, 1973. pp. 113. *bibliog.*

— **Finland.**

HANNI (EILA) Inflation in postwar Finland. Helsinki, 1972. pp. 225. *bibliog. (Kansantaloudellinen Yhdistys. Kansantaloudellisia Tutkimuksia. 31)*

— **Germany.**

GREULICH (GEORG) Dritte deutsche Inflation und Notenbankpolitik: eine Analyse seit 1948. 2nd ed. Weinheim/Bergstrasse, 1973. pp. 237. *bibliog.*

BLECHSCHMIDT (AIKE) Löhne, Preise und Gewinne, 1967-1973: Materialien zur "Lohn-Preis-Spirale" und Inflation. Lampertheim, 1974. pp. 270. *bibliog.*

— **India.**

DELHI. Institute of Economic Growth. Inflation and India's economic crisis; by V.K.R.V. Rao [and others]. Delhi, [1973]. pp. 71.

— **Italy.**

CONTRO l'inflazione. Roma, 1973. pp. 126. *(Centro Operaio. Quaderni. N.3)*

— **Pakistan.**

FAROOQ (DANIAL M.) Inflation, money and credit in Pakistan. Islamabad, United States Agency for International Development, 1973. 1 pamphlet (various pagings).

AUCHTER (EDMUND L.) and DURRANI (TARIQ) Import costs and Pakistan's inflation. Islamabad, United States Agency for International Development, 1974. fo. 7.

— **Turkey.**

AKYÜZ (YILMAZ) Money and inflation in Turkey 1950-1968. Ankara, 1973. pp. 212. *bibliog. (Ankara. Üniversitesi. Siyasal Bilgiler Fakültesi. Yayinlari. No. 361)*

— **United Kingdom.**

DERRICK (PAUL) Socialism and inflation: the relevance of co-operative principles. London, 1973. pp. 22.

ECONOMIC DEVELOPMENT COMMITTEE FOR THE MECHANICAL ENGINEERING INDUSTRY. Inflation and company accounts in mechanical engineering. London, National Economic Development Office, 1973. pp. 56.

FRIEDMAN (MILTON) Monetary correction: a proposal for escalator clauses to reduce the costs of ending inflation. London, 1974. pp. 54. *bibliog. (Institute of Economic Affairs. Occasional Papers. 41)*

LAIDLER (DAVID E.W.) and PURDY (DAVID) eds. Inflation and labour markets. Manchester, [1974]. pp. 258. *bibliogs.*

PARDOE (JOHN WENTWORTH) We must conquer inflation: a Liberal approach to the greatest danger of the age. London, [1974]. pp. 49.

— **United States.**

JOHNSEN (JULIA EMILY) compiler. Wage stabilization and inflation. New York, 1943. pp. 187. *bibliog.*

COMMITTEE FOR ECONOMIC DEVELOPMENT. Research and Policy Committee. Further weapons against inflation: measures to supplement general fiscal and monetary policies; a statement on national policy. New York, 1970 repr. 1971. pp. 90.

LEKACHMAN (ROBERT) Inflation: the permanent problem of boom and bust. New York, [1973]. pp. 121.

MORRISON (RODNEY J.) Expectations and inflation: Nixon, politics and economics. Lexington, 1973. pp. 167.

A NEW look at inflation: economic policy in the early 1970s; [by] Phillip Cagan [and others]. Washington, D.C., [1973]. pp. 172. *(American Enterprise Institute for Public Policy Research. Domestic Affairs Studies. 17)*

PALMER (JOHN L.) Inflation, unemployment and poverty. Lexington, Mass., [1973]. pp. 170. *bibliog.*

BARRETT (NANCY SMITH) and others. Prices and wages in U.S. manufacturing: a factor analysis. Lexington, Mass., [1973]. pp. 212. *bibliog.*

INFLATION (FINANCE) AND ACCOUNTING.

CONFEDERATION OF BRITISH INDUSTRY. Inflation and company accounts: an interim report for discussion. London, 1973. pp. 14.

KIRKMAN (PATRICK (R.A.) Accounting under inflationary conditions. London, 1974. pp. 266.

INFORMATION PROCESSING, HUMAN.

See HUMAN INFORMATION PROCESSING.

INFORMATION SERVICES.

ORGANISATION FOR ECONOMIC CO-OPERATION AND DEVELOPMENT. Ad Hoc Group on Scientific and Technical Information. 1971. Information for a changing society: some policy considerations. Paris, 1971. pp. 48.

AMERICAN SOCIETY FOR INFORMATION SCIENCE. Mid-Year Regional Conference, 1st, Dayton, 1972. Cost reduction for special libraries and information centres; [papers]; Frank Slater, editor. Washington, D.C., 1973. pp. 187. *bibliogs.*

AMERICAN ACADEMY OF POLITICAL AND SOCIAL SCIENCE. Annals. vol. 412. The information revolution: special editor of this volume, Donald M. Lamberton. Philadelphia, 1974. pp. 234.

— **Bibliography.**

UNITED NATIONS. Geneva. Library. 1973. Technological information systems and services for innovation: a selective bibliography. (ST/GENEVA/LIB/SER. B/Ref. 5) (SC. TECH/SEM. 1/R. 56). Geneva, 1973. pp. 61. *(Reference lists. No. 5) In various languages.*

— **Europe.**

BRIGHTON. University of Sussex. Institute of Development Studies. Library. Occasional Guides. No. 4. West German, Swiss and Austrian sources of information on Third World countries. Brighton, [1973]. pp. 29.

— **United Kingdom.**

BURKETT (JACK) Industrial and related library and information services in the United Kingdom. 3rd ed. London, 1972. pp. 263. *bibliog.*

BURKETT (JACK) ed. Government and related library and information services in the United Kingdom. 3rd ed. London, 1974. pp. 217. *bibliogs.*

INFORMATION THEORY.

INFORMATION STORAGE AND RETRIEVAL SYSTEMS.

BENJAMIN (ROBERT I.) Control of the information system development cycle. New York, [1971]. pp. 94.

ORGANISATION FOR ECONOMIC CO-OPERATION AND DEVELOPMENT. Ad Hoc Group on Scientific and Technical Information. 1971. Information for a changing society: some policy considerations. Paris, 1971. pp. 48.

BELGIUM. Parlement. Bibliothèque. 1972. L'ordinateur et la sauvegarde des libertés individuelles. Bruxelles, 1972. pp. 58. *bibliog. (Dossiers documentaires. 6)*

JANCO (MANUEL) and FURJOT (DANIEL) Informatique et capitalisme. Paris, 1972. pp. 272. *bibliog.*

FIORELLO (MARCO R.) Management and design tools for document retrieval systems: a method for predicting quantity output. [Santa Monica], 1973. pp. 210. *bibliog. (Rand Corporation. [Papers]. 4980)*

— **Cities and towns.**

INTEGRATED municipal information systems: the use of the computer in local government; [by] Kenneth L. Kraemer [and others]. New York, 1974. pp. 105. *bibliog.*

— **Economics.**

DAVID (MARTIN HEIDENHAIN) and others. Linkage and retrieval of microeconomic data: a strategy for data development and use: a report on the Wisconsin assets and incomes archives. Toronto, [1974]. pp. 296. *bibliog.*

— — **Bibliography.**

ATRIAKHINA (N.V.) and others, compilers. Mekhanizatsiia obrabotki ekonomicheskoi informatsii: bibliograficheskii ukazatel' literatury, 1924-1967 gg. Moskva, 1969. pp. 471.

— **International organization.**

PRICE (N.H.) and others. On-line searching of Council of Europe conventions and agreements: a study in bilingual document retrieval. Harwell, 1974. pp. 13. *(U.K. Atomic Energy Authority. [Research Group. Reports.] AERE-R7673)*

— **Management.**

CLOOT (PETER L.) Management information: a systematic approach. 3rd ed. Henley-on-Thames, 1974. pp. 24. *bibliog. (Henley-on-Thames. Administrative Staff College. Occasional Papers. No. 7)*

— **Social sciences.**

UNITED NATIONS EDUCATIONAL, SCIENTIFIC AND CULTURAL ORGANIZATION. Reports and Papers in the Social Sciences. Paris, 1955 in progress.

DAVID (MARTIN HEIDENHAIN) and others. Linkage and retrieval of microeconomic data: a strategy for data development and use: a report on the Wisconsin assets and incomes archives. Toronto, [1974]. pp. 296. *bibliog.*

— **Space sciences.**

NORTH ATLANTIC TREATY ORGANIZATION. Advisory Group for Aerospace Research and Development. 1973. New developments in storage, retrieval and dissemination of aerospace information; papers presented at the... meeting... held... London... 2-3 October, 1973. [London], 1973. 1 vol. (various pagings). *(AGARD Conference Proceedings. No. 136)*

INFORMATION THEORY.

CHERNYSH (VLADIMIR IVANOVICH) Informatsionnye protsessy v obshchestve. Moskva, 1968. pp. 102. *bibliog.*

SUNDGREN (BO) An infological approach to data bases. Stockholm, 1973. pp. 478. *bibliog. (Sweden. Statistiska Centralbyrån. Urval. No. 7)*

INFORMATION THEORY IN ECONOMICS.

INFORMATION THEORY IN ECONOMICS.

MARSCHAK (JAKOB) Economic theory of information: lecture notes. Los Angeles, 1967. 1 vol. (various foliations). *(California University. Western Management Science Institute. Working Papers. No. 118)*

LAMBERTON (DONALD McL.) ed. Economics of information and knowledge: selected readings. Harmondsworth, 1971. pp. 384. *bibliog.*

PRED (ALLAN R.) and TÖRNQVIST (GUNNAR) Systems of cities and information flows: two essays. Lund, 1973. pp. 121. *bibliogs.* *(Lund. Universitet. Geografiska Institution. Lund Studies in Geography. Series B. Human Geography. No. 38)*

INHERITANCE AND SUCCESSION

— **Russia.**

NIKITIUK (PETR SEMENOVICH) Nasledstvennoe pravo i nasledstvennyi protsess: problemy teorii i praktiki. Kishinev, 1973. pp. 258.

— — **Ukraine.**

DRONIKOV (VLADIMIR KLAVDIEVICH) Nasledstvennoe pravo Ukrainskoi SSR. Kiev, 1974. pp. 159.

— **United Kingdom.**

BAILEY (STANLEY JOHN) The law of wills, including intestacy and administration of assets: an introduction to the rules of law, equity and construction relating to testamentary dispositions. 7th ed. London, [1973]. pp. 364.

SAMUELS (ROGER) Equity and succession. London, 1974. pp. 218.

INHERITANCE AND TRANSFER TAX.

KISSLING (HANS) Die Umverteilung bestehender Vermögenswerte als Mittel der Vermögenspolitik. [Zürich, imprint], 1973. pp. 191. *bibliog.*

SANDFORD (CEDRIC T.) Taxing inheritance and capital gains: towards a comprehensive system of capital taxation. London, 1965. pp. 69. *bibliog.* *(Institute of Economic Affairs. Hobart Papers. 32)*

SANDFORD (CEDRIC T.) and others. An accessions tax: a study of the desirability and feasibility of replacing the United Kingdom estate duty by a cumulative tax on recipients of gifts and inheritances. London, 1973. pp. 220. *(Institute for Fiscal Studies. Publications. No. 7)*

BEATTIE (CHARLES NOEL) Elements of estate duty; eighth edition by John Tiley. London, 1974. pp. 219.

— **United States.**

WAGNER (RICHARD E.) Death and taxes: some perspectives on inheritance, inequality, and progressive taxation. Washington, D.C., 1973. pp. 63. *(American Enterprise Institute for Public Policy Research. Domestic Affairs Studies. 13)*

INITIATIVE, RIGHT OF

— **France.**

BASTID-BURDEAU (GENEVIEVE) La genèse de l'initiative législative: un cas: l'agriculture, 1958-1968. Paris, 1973. pp. 107. *bibliog.* *(Paris. Université de Paris II. Travaux et Recherches. Série Science Politique. 3)*

INLAND NAVIGATION

— **Belgium.**

INSTITUT ECONOMIQUE ET SOCIAL DES CLASSES MOYENNES [BELGIUM]. Orientation du crédit à la flotte fluviale. [Brussels, 1960]. pp. 33..

— **United Kingdom.**

BRITISH WATERWAYS BOARD. The last ten years: progress and achievement 1963-72. [London, 1973]. pp. 36.

DUCKHAM (BARON F.) The inland waterways of East Yorkshire, 1700-1900. York, 1973. pp. 72. *bibliog.* *(East Yorkshire Local History Society. East Yorkshire Local History Series. No. 29)*

INLAND WATER TRANSPORTATION

— **India** — **Punjab.**

ARRORA (FAQIR CHAND) Commerce by river in the Punjab, or a survey of the activities of the Marine Department of the government of the Punjab, 1861-62 to 1871-72. [Lahore, 1930]. pp. 98,xxix. *(Punjab. Government Record Office. Monographs. No.9)*

— **United Kingdom.**

SAPSFORD (ALFRED) Economic aspects of the future development of British waterways under the control of the British transport commission; [London M.Sc.(Econ.) thesis]. 1962. fo. 171. *Typscript: unpublished.*

INSANE, CRIMINAL AND DANGEROUS

— **Italy.**

PAOLELLA (ALFREDO) and CITTERIO (CARLO) Manicomi giudiziari e case di cura e di custodia: analisi della popolazione secondo categorie psichiatriche e giuridiche. Roma, 1972. pp. 150. *(Italy. Direzione Generale per gli Istituti di Prevenzione e di Pena. Ufficio Studi e Ricerche. Quaderni. 2)*

— **United Kingdom.**

BLACK (D.A.) A decade of psychological investigation of the male patient population of Broadmoor. 1. General demographical information. [London, Special Hospitals Research Unit], 1973. pp. 35. *(Special Hospitals Research Reports. No. 8)*

BROWN (C. TREVES) Assessment of regional differences in rates of referral for special hospitals placement. [London, Special Hospitals Research Unit], 1973. pp. 75. *(Special Hospitals Research Reports. No. 7)*

PARKER (ELIZABETH) An inquiry into the reliability of special hospital case records with reference to the recording of previous psychiatric hospitalizations and criminal histories. [London, Special Hospitals Research Unit], 1973. pp. 14. *(Special Hospitals Research Reports. No. 9)*

INSTITUTE OF PACIFIC RELATIONS.

THOMAS (JOHN N.) The Institute of Pacific Relations: Asian scholars and American politics. Seattle, [1974]. pp. 187. *bibliog.*

INSTITUTIONAL INVESTMENTS

— **United Kingdom.**

INSTITUTIONAL investors and the London Stock Exchange; with special reference to the relationships between...investors and quoted companies: proceedings of a one-day seminar [organised by BAFA];...May 11, 1972. n.p., [1972?]. pp. 42. *(British Accounting and Finance Association. Occasional Papers. No. 1)*

INSURANCE

— **Finland** — **Taxation.**

FINLAND. Företagsbeskattningens Nydaningskommission. 1970. Betänkande 4: reformering av inkomstbeskattningen av försäkringsanstalter och pensionsstiftelser. Helsingfors, 1970. fo. 37. *(Finland. Komiteanmietinnöt. 1970. B.82)*

— **Italy.**

ITALY. Istituto Nazionale delle Assicurazioni. 1962. Le origini dell'Istituto Nazionale delle Assicurazioni: mostra grafica e documentaria allestita nella Sede dell' I.N.A. nel cinquantenario della legge 4 aprile 1912. n. 305. Roma, 1962. pp. [25].

— **Russia.**

DROZDKOV (IVAN PAVLOVICH) Organizatsiia raboty po lichnomu strakhovaniiu: posobie dlia rabotnikov inspektsii i upravlenii gosudarstvennogo strakhovaniia. 3rd ed. Moskva, 1973. pp. 112.

INSURANCE, AGRICULTURAL

— **Crops** — **Russia.**

GULIAEV (FILIPP SERGEEVICH) and KATSOV (M.IA.) Opredelenie strakhovogo vozmeshcheniia po sel'skokhoziaistvennym kul'turam i mnogoletnim nasazhdeniiam; pod redaktsiei...L.A. Motyleva. Moskva, 1969. pp. 208.

— **Russia.**

GLADKOV (NIKOLAI IVANOVICH) Gosudarstvennoe strakhovanie imushchestva kolkhozov. 2nd ed. Moskva, 1973. pp. 112.

INSURANCE, AUTOMOBILE

— **United Kingdom.**

U.K. Department of the Environment. 1972. Compensation of victims of uninsured drivers: text of an agreement dated the 22nd November 1972 between the Secretary of State for the Environment and the Motor Insurers' Bureau, together with some notes on its scope and purpose. London, 1972. pp. 7.

U.K. Department of the Environment. 1972. Compensation of victims of untraced drivers: text of an agreement dated the 22nd November 1972, between the Secretary of State for the Environment and the Motor Insurers' Bureau, together with some notes on its scope and purpose. London, 1972. pp. 14.

IVAMY (EDWARD RICHARD HARDY) Fire and motor insurance. 2nd ed. London, 1973. pp. 498.

INSURANCE, CREDIT

— **European Economic Community countries.**

GLOTZBACH (MICHAEL) Die staatliche Ausfuhrkreditversicherung in Frankreich und Deutschland: eine rechtsvergleichende Darstellung unter Berücksichtigung der Harmonisierungsbestrebungen im Gemeinsamen Markt. Berlin, [1973]. pp. 167. *bibliog.* *(Mainz. Universität. Institut für Internationales Recht des Spar-, Giro- und Kreditwesens. Untersuchungen über das Spar-, Giro- und Kreditwesen. Abteilung B: Rechtswissenschaft. Band 3)*

INSURANCE, DISABILITY

— **Denmark.**

DENMARK. Statutes, etc. 1969-72. The Invalidity Pension Act, [and] the Invalidity Pension (Amendment) Act, 1972. [Copenhagen, 1970-1972). 2 pts.

INSURANCE, FIRE

— **United Kingdom.**

IVAMY (EDWARD RICHARD HARDY) Fire and motor insurance. 2nd ed. London, 1973. pp. 498.

INSURANCE, HEALTH.

INSTITUT NATIONAL D'ASSURANCE MALADIE-INVALIDITE [BELGIUM]. Problèmes de l'assurance maladie-indemnités. Bruxelles, 1971. pp. 320. *bibliogs. Articles in French and Flemish.*

— **Australia.**

AUSTRALIA. Committee of Enquiry into Health Insurance. 1969. Health insurance; report. in AUSTRALIA. Parliament. Parliamentary papers, 1969, vol.4.

AUSTRALIA. Parliament. Senate. Select Committee on Medical and Hospital Costs. 1969. Report. in AUSTRALIA. Parliament. Parliamentary papers, 1969, vol.6.

AUSTRALIA. Department of Social Security. Annual report on the operations of the registered medical and hospital benefits organizations. a., 1970/71 (1st)- Canberra.

INSURANCE, SOCIAL.

— Denmark.

BETAENKNING om sikring af søfarende i sygdomstilfaelde; afgivet af det af socialministeren den 17. juni 1964 nedsatte udvalg. København, 1970. pp. 43. *(Denmark. Betaenkninger. Nr.568)*

DENMARK. Statutes, etc. 1972. The Daily Cash Benefit (Sickness or Maternity) Act, 1972. [Copenhagen?, 1972]. fo. 18.

— Germany.

LEISNER (WALTER) Zur Abgrenzung von gesetzlicher und privater Krankenversicherung: eine verfassungsrechtliche Untersuchung. Köln, 1974. pp. 57. *(Verband der Privaten Krankenversicherung. Dokumentationen. 3)*

— Netherlands.

LEDEBOER (L.V.) Heden en verleden van de ziekenfondsverzekering en de verzekering van bijzondere ziektekosten. 's-Gravenhage, Staatsuitgeverij, 1973. pp. 84.

— Switzerland.

SWITZERLAND. Office Fédéral des Assurances Sociales. 1971. Assurance-maladie: loi fédérale, dispositions d'exécution, index alhabétique: état au 1er avril 1971. [Bern, 1971]. pp. 180.

— United States.

NEWHOUSE (JOSEPH P.) and ACTON (JAN PAUL) Compulsory health planning laws and national health insurance. [Santa Monica], 1972. pp. 26. *bibliog. (Rand Corporation. [Papers]. 4846)*

PHELPS (CHARLES E.) and NEWHOUSE (JOSEPH P.) The effects of coinsurance on demand for physician services. Santa Monica, 1972. pp. 21. *bibliog. (Rand Corporation. [Rand Reports]. 976)*

PHELPS (CHARLES E.) Demand for health insurance: a theoretical and empirical investigation; prepared for the Office of Economic Opportunity. Santa Monica, 1973. pp. 187. *bibliog. (Rand Corporation. [Rand Reports]. 1054)*

LAW (SYLVIA A.) Blue Cross: what went wrong?...; prepared by the Health Law Project, University of Pennsylvania. New Haven, Conn., 1974. pp. 246.

— Uruguay.

MARGOLIS (EFRAIN) La asistencia medica colectivizada en el Uruguay: el seguro voluntario pre-pago de atencion medica, 1853-1972; (informe al Sindicato Medica del Uruguay). Montevideo, 1972. pp. 299. *bibliog.*

INSURANCE, HOSPITALIZATION

— Germany.

BRANDECKER (KARL) Zur Reform des Krankenhauswesens: das Interesse des Krankenhauses am Selbstzahler bisher und in Zukunft; Probleme, Analysen. Köln, 1974. pp. 64. *bibliog. (Verband der Privaten Krankenversicherung. Dokumentationen. 2)*

— United States.

LAW (SYLVIA A.) Blue Cross: what went wrong?...; prepared by the Health Law Project, University of Pennsylvania. New Haven, Conn., 1974. pp. 246.

INSURANCE, LIFE

— European Economic Community countries.

INSURANCE INSTITUTE OF LONDON. Advanced Study Group No. 200. Life assurance and pensions in the European Community: report. London, [1973]. pp. 110.

— United States.

ORREN (KAREN) Corporate power and social change: the politics of the life insurance industry. Baltimore, [1974]. pp. 204. *bibliog.*

INSURANCE, MATERNITY

— Denmark.

DENMARK. Socialministeriet. 1970. Moderskabsydelse [og] barseldagpenge. [Copenhagen?, 1970?]. pp. 14.

DENMARK. Statutes, etc. 1972. The Daily Cash Benefit (Sickness or Maternity) Act, 1972. [Copenhagen?, 1972]. fo. 18.

INSURANCE, SOCIAL.

DOUBLET (JACQUES) Sécurité sociale. 5th ed. Paris, 1972. pp. 816. *bibliogs.*

SAVY (ROBERT) Social security in agriculture and rural areas. Geneva, International Labour Office, 1972. pp. 268. *bibliog. (Studies and Reports. New Series. No. 78)*

— Research.

U.K. Department of Health and Social Security. Annual report on departmental research and development. a., 1973 [1st]- London.

— America, Latin.

KUZNETSOVA (EMMA EVDOKIMOVNA) Latinskaia Amerika: problemy sotsial'nogo obespecheniia. Moskva, 1973. pp. 207. *bibliog.*

— Argentine Republic.

GUEVARA (RAFAEL EDUARDO) La mujer y la seguridad social en la legislacion argentina...; trabajo encomendado por el Ministerio de Cultura y Educacion para la Conferencia Interamericana Especializada sobre Educacion Integral de la Mujer. Buenos Aires, Centro Nacional de Documentacion e Informacion Educativa, 1972. pp. 45.

— Australia.

KEWLEY (T.H.) Social security in Australia, 1900-72. 2nd ed. Sydney, 1973. pp. 586. *bibliog.*

AUSTRALIA. Commission of Inquiry into Poverty. 1974. Poverty in Australia; interim report; [Ronald F. Henderson, chairman]. Canberra, 1974. pp. 24.

— Belgium.

BELGIUM. Office National de Sécurité Sociale. 1968. L'Office National de Sécurité Sociale: sa mission, son fonctionnement. [Brussels?, 1968?]. pp. 35.

BELGIUM. Office National de Sécurité Sociale. 1969. Rendement de la perception des cotisations de sécurité sociale: analyse des arriérés de perception. Bruxelles, 1969. pp. 67.

BELGIUM. Ministère de la Prévoyance Sociale. Secrétariat Général. 1972. Aperçu de la sécurité sociale en Belgique. [Brussels?], 1972. pp. 215. *bibliog. (Etudes Juridiques)*

BELGIUM. Office National de Sécurité Sociale. 1972. L'Office National de Sécurité Sociale: sa mission, son fonctionnement. 3rd ed. [Brussels?], 1972. pp. 35.

DELEECK (HERMAN) Opstellen over inkomensverdeling sociale zekerheid en sociaal beleid. Antwerp, 1972. pp. 247.

SPITAELS (GUY) Réflexions sur la politique de sécurité sociale. Bruxelles, [1973]. pp. 233. *bibliog. (Brussels. Université Libre. Institut de Sociologie. Etudes d'Economie Sociale)*

— Brazil.

BRAZIL. Ministerio do Trabalho e Previdencia Social. Programa de Assistencia ao Trabalhador Rural. 1972. Lei complementar no. 11, de 25-5-71 - regulamento aprovado pelo Decreto noj 69.919 de 11-1-72: esclarecimentos sôbre os beneficios. [Brasilia? 1972?]. pp. 16.

— Denmark.

DENMARK. Socialreformkommission. 1972. 2. betaenkning: det sociale tryghedssystem, service og bistand. København, 1972. pp. 380. *(Denmark. Betaenkninger. Nr. 664)*

— European Economic Community countries.

EUROPEAN COMMUNITIES. Statistical Office. Social Statistics. Luxembourg, 1960 in progress.

ASPETTI internazionali comunitari e interni della sicurezza sociale: atti del convegno di studi promosso dalla Scuola di specializzazione in sicurezza, previdenza e assistenza sociali dell'Università di Macerata...Roma...1970. Milano, 1972. pp. 183.

FRANCE. Direction de la Documentation. La Documentation Française. Notes et Etudes Documentaires. Nos. 3,961-3, 962. Les prestations sociales dans les pays de la C.E.E.; [rédigée par André Laurent]. [Paris], 1973. pp. 68.

HANOTIAU (BERNARD) Les problèmes de securité sociale des travailleurs migrants. Bruxelles, 1973. pp. 178. *bibliog.*

— France.

FRANCE. Direction de la Sécurité Sociale. 1971. Statistiques de sécurité sociale. 4th ed. [Paris?], 1971. pp. 93.

FRANCE. Ministère de la Santé Publique et de la Sécurité Sociale. Direction de l'Administration Générale, du Personnel et du Budget. Division de la Documentation Générale, des Publications et de la Bibliothèque. 1971. La protection sanitaire et sociale en France. [Paris, 1971]. pp. 191.

DOUBLET (JACQUES) Sécurité sociale. 5th ed. Paris, 1972. pp. 816. *bibliogs.*

SAINT-JOURS (YVES) Le droit pénal de la sécurité sociale. Paris, 1973. pp. 137. *bibliog. (Paris. Université de Paris II. Travaux et Recherches. Série Sciences Criminelles. 1)*

THEVENET (AMEDEE) L'aide sociale en France. Paris, 1973. pp. 128. *bibliog.*

— Germany.

GERMANY (BUNDESREPUBLIK). Statistisches Bundesamt. Ausgaben der öffentlichen Haushalte für Soziale Sicherung. a., 1971- Wiesbaden. *(Finanzen und Steuern. Reihe 5. Sonderbeiträge zur Finanzstatistik)*

SCHEWE (DIETER) and others. Survey of Social Security in the Federal Republic of Germany. [Bonn, Federal Minister for Labour and Social Affairs, 1972]. pp. 270.

GERMANY (BUNDESREPUBLIK). Statistisches Bundesamt. 1973. Sozialaufwand von Bund, Ländern und Gemeinden (Gv.), 1966 bis 1969. Stuttgart, 1973. pp. 62. *(Finanzen und Steuern. Reihe 5. Sonderbeiträge zur Finanzstatistik)*

GERMANY (BUNDESREPUBLIK). Statistisches Bundesamt. 1973. Ausgaben der öffentlichen Haushalte für soziale Sicherung 1970. Stuttgart, 1973. pp. 116. *(Finanzen und Steuern. Reihe 5. Sonderbeiträge zur Finanzstatistik)*

MEYER-HARTER (RENATE) Die Stellung der Frau in der Sozialversicherung: Lageanalyse und Reformmöglichkeit. Berlin, [1974]. pp. 191. bibliog.

— Germany, Eastern.

FREIER DEUTSCHER GEWERKSCHAFTSBUND. Bundesvorstand. Social Insurance Administration. The social insurance system of the German Democratic Republic. Dresden, 1973. pp. 71.

— India.

HASAN (N.) The social security system of India. New Delhi, 1972. pp. 253. *bibliog.*

— Italy.

ISTITUTO NAZIONALE DELLA PREVIDENZA SOCIALE. Seventy years of the National Social Insurance Institute; fifty years of general compulsory insurance for disability and old- age: collection of studies. Rome, 1970. pp. 522.

INSURANCE, SOCIAL. (Cont.)

ASPETTI internazionali comunitari e interni della sicurezza sociale: atti del convegno di studi promosso dalla Scuola di specializzazione in sicurezza, previdenza e assistenza sociali dell'Università di Macerata...Roma...1970. Milano, 1972. pp. 183.

CLEMENTI (GIORGIO) and RUZZENENTI (GIUSEPPE) Sintesi dell'attività economica degli enti di previdenza e assistenza sociale in Italia dal 1960 al 1970. Roma, [Ministero del Lavoro e della Previdenza Sociale], 1972. pp. 76.

MONTESANO (LUIGI) and MAZZIOTTI (FABIO) Le controversie del lavoro e della sicurezza sociale: commento della legge 11 agosto 1973 n. 533. Napoli, 1974. pp. 311.

— Netherlands.

NETHERLANDS. Staatscommissie Vereenvoudiging en Codificatie van de Sociale-Zekerheidswetgeving. 1970- . Vereenvoudiging en codificatie van de sociale wetgeving. 's-Gravenhage, 1970 in progress. *(Netherlands. Ministerie van Sociale Zaken. Verslagen en Rapporten: Sociale Zaken. 1970. 3)*

— New Zealand.

NEW ZEALAND. Royal Commission to Inquire into and Report on Social Security, 1969. Social security in New Zealand; report of the Royal Commission; (Sir Thaddeus Pearcey McCarthy, chairman]. Wellington, 1972. pp. 617.

— Portugal.

PORTUGAL. Presidência do Conselho. 1955. 25 anos de administração publica: Ministerio das Corporações e Previdência Social. Lisboa, 1955. pp. 174.

PORTUGAL. Presidência do Conselho. 1955. 25 anos de administrações e Previdência Social. Lisboa, 1955. pp. 174.

— Russia.

BYKHOVSKII (N.I.) Sotsial'noe strakhovanie v SSSR: iz tsikla lektsii "Zaochnykh kursov sovetskogo stroitel'stva"; redaktsiia D.I. Efimova. Moskva, 1930. pp. 40. *Title page gives author's name as I.Bykhovskii.*

— Scandinavia.

[SCANDINAVIA]. Nordisk Statistisk Skriftserie. 24. Social security in the Nordic countries: expenditure on and scope of certain social security measures 1970 (1970/71); translation of...social trygghet i de nordiska länderna. Stockholm, 1973. pp. 162. *bibliog.*

— Sweden.

BROBERG (ROLF) Så formades tryggheten: socialförsäkringens historia, 1946- 1972. [Stockholm, 1973]. pp. 316.

— Switzerland.

SWITZERLAND. Conseil Fédéral. 1971. Rapport...à l'Assemblée fédérale sur l'encouragement de la prévoyance professionnelle pour les cas de vieillesse, d'invalidité et de décès (du 2 septembre 1970). [Berne? 1971]. pp. 144.

— United Kingdom.

U.K. Department of Health and Social Security. Annual report on departmental research and development. a., 1973 [1st]- London.

U.K. Statutes, etc. 1946- . The law relating to family allowances and national insurance: the statutes, regulations and orders as now in force, annotated and indexed;... compiled by J. St.L. Brockman; revised and edited by P.C. Nilsson; (with Supplements). [rev. ed.] London, 1973 in progress. 2 vols. (loose-leaf).

CALVERT (HARRY) Social security law. London, 1974. pp. 318.

LISTER (RUTH) Justice for the claimant: a study of supplementary benefit appeal tribunals. London, 1974. pp. 67. *(Child Poverty Action Group. Poverty Research Series. 4)*

LYNES (TONY ALFRED) The Penguin guide to supplementary benefits: supplementary benefits, the family income supplement and the Appeals Tribunal. 2nd ed. Harmondsworth, 1974. pp. 232.

STREATHER (JANE) and WEIR (STUART) Social insecurity: single mothers on benefit. London, 1974. pp. 62. *(Child Poverty Action Group. Poverty Pamphlets. 16)*

— — Ireland, Northern.

IRELAND, NORTHERN. Supplementary Benefits Commission. 1973. Supplementary benefits handbook. 2nd ed. Belfast, 1973. pp. 76.

— United States.

BOOTH (PHILIP) Social security in America. Ann Arbor, 1973. pp. 180. *bibliog. (Michigan University and Wayne State University. Institute of Labor and Industrial Relations. Policy Papers in Human Resources and Industrial Relations. No. 19)*

MICHIGAN SOCIAL SECURITY CONFERENCE, 7TH, 1972. Social security: policy for the seventies; proceedings of the...conference [sponsored by the School of Labor and Industrial Relations at Michigan State University, and others]; Philip Booth, editor. Ann Arbor, 1973. pp. 229.

SANDERS (DANIEL S.) The impact of reform movements on social policy change: the case of social insurance. Fair Lawn, N.J., [1973]. pp. 205. *bibliog.*

INSURANCE, STRIKE

— United Kingdom.

MOORE (PETER) Lawyer. Unemployed workers and strikers guide to social security. London, 1974. pp. 47. *(Child Poverty Action Group. CPAG Rights Guide. No. 1)*

INSURANCE, UNEMPLOYMENT

— Canada.

DODGE (DAVID A.) and SARGENT (JOHN H.) Towards a new tax-transfer system in Canada: an analysis of the changes proposed in the white papers on income security, unemployment insurance and taxation. Kingston, 1971. fo. 45. *(Kingston, Ontario. Queen's University. Institute for Economic Research. Discussion Papers. No.49)*

— European Economic Community countries.

La PROTECTION des travailleurs en cas de perte de l'emploi; par G. Boldt [and others]. Luxembourg, Communauté Européenne du Charbon et de l'Acier, 1961. pp. 489. *(European Coal and Steel Community. Collection du Droit du Travail)*

— Switzerland.

SWITZERLAND. Office Fédéral de l'Industrie, des Arts et Métiers et du Travail. 1970. Assurance-chômage: édition des prescriptions légales et des circulaires avec tables des matières. [Berne, 1970). pp. 225.

— United Kingdom.

EMMERSON (Sir HAROLD CORTI) and LASCELLES (EDWARD CHARLES PONSONBY) Guide to the Unemployment Insurance Acts. 5th ed. London, 1939. pp. 292.

MOORE (PETER) Lawyer. Unemployed workers and strikers guide to social security. London, 1974. pp. 47. *(Child Poverty Action Group. CPAG Rights Guide. No. 1)*

— United States.

IMPROVING unemployment insurance. Washington, D.C., [1954]. pp. 57-64. *(Reprinted from Economic Outlook, August 1954)*

BECKER (JOSEPH M.) Experience rating in unemployment insurance: virtue or vice. Kalamazoo, 1972. pp. 94. *(W.E. Upjohn Institute for Employment Research. Studies in Unemployment Insurance and Related Problems)*

MURRAY (MERRILL G.) The treatment of seasonal unemployment under unemployment insurance. Kalamazoo, Mich., 1972. pp. 84. *(W.E. Upjohn Institute for Employment Research. Studies in Unemployment Insurance and Related Problems)*

INSURANCE COMPANIES

— Employees — United Kingdom.

COMMISSION ON INDUSTRIAL RELATIONS [U.K.]. General Accident Fire and Life Assurance Corporation Limited: second report. London, H.M.S.O., 1973. pp. 47. *(Reports. No. 52) First report issued as British Parliamentary Paper, Cmnd. 4247, session 1969/70.*

— France.

FRANCE. Délégation à l'Aménagement du Territoire et à l'Action Régionale. 1972. La décentralisation du tertiaire: les banques et les assurances: documents. [Paris, 1972]. pp. 57.

— New Zealand.

NEW ZEALAND INSURANCE COMPANY. Bold century...1859-1959. [Auckland, 1959?]. pp. 111.

INSURGENCY

— Laos.

DAVIS (GEORGE ELLSWORTH) External intervention and mobilization of ethnic minorities in Laos, 1945-1973; [Ph.D. (London) thesis]. 1973. fo. 221. *bibliog. Typescript: unpublished. This thesis is the property of London University and may not be removed from the Library.*

— Rhodesia.

INTERNATIONAL INSTITUTE FOR STRATEGIC STUDIES. Adelphi Papers. No. 100. Insurgency in Rhodesia, 1957-1973: an account and assessment; by Anthony R. Wilkinson. London, 1973. pp. 47.

INTEGER PROGRAMMING.

ZIONTS (STANLEY) Linear and integer programming. Englewood Cliffs, [1974]. pp. 514. *bibliog.*

INTELLECT.

CALHOUN (DANIEL) The intelligence of a people. Princeton, [1973]. pp. 408. *bibliog.*

INTELLECTUAL LIFE.

UNITED NATIONS EDUCATIONAL, SCIENTIFIC AND CULTURAL ORGANIZATION. Studies and Documents on Cultural Policies . Paris, 1969 in progress.

INTELLECTUALS.

El INTELECTUAL y la sociedad; por Roque Dalton [and others]. Mexico, 1969. pp. 151.

SARTRE (JEAN PAUL) Between existentialism and marxism; translated from the French by John Matthews. London, 1974. pp. 302. *Essays and interviews from Situations VIII and IX.*

— China.

NAM (SVETLANA GEORGIEVNA) Formirovanie narodnoi intelligentsii v KNDR, 1945-1962 gg. Moskva, 1970. pp. 111. *bibliog.*

— Cuba.

El INTELECTUAL y la sociedad; por Roque Dalton [and others]. Mexico, 1969. pp. 151.

— Czechoslovakia.

FRANCE. Direction de la Documentation. La Documentation Française. Notes et Etudes Documentaires. Nos. 3,729-3, 730. La presse, les intellectuels et le pouvoir en Union Soviétique et dans les pays socialistes européens. 2. Pologne et Tchécoslovaquie; [by] Georges H. Mond. Paris, 1970. pp. 57. *bibliogs.*

— Europe, Eastern.

FRANCE. Direction de la Documentation. La Documentation Française. Notes et Etudes Documentaires. Nos. 3,736-3, 737. La presse, les intellectuels et le pouvoir en Union Soviétique et dans les pays socialistes européens. 3. Albanie, Allemagne de l'Est, Bulgarie, Hongrie, Roumanie, Yougoslavie; [by] Georges H. Mond [and others]. Paris, 1970. pp. 80. *bibliogs.*

— Germany.

SCHWENGER (HANNES) Das Ende der Unbescheidenheit: Intellektuelle auf dem Weg zur Gewerkschaft. Frankfurt am Main, [1974]. pp. 103.

— Italy.

CEREJA (FEDERICO) Intellettuali e politica dall'epoca giolittiana all'affermazione del fascismo. Torino, [1973]. pp. 167.

VACCA (GIUSEPPE) ed. P[artito] C[omunista] I[taliano], Mezzogiorno e intellettuali dalle alleanze all'organizzazione. Bari, [1973]. pp. 478.

GARIN (EUGENIO) Intellettuali italiani del XX secolo. Roma, 1974. pp. 370.

— Mexico.

CAREAGA (GABRIEL) Los intelectuales y la politica en Mexico. Mexico, [1971]. pp. 141. *bibliog.*

— Poland.

FRANCE. Direction de la Documentation. La Documentation Française. Notes et Etudes Documentaires. Nos. 3,729-3, 730. La presse, les intellectuels et le pouvoir en Union Soviétique et dans les pays socialistes européens. 2. Pologne et Tchécoslovaquie; [by] Georges H. Mond. Paris, 1970. pp. 57. *bibliogs.*

— Russia.

ASTAKHOVA (VALENTINA ILLARIONOVNA) V.I. Lenin o sushchnosti i sotsial'noi prirode sotsialisticheskoi intelligentsii. Khar'kov, 1970. pp. 84. *bibliog.*

BLIAKHMAN (LEONID SOLOMONOVICH) and SHKARATAN (OVSEI IRMOVICH) NTR, rabochii klass, intelligentsiia. Moskva, 1973. pp. 320.

— — Turkmenistan.

DURDYEV (TAGAN) Formirovanie i razvitie turkmenskoi sovetskoi intelligentsii, 1917- 1958 gg.; pod nauchnoi redaktsiei...K. Kerimi i...M. Mosheva. Ashkhabad, 1972. pp. 286.

— — White Russia.

MONICH (ZINAIDA IVANOVNA) Intelligentsiia v strukture sel'skogo naseleniia: na materialakh BSSR. Minsk, 1971. pp. 166.

— United Kingdom.

STOLLBERG (GUNNAR) Die soziale Stellung der intellektuellen Oberschicht im England des 12. Jahrhunderts. LÜBECK 1973. pp. 184. *bibliog.*

PAREKH (BHIKHUBHAI CHHOTALAL) ed. Colour, culture and consciousness: immigrant intellectuals in Britain; edited [on behalf of the Acton Society Trust]. London, 1974. pp. 249.

INTELLIGENCE LEVELS.

EYSENCK (HANS JÜRGEN) The inequality of man. London, 1973. pp. 288. *bibliog.*

— Denmark.

ØRUM (BENTE) Samspillet mellem social baggrund, intellektuelt niveau og placering i skolesystemet efter 7. klasse; [with English summary]; The relationship between social background, intellectual level, and the position in the school system at 14 years: rapport nr. 1 fra ungdomsforlØsundersOgelsen. KØbenhavn, 1971. pp. 144. *bibliog. (Socialforskningsinstituttet. Studier. Nr. 20)*

INTELLIGENCE SERVICE

— China.

DEACON (RICHARD) A history of the Chinese secret service. London, 1974. pp. 523. *bibliog.*

— Rhodesia.

ZAMBIA. Tribunal on Detainees. 1967. Report: tHOMAS pICKETT, CHAIRMAN!. lUSAKA, 1967. PP. 24.

— United States.

COWAN (PAUL) and others. State secrets: (police surveillance in America). New York, [1974]. pp. 333.

MARCHETTI (VICTOR) and MARKS (JOHN D.) The CIA and the cult of intelligence. London, 1974. pp. 398,xxi.

INTERCONTINENTAL BALLISTIC MISSILES.

TAMMEN (RONALD L.) MIRV and the arms race: an interpretation of defense strategy. New York, 1973. pp. 162. *bibliog.*

YORK (HERBERT FRANK) The origins of MIRV. Stockholm, 1973. pp. 28. *bibliog. (Stockholm International Peace Research Institute. Research Reports. No. 9)*

INTERDICT (CANON LAW).

TREXLER (RICHARD C.) The spiritual power: republican Florence under interdict. Leiden, 1974. pp. 208. *bibliog.*

INTEREST (PSYCHOLOGY).

NEUENDORFF (HARTMUT) Der Begriff des Interesses: eine Studie zu den Gesellschaftstheorien von Hobbes, Smith und Marx. Frankfurt am Main, 1973. pp. 163. *bibliog.*

INTEREST AND USURY.

HIRSHLEIFER (JACK) Investment, interest and capital. Englewood Cliffs, [1970]. pp. 320. *bibliogs.*

HENNINGS (K.H.) Böhm-Bawerk on the rate of interest: a reinterpretation. [Reading], 1973. fo. 25. *bibliog. (Reading. University. Department of Economics. Discussion Papers in Economics. No. 47)*

DODDS (J.C.) and FORD (JAMES LORNE) Expectations, uncertainty and the term structure of interest rates. London, 1974. pp. 314.

— Mathematical models.

FREEDMAN (CHARLES) International capital flows, interest rates, and the money supply. Minneapolis, 1973. fo. 37. *bibliog. (Minnesota University. Center for Economic Research. Discussion Papers. No. 32)*

PAZNER (ELISHA A.) and RAZIN (ASSAF) A model of investment under interest rate uncertainty. Minneapolis, 1973. fo. 13. *bibliog. (Minnesota University. Center for Economic Research. Discussion Papers. No. 33)*

— Canada — Mathematical models.

McCOLLUM (J.F.) Inflation and interest rates in Canada; a study prepared for the Prices and Incomes Commission. Ottawa, Information Canada, 1973. pp. 113. *bibliog.*

— Communist countries.

LASKI (KAZIMIERZ) The rate of growth and the rate of interest in the socialist economy.New York, 1972. pp. 238. *(Oesterreichisches Institut für Wirtschaftsforschung. Studien über Wirtschafts- und Systemvergleiche. Band 4) With German and Russian summaries.*

— India.

PANANDIKAR (D.H. PAI) Interest rates and flow of funds: a case study: India. Delhi, [1973]. pp. 180.

INTERGOVERNMENTAL FISCAL RELATIONS

— Australia.

GILBERT (R.S.) The Australian Loan Council in federal fiscal adjustments, 1890-1965. Canberra, 1973. pp. 337. *bibliog.*

— Germany.

THOMPSON (D.M.) The constitutional and financial relationship between Bund and Laender in the Federal German Republic. London, H.M. Treasury, 1972. 1 vol. (unpaged).

HUNTER (J.S.H.) Revenue sharing in the Federal Republic of Germany. Canberra, 1973. pp. 116. *bibliog. (Australian National University. Centre for Research on Federal Financial Relations. Research Monographs. No.2)*

— Switzerland — Bern (Canton).

BERN (CANTON). Regierungsrat. 1955. Le Jura et les finances de l'état de Berne. Bern, 1955. pp. 40.

INTERGOVERNMENTAL TAX RELATIONS

— United States.

MEYERS (EDWARD M.) and MUSIAL (JOHN J.) Urban incentive tax credits: a self-correcting strategy to rebuild central cities. New York, [1974]. pp. 140.

INTERINDUSTRY ECONOMICS.

UNITED NATIONS. Economic Commission for Asia and the Far East. Development Programming Techniques Series. Bangkok, 1960 in progress.

CHAKRAVERTI (A.K.) Structure of the Indian economy. Calcutta, 1968. pp. 330. *bibliog.*

STAEGLIN (REINER) Input-Output-Rechnung; Aufstellung von Input-Output- Tabellen; konzeptionelle und empirisch-statistische Probleme. Berlin, 1968. pp. 104. *bibliog. (Deutsches Institut für Wirtschaftsforschung. Beiträge zur Strukturforschung. Heft 4)*

EUROPEAN COMMUNITIES. Statistical Office. General Statistics. Série Spéciale: Tableaux Entrées-Sorties, 1965 . [Luxembourg], [1970-73].

BAKHTIN (A.E.) and others, eds. Optimal'noe otraslevoe planirovanie v promyshlennosti: materialy konferentsii 11-13 iiulia 1968 g. Novosibirsk, 1970. pp. 332.

AUSTRALIA. Commonwealth Bureau of Census and Statistics. 1972. Australian national accounts: input-output tables, 1962-63; prepared... by J.P. O'Neill. Canberra, [1972]. pp. 205. *Chart in end pocket.*

FORMOSA. Council for International Economic Cooperation and Development. 1972. Input-output tables, Taiwan, Republic of China, 1969. [Taipei, 1972]. fo.(22).

GAIHA (RAGHAV) and VASHISHTHA (PREM) An input-output analysis of key sectors in the Indian economy. Delhi, [1972]. fo. 24.

AUSTRIA. Statistisches Zentralamt. 1973. Input-Output-Tabelle 1964. Wien, 1973. pp. 152. *Folding table in end pocket.*

DENMARK. Danmarks Statistik. 1973. Input-output tabeller for Danmark 1966. KØbenhavn, 1973. 2 vols. (in 1). *(Statistiske UndersØgelser. Nr. 30) 8 tables in end pocket. With English summary.*

ERSHOV (E.B.) ed. Mezhotraslevye issledovaniia v Vengrii. Moskva, 1973. pp. 264.

IRELAND, NORTHERN. Ministry of Finance. Economic Section. 1973. Input-output tables for Northern Ireland, 1963. Belfast, 1973. 1 vol. (unpaged).

ISPOL'ZOVANIE mezhotraslevykh rezervov ekonomicheskogo raiona. Leningrad, 1973. pp. 192.

NIEDUSZYŃSKI (MIECZYSŁAW) Dynamiczna równowaga gospodarcza. Warszawa, 1973. pp. 215. *bibliog.*

INTERINDUSTRY ECONOMICS. (Cont.)

RODGERS (JOHN M.) State estimates of interregional commodity trade, 1963. Lexington, Mass., [1973]. pp. 447. *bibliog.*

ROSEFIELDE (STEVEN) Soviet international trade in Heckscher-Ohlin perspective: an input-output study. Lexington, Mass., [1973]. pp. 173. *bibliog.*

STAEGLIN (REINER) and WESSELS (HANS) Input-Output-Rechnung für die Bundesrepublik Deutschland, 1954, 1958, 1962, 1966. Berlin, 1973. pp. 169. *(Deutsches Institut für Wirtschaftsforschung. DIW-Beiträge zur Strukturforschung. Heft 27)* With summaries in English and French.

U.K. Central Statistical Office. 1973. Input-output tables for the United Kingdom, 1968. London, 1973. pp. 128. *(Studies in Official Statistics. No.22)*

BAUM (CLEMENS) Möglichkeiten und Grenzen der Entwicklung einer gesamtwirtschaftlichen Preistheorie. Berlin, [1974]. pp. 174. *bibliog.*

GHOSH (A.P.) Development planning in south-east Asia: an input-output approach;... in collaboration with D. Chakravarti and H. Sarkar. Rotterdam, 1974. pp. 118. *bibliog.*

HAIG (B.D.) and WOOD (M.P.) A dynamic input-output system for analysing price changes. Canberra, 1974. fo.34. *bibliog. (Australian National University. Research School of Social Sciences. Department of Economics. Working Papers in Economics and Econometrics. No.23)*

SENGER (JUERGEN) Technischer Fortschritt in Input-Output-Modellen. Berlin, [1974]. pp. 144. *bibliog.*

INTERNAL REVENUE

— European Economic Community countries.

EUROPEAN COMMUNITIES. Commission. 1972. Proposed Council directives on excise duties and similar taxes; transmitted on 7 March 1972. Brussels, 1972. pp. 82. *(Bulletin of the European Communities. Supplements. [1972/3])*

INTERNAL SECURITY

— South Africa.

SOUTH AFRICA. Commission of Inquiry into Certain Organisations. 1974. Fourth interim report (R.P. 33/1974). in SOUTH AFRICA. Parliament. House of Assembly. Votes and proceedings; (with Printed annexures).

SOUTH AFRICA. Commission of Inquiry into Certain Organisations. 1974. Fifth interim report (R.P. 62/1974). in SOUTH AFRICA. Parliament. House of Assembly. Votes and proceedings; (with Printed annexures).

— United States.

GRIFFITH (ROBERT) and THEOHARIS (ATHAN G.) eds. The specter: original essays on the cold war and the origins of McCarthyism. New York, 1974. pp. 366.

INTERNATIONAL, THE.

BROWN (H. RUNHAM) Cutting ice: a brief survey of war resistance and the International. Enfield, 1930. pp. 61. *Photographic reprint.*

BRUEGEL (FRITZ) Der Weg der Internationale. Wien, 1931. pp. 32.

GROOT (PAUL DE) De dertiger jaren 1930-(1939): herinneringen en overdenkingen. Amsterdam, 1965-67. 2 vols.

HEN-TOV (JACOB) The Communist International, the Palestine Communist Party, and the political unrest in Palestine in 1929;...paper submitted to the conference on "The Middle East in revolution"...April 1970. n.p., [1970?]. pp. 33.

DETTI (TOMMASO) Serrati e la formazione del Partito comunista italiano: storia della frazione terzinternazionalista, 1921-1924. Roma, 1972. pp. 547.

FAENZA (LILIANO) Marxisti e "riministi": la conferenza di Rimini e l'Internazionale italiana; vent'anni di storia del movimento operaio, 1872-1892. Rimini, [1972]. pp. 93. *bibliog.*

WEERDT (DENISE DE) De Belgische socialistische arbeidersbeweging op zoek naar een eigen vorm, 1872-1880. Antwerpen, [1972]. pp. 188. bibliog.

WEERDT (DENISE DE) De Belgische socialistische arbeidersbeweging op zoek naar een eigen vorm, 1872-1880. Antwerpen, [1972]. pp. 188.

FELICE (FRANCO DE) Fascismo, democrazia, fronte popolare: il movimento comunista alla svolta del VII Congresso dell'Internazionale. Bari, [1973]. pp. 569.

FOURTH INTERNATIONAL. Documents of the Fourth International: the formative years, 1933-40; (edited by Will Reisner). New York, 1973. pp. 448.

FOURTH INTERNATIONAL. International Committee. In defence of Trotskyism. London, 1973. pp. 80.

FRANK (PIERRE) La Quatrième Internationale: contribution à l'histoire du mouvement trotskyste. [2nd ed.]. Paris, 1973. pp. 180. *bibliog.*

GIELE (JACQUES J.) De Eerste Internationale in Nederland: een onderzoek naar het ontstaan van de nederlandse arbeidersbeweging van 1868 tot 1876. Nijmegen, 1973. pp. 273. *bibliog.*

KRIVINE (ALAIN) Questions sur la révolution; entretiens avec Roland Biard. [Paris, 1973]. pp. 319.

LAZITCH (BRANKO) and DRAŠKOVIĆ (MILORAD M.) Biographical dictionary of the Comintern. Stanford, 1973. pp. 458. *(Stanford University. Hoover Institution on War, Revolution and Peace. Hoover Institution Publications. 121)*

La QUESTION coloniale et la section française de la IVe Internationale. Paris, 1973. pp. 82.

The TRANSITIONAL program for socialist revolution; [programme by Leon Trotsky adopted at the Founding Conference of the Fourth International in 1938; with discussions with Trotsky and] introductory essays by Joseph Hansen and George Novack. New York, 1973. pp. 223.

COMMUNIST INTERNATIONAL World Congress, 1st, 1919. Les congrès de l'Internationale communiste: textes intégraux publiés sous la direction de Pierre Broué; le premier congrès, 2-6 mars 1919. Paris, [1974]. pp. 307.

COMMUNIST INTERNATIONAL. World Congress, 1st, 1919. Les congrès de l'Internationale communiste: textes intégraux publiés sous la direction de Pierre Broué; le premier congrès, 2-6 mars 1919. Paris, [1974]. pp. 307.

HABERL (OTHMAR NIKOLA) Die Emanzipation der KP Jugoslawiens von der Kontrolle der Komintern/KPdSU, 1941-1945. München, 1974. pp. 86. *bibliog. (Munich. Südost-Institut München. Untersuchungen zur Gegenwartskunde Südosteuropas. 8)*

NOVACK (GEORGE) and others. The first three Internationals: their history and lessons. New York, 1974. pp. 207. *bibliog.*

POULANTZAS (NICOS) Fascism and dictatorship: the Third International and the problem of fascism; translated from the French by Judith White. London, 1974. pp. 366.

PROBLEMI di storia dell'Internazionale Comunista, 1919-1939: relazioni tenute al Seminario di studi organizzato dalla Fondazione Luigi Einaudi, torino aprile 1972; contributi di Fernando Claudin [and others]; a cura di Aldo Agosti. Torino, 1974. pp. 255. *(Fondazione Luigi Einaudi. Studi. 16)*

INTERNATIONAL AGENCIES.

CARNEGIE ENDOWMENT FOR INTERNATIONAL PEACE. Groupe d'Etude sur l'Organisation Internationale. Les missions permanentes auprès des organisations internationales; [by] M. Virally [and others]. Bruxelles, 1971 in progress.

JORDAN (ROBERT S.) ed. Multinational cooperation: economic, social and scientific development. New York, 1972. pp. 392. *bibliog.*

BRIGHTON. University of Sussex. Institute of Development Studies. Library. Occasional Guides. No. 6. International agency aid and technical assistance programmes; a preliminary guide to documents. Brighton, [1973]. 1 pamphlet (unpaged).

SONDEREGGER (FRITZ) Geneva as a center of international organizations. Zurich, [1973]. pp. 15.

WIGHTMAN (DAVID R.) Economic diplomacy and international organisation: (an inaugural lecture delivered in the University of Birmingham on 22 March 1973). Birmingham, 1973. pp. 14.

AFRICA and international organization; [including papers given at a symposium held in 1970 under the auspices of the Center for African Studies, St. John's University, New York]; edited by Yassin El-Ayouty [and] Hugh C. Brooks. The Hague, 1974. pp. 250.

— Bibliography.

WINTON (HARRY NATHANIEL McQUILLIAN) compiler. Publications of the United Nations system: a reference guide. New York, 1972. pp. 202.

DIMITROV (THEODORE D.) compiler. Documents of international organisations: a bibliographic handbook covering the United Nations and other intergovernmental organisations. London, 1973. pp. 301.

— Documentation.

INTERNATIONAL SYMPOSIUM ON THE DOCUMENTATION OF THE UNITED NATIONS AND OTHER INTERGOVERNMENTAL ORGANIZATIONS, GENEVA, 1972. Sources, organization, utilization of international documentation: proceedings of the...Symposium...Geneva, 21-23 August 1972; organized by United Nations Institute for Training and Research [and others]. The Hague, International Federation for Documentation, 1974. pp. 586.

— Law and legislation.

ALEXANDROWICZ (CHARLES HENRY) The law-making functions of the specialised agencies of the United Nations. Sydney, 1973. pp. 181.

INTERNATIONAL AGENCIES IN EUROPE

— Periodicals.

PEMBERTON (JOHN E.) compiler. European materials in British university libraries: a bibliography and union catalogue;...with A survey by William E. Paterson. London, 1973. pp. 42.

INTERNATIONAL AND MUNICIPAL LAW

— European Economic Community countries.

EUROPEAN COMMUNITIES. Commission. 1972. Report on the Convention on jurisdiction and the enforcement of judgments in civil and commercial matters. Brussels, 1972. pp. 113. *(Bulletin of the European Communities. Supplements. [1972/12])*

La COMMUNAUTE et ses états membres: actes du sixième colloque de l'I[nstitut d'] E[tudes] J[uridiques] E[uropéennes] sur les Communautés européennes organisé à Liège...janvier 1973. Liège, 1973. pp. 325. *(Liège. Université. Faculté de Droit. Collection Scientifique. 36)*

— France.

BERGSTEN (ERIC E.) Community law in the French courts: the law of treaties in modern attire. The Hague, 1973. pp. 145.

— Italy.

SORRENTINO (FEDERICO) Corte costituzionale e Corte di giustizia delle Comunità europee. Milano, 1970-73. 2 vols. (in 1). *(Genoa. Università. Facoltà di Giurisprudenza. Annali. Collana. 27, 34)*

INTERNATIONAL BANK FOR ECONOMIC COOPERATION.

STELZL (DIETHARD) Die internationalen Banken des Rats für gegenseitige Wirtschaftshilfe. München, [1973]. pp. 191. *bibliog.* (*Osteuropa-Institut, München. Gegenwartsfragen der Ost-Wirtschaft. Band 7*)

INTERNATIONAL BANK FOR RECONSTRUCTION AND DEVELOPMENT.

FRANCE. Direction de la Documentation. La Documentation Française. Notes et Etudes Documentaires. Nos. 3,920-3, 921. La Banque Mondiale: vingt-cinq ans après. [Paris], 1972. pp. 63.

The WORLD Bank group, multilateral aid, and the 1970s; [contributions to a seminar held at the Woodrow Wilson School of Public and International Affairs, Princeton University, in 1971; edited by] John P. Lewis [and] Ishan Kapur. Lexington, Mass., [1973]. pp. 168. *bibliog.*

INTERNATIONAL BUSINESS ENTERPRISES.

FRANCE. Direction de la Documentation. La Documentation Française. Notes et Etudes Documentaires. Nos. 3,709-3, 710. Les sociétés internationales; [by] Roger Pichard du Page [and] Paul Turot. Paris, 1970. pp. 70. *bibliog.*

AMERICAN ARBITRATION ASSOCIATION. New strategies for peacefull resolution of international business disputes New York, 1971. pp. 252

COPPÉ (ALBERT) De multinationale onderneming: macht zonder grenzen. Antwerpen, [1972]. pp. 179. *bibliog.*

La CROISSANCE de la grande firme multinationale: the growth of the large multinational corporation; (actes du colloque international...organisé...à Rennes du 28 au 30 septembre, 1972). Paris, 1973. pp. 614. (*Centre National de la Recherche Scientifique. Colloques Internationaux. No. 549*) *In English or French.*

EUROPEAN COMMUNITIES. Commission. 1973. Multinational undertakings and Community regulations: communication...to the Council, presented on 8 November 1973. [Brussels], 1973. pp. 32. (*Bulletin of the European Communities. Supplements. [1973/15]*)

INTERNATIONAL LABOUR OFFICE. Studies and Reports. New Series. No. 79. Multinational enterprises and social policy. Geneva, 1973. pp. 182.

JAUMONT (BERNARD) and others. Le Marché commun contre l'Europe. Paris, [1973]. pp. 192.

KUJAWA (DUANE) ed. American labor and the multinational corporation. New York, 1973. pp. 285. *bibliog.*

LEA (SPERRY) and WEBLEY (SIMON) Multinational corporations in developed countries: a review of recent research and policy thinking. [London], 1973. pp. 71. (*British North-American Committee. Publications. 8*)

MULTINATIONAL corporations and labour unions; selected papers from a symposion in Nijmegen [held under the auspices of the Peace Research Centre and the Dutch labour unions] 17th- 19th May 1973; [edited by Kurt P. Tudyka]. [Nijmegen], 1973. pp. 326. *bibliogs.*

NATIONALISM and the multinational enterprise: legal, economic and managerial aspects; ([based on] an international conference held under the joint auspices of the Institute of Comparative Law, the Faculty of Management and the Department of Economics of McGill University in Montreal in August, 1971); edited by H.R. Hahlo [and others]. Leiden, 1973. pp. 373.

NEHLS (KATJA) Internationale Konzerne: Monopolmacht, Klassenkampf; die Rolle ... in der kapitalistischen Weltwirtschaft. Berlin, 1973. pp. 160. (*Institut für Internationale Politik und Wirtschaft. IPW-Forschungshefte. 1973, Heft 1*) *With table of contents in English and Russian.*

PALLOIX (CHRISTIAN) Les firmes multinationales et le procès d'internationalisation. Paris, 1973. pp. 194.

STAUFFER (ROBERT BURTON) Nation-building in a global economy: the role of the multinational corporation. Beverly Hills, [1973]. pp. 46. *bibliog.*

VAUPEL (JAMES W.) and CURHAN (JOAN P.) The world's multinational enterprises: a sourcebook of tables based on a study of the largest U.S. and non-U.S. manufacturing corporations. Boston, 1973. pp. 505.

WORKSHOP IN INTERNATIONAL BUSINESS-GOVERNMENT AFFAIRS, NEW YORK, 1972. International business-government affairs: toward an era of accommodation; edited by John Fayerweather. Cambridge, Mass., [1973]. pp. 131.

BAUM (DANIEL JAY) The banks of Canada in the Commonwealth Caribbean: economic nationalism and multinational enterprises of a medium power. New York, 1974. pp. 158.

DUESSELDORF CONFERENCE ON MULTINATIONAL CORPORATIONS, 1973. International control of investment: [sponsored by the Institute for International and Foreign Trade Law, Georgetown University Law Center]; edited by Don Wallace, Jr.. New York, 1974. pp. 275.

DUNNING (JOHN HARRY) ed. Economic analysis and the multinational enterprise. London, 1974. pp. 405. *bibliog.*

HELLMANN (RAINER) Puissance et limites des multinationales; traduit de l'allemand par Willy de Schepper. [Tours, 1974]. pp. 232. *bibliog.*

HOCHMUTH (MILTON S.) Organizing the transnational: the experience with transnational enterprise in advanced technology. Leiden, 1974. pp. 211.

HODGES (MICHAEL) Multinational corporations and national government: a case study of the United Kingdom's experience, 1964-1970. Farnborough, [1974]. pp. 307.

LABOUR RESEARCH DEPARTMENT. The menace of the multinationals. London, 1974. pp. 31.

MULTINATIONAL enterprises: financial and monetary aspects: [papers of a colloquium organized by the Société Universitaire Européenne de Recherches Financières at the University of Nottingham in 1973]; edited by J.S.G. Wilson and C.F. Scheffer; with contributions from Lord O'Brien [and others]. Leiden, 1974. pp. 241.

TURNER (LOUIS) Multinational companies and the third world. London, 1974. pp. 294. *bibliog.*

VAITSOS (CONSTANTINE V.) Intercountry income distribution and transnational enterprises. Oxford, 1974. pp. 198.

— Accounting.

AMERICAN ACCOUNTING ASSOCIATION. Committee on International Accounting. An introduction to financial control and reporting in multinational enterprises: modified version of a report by the Committee, etc. [George M. Scott, chairman]. Austin, Texas, 1973. pp. 89. *bibliog.* (*Texas University. Bureau of Business Research. Studies in International Business. No.1*)

— Finance.

ROBBINS (SIDNEY MARTIN) and STOBAUGH (ROBERT B.) Money in the multinational enterprise: a study of financial policy.London, 1974. pp. 231.

— — Mathematical models.

CHATEAU (JEAN PIERRE) Vers une programmation des politiques financières conflictuelles du budget de capital de la firme multinationale. Montréal, 1974. fo. 42. *bibliog.* (*Montréal. Universitité. Département des Sciences Economiques. Cahiers. No. 7406*)

— United States.

WARD (JAMES J.) The European approach to U.S. markets: product and promotion adaptation by European multinational corporations. New York, 1973. pp. 111. *bibliog.*

INTERNATIONAL COOPERATION.

ONE WORLD ONLY, 1967. One world only: a forum on international cooperation; (editor: Klaus W. Bender). Tokyo, [1968?]. pp. 84. (*Friedrich-Ebert-Stiftung. Asian Labour Institute. Reports. 1*)

— Societies.

SONDEREGGER (FRITZ) Geneva as a center of international organizations. Zurich, [1973]. pp. 15.

INTERNATIONAL ECONOMIC INTEGRATION.

COUNCIL FOR MUTUAL ECONOMIC ASSISTANCE. 1971. Comprehensive programme for the further extension and improvement of co-operation and the development of socialist economic integration by the CMEA member-countries. Moscow, 1971. pp. 99.

CHODOROWSKI (JERZY) Niemiecka doktryna gospodarki wielkiego obszaru: Grossraumwirtschaft, 1800-1945. Wrocław, 1972. pp. 423. *bibliog.* *With Russian, English and German summaries.*

See also subdivision Economic integration under continents and regions and under the heading UNDERDEVELOPED AREAS.

INTERNATIONAL ECONOMIC RELATIONS.

MYRDAL (GUNNAR) Economic conditions and policies in their relation to war and peace: lecture at the fourteenth International Seminar for Diplomats... 1971. [Stockholm, 1971?]. fo. 17.

HASLEMERE DECLARATION GROUP. The Haslemere declaration: a radical analysis of the relationships between the rich world and the poor world. 6th ed. London, 1972. pp. 28. *bibliog.*

ORGANISATION FOR ECONOMIC CO-OPERATION AND DEVELOPMENT. High Level Group on Trade and Related Problems. 1972. Policy perspectives for international trade and economic relations: report...to the Secretary-General of OECD. Paris, 1972. pp. 168.

BERGSTEN (C. FRED) The future of the international economic order: an agenda for research. Lexington, Mass., [1973]. pp. 357. *bibliogs.*

HUGHES (HELEN) ed. Prospects for partnership: industrialization and trade policies in the 1970s; a seminar held at the International Bank for Reconstruction and Development, October 5 and 6, 1972. Baltimore, 1973. pp. 289.

LEADING issues in international economic policy: essays in honor of George N. Halm; edited by C. Fred Bergsten [and] William G. Tyler. Lexington, [1973]. pp. 217. *bibliog.*

WIGHTMAN (DAVID R.) Economic diplomacy and international organisation: (an inaugural lecture delivered in the University of Birmingham on 22 March 1973). Birmingham, 1973. pp. 14.

CORBET (HUGH) and JACKSON (ROBERT VICTOR) eds. In search of a new world economic order. London, 1974. pp. 288.

EVANS (DOUGLAS) The politics of trade: the evolution of the superbloc. London, 1974. pp. 128.

SCAMMELL (WILLIAM McCONNELL) International trade and payments. London, 1974. pp. 607. *bibliog.*

See also subdivision Foreign economic relations under names of countries and under the heading UNDERDEVELOPED AREAS.

— Mathematical models.

FOMIN (BORIS SERGEEVICH) Ekonometricheskie teorii i modeli mezhdunarodnykh ekonomicheskikh otnoshenii. Moskva, 1970. pp. 268.

INTERNATIONAL FEDERATION OF COTTON AND ALLIED TEXTILE INDUSTRIES.

INTERNATIONAL FEDERATION OF COTTON AND ALLIED TEXTILE INDUSTRIES. Directory. 6th ed. Zürich, 1973. pp. 41.

INTERNATIONAL FINANCE.

GROUP OF TEN. Study Group on the Creation of Reserve Assets.1965. Report...to the Deputies of the Group of Ten; [R. Ossola, Chairman]. [Rome, 1965]. pp. 113.

U.K. Central Office of Information. Reference Division. 1965. Britain's financial services for overseas. London, 1965. pp. 38. *bibliog.*

GROUP OF TEN. 1966. Communiqué of ministers and governors and report of deputies "... on improvements needed in the international monetary system, etc". [Frankfurt?], 1966. pp. 25.

ORGANISATION FOR ECONOMIC CO-OPERATION AND DEVELOPMENT. Committee for Invisible Transactions. Country Capital- Market Series. [Paris], 1969 in progress.

GROUP OF TEN. 1971. Press communique of the ministerial meeting...on 17th-18th December, 1971 in Washington, D.C. [Washington], 1971. fo. 3.

VANES (F.R.) and VERHEIRSTRAETEN (A.) De geldkapitaalmarkt. 2nd ed, Leuven, 1972 in progress. *bibliog.*

GROVE (DAVID L.) A proposed solution for the dollar overhang problem. Tübingen, 1972. pp. 14. *(Kiel. Universität. institut für Weltwirtschaft. Kieler Vorträge. Neue Folge. 74)*

LUTZ (FRIEDRICH AUGUST) Das Problem der internationalen Währungsordnung. Erlenbach-Zürich, [1972]. pp. 29. *(Schweizerisches Institut für Auslandforschung. Schriftenreihe zu Aktuellen Problemen aus Politik und Wirtschaft. 6)*

WALLICH (HENRY CHRISTOPHER) and others. The monetary crisis of 1971: the lessons to be learned. Washington, D.C., 1972. pp. 79. *(Per Jacobsson Foundation.* [*Lectures*]. *1972)*

WASSERMAN (MAX JUDD) and others. International money management. [New York, 1972]. pp. 232. *bibliog.*

ALIBER (ROBERT Z.) The international money game. London, 1973. pp. 236.

ALIBER (ROBERT Z.) National preferences and the scope for international monetary reform.Princeton, [1973]. pp. 22. *(Princeton University. Department of Economics and Sociology. International Finance Section. Essays in International Finance. No. 101)*

BALLING (MORTEN) National pengepolitik i en international ökonomi. Köbenhavn, 1973. pp. 624. *bibliogs.*

EMMINGER (OTMAR) and others. L'inflation et le système monétaire international. Bâle, 1973. pp. 85. *(Per Jacobsson Foundation.* [*Lectures*]. *1973)*

EMMINGER (OTMAR) and others. Inflation and the international monetary system. Basle, 1973. pp. 78. *(Per Jacobsson Foundation.* [*Lectures*]. *1973)*

HIRSCH (FRED) Reform of the international monetary system with special reference to the interests of developing countries of the Commonwealth; a study. London, Commonwealth Secretariat, 1973. pp. 20. *(Commonwealth Economic Papers. No. 3)*

KONJUNKTURPOLITIK: Zeitschrift für angewandte Konjunkturforschung. Beihefte. Heft 20. Zur Neuordnung des internationalen Währungssystems: Bericht über den wissenschaftlichen Teil der 36. Mitgliederversammlung der Arbeitsgemeinschaft deutscher wirtschaftswissenschaftlicher Forschungsinstitute...1973. Berlin, [1973]. pp. 177. *In German or English.*

LEADING issues in international economic policy: essays in honor of George N. Halm; edited by C. Fred Bergsten [and] William G. Tyler. Lexington, [1973]. pp. 217. *bibliog.*

MENEGAZZI (GUIDO) The laws of the dynamics of economy and finance as the basis and objective of international monetary and credit reform. Verona, 1973. pp. 68.

NARPATI (B.) The monetary system: its components and some trade issues. Rotterdam, 1973. pp. 136. *bibliog.*

REVELL (JACK) Financial centres, financial institutions and economic change. Bangor, [1973]. pp. 20. *bibliog. (Wales. University. University College of North Wales. Economic Research Papers. FIN 4)*

BOECK (KLAUS) and GEHRMANN (DIETER) Die DM als internationale Reservewährung: Bedeutung, Ursachen und Probleme. Hamburg, 1974. pp. 75. *(Hamburg. Hamburgisches Welt-Wirtschafts-Archiv. Studien zur Aussenwirtschaft und Entwicklungspolitik)*

BOYER DE LA GIRODAY (FRÉDÉRIC) Myths and reality in the development of international monetary affairs. Princeton, 1974. pp. 31. *(Princeton University. Department of Economics and Sociology. International Finance Section. Essays in International Finance. No. 105)*

COFFEY (PETER) Economist. The world monetary crisis. London, 1974. pp. 115.

HIPPLE (F. STEB) The disturbances approach to the demand for international reserves. Princeton, 1974. pp. 41. *bibliog. (Princeton University. Department of Economics and Sociology. International Finance Section. Princeton Studies in International Finance. No. 35)*

JOHNSON (HARRY GORDON) The problem of international monetary reform. London, 1974. pp. 22. *(London. University. Stamp Memorial Lectures. 1973)*

LEES (FRANCIS A.) International banking and finance. London, 1974. pp. 419.

McKENZIE (GEORGE W.) The monetary theory of international trade. London, 1974. pp. 96. *bibliog.*

MAKIN (JOHN H.) Capital flows and exchange-rate flexibility in the post-Bretton Woods era. Princeton, 1974. pp. 25. *bibliog. (Princeton University. Department of Economics and Sociology. International Finance Section. Essays in International Finance. No. 103)*

MARSTON (RICHARD C.) American monetary policy and the structure of the Eurodollar market. Princeton, 1974. pp. 35. *bibliog. (Princeton University. Department of Economics and Sociology. International Finance Section. Princeton Studies in International Finance. No. 34)*

MAYER (HELMUT W.) The anatomy of official exchange-rate intervention systems. Princeton, N.J., 1974. pp. 34. *(Princeton University. Department of Economics and Sociology. International Finance Section. Essays in International Finance. No. 104)*

MEIER (GERALD MARVIN) Problems of a world monetary order. New York, 1974. pp. 305. *bibliogs.*

MIKESELL (RAYMOND FRECH) and FURTH (J. HERBERT) Foreign dollar balances and the international role of the dollar. New York, 1974. pp. 125. *(National Bureau of Economic Research. Studies in International Economic Relations. No. 7)*

MONROE (WILBUR F.) International monetary reconstruction: problems and issues. Lexington, Mass., [1974]. pp. 191.

ROLFE (SIDNEY E.) and BURTLE (JAMES L.) The great wheel: the world monetary system; a reinterpretation. London, 1974. pp. 279. *bibliog.*

INTERNATIONAL GEOPHYSICAL YEAR, 1957—1958

— United Kingdom.

LONDON. Royal Society of London. The United Kingdom contribution to the International Geophysical year 1957-58. London, 1957. pp. 72.

INTERNATIONAL INVESTMENT BANK.

STELZL (DIETHARD) Die internationalen Banken des Rats für gegenseitige Wirtschaftshilfe. München, [1973]. pp. 191. *bibliog. (Osteuropa-Institut, München. Gegenwartsfragen der Ost-Wirtschaft. Band 7)*

INTERNATIONAL LABOUR ORGANISATION.

NATIONAL LABOUR ADVISORY COUNCIL [AUSTRALIA]. Review of Australian law and practice relating to conventions adopted by the International Labour Conference. in AUSTRALIA. Parliament. Parliamentary papers, 1969, vol.4.

ALLIO (RENATA) L'Organizzazione Internazionale del Lavoro e il sindacalismo fascista. Bologna, [1973]. pp. 149.

GIANNOPOULOS (DEMETRIUS C.) La protection internationale de la liberté syndicale: la Commission d'Investigation et de Conciliation en matière de liberté syndicale de l'Organisation Internationale du Travail.Paris, 1973. pp. 274. *bibliog.*

HARARI (EHUD) The politics of labor legislation in Japan: national- international interaction. Berkeley, [1973]. pp. 221. *bibliog.*

INTERNATIONAL LABOUR CONFERENCE. 59th Session. Reports. 9. Structure of the ILO. Geneva, 1974. pp. 83.

— Bibliography.

CATALOGUE OF ILO PUBLICATIONS; [pd. by] International Labour Office; (with Supplements). irreg., 1969- Geneva.

INTERNATIONAL LAW.

KURS mezhdunarodnogo prava. Moskva, 1967-73. 6 vols.

LEPAWSKY (ALBERT) and others, eds. The search for world order: studies by students and colleagues of Quincy Wright. New York, [1971]. pp. 451. *bibliog.*

INTERNATIONAL LAW ASSOCIATION. The present state of international law, and other essays written in honour of the centenary celebration of the International Law Association, 1873-1973; editor Maarten Bos. Deventer, 1973. pp. 392. *In English or French.*

BOWIE (ROBERT RICHARDSON) Suez 1956. London, 1974. pp. 148. *(American Society of International Law. International Crises and the Role of Law)*

EHRLICH (THOMAS) Cyprus, 1958-1967. London, 1974. pp. 164. *(American Society of International Law. International Crises and the Role of Law)*

GAWENDA (J.A.B.) The Soviet domination of Eastern Europe in the light of international law. Richmond, 1974. pp. 220. *bibliog.*

INTERNATIONAL organization: law in movement: essays in honour of John McMahon; edited by J.E.S. Fawcett and Rosalyn Higgins. London, 1974. pp. 182.

LUKASHUK (IGOR' IVANOVICH) Otnosheniia mirnogo sosushchestvovaniia i mezhdunarodnoe pravo: problemy mezhdunarodno-pravovogo regulirovaniia. Kiev, 1974. pp. 207.

SHEIKH (AHMED) International law and national behavior: a behavioral interpretation of contemporary international law and politics. New York, [1974]. pp. 352. *bibliog.*

— History — China.

KAMINSKI (GERD) Chinesische Positionen zum Völkerrecht. Berlin, [1973]. pp. 369. *bibliog.*

COHEN (JEROME ALAN) and CHIU (HUNGDAH) People's China and international law: a documentary study. Princeton, [1974]. 2 vols. *bibliog. (Harvard University. Harvard Studies in East Asian Law)*

— — Russia.

MIRONOV (NIKOLAI VLADIMIROVICH) Law, progress and peace: a journalist's observations on the influence of Soviet law on the progressive development of international law. Moscow, 1971. pp. 136.

— **Philosophy.**

SZTUCKI (JERZY) Jus cogens and the Vienna Convention on the Law of Treaties: a critical appraisal. Wien, 1974. pp. 204. bibliog. (Österreichische Zeitschrift für Öffentliches Recht. Supplementa. 3)

INTERNATIONAL LAW, PRIVATE

SZÁSZY (ISTVÁN) Conflict of laws in the western, socialist and developing countries. Leiden, 1974. pp. 424.

— **Bankruptcy.**

PELLERIN (PIERRE) Barrister-at-Law. The French law of bankruptcy and winding up of limited companies: the conflict of laws arising therefrom. London, 1907. pp. 117.

— **Australia.**

SYKES (EDWARD I.) A textbook on the Australian conflict of laws. Melbourne, 1972. pp. 561.

— **Communist countries.**

PFAFF (DIETER) and others. Die Aussenhandelsschiedsgerichtbarkeit der sozialistischen Länder im Handel mit der Bundesrepublik Deutschland unter Berücksichtigung des internationalen Privatrechts. Heidelberg, [1973]. pp. 887.

— **United Kingdom.**

DICEY (ALBERT VENN) and MORRIS (JOHN HUMPHREY CARLILE) The conflict of laws; ninth edition [by] J.H.C. Morris [and others]. London, 1973. pp. 1205. bibliog.

CHESHIRE (GEOFFREY CHEVALIER) Private international law; ninth edition by P.M. North. London, 1974. pp. 740.

INTERNATIONAL LIQUIDITY.

CENTRO DE ESTUDIOS MONETARIOS LATINOAMERICANOS. America Latina y la liquidez internacional; [selected papers and documents for the years 1964 to 1969]. Mexico, 1970. pp. 376.

GUPTA (R.D.) International liquidity: problems, appraisals and perspectives. New Delhi, 1972. pp. 385. bibliog.

INTERNATIONAL MONETARY FUND.

GROUP OF TEN. Study Group on the Creation of Reserve Assets.1965. Report...to the Deputies of the Group of Ten; [R. Ossola, Chairman]. [Rome, 1965]. pp. 113.

INTERNATIONAL OBLIGATIONS.

PAZARCI (HÜSEYIN) Responsabilité internationale des états en matière contractuelle. Ankara, 1973. pp. 144. bibliog. (Ankara. Universitesi. Siyasal Bilgiler Fakültesi. Yayinlari. 350)

INTERNATIONAL ORGANIZATION.

MITRANY (DAVID) A working peace system: an argument for the functional development of international organization;...(with new appendix). London, 1943 repr. 1944. pp. 60. (Royal Institute of International Affairs. Post-War Problems)

KEOHANE (ROBERT O.) and NYE (JOSEPH S.) eds. Transnational relations and world politics. Cambridge, Mass., [1971] repr. 1973. pp. 428. bibliog.

RITTBERGER (VOLKER) Evolution and international organization: toward a new level of sociopolitical integration. Den Haag, 1973. pp. 120. bibliog.

INTERNATIONAL organization: law in movement: essays in honour of John McMahon; edited by J.E.S. Fawcett and Rosalyn Higgins. London, 1974. pp. 182.

U.K. Department of Education and Science. 1974. Sources of information on international organisations, 1974. [London, 1974]. pp. 55.

— **Bibliography.**

HAAS (MICHAEL) compiler. International organization: an interdisciplinary bibliography. Stanford, [1971]. pp. 944. (Stanford University. Hoover Institution on War, Revolution and Peace. Bibliographical Series. 41)

— **Information storage and retrieval systems.**

See INFORMATION STORAGE AND RETRIEVAL SYSTEMS — International organization.

INTERNATIONAL POLICE.

WAINHOUSE (DAVID WALTER) and others. International peacekeeping at the crossroads: national support; experience and prospects. Baltimore, [1973]. pp. 634.

INTERNATIONAL RELATIONS.

SPROUT (HAROLD HANCE) and SPROUT (MARGARET TUTTLE) The ecological perspective on human affairs: with special reference to international politics. Princeton, 1965. pp. 234.

McCLELLAND (CHARLES A.) Theory and the international system. London, [1966]. pp. 138. bibliogs.

JONES (ROY E.) Analysing foreign policy: an introduction to some conceptual problems. London, 1970. pp. 157. bibliogs.

LEPAWSKY (ALBERT) and others, eds. The search for world order: studies by students and colleagues of Quincy Wright. New York, [1971]. pp. 451. bibliog.

TENEKIDES (GEORGIOS) L'élaboration de la politique étrangère des états et leur sécurité. Paris, [1972]. 2 vols. (in 1).

CAMILLERI (JOSEPH ANTHONY) and TEICHMANN (MAX) Security and survival: the new era in international relations. South Yarra, Victoria, 1973. pp. 226. bibliog.

FERRIS (WAYNE H.) The power capabilities of nation-states: international conflict and war. Lexington, [1973]. pp. 191. bibliog.

FOOT (HUGH MACKINTOSH) Baron Caradon of St. Cleer. The need for new initiatives in international affairs. Colchester, 1973. pp. 23. (University of Essex. Noel Buxton Lectures. 1972)

HILTON (GORDON) A review of the Dimensionality of Nations project. Beverly Hills, [1973]. pp. 77. bibliog.

KATZ (ELIHU) and DANET (BRENDA) eds. Bureaucracy and the public: a reader in official-client relations.New York, [1973]. pp. 534. bibliog.

KEGLEY (CHARLES WILLIAM) A general empirical typology of foreign policy behavior. Beverly Hills, [1973]. pp. 73. bibliog.

LISKA (GEORGE) States in evolution: changing societies and traditional systems in world politics. Baltimore, 1973. pp. 184. (Johns Hopkins University. Washington Center of Foreign Policy Research. Studies in International Affairs, No. 19)

McGOWAN (PATRICK J.) and SHAPIRO (HOWARD B.) The comparative study of foreign policy: a survey of scientific findings. Beverly Hills, [1973]. pp. 256. bibliog.

PURNELL (ROBERT) The society of states: an introduction to international politics. London, 1973. pp. 332. bibliog.

STEVENS (Sir ROGER BENTHAM) Middle East oil in international relations. Leeds, 1973. pp. 29. (Leeds. University. Montague Burton Lectures on International Relations. No. 31)

WALLACE (MICHAEL DAVID) War and rank among nations. Lexington, Mass., [1973]. pp. 142. bibliog.

WALLENSTEEN (PETER) Structure and war: on international relations, 1920-1968. Stockholm, [1973]. pp. 266. bibliog. (Uppsala. Statsvetenskapliga Föreningen. Skrifter. 64)

WILKENFELD (JONATHAN) ed. Conflict behavior and linkage politics. New York, [1973]. pp. 388. bibliog.

INTERNATIONAL YEARBOOK OF FOREIGN POLICY ANALYSIS. a., 1974 (v.1)- London.

ABRAMSKY (CHIMEN) ed. Essays in honour of E.H. Carr; edited by C. Abramsky assisted by Beryl J. Williams. London, 1974. pp. 387. bibliog.

CAMPS (MIRIAM) The management of interdependence: a preliminary view. New York, [1974]. pp. 104. (Council on Foreign Relations. Council Papers on International Affairs. 4)

HAAS (MICHAEL) and others. International systems: a behavioral approach. New York, [1974]. pp. 433. bibliog.

LEVI (WERNER) International politics: foundations of the system. Minneapolis, [1974]. pp. 285. bibliog.

NORTHEDGE (FREDERICK SAMUEL) ed. The use of force in international relations. London, 1974. pp. 258.

QUESTER (GEORGE H.) The continuing problem of international politics. [Hinsdale, Ill., 1974]. pp. 342. bibliogs.

SHEIKH (AHMED) International law and national behavior: a behavioral interpretation of contemporary international law and politics. New York, [1974]. pp. 352. bibliog.

The STUDY of world society: a London perspective: [discussions among members of the Centre for the Analysis of Conflict]. Pittsburgh, [1974.] pp. 92. (International Studies Association. Occasional Papers. No.1)

— **Dictionaries and encyclopaedias.**

ELLIOTT (FLORENCE M.J.) A dictionary of politics. 7th ed. Harmondsworth, 1973. pp. 522.

— **Mathematical models.**

LUTERBACHER (URS) Dimensions historiques de modèles dynamiques de conflit: application aux processus de course aux armements, 1900-1965. Leiden, 1974. pp. 175. bibliog. (Geneva. Graduate Institute of International Studies. Collection de Relations Internationales. 2)

— **Psychological aspects.**

LAUTERBACH (ALBERT T.) Psychological challenges to modernization. Amsterdam, 1974. pp. 190.

— **Public opinion.**

HENDERSON (GREGORY) ed. Public diplomacy and political change: four case studies: Okinawa, Peru, Czechoslovakia, Guinea. New York, 1973. pp. 339. bibliogs.

— **Research.**

A DESIGN for international relations research: scope, theory, methods, and relevance: [proceedings of a conference held in Philadelphia, 1969]...; edited by Norman D. Palmer. Philadelphia, 1970. pp. 307. (American Academy of Political and Social Science. Monographs. [No.] 10)

WELTMAN (JOHN J.) Systems theory in international relations: a study in metaphoric hypertrophy. Lexington, Mass., [1973]. pp. 99.

— — **United States.**

ROSENAU (JAMES N.) International studies and the social sciences: problems, priorities and prospects in the United States. Beverly Hills, [1973]. pp. 147. bibliog.

— **Societies, etc.**

U.K. Department of Education and Science. 1973. Sources of information on international and Commonwealth organisations. [London, 1973]. pp. 45.

— **Study and teaching.**

INTERNATIONAL studies: present status and future prospects: [proceedings of a conference]..., editor, Fred W. Riggs. Philadelphia, 1971. pp. 271. (American Academy of Political and Social Science. Monographs. [No.] 12)

INTERNATIONAL RELATIONS. (Cont.)

ROSENAU (JAMES N.) International studies and the social sciences: problems, priorities and prospects in the United States. Beverly Hills, [1973]. pp. 147. *bibliog.*

INTERNATIONAL RELIEF.

INTERNATIONAL UNIVERSITY EXCHANGE FUND. Ten years of assistance to African refugees through international cooperation. [Geneva, 1972]. pp. 107.

— Africa, West.

SHEETS (HAL) and MORRIS (ROGER) Disaster in the desert: failures of international relief in the West African drought. Washington, [1974]. pp. 167. *(Carnegie Endowment for International Peace. Humanitarian Policy Studies Program. Special Reports)*

— Turkey.

KERR (STANLEY ELPHINSTONE) The lions of Marash: personal experiences with American Near East Relief, 1919-1922. Albany, N.Y., 1973. pp. 318. *bibliog.*

INTERNATIONAL UNIVERSITY EXCHANGE FUND.

INTERNATIONAL UNIVERSITY EXCHANGE FUND. Ten years of assistance to African refugees through international cooperation. [Geneva, 1972]. pp. 107.

INTERNATIONALISM.

CALDER (PETER RITCHIE) Baron Ritchie-Calder. The internationalist in the world of nationalism. Leeds, 1973. pp. 19. *(Leeds. University. Selig Brodetsky Memorial Lectures. No. 15)*

INTERNATSIONAL'NE i natsional'ne v sotsialistychnomu suspil'stvi. Kyïv, 1973. pp. 243.

INTERPERSONAL RELATIONS.

CONNECTICUT COLLEGE SYMPOSIUM ON THEORIES OF INTERPERSONAL ATTRACTION IN THE DYAD, 1970. Theories of attraction and love: [papers given at the Symposium] by Donn Byrne [and others]; editor, Bernard I. Murstein. New York, [1971]. pp. 179. *bibliogs.*

ALTMAN (IRWIN) and TAYLOR (DALMAS A.) Social penetration: the development of interpersonal relationships. New York, [1973]. pp. 212. *bibliog.*

DEUTSCH (MORTON) The resolution of conflict: constructive and destructive processes. New Haven, 1973. pp. 420. *bibliog. (Yale University. Carl Hovland Memorial Lectures)*

DUCK (STEVEN W.) Personal relationships and personal constructs: a study of friendship formation. London, [1973]. pp. 170. *bibliog.*

INTERPERSONAL dynamics: essays and readings on human interaction; edited by Warren G. Bennis [and others]. 3rd ed. Homewood, Ill., 1973. pp. 608.

COLEMAN (JOHN C.) Relationships in adolescence. London, 1974. pp. 214. *bibliog.*

INTERVENTION (INTERNATIONAL LAW).

BERGMANN (PHILIP) pseud. Self-determination: the case of Czechoslovakia, 1968-1969. Bellinzona, 1972. pp. 159. *bibliog.*

HUMANITARIAN intervention and the United Nations: [proceedings of a conference held in Charlottesville, Va. in 1972]; edited by Richard B. Lillich. Charlottesville, Va., 1973. pp. 240. *bibliog. (Virginia University. School of Law. Virginia Legal Studies)*

ZOUREK (JAROSLAV) L'interdiction de l'emploi de la force en droit international. Leiden, 1974. pp. 128. *bibliog. (Institut Henry Dunant. "Teneat Lex Gladium". No. 3)*

INTERVIEWING.

CROSS (CRISPIN PATRIC ROBERT) ed. Interviewing and communication in social work. London, 1974. pp. 176. *bibliog.*

INVENTORIES

— Canada — Mathematical models.

DEWALEYNE (C.) CANDIDE [Canadian Disaggregated Interdepartmental Econometric] model 1.0: inventories. Ottawa, Information Canada, 1973. pp. 12. *(CANDIDE Project Papers. No. 4)*

INVENTORY CONTROL

— Mathematical models.

GENUGTEN (B.B. VAN DER) A statistical view to the problem of the economic lot size. Tilburg, 1973. pp. 18. *bibliog. (Tilburg. Katholieke Hogeschool. Tilburg Institute of Economics. Research Memoranda. EIT 44)*

INVERGORDON MUTINY, 1931.

WINCOTT (LEN) Invergordon mutineer. London, [1974]. pp. 183.

INVESTMENT ADVISERS.

ALHAIQUE (CLAUDIO) Creation of an industrial promotion service. Paris, Organisation for Economic Co-operation and Development, 1972. pp. 67. *(Problems of Development)*

INVESTMENT BANKING

— Netherlands.

NEDERLANDSE INVESTERINGSBANK VOOR ONTWIKKELINGSLANDEN. Annual report. a., 1973- The Hague. *In-English.*

INVESTMENT CLUBS.

BOSS (CHRISTIAN) Die Investmentclubs in der Bundesrepublik Deutschland. [Erlangen, imprint, 1973?]. pp. 188, xxxvi. *bibliog.*

INVESTMENT OF PUBLIC FUNDS

— Denmark.

DENMARK. Statsrevisoratet. 1969. Beretning om de statslige investeringer i finansårene 1955-56 - 1967-68. København, 1969. pp. 44.

— United Kingdom.

HARRISON (A.J.) and MACKIE (P.J.) The comparability of cost benefit and financial rates of return;... [with] an annex by A. Peaker. London, H.M.S.O., 1973. pp. 17. *bibliog. (Government Economic Service Occasional Papers. 5)*

INVESTMENT TRUSTS.

ORGANISATION FOR ECONOMIC CO-OPERATION AND DEVELOPMENT. Committee on Financial Markets. 1972. Standard rules for the operations of institutions for collective investment in securities. Paris, 1972. pp. 77.

— Norway.

INNSTILLING om investeringsselskaper; fra et utvalg oppnevnt av Finansdepartementet 14. januar 1969; [Erling Borresen, chairman]. Bergen, 1970. pp. 65.

— United Kingdom.

GAMMELL (W.S.) The Association of Investment Trust Companies: the first 38 years, 1932-1970. London, [1973]. pp. 55.

DAY (MARTIN J.) and HARRIS (PAUL I.) Unit trusts: (the law and practice). London, 1974. pp. 206.

INVESTMENTS.

COHEN (JEROME BERNARD) and others. Investment analysis and portfolio management. rev. ed. Homewood, Ill., 1973. pp. 946. *bibliogs.*

— Bibliography.

ANDRIĆ (STANISLAVA) and others, compilers. Bibliografija o sistemu investiranja. Zagreb, 1972. pp. 110.

BREALEY (RICHARD A.) and PYLE (C.) compilers. A bibliography of finance and investment. London, 1973. pp. 361.

— Mathematical models.

FRANCIS (JACK CLARK) and ARCHER (STEPHEN H.) Portfolio analysis. Englewood Cliffs, N.J., [1971]. pp. 268.

CHAPMAN (C.B.) Basic modular portfolio selection: a first order interpretation;...paper...prepared for the Royal Economic Society Conference of Decision Analysis, held at...Lancaster...1973. 1973. fo. 50. *bibliog. (Southampton. University. Discussion Papers in Economics and Econometrics. No. 7301)*

CHAPMAN (C.B.) Modular portfolio selection: statistical estimation of return. [Southampton], 1973. fo. 45. *bibliog. (Southampton. University. Discussion Papers in Economics and Econometrics. No. 7307)*

CHAPMAN (C.B.) and PALMER (M.J.) Modular portfolio selection: statistical estimation of return: some preliminary results. [Southampton], 1973. fo. 46. *bibliog. (Southampton. University. Discussion Papers in Economics and Econometrics. No.7308)*

JORGENSON (DALE W.) Investment and production: a review; [presented at the Winter meetings of the Econometric Society in Toronto in 1972]. Stanford, 1973. pp. 44. *bibliog. (Stanford University. Institute for Mathematical Studies in the Social Sciences. Technical Reports. [New Series]. No. 97)*

PAZNER (ELISHA A.) and RAZIN (ASSAF) A model of investment under interest rate uncertainty. Minneapolis, 1973. fo. 13. *bibliog. (Minnesota University. Center for Economic Research. Discussion Papers. No. 33)*

PLASMANS (J.E.J.) Adjustment cost models for the demand of investment. Tilburg, 1973. pp. 34. *bibliog. (Tilburg. Katholieke Hogeschool. Tilburg Institute of Economics. Research Memoranda. EIT 37)*

SOLNIK (BRUNO H.) European capital markets: towards a general theory of international investment. Lexington, Mass., [1973]. pp. 114. *bibliog.*

ATKINS (DEREK R.) and ASHTON (DAVID) A re-examination of the Baumol and Quandt paradox. Coventry, 1974. pp. 22. *bibliog. (University of Warwick. Centre for Industrial Economic and Business Research. [Warwick Research in Industrial and Business Studies]. No.44)*

DAS (R.K.) Optimal investment planning: a reappraisal of Mahalonobis- Fel'dman strategy. Rotterdam, 1974. pp. 146. *bibliog.*

— Mathematics.

HIRSHLEIFER (JACK) Investment, interest and capital. Englewood Cliffs, [1970]. pp. 320. *bibliogs.*

BHATTACHARYYA (D.K.) A note on mean-variance portfolio analysis. [Stirling, 1972?]. fo. 10. *bibliog. (University of Stirling. Discussion Papers in Economics, Finance and Investment. No. 6)*

— Argentine Republic.

ARGENTINE REPUBLIC. Consejo Federal de Inversiones. Boletin. m., current issues only kept. Buenos Aires.

— France.

MARNATA (FRANÇOISE) La Bourse et le financement des investissements. Paris, 1973. pp. 125. *bibliog. (Fondation Nationale des Sciences Politiques. Travaux et Recherches de Sciences Economiques. Serie "Economie Française". 1)*

— Philippine Islands.

PHILIPPINE ISLANDS. Board of Investments. Annual report. a., 1971/2- Rizal.

— Sweden.

BERGSTRÖM (VILLY) Kapitalbildning och industriell demokrati: socialdemokratiska perspektiv. Stockholm, [1973]. pp. 182. *bibliog.*

INVESTMENTS, FOREIGN.

— Thailand.

THAILAND. Statutes, etc. 1960. Promotion of Industrial Investment Act, B.E. 2503. [Bangkok, 1960]. fo. 7.

— United Kingdom.

ASH (J.C.K.) Quarterly forecasting at the N[ational I[nstitute of] E[conomic and] S[ocial] R[esearch]: gross fixed investment. [Reading], 1973. fo.13. bibliog. *(Reading. University. Department of Economics. Discussion Papers in Economics. No.45)*

NURSAW (WILLIAM GEORGE) The art and practice of investment. 3rd ed. London, 1974. pp. 176.

INVESTMENTS, AMERICAN.

JAVITS (BENJAMIN A.) Peace by investment. New York, [1950]. pp. 242.

GREEN (ROBERT T.) Political instability as a determinant of U.S. foreign investment. Austin, 1972. pp. 122. bibliog. *(Texas University. Bureau of Business Research. Studies in Marketing. No.17)*

KUJAWA (DUANE) ed. American labor and the multinational corporation. New York, 1973. pp. 285. bibliog.

KUENTZEL (ULRICH) Der nordamerikanische Imperialismus: zur Geschichte der US- Kapitalausfuhr. Darmstadt, 1974. pp. 253. bibliog.

LAFFARGUE (JEAN PIERRE) Les investissements américains dans les pays industrialisés. [Paris], 1974. pp. 132. bibliog.

— America, Latin.

SCHILLING (PAULO R.) El imperio Rockefeller: America Latina documentos; [and] La estrategia norteamericana en America Latina: de la doctrina Monroe al informe Rockefeller; ensayo; [translated from the English by Rosario Lorente]. Montevideo, [1970]. pp. 129.

— Europe.

HU (Y.S.) The impact of U.S. investment in Europe: a case study of the automotive and computer industries. New York, 1973. pp. 291.

HELLMANN (RAINER) Puissance et limites des multinationales; traduit de l'allemand par Willy de Schepper. [Tours, 1974]. pp. 232. bibliog.

— France.

FRANCE. Direction de la Documentation. La Documentation Française. Notes et Etudes Documentaires. No. 3,770. Aperçu sur les investissements américains en France. Paris, 1971. pp. 24. bibliog.

— Italy.

LAMONT (DOUGLAS F.) Managing foreign investment in southern Italy: US business in developing areas of the EEC;... with the special assistance of Robert Purtshert. New York, 1973. pp. 169. bibliog.

— Japan.

DUNCAN (WILLIAM CHANDLER) U.S.-Japan automobile diplomacy: a study in economic confrontation. Cambridge, Mass., [1973]. pp. 202. bibliog.

— Russia.

SUTTON (ANTONY C.) Wall Street and the Bolshevik revolution. New Rochelle, N.Y., [1974]. pp. 228. bibliog.

INVESTMENTS, BRITISH

— Mathematical models.

BOATWRIGHT (B.D.) and RENTON (G.A.) An analysis of U.K. inflows and outflows of direct foreign investment. London, 1973. fo. 23. bibliog. *(London Graduate School of Business Studies. Econometric Forecasting Unit. Discussion Papers. No.27)*

— Spain.

AVERY (DAVID) Not on Queen Victoria's birthday: the story of the Rio Tinto mines. London, 1974. pp. 464. bibliog.

INVESTMENTS, DUTCH.

NETHERLANDS. Nationale Raad van Advies inzake Hulpverlening aan Minder Ontwikkelde Landen. 1969. Advies besluitvorming overzeese vestigingen, februari 1969, no.27. 's-Gravenhage, 1969. pp. 22. *Folding chart in end pocket.*

INVESTMENTS, EUROPEAN

— United States.

HELLMANN (RAINER) Puissance et limites des multinationales; traduit de l'allemand par Willy de Schepper. [Tours, 1974]. pp. 232. bibliog.

INVESTMENTS, FOREIGN.

LACROIX (ROBERT) Pour une théorie de l'investissement direct étranger dans l'industrie manufacturière. Louvain, 1970. pp. 268. bibliog. *(Louvain. Université. Faculté des Sciences Economiques, Sociales et Politiques. [Publications]. Nouvelle Série. No. 84)*

CAIRNCROSS (Sir ALEXANDER KIRKLAND) Control of long-term international capital movements. Washington, [1973]. pp. 104. bibliog. *(Brookings Institution. Brookings Staff Papers)*

SOLNIK (BRUNO H.) European capital markets: towards a general theory of international investment. Lexington, Mass., [1973]. pp. 114. bibliog.

DUESSELDORF CONFERENCE ON MULTINATIONAL CORPORATIONS, 1973. International control of investment: [sponsored by the Institute for International and Foreign Trade Law, Georgetown University Law Center]; edited by Don Wallace, Jr.. New York, 1974. pp. 275.

— Mathematical models.

FREEDMAN (CHARLES) International capital flows, interest rates, and the money supply. Minneapolis, 1973. fo. 37. bibliog. *(Minnesota University. Center for Economic Research. Discussion Papers. No. 32)*

BOS (HENDRICUS CORNELIS) and others. Private foreign investment in developing countries: a quantitative study on the evaluation of the macro-economic effects; (published for the Development Centre of the Organization for Economic Cooperation and Development). Dordrecht, [1974]. pp. 402.

— America, Latin.

HEYDENREICH (HORST DIETER) Problembereiche ausländischer privater Direktinvestitionen in Lateinamerika: eine empirische Untersuchung. Göttingen, [1974]. pp. 237. bibliog. *(Göttingen. Universität. Ibero-Amerika- Institut für Wirtschaftsforschung. Arbeitsberichte. Heft 15)*

— Asia, Southeast.

NEW directions in the international relations of southeast Asia: economic relations; papers presented at a conference organized by the Institute of Southeast Asian Studies; edited by Lee Soo Ann. Singapore, 1973. pp. 133. bibliog.

— Australia.

AUSTRALIA. Australian News and Information Bureau, [Canberra]. 1970. Australia: (an economic and investment reference). [new ed.]. [Canberra, 1970]. pp. 112. bibliog.

— — Directories.

AUSTRALIA. Department of Trade and Industry. Office of Secondary Industry. 1966. Directory of overseas investment in Australian manufacturing industry, 1966. Canberra, [1966]. pp. 159.

AUSTRALIA. Department of Trade and Industry. Office of Secondary Industry. 1971. Directory of overseas investment in Australian manufacturing industry, 1971. Canberra, [1971]. pp. 205.

— Belgium.

BULCKE (D. VAN DEN) and others. Les entreprises étrangères dans l'industrie belge: aspects généraux, régionaux et économiques;...avec la collaboration de J. De Sloovere [and others]. Gand, 1971. 1 vol. (various pagings).

La BELGIQUE face aux investissements étrangers: une approche sociologique; ([by] Marc Beckers [and others])... sous la direction de Pierre de Bie. Leuven, 1973. pp. 269.

THOMAN (G. RICHARD) Foreign investment and regional development: the theory and practice of investment incentives, with a case study of Belgium. New York, 1973. pp. 148. bibliog.

— Czechoslovakia.

TEICHOVA (ALICE) An economic background to Munich: international business and Czechoslovakia, 1918-1938. London, 1974. pp. 422. bibliog. *(National Association for Soviet and East European Studies. Soviet and East European Studies)*

— Greece.

COMMERCIAL BANK OF GREECE, and others. Investment guide to Greece.. 3rd ed. Athens, 1973. pp. 142.

GIANNITSIS (ANASTASIOS) Private Auslandskapitalien im Industrialisierungsprozess Griechenlands, 1953 bis 1970. Berlin, 1974. pp. 292. bibliog.

— Japan.

KAGAMI (N.) Foreign investments in Japanese securities. [Tokyo], 1973. fo. 7. *Photocopy of typescript.*

— Russia.

TSENTRAL'NYI ARKHIV RSFSR. Russkie finansy i evropeiskaia birzha v 1904-1906 gg.; pod redaktsiei i s predisloviem E.A. Preobrazhenskogo, etc. Moskva, 1926. pp. 400. *Xerographic reprint.*

— Singapore.

SINGAPORE in the international economy:...papers[of a symposium organized by the Economic Society of Singapore]; edited by Wong Kum Poh and Maureen Tan. Singapore, 1972. pp. 97.

— Sri Lanka.

SRI LANKA. Ministry of Planning and Employment.1972. Policy of the government of Sri Lanka (Ceylon) on private foreign investment. [Colombo], 1972. pp. 14.

— Switzerland.

LAMBELET (JOHN C.) and SCHILTKNECHT (KURT) On the importance of an elastic supply of foreign labor and capital: simulation results for the Swiss economy. Zürich, [1973]. pp. 77. bibliog. *(Zürich. Eidgenössische Technische Hochschule. Institut für Wirtschaftsforschung. Untersuchungen. Neue Folge. Band 8)*

— Trinidad and Tobago.

McINTYRE (ALISTER) and WATSON (BEVERLY) Trinidad and Tobago. [Mona], 1970. pp. 74. *(West Indies, University of the. Institute of Social and Economic Research. Studies in Foreign Investment in the Commonwealth Caribbean. No. 1)*

— Underdeveloped areas.

See UNDERDEVELOPED AREAS — Investments, Foreign.

INVESTMENTS, FOREIGN. (Cont.)

— United Kingdom — Mathematical models.

BOATWRIGHT (B.D.) and RENTON (G.A.) An analysis of U.K. inflows and outflows of direct foreign investment. London, 1973. fo. 23. *bibliog*. *(London Graduate School of Business Studies. Econometric Forecasting Unit. Discussion Papers. No.27)*

INVESTMENTS, FRENCH

— Russia.

GIRAULT (RENE) Emprunts russes et investissements français en Russie 1887-1914: recherches sur l'investissement international. Paris, 1973. pp. 624. *bibliog. (Paris. Université de Paris I (Panthéon-Sorbonne). Publications. Nouvelle Série. Recherches. 3)*

INVESTMENTS, GERMAN

— Indonesia.

KEBSCHULL (DIETRICH) and MAYER (OTTO G.) Deutsche Investitionen in Indonesien: eine Untersuchung über Umfang, Motive und Förderungsmöglichkeiten. Hamburg, 1974. pp. 174. *bibliog. (Hamburg. Hamburgisches Welt-Wirtschafts-Archiv. Studien zur Aussenwirtschaft und Entwicklungspolitik) With English summary.*

INVESTMENTS, SWEDISH

— South Africa.

MAGNUSSON (ÅKE) Swedish investments in South Africa. Uppsala, 1974. pp. 57. *(Nordiska Afrikainstitutet. Research Reports. No.23)*

IPSWICH

— Transit systems.

JAMIESON AND MACKAY. Ipswich and district transportation study; consultants' report [to Ipswich County Borough Council and the Department of the Environment]. London, 1973. fo. xxiii,82.

IRAN

— Boundaries — Iraq.

AL-IZZI (KHALID YAHYA) The Shatt al-Arab river dispute in terms of law. 2nd ed. Baghdad, Ministry of Information, 1972. pp. 159, 3 maps.*bibliog*.

— Economic conditions.

LOONEY (ROBERT E.) The economic development of Iran: a recent survey with projections to 1981. New York, 1973. pp. 199. *bibliog*.

— Economic policy.

FURTER (PIERRE) Possibilities and limitations of functional literacy: the Iranian experiment. Paris, United Nations Educational, Scientific and Cultural Organization, 1973. pp. 59. *bibliog. (Educational Studies and Documents. New Series. No. 9)*

LOONEY (ROBERT E.) The economic development of Iran: a recent survey with projections to 1981. New York, 1973. pp. 199. *bibliog*.

— Foreign relations — India.

ISLAM (RIAZUL) Indo-Persian relations: a study of the political and diplomatic relations between the Mughul empire and Iran. Teheran, [1970]. pp. 287. *bibliog. (Iranian Culture Foundation. Sources of the History and Geography of Iran. No.32)*

— Persian Gulf.

RAMAZANI (ROUHOLLAH KAREGAR) The Persian Gulf: Iran's role. Charlottesville, 1972 repr. 1973. pp. 157. *bibliog*.

— — Russia.

TUZMUKHAMEDOV (RAIS ABDULKHAKOVICH) Sovetsko-iranskie otnosheniia, 1917-1921. Moskva, 1960. pp. 95. *Author's name wrongly given in colophon as Rals.*

— — United States.

SHEEHAN (MICHAEL KAHL) Iran: the impact of United States interests and policies, 1941-1954. Brooklyn, N.Y., 1968. pp. 88. *bibliog*.

IRANIAN STUDENTS IN FOREIGN COUNTRIES.

NASSEFAT (MORTEZA) Le rôle des étudiants dans l'échange interculturel: une enquête de psychologie sociale. Teheran, 1973. pp. 319. *bibliog. With English summary.*

IRAQ

— Boundaries — Iran.

AL-IZZI (KHALID YAHYA) The Shatt al-Arab river dispute in terms of law. 2nd ed. Baghdad, Ministry of Information, 1972. pp. 159, 3 maps.*bibliog*.

— History.

WARNER (GEOFFREY) Iraq and Syria, 1941. London, 1974. pp. 180. *bibliog*.

IRELAND.

AKENSON (DONALD HARMAN) The United States and Ireland. Cambridge, Mass., 1973. pp. 311. *bibliog*.

— Civilization.

O'RAIFEARTAIGH (T. F.) Ireland and the E.E.C.: the cultural aspects; [expanded version of a speech given to a symposium on the E.E.C. in Dublin in 1972]. Dublin, [1972?]. 1 pamphlet (unpaged).

— History.

McGEE (THOMAS D'ARCY) Historical sketches of O'Connell and his friends...with a glance at the future destiny of Ireland. 2nd ed. Boston, 1845. pp. 208.

— — Sources.

IRELAND, NORTHERN. Public Record Office. 1973- Eighteenth century Irish official papers in Great Britain: private collections. Belfast, 1973 in progress.

— — To 1172.

THOMAS (CHARLES) b. 1928. Britain and Ireland in early Christian times, A.D. 400-800. London, [1971]. pp. 144. *bibliog*.

MACNIOCAILL (GEAROID) Ireland before the Vikings. Dublin, [1972]. pp. 172. *bibliog*.

O CORRAIN (DONNCHA) Ireland before the Normans. Dublin, [1972]. pp. 210. *bibliog*.

— — 1172—1603.

NICHOLLS (KENNETH) Gaelic and Gaelicised Ireland in the middle ages. Dublin, [1972]. pp. 197. *bibliog*.

BRADSHAW (BRENDAN) The dissolution of the religious orders in Ireland under Henry VIII. London, 1974. pp. 276. *bibliog*.

— — 1600—1699.

HEALY (TIMOTHY MICHAEL) The great fraud of Ulster; [reprint of the 1917 edition, with a new] foreword by Dennis Kennedy. Tralee, 1971. pp. 154. *bibliog*.

JAMES (FRANCIS GODWIN) Ireland in the Empire, 1688-1770: a history of Ireland from the Williamite wars to the eve of the American revolution. Cambridge, Mass., 1973. pp. 356. *bibliog. (Harvard University. Harvard Historical Monographs. 68)*

— — 1700—1799.

JAMES (FRANCIS GODWIN) Ireland in the Empire, 1688-1770: a history of Ireland from the Williamite wars to the eve of the American revolution. Cambridge, Mass., 1973. pp. 356. *bibliog. (Harvard University. Harvard Historical Monographs. 68)*

— — 1800, The Union.

O' SNODAIGH (PÁDRAIG) A second Act of Union?. Dublin, 1972. pp. 16. *(Common Market Study Group. Ireland and the Common Market. 7)*

— — 1800—1899.

DAUNT (WILLIAM JOSEPH O'NEILL) Ireland and her agitators. Dublin, 1845. pp. 376.

O'DONOVAN ROSSA (DIARMUID) Rossa's recollections, 1838-1898; [reprint of the first edition, New York 1898]; introduction by Sean O Luing and a new index. Shannon, [1972]. pp. 410. *bibliog*.

— Nationalism.

SPEECHES from the dock; or, Protests of Irish patriotism; containing, with introductory sketches and biographical notices, speeches delivered after conviction by Theobald Wolfe Tone [and others]. Dublin, 1867. pp. 192.

TONE (THEOBALD WOLFE) Freedom the Wolfe Tone way; ([compiled by] Sean Cronin and Richard Roche); with an introduction by Jack Bennett. Tralee, [1973]. pp. 242. *bibliog*.

— Politics and government.

SINN FEIN. Ard Fheis, Dublin, 1971. Report. [Dublin, 1971?]. pp. 38.

BUCKLAND (PATRICK) Irish unionism, 1885-1922. London, 1973. pp. 48. *bibliog. (Historical Association. General Series. G.81)*

MILLER (DAVID WILLIAM) Church, state and nation in Ireland 1898-1921. Dublin, 1973. pp. 579. *bibliog*.

— Religion.

NEW ULSTER MOVEMENT. Publications. [No. 9]. Tribalism or Christianity in Ireland?. Belfast, [1973?]. 1 pamphlet (unpaged).

— Social policy.

SINN FEIN. Ard Fheis, Dublin, 1971. Report. [Dublin, 1971?]. pp. 38.

IRELAND (REPUBLIC)

— Census.

EIRE. Census, 1971. Census of population, 1971: preliminary county results [and results for provinces and the state]: bulletin[s]. [Dublin, 1972? in progress].

— Commerce.

IRISH EXPORT BOARD. Annual report. a., 1961/2 (10th); 1964- Dublin.

— Constitution.

GANNON (JACK) Catholic political culture and the constitution of Ireland. Belfast, 1972. pp. 82. *First issued 1971.*

— Economic conditions.

SHANNON FREE AIRPORT DEVELOPMENT COMPANY and MUINTIR NA TIRE. The Mid-West Region Parish Resource Survey: report. [Shannon], 1972. fo. 76.

NATIONAL ECONOMIC AND SOCIAL COUNCIL [EIRE]. Report on the economy in [ ] and the prospects for [the next yr.]. a., 1973 (no.1)- Dublin.

— Economic policy.

NATIONAL ECONOMIC AND SOCIAL COUNCIL [EIRE]. Report on the economy in [ ] and the prospects for [the next yr.]. a., 1973 (no.1)- Dublin.

— Executive departments — Directories.

EIRE. [Department of Finance]. Directory of state services. a., current issue only kept. Dublin.

— Foreign relations.

KEATINGE (NEIL PATRICK) The formulation of Irish foreign policy. Dublin, [1973]. pp. 323. *bibliog.*

See also EUROPEAN ECONOMIC COMMUNITY — Ireland (Republic).

— Full employment policies.

HENRY (E.W.) Irish full employment structures 1968 and 1975. Dublin, 1974. pp. 109. *bibliog.* (*Economic and Social Research Institute. Papers. No. 74*)

— Government publications.

FORD (PERCY) and FORD (GRACE) A select list of reports of inquiries of the Irish Dáil and Senate, 1922-72. Dublin, [1974]. pp. 64. (*Southampton. University. Studies in Parliamentary Papers*)

— History.

ORLOVA (MARGARITA EVGEN'EVNA) Irlandiia v poiskakh putei nezavisimogo razvitiia, 1945-1948. Moskva, 1973. pp. 231. *bibliog.*

— Industries.

EIRE. Central Statistics Office. 1973. Analysis of the census of industrial production, 1968. Supplement to IRISH STATISTICAL BULLETIN, March 1973.

FOGARTY (MICHAEL PATRICK) Irish entrepreneurs speak for themselves. Dublin, 1973. pp. 141. (*Economic and Social Research Institute. Broadsheets. No.8*)

— Officials and employees — Directories.

EIRE. [Department of Finance]. Directory of state services. a., current issue only kept. Dublin.

— Oireachtas.

SMYTH (JOHN McGOWAN) The houses of the Oireachtas. 3rd ed. Dublin, 1973. pp. 69.

— — Elections.

KNIGHT (JAMES S.) and BAXTER-MOORE (NICOLAS) Republic of Ireland: the general elections of 1969 and 1973. London, [1973?]. pp. 181. *bibliog.*

— Politics and government.

EIRE. [Dáil Eireann and Seanad Eiraenn]. Joint Committee on the Secondary Legislation of the European Communities. Parliamentary debates: official report. sess., Ag 3 1973 (v.1, no.1)- Dublin.

KEATINGE (NEIL PATRICK) The formulation of Irish foreign policy. Dublin, [1973]. pp. 323. *bibliog.*

SCHMITT (DAVID E.) The irony of Irish democracy: the impact of political culture on administrative and democratic political development in Ireland. Lexington, [1973]. pp. 118. *bibliog.*

— Social conditions.

SHANNON FREE AIRPORT DEVELOPMENT COMPANY and MUINTIR NA TIRE. The Mid-West Region Parish Resource Survey: report. [Shannon], 1972. fo. 76.

SCHMITT (DAVID E.) The irony of Irish democracy: the impact of political culture on administrative and democratic political development in Ireland. Lexington, [1973]. pp. 118. *bibliog.*

GEARY (ROBERT CHARLES) and Ó MUIRCHEARTAIGH (F.S.) Equalization of opportunity in Ireland: statistical aspects. Dublin, 1974. pp. 122. (*Economic and Social Research Institute. Broadsheets. 10*)

IRELAND, NORTHERN

— Appropriations and expenditures.

IRELAND, NORTHERN. Department of Finance. Vote on account. a., 1974/5- Belfast. *Included in the file of IRELAND, NORTHERN. Northern Ireland Assembly. Assembly papers. 1921/2-1972/3 included in file of IRELAND, NORTHERN. Parliament. House of Commons. [Papers].*

— Assembly.

IRELAND, NORTHERN. Northern Ireland Assembly. Journals of the proceedings of the Assembly. sess., Jl/D 1973(v.1)- Belfast.

— — Privileges and immunities.

IRELAND, NORTHERN. NIA 19. Second report from the Committee of Privileges, together with the proceedings of the Committee and appendices: member's complaint that he was prevented in the corridors from approaching Mr. Speaker's room. Belfast, 1974. pp. 16.

— — Rules and practice.

IRELAND, NORTHERN. NIA 1. Report from the Presiding Officer's Committee on standing orders together with the proceedings of the Committee and appendices; (and Minutes of evidence). Belfast, 1973. 2 pts.

— Economic conditions.

CUTHBERT (NORMAN) The Northern Ireland economy:... an inaugural lecture delivered before the Queen's University of Belfast on 25 November 1970. Belfast, 1970. pp. 26. *bibliog.* (*Belfast. Queen's University. Lectures. New Series. No. 55*)

IRELAND, NORTHERN. Ministry of Finance. Economic Section. 1973. Input-output tables for Northern Ireland, 1963. Belfast, 1973. 1 vol. (unpaged).

— Economic policy.

NORTHERN IRELAND ECONOMIC COUNCIL. Area development in Northern Ireland. Belfast, 1969. pp. 49.

CUTHBERT (NORMAN) The Northern Ireland economy:... an inaugural lecture delivered before the Queen's University of Belfast on 25 November 1970. Belfast, 1970. pp. 26. *bibliog.* (*Belfast. Queen's University. Lectures. New Series. No. 55*)

— Emigration and immigration.

PERCEVAL-MAXWELL (MICHAEL) The Scottish migration to Ulster in the reign of James I. London, 1973. pp. 411. *bibliog.* (*Ulster-Scot Historical Society. Ulster-Scot Historical Series. 3.*)

— Government publications.

MALTBY (ARTHUR) The government of Northern Ireland 1922-72: a catalogue and breviate of parliamentary papers. Dublin, 1974. pp. 235.

— History.

BIGGS-DAVISON (JOHN ALEC) The hand is red. London, 1973. pp. 202.

— Industries.

REGIONAL policy and the attraction of manufacturing industry in Northern Ireland; by A.S. Murie [and others]. London, 1974. pp. 133. (*Centre for Environmental Studies. Research Papers.4*)

— Maps.

IRELAND, NORTHERN. [Ministry of Development]. 1972. [Local government boundaries maps]: final district electoral areas, 1972 [and General map]. [Belfast, 1972]. 27 maps.

— Politics and government.

NEW ULSTER MOVEMENT. Annual report. a., 1971/2- Belfast. *File also includes Interim report to members, April 1972.*

CONWAY (ANDY) There are no evil men: a fresh look at the Irish question and a suggested way forward: (a viewpoint from within the New Ireland Movement). Dublin, 1972. pp. 30.

FARRELL (MIKE) The struggle in the north. 2nd ed. London, 1972. pp. 37.

NEW ULSTER MOVEMENT. Publications. 6. Violence and Northern Ireland. Belfast, 1972. pp. (16).

ROBB (JOHN DANIEL ALEXANDER) New Ireland: sell-out or opportunity?. [Dublin, 1972]. pp. 50.

RUSSELL (JAMES LYON) Some aspects of the civic education of secondary schoolboys in Northern Ireland. [Belfast], Northern Ireland Community Relations Commission, 1972. fo. 34. (*Research Papers*)

DEUTSCH (RICHARD) and MAGOWAN (VIVIEN) Northern Ireland, 1968-73: a chronology of events. Belfast, 1973 in progress. *bibliog.*

IRELAND, NORTHERN. Northern Ireland Assembly. Assembly papers. sess., S 1973 (1)- Belfast.

IRELAND, NORTHERN. Northern Ireland Assembly. Journals of the proceedings of the Assembly. sess., Jl/D 1973(v.1)- Belfast.

BARZILAY (DAVID) The British army in Ulster. Belfast, 1973. pp. 253.

BIGGS-DAVISON (JOHN ALEC) The hand is red. London, 1973. pp. 202.

DILLON (MARTIN) and LEHANE (DENIS CHARLES) Political murder in Northern Ireland. Harmondsworth, 1973. pp. 318.

HARBINSON (JOHN F.) The Ulster Unionist Party, 1882-1973: its development and organisation. Belfast, 1973. pp. 252. *bibliog.*

INSTITUTE FOR THE STUDY OF CONFLICT. Research Department. Ulster: politics and terrorism. London, 1973. pp. 20. (*Institute for the Study of Conflict. Conflict Studies. No.36*)

IRISH REPUBLICAN ARMY. Provisional IRA. Freedom struggle. [London, 1973]. pp. 101.

RUSSELL (JAMES LYON) Some aspects of the civic education of secondary schoolboys in Northern Ireland. [Belfast], Northern Ireland Community Relations Commission, 1973. fo. 34. (*Research Papers*)

IRELAND, NORTHERN. Northern Ireland Assembly. Proposed measures. sess., F 6 1974 (no.1)- Belfast.

ARTHUR (PAUL) The People's Democracy, 1968-1973. Belfast, 1974. pp. 159. *bibliog.*

MAGEE (JOHN) Northern Ireland: crisis and conflict. London, 1974. pp. 196. *bibliog.*

— — Research.

DARBY (JOHN P.) Register of research into the Irish conflict. [Belfast], Northern Ireland Community Relations Commission, [1972]. 1 pamphlet (unpaged). (*Research Papers*)

— Statistics, Vital.

MACAFEE (CHARLES HORNER GREER) and others. A report on an enquiry into maternal deaths in Northern Ireland, 1964-1967. Belfast, H.M.S.O., 1968. pp. 31.

IRIAN BARAT

— Economic conditions.

GARNAUT (ROSS) and MANNING (CHRIS) Irian Jaya: the transformation of a Melanesian economy. Canberra, 1974. pp. 116.

IRIAN JAYA.

See IRIAN BARAT.

IRISH IN THE UNITED STATES.

BIRMINGHAM (STEPHEN) Real lace: America's Irish rich. London, 1974. pp. 322.

IRISH QUESTION.

DAUNT (WILLIAM JOSEPH O'NEILL) Ireland and her agitators. Dublin, 1845. pp. 376.

SPEECHES from the dock; or, Protests of Irish patriotism; containing, with introductory sketches and biographical notices, speeches delivered after conviction by Theobald Wolfe Tone [and others]. Dublin, 1867. pp. 192.

IRISH QUESTION. (Cont.)

O'DONOVAN ROSSA (DIARMUID) Rossa's recollections, 1838-1898; [reprint of the first edition, New York 1898]; introduction by Sean O Luing and a new index. Shannon, [1972]. pp. 410. *bibliog.*

HAMILTON (IAIN) and MOSS (ROBERT) The spreading Irish conflict. London, 1971. pp. 27. *(Institute for the Study of Conflict. Conflict Studies. No. 17)*

SINN FEIN. Ard Fheis, Dublin, 1971. Report. [Dublin, 1971?]. pp. 38.

BRITISH AND IRISH COMMUNIST ORGANISATION. The economics of partition. rev ed. [london], 1972. pp. 83.

CONWAY (ANDY) There are no evil men: a fresh look at the Irish question and a suggested way forward: (a viewpoint from within the New Ireland Movement). Dublin, 1972. pp. 30.

NEW ULSTER MOVEMENT. Publications. 5. Two Irelands or one?. Belfast, 1972. pp. 14.

ROBB (JOHN DANIEL ALEXANDER) New Ireland: sell-out or opportunity?. [Dublin, 1972]. pp. 50.

SWEETMAN (MICHAEL) The common name of Irishman. [Belfast, 1972]. pp. 16.

AKENSON (DONALD HARMAN) The United States and Ireland. Cambridge, Mass., 1973. pp. 311. *bibliog.*

IRISH REPUBLICAN ARMY. Provisional IRA. Freedom struggle. [London, 1973]. pp. 101.

TONE (THEOBALD WOLFE) Freedom the Wolfe Tone way; ([compiled by] Sean Cronin and Richard Roche); with an introduction by Jack Bennett. Tralee, [1973]. pp. 242. *bibliog.*

BLEAKLEY (DAVID) Crisis in Ireland: inter-Irish and Anglo-Irish relations. London, 1974. pp. 32. *(Fabian Society. Research Series. [No.] 318)*

STEELE (EDWARD DAVID) Irish land and British politics: tenant-right and nationality, 1865-1870. London, 1974. pp. 367. *bibliog.*

IRISH REPUBLICAN ARMY.

BARRY (TOM) Guerilla days in Ireland. Tralee, 1962 repr. 1971. pp. 207. *First published in 1949.*

RYAN (DESMOND) Michael Collins and the invisible army; [a novel]. Tralee, 1968 repr. 1971. pp. 164. *First published in 1932 as The invisible army.*

IRISH REPUBLICAN ARMY. Provisional IRA. Freedom struggle. [London, 1973]. pp. 101.

IRISH SEA.

DOBSON (M.R.) and others. The geology of the south Irish Sea. London, 1973. pp. 35. *bibliog. (U.K. Institute of Geological Sciences. Reports. No. 73/11) 2 maps in end pocket.*

IRISH WORKERS' PARTY.

IRISH WORKERS' PARTY. Ireland her own: the programme of the...Party adopted at its fourth national conference, held in Dublin in March 1962. Dublin, 1963. pp. 26.

IRKUTSK (OBLAST')

— Statistics.

IRKUTSK (OBLAST'). Statisticheskoe Upravlenie. Narodnoe khoziaistvo Irkutskoi oblasti: statisticheskii sbornik.Irkutsk, 1972. pp. 268.

IRON AGE.

CUNLIFFE (BARRINGTON WINDSOR) Iron Age communities in Britain: an account of England, Scotland and Wales from the seventh century B.C. until the Roman conquest. London, 1974. pp. 418. *bibliog.*

IRON AND STEEL WORKERS

— Sweden.

SJÖBERG (STAFFAN) Arbetare vid Surahammars järnverk: löneoch anställningsförhållanden, 1936-1969. Stockholm, [1973]. pp. 252. *bibliog. (Uppsala. Universitet. Ekonomisk-Historiska Institution. Ekonomisk-Historiska Studier. 9) With English summary.*

IRON INDUSTRY AND TRADE

— European Economic Community countries.

EUROPEAN COMMUNITIES. Commission. Cahiers de Reconversion Industrielle . Bruxelles, 1963 in progress.

— — Accidents.

EUROPEAN COMMUNITIES. Statistical Office. Social Statistics. Luxembourg, 1960 in progress.

— Germany.

RIEDEL (MATTHIAS) Eisen und Kohle für das Dritte Reich: Paul Pleigers Stellung in der NS-Wirtschaft. Göttingen, [1973]. pp. 375. *bibliog.*

— Russia.

LELIUKHINA (NINA DMITRIEVNA) Ekonomicheskaia effektivnost' razmeshcheniia chernoi metallurgii: na primere Zapadnykh i Vostochnykh raionov SSSR. Moskva, 1973. pp. 296. *bibliog.*

— — Russia (RSFSR).

SERBINA (KSENIIA NIKOLAEVNA) Krest'ianskaia zhelezodelatel'naia promyshlennost' Severo- Zapadnoi Rossii XVI - pervoi poloviny XIX v. Leningrad, 1971. pp. 264.

— United Kingdom.

BRITISH IRON AND STEEL RESEARCH ASSOCIATION. Plant Engineering Division and Operational Research Section. Conference on works transport; held at Ashorne Hill...July 6th and 7th, 1954; chairman, W.F. Cartwright. London, [1954]. pp. 44.

IRON AND STEEL INDUSTRY TRAINING BOARD [U.K.]. Annual report. a., 1972/3- London. *Formerly included in the file of British Parliamentary Papers.*

MUTTON (NORMAN) The Foster family: a study of a Midland industrial dynasty 1786-1899; [Ph. D. (London) thesis]. [1974]. fo. 352. *bibliog. Typescript: unpublished. Offprints of three articles bound in at end. This thesis is the property of London University and may not be removed from the Library.*

NATIONAL ECONOMIC DEVELOPMENT OFFICE. Industrial review to 1977: iron and steel castings. London, 1974. pp. 68.

IRON ORES.

FRANCE. Direction de la Documentation. La Documentation Française. Notes et Etudes Documentaires. No. 3,707. Le minerai de fer dans le monde. Paris, 1970. pp. 27.

— Russia — Kazakstan.

MEL'NIKOV (NIKOLAI VASIL'EVICH) ed. Perspektivy razvitiia Kustanaiskogo zhelezorudnogo basseina. Alma-Ata, 1972. pp. 346. *bibliog.*

— Sweden.

FRITZ (MARTIN) German steel and Swedish iron ore, 1939-1945. Göteborg, 1974. pp. 137. *bibliog. (Göteborgs Universitet. Ekonomisk-Historiska Institutionen. Meddelanden. 29)*

IROQUOIS INDIANS.

WEAVER (SALLY M.) Medicine and politics among the Grand River Iroquois: a study of the non-conservatives. Ottawa, National Museums of Canada, 1972. pp. 182. *bibliog. (National Museum of Man [Canada]. Publications in Ethnology. No. 4) With French summary.*

IRRIGATION.

BERGMANN (HELLMUTH) Guide to the economic evaluation of irrigation projects. Paris, Organisation for Economic Co-operation and Development, 1973. pp. 133. *bibliog. (Problems of Development)*

— Brazil.

TAHAL CONSULTING ENGINEERS LTD. and SONDOTECNICA ENGENHARIA DE SOLOS S.A. Pluriannual irrigation programme (PPI)...; studies prepared by Consortium. [Brasilia], Ministerio do Interior, 1971. 13 vols.

— Ecuador.

ECUADOR. Junta Nacional de Planificacion y Coordinacion Economica. 1964. Plan general de desarrollo economico y social (version preliminar). Tomo 4. Las obras y servicios publicos economicos. Libro tercero. Regadio. Quito, [1964?]. 1 vol. (various pagings).

— Ghana.

FOOD AND AGRICULTURE ORGANIZATION. 1963. Final report on survey of the Lower Volta river flood plain. Rome, 1963. 5 vols. Microfilm: 1 reel.

— India.

REGIONAL FARM MANAGEMENT RESEARCH CENTRE [BANGALORE]. Studies in the economics of farm management: Bangalore district (Mysore): report[s] for the year[s] 1960-61 [and] 1961-62. [Delhi, Manager of Publications, 1972]. 2 pts.

— Oman.

WILKINSON (J.C.) The organisation of the Falaj irrigation system in Oman. Oxford, 1974. pp. 47. *bibliog. (Oxford. University. School of Geography. Research Papers. No 10)*

ISERLOHN

— Politics and government.

PESCHKE (KLAUS) Die Bedeutung der liberalen Parteien und der Sozialdemokratie für das politische Leben im Wahlkreis Altena-Iserlohn von der Reichsgründung 1871 bis zum Jahre 1890. [Altena, 1973]. pp. 150. *bibliog. (Verein Freunde der Burg Altena. Altenaer Beiträge. Neue Folge. Band 8)*

ISLANDS

— Finland.

HUSTICH (ILMARI) Finlands skärgård: en ekonomisk-geografisk översikt. Helsingfors, 1964. pp. 154. *bibliog. (Svenska Handelshögskolan. Ekonomi och Samhälle. Nr. 10)*

ISOKO (AFRICAN PEOPLE).

IKIME (OBARO) The Isoko people: a historical survey;...with a section on the Isoko language by B.O.W. Mafeni. Ibadan, 1972. pp. 166. *bibliog.*

ISOSTASY.

ANDREWS (JOHN THOMAS) ed. Glacial isostasy. Stroudsburg, Pa., [1974]. pp. 491. *bibliogs.*

ISRAEL

— Boundaries.

LESCH (ANN MOSELY) Israel's occupation of the West Bank: the first two years; [prepared for the Advanced Research Projects Agency]. Santa Monica, 1970. pp. 113. *bibliog. (Rand Corporation. Research Memoranda. 6296)*

— Civilization.

HOROWITZ (IRVING LOUIS) Israeli ecstasies, Jewish agonies. New York, 1974. pp. 244.

— Defences.

TAHTINEN (DALE R.) The Arab-Israeli military balance today. Washington, [1973]. pp. 37. *(American Enterprise Institute for Public Policy Research. Foreign Affairs Studies. 9)*

ABIR (MORDECHAI) Sharm al-Sheikh: Bab al-Mandeb: the strategic balance and Israel's southern approaches. Jerusalem, 1974. pp. 29. bibliog. (Hebrew University. Leonard Davis Institute for International Relations. Jerusalem Papers on Peace Problems. No. 5)

TAHTINEN (DALE R.) The Arab-Israeli military balance since October 1973. Washington, [1974]. pp. 43. (American Enterprise Institute for Public Policy Research. Foreign Affairs Studies. 11)

— Description and travel.

ISRAEL pocket library: geography; (compiled from material originally published in the Encyclopaedia Judaica). Jerusalem, [1973]. pp. 263. bibliog.

— Economic conditions.

ISRAEL pocket library: economy; (compiled from material originally published in the Encyclopaedia Judaica). Jerusalem, [1973]. pp. 306. bibliog.

— — Statistics.

BARON (RAPHAEL RAYMOND V.) Analysis of seasonality and trends in statistical series: methodology and applications in Israel. Jerusalem, 1973. 3 vols. (in 1). bibliog. (Israel. Central Bureau of Statistics. Technical Publications. No.39)

— Foreign relations.

ROBERTS (SAMUEL J.) Survival or hegemony?: the foundations of Israeli foreign policy. Baltimore, 1973. pp. 163. bibliog. (Johns Hopkins University. Washington Center of Foreign Policy Research. Studies in International Affairs. No. 20)

— — Arab countries.

LADEIKIN (VLADIMIR PETROVICH) Istochnik opasnogo krizisa: rol' sionizma v razzhiganii konflikta na Blizhnem Vostoke. Moskva, 1973. pp. 296.

— — France.

CROSBIE (SYLVIA KOWITT) A tacit alliance: France and Israel from Suez to the six day war. Princeton, [1974]. pp. 277. bibliog. (Columbia University. Middle East Institute. Modern Middle East Series. [No.] 7)

— — United States.

SNETSINGER (JOHN) Truman, the Jewish vote, and the creation of Israel. Stanford, [1974]. pp. 208. bibliog. (Stanford University. Hoover Institution on War, Revolution and Peace. Hoover Institution Studies. 39)

— History.

KIMCHE (JON) Palestine or Israel: the untold story of why we failed; 1917- 1923, 1967-1973. London, 1973. pp. 360. bibliog.

— Knesset — Elections.

ARIAN (ALAN) ed. The elections in Israel, 1969. Jerusalem, 1972. pp. 311.

— Military policy.

LESCH (ANN MOSELY) Israel's occupation of the West Bank: the first two years; [prepared for the Advanced Research Projects Agency]. Santa Monica, 1970. pp. 113. bibliog. (Rand Corporation. Research Memoranda. 6296)

HANDEL (MICHAEL I.) Israel's political-military doctrine. [Cambridge, Mass.], 1973. pp. 94. (Harvard University. Center for International Affairs. Occasional Papers in International Affairs. No. 30)

— Politics and government.

GERIES (SABRI) Democratic freedoms in Israel;...translated by Meric Dobson. Beirut, 1972. pp. 109. (Institute for Palestine Studies. Monograph Series. No. 30)

ELIZUR (YUVAL) and SALPETER (ELIAHU) Who rules Israel?. New York, [1973]. pp. 342.

AVI-HAI (AVRAHAM) Ben Gurion, state-builder: principles and pragmatism, 1948-1963. New York, [1974]. pp. 354. bibliog.

GHILAN (MAXIM) How Israel lost its soul. Harmondsworth, 1974. pp. 290.

— Territorial expansion.

ABIR (MORDECHAI) Sharm al-Sheikh: Bab al-Mandeb: the strategic balance and Israel's southern approaches. Jerusalem, 1974. pp. 29. bibliog. (Hebrew University. Leonard Davis Institute for International Relations. Jerusalem Papers on Peace Problems. No. 5)

ISRAEL AND THE DIASPORA.

GOLDSTEIN (ISRAEL) Israel at home and abroad, 1962-1972. Jerusalem, [1973]. pp. 422.

ISRAEL—ARAB CONFLICT, 1948— .

TUMA (ELIAS H.) Peacemaking and the immoral war: Arabs and Jews in the Middle East. New York, 1972. pp. 126.

FRANKEL (DAVE) and others. War in the Middle East: the socialist view: [selected articles appearing in the October 19 and 26, and November 2 and 9, 1973, issues of The Militant]. New York, [1973]. pp. 31.

ALLEN (Sir RICHARD HUGH SEDLEY) Imperialism and nationalism in the fertile crescent: sources and prospects of the Arab-Israeli conflict. New York, 1974. pp. 686. bibliog.

— Maps.

GILBERT (MARTIN) The Arab-Israeli conflict: its history in maps. London, 1974. pp. 101.

ISRAEL—ARAB WAR, 1967.

SCHLEIFER (ABDULLAH) The fall of Jerusalem. Nottingham, [1972]. pp. 247.

ISRAEL—ARAB WAR, 1973.

KOHLER (FOY D.) and others. The Soviet Union and the October 1973 Middle East War: the implications for detente. Miami, [1974]. pp. 131. (Miami (Florida). University. Center for Advanced International Studies. Monographs in International Affairs)

LAQUEUR (WALTER ZE'EV) Confrontation: the Middle East war and world politics. London, 1974. pp. 245.

LESSONS from the Arab-Israeli war; report of a seminar held at the Royal United Services Institute for Defence Studies on Wednesday, 30 January 1974. London, 1974. pp. 16.

PALIT (D.K.) Return to Sinai: the Arab-Israeli war, 1973. Salisbury, Wilts., [1974]. pp. 172.

PRITTIE (TERENCE CORNELIUS FARMER) The fourth Arab-Israeli war: the propaganda battle. London, [1974]. pp. 16. (World Jewish Congress. British Section. Noah Barou Memorial Lectures. 1973)

SUNDAY TIMES. Insight Team. Insight on the Middle East War. London, 1974. pp. 256.

ISRAEL INSTITUTE OF APPLIED SOCIAL RESEARCH.

GRATCH (HAYA) ed. Twenty-five years of social research in Israel: a review of the work of the Israel Institute of Applied Social Research, 1947-1971. Jerusalem, 1973. pp. 292. bibliog.

ITALIAN LANGUAGE

— Syntax.

KESSLER (CAROLYN) The acquisition of syntax in bilingual children. Washington, [1971]. pp. 109. bibliog.

ITALIAN NEWSPAPERS.

ONOFRI (NAZARIO SAURO) I giornali bolognesi nel ventennio fascista. [Bologna, 1972]. pp. 295.

BECHELLONI (GIOVANNI) Informazione e potere: la stampa quotidiana in Italia. Roma, 1974. pp. 316.

FUSAROLI (GAETANO) Giornali in Italia: cambiare per sopravvivere. Parma, 1974. pp. 345. bibliog. (Centro di Studi sul Giornalismo "Gino Pestelli". Comitato Scientifico. Studi e Ricerche sul Giornalismo. 6)

ITALIAN PERIODICALS.

GALANTE (SEVERINO) La politica del PCI e il Patto Atlantico: "Rinascita" 1946-'49. Padova, [1973]. pp. 257. (Padua. Università. Istituto di Scienze Storiche, and Centro di Studi e Documentazioni per la Storia Contemporanea e le Relazioni Internazionali. Collana. 1)

ITALIANS IN CANADA.

ZIEGLER (SUZANNE) Characteristics of Italian householders in metropolitan Toronto. Toronto, 1972. fo. 125. bibliog. (York University (Toronto). Institute for Behavioural Research. Ethnic Research Programme. Research Reports)

ITALIANS IN SWITZERLAND.

HAGEN (ECKEHART) Arbeitsmotive von Gastarbeitern: Ergebnisse einer Befragung schweizerischer und italienischer Arbeitskräfte in der Schweiz. Bern, [1973]. pp. 319. bibliog. (Hochschule St.Gallen für Wirtschafts- und Sozialwissenschaften. Schriftenreihe Betriebswirtschaft. Band 2)

HOFFMANN-NOWOTNY (HANS JOACHIM) Soziologie des Fremdarbeiterproblems: eine theoretische und empirische Analyse am Beispiel der Schweiz. Stuttgart, 1973. pp. 377. bibliog. With summaries in various languages.

ITALO—ETHIOPIAN WAR, 1935—1936.

CHIAVARELLI (EMILIA) L'opera della Marina italiana nella guerra italo-etiopica. Milano, 1969. pp. 170. bibliog. (Roma. Università. Istituto di Studi Storici e Politici. [Publications]. 18)

COFFEY (THOMAS M.) Lion by the tail: the story of the Italian-Ethiopian war. London, 1974. pp. 369. bibliog.

HARDIE (FRANK) The Abyssinian crisis. London, 1974. pp. 294. bibliog.

ITALY

— Appropriations and expenditures.

ITALY. Camera dei Deputati. Commissioni Permanenti. V. Bilancio. 1972. Problemi della spesa e della contabilità pubblica: indagine conoscitiva. [Rome], 1972. pp. 780. (Italy. Servizio Commissioni Parlamentari. Indagini Conoscitive e Documentazioni Legislative. 14)

— Army — History.

ITALY. Stato Maggiore Esercito. Ufficio Storico. 1971. Il Corpo italiano di liberazione aprile-settembre 1944: narrazione, documenti. 2nd ed. Roma, 1971. pp. 342.

— Civilization.

NICHOLS (PETER) Correspondent of The Times. Italia, Italia. London, 1973 repr. 1974. pp. 346.

— Colonies — History.

ZAGHI (CARLO) L'Africa nella coscienza europea e l'imperialismo italiano. Napoli, [1973]. pp. 576.

— Commercial treaties — Austria.

SCHOBER (ERNST GEORG) Das regionale Handelsabkommen Trentino-Südtirol, Nordtirol-Vorarlberg. Innsbruck, 1971. pp. 127. bibliog.

— Constitutional history.

GHISALBERTI (CARLO) Storia costituzionale d'Italia, 1849-1948. Roma, 1974. pp. 460.

— Constitutional law.

CONTINI (GIUSEPPE) La revisione costituzionale in Italia. Milano, 1971. pp. 341. (Cagliari. Università. Facoltà di Giurisprudenza. Pubblicazioni. Serie 1. vol. 10)

ITALY. (Cont.)

CHIARELLI (RAFFAELE) Gli organi della pianificazione economica. Milano, 1973. pp. 272. *(Florence. Università degli Studi di Firenze. Istituto di Diritto Costituzionale Italiano e Comparato. La Persona e la Comunità nella Problematica del Potere Politico. 14)*

— Defences.

ITALY. Ministero della Difesa. Bureau de Presse. 1966. La sécurité dans la liberté: note d'information sur le Ministère de la Défense et les forces armées italiennes. [Rome, 1966?]. pp. 123.

— Economic conditions.

BORDINI (M.) and others. Contratti '72 e crisi economica: ricerca effettuata dalla ISRIL Co-operativa. 2nd ed. Roma, 1972. pp. 170.

GRAZIANI (AUGUSTO) ed. L'economia italiana: 1945-1970: [a collection of readings]. Bologna, [1972]. pp. 396. *bibliog.*

EINAUDI (LUIGI) and MENICHELLA (DONATO) Fine dell'autarchia e miracolo economico, 1946-1959. Roma, [1973?]. pp. 551. *(Reprinted from Banca d'Italia, Assemblea generale ordinaria dei partecipanti, Relazioni del governatore)*

GAY (FRANÇOIS) and WAGRET (PAUL) L'économie de l'Italie. 4th ed. Paris, 1973. pp. 127. *bibliog.*

LAMONT (DOUGLAS F.) Managing foreign investment in southern Italy: US business in developing areas of the EEC;... with the special assistance of Robert Purtshert. New York, 1973. pp. 169. *bibliog.*

— Economic history.

FRANCE. Direction de la Documentation. La Documentation Française. Notes et Etudes Documentaires. No. 3,071. Le midi italien: situation et problèmes, 1950-1963. Paris, 1964. pp. 24.

CAPECELATRO (EDMONDO M.) and CARLO (ANTONIO) eds. Per la critica del sottosviluppo meridionale: antologia di scritti. Firenze, 1973. pp. 374.

GUERIN (DANIEL) Fascism and big business; (translated from the French). New York, 1973. pp. 318.

— — Sources.

MELIS (FEDERIGO) Documenti per la storia economica dei secoli XIII-XVI; con una nota di paleografia commerciale a cura di Elena Cecchi. Firenze, 1972. pp. 628. *(Istituto Internazionale di Storia Economica "F. Datini". Pubblicazioni. Serie 1: Documenti. 1)*

— Economic policy.

FRANCE. Direction de la Documentation. La Documentation Française. Notes et Etudes Documentaires. No. 3,071. Le midi italien: situation et problèmes, 1950-1963. Paris, 1964. pp. 24.

ITALY. Ministero del Bilancio e della Programmazione Economica. 1967. Programma di sviluppo economico per il quinquennio 1966-1970. Roma, 1967. pp. 254.

SOCIETA ITALIANA DEGLI ECONOMISTI. Riunione Scientifica, 7a, Bari, 1966. Caratteristiche e prospettive dello sviluppo economico italiano: [proceedings]. Milano, 1971. pp. 205. *bibliog.*

CUOCO (LEONARDO) Il processo di sviluppo di un'area sovrapopolata: il Mezzogiorno d'Italia. Milano, 1971. pp. 181. *bibliog. (Associazione per lo Sviluppo dell'Industria nel Mezzogiorno. Centro per gli Studi sullo Sviluppo Economico. Collana Francesco Giordani)*

BALLONI (VALERIANO) ed. Lezioni sulla politica economica in Italia; ([given in 1970 in the] Istituto Superiore di Studi Economici "Adriano Olivetti"). Milano, [1972]. pp. 414. *bibliogs.*

MARELLI (LUIGI) ed. Sviluppo e sottosviluppo nel Mezzogiorno d'Italia dal 1945 agli anni 70: [readings]. Napoli, [1972]. pp. 223. *bibliogs.*

ANNESI (MASSIMO) Nuove tendenze dell'intervento pubblico nel Mezzogiorno. Milano, 1973. pp. 232. *(Associazione per lo Sviluppo dell'Industria nel Mezzogiorno. Centro per gli Studi sullo Sviluppo Economico. Collana Francesco Giordani)*

CAPECELATRO (EDMONDO M.) and CARLO (ANTONIO) eds. Per la critica del sottosviluppo meridionale: antologia di scritti. Firenze, 1973. pp. 374.

CHIARELLI (RAFFAELE) Gli organi della pianificazione economica. Milano, 1973. pp. 272. *(Florence. Università degli Studi di Firenze. Istituto di Diritto Costituzionale Italiano e Comparato. La Persona e la Comunità nella Problematica del Potere Politico. 14)*

DEMOCRAZIA CRISTIANA. Convegno Nazionale di Studi, Perugia, 1972. I problemi dell'economia italiana, superamento della crisi e nuove prospettive di sviluppo sociale. Roma, [1973]. 3 vols. (in 1).

L'ECONOMIA italiana in un triennio difficile: [proceedings of three round tables held in 1971, 1972 and 1973]. Roma, [1973]. pp. 141. *(Movimento Gaetano Salvemini. Quaderni del Salvemini. 9/11)*

GAY (FRANÇOIS) and WAGRET (PAUL) L'économie de l'Italie. 4th ed. Paris, 1973. pp. 127. *bibliog.*

PARRILLO (FRANCESCO) Politica creditizia e stabilizzazione economica. Roma, 1974. pp. 134. *(Estratto dalla rivista Credito Popolare, NN. 3-4, 1974)*

— Emigration and immigration.

ITALY. Consiglio Nazionale dell'Economia e del Lavoro. 1970. Osservazioni e proposte sui problemi dell'emigrazione. Roma, 1970. pp. 317.

TOEPFER (LORE) Die Abwanderung deutschsprachiger Bevölkerung aus Südtirol nach 1955. Innsbruck, 1973. pp. 135. *bibliog.*

— Executive departments.

ITALY. Istituto Nazionale delle Assicurazioni. 1962. Le origini dell'Istituto Nazionale delle Assicurazioni: mostra grafica e documentaria allestita nella Sede dell' I.N.A. nel cinquantenario della legge 4 aprile 1912. n. 305. Roma, 1962. pp. [25].

ITALY. Ministero della Difesa. Bureau de Presse. 1966. La sécurité dans la liberté: note d'information sur le Ministère de la Défense et les forces armées italiennes. [Rome, 1966?]. pp. 123.

ITALY. Ragioneria Generale dello Stato. 1969. La Ragioneria Generale dello Stato: centenario, 1869-1969. Roma, 1969. pp. 196.

GALUPPINI (GINO) Il Ministero della Marina, 1863-1966. [Rome], Stato Maggiore della Marina, 1970. pp. 70. *(Rivista Marittima, Luglio-Agosto, 1970. Supplemento)*

— Foreign economic relations — United Kingdom.

CUGIS (CARLO DE) ed. Italia e Inghilterra un secolo fa: il nuovo corso nelle relazioni economiche; appendice al Catalogo della mostra tenuta in occasione della settimana brittanica a Milano, 9-17 ottobre 1965. Milano, 1968. pp. 547. *In English, Italian or French.*

— Foreign relations.

PERTICONE (GIACOMO) ed. La politica estera dell'Italia negli atti, documenti e discussioni parlamentari dal 1861 al 1914. Roma, 1971 in progress.

FELICE (RENZO DE) ed. L'Italia fra tedeschi e alleati: la politica estera fascista e la seconda guerra mondiale. Bologna, [1973]. pp. 301.

MORI (RENATO) La politica estera di Francesco Crispi, 1887-1891. Roma, 1973. pp. 286.

— — Catholic Church.

GARZIA (ITALO) Il negoziato diplomatico per i Patti Lateranensi. Milano, 1974. pp. 127. *(Politico, Il. Quaderni. n.13) With English summary.*

— — Treaties.

CATHOLIC CHURCH. Treaties. 1929-1954. Patti Lateranensi, convenzioni e accordi successivi fra il Vaticano e l'Italia fino al 31 dicembre (1954). [Vatican City], 1955-72. 2 vols.(in 1).

— — Austria.

SIEGLER (HEINRICH) Die österreichisch-italienische Einigung über die Regelung des Südtirolkonflikts. Bonn, [1970]. pp. 35.

— — Malta.

SMITH (HARRISON) Mussolini and Strickland. Malta, 1974. pp. 42. *(Reprinted from Scientia, vol. 36, 1973)*

— — United Kingdom.

PETRICIOLI (MARTA) L'occupazione italiana del Caucaso: "un ingrato servizio" da rendere a Londra. Milano, 1972. pp. 93. *(Politico, Il. Quaderni. n.10) With English summary.*

— History — Sources.

ITALY. Camera dei Deputati. Segretariato Generale. Archivio Storico. 1967. Comitati segreti sulla condotta della guerra, giugno - dicembre 1917. [Roma, 1967]. pp. 249.

PERTICONE (GIACOMO) ed. La politica estera dell'Italia negli atti, documenti e discussioni parlamentari dal 1861 al 1914. Roma, 1971 in progress.

BEALES (DEREK EDWARD DAWSON) The risorgimento and the unification of Italy: [with selected historical documents]. London, 1971. pp. 176.

SONNINO (SIDNEY) Barone. Diario, 1866-(1922); a cura di Benjamin F. Brown ([and] Pietro Pastorelli). Bari, 1972. 3 vols. *(Opera Omnia di Sidney Sonnino)*

VITALE (ELIGIO) La riforma degli istituti di emissione e gli 'scandali bancari' in Italia, 1892-1896. Roma, Archivio Storico, 1972. 3 vols. (in 2).

— — 1789—1900.

MOSCATI (RUGGERO) Aspetti e momenti dell'Italia moderna. Assisi, [1973]. pp. 175.

— — 1789—1815.

NAPOLEONE e l'Italia: (atti del convegno...) Roma, 8-13 ottobre 1969. Roma, 1973 in progress. *(Accademia Nazionale dei Lincei. Problemi Attuali di Scienza e di Cultura. Quaderni. N. 179)*

— — 1800—1899.

GABRIELE (MARIANO) and FRIZ (GIULIANO) La flotta come strumento di politica nei primi decenni dello stato unitario italiano. Roma, Ufficio Storico della Marina Militare, 1973. pp. 367. *bibliog.*

— — 1815—1870.

BEALES (DEREK EDWARD DAWSON) The risorgimento and the unification of Italy: [with selected historical documents]. London, 1971. pp. 176.

PERUTA (FRANCO DELLA) Mazzini e i rivoluzionari italiani: il "partito d'azione", 1830- 1845. Milano, 1974. pp. 469.

— — 1849—1870.

LIBERTI (EGIDIO) ed. Tecniche della guerra partigiana nel Risorgimento: testi di autori mazziniani. [Firenze, 1972]. pp. 651. *(Centro per la Storia della Tecnica in Italia. Pubblicazioni. Sezione 1. vol.3)*

— — 1914—1945.

TRANFAGLIA (NICOLA) Dallo stato liberale al regime fascista: problemi e ricerche. Milano, 1973. pp. 297.

— — 1943—1947, Allied occupation.

SEROVA (OL'GA VASIL'EVNA) Italiia i antigitlerovskaia koalitsiia, 1943-1945. Moskva, 1973. pp. 272. *bibliog.*

— History, Naval.

CHIAVARELLI (EMILIA) L'opera della Marina italiana nella guerra italo-etiopica. Milano, 1969. pp. 170. *bibliog. (Roma. Università. Istituto di Studi Storici e Politici. [Publications]. 18)*

— **Industries.**

ITALY. Cassa per Opere Straordinarie di Pubblico Interesse nell'Italia Meridionale. 1963. Summary of measures to promote industrialization in southern Italy. Rome, 1963. pp. 47.

CONFEDERAZIONE GENERALE DELL'INDUSTRIA ITALIANA. Servizio Studi e Rilevazioni. Collana di Studi e Documentazione. 31. Prime indicazioni sugli interventi dell'industria privata a difesa dell'ambiente; (a cura di Francesco Galli and others). Roma, 1973. pp. 216.

RUGAFIORI (PARIDE) and others. Il triangolo industriale tra ricostruzione e lotta di classe, 1945-1948. Milano, 1974. pp. 308.

— **Intellectual life.**

CASTRIS (ARCANGELO LEONE DE) Il decadentismo italiano: Svevo, Pirandello, D'Annunzio. Bari, [1974]. pp. 262.

— **Navy.**

GALUPPINI (GINO) Il Ministero della Marina, 1863-1966. [Rome], Stato Maggiore della Marina, 1970. pp. 70. (*Rivista Marittima, Luglio-Agosto, 1970. Supplemento*)

ITALY. Marine Militare. Ufficio Storico. 1972- . La Marina italiana nella seconda guerra mondiale. vol. 21. L'organizzazione della Marina durante il conflitto: compilatore: Giuseppe Fioravanzo. Roma, 1972 in progress.

GABRIELE (MARIANO) and FRIZ (GIULIANO) La flotta come strumento di politica nei primi decenni dello stato unitario italiano. Roma, Ufficio Storico della Marina Militare, 1973. pp. 367. *bibliog.*

— **Officials and employees.**

MISSORI (MARIO) Governi, alte cariche dello Stato e prefetti del regno d'Italia. Roma, 1973. pp. 579. (*Italy. Archivi di Stato. Fonti e Sussidi. 3*)

— **Parliament.**

MANNINO (ARMANDO) Indirizzo politico e fiducia nei rapporti tra governo e parlamento. Milano, 1973. pp. 428. *bibliog.*

— — **Committees.**

BRUNO (FERNANDA) Le commissioni parlamentari in sede politica. Milano, 1972. pp. 306. (*Rome. Università. Istituto di Studi Giuridici. Pubblicazioni. Serie 5. n.12*)

— — **History.**

CERBONE (CARLO) ed. L'antiparlamentarismo italiano, 1870-1919. Roma, [1972]. pp. 110. *bibliog.*

ARALDI (VINICIO) Camicie nere a Montecitorio: storia parlamentare dell'avvento del fascismo. Milano, 1974. pp. 371. *bibliog.*

— **Politics and government.**

FISICHELLA (DOMENICO) L'alternativa rischiosa. Firenze, [1973]. pp. 92.

NICHOLS (PETER) Correspondent of The Times. Italia. London, 1973 repr. 1974. pp. 346.

— — **1799—1900.**

FERRARI (GIUSEPPE) Political writer. Scritti politici;...a cura di Silvia Rota Ghibaudi. Torina, 1973. pp. 117. *bibliog.*

— — **1849—1870.**

CONGRESSO CELEBRATIVO DEL CENTENARIO DELLE LEGGI AMMINISTRATIVE DI UNIFICAZIONE. L'unificazione amministrativa ed i suio protagonisti; a cura di Feliciano Benvenuti e Gianfranco Miglio; (atti del congresso, etc.). Milano, 1969. pp. 461.

— — **1870—1915.**

SONNINO (SIDNEY) Barone. Scritti e discorsi extraparlamentari, 1870(-1920); a cura di Benjamin F. Brown. Bari, 1972. 2 vols. (*Opera Omnia di Sidney Sonnino*)

MANZOTTI (FERNANDO) Partiti e gruppi politici dal Risorgimento al fascismo. Firenze, 1973. pp. 456. *bibliog.*

PARETO (VILFREDO) Oeuvres complètes; publiées sous la direction de Giovanni Busino. Genève, 1964 in progress. *bibliog.*

— — **1900—1999.**

CEREJA (FEDERICO) Intellettuali e politica dall'epoca giolittiana all'affermazione del fascismo. Torino, [1973]. pp. 167.

SALVEMINI (GAETANO) The origins of fascism in Italy: [based on a lecture course at Harvard and written in 1942]; edited... by Roberto Vivarelli. New York, [1973]. pp. 445. *bibliog.*

— — **1914—1945.**

MUSSOLINI (BENITO) Corrispondenza inedita; a cura di Duilio Susmel. Milano, [1972]. pp. 263.

CLARK (MARTIN) The failure of revolution in Italy, 1919-1920. Reading, 1973. pp. 34. (*Reading. University. Department of Italian Studies. Centre for the Advanced Study of Italian Society. Occasional Papers. No. 5*)

CURIEL (EUGENIO) Scritti, 1935-1945; a cura di Filippo Frassati. Roma, 1973. 2 vols.

ZINI (ZINO) La tragedia del proletariato in Italia: diario 1914-1926; [edited by] Giancarlo Bergami. Milano, 1973. pp. 275. *bibliog.*

— — **1922—1945.**

BOCCA (GIORGIO) L'Italia fascista. Milano, 1973. pp. 141. *bibliog.*

FEO (ITALO DE) Diario politico, 1943-1948. Milano, 1973. pp. 536.

LANDUYT (ARIANE) Le sinistre e l'Aventino. Milano, [1973]. pp. 495. (*Istituto Nazionale per la Storia del Movimento di Liberazione in Italia. [Publications. 5]*)

SARTI (ROLAND) ed. The ax within: Italian fascism in action. New York, 1974. pp. 278. *bibliog.*

UVA (BRUNO) La nascita dello stato corporativo e sindacale fascista. Assisi, [1974]. pp. 302.

— — **1945— .**

EARLE (JOHN) Journalist. Report on Italy. London, 1972. pp. 15. (*Institute for the Study of Conflict. Conflict Studies. No. 19*)

TEDESCHI (MARIO) Destra nazionale: sintesi di una politica nuova. Milano, [1972]. pp. 183.

AMENDOLA (GIORGIO) Fascismo e Mezzogiorno. Roma, [1973]. pp. 210.

FARNETI (PAOLO) ed. Il sistema politico italiano: (testi di A. Bagnasco [and others]. Bologna, [1973]. pp. 508.

FEO (ITALO DE) Diario politico, 1943-1948. Milano, 1973. pp. 536.

MANNINO (ARMANDO) Indirizzo politico e fiducia nei rapporti tra governo e parlamento. Milano, 1973. pp. 428. *bibliog.*

TAMBURRANO (GIUSEPPE) Storia e cronaca del centro-sinistra. 3rd ed. Milano, 1973. pp. 380.

— **Population.**

BARBAGALLO (FRANCESCO) Lavoro ed esodo nel sud, 1861-1971. Napoli, [1973]. pp. 267.

— **Presidents.**

VALENTINO (NINO) Il Presidente: elezione e poteri del capo dello stato. [Rome, 1973]. pp. 189.

— — **Staff.**

OCCHIOCUPO (NICOLA) Il Segretariato generale della Presidenza della Repubblica. Milano, 1973. pp. 441. *bibliog.* (*Parma. Università. Facoltà di Giurisprudenza. Pubblicazioni. 30*)

— **Relations (general) with the United Kingdom.**

INGHILTERRA e Italia nel '900: atti del convegno di Bagni di Lucca, ottobre 1972. Firenze, 1973. pp. 317.

— **Rural conditions.**

BOLAFFI (GUIDO) and VAROTTI (ADRIANO) Agricoltura capitalistica e classi sociali in Italia, 1948-1970. Bari, [1973]. pp. 323. *bibliog.*

— **Social history.**

SEMINARIO DI STORIA CONTEMPORANEA, 8', . 1972. Fascismo e società italiana; [papers] a cura di Guido Quazza. Torino, [1973]. pp. 253.

BURKE (PETER) Historian. Tradition and innovation in renaissance Italy: a sociological approach. [London], 1974. pp. 413. *Corrected paperback edition of Culture and society in renaissance Italy, 1420-1540.*

— **Social policy.**

BEVILACQUA (PIERO) Critica dell'ideologia meridionalistica: Salvemini, Dorso, Gramsci. Padova, [1972]. pp. 124.

IVANO—FRANKOVSK (OBLAST').

RADIANS'KE Prykarpattia: dovidnyk-putivnyk. Uzhhorod, 1969. pp. 240. *With English summary and captions.*

IVANOVO (OBLAST')

— **Statistics.**

IVANOVO (OBLAST'). Statisticheskoe Upravlenie. Ivanovskaia oblast' za 50 let: statisticheskii sbornik. Ivanovo, 1967. pp. 278.

IVORY COAST.

FRANCE. Direction de la Documentation. La Documentation Française. Notes et Etudes Documentaires. Nos. 3,989-3, 990. La République de Côte-d'Ivoire. [Paris], 1973. pp. 55. *bibliog.*

— **Economic conditions.**

AUTORITE POUR L'AMENAGEMENT DE LA REGION DU SUD-OUEST [IVORY COAST]. Esquisse du schéma directeur d'aménagement de la région du Sud-Ouest. [Abidjan?], 1970. 1 vol. (various pagings).

AUTORITE POUR L'AMENAGEMENT DE LA REGION DU SUD-OUEST [IVORY COAST]. Le sud-ouest ivoirien: effort de développement. [Abidjan?], 1970. pp. 149.

EDIAFRIC - SERVICE. Dictionnaire économique et politique de la Côte d'Ivoire. Paris, [1973]. pp. 201. (*Bulletin de l'Afrique Noire. Numéro Spécial*)

— **Economic policy.**

AUTORITE POUR L'AMENAGEMENT DE LA REGION DU SUD-OUEST [IVORY COAST]. Esquisse du schéma directeur d'aménagement de la région du Sud-Ouest. [Abidjan?], 1970. 1 vol. (various pagings).

AUTORITE POUR L'AMENAGEMENT DE LA REGION DU SUD-OUEST [IVORY COAST]. Le sud-ouest ivoirien: effort de développement. [Abidjan?], 1970. pp. 149.

AUTORITE POUR L'AMENAGEMENT DE LA REGION DU SUD-OUEST [IVORY COAST]. Note de présentation sur le développement de la région du Sud-Ouest et l'opération San Pédro. [Abidjan?], 1970. fo. 28.

IVORY COAST. (Cont.)

FRANCE. Office de la Recherche Scientifique et Technique Outre-Mer. Centre de Petit-Bassam. Section Economie. 1971. Problèmes posés par le développement à base régionale en Côte d'Ivoire. [Abidjan?], 1971. fo. 76. (*France. Office de la Recherche Scientifique et Technique Outre-Mer. Sciences Humaines. Vol. 4. No. 2*)

FRANCE. Office de la Recherche Scientifique et Technique Outre-Mer. Centre de Petit-Bassam. Section Economie. 1971. L'analyse économique spatiale: méthodes et indicateurs. [Abidjan, 1971]. fo. 47. (*France. Office de la Recherche Scientifique et Technique Outre-Mer. Sciences Humaines. Vol. 4. No. 3*)

IVORY COAST. Ministère du Plan. 1972. Plan quinquennal de développement économique, social et culturel, 1971-1975. [Abidjan?, 1972?]. pp. 465.

— Politics and government.

EDIAFRIC - SERVICE. Dictionnaire économique et politique de la Côte d'Ivoire. Paris, [1973]. pp. 201. (*Bulletin de l'Afrique Noire. Numéro Spécial*)

COHEN (MICHAEL A.) Urban policy and political conflict in Africa: a study of the Ivory Coast. Chicago, [1974]. pp. 262. *bibliog.*

— Rural conditions.

ANCEY (G.) Exploitations agricoles en pays Diamala - Djimini: aspects de la vie rurale. [Abidjan], 1969. pp. 177. (*France. Office de la Recherche Scientifique et Technique Outre-Mer. Sciences Humaines. Vol. 2. No. 6*)

— Social policy.

IVORY COAST. Ministère du Plan. 1972. Plan quinquennal de développement économique, social et culturel, 1971-1975. [Abidjan?, 1972?]. pp. 465.

JACKSON (ANDREW) President of the United States.

SNYDER (CHARLES McCOOL) The Jacksonian heritage: Pennsylvania politics, 1833-1848. Harrisburg, Pennsylvania Historical and Museum Commission, 1958. pp. 256. *bibliog.*

JACKSON (Sir GEOFFREY HOLT SEYMOUR).

JACKSON (Sir GEOFFREY HOLT SEYMOUR) People's prison. London, 1973. pp. 222.

JACOBINS.

MALLETT (MARC GEORGE) La politique financière des Jacobins. Paris, 1913. pp. 449. *bibliog.*

KENNEDY (MICHAEL L.) The Jacobin Club of Marseilles, 1790-1794. Ithaca, 1973. pp. 245. *bibliog.*

STEINER (GERHARD) Jakobinerschauspiel und Jakobinertheater. Stuttgart, [1973]. pp. 336. *bibliog.*

JAKSCH (WENZEL).

BACHSTEIN (MARTIN K.) Wenzel Jaksch und die sudetendeutsche Sozialdemokratie. München, 1974. pp. 306. *bibliog.* (*Ludwigshafen. Collegium Carolinum. Veröffentlichungen. Band 29*)

JAMAICA

— Politics and government.

STONE (CARL) Stratification and political change in Trinidad and Jamaica; [revised version of a paper presented at the meeting of the American Political Science Association, Los Angeles, 1970]. Beverly Hills, Calif., [1972]. pp. 39.

FONER (NANCY) Status and power in rural Jamaica: a study of educational and political change. New York, [1973]. pp. 172. *bibliog.*

MANLEY (MICHAEL) The politics of change: a Jamaican testament. London, 1974. pp. 223.

— Population.

ROSEN (ROBERT C.) Law and population growth in Jamaica. Medford, Mass., 1973. pp. 44. (*Tufts University. Fletcher School of Law and Diplomacy. Law and Population Monograph Series. No.10*)

— Race question.

STONE (CARL) Class, race and political behaviour in urban Jamaica. [Mona], 1973. pp. 188. *bibliog.*

— Rural conditions.

FONER (NANCY) Status and power in rural Jamaica: a study of educational and political change. New York, [1973]. pp. 172. *bibliog.*

JAPAN

— Civilization.

ABEGG (LILY) Japans Traum vom Musterland: der neue Nipponismus. München, [1973]. pp. 258.

— Commerce.

WHITE PAPER ON INTERNATIONAL TRADE, JAPAN; [pd. by] Japan External Trade Organization. a., 1972 [24th]- [Tokyo].

MUELLER-HILLEBRAND (VEIT) Das Vordringen der japanischen Konkurrenz auf den Weltmärkten im Vergleich zum deutschen Export. Nürnberg, 1972. pp. 337, xxii. (*Erlangen. Universität. Institut für Exportforschung. Berichte*)

FUKUDA (HARUKO) Japan and world trade: the years ahead. Farnborough, [1973]. pp. 155.

WOODTLI (ROBERT) Le Japon et la conquête minérale. Lausanne, 1973. pp. 170. *bibliog.* (*Lausanne. Université. Centre de Recherches Européennes. Publications. 5. L'Europe Face à la Concurrence Internationale*)

DISTRIBUTION ECONOMICS INSTITUTE OF JAPAN. Outline of Japanese distribution structures:... 1973-74: enlarged edition. Tokyo, [1974]. pp. 251. *bibliog.*

— — Portugal.

MOURA (CARLOS FRANCISCO) Macau e o comercio portuguûes com a China e o Japão nos seculos XVI e XVII: as viagens da China e do Japão; a nau do trato; as galeotas. Macau, Imprensa Nacional, 1973. pp. 35. *bibliog.* *Separata dos no. 1 do vol. vii do Boletim do Instituto Luis de Camões.*

— Commercial policy.

FUKUDA (HARUKO) Japan and world trade: the years ahead. Farnborough, [1973]. pp. 155.

— Defences.

WILLIAMS (SHELTON L.) Nuclear nonproliferation in international politics: the Japanese case. Denver, 1971-1972. pp. 74. (*Denver. University. Social Science Foundation and Graduate School of International Studies. Monograph Series in World Affairs. vol.9. no.3*)

EMMERSON (JOHN K.) and HUMPHREYS (LEONARD A.) Will Japan rearm?: a study in attitudes. Washington, D.C., 1973. pp. 165. (*American Enterprise Institute for Public Policy Research and Stanford University. Hoover Institution on War, Revolution and Peace. AEI-Hoover Policy Studies. 9*)

— Economic conditions.

The WORLD in 2000: repo[r]t of a JERC international conference. Tokyo, 1967. pp. 285. (*Japan Economic Research Center. Center Papers. No.8*)

CARDUCCI (GIORGIO) and PADOA-SCHIOPPA (TOMMASO) Rapporto sull'economia giapponese. [Rome, 1973]. pp. 107. *bibliog.* (*Ente per gli Studi Monetari, Bancari, e Finanziari Luigi Einaudi. Quaderni di Ricerche. N. 12*)

KAHN (HERMAN) The emerging Japanese superstate: challenge and response; [paperback edition of work first published in the United States in 1970]. Harmondsworth, 1973. pp. 318. *bibliog.*

NISHIYAMA (CHIAKI) and ALLEN (GEORGE CYRIL) The price of prosperity: lessons from Japan. London, 1974. pp. 66. *bibliog.* (*Institute of Economic Affairs. Hobart Papers. 58*)

— Economic history.

HAUSER (WILLIAM B.) Economic institutional change in Tokugawa Japan: Osaka and Kinai cotton trade. London, 1974. pp. 239. *bibliog.*

YAMAMURA (KOZO) A study of Samurai income and entrepreneurship: quantitative analyses of economic and social aspects of the Samurai in Tokugawa and Meiji Japan. Cambridge, Mass., 1974. pp. 243. *bibliog.* (*Harvard University. East Asian Research Center. Harvard East Asian Series. No.76*)

— Economic policy.

FRANCE. Direction de la Documentation. La Documentation Française. Notes et Etudes Documentaires. No. 3,431. Le plan économique japonais à moyen terme, 1964-68: [traduction intégrale de Medium-term economic plan, publié par Economic Planning Agency du gouvernement japonais]. Paris, 1967. pp. 38.

NISHIYAMA (CHIAKI) and ALLEN (GEORGE CYRIL) The price of prosperity: lessons from Japan. London, 1974. pp. 66. *bibliog.* (*Institute of Economic Affairs. Hobart Papers. 58*)

— Foreign economic relations.

LANGDON (FRANK C.) Japan's foreign policy. Vancouver, [1973]. pp. 231. *bibliog.*

ABE (ISAO) Le Japon et sa politique économique internationale; conférence. Bruxelles, 1974. pp. 24. (*Société Royale d'Economie Politique de Belgique. [Publications]. No. 377*)

— — Asia, Southeast.

NEW directions in the international relations of southeast Asia: economic relations; papers presented at a conference organized by the Institute of Southeast Asian Studies; edited by Lee Soo Ann. Singapore, 1973. pp. 133. *bibliog.*

— — United States.

UNITED STATES-JAPAN ECONOMIC CONFERENCE, WASHINGTON, D.C., 1973. Perspectives on U.S.-Japan economic relations; [proceedings of the conference sponsored by] United States-Japan Trade Council; edited by Allen Taylor. Cambridge, Mass., [1973]. pp. 274.

— Foreign relations.

KAHN (HERMAN) The emerging Japanese superstate: challenge and response; [paperback edition of work first published in the United States in 1970]. Harmondsworth, 1973. pp. 318. *bibliog.*

LANGDON (FRANK C.) Japan's foreign policy. Vancouver, [1973]. pp. 231. *bibliog.*

PETROV (DMITRII VASIL'EVICH) Iaponiia v mirovoi politike. Moskva, 1973. pp. 295. *bibliog.*

MORLEY (JAMES WILLIAM) ed. Japan's foreign policy, 1868-1941: a research guide. New York, 1974. pp. 618. *bibliog.* (*Columbia University. East Asian Institute. Studies*)

— — Treaties.

ADAMS (LOUIS JEROLD) Theory, law and policy of contemporary Japanese treaties. Dobbs Ferry, N.Y., 1974. pp. 270. *bibliog.*

— — Atlantic, The.

JAPAN and the Atlantic world: [papers of a conference organized by the Atlantic Institute in 1972; edited by Curt Gasteyger]. Farnborough, Hants, [1972]. pp. 88. (*Atlantic Institute. Atlantic Papers. 1972.3*)

— — China.

BAMBA (NOBUYA) Japanese diplomacy in a dilemma: new light on Japan's China policy, 1924-1929. Vancouver, 1972. pp. 440. *bibliog.*

KATO (SHUICHI) The Japan-China phenomenon: conflict or compatibility; ... translated from the Japanese by David Chibbett. London, 1974. pp. 103.

— — New Zealand.

LISSINGTON (MARY PATRICIA) New Zealand and Japan, 1900-1941. Wellington, Government Printer, 1972. pp. 206, 1 map. *bibliog.*

— — United States.

DISCORD in the Pacific: challenges to the Japanese-American alliance: [advance reading for the third Japanese-American Assembly, Shimoda, 1972]; edited by Henry Rosovsky. Washington, D.C., 1972. pp. 246.

HERZOG (JAMES H.) Closing the open door: American-Japanese diplomatic negotiations, 1936-1941. Annapolis, Md., [1973]. pp. 295. *bibliog.*

PEARL Harbor as history: Japanese-American relations, 1931-1941; (essays... presented at a binational conference held at Lake Kawaguchi, Japan... 1969); edited by Dorothy Borg and Shumpei Okamoto. New York, 1973. pp. 801. *(Columbia University. East Asian Institute. Studies)*

— Government publications — Bibliography.

JAPAN. National Diet. Library. 1959. List of Japanese government publications in European languages; revised and enlarged edition...; 1945-1958. Tokyo, 1959. pp. 82,9.

— History.

HALL (JOHN WHITNEY) and MASS (JEFFREY P.) eds. Medieval Japan: essays in institutional history. New Haven, 1974. pp. 269.

— Industries.

ORGANISATION FOR ECONOMIC CO-OPERATION AND DEVELOPMENT. Industry Committee. 1972. The industrial policy of Japan. Paris, 1972. pp. 195.

— — Statistics.

JAPAN. Establishment Census, 1972. 1972 establishment census of Japan. [Tokyo, 1973] in progress. :

— Navy.

DENLINGER (HARRY SUTHERLAND) and GARY (CHARLES BINFORD) War in the Pacific: a study of navies, peoples and battle problems; [reprint of work first published in New York in 1936]. New York, 1970. pp. 338.

FRANCE. Direction de la Documentation. La Documentation Française. Notes et Etudes Documentaires. Nos. 3,778-3, 779. Les activités maritimes du Japon; [by] Albert Boyer. Paris, 1971. pp. 52.

— Politics and government.

HALL (JOHN WHITNEY) and MASS (JEFFREY P.) eds. Medieval Japan: essays in institutional history. New Haven, 1974. pp. 269.

RICHARDSON (BRADLEY M.) The political culture of Japan. Berkeley, [1974]. pp. 271. *bibliog.*

— Population.

JAPAN. Institute of Population Problems. Anjrnports. a., current issues only kept. Tokyo. *In Japanese with English summaries.*

— Relations (general) with China.

KATO (SHUICHI) The Japan-China phenomenon: conflict or compatibility; ... translated from the Japanese by David Chibbett. London, 1974. pp. 103.

— Relations (military) with Burma.

YOON (WON Z.) Japan's scheme for the liberation of Burma: the role of the Minami Kikan and the "thirty comrades". Athens, Oh., 1973. fo. 54. *bibliog. (Ohio University. Center for International Studies. Papers in International Studies. Southeast Asia Series. No. 27)*

— Religion.

RAJANA (EIMI WATANABE) A sociological study of new religious movements: Chilean Pentecostalism and Japanese new religions; [Ph.D.(London) thesis]. 1974. fo. 288. *bibliog. Typescript: unpublished. This thesis is the property of London University and may not be removed from the Library.*

— Social conditions.

ABEGG (LILY) Japans Traum vom Musterland: der neue Nipponismus. München, [1973]. pp. 258.

NAKANE (CHIE) Japanese society. rev. ed. Harmondsworth, 1973. pp. 162.

— Social policy.

FRANCE. Direction de la Documentation. La Documentation Française. Notes et Etudes Documentaires. No. 3,431. Le plan économique japonais à moyen terme, 1964-68: [traduction intégrale de Medium-term economic plan, publié par Economic Planning Agency du gouvernement japonais]. Paris, 1967. pp. 38.

JAPANESE IN BRAZIL.

THIAGO CINTRA (JOSE) La migracion japonesa en Brasil, 1908-1958. Mexico, 1971. pp. 116 (4 fold.maps). *(Mexico City. Colegio de Mexico. Jornadas. 70)*

JAPANESE IN THE UNITED STATES.

CONRAT (MAISIE) and CONRAT (RICHARD) eds. Executive order 9066: the internment of 110,000 Japanese Americans: [photographs taken by Dorothea Lange and others].Cambridge, Mass., 1972. pp. 120.

JAUREGUI (ARTURO).

HAWKINS (CARROLL) Two democratic labor leaders in conflict: the Latin American revolution and the role of the workers. Lexington, Mass., [1973]. pp. 140. *bibliog.*

JAVA

— Social history.

KARTODIRDJO (SARTONO) Protest movements in rural Java: a study of agrarian unrest in the nineteenth and early twentieth centuries. Singapore, 1973. pp. 229. *bibliog.*

JENGHIS KHAN, Great Khan of the Moguls.

HAMBIS (LOUIS) Gengis-Khan. Paris, 1973. pp. 128. *bibliog.*

JERUSALEM

— History.

SCHLEIFER (ABDULLAH) The fall of Jerusalem. Nottingham, [1972]. pp. 247.

— — 1099—1244, Latin Kingdom.

RILEY-SMITH (JONATHAN) The feudal nobility and the Kingdom of Jerusalem, 1174-1277. London, 1973. pp. 351. *bibliog.*

— International status.

BLUM (YEHUDA ZVI) The juridical status of Jerusalem. Jerusalem, 1974. pp. 32. *(Hebrew University. Leonard Davis Institute for International Relations. Jerusalem Papers on Peace Problems. 2)*

JESUITS IN LATVIA.

DOROSHENKO (VASILII VASIL'EVICH) Myza i rynok: khoziaistvo Rizhskoi iezuitskoi kollegii na rubezhe XVI i XVII vv. Riga, 1973. pp. 187. *With English summary.*

JEWISH—ARAB RELATIONS.

INTERNATIONAL DOCUMENTS ON PALESTINE; [pd. by] Institute for Palestine Studies [and] the University of Kuwait. a., 1968 [2nd]- Beirut.

AUSTRALIA. Parliament. Joint Committee on Foreign Affairs. 1969. Report... on the Middle East situation. in AUSTRALIA. Parliament. Parliamentary papers, 1969, vol.6.

HEN-TOV (JACOB) The Communist International, the Palestine Communist Party, and the political unrest in Palestine in 1929;...paper submitted to the conference on "The Middle East in revolution"...April 1970. n.p., [1970?]. pp. 33.

SEARCH for peace in the Middle East; (a study prepared by a workers party, initiated by the American Friends Service Committee and the Canadian Friends Service Committee, and acting in association with the Friends Service Council, London, the Friends World Committee for Consultation and the Friends Peace and International Relations Committee, London). London, 1970. pp. 72.

CATTAN (HENRY) The Palestine problem in a nutshell. Beirut, [1971]. pp. 35. *(Palestine Research Center. Palestine Essays. No. 26)*

SAYEGH (FAYEZ A.) and SOUKKARY (SOHAIR A.) Palestine: concordance of United Nations resolutions 1967-1971.New York, 1971. pp. 93.

TESSIER (ARLETTE) Gaza. Beirut, [1971]. pp. 36. *(Palestine Research Center. Palestine Essays. No. 27)*

CARRE (OLIVIER) L'idéologie palestinienne de résistance: analyse de textes, 1964-1970. Paris, 1972. pp. 164. *(Fondation Nationale des Sciences Politiques. Travaux et Recherches de Science Politique. 20)*

PRISM PUBLICATIONS. Israeli peace...; words or deeds?. Cairo, [1972?]. 1 pamphlet (unpaged).

SCHLEIFER (ABDULLAH) The fall of Jerusalem. Nottingham, [1972]. pp. 247.

SHAHAK (ISRAEL) Civil rights in Israel today. London, [1972?]. pp. 14.

BEN-GURION (DAVID) My talks with Arab leaders;... translated from the Hebrew by Aryeh Rubinstein and Misha Louvish; edited by Misha Louvish. New York, 1973. pp. 342.

COOLEY (JOHN K.) Green March, Black September: the story of the Palestinian Arabs. London, 1973. pp. 263. *bibliog.*

FERGUSON (PAMELA) The Palestine problem. London, 1973. pp. 158. *bibliog.*

KIMCHE (JON) Palestine or Israel: the untold story of why we failed; 1917- 1923, 1967-1973. London, 1973. pp. 360. *bibliog.*

MALLISON (W.T.) and MALLISON (S.V.) An international law appraisal of the juridical characteristics of the resistance of the people of Palestine: the struggle for human rights. Beirut, 1973. pp. 38. *(Palestine Research Center. Palestine Essays. No. 31)*

The MIDDLE East: quest for an American policy; [papers of a conference held in 1970 at the 47th session of the Institute of World Affairs, sponsored by the University of Southern California]; edited by Willard A. Beling. Albany, N.Y., 1973. pp. 347.

MUSALLAM (SAMI) ed. United Nations resolutions on Palestine, 1947-1972. Beirut, 1973. pp. 225. *(Institute for Palestine Studies. Basic Documentary Series. No. 10)*

PALESTINE lives: interviews with leaders of the resistance: Khalid al-Hassan [and others]. Beirut, 1973. pp. 172. *(Palestine Research Center. Palestine Books. No. 40)*

SAYEGH (YUSEF) compiler. Palestine: background to conflict; (second edition revised...by Louis Eaks). London, [1973]. pp. 32. *bibliog.*

SHAHAK (ISRAEL) Israeli League for Human and Civil Rights: the Shahak papers; compiled and edited by Adnan Amad. Beirut, [1973]. pp. 262.

JEWISH — ARAB RELATIONS. (Cont.)

SOCIETY FOR MIDDLE EAST CONFEDERATION. Confederation in the Middle East: various proposals [by Hugh Schoenfield and others]. Haifa, 1973. pp. 24.

TERROR in Palestine. London, [1973?]. 1 pamphlet (unpaged).

ELON (AMOS) and HASSAN (SANA) Between enemies: an Arab-Israeli dialogue. London, 1974. pp. 151.

GHILAN (MAXIM) How Israel lost its soul. Harmondsworth, 1974. pp. 290.

HATEM (MOHAMED ABDEL KADER) Information and the Arab cause. London, 1974. pp. 320.

HERADSTVEIT (DANIEL) Arab and Israeli elite perceptions. Oslo, [1974]. pp. 148.

HOROWITZ (IRVING LOUIS) Israeli ecstasies, Jewish agonies. New York, 1974. pp. 244.

PORATH (YEHOSHUA) The emergence of the Palestinian-Arab national movement, 1918- 1929. London, 1974. pp. 406.

SMITH (GARY V.) ed. Zionism: the dream and the reality; a Jewish critique. Newton Abbot, 1974. pp. 325. *bibliog.*

JEWISH QUESTION.

NOVACK (GEORGE) How can the Jews survive?: a socialist answer to Zionism. New York, 1969 repr. 1970. pp. 22.

NEDAVA (JOSEPH) Trotsky and the Jews. Philadelphia, 1972. pp. 299. *bibliog.*

JEWS

— Converts to Christianity.

DOMINGUEZ ORTIZ (ANTONIO) Los judeoconversos en España y América. Madrid, [1971]. pp. 253.

— Political and social conditions.

WORLD politics and the Jewish condition; essays prepared for a task force on the world of the 1970s of the American Jewish Committee; edited...by Louis Henkin. New York, [1972]. pp. 342.

HOROWITZ (IRVING LOUIS) Israeli ecstasies, Jewish agonies. New York, 1974. pp. 244.

— Restoration.

SELZER (MICHAEL) ed. Zionism reconsidered: the rejection of Jewish normalcy. London, [1970]. pp. 259. *bibliog.*

SHARIF (MOHAMMED BADI) Strangers in Palestine. London, 1970. pp. 84. *bibliog.*

NUTTING (Sir ANTHONY) Britain and Palestine: a legacy of deceit. London, [1972?]. pp. 15.

STEVENS (RICHARD P.) ed. Zionism and Palestine before the mandate: a phase of Western imperialism; an essay with a selection of readings. Beirut, 1972. pp. 153. *(Institute for Palestine Studies. Anthology Series. No. 5)*

GOLDSTEIN (ISRAEL) Israel at home and abroad, 1962-1972. Jerusalem, [1973]. pp. 422.

KIMCHE (JON) Palestine or Israel: the untold story of why we failed; 1917- 1923, 1967-1973. London, 1973. pp. 360. *bibliog.*

LADEIKIN (VLADIMIR PETROVICH) Istochnik opasnogo krizisa: rol' sionizma v razzhiganii konflikta na Blizhnem Vostoke. Moskva, 1973. pp. 296.

ROBERTS (SAMUEL J.) Survival or hegemony?: the foundations of Israeli foreign policy. Baltimore, 1973. pp. 163. *bibliog. (Johns Hopkins University. Washington Center of Foreign Policy Research. Studies in International Affairs. No. 20)*

GHILAN (MAXIM) How Israel lost its soul. Harmondsworth, 1974. pp. 290.

PORATH (YEHOSHUA) The emergence of the Palestinian-Arab national movement, 1918- 1929. London, 1974. pp. 406.

RABINOWICZ (OSKAR K.) Arnold Toynbee on Judaism and Zionism: a critique. London, 1974. pp. 372.

SMITH (GARY V.) ed. Zionism: the dream and the reality; a Jewish critique. Newton Abbot, 1974. pp. 325. *bibliog.*

JEWS AS SOLDIERS.

OPPENHEIMER (FRANZ) Die Judenstatistik des preussischen Kriegsministeriums. München, 1922. pp. 48.

JEWS IN AUSTRIA.

SCHOLZ (WILHELM) Ein Weg ins Leben: das neue Österreich und die Judenfrage. London, 1943. pp. 16.

JEWS IN BELGIUM.

STEINBERG (LUCIEN) Le Comité de défense des Juifs en Belgique 1942-1944. [Brussels, 1973]. pp. 198. *bibliog.*

JEWS IN FRANCE.

CHAZAN (ROBERT) Medieval Jewry in northern France: a political and social history. Baltimore, [1973]. pp. 238. *bibliog. (Johns Hopkins University. Studies in Historical and Political Science. Series 91. [No.]2)*

JEWS IN GERMANY.

OPPENHEIMER (FRANZ) Die Judenstatistik des preussischen Kriegsministeriums. München, 1922. pp. 48.

ADLER (HANS GUENTHER) Der verwaltete Mensch: Studien zur Deportation der Juden aus Deutschland. Tübingen, 1974. pp. 1076. *bibliog.*

ADLER-RUDEL (SALOMON) Jüdische Selbsthilfe unter dem Naziregime, 1933-1939, im Spiegel der Berichte der Reichsvertretung der Juden in Deutschland. Tübingen, 1974. pp. 221. *(Leo Baeck Institute. Schriftenreihe Wissenschaftlicher Abhandlungen. 29)*

KROHN (HELGA) Die Juden in Hamburg: die politische, soziale und kulturelle Entwicklung einer jüdischen Grosstadtgemeinde nach der Emanzipation, 1848-1918. Hamburg, 1974. pp. 247. *bibliog.*

REICHMANN (EVA G.) Grösse und Verhängnis deutsch-jüdischer Existenz: Zeugnisse einer tragischen Begegnung; [selected essays and lectures, 1930-1971]; mit einem Geleitwort von Helmut Gollwitzer. Heidelberg, 1974. pp. 295. *bibliog.*

JEWS IN ITALY.

WAAGENAAR (SAM) The Pope's Jews. London, 1974. pp. 487. *bibliog.*

JEWS IN LATIN AMERICA.

EXPERTS CONFERENCE ON LATIN AMERICA AND THE FUTURE OF ITS JEWISH COMMUNITIES, NEW YORK, 1972. Proceedings, etc. London, [1973]. pp. 159. *bibliog.*

JEWS IN RUSSIA.

INSTITUTE OF JEWISH AFFAIRS. Background Papers. No. 24. The Soviet "diploma tax". [London], 1972. pp. 15.

NEDAVA (JOSEPH) Trotsky and the Jews. Philadelphia, 1972. pp. 299. *bibliog.*

SHAFFER (HARRY GEORGE) The Soviet treatment of Jews. New York, 1974. pp. 231.

JEWS IN SYRIA.

INTERNATIONAL CONFERENCE FOR THE DELIVERANCE OF JEWS IN THE MIDDLE EAST. The plight of Syrian Jewry. [Paris, 1974]. pp. 48.

JEWS IN THE NEAR EAST.

GOITEIN (SOLOMON DOB FRITZ) compiler. Letters of medieval Jewish traders; translated from the Arabic with introductions and notes by S.D. Goitein. Princeton, [1973]. pp. 359.

JEWS IN THE UNITED STATES.

GOLDSTEIN (ISRAEL) Israel at home and abroad, 1962-1972. Jerusalem, [1973]. pp. 422.

HOROWITZ (IRVING LOUIS) Israeli ecstasies, Jewish agonies. New York, 1974. pp. 244.

SNETSINGER (JOHN) Truman, the Jewish vote, and the creation of Israel. Stanford, [1974]. pp. 208. *bibliog. (Stanford University. Hoover Institution on War, Revolution and Peace. Hoover Institution Studies. 39)*

STEINBERG (STEPHEN) The academic melting pot: Catholics and Jews in American higher education;... a report prepared for the Carnegie Commission on Higher Education. New York, [1974]. pp. 183. *bibliog.*

JIK (KIM HYONG).

See KIM (HYONG JIK).

JIVARO INDIANS.

HARNER (MICHAEL J.) The Jivaro: people of the sacred waterfalls. Garden City, N.Y., [1972]. pp. 233. *bibliog.*

JOB ANALYSIS.

BUNTINX (HUBERT) Geëngageerd bedrijfsbeleid: evolutie van mens en arbeidsstructuur; (met medewerking van W. van Hoorick [and others]). Den Haag, 1970. pp. 166. *(Nederlands Instituut voor Efficiency. Publikaties. Nr. 500)*

PATERSON (THOMAS THOMSON) Job evaluation vol. 1. A new method. London, 1972. pp. 209. *bibliog.*

SHAFRITZ (JAY M.) Position classification: a behavioral analysis for the public service. New York, 1973. pp. 133. *bibliog.*

COOPER (ROBERT) Ph.D. Job motivation and job design. London, 1974. pp. 140.

JOB SATISFACTION.

COOPER (ROBERT) Ph.D. Job motivation and job design. London, 1974. pp. 140.

JOHANNESBURG

— Population.

JOHANNESBURG. City Engineer's Department. Forward Planning Branch. Greater Johannesburg area: population report. Johannesburg, 1970. fo. 70.

JOHNSON (ANDREW) President of the United States.

MANTELL (MARTIN E.) Johnson, Grant, and the politics of reconstruction. New York, 1973. pp. 209. *bibliog.*

JOHNSON (HARRY GORDON)

— Bibliography.

BIBLIOGRAPHY [of works by] Harry G. Johnson. [London, 1973]. 1 vol. (various foliations). *Typescript.*

JOHNSON (JAMES WELDON).

LEVY (EUGENE) Historian. James Weldon Johnson: black leader, black voice. Chicago, 1973. pp. 380. *bibliog.*

JOHNSON (LYNDON BAINES) President of the United States.

HARWOOD (RICHARD) and JOHNSON (HAYNES BONNER) Lyndon. New York, 1973. pp. 187.

JOURNALISM.

ORAGE (ALFRED RICHARD) Readers and writers, 1917-1921. New York, 1922. pp. 181.

— Social aspects.

BECHELLONI (GIOVANNI) Informazione e potere: la stampa quotidiana in Italia. Roma, 1974. pp. 316.

— Netherlands.

BRANTS (KEES) Journalistiek ondersteboven: afhankelijkheid en manipulatie in de media. Amsterdam, 1974. pp. 117. bibliog.

— United States.

MUCKRAKING: past, present and future; [including papers presented at a conference held at Pennsylvania State University, 1970]; edited by John M. Harrison and Harry H. Stein. University Park, [1973]. pp. 165.

BUNI (ANDREW) Robert L. Vann of the Pittsburgh Courier: politics and black journalism. Pittsburgh, [1974]. pp. 410. bibliog.

SAYRE (NORA) Sixties going on seventies. London, 1974. pp. 441.

JOY AND SORROW.

MARRIS (PETER) Loss and change. London, 1974. pp. 178. bibliog. (Institute of Community Studies. Reports)

JUDAISM.

RABINOWICZ (OSKAR K.) Arnold Toynbee on Judaism and Zionism: a critique. London, 1974. pp. 372.

JUDGEMADE LAW
— United Kingdom.

KEETON (GEORGE WILLIAMS) English law: the judicial contribution. Newton Abbot, [1974]. pp. 384.

JUDGES.

LASKIN (BORA) The institutional character of the judge. Jerusalem, 1972. pp. 24. (Hebrew University. Lionel Cohen Lectures. 17th Series)

— Australia.

NEUMANN (EDDY) The High Court of Australia: a collective portrait 1903-1972.2nd ed. Sydney, 1973. fo. 131. bibliog. (Sydney. University. Department of Government and Public Administration. Occasional Monographs. No.6)

— Italy.

PELLEGRINI (EDGARDO) Gli ermellini da guardia: (magistratura e repressione in Italia, 1968-1973). Roma, [1973]. pp. 159.

— United States.

ABRAHAM (HENRY JULIAN) Justices and presidents: a political history of appointments to the Supreme Court. New York, 1974. pp. 310. bibliog.

JUDGMENT.

EISER (JOHN RICHARD) and STROEBE (WOLFGANG) Categorization and social judgement. London, 1972. pp. 235. bibliog.

JUDICIAL ASSISTANCE
— Russia.

RUSSIA (U.S.S.R.) Treaties. 1954-1972. Dogovory ob okazanii pravovoi pomoshchi po grazhdanskim, semeinym i ugolovnym delam, zakliuchennye SSSR s drugimi sotsialisticheskimi gosudarstvami. 2nd ed. Moskva, 1973. pp. 392.

JUDICIAL REVIEW
— Russia.

TRUBNIKOV (PETR IAKOVLEVICH) Nadzornoe proizvodstvo po grazhdanskim delam. Moskva, 1967. pp. 144.

PROKURORSKII nadzor v SSSR. 3rd ed. Moskva, 1973. pp. 358.

JUDICIAL REVIEW OF ADMINISTRATIVE ACTS
— Russia.

NIKOLAEVA (LIDIIA ALEKSANDROVNA) Sudebnyi nadzor za zakonnost'iu v sovetskom gosudarstvennom upravlenii. Leningrad, 1973. pp. 64.

— United Kingdom.

DE SMITH (STANLEY ALEXANDER) Judicial review of administrative action. 3rd ed. London, 1973. pp. 549.

JUDICIAL STATISTICS
— Finland.

FINLAND. Tilastokeskus. Tuomioistuinten toiminta:... Function of courts. irreg., 1955/1969- Helsinki. In Finnish, Swedish and English.

— United Kingdom.

U.K. Lord Chancellor's Office. Statistics on judicial administration. a., [1972, 1st]- London.

JUNG (CHARLES GUSTAVE).

JUNG (CHARLES GUSTAVE) C.G. Jung: letters; selected and edited by Gerhard Adler in collaboration with Aniela Jaffé; translations from the German by R.F.C. Hull. London, 1973 in progress.

JURA
— Nationalism.

BERN (CANTON). Commission des 24. 1968. Les données actuelles du problème jurassien. [Berne, 1968]. pp. 235.

SCHWIERIGE Selbstbestimmung im Jura: Hintergründe eines Minderheitenproblems; ([series of articles by] Peter Forster [and others]). Zürich, 1974. pp. 111. (Neue Zürcher Zeitung. NZZ-Schriften zur Zeit. 30)

JURISDICTION
— United Kingdom.

JOHNSTON (W. ROSS) Sovereignty and protection: a study of British jurisdictional imperialism in the late nineteenth century. Durham, N.C., 1973. pp. 357. bibliog. (Duke University. Commonwealth Studies Center. Publications. No. 41)

JURISDICTION (INTERNATIONAL LAW).

EUROPEAN COMMUNITIES. Commission. 1972. Report on the Convention on jurisdiction and the enforcement of judgments in civil and commercial matters. Brussels, 1972. pp. 113. (Bulletin of the European Communities. Supplements. [1972/12])

JURISDICTION OVER AIRCRAFT.

SHUBBER (SAMI) Jurisdiction over crimes on board aircraft. The Hague, 1973. pp. 369. bibliog.

JURISPRUDENCE.

SHABALIN (VLADIMIR ALEKSANDROVICH) Metodologicheskie voprosy pravovedeniia: v sviazi s teoriei i praktikoi sotsialisticheskogo upravleniia. Saratov, 1972. pp. 226.

FINCH (JOHN D.) Introduction to legal theory. 2nd ed. London, 1974. pp. 211.

ZIEMBIŃSKI (ZYGMUNT) Metodologiczne zagadnienia prawoznawstwa. Warszawa, 1974. pp. 287. With French summary.

JURY
— United Kingdom.

GRIEW (EDWARD JAMES) Dishonesty and the jury: an inaugural lecture delivered in the University of Leicester, 6 November 1973. Leicester, 1974. pp. 24.

— United States.

SCHAUFELBERGER (ALFRED) Blacks and the trial by jury: the black man's experience in the courts. Bern, 1973. pp. 170. bibliog.

JUSTICE.

POUND (ROSCOE) Justice according to law. Port Washington, N.Y., [1951 repr. 1973]. pp. 98. (Westminster College. [Lectures])

BARRY (BRIAN M.) The liberal theory of justice: a critical examination of the principal doctrines in a theory of justice, by John Rawls. Oxford, 1973. pp. 169.

ECKHOFF (TORSTEIN) Justice: its determinants in social interaction. Rotterdam, 1974. pp. 414. bibliog.

JUSTICE, ADMINISTRATION OF
— Argentine Republic.

AREAL (LEONARDO JORGE) Organizacion judicial: Argentina. Madrid, 1970. pp. 58. bibliog. (Spain. Comision General de Codificacion. Cuadernos Informativos)

— Belgium.

INSTITUT BELGE D'INFORMATION ET DE DOCUMENTATION. Ce qu'il faut savoir...du Ministère de la Justice. Bruxelles, [1971]. fo. 38.

— Colombia.

ORGANIZACION judicial: Colombia, Ecuador, Venezuela; [by Hernando Devis Echandia and others]. Madrid, 1970. pp. 90. (Spain. Comision General de Codificacion. Cuadernos Informativos)

— Ecuador.

ORGANIZACION judicial: Colombia, Ecuador, Venezuela; [by Hernando Devis Echandia and others]. Madrid, 1970. pp. 90. (Spain. Comision General de Codificacion. Cuadernos Informativos)

— Eritrea.

ITALY. Ministero degli Affari Esteri. Comitato per la Documentazione dell'Opera dell'Italia in Africa. L'Italia in Africa. Serie Giuridico-Amministrativa. Vol. 2. L'amministrazione della giustizia nei territori oltremare. Tomo 1. L'amministrazione della giustizia in Eritrea e in Somalia, 1869-1936; testo di Vincenzo Mellana. Roma, 1971. pp. 446.

— France.

DURAND-BARTHEZ (PASCAL) Histoire des structures du Ministère de la Justice, 1789-1945. Paris, 1973. pp. 91. bibliog. (Paris. Université de Paris II. Travaux et Recherches. Série Science Administrative. 5)

— Guyana.

SHAHABUDDEEN (MUHAMMAD) The legal system of Guyana. Georgetown, 1973. pp. 523. bibliog.

— Netherlands.

HOEKEMA (A.J.) Vertrouwen in de justitie: resultaten van een vergelijkend onderzoek. Alphen aan den Rijn, 1971. pp. 100.

— Philippine Islands.

CONCEPCION (ROBERTO) Organizacion judicial: Filipinas. Madrid, 1970. pp. 70. (Spain. Comision General de Codificacion. Cuadernos Informativos)

— Somaliland.

ITALY. Ministero degli Affari Esteri. Comitato per la Documentazione dell'Opera dell'Italia in Africa. L'Italia in Africa. Serie Giuridico-Amministrativa. Vol. 2. L'amministrazione della giustizia nei territori oltremare. Tomo 1. L'amministrazione della giustizia in Eritrea e in Somalia, 1869-1936; testo di Vincenzo Mellana. Roma, 1971. pp. 446.

JUSTICE, ADMINISTRATION OF. (Cont.)

— South Africa.

SOUTH AFRICAN COUNCIL OF CHURCHES and CHRISTIAN INSTITUTE OF SOUTHERN AFRICA. Study Project on Christianity in Apartheid Society. Legal Commission. Law, justice and society;... report. Johannesburg, 1972. pp. 100. *bibliog.* (*South African Council of Churches and Christian Institute of Southern Africa. Study Project on Christianity in Apartheid Society. Publications. 9*)

— United Kingdom.

McCARTHY COMMITTEE. Who killed Stephen McCarthy?. London, [1972]. pp. (30).

U.K. Central Office of Information. Reference Division. Reference Pamphlets. 49. The English legal system. 4th ed. London, 1972. pp. 38. *bibliog.*

FREEMAN (MICHAEL D.A.) The legal structure. London, 1974. pp. 243. *bibliog.*

—— Ireland, Northern.

HADDEN (TOM) and HILLYARD (PADDY) Justice in Northern Ireland: a study in social confidence. London, [1973]. pp. 74.

— United States.

JUSTICE in America: [proceedings of a conference organized by the Fund for New Priorities in America in Washington, 1970]; edited by William Meyers [and others]. New York, [1972]. pp. 92.

FISH (PETER GRAHAM) The politics of federal judicial administration. Princeton, [1973]. pp. 528. *bibliog.*

JACOB (HERBERT) Urban justice: law and order in American cities. Englewood Cliffs, [1973]. pp. 145.

— Uruguay.

GELSI BIDART (ADOLFO) Organizacion judicial: Uruguay. Madrid, 1970. pp. 84. (*Spain. Comision General de Codificacion. Cuadernos Informativos*)

— Venezuela.

ORGANIZACION judicial: Colombia, Ecuador, Venezuela; [by Hernando Devis Echandia and others]. Madrid, 1970. pp. 90. (*Spain. Comision General de Codificacion. Cuadernos Informativos*)

JUSTICE AND POLITICS

— France.

MONTALDO (JEAN) Dossier S - comme Sanguinetti. Paris, [1973]. pp. 156.

— Italy.

TRANFAGLIA (NICOLA) Dallo stato liberale al regime fascista: problemi e ricerche. Milano, 1973. pp. 297.

— United Kingdom.

MORRISON (FRED L.) Courts and the political process in England. Beverly Hills, [1973]. pp. 224.

— United States.

COLE (GEORGE F.) Politics and the administration of justice. Beverly Hills, [1973]. pp. 234.

JUSTICES OF THE PEACE

— United Kingdom.

McLEAN (IAN GRAEME) and MORRISH (PETER) The magistrates' coourt: an index of common penalties and formalities in cases before justices. Chichester, 1973. pp. 156.

PUGH (LESLIE M.) Matrimonial proceedings before magistrates; third edition by L. M. Pugh and J.B. Horsman. London, 1974. pp. 658.

JUTE

— India.

BULLETIN ON JUTE STATISTICS IN INDIA (DISTRICT-WISE); [pd. by] Directorate of Economics and Statistics, Ministry of Agriculture. irreg., 1972[1st issue, covering 1928-9/1971-2]- New Delhi.

— United Kingdom.

WOOL, JUTE AND FLAX INDUSTRY TRAINING BOARD [U.K.]. Report and statement of accounts. a., 1972/3- Bradford. *Formerly included in the file of British Parliamentary Papers.*

JUVENILE COURTS

— Israel.

REIFEN (DAVID) The juvenile court in a changing society: young offenders in Israel. London, [1972]. pp. 214. *bibliog.*

— United Kingdom.

GOODMAN (LEO) Notes on juvenile court law. 9th ed. Chichester, 1973. pp. 36.

JUVENILE DELINQUENCY

— Research — United States.

HIRSCHI (TRAVIS) and SELVIN (HANAN CHARLES) Principles of survey analysis; formerly titled Delinquency research. 2nd ed. New York, 1973. pp. 280.

— Czechoslovakia.

CIC (MILAN) Ochranná výchova v československom trestnom práve. Bratislava, 1971. pp. 126. *bibliog.*

— Finland.

FINLAND. Ungdomsbrottskommittén. 1971. Ungdomsbrottskommitténs betänkande. Helsingfors, 1970 (or rather 1971). pp. 55. (*Kommittébetänkande 1970:A 9*)

RAUHALA (URHO) Later lives of approved school boys and young prisoners: the effect of their social background, personality traits and institutionalization on their later lives. Helsinki, 1973. pp. 55, 6.. *bibliog.* (*Finland. Suomen Virallinen Tilasto. 32. Sosiaalisia Erikoistutkimuksia. 31*)

— France.

FRANCE. Direction de la Documentation. La Documentation Francçaise. Notes et Etudes Documentaires. Nos. 3,987-3, 988. La délinquance des jeunes en France, par Henri Michard. [Paris], 1973. pp. 63. *bibliog.*

— Ireland (Republic).

HART (IAN) Factors relating to reconviction among young Dublin probationers. Dublin, 1974. pp. 124. *bibliog.* (*Economic and Social Research Institute. Papers. No.76*)

— Israel.

ACTION-RESEARCH PROJECT ON DELINQUENT STREET-CORNER GROUPS. Final report, research project on forces acting in street corner groups. vol.1. Jerusalem, 1967. fo. 221.

— Poland.

ZABRODZKA (HALINA) and KOSECKI (MIECZYSŁAW) Orzecznictwo Sądu Najwy'zszego w sprawach karnych nieletnich za okres od 1930 r. do 1971 r. Warszawa, 1973. pp. 48.

— Russia — Ukraine.

LEONENKO (VITALII VASYL'OVYCH) Rozhliad sprav pro zlochyny nepovnolitnikh u stadii viddannia do sudu. Kyïv, 1972. pp. 150. *With Russian summary.*

— United Kingdom.

COCKETT (R.) The crimes of detention centre boys. [London], 1972. 1 pamphlet (various pagings). (*U.K. Prison Department. Office of the Chief Psychologist. CP Reports. Series 1. No.3*)

ANTHONY (HELEN SYLVIA) Depression, psychopathic personality and attempted suicide in a borstal sample; (a Home Office Research Unit report). London, 1973. pp. 43. *bibliog.* (*U.K. Home Office. Home Office Research Studies. 19*)

CHILDREN still in trouble?: papers given in the 18th series of I.S.T.D. lectures... London, October 1972 - March 1973;... [by Shirley Becke [and others]. London, 1973. pp. 40. (*Institute for the Study and Treatment of Delinquency. Lectures. 18th series*)

U.K. Social Work Service. Developement Group. 1973. Intermediate treatment project: an account of a project set up to demonstrate some ways of providing intermediate treatment. London, 1973. pp. 61. *bibliog.*

WEST (DONALD JAMES) Who becomes delinquent?: second report of the Cambridge study in delinquent development;... in collaboration with D.P. Farrington. London, 1973. pp. 265. *bibliog.* (*Cambridge. University. Institute of Criminology. Cambridge Studies in Criminology. vol.34*)

ADVISORY COUNCIL ON THE PENAL SYSTEM. Young adult offenders; report. London, H.M.S.O., 1974. pp. 265.

BERLINS (MARCEL) and WANSELL (GEOFFREY) Caught in the act: children, society and the law. Harmondsworth, 1974. pp. 124.

PARKER (HOWARD J.) View from the boys: a sociology of downtown adolescents. Newton Abbot, [1974]. pp. 237.

TUTT (NORMAN) Care or custody: community homes and the treatment of delinquency. London, 1974. pp. 228.

— United States.

MENNEL (ROBERT M.) Thorns and thistles: juvenile delinquents in the United States, 1825-1940. Hanover, N.H., 1973. pp. 231. *bibliog.*

KABARDINOBALKARIAN REPUBLIC

— Economic history.

SHCHEGOLEV (ANDREI IVANOVICH) Krest'ianskoe dvizhenie v Kabarde i Balkarii v gody stolypinskoi reaktsii i novogo revoliutsionnogo pod'ema. Nal'chik, 1962. pp. 140.

KABYLES.

BOURDIEU (PIERRE) Esquisse d'une théorie de la pratique, precédé de Trois études d'ethnologie kabyle. Genève, 1972. pp. 269.

KADAR (JANOS).

SHAWCROSS (WILLIAM) Crime and compromise: Janos Kadar and the politics of Hungary since revolution. London, [1974]. pp. 311.

KAFIRS (AFRICAN PEOPLE).

PAUW (BERTHOLD ADOLF) The second generation: a study of the family among urbanized Bantu in East London. 2nd ed. Cape Town, 1973. pp. 241. (*Rhodes University. Institute of Social and Economic Research. Xhosa in Town. 3*)

KAFR EL—ELOW

— Social life and customs.

FAKHOURI (HANI) Kafr El-Elow: an Egyptian village in transition. New York, 1972. pp. 134. *bibliog.*

KALININGRAD (OBLAST')

— Statistics.

KALININGRAD (OBLAST'). Statisticheskoe Upravlenie. Kaliningradskaia oblast' v vos'moi piatiletke: statisticheskii sbornik. Kaliningrad, 1972. pp. 255.

KALMYK REPUBLIC.

GORODOVIKOV (BASAN BAD'MINOVICH) Ordenonosnaia Kalmykiia. 2nd ed. Elista, 1972. pp. 163.

KANO (STATE)

— Politics and government.

PADEN (JOHN N.) Religion and political culture in Kano. Berkeley, Calif., [1973]. pp. 461. *bibliog.*

— Religion.

PADEN (JOHN N.) Religion and political culture in Kano. Berkeley, Calif., [1973]. pp. 461. *bibliog.*

KANT (IMMANUEL).

ADORNO (THEODOR WIESENGRUND) Negative dialectics;...translated by E.B. Ashton. London, 1973. pp. 416.

ASMUS (VALENTIN FERDINANDOVICH) Immanuil Kant. Moskva, 1973. pp. 534.

RESCHER (NICHOLAS) The primacy of practice: essays towards a pragmatically Kantian theory of empirical knowledge. Oxford, 1973. pp. 156.

SANER (HANS) Kant's political thought: its origins and development; translated by E.B. Ashton. Chicago, 1973. pp. 374. *bibliog.*

KARAKALPAK REPUBLIC

— Politics and government.

KARAKALPAK REPUBLIC. Verkhovnyi Sovet. Zasedaniia: stenograficheskii otchet. sess., Jl 1970 (7th series, 8th session). Nukug.

KARELIA

— History — 1917—1921, Revolution.

BALAGUROV (IAKOV ALEKSEEVICH) Bor'ba za Sovety v Karel'skom Pomor'e. 2nd ed. Petrozavodsk, 1973. pp. 160.

KATANGA.

See SHABA.

KAZAKS IN RUSSIA.

IRMURATOV (KHAIDAR DISEMALIEVICH) Oktiabr' v aule. Volgograd, 1967. pp. 190.

KAZAKSTAN

— Description and travel.

PO Srednei Azii i Kazakhstanu: putevoditel'. Moskva, 1973. pp. 407.

— Economic conditions.

DEMKO (GEORGE J.) The Russian colonization of Kazakhstan 1896-1916. Bloomington, [1969]. pp. 271. *bibliog. (Indiana University. Graduate School. Publications. Uralic and Altaic Series. vol. 99)*

PETRUSHIN (NIKOLAI IVANOVICH) Elektrifikatsiia i proizvoditel'nye sily Kazakhstana. Alma-Ata, 1973. pp. 207.

— Economic history.

AKADEMIIA NAUK SSSR. Institut Etnografii. Trudy. Novaia Seriia. t.98. Ocherki po istorii khoziaistva narodov Srednei Azii i Kazakhstana. Leningrad, 1973. pp. 260.

— Emigration and immigration.

DEMKO (GEORGE J.) The Russian colonization of Kazakhstan 1896-1916. Bloomington, [1969]. pp. 271. *bibliog. (Indiana University. Graduate School. Publications. Uralic and Altaic Series. vol. 99)*

— History — Historiography.

DAKHSHLEIGER (GRIGORII FEDOROVICH) V.I. Lenin i problemy kazakhstanskoi istoriografii. Alma-Ata, 1973. pp. 215.

— Industries.

UPRAVLENIE promyshlennost'iu Kazakhskoi SSR: gosudarstvenno- pravovye problemy. Alma-Ata, 1972. pp. 298.

EFFEKTIVNOST' tekhnicheskogo progressa v promyshlennosti Kazakhstana. Alma-Ata, 1973. pp. 168.

FORMY otraslevoi organizatsii i effektivnost' proizvodstva. Alma-Ata, 1973. pp. 256. *bibliog.*

— Intellectual life.

SEGIZBAEV (ORAZ AMANGALIEVICH) Traditsii svobodomysliia i ateizma v dukhovnoi kul'ture kazakhskogo naroda. Alma-Ata, 1973. pp. 168.

— Population.

PROBLEMY truda i narodonaseleniia v Kazakhstane. Alma-Ata, 1973. pp. 174.

KEHRL (HANS).

KEHRL (HANS) Krisenmanager im Dritten Reich: 6 Jahre Frieden, 6 Jahre Krieg; Erinnerungen; mit kritischen Anmerkungen und einem Nachwort, von Erwin Viefhaus. Düsseldorf, 1973. pp. 552.

KENNEDY (JOHN FITZGERALD) President of the United States.

TOBIN (JAMES) The new economics : one decade older. Princeton, N.J., [1974]. pp. 15. *(Princeton University. Woodrow Wilson School of Public and International Affairs. Eliot Janeway Lectures on Historical Economics. 1972)*

KENSINGTON AND CHELSEA

— Civic improvement.

The COLVILLE Tavistock study: consultation report; a study of social and building conditions and recommendations for rehabilitation and redevelopment [by a study team, led by Frank Clinch, for the Royal Borough of Kensington and Chelsea]. London, Royal Borough of Kensington and Chelsea, 1972. pp. 326.

— Social conditions.

The COLVILLE Tavistock study: consultation report; a study of social and building conditions and recommendations for rehabilitation and redevelopment [by a study team, led by Frank Clinch, for the Royal Borough of Kensington and Chelsea]. London, Royal Borough of Kensington and Chelsea, 1972. pp. 326.

KENT STATE UNIVERSITY.

DAVIES (PETER) The truth about Kent State: a challenge to the American conscience; by Peter Davies and the Board of Church and Society of the United Methodist Church. London, 1974. pp. 242. *bibliog.*

KENYA

— Commerce.

PORTER (RICHARD C.) Some doubts about Kenya's future as an exporter of manufactures. Ann Arbor, 1973. pp. 28. *bibliog. (Michigan University. Center for Research on Economic Development. Discussion Papers. No. 31)*

— Economic history.

GUPTA (DESH BANDHU) Labour supplies and economic development in Kenya: [Ph.D. (London) thesis]. [1974]. fo. 423. *bibliog. Typescript: unpublished. Photocopy of article in end pocket. This thesis is the property of London University and may not be removed from the Library.*

WOLFF (RICHARD D.) The economics of colonialism: Britain and Kenya, 1870-1930. New Haven, 1974. pp. 203. *bibliog.*

— Economic policy.

KENYA. Town Planning Department. 1970. Western Province regional physical development plan. [Nairobi, 1970]. 1 vol. (various pagings).

BIENEN (HENRY) Kenya: the politics of participation and control. Princeton, [1974]. pp. 215. *bibliog.*

GUPTA (DESH BANDHU) Labour supplies and economic development in Kenya: [Ph.D. (London) thesis]. [1974]. fo. 423. *bibliog. Typescript: unpublished. Photocopy of article in end pocket. This thesis is the property of London University and may not be removed from the Library.*

— Emigration and immigration.

KENYA. Central Bureau of Statistics. Migration and tourism statistics. irreg., 1968/1971 [1st]- Nairobi.

— Manufactures.

PORTER (RICHARD C.) Some doubts about Kenya's future as an exporter of manufactures. Ann Arbor, 1973. pp. 28. *bibliog. (Michigan University. Center for Research on Economic Development. Discussion Papers. No. 31)*

— Nationalism.

BUIJTENHUIJS (ROBERT) Mau Mau: twenty years after; the myth and the survivors. The Hague, [1973]. pp. 170. *bibliog. (Afrika-Studiecentrum. Communications. 4)*

— Officials and employees.

NELLIS (JOHN R.) The ethnic composition of leading Kenyan government positions. Uppsala, 1974. pp. 26. *(Nordiska Afrikainstitutet. Research Reports. No.24)*

— — Salaries, allowances, etc.

KENYA. Public Service Structure and Remuneration Commission. 1971. Report...1970-71; chairman: D.N. Ndegwa. [Nairobi], 1971. pp. 397. *3 charts in end pocket.*

— Politics and government.

BUIJTENHUIJS (ROBERT) Mau Mau: twenty years after; the myth and the survivors. The Hague, [1973]. pp. 170. *bibliog. (Afrika-Studiecentrum. Communications. 4)*

ARNOLD (GUY) Kenyatta and the politics of Kenya. London, 1974. pp. 226. *bibliog.*

WOLFF (RICHARD D.) The economics of colonialism: Britain and Kenya, 1870-1930. New Haven, 1974. pp. 203. *bibliog.*

— Rural conditions.

RASMUSSON (RASMUS) Kenyan rural development and aid: a case study on effects of assistance on planning and implementation for the Special Rural Development Programme, etc. [Stockholm], 1972. pp. 53. *(Swedish International Development Authority. Information Division. Development Studies. 2/72)*

FORDHAM (PAUL) Rural development in the Kenya highlands: a report of geographical field work carried out during August 1971. Nottingham, [1973]. pp. 122. *(Nottingham. University. Department of Geography. Geographical Field Group. Regional Studies. No.17)*

— Social conditions.

BIENEN (HENRY) Kenya: the politics of participation and control. Princeton, [1974]. pp. 215. *bibliog.*

KENYATTA (JOMO).

ARNOLD (GUY) Kenyatta and the politics of Kenya. London, 1974. pp. 226. *bibliog.*

KEYNES (JOHN MAYNARD) 1st Baron Keynes.

MANTOUX (ETIENNE) La paix calomniée; ou, Les conséquences économiques de M. Keynes. [Paris, 1946]. pp. 333.

STEWART (MICHAEL JAMES) Keynes and after. 2nd ed. Harmondsworth, 1972 repr. 1973. pp. 317. *bibliog.*

WEINTRAUB (SIDNEY) b. 1914, and others. Keynes and the monetarists and other essays: [lectures delivered at the Graduate School of Business Administration of the University of Puerto Rico, 1970-71]. New Brunswick, [1973]. pp. 227.

KEYNES (JOHN MAYNARD) 1st Baron Keynes. (Cont.)

HICKS (Sir JOHN RICHARD) The crisis in Keynesian economics. Oxford, [1974]. pp. 85. (*Yrjö Jahnssonin Säätiö. Yrjö Jahnsson Lectures. 1973*)

MUELLER (KLAUS O.W.) Neokeynesianismus: kritische Untersuchung einer modernen staatsmonopolkapitalistischen Wirtschaftslehre. 2nd ed. Westberlin, 1974. pp. 260.

SHACKLE (GEORGE LENNOX SHARMAN) Keynesian kaleidics: the evolution of a general political economy. Edinburgh, [1974]. pp. 92.

UNIVERSITY OF KENT AT CANTERBURY. Keynes Seminar, 1st, 1972. Keynes: aspects of the man and his work...; edited by D.E. Moggridge. London, 1974. pp. 107.

KHARKOV.

KHARKIV u tsyfrakh i faktakh: dovidnyk. Kharkiv, 1967. pp. 199. *bibliog.*

KHRUSHCHEV (NIKITA SERGEEVICH).

KHRUSHCHEV (NIKITA SERGEEVICH) Khrushchev remembers: the last testament; translated and edited by Strobe Talbott. London, 1974. pp. 602.

KIANGSI

— Politics and government.

KIM (ILPYONG J.) The politics of Chinese communism: Kiangsi under the Soviets. Berkeley, [1973]. pp. 232. *bibliog.*

KIM (DAE—JUNG).

DEMOCRATIC FRONT FOR THE REUNIFICATION OF THE FATHERLAND [KOREA] and COMMITTEE FOR THE PEACEFUL REUNIFICATION OF THE FATHERLAND [KOREA]. The truth about the abduction and detention of Kim Dae Jung, a democratic personage of South Korea. Pyongyang, 1973. pp. 16.

KIM (HYONG JIK).

CHOSON NODONGDANG. Central Committee. Party History Institute. Kim Hyong Jik: indomitable anti-Japanese revolutionary fighter. Pyongyang, 1973. pp. 124.

KIM (IL—SUNG).

BONG (BAIK) Kim Il Sung: biography. Beirut, 1973. 3 vols.

PAN-AFRICAN SEMINAR ON THE JUCHE IDEA OF COMRADE KIM IL SUNG, FREETOWN, 1972. Documents and deliberations of the seminar. Beirut, 1973. pp. 184.

KINGS AND RULERS

— Succession.

BURLING (ROBBINS) The passage of power: studies in political succession. New York, [1974]. pp. 322. *bibliog.*

KINGS AND RULERS (IN RELIGION, FOLK—LORE, ETC.)

Le POUVOIR et le sacré; par Luc de Heusch [and others]. Bruxelles, 1962. pp. 186. (*Brussels. Université Libre. Institut de Sociologie. Centre d'Étude des Religions. Annales. 1*)

KINSHIP.

HOCART (ARTHUR MAURICE) The life-giving myth and other essays;...edited...by Lord Raglan; second impression edited with a foreword by Rodney Needham. London, 1970 repr. 1973. pp. 252.

TREMBLAY (MARC ADELARD) and LAPLANTE (MARC) Famille et parenté en Acadie: évolution des structures et des relations familiales et parentales à l'Anse-des-Lavallée. Ottawa, National Museums of Canada, 1971. pp. 174. *bibliog.* (*National Museum of Man [Canada]. Publications in Ethnology. No. 3*) With English summary.

FARBER (BERNARD) Family and kinship in modern society. Glenview, Ill., [1973]. pp. 179. *bibliog.*

GOODY (JOHN RANKINE) ed. The character of kinship. London, 1973. pp. 251.

SCHNEIDER (DAVID MURRAY) and SMITH (RAYMOND T.) Class differences and sex roles in American kinship and family structure. Englewood Cliffs, [1973]. pp. 132. *bibliog.*

CHEKKI (DANESH A.) Modernization and kin network. Leiden, 1974. pp. 184. *bibliog.*

NEEDHAM (RODNEY) Remarks and inventions: skeptical essays about kinship. London, 1974. pp. 181. *bibliog.*

KIRGHIZIA

See also Turkestan.

— Economic conditions.

TEMPY i proportsii rasshirennogo vosproizvodstva v Kirgizii. Frunze, 1973. pp. 61.

— Economic policy.

RAZVITIE ekonomiki Kirgizstana i voprosy sovershenstvovaniia planirovaniia na sovremennom etape. Frunze, 1972. pp. 196.

— — Mathematical models.

NEKOTORYE matematicheskie metody optimizatsii i ikh primenenie v narodnom khoziaistve Kirgizii. Frunze, 1973. pp. 106.

— Industries.

ABDURAZAKOV (ISHENBAI) Razvitie promyshlennosti Kirgizii. Frunze, 1965. pp. 100.

— Statistics.

KIRGHIZIA. Tsentral'noe Statisticheskoe Upravlenie. 1971. Kirgizstan v tsifrakh: statisticheskii sbornik. Frunze, 1971. pp. 280.

KIRKBY

— Social conditions.

PICKETT (KATHLEEN GORDON) and BOULTON (DAVID K.) Migration and social adjustment: Kirkby and Maghull; (with the assistance of Norman Rankin). Liverpool, 1974. pp. 179.

KIROV (SERGEI MIRONOVICH).

DOLUNTS (GURGEN KARAPETOVICH) Kirov na Severnom Kavkaze. Moskva, 1973. pp. 192.

KIROV (OBLAST')

— Economic history.

POPOVA (EMILIIA DMITRIEVNA) Krest'ianskie komitety Viatskoi gubernii v 1917 godu. Kirov, 1966. pp. 41.

KISSINGER (HENRY ALFRED).

CATLIN (Sir GEORGE EDWARD GORDON) Kissinger's Atlantic charter. Gerrards Cross, 1974. pp. 144.

KLAVER (IMKE).

KLAVER (IMKE) Herinneringen van een friese landarbeider: enkele opgetekende zaken uit het jongste verleden tot 1925: inkele oanteikene dingen út de jonge tiid oan 1925; ingeleid door Ger Harmsen. Nijmegen, [1974]. pp. 245. *Parallel Frisian and Dutch texts.*

KLIUCHEVSKII (VASILII OSIPOVICH).

VOPROSY istorii Sibiri dosovetskogo perioda: bakhrushinskie chteniia, 1969. Novosibirsk, 1973. pp. 463.

KNIT GOODS.

TOOKEY (DOUGLAS) The impact of knitwear imports: a survey of buyers' attitudes. London, National Economic Development Office, 1970. pp. 60.

KNIT GOODS INDUSTRY

— United Kingdom.

TOOKEY (DOUGLAS) The impact of knitwear imports: a survey of buyers' attitudes. London, National Economic Development Office, 1970. pp. 60.

KNITTING, LACE AND NET INDUSTRY TRAINING BOARD [U.K.]. Report and statement of accounts. a., 1973/4- Nottingham. *To 1971/2 included in the file of British Parliamentry Papers*

KNOWLEDGE, SOCIOLOGY OF.

MULLINS (NICHOLAS C.) Theories and theory groups in contemporary American sociology. New York, [1973]. pp. 337. *bibliogs.*

HAMILTON (PETER) Sociologist. Knowledge and social structure: an introduction to the classical argument in the sociology of knowledge. London, 1974. pp. 164.

LHOMME (JEAN) Pour une sociologie de la connaissance économique. Paris, [1974]. pp. 279.

KNOWLEDGE, THEORY OF.

GLASTRA VAN LOON (JAN F.) Facts are not facts. The Hague, 1973. pp. 11. (*Hague. Institute of Social Studies. Occasional Papers. No.35*)

LATOUCHE (SERGE) Epistémologie et économie: essai sur une anthropologie sociale freudo-marxiste. Paris, [1973]. pp. 583.

MILLER (LIBUSE LUKAS) Knowing, doing, and surviving: cognition in evolution. New York, [1973]. pp. 343. *bibliog.*

RESCHER (NICHOLAS) The primacy of practice: essays towards a pragmatically Kantian theory of empirical knowledge. Oxford, 1973. pp. 156.

TEENSMA (E.) Solipsism and induction. Assen, 1974. pp. 59. *bibliog.*

KOERNER (THEODOR).

KOLLMAN (ERIC C.) Theodor Körner: Militär und Politik. Wien, 1973. pp. 468. *bibliog.*

KONKU

— Rural conditions.

BECK (BRENDA E.F.) Peasant society in Konku: a study of right and left subcastes in south India. Vancouver, [1972]. pp. 334. *bibliog.*

KORAN.

KORAN. The Quran: the eternal revelation vouchsafed to Muhammad, the Seal of the Prophets; Arabic text with a new translation by Muhammad Zafrulla Khan. London, 1971. pp. 673. *In English and Arabic.*

KOREA

— Commerce — Statistics.

KOREA (REPUBLIC). Department of Customs Administration. Statistical yearbook of foreign trade. a., 1964[1st issue]- 1969, 1972- Seoul. *Title varies.*

— Constitution.

CHUNG (KYUNG CHO) Korea: the Third Republic. New York, [1971]. pp. 269. *bibliog.*

— Economic conditions.

BROWN (GILBERT T.) Korean pricing policies and economic development in the 1960s. Baltimore, [1973]. pp. 317.

— **Economic policy.**

KOREA (REPUBLIC). Economic Planning Board. Overall resources budget. a., 1971 (terminal year of the second Five-Year Economic Development Plan)- Seoul.

KIM (IL-SUNG) Let us develop the Chollima Workteam Movement in depth, a great impetus to socialist construction: speech delivered...May 11, 1968. Pyongyang, 1972. pp. 40.

KIM (IL-SUNG) Talk to delegation of Japan National Socialist Mayors Association, May 14, 1972. Pyongyang, 1972. pp. 26.

BROWN (GILBERT T.) Korean pricing policies and economic development in the 1960s. Baltimore, [1973]. pp. 317.

CHUNG (JOSEPH SANG-HOON) The North Korean economy: structure and development. Stanford, [1974]. pp. 212. *bibliog.* (*Stanford University. Hoover Institution on War, Revolution and Peace. Hoover Institution Publications. 132*)

KIM (NAK KWAN) The choice of technology and the full utilization of resources. Seoul, 1974. pp. 28. (*Research Institute of Asian Economies. Occasional Papers. No. 1*)

— **Foreign relations.**

KIM (IL-SUNG) Answers to the questions raised by foreign journalists. Pyongyang, 1970. pp. 137.

REES (DAVID) North Korea's growth as a subversive centre. London, 1972. pp. 19. (*Institute for the Study of Conflict. Conflict Studies. No. 28*)

MAJOR powers and Korea: [proceedings of a symposium sponsored by the Research Institute on Korean Affairs in 1972]; edited by Young C. Kim. Silver Spring, Md., [1973]. pp. 164.

— **Intellectual life.**

KIM (IL-SUNG) On creating revolutionary literature and art: speech to workers in the field of literature and art, November 7, 1964. Pyongyang, 1972. pp. 22.

— **Politics and government.**

KIM (IL-SUNG) Answers to the questions raised by foreign journalists. Pyongyang, 1970. pp. 137.

CHUNG (KYUNG CHO) Korea: the Third Republic. New York, [1971]. pp. 269. *bibliog.*

KIM (IL-SUNG) Talk to delegation of Japan National Socialist Mayors Association, May 14, 1972. Pyongyang, 1972. pp. 26.

CHONG GYONG MO. South Korean reality. Pyongyang, 1973. pp. 14. (*Reprinted from Sekai, No. 9, 1973*)

DEMOCRATIC FRONT FOR THE REUNIFICATION OF THE FATHERLAND [KOREA] and COMMITTEE FOR THE PEACEFUL REUNIFICATION OF THE FATHERLAND [KOREA]. The truth about the abduction and detention of Kim Dae Jung, a democratic personage of South Korea. Pyongyang, 1973. pp. 16.

KIM (IL-SUNG) Let us prevent a national split and reunify the country: speech at the Pyongyang mass rally to welcome the party and government delegation of the Czechoslovak Socialist Republic, June 23, 1973. Pyongyang, 1973. pp. 17.

HAN (SUNGJOO) The failure of democracy in South Korea. Berkeley, [1974]. pp. 240. *bibliog.*

— **Social policy.**

KIM (IL-SUNG) Talk to delegation of Japan National Socialist Mayors Association, May 14, 1972. Pyongyang, 1972. pp. 26.

— **Statistics.**

KOREA (REPUBLIC). Economic Planning Board. Major statistics in charts. a., current issues only kept. [Seoul]. *In Korean and English.*

KOREAN LITERATURE.

KIM (IL-SUNG) On creating revolutionary literature and art: speech to workers in the field of literature and art, November 7, 1964. Pyongyang, 1972. pp. 22.

KOREAN REUNIFICATION QUESTION (1945—).

INTERNATIONAL CONFERENCE ON THE PROBLEMS OF KOREAN UNIFICATION, SEOUL, 1970. Korean unification: problems and prospects; [papers of the conference]; edited by C.I. Eugene Kim. Kalamazoo, Mich., [1973]. 1 vol. (various pagings).

KÖRNER.

See KOERNER.

KORNILOV (LAVR GEORGIEVICH).

SAVINKOV (BORIS VIKTOROVICH) K delu Kornilova. Paris, 1919. pp. 29.

KRASNOYARSK (KRAI)

— **Politics and government.**

OCHERKI istorii Krasnoiarskoi partiinoi organizatsii. t.2. Krasnoiarsk, 1970. pp. 390.

KREFELD

— **History.**

BILLSTEIN (AUREL) ed. Der eine fällt, die anderen rücken nach...: Dokumente des Widerstandes und der Verfolgung in Krefeld, 1933-1945; zusammengestellt im Auftrag der Vereinigung der Verfolgten des Naziregimes, etc. Frankfurt/Main, [1973]. pp. 343. *bibliog.*

KREISKY (BRUNO).

VODOPIVEC (ALEXANDER) Die Quadratur des Kreisky: Österreich zwischen parlamentarischer Demokratie und Gewerkschaftsstaat. Wien, [1973]. pp. 368.

KRONACKER (PAUL).

KRONACKER (PAUL) Souvenirs de paix et de guerre. [Paris, 1973]. pp. 317.

KRONSTADT

— **History — 1921, Revolt.**

SEMANOV (SERGEI NIKOLAEVICH) Likvidatsiia antisovetskogo kronshtadtskogo miatezha 1921 goda. Moskva, 1973. pp. 232.

KRUGER (STEPHANUS JOHANNES PAULUS).

FISHER (JOHN) born 1909. Paul Kruger: his life and times. London, 1974. pp. 278. *bibliog.*

KRUPP FAMILY.

BARTEL (WALTER) Karl Liebknecht gegen Krupp. 2nd ed. Berlin, 1951. pp. 47.

KUBAN'

— **Economic history.**

BESLENEEV (ALI DZHEMAL'EVICH) and SHAMANOV (IBRAGIM MAGOMETOVICH) Ocherki istorii khoziaistva i khoziaistvennogo byta gortsev Kubanskoi oblasti, vtoraia polovina XIX veka. Cherkessk, 1972. pp. 68.

KUCKHOFF (GRETA).

KUCKHOFF (GRETA) Vom Rosenkranz zur Roten Kapelle: ein Lebensbericht. Frankfurt am Main, 1974. pp. 434.

KUECHENHOFF (ERICH).

Der FALL Küchenhoff; oder, Agitation mit falschem Etikett: wie politische Gegnerschaft zu "Bild" wissenschaftlich verbrämt werden sollte; (herausgegeben von der Axel Springer Verlag AG, Abteilung Information). Berlin, 1972. pp. 113.

KUIBYSHEV (OBLAST')

— **Politics and government.**

OCHERKI istorii Kuibyshevskoi organizatsii KPSS. Kuibyshev, 1967. pp. 642.

KUMAS (NEW GUINEA TRIBE).

HAYES (RITA THERESA) Sorcery and power among the Kwoma of Sepik New Guinea; [M. Phil. (London) thesis]. 1973[or rather 1974]. fo. 304. *bibliog. Typescript: unpublished. This thesis is the property of London University and may not be removed from the library.*

KUMBA

— **Social conditions.**

LAGERBERG (CORNELIS SERAFINUS IGNATIUS JOANNES) and WILMS (G.J.) Profile of a commercial town in West-Cameroon: research findings of a socio-anthropological enquire [sic] in Kumba. Tilburg, 1974. pp. 76. (*Tilburg. Katholieke Hogeschool. Tilburg Institute of Development Research. Studies on Development Research. 1*)

KUSTANAI (OBLAST')

— **Economic conditions.**

MEL'NIKOV (NIKOLAI VASIL'EVICH) ed. Perspektivy razvitiia Kustanaiskogo zhelezorudnogo basseina. Alma-Ata, 1972. pp. 346. *bibliog.*

KUUSINEN (AINO).

KUUSINEN (AINO) Before and after Stalin: a personal account of Soviet Russia from the 1920s to the 1960s;...translated from the German by Paul Stevenson. London, 1974. pp. 256.

KUWAIT FUND FOR ARAB ECONOMIC DEVELOPMENT.

STEPHENS (ROBERT) The Arabs' new frontier. London, 1973. pp. 256.

KWAZULU (TERRITORY)

— **Boundaries.**

BEST (ALAN C.G.) and YOUNG (BRUCE S.) Homeland consolidation: the case of KwaZulu. Stellenbosch, 1972. pp. 63-74. (*From South African Geographer, vol. 4, no. 1, September 1972) Xerox copy.*

— **Politics and government.**

SOUTH AFRICA. Report of the Controller and Auditor-General on the accounts of the kwaZulu Government and of the lower authorities in the area. a., 1972/3- Pretoria. *Included in the file of SOUTH AFRICA. Parliament. House of Assembly. Votes and proceedings; (with Printed annexures).*

KWOMAS.

See KUMAS (NEW GUINEA TRIBE).

LABOUR AND LABOURING CLASSES.

INTERNATIONAL LABOUR ORGANISATION. Labour-Management Relations Series. Geneva, 1957 in progress.

VERCAUTEREN (PAUL) Les sous-prolétaires: essai sur une forme de paupérisme contemporain. Bruxelles, [1970]. pp. 203. *bibliog.*

INTERNATIONAL COMMITTEE OF HISTORICAL SCIENCES. Commission Internationale d'Histoire des Mouvements Sociaux et des Structures Sociales. Mouvements nationaux d'indépendance et classes populaires aux XIXe et XXe siècles en Occident et en Orient: [published under the general direction of Ernest Labrousse]. Paris, 1971. 2 vols. (in 1). *bibliogs. In French or English.*

LABOUR AND LABOURING CLASSES. (Cont.)

URBANIZATSIIA, nauchno-tekhnicheskaia revoliutsiia i rabochii klass: nekotorye voprosy teorii, kritika burzhuaznykh kontseptsii; Urbanization, scientific and technological revolution, and working class: theory - some aspects, bourgeois conceptions: critical survey. Moskva, 1972. pp. 268. *With English table of contents.*

JAHRBUCH ARBEITERBEWEGUNG. a., 1973 (Bd.1)- Frankfurt am Main.

CHANGLI (IRINA IVANOVNA) Trud: sotsiologicheskie aspekty teorii i metodologii issledovaniia; Labour: sociological aspects of the theory and methodology of research. Moskva, 1973. pp. 588. *bibliog. With English table of contents.*

CRITIQUES DE L'ÉCONOMIE POLITIQUE. No. 10. Travail et emploi. Paris, 1973. pp. 151.

RABOCHII klass - glavnaia revoliutsionnaia sila. Moskva, 1973. pp. 400.

RABOCHII klass - vedushchaia sila mirovogo revoliutsionnogo protsessa: kritika burzhuaznykh i reformistskikh kontseptsii. Moskva, 1973. pp. 184.

SOREVNOVANIE dvukh sistem: ekonomika i trudiashchiesia. Moskva, 1973. pp. 400. *With brief English summaries and table of contents.*

INTERNATIONAL LABOUR OFFICE. Studies and Reports. New Series. No. 79. Multinational enterprises and social policy. Geneva, 1973. pp. 182.

ZUR Sozialstruktur der sozialistischen Gesellschaft: ([papers and discussion at a symposium]; herausgegeben vom Wissenschaftlichen Rat für Soziologische Forschung in der DDR). Berlin, 1974. pp. 221.

— Directories.

INTERNATIONAL ASSOCIATION OF LABOUR HISTORY INSTITUTIONS. Directory. [London?, 1974]. 1 vol. (looseleaf).

— History.

SCHWEIZERISCHES SOZIALARCHIV. Jahresbericht. a., 1973- Zürich.

— Language (new words, slang, etc.)

WRIGHT (PETER) The language of British industry. London, 1974. pp. 206. *bibliog.*

— Africa.

GUTKIND (PETER C.W.) The emergent African urban proletariat. Montreal, [1974]. pp. 79. *bibliog.* (*McGill University. Centre for Developing-Area Studies. Occasional Paper Series. No. 8*)

— America, Latin.

AMERICAN INSTITUTE FOR MARXIST STUDIES. Bibliographical Series. No. 1 A bibliography of the history of the Latin-American labor and trade union movements. [3rd ed.] New York, 1967. pp. 18.

DAVIS (STANLEY M.) and GOODMAN (LOUIS WOLF) eds. Workers and managers in Latin America. Lexington, Mass., [1972]. pp. 308.

— Argentine Republic.

SOLOMONOFF (JORGE N.) Ideologias del movimiento obrero y conflicto social: de la organizacion nacional hasta la Prima Guerra Mundial. Buenos Aires, [1971]. pp. 314. *bibliog.*

— Asia.

ONE WORLD ONLY, 1969. Industrialization and technological change in Asia: its implication for the Asian labour movement; (editor: Dieter Bielenstein). Tokyo, [1970?]. pp. 163. (*Friedrich-Ebert-Stiftung. Asian Labour Institute. Reports. 3*)

— Austria.

MASERATI (ENNIO) Il movimento operaio a Trieste dalle origini alla prima guerra mondiale. [Milan, 1973]. pp. 281.

HAUTMANN (HANS) and KROPF (RUDOLF) Die österreichische Arbeiterbewegung vom Vormärz bis 1945: sozialökonomische Ursprünge ihrer Ideologie und Politik. Wien, [1974]. pp. 214. *bibliog.* (*Ludwig-Boltzmann-Institut für Geschichte der Arbeiterbewegung. Schriftenreihe. 4*)

— Canada.

CANADA. Public Service Staff Relations Board. Pay Research Bureau. 1973. Employee benefits and conditions of employment in Canada: highlights of studies of prevalence, characteristics and costs from 1967 into 1972. Ottawa, 1973. pp. 93,(2).

— — New Brunswick.

NEW BRUNSWICK. Department of Labour. Survey of working conditions. a., 1971- Fredericton, N.B.

— — Quebec.

DRACHE (DANIEL) ed. Quebec: only the beginning: the manifestoes of the Common Front; [translations of manifestoes of various labour organizations]. Toronto, 1972. pp. 272.

— — Bibliography.

LEBLANC (ANDRE E.) and THWAITES (JAMES D.) compilers. Le monde ouvrier au Québec: bibliographie rétrospective...; en collaboration avec Hélène Espesset [and others]. Montréal, 1973. pp. 283. *bibliog.* (*Regroupement de Chercheurs en Histoire des Travailleurs Québécois. Collection Histoire des Travailleurs Québécois. 1*)

— Chile.

RAPTIS (MICHEL) Revolution and counter-revolution in Chile: a dossier on workers' participation in the revolutionary process; translated by John Simmonds. London, [1974]. pp. 174.

— China.

SHIH (PING) Life of workers under Chinese Communist persecution. [Taiwan], 1973. pp. 80. (*Asian Peoples' Anti-Communist League. Pamphlets. No. 174*)

— Colombia.

PECAUT (DANIEL) and PECAUT (MYRIAM) La classe ouvrière en Colombie: rapport de recherche. Paris, 1971. 2 vols.

VILLAZON DE ARMAS (CRISPIN) Nueva politica laboral: discursos. Bogota, Ministerio de Trabajo y Seguridad Social, 1972. pp. 34.

— — Statistics.

COLOMBIA. Departamento Administrativo Nacional de Estadistica. 1969. Sub-empleo en las 7 principales ciudades del pais, segun el censo de 1964. Bogota, 1969. pp. 166. *bibliog.*

— Communist countries.

RABOCHII klass i ego partiia v sovremennom sotsialisticheskom obshchestve: [polnye teksty vystuplenii i otvetov na voprosy uchastnikov konferentsii, 21-23 maia, 1973 g., v Varshave]. Praga, 1973. pp. 271.

— Ecuador.

ECUADOR. Junta Nacional de Planificacion y Coordinacion. 1970. Plan ecuatoriano para el desarrollo de los recursos humanos. Quito, 1970. 2 vols. (in 1).

— — Statistics.

ECUADOR. Direccion General de Estadistica y Censos. 1963. Estadisticas economicas y del trabajo: indices de empleo y salario, años 1959-1961. Quito, 1963. pp. 61.

ECUADOR. Division de Estadistica y Censos. 1965. Estadisticas del trabajo: indices de empleo y salarios, 1964. Quito, 1965. pp. 59.

— European Economic Community countries — Statistics.

EUROPEAN COMMUNITIES. Statistical Office. Social Statistics. Luxembourg, 1960 in progress.

— France.

MOTHE (DANIEL) Le métier de militant. Paris, [1973]. pp. 187.

MARX (KARL) and ENGELS (FRIEDRICH) Le mouvement ouvrier français; [texts selected with] introduction, traduction et notes de Roger Dangeville. Paris, 1974. 2 vols. (in l).

— Germany.

PROLETARIAT in der BRD: Reproduktion, Organisation, Aktion; ([by] Martin Anders [and others]). Berlin, 1974. pp. 633.

REULECKE (JUERGEN) ed. Arbeiterbewegung an Rhein und Ruhr: Beiträge zur Geschichte der Arbeiterbewegung in Rheinland-Westfalen. Wuppertal, [1974]. pp. 468. *bibliog.*

ROTH (KARL HEINZ) Die "andere" Arbeiterbewegung und die Entwicklung der kapitalistischen Repression von 1880 bis zur Gegenwart: ein Beitrag zum Neuverständnis der Klassengeschichte in Deutschland, etc. München, 1974. pp. 395. *bibliog.*

— Hungary.

A MAGYAR forradalmi munkásmozgalom története. kötet 1,2. 2nd ed. Budapest, 1970. pp. 563.

— India.

KUTHIALA (S.K.) From tradition to modernity. New Delhi, 1973. pp. 227. *bibliog.*

— — Bibliography.

INDIA. Ministry of Labour and Employment. Library. Bibliographical Series. 14. Catalogue of publications of the Ministry of Labour and Employment. New Delhi, [1962]. pp. 57.

— — India — Education.

KAKKAR (N.K.) Workers' education in India. New Delhi, 1973. pp. 404. *bibliog.*

— Ireland (Republic).

GEARY (ROBERT CHARLES) and Ó MUIRCHEARTAIGH (F.S.) Equalization of opportunity in Ireland: statistical aspects. Dublin, 1974. pp. 122. (*Economic and Social Research Institute. Broadsheets. 10*)

— Israel.

MERHAV (PERETZ) La gauche israélienne: histoire, problemes et tendances du mouvement ouvrier israélien. Paris, [1973]. pp. 498. *bibliog.*

— Italy.

LISI (ARCANGELO) Storia del movimento operaio di Locorotondo, dai miei ricordi. Locorotondo, [197-?]. pp. 63.

FAENZA (LILIANO) Marxisti e "riministi": la conferenza di Rimini e l'Internazionale italiana; vent'anni di storia del movimento operaio, 1872-1892. Rimini, [1972]. pp. 93. *bibliog.*

PANZIERI (RANIERO) La ripresa del marxismo-leninismo in Italia: [an anthology];...a cura di Dario Lanzardo. Milano, [1972]. pp. 365.

I PROBLEMI dell'occupazione in Lombardia: atti del Convegno svoltosi a Milano il 15 e il 16 ottobre 1971. [Milano], Giunta Regionale Lombardia, Assessorato al Lavoro e Movimenti Demografici, [1972]. pp. 448.

ALTIERI (LEONARDO) Sindacato e organizzazione di classe. Milano, 1973. pp. 158. *bibliog.*

CLASSE: Quaderni sulla Condizione e sulla Lotta Operaia. 7. 1972-73: crisi, ristrutturazione, lotte. Milano, 1973. pp. 396.

CURIEL (EUGENIO) Scritti, 1935-1945; a cura di Filippo Frassati. Roma, 1973. 2 vols.

MONTALE (BIANCA) Mazzini e le origini del movimento operaio italiano: appunti di storia del Risorgimento. Genova, 1973. pp. 135. *bibliog.*

LABOUR AND LABOURING CLASSES. (Cont.)

MOVIMENTO operaio e fascismo nell'Emilia-Romagna, 1919-1923; ([by] Luciano Casali [and others]). Roma, 1973. pp. 363.

PACI (MASSIMO) Mercato del lavoro e classi sociali in Italia: ricerche sulla composizione del proletariato. Bologna, 1973 repr. 1974. pp. 351.

FAVILLI (PAOLO) Capitalismo e classe operaia a Piombino, 1861-1918. Roma, 1974. pp. 256.

LIBERTINI (LUCIO) Tecnini, impiegati, classe operaia: inquadramento unico e 150 ore. Roma, [1974]. pp. 237.

— — Congresses.

PARTITO OPERAIO ITALIANO. Congresso. I congressi del Partito operaio italiano: [reports of the 1st to 5th congresses, 1885-1890, edited with a historical introduction by] Diana Perli. Padova, 1972. pp. 180.

— Korea.

KIM (IL-SUNG) Let us develop the Chollima Workteam Movement in depth, a great impetus to socialist construction: speech delivered...May 11, 1968. Pyongyang, 1972. pp. 40.

— Mexico.

CARR (BARRY) Organised labour and the Mexican revolution 1915-1928. [Oxford], 1972. fo.33. (*Oxford. University. St. Antony's College. Latin American Centre. Occasional Papers.* 2) Typescript.

— Netherlands.

SWAAN (ABRAM DE) Een boterham met tevredenheid: gesprekken met arbeiders. Amsterdam, 1972. pp. 144.

VAN onderen: brieven, interviews, gedichten en verhalen uit de arbeidswereld; met een nawoord van C. Poppe. Amsterdam, 1972. pp. 116.

GIELE (JACQUES J.) De Eerste Internationale in Nederland: een onderzoek naar het onstaan van de nederlandse arbeidersbeweging van 1868 tot 1876. Nijmegen, 1973. pp. 273. *bibliog.*

— Philippine Islands.

PHILIPPINE ISLANDS. Department of Labor. 1960. A report to the nation: labor today; by Angel M. Castaño. Manila, 1960. pp. 17.

— Poland.

IAZHBOROVSKAIA (INESSA SERGEEVNA) Ideinoe razvitie pol'skogo revoliutsionnogo rabochego dvizheniia, konets XIX - pervaia chetvert' XX v. Moskva, 1973. pp. 415.

MALINOWSKI (HENRYK) Szkice z dziejów klasy robotniczej: wybrane zagadnienia z lat 1917-1919. Warszawa, 1973. pp. 466.

— Russia.

TSENTRAL'NYI GOSUDARSTVENNYI ARKHIV OKTIABR'SKOI REVOLIUTSII, VYSSHIKH ORGANOV GOSUDARSTVENNOI VLASTI I ORGANOV GOSUDARSTVENNOGO UPRAVLENIIA SSSR. 1917 God v Dokumentakh i Materialakh. Rabochee dvizhenie v 1917 godu; podgotovili k pechati V.L. Meller i A.M. Pankratova, etc. Moskva, 1926. pp. 371.

BLIAKHMAN (LEONID SOLOMONOVICH) and SHKARATAN (OVSEI IRMOVICH) NTR, rabochii klass, intelligentsiia. Moskva, 1973. pp. 320.

BUIAN (IVAN VASIL'EVICH) Sotsial'no-ekonomicheskie osnovy truda pri sotsializme. Kiev, 1973. pp. 191.

PARTIIA i rabochii klass v usloviiakh stroitel'stva kommunizma. Moskva, 1973. pp. 303.

ZIMOGLIADOV (FELIKS ROMANOVICH) Kommunisticheskaia partiia Sovetskogo Soiuza vo glave trudovoi aktivnosti mass, 1928-1941 gg.: iz opyta raboty partiinykh organizatsii Donbassa. Moskva, 1973. pp. 160.

— — Education.

DIAMENT (KH.) Kul'trabota na novom etape. Moskva, 1930. pp. 49.

— — Caucasus.

SHIGABUDINOV (MAGOMED SHIGABUDINOVICH) Rabochee dvizhenie na Severnom Kavkaze v gody reaktsii, 1907- 1910 gg. Makhachkala, 1973. pp. 143.

— — Chechen—Ingush Republic.

KOLOSOV (LEONID NIKOLAEVICH) Pervoe pokolenie proletariata Checheno-Ingushetii, 1893-1917 gody. Groznyi, 1965. pp. 106.

— — Moldavian Republic.

RAZVITIE rabochego klassa Moldavskoi SSR, 1940-1965 gg. Kishinev, 1970. pp. 228.

— — Siberia.

DOKUCHAEV (GEORGII ANTONOVICH) Rabochii klass Sibiri i Dal'nego Vostoka v gody Velikoi Otechestvennoi voiny. Moskva, 1973. pp. 423.

— — Soviet Far East.

DOKUCHAEV (GEORGII ANTONOVICH) Rabochii klass Sibiri i Dal'nego Vostoka v gody Velikoi Otechestvennoi voiny. Moskva, 1973. pp. 423.

— — Tatar Republic.

NUGAEV (RASHID ALIMZHANOVICH) Sotsial'no-ekonomicheskie problemy zaniatosti i ispol'zovaniia rabochei sily: na primere Tatarskoi ASSR. Kazan', 1972. pp. 121.

— — Ukraine.

SUSPIL'NO-politychne zhyttia trudiashchykh Ukraïns'koï RSR.Kyïv, 1973 in progress.

PLIUSHCH (MYKOLA ROMANOVYCH) Tekhnichna tvorchist' robitnychoho klasu Ukraïns'koï RSR, 1959-1970 rr. Kyïv, 1973. pp. 183. *With Russian summary.*

— — — Education.

NIKITINA (ELENA IVANOVNA) and PRESS (TAMARA NATANOVNA) Rabochee obshchezhitie: opyt vospitatel'noi raboty. Moskva, 1971. pp. 111.

NIKITINA (ELENA IVANOVNA) and PRESS (TAMARA NATANOVNA) Rabochee obshchezhitie: opyt vospitatel'noi raboty. Moskva, 1971. pp. 111.

— Samoa.

DUNCAN (H.G.) Labour conditions in Western Samoa: report to the government of Western Samoa to be used as a basis for a suitable labour ordinance for the territory. [Apia?, 1953]. pp. 46.

— South Africa.

SOUTH AFRICAN CONGRESS OF TRADE UNIONS. Apartheid in South African industry. London, [1972?]. pp. 7.

MANAGEMENT responsibility and African employment in South Africa; report of a panel investigation; [edited by W.H. Thomas]. Johannesburg, 1973. pp. 142.

WORKSHOP ON ORGANISED LABOUR IN SOUTH AFRICAN SOCIETY, CAPE TOWN, 1973. Labour perspectives on South Africa: (proceedings...); edited by Wolfgang H. Thomas. Cape Town, 1974. pp. 259.

— Spain.

CANDEL (FRANCISCO) Inmigrantes y trabajadores. Barcelona, [1972]. pp. 239.

CALERO AMOR (ANTONIO MARIA) Historia del movimiento obrero en Granada, 1909-1923. Madrid, 1973. pp. 374. *bibliog.*

DURAN I SANPERE (AGUSTI) Barcelona i la seva historia: la societat i l'organitzacio del treball. Barcelona, 1973. pp. 698.

OLLE ROMEU (JOSEP M.) ed. El moviment obrer a Catalunya, 1840-1843: textos i documents. Barcelona, [1973]. pp. 428. *bibliog. In Catalan or Spanish.*

— — Congresses.

CONGRESO OBRERO ESPAÑOL, Iº, BARCELONA, 1870. I Congreso obrero español; estudio preliminar y notas de Victor Manuel Arbeloa. Madrid, 1972. pp. 376.

— Switzerland.

WULLSCHLEGER (EUGEN) Aus der Geschichte der Arbeiterbewegung in Basel: Vortrag, gehalten in den Volksbildungskursen des Arbeiterbundes. Basel, 1912. pp. 32.

GREULICH (HERMAN) Ein Kampf um die Menschwerdung: gegen die Verlängerung der Arbeitszeit, Art. 41 des Fabriksgesetzes. Aarau, [1922]. pp. 48.

SCHWEIZERISCHES SOZIALARCHIV. Jahresbericht. a., 1973- Zürich.

— United Kingdom.

RAZZELL (P.E.) and WAINWRIGHT (R.W.) eds. The Victorian working class: selections from letters to the Morning Chronicle (1849-1851). London, 1973. pp. 338.

ROZHKOV (BORIS ARKHIPOVICH) Angliiskoe rabochee dvizhenie, 1859-1864 gg. Moskva, 1973. pp. 236. *bibliog.*

U.K. Central Office of Information. Reference Division. 1973. Manpower and employment in Britain: the role of government. London, 1973. pp. 28. *bibliog.*

YOUNG SOCIALISTS. Racialism: a threat to all workers. London, [1973]. pp. 7.

BURNETT (JOHN) Ph.D., ed. Useful toil: autobiographies of working people from the 1820s to the 1920s. London, 1974. pp. 364.

FOSTER (JOHN) 1940- . Class struggle and the industrial revolution: early industrial capitalism in three English towns. London, [1974]. pp. 346. *bibliog.*

GORBIK (VIACHESLAV ALEKSANDROVICH) Antirabochaia politika pravitel'stva konservatorov i polozhenie trudiashchikhsia v poslevoennoi Anglii. Kiev, 1974. pp. 111.

LANE (ANTHONY D.) The union makes us strong: the British working class, its trade unionism and politics. London, 1974. pp. 320. *bibliog.*

TUC YOUTH CONFERENCE, LONDON, 1974. Trade union youth in conference: report of the first...conference, etc. London, [1974]. pp. 59.

— — Dwellings.

TARN (JOHN NELSON) Five per cent philanthropy: an account of housing in urban areas between 1840 and 1914. Cambridge, 1973. pp. 211. *bibliog.*

— — Medical care.

U.K. Department of Employment. 1972. Employment Medical Advisory Service Act, 1972: guide to the Service. [London, 1972]. pp. (5).

— — Statistics.

LABOUR statistics: report of a Conference held under the general auspices of the Standing Committee of Statistics Users, 3 April 1973, at the Royal Society, Carlton House Terrace, London. London, National Economic Development Office, 1973. pp. 141.

— United States.

MANDEL (ERNEST) and NOVACK (GEORGE) On the revolutionary potential of the working class. New York, 1969 repr. 1970. pp. 46.

GROSSMAN (JONATHAN PHILIP) The Department of Labor. New York, 1973. pp. 309. *bibliog.*

LABOUR AND LABOURING CLASSES. (Cont.)

LYND (ALICE) and LYND (ROBERT STAUGHTON) eds. Rank and file: personal histories by working-class organizers. Boston, [1973]. pp. 297.

MOORE (ROBERT LAURENCE) ed. The emergence of an American left: civil war to World War I. New York, [1973]. pp. 212. *bibliog.*

WORK in America; report of a special task force to the Secretary of Health, Education, and Welfare; prepared under the auspices of the W.E. Upjohn Institute for Employment Research; [James O'Toole, chairman]. Cambridge, Mass., 1973. pp. 262. *bibliog.*

CROWLEY (J.E.) This Sheba, self: the conceptualization of economic life in eighteenth-century America. Baltimore, [1974]. pp. 161. *(Johns Hopkins University. Studies in Historical and Political Science. Series 92. No.2)*

— — Massachusetts.

FRIED (MARC) The world of the urban working class. Cambridge, Mass., 1973. pp. 410. *bibliog.*

— Yugoslavia.

HRONOLOGIJA radničkog pokreta u Srbiji. knj.2. Od 1919. do 1941. godine. Beograd, 1969. pp. 397. *In Cyrillic.*

LABOUR AND LABOURING CLASSES IN LITERATURE.

PROZHOGIN (VASILII ELIZAROVICH) Problematika truda v tvorchestve M. Gor'kogo i sovremennost'. Kiev, 1974. pp. 271.

LABOUR CONTRACT

— Italy.

LIBERTINI (LUCIO) Tecnini, impiegati, classe operaia: inquadramento unico e 150 ore. Roma, [1974]. pp. 237.

— Russia — Azerbaijan.

ISMAILOV (IBRAGIM ISAEVICH) Kollektivnyi dogovor v Azerbaidzhane: istoriia vozniknoveniia i ego nekotorye voprosy. Baku, 1967. pp. 66.

LABOUR COSTS

— European Economic Community countries.

EUROPEAN COMMUNITIES. Statistical Office. Social Statistics. Luxembourg, 1960 in progress.

LABOUR COURTS

— Europe.

AARON (BENJAMIN) Labor courts: western European models and their significance for the United States. Los Angeles, 1970. pp. 847-882. *(California University. Institute of Industrial Relations. Reprints. No. 209)*

LABOUR DISCIPLINE

— Italy.

MONTUSCHI (LUIGI) Potere disciplinare e rapporto di lavoro. Milano, 1973. pp. 229. *(Bologna. Università. Seminario Giuridico. Pubblicazioni. 64)*

LABOUR DISPUTES.

INDUSTRIAL unrest: report of a conference at Ditchley Park, 1-4 December 1972; by Theodore R. Iserman, conference rapporteur. Enstone, [1973]. pp. 23. *(Ditchley Foundation. Ditchley Papers. No. 43)*

NATIONAL INDUSTRIAL CONFERENCE BOARD. Resolving labor-management disputes: a nine-country comparison. New York, [1973]. pp. 89. *bibliog.*

— Colombia.

RUEDA ROSERO (ULPIANO) Los conflictos de trabajo: la huelga; el arbitramento. Bogota, 1969. pp. 92. *bibliog.*

— India.

SINGH (GURBAKHSH) Industrial disputes and machinery for settlement in India. New Delhi, 1973. pp. 78. *bibliog.*

— Sierra Leone.

SIERRA LEONE. Board of Inquiry into the Docks Dispute. 1967. Report...; by G.S. Panda. Freetown, [1967]. pp. 11.xiv.

— United States.

The ROLE of the neutral in public employee disputes; a report on the joint conference of the Association of Labor Mediation Agencies and the National Association of State Labor Relations Agencies...1971; edited by Howard J. Anderson. Washington, D.C., [1972]. pp. 124.

LABOUR ECONOMICS.

FREEMAN (RICHARD BARRY) Labor economics. Englewood Cliffs, [1972]. pp. 136. *bibliogs.*

LABOUR EXCHANGES

— Belgium.

LAMBINON (MAURICE) Les indépendants face à l'O.N.E.M. [Bruxelles, Institut Economique et Social des Classes Moyennes, 1972]. fo. 24. *bibliog.*

— Sweden.

SWEDEN. Statskontoret. 1968. Arbetsmarknadsverket och arbetsmarknadspolitiken: huvudrapport; Statskontorets översyn av arbetsmarknadsverkets organisation. Stockholm, 1968. pp. 299. *(Sweden. Statens Offentliga Utredningar. 1968.60)*

SWEDEN. Statskontoret. 1968. Tio ekonomer om arbetsmarknadspolitiken: Statskontorets översyn av arbetsmarknadsverkets organisation. Stockholm, 1968. pp. 165. *(Sweden. Statens Offentliga Utredningar. 1968. 62)*

— United Kingdom.

U.K. Department of Employment. 1971. Services for employers: government employment services. [London, 1971]. pp. 13.

LABOUR LAWS AND LEGISLATION

— Andean Group Countries.

APARICIO VALDEZ (LUIS) Politica laboral en el Grupo Andino. Lima, 1972. pp. 262. *(Universidad del Pacifico. Centro de Investigacion. Coleccion Trabajos de Investigacion. Serie Derecho de Trabajo)*

— Australia.

NATIONAL LABOUR ADVISORY COUNCIL [AUSTRALIA]. Review of Australian law and practice relating to conventions adopted by the International Labour Conference. in AUSTRALIA. Parliament. Parliamentary papers, 1969, vol.4.

SYKES (EDWARD I.) and GLASBEEK (HARRY JACQUES) Labour law in Australia. Sydney, 1972. pp. 771.

GLASBEEK (HARRY JACQUES) and EGGLESTON (E.M.) Cases and materials on industrial law in Australia. Sydney, 1973. pp. 590.

— Austria.

SCHWARZ (WALTER) Arbeitsrecht und Verfassung: Antrittsvorlesung, gehalten am 26. November 1970 an der Universität Graz. Wien, [1972]. pp. 45. *bibliog.* *(Vienna. Kammer für Arbeiter und Angestellte. Schriftenreihe)*

— Belgium.

BELGIUM. Ministère de l'Emploi et du Travail. Direction Générale des Etudes. 1971. Aperçu de la législation du travail en Belgique. 3rd ed. Bruxelles, 1971. pp. 190. *bibliog.*

BELGIUM. Ministère des Classes Moyennes. 1972. Le statut social des travailleurs indépendants. [Bruxelles], 1972. pp. 78.

— Brazil.

BRAZIL. Statutes, etc. 1972. Programa nacional de valorização do trabalhador: melhor trabalho melhor solario. [Brasilia?] 1972. pp. 15.

— Denmark.

DENMARK. Statutes, etc. 1971. The Employers and Salaried Employees (Legal Relationship)Act, 1971. [Copenhagen, 1971]. fo. 9.

— France.

DESPAX (MICHEL) Le droit du travail. 3rd ed. Paris, 1973. pp. 128. *bibliog.*

— Germany.

PELTZER (MARTIN) The German Labour Management Relations Act. London, 1972. pp. 324. *In English and German.*

— Italy.

COTTINO (AMEDEO) Il mercato delle braccia e il problema dell'efficacia della legge: considerazioni teorico-empiriche. Torino, 1973. pp. 158. *(Turin. Università. Istituto di Scienze Politiche. Pubblicqzioni. vol. 27) With English summary.*

MONTESANO (LUIGI) and MAZZIOTTI (FABIO) Le controversie del lavoro e della sicurezza sociale: commento della legge 11 agosto 1973 n. 533. Napoli, 1974. pp. 311.

ROMAGNOLI (UMBERTO) Lavoratori e sindacati tra vecchio e nuovo diritto. Bologna, [1974]. pp. 293.

— Japan.

HARARI (EHUD) The politics of labor legislation in Japan: national- international interaction. Berkeley, [1973]. pp. 221. *bibliog.*

— Mexico.

MEXICO. Statutes, etc. 1970. Ley Federal del Trabajo, Mexico, 1970. pp. 488.

— Russia.

RUSSIA (R.S.F.S.R.). Statutes, etc. 1918. Russian code of laws of labour;... edited by the People's Commissariat of Justice. Petrograd, 1919. pp. 24.

PASHKOV (ALEKSEI STEPANOVICH) and KHRUSTALEV (BORIS FEDOROVICH) Obiazannost' trudit'sia po sovetskomu pravu. Moskva, 1970. pp. 192.

ROMMA (FEDOR DMITRIEVICH) and URZHINSKII (KONSTANTIN PAVLOVICH) Pravovye voprosy podbora i rasstanovki kadrov. Moskva, 1971. pp. 168.

ALEKSANDROV (NIKOLAI GRIGOR'EVICH) ed. Sovetskoe trudovoe pravo. Moskva, 1972. pp. 576.

GLOZMAN (VIL' ABRAMOVICH) and KARINSKII (SERGEI SERGEEVICH) eds. Osnovy trudovogo zakonodatel'stva SSSR. Minsk, 1973. pp. 238.

KLIUEV (ANATOLII ALEKSEEVICH) and MAVRIN (ALEKSANDR VENEDIKTOVICH) Rukovoditeliu predpriiatiia o trudovom zakonodatel'stve. 2nd ed. Moskva, 1973. pp. 277.

RUSSIA (U.S.S.R.). Statutes, etc. 1926-72. Normativnye akty o trude: kratkii sbornik ofitsial'nykh materialov. Moskva, 1973. pp. 542.

— — Estonia.

ESTONIA. Statutes, etc. 1973. Kodeks zakonov o trude Estonskoi SSR: ofitsial'nyi tekst. Tallin, 1973. pp. 174.

— — Lithuania.

LITHUANIA. Statutes, etc. 1973. Kodeks zakonov o trude Litovskoi Sovetskoi Sotsialisticheskoi Respubliki. Vil'nius, 1973. pp. 175.

— — **Moldavian Republic.**

MOLDAVIAN REPUBLIC. Statutes, etc. 1973. Kodeks zakonov o trude Moldavskoi SSR: ofitsial'nyi tekst. Kishinev, 1973. pp. 348. *In Moldavian and Russian.*

— — **Tajikistan.**

TAJIKISTAN. Statutes, etc. 1973. Kodeks zakonov o trude Tadzhikskoi SSR, etc. Dushanbe, 1973. pp. 170.

— **Spain.**

OJEDA AVILES (ANTONIO) Los trabajadores temporales: problemas juridicos de eventuales, interinos y temporeros en derecho español. Sevilla, 1973. pp. 301. *(Seville. Universidad. Publicaciones. Serie Derecho. No. 17)*

— **Sri Lanka.**

DE SILVA (S.R.) The legal framework of industrial relations in Ceylon. Colombo, [1973]. pp. 679.

— **Sweden.**

KOMMUNISTISK TIDSKRIFT. Skriftserie. 1971. Nr.3. De antifackliga klasslagarna. Stockholm, 1971. pp. 124. *bibliog.*

— **Switzerland.**

SWITZERLAND. Statutes, etc. 1964-1967. Textausgabe zum Arbeitsgesetz. Bern, 1967. pp. 220.

— **United Kingdom.**

DRAKE (CHARLES DOMINIC) Labour law. 2nd ed. London, 1973. pp. 358.

HENDERSON (JOAN) The Industrial Relations Act in the courts. London, 1973. pp. 38.

CRONIN (J.B.) and GRIME (R.P.) Introduction to industrial law. London, 1974. pp. 212.

— **United States.**

JOHNSON (JULIA EMILY) ed. The National Labor Relations Act: should it be amended?. New YORK, 1940..pp.416 *bibliog.*

LABOUR LAWS AND LEGISLATION, INTERNATIONAL.

INTERNATIONAL LABOUR ORGANISATION. Labour-Management Relations Series. Geneva, 1957 in progress.

INTERNATIONAL LABOUR CONFERENCE. 54th Session. Reports. 3. Third item on the agenda: information and reports on the application of conventions and recommendations. Geneva, 1970. 4 pts.

INTERNATIONAL LABOUR CONFERENCE. 56th Session. Reports. 3. Third item on the agenda: information and reports on the application of conventions and recommendations. Geneva, 1971. 5 pts. (in 1 vol.).

INTERNATIONAL LABOUR CONFERENCE. 57th Session. Reports. 3. Third item on the agenda: information and reports on the application of conventions and recommendations. Geneva, 1972. 7 pts. (in 1 vol.)

GIANNOPOULOS (DEMETRIUS C.) La protection internationale de la liberté syndicale: la Commission d'Investigation et de Conciliation en matière de liberté syndicale de l'Organisation Internationale du Travail.Paris, 1973. pp. 274. *bibliog.*

INTERNATIONAL LABOUR CONFERENCE. 58th Session. Reports. 3. Third item on the agenda: information and reports on the application of conventions and recommendations. Geneva, 1973. 5 pts. (in 1 vol.)

INTERNATIONAL LABOUR CONFERENCE. 59th Session. Reports. 3. Third item on the agenda: information and reports on the application of conventions and recommendations. Geneva, 1974. 5 pts. (in 1 vol.)

LABOUR MOBILITY.

ARBEJDSKRAFTENS mobilitet 1: litteraturstudiet, etc.; [by] Helge Tetzschner [and others]. København, 1974. pp. 177. *bibliog. (Socialforskningsinstituttet. Studier. Nr. 30) With English summary.*

WILLIS (KENNETH G.) Problems in migration analysis. Farnborough, Hants, [1974]. pp. 247. *bibliog.*

— **Austria.**

LIST (ALOIS) Analyse der Arbeitnehmermobilität und ihrer Einflussgrössen anhand empirischer Untersuchungen in Österreich. Wien, 1974. pp. 134. *bibliog. (Vienna. Hochschule für Welthandel. Dissertationen. 16)*

— **Canada.**

VANDERKAMP (JOHN) Mobility behaviour in the Canadian labour force. Ottawa, 1973. pp. 152. *bibliog. (Canada. Economic Council. Special Studies. No. 16)*

— **Denmark.**

ARBEJDSKRAFTENS mobilitet 1: litteraturstudiet, etc.; [by] Helge Tetzschner [and others]. København, 1974. pp. 177. *bibliog. (Socialforskningsinstituttet. Studier. Nr. 30) With English summary.*

GUNDELACH (PETER) and TETZSCHNER (HELGE) Arbejdskraftens mobilitet 2: forundersøgelsen, etc. København, 1974. pp. 150. *bibliog. (Socialforskningsinstituttet. Studier. Nr. 31) With English summary.*

— **European Economic Community countries.**

MAESTRIPIERI (CESARE) La libre circulation des personnes et des services dans la CEE. Heule, [1972]. pp. 200. *bibliog. (Luxembourg (City). Université Internationale de Sciences Comparées. Centre International d'Etudes et de Recherches Européennes. Cours. 1970-71)*

— **Sierra Leone.**

SWINDELL (KENNETH) Labour migration and mining in Sierra Leone; [Ph.D.(London) thesis]. 1973[or rather 1974]. fo. 287. *Typescript: unpublished. This thesis is the property of London University and may not be removed from the Library.*

— **Underdeveloped areas.**

See UNDERDEVELOPED AREAS — Labour mobility.

— **United Kingdom.**

JOHNSON (JAMES HENRY) and others. Housing and the migration of labour in England and Wales. Farnborough, Hants, [1974]. pp. 299. *bibliog.*

— — **Mathematical models.**

LINDLEY (ROBERT M.) Inter-industry mobility of male employees in Great Britain, 1959-68: a stochastic model framework. Coventry, 1973. pp. 51. *bibliog. (University of Warwick. Centre for Industrial Economic and Business Research. [Warwick Research in Industrial and Business Studies]. No. 34)*

LABOUR PARTY

— **Australia.**

ALBINSKI (HENRY STEPHEN) The Australian Labor Party and the aid to parochial schools controversy. University Park, Penn., 1966. pp. 55. *(Pennsylvania State University. Penn State Studies. No. 19)*

— **Ireland (Republic).**

MITCHELL (ARTHUR) M.A., Ph.D. Labour in Irish politics, 1890-1930: the Irish labour movement in an age of revolution. Dublin, [1974]. pp. 317. *bibliog.*

— **Norway.**

LORENZ (EINHART) Arbeiderbevegelsens historie: en innfóring; norsk sosialisme i internasjonalt perspektiv. Oslo, [1972-74]. 2 vols.(in 1). *bibliogs.*

NORSKE ARBEIDERPARTI. Arbeiderpartiet og valget 73: håndbok for valgarbeidere, og DNA's politiske regnskap, 1969-1973. [Oslo, 1973]. pp. 156. *bibliog.*

— **United Kingdom.**

FOSTER (D.B.) The logic of the alliance; or, The Labour Party analyzed and justified. Leeds, [191-?]. pp. 8.

COLE (GEORGE DOUGLAS HOWARD) The people's front. London, 1937. pp. 366.

BERRINGTON (HUGH) Backbench opinion in the House of Commons, 1945-55. Oxford, 1973. pp. 265.

FABIAN SOCIETY. Fabian Tracts. [No.] 420. Labour in Asia: a new chapter?; editor, Colin Jackson. London, 1973. pp. 52.

U.K. National Register of Archives. 1973. Archives of the Labour Party: Labour and Socialist International; listed by R.A. Storey and T.W.M. Jaine. London, 1973. fo. 132.

U.K. National Register of Archives. 1973. Archives of the Labour Party: Labour Representation Committee: Appendix; listed by T.W.M. Jaine. London, 1973. fo.12.

U.K. National Register of Archives. 1973. Labour Party archives: Daily Citizen, 1912-15. London, 1973. fo.2.

U.K. [National Register of Archives]. 1973. Labour Party archives: Labour Party Distressed Areas Commission: list of LP/DAC/1-13; compiled by S. Horrocks. London, 1973. fo. 19.

WILSON (HAROLD) Individual choice in democracy: a speech delivered at an East of Scotland Labour Party meeting at Leith on 20 January, 1973. [London, 1973]. pp. 19. *(Labour Party. Edinburgh Series of Policy Speeches. No. 1)*

AIMS OF INDUSTRY. The importance of being earnest: the case for Mr. Benn. London, [1974]. pp. 5.

BRAND (CARL FREMONT) The British Labour Party: a short history. rev. ed. Stanford, 1974. pp. 424. *bibliog.*

BROWN (KENNETH D.) ed. Essays in anti-labour history: responses to the rise of labour in Britain. London, 1974. pp. 409.

HALFWAY to 1984...1979. London, [1974]. pp. 15.

LABOUR PARTY. Labour's programme: campaign document 1974 agreed at a joint meeting of the Labour Party N[ational] E[xecutive] C[ommittee] and the P[arliamentary] L[abour] P[arty] Parliamentary Committee on Friday, January 11, 1974. London, [1974]. pp. 16.

LABOUR PARTY. Let us work together: Labour's way out of the crisis; the Labour Party manifesto, 1974. London, 1974. pp. 16.

PANITCH (LEO VICTOR) The Labour Party and the trade unions: a study of incomes policy since 1945 with special reference to 1964-70; [Ph. D. (London) thesis]. 1973[or rather 1974]. fo. 401. *bibliog. Typescript: unpublished. This thesis is the property of London University and may not be removed from the library. Offprint from "Political Studies: vol. 19, no. 2, in end pocket.*

STEWART (MARGARET) Protest or power?: a study of the Labour Party. London, 1974. pp. 133. *bibliog.*

TAVERNE (DICK) The future of the left: Lincoln and after. London, 1974. pp. 175.

LABOUR REST HOMES

— **Poland.**

POLAND. Główny Urząd Statystyczny. Statystyka Polski: Materiały Statystyczne. Nr.109(231) Hotele robotnicze, 1971. Warszawa, 1972. pp. 78.

LABOUR SERVICE

— **Ghana.**

GHANA. 1968. White Paper on the report of the Commission of Enquiry into the functions, operations and administration of the Workers Brigade. [Accra], 1968. pp. 11. *(W[hite] P[apers]. 1968. No. 8) Bound with the Report.*

LABOUR SUPPLY.

LABOUR SUPPLY.

UNITED NATIONS. Department of Economic and Social Affairs. Population Studies. New York, 1948 in progress.

INTERNATIONAL LABOUR ORGANISATION. Labour-Management Relations Series. Geneva, 1957 in progress.

INTERNATIONAL LABOUR CONFERENCE. 56th Session. Reports. 4. Fourth item on the agenda: the World Employment Programme. Geneva, 1971. pp. 86.

NAVILLE (PIERRE) Temps et technique: structures de la vie de travail. Genève, 1972. pp. 234.

VERNIERES (MICHEL) Travail et croissance: essai sur le rôle du facteur travail au cours du processus de croissance. Paris, [1972]. pp. 210. *bibliog.*

DEATON (DAVID) and THOMAS (BARRY) Adjustments to labour shortages. Coventry, 1973. pp. 43. *(U.K. Social Science Research Council. Industrial Relations Research Unit. Discussion Papers. No. 9)*

KALACHEK (EDWARD D.) Labor markets and unemployment. Belmont, Calif., [1973]. pp. 146.

TIMPERLEY (STUART R.) Personnel planning and occupational choice. London, 1974. pp. 236.

— Mathematical models.

CORINA (JOHN) Labour market models viewed from economic theory: a short appraisal; [prepared for the Labour Market Conference, 1971] . [Coventry, 1971]. fo. 70,(viii). *(U.K. Social Science Research Council. Industrial Relations Research Unit. Discussion Papers)*

LAIDLER (DAVID E.W.) and PURDY (DAVID) eds. Inflation and labour markets. Manchester, [1974]. pp. 258. *bibliogs.*

— Statistics.

JALLADE (JEAN-PIERRE) and others. Occupational and educational structures of the labour force and levels of economic development. Paris, Organisation for Economic Co-operation and Development, 1970-71. 2 vols.

— Africa, Subsaharan.

FRANCE. Direction de l'Aide au Développement des Etats Francophones d'Afrique au Sud du Sahara et de la République Malgache. Bureau des Programmes. Secteur Synthèse. 1973. Eléments de Statistiques de l'emploi rétrospective 1957- 1970: statistiques décennales de l'emploi salarié. [Paris], 1973. pp. 72. *(Structures et Statistiques dans 14 Etats Africains et Malgache. Série B.1. No.1)*

— Argentine Republic — Santiago del Estero (Province).

CABELLO (PLACIDO) and SPEKTOR (SUSANA) Estructura demografica y socio-ocupacional de la provincia de Santiago del Estero. Buenos Aires, 1973. pp. 211. *(Argentine Republic. Consejo Federal de Inversiones. Serie Tecnica. No. 21)*

— Australia.

AUSTRALIA. Commonwealth Bureau of Census and Statistics. 1971. Survey of leavers from schools, universities or other educational institutions, February 1971. Canberra, 1971. pp. 7.

— Austria.

BEIRAT FÜR WIRTSCHAFTS- UND SOZIALFRAGEN. [Publikationen. 20].Untersuchung über die Abwanderung von Arbeitskräften aus Österreich nach Süddeutschland und in die Schweiz. Wien, 1972. pp. 107.

— Belgium.

VERSICHELEN (MARTHE) Verlaten beroepen?: oorzaken en achtergronden van het aanhoudend tekort aan arbeidskrachten in de bouwnijverheid. Gent, [1970?]. pp. 231. *bibliog. With summary in French.*

NEESEN (VICTOR) and others. Vraag en aanbod van geschoolde arbeidskrachten in Limburg;... algemene leiding: V. Neesen. Hasselt, 1971. pp. 232.

PONTANUS (FERNAND) La population active en Belgique: 1910-1961 et tendances récentes; un demi-siècle d'évolution. Bruxelles, 1974. pp. 243. *bibliog. (Brussels. Université Libre. Institut de Sociologie. Groupe d'Etude de la Population Active. Etudes Démographiques)*

— Cameroons.

MANDENG (PATRICE) Auswirkungen der deutschen Kolonialherrschaft in Kamerun: die Arbeitskräftebeschaffung in den Südbezirken Kameruns... 1884-1914. Hamburg, [1973]. pp. 204. *bibliog. (Vereinigung von Afrikanisten in Deutschland. Schriften. Band 4)*

— Canada.

DODGE (DAVID A.) and SWAN (NEIL M.) Factors influencing career choices of students: an empirical examination of some aspects of the neoclassical theory of choice in labour markets. Kingston, 1971. 1 vol. (various foliations). *(Kingston, Ontario. Queen's University. Institute for Economic Research. Discussion Papers. No. 48)*

CANADA. Statistics Canada. Manufacturing and Primary Industries Division. 1973. Growth patterns in manufacturing employment by counties and census divisions; La croissance de l'emploi dans les industries manufacturières, par comtés et par divisions de recensement; 1961-1970. Ottawa, 1973. pp. 134. *bibliog. In English and French.*

CANADA. Census, 1971. Advance bulletin[s]: [series AE: economic characteristics] . [Ottawa], 1974 in progress. *In English and French.*

HARVEY (EDWARD) Educational systems and the labour market. Don Mills, Ont., [1974]. pp. 223.

— — Mathematical models.

SWAN (NEIL M.) Differences in the response of the demand for labour to variations in output among Canadian regions: a preliminary interpretation. Kingston, Ontario, [1971]. fo. 35. *(Kingston, Ontario. Queen's University. Institute for Economic Research. Discussion Papers. No. 41)*

— — British Columbia.

B.C. LABOUR MARKET INFORMATION; [pd. by] Research and Planning Branch, Department of Labour [British Columbia] a., 1973- Victoria, B.C. *Similar information for previous years pd. as a suppl. to the Department's Annual report.*

— Cuba.

RITTER (ARCH R.M.) Human resource mobilization strategies in revolutionary Cuba. [Ottawa], 1973. fo. 62. *(Carleton University. Carleton Economic Papers)*

— Ecuador.

ECUADOR. Junta Nacional de Planificacion y Coordinacion. 1970. Plan ecuatoriano para el desarrollo de los recursos humanos. Quito, 1970. 2 vols. (in 1).

ECUADOR. Junta Nacional de Planificacion y Coordinacion. 1970. Plan ecuatoriano para el desarrollo de los recursos humanos. Quito, 1970. 2 vols. (in 1).

— Europe.

GESELLSCHAFT FÜR SOZIAL- UND WIRTSCHAFTSGESCHICHTE. 4. Arbeitstagung, 1971. Wirtschaftspolitik und Arbeitsmarkt: Bericht...in Wien am 14. und 15. April 1971;...herausgegeben von Hermann Kellenbenz. Wien, 1974. pp. 328. *(Vienna. Universität. Institut für Wirtschafts- und Sozialgeschichte. Sozial- und Wirtschaftshistorische Studien)*

— European Economic Community countries.

EUROPEAN COMMUNITIES. Statistical Office. Social Statistics. Luxembourg, 1960 in progress.

PAULUS (DANIEL) La création du Comité permanent de l'emploi des Communautés européennes. Bruxelles, 1972. pp. 129. *(Brussels. Université Libre. Institut d'Etudes Européennes. Travaux)*

— France.

FRANCE. Institut National de la Statistique et des Etudes Economiques. Collections de l'I.N.S.E.E. Série D. Démographie et Emploi . Paris, 1969 in progress.

FRANCE. Institut National de la Statistique et des Etudes Economiques. Collections de l'I.N.S.E.E. Série. R. Régions . Paris, 1970 in progress.

OFFICE NATIONAL D'INFORMATION SUR LES ENSEIGNEMENTS ET LES PROFESSIONS [FRANCE]. Tendances d'évolution de l'emploi en France jusqu'en 1975.[Paris, 1972]. pp. 47. *bibliog.*

L'ANALYSE de l'emploi par région et par département. [Paris, 1973]. pp. 215. *(France. Centre d'Etudes de l'Emploi. Cahiers. 1) With summaries in English and German.*

FRANCE. Echelon Regional de l'Emploi de Toulouse. 1973. Structure des emplois... au 31 mars 1973. Toulouse, 1973. pp. 162.

FRANCE. Institut National de la Statistique et des Etudes Economiques. Direction Régionale de Lille. 1973. Région Nord 1962-1972: population, emploi, établissements, données comparées suivant les arrondissements. [Lille, 1973]. pp. 96.

HUGUES (PHILIPPE D') and others. Les emplois industriels: nature, formation, recrutement. Paris, [1973]. pp. 515. *(France. Centre d'Etudes de l'Emploi. Cahiers. 4) With English summary.*

FRANCE. Centre d'Etudes de l'Emploi. 1974. Les besoins en main-d'oeuvre dans la région parisienne au cours de la période 1968-1975 par catégories socio-professionnelles. [Paris], 1974. [fo.73].

— Germany — Bavaria.

KORNRUMPF (MARTIN) 25 Jahre Arbeit und Wirtschaft in Bayern: ein dokumentarischer Rückblick auf die Entwicklung des Arbeitsmarktes in Bayern vom Zusammenbruch 1945 bis zur "Bestkonjunktur" im Sommer 1970. [München, 1970]. pp. 91. *(Arbeit und Wirtschaft in Bayern. Jahrgang 25. Sondernummer. September 1970)*

— Ghana — Mathematical models.

BRECHER (RICHARD A.) Summary of The labor-and-land surplus economy (Ghana). [New Haven], 1972. pp. 19. *bibliog.*

— Greece.

KINTIS (ANDREAS A.) The demand for labour in Greek manufacturing: an econometric analysis. Athens, 1973. pp. 179. *bibliog. (Center of Planning and Economic Research, [Athens]. Research Monograph Series. 20)*

— India — Mathematical models.

EVENSON (ROBERT EUGENE) Labor in the Indian agriculture sector. [New Haven], 1972. pp. 53. *bibliog.*

— Ireland (Republic).

HENRY (E.W.) Irish full employment structures 1968 and 1975. Dublin, 1974. pp. 109. *bibliog. (Economic and Social Research Institute. Papers. No. 74)*

— Italy.

BARBAGALLO (FRANCESCO) Lavoro ed esodo nel sud, 1861-1971. Napoli, [1973]. pp. 267.

PACI (MASSIMO) Mercato del lavoro e classi sociali in Italia: ricerche sulla composizione del proletariato. Bologna, 1973 repr. 1974. pp. 351.

— Ivory Coast.

IVORY COAST. Office National de Formation Professionnelle. 1972. Le secteur privé et para-public en Côte d'Ivoire, 1971: résultats de l'enquête main d'oeuvre, 1971. 2e partie: les données individuelles de la main d'oeuvre salariée. [Abidjan], 1972. fo. 245.

LABOUR SUPPLY. (Cont.)

— Jamaica.

JAMAICA. Department of Statistics. Continuous Social and Demographic Survey Unit. 1972. The labour force, 1968, 1969. [Kingston], 1971 [or rather 1972]. pp. 61.

JAMAICA. Department of Statistics. [Continuous Social and Demographic Survey Unit]. 1973. The labour force, 1972. [Kingston, 1973]. pp. 58.

— Kenya.

GUPTA (DESH BANDHU) Labour supplies and economic development in Kenya: [Ph.D. (London) thesis]. [1974]. fo. 423. *bibliog. Typescript: unpublished. Photocopy of article in end pocket. This thesis is the property of London University and may not be removed from the Library.*

— Netherlands.

NETHERLANDS. Centraal Planbureau. 1972. Regionale ontwikkeling van de werkgelegenheid en het spreidingsbeleid, 1970-2000, toegespitst op het Noorden des Lands.'s-Gravenhage, 1972. pp. 16. *(Monografieën. No. 15)*

— Netherlands Antilles.

NETHERLANDS ANTILLES. Bureau voor de Statistiek. 1971. De werkgelegenheidssituatie op Curacao en Aruba in juli 1971 op grond van een gehouden steekproef onderzoek en een vergelijking met 1966. Curacao, 1971. fo. 7.

— New Zealand.

NEW ZEALAND. Department of Labour. Research and Planning Division. 1972. Labour supply and demand in the national development context. [Wellington], 1972. pp. 18. *(Reports Series)*

— — Mathematical models.

HAZELDINE (TIM) Employment and output functions for New Zealand manufacturing industries. Coventry, 1973. pp. 67. *bibliog. (University of Warwick. Department of Economics. Warwick Economic Research Papers. No. 33)*

— Nigeria.

NIGERIA. National Manpower Board. Manpower Studies. No. 15. Survey of manpower shortages and surpluses, 1968-1969. Lagos, 1973. pp. 73.

— Norway.

NORWAY. Arbeidsdirektoratet. Kontoret for Statistikk og Utredninger. 1971. Framskriving av den totale sysselsetting til 1990 for riket, de enkelte fylker og arbeidskontordistrikter. [Oslo], 1971. *fo. 114.*

VISTE (JON OLAV) Utviklingsmønstre for bosetting og sysselsetting i Agder og Rogaland: oppdragsrapport utført for Landsdelskomitéen for Agder og Rogaland: hovedrapport. Oslo, 1972 in progress.

— Pakistan.

SOLIGO (RONALD) Factor intensity of consumption patterns, income distribution and employment growth in West Pakistan (a report to A.I.D.). [New Haven], 1972. pp. 29. *bibliog. Typescript.*

— Poland.

SZKURŁATOWSKI (ZYGMUNT) Siła robocza na wsi lubińskiej i jej produkcyjne wykorzystanie w okresie silnego uprzemysłowienia. Wrocław, 1972. pp. 105. *(Politechnika Wrocławska. Instytut Nauk Społecznych. Prace Naukowe. Nr.5 [being also] Monografie. Nr.2) With English and Russian summaries.*

POLAND. Główny Urząd Statystyczny. Statystyka Polski. [2nd series]. Nr.8. Nowe kadry pracownicze: pracownicy podejmujący pierwszą pracę w gospodarce uspołecznionej w 1971 r. Warszawa, 1973. pp. 174.

— Reunion Island.

FRANCE. Institut National de la Statistique et des Etudes Economiques. Service Départemental de la Réunion. 1970. La situation de l'emploi à la Réunion, 1967-1969. Paris, [1970?]. pp. 38.

— Russia.

FRANCE. Direction de la Documentation. La Documentation Française. Notes et Etudes Documentaires. No. 3,796. L'emploi en U.R.S.S., 1959-1984; [by] Chantal Beaucourt [and] Anton Brender. Paris, 1971. pp. 38. *bibliog.*

CHEMBROVSKII (VLADISLAV VIKENT'EVICH) Problemy zaniatosti v sotsialisticheskom obshchestve; pod redaktsiei...N.P. Frolova. Kishinev, 1973. pp. 274.

— — Bashkir Republic.

ISPOL'ZOVANIE trudovykh resursov malykh, srednikh gorodov i sel'skoi mestnosti: na materialakh Bashkirskoi ASSR. Ufa, 1970. pp. 177.

— Sierra Leone.

SIERRA LEONE. Central Statistics Office. 1971. Household survey of the Northern Province, urban areas, March, 1968-December 1969: final report: household expenditure and income and economic characteristics. Freetown, [1971]. pp. 104.

— South Africa.

SOUTH AFRICA. Department of Labour. Manpower survey: all industries and occupations. bien., 1969 (no.8)- Pretoria. *In English and Afrikaans; nos.1-7 undertaken for departmental purpose only and not available.*

PHILLIPS (BRUCE D.) Secondary industry in the Port Elizabeth/Uitenhage region: an employment study. Port Elizabeth, 1969. pp. 143. *(University of Port Elizabeth. Institute for Planning Research. Research Reports. No.3) With Afrikaans summary.*

— Sweden.

SWEDEN. Statskontoret. 1968. Arbetsmarknadsverket och arbetsmarknadspolitiken: huvudrapport; Statskontorets översyn av arbetsmarknadsverkets organisation. Stockholm, 1968. pp. 299. *(Sweden. Statens Offentliga Utredningar. 1968.60)*

SWEDEN. Statskontoret. 1968. Tio ekonomer om arbetsmarknadspolitiken: Statskontorets översyn av arbetsmarknadsverkets organisation. Stockholm, 1968. pp. 165. *(Sweden. Statens Offentliga Utredningar. 1968. 62)*

SWEDEN. Statistiska Centralbyrån. 1969. Regionala arbetskrafts- och befolkningsförändringar 1960-1965 med projektion till 1980, etc. Stockholm, 1969. pp. 222. *(Information i Prognosfrågor. 1969.5)*

SWEDEN. Statistiska Centralbyrån. Region, förvärvsarbete och inkomst: Region, employment status and income. a., 1971- Stockholm. *(Statistiska Meddelanden: N) With summary and headings of tables in English.*

SWEDEN. Finansdepartementet. Långtidsutredningen. 1971. [Svensk ekonomi fram till 1977]; 1970 års långtidsutredning. Bilaga. 1. Arbetskraftsresurserna 1965-1990; utarbetad inom Statistiska Centralbyråns Prognosinstitut. Stockholm, 1971. pp. 92. *(Sweden. Statens Offentliga Utredningar. 1971.8)*

NYBERG (JAN ERIK) Arbetsmarknad och sysselsättning: en skrift om arbetsmarknadspolitik, utarbetad inom T[jänstemännens] C[entral] O[rganisation]. Stockholm, [1972]. pp. 144.

SWEDEN. Prognosinstitut. 1972. Trender och prognoser: befolkning, utbildning och arbetsmarknad, etc. Stockholm, 1972. pp. 179. *(Information i Prognosfrågor. 1972.10)*

GONÄS (LENA) Företagsnedläggning och arbetsmarknadspolitik: en studie av sysselsättningskriserna vid Oskarshamns Varv. Uppsala, 1974. pp. 240. *bibliog. (Uppsala. Universitet. Kulturgeografiska Institutionen. Geografiska Regionstudier. Nr. 10) With English summary.*

— Switzerland.

BERN (CANTON). Statistisches Bureau. 1970. Beschäftigte in den Gemeinden nach Betriebszählung 1965, etc. Bern, 1970. fo.41, 19. *(Beiträge zur Statistik des Kantons Bern. Produktionsgrundlagen. Reihe E. Heft 1) In German and French.*

— Trinidad and Tobago.

THOMAS (ROY DARROW) The adjustment of displaced workers in a labour-surplus economy: a case study of Trinidad and Tobago. [Mona, 1972]. pp. 118. *bibliog.*

— Turkey.

HJARNØ (JAN) Fremmedarbejdere: en etnologisk undersøgelse af arbejdskraftseksportens virkninger i Tyrkiet. København, Nationalmuseet, 1971. pp. 76.

PAINE (SUZANNE) Exporting workers: the Turkish case. London, 1974. pp. 227. *bibliog. (Cambridge. University. Department of Applied Economics. Occasional Papers. 41)*

— Underdeveloped areas.

See UNDERDEVELOPED AREAS — Labour supply.

— United Kingdom.

MANPOWER IN AIR TRANSPORT AND TRAVEL: a report from the Air Transport and Travel Industry Training Board. a., 1972/1975 [3rd]- Staines. *Each issue covers 3 yrs.*

U.K. Department of Employment. Research: (annual report). a., 1972/3 [1st]- London.

CHISHOLM (MICHAEL) and OEPPEN (JIM) The changing pattern of employment: regional specialisation and industrial localisation in Britain. London, 1973. pp. 127. *bibliog.*

U.K. Census, 1971. Census, 1971: Great Britain: economic activity. London, 1973. pp. 102.

U.K. Central Office of Information. Reference Division. 1973. Manpower and employment in Britain: the role of government. London, 1973. pp. 28. *bibliog.*

FROST (MARTIN EUGENE) Regional employment change in Great Britain, 1952-68, with special reference to the influence of government policy on the northern region; [Ph.D.(London) thesis]. [1974]. 2 vols. *bibliog. Typescript: unpublished. This thesis is the property of London University and may not be removed from the Library.*

LAIDLER (DAVID E.W.) and PURDY (DAVID) eds. Inflation and labour markets. Manchester, [1974]. pp. 258. *bibliogs.*

SPENCE (NIGEL ANTHONY) Spatial dynamics of English regional employment change: 1951 and 1961; [Ph.D.(London) thesis]. 1974. fo. 594. *bibliog. Typescript: unpublished. This thesis is the property of London University and may not be removed from the Library.*

— — Ireland, Northern.

BLACK (WILLIAM) Economist and JEFFERSON (CLIFFORD W.) Regional employment patterns in Northern Ireland. Dublin, 1974. pp. 31. *(Economic and Social Research Institute. Papers. No. 73)*

— United States.

CONFERENCE ON THE UTILIZATION OF SCIENTIFIC AND PROFESSIONAL MANPOWER, COLUMBIA UNIVERSITY, 1953. Proceedings of a conference...;[(convened by the] National Manpower Council). New York, 1954. pp. 197.

MANPOWER in the United States: problems and policies;... [edited by] William Haber [and others]. New York, [1954]. pp. 225. *(Industrial Relations Research Association. Publications. No. 11)*

FREEMAN (RICHARD BARRY) The market for college-trained manpower: a study in the economics of career choice. Cambridge, Mass., 1971. pp. 264.

GREENBERG (DAVID H.) Income guarantees and the working poor in New York City: the effects of income maintenance programs on the hours of work of male family heads. New York, 1971. pp. 103. *(Rand Corporation. [Rand Reports]. 658)*

LABOUR SUPPLY. (Cont.)

MORTON (JOSEPH EDWARD) Handbook for community manpower surveys. Kalamazoo, 1972. pp. 116. (*W.E. Upjohn Institute for Employment Research. Methods for Manpower Analysis. No. 5*)

KNIGHT (RICHARD VICTOR) Employment expansion and metropolitan trade. New York, 1973. pp. 108. (*Columbia University. Graduate School of Business. Conservation of Human Resources Project. Conservation of Human Resources Studies*)

MANGUM (GARTH LEROY) and ROBSON (R. THAYNE) eds. Metropolitan impact of manpower programs: a four-city comparison. Salt Lake City, [1973]. pp. 304. *bibliog.*

NEW directions in employability: reducing barriers to full employment; [papers of a conference sponsored by the National Graduate University in 1972]; edited by David B. Orr. New York, 1973. pp. 244.

O'NEILL (DAVE M.) The Federal government and manpower: a critical look at the MDTA-Institutional and Job Corps programs. Washington, D.C., 1973. pp. 65. (*American Enterprise Institute for Public Policy Research. Evaluative Studies. 9*)

PUBLIC service employment: an analysis of its history, problems and prospects: [essays originally presented at a conference held in 1972, jointly sponsored by the National Conference on Public Service Employment, the New Careers Development Center, and Social Policy magazine]; edited by Alan Gartner [and others]). New York, 1973. pp. 230.

FOGEL (WALTER A.) and MITCHELL (DANIEL J.B.) Higher education decision making and the labor market. Los Angeles, 1974. pp. 49. *bibliog.* (*California University. Institute of Industrial Relations. Reprints. No. 239*)

NATIONAL PLANNING ASSOCIATION. Reports. No.137. A public service employment program: effective manpower strategy: a N.P.A. joint statement by the N.P.A. Board of Trustees [and others]. Washington, D.C., [1974]. pp. 22.

SORKIN (ALAN L.) Education, unemployment, and economic growth. Lexington, Mass., [1974]. pp. 186.

— — New York.

NEW YORK (STATE). Department of Labor. Division of Research and Statistics. 1973. Employment statistics. Vol. 10. Civilian work force, New York State, major areas and counties, 1966-1970; employees in nonagricultural establishments, by industry..., by month, 1966-1970...[and] annual averages, 1966-1970; earnings and hours in nonagricultural establishments..., 1966-1970. Albany, 1973. pp. 214.

— — Venezuela — Carabobo.

VENEZUELA. Direccion General de Estadistica. Division de Muestreo. 1973. Investigacion conjunta: encuesta regional de hogares por muestreo, Estado Carabobo, agosto 1968...:empleo, desempleo y analfabetismo. Caracas, 1973. pp. 242.

— Zambia.

ZAMBIA. Central Statistical Office. Employment and earnings. irreg., 1966/1968- Lusaka.

LABRIOLA (ANTONIO).

LABRIOLA (ANTONIO) Scritti filosofici e politici...; a cura di Franco Sbarberi. Torino, 1973. 2 vols.

LACE AND LACE MAKING

— United Kingdom.

KNITTING, LACE AND NET INDUSTRY TRAINING BOARD [U.K.]. Report and statement of accounts. a., 1973/4- Nottingham. *To 1971/2 included in the file of British Parliamentry Papers*

LA FAYETTE (MARIE JEAN PAUL ROCH YVES GILBERT MOTIER DE) Marquis.

See MOTIER (MARIE JEAN PAUL ROCH YVES GILBERT) Marquis de la Fayette.

LAGOS

— Harbour.

PORT OF LAGOS, THE: (annual report of the Lagos Port Complex). [Nigeria]. a., 1972/3 (3rd)- Apapa Quay, Nigeria.

LAING (RONALD DAVID).

MARTIN (DAVID ALFRED) Tracts against the times. Guildford, 1973. pp. 186.

LAIR VON SIEGBURG (JOHANN).

See SIBERCH (JOHN).

LAKE DISTRICT, UNITED KINGDOM.

U.K. Countryside Commission. 1972. West Cumberland trunk road study. [London], 1972. fo. 44,xxiii. *bibliog.*

ROLLINSON (WILLIAM) Life and tradition in the Lake District. London, 1974. pp. 205. *bibliog.*

LAMBETH

— Civic improvement.

SHANKLAND-COX PARTNERSHIP AND INSTITUTE OF COMMUNITY STUDIES. Inner area study: Lambeth: project report. [London], Department of the Environment, [1974]. pp. 39.

— Social conditions.

SHANKLAND-COX PARTNERSHIP AND INSTITUTE OF COMMUNITY STUDIES. Inner area study: Lambeth: project report. [London], Department of the Environment, [1974]. pp. 39.

LAMBTON (ANTONY CLAUD FREDERICK) Viscount Lambton.

[GENERAL COUNCIL OF THE PRESS]. Press conduct in the Lambton affair; a report by the Press Council. London, [1974]. pp. 37. (*Press Council Booklets. No.5*)

LAMPIÃO.

See FERREIRA DA SILVA (VIRGOLINO) known as Lampião.

LANCASHIRE

— Historical geography.

PORTER (JOHN) Ph.D. The reclamation and settlement of Bowland, with special reference to the period 1500-1650; [Ph.D.(London) thesis]. 1973[or rather 1974]. fo. 267. *Typescript: unpublished. This thesis is the property of London University and may not be removed from the library.*

— Social history.

ELBOURNE (ROGER PHILLIP) Industrialization and popular culture: a case study of Lancashire handloom weavers, 1780-1840; [M. Phil. (London) thesis]. [1974]. fo. 243. *bibliog. Typscript: unpublished. This thesis is the property of London University and may not be removed from the library.*

— — Sources.

VICTORIAN and Edwardian Manchester and east Lancashire from old photographs; introduction and commentaries by George Chandler. London, 1974. pp. (128).

— Transit systems.

SOUTH EAST LANCASHIRE AND NORTH EAST CHESHIRE PASSENGER TRANSPORT EXECUTIVE. Public transport plan for the future. [Manchester], 1973. pp. 107.

LAND

— Taxation — China.

WANG (YEH-CHIEN) An estimate of the land-tax collection in China, 1753 and 1908. Cambridge, Mass., 1973. pp. 57. *bibliog.* (*Harvard University. East Asian Research Center. Harvard East Asian Monographs. 52*)

— — Finland.

VARJO (UUNO) Uber die Produktivität der Acker- und Waldböden Finnlands. Helsinki, 1972. pp. 50. *bibliog.* (*Suomen Maantieteellinen Seura. Fennia. 113*) *With English summary.*

— — Mexico.

MERINO MAÑON (JOSE) La fiscalidad del suelo y el desarrollo urbano. Toluca, Direccion General de Hacienda del Estado de Mexico, 1972. pp. 110. (*Coleccion Estudios Fiscales. 4*)

— — United Kingdom.

JONES (TUDOR) M. Phil. The case for land-value taxation. London, 1973. pp. 15. (*Liberal Publication Department. Liberal Focus. No.5*)

— Australia.

AUSTRALIA. Commonwealth Scientific and Industrial Research Organization. Land Research Series. Melbourne, 1953 in progress.

— British Virgin Islands.

KLUMB (HENRY) Firm and ROBBINS (STANTON) AND COMPANY. Development and land use in program for the British Virgin Islands; report prepared... in consultation with Herbert Croucher. [Tortola, Administrator's Office, 1960]. fo. 46.

— Canada — Prince Edward Island.

BRADLEY (L.F.) and BEAULIEU (ANDREE) Social and geographical aspects of agricultural land use in Prince Edward Island: a case study of the O'Leary area. Ottawa, 1973. pp. 32. *bibliog.* (*Canada. Lands Directorate. Geographical Papers. No. 54*)

— Ghana — Mathematical models.

BRECHER (RICHARD A.) Summary of The labor-and-land surplus economy (Ghana). [New Haven], 1972. pp. 19. *bibliog.*

— Greece, Ancient.

FINLEY (MOSES I.) ed. Problèmes de la terre en Grèce ancienne: recueil de travaux. Paris, 1973. pp. 330. (*Paris. Ecole Pratique des Hautes Etudes. Section des Sciences Economiques et Sociales. Centre de Recherches Historiques. Civilisations et Sociétés. 33*). *In various languages.*

— India.

KHUSRO (ALI M.) The economics of land reform and farm size in India. Madras, 1973. pp. 162. *bibliog.* (*Delhi. Institute of Economic Growth. Studies in Economic Growth. No. 14*)

— Papua New Guinea.

AUSTRALIA. Commonwealth Scientific and Industrial Research Organization. Land Research Series. Melbourne, 1953 in progress.

SACK (PETER G.) ed. Problem of choice: land in Papua New Guinea's future. Canberra, 1974. pp. 220. *bibliog.*

— Russia — Abkhazia.

GUNIA (CHICHIKO KHARUNOVICH) Zemlepol'zovanie v Abkhazii. Sukhumi, 1972. pp. 84.

— — Ukraine.

NOVAKOVS'KYI (LEONID IAKOVYCH) and PYLYPENKO (MYKOLA ANDRIIOVYCH) Zemel'ni resursy Ukraïns'koï RSR. Kyïv, 1973. pp. 238.

— South Africa.

BOTHA (D.J.J.) Urban taxation and land use: report of a one-man commission appointed by the City Council of Port Elizabeth. [Port Elizabeth, 1970]. pp. 192.

— Swaziland.

SWAZILAND. Central Statistical Office. Report on annual survey of Swazi Nation Land. a., 1972/3- Mbabane.

LAND TENURE

— Underdeveloped areas

See UNDERDEVELOPED AREAS — Land.

— United Kingdom.

SOUTH HAMPSHIRE PLAN ADVISORY COMMITTEE. Study Reports. Group C. Urban Form. No. 3. Land commitments. Winchester, 1969. pp. 13.

U.K. Ministry of Agriculture, Fisheries and Food. Agricultural Land Service. Technical Reports. 25. An enquiry into the expenses of agricultural land ownership, England and Wales, 1967-68. [London], 1970. pp. 29.

U.K. Countryside Commission. 1971. Changing countryside project; a report. London, [1971]. pp. 206. *4 maps in end pocket.*

LINDSEY. County Council. Lindsey countryside recreational survey. [Lincoln, 1972]. pp. 86. *Maps in end paper.*

STANDING CONFERENCE ON LONDON AND SOUTH EAST REGIONAL PLANNING. Land availability for residential development; report by the technical panel on a recent publication by the Shankland Cox Partnership for the Housing Research Foundation. [London], 1972. pp. 5.

DOBRY (GEORGE) Review of the development control system: interim report; presented to the Secretary of State for the Environment and the Secretary of State for Wales. London, H.M.S.O., 1974. pp. 102.

ELKIN (STEPHEN L.) Politics and land use planning: the London experience. London, [1974]. pp. 196.

GOVERNMENT and the land...; [by] A.A. Walters [and others]. London, 1974. pp. 95. *(Institute of Economic Affairs. Readings. 13)*

RURAL resource development; [by] M.C. Whitby [and others]. London, 1974. pp. 244. *bibliog.*

— — Wales.

MERIONETH. County Planning Office. Merioneth structure plan: (subject report no. 15): derelict land. Dolgellau, [1973]. fo. 35. *bibliog.*

U.K. Welsh Office. 1973. Land availability for housing, etc. Cardiff, 1973. pp. 6. *(Circulars. 241/73)*

— United States.

BOSCHKEN (HERMAN L.) Corporate power and the mismarketing of urban development: Boise Cascade recreation communities. New York, 1974. pp. 283. *bibliog.*

LAND use, urban form and environmental quality: [report of a study conducted at the University of Chicago for the Office of Research and Development of the U.S. Environmental Protection Agency]; [by] Brian J.L. Berry [and others]. Chicago, 1974. pp. 440. *bibliog. (Chicago. University. Department of Geography. Research Papers. No. 155)*

LAND REFORM.

CRITIQUES DE L'ECONOMIE POLITIQUE. No. 15. Paysannerie et réformes agraires. Paris, 1974. pp. 144.

LE COZ (JEAN) Les réformes agraires: de Zapata à Mao Tsé-toung et la F.A.O.. Paris, 1974. pp. 308. *bibliog.*

TAI (HUNG-CHAO) Land reform and politics: a comparative analysis. Berkeley, [1974]. pp. 565.

— America, Latin.

GARCIA (ANTONIO) Sociologia de la reforma agraria en America latina. Buenos Aires, 1973. pp. 239.

— — Terminology.

SANTOS DE MORAIS (CLODOMIR) Diccionario de reforma agraria: latinoamerica. San Jośe, 1973. pp. 552. *bibliog.*

— Bolivia.

ANTEZANA E. (LUIS) El feudalismo de Melgarejo y la reforma agraria: proceso de la propiedad territorial y de la politica de Bolivia. [Cochabamba], 1970 [or rather 1971]. pp. 174.

— Brazil.

CANA e reforma agraria; [by] Gilberto Freyre [and others]. [2nd ed.] Recife, Instituto Joaquim Nabuco de Pesquisas Sociais, 1970. pp. 372.

— Chile.

CHILE: reforma agraria y gobierno popular; [by] Solon Barraclough [and others]. Buenos Aires, [1973]. pp. 247.

— China.

YEH (KUNG-CHIA) Land reform and the revolutionary war: a review of Mao's concepts and doctrines. Santa Monica, 1971. pp. 125. *bibliog. (Rand Corporation. Rand Reports. 744)*

— Germany, Eastern.

MATTHESS (ERICH) and NAUMANN (HEINZ) Demokratische Bodenreform und antifaschistisch-demokratische Justizentwicklung im Kreis Plauen, 1945-1946, etc. Plauen, 1969. pp. 79. *(Vogtländisches Kreismuseum Plauen. Museumsreihe. Heft 35)*

— India — Bihar.

JANNUZI (FRANK TOMASSON) Agrarian crisis in India: the case of Bihar. Austin, [1974]. pp. 233. *bibliog.*

— Iran.

DENMAN (DONALD ROBERT) The king's vista: a land reform which has changed the face of Persia. Berkhamsted, Herts., [1973]. pp. 368. *bibliog.*

— Lesotho.

WILLIAMS (JOHN COX) Lesotho: land tenure and economic development. Pretoria, 1972. pp. 52. *(Africa Institute. Communications. No. 19)*

— Mexico.

LEMUS GARCIA (RAUL) Panoramica actual de la reforma agraria en Mexico. Mexico, 1968. pp. 83.

REFORMA agraria; [by] Sergio Reyes Osorio [and others; three papers presented at the Primera Reunion Naional de Ciencia y Tecnologia en la Reforma Agraria organized by the Centro Nacional de Productividad]. Mexico, 1969. pp. 150.

STAVENHAGEN (RODOLFO) Land reform and institutional alternatives in agriculture: the case of the Mexican ejido. Vienna, [1973]. pp. 33. *(Wiener Institut für Entwicklungsfragen. Occasional Papers. 73/9)*

— Nepal.

NEPAL. Land Reform Department. Planning, Analysis and Publicity Division. 1973. Evaluation of land reform in Nepal; based on the work of M. A. Zaman. Kathmandu, 1973. pp. 124. *bibliog.*

— Paraguay.

PASTORE (CARLOS) La lucha por la tierra en el Paraguay. Montevideo, 1972. pp. 526.

— Peru.

PERU. Direccion de Comunidades Campesinas. 1970. Chuyama-Chacchahua y Rio Blanco: historia de una "reivindicacion". [Lima, 1970]. pp. 77. *bibliog. (Zac-Andahuaylas. No. 1)*

— Puerto Rico.

BAGUE RAMIREZ (JAIME) Movimientos de reforma agraria en Puerto Rico (1510-1961). [San Juan, Departamento de Agricultura, 1968]. pp. 313. *bibliog. Issued as Revista de Agricultura de Puerto Rico, vol. 55, 1968, nos. 1-2.*

— Russia.

ZEMSKII, pseud. Zemlia - daiushchim khleb. Moskva, 1919. pp. 19.

— Spain.

CARRION (PASCUAL) La reforma agraria de la segunda republica y la situacion actual de la agricultura española. Barcelona, [1973]. pp. 278.

— Uganda.

MAFEJE (ARCHIE) Agrarian revolution and the land question in Buganda. The Hague, 1973. pp. 27. *bibliog. (Hague. Institute of Social Studies. Occasional Papers. No.32)*

— Underdeveloped AREAS.

See UNDERDEVELOPED AREAS — Land reform.

— Uruguay.

INTER-AMERICAN INSTITUTE OF AGRICULTURAL SCIENCES. 1968. Curso de capacitacion en elaboracion de projectos de subdivision de tierras (1968-69): parte práctica; projecto de desarrollo y ampliación de la Colonia Tomas Berreta, Depto. de Rio Negro, Uruguay; presentación resumida. Montevideo, [1968?]. fo. 227.

— Venezuela.

PLAZA (SALVADOR DE LA) El problema de la tierra. Caracas, 1973. 2 vols (in 1).

LAND SETTLEMENT

— United States — Pennsylvania.

WOLF (GEORGE D.) The Fair Play settlers of the West Branch Valley, 1769- 1784: a study of frontier ethnography. Harrisburg, Pennsylvania Historical and Museum Commission, 1969. pp. 122. *bibliog.*

LAND TENURE

— America, Latin.

INTER-AMERICAN COMMITTEE FOR AGRICULTURAL DEVELOPMENT. 1973. Agrarian structure in Latin America: a resume of the CIDA land tenure studies...; edited by Solon Barraclough...with Juan Carlos Collarte. Lexington, Mass., [1973]. pp. 351.

— Cameroun — Law.

MELONE (STANISLAS) La parenté et la terre dans la stratégie du développement: l'expérience camerounaise; étude critique. Paris, 1972. pp. 201. *bibliog.*

— Chile.

BORDE (JEAN) and GONGORA (MARIO) Evolucion de la propiedad rural en el Valle del Puangue. Santiago de Chile, 1956. 2 vols. *(Santiago de Chile. Universidad de Chile. Instituto de Sociologia. [Publications]. 1-2)*

— Ethiopia.

HOBEN (ALLAN) Land tenure among the Amhara of Ethiopia: the dynamics of cognatic descent. Chicago, 1973. pp. 273. *bibliog. (Haile Sellassie I University. Institute of Ethiopian Studies and Faculty of Law. Monographs in Ethiopian Land Tenure. vol. 4)*

— India

— — Gujarat.

BREMAN (JAN) Patronage and exploitation: changing agrarian relations in South Gujarat, India. Berkeley, [1974]. pp. 287. *bibliog.*

— Mexico

— — Mexico (State).

HUITRON H. (ANTONIO) Bienes comunales en el Estado de Mexico. Toluca, Direccion General de Hacienda del Estado de Mexico, 1972. pp. 153. *(Coleccion Estudios Historicos. 2)*

LAND TENURE. (Cont.)

— Nigeria.

NIGERIA. Agricultural Statistics Unit. 1973. Consolidated report of the land tenure enquiries, 1968/69, 1969/70 and 1970/71. Lagos, 1973. pp. 15. (*Rural Economic Surveys of Nigeria. 1973/2*)

— Papua New Guinea.

SACK (PETER G.) ed. Problem of choice: land in Papua New Guinea's future. Canberra, 1974. pp. 220. *bibliog.*

— Peru.

PERU. Direccion de Comunidades Campesinas. 1971. Datos basicos e inventario del patrimonio comunal de las comunidades de la provincia de Andahuaylas. [Lima, 1971]. pp. 59. (*Zac-Andahuaylas. No.2*)

— Russia.

PROBLEMY krest'ianskogo zemlevladeniia i vnutrennei politiki Rossii: dooktiabr'skii period. Leningrad, 1972. pp. 365. (*Akademiia Nauk SSSR. Institut Istorii SSSR. Leningradskoe Otdelenie. Trudy. vyp.13*)

— — Law.

BORODANOV (NIKOLAI MATVEEVICH) Osnovy zemel'nogo prava. Moskva, 1970. pp. 71.

RUSSIA (U.S.S.R.) Statutes, etc. 1968. Fundamentals of legislation of the USSR and the Union Republics on marriage and the family; Fundamentals of land legislation of the USSR and the Union Republics. Moscow, 1972. pp. 77.

— — Lithuania — Law.

LITHUANIA. Statutes, etc. 1922. Zakon o zemel'noi reforme, priniatyi Litovskim Uchreditel'nym Seimom 15-go fevralia 1922 g....; perevel [s litovskogo] An.Rg. Kovno, [1922]. pp. 24.

— — Ukraine — Law.

UKRAINE. Statutes, etc. 1972. Zemel'nyi kodeks Ukrainskoi SSR; s postateinymi materialami v redaktsii po sostoianiiu na 1 sentiabria 1972 goda. Kiev, 1973. pp. 211.

— South Africa. — Natal.

GREYLING (JACOB JOHANNES CAROLUS) and DAVIES (RONALD JOHN) Indian agricultural holdings on the Natal North Coast. Report 1. Land-subdivision, land-ownership and land-occupation. Natal, Town and Regional Planning Commission, 1970. 3 vols. *bibliog. Vol. 3 is Atlas.*

— Sweden.

HERLITZ (LARS) Jordegendom och ränta: omfördelningen av jordbrukets merprodukt i Skaraborgs län under frihetstiden. Lund, 1974. pp. 387. *bibliog.* (*Göteborgs Universitet. Ekonomisk-Historiska Institutionen. Meddelanden. 31*) *With English summary.*

— Switzerland — Zürich (Canton) — Law.

ZUERICH (CANTON). Kommission für die Reform der Zürcherischen Bodenrechts. 1972. Schlussbericht. [Zürich], 1972. pp. 345, map and 13 charts in end pocket.

— United Kingdom.

DEWINDT (EDWIN BREZETTE) Land and people in Holywell-cum-Needingworth: structures of tenure and patterns of social organization in an East Midlands village, 1252-1457. Toronto, 1972. pp. 299. *bibliog.* (*Pontifical Institute of Mediaeval Studies. Studies and Texts. 22*)

— — Law.

DALTON (PATRICK J.) Land law. London, 1972. pp. 316.

POOLE (ERIC) English property law. London, 1973. pp. 413.

RIDDALL (JOHN GERVASE) Introduction to land law. London, 1974. pp. 351.

— — Ireland.

O'NEILL (BRIAN) The war for the land in Ireland. London, 1933. pp. 201.

STEELE (EDWARD DAVID) Irish land and British politics: tenant-right and nationality, 1865-1870. London, 1974. pp. 367. *bibliog.*

LAND TITLES

— Registration and transfer — Mexico.

ROMERO GONZALEZ (GREGORIO) Cien años del registro publico en el distrito de Toluca. 1970. Toluca, Direccion General de Hacienda del Estado de Mexico, 1972. pp. 444. (*Coleccion Estudios Historicos. 1*)

— — Sweden

KULLBERG (ANDERS) Johan Gabriel Stenbock och reduktionen: godspolitik och ekonomiförvaltning, 1675-1705. Stockholm, [1973]. pp. 174. *bibliog.* (*Uppsala. Universitet. Historiska Institutionen. Studia Historica Upsaliensia. 51*) *With German summary.*

LANDLORD AND TENANT

— Netherlands.

JANSSEN (J.M.J.F.) Nota/witboek over de positie van de huurder. Groningen, 1974. pp. 119.

— United Kingdom.

DAVIES (RONALD) Landlords and tenants. London, 1951. pp. 20. *bibliog.* (*Current Affairs. No. 129*)

U.K. Lord Chancellor's Office. 1968. Landlord and Tenant Act 1954: security of tenure of business premises: how landlord and tenant are affected. 3rd ed. London, 1968. pp. 19.

ADKIN (BENAIAH WHITELEY) Landlord and tenant; seventeenth edition by Raymond Walton and Michael Essayan. London, 1973. pp. 454.

LANDSCAPE.

U.K. Countryside Commission. 1971. Changing countryside project; a report. London, [1971]. pp. 206. *4 maps in end pocket.*

LANDSCAPE PROTECTION.

NEEDHAM (BARRIE) An experiment with landscape evaluation techniques. [Oxford], 1973. pp. 89. *bibliog.* (*Oxford Polytechnic. Department of Town Planning. Oxford Working Papers in Planning Education and Research. 15*)

SOUTH HAMPSHIRE PLAN ADVISORY COMMITTEE. Study Reports. Group A. Rural Conservation. No. 5. Rural landscape. Winchester, 1969. pp. 32.

— — Scotland.

LAND USE CONSULTANTS. A planning classification of Scottish landscape resources. Perth, Countryside Commission for Scotland, [1972]. pp. 124. *bibliog.* (*Occasional Papers. No. 1*)

LANDSHUT

— Economic history.

PREISSLER (PETER REINHOLD) Wirtschaft und Gesellschaft Landshuts in der Zeit von 1834- 1914. [Erlangen-Nürnberg?, 1973?]. pp. 309,xxvii. *bibliog.*

— Social history.

PREISSLER (PETER REINHOLD) Wirtschaft und Gesellschaft Landshuts in der Zeit von 1834- 1914. [Erlangen-Nürnberg?, 1973?]. pp. 309,xxvii. *bibliog.*

LANG (OTTO).

SPILLMANN (CHARLES) Otto Lang, 1863-1936: Sozialismus und Individuum. Bern, 1974. pp. 140. *bibliog.*

LANGOS.

CURLEY (RICHARD T.) Elders, shades and women: ceremonial change in Lango, Uganda. Berkeley, [1973]. pp. 223. *bibliog.*

LANGUAGE AND LANGUAGES.

WHITAKER (HARRY A.) On the representation of language in the human brain: problems in the neurology of language and the linguistic analysis of aphasia. Edmonton, [1971]. pp. 224. *bibliog.*

LAMBERT (WALLACE EARL) Language, psychology, and culture: essays...; selected and introduced by Anwar S. Dil. Stanford, Calif., 1972. pp. 362. *bibliogs.* (*Linguistic Research Group of Pakistan. Language Science and National Development*)

HENSON (HILARY) British social anthropologists and language: a history of separate development. Oxford, 1974. pp. 147. *bibliog.*

LANGUAGES

— Philosophy.

SEARLE (JOHN ROGERS) ed. The philosophy of language. London, 1971 repr. 1972. pp. 149. *bibliog.*

DUMMETT (MICHAEL ANTHONY EARDLEY) Frege: philosophy of language. London, 1973. pp. 698. *bibliog.*

SCHAFF (ADAM) Language and cognition: introduction by Noam Chomsky; edited by Robert S. Cohen; based on a translation by Olgierd Wojtasiewicz. New York, [1973]. pp. 194. *bibliog.*

— Political aspects.

HEATH (SHIRLEY BRICE) Telling tongues: language policy in Mexico: colony to nation. New York, [1972]. pp. 300. *bibliog.*

LANGUAGES, MODERN

— Study and teaching.

U.K. National Committee for Commonwealth Immigrants. Education Panel. 1966. Problems of language for immigrants: the choice of languages in the curriculum in English schools. [London, 1966 repr. 1970]. pp. 5.

— — Bibliography.

CENTRE FOR INFORMATION ON LANGUAGE TEACHING, and BRITISH COUNCIL. English-Teaching Information Centre. A language-teaching bibliography. 2nd ed. Cambridge, 1972. pp. 242.

LANGUEDOC

— Economic history.

LE ROY LADURIE (EMMANUEL) The peasants of Languedoc;...translated with an introduction by John Day. Urbana, [1974]. pp. 370. *bibliog.*

LAOS

— Foreign relations.

FRANCE. Direction de la Documentation. La Documentation Française. Notes et Etudes Documentaires. No. 3,189. L'evolution de la situation au Laos: chronologie, juin 1962- avril 1963. Paris, 1965. pp. 27. *bibliog.*

— History.

LEVY (PAUL) Archaeologist. Histoire du Laos. Paris, 1974. pp. 128. *bibliog.*

— Politics and government.

FRANCE. Direction de la Documentation. La Documentation Française. Notes et Etudes Documentaires. No. 3,189. L'evolution de la situation au Laos: chronologie, juin 1962- avril 1963. Paris, 1965. pp. 27. *bibliog.*

DAVIS (GEORGE ELLSWORTH) External intervention and mobilization of ethnic minorities in Laos, 1945-1973; [Ph.D. (London) thesis]. 1973. fo. 221. *bibliog. Typescript: unpublished. This thesis is the property of London University and may not be removed from the Library.*

LA PAMPA

— Statistics.

ARGENTINE REPUBLIC. Consejo Federal de Inversiones. 1963. Analisis economico de la provincia de La Pampa. [Vol.] 2. Apendice estadistico. [Buenos Aires, 1963]. 1 vol. (unpaged).

LAPPS.

INNSTILLING om Samisk husflid som stottenaering; fra en komité oppnevnt ved kongelig resolusjon av 13. juni 1969. Orkanger, 1970. pp. 32.

EIDHEIM (HARALD) Aspects of the Lappish minority situation. Oslo, [1971]. pp. 86. *bibliog.*

LARCENY

— United Kingdom.

GRIEW (EDWARD JAMES) The Theft Act 1968. 2nd ed. London, 1974. pp. 181.

LARSSON FAMILY.

BRATTNE (BERT) Bröderna Larsson: en studie i svensk emigrantagentverksamhet under 1880-talet. Stockholm, [1973]. pp. 298. *bibliog. (Uppsala. Universitet. Historiska Institutionen. Studia Historica Upsaliensia. 50) With English summary.*

LASSALLE (FERDINAND JOHANN GOTTLIEB).

UEXKUELL (GÖSTA VON) Ferdinand Lassalle in Selbstzeugnissen und Bilddokumenten. Reinbek bei Hamburg, 1974. pp. 158. *bibliog.*

LASTENAUSGLEICH (1949—).

KRUMPER (ARTUR) Die Hauptentschädigung im Lastenausgleich der Bundesrepublik Deutschland in finanzwissenschaftlicher und rechtswissenschaftlicher Sicht, etc. [Erlangen, imprint, 1973]. pp. 187. *bibliog.*

LATIN AMERICAN FREE TRADE ASSOCIATION COUNTRIES

— Commerce — Ecuador.

ECUADOR. Ministerio de Industrias y Comercio. Direccion de Integracion. 1969. Intercambio comercial del Ecuador con los paises miembros de la ALALC, 1962-1967. Quito, 1969. pp. 139. *(Boletines. No. 65)*

LATIN AMERICAN STUDIES.

BYARS (ROBERT S.) and LOVE (JOSEPH L.) eds. Quantitative social science research on Latin America. Urbana, [1973]. pp. 270. *bibliogs. (Illinois University. Center for Latin American and Caribbean Studies. [Publications]. No.1)*

— Russia.

ORTEGA Y MEDINA (JUAN A.) Historiografia sovietica iberoamericanista, 1945-1960. Mexico, 1961. pp. 195. *(Mexico City. Universidad Nacional Autonoma de Mexico. Facultad de Filosofia y Letras. Seminario de Historiografia Mexicana Moderna)*

LATVIA

— Commerce.

PRAUDE (VALERII ROBERTOVICH) Ekonomicheskaia reforma v torgovle, ee tseli, osushchestvlenie i problemy. Riga, 1973. pp. 79.

— Economic policy.

SOVERSHENSTVOVANIE ekonomicheskikh otnoshenii v deviatoi piatiletke: respublikanskii mezhvuzovskii sbornik nauchnykh trudov. vyp.1. Riga, 1973. pp. 154.

— History.

KAPENIECE (ILGA) The year of change; (translated from the Latvian by J. Vejš). Riga, 1973. pp. 80. *bibliog.*

— Religion.

PODMAZOV (ARNOL'D ANDREEVICH) Tserkov' bez sviashchenstva. Riga, 1973. pp. 167.

— Social conditions.

IZMENENIIA sotsial'noi struktury sotsialisticheskogo obshchestva: na primere Latviiskoi SSR; materialy ko vtoroi vsesoiuznoi nauchnoi konferentsii. Riga, 1971. pp. 93.

— Statistics, Vital.

SHLINDMAN (SHEFTEL' ISAAKOVICH) and ZVIDRIN'SH (PETR PAVLOVICH) Izuchenie rozhdaemosti: po materialam spetsial'nogo issledovaniia v Latviiskoi SSR. Moskva, 1973. pp. 176. *bibliog.*

LATVIANS IN GERMANY.

LATVIISKII GOSUDARSTVENNYI UNIVERSITET. Uchenye Zapiski. t.185. Germaniia i Pribaltika. 2. Riga, 1973. pp. 99.

LAURIER (Sir WILFRED).

NEATBY (H. BLAIR) Laurier and a Liberal Quebec: a study in political management;edited...by Richard T. Clippingdale. Toronto, [1973]. pp. 244. *bibliog. (Carleton University. Institute of Canadian Studies. Carleton Library. No. 63)*

LAW.

CENTRE INTERNATIONAL DE SYNTHÈSE. Semaine de Synthèse, 29e, 1970. Le droit, les sciences humaines et la philosophie: communications et échanges de vues. Paris, 1973. pp. 405.

TAPPER (COLIN) Computers and the law. London, [1973]. pp. 314. *bibliog.*

— Philosophy.

JAMES (M.H.) ed. Bentham and legal theory. [Belfast, 1973]. pp. 154. *(Reprinted from Northern Ireland Legal Quarterly, 1973)*

LUKASHEVA (ELENA ANDREEVNA) Sotsialisticheskoe pravosoznanie i zakonnost'. Moskva, 1973. pp. 344.

PENNOCK (JAMES ROLAND) and CHAPMAN (JOHN WILLIAM) eds. The limits of law. New York, 1974. pp. 276. *(American Society for Political and Legal Philosophy. Nomos. 15)*

STEIN (PETER) and SHAND (JOHN) Legal values in western society. Edinburgh, [1974]. pp. 280.

— Study and teaching — Germany.

GERMANY (BUNDESREPUBLIK). Deutscher Bundestag. Wissenschaftliche Dienste. 1972. Studierende der Rechtswissenschaft und Bedarf an Juristen in der Bundesrepublik Deutschland: eine Analyse vorliegender Planungen und Prognosen. Bonn, 1972. pp. 66. *(Materialien. 29)*

— Austria — History and criticism.

UHL (HARALD) Handwerk und Zünfte in Eferding: Materialien zum grundherrschaftlichen Zunfttypus. Wien, 1973. pp. 159. *bibliog. (Oesterreichische Akademie der Wissenschaften. Philosophisch-Historische Klasse. Kommission für die Savigny-Stiftung. Fontes Rerum Austriacarum. 3.Abteilung. Fontes Iuris. 3.Band)*

— Canada — Alberta.

CANADIAN BAR ASSOCIATION. Alberta Branch. Annual Mid-Winter Meeting, 1st, 1973. Selected proceedings. [Edmonton, 1973]. pp. 277.

— China.

KITAISKAIA Narodnaia Respublika: ekonomika, gosudarstvo i pravo, kul'tura. Moskva, 1970. pp. 227.

— Communist countries.

PRAVO i sotsiologiia. Moskva, 1973. pp. 359.

— European Economic Community Countries.

EIRE. [Dáil Eireann and Seanad Eiraenn]. Joint Committee on the Secondary Legislation of the European Communities. Parliamentary debates: official report. sess., Ag 3 1973 (v.1, no.1)- Dublin.

BERGSTEN (ERIC E.) Community law in the French courts: the law of treaties in modern attire. The Hague, 1973. pp. 145.

KAHN-FREUND (OTTO) European Community law and the British legal system; (transcript of... lecture held on 7 February 1972). [London], Civil Service College, [1973?]. fo. (31). *(Lectures on the European Community. Series A. No.5)*

MEISSNER (FRIEDRICH) Das Recht der Europäischen Wirtschaftsgemeinschaft im Verhältnis zur Rheinschiffahrtsakte von Mannheim: ein Beitrag des völkervertragsrechtlichen Bedeutung des Artikels 234 EWGV. Berlin, [1973]. pp. 158. *bibliog.*

KEETON (GEORGE WILLIAMS) and FROMMEL (S.N.) eds. British industry and European law. London, 1974. pp. 206.

LIPSTEIN (KURT) The law of the European Economic Community. London, 1974. pp. 368.

PESCATORE (PIERRE) The law of integration: emergence of a new phenomenon in international relations, based on the experience of the European Communities. Leiden, 1974. pp. 117. *(Council of Europe. European Aspects. Series E: Law. No. 13)*

WORTLEY (BEN ATKINSON) ed. The law of the common market. Manchester, [1974]. pp. 248.

— — Bibliography.

BRITISH INSTITUTE OF INTERNATIONAL AND COMPARATIVE LAW. Guides to Common Market Law. No.1. Where to find your Community law. 2nd ed. London, 1973. pp. 13.

— — Sources.

REINERS (EDGAR) Die Normenhierarchie in den Mitgliedstaaten der europäischen Gemeinschaften: eine rechtsvergleichende Darstellung, etc. Hamburg, 1971. 2 vols.(in 1). BIBLIOG.

— France.

FRANCE. Premier Ministre. Secrétariat Général du Gouvernement. 1972. Bilan de la IVe législature: principales lois votées par le Parlement de 1968 à 1972. [Paris], 1972. pp. 11.

— — Dictionaries and encyclopaedias.

BARRAINE (RAYMOND) Nouveau dictionnaire de droit et de sciences économiques. 4th ed. Paris, 1974. pp. 508,32.

— Ghana.

GHANA. Statutes, etc. 1961-73. Acts of Ghana; (with Index to the statutes... in force on 1st August, 1970). [Accra, 1961-73]. 10 vols. (loose-leaf) and Index.

— Ireland (Republic).

EIRE. [Dáil Eireann and Seanad Eiraenn]. Joint Committee on the Secondary Legislation of the European Communities. Parliamentary debates: official report. sess., Ag 3 1973 (v.1, no.1)- Dublin.

— Italy — Colonies.

ITALY. Ministero degli Affari Esteri. Comitato per la Documentazione dell'Opera dell'Italia in Africa. L'Italia in Africa. Serie Giuridico-Amministrativa. Vol. 3. Repertorio delle disposizioni legislative e regolamentari vigenti nelle colonie italiane; a cura di Cesare Marinucci. Roma, 1969. pp. 307.

LAW. (Cont.)

— Malaya.

HOOKER (M.B.) Adat laws in modern Malaya: land tenure, traditional government and religion. Kuala Lumpur, 1972. pp. 294. *bibliog.*

— Netherlands.

NETHERLANDS. Staatscommissie Vereenvoudiging en Codificatie van de Sociale-Zekerheidswetgeving. 1970- . Vereenvoudiging en codificatie van de sociale wetgeving. 's-Gravenhage, 1970 in progress. *(Netherlands. Ministerie van Sociale Zaken. Verslagen en Rapporten: Sociale Zaken. 1970. 3)*

— Russia.

RUSSIA (EMPIRE). Statutes, etc. 1649-1911. Polnyi svod zakonov Rossiiskoi Imperii: vse 16 tomov so vsemi otnosiashchimisia k nim Prodolzheniiami i s dopolnitel'nymi uzakoneniiami po 1 Sentiabria 1910 goda v 2-kh knigakh; pod redaktsiei...A.A. Dobrovol' skogo...sostavil A.L. Saatchian. S.-Petersburg, 1911. 2 vols.

KOZIUBRA (MYKOLA IVANOVYCH) Perekonannia i prymus v radians'komu pravi. Kyiv, 1970. pp. 152. *With Russian summary.*

MIRONOV (NIKOLAI VLADIMIROVICH) Law, progress and peace: a journalist's observations on the influence of Soviet law on the progressive development of international law. Moscow, 1971. pp. 136.

XXIV s''ezd KPSS i voprosy teorii gosudarstva i prava. Moskva, 1972. pp. 399.

GORSHENEV (VIKTOR MIKHAILOVICH) Sposoby i organizatsionnye formy pravovogo regulirovaniia v sotsialisticheskom obshchestve. Moskva, 1972. pp. 258.

SHABALIN (VLADIMIR ALEKSANDROVICH) Metodologicheskie voprosy pravovedeniia: v sviazi s teoriei i praktikoi sotsialisticheskogo upravleniia. Saratov, 1972. pp. 226.

LUKASHEVA (ELENA ANDREEVNA) Sotsialisticheskoe pravosoznanie i zakonnost'. Moskva, 1973. pp. 344.

SPIRIDONOV (LEV IVANOVICH) Sotsial'noe razvitie i pravo. Leningrad, 1973. pp. 205.

CHAMBRE (HENRI) L'évolution du marxisme soviétique: théorie économique et droit. Paris, [1974]. pp. 476.

— — Codification.

KORENEV (ALEKSEI PETROVICH) Kodifikatsiia sovetskogo administrativnogo prava: teoreticheskie problemy. Moskva, 1970. pp. 134.

DAVYDOV (VLADIMIR IVANOVICH) Problemy kodifikatsii grazhdanskogo zakonodatel'stva. Kishinev, 1973. pp. 207.

— — Dictionaries and encyclopedias.

FELDBRUGGE (F.J.) ed. Encyclopedia of Soviet law. Leiden, 1973. 2 vols. *With Analytical Table in end pocket.*

— — History and criticism.

ZILE (ZIGURDS L.) Ideas and forces in Soviet legal history: statutes, decisions and other materials on the development and processes of Soviet law. 2nd ed. Madison, Wisc., 1970. pp. 456.

GAL'PERIN (GRIGORII BORISOVICH) and KOROLEV (ALEKSEI IVANOVICH) Metodologicheskie i teoreticheskie voprosy nauki istorii gosudarstva i prava SSSR. Leningrad, 1974. pp. 103.

— — Mathematical models.

PRAVOVAIA kibernetika. [sb.2]. Moskva, 1973. pp. 248.

— — Azerbaijan — History and criticism.

ISTORIIA gosudarstva i prava Azerbaidzhanskoi SSR, 1920-1934 gg. Baku, 1973. pp. 552.

— — Russia (RSFSR).

RUSSIA (RSFSR). Statutes, etc. 1923. Sobranie Kodeksov RSFSR. t.1. Moskva, 1923. pp. 560.

— — White Russia.

OCHERKI istorii gosudarstva i prava BSSR. vyp.2. Minsk, 1969. pp. 382.

— Sicily — History and criticism.

MALINOWSKA-KWIATKOWSKA (IRENA) Prawo prywatne w ustawodawstwie Królestwa Sycylii, 1140-1231. Wrocław, 1973. pp. 215. *bibliog.* *With English summary.*

— South Africa.

SOUTH AFRICAN COUNCIL OF CHURCHES and CHRISTIAN INSTITUTE OF SOUTHERN AFRICA. Study Project on Christianity in Apartheid Society. Legal Commission. Law, justice and society;... report. Johannesburg, 1972. pp. 100. *bibliog.* *(South African Council of Churches and Christian Institute of Southern Africa. Study Project on Christianity in Apartheid Society. Publications. 9)*

— Sweden.

SWEDEN. Justitiedepartementet. Utredningen om Författningspublicering. 1970. Svensk författningssamling. Stockholm, 1970. pp. 140. *(Sweden. Statens Offentliga Utredningar. 1970.48)*

— Uganda.

FALLERS (LLOYD A.) Law without precedent: legal ideas in action in the courts of colonial Busoga. Chicago, 1969. pp. 365. *bibliog.*

— United Kingdom.

AITKEN (WILLIAM) of the Edinburgh Regional Computing Centre, and others. Computers for lawyers: a report presented to the Scottish Legal Computer Research Trust, etc. [Edinburgh], 1972. pp. 159. *bibliog.*

KEETON (GEORGE WILLIAMS) English law: the judicial contribution. Newton Abbot, [1974]. pp. 384.

THEN and now, 1799-1974, commemorating 175 years of law bookselling and publishing. London, 1974. pp. 219.

— — Anecdotes, facetiae, satire, etc.

MEGARRY (Sir ROBERT EDGAR) A second miscellany-at-law: a further diversion for lawyers and others. London, 1973. pp. 420.

— — Study and teaching — Bibliography.

GREEN (ANDREW WILSON) Bibliography on British legal education. West Chester, Pa., [1973]. pp. 209. *(West Chester State College. Department of Business and Economics. Research Papers. No.1)*

— — Ireland — History and criticism.

CELTIC law papers: introductory to Welsh medieval law and government; (edited by Dafydd Jenkins). Bruxelles, 1973. pp. 213. *bibliog.* *(International Commission for the History of Representative and Parliamentary Institutions. Studies. No. 42)*

— — Wales — History and criticism.

CELTIC law papers: introductory to Welsh medieval law and government; (edited by Dafydd Jenkins). Bruxelles, 1973. pp. 213. *bibliog.* *(International Commission for the History of Representative and Parliamentary Institutions. Studies. No. 42)*

— United States.

HOYT (HOMER) According to Hoyt: 53 years of Homer Hoyt: articles on law, real estate cycle, economic base, sector theory, shopping centers, urban growth, 1916-1969. [2nd ed.] [Washington, 1970?]. pp. 855. *bibliog.*

— West Indies — Bibliography.

PATCHETT (KEITH W.) and JENKINS (VALERIE) A bibliographical guide to law in the Commonwealth Caribbean. [Kingston, Jamaica], 1973. pp. 80. *(West Indies, University of the. Institute of Social and Economic Research. Law and Society in the Caribbean. No. 2)*

LAW, CELTIC.

CELTIC law papers: introductory to Welsh medieval law and government; (edited by Dafydd Jenkins). Bruxelles, 1973. pp. 213. *bibliog.* *(International Commission for the History of Representative and Parliamentary Institutions. Studies. No. 42)*

LAW, COMPARATIVE.

INTERNATIONAL encyclopedia of comparative law...; K. Zweigert responsible editor. Tübingen, 1972 in progress.

LAW, MOHAMMEDAN

— Africa.

HAZARD (JOHN NEWBOLD) Socializing Islamic law in Africa. [New York, 1973]. pp. 543-554. *(Extraits des Mélanges offerts à Pierre Andrieu-Guitrancourt, tome XVII)*

LAW AND FACT

— Russia.

MUKHIN (IVAN IOSIFOVICH) Ob''ektivnaia istina i nekotorye voprosy otsenki sudebnykh dokazatel'stv pri osushchestvlenii pravosudiia. Leningrad, 1971. pp. 184.

ELISEIKIN (PETR FEDOROVICH) Sudebnoe ustanovlenie faktov, imeiushchikh iuridicheskoe znachenie. Moskva, 1973. pp. 128.

LAW AND POLITICS.

HARBAUGH (WILLIAM HENRY) Lawyer's lawyer: the life of John W. Davis. New York, 1973. pp. 648.

JACOB (HERBERT) Urban justice: law and order in American cities. Englewood Cliffs, [1973]. pp. 145.

LAW ENFORCEMENT

— United States.

CULL (JOHN G.) and HARDY (RICHARD E.) eds. Law enforcement and correctional rehabilitation: [readings]. Springfield, Ill., [1973]. pp. 266.

BENT (ALAN EDWARD) The politics of law enforcement: conflict and power in urban communities. Lexington, Mass., [1974]. pp. 203.

LAW REFORM

— United Kingdom.

FABIAN SOCIETY. Fabian Tracts. [No.] 427. Tribunals: a social court?; [by] Julian Fulbrook [and others]; Society of Labour Lawyers report. London, 1973. pp. 16.

U.K. Law Commission. Working Papers. No. 53. Family law: matrimonial proceedings in magistrates' courts. London, 1973. pp. 121.

FARRAR (JOHN H.) Law reform and the Law Commission. London, 1974. pp. 151.

— — Scotland.

SCOTLAND. Working Party on Insolvency, Bankruptcy and Liquidation. 1971. Insolvency, bankruptcy and liquidation in Scotland; [Lord Kilbrandon, chairman]. Edinburgh, 1971. pp. 151. *(Scotland. Scottish Law Commission. Memoranda. No.16)*

LAW REPORTS, DIGESTS, ETC.

RUSSIA (USSR). Statutes, etc. 1959-71. Sbornik postanovlenii Plenuma i opredelenii kollegii Verkhovnogo Suda SSSR po ugolovnym delam, 1959-1971 gg.; pod redaktsiei... G.Z. Anashkina. Moskva, 1973. pp. 412.

ZABRODZKA (HALINA) and KOSECKI (MIECZYSŁAW) Orzecznictwo Sądu Najwy'zszego w sprawach karnych nieletnich za okres od 1930 r. do 1971 r. Warszawa, 1973. pp. 48.

LAWRENCE (THOMAS EDWARD).

ALDANOV (MARK ALEKSANDROVICH) pseud. [i.e. LANDAU (MARK ALEKSANDROVICH)] Iunost' Pavla Stroganova i drugie kharakteristiki. Belgrad, [1935?]. pp. 188.

LAWYERS

— Germany.

GERMANY (BUNDESREPUBLIK). Deutscher Bundestag. Wissenschaftliche Dienste. 1972. Studierende der Rechtswissenschaft und Bedarf an Juristen in der Bundesrepublik Deutschland: eine Analyse vorliegender Planungen und Prognosen. Bonn, 1972. pp. 66. *(Materialien. 29)*

— Ireland (Republic).

EIRE. Committee on Court Practice and Procedure. 1971. Fourteenth interim report...: liability of barristers and solicitors for professional negligence. Dublin, [1971]. pp. 14.

EIRE. Committee on Court Practice and Procedure. 1971. Thirteenth interim report...: the solicitor's right of audience. Dublin, [1971]. pp. 20.

— United States — Directories.

MARTINDALE-HUBBELL LAW DIRECTORY. a., 1972 (104th ed.). Summit, N.J. *In 5 vols.*

LAZIO

— History.

TOUBERT (PIERRE) Les structures du Latium médiéval: le Latium méridional et la Sabine du IXe siècle à la fin du XIIe siècle. Rome, 1973. 2 vols. *bibliog. (Ecoles Françaises d'Athènes et de Rome. Bibliothèque. Fasc. 221)* 7 maps in end pocket of vol. 2.

LEAD MINES AND MINING

— United Kingdom.

BROOK (FRED) and ALLBUTT (MARTIN) The Shropshire lead mines. Cheddleton, [1973]. pp. 95. *bibliog.*

LEADERSHIP.

CAVALLI (LUCIANO) ed. Classe dirigente e sviluppo regionale: ricerca sulla classe dirigente toscana di Gianfranco Bettin [and others]. Bologna, [1973]. pp. 196.

COURTNEY (JOHN C.) The selection of national party leaders in Canada. Hamden, Conn., 1973. pp. 278. *bibliog.*

JONES (REGINALD VICTOR) Command and complementarity. London, [1973]. pp. 17. *(London. University. Birkbeck College. Bernal Lectures. 1973)*

VROOM (VICTOR HAROLD) and YETTON (PHILIP W.) Leadership and decision-making. Pittsburgh, [1973]. pp. 233. *bibliog.*

KAVANAGH (DENNIS A.) Crisis, charisma and British political leadership: Winston Churchill as the outsider. London, [1974]. pp. 42. *bibliog.*

TILLEY (K.W.) ed. Leadership and management appraisal: the proceedings of a NATO conference held in Brussels. London, 1974. pp. 432. *bibliogs.*

LEAGUE OF NATIONS.

PEROTIN (YVES) L'ouverture des archives de la Société des Nations. [Geneva, 1970]. pp. 180-190. *(From Annales d'Etudes Internationales, vol. 1,1970) Xerox copy.*

SCOTT (GEORGE) 1925- . The rise and fall of the League of Nations. London, 1973. pp. 432.

MADARIAGA (SALVADOR DE) Morning without noon: memoirs. Farnborough, 1974. pp. 441.

— Bibliography.

GHEBALI (VICTOR YVES) and GHEBALI (CATHERINE) compilers. A repertoire of League of Nations serial documents, 1919-1947. Dobbs Ferry, N.Y., 1973. 2 vols.

LEARNING, PSYCHOLOGY OF.

HOLT (JOHN CALDWELL) How children learn; [first published in the United States in 1967]. Harmondsworth, 1970 repr. 1973. pp. 173.

ESSMAN (WALTER B.) and NAKAJIMA (SHINSHU) eds. Current biochemical approaches to learning and memory. Flushing, N.Y., [1973]. pp. 205. *bibliogs.*

ROHWER (WILLIAM D.) and others. Understanding intellectual development: three approaches to theory and practice. Hinsdale, Ill., [1974]. pp. 429. *bibliog.*

LEARY (TIMOTHY).

LEARY (TIMOTHY) Confessions of a hope fiend. New York, 1973. pp. 296.

LEAST SQUARES.

PARK (SOO-BIN) An indirect least squares interpretation of two-stage least squares estimation. Ottawa, 1973. fo. 9. *bibliog. (Carleton University. Carleton Economic Papers)*

— Computer programs.

MATRONE (LUCIANO) Programma di regressione multipla. Portici, [1973]. pp. 71. *bibliog. (Naples. Università. Centro di Specializzazione e Ricerche Economico-Agrarie per il Mezzogiorno. Informatica ed Econometrica.1)* With English summary.

LEATHER INDUSTRY AND TRADE

— France.

FRANCE. Direction de la Documentation. La Documentation Française. Notes et Etudes Documentaires. Nos. 3,918-3, 919. Les industries françaises du cuir. [Paris], 1972. pp. 56.

— United Kingdom.

FOOTWEAR, LEATHER AND FUR SKIN INDUSTRY TRAINING BOARD [U.K.]. Report and statement of accounts. a., 1972/3- Sutton Coldfield. *Formerly included in the file of British Parliamentary Papers.*

LEATHER WORKERS

— Germany.

SCHUSTER (DIETER) 1872-1972, "Schritt für Schritt": ein Jahrhundert Leder- Gewerkschaften. Stuttgart, [1972]. pp. 239. *bibliog.*

LEBANON

— Biography.

WHO'S who in Lebanon...1973-1974. 5th ed. Beyrouth, [1973]. pp. 820.

LEE (ARTHUR HAMILTON) 1st Viscount Lee of Fareham.

LEE (ARTHUR HAMILTON) 1st Viscount Lee of Fareham. 'A good innings': the private papers of Viscount Lee of Fareham...; edited by Alan Clark. London, [1974]. pp. 360.

LEE (KUAN YEW).

JOSEY (ALEX) Lee Kuan Yew and the Commonwealth. Singapore, 1969. pp. 112.

JOSEY (ALEX) Lee Kuan Yew: the struggle for Singapore. Sydney, 1974. pp. 334.

LEEDS

— History.

HENNOCK (E.P.) Fit and proper persons: ideal and reality in nineteenth-century urban government. Montreal, 1973. pp. 395. *bibliog.*

LEFEBVRE (GEORGES)

— Bibliography.

FRIGUGLIETTI (JAMES) compiler. Bibliographie de Georges Lefebvre. Paris, 1972. pp. 95.

LEGAL AID.

COMMITTEE ON LEGAL SERVICES TO THE POOR IN THE DEVELOPING COUNTRIES. Legal aid and world poverty: a survey of Asia, Africa and Latin America. New York, 1974. pp. 309. *bibliog.*

— Hong Kong.

HONG KONG. Legal Aid [Department]. Annual departmental report. a., 1973/4- Hong Kong.

— United Kingdom.

BORRIE (GORDON JOHNSON) and VARCOE (J.R.) Legal aid in criminal proceedings: a regional survey. Birmingham, [1970]. pp. 101.

LEGAL RESEARCH

— United Kingdom — Directories.

BRITISH RESEARCH DIRECTORY OF LAW AND SOCIETY. a., current issue only kept. London.

LEGENDS

— Peru.

HOWKINS (DOUGLAS W.) A Quechua legend of Peru: Yaku Runa or River Man. Glasgow, 1973. fo.19. *(Glasgow. University. Institute of Latin American Studies. Occasional Papers. No.5)*

LEGISLATION

— European Economic Community countries.

EUROPEAN COMMUNITIES. Commission. 1972. Community measures for the alignment of legislation 1958-1971. Brussels, 1972. pp. 49. *(Bulletin of the European Communities. Supplements. [1972/9])*

— Germany.

GERMANY (BUNDESREPUBLIK). Deutscher Bundestag. Wissenschaftliche Dienste. 1973. Die Gesetzgebung des deutschen Bundestages in der VI. Wahlperiode 1969-1972. Bonn, 1973. pp. 103. *(Materialien. 32)*

— Ireland (Republic).

EIRE. Seanad Eireann. Select Committee on Statutory Instruments. 1971. Interim report of the Select Committee on Statutory Instruments appointed 10th December, 1969. Dublin, 1971. pp. 8.

— United Kingdom.

GRIFFITH (JOHN ANEURIN GREY) Parliamentary scrutiny of Government bills. London, 1974. pp. 285.

LEGISLATIVE BODIES.

BLONDEL (JEAN) 1929- . Comparative legislatures. Englewood Cliffs, N.J., [1973]. pp. 173. *bibliog.*

— Africa, Subsaharan.

HAKES (JAY E.) Weak parliaments and military coups in Africa: a study in regime instability. Beverly Hills, [1973]. pp. 37. *bibliog.*

LEGISLATIVE BODIES. (Cont.)

— Europe — Congresses.

HUOPANIEMI (JUKKA) Parliaments and European rapprochement: [report on] the conference of the Inter-Parliamentary Union on European Co-operation and Security, Helsinki, January 1973. Leiden, 1973. pp. 138.

— Germany.

VEREINIGUNG DER DEUTSCHEN PARLAMENTSDIREKTOREN. Parlamentspraxis in der Weimarer Republik: die Tagungsberichte der Vereinigung der deutschen Parlamentsdirektoren, 1925 bis 1933; bearbeitet von Martin Schumacher. Düsseldorf, [1974]. pp. 272. bibliog. (Germany (Bundesrepublik). Quellen zur Geschichte des Parlamentarismus und der Politischen Parteien. 3. Reihe. Band 2)

— Russia.

KRAVCHUK (S.S.) ed. Pravovye problemy dal'neishego sovershenstvovaniia predstavitel'nykh organov gosudarstvennoi vlasti. Moskva, 1973. pp. 154.

— United States.

ROBINSON (JAMES ARTHUR) ed. State legislative innovation: case studies of Washington, Ohio, Florida, Illinois, Wisconsin, and California. New York, 1973. pp. 278.

LEGISLATORS.

ROSSI-LANDI (GUY) Les hommes politiques. [Paris], 1973. pp. 114. bibliog.

— Denmark.

HVIDT (KRISTIAN) and NEMETH (CSABA) eds. Folketinget håndbog 1973; (efter valget 4. December: biografier, partiprogrammer, valgstatistik m.m.). København, 1974. pp. 408.

— France.

CAYROL (ROLAND) and others. Le député français. Paris, 1973. pp. 159. (Fondation Nationale des Sciences Politiques. Travaux et Recherches de Science Politique. 23)

WOSHINSKY (OLIVER H.) The French deputy: incentives and behavior in the National Assembly. Lexington, Mass., [1973]. pp. 232. bibliog.

LOCKE (ROBERT R.) French legitimists and the politics of moral order in the early Third Republic. Princeton, [1974]. pp. 321. bibliog.

— Germany.

BERTSCH (HERBERT) Wer sitzt im Bonner Bundestag?: eine dokumentarische Analyse der Bundestagswahlen, 1961. Berlin, [1961 repr. 1962]. pp. 127.

APEL (HANS) Bonn, den ...: Tagebuch eine Bundestagsabgeordneten. Köln, [1972]. pp. 180.

GERMANY (BUNDESREPUBLIK). Deutscher Bundestag. Wissenschaftliche Dienste. 1974. Zum Mandatsverlust bei Ausscheiden eines Abgeordneten aus seiner Fraktion: Stand der Diskussion. Bonn, 1974. pp. 29. (Materialien. 35)

— — Bibliography.

GERMANY (BUNDESREPUBLIK). Deutscher Bundestag. Wissenschaftliche Dienste. 1973. Das Abgeordnetenmandat in der parteienstaatlichen Demokratie: Auswahlbibliographie. Bonn, 1973. pp. 40. (Bibliographien. 33)

— India.

INDIA. Parliament. Lok Sabha. Secretariat. 1967. Parliament of India: fourth Lok Sabha; Who's who, 1967. New Delhi, 1967. pp. 680.

— — Haryana.

HARYANA. Vidhan Sabha. Secretariat. 1972. Who's who, 1972. Chandigarh, 1972. pp. 355.

— Russia — Azerbaijan.

AZERBAIJAN. Verkhovnyi Sovet. 1968. Deputaty Verkhovnogo Soveta Azerbaidzhanskoi SSR: sed'moi sozyv. Baku, 1968. pp. 400. In Azerbaijani and Russian.

— Sweden.

HOLMBERG (SÖREN) 'Riksdagen representerar svenska folket': empiriska studier i representativ demokrati. Lund, [1974]. pp. 452. bibliog. With English summary.

— Switzerland.

GRUNER (ERICH) Politische Führungsgruppen im Bundesstaat. Bern, [1973]. pp. 104. (Allgemeine Geschichtsforschende Gesellschaft der Schweiz. Monographien zur Schweizer Geschichte. Band 7)

— United Kingdom.

ABSE (LEO) Private member. London, 1973. pp. 296. bibliog.

ELLIS (JOHN) b. 1930, and JOHNSON (RICHARD WILLIAM) Members from the unions. London, 1974. pp. 31. (Fabian Society. Research Series. [No.] 316)

ELLIS (NESTA WYN) Dear elector: the truth about MPs. London, 1974. pp. 236.

GRANT (JOHN DOUGLAS) Member of Parliament. London, 1974. pp. 190.

— United States.

BARONE (MICHAEL) and others. The almanac of American politics: the senators, the representatives, their records, states and districts, 1974. 2nd ed. London, 1974. pp. 1240.

MAYHEW (DAVID R.) Congress: the electoral connection. New Haven, 1974. pp. 194.

LEHÁR (ANTON).

LEHÁR (ANTONO) eRINNERUNGEN: gEGENREVOLUTION UND rESTAURATIONSVERSUCHE IN uNGARN, 1918-1921; HERAUSGEGEBEN VON pETER bROUCEK. wIEN, 1973. PP. 280.

LEICESTER

— Civic improvement.

LEICESTER. City Council, and LEICESTERSHIRE. County Council. Leicester and Leicestershire structure plan: report of survey; ([with] Addendum). [Leicester], 1974. 2 vols. (in 1).

— Social policy.

P.A. MANAGEMENT CONSULTANTS LTD. Economic Studies Division. An evaluation of future social services expenditure on behalf of the city of Leicester. [London, 1974]. pp. 157.

LEICESTERSHIRE

— Economic policy.

LEICESTER. City Council, and LEICESTERSHIRE. County Council. Leicester and Leicestershire structure plan: report of survey; ([with] Addendum). [Leicester], 1974. 2 vols. (in 1).

— Social policy.

LEICESTER. City Council, and LEICESTERSHIRE. County Council. Leicester and Leicestershire structure plan: report of survey; ([with] Addendum). [Leicester], 1974. 2 vols. (in 1).

LEIPZIG

— Statistics.

STATISTISCHES JAHRBUCH DER STADT LEIPZIG; bearbeit im Statistischen Amt. 1919/29(7.Bd.). Leipzig.

LEISURE.

UNITED NATIONS. Department of Economic and Social Affairs. European Social Development Programme. Reports. New York, 1967 in progress.

GOLDRING (PATRICK) Multipurpose man. London, 1973. pp. 120.

PEARSON (JOHN WARD) The 8-day week. New York, [1973]. pp. 161. bibliog.

ANDERSON (NELS) Man's work and leisure. Leiden, 1974. pp. 146.

CLAYRE (ALASDAIR) Work and play: ideas and experience of work and leisure. London, [1974]. pp. 261.

DUMAZEDIER (JOFFRE) Sociologie empirique du loisir: critique et contre-critique de la civilisation du loisir. Paris, [1974]. pp. 270.

SALAMAN (GRAEME) Community and occupation: an exploration of work/leisure relationships. London, 1974. pp. 136. bibliog. (Cambridge. University. Department of Applied Economics. Cambridge Papers in Sociology. No.4)

— Bibliography.

RECREATION, leisure and tourism: sources of information; proceedings of a...conference held at the Library Association, London...1972; edited by Ken Bradbury. London, 1973. pp. 85. bibliog.

— Israel.

TEL-AVIV. Department of Research and Statistics. Special Surveys. No.44. Leisure patterns of the inhabitants of Tel Aviv-Yafo. Tel-Aviv, 1974. pp. 1vi, 109. In English and Hebrew.

— Russia.

GORDON (LEONID ABRAMOVICH) and KLOPOV (EDUARD VIKTOROVICH) Chelovek posle raboty: sotsial'nye problemy byta i vnerabochego vremeni; po materialam izucheniia biudzhetov vremeni rabochikh v krupnykh gorodakh Evropeiskoi chasti SSSR; [s prilozheniem tablits]. Moskva, 1972. 2 pts (in 1).

— United Kingdom.

NORTH WEST SPORTS COUNCIL. Leisure in the North West: the technical report of the Leisure Activities Survey of the...Council. Salford, [1972]. pp. 257.

PLUMB (JOHN HAROLD) The commercialisation of leisure in eighteenth-century England. Reading, 1973. pp. 20. (Reading. University. Stenton Lectures. 1972)

LENIN (VLADIMIR IL'ICH).

NOL'DE (BORIS) Baron. Lenins Räte-Republik: ein Beitrag zur Geschichte der politischen und wirtschaftlichen Entwicklung im neuen Russland; aus dem Französischen übersetzt von R. Paderstein. Berlin, 1920. pp. 44.

V.I. Lenin i sovremennaia statistika. Moskva, 1970-73. 3 vols.

DIPLOMATICHESKAIA deiatel'nost' V.I. Lenina. Moskva, 1970. pp. 136.

POTULOV (BORIS MIKHAILOVICH) Leninskaia zabota o zdorov'e trudiashchikhsia. Moskva, 1970. pp. 135.

SAVASTIUK (ANTON IVANOVICH) V.I. Lenin o pobede sotsializma v SSSR; pod redaktsiei ... K.P. Buslova. Minsk, 1970. pp. 222. bibliog.

SHIRENDYB (BAZARYN) V.I. Lenin i mongol'skii narod. Moskva, 1970. pp. 60.

KOMMUNISTISCHER STUDENTENBUND GÖTTINGEN. Die Differenzen zwischen Lenin und Rosa Luxemburg im Kampf gegen Revisionismus und Opportunismus in der Sozialdemokratie. 2nd ed. Göttingen, 1971. pp. 59.

V.I. Lenin i Stavropol'e: sbornik dokumentov i materialov. Stavropol', 1971. pp. 208.

BERNOV (IURII VLADIMIROVICH) and MANUSEVICH (ALEKSANDR IAKOVLEVICH) Lenin v Krakove. Moskva, 1972. pp. 239.

FARUKSHIN (MIDKHAT KHABIBOVICH) Leninskie printsipy kritiki antimarksizma. Kazan', 1972. pp. 115.

NOVIKOV (VIKTOR IVANOVICH) V.I. Lenin i pskovskie iskrovtsy. 2nd ed. Leningrad, 1972. pp. 267.

WOODS (ALAN) and others. Lenin and Trotsky: what they really stood for. Colombo, 1972. pp. 173. *bibliogs.*

BOCHKAREV (NIKOLAI IVANOVICH) V.I. Lenin i burzhuaznaia sotsiologiia v Rossii. Moskva, 1973. pp. 251.

BOLOTNIKOV (IGOR' MIKHAILOVICH) and VAVILOV (KONSTANTIN KUZ'MICH) Leninizm i nauchnoe upravlenie sotsialisticheskim obshchestvom. Leningrad, 1973. pp. 256. *bibliog.*

FOMIN (VASILII VASIL'EVICH) Lenin i transport. Moskva, 1973. pp. 71.

GAUTSCHI (WILLI) Lenin als Emigrant in der Schweiz. Zürich, [1973]. pp. 383. *bibliog.*

GUROV (PETR IAKOVLEVICH) and GONCHAROV (ALEKSANDR DMITRIEVICH) Leninskaia agrarnaia politika. Moskva, 1973. pp. 190.

IATSUNSKII (VIKTOR KORNEL'EVICH) Sotsial'no-ekonomicheskaia istoriia Rossii XVIII-XIX vv.: izbrannye trudy. Moskva, 1973. pp. 302.

LECOURT (DOMINIQUE) Une crise et son enjeu: essai sur la position de Lénine en philosophie. Paris, 1973. pp. 142.

LENINSKIE idei v nauke ugolovnogo prava: sbornik statei. Leningrad, 1973. pp. 100.

LIEBMAN (MARCEL) Le léninisme sous Lénine. Paris, [1973]. 2 vols.

LUXEMBURG (ROSA) Leninism or marxism?: originally entitled Organisational questions of Russian social democracy;... a new translation by Ken Eaton. Leeds, [1973]. pp. 20. (*Independent Labour Party. Square One Pamphlets.* 2)

NECHIPURENKO (VASILII IGNAT'EVICH) V.I. Lenin o zashchite sotsialisticheskogo Otechestva: printsipy internatsionalizma i zashchita Otechestva. Moskva, 1973. pp. 223. *bibliog.*

NIL'VE (ANNA IL'INICHNA) Bor'ba V.I. Lenina s revizionizmom v agrarnom voprose i ee mezhdunarodnoe znachenie; pod redaktsiei E.L. Boginoi. Moskva, 1973. pp. 147.

STEKLOV (IURII MIKHAILOVICH) Izbrannoe. Moskva, 1973. pp. 262. *bibliog.*

VARLAMOV (KONSTANTIN IVANOVICH) Leninskaia kontseptsiia sotsialisticheskogo upravleniia: genezis, stanovlenie. Moskva, 1973. pp. 398.

VOPROSY istorii partii v trudakh V.I. Lenina. Moskva, 1973. pp. 316.

ZAPADOV (ALEKSANDR VASIL'EVICH) Mysl' i slovo: iz nabliudenii nad literaturnoi rabotoi V.I. Lenina. 2nd ed. Moskva, 1973. pp. 392.

GINSBORG (PAUL) The politics of Lenin. [London], 1974. pp. 31.

LENINE et la pratique scientifique: colloque d'Orsay; [papers of a meeting held in 1971]. Paris, [1974]. pp. 606.

SHITOV (NIKOLAI FEDOROVICH) V.I. Lenin i proletarskii internatsionalizm, 1917-1924 gg. Moskva, 1974. pp. 359.

STROBEL (GEORG WALDEMAR) Die Partei Rosa Luxemburgs, Lenin und die SPD: der polnische "europäische" Internationalismus in der russischen Sozialdemokratie. Wiesbaden, 1974. pp. 759. *bibliog.*

VISHNIAKOV-VISHNEVETSKII (KONSTANTIN ANATOL'EVICH) V.I. Lenin i revoliutsionnye sviazi rossiiskogo i germanskogo proletariata, 1903-1910 gg. Leningrad, 1974. pp. 220.

— Bibliography.

RUSSIA (U.S.S.R.). Vsesoiuznaia Knizhnaia Palata. 1972. Lenin v pechati, 1894-1970: izdanie proizvedenii V.I. Lenina, knig i broshiur o nem; nauchno-statisticheskii sbornik. 2nd ed. Moskva, 1972. pp. 244.

LEVIN (LEV ABRAMOVICH) compiler. K. Marks, F. Engel's, V.I. Lenin: ukazatel' bibliograficheskikh rabot, 1961-1972. Moskva, 1973. pp. 288.

LENINGRAD

— Civic improvement.

KRUGLIAKOV (IULII GDAL'EVICH) Kompleksnaia rekonstruktsiia zhilykh kvartalov staroi zastroiki: opyt Leningrada. Leningrad, 1971. pp. 89.

KAMENSKII (VALENTIN ALEKSANDROVICH) and NAUMOV (ALEKSANDR IVANOVICH) Leningrad: gradostroitel'nye problemy razvitiia. Leningrad, 1973. pp. 360.

KHROMOV (IURII BORISOVICH) Novoe v blagoustroistve Leningrada. Leningrad, 1973. pp. 128.

— Economic conditions.

CHERTOV (LEONID GEORGIEVICH) Leningrad: ekonomiko-geograficheskii ocherk. Moskva, 1972. pp. 127. *bibliog.*

— Industries.

POLOZOV (VLADIMIR ROMANOVICH) and KOMAROV (GEORGII FILIPPOVICH) Problemy planomernogo formirovaniia i ispol'zovaniia promyshlennykh rabochikh: opyt sotsial'no-ekonomicheskogo issledovaniia v g. Leningrade. Leningrad, 1968. pp. 124.

DUMACHEV (ANATOLII PANTELEEVICH) Khozraschetnye ob"edineniia v promyshlennosti. Leningrad, 1972. pp. 195.

— Social conditions.

VASIL'EVA (EVELINA KARLOVNA) Sotsial'no-professional'nyi uroven' gorodskoi molodezhi: po materialam vyborochnogo obsledovaniia shkol'nikov i molodezhi Leningrada. Leningrad, 1973. pp. 142.

LENINGRAD (OBLAST')

— Politics and government.

UCHENYE ZAPISKI KAFEDR OBSHCHESTVENNYKH NAUK VUZOV LENINGRADA. Istoriia KPSS. vyp.12. Leninskim kursom. Leningrad, 1972. pp. 184.

LEOPOLD II, King of the Belgians.

KURGAN-VAN HENTENRYK (GINETTE) Léopold II et les groupes financiers belges en Chine: la politique royale et ses prolongements, 1895-1914. Bruxelles, [1972]. pp. 969. *bibliog.* (*Académie Royale de Belgique. Classe des Lettres et des Sciences Morales et Politiques. Mémoires. Collection in-8°. 2e série. Tome 61. Fasc. 2*)

LESOTHO

— Economic conditions.

WILLIAMS (JOHN COX) Lesotho: land tenure and economic development. Pretoria, 1972. pp. 52. (*Africa Institute. Communications. No. 19*)

ONADO (MARCO) and PORTERI (ANTONIO) The banking system and the formation of savings in Lesotho. Milan, 1974. pp. 139. (*Cassa di Risparmio delle Provincie Lombarde. The Credit Markets of Africa. 9*)

— Industries.

SELWYN (PERCY) The dual economy transcending national frontiers: the case of industrial development in Lesotho. Brighton, [1972]. pp. 24. (*Brighton. University of Sussex. Institute of Development Studies. Communications. No.105*)

— Kings and rulers.

WEISFELDER (RICHARD F.) The Basotho monarchy: a spent force or a dynamic political factor. Athens, Ohio, [1972]. pp. 97. (*Ohio University. Center for International Studies. Papers in International Studies. Africa Series. No.16*)

— Politics and government.

WEISFELDER (RICHARD F.) Defining national purpose in Lesotho. [Athens, Oh.], 1969. pp. 28. (*Ohio University. Center for International Studies. Papers in International Studies. Africa Series. No. 3*)

— Population.

WILLIAMS (JOHN COX) Lesotho: three manpower problems: education, health, population growth. Pretoria, 1971. pp. 70. (*Africa Institute. Communications. No. 16*)

LE VAUDREUIL.

FRANCE. Mission d'Etudes de la Ville Nouvelle du Vaudreuil. 1971-1972. Ville nouvelle du Vaudreuil. [Le Vaudreuil?], 1971-72. pp. 7 pts. (in 1).

Une VILLE pilote pour la lutte contre les pollutions et les nuisances: la ville nouvelle du Vaudreuil. Paris, 1973. pp. 181. (*Environnement. 14*)

LEVELLERS.

WINSTANLEY (GERARD) The law of freedom and other writings; edited...by Christopher Hill. Harmondsworth, 1973. pp. 395. *bibliog.*

LEVERIDGE (ANNA MARIA).

LEVERIDGE (ANNA MARIA) Your loving Anna: letters from the Ontario frontier; [edited by] Louis Tivy. Toronto, [1972]. pp. 120.

LEVIN (SHNEER MENDELEVICH).

LEVIN (SHNEER MENDELEVICH) Ocherki po istorii russkoi obshchestvennoi mysli, vtoraia polovina XIX - nachalo XX veka: [glavy iz dvukh nezavershennykh rukopisei, Raznochinskii period russkogo osvoboditel'nogo dvizheniia v osveshchenii dorevoliutsionnoi istoriografii i Krymskaia voina i russkoe obshchestvo; otv. redaktor S.N. Valk]. Leningrad, 1974. pp. 442.

LÉVI—STRAUSS (CLAUDE).

FAGES (J.B.) Comprendre Lévi-Strauss. Toulouse, [1972]. pp. 130. *bibliog.*

COURTES (JOSEPH) Lévi-Strauss et les contraintes de la pensée mythique: une lecture sémiotique des "Mythologiques". [Tours, 1973]. pp. 187.

DELFENDAHL (BERNHARD) Le clair et l'obscur: critique de l'anthropologie savante; défense de l'anthropologie amateur. Paris, [1973]. pp. 222.

MAKARIUS (RAOUL) and MAKARIUS (LAURA) Structuralisme ou ethnologie: pour une critique radicale de l'anthropologie de Levi-Strauss. Paris, [1973]. pp. 375. *bibliog.*

GLUCKSMANN (MIRIAM ANNE) Structuralist analysis in contemporary social thought: a comparison of the theories of Claude Lévi-Strauss and Louis Althusser. London, 1974. pp. 197. *bibliog.*

LEVY—BRUHL (LUCIEN).

DAVY (GEORGES) L'homme, le fait social et le fait politique: [collection of articles and other writings originally published 1919-1969]. Paris, [1973]. pp. 324. (*Paris. Ecole Pratique des Hautes Etudes. Section des Sciences Economiques et Sociales. Textes de Sciences Sociales. 9*)

LEWIN (HUGH).

LEWIN (HUGH) Bandiet: seven years in a South African prison. London, 1974. pp. 223.

LEWISHAM.

LEWISHAM — Playgrounds.
LEWISHAM. Planning Department. Development Plan and Research Group. A report on the provision of playground facilities in the London borough of Lewisham;...compiled by W.F. Stanley and H.F. Pollitzer. [London], 1972. pp. 31. (*Lewisham. Planning Department. Research Reports. 1*)

LEYH (GEORG).
DOSA (MARTA LESZLEI) Libraries in the political scene. Westport, Conn., [1974]. pp. 226. *bibliog.*

LIABILITY FOR ROAD ACCIDENTS.
JUSTICE (BRITISH SECTION OF THE INTERNATIONAL COMMISSION OF JURISTS). No fault on the roads: (a report); chairman of committee, Paul Sieghart. London, 1974. pp. 58. *bibliog.*

LIANG (CHI—CHAO).
HUANG (PHILIP C.) Liang Ch'i-ch'ao and modern Chinese liberalism. Seattle, [1972]. pp. 231. *bibliog.* (*Washington State University. Institute for Comparative and Foreign Area Studies. Publications on Asia. No.22*)

LIBEL AND SLANDER
— **United Kingdom.**

GENERAL COUNCIL OF THE PRESS. Reforming the law of defamation: a memorandum (to the Committee on Defamation). London, [1973]. pp. 43. (*Press Council Booklets. No.4*)

GATLEY (JOHN CLEMENT CARPENTER) On libel and slander: seventh edition by Robert McEwen and Philip Lewis. London, 1974. pp. 719.

LIBERAL PARTY
— **Canada.**

NEATBY (H. BLAIR) Laurier and a Liberal Quebec: a study in political management;edited...by Richard T. Clippingdale. Toronto, [1973]. pp. 244. *bibliog.* (*Carleton University. Institute of Canadian Studies. Carleton Library. No. 63*)

— **France.**

GRIGNON (MAX) Le parti libéral dans la Sarthe sous la Restauration. Le Mans, 1927. pp. 84.

— **Germany.**

NATIONALLIBERALE PARTEI DEUTSCHLANDS. Allgemeiner Delegirtentag, 1896. Allgemeiner Delegirtentag ...: zweiter Tag. Berlin, 1896. pp. 52.

PESCHKE (KLAUS) Die Bedeutung der liberalen Parteien und der Sozialdemokratie für das politische Leben im Wahlkreis Altena-Iserlohn von der Reichsgründung 1871 bis zum Jahre 1890. [Altena, 1973]. pp. 150. *bibliog.* (*Verein Freunde der Burg Altena. Altenaer Beiträge. Neue Folge. Band 8*)

— **United Kingdom.**

HAIN (PETER) Radical liberalism and youth politics. London, [1973]. pp. 20. (*Liberal Party. Strategy 2,000. 1st Series. No. 3*)

LIBERAL PUBLICATION DEPARTMENT. Forward with the Liberals: a statement of Liberal policy. London, 1973. pp. (28).

LIBERAL PARTY. You can change the face of Britain: the Liberal programme for national reconstruction. London, [1974]. pp. 28.

LIBERAL PARTY. Why Britain needs Liberal government. London, [1974]. pp. 16.

PARDOE (JOHN WENTWORTH) We must conquer inflation: a Liberal approach to the greatest danger of the age. London, [1974]. pp. 49.

LIBERALISM.
BARRY (BRIAN M.) The liberal theory of justice: a critical examination of the principal doctrines in a theory of justice, by John Rawls. Oxford, 1973. pp. 169.

BUDE (JACQUES) L'obscurantisme libéral et l'investigation sociologique. Paris, [1973]. pp. 223.

BLUHM (WILLIAM THEODORE) Ideologies and attitudes: modern political culture. Englewood Cliffs, [1974]. pp. 385. *bibliogs.*

LIBERALISM IN BELGIUM.
PAEPE (JEAN LUC DE) "La Réforme", organe de la démocratie libérale, 1884-1907. Leuven, 1972. pp. 179. *bibliog.* (*Centre Interuniversitaire d'Histoire Contemporaine. Cahiers. 64*)

LIBERALISM IN CHINA.
HUANG (PHILIP C.) Liang Ch'i-ch'ao and modern Chinese liberalism. Seattle, [1972]. pp. 231. *bibliog.* (*Washington State University. Institute for Comparative and Foreign Area Studies. Publications on Asia. No.22*)

LIBERALISM IN FRANCE.
HARDY (CHARLES NOEL) Imaginer l'avenir: propositions libérales établies par les clubs Perspectives et Realités. Paris, [1972]. pp. 253.

LIBERALISM IN GERMANY.
OPITZ (REINHARD) Der deutsche Sozialliberalismus, 1917-1933. Köln, [1973]. pp. 310. *bibliog.*

BAUMGARTEN (HERMANN) Der deutsche Liberalismus: ein Selbstkritik, herausgegeben und eingeleitet von Adolf M. Birke. Frankfurt/M, [1974]. pp. 199. *bibliog.*

LIBERALISM IN THE UNITED STATES.
BUENKER (JOHN D.) Urban liberalism and progressive reform. New York, [1973]. pp. 299. *bibliog.*

HAMBY (ALONZO L.) Beyond the New Deal: Harry S. Truman and American liberalism. New York, 1973. pp. 635. *bibliog.*

YARNELL (ALLEN) Democrats and progressives: the 1948 presidential election as a test of postwar liberalism. Berkeley, 1974. pp. 155. *bibliog.*

LIBERIA
— **Economic conditions.**

SCHULZE (WILLI) A new geography of Liberia. London, 1973. pp. 218. *bibliogs.*

— **History.**

YANCY (ERNEST JEROME) The republic of Liberia. London, 1959. pp. 154.

LIBERMAN (EVSEI GRIGOR'EVICH).
LAW (P.J.) On a proposal by Liberman for enterprise incentive funds. Coventry, 1973. pp. 25. *bibliog.* (*University of Warwick. Department of Economics. Warwick Economic Research Papers. No. 34*)

LIBERTY.
The LEGION of liberty.' and force of truth, containing the thoughts, words, and deeds, of some prominent apostles, champions and martyrs. 2nd ed. [New York], 1843. 1 vol. (unpaged).

RE-BARTLETT (LUCY) Towards liberty. London, 1913. pp. 74.

LOPEZ MEJIA (CARLOS ARTURO) Actividad de policia y libertad. Bogota, 1970. pp. 65. *bibliog.*

BITSAXIS (EVAN) Welfare versus freedom. Athens, 1972. pp. 383.

ZAVALA (SILVIO ARTURO) La filosofia politica en la conquista de America. 2nd ed. Mexico, 1972. pp. 145. *bibliog.*

HAYEK (FRIEDRICH AUGUST) Economic freedom and representative government; fourth Wincott Memorial Lecture...1973. London, 1973. pp. 22. (*Institute of Economic Affairs. Occasional Papers. 39*)

IMMINK (P.W.A.) La liberté et la peine: étude sur la transformation de la liberté et sur le développement du droit pénal public en Occident avant le XIIe siècle; éditée d'après le manuscrit et les notes de lauteur par P. Sarolea. Assen, 1973. pp. 289. *bibliog.*

FONDAZIONE GIOACCHINO VOLPE. Incontro Romano, I', 1973. Autorità e libertà: [papers]. Roma, [1974]. pp. 282.

O'ROURKE (JAMES J.) The problem of freedom in Marxist thought: an analysis of the treatment of human freedom by Marx, Engels, Lenin and contemporary Soviet philosophy. Dordrecht, [1974]. pp. 231. *bibliog.* (*Freiburg (Switzerland). Universität. Ost- Europa Institut. Sovietica. vol. 32*)

LIBERTY OF INFORMATION
— **Italy.**

RADIOTELEVISIONE, informazione, democrazia: atti del convegno del P[artito] C[omunista] I[taliano] tenuto a Roma dal 29 al 31 marzo 1973. Roma, 1973. pp. 545.

LIBERTY OF SPEECH
— **Germany.**

BRENNER (HILDEGARD) ed. Ende einer bürgerlichen Kunst-Institution: die politische Formierung der Preussischen Akademie der Künste ab 1933; (eine Dokumentation). Stuttgart, [1972]. pp. 174. (*Vierteljahrshefte für Zeitgeschichte. Schriftenreihe. Nr. 24*)

LIBERTY OF THE PRESS
— **Czechoslovakia.**

FRANCE. Direction de la Documentation. La Documentation Française. Notes et Etudes Documentaires. Nos. 3,729-3, 730. La presse, les intellectuels et le pouvoir en Union Soviétique et dans les pays socialistes européens. 2. Pologne et Tchécoslovaquie; [by] Georges H. Mond. Paris, 1970. pp. 57. *bibliogs.*

— **Europe, Eastern.**

FRANCE. Direction de la Documentation. La Documentation Française. Notes et Etudes Documentaires. Nos. 3,736-3, 737. La presse, les intellectuels et le pouvoir en Union Soviétique et dans les pays socialistes européens. 3. Albanie, Allemagne de l'Est, Bulgarie, Hongrie, Roumanie, Yougoslavie; [by] Georges H. Mond [and others]. Paris, 1970. pp. 80. *bibliogs.*

— **Germany.**

ATZROTT (OTTO) Sozialdemokratische Druckschriften und Vereine, (verboten auf Grund des Reichsgesetzes gegen die gemeingefährlichen Bestrebungen der Sozialdemokratie vom 21.Oktober 1878... Neudruck der Ausgabe Berlin, 1886; [with] Nachtrag, 1888). Glashütten im Taunus, 1971. 1 vol.(various pagings).

— **Italy.**

FIENGO (RAFFAELE) Libertà di stampa: anno zero; una terza via al diritto per tutti di manifestare il pensiero. Firenze, 1974. pp. 261.

— **Poland.**

FRANCE. Direction de la Documentation. La Documentation Française. Notes et Etudes Documentaires. Nos. 3,729-3, 730. La presse, les intellectuels et le pouvoir en Union Soviétique et dans les pays socialistes européens. 2. Pologne et Tchécoslovaquie; [by] Georges H. Mond. Paris, 1970. pp. 57. *bibliogs.*

— **United Kingdom.**

AIMS OF INDUSTRY. Ban: the attack on press freedom. London, [1974]. pp. 5.

SMITH (ANTHONY) b. 1938, ed. The British press since the war. Newton Abbot, [1974]. pp. 320. *bibliog.*

— **United States.**

ASHMORE (HARRY SCOTT) Fear in the air: broadcasting and the first amendment; the anatomy of a constitutional crisis. New York, [1973]. pp. 180.

WORKSHOP ON GOVERNMENT AND THE MEDIA, ASPEN, COLORADO, 1972. Aspen notebook on government and the media: [proceedings of the meetings]; edited by William L. Rivers [and] Michael J. Nyhan. New York, 1973. pp. 192.

LIBRARIANS

— Job descriptions.

LIBRARY ASSOCIATION. Research and Development Committee. Professional and non-professional duties in libraries...: a descriptive list compiled by a working party of the...Committee. 2nd ed. London, 1974. pp. 86.

LIBRARIES

HARDY (E.A.) The public library: its place in our educational system. Toronto, 1912. pp. 223.

— Automation — Bibliography.

TINKER (LYNNE) compiler. An annotated bibliography of library automation, 1968-1972. London, 1973. pp. 85. *Continuation of CAYLESS (C.F.) and POTTS (HILARY) compilers. Bibliography of library automation, 1964-1967.*

— History — Bibliography.

ABHB: annual bibliography of the history of the printed book and libraries; edited by Hendrik D.L. Vervliet. The Hague, 1973.(vol.1).

— Canada.

HARDY (E.A.) The public library: its place in our educational system. Toronto, 1912. pp. 223.

CANADA. Statistics Canada. Public libraries in Canada. a., 1970 [1st]- Ottawa.

— Germany — History.

DOSA (MARTA LESZLEI) Libraries in the political scene. Westport, Conn., [1974]. pp. 226. *bibliog.*

— India.

DUTT (NEWTON MOHUN) Baroda and its libraries. Baroda, 1928. pp. 191. *bibliog.*

— Russia.

VASIL'CHENKO (VLADIMIR EVSTAF'EVICH) Istoriia bibliotechnogo dela v SSSR: uchebnik dlia bibliotechnykh institutov; pod redaktsiei... E.V. Seglin. Moskva, 1958. pp. 216.

— United Kingdom.

PEMBERTON (JOHN E.) The national provision of printed ephemera in the social sciences; a report prepared for the Social Science and Government Committee of the Social Science Research Council. [Coventry], 1971. fo. 56. *(University of Warwick. Library. Occasional Publications. No. 1)*

LIBRARY ADVISORY COUNCIL (ENGLAND). Aspects of public library management: the application of new management processes to the public library service; the report of a Working Party of the... Council; [J.D. Stewart, chairman]. London, H.M.S.O., 1973. pp. 22. *(Library Information Series. No. 3)*

U.K. Department of Education and Science. Libraries Division. 1973. The public library service: reorganisation and after. London, 1973. pp. 29. *(Library Information Series. No. 2)*

LIBRARIES, GOVERNMENTAL, ADMINISTRATIVE, ETC.

BURKETT (JACK) ed. Government and related library and information services in the United Kingdom. 3rd ed. London, 1974. pp. 217. *bibliogs.*

LIBRARIES, SPECIAL.

AMERICAN SOCIETY FOR INFORMATION SCIENCE. Mid-Year Regional Conference, 1st, Dayton, 1972. Cost reduction for special libraries and information centres; [papers]; Frank Slater, editor. Washington, D.C., 1973. pp. 187. *bibliogs.*

BURKETT (JACK) Industrial and related library and information services in the United Kingdom. 3rd ed. London, 1972. pp. 263. *bibliog.*

BURKETT (JACK) ed. Government and related library and information services in the United Kingdom. 3rd ed. London, 1974. pp. 217. *bibliogs.*

LIBRARIES, UNIVERSITY AND COLLEGE

— Canada — Statistics.

CANADA. Statistics Canada. University and college libraries in Canada. a., 1970/71 [1st]- Ottawa.

— United Kingdom.

CAMBRIDGE. University. Library Management Research Unit. A report to the Office for Scientific and Technical Information covering the period January 1969-June 1972. Cambridge, 1973. pp. 63.

— United States.

BAUMOL (WILLIAM JACK) and MARCUS (MATITYAHU) Economics of academic libraries; prepared for Council on Library Resources by Mathematica, Inc. Washington, [1973]. pp. 98.

BURDICK (CHARLES BURTON) Ralph H. Lutz and the Hoover Institution. Stanford, [1974]. pp. 185. *(Stanford University. Hoover Institution on War, Revolution and Peace. Hoover Institution Publications. 131)*

LIBRARIES AND STATE

— Germany.

DOSA (MARTA LESZLEI) Libraries in the political scene. Westport, Conn., [1974]. pp. 226. *bibliog.*

LIBRARY ADMINISTRATION.

THOMAS (PAULINE ANN) Bibliographic information in library systems. London, [1973]. pp. 52. *bibliog. (Association of Special Libraries and Information Bureaux. Aslib Occasional Publications. No. 13)*

THOMAS (PAULINE ANN) and WARD (VALERIE A.) Where the time goes: librarians as managers: an exploratory survey. London, [1973]. pp. 43. *(Association of Special Libraries and Information Bureaux. Aslib Occasional Publications. No. 12)*

LIBRARY FINANCE.

AMERICAN SOCIETY FOR INFORMATION SCIENCE. Mid-Year Regional Conference, 1st, Dayton, 1972. Cost reduction for special libraries and information centres; [papers]; Frank Slater, editor. Washington, D.C., 1973. pp. 187. *bibliogs.*

— United States.

BAUMOL (WILLIAM JACK) and MARCUS (MATITYAHU) Economics of academic libraries; prepared for Council on Library Resources by Mathematica, Inc. Washington, [1973]. pp. 98.

LIBRARY OF CONGRESS.

GOODRUM (CHARLES A.) The Library of Congress. New York, 1974. pp. 292. *bibliog.*

LIBRARY SCHOOLS AND TRAINING.

BRITISH LIBRARY. Research and Development Department. Directory of short courses in librarianship and information work. q., current issue only kept. London.

LIBRARY SCIENCE.

CAMBRIDGE. University. Library Management Research Unit. A report to the Office for Scientific and Technical Information covering the period January 1969-June 1972. Cambridge, 1973. pp. 63.

LIBYA.

FRANCE. Direction de la Documentation. La Documentation Française. Notes et Etudes Documentaires. Nos. 3,740-3, 741. La République Arabe Libyenne; [by] Attilio Gaudio. Paris, 1970. pp. 52. *bibliog.*

— Foreign relations.

INSTITUTE FOR THE STUDY OF CONFLICT. Research Studies. Libya's foreign adventures. London, 1973. pp. 16. *(Institute for the Study of Conflict. Conflict Studies. No. 41)*

LIEBKNECHT (KARL).

BARTEL (WALTER) Karl Liebknecht gegen Krupp. 2nd ed. Berlin, 1951. pp. 47.

SCHMIDT (GISELHER) Spartakus: Rosa Luxemburg und Karl Liebknecht. Frankfurt am Main, [1971]. pp. 175. *bibliog.*

WOHLGEMUTH (HEINZ) Karl Liebknecht: eine Biographie. Berlin, 1973. pp. 533.

LIEBKNECHT (WILHELM PHILIPP MARTIN CHRISTIAN LUDWIG).

AVELING (EDWARD BIBBINS) Wilhelm Liebknecht and the social-democratic movement in Germany;...on behalf of the Zürich Committee for the International Socialist Workers and Trade Union Congress, London, July 26 to August 1, 1896. London, [1896]. pp. 7.

CHUBINSKII (VADIM VASIL'EVICH) Wilhelm Liebknecht: eine Biographie. Berlin, 1973. pp. 387. *bibliog.*

LIECHTENSTEIN

— Census.

LIECHTENSTEIN. Census, 1960. Liechtensteinische Volkszählung, 1. Dezember 1960. Vaduz, 1963. 1 vol. (unpaged).

— Economic history.

OSPELT (ALOIS) Wirtschaftsgeschichte des Fürstentums Liechtenstein im 19. Jahrhundert: von den napoleonischen Kriegen bis zum Ausbruch des Ersten Weltkrieges. [Schaan, imprint], 1974. pp. 424, 267. *bibliog. (Erschienen in: Jahrbuch des Historischen Vereins für das Fürstentum Liechtenstein, Band 72)*

LIEGE (PROVINCE)

— Economic conditions.

BELGIUM. Administration de l'Urbanisme et de l'Aménagement du Territoire. 1971. Développement et aménagement de la province de Liège. [Liège?], 1971. pp. 264. *(Atlas in end pocket)*

— Economic policy.

BELGIUM. Administration de l'Urbanisme et de l'Aménagement du Territoire. 1971. Développement et aménagement de la province de Liège. [Liège?], 1971. pp. 264. *(Atlas in end pocket)*

LIFE.

KOHL (MARVIN) The morality of killing: sanctity of life, abortion and euthanasia. London, 1974. pp. 112. *bibliog.*

LIFE SPAN, PRODUCTIVE.

NAVILLE (PIERRE) Temps et technique: structures de la vie de travail. Genève, 1972. pp. 234.

LIGUE DES DROITS DE L'HOMME.

LEVINE (MICHAEL) Affaires non classées: enquêtes et dossiers de la Ligue des Droits de l'Homme. [Paris, 1973]. pp. 392.

LIGURIA

— History.

LAZAGNA (GIOVANNI BATTISTA) Ponte rotto: la lotta al fascismo; dalla cospirazione all'insurrezione armata. Milano, [1972]. pp. 333.

LILONGWE

— Markets.

MALAWI. Agro-Economic Survey. 1974. Agro-economic survey: report no. 14: the town markets of Lilongwe: a study of the Lilongwe town markets, its customers, their purchasing behaviour and expenditure; prepared by O. Lavrijsen. Lilongwe, 1974. fo. 22.

LIMA

— Growth.

LEWIS (ROBERT ALDEN) Employment, income and the growth of the barriadas in Lima, Peru.[Ithaca], 1973. pp. 359. *bibliog. (Cornell University. Latin American Studies Program. Dissertation Series. No.46)*

LIMBURG (PROVINCE)

— Economic conditions.

NEESEN (VICTOR) and BALLAER (R.VAN) De economische ontwikkeling van Zuid-Limburg. Hasselt, Limburgse Economische Raad, 1973. pp. 457, 21 maps.

— Economic history.

NEESEN (VICTOR) and BALLAER (R.VAN) De economische ontwikkeling van Zuid-Limburg. Hasselt, Limburgse Economische Raad, 1973. pp. 457, 21 maps.

LIMOUSIN

— Economic policy.

BRUECHER (WOLFGANG) Die Industrie im Limousin: ihre Entwicklung und Förderung in einem Problemgebiet Zentralfrankreichs. Wiesbaden, 1974. pp. 45. *bibliog. (Geographische Zeitschrift. Beihefte. Erdkundliches Wissen. Heft 37)*

— Industries.

BRUECHER (WOLFGANG) Die Industrie im Limousin: ihre Entwicklung und Förderung in einem Problemgebiet Zentralfrankreichs. Wiesbaden, 1974. pp. 45. *bibliog. (Geographische Zeitschrift. Beihefte. Erdkundliches Wissen. Heft 37)*

LINCOLNSHIRE

— Description and travel.

LINDSEY. County Council. Countryside recreation: the ecological implications:...lowland Britain with particular reference to the countryside of Lindsey; [compiled by R.J. Lloyd]. [Lincoln], 1970. pp. 125.

— Rural conditions.

LINDSEY. County Council. Communities in rural Lindsay, present and future. Lincoln, 1973. pp. 52.

RURAL transport problems in Lincolnshire and East Nottinghamshire; [part 1 by members of the Lincolnshire Geographical Research Group; part 2 by Mark Evans; with the assistance of the East Midlands Region of the Open University]. [Nottingham, 1973]. 1 vol. (various pagings). *bibliog.*

LINEAR PROGRAMMING.

ORCHARD-HAYS (WILLIAM) Advanced linear-programming computing techniques. New York, [1968]. pp. 355. *bibliog.*

LARGE sparse sets of linear equations: proceedings of the Oxford conference of the Institute of Mathematics and its Applications held in April, 1970; edited by J.K. Reid. London, 1971. pp. 284.

EVERS (J.J.M.) Linear infinite horizon programming and Lemke's complementarity algorithm for the calculation of equilibrium combinations. Tilburg, 1973. pp. 20. *(Tilburg. Katholieke Hogeschool. Tilburg Institute of Economics. Research Memoranda. EIT 45)*

EVERS (J.J.M.) Linear programming over an infinite horizon. [Tilburg], 1973. pp. 187. *bibliog. (Tilburg. Katholieke Hogeschool. Tilburg Institute of Economics. Tilburg Studies on Economics. 8)*

HO (JAMES K.) and MANNE (ALAN S.) Nested decomposition for dynamic models. Stanford, 1973. 1 vol. (various pagings). *bibliog. (Stanford University. Institute for Mathematical Studies in the Social Sciences. Technical Reports. [New Series]. No. 96)*

BEARD (C.N.) The use of linear programming for analysis and planning. London, H.M.S.O., 1974. pp. 58. *(Civil Service College [U.K.]. Occasional Papers. No. 19)*

ZIONTS (STANLEY) Linear and integer programming. Englewood Cliffs, [1974]. pp. 514. *bibliog.*

LINGUISTIC CHANGE.

BARON (DENNIS E.) Case grammar and diachronic English syntax. The Hague, 1974. pp. 132. *bibliog.*

LINGUISTIC GEOGRAPHY.

KURATH (HANS) Studies in area linguistics. Bloomington, Ind., [1972]. pp. 202. *bibliog. (Indiana University. Studies in the History and Theory of Linguistics)*

MYERS (SARAH K.) Language shift among migrants to Lima, Peru. Chicago, 1973. pp. 203. *bibliog. (Chicago. University. Department of Geography. Research Papers. No. 147)*

LINGUISTICS.

ANNUAL ROUND TABLE MEETING ON LINGUISTICS AND LANGUAGE STUDIES, GEORGETOWN UNIVERSITY. Georgetown University Round Table selected papers on linguistics, 1961-1965; compiled by Richard O'Brien. Washington, [1968]. pp. 501. *bibliogs.*

CHICAGO LINGUISTIC SOCIETY. Regional Meeting, 8th, 1972. Papers...; edited by Paul M. Peranteau [and others]. Chicago, [1972]. pp. 615. *bibliogs.*

CHICAGO LINGUISTIC SOCIETY. Regional Meeting, 9th, 1973. Papers...; edited by Claudia Corum [and others]. Chicago, [1973]. pp. 709. *bibliogs.*

INTERNATIONAL CONFERENCE ON THE FORMAL ANALYSIS OF NATURAL LANGUAGES, 1ST, ROCQUENCOURT, 1970. The formal analysis of natural languages: proceedings...; edited by Maurice Gross [and others]. The Hague, 1973. pp. 388. *bibliogs. In English or French.*

SEBEOK (THOMAS ALBERT) ed. Current trends in linguistics... vol. 11. Diachronic, areal and typological linguistics;... editors, Henry M. Hoenigswald [and] Robert E. Longacre. The Hague, 1973. pp. 604. *bibliogs.*

SOME new directions in linguistics: (six lectures delivered at the School of Languages and Linguistics, Georgetown University... 1971-72); Roger W. Shuy, editor. Washington, [1973]. pp. 149. *bibliogs.*

SOUTHEAST CONFERENCE ON LINGUISTICS, 8TH, GEORGETOWN UNIVERSITY, 1972. Towards tomorrow's linguistics; [papers of the meetings held in combination with the first Conference on New Ways of Analyzing Variability in English]; Roger W. Shuy, Charles-James N. Bailey, editors. Washington, D.C., [1974]. pp. 351. *bibliogs.*

— Bibliography.

CENTRE FOR INFORMATION ON LANGUAGE TEACHING, and BRITISH COUNCIL. English-Teaching Information Centre. A language-teaching bibliography. 2nd ed. Cambridge, 1972. pp. 242.

LINTON (WILLIAM JAMES).

SMITH (FRANCIS BARRYMORE) Radical artisan: William James Linton, 1812-97. Manchester, [1973]. pp. 254. *bibliog.*

LIQUIDATION

— United Kingdom.

LOOSE (PETER) On liquidators: the role of a liquidator in a voluntary winding-up. Bristol, 1972. pp. 216.

— — Scotland.

SCOTLAND. Working Party on Insolvency, Bankruptcy and Liquidation. 1971. Insolvency, bankruptcy and liquidation in Scotland; [Lord Kilbrandon, chairman]. Edinburgh, 1971. pp. 151. *(Scotland. Scottish Law Commission. Memoranda. No.16)*

LIQUIDITY (ECONOMICS).

NORWAY. Statistiske Centralbyrå. 1972. Rentabilitet og kapitalstruktur i store industriforetak, etc. Oslo, 1972. fo. 55. *(Statistiske Analyser. 3) Tables in Norwegian and English.*

RUEHL (FRANK) Zur Nachfrage der Schweizer Banken nach Liquiditätsreserven, 1959-1970. Zürich, [1974]. pp. 226. *bibliog. With English summary.*

LIQUOR PROBLEM

— France.

FRANCE. Haut Comité d'Etude et d'Information sur l'Alcoolisme. 1972. Rapport au Premier Ministre sur l'activité du...Comité, etc. Paris, 1972. pp. 148.

— South Africa.

LÖTTER (JOHANN MORGENDALL) and DE VOS (H.V.N.) Die drinkpatroon van die Indiërs in Natal. [Pretoria], 1966. pp. 70. *bibliog. (South Africa. National Bureau of Educational and Social Research. Research Series. No. 35)*

VENTER (J.D.) and GOOSEN (D.S.) The drinking pattern of the Coloureds in the Transvaal and the Orange Free State. [Pretoria], 1966. pp. 97. *bibliog. (South Africa. National Bureau of Educational and Social Research. Research Series. No. 20)*

— United States.

FORT (JOEL) Alcohol: our biggest drug problem. New York, [1973]. pp. 180. *bibliog.*

GOSHEN (CHARLES E.) Drinks, drugs, and do-gooders. New York, [1973]. pp. 268. *bibliog.*

LIQUOR TRAFFIC

— Canada.

ACHESON (A.L. KEITH) Revenue vs. protection: the discretionary behaviour of the Liquor Control Board of Ontario. Ottawa, [1972]. fo. 28. *(Carleton University. Carleton Economic Papers)*

— Guatemala.

GUATEMALA. Comision Nacional del Salario. 1966. Monografia para la determinacion del salario minimo en la industria de alcoholes, bebidas alcoholicas, destiladas y fermentadas. Guatemala, 1966. pp. 59.

LIST (GEORG FRIEDRICH).

GEHRING (PAUL) Friedrich List bei der Neuordnung der Reutlinger Stadtverwaltung, 1816-1819. Reutlingen, 1967. pp. 28-75. *(Reutlinger Geschichtsblätter, 1967: Sonderdruck)*

SEIDEL (FRIEDRICH) Das Armutsproblem im deutschen Vormärz bei Friedrich List. Köln, 1971. pp. 56. *(Cologne. Universität. Forschungsinstitut für Sozial- und Wirtschaftsgeschichte. Kölner Vorträge zur Sozial- und Wirtschaftsgeschichte. Heft 13)*

LITERARY SOCIETIES

— United Kingdom.

WILLIAMS (Sir HAROLD HERBERT) Book clubs and printing societies of Great Britain and Ireland. London, 1929. pp. 127.

LITERATURE.

ORAGE (ALFRED RICHARD) Readers and writers, 1917-1921. New York, 1922. pp. 181.

— History and criticism.

SARTRE (JEAN PAUL) Situations. [Paris, 1947, repr. 1973 in progress].

LITERATURE, IMMORAL.

HOLBROOK (DAVID) The pseudo-revolution: a critical study of extremist 'liberation' in sex. London, 1972. pp. 202. *bibliog.*

TRIBE (DAVID) Questions of censorship. London, 1973. pp. 368. *bibliog.*

— Bibliography.

ASHBEE (HENRY SPENCER) Forbidden books of the Victorians: Henry Spencer Ashbee's bibliographies of erotica; abridged and edited, with an introduction and notes, by Peter Fryer. London, 1970. pp. 239.

LITERATURE AND SOCIETY.

CARPENTIER (ALEJO) Literatura y conciencia politico en America Latina. Madrid, [1969]. pp. 143.

KUCZYNSKI (JUERGEN) Gestalten und Werke. (Band 2). Soziologische Studien zur englischsprachigen und französischen Literatur. Berlin, 1971. pp. 499.

CRAIG (DAVID M.) Ph. D. The real foundations: literature and social change. London, 1973. pp. 318.

CAUTE (DAVID) Collisions: essays and reviews. London, 1974. pp. 231.

MUTISO (G.C.M.) Socio-political thought in African literature: weusi?. London, 1974. pp. 182. *bibliog.*

ROCKWELL (JOAN) Fact in fiction: the use of literature in the systematic study of society. London, 1974. pp. 211. *bibliog.*

LITHUANIA

— Industries.

LITHUANIA. Tsentral'noe Statisticheskoe Upravlenie. 1973. Promyshlennost' Litovskoi SSR: statisticheskii sbornik. Vil'nius, 1973. pp. 418.

LITTLE ENTENTE, 1920—1939.

CARMI (OZER) La Grande-Bretagne et la petite entente. Genève, 1972. pp. 381. *bibliog.*

LITTLE MAGAZINES

— United States — Directories.

INTERNATIONAL DIRECTORY OF LITTLE MAGAZINES AND SMALL PRESSES. a., 1965 [1st]- Paradise, California (formerly El Cerrito, California). *Title varies.*

LITTLE PRESSES

— United States — Bibliography.

SMALL PRESS RECORD OF BOOKS: a listing of books, pamphlets and broadsides pd. by the small presses. irreg., 1966/1968 (1st ed.)- Paradise, California.

— — Directories.

INTERNATIONAL DIRECTORY OF LITTLE MAGAZINES AND SMALL PRESSES. a., 1965 [1st]- Paradise, California (formerly El Cerrito, California). *Title varies.*

LIVERPOOL

— Civic improvement.

CIVIC TRUST FOR THE NORTH WEST. Environmental quality: a measuring system; a report prepared... for the Environment[al] Health and Protection Administration, City of Liverpool. [Manchester], 1971. fo. 36.

LIVERPOOL. City Planning Department. Liverpool city centre plan review, 1972. Liverpool, 1972. pp. 56.

SHELTER NEIGHBOURHOOD ACTION PROJECT. Another chance for cities: SNAP 69/72. Liverpool, 1972. pp. 225.

WILSON (HUGH) AND WOMERSLEY (LEWIS) Firm, and others. Inner area study: Liverpool: study review: proposals for action and research. [London], Department of the Environment, [1974]. 1 vol. (various pagings).

WILSON (HUGH) AND WOMERSLEY (LEWIS) Firm, and others. Inner area study: Liverpool: project report. [London], Department of the Environment, [1974]. pp. 53.

— Social conditions.

LIVERPOOL. Liverpool Council of Social Service. Social and community services: community work and education for adults; the N.O.C. handbook, editor Robin Little. Liverpool, 1973. pp. 33.

WILSON (HUGH) AND WOMERSLEY (LEWIS) Firm, and others. Inner area study: Liverpool: study review: proposals for action and research. [London], Department of the Environment, [1974]. 1 vol. (various pagings).

WILSON (HUGH) AND WOMERSLEY (LEWIS) Firm, and others. Inner area study: Liverpool: project report. [London], Department of the Environment, [1974]. pp. 53.

— Social history.

TAPLIN (E.L.) Liverpool dockers and seamen, 1870-1890. Hull, 1974. pp. 96. *bibliog.* (Hull. University. Occasional Papers in Economic and Social History. No. 6)

LLIGA CATALANA.

MOLAS (ISIDRE) Lliga catalana: un estudi d'estasiologia. Barcelona, 1972 repr. 1973. 2 vols. *bibliog.*

LO (JUI—CHING).

harding (harry) AND gurton (melvin) tHE PURGE OF lO jUI-CH'ING: THE POLITICS OF cHINESE STRATEGIC PLANNING...A REPORT PREPARED FOR uNITED sTATES aIR fORCE pROJECT rAND. sANTA mONICA, 1971. PP. 63. *(rAND cORPORATION. ?rAND rEPORTS!. 548)*

LOAD—LINE.

INTERNATIONAL CONFERENCE ON LOAD LINES, 1966. Final act of the Conference with attachments including the International Convention on Load Lines, 1966, signed in London 5 April 1966. London, Inter-Governmental Maritime Consultative Organization, 1972. pp. 213. *In English and French.*

LOANS

— Mathematical models.

WREAN (WILLIAM HAMILTON) The demand for business loan credit. Lexington, Mass., [1974]. pp. 224. *bibliog.*

LOANS, AMERICAN.

SLIGHTON (ROBERT L.) and others. The effect of untied development loans on the U.S. balance of payments. Santa Monica, 1972. pp. 92. *(Rand Corporation. Rand Reports. R.973)*

LOBBYING.

WALTERS (ALAN A.) The politicisation of economic decisions. London, [1973]. pp. 8. *(Aims of Industry. The Future of Capitalism)*

LOBBYISTS

— United States.

BURMAN (IAN D.) Lobbying at the Illinois Constitutional Convention. Urbana, Ill., [1973]. pp. 119. *(Illinois University. Institute of Government and Public Affairs. Studies in Illinois Constitution Making)*

LOCAL FINANCE

— Austria.

KUBIN (ERNST) Die Gemeindeaufgaben und ihre Finanzierung: das zentrale Problem der Kommunen. [Linz, 1972]. pp. 343. *bibliog.* (Linz. Hochschule für Sozial- und Wirtschaftswissenschaften. Institut für Kommunalwissenschaften and others. Kommunale Forschung in Österreich. 8)

— Canada — British Columbia — Statistics.

BRITISH COLUMBIA. Department of Municipal Affairs. Municipal statistics, including regional districts. a., 1972- Victoria, B.C.

— France.

ATELIER CENTRAL D'ETUDES D'AMENAGEMENT RURAL. L'étude des finances communales. [Paris], 1972. pp. 208. *bibliog.*

— — Statistics.

FRANCE. Ministère de l'Intérieur. Direction Générale des Collectivités Locales. Statistique des comptes administratifs départementaux. a., 1968- Paris.

— Ireland (Republic).

DE BUITLEIR (DONAL) Problems of Irish local finance. Dublin, 1974. pp. 81. *bibliog.*

— Kenya.

KENYA. Local government Loans Authority. Annual report. a., 1967/1969- Nairobi.

KENYA. Local Government Loans Authority. Annual report. a., 1967/1969- Nairobi.

— Norway — Accounting.

NORWAY. Statistiske Centralbyrå. 1973. Kommunerekneskapar 1971. Oslo, 1973. pp. 115. *(Norges Offisielle Statistikk. Rekke A. 567)*

— Russia.

FILIMONOV (BORIS IVANOVICH) Ukreplenie dokhodnoi bazy mestnykh biudzhetov. Moskva, 1973. pp. 103.

— South Africa.

BOTHA (D.J.J.) Urban taxation and land use: report of a one-man commission appointed by the City Council of Port Elizabeth. [Port Elizabeth, 1970]. pp. 192.

— Switzerland — Bern (Canton).

MEYER (HANS RUDOLF) Entwicklung und Struktur der Gemeindefinanzen der Agglomeration Bern, 1950-1967. Bern, 1969. pp. 100, (10). *(Bern (Canton). Statistisches Bureau. Sonderhefte. 17)*

— United Kingdom.

HOLLINRAKE (W.) The central control of local government expenditure; (transcript of ... lecture held on 19 February 1973). [London], Civil Service College, [1973]. fo. 27. *(Lectures on the Control of Public Expenditure. No. 1)*

PROCEEDINGS of a conference on local government finance [arranged by the] Institute for Fiscal Studies. London, 1973. pp. 141. *(Institute for Fiscal Studies. Publications. No.10)*

SOCIETY OF COUNTY TREASURERS. Local Government Act. 1972: finances of the new authorities. Taunton, [1973]. pp. 50.

LOCAL FINANCE. (Cont.)

U.K. Department of the Environment. 1973. Local government finance in England and Wales: consultation paper. London, 1973. fo. 6.

U.K. Department of the Environment. 1973. Local government finance in England and Wales: new rate rebate scheme. [London, 1973]. fo. 11.

CHARTERED INSTITUTE OF PUBLIC FINANCE AND ACCOUNTANCY. The medium-term financial plan in local authorities: a practical guide. London, [1974]. pp. 44.

MARSHALL (ARTHUR HEDLEY) Financial management in local government. London, 1974. pp. 303.

— Statistics.

CHARTERED INSTITUTE OF PUBLIC FINANCE AND ACCOUNTANCY and SOCIETY OF COUNTY TREASURERS. Welfare services statistics. a., 1949/50 (1st issue)- 1970/71; ceased pbln. London.

— United States.

HOUSING development and municipal costs; [by] George Sternlieb [and others]. New Brunswick, N.J., [1973]. pp. 378. bibliog.

— — Accounting.

TENNER (IRVING) and LYNN (EDWARD S.) Municipal and governmental accounting. 4th ed. Englewood Cliffs, [1960]. pp. 592. bibliog.

LOCAL GOVERNMENT.

MADDICK (HENRY) Mud walls and metropolises; an inaugural lecture delivered in the University of Birmingham on 12 May 1970. Birmingham, 1973. pp. 15.

MLINAR (ZDRAVKO) and others. Alternative local organizational policies in development. Vienna, [1973]. pp. 24. (Wiener Institut für Entwicklungsfragen. Occasional Papers. 73/1)

STEWART (JOHN DAVID) Management, local, environment, urban, government: a few words considered;... (an inaugural lecture delivered in the University of Birmingham on 5 December 1972). Birmingham, 1973. pp. 15.

WIATR (JERZEY J.) Alternative goals and policies in local administration. Vienna, [1973]. pp. 17. (Wiener Institut für Entwicklungsfragen. Occasional Papers. 73/10)

— Africa.

U.K. Colonial Office. Summer Conference on African Administration. [Papers, reports, etc.]. a., 1947-1960 (1st-11th sessions); ceased pbln. Cambridge. Not held 1950, 1952, 1955. (African [Publications]).

— Africa, Subsaharan.

VOSLOO (WILLEM BENJAMIN) and others. Local government in Southern Africa. Pretoria, 1974. pp. 291.

— Africa, West.

CAMPBELL (MICHAEL J.) and others. The structure of local government in West Africa. The Hague, 1965. pp. 421. bibliog. (International Union of Local Authorities. [Publications]. 84)

— — Bibliography.

[ASIEDU (E.S.) compiler]. Local administration and indirect rule: West Africa (general): [a bibliography]. [1972]. fo. 12. Xerographic copy.

— Australia — New South Wales.

CLARK (R.G.) and McPHAIL (I.R.) A preliminary examination of the urban system and alternative forms of local government of Coffs Harbour and District. Armidale, N.S.W., 1973. pp. 63. bibliog. (University of New England, Armidale. Department of Geography. Research Series in Applied Geography. No. 37)

— — Western Australia.

WESTERN AUSTRALIA. Local Government Assessment Committee. 1968. Reports on aspects of local government in Western Australia; [G.F. Mathea, chairman]. Perth, 1968. pp. 86, 6 maps.

— Bangladesh.

ABEDIN (NAJMUL) Local administration and politics in modernising societies: Bangladesh and Pakistan. Dacca, 1973. pp. 458. bibliog.

— Burma.

MYA SEIN, Daw. The administration of Burma: (Sir Charles Crosthwaite and the consolidation of Burma); [reprint of the first edition of 1938] with an introduction by Josef Silverstein. Kuala Lumpur, 1973. pp. 186. bibliog.

— Chile.

CLEAVES (PETER S.) Developmental processes in Chilean local government. Berkeley, [1969]. pp. 63. bibliog. (California University. Institute of International Studies. Politics of Modernization Series. No. 8)

— France.

FRANCE. Direction de la Documentation. La Documentation Française. Notes et Etudes Documentaires. Nos. 3,899-3, 900. Libertés, fusions et regroupements des communes, par Pierre Abrial. [Paris], 1972. pp. 49.

YVELINES. Préfecture. Spécial communes. Versailles, [imprint], 1972. pp. 15. (Bulletin d'Information et Recueil des Actes Administratifs. Suppléments)

MADIOT (YVES) Les fusions et regroupements de communes: problèmes posés par la réforme des structures communales. Paris, 1973. pp. 284. bibliog.

— Germany.

SCHNUR (ROMAN) Regionalkreise?: grundsätzliche Bemerkungen zur Schaffung von sogenannten Regionalkreisen, insbesondere in Nordrhein- Westfalen. Köln, [1971]. pp. 47. (Nordrhein-Westfälischer Städte- und Gemeindebund. Abhandlungen zur Kommunalpolitik. Band 1)

— Ghana.

DUNN (JOHN) and ROBERTSON (A.F.) Dependence and opportunity: political change in Ahafo. London, 1973. pp. 400.

— India.

INDIA. Committee on Plan Projects. Development Administration Unit. 1966. Role and function of panchayati raj institutions in planning and development. [New Delhi], 1966. pp. 73, 3. bibliog.

INDIA. Administrative Reforms Commission. Study Team on District Administration. 1970. Report...Vol. 2, September 1967. Delhi, [1970]. pp. 248.

MILLER (DONALD F.) Pervasive politics: a study of the Indian district. Melbourne, 1972. pp. 226. (Melbourne. University. Department of Political Science. Melbourne Politics Monographs)

— — Rajasthan.

GROVER (V.P.) and others. Panchayati raj administration in Rajasthan: a study of the media of supervision and control. Agra, 1973. pp. 215. A research project of the Administrative Reforms Commission carried out by the Department of Political Science, Rajasthan University.

— Italy.

BELTRAME (CARLO) Il discorso dei comprensori nell'esperienza italiana. Alessandria, 1969. pp. 68. (Alessandria (Province). Centro Documentazione e Ricerche Economico-Sociali. Quaderni. n.46)

Il FASCISMO e le autonomie locali [papers given at a seminar in 1972]; a cura di Sandro Fontana. Bologna, [1973]. pp. 435.

— New Zealand.

NEW ZEALAND. Local Government Commission. 1970. Wellington local government area: final scheme. [Wellington], 1970. pp. 10. Map in end pocket.

— Nigeria.

NIGERIA (WESTERN STATE). Ministry of Home Affairs and Information. Information Division. 1973. The new local government council system. [Ibadan, 1973]. pp. 27.

— Pakistan.

ABEDIN (NAJMUL) Local administration and politics in modernising societies: Bangladesh and Pakistan. Dacca, 1973. pp. 458. bibliog.

— Papua New Guinea.

MORAUTA (LOUISE HELEN MARGARET) Beyond the village: local politics in Madang, Papua New Guinea. London, 1974. pp. 194. bibliog. (London. University. London School of Economics and Political Science. Monographs on Social Anthropology. No. 49)

— Poland.

DZIABAŁA (STEFAN) Autorytety wiejskie: studium socjologiczne. Warszawa, 1973. pp. 349. bibliog.

— — Bibliography.

BIBLIOGRAFIA rad narodowych 1944-1969. Wrocław, 1973. pp. 339.

— Rhodesia.

PASSMORE (GLORIA C.) Theoretical aspects of local government and community action in the African rural areas of Rhodesia. Salisbury, 1971.pp. 95. (University of Rhodesia. Department of Political Science. Monographs in Political Science. No. 3)

— Russia.

AGEEVA (ELIZAVETA ALEKSANDROVNA) Formy upravlencheskoi deiatel'nosti ispolkomov mestnykh Sovetov. Moskva, 1973. pp. 104.

— — Ukraine.

BUTKO (IHOR PYLYPOVYCH) and SHEMSHUCHENKO (IURII SERHIIOVYCH) Mistsevi Rady i zabezpechennia zakonnosti. Kyïv, 1973. pp. 232. With Russian summary.

TERESHCHENKO (IURII ILARIONOVYCH) Politychna borot'ba na vyborakh do mis'kykh dum Ukraïny v period pidhotovky Zhovtnevoï revoliutsiï. Kyïv, 1974. pp. 143.

— Senegal.

SENEGAL. Ministère de l'Intérieur. 1960. Communication du Ministre de l'Intérieur sur la réforme administrative et discours prononcé à l'occasion de la réunion des chefs d'arrondissements à Dakar. Saint-Louis, 1960. pp. 30.

— Spain.

TUSELL GOMEZ (JAVIER) and CHACON ORTIZ (DIEGO) La reforma de la administracion local en España, 1900-1936. Madrid, 1973. pp. 449. bibliog. (Instituto de Estudios Administrativos. Estudios de Historia de la Administracion. 10)

— Sri Lanka.

LEITAN (GENEVIEVE RITA TRESSIBELLE) Local government and administration in Ceylon; [Ph.D. (London) thesis]. 1973. fo. 319. bibliog. Typescript: unpublished. This thesis is the property of London University and may not be removed from the Library.

— Switzerland.

RATIONALISIERUNG der öffentlichen Verwaltung; ([by] Hans Künzi [and others]). Bern, [1971]. pp. 50. (Zürich. Universität. Institut für Betriebswirtschaftliche Forschung. Schriftenreihe. Band 3)

MEYLAN (JEAN) and others. Communes suisses et autonomie communale; ([by] Groupe d'Etude de l'Autonomie Communale en Suisse). [Lausanne], 1972. pp. 387. bibliog.

— Tanzania.

SAMOFF (JOEL) Tanzania: local politics and the structure of power. Madison, 1974. pp. 286. *bibliog*.

— Thailand.

NEHER (CLARK D.) The dynamics of politics and administration in rural Thailand. Athens, [1974]. pp. 105. *(Ohio University. Center for International Studies. Papers in International Studies. Southeast Asia Series. No. 30)*

— United Kingdom.

BUILDER, THE. Consortia of local authorities: advantages and disadvantages; a survey by [O.W. Roskill, industrial consultants for] The Builder. [London], 1964. pp. 68.

FRANCE. Direction de la Documentation. La Documentation Française. Notes et Etudes Documentaires. No. 3,768. La réforme de l'administration locale en Angleterre: rapport de la Commission Maud. Paris, 1971. pp. 46. *bibliog*.

LOCAL TEST BEDS CONFERENCE, LONDON, 1972. Report. [London, Central Statistical Office, 1972?]. 1 pamphlet (various pagings).

BUXTON (RICHARD) Local government. 2nd ed. Harmondsworth, 1973. pp. 301. *bibliog*.

EDDISON (TONY) Local government: management and corporate planning. Aylesbury, 1973. pp. 225.

U.K. Department of the Environment. 1973. Local government reorganisation in England: transfer of property: memorandum. 2nd ed. London, 1973. pp. 74.

U.K. Department of the Environment. 1973. Local government reorganisation: transfer of property: airports. London, 1973. fo. 5.

U.K. Department of the Environment. 1973. Local Government Act 1972: local authority records. London, 1973. fo. 9.

U.K. Working Party on Collaboration between the National Health Service and Local Government. 1973. Reorganisation of the National Health Service and local government in England and Wales: a report from the Working Party... on its activities from January to July 1973; [A.R.W. Bavin, chairman]. London, 1973. pp. 86.

CROSS (CHARLES ALBERT) Principles of local government law. 5th ed. London, 1974. pp. 577.

FABIAN SOCIETY. Fabian Tracts. [No.] 429. Building better communities; [by] Chris Cossey. London, 1974. pp. 27. *(Fabian Society. Initiatives in Local Government. 1)*

FRIEND (JOHN K.) and others. Public planning: the inter-corporate dimension. London, 1974. pp. 534. *bibliog*.

GREENWOOD (ROYSTON) and STEWART (JOHN DAVID) Corporate planning in English local government: an analysis with readings, 1967-72. London, [1974]. pp. 584.

GRIFFITH (JOHN ANEURIN GREY) Local authorities and central control. Chichester, [1974]. pp. 29.

HILL (DILYS M.) Democratic theory and local government. London, 1974. pp. 243.

MAUD (JOHN PRIMATT REDCLIFFE) Baron Redcliffe-Maud and WOOD (BRUCE) English local government reformed. London, 1974. pp. 186. *bibliog*.

STEWART (JOHN DAVID) The responsive local authority. London, 1974. pp. 168.

— — Scotland.

YOUNG (RONALD G.) Crisis for democracy?: an essay on the state of policy-making in Scottish local government. Paisley, 1972. fo. 67. bibliog. *(Paisley College of Technology. Local Government Research Unit. Occasional Papers. 1)*

WORKING GROUP ON SCOTTISH LOCAL GOVERNMENT MANAGEMENT STRUCTURES. The new Scottish local authorities: organisation and management structures; report; [J.F. Niven, chairman]. Edinburgh, H.M.S.O., 1973. pp. 127.

— — Wales.

U.K. Welsh Office. 1973. Local government reorganisation in Wales: general contact points in government departments. Cardiff, 1973. pp. 7. *(Circulars. 190/73)*

U.K. Welsh Office. 1973. Local government reorganisation in Wales: transfer of property. Cardiff, 1973. single sheet. *(Circulars. 160/73)*

— United States.

ALESCH (DANIEL J.) and DOUGHARTY (L.A.) Economies-of-scale analysis in state and local government...: a report prepared for Council on Intergovernmental Relations, State of California. Santa Monica, 1971. pp. 56. *bibliog. (Rand Corporation. [Rand Reports]. 748)*

ALESCH (DANIEL J.) Intergovernmental communication in the New York-New Jersey- Connecticut metropolitan region;... prepared for the Metropolitan Regional Council. Santa Monica, 1972. pp. 141. *bibliogs. (Rand Corporation. Rand Reports. 977)*

WEBB (KENNETH) and HATRY (HARRY P.) Obtaining citizen feedback: the application of citizen surveys to local governments. Washington, D.C., [1973]. pp. 105. *bibliog*.

— — Bibliography.

TOMPKINS (DOROTHY LOUISE CAMPBELL) compiler. Research and service: a fifty year record; [publications of the]...Institute of Governmental Studies, University of California, etc. Berkeley, 1971. pp. 154.

LOCAL GOVERNMENT OFFICIALS AND EMPLOYEES

— India — Mysore.

REPORT ON THE CENSUS OF EMPLOYEES IN MUNICIPALITIES IN MYSORE STATE; issued by Department of Statistics, Government of Mysore. a., 1955-6/1959-60. Bangalore.

— Nigeria.

DADA (PAUL O.A.) Evaluation of local government courses in relation to careers of staff trained in Zaria, 1954-1964. Zaria, 1966. fo. 49. *(Ahmadu Bello University. Institute of Administration. Research Memoranda Series)*

— United Kingdom.

U.K. Department of the Environment. 1973. Local government reorganisation in England and Wales: transfer and protection of staff: memorandum. [London, 1973]. pp. 33.

— — Salaries, pensions, etc.

LOCAL AUTHORITIES' CONDITIONS OF SERVICE ADVISORY BOARD. Survey of local authorities' salaries. London, 1974. pp. 256.

— United States.

SPERO (STERLING DENHARD) and CAPOZZOLA (JOHN M.) The urban community and its unionised bureaucracies: pressure politics in local government labor relations. New York, [1973]. pp. 361. *bibliog*.

LOCAL TRANSIT.

DE LEUW, CHADWICK, O hEOCHA. A study of intermediate capacity rapid transit systems; a report prepared for the Department of the Environment. [London, Department of the Environment], 1972. pp. (125).

LOGIC.

GRANT (BRIAN E.) and RUSSELL (WALLACE J.) Opportunities in automated urban transport...; prepared under contract to the Transport and Road Research Laboratory by Robert Matthew, Johnson-Marshall and Partners for the Transport Research Assessment Group. [Crowthorne, Transport and Road Research Laboratory, 1973] . pp. 46.

— Australia.

AUSTRALIA. Commonwealth Bureau of Census and Statistics. 1971. Journey to work and journey to school, May 1970: preliminary statement. Canberra, 1971. pp. 10.

— Austria — Rates.

MATZNER (EGON) and NOVY (MANFRED) Zur Frage der Tarifgestaltung der öffentlichen Personen- Nahverkehrsunternehmungen. Wien, [1973]. pp. 60. *bibliog. (Kommunalwissenschaftliches Dokumentationszentrum. Kommunale Forschung in Österreich. 6)*

— Canada.

REYNOLDS (D.J.) The urban transport problem in Canada, 1970-2000; [prepared] for the... Minister responsible for Housing, government of Canada. Ottawa, Central Mortgage and Housing Corporation, 1971. pp. 105. *(Urban Canada: problems and prospects. Research Monographs. No. 3)*

— United Kingdom.

JAMIESON AND MACKAY. Ipswich and district transportation study; consultants' report [to Ipswich County Borough Council and the Department of the Environment]. London, 1973. fo. xxiii,82.

RURAL transport problems in Lincolnshire and East Nottinghamshire; [part 1 by members of the Lincolnshire Geographical Research Group; part 2 by Mark Evans; with the assistance of the East Midlands Region of the Open University]. [Nottingham, 1973]. 1 vol. (various pagings). *bibliog*.

— United States — Finance.

SHELDON (NANCY W.) and BRANDWEIN (ROBERT) The economic and social impact of investments in public transit. Lexington, Mass., [1973]. pp. 170. *bibliog*.

LOCKE (JOHN).

BENNETT (JONATHAN) Locke, Berkeley, Hume: central themes. Oxford, 1971. pp. 361. *bibliog*.

ZAICHENKO (GEORGII ANTONOVICH) Dzhon Lokk. Moskva, 1973. pp. 204. *bibliog*.

LOCOMOTIVES

— Construction.

EFREMTSEV (GRIGORII PETROVICH) Istoriia Kolomenskogo zavoda: ocherk istorii Kolomenskogo teplovozostroitel'nogo zavoda imeni V.V. Kuibysheva za 110 let, 1863-1973. Moskva, 1973. pp. 351. *bibliog*.

— Repairs.

ETAPY bol'shogo puti: k 75-letiiu lokomotivnogo depo Kurgan. Kurgan, 1971. pp. 31.

LODGING HOUSES

— Russia — Ukraine.

NIKITINA (ELENA IVANOVNA) and PRESS (TAMARA NATANOVNA) Rabochee obshchezhitie: opyt vospitatel'noi raboty. Moskva, 1971. pp. 111.

LOEFFLER (TOBIAS).

REINICKE (HANS) Tobias Loeffler: ein Kapitel zur Geschichte Mannheims in der Zeit Karl Theodors. Mannheim, 1966. pp. 40. *bibliog*.

LOGIC.

SOLLY (THOMAS) A syllabus of logic in which the views of Kant are generally adopted, and the laws of syllogism symbolically expressed. Cambridge, Deighton, 1839. pp. x, 164.

LOGIC. (Cont.)

FANN (K.T.) Peirce's theory of abduction. The Hague, 1970. pp. 62. *bibliog.*

LEDNIKOV (EVGENII EVGEN'EVICH) Kriticheskii analiz nominalisticheskikh i platonistskikh tendentsii v sovremennoi logike. Kiev, 1973. pp. 223.

LOGIC, SYMBOLIC AND MATHEMATICAL.

CRESSWELL (M.J.) Logics and languages. London, 1973. pp. 273. *bibliog.*

LOIRE (REGION)

— Economic policy.

PAYS DE LA LOIRE. VIème plan: plan régional de développement et d'équipement. [Nantes?], 1972. pp. 172.

— Social policy.

PAYS DE LA LOIRE. VIème plan: plan régional de développement et d'équipement. [Nantes?], 1972. pp. 172.

LOMBARDY

— Economic history.

ASPETTI di vita agricola lombarda, secoli XVI-XIX. Milano, 1973. pp. 307. *(Milan. Università Cattolica del Sacro Cuore. Istituto di Storia Economica e Sociale. Contributi. vol. 1)*

— Politics and government.

LOMBARDY. Consiglio Regionale. 1971. Osservazioni sugli schemi dei decreti delegati concernenti il trasferimento di funzioni amministrative statali alle Regioni a statuto ordinario. Milano, 1971. pp. 405.

LONDON

— Census.

TROWBRIDGE (BARRY) 1966 census: basic summaries for Greater London and the Greater London conurbation. [London], 1972. pp. 35. *(London,. Greater London Council. Department of Planning and Transportation. Research Memoranda. 369)*

DAVIES (HYWEL) and MORREY (C.R.) 1971 census: constituency data for Greater London. [London], 1974. pp. 373. *(London. Greater London Council. Department of Planning and Transportation. Research Memoranda. 437)*

LONDON. Greater London Council. Intelligence Unit. 1971 census data for London. [London], 1974. pp. 62. Reprinted from the Annual Abstract of Greater London Statistics.

LONDON. Greater London Council. Intelligence Unit. 1971 census data on London's overseas-born population and their children; by A.M. Field [and others]. London, 1974. pp. 119. *bibliog. (Greater London Council. Department of Planning and Transportation. Research Memoranda. 425)*

— Civic improvement.

LONDON. Greater London Council. [Greater London development plan: background documents, series B]. London, 1970-72. 46 pts. *Incomplete run from B 600-B 659.*

LONDON. Greater London Council. Valuation and Estates Department. Work of the Valuation and Estates Department, 1965-1970. [London, 1970]. pp. 66.

LONDON. Greater London Council. Traffic and Development Branch. The south east London study: an outline of the implications of the Greater London development plan for secondary road network and environmental area planning in south-east London. [London], 1972. pp. 58. *(London. Greater London Council. Greater London Development Plan. Background Papers. No.548)*

WESTMINSTER. City Council. The future of Piccadilly Circus; a public consultation paper. [London, 1972!]. pp. 42.

LONDON. Greater London Council. Thamesmead annual report. a., 1973/4- London.

DROVER (GLENN GORDON) Urban residential densities: a comparison of policies with particular reference to London and New York, 1945-1970; [Ph. D.(London) thesis]. 1973. fo. 276. *Typescript: unpublished. This thesis is the property of London University and may not be removed from the Library.*

LLEWELYN-DAVIES WEEKS [AND PARTNERS[. SE London and the Fleet Line: a study of land use potential carried out for London Transport Executive. London, 1973. pp. 172.

LONDON. Greater London Council. Valuation and Estates Department. Land for London: work of the Valuation and Estates Department, 1970-73. [London, 1973]. pp. 72.

LONDON DOCKLANDS STUDY TEAM. Docklands: redevelopment proposals for east London; a report to the Greater London Council and the Department of the Environment. [London, 1973]. 2 vols. (in 1).

PAHL (RAYMOND EDWARD) London: what next? the case for a Joint Inner London Rehabilitation Organisation; [a] lecture. London, 1973. pp. 30.

U.K. Department of the Environment. 1973. Greater London development plan: statement by Geoffrey Rippon, Secretary of State for the Environment. London, 1973. fo. 14. *Photocopy.*

ELKIN (STEPHEN L.) Politics and land use planning: the London experience. London, [1974]. pp. 196.

— Commerce.

U.K. Central Office of Information. Reference Division. 1965. Britain's financial services for overseas. London, 1965. pp. 38. *bibliog.*

GODDARD (JOHN BURGESS) Office linkages and location: a study of communications and spatial patterns in Central London; [Ph.D.(London) thesis] . 1973. fo. 124. *bibliog. Unpublished. This thesis is the property of London University and may not be removed from the Library.*

HILTON (RICHARD NOEL) Office employment and the demand for retail services in central London; [Ph. D. (London) thesis]. [1973]. fo. 278. *Typescript: unpublished. This thesis is the property of London University and may not be removed from the library.*

REVELL (JACK) Financial centres, financial institutions and economic change. Bangor, [1973]. pp. 20. *bibliog. (Wales. University. University College of North Wales. Economic Research Papers. FIN 4)*

— Docks.

LONDON DOCKLANDS STUDY TEAM. Docklands: redevelopment proposals for east London; a report to the Greater London Council and the Department of the Environment. [London, 1973]. 2 vols. (in 1).

— Foreign population.

LONDON. Greater London Council. Intelligence Unit. 1971 census data on London's overseas-born population and their children; by A.M. Field [and others]. London, 1974. pp. 119. *bibliog. (Greater London Council. Department of Planning and Transportation. Research Memoranda. 425)*

— Growth.

DROVER (GLENN GORDON) Urban residential densities: a comparison of policies with particular reference to London and New York, 1945-1970; [Ph. D.(London) thesis]. 1973. fo. 276. *Typescript: unpublished. This thesis is the property of London University and may not be removed from the Library.*

JACKSON (ALAN ARTHUR) Semi-detached London: suburban development, life and transport, 1900-39. London, 1973. pp. 381. *bibliog.*

— Hospitals.

FAIRFIELD (JOSEPHINE LETITIA DENNY) Maternity work in L.C.C. hospitals, 1931-1936. London, 1938. pp. 21. *(From Proceedings of the Royal Society of Medicine, vol. XXXI, 1938)*

— Politics and government.

ELKIN (STEPHEN L.) Politics and land use planning: the London experience. London, [1974]. pp. 196.

YOUNG (KENNETH GEORGE) The London Municipal Society, 1894-1963: a study in conservatism and local government; [Ph.D. (London) thesis]. 1973 [or rather 1974]. fo. 399 .*bibliog. With two previously published items bound in at end. Typescript: unpublished. This thesis is the property of London University and may not be removed from the Library.*

— — Information services.

PRATT (GORDON E.C.) and FERGUSON (HILARY A.) A study of the information needs of London's local government officers. [London], 1973. pp. 78. *bibliog. (London. Greater London Council. Department of Planning and Transportation. Research Memoranda. 433)*

— Poor.

ISLINGTON POVERTY ACTION GROUP. Working Papers. 1. Homeless in Islington. [London?, 1972?]. fo. 34. *Xerox copy.*

HEREN (LOUIS) Growing up poor in London. London, 1973. pp. 208.

— Population.

DROVER (GLENN GORDON) Urban residential densities: a comparison of policies with particular reference to London and New York, 1945-1970; [Ph. D.(London) thesis]. 1973. fo. 276. *Typescript: unpublished. This thesis is the property of London University and may not be removed from the Library.*

DUGMORE (KEITH) a GUIDE TO NON-CENSUS SOURCES OF POPULATION STATISTICS FOR gREATER lONDON. ?lONDON!, 1973. PP. 44. BIBLIOG. (lONDON. gREATER lONDON cOUNCIL. dEPARTMENT OF pLANNING AND tRANSPORTATION. rESEARCH mEMORANDA. 420)

GILJE (E.K.) and ARMSTRONG (WILLIAM) Revised demographic projections for Greater London and the London boroughs, 1973. [London], 1973. pp. 111. *bibliog. (London. Greater London Council. Department of Planning and Transportation. Research Memoranda. 430)*

HOCKLEY (D.) Population projections for the South-East sub-regions. [London], 1973. pp. 30. *bibliog. (London. Greater London Council. Department of Planning and Transportation. Research Memoranda. 417)*

MORREY (C.R.) The changing population of the London boroughs. [London], 1973. pp. 56. *(London. Greater London Council. Department of Planning and Transportation. Research Memoranda. 413)*

NORMAN (K.) and GILJE (E.K.) Analytic graduation of age specific fertility rates in the London boroughs. [London], 1973. pp. 118. *bibliog. (London. Greater London Council. Department of Planning and Transportation. Research Memoranda. 423)*

— Port.

LONDON. Port of London Authority. Notes on the Port of London. rev. ed. Gerrards Cross, Bucks., 1973. pp. 34.

— Schools.

ARROWSMITH (PAT) The colour of six schools. London, 1972. pp. 132. *Not available for consultation.*

TRUEFITT (ALISON) How to set up a free school: alternative education and the law. London, [1973?]. pp. 42. *bibliog.*

— Social conditions.

GRANT (CLARA ELLEN) From 'me' to 'we': forty years on Bow Common. London, [c.1940]. pp. 197.

— Transit systems.

LONDON TRANSPORT PASSENGERS COMMITTEE. Annual report. a., 1970[1st]- London.

CROYDON. Borough Council. The Croydon transportation study: an interim report: data collection. [Croydon], 1972. 1 vol. (various pagings). With maps.

WEBSTER (F.V.) and OLDFIELD (R.H.) A theoretical study of bus and car travel in central London. Crowthorne, 1972. pp. 22. *(U.K. Transport and Road Research Laboratory. Reports. LR 451)*

CROWTHER (G.L.) and others. A new RingRail for London: the key to an integrated public transport system. London, 1973. pp. 67.

EDMONDS (ALEXANDER) History of the Metropolitan District Railway Company to June 1908;... prepared for publication, with preface, notes and an epilogue by Charles E. Lee. London, 1973. pp. 243.

ELDRIDGE (DEREK A.) and CHAKRABORTI (S.) Thamesmead transportation study. [London], 1973. pp. 66. *(London. Greater London Council. Department of Planning and Transportation. Research Memoranda. 346)*

FAIRHURST (M.H.) An analysis of factors affecting bus and rail receipts (1970-72). [London], London Transport Executive, 1973. 1 pamphlet (various pagings). *(Department of Operational Research. Operational Research Reports. 201)*

COLLINS (MICHAEL F.) and PHAROAH (TIMOTHY M.) Transport organisation in a great city: the case of London. London, 1974. pp. 660.

FAIRHURST (M.H.) The influence of public transport on car ownership in London. [London], London Transport Executive, 1974. pp. 22. *(Economic and Operational Research Office. Operational Research Reports. 203)*

— Water supply.

LONDON. Metropolitan Water Board. A brief description of the undertaking. [London], 1972. pp. 28, 1 diagram.

LONDON MUNICIPAL SOCIETY.

YOUNG (KENNETH GEORGE) The London Municipal Society, 1894-1963: a study in conservatism and local government; [Ph.D. (London) thesis]. 1973 [or rather 1974]. fo. 399 .*bibliog*. *With two previously published items bound in at end. Typescript: unpublished. This thesis is the property of London University and may not be removed from the Library.*

LONELINESS.

SEABROOK (JEREMY) Loneliness; (text by Jeremy Seabrook, picture sequences by Bryn Campbell). London, 1973. pp. 191.

WEISS (ROBERT STUART) Loneliness: the experience of emotional and social isolation. Cambridge, Mass., [1973]. pp. 236.

LONG LARTIN PRISON.

A RESEARCH into consultative management at Long Lartin Prison; by P. Shapland [and others]. [London], 1972. fo. 122. *bibliog*. *(U.K. Prison Department. Office f the Chief Psychologist. CP Reports. Series 1. No. 2)*

LONG—TERM CARE OF THE SICK.

LANGTIDSBEHANDLING på sygehuse: betaenkning I afgivet af det af Sundhedsstyrelsen den 3. marts 1969 nedsatte udvalg, etc. København, 1970. pp. 79. *bibliog*.

SPECIALLAEGEUDDANNELSE i langtidsmedicin og i fysiurgi og genoptraening: betaenkning 2 afgivet af det af Sundhedsstyrelsen den 3. marts 1969 nedsatte udvalg. København, 1971. fo. 22, [11].

LONGEVITY.

SULTANOV (MEKHDI NECHEFOVICH) Kak prodlit' nashu zhizn'. Baku, 1973. pp. 69.

LONGSHOREMEN

— United Kingdom.

CLARK (ROY) The longshoremen. Newton Abbot, [1974]. pp. 201. *bibliog*.

LOPEZ (ESTANISLAO).

BUSANICHE (JOSE LUIS) Estanislao Lopez y el federalismo del litoral. Buenos Aires, [1969]. pp. 174.

LORAINE (Sir PERCY LYHAM).

WATERFIELD (GORDON) Professional diplomat: Sir Percy Loraine of Kirkharle Bt., 1880-1961. London, [1973]. pp. 312.

LOS ANGELES

— Race question.

BULLOCK (PAUL) Aspiration vs. opportunity: "careers" in the inner city. Ann Arbor, 1973. pp. 177. *(Michigan University, and Wayne State University. Institute of Labor and Industrial Relations. Policy Papers in Human Resources and Industrial Relations. 20)*

— Social conditions.

SANDBERG (NEIL C.) Ethnic identity and assimilation: the Polish-American community; case study of Metropolitan Los Angeles. New York, 1974. pp. 88. *bibliog*.

LOUIS XIV, King of France.

MOUSNIER (ROLAND) Louis XIV...; translated by J.W. Hunt. London, 1973. pp. 32. *bibliog*. *(Historical Association. General Series. G.83)*

THIREAU (JEAN LOUIS) Les idées politiques de Louis XIV. Paris, 1973. pp. 127. *bibliog*. *(Paris. Université de Paris II. Travaux et Recherches. Série Sciences Historiques. 4)*

LOUIS XVI, King of France.

WALZER (MICHAEL) ed. Regicide and revolution: speeches at the trial of Louis XVI;...translated by Marian Rothstein. London, 1974. pp. 219.

LOVE.

CONNECTICUT COLLEGE SYMPOSIUM ON THEORIES OF INTERPERSONAL ATTRACTION IN THE DYAD, 1970. Theories of attraction and love: [papers given at the Symposium] by Donn Byrne [and others]; editor, Bernard I. Murstein. New York, [1971]. pp. 179. *bibliogs*.

LOWE (ROBERT) 1st Viscount Sherbrooke.

SYLVESTER (DAVID WILLIAM) Robert Lowe and education. Cambridge, 1974. pp. 240. *bibliog*.

LOYALTY—SECURITY PROGRAM, 1947— .

COOK (FRED J.) The nightmare decade: the life and times of Senator Joe McCarthy. New York, [1971]. pp. 626.

THOMAS (LATELY) When even angels wept: the Senator Joseph McCarthy affair: a story without a hero. New York, 1973. pp. 654.

REES (DAVID) Harry Dexter White: a study in paradox. London, 1974. pp. 506. *bibliog*.

THOMAS (JOHN N.) The Institute of Pacific Relations: Asian scholars and American politics. Seattle, [1974]. pp. 187. *bibliog*.

LUANDA.

AMARAL (ILIDIO DO) Luanda: estudo de geografia urbana. Lisboa, 1968. pp. 152, 4 maps. *bibliog*. *(Portugal. Junta de Investigações do Ultramar. Memorias. Segunda Serie. 53)*

LUBIN

— Social conditions.

SZKURŁATOWSKI (ZYGMUNT) Siła robocza na wsi lubińskiej i jej produkcyjne wykorzystanie w okresie silnego uprzemysłowienia. Wrocław, 1972. pp. 105. *(Politechnika Wrocławska. Instytut Nauk Społecznych. Prace Naukowe. Nr.5 [being also] Monografie. Nr.2) With English and Russian summaries.*

LUCERNE (CANTON)

— Economic history.

BUCHER (SILVIO) Bevölkerung und Wirtschaft des Amtes Entlebuch im 18. Jahrhundert: eine Regionalstudie...der Schweiz im Ancien Régime. Luzern, [1974]. pp. 280. *bibliog*. *(Lucerne (Canton). Staatsarchiv. Luzerner Historische Veröffentlichungen. Band 1) With summaries in English and French.*

LUCERNE (CITY)

— Police.

JENNY (THEO) ed. 100 Jahre Stadtpolizei Luzern. Luzern, 1968. pp. 82. *(Lucerne. Stadtpräsidium. Luzern im Wandel der Zeiten. Heft 43)*

— Politics and government.

HELLER (HERMANN) Amtsrichter in Lucerne. Die Geschichte der Korporationsgemeinde von Luzern. Luzern, 1966. pp. 30. *bibliog*. *(Lucerne. Stadtpräsidium. Luzern im Wandel der Zeiten. Heft 38)*

LUDHIANA

— Rural conditions.

AGGARWAL (PARTAP C.) The green revolution and rural labour: a study of Ludhiana. New Delhi, [1973]. pp. 148. *bibliog*.

LUEBECK

— Commerce.

STARK (WALTER) Lübeck und Danzig in der zweiten Hälfte des 15. Jahrhunderts: Untersuchungen zum Verhältnis der wendischen und preussischen Hansestädte, etc. Weimar, 1973. pp. 275. *bibliog*. *(Historiker-Gesellschaft der Deutschen Demokratischen Republik. Hansische Arbeitsgemeinschaft. Abhandlungen zur Handels- und Sozialgeschichte. Band 11)*

LUECHOW—DANNENBERG

— Economic conditions.

SCHWENKE (HELMUT) Die Förderung und Entwicklung der Wirtschaft im Landkreis Lüchow-Dannenberg: eine Betrachtung und Beurteilung regionaler Förderungspolitik. Berlin, 1970. pp. 305. *bibliog*.

LUKÁCS (GEORG).

GOLDMANN (LUCIEN) Lukacs et Heidegger; fragments posthumes établis et présentés par Youssef Ishaghpour. [Paris, 1973]. pp. 177.

KAMMLER (JOERG) Politische Theorie von Georg Lukács: Struktur und historischer Praxisbezug bis 1929. Darmstadt, [1974]. pp. 382. *bibliog*.

LUMBER TRADE

— United States.

CARROLL (CHARLES F.) The timber economy of Puritan New England. Providence, [1973]. pp. 221.

LUMBERMEN

— Argentine Republic.

VICAT (BLANCA ELENA) Tres familias en un obraje del norte argentino. Buenos Aires, 1972. pp. 326.

LUMUMBA (PATRICE).

LUMUMBA (PATRICE) Lumumba speaks: the speeches and writings of Patrice Lumumba, 1958-1961; edited by Jean Van Lierde; translated... by Helen R. Lane; introduction by Jean-Paul Sartre. Boston, [1972]. pp. 433.

LUNACHARSKII (ANATOLII VASIL'EVICH).

BUGAENKO (PAVEL ANDREEVICH) A.V. Lunacharskii i sovetskaia literaturnaia kritika. Saratov, 1972. pp. 408.

LUR'E (ALEKSANDR L'VOVICH).

LUR'E (ALEKSANDR L'VOVICH) Ekonomicheskii analiz modelei planirovaniia sotsialisticheskogo khoziaistva. Moskva, 1973. pp. 435. *bibliog*. Contains *O matematicheskikh metodakh resheniï zadach na optimum pri planirovanii sotsialisticheskogo khoziaistva* and some other papers.

LUTHERAN CHURCH IN DENMARK.

DENMARK. Kirkeministeriet. Strukturkommission. 1971. Betaenkning om folkekirken i det moderne samfund. København, 1971. 2 vols. (*Denmark. Betaenkninger. Nr. 610*)

LUTHERAN CHURCH IN FINLAND.

ÅBO. Akademi. Acta Academiae Aboensis. Humaniora. 45. 2. Religion och politik: studier i finländsk politisk idéevärld och politisk miljö vid 1900-talets början; av Heimer Lindström. Åbo, 1973. pp. 224. *bibliog*.

LUTHERAN CHURCH IN POLAND.

MEISSLER (WOLFGANG) Kirche unter dem Kreuz: Beiträge und Erinnerungen über 17 Jahre "hinter Oder und Neisse". Leer (Ostfriesland), [1971]. pp. 40. *bibliog*.

LUTHERAN CHURCH IN RUSSIA.

KAHLE (WILHELM) Geschichte der evangelisch-lutherischen Gemeinden in der Sovetunion, 1917-1938. Leiden, 1974. pp. 625. *bibliog*.

LUTZ (RALPH HASWELL).

BURDICK (CHARLES BURTON) Ralph H. Lutz and the Hoover Institution. Stanford, [1974]. pp. 185. (*Stanford University. Hoover Institution on War, Revolution and Peace. Hoover Institution Publications. 131*)

LUXEMBOURG

— Census.

LUXEMBOURG. Census, 1970. Recensement de la population au 31 décembre 1970. [Luxembourg], 1974 in progress.

— Government publications.

LUXEMBOURG. Service Central de la Statistique et des Etudes Economiques. 1970. Répertoire analytique des publications. 2nd ed. [Luxembourg], 1970. pp. 135. (*Collection (Définitions et Méthodes'. 3*)

LUXEMBURG (ROSA).

OELSSNER (FRED) Rosa Luxemburg: eine kritische biographische Skizze. Berlin, 1951. pp. 216.

HIRSCH (HELMUT) Rosa Luxemburg in Selbstzeugnissen und Bilddokumenten. Reinbek bei Hamburg, 1969 repr. 1974. pp. 157. *bibliog*.

KOMMUNISTISCHER STUDENTENBUND GÖTTINGEN. Die Differenzen zwischen Lenin und Rosa Luxemburg im Kampf gegen Revisionismus und Opportunismus in der Sozialdemokratie. 2nd ed. Göttingen, 1971. pp. 59.

SCHMIDT (GISELHER) Spartakus: Rosa Luxemburg und Karl Liebknecht. Frankfurt am Main, [1971]. pp. 175. *bibliog*.

STROBEL (GEORG WALDEMAR) Die Partei Rosa Luxemburgs, Lenin und die SPD: der polnische "europäische" Internationalismus in der russischen Sozialdemokratie. Wiesbaden, 1974. pp. 759. *bibliog*.

LYONS

— Religion.

LAPERRIERE (GUY) La "Séparation" à Lyon, 1904-1908: étude d'opinion publique. Lyon, 1973. pp. 220. *bibliog*. (*Centre d'Histoire du Catholicisme. Collection. No. 9*)

MAASAI.

See MASAI.

MACAO

— Economic history.

MOURA (CARLOS FRANCISCO) Macau e o comercio português com a China e o Japão nos seculos XVI e XVII: as viagens da China e do Japão; a nau do trato; as galeotas. Macau, Imprensa Nacional, 1973. pp. 35. *bibliog*. Separata dos no. 1 do vol. vii do Boletim do Instituto Luis de Camões.

MACAULAY (THOMAS BABINGTON) Baron Macaulay.

MACAULAY (THOMAS BABINGTON) Baron Macaulay. The letters of Thomas Babington Macaulay; edited by Thomas Pinney. Cambridge, 1974 in progress.

MACAULAY FAMILY.

U.K. [National Register of Archives]. 1973. Report on the correspondence of Charles Booth (1840-1916), Mary Catherine Booth (1847-1939) and other members of the Booth and Macaulay families; (a handlist of the personal correspondence... in the University of London Library; compiled by T.D. Rogers and H.M. Young). London, 1973. fo. 317.

McCARTHY (JOSEPH RAYMOND).

COOK (FRED J.) The nightmare decade: the life and times of Senator Joe McCarthy. New York, [1971]. pp. 626.

GRIFFITH (ROBERT) and THEOHARIS (ATHAN G.) eds. The specter: original essays on the cold war and the origins of McCarthyism. New York, 1974. pp. 366.

THOMAS (LATELY) When even angels wept: the Senator Joseph McCarthy affair: a story without a hero. New York, 1973. pp. 654.

McCARTHY (STEPHEN).

McCARTHY COMMITTEE. Who killed Stephen McCarthy?. London, [1972]. pp. (30).

MACDONALD (Sir JOHN ALEXANDER).

CREIGHTON (DONALD GRANT) Towards the discovery of Canada: selected essays. Toronto, [1972]. pp. 315.

MACEK (VLADKO).

MAČEK (VLADKO) Vodja govori: ličnost, izjave, govori i politički rad vodje Hrvata, Dra. Vladka Mačka; sabrao i uredio Mirko Glojnarić. Zagreb, 1936. pp. 349.

McGOVERN (GEORGE STANLEY).

HART (GARY WARREN) Right from the start: a chronicle of the McGovern campaign. New York, [1973]. pp. 334.

WEIL (GORDON LEE) The long shot: George McGovern runs for president. New York, [1973]. pp. 253.

MACHINE TOOLS.

BACON (R.W.) and ELTIS (WALTER ALFRED) The age of US and UK machinery. London, National Economic Development Office, 1974. pp. 53. (*NEDO Monographs. 3*)

— History.

WOODBURY (ROBERT SMITH) Studies in the history of machine tools; [reprints of four monographs published between 1958 and 1961]. Cambridge, Mass., [1972]. 1 vol. (various pagings). *bibliogs*.

— Trade and manufacture — United Kingdom.

ECONOMIC DEVELOPMENT COMMITTEE FOR MACHINE TOOLS. A financial study of British machine tool companies; [by Peat, Marwick, Mitchell and Company]. London, National Economic Development Office, 1974. pp. 129.

MACHINERY

— Trade and manufacture — Roumania.

ROTARU (PETRE) Introducerea tehnicii moderne în construcțiile de mașini: orientări, rezultate, calcule de eficiență. București, 1973. pp. 278. *bibliog*. (*Academia de Științe Sociale și Politice a Republicii Socialiste România. Institutul de Cercetări Economice. Bibliotheca Oeconomica. 24*) With English, Russian, French and German tables of contents.

— — Russia.

BREKHOV (KONSTANTIN IVANOVICH) Khimicheskoe i neftianoe mashinostroenie v vos'moi piatiletke. Moskva, 1971. pp. 56.

— — — Russia (RSFSR).

VOLOKHOV (VALENTIN PETROVICH) Brianskii ordena Trudovogo Krasnogo Znameni mashinostroitel'nyi zavod: ocherk revoliutsionnykh i trudovykh traditsii kollektiva. Tula, 1966. pp. 230.

— — — Ukraine.

KUCHERIAVYI (IVAN MYKOLAIOVYCH) Shliakhy pidvyshchennia efektyvnosti zahotovchoho vyrobnytstva u mashynobuduvanni. Kyïv, 1973. pp. 184.

MIROSHNIKOV (PETR SEMENOVICH) and others. Material'noe stimulirovanie nauchno-tekhnicheskogo progressa. Kiev, 1973. pp. 159. *bibliog*.

MACKENZIE RIVER.

The MACKENZIE basin: proceedings of the intergovernmental seminar held at Inuvik, N.W.T., June 24-27, 1972. Ottawa, Information Canada, 1973. pp. 131.

MACLEAN (JOHN).

MILTON (NAN) John Maclean. [London], 1973. pp. 318. *bibliog*.

MADAGASCAR

— History.

DESCHAMPS (HUBERT) Histoire de Madagascar. 4th ed. Paris, 1972. pp. 358. *bibliog*.

— Statistics.

ANNUAIRE STATISTIQUE DE MADAGASCAR; [pd. by] Service de Statistique Générale. 1938/1951 (v.1). Tananarive.

MADARIAGA (SALVADOR DE).

MADARIAGA (SALVADOR DE) Morning without noon: memoirs. Farnborough, 1974. pp. 441.

MADEIRA

— Industries.

PORTUGAL. Instituto Nacional de Estatistica. 1966. Inquerito industrial..., 1.° semestre de 1964; Enquête industrielle..., 1er semestre 1964: 1. Arquipelago da Madeira, distrito do Funchal. 2. Arquipelago dos Açores. [Lisbon, 1966]. 2 pts.

MADRID.

FRANCE. Direction de la Documentation. La Documentation Française. Notes et Etudes Documentaires. Nos. 3,854-3, 855. Les grandes villes du monde: Madrid; [rédigée par A. Huetz de Lemps]. [Paris], 1972. pp. 92. *bibliog*.

MAFIA.

ITALY. Camera dei Deputati. Commissione Parlamentare di Inchiesta sul Fenomeno della Mafia in Sicilia. 1972. Relazione sui lavori svolti e sullo stato del fenomeno mafioso al termine della V. legislatura. [Rome], 1972. pp. 1262.

BARRESE (ORAZIO) I complici: gli anni dell'antimafia. Milano, 1973. pp. 342.

HESS (HENNER) Mafia and mafiosi: the structure of power; translated from the German by Ewald Osers. Farnborough, Hants, [1973]. pp. 233. *bibliog.*

PETRUCCI (LUIGI) Io accusa mafia e polizia. [Rome, 1973]. pp. 509.

BLOK (ANTON) The Mafia of a Sicilian village, 1860-1960: a study of violent peasant entrepreneurs. Oxford, [1974]. pp. 293. *bibliog.*

MAGHULL
— **Social conditions.**

PICKETT (KATHLEEN GORDON) and BOULTON (DAVID K.) Migration and social adjustment: Kirkby and Maghull; (with the assistance of Norman Rankin). Liverpool, 1974. pp. 179.

MAGNESIUM INDUSTRY AND TRADE
— **Russia — Russia (RSFSR).**

GOD rozhdeniia 1943-i: istoricheskii ocherk o Bereznikovskom ordena Trudovogo Krasnogo Znameni titano-magnievom kombinate. Perm', 1968. pp. 259.

MAGNITOGORSK
— **History.**

STANOVLENIE i razvitie goroda Magnitogorska: gorodskaia nauchno-tekhnicheskaia konferentsiia; doklady. Magnitogorsk, 1968. pp. 220. *bibliog.*

MAIN, RIVER (NORTHERN IRELAND).

HUTTON (J.B.E.) Report of a public inquiry into the proposed River Main drainage scheme. Belfast, H.M.S.O., 1972. pp. 49, 1 map.

MAINZ
— **History.**

FALCK (LUDWIG) Mainz in seiner Blütezeit als freie Stadt, 1244 bis 1328. Düsseldorf, [1973]. pp. 234. *bibliog.*

BLANNING (TIMOTHY CHARLES WILLIAM) Reform and revolution in Mainz, 1743-1803. London, 1974. pp. 355. *bibliog.*

MAISEL (KARL).

[BRUCKNER (WINIFRED)] Karl Maisel: der Mann, der niemals aufgab. [Wien, 1971]. 1 pamphlet (unpaged).

MAISKII (IVAN MIKHAILOVICH).

MAISKII (IVAN MIKHAILOVICH) Liudi, sobytiia, fakty. Moskva, 1973. pp. 216.

MAKARIOS III, Archbishop and Ethnarch of Cyprus.

VANEZIS (P.N.) Makarios: pragmatism v. idealism. London, 1974. pp. 203. *bibliog.*

MAKAROV (PAVEL VASIL'EVICH).

MAKAROV (PAVEL VASIL'EVICH) Ad''iutant Generala Mai-Maevskogo: iz vospominanii nachal'nika otriada krasnykh partizanov v Krymu, etc. Leningrad, [1925?]. pp. 197.

MALAITA
— **Social conditions.**

ROSS (HAROLD M.) Baegu: social and ecological organization in Malaita, Solomon Islands. Urbana, Ill., [1973]. pp. 334. *bibliog. (Illinios University. Illinois Studies in Anthropology. No. 8)*

MALAWI
— **Economic policy.**

MALAWI. Economic Planning Division. 1971. Statement of development policies, 1971-1980. [Zomba, 1971]. pp. 140, map. *bibliog.*

— **Government publications.**

MALAWI. Publications. irreg., S 1974 (no.1)- Zomba.

— **Politics and government.**

AFRICA PUBLICATIONS TRUST. Malawi: dialogue and development. London, 1973. pp. 24.

SHORT (PHILIP) Banda. London, 1974. pp. 357. *bibliog.*

— **Social policy.**

MALAWI. Economic Planning Division. 1971. Statement of development policies, 1971-1980. [Zomba, 1971]. pp. 140, map. *bibliog.*

MALAY LANGUAGE
— **Grammar.**

LEWIS (M. BLANCHE) Sentence analysis in modern Malay…: with examples drawn from two plays by Za'ba. Cambridge, 1969. pp. 345.

MALAYA
— **History.**

U.K. Central Office of Information. Reference Division. 1957. Malaya: the making of a nation. London, 1957. pp. 67. *bibliog.*

MALAYSIA
— **Commerce.**

ARIFF (K.A.MOHAMED) Export trade and the West Malaysian economy: an enquiry into the economic implications of export instability. Kuala Lumpur, 1972. pp. 246. *bliog. (University of Malaya. Faculty of Economics and Administration. Monograph Series on Malaysian Economic Affairs. 3)*

— **Foreign relations — United Kingdom.**

SULITSKAIA (TAT'IANA IVANOVNA) Angliia i Malaiziia, 1961-1971. Moskva, 1973. pp. 182. *bibliog.*

— **Officials and employees — Salaries, allowances etc.**

FEDERATION OF MALAYSIA. Royal Commission on the Revision of Salaries and Conditions of Service in the Public Services, 1964. Report…July, 1967; (under the chairmanship of Mr. Justice Suffian). Kuala Lumpur, 1969. pp. 320.

— **Politics and government.**

ONGKILI (JAMES P.) Modernization in East Malaysia, 1960-1970. Kuala Lumpur, 1972. pp. 123. *bibliog.*

MILNE (ROBERT STEVEN) and RATNAM (K.J.) Malaysia: new states in a new nation; political development of Sarawak and Sabah in Malaysia. London, 1974. pp. 501. *bibliog.*

— **Social policy.**

LEFTWICH (ADRIAN) ed. South Africa: economic growth and political change; with comparative studies of Chile, Sri Lanka and Malaysia. London, 1974. pp. 357.

MALCOLM X, pseud.

BREITMAN (GEORGE) and PORTER (HERMAN) The assassination of Malcolm X: 1. Unanswered questions…2. The trial. New York, 1969 repr. 1971. pp. 31. *Articles reprinted from The Militant, 1965 and 1966.*

GOLDMAN (PETER L.) The death and life of Malcolm X. London, 1974. pp. 438.

MALDON
— **Civic improvement.**

ESSEX. Town Design Group. Maldon: a comparative study. [Chelmsford, 1966]. 2 vols.(in 1).

MALINOWSKI (BRONISŁAW).

McLEISH (JOHN) The theory of social change: four views considered. London, Routledge and Kegan Paul, 1969 repr. 1972. pp. xiii, 95. *bibliog. (International Library of Sociology and Social Reconstruction)*

MALNUTRITION.

MAY (JACQUES M.) The ecology of malnutrition in the French speaking countries of West Africa and Madagascar, etc. New York, 1968. pp. 433. *bibliogs. (Studies in Medical Geography. vol. 8)*

MAY (JACQUES M.) and McLELLAN (DONNA L.) The ecology of malnutrition in seven countries of southern Africa and in Portuese Guinea: the Republic of South Africa, South West Africa etc. New York, 1971. pp. 432. *bibliogs. (American Geographical Society. Studies in Medical Geography. vol.10)*

PALMER (INGRID) Food and the new agricultural technology. (UNRISD Reports. No.72.9). Geneva, United Nations Research Institute for Social Development, 1972. pp. 85. *(Studies on the Green Revolution. No.5)*

U.K. Advisory Committee on Protein. 1974. British aid and the relief of malnutrition; report; [Sir Joseph Hutchinson, chairman]. [London], 1974. pp. 30. *bibliog.*

MALRAUX (ANDRE).

LACOUTURE (JEAN) André Malraux: une vie dans le siècle. Paris, [1973]. pp. 428.

MALTA
— **Constitutional history.**

LEE (HILDA I.) Malta 1813-1914: a study in constitutional and strategic development. Valletta, [imprint, 1973?]. pp. 292. *bibliog.*

— **Economic policy.**

MALTA. Ministry for the Treasury. 1927. Report by C. Mifsud Bonnici, Minister for the Treasury, on the work performed in the several ministerial divisions during the legislature which has just expired. [Valletta], 1927. pp. 23. *(Malta. Government Gazette. Supplements. No. 104)*

MALTA. 1961. Review of development plan for the Maltese Islands, 1959-64. [Valletta], 1961. pp. 110.

— **Foreign relations — Italy.**

SMITH (HARRISON) Mussolini and Strickland. Malta, 1974. pp. 42. *(Reprinted from Scientia, vol. 36, 1973)*

— **Politics and government.**

LEE (HILDA I.) Malta 1813-1914: a study in constitutional and strategic development. Valletta, [imprint, 1973?]. pp. 292. *bibliog.*

SMITH (HARRISON) Mussolini and Strickland. Malta, 1974. pp. 42. *(Reprinted from Scientia, vol. 36, 1973)*

— **Social policy.**

MALTA. Ministry for the Treasury. 1927. Report by C. Mifsud Bonnici, Minister for the Treasury, on the work performed in the several ministerial divisions during the legislature which has just expired. [Valletta], 1927. pp. 23. *(Malta. Government Gazette. Supplements. No. 104)*

MALTA. 1961. Review of development plan for the Maltese Islands, 1959-64. [Valletta], 1961. pp. 110.

— **Statistics, Vital.**

VITAL STATISTICS AND STATISTICAL INFORMATION ON THE INCIDENCE AND MORTALITY OF DISEASE IN THE MALTESE ISLANDS; [pd. by Department of Health] Malta. a., 1972- Valletta.

MAN (HENRI DE).

CLAEYS-VAN HAEGENDOREN (MIEKE) Hendrik de Man: een biografie. Antwerpen, [1972]. pp. 440. *bibliog.*

MAN (HENRI DE). (Cont.)

COLLOQUE INTERNATIONAL SUR L'OEUVRE D'HENRI DE MAN, GENEVA, 1973. Actes du Colloque...organisé par la Faculté de droit de l'Université de Genève. [Geneva, 1974]. 3 vols. (in 1).

MAN.

MILLER (LIBUSE LUKAS) Knowing, doing, and surviving: cognition in evolution. New York, [1973]. pp. 343. *bibliog.*

LEWIS (JOHN) B.Sc., Ph.D. The uniqueness of man. London, 1974. pp. 197.

STEVENSON (LESLIE) Seven theories of human nature. Oxford, 1974. pp. 128. *bibliogs.*

— Influence of environment — Bibliography.

WINTON (HARRY NATHANIEL MCQUILLIAN) ed. Man and the environment: a bibliography of selected publications of the United Nations system, 1946-1971. New York, 1972. pp. 305.

— Influence on nature.

CHELOVEK, obshchestvo i okruzhaiushchaia sreda: geograficheskie aspekty ispol'zovaniia estestvennykh resursov i sokhraneniia okruzhaiushchei sredy. Moskva, 1973. pp. 436. *bibliog.*

PASSMORE (JOHN ARTHUR) Man's responsibility for nature: ecological problems and western traditions. London, 1974. pp. 213.

MAN, PREHISTORIC

— South Africa.

CALIFORNIA UNIVERSITY. Anthropological Records. vol. 28. Montagu Cave in prehistory: a descriptive analysis; by Charles M. Keller. Berkeley, 1973. pp. 98, (30), 53 plates. *bibliog.*

MAN—MACHINE SYSTEMS.

SINGLETON (WILLIAM THOMAS) Man-machine systems. Harmondsworth, 1974. pp. 178. *bibliog.*

MANA.

PITT-RIVERS (JULIAN ALFRED LANE-FOX) Mana: an inaugural lecture (delivered at the London School of Economics on 1 November 1973). London, [1974]. pp. 37.

MANAGEMENT.

U.K. Working Party on Management Structure in the Local Authority Nursing Services. 1969. Report; [E.L. Mayston, chairman]. [London], 1969. pp. 61, 29.

BUNTINX (HUBERT) Geëngageerd bedrijfsbeleid: evolutie van mens en arbeidsstructuur; (met medewerking van W. van Hoorick [and others]). Den Haag, 1970. pp. 166. *(Nederlands Instituut voor Efficiency. Publikaties. Nr. 500)*

P.A. MANAGEMENT CONSULTANTS LTD. Company organization: theory and practice;...written by M.C. Barnes [and others]. London, 1970. pp. 235. *bibliog.*

VROOM (VICTOR HAROLD) and DECI (EDWARD L.) eds. Management and motivation: selected readings. Harmondsworth, 1970 repr. 1973. pp. 399. *bibliogs.*

GVISHIANI (DZHERMEN MIKHAILOVICH) Organizatsiia i upravlenie. 2nd ed. Moskva, 1972. pp. 536. *1st ed. has subtitle: sotsiologicheskii analiz burzhuaznykh teorii.*

THOMAS (JOHN M.) and BENNIS (WARREN G.) eds. The management of change and conflict: selected readings. Harmondsworth, 1972. pp. 507. *bibliogs.*

YOUNG (JAMES ALEXANDER) Agricultural progress and future trends in Northern Ireland. [Belfast, 1972]. pp. 36. *(Belfast. Queen's University. George Scott Robertson Memorial Lectures. No. 22)*

ATKINS (DEREK R.) Decentralisation in management. Coventry, 1973. pp. 41. *bibliog. (University of Warwick. Centre for Industrial Economic and Business Research. [Warwick Research in Industrial and Business Studies]. N0.36)*

HOPWOOD (ANTHONY G.) An accounting system and managerial behaviour. Farnborough, Hants, [1973]. pp. 237. *bibliog.*

LANSBURY (RUSSELL DUNCAN) Management services in a British airline: a study of occupational specialisation; [Ph.D. (London) thesis]. 1973. fo. 529. *bibliog. Typescript: unpublished. This thesis is the property of London University and may not be removed from the Library.*

MANAGEMENT research: a cross-cultural perspective; (a symposium of papers and discussions held at Eersel, Holland in 1970); edited by Desmond Graves. Amsterdam, 1973. pp. 349. *bibliogs.*

MENZ (WOLF DIETER) Die Profit Center Konzeption: theoretische Darstellung und praktische Anwendung. Bern, 1973. pp. 288. *bibliog.*

MINKES (ARON LEONARD) Business and a behavioural tradition: (an inaugural lecture delivered in the University of Birmingham on 21 November 1972).Birmingham, 1973. pp. 20. *bibliog.*

POPOV (GAVRIIL KHARITONOVICH) ed. Funktsii i struktura organov upravleniia, ikh sovershenstvovanie. Moskva, 1973. pp. 255.

U.K. Department of Health and Social Security. 1973. Management structure in the local authority nursing services: the implementation of Mayston. [London], 1973. pp. 49.

WOLF (WILLIAM B.) Conversations with Chester I. Barnard. New York, 1973. pp. 58. *(Cornell University. New York State School of Industrial and Labor Relations. ILR Paperbacks. No. 12)*

WORKING GROUP ON SCOTTISH LOCAL GOVERNMENT MANAGEMENT STRUCTURES. The new Scottish local authorities: organisation and management structures; report; [J.F. Niven, chairman]. Edinburgh, H.M.SO., 1973. pp. 127.

CLOOT (PETER L.) Management information: a systematic approach. 3rd ed. Henley-on-Thames, 1974. pp. 24. *bibliog. (Henley-on-Thames. Administrative Staff College. Occasional Papers. No. 7)*

CURWEN (PETER J.) Managerial economics. London, 1974. pp. 245. *bibliogs.*

DOW (R.) Computers and management today and tomorrow: a 1970's reassessment. [Berkhamsted, 1974]. pp. 14. *(Ashridge Management College. Papers in Management Studies)*

JERVIS (FRANK ROBERT JOSEPH) Bosses in British business: managers and management from the industrial revolution to the present day. London, 1974. pp. 184. *bibliog.*

LEWIS (RALPH F.) Planning and control for profit;... UK and Commonwealth edition. London, 1974. pp. 208. *bibliog.*

MANAGEMENT in the social and safety services: (contributions to a seminar organised by the Faculty of Social Sciences of Edinburgh University... 1972); edited by W.D. Reekie and Norman C. Hunt. London, 1974. pp. 198. *bibliogs. (Edinburgh. University. Faculty of Social Sciences. Seminars Committee. Social Issues in the Seventies. 3)*

MARTIN (MICHAEL J.C.) Management science and urban problems;... in collaboration with W.B. Wells [and others]. Farnborough, Hants, [1974]. pp. 209. *bibliogs.*

ROBERTS (TOM JOHN) Developing effective managers. rev. ed. London, 1974. pp. 166. *bibliog.*

TILLEY (K.W.) ed. Leadership and management appraisal: the proceedings of a NATO conference held in Brussels. London, 1974. pp. 432. *bibliogs.*

— Study and teaching — India.

HILL (THOMAS M.) and others. Institution building in India: a study of international collaboration in management education. Boston, 1973. pp. 381. *bibliog.*

— — Netherlands.

BEENHAKKER (MARTINUS) Groepsbijeenkomsten ten dienste van het management development: een onderzoek naar de effecttiviteit(sbepaling) van externe cursusgroepen. Rotterdam, 1973. pp. 370. *bibliog. With an English summary.*

— — United Kingdom.

WORKING PARTY TO REVIEW HIGHER TRAINING IN THE FIRE SERVICE [U.K.]. Reports; [R.F.D. Shuffrey, chairman]. [London], 1973. fo. 52.

— Terminology.

U.K. Department of Employment. Industrial Relations Division. Central Information Service. 1973. A glossary of management terms. rev. ed. London, 1973. fo. 37. *(Information Papers. [New Series]. No. 5)*

MANAGEMENT GAMES.

HALL (ANTHONY S.) and ALGIE (JIMMY) A management game for social services. London, [1974]. pp. 55.

MANCHESTER

— Economic history.

MARCUS (STEVEN) Engels, Manchester, and the working class. New York, [1974]. pp. 271. *bibliog.*

— Poor.

DUNKLEY (RUTH) Ten families: (a study of poverty in Manchester by the Child Poverty Action Group); [originally published in the Manchester Evening News in 1971]. London, [1972?]. pp. 35.

— Social history.

REACH (ANGUS BETHUNE) Manchester and the textile districts in 1849; edited by C. Aspin.Helmshore, 1972. pp. 122.

— — Sources.

VICTORIAN and Edwardian Manchester and east Lancashire from old photographs; introduction and commentaries by George Chandler. London, 1974. pp. (128).

MANCHURIA

— History.

HUNT (MICHAEL H.) Frontier defense and the open door: Manchuria in Chinese-American relations, 1895-1911. New Haven, 1973. pp. 281. *bibliog.*

MANDINGO (AFRICAN PEOPLE).

QUINN (CHARLOTTE A.) Mandingo kingdoms of the Senegambia: traditionalism, Islam, and European expansion. London, 1972. pp. 211. *bibliog.*

MANITOBA

— Bibliography.

MORLEY (MARJORIE) compiler. A bibliography of Manitoba from holdings in the Legislative Library of Manitoba. Winnipeg, 1970. pp. 267.

— Economic conditions.

MANITOBA. Department of Industry and Commerce. 1970. The economy of the province of Manitoba, 1970. [Winnipeg, 1970]. pp. 59.

MANITOBA. Regional Development Branch. 1972- Regional analysis program, southern Manitoba; Carvalho-Page group, program advisors. [Winnipeg, 1972 in progress].

— Economic policy.

CONFERENCE ON ECONOMIC DEVELOPMENT IN MANITOBA, WINNIPEG, 1971. The challenge: [proceedings of the Conference] sponsored by the Economic Development Advisory Board of Manitoba. [Winnipeg, 1972]. pp. 160.

— **Government publications.**

MANITOBA. Legislative Library. Publications of the Government of Manitoba received in the ... Library: checklist. 3 a yr. Ja/Ap 1973 (no.8)- Winnipeg.

— **Population.**

MANITOBA. Regional Development Branch. 1972- . Regional analysis program, southern Manitoba; Carvalho-Page group, program advisors. [Winnipeg, 1972 in progress].

— **Social conditions.**

MANITOBA. Regional Development Branch. 1972- . Regional analysis program, southern Manitoba; Carvalho-Page group, program advisors. [Winnipeg, 1972 in progress].

MANNHEIM

— **History.**

SALM (FRITZ) Im Schatten des Henkers: vom Arbeitswiderstand in Mannheim gegen faschistische Diktatur und Krieg. Frankfurt/Main, [1973]. pp. 301.

MANNINGTREE

— **Civic improvement.**

ESSEX. County Planning Department. Manningtree: study and proposals: 1970. [Chelmsford], 1970. fo. 37.

MANORS

— **France.**

GOUBERVILLE (GILLES DE) Un sire de Gouberville: gentilhomme campagnard au Cotentin de 1553 à 1562; publié par Abbé A. Tollemer; précédé d'une introduction par E. Le Roy Ladurie. 2nd ed. Paris, 1873 repr. 1972. pp. 841. (Maison des Sciences de l'Homme. Rééditions. 10) Material from the Journal arranged by subject with comment by Abbé Tollemer.

— **Russia — Latvia.**

DOROSHENKO (VASILII VASIL'EVICH) Myza i rynok: khoziaistvo Rizhskoi iezuitskoi kollegii na rubezhe XVI i XVII vv. Riga, 1973. pp. 187. *With English summary.*

MANPOWER

— **Mathematical models.**

CLOUGH (DONALD J.) and others, eds. Manpower planning models; proceedings of a conference held in Cambridge, U.K., under the aegis of the NATO Science Committee and the NATO Advisory Panel on Operational Research. London, 1974. pp. 504. *bibliogs.*

MANUFACTURERS

— **United States.**

PORTER (GLENN) and LIVESAY (HAROLD C.) Merchants and manufacturers: studies in the changing structure of nineteenth-century marketing. Baltimore, [1971]. pp. 257. *bibliog.*

MANUSCRIPTS

— **United Kingdom**

— — **Catalogues.**

SOTHEBY AND COMPANY. Bibliotheca Phillippica, medieval manuscripts, new series, eighth part: catalogue of manuscripts on vellum, paper and papyrus of the 4th to the 17th century from the celebrated collection formed by Sir Thomas Phillips, 1792-1872, etc. London, [1973]. pp. 127.

SOTHEBY AND COMPANY. Bibliotheca Phillippica, new series...part 9: catalogue of oriental manuscripts, Indian and Persian miniatures (from the celebrated collection formed by Sir Thomas Phillips, Bt., 1792-1872, etc). London, [1974]. pp. 126.

SOTHEBY AND COMPANY. Bibliotheca Phillippica, new series, twelfth part: catalogue of English manuscripts, autograph letters and charters from the celebrated collection formed by Sir Thomas Phillips, Bt., 1792-1872, etc. London, [1974]. pp. 154.

MAO (TSE—TUNG).

GEL'BRAS (VILIA GDALIVICH) Mao's pseudo-socialism. Moscow, [1967?]. pp. 156.

GRAY (JACK) and CAVENDISH (PATRICK) Chinese communism in crisis: Maoism and the cultural revolution. London, Pall Mall Press, 1968 repr. 1970. pp. viii, 279.

YEH (KUNG-CHIA) Land reform and the revolutionary war: a review of Mao's concepts and doctrines. Santa Monica, 1971. pp. 125. *bibliog.* (Rand Corporation. Rand Reports. 744)

DEICH (TAT'IANA LAZAREVNA) Maoizm - ugroza Afrike. Moskva, 1972. pp. 168.

MAOISM unmasked: collection of Soviet press articles; (compiled by V.F. Feoktistov). Moscow, 1972. pp. 246.

VLADIMIROV (OLEG EVGEN'EVICH) and RIAZANTSEV (VLADIMIR IVANOVICH) Stranitsy politicheskoi biografii Mao Tsze-duna. 2nd ed. Moskva, 1973. pp. 112.

CHEN (THEODORE HSI-EN) The Maoist educational revolution. New York, 1974. pp. 295.

MAO (TSE-TUNG) Mao Tse-tung unrehearsed: talks and letters, 1956-1971; edited and introduced by Stuart Schram; translated by John Chinnery and Tieyun. Harmondsworth, [1974]. pp. 352.

SIAO-YU Mao Tse-tung and I were beggars: a personal memoir of the early years of Chairman Mao. London, 1974. pp. 266.

— **Bibliography.**

SHU (AUSTIN C.W.) compiler. On Mao Tse-Tung: a bibliographic guide. East Lansing, 1972. pp. 78. *(Michigan State University. Asian Studies Center. East Asia Series. Occasional Papers. No. 2)*

MAORIS.

WARD ALAN) A show of justice: racial 'amalgamation' in nineteenth century New Zealand. Canberra, 1974. pp. 382. *bibliog.*

MARC (ALEXANDRE).

Le FEDERALISME et Alexandre Marc. Lausanne, 1974. pp. 235. *bibliog. (Lausanne. Université. Centre de Recherches Européennes. Publications. 1. Histoire, Précurseurs et Promoteurs de l'Union de l'Europe)*

MARCHES

— **Politics and government.**

SERRANI (DONATELLO) ed. Commento allo statuto della regione Marche. Milano, 1972. pp. 283.

MARGINAL PRODUCTIVITY.

OORT (COENRAAD JAN) La théorie marginaliste et les prix de transport: une analyse. Rotterdam, 1960. pp. 93. *bibliog.*

MARI REPUBLIC

— **Politics and government.**

MARI REPUBLIC. Verkhovnyi Sovet. Zasedaniia: stenograficheskii otchet. sess., D 1970 (7th series, 10th session). Ioshkar-Ola.

MARIGHELA (CARLOS).

CARLOS Marighella; [a brief biography with extracts from his writings]. [Havana, 1970]. pp. 101.

MARIGHELA (CARLOS) La guerra revolucionaria. Mexico, 1970. pp. 101. *bibliog.*

MARIHUANA.

GRUPP (STANLEY E.) The marihuana muddle. Lexington, [1973]. pp. 181.

BONNIE (RICHARD J.) and WHITEBREAD (CHARLES H.) The marihuana conviction: a history of marihuana prohibition in the United States. Charlottesville, 1974. pp. 368. *bibliog.*

MARINE ACCIDENTS.

CASUALTIES TO VESSELS AND ACCIDENTS TO MEN: vessels registered in the United Kingdom; ([pd. by] Department of Industry [U. K.]). a., 1972[1st]- London. *Supersedes* DEEP SEA TRAWLERS: *casualties to vessels and accidents to men: statistics, and* SHIPPING CASUALTIES AND DEATHS: *vessels registered in the United Kingdom, both of which see.*

MARINE ALGAE

— **New Zealand — Economic aspects.**

MOORE (LUCY BEATRICE) The economic importance of seaweeds. Wellington, 1941 repr. 1966. pp. 40. *bibliog. (New Zealand. Department of Scientific and Industrial Research. Bulletins. No. 85.) (New Zealand. Botany Division. Publications. No.5.) Reprinted without revision but with an Addendum of selected titles of papers published 1940-64.*

MARINE POLLUTION.

FRANCE. Groupe Interministériel des Problèmes de Pollution de la Mer. 1973. Pour une politique de lutte contre la pollution des mers: rapport. Paris, 1973. pp. 271. (Environnement. 12)

BELLAN (GERARD) and PERES (JEAN MARIE) La pollution des mers. Paris, 1974. pp. 127. *bibliog.*

SHINN (ROBERT A.) The international politics of marine pollution control. New York, 1974. pp. 200. *bibliog.*

— **Law and legislation.**

INTERNATIONAL CONFERENCE ON PREVENTION OF POLLUTION OF THE SEA BY OIL, 1962. (Final act of the 1962 Conference and its Annexes...[and] complete text of the amended 1954 Convention... [and] charts indicating the extent of the probibited zones). London, Inter-governmental Maritime Consultative Organization, 1962. pp. 93. *In English and French.*

INTER-GOVERNMENTAL MARITIME CONSULTATIVE ORGANIZATION. 1967. Charts of prohibited zones: International Convention for the Prevention of Pollution of the Sea by Oil. London, [1967]. pp. 7 (and charts). *In English and French.*

INTER-GOVERNMENTAL MARITIME CONSULTATIVE ORGANIZATION. 1967. International Convention for the Prevention of Pollution of the Sea by Oil, 1954, including the amendments adopted in 1962. London, [1967]. pp. 47. *In English and French.*

INTERNATIONAL LEGAL CONFERENCE ON MARINE POLLUTION DAMAGE, 1969. Final act of the Conference with attachments including the texts of the adopted Conventions. London, [1970]. pp. 88. *In English and French.*

CONFERENCE ON THE ESTABLISHMENT OF AN INTERNATIONAL COMPENSATION FUND FOR OIL POLLUTION DAMAGE, 1971. Final act of the Conference with attachments including the text of the adopted Convention. London, Inter-Governmental Maritime Consultative Organization, [1972]. pp. 84. *In English and French.*

INTER-GOVERNMENTAL MARITIME CONSULTATIVE ORGANIZATION. 1972. Charts of prohibited zones: International Convention for the Prevention of Pollution of the Sea by Oil. London, 1972. pp. 7 (and charts). *In English and French.*

MARINE POLLUTION. (Cont.)

INTER-GOVERNMENTAL MARITIME CONSULTATIVE ORGANIZATION. 1972. International Convention for the Prevention of Pollution of the Sea by Oil, 1954, including the amendments adopted in 1962. London, [1972]. pp. 77. *In English and French.*

INTERNATIONAL CONFERENCE ON MARINE POLLUTION, 1973. Final act of the Conference with attachments, including International Convention for the Prevention of Pollution from Ships, 1973, and Protocol relating to Intervention on the HighSeas in Cases of Marine Pollution by Substances other than Oil. London, Inter-Governmental Maritime Consultative Organization, 1973. pp. 171.

INTERNATIONAL LEGAL CONFERENCE ON MARINE POLLUTION DAMAGE, 1969. Official records of the ... Conference etc. London, Inter-governmental Maritime Consultative Organization, 1973. pp. 819.

MARINE RESOURCES.

OCEAN resources and public policy: [based on a series of seminars organized by the Graduate School of Public Affairs of the University of Washington]; edited by T. Saunders English. Seattle, [1973]. pp. 184. *bibliogs.*

MARINE RESOURCES CONSERVATION

— Law and legislation.

CANADA. International Fisheries Branch. 1973. The marine environment and renewable resources: law of the sea discussion paper. [Ottawa, 1973]. fo. 10.

MARITIME LAW.

INTERNATIONAL CONFERENCE ON FACILITATION OF MARITIME TRAVEL AND TRANSPORT, 1965. [Final act, convention and resolutions of the Conference]. London, Intergovernmental Maritime Consultative Organization, 1966. pp. 135. *In various languages.*

INTER-GOVERNMENTAL MARITIME CONSULTATIVE ORGANIZATION. 1968. Convention on Facilitation of International Maritime Traffic, 1965: notifications by contracting governments under Article 8 of the Convention. London, [1968]. pp. 33. *In English and French.*

INTERNATIONAL CONFERENCE ON SAFETY OF LIFE AT SEA, 1960. Final act of the Conference with Annexes including the text of the adopted Convention; (with Supplement). London, Inter-Governmental Maritime Consultative Organization, [1970]. 2 parts. *In English and French.*

INTER-GOVERNMENTAL MARITIME CONSULTATIVE ORGANIZATION. 1972. Convention on Facilitation of International Maritime Traffic, 1965; supplement to the Annex. London, [1972]. pp. 75. *In English and French.*

HILTON-YOUNG (ELIZABETH) Baroness Kennet, and JOHNSON (BRIAN) The law of the sea. London, 1973. pp. 48. (Fabian Society. Research Series. [No.] 313)

PHARAND (DONAT) The law of the sea of the Arctic, with special reference to Canada. Ottawa, 1973. pp. 367. *bibliog.* (Ottawa. Université. Faculté de Droit. Collection des Travaux. Monographies Juridiques. No. 7)

SYMPOSIUM ON THE FUTURE OF THE SEA, 1972. The future of the law of the sea: (proceedings)...; edited by L.J. Bouchez and L. Kaijen. The Hague, 1973. pp. 164.

DUPUY (RENE JEAN) The law of the sea: current problems. Leiden, 1974. pp. 210. *bibliog.*

LOGAN (R.M.) Canada, the United States and the third Law of the Sea Conference. [Montreal, 1974]. pp. 117. *bibliog.*

SOCIETY OF CONSERVATIVE LAWYERS. Whose sea?: a study of maritime jurisdiction. London, 1974. pp. 31. (Conservative Political Centre. [Publications]. No. 547)

— Sources.

LAY (S. HOUSTON) and others. New directions in the law of the sea: documents. Dobbs Ferry, N.Y., 1973. 2 vols. *bibliog.*

— America.

ZACKLIN (RALPH) ed. The changing law of the sea: western hemisphere perspectives; [papers by members of the Inter-American Study Group of International Law]. Leiden, 1974. pp. 272.

— Russia.

RUSSIA (U.S.S.R.) Statutes, etc., 1968. The Merchant Shipping Code of the USSR (1968); translated and edited by William E. Butler and John B. Quigley. Baltimore, [1970]. pp. 169. *bibliog.*

MARKETING.

DELEAGE (JEAN) and CASMECASSE ( ) La fonction commerciale dans l'industrie. [Paris?], Ministère du Développement Industriel et Scientifique, 1971. fo.78.

GREER (THOMAS V.) Marketing in the Soviet Union. New York, 1973. pp. 188.

HUYNEN (J.M.H) Trends in trade fairs...: history, environment, marketing, motivation. Valkenburg, [1973]. pp. 372. *bibliog. With summaries in English and Dutch.*

Det KOMMUNIKATIONSBEVIDSTE salg; [by] Otto Ottesen, red., Johan Arndt [and others]. København, 1973. pp. 91. (Copenhagen. Handelshøjskolen. Skriftraekke F. 45)

WARD (JAMES J.) The European approach to U.S. markets: product and promotion adaptation by European multinational corporations. New York, 1973. pp. 111. *bibliog.*

VALDELIN (JAN) Produktutveckling och marknadsföring: en undersökning av produktutvecklingsprocesser i svenska företag. Stockholm, 1974. pp. 249. *bibliog. With English summary.*

— History.

PORTER (GLENN) and LIVESAY (HAROLD C.) Merchants and manufacturers: studies in the changing structure of nineteenth-century marketing. Baltimore, [1971]. pp. 257. *bibliog.*

— Mathematical models.

FISHER (R.W.) and HIRST (M.) Marketing models in British industry. Coventry, 1973. pp. 72. *bibliog.* (University of Warwick. Centre for Industrial Economic and Business Research. [Warwick Research in Industrial and Business Studies]. No.39)

MUNIER (BERTRAND) Jeux et marchés. Paris, 1973. pp. 172. *bibliogs.*

LEEFLANG (PIETER SAMUEL HENDRIK) Mathematical models in marketing: a survey, the stage of development, some extensions and applications. Leiden, 1974. pp. 216. *bibliog.*

MARKETING MANAGEMENT.

BOSCHKEN (HERMAN L.) Corporate power and the mismarketing of urban development: Boise Cascade recreation communities. New York, 1974. pp. 283. *bibliog.*

MARKETING OF LIVESTOCK

— United Kingdom.

CAPIE (FORREST HUNTER) The British market for livestock products, 1920-1939; [Ph.d. (London) thesis]. 1973. 2 vols.. *bibliog. Typescript: unpublished. This thesis is the property of London University and may not be removed from the Library.*

CAPIE (FORREST HUNTER) The British market for livestock products, 1920-1939; [Ph.D. (London) thesis]. 1973. 2 vols. *bibliog. Typescript: unpublished. This thesis is the property of London University and may not be removed from the Library.*

MARKETING RESEARCH.

ZALTMAN (GERALD) and others. Metatheory and consumer research. New York, [1973]. pp. 226. *bibliog.*

MARKETS.

See also subdivision Markets under names of cities.

MARKOV PROCESSES.

SCHAICH (EBERHARD) Die Intergenerationenmobilität in Westdeutschland: eine dynamische Analyse auf der Basis Markovscher Ketten. Meisenheim am Glan, 1973. pp. 120. *bibliog.*

MUSTERT (G.R.) The development of the income distribution in the Netherlands after the second world war: a Markovian approach. Tilburg, 1974. pp. 20,9,5. (Tilburg. Katholieke Hogeschool. Tilburg Institute of Economics. Research Memoranda. EIT 47)

MARKS OF ORIGIN.

EIRE. Merchandise Marks Commission. 1971. Report on carpets. Dublin, [1971]. pp. 8. (Reports. No. 13)

EIRE. Merchandise Marks Commission. 1971. Report on footwear. Dublin, [1971]. pp. 7. (Reports. No. 14)

EIRE. Merchandise Marks Commission. 1971. Report on jewellery. Dublin, [1971]. pp. 22. (Reports. No. 15)

EIRE. Merchandise Marks Commission. 1972. Report on lead acid accumulators. Dublin, [1972]. pp. 12. (Reports. No. 16)

EIRE. Merchandise Marks Commission. 1972. Report on question of amending the Merchandise Marks (Restriction on Importation of Ceramic Ware) Order, 1969. Dublin, [1972]. pp. 3. (Reports. No. 17)

EIRE. Merchandise Marks Commission. 1973. Report on question of amending the Merchandise Marks (Restriction on Importation of Ceramic Ware) Order, 1969. Dublin, [1973]. pp. 5. (Reports. No.18)

MARRIAGE.

YAUKEY (DAVID) Marriage reduction and fertility. Lexington, [1973]. pp. 115.

SMITH (JAMES R.) and SMITH (LYNN G.) eds. Beyond monogamy: recent studies of sexual alternatives in marriage. Baltimore, [1974]. pp. 336. *bibliogs.*

— Africa, Subsaharan.

HASTINGS (ADRIAN) Christian marriage in Africa: being a report commissioned by the archbishops of Cape Town, Central Africa, Kenya, Tanzania, and Uganda. London, 1973. pp. 185.

— Australia.

McDONALD (PETER F.) Marriage in Australia: age at first marriage and proportions marrying, 1860-1971. Canberra, 1974. pp. 311. *bibliog.* (Australian National University. Research Scool of Social Sciences. Department of Demography. Australian Family Formation Project. Monographs. No.2)

McDONALD (PETER F.) Marriage in Australia: age at first marriage and proportions marrying, 1860-1971. Canberra, 1974. pp. 311. *bibliog.* (Australian National University. Research School of Social Sciences. Department of Demography. Australian Family Formation Project. Monographs. No.2)

— Cuba.

MARTINEZ-ALIER (VERENA) Marriage, class and colour in nineteenth century Cuba: a study of racial attitudes and sexual values in a slave society. London, 1974. pp. 202. *bibliog.*

— Ghana.

OPPONG (CHRISTINE) Marriage among a matrilineal elite: a family study of Ghanaian senior civil servants. London, 1974. pp. 187. *bibliog.*

— **India.**

VEEN (KLAAS W. VAN DER) I give thee my daughter: a study of marriage and hierarchy among the Anavil Brahmans of South Gujarat; [translated by Nanette Jockin]. Assen, 1972. pp. 297. *bibliog.*

SUR (A.K.) Sex and marriage in India: an ethnohistorical survey. Bombay, 1973. pp. 194. *bibliog.*

GUPTA (GIRI RAJ) Marriage, religion and society: pattern of change in an Indian village. Delhi, [1974]. pp. 187. *bibliog.*

— **Netherlands.**

INSTITUUT VOOR PSYCHOLOGISCH MARKTONDERZOEK. Rapport van een oriënterend onderzoek naar problemen onder jonggehuwden...in opdracht van het Ministerie van Cultuur, Recreatie en Maatschappelijk Werk. 's-Gravenhage, 1970. pp. 336.

NETHERLANDS. Centraal Bureau voor de Statistiek. 1970. Huwelijks- en hertrouwtafels voor Nederland, afgeleid uit waarnemingen over de perioden 1948-1949, 1950-1955, 1956-1960 en 1961-1965: aanhangsel: huwelijksontbindingskansen sedert 1948. 's- Gravenhage, 1970. pp. 69.

HEEREN (HENDRIK JAN) ed. Huwelijksleeftijd in Nederland: demografische en sociologische beschouwingen over de dalende huwelijksleeftijd in Nederland. Meppel, 1973. pp. 163.

— **Thailand.**

MAURER (KENNETH) and others. Marriage, fertility, and labor force participation of Thai women: an econometric study;... a report prepared for Agency for International Development. Santa Monica, 1973. pp. 54. *bibliog. (Rand Corporation. [Rand Reports]. 829)*

MARRIAGE GUIDANCE.

HEISLER (JILL) Why counsellors resign; a report. Rugby, 1974. pp. 32.

MARRIAGE LAW

— **Russia.**

RUSSIA (U.S.S.R.) Statutes, etc. 1968. Fundamentals of legislation of the USSR and the Union Republics on marriage and the family; Fundamentals of land legislation of the USSR and the Union Republics. Moscow, 1972. pp. 77.

MARRIED WOMEN

— **Netherlands.**

NETHERLANDS. Staatssecretaris van Financiën. 1970. Nota fiscale positie van de werkende gehuwde vrouw. 's-Gravenhage, 1970. pp. 37.

MARSEILLES

— **History.**

KENNEDY (MICHAEL L.) The Jacobin Club of Marseilles, 1790-1794. Ithaca, 1973. pp. 245. *bibliog.*

MARSHALL (THURGOOD).

BLAND (RANDALL W.) Private pressure on public law: the legal career of Justice Thurgood Marshall. Port Washington, N.Y., 1973. pp. 206. *bibliog.*

MARTIN (BASIL KINGSLEY).

ROLPH (C.H.) pseud. [i.e. Cecil Rolph HEWITT] Kingsley: the life, letters and diaries of Kingsley Martin. London, 1973. pp. 413.

MARTINIQUE.

FRANCE. Direction de la Documentation. La Documentation Française. Notes et Etudes Documentaires. No. 4,060. Les départements d'outre-mer: la Martinique; par Augusta Lagrosillière. Paris, 1974. pp. 30. *bibliog.*

— **Commerce.**

FRANCE. Institut National de la Statistique et des Etudes Economiques. Direction Générale. 197x. Une enquête sur les établissements commerciaux à la Réunion et à la Martinique 1967-1968. Paris, [1970?]. pp. 43.

— **Population.**

FRANCE. Institut National de la Statistique et des Etudes Economiques. 1972. Tendances démographiques dans les départements insulaires d'outre-mer: Martinique, Guadeloupe et Réunion. Paris, [1972?]. pp. 261.

MARTY (ANDRE).

LE BRAZ (YVES) Les rejetés: l'affaire Marty-Tillon; pour une histoire différente du PCF. Paris, [1974]. pp. 281. *bibliog.*

MARX (KARL).

LIFSHITS (MIKHAIL ALEKSANDROVICH) The philosophy of art of Karl Marx;...translated from the Russian by Ralph N. Winn; [reprint of translation first published in 1938]. London, 1973. pp. 118.

FISCHER (ERNST) of the Austrian Communist Party. Marx in his own words;...in collaboration with Franz Marek; translated by Anna Bostock. Harmondsworth, 1973, pp. 187. *This translation first published in 1970.*

NIKONENKO (STANISLAV STEPANOVICH) and RIABOV (FELIKS GRIGOR'EVICH) Velikii soratnik Marksa. Moskva, 1970. pp. 96.

PRINTSIP istorizma v poznanii sotsial'nykh iavlenii. Moskva, 1972. pp. 291.

FOUGEYROLLAS (PIERRE) Marx, Freud et la révolution totale. Paris, [1972]. pp. 642.

FREIRE (ANTONIO DE ABREU) La révolution désaliénante: fondements de la pensée de Karl Marx. Tournai, 1972. pp. 260. *(Facultés de la Compagnie de Jésus au Québec. Hier- Aujourd'hui. 7)*

PRA (MARIO DAL) La dialettica in Marx, dagli scritti giovanili all'Introduzione alla critica dell'economia politica. 2nd ed. Bari, 1972. pp. 327.

MARX (KARL) Political writings; edited by David Fernbach. London, 1973 in progress. *bibliogs.*

BEVAN (RUTH A.) Marx and Burke: a revisionist view. La Salle, [1973]. pp. 197. *bibliog.*

BOTTOMORE (THOMAS BURTON) ed. Karl Marx. Englewood Cliffs, [1973]. pp. 186. *bibliog.*

DUNCAN (GRAEME) Marx and Mill: two views of social conflict and social harmony. Cambridge, 1973. pp. 386. *bibliog.*

HARVEY (DAVID) A question of method for the matter of survival. Reading, 1973. pp. 44. *bibliog. (Reading. University. Department of Geography. Reading Geographical Papers. No.23)*

HERRE (GUENTHER) Verelendung und Proletariat bei Karl Marx: Entstehung einer Theorie und ihre Quellen. Düsseldorf, [1973]. pp. 200. *bibliog. (Tübingen. Universität. Seminar für Zeitgeschichte. Tübinger Schriften zur Sozial-und Zeitgeschichte. 2)*

KURUMA (SAMEZO) ed. Marx-Lexikon zur politischen Ökonomie. Glashütten im Taunus, 1973. 3 vols. *bibliogs.*

McLELLAN (DAVID) of the University of Kent. Karl Marx: his life and thought. London, 1973. pp. 498. *bibliog.*

NEUENDORFF (HARTMUT) Der Begriff des Interesses: eine Studie zu den Gesellschaftstheorien von Hobbes, Smith und Marx. Frankfurt am Main, 1973. pp. 163. *bibliog.*

SHKREDOV (VLADIMIR PETROVICH) Metod issledovaniia sobstvennosti v "Kapitale" K. Marksa. Moskva, 1973. pp. 262.

Der UNBEKANNTE junge Marx: neue Studien zur Entwicklung des Marxschen Denkens, 1835-1847; [by Heinz Monz and others]. Mainz, 1973. pp. 311.

VECA (SALVATORE) Marx e la critica dell'economia politica. Milano, 1973. pp. 244. *bibliog.*

VYGODSKII (VITALII SOLOMONOVICH) The story of a great discovery: how Karl Marx wrote "Capital"; (translated by Christopher S.V. Salt and revised by Maurice Dobb [and others]). Berlin, 1973. pp. 150.

DUCLOS (JACQUES) Bakounine et Marx: ombre et lumière; en annexe: La confession de Bakounine à Nicholas 1er; traduit du russe, etc.[Paris, 1974]. pp. 479.

GRANDJONC (JACQUES) Marx et les communistes allemands à Paris, 1844: contribution à l'étude de la naissance du marxisme. Paris, 1974. pp. 264. *bibliog.*

MERKEL (RENATE) Marx und Engels über Sozialismus und Kommunismus: zur Herausbildung der Auffassung...in der Entstehungsperiode des wissenschaftlichen Kommunismus, 1842-1846. Berlin, 1974. pp. 311.

PUSTARNAKOV (VLADIMIR FEDOROVICH) "Kapital" K. Marksa i filosofskaia mysl' v Rossii, konets XIX - nachalo XX v. Moskva, 1974. pp. 383.

SETTEMBRINI (DOMENICO) Due ipotesi per il socialismo in Marx ed Engels. Bari, 1974. pp. 317.

— **Bibliography.**

LEVIN (LEV ABRAMOVICH) compiler. K. Marks, F. Engel's, V.I. Lenin: ukazatel' bibliograficheskikh rabot, 1961-1972. Moskva, 1973. pp. 288.

MARXISM.

INSTITUT MARKSIZMA-LENINIZMA. La guerra partigiana vista dai classici del marxismo-leninismo; [edited by B. Ponomarev]. Mosca, [1945]; Milano, [1971?]. pp. 119.

PONCE (ANIBAL) El viento en el mundo: examen de la España actual en el centenario de Fourier. Buenos Aires, 1963. pp. 188.

KEMPER (MAX) Marxismus und Landwirtschaft; [reprint of work originally published in 1929]. Stuttgart, [1973]. pp. 117. *bibliog.*

CORNFORTH (MAURICE CAMPBELL) Marxism and the linguistic philosophy. 2nd ed. London, 1967 repr. 1971. pp. 384.

CORNFORTH (MAURICE CAMPBELL) The open philosophy and the open society: a reply to Dr. Karl Popper's refutations of marxism. London, 1968. pp. 396.

LESER (NORBERT) Zwischen Reformismus und Bolschewismus: der Austromarxismus als Theorie und Praxis. Wien, [1968]. pp. 600.

LISTEN marxist'.: [a reprint , by Leeds Anarchist Group, of the article published in Anarchos, May 1969]. Leeds, [1973?]. pp. 30.

McLEISH (JOHN) The theory of social change: four views considered. London, Routledge and Kegan Paul, 1969 repr. 1972. pp. xiii, 95. *bibliog. (International Library of Sociology and Social Reconstruction)*

HYMAN (RICHARD) Marxism and the sociology of trade unionism. London, 1971 repr. 1973. pp. 53.

BOSSLE (LOTHAR) Marxismus: demokratischer Sozialismus. Bonn, [1972]. pp. 39. *(Christlich-Demokratische Union Deutschlands. Wirtschaftsrat. Information. 8)*

FARUKSHIN (MIDKHAT KHABIBOVICH) Leninskie printsipy kritiki antimarksizma. Kazan', 1972. pp. 115.

GUICHARD (JEAN) Le marxisme: théorie et pratique de la révolution. 3rd ed. Lyon, [1972]. pp. 303. *bibliog.*

ISTORICHESKII materializm kak teoriia sotsial'nogo poznaniia i deiatel'nosti. Moskva, 1972. pp. 320.

PANZIERI (RANIERO) La ripresa del marxismo-leninismo in Italia: [an anthology];...a cura di Dario Lanzardo. Milano, [1972]. pp. 365.

REICH (WILHELM) Dialectical materialism and psychoanalysis. London, [1972]. pp. 71.

MARXISM. (Cont.)

SOCIALISTIES ONDERWIJSFRONT. Marx voor scholieren. 12th ed. [Nijmegen, 1972?]. pp. 47. *bibliog.*

SUL marxismo le scienze. Roma, 1972. pp. 286. *(Critica Marxista. Quaderni. n.6)*

LANGE (OSKAR) Dzieła. Warszawa, 1973 in progress.

MARX (KARL) Political writings; edited by David Fernbach. London, 1973 in progress. *bibliogs.*

ALBÈRGAMO (FRANCESCO) La teoria dello sviluppo in Marx ed Engels. Napoli, [1973]. pp. 267.

BATALOV (EDUARD IAKOVLEVICH) Filosofiia bunta: kritika ideologii levogo radikalizma. Moskva, 1973. pp. 222.

BROWN (BRUCE) b. 1944. Marx, Freud, and the critique of everyday life: toward a permanent cultural revolution. New York, [1973]. pp. 202.

CAMPORESI (CRISTIANO) Il marxismo teorico negli USA, 1900-1945. Milano, 1973. pp. 170.

CASSANO (FRANCO) ed. Marxismo e filosofia in Italia, 1958-1971: i dibattiti e le inchieste su Rinascita e il Contemporaneo. Bari, [1973]. pp. 401.

CRITIQUES DE L'ÉCONOMIE POLITIQUE. No. 10. Travail et emploi. Paris, 1973. pp. 151.

DEGROOD (DAVID H.) and others, eds. East-West dialogues: foundations and problems of revolutionary praxis. Amsterdam, 1973. pp. 179.

DUPRAT (GERARD) Marx Proudhon: théorie du conflit social. Paris, [1973]. pp. 176. *bibliog. (Strasbourg. Université de Strasbourg 3. Institut d'Etudes Politiques. Cahiers. Nouvelle Série. 1)*

FEDOSEEV (PETR NIKOLAEVICH) Kommunismus und Philosophie; (übersetzt [from the Russian] von Leon Nebenzahl). Berlin, 1973. pp. 594.

FOURTH INTERNATIONAL. International Committee. In defence of Trotskyism. London, 1973. pp. 80.

HERRE (GUENTHER) Verelendung und Proletariat bei Karl Marx: Entstehung einer Theorie und ihre Quellen. Düsseldorf, [1973]. pp. 200. *bibliog. (Tübingen. Universität. Seminar für Zeitgeschichte. Tübinger Schriften zur Sozial-und Zeitgeschichte. 2)*

HRZAL (LADISLAV) Die Auseinandersetzung mit dem Revisionismus und dem Antikommunismus während der krisenhaften Entwicklung in der ČSSR 1968/69. Frankfurt/Main, 1973. pp. 47.

IVANOV (VLADIMIR VASIL'EVICH) Sootnoshenie istorii i sovremennosti kak metodologicheskaia problema: ocherki po marksistsko-leninskoi metodologii istoricheskogo issledovaniia. Moskva, 1973. pp. 288. *bibliog.*

JAY (MARTIN) The dialectical imagination: a history of the Frankfurt School and the Institute of Social Research, 1923-1950. London, 1973. pp. 382. *bibliog.*

LABICA (GEORGES) Le marxisme d'aujourd'hui. [Paris, 1973]. pp. 96.

LABRIOLA (ANTONIO) Scritti filosofici e politici...; a cura di Franco Sbarberi. Torino, 1973. 2 vols.

LIEBMAN (MARCEL) Le léninisme sous Lénine. Paris, [1973]. 2 vols.

LUKÁCS (GEORG) Marxist. Marxism and human liberation: essays on history, culture and revolution;... edited and with an introduction by E. San Juan, Jr. New York, [1973]. pp. 332. *bibliog.*

LUXEMBURG (ROSA) Leninism or marxism?: originally entitled Organisational questions of Russian social democracy;... a new translation by Ken Eaton. Leeds, [1973]. pp. 20. *(Independent Labour Party. Square One Pamphlets. 2)*

MARX (KARL) Karl Marx on society and social change, with selections by Friedrich Engels; edited and with an introduction by Neil J. Smelser. Chicago, 1973. pp. 206.

METODICHESKOE posobie po nauchnomu kommunizmu; dlia shkol osnov marksizma-leninizma. 2nd ed. Moskva, 1973. pp. 319.

PABST (WILM K.) Arbeitsproduktivität als politökonomische Frage für Marxismus-Leninismus, UdSSR und DDR. Berlin, 1973. pp. 351. *(Berlin. Freie Universität. Osteuropa-Institut. Berichte: Reihe Wirtschaft und Recht. Heft 96)*

PARIZHSKAIA Kommuna i marksizm: ocherki. Moskva, 1973. pp. 248.

REY (PIERRE PHILIPPE) Les alliances de classes: sur l'articulation des modes de production; suivi de Matérialisme historique et luttes de classes. Paris, 1973. pp. 221.

SHIH (CHUN) On studying some world history. Peking, 1973. pp. 59.

SIK (OTA) Argumente für den dritten Weg. Hamburg, 1973. pp. 213.

THOMSON (GEORGE DERWENT) Capitalism and after: the rise and fall of commodity production. London, [1973]. pp. 148. *bibliog.*

TSAGOLOV (NIKOLAI ALEKSANDROVICH) ed. O sisteme kategorii i zakonov politicheskoi ekonomii. Moskva, 1973. pp. 271.

VERCELLI (ALESSANDRO) Teoria della struttura economica capitalistica: il metodo di Marx e i fondamenti della critica all'economia politica. Torino, 1973. pp. 262. *bibliogs. (Fondazione Luigi Einaudi. Studi. 15)*

ARMANSKI (GERHARD) Entstehung des wissenschaftlichen Sozialismus. Darmstadt, 1974. pp. 243. *bibliog.*

CHAMBRE (HENRI) L'évolution du marxisme soviétique: théorie économique et droit. Paris, [1974]. pp. 476.

DUNCKER (HERMANN) Road to the future: an introduction to marxism; selected speeches and articles. Dresden, 1974. pp. 43.

EINFUEHRUNG in die politische Ökonomie des Sozialismus; (Autoren: Willy Becker [and others]). Berlin, 1974. pp. 503.

GREGOR (A.JAMES) The fascist persuasion in radical politics. Princeton, [1974]. pp. 472. *bibliog.*

GUENTHER (HENNING) Walter Benjamin und der humane Marxismus: (zwischen Marxismus und Theologie). Olten, [1974]. pp. 188.

JALEE (PIERRE) L'exploitation capitaliste: initiation au marxisme. Paris, 1974. pp. 137.

JOHNSON (OAKLEY C.) Marxism in United States history before the Russian Revolution, 1876-1917. New York, 1974. pp. 196. *bibliog. (American Institute for Marxist Studies. History Series. No.9)*

KORSCH (KARL) Politische Texte; herausgegeben und eingeleitet von Erich Gerlach und Jürgen Seifert. Frankfurt am Main, [1974]. pp. 400.

LEONHARD (WOLFGANG) Three faces of marxism; the political concepts of Soviet ideology, maoism, and humanist marxism; (translated by Ewald Osers). New York, [1974]. pp. 497. *bibliog.*

LEVITAS (MAURICE) Marxist perspectives in the sociology of education. London, 1974. pp. 208. *bibliog.*

MARCUSE (HERBERT) Die Gesellschaftslehre des sowjetischen Marxismus; (Übersetzung [from the English]: Alfred Schmidt). Darmstadt, 1974. pp. 256.

MARKOVIĆ (MIHAILO) From affluence to praxis: philosophy and social criticism. Ann Arbor, Mich., [1974]. pp. 265.

O'ROURKE (JAMES J.) The problem of freedom in Marxist thought: an analysis of the treatment of human freedom by Marx, Engels, Lenin and contemporary Soviet philosophy. Dordrecht, [1974]. pp. 231. *bibliog. (Freiburg (Switzerland). Universität. Ost- Europa Institut. Sovietica. vol. 32)*

SOCIETY FOR THE PHILOSOPHICAL STUDY OF DIALECTICAL MATERIALISM. Dialogues on the philosophy of Marxism from the proceedings of the society...; edited by John Somerville and Howard L. Parsons. Westport, Conn., 1974. pp. 420. *(Contributions in Philosophy. No. 6)*

SOLZHENITSYN (ALEKSANDR ISAEVICH) Letter to Soviet leaders; translated by Hilary Sternberg [from an unpublished letter written in 1973]. London, 1974. pp. 59.

ZOLO (DANILO) La teoria comunista dell'estinzione dello stato. Bari, [1974]. pp. 316. *bibliog.*

ZUR Sozialstruktur der sozialistischen Gesellschaft: ([papers and discussion at a symposium]; herausgegeben vom Wissenschaftlichen Rat für Soziologische Forschung in der DDR). Berlin, 1974. pp. 221.

— **Dictionaries and encyclopaedias.**

KURUMA (SAMEZO) ed. Marx-Lexikon zur politischen Ökonomie. Glashütten im Taunus, 1973. 3 vols. *bibliogs.*

— **Periodicals.**

WORLD MARXIST REVIEW. For peace and socialism. Prague, 1973. pp. 152. *bibliog.*

MARYLAND

— **History.**

HOFFMAN (RONALD) A spirit of dissension: economics, politics and the revolution in Maryland. Baltimore, [1973]. pp. 280.

— **Politics and government.**

EVITTS (WILLIAM J.) A matter of allegiances: Maryland from 1850 to 1861. Baltimore, [1974]. pp. 212. *bibliog. (Johns Hopkins University. Studies in Historical and Political Science. Series 92. [No.] 1)*

— **Social history.**

EVITTS (WILLIAM J.) A matter of allegiances: Maryland from 1850 to 1861. Baltimore, [1974]. pp. 212. *bibliog. (Johns Hopkins University. Studies in Historical and Political Science. Series 92. [No.] 1)*

MASAI.

SANKAN (S.S. OLE) The Maasai. Nairobi, [c. 1968]. pp. 102.

MASPERO (EMILIO).

HAWKINS (CARROLL) Two democratic labor leaders in conflict: the Latin American revolution and the role of the workers. Lexington, Mass., [1973]. pp. 140. *bibliog.*

MASS MEDIA.

RONNENBERGER (FRANZ) Wege der Meinungsbildung in der komplexen Gesellschaft. Hannover, Niedersächsische Landeszentrale für Politische Bildung, 1972. pp. 84. *bibliog.*

CAYROL (ROLAND) La presse écrite et audio-visuelle. Paris, [1973]. pp. 628. *bibliogs.*

HENDERSON (GREGORY) ed. Public diplomacy and political change: four case studies: Okinawa, Peru, Czechoslovakia, Guinea. New York, 1973. pp. 339. *bibliogs.*

SCHRAMM (WILBUR LANG) Men, messages, and media: a look at human communication. New York, [1973]. pp. 341.

SERVAN-SCHREIBER (JEAN LOUIS) The power to inform: media, the information business;... translated...with the cooperation of Paris Research Associates. New York, [1974]. pp. 297.

— **Political aspects.**

SEYMOUR-URE (COLIN) The political impact of mass media. London, 1974. pp. 296. *bibliog.*

— — United States.

WORKSHOP ON GOVERNMENT AND THE MEDIA, ASPEN, COLORADO, 1972. Aspen notebook on government and the media: [proceedings of the meetings]; edited by William L. Rivers [and] Michael J. Nyhan. New York, 1973. pp. 192.

— Social aspects.

HALLORAN (JAMES D.) Mass media and society: the challenge of research: an inaugural lecture delivered in the University of Leicester, 25 October 1973. Leicester, 1974. pp. 30. *bibliog.*

— — United Kingdom.

HARTMANN (PAUL G.) and HUSBAND (CHARLES H.) Racism and the mass media: a study of the role of the mass media in the formation of white beliefs and attitudes in Britain. London, 1974. pp. 279.

— — United States.

WORKSHOP ON GOVERNMENT AND THE MEDIA, ASPEN, COLORADO, 1972. Aspen notebook on government and the media: [proceedings of the meetings]; edited by William L. Rivers [and] Michael J. Nyhan. New York, 1973. pp. 192.

— Denmark.

TEGLERS (HANS EDVARD) Penge og positioner: rapport om det private Danmark. København, 1973. pp. 206.

— France.

DIVIER (PIERRE FRANÇOIS) Le mensonge en publicité: sa répression et sa prévention en France. [Paris, 1972]. pp. 246.

— Mexico.

CINQ aspects de sociétés latino-américaines; [by Carlos M. Rama and others]. Paris, [1965]. pp. 151. *(Paris. Université. Institut des Hautes Etudes de l'Amérique Latine. Cahiers. No. 7)*

— Russia.

HOPKINS (MARK W.) Mass media in the Soviet Union. New York, [1970]. pp. 384. *bibliog.*

— Sweden.

TÖRNQVIST (KURT) Attityder till några internationella problem och massmedier: en opinionsundersökning hösten 1969. Stockholm, 1970. fo. 23. *(Psykologiskt Försvar. Nr. 47)*

— United Kingdom.

DOWNING (JOHN DEREK HALL) Some aspects of the presentation of industrial relations and race relations in some major British news media; [Ph. D. (London) thesis]. [1974]. fo. 287. *Typescript: unpublished. This thesis is the property of London University and may not be removed from the Library.*

— United States.

LEWELS (FRANCISCO JOSE) The uses of the media by the Chicano movement: a study in minority access. New York, 1974. pp. 185. *bibliog.*

MASS SOCIETY.

BOBROVSKII (VLADIMIR SERGEEVICH) Teoriia "massovogo obshchestva" na sluzhbe amerikanskogo imperializma. Minsk, 1973. pp. 175.

MASSA

— History.

MASSA. Amministrazione Comunale. La resistenza continua...... Massa, 1968. 1 vol. (unpaged).

MASSACHUSETTS

— Politics and government.

PATTERSON (STEPHEN E.) Political parties in revolutionary Massachusetts. Madison, 1973. pp. 299. *bibliog.*

MASSIGLI (RENE).

MASSIGLI (RENE) La Turquie devant la guerre: mission à Ankara. [Paris, 1964]. pp. 511.

MASSINGHAM (HENRY WILLIAM).

HAVIGHURST (ALFRED FREEMAN) Radical journalist: H.W. Massingham, 1860-1924. London, 1974. pp. 350. *bibliog. (Conference on British Studies. Biographical Series)*

MATABELE.

MOYO (EDGAR) 'Big' mother and 'little' mother in Matebeleland. [Oxford, 1973]. pp. 52. *(History Workshop. Pamphlets. No. 12)*

MATAKAM (AFRICAN PEOPLE).

MARTIN (JEAN YVES) Les Matakam du Cameroun: essai sur la dynamique d'une société pré-industrielle. Paris, Office de la Recherche Scientifique et Technique Outre-Mer, 1970. pp. 215. *bibliog. (Mémoires O.R.S.T.O.M. 41)*

MATERIALISM.

HALDANE (JOHN SCOTT) Materialism; [a collection of essays, addresses, etc.]. London, [1932]. pp. 221.

KOESTLER (ARTHUR) The heel of Achilles: essays, 1968-1973. London, 1974. pp. 254.

MATERIALS

— Research.

GUERON (J.) and RUARK (A.) Problems and prospects of fundamental research in multi-dusciplinary fields: materials. Paris, Organisation for Economic Co-operation and Development, 1972. pp. 63. *(Science Policy Studies)*

MATERIALS MANAGEMENT.

Die MATERIALWIRTSCHAFT der Deutschen Demokratischen Republik; [by an] Autorenkollektiv unter Leitung von Carl-Jürgen Strauss. 3rd ed. Berlin, 1973. pp. 570. *bibliog.*

MATERNAL AND INFANT WELFARE

— Netherlands.

LAPRÉ (RUDY M.) Maternity care: a socio-economic analysis; (translated by Margaret van den Bergh-Marshall). Tilburg, 1973. pp. 99. *bibliog. (Tilburg. Katholieke Hogeschool. Institute for Health Care Research. Tilburg Studies on Health Care. 1)*

— Russia — Latvia.

VOPROSY okhrany materinstva i detstva. Riga, 1972. pp. 185.

— United Kingdom — Scotland.

MATERNITY services: integration of maternity work; [report of a joint sub-committee of the Standing Nursing and Midwifery Advisory Committee and the Standing Medical Advisory Committee of the Scottish Health Services Council; R.A. Tennent, chairman]. Edinburgh, H.M.S.O., 1973. pp. 56.

MATHEMATICAL OPTIMIZATION.

KATSENELINBOIGEN (ARON IOSIFOVICH) and others. Metodologicheskie voprosy optimal'nogo planirovaniia sotsialisticheskoi ekonomiki. Moskva, 1966. pp. 246. *bibliog.*

LASDON (LEON S.) Optimization theory for large systems. London, [1970] repr. 1972. pp. 523.

HOLBROOK (ROBERT S.) An approach to the choice of optimal policy using large econometric models. [Ottawa], 1973. pp. 105. *bibliog. (Bank of Canada. Staff Research Studies. No. 8)*

COTTLE (RICHARD W.) and KRARUP (JACOB G.) eds. Optimization methods for resource allocation; the proceedings of a NATO conference held in Elsinore, Denmark. London, 1974. pp. 440. *bibliogs.*

MATHEMATICS.

ROBINSON (PETER D.) The oldest and the youngest science; an inaugural lecture delivered at University of Bradford on 17 October 1972. [Bradford, 1973]. pp. 12.

— Philosophy.

KLUEVER (JUERGEN) Operationalismus: Kritik und Geschichte einer Philosophie der exakten Wissenschaften. Stuttgart-Bad Cannstatt, 1971. pp. 220. *bibliog.* With English summary.

— Study and teaching — United Kingdom.

McLONE (R.R.) The training of mathematicians: a research report. London, Social Science Research Council, [1973]. pp. 94.*bibliog.*

— Study and teaching — United Kingdom — Scotland.

SCOTLAND. Scottish Education Department. 1973. Primary education in Scotland: mathematics. Edinburgh, 1973. pp. 48. *(Curriculum Papers. 13)*

MATRILINEAL KINSHIP.

NSUGBE (PHILIP O.) Ohaffia: a matrilineal Ibo people. Oxford, 1974. pp. 136. *bibliog.*

MATRIMONIAL ACTIONS

— United Kingdom.

U.K. Law Commission. Working Papers. No. 53. Family law: matrimonial proceedings in magistrates' courts. London, 1973. pp. 121.

PASSINGHAM (BERNARD) Law and practice in matrimonial cases. 2nd ed. London, 1974. pp. 452.

MATTEOTTI (GIACOMO).

GEROSA (GUIDO) and VENÉ (GIAN FRANCO) eds. Il delitto Matteotti. [Verona, 1973]. pp. 171.

MATVEEV (ANDREI ARTAMONOVICH).

MATVEEV (ANDREI ARTAMONOVICH) Russkii diplomat vo Frantsii: zapiski Andreia Matveeva; publikatsiia podgotovlena I.S. Sharkovoi, pod redaktsiei A.D. Liublinskoi. Leningrad, 1972. pp. 296.

MAUDLING (REGINALD).

GILLARD (MICHAEL) A little pot of money: the story of Reginald Maudling and the Real Estate Fund of America. London, 1974. pp. 170.

MAURITANIA

— Social policy.

STEWART (C.C.) and STEWART (E.K.) Islam and social order in Mauritania: a case study from the nineteenth century. Oxford, 1973. pp. 204. *bibliog.*

MAURITIUS.

FRANCE. Direction de la Documentation. La Documentation Française. Notes et Etudes Documentaires. No. 3,794. L'Ile Maurice et ses dépendances; [by] Louis Dollot. Paris, 1971. pp. 36. *bibliog.*

MAY DAY (LABOUR HOLIDAY).

TROTSKII (LEV DAVYDOVICH) May Day in the West and the East: (on the 35th anniversary of the May Day holiday; speech at the commemorative plenum of the Moscow Soviet, April 25, 1924). London, 1973. pp. 24.

MAZZINI (GIUSEPPE).

GHISALBERTI (ALBERTO MARIA) Attorno e accanto a Mazzini. Milano, 1972. pp. 169.

MONTALE (BIANCA) Mazzini e le origini del movimento operaio italiano: appunti di storia del Risorgimento. Genova, 1973. pp. 135. *bibliog.*

PERUTA (FRANCO DELLA) Mazzini e i rivoluzionari italiani: il "partito d'azione", 1830- 1845. Milano, 1974. pp. 469.

MBALE

— Social conditions.

JACOBSON (DAVID) Anthropologist. Itinerant townsmen: friendship and social order in urban Uganda.Menlo Park, Calif., [1973]. pp. 150. *bibliog.*

MEAD (GEORGE HERBERT).

NATANSON (MAURICE) The social dynamics of George H. Mead: [reprint, with additional bibliography, of work originally published in 1956]. The Hague, 1973. pp. 108. *bibliog.*

MEANING.

BENNETT (JONATHAN) Locke, Berkeley, Hume: central themes. Oxford, 1971. pp. 361. *bibliog.*

SYNTAX AND SEMANTICS; ed. by John P. Kimball. a., 1972-1973 (v.1-2). New York.

BARTSCH (RENATE) and VENNEMANN (THEO) Semantic structures: a study in the relation between semantics and syntax. Frankfurt/Main, [1972] repr. 1973. pp. 186. *bibliogs.*

JACKENDOFF (RAY S.) Semantic interpretation in generative grammar. Cambridge, Mass., [1972]. pp. 400. *bibliog.*

COURTES (JOSEPH) Lévi-Strauss et les contraintes de la pensée mythique: une lecture sémiotique des "Mythologiques". [Tours, 1973]. pp. 187.

MEAT INDUSTRY AND TRADE

— Australia.

LONGWORTH (JOHN W.) The problem of meat marketing: are marketing boards the answer?. [Sydney, 1972?]. pp. 52-63a. *(Sydney. University. Department of Agricultural Economics. Miscellaneous Papers. No. 57) (Reprinted from the Australian Quarterly, March, 1972)*

— Belgium.

VERBEKE (N.) Etude méthodologique du bilan "viande". Bruxelles, 1972. [fo. 41]. *(Belgium. Institut Economique Agricole. Cahiers. No. 149)*

— Russia.

KRASNOV (SERGEI EVDOKIMOVICH) and STERLIGOV (BORIS IL'ICH) Ekonomika miasnoi promyshlennosti. Moskva, 1973. pp. 480. *bibliog.*

— Uruguay.

MUÑOZ DURAN (ROBERTO) Aspectos basicos de la industria de la carne en Uruguay: produccion, industria, mercados. [Montevideo?], Instituto Nacional de Carnes, 1973. fo. 102. *bibliog.*

MECHANICAL ENGINEERING

— United Kingdom.

COMPANY FINANCIAL RESULTS; (prepared by the National Economic Development Office on behalf of the E[conomic] D[evelopment] C[ommittee] for Mechanical Engineering). a., 1968-9/1972-3(5th)- London.

ECONOMIC DEVELOPMENT COMMITTEE FOR THE MECHANICAL ENGINEERING INDUSTRY Company financial results, 1967/68-1971/72. [London, National Economic Developement Office, 1973] pp. 96.

ECONOMIC DEVELOPMENT COMMITTEE FOR THE MECHANICAL ENGINEERING INDUSTRY. Inflation and company accounts in mechanical engineering. London, National Economic Development Office, 1973. pp. 56.

NATIONAL ECONOMIC DEVELOPMENT OFFICE. Industrial review to 1977: mechanical engineering; (with Supplementary note on the new energy situation). London, 1974. pp. 87, 5.

MEDIATION, INTERNATIONAL.

GULHATI (NIRANJAN D.) Indus waters treaty: an exercise in international mediation. Bombay, 1973. pp. 472.

MEDIATION AND CONCILIATION, INDUSTRIAL

— France.

GIRAUD (HENRY) Mon été chez LIP. Paris, [1974]. pp. 173.

MEDICAL AUXILIARIES

— Germany.

GERMANY (BUNDESREPUBLIK). Wissenschaftsrat. 1973. Dreijährige Studiengänge im Gesundheitswesen: Vorschläge für Modellversuche. [Cologne?], 1973. pp. 40.

MEDICAL CARE.

REINKE (WILLIAM A.) ed. Health planning: qualitative aspects and quantitative techniquea. Baltimore, 1972. pp. 350. *bibliogs. (Johns Hopkins University. School of Hygiene and Public Health. Department of International Health. Johns Hopkins Monographs in International Health)*

DOUGLAS-WILSON (IAN) and McLACHLAN (GORDON) eds. Health service prospects: an international survey; published on The Lancet's 150th anniversary in October 1973. London, 1973. pp. 346. *bibliogs.*

ROBINSON (DAVID) 1941- . Patients, practitioners, and medical care: aspects of medical sociology. [London], 1973. pp. 178. *bibliogs.*

MECHANIC (DAVID) Politics, medicine, and social science. New York, [1974]. pp. 306.

SHANNON (GARY WILLIAM) and DEVER (G.E. ALAN) Health care delivery: spatial perspectives. New York, [1974]. pp. 141.

— Bangladesh.

CHEN (LINCOLN C.) ed. Disaster in Bangladesh. New York, 1973. pp. 290. *bibliogs.*

— Canada — Ontario.

WEAVER (SALLY M.) Medicine and politics among the Grand River Iroquois: a study of the non-conservatives. Ottawa, National Museums of Canada, 1972. pp. 182. *bibliog. (National Museum of Man [Canada]. Publications in Ethnology. No. 4) With French summary.*

— Germany.

SCHOLMER (JOSEPH) Patient und Profitmedizin: das Gesundheitswesen in der Bundesrepublik zwischen Krise und Reform. Opladen, 1973. pp. 222.

— Lesotho.

WILLIAMS (JOHN COX) Lesotho: three manpower problems: education, health, population growth. Pretoria, 1971. pp. 70. *(Africa Institute. Communications. No. 16)*

— Russia.

HYDE (GORDON) The Soviet health service: historical and comparative study. London, 1974. pp. 352.

— Sweden.

SJUKVÅRDENS OCH SOCIALVÅRDENS PLANERINGS- OCH RATIONALISERINGSINSTITUT. Conference, Stockholm, 1970. Sjukvårdsrationalisering under 70-talet: referat av SPRIs rikskonferens, 9.6.1970. [Stockholm, 1970]. pp. 32. *(Rapporter. 1970. 14)*

— Switzerland.

VAUD (CANTON). Service de la Santé Publique. 1972. Démographie, sociologie, économie et prospective médicales: études...fondées sur les données de la Suisse et du canton de Vaud: rapport technique. Lausanne, 1972. pp. 268.

— Underdeveloped areas.

See UNDERDEVELOPED AREAS — Medical care.

— United Kingdom.

McLACHLAN (GORDON) ed. Problems and progress in medical care: ninth series: essays in current research: (The future - and present indicatives). London, 1973. pp. 193. *bibliogs.*

MANAGEMENT in the social and safety services: (contributions to a seminar organised by the Faculty of Social Sciences of Edinburgh University... 1972); edited by W.D. Reekie and Norman C. Hunt. London, 1974. pp. 198. *bibliogs. (Edinburgh. University. Faculty of Social Sciences. Seminars Committee. Social Issues in the Seventies. 3)*

OFFICE OF HEALTH ECONOMICS. [Studies in Current Health Problems]. No. 49. The work of primary medical care. London, [1974]. pp. 44.

— United States.

PHELPS (CHARLES E.) and NEWHOUSE (JOSEPH P.) The effects of coinsurance on demand for physician services. Santa Monica, 1972. pp. 21. *bibliog. (Rand Corporation. [Rand Reports]. 976)*

SOMERS (ANNE RAMSAY) The hospital in the evolving health care system. San Francisco, 1972. pp. 21. *(Mount Zion Hospital and Medical Center. Mark Berke Memorial Lectures. 1972)*

COMMITTEE FOR ECONOMIC DEVELOPMENT. Research and Policy Committee. Statements on National Policy. Building a national health-care system. New York, 1973. pp. 105.

SEHAM (MAX) Blacks and American medical care. Minneapolis, [1973]. pp. 136.

CONFERENCE ON CONSUMER INCENTIVES IN HEALTH CARE USES, WASHINGTON, 1973. Consumer incentives for health care: [papers of the conference held by the Public Services Laboratory]; edited by Selma J. Mushkin. New York, 1974. pp. 431. *bibliogs.*

LEVIN (TOM) American health: professional privilege vs. public need. New York, 1974. pp. 115.

RUTSTEIN (DAVID D.) Blueprint for medical care. Cambridge, Mass., [1974]. pp. 384.

— — Statistics.

AMERICAN MEDICAL ASSOCIATION. Center for Health Services Research and Development. Reference data on socioeconomic issues of health;...compiled and edited by Robert J. Walsh. Chicago, 1972. pp. 148.

MEDICAL CARE, COST OF

— Australia.

AUSTRALIA. Parliament. Senate. Select Committee on Medical and Hospital Costs. 1969. Report. in AUSTRALIA. Parliament. Parliamentary papers, 1969. vol.6.

— Canada.

EVANS (ROBERT G.) Price formation in the market for physician services in Canada, 1957-1969;... prepared for the Prices and Incomes Commission. Ottawa, Information Canada, 1973. pp. 131.

— Greenland.

GREENLAND. Statutes, etc. 1960. Regulations of 29th October 1960 on rates of charge for hospital stays, medical care, etc. under the public health service in Greenland. [Copenhagen?, 1960]. fo. 5.

— Morocco.

BARLOW (ROBIN) Planning public health expenditures with special reference to Morocco. Ann Arbor, 1972. pp. 68. (Michigan University. Center for Research on Economic Development. Discussion Papers. No. 27)

— Netherlands.

NETHERLANDS. Centraal Bureau voor de Statistiek. 1972. Kosten en financiering van de gezondheidszorg in Nederland 1968. 's-Gravenhage, 1972. pp. 69.

— United Kingdom.

KING EDWARD'S HOSPITAL FUND FOR LONDON. Accounting for health: report of a...working party on the application of economic principles to health service management. London, 1973. pp. 63. bibliog.

MEDICAL CENTRES.

ROEMER (MILTON IRWIN) Evaluation of community health centres. Geneva, World Health Organization, 1972. pp. 42. bibliog. (Public Health Papers. No. 48)

— Canada.

CANADA. Community Health Centre Project. 1972-73. The community health centre in Canada; report... to the Conference of Health Ministers; [John E.F. Hastings, chairman]. Ottawa, 1972-73. 3 vols. (in 1).

— United Kingdom.

mentation. La Documentation Française. Notes et Etudes Documentaires. Nos. 4,034-4, 035-4,036. Les besoins réels du grand public en matiere d'information médicale et sanitaire. [Paris], 1973. pp. 69.

MEDICAL ECONOMICS.

GREENFIELD (HARRY I.) Hospital efficiency and public policy. New York, 1973. pp. 80.

INTERNATIONAL ECONOMIC ASSOCIATION. Conference, 1973. The economies of health and medical care: proceedings...; edited by Mark Perlman. London, 1974. pp. 547.

— United States.

CONLEY (RONALD W.) The economics of mental retardation. Baltimore, [1973]. pp. 377.

MEDICAL FEES

— Canada.

CANADA. Department of National Health and Welfare. Research and Statistics Directorate. Health Care Series. [Memoranda]. No. 28. Earnings of physicians in Canada, 1959-1969. [Ottawa, 1971]. pp. 41.

CANADA. Department of National Health and Welfare. Health Economics and Statistics Directorate. Health Care Series. [Memoranda]. No. 30. Earnings of physicians in Canada, 1961-1971. [Ottawa, 1972]. pp. 59.

EVANS (ROBERT G.) Price formation in the market for physician services in Canada, 1957-1969;... prepared for the Prices and Incomes Commission. Ottawa, Information Canada, 1973. pp. 131.

— Germany.

GESELLSCHAFT FÜR SOZIALEN FORTSCHRITT. Schriften. Band 20. Der Wandel der Stellung des Arztes im Einkommensgefüge: Arzteinkommen, Honorierungssystem und ärztliche Tätigkeit; Bericht eines Arbeitskreises, etc. Berlin, [1974]. pp. 139. bibliog.

MEDICAL GEOGRAPHY.

SHANNON (GARY WILLIAM) and DEVER (G.E. ALAN) Health care delivery: spatial perspectives. New York, [1974]. pp. 141.

— Africa, Subsaharan.

MAY (JACQUES M.) The ecology of malnutrition in the French speaking countries of West Africa and Madagascar, etc. New York, 1968. pp. 433. bibliog. (Studies in Medical Geography. vol. 8)

MAY (JACQUES M.) and McLELLAN (DONNA L.) The ecology of malnutrition in seven countries of southern Africa and in Portuese Guinea: the Republic of South Africa, South West Africa etc. New York, 1971. pp. 432. bibliogs. (American Geographical Society. Studies in Medical Geography. vol.10)

— United Kingdom.

YOUNG (JOHNATHAN C.) Suspected food poisoning in Consett, County Durham. Durham, 1974. pp. 21. bibliog. (Durham. University. Department of Geography. Occasional Publications (New Series). No. 3)

MEDICAL JURISPRUDENCE.

INTERNATIONAL SYMPOSIUM ON SOCIETY, MEDICINE AND LAW, 1972. International Symposium on Society, Medicine and Law, Jerusalem, March 1972: [papers]; edited by H. Karplus. Amsterdam, 1973. pp. 204.

SIMPSON (KEITH) Professor of Forensic Medicine. Forensic medicine. 7th ed. London, 1974. pp. 362.

MEDICAL LAWS AND LEGISLATION

— Czechoslovakia.

ŠTĚPÁN (JARO MÍR) Právní odpovědnost ve zdravotnictví. 2nd ed. Praha, 1970. pp. 370.

— United Kingdom.

HEALTH CENTRE CONFERENCE, LONDON, 1972. [Report]. [London], Department of Health and Social Security, [1972]. 1 pamphlet (various pagings).

MEDICAL PERSONNEL

— United Kingdom — Salaries, pensions, etc.

U.K. Government Actuary's Department. 1973. National Health Service Act, 1946: report by the Government Actuary on the National Health Service superannuation scheme, 1962-1969. London, 1973. pp. 19.

— United States.

STEWART (CHARLES T.) Economist, and SIDDAYAO (CORAZON M.) Increasing the supply of medical personnel: needs and alternatives. Washington, 1973. pp. 81. (American Enterprise Institute for Public Policy Research. Evaluative Studies. 6)

MEDICAL RESEARCH

— United Kingdom.

U.K. Department of Health and Social Security. Annual report on departmental research and development. a., 1973 [1st]- London.

MEDICAL STATISTICS.

WORLD HEALTH ORGANIZATION. Technical Report Series. Geneva, 1950 in progress.

MEDICAL TECHNOLOGISTS.

GERMANY (BUNDESREPUBLIK). Wissenschaftsrat. 1973. Dreijährige Studiengänge im Gesundheitswesen: Vorschläge für Modellversuche. [Cologne?], 1973. pp. 40.

MEDICINE

— Study and teaching.

WORLD HEALTH ORGANIZATION. Technical Report Series. Geneva, 1950 in progress.

WORLD HEALTH ORGANIZATION. Public Health Papers.. Geneva, 1959 in progress.

CRAMOND (W.A.) Prescription for a doctor: an inaugural lecture delivered in the University of Leicester, 30 January 1973. Leicester, 1973. pp. 30.

— — Canada.

HORNE (J.M.) and others. Medical education in Canadian teaching hospitals: a statistical cost analysis. Ottawa, 1970 [or rather 1971]. fo. 74. bibliog. (Carleton University. Carleton Economic Papers)

— — Denmark.

SPECIALLAEGEUDDANNELSE i langtidsmedicin og i fysiurgi og genoptraening: betaenkning 2 afgivet af det af Sundhedsstyrelsen den 3. marts 1969 nedsatte udvalg. København, 1971. fo. 22, [11].

— — Underdeveloped areas.

See UNDERDEVELOPED AREAS — Medicine — Study and teaching.

— Botswana.

SEELEY (CAROLINE FRASER) The reaction of the Batswana to the practice of western medicine; [M. Phil.(London) thesis]. 1973. fo. 259. bibliog. Typescript: unpublished. This thesis is the property of London University and may not be removed from the Library.

— Europe.

RETI (LADISLAO) and GIBSON (WILLIAM C.) Some aspects of seventeenth-century medicine and science; papers read at a Clark Library seminar [at Los Angeles], October 12, 1968. Los Angeles, 1969. pp. 46.

— France — Public opinion.

FRANCE. Direction de la Doc
MARTIN (CHARLES RUPERT ARTHUR) Law relating to medical practice. London, 1973. pp. 555.

SPELLER (SYDNEY REGINALD) Law of doctor and patient. London, 1973. pp. 202.

— Germany.

TERNON (YVES) and HELMAN (SOCRATE) Les médecins allemands et le national-socialisme: les métamorphoses du darwinisme. [Tournai, 1973]. pp. 219. bibliog.

— — Practice.

BOEGE (ULF) Kassenpraxis und Privatpraxis: eine wirtschaftswissenschaftliche Studie über freiberufliche ärztliche Leistungen. Berlin, [1973]. pp. 197. bibliog. (Mainz. Universität. Forschungsinstitut für Wirtschaftspolitik. Veröffentlichungen. Band 32)

SCHOLMER (JOSEPH) Patient und Profitmedizin: das Gesundheitswesen in der Bundesrepublik zwischen Krise und Reform. Opladen, 1973. pp. 222.

— United States.

KAUFMAN (MARTIN) Homeopathy in America: the rise and fall of a medical heresy. Baltimore, [1971]. pp. 205. bibliog.

ROTHSTEIN (WILLIAM G.) American physicians in the nineteenth century: from sects to science. Baltimore, [1972]. pp. 362.

MEDICINE, PRIMITIVE.

BOUQUET (ARMAND) Féticheurs et médecines traditionnelles du Congo (Brazzaville). Paris, Office de la Recherche Scientifique et Technique Outre-Mer, 1969. pp. 282. (Mémoires O.R.S.T.O.M. 36)

COMMUNITY culture and national change: [essays by] Richard N. Adams [and others]; (Margaret A.L. Harrison, Robert Wauchope, editors). New Orleans, 1972. pp. 275. bibliogs. (Tulane University of Louisiana. Middle American Research Institute. Publications. No.24)

MEDICINE, STATE.

WORLD HEALTH ORGANIZATION. Technical Report Series. Geneva, 1950 in progress.

WORLD HEALTH ORGANIZATION. Public Health Papers. Geneva, 1959 in progress.

MEDICINE, STATE. (Cont.)

— Canada — Manitoba.

MANITOBA. Committee on Health, Education and Social Policy. 1972. White Paper on health policy; (with Appendices). [Winnipeg], 1972. 3 pts.

— European Economic Community countries.

WADE (DONALD WILLIAM) Baron Wade. Europe and the British Health Service. London, [1974]. pp. 95.

— New Zealand.

MAPLES (EDWARD WILLIAM) Social security services in New Zealand: what we may learn from them. Oxford, 1949. pp. 34.

— Russia.

HYDE (GORDON) The Soviet health service: historical and comparative study. London, 1974. pp. 352.

— United Kingdom.

MARKS (JOHN HENRY) The Conference of Local Medical Committees and its executive: a review of sixty years. [London], 1972. pp. 20.

FORSYTH (GORDON) Doctors and state medicine: a study of the British Health Service. 2nd ed. London, 1973. pp. 224. *bibliogs.*

McLACHLAN (GORDON) ed. Problems and progress in medical care: ninth series: essays in current research: (The future - and present indicatives). London, 1973. pp. 193. *bibliogs.*

U.K. Working Party on Collaboration between the National Health Service and Local Government. 1973. Reorganisation of the National Health Service and local government in England and Wales: a report from the Working Party... on its activities from January to July 1973; [A.R.W. Bavin, chairman]. London, 1973. pp. 86.

DOLL (Sir WILLIAM RICHARD SHABOE) To measure N[ational] H[ealth] S[ervice] progress. London, 1974. pp. 12. *(Fabian Society. Fabian Occasional Papers. 8)*

HAYWOOD (S.C.) Managing the Health Service. London, 1974. pp. 207.

MANAGEMENT in the social and safety services: (contributions to a seminar organised by the Faculty of Social Sciences of Edinburgh University... 1972); edited by W.D. Reekie and Norman C. Hunt. London, 1974. pp. 198. *bibliogs. (Edinburgh. University. Faculty of Social Sciences. Seminars Committee. Social Issues in the Seventies. 3)*

OFFICE OF HEALTH ECONOMICS. [Studies in Current Health Problems]. No.48. The N[ational] H[ealth] S[ervice] reorganisation. London, [1974]. pp. 41. *bibliog.*

WADE (DONALD WILLIAM) Baron Wade. Europe and the British Health Service. London, [1974]. pp. 95.

— — Scotland.

NURSES in an integrated health service; report of a Working Group appointed by the Scottish Home and Health Department;[Muriel Powell, chairman]. Edinburgh, H.M.S.O., 1972. pp. 37.

MEDINA (Sir SOLOMON DE).

RABINOWICZ (OSKAR K.) Sir Solomon de Medina;...and a biography of the author by Judith K. Tapiero and Theodore K. Rabb. London, 1974. pp. 155.

MEDITERRANEAN.

CONFERENCE ON THE WESTERN MEDITERRANEAN, PALMA, 1972. The western Mediterranean: its political, economic, and strategic importance: [papers of the conference sponsored by the Center for Strategic and International Studies, Georgetown University]; (edited by Alvin J. Cottrell [and] James D. Theberge]. New York, 1974. pp. 249.

— Economic history.

MELANGES en l'honneur de Fernand Braudel. Toulouse, [1973]. 2 vols. *bibliog. In various languages.*

— Economic policy.

TOURISM, development and economic growth; seminar held under the auspices of the Technical Assistance Programme of the OECD, Estoril, Portugal, 8th-14th May, 1966. Paris, Organisation for Economic Co-operation and Development, 1967. pp. 46.

— History.

BRAUDEL (FERNAND) The Mediterranean and the Mediterranean world in the age of Philip II; translated from the French by Sian Reynolds. London, 1972-73. 2 vols. *bibliog.*

— Politics and government.

BURRELL (R.M.) and COTTRELL (ALVIN J.) Politics, oil and the Western Mediterranean. Beverly Hills, [1973]. pp. 80. *(Georgetown University. Center for Strategic and International Studies. Washington Papers. vol. 1/7)*

MEINBERG (ADOLF).

MEINBERG (ADOLF) Aufstand an der Ruhr: Reden und Aufsätze; herausgegeben von Hellmut G. Haasis und Erhard Lucas. Frankfurt M., [1973]. pp. 232. *bibliog.*

MEKONG RIVER

— Regulation.

GAITSKELL (Sir ARTHUR) Alternative choices in development strategy and tactics: the Mekong river project in South East Asia as a case study. Vienna, [1973]. pp. 23. *(Wiener Institut für Entwicklungsfragen. Occasional Papers. 73/7)*

MELBOURNE

— Civic improvement.

MELBOURNE AND METROPOLITAN BOARD OF WORKS. Planning policies for the Melbourne metropolitan region. [Melbourne], 1971. pp. 113.

— Growth.

MELBOURNE AND METROPOLITAN BOARD OF WORKS. Planning policies for the Melbourne metropolitan region. [Melbourne], 1971. pp. 113.

MELGAREJO (MARIANO).

ANTEZANA E. (LUIS) El feudalismo de Melgarejo y la reforma agraria: proceso de la propiedad territorial y de la política de Bolivia. [Cochabamba], 1970 [or rather 1971]. pp. 174.

MELROSE (WILLIAM).

SCOTTISH HISTORY SOCIETY. [Publications] 4th series. vol. 10. William Melrose in China, 1845-1855: the letters of a Scottish tea merchant; edited by Hoh-cheung Mui and Lorna H. Mui. Edinburgh, 1973. pp. 301. *6 papers in end pocket.*

MEMORY.

ESSMAN (WALTER B.) and NAKAJIMA (SHINSHU) eds. Current biochemical approaches to learning and memory. Flushing, N.Y., [1973]. pp. 205. *bibliogs.*

FILLENBAUM (SAMUEL) Syntactic factors in memory. tHE hAGUE, 1973. PP. 98. *BIBLIOG.*

MURDOCK (BENNET BRONSON) Human memory: theory and data. Potomac, Md., [1974]. pp. 362. *bibliog.*

MEN.

KORDA (MICHAEL) Male chauvinism: how it works. London, 1974. pp. 235. *bibliog. First published in New York in 1972.*

MENDÈS—FRANCE (PIERRE).

BOTHOREL (JEAN) Choisir: (Pierre Mendès France); conversations avec J. Bothorel. [Paris, 1974]. pp. 400. *bibliog.*

MENDIETA Y NUÑEZ (LUCIO).

AGRAMONTE (ROBERTO) Mendieta y Nuñez y su magisterio sociologico. Mexico, 1961. pp. 224.

MENDOZA (PROVINCE)

— Economic conditions.

MENDOZA (PROVINCE). Direccion de Estadisticas e Investigaciones Economicas. 1972. Producto bruto interno 1961/69. [Mendoza, 1972?]. fo. 30. *(Mendoza (Province). Direccion de Estadisticas e Investigaciones Economicas. Estudios Especiales. No.83)*

MENDOZA (PROVINCE). Direccion de Estadisticas e Investigaciones Economicas. 1972. Producto bruto interno 1970/1971. [Mendoza, 1972?]. fo.38. *(Mendoza (Province). Direccion de Estadisticas e Investigaciones Economicas. Estudios Especiales. No.85)*

MENTAL DEFICIENCY.

GENETIC studies in mental subnormality;...[collected papers] by B.C. Clare Davison [and others]. Ashford, Kent, [1973]. pp. 82. *bibliogs. (British Journal of Psychiatry. Special Publications. No.8)*

MENTAL HYGIENE.

WORLD HEALTH ORGANIZATION. Technical Report Series. Geneva, 1950 in progress.

WORLD HEALTH ORGANIZATION. Public Health Papers.. Geneva, 1959 in progress.

MAY (ANTHONY R.) and others. Mental health of adolescents and young persons: report on a technical conference, Stockholm, 9-13 June, 1969. Geneva, World Health Organization, 1971. pp. 72. *(Public Health Papers. No.41)*

— Scandinavia.

KATA (KEIJO) and UUSITALO (HANNU) On the data, sampling and representativeness of the Scandinavian survey [on welfare, need-satisfaction and mental health] in 1972. Helsinki, 1974. pp. 64. *(Helsinki. Yliopisto. Research Group for Comparative Sociology. Research Reports. No.4)*

— United States.

CONFERENCE ON ANTHROPOLOGY AND MENTAL HEALTH, STANFORD, 1971. Cultural illness and health: essays in human adaptation; edited by Laura Nader and Thomas W. Maretzki. Washington, [1973]. pp. 145. *bibliogs. (American Anthropological Association. Anthropological Studies. No. 9)*

MENTAL ILLNESS.

LAUTERBACH (ALBERT T.) Psychological challenges to modernization. Amsterdam, 1974. pp. 190.

— Russia.

SAARMA (IURII MARTINOVICH) Psikhicheskie zabolevaniia. Tallin, 1973. pp. 72.

— United States.

BRENNER (M. HARVEY) Mental illness and the economy. Cambridge, Mass., 1973. pp. 287.

MENTALLY HANDICAPPED.

WORLD HEALTH ORGANIZATION. Expert Committee on Mental Health. 1968. Organization of services for the mentally retarded; fifteenth report of the ...Committee, etc. Geneva, 1968. pp. 55. *(Technical Report Series. No. 392)*

— Finland.

TARVAINEN (LAURI) Suomen vajaamieliset ja heidän huollontarpeensa, 1962: I: sosiaalinen osa, etc. Helsinki, 1966-67. 2 parts. *(Finland. Suomen Virallinen Tilasto. Finlands Officiella Statistik. 32. Sosiaalisia Erikoistutkimuksia. 26) In Finnish and Swedish. With English summaries of social, psychological and medical parts.*

— United Kingdom.

CAMPAIGN FOR THE MENTALLY HANDICAPPED. Central Action Group. Even better services for the mentally handicapped; a policy statement. [London], 1972. fo. 32.

HILLINGDON. [Social Services Department]. Mentally handicapped in Hillingdon: a survey of the needs, both present and future, and capabilities of the mentally handicapped in Hillingdon. [London, 1972?]. 1 vol. (various pagings).

BAYLEY (MICHAEL) Mental handicap and community care: a study of mentally handicapped people in Sheffield. London, 1973. pp. 404. *bibliog.*

FORWARD planning of services for the mentally handicapped in Wessex; report of a Joint Planning Group;[J.J. Clugston, chairman]. Winchester, [Wessex Regional Hospital Board], 1973. pp. 133.

FRANCKLIN (SANDRA) Homes for mentally handicapped people. London, 1974. pp. 41. *(Campaign for the Mentally Handicapped. Discussion Papers. No. 4)*

— — Scotland.

The TRAINING of staff for centres for the mentally handicapped; report of the Committee appointed by the Secretary of State for Scotland; [Charles Melville, chairman]. Edinburgh, H.M.S.O., 1973. pp. 47.

— United States.

CONLEY (RONALD W.) The economics of mental retardation. Baltimore, [1973]. pp. 377.

MERCER (JANE R.) Labeling the mentally retarded: clinical and social system perspectives on mental retardation. Berkeley, [1973]. pp. 319. *bibliog.*

WILLS (RICHARD H.) The institutionalized severely retarded: a study of activity and interaction. Springfield, Ill., [1973]. pp. 157. *bibliog.*

MENTALLY HANDICAPPED CHILDREN

— Education.

WATSON (LUKE S.) Child behavior modification: a manual for teachers, nurses, and parents. New York, [1973]. pp. 147. *bibliog.*

— — United Kingdom.

The EDUCATION of mentally handicapped children: papers given at a one-day conference on 24 March 1973 by W.K. Brennan...[and others]; edited by R. Hermelin. London, [1974]. pp. 30. *(National Society for Mentally Handicapped Children. Education and Training Series. No.1)*

— United Kingdom.

KENDALL (ALAN) b. 1943, and MOSS (PETER) Integration or segregation?; the future of educational and residential services for mentally handicapped children. London, 1972. fo. 14. *(Campaign for the Mentally Handicapped. Discussion Papers. No. 1)*

MENTALLY ILL

— Care and treatment — India.

MOHAN (BRIJ) Social psychiatry in India: a treatise on the mentally ill. Calcutta, 1973. pp. 216.

— New Zealand.

NEW ZEALAND. Department of Health. National Health Statistics Centre. 1972. Psychiatric illness causing hospitalization or death, 1967. Wellington, 1972. pp. 46. *(Department of Health. Special Report Series. 39)*

— — United Kingdom.

ENNALS (DAVID) Out of mind. London, 1973. pp. 96.

— Care and treatment — United States.

SLOAN (FRANK A.) Planning public expenditures on mental health service delivery. New York, 1971. pp. 118. *bibliog. (Rand Corporation. [Research Memoranda]. 6339)*

— New Zealand.

NEW ZEALAND. Department of Health. National Health Statistics Centre. 1973. Census of mental hospital patients, 1971. Wellington, 1973. pp. 95. *(Department of Health. Special Report Series. 40)*

MERCANTILE SYSTEM

— Bibliography.

SEGERS (AGNES) compiler. Het industrieel aspect in het Engels commercialistisch mercantilisme ...: The industrial aspect of English commercial mercantilism, 1660-1727. Brussel, 1973. pp. 176. *(Commission Belge de Bibliographie. Bibliographia Belgica. 119)*

MERCHANT MARINE

— Congresses.

INTERNATIONAL CONFERENCE ON FACILITATION OF MARITIME TRAVEL AND TRANSPORT, 1965. [Final act, convention and resolutions of the Conference]. London, Intergovernmental Maritime Consultative Organization, 1966. pp. 135. *In various languages.*

— Safety measures.

INTERNATIONAL CONFERENCE ON SPECIAL TRADE PASSENGER SHIPS, 1971. Final act of the Conference with attachments including the text of the adopted Agreement. London, Inter-Governmental Maritime Consultative Organization, [1972]. pp. 60. *In English and French.*

— Safety regulations.

See SHIPS — Safety regulations.

— Brazil.

VALENTE (MURILLO GURGEL) A politica de transportes maritimos no Brasil: crônica de uma batalha. 2nd ed. [Rio de Janeiro], Ministerio dos Transportes, Serviço de Documentação, 1972. pp. 114.

— Germany.

BROERS (PETER) Die Strukturwandlungen in der deutschen Seeschiffahrt. Berlin, [1974]. pp. 255. *bibliog. (Bonn. Universität. Institut für Industrie- und Verkehrspolitik. Verkehrswissenschaftliche Forschungen. Band 27)*

— Japan.

FRANCE. Direction de la Documentation. La Documentation Française. Notes et Etudes Documentaires. Nos. 3,778-3, 779. Les activités maritimes du Japon; [by] Albert Boyer. Paris, 1971. pp. 52.

— United Kingdom.

FRANCE. Direction de la Documentation. La Documentation Française. Notes et Etudes Documentaires. No. 3,727. Les activités maritimes du Royaume-Uni de Grande-Bretagne et d'Irlande du Nord. Paris, 1970. pp. 47.

MERCHANT SHIPS

— Passenger accommodation.

INTER-GOVERNMENTAL MARITIME CONSULTATIVE ORGANIZATION. 1969. Recommendation on intact stability for passenger and cargo ships under 100 metres in length. London, [1969]. pp. 18.

INTERNATIONAL CONFERENCE ON SPECIAL TRADE PASSENGER SHIPS, 1971. Final act of the Conference with attachments including the text of the adopted Agreement. London, Inter-Governmental Maritime Consultative Organization, [1972]. pp. 60. *In English and French.*

INTERNATIONAL CONFERENCE ON SPACE REQUIREMENTS FOR SPECIAL TRADE PASSENGER SHIPS, 1973. Final act of the Conference with attachments including the text of the adopted Protocol. London, Inter-Governmental Maritime Consultative Organization, [1973]. pp. 57. *In English and French.*

MERCHANTS.

SILBERSTEIN (ENRIQUE) Los asaltantes de caminos. Buenos Aires, [1969]. pp. 120.

MERCHANTS, AMERICAN.

PORTER (GLENN) and LIVESAY (HAROLD C.) Merchants and manufacturers: studies in the changing structure of nineteenth-century marketing. Baltimore, [1971]. pp. 257. *bibliog.*

MERCHANTS, BELGIAN.

STOLS (EDDY) De Spaanse Brabanders of de handelsbetrekkingen der Zuidelijke Nederlanden met de Iberische wereld, 1598-1648. Brussel, 1971. 2 vols. *bibliog. (Vlaamse Academie voor Wetenschappen, Letteren en Schone Kunsten van Belgie. Klasse der Letteren. Verhandelingen. Nr. 70)*

MERCHANTS, GERMAN.

BOEHM (EKKEHARD) Überseehandel und Flottenbau: hanseatische Kaufmannschaft und deutsche Seerüstung, 1879-1902. Düsseldorf, [1972]. pp. 417. *bibliog. (Hamburg. Hansische Universität. Studien zur Modernen Geschichte. Band 8)*

MERCHANTS, JEWISH.

GOITEIN (SOLOMON DOB FRITZ) compiler. Letters of medieval Jewish traders; translated from the Arabic with introductions and notes by S.D. Goitein. Princeton, [1973]. pp. 359.

MERIONETH

— Industries.

MERIONETH. County Planning Office. Merioneth structure plan: (subject report no. 4): industry. Dolgellau, [1973]. fo. 49.

MESKHETIANS.

SHEEHY (ANN) The Crimean Tatars, Volga Germans and Meskhetians: Soviet treatment of some national minorities. new ed. London, 1973. pp. 36. *bibliog. (Minority Rights Group. Reports. No. 6)*

METAL TRADE

— United States.

ELLIOTT-JONES (M.F.) Long-term projections of primary metals markets. New York, [1972]. pp. 52. *(National Industrial Conference Board. Conference Board Reports. No.572)*

METAL WORKERS

— Netherlands.

BINNEVELD (JOHANNES MARTINUS WOUTER) De stakingen in de Rotterdamse metaalindustrie in 1965: een sociologische analyse van de ontwikkelingen binnen een systeem van industriële verhoudingen. Groningen, 1974. pp. 111. *bibliog. With English summary.*

— Switzerland.

SCHWEIZERISCHER METALL- UND UHRENARBEITER-VERBAND. Ein Tatsachenbericht über den Christlichen Metallarbeiter- Verband; zur Aufklärung der Funktionäre und der Vertrauensleute des Schweizerischen Metall- und Uhrenarbeiter-Verbandes, SMUV. [Bern], 1950. pp. 69.

— United Kingdom.

HEY (DAVID G.) The rural metalworkers of the Sheffield region: a study of rural industry before the Industrial Revolution. [Leicester], 1972. pp. 60. *(Leicester. University. Department of English Local History. Occasional Papers. 2nd Series. No. 5)*

COMMISSION ON INDUSTRIAL RELATIONS [U.K.]. Keg and Drum Wages Council. London, H.M.S.O., 1973. pp. 36. *(Reports. No. 48)*

COMMISSION ON INDUSTRIAL RELATIONS [U.K.]. Coffin Furniture and Cerement-making Wages Council. London, H.M.S.O., 1973. pp. 32. *(Reports. No. 46)*

METAPHYSICS.

MACKINNON (DONALD MACKENZIE) The problem of metaphysics; [revised version of the Gifford Lectures delivered in 1965 and 1966]. London, 1974. pp. 172.

METAPHYSICS. (Cont.)

SUPPES (PATRICK) Probabilistic metaphysics. Uppsala, 1974. fo. 160. *bibliog.* (*Uppsala. Universitet. Filosofiska Föreningen, and Filosofiska Institutionen. Filosofiska Studier. Nr. 22*)

METEOROLOGY

— Zambia.

ZAMBIA. Department of Meteorology. Annual report. a., 1970, 1973- Lusaka.

METHODISM.

BRAKE (GEORGE THOMPSON) Drink: ups and downs of Methodist attitudes to temperance. London, 1974. pp. 150.

METHODIST CHURCH IN THE UNITED KINGDOM.

COOPER (WILLIAM DONALD) Methodism in Portsmouth, 1750-1932. Portsmouth, 1973. pp. 21. (*Portsmouth. City Council. Portsmouth Papers. No.18*)

SEMMEL (BERNARD) The Methodist revolution. London, 1974. pp. 273. e *bibliog.*

METHODIST CHURCH IN TONGA.

LATUKEFU (SIONE) Church and state in Tonga: the Wesleyan Methodist missionaries and political development, 1822-1875. Canberra, 1974. pp. 302. *bibliog.*

METHODISTS IN THE UNITED KINGDOM.

MOORE (ROBERT) Pit-men, preachers and politics: the effects of Methodism in a Durham mining community. London, 1974. pp. 292. *bibliog.*

METHODOLOGY.

MAESTRE (CLAUDE) and PAVITT (KEITH) Analytical methods in government science policy: an evaluation. Paris, Organisation for Economic Co-operation and Development, 1972. pp. 89. *bibliog.* (*Science Policy Studies*)

METRIC SYSTEM.

TEMPLETON (J.) Going metric in the fish industry. [Aberdeen], Torry Research Station, [1969]. pp. 8. (*Torry Advisory Notes. No.40*)

METRICATION BOARD [U.K.]. Going metric: [information leaflets; with additional pamphlet material]. London, 1970 in progress.

CANADA. Metric Commission. Report. a., Je 1971/Mr 1973 (1st)- Ottawa. *In English and French.*

HOLT (SUSAN FRAKER) The United States and the metric system. Minneapolis, 1972. pp. 35. *bibliog.* (*Federal Reserve Bank of Minneapolis. Ninth District Exponent. vol. 2, no.11*)

BUREAU INTERNATIONAL DES POIDS ET MESURES. S.I.: the international system of units; [translated from the French; prepared jointly by the National Physical Laboratory and the National Bureau of Standards, USA]; editors: Chester H. Page [and] Paul Vigoureux. 2nd ed. London, H.M.S.O., 1973. pp. 47.

METROPOLITAN AREAS

FAIR (T.J.D.) The metropolitan imperative: inaugural lecture...delivered 27 October 1971 [at the University of Witwatersrand]. Johannesburg, 1972. pp. 24. *bibliog.*

— Australia.

HARRISON (PETER) Post-war planning in the capital cities of the mainland states. Canberra, 1972. fo. 25. *bibliog.*

— France.

FRANCE. Ministère de l'Equipement et du Logement. Direction Départementale du Rhône. Groupe d'Etude et de Programmation. 1969. Lyon 2000: schéma directeur d'aménagement et d'urbanisme de l'agglomération lyonnaise. [Lyons?], 1969.pp. 129.

SCHEMA général d'aménagement de la France: régions urbaines, régions de villes. Paris, 1973. pp. 166. (*France. Délégation à l'Aménagement du Territoire et à l'Action Régionale. Travaux et Recherches de Prospective. 44*)

— Venezuela.

BREWER-CARIAS (ALLAN RANDOLPH) Problemas institucionales del area metropolitana de Caracas y del desarrollo regional y urbano. Caracas, Comision de Administracion Publica, 1971. fo. 60.

METROPOLITAN FINANCE

— United States.

KAVANAGH (J. MICHAEL) and others. Program budgeting for urban recreation: current status and prospects in Los Angeles. New York, 1973. pp. 107. (*California University. Institute of Government and Public Affairs. Local Government Program Budgeting Series*)

METROPOLITAN GOVERNMENT

— United Kingdom.

REFORM as reorganization: papers by Royce Hanson [and others]. Washington, D.C., [1974]. pp. 131. (*Resources for the Future, Inc. The Governance of Metropolitan Regions. No. 4*)

— United States.

HAWLEY (WILLIS D.) Blacks and metropolitan governance: the stakes of reform. Berkeley, Calif., 1972. pp. 34.

BISH (ROBERT L.) and OSTROM (VINCENT) Understanding urban government: metropolitan reform reconsidered. Washington, [1973]. pp. 111. *bibliog.* (*American Enterprise Institute for Public Policy Research. Domestic Affairs Studies. 20*)

DAVID (STEPHEN M.) and PETERSON (PAUL E.) eds. Urban politics and public policy: the city in crisis. New York, 1973. pp. 337. *bibliogs.*

REFORM as reorganization: papers by Royce Hanson [and others]. Washington, D.C., [1974]. pp. 131. (*Resources for the Future, Inc. The Governance of Metropolitan Regions. No. 4*)

METTERNICH—WINNEBURG (CLEMENS WENZESLAUS NEPOMUK LOTHAR VON) PRINCE

ANDICS (ERZSÉBET) Metternich und die Frage Ungarns; (aus dem Ungarischen übersetzt von Zoltán Jókai). Budapest, 1973. pp. 514.

MEUSE (DEPARTMENT)

— Economic history.

MEEH (KUNO) Struktur und Entwicklung des Wirtschaftsraums Verdun: ein Betrachtung und Beurteilung eines französischen Passivraums. Berlin, 1972. pp. 343. *bibliog.*

MEXICANS IN THE UNITED STATES.

La RAZA!: why a Chicano party?; why Chicano studies?; by Roger Alvarado [and others]. New York, 1970. pp. 15. (*Reprinted from The Militant, January 23 and March 30, 1970*)

DOCUMENTS of the Chicano struggle. New York, 1971. pp. 15.

CORONA (BERT) Bert Corona speaks on La Raza Unida Party and the 'illegal alien' scare. New York, 1972. pp. 23.

DE LA GARZA (RUDOLPH O.) and others, eds. Chicanos and native Americans: the territorial minorities; [including papers presented at the Workshop on Southwest Ethnic Groups: Sociopolitical Environment and Education, El Paso, 1972]. Englewood Cliffs, N. J., [1973]. pp. 205.

GARCIA (F. CHRIS) Political socialization of Chicano children: a comparative study with Anglos in California schools. New York, 1973. pp. 255. *bibliog.*

GARCIA (F. CHRIS) ed. Chicano politics: readings. New York, [1973]. pp. 225.

KURTZ (DONALD V.) The politics of a poverty habitat. Cambridge, Massachussetts, [1973]. pp. 243. *bibliog.*

LOPEZ Y RIVAS (GILBERTO) The Chicanos: life and struggles of the Mexican minority in the United States;... with readings translated and edited by Elizabeth Martinez and Gilberto López y Rivas. New York, [1973]. pp. 187. *bibliog.*

PEREZ (JOSÉ G.) Viva la huelga'. the struggle of the farm workers. New York, [1973]. pp. 15.

ROSALDO (RENATO) and others. Chicano: the evolution of a people. Minneapolis, [1973]. pp. 461.

SHANNON (LYLE WILLIAM) and SHANNON (MAGDALINE) Minority migrants in the urban community: Mexican-American and negro adjustment to industrial society. Beverly Hills, [1973]. pp. 351.

LEWELS (FRANCISCO JOSE) The uses of the media by the Chicano movement: a study in minority access. New York, 1974. pp. 185. *bibliog.*

MEXICO

— Census.

MEXICO. Census, 1970. 9° censo general de poblacion, 1970: 28 de enero de 1970; resumen general. Mexico, 1972. pp. 1140.

— Economic conditions.

BANCO NACIONAL DE COMERCIO EXTERIOR, S.A. Mexico 1970: facts, figures and trends. 5th ed. Mexico [City], 1970. pp. 254. *bibliog.*

DEROSSI (FLAVIA ZACCONE) The Mexican entrepreneur. Paris, Organisation for Economic Co-operation and Development, 1971. pp. 428. *bibliog.* (*Development Centre. Studies*)

— Economic history.

PADILLA ARAGON (ENRIQUE) Mexico: desarrollo con pobreza. Mexico, 1969 repr. 1970. pp. 179.

La ECONOMIA mexicana en la epoca de Juarez; [by] Luis Gonzalez [and others]. [Mexico], Secretaria de Industria y Comercio, 1972. pp. 221.

— Economic policy.

PADILLA ARAGON (ENRIQUE) Mexico: desarrollo con pobreza. Mexico, 1969 repr. 1970. pp. 179.

— Foreign relations

See also UNITED NATIONS — Mexico.

— — United States.

SCHMITT (KARL MICHAEL) Mexico and the United States, 1821-1973: conflict and coexistence. New York, [1974]. pp. 288. *bibliog.*

— History — Sources.

FLORES MAGON (RICARDO) La revolucion mexicana: seleccion y nota preliminar de Adolfo Sanchez Rebolledo. Mexico, 1970. pp. 158.

— History — 1910—1929, Revolution.

LANGLE (ARTURO) Vocabulario, apodos, seudonimos, sobrenombres y hemerografia de la Revolucion. Mexico, 1966. pp. 153. *bibliog.*

FLORES MAGON (RICARDO) La revolucion mexicana: seleccion y nota preliminar de Adolfo Sanchez Rebolledo. Mexico, 1970. pp. 158.

CARR (BARRY) Organised labour and the Mexican revolution 1915-1928. [Oxford], 1972. fo.33. (*Oxford. University. St. Antony's College. Latin American Centre. Occasional Papers. 2*) Typescript.

QUIRK (ROBERT EMMETT) The Mexican revolution and the Catholic Church 1910-1929. Bloomington, Ind., [1973]. pp. 276.

BAILEY (DAVID C.) Viva Cristo Rey!: the Cristero rebellion and the church- state conflict in Mexico. Austin, [1974]. pp. 346. *bibliog.*

— Industries.

DEROSSI (FLAVIA ZACCONE) The Mexican entrepreneur. Paris, Organisation for Economic Co-operation and Development, 1971. pp. 428. *bibliog.* *(Development Centre. Studies)*

MEXICO. Direccion General de Estadistica. Estadistica industrial mensual. a., 1972- Mexico.

— Languages.

HEATH (SHIRLEY BRICE) Telling tongues: language policy in Mexico: colony to nation. New York, [1972]. pp. 300. *bibliog.*

— Officials and employees.

COMMUNITY culture and national change: [essays by] Richard N.Adams [and others]; (Margaret A.L. Harrison, Robert Wauchope, editors). New Orleans, 1972. pp. 275. *bibliogs. (Tulane University of Louisiana. Middle American Research Institute. Publications. No.24)*

— Politics and government.

TRES culturas en agonia; [by] Jorge Carrion [and others]. Mexico, 1969 repr. 1970. pp. 290.

CAREAGA (GABRIEL) Los intelectuales y la politica en Mexico. Mexico, [1971]. pp. 141. *bibliog.*

— Rural conditions.

GARCIA RUIZ (RAMON) Educacion, cambios y desarrollo de la comunidad. Mexico, 1970. pp. 183. *bibliog.*

ROMANUCCI-ROSS (LOLA) Conflict, violence, and morality in a Mexican village. Palo Alto, Calif., 1973. pp. 202. *bibliog.*

— Social conditions.

BANCO NACIONAL DE COMERCIO EXTERIOR, S.A. Mexico 1970: facts, figures and trends. 5th ed. Mexico [City], 1970. pp. 254. *bibliog.*

MEXICO CITY.

FRANCE. Direction de la Documentation. La Documentation Française. Notes et Etudes Documentaires. Nos. 3,963-3, 964. Les grandes villes du monde: Mexico. [Paris], 1973. pp. 76. *bibliog.*

MEXICO UNIVERSITY

— Finance.

ATTOLINI (JOSE) Las finanzas de la Universidad a traves del tiempo. [Mexico], 1951. pp. 91. *bibliog. (Mexico City. Universidad Nacional Autonoma de Mexico. Ediciones del IV Centenario. 11)*

MICHELS (ROBERT).

MITZMAN (ARTHUR B.) Sociology and estrangement: three sociologists of imperial Germany. New York, 1973. pp. 375, viii.

MICRONESIA

— Politics and government.

HEINE (CARL) Micronesia at the crossroads: a reappraisal of the Micronesian political dilemma. Canberra, [1974]. pp. 210. *bibliog.*

MIDDLE CLASSES

— America, Latin.

GARCIA (ANTONIO) Estructura social y desarrollo latinoamericanos. Santiago de Chile, Instituto de Capacitacion e Investigacion en Reforma Agraria, 1969. pp. 134.

— France.

BAUDELOT (CHRISTIAN) and others. La petite bourgeoisie en France. Paris, 1974. pp. 305.

— Italy.

BAGLIONI (GUIDO) L'ideologia della borghesia industriale nell' Italia liberale. Torino, [1974]. pp. 565.

— Switzerland.

SOZIALDEMOKRATISCHE PARTEI DER SCHWEIZ. Wählt der Mittelstand sozialdemokratisch?. Zürich, [1939?]. pp. 48. *(Kultur und Arbeit)*

— United States.

CUTLER (RICHARD L.) The liberal middle class: maker of radicals. New Rochelle, [1973]. pp. 255.

MIDOL (LUCIEN).

MIDOL (LUCIEN) La voie que j'ai suivie: un ingénieur au coeur des batailles sociales, 1900-1970. Paris, [1973]. pp. 221.

MIGRANT LABOUR.

INTERNATIONAL LABOUR CONFERENCE. 59th Session. Reports. 7. Migrant workers: seventh item on the agenda. Geneva, 1973-74. 2 pts.

— Africa, West.

INTERNATIONAL AFRICAN SEMINAR. 11th Seminar, Dakar, 1972. Modern migrations in western Africa: studies presented and discussed at the...seminar...; edited with an introduction by Samir Amin. London, 1974. pp. 426. *Text in French and English with a summary in the other language.*

— Europe.

KAYSER (BERNARD) Cyclically-determined homeward flows of migrant workers and the effects of emigration. Paris, Organisation for Economic Co-operation and Development, 1972. pp. 56. *bibliog.*

— European Economic Community countries.

HANOTIAU (BERNARD) Les problèmes de securité sociale des travailleurs migrants. Bruxelles, 1973. pp. 178. *bibliog.*

— South Africa.

WILSON (FRANCIS) Economist. Migrant labour;... report to the South African Council of Churches. Johannesburg, 1972. pp. 281. *bibliog. (South African Council of Churches and Christian Institute of Southern Africa. Special Programme for Christian Action in Society. [Publications. No. 3])*

— Zambia.

HEISLER (HELMUTH) Urbanisation and the government of migration: the inter-relation of urban and rural life in Zambia. London, [1974]. pp. 166. *bibliog.*

MIGRATION.

For Population movement across frontiers see heading EMIGRATION AND IMMIGRATION and subdivision Emigration and immigration under countries. For movement within a country see subdivision Population under countries, etc.

MIHAILOVIĆ (DRAŽA).

ŽIVANOVIĆ (SERGIJE M.) Treći srpski ustanak, 1941. Cikago, 1962-66. 3 vols(in 1). *Cover has title: Djeneral Mihailović i njegovo delo.*

MILAN (CITY)

— Statistics.

MILAN. Servizio Lavoro e Statistica. Annuario statistico: vol. 1. Statische demografiche... 1940- 1955; vol.2. Statistiche economiche e sociali... 1940-1955; pt. 1. Milano, 1957-60. 3 pts. (in 1 vol.)

MILAN (PROVINCE)

— History.

MILAN (PROVINCE). Amministrazione Provinciale. Dalla Resistenza: uomini, eventi, idee della lotta di liberazione in Provincia di Milano; a cura di Gianfranco Bianchi. Milano, [1969]. pp. 247.

MILITARISM

— Germany.

KRAUSE (FRITZ) Writer on politics. Antimilitaristische Opposition in der BRD, 1949-55. Frankfurt am Main, [1971]. pp. 185.

— Switzerland.

GERBER (MAX) Demokratie und Militarismus: Betrachtungen über die Voraussetzungen schweizerischer Militärpolitik. Zürich, 1913. pp. 95.

— United States.

CUNLIFFE (MARCUS) Soldiers and civilians: the martial spirit in America, 1775-1865.[2nd ed.] New York, 1973. pp. 499.

MILITARY ASSISTANCE, AMERICAN

WOLPIN (MILES D.) Military indoctrination and United States imperialism. New York, [1973]. pp. 56. *bibliog.* *(American Institute for Marxist Studies. Occasional Papers. No. 13)*

— Russia.

SUTTON (ANTONY C.) National suicide: military aid to the Soviet Union. New Rochelle, N.Y., [1973]. pp. 283. *bibliog.*

MILITARY ASSISTANCE, BELGIAN

— Zaire.

BRASSINNE (J.) Douze années de coopération technique militaire belgo-zairoise. Bruxelles, 1972. fo. 40. *bibliog. (Centre de Recherche et d'Information Socio- Politiques. Etudes Africaines du CRISP)*

MILITARY BASES, AMERICAN

— Philippine Islands.

LOVEDAY (DOUGLAS F.) The role of U.S. military bases in the Philippine economy;... prepared for the Assistant Secretary of Defense/International Security Affairs. Santa Monica, 1971. pp. 60. *(Rand Corporation. Research Memoranda. 5801)*

MILITARY EDUCATION

— Russia.

GOURE (LEON) The military indoctrination of Soviet youth. New York, [1973]. pp. 75. *bibliog. (National Strategy Information Center. Strategy Papers. No. 16)*

MILITARY HISTORY

— Bibliography.

HIGHAM (ROBIN) ed. Official histories: essays and bibliographies from around the world. Manhattan, Ka., 1970. pp. 644. *(Kansas State University of Agriculture and Applied Science. Library. Bibliography Series. No.8)*

— Maps.

BANKS (ARTHUR) A world atlas of military history. London, 1973 in progress.

MILITARY LAW

— Russia.

RUSSIA (U.S.S.R.) Ministerstvo Oborony. 1973. Osnovy sovetskogo voennogo zakonodatel'stva: uchebnoe posobie dlia kursantov vysshikh voenno-politicheskikh uchilishch. Moskva, 1973. pp. 270.

MILITARY SERVICE, COMPULSORY

— France.

PENNAC (DANIEL) Le service militaire au service de qui?. Paris, [1973]. pp. 176.

— Germany.

BIHR (DIETRICH) Die Durchführung der Wehrpflicht in der Bundesrepublik Deutschland und die mögliche Erhebung einer Wehrdienstausgleichsabgabe, etc. [Augsburg, imprint], 1973. pp. 203. *bibliog.*

— Netherlands.

GEESTELIJKE VERZORGING BIJ DE KRIJGSMACHT. Werkgroep Oorlog en Vrede. Militaire dienstplicht, vrijstelling, gewetensbezwaarden, alternatieve dienstplicht, vredesbeweging, pacifisme. Haarlem, [1971]. pp. 159.

— United States.

USEEM (MICHAEL) Conscription, protest, and social conflict: the life and death of a draft resistance movement. New York, [1973]. pp. 329. *bibliog.*

MILITARY SERVICE AS A PROFESSION.

INTERNATIONAL INSTITUTE FOR STRATEGIC STUDIES. Adelphi Papers. No. 103. Force in modern societies: the military profession; [papers given at the 15th annual conference, Travemünde, 1973]. London, 1973. pp. 45.

TEITLER (GERKE) De wording van het professionele officierskorps: een sociologisch- historische analyse. Rotterdam, 1974. pp. 309. *bibliog. With an English summary.*

MILK

— Analysis and examination.

FAO/WHO EXPERT PANEL ON MILK QUALITY. 1972. Payment for milk on quality. Rome, Food and Agriculture Organization, 1972. pp. 82. (*Agricultural Studies. No. 89*)

— Transportation.

HEGHE (G. VAN) and VERTESSEN (J.) Analyse du travail requis par le ramassage du lait. Bruxelles, 1973. pp. 46. (*Belgium. Institut Economique Agricole. Cahiers. No. 160*)

MILK SUPPLY

— Underdeveloped areas.

See UNDERDEVELOPED AREAS — Milk Supply.

— United Kingdom — Ireland, Northern.

IRELAND, NORTHERN. Ministry of Agriculture. Economics and Statistics Division. 1970. An economic survey of summer and winter milk producers. Belfast, 1970. fo. 30.

— — Scotland.

SCOTLAND. Scottish Milk Marketing Board. Marketing Services Department. 1969. Milk production '69: a comment on the results of the 1969 Scottish dairy farm census. [Paisley, 1969]. pp. 78.

MILK TRADE

— Belgium.

HEGHE (G. VAN) and VERTESSEN (J.) Analyse du travail requis par le ramassage du lait. Bruxelles, 1973. pp. 46. (*Belgium. Institut Economique Agricole. Cahiers. No. 160*)

MILL (JOHN STUART).

MILL (JOHN STUART) (Collected works of John Stuart Mill. vols.14-17). The later letters of John Stuart Mill, 1849-1873; edited by Francis E. Mineka and Dwight N. Lindley. Toronto, [1972]. 4 vols.

DUNCAN (GRAEME) Marx and Mill: two views of social conflict and social harmony. Cambridge, 1973. pp. 386. *bibliog.*

MILLENNIUM.

BARKUN (MICHAEL) Disaster and the millennium. New Haven, 1974. pp. 246. *bibliog.*

MILLS AND MILL WORK.

ZIMILES (MARTHA) and ZIMILES (MURRAY) Early American mills. New York, [1973]. pp. 290. *bibliog.*

MILNER (ALFRED) 1st Viscount Milner.

HALPERIN (VLADIMIR) Lord Milner and the Empire: the evolution of British imperialism. London, 1952. pp. 256. *bibliog.*

MIND AND BODY.

The DEVELOPMENT of mind; [by] A.J.P. Kenny [and others] . Edinburgh, [1973]. pp. 152. (*Gifford Lectures. 1972-1973*)

MINE DUSTS.

CONFERENCE ON TECHNICAL MEASURES OF DUST PREVENTION AND SUPPRESSION IN MINES, LUXEMBURG, 1972. Proceedings of the Conference...Luxemburg, 11-13th October 1972. Luxemburg, European Communities, 1973. pp. 693,xxxiv.

MINERAL INDUSTRIES

— Ecuador.

ECUADOR. Instituto Nacional de Estadistica. Encuesta de manufactura y mineria. a., 1968, 1969, 1971- Quito.

BRITISH PRINTING INDUSTRIES FEDERATION. Annual report ([and] Annual accounts). a., 1973/4- London.

— European Economic Community countries.

SOUTH AFRICA. Planning Advisory Council. Subsidiary Committee for the Optimum Utilization of Mineral Resources in the Republic of South Africa and in South West Africa, 1970. The mineral trade between South Africa and the European Economic Community; a report. Pretoria, 1970. pp. 132. *bibliog.*

— Iraq.

OIL AND MINERALS IN IRAQ; [pd. annually under supervision of a permanent committee from the Ministry of Oils and Minerals, the Iraqi National Oil Company and the Iraqi National Minerals Company]. a., 1970 (1st)- Baghdad.

— Mexico.

MEXICO. Consejo de Recursos Naturales No Renovables. Departamento de Estudios Economicos, 1968. Sumario estadistico de la mineria mexicana, 1967. Mexico, [1968?]. fo. 113.

— South Africa.

SOUTH AFRICA. Planning Advisory Council. Subsidiary Committee for the Optimum Utilization of Mineral Resources in the Republic of South Africa and in South West Africa, 1970. The mineral trade between South Africa and the European Economic Community; a report. Pretoria, 1970. pp. 132. *bibliog.*

— United Kingdom.

CERAMICS, GLASS AND MINERAL PRODUCTS INDUSTRY TRAINING BOARD [U.K.]. Report and statement of accounts. a., 1972/3- Harrow. *Formerly included in the file of British Parliamentary Papers.*

— — Directories.

U.K. Mines Inspectorate Division. 1972. List of miscellaneous mines in Great Britain. [London, 1972]. pp. 12, 2.

MINERAL RESOURCES IN SUBMERGED LANDS.

INTERREGIONAL SEMINAR ON THE DEVELOPMENT OF THE MINERAL RESOURCES OF THE CONTINENTAL SHELF, PORT-OF-SPAIN, 1971. Interregional seminar...[held at] Port-of-Spain, Trinidad and Tobago, 5-16 April, 1971: technical papers, (ST/TAO/SER. C/138). New York, United Nations, 1972. pp. 172. *In English and French.*

MINERS

— Bolivia.

IRIARTE (GREGORIO) Galerias de muerte: vida de los mineros bolivianos. Montevideo, 1972. pp. 214.

— South Africa.

MANAGEMENT responsibility and African employment in South Africa; report of a panel investigation; [edited by W.H. Thomas]. Johannesburg, 1973. pp. 142.

— United Kingdom.

UNOFFICIAL REFORM COMMITTEE. The miners' next step: being a suggested scheme for the reorganisation of the Federation; [reprint of work] first published [at Tonypandy] in 1912:...with a new introduction by R. Merfyn Jones. London, 1973. pp. 34. (*International Socialists. History Group. Reprints in Labour History. No. 4*)

GREGORY (ROY) The miners and British politics, 1906-1914. Oxford, 1968. pp. 207.

MOORE (ROBERT) Pit-men, preachers and politics: the effects of Methodism in a Durham mining community. London, 1974. pp. 292. *bibliog.*

— United States.

ROWE (WILLIAM JOHN) The hard-rock men: Cornish immigrants and the North American mining frontier. Liverpool, 1974. pp. 322. *bibliog.*

MINES AND MINERAL RESOURCES

— Asia.

UNITED NATIONS. Economic Commission for Asia and the Far East. Mineral Resources Development Series . New York, 1952 in progress.

— Australasia.

UNITED NATIONS. Economic Commission for Asia and the Far East. Mineral Resources Development Series . New York, 1952 in progress.

— Brazil.

ANUARIO MINERAL BRASILEIRO; [pd. by] Departamento Nacional da Produção Mineral [Brazil]. a., 1973- Rio de Janeiro.

— Japan.

WOODTLI (ROBERT) Le Japon et la conquête minérale. Lausanne, 1973. pp. 170. *bibliog.* (*Lausanne. Université. Centre de Recherches Européennes. Publications. 5. L'Europe Face à la Concurrence Internationale*)

— Peru.

SAMAME BOGGIO (MARIO) Mineria peruana: biografia y estrategia de una actividad decisiva. 2nd ed. Lima, 1974. pp. 712.

— Russia.

CLEMENT (HERMANN) Die Roh- und Grundstoffwirtschaft der Sowjetunion: die Stellung ... in der internen sowjetischen Entwicklungspolitik. Hamburg, 1974. pp. 466. *bibliog.* (*Hamburg. Hamburgisches Welt-Wirtschafts-Archiv. Veröffentlichungen*)

— — Soviet North.

D'IAKOV (IURII LEONT'EVICH) Severnaia ugol'no-metallurgicheskaia baza SSSR: vozniknovenie i razvitie. Moskva, 1973. pp. 255. *bibliog.*

— **United Kingdom.**

SOUTH HAMPSHIRE PLAN ADVISORY COMMITTEE. Study Reports. Group A. Rural Conservation. No. 3. Mineral workings. Winchester, 1969. pp. 21.

COMMISSION ON MINING AND THE ENVIRONMENT. Report of the commission...; [S. Zuckerman, chairman]; ([and] The exploration , evaluation and mining of non-ferrous metallic ores:... supplement to chapter 4). London, 1972. pp. 92. Map and supplement to chapter 4 in end pocket.

— — **Ireland, Northern.**

IRELAND, NORTHERN. Ministry of Commerce. Mineral Development Act (Northern Ireland) 1969: statement. a., 1971/2 [2nd]- Belfast. *1970/71 [1st] included in the file of IRELAND, NORTHERN. Parliament. House of Commons. [Papers] as H.C.2110.*

MINIATURE PAINTINGS, INDIC

— **Catalogues.**

SOTHEBY AND COMPANY. Bibliotheca Phillippica, new series...part 9: catalogue of oriental manuscripts, Indian and Persian miniatures (from the celebrated collection formed by Sir Thomas Phillipps, Bt., 1792-1872, etc). London, [1974]. pp. 126.

MINIATURE PAINTINGS, PERSIAN

— **Catalogues.**

SOTHEBY AND COMPANY. Bibliotheca Phillippica, new series...part 9: catalogue of oriental manuscripts, Indian and Persian miniatures (from the celebrated collection formed by Sir Thomas Phillipps, Bt., 1792-1872, etc). London, [1974]. pp. 126.

MINING CORPORATIONS

— **United Kingdom.**

CENTRAL MINING AND INVESTMENT CORPORATION. Fiftieth anniversary. London, [1955?]. 1 vol. (unpaged).

MINING INDUSTRY AND FINANCE

— **Sierra Leone.**

SWINDELL (KENNETH) Labour migration and mining in Sierra Leone; [Ph.D.(London) thesis]. 1973[or rather 1974]. fo. 287. *Typescript: unpublished. This thesis is the property of London University and may not be removed from the Library.*

— **South Africa.**

SOUTH AFRICA. Bureau of Statistics. Mining: financial statistics. a., 1966/1969 (1st)- Pretoria. *In English and Afrikaans.*

— **Zambia.**

NORTHERN RHODESIA. 1964. The British South Africa Company's claims to mineral royalties in Northern Rhodesia. Lusaka, 1964. pp. 33.

MULEMBA (H.) The progress of Zambianisation in the mining industry (December, 1968). Lusaka, Ministry of Labour, 1969. pp. 11.

MINING LAW.

UNITED NATIONS. Economic Commission for Asia and the Far East. Mineral Resources Development Series . New York, 1952 in progress.

— **Peru.**

SAMAME BOGGIO (MARIO) Mineria peruana: biografia y estrategia de una actividad decisiva. 2nd ed. Lima, 1974. pp. 712.

MINNESOTA

— **Politics and government.**

CHRISLOCK (CARL H.) The Progressive era in Minnesota, 1899-1918. St. Paul, 1971. pp. 242.

MINORITIES.

MARTIN (JAMES GILBERT) and FRANKLIN (CLYDE W.) Minority group relations. Columbus, Ohio, [1973]. pp. 338.

— **Education — United Kingdom.**

TAYLOR (FRANCINE) Race, school and community: (a survey of research and literature on education in multi-racial Britain). Windsor, 1974. pp. 200. *bibliog.*

— — **United States.**

EDUCATIONAL TESTING SERVICE. Graduate and professional school opportunities for minority students...1973-74. 5th ed. Princeton, N.J., [1973]. pp. 211.

— **Employment — United States.**

BULLOCK (PAUL) Aspiration vs. opportunity: "careers" in the inner city. Ann Arbor, 1973. pp. 177. *(Michigan University, and Wayne State University. Institute of Labor and Industrial Relations. Policy Papers in Human Resources and Industrial Relations. 20)*

— **Canada — British Columbia.**

PEOPLES of the living land: geography of cultural diversity in British Columbia: [prepared in connection with a symposium on Cultural discord in the modern world, organized by the Department of Geography, Simon Fraser University, as part of the 22nd International Geographical Congress, Montreal, 1972]; edited by Julian V. Minghi. Vancouver, [1972]. pp. 242. *(Canadian Association of Geographers. British Columbia Division. Occasional Papers. No. 15)*

— **China.**

MOSELEY (GEORGE V.H.) The consolidation of the south China frontier. Berkeley, Calif., 1973. pp. 192. *bibliog.*

— **Europe.**

SALVI (SERGIO) Le nazioni proibite: guida a dieci colonie "interne" dell'Europa occidentale. Firenze, [1973]. pp. 623. *bibliog.*

— **Europe, Eastern.**

KING (ROBERT R.) Minorities under Communism: nationalities as a source of tension among Balkan communist states. Cambridge, Mass., 1973. pp. 326. *bibliog.*

— **Laos.**

DAVIS (GEORGE ELLSWORTH) External intervention and mobilization of ethnic minorities in Laos, 1945-1973; [Ph.D. (London) thesis]. 1973. fo. 221. *bibliog. Typescript: unpublished. This thesis is the property of London University and may not be removed from the Library.*

— **Netherlands.**

AMERSFOORT (J.M.M. VAN) Immigratie en minderheidsvorming: een analyse van de Nederlandse situatie 1945-1973. Alphen aan den Rijn, 1974. pp. 242. *bibliog.*

— **Norway.**

EIDHEIM (HARALD) Aspects of the Lappish minority situation. Oslo, [1971]. pp. 86. *bibliog.*

— **Russia.**

SWOBODA (VICTOR) and SHEEHY (ANN) Ethnic pressures in the Soviet Union. London, 1972. pp. 27. *(Institute for the Study of Conflict. Conflict Studies. No.30)*

SHEEHY (ANN) The Crimean Tatars, Volga Germans and Meskhetians: Soviet treatment of some national minorities. new ed. London, 1973. pp. 36. *bibliog. (Minority Rights Group. Reports. No. 6)*

TSAMERIAN (IVAN PETROVICH) Teoreticheskie problemy obrazovaniia i razvitiia Sovetskogo mnogonatsional'nogo gosudarstva. Moskva, 1973. pp. 295.

— **United Kingdom.**

PERRY (JANE) The fair housing experiment: community relations councils and the housing of minority groups. London, 1973. pp. 53.

WILSON (DES) Minority report: a diary of protest 1970-73. London, 1973. pp. 168.

— **United States.**

FICKER (VICTOR B.) and GRAVES (HERBERT S.) eds. Deprivation in America. Beverly Hills, [1971]. pp. 149.

HUNT (ISAAC C.) and COHEN (BERNARD) Criminologist. Minority recruiting in the New York City Police Department. New York, 1971. pp. 92. *(Rand Corporation. [Rand Reports]. 702)*

BERNARD (WILLIAM S.) ed. Immigrants and ethnicity: ten years of changing thought; an analysis based on the special [Integration] Seminars of the American Immigration and Citizenship Conference, 1960-1970. New York, [1972]. pp. 73.

ABRAMSON (HAROLD J.) Ethnic diversity in Catholic America. New York, [1973]. pp. 207. *bibliog.*

BREMBECK (COLE SPEICHER) and HILL (WALKER H.) eds. Cultural challenges to education: the influence of cultural factors in school learning. Lexington, Mass., [1973]. pp. 160.

GABRIEL (RICHARD A.) The ethnic factor in the urban polity. New York, 1973. pp. 149.

McCOY (DONALD RICHARD) and RUETTEN (RICHARD T.) Quest and response: minority rights and the Truman administration. Lawrence, Kansas, [1973]. pp. 427. *bibliog.*

OGBU (JOHN U.) The next generation: an ethnography of education in an urban neighborhood. New York, 1974. pp. 275. *bibliog.*

MINORITY BUSINESS ENTERPRISES

— **United States.**

DOCTORS (SAMUEL I.) and HUFF (ANNE SIGISMUND) Minority enterprise and the Resident's Council. Cambridge, Mass., [1973]. pp. 201. *bibliog.*

MINTS

— **South Africa.**

SOUTH AFRICAN MINT. Annual report of the Director. a., 1972/3- Pretoria.

— **United Kingdom.**

GRINSELL (L.V.) The Bath mint: an historical outline;...with a section on The moneyers' names, by Mrs. V.J. Smart. London, 1973. pp. 52.

MISCEGENATION.

SOLAUN (MAURICIO) and KRONUS (SIDNEY) Discrimination without violence: miscegenation and racial conflict in Latin America. New York, [1973]. pp. 240. *bibliog.*

HENRIQUES (LOUIS FERNANDO) Children of Caliban: miscegenation. London, 1974. pp. 196.

MARTINEZ-ALIER (VERENA) Marriage, class and colour in nineteenth century Cuba: a study of racial attitudes and sexual values in a slave society. London, 1974. pp. 202. *bibliog.*

MISCONDUCT IN OFFICE

— **Sierra Leone.**

SIERRA LEONE. Beoku-Betts Commission of Inquiry into the Sierra Leone Produce Marketing Board. 1968. Report...with particular reference to the sale of palm oil, rice and coffee haulers, nut-cracking machine and the industrialisation programme undertaken by the Board during the period January, 1961 to March, 1967; [R.W. Beoku-Betts, chairman]. [Freetown, 1968]. pp. 120.

MISKITO INDIANS.

See MOSQUITO INDIANS.

MISSIONARIES, AMERICAN.

MISSIONARIES, AMERICAN.
GULICK (EDWARD VOSE) Peter Parker and the opening of China. Cambridge, Mass., 1973. pp. 282. bibliog. (Harvard University. Harvard Studies in American East Asian Relations. 3)

MISSIONS
— Africa, East.

STRAYER (ROBERT W.) and others. Protest movements in colonial East Africa: aspects of early African response to European rule. Syracuse, 1973. pp. 96. (Syracuse University. Maxwell Graduate School of Citizenship and Public Affairs. Program of Eastern African Studies. Eastern African Studies. 12)

— Ethiopia.

CRUMMEY (DONALD) Priests and politicians: protestant and catholic missions in orthodox Ethiopia 1830-1868. Oxford, 1972. pp. 176. bibliog.

— Tonga.

LATUKEFU (SIONE) Church and state in Tonga: the Wesleyan Methodist missionaries and political development, 1822-1875. Canberra, 1974. pp. 302. bibliog.

MISSIONS, MEDICAL
— China.

GULICK (EDWARD VOSE) Peter Parker and the opening of China. Cambridge, Mass., 1973. pp. 282. bibliog. (Harvard University. Harvard Studies in American East Asian Relations. 3)

MISSISSIPPI
— Economic conditions.

BARNEY (WILLIAM L.) The secessionist impulse: Alabama and Mississippi in 1860. Princeton, [1974]. pp. 371. bibliog.

— Politics and government.

BARNEY (WILLIAM L.) The secessionist impulse: Alabama and Mississippi in 1860. Princeton, [1974]. pp. 371.

MOBILE SHOPS.
See STORES, TRAVELLING.

MODEL THEORY.
SHUBIK (MARTIN) and BREWER (GARRY D.) Models, simulations and games: a survey;...a report prepared for Advanced Research Projects Agency. Santa Monica, 1972. pp. 160. (Rand Corporation. [Rand Reports]. 1060)

— Bibliography.

SHUBIK (MARTIN) and others. The literature of gaming, simulation and model-building: index and critical abstracts;...a report prepared for Advanced Research Projects Agency. Santa Monica, 1972. pp. 121. (Rand Corporation. [Rand Reports]. 620)

MOHAMMED REZA PAHLAVI, Shahanshah of Iran.
DENMAN (DONALD ROBERT) The king's vista: a land reform which has changed the face of Persia. Berkhamsted, Herts., [1973]. pp. 368. bibliog.

MOHAMMEDAN EMPIRE.
LOMBARD (MAURICE) Espaces et réseaux du haut moyen âge. Paris, [1972]. pp. 231. bibliog. (Paris. Ecole Pratique des Hautes Etudes. Section des Sciences Economiques et Sociales. Le Savoir Historique. 2)

MOHAMMEDANISM.
RODINSIN (MAXIME) Islam and capitalism; translated by Brian Pearce. London, 1974. pp. 308.

RODINSON (MAXIME) Islam and capitalism; translated by Brian Pearce. London, 1974. pp. 308.

MOHAMMEDANISM AND STATE.
STEWART (C.C.) and STEWART (E.K.) Islam and social order in Mauritania: a case study from the nineteenth century. Oxford, 1973. pp. 204. bibliog.

MOHAMMEDANS IN INDIA.
AHMAD (IMTIAZ) ed. Caste and social stratification among the Muslims. Delhi, 1973. pp. 256. bibliog.

MOHAMMEDANS IN NIGERIA.
PADEN (JOHN N.) Religion and political culture in Kano. Berkeley, Calif., [1973]. pp. 461. bibliog.

MOHAMMEDANS IN THE GAMBIA.
QUINN (CHARLOTTE A.) Mandingo kingdoms of the Senegambia: traditionalism, Islam, and European expansion. London, 1972. pp. 211. bibliog.

MOHAMMEDANS IN THE PHILIPPINE ISLANDS.
KIEFER (THOMAS M.) The Tausug: violence and law in a Philippine Moslem society. New York, [1972]. pp. 145. bibliog.

MOHAVE INDIANS.
KROEBER (ALFRED LOUIS) and KROEBER (CLIFTON BROWN) A Mohave war reminiscence, 1854-1880. Berkeley, 1973. pp. 97. (California University. Publications in Anthropology. vol. 10) 2 maps in end pocket.

MOLDAVIA.
DIMITRIE CANTEMIR, Prince of Moldavia. Descrierea Moldovei; Descriptio antiqui et hodierni status Moldaviae, etc.; traducere după originalul latin, etc. Bucureşti, 1973. pp. 401. Original Latin text of 1714 with modern Roumanian translation.

— Population.

DMITRIEV (PAVEL GEORGIEVICH) Narodonaselenie Moldavii: po materialam perepisei 1772-1773, 1774 i 1803 gg. Kishinev, 1973. pp. 155.

MOLDAVIAN REPUBLIC
— Economic conditions.

KIRKE (SERGEI IVANOVICH) Tempy i proportsii ekonomicheskogo razvitiia soiuznoi respubliki: na primere Moldavskoi SSR. Kishinev, 1973. pp. 183.

— History — Historiography.

PROTIV burzhuaznykh fal'sifikatorov istorii i kul'tury moldavskogo naroda: sbornik statei. Kishinev, 1972. pp. 225.

— Politics and government.

KOMPARTIIA Moldavii v gody sotsialisticheskogo i kommunisticheskogo stroitel'stva. Kishinev, 1973. pp. 91.

— Religion.

STRANITSY istorii religii i ateizma v Moldavii. Kishinev, 1970. pp. 132.

MOLUCCANS IN THE NETHERLANDS.
AMERSFOORT (J.M.M. VAN) De sociale positie van de Molukkers in Nederland. 's-Gravenhage, Staatsuitgeverij, 1971. pp. 74. bibliog.

MONARCHY.
LOKOT' (TIMOFEI VASIL'EVICH) "Zavoevanie revoliutsii" i ideologiia russkogo monarkhizma; doklad...T.V. Lokotia. [Vienna?, 1921]. pp. 24.

JUSEU (JORGE) Monarquia a la española: un Cesar con fueros. Madrid, 1971. pp. 123.

THIREAU (JEAN LOUIS) Les idées politiques de Louis XIV. Paris, 1973. pp. 127. bibliog. (Paris. Université de Paris II. Travaux et Recherches. Série Sciences Historiques. 4)

MONASTICISM AND RELIGIOUS ORDERS
— United Kingdom — Ireland.

BRADSHAW (BRENDAN) The dissolution of the religious orders in Ireland under Henry VIII. London, 1974. pp. 276. bibliog.

MONETARY UNIONS.
CONFERENCE ON THE IMPLICATIONS OF EUROPEAN MONETARY INTEGRATION FOR THE UNITED STATES, BROOKINGS INSTITUTION, 1972. European monetary unification and its meaning for the United States; (Lawrence B. Krause and Walter S. Salant, editors).Washington, D.C., [1973]. pp. 322.

MONEY.
VARGA (ISTVÁN) Wesen und Funktionen des Geldes im Sozialismus: Vortrag gehalten am 6.Juni 1961, etc. München, 1962. pp. 35. bibliog. (Südosteuropa-Gesellschaft. Südosteuropa- Studien. 3)

SAHARA (TAKAOMI) Synthesis of monetary theories; [translated from the revised Japanese edition of 1962]. Rutland, Vt., 1964. pp. 438.

GROUP OF TEN. 1966. Communiqué of ministers and governors and report of deputies "... on improvements needed in the international monetary system, etc". [Frankfurt?], 1966. pp. 25.

ORGANISATION FOR ECONOMIC CO-OPERATION AND DEVELOPMENT. Committee for Invisible Transactions. Country Capital- Market Series. [Paris], 1969 in progress.

MONNAIE et quasi-monnaie: rôle dans les circuits économiques et financiers; (colloque d'information) 15 et 16 juin 1970; [sponsored by the Banque de France]. [Paris, 1970]. 1 vol. (various pagings).

GERMANY (BUNDESREPUBLIK). Sachverständigenrat zur Begutachtung der Gesamtwirtschaftlichen Entwicklung. 1971. Währung, Geldwert, Wettbewerb: Entscheidungen für morgen:Jahresgutachten 1971-72. Stuttgart, 1971. pp. 240.

WALTERS (ALAN A.) Monetary myths, freedom, and reality. St. Lucia, Queensland, [1971]. pp. 14. (Australia and New Zealand Banking Group Limited. Research Lectures. 1971)

BORDO (MICHAEL DAVID) The first round effects of monetary change: an historical approach.[Ottawa, 1972]. fo. 68. bibliog. (Carleton University. Carleton Economic Papers)

DENIZET (JEAN) Monnaie et financement: essai de théorie dans un cadre de comptabilité économique. 3rd ed. Paris, 1972. pp. 252. bibliog.

LUTZ (FRIEDRICH AUGUST) Das Problem der internationalen Währungsordnung. Erlenbach-Zürich, [1972]. pp. 29. (Schweizerisches Institut für Auslandforschung. Schriftenreihe zu Aktuellen Problemen aus Politik und Wirtschaft. 6)

RYMES (THOMAS K.) The logical impossibility of optimum money supply policies. [Ottawa, 1972]. fo. 21. (Carleton University. Carleton Economic Papers)

WALLICH (HENRY CHRISTOPHER) and others. The monetary crisis of 1971: the lessons to be learned. Washington, D.C., 1972. pp. 79. (Per Jacobsson Foundation. [Lectures]. 1972)

CLARKE (STEPHEN V.O.) The reconstruction of the international monetary system: the attempts of 1922 and 1933. Princeton, 1973. pp. 44. bibliog. (Princeton University. Department of Economics and Sociology. International Finance Section. Princeton Studies in International Finance. No.33)

ALIBER (ROBERT Z.) The international money game. London, 1973. pp. 236.

MONEY.

ALIBER (ROBERT Z.) Monetary reform and world inflation. Beverley Hills, [1973]. pp. 82. *bibliog.*

AMERICAN INTERNATIONAL INVESTMENT CORPORATION. World currency charts. 7th ed. San Francisco, 1973. pp. 71.

ATALA (CHARLES) De Bretton Woods à Watergate: où va la monnaie?. Ottawa, [1973]. pp. 244. *bibliog.*

BAFFI (PAOLO) Nuovi studi sulla moneta. Milano, 1973. pp. 138. (*Rome. Università. Istituto di Politica Economica e Finanziaria. Pubblicazioni. 16*)

BALAT (ALAIN) Sens et formes de l'économie monétaire: le langage de la monnaie. Paris, [1973]. pp. 487. *bibliog.*

BALL (ROBERT JAMES) Inflation and the theory of money. 2nd ed. London, 1973. pp. 313.

BALLING (MORTEN) National pengepolitik i en international økonomi. Kóbenhavn, 1973. pp. 624. *bibliogs.*

BERGER (PIERRE) Le marché monétaire: marché de l'argent à court terme et marché de la monnaie; banque centrale. Paris, 1973. pp. 128.

BORDO (MICHAEL DAVID) The monetary theory and policy of John E. Cairnes. [Ottawa, 1973]. fo. 33. ii. *bibliog. Carleton University. Carleton Economic Papers)*

CHICK (VICTORIA) The theory of monetary policy. London, 1973. pp. 163. *bibliog.*

CROCKETT (ANDREW) Money, theory, policy and institutions. London, 1973. pp. 258. *bibliogs.*

EMMINGER (OTMAR) and others. L'inflation et le système monétaire international. Bâle, 1973. pp. 85. (*Per Jacobsson Foundation.* [*Lectures*]. *1973*)

EMMINGER (OTMAR) and others. Inflation and the international monetary system. Basle, 1973. pp. 78. (*Per Jacobsson Foundation.* [*Lectures*]. *1973*)

FISCHER (JOSEF A.) Zur Theorie der optimalen Währungsräume. [Erlangen, imprint, 1973?]. pp. 201,xxiii. *bibliog.*

FLANNERY (MARK J.) and JAFFEE (DWIGHT M.) The economic implications of an electronic monetary transfer system. Lexington, Mass., [1973]. pp. 209. *bibliog.*

FRAZER (WILLIAM JOHNSON) Crisis in economic theory: a study of monetary policy, analysis, and economic goals. Gainesville, Fla., 1973. pp. 526. *bibliog.*

GUGLIELMI (JEAN LOUIS) Les expériences de la politique monétaire. Paris, 1973. pp. 228. *bibliog.*

HIRSCH (FRED) Reform of the international monetary system with special reference to the interests of developing countries of the Commonwealth; a study. London, Commonwealth Secretariat, 1973. pp. 20. (*Commonwealth Economic Papers. No. 3*)

KONJUNKTURPOLITIK: Zeitschrift für angewandte Konjunkturforschung. Beihefte. Heft 20. Zur Neuordnung des internationalen Währungssystems: Bericht über den wissenschaftlichen Teil der 36. Mitgliederversammlung der Arbeitsgemeinschaft deutscher wirtschaftswissenschaftlicher Forschungsinstitute...1973. Berlin, [1973]. pp. 177. *In German or English.*

MENEGAZZI (GUIDO) The laws of the dynamics of economy and finance as the basis and objective of international monetary and credit reform. Verona, 1973. pp. 68.

NARPATI (B.) The monetary system: its components and some trade issues. Rotterdam, 1973. pp. 136. *bibliog.*

RITTER (LAWRENCE S.) and SILBER (WILLIAM L.) Money. 2nd ed. New York, [1973]. pp. 293. *bibliog.*

RUEFF (JACQUES) La réforme du système monétaire international: (pour un succès immédiat et certain). [Paris, 1973]. pp. 61.

STANFORD (JON D.) Money, banking and economic activity. Sydney, [1973]. pp. 130. *bibliogs.*

WEINTRAUB (SIDNEY) b. 1914, and others. Keynes and the monetarists and other essays: [lectures delivered at the Graduate School of Business Administration of the University of Puerto Rico, 1970-71]. New Brunswick, [1973]. pp. 227.

COFFEY (PETER) Economist. The world monetary crisis. London, 1974. pp. 115.

GEIGER (HELMUT) Herausforderungen für Stabilität und Fortschritt: [collection of lectures, 1970-1974]. Stuttgart, [1974]. pp. 211.

JOHNSON (HARRY GORDON) The problem of international monetary reform. London, 1974. pp. 22. (*London. University. Stamp Memorial Lectures. 1973*)

KLEIN (JOHN J.) Money and the economy. 3rd ed. New York, [1974]. pp. 556. *bibliogs.*

MARSHALL (ROBERT HERMAN) and SWANSON (RODNEY B.) The monetary process: essentials of money and banking. Boston, [Mass., 1974]. pp. 484. *bibliogs.*

MEIER (GERALD MARVIN) Problems of a world monetary order. New York, 1974. pp. 305. *bibliogs.*

MONEY STUDY GROUP. Conference, 1972. Issues in monetary economics: proceedings of the ... conference; edited by H.G. Johnson and A.R. Nobay. London, 1974. pp. 595. *bibliogs.*

MONROE (WILBUR F.) International monetary reconstruction: problems and issues. Lexington, Mass., [1974]. pp. 191.

PIERCE (DAVID G.) and SHAW (DAVID M.) Monetary economics: theories, evidence and policy. London, 1974. pp. 454. *bibliogs.*

ROLFE (SIDNEY E.) and BURTLE (JAMES L.) The great wheel: the world monetary system; a reinterpretation. London, 1974. pp. 279. *bibliog.*

— **Mathematical models.**

HOSAKA (NAOMICHI) Money supply and monetary policy indicator. [Kobe], [1972?]. fo.30. *bibliog.* (*Kobe. University. Institute of Economic Research. Working Papers in Economics and Management Science. No. 13*)

ENGERING (F.A.) The monetary multiplier and the monetary model. Tilburg, 1973. pp. 37. (*Tilburg. Katholieke Hogeschool. Tilburg Institute of Economics. Research Memoranda. EIT 40*)

FRAZER (WILLIAM JOHNSON) Crisis in economic theory: a study of monetary policy, analysis, and economic goals. Gainesville, Fla., 1973. pp. 526. *bibliog.*

HAYASHI (TOSHIHIKO) Monetary equilibria in some infinite transaction economies. Stanford, 1973. pp. 38. *bibliog.* (*Stanford University. Institute for Mathematical Studies in the Social Sciences. Technical Reports.* [*New Series*]. *No. 101*)

— **Africa, Subsaharan.**

DIARRA (MAMADOU) Les états africains et la garantie monétaire de la France: où va l'argent des français?. Dakar, [1972]. pp. 76.

STOLPER (WOLFGANG FRIEDRICH) Internal effects of devaluation. Michigan, [1972]. pp. 411-419. (*Michigan University. Center for Research on Economic Development. Cred Reprints. New Series. 34*) (*From Africa and Monetary Integration, 6*)

— **America, Latin.**

CENTRO DE ESTUDIOS MONETARIOS LATINOAMERICANOS. America Latina y la liquidez internacional; [selected papers and documents for the years 1964 to 1969]. Mexico, 1970. pp. 376.

FERNANDEZ HOLMANN (ERNESTO) Politica monetaria, estabilidad financiera y desarrollo economico en Centroamerica. Mexico, 1970. pp. 194.

MAX (HERMANN) El valor de la moneda: la funcion del dinero, la funcion del credito, la funcion de los cambios. Buenos Aires, 1970. pp. 326. *bibliog.*

— **Argentine Republic.**

CARBONELL TUR (ANTONIO) La estabilidad monetaria y la banca comercial en la Republica Argentina: periodo 1935-1969. Buenos Aires, [1970 repr.] 1971. pp. 302. *bibliog.*

BANCO CENTRAL DE LA REPUBLICA ARGENTINA. La creacion del Banco Central y la experiencia monetaria argentina entre los años 1935-1943. [Buenos Aires, 1972]. 2 vols. *Apendices in end pocket.*

— **Australia.**

BUTLIN (SYDNEY JAMES) and others. Australian banking and monetary statistics, 1817-1945. Sydney, 1971. pp. 562. (*Reserve Bank of Australia. Occasional Papers. No. 4A*)

WHITE (R.C.) Australian banking and monetary statistics, 1945-1970. Sydney, 1973. pp. 681. (*Reserve Bank of Australia. Occasional Papers. No. 4B*)

— **Belgium.**

FRANCE. Direction de la Documentation. La Documentation Française. Notes et Etudes Documentaires. Nos. 3,747-3, 748. Le franc belge et le florin. Paris, 1970. pp. 55. *bibliog.*

VANES (F.R.) and VERHEIRSTRAETEN (A.) De geldkapitaalmarkt. 2nd ed, Leuven, 1972 in progress. *bibliog.*

— **Burgundy.**

MUNRO (JOHN H.A.) Wool, cloth, and gold: the struggle for bullion in Anglo-Burgundian trade, 1340-1478. Brussels, 1972. pp. 241. *bibliog.*

— **Communist countries.**

MEZHDUNARODNAIA sotsialisticheskaia valiuta stran-chlenov SEV. Moskva, 1973. pp. 96.

INTERNATIONALE sozialistische Währung der Mitgliedsländer des RGW: Übersetzung ([by] Peter Freide [and] Gerhard Huber) aus dem Russischen. Berlin, 1974. pp. 83.

— **Denmark.**

BALLING (MORTEN) National pengepolitik i en international økonomi. Kóbenhavn, 1973. pp. 624. *bibliogs.*

— **Europe.**

INTERNATIONAL CENTER FOR MONETARY AND BANKING STUDIES. Conference, 1st, Geneva, 1972. Europe and the evolution of the international monetary system: proceedings...; edited by Alexander K. Swoboda. Leiden, 1973. pp. 172. (*Geneva. Graduate Institute of International Studies. International Economics Series. 1*)

— **Europe, Eastern.**

CENTRO STUDI E RICERCHE SUI PROBLEMI ECONOMICO-SOCIALI. Seminario Internazionale, 5o, 1969. Piano e moneta nelle economie dell'Est: [proceedings]. Milano, [1972]. pp. 213. (*Est, L'. Quaderni. 1*)

— **European Economic Community countries.**

EUROPEAN COMMUNITIES. Monetary Committee. 1972-74. Monetary policy in the countries of the European Economic Community: institutions and instruments. [Luxembourg], 1972-74. 2 vols.

CONFERENCE ON THE IMPLICATIONS OF EUROPEAN MONETARY INTEGRATION FOR THE UNITED STATES, BROOKINGS INSTITUTION, 1972. European monetary unification and its meaning for the United States; (Lawrence B. Krause and Walter S. Salant, editors).Washington, D.C., [1973]. pp. 322.

DEUTSCHES INSTITUT FÜR WIRTSCHAFTSFORSCHUNG. Sonderhefte. [Neue Folge]. Nr. 96. Wirtschaftspolitische Prioritätsunterschiede in der EG als Hindernisse für die Errichtung der Wirtschafts- und Währungsunion und Instrumente zu ihrer Überwindung; ([by] Fritz Franzmeyer und Bernhard Seidel). Berlin, 1973. pp. 162. *With English summary.*

MONEY. (Cont.)

OPPENHEIMER (PETER MORRIS) The problem of monetary union. [London], Civil Service College, 1973. fo. 29. (*Lectures on the European Community. Series A. No. 6. Series B. No.8*)

— Finland.

RUEHL (HARALD) Das währungspolitische Instrumentarium der nordischen Zentralbanken. Bern, 1972. pp. 250, xxxviii. *bibliog.*

— France.

NETTER (MARCEL) Les institutions monétaires en France. 3rd ed. Paris, 1973. pp. 128.

— — Colonies.

DIARRA (MAMADOU) Les états africains et la garantie monétaire de la France: où va l'argent des français?. Dakar, [1972]. pp. 76.

— Germany.

GREULICH (GEORG) Dritte deutsche Inflation und Notenbankpolitik: eine Analyse seit 1948. 2nd ed. Weinheim/Bergstrasse, 1973. pp. 237. *bibliog.*

VOCKE (WILHELM) Bundesbankpräsident. Memoiren. Stuttgart, [1973]. pp. 223.

BOECK (KLAUS) and GEHRMANN (DIETER) Die DM als internationale Reservewährung: Bedeutung, Ursachen und Probleme. Hamburg, 1974. pp. 75. (*Hamburg. Hamburgisches Welt-Wirtschafts-Archiv. Studien zur Aussenwirtschaft und Entwicklungspolitik*)

DIWOK (FRITZ) Die DM-Legende: deutsche Währung in kritischer Phase. Wien, [1974]. pp. 272.

— — Mathematical models.

BARTOLOMEI (J.A.) Balance des paiements et politique monétaire: l'expérience allemande entre 1958 et 1968. Louvain, 1972. pp. 107. *bibliog.* (*Louvain. Université. Faculté des Sciences Economiques, Sociales et Politiques. [Publications]. Nouvelle Série. No. 96*)

— Iceland.

RUEHL (HARALD) Das währungspolitische Instrumentarium der nordischen Zentralbanken. Bern, 1972. pp. 250, xxxviii. *bibliog.*

— India.

GHOSH (ALAK) Control techniques in Indian monetary management. Calcutta, 1971. pp. 119. (*Patna University. Banaili Readership Lectures in Indian Economics. 1969*)

MITTRA (SID) Monetary politics in India. Bombay, 1972. pp. 250.

— — Kerala.

PILLAI (VELU PILLAI RAMAN) and PANIKAR (PUTHENVEETIL GOVINDA KESAVA) Monetisation in Kerala. New Delhi, Research Programmes Committee, Planning Commission, 1970. pp. 161.

— Italy.

ORGANISATION FOR ECONOMIC CO-OPERATION AND DEVELOPMENT. Monetary Studies Series. Monetary policy in Italy. [Paris], 1973. pp. 90.

— Japan.

ORGANISATION FOR ECONOMIC CO-OPERATION AND DEVELOPMENT. Monetary Studies Series. Monetary policy in Japan. Paris, 1972. pp. 105.

BANK OF JAPAN. Economic Research Department. Money and banking in Japan;... translated by S. Nishimura; edited by L.S. Pressnell. London, 1973. pp. 456.

— Malaysia.

LEE (SHENG-YI) The monetary and banking development of Malaysia and Singapore. Singapore, [1974]. pp. 404. *bibliog.*

— Netherlands.

FRANCE. Direction de la Documentation. La Documentation Française. Notes et Etudes Documentaires. Nos. 3,747-3, 748. Le franc belge et le florin. Paris, 1970. pp. 55. *bibliog.*

TIMMERS (JACOBUS) Geld en geldpolitiek: enige beschouwingen over het werkterrein van het monetaire beleid in het bijzonder ten aanzien van de Nederlandse economie met een semi-geleid en open karakter. Arnhem, 1971. pp. 207. *bibliog. With English summary.*

— New Zealand.

DEANE (RODERICK S.) Papers on monetary policy, credit creation, economic objectives and the Reserve Bank. Wellington, 1972. pp. 35. (*Reserve Bank of New Zealand. Research Papers. No. 9*)

— Norway.

EIDE (LEIF) The Norwegian monetary and credit system. Oslo, 1973. pp. 62. (*Norges Bank. Skriftserie. No.1*)

SEJERSTED (FRANCIS) Ideal, teori og virkelighet: Nicolai Rygg og pengepolitikken i 1920-årene. [Oslo, 1973]. pp. 134.

— Pakistan.

FAROOQ (DANIAL M.) Inflation, money and credit in Pakistan. Islamabad, United States Agency for International Development, 1973. 1 pamphlet (various pagings).

— Portugal.

SOARES (L. RIBEIRO) Money in Portugal: a short history; [translated by Matilde Paes Parente and Maria Aguiar]. [Lisbon], 1971. pp. 86.

— Russia.

FEDORENKO (ALEKSANDR IVANOVICH) Denezhnoe obrashchenie v sotsialisticheskom khoziaistve: voprosy teorii i metodologii; pod redaktsiei... G.A. Shvartsa. Moskva, 1973. pp. 127.

PRAVOTOROV (GEORGII BORISOVICH) Stoimostnye kategorii i sposob proizvodstva: problemy teorii i metodologii. Moskva, 1974. pp. 303.

— Scandinavia.

RUEHL (HARALD) Das währungspolitische Instrumentarium der nordischen Zentralbanken. Bern, 1972. pp. 250, xxxviii. *bibliog.*

— Singapore.

LEE (SHENG-YI) The monetary and banking development of Malaysia and Singapore. Singapore, [1974]. pp. 404. *bibliog.*

— Sri Lanka.

KARUNATILAKE (HALWALAGE NEVILLE SEPALA) Central banking and monetary policy in Sri Lanka. Colombo, 1973. pp. 209. *bibliog.*

— Switzerland.

JENNY (KLAUS) Der schweizerische Geldmarkt. Bern, [1973]. pp. 307. *bibliog.* (*Zürich. Universität. Institut für Schweizerisches Bankwesen, and Hochschule St.Gallen für Wirtschafts- und Sozialwissenschaften. Institut für Bankwirtschaft. Bankwirtschaftliche Forschungen. Band 15*)

WINTERBERGER (GERHARD) Gedanken zur schweizerischen Währungs-und Konjunkturpolitik. [Zürich, 1973]. pp. 13. (*Wirtschaftsförderung: Gesellschaft zur Förderung der Schweizerischen Wirtschaft. Stimmen zur Staats- und Wirtschaftspolitik. 55*) (*Sonderdruck aus Schweizer Monatshefte, Heft 4, Juli 1973*)

— Syria.

OFFICE ARABE DE PRESSE ET DE DOCUMENTATION. Serie "Etudes". 150. La nouvelle politique monétaire et bancaire en Syrie. Damas, [1973?]. fo. 42.

— Underdeveloped areas.

See UNDERDEVELOPED AREAS — Money.

— United Kingdom.

BARBON (NICHOLAS) A discourse concerning coining the new money lighter in answer to Mr. Lock's considerations about raising the value of money. London, Chiswell, 1696; Farnborough, Hants., 1971. pp. 96. *Facsimile reprint.*

CROCKETT (ANDREW) Money, theory, policy and institutions. London, 1973. pp. 258. *bibliogs.*

CHALMERS (ERIC B.) The money world: a guide to money and banking in the age of inflation. London, 1974. pp. 211.

— United States.

RITTER (LAWRENCE S.) ed. Money and economic activity: readings in money and banking. 3rd ed. New York, [1967]. pp. 450.

MONETARY CONFERENCE, 1ST, NANTUCKET ISLAND, 1969. Controlling monetary aggregates: proceedings of the...conference...sponsored by the Federal Reserve Bank of Boston. [Boston, 1969]. pp. 174.

SMITH (WARREN LOUNSBURY) and TEIGEN (RONALD L.) eds. Readings in money, national income and stabilization policy. rev. ed. Homewood, Illinois, 1970 repr. 1971. pp. 647.

ERNST (JOSEPH ALBERT) Money and politics in America, 1755-1775: a study in the Currency Act of 1764 and the political economy of revolution. Chapel Hill, N.C., [1973]. pp. 403. *bibliog.*

ERNST (JOSEPH ALBERT) Money in America, 1755-1775: a study in The Currency Act of 1964 and the political economy of revolution. Chapel Hill, N.C., [1973]. pp. 403. bibliog.

WILLIAMS (HAROLD R.) and WOUDENBERG (HENRY W.) Money, banking, and monetary theory: problems and concepts... a study guide to accompany Chandler, The economics of money and banking, 6th ed. 2nd ed. New York, [1973]. pp. 324.

— — Mathematical models.

FISHER (GORDON R.) and SHEPPARD (DAVID K.) Inter-relationships between real and monetary variables: some evidence from recent U.S. empirical studies; (revised version of a paper read to the Money Study Group Conference held in Bournemouth...1972). Southampton, 1972. fo.100. *bibliog.* (*Southampton. University. Discussion Papers in Economics and Econometrics. No. 7213*)

COOPER (JEROME PHILLIP) Development of the monetary sector, prediction and policy analysis in the FRB-MIT-Penn model. Lexington, Mass., [1974]. pp. 225. *bibliog.*

— Yugoslavia.

DIMITRIJEVIC (DIMITRIJE) and MACESICH (GEORGE) Money and finance in contemporary Yugoslavia. New York, 1973. pp. 261. *bibliog.*

MONGOLIA

— Constitution.

FRANCE. Direction de la Documentation. La Documentation Française. Notes et Etudes Documentaires. No. 3,795. Constitution de la République populaire mongole, 6 juillet 1960: les institutions et les forces politiques de la Mongolie extérieure; [by] Patrice Gélard. Paris, 1971. pp. 18. *bibliog.*

— Foreign relations — Russia.

SHIRENDYB (BAZARYN) V.I. Lenin i mongol'skii narod. Moskva, 1970. pp. 60.

— Industries.

ZAGASBALDAN (D.) Problemy sotsialisticheskoi industrializatsii Mongol'skoi Narodnoi Respubliki. Moskva, 1973. pp. 216.

MONGOLS

— History.

SAUNDERS (JOHN JOSEPH) The history of the Mongol conquests. London, 1971. pp. 275. *bibliog.*

MONNET (JEAN).

La GREFFE européenne; ([by] Henri Rieben [and others]). Lausanne, 1973. pp. 133. *(Lausanne. Université. Centre de Recherches Européennes. Publications)*

FONTAINE (PASCAL) Le Comité d'Action pour les Etats-Unis d'Europe de Jean Monnet. Lausanne, 1974. pp. 242. *bibliog.* *(Lausanne. Université. Centre de Recherches Européennes. Publications. 2. Le Processus d'Union de l'Europe)*

MONOPOLIES.

GOSUDARSTVENNAIA sobstvennost' i antimonopolisticheskaia bor'ba v stranakh razvitogo kapitalizma. Moskva, 1973. pp. 391. *bibliog.*

TORKANOVSKII (VIKTOR SEMENOVICH) Novye iavleniia v razvitii monopolisticheskogo kapitala. Leningrad, 1973. pp. 196.

— Europe — Bibliography.

U.K. Department of Trade and Industry. Library Services. Economics Division. 1974. Monopolies and mergers in Great Britain and Europe: recent information. London, 1974. fo. 5. *(Bibliographical Series. No. 74/1)*

— Germany.

TAMMER (HANS) BRD-Monopole auf Kurs zu internationalen Dimensionen. Frankfurt/Main, 1974. pp. 186.

— Japan.

FRANCE. Direction de la Documentation. La Documentation Française. Notes et Etudes Documentaires. No. 3,724. Fusions et concentrations au Japon: les grandes entreprises; [by] Marie-Agnès Blanchon. Paris, 1970. pp. 43. *bibliog.*

— United Kingdom.

POLANYI (GEORGE) Which way monopoly policy?: some questions raised by recent reports of the Monopolies Commission. London, 1973. pp. 65. *(Institute of Economic Affairs. Research Monographs. 30)*

— — Bibliography.

U.K. Department of Trade and Industry. Library Services. Economics Division. 1974. Monopolies and mergers in Great Britain and Europe: recent information. London, 1974. fo. 5. *(Bibliographical Series. No. 74/1)*

— United States.

GREEN (MARK J.) ed. The monopoly makers: Ralph Nader's study group report on regulation and competition. New York, 1973. pp. 400.

MONSOONS.

RURAL settlements in monsoon Asia: proceedings of I[nternational] G[eographical] U[nion] symposia at Varanasi and Tokyo [in 1971, organized by the IGU Commission on Rural Settlements in Monsoon Asia]; edited by R.L. Singh. Varanasi, 1972. pp. 510.

MONTAGNARDS (VIETNAMESE TRIBES).

The MONTAGNARDS of South Vietnam. London, 1974. pp. 28. *bibliog.* *(Minority Rights Group. Reports. No. 18)*

MONTE CARLO METHOD.

SMITH (V. KERRY) Monte Carlo methods: their role for econometrics. Lexington, Mass., [1973]. pp. 153. *bibliog.*

MONTGOMERY (BERNARD LAW) 1st Viscount Montgomery of Alamein.

MONTGOMERY (BRIAN) A field-marshal in the family. London, 1973. pp. 372.

MONTGOMERY FAMILY.

MONTGOMERY (BRIAN) A field-marshal in the family. London, 1973. pp. 372.

MONTPELLIER.

FRANCE. Direction de la Documentation. La Documentation Française. Notes et Etudes Documentaires. Nos. 3,801-3, 802. Les villes françaises: Montpellier; [by] S. Savey [and] J.P. Volle. Paris, 1971. pp. 59. *bibliog.*

MONTREAL

— Politics and government.

ADAM (MARCEL) La démocratie à Montréal; ou, Le vaisseau dort. Montréal, [1972]. pp. 170.

— Social conditions.

AMES (Sir HERBERT BROWN) The city below the hill: (a sociological study of a portion of the city of Montreal, Canada [first published in 1897]); with an introduction by P.F.W. Rutherford. Toronto, [1972]. pp. 116.

MORAL EDUCATION.

DURKHEIM (EMILE) Moral education: a study in the theory and application of the sociology of education;...translated by Everett K. Wilson and Herman Schnurer; edited...: by Everett K. Wilson. London, [1973]. pp. 288.

SUGARMAN (BARRY) The school and moral development. London, 1973. pp. 285. *bibliogs.*

— Bibliography.

BLACKHAM (HAROLD JOHN) compiler. Moral education: an annotated list; selected by...Secretary of the Campaign for Moral Education. London, 1971. pp. 46.

MORE (Sir THOMAS) Saint.

FLEISHER (MARTIN) Radical reform and political persuasion in the life and writings of Thomas More. Genève, 1973. pp. 183. *bibliog.*

MORGAN (JOHN PIERPONT).

WHEELER (GEORGE) Pierpont Morgan and friends: the anatomy of a myth. Englewood Cliffs, [1973]. pp. 338. *bibliog.*

MOROCCO

— Foreign relations — Spain.

MARTÍN (MIGUEL) El colonialismo español en Marruecos, 1860-1956. [Paris, 1973]. pp. 263. *bibliog.*

— Industries.

MOROCCO. Direction de la Statisque. 1973. Etude de structure sur l'industrie, les mines l'artisanat, l'énergie, le bâtiment, les travaux publics, les transports et le commerce de gros, 1969. Rapports[s] no[s.] 1—[12]. [Rabat? 1973?]. 12 parts (3).

— Relations (general) with Russia.

CONSTANT (JEAN PAUL) Les relations maroco-soviétiques, 1956-1971. Paris, 1973. pp. 136.

— Social policy.

MORLA (VIAL DE) España en Marruecos: la obra social. Madrid, 1947. pp. 173.

MORRIS (HENRY).

RÉE (HARRY) Educator extraordinary: the life and achievement of Henry Morris, 1889-1961. London, 1973. pp. 163.

MORTALITY.

BOLANDER (ANNE MARIE) and others. Cohort mortality of Sweden: three studies describing past, present, and future trends in mortality. Stockholm, 1970. pp. 86. *(Sweden. Statistiska Centralbyrån. Statistiska Meddelanden. Be/1970/3) With Swedish summaries.*

DAVIS (KINGSLEY) Cities and mortality; [reprint of a paper delivered at the International Population Conference, Liege, 1973]. Berkeley, Ca., [1973]. pp. 22. *(California University. Institute of International Studies. Population Reprint Series. No. 433) With French summary.*

VALLIN (JACQUES) La mortalité par génération en France, depuis 1899. [Paris], 1973. pp. 483. *bibliog.* *(France. Institut National d'Etudes Démographiques. Travaux et Documents. Cahiers. No. 63)*

FRANKENSTEIN (PETER FRITZ) Die Sterblichkeit nach Todesursache und Zivilstand in der schweizerischen Wohnbevölkerung von 1941 bis 1960: eine statistische Analyse, etc. Zürich, 1974. pp. 204. *bibliog.*

— Tables.

GUATEMALA. Direccion General de Estadistica. Departamento de Estudios Especiales y Estadisticas Continuas. 1967. Tablas de vida, Republica de Guatemala, 1964; preparadas... por J. Antonio Barrera Tunchez... bajo la direccion y supervision [de] Luis Eduardo Contreras R. Guatemala, [1967]. pp. 67.

ARGENTINE REPUBLIC. Departamento de Atencion Medica. 1969. Mortalidad en la Republica Argentina: tasas especificas y ajustadas por edad y sexo y otros indicadores derivados de las estadisticas de mortalidad, 1959-1961. [Buenos Aires], 1969. pp. 79. *(Publicaciones. No.4)*

ARGENTINE REPUBLIC. Departamento de Atencion Medica. 1969. Mortalidad por causa, edad y sexo en la Republica Argentina, 1959-1961. [Buenos Aires, 1969]. pp. 197.

SWEDEN. Statistiska Centralbyrån. 1969. Dödsorsaksmönstret för perioden 1964-1966: frekvenser, dödstal, proportioner och indextal över den orsaksspecifika dödligheten; Mortality patterns by cause in 1964-1966: frequencies, death rates, proportions, and indexes of cause-specific mortality. Stockholm, 1969. pp. 109. *(Statistiska Meddelanden. Be/1969/3) In English and Swedish.*

SWEDEN. Statistiska Centralbyrån. 1969. Dödsorsaksmönstret och dödlighetsutvecklingen 1951-1966; Cause-of-death patterns and mortality trends in Sweden. Stockholm, 1969. 2 parts. *(Statistiska Meddelanden. Be/1969/2) In English and Swedish.*

ARGENTINE REPUBLIC. Departamento de Atencion Medica. 1970. Mortalidad en la Republica Argentina: tasas especificas y ajustadas por edad y sexo y otros indicadores derivados de las estadisticas de mortalidad, 1962-1965: comparacion trienio 1959- 1961 con cuatrienio 1962-1965. [Buenos Aires], 1970. pp. 95. *(Publicaciones. No.5)*

SOUTH AFRICA. Bureau of Statistics. Reports. No. 07-03-01. Report on deaths, 1963-1966, South Africa. Pretoria, [1971]. pp. 279. *In English and Afrikaans.*

SWEDEN. Statistiska Centralbyrån. 1971. Dödlighet och dödsorsaker med regional fördelning, 1964-1967; Mortality and causes of death by regions, 1964-1967. Stockholm, 1971. pp. 79. *(Sveriges Officiella Statistik) With summary and table headings etc. in English.*

MORTALITY. (Cont.)

SWITZERLAND. Bureau Fédéral de Statistique. 1973. Schweizerische Sterbetafel 1960-1970: Grundzahlen und Nettowerte, etc. Bern, 1973. pp. 89. (*Statistiques de la Suisse. 521e fasc.*) *In French and German.*

VALLIN (JACQUES) La mortalité par génération en France, depuis 1899. [Paris], 1973. pp. 483. *bibliog.* (*France. Institut National d'Etudes Démographiques. Travaux et Documents. Cahiers. No. 63*)

MOSCA (GAETANO).

ALBERTONI (ETTORE A.) Il pensiero politico di Gaetano Mosca: valori, miti, ideologia. Milano, 1973. pp. 166.

TANTURRI (RICCARDO) Pensiero e significato di Gaetano Mosca ed altri scritti. Padova, 1973. pp. 108.

MOSCOW

— Civic improvement.

FROLIC (B.M.) Moscow: the socialist alternative. 1972. fo. 109. *Typescript: unpublished.*

PASHCHENKO (N.E.) and SEGEDINOV (A.A.) Ekonomika gradostroitel'stva: na moskovskom opyte. Moskva, 1973. pp. 264.

— Directories.

MOSCOW. Moskovskaia Gorodskaia Spravochno-Informatsionnaia Kontora. Moskva, 1973: kratkaia adresno-spravochnaia kniga. Moskva, 1973. pp. 738.

MOSCOW UNIVERSITY.

PETROVSKII (IVAN GEORGIEVICH) Moscow University. London, 1955. pp. 52. (*[Russia. Soviet Embassy in London. Press Department]. Soviet Booklets. [2nd Series]. 18*)

MOSQUITO INDIANS.

NIETSCHMANN (BERNARD) Between land and water: the subsistence ecology of the Miskito Indians, Eastern Nicaragua. New York, 1973. pp. 279. *bibliog.*

MOTHERS.

MARSDEN (DENNIS) Mothers alone: poverty and the fatherless family. rev. ed. Harmondsworth, 1973. pp. 412.

STREATHER (JANE) and WEIR (STUART) Social insecurity: single mothers on benefit. London, 1974. pp. 62. (*Child Poverty Action Group. Poverty Pamphlets. 16*)

— Mortality.

MACAFEE (CHARLES HORNER GREER) and others. A report on an enquiry into maternal deaths in Northern Ireland, 1964-1967. Belfast, H.M.S.O., 1968. pp. 31.

MOTIER (MARIE JEAN PAUL ROCH YVES GILBERT) Marquis de la Fayette.

GOTTSCHALK (LOUIS REICHENTHAL) and MADDOX (MARGARET) Lafayette in the French revolution: from the October days through the Federation. Chicago, 1973. pp. 586.

MOTIVATION (PSYCHOLOGY).

VROOM (VICTOR HAROLD) and DECI (EDWARD L.) eds. Management and motivation: selected readings. Harmondsworth, 1970 repr. 1973. pp. 399. *bibliogs.*

SOCIETY FOR RESEARCH INTO HIGHER EDUCATION. Annual Conference, 8th, 1972. Motivation: non-cognitive aspects of student performance: papers... edited by Colin Flood Page and Jill Gibson. London, 1973. pp. 118. *bibliogs.*

TURNER (HOWARD M.) The people motivators: consumer and sales incentives in modern marketing. New York, [1973]. pp. 269.

MOTOR ABILITY

— Testing.

ANTHONY (HELEN SYLVIA) Depression, psychopathic personality and attempted suicide in a borstal sample; (a Home Office Research Unit report). London, 1973. pp. 43. *bibliog.* (*U.K. Home Office. Home Office Research Studies. 19*)

MOTOR BUS LINES

— United Kingdom.

KITCHIN (LESLIE DEANS) Bus operation: principles and practice for the transport student. London, 1947. pp. 164.

NATIONAL BUS COMPANY [U.K.]. Public transport after the Local Government Act: the role of the National Bus Company: organisation, planning, staff, training, maintenance, administration, and all associated requirements. [London, 1972]. 1 pamphlet (unpaged).

TURNS (KEITH L.) The independent bus: a historical survey of some independent bus operators. Newton Abbot, [1974]. pp. 208.

— — London.

WEBSTER (F.V.) and OLDFIELD (R.H.) A theoretical study of bus and car travel in central London. Crowthorne, 1972. pp. 22. (*U.K. Transport and Road Research Laboratory. Reports. LR 451*)

BRUCE (JAMES GRAEME) and CURTIS (COLIN HARTLEY) The London motor bus: its origins and development. London, [1973]. pp. 138. *bibliog.*

DAY (JOHN ROBERT) The story of the London bus: London and its buses from the horse bus to the present day. London, [1973]. pp. 148. *bibliog.*

MOTOR BUSES.

WIGAN (M. RAMSAY) and BAMFORD (T.J.G.) An equilibrium model of bus and car travel over a road network. Crowthorne, 1973. pp. 43. (*U.K. Transport and Road Research Laboratory. Reports. LR 559*)

MOTOR TRUCKS.

LORRIES and the world we live in; a report to the...Minister for Transport Industries; [D.E.A. Pettit, chairman of the Committee]. London, H.M.S.O., 1973. pp. 72.

SHARP (CLIFFORD H.) Living with the lorry: a study of the goods vehicle in the environment. [Mansfield, imprint, 1973]. pp. 194.

DAUTEL (PETER) Konzentration und Wettbewerb in der Herstellung und im Vertrieb von Lastkraftwagen in der Bundesrepublik Deutschland. Berlin, [1974]. pp. 226. *bibliog.*

MOTOR VEHICLES.

WORLD HEALTH ORGANIZATION. Expert Committee on Urban Air Pollution with Particular Reference to Motor Vehicles. 1969. Urban air pollution with particular reference to motor vehicles: report, etc. Geneva, 1969. pp. 53. (*Technical Report Series. No. 410*)

MOUNTAINS

— Switzerland.

FLUEKIGER (H.) Concetto generale dello sviluppo economico delle regioni di montagna in Svizzera: riassunto dei principali risultati di una perizia. Bellinzona, 1974. pp. 70. (*Ticino (Canton). Ufficio delle Ricerche Economiche. Documenti Economia di Montagna. 2*)

— — Ticino.

TICINO (CANTON). Ufficio delle Ricerche Economiche. 1973. Studi per il promovimento delle regioni di montagna: studi preliminari relativi all'applicazione delle direttive federali per il promovimento delle regioni di montagna. Bellinzona, 1973. 1 vol. (various pagings). (*Documenti Economia di Montagna. 1*)

MOUNTFORD (CHARLES PEARCY).

LAMSHED (MAX) 'Monty': the biography of C.P. Mountford. London, 1973. pp. 222.

MOURIDES.

ROCH (JEAN) Eléments d'analyse du système agricole en milieu wolof mouride: l'exemple de Darou Rahmane II. [Dakar], Office de la Recherche Scientifique et Technique Outre-Mer, Centre de Dakar-Hann, 1968. fo. 56. *bibliog.*

ROCH (JEAN) Les Mourides du vieux bassin arachidier sénégalais: entretiens recueillis dans la région du Baol. [Dakar], Office de la Recherche Scientifique et Technique Outre-Mer, Centre ORSTOM de Dakar-Hann, 1971. fo. 112.

MOVIMIENTO NACIONALISTA REVOLUCIONARIO.

MALLOY (JAMES M.) Bolivia's MNR: a study of a national popular movement in Latin America. Buffalo, N.Y., 1971. fo. 55. (*New York State University. Council on International Studies. Special Studies. No. 8*)

MOVING PICTURE INDUSTRY

— Finance.

FRANCE. Direction de la Documentation. La Documentation Française. Notes et Etudes Documentaires. Nos. 3,861-3, 862. L'aide dans le financement du film en France et à l'étranger; [par Claude Degand]. [Paris], 1972. pp. 60.

MOVING PICTURES.

UNITED NATIONS EDUCATIONAL, SCIENTIFIC AND CULTURAL ORGANIZATION. Department of Mass Communication. Reports and Papers on Mass Communication. Paris, 1953 in progress.

— Censorship — United Kingdom.

TREVELYAN (JOHN) O.B.E., M.A. What the censor saw. London, 1973. pp. 276.

MOVING PICTURES IN PROPAGANDA.

PIVASSET (JEAN) Essai sur la signification politique du cinéma: l'exemple français, de la libération aux événements de mai 1968. Paris, [1971]. pp. 637. *bibliog.*

MOYO (TEMBA).

MOYO (TEMBA) The organizer: story of Temba Moyo; (recorded and edited by Ole Gjerstad). Richmond, B.C., [1974]. pp. 86.

MOZAMBIQUE.

ABSHIRE (DAVID M.) and SAMUELS (MICHAEL A.) eds. Portuguese Africa: a handbook. New York, 1969. pp. 480.

— Nationalism.

COMMITTEE FOR FREEDOM IN MOZAMBIQUE, ANGOLA AND GUINE, and AFRICA RESEARCH GROUP. War on three fronts: the fight against Portuguese colonialism. London, [1972?]. pp. (44).

MACHEL (SAMORA MOISES) Mozambique: sowing the seeds of revolution. [London, 1974]. pp. 68.

— Politics and government.

INTERNATIONAL DEFENCE AND AID FUND [FOR SOUTHERN AFRICA]. Special Reports. No. 2. Terror in Tete: a documentary report of Portuguese atrocities in Tete district, Mozambique, 1971-1972. London, 1973. pp. 48.

HASTINGS (ADRIAN) Wiriyamu. London, 1974. pp. 158.

MUELLER (HERMANN).

MAURER (ILSE) Reichsfinanzen und Grosse Koalition: zur Geschichte des Reichskabinetts Müller, 1928-1930. Bern, 1973. pp. 269. *bibliog.*

MULTILINGUALISM.

LEWIS (E. GLYN) Multilingualism in the Soviet Union: aspects of language policy and its implementation. The Hague, 1972. pp. 332. *bibliog.*

MULTIPLIER (ECONOMICS).

ENGERING (F.A.) The monetary multiplier and the monetary model. Tilburg, 1973. pp. 37. *(Tilburg. Katholieke Hogeschool. Tilburg Institute of Economics. Research Memoranda. EIT 40)*

ORTMANN (FRIEDRICH) Überlegungen zur regionalpolitischen Anwendbarkeit des Multiplikatorkonzeptes. Tübingen, 1973. pp. 184. *bibliog. (Kiel. Universität. Institut für Weltwirtschaft. Kieler Studien. 122)*

SADLER (PETER G.) and others. Regional income multipliers: the Anglesey study. [Bangor], 1973. pp. 109. *(Wales. University. University College of North Wales. Bangor Occasional Papers in Economics. No.1)*

MULVANY (WILLIAM THOMAS).

HENDERSON (WILLIAM OTTO) William Thomas Mulvany: ein irischer Unternehmer im Ruhrgebiet, 1806-1885. Köln, 1970. pp. 20. *(Cologne. Universität. Forschungsinstitut für Sozial- und Wirtschaftsgeschichte. Kölner Vorträge zur Sozial- und Wirtschaftsgeschichte. Heft 12)*

MUNICH FOUR POWER AGREEMENT, 1938.

DOHERTY (JULIAN CAMPBELL) Das Ende des Appeasement: die britische Aussenpolitik, die Achsenmächte und Osteuropa nach dem Münchener Abkommen. Berlin, [1973]. pp. 284. *bibliog.*

MUNICIPAL COURTS

— United States.

JACOB (HERBERT) Urban justice: law and order in American cities. Englewood Cliffs, [1973]. pp. 145.

MUNICIPAL GOVERNMENT

— Austria.

KUBIN (ERNST) Die Gemeindeaufgaben und ihre Finanzierung: das zentrale Problem der Kommunen. [Linz, 1972]. pp. 343. *bibliog. (Linz. Hochschule für Sozial- und Wirtschaftswissenschaften. Institut für Kommunalwissenschaften and others. Kommunale Forschung in Österreich. 8)*

— Belgium.

WITTE (ELS) Politieke machtsstrijd in en om de voornaamste Belgische steden, 1830-1848. [Brussels], 1973. 2 vols. (in 1). *bibliog. (Pro Civitate. Collection Histoire. Série in-8.° No. 37) With English and French summaries.*

— Canada.

MASSON (JACK K.) and ANDERSON (JAMES D.) Emerging party politics in urban Canada. Toronto, [1972]. pp. 212. *bibliog.*

— — British Columbia.

BRITISH COLUMBIA. Department of Municipal Affairs. Municipal statistics, including regional districts. a., 1972- Victoria, B.C.

— France.

FRANCE. Direction de la Documentation. La Documentation Française. Notes et Etudes Documentaires. No. 3,758. Le conseil municipal; [by] J.L. Langlais. Paris, 1971. pp. 40.

FRANCE. French Embassy, London. Service de Presse et d'Information. 1972. Municipal organization in France. London, [1972]. pp. 35.

INSTITUTION communale et pouvoir politique: le cas de Roanne; [by] Sylvie Biarez [and others]. Paris, [1973]. pp. 208. *bibliog.*

— Guatemala.

COMMUNITY culture and national change: [essays by] Richard N.Adams [and others]; (Margaret A.L. Harrison, Robert Wauchope, editors). New Orleans, 1972. pp. 275. *bibliogs. (Tulane University of Louisiana. Middle American Research Institute. Publications. No.24)*

— Netherlands.

FRIESWIJK (JOHAN) Gemeentepolitiek en opbouwwerk: een verkenning van de problematiek aan de hand van de gebeurtenissen rond het opbouwwerk in Heerhugowaard. Deventer, 1973. pp. 77. *(Nederlands Instituut voor Maatschappelijke Opbouw. Nimocahiers. 13)*

— United Kingdom.

HENNOCK (E.P.) Fit and proper persons : ideal and reality in nineteenth-century urban government. Montreal, 1973. pp. 395. *bibliog.*

MARTIN (MICHAEL J.C.) Management science and urban problems;... in collaboration with W.B. Wells [and others]. Farnborough, Hants, [1974]. pp. 209. *bibliogs.*

— United States.

DAVID (STEPHEN M.) and PETERSON (PAUL E.) eds. Urban politics and public policy: the city in crisis. New York, 1973. pp. 337. *bibliogs.*

GABRIEL (RICHARD A.) The ethnic factor in the urban polity. New York, 1973. pp. 149.

GREENSTONE (J. DAVID) and PETERSON (PAUL E.) Race and authority in urban politics: community participation and the war on poverty. New York, [1973]. pp. 364.

YATES (DOUGLAS) Neighborhood democracy: the politics and impacts of decentralization. Lexington, Mass., [1973]. pp. 202. *bibliog.*

COLE (RICHARD L.) Citizen participation and the urban policy process. Lexington, Mass., [1974]. pp. 178. *bibliog.*

GRIFFITH (ERNEST STACEY) A history of American city government: the conspicuous failure, 1870-1900. New York, 1974. pp. 308.

INTEGRATED municipal information systems: the use of the computer in local government; [by] Kenneth L. Kraemer [and others]. New York, 1974. pp. 105. *bibliog.*

WASHNIS (GEORGE J.) Community development strategies: case studies of major model cities. New York, 1974. pp. 415.

MUNICIPAL POWERS AND SERVICES BEYOND CORPORATE LIMITS

— United States.

COSTIKYAN (EDWARD N.) and LEHMAN (MAXWELL) New strategies for regional cooperation: a model for the tri-state New York-New Jersey-Connecticut area. New York, 1973. pp. 93. *bibliog.*

MUNICIPAL RESEARCH.

CENTRE FOR ENVIRONMENTAL STUDIES. Information Papers. 23. Urban and regional research in the United Kingdom, 1972: an annotated list. London, 1972. pp. 125.

MUNICIPAL SERVICES

— United States — New York (City).

BERKOWITZ (MARVIN) The social costs of human underdevelopment: case study of seven New York City neighbourhoods. New York, 1974. pp. 299. *bibliog.*

MUNITIONS.

ENGELHARDT (KLAUS) and HEISE (KARL HEINZ) Militär-Industrie-Komplex im staatsmonopolistischen Herrschaftssystem. Berlin, 1974. pp. 304.

— Trade and manufacture — Russia.

ISTORIIA Tul'skogo oruzheinogo zavoda, 1712-1972, etc. Moskva, 1973. pp. 494. *bibliog.*

— Germany.

ENGELHARDT (KLAUS) and HEISE (KARL HEINZ) Militär-Industrie-Komplex im staatsmonopolistischen Herrschaftssystem. Berlin, 1974. pp. 304.

MURSI.

TURTON (DAVID ANTHONY) The social organisation of the Mursi: a pastoral tribe of the lower Omo valley, south west Ethiopia; [Ph.D. (London) thesis]. 1973. fo. 425. *bibliog. Typescript: unpublished. This thesis is the property of London University and may not be removed from the Library.*

MUSCAT AND OMAN.

See OMAN.

MUSEUMS

— Belgium.

MARTYNOW-REMICHE (ANNE) and WERY (CLAIRE) Le musée interdit: enquête sociologique sur le fait muséologique en milieu ouvrier dans la région liégeoise. Bruxelles, 1971. pp. 67. *bibliog. (Belgium. Direction Générale des Arts et des Lettres. Documentation et Enquêtes. No. 2)*

MUSIC AND SOCIETY.

GANE (MICHAEL JOHN) Social changes in English music and music-making, 1800-1970, with special reference to the symphony orchestra; [Ph.D. (London) thesis]. 1972 [or rather 1973]. fo. 233. *bibliog. Typescript: unpublished. This thesis is the property of London University and may not be removed from the Library.*

MUSIC FESTIVALS.

U.K. Advisory Committee on Pop Festivals. 1973. Pop festivals...: report and code of practice; [Dennis Stevenson, chairman]. London, 1973. pp. 147. *bibliog.*

MUSSOLINI (BENITO).

MUSSOLINI (BENITO) Corrispondenza inedita; a cura di Duilio Susmel. Milano, [1972]. pp. 263.

GALLO (MAX) Mussolini's Italy: twenty years of the fascist era;... translated by Charles Lam Markmann. New York, [1973]. pp. 452. *bibliog.*

LESSONA (ALESSANDRO) Un ministro di Mussolini racconta. Milano, 1973. pp. 223.

MUTASA (DIDYMUS NOEL EDWIN).

MUTASA (DIDYMUS NOEL EDWIN) Rhodesian black behind bars. London, 1974. pp. 150.

MUTINY

— Zaire.

STORME (MARCEL) La mutinerie militaire au Kasai en 1895: introduction. Bruxelles, 1970. pp. 162. *bibliog. (Académie Royale des Sciences d'Outre-Mer. Classe des Sciences Morales et Politiques. Meémoires in -8?. Nouvelle Série. [Tome] 38. [Fasc.] 4)*

MYDDLE

— History.

HEY (DAVID G.) An English rural community: Myddle under the Tudors and Stuarts. Leicester, 1974. pp. 260. *bibliog.*

— Rural conditions.

HEY (DAVID G.) An English rural community: Myddle under the Tudors and Stuarts. Leicester, 1974. pp. 260. *bibliog.*

MYSORE

— Rural conditions.

VENKATARAYAPPA (K.N.) Rural society and social change: (a study of some villages in Mysore). Bombay, 1973. pp. 264.

MYTHOLOGY.

HOCART (ARTHUR MAURICE) The life-giving myth and other essays;...edited...by Lord Raglan; second impression edited with a foreword by Rodney Needham. London, 1970 repr. 1973. pp. 252.

COURTES (JOSEPH) Lévi-Strauss et les contraintes de la pensée mythique: une lecture sémiotique des "Mythologiques". [Tours, 1973]. pp. 187.

NABARRO (Sir GERALD DAVID NUNES).

NABARRO (Sir GERALD DAVID NUNES) Exploits of a politician. London, [1973]. pp. 308.

NAESTVED

— Economic history.

HOLST (SVEND) Naestved Diskontobank 1871-1971: utraditionel byhistorie;... i anledning af... 100 aars jubilaeum, etc. Naestved, 1971. pp. 63.

NAGAS.

MAXWELL (NEVILLE G.A.) India and the Nagas. London, 1973. pp. 32. (*Minority Rights Group. Reports. No.17*)

NAGLER (ISIDORE).

HASKEL (HARRY) A leader of the garment workers: the biography of Isidore Nagler. New York, 1950. pp. 351. *bibliog.*

NAMES, GEOGRAPHICAL

— Russia — White Russia.

OSTROWSKI (WIKTOR) ed. The ancient names and early cartography of Byelorussia...material for historical research and study, etc. 2nd ed. London, 1971. pp. 24, 33 plates.

— United Kingdom.

U.K. Local Government Boundary Commission for England. 1972. Names for non-metropolitan districts. London, 1972. pp. (2). (*Circulars. 72/1*)

— — Yorkshire.

JENSEN (GILLIAN FELLOWS) Scandinavian settlement names in Yorkshire. Copenhagen, 1972. pp. 276. *bibliog.* (*Institut for Navneforskning. Navnestudier. Nr. 11*)

NAMUR (PROVINCE)

— Economic conditions.

BELGIUM. Administration de l'Urbanisme et de l'Aménagement du Territoire. 1971. Programme de développement et d'aménagement de la Province de Namur: pour une croissance humanisée. Namur, Bureau Economique de la Province de Namur, 1971. pp. 172. Atlas in end pocket.

— Economic policy.

BELGIUM. Administration de l'Urbanisme et de l'Aménagement du Territoire. 1971. Programme de développement et d'aménagement de la Province de Namur: pour une croissance humanisée. Namur, Bureau Economique de la Province de Namur, 1971. pp. 172. Atlas in end pocket.

NANAI.

See GOLDS.

NANCY.

FRANCE. Direction de la Documentation. La Documentation Française. Notes et Etudes Documentaires. Nos. 4,039-4, 040. Les villes françaises: Nancy et son agglomération, par Jean-Claude Bonnefont. [Paris], 1973. pp. 68. *bibliog.*

— Politics and government.

La CRISE politique nancéienne, 1969-1971; ([by] Serge Bonnet [and others]). Nancy, [1972]. pp. 268. *bibliog.* (*Nancy. Université 2. Faculte de Droit et des Sciences Economiques. Etudes et Travaux. Série "Sciences Politiques"*)

NANSA VALLEY.

CHRISTIAN (WILLIAM A.) Person and God in a Spanish valley. New York, [1972]. pp. 215. *bibliog.*

NANTES

— Growth.

ASSOCIATION DE RECHERCHES EN SCIENCES HUMAINES. Nantes, le centre-ville: étude des conditions sociologiques de la création du centre principal de fonctions tertiaires supérieures de la métropole Nantes-Saint-Nazaire. [Nantes, 1970-71]. 2 vols.

NAPALM.

STOCKHOLM INTERNATIONAL PEACE RESEARCH INSTITUTE. Napalm and incendiary weapons: legal and humanitarian aspects; SIPRI interim report [prepared by Malvern Lumsden from the papers of the SIPRI Symposium on Napalm and Incendiary Weapons held in Stockholm in 1972]. Stockholm, [1972]. fo. 125. *bibliog.*

NAPLES

— History.

COLAPIETRA (RAFFAELE) Dal Magnanimo a Masaniello: studi di storia meridionale nell'età moderna. Salerno, [1972-73]. 2 vols.

JACO (ALDO DE) Le quattro giornate di Napoli: la città insorge. 3rd ed. Roma, 1972. pp. 321.

BATTAGLINI (MARIO) ed. La rivoluzione giacobina del 1799 a Napoli: testi antologici da G.M. Galanti [and others]. Messina, 1973. pp. 185. *bibliog.*

VILLANI (PASQUALE) Mezzogiorno tra riforme e rivoluzione. 2nd ed. Bari, 1973. pp. 340.

— Industries.

VITIELLO (ANTONIO) Come nasce l'industria subalterna: il caso Alfasud a Napoli 1966-1972. Napoli, [1973]. pp. 99.

— Politics and government.

SCIROCCO (ALFONSO) Democrazia e socialismo a Napoli dopo l'unità, 1860-1878. Napoli, [1973]. pp. 365.

— Social history.

SERAO (MATILDE) Il ventre di Napoli; [reprint of work originally published in 1905] con introduzione di Gianni Infusino. [Naples, 1973]. pp. 125.

NAPOLÉON I, Emperor of the French.

FRANCE. Archives Nationales. 1969. Napoléon, tel qu'en lui-même; [exhibition held at the] Hôtel de Rohan, Paris, juin- décembre, 1969. Paris, 1969. pp. 144.

NAPOLEONE e l'Italia: (atti del convegno...) Roma, 8-13 ottobre 1969. Roma, 1973 in progress. (Accademia Nazionale dei Lincei. Problemi Attuali di Scienza e di Cultura. Quaderni. N. 179)

NARCOTIC ADDICTS

— United States.

WALDORF (DAN) Careers in dope. Englewood Cliffs, N.J., [1973]. pp. 186. *bibliog.*

NARCOTIC HABIT.

KAPLAN (R.G.) How to roll a perfect joint: an informative guide for the avid head; (... photos by Spo, etc.) San Francisco, [1966]. pp. 13.

SWEDEN. Narkomanvårdskommitté. 1967-1969. Narkotikaproblemet. Stockholm, 1967-1969. 4 vols. (*Sweden. Statens Offentliga Utredningar. 1967. 25, etc.*)

WORLD HEALTH ORGANIZATION. Expert Committee on Mental Health. 1967. Services for the prevention and treatment of dependence on alcohol and other drugs: fourteenth report of the...Committee, etc. Geneva, 1967. pp. 45. (*Technical Report Series. No. 363*)

BIEBERMAN (LISA) Phanerothyme: a western approch to the religious use of psychochemicals. Cambridge, Mass., [1968]. pp. 32.

FAKTA on narkotika och narkomani; [report of a working party set up by the Samarbetsorgan för Bekämpande av Narkotikamissbruk]. Stockholm, 1969. pp. 68.

SUPERWEED (MARY JANE) pseud. Herbal highs. n.p., Stone Kingdom Syndicate, [1970]. pp. 16. *Reissued by Unicorn Bookshop, Brighton.*

MITCHELL (ALEXANDER ROSS KERR) Drugs: the parents' dilemma;... with additional sections by Kenneth Myers [and] Terence Jones. 4th ed. London, 1972. pp. 158. *bibliog.*

NETHERLANDS. Werkgroep Verdovende Middelen. 1972. Background and risks of drug use: report of the Narcotics Working Party. The Hague, 1972. pp. 101.

ANGLO-AMERICAN CONFERENCE ON DRUG ABUSE, LONDON, 1973. Society's reaction: medicine's responsibility; proceedings of a conference sponsored jointly by the Royal Society of Medicine and the Royal Society of Medicine Foundation Inc...; editor R.A. Bowen. London, 1973. pp. 138.

CANADA. Commission of Inquiry into the Non-Medical Use of Drugs. 1973. Final report; [Gerald Le Dain, chairman]. Ottawa, 1973. pp. 1148. *bibliogs.*

GUINNESS (OS) The dust of death:... a critique of the establishment and the counter culture, and a proposal for a third way. London, 1973. pp. 416.

— Bibliography.

ITALY. Direzione Generale per gli Istituti di Prevenzione e di Pena. Ufficio Studi e Ricerche. 1971. La droga: aspetti sociologici e criminologici: bibliografia, 1950-1970. Roma, 1971. pp. 288. (*Quaderni. 1*)

— Australia — New South Wales.

NEW SOUTH WALES. Bureau of Crime Statistics and Research Drug offences. a., 1971 (1)- Sydney. (*Statistical Reports*)

— Canada.

CANADA. Commission of Inquiry into the Non-Medical Use of Drugs. 1973. Final report; [Gerald Le Dain, chairman]. Ottawa, 1973. pp. 1148. *bibliogs.*

— Sweden.

SWEDEN. Narkomanvårdskommitté. 1967-1969. Narkotikaproblemet. Stockholm, 1967-1969. 4 vols. (*Sweden. Statens Offentliga Utredningar. 1967. 25, etc.*)

FAKTA on narkotika och narkomani; [report of a working party set up by the Samarbetsorgan för Bekämpande av Narkotikamissbruk]. Stockholm, 1969. pp. 68.

— United Kingdom — Scotland.

CONSULTATIVE COMMITTEE OF MEDICAL OFFICERS OF HEALTH [SCOTLAND]. Misuse of drugs in Scotland; the second report of a Sub- Committee; [J.A. Ward, chairman]. Edinburgh, H.M.S.O., 1972. pp. 22.

— United States.

GOSHEN (CHARLES E.) Drinks, drugs, and do-gooders. New York, [1973]. pp. 268. *bibliog.*

GRUPP (STANLEY E.) The marihuana muddle. Lexington, [1973]. pp. 181.

SCHER (JORDAN M.) ed. Drug abuse in industry: growing corporate dilemma. Springfield, Ill., [1973]. pp. 312.

NARCOTIC LAWS — Bibliography.

ITALY. Direzione Generale per gli Istituti di Prevenzione e di Pena. Ufficio Studi e Ricerche. 1971. La droga: aspetti sociologici e criminologici: bibliografia, 1950-1970. Roma, 1971. pp. 288. *(Quaderni. 1)*

— Canada.

CANADA. Commission of Inquiry into the Non-Medical Use of Drugs. 1973. Final report; [Gerald Le Dain, chairman]. Ottawa, 1973. pp. 1148. *bibliogs.*

— United States.

BONNIE (RICHARD J.) and WHITEBREAD (CHARLES H.) The marihuana conviction: a history of marihuana prohibition in the United States. Charlottesville, 1974. pp. 368. *bibliog.*

NARCOTICS.

WORLD HEALTH ORGANIZATION. Technical Report Series. Geneva, 1950 in progress.

WORLD HEALTH ORGANIZATION. Expert Committee on Dependence- Producing Drugs. 1966. Fifteenth report. Geneva, 1966. pp. 18. *(Technical Report Series. No. 343)*

NARCOTICS, CONTROL OF.

PACE (DENNY F.) and STYLES (JIMMIE C.) Handbook of narcotics control. Englewood Cliffs, [1972]. pp. 95. *bibliog.*

TRUCKER'S Bible, summer 1974. [London], 1974. pp. 112.

NARCOTICS AND YOUTH

— Denmark.

DENMARK. Kontaktudvalget vedrørende Ungdomsnarkomanien. Forskningsunderudvalg. 1971. Udbredelse af stofbrug blandt danske skoleelever, af Boel Ulff- Møller [and others]. København, 1971. pp. 182.

ULFF-MØLLER (BOEL) Stofbrug blandt studerende: en redegørelse for brug af euforiserende stoffer bygget på svar fra 2812 studerende ved universiteter og højere laereanstalter, etc. København, 1973. pp. 294. *bibliog. (Socialforskningsinstituttet. Publikationer. 58)*

— United States.

JOHNSTON (LLOYD) Drugs and American youth;... a report from the youth in transition project. Ann Arbor, 1973. pp. 273. *bibliog.*

SPECK (ROSS V.) and others. The new families: youth, communes, and the politics of drugs. London, 1974. pp. 190. *First published in New York in 1972.*

NATAL

— History.

ROBERTS (BRIAN) The Zulu kings. London, 1974. pp. 388. *bibliog.*

— Population.

GRICE (DUCHESNE COWLEY) The approaching crisis: land and population in the Transvaal and Natal. Johannesburg, [1973]. pp. 22. *(South African Institute of Race Relations. Presidential Addresses. 1973)*

NATIONAL ASSOCIATION FOR MENTAL HEALTH.

ROLPH (C.H.) pseud. [i.e. Cecil Rolph HEWITT] Believe what you like: what happened between the Scientologists and the National Association for Mental Health. London, 1973. pp. 172.

NATIONAL CHARACTERISTICS, JAPANESE.

DE VOS (GEORGE A.) Socialization for achievement: essays on the cultural psychology of the Japanese...; with contributions by Hiroshi Wagatsuma [and others]. Berkeley, [1973]. pp. 597. *bibliog.*

KAHN (HERMAN) The emerging Japanese superstate: challenge and response; [paperback edition of work first published in the United States in 1970]. Harmondsworth, 1973. pp. 318. *bibliog.*

NATIONAL FRONT.

NATIONAL FRONT. For a new Britain: the manifesto of the National Front. Croydon, [1974]. pp. 26.

NATIONAL GREENBACK PARTY.

RICKER (RALPH ROSS) The Greenback-Labor movement in Pennsylvania. Bellefonte, [1966]. pp. 141. *bibliog.*

NATIONAL INCOME.

VAITSOS (CONSTANTINE V.) Intercountry income distribution and transnational enterprises. Oxford, 1974. pp. 198.

— Accounting.

ORGANISATION FOR ECONOMIC CO-OPERATION AND DEVELOPMENT. Department of Economics and Statistics. 1971. National accounts statistics, 1953-1969. [Paris, 1971]. pp. 453. *In English and French.*

CZAMANSKI (STANISLAW) Regional and interregional social accounting. Lexington, Mass., [1973]. pp. 204. *bibliog.*

— Australia — Accounting.

AUSTRALIA. Commonwealth Bureau of Census and Statistics. 1972. Australian national accounts: input-output tables, 1962-63; prepared... by J.P. O'Neill. Canberra, [1972]. pp. 205. *Chart in end pocket.*

— Austria — Accounting.

AUSTRIA. Statistisches Zentralamt. 1973. Input-Output-Tabelle 1964. Wien, 1973. pp. 152. *Folding table in end pocket.*

— Belgium.

BELGIUM. Institut National de Statistique. 1970. Les comptes nationaux de la Belgique, 1963-1969. [Brussels], 1970. pp. 39.

— Bolivia.

BOLIVIA. Ministerio de Planificacion y Coordinacion. 1970. Cuentas nacionales, 1950-1969. La Paz, [1970]. pp. 86. *(Revista de Planificacion y Desarrollo. 1)*

— Chile — Accounting.

CHILE. Oficina de Planificacion Nacional. 1973. Balances economicos de Chile, 1960-1970. Santiago, 1973. pp. 258. *(Serie 4. No.2. Balances Economicos)*

— Fiji Islands — Accounting.

FIJI. Bureau of Statistics. 1973. The national accounts of Fiji, 1968-1972. Suva, 1973. pp. 80. *(National Accounts Studies. Vol. 3)*

— Finland — Accounting.

FINLAND. Tilastokeskus. 1971. Kansantalouden tilinpito vuosina 1964-1971, I-II, etc. Helsinki, 1971. pp. 91. *(Tilastotiedotus. KT.1971.4)*

— France — Accounting.

FRANCE. Institut National de la Statistique et des Etudes Economiques. Collections de l'I.N.S.E.E. Série C. Comptes et Planification . Paris, 1969 in progress.

BAUCHET (PIERRE) Comptabilité nationale et analyse économique. [Paris, 1971]. pp. 283. *bibliog.*

FRANCE. Institut National de la Statistique et des Etudes Economiques. 1972. Les comptes de la nation, base 1962: les comptes des années 1949-1959. [Paris], 1972. pp. 60. *(France. Institut National de la Statistique et des Etudes Economiques. Collections de l'INSEE. Série C. Comptes et Planification. 13) Summaries in English and Spanish.*

NATIONAL INCOME.

— French Territory of the Afars and the Issas — Accounting.

FRANCE. Institut National de la Statistique et des Etudes Economiques. Direction Générale. 1970. Etude sur les comptes économiques du Territoire Français des Afars et des Issas, 1965-1966 - 1967-1968. Paris, 1970. pp. 51.

— Gabon — Accounting.

GABON. Direction de la Statistique et des Etudes Economiques. Comptes économiques. a., 1972- Libreville.

— Germany — Accounting.

GERMANY (BUNDESREPUBLIK). Statistisches Bundesamt. Ausgaben der öffentlichen Haushalte für Wirtschaftsförderung. bien., 1970/1971- Wiesbaden. *(Finanzen und Steuern. Reihe 5. Sonderbeiträge zur Finanzstatistik)*

— Germany, Eastern.

KECK (ALFRED) Leistung, Wachstum, Wohlstand: unser Nationaleinkommen, Quelle des gesellschaftlichen Reichtums. Berlin, 1973. pp. 152.

— Guadeloupe — Accounting.

FRANCE. Institut National de la Statistique et des Etudes Economiques. Direction Générale. 1970. Comptes économiques de la Guadeloupe. 1968. Paris, [1970?]. pp. 23.

— Italy — Accounting.

ITALY. Camera dei Deputati. Commissioni Permanenti. V. Bilancio. 1972. Problemi della spesa e della contabilità pubblica: indagine conoscitiva. [Rome], 1972. pp. 780. *(Italy. Servizio Commissioni Parlamentari. Indagini Conoscitive e Documentazioni Legislative. 14)*

— New Caledonia — Accounting.

FRANCE. Institut National de la Statistique et des Etudes Economiques. 1971. Etude sur les comptes économiques de la Nouvelle-Calédonie, 1960-1969. [Paris], 1971. pp. 115.

FRANCE. Institut National de la Statistique et des Etudes Economiques. 1972. Comptes économiques de la Nouvelle-Calédonie 1970. Paris, [1972?]. pp. 31.

— Pakistan.

KHAN (TAUFIQ M.) ed. Studies on national income and its distribution. Karachi, [1970]. pp. 191. *(Pakistan Institute of Development Economics. Readings in Development Economics. No.5)*

— Reunion Island — Accounting.

FRANCE. Institut National de la Statistique et des Etudes Economiques. Direction Générale. 1970. Comptes économiques de la Réunion 1968. Paris, [1970?]. pp. 27.

FRANCE. Institut National de la Statistique et des Etudes Economiques. Direction Générale. 1972. Comptes économiques de la Réunion 1970. Paris, [1972?]. pp. 25.

— Saint—Pierre and Miquelon — Accounting.

FRANCE. Institut National de la Statistique et des Etudes Economiques. 1964. Comptes économiques de Saint-Pierre et Miquelon 1960-1961. Paris, [1964?]. pp. 33.

— Samoa.

FAIRBAIRN (IAN J.) The national income of Western Samoa. Melbourne, 1973. pp. 215. *bibliog.*

— Senegal — Accounting.

SENEGAL. Direction de la Statistique. 1972. Comptes économiques, année 1969-70. Dakar, 1972. fo. 102.

— Thailand.

GOULD (JOSEPH S.) Estimates of gross national product and net national income of Thailand 1938/39, 1946, 1947 and 1948. [Bangkok], 1950. fo. 5.

NATIONAL INCOME (Cont.)

— United States — Accounting.

NATIONAL BUREAU OF ECONOMIC RESEARCH. Conference on Research in Income and Wealth. Studies in Income and Wealth. vol. 38. The measurement of economic and social performance: [papers presented in 1971]; Milton Moss, editor. New York, 1973. pp. 605.

DENISON (EDWARD FULTON) Accounting for United States economic growth, 1929-1969. Washington, D.C., [1974]. pp. 355.

— Upper Volta — Accounting.

UPPER VOLTA. Direction de la Statistique et de la Mécanographie. 1971. Comptes économiques de la Haute Volta 1968. [Paris], 1971. pp. 176. *2 tables in end pocket.*

— Yugoslavia — Accounting.

YUGOSLAVIA. Savezni Zavod za Statistiku. Studije, Analize i Prikazi. 61. Privredni bilansi Jugoslavije, 1966-1971; Economic balances of Yugoslavia, 1966-1971. Beograd, 1973. pp. 257. *With English summary.*

NATIONAL LIBERAL PARTY (GERMANY).

See LIBERAL PARTY — Germany.

NATIONAL PARKS AND RESERVES

— Switzerland.

URBAPLAN. Valorizzazione naturale dell'alta Valle Maggia: apporto economico e principi di organizzazione. Bellinzona, 1974. pp. 98. *bibliog. (Ticino (Canton). Ufficio delle Ricerche Economiche. Documenti Economia di Montagna. 10)*

— United Kingdom.

JACOBS (COLIN A.J.) The national parks in England and Wales. London, 1973. pp. 20. *(Institution of Municipal Engineers. Monographs. No. 16)*

— — Ireland, Northern.

IRELAND, NORTHERN. Nature Reserves Committee. Annual report.a., 1970/71 (5th)- Belfast.

— United States — Alaska.

RICH (PAMELA E.) and TUSSING (ARLON R.) The national park system in Alaska: an economic impact study. [Fairbanks], 1973. pp. 88. *(University of Alaska. Institute of Social, Economic and Government Research. ISEGR Reports. No. 35)*

NATIONAL SOCIALISM.

RASSE in Wissenschaft und Politik; ([essays by] Hugo Iltis [and others]). Prag, [1935]. pp. 48.

HENKYS (REINHARD) Die nationalsozialistischen Gewaltverbrechen: Geschichte und Gericht; mit...einem Beitrag von Jürgen Baumann; herausgegeben von Dietrich Goldschmidt. Stuttgart, [1964]. pp. 392. *bibliog.*

BOLLMUS (REINHARD) Das Amt Rosenberg und seine Gegner: Studien zum Machtkampf im nationalsozialistischen Herrschaftssystem. Stuttgart, 1970. pp. 360. *bibliog. (Institut für Zeitgeschichte. Studien zur Zeitgeschichte)*

PLESSE (SIGURD) Die nationalsozialistische Machtergreifung im Oberharz: Clausthal-Zellerfeld, 1929-1933. Clausthal-Zellerfeld, 1970. pp. 95.

RAMME (ALWIN) Der Sicherheitsdienst der SS: zu seiner Funktion im faschistischen Machtapparat und im Besatzungsregime des sogenannten Generalgouvernements Polen. [Berlin, 1970]. pp. 325. *bibliog. (Deutsche Akademie der Wissenschaften zu Berlin. Institut für Geschichte. Abteilung Militärgeschichte. Militärhistorische Studien. Neue Folge. 12) 8 tables and 1 map in end pocket.*

BRENNER (HILDEGARD) ed. Ende einer bürgerlichen Kunst-Institution: die politische Formierung der Preussischen Akademie der Künste ab 1933; (eine Dokumentation). Stuttgart, [1972]. pp. 174. *(Vierteljahrshefte für Zeitgeschichte. Schriftenreihe. Nr. 24)*

FAYE (JEAN PIERRE) Langages totalitaires. Paris, [1972]. pp. 771.

KRUEGER (ARND) Die Olympischen Spiele 1936 und die Weltmeinung: ihre aussenpolitische Bedeutung, unter besonderer Berücksichtigung der USA. Berlin, [1972]. pp. 255. *bibliog.*

BLEUEL (HANS PETER) Strength through joy: sex and society in Nazi Germany; edited... by Heinrich Fraenkel: translated from the German by J. Maxwell Brownjohn. London, 1973. pp. 272.

FAUST (ANSELM) Der Nationalsozialistische Deutsche Studentenbund: Studenten und Nationalsozialismus in der Weimarer Republik. Düsseldorf, 1973. 2 vols. (in 1). *bibliog.*

GRUPPE ARBEITERPOLITIK. Der Faschismus in Deutschland: Analysen der KPD-Opposition aus den Jahren 1928-1933: [selected articles from the periodical "Gegen den Strom", mainly by August Thalheimer]. Frankfurt am Main, [1973]. pp. 220. *bibliog.*

GUERIN (DANIEL) Fascism and big business; (translated from the French). New York, 1973. pp. 318.

HENNIG (EIKE) Thesen zur deutschen Sozial- und Wirtschaftsgeschichte, 1933 bis 1938. Frankfurt am Main, 1973. pp. 264. *bibliog.*

HILDEBRAND (KLAUS) The foreign policy of the Third Reich;... translated [from the German] by Anthony Fothergill. London, 1973. pp. 209. *bibliog.*

JACOBY (FRITZ) Die nationalsozialistische Herrschaftsübernahme an der Saar: die innenpolitischen Probleme der Rückgliederung des Saargebietes bis 1935. Saarbrücken, 1973. pp. 275. *bibliog. (Kommission für Saarländische Landesgeschichte und Volksforschung. Veröffentlichungen. 6)*

KEHRL (HANS) Krisenmanager im Dritten Reich: 6 Jahre Frieden, 6 Jahre Krieg; Erinnerungen; mit kritischen Anmerkungen und einem Nachwort, von Erwin Viefhaus. Düsseldorf, 1973. pp. 552.

KERN (ERICH) pseud. [i.e. Erich Knud KERNMAYR] Adolf Hitler und der Krieg: der Feldherr. Preuss. Oldendorf (Westf), 1973. pp. 462. *bibliog.*

KETTENACKER (LOTHAR) Nationalsozialistische Volkstumspolitik im Elsass. Stuttgart , 1973. pp. 389. *bibliog. (Institut für Zeitgeschichte. Studien zur Zeitgeschichte)*

LEVINE (HERBERT S.) Hitler's free city: a history of the Nazi party in Danzig, 1925-39. Chicago, 1973. pp. 223. *bibliog.*

MERSON (ALLAN LESLIE) Nazis and monopoly capital: new evidence reviewed;...(paper originally read in the history course of the Communist University in 1972). London, 1973. pp. 19. *(Communist Party of Great Britain. History Group. Our History. No.57)*

MYLLYNIEMI (SEPPO) Die Neuordnung der baltischen Länder 1941-1944: zum nationalsozialistischen Inhalt der deutschen Besatzungspolitik. Helsinki, 1973. pp. 308. *bibliog. (Suomen Historiallinen Seura. Historiallisia Tutkimuksia. 90)*

REICH (WILHELM) What is class consciousness?; [originally published in German in 1934 under the pseudonym of Ernst Parell]. 2nd ed. [London], 1973. pp. 76.

RIEDEL (MATTHIAS) Eisen und Kohle für das Dritte Reich: Paul Pleigers Stellung in der NS-Wirtschaft. Göttingen, [1973]. pp. 375. *bibliog.*

SOHN-RETHEL (ALFRED) Ökonomie und Klassenstruktur des deutschen Faschismus: Aufzeichnungen und Analysen; herausgegeben von Johannes Agnoli [and others]. Frankfurt am Main, 1973. pp. 210.

STEPHENS (FREDERICK J.) Hitler youth: history, organisation, uniforms and insignia. London, 1973. pp. 88. *bibliog.*

TERNON (YVES) and HELMAN (SOCRATE) Les médecins allemands et le national-socialisme: les métamorphoses du darwinisme. [Tournai, 1973]. pp. 219. *bibliog.*

VON MALTITZ (HORST) The evolution of Hitler's Germany: the ideology, the personality, the moment. New York, [1973]. pp. 479. *bibliog.*

WOLLSTEIN (GUENTER) Vom Weimarer Revisionismus zu Hitler: das Deutsche Reich und die Grossmächte in der Anfangsphase der nationalsozialistischen Herrschaft in Deutschland. Bonn, [1973]. pp. 325. *bibliog.*

ADLER (HANS GUENTHER) Der verwaltete Mensch: Studien zur Deportation der Juden aus Deutschland. Tübingen, 1974. pp. 1076. *bibliog.*

DIAMOND (SANDER A.) The Nazi movement in the United States, 1924-1941. Ithaca, 1974. pp. 380. *bibliog.*

FRANZ-WILLING (GEORG) Ursprung der Hitlerbewegung, 1919-1922. 2nd ed. Preussisch Oldendorf, 1974. pp. 391. *bibliog.*

KATER (MICHAEL H.) Das "Ahnenerbe" der SS, 1935-1945: ein Beitrag zur Kulturpolitik des Dritten Reiches. Stuttgart, 1974. pp. 523. *bibliog. (Institut für Zeitgeschichte. Studien zur Zeitgeschichte)*

LAACK-MICHEL (URSULA) Albrecht Haushofer und der Nationalsozialismus: ein Beitrag zur Zeitgeschichte. Stuttgart, [1974]. pp. 407. *bibliog.*

MASER (WERNER VIKTOR) Adolf Hitler: Mein Kampf; der Fahrplan eines Welteroberers: Geschichte, Auszüge, Kommentare. Esslingen, [1974]. pp. 454. *bibliog.*

SCHULZ (GERHARD) Faschismus, Nationalsozialismus: Versionen und theoreische Kontroversen, 1922-1972. Frankfurt/M, [1974]. pp. 222. *bibliog.*

TAYLOR (ROBERT R.) The word in stone: the role of architecture in the National Socialist ideology. Berkeley, [1974]. pp. 298. *bibliog.* Soviet Russia. London, 1974. pp. 286. *bibliog. (London. University. London School of Economics and Political Science. Centre for International Studies. International Studies)*

NATIONAL URBAN LEAGUE.

WEISS (NANCY JOAN) The National Urban League, 1910-1940. New York, 1974. pp. 402. *bibliog.*

NATIONALDEMOKRATISCHE PARTEI DEUTSCHLANDS [BUNDESREPUBLIK].

FINK (WILLIBALD) Die NPD bei der Bayerischen Landtagswahl, 1966: eine ökologische Wahlstudie. München, [1969]. pp. 110. *bibliog. (Hanns-Seidel-Stiftung. Berichte und Studien. Band 2)*

NATIONALISM.

INTERNATIONAL COMMITTEE OF HISTORICAL SCIENCES. Commission Internationale d'Histoire des Mouvements Sociaux et des Structures Sociales. Mouvements nationaux d'indépendance et classes populaires aux XIXe et XXe siècles en Occident et en Orient: [published under the general direction of Ernest Labrousse]. Paris, 1971. 2 vols. (in 1). *bibliogs. In French or English.*

Le NATIONALISME: facteur belligène; colloque des 4,5,6 mai 1971. Bruxelles, 1972. pp. 387. *(Brussels. Université Libre. Institut de Sociologie. Centre de Sociologie de la Guerre. Etudes de Sociologie de la Guerre)*

ZAGLADIN (V.V.) and RYZHENKO (F.D.) eds. Sovremennoe revoliutsionnoe dvizhenie i natsionalizm. Moskva, 1973. pp. 320.

BELL (WENDELL) and FREEMAN (WALTER E.) eds. Ethnicity and nation-building: comparative, international, and historical perspectives. Beverly Hills, [1974]. pp. 400. *bibliogs. Consists mainly of papers of the 12th Annual Convention of the International Studies Association.*

JONES (ROBERT TUDUR) The desire of nations. Llandybie, 1974. pp. 207.

NATIONALISM AND SOCIALISM.

DAVIS (HORACE BANCROFT) Nationalism and socialism: marxist and labor theories of nationalism to 1917. New York, [1967]. pp. 258. *bibliog.*

LIESS (OTTO RUDOLF) Sowjetische Nationalitätenstrategie als weltpolitisches Konzept. Wien, [1972]. pp. 226. *bibliog. (Forschungsstelle für Nationalitäten- und Sprachenfragen. Ethnos. Band 12)*

NATURAL RESOURCES.

CHELOVEK, obshchestvo i okruzhaiushchaia sreda: geograficheskie aspekty ispol'zovaniia estestvennykh resursov i sokhraneniia okruzhaiushchei sredy. Moskva, 1973. pp. 436. *bibliog.*

EUGENICS SOCIETY. Annual Symposium, 9th, 1972. Resources and population: proceedings...; edited by Bernard Benjamin [and others]. London, 1973. pp. 181. *bibliogs.*

— Bibliography.

WINTON (HARRY NATHANIEL MCQUILLIAN) ed. Man and the environment: a bibliography of selected publications of the United Nations system, 1946-1971. New York, 1972. pp. 305.

— Australia — Queensland.

AUSTRALIA. Department of National Development. 1969. Resources and industry of central Queensland; report. Canberra, 1969. pp. 131.

AUSTRALIA. Department of National Development. 1971. Resources and industry of far north Queensland; report. Canberra, 1971. pp. 199. *bibliogs.*

— Canada.

BURTON (THOMAS L.) Natural resource policy in Canada: issues and perspectives. Toronto, [1972]. pp. 174. *bibliog.*

NATURAL resource development in Canada: multi-disciplinary seminar [held at the University of Ottawa in 1970-71]; edited by Philippe Crabbé [and] Irene M. Spry. Ottawa, 1973. pp. 340. *bibliogs. (Ottawa. Université. Cahiers des Sciences Sociales. No.8) In English and French, with abstract in the alternative language.*

— Chile.

GALDAMES G. (JUAN) and AUDA J. (JAIME) Chile: un pais andino del Pacifico Sur. Santiago de Chile, [1972]. pp. 176.

— Norway.

NORWAY. Ressursutvalget. 1971 Innstilling nr. 2. [Oslo, 1971]. pp. 272, 104.

NORWAY. Ressursutvalget. 1972. Bruken av Norges naturressurser: prinsipper, krefter, problemer, retningslinjer; Norge gjennom 10,000 år: utredning nr. 3, etc. Oslo, 1972. pp. 132. *bibliog. (Norway. Norges Offentlige Utredninger. 1972.1)*

— Russia.

FEDORENKO (NIKOLAI PROKOF'EVICH) ed. Ekonomicheskie problemy optimizatsii prirodopol'zovaniia. Moskva, 1973. pp. 157.

CLEMENT (HERMANN) Die Roh- und Grundstoffwirtschaft der Sowjetunion: die Stellung ... in der internen sowjetischen Entwicklungspolitik. Hamburg, 1974. pp. 466. *bibliog. (Hamburg. Hamburgisches Welt-Wirtschafts-Archiv. Veröffentlichungen)*

— — Moldavian Republic.

TON (D.S.) and others. Prirodnye faktory i ekonomika proizvodstva. Kishinev, 1970. pp. 188. *bibliog.*

— United Kingdom — Scotland.

TIVY (JOY) ed. The organic resources of Scotland: their nature and evaluation. Edinburgh, 1973. pp. 227. *bibliog.*

— United States.

The AMERICAN environment: [papers from a seminar held at the Institute of United States Studies in the University of London]; edited by W.R. Mead. London, 1974. pp. 69. *(London. University. Institute of United States Studies. Monographs. 1)*

NATURAL RESOURCES, CONSERVATION OF.

See CONSERVATION OF NATURAL RESOURCES.

NATURE CONSERVATION

— United Kingdom.

U.K. Countryside Commission. 1971. Submission to Defence Lands Review Committee on the conservation of natural beauty and the use of the countryside for open-air recreation. [London], 1971. pp. 16.

TOURISM and conservation; report of a one-day conference sponsored by the English Tourist Board and the Countryside Commission in association with the Civic Trust and the Council for the Protection of Rural England..., 6 June, 1974. London, English Tourist Board, [1974]. fo. 42. *(Discussion Papers)*

NAVAHO INDIANS.

GILBREATH (KENT) Red capitalism: an analysis of the Navajo economy. Norman, Okla., [1973]. pp. 157. *bibliog.*

NAVAL ARCHITECTURE.

GOODRICH (G.J.) A quiet revolution: an inaugural lecture delivered at the University [of Southampton], 4th December 1973. Southampton, 1974. pp. 18.

NAVAL ART AND SCIENCE.

DENLINGER (HARRY SUTHERLAND) and GARY (CHARLES BINFORD) War in the Pacific: a study of navies, peoples and battle problems; [reprint of work first published in New York in 1936]. New York, 1970. pp. 338.

NAVAL HISTORY

— Bibliography.

HIGHAM (ROBIN) ed. Official histories: essays and bibliographies from around the world. Manhattan, Ka., 1970. pp. 644. *(Kansas State University of Agriculture and Applied Science. Library. Bibliography Series. No.8)*

NAVAL MUSEUMS.

MUZEI ISTORII GORODA RIGI I MOREKHODSTVA. Tezisy dokladov nauchnoi konferentsii, posviashchennoi 200-letiiu Muzeia istorii gor.Rigi i morekhodstva, Riga, 20/XI 1973 g. Riga, 1973. pp. 38.

NAVAL TACTICS.

DENLINGER (HARRY SUTHERLAND) and GARY (CHARLES BINFORD) War in the Pacific: a study of navies, peoples and battle problems; [reprint of work first published in New York in 1936]. New York, 1970. pp. 338.

NAVARRE

— Population.

CARRASCO PEREZ (JUAN) La poblacion de Navarra en el siglo XIV. Pamplona, 1973. pp. 703. *(Universidad de Navarra. Facultad de Filosofia y Letras. Coleccion Historica. 29)*

NEALE (EDWARD VANSITTART).

BACKSTROM (PHILIP N.) Christian Socialism and co-operation in Victorian England: Edward Vansittart Neale and the co-operative movement. London, 1974. pp. 238. *bibliog.*

NEBRASKA

— Politics and government.

PARSONS (STANLEY B.) The populist context: rural versus urban power on a Great Plains frontier. Westport, Conn., 1973. pp. 205. *bibliog.*

WYNER (ALAN J.) The Nebraska ombudsman: innovation in state government. Berkeley, 1974. pp. 160. *(California University. Institute of Governmental Studies. Ombudsman Research. Monographs)*

NECESSITY (LAW)

— Russia.

OVEZOV (NIKOLAI AGAMURADOVICH) K voprosu ob obstoiatel'stvakh, ustraniaiushchikh obshchestvennuiu opasnost' i protivopravnost' deianiia v sovetskom ugolovnom prave; otvetstvennyi redaktor... M.P. Karpushin. Ashkhabad, 1972. pp. 103.

NECHAEV (SERGEI GENNADIEVICH).

CONFINO (MICHAEL) ed. Daughter of a revolutionary: Natalie Herzen and the Bakunin- Nechayev circle;...translated by Hilary Sternberg and Lydia Bott. London, 1974. pp. 416.

NECKER (JACQUES).

GRANGE (HENRI) Les idées de Necker. Paris, 1974. pp. 669. *bibliog.*

NEGLIGENCE

— Ireland (Republic).

EIRE. Committee on Court Practice and Procedure. 1971. Fourteenth interim report...: liability of barristers and solicitors for professional negligence. Dublin, [1971]. pp. 14.

NEGOTIATION.

ILICH (JOHN) The art and skill of successful negotiation. Englewood Cliffs, [1973]. pp. 205.

— Mathematical models.

BARTOS (OTOMAR J.) Process and outcome of negotiations. New York, 1974. pp. 451. *bibliog.*

NEGRELLI (LUIGI).

ITALY. Ministero degli Affari Esteri. Comitato per la Documentazione dell'Opera dell'Italia in Africa. L'Italia in Africa. Serie Storica. Vol. 4. Luigi Negrelli e il Canale di Suez nelle carte del Fondo Maria Grois Negrelli. Tomi 1-2. 1846-1858, 1859-1869; a cura di Francesco Attilio Scaglione. Rome, 1971-72. 2 vols.

NEGRO—ENGLISH DIALECTS.

DILLARD (JOEY LEE) Black English: its history and usage in the United States. New York, [1972]. pp. 361. *bibliog.*

KOCHMAN (THOMAS) ed. Rappin' and stylin' out: communication in urban black America. Urbana, Ill., [1972]. pp. 424.

LABOV (WILLIAM) Language in the inner city: studies in the black English vernacular. Philadelphia, [1972]. pp. 412. *bibliog.*

NEGRO RACE

— Race identity.

NWIGWE (HENRY EMEZUEM) Black power re-examined: (new concept of black power). [Tadworth, Surrey, 1973]. pp. 17.

NEGRO TEACHERS.

SILVER (CATHERINE BODARD) Black teachers in urban schools: the case of Washington, D.C.. New York, 1973. pp. 222. *bibliog.*

MOORE (WILLIAM) Educationist, and WAGSTAFF (LONNIE H.) Black educators in white colleges. San Francisco, 1974. pp. 226. *bibliog.*

NEGRO UNIVERSITIES AND COLLEGES.

JONES (ANN) Uncle Tom's campus. New York, 1973. pp. 225.

NEGRO YOUTH

— United Kingdom.

HINES (VINCE) Black youth and the survival game in Britain. London, [1973]. pp. 50.

NEGROES.

NEGROES.

BROWN (INA CORINNE) Understanding race relations. Englewood Cliffs, [1973]. pp. 275. *bibliog.*

QUARLES (BENJAMIN) Allies for freedom: blacks and John Brown. New York, 1974. pp. 244. *bibliog.*

— Civil rights.

BLAND (RANDALL W.) Private pressure on public law: the legal career of Justice Thurgood Marshall. Port Washington, N.Y., 1973. pp. 206. *bibliog.*

SHERMAN (RICHARD B.) The Republican Party and black America: from McKinley to Hoover, 1896-1933. Charlottesville, Va., 1973. pp. 274.

WEISS (NANCY JOAN) The National Urban League, 1910-1940. New York, 1974. pp. 402. *bibliog.*

— Economic conditions.

BELL (CAROLYN SHAW) The economics of the ghetto. New York, [1970]. pp. 267.

BATES (TIMOTHY MASON) Black capitalism: a quantitative analysis. New York, 1973. pp. 140.

FUSFELD (DANIEL ROLAND) The basic economics of the urban racial crisis. New York, [1973]. pp. 122. *bibliog.*

— Education.

PIFER (ALAN J.) The higher education of blacks in the United States. Johannesburg, 1973. pp. 44. *bibliog. (South African Institute of Race Relations. Hoernlé Memorial Lectures. 1973)*

RIST (RAY C.) The urban school: a factory for failure; a study of education in American society. Cambridge, Mass., [1973]. pp. 265. *bibliog.*

LINDSEY (PAUL) and LINDSEY (OUIDA) Breaking the bonds of racism. Homewood, Ill., 1974. pp. 242. *bibliog.*

YOHALEM (ALICE M.) Desegregation and career goals: children of Air Force families. New York, 1974. pp. 140. *(Columbia University. Graduate School of Business. Conservation of Human Resources Studies)*

— Employment.

DUBINSKY (IRWIN) Reform in trade union discrimination in the construction industry: operation dig and its legacy. New York, 1973. pp. 311. *bibliog.*

SHANNON (LYLE WILLIAM) and SHANNON (MAGDALINE) Minority migrants in the urban community: Mexican-American and negro adjustment to industrial society. Beverly Hills, [1973]. pp. 351.

FONER (PHILIP SHELDON) Organized labor and the black worker, 1619-1973. New York, 1974. pp. 489. *bibliog.*

RUBIN (LESTER) The negro in the longshore industry. Philadelphia, [1974]. pp. 164. *(Pennsylvania University. Wharton School of Finance and Commerce. Industrial Research Unit. Racial Policies of American Industry. Report No. 29)*

SWIFT (WILLIAM S.) The negro in the offshore maritime industry. Philadelphia, [1974]. pp. 204. *(Pennsylvania University. Wharton School of Finance and Commerce. Industrial Research Unit. Racial Policies of American Industry. Report No. 30)*

WEISS (NANCY JOAN) The National Urban League, 1910-1940. New York, 1974. pp. 402. *bibliog.*

WRONG (ELAINE GALE) The negro in the apparel industry. Philadelphia, [1974]. pp. 170. *(Pennsylvania University. Wharton School of Finance and Commerce. Industrial Research Unit. Racial Policies of American Industry. Report No. 31)*

YOHALEM (ALICE M.) Desegregation and career goals: children of Air Force families. New York, 1974. pp. 140. *(Columbia University. Graduate School of Business. Conservation of Human Resources Studies)*

— Health and hygiene.

SEHAM (MAX) Blacks and American medical care. Minneapolis, [1973]. pp. 136.

— History.

PORTER (KENNETH WIGGINS) The negro on the American frontier. New York, 1971. pp. 529.

COX (LAWANDA C.) and COX (JOHN HENRY) eds. Reconstruction, the negro, and the new South. Columbia, S.C., 1973. pp. 425.

LEVY (EUGENE) Historian. James Weldon Johnson: black leader, black voice. Chicago, 1973. pp. 380. *bibliog.*

LYNCH (HOLLIS R.) The black urban condition: a documentary history, 1866-1971. New York, [1973]. pp. 469. *bibliog.*

ELLISON (MARY) The black experience: American blacks since 1865. London, 1974. pp. 334. *bibliog.*

JORDAN (WINTHROP D.) The white man's burden: historical origins of racism in the United States. New York, 1974. pp. 229. *bibliog.*

— — Sources.

HORNSBY (ALTON) ed. In the cage: eyewitness accounts of the freed Negro in Southern society, 1877-1929. Chicago, 1971. pp. 272.

— — Study and teaching.

FORD (NICK AARON) Black studies: threat or challenge. Port Washington, N.Y., 1973. pp. 217. *bibliog.*

— Legal status, laws, etc.

BALBUS (ISAAC D.) The dialectics of legal repression: black rebels before the American criminal courts. New York, [1973]. pp. 269.

SCHAUFELBERGER (ALFRED) Blacks and the trial by jury: the black man's experience in the courts. Bern, 1973. pp. 170. *bibliog.*

— Politics and suffrage.

HAWLEY (WILLIS D.) Blacks and metropolitan governance: the stakes of reform. Berkeley, Calif., 1972. pp. 34.

BUNCHE (RALPH JOHNSON) The political status of the negro in the age of FDR; edited... by Dewey W. Grantham. Chicago, 1973. pp. 682. *bibliog.*

WILLIAMS (JOYCE E.) Black community control: a study of transition in a Texas ghetto. New York, 1973. pp. 277. *bibliog.*

BUNI (ANDREW) Robert L. Vann of the Pittsburgh Courier: politics and black journalism. Pittsburgh, [1974]. pp. 410. *bibliog.*

THOMAS (TONY) ed. Black liberation and socialism. New York, 1974. pp. 207.

— Psychology.

CRAIN (ROBERT L.) and WEISMAN (CAROL SACHS) Discrimination, personality and achievement: a survey of northern blacks. New York, 1972. pp. 225.

— Segregation.

BLASSINGAME (JOHN W.) Black New Orleans, 1860-1880. Chicago, 1973. pp. 301. *bibliog.*

— Social conditions.

RAINWATER (LEE) and YANCEY (WILLIAM L.) The Moynihan Report and the politics of controversy:... including the full text of The negro family: the case for national action; by Daniel Patrick Moynihan. Cambridge, Mass., [1967] repr. 1969. pp. 493. *(Trans-action-Social Science and Modern Society. Social Science and Public Policy Reports)*

CRAIN (ROBERT L.) and WEISMAN (CAROL SACHS) Discrimination, personality and achievement: a survey of northern blacks. New York, 1972. pp. 225.

HALPERN (FLORENCE) Survival: black/white. New York, [1973]. pp. 238. *bibliog.*

O'TOOLE (JAMES) Watts and Woodstock: identity and culture in the United States and South Africa. New York, [1973]. pp. 154. *bibliog.*

— — Study and teaching.

FORD (NICK AARON) Black studies: threat or challenge. Port Washington, N.Y., 1973. pp. 217. *bibliog.*

— Social life and customs.

KOCHMAN (THOMAS) ed. Rappin' and stylin' out: communication in urban black America. Urbana, Ill., [1972]. pp. 424.

— Detroit.

KATZMAN (DAVID M.) Before the ghetto: black Detroit in the nineteenth century. Urbana, Ill., [1973]. pp. 254. *bibliog.*

— Los Angeles.

O'TOOLE (JAMES) Watts and Woodstock: identity and culture in the United States and South Africa. New York, [1973]. pp. 154. *bibliog.*

— New Orleans.

BLASSINGAME (JOHN W.) Black New Orleans, 1860-1880. Chicago, 1973. pp. 301. *bibliog.*

— Texas.

WILLIAMS (JOYCE E.) Black community control: a study of transition in a Texas ghetto. New York, 1973. pp. 277. *bibliog.*

— Virginia.

CRAVEN (WESLEY FRANK) White, red, and black: the seventeenth-century Virginian. Charlottesville, 1971. pp. 114. *(Virginia University. Richard Lectures. 1970)*

NEGROES AS BUSINESSMEN.

BATES (TIMOTHY MASON) Black capitalism: a quantitative analysis. New York, 1973. pp. 140.

CAPLOVITZ (DAVID) The merchants of Harlem: a study of small business in a black community. Beverly Hills, [1973]. pp. 191. *bibliog.*

PURYEAR (ALVIN N.) and WEST (CHARLES A.) Black enterprise, inc.: case studies of a new experiment in black business development. Garden City, N.Y., 1973. pp. 462. *bibliog.*

NEGROES AS SOLDIERS.

MULLEN (ROBERT W.) Blacks in America's wars: the shift in attitudes from the revolutionary war to Vietnam. New York, 1973. pp. 96. *bibliog.*

NEGROES IN BRAZIL.

FERNANDES (FLORESTAN) O negro no mundo dos brancos. São Paulo, 1972. pp. 285.

NEGROES IN PORTUGAL.

BRASIO (ANTONIO) Os pretos em Portugal. Lisboa, 1944. pp. 123. *(Portugal. Agência Geral das Colonias. Divisão de Publicações e Biblioteca. Colecção Pelo Imperio. No. 101)*

NEGROES IN SOUTH AFRICA.

BLACK review 1972; editor B.A. Khoapa; published by Black Community Programmes. Durban, 1973. pp. 227.

MANAGEMENT responsibility and African employment in South Africa; report of a panel investigation; [edited by W.H. Thomas]. Johannesburg, 1973. pp. 142.

PILLAY (P. NESEN) Poverty datum line study among Africans in Durban. Durban, 1973. pp. 34. *(Natal. University. Department of Economics. Occasional Papers. No. 3)*

MAASDORP (GAVIN G.) Economic development strategy in the African homelands: the rôle of agriculture and industry;... paper given at the 44th council meeting of the S[outh] A[frican] Institute of Race Relations, Cape Town, January 1974. Johannesburg, 1974. pp. 38. *bibliog.*

NEGROES IN THE UNITED KINGDOM.

HINES (VINCE) Britain, the black man and the future. 2nd ed. London, 1972. pp. 47. *bibliog.*

ONYEAMA (DILLIBE) John Bull's nigger. London, 1974. pp. 159.

SHYLLON (F.O.) Black slaves in Britain. London, 1974. pp. 252. *bibliog.*

NEHRU (JAWAHARLAL).

NANDA (B.R.) Gokhale, Gandhi and the Nehrus: studies in Indian nationalism. London, 1974. pp. 203.

NEHRU (MOTILAL).

NANDA (B.R.) Gokhale, Gandhi and the Nehrus: studies in Indian nationalism. London, 1974. pp. 203.

NEOSCHOLASTICISM.

THIBAULT (PIERRE) Savoir et pouvoir: philosophie thomiste et politique cléricale au XIXe siècle. Québec, 1972. pp. 252. *bibliog.*

NEPAL

— **Economic conditions.**

ECONOMIC AFFAIRS REPORT, THE; pd. by the Ministry of Economic Planning [Nepal]. q., Ag 1966 - F 1968 (v.4, no.3 - v.6, no.1); ceased pbln. Kathmandu.

— **Economic policy.**

ECONOMIC AFFAIRS REPORT, THE; pd. by the Ministry of Economic Planning [Nepal]. q., Ag 1966 - F 1968 (v.4, no.3 - v.6, no.1); ceased pbln. Kathmandu.

SEMINAR ON POPULATION AND DEVELOPMENT, KATHMANDU, 1971. Population and development; proceedings of the seminar... organized by Centre for Economic Development and Administration, etc. Kathmandu, [1971]. pp. 201. *bibliogs. (Kathmandu. Centre for Economic Development and Administration. Study Series. Seminar Papers. No.2)*

— **Foreign economic relations — India.**

RAWAT (POORAN CHAND) Indo-Nepal economic relations. Delhi, 1974. pp. 287.

— **Foreign relations.**

MUNI (S.D.) Foreign policy of Nepal. Delhi, 1973. pp. 320. *bibliog.*

— **Population.**

SEMINAR ON POPULATION AND DEVELOPMENT, KATHMANDU, 1971. Population and development; proceedings of the seminar... organized by Centre for Economic Development and Administration, etc. Kathmandu, [1971]. pp. 201. *bibliogs. (Kathmandu. Centre for Economic Development and Administration. Study Series. Seminar Papers. No.2)*

— **Social policy.**

SEMINAR ON POPULATION AND DEVELOPMENT, KATHMANDU, 1971. Population and development; proceedings of the seminar... organized by Centre for Economic Development and Administration, etc. Kathmandu, [1971]. pp. 201. *bibliogs. (Kathmandu. Centre for Economic Development and Administration. Study Series. Seminar Papers. No.2)*

NER (JACQUES ELIE HENRI AMBROISE MATHIEU ERNEST). See RYNER (HAN) pseud.

NETHERLANDS

— **Armed forces.**

NETHERLANDS. Commissie van Civiele en Militaire Deskundigen. 1972. De toekomst van de Nederlandse defensie: bevindingen en aanbevelingen van de Commissie, etc. [with] Bijlage: Dienstvervulling naar keuze: een weg tot vergroting van het vrijwilligersaandeel bij de Nederlandse krijgsmacht. 's-Gravenhage, 1972. 2 pts.

— **Boundaries.**

MROHS (EDMUND) and HUEKELS (J.M.) Die Grenze: Trennung oder Begegnung: eine Untersuchung über die Bedeutung der Grenze und der Grenzverwischung im deutsch-niederländischen Grenzraum Achterhoek und Borken/Bocholt. 's-Gravenhage, Staatsuitgeverij, 1970. 2 pts. *In German and Dutch, with summaries in English and French.*

— **Colonies — History.**

SMITH (GEORGE L.) Religion and trade in New Netherland: Dutch origins and American development. Ithaca, 1973. pp. 266. *bibliog.*

— **Commerce.**

SPADING (KLAUS) Holland und die Hanse im 15. Jahrhundert: zur Problematik des Übergangs vom Feudalismus zum Kapitalismus. Weimar, 1973. pp. 189. *bibliog. (Historiker-Gesellschaft der Deutschen Demokratischen Republik. Hansische Arbeitsgemeinschaft. Abhandlungen zur Handels- und Sozialgeschichte. Band 12)*

— — **Germany.**

ROEHLK (FRAUKE) Schiffahrt und Handel zwischen Hamburg und den Niederlanden in der zweiten Hälfte des 18. und zu Beginn des 19. Jahrhunderts. Wiesbaden, 1973. 2 vols. (in 1). *bibliog. (Vierteljahrschrift für Sozial- und Wirtschaftsgeschichte. Beihefte. Nr.60) Table in end pocket.*

— **Constitution.**

NETHERLANDS. Ministerie van Binnenlandse Zaken. Naar een nieuwe grondwet? Documentatiereeks. Deel 3. Adviezen van politieke en maatschappelijke organen over vernieuwing van grondwet en kieswet (juni 1968-juli 1969); onder redactie van H.Th.J.F. van Maarseveen met medewerking van J.L. Bouwens. 's-Gravenhage, 1969. pp. 198.

NETHERLANDS. Ministerie van Binnenlandse Zaken. Naar een nieuwe grondwet? Documentatiereeks. Deel 4. Adviezen van politieke en maatschappelijke organen over vernieuwing van grondwet en kieswet (augustus 1969-januari 1970); onder redactie van H. Th. J. F. van Maarseveen met medewerking van J.L. Bouwens. 's-Gravenhage, 1970. pp. 76.

NETHERLANDS. Constitution. 1972. Grondwet voor het Koninkrijk der Nederlanden: tekst zoals deze luidt na de laatstelijk blijkens de wetten van 10 februari 1972...en 11 maart 1972 aangebrachte veranderingen. 's-Gravenhage, Staatsuitgeverij, 1972. pp. 45.

— **Constitutional history.**

LEEB (I. LEONARD) The ideological origins of the Batavian revolution; history and politics in the Dutch republic 1747-1800. The Hague, 1973. pp. 300. *bibliog.*

— **Defences.**

NETHERLANDS. Commissie van Civiele en Militaire Deskundigen. 1972. De toekomst van de Nederlandse defensie: bevindingen en aanbevelingen van de Commissie, etc. [with] Bijlage: Dienstvervulling naar keuze: een weg tot vergroting van het vrijwilligersaandeel bij de Nederlandse krijgsmacht. 's-Gravenhage, 1972. 2 pts.

— **Economic conditions.**

BEGEER (WILLEM) and others, eds. Economie dezer dagen: (opstellen aangeboden aan prof. drs. H.W. Lambers ter gelegenheid van zijn 25-jarig hoogleraarschap aan de Nederlandse Economische Hogeschool). Rotterdam, 1973. pp. 345. *bibliog.*

— **Economic history.**

DE VRIES (JAN) The Dutch rural economy in the golden age, 1500-1700. New Haven, Conn., 1974. pp. 316. *bibliog.*

— **Economic policy.**

TIMMERS (JACOBUS) Geld en geldpolitiek: enige beschouwingen over het werkterrein van het monetaire beleid in het bijzonder ten aanzien van de Nederlandse economie met een semi-geleid en open karakter. Arnhem, 1971. pp. 207. *bibliog. With English summary.*

ZANEN (TEUN JAN) Noord Nederland, een kolonie?. Amsterdam, 1973. pp. 143. *bibliog.*

— **Emigration and immigration.**

AMERSFOORT (J.M.M. VAN) Immigratie en minderheidsvorming: een analyse van de Nederlandse situatie 1945-1973. Alphen aan den Rijn, 1974. pp. 242. *bibliog.*

— **Foreign relations — Europe.**

TAMSE (C.A.) Nederland en België in Europa, 1859-1871: de zelfstandigheidspolitiek van twee kleine staten. Den Haag, 1973. pp. 371. *bibliog.*

— **Government publications.**

NETHERLANDS. Ministerie van Volksgezondheid en Milieuhygiëne. 1971. Vijftig jaar Verslagen en mededelingen. 's-Gravenhage, 1971. pp. 209. *(Verslagen en Mededelingen [betreffende de] Volksgezondheid. 1971. 1)*

— **History — 1714—1795.**

LEEB (I. LEONARD) The ideological origins of the Batavian revolution; history and politics in the Dutch republic 1747-1800. The Hague, 1973. pp. 300. *bibliog.*

— — **1945— .**

HOFLAND (H.J.A.) Tegels lichten, of ware verhalen over de autoriteiten in het land van de voldongen feiten. Amsterdam, 1972. pp. 224.

— **Industries.**

JANSEN (A.C.M.) and SMIDT (M. DE) Industrie en ruimte: de industriële ontwikkeling van Nederland in een veranderend sociaal-ruimtelijk bestel. Assen, 1974. pp. 202.

— **Parliament.**

NETHERLANDS. Staten-Generaal. Tweede Kamer. 1970. De Tweede Kamer der Staten-Generaal. 's-Gravenhage, 1970. 1 pamphlet (unpaged).

— — **Elections.**

WERKGROEP NATIONAAL VERKIEZINGSONDERZOEK. De Nederlandse kiezer '73. Alphen aan den Rijn, 1973. pp. 161.

— **Politics and government.**

NETHERLANDS. Ministerie van Binnenlandse Zaken. 1969. Nota bestuurlijke organisatie, etc. 's-Gravenhage, 1969. pp. 16.

HOOGERWERF (A.) Politiek in beweging: een bundel politicologische schetsen. Alphen aan den Rijn, 1971. pp. 161.

INSTITUUT VOOR BESTUURSWETENSCHAPPEN [NETHERLANDS]. Onderzoek naar de bestuurlijke organisatie. Rijswijk, 1972 in progress.

SINNER (LOUIS) De wortels van de Nederlandse politiek: de tweeënveertig politieke partijen sinds 1848. Amsterdam, 1973. pp. 229.

BERG (J.TH.J.VAN DEN) and MOLLEMAN (H.A.A.) Crisis in de Nederlandse politiek. Alphen aan den Rijn, 1974. pp. 226.

DAALDER (HANS) Politisering en lijdelijkheid in de Nederlandse politiek. Assen, 1974. pp. 78.

NETHERLANDS. (Cont.)

— Population.

NETHERLANDS. Centraal Bureau voor de Statistiek. 1973. De toekomstige nederlandse bevolkingsontwikkeling na 1972. 's-Gravenhage, 1973. pp. 76.

— Social conditions.

HOFLAND (H.J.A.) Tegels lichten, of ware verhalen over de autoriteiten in het land van de voldongen feiten. Amsterdam, 1972. pp. 224.

SWAAN (ABRAM DE) Een boterham met tevredenheid: gesprekken met arbeiders. Amsterdam, 1972. pp. 144.

VAN onderen: brieven, interviews, gedichten en verhalen uit de arbeidswereld; met een nawoord van C. Poppe. Amsterdam, 1972. pp. 116.

— Social history.

DE VRIES (JAN) The Dutch rural economy in the golden age, 1500-1700. New Haven, Conn., 1974. pp. 316. *bibliog.*

— Social policy.

OMMEN (L.B. VAN) Cultural aspects of welfare policy: a collection of introductions. Rijswijk, Ministry of Cultural Affairs, Recreation and Social Welfare, 1969. pp. 45.

NETHERLANDS. Commissie Voorbereiding Onderzoek Toekomstige Maatschappij-Structuur. 1970. Rapport. 's-Gravenhage, 1970. pp. 25.

— Statistics, Vital.

KERSSEBOOM (WILLEM) Essais d'arithmétique politique: contenant trois traités sur la population de la province de Hollande et Frise occidentale, la durée de survie des veuves, la durée des mariages, la relation entre la population et le nombre de naissances, le nombre de couples, etc.;...[and] Kersseboom et son oeuvre: la table de mortalité; par M. van Haaften. [Paris], Institut National d'Etudes Démographiques, 1970. pp. 171. *bibliog.*

NETHERLANDS ANTILLES.

NETHERLANDS ANTILLES. 1956. Netherlands Antilles. [Willemstad, 1956]. fo. 7.

— History — Sources.

MEILINK-ROELOFSZ (M. ANTOINETTE P.) A survey of archives in the Netherlands pertaining to the history of the Netherlands Antilles. [The Hague, Algemeen Rijksarchief, 1968]. pp. 53. *Reprinted from 'De West-Indische Gids', XXXV, 1954/5.*

NETWORK ANALYSIS (PLANNING).

STEENBRINK (PETER ANTONIUS) Optimization of transport networks. [Rotterdam, 1974]. pp. 328. *bibliogs. With Dutch summary.*

NEURATH (OTTO).

NEURATH (OTTO) Empiricism and sociology; [selections from his writings]; edited by Marie Neurath and Robert S. Cohen; with a selection of biographical and autobiographical sketches. Dordrecht, [1973]. pp. 473. *bibliog.*

NEUROLOGY.

WHITAKER (HARRY A.) On the representation of language in the human brain: problems in the neurology of language and the linguistic analysis of aphasia. Edmonton, [1971]. pp. 224. *bibliog.*

NEUTRALITY.

CONFERENCE OF HEADS OF STATE OR GOVERNMENT OF NON-ALIGNED COUNTRIES. Neither East nor West: the basic documents of non-alignment [selected from the proceedings of the 1st-3rd conferences, 1961, 1964 and 1970]; edited by Henry M. Christman. New York, [1973]. pp. 206.

NEVADA (STATE)

— Foreign population.

ETEROVICH (ADAM SLAV.) Yugoslavs in Nevada 1859-1900: Croatians, Dalmatians, Montenegrins, Hercegovinians. San Francisco, 1973. pp. 263. *bibliog.*

NEW BRUNSWICK

— Social policy.

NEW BRUNSWICK. Task Force on Social Development. 1971. Participation and development;...report; [Emery LeBlanc and Harold L. Nutter, chairmen]. [Fredericton], 1971. 3 vols. (in 1) *bibliog.*

NEW CALEDONIA

— Economic conditions.

ROCHETEAU (G.) Le nord de la Nouvelle-Calédonie région économique. Paris, Office de la Recherche Scientifique et Technique Outre-Mer, 1968 [or rather 1969]. pp. 132. *(Mémoires O.R.S.T.O.M. 32)*

NEW DURHAM

— Politics and government.

NEW DURHAM. County Council. Minutes; [and Reports]. irreg., F 5 1974[1st]- [Durham].

NEW ENGLAND

— Economic history.

CARROLL (CHARLES F.) The timber economy of Puritan New England. Providence, [1973]. pp. 221.

— Economic policy.

NEW ENGLAND REGIONAL COMMISSION. Regional development plan: summary. Boston, [1973?]. pp. 98.

— Intellectual life.

MORISON (SAMUEL ELIOT) The intellectual life of colonial New England. New York, 1956. pp. 288.

— Social policy.

NEW ENGLAND REGIONAL COMMISSION. Regional development plan: summary. Boston, [1973?]. pp. 98.

NEW GUINEA

— Economic policy.

PAPUA AND NEW GUINEA, TERRITORY OF. Central Planning Office. 1973. Papua New Guinea's improvement plan for 1973-74; (with Districts supplement); prepared...by authority of the Cabinet Committee on Planning. Port Moresby, 1973. 2 pts. (in 1).

— Social policy.

PAPUA AND NEW GUINEA, TERRITORY OF. Central Planning Office. 1973. Papua New Guinea's improvement plan for 1973-74; (with Districts supplement); prepared...by authority of the Cabinet Committee on Planning. Port Moresby, 1973. 2 pts. (in 1).

— Statistics.

PAPUA AND NEW GUINEA, TERRITORY OF. Bureau of Statistics. Statistical bulletin: monthly abstract of statistics. m. (approx.) Ja - Oc/N 1971 (with certain figures from Je 1966). Konedobu.

NEW HAVEN

— Civic improvement.

PATTERNS of urban change: the New Haven experience; [by] David Birch [and others]. Lexington, [1974]. pp. 161. *bibliogs.*

NEW HEBRIDES

— Census.

NEW HEBRIDES. Census, 1967. Le recensement du Condominium des Nouvelles-Hébrides 1967: principaux résultats. Paris, Institut National de la Statistique et des Etudes Economiques, [1973?]. pp. 49.

— Commerce — Statistics.

NEW HEBRIDES. Condominium Bureau of Statistics. Statistical bulletin: Principal exports: tonnages by port and country [and]: Copra: stocked and received for export at Vila and Santo. m., F 1974- Vila. *In English and French.*

— Politics and government.

BENOIST (HUBERT) Le condominium des Nouvelles-Hébrides et la société mélanésienne. Paris, [1972]. pp. 230. *bibliog.*

— Population.

BEDFORD (R.D.) New Hebridean mobility: a study of circular migration. Canberra, 1973. pp. 164. *bibliog. (Australian National University. Research School of Pacific Studies. Department of Human Geography. Publications. HG/9)*

— Social conditions.

BENOIST (HUBERT) Le condominium des Nouvelles-Hébrides et la société mélanésienne. Paris, [1972]. pp. 230. *bibliog.*

NEW MEXICO

— Economic conditions.

VAN DRESSER (PETER) Development on a human scale. New York, 1973. pp. 116.

NEW ORLEANS

— Social history.

BLASSINGAME (JOHN W.) Black New Orleans, 1860-1880. Chicago, 1973. pp. 301. *bibliog.*

NEW SOUTH WALES

— Economic conditions.

WOOLMINGTON (E.R.) Symptoms of underdevelopment in northern New South Wales; (a study undertaken by the Department of Geography, University of New England, Armidale N.S.W. for the Clarence and Richmond-Tweed regional development committees and the N.S.W. Department of Decentralisation. [Sydney], 1968. pp. 102. *(University of New England, Armidale. Department of Geography. Research Series in Applied Geography. No. 8)*

— Economic policy.

NEW SOUTH WALES. Premier's Department. Upper Hunter Regional Development Committee. 1968. Report on development of the upper Hunter region. [Sydney, 1968]. pp. 58, 1 map. *Loose-leaf binder.*

— History.

MOLONY (JOHN N.) An architect of freedom: John Hubert Plunkett in New South Wales, 1832-1869. Canberra, 1973. pp. 313. *bibliog.*

— Parliament — Elections.

MACKERRAS (MALCOLM) New South Wales elections. Canberra, 1973. pp. 209.

NEW WINDSOR

— History — Sources.

NEW WINDSOR. The fifth hall book of the Borough of New Windsor, 1828-1852; edited, with an introduction, by Raymond South. New Windsor, 1974. pp. 210. *(New Windsor. Windsor Borough Historical Records Publications. vol. 3)*

— Politics and government.

NEW WINDSOR. The fifth hall book of the Borough of New Windsor, 1828-1852; edited, with an introduction, by Raymond South. New Windsor, 1974. pp. 210. (New Windsor. Windsor Borough Historical Records Publications. vol. 3)

NEW YORK (CITY).

FRANCE. Direction de la Documentation. La Documentation Française. Notes et Etudes Documentaires. Nos. 3,872-3, 873-3,874. Les grandes villes du monde: New York; [by] Jean Heffer.Paris, 1972. pp. 138. bibliog.

— Civic improvement.

DROVER (GLENN GORDON) Urban residential densities: a comparison of policies with particular reference to London and New York, 1945-1970; [Ph. D.(London) thesis]. 1973. fo. 276. Typescript: unpublished. This thesis is the property of London University and may not be removed from the Library.

SCHWARTZ (HARRY) and ABELES (PETER LEE) Planning for the Lower East Side. New York, 1973. pp. 204. bibliog.

— Civilization.

SAYRE (NORA) Sixties going on seventies. London, 1974. pp. 441.

— Foreign population.

ROSENBERG (TERRY J.) Residence, employment, and mobility of Puerto Ricans in New York City. Chicago, 1974. pp. 230. bibliog. (Chicago. University. Department of Geography. Research Papers. No. 151)

— Growth.

DROVER (GLENN GORDON) Urban residential densities: a comparison of policies with particular reference to London and New York, 1945-1970; [Ph. D.(London) thesis]. 1973. fo. 276. Typescript: unpublished. This thesis is the property of London University and may not be removed from the Library.

— Harbour.

JENSEN (VERNON H.) Strife on the waterfront: the port of New York since 1945. Ithaca, 1974. pp. 478. bibliog.

— Hospitals.

KAPLAN (SEYMOUR R.) and ROMAN (MELVIN) The organization and delivery of mental health services in the ghetto: the Lincoln Hospital experience. New York, 1973. pp. 315.

— Police.

HUNT (ISAAC C.) and COHEN (BERNARD) Criminologist. Minority recruiting in the New York City Police Department. New York, 1971. pp. 92. (Rand Corporation. [Rand Reports]. 702)

VITERITTI (JOSEPH P.) Police, politics, and pluralism in New York City: a comparative case study. Beverly Hills, [1973]. pp. 72. bibliog.

— Politics and government.

NEW YORK (CITY). Temporary Commission to Make a Study of the Governmental Operations of the City of New York. Task Force on Jurisdiction and Structure. Re-structuring the government of New York City: report...; [by Edward N. Costikyan and Maxwell Lehman]. New York, 1972. pp. 198. bibliog.

GORDON (DIANA R.) City limits: barriers to change in urban government. New York, [1973]. pp. 329.

VITERITTI (JOSEPH P.) Police, politics, and pluralism in New York City: a comparative case study. Beverly Hills, [1973]. pp. 72. bibliog.

— Poor.

GREENBERG (DAVID H.) Income guarantees and the working poor in New York City: the effect of income maintenance programs on the hours of work of male family heads. New York, 1971. pp. 103. (Rand Corporation. [Rand Reports]. 658)

STERNLIEB (GEORGE S.) and INDIK (BERNARD P.) The ecology of welfare: housing and the welfare crisis in New York city. New Brunswick, N.J., [1973]. pp. 292.

— Population.

ROSENWAIKE (IRA) Population history of New York City. Syracuse, 1972. pp. 224. bibliog.

DROVER (GLENN GORDON) Urban residential densities: a comparison of policies with particular reference to London and New York, 1945-1970; [Ph. D.(London) thesis]. 1973. fo. 276. Typescript: unpublished. This thesis is the property of London University and may not be removed from the Library.

— Race question.

BENJAMIN (GERALD) Race relations and the New York City Commission on Human Rights. Ithaca, 1991974474. pp. 274. bibliog.

— Riots.

COOK (ADRIAN) The armies of the streets: the New York City draft riots of 1863. Lexington, Ky., [1974]. pp. 323. bibliog.

— Schools.

KAESTLE (CARL F.) The evolution of an urban school system: New York City, 1750-1850. Cambridge, Mass., 1973. pp. 205. bibliog.

SKJEI (STEPHEN S.) Information for collective action: a microanalytic view of plural decision-making. Lexington, [1973]. pp. 188.

NEW YORK (STATE)

— Economic history.

BRENNER (M. HARVEY) Mental illness and the economy. Cambridge, Mass., 1973. pp. 287.

SMITH (GEORGE L.) Religion and trade in New Netherland: Dutch origins and American development. Ithaca, 1973. pp. 266. bibliog.

NEW ZEALAND

— Economic conditions.

NEW ZEALAND GEOGRAPHY CONFERENCE, 7TH, HAMILTON, 1972. Proceedings...; edited by Evelyn Stokes. [Christchurch], 1973. pp. 298. bibliogs. (New Zealand Geographical Society. Conference Series. No. 7)

ROYAL SOCIETY OF NEW ZEALAND, WELLINGTON. Science Congress, 12th, 1972. Contemporary New Zealand: essays on the human resource, urban growth and problems of society; [papers presented by social scientists]; edited by K.W. Thomson and A.D. Trlin. Wellington, N.Z., 1973. pp. 218.

— — Mathematical models.

DEANE (RODERICK S.) ed. A New Zealand model: structure, policy uses and some simulation results. Wellington, 1972. pp. 92. bibliogs. (Reserve Bank of New Zealand. Research Papers. No. 8)

— Economic policy.

DEANE (RODERICK S.) Papers on monetary policy, credit creation, economic objectives and the Reserve Bank. Wellington, 1972. pp. 35. (Reserve Bank of New Zealand. Research Papers. No. 9)

— Foreign relations.

NEW ZEALAND. Ministry of Foreign Affairs. 1972. New Zealand foreign policy: statements and documents, 1943-1957/Wellington, 1972. pp. 495.

See also EUROPEAN ECONOMIC COMMUNITY — New Zealand.

— — Japan.

LISSINGTON (MARY PATRICIA) New Zealand and Japan, 1900-1941. Wellington, Government Printer, 1972. pp. 206, 1 map. bibliog.

— — United States.

LISSINGTON (MARY PATRICIA) New Zealand and the United States, 1840-1944. Wellington, Government Printer, 1972. pp. 114, 1 map. bibliog.

— Government Publications.

NEW ZEALAND. Department of Statistics. 1972. Catalogue of New Zealand statistics. 3rd ed. Wellington, 1972. pp. 286.

— History.

WARD ALAN) A show of justice: racial 'amalgamation' in nineteenth century New Zealand. Canberra, 1974. pp. 382. bibliog.

— Sources.

McNAB (ROBERT) ed. Historical records of New Zealand. Wellington, 1908-14 [repr. 1973]. 2 vols.

— Officials and employees — Salaries, allowances, etc.

NEW ZEALAND. Royal Commission on Salary and Wage Fixing Procedures in the New Zealand State Services, 1972. Salary and wage fixing procedures in the New Zealand State Services, 1972; report; [Sir Thaddeus McCarthy, chairman]. Wellington, 1972. pp. 112.

— Population.

NEW ZEALAND. Ministry of Works. Town and Country Planning Branch. 1972. Population forecasts, 1971-1991: recent population trends and forecasts of future growth of regional and local areas. [Wellington], 1972. pp. 84.

JAIN (SHAILENDRA K.) Source book of population data: New Zealand non-Maori population 1921-1967. Canberra, [1973?]. 3 vols. (in 1).

— Race question.

WARD ALAN) A show of justice: racial 'amalgamation' in nineteenth century New Zealand. Canberra, 1974. pp. 382. bibliog.

— Relations (general) with South Africa.

NATIONAL ANTI-APARTHEID COORDINATING COMMITTEE [NEW ZEALAND]. Fight apartheid: a manual for action; editorial committee: Christopher Wainwright, Lindsay Wright. rev. ed. Wellington, N.Z., [1972]. pp. 57. bibliog.

— Social conditions.

NEW ZEALAND GEOGRAPHY CONFERENCE, 7TH, HAMILTON, 1972. Proceedings...; edited by Evelyn Stokes. [Christchurch], 1973. pp. 298. bibliogs. (New Zealand Geographical Society. Conference Series. No. 7)

ROYAL SOCIETY OF NEW ZEALAND, WELLINGTON. Science Congress, 12th, 1972. Contemporary New Zealand: essays on the human resource, urban growth and problems of society; [papers presented by social scientists]; edited by K.W. Thomson and A.D. Trlin. Wellington, N.Z., 1973. pp. 218.

— Statistics — Bibliography.

NEW ZEALAND. Department of Statistics. 1972. Catalogue of New Zealand statistics. 3rd ed. Wellington, 1972. pp. 286.

NEWARK, NEW JERSEY

— Politics and government.

GWYN (WILLIAM BRENT) Barriers to establishing urban ombudsmen: the case of Newark. Berkeley, 1974. pp. 93. (California University. Institute of Governmental Studies. Ombudsman Research. Monographs)

NEWARK, NEW JERSEY. (Cont.)

— Poor.

STERNLIEB (GEORGE S.) and BURCHELL (ROBERT WILLIAM) Residential abandonment: the tenement landlord revisited. New Brunswick, 1973. pp. 444. *bibliog.*

NEWCASTLE—UPON—TYNE

— Social conditions.

The SCHOOL years in Newcastle upon Tyne, 1952-62: being a further contribution to the study of a thousand families; by F.J.W. Miller [and others]. London, 1974. pp. 362. *bibliog.*

NEWFOUNDLAND

— Politics and government.

GWYN (RICHARD J.) Smallwood: the unlikely revolutionary. rev. ed. Toronto, 1972 repr. 1974. pp. 364.

NEWRY

— Civic improvement.

NEWRY area plan; [Patrick McArdle, chairman of the Steering Committee]. Belfast, H.M.S.O., 1973. pp. 86. *Map in end pocket.*

NEWS AGENCIES.

INGMAR (GUNILLA) Monopol på nyheter: ekonomiska och politiska aspekter på svenska och internationella nyhetsbyråers verksamhet, 1870-1919. Stockholm, [1973]. pp. 240. *bibliog. (Uppsala. Universitet. Historiska Institutionen. Studia Historica Upsaliensia. 52) With German summary.*

NEWSPAPER AND PERIODICAL WHOLESALERS

— Germany.

MOESTL (REINHARD) Der Absatz von Zeitungen und Zeitschriften als Kommunikationsmittlerleistung. [Erlangen-Nürnberg?, 1974]. pp. 371, xix. *bibliog.*

NEWSPAPER PUBLISHING

— Norway — Finance.

INNSTILLING om Statens lånekasse for aviser; fra et utvalg oppnevnt...av 17. oktober 1969. Orkanger, 1971. pp. 65.

NEWTON (Sir ISAAC).

MANUEL (FRANK EDWARD) A portrait of Isaac Newton. Cambridge, Mass., 1968. pp. 478.

NICARAGUA

— Foreign relations — United States.

SELSER (GREGORIO) Sandino; [with texts of political manifestoes, speeches etc.]. Montevideo, [1970]. pp. 125. *bibliog.*

— Politics and government.

SELSER (GREGORIO) Sandino; [with texts of political manifestoes, speeches etc.]. Montevideo, [1970]. pp. 125. *bibliog.*

NICHOLAS II, Emperor of Russia.

ZAITSEV (KIRILL IOSIFOVICH) Pamiati poslednego Tsaria, etc. Shankhai, 1948. pp. 86. *Rev. version of article published in Khleb nebesnyi, 1943.*

NIEKISCH (ERNST).

NIEKISCH (ERNST) Erinnerungen eines deutschen Revolutionärs. 2. Band. Gegen den Strom, 1945-1967. Köln, 1974. pp. 310.

NIEUWENHUIS (FERDINAND DOMELA).

JONG (ALBERT DE) Writer on Socialism. Domela Nieuwenhuis. 2nd ed. Den Haag, [1972]. pp. 88. *bibliog.*

NIGER

— Economic conditions.

FRANCE. Direction de l'Aide au Développement des Etats Francophones d'Afrique au Sud du Sahara et de la République Malgache. Secteur Information Economique et Conjoncture. 1973. Niger 1971-72: dossier d'information économique. Paris, 1973. fo. 61,78.

NIGERIA

— Climate.

KOWAL (JAN M.) and KNABE (DANUTA T.) An agroclimatological atlas of the northern states of Nigeria; with explanatoprry notes. Samaru-Zaria, [1972]. pp. 111, 17 maps.

— Commerce.

OKURUME (GODWIN E.) Foreign trade and the subsistence sector in Nigeria: the impact of agricultural exports on domestic food supplies in a peasant economy. New York, 1973. pp. 136. *bibliog.*

— Constitutional history.

OLUSANYA (G.O.) The Second World War and politics in Nigeria, 1939-1953. Lagos, 1973. pp. 181. *bibliog.*

— Economic conditions.

DAMACHI (UKANDI GODWIN) and SEIBEL (HANS DIETER) eds. Social change and economic development in Nigeria. New York, 1973. pp. 252. *bibliogs.*

— — Statistics.

NIGERIA. Central Planning Office. Economic and statistical review. a., 1971 [2nd]- Lagos.

— Economic policy.

NIGERIA (MID-WESTERN REGION). 1965. Mid-Western Nigeria development plan, 1964-68. [Benin City, 1965]. pp. 78.

MABOGUNJE (AKIN L.) Growth poles and growth centres in the regional development of Nigeria. (UNRISD Reports. No. 71.3) (UNRISD/71/C.78). Geneva, United Nations Research Institute for Social Development, 1971. pp. 85. *bibliog.*

DEAN (EDWIN) Plan implementation in Nigeria: 1962-1966. Ibadan, 1972. pp. 294. *bibliog.*

NIGERIA. Central Planning Office. 1973. Guidelines for the third national development plan, 1975-80. Lagos, [1973]. pp. 61.

NIGERIAN ECONOMIC SOCIETY. Annual Conference, 1972. Rural development in Nigeria: proceedings, etc. Ibadan, [1973]. pp. 300.

— Foreign relations.

IDANG (GORDON J.) Nigeria: internal politics and foreign policy, 1960-1966. Ibadan, 1973. pp. 171. *bibliog.*

— History.

ISICHEI (ELIZABETH ALLO) The Ibo people and the Europeans: the genesis of a relationship - to 1906. London, 1973. pp. 207. *bibliog.*

— — 1967—1970, Civil War.

OKPAKU (JOSEPH) ed. Nigeria: dilemma of nationhood: an African analysis of the Biafran conflict. New York, [1972]. pp. 426.

BALOGUN (OLA) The tragic years: Nigeria in crisis, 1966-1970. Benin City, 1973. pp. 125. *bibliog.*

HENTSCH (THIERRY) Face au blocus: la Croix-Rouge internationale dans le Nigéria en guerre, 1967-1970. Genève, 1973. pp. 307. *bibliog.*

— Industries.

INDUSTRIAL STATISTICS OF WESTERN STATE OF NIGERIA; [pd. by] Ministry of Economic Planning and Social Development, Statistics Division (Western State of Nigeria). N 1968 (v.2, no.1). Ibadan.

SCHAETZL (LUDWIG) Industrialization in Nigeria: a spatial analysis. München, [1973]. pp. 262. *bibliog. (Ifo-Institut für Wirtschaftsforschung. Afrika- Studien. 81) 2 maps in end pocket.*

— Maps.

KOWAL (JAN M.) and KNABE (DANUTA T.) An agroclimatological atlas of the northern states of Nigeria; with explanatoprry notes. Samaru-Zaria, [1972]. pp. 111, 17 maps.

— Nationalism.

OLUSANYA (G.O.) The Second World War and politics in Nigeria, 1939-1953. Lagos, 1973. pp. 181. *bibliog.*

— Officials and employees.

NIGERIA (WESTERN STATE). Statutory Corporations Service Commission. Report. a., 1970/71 [2nd]- Ibadan.

— — Salaries, allowances, etc.

NIGERIA. Wages and Salaries Review Commission. 1971. Second and final report; [S.O. Adebo, chairman]. [Lagos, 1971]. pp. 84. *Bound with White Paper on the report.*

NIGERIA. 1971. White Paper on the second and final report of the Wages and Salaries Review Commission, 1970-71. Lagos, 1971. pp. 15. *Bound with the Report.*

— Politics and government.

NIGERIAN PEOPLE'S UNION. Programme of the... Union, etc. London, [imprint, 197-]. pp. 30.

AKINSANYA (OLU) A mini biography of Chief Obafemi Awolowo. Lagos, 1972. pp. 28.

OKPAKU (JOSEPH) ed. Nigeria: dilemma of nationhood: an African analysis of the Biafran conflict. New York, [1972]. pp. 426.

DAMACHI (UKANDI GODWIN) and SEIBEL (HANS DIETER) eds. Social change and economic development in Nigeria. New York, 1973. pp. 252. *bibliogs.*

DUDLEY (BILLY JOSEPH) Instability and political order: politics and crisis in Nigeria. Ibadan, 1973. pp. 265.

IDANG (GORDON J.) Nigeria: internal politics and foreign policy, 1960-1966. Ibadan, 1973. pp. 171. *bibliog.*

OLUSANYA (G.O.) The Second World War and politics in Nigeria, 1939-1953. Lagos, 1973. pp. 181. *bibliog.*

COHEN (ROBIN) Labour and politics in Nigeria, 1945-71. London, 1974. pp. 302. *bibliog.*

ROBERTSON (Sir JAMES WILSON) Transition in Africa: from direct rule to independence; a memoir. London, [1974]. pp. 272.

— Population.

NIGERIA. Federal Office of Statistics. 1968. Rural demographic sample survey, 1965-1966. Lagos, 1968. fo. 46.

ADEPOJU (JOHN ADERANTI) Internal migration in south-west Nigeria: a demographic and socio-economic study of recent in-migration to the towns of Ife and Oshogbo; [Ph.D.(London) thesis]. 1973. fo. 354. *bibliog. Typescript: unpublished. This thesis is the property of London University and may not be removed from the Library.*

— Rural conditions.

NIGERIAN ECONOMIC SOCIETY. Annual Conference, 1972. Rural development in Nigeria: proceedings, etc. Ibadan, [1973]. pp. 300.

— Social conditions.

DAMACHI (UKANDI GODWIN) and SEIBEL (HANS DIETER) eds. Social change and economic development in Nigeria. New York, 1973. pp. 252. *bibliogs.*

— **Social policy.**

NIGERIA (MID-WESTERN REGION). 1965. Mid-Western Nigeria development plan, 1964-68. [Benin City, 1965]. pp. 78.

NIGERIA. Central Planning Office. 1973. Guidelines for the third national development plan, 1975-80. Lagos, [1973]. pp. 61.

— **Statistics.**

NIGERIA (EAST-CENTRAL STATE). Ministry of Economic Development and Reconstruction. Statistics Division. Statistical digest. a., 1970 [1st]- Enugu.

NIGERIA (BENUE-PLATEAU STATE). Military Governor's Office. Economic Development and Reconstruction Division. Statistics Section. Statistical yearbook. a., 1971- Jos.

— **Statistics, Vital.**

NIGERIA. Federal Office of Statistics. 1968. Rural demographic sample survey, 1965-1966. Lagos, 1968. fo. 46.

— **Yearbooks.**

NIGERIA YEAR BOOK. a., 1969, 1973- Apapa.

NIGERIAN PEOPLE'S UNION.

NIGERIAN PEOPLE'S UNION. Programme of the... Union, etc. London, [imprint, 197-]. pp. 30.

NIJMEGEN UNIVERSITY.

SCHOPMAN (JAN) Kritiese universiteit: de ruk naar links in de nijmeegse studentenbeweging. Nijmegen, [1974]. pp. 106. bibliog.

NITRATES.

BLAKEMORE (HAROLD) British nitrates and Chilean politics, 1886-1896: Balmaceda and North. London, 1974. pp. 260. (London. University. Institute of Latin American Studies. Monographs. 4)

NIVKHS.

See GILYAKS.

NIXON (RICHARD MILHOUS) President of the United States.

HANSEN (JOSEPH) Marxist, and LUND (CAROLINE) Nixon's Moscow and Peking summits: their meaning for Vietnam. New York, [1972]. pp. 31.

GARDNER (LLOYD C.) ed. The great Nixon turn-around: America's new foreign policy in the post-liberal era...; essays and articles. New York, 1973. pp. 350.

GARTNER (ALAN) and others, eds. What Nixon is doing to us. New York, 1973. pp. 258.

KAMMERMAN (ROY) Poor Richard's Watergate. Los Angeles, 1973. 1 vol. (unpaged).

MANKIEWICZ (FRANK) Nixon's road to Watergate. London, 1973. pp. 271.

NOISE.

Une VILLE pilote pour la lutte contre les pollutions et les nuisances: la ville nouvelle du Vaudreuil. Paris, 1973. pp. 181. (Environnement. 14)

NOISE ADVISORY COUNCIL [U.K.]. Panel on Noise in the Seventies. Noise in the next ten years; report; [E.J. Richards, chairman]. London, H.M.S.O., 1974. pp. 15.

NOMADS.

The DESERT and the sown: nomads in the wider society: [papers of an international conference held at the American University in Cairo in 1972]; Cynthia Nelson, editor. Berkeley, [1973]. pp. 173. (California University. Institute of International Studies. Research Series. No. 21)

NOMINALISM.

LEDNIKOV (EVGENII EVGEN'EVICH) Kriticheskii analiz nominalisticheskikh i platonistskikh tendentsii v sovremennoi logike. Kiev, 1973. pp. 223.

NONFERROUS METAL INDUSTRIES

— **United Kingdom.**

LITTLE (BRYAN) (Capper Pass): the first hundred and fifty years. London, [1963]. pp. 33. bibliog.

NONWAGE PAYMENTS

— **Canada.**

CANADA. Public Service Staff Relations Board. Pay Research Bureau. 1973. Employee benefits and conditions of employment in Canada: highlights of studies of prevalence, characteristics and costs from 1967 into 1972. Ottawa, 1973. pp. 93,(2).

— **United Kingdom.**

MOONMAN (JANE) The effectiveness of fringe benefits in industry, including a survey of current practice undertaken by an independent study group. Epping, Essex, 1973. pp. 222. bibliog.

NOONAN (ROBERT).

See TRESSELL (ROBERT) pseud.

NORD (DEPARTMENT)

— **Foreign population.**

SALAH (ALI) La communauté algérienne: étude sur l'immigration algérienne dans le Département du Nord, 1945-1972. Lille, [1973]. pp. 213. bibliog.

— **Population.**

L'HOMME, la vie et la mort dans le Nord au 19e siècle; ([by] M.-P. Buriez [and others]); études présentées par Marcel Gillet. Lille, [1972]. pp. 215.

NORDISK RÅD.

NORDISK RÅD. Nordic Organisations Committee. 1970. The organisation of Nordic co-operation: proposals. Stockholm, 1970. pp. 31. (Nordisk Råd. Nordisk Udredningsserie. 1970.13)

NORIL'SK.

NAZAROVA (LARISA GRIGOR'EVNA) and POLUEKTOV (VLADIMIR EVGEN'EVICH) Opyt proektirovaniia i stroitel'stva gorodov Krainego Severa: na primere Noril'ska. Moskva, 1973. pp. 176. bibliog.

NORMANDY

— **Economic conditions.**

FRANCE. Direction de la Documentation. La Documentation Française. Notes et Etudes Documentaires. Nos. 3,835-3, 836. Les économies régionales: l'économie de la Haute- Normandie; [by] le Comité régional d'expansion économique de Haute-Normandie. Paris, 1971. pp. 96.

FRANCE. Direction de la Documentation. La Documentation Française. Notes et Etudes Documentaires. Nos. 3,856-3, 857. L'économie de la Basse-Normandie; [by] l'Institut de Géographie de l'Université de Caen en liaison avec la Mission régionale et le Service régional de l'Equipement et du Logement de Basse-Normandie. Paris, 1972. pp. 87.

NORRLAND

— **Economic policy.**

GERARD (OVE) The Norrland question: part 1: studies in the government's and the parliament's treatment of the Norrland question 1892- 1901; [translated from the Swedish]. Lund, 1971. pp. 164. (Economy and History. Supplements)

NORSKE ARBEIDERPARTI.

See LABOUR PARTY — Norway.

NORTH (JOHN THOMAS).

BLAKEMORE (HAROLD) British nitrates and Chilean politics, 1886-1896: Balmaceda and North. London, 1974. pp. 260. (London. University. Institute of Latin American Studies. Monographs. 4)

NORTH ATLANTIC TREATY ORGANIZATION.

NORTH ATLANTIC ASSEMBLY. Addresses, reports, texts adopted. [title varies]. a., 1960 (6th conf.)- 1964, 1966- [Brussels]. *1960 reports were the first printed version; 1960-1968 are in 2 pts.; for 1971-1972 only Texts adopted were pd.*

WILLIAMS (GEOFFREY) Natural alliance for the West: flexibility and global security. London, 1969. pp. 109.

NELIN (IURII GRIGOR'EVICH) Atom i NATO. Moskva, 1970. pp. 131.

NORTH ATLANTIC TREATY ORGANIZATION. Information Service. 1971. NATO: facts and figures. Brussels, 1971. pp. 413.

NATO HANDBOOK; [pd. by] NATO Information Service. a., 1972- Brussels. *Every fifth issue only kept permanently.*

EUROPEAN security and the Soviet problem: report of a study group of the Institute for the Study of Conflict, London, July-November 1971; rapporteur, Brian Crozier; participants, Max Beloff [and others]. [London], 1972. pp. 64. (Institute for the Study of Conflict. Special Reports)

GALANTE (SEVERINO) La politica del PCI e il Patto Atlantico: "Rinascita" 1946-'49. Padova, [1973]. pp. 257. (Padua. Università. Istituto di Scienze Storiche, and Centro di Studi e Documentazioni per la Storia Contemporanea e le Relazioni Internazionali. Collana. 1)

INTERNATIONAL INSTITUTE FOR STRATEGIC STUDIES. Adelphi Papers. No. 96. The Alliance and Europe: part 1: crisis stability in Europe and theatre nuclear weapons; by Wolfgang Heisenberg. London, 1973. pp. 35.

INTERNATIONAL INSTITUTE FOR STRATEGIC STUDIES. Adelphi Papers. No. 98. The Alliance and Europe: part 2: defence with fewer men; by Kenneth Hunt. London, 1973. pp. 42.

INSTITUTE ON NATO AND DISSUASION, CHICAGO, 1972. NATO and dissuasion: [papers presented at the Institute; edited by] Morton A. Kaplan. [Chicago, 1974]. pp. 151.

— **Germany.**

DEUTSCHE GESELLSCHAFT FUR AUSWARTIGE POLITIK. Forschungsinstitut. Regionale Verflechtung der Bundesrepublik Deutschland: empirische Analysen und theoretische Probleme. München, 1973. pp. 311. (Schriften. Band 33)

— **Portugal.**

BOSGRA (S.J.) and KRIMPEN (CHR. VAN) Portugal and NATO. 3rd ed. Amsterdam, [1972]. pp. 80.

CROLLEN (LUC) Portugal, the U.S. and NATO. Leuven, [1973]. pp. 163. bibliog. (Katholieke Universiteit te Leuven. Departement Politieke Wetenschappen. Studies in International Relations. No.1)

— **United Kingdom.**

NEWENS (STAN) The case against N.A.T.O.: the danger of nuclear alliances. [London, 1972]. pp. 17.

— **United States.**

LAWRENCE (RICHARD D.) and RECORD (JEFFREY) U.S. force structure in NATO: an alternative: a staff paper. Washington, [1974]. pp. 136. (Brookings Institution. Studies in Defense Policy)

NORTH CAROLINA

— **Economic policy.**

COASTAL PLAINS REGIONAL COMMISSION. Economic development plan. Washington, the Commission, 1971. pp. 111.

NORTH CAROLINA. (Cont.)

COASTAL PLAINS REGIONAL COMMISSION [UNITED STATES]. Regional plan in brief. [Washington, the Commission], 1973. pp. 20.

NORTH HOLLAND

— Population.

AMSTERDAM. Bureau van Statistiek. Statistische Mededelingen. No.189. De bevolkingsontwikkeling in de Noordhollandse regio's, 1962- 1971. Amsterdam, 1973. pp. 52.

NORTH OSSETIAN REPUBLIC

— History — 1917—1921, Revolution — Sources.

BOR'BA za Sovetskuiu vlast' v Severnoi Osetii: sbornik dokumentov i materialov. Ordzhonikidze, 1972. pp. 542.

— Politics and government.

NORTH OSSETIAN REPUBLIC. Verkhovnyi Sovet. Zasedaniia: stenograficheskii otchet. sess., D 1971(series 8, session 3). Ordzhonikidze.

NORTH RHINE—WESTPHALIA

— Census.

NORTH RHINE-WESTPHALIA. Statistisches Landesame. Beiträge zur Statistik des Landes Nordrhein-Westfalen. Sonderreihe Volkszählung 1970. Heft 3b. Gemeindestatistik 1970: Bevölkerung und Erwerbstätigkeit. Düsseldorf, 1973. pp. 455.

NORTH RHINE-WESTPHALIA. Statistisches Landesamt. Beiträge zur Statistik des Landes Nordrhein-Westfalen. Sonderreihe Volkszählung 1970. Heft 13. Die Haushalte in Nordrhein-Westfalen nach Art und Grösse am 27.Mai 1970. Düsseldorf, 1973. pp. 279.

NORTH RHINE-WESTPHALIA. Statistisches Landesamt. Beiträge zur Statistik des Landes Nordrhein-Westfalen. [Sonderreihe Volkszählung 1970]. Heft 2a. Amtliches Verzeichnis der Gemeinden und Wohnplätze (Ortschaften) in Nordrhein-Westfalen 1970: Bevölkerung und Erwerbstätigkeit. Düsseldorf, 1973. pp. 1277.

NORTH RHINE-WESTPHALIA. Statistisches Landesamt. Beiträge zur Statistik des Landes Nordrhein-Westfalen. Sonderreihe Volkszählung 1970. Heft 17a. Die Arbeitsstätten in Nordrhein-Westfalen 1970: Landes-, Kreis- und Gemeindeergebnisse in wirtschaftssystematischer Gliederung. Düsseldorf, 1973. pp. 694.

NORTH RHINE-WESTPHALIA. Statistisches Landesamt. Beiträge zur Statistik des Landes Nordrhein-Westfalen. Sonderreihe Volkszählung 1970. Heft 12a. Verkehrsmittel und Zeitaufwand der Pendelwanderer in Nordrhein-Westfalen am 27. Mai 1970: Landes- und Kreisergebnisse. Düsseldorf, 1974. pp. 351.

NORTH RHINE-WESTPHALIA. Statistisches Landesamt. Beiträge zur Statistik des Landes Nordrhein-Westfalen. Sonderreihe Volkszählung 1970. Heft 2b. Amtliches Verzeichnis der Gemeinden und Wohnplätze (Ortschaften) in Nordrhein-Westfalen 1970: Arbeitsstätten und Beschäftigte. Düsseldorf, 1974. pp. 674.

— Occupations.

NORTH RHINE-WESTPHALIA. Statistisches Landesamt. Beiträge zur Statistik des Landes Nordrhein-Westfalen. Sonderreihe Volkszählung 1970. Heft 3c. Gemeindestatistik 1970: Arbeitsstätten und Beschäftigte. Düsseldorf, 1973. pp. 238.

NORTH RHINE-WESTPHALIA. Statistisches Landesamt. Beiträge zur Statistik des Landes Nordrhein-Westfalen. Sonderreihe Volkszählung 1970. Heft 17a. Die Arbeitsstätten in Nordrhein-Westfalen 1970: Landes-, Kreis- und Gemeindeergebnisse in wirtschaftssystematischer Gliederung. Düsseldorf, 1973. pp. 694.

NORTH RHINE-WESTPHALIA. Statistisches Landesamt. Beiträge zur Statistik des Landes Nordrhein-Westfalen. Sonderreihe Volkszählung 1970. Heft 2b. Amtliches Verzeichnis der Gemeinden und Wohnplätze (Ortschaften) in Nordrhein-Westfalen 1970: Arbeitsstätten und Beschäftigte. Düsseldorf, 1974. pp. 674.

— Politics and government.

SCHNUR (ROMAN) Regionalkreise?: grundsätzliche Bemerkungen zur Schaffung von sogenannten Regionalkreisen, insbesondere in Nordrhein- Westfalen. Köln, [1971]. pp. 47. (Nordrhein-Westfälischer Städte- und Gemeindebund. Abhandlungen zur Kommunalpolitik. Band 1)

— Population.

NORTH RHINE-WESTPHALIA. Statistisches Landesamt. Beiträge zur Statistik des Landes Nordrhein-Westfalen. Sonderreihe Volkszählung 1970. Heft 3e. Gemeindestatistik 1970: Entwicklung der kreisfreien Städte, Kreise und Gemeinden 1961 bis 1975. Düsseldorf, 1973. pp. 215,44 matrices.

— Statistics.

NORTH RHINE-WESTPHALIA. Statistisches Landesamt. Beiträge zur Statistik des Landes Nordrhein-Westfalen. Sonderreihe Volkszählung 1970. Heft 3 d. Gemeindestatistik 1970: weitere Strukturdaten. Düsseldorf, 1973. pp. 158.

NORTHAMPTON

— Social history.

FOSTER (JOHN) 1940- . Class struggle and the industrial revolution: early industrial capitalism in three English towns. London, [1974]. pp. 346. bibliog.

NORTHERN IRELAND STUDIES.

DARBY (JOHN P.) Register of research into the Irish conflict. [Belfast], Northern Ireland Community Relations Commission, [1972]. 1 pamphlet (unpaged). (Research Papers)

NORTHERN TERRITORY

— Constitution.

AUSTRALIA. Northern Territory. Legislative Council. Select Committee... appointed to Inquire into Necessity or Otherwise for Constitutional Reform in the Northern Territory. 1958. Report; [R.J. Withnall, chairman]. Canberra, [1958]. pp. 20.

NORTHERN WAR, 1700—1721.

NORDMANN (CLAUDE J.) La crise du Nord au début du XVIIIe siècle. Paris, 1962. pp. 318. bibliog.

NORTHUMBERLAND

— Industries.

McCORD (NORMAN) and ROWE (D.T.) Northumberland and Durham: industry in the nineteenth century. Newcastle upon Tyne, 1971. pp. 80.

NORWAY

— Defences.

ANDREASSEN (TORMOD) Forsvarets virkninger på norsk økonomi etc. Oslo, 1972. pp. 141. (Norway. Statistiske Centralbyrå. Samfunnsøkonomiske Studier. 22)

— Diplomatic and consular service.

INNSTILLING om utenrikstjenesten: hovedoppgaver og organisasjon; fra et utvalg oppnevnt av Utenriksdepartementet 5. mars 1969.; [Erik Dons, chairman]. [Oslo], 1970. pp. 80.

— Economic history.

LIEBERMAN (SIMA) The industrialization of Norway 1800-1920. Oslo, [1970]. pp. 222. bibliog. (Norges Almenvitenskapelige Forskningsråd. Gruppe: Økonomi)

SVENDSEN (ARNLJOT STRØMME) Den naeringsøkonomiske utvikling i Norge i efterkrigstiden. Bergen, [1973]. pp. 9-28. (Norges Handelshøyskole. Saertrykk-Serie. Nr. 103) (Saertrykk av "Aktieselskabet Hafslund 1948-1973", Oslo, 1973)

— Economic policy.

GJEDE (TORBEN) Det makroøkonomiske prognosearbejde i Sverige og Norge. København, 1970. fo. 68. (Denmark. Danmarks Statistik. Arbejdsnotater. 1)

HAARR (ARNE) The industrial policy of Norway. Oslo, 1970. pp. 32.

INNSTILLING om planleggings- og budsjetteringsorganene i staten; fra en komité oppnevnt ved kongelig resolusjon 16. juni 1967. Orkanger, 1970. pp. 103.

NORWAY. Komitéen for Langtidsplanlegging og Langtidsbudsjettering i Kommunene og Fylkene. 1970. Innstilling om langtidsplanlegging og langtidsbudsjettering i kommunene og fylkene; fra et utvalg oppnevnt ved kongelig resolusjon 7. januar 1966. Orkanger, 1970. pp. 78.

VISTE (JON OLAV) Utviklingsmønster for bosetting og sysselsetting i Agder og Rogaland: oppdragsrapport utført for Landsdelskomitéen for Agder og Rogaland: hovedrapport. Oslo, 1972 in progress.

WYLLER (THOMAS CHRISTIAN) ed. Norge som oljestat: artikler av Thomas Chr. Wyller [and others]. Oslo, 1973. pp. 141.

— Emigration and Immigration.

NORWAY. Statistiske Centralbyrå. 1972. Folkemengdens bevegelse oversikt 1966-1970, etc. Oslo, 1972. pp. 81. (Statistiske Analyser. 1)

— Foreign economic relations.

NORWAY. Utenriksdepartementet. 1970. Om Norges deltakelse i Organisasjonen for Økonomisk Samarbeid og Utvikling (OECD). [Oslo?, 1970?]. pp. 24. (Norway. Stortinget. Stortingsmeldinger. 1969-70, nr. 12)

— Foreign relations

See also EUROPEAN ECONOMIC COMMUNITY — Norway; UNITED NATIONS — Norway.

— Denmark.

BLOM (IDA) Kampen om Eirik Raudes land: pressgruppepolitikk i grønlandsspørsmålet, 1921-1931. Oslo, 1973. pp. 439. bibliog.

— History — 1940—1945, German Occupation.

[MANNHEIMER (KAJ)] Norge och den norska exilregeringen under andra världskriget: undersökning utförd på uppdrag av Grundlagberedningen. Stockholm, 1972. pp. 165. (Sweden. Statens Offentliga Utredningar. 1972. 18)

— Industries.

AUKRUST (ODD) The role of manufacturing industry in the Norwegian economy. Oslo, 1970. pp. 17. (Norway. Utenriksdepartementet. Presseavdelingen. Reference Papers. 1970.88)

HAARR (ARNE) The industrial policy of Norway. Oslo, 1970. pp. 32.

NORWAY. Statistiske Centralbyrå. 1972. Rentabilitet og kapitalstruktur i store industriforetak, etc. Oslo, 1972. fo. 55. (Statistiske Analyser. 3) Tables in Norwegian and English.

LAFFERTY (WILLIAM M.) Industrialization, community structure, and socialism: an ecological analysis of Norway, 1875-1924. Oslo, [1974]. pp. 364. bibliog.

— Officials and employees.

INNSTILLING om Saksbehandlerproblemene m.v. i sentraladministrasjonen; fra en komité oppnevnt av Lønns- og Prisdepartementet 3.januar 1968. Otta, 1970. pp. 57.

VELFERDSTILTAK for de ansatte i staten; fra et utvalg oppnevnt av Lønns- og Prisdepartementet 6. juni 1969. Oslo, 1972. pp. 20. (Norway. Norges Offentlige Utredninger. 1972.43)

— — Salaries, allowances, etc.

NORWAY. Lønns- og Prisdepartementet. 1971. Om statens lønns- og personalpolitikk. [Oslo?, 1971?]. pp. 54. (Norway. Stortinget. Stortingsmeldinger. 1970-71. Nr. 25)

INNSTILLING om voldgiftsordning for statstjenestemenn som ikke har streikerett; avgitt av en komité oppnevnt av Lønn-og Prisdepartementet 30. november 1970. Orkanger, 1971. pp. 11.

NORWAY. Statistiske Centralbyrå. 1974. Lønnsstatistikk for statens embets- og tjenestemenn 1. oktober 1973, etc. Oslo, 1974. pp. 71. (Norges Offisielle Statistikk. Rekke A. 631) With English summary.

— Population.

NORWAY. Statistiske Centralbyrå. 1972. Folkemengdens bevegelse oversikt 1966-1970, etc. Oslo, 1972. pp. 81. (Statistiske Analyser. 1)

NORWAY. Statistiske Centralbyrå. 1972. Framskriving av folkemengden 1971-2000 etc. Oslo, 1972. pp. 129. (Norges Offisielle Statistikk. Rekke A. 468) In Norwegian and English.

NORWAY. Statistiske Centralbyrå. 1972. Framskriving av folkemengden 1972-2000: regionale tall, etc. Oslo. 1972. pp. 157. (Norges Offisielle Statistikk. Rekke A.523) In Norwegian and English.

NORWAY. Statistiske Centralbyr'a. 1974. Flyttemotivundersøkelsen 1972, etc. Oslo, 1974. pp. 162. (Norges Offisielle Statistikk. Rekke A. 617)

— Relations (general) with Russia.

GILBERG (TROND) The Soviet Communist party and Scandinavian communism: the Norwegian case. Oslo, [1973]. pp. 271. bibliog.

— Social conditions.

RAMSØY (NATALIE ROGOFF) ed. Norwegian society. Oslo, [1974]. pp. 452. bibliog.

— Social policy.

NORWAY. Komitéen for Langtidsplanlegging og Langtidsbudsjettering i Kommunene og Fylkene. 1970. Innstilling om langtidsplanlegging og langtidsbudsjettering i kommunene og fylkene; fra et utvalg oppnevnt ved kongelig resolusjon 7. januar 1966. Orkanger, 1970. pp. 78.

— Statistics.

NORWAY. Utvalget for Regionalstatistikk. 1972. Regionalstatistikk: om statistikkbehovet i regional planlegging: utredning fra utvalg, etc. Oslo, 1972. pp. 165. (Norway. Norges Offentlige Utredninger. 1972. 44)

— Statistics, Vital.

NORWAY. Statistiske Centralbyrå. 1972. Folkemengdens bevegelse oversikt 1966-1970, etc. Oslo, 1972. pp. 81. (Statistiske Analyser. 1)

NOTARIES

— United Kingdom.

HAMPSON (GEOFFREY) ed. Southampton notarial protest books 1756-1810. Southampton, 1973. pp. 133. bibliog. (Southampton. University of Southampton. Southampton Records Series. vol. 16)

NOTTINGHAM

— Race question.

LAWRENCE (DANIEL) Black migrants, white natives: a study of race relations in Nottingham. London, 1974. pp. 251. bibliog.

NOVOSIL'TSEV (NIKOLAI NIKOLAEVICH).

ALDANOV (MARK ALEKSANDROVICH) pseud. [i.e. Mark Alexandrovich LANDAU] Iunost' Pavla Stroganova i drugie kharakteristiki. Belgrad, [1935?]. pp. 188.

NUBIA

— Social life and customs.

FERNEA (ROBERT ALAN) Nubians in Egypt: peaceful people; notes on Nubian architecture and architectural drawings by Horst Jaritz; (photographs by Georg Gerster). Austin, Texas, [1973]. pp. 146. bibliog.

NUCLEAR PHYSICS.

GASTON (JERRY) Originality and competition in science: a study of the British high energy physics community. Chicago, [1973]. pp. 210. bibliog.

NUCLEAR REACTORS

— Materials — Transportation.

INTERNATIONAL LEGAL CONFERENCE ON MARITIME CARRIAGE OF NUCLEAR SUBSTANCES, BRUSSELS, 1971. Final act of the Conference including the text of the adopted Convention. London, Inter-Governmental Maritime Consultative Organization, 1972. pp. 39. In English and French.

NUREMBERG

— Commerce.

SCHAPER (CHRISTA) Die Hirschvogel von Nürnberg und ihr Handelshaus. Nürnberg, 1973. pp. 351. bibliog. (Nuremberg. Verein für Geschichte der Stadt Nürnberg. Nürnberger Forschungen. 18. Band)

NURSERY SCHOOLS.

BRITISH HUMANIST ASSOCIATION. Women's Liberation Project Group. Survey of local authority day nurseries and nursery schools/classes in the 32 London boroughs; carried out by Pat Knight. London, [1972?]. fo. 14.

GREENWICH. [Department of Social Services]. Programme Planning Section. Day care and play for under-5's in Greenwich: (key issue report). [London], 1972. fo. 62.

SJØLUND (ARNE) Daycare institutions and children's development;... translated from the Danish by W. Glyn Jones. Farnborough, [1973]. pp. 308. bibliog.

NURSES AND NURSING.

WORLD HEALTH ORGANIZATION. Public Health Papers. No. 44. Planning and programming for nursing services. Geneva, 1971. pp. 123. bibliog.

— United Kingdom.

U.K. Working Party on Management Structure in the Local Authority Nursing Services. 1969. Report; [E.L. Mayston, chairman]. [London], 1969. pp. 61, 29.

U.K. Department of Health and Social Security. 1973. Management structure in the local authority nursing services: the implementation of Mayston. [London], 1973. pp. 49.

— — Scotland.

NURSES in an integrated health service; report of a Working Group appointed by the Scottish Home and Health Department;[Muriel Powell, chairman]. Edinburgh, H.M.S.O., 1972. pp. 37.

— United States.

ARCHIBALD (K.A.) The supply of professional nurses and their recruitment and retention by hospitals. New York, 1971. pp. 95. bibliogs. (Rand Corporation. [Rand Reports]. 836)

NUTRITION.

WHYTE (ROBERT ORR) Rural nutrition in China. Hong Kong, 1972. pp. 54. bibliog.

OCCUPATIONAL DISEASES.

— Underdeveloped areas.

See UNDERDEVELOPED AREAS — Nutrition.

NUTRITION SURVEYS

— Ethiopia.

WORLD LAND USE SURVEY. Occasional Papers. No. 11. Welenkomi: a socio-economic and nutritional survey of a rural community in the Central Highlands of Ethiopia; by Mesfin Wolde-Mariam [and others]. Berkhamsted, 1971. pp. 67. Map in end pocket.

NYERERE (JULIUS KAMBARAGE).

NYERERE (JULIUS KAMBARAGE) Freedom and development; Uhuru na maendeleo: a selection from writings and speeches, 1968-1973. Dar es Salaam, 1973. pp. 400.

OATS.

ABERDEEN. University. North of Scotland College of Agriculture. Agricultural Economics Division, and others. The economics of oat production in Scotland: a joint study carried out by the Economics Departments of the three Scottish agricultural colleges. Aberdeen, 1973. pp. 53. (Economic Reports. No.130)

OBEDIENCE.

MILGRAM (STANLEY) Obedience to authority: an experimental view. London, 1974. pp. 224. bibliog.

OBEREMMENTAL.

See EMME VALLEY.

OBLIGATIONS (LAW)

— Russia.

TOLSTOI (VLADIMIR STEPANOVICH) Ispolnenie obiazatel'stv. Moskva, 1973. pp. 207.

O'BRIEN (LAWRENCE FRANCIS).

O'BRIEN (LAWRENCE FRANCIS) No final victories: a life in politics, from John F. Kennedy to Watergate. New York, 1974. pp. 394.

OBSCENITY (LAW)

— United Kingdom.

HALLIS (FREDERICK) The law and obscenity. London, 1932. pp. 40.

OBSESSIVE—COMPULSIVE NEUROSES.

BEECH (HAROLD REGINALD) ed. Obsessional states. London, 1974. pp. 352. bibliog.

OBSTETRICS.

CIBA FOUNDATION. Symposia. New Series. 17. Law and ethics of A[rtificial] I[nsemination by] D[onor] and embryo transfer. Amsterdam, 1973. pp. 110. bibliogs.

MATERNITY services: integration of maternity work; [report of a joint sub-committee of the Standing Nursing and Midwifery Advisory Committee and the Standing Medical Advisory Committee of the Scottish Health Services Council; R.A. Tennent, chairman]. Edinburgh, H.M.S.O., 1973. pp. 56.

OCCUPATIONAL DISEASES.

INTERNATIONAL LABOUR CONFERENCE. 58th Session. Reports. 7. Control and prevention of occupational cancer: seventh item on the agenda. Geneva, 1972-73. 2 pts.

INTERNATIONAL LABOUR CONFERENCE. 59th Session. Reports. 5. Control and prevention of occupational hazards caused by carcinogenic substances and agents; fifth item on the agenda. Geneva, 1973-74. 2 pts.

KINNERSLY (PATRICK) The hazards of work: how to fight them. London, 1973. pp. 394.

OCCUPATIONAL MOBILITY.

INTERNATIONAL WORKSHOP ON CAREER MOBILITY, KONSTANZ, 1971. Social stratification and career mobility; [papers presented at the workshop]; edited by Walter Müller and Karl Ulrich Mayer. Paris, [1973]. pp. 390. *bibliogs.* (*International Social Science Council. Publications. 16*)

GEARY (ROBERT CHARLES) and Ó MUIRCHEARTAIGH (F.S.) Equalization of opportunity in Ireland: statistical aspects. Dublin, 1974. pp. 122. (*Economic and Social Research Institute. Broadsheets. 10*)

OCCUPATIONAL THERAPISTS

— United Kingdom.

The REMEDIAL professions; a report by a Working Party set up in March 1973 by the Secretary of State for Social Services; [E.L. McMillan, chairman]. London, H.M.S.O., 1973. pp. 24.

OCCUPATIONAL TRAINING

— Canada.

FEDERALISM and policy development: the case of adult occupational training in Ontario; ([by] J. Stefan Dupré [and others]). Toronto, [1973]. pp. 248.

— Germany, Eastern.

GERMANY (DEUTSCHE DEMOKRATISCHE REPUBLIK). Staatsrat. Abteilung Presse und Information. 1970. Grundsätze für die Aus- und Weiterbildung der Werktätigen: Materialien der 18. Tagung der Volkskammer der DDR am 16. September 1970, etc. [Berlin], 1970. pp. 79. (*Aus der Taetigkeit der Volkskammer und ihrer Ausschüsse. 5. Wahlperiode. Heft 19*)

— Russia.

NOVGORODSKII (IURII FEDOROVICH) and others. Technicheskii progress i sovershenstvovanie podgotovki kadrov. Moskva, 1973. pp. 151.

— United Kingdom.

SALFORD. University. Department of Sociology, Government and Administration. Unemployment and occupational training: [a number of papers delivered for a course at the university, 1971-1972; course organiser, Miss M.P. Reay]. Salford, [1972]. pp. 63.

— United States.

MANGUM (GARTH LEROY) and ROBSON (R. THAYNE) eds. Metropolitan impact of manpower programs: a four-city comparison. Salt Lake City, [1973]. pp. 304. *bibliog.*

NEW directions in employability: reducing barriers to full employment; [papers of a conference sponsored by the National Graduate University in 1972]; edited by David B. Orr. New York, 1973. pp. 244.

O'NEILL (DAVE M.) The Federal government and manpower: a critical look at the MDTA-Institutional and Job Corps programs. Washington, D.C., 1973. pp. 65. (*American Enterprise Institute for Public Policy Research. Evaluative Studies. 9*)

OCCUPATIONS.

SALAMAN (GRAEME) Community and occupation: an exploration of work/leisure relationships. London, 1974. pp. 136. *bibliog.* (*Cambridge. University. Department of Applied Economics. Cambridge Papers in Sociology. No.4*)

— Classification.

JALLADE (JEAN-PIERRE) and others. Occupational and educational structures of the labour force and levels of economic development. Paris, Organisation for Economic Co-operation and Development, 1970-71. 2 vols.

AUSTRIA. Statistisches Zentralamt. 1972. Systematisches Verzeichnis der Berufe: überarbeitete Neuauflage des systematischen Verzeichnisses der Berufe 1961, mit einem alphabetischen Anhang. Ausgabe 1971. Wien, 1972. pp. 216.

— Diseases and hygiene.

See OCCUPATIONAL DISEASES.

OCEAN BOTTOM.

LUARD (DAVID EVAN TRANT) The control of the sea-bed: a new international issue. London, 1974. pp. 309.

OCEANIA

— Biography.

DAVIDSON (JAMES WIGHTMAN) and SCARR (DERYCK ANTONY) eds. Pacific islands portraits. Canberra, 1970. pp. 346.

— History.

DAVIDSON (JAMES WIGHTMAN) and SCARR (DERYCK ANTONY) eds. Pacific islands portraits. Canberra, 1970. pp. 346.

O'CONNELL (DANIEL).

McGEE (THOMAS D'ARCY). hISTORICAL SKETCHES OF o'cONNELL AND HIS FRIENDS...WITH A GLANCE AT THE FUTURE DESTINY OF iRELAND. 2ND ED. bOSTON, 1845. PP. 208.

O'CONNELL (DANIEL) The correspondence of Daniel O'Connell...; edited by Maurice R. O'Connell. Shannon, 1972 in progress.

OCTOBRISTS.

See SOIUZ SEMNADTSATOGO OKTIABRIA.

ODER RIVER.

BIERMAN (DON EDWARD) The Oder river: transport and economic development. Evanston, Ill., [1973]. pp. 247. *bibliog.* (*Northwestern University. Transportation Center. Monographs. No. 1*)

ODESSA

— History — 1917—1921, Revolution.

AVERBUKH (N.I.) Odesskaia "chrezvychaika", bol'shevistskii zastenok: fakty i nabliudeniia N.I. Averbukha (Averiusa). ch.1. Kishinev, 1920. pp. 39.

O'DONOVAN ROSSA (DIARMUID).

O'DONOVAN ROSSA (DIARMUID) Rossa's recollections, 1838-1898; [reprint of the first edition, New York 1898]; introduction by Sean O Luing and a new index. Shannon, [1972]. pp. 410. *bibliog.*

ODOUR CONTROL.

U.K. Working Party on the Suppression of Odours from Offensive and Selected Other Trades. 1974- . Odours; report; [F.H.H. Valentin, chairman]. Stevenage, 1974 in progress.

OFFENCES AGAINST PROPERTY

— Finland.

AROMAA (KAUKO) and LEPPÄ (SEPPO) Omaisuusrikosten yksilöuhrien tarkastelua, etc. Helsinki, 1973. fo. 57. *bibliog.* (*Kriminologinen Tutkimuslaitos. Sarja M. 26*) *With English summary.*

MÄKINEN (TUIJA) Rikosvahinkotilastointikokeilu, etc. Helsinki, 1973. fo. 68. *bibliog.* (*Kriminologinen Tutkimuslaitos. Sarja M. 28*) *With English summary.*

OFFENCES AGAINST THE PERSON

— Finland.

MÄKINEN (TUIJA) Rikosvahinkotilastointikokeilu, etc. Helsinki, 1973. fo. 68. *bibliog.* (*Kriminologinen Tutkimuslaitos. Sarja M. 28*) *With English summary.*

AROMAA (KAUKO) The replication of a survey on victimization to violence: a report on changes in the violence situation from 1970 to 1973 in Finland. Helsinki, 1974. fo. 30. (*Kriminologinen Tutkimuslaitos. Sarja M. 36*)

OFFICE BUILDINGS.

INSTITUTE OF PERSONNEL MANAGEMENT. Living in an office landscape; [by Annette Thies and Margaret Barnard]. London, 1971. pp. 89. *bibliog.* (*Information Reports. New Series. 8*)

OFFICES

— Location — United Kingdom.

MANCHESTER. City Planning Department. Central Manchester office survey 1971; [J.S. Millar, City Planning Officer]. Manchester, [1972?]. pp. 56.

GODDARD (JOHN BURGESS) Office linkages and location: a study of communications and spatial patterns in Central London; [Ph.D.(London) thesis] . 1973. fo. 124. *bibliog.* *Unpublished. This thesis is the property of London University and may not be removed from the Library.*

OFFICIAL SECRETS

— United Kingdom.

NONE of your business: (government secrecy in America): [proceedings of a conference held in New York in 1973, sponsored jointly by the Committee for Public Justice and the Arthur Garfield Hays Civil Liberties Program at New York University School of Law]; edited by Norman Dorsen and Stephen Gillers. New York, 1974. pp. 362.

— United States.

NONE of your business: (government secrecy in America): [proceedings of a conference held in New York in 1973, sponsored jointly by the Committee for Public Justice and the Arthur Garfield Hays Civil Liberties Program at New York University School of Law]; edited by Norman Dorsen and Stephen Gillers. New York, 1974. pp. 362.

OIL INDUSTRIES

— Information services.

UNITED NATIONS INDUSTRIAL DEVELOPMENT ORGANIZATION. Guides to Information Sources. No. 7. Information sources on the vegetable oil processing industry. (UNIDO/LIB/SER.D/7). New York, United Nations, 1973. pp. 90. *bibliog.*

— Iraq.

OIL AND MINERALS IN IRAQ; [pd. annually under supervision of a permanent committee from the Ministry of Oils and Minerals, the Iraqi National Oil Company and the Iraqi National Minerals Company]. a., 1970 (1st)- Baghdad.

OIL POLLUTION OF RIVERS, HARBOURS, ETC.

INTERNATIONAL CONFERENCE ON PREVENTION OF POLLUTION OF THE SEA BY OIL, 1962. (Final act of the 1962 Conference and its Annexes...[and] complete text of the amended 1954 Convention... [and] charts indicating the extent of the probibited zones). London, Inter-governmental Maritime Consultative Organization, 1962. pp. 93. *In English and French.*

INTER-GOVERNMENTAL MARITIME CONSULTATIVE ORGANIZATION. 1967. Charts of prohibited zones: International Convention for the Prevention of Pollution of the Sea by Oil. London, [1967]. pp. 7 (and charts). *In English and French.*

INTER-GOVERNMENTAL MARITIME CONSULTATIVE ORGANIZATION. 1967. International Convention for the Prevention of Pollution of the Sea by Oil, 1954, including the amendments adopted in 1962. London, [1967]. pp. 47. *In English and French.*

CONFERENCE ON THE ESTABLISHMENT OF AN INTERNATIONAL COMPENSATION FUND FOR OIL POLLUTION DAMAGE, 1971. Final act of the Conference with attachments including the text of the adopted Convention. London, Inter-Governmental Maritime Consultative Organization, [1972]. pp. 84. *In English and French.*

INTER-GOVERNMENTAL MARITIME CONSULTATIVE ORGANIZATION. 1972. Charts of prohibited zones: International Convention for the Prevention of Pollution of the Sea by Oil. London, 1972. pp. 7 (and charts). *In English and French.*

INTER-GOVERNMENTAL MARITIME CONSULTATIVE ORGANIZATION. 1972. Manual on oil pollution: practical information on means of dealing with oil spillages. London, [1972]. pp. 84.

INTER-GOVERNMENTAL MARITIME CONSULTATIVE ORGANIZATION. 1972. International Convention for the Prevention of Pollution of the Sea by Oil, 1954, including the amendments adopted in 1962. London, [1972]. pp. 77. *In English and French.*

INTERNATIONAL LEGAL CONFERENCE ON MARINE POLLUTION DAMAGE, 1969. Official records of the ... Conference etc. London, Inter-governmental Maritime Consultative Organization, 1973. pp. 819.

ROSS (WILLIAM MICHAEL) Oil pollution as an international problem: a study of Puget Sound and the Strait of Georgia. Seattle, 1973. pp. 278. *bibliog.*

OILS AND FATS

— Information services.

UNITED NATIONS INDUSTRIAL DEVELOPMENT ORGANIZATION. Guides to Information Sources. No. 7. Information sources on the vegetable oil processing industry. (UNIDO/LIB/SER.D/7). New York, United Nations, 1973. pp. 90. *bibliog.*

OILS AND FATS, EDIBLE.

KUHL (ESTHER ELISABETH) Der schweizerische Buttermarkt unter besonderer Berücksichtigung der Konkurrenzprodukte, Speiseöle, Speisefette und Margarine. Zürich, 1974. pp. 181. *bibliog.*

OKPE

— Politics and government.

OTITE (ONIGU) Autonomy and dependence: the Urhobo Kingdom of Okpe in modern Nigeria. London, [1973]. pp. 215. *bibliog.*

OLD AGE

— Hospital care — United Kingdom.

PARNELL (JOAN W.) and NAYLOR (ROGER) Home for the weekend - back on Monday: a study of a five-day ward for the rehabilitation of geriatric patients. London, [1973]. pp. 153.

— — — Scotland.

SCOTTISH HOSPITAL CENTRE.Centrepiece Series. Day hospitals for geriatric patients. Edinburgh, 1973. pp. 98.

— Austria.

AUSTRIA. Statistisches Zentralamt. 1972. Lebensverhältnisse älterer Menschen: Ergebnisse des Mikrozensus, Dezember 1971. Wien, 1972.'pp. 138. *(Beiträge zur Österreichischen Statistik. Heft 310)*

— Denmark — Care and hygiene.

FÜRSTNOW-SØRENSEN (BENT) Samfundet og de aeldre. [Copenhagen], 1969. pp. 30.

DENMARK. Udvalget om Omsorg for Aeldre og for Pensionister. 1972. Betaenkning om omsorgen for aeldre og for pensionister. [Copenhagen], 1972. pp. 80. *(Denmark. Betaenkninger. Nr. 630)*

OLSEN (HENNING) Aeldre på pleje- og alderdomshjem, etc. København, 1973. pp. 396. *(Socialforskningsinstituttet. Publikationer. 57) With English summary.*

— Europe.

UNITED NATIONS. Department of Economic and Social Affairs. European Social Development Programme. Reports . New York, 1967 in progress.

— Finland — Care and hygiene.

SINTONEN (HARRI) Vanhusten huoltomuodon valinnasta, etc. Helsinki, 1973. pp. 86. *bibliog. (Finland. Suomen Virallinen Tilasto. Finlands Officiella Statistik. 32. Sosiaalisia Erikoistutkimuksia. 36) With English summary.*

— France.

MASLOWSKI (JACQUELINE) and PAILLAT (PAUL) Conditions de vie et besoins des personnes agées en France. III. Les ruraux agés non agricoles. [Paris], 1973. pp. 246. *(France. Institut National d'Etudes Démographiques. Travaux et Documents. Cahiers. No. 68)*

— Netherlands.

NETHERLANDS. Ministerie van Cultuur, Recreatie en Maatschappelijk Werk. 1970. Nota bejaardenbeleid 1970. 's-Gravenhage, 1970. pp. 41.

MAST (FRANS A.C.DE) and others. Atlas van de ouder wordende Nederlandse bevolking. Nijmegen, 1972. pp. 126. *bibliog.*

— Norway.

MIDRÉ (GEORGES) Å bli gammel: en sosiologisk beskrivelse av aldring i en utkantkommune. Oslo, [1973]. pp. 152. *bibliog.*

NORWAY. Komitéen for Eldreomsorgen. 1973. Eldres helse, aktivitet og trivsel: utredning 4 fra Komitéen, etc. Oslo, 1973. pp. 119. *(Norway. Norges Offentlige Utredninger. 1973.26)*

Å vaere pensjonist; utgitt av Rådet for Eldreomsorgen, [and others]. [Oslo, 1971]. pp. 32.

— — Dwellings.

NORWAY. Komitéen for Eldreomsorgen. 1971. Innstilling om boliger for eldre: innstilling 3...avgitt 30. desember 1970. Oslo, 1971. pp. 116.

— South Africa.

SOUTH AFRICA. National Bureau of Educational and Social Research. 1962. The living conditions of the aged. [Pretoria], 1962. pp. 115. *bibliog.*

— Switzerland.

COMMISSION D'ETUDE DES PROBLEMES DE LA VIEILLESSE [SWITZERLAND]. Les problèmes de la vieillesse en Suisse: rapport de la Commission, etc.; [A. Saxer, chairman]. Berne, 1967. pp. 341. *bibliog.*

— United Kingdom.

U.K. Social Survey. [Reports. New Series.] 327. Health and welfare of older people in Lewisham;...an inquiry carried out on behalf of the Lewisham Co-ordinating Committee sponsored by the King Edward's Hospital Fund for London. [London], 1962. 1 vol. (various pagings).

REDBRIDGE. Health and Welfare Department. Survey of the elderly in the London Borough of Redbridge, 1968; report. [London], Greater London Council, 1970. pp. 22.

CARE of the elderly; the report of a Working Party. Vols. 1-2; (with A summary of main recommendations); [M.R.P. Hall, chairman]. Winchester, Wessex Regional Hospital Board, [1972?]. 3 pts.(in 1). *Vol. 3 produced for limited circulation only and not in Library.*

GREENWICH. Chief Executive and Town Clerk's Department. Programme Planning Section. The elderly in Greenwich: report of a survey. [London], 1972. pp. 52.

KENSINGTON AND CHELSEA. Social Services Department. Survey of handicapped and impaired persons and persons aged 75 or over and living alone in the...Borough...; research...by Judith Buckle and Philip Baldwin. London, 1972. pp. 103.

NEEDS of the elderly for health and welfare services: proceedings of a seminar held at the University of Exeter 1-3 March 1972; edited by R.W. Canvin and N.G. Pearson. Exeter, 1973. pp. 106. *bibliogs. (Exeter. University. Institute of Biometry and Community Medicine. Publications. No. 2)*

U.K. Census, 1971. Census, 1971: Great Britain: persons of pensionable age. London, 1974. pp. 329.

— — Care and hygiene.

PARNELL (JOAN W.) and NAYLOR (ROGER) Home for the weekend - back on Monday: a study of a five-day ward for the rehabilitation of geriatric patients. London, [1973]. pp. 153.

— — Dwellings.

GREENWICH. Chief Executive and Town Clerk's Department. Programme Planning Section. Old people's homes and sheltered housing in Greenwich: (key issue report). Greenwich, 1972. fo. 27.

— United States.

BUCKLEY (MARY) The aged are people, too: about William Posner and social work with the old. Port Washington, N.Y., 1972. pp. 174. *bibliog.*

BAHR (HOWARD M.) and CAPLOW (THEODORE) Old men drunk and sober. New York, 1973. pp. 407. *bibliog.*

— — Care and hygiene.

CULL (JOHN G.) and HARDY (RICHARD E.) The neglected older American: social and rehabilitation services.Springfield, Ill., [1973]. pp. 263.

— — Dwellings.

COGGESHALL (JOHN H.) Management of retirement homes and long-term care facilities. Saint Louis, 1973. pp. 200.

— — Georgia — Dwellings.

CRAWFORD (FRED R.) and SPARKS (JUNELLE) Housing aid to the aged in Atlanta's model cities: a systematic evaluation. Atlanta, 1973. pp. 146. *(Emory University. Center for Research in Social Change. Publications. Series B. Report No. 3)*

— — Maryland.

MARYLAND. Commission on Aging. 1971-72. Maryland's older population: an assessment of needs and services; [by Robert T. Landsdale and William D. Bechill].[Baltimore], 1971-72. 4 pts. (in 1 vol.).

OLD AGE HOMES

— Denmark.

OLSEN (HENNING) Aeldre på pleje- og alderdomshjem, etc. København, 1973. pp. 396. *(Socialforskningsinstituttet. Publikationer. 57) With English summary.*

— New Zealand.

HARVEY (THOMAS BLAIR) A clinical study of aged persons in old people's homes and hospitals in Hawke's Bay. [Wellington, Government Printer, 1970]. pp. 32.

NEW ZEALAND. Department of Health. National Health Statistics Centre. 1973. Census of public, private and maternity hospital patients, and old people's homes, 1971. Wellington, 1973. pp. 58. *(Department of Health. Special Report Series. No. 41)*

— United Kingdom.

GREENWICH. Chief Executive and Town Clerk's Department. Programme Planning Section. Old people's homes and sheltered housing in Greenwich: (key issue report). Greenwich, 1972. fo. 27.

BOLDY (DUNCAN) and others. The elderly in grouped dwellings: a profile. Exeter, 1973. pp. 50. *bibliog. (Exeter. University. Institute of Biometry and Community Medicine. Publications. No.3)*

— United States.

COGGESHALL (JOHN H.) Management of retirement homes and long-term care facilities. Saint Louis, 1973. pp. 200.

OLD AGE PENSIONS

— Europe.

WILSON (THOMAS) Ph.D., ed. Pensions, inflation and growth: a comparative study of the elderly in the welfare state. London, 1974. pp. 422.

— Germany.

SCHMAEHL (WINFRIED) Systemänderung in der Altersvorsorge: von der einkommensabhängigen Altersrente zur Staatsbürger- Grundrente, etc. Opladen, [1974]. pp. 294. *bibliog.*

— United Kingdom.

JONES (JAMES LARKIN) What about the pensioners?. London, 1973. pp. 20.

LABOUR RESEARCH DEPARTMENT. Services for pensioners. London, 1973. pp. 30.

OLD BELIEVERS.

See RASKOLNIKS.

OLDHAM

— Civic improvement.

LICHFIELD (NATHANIEL) AND ASSOCIATES and INBUCON/AIC MANAGEMENT CONSULTANTS LIMITED. The Oldham study: environmental planning and management. London, H.M.S.O., 1973. pp. 59. *bibliog.*

— Poor.

U.K. Ministry of Housing and Local Government. Sociological Research Station. 1963. Living in a slum: a study of people in a central slum clearance area in Oldham. [London], 1963. fo. 59. *bibliog.*

— Social history.

FOSTER (JOHN) 1940- . Class struggle and the industrial revolution: early industrial capitalism in three English towns. London, [1974]. pp. 346. *bibliog.*

OLIGOPOLIES.

MUNIER (BERTRAND) Jeux et marchés. Paris, 1973. pp. 172. *bibliogs.*

OLORON—SAINTE—MARIE

— Politics and government.

BOUSQUET-MELOU (JEAN) Louis Barthou et la circonscription d'Oloron, 1889-1914. Paris, [1972]. pp. 268. *bibliog.* (Bordeaux. Université. Institut d'Etudes Politiques. Centre d'Etude et de Recherche sur la Vie Locale. Série Vie Locale. 3)

OLYMPIC GAMES.

KRUEGER (ARND) Die Olympischen Spiele 1936 und die Weltmeinung: ihre aussenpolitische Bedeutung, unter besonderer Berücksichtigung der USA. Berlin, [1972]. pp. 255. *bibliog.*

OMAN

— Description and travel.

SKEET (IAN) Muscat and Oman: the end of an era. London, 1974. pp. 224.

— History.

SKEET (IAN) Muscat and Oman: the end of an era. London, 1974. pp. 224.

— Politics and government.

SKEET (IAN) Muscat and Oman: the end of an era. London, 1974. pp. 224.

— Relations (military) with the United Kingdom.

GULF COMMITTEE. Dhofar: Britain's colonial war in the Gulf; a collection of documents and articles. London, 1972. pp. 72.

Statistics.

GERMANY (BUNDESREPUBLIK). Statistisches Bundesamt. Länderkurzberichte: Oman. irreg., 1974- Wiesbaden.

OMBUDSMAN.

ROWAT (DONALD CAMERON) The ombudsman plan: essays on the worldwide spread of an idea. Toronto, [1973]. pp. 314. *bibliog.*

WEEKS (KENT M.) Ombudsmen around the world: a comparative chart. Berkeley, 1973. pp. 101. (California University. Institute of Governmental Studies. Ombudsman Research. Monographs)

— Finland.

HIDÉN (MIKAEL) The Ombudsman in Finland: the first fifty years;... translated by Aaron Bell; edited and with a foreword by Donald C. Rowat. Berkeley, 1973. pp. 198. *bibliog.* (California University. Institute of Governmental Studies. Ombudsman Research. Monographs)

— United States.

FITZHARRIS (TIMOTHY L.) The desirability of a correctional ombudsman. Berkeley, Ca., 1973. pp. 114.

GWYN (WILLIAM BRENT) Barriers to establishing urban ombudsmen: the case of Newark. Berkeley, 1974. pp. 93. (California University. Institute of Governmental Studies. Ombudsman Research. Monographs)

WYNER (ALAN J.) The Nebraska ombudsman: innovation in state government. Berkeley, 1974. pp. 160. (California University. Institute of Governmental Studies. Ombudsman Research. Monographs)

OMSK (OBLAST')

— Statistics.

OMSK (OBLAST'). Statisticheskoe Upravlenie. Narodnoe khoziaistvo Omskoi oblasti: statisticheskii sbornik. Omsk, 1971. pp. 261.

ONTARIO

— Emigration and immigration.

LEVERIDGE (ANNA MARIA) Your loving Anna: letters from the Ontario frontier; [edited by] Louis Tivy. Toronto, [1972]. pp. 120.

— Government publications.

ONTARIO GOVERNMENT PUBLICATIONS; (pd. by the Ministry of Government Services... Ontario). a., 1972 (1st)- Toronto.

ONTARIO GOVERNMENT PUBLICAYIONS; (pd. by the Ministry of Government Services... Ontario). a., 1972 (1st)- Toronto.

— Population.

AMYOT (MICHEL) and GEORGE (M.V.) Intraprovincial migration streams in Quebec and Ontario, 1956- 1961. Ottawa, 1973. pp. 51. *bibliog.* (Canada. Statistics Canada. [Census Division]. Analytical and Technical Memoranda. No. 8)

ONYEAMA (DILLIBE).

ONYEAMA (DILLIBE) John Bull's nigger. London, 1974. pp. 159.

OPEN UNIVERSITY.

TUNSTALL (JEREMY) ed. The Open University opens. London, 1974. pp. 191. *bibliog.*

OPERATIONS RESEARCH.

CETRON (MARVIN J.) and others, eds. Quantitative decision aiding techniques for research and development management; [papers presented at the Military Operations Research Society Working Group on Research Management]. New York, [1972]. pp. 205.

INTERNATIONAL CONFERENCE ON OPERATIONAL RESEARCH. 6th Conference, Dublin, 1972. Operational research '72: proceedings...; edited by Miceal Ross. Amsterdam, 1973. pp. 732.

BOOTHROYD (HYLTON) On the theory of operational research. Coventry, 1974. pp. 77. (University of Warwick. Centre for Industrial, Economic and Business Research. [Warwick Research in Industrial and Business Studies]. No.51)

LEWIS (RALPH F.) Planning and control for profit;... UK and Commonwealth edition. London, 1974. pp. 208. *bibliog.*

OPIUM TRADE.

LAMOUR (CATHERINE) and LAMBERTI (MICHEL R.) pseud. The second opium war; translated by Peter and Betty Ross. London, 1974. pp. 278.

OPPENHEIMER (Sir ERNEST).

HOCKING (ANTHONY) Oppenheimer and son. New York, [1973]. pp. 526. *bibliog.*

OPPENHEIMER (HARRY FREDERICK).

HOCKING (ANTHONY) Oppenheimer and son. New York, [1973]. pp. 526. *bibliog.*

OPPOSITION (POLITICAL SCIENCE).

PATERSON (WILLIAM EDGAR) The German Social Democratic Party and European integration, 1949-57: a case-study of opposition in foreign affairs; [Ph.D. (London) thesis]. 1972. fo. 239. *bibliog. Typescript: unpublished. This thesis is the property of London University and may not be removed from the Library.*

FACH (WOLFGANG) Koalition und Opposition in spieltheoretischer Sicht: ein Beitrag zur Analyse und Kritik der neuen politischen Ökonomie. Berlin, [1974]. pp. 200. *bibliog.*

PATERSON (WILLIAM EDGAR) The SPD and European integration. Farnborough, [1974]. pp. 177. *bibliog.*

OPTICAL ILLUSIONS.

ROBINSON (J.O.) The psychology of visual illusion. London, 1972. pp. 288. *bibliog.*

GREGORY (RICHARD LANGTON) and GOMBRICH (Sir ERNST HANS) eds. Illusion in nature and art. London, 1973. pp. 288. *bibliogs.*

OPUS DEI.

THIERRY (JEAN JACQUES) L'Opus Dei: mythe et réalité. [Paris, 1973]. pp. 179. *bibliog.*

ORCHESTRA.

GANE (MICHAEL JOHN) Social changes in English music and music-making, 1800-1970, with special reference to the symphony orchestra; [Ph.D. (London) thesis]. 1972 [or rather 1973]. fo. 233. *bibliog. Typescript: unpublished. This thesis is the property of London University and may not be removed from the Library.*

ORELLI—RINDERKNECHT (SUSANNA).

VEREIN FÜR WIRTSCHAFTSHISTORISCHE STUDIEN. Schweizer Pioniere der Wirtschaft und Technik. 26. Zwei Pionierinnen der Volksgesundheit: Susanna Orelli- Rinderknecht, 1845-1939; Else Züblin-Spiller, 1881-1948. Zürich, 1973. pp. 103. *bibliog.*

ORGANISATION FOR ECONOMIC COOPERATION AND DEVELOPMENT

— Norway.

NORWAY. Utenriksdepartementet. 1970. Om Norges deltakelse i Organisasjonen for Økonomisk Samarbeid og Utvikling (OECD). [Oslo?, 1970?]. pp. 24. (Norway. Stortinget. Stortingsmeldinger. 1969-70, nr. 12)

ORGANIZATION.

SEASHORE (STANLEY E.) and BOWERS (DAVID G.) Changing the structure and functioning of an organization: report of a field experiment. Ann Arbor, Mich., [1963]. pp. 113.

FERGUS (H.K.) Selected aspects of the organization of Brockhill. [London], 1972. fo. 102. *bibliog.* (*U.K. Prison Department. Office of the Chief Psychologist. CP Reports. Series. 1. No. 1*)

CROZIER (MICHEL) The stalled society. New York, 1973. pp. 177.

NEGANDHI (ANANT R.) ed. Modern organizational theory: contextual, environmental, and socio-cultural variables; [selection of papers first presented at annual conferences of the Comparative Administration Research Institute, Kent State University, 1968-71]. Kent, Ohio, [1973]. pp. 404.

PETTIGREW (ANDREW M.) The politics of organizational decision-making. London, 1973. pp. 302. *bibliog.*

SMITH (PETER B.) Groups within organizations: applications of social psychology to organizational behaviour. London, 1973. pp. 134. *bibliog.*

VICKERS (Sir CHARLES GEOFFREY) Making institutions work. London, 1973. pp. 187.

VROOM (VICTOR HAROLD) and YETTON (PHILIP W.) Leadership and decision-making. Pittsburgh, [1973]. pp. 233. *bibliog.*

WAMSLEY (GARY L.) and ZALD (MAYER NATHAN) The political economy of public organizations: a critique and approach to the study of public administration. Lexington, [1973]. pp. 110.

BRADLEY (DAVID A.) and WILKIE (ROY) The concept of organization: an introduction to organizations. Glasgow, [1974]. pp. 123. *bibliog.*

ORGANIZATION OF AMERICAN STATES.

CHAYES (ABRAM) The Cuban missile crisis. London, 1974. pp. 157. (*American Society of International Law. International Crises and the Role of Law*)

— Bibliography.

ORGANIZATION OF AMERICAN STATES. 1961. Official records series of the Organization of American States: guide, outline and expanded tables, etc. Washington, 1961. pp. 68. (*Official Records. Series Y/I.1 Rev, etc.*)

ORGANIZATION OF CENTRAL AMERICAN STATES.

INSTITUTO CENTROAMERICANO DE ADMINISTRACION PUBLICA. Documentos sobre aspectos institucionales de la integracion centroamericana. San José, 1973. 1 vol. (various pagings).

ORGANIZATION OF THE PETROLEUM EXPORTING COUNTRIES.

ISKANDAR (MARWAN) The Arab oil question. [Beirut, 1973]. pp. 109.

ORGANIZATIONAL CHANGE.

THOMAS (JOHN M.) and BENNIS (WARREN G.) eds. The management of change and conflict: selected readings. Harmondsworth, 1972. pp. 507. *bibliogs.*

JOHNS (EDWARD ALISTAIR) The sociology of organizational change. Oxford, 1973. pp. 173. *bibliog.*

ZALTMAN (GERALD) and others. Innovations and organizations. New York, [1973]. pp. 212. *bibliog.*

ORGANIZATIONAL RESEARCH.

HAGE (JERALD) Communication and organizational control: cybernetics in health and welfare settings. New York, [1974]. pp. 273. *bibliog.*

HERBST (PHILIP G.) Socio-technical design: strategies in multidisciplinary research. London, 1974. pp. 242. *bibliog.*

ORIENTAL STUDIES

— Russia.

DANTSIG (BORIS MOISEEVICH) Blizhnii Vostok v russkoi nauke i literature: dooktiabr'skii period. Moskva, 1973. pp. 434. *bibliog.*

— United Kingdom — Bibliography.

CURRENT BRITISH RESEARCH IN MIDDLE EASTERN AND ISLAMIC STUDIES; ([pd. by] Centre for Middle Eastern and Islamic Studies, University of Durham). a., 1971 (no.2)- Durham.

ORIGIN AND DESTINATION TRAFFIC SURVEYS

— Sweden — Uppsala.

WESTELIUS (ORVAR) The individual's pattern of travel in an urban area. Stockholm, 1972. pp. 202. *bibliog.* (*Sweden. Statens Institut for Byggnadsforskning. Documents. 1972. D2) With Swedish summary.*

— United Kingdom.

U.K. Department of Trade and Industry. 1972. Passengers in Wales, West, Midlands, North East and Northern Ireland: origin and destination survey, 7 June-4 October 1971. London, 1972. pp. 55.

ORISSA

— Rural conditions.

NAGIN: story of the short life of Nagin Parekh which ended as a lance broken in the service of the tribesfolk of South Orissa; edited by Evelyn Wood from contributions by Nagin's friends and colleagues, and especially Annasaheb Sahasrabudhe. Bombay, [1965]. pp. 170.

ORMUZ.

See HORMUZ.

OROKAIVAS.

SCHWIMMER (ERIK) Exchange in the social structure of the Orokaiva: traditional and emergent ideologies in the Northern District of Papua. London, [1973]. pp. 244. *bibliog.*

ORTHOPAEDIA.

ELLIS (JAMES) Getting it straight: an inaugural lecture delivered at the University [of Southampton], 2nd May 1974. Southampton, 1974. pp. 14.

OSAKA

— Commerce.

HAUSER (WILLIAM B.) Economic institutional change in Tokugawa Japan: Osaka and Kinai cotton trade. London, 1974. pp. 239. *bibliog.*

OSLO

— Transit systems.

NORWAY. Naertrafikk-Komitéen for Oslo-Området. 1971. Innstilling om naertrafikken i Oslo-området. [Oslo, 1971]. pp. 222.

OTTO, Archduke of Austria.

La VOCATION européenne d'Otto de Hapsbourg-Lorraine; ([by] Marcel Regamey [and others]). Lausanne, 1973. pp. 183. (*Lausanne. Université. Centre de Recherches Européennes. Publications. 1. Histoire, Précurseurs et Promoteurs de l'Union de l'Europe*)

OUAGADOUGOU

— Census.

UPPER VOLTA. Service de la Statistique Générale. 1964. Recensement démographique, Ouagadougou, 1961-1962: résultats définitifs. Paris, 1964. pp. 93.

— Social conditions.

SKINNER (ELLIOTT PERCIVAL) African urban life: the transformation of Ouagadougou. Princeton, [1974]. pp. 487. *bibliog.*

OUDENAARDE

— Economic conditions.

GHENT. Université. Hogere School voor Handels- en Economische Wetenschappen. Seminar for Applied Economics. Het arrondissement Oudenaarde: een regionaal-economische studie [uitgevoerd op initiatief van het Staatssecretariaat voor Streekeconomie en het Provinciebestuur van Oost-Vlaanderen]; algemene leiding: A.J. Vlerick. Gent, [1973]. pp. 413. (*Reeks Regionaal-Economische Studien*)

— Social conditions.

GHENT. Université. Hogere School voor Handels- en Economische Wetenschappen. Seminar for Applied Economics. Het arrondissement Oudenaarde: een regionaal-economische studie [uitgevoerd op initiatief van het Staatssecretariaat voor Streekeconomie en het Provinciebestuur van Oost-Vlaanderen]; algemene leiding: A.J. Vlerick. Gent, [1973]. pp. 413. (*Reeks Regionaal-Economische Studien*)

OUTDOOR RECREATION

— United Kingdom.

U.K. Countryside Commission. Research Branch. 1969. Digest of countryside recreation statistics, 1969. [London, 1969]. pp. 31.

LINDSEY. County Council. Countryside recreation: the ecological implications:...lowland Britain with particular reference to the countryside of Lindsey; [compiled by R.J. Lloyd]. [Lincoln], 1970. pp. 125.

INLAND WATERWAYS AMENITY ADVISORY COUNCIL [U.K.]. Remainder waterways: a report to the Secretary of State for the Environment containing the recommendations of the Advisory Council in respect of proposals received between 1968 and 1971 for the addition of certain of the 'remainder' waterways to the cruising waterway system. [London], 1971. pp. 60.

INLAND WATERWAYS AMENITY ADVISORY COUNCIL [U.K.]. Waterway facilities: a report to the Secretary of State for the Environment on the leisure potential of the inland waterway system. [London], 1972. pp. 24.

— United States.

CICCHETTI (CHARLES J.) Forecasting recreation in the United States: an economic review of methods and applications to plan for the required environmental resources. Lexington, [1973]. pp. 200. *bibliog.*

OVAMBOLAND.

SOUTH AFRICA. Department of Foreign Affairs. 1971. Owambo. [Pretoria], 1971. pp. 37.

OVANDO CANDIA (ALFREDO).

OBLITAS FERNANDEZ (EDGAR) Un perfil, una revolucion: breve ensayo biografico del Gral. Alfredo Ovando Candia. La Paz, 1970. pp. 134.

OVERTIME

— United Kingdom.

TRADES UNION CONGRESS. Overtime and shift-working: (a guide for negotiators). London, 1973. pp. 35. *bibliog.*

OWEN (ROBERT).

ROBERT OWEN BICENTENNIAL CONFERENCE, NEW HARMONY, INDIANA, 1971. Robert Owen's American legacy: proceedings...; edited by Donald E. Pitzer; [sponsored by the Department of History, Indiana State University, Evansville, and by Harmonie Associates, New Harmony, Indiana]. Indianapolis, 1972. pp. 88.

TORITSYN (TIMOFEI MIKHAILOVICH) Uchenie Roberta Ouena i ego vliianie nna rasprostranenie i razvitie sotsialisticheskikh idei. Riazan', 1972. pp. 174. *bibliog.*

OXFORD

OXFORD

— Transit systems.

OXFORD. University. University travel and parking survey; [carried out jointly with the City Council]. Oxford, 1972. pp. 178.

OXFORD UNIVERSITY.

OXFORD. Oxford Historical Society. [Publications]. New Series. vol. 22. The register of Congregation, 1448-1463; edited by W.A. Pantin and W.T. Mitchell with an epilogue by Graham Pollard. Oxford, 1972. pp. 478.

GREEN (VIVIAN HUBERT HOWARD) A history of Oxford University. London, 1974. pp. 214. *bibliog.*

— Merton College.

OXFORD. Oxford Historical Society. [Publications]. New Series. vol. 23. Registrum annalium Collegii Mertonensis, 1521-1567; edited by John M. Fletcher. Oxford, 1974. pp. 297.

OXFORDSHIRE

— Social life and customs.

HOWKINS (ALUN) Whitsun in 19th century Oxfordshire. Oxford, [1973]. pp. 68. *(History Workshop. Pamphlets. No. 8)*

OZOLIN (KONSTANTIN IVANOVICH).

SEMENOV (ALEKSEI PETROVICH) Put' komissara. Riga, 1974. pp. 182.

PACIFIC, THE.

CROCOMBE (RONALD GORDON) The new South Pacific. Canberra, 1973. pp. 130. *bibliog.*

— Commerce.

NEW ZEALAND. Ministry of Foreign Affairs. 1971. South Pacific trade, 1971; a study prepared for a meeting of officials from the members of the South Pacific Forum, held in Wellington from 9 to 11 November 1971. Wellington, 1971. pp. 132.

— — Asia.

PACIFIC TRADE AND DEVELOPMENT CONFERENCE, 5TH, TOKYO, 1973. Structural adjustments in Asian-Pacific trade: papers and proceedings...; edited by Kiyoshi Kojima. Tokyo, 1973. 2 vols. (in 1). *(Japan Economic Research Center. Center Papers. No.21) Paged continuously.*

— Commercial policy.

PACIFIC TRADE AND DEVELOPMENT CONFERENCE, 4TH, OTTAWA, 1971. Obstacles to trade in the Pacific area; proceedings...; edited by H.E. English and Keith A.J. Hay. Ottawa, 1972. pp. 296.

— Social conditions.

BROOKFIELD (HAROLD CHILLINGWORTH) ed. The Pacific in transition: geographical perspectives on adaptation and change. London, 1973. pp. 332. *bibliog.*

NEW ZEALAND GEOGRAPHY CONFERENCE, 7TH, HAMILTON, 1972. Proceedings...; edited by Evelyn Stokes. [Christchurch], 1973. pp. 298. *bibliogs. (New Zealand Geographical Society. Conference Series. No. 7)*

— Social life and customs.

BROOKFIELD (HAROLD CHILLINGWORTH) ed. The Pacific in transition: geographical perspectives on adaptation and change. London, 1973. pp. 332. *bibliog.*

PACIFIC OCEAN.

DENLINGER (HARRY SUTHERLAND) and GARY (CHARLES BINFORD) War in the Pacific: a study of navies, peoples and battle problems; [reprint of work first published in New York in 1936]. New York, 1970. pp. 338.

PACIFIC SETTLEMENT OF INTERNATIONAL DISPUTES.

WAART (P.J.I.M.DE) The element of negotiation in the pacific settlement of disputes between states: an analysis of provisions made and/or applied since 1918, etc. The Hague, 1973. pp. 229. *bibliog.*

PACIFISM.

TREVELYAN (Sir CHARLES PHILIPS) Mass resistance to war. London, [1933?]. pp. 10. *(Socialist League. Capitalism in Crisis: Forum Series, 1933-4. No.2)*

GEESTELIJKE VERZORGING BIJ DE KRIJGSMACHT. Werkgroep Oorlog en Vrede. Militaire dienstplicht, vrijstelling, gewetensbezwaarden, alternatieve dienstplicht, vredesbeweging, pacifisme. Haarlem, [1971]. pp. 159.

MILLER (WILLIAM D.) A harsh and dreadful love: Dorothy Day and the Catholic Worker movement. London, [1973]. pp. 370. *bibliog.*

PAEPE (CESAR DE).

PAEPE (CESAR DE) Entre Marx et Bakounine: César de Paepe; correspondance;texte de présentation et notes par Bernard Dandois. Paris, 1974. pp. 316. *bibliog. (Centre d'Histoire du Syndicalisme. Collection)*

PAGET (WILLIAM) 1st Baron Paget.

CAMDEN SOCIETY. [Publications]. 4th Series. vol. 13. Camden miscellany. vol. 25. London, 1974. pp. 278.

PAIN.

MILLER (JONATHAN WOLFE) The uses of pain. London, [1974?]. pp. 20. *(South Place Ethical Society. Conway Memorial Lectures. 1973)*

PAISLEY (IAN).

MARRINAN (PATRICK) Paisley: man of wrath. Tralee, [1973]. pp. 260.

PAKENHAM (FRANCIS AUNGIER) 7th Earl of Longford.

PAKENHAM (FRANCIS AUNGIER) 7th Earl of Longford. The grain of wheat. London, 1974. pp. 286.

PAKISTAN

— Commerce.

AUCHTER (EDMUND L.) and DURRANI (TARIQ) Import costs and Pakistan's inflation. Islamabad, United States Agency for International Development, 1974. fo. 7.

— Constitution.

PAKISTAN. Constitution. 1972. The interim constitution of the Islamic Republic of Pakistan. Karachi, [1972]. pp. 114.

PAKISTAN. Constitution. 1973. The constitution of the Islamic Republic of Pakistan. Karachi, 1973. pp. 179.

— Constitutional history.

HUSAIN (AHMED) Politics and people's representation in Pakistan. Karachi, 1972. pp. 243. *bibliog.*

— Economic policy.

NAQVI (SYED NAWAB HAIDER) Egalitarianism versus growthmanship. Karachi, [1971]. pp. 10. *(Pakistan Institute of Development Economics. Essays in Development Economics. No. 1)*

PAKISTAN. Department of Films and Publications. 1972. A new beginning: reforms introduced by the People's government in Pakistan, December 20, 1971 - April 20, 1972. [Karachi, 1972]. pp. 68.

BAQAI (MOIN) and BRECHER (IRVING) eds. Development planning and policy in Pakistan, 1950-1970. Karachi, 1973. pp. 186. *bibliog.*

— Foreign relations.

BHUTTO (ZULFIKAR ALI) A compendium of speeches and press statements made from October 1957 to June 1966. Karachi, 1966. pp. 760.

BURKE (SAMUEL MARTIN) Mainsprings of Indian and Pakistani foreign policies. Minneapolis, [1974]. pp. 308. *bibliog.*

— Government publications.

PAKISTAN. 1962. Catalogue of the government of Pakistan publications. Karachi, 1962. pp. 168.

BRIGHTON. University of Sussex. Institute of Development Studies. Library. Occasional Guides. No.5. Pakistan central government and quasi-governmental organisations: a preliminary directory and list of IDS library holdings, 1947- 1971. Brighton, [1973]. 1 vol.(various pagination).

— Industries.

WHITE (LAWRENCE J.) Industrial concentration and economic power in Pakistan. Princeton, [1974]. pp. 212. *bibliog.*

— Politics and government.

HUSAIN (AHMED) Politics and people's representation in Pakistan. Karachi, 1972. pp. 243. *bibliog.*

MUKERJEE (DILIP) Zulfiqar Ali Bhutto: quest for power. Delhi, [1972]. pp. 240.

PAKISTAN. Department of Films and Publications. 1972. A new beginning: reforms introduced by the People's government in Pakistan, December 20, 1971 - April 20, 1972. [Karachi, 1972]. pp. 68.

AZIZ (QUTUBUDDIN) Mission to Washington: an expose of India's intrigues in the United States of America in 1971 to dismember Pakistan. Karachi, 1973. pp. 234.

— Population.

HASHMI (SULTAN S.) Main features of the demographic conditions in Pakistan; country background paper presented to the Asian Population Conference, New Delhi, December 10-20, 1963. [Karachi, Central Statistical Office, 1963]. fo. 154.

POPULATION GROWTH SURVEY; [pd. by] Statistical Division. Ministry of Finance, Planning and Development, Government of Pakistan. a., 1968[1st]- Karachi.

— Rural conditions.

GOTSCH (CARL H.) Tractor mechanization and rural development in Pakistan. Cambridge, Mass., 1972. pp. 65. *(Harvard University. Center for International Affairs. Development Research Group. Economic Development Reports. No. 227)*

— Social policy.

NAQVI (SYED NAWAB HAIDER) Egalitarianism versus growthmanship. Karachi, [1971]. pp. 10. *(Pakistan Institute of Development Economics. Essays in Development Economics. No. 1)*

PAKISTAN. Department of Films and Publications. 1972. A new beginning: reforms introduced by the People's government in Pakistan, December 20, 1971 - April 20, 1972. [Karachi, 1972]. pp. 68.

— Statistics, Vital.

HASHMI (SULTAN S.) Main features of the demographic conditions in Pakistan; country background paper presented to the Asian Population Conference, New Delhi, December 10-20, 1963. [Karachi, Central Statistical Office, 1963]. fo. 154.

PALAEOGRAPHY, ITALIAN.

MELIS (FEDERIGO) Documenti per la storia economica dei secoli XIII-XVI; con una nota di paleografia commerciale a cura di Elena Cecchi. Firenze, 1972. pp. 628. *(Istituto Internazionale di Storia Economica "F. Datini". Pubblicazioni. Serie I: Documenti. 1)*

PALESTINE

— Description and travel.

HALBWACHS (MAURICE) La topographie légendaire des Evangiles en Terre Sainte: étude de mémoire collective. 2nd ed. Paris, 1971. pp. 173. *bibliog.*

— History.

SHARIF (MOHAMMED BADI) Strangers in Palestine. London, 1970. pp. 84. *bibliog.*

STEVENS (RICHARD P.) ed. Zionism and Palestine before the mandate: a phase of Western imperialism; an essay with a selection of readings. Beirut, 1972. pp. 153. *(Institute for Palestine Studies. Anthology Series. No. 5)*

COOLEY (JOHN K.) Green March, Black September: the story of the Palestinian Arabs. London, 1973. pp. 263. *bibliog.*

FERGUSON (PAMELA) The Palestine problem. London, 1973. pp. 158. *bibliog.*

PORATH (YEHOSHUA) The emergence of the Palestinian-Arab national movement, 1918-1929. London, 1974. pp. 406.

— Politics and government.

DUA (GERSZON) Belyi terror v Palestine; predislovie M. Litvakova; perevel s evreiskogo M. Zel'manov. Moskva, 1926. pp. 40.

CATTAN (HENRY) The Palestine problem in a nutshell. Beirut, [1971]. pp. 35. *(Palestine Research Center. Palestine Essays. No. 26)*

PALM OIL.

LABYS (WALTER C.) Dynamic commodity models: specification, estimation, and simulation. Lexington, [1973]. pp. 350. *bibliog.*

PAMPA, LA.

See LA PAMPA.

PANAFRICANISM.

MAZRUI (ALI A.) Towards a pax Africana: a study of ideology and ambition. Chicago, 1967. pp. 287.

MAZRUI (ALI A.) and PATEL (HASU H.) eds. Africa in world affairs: the next thirty years. New York, [1973]. pp. 265.

GEISS (IMANUEL) The Pan-African movement;...translated by Ann Keep. London, [1974]. pp. 575. *bibliog.*

PANAMA.

FRANCE. Direction de la Documentation. La Documentation Française. Notes et Etudes Documentaires. No. 3,173. La République de Panama. Paris, 1965. pp. 32.

TORRIJOS HERRERA (OMAR) La batalla de Panama. Buenos Aires, [1973]. pp. 125.

PAPACY

— History.

ULLMANN (WALTER) A short history of the Papacy in the middle ages. London, 1972 repr. 1974. pp. 393. *bibliog.*

PAPER MAKING AND TRADE.

UNITED NATIONS EDUCATIONAL, SCIENTIFIC AND CULTURAL ORGANIZATION. Department of Mass Communication. Reports and Papers on Mass Communication. Paris, 1953 in progress.

SIMULA (MARKKU) An econometric model of the sales of printing and writing paper. Helsinki, 1971. pp. 28. *(Folia Forestalia. 124)*

— Germany.

SUPTHUT (CHRISTIAN ROBERT) Der Einfluss der europäischen Wirtschaftsintegration auf die Papierindustrie der BRD unter besonderer Berücksichtigung des Aussenhandels. Berlin, 1972. pp. 199. *bibliog.*

— Norway.

MYHRER (ERIK) The Norwegian pulp and paper industry. Oslo, 1971. pp. 15. *(Norway. Utenriksdepartementet. Presseavdelingen. Reference Papers. 1971. 220)*

— Russia.

UCHASTKINA (ZOIA VASIL'EVNA) Ekonomika tselliulozno-bumazhnoi promyshlennosti. 2nd ed. Moskva, 1973. pp. 206. *bibliog.*

— United Kingdom.

HAMPSON (CYRIL GARFORTH) 150th anniversary history of Robert Fletcher and Son Ltd. Manchester, [1973]. pp. 69.

PAPUA NEW GUINEA

— Census.

PAPUA NEW GUINEA. Census, 1971. Papua New Guinea population census, July 1971: preliminary bulletin[s]. Konedobu, 1972 in progress.

— Economic conditions.

FINNEY (BEN R.) Big-men and business: entrepreneurship and economic growth in the New Guinea highlands. Honolulu, [1973]. pp. 206. *bibliog.*

— Economic policy.

ROSS (ANTHONY CLUNIES) and LANGMORE (JOHN) eds. Alternative strategies for Papua New Guinea. Melbourne, 1973. pp. 263. *bibliog.*

— Politics and government.

EPSTEIN (ARNOLD LEONARD) and others, eds. The politics of dependence: Papua New Guinea 1968. Canberra, 1971. pp. 398. *bibliog.*

BERNDT (RONALD MURRAY) and LAWRENCE (PETER) eds. Politics in New Guinea: traditional and in the context of change; some anthropological perspectives. Washington, 1973. pp. 430. *bibliogs.*

ROSS (ANTHONY CLUNIES) and LANGMORE (JOHN) eds. Alternative strategies for Papua New Guinea. Melbourne, 1973. pp. 263. *bibliog.*

— Social life and customs.

BERNDT (RONALD MURRAY) and LAWRENCE (PETER) eds. Politics in New Guinea: traditional and in the context of change; some anthropological perspectives. Washington, 1973. pp. 430. *bibliogs.*

— Social policy.

ROSS (ANTHONY CLUNIES) and LANGMORE (JOHN) eds. Alternative strategies for Papua New Guinea. Melbourne, 1973. pp. 263. *bibliog.*

— Statistics.

PAPUA NEW GUINEA. Bureau of Statistics. Statistical bulletin: monthly abstract of statistics. m.(approx.) Ja-Oc/N 1971 (with certain figures from Je 1966). Konedobu.

PARAGUAY

— Emigration and immigration.

PARAGUAY. Direccion General de Inmigracion y Colonizacion. 1908. Datos estadisticos sobre el movimiento de inmigracion en el Paraguay desde 1882 hasta 1907, etc. Asuncion, 1908. pp. 16.

— Foreign relations.

BENITEZ (LUIS G.) Historia diplomatica del Paraguay. Asuncion, 1972. pp. 496. *bibliog.*

— — America, Latin.

SALUM-FLECHA (ANTONIO) Historia diplomatica del Paraguay de 1869 a 1938. Asuncion, 1972. pp. 215. *bibliog.*

— History — Dictionaries and encyclopaedias.

KOLINSKI (CHARLES J.) Historical dictionary of Paraguay. Metuchen, N.J., 1973. pp. 282. *bibliog.*

— History, Military.

BEJARANO (RAMON CESAR) Vencer o morir: formacion guerrera del pueblo paraguayo antes de 1932. Asuncion, 1970. pp. 93. *bibliog.*

— Social conditions.

ANGEL PANGRAZIO (MIGUEL) Indicadores de la estructura social del Paraguay. Asuncion, 1973. pp. 370. *bibliog.*

— Statistics.

PARAGUAY. Servicio Tecnico Interamericano de Cooperacion Agricola. 1958. Manual estadistico del Paraguay; 1951/1957;...datos compiladospor Maximo V.A. Ortiz. Asuncion, 1958. pp. 141. *(Boletines. No. 218)*

PARE (WILLIAM).

GARNETT (RONALD GEORGE) William Pare, 1805-1873: co-operator and social reformer. Loughborough, 1973. pp. 56. *(Loughborough. Co-operative College. Co-operative College Papers. No. 16)*

PAREKH (NAGIN).

NAGIN: story of the short life of Nagin Parekh which ended as a lance broken in the service of the tribesfolk of South Orissa; edited by Evelyn Wood from contributions by Nagin's friends and colleagues, and especially Annasaheb Sahasrabudhe. Bombay, [1965]. pp. 170.

PARENT AND CHILD.

NATIONAL CHILDREN'S BUREAU. Annual Conference, Sheffield, 1972. The parental role: papers given at the...conference. London, [1972]. pp. 42. *bibliog.*

RENVOIZE (JEAN) Children in danger: the causes and prevention of baby battering. London, 1974. pp. 193. *bibliog.*

PARENT AND CHILD (LAW)

— France.

FRANCE. Direction de la Documentation. La Documentation Française. Notes et Etudes Documentaires. Nos. 3,897-3, 898. L'autorité parentale; [rédigée par J.-C. Javillier]. [Paris], 1972. pp. 58.

PARETO (VILFREDO).

MONGARDINI (CARLO) Vilfredo Pareto dall'economia alla sociologia; con un'antologia dei primi scritti sociologici di Pareto. Roma, [1973]. pp. 311.

SAMUELS (WARREN J.) Pareto on policy. Amsterdam, 1974. pp. 232. *bibliog.*

PARIS.

FRANCE. Direction de la Documentation. La Documentation Française. Notes et Etudes Documentaires. Nos. 3,982-3, 983. Les grandes villes du monde: Paris, la vie quotidienne de l'agglomération; par Antoine Haumont. [Paris], 1973. pp. 61. *bibliog.*

SYSTEME D'ETUDES DU SCHEMA GENERAL D'AMENAGEMENT DE LA FRANCE. Groupe de Coordination. Schéma général d'aménagement de la France: Paris, ville internationale: rôles et vocation. Paris, 1973. pp. 143. *(France. Délégation à l'Aménagement du Territoire et à l'Action Régionale. Travaux et Recherches de Prospective. 39) Map in end pocket.*

PARIS. (Cont.)

— Civic improvement.

GODARD (FRANCIS) ed. La renovation urbaine à Paris: structure urbaine et logique de classe; enquête et analyse [by] Manuel Castells [and others]. Paris, [1973]. pp. 148. *bibliog.*

— Growth.

LOJKINE (JEAN) La politique urbaine dans la région parisienne, 1945-1971. Paris, [1972]. pp. 281.

— History.

AUDIAT (PIERRE) Paris pendant la guerre, juin 1940 - août 1944. [Paris, 1946]. pp. 333.

— — 1871, Commune.

TROTSKII (LEV DAVYDOVICH) Leon Trotsky on the Paris Commune. New York, 1970 repr. 1972. pp. 63.

ALVAREZ JUNCO (JOSE) ed. La Comuna en España. Madrid, 1971. pp. 252.

BIBLIOTHEQUE ROYALE ALBERT Ier. La Commune de Paris 1871 dans le livre et l'image: [exposition organisée à l'occasion du centenaire de la commune de Paris]. Bruxelles, 1971. pp. 94.

KRAUSE (FRITZ) Writer on politics. Pariser Commune, 1871. Frankfurt am Main, [1971]. pp. 92. *bibliog.*

VOICI l'aube: l'immortelle Commune de Paris: compte rendu analytique du colloque scientifique international organisé par l'Institut Maurice Thorez...1971. Paris, [1972]. pp. 458.

— — — Foreign public opinion.

PARIZHSKAIA Kommuna i marksizm: ocherki. Moskva, 1973. pp. 248.

— Politics and government.

ROUSSIER (MICHEL) Le conseil municipal de Paris, 1800-1970. Paris, 1968. pp. 109-121. (*Extrait du Bulletin de la Société de l'Histoire de Paris et de l'Ile-de-France, 1966*)

— Social conditions.

LOJKINE (JEAN) La politique urbaine dans la région parisienne, 1945-1971. Paris, [1972]. pp. 281.

PARKER (PETER).

GULICK (EDWARD VOSE) Peter Parker and the opening of China. Cambridge, Mass., 1973. pp. 282. *bibliog.* (*Harvard University. Harvard Studies in American East Asian Relations. 3*)

PARKS

— Russia.

MASHINSKII (L.O.) Gorod i priroda: gorodskie zelenye nasazhdeniia. Moskva, 1973. pp. 228. *bibliog.*

— United Kingdom.

ZETTER (J.A.) The evolution of country park policy. London, Countryside Commission, 1971. pp. 10.

WATERHOUSE (SUZETTE) Country parks and the West Midlands: an examination of the operation of the 1968 Countryside Act in the West Midlands, with particular reference to country park policy. [Birmingham], 1972. fo. 41,iv (*Birmingham. University. Centre for Urban and Regional Studies. Research Memoranda. No.17*)

PARLIAMENTARY PRACTICE.

CONFERENCE OF PRESIDING OFFICERS AND CLERKS-AT-THE-TABLE OF THE PARLIAMENTS OF AUSTRALIA, PAPUA AND NEW GUINEA, NEW ZEALAND, FIJI, NAURU AND WESTERN SAMOA, 2nd, BRISBANE, 1969. [Report]. in AUSTRALIA. Parliament. Parliamentary papers, 1969, vol.5.

— Australia.

CONFERENCE OF PRESIDING OFFICERS AND CLERKS-AT-THE-TABLE OF THE PARLIAMENTS OF AUSTRALIA, PAPUA AND NEW GUINEA, NEW ZEALAND, FIJI, NAURU AND WESTERN SAMOA, 2nd, BRISBANE, 1969. [Report]. in AUSTRALIA. Parliament. Parliamentary papers, 1969, vol.5.

— Germany.

VEREINIGUNG DER DEUTSCHEN PARLAMENTSDIREKTOREN. Parlamentspraxis in der Weimarer Republik: die Tagungsberichte der Vereinigung der deutschen Parlamentsdirektoren, 1925 bis 1933; bearbeitet von Martin Schumacher. Düsseldorf, [1974]. pp. 272. *bibliog.* (*Germany (Bundesrepublik). Quellen zur Geschichte des Parlamentarismus und der Politischen Parteien. 3. Reihe. Band 2*)

PARMA (PROVINCE)

— History.

SAVANI (PRIMO) Antifascismo e guerra di liberazione a Parma: cronache dei tempi.Parma, 1972. pp. 261.

PAROLE

— Canada.

WALLER (IRVIN) Men released from prison. Toronto, [1974]. pp. 273. *bibliog.* (*Toronto. University. Centre of Criminology. Canadian Studies in Criminology. 2*)

— Russia.

SVIRIDOV (MIKHAIL KONSTANTINOVICH) Poriadok razresheniia del ob uslovno-dosrochnom osvobozhdenii ot nakazaniia: uchebnoe posobie. Tomsk, 1972. pp. 136.

— United States — Bibliography.

TOMPKINS (DOROTHY LOUISE CAMPBELL) and BUSHER (WALTER H.) compilers. Furlough from prison. Berkeley, 1973. pp. 61. (*California University. Institute of Governmental Studies. Public Policy Bibliographies. No. 5*)

PARSONS (TALCOTT).

McLEISH (JOHN) The theory of social change: four views considered. London, Routledge and Kegan Paul, 1969 repr. 1972. pp. xiii, 95. *bibliog.* (*International Library of Sociology and Social Reconstruction*)

CHAZEL (FRANÇOIS) La théorie analytique de la société dans l'oeuvre de Talcott Parsons. Paris, [1974]. pp. 200. *bibliog.* (*Paris. Ecole Pratique des Hautes Etudes. Section des Sciences Economiques et Sociales. Société, Mouvements Sociaux et Idéologies. 1e Série. Etudes. 16*)

PART—TIME EMPLOYMENT

— United States.

CARROLL (STEPHEN J.) Part-time experience and the transition from school to work...: a report prepared for Office of Economic Opportunity. Santa Monica, 1970. pp. 71. *bibliog.* (*Rand Corporation. [Rand Reports]. 575*)

PART—TIME FARMING

— Australia.

SHILTON (PETER) Urban influences on the agricultural areas of the central coast with particular reference to part-time farming. Armidale, N.S.W., 1973. pp. 192. *bibliog.* (*University of New England, Armidale. Department of Geography. Research Series in Applied Geography. No. 35*)

PARTI QUEBECOIS.

PARTI QUEBECOIS. Conseil Exécutif. Prochaine étape...quand nous serons vraiment chez nous. [Montréal, 1972]. pp. 139.

PARTI SOCIALISTE UNIFIE.

NANIA (GUY) Le P[arti] S[ocialiste] U[nifié] avant Rocard. Paris, [1973]. pp. 253. *bibliog.*

PARTI SOCIALISTE UNIFIE. Congrès National, 8e, Toulouse, 1972. Manifeste: contrôler aujourd'hui pour décider demain, etc. Paris, [1973]. pp. 231. *bibliog.*

PARTIDO APRISTA PERUANO.

KLAREN (PETER F.) Modernization, dislocation and Aprismo: origins of the Peruvian Aprista party, 1870-1932. Austin, [1973]. pp. 189. *bibliog.* (*Texas University. Institute of Latin American Studies. Latin American Monographs. No.32*)

PARTIDO DEMOCRATA CRISTIANO (CHILE).

VUSKOVIC (SERGIO) Problematica D[emocrata] C[ristiana]: propiedad, revolucion, estado. [Santiago, Chile, 1968]. pp. 130.

PARTIDO NACIONAL DEL URUGUAY.

CALATAYUD BOSCH (JOSE) Grandeza y decadencia del Partido Nacional. Montevideo, 1971. pp. 199.

PARTIDO RADICAL (CHILE).

SNOW (PETER GORDON) Historia y doctrina del Partido Radical; [translated from the English by Ana Noboa de Dufaux]. Buenos Aires, 1972. pp. 163. *bibliog.*

PARTIES TO ACTIONS

— Russia.

ORLOVA (LIUDMILA MIKHAILOVNA) Prava storon v grazhdanskom protsesse. Minsk, 1973. pp. 192.

PARTIJ VAN DE ARBEID.

SCHEPS (J.H.) Kink in de kabel: scheuring en polarisatie P[artij] v[an] d[e] A[rbeid]-D[emocratische S[ocialisten] '70. Apeldoorn, [1972]. pp. 96.

PARTITO COMUNISTA D'ITALIA (MARXISTA—LENINISTA).

PARTITO COMUNISTA D'ITALIA (MARXISTA-LENINISTA). La linea politica del Partito, etc. [Naples, 1973]. pp. 155.

PARTITO OPERAIO ITALIANO.

PARTITO OPERAIO ITALIANO. Congresso. I congressi del Partito operaio italiano: [reports of the 1st to 5th congresses, 1885-1890, edited with a historical introduction by] Diana Perli. Padova, 1972. pp. 180.

PARTNERSHIP

— United States.

CRANE (JUDSON A.) and BROMBERG (ALAN R.) On partnership. St. Paul, Minn., 1968. pp. 695.

PARTY DISCIPLINE

— Germany.

GERMANY (BUNDESREPUBLIK). Deutscher Bundestag. Wissenschaftliche Dienste. 1974. Zum Mandatsverlust bei Ausscheiden eines Abgeordneten aus seiner Fraktion: Stand der Diskussion. Bonn, 1974. pp. 29. (*Materialien. 35*)

GERMANY (BUNDESREPUBLIK). Deutscher Bundestag. Wissenschaftliche Dienste. 1973. Das Abgeordnetenmandat in der parteienstaatlichen Demokratie: Auswahlbibliographie. Bonn, 1973. pp. 40. (*Bibliographien. 33*)

PASSIVE RESISTANCE.

LAKEY (GEORGE) Strategy for a living revolution. San Francisco, 1973. pp. 234.

BOSERUP (ANDERS) and MACK (ANDREW) War without weapons: non-violence in national defence. London, 1974. pp. 194. *bibliog.*

— Periodicals — Bibliography.

BLUMBERG (HERBERT H.) compiler. Periodicals concerned with nonviolence and social change; with organisation, geographic and subject indexes. Haverford, Pa., 1973. 1 vol. (unfoliated). *(Haverford College. Center for Nonviolent Conflict Resolution. Nonviolent Action Research Project. Monograph Series on Nonviolent Action. No.21)*

PASTORAL COUNSELLING.

CAPLAN (RUTH B.) Helping the helpers to help: mental health consultation to aid clergymen in pastoral work;...in collaboration with Gerald Caplan [and others]. New York, [1972]. pp. 241.

PASTORAL THEOLOGY.

SHORTER (AYLWARD) African culture and the Christian church: an introduction to social and pastoral anthropology. London, 1973. pp. 229. *bibliog.*

PATENT LAWS AND LEGISLATION

— Europe.

EUROPEAN PATENT CONVENTION. Ubereinkommen über die Erteilung europäischer Patente, Europäisches Patentübereinkommen und dazugehörige Dokumente; herausgegeben von der Regierung der Bundesrepublik Deutschland, etc. [München], 1973. pp. 343. *Parallel texts in English, French and German.*

— Germany.

GERMANY (BUNDESREPUBLIK). Patentamt. 1973. Federal German patent examining practice and patent law: a translation by E.F. Thomson of 'Guidelines for the examination of patent applications' and 'Guidelines for carrying out opposition proceedings'. London, 1973. pp. 64. *(National Reference Library of Science and Invention. Occasional Publications.) Xerox copy.*

VOSSIUS (VOLKER) and HALLMANN (ULRICH) eds. Patent granting procedure, utility model registration in the Federal Republic of Germany: official texts of the laws, regulations, etc. München, 1974. pp. 259.

— Germany, Eastern.

ADRIAN (JOHANN) and SCHOENFELD (GUENTER) Die Anmeldung, Erteilung und Bestätigung von Patenten. Berlin, 1967. pp. 255. *(Schriftenreihe Patentrecht. Heft 2)*

KAWALLE (OTTO) and SCHOENFELD (GUENTER) Der Patentverletzungsstreit und die Nichtigerklärung von Patenten. Berlin, 1967. pp. 168. *(Schriftenreihe Patentrecht. Heft 3)*

— United Kingdom.

WHITE (THOMAS ANTHONY BLANCO) Patents for inventions and the protection of industrial designs. 4th ed. London, 1974. pp. 749.

PATENTS

— Canada.

CANADA. Bureau of Intellectual Property. Annual report. a., 1972/3 [1st]- Hull, Canada. *In English and French.*

— European Economic Community countries.

The NEW European patent system and its implications for industry; a report of four papers delivered at a one-day conference held at the Confederation of British Industry in London on Tuesday 8 January 1974. London, 1974. pp. 44.

— Germany.

GERMANY (BUNDESREPUBLIK). Patentamt. 1973. Federal German patent examining practice and patent law: a translation by E.F. Thomson of 'Guidelines for the examination of patent applications' and 'Guidelines for carrying out opposition proceedings'. London, 1973. pp. 64. *(National Reference Library of Science and Invention. Occasional Publications.) Xerox copy.*

— United Kingdom.

TAYLOR (C.T.) Do we still need a patent system?. Cambridge, 1973. pp. 17. *(Cambridge. University. Department of Applied Economics. Reprint Series. No. 384)*

TAYLOR (C.T.) and SILBERSTON (ZANGWILL AUBREY) The economic impact of the patent system: a study of the British experience. Cambridge, 1973. pp. 408. *bibliog. (Cambridge. University. Department of Applied Economics. Monographs. 23)*

PATERSON (EMMA).

GOLDMAN (HAROLD) Emma Paterson: she led woman into a man's world. London, 1974. pp. 127. *bibliog.*

PATIDARS.

POCOCK (DAVID FRANCIS) Mind, body and wealth: a study of belief and practice in an Indian village. Oxford, [1973]. pp. 187.

PATON (ALAN).

PATON (ALAN) Case history of a pinky. Johannesburg, [c.1971]. pp. 16. *(South African Institute of Race Relations. Topical Talks. 28)*

PATRIOTISM

— Germany.

SCHWEIGLER (GEBHARD) Nationalbewusstsein in der BRD und der DDR. Düsseldorf, [1973]. pp. 235. *bibliog.*

— Germany, Eastern.

SCHWEIGLER (GEBHARD) Nationalbewusstsein in der BRD und der DDR. Düsseldorf, [1973]. pp. 235. *bibliog.*

— United States.

LANG (DANIEL) Patriotism without flags. New York, [1974]. pp. 209. *Articles originally published in The New Yorker.*

PATRONAGE, POLITICAL

— Canada.

PAQUET (GILLES) and WALLOT (JEAN PIERRE) Patronage et pouvoir dans le Bas-Canada, 1794-1812: un essai d'économie historique. Montréal, 1973. pp. 185. *bibliog.*

PAVIA UNIVERSITY.

SCARAMOZZINO (PASQUALE) La popolazione universitaria di Pavia: indagine di statistica sociale. Milano, [1970]. pp. 258. *(Pavia. Università. Istituto di Statistica. Pubblicazioni. 9)*

PAYMENT.

HÄGG (CLAES) Periodiska betalningsvariationer: en studie i företagsekonomisk tidsserieanalys. Stockholm, [1974]. pp. 143. *bibliog. With English summary.*

PAYS DE LOIRE.

See LOIRE (REGION).

PEACE.

JAVITS (BENJAMIN A.) Peace by investment. New York, [1950]. pp. 242.

BEITZ (CHARLES R.) and HERMAN (THEODORE) eds. Peace and war. San Francisco, [1973]. pp. 435. *bibliogs.*

PROTOPOPOV (ANATOLII SERGEEVICH) SSSR i mezhdunarodnyi rabochii klass v bor'be za mir. Moskva, 1973. pp. 212. *bibliog.*

LUKASHUK (IGOR' IVANOVICH) Otnosheniia mirnogo sosushchestvovaniia i mezhdunarodnoe pravo: problemy mezhdunarodno-pravovogo regulirovaniia. Kiev, 1974. pp. 207.

SCHWABE (ERNST OTTO) We want to live in peace: but how?: the G[erman] D[emocratic] R[epublic] presents its views. Berlin, 1974. pp. 63.

— Congresses.

COHEN (RAYMOND) and COHEN (STUART) Peace conferences: the formal aspects. Jerusalem, 1974. pp. 28. *bibliog. (Hebrew University. Leonard Davis Institute for International Relations. Jerusalem Papers on Peace Problems. No. 1)*

— Research.

BOENISCH (ALFRED) and STEINKE (WOLFGANG) Bürgerliche Friedensforschung: Probleme, Widersprüche, Tendenzen. Berlin, 1973. pp. 167.

— Study and teaching.

WULF (CHRISTOPH) ed. Handbook on peace education. Frankfurt/Main, [1974]. pp. 378. *bibliog.*

PEACE SOCIETIES.

BROWN (H. RUNHAM) Cutting ice: a brief survey of war resistance and the International. Enfield, 1930. pp. 61. *Photographic reprint.*

BUZAN (BARRY GORDON) The British peace movement from 1919 to 1939; [Ph.D. (London) thesis]. 1973. fo. 460. *bibliog. Typescript: unpublished. This thesis is the property of London University and may not be removed from the Library.*

CHATFIELD (CHARLES) ed. Peace movements in America. New York, 1973. pp. 191.

PEACE TREATIES.

RYDER (TIMOTHY THOMAS BENNETT) Koine eirene: general peace and local independence in ancient Greece. London, 1965. pp. 184. *bibliog.*

PEACEFUL CHANGE (INTERNATIONAL RELATIONS).

GEWELDLOZE actie en sociale verdediging; [by] F. Bekkers [and others]. Rotterdam, 1971. pp. 153. *(Mens en Maatschappij. Boekafleveringen. 1971)*

BUCHAN (ALASTAIR) Change without war: the shifting structures of world power. London, 1974. pp. 112. *(British Broadcasting Corporation. Reith Lectures. 1973)*

PEAK NATIONAL PARK.

MILES (JOHN C.) The Goyt valley traffic experiment, 1970-1971; a report written for the Countryside Commission. London, Countryside Commission, [1972]. pp. 114.

PEARL HARBOR, ATTACK ON, 1941.

PEARL Harbor as history: Japanese-American relations, 1931- 1941; (essays... presented at a binational conference held at Lake Kawaguchi, Japan... 1969); edited by Dorothy Borg and Shumpei Okamoto. New York, 1973. pp. 801. *(Columbia University. East Asian Institute. Studies)*

PEARSON (LESTER BOWLES).

PEARSON (LESTER BOWLES) Memoirs 1948-1957: the international years;...edited by John A. Munro and Alex I. Inglis. London, 1974. pp. 344.

PEASANT UPRISINGS.

LANDSBERGER (HENRY A.) ed. Rural protest: peasant movements and social change. London, 1974. pp. 430.

— China.

CHESNEAUX (JEAN) Peasant revolts in China, 1840-1949;... translated by C.A. Curwen. [New York], 1973. pp. 180. *bibliog.*

— India.

SUNDARAYYA (P.) Telangana people's struggle and its lessons. Calcutta, 1972. pp. 592.

PEASANT UPRISINGS. (Cont.)

— **Indonesia.**

KARTODIRDJO (SARTONO) Protest movements in rural Java: a study of agrarian unrest in the nineteenth and early twentieth centuries. Singapore, 1973. pp. 229. *bibliog.*

— **Roumania.**

EIDELBERG (PHILIP GABRIEL) The great Rumanian peasant revolt of 1907: origins of a modern jacquerie. Leiden, 1974. pp. 259. *bibliog. (Columbia University. East Central European Studies)*

PEASANTRY.

CRITIQUES DE L'ECONOMIE POLITIQUE. No. 15. Paysannerie et réformes agraires. Paris, 1974. pp. 144.

— **Bukovina.**

KRAVETS' (MYKOLA MYKOLAIOVYCH) Selianstvo Skhidnoï Halychyny i Pivnichnoï Bukovyny u druhii polovyni XIX st. L'viv, 1964. pp. 239.

— **Ecuador.**

SCHWEFEL (DETLEF) Situationsdefinition und Situationsanalyse der landlosen und landarmen Agrarbevölkerung in einem Kolonisationsgebiet Ecuadors. Bielefeld, 1972. pp. 90. *(Kontaktprogramm zur Sozialwissenschaftlichen Forschung in Lateinamerika. Arbeitsunterlagen zur Lateinamerikaforschung. 47)*

— **Egypt.**

HARIK (ILIYA F.) The political mobilization of peasants: a study of an Egyptian community. Bloomington, Ind., [1974]. pp. 309. *bibliog. (Indiana University. International Development Research Center. Studies in Development. No.8)*

— **Europe.**

BAILEY (FREDERICK GEORGE) ed. Debate and compromise: the politics of innovation. Oxford, 1973. pp. 343. *bibliog.*

— **France.**

COLLOQUE FRANCO-HONGROIS D'HISTOIRE SOCIALE, BUDAPEST, 1972. Paysannerie française, paysannerie hongroise, XVIe-XXe siècles; volume 1 publié sous la direction de Béla Köpeczi et Eva H. Balázs. Budapest, 1973. pp. 319.

LE ROY LADURIE (EMMANUEL) The peasants of Languedoc;...translated with an introduction by John Day. Urbana, [1974]. pp. 370. *bibliog.*

— **Galicia (Eastern Europe).**

KRAVETS' (MYKOLA MYKOLAIOVYCH) Selianstvo Skhidnoï Halychyny i Pivnichnoï Bukovyny u druhii polovyni XIX st. L'viv, 1964. pp. 239.

— **Guatemala.**

SNEE (CAROLE A.) Current types of peasant-agricultural worker coalitions and their historical development in Guatemala. Cuernavaca, 1969. pp. 129. *bibliog. (Centro Intercultural de Documentacion. Cidoc Cuadernos. No. 31)*

— **Hungary.**

COLLOQUE FRANCO-HONGROIS D'HISTOIRE SOCIALE, BUDAPEST, 1972. Paysannerie française, paysannerie hongroise, XVIe-XXe siècles; volume 1 publié sous la direction de Béla Köpeczi et Eva H. Balázs. Budapest, 1973. pp. 319.

— **India.**

BECK (BRENDA E.F.) Peasant society in Konku: a study of right and left subcastes in south India. Vancouver, [1972]. pp. 334. *bibliog.*

CRITCHFIELD (RICHARD) The golden bowl be broken: peasant life in four cultures. Bloomington, [1973]. pp. 312.

MULAY (SUMATI) and RAY (G.L.) Towards modernization: a study of peasantry in rural Delhi. Delhi, 1973. pp. 159. *bibliog.*

— **Indonesia.**

CRITCHFIELD (RICHARD) The golden bowl be broken: peasant life in four cultures. Bloomington, [1973]. pp. 312.

— **Iraq.**

CRITCHFIELD (RICHARD) The golden bowl be broken: peasant life in four cultures. Bloomington, [1973]. pp. 312.

— **Italy.**

COTTONE (ELVIRA) ed. Riorganizzazione capitalistica e lotta di classe nelle campagne. Roma, [1972]. pp. 126.

CHIAROMONTE (GERARDO) Agricoltura, sviluppo economico, democrazia: la politica agraria e contadina dei comunisti, 1965-1972. Bari, [1973]. pp. 370.

— **Madagascar.**

ROUVEYRAN (JEAN CLAUDE) La logique des agricultures de transition: l'exemple des sociétés paysannes malgaches. [Tananarive], 1972. pp. 277. *bibliog.*

— **Malaysia.**

NASH (MANNING) Peasant citizens: politics, religion and modernization in Kelantan, Malaysia. Athens, [1974]. pp. 153. *bibliog. (Ohio University. Center for International Studies. Papers in International Studies. Southeast Asia Series. No. 31)*

— **Mauritius.**

CRITCHFIELD (RICHARD) The golden bowl be broken: peasant life in four cultures. Bloomington, [1973]. pp. 312.

— **Peru.**

BLANCJLDOS (HUGO) El camino de nuestra revolucion. Lima, 1964. pp. 64.

— **Poland.**

ADAMSKI (WŁADYSŁAW) Chłopi i przyszłość wsi: postawy, dą'zenia, aspiracje. Warszawa, 1974. pp. 302.

— **Roumania.**

MAREA răscoală a ţăranilor din 1907. București, 1967. pp. 909.

— **Russia.**

TSENTRAL'NYI GOSUDARSTVENNYI ARKHIV OKTIABR'SKOI REVOLIUTSII, VYSSHIKH ORGANOV GOSUDARSTVENNOI VLASTI I ORGANOV GOSUDARSTVENNOGO UPRAVLENIIA SSSR. 1917 God v Dokumentakh i Materialakh. Krest'ianskoe dvizhenie v 1917 godu; podgotovili k pechati K.G. Kotel'nikov i V.L. Meller, etc. Moskva, 1927. pp. 444.

POPOVA (EMILIIA DMITRIEVNA) Krest'ianskie komitety Viatskoi gubernii v 1917 godu. Kirov, 1966. pp. 41.

PROBLEMY krest'ianskogo zemlevladeniia i vnutrennei politiki Rossii: dooktiabr'skii period. Leningrad, 1972. pp. 365. *(Akademiia Nauk SSSR. Institut Istorii SSSR. Leningradskoe Otdelenie. Trudy. vyp.13)*

CHERNUKHA (VALENTINA GRIGOR'EVNA) Krest'ianskii vopros v pravitel'stvennoi politike Rossii, 60- 70 gody XIX v. Leningrad, 1972. pp. 226.

RÉVÉSZ (LÁSZLÓ) Der Bauer in der Sowjetunion. Bern, [1972]. pp. 127.

GUROV (PETR IAKOVLEVICH) and GONCHAROV (ALEKSANDR DMITRIEVICH) Leninskaia agrarnaia politika. Moskva, 1973. pp. 190.

SCHEIBERT (PETER) Die russische Agrarreform von 1861: ihre Probleme und der Stand ihrer Erforschung. Köln, 1973. pp. 195. *bibliog.*

SUSLOV (IVAN FEDOROVICH) Ekonomicheskie interesy i sotsial'noe razvitie kolkhoznogo krest'ianstva. Moskva, 1973. pp. 256.

IGNATOVSKII (PAVEL ARTEM'EVICH) Die Bauernschaft und die Wirtschaftspolitik der Partei auf dem Lande; (Übersetzer [from the Russian]: Hans Bär). Berlin, 1974. pp. 299.

— — **Kabardinobalkarian Republic.**

SHCHEGOLEV (ANDREI IVANOVICH) Krest'ianskoe dvizhenie v Kabarde i Balkarii v gody stolypinskoi reaktsii i novogo revoliutsionnogo pod'ema. Nal'chik, 1962. pp. 140.

— — **Moldavian Republic.**

KODITSA (N.) Ekonomicheskie problemy ispol'zovaniia trudovykh resursov v sel'skom khoziaistve Moldavii. Kishinev, 1973. pp. 183.

SYTNIK (MIKHAIL KONDRAT'EVICH) Perelomnyi god v zhizni krest'ianstva Pravoberezhnoi Moldavii: iz istorii revoliutsionnykh preobrazovanii v derevne osvobozhdennykh raionov Moldavii v 1940-1941 gg. Kishinev, 1973. pp. 124.

— — **Turkestan.**

VOZNIKNOVENIE i razvitie revoliutsionnogo dvizheniia v Kirgizii v kontse XIX - nachale XX vv.; pod redaktsiei K.U. Usenbaeva. Frunze, 1973. pp. 230.

— **Spain.**

RODRIGUEZ VILAMOR (JOSE) La rebelion de los campesinos gallegos. Algorta, Spain, 1970. pp. 77. *bibliog.*

— **Underdeveloped areas.**

See UNDERDEVELOPED AREAS — Peasantry.

— **Vietnam.**

NGO VINH LONG Before the revolution: the Vietnamese peasants under the French. Cambridge, Mass., [1973]. pp. 292. *bibliog.*

— **Yugoslavia — Croatia.**

MAČEK (VLADKO) Vodja govori: ličnost, izjave, govori i politički rad vodje Hrvata, Dra. Vladka Mačka; sabrao i uredio Mirko Glojnaric. Zagreb, 1936. pp. 349.

PEDESTRIANS

— **United Kingdom.**

DALBY (E.) Pedestrians and shopping centre layout: a review of the current situation. Crowthorne, 1973. pp. 25. *(U.K. Transport and Road Research Laboratory. Reports. LR 577)*

MITCHELL (C.G.B.) Pedestrian and cycle journeys in English urban areas. Crowthorne, 1973. pp. 41. *(U.K. Transport and Road Research Laboratory. Reports. LR 497)*

PEIRCE (CHARLES SANTIAGO SANDERS).

FANN (K.T.) Peirce's theory of abduction. The Hague, 1970. pp. 62. *bibliog.*

PELHAM—HOLLES (THOMAS) 1st Duke of Newcastle.

KELCH (RAY A.) Newcastle: a duke without money: Thomas Pelham-Holles, 1693- 1768. London, 1974. pp. 222. *bibliog.*

PEÑALOZA (ANGEL VICENTE).

COMISION CENTRAL DE HOMENAJE A ANGEL VICENTE PEÑALOZA. Angel Vicente Peñaloza; [by Pedro Santos Martinez and others]. Buenos Aires, 1969. pp. 301.

PENG (MING—MIN).

PENG (MING-MIN) A taste of freedom: memoirs of a Formosan independence leader. New York, [1972]. pp. 270.

PENN (WILLIAM).

FANTEL (HANS) William Penn: apostle of dissent. New York, 1974. pp. 298. bibliog.

PENNINE CHAIN.

WILLIS (KENNETH G.) Economic policy determination and evaluation in the North Pennines. [Newcastle], 1973. pp. 60,vii. bibliog. (Newcastle-upon-Tyne. University. Department of Agricultural Economics. Agricultural Adjustment Unit. Research Monographs. No. 3)

PENNSYLVANIA

— Boundaries.

RUSS (WILLIAM ADAM) How Pennsylvania acquired its present boundaries. University Park, Pa., 1966. pp. 76. bibliog. (Pennsylvania History Studies. No. 8)

— Government publications.

CHECKLIST OF OFFICIAL PENNSYLVANIA PUBLICATIONS; [pd. by] State Library of Pennsylvania. m., S 1963 (v.1, no.1)- , with gap (F 1965: v.2, no.7). Harrisburg.

— History.

COMFORT (WILLIAM WISTAR) The Quakers: a brief account of their influence on Pennsylvania. [rev. ed.] Gettysburg, 1948 [repr. with revisions 1963?]. pp. 65. bibliog. (Pennsylvania History Studies. No. 2)

KENT (DONALD H.) and RICHMAN (IRWIN) Pennsylvania and the federal constitution. Harrisburg, Pennsylvania Historical and Museum Commission, 1964. pp. 16. bibliog.

— Politics and government.

TINKCOM (HARRY MARLIN) The Republicans and Federalists in Pennsylvania, 1790-1801: a study in national stimulus and local response. Harrisburg, Pennsylvania Historical and Museum Commission, 1950. pp. 354. bibliog.

HIGGINBOTHAM (SANFORD WILSON) The keystone in the democratic arch: Pennsylvania politics, 1800-1816. Harrisburg, Pennsylvania Historical and Museum Commission, 1952. pp. 417.

THAYER (THEODORE) Pennsylvania politics and the growth of democracy, 1740-1776. Harrisburg, Pennsylvania Historical and Museum Commission, 1953. pp. 234.

SNYDER (CHARLES McCOOL) The Jacksonian heritage: Pennsylvania politics, 1833-1848. Harrisburg, Pennsylvania Historical and Museum Commission, 1958. pp. 256. bibliog.

RICKER (RALPH ROSS) The Greenback-Labor movement in Pennsylvania. Bellefonte, [1966]. pp. 141. bibliog.

WOLF (GEORGE D.) The Fair Play settlers of the West Branch Valley, 1769- 1784: a study of frontier ethnography. Harrisburg, Pennsylvania Historical and Museum Commission, 1969. pp. 122. bibliog.

— Social history.

BROWN (IRA VERNON) Pennsylvania reformers: from Penn to Pinchot. University Park, Pa., 1966. pp. 68. bibliog. (Pennsylvania History Studies. No. 9)

PENSION TRUSTS

— Taxation — Finland.

FINLAND. Företagsbeskattningens Nydaningskommission. 1970. Betänkande 4: reformering av inkomstbeskattningen av försäkringsanstalter och pensionsstiftelser. Helsingfors, 1970. fo. 37. (Finland. Komiteanmietinnöt. 1970. B.82)

— United States.

MALCA (EDWARD) Bank-administered, commingled pension funds: performance and characteristics, 1962-1970. Lexington, [1973]. pp. 93. bibliog.

PENSIONS

— Belgium.

BELGIUM. Office National d'Assurances Sociales pour Travailleurs Indépendants. Rapport annuel. a., 1969; ceased pbln. Bruxelles.

— Caribbean area.

ODLE (MAURICE A.) Pension funds in labour surplus economies: an analysis of the developmental role of pension plans in the Caribbean. Mona, 1974. pp. 150. bibliog.

— Denmark.

FÜRSTNOW-SØRENSEN (BENT) Samfundet og invalidepensionisterne. [Copenhagen], 1969. pp. 28.

DENMARK. Statutes, etc. 1969-72. The Invalidity Pension Act, [and] the Invalidity Pension (Amendment) Act, 1972. [Copenhagen, 1970-1972]. 2 pts.

— European Economic Community countries.

INSURANCE INSTITUTE OF LONDON. Advanced Study Group No. 200. Life assurance and pensions in the European Community: report.London, [1973]. pp. 110.

— Russia.

ACHARKAN (VIKTOR ADOL'FOVICH) Gosudarstvennye pensii. Moskva, 1967. pp. 165.

RUSSIA (USSR). Statutes, etc. 1964-1971. Sbornik ofitsial'nykh materialov o pensiiakh i posobiiakh chlenam kolkhozov; [sostavili Sheferova G.S. i Mikhalkevich V.N.]. Moskva, 1972. pp. 191.

— Sweden.

SWEDEN. Socialdepartementet. Pensionsförsäkringskommittén. 1971. Familjepensionsfrågor m.m. Stockholm, 1971. pp. 106. (Sweden. Statens Offentliga Utredningar. 1971. 19)

— Switzerland.

SWITZERLAND. Bureau Fédéral de Statistique. 1972. Vorsorgeeinrichtungen in der Schweiz: schweizerische Pensionskassenstatistik 1970, etc. Bern, 1972. pp. 93. (Statistiques de la Suisse. 489e fasc.)

— United Kingdom.

PETCH (ARTHUR W.) Co-operative employees and superannuation funds. Manchester, [imprint], 1928. pp. 63.

PETCH (ARTHUR W.) Co-operative employees and superannuation funds. rev. ed. [Manchester], 1930. pp. 92.

CROSSMAN (RICHARD HOWARD STAFFORD) The politics of pensions. Liverpool, 1972. pp. 26. (Eleanor Rathbone Memorial Trust. Eleanor Rathbone Memorial Lectures. 19)

CONFEDERATION OF BRITISH INDUSTRY. Guidance on provision of information to members of occupational pension schemes. London, 1973. pp. 10.

GILLING-SMITH (G. DRYDEN) The manager's guide to pensions. London, 1974. pp. 147. bibliog.

PENSIONS, MILITARY

— Canada.

CANADA. Pension Review Board. Reports. irreg., 1972 (v.1, no.1)- Ottawa. In English and French.

— Russia.

PARSHIN (M.IA.) and KRIVTSOV (G.F.) L'goty, pensii i posobiia voennosluzhashchim srochnoi i sverkhsrochnoi sluzhby i ikh sem'iam: spravochnik. Moskva, 1971. pp. 328.

PENTECOST FESTIVAL.

See WHITSUNTIDE.

PENTECOSTAL CHURCHES

— Chile.

RAJANA (EIMI WATANABE) A sociological study of new religious movements: Chilean Pentecostalism and Japanese new religions; [Ph.D.(London) thesis]. 1974. fo. 288. bibliog. Typescript: unpublished. This thesis is the property of London University and may not be removed from the Library.

PEPPER.

BRESLIN (PATRICK) and JONES (ANDREW) of the Tropical Products Institute. The structure of the pepper market in the United Kingdom, the Federal Republic of Germany, the Netherlands and France. London, Tropical Products Institute, 1973. pp. 61. ([Reports]. G84) With summaries in French and Spanish.

PEPPERELL (ELIZABETH).

REED (MAUD D.) Elizabeth Pepperell, 21 June 1914 to 24 May 1971. London, 1973. pp. 115.

PERCEPTION.

BENNETT (JONATHAN) Locke, Berkeley, Hume: central themes. Oxford, 1971. pp. 361. bibliog.

DONNELLY (DENNIS) and others. Perception-related survey for local authorities: a pilot study in Sunderland. Birmingham, 1973. 1 vol. (various foliations). bibliog. (Birmingham. University. Centre for Urban and Regional Studies. Research Memoranda. No.20)

BRUNER (JEROME SEYMOUR) Beyond the information given: studies in the psychology of knowing; selected, edited and introduced by Jeremy M. Anglin. London, 1974. pp. 502. bibliog.

BRYANT (PETER) Perception and understanding in young children: an experimental approach. London, [1974]. pp. 195. bibliog.

POWERS (WILLIAM T.) Behavior: the control of perception. London, 1974. pp. 296. bibliogs.

ROSS (HELEN E.) Behaviour and perception in strange environments. London, 1974. pp. 171.

PERFORMING ARTS

— United States.

KLEINGARTNER (ARCHIE) and LLOYD (KENNETH) Labor-management relations in the performing arts: the case of Los Angeles. Los Angeles, 1973. pp. 5. (California University. Institute of Industrial Relations. Reprints. No. 233) (Reprinted from California Management Review, Vol. 15, No. 2, winter 1972)

PERFUSION PUMP (HEART).

Un EXEMPLE d'utilisation de la méthode Delphi: perspectives de développement en France des techniques de coeur artificiel; par Jean-Claude Derian [and others]. Gif-sur-Yvette, 1971. pp. 80. bibliog. (France. Commissariat à l'Energie Atomique. Etudes Economiques)

PERIODICALS

— Bibliography.

ULRICH (CAROLYN FARQUHAR) ed. International periodicals directory: (a classified guide to current periodicals, foreign and domestic). 15th ed. New York, [1973]. pp. 2706.

BRITISH LIBRARY. Lending Division. Current serials received by the BLL, March 1974. Boston Spa, 1974. pp. 376.

U.K. Department of Health and Social Security. Library. Periodicals currently received. London, 1974. pp. 28.

URWICK, ORR AND PARTNERS. Management Intelligence Services. Periodicals list, 1974. Slough, 1974. pp. 29.

PERON (JUAN DOMINGO).

CONCATTI (ROLANDO) Nuestra opcion por el Peronismo. 2nd ed. Mendoza, [1972]. pp. 173.

PERON (JUAN DOMINGO). (Cont.)

MAFUD (JULIO) Sociologia del Peronismo. Buenos Aires, [1972]. pp. 182. *bibliog.*

CAMPORA (HECTOR J.) La revolucion Peronista. Buenos Aires, [1973]. pp. 205.

CERESOLE (NORBERTO) and MASTRORILLI (CARLOS P.) Peronismo: teoria e historia del socialismo nacional. Buenos Aires, [1973]. pp. 432.

JOHNSON (KENNETH F.) Peronism: the final gamble. London, 1974. pp. 18. *(Institute for the Study of Conflict. Conflict Studies. No. 42)*

PERON (JUAN DOMINGO) Juan Peron en la Argentina, 1973: sus discursos, sus dialogos, sus conferencias; plan trienal 1974-77. [Buenos Aires, 1974]. pp. 395.

PERSIAN GULF.

BURRELL (R.M.) and COTTRELL (ALVIN J.) Iran, the Arabian peninsula, and the Indian ocean. New York, [1972]. pp. 46. *bibliog.* *(National Strategy Information Center. Strategy Papers. No. 14)*

LABROUSSE (HENRI) Le Golfe et le Canal: la réouverture du canal de Suez et la paix internationale. [Paris], 1973. pp. 164. *bibliog.*

— Defences.

TAHTINEN (DALE R.) Arms in the Persian Gulf. Washington, [1974]. pp. 31. *(American Enterprise Institute for Public Policy Research. Foreign Affairs Studies. 10)*

— Economic conditions.

GUINE (ANTOINE) ed. Etude sur les états du Golfe Arabe. [Damascus, 1973]. fo. 117.

— Foreign relations — Iran.

RAMAZANI (ROUHOLLAH KAREGAR) The Persian Gulf: Iran's role. Charlottesville, 1972 repr. 1973. pp. 157. *bibliog.*

— — United Kingdom.

MEDVEDKO (LEONID IVANOVICH) Vetry peremen v Persidskom zalive. Moskva, 1973. pp. 208.

— Politics and government.

BURRELL (R.M.) The Persian gulf. New York, 1972. pp. 81. *(Georgetown University. Center for Strategic and International Studies. Washington Papers. vol.[1]/1)*

PERSONAL INJURIES

— United Kingdom.

MUNKMAN (JOHN HENRY) Damages for personal injuries and death. 5th ed. London, 1973. pp. 292.

PERSONAL PROPERTY.

SAUVEPLANNE (J.G.) ed. Security over corporeal movables: (papers presented to a Colloquium, Edinburgh, 1971). Leiden, 1974. pp. 308. *(Netherlands Association of Comparative Law. Studies in Comparative Law. No.1)*

— Russia.

EROSHENKO (ALEKSANDR ARSEN'EVICH) Lichnaia sobstvennost' v grazhdanskom prave. Moskva, 1973. pp. 207.

PERSONALISM.

LACROIX (JEAN PAUL) 1900- . Le personnalisme comme antiidéologie. [Paris], 1972. pp. 164. *bibliog.*

PERSONALITY.

EYSENCK (HANS JÜRGEN) The inequality of man. London, 1973. pp. 288. *bibliog.*

KRASNER (LEONARD) and ULLMANN (LEONARD P.) Behavior influence and personality: the social matrix of human action. New York, [1973]. pp. 560. *bibliog.*

LEVINE (ROBERT ALAN) Culture, behaviour and personality. London, 1973. pp. 319. *bibliog.*

McKINNEY (DAVID W.) The authoritarian personality studies: an inquiry into the failure of social science research to produce demonstrable knowledge. The Hague, 1973. pp. 304. *bibliogs.*

La NOTION de personne en Afrique noire; [papers of a conference held in] Paris, 11-17 octobre 1971. Paris, 1973. pp. 596. *bibiogs.* *(Centre National de la Recherche Scientifique. Colloques Internationaux. No. 544) In French and English.*

BERNE (ERIC LENNARD) What do you say after you say hello?: the psychology of human destiny. London, 1974. pp. 457.

PERSONNEL SERVICE IN EDUCATION.

NEWSOM (AUDREY) and others. Student counselling in practice. London, [1973]. pp. 196. *bibliog.*

— United Kingdom.

CONFERENCE ON STUDENT COUNSELLING, 2nd, LONDON, 1971. Student counselling and student progress; proceedings of the... conference...convened under the auspices of the Department of Higher Education, University of London Institute of Education. [London], 1971. pp. 53.

PERSONS (INTERNATIONAL LAW).

CHERNICHENKO (STANISLAV VALENTINOVICH) Lichnost' i mezhdunarodnoe pravo. Moskva, 1974. pp. 166.

OKEKE (CHRIS N.) Controversial subjects of contemporary international law: an examination of the new entities of international law and their treaty-making capacity. Rotterdam, 1974. pp. 243.

PERU

— Armed forces — Political activity.

PALMER (DAVID SCOTT) Revolution from above: military government and popular participation in Peru, 1968-1972. [Ithaca], 1973. pp. 307. *bibliog.* *(Cornell University. Latin American Studies Program. Dissertation Series. No.47)*

VILLANUEVA (VICTOR) Ejercito peruano: del caudillaje anarquico al militarismo reformista. Lima, 1973. pp. 439. *bibliog.*

— Army — History.

VILLANUEVA (VICTOR) 100 años del ejercito peruano: frustraciones y cambios. Lima, 1972. pp. 187.

— Boundaries — Ecuador.

CHIRINOS SOTO (ENRIQUE) Peru y Ecuador. Lima, 1968. pp. 55.

— Economic history.

KLAREN (PETER F.) Modernization, dislocation and Aprismo: origins of the Peruvian Aprista party, 1870-1932. Austin, [1973]. pp. 189. *bibliog.* *(Texas University. Institute of Latin American Studies. Latin American Monographs. No.32)*

— Economic policy.

PERU. Instituto Nacional de Planificacion. 1972. Plan nacional de desarrollo para 1971-1975. [Lima, 1972?]. 11 vols. (in 2). *11 volumes originally issued in 5 tomos.*

— Industries.

PERU. Direccion Nacional de Estadistica y Censos. 1967. (Primer censo nacional economico, 1963): suplemento al primer censo de industria manufacturera. Lima, [1967?]. pp. 533.

— Manufactures .

PERU. Direccion Nacional de Estadistica y Censos. 1967. (Primer censo nacional economico, 1963): suplemento al primer censo de industria manufacturera. Lima, [1967?]. pp. 533.

— Native races.

DAVIES (THOMAS M.) Indian integration in Peru: a half century of experience, 1900- 1948. Lincoln, Neb., [1974]. pp. 204. *bibliog.*

— Politics and government.

PERU. President. Mensaje presidencial. a., 1967. Lima.

KLAREN (PETER F.) Modernization, dislocation and Aprismo: origins of the Peruvian Aprista party, 1870-1932. Austin, [1973]. pp. 189. *bibliog.* *(Texas University. Institute of Latin American Studies. Latin American Monographs. No.32)*

PALMER (DAVID SCOTT) Revolution from above: military government and popular participation in Peru, 1968-1972. [Ithaca], 1973. pp. 307. *bibliog.* *(Cornell University. Latin American Studies Program. Dissertation Series. No.47)*

— Population.

MARTINEZ (HECTOR) Las migraciones altiplanicas y la colonizacion del Tambopata. Lima, 1969. pp. 278. *bibliog.*

— Presidents — Election.

CINQ aspects de sociétés latino-américaines; [by Carlos M. Rama and others]. Paris, [1965]. pp. 151. *(Paris. Université. Institut des Hautes Etudes de l'Amérique Latine. Cahiers. No. 7)*

— Rural conditions.

MARTINEZ (HECTOR) Las migraciones altiplanicas y la colonizacion del Tambopata. Lima, 1969. pp. 278. *bibliog.*

PERU. Direccion de Comunidades Campesinas. 1970. Chuyama-Chacchahua y Rio Blanco: historia de una ''reivindicacion''. [Lima, 1970]. pp. 77. *bibliog.* *(Zac-Andahuaylas. No. 1)*

PERU. Direccion de Comunidades Campesinas. 1971. Segundo proyecto ''Lampa-Capachica'': datos para el desarrollo. [Lima, 1971]. fo. 86. *(Zac-Puno. No. 5)*

PERU. Direccion de Comunidades Campesinas. 1971. S[ociedad] A[gricola de] I[nteres] S[ocial] ''Pachacutec'': datos para el desarrollo. [Lima, 1971]. pp. 349. *(Zac-Mantaro. No.3)*

PERU. Direccion de Comunidades Campesinas. Division de Estudios Sociales. 1971. S[ociedad] A[gricola de] I[nteres] S[ocial] Tawantinsuyo: datos para el desarrollo. Lima, 1971. pp. 221. *(Z[ona] A[graria] 3-Trujillo. No. 2)*

— Social conditions.

KUITENBROUWER (JOOST B.W.) The function of social mobilization in the process towards a new society in Peru. The Hague, 1973. pp. 82. *(Hague. Institute of Social Studies. Occasional Papers. No. 36)*

— Social policy.

PERU. Instituto Nacional de Planificacion. 1972. Plan nacional de desarrollo para 1971-1975. [Lima, 1972?]. 11 vols. (in 2). *11 volumes originally issued in 5 tomos.*

PESCH (HEINRICH).

HAURAND (PETER WILHELM) Das nationalökonomische System von Heinrich Pesch, S.J.; in seinen Grundzügen dargestellt. M. Gladbach, 1922. pp. 104. *bibliog.*

PESTICIDES.

WELLFORD (HARRISON) Sowing the wind: (a report from Ralph Nader's Center for Study of Responsive Law on Food Safety and the Chemical Harvest). New York, 1973. pp. 384.

— Safety regulations.

INTER-GOVERNMENTAL MARITIME CONSULTATIVE ORGANIZATION. 1973. Recommendations on the safe use of pesticides in ships. London, [1973]. pp. 14.

PETAIN (HENRI PHILIPPE BENONI OMER JOSEPH).

PEDRONCINI (GUY) Pétain: général en chef, 1917-1918. Paris, 1974. pp. 463. *bibliog. (Paris. Université de Paris I (Panthéon- Sorbonne). Publications. Nouvelle Série. Recherches. 8)*

PETER I, called the Great, Emperor of Russia.

PLATONOV (SERGEI FEDOROVICH) Petr Velikii: lichnost' i deiatel'nost'. [Leningrad, 1926]. pp. 115.

PETERBOROUGH

— Growth.

PETERBOROUGH DEVELOPMENT CORPORATION. Greater Peterborough. [Peterborough, 1972]. pp. 20.

— Transit systems.

SLEVIN (ROGER) Citywide in Peterborough: the effects of introducing ordinary and unlimited-travel bus season tickets. Cranfield, 1973. pp. 58. *(Cranfield Institute of Technology. Centre for Transport Studies. Reports. 4)*

PETERLEE

— Social conditions.

RANKIN (HELEN) New towns for old: the Peterlee social survey. London, 1949. pp. 20. *bibliog. (Current Affairs. No. 75)*

PETERS (RICHARD STANLEY).

PETERS (RICHARD STANLEY) Psychology and ethical development: a collection of articles on psychological theories, ethical development and human understanding. London, 1974. pp. 480.

PETITOT (EMILE).

PETITOT (EMILE) The Amerindians of the Canadian northwest in the 19th century, as seen by Emile Petitot...; edited by Donat Savoie. Ottawa, 1971. 2 vols. (in 1). *bibliog. (Canada. Northern Science Research Group. MDRP [Reports]. 9-10)*

PETROLEUM.

TIRATSOO (E.N.) Oilfields of the world. Beaconsfield, 1973. pp. 376.

— Asia .

UNITED NATIONS. Economic Commission for Asia and the Far East. Mineral Resources Development Series . New York, 1952 in progress.

— Australasia.

UNITED NATIONS. Economic Commission for Asia and the Far East. Mineral Resources Development Series . New York, 1952 in progress.

— Nigeria.

NIGERIA. Petroleum Division. Annual report. a., 1968/9- Lagos.

PETROLEUM CONSERVATION.

SCHULZ (WALTER) Ökonomische Probleme der Politik der Erdölkonservierung in den USA. München, 1972. pp. 406. *(Cologne. Universität. Energiewirtschaftliches Institut. Schriftenreihe. Band 17)*

POLE (NICHOLAS) Oil and the future of personal mobility. Cambridge, 1973. pp. 64.

PETROLEUM IN SUBMERGED LANDS

— North Sea.

NORTH Sea oil: the challenge and the implications. Edinburgh, 1973. pp. 77. *(Heriot-Watt University. Lectures. 1973)*

— — Bibliography.

EDINBURGH COLLEGE OF COMMERCE. Library. North Sea oil, 1972; select list: periodical and newspaper articles; compiler A.J. Macaulay. Edinburgh, 1973. pp. 39.

— United Kingdom.

CONFEDERATION OF BRITISH INDUSTRY. United Kingdom oil: the opportunity for Welsh industry; a report on the opportunities for Welsh industry arising from oil exploration off the U.K. coast, by a team of industrialists from CBI Wales. Cardiff, 1972. pp. 40.

U.K. Department of Trade and Industry. Offshore Supplies Office. 1973. Offshore supplies interest relief grants: a guide for industry. London, 1973. pp. 14.

U.K. Interdepartmental Working Party on Education and Training for Offshore Development. 1973. Education and training for offshore development; report; [B.A. Smith, chairman]. London, Department of Employment, Training Division, [1973]. 1 vol. (various pagings).

— — Directories.

NORTH EAST DEVELOPMENT COUNCIL and UNITED KINGDOM. Department of Trade and Industry. Oilfield: (directory of industrial resources in the north east of England). Newcastle upon Tyne, [1972 repr.1973?]. pp. 159. *bibliog.*

PETROLEUM INDUSTRY AND TRADE.

GRAF (GEORG ENGELBERT) Erdöl, Erdölkapitalismus und Erdölpolitik. Jena, [1925]. pp. 96. *bibliog.*

UNITED NATIONS. Economic Commission for Asia and the Far East. Mineral Resources Development Series . New York, 1952 in progress.

ITALY. Ente Nazionale Idrocarburi. Energy and petroleum. irreg., 1964- Roma. *In English or Italian, with index and glossary in English.*

EVENSEN (JENS) Report on oil policy problems viewed against the background of oil legislation and concession policies of other nations. [Oslo?], Norwegian Ministry of Industry, 1971. pp. 250.

INTERNATIONAL OIL SYMPOSIUM, LONDON, 1972. Selected papers presented at the...symposium [organized by the Economist Intelligence Unit]. London, [1973]. pp. 160.

ORGANISATION FOR ECONOMIC CO-OPERATION AND DEVELOPMENT. Oil Committee. 1973. Oil: the present situation and future prospects. Paris, 1973. pp. 293.

WHITE (NORMAN ARTHUR) The economics of scale in the international petroleum industry; [Ph.D.(London) thesis]. 1973. 1 vol. (various foliations). *bibliog. Typescript: unpublished. This thesis is the property of London University and may not be removed from the Library.*

MEHTA (BALRAJ) India and the world oil crisis. New Delhi, 1974. pp. 148.

MICHAELIS (ALFRED) 1901- . Erdöl in der Weltwirtschaft und Weltpolitik. Berlin, [1974]. pp. 240. *bibliog.*

ODELL (PETER R.) Oil and world power: background to the oil crisis. 3rd ed. Harmondsworth, 1974. pp. 245. *bibliog.*

PERLO (VICTOR) The economics of oil production: (paper prepared for a seminar on oil held in Baghdad in November 1972). New York, 1974. pp. 44. *(American Institute for Marxist Studies. Occasional Papers. No.14)*

RIFAÏ (TAKI) The pricing of crude oil: economic and strategic guidelines for an international energy policy. New York, 1974. pp. 356. *bibliog.*

— America, Latin.

INGRAM (GEORGE M.) Expropriation of U.S. property in South America: nationalization of oil and copper companies in Peru, Bolivia, and Chile. New York, 1974. pp. 392. *bibliog.*

— East (Near East).

ISSAWI (CHARLES PHILIP) Oil, the Middle East and the world. New York, 1972. pp. 86. *bibliog. (Georgetown University. Center for Strategic and International Studies. Washington Papers. 4)*

ISKANDAR (MARWAN) The Arab oil question. [Beirut, 1973]. pp. 109.

LANDIS (LINCOLN) Politics and oil: Moscow in the Middle East. New York, 1973. pp. 201. *bibliog.*

SHWADRAN (BENJAMIN) The Middle East, oil and the great powers. 3rd ed. New York, 1973. pp. 630. *bibliog. (Tel Aviv. University. Shiloah Center for Middle Eastern and African Studies. Monograph Series)*

STEVENS (Sir ROGER BENTHAM) Middle East oil in international relations. Leeds, 1973. pp. 29. *(Leeds. University. Montague Burton Lectures on International Relations. No. 31)*

KLEBANOFF (SHOSHANA) Middle east oil and U.S. foreign policy, with special reference to the U.S. energy crisis. New York, 1974. pp. 288. *bibliog.*

— Ecuador.

TAMA PAZ (CYRANO) Petroleo, drama ecuatoriano. Grayaquil, 1970. pp. 207.

— India.

MEHTA (BALRAJ) India and the world oil crisis. New Delhi, 1974. pp. 148.

— Iraq.

OIL AND MINERALS IN IRAQ; [pd. annually under supervision of a permanent committee from the Ministry of Oils and Minerals, the Iraqi National Oil Company and the Iraqi National Minerals Company]. a., 1970 (1st)- Baghdad.

— Italy.

ITALY. Ente Nazionale Idrocarburi. Energy and petroleum. irreg., 1964- Roma. *In English or Italian, with index and glossary in English.*

— Mediterranean.

BURRELL (R.M.) and COTTRELL (ALVIN J.) Politics, oil and the Western Mediterranean. Beverly Hills, [1973]. pp. 80. *(Georgetown University. Center for Strategic and International Studies. Washington Papers. vol. 1/7)*

— Norway.

NORWAY. Bensinomsetningsutvalget. 1972. Bensinomsetningen: utredning fra et utvalg oppnevnt...av 11. oktober 1968. Oslo, 1972. pp. 122. *(Norway. Norges Offentlige Utredninger. 1972. 35)*

WYLLER (THOMAS CHRISTIAN) ed. Norge som oljestat: artikler av Thomas Chr. Wyller [and others]. Oslo, 1973. pp. 141.

— Russia.

BREKHOV (KONSTANTIN IVANOVICH) Khimicheskoe i neftianoe mashinostroenie v vos'moi piatiletke. Moskva, 1971. pp. 56.

ECONOMIST INTELLIGENCE UNIT. Q[uarterly] E[conomic] R[eview] Specials. No. 14. Soviet oil to 1980. London, [1973]. pp. 49.

— — Ukraine.

KORCHAGINA (VALENTINA IVANOVNA) and LUGOVSKOI (IVAN GAVRILOVICH) Neftianiki Prichernomor'ia. Odessa, 1966. pp. 23.

— United Kingdom.

CONFEDERATION OF BRITISH INDUSTRY. United Kingdom oil: the opportunity for Welsh industry; a report on the opportunities for Welsh industry arising from oil exploration off the U.K. coast, by a team of industrialists from CBI Wales. Cardiff, 1972. pp. 40.

PETROLEUM INDUSTRY AND TRADE. (Cont.)

WOODWARD (GUY H.) and WOODWARD (GRACE STEELE) The secret of Sherwood Forest: oil production in England during World War II. Norman, Okla., [1973]. pp. 266. *bibliog.*

MITCHISON (NAOMI MARGARET) Oil for the Highlands?. London, 1974. pp. 32. *(Fabian Society. Research Series. [No.] 315)*

NORTH sea report: exploration, production, financing, investment; produced jointly by the Investors Chronicle and Petroleum Times. London. *Supplement to INVESTORS CHRONICLE, My 3 1974.*

— — **Bibliography.**

EDINBURGH COLLEGE OF COMMERCE. Library. North Sea oil, 1972; select list: periodical and newspaper articles; compiler A.J. Macaulay. Edinburgh, 1973. pp. 39.

— **United States.**

SCHULZ (WALTER) Okonomische Probleme der Politik der Erdölkonservierung in den USA. München, 1972. pp. 406. *(Cologne. Universität. Energiewirtschaftliches Institut. Schriftenreihe. Band 17)*

RUTTENBERG (STANLEY H.) AND ASSOCIATES, INC. The American oil industry: a failure of anti-trust policy. New York, 1973. pp. 160.

KLEBANOFF (SHOSHANA) Middle east oil and U.S. foreign policy, with special reference to the U.S. energy crisis. New York, 1974. pp. 288. *bibliog.*

— — **Pennsylvania.**

GIDDENS (PAUL HENRY) Pennsylvania petroleum 1750-1872: a documentary history. Titusville, Drake Well Memorial Park, 1947. pp. 420.

MILLER (ERNEST CONRAD) Pennsylvania's oil industry. rev. ed. Gettysburg, 1959. pp. 55. *bibliog. (Pennsylvania History Studies. No. 4)*

PETROLEUM LAW AND LEGISLATION.

EVENSEN (JENS) Report on oil policy problems viewed against the background of oil legislation and concession policies of other nations. [Oslo?], Norwegian Ministry of Industry, 1971. pp. 250.

PETROLEUM PRODUCTS

— **Prices.**

RIFAÏ (TAKI) Les prix du pétrole: économie du marché ou stratégie de puissance. Paris, 1974. pp. 424. *bibliog.*

RIFAÏ (TAKI) The pricing of crude oil: economic and strategic guidelines for an international energy policy. New York, 1974. pp. 356. *bibliog.*

PETROLEUM REFINERIES

— **Mathematical models.**

RUSSELL (CLIFFORD S.) Residuals management in industry: a case study of petroleum refining. Baltimore, [1973]. pp. 193.

— **Waste disposal.**

RUSSELL (CLIFFORD S.) Residuals management in industry: a case study of petroleum refining. Baltimore, [1973]. pp. 193.

— **Canada.**

CANADA. Statistics Canada. Productivity Research and Analysis Section. 1971. Productivity trends in industry: indexes of output per person employed and per man-hour: petroleum refineries... 1959-1969. Ottawa, 1971. pp. 24. *In English and French.*

PEWTER, BRITISH.

HATCHER (JOHN) and BARKER (THEODORE CARDWELL) A history of British pewter. London, 1974. pp. 363. *bibliog.*

PEYER IM HOF (JOHANN FRIEDRICH).

VEREIN FÜR WIRTSCHAFTSHISTORISCHE STUDIEN. Schweizer Pioniere der Wirtschaft und Technik. 27. Zwei Schaffhauser Pioniere: Friedrich Peyer im Hof, 1817- 1900; Heinrich Theophil Bäschlin, 1845-1887. Zürich, 1973. pp. 107. *bibliog.*

PFUNDS

— **Economic history.**

WISCHHAUSEN (HANS) Pfunds: ein Bergdorf wandelt sich zum Fremdenplatz. Innsbruck, 1972. pp. 96. *bibliog.*

PHARMACY

— **Laws and legislation — France.**

CRISTAU (BERNARD) Le droit de la pharmacie. Paris, 1973. pp. 125. *bibliog.*

PHENOMENOLOGY.

NATANSON (MAURICE) ed. Phenomenology and the social sciences. Evanston, 1973. 2 vols. *bibliogs. (Northwestern University. Studies in Phenomenology and Existential Philosophy)*

PHENOMENOLOGICAL sociology: issues and applications; edited by George Psathas. New York, [1973]. pp. 369.

SCHUTZ (ALFRED) and LUCKMANN (THOMAS) The structures of the life-world; translated by Richard M. Zaner and H. Tristram Engelhardt, Jr. London, 1974. pp. 335.

PHILADELPHIA

— **Economic conditions.**

WEILER (CONRAD J.) Philadelphia: neighborhood, authority and the urban crisis. New York, 1974. pp. 218.

— **Politics and government.**

WEILER (CONRAD J.) Philadelphia: neighborhood, authority and the urban crisis. New York, 1974. pp. 218.

— **Social conditions.**

WEILER (CONRAD J.) Philadelphia: neighborhood, authority and the urban crisis. New York, 1974. pp. 218.

PHILBY (HAROLD ADRIAN RUSSELL).

SEALE (PATRICK) and McCONVILLE (MAUREEN) Philby: the long road to Moscow. New York, [1973]. pp. 282.

PHILIP, Duke of Burgundy, called the Good.

VAUGHAN (RICHARD) Professor of Medieval History, University of Hull. Philip the Good: the apogee of Burgundy. London, 1970. pp. 456. *bibliog.*

PHILIPPINE ISLANDS

— **Commerce — Africa.**

PHILIPPINE ISLANDS. Department of Commerce and Industry. Research and Information Division. 1965. Philippine trade with the EFTA countries; editor Socorro B. Ramos. Manila, 1965. pp. 45.

— — **European Free Trade Association countries.**

PHILIPPINE ISLANDS. Department of Commerce and Industry. Research and Information Division. 1965. Philippine trade with the African countries; editor, Socorro B. Ramos. rev. ed. Manila, 1965. pp. 32.

— **Economic conditions.**

PHILIPPINE ISLANDS. Department of Commerce and Industry. Research and Information Division. 1966. The Philippines: a handbook of economic facts and general information; [edited by Socorro B. Ramos and Salvador M. Quiniquini]. [Manila, 1966]. pp. 170.

FRANCE. Direction de la Documentation. La Documentation Française. Notes et Etudes Documentaires. Nos. 3,831-3, 832. L'économie philippine. Paris, 1971. pp. 58.

SICAT (GERARDO P.) Economic policy and Philippine development. [Quezon City], 1972. pp. 461. *bibliog.*

LICHAUCO (ALEJANDRO) The Lichauco paper: imperialism in the Philippines. New York, 1973. pp. 111.

— **Economic policy.**

PHILIPPINE ISLANDS. President, 1957-61 (Garcia). 1958. In the Philippines: stability through sacrifice: the inaugural address and the state-of-the-nation address to the Congress of the Philippines, etc. London, 1958. pp. 24.

PHILIPPINE ISLANDS. Council of Administrative Management. 1962. Primer on President Macapagal's socio-economic program. FY- 1962 to FY-1967. [Manila, 1962?]. pp. (36).

SICAT (GERARDO P.) Economic policy and Philippine development. [Quezon City], 1972. pp. 461. *bibliog.*

— **Foreign economic relations — United States.**

LICHAUCO (ALEJANDRO) The Lichauco paper: imperialism in the Philippines. New York, 1973. pp. 111.

— **Foreign relations — United States.**

STANLEY (PETER W.) A nation in the making: the Philippines and the United States, 1899-1921. Cambridge, Mass., 1974. pp. 340. *bibliog. (Harvard University. Harvard Studies in American- East Asian Relations. 4)*

— **History — 1898— .**

STANLEY (PETER W.) A nation in the making: the Philippines and the United States, 1899-1921. Cambridge, Mass., 1974. pp. 340. *bibliog. (Harvard University. Harvard Studies in American- East Asian Relations. 4)*

— **Industries.**

PHILIPPINE ISLANDS. Department of Commerce and Industry. Research and Information Division. 1965. Philippine industry; [edited by Socorro B. Ramos and Salvador M. Quiniquini]. [Manila, 1965?]. pp. 149.

— **Politics and government.**

STOWE (JUDITH) Philippines: the need for a new society. London, 1973. pp. 20. *(Institute for the Study of Conflict. Conflict Studies. No. 37)*

WEINTRAUB (DOV) Development and modernization in the Philippines: the problem of change in the context of political stability and social continuity. Beverly Hills, [1973]. pp. 32. *bibliog.*

— **Social conditions.**

WEINTRAUB (DOV) Development and modernization in the Philippines: the problem of change in the context of political stability and social continuity. Beverly Hills, [1973]. pp. 32. *bibliog.*

— **Social life and customs.**

KIEFER (THOMAS M.) The Tausug: violence and law in a Philippine Moslem society. New York, [1972]. pp. 145. *bibliog.*

— **Social policy.**

PHILIPPINE ISLANDS. President, 1957-61 (Garcia). 1958. In the Philippines: stability through sacrifice: the inaugural address and the state-of-the-nation address to the Congress of the Philippines, etc. London, 1958. pp. 24.

PHILIPPINE ISLANDS. Council of Administrative Management. 1962. Primer on President Macapagal's socio-economic program. FY- 1962 to FY-1967. [Manila, 1962?]. pp. (36).

— **Statistics.**

PHILIPPINE ISLANDS. Bureau of the Census and Statistics. Special Releases . Manila, 1966 in progress.

PHILOSOPHICAL ANTHROPOLOGY.

ANAN'EV (B.G.) Der Mensch als Gegenstand der Erkenntnis; (Übersetzung aus dem Russischen [by] Maria Uhlmann; für die Redaktion der Ausgabe in deutscher Sprache verantwortlich: Manfred Vorwerg. Berlin, 1974. pp. 315. *bibliog.*

KOESTLER (ARTHUR) The heel of Achilles: essays, 1968-1973. London, 1974. pp. 254.

STEVENSON (LESLIE) Seven theories of human nature. Oxford, 1974. pp. 128. *bibliogs.*

PHILOSOPHY.

AYER (Sir ALFRED JULES) The central questions of philosophy. London, 1973. pp. 243. (*Gifford Lectures. 1972-1973*)

— History.

STIEHLER (GOTTFRIED) ed. Veränderung und Entwicklung: Studien zur vormarxistischen Dialektik. Berlin, 1974. pp. 310.

PHILOSOPHY, AMERICAN.

CAMPORESI (CRISTIANO) Il marxismo teorico negli USA, 1900-1945. Milano, 1973. pp. 170.

PHILOSOPHY, ARMENIAN.

KHACHATURIAN (ASHOT BOGDANOVICH) Istoriia progressivnoi armianskoi filosofskoi i obshchestvenno- politicheskoi mysli kontsa XVIII - serediny XIX veka. Moskva, 1973. pp. 261.

PHILOSOPHY, BRITISH.

BOGOMOLOV (ALEKSEI SERGEEVICH) Angliiskaia burzhuaznaia filosofiia XX veka. Moskva, 1973. pp. 317. *bibliog.*

FERGUSON (JAMES P.) The philosophy of Dr. Samuel Clarke and its critics. New York, [1974]. pp. 292. *bibliog.*

PHILOSOPHY, CHINESE.

THREE major struggles on China's philosophical front, 1949-64. Peking, 1973. pp. 66.

PHILOSOPHY, ENGLISH.

See PHILOSOPHY, BRITISH.

PHILOSOPHY, ITALIAN.

CASSANO (FRANCO) ed. Marxismo e filosofia in Italia, 1958-1971: i dibattiti e le inchieste su Rinascita e il Contemporaneo. Bari, [1973]. pp. 401.

PHILOSOPHY, MODERN.

SARTRE (JEAN PAUL) Situations. [Paris, 1947, repr. 1973, in progress].

ALBRECHT (REINHARDT) Sozialtechnologie und ganzheitliche Sozialphilosophie: zu Karl R. Poppers Kritik der ganzheitlichen Sozialphilosophie. Bonn, 1973. pp. 235.

CENTRE INTERNATIONAL DE SYNTHÈSE. Semaine de Synthèse, 29e, 1970. Le droit, les sciences humaines et la philosophie: communications et échanges de vues. Paris, 1973. pp. 405.

HUNTER (J.F.M.) Essays after Wittgenstein. London, 1973. pp. 202.

MANSER (ANTHONY R.) The end of philosophy: Marx and Wittgenstein; an inaugural lecture delivered at the University [of Southampton] 1st May, 1973. [Southampton], 1973. pp. 14.

GELLNER (ERNEST ANDRE) The devil in modern philosophy; edited with a preface by I.C. Jarvie and Joseph Agassi. London, 1974. pp. 262. *bibliog.*

SARTRE (JEAN PAUL) Between existentialism and marxism; translated from the French by John Matthews. London, 1974. pp. 302. *Essays and interviews from Situations VIII and IX.*

STRAWSON (PETER FREDERICK) Freedom and resentment and other essays. London, 1974. pp. 214.

SPECHT (RAINER) Innovation und Folgelast: Beispiele aus der neueren Philosophie- und Wissenschaftsgeschichte. Stuttgart-Bad Cannstatt, [1972]. pp. 237. *With English summary.*

PHILOSOPHY, ROUMANIAN.

MAZYLU (ALEKSANDR DEM'IANOVICH) Razvitie istoriko-filosofskoi nauki v Sotsialisticheskoi Respublike Rumynii, 1944- 1969. Kishinev, 1973. pp. 158. *bibliog.*

PHILOSOPHY, RUSSIAN.

UCHENYE ZAPISKI KAFEDR OBSHCHESTVENNYKH NAUK VUZOV G.LENINGRADA. Filosofiia. vyp. 13. Filosofskie i sotsiologicheskie issledovaniia. Leningrad, 1972. pp. 238.

FEDOSEEV (PETR NIKOLAEVICH) Kommunismus und Philosophie; (übersetzt [from the Russian] von Leon Nebenzahl). Berlin, 1973. pp. 594.

UCHENYE ZAPISKI KAFEDR OBSHCHESTVENNYKH NAUK VUZOV LENINGRADA. Filosofiia. vyp.14. Filosofskie i sotsiologicheskie issledovaniia. Leningrad, 1973. pp. 212.

PUSTARNAKOV (VLADIMIR FEDOROVICH) "Kapital" K. Marksa i filosofskaia mysl' v Rossii, konets XIX - nachalo XX v. Moskva, 1974. pp. 383.

PHILOSOPHY, URUGUAYAN.

ARDAO (ARTURO) Origenes de la influencia de Renan en el Uruguay. Montevideo, 1955. pp. 34. (*Instituto Nacional de Investigaciones y Archivos Literarios. Estudios y Testimonios. 1*)

PHILOSOPHY, WHITE RUSSIAN.

OCHERKI istorii filosofskoi i sotsiologichekoi mysli Belorussii do 1917 g. Minsk, 1973. pp. 557.

PHOSPHATE INDUSTRY

— Nauru.

NAURU. 1969. Nauru Island phosphate industry, 1967: agreed minute. in AUSTRALIA. Parliament. Parliamentary papers, 1969, vol.10.

— United States.

BLAKEY (ARCH FREDRIC) The Florida phosphate industry: a history of the development and use of a vital mineral. Cambridge, Mass., 1973. pp. 197.

PHYSICAL GEOGRAPHY.

POLSKA AKADEMIA NAUK. Instytut Geografii. Geographia Polonica. 28. [Papers on physical and economic geography]. Warszawa, 1974. pp. 144. *bibliogs.*

— Africa, East.

MORGAN (WILLIAM THOMAS WILSON) East Africa. London, 1973. pp. 410. *bibliogs.*

— Africa, West.

HARRISON-CHURCH (RONALD JAMES) West Africa: a study of the environment and of man's use of it;... with a chapter on soils and soil management [by] P.R. Moss. 7th ed. London, 1974. pp. 526. *bibliog.*

— America, North.

WHITE (CHARLES LANGDON) and others. Regional geography of Anglo-America. 4th ed. Englewood Cliffs, [1974]. pp. 617. *bibliogs.*

— Cameroun.

IMBERT (JEAN) Le Cameroun. Paris, 1973. pp. 127. *bibliog.*

— Chad.

CABOT (JEAN) and BOUQUET (CHRISTIAN) Le Tchad. Paris, 1973. pp. 128. *bibliog.*

— Europe.

MONKHOUSE (FRANCIS JOHN) A regional geography of western Europe. 4th ed. London, 1974. pp. 704. *bibliog.*

— France.

GEORGE (PIERRE) France: a geographical study;... translated by I.B. Thompson. London, 1973. pp. 228. *bibliog.*

— Israel.

ISRAEL pocket library: geography; (compiled from material originally published in the Encyclopaedia Judaica). Jerusalem, [1973]. pp. 263. *bibliog.*

— Liberia.

SCHULZE (WILLI) A new geography of Liberia. London, 1973. pp. 218. *bibliogs.*

— New Zealand.

NEW ZEALAND GEOGRAPHY CONFERENCE, 7TH, HAMILTON, 1972. Proceedings...; edited by Evelyn Stokes. [Christchurch], 1973. pp. 298. *bibliogs.* (*New Zealand Geographical Society. Conference Series. No. 7*)

— Puerto Rico.

PICO (RAFAEL) The geography of Puerto Rico. Chicago, 1974. pp. 439. *bibliog.*

— Roumania.

TURNOCK (DAVID) An economic geography of Romania. London, 1974. pp. 319. *bibliog.*

— Russia — Tatar Republic.

GEOGRAFICHESKAIA kharakteristika administrativnykh raionov Tatarskoi ASSR. Kazan', 1972. pp. 252. *bibliog.*

PHYSICAL THERAPISTS

— United Kingdom.

The REMEDIAL professions; a report by a Working Party set up in March 1973 by the Secretary of State for Social Services; [E.L. McMillan, chairman]. London, H.M.S.O., 1973. pp. 24.

PHYSICALLY HANDICAPPED

— Rehabilitation.

GARRETT (JAMES F.) and LEVINE (EDNA SIMON) eds. Rehabilitation practices with the physically disabled. New York, [1973]. pp. 569. *bibliogs.*

PHYSICALLY HANDICAPPED CHILDREN

— Bibliography.

PILLING (DORIA) compiler. The orthopaedically handicapped child: social, emotional and educational adjustment; an annotated bibliography. Windsor, 1972. pp. 56.

— United States.

DIBNER (SUSAN SCHMIDT) and DIBNER (ANDREW S.) Integration or segregation for the physically handicapped child?. Springfield, Ill., [1973]. pp. 201.

PHYSICIAN AND PATIENT.

FRANCE. Direction de la Documentation. La Documentation Française. Notes et Etudes Documentaires. Nos. 4,034-4, 035-4,036. Les besoins réels du grand public en matiere d'information médicale et sanitaire. [Paris], 1973. pp. 69.

PHYSICIANS.

SHANNON (GARY WILLIAM) and DEVER (G.E. ALAN) Health care delivery: spatial perspectives. New York, [1974]. pp. 141.

PHYSICIANS. (Cont.)

— Ireland (Republic).

EIRE. Consultative Council on General Medical Practice. 1974. The general practitioner in Ireland; report; [James McCormick, chairman]. Dublin, [1974]. pp. 104. *bibliog.*

— Norway.

NORWAY. Statistiske Centralbyrå. 1973. Legestatistikk 1972, etc. Oslo, 1973. pp. 69. (*Norges Offisielle Statistikk. Rekke A. 538*)

— Switzerland.

VAUD (CANTON). Service de la Santé Publique. 1972. Démographie, sociologie, économie et prospective médicales: études...fondées sur les données de la Suisse et du canton de Vaud: rapport technique. Lausanne, 1972. pp. 268.

— United Kingdom.

ATKINSON (PAUL) and others. Medical mystique: indeterminacy and models of professional process. Edinburgh, 1973. fo. 42. *bibliog.* (*Edinburgh. University. Centre for Research in the Educational Sciences. Occasional Papers. 14*)

BUTLER (JOHN R.) and others. Family doctors and public policy: a study of manpower distribution. London, 1973. pp. 198.

— — Scotland

BUCHAN (IAN CARPENTER) and RICHARDSON (IAN MILNE) Time study of consultations in general practice. [Edinburgh], Scottish Home and Health Department, 1973. pp. 42. *bibliog.* (*Scottish Health Service Studies. No.27*)

— United States.

LUFT (HAROLD) Determinants of the flow of physicians to the United States. Santa Monica, 1970. pp. 118. *bibliog.* (*Rand Corporation.* [*Papers*]. *4538*)

ROTHSTEIN (WILLIAM G.) American physicians in the nineteenth century: from sects to science. Baltimore, [1972]. pp. 362.

SLOAN (FRANK A.) Supply responses of young physicians: an analysis of physicians in residency programs; prepared for the Office of Economic Opportunity. Santa Monica, 1973. pp. 85. *bibliog.* (*Rand Corporation.* [*Rand Reports*]. *1131*)

PHYSICISTS

— United Kingdom.

GASTON (JERRY) Originality and competition in science: a study of the British high energy physics community. Chicago, [1973]. pp. 210. *bibliog.*

PHYSICS

— Philosophy.

COHEN (ROBERT SONNE) and WARTOFSKY (MARX W.) eds. Logical and epistemological studies in contemporary physics. Dordrecht, [1974]. pp. 462. *bibliogs.* (*Boston Colloquium for the Philosophy of Science. Boston Studies in the Philosophy of Science. vol. 13*)

PHYSIOCRATS.

GRANDAMY (RENE) La Physiocratie: théorie générale du développement économique. Paris, [1973]. pp. 148.

PHYSIOGNOMY.

EKMAN (PAUL) and others. Emotion in the human face: guidelines for research and an integration of findings. New York, [1972]. pp. 191. *bibliog.*

PHYSIOLOGY.

WORLD HEALTH ORGANIZATION. Public Health Papers. Geneva, 1959 in progress.

PIAGET (JEAN).

BOYLE (D.G.) A students' guide to Piaget. Oxford, 1969 repr. 1970. pp. 156. *bibliog.*

McNALLY (D.W.) Piaget, education and teaching. Lewes, 1974. pp. 171. *bibliog.*

PIATNITSKII (OSIP ARONOVICH) pseud.

PIATNITSKII (OSIP ARONOVICH) pseud. [i.e. Iosif Aronovich TARSHIS] Memoirs of a Bolshevik; [reprint of the work first published in London, 1933]. Westport, Conn., 1973. pp. 224.

PICKETING

— United Kingdom.

BROADWAY (FRANK) Stop and listen: licence for extremists. London, [1974]. pp. 7.

PIEDMONT

— Economic history.

ROTELLI (CLAUDIO) Una campagna medievale: storia agraria del Piemonte fra il 1250 e il 1450. Torino, [1973]. pp. 378.

— Social history.

PAPA (EMILIO RAFFAELE) Origini delle società operaie: libertà di associazione e organizzazioni operaie di mutuo soccorso in Piemonte, 1848-1861. Milano, [1967]. pp. 368.

PILLER (NORMAN).

PILLER (NORMAN) Instead of the butler's apron. Luton, 1974. pp. 433.

PINCHOT (GIFFORD).

PINKETT (HAROLD T.) Gifford Pinchot: private and public forester. Urbana, [1970]. pp. 167. *bibliog.*

PINTO (RUI DE).

PINTO (RUI DE) The making of a middle cadre: the story of Rui de Pinto; taped and edited by Don Barnett. Richmond, B.C., [1973]. pp. 107. (*Liberation Support Movement. Information Center. Life Histories from the Revolution. Angola, MPLA.1*)

PIOMBINO

— Economic history.

FAVILLI (PAOLO) Capitalismo e classe operaia a Piombino, 1861-1918. Roma, 1974. pp. 256.

PIRANDELLO (LUIGI).

CASTRIS (ARCANGELO LEONE DE) Il decadentismo italiano: Svevo, Pirandello, D'Annunzio. Bari, [1974]. pp. 262.

PISA

— History.

TANGHERONI (MARCO) Politica, commercio, agricoltura a Pisa nel trecento. [Pisa, 1973]. pp. 243. *bibliog.* (*Pisa. Università. Istituto di Storia. Pubblicazioni. 5*)

PISEMSKII (ALEKSEI FEOFILAKTOVICH).

BLANKOFF (JEAN) La société russe de la seconde moitié du XIXe siècle: trois témoignages littéraires: M.E. Saltykov-Ščedrin, Gleb Uspenskij, A.F. Pisemskij. Bruxelles, [1972]. pp. 248. *bibliog.*

PITT (Right Hon. WILLIAM).

JARRETT (JOHN DEREK) Pitt the Younger. London, [1974]. pp. 224. *bibliog.*

PLANNING.

JACOBSEN (BERTIL) and ANDERSEN (BENT ROLD) Den departementale planlaegningsvirksomhed. [Copenhagen?, Arbejdsministeriet], 1970. pp. 48. *bibliog.*

ASSESSING the future and policy planning: [based on a conference held at the National Bureau of Standards, Gaithersburg, Maryland in 1970]; editors, Walter A. Hahn and Kenneth F. Gordon. New York, [1973]. pp. 344.

BREEV (MIKHAIL VIKTOROVICH) Ekonomicheskie i metodologicheskie osnovy planirovaniia. Moskva, 1973. pp. 150.

HEYWOOD (PHIL) Planning and human need. Newton Abbot, [1974]. pp. 192.

— Directories.

EUROPEAN directory of economic and corporate planning, 1973-74. Epping, 1973. pp. 442.

PLANTATION LIFE

— United States.

SMITH (JULIA FLOYD) Slavery and plantation growth in antebellum Florida, 1821-1860. Gainesville, [1973]. pp. 249. *bibliog.*

PLANTATIONS.

TINKER (HUGH) A new system of slavery: the export of Indian labour overseas, 1830-1920. London, 1974. pp. 432. *bibliog.*

— Ivory Coast.

IVORY COAST. Bureau National d'Etudes Techniques de Développement. 1970. Barrage du Bandama: recensement foncier. [Abidjan?, 1970?]. pp. [75].

PLASTICS INDUSTRY AND TRADE

— United Kingdom.

RUBBER AND PLASTICS PROCESSING INDUSTRY TRAINING BOARD [U.K.]. Report and statement of accounts. a., 1972/3- Brentford. *Formerly included in the file of British Parliamentary Papers.*

PLATO.

BARROW (JOHN PENROSE) The noble lie and the politics of reaction; [an] inaugural lecture... at University of London King's College June 5th 1972. [London, 1972]. pp. 19.

GOSLING (J.C.B.) Plato. London, 1973. pp. 319. *bibliog.*

LEDNIKOV (EVGENII EVGEN'EVICH) Kriticheskii analiz nominalisticheskikh i platonistskikh tendentsii v sovremennoi logike. Kiev, 1973. pp. 223.

FINDLAY (JOHN NIEMEYER) Plato: the written and unwritten doctrines. London, 1974. pp. 484.

PLAY.

ELLIS (MICHAEL J.) Why people play. Englewood Cliffs, [1973]. pp. 173. *bibliog.*

PLAY SCHOOLS.

CENTRAL TRAINING COUNCIL IN CHILD CARE [U.K.]. Study Group on Fieldwork Training. Playgroups: the development of dual purpose groups in social work education. [London], 1970. fo. 12. (*Discussion Papers. No. 3*)

PLEBISCITE

— Germany.

HEUER (JUERGEN) Zur politischen, sozialen und ökonomischen Problematik der Volksabstimmungen in Schleswig, 1920. Kiel, 1973. pp. 238. *bibliog.*

— Puerto Rico.

ESTEFANO (MIGUEL A.D') Puerto Rico: analisis de un plebiscito. La Habana, 1967. pp. 126.

PLEIGER (PAUL).

RIEDEL (MATTHIAS) Eisen und Kohle für das Dritte Reich: Paul Pleigers Stellung in der NS-Wirtschaft. Göttingen, [1973]. pp. 375. *bibliog.*

PLEKHANOV (GEORGII VALENTINOVICH).

ISTORIKO-revoliutsionnyi vestnik. no. 1(4). Moskva, 1922. pp. 103.

KOZHURIN (IAKOV IAKOVLEVICH) Iz istorii bor'by za nauchnyi ateizm: A. Bebel' i G.V. Plekhanov. Leningrad, 1972. pp. 84.

CHAGIN (BORIS ALEKSANDROVICH) and KURBATOVA (IRINA NIKOLAEVNA) Plekhanov. Moskva, 1973. pp. 220. *bibliog.*

PLUMB (JOHN HAROLD).

McKENDRICK (NEIL) ed. Historical perspectives: studies in English thought and society in honour of J.H. Plumb. London, [1974]. pp. 319. *bibliog.*

PLUNKETT (JOHN HUBERT).

MOLONY (JOHN N.) An architect of freedom: John Hubert Plunkett in New South Wales, 1832-1869. Canberra, 1973. pp. 313. *bibliog.*

PLURALISM (SOCIAL SCIENCES).

EDUCATION for cultural pluralism; papers from a conference held in London, December 15-17, 1970 under the auspices of the Cultural Department, World Jewish Congress...; edited by E.M. Eppel. London, 1972. pp. 133.

POINTE—NOIRE.

VENNETIER (PIERRE) Pointe-Noire et la façade maritime du Congo-Brazzaville. Paris, Office de la Recherche Scientifique et Technique Outre-Mer, 1968. pp. 458. *bibliog. (Mémoires O.R.S.T.O.M. 26)*

POITOU

— **Economic conditions.**

FRANCE. Direction de la Documentation. La Documentation Française. Notes et Etudes Documentaires. Nos. 3,731-3, 732-3,733. Les économies régionales: l'économie de la région Poitou-Charentes. Paris, 1970. pp. 120. *bibliog.*

— **Industries.**

PINARD (JACQUES) Les industries du Poitou et des Charentes: étude de l'industrialisation d'un milieu rural et de ses villes. Poitiers, 1972. pp. 516. *bibliog. Maps in end pocket.*

POLAND.

POLAND: a handbook; ([with appendix:] Poland 1974). Warsaw, 1974. pp. 575.

— **Boundaries.**

WESTERN and Northern Poland: historical outline, nationality problems, legal aspect, new society, economic survey; (elaborated by T. Derlatka [and others]; editor: Maria Kornilowicz). Poznan, 1962. pp. 534.

— **Clubs.**

JEDLICKI (WITOLD) Klub Krzywego Koła. Pary'z, 1963. pp. 168.

— **Commerce.**

ŁADYKA (STANISŁAW) 'Zegluga morska i morski handel zagraniczny. cz. 3. Gdańsk, 1972. pp. 136. *bibliog. Pts. 1, 2 appeared as nos. 16, 27 of Zeszyty naukowe Wy'zszej Szkoły Ekonomicznej w Sopocie. Seria A.*

POLAND. Główny Urząd Statystyczny. Rocznik statystyczny handlu wewnętrznego. a., 1973- Warszawa. *(Statystyka Polski. [2nd series])*

ATTMAN (ARTUR) The Russian and Polish markets in international trade, 1500-1650. Göteborg, 1973. pp. 232. *(Göteborgs Universitet. Ekonomisk-Historiska Institutionen. Meddelanden. 26)*

— **Constitutional history.**

HOENSCH (JOERG K.) Sozialverfassung und politische Reform: Polen im vorrevolutionären Zeitalter. Köln, 1973. pp. 500. *bibliog.*

— **Economic conditions.**

WESTERN and Northern Poland: historical outline, nationality problems, legal aspect, new society, economic survey; (elaborated by T. Derlatka [and others]; editor: Maria Kornilowicz). Poznan, 1962. pp. 534.

ROCZNIK POLITYCZNY I GOSPODARCZY. a., 1971- Warszawa. *'Contents' in Polish, Russian, English, French and German.*

ZIELINSKI (JANUSZ G.) Economic reforms in Polish industry. London, 1973. pp. 333. *(Glasgow. University. Institute of Soviet and East European Studies. Economic Reforms in East European Industry)*

— — **Mathematical models.**

NIEDUSZYŃSKI (MIECZYSŁAW) Dynamiczna równowaga gospodarcza. Warszawa, 1973. pp. 215. *bibliog.*

— **Economic policy.**

POLSKA ZJEDNOCZONA PARTIA ROBOTNICZA. Komitet Centralny. Report...on the period between the 5th and 6th congresses. Warsaw, 1971. pp. 47.

JAROSJEWICZ (PIOTR) The principal trends of the socio-economic development of the Polish People's Republic in the years 1971-1975: report for the 6th PUWP Congress delivered...December 7th, 1971. [Warsaw, 1972?]. pp. 27.

LEWANDOWSKI (JĘDRZEJ) ed. System funkcjonowania gospodarki socjalistycznej, etc. Warszawa, 1973. pp. 378. *With English and Russian summaries.*

WYROBISZ (STANISŁAW) Polska czterdziestomilionowa: wybrane przesłanki i elementy prognozy. Warszawa, 1973. pp. 217.

ZIELINSKI (JANUSZ G.) Economic reforms in Polish industry. London, 1973. pp. 333. *(Glasgow. University. Institute of Soviet and East European Studies. Economic Reforms in East European Industry)*

— **Foreign relations — Treaties.**

GELBERG (LUDWIK) Układ PRL-NRF z 7 grudnia 1970 r.: analiza prawna. Wrocław, 1974. pp. 124. *bibliog. With Russian, English and German tables of contents.*

— — **Germany.**

RACHOCKI (JANUSZ) ed. Polska - NRF: przesłanki i proces normalizacji stosunków, etc. Poznań, 1972. pp. 435. *(Poznań. Instytut Zachodni. Studia Niemcoznawcze. Nr. 21)*

KELLERMANN (VOLKMAR) Brücken nach Polen: die deutsch-polnischen Beziehungen und die Weltmächte 1939-1973. Stuttgart, [1973]. pp. 227. *bibliog.*

KREKELER (NORBERT) Revisionsanspruch und geheime Ostpolitik der Weimarer Republik: die Subventionierung der deutschen Minderheit in Polen. Stuttgart, [1973]. pp. 158. *bibliog. (Vierteljahrshefte für Zeitgeschichte. Schriftenreihe. Nr.27)*

— — **Russia.**

JUZWENKO (ADOLF) Polska a "biała" Rosja, od listopada 1918 do kwietnia 1920 r. Wrocław, 1973. pp. 296. *bibliog. With French summary.*

— **History — Bibliography.**

SKWIROWSKA (STEFANIA) compiler. Bibliographie des travaux des historiens polonais en langues étrangères [sic] parus dans les années 1945-1968 / Bibliografia prac historyków polskich w językach obcych za lata 1945-1968. Wrocław, 1971. pp. 91.

— — **1830—1832, Revolution.**

SOKOLNICKI (MICHEL) Les origines de l'émigration polonaise en France, 1831-1832. Paris, 1910. pp. 239.

— **History — 1939—1945, Occupation.**

RAMME (ALWIN) Der Sicherheitsdienst der SS: zu seiner Funktion im faschistischen Machtapparat und im Besatzungsregime des sogenannten Generalgouvernements Polen. [Berlin, 1970]. pp. 325. *bibliog. (Deutsche Akademie der Wissenschaften zu Berlin. Institut für Geschichte. Abteilung Militärgeschichte. Militärhistorische Studien. Neue Folge. 12)* 8 tables and 1 map in end pocket.

— **History, Military.**

ARCISZEWSKI (FRANCISZEK ADAM) Patrząc krytycznie, etc. London, 1972. pp. 310.

— **Intellectual life.**

JEDLICKI (WITOLD) Klub Krzywego Koła. Pary'z, 1963. pp. 168.

— **Nationalism.**

BROCK (PETER DE BEAUVOIR) Nationalism and populism in partitioned Poland: selected essays. London, [1973]. pp. 219.

— **Politics and government.**

ZARYS historii polskiego ruchu ludowego. Warszawa, 1963-70. 2 vols. *bibliog.*

PRAGIER (ADAM) Czas przeszły dokonany. Londyn, 1966. pp. 943.

ROCZNIK POLITYCZNY I GOSPODARCZY. a., 1971- Warszawa. *'Contents' in Polish, Russian, English, French and German.*

HOENSCH (JOERG K.) Sozialverfassung und politische Reform: Polen im vorrevolutionären Zeitalter. Köln, 1973. pp. 500. *bibliog.*

IAZHBOROVSKAIA (INESSA SERGEEVNA) Ideinoe razvitie pol'skogo revoliutsionnogo rabochego dvizheniia, konets XIX - pervaia chetvert' XX v. Moskva, 1973. pp. 415.

— **Population.**

POLAND. Główny Urząd Statystyczny. Studia i Prace Statystyczne. nr.40. Zmiany w strukturze ludności według płci i wieku w latach 1950, 1960, 1970; opracował... Władysław Kondrat. Warszawa, 1972. pp. 64.

POLAND. Główny Urząd Statystyczny. Statystyka Polski. [2nd series]. Nr.3. Perspektywy rozwoju ludności do 2000 r.; opracowała jANINA aLEKSIŃSKA. wARSZAWA, 1973. PP. 97.

WYROBISZ (STANISŁAW) Polska czterdziestomilionowa: wybrane przesłanki i elementy prognozy. Warszawa, 1973. pp. 217.

— **Relations (general) with France.**

FRANCE. Direction de la Documentation. La Documentation Française. Notes et Etudes Documentaires. No. 3,922. Les relations franco-polonaises, 1945-1972, par Jadwiga Castagné. [Paris], 1972. pp. 48. *bibliog.*

— **Rural conditions.**

DZIABAŁA (STEFAN) Autorytety wiejskie: studium socjologiczne. Warszawa, 1973. pp. 349. *bibliog.*

ADAMSKI (WŁADYSŁAW) Chłopi i przyszłość wsi: postawy, dążenia, aspiracje. Warszawa, 1974. pp. 302.

— **Social conditions.**

WESTERN and Northern Poland: historical outline, nationality problems, legal aspect, new society, economic survey; (elaborated by T. Derlatka [and others]; editor: Maria Kornilowicz). Poznan, 1962. pp. 534.

DYONIZIAK (RYSZARD) and others. Współczesne społeczeństwo polskie: wstęp do socjologii. Warszawa, 1974. pp. 248. *bibliog.*

POLAND. (Cont.)

— Social history.

HOENSCH (JOERG K.) Sozialverfassung und politische Reform: Polen im vorrevolutionären Zeitalter. Köln, 1973. pp. 500. *bibliog.*

— Social policy.

POLSKA ZJEDNOCZONA PARTIA ROBOTNICZA. Komitet Centralny. Report...on the period between the 5th and 6th congresses. Warsaw, 1971. pp. 47.

JAROSJEWICZ (PIOTR) The principal trends of the socio-economic development of the Polish People's Republic in the years 1971-1975: report for the 6th PUWP Congress delivered...December 7th, 1971. [Warsaw, 1972?]. pp. 27.

ROSNER (JAN) ed. Polityka społeczna i służby społeczne w PRL. Warszawa, 1972. pp. 439. *bibliog. (Towarzystwo Wolnej Wszechnicy Polskiej. Komisja Naukowo-Badawsza. Studia z Pedagogiki Społecznej i Polityki Społecznej. t.2)*

— Statistics.

POLAND. Główny Urząd Statystyczny. Rocznik statystyczny powiatów. a., 1973 [1st]- Warszawa. *(Statystyka Polski. [2nd series])*

— Statistics, Vital.

POLAND. Główny Urzad Statystyczny. Studia i Prace Statystyczny. nr. 43. Umieralność według przyczyn w latach 1951-1970. Warszawa, 1972. pp. 159.

POLES IN FRANCE.

SOKOLNICKI (MICHEL) Les origines de l'émigration polonaise en France, 1831-1832. Paris, 1910. pp. 239.

POLES IN KAZAKSTAN.

SAPARGALIEV (GAIRAT SAPARGALIEVICH) and D'IAKOV (VLADIMIR ANATOL'EVICH) Obshchestvenno-politicheskaia deiatel'nost' ssyl'nykh poliakov v dorevoliutsionnom Kazakhstane. Alma-Ata, 1971. pp. 252.

POLES IN THE UNITED STATES.

SANDBERG (NEIL C.) Ethnic identity and assimilation: the Polish-American community; case study of Metropolitan Los Angeles. New York, 1974. pp. 88. *bibliog.*

POLESINE

— Economic policy.

CONTINI (BRUNO) and PACI (MASSIMO) Difesa del suolo e sviluppo dell'agricoltura: un'analisi di sistemi applicata al Polesine. Bologna, [1973]. pp. 343. *bibliog.*

POLICE.

LOPEZ MEJIA (CARLOS ARTURO) Actividad de policia y libertad. Bogota, 1970. pp. 65. *bibliog.*

CASAMAYOR ( ) La police. [Paris, 1973]. pp. 199.

CHIAPPETTI (ACHILLE) L'attività di polizia: aspetti storici e dogmatici. Padova, 1973. pp. 163. *bibliog. (Rome. Università. Istituto di Diritto Pubblico. Pubblicazioni. Serie 3. vol.7)*

— Australia — Northern Territory.

AUSTRALIA. Department of the Interior. 1969. Northern Territory (Administration) Act: Police and Police Offences Ordinance (No.2) 1968 together with statement of reasons for withholding assent to the Ordinance. in AUSTRALIA. Parliament. Parliamentary papers, 1969, vol.10.

— Denmark.

BETAENKNING om aldersfordelingen i politikorpset; afgivet af det af justitsministeriet den 17. januar 1964 nedsatte udvalg; [E. Heide-JØgensen, chairman]. København, 1970. pp. 106. *(Denmark. Betaenkninger. Nr. 555)*

BETAENKNING om politikredsinddelingen i Danmark; afgivet af det af Justitsministeriet den 10. maj 1967 nedsatte strukturudvalg vedrorende politiet. København, 1971. pp. 125. *(Denmark. Betaenkninger. Nr. 605)*

— Germany, Eastern.

LUEERS (HARTWIG) Das Polizeirecht in der DDR: Aufgaben, Befugnisse und Organisation der Deutschen Volkspolizei. Köln, [1974]. pp. 156. *bibliog. (Cologne. Universität. Institut für Ostrecht, and others. Abhandlungen zum Ostrecht. Band 12)*

— India.

INDIAN CONFERENCE OF SOCIAL WORK. The role of police in social welfare work: Social Welfare Day, 1966. Bombay, 1966. pp. 24.

— Italy.

ITALY. Direzione Generale della Pubblica Sicurezza. Divisione Affari Legislativi e Documentazione. 1969. La polizia italiana negli anni 60: una polizia moderna per uno stato moderno. [Rome, 1969]. pp. 33.

— Netherlands.

NETHERLANDS. Ministerie van Justitie. 1969. Herziening politiewet. 's-Gravenhage, 1969. pp. 85.

— Sweden.

SWEDEN. Justitiedepartementet. Polisutredningen. 1970. Polisen i samhället: betänkandet avgivet av 1967 års polisutredning. Stockholm, 1970. pp. 236. *(Sweden. Statens Offentliga Utredningar. 1970. 32)*

— United Kingdom.

BLACK UNITY AND FREEDOM PARTY. Issues. No. 1. Who killed Aseta Simms?: she was murdered. London, 1972. pp. 12.

McCARTHY COMMITTEE. Who killed Stephen McCarthy?. London, [1972]. pp. (30).

PULLÉ (STANISLAUS) Police immigrant relations in Ealing: report of an investigation conducted on behalf of the Ealing C[ommunity] R[elations] C[ouncil]. London, [1973]. pp. 88.

EVANS (PETER C.C.) The police revolution. London, 1974. pp. 192. *bibliog.*

FRIEDLANDER (C.P.) and MITCHELL (EDWARD) The police: servants or masters?. London, 1974. pp. 144.

PURCELL (WILLIAM ERNEST) British police in a changing society. London, 1974. pp. 175.

— United States.

KOSTIN (P.V.) FBR - portret vo ves' rost. Moskva, 1970. pp. 230.

NORRIS (DONALD F.) Police-community relations: a program that failed. Lexington, Mass., [1973]. pp. 136. *bibliog.*

PERRY (DAVID C.) and SORNOFF (PAULA A.) Politics at the street level: the select case of police administration and the community. Beverly Hills, [1973]. pp. 39. *bibliog.*

BENT (ALAN EDWARD) The politics of law enforcement: conflict and power in urban communities. Lexington, Mass., [1974]. pp. 203.

— — Georgia.

MATHIAS (WILLIAM J.) and ANDERSON (STUART) Horse to helicopter: first century of the Atlanta Police Department. Atlanta, 1973. pp. 192. *bibliog. (Georgia State University (United States). School of Urban Life. Community Life Publications. Criminal Justice Series)*

POLICE, POLITICAL AND SECRET

— Germany.

POELS (WERNER) Staat und Sozialdemokratie im Bismarckreich: die Tätigkeit der Politischen Polizei beim Polizeipräsidenten in Berlin in der Zeit des Sozialistengesetzes, 1878- 1890. Berlin, [1964]. pp. 24. *(Sonderdruck aus dem Jahrbuch für die Geschichte Mittel- und Ostdeutschlands...Band 13, 1964)*

RAMME (ALWIN) Der Sicherheitsdienst der SS: zu seiner Funktion im faschistischen Machtapparat und im Besatzungsregime des sogenannten Generalgouvernements Polen. [Berlin, 1970]. pp. 325. *bibliog. (Deutsche Akademie der Wissenschaften zu Berlin. Institut für Geschichte. Abteilung Militärgeschichte. Militärhistorische Studien. Neue Folge. 12)* 8 tables and 1 map in end pocket.

— Russia — Ukraine.

AVERBUKH (N.I.) Odesskaia "chrezvychaika", bol'shevistskii zastenok: fakty i nabliudeniia N.I. Averbukha (Averiusa). ch.1. Kishinev, 1920. pp. 39.

POLISH LITERATURE.

WYGODZKI (STANISŁAW) Zatrzymany do wyjaśnienia. Pary'z, 1968. pp. 205.

POLISH QUESTION.

WESTERN and Northern Poland: historical outline, nationality problems, legal aspect, new society, economic survey; (elaborated by T. Derlatka [and others]; editor: Maria Kornilowicz). Poznan, 1962. pp. 534.

GRABSKI (WŁADYSŁAW) Wspomnienia ze Spa; wstęp i przypisy opracował Stanisław Kirkor. Londyn, 1973. pp. 54.

POLISHES.

COMMISSION ON INDUSTRIAL RELATIONS [U.K.]. Boot and Floor Polish Wages Council (Great Britain). London, H.M.S.O., 1973. pp. 17. *(Reports. No. 51)*

POLITICAL BALLADS AND SONGS, ITALIAN.

MERCURI (LAMBERTO) and TUZZI (CARLO) Canti politici italiani, 1793-1945. 2nd ed. Roma, 1973. pp. 399.

POLITICAL CONVENTIONS.

CHASE (JAMES S.) Emergence of the presidential nominating convention, 1789-1832. Urbana, [1973]. pp. 332. *bibliog.*

POLITICAL CRIMES AND OFFENCES

SCHAFER (STEPHEN) The political criminal: the problem of morality and crime. New York, [1974]. pp. 179. *bibliog.*

— Italy.

Il REGIME contro la Destra: [debates in the Italian Parliament concerning the prosecution of Giorgio Almirante]. Milano, [1973]. pp. 344.

— Mexico.

ACADEMIA MEXICANA DE CIENCIAS PENALES. Los delitos de disolucion social. Mexico, 1969. pp. 166.

POLITICAL ETHICS.

NORONHA (SANCHO DE) Tratado moral de louvores e perigos de alguns estados seculares; introdução e notas por Martim de Albuquerque. Lisboa, 1969. pp. 149. *(Portugal. Junta de Investigações do Ultramar. Centro de Estudos Politicos e Sociais. Estudos de Ciencias Politicas e Sociais. 83)* Reprint of edition of 1549.

TITARENKO (ALEKSANDR IVANOVICH) Morality and politics: critical essays on contemporary views about the relationship between morality and politics in bourgeois sociology. Moscow, 1972. pp. 260.

POLITICAL PARTICIPATION.

ASHFORD (DOUGLAS ELLIOTT) Ideology and participation. Beverly Hills, [1972]. pp. 300. *bibliog.*

PUSIĆ (EUGEN) Participation and the multidimensional development of complexity. Vienna, [1972]. pp. 30. *(Wiener Institut für Entwicklungsfragen. Occasional Papers. 72/2)*

CITIZEN organizations: increasing client control over services; prepared for the Department of Health, Education and Welfare [by] Robert K. Yin [and others]. Santa Monica, 1973. pp. 215. *(Rand Corporation. [Rand Reports]. 1196)*

CORNELIUS (WAYNE A.) Political learning among the migrant poor: the impact of residential context. Beverly Hills, [1973]. pp. 88. *bibliog.*

GREENSTONE (J. DAVID) and PETERSON (PAUL E.) Race and authority in urban politics: community participation and the war on poverty. New York, [1973]. pp. 364.

MACKINNON (FRANK) Postures and politics: some observations on participatory democracy. Toronto, [1973]. pp. 275.

NELLES (VIV) and ROTSTEIN (ABRAHAM) eds. Nationalism or local control: responses to George Woodcock; [first published in the October 1972 issue of The Canadian Forum]. Toronto, 1973. pp. 95.

ROSSI-LANDI (GUY) Les hommes politiques. [Paris], 1973. pp. 114. *bibliog.*

SKJEI (STEPHEN S.) Information for collective action: a microanalytic view of plural decision-making. Lexington, [1973]. pp. 188.

— Bibliography.

U.K. Department of the Environment. Library. 1971. Participation in planning. [London, 1971]. fo. 7. *(Bibliographies. No. 151)*

— Canada — New Brunswick.

NEW BRUNSWICK. Task Force on Social Development. 1971. Participation and development;...report; [Emery LeBlanc and Harold L. Nutter, chairmen]. [Fredericton], 1971. 3 vols. (in 1) *bibliog.*

— Egypt.

HARIK (ILIYA F.) The political mobilization of peasants: a study of an Egyptian community. Bloomington, Ind., [1974]. pp. 309. *bibliog. (Indiana University. International Development Research Center. Studies in Development. No.8)*

— France.

CAPITANT (RENE) Démocratie et participation politique dans les institutions françaises de 1875 à nos jours. Paris, [1972]. pp. 185.

WOSHINSKY (OLIVER H.) The French deputy: incentives and behavior in the National Assembly. Lexington, Mass., [1973]. pp. 232. *bibliog.*

— Jamaica.

STONE (CARL) Class, race and political behaviour in urban Jamaica. [Mona], 1973. pp. 188. *bibliog.*

— Kenya.

BIENEN (HENRY) Kenya: the politics of participation and control. Princeton, [1974]. pp. 215. *bibliog.*

— Netherlands.

DAALDER (HANS) Politisering en lijdelijkheid in de Nederlandse politiek. Assen, 1974. pp. 78.

— Norway.

MARTINUSSEN (WILLY) Fjerndemokratiet: sosial ulikhet, politiske ressurser og politisk medvirkning i Norge. Oslo, 1973. pp. 299.

— Peru.

PALMER (DAVID SCOTT) Revolution from above: military government and popular participation in Peru, 1968-1972. [Ithaca], 1973. pp. 307. *bibliog. (Cornell University. Latin American Studies Program. Dissertation Series. No.47)*

— Singapore.

SEAH CHEE MEOW. Community centres in Singapore: their political involvement. Singapore, 1973. pp. 142. *bibliog.*

— United Kingdom.

U.K. Department of the Environment. 1973. Public participation in general improvement areas. London, 1973. pp. 50. *(Area Improvement Notes. 8)*

— United States.

GARCIA (F. CHRIS) ed. Chicano politics: readings. New York, [1973]. pp. 225.

LADD (EVERETT CARLL) and LIPSET (SEYMOUR MARTIN) Academics, politics and the 1972 election. Washington, D.C., [1973]. pp. 99. *(American Enterprise Institute for Public Policy Research. Domestic Affairs Studies. 15)*

COLE (RICHARD L.) Citizen participation and the urban policy process. Lexington, Mass., [1974]. pp. 178. *bibliog.*

GREENBERG (STANLEY B.) Politics and poverty: modernization and response in five poor neighborhoods. London, [1974]. pp. 282.

ROSENAU (JAMES N.) Citizenship between elections: an inquiry into the mobilizable American. New York, [1974]. pp. 526.

POLITICAL PARTIES.

See also the names of political parties and of types of political parties.

NORWAY. Partifinansieringsutvalget. 1969. Innstilling fra Partifinansieringsutvalget av 1968. Oslo, 1969. pp. 53.

MACKIE (THOMAS T.) and ROSE (RICHARD) The international almanac of electoral history. London, 1974. pp. 434. *bibliogs.*

— Africa, Subsaharan.

WELFLING (MARY B.) Political institutionalization: comparative analyses of African party systems. Beverly Hills, [1973]. pp. 63. *bibliog.*

— America, Latin.

BERNARD (JEAN PIERRE) and others. Guide to the political parties of South America; translated by Michael Perl. Harmondsworth, 1973. pp. 574.

— Argentine Republic.

PASO (LEONARDO) Historia del origen de los partidos politicos en la Argentina, 1810-1918. Buenos Aires, [1972]. pp. 518.

CANTON (DARIO) Elecciones y partidos politicos en la Argentina: historia, interpretacion y balance, 1910-1966. Buenos Aires, 1973. pp. 277.

— Austria.

MIGSCH (ERWIN) Sozialprogramme und Wirklichkeit: (Analyse und Vergleich der für Österreich wesentlichen Ideologien). Wien, [1962]. pp. 62. *(Österreichischer Gewerkschaftsbund. Aktuelle Probleme unserer Zeit)*

— Canada.

MASSON (JACK K.) and ANDERSON (JAMES D.) Emerging party politics in urban Canada. Toronto, [1972]. pp. 212. *bibliog.*

THORBURN (HUGH GARNET) ed. Party politics in Canada. 3rd ed. Scarborough, Ontario, [1972]. pp. 249.

COURTNEY (JOHN C.) The selection of national party leaders in Canada. Hamden, Conn., 1973. pp. 278. *bibliog.*

MEISEL (JOHN) Cleavages, parties and values in Canada. London, [1974]. pp. 55. *bibliog.*

— — Quebec.

BELLAVANCE (LIONEL) Les partis indépendantistes québécois de 1960-73. [Montréal, 1973]. pp. 98.

STEIN (MICHAEL BERNARD) The dynamics of right-wing protest: a political analysis of Social Credit in Quebec. Toronto, [1973]. pp. 256.

— Colombia.

SEPULVEDA NIÑO (SATURNINO) Las elites colombianas en crisis: de partidos policlasistas a partidos monoclasistas. [Bogota], 1970. pp. 196. *bibliog.*

— Denmark.

THOMAS (ALASTAIR H.) Parliamentary parties in Denmark 1945-1972. Glasgow, 1973. pp. 114. *bibliog. (Glasgow. University of Strathclyde. Survey Research Centre. Occasional Papers. No.13)*

— Finland.

ÅBO. Akademi. Acta Academiae Aboensis. Humaniora. 48.1. Analys av partiers beteende: en fallstudie i partistrategi; av Dag Anckar. Åbo, 1974. pp. 152. *bibliog.*

— France.

DUIGOU (DANIEL) Guide des élections; (avec la collaboration de Jean-François Thoraval). Paris, [1973]. pp. 243.

KRAEHE (RAINER) Le financement des partis politiques: contribution à l'étude du statut constitutionnel des partis politiques. Paris, [1973]. pp. 126. *bibliog. (Rouen. Université. Publications. 18)*

TARROW (SIDNEY G.) Partisanship and political exchange in French and Italian local politics: a contribution to the typology of party systems. London, [1974]. pp. 54. *bibliog.*

— Germany.

BERNSTEIN (HERBERT) and ZWEIGERT (KONRAD) Die Rehabilitierung einer aufgelösten politischen Partei: verfassungsrechtliche und prozessuale Betrachtungen. Tübingen, 1972. pp. 34.

DITTBERNER (JUERGEN) and EBBIGHAUSEN (ROLF) eds. Parteiensystem in der Legitimationskrise: Studien und Materialien zur Soziologie der Parteien in der Bundesrepublik Deutschland. Opladen, 1973. pp. 526. *bibliog. (Berlin. Freie Universität. Zentralinstitut für Sozialwissenschaftliche Forschung. Schriften. Band 24)*

ESTIEVENART (GEORGES) Les partis politiques en Allemagne fédérale. Paris, 1973. pp. 128.

HERGT (SIEGFRIED) ed. Parteiprogramme: SPD, CDU, CSU, FDP, DKP, NPD; eine Dokumentation der Grundsatzprogramme und aktueller politischer Ziele. Opladen, [1973]. pp. 337. *bibliog.*

KUEHR (HERBERT) Parteien und Wahlen im Stadt- und Landkreis Essen in der Zeit der Weimarer Republik, etc. Düsseldorf, [1973]. pp. 309. *bibliog. (Germany (Bundesrepublik Deutschland). Kommission für Geschichte des Parlamentarismus und der Politischen Parteien. Beiträge zur Geschichte des Parlamentarismus und der Politischen Parteien. Band 49)*

OLZOG (GUENTER) and HERZIG (ARTHUR) Die politischen Parteien in der Bundesrepublik Deutschland. 8th ed. München, 1973. pp. 170. *bibliog.*

ROTH (REINHOLD) Parteiensystem und Aussenpolitik: zur Bedeutung des Parteiensystems für den aussenpolitischen Entscheidungsprozess in der BRD. Meisenheim am Glan, 1973. pp. 159. *bibliog.*

SCHLETH (UWE) Parteifinanzen: eine Studie über Kosten und Finanzierung der Parteitätigkeit, etc. Meisenheim am Glan, 1973. pp. 542. *bibliog.*

ZIERER (DIETMAR) Niedergang und Zusammenbruch der Weimarer Parteien von 1930 bis 1933. München, [1973]. pp. 72. *bibliog.*

POLITICAL PARTIES. (Cont.)

— — Bavaria.

THRAENHARDT (DIETRICH) Wahlen und politische Strukturen in Bayern, 1848-1953: historisch-soziologische Untersuchungen zum Entstehen und zur Neuerrichtung eines Parteiensystems. Düsseldorf, 1973. pp. 360. *bibliog.* *(Germany (Bundesrepublik). Kommission für Geschichte des Parlamentarismus und der Politischen Parteien. Beiträge zur Geschichte des Parlamentarismus und der Politischen Parteien. Band 51)*

— Hungary.

TOTH (ADALBERT) Parteien und Reichstagswahlen in Ungarn, 1848-1892. München, 1973. pp. 383. *bibliog.* *(Munich. Südost-Institut München. Südosteuropäische Arbeiten. 70)*

— Israel.

MERHAV (PERETZ) La gauche israélienne: histoire, problemes et tendances du mouvement ouvrier israélien. Paris, [1973]. pp. 498. *bibliog.*

— Italy.

MEYNAUD (JEAN) Les partis politiques en Italie. Paris, 1965. pp. 128. *bibliog.*

CECCHINI (VINCENZO) La crisi dello Stato: partitocrazia e sindacati. Milano, [1972]. pp. 199.

LANDUYT (ARIANE) Le sinistre e l'Aventino. Milano, [1973]. pp. 495. *(Istituto Nazionale per la Storia del Movimento di Liberazione in Italia. [Publications. 5]*

MANZOTTI (FERNANDO) Partiti e gruppi politici dal Risorgimento al fascismo. Firenze, 1973. pp. 456. *bibliog.*

TAMBURRANO (GIUSEPPE) Storia e cronaca del centro-sinistra. 3rd ed. Milano, 1973. pp. 380.

TARROW (SIDNEY G.) Partisanship and political exchange in French and Italian local politics: a contribution to the typology of party systems. London, [1974]. pp. 54. *bibliog.*

— Kenya.

BIENEN (HENRY) Kenya: the politics of participation and control. Princeton, [1974]. pp. 215. *bibliog.*

— Lebanon.

ENTELIS (JOHN P.) Pluralism and party transformation in Lebanon: Al-Kata'ib, 1936-1970. Leiden, 1974. pp. 227. *bibliog.*

— Mexico.

ANLEN (JESUS) Origen y evolucion de los partidos politicos en Mexico. Mexico, [1973]. pp. 149. *bibliog.*

— Netherlands.

SINNER (LOUIS) De wortels van de Nederlandse politiek: de tweeënveertig politieke partijen sinds 1848. Amsterdam, 1973. pp. 229.

— Norway.

NORWAY. Partifinansieringsutvalget. 1969. Innstilling fra Partifinansieringsutvalget av 1968. Oslo, 1969. pp. 53.

NORWAY. Lønns- og Prisdepartementet. 1970. Om generell støtte til de politiske partiers organisasjoner. [Oslo?, 1970]. pp. 20. *(Norway. Stortinget. Stortingsproposisjoner. 1969-70, nr.108)*

— Russia.

VIKTOROV (V.P.) ed. Soiuz russkogo naroda po materialam Chrezvychainoi sledstvennoi komissii vremennogo pravitel'stva 1917 g.; sostavil A. Chernovskii. Moskva, 1929. pp. 444.

SIVOKHINA (TAT'IANA ALEKSANDROVNA) Krakh melkoburzhuaznoi oppozitsii. Moskva, 1973. pp. 232.

— Sweden.

SWEDEN. Justitiedepartementet. Grundlagberedningen. 1970. Riksdagsgrupperna: Regeringsbildningen: studier utförda på uppdrag, etc. Stockholm, 1970. pp. 152. *bibliogs. (Sweden. Statens Offentliga Utredningar. 1970.16)*

PARTIERNA inför väljarna: svensk valpropaganda, 1960-1966; ([by] Magnus Isberg [and others]). Stockholm, 1974. pp. 492. *(Stockholms Universitet. Statsvetenskapliga Institutionen. Stockholm Studies in Politics. 6)* With English summary.

— Switzerland.

SCHWEIZERISCHE Parteiprogramme, etc. Bern, 1973. pp. 142.

KERR (HENRY H.) Switzerland: social cleavages and partisan conflict. London, 1974. pp. 39. *bibliog.*

STEINER (JUERG) Amicable agreement versus majority rule: conflict resolution in Switzerland;...translated from the German by Asger Braendgaard and Barbara Braendgaard. rev. ed. Chapel Hill, [1974]. pp. 312.

— United Kingdom.

BROWN (KENNETH D.) ed. Essays in anti-labour history: responses to the rise of labour in Britain. London, 1974. pp. 409.

ROSE (RICHARD) The problem of party government. London, 1974. pp. 502. *bibliog.*

— United States.

TINDALL (GEORGE BROWN) The disruption of the solid South. Athens, Ga., [1972]. pp. 98. *bibliog. (Mercer University. Eugenia Dorothy Blount Lamar Memorial Lectures. No. 14)*

BELL (RUDOLPH M.) Party and faction in American politics: the House of Representatives, 1789-1801. Westport, Conn., 1973. pp. 311. *bibliog.*

BORDEN (MORTON) ed. Political parties in American history. New York, [1973-4]. 3 vols. *bibliogs.*

HAWLEY (WILLIS D.) Nonpartisan elections and the case for party politics. New York, [1973]. pp. 202. *bibliog.*

JOHNSON (DONALD BRUCE) and PORTER (KIRK HAROLD) eds. National party platforms, 1840-1972. [5th ed.] Urbana, Ill., [1973]. pp. 889.

SILBEY (JOEL HENRY) ed. Political ideology and voting behavior in the age of Jackson. Englewood Cliffs, [1973]. pp. 189. *bibliog.*

MAZMANIAN (DANIEL A.) Third parties in presidential elections. Washington, D.C., [1974]. pp. 163.

— — California.

OWENS (JOHN ROBERT) Trends in campaign spending in California, 1958-1970: tests of factors influencing costs. Princeton, 1973. pp. 84. *(Citizens' Research Foundation. Studies. No. 22)*

— — Massachusetts.

PATTERSON (STEPHEN E.) Political parties in revolutionary Massachusetts. Madison, 1973. pp. 299. *bibliog.*

— — Pennsylvania.

TINKCOM (HARRY MARLIN) The Republicans and Federalists in Pennsylvania, 1790-1801: a study in national stimulus and local response. Harrisburg, Pennsylvania Historical and Museum Commission, 1950. pp. 354. *bibliog.*

POLITICAL POETRY, ENGLISH.

COLE (GEORGE DOUGLAS HOWARD) The crooked world. London, 1933. pp. 135.

POLITICAL POETRY, PORTUGUESE.

RIO (MANUEL) pseud. [i.e. Manuel Coelho da SILVA] Caverne aux esclaves. Paris, 1973. pp. (28), 12-66,(6).

POLITICAL POSTERS, FRENCH.

ROSSEL (ANDRE) Editor of Journaux du temps passé, ed. Mai 68: (images, affiches, etc.);...réalisé sur une maquette de François Doat. [Paris], 1968. 8 pts.

POLITICAL POSTERS, GERMAN.

LINHARDT (HANNS) Das Plakat der politischen Parteien: (Vortrag...am 4.Juni 1971 [in the] mUSEUM fOLKWANG iN eSSEN). bONN-bAD gODESBERG, ?1972!. PP. 54.

DIALOG: Magazin für Politik, Wirtschaft und Kultur. Wahlkampf '72: Fakten und Zahlen. Bonn, 1973. pp. 203.

RICHTER (JOERG) 1941- , ed. Klassenkampf von oben?; oder, Angstmacher von rechts: Dokumente und Analysen eines gescheiterten Wahlkampfes. Reinbek bei Hamburg, 1973. pp. 206.

SOZIALDEMOKRATISCHE PARTEI DEUTSCHLANDS. Vorstand. Dokumentation über die Werbekampagnen der CDU/CSU und der CDU/CSU-Hilfsorganisationen im Bundestagswahlkampf 1972. Bonn, 1973. pp. 228. *Diagram in end pocket.*

POLITICAL PRISONERS

— Poland.

WYGODZKI (STANISŁAW) Zatrzymany do wyjaśnienia. Pary'z, 1968. pp. 205.

— Russia.

SOLZHENITSYN (ALEKSANDR ISAEVICH) Arkhipelag GULag, 1918-1956: opyt khudozhestvennogo issledovaniia. Paris, 1973 in progress.

— — Ukraine.

AVERBUKH (N.I.) Odesskaia "chrezvychaika", bol'shevistskii zastenok: fakty i nabliudeniia N.I. Averbukha (Averiusa). ch.1. Kishinev, 1920. pp. 39.

— South Africa.

LEWIN (HUGH) Bandiet: seven years in a South African prison. London, 1974. pp. 223.

— Turkey.

COUSINS (JANE) Turkey: torture and political persecution. London, 1973. pp. 106.

— Zambia.

ZAMBIA. Tribunal on Detainees. 1967. Report: tHOMAS pICKETT, CHAIRMAN!. lUSAKA, 1967. PP. 24.

POLITICAL PSYCHOLOGY.

BONDURANT (JOAN VALERIE) ed. Conflict: violence and nonviolence. Chicago, 1971. pp. 206.

TERRA (JUAN PABLO) Mistica, desarrollo y revolucion. Santiago de Chile, 1971. pp. 210.

ABSE (LEO) Private member. London, 1973. pp. 296. *bibliog.*

ANDERSON (WALT) Politics and the new humanism. Pacific Palisades, Calif., [1973]. pp. 149.

DAVIES (ALAN FRASER) Politics as work. Melbourne, 1973. pp. 227. *(Melbourne. University. Department of Political Science. Melbourne Politics Monographs)*

KNUTSON (JEANNE NICKELL) ed. Handbook of political psychology. San Francisco, 1973. pp. 542. *bibliog.*

WOSHINSKY (OLIVER H.) The French deputy: incentives and behavior in the National Assembly. Lexington, Mass., [1973]. pp. 232. *bibliog.*

ROSENAU (JAMES N.) Citizenship between elections: an inquiry into the mobilizable American. New York, [1974]. pp. 526.

POLITICAL SATIRE, AUSTRIAN.

BROER (WOLFGANG) Wort als Waffe: politischer Witz und politische Satire in der Republik Österreich, 1918-1927; Versuch einer Darstellung und Auswertung. Wien, 1973. 2 vols. *bibliogs.* (*Vienna. Universität. Dissertationen. 100*)

POLITICAL SATIRE, ITALIAN.

[MELLONI (MARIO)] Lor signori: corsivi 1971-1972; ([by] Fortebraccio [pseud.]). Roma, 1972. pp. 263.

POLITICAL SATIRE, RUSSIAN.

BURD-VOSKHODOV (ALEKSANDR PAVLOVICH) Moskva dalekaia.... Moscow, the wide.... Moscou, la lointanie [sic]... [New York?, 1950]. pp. 219. *Added title page has subtitle: The immortals [sic] Russian's [sic] "liberators".*

POLITICAL SCIENCE.

LOCAL-level politics: social and cultural perspectives; edited by Marc J. Swartz; [result of a conference sponsored by the Wenner-Gren Foundation for Anthropological Research, held at Burg Wartenstein, July, 1966]. Chicago, 1968. pp. viii, 437. *bibliogs.*

BARRERA (MARIO) Modernization and coercion. Berkeley, [1969]. pp. 58. *bibliog.* (*California University. Institute of International Studies. Politics of Modernization Series. No. 6*)

CORNFORD (JAMES PETERS) The political theory of scarcity;... delivered on Thursday, 17th April, 1969. Edinburgh, [1969?]. pp. 20. (*Edinburgh. University. Inaugural Lectures. No.50*)

HOOGERWERF (A.) Politiek in beweging: een bundel politicologische schetsen. Alphen aan den Rijn, 1971. pp. 161.

BECKWITH (BURNHAM PUTNAM) Government by experts: the next stage in political evolution. New York, [1972]. pp. 166. *bibliog.*

GROSSER (ALFRED) L'explication politique: une introduction à l'analyse comparative. Paris, 1972. pp. 144. (*Fondation Nationale des Sciences Politiques. Cahiers. 183*)

JOUVENEL (BERTRAND DE) Du principat, et autres réflexions politiques. [Paris, 1972]. pp. 293.

WALDMAN (SIDNEY R.) Foundations of political action: AN EXCHANGE THEORY OF POLITICS. bOSTON, ?mASS., 1972!. PP. 256.

DUVERGER (MAURICE) Institutions politiques et droit constitutionnel. 13th ed. Paris, [1973 in progress].

MARX (KARL) Political writings; edited by David Fernbach. London, 1973 in progress. *bibliogs.*

SCHMID (CARLO) Gesammelte Werke in Einzelausgaben. Bern, 1973 in progress. *bibliogs.*

BAKUNIN (MIKHAIL ALEKSANDROVICH) Selected writings; edited and introduced by Arthur Lehning; translations from the French by Steven Cox; translations from the Russian by Olive Stevens. London, 1973. pp. 288. *bibliog.*

BILL (JAMES ALBAN) and HARDGRAVE (ROBERT L.) Comparative politics: the quest for theory. Columbus, [1973]. pp. 261. *bibliog.*

COTTERET (JEAN MARIE) Gouvernants et gouvernés: la communication politique. [Paris], 1973. pp. 178. *bibliog.*

DAVY (GEORGES) L'homme, le fait social et le fait politique: [collection of articles and other writings originally published 1919-1969]. Paris, [1973]. pp. 324. (*Paris. Ecole Pratique des Hautes Etudes. Section des Sciences Economiques et Sociales. Textes de Sciences Sociales. 9*)

DE GRAZIA (ALFRED) Politics for better or worse. Glenview, Ill., [1973]. pp. 377. *bibliog.*

DODD (CLEMENT HENRY) Political change. Hull, 1973. pp. 20. (*Hull. University. Inaugural Lectures*)

DUVERGER (MAURICE) Sociologie de la politique: éléments de science politique. Paris, [1973]. pp. 452. *bibliogs.*

EISENSTADT (SHMUEL N.) Traditional patrimonialism and modern neopatrimonialism. Beverly Hills, [1973]. pp. 93. *bibliog.*

FAURE (EDGAR) Pour un nouveau contrat social. Paris, [1973]. pp. 101.

FERRARI (GIUSEPPE) Political writer. Scritti politici;...a cura di Silvia Rota Ghibaudi. Torina, 1973. pp. 117. *bibliog.*

LABRIOLA (ANTONIO) Scritti filosofici e politici...; a cura di Franco Sbarberi. Torino, 1973. 2 vols.

LANE (RUTH) Political man: toward a conceptual base. Beverly Hills, [1973]. pp. 71. *bibliog.*

PESTIEAU (JOSEPH) Essai contre le défaitisme politique: imagination politique et intelligence économique. Montréal, 1973. pp. 255. *bibliog.*

ROSENAU (JAMES N.) The dramas of politics: an introduction to the joys of inquiry. Boston, [Mass., 1973]. pp. 250.

SCHAFFER (BENJAMIN BERNARD) The administrative factor: papers in organization, politics and development. London, 1973. pp. 329.

ŠIK (OTA) Argumente für den dritten Weg. Hamburg, 1973. pp. 213.

SPRAGENS (THOMAS A.) The dilemma of contemporary political theory: toward a postbehavioral science of politics. New York, [1973]. pp. 181. *bibliog.*

GELLNER (ERNEST ANDRE) Contemporary thought and politics;... edited with a preface by I. C. Jarvie and Joseph Agassi. London, 1974.. pp. 207.

ROSE (GUENTHER) "Industriegesellschaft" und Konvergenztheorie: Genesis, Strukturen, Funktionen. 2nd ed. Berlin, 1974. pp. 412.

ŠIK (OTA) Für eine Wirtschaft ohne Dogma: [collection of three articles and four interviews]. München, [1974]. pp. 209. *bibliog.*

See also subdivisions Constitution; Politics and government under names of countries, states, etc., also UNDERDEVELOPED AREAS — Politics.

— Bibliography.

TARAMANOV (DMITRII DMITRIEVICH) Vydy bibliohrafii suspil'no-politychnoï literatury. Kharkiv, 1968. pp. 64.

BRACHER (KARL DIETRICH) and JACOBSEN (HANS ADOLF) eds. Bibliographie zur Politik in Theorie und Praxis: Ergänzungsband... Juni 1969 bis Oktober 1972...; unter Mitarbeit von Wilfried v. Bredow [and others]. Düsseldorf, 1973. pp. 207. (*Bonn. Universität. Seminar für Politische Wissenschaft. Bonner Schriften zur Politik und Zeitgeschichte. 8*)

— History.

LARIS CASILLAS (JORGE) Ensayos sobre teoria politica; [translated from English by Martha Hernandez Laris]. [Toluca], 1973. pp. 121. (*Cuadernos del Estado de Mexico*)

SANTONASTASO (GIUSEPPE) Studi di pensiero politico. Napoli, 1973. pp. 322.

TANTURRI (RICCARDO) Pensiero e significato di Gaetano Mosca ed altri scritti. Padova, 1973. pp. 108.

HABERMAS (JUERGEN) Theory and practice;... [4th ed. abridged of Theorie und Praxis [with] Arbeit und Interaktion from Technik und Wissenschaft als Ideologie]; translated by John Viertel. London, 1974. pp. 310.

POLITICAL SOCIALIZATION.

NISBET (ROBERT ALEXANDER) The social philosophers: community and conflict in western thought.London, 1974. pp. 466.

— — Germany.

STRUVE (WALTER) Elites against democracy: leadership ideals in bourgeois political thought in Germany, 1890-1933. Princeton, [1973]. pp. 486. *bibliog.*

BEETHAM (DAVID) Max Weber and the theory of modern politics. London, 1974. pp. 287. *bibliog.*

— — India.

APPADORAI (ANGADIPURAM) Documents on political thought in modern India. Bombay, 1973 in progress.

— — Italy.

TANTURRI (RICCARDO) Pensiero e significato di Gaetano Mosca ed altri scritti. Padova, 1973. pp. 108.

ZEPPI (STELIO) Il pensiero politico dell'idealismo italiano e il nazionalfascismo.Firenze, 1973. pp. 303.

— — Netherlands.

LEEB (I. LEONARD) The ideological origins of the Batavian revolution; history and politics in the Dutch republic 1747-1800. The Hague, 1973. pp. 300. *bibliog.*

— — Russia.

DOWLER (ERIC WAYNE) The "native soil" (pochvennichestvo) movement in Russian social and political thought, 1850-1870; [Ph.D. (London) thesis]. [1973]. fo. 348. *bibliog.* Typescript: *unpublished. This thesis is the property of London University and may not be removed from the Library.*

— — United States.

THIGPEN (ROBERT BYRON) Liberty and community: the political philosophy of William Ernest Hocking. The Hague, 1972. pp. 121. *bibliog.*

— Methodology.

SMITH (ARTHUR) Writer on heuristics. Four uses of heuristics; [models for project design and large idea-systems]. Rochdale, [1973]. pp. 207. *bibliog.*

— Study and teaching.

NUERNBERGER (RICHARD) Die Lehre von der Politik an der Universität Göttingen während der französischen Revolution. Göttingen, [1971]. pp. 29. (*Göttingen. Akademie der Wissenschaften. Nachrichten. Philologisch-Historische Klasse. Jahrgang 1971, Nr. 2*)

MILLETT (JOHN DAVID) Why political science?: (explorations in undergraduate education); report of a study. New York, 1973. pp. 70. (*Carnegie Foundation for the Advancement of Teaching. Bulletins. No.35*)

POLITICAL SCIENCE RESEARCH.

U.K. Social Science Research Council. Political science theses: an annual register of research theses, supported from all sources and being prepared for British higher degrees in all aspects of political science. a., current issue only kept. London.

CLINTON (RICHARD L.) ed. Population and politics: new directions in political science research. Lexington, Mass., [1973]. pp. 298.

POLITICAL SOCIALIZATION.

GOTTSCHALCH (WILFRIED) Bedingungen und Chancen politischer Sozialisation: Aufsätze. Frankfurt am Main, 1972. pp. 143.

GARCIA (F. CHRIS) Political socialization of Chicano children: a comparative study with Anglos in California schools. New York, 1973. pp. 255. *bibliog.*

JAROS (DEAN) Socialization to politics. New York, 1973. pp. 160.

MARTIKAINEN (TUOMO) Political activity: structure, determinants and dynamics. Helsinki, 1973. pp. 117. *bibliog.* (*Societas Scientiarum Fennica. Commentationes Scientiarum Socialium. 6*)

POLITICAL SOCIALIZATION. (Cont.)

MERCER (GEOFFREY) Political education and socialization to democratic norms. Glasgow, 1973. pp. 30,4. *(Glasgow. University of Strathclyde. Survey Research Centre. Occasional Papers. No. 11)*

COLES (ROBERT) Children and political authority. Cape Town, 1974. pp. 34. *(Cape Town. University. T.B. Davie Memorial Lectures. 15)*

KHARE (BRIJ B.) India: political attitudes and social change. New Delhi, [1974]. pp. 264. *bibliog.*

POLITICAL SOCIOLOGY.

BLONDEL (JEAN) 1929- . Voters, parties, and leaders: the social fabric of British politics. rev. ed. Harmondsworth, 1969 repr. 1972. pp. 272. *bibliog.*

CARDOSO (FERNANDO HENRIQUE) Ideologias de la burguesia industrial en sociedades dependientes: Argentina y Brasil. Mexico, 1969 repr. 1972. pp. 239. *bibliog.*

RUNCIMAN (WALTER GARRISON) Social science and political theory. 2nd ed. Cambridge, 1969. pp. 200.

SEILER (DANIEL) and RAES (JEAN) Idéologie et citoyens: analyse des attitudes politiques d'un échantillon de l'électorat wallon. Bruxelles, [1970]. pp. 219. *bibliog. (Namur. Facultés Universitaires Notre Dame de la Paix. Collection Questions Economiques, Sociales et Politiques)*

TERRA (JUAN PABLO) Mistica, desarrollo y revolucion. Santiago de Chile, 1971. pp. 210.

COMMUNITY culture and national change: [essays by] Richard N.Adams [and others]; (Margaret A.L. Harrison, Robert Wauchope, editors). New Orleans, 1972. pp. 275. *bibliogs. (Tulane University of Louisiana. Middle American Research Institute. Publications. No.24)*

MAFUD (JULIO) Sociologia del Peronismo. Buenos Aires, [1972]. pp. 182. *bibliog.*

STONE (CARL) Stratification and political change in Trinidad and Jamaica; [revised version of a paper presented at the meeting of the American Political Science Association, Los Angeles, 1970]. Beverly Hills, Calif., [1972]. pp. 39.

DITTBERNER (JUERGEN) and EBBIGHAUSEN (ROLF) eds. Parteiensystem in der Legitimationskrise: Studien und Materialien zur Soziologie der Parteien in der Bundesrepublik Deutschland. Opladen, 1973. pp. 526. *bibliog. (Berlin. Freie Universität. Zentralinstitut für Sozialwissenschaftliche Forschung. Schriften. Band 24)*

DUVERGER (MAURICE) Sociologie de la politique: éléments de science politique. Paris, [1973]. pp. 452. *bibliogs.*

FRANK (ROBERT SHELBY) Linguistic analysis of political elites: a theory of verbal kinesics. Beverly Hills, [1973]. pp. 59. *bibliog.*

GAXIE (DANIEL) Les professionnels de la politique. [Paris, 1973]. pp. 96. *bibliog.*

HIRSCH (HERBERT) and PERRY (DAVID C.) eds. Violence as politics: a series of original essays. New York, [1973]. pp. 262. *bibliog.*

LAGROYE (JACQUES) Société et politique: J. Chaban-Delmas à Bordeaux. [Paris, 1973]. pp. 345. *bibliog. (Bordeaux. Université. Institut d'Etudes Politiques. Centre d'Etude et de Recherche sur la Vie Locale. Série Vie Locale. 4)*

MUELLER (CLAUS) The politics of communication : a study in the political sociology of language, socialization, and legitimation. New York, 1973. pp. 226. *bibliog.*

PERSPECTIVES in political sociology; [articles which originally appeared in Sociological Inquiry, v.42, nos.3 and 4, 1972]. Indianapolis, [1973]. pp. 311.

VICKERS (Sir CHARLES GEOFFREY) Making institutions work. London, 1973. pp. 187.

BRITISH POLITICAL SOCIOLOGY YEARBOOK. a., 1974 (v.1)- London.

BLUME (STUART S.) Toward a political sociology of science. New York, [1974]. pp. 288.

LOCKE (ROBERT R.) French legitimists and the politics of moral order in the early Third Republic. Princeton, [1974]. pp. 321. *bibliog.*

MEISEL (JOHN) Cleavages, parties and values in Canada. London, [1974]. pp. 55. *bibliog.*

MOMMSEN (WOLFGANG JUSTIN) The age of bureaucracy: perspectives on the political sociology of Max Weber. Oxford, [1974]. pp. 124. *bibliog.*

RICHARDSON (BRADLEY M.) The political culture of Japan. Berkeley, [1974]. pp. 271. *bibliog.*

POLITICS, PRACTICAL.

DIALOG: Magazin für Politik, Wirtschaft und Kultur. Wahlkampf '72: Fakten und Zahlen. Bonn, 1973. pp. 203.

BRAYBROOKE (DAVID) Traffic congestion goes through the issue-machine: a case-study in issue processing, illustrating a new approach. London, 1974. pp. 62.

CONSERVATIVE POLITICAL CENTRE. [Publications]. 542. CPC: the vote catchers. London, 1974. 1 pamphlet (unpaged). *bibliog.*

POLITICS AND EDUCATION.

HENNESSY (BERNARD CHARLES) Political internships: theory, practice, evaluation. University Park, Penn., [1970] repr. 1972. pp. 129. *(Pennsylvania State University. Penn State Studies. No. 28)*

LOCKE (MICHAEL) Power and politics in the school system: a guidebook. London, 1974. pp. 184. *bibliog.*

POLITICS AND WAR.

BRODIE (BERNARD) War and politics. London, 1974. pp. 514.

POLITICS IN LITERATURE.

RADDATZ (FRITZ J.) Erfolg oder Wirkung: Schicksale politischer Publizisten in Deutschland. München, [1972]. pp. 137. *bibliog.*

STEINER (GERHARD) Jakobinerschauspiel und Jakobinertheater. Stuttgart, [1973]. pp. 336. *bibliog.*

MUTISO (G.C.M.) Socio-political thought in African literature: weusi?. London, 1974. pp. 182. *bibliog.*

WILLIAMS (CEDRIC ELLIS) The broken eagle: the politics of Austrian literature from empire to Anschluss. London, 1974. pp. 281. *bibliog.*

POLITICS IN MOVING PICTURES.

PIVASSET (JEAN) Essai sur la signification politique du cinéma: l'exemple français, de la libération aux événements de mai 1968. Paris, [1971]. pp. 637. *bibliog.*

BOBROWSKI (EDOUARD) Aux urnes, citoyens...: [municipal elections, Arras, 1971]. Paris, [1973]. pp. 259.

POLLUTION.

C.C. FURNAS MEMORIAL CONFERENCE, 2ND, BUFFALO, 1971. The steel industry and the environment: (proceedings); edited by Julian Szekely. New York, 1973. pp. 285. *bibliogs.*

POLLUTION abatement: (record of a seminar held at the University of East Anglia in October 1971); edited by K.M. Clayton and R.C. Chilver. Newton Abbot, [1973]. pp. 203.

BARROS (JAMES) and JOHNSTON (DOUGLAS M.) The international law of pollution. New York, [1974]. pp. 476. *bibliogs. In English or French.*

— Economic aspects.

MEADE (JAMES EDWARD) The theory of economic externalities: the control of environmental pollution and similar social costs. Leiden, 1973. pp. 92. *(Geneva. Graduate Institute of International Studies. International Economics Series. 2)*

PAGE (TALBOT) Economics of involuntary transfers: a unified approach to pollution and congestion externalities. Berlin, 1973. pp. 159. *bibliog.*

— — United States.

SMITH (GRAHAME J.) and others. Our ecological crisis: its biological, economic, and political dimensions. New York, [1974]. pp. 198. *bibliogs.*

— International cooperation.

BAUMOL (WILLIAM JACK) Environmental protection, international spillovers and trade. Stockholm, [1971]. pp. 59. *(Wicksell Lecture Society. Wicksell Lectures. 1971)*

— Mathematical models.

MIDDLETON (DAVID) A mathematical approach to analysis of environmental pollution generated by mixes of transportation modes: the case of electrical interference...: a report prepared for U.S. Department of Transportation [and others]. Santa Monica, 1971. pp. 60. *(Rand Corporation. [Rand Reports]. 762)*

PAGE (TALBOT) Economics of involuntary transfers: a unified approach to pollution and congestion externalities. Berlin, 1973. pp. 159. *bibliog.*

— Research.

WORLD HEALTH ORGANIZATION. Technical Report Series. No. 406. Research into environmental pollution: report of five WHO scientific groups. Geneva, 1968. pp. 83.

— France.

RICHARD (RENE) and BARTOLI (CAMILLE) La Côte d'Azur assassinée?. Paris, [1971]. pp. 137.

Une VILLE pilote pour la lutte contre les pollutions et les nuisances: la ville nouvelle du Vaudreuil. Paris, 1973. pp. 181. *(Environnement. 14)*

— Italy.

ISTITUTO PER GLI STUDI SULLO SVILUPPO ECONOMICO E IL PROGRESSO TECNICO. Economic costs and benefits of an antipollution project in Italy: summary report of a preliminary evaluation: special issue for the United Nations Conference on the Human Environment, Stockholm, June 5-16, 1972. [Rome, 1972?]. pp. 244.

— Japan.

TOKYO. Metropolitan Government. Ordinances, local laws, etc. The Tokyo metropolitan environmental pollution control ordinance and its enforcement regulation. Tokyo, 1971. pp. 84.

— Netherlands.

LEK (BRAM VAN DER) Het milieuboekje: over produktie, vervuiling en actie. Amsterdam, 1972. pp. 109. *bibliog.*

MILIEU AKTIECENTRUM NEDERLAND. De mens moet blijven. [Rotterdam, 1973]. pp. 57.

BOERENGROEP WAGENINGEN. Agri-business of binnenlandse kolonie II: (sociaal-ekonomische positie van de boer; landbouw en milieu). Wageningen, [1974]. pp. 133.

— Norway.

SMITH (DOUGLAS V.) Technology, ecosystems, and planning: thoughts on contradictions in industrial Norway and a procedure for planning. Oslo, 1972. fo. 100.

— South Africa.

CLARKE (JAMES) Journalist. Our fragile land: South Africa's environmental crisis. Johannesburg, [1974]. pp. 134.

— Tasmania.

TASMANIA. Department of the Environment. 1972. Environmental pollution in Tasmania. in TASMANIA. Parliament. Journals and Printed Papers. 1972. no. 74.

— United Kingdom.

U.K. Central Unit on Environmental Pollution. 1973. Pollution control in England. [London, 1973]. fo. 7. *bibliog.*

The GEOGRAPHY of pollution: a study of Greater Manchester; [by] C.M. Wood [and others]. Manchester, [1974]. pp. 150.

BROOKS (PETER F.) Problems of the environment: an introduction. London, 1974. pp. 223. *bibliogs.*

McKNIGHT (ALLAN D.) and others, eds. Environmental pollution control: technical, economic and legal aspects. London, 1974. pp. 324. *bibliogs.*

— United States.

VAN TASSEL (ALFRED J.) ed. Our environment: the outlook for 1980. Lexington, Mass., [1973]. pp. 589. *bibliogs.*

CANNON (JAMES SPENCER) Environmental steel: pollution in the iron and steel industry; edited [for the Council on Economic Priorities] by Jean M. Halloran). New York, 1974. pp. 521.

POLYGAMY.

CAIRNCROSS (JOHN) After polygamy was made a sin: the social history of Christian polygamy. London, 1974. pp. 236. *bibliog.*

POOR.

VERCAUTEREN (PAUL) Les sous-prolétaires: essai sur une forme de paupérisme contemporain. Bruxelles, [1970]. pp. 203. *bibliog.*

CORNELIUS (WAYNE A.) Political learning among the migrant poor: the impact of residential context. Beverly Hills, [1973]. pp. 88. *bibliog.*

— Australia.

AUSTRALIA. Commission of Inquiry into Poverty. 1974. Poverty in Australia; interim report; [Ronald F. Henderson, chairman]. Canberra, 1974. pp. 24.

— Belgium.

VRANKEN (JAN) ed. Armoede in België. Antwerpen, [1974]. pp. 56.

— Egypt.

FATHY (HASSAN) Architecture for the poor: an experiment in rural Egypt. Chicago, 1973. pp. 233.

— Europe.

ABEL (WILHELM) Massenarmut und Hungerkrisen im vorindustriellen Europa: Versuch einer Synopsis. Hamburg, 1974. pp. 427.

GUTTON (JEAN PIERRE) La société et les pauvres en Europe, XVIe-XVIIIe siècles. Paris, 1974. pp. 207. *bibliog.*

— France.

PETONNET (COLETTE) Those people: the subculture of a housing project;...translated from the French by Rita Smidt. Westport, Conn., [1973]. pp. 293. *bibliog.*

— Germany.

ABEL (WILHELM) Der Pauperismus in Deutschland am Vorabend der industriellen Revolution. [Hannover, Niedersächsische Landeszentrale für Politische Bildung], 1970. pp. 60.

SEIDEL (FRIEDRICH) Das Armutsproblem im deutschen Vormärz bei Friedrich List. Köln, 1971. pp. 56. *(Cologne. Universität. Forschungsinstitut für Sozial- und Wirtschaftsgeschichte. Kölner Vorträge zur Sozial- und Wirtschaftsgeschichte. Heft 13)*

CHRISTIANSEN (URSULA) Obdachlos weil arm: gesellschaftliche Reaktionen auf die Armut. Giessen, 1973. pp. 209. *bibliog.*

ROTH (JUERGEN) Armut in der Bundesrepublik: über psychische und materielle Verelendung. Frankfurt am Main, 1974. pp. 223.

— South Africa.

POTGIETER (J.F.) The poverty datum line in two cities and three towns in the Eastern province/border area. [Port Elizabeth], 1972. pp. 36. *bibliog. (University of Port Elizabeth. Institute for Planning Research. Research Reports. No.11)*

POTGIETER (J.F.) The household subsistence level in the major urban centres of the Republic (October, 1973). Port Elizabeth, 1973. fo. 24. *(University of Port Elizabeth. Institute for Planning Research. Fact Papers. No. 8)*

— United Kingdom.

FIELD (FRANK) 1942- . One nation: the Conservatives' record since June 1970. London, 1972. pp. 12. *(Child Poverty Action Group. Poverty Pamphlets. 12)*

FIELD (FRANK) 1942- . An incomes policy for poor families: a memorandum to the Chancellor of the Exchequer. London, 1973. pp. 12. *(Child Poverty Action Group. Poverty Pamphlets. 14)*

FIELD (FRANK) 1942- , ed. Low pay; Acton Society Trust essays. London, 1973. pp. 141.

MARSDEN (DENNIS) Mothers alone: poverty and the fatherless family. rev. ed. Harmondsworth, 1973. pp. 412.

FIELD (FRANK) 1942- . Housing and poverty. London, [1974]. pp. 10.

JORDAN (WILLIAM) Poor parents: social policy and the 'cycle of deprivation'. London, 1974. pp. 200.

LYNES (TONY ALFRED) The Penguin guide to supplementary benefits: supplementary benefits, the family income supplement and the Appeals Tribunal. 2nd ed. Harmondsworth, 1974. pp. 232.

OXLEY (GEOFFREY W.) Poor relief in England and Wales, 1601-1834. Newton Abbot, [1974]. pp. 159. *bibliog.*

PIACHAUD (DAVID F.J.) Do the poor pay more?. London, 1974. pp. 24. *(Child Poverty Action Group. Poverty Research Series. 3)*

WEDDERBURN (DOROTHY) ed. Poverty, inequality and class structure. London, 1974. pp. 247.

YOUNG (MICHAEL DUNLOP) ed. Poverty report 1974: a review of policies and problems in the last year. London, 1974. pp. 266. *bibliogs. (Institute of Community Studies. Reports)*

— United States.

GREENBERG (DAVID H.) and KOSTERS (MARVIN) Income guarantees and the working poor: the effect of income maintenance programs on the hours of work of male family heads. Santa Monico, 1970. pp. 134. *(Rand Corporation. [Rand Reports]. 579)*

AMERICAN ENTERPRISE INSTITUTE FOR PUBLIC POLICY RESEARCH. Legislative Analyses. 92nd Congress. No. 4. Welfare reform proposals. Washington, D.C., 1971. pp. 102.

FICKER (VICTOR B.) and GRAVES (HERBERT S.) eds. Deprivation in America. Beverly Hills, [1971]. pp. 149.

PILISUK (MARC) and PILISUK (PHYLLIS) eds. Poor Americans: how the white poor live. [Chicago, 1971]. pp. 189. *bibliogs.*

MARRIS (PETER) and REIN (MARTIN) Dilemmas of social reform: poverty and community action in the United States. 2nd ed. London, 1972. pp. 309. *bibliog. (Institute of Community Studies. Reports. 15)*

BAHR (HOWARD M.) and CAPLOW (THEODORE) Old men drunk and sober. New York, 1973. pp. 407. *bibliog.*

BLUESTONE (BARRY) and others. Low wages and the working poor. Ann Arbor, 1973. pp. 215. *(Michigan University, and Wayne State University. Institute of Labor and Industrial Relations. Policy Papers in Human Resources and Industrial Relations. 22)*

BRECHER (CHARLES) The impact of Federal antipoverty policies. New York, 1973. pp. 126. *bibliog. (Columbia University. Graduate School of Business. Conservation of Human Resources Project. Conservation of Human Resources Studies)*

DUGAN (DENNIS J.) and LEAHY (WILLIAM HARRALL) eds. Perspectives on poverty. New York, 1973. pp. 198. *bibliogs.*

FORD (ARTHUR M.) Political economics of rural poverty in the South. Cambridge, Mass., [1973]. pp. 101. *bibliog.*

GRAHAM (DAVID RALPH) and LUFT (KATHLEEN) The role of business in the economic redevelopment of the rural community. Austin, Tex., 1973. pp. 114. *bibliog. (Texas University. Bureau of Business Research. Research Monographs. No. 36)*

GREENSTONE (J. DAVID) and PETERSON (PAUL E.) Race and authority in urban politics: community participation and the war on poverty. New York, [1973]. pp. 364.

HUBER (JOAN) and FORM (WILLIAM HUMBERT) Income and ideology: an analysis of the American political formula. New York, [1973]. pp. 226. *bibliog.*

JACKSON (LARRY R.) and JOHNSON (WILLIAM A.) Protest by the poor: the welfare rights movement in New York City. New York, 1973. pp. 35. *bibliog. (Rand Corporation. [Rand Reports]. 791)*

KURTZ (DONALD V.) The politics of a poverty habitat. Cambridge, Massachusetts, [1973]. pp. 243. *bibliog.*

LEVITAN (SAR A.) Programs in aid of the poor for the 1970s. rev. ed. Baltimore, [1973]. pp. 146. *bibliog.*

McCALL (JOHN JOSEPH) Income, mobility, racial discrimination, and economic growth. Lexington, [1973]. pp. 212. *bibliog.*

PALMER (JOHN L.) Inflation, unemployment and poverty. Lexington, Mass., [1973]. pp. 170. *bibliog.*

SHOSTAK (ARTHUR B.) and others. Privilege in America: an end to inequality?. Englewood Cliffs, N.J., [1973]. pp. 150. *bibliog.*

GOTTLIEB (NAOMI) The welfare bind. New York, 1974. pp. 206.

GREENBERG (STANLEY B.) Politics and poverty: modernization and response in five poor neighborhoods. London, [1974]. pp. 282.

— — California.

STONE (ROBERT C.) and SCHLAMP (FREDRIC T.) Welfare and working fathers: low-income family life styles. Lexington, Mass., [1971]. pp. 284. *bibliog.*

POOR LAWS

— United Kingdom.

U.K. Royal Commission on the Poor Laws, 1834. The Poor Law Report of 1834; edited...by S.G. and E.O.A. Checkland. Harmondsworth, 1974. pp. 518.

POPPER (Sir KARL RAIMUND).

CORNFORTH (MAURICE CAMPBELL) The open philosophy and the open society: a reply to Dr. Karl Popper's refutations of marxism. London, 1968. pp. 396.

ALBRECHT (REINHARDT) Sozialtechnologie und ganzheitliche Sozialphilosophie: zu Karl R. Poppers Kritik der ganzheitlichen Sozialphilosophie. Bonn, 1973. pp. 235.

SCHILPP (PAUL ARTHUR) ed. The philosophy of Karl Popper. La Salle, Ill.; [1974]. 2 vols.

POPULAR FRONTS.

CONSTANTINESCU-IAȘI (PETRU) La lutte pour la création du front populaire en Roumanie. Bucarest, 1972. pp. 181. *(Academia Republicii Socialiste România. Secția de Științe Istorice, Filozofice și Economico-Juridice. Bibliotheca Historica Romaniae. Studies. 21)*

POPULAR FRONTS. (Cont.)

FREYBERG (JUTTA VON) Sozialdemokraten und Kommunisten: die Revolutionären Sozialisten Deutschlands vor dem Problem der Aktionseinheit 1934-1937. Köln, [1973]. pp. 186.

HEMJE-OLTMANNS (DIRK) Arbeiterbewegung und Einheitsfront: zur Diskussion der Einheitsfronttaktik in der KPD, 1920/21. Westberlin, 1973. pp. 139. bibliog.

RIOUX (JEAN PIERRE) Revolutionnaires du Front populaire: choix de documents, 1935- 1938. [Paris, 1973]. pp. 444. bibliog.

POPULATION.

UNITED NATIONS. Department of Economic and Social Affairs. Population Studies. New York, 1948 in progress.

UNITED NATIONS. Department of Economic and Social Affairs. Population Studies. No.44. Growth of the world's urban and rural population, 1920-2000. (ST/SOA/SER.A/44) New York, 1969. pp. 124.

BARRETO (ANTONIO) ed. A study of the social and economic implications of the large scale introduction of high-yielding varieties of foodgrain: a selection of readings; an Institute staff study. (UNRISD Reports. No.71.6) (UNRISD/72/C.3). Geneva, United Nations Research Institute for Social Development, 1971. pp. 173. ([Studies on the Green Revolution. No.2])

SCHULTZ (T. PAUL) The changing balance of births and deaths: a comment. Santa Monica, 1971. pp. 10. (Rand Corporation. [Papers]. 4575)

MORRISON (PETER A.) Uses of the social security work history sample in studying metropolitan migration. [Santa Monica], 1972. pp. 9. (Rand Corporation. [Papers]. 4869)

POPULATION CONFERENCE, 4TH, PARIS, 1971. An assessment of family planning programmes: summary proceedings of the fourth annual population conference of the Development Centre, Paris, 20-22nd October, 1971. Paris, Organisation for Economic Co-operation and Development, 1972. pp. 193.

BORRIE (WILFRED DAVID) Population, environment, and society. Auckland, [1973]. pp. 106. (Auckland. University. Sir Douglas Robb Lectures. 1972)

COMPUTER simulation in human population studies; [proceedings of a conference held at Pennsylvania State University, 1972, sponsored by the Social Science Research Council]; edited by Bennett Dyke [and] Jean Walters MacCluer. New York, 1973. pp. 518. bibliog.

FOOD, population and employment: the impact of the green revolution: [papers from a workshop sponsored by Cornell University Program on Science, Technology and Society]; edited by Thomas T. Poleman and Donald K. Freebairn. New York, 1973. pp. 272.

EUGENICS SOCIETY. Annual Symposium, 9th, 1972. Resources and population: proceedings...; edited by Bernard Benjamin [and others]. London, 1973. pp. 181. bibliogs.

GEORGE (PIERRE) Géographie de la population. 4th ed. Paris, 1973. pp. 128. bibliog.

HARVEY (DAVID) A question of method for the matter of survival. Reading, 1973. pp. 44. bibliog. (Reading. University. Department of Geography. Reading Geographical Papers. No.23)

INTERNATIONAL ADVISORY COMMITTEE ON POPULATION AND LAW. Annual Meetings, 2nd, 1972. Human rights and population from the perspectives of law, policy and organization: proceedings. Medford, Mass., 1973. pp. 101. (Tufts University. Fletcher School of Law and Diplomacy. Law and Population Book Series. No. 5)

INTERNATIONAL PLANNED PARENTHOOD FEDERATION. Population. London, 1973. pp. 38. bibliog.

MORRIS (GEORGE MICHAEL) Overpopulation: everyone's baby. London, 1973. pp. 192. bibliog.

McCORMACK (ARTHUR) The population explosion: a Christian concern. New York, 1973. pp. 78.

UTZINGER (ROLF PETER) Bevölkerungspolitik, Kontrazeption, Geburtenkontrollprogramme. Zürich, 1973. pp. 294. bibliog.

BROWN (LESTER RUSSELL) In the human interest: a strategy to stabilize world population. New York, [1974]. pp. 190. bibliog.

KUZNETS (SIMON SMITH) Population, capital, and growth: selected essays. London, 1974. pp. 342.

MORAES (DOM) A matter of people. London, 1974. pp. 226.

OVERBEEK (J.) History of population theories. Rotterdam, 1974. pp. 232. bibliog.

PITCHFORD (JOHN DAVID) Population in economic growth. Amsterdam, 1974. pp. 280. bibliogs.

POPULATION and its problems: a plain man's guide...; edited by H.B. Parry. Oxford, 1974. pp. 422. bibliogs.(Oxford. University. Wolfson College. Wolfson College Lectures. 1973)

SPENGLER (JOSEPH JOHN) Population change, modernization, and welfare. Englewood Cliffs, [1974]. pp. 182. bibliog.

— Bibliography.

POPULATION, POPULATION AND FAMILY EDUCATION AND FAMILY PLANNING: accessions list; [pd.by] Population Education Clearing House Section of the Unesco Regional Office for Education in Asia. q.(approx.), current issues only kept. Bangkok.

WINTON (HARRY NATHANIEL MCQUILLIAN) ed. Man and the environment: a bibliography of selected publications of the United Nations system, 1946-1971. New York, 1972. pp. 305.

— History.

PRESSAT (ROLAND) L'analyse démographique: concepts, méthodes, résultats. 3rd ed. Paris, 1973. pp. 321.

— Statistics.

UNITED NATIONS. Department of Economic and Social Affairs. Population Studies. New York, 1948 in progress.

— Study and teaching.

POPULATION education and the younger generation; [papers of a course organized by the International Planned Parenthood Federation in October 1969]; edited by Denis Lawton. London, 1971. pp. 85.

— Underdeveloped areas.

See UNDERDEVELOPED AREAS — Population.

POPULATION FORECASTING.

UNITED NATIONS. Department of Economic and Social Affairs. Population Studies. New York, 1948 in progress.

UNITED NATIONS. Department of Economic and Social Affairs. Population Studies. No.44. Growth of the world's urban and rural population, 1920-2000. (ST/SOA/SER.A/44) New York, 1969. pp. 124.

INTERNATIONAL INSTITUTE FOR EDUCATIONAL PLANNING. Fundamentals of Educational Planning. Paris, Unesco, 1970 in progress.

MORRISON (PETER A.) Demographic information for cities: a manual for estimating and projecting local population characteristics. Santa Monica, 1971. pp. 164. bibliog. (Rand Corporation. Rand Reports. 618)

— Colombia.

OLIVARES M. (JUAN) Proyecciones de la poblacion del Distrito Especial de Bogota, 1965-1985. Bogota, 1970. pp. 91.

— France.

FRANCE. Institut National de la Statistique et des Etudes Economiques. Collections de l'I.N.S.E.E. Série D. Démographie et Emploi. Paris, 1969 in progress.

— Germany.

HECHELTJEN (PETER) Bevölkerungsentwicklung und Erwerbstätigkeit: ein Beitrag zur Simulation sozioökonomischer Systeme, mit Prognosen für die Bundesrepublik Deutschland. Opladen, [1974]. pp. 319. bibliog.

— Netherlands

NETHERLANDS. Centraal Planbureau. 1972. Regionale ontwikkeling van de werkgelegenheid en het spreidingsbeleid, 1970-2000, toegespitst op het Noorden des Lands.'s-Gravenhage, 1972. pp. 16. (Monografieën. No. 15)

NETHERLANDS. Centraal Bureau voor de Statistiek. 1973. De toekomstige nederlandse bevolkingsontwikkeling na 1972. 's-Gravenhage, 1973. pp. 76.

— New Zealand

NEW ZEALAND. Ministry of Works. Town and Country Planning Branch. 1972. Population forecasts, 1971-1991: recent population trends and forecasts of future growth of regional and local areas. [Wellington], 1972. pp. 84.

— Norway

NORWAY. Statistiske Centralbyrå. 1972. Framskriving av folkemengden 1971-2000 etc. Oslo, 1972. pp. 129. (Norges Offisielle Statistikk. Rekke A. 468) In Norwegian and English.

— Poland

POLAND. Główny Urząd Statystyczny. Statystyka Polski. [2nd series]. Nr.3. Perspektywy rozwoju ludności do 2000 r.; opracowaRŁa jANINA aLEKSIŃSKA. wARSZAWA, 1973. PP. 97.

— Sweden

SWEDEN. Statistiska Centralbyrån. 1968. Befolkningsprojektion för riket, 1967-1980; etc. Stockholm, 1968. pp. 41. (Statistiska Meddelanden. Be/1968/3)

SWEDEN. Statistiska Centralbyrån. Befolkningsprognos för riket (formerly Befolkningsprojektion för riket): Population projection for Sweden. a., 1969/1990- Stockholm. With contents and headings in English.

SWEDEN. Statistiska Centralbyrån. 1969. Regionala arbetskrafts- och befolkningsförändringar 1960-1965 med projektion till 1980, etc. Stockholm, 1969. pp. 222. (Information i Prognosfrågor. 1969.5)

— United Kingdom

WILLIS (KENNETH G.) Models of population and income: economic planning in rural areas. Newcastle upon Tyne, 1971. pp. 65. (Newcastle-upon-Tyne. University. Department of Agricultural Economics. Agricultural Adjustment Unit. Research Monographs. No. 1)

GILJE (E.K.) and ARMSTRONG (WILLIAM) Revised demographic projections for Greater London and the London boroughs, 1973. [London], 1973. pp. 111. bibliog. (London. Greater London Council. Department of Planning and Transportation. Research Memoranda. 430)

HOCKLEY (D.) Population projections for the South-East sub-regions. [London], 1973. pp. 30. bibliog. (London. Greater London Council. Department of Planning and Transportation. Research Memoranda. 417)

POPULATION RESEARCH.

BUTZ (WILLIAM P.) Research and information strategies to improve population policy in less developed countries. Santa Monica, 1972. pp. 82. bibliog. (Rand Corporation. [Rand Reports]. 952)

CLINTON (RICHARD L.) ed. Population and politics: new directions in political science research. Lexington, Mass., [1973]. pp. 298.

POPULATION TRANSFERS

— Germans.

ZIEMER (GERHARD) Deutscher Exodus: Vertreibung und Eingliederung von 15 Millionen Ostdeutschen. Stuttgart, 1973. pp. 246. *bibliog.*

POPULISM IN POLAND.

BROCK (PETER DE BEAUVOIR) Nationalism and populism in partitioned Poland: selected essays. London, [1973]. pp. 219.

POPULISM IN RUSSIA.

UCHENYE ZAPISKI KAFEDR OBSHCHESTVENNYKH NAUK VUZOV LENINGRADA. Filosofiia. vyp.14. Filosofskie i sotsiologicheskie issledovaniia. Leningrad, 1973. pp. 212.

POPULISM IN THE UKRAINE.

RUD'KO (MYKOLA PORFYRIIOVYCH) Revoliutsiini narodnyky na Ukraïni, 70-ti roky XIX st. Kyïv, 1973. pp. 206.

POPULISM IN THE UNITED STATES.

PARSONS (STANLEY B.) The populist context: rural versus urban power on a Great Plains frontier. Westport, Conn., 1973. pp. 205. *bibliog.*

PORT ELIZABETH.

PHILLIPS (BRUCE D.) and DE CONING (C.) Secondary industry in the Port Elizabeth/Uitenhage region: a structural analysis. Port Elizabeth, 1969. pp. 189. *(University of Port Elizabeth. Institute for Planning Research. Research Reports. No. 2)*

— Commerce.

VAN NIEKERK (W.P.) Die handelstruktuur van Port Elizabeth. Port Elizabeth, 1968. pp. 103. *bibliog.* *(University of Port Elizabeth. Institute for Planning Research. Research Reports. No.1)*

— Industries.

PHILLIPS (BRUCE D.) Secondary industry in the Port Elizabeth/Uitenhage region: an employment study. Port Elizabeth, 1969. pp. 143. *(University of Port Elizabeth. Institute for Planning Research. Research Reports. No.3) With Afrikaans summary.*

PORT LOUIS, MAURITIUS

— History.

TOUSSAINT (AUGUSTE) Port Louis: a tropical city;...translated by W.E.F. Ward. London, 1973. pp. 144. *bibliog.*

PORTLAND, OREGON

— Schools.

CONANT (EATON H.) Teacher and paraprofessional work productivity: a public school cost effectiveness study. Lexington, Mass., [1973]. pp. 149.

PORTUGAL

— Army.

PORTUGAL. Presidência do Conselho. 1954. 25 anos de administração publica: Ministerio do Exército. Lisboa, 1954. pp. 107.

— Census.

PORTUGAL. Censo, 1970. 11 recenseamento da população, 1970: continente e ilhas adjacentes: lista alfabetica de concelhos e freguesias. [Lisbon, 1971]. pp. 50.

— Colonies.

ABSHIRE (DAVID M.) and SAMUELS (MICHAEL A.) eds. Portuguese Africa: a handbook. New York, 1969. pp. 480.

CAETANO (MARCELLO) Portugal's reasons for remaining in the overseas provinces: excerpts from speeches, etc. [Lisbon], Office of the Secretary of State for Information and Tourism, General Direction for Information, [1971?]. pp. 54.

BOSGRA (S.J.) and KRIMPEN (CHR. VAN) Portugal and NATO. 3rd ed. Amsterdam, [1972]. pp. 80.

COMMITTEE FOR FREEDOM IN MOZAMBIQUE, ANGOLA AND GUINE, and AFRICA RESEARCH GROUP. War on three fronts: the fight against Portuguese colonialism. London, [1972?]. pp. (44).

BRUCE (NEIL) Portugal's African wars. London, 1973. pp. 22. *(Institute for the Study of Conflict. Conflict Studies. No. 34)*

MAXWELL (KENNETH R.) Conflicts and conspiracies: Brazil and Portugal 1750-1808. Cambridge, 1973. pp. 289. *bibliog.*

— — Administration.

PORTUGAL. Presidência do Conselho. 1955. 25 anos de administração publica: Ministerio do Ultramar. Lisboa, 1955. pp. 358.

— — Politics and government.

PORTUGAL. Statutes, etc. 1969. Conselho Ultramarino: Decreto-Lei N.o 49146 (Lei Orgânica), Decreto N.o 49147 (Regimento) e Portaria N.o 24204 (Tabela das custas), de 25 de Julho de 1969, anotados (by) J. Pinto Furtado; em apêndice: Decreto- Lei N.o 49145. Lisboa, 1969. pp. 163.

SANTOS (ANTONIO DE ALMEIDA) Mensagem aos portugueses do ultramar: mensagem do Ministro da Coordenação Interterritorial...em 17 de Maio de 1974. Lisboa, 1974. pp. 12.

— Commerce.

CORREIA (HERMINIA GALVÃO) Inquerito "remunerações/1969" (Comercio) resultados e análise. Lisboa, 1970. pp. 119. *(Fundo de Desenvolvimento da Mão-de-Obra. Cadernos. 35) With abstracts in English, French and German.*

— — Belgium.

STOLS (EDDY) De Spaanse Brabanders of de handelsbetrekkingen der Zuidelijke Nederlanden met de Iberische wereld, 1598-1648. Brussel, 1971. 2 vols. *bibliog. (Vlaamse Academie voor Wetenschappen, Letteren en Schone Kunsten van Belgie. Klasse der Letteren. Verhandelingen. Nr. 70)*

— — China.

MOURA (CARLOS FRANCISCO) Macau e o comercio portuguûes com a China e o Japão nos seculos XVI e XVII: as viagens da China e do Japão; a nau do trato; as galeotas. Macau, Imprensa Nacional, 1973. pp. 35. *bibliog. Separata dos no. 1 do vol. vii do Boletim do Instituto Luis de Camões.*

— — Japan.

MOURA (CARLOS FRANCISCO) Macau e o comercio portuguûes com a China e o Japão nos seculos XVI e XVII: as viagens da China e do Japão; a nau do trato; as galeotas. Macau, Imprensa Nacional, 1973. pp. 35. *bibliog. Separata dos no. 1 do vol. vii do Boletim do Instituto Luis de Camões.*

— Constitution.

CAETANO (MARCELLO) Revision of the Portuguese constitution: speech...before the National Assembly on 2 December 1970. [Lisbon], Secretaria de Estado da Informação e Turismo, 1970. pp. 28.

PORTUGAL. Ministerio da Comunicação Social. 1974. Provisional government: the men and the programme. [Lisbon], 1974. pp. 49.

— Economic conditions.

PORTUGAL. Secretaria de Estado da Informação e Turismo. Direcção Geral de Informação. 1971. Survey of the Portuguese economy. [Lisbon?], 1971. pp. 34.

PORTUGAL. Ministerio do Trabalho. Gabinete de Planeamento. 1973. Atlas socio-economico. Lisboa, [1973?]. 1 vol. (unpaged). *Transparency in end pocket.*

— Emigration and immigration.

BETTENCOURT (JOSE DE SOUSA) O fenomeno da emigração portuguesa. Luanda, Instituto de Investigação Cientifica de Angola, 1961 [or rather 1962]. pp. 95. *bibliog.*

— Executive departments.

PORTUGAL. Presidência do Conselho. 1953. 25 anos de administração publica: Ministerio das Comunicações. Lisboa, 1953. pp. 67.

PORTUGAL. Presidência do Conselho. 1953. 25 anos de administração publica: Ministerio das Finanças. Lisboa, 1953. pp. 75.

PORTUGAL. Presidência do Conselho. 1953. 25 anos de administração publica: Ministerio das Obras Publicas. Lisboa, 1953. pp. 116.

PORTUGAL. Presidência do Conselho. 1953. 25 anos de administração publica: Ministerio do Interior. Lisboa, 1953. pp. 67.

PORTUGAL. Presidência do Conselho. 1953. 25 anos de administração publica: Presidência do Conselho. Lisboa, 1953. pp. 155.

PORTUGAL. Presidência do Conselho. 1954. 25 anos de administração publica: Ministerio da Educação Nacional. Lisboa, 1954. pp. 211.

PORTUGAL. Presidência do Conselho. 1954. 25 anos de administração publica: Ministerio do Exército. Lisboa, 1954. pp. 107.

PORTUGAL. Presidência do Conselho. 1955. 25 anos de administração publica: Ministerio das Corporações e Previdência Social. Lisboa, 1955. pp. 174.

PORTUGAL. Presidência do Conselho. 1955. 25 anos de administração publica: Ministerio do Ultramar. Lisboa, 1955. pp. 358.

PORTUGAL. Presidência do Conselho. 1955. 25 anos de administrações e Previdência Social. Lisboa, 1955. pp. 174.

PORTUGAL. Ministerio da Comunicação Social. 1974. Provisional government: the men and the programme. [Lisbon], 1974. pp. 49.

— Foreign opinion.

PORTUGAL and the press, 1961-1972: [a selection of newspaper articles]. Lisbon, [1973]. pp. 586. *In various languages.*

— Foreign relations — Brazil.

MAXWELL (KENNETH R.) Conflicts and conspiracies: Brazil and Portugal 1750-1808. Cambridge, 1973. pp. 289. *bibliog.*

— — United States.

CROLLEN (LUC) Portugal, the U.S. and NATO. Leuven, [1973]. pp. 163. *bibliog. (Katholieke Universiteit te Leuven. Departement Politieke Wetenschappen. Studies in International Relations. No.1)*

— Gazetteers.

PORTUGAL. Censo, 1970. 11 recenseamento da população, 1970: continente e ilhas adjacentes: lista alfabetica de concelhos e freguesias. [Lisbon, 1971]. pp. 50.

— Maps.

PORTUGAL. Ministerio do Trabalho. Gabinete de Planeamento. 1973. Atlas socio-economico. Lisboa, [1973?]. 1 vol. (unpaged). *Transparency in end pocket.*

— Politics and government.

PORTUGAL. Presidência do Conselho. 1953. 25 anos de administração publica: Presidência do Conselho. Lisboa, 1953. pp. 155.

PORTUGAL. (Cont.)

CAETANO (MARCELLO) For the safety, the welfare and the progress of the Portuguese people: speech delivered at the annual conference of the People's National Action Movement,...Estoril, on 28 February, 1972. [Lisbon], Secretaria de Estado da Informação e Turismo, 1972. pp. 21.

PORTUGAL. Ministerio da Comunicação Social. 1974. Provisional government: the men and the programme. [Lisbon], 1974. pp. 49.

SPINOLA (ANTONIO SEBASTIÃO RIBEIRO DE) Portugal e o futuro: analise da conjuntura nacional. 3rd ed. [Lisbon, 1974]. pp. 247.

— Public works.

PORTUGAL. Presidência do Conselho. 1953. 25 anos de administração publica: Ministerio das Obras Publicas. Lisboa, 1953. pp. 116.

— Social conditions.

PORTUGAL. Ministerio do Trabalho. Gabinete de Planeamento. 1973. Atlas socio-economico. Lisboa, [1973?]. 1 vol. (unpaged). *Transparency in end pocket.*

— Statistics — Bibliography.

PORTUGAL. Instituto Nacional de Estatistica. Serviços Centrais. 1970. Inventario das estatisticas disponiveis no continente e ilhas adjacentes. [Lisbon, 1970]. pp. 273.

PORTUGUESE GUINEA.

ABSHIRE (DAVID M.) and SAMUELS (MICHAEL A.) eds. Portuguese Africa: a handbook. New York, 1969. pp. 480.

— Nationalism.

COMMITTEE FOR FREEDOM IN MOZAMBIQUE, ANGOLA AND GUINE, and AFRICA RESEARCH GROUP. War on three fronts: the fight against Portuguese colonialism. London, [1972?]. pp. (44).

CABRAL (AMILCAR) The struggle in Guinea; [based on speeches made at the Frantz Fanon Center in Milan in May 1964]. [Cambridge, Mass., 1973?]. pp. 429-446. *(Africa Research Group. Reprints. 1)*

— Social conditions.

CABRAL (AMILCAR) The struggle in Guinea; [based on speeches made at the Frantz Fanon Center in Milan in May 1964]. [Cambridge, Mass., 1973?]. pp. 429-446. *(Africa Research Group. Reprints. 1)*

PORTUGUESE IN ANGOLA.

BOAVIDA (AMERICO) Angola: five centuries of Portuguese exploitation. Richmond, B.C., 1972. pp. 124.

POSITIVISM.

GIDDENS (ANTHONY) ed. Positivism and sociology. London, 1974. pp. 244.

POSNER (WILLIAM).

BUCKLEY (MARY) The aged are people, too: about William Posner and social work with the old. Port Washington, N.Y., 1972. pp. 174. *bibliog.*

POSTAL SAVINGS BANKS

— Austria.

AUSTRIA. Statutes, etc. 1969. Postsparkassengesetz (BGBl. 458/1969). Wien, 1969. fo. 16.

FREMUTH (WALTER) Die Österreichische Postsparkasse: vom Amt zum Unternehmen. Wien, 1974. pp. 32.

POSTAL SERVICE

— France — Postal cheques.

VILLENEUVE (ANDRE) Comportements de gestion d'un compte chèque postal: [and] Evolution de l'équipement des ménages jusqu'au début de 1970. [Paris], 1970. pp. 83. *(France. Institut National de la Statistique et des Etudes Economiques. Collections de l'INSEE. Série M. Ménages. 4)* With summaries in English and Spanish.

— India.

INDIA. Administrative Reforms Commission.1970. Report on posts and telegraphs. [Delhi], 1970. pp. 82.

— United Kingdom — Employees.

MORAN (MICHAEL) The Union of Post Office Workers: a study in political sociology. London, 1974. pp. 184.

— United States — History.

CULLINAN (GERALD) The United States Postal Service. New York, [1973]. pp. 271. *bibliog.*

POTASH INDUSTRY AND TRADE.

KOEPKE (WRAY E.) Structure, behaviour and performance of the world potash industry. Ottawa, 1973. pp. 98. *bibliog. (Canada. Mineral Development Sector. Mineral Bulletins. 139)*

POTTER FAMILY.

PLAYNE (MARY ELIZABETH) compiler. 1896: a happy New Year to my sisters; [letters and papers concerning the Potter family and Lawrence Heyworth]. [Stroud, imprint, 1896]. pp. 34.

POTTERY

— United Kingdom.

MYRES (JOHN NOWELL LINTON) Anglo-Saxon pottery and the settlement of England. Oxford, 1969. pp. 259. *(Rhind Lectures in Archaeology. 1965)*

GAY (PHILIP W.) and SMYTH (ROBERT LESLIE) The British pottery industry. London, 1974. pp. 293.

POUGET (EMILE).

GOUSTINE (CHRISTIAN DE) Pouget: les matins noirs du syndicalisme. [Paris, 1972]. pp. 246. *bibliog.*

POULTRY

— European Economic Community countries.

ECONOMIC DEVELOPMENT COMMITTEE FOR THE AGRICULTURAL INDUSTRY. Common Market Sub-Committee. UK farming and the Common Market: poultry meat; a report. London, National Economic Development Office, 1974. pp. 30.

— United Kingdom.

ECONOMIC DEVELOPMENT COMMITTEE FOR THE AGRICULTURAL INDUSTRY. Common Market Sub-Committee. UK farming and the Common Market: poultry meat; a report. London, National Economic Development Office, 1974. pp. 30.

POVERTY.

GORDON (DAVID M.) Theories of poverty and under-employment: orthodox, radical, and dual labor market perspectives. Lexington, [1972]. pp. 177. *bibliog.*

HAZLITT (HENRY) The conquest of poverty. New Rochelle, [1973]. pp. 240.

KUITENBROUWER (JOOST B.W.) On the concept and process of marginalization. The Hague, 1973. pp. 15. *(Hague. Institute of Social Studies. Occasional Papers. No. 37)*

KUITENBROUWER (JOOST B.W.) On the practice and theory of affluence and poverty: some reflections. The Hague, 1973. pp. 26. *(Hague. Institute of Social Studies. Occasional Papers. No. 33)*

MAGEE (BRYAN EDGAR) and others. The long debate on poverty; [transcript of a discussion with] Max Hartwell [and] Eric Hobsbawm;...transmitted: 17 May 1973. [London, 1973]. fo.28. *(Thames Television. Something to Say)*

PSYCHIATRIC REHABILITATION ASSOCIATION. Poverty and schizophrenia: an examination of the relationship between environmental factors and the schizophrenia discharge rate; the development of a predictive formula; research team: Gillian Lomas [and others]. London, 1973. fo. 28. *bibliog.*

MOLLAT (MICHEL) ed. Etudes sur l'histoire de la pauvreté. Paris, 1974. 2 vols. (in 1). *(Paris. Université de Paris I (Panthéon-Sorbonne), and others. Publications de la Sorbonne. Série "Etudes". tome 8)*

POWELL (JOHN ENOCH).

POWELL (JOHN ENOCH) No easy answers. London, 1973 repr. 1974. pp. 135.

POWER (SOCIAL SCIENCES).

Le POUVOIR et le sacré; par Luc de Heusch [and others]. Bruxelles, 1962. pp. 186. *(Brussels. Université Libre. Institut de Sociologie. Centre d'Étude des Religions. Annales. 1)*

BOSSLE (LOTHAR) Der Autoritäts- und Machtanspruch des Politikers und Staatsmannes. Hannover, 1973. pp. 51. *(Niedersaechsische Landeszentrale für Politische Bildung. Schriftenreihe. Das Autoritätsproblem. 3)*

FERRIS (WAYNE H.) The power capabilities of nation-states: international conflict and war. Lexington, [1973]. pp. 191. *bibliog.*

HUBER (JOAN) and FORM (WILLIAM HUMBERT) Income and ideology: an analysis of the American political formula. New York, [1973]. pp. 226. *bibliog.*

JAEGGI (URS) Kapital und Arbeit in der Bundesrepublik: Elemente einer gesamtgesellschaftlichen Analyse. Frankfurt am Main, 1973. pp. 406. *bibliog.*

KEIZEROV (NIKOLAI MIRONOVICH) Vlast' i avtoritet: kritika burzhuaznykh teorii. Moskva, 1973. pp. 264.

TEDESCHI (JAMES T.) and others. Conflict, power and games: the experimental study of interpersonal relations. Chicago, 1973. pp. 270. *bibliog.*

VEREIN FÜR SOZIALPOLITIK. Schriften. Neue Folge. Band 74. Macht und ökonomisches Gesetz: (Verhandlungen auf der Jubiläumstagung in Bonn...1972, aus Anlass des Eisenacher Kongresses von 1872; herausgegeben von Hans K. Schneider und Christian Watrin). Berlin, [1973]. 2 vols.

BURLING (ROBBINS) The passage of power: studies in political succession. New York, [1974]. pp. 322. *bibliog.*

COLEMAN (JAMES SAMUEL) Power and the structure of society. New York, [1974]. pp. 112. *bibliog. (Pennsylvania University. Fels Center of Government. Fels Lectures on Public Policy Analysis)*

POWER RESOURCES.

GRENON (MICHEL) Pour une politique de l'énergie: charbon? pétrole? atome?. [Verviers, 1972]. pp. 352. *bibliog.*

ORGANISATION FOR ECONOMIC CO-OPERATION AND DEVELOPMENT. Oil Committee. 1973. Oil: the present situation and future prospects. Paris, 1973. pp. 293.

CRESCENZO (BERNARD DI) Crise de l'énergie ou crise politique?. Paris, [1974]. pp. 203. *bibliog.*

Die ENERGIEKRISE: Episode oder Ende einer Ära?; eine Diskussion zwischen Ralf Dahrendorf [and others]. Hamburg, 1974. pp. 125. *(Zeit, Die: Wochenzeitung für Politik, Wirtschaft, Handel und Kultur. Bücher)*

ENERGY: demand, conservation, and institutional problems; edited by Michael S. Macrakis; (proceedings of a conference held at the Massachusetts Institute of Technology, February 12-14, 1973, by the Massachusetts Institute of Technology Energy Laboratory). Cambridge, Mass., [1974]. pp. 556. *bibliogs.*

ENERGY in the 1980s: a Royal Society discussion organized by Sir Peter Kent. London, 1974. pp. 209. *(Reprinted from Philosophical Transactions of the Royal Society, series A, vol. 276, no. 1261)*

ROBINSON (COLIN) The energy 'crisis' and British coal: the economics of the fuel market in the 1970s and beyond. London, 1974. pp. 61. *bibliog. (Institute of Economic Affairs. Hobart Papers. 59)*

SZCZELKUN (STEFAN A.) Survival scrapbook 5: energy. Brighton, [1974]. 1 vol. (unpaged). *bibliog.*

THOMAS (D.I.) Resources and energy: a global study of the factors influencing their acquisition. [Grange-Over-Sands?], 1974. pp. 14. *(Merlewood Research and Development Papers. No. 57)*

The WESTERN world and energy; [revised versions of papers presented at a conference held by the Atlantic Institute in Tokyo in 1973]; edited by Curt Gasteyger. Farnborough, [1974]. pp. 104. *(Atlantic Institute. Atlantic Papers. 1974.1)*

— Belgium.

BELGIUM. Bureau du Plan. 1971. Plan 1971-1975: énergie. [Brussels], 1971. pp. [113].

— Communist countries.

KOZLOV (IGOR' DMITRIEVICH) and SHMAKOVA (ELENA KONSTANTINOVNA) Sotrudnichestvo stran-chlenov SEV v energetike. Moskva, 1973. pp. 141.

— European Economic Community countries.

EUROPEAN COMMUNITIES. Commission. 1972. Necessary progress in community energy policy: communication...to the Council forwarded on 13 October 1972. Brussels, 1972. pp. 27. *(Bulletin of the European Communities. Supplements. [1972/11])*

EUROPEAN COMMUNITIES. Commission. 1973. Guidelines and priority actions under the Community energy policy: communication... to the Council presented on 27 April 1973. [Brussels], 1973. pp. 9. *(Bulletin of the European Communities. Supplements. [1973/6])*

COMITE D'ETUDE DES PRODUCTEURS DE CHARBON D'EUROPE OCCIDENTALE. Energy in Europe: the importance of coal; a report. [London, National Coal Board], 1974. pp. 48.

— France.

FRANCE. Commissariat Général du Plan. 1972. L'énergie. [Paris, 1972]. pp. 205. *(Plan et prospectives. 6)*

OIZON (RENE) L'évolution récente de la production énergétique française.Paris, [1973]. pp. 588. *bibliog.*

— Germany.

GERMANY (BUNDESREPUBLIK). Bundesministerium für Wirtschaft. 1973. Daten zur Entwicklung der Energiewirtschaft in der Bundesrepublik Deutschland. [Bonn?], 1973. pp. 41.

— Italy.

ITALY. Ente Nazionale Idrocarburi. Energy and petroleum. irreg., 1964- Roma. *In English or Italian, with index and glossary in English.*

— Russia.

BEAUCOURT (CHANTAL) Le potentiel énergétique de l'URSS: perspectives 1975-1980. [Paris, 1972]. pp. 50. *bibliog. (France. Direction de la Documentation. La Documentation Française. Notes et Etudes Documentaires. Nos. 3926-3927)*

— — Kazakstan.

OSNOVY razvitiia energetiki Kazakhstana. Alma-Ata, 1971. pp. 279.

— — Tajikistan.

PIROGOVA (ZOIA ALEKSANDROVNA) Energetika Tadzhikistana. Dushanbe, 1966. pp. 60.

— Saudi Arabia.

SEIFERT (WILLIAM W.) and others, eds. Energy and development: a case study; based upon an interdepartmental student project...at the Massachusetts Institute of Technology...and a study at the College of Petroleum and Minerals, Dhahran, Saudi Arabia. Cambridge, Mass., [1973]. pp. 300. *(Massachusetts Institute of Technology. M.I.T. Reports. No. 25)*

— Sweden.

SWEDEN. Industridepartementet. Energikommittén. 1970. Sveriges energiförsörjning: energipolitik och organisation. Stockholm, 1970. pp. 129. *(Sweden. Statens Offentliga Utredningar. 1970. 13)*

— United Kingdom.

WAYNE (FRANCIS) Energy sources for Scottish transport. [Aberdeen, imprint], 1973. pp. 22. *bibliog.*

ROBINSON (COLIN) The energy 'crisis' and British coal: the economics of the fuel market in the 1970s and beyond. London, 1974. pp. 61. *bibliog. (Institute of Economic Affairs. Hobart Papers. 59)*

— United States.

GARVEY (GERALD) Energy, ecology, economy:...a project of the Center of International Studies, Princeton University. Princeton, 1972; London, 1974. pp. 235.

AMERICAN ACADEMY OF POLITICAL AND SOCIAL SCIENCE. Annals. vol. 410. The energy crisis: reality or myth: special editors of this volume Robert M. Lawrence [and] Norman I. Wengert. Philadelphia, 1973. pp. 264.

BREYER (STEPHEN G.) and MACAVOY (PAUL WEBSTER) Energy regulation by the Federal Power Commission. Washington, [1974]. pp. 163. *(Brookings Institution. Studies in the Regulation of Economic Activity)*

ENERGY: demand, conservation, and institutional problems; edited by Michael S. Macrakis; (proceedings of a conference held at the Massachusetts Institute of Technology, February 12-14, 1973, by the Massachusetts Institute of Technology Energy Laboratory). Cambridge, Mass., [1974]. pp. 556. *bibliogs.*

BREYER (STEPHEN G.) and MACAVOY (PAUL WEBSTER) Energy regulation by the Federal Power Commission. Washington, [1974]. pp. 163. *(Brookings Institution. Studies in the Regulation of Economic Activity)*

MANCKE (RICHARD B.) The failure of U.S. energy policy. New York, 1974. pp. 189. *bibliog.*

POZNAŃ UNIVERSITY.

WIKARJAK (JAN) ed. Uniwersytet Ziem Zachodnich i tajne kursy uniwersyteckie 1939- 1945: pokłosie wspomnień. Poznań, 1972. pp. 292. *(Poznań. Uniwersytet. Seria Dzieje UAM. Nr.8). With English and German summaries.*

PRAGIER (ADAM).

PRAGIER (ADAM) Czas przeszły dokonany. Londyn, 1966. pp. 943.

PRAT DE LA RIBA (ENRIC).

AINAUD DE LASARTE (JOSEP MARIA) and JARDI I CASANY (ENRIC) Prat de la Riba: home de govern. Barcelona, [1973]. pp. 320. *bibliog.*

PRECARPATHIA.

See IVANO—FRANKOVSK (OBLAST').

PRECEDENCE

— Thailand.

JONES (ROBERT BURTON) Thai titles and ranks; including a translation of Traditions of royal lineage in Siam, by King Chulalongkorn. Ithaca, N.Y., 1971. pp. 147. *bibliog. (Cornell University. Department of Asian Studies. Southeast Asia Program. Data Papers. No. 81) Includes original text.*

PRECIOUS METALS.

ASHTOR (ELIYAHU) Les métaux précieux et la balance des payements du Proche- Orient à la basse époque. Paris, 1971. pp. 125. *bibliog. (Paris. Ecole Pratiquè des Hautes Etudes. Section des Sciences Economiquès et Sociales. Centre de Recherches Historiques. Monnaie, Prix, Conjoncture. 10)*

PREFECTS (FRENCH GOVERNMENT).

LE CLERE (BERNARD) and WRIGHT (VINCENT) Les préfets du Second Empire. Paris, 1973. pp. 411. *bibliog. (Fondation Nationale des Sciences Politiques. Cahiers. 187)*

RIDLEY (FREDERICK FERNAND) The French prefectoral system: an example of integrated administrative decentralisation. London, 1973. pp. 42. *(U.K. Commission on the Constitution, 1969. Research Papers. 4)*

PREFERENTIAL BALLOT.

NEWLAND (ROBERT A.) and BRITTON (FRANK S.) How to conduct an election by the single transferable vote. London, 1973. pp. 32. *bibliog. With 4 specimen forms.*

PREGNANCY.

BOGUE (DONALD JOSEPH) and BOGUE (ELIZABETH J.) Techniques of pregnancy history analysis. Chicago, 1970. pp. 156. *(Chicago. University. Community and Family Study Center. R.F.F.P.I. Family Planning Evaluation Manuals. No. 4)*

PRESIDENTS.

DUVERGER (MAURICE) La monarchie républicaine. Paris, [1974]. pp. 284.

PRESS.

UNITED NATIONS EDUCATIONAL, SCIENTIFIC AND CULTURAL ORGANIZATION. Department of Mass Communication. Reports and Papers on Mass Communication. Paris, 1953 in progress.

CAYROL (ROLAND) La presse écrite et audio-visuelle. Paris, [1973]. pp. 628. *bibliogs.*

— Czechoslovakia.

FRANCE. Direction de la Documentation. La Documentation Française. Notes et Etudes Documentaires. Nos. 3,729-3, 730. La presse, les intellectuels et le pouvoir en Union Soviétique et dans les pays socialistes européens. 2. Pologne et Tchécoslovaquie; [by] Georges H. Mond. Paris, 1970. pp. 57. *bibliogs.*

— Europe, Eastern.

FRANCE. Direction de la Documentation. La Documentation Française. Notes et Etudes Documentaires. Nos. 3,736-3, 737. La presse, les intellectuels et le pouvoir en Union Soviétique et dans les pays socialistes européens. 3. Albanie, Allemagne de l'Est, Bulgarie, Hongrie, Roumanie, Yougoslavie; [by] Georges H. Mond [and others]. Paris, 1970. pp. 80. *bibliogs.*

— France.

RADER (DANIEL L.) The journalists and the July Revolution in France: the role of the political press in the overthrow of the Bourbon restoration, 1827-1830. The Hague, 1973. pp. 283. *bibliog.*

— Italy.

MURIALDI (PAOLO) La stampa italiana del dopoguerra, 1943-1972. Bari, 1973. pp. 644. *bibliog.*

ERAMO (LUCE D') Cruciverba politico: come funziona in Italia la strategia della diversione; (topografia politico-economica dei più noti quotidiani italiani esaminati all'epoca dell' affare Feltrinelli. Firenze, [1974]. pp. 341.

MACCHI (PIER AUGUSTO) Informazione e libertà: indagine sulla crisi della stampa. Firenze, [1974]. pp. 254. *(Fondazione Luigi Einaudi. Attualità Politica)*

PRESS. (Cont.)

— Poland.

FRANCE. Direction de la Documentation. La Documentation Française. Notes et Etudes Documentaires. Nos. 3,729-3, 730. La presse, les intellectuels et le pouvoir en Union Soviétique et dans les pays socialistes européens. 2. Pologne et Tchécoslovaquie; [by] Georges H. Mond. Paris, 1970. pp. 57. *bibliogs.*

— Russia.

VOPROSY teorii i praktiki massovykh sredstv propagandy. vyp.4. Moskva, 1971. pp. 415.

KOMMUNISTICHESKAIA PARTIIA SOVETSKOGO SOIUZA. O partiinoi i sovetskoi pechati, radioveshchanii i televidenii: sbornik dokumentov i materialov. Moskva, 1972. pp. 635.

— — Caucasus.

VATEISHVILI (DZHUANSHER LEVANOVICH) Russkaia obshchestvennaia mysl' i pechat' na Kavkaze v pervoi treti XIX veka. Moskva, 1973. pp. 460. *With English summary.*

— — Turkmenistan — Statistics.

PECHAT' TURKMENSKOI SSR V... GODU: statisticheskie materialy; ([pd. by] Gosudarstvennyi Komitet po Pechati [and] Gosudarstvennaia Knizhnaia Palata [Turkmenistan]. a., 1967, 1969. Ashkhabad.

— — Ukraine, Western.

OLEKSIUK (MYROSLAV MYRONOVYCH) Prohresyvna presa Zakhidnoï Ukraïny v borot'bi na zakhyst SRSR, 20-30-ti roky. Kyïv, 1973. pp. 228.

— Tanzania.

PIPPING (IDA) An episode of colonial history: the German press in Tanzania 1901-1914. Uppsala, 1974. pp. 47. *(Nordiska Afrikainstitutet. Research Reports. No. 22)*

— United Kingdom.

INDOCHINA SOLIDARITY CONFERENCE. Media Group. The British press and Vietnam. London, 1973. pp. 31. *(Indochina Solidarity Conference. Indochina Information [Series]. No. 3)*

SMITH (ANTHONY) b. 1938, ed. The British press since the war. Newton Abbot, [1974]. pp. 320. *bibliog.*

PRESS, CATHOLIC.

BEDESCHI (LORENZO) ed. La terza pagina de Il Popolo, 1923-1925; cattolici democratici e clerico-fascisti. Roma, 1973. pp. 463.

— Germany.

ROEDER (ELMAR) Der konservative Journalist Ernst Zander und die politischen Kämpfe seines "Volksboten". München, 1972. pp. 339. *bibliog. (Munich. Stadtarchiv. Neue Schriftenreihe. Band 58)*

PRESS AND POLITICS

— Austria.

FABER (PETER) Die Nationalratswahlen 1970 in den Wiener Tageszeitungen: eine inhaltsanalytische Untersuchung. Wien, 1973. pp. 255. *bibliog. (Vienna. Universität. Institut für Publizistik. Schriftenreihe. Band 3)*

— Germany.

Der FALL Küchenhoff; oder, Agitation mit falschem Etikett: wie politische Gegnerschaft zu "Bild" wissenschaftlich verbrämt werden sollte; (herausgegeben von der Axel Springer Verlag AG, Abteilung Information). Berlin, 1972. pp. 113.

GURATZSCH (DANKWART) Macht durch Organisation: die Grundlegung des Hugenbergschen Presseimperiums. Düsseldorf, [1974]. pp. 486. *bibliog. (Hamburg. Hansische Universität. Studien zur Modernen Geschichte. Band 7)*

— Sweden.

[BRÄNDSTRÖM (DAN)] Nomineringsförfarande vid riksdagsval; [and] Riksdagen i pressen, [by Stig Hadenius]; undersökningar utförda på uppdrag av Grundlagberedningen. Stockholm, 1972. pp. 126. *(Sweden. Statens Offentliga Utredningar. 1972. 17)*

— United Kingdom.

[GENERAL COUNCIL OF THE PRESS]. Press conduct in the Lambton affair; a report by the Press Council. London, [1974]. pp. 37. *(Press Council Booklets. No.5)*

PRESS LAW

— Brazil.

COSTELLA (ANTÔNIO F.) O contrôle da informação no Brasil: evolução historica da legislação brasileira de imprensa. Petrópolis, 1970. pp. 156. *bibliog.*

— Spain.

FERNANDEZ AREAL (MANUEL) El control de la prensa en España. Madrid, [1973]. pp. 324.

— United Kingdom.

SMITH (ANTHONY) b. 1938, ed. The British press since the war. Newton Abbot, [1974]. pp. 320. *bibliog.*

PRESSURE GROUPS

AMERICAN ACADEMY OF POLITICAL AND SOCIAL SCIENCE. Annals. vol. 413. Interest groups in international perspective; special editor of this volume, Robert Presthus. Philadelphia, 1974. pp. 251.

— America, Latin.

ADIE (ROBERT F.) and POITRAS (GUY E.) Latin America: the politics of immobility. Englewood Cliffs, [1974]. pp. 278. *bibliogs.*

— Canada.

PRESTHUS (ROBERT V.) Elites in the policy process. London, 1974. pp. 525.

— European Economic Community countries.

MEYNAUD (JEAN) and SIDJANSKI (DUSAN) Les groupes de pression dans la Communauté européenne, 1958- 1968: structure et action des organisations professionnelles. Bruxelles, 1971. pp. 728. *(Brussels. Université Libre. Institut d'Etudes Européennes. Thèses et Travaux Politiques)*

— Germany.

HENSEL (RAINER) Der Einfluss der wirtschaftspolitischen Verbände auf die parlamentarische Arbeit. Göttingen, 1973. pp. 190. *bibliog.*

GURATZSCH (DANKWART) Macht durch Organisation: die Grundlegung des Hugenbergschen Presseimperiums. Düsseldorf, [1974]. pp. 486. *bibliog. (Hamburg. Hansische Universität. Studien zur Modernen Geschichte. Band 7)*

— Norway.

BLOM (IDA) Kampen om Eirik Raudes land: pressgruppepolitikk i grønlandsspørsmålet, 1921-1931. Oslo, 1973. pp. 439. *bibliog.*

— United Kingdom.

JERMAN (BETTY) Do something!: a guide to self-help organisations. London, [1971]. pp. 203.

BUZAN (BARRY GORDON) The British peace movement from 1919 to 1939; [Ph.D. (London) thesis]. 1973. fo. 460. *bibliog. Typescript: unpublished. This thesis is the property of London University and may not be removed from the Library.*

KIMBER (RICHARD) and RICHARDSON (JEREMY JOHN) eds. Campaigning for the environment. London, 1974. pp. 228. *bibliog.*

KIMBER (RICHARD) and RICHARDSON (JEREMY JOHN) eds. Pressure groups in Britain: a reader. London, 1974. pp. 304. *bibliog.*

PYM (BRIDGET) Pressure groups and the permissive society. Newton Abbot, [1974]. pp. 183. *bibliog.*

RIVERS (PATRICK) Politics by pressure. London, 1974. pp. 240. *bibliog.*

— United States.

WILSON (JAMES Q.) Political organizations. New York, [1973]. pp. 359.

PRESTHUS (ROBERT V.) Elites in the policy process. London, 1974. pp. 525.

PREUSSISCHE AKADEMIE DER KÜNSTE.

BRENNER (HILDEGARD) ed. Ende einer bürgerlichen Kunst-Institution: die politische Formierung der Preussischen Akademie der Künste ab 1933; (eine Dokumentation). Stuttgart, [1972]. pp. 174. *(Vierteljahrshefte für Zeitgeschichte. Schriftenreihe. Nr. 24)*

PREVENTIVE DENTISTRY.

WORKING PARTY ON THE DENTAL SERVICES [U.K.]. Preventive dentistry: interim report to: Secretary of State for Social Services, Secretary of State for Scotland, Secretary of State for Wales. London, H.M.S.O., 1973. pp. 5.

PRICE INDEXES.

UNITED NATIONS. Statistical Office. Statistical Papers. Series M. No. 29. Rev.1. Add.1. Price movements of basic commodities in international trade: 1950-1970. (ST/STAT/SER.M/29/Rev.1/Add.1) New York, 1971. pp. 91.

— Netherlands Antilles.

NETHERLANDS ANTILLES. Bureau voor de Statistiek. 1970. De verlegging van het basisjaar van het prijsindexcijfer van de kosten van het levensonderhoud. Curaçao, 1970. fo. 6.

PRICE REGULATION

— Communist countries.

FRANCE. Direction de la Documentation. La Documentation Française. Notes et Etudes Documentaires. No. 4,002. La fixation des prix du commerce international dans les économies socialistes, par Françoise Lemoine. [Paris], 1973. pp. 30.

— India.

SINGH (VIDYA BHUSAN) An evaluation of fair price shops. New Delhi, [1973]. pp. 132.

— United Kingdom.

U.K. Price Commission. 1973- . Data sheets. [London, 1973 in progress].

U.K. Price Commission. 1973. The price code in stage 3: a guide to the new obligations. [London, 1973]. pp. 22.

U.K. [Treasury]. 1974. Changes in price control: consultative document. [London, 1974]. pp. 4,2.

PRICES.

COMMODITY TRADE AND PRICE TRENDS (formerly Commodity price trends); ([pd. by] International Bank for Reconstruction and Development [and] International Development Association). a., 1970, 1971, 1973- [Washington]. *In English, French and Spanish.*

KOZLOVA (KAMA BORISOVNA) and ENTOV (REVOL'D MIKHAILOVICH) Teoriia tseny. Moskva, 1972. pp. 239.

ATKINS (DEREK R.) The hybridisation of administered price and administered budget controls. Coventry, 1973. pp. 22. *bibliog. (University of Warwick. Centre for Industrial Economic and Business Research. [Warwick Research in Industrial and Business Studies]. No.41)*

EARL (PAUL H.) Inflation and the structure of industrial prices. Lexington, [1973]. pp. 257. *bibliog.*

GONZALEZ PAZ (JOSE) Evolucion de los presios e inflacion. Salamanca, 1973. pp. 190.

LEFTWICH (RICHARD HENRY) The price system and resource allocation. 5th ed. Hinsdale, Ill., [1973]. pp. 433. *bibliogs.*

BAUM (CLEMENS) Möglichkeiten und Grenzen der Entwicklung einer gesamtwirtschaftlichen Preistheorie. Berlin, [1974]. pp. 174. *bibliog.*

COWLING (KEITH) and WATERSON (MICHAEL) Price-cost margins and market structure. Coventry, 1974. pp. 22. *bibliog.* *(University of Warwick. Department of Economics. Warwick Economic Research Papers. No. 44)*

HAIG (B.D.) and WOOD (M.P.) A dynamic input-output system for analysing price changes. Canberra, 1974. fo.34. *bibliog.* *(Australian National University. Research School of Social Sciences. Department of Economics. Working Papers in Economics and Econometrics. No.23)*

RUYS (P.H.M.) Public goods and decentralization: the duality approach in the theory of value. Tilburg, 1974. pp. 236. *bibliog.* *(Tilburg. Katholieke Hogeschool. Tilburg Institute of Economics. Tilburg Studies on Economics. 10)*

— **Dictionaries and encyclopaedias.**

LEXIKON der Wirtschaft: Preise; (Herausgeber und Redaktionskollektiv: Kurt Ambrée [and others]). Berlin, 1973. pp. 276.

— **Mathematical models.**

EARL (PAUL H.) Inflation and the structure of industrial prices. Lexington, [1973]. pp. 257. *bibliog.*

— **Belgium.**

VERLINDEN (CHARLES) and others, eds. Dokumenten voor de geschiedenis van prijzen en lonen in Vlaanderen en Brabant...(XIVe-XIXe eeuw). Brugge, 1959 in progress. *bibliogs.* *(Ghent. Université. Faculté de Philosophie et Lettres. Recueil de Travaux. Fascicules 125, etc.)*

— **Canada.**

PORTER (ALLAN A.) Productivity, costs and prices: an examination of trends in selected manufacturing industries. Ottawa, 1973. pp. 366. *(Canada. Department of Labour. Economics and Research Branch. Occasional Papers. No. 7)*

— **Communist countries.**

TSENY i stimulirovanie nauchno-tekhnicheskogo progressa v sotsialisticheskikh stranakh. Moskva, 1973. pp. 272.

— **Europe.**

MADDALENA (ALDO DE) Moneta e mercato nel '500: la rivoluzione dei prezzi. Firenze, [1973]. pp. 126. *bibliog.*

— **Europe, Eastern.**

MARER (PAUL) Postwar pricing and price patterns in socialist foreign trade, 1946- 1971. [Bloomington], [1972]. pp. 99. *bibliog.* *(Indiana University. International Development Research Center. IDRC Reports. 1)*

HEWETT (EDWARD A.) Foreign trade prices in the Council for Mutual Economic Assistance. London, 1974. pp. 196. *(National Association for Soviet and East European Studies. Soviet and East European Studies)*

— **France.**

FRANCE. Centre d'Etude des Revenus et des Coûts. 1969. Prix, coûts et revenus en France de 1949 à 1968. Paris, 1969. pp. 62. *(Documents. No. 2)*

— **Germany — Mathematical models.**

POHL (RUEDIGER) Lohnkosten und Preisentwicklung in der Industrie der Bundesrepublik Deutschland. Berlin, [1972]. pp. 39. *(Institut für Empirische Wirtschaftsforschung. Arbeitspapiere. Heft 2)*

— **India.**

GHOSH (AMIYA BHUSHAN) Price trends and policies in India. Delhi, [1974]. pp. 255. *bibliog.*

— **Korea.**

BROWN (GILBERT T.) Korean pricing policies and economic development in the 1960s. Baltimore, [1973]. pp. 317.

— **Poland.**

SZTYBER (WŁADYSŁAW BOGDAN) Teoria i polityka cen w gospodarce socjalistycznej. 2nd ed. Warszawa, 1973. pp. 456. *bibliog.* With English and Russian summaries.

— **Roumania.**

ŞICĂ (GHEORGHE) Prognoza şi planul preţurilor de producţie. Bucureşti, 1973. pp. 259. *bibliog.* *(Academia de Ştiinţe Sociale şi Politice a Republicii Socialiste România. Institutul de Cercetări Economice. Bibliotheca Oeconomica. 23)*

— **Russia.**

ZAIKOV (GELII IVANOVICH) and ROMANOV (RAFAIL GAVRILOVICH) Uroven' kachestva i stoimost' produktsii. Moskva, 1970. pp. 119.

VAINSHTEIN (AL'BERT L'VOVICH) Tseny i tsenoobrazovanie v SSSR v vosstanovitel'nyi period, 1921-1928 gg. Moskva, 1972. pp. 190.

KHUDOKORMOV (GEORGII NIKOLAEVICH) Obshchestvennaia stoimost' i zakupochnye tseny. Moskva, 1973. pp. 263.

— **Tanzania.**

UNITED REPUBLIC OF TANZANIA. Bureau of Statistics. Prices and price index numbers for eighteen towns in Tanzania. a., 1968/9- Dar es Salaam.

— **United States — Mathematical models.**

BARRETT (NANCY SMITH) and others. Prices and wages in U.S. manufacturing: a factor analysis. Lexington, Mass., [1973]. pp. 212. *bibliog.*

— **Yugoslavia — Mathematical models.**

SEKULIĆ (MIJO) Analiza kretanja sistema cijena: primjena medjusektorskog modela. Zagreb, 1974. pp. 63. *bibliog.*

PRIEST WORKERS.

DELIAT (ROGER) Vingt ans O.S. chez Renault: l'évolution d'un enfant du peuple prêtre-ouvrier. Paris, [1973]. pp. 207.

PRIMAKOV (VITALII MARKOVICH).

PRIMAKOV (VITALII MARKOVICH) Zapiski volontera: grazhdanskaia voina v Kitae; (otvetstvennyi redaktor L.P. Deliusin, vstupitel'naia stat'ia i primechaniia R.A. Mirovitskoi). Moskva, 1967. pp. 215. First published 1930.

PRIMO DE RIVERA Y SAENZ DE HEREDIA (JOSE ANTONIO).

NIN DE CARDONA (JOSE MARIA) Jose Antonio: la posibilidad politica truncada. Madrid, 1973. pp. 251. *bibliog.*

PRINCIPE.

See SÃO TOMÉ E PRINCIPE.

PRINTED EPHEMERA.

PEMBERTON (JOHN E.) The national provision of printed ephemera in the social sciences; a report prepared for the Social Science and Government Committee of the Social Science Research Council. [Coventry], 1971. fo. 56. *(University of Warwick. Library. Occasional Publications. No. 1)*

PRINTERS

— **France.**

[DUFRENE ( )] La misère des apprentifs imprimeurs, appliquée par le détail à chaque fonction de ce pénible état: vers burlesques; [reprint of work originally published 1710; issued by E. Morin] . Paris, 1900. pp. 14.

— **Italy.**

CENTRO STUDI FEDERLIBRO, FIM, SISM-CISL di VERONA. Mondadori per noi: monopolio e classe operaia. Verona, [1974]. pp. 198.

— **United Kingdom.**

ROSNER (CHARLES) ed. The world of De La Rue: the Old World and the New; presented on the occasion of the one hundred and fiftieth anniversary of the house of De la Rue, 1813-1963. [London, 1963]. 1 vol. (unpaged).

PRINTING

— **Anecdotes, facetiae, satire, etc.**

[DUFRENE ( )] La misère des apprentifs imprimeurs, appliquée par le détail à chaque fonction de ce pénible état: vers burlesques; [reprint of work originally published 1710; issued by E. Morin] . Paris, 1900. pp. 14. - **History - Bibliography.**

MANCHESTER. Public Libraries. Reference Library subject catalogue. Section 655. Printing. Part 1. General works, history of printing; edited by G.E. Haslam. Manchester, 1961. 1 vol. (unpaged).

— **History — United Kingdom.**

TREPTOW (OTTO) John Siberch: Johann Lair von Siegburg; translated by Trevor Jones; abridged and edited by John Morris and Trevor Jones. Cambridge, 1970. pp. 73. *bibliog.* *(Cambridge. Bibliographical Society. Monographs. No.6)*

— — — **Exhibitions.**

STANBROOK ABBEY. An exhibit of productions from Stanbrook Abbey Press, 1876- 1966: 22 April - May 1968. London, [1968]. pp. 8.

PRINTING, PRACTICAL

— **Bibliography.**

MANCHESTER. Public Libraries. Reference Library subject catalogue. Section 655. Printing. Part 1. General works, history of printing; edited by G.E. Haslam. Manchester, 1961. 1 vol. (unpaged).

PRINTING INDUSTRY

— **Italy.**

CENTRO STUDI FEDERLIBRO, FIM, SISM-CISL di VERONA. Mondadori per noi: monopolio e classe operaia. Verona, [1974]. pp. 198.

— **United Kingdom.**

BRITISH PRINTING INDUSTRIES FEDERATION. Storage and handling charges for printed sheets and bound stock. London, [1968]. pp. (2).

[ECONOMIC DEVELOPMENT COMMITTEE FOR PRINTING AND PUBLISHING]. Printing and publishing exports and imports in 1970. [London, National Economic Development Office, 1971?]. 1 pamphlet (unpaged).

PRINTING AND PUBLISHING INDUSTRY TRAINING BOARD [U.K.]. Report and statement of accounts. a., 1972/3- London. *Formerly included in the file of British Parliamentary Papers.*

BRITISH PRINTING INDUSTRIES FEDERATION. Annual report ([and] Annual accounts). a., 1973/4- London.

PRISONERS.

— Legal status, laws, etc.

— — United States.

FITZHARRIS (TIMOTHY L.) The desirability of a correctional ombudsman. Berkeley, Ca., 1973. pp. 114.

— Recreation.

ITALY. Direzione Generale per gli Istituti di Prevenzione e di Pena. Ufficio Studi e Ricerche. 1973. Lo sport nelle carceri: indagine comparata sulle attività ginniche e sportive negli istituti penitenziari. Roma, 1973. pp. 123. (*Quaderni. 5*)

— Canada.

WALLER (IRVIN) Men released from prison. Toronto, [1974]. pp. 273. *bibliog.* (*Toronto. University. Centre of Criminology. Canadian Studies in Criminology. 2*)

— United Kingdom.

FLETCHER (JOHN WILLIAM) A menace to society: my 35 years in prison - for stealing... 40[pounds]. London, 1972. pp. 142.

CURTIS (DOUGLAS) Dartmoor to Cambridge: the autobiography of a prison graduate. London, [1973]. pp. 191.

PRISONERS OF WAR, GERMAN.

BOEHME (KURT WILLI) and WOLFF (HELMUT) eds. Aufzeichnungen über die Kriegsgefangenschaft im Westen. München, 1973. pp. 552. (*Zur Geschichte der deutschen Kriegsgefangenen des zweiten Weltkrieges. Beihefte. 2*) Use restricted.

RATZA (WERNER) Die deutschen Kriegsgefangenen in der Sowjetunion: der Faktor Arbeit; mit einer Einleitung des Herausgebers. München, 1973. pp. 384. (*Zur Geschichte der deutschen Kriegsgefangenen des zweiten Weltkrieges. Band 4*) Use restricted.

PRISONERS OF WAR, NORWEGIAN.

APALSET (JAKOB) Heimsending av norske fangar frå Tyskland 1945: planar og forhandlingar 1944-45. [Oslo, 1970]. pp. 42. *bibliog.*

PRISONERS OF WAR, RUSSIAN.

BETHELL (NICHOLAS WILLIAM) 4th Baron Bethell. The last secret: forcible repatriation to Russia, 1944-7. London, 1974. pp. 224.

PRISONS.

See also the names of prisons.

CUSTODIAL treatment of offenders: report of a conference at Ditchley Park, 27-30 April 1973; by T.P. Morris, conference rapporteur. Enstone, [1973]. pp. 34. (*Ditchley Foundation. Ditchley Papers. No. 45*)

— Medical care.

CIBA FOUNDATION. Symposia. New Series. 16. Medical care of prisoners and detainees. [Amsterdam], 1973. pp. 238.

— Canada.

ADVISORY BOARD OF PSYCHIATRIC CONSULTANTS [CANADA]. The general program for the development of psychiatric services in federal correctional services in Canada; Plan d'ensemble de développement des services psychiatriques dans les services correctionnels fédéraux au Canada. Ottawa, Information Canada, 1973. pp. 60, 62. In English and French.

CANADA. Department of the Solicitor General. 1973. The criminal in Canadian society: a perspective on corrections. Ottawa, 1973. pp. 46, 49. *bibliog.* In English and French.

— Denmark.

DENMARK. Direktoratet for Faengselsvaesenet. 1972. The penal system of Denmark. [Copenhagen, 1972]. pp. 52.

— Italy.

INVERNIZZI (IRENE) Il carcere come scuola di rivoluzione. Torino, [1973]. pp. 379.

GIUSTIZIA penale e riforma carceraria in Italia: atti del seminario organizzato dal Centro di Studi e Iniziative ... Roma, 1973; [by] Gianfilippo Benedetti [and others]. Roma, 1974. pp. 382. (*Centro di Studi e Iniziative per la Riforma dello Stato. Quaderni. 1*)

— Russia.

KUUSINEN (AINO) Before and after Stalin: a personal account of Soviet Russia from the 1920s to the 1960s;...translated from the German by Paul Stevenson. London, 1974. pp. 256.

— South Africa.

INTERNATIONAL DEFENCE AND AID FUND FOR SOUTHERN AFRICA. South African prisons and the Red Cross investigation; an examination...with prisoners' testimony. London, 1967. pp. 63.

— United Kingdom.

PAUL (Sir GEORGE ONESIPHORUS) Address to His Majesty's justices of the peace for the County of Glocester, on the subject of forming rules, orders, and bye-laws, for the regulation and government of the prisons of the said county; delivered at their Michaelmas general quarter-sessions, 1789. 3rd ed. Glocester, Walker, 1808. pp. 59.

PAUL (Sir GEORGE ONESIPHORUS) Proceedings of the grand juries, magistrates, and other noblemen and gentlemen of the county of Glocester, on designing and executing a general reform in the construction and regulation of the prisons for the said county. 3rd ed. Glocester, Walker, 1808. 3 pts.

PAUL (Sir GEORGE ONESIPHORUS) Address to His Majesty's justices of the peace for the County of Glocester, on the administration and practical effects of the system of prison regulation, established in that county, delivered at their Epiphany general quarter sessions 1809. Glocester, Walker, 1809. pp. 158.

PAUL (Sir GEORGE ONESIPHORUS) Rules, orders, and regulations for the controul and government of the prisons of the county of Glocester, revised and recommended to the magistrates of the said county; with abstracts of the laws relating thereto. Glocester, Walker, 1810. 2 pts.

SOCIETY FOR THE IMPROVEMENT OF PRISON DISCIPLINE AND FOR THE REFORMATION OF JUVENILE OFFENDERS. Report of the committee...with an appendix. London, printed by T. Bensley...and sold by J. and A. Arch, etc., 1820. pp. xxxix, 171.

STRATTON (BRIAN) Who guards the guards?. London, [1973]. pp. 143.

COOK (TIMOTHY) and GUNN (JOHN) Psychiatrist. Penal reform. London, [1974?]. pp. 44. (*Liberal Party. Strategy 2,000. 1st Series. No.4*)

HOWARD LEAGUE FOR PENAL REFORM. Ill-founded premisses: the logic of penal policy and the prison building programme. London, 1974. pp. 9.

— United States.

ORLAND (LEONARD) Justice, punishment, treatment: the correctional process. New York, [1973]. pp. 579.

PRIVACY, RIGHT OF.

BELGIUM. Parlement. Bibliothèque. 1972. L'ordinateur et la sauvegarde des libertés individuelles. Bruxelles, 1972. pp. 58. *bibliog.* (*Dossiers documentaires. 6*)

INTERNATIONAL OSLO SYMPOSIUM ON DATA BANKS AND SOCIETY, 1ST, 1971. The first International Oslo Symposium on Data Banks and Society: the proceedings, etc. Oslo, 1972. pp. 150. (*Institutt for Privatrett. Avdeling for EDB-spørsmål. Publikasjoner. Nr. 2*)

SOCIAL AND COMMUNITY PLANNING RESEARCH. Survey research and privacy: report of a working party. London, [1973]. fo. 61. *bibliog.*

JONES (MERVYN) ed. Privacy. Newton Abbot, [1974]. pp. 230. *bibliog.*

— Denmark.

DENMARK. Straffelovrådet. 1971. Straffelovr ådets betaenkning om privatlivets fred. København, 1971. pp. 92. (*Denmark. Betaenkninger. Nr. 601*) With English summary.

— United Kingdom.

[GENERAL COUNCIL OF THE PRESS]. Press conduct in the Lambton affair; a report by the Press Council. London, [1974]. pp. 37. (*Press Council Booklets. No.5*)

JONES (MERVYN) ed. Privacy. Newton Abbot, [1974]. pp. 230. *bibliog.*

MADGWICK (DONALD) and SMYTHE (TONY) The invasion of privacy. London, 1974. pp. 197. *bibliog.*

— United States.

COWAN (PAUL) and others. State secrets: (police surveillance in America). New York, [1974]. pp. 333.

PRIVATE PROPERTY

— Russia.

MAKAROVA (ISKRA VLADIMIROVNA) Podsobnoe khoziaistvo kolkhoznikov. Moskva, 1973. pp. 64.

PROBABILITIES.

BJØNSTAD (JAN F.) A note on comparison of marginal probabilities in the 2x2 - table. Oslo, 1973. fo. 3. *bibliog.* (*Oslo. Universitet. Socialøkonomiske Institutt. Memoranda*)

STEMPELL (DIETER) A programmed introduction to the theory of probability; (translated by George L. Baurley on the basis of the 4th revised [German] edition). Berlin, 1973. pp. 168.

WIGGINS (LEE M.) Panel analysis: latent probability models for attitude and behavior processes. Amsterdam, 1973. pp. 255. *bibliog.*

BARTHOLOMEW (DAVID JOHN) Social probability: an inaugural lecture. [London, 1974]. pp. 19. *bibliog.*

SUPPES (PATRICK) Probabilistic metaphysics. Uppsala, 1974. fo. 160. *bibliog.* (*Uppsala. Universitet. Filosofiska Föreningen, and Filosofiska Institutionen. Filosofiska Studier. Nr. 22*)

PROBATE LAW AND PRACTICE

— United Kingdom.

TRISTRAM (THOMAS HUTCHINSON) and COOTE (HENRY CHARLES) Probate practice; twenty-fourth edition [by] W.J. Pickering [and others]. London, 1973. pp. 1373,55.

PROBATION

— Ireland (Republic).

HART (IAN) Factors relating to reconviction among young Dublin probationers. Dublin, 1974. pp. 124. *bibliog.* (*Economic and Social Research Institute. Papers. No.76*)

— Poland.

MAREK (ANDRZEJ) Warunkowe umorzenie postępowania karnego. Warszawa, 1973. pp. 283. *bibliog.* With English and Russian summaries.

— United Kingdom.

U.K. Home Office. 1973. The probation and after-care service in England and Wales. 5th ed. London, 1973. pp. 29.

PROBLEM CHILDREN

— Finland.

MÄÄTTÄNEN (MATTI) The relation between psychological and social factors affecting maladjustment. Helsinki, 1972. pp. 49. *(Finland. Suomen Virallinen Tilasto. Finlands Officiella Statistik. 32. Sosiaalisia Erikoistutkimuksia. 28)*

PRODUCE TRADE

— European Economic Community countries.

POELMANS (JACQUELINE) and LECOMTE (JACQUES) L'agriculture européenne et les pays tiers. Bruxelles, 1972. pp. 180. *bibliog. (Brussels. Université Libre. Institut d'Etudes Européennes. Thèses et Travaux Economiques. 7)*

ELLIS (FRANK) and others. Farmers and foreigners: impact of the Common Agricultural Policy on the associates and associables. London, [1973]. pp. 86.

— Underdeveloped areas.

See UNDERDEVELOPED AREAS — Produce trade.

— United States.

U.S. trade policy and agricultural exports: [based on papers of a conference organized by the Iowa State University Center for Agricultural and Rural Development]. Ames, Iowa, 1973. pp. 228.

PRODUCTION (ECONOMIC THEORY).

CASSON (MARK C.) Dynamic production functions and the theory of the firm. [Reading], [1973]. fo. 35. *bibliog. (Reading. University. Department of Economics. Discussion Papers in Economics. No. 41)*

CASSON (MARK C.) A dynamic theory of the productive process. [Reading], 1973. 2 pts. *bibliog. (Reading. University. Department of Economics. Discussion Papers in Economics. Nos. 43-44)*

CASSON (MARK C.) Training labour and management: an extension of the theory of production. [Reading], 1973. fo. 18. *bibliog. (Reading. University. Department of Economics. Discussion Papers in Economics. No. 48)*

AFRIAT (S.N.) Production duality and the von Neumann theory of growth and interest. Meisenheim am Glan, [1974]. pp. 78. *bibliog.*

— Mathematical models.

CASSON (MARK C.) The time profile of production. [Reading], 1973. fo. 37. *bibliog. (Reading. University. Department of Economics. Discussion Papers in Economics. No. 42)*

DIEWERT (W.E.) Separability and a generalization of the Cobb-Douglas cost, production and indirect utility functions. Stanford, 1973. pp. 45. *bibliog. (Stanford University. Institute for Mathematical Studies in the Social Sciences. Technical Reports. [New Series]. No. 86)*

GOORBERGH (W.M. VAN DEN) Productionstructures and external diseconomies. Tilburg, 1973. pp. 33. *bibliog. (Tilburg. Katholieke Hogeschool. Tilburg Institute of Economics. Research Memoranda. EIT 42)*

JORGENSON (DALE W.) Investment and production: a review; [presented at the Winter meetings of the Econometric Society in Toronto in 1972]. Stanford, 1973. pp. 44. *bibliog. (Stanford University. Institute for Mathematical Studies in the Social Sciences. Technical Reports. [New Series]. No. 97)*

JORGENSON (DALE W.) and LAU (LAWRENCE J.) Duality and differentiability in production. Stanford, 1973. pp. 43. *bibliog. (Stanford University. Institute for Mathematical Studies in the Social Sciences. Technical Reports. [New Series]. No. 100)*

JORGENSON (DALE W.) and LAU (LAWRENCE J.) The duality of technology and economic behavior. Stanford, 1973. pp. 42. *bibliog. (Stanford University. Institute for Mathematical Studies in the Social Sciences. Technical Reports. [New Series]. No. 85)*

KNUDSEN (NIELS CHR.) Production and cost models of a multi-product firm: a mathematical programming approach. Odense, 1973. pp. 300. *bibliog. (Odense Universitet. Studies in History and Social Sciences. vol.13)*

NADIRI (M. ISHAQ) and ROSEN (SHERWIN) A disequilibrium model of demand for factors of production. New York, 1973. pp. 200. *bibliog. (National Bureau of Economic Research. [Publications]. No. 99)*

PYATT (FRANK GRAHAM) Investment decisions in vintage models. Coventry, 1973. pp. 81. *bibliog. (University of Warwick. Department of Economics. Warwick Economic Research Papers. No. 31)*

BOSWORTH (DEREK L.) Some preliminary thoughts on the concept of the ex-ante function. Coventry, 1974. pp. 32. *bibliog. (University of Warwick. Centre for Industrial Economic and Business Research. [Warwick Research in Industrial and Business Studies]. No. 47)*

BOSWORTH (DEREK L.) The demand for labour: a putty-clay approach. Coventry, 1974. pp. 25. *bibliog. (University of Warwick. Centre for Industrial Economic and Business Research. [Warwick Research in Industrial and Business Studies]. No. 46)*

PRODUCTION MANAGEMENT.

McMANUS (JOHN C.) The organization of production. Ottawa, [1971]. fo. 25. *(Carleton University. Carleton Economic Papers)*

ZIMMERMANN (HANS JUERGEN) and SOVEREIGN (MICHAEL G.) Quantitative models for production management. Englewood Cliffs, [1974]. pp. 650.

PRODUCTION PLANNING.

ALESSANDRO (LUIGI D') Plant and stocks in the production of goods in seasonal demand; translated from Italian by J.W. Franklin; English text revised by F.M. Reid. Oxford, 1963. pp. 88.

KRAAY (J.M.A. VAN) An application of the product life cycle concept in international marketing, in particular regarding the wall paper market. Tilburg, 1973. pp. 33. *bibliog. (Tilburg. Katholieke Hogeschool. Tilburg Institute of Economics. Research Memoranda. EIT 41)*

PRODUCTIVITY.

BURNHAM (DONALD C.) Productivity improvement. New York, [1973]. pp. 73. *(Carnegie-Mellon University. Benjamin F. Fairless Memorial Lectures. 1972)*

PABST (WILM K.) Arbeitsproduktivität als politökonomische Frage für Marxismus-Leninismus, UdSSR und DDR. Berlin, 1973. pp. 351. *(Berlin. Freie Universität. Osteuropa-Institut. Berichte: Reihe Wirtschaft und Recht. Heft 96)*

SMITH (IAN G.) The measurement of productivity: a systems approach in the context of productivity agreements. Epping, 1973. pp. 167.

STEFANI (GIORGIO) ed. La produttività delle imprese pubbliche. Milano, [1973]. pp. 521. *(Centro Italiano di Ricerche e d'Informazione sull'Economia delle Imprese Pubbliche e di Pubblico Interesse. Studi e Documenti sul Settore Pubblico dell'Economia. 12)*

FALLON (PETER ROBERT) The productive roles of workers with different levels of education: an international cross-sectional study; [Ph.D. (London) thesis]. 1974. fo. 248. *bibliog. Typescript: unpublished. This thesis is the property of London University and may not be removed from the library.*

— Asia.

REGIONAL CONFERENCE ON PRODUCTIVITY AND EMERGING ECONOMIES, SINGAPORE, 1968. Report on the... conference (organized by the National Productivity Centre... Singapore; sponsored by the Friedrich-Ebert-Stiftung, etc.). Singapore, [1968?]. pp. 132.

— Canada.

CANADA. Statistics Canada. Productivity Research and Analysis Section. 1971. Productivity trends in industry: indexes of output per person employed and per man-hour: petroleum refineries... 1959-1969. Ottawa, 1971. pp. 24. *In English and French.*

PORTER (ALLAN A.) Productivity, costs and prices: an examination of trends in selected manufacturing industries. Ottawa, 1973. pp. 366. *(Canada. Department of Labour. Economics and Research Branch. Occasional Papers. No. 7)*

— — Mathematical models.

SWAN (NEIL M.) Differences in the response of the demand for labour to variations in output among Canadian regions: a preliminary interpretation. Kingston, Ontario, [1971]. fo. 35. *(Kingston, Ontario. Queen's University. Institute for Economic Research. Discussion Papers. No. 41)*

— Germany, Eastern.

PABST (WILM K.) Arbeitsproduktivität als politökonomische Frage für Marxismus-Leninismus, UdSSR und DDR. Berlin, 1973. pp. 351. *(Berlin. Freie Universität. Osteuropa-Institut. Berichte: Reihe Wirtschaft und Recht. Heft 96)*

— India.

GAIHA (RAGHAV) Sector and system measures of labour productivity in the Indian economy. Delhi, [1972]. fo. 11.

NATIONAL PRODUCTIVITY COUNCIL, [INDIA]. Productivity trends in iron and steel industry in India. New Delhi, 1974. pp. 76.

— Jamaica.

JAMAICA. Department of Statistics. 1974. Production statistics, 1973 [i.e. 1960-73]. [Kingston, 1974]. pp. 35.

— New Zealand — Mathematical models.

HAZELDINE (TIM) Employment and output functions for New Zealand manufacturing industries. Coventry, 1973. pp. 67. *bibliog. (University of Warwick. Department of Economics. Warwick Economic Research Papers. No. 33)*

— Russia.

FILIPPOVA (GALINA DMITRIEVNA) Planirovanie proizvoditel'nosti truda v promyshlennosti. Moskva, 1973. pp. 152.

PABST (WILM K.) Arbeitsproduktivität als politökonomische Frage für Marxismus-Leninismus, UdSSR und DDR. Berlin, 1973. pp. 351. *(Berlin. Freie Universität. Osteuropa-Institut. Berichte: Reihe Wirtschaft und Recht. Heft 96)*

— United Kingdom.

U.K. Treasury. Information Division. 1949. The Productivity Campaign 1949: productivity pays... and how. [London, 1949?]. pp. 18.

U.K. National Board for Prices and Incomes. NBPI Guides. 4. Efficiency and productivity. London, [1969]. pp. 13. *bibliog.*

CHEMICAL AND ALLIED PRODUCTS INDUSTRY TRAINING BOARD [U.K.]. Working Party on the Training Implications of Productivity Agreements. The training implications of manpower productivity agreements; [C. Denard, chairman]. [Staines], 1970. pp. 13. *bibliog. (Information Papers. No. 4)*

ECONOMIC DEVELOPMENT COMMITTEE FOR THE AGRICULTURAL INDUSTRY. Productivity Steering Group. Farm productivity; a report on factors affecting productivity at the farm level; [Edmund Bacon, chairman]. London, H.M.S.O., 1973. pp. 15.

— United States.

KENDRICK (JOHN W.) Postwar productivity trends in the United States, 1948-1969. New York, 1973. pp. 369. *(National Bureau of Economic Research. Publications. No. 98)*

TURE (NORMAN B.) Tax policy, capital formation and productivity. New York, 1973. pp. 40.

PROFESSIONAL EDUCATION

— United Kingdom.

EDUCATION and the professions: [papers delivered at a conference of the History of Education Society, Manchester, 1972]; edited...by T.G. Cook. London, 1973. pp. 88.

— — British Empire.

JOHNSON (TERENCE JAMES) and CAYGILL (MARJORIE) Community in the making: aspects of Britain's role in the development of professional education in the Commonwealth. London, 1972. pp. 308. *bibliog.*

PROFESSIONS.

INTERNATIONAL LABOUR ORGANISATION. Advisory Committee on Salaried Employees and Professional Workers. 6th Session. Reports. 1. Item 1(c). General report: recent events and developments affecting salaried employees and professional workers; first item on the agenda. Geneva, 1967. pp. 84.

INTERNATIONAL LABOUR ORGANISATION. Advisory Committee on Salaried Employees and Professional Workers. 6th Session. Reports. 1. Item 1(a) and (b). General report: effect given to the conclusions of the previous sessions; first item on the agenda. Geneva, 1967. pp. 148.

LAMBINON (MAURICE) Pour une approche des professions libérales. [Bruxelles, Institut Economique et Social des Classes Moyennes, 1972]. fo. 61.

SOCIOLOGICAL REVIEW, THE; [published by] University of Keele. Monographs. [No.] 20 Professionalisation and social change; edited by Paul Halmos. Keele, 1973. pp. 338. *bibliogs.*

WYATT (RAYMOND G.) Is planning a profession?. Oxford, 1973. pp. 33. *bibliog. (Oxford Polytechnic. Department of Town Planning. Oxford Working Papers in Planning Education and Research. 18)*

INTERNATIONAL LABOUR ORGANISATION. Advisory Committee on Salaried Employees and Professional Workers. 7th Session. Reports. 1. Item 1(a) and (b). Effect given to the conclusions of the previous sessions: (first item on the agenda). Geneva, 1974. pp. 162.

INTERNATIONAL LABOUR ORGANISATION. Advisory Committee on Salaried Employees and Professional Workers. 7th Session. Reports. 1 Item 1(c). Recent events and developments affecting salaried employees and professional workers: (first item on the agenda). Geneva, 1974. pp. 81.

— Bibliography.

MOHN (N. CARROLL) Compensation of professionals: a selected and annotated bibliography. Austin, 1972. pp. 90. *(Texas University. Bureau of Business Research. Bibliography Series. No. 16)*

— France.

FRANCE. Direction de la Documentation. La Documentation Française. Notes et Etudes Documentaires. Nos. 3,792-3, 793. Les professions libérales en France; [by] Jean Defrasne. Paris, 1971. pp. 72.

FOURRE (JEAN) Les professions face aux réformes. Paris, [1972]. pp. 359.

— Russia.

BLIAKHMAN (LEONID SOLOMONOVICH) and SHKARATAN (OVSEI IRMOVICH) NTR, rabochii klass, intelligentsiia. Moskva, 1973. pp. 320.

— United States.

CONFERENCE ON THE UTILIZATION OF SCIENTIFIC AND PROFESSIONAL MANPOWER, COLUMBIA UNIVERSITY, 1953. Proceedings of a conference...;([convened by the] National Manpower Council). New York, 1954. pp. 197.

FREIDSON (ELIOT) ed. The professions and their prospects. Beverly Hills, [1973]. pp. 333. *bibliogs.*

PROFIT.

ROBBINS (HORACE H.) Fictive capital and fictive profit: the welfare-military state; a political economy based on economic fictions. New York, [1974]. pp. 417.

— Mathematical models.

LELAND (HAYNE E.) Why profit maximization may be a better assumption than you think. Stanford, 1972. fo. 35. *bibliog. (Stanford University. Institute for Mathematical Studies in the Social Sciences. Technical Reports. [New Series]. No. 80)*

— Russia.

MOLIAKOV (DMITRII STEPANOVICH) Pribyl' i rentabel'nost' promyshlennogo predpriiatiia. Moskva, 1967. pp. 146.

SELEZNEV (ALEKSANDR ZAKHAROVICH) Stimulirovanie effektivnosti proizvodstva i pribyl'. Moskva, 1973. pp. 159.

— United Kingdom.

U.K. Price Commission. 1973- . Data sheets. [London, 1973 in progress].

— United States.

AXILROD (ERIC) The U.S. rate of profit and national income accounts 1946-1965. Hong Kong, 1971. pp. 88. *(Hong Kong. Chinese University. Economic Research Centre. Industrial Country Series. Occasional Papers. 2)*

PROFIT SHARING.

COPEMAN (GEORGE HENRY) Employee share participation in nationalized and other enterprises. London, [1974]. pp. 18. *bibliog.*

— France.

FRANCE. Direction de la Documentation. La Documentation Française. Notes et Etudes Documentaires. Nos. 3,866-3, 867. L'actionnariat des salariés. [Paris], 1972. pp. 89. *bibliog.*

— United Kingdom.

BELL (D. WALLACE) Financial participation: wages, profit sharing and employee shareholding. London, 1973. pp. 84. *bibliog.*

ROBERTSON (JAMES HUGH) Common sense about profits. London, [1974]. pp. 32. *bibliog. (Liberal Party. Strategy 2,000. 1st Series. No. 5)*

PROFITS TAX

— Russia.

KUPRIIANOV (ANATOLII SERGEEVICH) Podokhodnyi nalog s pribyli. Moskva, 1973. pp. 126.

PROGRAMME BUDGETING.

FRANCE. Direction de la Documentation. La Documentation Française. Notes et Etudes Documentaires. Nos. 3,815-3, 816. Rationalisation des choix budgétaires: vers une nouvelle raison d'état?; [by] Philippe Huet [and others]. Paris, 1971. pp. 77.

HEGHE (G. VAN) Planning Programming Budgeting System: le planning par l'analyse de systèmes. Bruxelles, 1972. fo. 18. *bibliog. (Belgium. Institut Economique Agricole. Notes. No. 28)*

LYDEN (FREMONT J.) and MILLER (ERNEST G.) eds. Planning, programming, budgeting: a systems approach to management. 2nd ed. Chicago, [1972]. pp. 423.

HETTICH (WALTER) Bureaucrats and public goods. [Ottawa, 1973]. fo. 28. *(Carleton University. Carleton Economic Papers)*

NOVICK (DAVID) ed. Current practice in program budgeting (PPBS): analysis and case studies covering government and business. London, [1973]. pp. 241. *bibliog.*

— France.

FRANCE. Direction de la Documentation. La Documentation Française. Notes et Etudes Documentaires. Nos. 3,815-3, 816. Rationalisation des choix budgétaires: vers une nouvelle raison d'état?; [by] Philippe Huet [and others]. Paris, 1971. pp. 77.

HUET (PHILIPPE) and others. L'expérience française de rationalisation des choix budgétaires (R.C.B.). Paris, 1973. pp. 295.

— Italy.

CAPALDO (PELLEGRINO) Il bilancio dello stato nel sistema della programmazione economica. Milano, 1973. pp. 334.

— Nepal.

BEYER (JOHN C.) Budget innovations in developing countries: the experience of Nepal. New York, 1973. pp. 185. *bibliog.*

— Norway.

PROGRAMBUDSJETTERING: utredning I om utvikling og innføring av programbudsjettering i staten fra et utvalg oppnevnt av det kgl. Finans- og Tolldepartement den 26. april 1967. Oslo, 1972. pp. 162. *bibliog. (Norway. Norges Offentlige Utredninger. 1972.5)*

— Sweden.

SWEDEN. Försvarsdepartementet. Programbudgetgrupp. 1969. Planering och programbudgetering inom försvaret. Stockholm, 1969. pp. 315. *(Sweden. Statens Offentliga Utredningar. 1969.25)*

SWEDEN. Riksrevisionsverket. M-Kommitté. 1970. Förvaltningsrevision i staten: mål och statsförvaltningen. [Stockholm], 1970. pp. 224. *bibliog.*

SWEDEN. Riksrevisionsverket. M-Kommitté. 1971. Effectiveness auditing in government administration: goals and methods for examining the effectiveness of central government in Sweden: summary of a report by the Swedish National Audit Bureau, 1970. [Stockholm], 1971. pp. 99.

— United States.

LEE (ROBERT D.) and JOHNSON (RONALD W.) Public budgeting systems. Baltimore, [1973] repr. 1974. pp. 356. *bibliog.*

ROVETCH (WARREN) and GASKIE (JOHN J.) Program budgeting for planners: a case study of Appalachia with projections through 1985. New York, 1974. pp. 136.

SONENBLUM (SIDNEY) and others. Program budgeting for urban health and welfare services, with special reference to Los Angeles. New York, 1974. pp. 226. *(California University. Institute of Government and Public Affairs. Local Government Program Budgeting Series)*

PROGRAMMING (ELECTRONIC COMPUTERS).

ORCHARD-HAYS (WILLIAM) Advanced linear-programming computing techniques. New York, [1968]. pp. 355. *bibliog.*

SONQUIST (JOHN A.) and others. Searching for structure (alias, AID-III): an approach to analysis of substantial bodies of micro-data and documentation for a computer program (successor to the Automatic Interaction Detector program). Ann Arbor, Mich., 1971. pp. 287.

BAKER (LAURIE) A selection of geographical computer programs. London, 1973 [or rather 1974]. pp. 118. *bibliog. (London. University. London School of Economics and Political Science. Department of Geography. Geographical Papers. No. 6)*

PROGRAMMING (MATHEMATICS).

DYSON (ROBERT) Mathematical programming under uncertainty. Coventry, 1973. fo. 18. *bibliog. (University of Warwick. Centre for Industrial Economic and Business Research. [Warwick Research in Industrial and Business Studies]. No. 40)*

FATSEAS (VICTOR A.) Multi-goal decision model solutions by goal programming. [Sydney], 1973. pp. 84. bibliog. (New South Wales, University of. School of Accountancy. Research Monograph Series. 4)

PROGRAMMING, DYNAMIC.

See DYNAMIC PROGRAMMING.

PROGRESS.

EISENSTADT (SHMUEL N.) Modernization: protest and change. Jerusalem, [1966]. pp. 166.

EL'MEEV (VASILII IAKOVLEVICH) and KAZAKOV (ANATOLII PAVLOVICH) eds. Kommunizm i sotsial'nyi progress. Leningrad, 1973. pp. 326.

PROGRESSIVISM (UNITED STATES POLITICS).

CHRISLOCK (CARL H.) The Progressive era in Minnesota, 1899-1918. St. Paul, 1971. pp. 242.

KIRBY (JACK TEMPLE) Darkness at the dawning: race and reform in the Progressive South. Philadelphia, [1972]. pp. 210. bibliog.

THELEN (DAVID P.) The new citizenship: origins of progressivism in Wisconsin, 1885-1900. Columbia, Mo., [1972]. pp. 340. bibliog.

PROHIBITED BOOKS.

ATZROTT (OTTO) Sozialdemokratische Druckschriften und Vereine, (verboten auf Grund des Reichsgesetzes gegen die gemeingefährlichen Bestrebungen der Sozialdemokratie vom 21.Oktober 1878... Neudruck der Ausgabe Berlin, 1886; [with] Nachtrag, 1888). Glashütten im Taunus, 1971. 1 vol.(various pagings).

PROJECT METHOD IN TEACHING.

CUDDY (MICHAEL) Perspectives in the design and evaluation of educational projects. [Oxford], 1973. pp. 46. (Oxford Polytechnic. Department of Town Planning. Oxford Working Papers in Planning Education and Research. 16)

PROJECTILES, INCENDIARY.

STOCKHOLM INTERNATIONAL PEACE RESEARCH INSTITUTE. Napalm and incendiary weapons: legal and humanitarian aspects; SIPRI interim report [prepared by Malvern Lumsden from the papers of the SIPRI Symposium on Napalm and Incendiary Weapons held in Stockholm in 1972]. Stockholm, [1972]. fo. 125. bibliog.

PROLETARIAT.

MANDEL (ERNEST) and NOVACK (GEORGE) On the revolutionary potential of the working class. New York, 1969 repr. 1970. pp. 46.

SALIERNO (GIULIO) Il sottoproletariato in Italia: per un approccio politico e metodologico al problema dell'alleanza tra classe operaia e "Lumpenproletariat". Roma, [1972]. pp. 139. bibliog.

HERRE (GUENTHER) Verelendung und Proletariat bei Karl Marx: Entstehung einer Theorie und ihre Quellen. Düsseldorf, [1973]. pp. 200. bibliog. (Tübingen. Universität. Seminar für Zeitgeschichte. Tübinger Schriften zur Sozial- und Zeitgeschichte. 2)

PROLETARIAT in der BRD: Reproduktion, Organisation, Aktion; ([by] Martin Anders [and others]). Berlin, 1974. pp. 633.

PROMOTERS.

GROSS (JOSEPH H.) Company promoters. Tel-Aviv, 1972. pp. 264. (Tel-Aviv. University. Faculty of Law. Legal Studies. No. 2)

PROPAGANDA.

QUALTER (TERENCE HALL) Propaganda and psychological warfare. New York, [1962]. pp. 176. bibliog.

BARROW (JOHN PENROSE) The noble lie and the politics of reaction; [an] inaugural lecture... at University of London King's College June 5th 1972. [London, 1972]. pp. 19.

DOMENACH (JEAN MARIE) La propagande politique. 7th ed. Paris, 1973. pp. 128.

STOTT (WILLIAM) Documentary expression and thirties America. New York, 1973. pp. 361. bibliog.

PROPAGANDA, ANTIRUSSIAN.

STUK (ANATOLII IVANOVYCH) and TKACHUK (REM ANDREEVYCH) Dyversanty ŭ efiry. Minsk, 1970. pp. 78.

PROPAGANDA, ARAB.

PRITTIE (TERENCE CORNELIUS FARMER) The fourth Arab-Israeli war: the propaganda battle. London, [1974]. pp. 16. (World Jewish Congress. British Section. Noah Barou Memorial Lectures. 1973)

PROPAGANDA, COMMUNIST.

VOPROSY teorii i praktiki massovykh sredstv propagandy. vyp.4. Moskva, 1971. pp. 415.

AKADEMIIA OBSHCHESTVENNYKH NAUK. Kafedra Teorii i Metodov Ideologicheskoi Raboty. Voprosy teorii i metodov ideologicheskoi raboty. vyp.1. Moskva, 1972. pp. 454.

SPRAVOCHNIK propagandista. [vyp.6]. Moskva, 1973. pp. 271.

PROPAGANDA, ISRAELI.

PRITTIE (TERENCE CORNELIUS FARMER) The fourth Arab-Israeli war: the propaganda battle. London, [1974]. pp. 16. (World Jewish Congress. British Section. Noah Barou Memorial Lectures. 1973)

PROPAGANDA, RUSSIAN.

GOURE (LEON) The military indoctrination of Soviet youth. New York, [1973]. pp. 75. bibliog. (National Strategy Information Center. Strategy Papers. No. 16)

PROPERTY

TOENNIES (FERDINAND) Das Eigentum. Wien, 1926. pp. 50. (Vienna. Soziologische Gesellschaft in Wien. Soziologie und Sozialphilosophie. 5)

PRYOR (FREDERIC L.) Property and industrial organization in communist and capitalist nations. Bloomington, [1973]. pp. 513. bibliog. (Indiana University. International Development Research Center. Studies in Development. No.7)

— **Communist countries.**

STARODUBROVSKAIA (VERA NIKOLAEVNA) Kooperativnaia sobstvennost' v sel'skom khoziaistve sotsialisticheskikh stran. Moskva, 1970. pp. 352.

— **Norway.**

NORWAY. Statistiske Centralbyrå. 1973. Formuesstatistikk 1970: personlige inntektstakere og husholdninger, etc. Oslo, 1973. pp. 65. (Norges Offisielle Statistikk. Rekke A. 542)

— **Russia.**

EREMIN (AL'BERT MIKHAILOVICH) Otnosheniia sotsialisticheskoi sobstvennosti i ekonomicheskoe upravlenie: ocherk teorii. Moskva, 1973. pp. 119.

— **United Kingdom.**

POOLE (ERIC) English property law. London, 1973. pp. 413.

MILLER (JOHN GARETH) Family property and financial provision. London, 1974. pp. 310.

PROPERTY TAX

— **Denmark.**

DENMARK. Statens Ligningsdirektorat. 1973. Indkomst- og formueskat. København, 1973. pp. 266. (Meddelelser. 1)

PROPORTIONAL REPRESENTATION.

U.K. Parliament. House of Commons. Library. Research Division. Background Papers. No. 37. Proportional representation. [London, 1974]. fo. 8.

PROSPECTING.

UNITED NATIONS. Economic Commission for Asia and the Far East. Mineral Resources Development Series. New York, 1952 in progress.

PROSTITUTION

— **Belgium.**

HAECHT (ANNE VAN) La prostituée: statut et image. Bruxelles, [1973]. pp. 213. bibliog.

— **United States.**

PIVAR (DAVID J.) Purity crusade: sexual morality and social control, 1868-1900. Westport, Conn., 1973. pp. 308. bibliog.

PROTECTORATES.

JOHNSTON (W. ROSS) Sovereignty and protection: a study of British jurisdictional imperialism in the late nineteenth century. Durham, N.C., 1973. pp. 357. bibliog. (Duke University. Commonwealth Studies Center. Publications. No. 41)

PROTEINS.

U.K. Advisory Committee on Protein. 1974. British aid and the relief of malnutrition; report; [Sir Joseph Hutchinson, chairman]. [London], 1974. pp. 30. bibliog.

PROUDHON (PIERRE JOSEPH).

DUPRAT (GERARD) Marx Proudhon: théorie du conflit social. Paris, [1973]. pp. 176. bibliog. (Strasbourg. Université de Strasbourg 3. Institut d'Etudes Politiques. Cahiers. Nouvelle Série. 1.)

SAMPSON (RONALD VICTOR) Tolstoy: the discovery of peace. London, 1973. pp. 205.

PRUSSIA

— **Foreign relations — Bavaria.**

SCHMIDT (JOCHEN) Bayern und das Zollparlament: Politik und Wirtschaft in den letzten Jahren vor der Reichsgründung, 1866/67-1870: zur Strukturanalyse Bayerns im Industriezeitalter. München, 1973. pp. 442. bibliog. (Munich. Stadtarchiv. Neue Schriftenreihe. Band 64)

PSKOV

— **Politics and government.**

NOVIKOV (VIKTOR IVANOVICH) V.I. Lenin i pskovskie iskrovtsy. 2nd ed. Leningrad, 1972. pp. 267.

— **Social conditions.**

OB osnovnykh itogakh izucheniia biudzheta vremeni zhitelei gor. Pskova: doklad o rezul'tatakh issledovaniia, provedennogo v 1964-1967 gg. v sootvetstvii s programmoi sravnitel'nogo mezhdunarodnogo izucheniia biudzhetov vremeni v sotsialisticheskikh i kapitalisticheskikh stranakh. Novosibirsk, 1968. pp. 85.

PSKOV (OBLAST')

— **Statistics.**

PSKOV (OBLAST'). Statisticheskoe Upravlenie. Narodnoe khoziaistvo Pskovskoi oblasti: statisticheskii sbornik.[Pskov], 1972. pp. 256.

PSYCHIATRIC CLINICS
— Sociological aspects.

MOOS (RUDOLF H.) Evaluating treatment environments: a social ecological approach. New York, [1974]. pp. 388. *bibliogs.*

PSYCHIATRIC HOSPITALS
— Sociological aspects.

MOOS (RUDOLF H.) Evaluating treatment environments: a social ecological approach. New York, [1974]. pp. 388. *bibliogs.*

PSYCHIATRIC SOCIAL WORK.

CAPLAN (RUTH B.) Helping the helpers to help: mental health consultation to aid clergymen in pastoral work;...in collaboration with Gerald Caplan [and others]. New York, [1972]. pp. 241.

PSYCHIATRY.

FORREST (ALISTAIR) ed. Companion to psychiatric studies. Edinburgh, 1973. 2 vols. *bibliogs.*

GAY INFORMATION. Gay Liberation Pamphlets. No. 1: Psychiatry and the homosexual: a brief analysis of oppression. London, [1973]. pp. 32.

HONIGFELD (GILBERT) and HOWARD (ALFREDA) Psychiatric drugs: a desk reference. New York, 1973. pp. 227. *bibliog.*

SYMPOSIUM ON PSYCHIATRIC EPIDEMIOLOGY, 2ND, MANNHEIM, 1972. Roots of evaluation: the epidemiological basis for planning psychiatric services: proceedings...; edited by J.K. Wing and H. Häfner. London, 1973. pp. 360. *bibliogs.*

— Canada.

ADVISORY BOARD OF PSYCHIATRIC CONSULTANTS [CANADA]. The general program for the development of psychiatric services in federal correctional services in Canada; Plan d'ensemble de développement des services psychiatriques dans les services correctionnels fédéraux au Canada. Ottawa, Information Canada, 1973. pp. 60, 62. *In English and French.*

PSYCHOANALYSIS.

RACHMAN (STANLEY) ed. Critical essays on psychoanalysis. New York, 1963. pp. 284. *bibliogs.*

REICH (WILHELM) Dialectical materialism and psychoanalysis. London, [1972]. pp. 71.

BROWN (BRUCE) b. 1944. Marx, Freud, and the critique of everyday life: toward a permanent cultural revolution. New York, [1973]. pp. 202.

EYSENCK (HANS JÜRGEN) and WILSON (GLENN D.) eds. The experimental study of Freudian theories. London, 1973. pp. 405. *bibliogs.*

COLIN (HELENE) and PARADELLE (MICHEL) Les jeunes et le mouvement communautaire: approche sociopsychanalytique. Bruxelles, 1974. pp. 192.

SARTRE (JEAN PAUL) Between existentialism and marxism; translated from the French by John Matthews. London, 1974. pp. 302. *Essays and interviews from Situations VIII and IX.*

PSYCHOBIOLOGY.

DENENBERG (VICTOR H.) ed. Readings in the development of behavior. Stamford, Conn., [1972]. pp. 483. *bibliogs.*

The NATURE and nurture of behavior: developmental psychobiology: (readings from Scientific American); with introductions by William T. Greenough. San Francisco, [1973]. pp. 143. *bibliogs.*

PSYCHOLINGUISTICS.

LAMBERT (WALLACE EARL) Language, psychology, and culture: essays...; selected and introduced by Anwar S. Dil. Stanford, Calif., 1972. pp. 362. *bibliogs. (Linguistic Research Group of Pakistan. Language Science and National Development)*

ANNUAL ROUND TABLE MEETING ON LINGUISTICS AND LANGUAGE STUDIES, 23RD, GEORGETOWN UNIVERSITY. Language attitudes: current trends and prospects; Roger W. Shuy and Ralph W. Fasold, editors. Washington, [1973]. pp. 201. *bibliogs.*

ERVIN-TRIPP (SUSAN M.) Language acquisition and communicative choice: essays...; selected and introduced by Anwar S. Dil. Stanford, 1973. pp. 383. *bibliog. (Linguistic Research Group of Pakistan. Language Science and National Development)*

FRANK (ROBERT SHELBY) Linguistic analysis of political elites: a theory of verbal kinesics. Beverly Hills, [1973]. pp. 59. *bibliog.*

GOODGLASS (HAROLD) and BLUMSTEIN (SHEILA) eds. Psycholinguistics and aphasia. Baltimore, [1973]. pp. 346. *bibliogs.*

FODOR (JERRY ALAN) and others. The psychology of language: an introduction to psycholinguistics and generative grammar. New York, [1974]. pp. 537. *bibliog.*

PSYCHOLOGICAL RESEARCH.

ADAIR (JOHN G.) The human subject: the social psychology of the psychological experiment. Boston, [1973]. pp. 109. *bibliog.*

— Russia.

RAHMANI (LEVY) Soviet psychology: philosophical, theoretical, and experimental issues. New York, [1973]. pp. 440. *bibliog.*

PSYCHOLOGY.

BOYLE (D.G.) A students' guide to Piaget. Oxford, 1969 repr. 1970. pp. 156. *bibliog.*

LINDSAY (PETER H.) and NORMAN (DONALD A.) Human information processing: an introduction to psychology. New York, [1972]. pp. 737. *bibliog.*

BERNE (ERIC LENNARD) What do you say after you say hello?: the psychology of human destiny. London, 1974. pp. 457.

PETERS (RICHARD STANLEY) Psychology and ethical development: a collection of articles on psychological theories, ethical development and human understanding. London, 1974. pp. 480.

— History — Russia.

RAHMANI (LEVY) Soviet psychology: philosophical, theoretical, and experimental issues. New York, [1973]. pp. 440. *bibliog.*

— Mathematical models.

LAMING (DONALD) Mathematical psychology. London, 1973. pp. 388. *bibliog.*

— Methodology.

The STRUCTURAL approach in psychological testing; by Marvin L. Kaplan [and others]. New York, [1970]. pp. 195.

PSYCHOLOGY, COMPARATIVE.

PSYCHOLOGIE comparative et art: hommage à I. Meyerson. [Paris], 1972. pp. 306.

PSYCHOLOGY, FORENSIC.

DULOV (ATEIST VASIL'EVICH) Vvedenie v sudebnuiu psikhologiiu. Moskva, 1970. pp. 157.

DULOV (ATEIST VASIL'EVICH) Osnovy psikhologicheskogo analiza na predvaritel'nom sledstvii. Moskva, 1973. pp. 168.

PSYCHOLOGY, INDUSTRIAL.

BOLINDER (ERIK) and OHLSTRÖM (BO) Stress på svenska arbetsplatser: en enkätundersökning bland LO-medlemmarna rörande psykiska påfrestningar i arbetsmiljön. [Stockholm, 1971]. pp. 123. *bibliog.*

SILLS (PATRICK A.) The behavioural sciences: techniques of application. London, 1973. pp. 45. *bibliogs.*

PSYCHOLOGY, MILITARY.

JANOWITZ (MORRIS) ed. The new military:changing patterns of organization; research studies [resulting from the Inter-University Seminar on Armed Forces and Society sponsored by the Russell Sage Foundation]. New York, 1964 [repr. 1969]. pp. 369. *bibliog.*

PSYCHOLOGY, PATHOLOGICAL.

ANTHONY (HELEN SYLVIA) Depression, psychopathic personality and attempted suicide in a borstal sample; (a Home Office Research Unit report). London, 1973. pp. 43. *bibliog. (U.K. Home Office. Home Office Research Studies. 19)*

PSYCHOMETRICS.

GREEN (PAUL EDGAR) and RAO (VITHALA R.) Applied multidimensional scaling: a comparison of approaches and algorithms. New York, [1972]. pp. 292. *bibliog.*

KLINE (PAUL) ed. New approaches in psychological measurement. London, [1973]. pp. 269. *bibliogs.*

MEHRENS (WILLIAM A.) and LEHMANN (IRVIN J.) Measurement and evaluation in education and psychology. New York, [1973]. pp. 718. *bibliogs.*

PSYCHOTHERAPY.

TRUAX (CHARLES B.) and CARKHUFF (ROBERT R.) Toward effective counseling and psychotherapy: training and practice. Chicago, 1967 repr. 1973. pp. 416. *bibliog.*

PUANGUE VALLEY.

BORDE (JEAN) and GONGORA (MARIO) Evolucion de la propiedad rural en el Valle del Puangue. Santiago de Chile, 1956. 2 vols. *(Santiago de Chile. Universidad de Chile. Instituto de Sociologia. [Publications]. 1-2)*

PUBLIC CONTRACTS
— France.

LEBRETON (JEAN PIERRE) and ROBINET (ANDRE PAUL) La Commission centrale des Marchés: politiquè économique et réforme administrative. Paris, 1973. pp. 98. *bibliog. (Paris. Université de Paris II. Travaux et Recherches. Série Science Administrative. 6)*

PUBLIC DEFENDERS
— Russia.

GOL'DINER (VIKTOR DAVIDOVICH) Zashchititel'naia rech'. Moskva, 1970. pp. 167.

AVRAKH (IAKOV SOLOMONOVICH) Psikhologicheskie problemy zashchity po ugolovnym delam. Kazan', 1972. pp. 106.

PUBLIC HEALTH.

See HYGIENE, PUBLIC.

PUBLIC HEALTH RESEARCH
— Sweden.

SJUKVÅRDENS OCH SOCIALVÅRDENS PLANERINGS- OCH RATIONALISERINGSINSTITUT. Attitydundersökningar som medel för organisationsutveckling inom sjukvården; [with English summary; attitude surveys as a means of developing the organization in the National Swedish Health Service]. [Stockholm, 1972]. pp. 63. *(Råd. 1.1)*

PUBLIC HOUSING

— Europe.

FUERST (J.S.) ed. Public housing in Europe and America. London, 1974. pp. 216. *bibliog.*

— France.

PETONNET (COLETTE) Those people: the subculture of a housing project;...translated from the French by Rita Smidt. Westport, Conn., [1973]. pp. 293. *bibliog.*

— Italy.

— — Friuli—Venezia Giulia.

FRIULI-VENEZIA GIULIA. Assessorato dei Lavori Pubblici. 1965. L'edilizia popolare nel Friuli-Venezia Giulia. [Trieste, 1965]. pp. 62, 9 tables in end pocket.

CONVEGNO REGIONALE SULL'EDILIZIA POPOLARE, TRIESTE, 1965. [Atti]. [Udine, Regione Friuli-Venezia Giulia, Assessorato dei Lavori Pubblici, 1967]. pp. 149.

— United Kingdom.

REYNOLDS (INGRID) and others. Quality monitoring: a pilot survey of the quality and performance of local authority housing in England and Wales. [London], Department of the Environment, 1972. 3 vols.

SUTCLIFFE (ANTHONY) ed. Multi-storey living: the British working-class experience. New York, 1974. pp. 249.

WARD (COLIN) Tenants take over. London, 1974. pp. 176. *bibliog.*

— — London.

CHAPMAN (J.S.) Sample survey of London's housing waiting list, 1971/1972. [London], 1973. pp. 34. (*London. Greater London Council. Department of Planning and Transportation. Research Memoranda. 431*)

HAMMERSMITH. Department of the Borough Architect and Director of Borough Development. Living in a council flat: a survey of attitudes on five estates; (prepared... by Janet Thomson). London, 1974. pp. 68,fo.14.

— United States.

FUERST (J.S.) ed. Public housing in Europe and America. London, 1974. pp. 216. *bibliog.*

PUBLIC LENDING RIGHTS (OF AUTHORS)

— United Kingdom.

WRITERS ACTION GROUP. Ex libris: the working writers' report on PLR. London, [1972]. pp. 14.

PUBLIC OPINION

RONNENBERGER (FRANZ) Wege der Meinungsbildung in der komplexen Gesellschaft. Hannover, Niedersächsische Landeszentrale für Politische Bildung, 1972. pp. 84. *bibliog.*

— France.

FRANCE. Centre d'Etude des Revenus et des Coûts. 1971. Les Français et le vocabulaire économique: résultats et leçons d'une enquête. Paris, 1971. pp. 82. (*Documents. No. 9*)

LAPERRIERE (GUY) La "Séparation" à Lyon, 1904-1908: étude d'opinion publique. Lyon, 1973. pp. 220. *bibliog.* (*Centre d'Histoire du Catholicisme. Collection. No. 9*)

— South Africa.

SCHLEMMER (LAWRENCE) Privilege, prejudice and parties: a study of political motivation among white voters in Durban. Johannesburg, 1973. pp. 85.

— Sweden.

TÖRNQVIST (KURT) Attityder till några internationella problem och massmedier: en opinionsundersökning hösten 1969. Stockholm, 1970. fo. 23. (*Psykologiskt Försvar. Nr. 47*)

— Tanzania.

LEMA (A.A.) National attitude and educational innovation: a case study of change of attitude of the Tanzanian society towards education for self-reliance. Vienna, [1973]. pp. 34. (*Wiener Institut für Entwicklungsfragen. Occasional Papers. 73/8*)

— United Kingdom.

SOCIAL AND COMMUNITY PLANNING RESEARCH. Devolution and other aspects of government: an attitudes survey; prepared for the Office of Population Censuses and Surveys; [by Jean Morton-Williams]. London, 1973. pp. 158. (*U.K. Commission on the Constitution, 1969. Research Papers. 7*)

N.O.P. MARKET RESEARCH. Social Research Unit. Electors' preferences between working for private or nationalized industry; a report prepared for Aims of Industry... (synopsis by Aims of Industry). London, [1974]. pp. 2.

— United States.

HERO (ALFRED OLIVIER) American religious groups view foreign policy: trends in rank-and-file opinion, 1937-1969. Durham, N.C., 1973. pp. 552.

HIKEL (GERALD KENT) Beyond the polls: political ideology and its correlates. Lexington, Mass., [1973]. pp. 150. *bibliog.*

LAUDICINA (PAUL A.) World poverty and development: a survey of American opinion. Washington, D.C., 1973. pp. 126. *bibliog.* (*Overseas Development Council. Monographs. No. 8*)

MURPHY (WALTER F.) and others. Public evaluations of constitutional courts: alternative explanations. Beverly Hills, [1973]. pp. 63. *bibliog.*

PUBLIC OPINION POLLS.

NOELLE-NEUMANN (ELISABETH) Die Politiker und die Demoskopie: (Vortrag, gehalten...1967). Allensbach, [1968]. pp. 41.

GALLUP (GEORGE HORACE) The sophisticated poll watcher's guide. Princeton, [1972]. pp. 232. *bibliog.*

PUBLIC POLICY (LAW)

— United Kingdom.

JACKSON (DAVID C.) Law and public policy: the English connection; an inaugural lecture delivered... 23rd October 1973. Southampton, 1974. pp. 32.

PUBLIC RELATIONS

— Police.

EISENBERG (TERRY) and others. Police-community action: a program for change in police-community behavior patterns. New York, 1973. pp. 201.

— Social service.

SLADEN (CHRISTOPHER) Getting across: a publicity primer for voluntary organisations. London, [1973]. pp. 62. *bibliogs.*

PUBLIC RELATIONS AND POLITICS.

BLOOM (MELVYN H.) Public relations and presidential campaigns: a crisis in democracy. New York, [1973]. pp. 349. *bibliog.*

PUBLIC SERVICE.

PUBLIC service employment: an analysis of its history, problems and prospects: [essays originally presented at a conference held in 1972, jointly sponsored by the National Conference on Public Service Employment, the New Careers Development Center, and Social Policy magazine]; edited by Alan Gartner [and others]). New York, 1973. pp. 230.

NATIONAL PLANNING ASSOCIATION. Reports. No.137. A public service employment program: effective manpower strategy: a N.P.A. joint statement by the N.P.A. Board of Trustees [and others]. Washington, D.C., [1974]. pp. 22.

PUBLIC SERVICE COMMISSIONS — United States — District of Columbia.

COLUMBIA, DISTRICT OF. Public Service Commission. Annual report. a., 1968(56th)- Washington.

PUBLIC UTILITIES.

STEFANI (GIORGIO) ed. La produttività delle imprese pubbliche. Milano, [1973]. pp. 521. (*Centro Italiano di Ricerche e d'Informazione sull'Economia delle Imprese Pubbliche e di Pubblico Interesse. Studi e Documenti sul Settore Pubblico dell'Economia. 12*)

— Mathematical models.

BAILEY (ELIZABETH E.) Economic theory of regulatory constraint. Lexington, [1973]. pp. 200. *bibliog.*

— India.

ESSKEN ENGINEERING ENTERPRISES (P) LTD. and HAJRA (S.) Civic amenities in Greater Bombay: a survey... [for the] Economic and Scientific Research Foundation. New Delhi, 1972. pp. 176.

— Italy.

ZUELLI (FULVIO) Servizi pubblici e attività imprenditoriale. Milano, 1973. pp. 234. (*Bologna. Università. Seminario Giuridico. Pubblicazioni. 62*)

— United Kingdom.

MARTIN (MICHAEL J.C.) Management science and urban problems;... in collaboration with W.B. Wells [and others]. Farnborough, Hants, [1974]. pp. 209. *bibliogs.*

— United States — Finance.

FEREJOHN (JOHN A.) Pork barrel politics: rivers and harbors legislation, 1947-1968. Stanford, 1974. pp. 288. *bibliog.*

PUBLISHERS AND PUBLISHING.

MANGADA SANZ (ALFONSO) Calculo editorial: fundamentos economicos de la edicion. Madrid, 1972. pp. 580.

— Canada.

ONTARIO. Royal Commission on Book Publishing, 1970. Background papers. Toronto, 1972. pp. 395.

ONTARIO. Royal Commission on Book Publishing, 1970. Canadian publishers and Canadian publishing: [final report of the Commission; Richard Rohmer, chairman]. [Toronto, 1973]. pp. 371. *bibliog.*

— France.

LAFFONT (ROBERT) Editeur. Paris, [1974]. pp. 378.

— Germany.

DEUTSCHES BUCHARCHIV MÜNCHEN. Das Verlagswesen in der Bundesrepublik Deutschland. Rastatt, [1971]. pp. 72. (*Deutschland Report. 4*)

— Ireland (Republic) — Directories.

CASSELL AND COMPANY Cassell's directory of publishing in Great Britain, the Commonwealth, Ireland, South Africa and Pakistan, 1973-1974. 7th ed. London, 1973. pp. 560.

— Italy.

CENTRO STUDI FEDERLIBRO, FIM, SISM-CISL di VERONA. Mondadori per noi: monopolio e classe operaia. Verona, [1974]. pp. 198.

— New Zealand.

REED (ALEXANDER WYCLIF) Books are my business: the life of a publisher. Reading, 1966. pp. 131.

PUBLISHERS AND PUBLISHING. (Cont.)

— Pakistan — Directories.

CASSELL AND COMPANY Cassell's directory of publishing in Great Britain, the Commonwealth, Ireland, South Africa and Pakistan, 1973-1974. 7th ed. London, 1973. pp. 560.

— South Africa — Directories.

CASSELL AND COMPANY Cassell's directory of publishing in Great Britain, the Commonwealth, Ireland, South Africa and Pakistan, 1973-1974. 7th ed. London, 1973. pp. 560.

— Switzerland.

KROPF (LINDA S.) Publishing in Switzerland: the press and the book trade. Littleton, Colo., 1973. pp. 139. *bibliog.*

— United Kingdom.

JOSEPH (MICHAEL) The commercial side of literature. London, [1925]. pp. 254.

[ECONOMIC DEVELOPMENT COMMITTEE FOR PRINTING AND PUBLISHING]. Printing and publishing exports and imports in 1970. [London, National Economic Development Office, 1971?]. 1 pamphlet (unpaged).

PRINTING AND PUBLISHING INDUSTRY TRAINING BOARD [U.K.]. Report and statement of accounts. a., 1972/3- London. *Formerly included in the file of British Parliamentary Papers.*

STABLE (RONDLE OWEN CHARLES) and LEACH (Sir RONALD GEORGE) Report on the affairs of Maxwell Scientific International (Distribution Services) Limited, Robert Maxwell and Co. Limited and final report on the affairs of Pergamon Press Limited: investigation under section 165(b) of the Companies Act 1948. London, H.M.S.O., 1973. pp. 351-664,(15).

WARNER (OLIVER) Chatto and Windus: a brief account of the firm's origin, history and development. London, 1973. pp. 33.

BRIGGS (ASA) ed. Essays in the history of publishing in celebration of the 250th anniversary of the House of Longman, 1724-1974. London, [1974]. pp. 468.

THEN and now, 1799-1974, commemorating 175 years of law bookselling and publishing. London, 1974. pp. 219.

WALLIS (PHILIP) At the sign of the Ship: notes on the House of Longman, 1724-1974. Harlow, Essex, 1974. pp. 79.

— — Directories.

CASSELL AND COMPANY Cassell's directory of publishing in Great Britain, the Commonwealth, Ireland, South Africa and Pakistan, 1973-1974. 7th ed. London, 1973. pp. 560.

— — British Empire — Directories.

CASSELL AND COMPANY Cassell's directory of publishing in Great Britain, the Commonwealth, Ireland, South Africa and Pakistan, 1973-1974. 7th ed. London, 1973. pp. 560.

— United States.

EXMAN (EUGENE) The House of Harper: one hundred and fifty years of publishing. New York, [1967]. pp. 326.

PUERTO RICANS IN THE UNITED STATES.

FITZPATRICK (JOSEPH PARNELL) Puerto Rican Americans: the meaning of migration to the mainland. New Jersey, [1971]. pp. 192.

GARCIA OLIVERO (CARMEN SYLVIA) Study of the initial involvement in the social services by the Puerto Rican migrants in Philadelphia. New York, 1968 [or rather 1971]. pp. 316. *bibliog.*

LOPEZ (ALFREDO) The Puerto Rican papers: notes on the re-emergence of a nation. Indianapolis, [1973]. pp. 383.

WAGENHEIM (KAL) and WAGENHEIM (OLGA JIMENEZ DE) eds. The Puerto Ricans: a documentary history. New York, 1973. pp. 332. *bibliog.*

ROSENBERG (TERRY J.) Residence, employment, and mobility of Puerto Ricans in New York City. Chicago, 1974. pp. 230. *bibliog.* (*Chicago. University. Department of Geography. Research Papers. No. 151*)

PUERTO RICO

— Commerce.

PUERTO RICO. Department of Commerce. Boletin de estadisticas del comercio. a., Ap 1971 (v.2, no.2)- , with gap (no.3). San Juan.

— Constitution.

ESTEFANO (MIGUEL A.D') Puerto Rico: analisis de un plebiscito. La Habana, 1967. pp. 126.

— Economic conditions.

PICO (RAFAEL) The geography of Puerto Rico. Chicago, 1974. pp. 439. *bibliog.*

— Foreign relations — United States.

ESTEFANO (MIGUEL A.D') Puerto Rico: analisis de un plebiscito. La Habana, 1967. pp. 126.

— History.

LOPEZ (ALFREDO) The Puerto Rican papers: notes on the re-emergence of a nation. Indianapolis, [1973]. pp. 383.

— — Sources.

WAGENHEIM (KAL) and WAGENHEIM (OLGA JIMENEZ DE) eds. The Puerto Ricans: a documentary history. New York, 1973. pp. 332. *bibliog.*

— Population.

NERLOVE (MARC) and SCHULTZ (T. PAUL) Love and life between the censuses: a model of family decision making in Puerto Rico, 1950-1960. Santa Monica, 1970. pp. 105. *bibliog.* (*Rand Corporation.* [*Research Memoranda*]. 6322)

PUNISHMENT.

CUSTODIAL treatment of offenders: report of a conference at Ditchley Park, 27-30 April 1973; by T.P. Morris, conference rapporteur. Enstone, [1973]. pp. 34. (*Ditchley Foundation. Ditchley Papers. No. 45*)

INTERAMERICAN CONGRESS OF CRIMINOLOGY, 2ND, CARACAS, 1972. Corrections: problems of punishment and rehabilitation: [selected papers]; [edited by Edward Sagarin [and] Donal E.J. MacNamara]. New York, 1973. pp. 152. *bibliogs.*

MAESTRO (MARCELLO T.) Cesare Beccaria and the origins of penal reform. Philadelphia, 1973. pp. 179. *bibliog.*

— Russia.

NOI (IOSIF SOLOMONOVICH) Sushchnost' i funktsii ugolovnogo nakazaniia v Sovetskom gosudarstve: politiko-iuridicheskoe issledovanie. Saratov, 1973. pp. 193.

SHARGORODSKII (MIKHAIL DAVYDOVICH) Nakazanie, ego tseli i effektivnost'. Leningrad, 1973. pp. 160.

TITOV (NIKOLAI IVANOVICH) and ASATRIAN (GAGIK ZAVENOVICH) Vospitatel'noe vozdeistvie ugolovnogo nakazaniia. Erevan, 1973. pp. 103.

— South Africa.

STEYN (JAN HENDRIK) The role of punishment in the maintenance of law and order; an address delivered at the University of the Witwatersrand, May 1972. Johannesburg, [1972]. pp. 13. (*South African Institut of Race Relations. Topical Talks. 29*)

— United Kingdom.

BOTTOMLEY (A. KEITH) Decisions in the penal process. London, 1973. pp. 252. *bibliog.*

ADVISORY COUNCIL ON THE PENAL SYSTEM. Young adult offenders; report. London, H.M.S.O., 1974. pp. 265.

COOK (TIMOTHY) and GUNN (JOHN) Psychiatrist. Penal reform. London, [1974?]. pp. 44. (*Liberal Party. Strategy 2,000. 1st Series. No.4*)

— United States.

BECKER (GARY S.) and LANDES (WILLIAM M.) eds. Essays in the economics of crime and punishment. New York, 1974. pp. 268. (*National Bureau of Economic Research. Human Behavior and Social Institutions. 3*)

PUNJAB

— Appropriations and expenditures.

PUNJAB. Resources and Retrenchment Committee. 1939. Report; [Manohar Lal, chairman]. Lahore, 1939. pp. 503.

— Executive departments.

ARRORA (FAQIR CHAND) Commerce by river in the Punjab, or a survey of the activities of the Marine Department of the government of the Punjab, 1861-62 to 1871-72. [Lahore, 1930]. pp. 98,xxix. (*Punjab. Government Record Office. Monographs. No.9*)

PUNJAB. Resources and Retrenchment Committee. 1939. Report; [Manohar Lal, chairman]. Lahore, 1939. pp. 503.

PUNJAB (INDIA)

— Appropriations and expenditures.

PUNJAB (INDIA). Resources and Retrenchment Committee. 1950. Report; [Gopi Chand Bhargava, chairman]. Simla, 1950. pp. 161.

— Economic conditions.

HAJRA (S.) Bihar and Punjab: a study in regional economic disparity. New Delhi, [1973]. pp. 122.

— Executive departments.

PUNJAB (INDIA). Resources and Retrenchment Committee. 1950. Report; [Gopi Chand Bhargava, chairman]. Simla, 1950. pp. 161.

PURCHASING POWER

— France.

GOULENE (PIERRE) Evolution des pouvoirs d'achat en France, 1830-1972. Paris, [1974]. pp. 125. *bibliog.*

PURITANS.

WALLER (GEORGE M.) ed. Puritanism in early America. 2nd ed. Lexington, Mass., [1973]. pp. 204. *bibliog.*

ZIFF (LARZER) Puritanism in America: new culture in a new world. New York, [1973]. pp. 338.

QUALITY CONTROL.

ZAIKOV (GELII IVANOVICH) and ROMANOV (RAFAIL GAVRILOVICH) Uroven' kachestva i stoimost' produktsii. Moskva, 1970. pp. 119.

LAPIKUS (S.T.) Ekonomicheskie problemy povysheniia kachestva mashin. Kishinev, 1973. pp. 158.

OGRYZKOV (VITALII MIKHAILOVICH) Pravovoe regulirovanie kachestva produktsii. Moskva, 1973. pp. 288.

QUARRIES AND QUARRYING
— Environmental aspects.

DENBIGHSHIRE. County Planning Officer. Quarrying and the environment: a study of bulk mineral extraction: Denbighshire's status as a quarrying county: the aims of a planning policy on quarrying. [Ruthin, 1973?].. pp. 110,ix. *bibliog.*

— United Kingdom.

TILBURY GROUP. The Tilbury Group. [London], 1960. pp. 41.

— — Wales.

DENBIGHSHIRE. County Planning Officer. Quarrying and the environment: a study of bulk mineral extraction: Denbighshire's status as a quarrying county: the aims of a planning policy on quarrying. [Ruthin, 1973?].. pp. 110,ix. *bibliog.*

QUEBEC (PROVINCE)
— Economic conditions.

DRACHE (DANIEL) ed. Quebec: only the beginning: the manifestoes of the Common Front; [translations of manifestoes of various labour organizations]. Toronto, 1972. pp. 272.

SAINT-GERMAIN (MAURICE) Une économie à libérer: le Québec analysé dans ses structures économiques. Montréal, 1973. pp. 471. *bibliog.*

— Economic history.

FAUCHER (ALBERT) Québec en Amérique au XIXe siècle: essai sur les caractères économiques de la Laurentie. Montréal, [1973]. pp. 247. *(Centre de Recherche en Histoire Economique du Canada Français. Histoire Economique et Sociale du Canada Français)*

— Economic policy.

PARTI QUEBECOIS. Conseil Exécutif. Prochaine étape...quand nous serons vraiment chez nous. [Montréal, 1972]. pp. 139.

— Nationalism.

BERGERON (LEANDRE) Pourquoi une révolution au Québec?. [Montréal, 1972]. pp. 185.

DRACHE (DANIEL) ed. Quebec: only the beginning: the manifestoes of the Common Front; [translations of manifestoes of various labour organizations]. Toronto, 1972. pp. 272.

QUEBEC: the challenge from within; by a Canadian correspondent.London, 1972. pp. 16. *(Institute for the Study of Conflict. Conflict Studies. No.20)*

MORIN (CLAUDE) Le combat québécois. Montréal, [1973]. pp. 189. *bibliog.*

REGUSH (NICHOLAS M.) Pierre Vallières: the revolutionary process in Quebec. New York, 1973. pp. 211. *bibliog.*

— Politics and government.

QUEBEC: the challenge from within; by a Canadian correspondent.London, 1972. pp. 16. *(Institute for the Study of Conflict. Conflict Studies. No.20)*

NEATBY (H. BLAIR) Laurier and a Liberal Quebec: a study in political management;edited...by Richard T. Clippingdale. Toronto, [1973]. pp. 244. *bibliog. (Carleton University. Institute of Canadian Studies. Carleton Library. No. 63)*

RUMILLY (ROBERT) Maurice Duplessis et son temps. Montreal, [1973]. 2 vols.

RIOUX (MARCEL) Les Québécois. [Paris, 1974]. pp. 189. *bibliog.*

— Population.

AMYOT (MICHEL) and GEORGE (M.V.) Intraprovincial migration streams in Quebec and Ontario, 1956- 1961. Ottawa, 1973. pp. 51. *bibliog. (Canada. Statistics Canada. [Census Division]. Analytical and Technical Memoranda. No. 8)*

CHARBONNEAU (HUBERT) ed. La population du Québec: études rétrospectives. [Montreal, 1973]. pp. 111.

— Rural conditions.

VERDON (MICHEL) Anthropologie de la colonisation au Québec: le dilemme d'un village du Lac-Saint-Jean. Montréal, 1973. pp. 283.

— Social conditions.

RIOUX (MARCEL) Les Québécois. [Paris, 1974]. pp. 189. *bibliog.*

— Social policy.

PARTI QUEBECOIS. Conseil Exécutif. Prochaine étape...quand nous serons vraiment chez nous. [Montréal, 1972]. pp. 139.

QUEENSLAND
— Economic conditions.

AUSTRALIA. Department of National Development. 1969. Resources and industry of central Queensland; report. Canberra, 1969. pp. 131.

AUSTRALIA. Department of National Development. 1971. Resources and industry of far north Queensland; report. Canberra, 1971. pp. 199. *bibliogs.*

— Industries.

AUSTRALIA. Department of National Development. 1969. Resources and industry of central Queensland; report. Canberra, 1969. pp. 131.

AUSTRALIA. Department of National Development. 1971. Resources and industry of far north Queensland; report. Canberra, 1971. pp. 199. *bibliogs.*

QUIETISM.

ARMOGATHE (JEAN ROBERT) Le quiétisme. Paris, 1973. pp. 128. *bibliog.*

RABBE (ALPHONSE).

WIECLAWIK (LUCIENNE DE) Alphonse Rabbe dans la mêlée politique et littéraire de la Restauration. Paris, 1963. pp. 598. *bibliogs.*

RABINOWICZ (OSKAR K.)

RABINOWICZ (OSKAR K.) Sir Solomon de Medina,...and a biography of the author by Judith K. Tapiero and Theodore K. Rabb. London, 1974. pp. 155.

RACE.

RASSE in Wissenschaft und Politik; ([essays by] Hugo Iltis [and others]). Prag, [1935]. pp. 48.

BOISSEL (JEAN) Victor Courtet, 1813-1867: premier théoricien de la hiérarchie des races; contribution à l'histoire de la philosophie politique du romantisme. Paris, 1972. pp. 226. *(Montpellier. Université. Faculté des Lettres et Sciences Humaines. Publications. 36)*

BROWN (INA CORINNE) Understanding race relations. Englewood Cliffs, [1973]. pp. 275. *bibliog.*

BAKER (JOHN RANDAL) Race. London, 1974. pp. 625. *bibliog.*

POLIAKOV (LEON) The Aryan myth: a history of racist and nationalist ideas in Europe; translated [from the French] by Edmund Howard. London, 1974. pp. 388. *(Brighton. University of Sussex. Columbus Centre. Studies in the Dynamics of Persecution and Extermination)*

RACE DISCRIMINATION
— Law and legislation — United Kingdom.

WILSON (Sir GEOFFREY MASTERMAN) Amendments to the [Race Relations] Act: [address to a conference organised by the Bow Group and the National Association of Conservative Graduates, 10 November 1973]. [London, Race Relations Board, 1973?]. pp. 9.

— United States.

BOWERS (WILLIAM J.) Executions in America. Lexington, Mass., [1974]. pp. 489. *bibliog.*

RACE PROBLEMS.

ASAD (TALAL) ed. Anthropology and the colonial encounter. London, [1973]. pp. 286. *bibliog.*

BELL (WENDELL) and FREEMAN (WALTER E.) eds. Ethnicity and nation-building: comparative, international, and historical perspectives. Beverly Hills, [1974]. pp. 400. *bibliogs. Consists mainly of papers of the 12th Annual Convention of the International Studies Association.*

RABUSHKA (ALVIN) A theory of racial harmony. Columbia, S.C., 1974. pp. 106. *bibliogs. (South Carolina University. Institute of International Studies. Studies in International Affairs. No. 11)*

— Study and teaching.

TOWNSEND (HERBERT ELLWOOD ROUTLEDGE) and BRITTAN (E.M.) Multiracial education: need and innovation; the preliminary report of the Schools Council Education for a Multiracial Society Project. London, 1973. pp. 104. *(U.K. Department of Education and Science. Schools Council. Working Papers. 50)*

— Underdeveloped areas.

See UNDERDEVELOPED AREAS —
 Race question.

RADIĆ (STJEPAN).

KULUNDŽIĆ (ZVONIMIR) Atentat na Stjepana Radića i njegova prava pozadina. Zagreb, 1962. unpaged. *Offprints from Slobodni dom.*

RADICALISM.

HAMBURGER (GERD) Das kleine gelbe Schülerbuch. Graz, [1971]. pp. 160.

BROWN (BRUCE) b. 1944. Marx, Freud, and the critique of everyday life: toward a permanent cultural revolution. New York, [1973]. pp. 202.

LAKEY (GEORGE) Strategy for a living revolution. San Francisco, 1973. pp. 234.

NENNING (GUENTHER) Rot und realistisch: gesamtsozialistische Strategie und Sozialdemokratie. Wien, [1973]. pp. 420.

GREGOR (A.JAMES) The fascist persuasion in radical politics. Princeton, [1974]. pp. 472. *bibliog.*

RADICALISM IN BANGLADESH.

BRASS (PAUL R.) and FRANDA (MARCUS F.) eds. Radical politics in south Asia. Cambridge, Mass., [1973]. pp. 449. *(Massachusetts Institute of Technology. Center for International Studies. Studies in Communism, Revisionism and Revolution. 19)*

RADICALISM IN BELGIUM.

COLLARD (LEO) Front des progressistes et crise de la démocratie. [Nivelles, 1972]. pp. 156.

RADICALISM IN FRANCE.

NICOLET (CLAUDE) Le radicalisme. 4th ed. Paris, 1974. pp. 128. *bibliog.*

NORDMANN (JEAN THOMAS) Histoire des radicaux. 1820-1973. Paris, [1974]. pp. 529. *bibliog.*

RADICALISM IN GERMANY.

MANN (GOLO) Radikalisierung und Mitte: zwei Vorträge. Stuttgart, [1971]. pp. 48.

RADICALISM IN GERMANY. (Cont.)

HORCHEM (HANS JOSEF) West Germany: "the Long March through the institutions". London, 1973. pp. 20. *(Institute for the Study of Conflict. Conflict Studies. No. 33)*

— **Bibliography.**

SPALL (PETER VAN) compiler. Übersicht deutschsprachiger Periodika der unabhängigen sozialistischen Linken. Offenbach, 1973. pp. 40.

RADICALISM IN INDIA.

BRASS (PAUL R.) and FRANDA (MARCUS F.) eds. Radical politics in south Asia. Cambridge, Mass., [1973]. pp. 449. *(Massachusetts Institute of Technology. Center for International Studies. Studies in Communism, Revisionism and Revolution. 19)*

RADICALISM IN JAPAN.

KRAUSS (ELLIS S.) Japanese radicals revisited: student protest in postwar Japan. Berkeley, [1974]. pp. 192. *bibliog.*

RADICALISM IN RUSSIA.

LANG (DAVID MARSHALL) The first Russian radical: Alexander Radishchev, 1749-1802. London, 1959. pp. 298. *bibliog.*

ORLIK (OL'GA VASIL'EVNA) Peredovaia Rossiia i revoliutsionnaia Frantsiia, I polovina XIX v. Moskva, 1973. pp. 299.

LEVIN (SHNEER MENDELEVICH) Ocherki po istorii russkoi obshchestvennoi mysli, vtoraia polovina XIX - nachalo XX veka: [glavy iz dvukh nezavershennykh rukopisei, Raznochinskii period russkogo osvoboditel'nogo dvizheniia v osveshchenii dorevoliutsionnoi istoriografii i Krymskaia voina i russkoe obshchestvo; otv. redaktor S.N. Valk]. Leningrad, 1974. pp. 442.

SZAMUELY (TIBOR) The Russian tradition;...edited and with an introduction by Robert Conquest. London, 1974. pp. 443.

RADICALISM IN SRI LANKA.

BRASS (PAUL R.) and FRANDA (MARCUS F.) eds. Radical politics in south Asia. Cambridge, Mass., [1973]. pp. 449 *(Massachusetts Institute of Technology, Center for International Studies. Studies in Communism, Revisionism and Revolution. 19)*

RADICALISM IN SWITZERLAND.

JOST (HANS ULRICH) Linksradikalismus in der deutschen Schweiz, 1914-1918. Bern, [1973]. pp. 206. *bibliog.*

RADICALISM IN THE UNITED KINGDOM.

RUBINSTEIN (DAVID) ed. People for the people: radical ideas and personalities in British history. London, 1973. pp. 254. *bibliogs.*

SMITH (FRANCIS BARRYMORE) Radical artisan: William James Linton, 1812-97. Manchester, [1973]. pp. 254. *bibliog.*

MORRIS (ANDREW JAMES ANTHONY) ed. Edwardian radicalism 1900-1914: some aspects of British radicalism. London, 1974. pp. 277. *bibliog.*

RADICALISM IN THE UNITED STATES.

NEUHAUS (RICHARD) In defense of people: ecology and the seduction of radicalism. New York, [1971]. pp. 315.

POPOV (MILORAD I.) The American extreme left: a decade of conflict. London, 1972. pp. 19. *(Institute for the Study of Conflict. Conflict Studies. No. 29)*

CUTLER (RICHARD L.) The liberal middle class: maker of radicals. New Rochelle, [1973]. pp. 255.

DIGGINS (JOHN P.) The American left in the twentieth century. New York, [1973]. pp. 210.

MILLER (WILLIAM D.) A harsh and dreadful love: Dorothy Day and the Catholic Worker movement. London, [1973]. pp. 370. *bibliog.*

MOORE (ROBERT LAURENCE) ed. The emergence of an American left: civil war to World War I. New York, [1973]. pp. 212. *bibliog.*

SIRACUSA (JOSEPH M.) New Left diplomatic histories and historians: the American revisionists. Port Washington, N.Y., 1973. pp. 138. *bibliog.*

VEYSEY (LAURENCE R.) The communal experience: anarchist and mystical counter-cultures in America. New York, [1973]. pp. 495.

WATERGATE: the view from the Left; introduction by Linda Jenness and Andrew Pulley. New York, 1973. pp. 95.

BACCIOCCO (EDWARD J.) The new left in America: reform to revolution, 1956 to 1970. Stanford, Cal., [1974]. pp. 300. *bibliog. (Stanford University. Hoover Institution on War, Revolution and Peace. Hoover Institution Publications. 130)*

BAILEY (ROBERT) Radicals in urban politics: the Alinsky approach. Chicago, 1974. pp. 187. *bibliog.*

MILLER (SALLY M.) The radical immigrant. New York, [1974]. pp. 212. *bibliog.*

SAYRE (NORA) Sixties going on seventies. London, 1974. pp. 441.

RADIO.

UNITED NATIONS EDUCATIONAL, SCIENTIFIC AND CULTURAL ORGANIZATION. Department of Mass Communication. Reports and Papers on Mass Communication. Paris, 1953 in progress.

— **Germany — Laws and regulations.**

BERENDES (KONRAD) Die Staatsaufsicht über den Rundfunk. Berlin, [1973]. pp. 272. *bibliog.*

— **United States — Laws and regulations.**

ASHMORE (HARRY SCOTT) Fear in the air: broadcasting and the first amendment; the anatomy of a constitutional crisis. New York, [1973]. pp. 180.

RADIO ADVERTISING

— **United Kingdom.**

INDEPENDENT BROADCASTING AUTHORITY. The IBA code of advertising standards and practice. London, 1972. pp. 20.

RADIO AUDIENCES

— **Malawi.**

MALAWI. National Statistical Office. 1971-72. Radio listenership survey, August 1970 - January 1971 (and February 1971 - July 1971) (African households only, rural and non-rural areas). [Zomba], 1971-72. 2 pts.

RADIO BROADCASTING.

SMITH (ANTHONY) b.1938. The shadow in the cave: a study of the relationship between the broadcaster, his audience and the state. London, 1973. pp. 351. *bibliog.*

— **Austria.**

MAGENSCHAB (HANS) Demokratie und Rundfunk: Hörfunk und Fernsehen im politischen Prozess Österreichs. Wien, [1973]. pp. 472. *bibliog.*

— **India.**

ALL INDIA RADIO. Report on the progress of broadcasting in India up to the 31st March, 1939. Delhi, Manager of Publications, 1940. pp. 230.

— **Ireland (Republic).**

EIRE. Broadcasting Review Committee. 1974. Report. Dublin, 1974. pp. 198.

— **Italy.**

RADIOTELEVISIONE, informazione, democrazia: atti del convegno del P[artito] C[omunista] I[taliano] tenuto a Roma dal 29 al 31 marzo 1973. Roma, 1973. pp. 545.

— **Netherlands.**

VERKIJK (DICK) Radio Hilversum, 1940-1945: de omroep in de oorlog. Amsterdam, [1974]. pp. 832.

— **Russia.**

KOMMUNISTICHESKAIA PARTIIA SOVETSKOGO SOIUZA. O partiinoi i sovetskoi pechati, radioveshchanii i televidenii: sbornik dokumentov i materialov. Moskva, 1972. pp. 635.

— **Azerbaijan.**

RUSTANOV (TOFIG) Shagi v efire. Baku, 1968. pp. 15.

— **United Kingdom.**

GEDDES (KEITH) Broadcasting in Britain, 1922-1972: a brief account of its engineering aspects. London, H.M.S.O., 1972. pp. 63.

CHURCH OF ENGLAND. General Synod. Broadcasting Commission. Broadcasting, society, and the church; report of the... Commission. London, 1973. pp. 119. *bibliog.*

The FUTURE of broadcasting: a report presented to the Social Morality Council, October 1973 [by a commission under the chairmanship of Dame Margaret Miles]. London, 1974. pp. 100.

SMITH (ANTHONY) b.1938, ed. British broadcasting. Newton Abbot, [1974]. pp. 271. *bibliog.*

— **United States.**

SANGER (ELLIOTT M.) Rebel in radio: the story of New York Times 'commercial' radio station. London, [1973]. pp. 190.

RADIO IN ADULT EDUCATION.

PERRATON (HILARY DAVID) Broadcasting and correspondence. Cambridge, [1973]. pp. 42. *bibliog. (National Extension College. Reports. Series 2. No. 2)*

RADIO IN EDUCATION.

HALL (BUDD L.) Wakati wa Furaha: an evaluation of a radio study group campaign. Uppsala, 1973. pp. 47. *(Nordiska Afrikainstitutet. Research Reports. No. 13)*

RADIO IN POLITICS

— **Austria.**

MAGENSCHAB (HANS) Demokratie und Rundfunk: Hörfunk und Fernsehen im politischen Prozess Österreichs. Wien, [1973]. pp. 472. *bibliog.*

RADIO IN PROPAGANDA.

STUK (ANATOLII IVANOVYCH) and TKACHUK (REM ANDREEVYCH) Dyversanty ŭ efiry. Minsk, 1970. pp. 78.

RADIO IN RELIGION.

CHURCH OF ENGLAND. General Synod. Broadcasting Commission. Broadcasting, society, and the church; report of the... Commission. London, 1973. pp. 119. *bibliog.*

RADIOACTIVE FALLOUT.

NATIONAL RADIATION ADVISORY COMMITTEE [AUSTRALIA]. Biological aspects of fallout in Australia from French nuclear weapons explosions in the Pacific, July-September 1968. in AUSTRALIA. Parliament. Parliamentary papers, 1969, vol.1.

RADIOACTIVE WASTE DISPOSAL.

THIRIET (LUCIEN) and others. Problèmes techniques et économiques liés au développement des méthodes de traitement et d'utilisation des déchets radioactifs. Gif-sur-Yvette, 1968. pp. 46. *(France. Commissariat à l'Energie Atomique. Etudes Economiques) In English and French*

RADISHCHEV (ALEKSANDR NIKOLAEVICH).

LANG (DAVID MARSHALL) The first Russian radical: Alexander Radishchev, 1749-1802. London, 1959. pp. 298. *bibliog.*

RAILWAYS

— Construction.

SWITZERLAND. Kommission Eisenbahntunnel durch die Alpen. 1971. Eisenbahntunnel durch die Alpen: Schlussbericht der Kommission, etc.; [with Dokumentationsanhang]. Bern, 1971. 2 pts.

— Costa Rica.

TRANSPORTATION CONSULTANTS, INC. Republic of Costa Rica: report on port and railway study; prepared with the assistance of United Nations. Special Fund; executing agency: International Bank for Reconstruction and Development. [Washington, 1964]. 1 vol. (various pagings). *bibliog. Microfilm: 1 reel.*

— France.

GEOGRAPHIE économique et ferroviaire des pays de la C.E.E. et de la Suisse. Fascicule 6. France, géographie économique et ferroviaire, etc. [Paris. S.N.C.F., 1973]. pp. 335, 48.

— — History.

CARON (FRANÇOIS) Histoire de l'exploitation d'un grand réseau: la Compagnie du Chemin der Fer du Nord, 1846-1937. Paris, 1973. pp. 619. *bibliog. (Paris. Ecole Pratique des Hautes Etudes. Section des Sciences Economiques et Sociales. Centre de Recherches Historiques. Industrie et Artisanat. 7)*

— Germany — Employees.

BUSS (HANS JOACHIM) Dreimal Stunde Null: Gewerkschaft am Schienenstrang; Aufstieg und Wandlungen 1897-1972. Frankfurt/M., [1973]. pp. 187.

— Luxembourg.

SOCIETE NATIONALE DES CHEMINS DE FER LUXEMBOURGEOIS. Rapport annuel.a., 1970- Luxembourg.

— Netherlands.

NETHERLANDS. Werkgroep 'Spoorlijn Amsterdam-Den Haag'. 1969. Schiphollijn: eindrapport van de werkgroep. ['s-Gravenhage, 1970]. pp. 102.

— Norway.

NORWAY. Hovedstyret for Statsbanene, 1966. Statsbanenes moderniserings- og rasjonaliseringsplan, 1960-69; (oversikt pr. 31.12.1965). [Oslo], 1966. pp. 142.

NORWAY. Samferdselsdepartementet. 1972. Langtidsplan for NSB fram til 1980. Oslo, 1972. pp. 91. *(Norway. Norges Offentlige Utredninger. 1972.18)*

— Russia — Employees.

SILIN (IL'IA L'VOVICH) Kommentarii k Polozheniiu o rabochem vremeni i vremeni otdykha rabotnikov zheleznodorozhnogo transporta. Moskva, 1973. pp. 159.

— — Passenger traffic.

VLAIKOVA (IRINA ALEKSANDROVNA) and others. Zheleznodorozhnye passazhirskie perevozki i ikh effektivnost'. Moskva, 1973. pp. 176. *bibliog.*

— — Kazakstan — Employees.

ASYLBEKOV (MALIK KHANTEMIRULY) Formirovanie i razvitie kadrov zheleznodorozhnikov Kazakhstana, 1917-1970 gg. Alma-Ata, 1973. pp. 327. *bibliog.*

— — Turkmenistan — History.

STADELBAUER (JOERG) Bahnbau und kulturgeographischer Wandel in Turkmenien: Einflüsse der Eisenbahn ... in einem Grenzgebiet des russischen Machtbereichs. Berlin, 1973. pp. 520. *bibliog. (Berlin. Freie Universität. Osteuropa-Institut. Wirtschaftswissenschaftliche Veröffentlichungen. Band 34) With summaries in various languages; 11 maps in end pocket.*

— Uganda — Employees.

GRILLO (R.D.) African railwaymen: solidarity and opposition in an East African labour force. Cambridge, 1973. pp. 215. *bibliog. (Cambridge. University. African Studies Centre. African Studies Series. 10)*

— United Kingdom.

CALVERT (ROGER) Transport disintegrated: [with Improving London's rail transport]. London, 1973. pp. 144, 7.

U.K. British Railways Board. 1974. Channel tunnel: London-tunnel new rail link: a document for consultation. [London], 1974. pp. 23.

— — Finance.

JOY (STEWART CAMERON) The train that ran away: a business history of British Railways, 1948-1968. London, 1973. pp. 160.

— — History.

NEWTON (SURR CARL) Rails across the weald. Lewes, 1972. pp. 26. *bibliog. (East Sussex Record Office. Handbooks. No.4)*

JOY (STEWART CAMERON) The train that ran away: a business history of British Railways, 1948-1968. London, 1973. pp. 160.

— — Management.

LAMB (DAVID R.) Modern railway operation. 3rd ed. London, 1941. pp. 243.

— — Stations.

SARICKS (CHRISTOPHER LEE) Commuter choice and station catchment areas in metropolitan rail transport, with special reference to the London region; [M. Phil. (London) thesis]. 1973. fo. 154. *bibliog. Typescript: unpublished. This thesis is the property of London University and may not be removed from the Library.*

— — Ireland, Northern.

IRELAND, NORTHERN. Ministry of Commerce. 1956. Report of inquiry dated 11th September, 1956: Great Northern Railway Board: termination of certain services. Belfast, 1956. pp. 71.

— — London.

CROWTHER (G.L.) and others. A new RingRail for London: the key to an integrated public transport system. London, 1973. pp. 67.

SARICKS (CHRISTOPHER LEE) Commuter choice and station catchment areas in metropolitan rail transport, with special reference to the London region; [M. Phil. (London) thesis]. 1973. fo. 154. *bibliog. Typescript: unpublished. This thesis is the property of London University and may not be removed from the Library.*

ROBERTS (J.R.S.) Ringrail reviewed. [London], 1974. pp. 79. *bibliog.*

— United States — History.

FOGEL (ROBERT WILLIAM) Railroads and American economic growth: essays in econometric history. Baltimore, 1964 repr. 1970. pp. 296. *bibliog.*

MARTIN (ALBRO) Enterprise denied: origins of the decline of American railroads, 1897-1917. New York, 1971. pp. 402. *bibliog.*

— Zaire.

KATZENELLENBOGEN (S.E.) Railways and the copper mines of Katanga. Oxford, 1973. pp. 165. *bibliog.*

RAILWAYS, ELEVATED.

DE LEUW, CHADWICK, O hEOCHA. A study of intermediate capacity rapid transit systems; a report prepared for the Department of the Environment. [London, Department of the Environment], 1972. pp. (125).

RAILWAYS, INDUSTRIAL

— United Kingdom.

BRITISH IRON AND STEEL RESEARCH ASSOCIATION. Plant Engineering Division and Operational Research Section. Conference on works transport; held at Ashorne Hill...July 6th and 7th, 1954; chairman, W.F. Cartwright. London, [1954]. pp. 44.

RAILWAYS AND STATE

— France.

ADAM (JEAN PAUL) Instauration de la politique des chemins de fer en France. Paris, [1972]. pp. 207. *bibliog. (Rouen. Université. Publications. [Série Juridique. 14])*

DROUOT (GUY) and BONNAUD (JACQUES) Deux entreprises publiques devant leur avenir: Air-France et SNCF. Paris, 1973. pp. 240. *bibliog. (Université d'Aix-Marseille II. Faculté de Droit et de Science Politique. Travaux et Mémoires. No. 18)*

— Italy.

PAPA (ANTONIO) Classe politica e intervento pubblico nell'età giolittiana: la nazionalizzazione delle ferrovie. Napoli, [1973]. pp. 166.

RAND CORPORATION.

RAND CORPORATION. Rand 25th anniversary volume. Santa Monica, Ca., [1973]. pp. 239. *bibliog.*

RAPE

— Finland.

ANTTILA (INKERI) and others. Selvitys väkisinmakaamis: rikollisuuden lisääntymisestä; Forcible rape: an evaluation of the crime trend. Helsinki, 1968. fo. 31. *bibliog. (Kriminologinen Tutkimuslaitos. Sarja M.2) With English summary.*

RASKOLNIKS.

PODMAZOV (ARNOL'D ANDREEVICH) Tserkov' bez sviashchenstva. Riga, 1973. pp. 167.

RATHENAU (WALTHER).

ALDANOV (MARK ALEKSANDROVICH) pseud. [i.e. LANDAU (MARK ALEKSANDROVICH)] Iunost' Pavla Stroganova i drugie kharakteristiki. Belgrad, [1935?]. pp. 188.

RATIONING, CONSUMER

— India.

SINGH (VIDYA BHUSAN) An evaluation of fair price shops. New Delhi, [1973]. pp. 132.

RAVERA (CAMILLA).

RAVERA (CAMILLA) Diario di trent'anni, 1913-1943. Roma, 1973. pp. 698.

RAW MATERIALS

— Germany.

ROLSHOVEN (HUBERTUS) Mineralrohstoffe: Grundlage der Industriewirtschaft; die gegenwärtige Versorgung der Bundesrepublik Deutschland, etc. Essen, 1972. pp. 48. *bibliog.*

RAWLS (JOHN).

BARRY (BRIAN M.) The liberal theory of justice: a critical examination of the principal doctrines in a theory of justice, by John Rawls. Oxford, 1973. pp. 169.

RAZA UNIDA PARTY.

DOCUMENTS of the Chicano struggle. New York, 1971. pp. 15.

REACTOR FUEL REPROCESSING.

THIRIET (LUCIEN) Tailles et localisations optimales des usines de retraitement des combustibles nucléaires, etc. Gif-sur-Yvette, 1967. pp. (iii), 60bis. *bibliog. (France. Commissariat à l'Energie Atomique. Etudes Economiques)*. In English and French.

READING, PSYCHOLOGY OF.

TALOVOV (VALENTIN PAVLOVICH) O chitatel'skoi psikhologii i teoreticheskikh osnovakh ee izucheniia: opyt analiza materialov otechestvennoi literatury. Leningrad, 1973. pp. 77. *bibliog.*

REAL ESTATE BUSINESS

— Belgium.

VANDERMOTTEN (CHRISTIAN) Le marché des terrains à bâtir dans la région bruxelloise, 1912-1968. Bruxelles, 1971. pp. 257. *bibliog.*

— Italy.

PARRILLO (FRANCESCO) Il risparmio e l'intermediazione finanziaria nell'investimento immobiliare. Milano, 1973. pp. 111. *bibliog.*

— New Zealand.

URBAN REAL ESTATE MARKET IN NEW ZEALAND; [pd. by] Valuation Department, New Zealand. irreg., 1967/1969 [1st]- Wellington.

— United Kingdom.

U.K. Parliament. House of Commons. Library. Research Division. Background Papers. No. 35. Property companies and taxation. [London, 1974]. fo. 12.

REAL ESTATE INVESTMENT.

COOPER (JAMES R.) Real estate investment analysis. Lexington, Mass., [1974]. pp. 377. *bibliog.*

REAL ESTATE INVESTMENT TRUSTS

— France.

GUYÉNOT (JEAN) Les sociétés civiles immobilières de capitaux. Paris, 1972. pp. 267. *bibliogs.*

— United States.

GILLARD (MICHAEL) A little pot of money: the story of Reginald Maudling and the Real Estate Fund of America. London, 1974. pp. 170.

REAL PROPERTY

— Valuation.

DOBNER E. (HORST K.) Sistema y procedimientos de la tasacion aplicados al planeamiento de nuevos sistemas catastrales. Toluca, Direccion General de Hacienda del Estado de Mexico, 1972. pp. 103. *(Coleccion Estudios Fiscales. 2)*

— Denmark — Prices.

JØRGENSEN (AAGE) and JØRGENSEN (NIELS C.) Nogre faktorers indvirkning p'a ejendomspriserne i landbruget. København, 1971. pp. 70. *(Denmark. Landøkonomiske Driftsbureau. Memoranda. 3)* With English summary.

— Denmark — Valuation.

DENMARK. Statens Ligningsdirektorat. 1972. Vurdering af fast ejendom. København, 1972. pp. 76. *(Meddelelser. 2)*

— Ethiopia.

BERHANOU ABBEBE. Evolution de la propriété foncière au Choa, Ethiopie, du règne de Ménélik à la constitution de 1931. Paris, 1971. pp. 270. *bibliog. (Ecole des Langues Orientales Vivantes. Bibliothèque. 23)*

— France.

LIPIETZ (ALAIN) Le tribut foncier urbain: circulation du capital et propriété foncière dans la production du cadre bâti. Paris, 1974. pp. 297.

— Ireland (Republic) — Prices.

EIRE. Committee on the Price of Building Land. 1974. Report to the Minister for Local Government; [John Kenny, chairman]. Dublin, [1974]. pp. 125.

— South Africa.

ERWEE (J.A.) and BARNARD (J.) Trends in property sales in Port Elizabeth, Uitenhage and Despatch, Jan.-June 1972. Port Elizabeth, 1973. fo. 45. *(University of Port Elizabeth. Institute for Planning Research. Fact Papers. No. 5)*

— United Kingdom.

DALTON (PATRICK J.) Land law. London, 1972. pp. 316.

FORBES (Sir HUGH H.V.) Real property law. 3rd ed. London, 1974. pp. 198.

RIDDALL (JOHN GERVASE) Introduction to land law. London, 1974. pp. 351.

— — Prices.

DIFFEY (JAY) An investigation into the effect of high traffic noise on house prices in a homogenous sub-market. Keele, 1972. pp. 14. *(Keele. University. Statistical Research Unit in Sociology. Occasional Papers. No.1)*

— — Valuation.

LONDON. Greater London Council. Valuation and Estates Department. Work of the Valuation and Estates Department, 1965-1970. [London, 1970]. pp. 66.

LONDON. Greater London Council. Valuation and Estates Department. Land for London: work of the Valuation and Estates Department, 1970-73. [London, 1973]. pp. 72.

— United States — Valuation.

GOVERNMENT spending and land values: public money and private gain: (proceedings of a symposium sponsored by the Committee on Taxation, Resources and Economic Development...at the University of Wisconsin, Madison, 1971); edited by C. Lowell Harriss. Madison, 1973. pp. 239. *(Committee on Taxation, Resources and Economic Development. Publications. 6)*

REAL PROPERTY TAX

— Mexico.

LARIS CASILLAS (JORGE) and others. Sobre el impuesto predial. Toluca, Direccion General de Hacienda del Estado de Mexico, 1972. pp. 172. *(Coleccion Estudios Fiscales. 1)*

— Netherlands.

RAAD VOOR HET MIDDEN- EN KLEINBEDRIJF. Gemeentelijke onroerend goed-belastingen. [The Hague?, 1973?]. pp. 24.

— United Kingdom.

U.K. Parliament. House of Commons. Library. Research Division. Background Papers. No. 35. Property companies and taxation. [London, 1974]. fo. 12.

— United States.

PROPERTY taxes, housing and the cities; [by] George E. Peterson [and others]. Lexington, [1973]. pp. 203.

DOUGHARTY (L.A.) Forces shaping urban development: the property tax. Santa Monica, 1973. pp. 51. *bibliog. (Rand Corporation. [Papers]. 5022)*

REASONING.

DIETZGEN (JOSEPH) Pièces pour un dossier: L'essence du travail intellectuel; Ecrits philosophiques annotés par Lénine; [edited by] Jean Pierre Osier. Paris, 1973. pp. 249.

REBELO DA SILVA (LUIS AUGUSTO).

PAIXÃO (BRAGA) O historiador Rebelo da Silva, Ministro da Marinha e Ultramar, etc. Lisboa, Agência Geral do Ultramar, 1970. pp. 76.

RECIDIVISTS

— Italy.

ITALY. Direzione Generale per gli Istituti di Prevenzione e di Pena. Ufficio Studi e Ricerche. 1973. La recidiva postpenitenziaria: contributo a un'indagine comparativa internazionale. Roma, 1973. pp. 45. *(Quaderni. 6)*

RECLAMATION OF LAND

— Netherlands.

THIJSSE (J. TH.) Een halve eeuw Zuiderzeewerken, 1920-1970. Groningen, 1972. pp. 470. *bibliog.*

— United Kingdom

— — Wales.

DENBIGHSHIRE. County Planning Officer. Derelict land in Denbighshire: a report on the extent, nature and distribution of derelict land and the scope for reclamation. Ruthin, 1972. pp. 29.

MERIONETH. County Planning Office. Merioneth structure plan: (subject report no. 15): derelict land. Dolgellau, [1973]. fo. 35. *bibliog.*

— United States.

BERKMAN (RICHARD LYLE) and VISCUSI (W. KIP) Damming the West: (Ralph Nader's study group report on the Bureau of Reclamation). New York, 1973. pp. 272.

RECOGNITION (INTERNATIONAL LAW).

BELKHERROUBI (ABDELMADJID) La naissance et la reconnaissance de la République algérienne. Bruxelles, 1972. pp. 176. *bibliog.*

RECONSTRUCTION (1939—1951)

— France.

CAHIERS FRANÇAIS D'INFORMATION. [Paris], 1945-48. 12 parts.

— Germany.

LATOUR (CONRAD F.) and VOGELSANG (THILO) Okkupation und Wiederaufbau: die Tätigkeit der Militärregierung in der amerikanischen Besatzungszone Deutschlands, 1944-1947. Stuttgart, 1973. pp. 227. *bibliog. (Institut für Zeitgeschichte. Studien zur Zeitgeschichte)*

POHL (MANFRED) Wiederaufbau: Kunst und Technik der Finanzierung, 1947-1953; die ersten Jahre der Kreditanstalt für Wiederaufbau. Frankfurt/Main, [1973]. pp. 240. *bibliog.*

— Russia.

PRIKHOD'KO (IURII ALEKSANDROVICH) Vosstanovlenie industrii, 1942-1950. Moskva, 1973. pp. 287. *bibliog.*

RECONSTRUCTION (UNITED STATES).

TRELEASE (ALLEN WILLIAM) Reconstruction: the great experiment. New York, [1971]. pp. 224. *bibliog.*

COX (LAWANDA C.) and COX (JOHN HENRY) eds. Reconstruction, the negro, and the new South. Columbia, S.C., 1973. pp. 425.

MANTELL (MARTIN E.) Johnson, Grant, and the politics of reconstruction. New York, 1973. pp. 209. *bibliog.*

RECREATION

— Canada.

CANADA. Statistics Canada. Accommodation, food and recreational services: employment, earnings and hours of work. irreg., 1972- Ottawa. In English and French.

— — Newfoundland.

NEWFOUNDLAND. Department of Rehabilitation and Recreation. Annual report. a., 1973/4 [1st]- St. John's, Newfoundland.

— Germany — Bavaria.

BAVARIA. Staatsministerium für Landesentwicklung und Umweltfragen. 1973. Ergebnisse und Forschungen über das Freizeitverhalten. [Munich], 1973. pp. 52.

— United Kingdom.

NORTH WEST SPORTS COUNCIL. Leisure in the North West: the technical report of the Leisure Activities Survey of the...Council. Salford, [1972]. pp. 257.

— Bibliography.

RECREATION, leisure and tourism: sources of information; proceedings of a...conference held at the Library Association, London,...1972; edited by Ken Bradbury. London, 1973. pp. 85. *bibliog.*

— — Wales.

STANDING CONFERENCE ON REGIONAL PLANNING IN SOUTH WALES AND MONMOUTHSHIRE. Recreation in South Wales. n.p., 1973. pp. 64.

— United States.

BANNON (JOSEPH J.) ed. Outreach: extending community service in urban areas. Springfield, Ill., [1973]. pp. 219. *bibliogs.*

BOSCHKEN (HERMAN L.) Corporate power and the mismarketing of urban development: Boise Cascade recreation communities. New York, 1974. pp. 283. *bibliog.*

RECREATION AREAS

— Switzerland — Ticino.

TICINO (CANTON). Ufficio delle Ricerche Economiche. 1974. La posizione concorrenziale delle stazioni sciistiche ticinesi: studio comparativo della situazione del Ticino, dei Cantoni confederati e dell' Italia del nord sul 'Mercato della neve' nazionale e internazionale. Bellinzona, 1974. pp. 105. *(Documenti Economia di Montagna. 3)*

— United Kingdom.

SOUTH HAMPSHIRE PLAN ADVISORY COMMITTEE. Study Reports. Group D. People, Activities and Housing. No.5. Recreation. [Winchester], 1969. pp. 33, xvi.

U.K. Countryside Commission. 1971. Submission to Defence Lands Review Committee on the conservation of natural beauty and the use of the countryside for open-air recreation. [London], 1971. pp. 16.

SOUTHERN SPORTS COUNCIL. A discussion strategy for major recreational development in New Oxfordshire under local government re-organisation 1974. Reading, 1972. pp. 71.

DUNN (MICHAEL C.) Scenic routes and recreation planning: the Teme valley experiment, 1973. Birmingham, 1973. fo. 36. *bibliog. (Birmingham. University. Centre for Urban and Regional Studies. Research Memoranda. No. 27)*

— United States.

BURBY (RAYMOND J.) Household decision processes in the purchase and use of reservoir recreation land. Raleigh, 1971. pp. 213. *bibliog. (North Carolina University. Water Resources Research Institute. Reports. No. 51)*

KAVANAGH (J. MICHAEL) and others. Program budgeting for urban recreation: current status and prospects in Los Angeles. New York, 1973. pp. 107. *(California University. Institute of Government and Public Affairs. Local Government Program Budgeting Series)*

RECREATION RESEARCH.

CICCHETTI (CHARLES J.) Forecasting recreation in the United States: an economic review of methods and applications to plan for the required environmental resources. Lexington, [1973]. pp. 200. *bibliog.*

RECRUITING OF EMPLOYEES

— United Kingdom.

PLUMBLEY (PHILIP RODNEY) Recruitment and selection. new ed. London, 1974. pp. 211. *bibliog.*

RED CROSS.

HENTSCH (THIERRY) Face au blocus: la Croix-Rouge internationale dans le Nigéria en guerre, 1967-1970. Genève, 1973. pp. 307. *bibliog.*

— France.

FRANCE. Direction de la Documentation. La Documentation Française. Notes et Etudes Documentaires. Nos. 3,971-1, 972. La Croix Rouge française. [Paris], 1973. pp. 55.

RED SEA.

ABIR (MORDECHAI) Sharm al-Sheikh: Bab al-Mandeb: the strategic balance and Israel's southern approaches. Jerusalem, 1974. pp. 29. *bibliog. (Hebrew University. Leonard Davis Institute for International Relations. Jerusalem Papers on Peace Problems. No. 5)*

REED (ALEXANDER WYCLIF).

REED (ALEXANDER WYCLIF) Books are my business: the life of a publisher. Reading, 1966. pp. 131.

REFERENDUM

— Germany.

SCHAMBECK (HERBERT) Das Volksbegehren. Tübingen, 1971. pp. 41.

— Italy.

BONETTI (ALBERTO) and MONDUCCI (MARIO) 12 maggio '74: fine dell'ipoteca clericale; cronaca di un referendum. Manduria, 1974. pp. 133. *bibliog.*

REFORMATORIES

— United Kingdom.

GILL (OWEN) Whitegate: an approved school in transition. Liverpool, 1974. pp. 139.

TUTT (NORMAN) Care or custody: community homes and the treatment of delinquency. London, 1974. pp. 228.

— United States — Massachusetts.

CLOSING correctional institutions: new strategies for youth services; edited by Yitzhak Bakal. Lexington, Mass., [1973]. pp. 186. *bibliogs.*

REFORMATORIES FOR WOMEN

— United Kingdom.

RADICAL ALTERNATIVES TO PRISON. Holloway Campaign Group. Alternatives to Holloway. London, [1972]. pp. 71.

— United States.

GIALLOMBARDO (ROSE) The social world of imprisoned girls: a comparative study of institutions for juvenile delinquents. New York, [1974]. pp. 317.

REFUGEES, AFRICAN.

INTERNATIONAL UNIVERSITY EXCHANGE FUND. Ten years of assistance to African refugees through international cooperation. [Geneva, 1972]. pp. 107.

REFUGEES, ARAB.

TOMEH (GEORGE J.) Legal status of Arab refugees. Beirut, 1969. pp. 26. *(Institute for Palestine Studies. Monograph Series. No. 20) (Reprinted from Law and Contemporary Problems, 1968)*

BEN-PORATH (YORAM) and MARX (EMANUEL) Some sociological and economic aspects of refugee camps on the West Bank. Santa Monica, 1971. pp. 78. *(Rand Corporation. [Rand Reports]. 835)*

TESSIER (ARLETTE) Gaza. Beirut, [1971]. pp. 36. *(Palestine Research Center. Palestine Essays. No. 27)*

COOLEY (JOHN K.) Green March, Black September: the story of the Palestinian Arabs. London, 1973. pp. 263. *bibliog.*

REFUGEES, AUSTRIAN.

MUESSENER (HELMUT) Exil in Schweden: politische und kulturelle Emigration nach 1933. München, [1974]. pp. 604. *bibliog.*

STADLER (KARL RUDOLF) Opfer verlorener Zeiten: Geschichte der Schutzbund- Emigration, 1934. Wien, [1974]. pp. 397. *(Ludwig-Boltzmann-Institut für Geschichte der Arbeiterbewegung. Veröffentlichungen)*

REFUGEES, DUTCH.

SCHILLING (HEINZ) Niederländische Exulanten im 16. Jahrhundert: ihre Stellung im Sozialgefüge und im religiösen Leben deutscher und englischer Städte. Gütersloh, [1972]. pp. 200. *bibliog. (Verein für Reformationsgeschichte. Schriften. Nr.187)*

REFUGEES, GERMAN.

ROEDER (WERNER) Die deutschen Exilgruppen in Grossbritannien, 1940-1945: ein Beitrag zur Geschichte des Widerstandes gegen den Nationalsozialismus. 2nd ed. Bonn-Bad Godesberg, [1973]. pp. 322. *bibliog. (Friedrich-Ebert-Stiftung. Forschungsinstitut. Schriftenreihe. Band 58)*

MUESSENER (HELMUT) Exil in Schweden: politische und kulturelle Emigration nach 1933. München, [1974]. pp. 604. *bibliog.*

REFUGEES, JEWISH.

SCHOLZ (WILHELM) Ein Weg ins Leben: das neue Österreich und die Judenfrage. London, 1943. pp. 16.

REFUGEES, RELIGIOUS.

SCHILLING (HEINZ) Niederländische Exulanten im 16. Jahrhundert: ihre Stellung im Sozialgefüge und im religiosen Leben deutscher und englischer Städte. Gütersloh, [1972]. pp. 200. *bibliog. (Verein für Reformationsgeschichte. Schriften. Nr.187)*

MAGEN (BEATE) Die Wallonengemeinde in Canterbury von ihrer Gründung bis zum Jahre 1635. Bern, 1973. pp. 287. *bibliog.*

REFUGEES, RUSSIAN.

YOUNG Russia. [Paris, imprint], 1933. pp. 8.

REFUGEES IN AFRICA.

BROOKS (HUGH C.) and EL-AYOUTY (YASSIN) eds. Refugees south of the Sahara: an African dilemma. Westport, conn [1970]. pp. 307.

REFUGEES IN GERMANY.

SCHILLING (HEINZ) Niederländische Exulanten im 16. Jahrhundert: ihre Stellung im Sozialgefüge und im religiösen Leben deutscher und englischer Städte. Gütersloh, [1972]. pp. 200. *bibliog. (Verein für Reformationsgeschichte. Schriften. Nr.187)*

ZIEMER (GERHARD) Deutscher Exodus: Vertreibung und Eingliederung von 15 Millionen Ostdeutschen. Stuttgart, 1973. pp. 246. *bibliog.*

REFUGEES IN RUSSIA.

REFUGEES IN RUSSIA.
STADLER (KARL RUDOLF) Opfer verlorener Zeiten: Geschichte der Schutzbund- Emigration, 1934. Wien, [1974]. pp. 397. (*Ludwig-Boltzmann-Institut für Geschichte der Arbeiterbewegung. Veröffentlichungen*)

REFUGEES IN SWEDEN.
MUESSENER (HELMUT) Exil in Schweden: politische und kulturelle Emigration nach 1933. München, [1974]. pp. 604. *bibliog.*

REFUGEES IN THE CENTRAL AFRICAN REPUBLIC.
GOSSELIN (G.) Le changement social et les institutions du développement dans une population réfugiée;... avec une introduction par Raymond Apthorpe. (UNRISD Reports. No.70.17) (UNRISD/70/C.61). Genève, Institut de Recherche des Nations Unies pour le Développement Social, 1970. pp. 112. *bibliog.*

REFUGEES IN THE UNITED KINGDOM.
BRITISH COUNCIL FOR AID TO REFUGEES. Annual report. a., 1967/8- London.

SCHILLING (HEINZ) Niederländische Exulanten im 16. Jahrhundert: ihre Stellung im Sozialgefüge und im religiosen Leben deutscher und englischer Städte. Gütersloh, [1972]. pp. 200. *bibliog. (Verein für Reformationsgeschichte. Schriften. Nr.187)*

MAMDANI (MAHMOOD) From citizen to refugee: Uganda Asians come to Britain. London, 1973. pp. 127.

ROEDER (WERNER) Die deutschen Exilgruppen in Grossbritannien, 1940-1945: ein Beitrag zur Geschichte des Widerstandes gegen den Nationalsozialismus. 2nd ed. Bonn-Bad Godesberg, [1973]. pp. 322. *bibliog. (Friedrich-Ebert-Stiftung. Forschungsinstitut. Schriftenreihe. Band 58)*

REFUGEES IN UGANDA.
TRAPPE (PAUL) Social change and development institutions in a refugee population: development from below as an alternative; the case of the Nakapiripirit settlement scheme in Uganda. (UNRISD Reports. No.71.2) (UNRISD/71.C.87). Geneva, United Nations Research Institute for Social Development, 1971. pp. 102. *bibliog.*

REFUSE AND REFUSE DISPOSAL
— Germany — Hesse.

FRANKFURT AM MAIN. Stadtreinigungsamt. 100 Jahre Stadtreinigung Frankfurt am Main, 1872-1972. Frankfurt am Main, [1972]. pp. 68.

— United Kingdom.

REPORT on litter in the countryside: [by a steering committee of surveyors and public health inspectors employed by Bedford County Council and local authorities in the county]. Bedford, 1971. pp. 20.

— United States.

DICKEY (JOHN W.) and others. Technology assessment: its application to the solid waste management programs of urban governments. Lexington, Mass., [1973]. pp. 194. *bibliog.*

VAN TASSEL (ALFRED J.) ed. Our environment: the outlook for 1980. Lexington, Mass., [1973]. pp. 589. *bibliogs.*

REGGIO NELL'EMILIA (PROVINCE)
— History.

REGGIO NELL'EMILIA (PROVINCE). Amministrazione Provinciale. La donna reggiana nella Resistenza: atti del convegno tenuta... 5 aprile 1965. [Reggio Emilia, 1967]. pp. 122.

CAVANDOLI (ROLANDO) Le origini del fascismo a Reggio Emilia. Roma, [1972]. pp. 271. *bibliog.*

REGICIDES.
WALZER (MICHAEL) ed. Regicide and revolution: speeches at the trial of Louis XVI;...translated by Marian Rothstein. London, 1974. pp. 219.

REGIONAL PLANNING.
POLISH-EGYPTIAN SEMINAR, 2nd SESSION, WARSAW, 1970. Long-range and regional planning: papers delivered at the. Warszawa, 1971. pp. 259. (*Instytut Gospodarki Krajow Rozwijajacych Sie. Prace i Materialy. No. 5*)

FALUDI (ANDREAS K.F.) Planning theory. Oxford, 1973. pp. 306. *bibliogs.*

KOZŁOWSKI (JERZY) Analiza progowa za granicą: próba oceny i rozwinięcia. Warszawa, 1973. pp. 123. *bibliog. (Polska Akademia Nauk. Komitet Przestrzennego Zagospodarowania Kraju. Studia. t. 42)* With Russian and English summaries.

NORTH ATLANTIC TREATY ORGANIZATION. Committee on the Challenge of Modern Society. 1973. Environment and regional planning: a pilot study, etc. [Brussels?, 1973?]. 1 vol. (various pagings). (*Environmental Studies. No. 17*)

ORTMANN (FRIEDRICH) Überlegungen zur regionalpolitischen Anwendbarkeit des Multiplikatorkonzeptes. Tübingen, 1973. pp. 184. *bibliog. (Kiel. Universität. Institut für Weltwirtschaft. Kieler Studien. 122)*

PLANNING regional development programs: five case studies from Ethiopia, Bolivia, Nepal, Peru, Zambia; [by] Christian Heimpel [and others]. Berlin, 1973. pp. 317. *bibliog. (Deutsches Institut für Entwicklungspolitik. Occasional Papers. No.15)*

GLASSON (JOHN) An introduction to regional planning : concepts, theory and practice. London, 1974. pp. 337. *bibliog.*

RATCLIFFE (JOHN) An introduction to town and country planning. London, 1974. pp. 378. *bibliogs.*

— Mathematical models.

MOGRIDGE (MARTIN J.H.) The use and misuse of entropy in urban and regional modelling of economic and spatial systems. London, 1972. pp. 46. *bibliog. (Centre for Environmental Studies. Working Papers. 80)*

BROADBENT (T.A.) Activity analysis of spatial allocation models. London, 1973. pp. 41. *bibliog. (Centre for Environmental Studies. Working Papers. 82)*

HARRIS (CURTIS C.) The urban economies, 1985: a multiregional multi-industry forecasting model. Lexington, Mass., [1973]. pp. 230.

REIF (BENJAMIN) Models in urban and regional planning. Aylesbury, 1973. pp. 246. *bibliog.*

WILSON (ALAN GEOFFREY) Urban and regional models in geography and planning. London, [1974]. pp. 418. *bibliogs.*

— Research.

FORBES (JEAN) ed. Studies in social science and planning. Edinburgh, 1974. pp. 321. *bibliogs.*

— — Sweden.

SWEDEN. Statens Råd för Byggnadsforskning. 1971. Urban and regional research in Sweden; etc. Stockholm, 1971. pp. 145. (*Sweden. Statens Institut för Byggnadsforskning. Documents. 1971. 4*) In English, French and Russian.

— — United Kingdom.

CENTRE FOR ENVIRONMENTAL STUDIES. Information Papers. 28. Urban and regional research in the United Kingdom 1972-1973: an annotated list. London, 1973. 1 vol. (unpaged).

— Africa.

URBANIZATION, national development, and regional planning in Africa: [papers of an interdisciplinary panel presented as part of the African Studies Association's fifteenth annual meeting, 1972]; (edited by Salah El-Shakhs [and] Robert Obudho). New York, 1974. pp. 227. *bibliog.*

— America, Latin.

LATIN American urban research; [series editors] Francine F. Rabinovitz and Felicity M. Trueblood. Beverly Hills, [1971 in progress]. *bibliogs.*

— Australia.

HARRISON (PETER) Post-war planning in the capital cities of the mainland states. Canberra, 1972. fo. 25. *bibliog.*

— — New South Wales.

NEW SOUTH WALES. Premier's Department. Upper Hunter Regional Development Committee. 1968. Report on development of the upper Hunter region. [Sydney, 1968]. pp. 58, 1 map. *Loose-leaf binder.*

— — Victoria.

MELBOURNE AND METROPOLITAN BOARD OF WORKS. Planning policies for the Melbourne metropolitan region. [Melbourne], 1971. pp. 113.

— Austria.

WURZER (RUDOLF) Raumordnung Vorarlberg. [Bregenz], Amt der Vorarlberger Landesregierung, 1971. 2 vols.

— Belgium.

DORNBURG (CHRISTIAN) Regionale Struktur und staatliche Entwicklungsplanung im Problemgebiet Westhoek, Provinz Westflandern/Belgien. Bonn, 1971. pp. 65. *bibliog. (Deutscher Verband für Wohnungswesen, Städtebau und Raumplanung. Kleine Schriften. 41)*

— Brazil.

BRAZIL. Superintendência do Desenvolvimento do Nordeste. Assessoria Tecnica. Relatorio anual. a., 1970- Recife.

— Canada — Quebec.

QUEBEC (PROVINCE). Office de Planification et de Développement. Rapport. a., 1971/2- Québec.

— Colombia.

PAETZ (HANS JUERGEN) Regionale Entwicklungsgesellschaften in Kolumbien. Göttingen, [1970]. pp. 133. *bibliog. (Göttingen. Universität. Ibero-Amerika- Institut für Wirtschaftsforschung. Arbeitsberichte. Heft 8)*

— Denmark.

ILLERIS (SVEN) and PEDERSEN (POUL OVE) eds. Regionaludvikling i Danmark: en artikelsamling om anvendelsen af regionalanalytiske metoder på danske forhold. [Copenhagen], 1973. pp. 261. *bibliogs.*

— Europe.

REGIONAL policy and planning for Europe: [papers of a seminar held at the University of East Anglia in September 1973]; edited by Morgan Sant. Farnborough, Hants, [1974]. pp. 268.

— France.

GODCHOT (JACQUES E.) Les sociétés d'économie mixte et l'aménagement du territoire. Paris, 1958. pp. 223. *bibliog.*

BOUDEVILLE (JACQUES R.) Aménagement du territoire et polarisation. Paris, [1972]. pp. 279.

FRANCE. Ministère de l'Equipement et du Logement. Direction départementale de la Loire-Atlantique. 1972. Livre blanc d'agglomération Saint Nazaire-La Baule 1971. [Nantes, 1972?]. pp. 115.

REGIONAL PLANNING.

FRANCE. Secrétariat Général de la Zone d'Appui Nord Champenoise. 1972. Perspectives de développement: l'espace Nord Champenoise. [Paris, 1972]. pp. 128. bibliog. (France. Délégation à l'Aménagement du Territoire et à l'Action Régionale. Travaux et Recherches de Prospective. 24)

— Germany.

SCHWENKE (HELMUT) Die Förderung und Entwicklung der Wirtschaft im Landkreis Lüchow-Dannenberg: eine Betrachtung und Beurteilung regionaler Förderungspolitik. Berlin, 1970. pp. 305. bibliog.

FORSCHUNGSGESELLSCHAFT FÜR AGRARPOLITIK UND AGRARSOZIOLOGIE. Forschungsstelle. Strukturwandel und Strukturpolitik: Beiträge zur agrarischen und regionalen Entwicklung in der Bundesrepublik Deutschland; ... (Heinrich Niehaus ...zum 75.Geburtstag...zugeeignet). Bonn, 1973. pp. 271. bibliogs.

— — Baden—Württemberg.

KREUTER (HANSHEINZ) Industrielle Standortaffinität und regionalpolitische Standortlenkung, dargestellt am Beispiel Baden-Württembergs.Berlin, [1974]. pp. 426. bibliog. With summaries in English and French.

— — Bavaria.

BAVARIA. Staatsministerium für Landesentwicklung und Umweltfragen. 1973. Landesplanung in Bayern: eine Einführung. [Munich], 1973. pp. 64.

— India.

SHARMA (PREM S.) Agricultural regionalisation of India. Delhi, 1973. pp. 190. bibliog.

— — Maharashtra.

SATHE (MADHUSUDAN DATTATRAYA) Regional planning: an areal exercise. Poona, 1973. pp. 229.

— Ireland (Republic).

SHANNON FREE AIRPORT DEVELOPMENT COMPANY and MUINTIR NA TIRE. The Mid-West Region Parish Resource Survey: report. [Shannon], 1972. fo. 76.

— Italy.

I COMPRENSORI nella provincia de Bologna: studi, documenti, statistiche e bibliografia; [by a study group]. Bologna, 1968. pp. 236. bibliog. (Bologna (Province). Collana di Studi e Monografie)

— Kenya.

KENYA. Town Planning Department. 1970. Western Province regional physical development plan. [Nairobi, 1970]. 1 vol. (various pagings).

— Netherlands.

WEST-Nederland, chaotische planning of geplande chaos?; met bijdragen van W. Steigenga [and others; papers of a congress held in October 1972 by the Vereniging van Utrechtse Geografische Studenten]. Assen, 1973. pp. 240. bibliogs.

ZANEN (TEUN JAN) Noord Nederland, een kolonie?. Amsterdam, 1973. pp. 143. bibliog.

NETHERLANDS. Ministerie van Volkshuisvesting en Ruimtelijke Ordening. 1974- . Oriënteringsnota ruimtelijke ordening: achtergronden, uitgangspunten en beleidsvoornemens van de regering; derde nota over de ruimtelijke ordening in Nederland. 's-Gravenhage, 1974 in progress.

— New Zealand.

WELLINGTON REGIONAL PLANNING AUTHORITY. Towards a metropolitan development strategy: a presentation of a metropolitan planning methodology. Wellington, 1971. pp. 115.

— Norway.

JOHNSEN (YNGVAR) Survey of Norwegian planning legislation and organization. [Oslo, Kommunal- og arbeidsdepartementet, 1970]. pp. 34.

NORWAY. Distriktenes Utbyggingsfond. Årsmelding. a., 1972- Oslo.

NORWAY. Distriktenes Utbyggingsfond. 1972. Regional development in Norway: the Regional Development Fund. [Oslo, 1972]. pp. 23.

NORWAY. Kommunal- og Arbeidsdepartementet. 1972. Om mål og midler i distriktsutbyggingen. [Oslo, 1972?]. pp. 53. (Norway. Stortinget. Stortingsmeldinger. 1972-73. Nr.13)

NORWAY. Kommunal- og Arbeidsdepartementet. 1972. Om regionalpolitikken og lands- og landsdelsplanleggingen. [Oslo, 1972]. pp. 185. Map in end pocket. (Norway. Stortinget. Stortingsmeldinger. 1971-72. Nr.27)

NORWAY. Landsdelskomitéen for Nord-Norge. 1972. Om landsdelsplan for Nord-Norge: forslag til plan for utvikling av landsdelen. Oslo, 1972. pp. 363, 6 maps. (Norway. Norges Offentlige Utredninger. 1972. 33)

NORWAY. Utvalget for Regionalstatistikk. 1972. Regionalstatistikk: om statistikkbehovet i regional planlegging: utredning fra Utvalg, etc. Oslo, 1972. pp. 165. (Norway. Norges Offentlige Utredninger. 1972. 44)

MARGINAL regions: essays on social planning: [papers from a seminar held in Swansea in 1972); edited by Maurice Broady. London, [1973]. pp. 120. bibliog.

— Poland.

CELE polityki regionalnej a przedmiot planowania regionalnego. Warszawa, 1971. pp. 165. (Polska Akademia Nauk. Komitet Przestrzennego Zagospodarowania Kraju. Studia. t.37) With Russian and English summaries.

— Russia.

PAVLENKO (VIKTOR FEDOROVICH) Territorial'noe i otraslevoe planirovanie: territorial'noe planirovanie v usloviiakh otraslevogo upravleniia khoziaistvom. Moskva, 1971. pp. 103.

EL'MEEV (VASILII IAKOVLEVICH) and others. Kompleksnoe planirovanie ekonomicheskogo i sotsial'nogo razvitiia raiona. Leningrad, 1972. pp. 126.

PERTSIK (EVGENII NAUMOVICH) Raionnaia planirovka: geograficheskie aspekty. Moskva, 1973. pp. 271. bibliog.

— Saudi Arabia.

SEIFERT (WILLIAM W.) and others, eds. Energy and development: a case study; based upon an interdepartmental student project...at the Massachusetts Institute of Technology...and a study at the College of Petroleum and Minerals, Dhahran, Saudi Arabia. Cambridge, Mass., [1973]. pp. 300. (Massachusetts Institute of Technology. M.I.T. Reports. No. 25)

— Spain.

BUTTLER (FRIEDRICH) Einkommensredistributive und raumstrukturelle Regionalpolitik im Rahmen der spanischen Entwicklungspläne. Göttingen, [1969]. pp. 83. bibliog. (Göttingen. Universität. Ibero-Amerika- Institut für Wirtschaftsforschung. Arbeitsberichte. Heft 5)

MEILAN (JOSE LUIS) España 71: el territorio, protagonista del desarrollo. Madrid, 1971. pp. 219.

— Sweden.

SWEDEN. Finansdepartementet. Långtidsutredningen. 1971. [Svensk ekonomi fram till 1977]; 1970 års långtidsutredning. Bilaga . 7. Regional utveckling och planering; utarbetad inom Expertgruppen för Regional Utredningsverksamhet, Inrikesdepartementet. Stockholm, 1971. pp. 174. (Sweden. Statens Offentliga Utredningar. 1971.16)

PRED (ALLAN R.) and TÖRNQVIST (GUNNAR) Systems of cities and information flows: two essays. Lund, 1973. pp. 121. bibliogs. (Lund. Universitet. Geografiska Institution. Lund Studies in Geography. Series B. Human Geography. No. 38)

— Switzerland.

SWITZERLAND. Groupe de Travail de la Confédération pour l'Aménagement du Territoire. 1970. Aménagement en Suisse: les tâches de l'aménagement et son organisation au niveau de la Confédération: rapport du Groupe, etc. [Bern], 1970. 2 vols.

INITIATIVEN der Gegenwart, Chancen der Zukunft: Bevölkerung und Wirtschaft in der Region Zürich; herausgegeben von der Zürcher Handelskammer anlässlich ihres 100 jährigen Bestehens; [by] Harald Jürgensen [and others]. Zürich, 1973. pp. 265.

FISCHER (GEORGES) Schaffhausen: Zukunft einer Region; sozio-ökonomische Strukturanalyse der Stadt und Region Schaffhausen als Grundlage zur Erarbeitung eines Leitbildes. Schaffhausen, 1973. 1 vol.(various pagings). (Hochschule St.Gallen für Wirtschafts- und Sozialwissenschaften. Schweizerisches Institut für Aussenwirtschafts-, Struktur- und Marktforschung. Struktur- und Regionalwirtschaftliche Studien. Band 4)

— United Kingdom.

MORRISON (RACHEL) Town and country planning. London, 1949. pp. 16. bibliog. (Current Affairs. No. 76)

BINNIE AND PARTNERS and MAUNSELL (G.) AND PARTNERS. Dee estuary scheme phase IIa: [report] (and Supplementary report). [London], H.M.S.O., 1971[-74]. 3 vols. bibliog.

COVENTRY. City Council, and others. Study Team. Coventry-Solihull-Warwickshire: a strategy for the sub-region; the report on the sub-regional planning study; ([with] Supplementary report 1: data, [and] Supplementary report 6: transportation). Coventry, 1971. 3 pts. (in 1 vol.) Supplementary reports Nos. 2-5 out of print.

ASHWORTH (GRAHAM) Designing for survival; paper delivered to the annual conference of the Royal Institute of British Architects at Lancaster University, July 1972. Manchester, 1972, repr. 1973. fo. 18.

DERBYSHIRE. County Planning Department. Countryside plan: an interim strategy for the countryside. [Derby, 1972?]. pp. 60. Maps in end pocket.

McLOUGHLIN (JOHN BRIAN) and THORNLEY (JENNIFER) Some problems in structure planning: a literature review. London, 1972. pp. 80. bibliog. (Centre for Environmental Studies. Information Papers. 27)

REGIONAL PLANNING DISCUSSION PAPERS. London, Department of the Environment, [1973? in progress].

COWLING (T. MALCOLM) and STEELEY (GEOFFREY C.) Sub-regional planning studies: an evaluation. Oxford, 1973. pp. 202. bibliog.

HOUSE (JOHN WILLIAM) ed. The UK space: resources, environment and the future. London, [1973]. pp. 371.

LINDSEY. County Council. The Lindsey coast: a policy for holiday development. [Lincoln], 1973. pp. 21.

McLOUGHLIN (JOHN BRIAN) and THORNLEY (JENNIFER) Structure planning: a preliminary testing of some research hypotheses in relation to current practice. London, 1973. pp. 61. bibliog. (Centre for Environmental Studies. Working Papers. 79)

MARGINAL regions: essays on social planning: [papers from a seminar held in Swansea in 1972); edited by Maurice Broady. London, [1973]. pp. 120. bibliog.

SOUTH HAMPSHIRE PLAN ADVISORY COMMITTEE. South Hampshire structure plan for the south east part of the county of Hampshire: city of Portsmouth, city of Southampton. [Winchester], 1973. pp. 334,60a,(29). Maps in end pocket.

REGIONAL PLANNING. (Cont.)

THOMSON (CHARLES W.) The industrial selection scheme: a study of conflicting objectives in urban and regional planning. London, 1973. pp. 46. *bibliog. (Centre for Environmental Studies. Working Papers. 81)*

U.K. Department of the Environment. 1973. Structure plans: the examination in public. [London, 1973]. pp. 13.

WARWICKSHIRE. County Council. County structure plan, 1973. Warwick, 1973. 8 pts. (in 1 vol.). *Comprises Written statement; Report of survey; Supplementary reports 1-6.*

WORCESTERSHIRE. Planning Department. Worcestershire structure plan; ([with Report of survey [and] Supporting information). [Worcester, 1973]. 5 vols. (in 3).

GLASSON (JOHN) An introduction to regional planning : concepts, theory and practice. London, 1974. pp. 337. *bibliog.*

LEICESTER. City Council, and LEICESTERSHIRE. County Council. Leicester and Leicestershire structure plan: report of survey; ([with] Addendum). [Leicester], 1974. 2 vols. (in 1).

— — Mathematical models.

U.K. Department of the Environment. 1973. Using predictive models for structure plans. London, 1973. pp. 72. *bibliogs.*

— — Ireland, Northern.

NORTHERN IRELAND ECONOMIC COUNCIL. Area development in Northern Ireland. Belfast, 1969. pp. 49.

ARMAGH area plan; [Samuel H. Moore, chairman of the Steering Committee]. Belfast, H.M.S.O., 1973. pp. 131. *2 maps in end pocket.*

NEWRY area plan; [Patrick McArdle, chairman of the Steering Committee]. Belfast, H.M.S.O., 1973. pp. 86. *Map in end pocket.*

REGIONAL policy and the attraction of manufacturing industry in Northern Ireland; by A.S. Murie [and others]. London, 1974. pp. 133. *(Centre for Environmental Studies. Research Papers.4)*

— — Scotland.

EDINBURGH. University. Department of Urban Design and Regional Planning. Tayside regional study '73: (main practical study in regional planning). Edinburgh, 1973. pp. 197.

— — Wales.

FLINTSHIRE. County Planning Department. Flintshire countryside report. Mold, Flintshire, 1972. pp. 50.

DENBIGHSHIRE. County Planning Officer. Structure plan: report of survey; [submitted to the County of Clwyd in February, 1974]. Ruthin, 1973 [or rather 1974]. pp. 97,iii.

DEVELOPMENT PLANNING PARTNERSHIP. Anglesey county structure plan: report of survey and discussion of alternatives; ([and] written statement); prepared on behalf of the County. Llangefni, 1974. 2 vols. (in 1).

— United States.

COASTAL PLAINS REGIONAL COMMISSION [UNITED STATES]. Annual report.a., 1967/8[1st], 1969/70[3rd]- Washington.

FOUR CORNERS REGIONAL COMMISSION [UNITED STATES]. Annual report. a., 1970/71 (4th)- Washington.

UPPER GREAT LAKES REGIONAL COMMISSION [UNITED STATES]. Annual report. a., Ja 1972 [covering 1970/71]- Washington.

OLD WEST REGIONAL COMMISSION [UNITED STATES]. Annual report. a., 1972/3 (1st)- Washington.

OZARKS REGIONAL COMMISSION. Annual report. a., 1973- Washington.

PACIFIC NORTHWEST REGIONAL COMMISSION. Annual report. a., 1973 [1st]- Washington.

BERRY (BRIAN JOE LOBLEY) Growth centers in the American urban system. Cambridge, Mass., [1973]. 2 vols. *bibliog.*

COSTIKYAN (EDWARD N.) and LEHMAN (MAXWELL) New strategies for regional cooperation: a model for the tri-state New York-New Jersey-Connecticut area. New York, 1973. pp. 93. *bibliog.*

CUMBERLAND (JOHN HAMMETT) Regional development: experiences and prospects in the United States of America. 2nd ed. Paris, 1973. pp. 170. *bibliog. (United Nations Research Institute for Social Development. Regional Planning. vol. 2)*

REGIONAL growth and water resource investment; [by] W. Cris Lewis [and others]. Lexington, mass [1973]. pp. 172.

DERTHICK (MARTHA) Between state and nation; regional organizations of the United States. Washington, [1974]. pp. 242.

— — Connecticut.

PATTERNS of urban change: the New Haven experience; [by] David Birch [and others]. Lexington, [1974]. pp. 161. *bibliogs.*

— — New Mexico.

VAN DRESSER (PETER) Development on a human scale. New York, 1973. pp. 116.

REGIONALISM.

UNITED NATIONS. Department of Economic and Social Affairs. 1970. Selected experiences in regional development. (ST/SOA/101). New York, 1970. pp. 146.

WEST (E.G.) 'Pure' versus 'operational' economics in regional policy. [Ottawa, 1972]. fo. 60. *(Carleton University. Carleton Economic Papers)*

EMANUEL (A.) Issues of regional policies: a report. Paris, Organisation for Economic Co-operation and Development, 1973. pp. 274.

INTERREGIONAL SEMINAR ON DEVELOPMENT PLANNING, 6TH, QUITO, 1971. Regional planning: report of the...seminar... [held at] Quito, Ecuador, 20 September-1 October 1971. (STTAO/SER. C/143). New York, United Nations, 1973. pp. 52.

REGIONAL analysis and development; edited by John Blunden [and others] at the Open University. London, 1973. pp. 318. *bibliogs.*

DERTHICK (MARTHA) Between state and nation; regional organizations of the United States. Washington, [1974]. pp. 242.

— Belgium.

SEMAINE SOCIALE WALLONNE. 54me Semaine. La Wallonie et la répartition du pouvoir; [by] M. Galderoux [and others]. Bruxelles, 1972. pp. 256.

— Canada.

SCHWARTZ (MILDRED A.) Politics and territory: the sociology of regional persistence in Canada. . Montreal, 1974. pp. 344.

— Europe.

REGIONAL policy and planning for Europe: [papers of a seminar held at the University of East Anglia in September 1973]; edited by Morgan Sant. Farnborough, Hants, [1974]. pp. 268.

— European Economic Community countries.

EUROPEAN COMMUNITIES. Commission. 1973. Report on the regional problems in the enlarged community. Brussels, 1973. pp. 289.

— France.

PICCHI (ANTONIO) Le regioni e l'agricoltura in Francia. Bologna, [1973]. pp. 82. *(Istituto Nazionale di Economia Agraria and Istituto per la Scienza dell'amministrazione Pubblica. Agricoltura e Regioni. 10)*

— India.

ALAGH (YOGINDER K.) Regional aspects of Indian industrialization. Bombay, 1972. pp. 79. *(Bombay (City). University. Economics Series. No. 21)*

— Italy.

Il FASCISMO e le autonomie locali [papers given at a seminar in 1972]; a cura di Sandro Fontana. Bologna, [1973]. pp. 435.

— Sweden.

ELDER (NEIL COLBERT MCAULEY) Regionalism and the publicity principle in Sweden. London, 1973. pp. 31. *(U.K. Commission on the Constitution, 1969. Research Papers. 3)*

— United Kingdom.

ASPECTS of parliamentary reform; by members of the Study of Parliament Group. London, 1973. pp. 62.

KING (DAVID N.) Financial and economic aspects of regionalism and separatism. London, 1973. pp. 99. *(U.K. Commission on the Constitution, 1969. Research Papers. 10)*

SOCIAL AND COMMUNITY PLANNING RESEARCH. Devolution and other aspects of government: an attitudes survey; prepared for the Office of Population Censuses and Surveys; [by Jean Morton-Williams]. London, 1973. pp. 158. *(U.K. Commission on the Constitution, 1969. Research Papers. 7)*

SPENCE (NIGEL ANTHONY) Spatial dynamics of English regional employment change: 1951 and 1961; [Ph.D.(London) thesis]. 1974. fo. 594. *bibliog.* Typescript: unpublished. This thesis is the property of London University and may not be removed from the Library.

— — Wales.

WELSH COUNCIL. Observation on the Kilbrandon report. [Cardiff?], 1974. pp. 13.

— United States.

DERTHICK (MARTHA) Between state and nation; regional organizations of the United States. Washington, [1974]. pp. 242.

— Venezuela.

BREWER-CARIAS (ALLAN RANDOLPH) Problemas institucionales del area metropolitana de Caracas y del desarrollo regional y urbano. Caracas, Comision de Administracion Publica, 1971. fo. 60.

REGIONALISM (INTERNATIONAL ORGANIZATION).

FALK (RICHARD A.) and MENDLOVITZ (SAUL H.) eds. Regional politics and world order. San Francisco, [1973]. pp. 475.

REGISTERS OF BIRTH, ETC.

GREATER LONDON RECORD OFFICE. A survey of the parish registers of the diocese of Southwark, inner London area. [London, Greater London Council, 1970]. pp. 66.

GREATER LONDON RECORD OFFICE. A survey of the parish registers of the diocese of London, inner London area. rev. ed. [London, Greater London Council, 1972]. pp. 80.

REGISTRATION TAX

— Italy.

GALLO (SALVATORE) Le nuove imposte tipo registro:...testo con commento teorico- pratico, etc. Piacenza, [1973]. pp. 571. *bibliog.*

REGRESSION ANALYSIS.

AMUNDSEN (HERDIS THORÉN) Binary variable multiple regressions. [Oslo], 1972. fo. 32. *bibliog. (Oslo. Universitet. Sosialøkonomisk Institutt. Memoranda)*

PARK (SOO-BIN) Some small-sample properties of Durbin's h statistic. [Ottawa, 1972]. fo. 22. *bibliog. (Carleton University. Carleton Economic Papers)*

GOLDSTEIN (HARALD) On the concept of simultaneous significance level in stepwise regression problems. Oslo, 1973. 1 vol. (various foliations) *bibliog. (Oslo. Universitet. Sosialøkonomiske Institutt. Memoranda)*

MAY (S.J.) Choosing a single equation estimator. [Ottawa, 1973]. fo. 35. *bibliog. (Carleton University. Carleton Economic Papers)*

DEWHURST (R.F.J.) An investigation of the possibility of using regression analysis to evaluate in money terms the routine outputs of the accounts department of a business organisation. Coventry, 1974. pp. 21, xxiii. *bibliog. (University of Warwick. Centre for Industrial Economic and Business Research. [Warwick Research in Industrial and Business Studies]. No. 48)*

LEECH (DENNIS) A note on testing the error specification in nonlinear regression. Coventry, 1974. fo. 11. *bibliog. (University of Warwick. Department of Economics. Warwick Economic Research Papers. No. 48)*

REHABILITATION

— Belgium.

Le RECLASSEMENT des handicapés: campagne nationale 1970-71. [Bruxelles, Commissariat Général à la Promotion du Travail, 1972]. pp. 312.

— Canada — Newfoundland.

NEWFOUNDLAND. Department of Rehabilitation and Recreation. Annual report. a., 1973/4 [1st]- St. John's, Newfoundland.

— Denmark.

LANGTIDSBEHANDLING på sygehuse: betaenkning I afgivet af det af Sundhedsstyrelsen den 3. marts 1969 nedsatte udvalg, etc. København, 1970. pp. 79. *bibliog.*

— Finland.

PUROLA (TAPANI) and others. Quantitative needs for rehabilitation in Finland in the light of an interview survey and clinical examinations. [Helsinki], 1971. pp. [8]. *bibliog. (Finland. Kansaneläkelaitos. Julkaisuja. E. 43/1971) Reprinted from Acta Socio-Medica Scandinavica. 1970.2.*

SOURANDER (LEIF B.) and others. Pitkäaikaisesti työkyvyttömien kuntoutustarve...[English summary: Need of rehabilitation in a group of subjects with long term disability]. Helsinki, 1972. pp. 45. *(Sosiaalinen Aikakauskiya. Lütteitä. 1972. 6)*

— Norway.

NORWAY. Komitéen for Internasjonale Sosialpolitiske Saker. Social and Labour News from Norway. 1963. No. 1. Employment of the disabled under sheltered conditions in Norway. [Oslo], 1963. fo. 11. *Reprinted from International Labour Review.*

— United States.

CULL (JOHN G.) and HARDY (RICHARD E.) Understanding disability for social and rehabilitation services. Springfield, Ill., [1973]. pp. 205. *bibliogs.*

REHABILITATION, RURAL

— Canada.

WILSON (JAMES WOOD) People in the way: the human aspects of the Columbia River project. Toronto, [1973]. pp. 200. *bibliog.*

— France.

FRANCE. Direction de la Documentation. La Documentation Française. Notes et Etudes Documentaires. No. 3,708. Aménagement du territoire: la politique de rénovation rurale; [by G. Rimareix]. Paris, 1970. pp. 44.

— Jamaica.

YALLAHS VALLEY LAND AUTHORITY. Yallahs Valley Land Authority, 1951-1966: 15th anniversary brochure. [Kingston?, 1966?]. pp. 52.

— South Africa.

BOARD (CHRISTOPHER) A sample survey to assess the effect on Bantu agriculture of the rehabilitation programme. Johannesburg, 1964. pp. 229-235. *(From South African Journal of Science, vol. 60, no.8)*

— United States.

NATIONAL PLANNING ASSOCIATION. Reports. No. 134. Toward a rural development policy; by James G. Maddox. Washington, D.C., [1973]. pp. 24. *(National Planning Association. Reports. No. 134)*

REHABILITATION OF CRIMINALS.

INTERAMERICAN CONGRESS OF CRIMINOLOGY, 2ND, CARACAS, 1972. Corrections: problems of punishment and rehabilitation: [selected papers]; [edited by Edward Sagarin [and] Donal E.J. MacNamara]. New York, 1973. pp. 152. *bibliogs.*

— United Kingdom.

U.K. Home Office. 1973. The probation and after-care service in England and Wales. 5th ed. London, 1973. pp. 29.

SOOTHILL (KEITH LEONARD) The prisoner's release: a study of the employment of ex-prisoners. London, 1974. pp. 319.

— United States.

MILLER (HERBERT S.) The closed door: the effect of a criminal record on employment with state and local public agencies. Washington, 1972. pp. 252. *Prepared at Georgetown University for the Manpower Administration, U.S. Department of Labor.*

REHABILITATION OF JUVENILE DELINQUENTS

— United Kingdom.

U.K. Department of Health and Social Security. 1972. Intermediate treatment: a guide for the regional planning of new forms of treatment for children in trouble. London, 1972. pp. 39.

— United States.

CULL (JOHN G.) and HARDY (RICHARD E.) eds. Law enforcement and correctional rehabilitation: [readings]. Springfield, Ill., [1973]. pp. 266.

— — Massachusetts.

CLOSING correctional institutions: new strategies for youth services; edited by Yitzhak Bakal. Lexington, Mass., [1973]. pp. 186. *bibliogs.*

REIMANN (MAX).

REIMANN (MAX) Entscheidungen 1945-1956. Frankfurt am Main, 1973. pp. 227.

RELATIVITY.

STANKIEWICZ (WLADYSLAW JOZEF) Relativism: thoughts and aphorisms. West Chesterfield, N.H., 1972. 1 vol. (unpaged).

RELIGION.

RELIGION, culture and methodology: papers of the Groningen Working-group for the Study of Fundamental Problems and Methods of Science of Religion; edited by Th. P. van Baaren and H.J.W. Drijvers. The Hague, [1973]. pp. 171. *bibliogs.*

— History.

ZIEGLER (ADOLF WILHELM) Religion, Kirche und Staat in Geschichte und Gegenwart: (ein Handbuch). München, 1969-74. 3 vols. *bibliogs.*

— Philosophy.

SUKHOV (ANDREI DMITRIEVICH) Religiia kak obshchestvennyi fenomen: filosofskie problemy issledovaniia. 2nd ed. Moskva, 1973. pp. 144.

RELIGION AND POLITICS.

HERO (ALFRED OLIVIER) American religious groups view foreign policy: trends in rank-and-file opinion, 1937-1969. Durham, N.C., 1973. pp. 552.

CONRAD (WOLFGANG) Ressentiment in der Klassengesellschaft: zur Diskussion um einen Aspekt religiösen Bewusstseins. Göttingen, [1974]. pp. 99. *bibliog.*

LEWY (GUENTER) Religion and revolution. New York, 1974. pp. 694.

RELIGION AND SOCIOLOGY.

DESROCHES (HENRI CHARLES) L'homme et ses religions: sciences humaines et expériences religieuses. Paris, 1972. pp. 239. *bibliog.*

SUKHOV (ANDREI DMITRIEVICH) Religiia kak obshchestvennyi fenomen: filosofskie problemy issledovaniia. 2nd ed. Moskva, 1973. pp. 144.

VOYE (LILIANE) Sociologie du geste religieux: de l'analyse de la pratique dominicale en Belgique à une interprétation théorique. Bruxelles, [1973]. pp. 314. *bibliog.*

EISTER (ALLAN W.) ed. Changing perspectives in the scientific study of religion. New York, [1974]. pp. 370. *bibliogs.*

FALLDING (HAROLD) The sociology of religion: an explanation of the unity and diversity in religion. London, [1974]. pp. 240.

MOORE (ROBERT) Pit-men, preachers and politics: the effects of Methodism in a Durham mining community. London, 1974. pp. 292. *bibliog.*

RAJANA (EIMI WATANABE) A sociological study of new religious movements: Chilean Pentecostalism and Japanese new religions; [Ph.D.(London) thesis]. 1974. fo. 288. *bibliog. Typescript: unpublished. This thesis is the property of London University and may not be removed from the Library.*

RELIGION AND STATE

LEWY (GUENTER) Religion and revolution. New York, 1974. pp. 694.

— Europe, Eastern.

BEESON (TREVOR) Discretion and valour: religious conditions in Russia and Eastern Europe; [report of a working party appointed by the British Council of Churches]. [London], 1974. pp. 348. *bibliog.*

— Russia.

BEESON (TREVOR) Discretion and valour: religious conditions in Russia and Eastern Europe; [report of a working party appointed by the British Council of Churches]. [London], 1974. pp. 348. *bibliog.*

RELIGIONS.

GUINNESS (OS) The dust of death:... a critique of the establishment and the counter culture, and a proposal for a third way. London, 1973. pp. 416.

RELIGIOUS EDUCATION

— United Kingdom.

BRITISH COUNCIL OF CHURCHES. Education Department. Religious education in a multi-religious society; report on a consultation in the West Riding of Yorkshire organised in collaboration with the Community Relations Commission. [London], Community Relations Commission, [1969]. pp. 6.

RELIGIOUS EDUCATION. (Cont.)

LONDON. Greater London Council. Inner London Education Authority. Standing Advisory Council on Religious Education. Religious education in local studies. London, 1971. pp. 37.

RELOCATION (HOUSING)

— Canada.

BARRETT (FRANK A.) Residential search behavior: a study of intra-urban relocation in Toronto. Toronto, 1973. pp. 257. bibliog. (York University (Toronto). Department of Geography. Geographical Monographs. No.1)

— United States.

MODELS of residential location and relocation in the city: [based on a seminar held at Northwestern University in 1972 sponsored by the Mathematical Social Science Board]; edited by Eric G. Moore. Evanston, Ill., 1973. pp. 197. bibliogs.(Northwestern University. Studies in Geography. No. 20)

REMAND HOMES

— Czechoslovakia.

ČIC (MILAN) Ochranná výchova v československom trestnom práve. Bratislava, 1971. pp. 126. bibliog.

— United Kingdom.

FERGUS (H.K.) Selected aspects of the organization of Brockhill. [London], 1972. fo. 102. bibliog. (U.K. Prison Department. Office of the Chief Psychologist. CP Reports. Series. 1. No. 1)

REMOTE SENSING SYSTEMS.

CANADA. Program Planning Office for Resource Satellites and Remote Airborne Sensing. Working Group on Agriculture and Geography. 1971. Resource satellites and remote airborne sensing for Canada. Report no.2. Agriculture and Geography; [C.V. Parker, chairman]. Ottawa, 1971. pp. 23. With French summary.

CANADA. Program Planning Office for Resource Satellites and Remote Airborne Sensing. Working Group on Atmospheric Constituents. 1971. Resource satellites and remote airborne sensing for Canada. Report no.3. Atmospheric constituents; [S.O. Winthrop, chairman]. Ottawa, 1971. pp. 32. bibliogs. With French summary.

CANADA. Program Planning Office for Resource Satellites and Remote Airborne Sensing. Working Group on Cartography and Photogrammetry. 1971. Resource satellites and remote airborne sensing for Canada. Report no.4. Cartography and Photogrammetry; [R.E. Moore, chairman]. Ottawa, 1971. pp. 8. With French summary.

CANADA. Program Planning Office for Resource Satellites and Remote Airborne Sensing. Working Group on Forestry and Wildlands. 1971. Resource satellites and remote airborne sensing for Canada. Report no.5. Forestry and wildlands; [L. Sayn-Wittgenstein, chairman]. Ottawa, 1971. pp. 17. With French summary.

CANADA. Program Planning Office for Resource Satellites and Remote Airborne Sensing. Working Group on Geology. 1971. Resource satellites and remote airborne sensing for Canada. Report no.6. Geology; [Alan F. Gregory, chairman]. Ottawa, 1971. pp. 26. With French summary.

CANADA. Program Planning Office for Resource Satellites and Remote Airborne Sensing. Working Group on Ice Reconnaissance and Glaciology. 1971. Resource satellites and remote airborne sensing for Canada. Report no.7. Ice reconnaissance and glaciology; [D.C. Archibald, chairman]. Ottawa, 1971. pp. 37. With French summary.

CANADA. Program Planning Office for Resource Satellites and Remote Airborne Sensing. Working Group on Water Resources. 1971. Resource satellites and remote airborne sensing for Canada. Report no.8. Water resources; [R.K. Lane, chairman]. Ottawa, 1971. pp. 25. bibliog. With French summary.

RENAISSANCE

— Italy.

BURKE (PETER) Historian. Tradition and innovation in renaissance Italy: a sociological approach. [London], 1974. pp. 413. Corrected paperback edition of Culture and society in renaissance Italy, 1420-1540.

RENAN (ERNEST).

ARDAO (ARTURO) Origenes de la influencia de Renan en el Uruguay. Montevideo, 1955. pp. 34. (Instituto Nacional de Investigaciones y Archivos Literarios. Estudios y Testimonios. 1)

RENNER (KARL).

LESER (NORBERT) Zwischen Reformismus und Bolschewismus: der Austromarxismus als Theorie und Praxis. Wien, [1968]. pp. 600.

KANN (ROBERT ADOLF) Renners Beitrag zur Lösung nationaler Konflikte im Lichte nationaler Probleme der Gegenwart. Wien, 1973. pp. 18. (Österreichische Akademie der Wissenschaften. Philosophisch-Historische Klasse. Sitzungsberichte. 279. Band. 4. Abhandlung)

RENT

— France.

POSTEL-VINAY (GILLES) La rente foncière dans le capitalisme agricole: analyse de la voie "classique" du développement du capitalisme dans l'agriculture à partir de l'exemple du soissonnais. Paris, 1974. pp. 286. bibliog.

— Sweden.

HERLITZ (LARS) Jordegendom och ränta: omfördelningen av jordbrukets merprodukt i Skaraborgs län under frihetstiden. Lund, 1974. pp. 387. bibliog. (Göteborgs Universitet. Ekonomisk-Historiska Institutionen. Meddelanden. 31) With English summary.

— United Kingdom.

U.K. Parliament. House of Commons. Library. Research Division. Background Papers. No. 33. Rent rebates and allowances. [London, 1973]. fo. 4.

— — London.

NEVITT (ADELA ADAM) Thamesmead rents; a report to the Greater London Council...; with a foreword by Sir Reg Goodwin, leader of the GLC, and Richard Balfe, chairman of the Thamesmead Committee, and comments by officers of the Council. London, [Greater London Council], 1973. pp. 48.

RENT (ECONOMIC THEORY).

CLARK (COLIN) The value of agricultural land. Oxford, 1973. pp. 117.

RENT SUBSIDIES

— United Kingdom.

MANDELKER (DANIEL ROBERT) Housing subsidies in the United States and England. Indianapolis, [1973]. pp. 246. bibliog.

— United States.

MANDELKER (DANIEL ROBERT) Housing subsidies in the United States and England. Indianapolis, [1973]. pp. 246. bibliog.

— — New York (City).

LOWRY (IRA S.) and others. Welfare housing in New York City. New York, 1972. pp. 265. (Rand Corporation. [Rand Reports]. 1164)

REPARATION.

EDELHERTZ (HERBERT) and GEIS (GILBERT) Public compensation to victims of crime. New York, 1974. pp. 309. bibliog.

— Ireland (Republic).

EIRE. Department of Justice. 1974. Scheme of compensation for personal injuries criminally inflicted; laid by the Minister for Justice before each House of the Oireachtas, February, 1974. Dublin, [1974]. pp. 6.

— United States.

EDELHERTZ (HERBERT) and GEIS (GILBERT) Public compensation to victims of crime. New York, 1974. pp. 309. bibliog.

REPLACEMENT OF INDUSTRIAL EQUIPMENT.

HUETTNER (DAVID) Plant size,technological change, and investment requirements: a dynamic framework for the long-run average cost curve. New York, 1974. pp. 183. bibliog.

REPRESENTATIVE GOVERNMENT AND REPRESENTATION.

JAEGER (WOLFGANG) Offentlichkeit und Parlamentarismus: eine Kritik an Jürgen Habermas. Stuttgart, [1973]. pp. 107.

ZAMPETTI (PIER LUIGI) Dallo stato liberale allo stato dei partiti: la rappresentanza politica. 2nd ed. Milano, 1973. pp. 223.

REPUBLICAN PARTY (UNITED STATES).

SHERMAN (RICHARD B.) The Republican Party and black America: from McKinley to Hoover, 1896-1933. Charlottesville, Va., 1973. pp. 274.

RIPON SOCIETY and BROWN (CLIFFORD WATERS) Jaws of victory: the game-plan politics of 1972, the crisis of the Republican Party, and the future of the constitution. Boston, [1974]. pp. 394. bibliog.

RESEARCH.

UNITED NATIONS EDUCATIONAL, SCIENTIFIC AND CULTURAL ORGANIZATION. Science Policy Studies and Documents. Paris, 1965 in progress.

ORGANISATION FOR ECONOMIC CO-OPERATION AND DEVELOPMENT. Information Service. 1967. Science and the OECD: science and the policies of government; cooperation in research: a joint approach by 21 nations. Paris, 1967. pp. 40.

— Economic aspects.

MEDFORD (R.D.) Curiosity oriented research: an experimental study: x-ray holography. Chilton, Programmes Analysis Unit, 1974. pp. 24. ([Publications]. P.A.U. M.21)

— Management.

MAESTRE (CLAUDE) and PAVITT (KEITH) Analytical methods in government science policy: an evaluation. Paris, Organisation for Economic Co-operation and Development, 1972. pp. 89. bibliog. (Science Policy Studies)

SEMINAR ON R[ESEARCH] AND D[EVELOPMENT] MANAGEMENT, ISTANBUL, 1970. Management of research and development; papers presented at a Seminar organised by the Scientific and Technical Research Council of Turkey, [held at] Istanbul 4-8 May 1970. Paris, Organisation for Economic Co-operation and Development, 1972. pp. 329. (Problems of Development).

— Statistics.

FREEMAN (CHRISTOPHER) Measurement of output of research and experimental development: a review paper. Paris, United Nations Educational, Scientific and Cultural Organization, [1970]. pp. 43. (Statistical Reports and Studies. [No. 16])

— Canada.

CANADA. Statistics Canada. Research and development expenditure in Canada. bien. 1963/1971(1st)- Ottawa. In English and French.

— **Communist countries.**

IUZUFOVICH (GERMAN KARLOVICH) Ekonomicheskie metody upravleniia nauchnymi issledovaniiami v stranakh-chlenakh SEV. Moskva, 1973. pp. 120.

— **Europe, Eastern.**

OSERS (JAN) Forschung und Entwicklung in sozialistischen Staaten Osteuropas. Berlin, [1974]. pp. 317. *bibliog.* (*Osteuropa-Institut, München. Reihe: Wirtschaft und Gesellschaft. Heft 14*) *With English summary.*

— **European Economic Community countries.**

EUROPEAN COMMUNITIES. Commission. 1972. Objectives and instruments of a common policy for scientific research and technological development; communication of the Commission to the Council; transmitted the 14th of June 1972. Brussels, 1972. pp. 58. (*Bulletin of the European Communities. Supplements. [1972/6]*)

— **France.**

FRANCE. Direction de la Documentation. La Documentation Française. Notes et Etudes Documentaires. No. 3,863. L'organisation administrative de la recherche scientifique en France: [rédigée par Gérard Druesne]. [Paris], 1972. pp. 48. *bibliog.*

— **Germany.**

GERMANY (BUNDESREPUBLIK). Wissenschaftsrat. Empfehlungen und Stellungnahmen. a., 1972- [Köln].

— **India.**

CHOWDHURY (P.N.) Economics of research and development. New Delhi, 1973. pp. 163. *bibliog.*

— **Netherlands.**

ORGANISATION FOR ECONOMIC CO-OPERATION AND DEVELOPMENT. Directorate for Scientific Affairs. 1973. Netherlands. Paris, 1973. pp. 375. (*Reviews of National Science Policy. [No. 16]*)

— **Russia — Finance.**

ALESHIN (SERGEI MAKAROVICH) and others. Finansirovanie nauchno-issledovatel'skikh uchrezhdenii. Moskva, 1973. pp. 144.

— **Scandinavia.**

[SCANDINAVIA]. Nordisk Statistisk Skriftserie. 27. Forskningsvirksomhet i Norden i 1971: utgifter og personale, etc. Oslo, 1974. pp. 91. *bibliog. With English and Finnish summaries.*

— **Sweden.**

SWEDEN. Statens Råd för Byggnadsforskning. 1971. Urban and regional research in Sweden; etc. Stockholm, 1971. pp. 145. (*Sweden. Statens Institut för Byggnadsforskning. Documents. 1971. 4*) *In English, French and Russian.*

— **United Kingdom.**

NATIONAL RESEARCH DEVELOPMENT CORPORATION [U.K.]. Annual report and statement of accounts. a., 1972/3 (24th)- London. *Formerly included in the file of British Parliamentary Papers.*

BEVAN (ERIC GILBERT) An analysis of equipment costs in university science and engineering departments. London, H.M.S.O., 1972. pp. 39. (*Science Policy Studies. No. 5*)

— — **Wales.**

RESEARCH, WALES: report; ([pd. by] Welsh Office [U.K.]). a., 1973/4 (1st)- Cardiff. *In Welsh and English.*

RESEARCH, INDUSTRIAL.

CETRON (MARVIN J.) and others, eds. Quantitative decision aiding techniques for research and development management; [papers presented at the Military Operations Research Society Working Group on Research Management]. New York, [1972]. pp. 205.

— **Canada.**

CANADA. Statistics Canada. Expenditures of provincial non- profit industrial research institutes. a., 1972 (1st)- Ottawa. *In English and French.*

— **Sweden.**

REHNVALL (HANS) Technical development activity in Sweden. [Stockholm], Royal Ministry for Foreign Affairs, Information Service, 1972. fo. 6.

DALBORG (HANS) Research and development: organization and location. Stockholm, 1974. pp. 152. *bibliog.*

— **United Kingdom.**

U.K. Department of Employment. Research: (annual report). a., 1972/3 [1st]- London.

U.K. Department of Industry. Reports of the Research Requirements Boards. a., 1973 [1st]- London.

RESERVE BANK OF NEW ZEALAND.

DEANE (RODERICK S.) Papers on monetary policy, credit creation, economic objectives and the Reserve Bank. Wellington, 1972. pp. 35. (*Reserve Bank of New Zealand. Research Papers. No. 9*)

HAWKE (G.R.) Between governments and banks: a history of the Reserve Bank of New Zealand. Wellington, Government Printer, 1973. pp. 244.

RESERVOIRS

— **India.**

MINHAS (BAGICHA SINGH) and others. Scheduling the operations of the Bhakra system: studies in technical and economic evaluation. Calcutta, 1972. pp. 89.

— **United States.**

BURBY (RAYMOND J.) Household decision processes in the purchase and use of reservoir recreation land. Raleigh, 1971. pp. 213. *bibliog.* (*North Carolina University. Water Resources Research Institute. Reports. No. 51*)

RESIDENTIAL MOBILITY

— **United Kingdom.**

MURIE (ALAN) Household movement and housing choice: a study based on the West Yorkshire Movers Survey, 1969. Birmingham, 1974. pp. 131. (*Birmingham. University. Centre for Urban and Regional Studies. Occasional Papers. No. 28*)

— **United States.**

MODELS of residential location and relocation in the city: [based on a seminar held at Northwestern University in 1972 sponsored by the Mathematical Social Science Board]; edited by Eric G. Moore. Evanston, Ill., 1973. pp. 197. *bibliogs.*(*Northwestern University. Studies in Geography. No. 20*)

REST HOMES, LABOUR.

See **LABOUR REST HOMES.**

RESTITUTION AND INDEMNIFICATION CLAIMS (1933—)

— **Germany.**

SCHWARZ (WALTER) Rückerstattung nach den Gesetzen der Alliierten Mächte. München, 1974. pp. 394. (*Die Wiedergutmachung nationalsozialistischen Unrechts durch die Bundesrepublik Deutschland. Band 1*)

RESTRAINT OF TRADE

— **Canada.**

CANADA. Department of Consumer and Corporate Affairs. 1973- . [Notes for addresses, etc. by the Hon. Herb Gray]. [Ottawa], 1973 in progress.

— **EUROPE.**

SZOKOLÓCZY-SYLLABA (ADRIENNE) EFTA: restrictive business practices. Bern, 1973. pp. 270. *bibliog.* (*Institut für Europäisches und Internationales Wirtschafts- und Sozialrecht and Centre d'Etudes Juridiques Européennes. Schweizerische Beiträge zum Europarecht. Band 13*)

— **Ireland (Republic).**

EIRE. Examiner of Restrictive Practices. Annual report. a., 1972 (1st)- Dublin.

EIRE. Restrictive Practices Commission. 1972. Report of enquiry into the conditions which obtain in regard to the supply and distribution of iron and steel scrap. Dublin, [1972]. pp. 79.

— **United Kingdom.**

COMPETITION in British industry: case studies of the effects of restrictive practices legislation; [by] Dennis Swann [and others]. Loughborough, 1973. pp. 413.

COMPETITION in British industry: restrictive practices legislation in theory and practice; [by] Dennis Swann [and others]. London, 1974. pp. 232.

RETAIL TRADE.

INTERNATIONAL LABOUR ORGANISATION. Advisory Committee on Salaried Employees and Professional Workers. 6th Session. Reports. 2. The impact of social and economic developments on working and living conditions in the distributive trades: second item on the agenda. Geneva, 1967. pp. 100.

TUCKER (KENNETH ARTHUR) And YAMEY (BASIL SELIG) eds. Economics of retailing: selected readings. Harmondsworth, 1973. pp. 377. *bibliogs.*

— **Denmark.**

DENMARK. Danmarks Statistik. 1971. Detailhandelstaellingen, 1969: Handelsområder og distrikter samt kommuner. København, 1971. pp. 85. (*Statistisk Tabelvaerk. 1971.2*)

DENMARK. Danmarks Statistik. 1971. Detailhandelstaellingen, 1969: Handelsområder og distrikter samt kommuner. København, 1971. pp. 85. (*Statistisk Tabelvaerk. 1971.2*)

— **European Economic Community countries.**

ECONOMIC DEVELOPMENT COMMITTEE FOR THE DISTRIBUTIVE TRADES. Common Market Working Group. The distributive trades in the Common Market; a report; [J. Jefferys, chairman]. London, H.M.S.O., 1973. pp. 134. *bibliog.*

— **Germany.**

GELLATELY (ROBERT JOHN) The economic position and the political activity of independent retailers in Germany, 1890-1914; [Ph.D. (London) thesis]. 1973 [or rather 1974]. fo. 367. *bibliog. Typescript: unpublished. This thesis is the property of London University and may not be removed from the library.*

GELLATELY (ROBERT JOHN) The politics of economic despair: shopkeepers and German politics, 1890-1914. London, [1974]. pp. 317. *bibliog.*

— **Japan.**

DISTRIBUTION ECONOMICS INSTITUTE OF JAPAN. Outline of Japanese distribution structures:... 1973-74: enlarged edition. Tokyo, [1974]. pp. 251. *bibliog.*

RETAIL TRADE. (Cont.)

— South Africa.

SOUTH AFRICA. Bureau of Statistics. 1973- . Census of wholesale and retail trade, 1966-67. Pretoria, [1973 in progress]. (Reports. No. 04-11-01 and 04-41-01, etc.) iN eNGLISH AND aFRIKAANS.

— Underdeveloped areas

See UNDERDEVELOPED AREAS — Retail trade.

— United Kingdom.

HILTON (RICHARD NOEL) Office employment and the demand for retail services in central London; [Ph. D. (London) thesis]. [1973]. fo. 278. *Typescript: unpublished. This thesis is the property of London University and may not be removed from the library.*

REES (GORONWY) St. Michael: a history of Marks and Spencer. rev. ed. London, 1973. pp. 284.

— — Security measures.

U.K. Working Party on Internal Shop Security. 1973. Shoplifting, and thefts by shop staff; report; [E.S. Pritchard, chairman]. London, 1973. pp. 73.

RETIREMENT.

GUILLEMARD (ANNE MARIE) La retraite: une mort sociale; sociologie des conduites en situation de retraite. Paris, [1972]. pp. 303. *bibliog. (Paris. Ecole Pratique des Hautes Etudes. Section des Sciences Economiques et Sociales. Société Mouvements Sociaux et Idéologies. 1e Série. Etudes. 14)*

RETZLAW (KARL).

RETZLAW (KARL) Spartakus: Aufstieg und Niedergang; Erinnerungen eines Parteiarbeiters. 2nd ed. Frankfurt, 1972. pp. 511.

REUNION ISLAND

— Commerce.

FRANCE. Institut National de la Statistique et des Etudes Economiques. Direction Générale. 197x. Une enquête sur les établissements commerciaux à la Réunion et à la Martinique 1967-1968. Paris, [1970?]. pp. 43.

— Population.

FRANCE. Institut National de la Statistique et des Etudes Economiques. 1972. Tendances démographiques dans les départements insulaires d'outre-mer: Martinique, Guadeloupe et Réunion. Paris, [1972?]. pp. 261.

REUTLINGEN

— Politics and government.

WAHLKAMPF und Parteiorganisation: eine Regionalstudie zum Bundestagswahlkampf, 1969; ([by] Klaus von Beyme [and others]). *Tübingen, 1974. pp. 314.*

REVENUE

— Russia.

MIROSHCHENKO (S.M.) ed. Gosudarstvennye dokhody. 3rd ed. Moskva, 1972. pp. 335.

REVOLUTION (THEOLOGY).

EPPSTEIN (JOHN) The cult of revolution in the Church. New Rochelle, [1974]. pp. 160.

REVOLUTIONISTS.

DALY (WILLIAM T.) The revolutionary: a review and synthesis. Beverly Hills, [1972]. pp. 40. *bibliog.*

HALLIER (JEAN EDERN) La cause des peuples. Paris, [1972]. pp. 251.

REVOLUTIONISTS, FRENCH.

RIOUX (JEAN PIERRE) Revolutionnaires du Front populaire: choix de documents, 1935- 1938. [Paris, 1973]. pp. 444. *bibliog.*

REVOLUTIONISTS, KOREAN.

CHOSON NODONGDANG. Central Committee. Party History Institute. Kim Hyong Jik: indomitable anti-Japanese revolutionary fighter. Pyongyang, 1973. pp. 124.

REVOLUTIONISTS, RUSSIAN.

GROSUL (VLADISLAV IAKIMOVICH) Rossiiskie revoliutsionery v Iugo-Vostochnoi Evrope, 1859-1874 gg. Kishinev, 1973. pp. 539. *bibliog.*

CONFINO (MICHAEL) ed. Daughter of a revolutionary: Natalie Herzen and the Bakunin- Nechayev circle;...translated by Hilary Sternberg and Lydia Bott. London, 1974. pp. 416.

REVOLUTIONS.

SARTRE (JEAN PAUL) Situations. [Paris, 1947, repr. 1973, in progress].

GROSS (FELIKS) and HOPPER (REX D.) Un siglo de revolucion. Mexico, [1959]. pp. 412. *(Mexico City. Universidad Nacional Autonoma de Mexico. Instituto de Investigaciones Sociales. Cuadernos de Sociologia)*

WOLFF (GEORG) Journalist, ed. Wir leben in der Weltrevolution: Gespräche mit Sozialisten; (Sammlung von "Spiegel"-Gesprächen). München, 1971. pp. 191.

PRINTSIP istorizma v poznanii sotsial'nykh iavlenii. Moskva, 1972. pp. 291.

FOUGEYROLLAS (PIERRE) Marx, Freud et la révolution totale. Paris, [1972]. pp. 642.

BROWN (BRUCE) b. 1944. Marx, Freud, and the critique of everyday life: toward a permanent cultural revolution. New York, [1973]. pp. 202.

KAPLAN (LAWRENCE SAMUEL) ed. Revolutions: a comparative study. New York, [1973]. pp. 482. *bibliog.*

DEBRAY (REGIS) La critique des armes. Paris, [1974 in progress].

CROZIER (BRIAN) A theory of conflict. London, 1974. pp. 245.

JONES (HOWARD MUMFORD) Revolution and romanticism. Cambridge, Mass., 1974. pp. 487.

KUTNER (LUIS) Due process of rebellion. Chicago, [1974]. pp. 169. *bibliog.*

LEWY (GUENTER) Religion and revolution. New York, 1974. pp. 694.

WERTHEIM (WILLEM FREDERIK) Evolution and revolution: the rising waves of emancipation. Harmondsworth, 1974. pp. 416. *An abridged and updated English ed.*

— America, Latin.

HALPERIN DONGHI (TULIO) The aftermath of revolution in Latin America;... translated from the Spanish by Josephine de Bunsen. New York, 1973. pp. 149. *bibliog.*

HODGES (DONALD CLARK) The Latin American revolution: politics and strategy from apro-marxism to guevarism. New York, 1974. pp. 287. *bibliog.*

— Canada.

PROTEST, violence and social change; [edited by] Richard P. Bowles [and others]. Scarborough, Ont., [1972]. pp. 209. *bibliog.*

— China.

FRIEDMAN (EDWARD) Backward toward revolution: the Chinese Revolutionary Party. Berkeley, [1974]. pp. 237. *(Michigan University. Center for Chinese Studies. Michigan Studies on China)*

— Europe.

RUEHLE (OTTO) Die Revolutionen Europas: [reprint of work originally published in 1927]. Wiesbaden, 1973. 3 vols. *bibliogs.*

— Spain.

BROUE (PIERRE) La révolution espagnole, 1931-1939. [Paris, 1973]. pp. 190. *bibliog.*

— Sudan.

BESHIR (MOHAMED OMER) Revolution and nationalism in the Sudan. London, 1974. pp. 314. *bibliog.*

— Zaire.

MARTYR, LE: organe de combat du Conseil Nationale de Libération; ([pd. by] Gouvernement Révolutionnaire de la Province Orientale). irreg., Ag 22/23 - N 22 1964 (nos.1-19); ceased pbln. Stanleyville. *Microfilm: 1 reel.*

RHEUMATISM.

OFFICE OF HEALTH ECONOMICS. [Studies in Current Health Problems]. No. 45. Rheumatism and arthritis in Britain. London, [1973]. pp. 44. *bibliog.*

RHINE

— Navigation — Laws and regulations.

MEISSNER (FRIEDRICH) Das Recht der Europäischen Wirtschaftsgemeinschaft im Verhältnis zur Rheinschiffahrtsakte von Mannheim: ein Beitrag zur völkervertragsrechtlichen Bedeutung des Artikels 234 EWGV. Berlin, [1973]. pp. 158. *bibliog.*

RHODE ISLAND

— Politics and government.

GETTLEMAN (MARVIN E.) The Dorr rebellion: a study in American radicalism, 1833-1849. New York, [1973]. pp. 257. *bibliog.*

RHODES (CECIL JOHN)

— Bibliography.

FEDERATION OF RHODESIA AND NYASALAND. Central African Archives. 1952. A bibliography of Cecil John Rhodes, 1853-1902. Salisbury, 1952. pp. 117-192. *(Bibliographical Series. 1)*

RHODESIA

— Foreign economic relations.

BALDWIN (ALAN) Token sanctions or total economic warfare?. London, [1972?]. pp. 20. *bibliog.*

— Nationalism.

WILMER (S.E.) ed. Zimbabwe now. London, 1973. pp. 141.

— Politics and government.

AFRICAN NATIONAL COUNCIL. No future without us: the story of the African National Council in Zimbabwe (Southern Rhodesia). London, [1973?]. pp. 48.

BOWMAN (LARRY W.) Politics in Rhodesia: white power in an African state. Cambridge, Mass., 1973. pp. 206. *bibliog.*

HIRSCH (MORRIS I.) A decade of crisis: ten years of Rhodesian Front rule, 1963- 1972. Salisbury, Rhodesia, 1973. pp. 186.

INTERNATIONAL INSTITUTE FOR STRATEGIC STUDIES. Adelphi Papers. No. 100. Insurgency in Rhodesia, 1957-1973: an account and assessment; by Anthony R. Wilkinson. London, 1973. pp. 47.

WILMER (S.E.) ed. Zimbabwe now. London, 1973. pp. 141.

MUTASA (DIDYMUS NOEL EDWIN) Rhodesian black behind bars. London, 1974. pp. 150.

TUPOV (BORIS SERGEEVICH) Rodeziiskii krizis. Moskva, 1974. pp. 163. *bibliog.*

— Public works.

RHODESIA. Department of Works. Report of the Controller of Works. a., 1972/3- Salisbury.

— Race question.

BOWMAN (LARRY W.) Politics in Rhodesia: white power in an African state. Cambridge, Mass., 1973. pp. 206. *bibliog.*

WILMER (S.E.) ed. Zimbabwe now. London, 1973. pp. 141.

MUTASA (DIDYMUS NOEL EDWIN) Rhodesian black behind bars. London, 1974. pp. 150.

RHODESIA AND NYASALAND, FEDERATION OF.

SHORT (ROBIN) African sunset. London, 1973. pp. 280.

— Politics and government.

NORTHERN RHODESIA, 1963. Report of the Central Africa Conference held at the Victoria Falls, 28th June-3rd July, 1963. Lusaka, [1963]. pp. 15.

RHONE RIVER.

FRANCE. Direction de la Documentation. La Documentation Française. Notes et Etudes Documentaires. Nos. 3,842-3, 843. L'aménagement du Rhône; [by] Charles Barrière. Paris, 1971. pp. 54.

RITTER (JEAN) Le Rhône. Paris, 1973. pp. 128. *bibliog.*

RIBBONS.

TROXLER (WERNER P.) Johann Rudolf Forcart-Weiss Söhne: ein Beitrag zur Unternehmergeschichte. Bern, 1973. pp. 128. *bibliog.* (Zürich. Universität. Historisches Seminar. Geist und Werk der Zeiten. No. 36)

RICE

— Burma.

ADAS (MICHAEL) The Burma delta: economic development and social change on an Asian rice frontier, 1852-1941. Madison, Wisc., 1974. pp. 256. *bibliog.*

RIGA

— Galleries and museums.

MUZEI ISTORII GORODA RIGI I MOREKHODSTVA. Tezisy dokladov nauchnoi konferentsii, posviashchennoi 200-letiiu Muzeia istorii gor.Rigi i morekhodstva, Riga, 20/XI 1973 g. Riga, 1973. pp. 38.

RIGHT AND LEFT (POLITICAL SCIENCE).

TAYLOR (PHILIP BATES) Thoughts on comparative effectiveness: leadership and the democratic left in Colombia and Venezuela. Buffalo, N.Y., 1971. fo. 42,xvi. *(New York State University. Council on International Studies. Special Studies. No. 2)*

PFISTER (THIERRY) Tout savoir sur le gauchisme. [Paris, 1972]. pp. 157.

TEDESCHI (MARIO) Destra nazionale: sintesi di una politica nuova. Milano, [1972]. pp. 183.

MERHAV (PERETZ) La gauche israélienne: histoire, problemes et tendances du mouvement ouvrier israélien. Paris, [1973]. pp. 498. *bibliog.*

VETTORI (GIUSEPPE) ed. La sinistra extraparlamentare in Italia: storia, documenti, analisi politica. Roma, 1973. pp. 377. *bibliog.*

RINDERKNECHT (SUSANNA ORELLI—).

See
ORELLI—RINDERKNECHT(SUSANNA).

RINGMER

— Social conditions.

AMBROSE (PETER JOHN) The quiet revolution: social change in a Sussex village, 1871- 1971. London, 1974. pp. 239.

— Social history.

AMBROSE (PETER JOHN) The quiet revolution: social change in a Sussex village, 1871- 1971. London, 1974. pp. 239.

RIO GRANDE DO SUL

— Economic history.

DELHAES-GUENTHER (DIETRICH VON) Industrialisierung in Südbrasilien: die deutsche Einwanderung und die Anfänge der Industrialisierung in Rio Grande do Sul. Köln, 1973. pp. 346. *bibliog. With summaries in various languages.*

RIOTS

— France.

FOHLEN (CLAUDE) ed. Mai 1968: révolution ou psychodrame?. [Paris, 1973]. pp. 95. *bibliog.*

— — Pictures, illustrations, etc.

ROSSEL (ANDRE) Editor of Journaux du temps passé, ed. Mai 68: (images, affiches, etc.);...réalisé sur une maquette de François Doat. [Paris], 1968. 8 pts.

— United States.

BASKIN (JANE A.) and others. The long, hot summer?; an analysis of summer disorders, 1967-1971.Waltham, Mass., [1972]. pp. 51. *bibliog. (Lemberg Center for the Study of Violence. Reports. No. 2)*

— Zambia.

NORTHERN RHODESIA. Commission of Inquiry into Unrest on the Copperbelt. 1963. Report: [F.J. Whelan, chairman]. Lusaka, 1963. pp. 16.

RISK.

HAGEN (OLE) Testing av nytteforventningshypotesen. Bergen, [1973]. pp. 11. *bibliog. (Norges Handelshøyskole. Saertrykk-Serie. Nr. 105) (Saertrykk av Sosialøkonomen, Nr. 5/73)*

SEMIN (GÜN REFIK) Risk-taking in group decision making; [Ph. D. (London) thesis]. 1973[or rather 1974]. fo. 282. *bibliog. Typescript: unpublished. This thesis is the property of London University and may not be removed from the Library.*

WOODROOFE (Sir ERNEST GEORGE) Catering for uncertainty. [London], 1974. pp. 14. *(London. University. Birkbeck College. Haldane Memorial Lectures. 37)*

RITES AND CEREMONIES.

HOCART (ARTHUR MAURICE) The life-giving myth and other essays;...edited...by Lord Raglan; second impression edited with a foreword by Rodney Needham. London, 1970 repr. 1973. pp. 252.

— Laos.

ARCHAIMBAULT (CHARLES) The New Year ceremony at Basăk, South Laos;...abridged translation by Simone B. Boas. Ithaca, N.Y., 1971. pp. 151. *(Cornell University. Department of Asian Studies. Southeast Asia Program. Data Papers. No. 78) Includes French text.*

— Uganda.

CURLEY (RICHARD T.) Elders, shades and women: ceremonial change in Lango, Uganda. Berkeley, [1973]. pp. 223. *bibliog.*

— United Kingdom.

BOCOCK (ROBERT) Ritual in industrial society: a sociological analysis of ritualism in modern England. London, 1974. pp. 209.

RIVAS VICUÑA (MANUEL).

RIVAS VICUÑA (MANUEL) Historia politica y parlamentaria de Chile. I. Las administraciones de 1891 a 1910. II. La administracion de Ramon Barros Luco (1910-1915). III. La administracion de Juan Luis Sanfuentes (1915-1920); ordenada segun diversos manuscritos del autor, con varios apendices relativos a dicha "historia", a los sucesos de 1920 a 1934 y documentos concernientes a Rivas Vicuña. Santiago de Chile, Ediciones de Biblioteca Nacional, 1964. 3 vols.

RIVERS.

UNITED NATIONS. Economic Commission for Asia and the Far East. Water Resources Series. Nos. 23 onwards . New York, 1963 in progress.

SCHUMM (STANLEY A.) ed. River morphology. Stroudsburg, Pa., [1972]. pp. 429. *bibliogs.*

MANN (ROY) Rivers in the city. New York, 1973. pp. 256.

— Iran.

BEAUMONT (PETER) River regimes in Iran. Durham, 1973. pp. 29. *bibliog. (Durham. University. Department of Geography. Occasional Publications (New Series). No. 1)*

— Russia.

L'VOVICH (MARK ISAAKOVICH) Reki SSSR. Moskva, 1971. pp. 348. *bibliog.*

— United States.

FEREJOHN (JOHN A.) Pork barrel politics: rivers and harbors legislation, 1947-1968. Stanford, 1974. pp. 288. *bibliog.*

ROAD ACCIDENTS

— Statistics.

SYMPOSIUM ON THE USE OF STATISTICAL METHODS IN THE ANALYSIS OF ROAD ACCIDENTS, CROWTHORNE, 1969. Proceedings of the symposium... held at the Road Research Laboratory, Crowthorne, U.K. on 14th, 15th and 16th April 1969. Paris, Organisation for Economic Co-operation and Development, 1970. pp. 210. *(Road Research)*

— Austria.

AUSTRIA. Statistisches Zentralamt. 1972. 10-Jahresbilanz der Strassenverkehrsunfälle. Wien, 1972. pp. 27. *(Beiträge zur Österreichischen Statistik. Heft 285)*

— — Mathematical models.

AUSTRIA. Statistisches Zentralamt. 1969. Verkehrsleistung und Unfallhäufigkeit: eine methodische Untersuchung. Wien, 1969. pp. 51. *(Beiträge zur Österreichischen Statistik. Heft 199) Map in end pocket.*

— South Africa.

SOUTH AFRICA. Bureau of Statistics. Reports. No. 12-01-01. Road vehicle accidents 1964. Pretoria, [1966?]. pp. 77. *In Afrikaans and English.*

— Switzerland.

SWITZERLAND. Groupe d'Etude pour la Lutte contre les Accidents de la Circulation Routière. 1969. La prévention des accidents de la circulation routière en Suisse, etc. [Lucerne, 1969]. pp. 200.

— United Kingdom.

A PRELIMINARY report on an on-the-spot survey of accidents; by R.N. Kemp [and others]. Crowthorne, 1972. pp. 25. *(U.K. Transport and Road Research Laboratory. Reports. LR 434)*

— United States.

TRAVELERS INSURANCE COMPANY. Voices in Society. Voice behind the wheel. Hartford, Conn., 1971. pp. 12.

TRAVELERS INSURANCE COMPANY. Voices in Society. Death by ounces. Hartford, Conn., 1972. pp. 20.

ROAD CONSTRUCTION
— Spain.

SPAIN. Servicio Nacional de Concentracion Parcelaria y Ordenacion Rural. 1967. Caminos rurales, dimensionado y construccion. Madrid, 1967. pp. 122. *bibliog. With summary in French and English.*

ROAD SAFETY
— United Kingdom.

LEWIS (G.D.) Children's use of aids to conspicuity. Crowthorne, 1973. pp. 32. *(U.K. Transport and Road Research Laboratory. Reports. LR 534)*

ROAD TRANSPORT WORKERS
— United Kingdom.

SMITH (GEORGE WILLIAM QUICK) Lorry drivers' wages and conditions of employment: a practical guide which includes points on the law relating to employment together with a ready reckoner based on the 44-hour week. London, 1948. pp. 74.

ROAD TRANSPORT INDUSTRY TRAINING BOARD [U.K.]. Report and statement of accounts. a., 1972/3- Wembley. *Formerly included in the file of British Parliamentary Papers.*

ROADS
— America, Latin — Finance.

CHURCHILL (ANTHONY) and others. Road user charges in Central America. [Washington], International Bank for Reconstruction and Development, [1972]. pp. 176. *bibliog. (World Bank Staff Occasional Papers. No. 15)*

— Canada — Finance.

ARCHAMBAULT (CAMILLE) Theories, objectives and practical problems of road finance: the truckers' viewpoint. [Quebec?, 1956]. fo. 65.

— Europe.

O'REILLY (M.P.) Some examples of underground development in Europe. Crowthorne, 1974. pp. 31. *(U.K. Transport and Road Research Laboratory. Reports. LR 592)*

— France.

FRANCE. Direction des Routes et de la Circulation Routière. Section des Relations Publiques. 1970. Le réseau routier national, 1970. [Paris, 1970]. pp. 56.

FRANCE. Délégation à l'Aménagement du Territoire et à l'Action Régionale. 1972. Les grandes liaisons routières: histoire d'un schéma. [Paris], 1972. pp. 103. *(Travaux et Recherches de Prospective. 31)*

FRANCE. Direction des Routes et de la Circulation Routière. 1972. Le réseau routier français: routes et autoroutes. Paris, 1972. pp. 222,CXX. *(Regards sur la France. Avril, 1972)*

JARDIN (ANTONIA) and FLEURY (PHILIPPE) La révolution de l'autoroute: l'autoroute dans la vie quotidienne des Français. [Paris, 1973]. pp. 256. *bibliog.*

— Germany — Hesse.

HESSE. Statistisches Landesamt. Beiträge zur Statistik Hessens. Neue Folge. Nr. 51. Die Gemeindestrassen am 1. Januar 1971. Wiesbaden, 1973. pp. 124.

— India — Finance.

NANJUNDAPPA (DOGGANAHAL MAHADEVAPPA) Road user taxation and road finance in Indian economy. Bombay, 1973. pp. 253.

— Norway.

NORWAY. Vegplankomitéen. 1970. Innstilling om Norsk vegplan [Karl Olsen, chairman] med Vegplanrådets uttalelse om innstilingen. Oslo, 1970. pp. 144.

TVEIT (NORVALD) Eit vegopprør i Bygde-Norge: Fjaerland. Oslo, 1973. pp. 118.

— Switzerland — Zürich (Canton).

ZUERICH (CANTON). Direktion der Öffentlichen Bauten. 1964. Aktuelle Probleme des zürcherischen Strassenbaues: das technische Konzept, die Verwirklichung. [Zürich?, 1964?]. pp. 29, fo.9.

ZUERICH (CANTON). Direktion der Öffentlichen Bauten. 1970. Zürcher Expressstrassen. [Zürich, 1970]. pp. 24.

ZUERICH (CANTON). Direktion der Öffentlichen Bauten. 1970. Zürcher Nationalstrassen. [Zürich, 1970]. pp. 16.

— Underdeveloped areas.

See UNDERDEVELOPED AREAS — Roads.

— United Kingdom.

BOOZ, ALLEN AND HAMILTON. Roads in Britain: an organisation review; a report...for the British Road Federation [reviewing recommendations contained in the Federation's report Roads: A New Approach]. London, [1970?]. pp. 59.

U.K. Parliament. House of Lords. Committee on the Highways Bill. Official report. Ap 28, My 3 1971 (1st-2nd sittings). London. *Photocopies.*

FREEMAN FOX AND ASSOCIATES. Speed/flow relationships on suburban main roads; a report on a study carried out for the Road Research Laboratory. London, 1972. pp. 25.

PEARCE (DAVID WILLIAM) and NASH (CHRISTOPHER A.) The evaluation of urban motorway schemes: a case study, Southampton. [Southampton], 1972. fo. 31. *(Southampton. University. Discussion Papers in Economics and Econometrics. No. 7214)*

U.K. Countryside Commission. 1972. West Cumberland trunk road study. [London], 1972. fo. 44,xxiii. *bibliog.*

U.K. Department of the Environment. 1973. Public inquiries into road proposals: what you will need to know... [London, 1973]. pp. 18.

U.K. Urban Motorways Project Team. 1973. Report...to the Urban Motorways Committee. London, 1973. pp. 287.

— — Finance.

BRITISH ROAD FEDERATION and BRITISH INDUSTRY ROADS CAMPAIGN. Finance and roads 1972;... [joint] study. London, [1972]. pp. 20.

NASH (CHRISTOPHER A.) The treatment of capital costs of vehicles in evaluating road schemes. [Southampton], 1973. fo. 22. *bibliog. (Southampton. University. Discussion Papers in Economics and Econometrics. No. 7313)*

— — London.

LONDON. Greater London Council. Traffic and Development Branch. The south east London study: an outline of the implications of the Greater London development plan for secondary road network and environmental area planning in south-east London. [London], 1972. pp. 58. *(London. Greater London Council. Greater London Development Plan. Background Papers. No.548)*

WEST LONDON STEERING GROUP. West London study; report of the steering group; (with Joint statement and Individual statements by the four participating authorities). [London, Greater London Council], 1973[-74]. pp. (28);5.

HALCROW (Sir WILLIAM THOMSON) AND PARTNERS and MOTT, HAY AND ANDERSON. Report on roads in tunnel for the Greater London Council. [London], Greater London Council, 1974. 1 vol. (various pagings).

— — Wales.

WELSH COUNCIL. Roads in Wales. [Cardiff?], 1974. pp. 51, 2 maps.

— United States — Finance.

STONE (ALASTAIR J.) Temporal costing and pricing of highway service. Berkeley, Calif., 1970. fo. 103. *(California University. Institute of Transportation and Traffic Engineering. Dissertation Series)*

— Zambia.

ZAMBIA. Roads Branch. Annual report. a., 1965/6, 1968- Lusaka.

ROANNE
— Politics and government.

INSTITUTION communale et pouvoir politique: le cas de Roanne; [by] Sylvie Biarez [and others]. Paris, [1973]. pp. 208. *bibliog.*

ROBERTSON (Sir JAMES WILSON).

ROBERTSON (Sir JAMES WILSON) Transition in Africa: from direct rule to independence; a memoir. London, [1974]. pp. 272.

ROCKEFELLER FAMILY.

SCHILLING (PAULO R.) El imperio Rockefeller: America Latina documentos; [and] La estrategia norteamericana en America Latina: de la doctrina Monroe al informe Rockefeller; ensayo; [translated from the English by Rosario Lorente]. Montevideo, [1970]. pp. 129.

KUTZ (MYER) Rockefeller power. New York, [1974]. pp. 288. *bibliog.*

ROLPH (C. H.) pseud.

ROLPH (C.H.) pseud. [i.e. Cecil Rolph HEWITT] Living twice: an autobiography. London, 1974. pp. 187.

ROMANCE LANGUAGES.

LINGUISTIC SYMPOSIUM ON ROMANCE LANGUAGES, 3RD, INDIANA UNIVERSITY, 1973. Linguistic studies in Romance languages: proceedings of the... symposium; R. Joe Campbell [and others] editors. Washington, [1974]. pp. 265. *bibliogs.*

ROMANTICISM.

JONES (HOWARD MUMFORD) Revolution and romanticism. Cambridge, Mass., 1974. pp. 487.

— Spain.

ZAVALA (IRIS M.) Romanticos y socialistas: prensa española del XIX. Madrid, 1972. pp. 208.

ROME (CITY).
— Politics and government.

ULLRICH (HARTMUT) Le elezioni del 1913 a Roma: i liberali fra massoneria e Vaticano. Milano, 1972. pp. 119. *(Nuova Rivista Storica. Biblioteca. N. 32)*

ROME, ANCIENT
— Economic history.

DUNCAN-JONES (RICHARD) The economy of the Roman Empire: quantitative studies. Cambridge, 1974. pp. 396. *bibliog.*

JONES (ARNOLD HUGH MARTIN) The Roman economy: studies in ancient economic and administrative history; edited by P.A. Brunt. Oxford, 1974. pp. 450.

— History.

GRUEN (ERICH S.) The last generation of the Roman Republic. Berkeley, Ca., [1974]. pp. 596. *bibliog.*

JONES (ARNOLD HUGH MARTIN) The Roman economy: studies in ancient economic and administrative history; edited by P.A. Brunt. Oxford, 1974. pp. 450.

— Social history.

FINLEY (MOSES I.) Studies in ancient society. London, 1974. pp. 324.

MACMULLEN (RAMSAY) Roman social relations, 50 B.C. to A.D. 284. New Haven, 1974. pp. 212. *bibliog.*

ROMMEL (ERWIN).

DOUGLAS-HOME (CHARLES) Rommel. London, [1973]. pp. 224. *bibliog.*

ROOSEVELT (FRANKLIN DELANO) President of the United States.

ASBELL (BERNARD) The F.D.R. memoirs; as written by Bernard Asbell. Garden City, N.Y., 1973. pp. 461. *bibliog.*

BARRON (GLORIA J.) Leadership in crisis: FDR and the path to intervention. Port Washington, N.Y., 1973. pp. 145. *bibliog.*

FREIDEL (FRANK BURT) Franklin D. Roosevelt: launching the New Deal. Boston, [1973]. pp. 574. *bibliog.*

BISHOP (JIM) FDR's last year: April 1944-April 1945. New York, 1974. pp. 690. *bibliog.*

ROSAS (JUAN MANUEL DE).

IBARGUREN (CARLOS) the Younger. Juan Manuel de Rosas: su vida, su drama, su tiempo. Buenos Aires, 1948. pp. 354.

ROSAS (JUAN MANUEL DE) defendant. Juicio criminal a Don Juan Manuel de Rosas; [documents compiled, with notes, by Vicente Zito Lema]. Buenos Aires, [1969]. pp. 111.

ROSENBERG (ALFRED).

BOLLMUS (REINHARD) Das Amt Rosenberg und seine Gegner: Studien zum Machtkampf im nationalsozialistischen Herrschaftssystem. Stuttgart, 1970. pp. 360. *bibliog.* (*Institut für Zeitgeschichte. Studien zur Zeitgeschichte*)

ROSSELLI (CARLO).

GAROSCI (ALDO) Vita di Carlo Rosselli. 2nd ed. Firenze, [1973]. 2 vols.

ROSTOCK

— Economic history.

HAUSCHILD (URSULA) Studien zu Löhnen und Preisen in Rostock im Spätmittelalter. Köln, 1973. pp. 229. *bibliog.* (*Hansischer Geschichtsverein. Quellen und Darstellungen zur Hansischen Geschichte. Neue Folge. Band 19*)

ROTHERHAM

— Civic improvement.

URWICK, ORR AND PARTNERS and ASHWORTH (GRAHAM) The Rotherham study. London, H.M.S.O., 1973. 2 pts.

ROUMANIA

— Economic conditions.

WILD (GERARD) Le développement économique de la Roumanie. [Paris, 1972]. pp. 63. *bibliog.* (*France. Direction de la Documentation. La Documentation Française. Notes et Etudes Documentaires. Nos. 3943-3944*)

CONSTANTINESCU (OLGA) Critica teoriei "România țară eminamente agricolă". București, 1973. pp. 323. *bibliog.* (*Academia de Științe Sociale și Politice a Republicii Socialiste România. Institutul de Cercetări Economice. Bibliotheca Oeconomica. 26*). With English, French and Russian tables of contents.

SPIGLER (IANCU) Economic reform in Rumanian industry. London, 1973. pp. 176. (*Glasgow. University. Institute of Soviet and East European Studies. Economic Reforms in East European Industry*)

TURNOCK (DAVID) An economic geography of Romania. London, 1974. pp. 319. *bibliog.*

— Economic history.

EIDELBERG (PHILIP GABRIEL) The great Rumanian peasant revolt of 1907: origins of a modern jacquerie. Leiden, 1974. pp. 259. *bibliog.* (*Columbia University. East Central European Studies*).

— Economic policy.

SPIGLER (IANCU) Economic reform in Rumanian industry. London, 1973. pp. 176. (*Glasgow. University. Institute of Soviet and East European Studies. Economic Reforms in East European Industry*)

— Fairs.

PENELEA (GEORGETA) Les foires de la Valachie pendant la période 1774-1848. Bucarest, 1973. pp. 189. (*Academia de Științe Sociale și Politice a Republicii Socialiste România. Bibliotheca Historica Romaniae. Studies. 44*)

— History.

GEORGESCU (TITU) Progress and revolution in the tradition of the Romanian people, 1848-1971. Bucharest, 1971. pp. 132.

CÎMPINA (BARBU) Scrieri istorice. București, 1973 in progress.

BERINDEI (DAN) L'année révolutionnaire 1821 dans les pays roumains. Bucarest, 1973. pp. 246. *bibliog.* (*Academia de Științe Sociale și Politice a Republicii Socialiste România. Bibliotheca Historica Romaniae. Studies. 46*)

— Industries.

ZANE (G.) L'industrie roumaine au cours de la seconde moitié du XIXe siècle: sur les origines historiques de l'industrie de fabrique.[Bucharest], 1973. pp. 261. (*Academia de Științe Sociale și Politice a Republicii Socialiste România. Bibliotheca Historica Romaniae. Studies. 43*)

— Intellectual life.

CURTICĂPEANU (V.) Le mouvement culturel pour le parachèvement de l'état national roumain, 1918. Bucarest, 1973. pp. 264. (*Academia Republicii Socialiste România. Secția de Științe Istorice, Filozofice și Economico-Juridice. Bibliotheca Historica Romaniae. Monographies. 12*)

— Politics and government.

CONSTANTINESCU-IAȘI (PETRU) La lutte pour la création du front populaire en Roumanie. Bucarest, 1972. pp. 181. (*Academia Republicii Socialiste România. Secția de Științe Istorice, Filozofice și Economico-Juridice. Bibliotheca Historica Romaniae. Studies. 21*)

ROUMANIANS IN AUSTRIA—HUNGARY.

CURTICĂPEANU (V.) Le mouvement culturel pour le parachèvement de l'état national roumain, 1918. Bucarest, 1973. pp. 264. (*Academia Republicii Socialiste România. Secția de Științe Istorice, Filozofice și Economico-Juridice. Bibliotheca Historica Romaniae. Monographies. 12*)

ROUSSEAU (JEAN JACQUES).

CHARVET (JOHN) The social problem in the philosophy of Rousseau. Cambridge, 1974. pp. 148.

ROVERUD

— Social conditions.

BROFOSS (INGER MARIE) Roverud: en sosiologisk analyse av endringsprosessene i et lokalsamfunn. Oslo, Distriktenes Utbyggingsfond, 1972. fo. 93, [18]. *bibliog.*

ROY (MANABENDRA NATH).

GROVER (D.C.) M.N. Roy: a study of revolution and reason in Indian politics. Calcutta, 1973. pp. 187. *bibliog.*

ROYAL NATIONAL LIFE—BOAT INSTITUTION.

WARNER (OLIVER) The life-boat service:... a history of the Royal National Life-boat Institution, 1824-1974. London, 1974. pp. 321. *bibliog.*

ROYAL TOUCH.

BLOCH (MARC LEOPOLD BENJAMIN) The royal touch: sacred monarchy and scrofula in England and France;... translated by J.E. Anderson. London, 1973. pp. 441. *bibliog.*

ROYAL WANSTEAD SCHOOL.

GRIST (DONALD HONEY) A Victorian charity: the Infant Orphan Asylum at Wanstead. London, [1974]. pp. 109,xxxviii.

RUBBER.

INTERNATIONAL RUBBER STUDY GROUP. Assembly, 19th, São Paulo, 1967. Documents. [Rio de Janeiro, Superintendência da Borracha, 1968?]. 1 vol. (various pagings). In English, French and Portuguese.

RUBBER INDUSTRY AND TRADE

— Europe.

FRANCE. Direction de la Documentation. La Documentation Française. Notes et Etudes Documentaires. No. 3,237. L'industrie du caoutchouc en Europe occidentale. Paris, 1965. pp. 33. *bibliog.*

— India.

CHITALE (V.P.) and ROY (P.K.) Natural and synthetic rubber: perspectives for the seventies; a study of the basic raw material requirements of the Indian rubber industry, etc. New Delhi, [1971]. pp. 96. (*Economic and Scientific Research Foundation. Natural Resources and Industrial Development. 3*)

— United Kingdom.

RUBBER REGENERATING COMPANY. The Rubber Regenerating Company Limited, Manchester, England: 1909-1959. Manchester, [1959]. pp. 38.

RUBBER AND PLASTICS PROCESSING INDUSTRY TRAINING BOARD [U.K.]. Report and statement of accounts. a., 1972/3- Brentford. *Formerly included in the file of British Parliamentary Papers.*

RUG AND CARPET INDUSTRY

— Russia — White Russia.

BORODULIN (MARK MOISEEVICH) and others. Rovesnik veka. Minsk, 1969. pp. 102.

— United Kingdom.

CARPET INDUSTRY TRAINING BOARD [U.K.]. Report and statement of accounts. a., 1972/3- Wilmslow, Cheshire. *Formerly included in the file of British Parliamentary Papers.*

RUGELEY

— Economic conditions.

SMITH (BARBARA M.D.) and PARSONS (HELEN K.) The Rugeley study: a report to Rugeley Urban District Council on employment opportunities in Rugeley and district. Birmingham, 1971. fo. 170. (*Birmingham. University. Centre for Urban and Regional Studies. Research Memoranda. No.8*)

RUHR

— Economic history.

HENDERSON (WILLIAM OTTO) William Thomas Mulvany: ein irischer Unternehmer im Ruhrgebiet, 1806-1885. Köln, 1970. pp. 20. (*Cologne. Universität. Forschungsinstitut für Sozial- und Wirtschaftsgeschichte. Kölner Vorträge zur Sozial- und Wirtschaftsgeschichte. Heft 12*)

BAUER (WILHELM) 1904- . Strukturveränderungen im Ruhrgebiet: das Ruhrgebiet, gestern und heute. Düsseldorf, [1972]. pp. 20. (*Volks- und Betriebswirtschaftliche Vereinigung im Rheinisch-Westfälischen Industriegebiet. Schriften. Sonderveröffentlichungen. 13*)

RUHR. (Cont.)

— History.

LUCAS (ERHARD) Märzrevolution 1920: der bewaffnete Arbeiteraufstand im Ruhrgebiet in seiner inneren Struktur und in seinem Verhältnis zu den Klassenkämpfen in den verschiedenen Regionen des Reiches. Frankfurt am Main, [1973]. pp. 251. *bibliog.*

MEINBERG (ADOLF) Aufstand an der Ruhr: Reden und Aufsätze; herausgegeben von Hellmut G. Haasis und Erhard Lucas. Frankfurt M., [1973]. pp. 232. *bibliog.*

TEUBER (HEINRICH) Für die Sozialisierung des Ruhrbergbaus: [new ed. of series of articles originally published in 1926]; herausgegeben von Hellmut G. Haasis und Erhard Lucas. Frankfurt, [1973]. pp. 131.

ELIASBERG (GEORGE) Der Ruhrkrieg von 1920; mit einer Einführung von Richard Löwenthal. Bonn-Bad Godesberg, [1974]. pp. 304. *bibliog.* *(Friedrich-Ebert-Stiftung. Forschungsinstitut. Schriftenreihe. Band 100)*

RULE OF LAW
— Russia — Ukraine.

BUTKO (IHOR PYLYPOVYCH) and SHEMSHUCHENKO (IURII SERHIIOVYCH) Mistsevi Rady i zabezpechennia zakonnosti. Kyïv, 1973. pp. 232. *With Russian summary.*

RUMBOLD (Sir HORACE MONTAGUE).

GILBERT (MARTIN) Sir Horace Rumbold: portrait of a diplomat, 1869-1941. London, 1973. pp. 496.

RURAL CONDITIONS.

CLOUT (HUGH D.) Rural geography: an introductory survey. Oxford, 1972. pp. 204. *bibliogs.*

RURAL CONDITIONS.

See also subdivision Rural conditions under names of countries, states, etc. and under the heading UNDERDEVELOPED AREAS.

RURAL FAMILIES
— Germany.

KNIRIM (CHRISTA) Erziehungsleitbilder in Stadt- und Landfamilien der Bundesrepublik Deutschland. Bonn, 1974. pp. 248. *bibliog. (Forschungsgesellschaft für Agrarpolitik und Agrarsoziologie. [Publications]. 223)*

RURAL SCHOOLS
— Mexico.

GARCIA RUIZ (RAMON) Educacion, cambios y desarrollo de la comunidad. Mexico, 1970. pp. 183. *bibliog.*

RURAL—URBAN MIGRATION.

BUSSEY (ELLEN M.) The flight from rural poverty: how nations cope. Lexington, Mass., [1973]. pp. 132.

CORNELIUS (WAYNE A.) Political learning among the migrant poor: the impact of residential context. Beverly Hills, [1973]. pp. 88. *bibliog.*

— Bibliography.

BRIGHTON. University of Sussex. Institute of Development Studies. Library. Occasional Guides. No. 3. Rural migration in less developed countries: a preliminary bibliography. Brighton, [1973]. pp. 62.

— Mathematical models.

GAUDE (JACQUES) Emploi agricole et migrations dans une économie dualiste. Genève, 1972. pp. 224. *(International Labour Office. Travaux et Recherches)*

— Africa, Subsaharan.

ROSSER (COLIN) Urbanization in tropical Africa: a demographic introduction. [New York, 1972?]. pp. 74. *(Ford Foundation. International Urbanization Survey. Working Papers. 272)*

— Africa, West.

INTERNATIONAL AFRICAN SEMINAR. 11th Seminar, Dakar, 1972. Modern migrations in western Africa: studies presented and discussed at the...seminar...; edited with an introduction by Samir Amin. London, 1974. pp. 426. *Text in French and English with a summary in the other language.*

— America, Latin.

CONSEJO LATINOAMERICANO DE CIENCIAS SOCIALES. Comision de Poblacion y Desarrollo. Grupo de Trabajo sobre Migraciones Internas. Migracion y desarrollo. Buenos Aires, 1972 in progress. *(Consejo Latinoamericano de Ciencias Sociales. Serie Poblacion. Informe de Investigacion)* Library has vols. 1 and 2.

— Austria.

GISSER (RICHARD) Die Zuwanderung nach Wien: eine Untersuchung zur Situation der Bundeshauptstadt in der regionalen Bevölkerungsentwicklung. Wien, 1969. 1 vol.(various pagings). *(Österreichisches Institut für Raumplanung. Veröffentlichungen. Nr. 34)*

— France.

VINCIENNE (MONIQUE) Du village à la ville: le système de mobilité des agriculteurs. Paris, [1972]. pp. 358. *bibliog. (Paris. École Pratique des Hautes Études. Section des Sciences Economiques et Sociales. Recherches Coopératives. 7)*

— Ivory Coast.

GIBBAL (JEAN MARIE) Citadins et paysans dans la ville africaine: l'exemple d'Abidjan. Grenoble, 1974. pp. 403.

— Japan.

WHITE (JAMES W.) Political implications of cityward migration: Japan as an exploratory test case. Beverly Hills, [1973]. pp. 59. *bibliog.*

— Kenya.

LAURENTI (LUIGI) and GERHART (JOHN) Urbanization in Kenya: urbanization trends and prospects; by Luigi Laurenti; Rural development and urban growth; by John Gerhart. [New York, 1972?]. pp. 45,19. *bibliog. (Ford Foundation. International Urbanization Survey. Working Papers. 274)*

— New Hebrides.

BEDFORD (R.D.) New Hebridean mobility: a study of circular migration. Canberra, 1973. pp. 164. *bibliog. (Australian National University. Research School of Pacific Studies. Department of Human Geography. Publications. HG/9)*

— Nigeria.

OLUSANYA (PHILIP OLUFEMI) Socio-economic aspects of rural-urban migration in western Nigeria.Ibadan, 1969. pp. 164. *bibliog.*

ADEPOJU (JOHN ADERANTI) Internal migration in south-west Nigeria: a demographic and socio-economic study of recent in-migration into the towns of Ife and Oshogbo; [Ph.D.(London) thesis]. 1973. fo. 354. *bibliog. Typescript: unpublished. This thesis is the property of London University and may not be removed from the Library.*

— Puerto Rico.

SAFA (HELEN ICKEN) The urban poor of Puerto Rico: a study in development and inequality. New York, [1974]. pp. 116. *bibliog.*

— Spain.

MATAS PERICE (ALFRED) Al sud-oest del riu Besos: deu anys de la vida d'un barri barceloni. Barcelona, 1970. pp. 204.

— Sudan.

GALAL EL DIN (MOHED ELAWAD) Internal migration in the Sudan since World War II, with special reference to migration to Greater Khartoum; [Ph.D. (London) thesis]. 1973. fo. 301. *bibliog. Typescript: unpublished. This thesis is the property of London University and may not be removed from the Library.*

— Trinidad and Tobago.

SIMPSON (JOY M.) A demographic analysis of internal migration in Trinidad and Tobago: a descriptive and theoretical orientation. [Kingston, Jamaica, 1973]. pp. 63.

— Uganda.

HUTTON (CAROLINE) Reluctant farmers?: a study of unemployment and planned rural development in Uganda. Nairobi, 1973. pp. 331. *bibliog. (Makerere Institute of Social Research. East African Studies. No.33)*

— United Kingdom.

PATTEN (JOHN) Rural-urban migration in pre-industrial England. Oxford, 1973. pp. 61. *(Oxford. University. School of Geography. Research Papers. No. 6)*

— Zambia.

SIMMANCE (ALAN J.F.) Urbanization in Zambia. [New York, 1972]. pp. 52. *(Ford Foundation . International Urbanization Survey. Working Papers. 275)*

HEISLER (HELMUTH) Urbanisation and the government of migration: the inter-relation of urban and rural life in Zambia. London, [1974]. pp. 166. *bibliog.*

RURAL YOUTH
— Russia.

PROFESSIONAL'NAIA orientatsiia sel'skoi molodezhi. Moskva, 1973. pp. 95. *bibliog.*

RUSKIN (JOHN).

JAUDEL (PHILIPPE) La pensée sociale de John Ruskin. Paris, 1972. pp. 446. *bibliog.*

RUSSELL (BERTRAND ARTHUR WILLIAM) 3rd Earl Russell.

FEINBERG (BARRY) and KASRILS (RONALD) Bertrand Russell's America: his transatlantic travels and writings;... a documented account. London, 1973 in progress. *bibliog.*

RUSSIA
— Annexation — Bessarabia.

KOPANSKII (IAKOV MIKHAILOVICH) Internatsional'nye traditsii bor'by za vossoedinenie Bessarabii s Sovetskoi Rodinoi, 1918-1940 gg. Kishinev, 1973. pp. 110.

— Armed forces — Political activity.

RUSSIA (U.S.S.R.). Ministerstvo Oborony. 1973. Spravochnik propagandista i agitatora armii i flota. 2nd ed. Moskva, 1973. pp. 349.

— Army — History.

DAVATTS (VLADIMIR KHRISTIANOVICH) and L'VOV (N.N.) Russkaia armiia na chuzbine. Belgrad, 1923. pp. 123.

GUSEV (SERGEI IVANOVICH) pseud. [i.e. Iakov Davydovich DRABKIN] Grazhdanskaia voina i Krasnaia Armiia: sbornik voenno- teoreticheskikh i voenno-politicheskikh statei, 1918-1924. Moskva, 1925. pp. 220. *Contains 25 articles.*

ISTRATI (EVGENIIA NIKOLAEVNA) Demokraticheskoe dvizhenie za mir na Rumynskom fronte v 1917 godu; pod redaktsiei... A.S. Esaulenko. Kishinev, 1973. pp. 148. *bibliog.*

SELIVANOV (PANTELEIMON ALEKSEEVICH) Voennoe stroitel'stvo v Belorussii v period razgroma pokhodov Antanty. Minsk, 1973. pp. 208.

RUSSIA.

ZAIONCHKOVSKII (PETR ANDREEVICH) Samoderzhavie i russkaia armiia na rubezhe XIX-XX stoletii, 1881-1903. Moskva, 1973. pp. 351.

— — — Sources.

GAPONENKO (LUKA STEPANOVICH) ed. Oktiabr'skaia revoliutsiia i armiia, 25 oktiabria 1917 g. - mart 1918 g.: sbornik dokumentov. Moskva, 1973. pp. 455.

— Bibliography.

UNIVERSITY OF ESSEX. Library. Reference Booklets. No. 2. Soviet materials: a guide for social scientists. 2nd ed. [Colchester], 1973. pp. 58.

— Census.

RUSSIA (U.S.S.R.). Census, 1970. Itogi Vsesoiuznoi perepisi naseleniia 1970 goda. Moskva, 1972-74. 7 vols.

— Commerce.

PATOLICHEV (NIKOLAI SEMENOVICH) (USSR yesterday, today, tomorrow): foreign trade. [Moscow, 1971?]. pp. 179.

ATTMAN (ARTUR) The Russian and Polish markets in international trade, 1500-1650.Göteborg, 1973. pp. 232. (*Göteborgs Universitet. Ekonomisk-Historiska Institutionen. Meddelanden. 26*)

GREER (THOMAS V.) Marketing in the Soviet Union. New York, 1973. pp. 188.

LEVIN (ALEKSANDR IVANOVICH) Sotsialisticheskii vnutrennii rynok: zakonomernosti i problemy razvitiia. Moskva, 1973. pp. 270.

LEVIN (ALEKSANDR IVANOVICH) and IARKIN (ANATOLII PAVLOVICH) Ekonomicheskie problemy funktsionirovaniia vnutrennei torgovli. Moskva, 1973. pp. 167.

McMILLAN (C.H.) The bilateral character of Soviet and Eastern European foreign trade. [Ottawa], 1973. fo. 38. bibliog. (*Carleton University. Carleton Economic Papers*)

OSNOVY ekonomiki torgovli. Moskva, 1973. pp. 231.

ROSEFIELDE (STEVEN) Soviet international trade in Heckscher-Ohlin perspective: an input-output study. Lexington, Mass., [1973]. pp. 173. bibliog.

— — Mathematical models.

ROSEFIELDE (STEVEN) Soviet international trade in Heckscher-Ohlin perspective: an input-output study. Lexington, Mass., [1973]. pp. 173. bibliog.

NOVOZHILOVA (ELENA MIKHAILOVNA) Indeksnyi metod analiza v torgovle. Moskva, 1974. pp. 128.

— Constitution.

CHIRKIN (VENIAMIN EVGEN'EVICH) Formy sotsialisticheskogo gosudarstva. Moskva, 1973. pp. 270.

KOPEICHIKOV (VLADIMIR VLADIMIROVICH) Mekhanizm gosudarstva v sovetskoi federatsii. Moskva, 1973. pp. 200.

TIKHOMIROV (IURII ALEKSANDROVICH) Pouvoir et administration dans la société socialiste. Paris, 1973. pp. 193.

VASIL'EV (VSEVOLOD IVANOVICH) Demokratichskii tsentralizm v sisteme Sovetov. Moskva, 1973. pp. 231.

— Constitutional history.

ISTORIIA natsional'no-gosudarstvennogo stroitel'stva v SSSR: natsional'no-gosudarstvennoe stroitel'stvo v SSSR v period sotsializma i stroitel'stva kommunizma, 1937-1967 gg. Moskva, 1970. pp. 276.

PROBLEMY gosudarstvennogo stroitel'stva v pervye gody Sovetskoi vlasti. Leningrad, 1973. pp. 363. bibliog. (*Akademiia Nauk SSSR. Institut Istorii. Leningradskoe Otdelenie. Trudy. vyp.14*)

SOVETSKOE gosudarstvo - god pervyi. Moskva, 1973. pp. 263.

GAL'PERIN (GRIGORII BORISOVICH) and KOROLEV (ALEKSEI IVANOVICH) Metodologicheskie i teoreticheskie voprosy nauki istorii gosudarstva i prava SSSR. Leningrad, 1974. pp. 103.

— — Sources.

TSENTRAL'NYI GOSUDARSTVENNYI ARKHIV OKTIABR'SKOI REVOLIUTSII, VYSSHIKH ORGANOV GOSUDARSTVENNOI VLASTI I ORGANOV GOSUDARSTVENNOGO UPRAVLENIIA SSSR. 1917 God v Dokumentakh i Materialakh. Petrogradskii Sovet rabochikh i soldatskikh deputatov: protokoly zasedanii Ispolnitel'nogo Komiteta i Biuro I.K.; podgotovleno k pechati B.Ia. Nalivaiskim. Moskva, 1925. pp. 375.

TSENTRAL'NYI GOSUDARSTVENNYI ARKHIV OKTIABR'SKOI REVOLIUTSII, VYSSHIKH ORGANOV GOSUDARSTVENNOI VLASTI I ORGANOV GOSUDARSTVENNOGO UPRAVLENIIA SSSR. 1917 God v Dokumentakh i Materialakh. Vserossiiskoe Soveshchanie Sovetov rabochikh i soldatskikh deputatov: stenograficheskii otchet; podgotovil k pechati M.N. Tsapenko, etc.. Moskva, 1927. pp. 356.

TSENTRAL'NYI GOSUDARSTVENNYI ARKHIV OKTIABR'SKOI REVOLIUTSII, VYSSHIKH ORGANOV GOSUDARSTVENNOI VLASTI I ORGANOV GOSUDARSTVENNOGO UPRAVLENIIA SSSR. 1917 God v Dokumentakh i Materialakh. Gosudarstvennoe Soveshchanie: (stenograficheskii otchet) s predisloviem Ia.A. Iakovleva. Moskva, 1930. pp. 372.

OBRAZOVANIE i razvitie Soiuza Sovetskikh Sotsialisticheskikh Respublik v dokumentakh. Moskva, 1973. pp. 735.

— Constitutional law.

KRAVCHUK (S.S.) ed. Pravovye problemy dal'neishego sovershenstvovaniia predstavitel'nykh organov gosudarstvennoi vlasti. Moskva, 1973. pp. 154.

— Defences.

BOOTH (KEN) The military instrument in Soviet foreign policy, 1917-1972. London, [1973]. pp. 65.

SUTTON (ANTONY C.) National suicide: military aid to the Soviet Union. New Rochelle, N.Y., [1973]. pp. 283. bibliog.

— Description and travel.

GEORGE (PIERRE) Géographie de l'U.R.S.S. 4th ed. Paris, 1974. pp. 127. bibliog.

— Discovery and exploration.

LANTZEFF (GEORGE VJATCHESLAU) and PIERCE (RICHARD A.) Eastward to empire: exploration and conquest on the Russian open frontier to 1750. Montreal, 1973. pp. 276. bibliog.

— Economic conditions.

SAUSHKIN (IULIAN GLEBOVICH) and others, eds. Ekonomicheskaia geografiia Sovetskogo Soiuza. Moskva, 1967-73. 2 vols.

FEODORITOV (VOLODAR IAKOVLEVICH) Problemy povysheniia ekonomicheskoi effektivnosti proizvodstva. Leningrad, 1970. pp. 192. bibliog.

LIBERMAN (EVSEI GRIGOR'EVICH) Ekonomicheskie metody povysheniia effektivnosti obshchestvennogo proizvodstva. Moskva, 1970. pp. 175.

SAVASTIUK (ANTON IVANOVICH) V. I. Lenin o pobede sotsializma v SSSR; pod redaktsiei ... K.P. Buslova. Minsk, 1970. pp. 222. bibliog.

EKONOMICHESKIE i sotsial'no-politicheskie problemy kommunisticheskogo stroitel'stva v SSSR: materialy nauchnoi konferentsii Instituta marksizma-leninizma pri TsK KPSS, Akademii obshchestvennykh nauk pri TsK KPSS, Vysshei partiinoi shkoly pri TsK KPSS, sektsii obshchestvennykh nauk AN SSSR na temu: "XXIV s"ezd KPSS i razvitie marksistsko-leninskoi teorii", 29 sentiabria 1 oktiabria 1971 g. Moskva, 1972. pp. 351.

UCHENYE ZAPISKI KAFEDR OBSHCHESTVENNYKH NAUK VUZOV LENINGRADA. Politicheskaia Ekonomiia. vyp.13. Protsess obobshchestvleniia sotsialisticheskogo proizvodstva v usloviiakh sovremennoi nauchno-tekhnicheskoi revoliutsii. Leningrad, 1972. pp. 198.

XXIV s"ezd KPSS i aktual'nye problemy politicheskoi ekonomii. Moskva, 1973. pp. 239.

AGEEV (VALENTIN MIKHAILOVICH) Metodologicheskie i teoreticheskie problemy osnovnogo ekonomicheskogo zakona sotsializma. Moskva, 1973. pp. 208.

AGENTSTVO PECHATI NOVOSTI. USSR'73: Novosti Press Agency Year Book. Moscow, 1973. pp. 304.

KOLESOV (NIKOLAI DMITRIEVICH) Zakon sootvetstviia proizvoditel'nykh sil i proizvodstvennykh otnoshenii pri sotsializme. Leningrad, 1973. pp. 159.

MALYSHEV (PAVEL ALEKSEEVICH) and SHILIN (IVAN GRIGOR'EVICH) Kriterii effektivnosti sotsialisticheskogo vosproizvodstva: sotsial'no-ekonomicheskii aspekt. Moskva, 1973. pp. 382.

MEDVEDEV (VLADIMIR AFINOGENOVICH) Sotsialisticheskoe vosproizvodstvo i strukturnye sdvigi v ekonomike. Moskva, 1973. pp. 183.

PIVTSAIKIN (GEORGII IVANOVICH) Obshchestvennye otnosheniia razvitogo sotsializma. Minsk, 1973. pp. 261.

SEMIN (SERGEI IVANOVICH) Preodolenie sotsial'no-ekonomicheskikh razlichii mezhdu gorodom i derevnei. Moskva, 1973. pp. 159.

CAMPBELL (ROBERT WELLINGTON) Soviet-type economies: performance and evolution. rev ed. London, 1974. pp. 259. bibliog.

GEORGE (PIERRE) Géographie de l'U.R.S.S. 4th ed. Paris, 1974. pp. 127. bibliog.

GORBUNOV (EDUARD PETROVICH) Struktura i effektivnost' obshchestvennogo proizvodstva. Moskva, 1974. pp. 199.

PASHKOV (ANATOLII IGNAT'EVICH) Ökonomische Probleme des Sozialismus; Übersetzung aus dem Russischen ([by] Cay-Harro Dahl [and others]). Berlin, 1974. pp. 470.

PRAVOTOROV (GEORGII BORISOVICH) Stoimostnye kategorii i sposob proizvodstva: problemy teorii i metodologii. Moskva, 1974. pp. 303.

— — Mathematical models.

STRUKTURA i tempy rosta obshchestvennogo proizvodstva. Kishinev, 1972. pp. 132.

ANCHISHKIN (ALEKSANDR IVANOVICH) Prognozirovanie rosta sotsialisticheskoi ekonomiki. Moskva, 1973. pp. 294.

IL'ENKOVA (SVETLANA DMITRIEVNA) Rezervy proizvodstva: statistiko-matematicheskoe issledovanie. Moskva, 1973. pp. 96. bibliog.

LUR'E (ALEKSANDR L'VOVICH) and NIT (IGOR' VASIL'EVICH) Ekonomiko-matematicheskoe modelirovanie sotsialisticheskogo khoziaistva; pod redaktsiei... A.I. Katsenelinboigena. Moskva, 1973. pp. 284. bibliog.

NAUMOVA (VALENTINA IVANOVNA) Sistema ekonomicheskikh zakonov sotsializma i mekhanizm ee deistviia: teoriia i metodologiia. Leningrad, 1973. pp. 176.

RUSSIA. (Cont.)

— Economic history.

LEL'CHUK (VITALII SEMENOVICH) and others. A short history of Soviet society; edited by Y. Polyakov. Moscow, 1971. pp. 445.

GIMPEL'SON (EFIM GILEVICH) "Voennyi kommunizm": politika, praktika, ideologiia. Moskva, 1973. pp. 296.

IATSUNSKII (VIKTOR KORNEL'EVICH) Sotsial'no-ekonomicheskaia istoriia Rossii XVIII-XIX vv.: izbrannye trudy. Moskva, 1973. pp. 302.

LENINSKOE uchenie o nepe i ego mezhdunarodnoe znachenie. Moskva, 1973. pp. 326.

ABRAMSKY (CHIMEN) ed. Essays in honour of E.H. Carr; edited by C. Abramsky assisted by Beryl J. Williams. London, 1974. pp. 387. bibliog.

BLACKWELL (WILLIAM LESLIE) ed. Russian economic development from Peter the Great to Stalin. New York, 1974. pp. 459. bibliog.

— — Historiography.

KAS'IANENKO (VASILII IGNAT'EVICH) Problemy sozdaniia material'no-tekhnicheskoi bazy kommunizma: istoriograficheskii ocherk. Moskva, 1973. pp. 182.

— Economic policy.

RYKOV (ALEKSEI IVANOVICH) Sotsialisticheskoe stroitel'stvo i mezhdunarodnaia politika SSSR: doklad na IV S"ezde Sovetov SSSR. Moskva, 1927. pp. 118. Bound in with Prokopovich (sergei Nikolaevich) Ocherki khoziaistva Sovetskoi Rossii.

MOLIAKOV (DMITRII STEPANOVICH) Pribyl' i rentabel'nost' promyshlennogo predpriiatiia. Moskva, 1967. pp. 146.

BERKHIN (IL'IA BORISOVICH) Ekonomicheskaia politika Sovetskogo gosudarstva v pervye gody Sovetskoi vlasti. Moskva, 1970. pp. 239. (Akademiia Nauk SSSR. Nauchno-Populiarnaia Seriia)

Le DEBAT soviétique sur la loi de la valeur; [by] L. Trotsky [and others]. Paris, 1972. pp. 258.

EL'MEEV (VASILII IAKOVLEVICH) and others. Kompleksnoe planirovanie ekonomicheskogo i sotsial'nogo razvitiia raiona. Leningrad, 1972. pp. 126.

SLADKEVICH (NAUM GRIGOR'EVICH) ed. Problemy obshchestvennoi mysli i ekonomicheskoi politika Rossii XIX-XX vekov; pamiati professora S.B. Okunia: sbornik statei. Leningrad, 1972. pp. 198.

SOVIET economic reform: progress and problems; [by Nikolai Fedoryenko, and others]. Moscow, 1972. pp. 247.

SOVIET planning: principles and techniques; (translated from the Russian by Leo Lempert). Moscow, 1972. pp. 194.

TSAPKIN (N.V.) ed. Planirovanie narodnogo khoziaistva SSSR: uchebnoe posobie. [2nd ed.] Moskva, 1972. pp. 479.

UCHENYE ZAPISKI KAFEDR OBSHCHESTVENNYKH NAUK VUZOV LENINGRADA. Problemy Nauchnogo Kommunizma. vyp. 6. XXIV s"ezd KPSS i aktual'nye problemy nauchnogo kommunizma. Leningrad, 1972. pp. 160.

VOPROSY ekonomicheskoi politiki KPSS na sovremennom etape: dlia sistemy partiinoi ucheby i ekonomicheskogo obrazovaniia. 2nd ed. Moskva, 1972. pp. 407.

ABALKIN (LEONID IVANOVICH) Khoziaistvennyi mekhanizm razvitiia sotsialisticheskogo obshchestva. Moskva, 1973. pp. 263.

BACHURIN (ALEKSANDR VASIL'EVICH) Planovo-ekonomicheskie metody upravleniia. Moskva, 1973. pp. 455.

BARKER (ENNO) Die Rolle der Parteiorgane in der sowjetischen Wirtschaftslenkung, 1957-1965: zum Verhältnis von Partei und Staat in der Periode der Chruščevschen Wirtschaftsreformen. Berlin, 1973. pp. 252. bibliog. (Berlin. Freie Universität. Osteuropa-Institut. Philosophische und Soziologische Veröffentlichungen. Band 12)

BIALKOVSKAIA (VERA SERGEEVNA) Perspektivnoe planirovanie napravlenii tekhnicheskogo progressa. Moskva, 1973. pp. 191. bibliog.

BREEV (MIKHAIL VIKTOROVICH) Ekonomicheskie i metodologicheskie osnovy planirovaniia. Moskva, 1973. pp. 150.

ELLMAN (MICHAEL JOHN) Planning problems in the USSR: the contribution of mathematical economics to their solution, 1960-1971. Cambridge, 1973. pp. 222. bibliog. (Cambridge. University. Department of Applied Economics. Monographs. 24)

EREMIN (AL'BERT MIKHAILOVICH) Otnosheniia sotsialisticheskoi sobstvennosti i ekonomicheskoe upravlenie: ocherk teorii. Moskva, 1973. pp. 119.

GOLOBOROD'KO (ALEKSEI NIKONOVICH) Obshchestvennyi kontrol' nad proizvodstvom i raspredeleniem pri sotsializme. Kiev, 1973. pp. 295.

ISPOL'ZOVANIE mezhotraslevykh rezervov ekonomicheskogo raiona. Leningrad, 1973. pp. 192.

OKTIABR'SKII (PAVEL IAKOVLEVICH) Sushchnost' i kriterii ekonomicheskoi effektivnosti obshchestvennogo proizvodstva. Leningrad, 1973. pp. 54. bibliog.

PREOBRAZHENSKII (EVGENII ALEKSEEVICH) From New Economic Policy to socialism: a glance into the future of Russia and Europe; (translated from the Russian, 1962, by Brian Pearce). London, 1973. pp. 116.

VOPROSY ekonomicheskoi politiki KPSS na sovremennom etape: dlia sistemy partiinoi ucheby i ekonomicheskogo obrazovaniia. 3rd ed. Moskva, 1973. pp. 350.

BLACKWELL (WILLIAM LESLIE) ed. Russian economic development from Peter the Great to Stalin. New York, 1974. pp. 459. bibliog.

CAMPBELL (ROBERT WELLINGTON) Soviet-type economies: performance and evolution. rev ed. London, 1974. pp. 259. bibliog.

CHAMBRE (HENRI) L'évolution du marxisme soviétique: théorie économique et droit. Paris, [1974]. pp. 476.

CLEMENT (HERMANN) Die Roh- und Grundstoffwirtschaft der Sowjetunion: die Stellung ... in der internen sowjetischen Entwicklungspolitik. Hamburg, 1974. pp. 466. bibliog. (Hamburg. Hamburgisches Welt-Wirtschafts-Archiv. Veröffentlichungen)

JEFFRIES (IAN) The Stalinist economic system as a model for underdeveloped countries: the development of Soviet thought since 1953; [Ph.D.(London) thesis]. [1974]. fo. 301. bibliog. Typescript: unpublished. This thesis is the property of London University and may not be removed from the Library.

KLINSKII (ANATOLII IVANOVICH) Planirovanie ekonomicheskogo i sotsial'nogo razvitiia. Moskva, 1974. pp. 216. bibliog.

MATTHEWS (MERVYN) ed. Soviet government: a selection of official documents on internal policies. London, 1974. pp. 472.

PASHKOV (ANATOLII IGNAT'EVICH) Ökonomische Probleme des Sozialismus; Übersetzung aus dem Russischen ([by] Cay-Harro Dahl [and others]). Berlin, 1974. pp. 470.

POLITISCHE Ökonomie und Wirtschaftsleitung; (Autorenkollektiv: R. Beloussow [and others]). Berlin, 1974. pp. 354.

SOLZHENITSYN (ALEKSANDR ISAEVICH) Letter to Soviet leaders; translated by Hilary Sternberg [from an unpublished letter written in 1973]. London, 1974. pp. 59.

— — Mathematical models.

KATSENELINBOIGEN (ARON IOSIFOVICH) and others. Metodologicheskie voprosy optimal'nogo planirovaniia sotsialisticheskoi ekonomiki. Moskva, 1966. pp. 246. bibliog.

BAGRINOVSKII (KIRILL ANDREEVICH) and BERLIAND (EFIM LEIBOVICH) eds. Matematicheskie voprosy formirovaniia ekonomicheskikh modelei. Novosibirsk, 1973. pp. 138. bibliog.

BESEDIN (VASILII FEDOROVICH) ed. Avtomatizirovannaia sistema planirovaniia material'nykh resursov. Kiev, 1973. pp. 199. bibliog.

CHERNIAVSKII (VASILII OSIPOVICH) Effektivnost' proizvodstva i optimal'nost' planirovaniia. Moskva, 1973. pp. 191.

GERONIMUS (BORIS L'VOVICH) Puti sovershenstvovaniia planirovaniia material'no-tekhnicheskogo snabzheniia narodnogo khoziaistva: na osnove primeneniia ekonomiko-matematicheskikh metodov i vychislitel'noi tekhniki. Moskva, 1973. pp. 181.

KHRUTSKII (EVGENII AFANAS'EVICH) Optimizatsiia khoziaistvennykh sviazei. Moskva, 1973. pp. 95. bibliog.

KRUSHEVSKII (ARKADII VLADIMIROVICH) and others. Ekonomiko-matematicheskie modeli v planirovanii i upravlenii narodnym khoziaistvom, etc. Kiev, 1973. pp. 311. bibliog.

LEMESHEV (MIKHAIL IAKOVLEVICH) and PANCHENKO (ALEKSANDR IVANOVICH) Kompleksnye programmy v planirovanii narodnogo khoziaistva. Moskva, 1973. pp. 167. bibliog.

LUR'E (ALEKSANDR L'VOVICH) Ekonomicheskii analiz modelei planirovaniia sotsialisticheskogo khoziaistva. Moskva, 1973. pp. 435. bibliog. Contains O matematicheskikh metodakh reshenii zadach na optimum pri planirovanii sotsialisticheskogo khoziaistva and some other papers.

MIROSHNIKOV (PETR SEMENOVICH) and BABICH (VLADIMIR P.) eds. Avtomatizirovannaia sistema tekhniko-ekonomicheskogo planirovaniia: nekotorye voprosy sozdaniia i vnedreniia. Kiev, 1973. pp. 243. bibliog.

SATUNOVSKII (LEON MIKHAILOVICH) Mezhotraslevye modeli territorial'nogo planirovaniia. Vil'nius, 1973. pp. 142.

VAL'TUKH (KONSTANTIN KURTOVICH) ed. Problemy narodnokhoziaistvennogo optimuma. Novosibirsk, 1973. pp. 384.

— Executive departments.

IUSUPOV (VITALII ANDREEVICH) and VOLKOV (NIKOLAI ANDREEVICH) Nauchnye osnovy gosudarstvennogo upravleniia v SSSR: uchebnoe posobie. Kazan', 1972. pp. 97.

GOLOBOROD'KO (ALEKSEI NIKONOVICH) Obshchestvennyi kontrol' nad proizvodstvom i raspredeleniem pri sotsializme. Kiev, 1973. pp. 295.

LUNEV (ALEKSANDR EFREMOVICH) Teoreticheskie problemy gosudarstvennogo upravleniia. Moskva, 1974. pp. 247.

— Foreign economic relations — Mathematical models.

SHAGALOV (GRIGORII LAZAREVICH) Problemy optimal'nogo planirovaniia vneshneekonomicheskikh sviazei: voprosy teorii i metodologii. Moskva, 1973. pp. 295.

— — France.

GIRAULT (RENE) Emprunts russes et investissements français en Russie 1887-1914: recherches sur l'investissement international. Paris, 1973. pp. 624. bibliog. (Paris. Université de Paris I (Panthéon-Sorbonne). Publications. Nouvelle Série. Recherches. 3)

RUSSIA. (Cont.)

— — **United States.**

SOREVNOVANIE dvukh sistem: ekonomika i trudiashchiesia. Moskva, 1973. pp. 400. *With brief English summaries and table of contents.*

— **Foreign relations.**

RYKOV (ALEKSEI IVANOVICH) Sotsialisticheskoe stroitel'stvo i mezhdunarodnaia politika SSSR: doklad na IV S"ezde Sovetov SSSR. Moskva, 1927. pp. 118. *Bound in with Prokopovich (sergei Nikolaevich) Ocherki khoziaistva Sovetskoi Rossii.*

GRIMSTED (PATRICIA KENNEDY) The foreign ministers of Alexander I: political attitudes and the conduct of Russian diplomacy, 1801-1825. Berkeley, Ca., 1969. pp. 367. *bibliog.*

DIPLOMATICHESKAIA deiatel'nost' V.I. Lenina. Moskva, 1970. pp. 136.

VNESHNIAIA politika Sovetskogo Soiuza: aktual'nye problemy, 1967-1970. Moskva, 1970. pp. 262.

EUROPEAN security and the Soviet problem: report of a study group of the Institute for the Study of Conflict, London, July-November 1971; rapporteur, Brian Crozier; participants, Max Beloff [and others]. [London], 1972. pp. 64. *(Institute for the Study of Conflict. Special Reports)*

HANSEN (JOSEPH) Marxist, and LUND (CAROLINE) Nixon's Moscow and Peking summits: their meaning for Vietnam. New York, [1972]. pp. 31.

LIPPMANN (WALTER) The Cold War: a study in U.S. foreign policy: [with The sources of Soviet conduct by George Kennan]. New York, 1972. pp. 81. *bibliog.*

TATU (MICHEL) Le triangle Washington-Moscou-Pékin et les deux Europe(s). [Paris, 1972]. pp. 149.

McLANE (CHARLES B.) Soviet-Third World relations. London, 1973 in progress. *bibliog.*

BAZILI (NIKOLAI ALEKSANDROVICH) Nicolas de Basily, diplomat of Imperial Russia, 1903-1917: memoirs. Stanford, [1973]. pp. 201. *(Stanford University. Hoover Institution on War, Revolution and Peace. Hoover Institution Publications. 125)*

BLINOV (S.I.) Vneshniaia politika Sovetskoi Rossii: pervyi god proletarskoi diktatury. Moskva, 1973. pp. 247. *bibliog.*

BOOTH (KEN) The military instrument in Soviet foreign policy, 1917-1972. London, [1973]. pp. 65.

BREZHNEV (LEONID IL'ICH) O vneshnei politike KPSS i Sovetskogo gosudarstva: rechi i stat'i. Moskva, 1973. pp. 599.

GRIFFITH (WILLIAM E.) Peking, Moscow, and beyond: the Sino-Soviet-American triangle. Washington, D.C., 1973. pp. 71. *(Georgetown University. Center for Strategic and International Studies. Washington Papers. vol.[1]/6)*

INSTITUTE FOR THE STUDY OF CONFLICT. The peacetime strategy of the Soviet Union. London, [1973]. pp. 83. *(Institute for the Study of Conflict. Special Reports)*

INTERNATIONAL INSTITUTE FOR STRATEGIC STUDIES. Adelphi Papers. No. 101. Soviet risk-taking and crisis behaviour: from confrontation to coexistence?; by Hannes Adomeit. London, 1973. pp. 40.

NECHIPURENKO (VASILII IGNAT'EVICH) V.I. Lenin o zashchite sotsialisticheskogo Otechestva: printsipy internatsionalizma i zashchita Otechestva. Moskva, 1973. pp. 223. *bibliog.*

PROTOPOPOV (ANATOLII SERGEEVICH) SSSR i mezhdunarodnyi rabochii klass v bor'be za mir. Moskva, 1973. pp. 212. *bibliog.*

SOVIET strategy for the seventies: from cold war to peaceful coexistence; ([by] Foy D. Kohler [and others]). Miami, 1973. pp. 241. *(Miami (Florida). University. Center for Advanced International Studies. Monographs in International Affairs)*

ABRAMSKY (CHIMEN) ed. Essays in honour of E.H.Carr; edited by C. Abramsky assisted by Beryl J. Williams. London, 1974. pp. 387. *bibliog.*

JELAVICH (BARBARA) St. Petersburg and Moscow: tsarist and Soviet foreign policy, 1814-1974. Bloomington, [1974]. pp. 480. *bibliog.*

KANET (ROGER E.) ed. The Soviet Union and the developing nations. Baltimore, [1974]. pp. 302.

KHRUSHCHEV (NIKITA SERGEEVICH) Khrushchev remembers: the last testament; translated and edited by Strobe Talbott. London, 1974. pp. 602.

SHITOV (NIKOLAI FEDOROVICH) V.I. Lenin i proletarskii internatsionalizm, 1917-1924 gg. Moskva, 1974. pp. 359.

SOLZHENITSYN (ALEKSANDR ISAEVICH) Letter to Soviet leaders; translated by Hilary Sternberg [from an unpublished letter written in 1973]. London, 1974. pp. 59.

— — **Treaties.**

RUSSIA (U.S.S.R.). Treaties. 1954-1972. Dogovory ob okazanii pravovoi pomoshchi po grazhdanskim, semeinym i ugolovnym delam, zakliuchennye SSSR s drugimi sotsialisticheskimi gosudarstvami. 2nd ed. Moskva, 1973. pp. 392.

— — **Africa, Subsaharan.**

STEVENS (CHRISTOPHER ANTHONY) Relations between the U.S.S.R. and Africa between 1953 and 1972, with special reference to Ghana, Guinea, Kenya, Mali, Nigeria, Somalia and Tanzania; [Ph.D. (london) thesis]. [1973]. 1 vol. (various foliation). Typescript: unpublished. *This thesis is the property of London University and may not be removed from the Library.*

— — **Arab countries.**

SMOLANSKY (OLES M.) The Soviet Union and the Arab East under Khrushchev. Lewisburg, [1974]. pp. 326. *bibliog. (Columbia University. Middle East Institute. Modern Middle East Series. vol. 6)*

— — **China.**

GEL'BRAS (VILIA GDALIVICH) Kitai: krizis prodolzhaetsia. Moskva, 1973. pp. 223.

KAPUR (HARISH) The embattled tringele: Moscow, Peking, New Delhi. New York, 1973. pp. 175. *bibliog.*

THORNTON (RICHARD C.) China, the struggle for power 1917-1972. Bloomington, [1973]. pp. 403.

SULZBERGER (CYRUS LEO) The coldest war: Russia's game in China. New York, [1974]. pp. 113.

— — **Cuba.**

TORRES RAMIREZ (BLANCA) Las relaciones cubano-sovieticas, 1959-1968. Mexico, 1971. pp. 142. *bibliog. (Mexico City. Colegio de Mexico. Jornadas. 71)*

CROZIER (BRIAN) Soviet pressures in the Caribbean: the satellisation of Cuba. London, 1973. pp. 20. *(Institute for the Study of Conflict. Conflict Studies. No. 35)*

— — **Czechoslovakia.**

DOKUMENTY i materialy po istorii sovetsko-chekhoslovatskikh otnoshenii. Moskva, 1973 in progress.

— — **East (Near East).**

LANDIS (LINCOLN) Politics and oil: Moscow in the Middle East. New York, 1973. pp. 201. *bibliog.*

INSTITUTE FOR THE STUDY OF CONFLICT. Study Group. Soviet objectives in the Middle East. London, 1974. pp. 27. *(Institute for the Study of Conflict. Special Reports)*

KOHLER (FOY D.) and others. The Soviet Union and the October 1973 Middle East War: the implications for detente. Miami, [1974]. pp. 131. *(Miami (Florida). University. Center for Advanced International Studies. Monographs in International Affairs)*

MA'OZ (MOSHE) Soviet and Chinese relations with the Palestinian guerrilla organizations. Jerusalem, 1974. pp. 35. *bibliog. (Hebrew University. Leonard Davis Institute for International Relations. Jerusalem Papers on Peace Problems. No. 4)*

The SOVIET Union and the Middle East: the post-World War II era; [papers presented at a conference organized by the Center for Russian and East European Studies at Stanford University, 1969]; edited by Ivo J. Lederer and Wayne S. Vucinich. Stanford, [1974]. pp. 302. *(Stanford University. Hoover Institution on War, Revolution and Peace. Hoover Institution Publications. 133).*

— — **Europe, Eastern.**

GAWENDA (J.A.B.) The Soviet domination of Eastern Europe in the light of international law. Richmond, 1974. pp. 220. *bibliog.*

— — **Finland.**

VAYRYNEN (RAIMO) Conflicts in Finnish-Soviet relations: three comparative case studies. Tampere, 1972. pp. 270. *(Tampere. Yliopisto. Acta Universitatis Tamperensis. Ser. A. vol. 47)*

— — **Hungary.**

RUSSIA (U.S.S.R.). Ministerstvo Inostrannykh Del. 1974. Sovetsko-vengerskie otnosheniia, 1948-1970 gg.: dokumenty i materialy. Moskva, 1974. pp. 726.

— — **India.**

KAPUR (HARISH) The embattled tringele: Moscow, Peking, New Delhi. New York, 1973. pp. 175. *bibliog.*

RAY (HEMEN) Indo-Soviet relations, 1955-1971. Bombay, 1973. pp. 302.

— — **Iran.**

TUZMUKHAMEDOV (RAIS ABDULKHAKOVICH) Sovetsko-iranskie otnosheniia, 1917-1921. Moskva, 1960. pp. 95. *Author's name wrongly given in colophon as Rals.*

— — **Mongolia.**

SHIRENDYB (BAZARYN) V.I. Lenin i mongol'skii narod. Moskva, 1970. pp. 60.

— — **Poland.**

JUZWENKO (ADOLF) Polska a "biała" Rosja, od listopada 1918 do kwietnia 1920 r. Wrocław, 1973. pp. 296. *bibliog. With French summary.*

— — **United Kingdom.**

RYZHIKOV (VLADIMIR ALEKSANDROVICH) Zigzagi diplomatii Londona: iz istorii sovetsko-angliiskikh otnoshenii. Moskva, 1973. pp. 215.

KAISER (ROBERT G.) Cold winter, cold war. London, 1974. pp. 226. *bibliog.*

— — **United States.**

LIPPMANN (WALTER) The Cold War: a study in U.S. foreign policy: [with The sources of Soviet conduct by George Kennan]. New York, 1972. pp. 81. *bibliog.*

CLEMENS (WALTER CARL) The superpowers and arms control: from cold war to interdependence. Lexington, Mass., [1973]. pp. 180. *bibliog.*

PATERSON (THOMAS GRAHAM) Soviet-American confrontation: postwar reconstruction and the origins of the cold war. Baltimore, [1973]. pp. 287. *bibliog.*

AMERICAN ACADEMY OF POLITICAL AND SOCIAL SCIENCE. Annals. vol. 414. USA - USSR: agenda for communication; special editor of this volume Marvin E. Wolfgang. Philadelphia, [1974]. pp. 239.

CHAYES (ABRAM) The Cuban missile crisis. London, 1974. pp. 157. *(American Society of International Law. International Crises and the Role of Law)*

KAISER (ROBERT G.) Cold winter, cold war. London, 1974. pp. 226. *bibliog.*

WILLRICH (MASON) and RHINELANDER (JOHN B.) eds. SALT: the Moscow agreements and beyond. New York, [1974]. pp. 361. *bibliog.*

RUSSIA. (Cont.)

— — Vietnam.

BOEVAIA solidarnost", bratskaia pomoshch': sbornik vazhneishikh vneshnepoliticheskikh dokumentov SSSR po v'etnamskomu voprosu, etc. Moskva, 1970. pp. 219.

— History — Historiography.

LEVIN (SHNEER MENDELEVICH) Ocherki po istorii russkoi obshchestvennoi mysli, vtoraia polovina XIX - nachalo XX veka: [glavy iz dvukh nezavershennykh rukopisei, Raznochinskii period russkogo osvoboditel'nogo dvizheniia v osveshchenii dorevoliutsionnoi istoriografii i Krymskaia voina i russkoe obshchestvo; otv. redaktor S.N. Valk]. Leningrad, 1974. pp. 442.

— — Philosophy.

SZAMUELY (TIBOR) The Russian tradition;...edited and with an introduction by Robert Conquest. London, 1974. pp. 443.

— — Sources.

GERTSEN (ALEKSANDR IVANOVICH) Byloe i dumy: pervoe polnoe izdanie. Berlin, 1921. 5 vols.

KREST'IANSKAIA voina 1773-1775 gg. v Rossii: dokumenty iz sobraniia Gosudarstvennogo Istoricheskogo muzeia. Moskva, 1973. pp. 440.

LEVYTSKY (BORIS) ed. The Stalinist terror in the thirties: documentation from the Soviet press. Stanford, [1974]. pp. 521. *bibliog. (Stanford University. Hoover Institution on War, Revolution and Peace. Hoover Institution Publications. 126)*

MATTHEWS (MERVYN) ed. Soviet government: a selection of official documents on internal policies. London, 1974. pp. 472.

— — 1667—1671, Rebellion of Stenka Razin.

STEPANOV (IVAN VASIL'EVICH) Krest'ianskaia voina v Rossii v 1670-1671 gg. Leningrad, 1966 in progress.

— — 1773—1775, Pugachev Uprising.

KREST'IANSKAIA voina 1773-1775 gg. v Rossii: dokumenty iz sobraniia Gosudarstvennogo Istoricheskogo muzeia. Moskva, 1973. pp. 440.

— — 1853—1856, Crimean War.

See CRIMEAN WAR, 1853—1856.

— — 1900—1999.

ULAM (ADAM BRUNO) Stalin: the man and his era. London, 1974. pp. 760. *First published in the United States in 1973.*

ABRAMSKY (CHIMEN) ed. Essays in honour of E.H. Carr; edited by C. Abramsky assisted by Beryl J. Williams. London, 1974. pp. 387. *bibliog.*

— — 1917— .

LEL'CHUK (VITALII SEMENOVICH) and others. A short history of Soviet society; edited by Y. Polyakov. Moscow, 1971. pp. 445.

See also REVOLUTIONS — Russia.

— — 1917—1921, Revolution.

DENIKIN (ANTON IVANOVICH) Ocherki russkoi smuty. Paris, [1921-26]. 5 vols. *Vols. 3-5 published in Berlin.*

MINTS (ISAAK IZRAILEVICH) Istoriia Velikogo Oktiabria. Moskva, 1967-73. 3 vols.

GIMPEL'SON (EFIM GILEVICH) "Voennyi kommunizm": politika, praktika, ideologiia. Moskva, 1973. pp. 296.

KANEV (SERAFIM NIKOLAEVICH) Oktiabr'skaia revoliutsiia i krakh anarkhizma: bor'ba partii bol'shevikov protiv anarkhizma 1917-1922 gg. Moskva, 1974. pp. 415, [xv].

SUTTON (ANTONY C.) Wall Street and the Bolshevik revolution. New Rochelle, N.Y., [1974]. pp. 228. *bibliog.*

— — — Campaigns.

DENIKIN (ANTON IVANOVICH) Ocherki russkoi smuty. Paris, [1921-26]. 5 vols. *Vols. 3-5 published in Berlin.*

GUSEV (SERGEI IVANOVICH) pseud. [i.e. Iakov Davydovich DRABKIN] Grazhdanskaia voina i Krasnaia Armiia: sbornik voenno- teoreticheskikh i voenno-politicheskikh statei, 1918-1924. Moskva, 1925. pp. 220. *Contains 25 articles.*

LIPITSKII (SEMEN VASIL'EVICH) Voennaia deiatel'nost' Tsk RKP/b/, 1917-1920. Moskva, 1973. pp. 317.

— — — Chronology.

KOMMUNISTICHESKAIA PARTIIA SOVETSKOGO SOIUZA. Tsentral'nyi Komitet. Otdel po Izucheniiu Istorii Oktiabr'skoi Revoliutsii i VKP(b). Revoliutsiia 1917 goda: khronika sobytii. Moskva, 1923-26. 5 vols.

— — — Foreign participation, Bulgarian.

OKTIABR' i bolgarskie internatsionalisty. Moskva, 1973. pp. 334. *bibliog.*

— — — Foreign participation, Latvian.

GERMANIS (ULDIS) Oberst Vacietis und die lettischen Schützen im Weltkrieg und in der Oktoberrevolution. Stockholm, 1974. pp. 336. *bibliog. (Stockholms Universitet. Acta Universitatis Stockholmiensis. Stockholm Studies in History. 20) With English summary.*

— — — Sources.

TSENTRAL'NYI GOSUDARSTVENNYI ARKHIV OKTIABR'SKOI REVOLIUTSII, VYSSHIKH ORGANOV GOSUDARSTVENNOI VLASTI I ORGANOV GOSUDARSTVENNOGO UPRAVLENIIA SSSR. 1917 God v Dokumentakh i Materialakh. Rabochee dvizhenie v 1917 godu; podgotovili k pechati V.L. Meller i A.M. Pankratova, etc. Moskva, 1926. pp. 371.

TSENTRAL'NYI GOSUDARSTVENNYI ARKHIV OKTIABR'SKOI REVOLIUTSII, VYSSHIKH ORGANOV GOSUDARSTVENNOI VLASTI I ORGANOV GOSUDARSTVENNOGO UPRAVLENIIA SSSR. 1917 God v Dokumentakh i Materialakh. Krest'ianskoe dvizhenie v 1917 godu; podgotovili k pechati K.G. Kotel'nikov i V.L. Meller, etc. Moskva, 1927. pp. 444.

GAPONENKO (LUKA STEPANOVICH) ed. Oktiabr'skaia revoliutsiia i armiia, 25 oktiabria 1917 g. - mart 1918 g.: sbornik dokumentov. Moskva, 1973. pp. 455.

— — 1918—1920, Allied Intervention.

PETRICIOLI (MARTA) L'occupazione italiana del Caucaso: "un ingrato servizio" da rendere a Londra. Milano, 1972. pp. 93. *(Politico, Il. Quaderni. n.10) With English summary.*

FISCHER (KURT) Historian. Deutsche Truppen und Entente-Intervention in Südrussland 1918-19. Boppard am Rhein, 1973. pp. 160. *bibliog. (Militärgeschichtliches Forschungsamt. Militärgeschichtliche Studien. 16)*

— — 1921, Kronstadt Revolt.

See KRONSTADT — History — 1921, Revolt.

— History, Military.

WAR and society in nineteenth century Russian empire: selected papers presented in a seminar held at McGill University, 1969- 1971; editors, J.G. Purves and D.A. West. Toronto, 1972. pp. 188.

— History, Naval.

MITCHELL (DONALD WILLIAM) A history of Russian and Soviet sea power. New York, 1974. pp. 657. *bibliog.*

— Industries.

MOLIAKOV (DMITRII STEPANOVICH) Pribyl' i rentabel'nost' promyshlennogo predpriiatiia. Moskva, 1967. pp. 146.

AGAFONOV (NIKOLAI TIMOFEEVICH) Osnovnye problemy formirovaniia promyshlennykh kompleksov v vostochnykh raionakh SSSR. ch.1. Osobennosti razvitiia i razmeshcheniia promyshlennosti. Leningrad, 1970. pp. 168. *bibliog.*

SOTSIAL'NI problemy vyrobnychoho kolektyvu: z dosvidu sotsiolohichnykh doslidzhen'. Kyïv, 1972. pp. 159.

SHOKHIN (ANATOLII ALEKSANDROVICH) Pravovoe polozhenie promyshlennykh ob"edinenii v SSSR. Kazan', 1972. pp. 114.

ADAMESKU (ALEKO ALEKSANDROVICH) Kompleksnoe issledovanie promyshlennykh predpriiatii. Moskva, 1973. pp. 128. *bibliog.*

FINANSY i effektivnost' proizvodstvennykh fondov; avtorskii kollektiv pod rukovodstvom V.K. Senchagova. Moskva, 1973. pp. 176.

INDUSTRIALIZATSIIA SSSR, 1938-1941 gg.: dokumenty i materialy. Moskva, 1973. pp. 424.

PODMARKOV (VALENTIN GEORGIEVICH) Vvedenie v promyshlennuiu sotsiologiiu: sotsial'nye problemy sotsialisticheskogo promyshlennogo proizvodstva. Moskva, 1973. pp. 318. *bibliog.*

PRIKHOD'KO (IURII ALEKSANDROVICH) Vosstanovlenie industrii, 1942-1950. Moskva, 1973. pp. 287. *bibliog.*

SHUMOV (NIKOLAI SERGEEVICH) Finansirovanie i kreditovanie promyshlennosti. 2nd ed. Moskva, 1973. pp. 288.

SYCHEV (N.G.) ed. Finansy predpriiatii i otraslei narodnogo khoziaistva. 2nd ed. Moskva, 1973. pp. 470.

— — Mathematical models.

BAKHTIN (A.E.) and others, eds. Optimal'noe otraslevoe planirovanie v promyshlennosti: materialy konferentsii 11-13 iiulia 1968 g. Novosibirsk, 1970. pp. 332.

— Intellectual life.

IVANOV-RAZUMNIK (RAZUMNIK VASIL'EVICH) pseud. [i.e. Razumnik Vasil'evich IVANOV] Istoriia russkoi obshchestvennoi mysli. t.2. S.-Peterburg, 1908. pp. 520. *Xerographic reprint. Lacks title page.*

IZ istorii sovetskoi kul'tury. Moskva, 1972. pp. 167.

PARTIIA i sotsialisticheskaia kul'tura: XXIV s"ezd KPSS i problemy dukhovnoi kul'tury sotsializma. Moskva, 1972. pp. 287.

KUMANEV (VIKTOR ALEKSANDROVICH) Revoliutsiia i prosveshchenie mass. Moskva, 1973. pp. 335. *bibliog.*

ABRAMSKY (CHIMEN) ed. Essays in honour of E.H. Carr; edited by C. Abramsky assisted by Beryl J. Williams. London, 1974. pp. 387. *bibliog.*

— Kings and rulers.

LOKOT' (TIMOFEI VASIL'EVICH) "Zavoevanie revoliutsii" i ideologiia russkogo monarkhizma: doklad...T.V. Lokotia. [Vienna?, 1921]. pp. 24.

RUSSIA. (Cont.)

— Languages.

LEWIS (E. GLYN) Multilingualism in the Soviet Union: aspects of language policy and its implementation. The Hague, 1972. pp. 332. bibliog.

— Military policy.

WOLFE (THOMAS W.) Soviet attitudes toward MBFR and the USSR's military presence in Europe. [Santa Monica], 1972. pp. 17. (Rand Corporation. [Papers]. 4819)

MOULTON (HARLAND B.) From superiority to parity: the United States and the strategic arms race, 1961-1971. Westport, Conn., [1973]. pp. 333. bibliog.

NECHIPURENKO (VASILII IGNAT'EVICH) V.I. Lenin o zashchite sotsialisticheskogo Otechestva: printsipy internatsionalizma i zashchita Otechestva. Moskva, 1973. pp. 223. bibliog.

SOVIET naval developments: capability and context; papers relating to Russia's maritime interests [deriving from a seminar held at Dalhousie University, Halifax, Nova Scotia in 1972]; edited by Michael MccGuire. New York, 1973. pp. 554.

— Moral conditions.

ZHURAVKOV (MIKHAIL GAVRILOVICH) Sotsializm i moral': nekotorye cherty i osobennosti formirovaniia morali sovetskogo obshchestva. Moskva, 1974. pp. 263.

— Nationalism.

LIESS (OTTO RUDOLF) Sowjetische Nationalitätenstrategie als weltpolitisches Konzept. Wien, [1972]. pp. 226. bibliog. (Forschungsstelle für Nationalitäten- und Sprachenfragen. Ethnos. Band 12)

DOWLER (ERIC WAYNE) The "native soil" (pochvennichestvo) movement in Russian social and political thought, 1850-1870; [Ph.D. (London) thesis]. [1973]. fo. 348. bibliog. Typescript: unpublished. This thesis is the property of London University and may not be removed from the Library.

INTERNATSIONAL'NE i natsional'ne v sotsialistychnomu suspil'stvi. Kyïv, 1973. pp. 243.

SERTSOVA (ANISIIA PETROVNA) Sotsializm i razvitie natsii: ob opyte SSSR i ChSSR. Moskva, 1973. pp. 304.

TORZHESTVO leninskoi natsional'noi politiki KPSS: materia-ly Mezhrespublikanskoi nauchno-teoreticheskoi konferentsii, posviashchennoi 50-letiiu obrazovaniia SSSR, 11-13 oktiabria 1972 goda. Alma-Ata, 1973. pp. 531.

TSAMERIAN (IVAN PETROVICH) Teoreticheskie problemy obrazovaniia i razvitiia Sovetskogo mnogonatsional'nogo gosudarstva. Moskva, 1973. pp. 295.

UCHENYE ZAPISKI KAFEDR OBSHCHESTVENNYKH NAUK VUZOV LENINGRADA. Istoriia KPSS. vyp.13. KPSS - organizator bratskoi druzhby narodov SSSR. Leningrad, 1973. pp. 154.

— Native races.

BOIKO (VLADIMIR IVANOVICH) Opyt sotsiologicheskogo issledovaniia problem razvitiia narodov Nizhnego Amura; otvetstvennyi redaktor...A.P. Okladnikov. Novosibirsk, 1973. pp. 211.

— Navy.

SOVIET naval developments: capability and context; papers relating to Russia's maritime interests [deriving from a seminar held at Dalhousie University, Halifax, Nova Scotia in 1972]; edited by Michael MccGuire. New York, 1973. pp. 554.

WALL (PATRICK) Europe's back door: the Soviet maritime threat. London, [1974]. pp. 22.

— — History.

MITCHELL (DONALD WILLIAM) A history of Russian and Soviet sea power. New York, 1974. pp. 657. bibliog.

— Non—Russian territories.

ISTORIIA natsional'no-gosudarstvennogo stroitel'stva v SSSR: natsional'no-gosudarstvennoe stroitel'stvo v SSSR v period sotsializma i stroitel'stva kommunizma, 1937-1967 gg. Moskva, 1970. pp. 276.

TORZHESTVO leninskoi natsional'noi politiki KPSS: materia-ly Mezhrespublikanskoi nauchno-teoreticheskoi konferentsii, posviashchennoi 50-letiiu obrazovaniia SSSR, 11-13 oktiabria 1972 goda. Alma-Ata, 1973. pp. 531.

— — Constitution.

RUSSIA (RSFSR). Constitution. 1972. Konstitutsiia (Osnovnoi Zakon) Rossiiskoi Sovetskoi Federativnoi Sotsialisticheskoi Respubliki; Konstitutsii (Osnovnye Zakony) Avtonomnykh Sovetskikh Sotsialisticheskikh Respublik, vkhodiashchikh v sostav RSFSR. Moskva, 1972. pp. 419.

— Occupations.

PROFESSIONAL'NAIA orientatsiia sel'skoi molodezhi. Moskva, 1973. pp. 95. bibliog.

— Officials and employees.

HODNETT (GREY) and OGAREFF (VAL) Leaders of the Soviet republics 1955-1972: a guide to posts and occupants. Canberra, 1973. pp. 454.

— Politics and government.

XXIV s"ezd KPSS i voprosy teorii gosudarstva i prava. Moskva, 1972. pp. 399.

BOLOTNIKOV (IGOR' MIKHAILOVICH) and VAVILOV (KONSTANTIN KUZ'MICH) Leninizm i nauchnoe upravlenie sotsialisticheskim obshchestvom. Leningrad, 1973. pp. 256. bibliog.

KERIMOV (DZHANGIR ALI-ABASOVICH) ed. XXIV s"ezd KPSS ob ukreplenii Sovetskogo gosudarstva i razvitii sotsialisticheskoi demokratii. Moskva, 1973. pp. 276.

STEKLOV (IURII MIKHAILOVICH) Izbrannoe. Moskva, 1973. pp. 262. bibliog.

VARLAMOV (KONSTANTIN IVANOVICH) Leninskaia kontseptsiia sotsialisticheskogo upravleniia: genezis, stanovlenie. Moskva, 1973. pp. 398.

YANEY (GEORGE L.) The systemization of Russian government: social evolution in the domestic administration of imperial Russia, 1711-1905. Urbana, [1973]. pp. 430. bibliog.

EREMIN (IURII ELEAZAROVICH) Klassy i demokratiia. Moskva, 1974. pp. 206.

LUNEV (ALEKSANDR EFREMOVICH) Teoreticheskie problemy gosudarstvennogo upravleniia. Moskva, 1974. pp. 247.

SZAMUELY (TIBOR) The Russian tradition;...edited and with an introduction by Robert Conquest. London, 1974. pp. 443.

— — Research.

BROWN (A.H.) Soviet politics and political science. London, 1974. pp. 128.

— — 1800—1899.

IVANOV-RAZUMNIK (RAZUMNIK VASIL'EVICH) pseud. [i.e. Razumnik Vasil'evich IVANOV] Istoriia russkoi obshchestvennoi mysli. t.2. S.-Peterburg, 1908. pp. 520. Xerographic reprint. Lacks title page.

— — 1894—1917.

SAVINKOV (BORIS VIKTOROVICH) K delu Kornilova. Paris, 1919. pp. 29.

VIKTOROV (V.P.) ed. Soiuz russkogo naroda po materialam Chrezvychainoi sledstvennoi komissii vremennogo pravitel'stva 1917 g.; sostavil A. Chernovskii. Moskva, 1929. pp. 444.

BAZILI (NIKOLAI ALEKSANDROVICH) Nicolas de Basily, diplomat of Imperial Russia, 1903-1917: memoirs. Stanford, [1973]. pp. 201. (Stanford University. Hoover Institution on War, Revolution and Peace. Hoover Institution Publications. 125)

SOBOLEV (GENNADII LEONT'EVICH) Revoliutsionnoe soznanie rabochikh i soldat Petrograda v 1917 g.: period dvoevlastiia. Leningrad, 1973. pp. 330.

SOVOKIN (ALEKSANDR MIKHAILOVICH) V preddverii Oktiabria: podgotovka pobedy vooruzhennogo vosstaniia. Moskva, 1973. pp. 348.

— — 1917— .

YOUNG Russia. [Paris, imprint], 1933. pp. 8.

ARMSTRONG (JOHN ALEXANDER) Ideology, politics, and government in the Soviet Union: an introduction. 3rd ed. London, [1974]. pp. 236.

KUUSINEN (AINO) Before and after Stalin: a personal account of Soviet Russia from the 1920s to the 1960s;...translated from the German by Paul Stevenson. London, 1974. pp. 256.

MATTHEWS (MERVYN) ed. Soviet government: a selection of official documents on internal policies. London, 1974. pp. 472.

SAUNDERS (GEORGE) ed. Samizdat: voices of the Soviet opposition. New York, 1974. pp. 464.

— — 1917—1953.

SVOBODNYI golos. sb 1-(14). Paris, 1946-48. 2 vols.

— — 1917—1936.

POPOV (GEORGII) Stremiashchimsia v Rossiiu...; zhizn' v Sovetskoi respublike, s 31 original'nymi fotografiiami. Berlin, 1924. pp. 232.

ARTSYBASHEV (MIKHAIL PETROVICH) Cheremukha: zapiski pisatelia. t.2. Varshava, 1927. pp. 179. Articles originally published in "Za svobodu". Vol.1 entitled Zapiski pisatelia.

COHEN (STEPHEN F.) Bukharin and the Bolshevik revolution: a political biography, 1888-1938. New York, 1973. pp. 498,xvii. bibliog.

ODOM (WILLIAM E.) The Soviet volunteers: modernization and bureaucracy in a public mass organization. Princeton, [1973]. pp. 360. bibliog.

SIVOKHINA (TAT'IANA ALEKSANDROVNA) Krakh melkoburzhuaznoi oppozitsii. Moskva, 1973. pp. 232.

PETHYBRIDGE (ROGER WILLIAM) The social prelude to Stalinism. London, 1974. pp. 343. bibliog.

— — 1953— .

KIRSTEIN (TATJANA) Die Konsultation von "Aussenstehenden" durch den Partei- und Staatsapparat sowie den Obersten Sowjet der UdSSR als stabilisierender Faktor des sowjetischen Herrschaftssystems. Berlin, 1972. pp. 131. bibliog. (Berlin. Freie Universität. Osteuropa-Institut. Philosophische und Soziologische Veröffentlichungen. Band 11)

KHRUSHCHEV (NIKITA SERGEEVICH) Khrushchev remembers: the last testament; translated and edited by Strobe Talbott. London, 1974. pp. 602.

MORTON (HENRY WALTER) and TÖKÉS (RUDOLF L.) eds. Soviet politics and society in the 1970's; [dedicated to John N. Hazard on the occasion of his 65th birthday]. New York, [1974]. pp. 401. (Columbia University. Russian Institute. Studies)

SAKHAROV (ANDREI DMITRIEVICH) Sakharov speaks;...edited and with a foreword by Harrison E. Salisbury. London, 1974. pp. 245.

RUSSIA. (Cont.)

— — 1964— .

EKONOMICHESKIE i sotsial'no-politicheskie problemy kommunisticheskogo stroitel'stva v SSSR: materialy nauchnoi konferentsii Instituta marksizma-leninizma pri TsK KPSS, Akademii obshchestvennykh nauk pri TsK KPSS, Vysshei partiinoi shkoly pri TsK KPSS, sektsii obshchestvennykh nauk AN SSSR na temu: "XXIV s"ezd KPSS i razvitie marksistko-leninskoi teorii", 29 sentiabria 1 oktiabria 1971 g. Moskva, 1972. pp. 351.

AGENTSTVO PECHATI NOVOSTI. USSR'73: Novosti Press Agency Year Book. Moscow, 1973. pp. 304.

SAVKO (ALEKSANDR PAVLOVICH) Partiinoe rukovodstvo Sovetami v period stroitel'stva kommunizma.Moskva, 1973. pp. 187.

— Population.

RYBAKOVSKII (LEONID LEONIDOVICH) Regional'nyi analiz migratsii. Moskva, 1973. pp. 148, [xi]. bibliog.

BZHILIANSKII (IURII ARONOVICH) Problemy narodonaseleniia pri sotsializme: politiko-ekonomicheskii analiz. Moskva, 1974. pp. 214.

— Relations (general) with Africa.

GORBATOV (OLEG MARKOVICH) and CHERKASSKII (LEONID IAKOVLEVICH) Sotrudnichestvo SSSR so stranami Arabskogo Vostoka i Afriki. Moskva, 1973. pp. 342. bibliog.

— Relations (general) with Arab countries.

GORBATOV (OLEG MARKOVICH) and CHERKASSKII (LEONID IAKOVLEVICH) Sotrudnichestvo SSSR so stranami Arabskogo Vostoka i Afriki. Moskva, 1973. pp. 342. bibliog.

— Relations (general) with Asia.

BULGANIN (NIKOLAI ALEKSANDROVICH) and KHRUSHCHEV (NIKITA SERGEEVICH) N.A. Bulganin and N.S. Khrushchov: full texts of speeches and statements in India, Burma and Afghanistan. London, Soviet News, 1955. pp. 47.

— Relations (general) with Bulgaria.

OKTIABR' i bolgarskie internatsionalisty. Moskva, 1973. pp. 334. bibliog.

— Relations (general) with China.

VLADIMIROV (OLEG EVGEN'EVICH) and RIAZANTSEV (VLADIMIR IVANOVICH) Stranitsy politicheskoi biografii Mao Tsze-duna. 2nd ed. Moskva, 1973. pp. 112.

— Relations (general) with France.

FRANCE. Direction de la Documentation. La Documentation Française. Notes et Etudes Documentaires. No. 3,746. Visite officielle de M. Georges Pompidou, Président de la République, en U.R.S.S., 6-13 octobre 1970. Paris, 1970. pp. 29.

ORLIK (OL'GA VASIL'EVNA) Peredovaia Rossiia i revoliutsionnaia Frantsiia, I polovina XIX v. Moskva, 1973. pp. 299.

— Relations (general) with Germany.

VISHNIAKOV-VISHNEVETSKII (KONSTANTIN ANATOL'EVICH) V.I. Lenin i revoliutsionnye sviazi rossiiskogo i germanskogo proletariata, 1903-1910 gg. Leningrad, 1974. pp. 220.

— Relations (general) with Morocco.

CONSTANT (JEAN PAUL) Les relations maroco-soviétiques, 1956-1971. Paris, 1973. pp. 136.

— Relations (general) with Norway.

GILBERG (TROND) The Soviet Communist party and Scandinavian communism: the Norwegian case. Oslo, [1973]. pp. 271. bibliog.

— Religion.

KOSTIUKOV (IVAN VASIL'EVICH) Bluzhdaiushchie dushi: razdum'ia o vere i zhizni. Moskva, 1971. pp. 136.

ATEIZM, religiia, sovremennost'. Leningrad, 1973. pp. 226.

VORONTSOV (GEORGII VASIL'EVICH) Leninskaia programma ateisticheskogo vospitaniia v deistvii, 1917-1937 gg. Leningrad, 1973. pp. 176.

BEESON (TREVOR) Discretion and valour: religious conditions in Russia and Eastern Europe; [report of a working party appointed by the British Council of Churches]. [London], 1974. pp. 348. bibliog.

— Rural conditions.

GONCHAROV (ALEKSANDR DMITRIEVICH) Pod"em kul'tury sela -delo partiinoe. Moskva, 1970. pp. 120.

SEMIN (SERGEI IVANOVICH) Preodolenie sotsial'no-ekonomicheskikh razlichij mezhdu gorodom i derevnei. Moskva, 1973. pp. 159.

— Social conditions.

POPOV (GEORGII) Stremiashchimsia v Rossiiu...; zhizn' v Sovetskoi respublike, s 31 original'nymi fotografiiami. Berlin, 1924. pp. 232.

SABIK-VOGULOV ( ) V pobezhdennoi Germanii. n.p., 1947. pp. 78.

PROBLEMY izmeneniia sotsial'noi struktury sovetskogo obshchestva.Rostov-na-Donu, 1972. pp. 111.

AGENTSTVO PECHATI NOVOSTI. USSR'73: Novosti Press Agency Year Book. Moscow, 1973. pp. 304.

FROMENT-MEURICE (GABRIELLE) La vie soviétique. 2nd ed. Paris, 1973. pp. 127.

KOLESOV (NIKOLAI DMITRIEVICH) Zakon sootvetstviia proizvoditel'nykh sil i proizvodstvennykh otnoshenii pri sotsializme. Leningrad, 1973. pp. 159.

PIVTSAIKIN (GEORGII IVANOVICH) Obshchestvennye otnosheniia razvitogo sotsializma. Minsk, 1973. pp. 261.

SIUSIUKALOV (BORIS IVANOVICH) Sotsialisticheskoe obshchestvo: problemy dialektiki razvitiia. Moskva, 1973. pp. 278.

UCHENYE ZAPISKI KAFEDR OBSHCHESTVENNYKH NAUK VUZOV LENINGRADA. Filosofiia. vyp.14. Filosofskie i sotsiologicheskie issledovaniia. Leningrad, 1973. pp. 212.

MORTON (HENRY WALTER) and TÖKÉS (RUDOLF L.) eds. Soviet politics and society in the 1970's; [dedicated to John N. Hazard on the occasion of his 65th birthday]. New York, [1974]. pp. 401. (Columbia University. Russian Institute. Studies)

— Social history.

BLANKOFF (JEAN) La société russe de la seconde moitié du XIXe siècle: trois témoignages littéraires: M.E. Saltykov-Ščedrin, Gleb Uspenskij, A.F. Pisemskij. Bruxelles, [1972]. pp. 248. bibliog.

PETHYBRIDGE (ROGER WILLIAM) The social prelude to Stalinism. London, 1974. pp. 343. bibliog.

— Social life and customs.

FROMENT-MEURICE (GABRIELLE) La vie soviétique. 2nd ed. Paris, 1973. pp. 127.

— Social policy.

OSBORN (ROBERT J.) Soviet social policies: welfare, equality and community. Homewood, 1970 repr. 1972. pp. 294. bibliog.

SOTSIAL'NAIA programma deviatoi piatiletki. Moskva, 1972. pp. 144.

UCHENYE ZAPISKI KAFEDR OBSHCHESTVENNYKH NAUK VUZOV LENINGRADA. Problemy Nauchnogo Kommunizma. vyp. 6. XXIV s"ezd KPSS i aktual'nye problemy nauchnogo kommunizma. Leningrad, 1972. pp. 160.

EL'MEEV (VASILII IAKOVLEVICH) Problemy sotsial'nogo planirovaniia. Leningrad, 1973. pp. 151.

KUZ'MIN (EVGENII SERGEEVICH) and BODALEV (ALEKSEI ALEKSANDROVICH) eds. Sotsial'naia psikhologiia i sotsial'noe planirovanie. Leningrad, 1973. pp. 167. bibliog.

KLINSKII (ANATOLII IVANOVICH) Planirovanie ekonomicheskogo i sotsial'nogo razvitiia. Moskva, 1974. pp. 216. bibliog.

MATTHEWS (MERVYN) ed. Soviet government: a selection of official documents on internal policies. London, 1974. pp. 472.

PROBLEMY sotsial'nogo planirovaniia: nekotorye aktual'nye voprosy teorii i praktiki. Moskva, 1974. pp. 215.

SOLZHENITSYN (ALEKSANDR ISAEVICH) Letter to Soviet leaders; translated by Hilary Sternberg [from an unpublished letter written in 1973]. London, 1974. pp. 59.

— Statistics.

RUSSIA (EMPIRE). Tsentral'nyi Statisticheskii Komitet. Statistika Rossiiskoi Imperii: Statistique de l'Empire de Russie. irreg., 1887-1916 (t.1-5,8,10-13,18;22(ch.10,14, 20, 44);24,25;27(ch.4,9,10,14);29(ch.10,11);33,38,40,41, 44, 45,47,48,50,53,56,58,61,65,68,70,72,74,82,84,85,87,88, 92). S.-Peterburg. 40 vols. Some captions, notes and tables of contents also in French. Microfilm: 8 reels.

— Territorial expansion.

LANTZEFF (GEORGE VJATCHESLAU) and PIERCE (RICHARD A.) Eastward to empire: exploration and conquest on the Russian open frontier to 1750. Montreal, 1973. pp. 276. bibliog.

RUSSIA (RSFSR)

— Constitution.

RUSSIA (RSFSR). Constitution. 1972. Konstitutsiia (Osnovnoi Zakon) Rossiiskoi Sovetskoi Federativnoi Sotsialisticheskoi Respubliki; Konstitutsii (Osnovnye Zakony) Avtonomnykh Sovetskikh Sotsialisticheskikh Respublik, vkhodiashchikh v sostav RSFSR. Moskva, 1972. pp. 419.

— Economic conditions.

TSENTRAL'NYI ekonomicheskii raion. Moskva, 1973. pp. 269. bibliog. (Akademiia Nauk SSSR. Sovet po Izucheniiu Proizvoditel'nykh Sil. Razvitie i Razmeshchenie Proizvoditel'nykh Sil SSSR)

— Economic policy.

DETINA (SAMUIL ISAAKOVICH) and others. Problemy razvitiia i razmeshcheniia proizvoditel'nykh sil Tsentral'nochernozemnogo raiona. Moskva, 1973. pp. 183.

— Population.

MAIKOV (A.Z.) ed. Migratsiia naseleniia RSFSR. Moskva, 1973. pp. 167.

RUSSIAN LITERATURE.

GERTSEN (ALEKSANDR IVANOVICH) Kto vinovat?: povesti. Berlin, 1921. pp. 607.

— History and criticism.

IVANOV-RAZUMNIK (RAZUMNIK VASIL'EVICH) pseud. [i.e. Razumnik Vasil'evich IVANOV] Istoriia russkoi obshchestvennoi mysli. t.2. S.-Peterburg, 1908. pp. 520. Xerographic reprint. Lacks title page.

BUGAENKO (PAVEL ANDREEVICH) A.V. Lunacharskii i sovetskaia literaturnaia kritika. Saratov, 1972. pp. 408.

TVARDOVSKII (ALEKSANDR TRIFONOVICH) O literature. Moskva, 1973. pp. 445. *Selected articles, reviews and editorial letters.*

RUSSIAN PERIODICALS.

SVOBODNYI golos. sb 1-(14). Paris, 1946-48. 2 vols.

IAMPOL'SKII (ISAAK GRIGOR'EVICH) Satiricheskie i iumoristicheskie zhurnaly 1860-kh godov. Leningrad, 1973. pp. 168.

RUSSIAN STUDIES.

BROWN (A.H.) Soviet politics and political science. London, 1974. pp. 128.

RUSSIANS IN CHINA.

VIDNYE sovetskie kommunisty - uchastniki kitaiskoi revoliutsii. Moskva, 1970. pp. 111.

RUSSIANS IN EASTERN EUROPE.

GROSUL (VLADISLAV IAKIMOVICH) Rossiiskie revoliutsionery v Iugo-Vostochnoi Evrope, 1859-1874 gg. Kishinev, 1973. pp. 539. *bibliog.*

RUSSIANS IN FOREIGN COUNTRIES.

SHCHETKIN (STEPAN PETROVICH) Pis'ma russkogo emigranta. Varshava, 1921. pp. 79.

DAVATTS (VLADIMIR KHRISTIANOVICH) and L'VOV (N.N.) Russkaia armiia na chuzbine. Belgrad, 1923. pp. 123.

SVITKOV (N.) Masonstvo v russkoi emigratsii, k 1 ianvaria 1932 g.: sostavlennoe na osnovanii mas. dokumentov. Parizh, 1932. pp. 32.

NATSIONAL'NO-TRUDOVOI SOIUZ NOVOGO POKOLENIIA. Programnye polozheniia i Ustav, etc. Belgrad, 1938. pp. 52.

POKROVSKII (ALEKSANDR) Russkie masony v emigratsii. Parizh, 1941. pp. 16.

SVOBODNYI golos. sb 1-(14). Paris, 1946-48. 2 vols.

BURD-VOSKHODOV (ALEKSANDR PAVLOVICH) Moskva dalekaia.... Moscow, the wide.... Moscou, la lointanie [sic]... [New York?, 1950]. pp. 219. *Added title page has subtitle: The immortals [sic] Russian's [sic] "liberators".*

HOLMSTON (A.) Izbrannye stat'i i rechi. Buenos Aires, 1953. pp. 224,13.

RUSSIANS IN KAZAKSTAN.

DEMKO (GEORGE J.) The Russian colonization of Kazakhstan 1896-1916. Bloomington, [1969]. pp. 271. *bibliog. (Indiana University. Graduate School. Publications. Uralic and Altaic Series. vol. 99)*

RUSSIANS IN SIBERIA.

RUSSKIE starozhily Sibiri: istoriko-antropologicheskii ocherk. Moskva, 1973. pp. 189.

RUSSIANS IN THE CAUCASUS.

VATEISHVILI (DZHUANSHER LEVANOVICH) Russkaia obshchestvennaia mysl' i pechat' na Kavkaze v pervoi treti XIX veka. Moskva, 1973. pp. 460. *With English summary.*

RUSSIANS IN THE TATAR REPUBLIC.

SOTSIAL'NOE i natsional'noe: opyt etnosotsiologicheskikh issledovanii po materialam Tatarskoi ASSR. Moskva, 1973. pp. 331.

RUSSO—FINNISH WAR, 1939—1940.

UPTON (ANTHONY FREDERICK) Finland, 1939-1940. London, 1974. pp. 174. *bibliog.*

RUSSO—JAPANESE WAR, 1904—1905.

WESTWOOD (JOHN N.) The illustrated history of the Russo-Japanese war. London, [1973]. pp. 126.

RWANDA

— Economic conditions.

RWANDA. Ministère du Plan et des Ressources Naturelles. 1973. Situation économique: données de base 1968-1972: situation au 31 décembre 1972. [Kigali?], 1973. fo. 34.

— History.

LA MAIRIEU (BAUDOUIN PATERNOSTRE DE) Le Rwanda: son effort de développement; antécédents historiques et conquêtes de la révolution rwandaise. Bruxelles, [1972]. pp. 413. *bibliog.*

RYDER (DUDLEY FRANCIS STUART) 3rd Earl of Harrowby.

RYDER (DUDLEY FRANCIS STUART) 3rd Earl of Harrowby. The Cabinet journal of Dudley Ryder, Viscount Sandon (later third Earl of Harrowby) 11 May - 10 August, 1878. London. *Special supplement, no.10, to BULLETIN OF THE INSTITUTE OF HISTORICAL RESEARCH, November 1974.*

RYGG (NICOLAI THEODORIUS NILSSEN).

SEJERSTED (FRANCIS) Ideal, teori og virkelighet: Nicolai Rygg og pengepolitikken i 1920-årene. [Oslo, 1973]. pp. 134.

RYNER (HAN) pseud.

SIMON (LOUIS) Un individualiste dans le social: Han Ryner. Paris, [1973]. pp. 143.

SAARLAND

— History.

JACOBY (FRITZ) Die nationalsozialistische Herrschaftsübernahme an der Saar: die innenpolitischen Probleme der Rückgliederung des Saargebietes bis 1935. Saarbrücken, 1973. pp. 275. *bibliog. (Kommission für Saarländische Landesgeschichte und Volksforschung. Veröffentlichungen. 6)*

— Politics and government.

SAARBRUECKEN. Universität. Annales Universitatis Saraviensis. Rechts- und Wirtschaftswissenschaftliche Abteilung. Band 71. Faktoren der Wahlentscheidung: eine wahlsoziologische Analyse am Beispiel der saarländischen Landtagswahl 1970... ; von Jürgen W. Falter. Köln, 1973. pp. 256. *bibliog.*

SABAH.

SABAH. 1973. Sabah's 10th anniversary of independence within Malaysia: a review of progress and achievements during the first decade of independence from 1963-1973. [Kota Kinabalu?, 1973?] pp. 316.

SABATE LLOPART (FRANCISCO).

TELLEZ (ANTONIO) La guerrilla urbana en España: Sabate. Paris, [1972]. pp. 213.

TELLEZ (ANTONIO) Sabate: guerrilla extraordinary; ... translated by Stuart Christie. London, 1974. pp. 183.

SAHARA

— Economic policy.

FRANCE. Direction de la Documentation. La Documentation Française. Notes et Etudes Documentaires. No. 2,801. Le cadre institutionnel du développement saharien. Paris, 1961. pp. 19.

— Politics and government.

FRANCE. Direction de la Documentation. La Documentation Française. Notes et Etudes Documentaires. No. 2,801. Le cadre institutionnel du développement saharien. Paris, 1961. pp. 19.

— Social policy.

FRANCE. Direction de la Documentation. La Documentation Française. Notes et Etudes Documentaires. No. 2,801. Le cadre institutionnel du développement saharien. Paris, 1961. pp. 19.

SAILING SHIPS.

FINCH (ROGER) Coals from Newcastle: the story of the north east coal trade in the days of sail. Lavenham, 1973. pp. 208. *bibliog.*

SAINT—ETIENNE.

FRANCE. Direction de la Documentation. La Documentation Française. Notes et Etudes Documentaires. Nos. 4,030-4, 031-4,032. Les villes françaises: Saint-Etienne et son agglomération. [Paris], 1973. pp. 88.

SAINT LAWRENCE RIVER.

CANADA-QUEBEC ST. LAWRENCE RIVER WORKING GROUP. Report for the fiscal year. a., 1972/3[1st]- Ottawa. *In English and French.*

SAKHAROV (ANDREI DMITRIEVICH).

SAKHAROV (ANDREI DMITRIEVICH) Sakharov speaks;...edited and with a foreword by Harrison E. Salisbury. London, 1974. pp. 245.

SALARIED EMPLOYEES.

INTERNATIONAL LABOUR ORGANISATION. Advisory Committee on Salaried Employees and Professional Workers. 6th Session. Reports. 1. Item 1(c). General report: recent events and developments affecting salaried employees and professional workers; first item on the agenda. Geneva, 1967. pp. 84.

INTERNATIONAL LABOUR ORGANISATION. Advisory Committee on Salaried Employees and Professional Workers. 6th Session. Reports. 1. Item 1(a) and (b). General report: effect given to the conclusions of the previous sessions; first item on the agenda. Geneva, 1967. pp. 148.

INTERNATIONAL LABOUR ORGANISATION. Advisory Committee on Salaried Employees and Professional Workers. 7th Session. Reports. 1 Item 1(c). Recent events and developments affecting salaried employees and professional workers: (first item on the agenda). Geneva, 1974. pp. 81.

INTERNATIONAL LABOUR ORGANISATION. Advisory Committee on Salaried Employees and Professional Workers. 7th Session. Reports. 1. Item 1(a) and (b). Effect given to the conclusions of the previous sessions: (first item on the agenda). Geneva, 1974. pp. 162.

— Underdeveloped areas.

See UNDERDEVELOPED AREAS — Salaried employees.

— United Kingdom.

U.K. National Board for Prices and Incomes. NBPI Guides. 5. Salary structures. [London, 1970]. pp. 9.

SALE OF PUBLIC OFFICE

— America, Latin.

TOMAS Y VALIENTE (FRANCISCO) La venta de oficios en Indias, 1492-1606. Madrid, 1972. pp. 180.

SALEM, MASSACHUSETTS

— History.

BOYER (PAUL) Historian, and NISSENBAUM (STEPHEN) Salem possessed: the social origins of witchcraft. Cambridge, Mass., 1974. pp. 231.

SALES

— United Kingdom.

IVAMY (EDWARD RICHARD HARDY) Casebook on sale of goods. 3rd ed. London, 1973. pp. 214.

BENJAMIN (JUDAH PHILIP) Sale of goods; [edited by] A.G. Guest [and others]. London, 1974. pp. 1287.

SALES FORECASTING

— Mathematical models.

BRISCOE (GEOFFREY) and HIRST (M.) An appreciation of alternative sales forecasting models: recent techniques based on historical data. Coventry, 1972. pp. 36,iv. *(University of Warwick. Centre for Industrial Economic and Business Research. [Warwick Research in Industrial and Business Studies].* No. 32)

SALES PROMOTION.

TURNER (HOWARD M.) The people motivators: consumer and sales incentives in modern marketing. New York, [1973]. pp. 269.

SALES TAX

— Switzerland.

LIPPUNER (HANS) Die Bundesfinanzen und die EWG-Steuerharmonisierung, unter besonderer Berücksichtigung der Umsatzsteuer. Bern, 1970. pp. 148. *bibliog.*

SALINE WATER CONVERSION.

DUTHEIL (FRANÇOISE) and MALISSEN (MARCEL) Aperçu sur le marché de l'eau dessalée en France pour de petites unites. Gif-sur-Yvette, 1969. pp. 14. *bibliog.* *(France. Commissariat à l'Energie Atomique. Etudes Economiques.) In English and French.*

THIRIET (LUCIEN) and LIEVRE (PAUL) Facteurs et incertitudes de la rentabilité du recours à l'énergie nucléaire dans le dessalement des eaux. Gif-sur-Yvette, 1969. pp. 30. *bibliog. (France. Commissariat à l'Energie Atomique. Etudes Economiques) In English and French.*

WATER, growth and politics in coastal California: the Diablo Canyon desalting facility; by K.N. Lee [and others]. Berkeley, 1972. pp. 145. *bibliog. (California University. Institute of Governmental Studies. Working Papers. No. 2)*

SALMON FISHERIES.

INTERNATIONAL PACIFIC SALMON FISHERIES COMMISSION. Annual report. a., 1939 [2nd]-1950,1952, 1954, 1956- New Westminster, B. C.

SALT

— Taxation — India.

INDIAN PARLIAMENTARY COMMITTEE. Memoranda on the proposed imposition of the salt tax, 1923. [London, imprint, 1923?]. 1 vol. (various foliations).

SALTYKOV—SHCHEDRIN (MIKHAIL EVGRAFOVICH).

BLANKOFF (JEAN) La société russe de la seconde moitié du XIXe siècle: trois témoignages littéraires: M.E. Saltykov-Ščedrin, Gleb Uspenskij, A.F. Pisemskij. Bruxelles, [1972]. pp. 248. *bibliog.*

SALVADOR

— Foreign relations — Honduras.

CARIAS (MARCO VIRGILIO) and SLUTZKY (DANIEL) eds. La guerra inutil: analisis socio-economico del conflicto entre Honduras y El Salvador. San Jose, C.R., 1971. pp. 338.

— Politics and government.

SALVADOR. Departamento de Relaciones Publicas. Mensajes y discursos del Señor Presidente de la Republica. s-a., Jl/D 1972(t.1)- San Salvador.

— Yearbooks.

SALVADOR, EL; [pd. by] Departamento de Relaciones Publicas... El Salvador. a., 1973(2a. ed.)- San Salvador.

SAMOA

— Politics and government.

WESTERN SAMOA. 1952. Meeting between the Hon. T. Clifton Webb and the Council of State, the Legislative Assembly and the Fono of Faipule on Thursday, 7th February, 1952. [Apia?], 1952. fo. 61.

SAMPLING (STATISTICS).

CLARK (PETER KING) The use of operational time to correct for sampling interval misspecification. Minneapolis, 1973. fo. 15. *bibliog. (Minnesota University. Center for Economic Research. Discussion Papers. No. 31)*

HOEM (JAN M.) Statistisk Sentralbyrås utvalgsundersøkelser: elementer av det matematiske grunnlaget. Oslo, 1973. pp. 55. *(Norway. Statistiske Centralbyrå. Artikler. Nr. 58)*

SAN FRANCISCO

— Police.

EISENBERG (TERRY) and others. Police-community action: a program for change in police-community behavior patterns. New York, 1973. pp. 201.

SAN JOSE DE GRACIA.

GONZALEZ Y GONZALEZ (LUIS) San José de Gracia: Mexican village in transition;... translated by John Upton. Austin, [1974]. pp. 362. *bibliog.*

SAN JUAN, PUERTO RICO

— Poor.

SAFA (HELEN ICKEN) The urban poor of Puerto Rico: a study in development and inequality. New York, [1974]. pp. 116. *bibliog.*

SAN JUAN LA LAGUNA

— Social conditions.

SEXTON (JAMES D.) Education and innovation in a Guatemalan community: San Juan la Laguna. Los Angeles, 1972. pp. 72. *bibliog. (California University. Latin American Center. Latin American Studies. vol. 19)*

SAN PEDRO (IVORY COAST)

— Growth.

AUTORITE POUR L'AMENAGEMENT DE LA REGION DU SUD-OUEST [IVORY COAST]. Note de présentation sur le développement de la région du Sud-Ouest et l'opération San Pédro. [Abidjan?], 1970. fo. 28.

SANCTIONS (INTERNATIONAL LAW).

BALDWIN (ALAN) Token sanctions or total economic warfare?. London, [1972?]. pp. 20. *bibliog.*

AMERICAN ASSOCIATION FOR THE UNITED NATIONS. Student and Young Adult Division. Rhodesian chrome. New York, 1973. pp. 96.

SAND

— United Kingdom.

ALLENDER (RONALD) and HOLLYER (STUART EDWIN) The sand and gravel resources of the area south and west of Woodbridge, Suffolk: description of 1 : 25 000 resource sheet TM 24. London, 1972. pp. 128. *bibliog. (U.K. Institute of Geological Sciences. Reports. No. 72/9) (Assessments of British Sand and Gravel Resources. No. 3) Map in end pocket.*

HAGGARD (HUMPHREY JAMES EDGCOMBE) The sand and gravel resources of the country around Witham, Essex: description of 1 : 25 000 resource sheet TL 81. London, 1972. pp. 90. *bibliog. (U.K. Institute of Geological Sciences. Reports. No. 72/6) (Assessments of British Sand and Gravel Resources. No. 2) Map in end pocket.*

AMBROSE (J.D.) The sand and gravel resources of the country around Layer Breton and Tolleshunt D'Arcy, Essex: description of 1 : 25 000 resource sheet TL 91 and part of TL 90. London, 1973. pp. 34. *bibliog. (U.K. Institute of Geological Sciences. Reports. No. 73/8) (Assessments of British Sand and Gravel Resources. No. 7) Map in end pocket.*

AMBROSE (J.D.) The sand and gravel resources of the country around Maldon, Essex: description of 1 : 25 000 resource sheet TL 80. London, 1973. pp. 60. *bibliog. (U.K. Institute of Geological Sciences. Reports. No. 73/1) (Assessments of British Sand and Gravel Resources. No.4) Map in end pocket.*

EATON (C.H.) The sand and gravel resources of the country around Terling, Essex: description of 1 : 25 000 resource sheet TL 71. London, 1973. pp. 120. *bibliog. (U.K. Institute of Geological Sciences. Reports. No. 73/5) (Assessments of British Sand and Gravel Resources. No.6) Map in end pocket.*

NICKLESS (E.F.P.) The sand and gravel resources of the country around Hethersett, Norfolk: description of 1: 25 000 sheet TG 10. London, 1973. pp. 80. *bibliog. (U.K. Institute of Geological Sciences. Reports. No. 73/4) (Assessments of British Sand and Gravel Resources. No.5) Map in end pocket.*

SANDINO (AUGUSTO CESAR).

SELSER (GREGORIO) Sandino; [with texts of political manifestoes, speeches etc.]. Montevideo, [1970]. pp. 125. *bibliog.*

SANSCULOTTES.

SOBOUL (ALBERT) Mouvement populaire et gouvernement révolutionnaire en l'an II, 1793-1794. [Paris, 1973]. pp. 510. *bibliog.*

SANTANDER (COLOMBIA)

— Economic policy.

SANTANDER (COLOMBIA). Comision Planificador. 1963. Plan de desarrollo economico y social de Santander, 1964-1967; por Alvaro Ortiz Lozano [and] Jacques Torfs. Bucaramanga, 1963. 2 vols.

— Social policy.

SANTANDER (COLOMBIA). Comision Planificador. 1963. Plan de desarrollo economico y social de Santander, 1964-1967; por Alvaro Ortiz Lozano [and] Jacques Torfs. Bucaramanga, 1963. 2 vols.

SANTIAGO DEL ESTERO (PROVINCE)

— Population.

CABELLO (PLACIDO) and SPEKTOR (SUSANA) Estructura demografica y socio-ocupacional de la provincia de Santiago del Estero. Buenos Aires, 1973. pp. 211. *(Argentine Republic. Consejo Federal de Inversiones. Serie Tecnica. No. 21)*

— Social conditions.

CABELLO (PLACIDO) and SPEKTOR (SUSANA) Estructura demografica y socio-ocupacional de la provincia de Santiago del Estero. Buenos Aires, 1973. pp. 211. *(Argentine Republic. Consejo Federal de Inversiones. Serie Tecnica. No. 21)*

SÃO TOMÉ E PRINCIPE

— History.

TENREIRO (FRANCISCO) Cabo Verde e S. Tomé e Principe: esquema de uma evolução conjunta. Praia, Imprensa Nacional, 1956. pp. 16. *Separata do Boletim de Propaganda e Informação Cabo Verde.*

RIBAS (TOMAZ) A Ilha do Principe: breve memoria descritiva e historica; extractos de um trabalho; [with] Sintese estatistica da provincia de S. Tomé e Principe, ano de 1963. [S. Tomé, 1964]. pp. 25.

— Statistics.

RIBAS (TOMAZ) A Ilha do Principe: breve memoria descritiva e historica; extractos de um trabalho; [with] Sintese estatistica da provincia de S. Tomé e Principe, ano de 1963. [S. Tomé, 1964]. pp. 25.

SARAGOSSA (PROVINCE)

— Economic conditions.

MARIN CANTALAPIEDRA (MANUEL) Movimientos de poblacion y recursos de la provincia de Zaragoza, 1860-1967: un siglo de historia demografica; estudio geografico. Zaragoza, 1973. pp. 377. *bibliog.*

— Population.

MARIN CANTALAPIEDRA (MANUEL) Movimientos de poblacion y recursos de la provincia de Zaragoza, 1860-1967: un siglo de historia demografica; estudio geografico. Zaragoza, 1973. pp. 377. *bibliog.*

SARDINIA

— History.

CORRIAS CORONA (MARIA) Stato e chiesa nelle valutazioni dei politici sardi, 1848-1853. Milano, [1972]. pp. 202. *(Cagliari. Università. Seminario di Scienze Politiche. Quaderni. Serie dell' Istituto di Filosofia Politica e Giuridica)*

— Maps.

PRACCHI (R.) and others. Atlante della Sardegna, sotto gli auspici dell'Assessorato all'Industria e Commercio della Regione Autonoma della Sardegna. Cagliari, 1971 in progress. *Library has fasc. 1.*

SARTHE (DEPARTMENT)

— Economic conditions.

FRANCE. Direction Départementale de l'Agriculture de la Sarthe. 1973. La Sarthe et son espace rural: éléments pour un programme d'aménagement. [Paris, 1973?]. pp. 287. *Transparency in end pocket.*

— History — 1814—1830, Restoration.

GRIGNON (MAX) Le parti libéral dans la Sarthe sous la Restauration. Le Mans, 1927. pp. 84.

SARTRE (JEAN PAUL).

JEANSON (FRANCIS) Sartre dans sa vie. Paris, [1974]. pp. 301.

SARTRE (JEAN PAUL) Between existentialism and marxism; translated from the French by John Matthews. London, 1974. pp. 302. *Essays and interviews from Situations VIII and IX.*

SASKATOON

— Social conditions.

DOSMAN (EDGAR J.) Indians: the urban dilemma. Toronto, [1972]. pp. 192.

SASTRI (V. S. SRINIVASA)

JAGADISAN (T.N.) V.S. Srinivasa Sastri. New Delhi, 1969. pp. 231. *bibliog. (Builders of Modern India)*

SATIRE, RUSSIAN.

ERSHOV (LEONID FEDOROVICH) Iz istorii sovetskoi satiry: M. Zoshchenko i satiricheskaia proza 20-40-kh godov. Leningrad, 1973. pp. 155.

IAMPOL'SKII (ISAAK GRIGOR'EVICH) Satiricheskie i iumoristicheskie zhurnaly 1860-kh godov. Leningrad, 1973. pp. 168.

SATISFACTION.

ALLARDT (ERIK) About dimensions of welfare: an exploratory analysis of a comparative Scandinavian survey. Helsinki, 1973. pp. 128. *(Helsinki. Yliopisto. Research Group for Comparative Sociology. Research Reports. No. 1)*

SAUD 1, King of Saudi Arabia.

BENOIST-MECHIN (JACQUES) Le roi Saud; ou, L'Orient à l'heure des relèves. Paris, [1960]. pp. 575.

SAUDI ARABIA.

In previous volumes of this bibliography similar works have been entered under ARABIA.

U.K. Central Office of Information. Reference Division. 1966. Aden and South Arabia. London, 1966. pp. 39. *bibliog.*

— Economic conditions.

SEIFERT (WILLIAM W.) and others, eds. Energy and development: a case study; based upon an interdepartmental student project…at the Massachusetts Institute of Technology…and a study at the College of Petroleum and Minerals, Dhahran, Saudi Arabia. Cambridge, Mass., [1973]. pp. 300. *(Massachusetts Institute of Technology. M.I.T. Reports. No. 25)*

SAVING AND INVESTMENT.

BURNS (JOSEPH M.) The saving-investment process in a theory of finance: a dissertation, etc. Chicago, 1967. fo. 121. *bibliog.*

ORGANISATION FOR ECONOMIC CO-OPERATION AND DEVELOPMENT. Committee for Invisible Transactions. Country Capital- Market Series. [Paris], 1969 in progress.

SOKOLINSKII (ZALMAN VENIAMINOVICH) Teorii nakopleniia. Moskva, 1973. pp. 150.

ANDERSON (BRUCE LOUIS) ed. Capital accumulation in the industrial revolution. London, 1974. pp. 212. *bibliogs.*

LAMBRINIDES (MATTHEW J.) Saving and social choice: an analysis of the relationship between corporate and personal saving. Coventry, 1974. pp. 33. *(University of Warwick. Department of Economics. Warwick Economic Research Papers. No. 42)*

THIRLWALL (ANTHONY PHILIP) Inflation, saving and growth in developing economies. London, 1974. pp. 256.

— Mathematical models.

LAMBRINIDES (MATTHEW J.) Private saving and the macro-economic distribution of income: the 'classical' and the 'managerial' savings functions. Coventry, 1973. pp. 48. *(University of Warwick. Department of Economics. Warwick Economic Research Papers. No. 36)*

— Africa.

ALBERICI (ADALBERTO) and BARAVELLI (MAURIZIO) eds. Savings banks and savings facilities in African countries; [replies to a questionnaire sent out on the occasion of the Conference on the Mobilization of Savings in African Countries, Milan, 1971]. Milan, 1973. pp. 131. *(Cassa di Risparmio delle Provincie Lombarde. The Credit Markets of Africa. 7)*

— Canada — Mathematical models.

SCHWEITZER (THOMAS T.) and SIEDULE (TOM) CANDIDE [Canadian Disaggregated Interdepartmental Econometric] model 1.0: savings and consumption. Ottawa, Information Canada, 1973. pp. 71. *(CANDIDE Project Papers. No. 2)*

— Fiji Islands.

FIJI. Bureau of Statistics. 1972. Gross capital formation, Fiji, 1968-1970. Suva, 1972. fo. 19. *(National Accounts Studies. Vol. 2)*

— France.

FRANCE. Institut National de la Statistique et des Etudes Economiques. Collections de l'I.N.S.E.E. SÉRIE M. Ménages . Paris, 1970 in progress.

PETIT-DUTAILLIS (GEORGES) Epargne, investissement et Bourse. [Paris], 1972. pp. 90. *bibliog. (France. Direction de la Documentation. La Documentation Française. Notes et Etudes Documentaires. Nos. 3937-3938)*

RENCONTRE UNIVERSITE-ENTREPRISE, 1E, 1971. Les incitations des particuliers à l'épargne;…rencontre…organisée les 10 et 11 juin 1971…par le Centre de Droit des Affaires…d'Aix-Marseille et Centre de Perfectionnement dans l'Administration des Affaires …Paris. Paris, [1972]. pp. 206.

— Germany.

BOSS (CHRISTIAN) Die Investmentclubs in der Bundesrepublik Deutschland. [Erlangen, imprint, 1973?]. pp. 188, xxxvi. *bibliog.*

— Italy.

PARRILLO (FRANCESCO) Il risparmio e l'intermediazione finanziaria nell'investimento immobiliare. Milano, 1973. pp. 111. *bibliog.*

— Lesotho.

ONADO (MARCO) and PORTERI (ANTONIO) The banking system and the formation of savings in Lesotho. Milan, 1974. pp. 139. *(Cassa di Risparmio delle Provincie Lombarde. The Credit Markets of Africa. 9)*

— Malaysia.

LEE (HOCK LOCK) Household saving in West Malaysia and the problem of financing economic development. Kuala Lumpur, 1971. pp. 324. *bibliog. (University of Malaya. Faculty of Economics and Administration. Monograph Series on Malaysian Economic Affairs. 1)*

— Netherlands.

NETHERLANDS. Centraal Bureau voor de Statistiek. Statistiek van de investeringen in vaste activa in de nijverheid: (Statistics on fixed capital formation in industry). a., 1971- 's-Gravenhage.

— **Underdeveloped areas.**

See UNDERDEVELOPED AREAS — Saving and investment.

— United Kingdom.

ANDERSON (BRUCE LOUIS) ed. Capital accumulation in the industrial revolution. London, 1974. pp. 212. *bibliogs.*

— — **Mathematical models.**

EL-MOKADEM (A.M.) Econometric models of personal saving: the United Kingdom, 1948-1966. London, 1973. pp. 196. *bibliog.*

— United States.

TURE (NORMAN B.) Tax policy, capital formation and productivity. New York, 1973. pp. 40.

SAVINGS BANKS

— Africa.

ALBERICI (ADALBERTO) and BARAVELLI (MAURIZIO) eds. Savings banks and savings facilities in African countries; [replies to a questionnaire sent out on the occasion of the Conference on the Mobilization of Savings in African Countries, Milan, 1971]. Milan, 1973. pp. 131. *(Cassa di Risparmio delle Provincie Lombarde. The Credit Markets of Africa. 7)*

— Germany.

VOGT (KLAUS DIETER) Die Sparkasse und ihr Wirken: (50 Jahre Kreissparkasse Gifhorn), 1921-1971; im Dienst der heimischen Wirtschaft. [Gifhorn, 1971]. pp. 180. *bibliog.*

GEIGER (HELMUT) Herausforderungen für Stabilität und Fortschritt: [collection of lectures, 1970-1974]. Stuttgart, [1974]. pp. 211.

SAVINGS BANKS. (Cont.)

— Norway.

HEGGLAND (JOHANNES) Fjaler Sparebank, 1873-1973. [Bergen, imprint], 1973. pp. 164.

— United Kingdom.

GOSDEN (PETER HENRY JOHN HEATHER) Self-help: voluntary associations in the 19th century. London, 1973. pp. 295. bibliog.

SCANDICCI

— Economic policy.

SCANDICCI. Note sullo stato di attuazione del piano quadriennale; [and] Schema orientativo per il 20 piano pluriennale 1970-1974, approvato dalla Commissione Economica nella seduta del 24 aprile 1969. [Scandicci, 1969]. pp. 97,fo. 45.

SCANDINAVIA.

WILSON (ALAN) Nordic cooperation: common solutions to common problems. [Stockholm], Royal Ministry for Foreign Affairs, 1972. fo. 6.

See also EUROPEAN ECONOMIC COMMUNITY — Scandinavia.

— Emigration and immigration.

NORDISK HISTORIKERMØDE, 1971. Emigrationen fra Norden indtil I. Verdenskrig: rapporter til... i København, 1971, 9-12 august; [edited by Kristian Hvidt]. [Copenhagen, 1971]. pp. 168. bibliogs. In various Scandinavian languages.

— Population.

NORDISK HISTORIKERMØDE, 1971. Emigrationen fra Norden indtil I. Verdenskrig: rapporter til... i København, 1971, 9-12 august; [edited by Kristian Hvidt]. [Copenhagen, 1971]. pp. 168. bibliogs. In various Scandinavian languages.

— Social conditions.

ALLARDT (ERIK) About dimensions of welfare: an exploratory analysis of a comparative Scandinavian survey. Helsinki, 1973. pp. 128. (Helsinki. Yliopisto. Research Group for Comparative Sociology. Research Reports. No. 1)

— Statistics.

[SCANDINAVIA]. Nordisk Statistisk Skriftserie. 25. Det nordiske chefstatistikermøde i Helsingfors 1973, etc. København, 1974. pp. 143.

SCHAFFHAUSEN

— Civic improvement.

FISCHER (GEORGES) Schaffhausen: Zukunft einer Region; sozio-ökonomische Strukturanalyse der Stadt und Region Schaffhausen als Grundlage zur Erarbeitung eines Leitbildes. Schaffhausen, 1973. 1 vol.(various pagings). (Hochschule St.Gallen für Wirtschafts- und Sozialwissenschaften. Schweizerisches Institut für Aussenwirtschafts-, Struktur- und Marktforschung. Struktur- und Regionalwirtschaftliche Studien. Band 4)

SCHEEL (WALTER).

ZIRNGIBL (WILLY) Gefragt: Walter Scheel. Bonn, [1972]. pp. 94.

SCHIZOPHRENIA.

GOTTESMAN (IRVING I.) and SHIELDS (JAMES) Schizophrenia and genetics: a twin study vantage point. New York, 1972. pp. 433. bibliog.

PSYCHIATRIC REHABILITATION ASSOCIATION. Poverty and schizophrenia: an examination of the relationship between environmental factors and the schizophrenia discharge rate; the development of a predictive formula; research team: Gillian Lomas [and others]. London, 1973. fo. 28. bibliog.

SCHIZOPHRENICS.

SUOMINEN (JAAKKO) and SIEVERS (KAI) Aspects of disabling schizophrenia in various population groups. [Helsinki], 1971. pp. [8]. bibliog. (Finland. Kansaneläkelaitos. Julkaisuja. E. 48/1971) Reprint from Psychiatria Fennica. 1971.

SCHLESWIG—HOLSTEIN QUESTION.

HEUER (JUERGEN) Zur politischen, sozialen und ökonomischen Problematik der Volksabstimmungen in Schleswig, 1920. Kiel, 1973. pp. 238. bibliog.

SCHLIEFFEN (ALFRED VON) Graf.

WALLACH (JEHUDA L.) Das Dogma der Vernichtungsschlacht: die Lehren von Clausewitz und Schlieffen und ihre Wirkungen in zwei Weltkriegen; (aus dem Englischen von Hans Jürgen Baron von Koskull). Frankfurt am Main, 1967. pp. 475. bibliog.

SCHMID (WERNER).

MERZ (JOHANNES) Werner Schmid, 1/4Jahrhundert Parlamentsarbeit. [Bern, 1972]. pp. 48.

SCHOLARSHIPS

— South Africa.

AWARDS AVAILABLE FOR POST-GRADUATE STUDY IN THE REPUBLIC OF SOUTH AFRICA AND OVERSEAS: Toekennings beskikbaar vir nagraadse studie in die Republiek van Suid-Afrika en in die buiteland; [pd. by] Human Sciences Research Council [South Africa]. irreg., current issue only kept. Pretoria. In English and Afrikaans.

— Switzerland.

SWITZERLAND. Commission Intercantonale des Bourses d'Etudes. 1970. Projekt für die Verbesserung der Ausbildungsfinanzierung in der Schweiz, etc. [Bern, 1970]. pp. 27bis.

SWITZERLAND. Commission Intercantonale des Bourses d'Etudes. 1971. Die Ausbildungsfinanzierung durch die Kantone, Stand 31, Dezember 1970, etc. [Bern, 1971]. pp. 48. In German and French.

— United Kingdom.

NATIONAL UNION OF STUDENTS. Educational charities. [5th ed.] London, 1972. pp. 26.

SCHOLASTICISM.

SMALLEY (BERYL) The Becket conflict and the schools: a study of intellectuals in politics. Oxford, 1973. pp. 258.

SCHOOL BUILDINGS

— Denmark.

DENMARK. Undervisningsministeriet. International Relations Division. 1967. School building in Denmark: administration and financing of private and public school building programmes. Copenhagen, 1967. fo. 17.

SCHOOL CHILDREN.

HANSEN (SØREN) AND JENSEN (JESPER) The little red school-book;...translated from Danish by Berit Thornberry. London, 1971. pp. 208. Unexpurgated edition.

HANSEN (SØREN) and JENSEN (JESPER) The little red school-book;...translated from Danish by Berit Thornberry. rev. ed. London, 1971. pp. 208. Expurgated edition.

— Food.

U.K. Department of Health and Social Security. Reports on Health and Social Subjects. No.6. First report by the Sub-Committee on Nutritional Surveillance; [Sir Frank Young, chairman]. London, 1973. pp. 25. bibliog.

— Transportation.

— — Canada.

CANADA. Statistics Canada. Pupil transportation in Canada. a., 1970/71- Ottawa. In English and French.

— — United Kingdom.

SCHOOL transport; report of the Working Party appointed by the Secretary of State for Education and Science and the Secretary of State for Wales; [M.W. Hodges, chairman].London, H.M.S.O., 1973. pp. 74.

— — United States.

TEELE (JAMES E.) Evaluating school busing: case study of Boston's Operation Exodus. New York, 1973. pp. 149.

— Australia.

KEEVES (JOHN P.) Educational environment and student achievement: a multivariate study of the contributions of the home, the school and the peer group to change in mathematics and science performance during the first year at secondary school. Stockholm, [1972]. pp. 311. bibliog. (Stockholms Universitet. Acta Universitatis Stockholmiensis. Stockholm Studies in Educational Psychology. 20)

— Denmark.

DENMARK. Kontaktudvalget vedrørende Ungdomsnarkomanien. Forskningsunderudvalg. 1971. Udbredelse af stofbrug blandt danske skoleelever, af Boel Ulff- Møller [and others]. København, 1971. pp. 182.

ØRUM (BENTE) Kønsforskelle blandt skoleungdom: rapport nr. 4 fra ungdomsforløbsunders/ogelsen, etc. København, 1973. pp. 216. bibliog. (Socialforskningsinstituttet. Publikationer. 59)

— France.

FRANCE. Institut National d'Etudes Démographiques. 1973. Enquête nationale sur le niveau intellectuel des enfants d'âge scolaire. Paris, 1973. pp. 197. (Travaux et Documents. Cahiers. No. 64)

— New Zealand.

NEW ZEALAND. Family Health Branch. 1971. Physical development of New Zealand school children, 1969; a survey. Wellington, 1971. pp. 119. (Department of Health. Special Report Series. 38)

— Russia.

VASIL'EVA (EVELINA KARLOVNA) Sotsial'no-professional'nyi uroven' gorodskoi molodezhi: po materialam vyborochnogo obsledovaniia shkol'nikov i molodezhi Leningrada. Leningrad, 1973. pp. 142.

— United Kingdom.

SWERLING (SAM) Who's getting at our kids?; an analysis of the organisations and personalities attempting to bring about revolution in our schools. [London, 1972]. fo. 23.

MARSON (DAVE) Children's strikes in 1911. [Oxford, 1973]. pp. 35. (History Workshop. Pamphlets. No 9)

— — Ireland, Northern.

RUSSELL (JAMES LYON) Some aspects of the civic education of secondary schoolboys in Northern Ireland. [Belfast], Northern Ireland Community Relations Commission, 1972. fo. 34. (Research Papers)

SCHOOL HYGIENE

— United Kingdom.

The SCHOOL health service: report of a Study Group set up by the Secretary of State for Scotland: [J.H.F. Brotherston, chairman]. [Edinburgh], Scottish Home and Health Department, 1968. pp. 55. bibliog.

SCHOOL INTEGRATION

— United States.

KIRBY (DAVID J.) and others. Political strategies in northern school desegregation. Lexington, Mass., [1973]. pp. 262. bibliog.

SMITH (AL) 1940- , and others. Achieving effective desegregation. Lexington, [1973]. pp. 248. bibliogs.

TEELE (JAMES E.) Evaluating school busing: case study of Boston's Operation Exodus. New York, 1973. pp. 149.

SCIENCE.

WILLIE (CHARLES VERT) and BEKER (JEROME) Race mixing in the public schools. New York, 1973. pp. 97.

LINDSEY (PAUL) and LINDSEY (OUIDA) Breaking the bonds of racism. Homewood, Ill., 1974. pp. 242. *bibliog.*

SCHOOL MANAGEMENT AND ORGANIZATION.

BENNETT (STEPHEN J.) The school: an organizational analysis. Glasgow, [1974]. pp. 128. *bibliog.*

— United Kingdom.

TRUEFITT (ALISON) How to set up a free school: alternative education and the law. London, [1973?]. pp. 42. *bibliog.*

BARON (GEORGE) and HOWELL (DAVID ANTONY) 1927- . The government and management of schools. London, 1974. pp. 245.

GORDON (PETER) The Victorian school manager: a study in the management of education, 1800-1902. London, 1974. pp. 337. *bibliog.*

— — Wales.

MORGAN (T.M.) Power in education. Swansea, [1973]. pp. 24. *(Wales. University. University College of Swansea. Charles Gittins Memorial Lectures. 1973)*

— United States.

LA NOUE (GEORGE R.) and SMITH (BRUCE L.R.) The politics of school decentralization. Lexington, Mass., [1973]. pp. 284.

SCHOOL SOCIAL WORK

— United Kingdom.

LYONS (K.H.) Social work and the school: a study of some aspects of the role of an education social worker. London, H.M.S.O., 1973. pp. 54.

SCHOOLS.

HANSEN (SØREN) AND JENSEN (JESPER) The little red school-book;...translated from Danish by Berit Thornberry. London, 1971. pp. 208. *Unexpurgated edition.*

HANSEN (SØREN) and JENSEN (JESPER) The little red school-book;...translated from Danish by Berit Thornberry. rev. ed. London, 1971. pp. 208. *Expurgated edition.*

OPEN UNIVERSITY. Faculty of Educational Studies. School and Society Course Team. School and society: a sociological reader. London, 1971. pp. 240. *bibliogs.*

— Australia.

CLAYDON (L. F.) Renewing urban teaching. Cambridge, 1973. pp. 190. *bibliog.*

— South Africa.

SOUTH AFRICA. Bureau of Statistics. 1973. Education: schools for Coloured and Asians, 1970. Pretoria, 1973. pp. 83. *(Reports. No.21-03-04) In English and Afrikaans.*

— United Kingdom.

BUCKS STEP. Our schools at the crossroads: the story of Buckinghamshire's search for a secondary education policy. Chesham, Bucks., [1973]. pp. 56.

BULLIVANT (ANTHONY) Schools for all our children - comprehensives. Billericay, [1973]. pp. 24. *bibliog. (Home and School Council of Great Britain. Working Papers)*

HALCROW (MORRISON) Schools of our choice. London, [1973]. pp. 22.

RUBINSTEIN (DAVID) and SIMON (BRIAN) The evolution of the comprehensive school, 1926-1972. 2nd ed. London, 1973. pp. 136. *bibliog.*

SHARP (JOHN ROBERT INGLE) Open school: the experience of 1964-1970 at Wyndham School, Egremont, Cumberland. London, 1973. pp. 132.

— — Scotland.

MILLAR (HUGH) and WHITE (DAVID) Depute Rector of the Auchenharvie Academy. Comprehensive education - has it changed anything?: a study of secondary schools in Ayrshire. Saltcoats, Ayrshire, [1973]. pp. 28.

— — Wales.

MERIONETH. County Planning Office. Merioneth structure plan: (subject report no. 5): education. Dolgellau, [1973]. pp. 39.

— United States.

HALL (FRED L.) Location criteria for high schools: student transportation and racial integration. Chicago, Ill., 1973. pp. 156. *bibliog. (Chicago. University. Department of Geography. Research Papers. No. 150)*

HUMMEL (RAYMOND C.) and NAGLE (JOHN M.) Urban education in America: problems and prospects. New York, 1973. pp. 298.

McDILL (EDWARD L.) and RIGSBY (LEO C.) Structure and process in secondary schools: the academic impact of educational climates. Baltimore, [1973]. pp. 201. *bibliog.*

POUNDS (RALPH LINNAEUS) and BRYNER (JAMES R.) The school in American society. 3rd ed. New York, [1973]. pp. 618. *bibliog.*

SIEBER (SAM D.) and WILDER (DAVID E.) eds. The school in society: studies in the sociology of education. New York, [1973]. pp. 440. *bibliogs.*

— — Centralization.

LA NOUE (GEORGE R.) and SMITH (BRUCE L.R.) The politics of school decentralization. Lexington, Mass., [1973]. pp. 284.

SCHROEDER (GERHARD).

KUPER (ERNST) Frieden durch Konfrontation und Kooperation: die Einstellung von Gerhard Schröder und Willi [sic] Brandt zur Entspannungspolitik. Stuttgart, 1974. pp. 534. *biblio. (Hamburg. Hansische Universität. Seminar für Sozialwissenschaften. Sozialwissenschaftliche Studien. Heft 14)*

SCHUMACHER (KURT).

BUCZYLOWSKI (ULRICH) Kurt Schumacher und die deutsche Frage: Sicherheitspolitik und strategische Offensivkonzeption vom August 1950 bis September 1951. Stuttgart-Degerloch, 1973. pp. 228. *bibliog.*

SCIENCE.

GROWING points in science; [by A.W. Merrison and others].[London], H.M.S.O., 1972. pp. 215.

— History.

RETI (LADISLAO) and GIBSON (WILLIAM C.) Some aspects of seventeenth-century medicine and science; papers read at a Clark Library seminar [at Los Angeles], October 12, 1968. Los Angeles, 1969. pp. 46.

SPECHT (RAINER) Innovation und Folgelast: Beispiele aus der neueren Philosophie- und Wissenschaftsgeschichte. Stuttgart-Bad Cannstatt, [1972]. pp. 237. *With English summary.*

CHANGING perspectives in the history of science: essays in honour of Joseph Needham; edited by Mikuláš Teich and Robert Young. Dordrecht, 1973. pp. 490. *bibliog.*

HOLTON (GERALD JAMES) Thematic origins of scientific thought: Kepler to Einstein. Cambridge, 1973. pp. 495.

BOSTON COLLOQUIUM FOR THE PHILOSOPHY OF SCIENCE. Proceedings, 1969- 1972. Boston studies in the philosophy of science, vol. 14: methodological and historical essays in the natural and social sciences; edited by Robert S. Cohen and Marx W. Wartofsky. Dordrecht, [1974]. pp. 405. *bibliogs.*

— — Russia — Baltic States.

IZ istorii estestvoznaniia i tekhniki Pribaltiki. t.2. Riga, 1970. pp. 379. *bibliog.*

— International cooperation.

DAHRENDORF (RALF) Towards a European science policy. Southampton, 1973. pp. 19. *(Southampton. University. Fawley Foundation. Lectures. 19)*

— Methodology.

The METHODOLOGICAL unity of science: [papers from the Bertrand Russell Colloquium on Exact Philosophy attached to the McGill University Foundations and Philosophy of Science Unit]; edited by Mario Bunge. Dordrecht, [1973]. pp. 264. *bibliogs.*

BOSTON COLLOQUIUM FOR THE PHILOSOPHY OF SCIENCE. Proceedings, 1969- 1972. Boston studies in the philosophy of science, vol. 14: methodological and historical essays in the natural and social sciences; edited by Robert S. Cohen and Marx W. Wartofsky. Dordrecht, [1974]. pp. 405. *bibliogs.*

— Philosophy.

FANN (K.T.) Peirce's theory of abduction. The Hague, 1970. pp. 62. *bibliog.*

KLUEVER (JUERGEN) Operationalismus: Kritik und Geschichte einer Philosophie der exakten Wissenschaften. Stuttgart-Bad Cannstatt, 1971. pp. 220. *bibliog. With English summary.* SUL marxismo e le scienze. Roma, 1972. pp. 286. *(Critica Marxista. Quaderni. n.6)*

SPECHT (RAINER) Innovation und Folgelast: Beispiele aus der neueren Philosophie- und Wissenschaftsgeschichte. Stuttgart-Bad Cannstatt, [1972]. pp. 237. *With English summary.*

EASLEA (BRIAN) Liberation and the aims of science: an essay on obstacles to the building of a beautiful world. London, 1973. pp. 370.

GRÜNFELD (JOSEPH) Science and values. Amsterdam, 1973. pp. 210.

KONTSEPTSII nauki v burzhuaznoi filosofii i sotsiologii, vtoraia polovina XIX-XX v. Moskva, 1973. pp. 352.

The METHODOLOGICAL unity of science: [papers from the Bertrand Russell Colloquium on Exact Philosophy attached to the McGill University Foundations and Philosophy of Science Unit]; edited by Mario Bunge. Dordrecht, [1973]. pp. 264. *bibliogs.*

NEURATH (OTTO) Empiricism and sociology; [selections from his writings]; edited by Marie Neurath and Robert S. Cohen; with a selection of biographical and autobiographical sketches. Dordrecht, [1973]. pp. 473. *bibliog.*

LENINE et la pratique scientifique: colloque d'Orsay; [papers of a meeting held in 1971]. Paris, [1974]. pp. 606.

LENZEN (WOLFGANG) Theorien der Bestätigung wissenschaftlicher Hypothesen. Stuttgart-Bad Cannstatt, [1974]. pp. 217. *bibliog. With English summary.*

— Social aspects.

UNITED NATIONS EDUCATIONAL, SCIENTIFIC AND CULTURAL ORGANIZATION. Science Policy Studies and Documents. Paris, 1965 in progress.

MELSEN (ANDREAS GERARDUS MARIA VAN) Science and responsibility. Pittsburgh, Pa., [1970]. pp. 172.

GASTON (JERRY) Originality and competition in science: a study of the British high energy physics community. Chicago, [1973]. pp. 210. *bibliog.*

MERTON (ROBERT KING) The sociology of science: theoretical and empirical investigations; edited and with an introduction by Norman W. Storer. Chicago, [1973]. pp. 605. *bibliog.*

SCIENTISTS in search of their conscience; Raymond Aron [and others; proceedings of a symposium organized by the European Committee of the Weizmann Institute of Science, Brussels, 1971]; edited by Anthony R. Michaelis and Hugh Harvey. Berlin, 1973. pp. 229.

SCIENCE. (Cont.)

SOCIAL processes of scientific development: [papers from a conference of the International Sociological Association's Research Committee on the Sociology of Science held in London in September 1972]; edited by Richard Whitley. London, 1974. pp. 286. *bibliogs.*

BLUME (STUART S.) Toward a political sociology of science. New York, [1974]. pp. 288.

— Study and teaching — Netherlands.

NETHERLANDS. Centraal Planbureau. 1972. Kwantitatieve en financiële effecten van de herstructurering van het wetenschappelijk onderwijs. 's-Gravenhage, 1972. pp. 24. *(Monografieën. No. 13)*

ORGANISATION FOR ECONOMIC CO-OPERATION AND DEVELOPMENT. Directorate for Scientific Affairs. 1973. Netherlands. Paris, 1973. pp. 375. *(Reviews of National Science Policy. [No. 16]*

— European Economic Community countries.

EUROPEAN COMMUNITIES COMMISSION. 1973. Scientific and technological policy programme: submitted to the Council on 1 August 1973. [Brussels], 1973. pp. 47. *(Bulletin of the European Communities. Supplements. [1973/14])*

SCIENCE AND ETHICS.

MELSEN (ANDREAS GERARDUS MARIA VAN) Science and responsibility. Pittsburgh, Pa., [1970]. pp. 172.

SCIENCE AND STATE.

UNITED NATIONS EDUCATIONAL, SCIENTIFIC AND CULTURAL ORGANIZATION. Science Policy Studies and Documents. Paris, 1965 in progress.

ORGANISATION FOR ECONOMIC CO-OPERATION AND DEVELOPMENT. Information Service. 1967. Science and the OECD: science and the policies of government; cooperation in research: a joint approach by 21 nations. Paris, 1967. pp. 40.

MAESTRE (CLAUDE) and PAVITT (KEITH) Analytical methods in government science policy: an evaluation. Paris, Organisation for Economic Co-operation and Development, 1972. pp. 89. *bibliog. (Science Policy Studies)*

SEMINAR ON R[ESEARCH] AND D[EVELOPMENT] MANAGEMENT, ISTANBUL, 1970. Management of research and development; papers presented at a Seminar organised by the Scientific and Technical Research Council of Turkey, [held at] Istanbul 4-8 May 1970. Paris, Organisation for Economic Co-operation and Development, 1972. pp. 329. *(Problems of Development).*

KUCZYNSKI (JUERGEN) Wissenschaft heute und morgen, etc. Köln, 1973. pp. 149.

ROUX (JEAN) Vers une démocratie scientifique. Paris, 1973. pp. 101.

BLUME (STUART S.) Toward a political sociology of science. New York, [1974]. pp. 288.

KING (ALEXANDER) Science and policy: the international stimulus. London, 1974. pp. 113. *bibliog.*

KUCZYNSKI (JUERGEN) Die vertauschte Eule der Minerva: der Wissenschaftler in der kapitalistischen Gesellschaft. Berlin, 1974. pp. 80.

— Canada.

HAYES (F. RONALD) The chaining of Prometheus: evolution of a power structure for Canadian science. Toronto, [1973]. pp. 217.

— India.

INDIA. Administrative Reforms Commission. Study Team on Scientific Departments. 1970. Report. [Delhi], 1970. pp. 130.

— Ireland (Republic).

CONFERENCE TO EVALUATE THE PILOT TEAMS PROJECT, 1967. Pilot teams project: evaluation conference. Paris, ORGANISATION FOR ECONOMIC CO-OPERATION AND DEVELOPMENT, 1968. pp. 260. *(Science and Development)*

— Mediterranean.

CONFERENCE TO EVALUATE THE PILOT TEAMS PROJECT, 1967. Pilot teams project: evaluation conference. Paris, ORGANISATION FOR ECONOMIC CO-OPERATION AND DEVELOPMENT, 1968. pp. 260. *(Science and Development)*

— Russia.

PROTSESS prevrashcheniia nauki v neposredstvennuiu proizvoditel'nuiu silu. Moskva, 1971. pp. 127.

HARVEY (MOSE L.) and others. Science and technology as an instrument of Soviet policy. Miami, 1972. pp. 219. *(Miami (Florida). University. Center for Advanced International Studies. Monographs in International Affairs)*

ORGANIZATSIONNO-pravovye voprosy rukovodstva naukoi v SSSR. Moskva, 1973. pp. 423.

— United States.

SCIENCE and the evolution of public policy: [based on a lecture- seminar series oeonsored by the Rockefeller University]; James A. Shannon, editor. New York, 1973. pp. 259.

ROSENTHAL (ALBERT HAROLD) ed. Public science policy and administration. Albuquerque, [1973]. pp. 322. *bibliog.*

SCIENCE AND THE HUMANITIES.

BLANSHARD (BRAND) The uses of a liberal education: and other talks to students;... [speeches and essays] edited by Eugene Freeman. London, 1974. pp. 415. *First published in the United States in 1973.*

SCIENCE AS A PROFESSION.

U.K. Civil Service Commission. 1970. The scientific civil service. rev. ed. [London], 1970. pp. 91.

SCIENTIFIC LIBRARIES.

ROZSA (GYÖRGY) Some considerations of the role of scientific libraries in the age of the scientific and technical revolution: an essay and approach to the problem. Budapest, 1970. pp. 25. *(Magyar Tudományos Akadémia. Könyvtar. Közlemények. 50)*

SCIENTISTS.

KUCZYNSKI (JUERGEN) Die vertauschte Eule der Minerva: der Wissenschaftler in der kapitalistischen Gesellschaft. Berlin, 1974. pp. 80.

— United Kingdom.

U.K. Department of Trade and Industry. 1973. The survey of professional scientists, 1971. London, 1973. pp. 79. *(Studies in Technological Manpower. No. 4)*

SCIENTOLOGY.

ROLPH (C.H.) pseud. [i.e. Cecil Rolph HEWITT] Believe what you like: what happened between the Scientologists and the National Association for Mental Health. London, 1973. pp. 172.

SCOTCH IN IRELAND.

PERCEVAL-MAXWELL (MICHAEL) The Scottish migration to Ulster in the reign of James I. London, 1973. pp. 411. *bibliog. (Ulster-Scot Historical Society. Ulster-Scot Historical Series. 3)*

SCOTLAND

— Census.

SCOTLAND. Census, 1971. Census, 1971: Scotland: population tables. Edinburgh, 1974. pp. 206.

SCOTLAND. Census, 1971. Census, 1971: Scotland: usual residence and birthplace tables. Edinburgh, 1974. pp. 129.

— Commerce — China.

SCOTTISH HISTORY SOCIETY. [Publications] 4th series. vol. 10. William Melrose in China, 1845-1855: the letters of a Scottish tea merchant; edited by Hoh-cheung Mui and Lorna H. Mui. Edinburgh, 1973. pp. 301. *6 papers in end pocket.*

— Economic conditions.

MITCHISON (NAOMI MARGARET) Oil for the Highlands?. London, 1974. pp. 32. *(Fabian Society. Research Series. [No.] 315)*

— Economic history.

SCOTTISH HISTORICAL CONFERENCE, 6TH, STIRLING, 1972. The union of 1707: its impact on Scotland; essays by P.W.J. Riley [and others] (first delivered as lectures at the... conference); edited by T.I. Rae. Glasgow, 1974. pp. 119.

— Emigration and immigration.

PERCEVAL-MAXWELL (MICHAEL) The Scottish migration to Ulster in the reign of James I. London, 1973. pp. 411. *bibliog. (Ulster-Scot Historical Society. Ulster-Scot Historical Series. 3)*

— History — Sources.

U.K. Parliament. House of Lords. Record Office. Memoranda. No. 47. Letters of the second Earl of Tweeddale, 1672 to 1692; a list compiled by D.J. Johnson. [London, 1972]. pp. 6.

— — To 1603.

NICHOLSON (RANALD) Scotland: the later middle ages. Edinburgh, 1974. pp. 695. *bibliog.*

— — 1707, The Union.

SCOTTISH HISTORICAL CONFERENCE, 6TH, STIRLING, 1972. The union of 1707: its impact on Scotland; essays by P.W.J. Riley [and others] (first delivered as lectures at the... conference); edited by T.I. Rae. Glasgow, 1974. pp. 119.

— Politics and government.

SCOTTISH COUNCIL (DEVELOPMENT AND INDUSTRY). International Forum, 1st, Aviemore, 1970. The influence of centralisation on the future; [proceedings]. Edinburgh, 1970]. pp. 123.

— Religion.

MACLAREN (A. ALLAN) Religion and social class: the disruption years in Aberdeen. London, 1974. pp. 268.

SCRAP METAL INDUSTRY

— Ireland (Republic).

EIRE. Restrictive Practices Commission. 1972. Report of enquiry into the conditions which obtain in regard to the supply and distribution of iron and steel scrap. Dublin, [1972]. pp. 79.

SEAMEN.

INTERNATIONAL LABOUR CONFERENCE. 55th Session. Reports. 6. Sixth item on the agenda: vocational training of seafarers. Geneva, 1970. pp. 41.

INTERNATIONAL LABOUR CONFERENCE. 55th Session. Reports. 7. Seventh item on the agenda: seafarers' welfare at sea and in port. Geneva, 1970. pp. 34.

SYMPOSIUM ON SEAFARER AND COMMUNITY. UNIVERSITY OF WALES INSTITUTE OF SCIENCE AND TECHNOLOGY, 1972. Seafarer and community: towards a social understanding of seafaring; [papers of the symposium] edited by Peter H. Fricke. London, 1973. pp. 164. *bibliog.*

— Accommodation on shipboard.

INTERNATIONAL LABOUR CONFERENCE. 55th Session. Reports. 2. Second item on the agenda: crew accommodation. Geneva, 1969-70. 2 pts.

— Salaries, pensions, etc.

INTERNATIONAL LABOUR CONFERENCE. 55th Session. Reports. 3. Third item on the agenda: recommendation No. 109, paragraph 2; revision of the 1958 wage figures... having regard solely to the fall in the value of money since 1958. Geneva, 1970. pp. 15.

— Denmark.

BETAENKNING om sikring af søfarende i sygdomstilfaelde; afgivet af det af socialministeren den 17. juni 1964 nedsatte udvalg. København, 1970. pp. 43. (Denmark. Betaenkninger. Nr.568)

— Finland.

FINLAND. Kommittén för Behandling av Sjöfarandes Välfärd till Sjöss och i Hamn. 1971. Betänkande, etc. Helsingfors, 1971. fo. 59. (Finland. Komiteanmietinnöt. 1971. B.95)

— Norway — Laws and regulations.

NORWAY. Departementet for Sociale Saker. Arbeiderkommisjonen av 1918. 1922. Innstilling...angående lov om sjømenns medvirkning i driftsledelsen. Kristiania, 1922. pp. 46.

NORWAY. Komitéen for Revisjon av Sjømannsloven. 1971. Instilling om ny sjømannslov: innstilling 4. Bergen, 1971. pp. 92.

— Sweden.

SWEDEN. Finansdepartementet. Skömansskattekommitté. 1969. Sjömansbeskattningen: betänkande av 1967 års...kommitté. Stockholm, 1969. pp. 158. (Sweden. Statens Offentliga Utredningar. 1969. 55)

— United Kingdom.

NATIONAL UNION OF SEAMEN. Rules. [London], 1972. pp. 80.

NOLAN (BRYAN) Social life in a merchant ship: a study of attitude change during assimilation into a total institution; [Ph.D. (London) thesis] . 1973 [or rather 1974]. fo. 306. bibliog. Typscript: unpublished. This thesis is the property of London University and may not be removed from the Library.

TAPLIN (E.L.) Liverpool dockers and seamen, 1870-1890. Hull, 1974. pp. 96. bibliog. (Hull. University. Occasional Papers in Economic and Social History. No. 6)

— United States.

SHERAR (MARIAM G.) Shipping out: a sociological study of the American merchant seaman. Cambridge, Md., 1973. pp. 84. bibliog.

SWIFT (WILLIAM S.) The negro in the offshore maritime industry. Philadelphia, [1974]. pp. 204. (Pennsylvania University. Wharton School of Finance and Commerce. Industrial Research Unit. Racial Policies of American Industry. Report No. 30)

SEARCH AND RESCUE OPERATIONS.

INTER-GOVERNMENTAL MARITIME CONSULTATIVE ORGANIZATION. 1970. Merchant ship search and rescue manual. (MERSAR). London, [1970]. pp. 54.

SEASONAL INDUSTRIES.

ALESSANDRO (LUIGI D') Plant and stocks in the production of goods in seasonal demand; translated from Italian by J.W. Franklin; English text revised by F.M. Reid. Oxford, 1963. pp. 88.

SEASONAL LABOUR

— Mexico.

CINQ aspects de sociétés latino-américaines; [by Carlos M. Rama and others]. Paris, [1965]. pp. 151. (Paris. Université. Institut des Hautes Etudes de l'Amérique Latine. Cahiers. No. 7)

SEASONAL VARIATIONS (ECONOMICS).

BARON (RAPHAEL RAYMOND V.) Analysis of seasonality and trends in statistical series: methodology and applications in Israel. Jerusalem, 1973. 3 vols. (in 1). bibliog. (Israel. Central Bureau of Statistics. Technical Publications. No.39)

NATH (S.K.) Seasonal variation in agricultural activity and estimating the marginal product of labour. Coventry, 1973. pp. 30. bibliog. (University of Warwick. Department of Economics. Warwick Economic Research Papers. No. 32)

SECESSION.

BARNEY (WILLIAM L.) The secessionist impulse: Alabama and Mississippi in 1860. Princeton, [1974]. pp. 371. bibliog.

SECONDAT (CHARLES LOUIS DE) Baron de Montesquieu.

PANGLE (THOMAS L.) Montesquieu's philosophy of liberalism: a commentary on The spirit of the laws. Chicago, 1973. pp. 336.

SECTS

— Russia.

LIVANOV (FEDOR VASIL'EVICH) Raskol'niki i ostrozhniki: ocherki i rasskazy. t.1, 2, 4. Sanktpeterburg, 1872-73. 3 vols. Vol.1 is of the 4th ed., vol.2 the 2nd.

SECURITIES

— Japan — Statistics.

NOMURA RESEARCH INSTITUTE OF TECHNOLOGY AND ECONOMICS. Manual of securities statistics, 1972. Tokyo, [1972]. pp. 354.

— New Zealand.

DEANE (RODERICK S.) and others. Financial asset behaviour and government financing transactions in New Zealand. Wellington, 1973. pp. 71. bibliogs. (Reserve Bank of New Zealand. Research Papers. No.11)

SECURITY (LAW).

SAUVEPLANNE (J.G.) ed. Security over corporeal movables: (papers presented to a Colloquium, Edinburgh, 1971). Leiden, 1974. pp. 308. (Netherlands Association of Comparative Law. Studies in Comparative Law. No.1)

SECURITY, INTERNATIONAL.

GRIBANOV (M.) Security for Europe: prospects for an all-European conference. Moscow, 1972. pp. 100.

TENEKIDES (GEORGIOS) L'élaboration de la politique étrangère des états et leur sécurité. Paris, [1972]. 2 vols. (in 1).

BERES (LOUIS RENE) The management of world power: a theoretical analysis. Denver, Col., [1973]. pp. 93. bibliog. (Denver. University. Social Science Foundation and Graduate School of International Studies. Monograph Series in World Affairs. vol. 10. no.3)

COMMISSION TO STUDY THE ORGANIZATION OF PEACE. Building peace: reports of the Commission... 1939-1972. Metuchen, N.J., 1973. 2 vols.

FRANCE. Ministère des Affaires Etrangères. Service d'Information et de Presse. 1973. La Conférence sur la Sécurité et la Coopération en Europe: pourparlers multilatéraux préliminaires de Helsinki, 22 novembre 1972-8 juin 1973. [Paris], 1973. pp. 128.

HISCOCKS (RICHARD) The Security Council: a study in adolescence. London, 1973. pp. 371. bibliog.

STEWART-SMITH (DUDLEY GEOFFREY) ed. Brandt and the destruction of NATO: [a collection of articles, two of which were previously published in Osteuropa, and Orbis]. Richmond, Surrey, 1973. pp. 101.

PICK (OTTO) and CRITCHLEY (JULIAN) Collective security. London, 1974. pp. 123. bibliog.

ZORGBIBE (CHARLES) L'insécurité européenne. Paris, 1974. pp. 127. bibliog.

SEDITION

— Russia.

KLIAGIN (VASILII SUDOROVICH) Otvetstvennost' za osobo opasnye gosudarstvennye prestupleniia. Minsk, 1973. pp. 268.

SEINE—SAINT—DENIS.

FRANCE. Direction de la Documentation. La Documentation Française. Notes et Etudes Documentaires. Nos. 3,892-3, 893-3,894. Les nouveaux départements de la région parisienne: le département de la Seine-Saint-Denis. [Paris], 1972. pp. 138.

SELF—DEFENCE.

GREENBANK (ANTHONY) Survival in the city. London, [1974]. pp. 352.

SELF—DEFENCE (INTERNATIONAL LAW).

SKAKUNOV (EDUARD IVANOVICH) Samooborona v mezhdunarodnom prave. Moskva, 1973. pp. 176.

CHAYES (ABRAM) The Cuban missile crisis. London, 1974. pp. 157. (American Society of International Law. International Crises and the Role of Law)

SELF—DEFENCE (LAW)

— Russia.

OVEZOV (NIKOLAI AGAMURADOVICH) K voprosu ob obstoiatel'stvakh, ustraniaiushchikh obshchestvennuiu opasnost' i protivopravnost' deianiia v sovetskom ugolovnom prave; otvetstvennyi redaktor... M.P. Karpushin. Ashkhabad, 1972. pp. 103.

SELF—DETERMINATION, NATIONAL.

BERGMANN (PHILIP) pseud. Self-determination: the case of Czechoslovakia, 1968-1969. Bellinzona, 1972. pp. 159. bibliog.

KANN (ROBERT ADOLF) Renners Beitrag zur Lösung nationaler Konflikte im Lichte nationaler Probleme der Gegenwart. Wien, 1973. pp. 18. (Österreichische Akademie der Wissenschaften. Philosophisch-Historische Klasse. Sitzungsberichte. 279. Band. 4. Abhandlung)

TORIGUIAN (SHAVARSH) The Armenian question and international law. Beirut, 1973. pp. 330. bibliog.

DOIMI DI DELUPIS (INGRID) International law and the independent state. Epping, Essex, 1974. pp. 252.

SELF—EMPLOYED

— Belgium.

BELGIUM. Ministère des Classes Moyennes. 1972. Le statut social des travailleurs indépendants. [Bruxelles], 1972. pp. 78.

LAMBINON (MAURICE) Les indépendants face à l'O.N.E.M. [Bruxelles, Institut Economique et Social des Classes Moyennes, 1972]. fo. 24. bibliog.

SELF—HELP GROUPS

— United Kingdom.

JERMAN (BETTY) Do something!: a guide to self-help organisations. London, [1971]. pp. 203.

SELF—INCRIMINATION
— United Kingdom.

WOLCHOVER (DAVID) The descent of the maxim Nemo tenetur seipsum prodere from Sanhedrin 9B: (a developmental aspect of the privilege against self-incrimination). London, 1973. pp. 21.

SEMIOLOGY.

GUIRAUD (PIERRE) La sémiologie. 2nd ed. Paris, 1973. pp. 125. *bibliog.*

SENEGAL
— Commerce.

SENEGAL. Direction de la Statistique. Commerce spécial: exportations [and] importations. s-a., 1973- Dakar.

— Constitution.

SENEGAL. Constitution. 1960. Constitution de la république du Sénégal. Saint-Louis, 1960. pp. 27.

— Economic conditions.

FRANCE. Direction de l'Aide au Développement des Etats Francophones d'Afrique au Sud du Sahara et de la République Malgache. Secteur Information Economique et Conjoncture. 1973. Šenégal 1971-1972: dossier d'information économique. Paris, 1973.fo. 37,47.

— Economic policy.

SENEGAL. Conseil de Gouvernement. 1958. Déclaration faite Mamadou Dia à l'ouverture de la session ordinaire de l'Assemblée Territoriale le 9 juin 1958.. Saint-Louis, 1958. pp. 16.

SENEGAL. Présidence du Conseil. 1959. Déclaration prononcée par Mamadou Dia devant l'Assemblée Législative du Sénégal reunie en session ordinaire à Dakar, le samedi 5 décembre 1959. Saint-Louis, 1959. pp. 35.

— Politics and government.

SENEGAL. Conseil de Gouvernement. 1958. Déclaration faite Mamadou Dia à l'ouverture de la session ordinaire de l'Assemblée Territoriale le 9 juin 1958.. Saint-Louis, 1958. pp. 16.

SENEGAL. Ministère de l'Intérieur. 1960. Communication du Ministre de l'Intérieur sur la réforme administrative et discours prononcé à l'occasion de la réunion des chefs d'arrondissements à Dakar. Saint-Louis, 1960. pp. 30.

SENSES AND SENSATION.

HARPER (ROLAND) Human senses in action. Edinburgh, 1972. pp. 358. *bibliog.*

SENTENCES (CRIMINAL PROCEDURE)
— United Kingdom.

BOTTOMLEY (A. KEITH) Decisions in the penal process. London, 1973. pp. 252. *bibliog.*

McLEAN (IAN GRAEME) and MORRISH (PETER) The magistrates' coourt: an index of common penalties and decisions in cases before justices. Chichester, 1973. pp. 156.

— United States.

ORLAND (LEONARD) Justice, punishment, treatment: the correctional process. New York, [1973]. pp. 579.

SEPARATION OF POWERS
— France.

TROPER (MICHEL) La séparation des pouvoirs et l'histoire constitutionnelle française. Paris, 1973. pp. 251. *bibliog.*

— Germany.

KARSCH (FRIEDERUN CHRISTA) Demokratie und Gewaltenteilung: zur Problematik der Verfassungsinterpretation in der BRD. Köln, [1973]. pp. 125. *bibliog.* (*Zeitschrift Demokratie und Recht. Beihefte. 3*)

SERBS IN RUSSIA.

KARASEV (VIKTOR GEORGIEVICH) Serbskii demokrat Zhivoin Zhuevich: publitsisticheskaia deiatel'nost' v Rossii v 60-kh godakh XIX v. Moskva, 1974. pp. 334.

SERERS.

GASTELLU (JEAN MARC) Lexique de termes Sérer ÀCONTENU économique en usage à Ngohe. [Dakar, Office de la Recherche Scientifique et Technique Outre-Mer], 1968. fo. 34.

SERFDOM
— Russia.

SCHEIBERT (PETER) Die russische Agrarreform von 1861: ihre Probleme und der Stand ihrer Erforschung. Köln, 1973. pp. 195. *bibliog.*

SERRATI (GIACINTO MENOTTI).

DETTI (TOMMASO) Serrati e la formazione del Partito comunista italiano: storia della frazione terzinternazionalista, 1921-1924. Roma, 1972. pp. 547.

SERVICE INDUSTRIES.

SOREVNOVANIE dvukh sistem: ekonomika i trudiashchiesia. Moskva, 1973. pp. 400. *With brief English summaries and table of contents.*

— Mathematical models.

WIRT (JOHN G.) Optimization of price and quality in service systems. Santa Monica, 1971. pp. 174. (*Rand Corporation.* [*Papers*]. *4590*)

— Brazil.

ALMEIDA (WANDERLY JOSE MANSO DE) and SILVA (MARIA DA CONCEIÇÃO) Dinâmica do setor serviços no Brasil: emprego e produto. Rio de Janeiro, 1973. pp. 207. (*Brazil. Instituto de Planejamento Econômico e Social. Instituto de Pesquisas. Relatorios de Pesquisa. No. 18*)

— France.

SYSTEME D'ETUDES DU SCHEMA GENERAL D'AMENAGEMENT DE LA FRANCE. Schéma général d'aménagement de la France: question à la société tertiaire. Paris, 1974. pp. 189. (*France. Délégation à l'Aménagement du Territoire et à l'Action Régionale. Travaux et Recherches de Prospective. 45*)

— Iraq.

IRAQ. Central Bureau of Statistics. 1958. Report on the census of services and service industries in Iraq for 1957. Baghdad, 1958. pp. 21,[31]. *In English and Arabic.*

— Russia — Moldavian Republic.

FORMIROVANIE trudovykh resursov i razvitie sfery uslug. Kishinev, 1972. pp. 272.

KOZHUKHAR' (A.F.) Razvitie neproizvodstvennoi sfery v Moldavskoi SSR. Kishinev, 1973. pp. 199.

— United States.

GERSUNY (CARL) and ROSENGREN (WILLIAM RUDOLPH) The service society. Cambridge, Mass., [1973]. pp. 156. *bibliog.*

SET FUNCTIONS.

AUMANN (ROBERT J.) and ROTHBLUM (URIEL G.) On orderable set functions and continuity II. Stanford, 1973. fo. 32. *bibliog.* (*Stanford University. Institute for Mathematical Studies in the Social Sciences. Technical Reports.* [*New Series*]. *No. 103*)

ROTHBLUM (URIEL G.) Orderable set functions and continuity III. Stanford, 1973. fo. 30. *bibliog.* (*Stanford University. Institute for Mathematical Studies in the Social Sciences. Technical Reports.* [*New Series*]. *No. 107*)

SET THEORY.

BOARDMAN (ELIZABETH M.) A quantitative estimate for the Steinhaus distance theorem. [London, 1970]. pp. 173-177. (*Offprint from Bull. London Math. Soc., 2, 1970*)

BOARDMAN (ELIZABETH M.) On extensions of the Steinhaus theorem for distance sets and difference sets. [London, 1972]. pp. 729-739. (*Offprint from J. London Math. Soc., 2, 1972*)

SEWARD (WILLIAM HENRY).

PAOLINO (ERNEST N.) The foundations of the American empire: William Henry Seward and the U.S. foreign policy. Ithaca, 1973. pp. 235. *bibliog.*

SEX.

McCABE (JOSEPH) The key to love and sex. vols. 1-4,7,8. Girard, Kansas, [1929]. 6 vols. (in 1).

SEX AND LAW
— United States.

BARNETT (WALTER) Sexual freedom and the constitution: an inquiry into the constitutionality of repressive sex laws. Albuquerque, [1973]. pp. 333.

SEX CUSTOMS.

SMITH (JAMES R.) and SMITH (LYNN G.) eds. Beyond monogamy: recent studies of sexual alternatives in marriage. Baltimore, [1974]. pp. 336. *bibliogs.*

— United Kingdom.

SCHOFIELD (MICHAEL) The sexual behaviour of young adults: a follow-up study to The sexual behaviour of young people. London, 1973. pp. 251. *bibliog.*

SEX INSTRUCTION.

[DENMARK. Undervisningsministeriet, 1966]. Sex education in primary and secondary schools in Denmark. [Copenhagen], 1966. fo.17.

SEX ROLE.

SCHNEIDER (DAVID MURRAY) and SMITH (RAYMOND T.) Class differences and sex roles in American kinship and family structure. Englewood Cliffs, [1973]. pp. 132. *bibliog.*

KRUELL (MARIANNE) Geschlechtsrollenleitbilder in Stadt- und Landfamilien der Bundesrepublik Deutschland. Bonn, 1974. pp. 284. *bibliog.* (*Forschungsgesellschaft für Agrarpolitik und Agrarsoziologie.* [*Publications*]. *224*)

SEXUAL PERVERSION.

HOLBROOK (DAVID) The pseudo-revolution: a critical study of extremist 'liberation' in sex. London, 1972. pp. 202. *bibliog.*

SHABA
— Economic history.

KATZENELLENBOGEN (S.E.) Railways and the copper mines of Katanga. Oxford, 1973. pp. 165. *bibliog.*

SHAIKH SIDIYYA AL—KABIR.

See SIDIYYA AL—KABIR, Shaikh.

SHAKERS.

ANDREWS (EDWARD DEMING) The people called Shakers: a search for the perfect society. new ed. New York, [1963]. pp. 351. *bibliog.*

SHAMANISM.

HARNER (MICHAEL J.) ed. Hallucinogens and shamanism. New York, 1973. pp. 200. *bibliogs.*

SHARANAHUA INDIANS.

SISKIND (JANET) To hunt in the morning. New York, 1973. pp. 214.

SHARE—CROPPING.

WARR (PETER) A subjective equilibrium theory of share tenancy. Cambridge, Mass., 1972. pp. 26. *bibliog. (Harvard University. Center for International Affairs. Economic Development Reports. No. 222)*

SHATT AL ARAB RIVER.

AL-IZZI (KHALID YAHYA) The Shatt al-Arab river dispute in terms of law. 2nd ed. Baghdad, Ministry of Information, 1972. pp. 159, 3 maps.*bibliog.*

SHAULL (RICHARD).

GRENHOLM (CARL HENRIC) Christian social ethics in a revolutionary age: an analysis of the social ethics of John C. Bennett, Heinz-Dietrich Wendland and Richard Shaull. Uppsala, 1973. pp. 351. *bibliog.*

SHCHETKIN (STEPAN PETROVICH).

SHCHETKIN (STEPAN PETROVICH) Pis'ma russkogo emigranta. Varshava, 1921. pp. 79.

SHEEP

— **Australia.**

AUSTRALIA. Bureau of Agricultural Economics. 1973. Statistical handbook of the sheep and wool industry. 4th ed. Canberra, 1973. 1 vol. (unpaged).

— **European Economic Community countries.**

ECONOMIC DEVELOPMENT COMMITTEE FOR THE AGRICULTURAL INDUSTRY. Common Market Sub-Committee. Livestock Group. UK farming and the Common Market: sheep and wool; a report. London, National Economic Development Office, 1974. pp. 61.

— **Sweden.**

ODENSTAD (GÖRAN) Fårskötselns ekonomi: företagsekonomiska synpunkter. Stockholm, 1973. pp. 113. *(Jordbrukets Utredningsinstitut. Meddelanden. 1973. Nr. 6)*

— **United Kingdom.**

JONES (W.DYFRI) and others. The economics of hill sheep farming: a study of hill flocks in Wales and the North of England. Aberystwyth, [1973]. pp. 54. *bibliog. (Wales. University. University College of Wales. Department of Agricultural Economics. Hill Sheep Reports. No. 20)*

ECONOMIC DEVELOPMENT COMMITTEE FOR THE AGRICULTURAL INDUSTRY. Common Market Sub-Committee. Livestock Group. UK farming and the Common Market: sheep and wool; a report. London, National Economic Development Office, 1974. pp. 61.

SHEFFIELD

— **Industries.**

HEY (DAVID G.) The rural metalworkers of the Sheffield region: a study of rural industry before the Industrial Revolution. [Leicester], 1972. pp. 60. *(Leicester. University. Department of English Local History. Occasional Papers. 2nd Series. No. 5)*

— **Social history.**

TRADES UNIONS COMMISSION. The Sheffield outrages: report presented to the Trades Unions Commissioners in 1867: with an introduction by Sidney Pollard. Bath, 1971. pp. 452. *(Documents of Social History)* Reprint of 1867 publication. Original also available in British Parliamentary Papers, 1867, vol. xxxii.

SHETLAND ISLANDS

— **Economic history.**

HEINEBERG (HEINZ) Changes in the economic-geographical structure of the Shetland Islands; translated from the German by Anne Menzies. [Inverness, Highlands and Islands Development Board, 1973?]. fo. 236. *bibliog. Map in end pocket. German original published in 1969 as vol. 5 of the Bochumer Geographische Arbeiten.*

SHIFT SYSTEMS.

NIGHT and shift work; (proceedings of an international symposium...) organized by the sub-committee on shift work of the Permanent Commission and International Association on Occupational Health, Oslo...1969; editor, Å. Swensson. Stockholm, [1970]. pp. 157. *(Arbetsmedicinska Institutet. Studia Laboris et Salutis. 4)*

TRADES UNION CONGRESS. Overtime and shift-working: (a guide for negotiators). London, 1973. pp. 35. *bibliog.*

U.K. Department of Employment. Industrial Relations Division. Central Information Service. 1973. Shiftworking: some problem areas. London, 1973. 1 vol. (various pagings). *bibliog. (Information Papers. [New Series]. No.9)*

FISHWICK (F.) and HARLING (C.J.) Shiftworking in the motor industry; a study carried out at the Cranfield School of Management...for the Economic Development Committee for the Motor Manufacturing Industry: summary report and conclusions. London, National Economic Development Office, 1974. pp. 37.

FISHWICK (F.) and HARLING (C.J.) Shiftworking in the motor industry; a study carried out at the Cranfield School of Management...for the Economic Development Committee for the Motor Manufacturing Industry: detailed study and assessment. London, National Economic Development Office, 1974. pp. 177.*bibliog.*

SCHICHTARBEIT in soziologischer Sicht: ([selected papers of a conference in 1972 on] Schichtarbeit und sozialistische Lebensweise); Herausgeber: R. Stollberg. Berlin, [1974]. pp. 135.

SHIPBUILDING

— **Sweden.**

EKSTRÖM (JOHN) Varvsindustrins problem: efterfrågan, konkurrens, framtidsutsikter. Stockholm, [1970]. pp. 243. *bibliog. With summary, list of diagrams and list of tables in English.*

— **United Kingdom.**

SHIPBUILDING INDUSTRY TRAINING BOARD [U.K.]. Report and statement of accounts. a., 1972/3- South Harrow. *Formerly included in the file of British Parliamentary Papers.*

LABOUR PARTY, and others. Nationalisation of shipbuilding, ship-repair and marine engineering:...statement...drawn up by a joint working party from the Labour Party, the Trades Union Congress and the Confederation of Shipbuilding and Engineering Unions, etc. London, [1973]. pp. 15.

— — **Scotland.**

McGILL (JACK) Crisis on the Clyde: the story of Upper Clyde Shipbuilders.London, 1973. pp. 143.

SHIPBUILDING WORKERS

— **Sweden.**

GONÄS (LENA) Företagsnedläggning och arbetsmarknadspolitik: en studie av sysselsättningskriserna vid Oskarshamns Varv. Uppsala, 1974. pp. 240. *bibliog. (Uppsala. Universitet. Kulturgeografiska Institutionen. Geografiska Regionstudier. Nr. 10) With English summary.*

— **United Kingdom.**

SHIPBUILDING INDUSTRY TRAINING BOARD [U.K.]. Manpower Forecasting Panel. Notes for guidance on the technique of manpower planning in the shipbuilding industry. South Harrow, [1973]. pp. 23. *bibliog. (Shipbuilding Industry Training Board [U.K.]. Information Papers. No. 2)*

SHIPPING

— **Belgium.**

ASAERT (G.) De Antwerpse scheepvaart in de XVe eeuw, 1394-1480: bijdrage tot de ekonomische geschiedenis van de stad Antwerpen. Brussel, 1973. pp. 505. *bibliog. (Academie voor Wetenschappen, Letteren en Schone Kunsten van België. Verhandelingen. Klasse der Letteren. Jaargang 35. nr. 72) With English summary.*

— **India.**

INDIA. Committee on Plan Projects. Management Group. 1965. The Shipping Corporation of India: a study of planning and control. Vol. 1. [New Delhi, 1965]. 1 vol. (various pagings). *bibliog. Vol.2 not required by Library.*

— **New Zealand.**

MILNE (G.S.) Industrial relations in the shipping industry: the role of government. Wellington, 1973. pp. 115. *bibliog. (Victoria University of Wellington. Industrial Relations Centre. Student Research Papers in Industrial Relations. No. 1)*

— **Underdeveloped areas.**

See UNDERDEVELOPED AREAS — Shipping.

— **United Kingdom.**

FISHER (H.E.S.) and MINCHINTON (WALTER EDWARD) eds. Transport and shipowning in the Westcountry. Exeter, 1973. pp. 71. *(Exeter. University. Department of Economic History. Exeter Papers in Economic History. No.7.)*

— — **Statistics.**

CASUALTIES TO VESSELS AND ACCIDENTS TO MEN: vessels registered in the United Kingdom; ([pd. by] Department of Industry [U. K.]). a., 1972[1st]- London. *Supersedes DEEP SEA TRAWLERS: casualties to vessels and accidents to men: statistics, and SHIPPING CASUALTIES AND DEATHS: vessels registered in the United Kingdom.*

SHIPPING BOUNTIES AND SUBSIDIES.

HENELL (OLOF) Flag discrimination: purposes, motives and economic consequences. Helsingfors, 1956. pp. 55. *bibliog. (Svenska Handelshögskolan. Ekonomi och Samhälle. Nr.3)*

SHIPPING CONFERENCES.

FASBENDER (KARL) and WAGNER (WOLFGANG) Economist. Shipping conferences, rate policy and developing countries: the argument of rate discrimination. Hamburg, 1973. pp. 357. *bibliog. (Hamburg. Hamburgisches Welt-Wirtschaft-Archiv Studien zur Aussenwirtschaft und Entwicklungspolitik) With German summary.*

SHIPS

— **Automation.**

INTERNATIONAL LABOUR CONFERENCE. 55th Session. Reports. 4. Fourth item on the agenda: employment problems arising from technical developments and modernisation on board ship. Geneva, 1969-70. 2 pts.

— **Disinfection.**

INTER-GOVERNMENTAL MARITIME CONSULTATIVE ORGANIZATION. 1973. Recommendations on the safe use of pesticides in ships. London, [1973]. pp. 14.

— **Manning.**

INTERNATIONAL LABOUR CONFERENCE. 55th Session. Reports. 4. Fourth item on the agenda: employment problems arising from technical developments and modernisation on board ship. Geneva, 1969-70. 2 pts.

SHIPS. (Cont.)

— Safety regulations.

INTERNATIONAL LABOUR CONFERENCE. 55th Session. Reports. 5. Fifth item on the agenda: accident prevention on board ship at sea and in port. Geneva, 1969-70. 2 pts.

INTERNATIONAL CONFERENCE ON SAFETY OF LIFE AT SEA, 1960. Final act of the Conference with Annexes including the text of the adopted Convention; (with Supplement). London, Inter-Governmental Maritime Consultative Organization, [1970]. 2 parts. *In English and French.*

INTER-GOVERNMENTAL MARITIME CONSULTATIVE ORGANIZATION. 1972. Code for the construction and equipment of ships carrying dangerous chemicals in bulk. London, [1972]. pp. 41.

INTERNATIONAL CONFERENCE ON SPACE REQUIREMENTS FOR SPECIAL TRADE PASSENGER SHIPS, 1973. Final act of the Conference with attachments including the text of the adopted Protocol. London, Inter-Governmental Maritime Consultative Organization, [1973]. pp. 57. *In English and French.*

SHOP ASSISTANTS.

INTERNATIONAL LABOUR ORGANISATION. Advisory Committee on Salaried Employees and Professional Workers. 6th Session. Reports. 2. The impact of social and economic developments on working and living conditions in the distributive trades: second item on the agenda. Geneva, 1967. pp. 100.

INTERNATIONAL LABOUR ORGANISATION. Advisory Committee on Salaried Employees and Professional Workers. 7th Session. Reports. 2. Conditions of work and life of employees in commerce and offices: (second item on the agenda). Geneva, 1974. pp. 81.

— United Kingdom.

DISTRIBUTIVE INDUSTRY TRAINING BOARD [U.K.]. Report and statement of accounts. a., 1972/3- Manchester. *Formerly included in the file of British Parliamentary Papers.*

U.K. Working Party on Internal Shop Security. 1973. Shoplifting, and thefts by shop staff; report; [E.S. Pritchard, chairman]. London, 1973. pp. 73.

SHOP STEWARDS

— Italy.

AGLIETA (ROBERTO) and others. I delegati operai: ricerca su nuove forme di rappresentanza operaia. Roma, [1970]. pp. 178. *(Istituto di Studi sulle Relazioni Industriali e di Lavoro. Quaderni ISRIL.2)*

TREU (TIZIANO) Sindacato e rappresentanze aziendali: modelli ed esperienze di un sindacato industriale, FIM-CISL, 1954-1970. Bologna, [1971]. pp. 297.

AGLIETA (ROBERTO) and others. Révolution dans l'entreprise: le mouvement des délégués ouvriers en Italie; préface du François Sellier. Paris, [1972]. pp. 131.

— United Kingdom.

MARSH (ARTHUR) Managers and shop stewards: shop floor revolution?. London, 1973. pp. 174.

SHOPLIFTING.

U.K. Working Party on Internal Shop Security. 1973. Shoplifting, and thefts by shop staff; report; [E.S. Pritchard, chairman]. London, 1973. pp. 73.

SHOPPING

— Singapore.

YEUNG (YUE-MAN) National development policy and urban transformation in Singapore: a study of public housing and the marketing system. Chicago, 1973. pp. 204. *bibliog. (Chicago. University. Department of Geography. Research Papers. No.149)*

— United Kingdom.

DAWS (LESLIE FREDERICK) and BRUCE (A.J.) Shopping in Watford. Garston, Building Research Station, 1971. pp. 143.

SHOPPING CENTRES.

DISCOUNT trading and hypermarkets; report of the proceedings of a conference held under the auspices of the corporation of Glasgow in... Glasgow...1971. Glasgow, Corporation, 1971. fo. 96.

GRUEN (VICTOR) Centers for the urban environment: survival of the cities. New York, [1973]. pp. 266.

URBAN LAND INSTITUTE. Technical Bulletins. [No]. 69. Shopping center zoning; by J. Ross McKeever. Washington, [1973]. pp. 73. 10-21-01, etc.)

BRISTOL. City Planning Department. The Cribbs Causeway out-of-town shopping (centre) enquiry, January-May 1972; a report of the proceedings. Bristol, 1972. pp. 212. *Maps at end.*

DEVELOPMENT CONTROL POLICY NOTES. 13. Out of town shops and shopping centres. London, H.M.S.O., 1972. pp. (4).

DALBY (E.) Pedestrians and shopping centre layout: a review of the current situation. Crowthorne, 1973. pp. 25. *(U.K. Transport and Road Research Laboratory. Reports. LR 577)*

URBAN freight distribution: studies of operations in shopping streets at Newbury and Camberley; by A.W. Christie [and others]. Crowthorne, 1973. pp. 81. *(U.K. Transport and Road Research Laboratory. Reports. LR 603)*

SHOPPING MALLS

BINKS (R.K.) Pedestrian precincts. London, 1973. pp. 12. *(Institution of Municipal Engineers. Monographs. No. 15)*

— United Kingdom.

DALBY (E.) Pedestrians and shopping centre layout: a review of the current situation. Crowthorne, 1973. pp. 25. *(U.K. Transport and Road Research Laboratory. Reports. LR 577)*

SHOPS, TRAVELLING.

See STORES, TRAVELLING.

SHROPSHIRE

— Economic history.

BROOK (FRED) and ALLBUTT (MARTIN) The Shropshire lead mines. Cheddleton, [1973]. pp. 95. *bibliog.*

SIBERCH (JOHN).

TREPTOW (OTTO) John Siberch: Johann Lair von Siegburg; translated by Trevor Jones; abridged and edited by John Morris and Trevor Jones. Cambridge, 1970. pp. 73. *bibliog. (Cambridge. Bibliographical Society. Monographs. No.6)*

SIBERIA

— History.

VOPROSY istorii Sibiri dosovetskogo perioda: bakhrushinskie chteniia, 1969. Novosibirsk, 1973. pp. 463.

— — Sources.

VAGIN (V.) ed. Istoricheskie svedeniia o deiatel'nosti grafa M.M. Speranskogo v Sibiri s 1819 po 1822 god. S.-Peterburg, 1872. 2 vols.

SIBERIANS.

RUSSKIE starozhily Sibiri: istoriko-antropologicheskii ocherk. Moskva, 1973. pp. 189.

SICILY

— Politics and government.

RENDA (FRANCESCO) Socialisti e cattolici in Sicilia, 1900-1904: le lotte agrarie. Caltanissetta, [1972]. pp. 463.

— Population.

INDAGINI bio-demografiche sulla popolazione siciliana; ([by] Carmelo Pennino [and others]). Palermo, [1969]. pp. 209. *(Palermo. Università. Istituto di Scienze Demografiche. Collana di Studi Demografici. 3) With summaries in English and French.*

— Rural conditions.

BLOK (ANTON) The Mafia of a Sicilian village, 1860-1960: a study of violent peasant entrepreneurs. Oxford, [1974]. pp. 293. *bibliog.*

SICK

— Denmark.

FÜRSTNOW-SØRENSEN (BENT) Samfundet og invalidepensionisterne. [Copenhagen], 1969. pp. 28.

SICKLE—CELL ANAEMIA.

KONOTEY-AHULU (F.I.D.) Medical considerations for legalizing voluntary sterilization: sickle cell disease as a case in point;... background paper presented at the 2nd International Conference on Voluntary Sterilization, 1973. Medford, Mass., 1973. pp. 28. *bibliog. (Tufts University. Fletcher School of Law and Diplomacy. Law and Population Monograph Series. No.13)*

SIDIYYA AL—KABIR, Shaikh.

STEWART (C.C.) and STEWART (E.K.) Islam and social order in Mauritania: a case study from the nineteenth century. Oxford, 1973. pp. 204. *bibliog.*

SIERRA LEONE

— Population.

SWINDELL (KENNETH) Labour migration and mining in Sierra Leone; [Ph.D.(London) thesis]. 1973[or rather 1974]. fo. 287. *Typescript: unpublished. This thesis is the property of London University and may not be removed from the Library.*

— Social conditions.

SIERRA LEONE. Central Statistics Office. 1967. Household survey of the Western Province, November, 1966- January, 1968: household characteristics and housing conditions. Freetown, [1967]. pp. 39.

SIERRA LEONE. Central Statistics Office. 1971. Household survey of the Northern Province, urban areas, March, 1968-December 1969: final report: household expenditure and income and economic characteristics. Freetown, [1971]. pp. 104.

SIKHS IN THE UNITED KINGDOM.

JAMES (ALAN G.) Sikh children in Britain. London, 1974. pp. 117. *bibliog.*

SIKKIM

— Foreign relations — India.

RAO (P.R.) India and Sikkim, 1814-1970. New Delhi, 1972. pp. 227. *bibliog.*

SIKORSKI (WŁADYSŁAW).

KUKIEL (MARJAN) General Sikorski: 'żołnierz i mąz stanu Polski walczącej. London, 1970. pp. 280. *bibliog.*

SILK MANUFACTURE AND TRADE

— Switzerland.

TROXLER (WERNER P.) Johann Rudolf Forcart-Weiss Söhne: ein Beitrag zur Unternehmergeschichte. Bern, 1973. pp. 128. *bibliog. (Zürich. Universität. Historisches Seminar. Geist und Werk der Zeiten. No. 36)*

— **United Kingdom.**

PAFFORD (ELIZABETH R.) and PAFFORD (JOHN HENRY PYLE) Employer and employed: Ford, Ayrton and Co. Ltd., silk spinners, with worker participation... 1870-1970. Edington, 1974. pp. 77. bibliog. (*Pasold Research Fund. Pasold Occasional Papers. vol. 2*)

SIMULATION METHODS.

SHUBIK (MARTIN) and BREWER (GARRY D.) Models, simulations and games: a survey;...a report prepared for Advanced Research Projects Agency. Santa Monica, 1972. pp. 160. (*Rand Corporation. [Rand Reports]. 1060*)

ALBRIGHT (W. PAUL) Collective bargaining: a Canadian simulation. Toronto, [1973]. pp. 92.

— **Bibliography.**

SHUBIK (MARTIN) and others. The literature of gaming, simulation and model-building: index and critical abstracts;...a report prepared for Advanced Research Projects Agency. Santa Monica, 1972. pp. 121. (*Rand Corporation. [Rand Reports]. 620*)

SIND

— **Foreign relations — United Kingdom.**

THAIRANI (KALA) British political missions to Sind: a narrative of negotiations from 1799 to 1843 leading up to the state's annexation. New Delhi, 1973. pp. 193. bibliog.

SINGAPORE

— **Census.**

SINGAPORE. Census, 1970. Report on the census of population, 1970, Singapore. Singapore, [1973]. 2 vols. bibliog.

— **Economic conditions.**

YOU (POH SENG) and LIM (CHONG-YAH) eds. The Singapore economy. Singapore, [1971]. pp. 417. bibliogs.

SINGAPORE in the international economy:...papers[of a symposium organized by the Economic Society of Singapore]; edited by Wong Kum Poh and Maureen Tan. Singapore, 1972. pp. 97.

GEIGER (THEODORE) Tales of two city-states: the development progress of Hong Kong and Singapore. Washington, D.C., [1973]. pp. 233. bibliog. (*National Planning Association. Studies in Development Progress. No. 3*)

— **Foreign economic relations.**

SINGAPORE in the international economy:...papers[of a symposium organized by the Economic Society of Singapore]; edited by Wong Kum Poh and Maureen Tan. Singapore, 1972. pp. 97.

— **Foreign relations.**

WU (YUAN-LI) Strategic significance of Singapore: a study in balance of power. Washington, 1972. pp. 28. (*American Enterprise Institute for Public Policy Research. Foreign Affairs Studies. 6*)

— **Politics and government.**

GEIGER (THEODORE) Tales of two city-states: the development progress of Hong Kong and Singapore. Washington, D.C., [1973]. pp. 233. bibliog. (*National Planning Association. Studies in Development Progress. No. 3*)

YEO (KIM WAH) Political development in Singapore, 1945-55. Singapore, [1973]. pp. 320. bibliog.

JOSEY (ALEX) Lee Kuan Yew: the struggle for Singapore. Sydney, 1974. pp. 334.

— **Population.**

HALL (PETER) Law and population growth in Singapore. Medford, Mass., 1973. pp. 57. (*Tufts University. Fletcher School of Law and Diplomacy. Law and Population Monograph Series. No.9*)

SINGLE PARENT FAMILY

— **Ireland (Republic).**

NATIONAL CONFERENCE ON COMMUNITY SERVICES FOR THE UNMARRIED PARENT, KILKENNY, 1970. The unmarried mother in the Irish community: a report. Kilkenny, 1971. pp. 65.

— **Netherlands.**

NETHERLANDS. Interdepartementale Werkgroep Onvolledige Gezinnen. 1972. Rapport betreffende de financiële positie van de gescheiden vrouwen en haar gezinnen. 's-Gravenhage, 1972. pp. 32.

— **United Kingdom.**

HOPKINSON (ANNE) Families without fathers. London, 1973. pp. 32. bibliog.

MARSDEN (DENNIS) Mothers alone: poverty and the fatherless family. rev. ed. Harmondsworth, 1973. pp. 412.

U.K. Social Survey. [Reports. New Series.] 466. Families and their needs, with particular reference to one-parent families; by Audrey Hunt [and others];...an enquiry carried out in 1970...on behalf of the Department of Health and Social Security. London, 1973. 2 vols.

STREATHER (JANE) and WEIR (STUART) Social insecurity: single mothers on benefit. London, 1974. pp. 62. (*Child Poverty Action Group. Poverty Pamphlets. 16*)

SINGLE PEOPLE.

REID (ELIZABETH) and ALTMAN (DENNIS) Equality: the new issues; [2 lectures originally delivered at the 1973 Fabian Winter Lecture Series Equality under Labor]. Melbourne, [1973?]. pp. 16. (*Victorian Fabian Society. Victorian Fabian Pamphlets. [No]. 28*)

SINGLE TAX.

POST (LOUIS FREELAND) Taxation of land values: an explanation with illustrative charts, notes and answers to typical questions of the land-labor-and-fiscal reform advocated by Henry George. 5th ed. Indianapolis, 1915. pp. 179.

SINGLE WOMEN.

NATIONAL COUNCIL FOR THE SINGLE WOMAN AND HER DEPENDANTS. Financial hardship and the single woman. London, 1973. fo. 6.

NETHERLANDS. Interdepartementale Werkgroep Oudere Ongehuwde Vrouw. 1973. Verbetering levensomstandigheden oudere ongehuwde vrouw, etc. 's-Gravenhage, 1973. pp. 55. (*Ministerie van Sociale Zaken. Verslagen en Rapporten: Sociale Zaken. 1973. 1*)

SINN FEIN.

DAVIS (RICHARD P.) Arthur Griffith and non-violent Sinn Fein. Dublin, 1974. pp. 232. bibliog.

SIT DOWN STRIKES

— **France.**

HOYLES (ANDRÉE) Imagination in power: the occupation of factories in France in 1968. Nottingham, 1973. pp. 72.

LIP 73; [by] Edmond Maire [and others]. Paris, [1973]. pp. 141.

PIAGET (CHARLES) and others. Lip: Charles Piaget et les LIP racontent. [Paris, 1973]. pp. 217.

Les TRAVAILLEURS de Lip: 53 photographies. [Paris, 1973]. 1 vol. (unpaged). (*Libération. Suppléments*)

GIRAUD (HENRY) Mon été chez LIP. Paris, [1974]. pp. 173.

— **Netherlands.**

CORTENBERGHE (AAD VAN) and TERLINGEN (JEROEN) Enka dossier: handboek voor bezetters. Uttrecht, [1972]. pp. 223.

SITUATIONIST INTERNATIONAL.

BRAU (ELIANE) Le situationnisme; ou, La nouvelle Internationale. Paris, [1968]. pp. 191.

SKELMERSDALE

— **Population.**

SKELMERSDALE DEVELOPMENT CORPORATION. Population and social survey, 1973. Skelmersdale, [1974]. pp. 44.

— **Social conditions.**

SKELMERSDALE DEVELOPMENT CORPORATION. Population and social survey, 1973. Skelmersdale, [1974]. pp. 44.

SKILLED LABOUR

— **Paraguay.**

MAS GARCIA (A.) Promocion profesional de trabajadores en Paraguay: un desafio, una respuesta. Asuncion, 1972. pp. 143. bibliog.

— **Russia.**

NOVGORODSKII (IURII FEDOROVICH) and others. Technicheskii progress i sovershenstvovanie podgotovki kadrov. Moskva, 1973. pp. 151.

OMEL'IANENKO (BORIS LUKICH) Tekhnicheskii progress i sovremennye trebovaniia k urovniu kvalifikatsii i podgotovke rabochikh kadrov. Moskva, 1973. pp. 128.

— — **Ukraine.**

KONOVALOV (MYKHAILO ANDRIIOVYCH) Vyrishal'na syla sotsialistychnoï rekonstruktsiï: diial'nist' KP Ukraïny po pidhotovtsi ta vykhovanniu industrial'no-tekhnichnykh kadriv, 1928-1937 rr. Kyïv, 1973. pp. 229.

— **United States.**

BURSTEIN (ABRAHAM C.) Changes in wage and salary employment, New York City, 1960- 1968, and problems of balance between demand and supply of skills. New York, 1970. fo. various.

MACKENZIE (GAVIN) The aristocracy of labor: the position of skilled craftsmen in the American class structure. London, 1973. pp. 208. bibliog. (*Cambridge. University. Department of Applied Economics. Cambridge Studies in Sociology. 7*)

— **Yugoslavia.**

BREKIĆ (JOVO) ed. Planiranje kadrova i obrazovanja u organizacijama udruženog rada. Zagreb, 1973. pp. 162. bibliog.

SKIS AND SKIING

— **Switzerland — Ticino.**

TICINO (CANTON). Ufficio delle Ricerche Economiche. 1974. La posizione concorrenziale delle stazioni sciistiche ticinesi: studio comparativo della situazione del Ticino, dei Cantoni confederati e dell' Italia del nord sul 'Mercato della neve' nazionale e internazionale. Bellinzona, 1974. pp. 105. (*Documenti Economia di Montagna. 3*)

SKYE

— **Transit systems.**

SCOTTISH COUNCIL (DEVELOPMENT AND INDUSTRY). By bridge to Skye. Inverness, 1969. pp. 15.

SKYJACKING.

See **HIJACKING OF AIRCRAFT.**

SLATE — United Kingdom — Wales.

LINDSAY (JEAN) A history of the North Wales slate industry. Newton 1973. pp. 620. bibliogs.

SLAVE TRADE

SLAVE TRADE

— Africa.

HOGG (PETER C.) The African slave trade and its suppression: a classified and annotated bibliography of books, pamphlets and periodical articles. London, 1973. pp. 409.

— Africa, West.

RODNEY (WALTER) West Africa and the Atlantic slave-trade. Cambridge, Mass., [1973?]. pp. 27. *bibliog.* (*Africa Research Group. Reprints. 6*)

SLAVERY.

NIEBOER (H.J.) Slavery as an industrial system: ethnological researches; [facsimile reprint of the edition first published in 1910]. 2nd ed. New York, 1971. pp. 474. *bibliog.*

MONTGOMERY (JOHN RUPERT PATRICK) The Anti-Slavery Society 1973. [London?, 1973?]. pp. (6). (*Reprinted from...the Contemporary Review, vol. 223, no.1291*)

SLAVERY IN AMERICA.

HOETINK (HARRY) Slavery and race relations in the Americas: comparative notes on their nature and nexus. New York, 1973. pp. 232. *bibliog.*

SLAVERY IN ANGOLA.

OLIVEIRA (MARIO ANTONIO FERNANDES DE) Para a historia do trabalho em Angola: (a escravatura luandense do terceiro quartel do seculo XIX). Luanda, Instituto do Trabalho, Providência e Acção Social, 1963. pp. 20. *bibliog. Separata do No.2 do boletim Trabalho.* With summaries in English and French.

SLAVERY IN CUBA.

MARTINEZ-ALIER (VERENA) Marriage, class and colour in nineteenth century Cuba: a study of racial attitudes and sexual values in a slave society. London, 1974. pp. 202. *bibliog.*

SLAVERY IN PEMBA.

LODHI (ABDULAIZ Y.) The institution of slavery in Zanzibar and Pemba. Uppsala, 1973. pp. 40. (*Skandinaviska Afrikainstitutet. Research Reports. No. 16*)

SLAVERY IN THE BRITISH EMPIRE.

CRATON (MICHAEL) Sinews of empire: a short history of British slavery. London, 1974. pp. 413. *bibliog.*

SLAVERY IN THE UNITED KINGDOM.

SHYLLON (F.O.) Black slaves in Britain. London, 1974. pp. 252. *bibliog.*

SLAVERY IN THE UNITED STATES.

MULLIN (GERALD W.) Flight and rebellion: slave resistance in eighteenth-century Virginia. London, [1972]. pp. 219. *bibliog.*

SMITH (JULIA FLOYD) Slavery and plantation growth in antebellum Florida, 1821-1860. Gainesville, [1973]. pp. 249. *bibliog.*

— Antislavery movements.

The LEGION of liberty.' and force of truth, containing the thoughts, words, and deeds, of some prominent apostles, champions and martyrs. 2nd ed. [New York], 1843. 1 vol. (unpaged).

— Personal narratives.

STAROBIN (ROBERT S.) ed. Blacks in bondage: letters of American slaves. New York, 1974. pp. 196.

SLAVERY IN THE WEST INDIES.

SHERIDAN (RICHARD BERT) Sugar and slavery: an economic history of the British West Indies, 1623-1775. Baltimore, 1974. pp. 529. *bibliog.*

SLAVERY IN ZANZIBAR.

LODHI (ABDULAIZ Y.) The institution of slavery in Zanzibar and Pemba. Uppsala, 1973. pp. 40. (*Skandinaviska Afrikainstitutet. Research Reports. No. 16*)

SLEEP.

HARTMANN (ERNEST L.) The functions of sleep. New Haven, 1973. pp. 198. *bibliog.*

SLOPES.

THORNES (JOHN B.) State, environment and attribute in scree-slope studies. [London, 1971?]. pp. 49-63. *bibliog.* (*Reprinted from Institute of British Geographers, Special Publication, No. 3*) With French and German summaries.

SLOVAKIA

— Learned institutions and societies.

WINKLER (TOMÁŠ) Matica slovenská v rokoch 1919-1945: z problémov a dokumentov ústredia MS. Martin, 1971. pp. 396.

— Nationalism.

DEAN (ROBERT W.) Nationalism and political change in eastern Europe: the Slovak question and the Czechoslovak reform movement. Denver, [1973]. pp. 67. (*Denver. University. Social Science Foundation and Graduate School of International Studies. Monograph Series in World Affairs. vol. 10, No. 1*)

SLUMS

— India.

DESAI (AKSHAYA R.) and PILLAI (S. DEVADAS) A profile of an Indian slum. Bombay, 1972. pp. 272.

— United States.

SEXTON (DONALD E.) Groceries in the ghetto. Lexington, Mass., [1973]. pp. 141. *bibliog.*

GREENBERG (STANLEY B.) Politics and poverty: modernization and response in five poor neighborhoods. London, [1974]. pp. 282.

SMALL BUSINESS.

ILO INTER-REGIONAL SEMINAR ON PROGRAMMES AND POLICIES FOR SMALL-SCALE INDUSTRY WITHIN THE FRAMEWORK OF OVER-ALL ECONOMIC DEVELOPMENT PLANNING, PRAGUE, 1966. Report on...seminar...held in Prague,...19 September-7 October 1966. (ILO/TAP/INT/R.14) Geneva, 1968. pp. ii, 191.

KROPOTKIN (PETR ALEKSEEVICH) Prince. Fields, factories and workshops tomorrow; edited, introduced and with additional material by Colin Ward. London, 1974. pp. 205.

— Australia.

AUSTRALIA. Committee on Small Business. 1971. Report; chairman: F.M. Wiltshire. [Canberra, 1971]. pp. 63.

NATIONAL SMALL BUSINESS SEMINAR, CAMBERRA, 1973. Topic papers; [by A.G. Moyes and others]. Canberra, Department of Secondary Industry, [1973]. 1 pamphlet (various pagings).

NATIONAL SMALL BUSINESS SEMINAR, CANBERRA, 1973. Report. Canberra, Department of Secondary Industry, 1973. 1 pamphlet (various pagings).

— Austria.

BEIRAT Fur wirtschafts- und sozialfragen. ?PUBLIKATIONEN. 24! . kLEIN- UND mITTELBETRIEBE IM wACHSTUMSPROZESS. wIEN, 1973. PP. 91.

— Belgium.

BELGIUM. Administration de la T.V.A., de l'Enregistrement et des Domaines. 1971. Les petites et moyennes entreprises et la T.V.A.. Bruxelles, [1971]. pp. 58.

— Canada — Nova Scotia.

SEARS (JOHN T.) Institutional financing of small business in Nova Scotia. Toronto, [1972]. pp. 248. *bibliog.* (*Social Science Research Council of Canada. Atlantic Provinces Studies. 3*)

— Ecuador.

ECUADOR. Secretaria General de Planeacion Economica. 1969. Programa de artesania y pequeñas industrias, 1969-1973; version preliminar para discusion; [by Danilo Bassi-Zambelli and Gustavo Chambers M.]. Quito, 1969. pp. 252. (*Documentos. No. 02-14*)

— European Economic Community countries.

RAAD VOOR HET MIDDEN- EN KLEINBEDRIJF. Werkgroep Europese N.V. Rapport inzake europese rechtsvormen en hun betekenis voor het midden- en kleinbedrijf: (Europese rechtsvormen). 's-Gravenhage, 1969. pp. 60. (*Raad voor het Midden- en Kleinbedrijf. [Publikaties]. 1969, no. 1*) With summaries in English, French, and German.

ADVIES inzake de Europese Groepering van economisch belang (EGEB): [report of a working party]; (Europese rechtsvormen 2). 's-Gravenhage, 1972. pp. 62. (*Raad voor het Midden- en Kleinbedrijf. [Publikaties]. 1972, no. 1*)

— Germany — Statistics.

BECKERMANN (THEO) Das Handwerk im Wachstum der Wirtschaft: eine statistische Analyse. Berlin, [1974]. pp. 141. (*Rheinisch-Westfälisches Institut für Wirtschaftsforschung, Essen. Schriftenreihe. Neue Folge. 34*)

— Netherlands.

RAAD VOOR HET MIDDEN- EN KLEINBEDRIJF. Enige korte adviezen en notities. 's-Gravenhage, 1973. pp. 44. ([*Publikaties*]. 1973, no. 2)

— — Taxation.

NETHERLANDS. Commissie Belastingen. 1970. Verzamelde fiscale aanbevelingen, 1958/1970. 's-Gravenhage, 1970. pp. 75. (*Raad voor het Midden- en Kleinbedrijf. [Publikaties]. 1970, no. 1*)

— United Kingdom.

SMALL FIRMS INFORMATION CENTRES PUBLICATIONS . [London, 1973 in progress].

MITCHELL (DAVID) M.P. The problems and potential of smaller businesses...seed corn. London, [1974]. pp. 16.

SMALL BUSINESS INVESTMENT COMPANIES.

KELLEY (ALBERT J.) and others. Venture capital: a guidebook for new enterprises. Chestnut Hill, Mass., 1971. pp. 150. *bibliog.*

SMALL CLAIMS COURTS.

BIRKS (MICHAEL) Small claims in the county court: how to sue and defend actions without a solicitor. [London, Lord Chancellor's Office, 1973]. pp. 74.

SMALL GROUPS.

OFSHE (RICHARD J.) ed. Interpersonal behavior in small groups. Englewood Cliffs, [1973]. pp. 792. *bibliogs.*

SMITH (PETER B.) Groups within organizations: applications of social psychology to organizational behaviour. London, 1973. pp. 134. *bibliog.*

SMALL HOLDINGS

— Africa, Subsaharan.

CLEAVE (JOHN H.) African farmers: labor use in the development of smallholder agriculture. New York, 1974. pp. 253. *bibliog.*

— Argentine Republic.

CARRERA (RODOLFO RICARDO) Regimen juridico aplicable a los minifundios de la provincia de La Rioja; informe final. Buenos Aires, 1973. pp. 131. *bibliog.* *(Argentine Republic. Consejo Federal de Inversiones. Serie Tecnica. No. 23)*

— Russia.

IASINSKAIA (GALINA FRANTSEVNA) Pravo zemlepol'zovaniia rabochikh i sluzhashchikh, prozhivaiushchikh v sel'skoi mestnosti. Moskva, 1973. pp. 111.

MAKAROVA (ISKRA VLADIMIROVNA) Podsobnoe khoziaistvo kolkhoznikov. Moskva, 1973. pp. 64.

SMALL PRESSES.

See LITTLE PRESSES.

SMALLEY (GEORGE WASHBURN).

MATHEWS (JOSEPH JAMES) George W. Smalley: forty years a foreign correspondent. Chapel Hill, [1973]. pp. 229.

SMALLWOOD (JOSEPH ROBERTS).

GWYN (RICHARD J.) Smallwood: the unlikely revolutionary. rev. ed. Toronto, 1972 repr. 1974. pp. 364.

SMITH (ADAM).

LINDGREN (J. RALPH) The social philosophy of Adam Smith. The Hague, 1973. pp. 164. *bibliog.*

NEUENDORFF (HARTMUT) Der Begriff des Interesses: eine Studie zu den Gesellschaftstheorien von Hobbes, Smith und Marx. Frankfurt am Main, 1973. pp. 163. *bibliog.*

SKINNER (ANDREW S.) Adam Smith and the role of the state; a paper delivered in Kirkcaldy on 5th June 1973, at a symposium, etc. Glasgow, 1974. pp. 28.

SMOG.

CARLIN (ALAN P.) and KOCHER (GEORGE E.) Environmental problems: their causes, cures, and evolution, using southern California smog as an example. Santa Monica, 1971. pp. 107. *(Rand Corporation. [Rand Reports]. 640)*

SMOKING.

McKENNELL (A.C.) A comparison of two smoking typologies. London, 1973. pp. 94. *(Tobacco Research Council. Research Papers. [No.] 12)*

See also TOBACCO HABIT.

SOBO (AFRICAN PEOPLE).

OTITE (ONIGU) Autonomy and dependence: the Urhobo Kingdom of Okpe in modern Nigeria. London, [1973]. pp. 215. *bibliog.*

SOCCER

— United Kingdom.

DOUGLAS (PETER) The football industry. London, 1973. pp. 175.

SOCIAL ACTION.

GOLDENBERG (I. IRA) ed. The helping professions in the world of action. Lexington, [1973]. pp. 273. *bibliogs.*

SOCIAL ADJUSTMENT.

PICKETT (KATHLEEN GORDON) and BOULTON (DAVID K.) Migration and social adjustment: Kirkby and Maghull; (with the assistance of Norman Rankin). Liverpool, 1974. pp. 179.

SOCIAL CASE WORK.

CARKHUFF (ROBERT R.) Helping and human relations: a primer for lay and professional helpers. New York, [1969]. 2 vols. *bibliogs.*

STREAN (HERBERT S.) ed. Social casework: theories in action. Metuchen, N.J., 1971. pp. 344. *bibliogs.*

CASEWORK within social work; [by] Helen H. Perlman [and others; papers of a study conference held at the Department of Social Studies, University of Newcastle upon Tyne, 1972]; Graham Parker, editor. Newcastle upon Tyne, 1973. pp. 42.

CROSS (CRISPIN PATRIC ROBERT) ed. Interviewing and communication in social work. London, 1974. pp. 176. *bibliog.*

SOCIAL CHANGE.

EISENSTADT (SHMUEL N.) Modernization: protest and change. Jerusalem, [1966]. pp. 166.

The WORLD in 2000: repo[r]t of a JERC international conference. Tokyo, 1967. pp. 285. *(Japan Economic Research Center. Center Papers. No.8)*

McLEISH (JOHN) The theory of social change: four views considered. London, Routledge and Kegan Paul, 1969 repr. 1972. pp. xiii, 95. *bibliog.* *(International Library of Sociology and Social Reconstruction)*

ASSOCIATION INTERNATIONALE DES SOCIOLOGUES DE LANGUE FRANÇAISE. 7e Colloque, Neuchâtel, 1968. Sociologie des mutations; sous la direction de Georges Balandier; édition préparée par Yvonne Roux. Paris, [1970]. pp. 531.

CAMPBELL (ALBERT ANGUS) and CONVERSE (PHILIP E.) eds. The human meaning of social change. New York, [1972]. pp. 547.

HALLIER (JEAN EDERN) La cause des peuples. Paris, [1972]. pp. 251.

HANQUET (HUBERTE) Travail professionnel des femmes et mutations sociales. Bruxelles, [1972]. pp. 405. *bibliog.*

ONE WORLD ONLY, 1972. Social aspects in the participation of rural and agricultural manpower in development: an international forum under the auspices of the Friedrich-Ebert-Stiftung, Manila, 1972; (editor: Klaus Pretzer). Rizal, [1972]. pp. 279. *(Friedrich-Ebert-Stiftung. [Asian Labour Institute]. Reports. 7)*

RAO (M.S.A.) Tradition, rationality, and change: essays in sociology of economic development and social change. Bombay, 1972. p. 182. *bibliog.*

BAILEY (FREDERICK GEORGE) ed. Debate and compromise: the politics of innovation. Oxford, 1973. pp. 343. *bibliog.*

CHODAK (SZYMON) Societal development: five approaches with conclusions from comparative analysis. New York, 1973. pp. 357. *bibliog.*

CLARK (TED) and JAFFE (DENNIS T.) Toward a radical therapy: alternate services for personal and social change. New York, [1973]. pp. 287. *bibliog.*

CRAIG (DAVID M.) Ph. D. The real foundations: literature and social change. London, 1973. pp. 318.

CROZIER (MICHEL) The stalled society. New York, 1973. pp. 177.

DUNCAN (GRAEME) Marx and Mill: two views of social conflict and social harmony. Cambridge, 1973. pp. 386. *bibliog.*

EISENSTADT (SHMUEL N.) Tradition, change and modernity. New York, [1973]. pp. 367.

GERMANI (GINO) ed. Modernization, urbanization and the urban crisis. Boston, [1973]. pp. 275.

KORNBERG (ALLAN) and others. Legislatures and societal change: the case of Canada. Beverly Hills, [1973]. pp. 64. *bibliog.*

KSHIBEKOV (DOSMUKHAMED) Perekhodnye obshchestvennye otnosheniia. Alma-Ata, 1973. pp. 283.

SOCIAL CLASSES.

KUITENBROUWER (JOOST B.W.) Societal processes and policies: some reflections on their nature and direction. The Hague, 1973. pp. 12. *(Hague. Institute of Social Studies. Occasional Papers. No. 31)*

KUITENBROUWER (JOOST B.W.) The function of social mobilization in the process towards a new society in Peru. The Hague, 1973. pp. 82. *(Hague. Institute of Social Studies. Occasional Papers. No. 36)*

LEECH (KENNETH) Youthquake: the growth of a counter-culture through two decades. London, 1973. pp. 246.

MARX (KARL) Karl Marx on society and social change, with selections by Friedrich Engels; edited and with an introduction by Neil J. Smelser. Chicago, 1973. pp. 206.

MULAY (SUMATI) and RAY (G.L.) Towards modernization: a study of peasantry in rural Delhi. Delhi, 1973. pp. 159. *bibliog.*

SHADE (WILLIAM L.) Social change and the electoral process. Gainesville, 1973. pp. 73. *(Florida University. Monographs. Social Sciences. No. 49)*

SOCIOLOGICAL REVIEW, THE; [published by] University of Keele. Monographs. [No.] 20 Professionalisation and social change; edited by Paul Halmos. Keele, 1973. pp. 338. *bibliogs.*

TESSLER (MARK A.) and others. Tradition and identity in changing Africa. New York, [1973]. pp. 363. *bibliog.*

AMBROSE (PETER JOHN) The quiet revolution: social change in a Sussex village, 1871- 1971. London, 1974. pp. 239.

CHEKKI (DANESH A.) Modernization and kin network. Leiden, 1974. pp. 184. *bibliog.*

HARANNE (MARKKU) and ALLARDT (ERIK) Attitudes toward modernity and modernization: an appraisal of an empirical study. Helsinki, 1974. pp. 109. *(Helsinki, Yliopisto. Research Group for Comparative Sociology. Research Reports. No.6)*

KADT (EMANUEL J. DE) and WILLIAMS (GAVIN) eds. Sociology and development. London, 1974. pp. 374. *bibliogs. (British Sociological Association. Explorations in Sociology. 4)*

LANDSBERGER (HENRY A.) ed. Rural protest: peasant movements and social change. London, 1974. pp. 430.

LAUTERBACH (ALBERT T.) Psychological challenges to modernization. Amsterdam, 1974. pp. 190.

MARRIS (PETER) Loss and change. London, 1974. pp. 178. *bibliog. (Institute of Community Studies. Reports)*

MARWICK (ARTHUR J.B.) War and social change in the twentieth century: a comparative study of Britain, France, Germany, Russia and the United States. London, 1974. pp. 258. *bibliog.*

RIBEILL (GEORGES) Tensions et mutations sociales. [Paris], 1974. pp. 220. *bibliog.*

WERTHEIM (WILLEM FREDERIK) Evolution and revolution: the rising waves of emancipation. Harmondsworth, 1974. pp. 416. *An abridged and updated English ed.*

— Periodicals — Bibliography.

BLUMBERG (HERBERT H.) compiler. Periodicals concerned with nonviolence and social change; with organisation, geographic and subject indexes. Haverford, Pa., 1973. 1 vol. (unfoliated). *(Haverford College. Center for Nonviolent Conflict Resolution. Nonviolent Action Research Project. Monograph Series on Nonviolent Action. No.21)*

SOCIAL CLASSES.

CERNEA (STELA) Protiv burzuaznykh izmyshlenii o klasskakh. Moskva, 1963. pp. 143.

DELMARLE (JEAN) Classes et lutte de classes: l'avenir de l'homme, de la société. Paris, [1973]. pp. 325. *bibliog.*

FALLERS (LLOYD A.) Inequality: social stratification reconsidered. Chicago, 1973. pp. 330. *bibliog.*

SOCIAL CLASSES. (Cont.)

GIDDENS (ANTHONY) The class structure of the advanced societies. London, 1973. pp. 336. *bibliog.*

INTERNATIONAL WORKSHOP ON CAREER MOBILITY, KONSTANZ, 1971. Social stratification and career mobility; [papers presented at the workshop]; edited by Walter Müller and Karl Ulrich Mayer. Paris, [1973]. pp. 390. *bibliogs.* *(International Social Science Council. Publications. 16)*

ORDRES et classes: colloque d'histoire sociale, Saint-Cloud, 24-25 mai 1967; communications réunies par D.Roche et présentées par C.E. Labrousse. Paris, [1973]. pp. 269. *(Paris. Ecole Pratique des Hautes Etudes. Section des Sciences Economiques et Sociales. Congrès et Colloques. 12)*

REY (PIERRE PHILIPPE) Les alliances de classes: sur l'articulation des modes de production; suivi de Matérialisme historique et luttes de classes. Paris, 1973. pp. 221.

EREMIN (IURII ELEAZAROVICH) Klassy i demokratiia. Moskva, 1974. pp. 206.

KELSALL (ROGER KEITH) and KELSALL (HELEN MARTIN) Stratification: an essay on class and inequality. London, 1974. pp. 156. *bibliog.*

— **America, Latin.**

GARCIA (ANTONIO) Estructura social y desarrollo latinoamericanos. Santiago de Chile, Instituto de Capacitacion e Investigacion en Reforma Agraria, 1969. pp. 134.

— **Caribbean Area.**

IMPERIALISMO y clases sociales en el Caribe; ([by Mercedes Acosta [and others]). Buenos Aires, [1973]. pp. 235.

— **Denmark.**

ØRUM (BENTE) Samspillet mellem social baggrund, intellektuelt niveau og placering i skolesystemet efter 7 . klasse; [with English summary]; The relationship between social background, intellectual level, and the position in the school system at 14 years: rapport nr. 1 fra ungdomsforlØsundersOgelsen. København, 1971. pp. 144. *bibliog.* *(Socialforskningsinstituttet. Studier. Nr. 20)*

— **East (Near East).**

NIEUWENHUIJZE (CHRISTOFFEL ANTHONIE OLIVIER VAN) On social stratification and societal articulation: prologomena to comparative stratification studies (with special reference to the Middle East). The Hague, 1973. pp. 19. *(Hague. Institute of Social Studies. Occasional Papers. No.40)*

— **Finland.**

RAUHALA (URHO) Sosiaalisten kerrostumien määrälliset vahvuudet, etc. [Helsinki, 1974]. pp. 146. *(Finland. Suomen Virallinen Tilasto. Finlands Officiella Statistik. 32. Sosiaalisia Erikoistutkimuksia. 37)*

— **France.**

LOJKINE (JEAN) La politique urbaine dans la région parisienne, 1945-1971. Paris, [1972]. pp. 281.

— **Italy.**

BOLAFFI (GUIDO) and VAROTTI (ADRIANO) Agricoltura capitalistica e classi sociali in Italia, 1948-1970. Bari, [1973]. pp. 323. *bibliog.*

— **Ivory Coast.**

COHEN (MICHAEL A.) Urban policy and political conflict in Africa: a study of the Ivory Coast. Chicago, [1974]. pp. 262. *bibliog.*

— **Jamaica.**

STONE (CARL) Class, race and political behaviour in urban Jamaica. [Mona], 1973. pp. 188. *bibliog.*

— **Nigeria.**

LLOYD (PETER CUTT) Power and independence: urban Africans' perception of social inequality. London, 1974. pp. 248. *bibliog.*

— **Russia.**

PROBLEMY izmeneniia sotsial'noi struktury sovetskogo obshchestva.Rostov-na-Donu, 1972. pp. 111.

YANOWITCH (MURRAY) and FISHER (WESLEY A.) eds. Social stratification and mobility in the U.S.S.R... with a commentary by S.M. Lipset. White Plains, N.Y., [1973]. pp. 402. *bibliog.*

— **Uganda.**

JACOBSON (DAVID) Anthropologist. Itinerant townsmen: friendship and social order in urban Uganda.Menlo Park, Calif., [1973]. pp. 150. *bibliog.*

— **United Kingdom.**

BAIN (GEORGE SAYERS) and others. Social stratification and trade unionism: a critique. London, 1973. pp. 174. *bibliog.* *(Warwick Studies in Industrial Relations)*

WEDDERBURN (DOROTHY) ed. Poverty, inequality and class structure. London, 1974. pp. 247.

— — **Scotland.**

MACLAREN (A. ALLAN) Religion and social class: the disruption years in Aberdeen. London, 1974. pp. 268.

— **United States.**

HUBER (JOAN) and FORM (WILLIAM HUMBERT) Income and ideology: an analysis of the American political formula. New York, [1973]. pp. 226. *bibliog.*

PESSEN (EDWARD) Riches, class, and power before the Civil War. Lexington, Mass., [1973]. pp. 378. *bibliog.*

SCHNEIDER (DAVID MURRAY) and SMITH (RAYMOND T.) Class differences and sex roles in American kinship and family structure. Englewood Cliffs, [1973]. pp. 132. *bibliog.*

NICHOLS (DAVID) Financing elections: the politics of an American ruling class. New York, 1974. pp. 191.

SOCIAL CONDITIONS.

KSHIBEKOV (DOSMUKHAMED) Perekhodnye obshchestvennye otnosheniia. Alma-Ata, 1973. pp. 283.

MARX (KARL) Karl Marx on society and social change, with selections by Friedrich Engels; edited and with an introduction by Neil J. Smelser. Chicago, 1973. pp. 206.

— **Underdeveloped areas.**

See UNDERDEVELOPED AREAS —
    Social conditions.

SOCIAL CONFLICT.

BEER (MAX) Socialist. Social struggles and thought, 1750-1860;...translated by H.J. Stenning and revised by the author. London, 1925. pp. 218.

VAN onderen: brieven, interviews, gedichten en verhalen uit de arbeidswereld; met een nawoord van C. Poppe. Amsterdam, 1972. pp. 116.

CASTELLS (MANUEL) Luttes urbaines et pouvoir politique. Paris, 1973. pp. 135.

DEUTSCH (MORTON) The resolution of conflict: constructive and destructive processes.New Haven, 1973. pp. 420. *bibliog.* *(Yale University. Carl Hovland Memorial Lectures)*

REICH (WILHELM) What is class consciousness?; [originally published in German in 1934 under the pseudonym of Ernst Parell]. 2nd ed. [London], 1973. pp. 76.

CONRAD (WOLFGANG) Ressentiment in der Klassengesellschaft: zur Diskussion um einen Aspekt religiösen Bewusstseins. Göttingen, [1974]. pp. 99. *bibliog.*

— **Africa, Subsaharan.**

AMIN (SAMIR) The class struggle in Africa. [Cambridge, Mass., 1973?]. pp. 23-47. *(Africa Research Group. Reprints. 2) (Reprinted from Revolution, vol. 1, no. 9, 1964)*

— **Canada.**

MEISEL (JOHN) Cleavages, parties and values in Canada. London, [1974]. pp. 55. *bibliog.*

— **Italy.**

COTTONE (ELVIRA) ed. Riorganizzazione capitalistica e lotta di classe nelle campagne. Roma, [1972]. pp. 126.

FERRARIS (PINO) Sviluppo industriale e lotta di classe nel Biellese. Torino, [1972]. pp. 189.

CLASSE: Quaderni sulla Condizione e sulla Lotta Operaia. 7. 1972-73: crisi, ristrutturazione, lotte. Milano, 1973. pp. 396.

FRABOTTA (BIANCAMARIA) ed. Femminismo e lotta di classe in Italia, 1970-1973: (analisi, documenti e prospettive). Roma, [1973]. pp. 256. *bibliog.*

RUGAFIORI (PARIDE) and others. Il triangolo industriale tra ricostruzione e lotta di classe, 1945-1948. Milano, 1974. pp. 308.

— **Mexico.**

ROMANUCCI-ROSS (LOLA) Conflict, violence, and morality in a Mexican village. Palo Alto, Calif., 1973. pp. 202. *bibliog.*

— **Switzerland.**

ULMER (HANS) Wollen wir den Klassenkampf?. St. Gallen, [1973]. pp. 63. *bibliog.* *(Landesverband Freier Schweizer Arbeiter. Soziale Schriftenreihe. Heft 52)*

KERR (HENRY H.) Switzerland: social cleavages and partisan conflict. London, 1974. pp. 39. *bibliog.*

— **United States.**

BERNSTEIN (IRVING) A comparison: industrial conflict in the thirties and race conflict in the sixties. Los Angeles, 1968. pp. 17-20. *(California University. Institute of Industrial Relations. Reprints. No. 179) (Reprinted from...proceedings of the IRRA 1967 annual spring meeting)*

SOCIAL CONTROL.

BARNSBY (GEORGE) Dictatorship of the bourgeoisie: social control in the nineteenth- century Black Country. London, 1972. 1 vol. (unpaged). *bibliog.* *(Communist Party of Great Britain. Historians' Group. Our History. No.55)*

SITES (PAUL) Control: the basis of social order. New York, [1973]. pp. 225.

TAYLOR (IAN) Criminologist, and TAYLOR (LAURIE) eds. Politics and deviance: [papers selected from the proceedings of the National Deviancy Conference]. Harmondsworth, 1973. pp. 208.

SOCIAL CREDIT.

STEIN (MICHAEL BERNARD) The dynamics of right-wing protest: a political analysis of Social Credit in Quebec. Toronto, [1973]. pp. 256.

SOCIAL DEMOCRATIC PARTY (GERMANY).

SOZIALDEMOKRATISCHE Bibliothek: Sammlung von Abhandlungen über Theorie und Geschichte des Sozialismus; (unveränderter fotomechanischer Nachdruck der Originalausgabe 1885-(90), [containing 36 pamphlets]). Leipzig, 1971. 3 vols.

ATZROTT (OTTO) Sozialdemokratische Druckschriften und Vereine, (verboten auf Grund des Reichsgesetzes gegen die gemeingefährlichen Bestrebungen der Sozialdemokratie vom 21.Oktober 1878... Neudruck der Ausgabe Berlin, 1886; [with] Nachtrag, 1888). Glashütten im Taunus, 1971. 1 vol.(various pagings).

AVELING (EDWARD BIBBINS) Wilhelm Liebknecht and the social-democratic movement in Germany;...on behalf of the Zürich Committee for the International Socialist Workers and Trade Union Congress, London, July 26 to August 1, 1896. London, [1896]. pp. 16.

LEGIEN (CARL) Warum müssen die Gewerkschaftsfunktionäre sich mehr am inneren Parteileben beteiligen?: ein Vortrag... in der Versammlung der Gewerkschaftskommission Berlins und Umgegend am 27.Januar 1915. Berlin, 1915. pp. 47.

OLLENHAUER (ERICH) 1953, das Jahr der Entscheidung: Referat des Vorsitzenden der Sozialdemokratischen Partei Deutschlands...auf dem Wahlkongress der SPD am 10.Mai 1953 in Frankfurt am Main. [Bonn, 1953]. pp. 38.

POELS (WERNER) Staat und Sozialdemokratie im Bismarckreich: die Tätigkeit der Politischen Polizei beim Polizeipräsidenten in Berlin in der Zeit des Sozialistengesetzes, 1878- 1890. Berlin, [1964]. pp. 24. (Sonderdruck aus dem Jahrbuch für die Geschichte Mittel- und Ostdeutschlands...Band 13, 1964)

WORM (MANFRED) SPD und Strafrechtsreform: (die Stellung der Sozialdemokratischen Partei Deutschlands zur Strafrechtsreform, etc.). München, [1968]. pp. 159. bibliog. (Politische Studien. Beihefte. 8)

BOSSLE (LOTHAR) Marxismus: demokratischer Sozialismus. Bonn, [1972]. pp. 39. (Christlich-Demokratische Union Deutschlands. Wirtschaftsrat. Information. 8)

FRANKE (KONRAD A.) Die SPD in Niedersachsen: Demokratie der ersten Stunde. [Hannover], Niedersächsische Landeszentrale für Politische Bildung, 1972. pp. 107. bibliog.

PATERSON (WILLIAM EDGAR) The German Social Democratic Party and European integration, 1949-57: a case-study of opposition in foreign affairs; [Ph.D. (London) thesis]. 1972. fo. 239. bibliog. Typescript: unpublished. This thesis is the property of London University and may not be removed from the Library.

SCHMID (CARLO) Gesammelte Werke in Einzelausgaben. Bern, 1973 in progress. bibliogs.

BERS (GUENTER) Wilhelm Hasselmann, 1844-1916: sozialrevolutionärer Agitator und Abgeordneter des Deutschen Reichstages. Köln, 1973. pp. 171. bibliog.

BRAUNMUEHL (CLAUDIA VON) Kalter Krieg und friedliche Koexistenz: die Aussenpolitik der SPD in der Grossen Koalition. Frankfurt am Main, 1973. pp. 161.

BUCZYLOWSKI (ULRICH) Kurt Schumacher und die deutsche Frage: Sicherheitspolitik und strategische Offensivkonzeption vom August 1950 bis September 1951. Stuttgart-Degerloch, 1973. pp. 228. bibliog.

FREYBERG (JUTTA VON) Sozialdemokraten und Kommunisten: die Revolutionären Sozialisten Deutschlands vor dem Problem der Aktionseinheit 1934-1937. Köln, [1973]. pp. 186.

KEMPE (MARTIN) SPD und Bundeswehr: Studien zum militärisch-industriellen Komplex. Köln, [1973]. pp. 278.

MAERKER (RUDOLF) and KRAUSE (PETER) Sozialismus ist das Ziel: Dokumente und Zeugnisse aus der Geschichte der Sozialdemokratie, 1863 bis 1933. München, [1973]. pp. 263.

MORAW (FRANK) Die Parole der "Einheit" und die Sozialdemokratie: zur parteiorganisatorischen und gesellschaftspolitischen Orientierung der SPD ... 1933-1948. Bonn-Bad Godesberg, [1973]. pp. 262. bibliog. (Friedrich-Ebert-Stiftung. Forschungsinstitut. Schriftenreihe. Band 94)

PESCHKE (KLAUS) Die Bedeutung der liberalen Parteien und der Sozialdemokratie für das politische Leben im Wahlkreis Altena-Iserlohn von der Reichsgründung 1871 bis zum Jahre 1890. [Altena, 1973]. pp. 150. bibliog. (Verein Freunde der Burg Altena. Altenaer Beiträge. Neue Folge. Band 8)

SCHULZE (HANS) Sozialdemokratismus zwischen Entideologisierung und Reideologisierung. Frankfurt/Main, 1973. pp. 118.

SCHUMACHER (KURT) 1895-1952. Der Kampf um den Staatsgedanken in der deutschen Sozialdemokratie; herausgegeben von Friedrich Holtmeier; mit einem Geleitwort von Herbert Wehner. Stuttgart, [1973]. pp. 144. bibliog.

WACHENHEIM (HEDWIG) Vom Grossbürgertum zur Sozialdemokratie: Memoiren einer Reformistin; [edited by Susanne Miller]. Berlin, 1973. pp. 155. (IWK: internationale wissenschaftliche Korrespondenz zur Geschichte der deutschen Arbeiterbewegung. Beihefte. 1)

WEISSER (GERHARD) Freiheit durch Sozialismus: zu wenig bekannte Arbeiten der Programmkommissionen und anderer Ausschüsse der SPD, etc. Göttingen, [1973]. pp. 46. (Forschungsinstitut für Gesellschaftspolitik und Beratende Sozialwissenschaft. Monographien zur Politik. Heft 11)

BRANDT (WILLY) Die Partei der Freiheit: Reden über August Bebel, Karl Marx, Friedrich Engels und Otto Wels. new ed. Bonn-Bad Godesberg, [1974]. pp. 69.

DEUTSCHER HISTORIKERTAG. Sektion "Geschichte der Arbeiterbewegung". Verhandlungen, 1972. Sozialdemokratie zwischen Klassenbewegung und Volkspartei: Verhandlungen... in Regensburg, Oktober 1972; ([edited by] Hans Mommsen]. Frankfurt am Main, [1974]. pp. 149.

ECKERT (RAINER) and SEIDERER (AXEL) Sozialdemokratie und Jungsozialisten: Politik, Programm und Gesellschaftstheorie; eine marxistische Kritik. Frankfurt/Main, 1974. pp. 194.

MISCH (AXEL) Das Wahlsystem zwischen Theorie und Taktik: zur Frage von Mehrheitswahl und Verhältniswahl in der Programmatik der Sozialdemokratie bis 1933. Berlin, [1974]. pp. 290. bibliog.

PATERSON (WILLIAM EDGAR) The SPD and European integration. Farnborough, [1974]. pp. 177. bibliog.

POTTHOFF (HEINRICH) and MILLER (SUSANNE) Kleine Geschichte der SPD. Bonn-Bad Godesberg, [1974]. 2 vols. (in 1). bibliogs.

RASCHKE (JOACHIM) Innerparteiliche Opposition: die Linke in der Berliner SPD. Hamburg, 1974. pp. 437.

REULECKE (JUERGEN) ed. Arbeiterbewegung an Rhein und Ruhr: Beiträge zur Geschichte der Arbeiterbewegung in Rheinland-Westfalen. Wuppertal, [1974]. pp. 468. bibliog.

STREITHOFEN (HEINRICH B.) SPD und katholische Kirche: eine Untersuchung über das Kirchenbild des Vorwärts. Stuttgart, [1974]. pp. 87. (Institut für Gesellschaftswissenschaften Walberberg. Walberberger Gespräche)

STROBEL (GEORG WALDEMAR) Die Partei Rosa Luxemburgs, Lenin und die SPD: der polnische "europäische" Internationalismus in der russischen Sozialdemokratie. Wiesbaden, 1974. pp. 759. bibliog.

VISHNIAKOV-VISHNEVETSKII (KONSTANTIN ANATOL'EVICH) V.I. Lenin i revoliutsionnye sviazi rossiiskogo i germanskogo proletariata, 1903-1910 gg. Leningrad, 1974. pp. 220.

Die WANDLUNG der deutschen Sozialdemokratie vom Erfurter Parteitag 1891 bis zum Ersten Weltkrieg; ([by an] Autorengruppe unter der Leitung von Georg Fülberth). Köln, [1974]. pp. 48. bibliog.

— Congresses.

SOZIALDEMOKRATISCHE PARTEI DEUTSCHLANDS. Parteitag, 1959. Protokoll der Verhandlungen des Ausserordentlichen Parteitages... vom 13.-15. November 1959 in Bad Godesberg. Bonn-Bad Godesberg, [1959? repr. 1972]. pp. 639.

SOCIAL DEMOCRATIC PARTY (LATVIA).

LATVIISKII GOSUDARSTVENNYI UNIVERSITET. Uchenye Zapiski. t.185. Germaniia i Pribaltika. 2. Riga, 1973. pp. 99.

SOCIAL DEMOCRATIC PARTY (SWEDEN).

SOCIAL DEMOCRATIC PARTY (NETHERLANDS).

OUTSHOORN (JOYCE) Vrouwenemancipatie en socialisme: een onderzoek naar de houding van de SDAP ten opzichte van het vrouwenvraagstuk tussen 1894 en 1919. [Nijmegen], 1973. pp. 111. bibliog.

COHEN (H.F.) Om de vernieuwing van het socialisme: de politieke oriëntatie van de Nederlandse sociaal-democratie, 1919-1930. Leiden, 1974. pp. 279. bibliog. With summary in English.

SOCIAL DEMOCRATIC PARTY (NORWAY).

See LABOUR PARTY — NORWAY.

SOCIAL DEMOCRATIC PARTY (POLAND).

STROBEL (GEORG WALDEMAR) Die Partei Rosa Luxemburgs, Lenin und die SPD: der polnische "europäische" Internationalismus in der russischen Sozialdemokratie. Wiesbaden, 1974. pp. 759. bibliog.

SOCIAL DEMOCRATIC PARTY (RUSSIA).

TSENTRAL'NYI GOSUDARSTVENNYI ARKHIV OKTIABR'SKOI REVOLIUTSII, VYSSHIKH ORGANOV GOSUDARSTVENNOI VLASTI I ORGANOV GOSUDARSTVENNOGO UPRAVLENIIA SSSR. 1917 God v Dokumentakh i Materialakh. Rabochee dvizhenie v 1917 godu; podgotovili k pechati V.L. Meller i A.M. Pankratova, etc. Moskva, 1926. pp. 371.

NOVIKOV (VIKTOR IVANOVICH) V.I. Lenin i pskovskie iskrovtsy. 2nd ed. Leningrad, 1972. pp. 267.

PLAMENNOE slovo bortsov revoliutsii: listovki arkhangel'skikh bol'shevikov, 1903-1917. Arkhangel'sk, 1972. pp. 99.

BOL'SHEVIZM i reformizm. Moskva, 1973. pp. 392.

SHIGABUDINOV (MAGOMED SHIGABUDINOVICH) Rabochee dvizhenie na Severnom Kavkaze v gody reaktsii, 1907- 1910 gg. Makhachkala, 1973. pp. 143.

SOVOKIN (ALEKSANDR MIKHAILOVICH) V preddverii Oktiabria: podgotovka pobedy vooruzhennogo vosstaniia. Moskva, 1973. pp. 348.

VOZNIKNOVENIE i razvitie revoliutsionnogo dvizheniia v Kirgizii v kontse XIX - nachale XX vv.; pod redaktsiei K.U. Usenbaeva. Frunze, 1973. pp. 230.

ZINOV'EV (GRIGORII EVSEEVICH) History of the Bolshevik party: a popular outline; translated by R. Chappell. London, 1973. pp. 229.

ELWOOD (RALPH CARTER) Russian social democracy in the underground: a study of the RSDRP in the Ukraine, 1907-1914. Assen, 1974. pp. 304. bibliog. (International Institute of Social History. Publications on Social History. 8)

STROBEL (GEORG WALDEMAR) Die Partei Rosa Luxemburgs, Lenin und die SPD: der polnische "europäische" Internationalismus in der russischen Sozialdemokratie. Wiesbaden, 1974. pp. 759. bibliog.

TERESHCHENKO (IURII ILARIONOVYCH) Politychna borot'ba na vyborakh do mis'kykh dum Ukraïny v period pidhotovky Zhovtnevoï revoliutsiï. Kyïv, 1974. pp. 143.

VISHNIAKOV-VISHNEVETSKII (KONSTANTIN ANATOL'EVICH) V.I. Lenin i revoliutsionnye sviazi rossiiskogo i germanskogo proletariata, 1903-1910 gg. Leningrad, 1974. pp. 220.

See also COMMUNIST PARTY — Russia.

SOCIAL DEMOCRATIC PARTY (SWEDEN).

FRÅN Palm till Palme: den svenska socialdemokratins program 1882-1960; kommentarer och dokument utgivna av Föreningen Socialistisk Debatt. Stockholm, [1972]. pp. 272.

SOCIAL DEMOCRATIC PARTY (SWEDEN). (Cont.)

TINGSTEN (HERBERT) The Swedish Social Democrats: their ideological development; translated by Greta Frankel and Patricia Howard-Rosen. Totowa, N.J., [1973]. pp. 719.

MOLIN (KARL) Försvaret, folkhemmet och demokratin: socialdemokratisk riksdagspolitik, 1939-1945. Stockholm, 1974. pp. 463. *bibliog. With English summary.*

SOCIAL DEMOCRATIC PARTY (SWITZERLAND).

SOZIALDEMOKRATISCHE PARTEI DER SCHWEIZ. Ein Wort an die schweiz. Landwirtschaft: zu den Nationalratswahlen im Oktober 1919. n.p., [1919]. 1 pamphlet (unpaged).

SOZIALDEMOKRATISCHE PARTEI DER SCHWEIZ. Wählt der Mittelstand sozialdemokratisch?. Zürich, [1939?]. pp. 48. *(Kultur und Arbeit)*

BRINGOLF (WALTHER) Perspektiven der sozialistischen Bewegung der Schweiz. [Schaffhausen, 1940]. pp. 26.

SOZIALISTISCHE JUGEND DER SCHWEIZ. Zeigt der Sozialismus einen Ausweg?: (unsere Antwort an Nationalrat Bringolf'.); Kapitulation vor dem Kapitalismus oder sozialistische Perspektiven?. [Zürich, 1940]. pp. 30.

BRINGOLF (WALTHER) Sozialismus in der Schweiz. [Zürich, 1956]. pp. 32.

BRINGOLF (WALTHER) Die Sozialdemokratie gestern, heute, morgen: Referat, gehalten am Parteitag der Sozialdemokratischen Partei der Schweiz in Winterthur vom 27./28.Juni 1959. [Zürich, 1959]. pp. 16.

AEMMER (ROBERT WALTER) Die Sozialdemokratie im Kanton Bern, 1890-1914. Zürich, 1973. pp. 302. *bibliog.*

JOST (HANS ULRICH) Linksradikalismus in der deutschen Schweiz, 1914-1918. Bern, [1973]. pp. 206. *bibliog.*

SOZIALDEMOKRATISCHE PARTEI DER SCHWEIZ. Arbeitsgruppe Sicherheitspolitik. Selbstbehauptung der Schweiz: Friedenssicherung, Kriegsverhütung, soziale und nationale Sicherheit; Grundfragen einer zeitgemässen Sicherheitspolitik. Bern, [1973]. pp. 87. *(SPS-Schriftenreihe. Nr.8)*

SOCIAL ETHICS.

DURKHEIM (EMILE) On morality and society: selected writings; edited...by Robert N. Bellah. Chicago, 1973. pp. 244. *bibliog.*

ACTON (HARRY BURROWS) The idea of a spiritual power. London, 1974. pp. 31. *(London. University. London School of Economics and Political Science. Auguste Comte Memorial Trust Lectures. 10)*

EPPSTEIN (JOHN) The cult of revolution in the Church. New Rochelle, [1974]. pp. 160.

SOCIAL EXCHANGE.

EKEH (PETER P.) Social exchange theory: the two traditions. London, 1974. pp. 237. *bibliog.*

SOCIAL GROUP WORK

— Study and teaching.

CENTRAL TRAINING COUNCIL IN CHILD CARE [U.K.]. Study Group on Fieldwork Training. Working with groups: the development of experience in group work as a basic part of social work education. [London], 1970. pp. 32. *(Discussion Papers. No. 5)*

SOCIAL GROUPS.

MARTIN (JAMES GILBERT) and FRANKLIN (CLYDE W.) Minority group relations. Columbus, Ohio, [1973]. pp. 338.

— Mathematical models.

HALLINAN (MAUREEN T.) The structure of positive sentiment. Amsterdam, 1974. pp. 115. *bibliog.*

SOCIAL HISTORY.

FISCHER (WOLFRAM) Wirtschaft und Gesellschaft im Zeitalter der Industrialisierung: Aufsätze, Studien, Vorträge. Göttingen, 1972. pp. 547.

SOCIAL INDICATORS

— Paraguay.

ANGEL PANGRAZIO (MIGUEL) Indicadores de la estructura social del Paraguay. Asuncion, 1973. pp. 370. *bibliog.*

SOCIAL INTERACTION.

BIRENBAUM (ARNOLD) and SAGARIN (EDWARD) eds. People in places: the sociology of the familiar. New York, 1973. pp. 301. *bibliogs.*

BRITTAN (ARTHUR) Meanings and situations. London, 1973. pp. 215.

CRANACH (MARIO VON) and VINE (IAN) eds. Social communication and movement: studies of interaction and expression in man and chimpanzee. London, 1973. pp. 489. *bibliogs. (European Association of Experimental Social Psychology. European Monographs in Social Psychology. 4)*

HELMER (JOHN) and EDDINGTON (NEIL A.) eds. Urbanman: the psychology of urban survival. London, [1973]. pp. 274. *bibliogs.*

ILLICH (IVAN D.) Tools for conviviality. London, 1973. pp. 110.

OFSHE (RICHARD J.) ed. Interpersonal behavior in small groups. Englewood Cliffs, [1973]. pp. 792. *bibliogs.*

SCHIFFER (IRVINE) Charisma: a psychoanalytic look at mass society. Toronto, [1973]. pp. 184. *bibliog.*

TEDESCHI (JAMES T.) and others. Conflict, power and games: the experimental study of interpersonal relations. Chicago, 1973. pp. 270. *bibliog.*

BOISSEVAIN (JEREMY FERGUS) Friends of friends: networks, manipulators and coalitions. Oxford, [1974]. pp. 285. *bibliog.*

MEHRABIAN (ALBERT) and KSIONZKY (SHELDON) A theory of affiliation. Lexington, [1974]. pp. 212. *bibliog.*

— Study and teaching.

DYAR (DAMIEN A.) and GILES (W. JOHN) Improving skills in working with people: interaction analysis. London, H.M.S.O., 1974. pp. 39. *bibliog. (Training Information Papers.7)*

SOCIAL ISOLATION.

FREIRE (ANTONIO DE ABREU) La révolution désaliénante: fondements de la pensée de Karl Marx. Tournai, 1972. pp. 260. *(Facultés de la Compagnie de Jésus au Québec. Hier- Aujourd'hui. 7)*

PAWLEY (MARTIN) The private future: causes and consequences of community collapse in the West. London, [1973]. pp. 208.

— United States.

SPIEGEL (DON) and KEITH-SPIEGEL (PATRICIA) eds. Outsiders USA: original essays on 24 outgroups in American society. San Francisco, [1973]. pp. 627,xxiv. *bibliogs.*

SOCIAL LEGISLATION

— Jamaica.

CUMPER (GLORIA) Survey of social legislation in Jamaica. [Kingston, Jamaica, 1972]. pp. 122. *(West Indies, University of the. Institute of Social and Economic Research. Law and Society in the Caribbean. No. 1)*

— Russia — Kazakstan.

CHELOVEK i zakony. Alma-Ata, 1973. pp. 327.

SOCIAL MEDICINE.

WORLD HEALTH ORGANIZATION. Technical Report Series. Geneva, 1950 in progress.

SPAIN. Direccion General de Sanidad. Coleccion de Folletos para Medicos sobre Temas de Caracter Sanitario. 57. La despobacion del agro y la medicina social; [by] Jose Alvarez-Sierra. Madrid, 1958. pp. 32.

WORLD HEALTH ORGANIZATION. Public Health Papers.. Geneva, 1959 in progress.

FOURNIER (ETIENNE) L'action médico-sociale dans les pays en voie de développement. Paris, 1961. pp. 311. *bibliog. (Paris. Université. Institut d'Etude du Développement Economique et Social.Collection Tiers-Monde)*

ROBINSON (DAVID) 1941- . Patients, practitioners, and medical care: aspects of medical sociology. [London], 1973. pp. 178. bibliogs.

WORLD HEALTH ORGANIZATION. Public Health Papers. No. 49. Interrelationships between health programmes and socio-economic development. Geneva, 1973. pp. 54. *bibliog.*

ELLIS (JAMES) Getting it straight: an inaugural lecture delivered at the University [of Southampton], 2nd May 1974. Southampton, 1974. pp. 14.

FABREGA (HORACIO) Disease and social behavior: an interdisciplinary perspective. Cambridge, Mass., [1974]. pp. 341. *bibliog.*

MECHANIC (DAVID) Politics, medicine, and social science. New York, [1974]. pp. 306.

SOCIAL MOBILITY.

BOUDON (RAYMOND) L'inégalité des chances: la mobilité sociale dans les sociétés industrielles. Paris, [1973]. pp. 237. *bibliog.*

— Mathematical models.

BOUDON (RAYMOND) Mathematical structures of social mobility. Amsterdam, 1973. pp. 168. *bibliog.*

— Belgium.

DELRUELLE-VOSSWINKEL (NICOLE) La mobilité sociale en Belgique: analyse des résultats d'un sondage national. [Brussels, 1970]. pp. 102, 4. *bibliog. (Brussels. Université Libre. Centre de Sociologie Générale et de Méthodologie. Collection)*

DELRUELLE-VOSSWINKEL (NICOLE) Les notables en Belgique: analyse des résultats d'une enquête. Bruxelles, [1972]. pp. 321. *(Brussels. Université Libre. Centre de Sociologie Générale et de Méthodologie. [Collection])*

— Germany.

SCHAICH (EBERHARD) Die Intergenerationenmobilität in Westdeutschland: eine dynamische Analyse auf der Basis Markovscher Ketten. Meisenheim am Glan, 1973. pp. 120. *bibliog.*

— Netherlands.

VAN ZEYL (CORNELIS J.) Ambition and social structure: educational structure and mobility orientation in the Netherlands and the United States. Lexington, [1974]. pp. 208. *bibliog.*

— Russia.

YANOWITCH (MURRAY) and FISHER (WESLEY A.) eds. Social stratification and mobility in the U.S.S.R... with a commentary by S.M. Lipset. White Plains, N.Y., [1973]. pp. 402. *bibliog.*

— United Kingdom.

RIDGE (J.M.) ed. Mobility in Britain reconsidered. Oxford, 1974. pp. 120. *bibliog. (Oxford Group for the Study of Social Mobility. Oxford Studies in Social Mobility. Working Papers. 2)*

— United States.

VAN ZEYL (CORNELIS J.) Ambition and social structure: educational structure and mobility orientation in the Netherlands and the United States. Lexington, [1974]. pp. 208. *bibliog.*

SOCIAL POLICY.

PAQUET (GILLES) Social science research as an evaluative instrument for social policy. Ottawa, 1971. fo. 32, xii. *(Carleton University. Carleton Economic Papers)*

INDUSTRIEGEWERKSCHAFT METALL FÜR DIE BUNDESREPUBLIK DEUTSCHLAND. Internationale Arbeitstagung, 4., 1972. Aufgabe Zukunft: Qualität des Lebens; Beiträge... 11. bis 14. April 1972 in Oberhausen...; Redaktion: Günter Friedrichs. Frankfurt am Main, 1973-74. 10 vols. *With summaries in English and French.*

ASSOCIATION FRANÇAISE DE SCIENCE ECONOMIQUE. Journées d'études des 24 et 25 septembre 1970, Faculté de Droit, Paris: (consommations collectives). Paris, 1973. pp. 166. *(Cahiers. No.1)*

COOPER (MICHAEL H.) ed. Social policy: a survey of recent developments. Oxford, [1973]. pp. 278. *bibliogs.*

HILLESTRØM (KARSTEN) Socialpolitikkens ideologi: et referat fra Socialpolitisk Forenings 47. sommermøde...1971. KØBENHAVN, 1973. PP. 42. *BIBLIOG. (sOCIALPOLITISK fORENING. sMÁSKRIFTER. nR.43)*

INTERNATIONAL LABOUR OFFICE. Studies and Reports. New Series. No. 79. Multinational enterprises and social policy. Geneva, 1973. pp. 182.

KUITENBROUWER (JOOST B.W.) Societal processes and policies: some reflections on their nature and direction. The Hague, 1973. pp. 12. *(Hague. Institute of Social Studies. Occasional Papers. No. 31)*

VEREIN FÜR SOZIALPOLITIK. Schriften. Neue Folge. Band 72. Leitbilder und Zielsysteme der Sozialpolitik; von Anton Burghardt [and others]; herausgegeben von Horst Sanmann. Berlin, [1973]. pp. 232. *With English summaries.*

SAMUELS (WARREN J.) Pareto on policy. Amsterdam, 1974. pp. 232. *bibliog.*

— Underdeveloped areas.

See UNDERDEVELOPED AREAS — Social policy.

SOCIAL PROBLEMS.

UNITED NATIONS EDUCATIONAL, SCIENTIFIC AND CULTURAL ORGANIZATION. Reports and Papers in the Social Sciences. Paris, 1955 in progress.

Het MILIEU van onze samenleving: (teksten...uitgesproken op 9 mei 1970 te Leiden tijdens een interdisciplinaire bijeenkomst); [by] V. Westhoff [and others]. Bussum, 1970. pp. 128. *bibliogs. (Annalen van het Thijmgenootschap. Jaargang 58, aflevering 2)*

ROSENBERG (BERNARD) and others, eds. Mass society in crisis: social problems and social pathology. 2nd ed. New York, [1971]. pp. 526.

GLINER (ROBERT) American society as a social problem. New York, [1973]. pp. 393.

NATIONAL ASSOCIATION OF SOCIAL WORKERS. Professional Symposium, 3rd, New Orleans, 1972. Social work practice and social justice...; selected papers [from the]...symposium...; editors Bernard Ross and Charles Shireman, editors. Washington, [1973]. pp. 152.

WALTHAM FOREST. Planning Department and Social Services Department. Survey of social stress. [London], 1973. pp. 23 with map.

WILSON (DES) Minority report: a diary of protest 1970-73. London, 1973. pp. 168.

CAUTE (DAVID) Collisions: essays and reviews. London, 1974. pp. 231.

LENOIR (RENE) Les exclus: un français sur dix. 2nd ed. Paris, [1974]. pp. 172.

LOWRY (RITCHIE PETER) Social problems: a critical analysis of theories and public policy. Lexington, Mass., [1974]. pp. 318. *bibliog.*

SHOSTAK (ARTHUR B.) Modern social reforms: solving today's social problems. New York, [1974]. pp. 411. *bibliog.*

SOCIAL PSYCHIATRY.

MOHAN (BRIJ) Social psychiatry in India: a treatise on the mentally ill. Calcutta, 1973. pp. 216.

SOCIAL PSYCHOLOGY.

ROKEACH (MILTON) Beliefs, attitudes and values: a theory of organization and change. San Francisco, 1968 repr. 1972. pp. 214. *bibliog.*

HOLLANDER (EDWIN PAUL) and HUNT (RAYMOND GEORGE) eds. Current perspectives in social psychology: readings with commentary. 3rd ed. New York, 1971. pp. 732. *bibliog.*

ARONSON (ELLIOT) The social animal. San Francisco, [1972]. pp. 324.

ADAIR (JOHN G.) The human subject: the social psychology of the psychological experiment. Boston, [1973]. pp. 109. *bibliog.*

KUZ'MIN (EVGENII SERGEEVICH) and BODALEV (ALEKSEI ALEKSANDROVICH) eds. Sotsial'naia psikhologiia i sotsial'noe planirovanie. Leningrad, 1973. pp. 167. *bibliog.*

ROWAN (JOHN) The social individual. London, 1973. pp. 247.

SCHIFFER (IRVINE) Charisma: a psychoanalytic look at mass society. Toronto, [1973]. pp. 184. *bibliog.*

ULEDOV (ALEKSANDR KONSTANTINOVICH) Die Struktur des gesellschaftlichen Bewusstseins: eine soziologisch-theoretische Untersuchung; herausgegeben von Werner Müller; (Übersetzung aus dem Russischen: Werner Rossade). Berlin, 1973. pp. 286.

ARMISTEAD (NIGEL) ed. Reconstructing social psychology. Harmondsworth, 1974. pp. 328. *bibliogs.*

NEAL (FRANK R.) Modal personality and sociocultural variation: cultural relativism and existential paralysis; with an empirical comparison of Italians and Mexican-Americans. Helsinki, 1974. pp. 62. *bibliog. (Helsinki. Yliopisto. Research Group for Comparative Sociology. Research Reports. No. 5)*

— Methodology.

BARON (ROBERT A.) and LIEBERT (ROBERT MANDEL) eds. Human social behavior: a contemporary view of experimental research. Homewood, Ill., 1971 repr. 1973. pp. 559. *bibliogs.*

SOCIAL REFORMERS

— United States.

RINGENBACH (PAUL T.) Tramps and reformers 1873-1916: the discovery of unemployment in New York. Westport, 1973. pp. 224. *bibliog.*

SOCIAL ROLE.

BIRENBAUM (ARNOLD) and SAGARIN (EDWARD) eds. People in places: the sociology of the familiar. New York, 1973. pp. 301. *bibliogs.*

ROSENMAYR (LEOPOLD) and KREUTZ (HENRIK) Rollenerwartung der weiblichen Jugend: eine empirische Untersuchung über Erwartungen und Dispositionen weiblicher Jugendlicher in Österreich. Wien, 1973. pp. 423. *bibliog. (Österreichisches Institut für Jugendkunde. Beiträge zur Jugendkunde. Band 16) With English summary.*

SOCIAL SCIENCE RESEARCH.

UNITED NATIONS EDUCATIONAL, SCIENTIFIC AND CULTURAL ORGANIZATION. Reports and Papers in the Social Sciences. Paris, 1955 in progress.

UNITED NATIONS EDUCATIONAL, SCIENTIFIC AND CULTURAL ORGANIZATION. Research Centre on Social and Economic Development in Southern Asia. 1959. Unesco Research Centre on the Social Implications of Industrialization in Southern Asia: organization and objectives. Calcutta, [1959]. pp. 17.

NITSCH (WOLFGANG) and WELLER (WALTER) Social science research on higher education and universities...; under the direction of Dietrich Goldschmidt. The Hague, 1970 in progress. *bibliog. (International Committee for Social Science Information and Documentation. Confluence. vols. 9, etc.)*

PAQUET (GILLES) Social science research as an evaluative instrument for social policy. Ottawa, 1971. fo. 32, xii. *(Carleton University. Carleton Economic Papers)*

BYARS (ROBERT S.) and LOVE (JOSEPH L.) eds. Quantitative social science research on Latin America. Urbana, [1973]. pp. 270. *bibliogs. (Illinois University. Center for Latin American and Caribbean Studies. [Publications]. No.1)*

COMPARATIVE social research: methodological problems and strategies: [selected papers of a faculty conference held by the Institute for Comparative Sociology in Bloomington, Indiana in 1971]; edited by Michael Armer [and] Allen D. Grimshaw. New York, [1973]. pp. 473. *bibliogs.*

FORCESE (DENNIS P.) and RICHER (STEPHEN) Social research methods. Englewood Cliffs, [1973]. pp. 280. *bibliogs.*

HUIZER (GERRIT) A research on social practice: some ethical considerations on research in the Third World. The Hague, 1973. pp. 10. *(Hague. Institute of Social Studies. Occasional Papers. No. 34)*

McKINNEY (DAVID W.) The authoritarian personality studies: an inquiry into the failure of social science research to produce demonstrable knowledge. The Hague, 1973. pp. 304. *bibliogs.*

MICHIGAN STATE UNIVERSITY SYMPOSIUM ON COMPARATIVE STUDIES IN THE SOCIAL SCIENCES, 1st-3rd, 1967-1969. Social science and the new societies: problems in cross-cultural research and theory building; edited by Nancy Hammond; contributors: Erik Allardt [and others]. East Lansing, 1973. pp. 245.

SHUL'HA (ZAKHARYI PETROVYCH) O metodike nauchno-issledovatel'skoi raboty: primenitel'no k issledovaniiam obshchestvovedov. Kiev, 1973. pp. 155. *bibliog.*

EASTHOPE (GARY) A history of social research methods. London, 1974. pp. 169. *bibliog.*

MANenvironment - a better fit?: is there a role for the social scientist?; [edited by] Dennis Donnelly; a conference under the auspices of the Occupational Section of the British Psychological Society...Oxford...1973. Birmingham, 1974. pp. 104,2. *(Birmingham. University. Centre for Urban and Regional Studies. Research Memoranda. No.26)*

— Bibliography.

NITSCH (WOLFGANG) and WELLER (WALTER) Social science research on higher education and universities...; under the direction of Dietrich Goldschmidt. The Hague, 1970 in progress. *bibliog. (International Committee for Social Science Information and Documentation. Confluence. vols. 9, etc.)*

— America, Latin.

The ROLE of the computer in economic and social research in Latin America: [selected papers of a conference held in Cuernavaca, Mexico, sponsored by the National Bureau of Economic Research and others]; edited by Nancy D. Ruggles. New York, 1974. pp. 399.

— India.

MUKHERJEE (RAMKRISHNA) and others. Data inventory on social sciences: India: first phase, 1967- 68; [a survey project carried out by the Sociological Research Unit of the Indian Statistical Institute]. Calcutta, [1971]. pp. 160.

SOCIAL SCIENCE RESEARCH. (Cont.)

— Israel.

GRATCH (HAYA) ed. Twenty-five years of social research in Israel: a review of the work of the Israel Institute of Applied Social Research, 1947-1971. Jerusalem, 1973. pp. 292. *bibliog.*

— United Kingdom.

COATES (KEN) and SILBURN (RICHARD) Adult education and social research: a case paper. Nottingham, 1968. pp. 22. *bibliog. (Nottingham. University. Department of Adult Education. Occasional Papers in Social Research. No.2)*

— — Directories.

BRITISH RESEARCH DIRECTORY OF LAW AND SOCIETY. a., current issue only kept. London.

— United States.

RAND CORPORATION. Rand 25th anniversary volume. Santa Monica, Ca., [1973]. pp. 239. *bibliog.*

SOCIAL SCIENCES.

CONFERENCE ON THE SOCIAL SCIENCES: THEIR RELATIONS IN THEORY AND IN TEACHING, LONDON, 1937. [Papers]. [London?, 1937?]. 1 vol. (variously paged).

UNITED NATIONS EDUCATIONAL, SCIENTIFIC AND CULTURAL ORGANIZATION. Reports and Papers in the Social Sciences . Paris, 1955 in progress.

PEMBERTON (JOHN E.) The national provision of printed ephemera in the social sciences; a report prepared for the Social Science and Government Committee of the Social Science Research Council. [Coventry], 1971. fo. 56. *(University of Warwick. Library. Occasional Publications. No. 1)*

BELIN-MILLERON (JEAN) Sciences humaines en dialogue. [Brussels, 1972]. pp. 189. *(Brussels. Université Libre. Institut de Sociologie. Sociologie Générale et Philosophie Sociale)*

CENTRE INTERNATIONAL DE SYNTHÈSE. Semaine de Synthèse, 29e, 1970. Le droit, les sciences humaines et la philosophie: communications et échanges de vues. Paris, 1973. pp. 405.

NATANSON (MAURICE) ed. Phenomenology and the social sciences. Evanston, 1973. 2 vols. *bibliogs. (Northwestern University. Studies in Phenomenology and Existential Philosophy)*

NEURATH (OTTO) Empiricism and sociology; [selections from his writings]; edited by Marie Neurath and Robert S. Cohen; with a selection of biographical and autobiographical sketches. Dordrecht, [1973]. pp. 473. *bibliog.*

SOZIALWISSENSCHAFTEN im Dienste der Wirtschaftspolitik: Wilhelm Bickel zum 70.Geburtstag; herausgegeben von Heinz Haller [and others]. Tübingen, [1973]. pp. 415. *bibliog. In German or English.*

ON the beginning of social inquiry; [by] Peter McHugh [and others]. London, 1974. pp. 184.

See also INFORMATION STORAGE AND RETRIEVAL SYSTEMS — Social sciences.

— Bibliography.

UNIVERSITY OF BATH. Library. Design of Information Systems in the Social Sciences. Working Papers. No. 7. Size and growth of monograph literature, with particular reference to the social sciences. Bath, 1974. 1 vol. (various pagings).

— Computer programs.

COMPUTERGUIDE 3: programs for social scientists: social data analysis programs in the UK; by J.Clyde Mitchell [and others]. Manchester, [1972]. pp. 88. *(National Computing Centre. Computers and the Professional)*

— History.

BOSTON COLLOQUIUM FOR THE PHILOSOPHY OF SCIENCE. Proceedings, 1969- 1972. Boston studies in the philosophy of science, vol. 14: methodological and historical essays in the natural and social sciences; edited by Robert S. Cohen and Marx W. Wartofsky. Dordrecht, [1974]. pp. 405. *bibliogs.*

— Mathematical models.

BARTHOLOMEW (DAVID JOHN) Stochastic models for social processes. 2nd ed. London, 1973. pp. 411. *bibliog.*

CONFERENCE ON STRUCTURAL EQUATION MODELS, UNIVERSITY OF WISCONSIN, 1970. Structural equation models in the social sciences; edited by Arthur S. Goldberger [and] Otis Dudley Duncan. New York, 1973. pp. 358. *bibliog.*

— Methodology.

INTEGRATION of the social sciences through policy analysis: [proceedings of a conference held in Philadelphia, 1971]; editor, James C. Charlesworth. Philadelphia, 1972. pp. 229. *(American Academy of Political and Social Science. Monographs. [No.] 14)*

SHEPARD (ROGER N.) and others, eds. Multidimensional scaling: theory and applications in the behavioral sciences. New York, 1972 repr. 1973. 2 vols. *bibliogs.*

CAPORASO (JAMES A.) and ROOS (LESLIE L.) eds. Quasi-experimental approaches: testing theory and evaluating policy. Evanston, 1973. pp. 368. *bibliog.*

LEVIN (JACK) Statistician. Elementary statistics in social research. New York, [1973]. pp. 279. *bibliog.*

McKINNEY (DAVID W.) The authoritarian personality studies: an inquiry into the failure of social science research to produce demonstrable knowledge. The Hague, 1973. pp. 304. *bibliogs.*

MELANGES en l'honneur de Fernand Braudel. Toulouse, [1973]. 2 vols. *bibliog. In various languages.*

PENNEY (G.) ed. Computers in the social sciences: a studyguide. Manchester, [1973]. pp. 48. *bibliog.*

U.K. Social Science Research Council. Panel on Computing and the Social Sciences. 1973. Computing and the social sciences: a report to the SSRC. London, [1973]. fo. 26.

BOSTON COLLOQUIUM FOR THE PHILOSOPHY OF SCIENCE. Proceedings, 1969- 1972. Boston studies in the philosophy of science, vol. 14: methodological and historical essays in the natural and social sciences; edited by Robert S. Cohen and Marx W. Wartofsky. Dordrecht, [1974]. pp. 405. *bibliogs.*

BRIER (ALAN) and ROBINSON (IAN) Lecturer in Sociology, Brunel University. Computers and the social sciences. London, 1974. pp. 285. *bibliogs.*

— Periodicals.

UNIVERSITY OF BATH. Library. Design of Information Systems in the Social Sciences. Working Papers. No. 5. Citation patterns in the social sciences: results of pilot citation study and selection of source journals for main citation study. [Bath], 1972. 1 vol. (various pagings).

— Philosophy.

RUNCIMAN (WALTER GARRISON) A critique of Max Weber's philosophy of social science. Cambridge, 1972 repr. 1973. pp. 106.

— Statistical methods.

BARTHOLOMEW (DAVID JOHN) Social probability: an inaugural lecture. [London, 1974]. pp. 19. *bibliog.*

KOHOUT (FRANK J.) Statistics for social scientists: a coordinated learning system. New York, [1974]. pp. 452.

— Study and teaching — Denmark.

SAMFUNDSVIDENSKABELIG teori og metode: rapport fra konferencen afholdt den 25. november 1971 af Udvalget for Samfundsvidenskabelige Basisuddannelser. [Copenhagen], 1972. pp. 146.

— — France.

CLARK (TERRY NICHOLS) Prophets and patrons: the French university and the emergence of the social sciences. Cambridge, Mass., 1973. pp. 282.

— — United Kingdom.

MARSH (ALAN) Postgraduate students' assessment of their social science training: a survey of the attitudes of SSRC-supported students towards their postgraduate training. London, Social Science Research Council Survey Unit, 1972. pp. 104. *(Occasional Papers in Survey Research.2)*

— Terminology.

ORGANISATION FOR ECONOMIC CO-OPERATION AND DEVELOPMENT. Development Centre. 1972. Macrothesaurus: a basic list of economic and social development terms. Paris, 1972. pp. 457.

SOCIAL SCIENTISTS.

MANenvironment - a better fit?: is there a role for the social scientist?; [edited by Dennis Donnelly; a conference under the auspices of the Occupational Section of the British Psychological Society...Oxford...1973. Birmingham, 1974. pp. 104,2. *(Birmingham. University. Centre for Urban and Regional Studies. Research Memoranda. No.26)*

SOCIAL SECURITY TAXES

— Denmark.

BETAENKNING vedrorende bidragsfonden; afgivet af en arbejdsgruppe nedsat af Socialministeriet. København, 1971. pp. 35. *(Denmark. Betaenkninger. Nr. 611)*

SOCIAL SERVICE.

WORLD HEALTH ORGANIZATION. Public Health Papers. Geneva, 1959 in progress.

MULLEN (EDWARD J.) and DUMPSON (JAMES R.) Evaluation of social intervention. San Francisco, 1972. pp. 267. *bibliog.*

SAVY (ROBERT) Social security in agriculture and rural areas. Geneva, International Labour Office, 1972. pp. 268. *bibliog. (Studies and Reports. New Series. No. 78)*

CASEWORK within social work; [by] Helen H. Perlman [and others; papers of a study conference held at the Department of Social Studies, University of Newcastle upon Tyne, 1972]; Graham Parker, editor. Newcastle upon Tyne, 1973. pp. 42.

GOLDSTEIN (HOWARD) Social work practice: a unitary approach. Columbia, S.C., 1973. pp. 288. *bibliog.*

FORDER (ROBERT ANTHONY DUNSTAN) Concepts in social administration: a framework for analysis. London, 1974. pp. 186.

HALL (ANTHONY S.) and ALGIE (JIMMY) A management game for social services. London, [1974]. pp. 55.

— Research.

SEMINAR ON SOCIAL WELFARE RESEARCH, LONDON, 1970. Report. [London], Council for Training in Social Work, [1970]. pp. 8. *bibliog.*

— Canada — Manitoba.

BARBER (CLARENCE LYLE) Welfare policy in Manitoba; a report to the Planning and Priorities Committee of Cabinet Secretariat, province of Manitoba. Winnipeg, 1972. pp. 74.

SOCIAL SERVICE.

— — **New Brunswick.**

NEW BRUNSWICK. Department of Social Services. Annual report. a., 1971/2- Fredericton, N.B. *In English and French.*

— — **Communist countries.**

NIEDUSZYŃSKI (MIECZYSŁAW) Analiza nakładów na usługi socjalne w krajach RWPG. Warszawa, 1973. pp. 303. *bibliog. With Russian and English summaries.*

— **Denmark.**

BETAENKNING om rådgivning inden for det sociale område; afgivet af et af Socialministeren nedsat udvalg. København, 1971. pp. 83. *(Denmark. Betaenkninger. Nr. 619)*

— **Europe.**

UNITED NATIONS. Department of Economic and Social Affairs. European Social Development Programme. Reports . New York, 1967 in progress.

— **Finland.**

LEHTO (MARKKU) Huoltoavun alueellinen vaihtelu, 1969, etc. Helsinki, 1972. pp. 153. *bibliog. (Finland. Suomen Virallinen Tilasto. Finlands Officiella Statistik. 32. Sosiaalisia Erikoistutkimuksia. 27) With English summary.*

— **Finland — Finance.**

LEHTO (MARKKU) Kuntien sosiaalihuollon menot 1969, etc. Helsinki, 1972. pp. 156. *bibliog. (Finland. Suomen Virallinen Tilasto. Finlands Officiella Statistik. 32. Sosiaalisia Erikoistutkimuksia. 29)*

— **France.**

FRANCE. Ministère de la Santé Publique et de la Sécurité Sociale. Direction de l'Administration Générale, du Personnel et du Budget. Division de la Documentation Générale, des Publications et de la Bibliothèque. 1971. La protection sanitaire et sociale en France. [Paris, 1971]. pp. 191.

FRANCE. Secretariat d'Etat à l'Action Sociale et à la Réadaptation. 1973. La prévention des inadaptations sociales: etudes de R[ationalisation des] C[hoix] B[udgétaires]. Paris, 1973. pp. 286. *bibliog.*

— **India.**

INDIAN CONFERENCE OF SOCIAL WORK. The social work forum 1947-1957: being a selective rendering of social work thought as reflected in the deliberations of the annual sessions of the... conference... between the years 1947-1957; [edited by M.S. Gore and others]. Bombay, 1958. pp. 320.

DUBEY (S.N.) Administration of social welfare programmes in India. Bombay, [1973]. pp. 214. *bibliogs. (Tata Institute of Social Sciences. Tata Institute of Social Sciences Series. No.27)*

— **Macao.**

SILVA (RODRIGUES DA) Assistência em Macau. [Macao, Imprensa Nacional], 1954. pp. 82.

— **Malta.**

MALTA. Charitable Institutions Committee. 1921. Charitable institutions; report; [A. Mercieca, chairman]. [Valletta], 1921. pp. 35. *(Malta. Government Gazette. Supplements. No.56)*

— **Netherlands.**

NETHERLANDS. Adviescommissie Voorlichting Algemene Bijstandswet. 1971. Rapport. 's- Gravenhage, 1971. pp. 108.

HAAK (C.P.M.VAN DER) Bekendmaken en bekend raken: evaluatie van de eerste vijf jaar overheidsvoorlichting over de Algemene Bijstandswet, 1962-1967, etc. 's-Gravenhage, Staatsuitgeverij, 1972. pp. 279. *bibliog. With English summary.*

— **New Zealand.**

NEW ZEALAND. Department of Social Welfare. Report. a., 1972/3 [1st]- Wellington.

— **Norway.**

NORWAY. Sosialreformkomitéen. 1972. Sosiale tjenester: utredning om de sosiale tjenester og det sosiale hjelpeapparat på kommune- og fylkesplanet: innstilling 2 fra Sosialreformkomiteen, etc. Oslo, 1972. pp. 171. *(Norway. Norges Offentlige Utredninger. 1972. 30)*

— **Poland.**

ROSNER (JAN) ed. Polityka społeczna i służby społeczne w PRL. Warszawa, 1972. pp. 439. *bibliog. (Towarzystwo Wolnej Wszechnicy Polskiej. Komisja Naukowo-Badawsza. Studia z Pedagogiki Społecznej i Polityki Społecznej. t.2)*

— **Portugal.**

PORTUGAL. Presidência do Conselho. 1953. 25 anos de administração publica: Ministerio do Interior. Lisboa, 1953. pp. 67.

— **Sweden.**

BREMBERG (LARS) Rätten till trygghet: debattbok om socialvårdens framtid. Stockholm, 1972. pp. 204.

— **United Kingdom.**

GRANT (CLARA ELLEN) From 'me' to 'we': forty years on Bow Common. London, [c.1940]. pp. 197.

TITMUSS (RICHARD MORRIS) Social administration in a changing society: (an inaugural lecture delivered...at the London School of Economics and Political Science...May 1951). [London], 1951. pp. 183-197. *(Offprint from British Journal of Sociology, vol. 2, no. 3, September 1951)*

HOLMAN (ROBERT) ed. Socially deprived families in Britain; (reprinted with supplement). London, 1970. repr. 1973. pp. 235, 28.

HILLINGDON. Social Services Department. Levels of service: a study of the current provision of social services in the London borough of Hillingdon; [study carried out by John Jevons]. [Hillingdon], 1972. pp. 130.

COVENTRY. Social Services Department. Helping people in need: (a manual of advice on welfare benefits in Coventry. a., My 1973 (2nd ed.)- Coventry.

EAST SUFFOLK. Social Services Committee. Social services: ten-year development plans 1973/83. [Ipswich], 1973. 1 pamphlet (unpaged).

BROWN (MALCOLM J.) ed. Social issues and the social services. London, 1974. pp. 251. *bibliogs.*

BRUNEL UNIVERSITY. Social Services Organization Research unit. Social services departments: developing patterns of work and organization;...principal contributors, Ralph Rowbottom [and others]. London, 1974. pp. 298. *bibliog.*

CUNNINGHAM (JOHN) Developments in social work; [published in conjunction with a BBC television series]; edited by John Brooke and John Radcliffe. London, 1974. pp. 64. *bibliog.*

KLEIN (RUDOLF EWALD) and HALL (PHOEBE) Caring for quality in the caring services: options for future policy. London, [1974]. pp. 47. *bibliog. (Centre for Studies in Social Policy. Doughty Street Papers. No. 2)*

MANAGEMENT in the social services: the team leader's task; a symposium of original papers [of a conference held at the University College of North Wales, Bangor in 1973]; edited by Rolf Olsen. Bangor, [1974]. pp. 101. *(Wales. University. University College of North Wales. Department of Social Theory and Institutions. Occasional Papers. No.1)*

MANAGEMENT in the social and safety services: (contributions to a seminar organised by the Faculty of Social Sciences of Canterbury, [1974]. pp. 149. Edinburgh University... 1972); edited by W.D. Reekie and Norman C. Hunt. London, 1974. pp. 198. *bibliogs. (Edinburgh. University. Faculty of Social Sciences. Seminars Committee. Social Issues in the Seventies. 3)*

NATIONAL INSTITUTE FOR SOCIAL WORK TRAINING. An introductory account 1961-1974. London, [1974]. pp. 32.

P.A. MANAGEMENT CONSULTANTS LTD. Economic Studies Division. An evaluation of future social services expenditure on behalf of the city of Leicester. [London, 1974]. pp. 157.

WESTMINSTER. Department of Architecture and Planning. Social and community services. London, [1974]. pp. 109. *(Westminster Development Plan Publications. Topic Papers. T2)*

— — **Directories.**

LIVERPOOL. Liverpool Council of Social Service. Social and community services: community work and education for adults; the N.O.C. handbook, editor Robin Little. Liverpool, 1973. pp. 33.

UNCAREERS. Directory of alternative work. rev. ed. Birmingham, 1973. pp. 40.

— — **Public opinion.**

HILLINGDON. Social Services Department. Report on a pilot survey to examine the publics' awareness of and attitude towards the Social Services Department. [London], 1973. fo. 29,5.

— — **Societies, etc.**

SHELTER HOUSING AID CENTRE, [EDINBURGH]. Progress report 1973: 2000 and on. Edinburgh, 1973. pp. 15.

— — **Statistics.**

U.K. Department of Health and Social Security. Statistics and Research Division. 1973. Local authority social services departments: aids to households: details of certain assistance provided to households by social services departments during the 12 months ending 31 March 1973: England. [London], 1973. pp. 74.

— — **Scotland.**

SCOTLAND. Scottish Office. Social Work Services Group. 1971. Social Work (Scotland) Act, 1968: proposals for developement of social work services. [Edinburgh, 1971]. fo. 60.

SCOTLAND. Scottish Office. Social Work Services Group 1971. Future developement of social work services. Edinburgh, 1971. fo. 3.(Circulars. No. SW 25/1971)

— — — **Societies, etc.**

SHELTER HOUSING AID CENTRE, [GLASGOW]. Report. Glasgow, [1973]. 1 vol. (unpaged).

— **United States.**

AMERICAN ENTERPRISE INSTITUTE FOR PUBLIC POLICY RESEARCH. Legislative Analyses. 92nd Congress. No. 4. Welfare reform proposals. Washington, D.C., 1971. pp. 102.

GARCIA OLIVERO (CARMEN SYLVIA) Study of the initial involvement in the social services by the Puerto Rican migrants in Philadelphia. New York, 1968 [or rather 1971]. pp. 316. *bibliog.*

THIEBLOT (ARMAND J.) and COWIN (RONALD M.) Welfare and strikes: the use of public funds to support strikers. Philadelphia, [1972]. pp. 276. *(Pennsylvania University. Wharton School of Finance and Commerce. Industrial Research Unit. Labor Relations and Public Policy Series. Reports. No. 6)*

CITIZEN organizations: increasing client control over services; prepared for the Department of Health, Education and Welfare [by] Robert K. Yin [and others]. Santa Monica, 1973. pp. 215. *(Rand Corporation. [Rand Reports]. 1196)*

FEDERICO (RONALD C.) The social welfare institution: an introduction. Lexington, [1973]. pp. 224.

GOLDENBERG (I. IRA) ed. The helping professions in the world of action. Lexington, [1973]. pp. 273. *bibliogs.*

SOCIAL SERVICE. (Cont.)

KAHN (ALFRED J.) ed. Shaping the new social work. New York, 1973. pp. 221. *(Columbia University. School of Social Work. Social Work and Social Issues. [vol. 3])*

NATIONAL ASSOCIATION OF SOCIAL WORKERS. Professional Symposium, 3rd, New Orleans, 1972. Social work practice and social justice...; selected papers [from the]...symposium...; Bernard Ross and Charles Shireman, editors. Washington, [1973]. pp. 152.

NATIONAL CONFERENCE OF LAWYERS AND SOCIAL WORKERS. Law and social work: statements. Washington, [1973]. pp. 56.

GOTTLIEB (NAOMI) The welfare bind. New York, 1974. pp. 206.

TRATTNER (WALTER I.) From poor law to welfare state: a history of social welfare in America. New York, [1974]. pp. 276. *bibliogs.*

— — California.

SONENBLUM (SIDNEY) and others. Program budgeting for urban health and welfare services, with special reference to Los Angeles. New York, 1974. pp. 226. *(California University. Institute of Government and Public Affairs. Local Government Program Budgeting Series)*

— — Massachusetts.

SAHLEIN (WILLIAM J.) A neighbourhood solution to the social services dilemma. Lexington, Mass., [1973]. pp. 120.

SOCIAL SETTLEMENTS.

JENNINGS (HILDA) University Settlement Bristol: sixty years of change, 1911- 1971. Bristol, [1973]. pp. 64.

SOCIAL SURVEYS.

SOCIAL AND COMMUNITY PLANNING RESEARCH. Survey research and privacy: report of a working party. London, [1973]. fo. 61. *bibliog.*

TRANSGAARD (HENNING) The cognitive component of attitudes and beliefs: structure and empirical methods: a review of some conceptualizations and of some empirical methods for discovering and assigning structure. København, 1973. pp. 89. *(Socialforskningsinstituttet. Studier. Nr. 27)*

CICOUREL (AARON VICTOR) Theory and method in a study of Argentine fertility. New York, [1974]. pp. 212. *bibliog.*

— India.

SEMINAR ON DATA COLLECTION TECHNIQUES IN THE NATIONAL SAMPLE SURVEY, CALCUTTA, 1969. Proceedings...; edited by M.N. Murthy. [New Delhi, 1971]. pp. 318. *bibliogs.*

— Scandinavia.

KATA (KEIJO) and UUSITALO (HANNU) On the data, sampling and representativeness of the Scandinavian survey [on welfare, need-satisfaction and mental health] in 1972. Helsinki, 1974. pp. 64. *(Helsinki. Yliopisto. Research Group for Comparative Sociology. Research Reports. No.4)*

— United Kingdom.

HOINVILLE (GERALD) and JOWELL (ROGER) Classification manual for household interview surveys in Great Britain. 2nd ed. London, 1971. pp. 73.

U.K. Social Survey. [Reports. New Series.] 457. The general household survey: introductory report; an inter-departmental survey sponsored by the Central Statistical Office; [by Louis Moss and others]. London, 1973. pp. 371,191.

SOCIOLOGICAL theory and survey research: institutional change and social policy in Great Britain: [papers of a seminar held in London 1972-73, sponsored by the Survey Unit of the Social Science Research Council]; edited by Timothy Leggatt. London, [1974]. pp. 334. *bibliogs.*

— United States.

HIRSCHI (TRAVIS) and SELVIN (HANAN CHARLES) Principles of survey analysis; formerly titled Delinquency research. 2nd ed. New York, 1973. pp. 280.

WEBB (KENNETH) and HATRY (HARRY P.) Obtaining citizen feedback: the application of citizen surveys to local governments. Washington, D.C., [1973]. pp. 105. *bibliog.*

— West Cameroon.

LAGERBERG (CORNELIS SERAFINUS IGNATIUS JOANNES) and WILMS (G.J.) Profile of a commercial town in West-Cameroon: research findings of a socio-anthropological enquire [sic] in Kumba. Tilburg, 1974. pp. 76. *(Tilburg. Katholieke Hogeschool. Tilburg Institute of Development Research. Studies on Development Research. 1)*

SOCIAL WORK AS A PROFESSION.

KAHN (ALFRED J.) ed. Shaping the new social work. New York, 1973. pp. 221. *(Columbia University. School of Social Work. Social Work and Social Issues. [vol. 3])*

SIMONOT (MICHEL) Les animateurs socio-culturels: étude d'une aspiration à une activité sociale. Paris, [1974]. pp. 238. *bibliog. (Rouen. Université. Publications. Série des Sciences du Comportement et de l'Education. 22)*

SOCIAL WORK EDUCATION

— Norway.

NORWAY. Rådet for Sosialarbeiderutdanning. 1970. Utredning om videreutdanning av sosionomer. Otta, 1970. pp. 92.

— United Kingdom.

TITMUSS (RICHARD MORRIS) Social administration in a changing society: (an inaugural lecture delivered...at the London School of Economics and Political Science...May 1951). [London], 1951. pp. 183-197. *(Offprint from British Journal of Sociology, vol. 2, no. 3, September 1951)*

COUNCIL FOR TRAINING IN SOCIAL WORK [U.K.]. Criteria for assessment of fieldwork. [London, 1968]. pp. 5.

VALK (M.A.) The place of fieldwork in the assessment of students in social work training; (paper...read before C[ertificate in] S[ocial] W[ork] tutors' annual conference...1967. [London], Council for Training in Social Work, [1968?] . pp. 10.

CENTRAL TRAINING COUNCIL IN CHILD CARE [U.K.]. Study Group on Fieldwork Training. 1st report. [London], 1970. pp. 24.

CENTRAL TRAINING COUNCIL IN CHILD CARE [U.K.]. Study Group on Fieldwork Training. Community placements: some experiments in social work education. [London], 1970. pp. 36. *(Discussion Papers. No. 4)*

CENTRAL TRAINING COUNCIL IN CHILD CARE [U.K.]. Study Group on Fieldwork Training. Playgroups: the development of dual purpose groups in social work education. [London], 1970. fo. 12. *(Discussion Papers. No. 3)*

CENTRAL TRAINING COUNCIL IN CHILD CARE [U.K.]. Study Group on Fieldwork Training. The residential placement in the training of social workers. [London], 1970. fo. 24. *(Discussion Papers. No. 2)*

CENTRAL TRAINING COUNCIL IN CHILD CARE [U.K.]. Study Group on Fieldwork Training. The structure of courses: some implications for the patterns of fieldwork training. [London], 1970. pp. 24. *(Discussion Papers. No. 1)*

CENTRAL TRAINING COUNCIL IN CHILD CARE [U.K.]. Study Group on Fieldwork Training. Working with groups: the development of experience in group work as a basic part of social work education. [London], 1970. pp. 32. *(Discussion Papers. No. 5)*

WRIGHT (REG. C.) Changing patterns in social work education; (with A curriculum discussion paper: the principles and practice of social work). [London, Council for Training in Social Work, 1970?]. pp. 2, 8.

CENTRAL TRAINING COUNCIL IN CHILD CARE [U.K.]. Study Group on Fieldwork Training. The supervision of fieldwork practice: some aspects of its adaptation to new developments in social work education. [London], 1971. pp. 39. *(Discussion Papers. No. 6)*

STUDY GROUP ON PLACEMENTS IN RESIDENTIAL ESTABLISHMENTS [U.K.]. Practical work placements in residential child care establishments as a resource in social work education; report; [K.M. Griffiths, chairman]. [London], Central Training Council in Child Care, 1971. pp. 28.

VALK (M.A.) The development of creativity in social work student training; based on material for a talk given to the Association of Tutors to Certificate in Social Work and Residential Social Work Courses. [London, Central Council for Education and Training in Social Work, 1972?]. pp. 20.

WORKING PARTY ON CRITERIA FOR SELECTION FOR QUALIFYING RESIDENTIAL CHILD CARE COURSES [U.K.]. Criteria for selection for qualifying residential child care courses; report; [Barbara Chumbley, chairman]. [London], Central Training Council in Child Care, 1972. pp. 40. *bibliog.*

WORKING PARTY ON EDUCATION FOR RESIDENTIAL SOCIAL WORK[U.K.]. Training for residential work; a new pattern suggested by the... party...with implications for training and education in the entire social services field. [London], 1973. fo. 61.

CENTRAL COUNCIL FOR EDUCATION AND TRAINING IN SOCIAL WORK [U.K.]. Social work: the way into the job. London, 1973. pp. 11. *(Leaflets. 1)*

CENTRAL COUNCIL FOR EDUCATION AND TRAINING IN SOCIAL WORK [U.K.]. Social work: setting the course for social work education, 1971- 1973. London, 1973. pp. 36. *(Reports. 1)*

CENTRAL COUNCIL FOR EDUCATION AND TRAINING IN SOCIAL WORK [U.K.]. Social work: the pattern of professional training. London, 1973. pp. 36. *(Leaflets. 2)*

CENTRAL COUNCIL FOR EDUCATION AND TRAINING IN SOCIAL WORK [U.K.]. Social work: the Central Council for Education and Training in Social Work. London, 1973. pp. 12. *(Leaflets. 3)*

WORKING PARTY ON EDUCATION FOR RESIDENTIAL SOCIAL WORK [U.K.]. Synopsis of discussion document...: Training for residential work: a new pattern suggested by the Working Party..., with implications for training and education in the entire social services field; [Denis Allen, chairman]. [London], Central Council for Education and Training in Social Work, 1973. fo. 8.

NATIONAL INSTITUTE FOR SOCIAL WORK TRAINING. An introductory account 1961-1974. London, [1974]. pp. 32.

SOCIAL WORK WITH CHILDREN

— United Kingdom.

U.K. Social Work Service. Development Group. 1973. Intermediate treatment project: an account of a project set up to demonstrate some ways of providing intermediate treatment. London, 1973. pp. 61. *bibliog.*

SOCIAL WORK WITH DELINQUENTS AND CRIMINALS

— Israel.

ACTION-RESEARCH PROJECT ON DELINQUENT STREET-CORNER GROUPS. Final report, research project on forces acting in street corner groups. vol.1. Jerusalem, 1967. fo. 221.

— United Kingdom.

U.K. Social Work Service. Development Group. 1973. Intermediate treatment project: an account of a project set up to demonstrate some ways of providing intermediate treatment. London, 1973. pp.61. *bibliog.*

— United States — Massachusetts.

CLOSING correctional institutions: new strategies for youth services; edited by Yitzhak Bakal. Lexington, Mass., [1973]. pp. 186. *bibliogs.*

SOCIAL WORK WITH SINGLE PEOPLE

— United Kingdom.

MATTHEWS (GORDON) Knowhere to go : (social services for the single homeless). Canterbury, [1974]. pp. 149.

SOCIAL WORK WITH THE BLIND

— United Kingdom.

SEMINAR ON SOCIAL WORK WITH BLIND PEOPLE AND THEIR FAMILIES, LONDON, 1970. Social work with blind people and their families; report. London, Council for Training in Social Work, [1971?]. pp. 11.

SOCIAL WORK WITH THE PHYSICALLY HANDICAPPED

— United Kingdom.

SEMINAR ON SOCIAL WORK WITH THE PHYSICALLY HANDICAPPED, LONDON, 1969. Social work with handicapped people; report. London, Council for Training in Social Work, [1969]. fo. 12.

SOCIAL WORK WITH YOUTH

— Norway.

NORWAY. Utredningskomitéen for Ungdomsarbeidet. 1971. Innstilling om ungdomsarbeidet i Norge. Oslo, 1971. pp. 146. *bibliog.*

— United Kingdom.

WORKING PARTY ON YOUTH AND ADULT SERVICES IN INNER LONDON. Report: (a chance to choose); [the Earl of Longford, chairman]. London, Inner London Education Authority, [1972]. pp. 97.

OXFORD (ALEC) Implications of youth work in Asian community: report of a conference organised by the National Association of Indian Youth,...Birmingham...1973. [Leicester], 1973. pp. 49. *(Youth Service Information Centre. Occasional Papers. 7)*

U.K. Central Office of Information. Reference Division. 1973. The youth service in Britain. London, 1973. pp. 30. *bibliog.*

HARKER (IAN) People adrift: a report on the activities of the Blenheim Project up to 1973. London, 1974. pp. 73.

— United States.

BANNON (JOSEPH J.) ed. Outreach: extending community service in urban areas. Springfield, Ill., [1973]. pp. 219. *bibliogs.*

SOCIAL WORKERS

— In—service training — United Kingdom.

CENTRAL TRAINING COUNCIL IN CHILD CARE [U.K.]. staff development and in-service study. Paper 2. Unqualified entrants and trainee social workers. [London, 1970]. pp. 16.

COUNCIL FOR TRAINING IN SOCIAL WORK [U.K.]. Graduate trainees in the health and welfare services. London, 1970. pp. (7). *(Discussion Papers. No.3)*

CENTRAL TRAINING COUNCIL IN CHILD CARE [U.K.]. Staff development and in-service study. Paper 3. Continuing needs for professional development. [London, 1971]. pp. 15.

WORKING PARTY ON THE STAFF DEVELOPMENT NEEDS OF RESIDENTIAL CHILD CARE STAFF WITHOUT PROFESSIONAL TRAINING [U.K.]. Draft report on progress of Working Party up to August 1971 for submission to the Central Council for Education and Training in Social Work; [J.R. Howells, chairman]. [London], Central Training Council in Child Care, [1971]. 1 pamphlet (various pagings).

CENTRAL COUNCIL FOR EDUCATION AND TRAINING IN SOCIAL WORK [U.K.]. Social work: creating opportunities for staff development. London, 1973. pp. 8. *(Papers. 1)*

CENTRAL COUNCIL FOR EDUCATION AND TRAINING IN SOCIAL WORK [U.K.]. Social work: in service study scheme for residential staff. London, 1973. pp. 22. *(Papers. 2)*

— France.

COURTECUISSE (N.) and BRAMS (LUCIEN) Les assistantes de service social 1970: contribution à la sociologie d'une profession. Le Vésinet, Division de la Recherche Médico-Sociale, [1972]. pp. 202. *bibliog.*

SIMONOT (MICHEL) Les animateurs socio-culturels: étude d'une aspiration à une activité sociale. Paris, [1974]. pp. 238. *bibliog. (Rouen. Université. Publications. Série des Sciences du Comportement et de l'Education. 22)*

— United Kingdom.

CARVER (VIDA) and EDWARDS (J.L.) Social workers and their workloads: the report of an investigation into work time and work patterns of 572 social work personnel employed in the health and/or welfare departments of 18 local authorities in England and Wales, etc. London, [1972]. pp. 84.

PARR (JOHN) First jobs: a study of students' experiences in applying for posts in the community and youth service. Birmingham, 1972. 1 pamphlet (unpaged). *(Westhill College of Education. Westhill Occasional Papers. No. 18)*

— — Ireland, Northern.

WALKER (REA) and others. Social workers and their workloads in Northern Ireland welfare departments. [London, 1972]. pp. 56, fo. xx. *bibliog.*

SOCIALISM.

SOZIALDEMOKRATISCHE Bibliothek: Sammlung von Abhandlungen über Theorie und Geschichte des Sozialismus; (unveränderter fotomechanischer Nachdruck der Originalausgabe 1885-(90), [containing 36 pamphlets]). Leipzig, 1971. 3 vols.

SPARGO (JOHN) The common sense of socialism: a series of letters addressed to Jonathan Edwards of Pittsburg. Chicago, 1911. pp. 184.

GREULICH (HERMAN) Vor hundert Jahren und heute: die Revolution des Bürgertums und der Befreiungskampf der arbeitenden Klasse; Vortrag, gehalten an der Märzfeier 1895 in Bern. 2nd ed. Zürich, 1912. pp. 31.

LASSALLE (FERDINAND JOHANN GOTTLIEB) Arbeiter-Programm: über den besonderen Zusammenhang der gegenwärtigen Geschichtsperiode mit der Idee des Arbeiterstandes;...herausgegeben von Eduard Bernstein. Berlin, 1919. pp. 47.

NEURATH (OTTO) Vollsozialisierung und Arbeiterorganisation: Vortrag, gehalten in der Reichenberger Turnhalle am 28.Juni 1920. Reichenberg, [1920]. pp. 27.

GRAF (GEORG ENGELBERT) Was muss der Arbeiter vom Kapitalismus una Sozialismus wissen?: Leitsätze. 3rd ed. Elberfeld, [1923]. pp. 16.

WEISS (FRIEDRICH) Argumente gegen den Sozialismus: bürgerliche Fragen und sozialistische Antworten; ... herausgegeben vom Parteivorstand der Deutschen sozialdemokratischen Arbeiterpartei in der Tschechoslowakischen Republik. Prag, 1925. pp. 43.

bibliog.

GRAF (GEORG ENGELBERT) Vom Kapitalismus zum Sozialismus: Leitsätze, Geschichtszahlen, Bücherverzeichnis. Berlin, [1931]. pp. 54. *bibliog.*

COLE (GEORGE DOUGLAS HOWARD) The working-class movement and the transition to socialism. London, [1934?]. pp. 16. *(Socialist League [1932-39]. Capitalism in Crisis: Forum Series, 1933-4. No.5)*

COLE (GEORGE DOUGLAS HOWARD) Socialist economics. London, 1950. pp. 158.

COUNCIL FOR MUTUAL ECONOMIC ASSISTANCE. 1962. Basic principles of international socialist division of labour. Moscow, 1962. pp. 31.

VARGA (ISTVÁN) Wesen und Funktionen des Geldes im Sozialismus: Vortrag gehalten am 6.Juni 1961, etc. München, 1962. pp. 35. *bibliog. (Südosteuropa-Gesellschaft. Südosteuropa- Studien. 3)*

ONE WORLD ONLY, 1967. One world only: a forum on international cooperation; (editor: Klaus W. Bender). Tokyo, [1968?]. pp. 84. *(Friedrich-Ebert-Stiftung. Asian Labour Institute. Reports. 1)*

GUILLORE (RAYMOND) Les trois phases de la révolution socialiste. Paris, [1972]. pp. 64.

VERMEYLEN (PIET) Mijn socialisme. [Brussels, 1972]. pp. 147.

BAKUNIN (MIKHAIL ALEKSANDROVICH) Selected writings; edited and introduced by Arthur Lehning; translations from the French by Steven Cox; translations from the Russian by Olive Stevens. London, 1973. pp. 288. *bibliog.*

BATALOV (EDUARD IAKOVLEVICH) Filosofiia bunta: kritika ideologii levogo radikalizma. Moskva, 1973. pp. 222.

BODINGTON (STEPHEN) Computers and socialism. Nottingham, 1973. pp. 245. *bibliog.*

BOL'SHEVIZM i reformizm. Moskva, 1973. pp. 392.

BOURGIN (NICOLAS GEORGES MARIE) and RIMBERT (PIERRE) Le socialisme. 11th ed. Paris, 1973. pp. 128. *bibliog.*

CERRONI (UMBERTO) Teoria politica e socialismo. Roma, 1973. pp. 227.

NENNING (GUENTHER) Rot und realistisch: gesamtsozialistische Strategie und Sozialdemokratie. Wien, [1973]. pp. 420.

PEGUY (CHARLES) Marcel, premier dialogue de la cité harmonieuse; [first published in 1897]; accompagné d'une serie d'articles publiés en 1897 et 1898 dans La Revue socialiste. [Paris, 1973]. pp. 206.

ŠIK (OTA) Argumente für den dritten Weg. Hamburg, 1973. pp. 213.

DRU (JEAN) pseud. Besoins contradictoires et projets révolutionnaires. Paris, [1974]. pp. 212.

EINFUEHRUNG in die politische Ökonomie des Sozialismus; (Autoren: Willy Becker [and others]). Berlin, 1974. pp. 503.

GREGOR (A.JAMES) The fascist persuasion in radical politics. Princeton, [1974]. pp. 472. *bibliog.*

JOUET (MICHEL) Le socialisme se porte bien. Paris, [1974]. pp. 128.

KREISKY (BRUNO) Aspekte des demokratischen Sozialismus: Aufsätze, Reden, Interviews; mit einem Vorwort von Ossip K. Flechtheim. München, [1974]. pp. 200. *bibliog.*

LAMONT (CORLISS) Voice in the wilderness: collected essays of fifty years. Buffalo, N.Y., [1974]. pp. 327.

LAOT (LAURENT) La croissance économique en question: le socialisme nécessaire?. Paris, [1974]. pp. 199.

MERKEL (RENATE) Marx und Engels über Sozialismus und Kommunismus: zur Herausbildung der Auffassung...in der Entstehungsperiode des wissenschaftlichen Kommunismus, 1842-1846. Berlin, 1974. pp. 311.

MINC (BRONISLAW) L'économie politique du socialisme...; traduit du polonais par Anna Posner. 2nd ed. , Paris, 1974. pp. 550.

SOCIALISM. (Cont.)

MOCH (JULES) Socialisme de l'ère atomique: nouvelles confrontations. [Paris, 1974]. pp. 488. *bibliog.*

SARTRE (JEAN PAUL) Between existentialism and marxism; translated from the French by John Matthews. London, 1974. pp. 302. *Essays and interviews from Situations VIII and IX.*

SETTEMBRINI (DOMENICO) Due ipotesi per il socialismo in Marx ed Engels. Bari, 1974. pp. 317.

ŠIK (OTA) Für eine Wirtschaft ohne Dogma: [collection of three articles and four interviews]. München, [1974]. pp. 209. *bibliog.*

The SOCIALIST idea: a reappraisal; [papers of an international meeting sponsored by Weidenfeld and Nicolson and the Graduate School of Contemporary European Studies of Reading University in April 1973]; edited by Leszek Kolakowski and Stuart Hampshire. London, [1974]. pp. 272. *bibliog.*

— History.

BEER (MAX) Socialist. Social struggles and thought, 1750-1860;...translated by H.J. Stenning and revised by the author. London, 1925. pp. 218.

TORITSYN (TIMOFEI MIKHAILOVICH) Uchenie Roberta Ouena i ego vliianie nna rasprostranenie i razvitie sotsialisticheskikh idei. Riazan', 1972. pp. 174. *bibliog.*

JAHRBUCH ARBEITERBEWEGUNG. a., 1973 (Bd.1)- Frankfurt am Main.

FORMAN (JAMES D.) Socialism: its theoretical roots and present-day development. New York, 1973. pp. 129. *bibliog.*

ALVAREZ DEL VAYO (JULIO) The march of socialism;...translated by Joseph M. Bernstein. London, 1974. pp. 426.

HYAMS (EDWARD SOLOMON) The millennium postponed. London, 1974. pp. 277.

— — Bibliography.

HARMSEN (GER) Idee en beweging: bibliografiese aanwijzingen bij de studie en het onderzoek van de geschiedenis van socialisme en arbeidersbeweging in Nederland. Nijmegen, 1972. pp. 101.

— — Sources.

U.K. National Register of Archives. 1973. Archives of the Labour Party: Labour and Socialist International; listed by R.A. Storey and T.W.M. Jaine. London, 1973. fo. 132.

— Maps.

JOXE (PIERRE) Atlas du socialisme. Paris, [1973]. pp. 114.

— Societies.

SCHWEIZERISCHES SOZIALARCHIV. Jahresbericht. a., 1973- Zürich.

SOCIALISM, CHRISTIAN.

BAUER (OTTO) Christian socialist, and RAGAZ (LEONHARD) Neuer Himmel und neue Erde]: ein religiös-sozialer Aufruf. Zürich, 1938. pp. 43.

The ARUSHA declaration and Christian Socialism: six papers presented at a seminar held at University College, Dar es Salaam in 1967 following the Arusha Declaration. Dar es Salaam, 1969. pp. 54. *bibliog.*

BACKSTROM (PHILIP N.) Christian Socialism and co-operation in Victorian England: Edward Vansittart Neale and the co-operative movement. London, 1974. pp. 238. *bibliog.*

SOCIALISM AND CATHOLIC CHURCH.

DIETZ (EDUARD) Wilhelm Hohoff und der Bund katholischer Sozialisten. Karlsruhe-Rüppurr, [1928]. pp. 19. *(Bund der Religiösen Sozialisten Deutschlands. Schriften der Religiösen Sozialisten. Nr. 6)*

SOCIALISM AND EDUCATION.

LANDELIJKE WERKGROEP ANTI-AUTORITAIRE EN SOCIALISTIESE OPVOEDING. Technies Kollektief. Anti-autoritaire en socialistiese opvoeding. Nijmegen, 1970. pp. 112. *bibliog.*

KLINKENBERG (PIETER) Socialistiese opvoedings- en onderwijsdenkbeelden; [facsimile reprint of the thesis published in Amsterdam, 1933, with an updated bibliography]. Nijmegen, 1973. pp. 264. *bibliog.*

STREITHOFEN (HEINRICH B.) SPD und katholische Kirche: eine Untersuchung über das Kirchenbild des Vorwärts. Stuttgart, [1974]. pp. 87. *(Institut für Gesellschaftswissenschaften Walberberg. Walberberger Gespräche)*

SOCIALISM AND RELIGION.

WENDEL (HERMANN MAX CARL LUDWIG) C Sozialdemokratie und antikirchliche Propaganda: ein erweiterter Vortrag. Leipzig, 1907. pp. 31.

SOCIALISM AND YOUTH.

BOEHNY (FERDINAND) Die sozialistische Jugendbewegung des Ersten Weltkrieges als politischer Faktor. ?bASEL[, 1964]. PP. 14. *(sONDERDRUCK AUS DEM oEFFENTLICHEN dIENST, jAHRGANG 1964, nRN.45 BIS 49)*

ECKERT (RAINER) and SEIDERER (AXEL) Sozialdemokratie und Jungsozialisten: Politik, Programm und Gesellschaftstheorie; eine marxistische Kritik. Frankfurt/Main, 1974. pp. 194.

SOCIALISM IN AUSTRIA.

PROFT (GABRIELE) Der Weg zu uns'.: die Frauenfrage im neuen Österreich. Wien, [1945]. pp. 24. *(Sozialistische Partei Österreichs. Sozialistische Hefte. Folge 4)*

LESER (NORBERT) Zwischen Reformismus und Bolschewismus: der Austromarxismus als Theorie und Praxis. Wien, [1968]. pp. 600.

HAUTMANN (HANS) and KROPF (RUDOLF) Die österreichische Arbeiterbewegung vom Vormärz bis 1945: sozialökonomische Ursprünge ihrer Ideologie und Politik. Wien, [1974]. pp. 214. *bibliog.* *(Ludwig-Boltzmann-Institut für Geschichte der Arbeiterbewegung. Schriftenreihe. 4)*

SOCIALISM IN BANGLADESH.

INTERNATIONAL ECONOMIC ASSOCIATION. Conference, [1973?], Dacca. The economic development of Bangladesh within a socialist framework: proceedings of a conference...; edited by E.A.G. Robinson and Keith Griffin. London, 1974. pp. 330.

SOCIALISM IN BELGIUM.

GROUPE B/Y. Quelle Wallonie? Quel socialisme?: les bases d'un rassemblement des progressistes. Liège, [1971]. pp. 234.

WEERDT (DENISE DE) De Belgische socialistische arbeidersbeweging op zoek naar een eigen vorm, 1872-1880. Antwerpen, [1972]. pp. 188. bibliog.

SOCIALISM IN BOLIVIA.

MAROF (TRISTAN) pseud. [i.e. Gustavo Adolfo NAVARRO] La verdaddd socialista en Bolivia. La Paz, 1938. pp. 96.

SOCIALISM IN CANADA.

COMMUNIST PARTY OF CANADA. The road to socialism in Canada: the program of the Communist party of Canada. Toronto, 1972. pp. 70.

SOCIALISM IN CHILE.

ALLENDE (SALVADOR) Chile's road to socialism;...edited by Joan E. Garces; translated by J.Darling. Harmondsworth, 1973. pp. 208.

MOSS (ROBERT) Chile's marxist experiment. Newton Abbot, [1973]. pp. 225. *bibliog.*

NAJMAN (MAURICE) ed. Le Chili est proche: révolution et contre-révolution dans le Chili de l'Unité populaire: textes. Paris, 1974. pp. 310.

RAPTIS (MICHEL) Revolution and counter-revolution in Chile: a dossier on workers' participation in the revolutionary process; translated by John Simmonds. London, [1974]. pp. 174.

WHITEHEAD (LAURENCE) The lesson of Chile. London, 1974. pp. 40. *(Fabian Society. Research Series. [No.] 317)*

SOCIALISM IN CUBA.

DUMONT (RENÉ) Is Cuba socialist?...translated by Stanley Hochman. London, 1974. pp. 159.

SOCIALISM IN CZECHOSLOVAKIA.

BACHSTEIN (MARTIN K.) Wenzel Jaksch und die sudetendeutsche Sozialdemokratie. München, 1974. pp. 306. *bibliog.* *(Ludwigshafen. Collegium Carolinum. Veröffentlichungen. Band 29)*

SOCIALISM IN EUROPE.

PATERSON (WILLIAM EDGAR) and CAMPBELL (IAN R.) Social democracy in post-war Europe. London, 1974. pp. 82. *bibliog.*

SOCIALISM IN FRANCE.

CHARLTON (SUE ELLEN M.) The French left and European integration. Denver, Col., [1972]. pp. 111. *bibliog.* *(Denver. University. Social Science Foundation and Graduate School of International Studies. Monograph Series in World Affairs. vol.9, no.4)*

GUIDONI (PIERRE) Histoire du nouveau parti socialiste. Paris, [1973]. pp. 406.

KRIVINE (ALAIN) Questions sur la révolution; entretiens avec Roland Biard. [Paris, 1973]. pp. 319.

MARCHAIS (GEORGES) Le défi démocratique. Paris, [1973]. pp. 249.

MIDOL (LUCIEN) La voie que j'ai suivie: un ingénieur au coeur des batailles sociales, 1900-1970. Paris, [1973]. pp. 221.

PARTI SOCIALISTE UNIFIE. Congrès National, 8e, Toulouse, 1972. Manifeste: contrôler aujourd'hui pour décider demain, etc. Paris, [1973]. pp. 231. *bibliog.*

PIERRE (ROGER) Les origines du syndicalisme et du socialisme dans la Drôme, 1850-1920. Paris, [1973]. pp. 254. *bibliog.*

SOCIALISM IN GERMANY.

SOZIALDEMOKRATISCHE Bibliothek: Sammlung von Abhandlungen über Theorie und Geschichte des Sozialismus; (unveränderter fotomechanischer Nachdruck der Originalausgabe 1885-90), [containing 36 pamphlets]). Leipzig, 1971. 3 vols.

HEINEMANN (BRUNO) Ziele und Gefahren der Sozialisierung. Berlin, 1919. pp. 23.

CHRISTLICH-DEMOKRATISCHE UNION DEUTSCHLANDS. Bundesgeschäftsstelle. Sozialdemokratische Legenden und die deutsche Wirklichkeit. Bonn, [1969]. pp. 30.

THOENNESSEN (WERNER) The emancipation of women: the rise and decline of the women's movement in German social democracy, 1863-1933; translated by Joris de Bres. [London], 1973. pp. 185. *bibliog.*

WEISSER (GERHARD) Freiheit durch Sozialismus: zu wenig bekannte Arbeiten der Programmkommissionen und anderer Ausschüsse der SPD, etc. Göttingen, [1973]. pp. 46. *(Forschungsinstitut für Gesellschaftspolitik und Beratende Sozialwissenschaft. Monographien zur Politik. Heft 11)*

ARMANSKI (GERHARD) Entstehung des wissenschaftlichen Sozialismus. Darmstadt, 1974. pp. 243. *bibliog.*

SOCIALISM IN HUNGARY.

KÁDÁR (JÁNOS) For a socialist Hungary: speeches, articles, interviews, 1968-1972; (translated by Gyula Gulyas and Karoly Ravasz). [Budapest, 1974]. pp. 404.

SOCIALISM IN INDIA.

BHULESHKAR (ASHOK V.) ed. Towards socialist transformation of Indian economy. Bombay, 1972. pp. 422.

SOCIALISM IN IRELAND (REPUBLIC).

IRISH WORKERS' PARTY. Ireland her own: the programme of the...Party adopted at its fourth national conference, held in Dublin in March 1962. Dublin, 1963. pp. 26.

SOCIALISM IN ITALY.

DAMIANI (FRANCO) Carlo Cafiero nella storia del primo socialismo italiano. Milano, [1974]. pp. 221. *bibliog*.

SOCIALISM IN LATIN AMERICA.

CINQ aspects de sociétés latino-américaines; [by Carlos M. Rama and others]. Paris, [1965]. pp. 151. *(Paris. Université. Institut des Hautes Etudes de l'Amérique Latine. Cahiers. No. 7)*

SOCIALISM IN NIGERIA.

NIGERIAN PEOPLE'S UNION. Programme of the... Union, etc. London, [imprint, 197-]. pp. 30.

SOCIALISM IN NORWAY.

LORENZ (EINHART) Arbeiderbevegelsens historie: en innføring; norsk sosialisme i internasjonalt perspektiv. Oslo, [1972-74]. 2 vols.(in 1). *bibliogs*.

LAFFERTY (WILLIAM M.) Industrialization, community structure, and socialism: an ecological analysis of Norway, 1875-1924. Oslo, [1974]. pp. 364. *bibliog*.

SOCIALISM IN POLAND.

BERNOV (IURII VLADIMIROVICH) and MANUSEVICH (ALEKSANDR IAKOVLEVICH) Lenin v Krakove. Moskva, 1972. pp. 239.

IAZHBOROVSKAIA (INESSA SERGEEVNA) Ideinoe razvitie pol'skogo revoliutsionnogo rabochego dvizheniia, konets XIX - pervaia chetvert' XX v. Moskva, 1973. pp. 415.

MALINOWSKI (HENRYK) Szkice z dziejów klasy robotniczej: wybrane zagadnienia z lat 1917-1919. Warszawa, 1973. pp. 466.

STROBEL (GEORG WALDEMAR) Die Partei Rosa Luxemburgs, Lenin und die SPD: der polnische "europäische" Internationalismus in der russischen Sozialdemokratie. Wiesbaden, 1974. pp. 759. *bibliog*.

SOCIALISM IN ROUMANIA.

COPOIU (NICOLAE) Le socialisme européen et le mouvement ouvrier et socialiste en Roumanie, 1835-1921. Bucureşti, 1973. pp. 208. *(Academia de Ştiinţe Sociale şi Politice a Republicii Socialiste România. Bibliotheca Historica Romaniae. Studies. 45)*

SOCIALISM IN RUSSIA.

ISTORIKO-revoliutsionnyi vestnik. no. 1(4). Moskva, 1922. pp. 103.

KRIVINE (ALAIN) Questions sur la révolution; entretiens avec Roland Biard. [Paris, 1973]. pp. 319.

SHAMARIN (EDUARD VIKTOROVICH) Gosudarstvenno-pravovye vzgliady predshestvennikov nauchnogo sotsializma v Rossii. Kiev, 1973. pp. 175.

SOBOLEV (GENNADII LEONT'EVICH) Revoliutsionnoe soznanie rabochikh i soldat Petrograda v 1917 g.: period dvoevlastiia. Leningrad, 1973. pp. 330.

SOCIALISM IN SICILY.

RENDA (FRANCESCO) Socialisti e cattolici in Sicilia, 1900-1904: le lotte agrarie. Caltanissetta, [1972]. pp. 463.

SOCIALISM IN SPAIN.

ZAVALA (IRIS M.) Romanticos y socialistas: prensa española del XIX. Madrid, 1972. pp. 208.

SOCIALISM IN SWEDEN.

BRAND 1905: illustrerad socialistisk tidning; organ för Socialistiska Ungdomsförbundet. Mölndal, 1971. 1 vol. (various pagings). *Facsimile reprint*.

BERGSTRÖM (VILLY) Kapitalbildning och industriell demokratie: socialdemokratiska perspektiv. Stockholm, [1973]. pp. 182. *bibliog*.

TINGSTEN (HERBERT) The Swedish Social Democrats: their ideological development; translated by Greta Frankel and Patricia Howard-Rosen. Totowa, N.J., [1973]. pp. 719.

PALME (OLOF) Att vilja gå vidare: [collection of speeches and articles]. [Stockholm, 1974]. pp. 272.

SOCIALISM IN SWITZERLAND.

WULLSCHLEGER (EUGEN) Aus der Geschichte der Arbeiterbewegung in Basel: Vortrag, gehalten in den Volksbildungskursen des Arbeiterbundes. Basel, 1912. pp. 32.

GREULICH (HERMAN) Zum Nachdenken: ein Wort an die schweiz[erische] Arbeiterschaft. St.Gallen, [1919]. pp. 32.

GRIMM (ROBERT) Schicksalsstunde der Schweiz. Bern, 1935. pp. 46.

SOZIALDEMOKRATISCHE PARTEI DER SCHWEIZ. Wählt der Mittelstand sozialdemokratisch?. Zürich, [1939?]. pp. 48. *(Kultur und Arbeit)*

BRINGOLF (WALTHER) Perspektiven der sozialistischen Bewegung der Schweiz. [Schaffhausen, 1940]. pp. 26.

SOZIALISTISCHE JUGEND DER SCHWEIZ. Zeigt der Sozialismus einen Ausweg?: (unsere Antwort an Nationalrat Bringolf.); Kapitulation vor dem Kapitalismus oder sozialistische Perspektiven?. [Zürich, 1940]. pp. 30.

BRINGOLF (WALTHER) Sozialismus in der Schweiz. [Zürich, 1956]. pp. 32.

BRINGOLF (WALTHER) Die Sozialdemokratie gestern, heute, morgen: Referat, gehalten am Parteitag der Sozialdemokratischen Partei der Schweiz in Winterthur vom 27./28.Juni 1959. [Zürich, 1959]. pp. 16.

SOCIALISM IN TANZANIA.

The ARUSHA declaration and Christian Socialism: six papers presented at a seminar held at University College, Dar es Salaam in 1967 following the Arusha Declaration. Dar es Salaam, 1969. pp. 54. *bibliog*.

CLIFFE (LIONEL) and SAUL (JOHN S.) eds. Socialism in Tanzania:...an interdisciplinary reader. Nairobi, afterwards Dar es Salaam, [1972-73]. 2 vols.

TOWARDS socialist planning; edited by Uchumi editorial board: J.F. Rweyemamu [and others]. Dar es Salaam, 1972. pp. 199.

WOLDETSADIK (TERREFE) Tanzania: the theoretical framework of development; self-reliance and socialism. The Hague, 1973. pp. 11. *(Hague. Institute of Social Studies. Occasional Papers. No. 29)*

SOCIALISM IN THE ARGENTINE REPUBLIC.

SOLOMONOFF (JORGE N.) Ideologias del movimiento obrero y conflicto social: de la organizacion nacional hasta la Prima Guerra Mundial. Buenos Aires, [1971]. pp. 314. *bibliog*.

SOCIALISM IN THE NETHERLANDS.

SCHEPS (J.H.) Kink in de kabel: scheuring en polarisatie P[artij] v[an] d[e] A[rbeid]-D[emocratische S[ocialisten] '70. Apeldoorn, [1972]. pp. 96.

COHEN (H.F.) Om de vernieuwing van het socialisme: de politieke oriëntatie van de Nederlandse sociaal-democratie, 1919-1930. Leiden, 1974. pp. 279. *bibliog. With summary in English*.

KLAVER (IMKE) Herinneringen van een friese landarbeider: enkele opgetekende zaken uit het jongste verleden tot 1925: inkele oanteikene dingen út de jonge tiid oan 1925; ingeleid door Ger Harmsen. Nijmegen, [1974]. pp. 245. *Parallel Frisian and Dutch texts*.

LOUW (ANDRE VAN DER) Rood als je hart: 'n geschiedenis van de AJC. Amsterdam, [1974]. pp. 296. *bibliog*.

— Bibliography.

HARMSEN (GER) Idee en beweging: bibliografiese aanwijzingen bij de studie en het onderzoek van de geschiedenis van socialisme en arbeidersbeweging in Nederland. Nijmegen, 1972. pp. 101.

SOCIALISM IN THE UNITED KINGDOM.

HOBHOUSE (LEONARD TRELAWNY) The labour movement;... [reprint of the third edition of 1912]; edited with an introduction and notes by Philip P. Poirier. Brighton, 1974. pp. xxiv, 159, xxv-xxx. *bibliog*.

COLE (GEORGE DOUGLAS HOWARD) The people's front. London, 1937. pp. 366.

STRACHEY (JOHN ST. LOE) Socialism looks forward. New York, [1945]. pp. 153.

DERRICK (PAUL) Socialism and inflation: the relevance of co-operative principles. London, 1973. pp. 22.

ROZHKOV (BORIS ARKHIPOVICH) Angliiskoe rabochee dvizhenie, 1859-1864 gg. Moskva, 1973. pp. 236. *bibliog*.

TERRILL (ROSS) R.H.Tawney and his times: socialism as fellowship. Cambridge, Mass., 1973. pp. 373. *bibliog*.

CROSLAND (CHARLES ANTHONY RAVEN) Socialism now and other essays; edited by Dick Leonard. London, 1974. pp. 260.

TAVERNE (DICK) The future of the left: Lincoln and after. London, 1974. pp. 175.

WINTER (J.M.) Socialism and the challenge of war: ideas and politics in Britain, 1912-18. London, 1974. pp. 310. *bibliog*.

SOCIALISM IN THE UNITED STATES.

CANNON (JAMES PATRICK) The history of American Trotskyism: from its origins, 1928, to the founding of the Socialist Workers Party, 1938; report of a participant. 2nd ed. New York, 1972. pp. 268.

ROBERT OWEN BICENTENNIAL CONFERENCE, NEW HARMONY, INDIANA, 1971. Robert Owen's American legacy: proceedings...; edited by Donald E. Pitzer; [sponsored by the Department of History, Indiana State University, Evansville, and by Harmonie Associates, New Harmony, Indiana]. Indianapolis, 1972. pp. 88.

MOORE (ROBERT LAURENCE) ed. The emergence of an American left: civil war to World War I. New York, [1973]. pp. 212. *bibliog*.

JOHNSON (OAKLEY C.) Marxism in United States history before the Russian Revolution, 1876-1917. New York, 1974. pp. 196. *bibliog. (American Institute for Marxist Studies. History Series. No.9)*

THOMAS (TONY) ed. Black liberation and socialism. New York, 1974. pp. 207.

SOCIALISM IN YUGOSLAVIA.

HRONOLOGIJA radničkog pokreta u Srbiji. knj.2. Od 1919. do 1941. godine. Beograd, 1969. pp. 397. *In Cyrillic*.

SOCIALIST COMPETITION.

SOCIALIST COMPETITION.

ELISEEV (GENNADII PAVLOVICH) Molodezh' i sotsialisticheskoe sorevnovanie: istoriia, opyt, problemy. Moskva, 1969. pp. 103. *bibliog.*

V.I. Lenin, KPSS o sotsialisticheskom sorevnovanii. Moskva, 1973. pp. 438.

SOCIALIST PARTY (AUSTRIA).

LESER (NORBERT) Zwischen Reformismus und Bolschewismus: der Austromarxismus als Theorie und Praxis. Wien, [1968]. pp. 600.

KREISKY (BRUNO) Aspekte des demokratischen Sozialismus: Aufsätze, Reden, Interviews; mit einem Vorwort von Ossip K. Flechtheim. München, [1974]. pp. 200. *bibliog.*

SOZIALISTISCHE PARTEI ÖSTERREICHS. Humankonferenz, 3., 1973. Humanpolitik im modernen Österreich: 3. Humankonferenz...27. September 1973. [Vienna], 1974. pp. 72.

STADLER (KARL RUDOLF) Opfer verlorener Zeiten: Geschichte der Schutzbund- Emigration, 1934. Wien, [1974]. pp. 397. *(Ludwig-Boltzmann-Institut für Geschichte der Arbeiterbewegung. Veröffentlichungen)*

SOCIALIST PARTY (FRANCE).

GUIDONI (PIERRE) Histoire du nouveau parti socialiste. Paris, [1973]. pp. 406.

See also PARTI SOCIALISTE UNIFIE.

SOCIALIST PARTY (ITALY).

PUNZO (MAURIZIO) Dalla Liberazione a Palazzo Barberini: storia del Partito Socialista Italiano dalla ricostruzione alla scissione del 1947. Milano, [1973]. pp. 337.

SOCIALIST PARTY (POLAND).

PRAGIER (ADAM) Czas przeszły dokonany. Londyn, 1966. pp. 943.

SOCIALIST PARTY (UNITED STATES).

MILLER (SALLY M.) Victor Berger and the promise of constructive socialism, 1910-1920. Westport, Conn., 1973. pp. 275. *bibliog.*

SOCIALISTS.

WOLFF (GEORG) Journalist, ed. Wir leben in der Weltrevolution: Gespräche mit Sozialisten; (Sammlung von "Spiegel"-Gesprächen). München, 1971. pp. 191.

SOCIALISTS, GERMAN.

INSTITUT FÜR MARXISMUS-LENINISMUS (BERLIN). Geschichte der deutschen Arbeiterbewegung: biographisches Lexikon; Redaktionskommission: R.Grau [and others]. Berlin, 1970. pp. 528.

MAERKER (RUDOLF) and KRAUSE (PETER) Sozialismus ist das Ziel: Dokumente und Zeugnisse aus der Geschichte der Sozialdemokratie, 1863 bis 1933. München, [1973]. pp. 263.

BRANDT (WILLY) Die Partei der Freiheit: Reden über August Bebel, Karl Marx, Friedrich Engels und Otto Wels. new ed. Bonn-Bad Godesberg, [1974]. pp. 69.

SOCIALISTS, YUGOSLAV.

PETROVIĆ (LAZAR) Versajska Jugoslavija: nekoliko marksističkih osvrta na njene političke borbe i borce. Cleveland, 1950. pp. 109. *Članci iz Radničke Borbe.*

SOCIALIZATION.

DE VOS (GEORGE A.) Socialization for achievement: essays on the cultural psychology of the Japanese...; with contributions by Hiroshi Wagatsuma [and others]. Berkeley, [1973]. pp. 597. *bibliog.*

FREY (HANS PETER) Theorie der Sozialisation: Integration von system- und rollentheoretischen Aussagen in einem mikrosoziologischen Ansatz. [Erlangen, imprint, 1973?]. pp. 257,xli. *bibliog.*

RUSHTEN (JOHN PHILIPPE) Social learning and cognitive development: alternative approaches to an understanding of generosity in 7 to 11 year olds: (Ph.D. [London] thesis). 1973. fo. 210. *bibliog. Typescript: unpublished. This thesis is the propery of London University and may not be removed from the Library*

RICHARDS (MARTIN PAUL MEREDITH) ed. The integration of a child into a social world. London, 1974. pp. 316. *bibliogs.*

WILSON (RICHARD W.) The moral state: a study of the political socialization of Chinese and American children. New York, [1974]. pp. 290. *bibliog.*

SOCIALLY HANDICAPPED

— Employment — United States — Bibliography.

PINTO (PATRICK R.) and BUCHMEIER (JEANNE O.) compilers. Problems and issues in the employment of minority, disadvantaged, and female groups: an annotated bibliography. Minneapolis, 1973. pp. 62. *(Minnesota University. Industrial Relations Center. Bulletins. 59)*

— Rehabilitation — Sweden.

SAMBERGS (ÅKE) Familjevård i landsbygdsmiljö. Stockholm, 1973. pp. 64. *bibliog. (Jordbrukets Utredningsinstitut. Meddelanden. 1973. Nr. 5) With English summary.*

— Germany.

SPIEGEL, DER. Underprivilegiert: eine Studie über sozial benachteiligte Gruppen in der Bundesrepublik Deutschland; herausgegeben von der Spiegel-Redaktion; [collection of reports originally published 1971-1973]. Neuwied, [1973]. pp. 325. *bibliog.*

— Sweden.

BERGLIND (HANS) and LINQUIST (ANNA LENA) Utslagningen på arbetsmarknaden: omfattning och utvecklingstendenser. Lund, 1973. pp. 136. *bibliog. With English summary.*

— United Kingdom.

HOLMAN (ROBERT) ed. Socially deprived families in Britain; (reprinted with supplement). London, 1970. repr. 1973. pp. 235, 28.

SOCIALLY HANDICAPPED CHILDREN.

KEDDIE (NELL) ed. Tinker, tailor: the myth of cultural deprivation. Harmondsworth, 1973. pp. 150. *bibliog.*

— Education — United States.

BEREITER (CARL EDWARD) and ENGELMANN (SIEGFRIED) Teaching disadvantaged children in the preschool. Englewood Cliffs, N.J., [1966]. pp. 312.

PASSOW (AARON HARRY) and others, eds. Education of the disadvantaged: a book of readings. New York, [1967]. pp. 503. *bibliogs.*

SOCIETY, PRIMITIVE.

LOCAL-level politics: social and cultural perspectives; edited by Marc J. Swartz; [result of a conference sponsored by the Wenner-Gren Foundation for Anthropological Research, held at Burg Wartenstein, July, 1966]. Chicago, 1968. pp. viii, 437. *bibliogs.*

PRINTSIP istorizma v poznanii sotsial'nykh iavlenii. Moskva, 1972. pp. 291.

SOCIOLINGUISTICS.

ESCOBAR (ALBERTO) Lenguaje y discriminacion social en America Latina. Lima, 1972. pp. 201.

LABOV (WILLIAM) Sociolinguistic patterns. Philadelphia, [1972]. pp. 344. *bibliog.*

LAMBERT (WALLACE EARL) Language, psychology, and culture: essays...; selected and introduced by Anwar S. Dil. Stanford, Calif., 1972. pp. 362. *bibliogs. (Linguistic Research Group of Pakistan. Language Science and National Development)*

ROBINSON (W. PETER) Language and social behaviour. Harmondsworth, 1972. pp. 223. *bibliog.*

SOCIOLINGUISTICS in cross-cultural analysis; [proceedings of a symposium held on the occasion of the 70th Annual Meeting of the American Anthropological Association, 1971; edited by] David M. Smith [and] Roger W. Shuy. Washington, [1972]. pp. 127. *bibliogs.*

ANNUAL ROUND TABLE MEETING ON LINGUISTICS AND LANGUAGE STUDIES, 23RD, GEORGETOWN UNIVERSITY. Language attitudes: current trends and prospects; Roger W. Shuy and Ralph W. Fasold, editors. Washington, [1973]. pp. 201. *bibliogs.*

ANNUAL ROUND TABLE MEETING ON LINGUISTICS AND LANGUAGE STUDIES, 23RD, GEORGETOWN UNIVERSITY. Language planning: current issues and research; Joan Rubin [and] Roger Shuy, editors. Washington, [1973]. pp. 111. *bibliogs.*

ERVIN-TRIPP (SUSAN M.) Language acquisition and communicative choice: essays...; selected and introduced by Anwar S. Dil. Stanford, 1973. pp. 383. *bibliog. (Linguistic Research Group of Pakistan. Language Science and National Development)*

FRANK (ROBERT SHELBY) Linguistic analysis of political elites: a theory of verbal kinesics. Beverly Hills, [1973]. pp. 59. *bibliog.*

MYERS (SARAH K.) Language shift among migrants to Lima, Peru. Chicago, 1973. pp. 203. *bibliog. (Chicago. University. Department of Geography. Research Papers. No. 147)*

TRUDGILL (PETER) Sociolinguistics: an introduction. Harmondsworth, 1974. pp. 189. *bibliog.*

TRUDGILL (PETER) The social differentiation of English in Norwich. Cambridge, 1974. pp. 211. *bibliog.*

WRIGHT (PETER) The language of British industry. London, 1974. pp. 206. *bibliog.*

SOCIOLOGICAL JURISPRUDENCE.

KUZNETSOVA (NINEL' FEDOROVNA) and MIKHAILOVSKAIA (INGA BORISOVNA) eds. Effektivnost' primeneniia ugolovnogo zakona. Moskva, 1973. pp. 208.

NATIONAL CONFERENCE OF LAWYERS AND SOCIAL WORKERS. Law and social work: statements. Washington, [1973]. pp. 56.

PRAVO i sotsiologiia. Moskva, 1973. pp. 359.

SPIRIDONOV (LEV IVANOVICH) Sotsial'noe razvitie i pravo. Leningrad, 1973. pp. 205.

ECKHOFF (TORSTEIN) Justice: its determinants in social interaction. Rotterdam, 1974. pp. 414. *bibliog.*

FREEMAN (MICHAEL D.A.) The legal structure. London, 1974. pp. 243. *bibliog.*

PENNOCK (JAMES ROLAND) and CHAPMAN (JOHN WILLIAM) eds. The limits of law. New York, 1974. pp. 276. *(American Society for Political and Legal Philosophy. Nomos. 15)*

RYFFEL (HANS) Rechtssoziologie: eine systematische Orientierung. Neuwied, 1974. pp. 414.

SOCIOLOGICAL RESEARCH.

FLETCHER (COLIN) Beneath the surface: an account of three styles of sociological research. London, 1974. pp. 221. *bibliog.*

— Communist countries.

ZUR Sozialstruktur der sozialistischen Gesellschaft: ([papers and discussion at a symposium]; herausgegeben vom Wissenschaftlichen Rat für Soziologische Forschung in der DDR). Berlin, 1974. pp. 221.

— Russia.

WEINBERG (ELIZABETH ANN) The development of sociology in the Soviet Union. London, 1974. pp. 173. *bibliog.*

— United States.

FICHTER (JOSEPH HENRY) One-man research: reminiscences of a Catholic sociologist. New York, [1973]. pp. 258.

SOCIOLOGY.

LE DANTEC (FELIX) L'égoïsme: seule base de toute société; étude des déformations résultant de la vie en commun. Paris, 1912. pp. 327.

COHEN (PERCY SAUL) Modern social theory. London, 1968 repr. 1970. pp. 247.

JACKSON (JOHN ARCHER) Neither fish, flesh, fowl nor good red herring;... an inaugural lecture delivered before the Queen's University of Belfast on 21 April 1971. Belfast, [1971]. pp. 22. *(Belfast. Queen's University. Lectures. New Series. No.58)*

JACKSON (JOHN ARCHER) Neither fish, flesh, fowl nor good red herring;...an inaugural lecture delivered before the Queen's University of Belfast on 21 April 1971. Belfast, [1971]. pp. 22. *(Belfast. Queen's University. Lectures. New Series. No.58)*

BEERLING (R.F.) and others, eds. Onderzocht en overdacht: sociologische opstellen voor prof. dr. F. van Heek, etc. Rotterdam, 1972. pp. 320. *bibliog. (Mens en Maatschappij. Boekafleveringen. 1972)*

DURKHEIM (EMILE) Selected writings; edited, translated, and with an introduction by Anthony Giddens. Cambridge, 1972. pp. 272.

GROSS (PETER) Reflexion, Spontaneität und Interaktion: zur Diskussion soziologischer Handlungstheorien. Stuttgart-Bad Cannstatt, [1972]. pp. 163. *bibliog.* With English summary.

BURGESS (ERNEST WATSON) On community, family, and delinquency: selected writings; edited by Leonard S. Cottrell [and others]. Chicago, [1973]. pp. 337. *bibliog.*

CALLOT (EMILE) Sociologie et politique: un art social, rationnel, est-il possible?. Paris, 1973. pp. 221.

CRUMP (STEPHEN THOMAS) Man and his kind. London, 1973. pp. 154. *bibliog.*

DAVY (GEORGES) L'homme, le fait social et le fait politique: [collection of articles and other writings originally published 1919-1969]. Paris, [1973]. pp. 324. *(Paris. Ecole Pratique des Hautes Etudes. Section des Sciences Economiques et Sociales. Textes de Sciences Sociales. 9)*

DION (MICHEL) Sociologie et idéologie. Paris, [1973]. pp. 174.

DOUGLAS (JACK D.) ed. Introduction to sociology: situations and structures. New York, [1973]. pp. 645. *bibliogs.*

MONGARDINI (CARLO) Vilfredo Pareto dall'economia alla sociologia; con un'antologia dei primi scritti sociologici di Pareto. Roma, [1973]. pp. 311.

MULLINS (NICHOLAS C.) Theories and theory groups in contemporary American sociology. New York, [1973]. pp. 337. *bibliogs.*

NEUENDORFF (HARTMUT) Der Begriff des Interesses: eine Studie zu den Gesellschaftstheorien von Hobbes, Smith und Marx. Frankfurt am Main, 1973. pp. 163. *bibliog.*

TOURAINE (ALAIN) Production de la société. Paris, [1973]. pp. 543.

WILLMS (BERNARD) Kritik und Politik: Jürgen Habermas; oder, Das politische Defizit der "Kritischen Theorie". Frankfurt am Main, 1973. pp. 207.

ZEITLIN (IRVING M.) Rethinking sociology: a critique of contemporary theory. New York, [1973]. pp. 263.

ALLEN (SHEILA) Sociology in a technological university; an inaugural lecture delivered at the University of Bradford on 19 February 1974. [Bradford, 1974]. pp. 12.

BANKS (OLIVE LUCY) Sociology and education: some reflections on the sociologist's role; an inaugural lecture delivered in the University of Leicester, 5 February 1974. Leicester, 1974. pp. 24.

BERRY (DAVID) Central ideas in sociology: an introduction. London, 1974. pp. 191.

COMTE (ISIDORE AUGUSTE MARIE FRANÇOIS XAVIER) The crisis of industrial civilization: the early essays...; introduced by Ronald Fletcher. London, 1974. pp. 251. *bibliog.*

FLETCHER (RONALD) ed. The science of society and the unity of mankind: a memorial volume for Morris Ginsberg. London, 1974. pp. 292. *bibliog.*

GIDDENS (ANTHONY) ed. Positivism and sociology. London, 1974. pp. 244.

GOLDTHORPE (JOHN ERNEST) An introduction to sociology. 2nd ed. Cambridge, 1974. pp. 222. *bibliogs.*

HABERMAS (JUERGEN) Theory and practice;... [4th ed. abridged of Theorie und Praxis [with] Arbeit und Interaktion from Technik und Wissenschaft als Ideologie]; translated by John Viertel. London, 1974. pp. 310.

KADT (EMANUEL J. DE) and WILLIAMS (GAVIN) eds. Sociology and development. London, 1974. pp. 374. *bibliogs. (British Sociological Association. Explorations in Sociology. 4)*

MARKOVIĆ (MIHAILO) From affluence to praxis: philosophy and social criticism. Ann Arbor, Mich., [1974]. pp. 265.

REX (JOHN ARDERNE) Sociology and the demystification of the modern world. London, 1974. pp. 271. *bibliog.*

REX (JOHN ARDERNE) ed. Approaches to sociology: an introduction to major trends in British sociology. London, 1974. pp. 302.

SMITH (MICHAEL GARFIELD) Corporations and society. London, 1974. pp. 383. *bibliog.*

TOURAINE (ALAIN) The post-industrial society: tomorrow's social history; classes, conflicts and culture in the programmed society;... translated by Leonard F.X. Mayhew. London, 1974. pp. 244.

— Bibliography.

HARVARD UNIVERSITY. Library. Widener Library Shelflists. [Nos.] 45-46. Sociology. Cambridge, Mass., 1973. 2 vols.

BRITISH SOCIOLOGICAL ASSOCIATION. Register of postgraduate theses, 1974; (compiled by Carl Riddell). [London], 1974. pp. 63.

— Dictionaries and encyclopaedias.

HARTFIEL (GUENTER) Wörterbuch der Soziologie. Stuttgart, [1972]. pp. 696.

— History.

AGULLA (JUAN CARLOS) Teoria sociologica. Mexico, 1964 [or rather 1965]. pp. 157. *(Mexico City. Universidad Nacional Autonoma de Mexico. Instituto de Investigaciones Sociales. Cuadernos de Sociologia)*

ABRAHAM (JOSEPH HAYIM) The origins and growth of sociology. Harmondsworth, 1973. pp. 648. *bibliog.*

— — Germany.

JAY (MARTIN) The dialectical imagination: a history of the Frankfurt School and the Institute of Social Research, 1923-1950. London, 1973. pp. 382. *bibliog.*

— — Russia.

BOCHKAREV (NIKOLAI IVANOVICH) V.I. Lenin i burzhuaznaia sotsiologiia v Rossii. Moskva, 1973. pp. 251.

WEINBERG (ELIZABETH ANN) The development of sociology in the Soviet Union. London, 1974. pp. 173. *bibliog.*

— — White Russia.

OCHERKI istorii filosofskoi i sotsiologicheskoi mysli Belorussii do 1917 g. Minsk, 1973. pp. 557.

— — United States.

JAY (MARTIN) The dialectical imagination: a history of the Frankfurt School and the Institute of Social Research, 1923-1950. London, 1973. pp. 382. *bibliog.*

— Mathematical models.

FARARO (THOMAS J.) Mathematical sociology: an introduction to fundamentals. New York, [1973]. pp. 802. *bibliog.*

— Methodology.

URIBE VILLEGAS (OSCAR) La matematica, la estadistica, y las ciencias sociales. Mexico, 1963. pp. 325. *bibliog. (Mexico City. Universidad Nacional Autonoma de Mexico. Instituto de Investigaciones Sociales. Cuadernos de Sociologia)*

CAPLOW (THEODORE) L'enquête sociologique. Paris, [1970]. pp. 267.

DOUGLAS (JACK D.) ed. Research on deviance. New York, [1972]. pp. 268.

BOUDON (RAYMOND) Les méthodes en sociologie. 3rd ed. Paris, 1973. pp. 128. *bibliog.*

COMPARATIVE social research: methodological problems and strategies: [selected papers of a faculty conference held by the Institute for Comparative Sociology in Bloomington, Indiana in 1971]; edited by Michael Armer [and] Allen D. Grimshaw. New York, [1973]. pp. 473. *bibliogs.*

FARARO (THOMAS J.) Mathematical sociology: an introduction to fundamentals. New York, [1973]. pp. 802. *bibliog.*

FORCESE (DENNIS P.) and RICHER (STEPHEN) Social research methods. Englewood Cliffs, [1973]. pp. 280. *bibliogs.*

LINDSEY (JAMES K.) Inferences from sociological survey data: a unified approach. Amsterdam, 1973. pp. 163. *bibliog.*

MULLINS (NICHOLAS C.) Theories and theory groups in contemporary American sociology. New York, [1973]. pp. 337. *bibliogs.*

EASTHOPE (GARY) A history of social research methods. London, 1974. pp. 169. *bibliog.*

FLETCHER (COLIN) Beneath the surface: an account of three styles of sociological research. London, 1974. pp. 221. *bibliog.*

SOCIOLOGICAL theory and survey research: institutional change and social policy in Great Britain: [papers of a seminar held in London 1972-73, sponsored by the Survey Unit of the Social Science Research Council]; edited by Timothy Leggatt. London, [1974]. pp. 334. *bibliogs.*

TURNER (ROY) ed. Ethnomethodology: selected readings. Harmondsworth, 1974. pp. 287. *bibliogs.*

— Philosophy.

ISTORICHESKII materializm kak teoriia sotsial'nogo poznaniia i deiatel'nosti. Moskva, 1972. pp. 320.

MARTIN (DAVID ALFRED) Two critiques of spontaneity: [two lectures given at the London School of Economics]. [London, 1973]. pp. 31.

PHENOMENOLOGICAL sociology: issues and applications; edited by George Psathas. New York, [1973]. pp. 369.

LESSNOFF (MICHAEL H.) The structure of social science: a philosophical introduction. London, 1974. pp. 173. *bibliog.*

PELZ (WERNER) The scope of understanding in sociology: towards a more radical reorientation in the social and humanistic sciences. London, 1974. pp. 283. *bibliog.*

SOCIOLOGY. (Cont.)

SCHUTZ (ALFRED) and LUCKMANN (THOMAS) The structures of the life-world; translated by Richard M. Zaner and H. Tristram Engelhardt, Jr. London, 1974. pp. 335.

— Statistics.

SHLIAPENTOKH (VLADIMIR EMMANUILOVICH) Problemy dostovernosti statisticheskoi informatsii v sotsiologicheskikh issledovaniiakh. Moskva, 1973. pp. 144. *bibliog.*

— Study and teaching.

BUDE (JACQUES) L'obscurantisme libéral et l'investigation sociologique. Paris, [1973]. pp. 223.

— — Germany.

ORTLIEB (HEINZ DIETRICH) ed. Destruktive Zeitzünder: asoziale Tendenzen in unserer Bildungsreform; ... mit weiteren Beiträgen von Max Liedtke [and others]. Hamburg, 1973. pp. 54. *(Hamburg. Hamburgisches Welt-Wirtschaft-Archiv. Veröffentlichungen)*

— — Hong Kong.

ANTHROPOLOGY and sociology in Hong Kong: field projects and problems of overseas scholars: proceedings of a symposium, February 8-9, 1969; compiled by Marjorie Topley. Hong Kong, 1969. pp. 143. *bibliog.*

— — Mexico.

AGRAMONTE (ROBERTO) Mendieta y Nuñez y su magisterio sociologico. Mexico, 1961. pp. 224.

— Terminology.

MERWE (CASPAR VAN DE) and others. Thesaurus of sociological research terminology. Rotterdam, 1974. pp. 471.

SOCIOLOGY, CHRISTIAN

— Catholic.

PESCH (HEINRICH) Neubau der Gesellschaft. Freiburg im Breisgau, 1919. pp. 24. *(Stimmen der Zeit. Flugschriften. 1. Heft)*

FICHTER (JOSEPH HENRY) One-man research: reminiscences of a Catholic sociologist. New York, [1973]. pp. 258.

SOCIOLOGY, MILITARY.

JANOWITZ (MORRIS) ed. The new military: changing patterns of organization; research studies [resulting from the Inter-University Seminar on Armed Forces and Society sponsored by the Russell Sage Foundation]. New York, 1964 [repr. 1969]. pp. 369. *bibliog.*

HAUSER (WILLIAM L.) America's army in crisis: a study in civil-military relations. Baltimore, [1973]. pp. 242. *bibliog.*

SOCIOLOGY, RURAL.

CHITAMBAR (J.B.) Introductory rural sociology: a synopsis of concepts and principles. New Delhi, [1973]. pp. 369. *bibliog.*

— Research.

HIERNAUX (J. PIERRE) Culture et maîtrise du devenir en milieu rural: quelques aspects d'une analyse culturelle réalisée au niveau des habitants de la vallée de l'Aisne. Bruxelles, 1972. pp. 94. *(Belgium. Direction Générale des Arts et des Lettres. Documentation et Enquêtes. No. 7)*

SOCIOLOGY, URBAN.

POWELL (ALAN) ed. The city: attacking modern myths; edited... for the University League for Social Reform. Toronto, [1972]. pp. 263.

ABERBACH (JOEL D.) and WALKER (JACK L.) Race in the city: political trust and public policy in the new urban system. Boston, [Mass., 1973]. pp. 293.

CORNELIUS (WAYNE A.) Political learning among the migrant poor: the impact of residential context. Beverly Hills, [1973]. pp. 88. *bibliog.*

HELMER (JOHN) and EDDINGTON (NEIL A.) eds. Urbanman: the psychology of urban survival. London, [1973]. pp. 274. *bibliogs.*

HUMMEL (RAYMOND C.) and NAGLE (JOHN M.) Urban education in America: problems and prospects. New York, 1973. pp. 298.

LOFLAND (LYN H.) A world of strangers: order and action in urban public space. New York, [1973]. pp. 223. *bibliog.*

BLAIR (THOMAS L.) The international urban crisis. London, 1974. pp. 176. *bibliog.*

BLOWERS (ANDREW) and others, eds. The future of cities; edited ... at the Open University. London, 1974. pp. 355. *bibliogs.*

GREENBANK (ANTHONY) Survival in the city. London, [1974]. pp. 352.

GUTKIND (PETER C.W.) Urban anthropology: perspectives on 'third world' urbanisation and urbanism. Assen, 1974. pp. 262. *bibliog.*

HEYWOOD (PHIL) Planning and human need. Newton Abbot, [1974]. pp. 192.

ROSSI (PETER HENRY) and others. The roots of urban discontent: public policy, municipal institutions and the ghetto. New York, [1974]. pp. 499.

See also CITIES AND TOWNS.

SOGAS.

FALLERS (LLOYD A.) Law without precedent: legal ideas in action in the courts of colonial Busoga. Chicago, 1969. pp. 365. *bibliog.*

SOIL EROSION

— Algeria.

BENCHETRIT (MAURICE) L'erosion actuelle et ses conséquences sur l'aménagement en Algérie. Paris, 1972 [or rather 1973]. pp. 217. *bibliog. (Poitiers. Université. Faculté des Lettres et Sciences Humaines. Publications. 11)*

SOIL PHYSICS.

WIT (C.T.DE) and KEULEN (H. VAN) Simulation of transport processes in soils. Wageningen, 1972. pp. 100. *bibliog.*

SOIL SURVEYS

— United Kingdom — Scotland.

SCOTLAND. Soil Survey of Great Britain. Scotland. Memoirs. Edinburgh, 1954 in progress.

SOILS.

BRIDGES (E.M.) World soils. Cambridge, 1970 repr. 1972. pp. 89. *bibliog.*

FITZPATRICK (EWART ADSIL) Pedology: a systematic approach to soil science. Edinburgh, 1971. pp. 306. *bibliog.*

CRUICKSHANK (J.G.) Soil geography. Newton Abbot, [1972]. pp. 256. *bibliogs.*

FOTH (H.D.) and TURK (LLOYD MILDON) Fundamentals of soil science. 5th ed. New York, [1972]. pp. 454.

HUNT (CHARLES B.) Geology of soils: their evolution, classification and uses. San Francisco, [1972]. pp. 344. *bibliogs.*

RUSSELL (Sir EDWARD JOHN) Soil conditions and plant growth: tenth edition by E. Walter Russell. 10th ed. London, 1973. pp. 849.

— United States — Illinois.

McGREGOR (JOHN R.) A delimitation of Indiana manufacturing regions;...Numerical analysis: a different approach to analysis of geographical data; [by] Howard W. Dennis [and others]; Agricultural productivity of prairie, forest, and prairie-forest transition soils in Illinois; [by] Paul W. Mausel. Terre Haute, Ind., 1973. pp. 67. *(Indiana State University. Department of Geography and Geology. Professional Papers. No. 4)*

SOIUZ RUSSKOGO NARODA.

VIKTOROV (V.P.) ed. Soiuz russkogo naroda po materialam Chrezvychainoi sledstvennoi komissii vremennogo pravitel'stva 1917 g.; sostavil A. Chernovskii. Moskva, 1929. pp. 444.

SOIUZ SEMNADTSATOGO OKTIABRIA.

BIRTH (ERNST) Die Oktobristen, 1905-1913: Zielvorstellungen und Struktur; ein Beitrag zur russischen Parteiengeschichte. Stuttgart, [1974]. pp. 203. *bibliog.*

PINCHUK (BEN-CION) The Octobrists in the third duma, 1907-1912. Seattle, [1974]. pp. 232. *bibliog. (Washington State University. Institute for Comparative and Foreign Area Studies. Publications on Russia and Eastern Europe. No. 4)*

SOLDIERS

— Education, Non—military — Netherlands.

BOND VOOR DIENSTPLICHTIGEN Het rode boekje voor soldaten. Amsterdam, 1971. pp. 132.

SOLOMON ISLANDS

See also MALAITA.

— Constitution.

BRITISH SOLOMON ISLANDS PROTECTORATE. Legislative Council. Special Select Committee on Constitutional Development. 1969. Report of the Special Select Committee appointed to examine Legislative Council Paper No. 119 of 1968 entitled 'Interim proposals on constitutional development'. Honiara, 1969. pp. 45. *(Legislative Council. Papers. 1969. No. 22)*

— Economic policy.

BRITISH SOLOMON ISLANDS PROTECTORATE. Sixth development plan, 1971- 1973: annual review of progress and revised project list. a., Ja 1971/F 1972(1st)- [Honiara]. *(Governing Council Paper)*

BRITISH SOLOMON ISLANDS PROTECTORATE. 1971. Sixth development plan, 1971-1973. [Honiara, 1971]. pp. 242, 1 map.

— Social policy.

BRITISH SOLOMON ISLANDS PROTECTORATE. Sixth development plan, 1971- 1973: annual review of progress and revised project list. a., Ja 1971/F 1972(1st)- [Honiara]. *(Governing Council Paper)*

BRITISH SOLOMON ISLANDS PROTECTORATE. 1971. Sixth development plan, 1971-1973. [Honiara, 1971]. pp. 242, 1 map.

SOLOTHURN

— Economic conditions.

BUERO FÜR ORTS- UND REGIONALPLANUNG [ZÜRICH]. Wachstumspolitik Kanton Solothurn: Notwendigkeit, Möglichkeiten und Grenzen. [Solothurn]. Finanzdepartement, 1970. fo. 134. *Folding map in end pocket.*

— Economic policy.

BUERO FÜR ORTS- UND REGIONALPLANUNG [ZÜRICH]. Wachstumspolitik Kanton Solothurn: Notwendigkeit, Möglichkeiten und Grenzen. [Solothurn]. Finanzdepartement, 1970. fo. 134. *Folding map in end pocket.*

SOUTH AFRICA

SOLZHENITSYN (ALEKSANDR ISAEVICH).

"AOÛT Quartorze" jugé par les lecteurs russes; traduit du russe par Lucile Nivat et Alfréda Aucouturier. Paris, [1973]. pp. 190.

SOMALILAND

— Economic policy.

PESTALOZZA (LUIGI) Somalia, cronaca della rivoluzione. Bari, 1973. pp. 361.

— History — Sources.

ITALY. Ministero degli Affari Esteri. Comitato per la Documentazione dell'Opera dell'Italia in Africa. L'Italia in Africa. Serie Storica. Vol. 2. Oceano Indiano. Tomo 3. Documenti relativi alla Somalia settentrionale, 1884-1891; a cura di Carlo Giglio. Roma, 1968. pp. 238.

— Politics and government.

PESTALOZZA (LUIGI) Somalia, cronaca della rivoluzione. Bari, 1973. pp. 361.

SOMBART (WERNER).

MITZMAN (ARTHUR B.) Sociology and estrangement: three sociologists of imperial Germany. New York, 1973. pp. 375, viii.

SONIC BOOM.

COMMITTEE FOR ENVIRONMENTAL CONSERVATION. Some effects of supersonic flight. London, 1972. pp. 63. *bibliogs.*

SONNINO (SIDNEY) Baron.

SONNINO (SIDNEY) Barone. Diario, 1866-(1922); a cura di Benjamin F. Brown ([and] Pietro Pastorelli). Bari, 1972. 3 vols. *(Opera Omnia di Sidney Sonnino)*

SORENSEN (REGINALD WILLIAM) Baron Sorensen.

ELLISON (S.K.) compiler. Handlist of the papers of Reginald, Lord Sorensen (the Rev. R.W. Sorensen, M.P.). [London, 1973]. pp. 10. *(U.K. Parliament. House of Lords. Record Office. Memoranda. No. 49)*

SOUTH AFRICA

— Commerce — European Economic Community countries.

SOUTH AFRICA. Planning Advisory Council. Subsidiary Committee for the Optimum Utilization of Mineral Resources in the Republic of South Africa and in South West Africa, 1970. The mineral trade between South Africa and the European Economic Community; a report. Pretoria, 1970. pp. 132. *bibliog.*

— Constitution.

SOUTH AFRICA. Constitution. 1961. Republic of South Africa Constitution Act, No.32 of 1961, as amended by Act No.28 of 1962, Act No.65 of 1962, Act No.9 of 1963, Act No.22 of 1963, Act No.47 of 1963, Act No.64 of 1963. [Pretoria, 1965?]. pp. 87. *In Afrikaans and English.*

— Economic conditions.

REPORTS ON THE STATE OF SOUTH AFRICA. No.22. An expanding economy. London, Department of Information, South African Embassy, 1962. pp. 19.

FASULO (G.) The powers behind apartheid. Cambridge, Mass., [1973?]. pp. 23. *(Africa Research Group. Reprints. 3)*

ACCELERATED development in Southern Africa (papers presented... at a conference..., Johannesburg,... March 1972); edited by John Barratt [and others]. London, 1974. pp. 706.

LEFTWICH (ADRIAN) ed. South Africa: economic growth and political change; with comparative studies of Chile, Sri Lanka and Malaysia. London, 1974. pp. 357.

— Economic history.

HOUGHTON (D. HOBART) The South African economy. 3rd ed. Cape Town, 1973. pp. 297. *bibliog.*

— — Sources.

DAVENPORT (THOMAS RODNEY HOPE) and HUNT (K.S.) eds. The right to the land: (documents on Southern African history). Cape Town, 1974. pp. 90. *bibliog.*

— Economic policy.

UNITED SOUTH AFRICAN NATIONAL PARTY. Statement... as approved by Union Congress of 1957. [Johannesburg], 1957. fo. (18).

LOMBARD (JOHANNES ANTHONIE) ed. Economic policy in South Africa: selected essays. Cape Town, [1973]. pp. 272.

ACCELERATED development in Southern Africa (papers presented... at a conference..., Johannesburg,... March 1972); edited by John Barratt [and others]. London, 1974. pp. 706.

MAASDORP (GAVIN G.) Economic development strategy in the African homelands: the rôle of agriculture and industry;... paper given at the 44th council meeting of the S[outh] A[frican] Institute of Race Relations, Cape Town, January 1974. Johannesburg, 1974. pp. 38. *bibliog.*

— Foreign relations — United States.

SEILER (JOHN J.) U.S. foreign policy toward Southern Africa: continuity and change. Johannesburg, 1973. pp. 15, iv.

— Industries.

SOUTH AFRICA. Bureau of Statistics. 1966. Industrial census, 1962-63: manufacturing; construction; electricity, gas and steam; laundries, dyeing and dry cleaning: South Africa and South West Africa. [Pretoria, 1966]. pp. 171. *(Reports. No. 302) In English and Afrikaans.*

SOUTH AFRICA. Bureau of Statistics. Reports. No. 291. Industrial census, 1959-60 and 1960-61, South Africa and South West Africa; private establishments: particulars of materials purchased and manufactures sold. Pretoria, 1966. pp. 369.

SOUTH AFRICA. Bureau of Statistics. 1970-71. Census of manufacturing, 1963-64.

[Pretoria, 1970-71]. 10pts.(in 1 vol.). (Reports. Nos. 10-21-01, etc.)

SOUTH AFRICA. Bureau of Statistics. 1971- . Census of manufacturing, 1967-68 and 1965-66. [Pretoria, 1971 in progress]. *(Reports. No. 10-21-14, etc.) In English and Afrikaans.*

— Manufactures.

SOUTH AFRICA. Bureau of Statistics. 1970-71. Census of manufacturing, 1963-64. [Pretoria, 1970-71]. 10 pts.(in 1 vol.). (Reports. Nos.

DAVIES (R.J.) and YOUNG (BRUCE .S.) Manufacturing in South African cities. [Cape Town, 1970]. pp. 595-605, 608-620. *(From Journal for Geography, vol. 3, no. 6, April 1970) Xerographic copy.*

DAVIES (R.J.) and YOUNG (BRUCE S.) Manufacturing and size of place in the South African urban system. [Cape Town, 1970]. pp. 699-713. *(From Journal for Geography, vol. 3, no. 7, Sept. 1970) Xerographic copy. Bound with their Manufacturing in South African cities.*

DAVIES (R.J.) and YOUNG (BRUCE S.) Manufacturing in South African cities. [Cape Town, 1970]. pp. 595-605, 608-620. *(From Journal for Geography, vol. 3, no. 6, April 1970) Xerographic copy.*

SOUTH AFRICA. Bureau of Statistics. 1971- . Census of manufacturing, 1967-68 and 1965-66. [Pretoria, 1971 in progress]. *(Reports. No. 10-21-14, etc.) In English and Afrikaans.*

SOUTH AFRICA. Bureau of Statistics. Manufacturing statistics: products manufactured. q., (formerly m.), F 1972- Pretoria. *In English and Afrikaans.*

— Native races.

BEST (ALAN C.G.) and YOUNG (BRUCE S.) Homeland consolidation: the case of KwaZulu. Stellenbosch, 1972. pp. 63-74. *(From South African Geographer, vol. 4, no. 1, September 1972) Xerox copy.*

BEST (ALAN C.G.) and YOUNG (BRUCE S.) Focus on Africa: capitals for the homelands. Stellenbosch, 1972. pp. 1043-1055. *(From Journal for Geography, vol. 3, no. 10, April,1972) Xerox copy.*

— Politics and government.

SOUTH AFRICA. Department of Information. 1962. A future for the coloured people. Pretoria, 1962. pp. 11. *(Digest of South African Affairs. Fact Papers. No.101)*

RANDALL (PETER) ed. Directions of change in South African politics. Johannesburg, 1971. pp. 73. *(South African Council of Churches and Christian Institute of Southern Africa. Study Project on Christianity in Apartheid Society. Publications. No. 3)*

GRAAFF (Sir DE VILLIERS) Sir De Villiers Graaff's opening address, Cape Congress, Port Elizabeth, 17.10.1972. Johannesburg, 1972. pp. 29.

VERWOERD (HENDRIK FRENSCH) Hoofartikels uit 'Die Transvaler', 1937-1948; saamgestel deur O. Geyser. Kaapstad, 1972. pp. 100.

SCHOEMAN (B.M.) Van Malan tot Verwoerd. Kaapstad, [1973]. pp. 261.

SOUTH AFRICAN COUNCIL OF CHURCHES and CHRISTIAN INSTITUTE OF SOUTHERN AFRICA. Study Project on Christianity in Apartheid Society. Political Commission. South Africa's political alternatives;... report. Johannesburg, 1973. pp. 252. *bibliog. (Study Project on Christianity in Apartheid Society. Publications. No. 10)*

MALHERBE (PAUL N.) Multistan: a way out of the South African dilemma. Cape Town, 1974. pp. 172. *bibliog.*

— Race question.

SCHOLTZ (GERT DANIEL) The origins and essence of the race pattern in South Africa: [address delivered at the annual congress of the South African Bureau of Social Affairs]. Pretoria, 1958. pp. 22. *(South Africa. Department of Information. Digest of South African Affairs. Fact Papers. No.61)*

REPORTS ON THE STATE OF SOUTH AFRICA. No.21. South Africa speaks. [London, Director of Information, South African Embassy, 1962]. pp. 30.

REPORTS ON THE STATE OF SOUTH AFRICA. No.24. South African realities. London, Department of Information, South African Embassy, 1962. pp. 23.

RANDALL (PETER) ed. Anatomy of apartheid. Johannesburg, 1970. pp. 88. *(South African Council of Churches and Christian Institute of Southern Africa. Study Project on Christianity in Apartheid Society. Publications. No. 1)*

PATON (ALAN) Case history of a pinky. Johannesburg, [c.1971]. pp. 16. *(South African Institute of Race Relations. Topical Talks. 28)*

RANDALL (PETER) ed. Some implications of inequality. Johannesburg, 1971. pp. 65. *(South African Council of Churches and Christian Institute of Southern Africa. Study Project on Christianity in Apartheid Society. Publications. No.4)*

SOUTH AFRICAN COUNCIL OF CHURCHES and CHRISTIAN INSTITUTE OF SOUTHERN AFRICA. Study Project on Christianity in Apartheid Society. Social Commission. Towards social change: (report); general editor Peter Randall. Johannesburg, 1971. pp. 197. *(Study Project on Christianity in Apartheid Society. Publications. 6)*

BLITTERSDORFF (WINRICH VON) Freiherr. Pluralismus der Bevölkerungsgruppen in der Verfassungsstruktur Südafrikas und Zyperns. Hamburg, 1972. pp. 135. *bibliog. (Hamburg. Institut für Auswärtige Politik. Darstellungen zur Auswärtigen Politik. Band 13)*

SOUTH AFRICA. (Cont.)

KLEINSCHMIDT (HORST) ed. White liberation: a collection of essays. Johannesburg, 1972. pp. 65. *(South African Council of Churches and Christian Institute of Southern Africa. Special Programme for Christian Action in Society. Publications. [No.4]*

NATIONAL ANTI-APARTHEID COORDINATING COMMITTEE [NEW ZEALAND]. Fight apartheid: a manual for action; editorial committee: Christopher Wainwright, Lindsay Wright. rev. ed. Wellington, N.Z., [1972]. pp. 57. *bibliog.*

SOUTH AFRICAN CONGRESS OF TRADE UNIONS. Apartheid in South African industry. London, [1972?]. pp. 7.

SOUTH AFRICAN COUNCIL OF CHURCHES and CHRISTIAN INSTITUTE OF SOUTHERN AFRICA. Study Project on Christianity in Apartheid Society. Economics Commission. Power, privilege and poverty;...report. Johannesburg, 1972. pp. 127. *(South African Council of Churches, and Christian Institute of Southern Africa. Study Project on Christianity in Apartheid Society. Publications. No. 7)*

AINSLIE (ROSALYNDE) Masters and serfs: farm labour in South Africa. London, 1973. pp. 55.

FASULO (G.) The powers behind apartheid. Cambridge, Mass., [1973?]. pp. 23. *(Africa Research Group. Reprints. 3)*

RANDALL (PETER) A taste of power: the final, co-ordinated Spro-cas report. Johannesburg, 1973. pp. 225. *(South African Council of Churches, and Christian Institute of Southern Africa. Study Project on Christianity in Apartheid Society. [Occasional] Publications. No. 11)*

SOUTH AFRICAN COUNCIL OF CHURCHES and CHRISTIAN INSTITUTE OF SOUTHERN AFRICA. Study Project on Christianity in Apartheid Society. Political Commission. South Africa's political alternatives;... report. Johannesburg, 1973. pp. 252. *bibliog. (Study Project on Christianity in Apartheid Society. Publications. No. 10)*

WILSON (FRANCIS) Economist, and PERROT (DOMINIQUE) eds. Outlook on a century: South Africa, 1870-1970. Lovedale, 1973. pp. 746.

MALHERBE (PAUL N.) Multistan: a way out of the South African dilemma. Cape Town, 1974. pp. 172. *bibliog.*

PATON (ALAN) Apartheid and the archbishop: the life and times of Geoffrey Clayton, Archbishop of Cape Town. London, 1974. pp. 311.

SOUTH AFRICA. Commission of Inquiry into Certain Organisations. 1974. Fifth interim report (R.P. 62/1974). in SOUTH AFRICA. Parliament. House of Assembly. Votes and proceedings; (with Printed annexures).

TUROK (BEN) Strategic problems in South Africa's liberation struggle: a critical analysis. Richmond, B.C., 1974. pp. 66.

WORKSHOP ON ORGANISED LABOUR IN SOUTH AFRICAN SOCIETY, CAPE TOWN, 1973. Labour perspectives on South Africa: (proceedings...); edited by Wolfgang H. Thomas. Cape Town, 1974. pp. 259.

— Relations (general) with New Zealand.

NATIONAL ANTI-APARTHEID COORDINATING COMMITTEE [NEW ZEALAND]. Fight apartheid: a manual for action; editorial committee: Christopher Wainwright, Lindsay Wright. rev. ed. Wellington, N.Z., [1972]. pp. 57. *bibliog.*

— Social conditions.

RANDALL (PETER) ed. Some implications of inequality. Johannesburg, 1971. pp. 65. *(South African Council of Churches and Christian Institute of Southern Africa. Study Project on Christianity in Apartheid Society. Publications. No.4)*

RANDALL (PETER) A taste of power: the final, co-ordinated Spro-cas report. Johannesburg, 1973. pp. 225. *(South African Council of Churches, and Christian Institute of Southern Africa. Study Project on Christianity in Apartheid Society. [Occasional] Publications. No. 11)*

WILSON (FRANCIS) Economist, and PERROT (DOMINIQUE) eds. Outlook on a century: South Africa, 1870-1970. Lovedale, 1973. pp. 746.

LEFTWICH (ADRIAN) ed. South Africa: economic growth and political change; with comparative studies of Chile, Sri Lanka and Malaysia. London, 1974. pp. 357.

— Social policy.

SOUTH AFRICAN COUNCIL OF CHURCHES and CHRISTIAN INSTITUTE OF SOUTHERN AFRICA. Study Project on Christianity in Apartheid Society. Social Commission. Towards social change: (report); general editor Peter Randall. Johannesburg, 1971. pp. 197. *(Study Project on Christianity in Apartheid Society. Publications. 6)*

RANDALL (PETER) A taste of power: the final, co-ordinated Spro-cas report. Johannesburg, 1973. pp. 225. *(South African Council of Churches, and Christian Institute of Southern Africa. Study Project on Christianity in Apartheid Society. [Occasional] Publications. No. 11)*

— Statistics, Vital.

SOUTH AFRICA. Bureau of Statistics. Reports. No. 07-03-01. Report on deaths, 1963-1966, South Africa. Pretoria, [1971]. pp. 279. *In English and Afrikaans.*

SOUTH AFRICA. Bureau of Statistics. 1973. Report on births, 1964 to 1971: South Africa. [Pretoria, 1973]. pp. 190. *(Reports. No. 07-01-01) In English and Afrikaans.*

— Yearbooks.

SOUTH AFRICA: official yearbook of the Republic of South Africa; (distributed by the South African Department of Information). a., 1974(1st)- Pretoria.

SOUTH AFRICAN WAR, 1899—1902

— Public opinion.

KOSS (STEPHEN E.) ed. The Pro-Boers: (the anatomy of an antiwar movement). Chicago, 1973. pp. 280. *bibliog.*

SOUTH CAROLINA

— Economic policy.

COASTAL PLAINS REGIONAL COMMISSION. Economic development plan. Washington, the Commission, 1971. pp. 111.

COASTAL PLAINS REGIONAL COMMISSION [UNITED STATES]. Regional plan in brief. [Washington, the Commission], 1973. pp. 20.

SOUTH SHIELDS

— Social history.

FOSTER (JOHN) 1940- . Class struggle and the industrial revolution: early industrial capitalism in three English towns. London, [1974]. pp. 346. *bibliog.*

SOUTH WEST AFRICA

— Economic policy.

WORLD COUNCIL OF CHURCHES. Programme to Combat Racism. Cunene Dam scheme and the struggle for the liberation of southern Africa. Geneva, 1971. pp. 45.

— Industries.

SOUTH AFRICA. Bureau of Statistics. 1966. Industrial census, 1962-63: manufacturing; construction; electricity, gas and steam; laundries, dyeing and dry cleaning: South Africa and South West Africa. [Pretoria, 1966]. pp. 171. *(Reports. No. 302) In English and Afrikaans.*

— Politics and government.

HIDAYATULLAH (MOHAMMAD) The South-West Africa case. Bombay, [1967]. pp. 144.

SOUTHAMPTON

— Economic history.

PLATT (COLIN) Medieval Southampton: the port and trading community, A.D. 1000-1600. London, 1973. pp. 309. *bibliog.*

— History — Sources.

HAMPSON (GEOFFREY) ed. Southampton notarial protest books 1756-1810. Southampton, 1973. pp. 133. *bibliog. (Southampton. University of Southampton. Southampton Records Series. vol. 16)*

— Social history.

PLATT (COLIN) Medieval Southampton: the port and trading community, A.D. 1000-1600. London, 1973. pp. 309. *bibliog.*

SOUTHERN YEMEN.

See YEMEN, SOUTHERN.

SOVEREIGNTY.

DOIMI DI DELUPIS (INGRID) International law and the independent state. Epping, Essex, 1974. pp. 252.

SOVIET CENTRAL ASIA

— Description and travel.

PO Srednei Azii i Kazakhstanu: putevoditel'. Moskva, 1973. pp. 407.

— Economic history.

AKADEMIIA NAUK SSSR. Institut Etnografii. Trudy. Novaia Seriia. t.98. Ocherki po istorii khoziaistva narodov Srednei Azii i Kazakhstana. Leningrad, 1973. pp. 260.

— Politics and government.

MASSELL (GREGORY J.) The surrogate proletariat: Moslem women and revolutionary strategies in Soviet Central Asia, 1919-1929. Princeton, [1974]. pp. 448. *bibliog.*

SOVIET NORTH

— Economic policy.

AKADEMIIA NAUK SSSR. Sovet po Izucheniiu Proizvoditel'nykh Sil. Mezhduvedomstvennaia Komissiia po Problemam Severa. vyp. 18. Razvitie proizvoditel'nykh sil i problemy okruzhaiushchei sredy. Moskva, 1973. pp. 247.

— History — 1917—1921, Revolution — Personal narratives.

KEDROV (M.S.) Za sovetskii Sever: lichnye vospominaniia i materialy o pervykh etapakh grazhdanskoi voiny 1918 g. Leningrad, 1927. pp. 202.

— Social life and customs.

FOL'KLOR i etnografiia Russkogo Severa. Leningrad, 1973. pp. 280.

SOVIETS

— Russia.

TSENTRAL'NYI GOSUDARSTVENNYI ARKHIV OKTIABR'SKOI REVOLIUTSII, VYSSHIKH ORGANOV GOSUDARSTVENNOI VLASTI I ORGANOV GOSUDARSTVENNOGO UPRAVLENIIA SSSR. 1917 God v Dokumentakh i Materialakh. Petrogradskii Sovet rabochikh i soldatskikh deputatov: protokoly zasedanii Ispolnitel'nogo Komiteta i Biuro I.K.; podgotovleno k pechati B.Ia. Nalivaiskim. Moskva, 1925. pp. 375.

TSENTRAL'NYI GOSUDARSTVENNYI ARKHIV OKTIABR'SKOI REVOLIUTSII, VYSSHIKH ORGANOV GOSUDARSTVENNOI VLASTI I ORGANOV GOSUDARSTVENNOGO UPRAVLENIIA SSSR. 1917 God v Dokumentakh i Materialakh. Vserossiiskoe Soveshchanie Sovetov rabochikh i soldatskikh deputatov: stenograficheskii otchet; podgotovil k pechati M.N. Tsapenko, etc.. Moskva, 1927. pp. 356.

CHKHIKVADZE (VIKTOR MIKHAILOVICH) ed. The Soviet form of popular government. Moscow, 1972. pp. 254.

SAVKO (ALEKSANDR PAVLOVICH) Partiinoe rukovodstvo Sovetami v period stroitel'stva kommunizma. Moskva, 1973. pp. 187.

VASIL'EV (VSEVOLOD IVANOVICH) Demokraticheskii tsentralizm v sisteme Sovetov. Moskva, 1973. pp. 231.

SPAAK (PAUL HENRI).

OUTERS (LUCIEN) Paul-Henri Spaak: son dernier combat. Bruxelles, [1972]. pp. 94.

SPACE AND TIME.

GRUENBAUM (ADOLF) Philosophical problems of space and time. 2nd ed. Dordrecht, [1973]. pp. 884. *bibliogs.* (*Boston Colloquium for the Philosophy of Science. Boston Studies in the Philosophy of Science. vol. 12*)

SPACE FLIGHT.

HIRSCH (RICHARD) and TRENTO (JOSEPH JOHN) The National Aeronautics and Space Administration. New York, 1973. pp. 245. *bibliog.*

LOVELL (Sir ALFRED CHARLES BERNARD) The origins and international economics of space exploration. Edinburgh, [1973]. pp. 104.

SPACE IN ECONOMICS.

LEFEBVRE (HENRI) Espace et politique: le droit à la ville. 2. Paris, [1972]. pp. 175.

GRUBBSTRÖM (ROBERT W.) Economic decisions in space and time: theoretical and experimental inquiries into the cause of economic motion. [Linköping, 1973]. pp. 379. *bibliog.*

KNIGHT (RICHARD VICTOR) Employment expansion and metropolitan trade. New York, 1973. pp. 108. (*Columbia University. Graduate School of Business. Conservation of Human Resources Project. Conservation of Human Resources Studies*)

STARRETT (DAVID A.) Principles of optimal location in a large homogeneous area. Stanford, 1973. pp. 48. *bibliog.* (*Stanford University. Institute for Mathematical Studies in the Social Sciences. Technical Reports.* [*New Series*]. *No. 90*)

SPENCE (NIGEL ANTHONY) Spatial dynamics of English regional employment change: 1951 and 1961; [Ph.D.(London) thesis]. 1974. fo. 594. *bibliog.* Typescript: unpublished. This thesis is the property of London University and may not be removed from the Library.

SPACE SCIENCES.

See also INFORMATION STORAGE AND RETRIEVAL SYSTEMS — Space sciences.

SPAIN

— Army — History.

SALAS LARRAZABAL (RAMON) Historia del Ejercito Popular de la Republica. Madrid, [1973]. 4 vols.

— Colonies.

SAEZ DE GOVANTES (LUIS) El africanismo español. Madrid, 1971. pp. 233.

ZAVALA (SILVIO ARTURO) La filosofia politica en la conquista de America. 2nd ed. Mexico, 1972. pp. 145. *bibliog.*

— — Administration.

MORLA (VIAL DE) España en Marruecos: la obra social. Madrid, 1947. pp. 173.

HANKE (LEWIS ULYSSES) Bartolome de las Casas: pensador politico, historiador, antropologo; [version española de Antonio Fernandez Travieso]. Buenos Aires, [1968]. pp. 125. *bibliog.*

BERNARD (GILDAS) Le secrétariat d'état et le conseil espagnol des Indes, 1700-1808. Genève, 1972. pp. 296. *bibliog.* (*Paris. Ecole Pratique des Hautes Etudes. Section des Sciences Historiques et Philologiques. Centre de Recherches d'Histoire et de Philologie. Hautes Etudes Medievales et Modernes. No. 14*)

TOMAS Y VALIENTE (FRANCISCO) La venta de oficios en Indias, 1492-1606. Madrid, 1972. pp. 180.

— — History.

RUMEU DE ARMAS (ANTONIO) España en el Africa atlantica. Madrid, 1956-57. 2 vols. (in 1).

YOUNG (RAYMOND ARTHUR) La influencia de Godoy en el desarrollo de los Estados Unidos de America, a costa de Nueva España. Mexico, 1968. pp. 146.

VILAR RAMIREZ (JUAN BAUTISTA) España en Argelia, Tunez, Ifni y Sahara, durante el siglo XIX. Madrid, 1970. pp. 174. *bibliog.*

MARTÍN (MIGUEL) El colonialismo español en Marruecos, 1860-1956. [Paris, 1973]. pp. 263. *bibliog.*

— Commerce — Belgium.

STOLS (EDDY) De Spaanse Brabanders of de handelsbetrekkingen der Zuidelijke Nederlanden met de Iberische wereld, 1598-1648. Brussel, 1971. 2 vols. *bibliog.* (*Vlaamse Academie voor Wetenschappen, Letteren en Schone Kunsten van Belgie. Klasse der Letteren. Verhandelingen. Nr. 70*)

— Constitution.

ZAFRA VALVERDE (JOSE) Regimen politico de España. Pamplona, 1973. pp. 534. (*Universidad de Navarra. Facultad de Derecho. Coleccion Juridica. 53*)

— Constitutional history.

OLTRA (JOAQUIN) La influencia norteamericana en la Constitucion Española de 1869. Madrid, 1972. pp. 194.

— Cortes.

GARCIA LAGUARDIA (JORGE MARIO) Origenes de la democracia constitucional en Centroamerica. San Jose, C.R., 1971. pp. 351. *bibliog.*

— Economic conditions.

FRANCE. Direction de la Documentation. La Documentation Française. Notes et Etudes Documentaires. Nos. 3,788-3, 789. L'économie de l'Espagne; [by] Yves Bravard. Paris, 1971. pp. 62.

COMENTARIO SOCIOLOGICO; elaborado por el Servicio de Estudios Sociologicos de la Confederacion Española de Cajas de Ahorros. Madrid, D 1973/Mr 1974 (año 2 no. 4/5). *bibliog.*

— Economic history.

RUIZ Y GONZALEZ DE LINARES (ERNESTO) Las Sociedades Economicas de los Amigos del Pais. Burgos, 1972. pp. 71. *bibliog.* (*Consejo Superior de Investigaciones Cientificas. Institucion Fernan Gonzalez. Publicaciones*)

— Economic policy.

BUTTLER (FRIEDRICH) Einkommensredistributive und raumstrukturelle Regionalpolitik im Rahmen der spanischen Entwicklungspläne. Göttingen, [1969]. pp. 83. *bibliog.* (*Göttingen. Universität. Ibero-Amerika-Institut für Wirtschaftsforschung. Arbeitsberichte. Heft 5*)

CIRCULO DE ECONOMIA. Hacia una nueva politica economica. Barcelona, 1970. pp. 100.

BUTTLER (FRIEDRICH) Entwicklungspole und räumliches Wirtschaftswachstum: Untersuchungen zur Identifikation und Inzidenz von Entwicklungspolen; das spanische Beispiel, 1964-1971. Tübingen, 1973. pp. 376. *bibliog.*

VELARDE FUERTES (JUAN) Politica economica de la Dictadura. Madrid, 1973. pp. 252.

— Emigration and immigration.

ATLAS DE LA EMIGRACION ESPAÑA; [pd. by] Instituto Español de Emigracion. a., 1970- Madrid.

SAGRERA (MARTIN) España peregrina: la influencia de las migraciones actuales en la transformacion sociocultural de España. Mexico, 1970. pp. 79.

— Executive departments.

BERNARD (GILDAS) Le secrétariat d'état et le conseil espagnol des Indes, 1700-1808. Genève, 1972. pp. 296. *bibliog.* (*Paris. Ecole Pratique des Hautes Etudes. Section des Sciences Historiques et Philologiques. Centre de Recherches d'Histoire et de Philologie. Hautes Etudes Medievales et Modernes. No. 14*)

— Foreign relations.

SPAIN. Oficina de Informacion Diplomatica. 1949. Notes for posterity: communist world offensive against Spain: a report on the "Spanish case" in the United Nations Organization, January-April, 1946; [by] Gonzalo Rodriguez Castillo. 2nd ed. Madrid, 1949. pp. 339.

YOUNG (RAYMOND ARTHUR) La influencia de Godoy en el desarrollo de los Estados Unidos de America, a costa de Nueva España. Mexico, 1968. pp. 146.

[CARRERO BLANCO (LUIS)] Comentarios de un español; las tribulaciones de Don Prudencio; diplomacia subterranea; ([by] "Juan de la Cosa" [pseud.]). Madrid, 1973. pp. 339.

MADARIAGA (SALVADOR DE) Morning without noon: memoirs. Farnborough, 1974. pp. 441.

See also EUROPEAN ECONOMIC COMMUNITY — Spain.

— — Germany.

PROCTOR (RAYMOND) Agonia de un neutral: las relaciones hispanoalemanas durante la segunda guerra mundial y la Division Azul. [Madrid, 1972]. pp. 354. *bibliog.*

ABENDROTH (HANS HENNING) Hitler in der spanischen Arena: die deutsch-spanischen Beziehungen...1936-1939. Paderborn, [1973]. pp. 411. *bibliog.*

— — Morocco.

MARTÍN (MIGUEL) El colonialismo español en Marruecos, 1860-1956. [Paris, 1973]. pp. 263. *bibliog.*

— — United Kingdom.

RODRIGUEZ-MOÑINO SORIANO (RAFAEL) La mision diplomatica de Don Jacobo Stuart Fitz James y Falco, XVII Duque de Alba en la Embajada de España en Londres, 1937-1945. [Madrid, 1971]. pp. 144. *bibliog.*

— History.

PONCE (ANIBAL) El viento en el mundo: examen de la España actual en el centenario de Fourier. Buenos Aires, 1963. pp. 188.

MENENDEZ-VALDES GOLPE (EDUARDO) Separatismo e unidade: una mitificacion historica. Vigo, [1970]. pp. 243.

— — 1516—1700, House of Austria.

GUARESTI (JUAN JOSE) the Younger. La guerra de las comunidades: el federalismo argentino. Buenos Aires, 1970. pp. 272. *bibliog.*

— — 1800—1899.

ARTOLA GALLEGO (MIGUEL) La burguesia revolucionaria, 1808-1869. Madrid, [1973]. pp. 434. *bibliog.*

— — 1868—1931.

MARTINEZ CUADRADO (MIGUEL) La burguesia conservadora, 1874-1931. Madrid, [1973]. pp. 592. *bibliog.*

— — 1873—1875, Republic.

FERRANDO BADIA (JUAN) Historia politico-parlamentaria de la Republica de 1873. Madrid, 1973. pp. 403.

SPAIN. (Cont.)

— — 1931—1939, Republic.

BRAVO MORATA (FEDERICO) La Republica...1931-(1935). [Madrid, 1973]. 2 vols. (in 1).

LOZANO GONZALEZ (JESUS) La segunda republica: imagenes, cronologia y documentos. Barcelona, [1973]. pp. 504. *bibliog.*

TAMAMES CÓMEZ (RAMÓN) La república: la era de Franco. Madrid, 1973 repr. 1974. pp. 623. *bibliog.*

— — 1931, Revolution.

GUZMAN (EDUARDO DE) 1930: historia politica de un año decisivo. Madrid, [1973]. pp. 643.

— — 1936—1939, Civil War.

COSTA DEU (G.) and BARCELLONA (ANTONIO MARIA DA) Martiri della rivoluzione del 1936 nella Catalogna. 2nd ed. Torino, [1937?]. pp. 201.

ROMERO (LUIS) Tres dias de julio: 18, 19 y 20 de 1936. Barcelona, 1967. pp. 639.

MARTINEZ BANDE (JOSE MANUEL) Los cien ultimos dias de la Republica. Barcelona, 1973. pp. 323. *bibliog.*

SALAS LARRAZABAL (RAMON) Historia del Ejercito Popular de la Republica. Madrid, [1973]. 4 vols.

JACKSON (GABRIEL) A concise history of the Spanish Civil War. London, [1974]. pp. 192. *bibliog.*

KISCH (RICHARD) They shall not pass: the Spanish people at war, 1936-39. London, [1974]. pp. 176. *bibliog.*

SEMPRUN-MAURA (CARLOS) Révolution et contre-révolution en Catalogne, 1936-1937. Tours, [1974]. pp. 307.

- - — — Foreign participation.

ABENDROTH (HANS HENNING) Hitler in der spanischen Arena: die deutsch-spanischen Beziehungen...1936-1939. Paderborn, [1973]. pp. 411. *bibliog.*

— — — Personal narratives.

JENKINS (MICK) George Brown: portrait of a communist leader. Manchester, [197-?]. pp. 30.

ARNAL (MOSEN JESUS) Por que fui secretario de Durruti: narracion. Tarrega, [1972]. pp. 266.

— — 1939— .

TAMAMES CÓMEZ (RAMÓN) La república: la era de Franco. Madrid, 1973 repr. 1974. pp. 623. *bibliog.*

— Kings and rulers.

JUSEU (JORGE) Monarquia a la española: un Cesar con fueros. Madrid, 1971. pp. 123.

— Nobility.

DOMINGUEZ ORTIZ (ANTONIO) Las clases privilegiadas en la España del Antiguo Regimen. Madrid, [1973]. pp. 464. *bibliog.*

— Politics and government.

[FRANCO BAHAMONDE (FRANCISCO)] El pequeño libro pardo del General. [Paris], 1972. pp. 191.

KERN (ROBERT) ed. The caciques: oligarchical politics and the system of caciquismo in the Luso-Hispanic world. Albuquerque, [1973]. pp. 202.

PIKE (FREDRICK BRAUN) and STRITCH (THOMAS) eds. The new corporation: social-political structures in the Iberian world. Notre Dame, [1974]. pp. 218. (*Notre Dame. University. Committee on International Relations. International Studies*).

— Relations (general) with Africa.

SAEZ DE GOVANTES (LUIS) El africanismo español. Madrid, 1971. pp. 233.

— Relations (general) with the United States.

OLTRA (JOAQUIN) La influencia norteamericana en la Constitucion Española de 1869. Madrid, 1972. pp. 194.

— Religion.

CHRISTIAN (WILLIAM A.) Person and God in a Spanish valley. New York, [1972]. pp. 215. *bibliog.*

— Social conditions.

COMENTARIO SOCIOLOGICO; elaborado por el Servicio de Estudios Sociologicos de la Confederacion Española de Cajas de Ahorros. Madrid. D 1973/Mr 1974 (año 2 no. 4/5). *bibliog.*

— Social history.

DOMINGUEZ ORTIZ (ANTONIO) Los judeoconversos en España y America. Madrid, [1971]. pp. 253.

DOMINGUEZ ORTIZ (ANTONIO) Las clases privilegiadas en la España del Antiguo Regimen. Madrid, [1973]. pp. 464. *bibliog.*

— Social policy.

GIRON DE VELASCO (JOSE ANTONIO) Orientaciones sociales del gobierno: discurso... ante el pleno de las Cortes Españolas, celebrado el 22 de noviembre de 1944. Madrid, 1945. pp. 58. (*Spain. Instituto Nacional de Prevision. Publicaciones. 598*)

SPANIARDS IN RUSSIA.

GROS (JOSE) Abriendo camino: relatos de un guerrillero comunista; prologo de Dolores Ibarruri. [Paris, 1972]. pp. 270.

SPANISH PERIODICALS.

ALVAREZ JUNCO (JOSE) ed. La Comuna en España. Madrid, 1971. pp. 252.

ZAVALA (IRIS M.) Romanticos y socialistas: prensa española del XIX. Madrid, 1972. pp. 208.

SPANN (OTHMAR).

SIEGFRIED (KLAUS JOERG) Universalismus und Faschismus: das Gesellschaftsbild Othmar Spanns; zur politischen Funktion seiner Gesellschaftslehre und Ständestaatskonzeption. Wien, [1974]. pp. 289. *bibliog.*

SPECIAL DRAWING RIGHTS.

HIRSCH (FRED) An SDR standard: impetus, elements, and impediments. Princeton, 1973. pp. 24. *bibliog.* (*Princeton University. Department of Economics and Sociology. International Finance Section. Essays in International Finance. No.99*)

PARK (YOON S.) The link between special drawing rights and development finance. Princeton, 1973. pp. 25. *bibliog.* (*Princeton University. Department of Economics and Sociology. International Finance Section. Essays in International Finance. No. 100*)

SPEECH.

FANT (C. GUNNAR M.) Speech sounds and features. Cambridge, Mass., [1973]. pp. 227. *bibliogs.*

SPERANSKII (MIKHAIL MIKHAILOVICH) Graf.

VAGIN (V.) ed. Istoricheskie svedeniia o deiatel'nosti grafa M.M. Speranskogo v Sibiri s 1819 po 1822 god. S.-Peterburg, 1872. 2 vols.

SPHERES OF INFLUENCE.

BERTRAND RUSSELL CENTENARY SYMPOSIUM ON SPHERES OF INFLUENCE IN THE AGE OF IMPERIALISM, LINZ, 1972. Spheres of influence in the age of imperialism; papers submitted to the Bertrand Russell Centenary Symposium...;[by] Noam Chomsky [and others]. Nottingham, 1972. pp. 144.

BERTRAND RUSSELL CENTENARY SYMPOSIUM ON SPHERES OF INFLUENCE IN THE AGE OF IMPERIALISM, LINZ, 1972. Spheres of influence and the third world; papers submitted to the Bertrand Russell Centenary Symposium...;[by] Vladimi Dedijer [and others]. Nottingham, 1973. pp. 123.

SPILLER (ELSE ZUEBLIN—).

See ZUEBLIN—SPILLER (ELSE).

SPINA BIFIDA

— Bibliography.

PILLING (DORIA) compiler. The child with spina bifida: social, emotional and educational adjustment; an annotated bibliography. Slough, 1973. pp. 46.

SPORTS

— Germany.

GERMANY (BUNDESREPUBLIK). Statistisches Bundesamt. Ausgaben der öffentlichen Haushalte für Gesundheit, Sport und Erholung. 1964/1969[1st]; a., 1970- Wiesbaden. *1964/1969 as Aufwendungen von Bund, Ländern und Gemeinden (Gv.) für Gesundheitspflege und Sport. (Finanzen und Steuern. Reihe 5. Sonderbeiträge zur Finanzstatistik).*

— United States.

EDWARDS (HARRY) Sociology of sport. Homewood, Ill., 1973. pp. 395. *bibliog.*

GOVERNMENT and the sports business: papers prepared for a conference of experts; (Roger G. Noll, editor). Washington, [1974]. pp. 445. *bibliog.* (*Brookings Institution. Studies in the Regulation of Economic Activity*)

— Venezuela.

VENEZUELA. Despacho del Ministro de Estado para la Juventud, la Ciencia y la Cultura. 1973. Primer informe sobre la juventud venezolana. [Tomo 1]. Documento de trabajo. Situacion del deporte. Caracas, 1973. 1 vol.(various pagings).

SQUATTERS

— Peru.

LEWIS (ROBERT ALDEN) Employment, income and the growth of the barriadas in Lima, Peru.[Ithaca], 1973. pp. 359. *bibliog.* (*Cornell University. Latin American Studies Program. Dissertation Series. No.46*)

SRAFFA (PIERO).

BOTTA (FRANCO) ed. Il dibattito su Sraffa: [a collection of readings]. Bari, [1974]. pp. 273.

SRI LANKA

— Commerce.

DUTTA (AMITA) International migration, trade, and real income: a case study of Ceylon, 1920-38. Calcutta, 1973. pp. 171. *bibliog.*

— Constitution.

KEARNEY (ROBERT N.) The politics of Ceylon (Sri Lanka). Ithaca, 1973. pp. 249. *bibliogs.*

— Economic policy.

INTERNATIONAL BANK FOR RECONSTRUCTION AND DEVELOPMENT. 1968. The problem of foreign exchange and long-term growth of Ceylon; [report submitted for meeting of Aid Ceylon Group, Paris, 1968; Manfred G. Blobel, chief of mission]. [Colombo, Ministry of Planning and Economic Affairs, 1968] . pp. 68.

SRI LANKA. Ministry of Planning and Employment. 1971. The five year plan, 1972-1976. [Colombo], 1971 repr. 1972. pp. 137.

— Emigration and immigration.

DUTTA (AMITA) International migration, trade, and real income: a case study of Ceylon, 1920-38. Calcutta, 1973. pp. 171. *bibliog.*

— **Executive departments.**

SRI LANKA. Ministry of Finance. Review of government activities.a., 1972 [1st issue]- [Colombo].

— **Foreign relations.**

PRASAD (DHIRENDRA MOHAN) Ceylon's foreign policy under the Bandaranaikes, 1956-65: a political analysis. New Delhi, 1973. pp. 465. *bibliog.*

— **Parliament — Elections.**

SRI LANKA. Department of Elections. 1971. Results of parliamentary general elections in Ceylon, 1947-1970. Colombo, 1971. pp. 120.

— **Politics and government.**

SRI LANKA. Ministry of Public Administration, Local Government and Home Affairs. 1970. Proposals for the establishment of people's committees. Colombo, 1970. pp. 9.

SRI LANKA. Constituent Assembly. Official report. sess., Ja 22 1971 (v.1, no.8)- Colombo. *In English or Sinhala. File includes Official reports of committees, F 20 1971 (v.1,no.6)-*

BRASS (PAUL R.) and FRANDA (MARCUS F.) eds. Radical politics in south Asia. Cambridge, Mass., [1973]. pp. 449. *(Massachusetts Institute of Technology. Center for International Studies. Studies in Communism, Revisionism and Revolution. 19)*

KEARNEY (ROBERT N.) The politics of Ceylon (Sri Lanka). Ithaca, 1973. pp. 249. *bibliogs.*

WILSON (A. JEYARATNAM) Politics in Sri Lanka, 1947-1973. London, 1974. pp. 347. *bibliog.*

— **Social policy.**

SRI LANKA. Ministry of Planning and Employment. 1971. The five year plan, 1972-1976. [Colombo], 1971 repr. 1972. pp. 137.

LEFTWICH (ADRIAN) ed. South Africa: economic growth and political change; with comparative studies of Chile, Sri Lanka and Malaysia. London, 1974. pp. 357.

STABILITY OF SHIPS.

INTER-GOVERNMENTAL MARITIME CONSULTATIVE ORGANIZATION. 1969. Recommendation on intact stability for passenger and cargo ships under 100 metres in length. London, [1969]. pp. 18.

INTER-GOVERNMENTAL MARITIME CONSULTATIVE ORGANIZATION. 1969. Recommendation on intact stability of fishing vessels. London, [1969]. pp. 24.

STAFFORDSHIRE

— **Social history — Sources.**

STAFFORDSHIRE. Education Department. Local History Source Books. No. 12. State of large towns in north Staffordshire; [sources]. [Stafford, 1972]. fo. 34.

STÄL—HOLSTEIN (ANNE LOUISE GERMAINE DE) Baronne.

ALDANOV (MARK ALEKSANDROVICH) pseud. [i.e. LANDAU (MARK ALEKSANDROVICH)] Iunost' Pavla Stroganova i drugie kharakteristiki. Belgrad, [1935?]. pp. 188.

STALIN (IOSIF VISSARIONOVICH).

BRINKMANN (HEINRICH) Stalin, Theoretiker der Bürokratie: eine Streitschrift gegen den offenen Stalinismus und gegen die verlegenen Entstalinisierer. 's Gravenhage, 1971 repr.1972. pp. 167. *bibliog.*

ULAM (ADAM BRUNO) Stalin: the man and his era. London, 1974. pp. 760. *First published in the United States in 1973.*

JEFFRIES (IAN) The Stalinist economic system as a model for underdeveloped countries: the development of Soviet thought since 1953; [Ph.D.(London) thesis]. [1974]. fo. 301. *bibliog. Typescript: unpublished. This thesis is the property of London University and may not be removed from the Library.*

LEVYTSKY (BORIS) ed. The Stalinist terror in the thirties: documentation from the Soviet press. Stanford, [1974]. pp. 521. *bibliog. (Stanford University. Hoover Institution on War, Revolution and Peace. Hoover Institution Publications. 126)*

STANDARDIZATION

— **Communist countries.**

STEPANENKO (STANISLAV IVANOVICH) Sotrudnichestvo stran-chlenov SEV v oblasti standartizatsii. 2nd ed. Moskva, 1973. pp. 168. *For 1st ed. see his Organizatsiia sotrudnichestva stran-chlenov SEV v oblasti standartizatsii.*

— **European Economic Community countries — Law and legislation.**

STARKOWSKI (REINHARD) Die Angleichung technischer Rechtsvorschriften und industrieller Normen in der Europäischen Wirtschaftsgemeinschaft. Berlin, [1973]. pp. 168. *bibliog.*

STANFORD UNIVERSITY.

BURDICK (CHARLES BURTON) Ralph H. Lutz and the Hoover Institution. Stanford, [1974]. pp. 185. *(Stanford University. Hoover Institution on War, Revolution and Peace. Hoover Institution Publications. 131)*

STATE, THE.

NORONHA (SANCHO DE) Tratado moral de louvores e perigos de alguns estados seculares; introdução e notas por Martim de Albuquerque. Lisboa, 1969. pp. 149. *(Portugal. Junta de Investigações do Ultramar. Centro de Estudos Politicos e Sociais. Estudos de Ciencias Politicas e Sociais. 83) Reprint of edition of 1549.*

REAL DE AZUA (CARLOS) Legitimidad, apoyo y poder politico: ensayo de tipologia. [Montevideo?], 1969. pp. 133.

CECCHINI (VINCENZO) La crisi dello Stato: partitocrazia e sindacati. Milano, [1972]. pp. 199.

FOURNOL (ETIENNE MAURICE) Bodin: prédécesseur de Montesquieu; étude sur quelques théories politiques de la République et de l'Esprit des lois; [originally published 1896]. New York, 1972. pp. 176.

CRICK (BERNARD ROWLAND) Basic forms of government:a sketch and a model. London, 1973. pp. 96. *bibliog.*

GULIEV (VLADIMIR EVGEN'EVICH) Sovremennoe imperialisticheskoe gosudarstvo: voprosy teorii. Moskva, 1973. pp. 207.

MILHAUD (JEAN) Mon ami l'état. [Paris], 1973. pp. 143.

SHAMARIN (EDUARD VIKTOROVICH) Gosudarstvenno-pravovye vzgliady predshestvennikov nauchnogo sotsializma v Rossii. Kiev, 1973. pp. 175.

ZAMPETTI (PIER LUIGI) Dallo stato liberale allo stato dei partiti: la rappresentanza politica. 2nd ed. Milano, 1973. pp. 223.

ZIPPELIUS (REINHOLD) Allgemeine Staatslehre, Politikwissenschaft: ein Studienbuch.4th ed. München, 1973. pp. 302.

SHENNAN (J.H.) The origins of the modern European state, 1450-1725. London, 1974. pp. 135.

SKINNER (ANDREW S.) Adam Smith and the role of the state; a paper delivered in Kirkcaldy on 5th June 1973, at a symposium, etc. Glasgow, 1974. pp. 28.

ZOLO (DANILO) La teoria comunista dell'estinzione dello stato. Bari, [1974]. pp. 316. *bibliog.*

STATE GOVERNMENTS

STATE ENCOURAGEMENT OF SCIENCE, LITERATURE AND ART.

UNITED NATIONS EDUCATIONAL, SCIENTIFIC AND CULTURAL ORGANIZATION. Studies and Documents on Cultural Policies. Paris, 1969 in progress.

STATE FARMS

See also AGRICULTURE, COOPERATIVE.

— **Russia.**

VOLKOV (VLADIMIR FEDOROVICH) and MALAKHOV (ALEKSANDR KIRILLOVICH) Zarabotnaia plata i premirovanie rabotnikov sovkhozov. Moskva, 1967. pp. 183.

PANKOVA (KLARA IVANOVNA) Voprosy intensifikatsii i ekonomicheskogo stimulirovaniia proizvodstva v sovkhozakh. Moskva, 1973. pp. 126.

SINEVA (LIUDMILA NIKOLAEVNA) Rentabel'nost' sovkhoznogo proizvodstva. Moskva, 1973. pp. 136.

VORONTSOV (ALEKSEI PAVLOVICH) Proizvoditel'nost' truda i zarabotnaia plata v sovkhozakh. Moskva, 1973. pp. 231.

— — **Accounting.**

DORMIDONTOV (MIKHAIL PETROVICH) Analiz khoziaistvennoi deiatel'nosti sovkhoza. Moskva, 1974. pp. 295.

— — **Finance.**

SEMENOV (VIKTOR NIKOLAEVICH) Finansy i kredit v sovkhozakh: ekonomicheskii eksperiment v sovkhozakh, perevedennykh na polnyi khoziaistvennyi raschet. Moskva, 1969. pp. 175.

SKALOZUBOVA (NELLI ALEKSANDROVNA) and SHTEINMAN (MIKHAIL IAKOVLEVICH) Finansovoe planirovanie v sovkhozakh. Moskva, 1973. pp. 143.

— — **Law and legislation.**

VEDENIN (NIKOLAI NIKIFOROVICH) Pravovoe polozhenie sovkhozov v usloviiakh ekonomicheskoi reformy. Moskva, 1973. pp. 260.

— — **Kazakhstan.**

MIKHAILOV (FEDOR KUZ'MICH) Sovkhoznoe stroitel'stvo v Kazakhstane, 1946-1970 gg. Alma-Ata, 1973. pp. 299.

STATE GOVERNMENTS

— **Canada.**

ROWAT (DONALD CAMERON) ed. Provincial government and politics: comparative essays. 2nd ed. [Ottawa, 1973]. pp. 577. *bibliog.*

— **India.**

INDIA. Administrative Reforms Commission. Study Team on State Level Administration. 1970. Report...1968. [Delhi, 1970]. pp. 187.

— **United States.**

ALESCH (DANIEL J.) and DOUGHARTY (L.A.) Economies-of-scale analysis in state and local government...: a report prepared for Council on Intergovernmental Relations, State of California. Santa Monica, 1971. pp. 56. *bibliog. (Rand Corporation. [Rand Reports]. 748)*

MAIN (JACKSON TURNER) The sovereign states, 1775-1783. New York, 1973. pp. 502. *bibliog.*

— — **Bibliography.**

TOMPKINS (DOROTHY LOUISE CAMPBELL) compiler. Research and service: a fifty year record; [publications of the]...Institute of Governmental Studies, University of California, etc. Berkeley, 1971. pp. 154.

STATE SUCCESSION.

ZAKHAROVA (NATAL'IA VASIL'EVNA) Pravopreemstvo gosudarstv. Moskva, 1973. pp. 126.

STATES, NEW.

WORSLEY (PETER MAURICE) The third world. 2nd ed. Chicago, 1970. pp. 373. *bibliog.*

JESSUP (PHILIP CARYL) The birth of nations; [incorporating and amplifying the Barnette Miller Lectures, Wellesley College, 1971]. New York, 1974. pp. 361.

STATES, SMALL.

BASILE (ANTOINE) Commerce extérieur et développement de la petite nation: essai sur les contraintes de l'exiguité économique. Beyrouth, 1972. pp. 396. *bibliog.*

TAMSE (C.A.) Nederland en België in Europa, 1859-1871: de zelfstandigheidspolitiek van twee kleine staten. Den Haag, 1973. pp. 371. *bibliog.*

STATESMEN.

ROSSI-LANDI (GUY) Les hommes politiques. [Paris], 1973. pp. 114. *bibliog.*

STATESMEN, BRITISH.

U.K. Central Office of Information. Reference Division. 1973-. Reference biography service: [notes on British ministers, secretaries of state, etc.]. [London], 1973 in progress. *Current issues only kept.*

SOUTHGATE (DONALD GEORGE) ed. The Conservative leadership, 1832-1932. London, 1974. pp. 277. *bibliog.*

STATESMEN, KENYAN.

NELLIS (JOHN R.) The ethnic composition of leading Kenyan government positions. Uppsala, 1974. pp. 26. *(Nordiska Afrikainstitutet. Research Reports. No.24)*

STATESMEN, RUSSIAN.

GRIMSTED (PATRICIA KENNEDY) The foreign ministers of Alexander I: political attitudes and the conduct of Russian diplomacy, 1801-1825. Berkeley, Ca., 1969. pp. 367. *bibliog.*

HODNETT (GREY) and OGAREFF (VAL) Leaders of the Soviet republics 1955-1972: a guide to posts and occupants. Canberra, 1973. pp. 454.

STATICS AND DYNAMICS (SOCIAL SCIENCES).

DALY (HERMAN E.) ed. Toward a steady-state economy. San Francisco, [1973]. pp. 332. *bibliogs.*

STATISTICAL DECISION.

PAQUETTE (NEIL) and FRANKLAND (PHILLIP) A discussion of decision making under conditions of environmental uncertainty. Iowa City, 1973. fo. 22. *bibliog. (Iowa University. Department of Geography. Discussion Paper Series. No. 21)*

STATISTICS

See also subdivision Statistics under the names of countries, cities, etc. also under the heading UNDERDEVELOPED AREAS.

— Bibliography.

MAGYAR KÖZGAZDASÁGI ÉS STATISZTIKAI IRODALOM BIBLIOGRÁFIA: Hungarian bibliography of economics and statistics; ([pd. by] Központi Statisztikai Hivatal Könyvtár és Dokumentációs Szolgálat [and] MTA Közgazdaságtudományi Intézetének Könyvtára). a., 1968[v.8]- Budapest. *In Hungarian, Russian and English.*

— Congresses.

NORWAY. Statistiske Centralbyrå. 1924. Det 13de Nordiske Statistiske Møte holdt i Kristiania 25- 26 August 1924. Kristiania, 1924. pp. 140.

[SCANDINAVIA]. Nordisk Statistisk Skriftserie. 25. Det nordiske chefstatistikermøde i Helsingfors 1973, etc. København, 1974. pp. 143.

— Dictionaries and encyclopaedias.

LEXIKON der Wirtschaft: Rechnungsführung und Statistik; (Herausgeber: Arno Donda). Berlin, [1974]. pp. 527.

— Graphic methods.

NORWAY. Geodatakomitéen. 1971. Innstilling om et forbedret regionalt informasjonssystem til samfunnsplanlegging og forvaltning. Otta, 1971. pp. 97.

— History.

MALYI (IL'IA GRIGOR'EVICH) Voprosy statistiki v trudakh Fridrikha Engel'sa. Moskva, 1973. pp. 140.

— — Netherlands.

DEURSEN (A.TH. VAN) Geschiedenis en toekomstverwachting: het onderwijs in de statistiek aan de universiteiten van de achttiende eeuw; rede uitgesproken ... aan de Vrije Universiteit te Amsterdam op 26 november 1971. Kampen, 1971. pp. 32.

— — Russia.

V.I. Lenin i sovremennaia statistika. Moskva, 1970-73. 3 vols.

— Problems, exercises, etc.

RAHMAN (N.A.) Practical exercises in probability and statistics...; with answers and hints on solutions. London, 1972. pp. 338.

— Theory, methods, etc.

ROBINSON (ENDERS ANTHONY) Selected papers. Uppsala, [196-?]. 1 vol.(various pagings). *(Uppsala. Universitet. Institute of Statistics. Selected publications. vol. 21)*

SPIEGEL (MURRAY RALPH) Schaum's outline of theory and problems of statistics. New York, [1961]. pp. 359.

URIBE VILLEGAS (OSCAR) La matematica, la estadistica, y las ciencias sociales. Mexico, 1963. pp. 325. *bibliog. (Mexico City. Universidad Nacional Autonoma de Mexico. Instituto de Investigaciones Sociales. Cuadernos de Sociologia)*

SHEPARD (ROGER N.) and others, eds. Multidimensional scaling: theory and applications in the behavioral sciences. New York, 1972 repr. 1973. 2 vols. *bibliogs.*

EDGERTON (DAVID L.) Nonlinear interdependent systems: a study of estimation and prediction in interdependent systems which contain nonlinearities in the variables. Uppsala, [1973]. pp. 174, 8. *(Uppsala. Universitet. Institute of Statistics. Selected Publications. vol. 30)*

FREUND (JOHN ERNST) Modern elementary statistics. 4th ed. Englewood Cliffs, [1973]. pp. 532.

LEVIN (JACK) Statistician. Elementary statistics in social research. New York, [1973]. pp. 279. *bibliog.*

LINDSEY (JAMES K.) Inferences from sociological survey data: a unified approach. Amsterdam, 1973. pp. 163. *bibliog.*

MAY (S.J.) Choosing a single equation estimator. [Ottawa, 1973]. fo. 35. *bibliog. (Carleton University. Carleton Economic Papers)*

POPHAM (W. JAMES) and SIROTNIK (KENNETH A.) Educational statistics: use and interpretation. 2nd ed. New York, [1973]. pp. 413. *bibliogs.*

THOMAS (JOHN JAMES) An introduction to statistical analysis for economists. London, [1973]. pp. 286. *bibliog. (London. University. London School of Economics and Political Science. LSE Handbooks in Economic Analysis)*

BERGSTRÖM (REINHOLD) Studies in the estimation of interdependent systems, especially the fix-point and iterative instrumental variables methods. Uppsala, [1974]. pp. 283. *bibliog. (Uppsala. Universitet. Institute of Statistics. Selected Publications. vol. 33)*

BODIN (LENNART) Recursive fix-point estimation: theory and applications. Uppsala, [1974]. pp. 343. *(Uppsala. Universitet. Institute of Statistics. Selected Publications. vol.32)*

CAMPBELL (STEPHEN KENT) Flaws and fallacies in statistical thinking. Englewood Cliffs, [1974]. pp. 200.

JOLLIFFE (F.R.) Commonsense statistics for economists and others. London, 1974. pp. 174. *bibliog.*

KOHOUT (FRANK J.) Statistics for social scientists: a coordinated learning system. New York, [1974]. pp. 452.

STATUTES

— United Kingdom.

STATUTE LAW SOCIETY. Statute law: the key to clarity; first report of the Committee appointed to propose solutions to the deficiencies of the statute law system in the United Kingdom. London, 1972. pp. 65.

STAVROPOL' (KRAI)

— History — Sources.

V.I. Lenin i Stavropol'e: sbornik dokumentov i materialov. Stavropol', 1971. pp. 208.

STEALING.

CARTER (R.L.) Theft in the market: an economic analysis of costs and incentives in improving prevention by government and private police and reducing loss by insurance. London, 1974. pp. 96. *bibliog. (Institute of Economic Affairs. Hobart Papers. 60)*

STEAM POWER PLANTS

— South Africa.

SOUTH AFRICA. Bureau of Statistics. Census of electricity, gas and steam. bien., 1963/4- Pretoria. *In English and Afrikaans.*

STEEL INDUSTRY AND TRADE.

FRIDÉN (LENNART) Instability in the international steel market: a study of import and export fluctuations;... translation, Roger Tanner. [Stockholm, 1972]. pp. 236. *bibliog.*

WOLTER (FRANK) Strukturelle Anpassungsprobleme der westdeutschen Stahlindustrie: zur Standortfrage der Stahlindustrie in hochindustrialisierten Ländern. Tübingen, 1974. pp. 182. *bibliog. (Kiel. Universität. Institut für Weltwirtschaft. Kieler Studien. 127)*

— Environmental aspects.

C.C. FURNAS MEMORIAL CONFERENCE, 2ND, BUFFALO, 1971. The steel industry and the environment: (proceedings); edited by Julian Szekely. New York, 1973. pp. 285. *bibliogs.*

— Canada.

ATLANTIC PROVINCES ECONOMIC COUNCIL. Background Papers. Steelmaking in the Atlantic provinces: a commentary. [Halifax], 1974. pp. 40. *bibliog.*

— China.

CLARK (MILLS GARDNER) Development of China's steel industry and Soviet technical aid.Ithaca, N.Y., 1973. pp. 160. *bibliog.*

— Europe.

ANNUAL BULLETIN OF STEEL STATISTICS FOR EUROPE; ([pd. by] Economic Commission for Europe) United Nations. a., 1973(v.1)- New York. *In English, French and Russian.*

— Germany.

FRITZ (MARTIN) German steel and Swedish iron ore, 1939-1945. Göteborg, 1974. pp. 137. bibliog. (Göteborgs Universitet. Ekonomisk-Historiska Institutionen. Meddelanden. 29)

WOLTER (FRANK) Strukturelle Anpassungsprobleme der westdeutschen Stahlindustrie: zur Standortfrage der Stahlindustrie in hochindustrialisierten Ländern. Tübingen, 1974. pp. 182. bibliog. (Kiel. Universität. Institut für Weltwirtschaft. Kieler Studien. 127)

— India.

NATIONAL PRODUCTIVITY COUNCIL, [INDIA]. Productivity trends in iron and steel industry in India. New Delhi, 1974. pp. 76.

— United Kingdom.

BRITISH STEEL CORPORATION. Annual report and accounts. a., 1971/2 (5th)- London. Formerly included in the file of British Parliamentary Papers.

IRON AND STEEL INDUSTRY TRAINING BOARD [U.K.]. Annual report. a., 1972/3- London. Formerly included in the file of British Parliamentary Papers.

HEAL (DAVID W.) The steel industry in post war Britain. Newton Abbot, [1974]. pp. 224. bibliog.

JONES (T.KEN) The human face of change: social responsibility and rationalization at British Steel. London, 1974. pp. 69. bibliog. (Institute of Personnel Management. Handbooks)

U.K. Central Office of Information. Reference Division. Reference Pamphlets. 116. British industry today: steel. London, 1974. pp. 52. bibliog.

VAIZEY (JOHN ERNEST) The history of British steel. London, [1974]. pp. 205. bibliog.

YOUNG FABIAN STEEL GROUP. Crisis in steel. London, 1974. pp. 40. (Young Fabian Group. Young Fabian Pamphlets. 38)

— United States.

HOGAN (WILLIAM THOMAS) The 1970s: critical years for steel. Lexington, 1973. pp. 132.

WARREN (KENNETH) The American steel industry 1850-1970: a geographical interpretation. Oxford, 1973. pp. 337.

CANNON (JAMES SPENCER) Environmental steel: pollution in the iron and steel industry; (edited [for the Council on Economic Priorities] by Jean M. Halloran). New York, 1974. pp. 521.

STEKLOV (IURII MIKHAILOVICH).

STEKLOV (IURII MIKHAILOVICH) Izbrannoe. Moskva, 1973. pp. 262. bibliog.

STENBOCK (JOHAN GABRIEL).

KULLBERG (ANDERS) Johan Gabriel Stenbock och reduktionen: godspolitik och ekonomiförvaltning, 1675-1705. Stockholm, [1973]. pp. 174. bibliog. (Uppsala. Universitet. Historiska Institutionen. Studia Historica Upsaliensia. 51) With German summary.

STENOGRAPHERS.

ALT (THEODOR RUDOLF) Hundert Jahre im Dienste der Österreichischen Volksvertretung. Wien, Österreichische Staatsdruckerei, 1948. pp. 204.

STEPNIAK (SERGEI) pseud.

TARATUTA (EVGENIIA ALEKSANDROVNA) Russkii drug Engel'sa. Moskva, 1970. pp. 143.

TARATUTA (EVGENIIA ALEKSANDROVNA) S.M. Stepniak-Kravchinskii - revoliutsioner i pisatel'. Moskva, 1973. pp. 541,[xvi].

STEPPES.

KARSHINSKAIA step' i geograficheskie problemy ee khoziaistvennogo osvoeniia. Tashkent, 1973. pp. 104. bibliog.

STERILIZATION (BIRTH CONTROL).

INTERNATIONAL PLANNED PARENTHOOD FEDERATION. Panel of Experts on Sterilization. Male and female sterilization: a report of the meeting of the IPPF Panel...; edited for the IPPF Central Medical Committee by R.L. Kleinman. London, 1973. pp. 40.

KONOTEY-AHULU (F.I.D.) Medical considerations for legalizing voluntary sterilization: sickle cell disease as a case in point;... background paper presented at the 2nd International Conference on Voluntary Sterilization, 1973. Medford, Mass., 1973. pp. 28. bibliog. (Tufts University. Fletcher School of Law and Diplomacy. Law and Population Monograph Series. No.13)

SOUTH AFRICA. Parliament. House of Assembly. Select Committee on the Abortion and Sterilization Bill 1973. Report (with Proceedings and Minutes of evidence); [C.V. van der Merwe, chairman] (S.C. 8 - 1973). in SOUTH AFRICA. Parliament. House of Assembly. Select Committee reports.

STEPAN (JAN) and KELLOGG (EDMUND H.) The world's laws on voluntary sterilization for family planning purposes. Medford, Mass., [1973]. pp. 69. (Tufts University. Fletcher School of Law and Diplomacy. Law and Population Monograph Series. No.8)

SOUTH AFRICA. Commission of Inquiry into the Abortion and Sterilization Bill. 1974. Report (R.P.68/1974). in SOUTH AFRICA. Parliament. House of Assembly. Votes and proceedings; (with Printed annexures) .

STETTINIUS (EDWARD REILLY).

FORBES (JOHN DOUGLAS) Stettinius, Sr.: portrait of a Morgan partner. Charlottesville, 1974. pp. 244. bibliog.

STIRLING

— Description.

TIMMS (DUNCAN W.G.) ed. The Stirling region. Stirling. (British Association for the Advancement of Science. Scientific survey, 1974)

— Economic conditions.

BROWNRIGG (MARK) A study of economic impact: the University of Stirling. Edinburgh, 1974. pp. 115. bibliog.

STIRLING UNIVERSITY.

BROWNRIGG (MARK) A study of economic impact: the University of Stirling. Edinburgh, 1974. pp. 115. bibliog.

STOCHASTIC PROCESSES.

BARTHOLOMEW (DAVID JOHN) Stochastic models for social processes. 2nd ed. London, 1973. pp. 411. bibliog.

NEWELL (GORDON F.) Approximate stochastic behavior of n-server service systems with large n. Berlin, 1973. pp. 118. bibliog.

SRINIVASAN (S.K.) Stochastic point processes and their applications. London, 1974. pp. 174. bibliog.

STOCK AND STOCK BREEDING

See also MARKETING OF LIVESTOCK.

— United Kingdom.

ECONOMIC DEVELOPMENT COMMITTEE FOR THE AGRICULTURAL INDUSTRY. Common Market Sub-Committee. Problem Areas Working Group. UK farming and the Common Market: hills and uplands; a report. London, National Economic Development Office, 1973. pp. 39.

— Uruguay.

BARRIOS PINTOS (ANIBAL) Historia de la ganaderia en el Uruguay, 1574-1971. Montevideo, [1973]. pp. 294. bibliog.

STOCK COMPANIES

— Russia.

SHEPELEV (LEONID EFIMOVICH) Aktsionernye kompanii v Rossii. Leningrad, 1973. pp. 347.

STOCK EXCHANGE

— Denmark — Law.

DENMARK. Udvalg til Revision af Fondsbørsordningen. 1971. Fondsbørsen og fondsbørsvekselererne: betaenkning II. [Copenhagen], 1971. pp. [148]. (Denmark. Betaenkninger. Nr.600)

— European Economic Community countries.

EUROPEAN COMMUNITIES. Commission. 1972. (Proposed directive and draft Council recommendation on a prospectus to be published when securities are admitted to official stock exchange quotation). Brussels, 1972. pp. 69. (Bulletin of the European Communities. Supplements. [1972/8])

— France.

PETIT-DUTAILLIS (GEORGES) Epargne, investissement et Bourse. [Paris], 1972. pp. 90. bibliog. (France. Direction de la Documentation. La Documentation Française. Notes et Etudes Documentaires. Nos. 3937-3938)

MARNATA (FRANÇOISE) La Bourse et le financement des investissements. Paris, 1973. pp. 125. bibliog. (Fondation Nationale des Sciences Politiques. Travaux et Recherches de Sciences Economiques. Serie "Economie Française". 1)

— United Kingdom.

THOMAS (W.A.) The provincial stock exchanges. London, 1973. pp. 335.

— United States.

NEEDHAM (JAMES J.) The threat to corporate growth. [Philadelphia], 1974. pp. 60.

STOCKHOLDERS

— Australia.

STANDING COMMITTEE OF STATE AND COMMONWEALTH ATTORNEYS-GENERAL [AUSTRALIA]. Company Law Advisory Committee. Second interim report. in AUSTRALIA. Parliament. Parliamentary papers, 1969. vol.1.

— United Kingdom.

VERNON (ROBIN A.) and others. Who owns the blue chips?: a study of shareholding in a leading company. Epping, Essex, 1973. pp. 198. bibliogs.

STOCKHOLM

— Civic improvement.

PASS (DAVID) Vällingby and Farsta - from idea to reality: the new community development process in Stockholm. Cambridge, Mass., [1973]. pp. 190. bibliog.

— Suburbs and environs.

PASS (DAVID) Vällingby and Farsta - from idea to reality: the new community development process in Stockholm. Cambridge, Mass., [1973]. pp. 190. bibliog.

STOCKS (MARY DANVERS) Baroness Stocks.

STOCKS (MARY DANVERS) Baroness Stocks. Still more commonplace. London, 1973. pp. 142.

STOCKS

— Prices.

DRAPER (P.R.) Sector influences on share price variability. [Stirling, 1972?]. fo. 28. (University of Stirling. Discussion Papers in Economics, Finance and Investment. No. 4)

STOCKS. (Cont.)

— Mexico.

CASO BERCHT (JORGE) El mercado de acciones en Mexico. Mexico, 1971. pp. 339.

— Netherlands.

PLATE (AUGUSTE) Niet volgestorte aandelen. Deventer, [1974]. pp. 172. *bibliog. With French summary.*

STORE HOURS.

See SHOPPING HOURS.

STORE LOCATION

— United Kingdom.

DEVELOPMENT CONTROL POLICY NOTES. 13. Out of town shops and shopping centres. London, H.M.S.O., 1972. pp. (4).

STORES, TRAVELLING.

ECONOMISCH INSTITUUT VOOR HET MIDDEN- EN KLEINBEDRIJF. Bedrijfseconomische Publikaties. De rijdende winkel, 1971-1972-1973. 's-Gravenhage, 1974. pp. 111.

STRAITS QUESTION.

JELAVICH (BARBARA) The Ottoman Empire, the great powers, and the Straits question, 1870-1887. Bloomington, [1973]. pp. 209. *bibliog. With appendices in French.*

STRASBOURG.

FRANCE. French Embassy, London. Service de Presse et d'Information. 1973. Strasbourg. London, [1973]. pp. 28.

— Economic history.

HERTNER (PETER) Stadtwirtschaft zwischen Reich und Frankreich: Wirtschaft und Gesellschaft Strassburgs 1650-1714. Köln, 1973. pp. 468. *bibliog.*

— Social history.

HERTNER (PETER) Stadtwirtschaft zwischen Reich und Frankreich: Wirtschaft und Gesellschaft Strassburgs 1650-1714. Köln, 1973. pp. 468. *bibliog.*

STRATEGY.

WALLACH (JEHUDA L.) Das Dogma der Vernichtungsschlacht: die Lehren von Clausewitz und Schlieffen und ihre Wirkungen in zwei Weltkriegen; (aus dem Englischen von Hans Jürgen Baron von Koskull). Frankfurt am Main, 1967. pp. 475. *bibliog.*

GEWELDLOZE actie en sociale verdediging; [by] F. Bekkers [and others]. Rotterdam, 1971. pp. 153. *(Mens en Maatschappij. Boekafleveringen. 1971)*

HAMMOND (JOHN S.) Defense decisionmaking: prudent versus excessive conservatism. Santa Monica, 1971. pp. 29. *(Rand Corporation. [Rand Reports]. 715)*

TAMMEN (RONALD L.) MIRV and the arms race: an interpretation of defense strategy. New York, 1973. pp. 162. *bibliog.*

BRODIE (BERNARD) War and politics. London, 1974. pp. 514.

STRAUSS (FRANZ JOSEF).

SCHWARZBUCH: Franz Josef Strauss; herausgegeben von Wolfgang Roth [and others]. Köln, [1972]. pp. 126.

BISCHOFF (DETLEF) Franz Josef Strauss, die CSU und die Uussenpolitik: Konzeption und Realität am Beispiel der Grossen Koalition. Meisenheim am Glan ,1973. pp. 346. bibliog.

STRESEMANN (GUSTAV).

BAUER (HEINRICH) Stresemann: ein deutscher Staatsmann. Berlin, 1930. pp. 268.

STRESS (PHYSIOLOGY).

GRAY (JEFFREY A.) The psychology of fear and stress. London, [1971]. pp. 256. *bibliog.*

LEVI (LENNART) Stress and distress in response to psychosocial stimuli: laboratory and real-life studies on sympatho-adrenomedullary and related reactions. Oxford, 1972 repr. 1973. pp. 166. *bibliogs. Summaries in various languages.*

WOLFF (SULAMMITH) Children under stress. rev. ed. Harmondsworth, 1973 repr. 1974. pp. 283. *bibliog.*

STRIKES AND LOCKOUTS.

HUTT (WILLIAM HAROLD) The strike-threat system: the economic consequences of collective bargaining. New Rochelle, N. Y., [1973]. pp. 294.

— Bolivia.

TABOADA TERAN (NESTOR) El precio del estaño: una tragedia boliviana. La Paz, 1960. pp. 271. *A fictionalised account of a true incident.*

— Canada.

ONTARIO FEDERATION OF LABOUR and LABOUR COUNCIL OF METROPOLITAN TORONTO. Strikebreaking Committee. The strikebreakers: the report of the...committee...written by Marc Zwelling. Toronto, 1972. pp. 161.

— — Manitoba.

MANN (MARGARET) The strike that wasn't: teachers' "strike", Brandon, 1922. Brandon, Manitoba, [1972]. pp. 136. *bibliog.*

— Colombia.

RUEDA ROSERO (ULPIANO) Los conflictos de trabajo: la huelga; el arbitramento. Bogota, 1969. pp. 92. *bibliog.*

— European Economic Community countries.

GRÈVE et lockout; par G. Boldt [and others]. Luxembourg, Communauté Européenne du Charbon et de l'Acier, 1961. pp. 399. *(European Coal and Steel Community. Collection du Droit du Travail)*

— France.

PERROT (MICHELLE) Les ouvriers en grève: France, 1871-1890. Paris, [1974]. 2 vols. *bibliog. (Paris. Ecole Pratique des Hautes Etudes. Section des Sciences Economiques et Sociales. Centre de Recherches Historiques. Civilisations et Sociétés. 31)*

SHORTER (EDWARD) and TILLY (CHARLES) Strikes in France, 1830-1968. London, 1974. pp. 428. *bibliog.*

— Germany.

GEWERKSCHAFTEN UND KLASSENKAMPF: kritisches Jahrbuch. a., 1972 [1st]- Frankfurt am Main.

ZEITLER (ADOLF FRANZ) Streikrecht und grundgesetz. [Ausburg, imprint, 1973]. pp. 170. *bibliog.*

— Italy.

MASSOLA (UMBERTO) Gli scioperi del '43: marzo-aprile; le fabbriche contro il fascismo. Roma, 1973. pp. 193.

SCALPELLI (ADOLFO) Dalmine 1919: storia e mito di uno sciopero "rivoluzionario". Roma, 1973. pp. 157.

— Netherlands.

BREIJ (BERT) Een kwestie van principe: getuigschrift voor stakers; (de fascinerende strijd van de Industriebonden in 1973). Baarn, [1973]. pp. 159.

— Scandinavia.

INGHAM (GEOFFREY K.) Strikes and industrial conflict: Britain and Scandinavia. London, 1974. pp. 95. *bibliog. (British Sociological Association. Studies in Sociology)*

— Sweden.

KOMMUNISTISK TIDSKRIFT. Skriftserie. 1971.Nr.2. 12-12 omröstningen: möte i 27-mannadelegationen den 1.2 1970. Stockholm, 1971. pp. 73.

— Switzerland.

TOBLER (MAX) Ein Stück Klassenkampf in der Schweiz: das Streikjahr 1906 in Zürich; (aus Zürichs Kosakenzeit). Zürich, [1912?]. pp. 46.

— United Kingdom.

JONES (ALAN) and THOMPSON (RON) After the miners' strike, what next? London, [1973?]. pp. 50.

MARSON (DAVE) Children's strikes in 1911. [Oxford, 1973]. pp. 35. *(History Workshop. Pamphlets. No. 9)*

BECK (TONY) The Fine Tubes strike. London, 1974. pp. 128.

INGHAM (GEOFFREY K.) Strikes and industrial conflict: Britain and Scandinavia. London, 1974. pp. 95. *bibliog. (British Sociological Association. Studies in Sociology)*

— United States.

THIEBLOT (ARMAND J.) and COWIN (RONALD M.) Welfare and strikes: the use of public funds to support strikers. Philadelphia, [1972]. pp. 276. *(Pennsylvania University. Wharton School of Finance and Commerce. Industrial Research Unit. Labor Relations and Public Policy Series. Reports. No 6)*

— Zambia.

NORTHERN RHODESIA. Committee of Inquiry into the Stoppage of Work among Teachers in the Western Province during the Months of July and August, 1963. 1963. Report. Lusaka, 1963. pp. 25.

STRONTIUM ORES

— United Kingdom.

THOMAS (I.A.) Celestite, including references to strontianite. London, H.M.S.O., 1973. pp. 26. *bibliog. (Mineral Dossiers. No. 6)*

STRUCTURAL ANTHROPOLOGY.

See ANTHROPOLOGY; STRUCTURALISM.

STRUCTURALISM.

WAHL (FRANÇOIS) ed. Qu'est-ce que le structuralisme?; [by] Oswald Ducrot [and others]. Paris, [1968]. pp. 446. *bibliogs.*

BOURDIEU (PIERRE) Esquisse d'une théorie de la pratique, precédé de Trois études d'ethnologie kabyle. Genève, 1972. pp. 269.

DELFENDAHL (BERNHARD) Le clair et l'obscur: critique de l'anthropologie savante; défense de l'anthropologie amateur. Paris, [1973]. pp. 222.

LEVI-STRAUSS (CLAUDE) Anthropologie structurale deux. [Paris, 1973]. pp. 450.

MAKARIUS (RAOUL) and MAKARIUS (LAURA) Structuralisme ou ethnologie: pour une critique radicale de l'anthropologie de Levi-Strauss. Paris, [1973]. pp. 375. *bibliog.*

GLUCKSMANN (MIRIAM ANNE) Structuralist analysis in contemporary social thought: a comparison of the theories of Claude Lévi-Strauss and Louis Althusser. London, 1974. pp. 197. *bibliog.*

STRUCTURALISM (PHILOSOPHY).

See STRUCTURE (PHILOSOPHY).

STRUCTURE (PHILOSOPHY).

SYMPOSIUM ON HIERARCHICAL STRUCTURE IN NATURE AND ARTIFACT, HUNTINGTON BEACH, CALIFORNIA, 1968.

STUART FITZ JAMES Y FALCO (JACOBO) 17th Duke of Alba.

RODRIGUEZ-MOÑINO SORIANO (RAFAEL) La mision diplomatica de Don Jacobo Stuart Fitz James y Falco, XVII Duque de Alba en la Embajada de España en Londres, 1937-1945. [Madrid, 1971]. pp. 144. *bibliog.*

STÜBER (FRITZ).

See STUEBER (FRITZ).

STUDENT AID

— Canada.

WEST (E.G.) Differential versus equal student subsidies in post-secondary education: a current Canadian dispute. [Ottawa, 1973]. fo. 29. *(Carleton University. Carleton Economic Papers)*

— Switzerland.

SWITZERLAND. Commission Intercantonale des Bourses d'Etudes. 1970. Projekt für die Verbesserung der Ausbildungsfinanzierung in der Schweiz, etc. [Bern, 1970]. pp. 27bis.

SWITZERLAND. Commission Intercantonale des Bourses d'Etudes. 1971. Die Ausbildungsfinanzierung durch die Kantone, Stand 31. Dezember 1970, etc. [Bern, 1971]. pp. 48. *In German and French.*

— United Kingdom.

BOOTH (JUDITH) compiler. Grants for higher education. rev.ed. London, 1973. pp. 250.

NATIONAL UNION OF STUDENTS. Grants yesterday, today, tomorrow?. [London, 1973]. pp. 8.

STUDENT COUNSELLORS, TRAINING OF.

CONFERENCE ON STUDENT COUNSELLING, 3rd, LONDON, 1972. Student counselling: scope and training; proceedings of the... conference. London, 1972. pp. 79. *bibliog.*

STUDENT HOUSING

— Denmark.

HANDS (JOHN) and BINGHAM (ROGER) Housing students in Scandinavia. London, [1973]. pp. 153. *(Student Co-operative Dwellings Limited. SCD Research Papers. No.1)*

— Finland.

HANDS (JOHN) and BINGHAM (ROGER) Housing students in Scandinavia. London, [1973]. pp. 153. *(Student Co-operative Dwellings Limited. SCD Research Papers. No.1)*

— Sweden.

HANDS (JOHN) and BINGHAM (ROGER) Housing students in Scandinavia. London, [1973]. pp. 153. *(Student Co-operative Dwellings Limited. SCD Research Papers. No.1)*

STUDENT STRIKES

— United States.

ROOT AND BRANCH. Pamphlets. 2. No class today, no ruling class tomorrow: lessons of the student strike. [Cambridge, Mass., 1970]. pp. 17.

STUDENT UNIONS.

SOUTH AFRICA. Commission of Inquiry into Certain Organisations. 1974. Fourth interim report (R.P. 33/1974). in SOUTH AFRICA. Parliament. House of Assembly. Votes and proceedings; (with Printed annexures).

STUDENTS

— Health and hygiene.

CONFERENCE ON STUDENT COUNSELLING, 2nd, LONDON, 1971. Student counselling and student progress; proceedings of the... conference...convened under the auspices of the Department of Higher Education, University of London Institute of Education. [London], 1971. pp. 53.

CAUTHERY (PHILIP) Student health. London, 1973. pp. 160. *bibliog.*

NEWSOM (AUDREY) and others. Student counselling in practice. London, [1973]. pp. 196. *bibliog.*

— America, Latin — Political activity.

SMITH (DAVID HORTON) Latin American student activism: participation in formal volunteer organizations by university students in six Latin cultures. Lexington, Mass., [1973]. pp. 169.

— Argentine Republic — Political activity.

BRIGNARDELLO (LUISA A.) El movimiento estudiantil argentino: corrientes ideologicas y opiniones de sus dirigentes. Buenos Aires, [1972]. pp. 362.

— Australia.

AUSTRALIA. Commonwealth Bureau of Census and Statistics. 1971. Survey of leavers from schools, universities or other educational institutions, February 1971. Canberra, 1971. pp. 7.

— Denmark.

[DENMARK. Undervisningsministeriet. 1969]. Student unrest in Denmark. [Copenhagen], 1969. fo. 4.

ULFF-MØLLER (BOEL) Stofbrug blandt studerende: en redegørelse for brug af euforiserende stoffer bygget på svar fra 2812 studerende ved universiteter og højere laereanstalter, etc. København, 1973. pp. 294. *bibliog. (Socialforskningsinstituttet. Publikationer. 58)*

— France.

CLAUSTRE (HENRI) Vivre dans l'université. Grenoble, [1973]. pp. 271.

— — Political activity

BACHY (JEAN PAUL) and BACHY (CLAUDINE) eds. Les étudiants et la politique: documents. Paris, [1973]. pp. 240. *bibliog.*

FOHLEN (CLAUDE) ed. Mai 1968: révolution ou psychodrame?. [Paris, 1973]. pp. 95. *bibliog.*

— — — Bibliography.

WYLIE (LAURENCE WILLIAM) and others. France: the events of May-June 1968; a critical bibliography. [Cambridge, Mass., 1973]. pp. 118.

— Germany — Political activity.

KREUTZBERGER (WOLFGANG) Studenten und Politik, 1918-1933: der Fall Freiburg im Breisgau. Göttingen, 1972. pp. 239. *bibliog.*

MARXISTISCHE AUFBAUORGANISATION. Die Krise der kommunistischen Parteien: Probleme der gegenwärtigen Revisionismuskritik. München, 1973. pp. 309. *bibliog.*

— India — Political activity.

NEELSEN (JOHN PETER) Student unrest in India: a typology and a socio-structural analysis. MÜNCHEN [1973]. pp. 101,xi. *bibliog. (Arnold-Bergstraesser-Institut für Kulturwissenschaftliche Forschung. Materialien zu Entwicklung und Politik. 1)*

— Italy.

SCARAMOZZINO (PASQUALE) La popolazione universitaria di Pavia: indagine di statistica sociale. Milano, [1970]. pp. 258. *(Pavia. Università. Istituto di Statistica. Pubblicazioni. 9)*

— Japan — Political activity.

KRAUSS (ELLIS S.) Japanese radicals revisited: student protest in postwar Japan. Berkeley, [1974]. pp. 192. *bibliog.*

— Mexico — Political activity.

TRES culturas en agonia; [by] Jorge Carrion [and others]. Mexico, 1969 repr. 1970. pp. 290.

— Netherlands.

SCHOPMAN (JAN) Kritiese universiteit: de ruk naar links in de nijmeegse studentenbeweging. Nijmegen, [1974]. pp. 106. *bibliog.*

— Nigeria.

NIGERIA. 1971. Comments of the federal military government on the report of the Commission of Inquiry into the disturbances on the campus of the University of Ibadan. Lagos, 1971. pp. 17.

— Turkey — Political activity.

SZYLIOWICZ (JOSEPH S.) A political analysis of student activism: the Turkish case. Beverley Hills, [1972]. pp. 77. *bibliog.*

— United Kingdom.

WANKOWSKI (J.A.) Temperament, motivation and academic achievement: studies of success and failure of a random sample of students in one university. Birmingham, [1972?]. 2 vols. (in 1). *bibliog. (Birmingham. University. Educational Survey)*

SOCIETY FOR RESEARCH INTO HIGHER EDUCATION. Annual Conference, 8th, 1972. Motivation: non-cognitive aspects of student performance: papers... edited by Colin Flood Page and Jill Gibson. London, 1973. pp. 118. *bibliogs.*

CAREERS RESEARCH AND ADVISORY CENTRE. Student life; (edited by J.P. O'Hanlon and Jenny Knight).Cambridge, 1974. pp. 281.

— Political activity.

MARTIN (DAVID ALFRED) Tracts against the times. Guildford, 1973. pp. 186.

— — Ireland, Northern — Political activity.

ARTHUR (PAUL) The People's Democracy, 1968-1973. Belfast, 1974. pp. 159. *bibliog.*

— United States.

SNYDER (BENSON R.) The hidden curriculum: [paperback edition of work first published in New York in 1971]. Cambridge, Mass., 1973. pp. 200.

— — Political activity.

ROOT AND BRANCH. Pamphlets. 2. No class today, no ruling class tomorrow: lessons of the student strike. [Cambridge, Mass., 1970]. pp. 17.

ALTBACH (PHILIP G.) Student politics in America: a historical analysis. New York, :1974].pp. 249.

BACCIOCCO (EDWARD J.) The new left in America: reform to revolution, 1956 to 1970. Stanford, Cal., [1974]. pp. 300. *bibliog. (Stanford University. Hoover Institution on War, Revolution and Peace. Hoover Institution Publications. 130)*

DAVIES (PETER) The truth about Kent State: a challenge to the American conscience; by Peter Davies and the Board of Church and Society of the United Methodist Church. London, 1974. pp. 242. *bibliog.*

TOURAINE (ALAIN) The academic system in American society;... third of a series of essays sponsored by the Carnegie Commission on Higher Education. New York, [1974]. pp. 319. *bibliog.*

STUDENTS. (Cont.)

— — — Abstracts.

KENISTON (KENNETH) Radicals and militants: an annotated bibliography of empirical research on campus unrest;... in collaboration with Mary-Kay Duffield [and] Sharon Martinek. Lexington, Mass., [1973]. pp. 219.

STUDENTS, FOREIGN

— Europe.

KLINEBERG (OTTO) and BEN BRIKA (JEANNE) Etudiants du tiers monde en Europe; problèmes d'adaptation; une étude effectuée en Autriche, en France, aux Pays-Bas et en Yougoslavie. Paris, [1972]. pp. 236. *bibliog. (European Coordination Centre for Research and Documentation in Social Sciences. Publications. 4) With English summaries.*

— United Kingdom.

UNITED KINGDOM COUNCIL FOR OVERSEAS STUDENT AFFAIRS. The situation of married overseas students in the U.K.; report of a pilot study undertaken in London and Leeds, etc. London, 1972. pp. 51. *bibliog.*

STUDENTS, INTERCHANGE OF.

NASSEFAT (MORTEZA) Le rôle des étudiants dans l'échange interculturel: une enquête de psycnologie sociale. Teheran, 1973. pp. 319. *bibliog. With English summary.*

STUDENTS, JEWISH

— United Kingdom.

UNION OF LIBERAL AND PROGRESSIVE SYNAGOGUES. Social Issues Committee. Jewish students: a question of identity. London, 1974. pp. 31. *bibliog.*

STUDENTS' SOCIETIES

— Germany.

FAUST (ANSELM) Der Nationalsozialistische Deutsche Studentenbund: Studenten und Nationalsozialismus in der Weimarer Republik. Düsseldorf, 1973. 2 vols. (in 1). *bibliog.*

STUEBER (FRITZ).

STUEBER (FRITZ) Ich war Abgeordneter: die Entstehung der freiheitlichen Opposition in Österreich. Graz, [1974]. pp. 304.

SUBJECT HEADINGS

— Sociology.

MERWE (CASPAR VAN DE) and others. Thesaurus of sociological research terminology. Rotterdam, 1974. pp. 471.

SUBMARINE GEOLOGY.

DOBSON (M.R.) and others. The geology of the south Irish Sea. London, 1973. pp. 35. *bibliog. (U.K. Institute of Geological Sciences. Reports. No. 73/11)* 2 maps in end pocket.

SUBSIDIES.

DENTON (GEOFFREY) and O'CLEIREACAIN (SEAMUS) Subsidy issues in international commerce. London, 1972. pp. 59. *(Trade Policy Research Centre. Thames Essays No. 5)*

— Canada — Quebec.

FEDERATION DES TRAVAILLEURS DU QUEBEC. Congrès, 12e, 1971. L'état, rouage de notre exploitation: documents de travail. [Montréal, 1971?]. pp. 143.

— India — Andhra Pradesh.

ANDHRA PRADESH. Law Commission. 1967. Laws relating to state aid to industries (April 1964). Hyderabad, 1967. pp. 46. *(Reports. 24)*

— United Kingdom.

U.K. Department of Trade and Industry. Offshore Supplies Office. 1973. Offshore supplies interest relief grants: a guide for industry. London, 1973. pp. 14.

PREST (ALAN RICHMOND) How much subsidy? a study of the economic concept and measurement of subsidies in the United Kingdom. London, 1974. pp. 38. *bibliog. (Institute of Economic Affairs. Research Monographs. 32)*

— United States.

DOWNS (ANTHONY) Federal housing subsidies: how are they working?. Lexington, Mass., [1973]. pp. 141. *bibliog.*

GOVERNMENT spending and land values: public money and private gain: (proceedings of a symposium sponsored by the Committee on Taxation, Resources and Economic Development...at the University of Wisconsin, Madison, 1971); edited by C. Lowell Harriss. Madison, 1973. pp. 239. *(Committee on Taxation, Resources and Economic Development. Publications. 6)*

SUBSTITUTION (ECONOMICS)

— Mathematical models.

THIRSK (WAYNE R.) Ease of factor substitution in agriculture. Houston, 1972. pp. 24. *(Rice University. Program of Development Studies. Papers. No. 34)*

LORANGER (JEAN GUY) Elasticité de substitution et rendements dans l'industrie manufacturière canadienne...; communication présentée au VIIIe congrès annuel de l'Association canadienne d'Economique, Université de Toronto, les 3, 4, 5 juin 1974. Montréal, [1974]. fo. 45. *bibliog. (Montreal. Université. Département des Sciences Economiques. Cahiers. No. 7408)*

SUBURBAN HOMES.

JACKSON (ALAN ARTHUR) Semi-detached London: suburban development, life and transport, 1900-39. London, 1973. pp. 381. *bibliog.*

SUBURBS.

JOHNSON (JAMES HENRY) ed. Suburban growth: geographical processes at the edge of the western city. London, [1974]. pp. 257. *bibliogs.*

SUBVERSIVE ACTIVITIES.

REES (DAVID) North Korea's growth as a subversive centre. London, 1972. pp. 19. *(Institute for the Study of Conflict. Conflict Studies. No. 28)*

INSTITUTE FOR THE STUDY OF CONFLICT. The peacetime strategy of the Soviet Union. London, [1973]. pp. 83. *(Institute for the Study of Conflict. Special Reports)*

— Chile.

INTERNATIONAL TELEPHONE AND TELEGRAPH CORPORATION. Subversion in Chile: a case study in U.S. corporate intrigue in the Third World; [memoranda of the Corporation with an introduction by a group representing the Bertrand Russell Peace Foundation and others]. Nottingham, 1972. pp. 114. *(Spokesman, The. Spokesman Books)*

SELSER (GREGORIO) Una empresa multinacional: la ITT en los Estados Unidos y en Chile. Buenos Aires, 1974. pp. 257.

— Germany.

SCHNEIDER (JOHANNES) Kommunistische Untergrundarbeit in der Bundesrepublik Deutschland. München, [1961]. pp. 49.

HORCHEM (HANS JOSEF) West Germany: "the Long March through the institutions". London, 1973. pp. 20. *(Institute for the Study of Conflict. Conflict Studies. No. 33)*

— United Kingdom.

SWERLING (SAM) Who's getting at our kids?; an analysis of the organisations and personalities attempting to bring about revolution in our schools. [London, 1972]. fo. 23.

COURTNEY (ANTHONY TOSSWILL) The enemies within. London, [1974?]. pp. 16.

— United States.

HOFFMAN (ABBIE) Steal this book. New York, [1971]. pp. 308. *bibliog.*

GRIFFITH (ROBERT) and THEOHARIS (ATHAN G.) eds. The specter: original essays on the cold war and the origins of McCarthyism. New York, 1974. pp. 366.

— Uruguay.

URUGUAY. Comision Investigadora de Actividades Antinacionales. 1943. Contralor de actividades subversivas en el Uruguay: manual de legislacion sobre contralor y transito de personas, expulsion...; ([by] Alejandro Rovira [and] Luis Segui Gonzalez). Montevideo, 1943. pp. 340.

— Zambia.

ZAMBIA. Tribunal on Detainees. 1967. Report: tHOMAS pICKETT, CHAIRMAN!. lUSAKA, 1967. PP. 24.

SUDAN

— Nationalism.

BESHIR (MOHAMED OMER) Revolution and nationalism in the Sudan. London, 1974. pp. 314. *bibliog.*

— Politics and government.

U.K. British Information Services (New York). Reference Division. 1952. The Sudan's progress towards self-government, 1951-52. New York, 1952. pp. 15.

EPRILE (CECIL) Sudan: the long war. London, 1972. pp. 19. *(Institute for the Study of Conflict. Conflict Studies. No. 21)*

BESHIR (MOHAMED OMER) Revolution and nationalism in the Sudan. London, 1974. pp. 314. *bibliog.*

EPRILE (CECIL) War and peace in the Sudan, 1955-1972. Newton Abbot, [1974]. pp. 192. *bibliog.*

MAHGOUB (MOHAMED AHMED) Democracy on trial: reflections on Arab and African politics. London, 1974. pp. 318.

ROBERTSON (Sir JAMES WILSON) Transition in Africa: from direct rule to independence; a memoir. London, [1974]. pp. 272.

— Population.

GALAL EL DIN (MOHED ELAWAD) Internal migration in the Sudan since World War II, with special reference to migration to Greater Khartoum; [Ph.D. (London) thesis]. 1973. fo. 301. *bibliog. Typescript: unpublished. This thesis is the property of London University and may not be removed from the Library.*

SUEZ CANAL.

ITALY. Ministero degli Affari Esteri. Comitato per la Documentazione dell'Opera dell'Italia in Africa. L'Italia in Africa. Serie Storica. Vol. 4. Luigi Negrelli e il Canale di Suez nelle carte del Fondo Maria Grois Negrelli. Tomi 1-2. 1846-1858, 1859-1869; a cura di Francesco Attilio Scaglione. Rome, 1971-72. 2 vols.

LABROUSSE (HENRI) Le Golfe et le Canal: la réouverture du canal de Suez et la paix internationale. [Paris], 1973. pp. 164. *bibliog.*

BOWIE (ROBERT RICHARDSON) Suez 1956. London, 1974. pp. 148. *(American Society of International Law. International Crises and the Role of Law)*

SUFFRAGE

— United Kingdom.

BROCK (MICHAEL) The great Reform Act. London, 1973. pp. 411. *bibliog.*

SUFISM.

GILSENAN (MICHAEL) Saint and Sufi in modern Egypt: an essay in the sociology of religion. Oxford, 1973. pp. 248. *bibliog.*

SUGAR

— Manufacture and refining — Antigua.

REPORT on the sugar industry and agriculture of Antigua; [C.J.M. Bennett, chairman]. London, Ministry of Overseas Development, 1966. fo.105. *bibliog.*

— — Brazil.

EISENBERG (PETER L.) The sugar industry in Pernambuco: modernization without change, 1840-1910. Berkeley, [1974]. pp. 289. *bibliog.*

— — United Kingdom.

GARBUTT (JOHN L.) Manbré and Garton Limited, 1855-1955: a hundred years of progress. [London, 1955]. pp. 51.

SUGAR GROWING

— Antigua.

REPORT on the sugar industry and agriculture of Antigua; [C.J.M. Bennett, chairman]. London, Ministry of Overseas Development, 1966. fo.105. *bibliog.*

— Brazil.

PEREIRA PINTO (JUAN CARLOS) La caña de azucar en la economia y la sociedad brasileña. Buenos Aires, [1968]. pp. 27. *bibliog.*

CANA e reforma agraria; [by] Gilberto Freyre [and others]. [2nd ed.] Recife, Instituto Joaquim Nabuco de Pesquisas Sociais, 1970. pp. 372.

— Guyana.

GUYANA. Commission of Inquiry into the Sugar Industry. 1968. Report; [G.L.B. Persaud, chairman]. Georgetown, 1968. pp. 166, 1 map.

SUGAR TRADE.

HARRIS (SIMON A.) and SMITH (IAN G.) World sugar markets in a state of flux. London, 1973. pp. 86. *(Trade Policy Research Centre. Agricultural Trade Papers. No. 4)*

WORLD DEVELOPMENT MOVEMENT. Cane sugar: the battle for survival. London, [1973]. 1 pamphlet (unpaged).

— Bulgaria.

SHCHORS (V.R.) Sakharnaia promyshlennost' narodnoi respubliki Bolgarii i perspektivy ee razvitiia. Moskva, 1969. pp. 11.

— United Kingdom.

SUGAR BOARD [U.K.].Report and accounts. a., 1972/3 (15th)- London. *Formerly included in the file of British Parliamentary Papers.*

— — British Empire.

NORTH LONDON HASELMERE GROUP. Sugar today, jam tomorrow?: a study of the sell-out over Commonwealth sugar in the Common Market negotiations. London, [1971]. pp. (11).

NORTH LONDON HASLEMERE GROUP. Sugar today, jam tomorrow?: a study of the sell-out over Commonwealth sugar in the Common Market negotiations. London, [1971]. pp. (11).

— United States.

JOHNSON (DAVID GALE) The sugar program: large costs and small benefits. Washington, 1974. pp. 90. *(American Enterprise Institute for Public Policy Research. Evaluative Studies. 14)*

SUGAR WORKERS

— Brazil.

PEREIRA PINTO (JUAN CARLOS) La caña de azucar en la economia y la sociedad brasileña. Buenos Aires, [1968]. pp. 27. *bibliog.*

— Dominican Republic.

CORTEN (ANDRE) La migration des travailleurs haitiens vers les centrales sucrières dominicaines. n.p., [1970]. pp. 713-731. *Xerox copy.*

— Guyana.

GUYANA. Commission of Inquiry into the Sugar Industry. 1968. Report; [G.L.B. Persaud, chairman]. Georgetown, 1968. pp. 166, 1 map.

SUICIDE.

ANTHONY (HELEN SYLVIA) Depression, psychopathic personality and attempted suicide in a borstal sample; (a Home Office Research Unit report). London, 1973. pp. 43. *bibliog.* (*U.K. Home Office. Home Office Research Studies. 19*)

SUKARNO, President of Indonesia.

PENDERS (C.L.M.) The life and times of Sukarno. London, 1974. pp. 224. *bibliog.*

SULZBERGER (CYRUS LEO).

SULZBERGER (CYRUS LEO) An age of mediocrity: memoirs and diaries, 1963-1972. New York, 1973. pp. 828.

SUMMER HOMES

— France.

BRISSON (CATHERINE) and BECHMANN (ROLAND) Les résidences secondaires en France dans le cadre de l'habitat de loisir. [Paris], 1972. pp. 88. *bibliog.* (*France. Direction de la Documentation La Documentation Française. Notes et Etudes Documentaires. Nos. 3939-3940*)

— Norway.

NORWAY. Statistiske Centralbyrå. 1972. Fritidshusundersøkelsen 1970, etc. Oslo, 1972. pp. 177. (*Norges Offisielle Statistikk. Rekke A. 509*)

SUNDERLAND

— Description.

DONNELLY (DENNIS) and others. Perception-related survey for local authorities: a pilot study in Sunderland. Birmingham, 1973. 1 vol. (various foliations). *bibliog.* (*Birmingham. University. Centre for Urban and Regional Studies. Research Memoranda. No. 20*)

SUOMEN PANKKI.

RUEHL (HARALD) Das währungspolitische Instrumentarium der nordischen Zentralbanken. Bern, 1972. pp. 250, xxxviii. *bibliog.*

SUPERMARKETS.

DISCOUNT trading and hypermarkets; report of the proceedings of a conference held under the auspices of the corporation of Glasgow in... Glasgow...1971. Glasgow, Corporation, 1971. fo. 96.

SUPPLEMENTARY EMPLOYMENT

— Australia.

AUSTRALIA. Commonwealth Bureau of Census and Statistics. 1972. Multiple jobholding, May 1971. Canberra, 1972. pp. 8.

SUPPLY AND DEMAND.

MIZHENSKAIA (EL'VINA FEDOROVNA) Lichnye potrebnosti pri sotsializme. Moskva, 1973. pp. 152.

HOPKIN (Sir BRYAN) The control of demand: an inaugural lecture given on 5 March 1974 at University College, Cardiff. Cardiff, [1974]. pp. 15. *bibliog.*

LEVIN (BORIS MIKHAILOVICH) Sotsial'no-ekonomicheskie potrebnosti: zakonomernosti formirovaniia i razvitiia. Moskva, 1974. pp. 316.

SIMMONS (PETER J.) Choice and demand. London, 1974. pp. 120. *bibliog.*

— Mathematical models.

MATTEI (AURELIO) La demande dynamique: théorie et estimation. Fribourg, [1972]. pp. 169. *bibliog.* (*Freiburg, Switzerland. Universität. Wirtschafts- und Sozialwissenschaftliches Institut. Veröffentlichungen. 24*)

BRISCOE (GEOFFREY) and HIRST (M.) A further appreciation of demand forecasting models: some methods based on survey information. Coventry, 1973. pp. 55,vii,d. *bibliog.* (*University of Warwick. Centre for Industrial Economic and Business Research.* [*Warwick Research in Industrial and Business Studies*]. *No. 43*)

CHRISTENSEN (LAURITS R.) and others. Transcendental logarithmic utility functions. Stanford, 1973. pp. 48. *bibliog.* (*Stanford University. Institute for Mathematical Studies in the Social Sciences. Technical Reports.* [*New Series*]. *No. 94*)

DIEWERT (W.E.) Hicks' aggregation theorem and the existence of a real value added function. Stanford, 1973. fo. 37. *bibliog.* (*Stanford University. Institute for Mathematical Studies in the Social Sciences. Technical Reports.* [*New Series*]. *No. 84*)

NADIRI (M. ISHAQ) and ROSEN (SHERWIN) A disequilibrium model of demand for factors of production. New York, 1973. pp. 200. *bibliog.* (*National Bureau of Economic Research.* [*Publications*]. *No. 99*)

RAZIN (ASSAF) A note on the elasticity of derived demand under decreasing returns. Minneapolis, 1973. fo. 11. *bibliog.* (*Minnesota University. Center for Economic Research. Discussion Papers. No. 30*)

SHVYRKOV (VLADISLAV VASIL'EVICH) and SHVYRKOVA (TAMARA SERGEEVNA) Modelirovanie vnutrigodichnykh kolebanii sprosa. Moskva, 1973. pp. 175. *bibliog.*

LORANGER (JEAN GUY) Estimation d'un modele dynamique d'equilibre non concurrentiel de la demande de capital. Montreal, 1974. fo. 41. *bibliog.* (*Montréal. Université. Département des Sciences Economiques. Cahiers. no. 7405*)

SUPPORT (DOMESTIC RELATIONS)

— Ireland (Republic).

EIRE. Committee on Court Practice and Procedure. 1974. Nineteenth interim report...: desertion and maintenance. Dublin, [1974]. pp. 20.

— United Kingdom.

MILLER (JOHN GARETH) Family property and financial provision. London, 1974. pp. 310.

SURINAMESE IN THE NETHERLANDS.

BRAAM (S.) Suriname en de Surinamers als maatschappelijke vreemdelingen in Nederland. Den Haag, [1973]. pp. 128.

SURVEYING.

U.K. Countryside Commission. 1971. Changing countryside project; a report. London, [1971]. pp. 206. *4 maps in end pocket.*

SURVIVORS' BENEFITS

— Denmark.

DENMARK. Statutes, etc. 1970-72. The Widow's Pension and Assistance Act, 1970 [and] the Widow's Pension and Assistance (Amendment) Act, 1972. [Copenhagen?, 1970-72]. 2 pts.

SVERDLOVSK (OBLAST')

— Statistics.

SVERDLOVSK (OBLAST'). Statisticheskoe Upravlenie. Sverdlovskaia oblast' v tsifrakh, 1966-1970 gg.: statisticheskii sbornik. Sverdlovsk, 1971. pp. 148.

SVEVO (ITALO) pseud.

CASTRIS (ARCANGELO LEONE DE) Il decadentismo italiano: Svevo, Pirandello, D'Annunzio. Bari, [1974]. pp. 262.

SWAZILAND

SWAZILAND
— Constitution.

SWAZILAND. Constitutional Committee. 1961. Report of Swaziland Constitutional Committee: note of reservation by the chairman and official members. Mbabane, 1961. fo. 6.

SWAZILAND. Constitutional Committee. 1962. Proposals for a Swaziland constitution: ([report of the]... Committee; B.A. Marwick, chairman). Mbabane, 1962. pp. 47.

— Economic conditions.

LIVERSAGE (VINCENT) Swaziland development. [Mbabane?, 1948?]. pp. 41.

— Economic policy.

SWAZILAND. 1964. Draft development plan, 1963/1966, revised January, 1964. [Mbabane?, 1964]. fo. ii, 90.

— Social policy.

SWAZILAND. 1964. Draft development plan, 1963/1966, revised January, 1964. [Mbabane?, 1964]. fo. ii, 90.

SWEDEN
— Biography.

VEM är det: svensk biografisk handbook 1973; redaktör: Eva Löwgren. Stockholm, [1972]. pp. 1139.

— Census.

SWEDEN. Census, 1970. Folk- och bostadsräkningen 1970: resultat från evalveringsstudierna avseende sysselsättning och utbildning, etc. Stockholm, 1974. pp. 84. (Sweden. Statistiska Centralbyrån. Statistiska Meddelanden. Be/1974/3)

— Commerce.

SWEDEN. Handelsdepartementet. 1971. Sveriges utrikeshandel under 1960-talet, mot bakgrund av marknadsbildningarna i Europa. Stockholm, 1971. pp. 58. (EEC Information)

CARLSSON (BO) and SUNDSTRÖM (ÅKE) Den svenska importen av industrivaror från låglöneländer. Stockholm, 1973. pp.189. bibliog. With table of contents and summary in English.

NORSTRÖM (GÖRAN) Transportgeografiska studier i svensk utrikeshandel. Stockholm, 1973. pp. 426. bibliog. With English summary.

STRINNHOLM (JAN) Varutransporter med flyg: flygfraktstudier med empirisk belysning af flygfrakt i Sveriges utrikeshandel samt flygfrakt över Arlanda. Uppsala, 1974. pp. 306. bibliog. (Uppsala. Universitet. Kulturgeografiska Institutionen. Geografiska Regionstudier. Nr. 11) With English summary.

— — Germany.

FRITZ (MARTIN) German steel and Swedish iron ore, 1939-1945. Göteborg, 1974. pp. 137. bibliog. (Göteborgs Universitet. Ekonomisk-Historiska Institutionen. Meddelanden. 29)

— Commercial policy.

SWEDEN. Finansdepartementet. Långtidsutredningen. 1971. [Svensk ekonomi fram till 1977]; 1970 års långtidsutredning. Bilaga. 5. Export och import 1971-1975; utarbetad inom konjunkturinstitutet. Stockholm, 1971. pp. 210. (Sweden. Statens Offentliga Utredningar. 1971.40)

SWEDEN. Finansdepartementet. Långtidsutredningen. 1971. [Svensk ekonomi fram till 1977]; 1970 års långtidsutredning. Bilaga. 3. Varuhandeln fram till 1975; [prepared by] Handelns Utredningsinstitut. Stockholm, 1971. pp. 55. (Sweden. Statens Offentliga Utredningar. 1971. 14)

— Constitutional history.

ROBERTS (MICHAEL) 1908- , Professor of History. Swedish and English parliamentarism in the eighteenth century. Belfast, 1973. pp. 42. (Oxford. University. James Ford Special Lectures. 1973)

— Defences.

SWEDEN. Försvarsdepartementet. Programbudgetgrupp. 1969. Planering och programbudgetering inom försvaret. Stockholm, 1969. pp. 315. (Sweden. Statens Offentliga Utredningar. 1969.25)

MOLIN (KARL) Försvaret, folkhemmet och demokratin: socialdemokratisk riksdagspolitik, 1939-1945. Stockholm, 1974. pp. 463. bibliog. With English summary.

— Economic conditions.

SWEDEN. Finansdepartementet. Långtidsutredningen. 1971. [Svensk ekonomi fram till 1977]; 1970 års långtidsutredning. Bilaga. 6. Utvecklingstendenser inom offentlig sektor. Stockholm, 1971. pp. 182. (Sweden. Statens Offentliga Utredningar. 1971. 13)

WILSON (ALAN) A look at Sweden's economy. [Stockholm], Royal Ministry for Foreign Affairs, Information Service, 1971. fo. 5.

SWEDEN. Finansdepartementet. Långtidsutredningen. 1973. Svensk ekonomi fram till 1977: 1970 års långtidsutredning avstämd och framskriven. Stockholm, 1973. pp. 456. (Sweden. Statens Offentliga Utredningar. 1973.21)

— Economic policy.

GJEDE (TORBEN) Det makroøkonomiske prognosearbejde i Sverige og Norge. København, 1970. fo. 68. (Denmark. Danmarks Statistik. Arbejdsnotater. 1)

TÖRNQVIST (GUNNAR) ed. Artiklar om svensk samhällsplanering. Lund, 1970. pp. 248. bibliogs.

SOCIALA mål i samhällsplaneringen: en kritisk kommentar till 1970 års långtidsutredning; ([by] Åke Burstedt [and others]). Stockholm, [1971]. pp. 132.

SWEDEN. Finansdepartementet. Långtidsutredningen. 1971. [Svensk ekonomi fram till 1977]; 1970 års långtidsutredning. Bilaga. 6. Utvecklingstendenser inom offentlig sektor. Stockholm, 1971. pp. 182. (Sweden. Statens Offentliga Utredningar. 1971. 13)

SWEDEN. Finansdepartementet. Långtidsutredningen. 1971. [Svensk ekonomi fram till 1977]; 1970 års långtidsutredning. Bilaga. 9. Plan och prognos: en studie i de svenska långtidsutredningarnas metodik, av Carl Johan Aberg. Stockholm, 1971. pp. 235. (Sweden. Statens Offentliga Utredningar. 1971. 70)

SWEDEN. Finansdepartementet. Sekretariatet för Ekonomisk Planering. 1971. The Swedish economy 1971-1975 and the general outlook up to 1990: the 1970 long-term economic survey: main report. Stockholm, 1971. pp. 339.

WILSON (ALAN) A look at Sweden's economy. [Stockholm], Royal Ministry for Foreign Affairs, Information Service, 1971. fo. 5.

BERGSTRÖM (VILLY) Kapitalbildning och industriell demokrati: socialdemokratiska perspektiv. Stockholm, [1973]. pp. 182. bibliog.

SWEDEN. Finansdepartementet. Långtidsutredningen. 1973. Svensk ekonomi fram till 1977: 1970 års långtidsutredning avstämd och framskriven. Stockholm, 1973. pp. 456. (Sweden. Statens Offentliga Utredningar. 1973.21)

SWEDEN. Inrikesdepartementet. 1973. Planning Sweden: regional development planning and management of land and water resources. Stockholm, 1973. pp. 142.

— Emigration and immigration.

BRATTNE (BERT) Bröderna Larsson: en studie i svensk emigrantagentverksamhet under 1880-talet. Stockholm, [1973]. pp. 298. bibliog. (Uppsala. Universitet. Historiska Institutionen. Studia Historica Upsaliensia. 50) With English summary.

— Executive departments.

SWEDEN. Byggnadsstyrelsen. 1969. The National Swedish Board of Public Building: a short introduction to its organization and work. [Stockholm], 1969. fo. 20.

— Foreign relations.

KOBLIK (STEVEN) Sweden: the neutral victor: Sweden and the Western powers, 1917-1918: a study of Anglo-American-Swedish relations. Stockholm, [1972]. pp. 233. bibliog. (Lund. Universitet. Historiska Institutionen. Lund Studies in International History. No. 3)

PALME (OLOF) Att vilja gå vidare: [collection of speeches and articles]. [Stockholm, 1974]. pp. 272.

— — Europe.

WILSON (ALAN) Labour market, working environment, adult education: some Swedish efforts to further European harmonization. [Stockholm], Royal Ministry for Foreign Affairs, Information Service, 1972. fo. 6.

— History.

GASSLANDER (OLLE) J.A. Gripenstedt: statsman och företagare. [Lund], [1949]. pp. 463. bibliog.

NORDMANN (CLAUDE J.) Grandeur et liberté de la Suède, 1660-1792. Paris, 1971. pp. 551. bibliog. (Paris. Université. Faculté des Lettres et Sciences Humaines. Publications. Série Recherches. Tome 63)

— Industries.

SWEDEN. Industridepartementet. Samarbetsutredningen. 1970. Företag och samhälle. Stockholm, 1970. 2 vols. (Sweden. Statens Offentliga Utredningar. 1970. 41-42)

SWEDEN. Finansdepartementet. Långtidsutredningen. 1971. [Svensk ekonomi fra m till 1977]; 1970 års långtidsutredning. Bilaga. 2. Svensk industri under 70-talet med utblick mot 80 - talet; [prepared by] Industriens Utredningsinstitut. Stockholm, 1971. pp. 271. (Sweden. Statens Offentliga Utredningar 1971.5)

BACK (ROLF) and others. Industrial location patterns: a multidimensional analysis of relationships between firms and regions;... translated from the Swedish by Nancy Adler. Stockholm, [1974]. fo.239.

— Neutrality.

KOBLIK (STEVEN) Sweden: the neutral victor: Sweden and the Western powers, 1917-1918: a study of Anglo-American-Swedish relations. Stockholm, [1972]. pp. 233. bibliog. (Lund. Universitet. Historiska Institutionen. Lund Studies in International History. No. 3)

— Occupations.

SWEDEN. Census, 1970. Folk- och bostadsräkningen 1970: resultat från evalveringsstudierna avseende sysselsättning och utbildning, etc. Stockholm, 1974. pp. 84. (Sweden. Statistiska Centralbyrån. Statistiska Meddelanden. Be/1974/3)

— Officials and employees.

MOLIN (BJÖRN) and others. Offentlig förvaltning: stats- och kommunalförvaltningens struktur och funktioner. 3rd ed. Stockholm, [1971]. pp. 383. bibliog.

— Politics and government.

BRAND 1905: illustrerad socialistisk tidning; organ för Socialistiska Ungdomsförbundet. Mölndal, 1971. 1 vol. (various pagings). Facsimile reprint.

MOLIN (BJÖRN) and others. Offentlig förvaltning: stats- och kommunalförvaltningens struktur och funktioner. 3rd ed. Stockholm, [1971]. pp. 383. bibliog.

FRIBERG (LENNART) Styre i kristid: studier i krisförvaltningens organisation och struktur, 1939-1945. Stockholm, 1973. pp. 444. bibliog. With English summary.

HATJE (ANN KATRIN) Befolkningsfrågan och välfärden: debatten om familjepolitik och nativitetsökning under 1930- och 1940-talen. Stockholm, 1974. pp. 285. bibliog. With English summary.

PALME (OLOF) Att vilja gå vidare: [collection of speeches and articles]. [Stockholm, 1974]. pp. 272.

— **Population.**

SWEDEN. Statistiska Centralbyrån. 1964. Folkmängden i kommuner och församlingar vid årsskiftet, 1963/64: preliminära uppgifter, etc. Stockholm, 1964. pp. 39. *(Statistiska Meddelanden. B/1964/4) With English summary.*

SWEDEN. Statistiska Centralbyrån. 1968. Befolkningsprojektion för riket, 1967-1980; etc. Stockholm, 1968. pp. 41. *(Statistiska Meddelanden. Be/1968/3)*

SWEDEN. Statistiska Centralbyrån. Befolkningsprognos för riket (formerly Befolkningsprojektion för riket): Population projection for Sweden. a., 1969/1990- Stockholm. *With contents and headings in English.*

SWEDEN. Statistiska Centralbyrån. 1969. Fertility for birth cohorts of Swedish women, 1870-1940. Stockholm, 1969. fo. 39. *(Statistiska Meddelanden. Be/1969/9) With Swedish summary.*

SWEDEN. Statistiska Centralbyrån. 1969. Regionala arbetskrafts- och befolkningsförändringar 1960-1965 med projektion till 1980, etc. Stockholm, 1969. pp. 222. *(Information i Prognosfrågor. 1969.5)*

BOLANDER (ANNE MARIE) and others. Cohort mortality of Sweden: three studies describing past, present, and future trends in mortality. Stockholm, 1970. pp. 86. *(Sweden. Statistiska Centralbyrån. Statistiska Meddelanden. Be/1970/3) With Swedish summaries.*

SWEDEN. Prognosinstitut. 1972. Trender och prognoser: befolkning, utbildning och arbetsmarknad, etc. Stockholm, 1972. pp. 179. *(Information i Prognosfrågor. 1972.10)*

ARISTOCRATS, farmers, proletarians: essays in Swedish demographic history; [by] Kurt Ågren [and others]. Stockholm, [1973]. pp. 119. *bibliogs. (Uppsala. Universitet. Historiska Institutionen. Studia Historica Ugpsaliensia. 47)*

HATJE (ANN KATRIN) Befolkningsfrågan och välfärden: debatten om familjepolitik och nativitetsökning under 1930- och 1940-talen. Stockholm, 1974. pp. 285. *bibliog. With English summary.*

SWEDEN. Statistiska Centralbyrån. 1974. Befolkningsförändringar 1961-1970: översikt för årtiondet, etc. Stockholm, 1974. pp. 137. *(Sveriges Officiella Statistik) With English summary.*

— **Public buildings.**

SWEDEN. Byggnadsstyrelsen. 1969. The National Swedish Board of Public Building: a short introduction to its organization and work. [Stockholm], 1969. fo. 20.

— **Relations (general) with Europe.**

SWEDEN in Europe, 1971; [by Kurt Samuelson and others]. [Stockholm], Royal Ministry for Foreign Affairs, 1971. pp. 94.

— **Riksdag.**

HOLMBERG (SÖREN) 'Riksdagen representerar svenska folket': empiriska studier i representativ demokrati. Lund, [1974]. pp. 452. *bibliog. With English summary.*

MOLIN (KARL) Försvaret, folkhemmet och demokratin: socialdemokratisk riksdagspolitik, 1939-1945. Stockholm, 1974. pp. 463. *bibliog. With English summary.*

— — **Elections.**

[BRÄNDSTRÖM (DAN)] Nomineringsförfarande vid riksdagsval; [and] Riksdagen i pressen, [by Stig Hadenius]; undersökningar utförda på uppdrag av Grundlagberedningen. Stockholm, 1972. pp. 126. *(Sweden. Statens Offentliga Utredningar. 1972. 17)*

— — **Reporters and Reporting.**

[BRÄNDSTRÖM (DAN)] Nomineringsförfarande vid riksdagsval; [and] Riksdagen i pressen, [by Stig Hadenius]; undersökningar utförda på uppdrag av Grundlagberedningen. Stockholm, 1972. pp. 126. *(Sweden. Statens Offentliga Utredningar. 1972. 17)*

— **Social conditions.**

BRAND 1905: illustrerad socialistisk tidning; organ för Socialistiska Ungdomsförbundet. Mölndal, 1971. 1 vol. (various pagings). *Facsimile reprint.*

SWEDEN. Finansdepartementet. Långtidsutredningen. 1971. [Svensk ekonomi fram till 1977]; 1970 års långtidsutredning. Bilaga. 6. Utvecklingstendenser inom offentlig sektor. Stockholm, 1971. pp. 182. *(Sweden. Statens Offentliga Utredningar. 1971. 13)*

— **Social history.**

ELMÉR (ÅKE) Från Fattigsverige till välfärdsstaten: sociala förhållanden och socialpolitik i Sverige under nittonhundratalet. 5th ed. Stockholm, 1972. pp. 144. *bibliog.*

— **Social policy.**

SOCIALA mål i samhällsplaneringen: en kritisk kommentar till 1970 års långtidsutredning; ([by] Åke Burstedt [and others]). Stockholm, [1971]. pp. 132.

SWEDEN. Finansdepartementet. Långtidsutredningen. 1971. [Svensk ekonomi fram till 1977]; 1970 års långtidsutredning. Bilaga. 6. Utvecklingstendenser inom offentlig sektor. Stockholm, 1971. pp. 182. *(Sweden. Statens Offentliga Utredningar. 1971. 13)*

BREMBERG (LARS) Rätten till trygghet: debattbok om socialvårdens framtid. Stockholm, 1972. pp. 204.

ELMÉR (ÅKE) Från Fattigsverige till välfärdsstaten: sociala förhållanden och socialpolitik i Sverige under nittonhundratalet. 5th ed. Stockholm, 1972. pp. 144. *bibliog.*

HATJE (ANN KATRIN) Befolkningsfrågan och välfärden: debatten om familjepolitik och nativitetsökning under 1930- och 1940-talen. Stockholm, 1974. pp. 285. *bibliog. With English summary.*

HECLO (HUGH) Modern social politics in Britain and Sweden: from relief to income maintenance. New Haven, 1974. pp. 349. *bibliog. (Yale University. Yale Studies in Political Science. 25)*

— **Statistics, Vital.**

SWEDEN. Statistiska Centralbyrån. 1969. Dödsorsaksmönstret för perioden 1964-1966: frekvenser, dödstal, proportioner och indextal över den orsaksspecifika dödligheten; Mortality patterns by cause in 1964-1966: frequencies, death rates, proportions, and indexes of cause-specific mortality. Stockholm, 1969. pp. 109. *(Statistiska Meddelanden. Be/1969/3) In English and Swedish.*

SWEDEN. Statistiska Centralbyrån. 1969. Dödsorsaksmönstret och dödlighetsutvecklingen 1951-1966; Cause-of-death patterns and mortality trends in Sweden. Stockholm, 1969. 2 parts. *(Statistiska Meddelanden. Be/1969/2) In English and Swedish.*

SWEDEN. Statistiska Centralbyrån. 1971. Dödlighet och dödsorsaker med regional fördelning, 1964-1967; Mortality and causes of death by regions, 1964-1967. Stockholm, 1971. pp. 79. *(Sveriges Officiella Statistik) With summary and table headings etc. in English.*

SWINE

— **Belgium.**

DEVISCH (N.) Aspects économiques de la speculation porcine. Bruxelles, 1972. fo. 17. *bibliog. (Belgium. Institut Economique Agricole. Notes. No. 29)*

FERRIN (L.) Analyse des résultats comptables d'une exploitation se livrant à la fois à l'élevage et à l'engraissement intensifs des porcs. Bruxelles, 1972. pp. 45. *(Belgium. Institut Economique Agricole. Cahiers. No. 147)*

— **United Kingdom.**

THOMAS (W.J.K.) and BURNSIDE (ESTELLE) Pig production: results of a study in South West England in 1971-72. Exeter, 1973. fo. 32. *(Agricultural Enterprise Studies in England and Wales. Economic Reports. No. 16)*

SWITZERLAND

— **Appropriations and expenditures.**

SWITZERLAND. Administration Fédérale des Contributions. Division de la Statistique et du Service Economique. 1973. Finanzhaushalt der Kantone, 1930-1971, etc. Bern, 1973. pp. 499. *(Switzerland. Bureau Fédéral de Statistique. Statisques de la Suisse. 520e fasc.) In French and German.*

— **Commerce.**

PARKLAND RESEARCH EUROPE. Guide to national practices in western Europe: a guide to commercial business and legal practices and attitudes in the continental EEC countries and Switzerland; [edited by Victor Selwyn]; research directed by Parkland Research Europe SA . London, [1973]. pp. 223.

SCHERER (THEODOR) Die Importfunktion der Schweiz: ein empirische Untersuchung für das Dezennium 1961-1970. Zürich, 1974. pp. 199. *bibliog.*

— **Commercial treaties — France.**

BRAND (URS) Die schweizerisch-französischen Unterhandlungen über einen Handelsvertrag und der Abschluss des Vertragswerkes von 1864, etc. Bern, 1968. pp. 321. *bibliog.*

— **Constitution.**

SWITZERLAND. Constitution. 1971. Bundesverfassung der Schweizerischen Eidgenossenschaft, vom 29. Mai 1874 mit den Änderungen bis 31.März 1971. Bern, 1971. pp. 77.

— **Defences.**

GERBER (MAX) Demokratie und Militarismus: Betrachtungen über die Voraussetzungen schweizerischer Militärpolitik. Zürich, 1913. pp. 95.

ALLGOEWER (WALTHER) Nationaler Widerstand, Herbst 1940. Aarau, [1940]. pp. 30. *(Jungliberale Bewegung der Schweiz. Schriften. Heft 6)*

SOZIALDEMOKRATISCHE PARTEI DER SCHWEIZ. Arbeitsgruppe Sicherheitspolitik. Selbstbehauptung der Schweiz: Friedenssicherung, Kriegsverhütung, soziale und nationale Sicherheit; Grundfragen einer zeitgemässen Sicherheitspolitik. Bern, [1973]. pp. 87. *(SPS-Schriftenreihe. Nr.8)*

SWITZERLAND. Office Fédéral de la Protection Civile. 1973. 10 ans Office fédéral de la protection civile, 1963-1972. [Bern? 1973?]. fo. 50.

— **Economic conditions.**

SWITZERLAND. Groupe de Travail des Etudes Prospectives. 1971-74. Perspectives relatives à l'évolution de l'économie suisse jusqu'en l'an 2000: [report of the working party, F. Kneschaurek, chairman]. Saint-Gall, 1971-1974. 4 vols.(in 1). *Vol. 3 in 2 pts. Vols. 1 2 of 2nd ed. Vols. 1 3 in French. Vol . 2 in German.*

BICKEL (WILHELM) Die Volkswirtschaft der Schweiz: Entwicklung und Struktur. Aarau, [1973]. pp. 464. *bibliog.*

— **Economic history.**

BRAND (URS) Die schweizerisch-französischen Unterhandlungen über einen Handelsvertrag und der Abschluss des Vertragswerkes von 1864, etc. Bern, 1968. pp. 321. *bibliog.*

BICKEL (WILHELM) Die Volkswirtschaft der Schweiz: Entwicklung und Struktur. Aarau, [1973]. pp. 464. *bibliog.*

VEREIN FÜR WIRTSCHAFTSHISTORISCHE STUDIEN. Schweizer Pioniere der Wirtschaft und Technik. 27. Zwei Schaffhauser Pioniere: Friedrich Peyer im Hof, 1817- 1900; Heinrich Theophil Bäschlin, 1845-1887. Zürich, 1973. pp. 107. *bibliog.*

BERGIER (JEAN FRANÇOIS) Naissance et croissance de la Suisse industrielle. Berne, [1974]. pp. 170. *bibliog. (Allgemeine Geschichtsforschende Gesellschaft der Schweiz. Monographien zur Schweizer Geschichte. Band 8)*

SWITZERLAND. (Cont.)

— Economic policy.

COLOMBO (GIOVANNI ANTONIO) Politique conjoncturelle en économie ouverte : les limites extérieures de la politique monétaire suisse. Berne, 1973. pp. 193. *bibliog.*

WINTERBERGER (GERHARD) Gedanken zur schweizerischen Währungs-und Konjunkturpolitik. [Zürich, 1973]. pp. 13. (*Wirtschaftsförderung: Gesellschaft zur Förderung der Schweizerischen Wirtschaft. Stimmen zur Staats- und Wirtschaftspolitik. 55*) (*Sonderdruck aus Schweizer Monatshefte, Heft 4, Juli 1973*)

WEILENMANN (JAKOB) Der Einfluss des Bundeshaushalts auf den schweizerischen Konjunkturverlauf: eine empirische Untersuchung des Zeitraums 1950-1970. Bern, 1974. pp. 192. *bibliog.*

— Executive departments.

SWITZERLAND. Office Fédéral de la Protection Civile. 1973. 10 ans Office fédéral de la protection civile, 1963-1972. [Bern? 1973?]. fo. 50.

— Foreign relations

See also EUROPEAN ECONOMIC COMMUNITY — Switzerland; UNITED NATIONS —Switzerland.

— — Austria

WITZIG (DANIEL) Die Vorarlberger Frage: die Vorarlberger Anschlussbewegung an die Schweiz,...1918-1922. Basel, 1974. pp. 527. *bibliog.*

— — France.

BRAND (URS) Die schweizerisch-französischen Unterhandlungen über einen Handelsvertrag und der Abschluss des Vertragswerkes von 1864, etc. Bern, 1968. pp. 321. *bibliog.*

— — Germany.

BOURGEOIS (DANIEL) Le troisième Reich et la Suisse, 1933-41. Neuchatel, [1974]. pp. 463. *bibliog.*

— Industries.

ABT (ROBERT) Agglomerationseffekte in der schweizerischen Industrie. [Zürich, 1974?]. pp. 69. *bibliog.*

BERGIER (JEAN FRANÇOIS) Naissance et croissance de la Suisse industrielle. Berne, [1974]. pp. 170. *bibliog.* (*Allgemeine Geschichtforschende Gesellschaft der Schweiz. Monographien zur Schweizer Geschichte. Band 8*)

— Nationalrat — Elections.

SWITZERLAND. Bureau Fédéral de Statistique. Statistiques de la Suisse. 529e fasc. Nationalratswahlen, 1971, etc. Bern, 1974. pp. 197. *In French and German.*

— Neutrality.

SCHOCH (JUERG) Die Oberstenaffäre: eine innenpolitische Krise, 1915/1916. Bern, 1972. pp. 169. *bibliog.*

— Politics and government.

GRIMM (ROBERT) Nationale Fronten und Arbeiterbewegung. n.p., [193-]. pp. 47.

SWITZERLAND. Conseil Fédéral. 1968. Rapport...à l'Assemblée Fédérale concernant les grandes lignes de la politique gouvernementale pendant la législature 1968-1971, du 15 mai 1968. [Berne, 1968]. pp. 44.

SWITZERLAND. Commission d'Experts Chargée de Préparer la Revision Totale de la Loi Fédérale sur l'Organisation de l'Administration Fédérale. 1971. Rapport et projet de loi. [Bern], 1971. 1 vol.(various pagings).

MERZ (JOHANNES) Werner Schmid, 1/4Jahrhundert Parlamentsarbeit. [Bern, 1972]. pp. 48.

SWITZERLAND. Conseil Fédéral. 1972. Rapport...à l'Assemblée Fédérale concernant les grandes lignes de la politique gouvernementale pendant la législature 1971-1975, du 13 mars 1972. [Berne], 1972. pp. 64.

ENGLER (URS) Stimmbeteiligung und Demokratie: Aspekte eines schweizerischen Problems. Bern, 1973. pp. 318. *bibliog.*

JOST (HANS ULRICH) Linksradikalismus in der deutschen Schweiz, 1914-1918. Bern, [1973]. pp. 206. *bibliog.*

STEINER (JUERG) Amicable agreement versus majority rule: conflict resolution in Switzerland;...translated from the German by Asger Braendgaard and Barbara Braendgaard. rev. ed. Chapel Hill, [1974]. pp. 312.

— Population.

SWITZERLAND. Groupe de Travail des Etudes Prospectives. 1971-74. Perspectives relatives à l'évolution de l'économie suisse jusqu'en l'an 2000: [report of the working party, F. Kneschaurek, chairman]. Saint-Gall, 1971-1974. 4 vols.(in 1). *Vol. 3 in 2 pts. Vols. 1 2 of 2nd ed. Vols. 1 3 in French. Vol . 2 in German.*

SWITZERLAND. Bureau Fédéral de Statistique. Statistiques de la Suisse. 474e fasc. Bevölkerungsentwicklung nach Kantonen und Gemeinden mit 1000 und mehr Einwohnern 1960-1970, etc. Bern, 1971. pp. 63, 13 maps. *In German and French.*

LEIMGRUBER (WALTER) Studien zur Dynamik und zum Strukturwandel der Bevölkerung im südlichen Umland von Basel. Basel, 1972. pp. 199. *bibliog.* (*Geographisch-Ethnologische Gesellschaft. Basler Beiträge zur Geographie. Heft 15*) *With summaries in various languages.*

— Relations (general) with Europe.

SWITZERLAND. Département Politique Fédéral. 1970. La Suisse et l'Europe. Berne, 1970. pp. 43.

— Statistics, Vital.

FRANKENSTEIN (PETER FRITZ) Die Sterblichkeit nach Todesursache und Zivilstand in der schweizerischen Wohnbevölkerung von 1941 bis 1960: eine statistische Analyse, etc. Zürich, 1974. pp. 204. *bibliog.*

SWORDS.

RICHARDSON (DAVID) The Shotley Bridge swordmakers: their strange history. Newcastle upon Tyne, [1973]. pp. 66. *bibliog.*

SYMBIONESE LIBERATION ARMY.

PEARSALL (ROBERT BRAINARD) ed. The Symbionese Liberation Army: documents and communications...with a commentary. Amsterdam, 1974. pp. 158.

SYMES (REGINALD ANTHONY COLMER).

HARRISON (FREDERICK MADDISON WILLIAM) Reginald Anthony Colmer Symes: one of Scunthorpe's greatest citizens, 1877-1933. [Wollaton, Notts., 1973]. pp. 46.

SYNDICALISM

— Colombia.

CAICEDO (EDGAR) Historia de las luchas sindicales en Colombia. Bogota, 1971. pp. 233.

— France.

GOUSTINE (CHRISTIAN DE) Pouget: les matins noirs du syndicalisme. [Paris, 1972]. pp. 246. *bibliog.*

SYRIA

— Commercial treaties.

OFFICE ARABE DE PRESSE ET DE DOCUMENTATION. Répertoire des accords et engagements conclus par la R[épublique] A[rabe] S[yrienne] de 1923 à 1971. 2nd ed. Damas, 1972. fo. 171.

— Economic conditions.

OFFICE ARABE DE PRESSE ET DE DOCUMENTATION. Série "Etudes". 149. Bilan de deux ans de réformes economiques en Syrie, 1971- 1972. Damas, [1973?]. fo. 51.

— Economic policy — Mathematical models.

MANAFIKHI (MOHAMAD FARIZ) Econometric models for economic growth, with application to the Syrian economy;...a Master of Science thesis [Cairo], etc.1973. fo. 178, 5. *With Arabic summary.*

— Foreign relations — Treaties.

OFFICE ARABE DE PRESSE ET DE DOCUMENTATION. Répertoire des accords et engagements conclus par la R[épublique] A[rabe] S[yrienne] de 1923 à 1971. 2nd ed. Damas, 1972. fo. 171.

— History.

WARNER (GEOFFREY) Iraq and Syria, 1941. London, 1974. pp. 180. *bibliog.*

SYSTEM ANALYSIS.

BELLMEN (RICHARD ERNEST) Adaptive control process: a guided tour. Princeton, 1961. pp. 255. *bibliogs.*

CHURCHMAN (CHARLES WEST) The systems approach. New York, [1968]. pp. 243. *bibliog.*

HERBST (PHILIP G.) Socio-technical design: strategies in multidisciplinary research. London, 1974. pp. 242. *bibliog.*

SYSTEM THEORY.

SMITH (ARTHUR) Writer on heuristics. Four uses of heuristics; [models for project design and large idea-systems]. Rochdale, [1973]. pp. 207. *bibliog.*

WELTMAN (JOHN J.) Systems theory in international relations: a study in metaphoric hypertrophy. Lexington, Mass., [1973]. pp. 99.

— Bibliography.

NEMEškal (vojtĕch) COMPILER. tEÓRIA SYSTÉMOV A JEJ APLIKÁCIE SO ŠPECIÁLNYM ZAMERANÍM NA EKONÓMIU: HODNOTIACA BIBLIOGRAFIA REFERÁTOVO SPRACOVAŇYMI VYBRANÝMI TEXTAMI; ZOSTAVIL vOJTĚCH nEMEŠKAL, KONZULTANT ľUDOVÍT rOMANČÍK. bRATISLAVA, 1973. PP. 195.

SYSTEMS ENGINEERING

— Mathematical models.

BEALL (RICHARD BURNAP) Properties of a systems model with applications to project management; [Ph.D. (London) thesis]. 1973. 1 vol. (various foliations). *Typescript: unpublished. This thesis is the property of London University and may not be removed from the Library.*

SZECHWAN

— Politics and government.

KAPP (ROBERT A.) Szechwan and the Chinese republic: provincial militarism and central power, 1911-1938. New Haven, 1973. pp. 188. *bibliog.* (*Yale University. Yale Historical Publications. Miscellany. 96*)

TABLE—CLOTHS.

ENCISO RECIO (LUIS MIGUEL) Los establecimientos industriales españoles en el siglo XVIII: la manteleria de la Coruña. Madrid, 1963. pp. 265. *bibliog.* (*Universidad de Navarra. Facultad de Filosofia y Letras. Coleccion Historica. 6*)

TAFT (WILLIAM HOWARD) President of the United States.

ANDERSON (DONALD F.) William Howard Taft: a conservative's conception of the presidency. Ithaca, 1973. pp. 355. *bibliog.*

TAIPING REBELLION, 1850—1864.

JEN (YU-WEN) The Taiping revolutionary movement New Haven, 1973. pp. 616. *bibliog.*

TAIWAN

— Economic conditions.

FORMOSA. Administrative Research and Evaluation Commission. 1973. A review of public administration [in] the Republic of China. [Taipei], 1973. pp. 98.

— Economic policy.

FORMOSA. Council for International Economic Cooperation and Development. 1969. Fifth four-year plan for economic development of Taiwan, 1969- 1972. [Taipei], 1969. pp. 286.

— Foreign relations — France.

FRANCE. Direction de la Documentation. La Documentation Française. Notes et Etudes Documentaires. Nos.4014-4015. Les relations franco-chinoises, 1945-1973. [Paris], 1973. pp. 57. *bibliog.*

— History.

TWENTY-sixth anniversary of the "February 28" uprising of the people of Taiwan province. Peking, 1973. pp. 23.

— Industries.

FORMOSA. Council for International Economic Cooperation and Development. 1972. Input-output tables, Taiwan, Republic of China, 1969. [Taipei, 1972]. fo.(22).

— Politics and government.

PENG (MING-MIN) A taste of freedom: memoirs of a Formosan independence leader. New York, [1972]. pp. 270.

FORMOSA. Administrative Research and Evaluation Commission. 1973. A review of public administration [in] the Republic of China. [Taipei], 1973. pp. 98.

— Social conditions.

FORMOSA. Administrative Research and Evaluation Commission. 1973. A review of public administration [in] the Republic of China. [Taipei], 1973. pp. 98.

— Social policy.

FORMOSA. Council for International Economic Cooperation and Development. 1969. Fifth four-year plan for economic development of Taiwan, 1969- 1972. [Taipei], 1969. pp. 286.

TAJIKISTAN

— History.

DZHALILOV (SHARIFDZHAN) Bor'ba s basmachestvom v Khodzhentskom uezde, 1918-1923 gg. Dushanbe, 1968. pp. 100.

— Politics and government.

SADYKOV (MARUF SADYKOVICH) Istoricheskii opyt KPSS po stroitel'stvu sotsializma v Tadzhikistane, 1917-1959 gg. Dushanbe, 1967. pp. 434. *bibliog.*

TAMBOPATA VALLEY, PERU.

MARTINEZ (HECTOR) Las migraciones altiplanicas y la colonizacion del Tambopata. Lima, 1969. pp. 278. *bibliog.*

TANGANYIKA AFRICAN NATIONAL UNION.

SAMOFF (JOEL) Tanzania: local politics and the structure of power. Madison, 1974. pp. 286. *bibliog.*

TANK—VESSELS.

KURZ (CHARLES) Oil tanker chartering: an economic and historical analysis. Philadelphia, Pa., [1969?]. fo. 102. *bibliog.*

INTER-GOVERNMENTAL MARITIME CONSULTATIVE ORGANIZATION. 1972. Construction and equipment of tankers. London, [1972]. pp. 16.

TANZANIA

— Bibliography.

HUNDSDOERFER (VOLKHARD) and KUEPER (WOLFGANG) compilers. Bibliographie zur sozialwissenschaftlichen Erforschung Tanzanias: Bibliography for social science research on Tanzania. München, [1974]. pp. 231. *(Arnold-Bergstraesser-Institut für Kulturwissenschaftliche Forschung. Materialien zu Entwicklung und Politik. 6) Table of contents, preface, etc. in German and English.*

— Economic policy.

TOWARDS socialist planning; edited by Uchumi editorial board: J.F. Rweyemamu [and others]. Dar es Salaam, 1972. pp. 199.

CLIFFE (LIONEL) and SAUL (JOHN S.) eds. Socialism in Tanzania:...an interdisciplinary reader. Nairobi, afterwards Dar es Salaam, [1972-73]. 2 vols.

— Industries.

SURVEY OF INDUSTRIAL PRODUCTION (formerly Survey of industries); [pd. by] Bureau of Statistics, Ministry of Economic Affairs and Development Planning, (United Republic of Tanzania). a., 1965- Dar es Salaam.

— Politics and government.

CLIFFE (LIONEL) and SAUL (JOHN S.) eds. Socialism in Tanzania:...an interdisciplinary reader. Nairobi, afterwards Dar es Salaam, [1972-73]. 2 vols.

BAILEY (MARTIN) The union of Tanganyika and Zanzibar: a study in political integration. Syracuse, N.Y., 1973. pp. 114. *(Syracuse University. Maxwell Graduate School of Citizenship and Public Affairs. Program of Eastern African Studies. Eastern African Studies.9)*

NYERERE (JULIUS KAMBARAGE) Freedom and development; Uhuru na maendeleo: a selection from writings and speeches, 1968-1973. Dar es Salaam, 1973. pp. 400.

— Population.

HENIN (ROUSHDI A.) and EGERO (BERTIL) The 1967 population census of Tanzania: a demographic analysis. Dar es Salaam, 1972. pp. 53. *(Dar es Salaam. University. Bureau of Resource Assessment and Land Use Planning. Research Papers. No. 19)*

— Rural conditions.

TANGANYIKA. Central Statistical Bureau, 1963. Village economic surveys, 1961/62. [Dar es Salaam], 1963. pp. 9,(xiv), viii.

CEDILLO (VALENTIN G.) Rural development through Ujamaa: a Tanzania case report. Vienna, [1973]. pp. 55,(25). *bibliog. (Wiener Institut für Entwicklungsfragen. Occasional Papers. 73/11)*

— Social policy.

CLIFFE (LIONEL) and SAUL (JOHN S.) eds. Socialism in Tanzania:...an interdisciplinary reader. Nairobi, afterwards Dar es Salaam, [1972-73]. 2 vols.

— Statistics.

TANGANYIKA. Central Statistical Bureau, 1963. Village economic surveys, 1961/62. [Dar es Salaam], 1963. pp. 9,(xiv), viii.

TARDIEU (ANDRÉ PIERRE GABRIEL AMÉDÉE).

ALDANOV (MARK ALEKSANDROVICH) pseud. [i.e. LANDAU (MARK ALEKSANDROVICH)] Iunost' Pavla Stroganova i drugie kharakteristiki. Belgrad, [1935?]. pp. 188.

TARIFFS.

UNITED NATIONS. Statistical Office. Statistical Papers. Series M. No. 30. Rev.1. Customs areas of the world. (ST/STAT/SER.M/30/Rev.1) New York, 1970. pp. 34.

STEFANO (FRANCESCO DE) Nixon-round e agricoltura comunitaria. [Portici, 1973]. pp. 51-55. *(Naples Università. Centro di Specializzazione e Ricerche Economico-Agrarie per il Mezzogiorno. Estratti. n. 123) (Estratto da Politica Agraria, anno xx,n.3)*

GOLT (SIDNEY) The GATT negotiations, 1973-75: a guide to the issues. London, 1974. pp. 82. *(British-North American Committee. Publications. 14)*

— Mathematical models.

STAELIN (CHARLES P.) A general equilibrium model of tariffs in a non-competitive economy. Ann Arbor, 1973. pp. 29. *bibliog. (Michigan University. Center for Research on Economic Development. Discussion Papers. No.26)*

— America, Latin.

ASOCIACION LATINOAMERICANA DE LIBRE COMERCIO. 1972. Recopilacion de normas sobre valoracion aduanera de las mercaderias en los paises de la ALALC. [Montevideo], 1972. 1 vol. (various pagings).

— Australia.

INTERNATIONAL CUSTOMS TARIFFS BUREAU. International Customs Journal. No. 166. Australia. 10th ed. Brussels, 1973. pp. 346.

— Bulgaria.

INTERNATIONAL CUSTOMS TARIFFS BUREAU. International Customs Journal. No. 74. Bulgarian People's Republic. 6th ed. Brussels, 1972. pp. 150.

— Dominican Republic.

INTERNATIONAL CUSTOMS TARIFFS BUREAU. International Customs Journal. No. 5. Dominican Republic. 7th ed. Brussels, 1972. pp. 213.

— Ecuador.

INTERNATIONAL CUSTOMS TARIFFS BUREAU. International Customs Journal. No. 59. Ecuador. 15th ed. Brussels, 1972. pp. 169.

— European Economic Community countries.

EWG-Zollpräferenzen und Welthandelsstruktur: die Auswirkungen der Assoziierungs- und Präferenzabkommen auf die Struktur des Welthandels; [by] Karl Fasbender [and others]; Projektleitung, Dietrich Kebschull. Hamburg, 1973. pp. 296. *bibliog. (Hamburg. Hamburgisches Welt-Wirtschafts-Archiv. Studien zur Aussenwirtschaft und Entwicklungspolitik) With English summary.*

— Netherlands Antilles.

INTERNATIONAL CUSTOMS TARIFFS BUREAU. International Customs Journal. No. 67. The Netherlands Antilles. 3rd ed. Brussels, 1972. pp. 57.

— New Zealand.

NATIONAL DEVELOPMENT COUNCIL [NEW ZEALAND]. Committee on Industrial Policy. Report on industrial protection in New Zealand: review of recommendation 209A. [Wellington, Government Printer], 1972. pp. 47.

— Portugal.

INTERNATIONAL CUSTOMS TARIFFS BUREAU. International Customs Journal. No. 9. Portugal. 10th ed. Brussels, 1973. pp. 195.

— Russia.

INTERNATIONAL CUSTOMS TARIFFS BUREAU. International Customs Journal. No. 23. U.S.S.R. 5th ed. Brussels, 1972. pp. 11.

— South Africa.

INTERNATIONAL CUSTOMS TARIFFS BUREAU. International Customs Journal. No. 42. South Africa (Republic of). 15th ed. Brussels, 1973. pp. 196.

TARIFFS. (Cont.)

— Spain.

SPAIN. Oficina de Coordinacion y Programacion Economica. Documentacion Economica. No. 17. Arancel de aduanas y tarifa fiscal. Madrid, 1960. pp. 471.

— Syria.

INTERNATIONAL CUSTOMS TARIFFS BUREAU. International Customs Journal. No. 50. Syria. 3rd ed. Brussels, 1972. pp. 147.

— Thailand.

INTERNATIONAL CUSTOMS TARIFFS BUREAU. International Customs Journal. No. 145. Thailand. 10th ed. Brussels, 1972. pp. 83.

— Underdeveloped areas.

See UNDERDEVELOPED AREAS — Tariffs.

— United States.

RATNER (SIDNEY) The tariff in American history. New York, [1972]. pp. 214. bibliog.

TERRILL (TOM E.) The tariff, politics and American foreign policy, 1874-1901. Westport, Conn., 1973. pp. 306. bibliog.

TASCA (ANGELO).

TROCCHI (FRANCESCO) Angelo Tasca e l'"Ordine Nuovo": la formazione del Partito Comunista Italiano. Milano, [1973]. pp. 191. bibliog.

TASMANIA

— Officials and employees.

TASMANIA. Parliament. Standing Committee on Subordinate Legislation 1972. Report on public service regulations; [L.H. Carins, chairman]. in TASMANIA. Parliament. Journals and Printed Papers. 1972, no. 57.

— Politics and government — Bibliography.

HEARD (DORA) and CHAPMAN (RALPH J.K.) compilers. A bibliography of literature on Tasmanian politics and government. Hobart. *Supplement to POLITICS, v.8, no.1, May 1974.*

TATAR REPUBLIC

— Economic conditions.

GEOGRAFICHESKAIA kharakteristika administrativnykh raionov Tatarskoi ASSR. Kazan', 1972. pp. 252. bibliog.

TABEEV (FIKRIAT AKHMEDZHANOVICH) Ekonomika Tatarii: itogi i perspektivy. Kazan', 1972. pp. 239.

— Intellectual life.

FASEEV (KAMIL' FATYKHOVICH) Natsional'noe i internatsional'noe v sotsialisticheskoi kul'ture. Kazan', 1970. pp. 80.

— Nationalism.

SOTSIAL'NOE i natsional'noe: opyt etnosotsiologicheskich issledovanii po materialam Tatarskoi AASSR. Moskva, 1973. pp. 331.

— Social conditions.

SOTSIAL'NOE i natsional'noe: opyt etnosotsiologicheskich issledovanii po materialam Tatarskoi ASSR. Moskva, 1973. pp. 331.

TATARS.

SHEEHY (ANN) The Crimean Tatars, Volga Germans and Meskhetians: Soviet treatment of some national minorities. new ed. London, 1973. pp. 36. bibliog. *(Minority Rights Group. Reports. No. 6)*

TAUSUG.

KIEFER (THOMAS M.) The Tausug: violence and law in a Philippine Moslem society. New York, [1972]. pp. 145. bibliog.

TAVERNE (DICK).

TAVERNE (DICK) The future of the left: Lincoln and after. London, 1974. pp. 175.

TAWNEY (RICHARD HENRY).

TERRILL (ROSS) R.H.Tawney and his times: socialism as fellowship. Cambridge, Mass., 1973. pp. 373. bibliog.

TAX AUDITING

— Vocational guidance.

U.K. Board of Inland Revenue. 1970. In command at thirty: a career in H.M. Inspectorate of Taxes. [London, 1970]. pp. 13.

TAX CREDITS

— United Kingdom.

IFS CONFERENCE ON PROPOSALS FOR A TAX-CREDIT SYSTEM, 1972. Conference on proposals for a tax-credit system. London, 1973. pp. 85. bibliogs. *(Institute for Fiscal Studies. Publications. No. 5)*

— United States.

MEYERS (EDWARD M.) and MUSIAL (JOHN J.) Urban incentive tax credits: a self-correcting strategy to rebuild central cities. New York, [1974]. pp. 140.

TAX DEDUCTIONS

— United States.

SURREY (STANLEY STERLING) Pathways to tax reform: the concept of tax expenditures. Cambridge, Mass., [1973] repr. 1974. pp. 418.

TAX EVASION.

MARGAIRAZ (ANDRE) La fraude fiscale et ses succédanés: comment on échappe à l'impôt. 2nd ed. Lausanne, [1973]. pp. 534. bibliog.

TAX PLANNING

EDWARDES-KER (MICHAEL) International tax strategy. Dublin, [1974]. loose-leaf.

— United Kingdom.

NELSON-JONES (JOHN A.) and SMITH (BERTRAM) Practical tax saving. 2nd ed. London, 1973. pp. 317.

POTTER (DONALD CHARLES) and MONROE (HUBERT HOLMES) Tax planning with precedents; seventh edition by D.A. Shirley and A.R. Thornhill. London, 1974. pp. 601.

TAXATION

— Mathematical models.

McLURE (CHARLES E.) A diagrammatic exposition of general equilibrium tax and expenditure incidence analysis with one immobile factor. Houston, Tex., 1972. pp. 37. bibliog. *(Rice University. Program of Development Studies. Papers. No. 31)*

McLURE (CHARLES E.) General equilibrium incidence analysis: the Harberger model after ten years. Houston, Tex., 1972. pp. 34. *(Rice University. Program of Development Studies. Papers. No. 37)*

BALLENTINE (J. GREGORY) and ERIS (IBRAHIM) On the general equilibrium analysis of tax incidence. Houston, 1973. pp. 34. *(Rice University. Program of Development Studies. Papers. No. 38)*

BRONSARD (CAMILLE) Two simple remarks on the structure of optimal taxation. Montréal, 1973. fo. 17. bibliog. *(Montreal. Université. Département des Sciences Economiques. Cahiers. no. 7307)*

KOELLREUTER (CHRISTOPH) Zur Theorie der internationalen Steuerinzidenz: ein neoklassischer und ein postkeynesianischer Beitrag. Zürich, [1973]. pp. 206. bibliog.

PITCHFORD (JOHN DAVID) and TURNOVSKY (STEPHEN J.) Some effects of taxes on inflation and income distribution. Canberra, 1974. fo. 40. bibliog. *(Australian National University. Research School of Social Sciences. Department of Economics. Working Papers in Economics and Econometrics. No.20)*

— Africa, East.

DAVEY (KENNETH J.) Taxing a peasant society: the example of graduated taxes in East Africa. London, 1974. pp. 226. bibliog.

— America, Latin.

McLURE (CHARLES E.) The proper use of indirect taxation in Latin America: the practice of economic marksmanship. Houston, Tex., 1972. pp. 46. *(Rice University. Program of Development Studies. Papers. No. 29)*

— Canada.

DODGE (DAVID A.) and SARGENT (JOHN H.) Towards a new tax-transfer system in Canada: an analysis of the changes proposed in the white papers on income security, unemployment insurance and taxation. Kingston, 1971. fo. 45. *(Kingston, Ontario. Queen's University. Institute for Economic Research. Discussion Papers. No.49)*

— Denmark.

DENMARK. Udvalget vedrørende Statsskatteadministrationen. 1972. Betaenkning vedr orende statsskatteadministrationen. København, 1972. pp. 131. *(Denmark. Betaenkninger. Nr. 651)*

— Ecuador.

ECUADOR. Junta Nacional de Planificacion y Coordinacion Economica. 1964. Plan general de desarrollo economico y social (version preliminar). Tomo 1. Fines y medios de una politica de desarrollo. Libro segundo. La transformacion: sus objectivos y medios (and Reforma tributaria). Quito, [1964]. 2 pts. (in 1 vol.)

— European Economic Community countries.

LIPPUNER (HANS) Die Bundesfinanzen und die EWG-Steuerharmonisierung, unter besonderer Berücksichtigung der Umsatzsteuer. Bern, 1970. pp. 148. bibliog.

DOSSER (DOUGLAS G.M.) Tax harmonisation and the value added tax; (transcript of... lecture held on 6 March 1972). [London], Civil Service College, [1973?]. fo. 18. *(Lectures on the European Community. Series A. No. 9)*

— France.

BOUVIER (JEAN) and WOLFF (JACQUES) eds. Deux siècles de fiscalité française, XIXe-XXe siècle: histoire, économie, politique; recueil d'articles... présentés par Jean Bouvier et Jacques Wolff. Paris, [1973]. pp. 323. *(Paris. Ecole Pratique des Hautes Etudes. Section des Sciences Economiques et Sociales. Le Savoir Historique. 5)*

BRIE (CHRISTIAN DE) and CHARPENTIER (PIERRE) L'inégalité par l'impôt. Paris, [1973]. pp. 191.

HALPERN (LIONEL) Taxes in France; ... adapted from... Les impôts en France [by Claude Gambier]. London, 1974. pp. 213.

— — Law.

ROBLOT (RENE) French business taxation. London, 1974. pp. 278.

— India.

MATHEW (T.) Economic objectives and tax-expenditure policies of India 1950- 1970. New Delhi, 1974. pp. 56. *(Economic and Scientific Research Foundation. Monographs. 5)*

— **Italy — Law.**

CUZZI (GIUSEPPE) La riforma tributaria: i decreti delegati sulle imposte indirette nella riforma. Roma, [1973]. pp. 502.

GALLO (SALVATORE) Le nuove imposte tipo registro:...testo con commento teorico- pratico, etc. Piacenza, [1973]. pp. 571. *bibliog.*

— **Japan — Law.**

HAYASHI (TAIZO) Guide to Japanese taxes 1973-74. Tokyo, [1973]. pp. 227.

— **Mexico.**

PICHARDO PAGAZA (IGNACIO) Ensayos sobre politica fiscal de Mexico. Toluca, Direccion General de Hacienda del Estado de Mexico, 1972. pp. 312. *(Coleccion Estudios Fiscales. 3)*

— **New Zealand.**

DEANE (RODERICK S.) and GRINDELL (D.) Quarterly taxation relationships for New Zealand. Wellington, 1972. pp. 35. *(Reserve Bank of New Zealand. Research Papers. No.7)*

— **Panama.**

McLURE (CHARLES E.) The distribution of income and tax incidence in Panama, 1969. Houston, Tex., 1972. pp. 39. *(Rice University. Program of Development Studies. Papers. No.36)*

— **Sri Lanka.**

SRI LANKA. Department of Inland Revenue. 1969. The new tax structure, 1969-70. Colombo, 1969. pp. 117.

— **Sweden.**

SWEDEN. Finansdepartementet. Skömansskattekommitté. 1969. Sjömansbeskattningen: betankande av 1967 års...kommitté. Stockholm, 1969. pp. 158. *(Sweden. Statens Offentliga Utredningar. 1969. 55)*

— **Switzerland.**

HIGY (CAMILLE) The Swiss tax system; adapted by the Federal Tax Administration. Bern, 1970. fo. 38.

— — **Bern (Canton).**

BERN (CANTON). Statistisches Bureau. 1971. Wachstum der Steuerkraft im Kanton Bern 1950-1968, etc. Bern, 1971. fo. 104, 37. *(Beiträge zur Statistik des Kantons Bern. Finanzstatistik. Reihe B. Heft 4)* Folding map in end pocket. In French and German.

— **Turkey.**

KRZYZANIAK (MARIAN) and ÖZMUCUR (SÜLEYMAN) The distribution of income and the short-run burden of taxes in Turkey, 1968. Houston, 1972. pp. 38. *bibliog. (Rice University. Program of Development Studies. Papers. No. 28)*

— **Uganda.**

DAVEY (KENNETH J.) Taxing a peasant society: the example of graduated taxes in East Africa. London, 1974. pp. 226. *bibliog.*

— **Underdeveloped areas.**

See **UNDERDEVELOPED AREAS — Taxation.**

— **United Kingdom.**

DOSSER (DOUGLAS G.M.) Tax harmonisation and the value added tax; (transcript of... lecture held on 6 March 1972. [London], Civil Service College, [1973?]. fo. 18. *(Lectures on the European Community. Series A. No. 9)*

JACKSON (PETER McLEOD) and McGILVRAY (JAMES WILLIAM) The impact of tax changes on income distribution: the 1973 budget. London, 1973. pp. 23. *(Institute for Fiscal Studies. Publications. No. 8)*

SANDFORD (CEDRIC T.) Hidden costs of taxation. London, 1973. pp. 206. *(Institute for Fiscal Studies. Publications. No. 6)*

U.K. Central Office of Information. Reference Division. 1973. A short guide to taxes in Britain. London, 1973. pp. 15.

— — **Law.**

IRONSIDE (DONALD JAMES) Personal taxation: the new unified system. [London, 1972]. pp. 78.

HEPKER (MICHAEL Z.) A modern approach to tax law. London, 1973. pp. 351.

— — **Mathematical models.**

DORRINGTON (J.C.) and RENTON (G.A.) A study of the effects of direct taxation on consumers' expenditure;... paper prepared for the conference on Modelling of the U.K. Economy... 3-6 July 1972. London, [1972?]. fo. 46. *bibliog. (London Graduate School of Business Studies. Econometric Forecasting Unit. Discussion Papers. No. 25)*

— **United States.**

BOULDING (KENNETH EWART) and others, eds. Transfers on an urbanized economy: theories and effects of the grants economy. Belmont, Calif., [1973]. pp. 376.

HYMAN (DAVID N.) The economics of governmental activity. New York, [1973]. pp. 333.

SURREY (STANLEY STERLING) Pathways to tax reform: the concept of tax expenditures. Cambridge, Mass., [1973] repr. 1974. pp. 418.

TURE (NORMAN B.) Tax policy, capital formation and productivity. New York, 1973. pp. 40.

WAGNER (RICHARD E.) Death and taxes: some perspectives on inheritance, inequality, and progressive taxation. Washington, D.C., 1973. pp. 63. *(American Enterprise Institute for Public Policy Research. Domestic Affairs Studies. 13)*

WALKER (CHARLES E.) and REUSS (HENRY S.) Major tax reform: urgent necessity or not?. Washington, [1973]. pp. 78. *(American Enterprise Institute for Public Policy Research. Rational Debate Seminars. 7th Series. 2)*

PECHMAN (JOSEPH A.) and OKNER (BENJAMIN A.) Who bears the tax burden?. Washington, D.C., [1974]. pp. 119. *(Brookings Institution. National Committee on Government Finance. Studies of Government Finance)*

— — **California.**

TAX and expenditure limitation by constitutional amendment: four perspectives on the California initiative; by William A. Niskanen [amd others]. Berkeley, 1973. pp. 70.

TAXATION, DOUBLE.

HEERDEN (KOENRAAD VAN DER) Dubbele belasting heffing van uitgedeelde winsten van besloten en open vennootschappen. Deventer, [1973]. pp. 210. *bibliog.* With English summary.

— **United Kingdom.**

DIBDEN (RONALD) Index to double taxation agreements. 5th ed. London, 1973. pp. 19.

STROBEL (JUERGEN) Die ertragsteuerliche Behandlung ausländischer Niederlassungen in Grossbritannien unter besonderer Berücksichtigung des deutsch-englischen Doppelbesteuerungsabkommens. Erlangen, 1973. pp. 169. *bibliog.*

TAXATION , EXEMPTION FROM

— **European Economic Community countries.**

EUROPEAN COMMUNITIES. Commission. 1972. Exemption from taxes granted to imports made by travellers. Brussels, 1972. pp. 10. *(Bulletin of the European Communities. Supplements. [1972/7])*

TAXATION, PROGRESSIVE.

VICKREY (WILLIAM SPENCER) Agenda for progressive taxation; [reprint of 1947 edition] with a new introduction. Clifton, N.J., 1972. pp. 496.

TAXATION OF ALIENS

— **France.**

MICHAUD (PATRICK) Régime fiscal des étrangers en France et des Français à l'étranger: impositions des membres des corps diplomatiques ou consulaires; conventions de Vienne. Paris, 1973. pp. 201.

TAYLOR (GORDON RATTRAY).

McLEISH (JOHN) The theory of social change: four views considered. London, Routledge and Kegan Paul, 1969 repr. 1972. pp. xiii, 95. *bibliog. (International Library of Sociology and Social Reconstruction)*

TEA.

RUNNER (JEAN) Le thé. 2nd ed. Paris, 1974. pp. 128. *bibliog.*

TEA TRADE

— **China.**

SCOTTISH HISTORY SOCIETY. [Publications] 4th series. vol. 10. William Melrose in China, 1845-1855: the letters of a Scottish tea merchant; edited by Hoh-cheung Mui and Lorna H. Mui. Edinburgh, 1973. pp. 301. *6 papers in end pocket.*

TEACHER—STUDENT RELATIONSHIPS.

BROPHY (JERE E.) and GOOD (THOMAS L.) Teacher-student relationships: causes and consequences. New York, [1974]. pp. 400. *bibliog.*

TEACHERS.

UNITED NATIONS EDUCATIONAL, SCIENTIFIC AND CULTURAL ORGANIZATION. Educational Studies and Documents. New Series . Paris, 1971 in progress.

[LADERRIÈRE (PIERRE) ed.] Training recruitment and utilization of teachers in primary and secondary education. Paris, Organisation for Economic Cooperation and Development, 1971. pp. 471.

MORRISON (ARNOLD) and McINTYRE (DONALD) Teachers and teaching. 2nd ed. Harmondsworth, 1973. pp. 246. *bibliog.*

The TEACHER in a changing society; edited by John D. Turner [and] J. Rushton. Manchester, [1974]. pp. 98. *bibliog.*

— **In—service training — United Kingdom.**

NATIONAL UNION OF TEACHERS. The induction of new teachers: a... policy statement. London, 1973. pp. 8.

UNIVERSITIES COUNCIL FOR THE EDUCATION OF TEACHERS. The inservice education and training of teachers in the light of the white paper, Education: a framework for expansion, Cmnd 5174. London, [1973]. pp. 24.

BRADLEY (HOWARD) In-service education after the white paper: a survey of the opinions of teachers about the form of release and kind of activities they would like provided under the scheme for a 3/r release of teachers in school time, etc. Nottingham, 1974. pp. 55.

— **Canada.**

CANADA. Statistics Canada. Citizenship of teachers in degree- granting institutions. a., 1971/2 [1st]- Ottawa. *In English and French.*

— — **Manitoba.**

MANN (MARGARET) The strike that wasn't: teachers' "strike", Brandon, 1922. Brandon, Manitoba, [1972]. pp. 136. *bibliog.*

— — **Quebec.**

DRACHE (DANIEL) ed. Quebec: only the beginning: the manifestoes of the Common Front; [translations of manifestoes of various labour organizations]. Toronto, 1972. pp. 272.

TEACHERS. (Cont.)

— Denmark.

BETAENKNING om stillingsstrukturen ved universiteterne og de hojere laereanstalter; afgivet af det af Undervisningsministeriet den 18. november 1969 nedsatte udvalg. [Copenhagen?], Statens Trykningskontor, 1970. pp. 91.

— European Economic Community countries.

NATIONAL ASSOCIATION OF SCHOOLMASTERS. The schoolmaster in the EEC. Hemel Hempstead, 1973. pp. 64.

— Italy.

BARBAGLI (MARZIO) and DEI (MARCELLO) Le vestali della classe media: ricerca sociologica sugli insegnanti. Bologna, 1969 repr. 1972. pp. 378. *(Istituto "Carlo Cattaneo". Studi e Ricerche. 1)*

CALABRIA (GIOSUÈ) and MONTI (GILBERTO) La pelle dei professori: per una tipologia della repressione nella scuola. Milano, 1972. pp. 244.

— Japan.

THURSTON (DONALD R.) Teachers and politics in Japan. Princeton, [1973]. pp. 334. *bibliog. (Columbia University. East Asian Institute. Studies)*

— United Kingdom.

NATIONAL UNION OF TEACHERS. National Union of Teachers war record, 1914-1919: a short account of duty and work accomplished during the war. London, 1920. pp. 207.

MORRIS (NORMAN) and others. How many teachers?: a report prepared for the National Union of Teachers. London, 1973. fo. 52.

WILLIAMS (GARETH L.) and others. The academic labour market: economic and social aspects of a profession. Amsterdam, 1974. pp. 566. *bibliog.*

— — Salaries, pensions, etc.

ASSISTANT MASTERS ASSOCIATION. Guide to the 1972 Burnham report. London, [1973]. pp. 22.

U.K. Department of Education and Science. 1973. Allocation of pension under the teacher's superannuation regulations. London, 1973. pp. 27.

— United States.

CARR (ROBERT KENNETH) and VAN EYCK (DANIEL K.) Collective bargaining comes to the campus. Washington, D.C., [1973]. pp. 314. *bibliog.*

CONANT (EATON H.) Teacher and paraprofessional work productivity: a public school cost effectiveness study. Lexington, Mass., [1973]. pp. 149.

LADD (EVERETT CARLL) and LIPSET (SEYMOUR MARTIN) Academics, politics and the 1972 election. Washington, D.C., [1973]. pp. 99. *(American Enterprise Institute for Public Policy Research. Domestic Affairs Studies. 15)*

— Zambia.

NORTHERN RHODESIA. Committee of Inquiry into the Stoppage of Work among Teachers in the Western Province during the Months of July and August, 1963. 1963. Report. Lusaka, 1963. pp. 25.

TEACHERS, TRAINING OF

— Australia.

CLAYDON (L. F.) Renewing urban teaching. Cambridge, 1973. pp. 190. *bibliog.*

— Belgium.

VROEDE (MAURITS DE) Van schoolmeester tot onderwijzer: de opleiding van de leerkrachten in België en Luxembourg, van het eind van de 18 de eeuw tot omstreeks 1842. Leuven, 1970. pp. 563. *bibliog. (Katholieke Universiteit te Leuven. Werken op het Gebied van het Geschiedenis en de Filologie. 5de Reeks. Deel 7)*

— France.

LYNCH (JAMES) and PLUNKETT (H. DUDLEY) Teacher education and cultural change: England, France, West Germany. London, 1973. pp. 197.

— Germany.

LYNCH (JAMES) and PLUNKETT (H. DUDLEY) Teacher education and cultural change: England, France, West Germany. London, 1973. pp. 197.

— Luxembourg.

VROEDE (MAURITS DE) Van schoolmeester tot onderwijzer: de opleiding van de leerkrachten in België en Luxembourg, van het eind van de 18 de eeuw tot omstreeks 1842. Leuven, 1970. pp. 563. *bibliog. (Katholieke Universiteit te Leuven. Werken op het Gebied van het Geschiedenis en de Filologie. 5de Reeks. Deel 7)*

— United Kingdom.

COLSTON RESEARCH SOCIETY. Symposium, 20th, 1968. Towards a policy for the education of teachers; edited by William Taylor. London, 1969. pp. 262. *bibliogs. (Colston Research Society and Bristol. University. Colston Papers. vol. 20)*

EDUCATION and the professions: [papers delivered at a conference of the History of Education Society, Manchester, 1972]; edited...by T.G. Cook. London, 1973. pp. 88.

LYNCH (JAMES) and PLUNKETT (H. DUDLEY) Teacher education and cultural change: England, France, West Germany. London, 1973. pp. 197.

NATIONAL UNION OF TEACHERS. The reform of teacher education: a...policy statement. London, 1973. pp. 12.

TEACHERS' UNIONS

— Australia.

BESSANT (BOB) and SPAULL (ANDREW DAVID) Teachers in conflict. Carlton, Vic., 1972. pp. 107.

— United States.

LADD (EVERETT CARLL) and LIPSET (SEYMOUR MARTIN) Professors, unions and American higher education;... prepared for the Carnegie Commission on Higher Education. Berkeley, Calif., [1973]. pp. 124. *bibliog.*

TEACHING.

CLAYDON (L. F.) Renewing urban teaching. Cambridge, 1973. pp. 190. *bibliog.*

INNOVATIONS dans l'enseignement en Afrique: orientations et administration; (documents présentés lors d'un colloque... Addis-Abéba...1971]; rédigé par J.A. Ponsioen. La Haye, [1973]. pp. 312.

— Aids and devices.

GARNETT (EMMELINE) Area resource centre: an experiment. London, 1972. pp. 116.

TEACHING, FREEDOM OF

— South Africa.

MARQUARD (LEOPOLD) Academic freedom and responsibility. Johannesburg, 1973. pp. 18. *(Johannesburg. University of the Witwatersrand. Chancellors' Lectures. No. 4)*

— United Kingdom.

THE CASE for academic freedom and democracy: [by] John Griffith [and others]. London, [1972]. pp. 15.

TECHNICAL ASSISTANCE.

UNITED NATIONS EDUCATIONAL, SCIENTIFIC AND CULTURAL ORGANIZATION. Science Policy Studies and Documents. Paris, 1965 in progress.

TERZO (FREDERICK C.) Urbanization in the developing countries: the response of international assistance. [New York, 1972?]. pp. 126. *(Ford Foundation. International Urbanization Survey. Working Papers. 286)*

BRIGHTON. University of Sussex. Institute of Development Studies. Library. Occasional Guides. No. 6. International agency aid and technical assistance programmes; a preliminary guide to documents. Brighton, [1973]. 1 pamphlet (unpaged).

La FORMATION des coopérants: actes du Colloque organisé par la Commission Nationale pour les Etudes Interethniques et Interculturelles...avril 1972 à Paris. Paris, [1973]. pp. 345. *(Nice. Université. Faculté des Lettres et Sciences Humaines. Institut d'Etudes et de Recherches Interethniques et Interculturelles. Publications. 3) In French or English.*

KLITGAARD (ROBERT E.) On assessing a gift horse: the evaluation of foreign aid by recipients. Santa Monica, 1973. pp. 59. *bibliog. (Rand Corporation. [Papers]. 5040)*

LOTTEM (EMANUAL) The evaluation of international technical assistance with special reference to Israeli technical assistance to Ghana, 1956-1966; [Ph.D. (London) thesis]. 1973. fo. 441. *bibliog. Typescript: unpublished. This thesis is the property of London University and may not be removed from the Library.*

MORRIS (ROBERT CRANE) Overseas volunteer programs: their evolution and the role of governments in their support. Lexington, Mass., [1973]. pp. 352. *bibliog. (Center for a Voluntary Society. Voluntary Action Research Series)*

SEGRE (D.V.) The high road and the low: a study in legitimacy, authority and technical aid. London, 1974. pp. 176.

TECHNICAL ASSISTANCE, AMERICAN

— Iran.

SHEEHAN (MICHAEL KAHL) Iran: the impact of United States interests and policies, 1941-1954. Brooklyn, N.Y., 1968. pp. 88. *bibliog.*

— Russia.

SUTTON (ANTONY C.) National suicide: military aid to the Soviet Union. New Rochelle, N.Y., [1973]. pp. 283. *bibliog.*

TECHNICAL ASSISTANCE, BRITISH.

SCHAFFER (BENJAMIN BERNARD) ed. Administrative training and development: a comparative study of East Africa, Zambia, Pakistan, and India. New York, 1974. pp. 445. *bibliog.*

TECHNICAL ASSISTANCE, DANISH.

DANISH INTERNATIONAL DEVELOPMENT AGENCY. Report on Denmark's participation in international development cooperation 1968-71. [Copenhagen], 1971. pp. 211.

— India.

FOLKE (STEEN) and others. An evaluation of the Danish Mysore project: an Indo- Danish agricultural-educational scheme. Copenhagen, Mellemfolkeligt Samvirke, 1969. pp. 255. *bibliog.*

TECHNICAL ASSISTANCE, EUROPEAN.

SOCIETY FOR INTERNATIONAL DEVELOPMENT. European Regional Conference, Oxford, 1973. Alternatives in development: is Europe responding to Third World needs?: (papers presented at the...conference); edited by Julian West. Oxford, 1974. pp. 153. *(Reprinted from World Development, vol. 2, no.2)*

TECHNICAL ASSISTANCE, FRENCH

— Africa.

FRANCE. Direction de la Documentation. La Documentation Française. Notes et Etudes Documentaires. No. 3,787. Le service de la coopération culturelle, scientifique et technique avec les états francophones africains et malgache: bilan et perspectives. Paris, 1971. pp. 34.

TECHNICAL ASSISTANCE, ISRAELI

— Ghana.

LOTTEM (EMANUAL) The evaluation of international technical assistance with special reference to Israeli technical assistance to Ghana, 1956-1966; [Ph.D. (London) thesis]. 1973. fo. 441. *bibliog.* Typescript: unpublished. This thesis is the property of London University and may not be removed from the Library.

TECHNICAL ASSISTANCE, NORWEGIAN.

ASARI (T.R. THANKAPPAN) The impact of the Indo-Norwegian project on the growth and development of Indian fisheries; submitted to the FAO International Conference on Investment in Fisheries, held in Rome 18th-24th September 1969. [Oslo? Norwegian Agency for International Development, 1969?]. pp. 11.

NORWAY. Direktoratet for Utviklingshjelp. 1970. Norway's aid to the developing countries: survey 1969. Oslo, [1970]. pp. 70.

NORWAY. Direktoratet for Utviklingshjelp. 1972. Norges utviklingshjelp: prinsipper og retningslinjer. [Oslo]. 1972. pp. 79.

NORWAY. Statistiske Centralbyrå. 1972. Attitudes to Norwegian development assistance, 1972. Oslo, 1972. pp. 78.

NORWAY. Direktoratet for Utviklingshjelp. 1973. On the main topics of Norway's co-operation with the developing countries. [Oslo], 1973. pp. 82.

TECHNICAL ASSISTANCE, RUSSIAN

— China.

CLARK (MILLS GARDNER) Development of China's steel industry and Soviet technical aid.Ithaca, N.Y., 1973. pp. 160. *bibliog.*

TECHNICAL ASSISTANCE IN EAST AFRICA.

TECHNICAL assistance administration in East Africa; edited by Yashpal Tandon; contributors, Reginald H. Green [and others]. Stockholm, 1973. pp. 209.

TECHNICAL ASSISTANCE IN KENYA.

RASMUSSON (RASMUS) Kenyan rural development and aid: a case study on effects of assistance on planning and implementation for the Special Rural Development Programme, etc. [Stockholm], 1972. pp. 53. (Swedish International Development Authority. Information Division. Development Studies. 2/72)

TECHNICAL ASSISTANCE IN PERU.

KLITGAARD (ROBERT E.) On assessing a gift horse: the evaluation of foreign aid by recipients. Santa Monica, 1973. pp. 59. *bibliog.* (Rand Corporation. [Papers]. 5040)

TECHNICAL ASSISTANCE IN ZAMBIA.

ZAMBIA. Ministry of Development Planning and National Guidance. Annual report. a., 1971(1st)- Lusaka.

TECHNICAL EDUCATION

— Belgium.

NEESEN (VICTOR) and others. Vraag en aanbod van geschoolde arbeidskrachten in Limburg;... algemene leiding: V. Neesen. Hasselt, 1971. pp. 232.

— Canada.

CANADA. Statistics Canada. Students in public trade schools and similar institutions. a., 1971/2(1st)- Ottawa. *In English and French.*

— France.

FRANCE. Direction de la Documentation. La Documentation Française. Notes et Etudes Documentaires. No. 4,001. L'enseignement supérieur court en France, par Janina Markiewicz-Lagneau. [Paris], 1973. pp. 42.

— United Kingdom.

U.K. Interdepartmental Working Party on Education and Training for Offshore Development. 1973. Education and training for offshore development; report; [B.A. Smith, chairman]. London, Department of Employment, Training Division, [1973]. 1 vol. (various pagings).

PRATT (JOHN) and BURGESS (TYRRELL) Polytechnics: a report. London, 1974. pp. 250. *bibliog.*

— — Scotland.

SCOTLAND. Scottish Education Department. 1972. Technical education in secondary schools; [D.G. Robertson, chairman of the Working Party]. Edinburgh, 1972. pp. 43. (*Curriculum Papers. 10*)

— United States.

RHINE (SHIRLEY H.) Technician education: who chooses it?. New York, [1972]. pp. 45. (*National Industrial Conference Board. Conference Board Reports. No. 543*)

TECHNICIANS IN INDUSTRY.

CAIN (GLEN GEORGE) and others. Labor market analysis of engineers and technical workers. Baltimore, [1973]. pp. 88. *bibliog.*

TECHNOCRACY.

THOENIG (JEAN CLAUDE) L'ère des technocrates: le cas des Ponts et Chaussées. Paris, 1973. pp. 281.

BAYLIS (THOMAS A.) The technical intelligentsia and the East German elite: legitimacy and social change in mature communism. Berkeley, [1974]. pp. 314. *bibliog.*

TECHNOLOGICAL FORECASTING.

LISICHKIN (VLADIMIR ALEKSANDROVICH) Teoriia i praktika prognostiki: metodologicheskie aspekty. Moskva, 1972. pp. 224.

THRING (MEREDITH W.) Man, machines and tomorrow. London, 1973. pp. 127.

TECHNOLOGICAL INNOVATIONS.

UNITED NATIONS EDUCATIONAL, SCIENTIFIC AND CULTURAL ORGANIZATION. Science Policy Studies and Documents. Paris, 1965 in progress.

RUSSO (GIUSEPPE) Progresso tecnologico e sviluppo economico. San Donato Milanese, [1967?]. pp. 103. (*Scuola Enrico Mattei di Studi Superiori sugli Idrocarburi. La scuola in azione. 8*)

NAVILLE (PIERRE) Temps et technique: structures de la vie de travail. Genève, 1972. pp. 234.

SINCLAIR (THOMAS CRAIG) and others. Innovation and human risk; the evaluation of human life and safety in relation to technical change;...[a project of the] Science Policy Research Unit, University of Sussex. London, [1972]. pp. 36. *bibliog.*

URBANIZATSIIA, nauchno-tekhnicheskaia revoliutsiia i rabochii klass: nekotorye voprosy teorii, kritika burzhuaznykh kontseptsii; Urbanization, scientific and technological revolution, and working class: theory - some aspects, bourgeois conceptions: critical survey. Moskva, 1972. pp. 268. *With English table of contents.*

L'ACQUISITION des techniques par les pays non-initiateurs: ([papers presented at a conference organized by the] Centre National de la Recherche Scientifique [and] International Cooperation in History of Technology Committee [held at Pont-à-Mousson in 1970]). Paris, 1973. pp. 624. (*Centre National de la Recherche Scientifique. Colloques Internationaux. No. 538*) *Papers in English and French, with a summary in the alternative language.*

NAUCHNO-tekhnicheskaia revoliutsiia i sotsializm. Moskva, 1973. pp. 366.

DICKSON (DAVID) Alternative technology and the politics of technical change. Glasgow, 1974. pp. 224.

NABSETH (LARS) and RAY (GEORGE F.) eds. The diffusion of new industrial processes: an international study.London, 1974. pp. 324. *bibliog.* (*National Institute of Economic and Social Research. Economic and Social Studies. 29*)

— Social aspects.

INTERNATIONAL LABOUR CONFERENCE. 57th Session. Reports. 6. Labour and social implications of automation and other technological developments: sixth item on the agenda. Geneva, 1972. pp. 75.

— Communist countries.

CHUKANOV (OLIMP ALEKSEEVICH) and others, eds. Nauchno-tekhnicheskii progress i sotrudnichestvo stran SEV. Moskva, 1973. pp. 207.

TSENY i stimulirovanie nauchno-tekhnicheskogo progressa v sotsialisticheskikh stranakh. Moskva, 1973. pp. 272.

STEPANENKO (STANISLAV IVANOVICH) Sovershenstvovanie nauchno-tekhnicheskogo sotrudnichestva stran SEV.Moskva, 1974. pp. 261.

— Europe.

BAILEY (FREDERICK GEORGE) ed. Debate and compromise: the politics of innovation. Oxford, 1973. pp. 343. *bibliog.*

— France.

FRANCE. Groupe de Prospective Technologique. 1972. Technologie et aménagement du territoire: premières réflexions. Paris, 1972. pp. 211. (*France. Délégation à l'Aménagement du Territoire et à l'Action Régionale. Travaux et Recherches de Prospective. 33*)

— Germany, Eastern.

GERMANY (DEUTSCHE DEMOKRATISCHE REPUBLIK). Statutes, etc. 1971-72. Neuererrecht: Textausgabe der wichtigsten gesetzlichen Bestimmungen mit Sachregister; herausgegeben vom Amt für Erfindungs- und Patentwesen. Berlin, 1973. pp. 79.

— India.

BHATTACHARYA (DEBESH) The role of technological progress in Indian economic development. Calcutta, 1972. pp. 276. *bibliog.*

BEHARI (BEPIN) Economic growth and technological change in India. Delhi, [1974]. pp. 274. *bibliog.*

— Korea.

KIM (NAK KWAN) The choice of technology and the full utilization of resources. Seoul, 1974. pp. 28. (*Research Institute of Asian Economies. Occasional Papers. No. 1*)

— Russia.

GATOVSKII (LEV MARKOVICH) ed. Planirovanie i stimulirovanie nauchno-tekhnicheskogo progressa. Moskva, 1972. pp. 239.

UCHENYE ZAPISKI KAFEDR OBSHCHESTVENNYKH NAUK VUZOV LENINGRADA. Politicheskaia Ekonomiia. vyp.13. Protsess obobshchestvleniia sotsialisticheskogo proizvodstva v usloviiakh sovremennoi nauchno-tekhnicheskoi revoliutsii. Leningrad, 1972. pp. 198.

TECHNOLOGICAL INNOVATIONS. (Cont.)

BIALKOVSKAIA (VERA SERGEEVNA) Perspektivnoe planirovanie napravlenii tekhnicheskogo progressa. Moskva, 1973. pp. 191. *bibliog.*

BLIAKHMAN (LEONID SOLOMONOVICH) and SHKARATAN (OVSEI IRMOVICH) NTR, rabochii klass, intelligentsiia. Moskva, 1973. pp. 320.

BUDAVEI (VSEVOLOD IUR'EVICH) and SITARIAN (STEPAN ARAMAISOVICH) eds. Finansy i nauchno-tekhnicheskii progress. Moskva, 1973. pp. 239.

DRONOV (FEDOR AMOSOVICH) Nauchno-tekhnicheskii progress i problemy ekonomiki; pod redaktsiei ... F.S. Martinkevicha. Minsk, 1973. pp. 381.

LITUNOVSKAIA (MARIIA KSENOFONTOVNA) Finansovo-kreditnye istochniki nauchno-tekhnicheskogo progressa. Moskva, 1973. pp. 159.

MARAKHOV (VLADIMIR GRIGOR'EVICH) and KORNEEV (MIKHAIL IAKOVLEVICH) eds. Problemy istoricheskogo materializma: filosofskie i sotsiologicheskie problemy nauchno-tekhnicheskoi revoliutsii. vyp.3. Leningrad, 1973. pp. 95.

MEDVEDEV (VLADIMIR AFINOGENOVICH) Sotsialisticheskoe vosproizvodstvo i strukturnye sdvigi v ekonomike. Moskva, 1973. pp. 183.

NOVGORODSKII (IURII FEDOROVICH) and others. Technicheskii progress i sovershenstvovanie podgotovki kadrov. Moskva, 1973. pp. 151.

OMEL'IANENKO (BORIS LUKICH) Tekhnicheskii progress i sovremennye trebovaniia k urovniu kvalifikatsii i podgotovke rabochikh kadrov. Moskva, 1973. pp. 128.

PROBLEMY ispol'zovaniia rabochei sily v usloviiakh nauchno- tekhnicheskoi revoliutsii. Moskva, 1973. pp. 263.

VAKHLAMOV (IVAN ALEKSEEVICH) and SEDLOV (PAVEL ALEKSEEVICH) Material'noe pooshchrenie v oblasti nauchno-tekhnicheskogo progressa: pravovye voprosy. Moskva, 1973. pp. 175.

— — Kazakstan.

EFFEKTIVNOST' tekhnicheskogo progressa v promyshlennosti Kazakhstana. Alma-Ata, 1973. pp. 168.

— — Ukraine.

MIROSHNIKOV (PETR SEMENOVICH) and others. Material'noe stimulirovanie nauchno-tekhnicheskogo progressa. Kiev, 1973. pp. 159. *bibliog.*

PLIUSHCH (MYKOLA ROMANOVYCH) Tekhnichna tvorchist' robitnychoho klasu Ukraïns'koï RSR, 1959-1970 rr. Kyïv, 1973. pp. 183. *With Russian summary.*

— United Kingdom.

WEALTH from knowledge: studies of innovation in industry; [by] J. Langrish [and others]. London, 1972. pp. 477. *bibliogs.*

SENKER (PETER) and HUGGETT (CHARLOTTE) Technology and manpower in the UK engineering industry: an interim report 1973; a report on a study by the Science Policy Research Unit, University of Sussex. Watford, Engineering Industry Training Board, 1973. pp. 44. *(Occasional Papers. No.3)*

ECONOMIC DEVELOPMENT COMMITTEE FOR THE CLOTHING INDUSTRY. The anatomy of purchasing clothing machinery: a study of the attitudes of clothing manufacturers towards the purchase of technologically advanced equipment. London, National Economic Development Office, 1974. pp. 52.

TECHNOLOGISTS
— Germany, Eastern.

BAYLIS (THOMAS A.) The technical intelligentsia and the East German elite: legitimacy and social change in mature communism. Berkeley, [1974]. pp. 314. *bibliog.*

TECHNOLOGY
— Communist countries.

WILCZYNSKI (JOZEF) Technology in Comecon: acceleration of technological progress through economic planning and the market. London, 1974. pp. 379.

— History — Russia — Baltic States.

IZ istorii estestvoznaniia i tekhniki Pribaltiki. t.2. Riga, 1970. pp. 379. *bibliog.*

— Information services — Bibliography.

UNITED NATIONS. Geneva. Library. 1973. Technological information systems and services for innovation: a selective bibliography. (ST/GENEVA/LIB/SER. B/Ref. 5) (SC. TECH/SEM. 1/R. 56). Geneva, 1973. pp. 61. *(Reference lists. No. 5) In various languages.*

— International cooperation.

HOCHMUTH (MILTON S.) Organizing the transnational: the experience with transnational enterprise in advanced technology. Leiden, 1974. pp. 211.

— Social aspects.

UNITED NATIONS EDUCATIONAL, SCIENTIFIC AND CULTURAL ORGANIZATION. Science Policy Studies and Documents. Paris, 1965 in progress.

INDUSTRIEGEWERKSCHAFT METALL FÜR DIE BUNDESREPUBLIK DEUTSCHLAND. Internationale Arbeitstagung, 4., 1972. Aufgabe Zukunft: Qualität des Lebens; Beiträge... 11. bis 14. April 1972 in Oberhausen...; Redaktion: Günter Friedrichs. Frankfurt am Main, 1973-74. 10 vols. *With summaries in English and French.*

BODINGTON (STEPHEN) Computers and socialism. Nottingham, 1973. pp. 245. *bibliog.*

CALLAHAN (DANIEL) The tyranny of survival, and other pathologies of civilized life. New York, 1973. pp. 284.

LAPP (RALPH EUGENE) The logarithmic century. Englewood Cliffs, [1973]. pp. 263.

THRING (MEREDITH W.) Man, machines and tomorrow. London, 1973. pp. 127.

CROSS (NIGEL) and others, eds. Man-made futures: readings in society, technology and design. London, 1974. pp. 365.

DICKSON (DAVID) Alternative technology and the politics of technical change. Glasgow, 1974. pp. 224.

THRING (MEREDITH W.) Machines - masters or slaves of man?. Stevenage, Herts, [1974]. pp. 115.

— — Denmark.

BUNNAGE (DAVID) and others. Teknikken og arbejderen. København, 1974 in progress. *(Socialforskningsinstituttet. Publikationer. 62, etc.) With English summary.*

— — United States.

SLOMICH (SIDNEY J.) The American nightmare. New York, [1971]. pp. 285.

— Europe.

SCIENCE policy and business: the changing relation of Europe and the United States;...David W. Ewing. Boston, 1973. pp. 110. *(Harvard University. Graduate School of Business Administration. John Diebold Lectures. 1971)*

— European Economic Community countries.

EUROPEAN COMMUNITIES COMMISSION. 1973. Scientific and technological policy programme: submitted to the Council on 1 August 1973. [Brussels], 1973. pp. 47. *(Bulletin of the European Communities. Supplements. [1973/14])*

— India.

CHITALE (V.P.) Foreign technology in India. New Delhi, [1973]. pp. 197.

— Japan.

SCIENCE policy and business: the changing relation of Europe and the United States;...David W. Ewing. Boston, 1973. pp. 110. *(Harvard University. Graduate School of Business Administration. John Diebold Lectures. 1971)*

SCIENCE policy and business: the changing relation of Europe and the United States;...David W. Ewing, editor. Boston, 1973. pp. 110. *(Harvard University. Graduate School of Business Administration. John Diebold Lectures. 1971)*

— United Kingdom.

BOSWORTH (DEREK L.) The changing international sources of U.K. technology. Coventry, 1973. pp. 32,x. *bibliog. (University of Warwick. Centre for Industrial Economic and Business Research. [Warwick Research in Industrial and Business Studies]. No. 35)*

— United States.

SCIENCE policy and business: the changing relation of Europe and the United States;...David W. Ewing. Boston, 1973. pp. 110. *(Harvard University. Graduate School of Business Administration. John Diebold Lectures. 1971)*

SCIENCE policy and business: the changing relation of Europe and the United States;...David W. Ewing, editor. Boston, 1973. pp. 110. *(Harvard University. Graduate School of Business Administration. John Diebold Lectures. 1971)*

TECHNOLOGY AND STATE.

UNITED NATIONS EDUCATIONAL, SCIENTIFIC AND CULTURAL ORGANIZATION. Science Policy Studies and Documents. Paris, 1965 in progress.

— Germany, Eastern.

HERSPRING (DALE ROY) East German civil-military relations: the impact of technology, 1949-72. New York, 1973. pp. 216. *bibliog.*

— Russia.

HARVEY (MOSE L.) and others. Science and technology as an instrument of Soviet policy. Miami, 1972. pp. 219. *(Miami (Florida). University. Center for Advanced International Studies. Monographs in International Affairs)*

TECHNOLOGY ASSESSMENT.

DICKEY (JOHN W.) and others. Technology assessment: its application to the solid waste management programs of urban governments. Lexington, Mass., [1973]. pp. 194. *bibliog.*

TECHNOLOGY TRANSFER.

CHITALE (V.P.) Foreign technology in India. New Delhi, [1973]. pp. 197.

TEHUANTEPEC (ISTHMUS)
— Economic conditions.

ORTIZ WADGYMAR (ARTURO) Aspectos de la economia del Istmo de Tehuantepec; revision y presentacion [by] Angel Bassols Batalla. Mexico, 1971. pp. 114.

TEL—AVIV
— Buildings.

TEL AVIV. Department of Research and Statistics. Census of Buildings. Publications. vol. 3. Census of buildings and area of housing units in Tel-Aviv- Yafo, 1968...: final data. [Tel Aviv], 1973. pp. xxxi,185. *(Tel Aviv. Department of Research and Statistics. Special Surveys. No.43) In English and Hebrew.*

— Population.

TEL AVIV. Department of Research and Statistics. Special Surveys. No. 42. Natural movement of the population in the last decade. [Tel Aviv], 1972. 1 vol. (various pagings).

— Social conditions.

TEL-AVIV. Department of Research and Statistics. Special Surveys. No.44. Leisure patterns of the inhabitants of Tel Aviv-Yafo. Tel-Aviv, 1974. pp. 1vi, 109. *In English and Hebrew*.

TELECOMMUNICATION.

The CABLE and wireless communications of the world: some lectures and papers on the subject 1924-1939 [by officers of Cable and Wireless Limited]. [Cambridge, 1939]. pp. 282.

UNITED NATIONS EDUCATIONAL, SCIENTIFIC AND CULTURAL ORGANIZATION. Department of Mass Communication. Reports and Papers on Mass Communication. Paris, 1953 in progress.

COMMUNICATIONS technology and social policy: understanding the new "cultural revolution": [based on papers discussed at a symposium held at the Annenberg School of Communications, University of Pennsylvania, 1972; edited by George Gerbner [and others]. New York, [1973]. pp. 573. *bibliogs*.

— France.

NORA (HERVE) and CHAUMONT (VICTOIRE) Schéma général d'aménagement de la France: services nouveaux de télécommunications: éléments pour un schéma directeur. Paris, 1973. pp. 83. *(France. Délégation à l'Aménagement du Territoire et à l'Action Régionale. Travaux et Recherches de Prospective. 42)*

TELEGRAPH

— India.

INDIA. Administrative Reforms Commission.1970. Report on posts and telegraphs. [Delhi], 1970. pp. 82.

TELEPHONE

— Austria.

AUSTRIA. Generaldirektion für die Post- und Telegraphenverwaltung. 1972. Die Vollautomatisierung des österreichischen Fernsprechnetzes.Wien, 1972. pp. 73.

TELEPHONE, AUTOMATIC.

AUSTRIA. Generaldirektion für die Post- und Telegraphenverwaltung. 1972. Die Vollautomatisierung des österreichischen Fernsprechnetzes.Wien, 1972. pp. 73.

TELEVISION

— Interference.

MIDDLETON (DAVID) A mathematical approach to analysis of environmental pollution generated by mixes of transportation modes: the case of electrical interference...: a report prepared for U.S. Department of Transportation [and others]. Santa Monica, 1971. pp. 60. *(Rand Corporation. [Rand Reports]. 762)*

— Law and legislation — United States.

ASHMORE (HARRY SCOTT) Fear in the air: broadcasting and the first amendment; the anatomy of a constitutional crisis. New York, [1973]. pp. 180.

TELEVISION AND CHILDREN.

CHILDREN'S television commercials: a content analysis; [by] Charles Winick [and others]. New York, 1973. pp. 155. *bibliog*.

TELEVISION AUDIENCES

— United States.

BOWER (ROBERT T.) Television and the public. New York, [1973]. pp. 205.

TELEVISION BROADCASTING.

SMITH (ANTHONY) b.1938. The shadow in the cave: a study of the relationship between the broadcaster, his audience and the state. London, 1973. pp. 351. *bibliog*.

— Social aspects.

DEKKER (JOHN) Business and television. London, [1973]. pp. 8. *(Foundation for Business Responsibilities. Seminar Papers. No. 3)*

MILGRAM (STANLEY) and SHOTLAND (R. LANCE) Television and antisocial behavior: field experiments. New York, 1973. pp. 183.

WILLIAMS (RAYMOND) Television: technology and cultural form. London, 1974. pp. 160. *bibliog*.

— Austria.

MAGENSCHAB (HANS) Demokratie und Rundfunk: Hörfunk und Fernsehen im politischen Prozess Österreichs. Wien, [1973]. pp. 472. *bibliog*.

— Germany, Eastern.

HEIL (KAROLUS HEINZ) Das Fernsehen in der sowjetischen Besatzungszone Deutschlands, 1953-1963. Bonn, 1967. pp. 168. *(Germany (Bundesrepublik). Bundesministerium für Gesamtdeutsche Fragen. Bonner Berichte aus Mittel- und Ostdeutschland)*

— Ireland (Republic).

EIRE. Broadcasting Review Committee. 1974. Report. Dublin, 1974. pp. 198.

— Italy.

RADIOTELEVISIONE, informazione, democrazia: atti del convegno del P[artito] C[omunista] I[taliano] tenuto a Roma dal 29 al 31 marzo 1973. Roma, 1973. pp. 545.

— Russia.

KOMMUNISTICHESKAIA PARTIIA SOVETSKOGO SOIUZA. O partiinoi i sovetskoi pechati, radioveshchanii i televidenii: sbornik dokumentov i materialov. Moskva, 1972. pp. 635.

— United Kingdom.

GEDDES (KEITH) Broadcasting in Britain, 1922-1972: a brief account of its engineering aspects. London, H.M.S.O., 1972. pp. 63.

CHURCH OF ENGLAND. General Synod. Broadcasting Commission. Broadcasting, society, and the church; report of the... Commission. London, 1973. pp. 119. *bibliog*.

WHELDON (HUW) British traditions in a world-wide medium. London, [1973]. pp. 12.

CURRAN (Sir CHARLES J.) The fourth television network: a question of priorities. London, 1974. pp. 18.

The FUTURE of broadcasting: a report presented to the Social Morality Council, October 1973 [by a commission under the chairmanship of Dame Margaret Miles]. London, 1974. pp. 100.

SMITH (ANTHONY) b.1938, ed. British broadcasting. Newton Abbot, [1974]. pp. 271. *bibliog*.

— United States.

BOWER (ROBERT T.) Television and the public. New York, [1973]. pp. 205.

MACY (JOHN WILLIAMS) To irrigate a wasteland: the struggle to shape a public television system in the United States; (expanded version of the Gaither Lectures given for the Centre for Research in Management Science, University of California). Berkeley, 1974. pp. 186.

TELEVISION BROADCASTING OF NEWS

— United States.

FRANK (ROBERT SHELBY) Message dimensions of television news. Lexington, Mass., [1973]. pp. 120.

TELEVISION IN ADULT EDUCATION.

PERRATON (HILARY DAVID) Broadcasting and correspondence. Cambridge, [1973]. pp. 42. *bibliog*. *(National Extension College. Reports. Series 2. No. 2)*

TELEVISION IN ADVERTISING.

INDEPENDENT BROADCASTING AUTHORITY. The IBA code of advertising standards and practice. London, 1972. pp. 20.

CHILDREN'S television commercials: a content analysis; [by] Charles Winick [and others]. New York, 1973. pp. 155. *bibliog*.

TELEVISION IN EDUCATION

— United States.

ASPEN WORKSHOP CONFERENCE ON THE CABLE AND CONTINUING EDUCATION, 1973. Aspen notebook: cable and continuing education: ([edited by] Richard Adler [and] Walter S. Baer). New York, 1973. pp. 193. *bibliog*.

TELEVISION IN POLITICS

— Austria.

MAGENSCHAB (HANS) Demokratie und Rundfunk: Hörfunk und Fernsehen im politischen Prozess Österreichs. Wien, [1973]. pp. 472. *bibliog*.

— United States.

FRANK (ROBERT SHELBY) Message dimensions of television news. Lexington, Mass., [1973]. pp. 120.

TELEVISION IN RELIGION.

CHURCH OF ENGLAND. General Synod. Broadcasting Commission. Broadcasting, society, and the church; report of the... Commission. London, 1973. pp. 119. *bibliog*.

TEMPERANCE.

FROEHLICH (RICHARD) Alkoholfrage und Arbeiterklasse. Berlin, 1904. pp. 32. *bibliog*.

VEREIN FÜR WIRTSCHAFTSHISTORISCHE STUDIEN. Schweizer Pioniere der Wirtschaft und Technik. 26. Zwei Pionierinnen der Volksgesundheit: Susanna Orelli- Rinderknecht, 1845-1939; Else Züblin-Spiller, 1881-1948. Zürich, 1973. pp. 103. *bibliog*.

BRAKE (GEORGE THOMPSON) Drink: ups and downs of Methodist attitudes to temperance. London, 1974. pp. 150.

TEMPORARY EMPLOYMENT

— Spain.

OJEDA AVILES (ANTONIO) Los trabajadores temporales: problemas juridicos de eventuales, interinos y temporeros en derecho español. Sevilla, 1973. pp. 301. *(Seville. Universidad. Publicaciones. Serie Derecho. No. 17)*

TERMINAL CARE.

U.K. Department of Health and Social Security. Reports on Health and Social Subjects. No. 5. Care of the dying; proceedings of a national symposium held on 29 November, 1972. London, 1973. pp. 98.

TERRITORIAL WATERS

— America, Latin.

HJERTONSSON (KARIN) The new law of the sea: influence of the Latin American states on recent developments of the law of the sea; a study of the law on coastal jurisdiction as it has emerged in Latin America and its impact on present and future law. Leiden, 1973. pp. 187. *bibliog*.

— Russia.

OLENICOFF (S.M.) Territorial waters in the Arctic: the Soviet position. Santa Monica, 1972. pp. 52. *bibliog*. *(Rand Corporation. [Rand Reports]. 907)*

TERRORISM.

TERRORISM.

RAPOPORT (DAVID C.) Assassination and terrorism; [expanded version of a series of talks broadcast by the Canadian Broadcasting Corporation]. Toronto, [1971]. pp. 88 .

REFLEXIONS sur la définition et la répression du terrorisme; actes du colloque..., Université Libre de Bruxelles, 19 et 20 mars 1973; ([sponsored by] Centre de droit international... et Association belge des juristes démocrates). Bruxelles, [1974]. pp. 292. *bibliog.*

WILKINSON (PAUL) Political terrorism. London, 1974. pp. 160. *bibliog.*

— Brazil.

EVANS (ROBERT DERVEL) Brazil: the road back from terrorism. London, [1974]. pp. 20. *bibliog.* (*Institute for the Study of Conflict. Conflict Studies. No. 47*)

— Canada — Quebec.

QUEBEC: the challenge from within; by a Canadian correspondent. London, 1972. pp. 16. (*Institute for the Study of Conflict. Conflict Studies. No.20*)

— East (Near East).

YAHALOM (DAN) File on Arab terrorism. Jerusalem, [1973]. pp. 48.

— Germany.

HORCHEM (HANS JOSEF) West Germany's Red Army anarchists. London, 1974. pp. 13. (*Institute for the Study of Conflict. Conflict Studies. No. 46*)

— Guatemala.

FUENTES MOHR (ALBERTO) Secuestro y prision: dos caras de la violencia en Guatemala. San Jose, 1971. pp. 213 .

JOHNSON (KENNETH F.) Guatemala: from terrorism to terror. London, 1972. pp. 19. (*Institute for the Study of Conflict. Conflict Studies. No. 23*)

— United Kingdom — Ireland, Northern.

INSTITUTE FOR THE STUDY OF CONFLICT. Research Department. Ulster: politics and terrorism. London, 1973. pp. 20. (*Institute for the Study of Conflict. Conflict Studies. No.36*)

— United States.

PEARSALL (ROBERT BRAINARD) ed. The Symbionese Liberation Army: documents and communications...with a commentary. Amsterdam, 1974. pp. 158.

— Uruguay.

MOSS (ROBERT) Uruguay: terrorism versus democracy. London, 1971. pp. 10. (*Institute for the Study of Conflict. Conflict Studies. No. 14*)

TEXAS

— Politics and government.

WILLIAMS (JOYCE E.) Black community control: a study of transition in a Texas ghetto. New York, 1973. pp. 277. *bibliog.*

TEXAS UNIVERSITY.

DUGGER (RONNIE) Our invaded universities: form, reform and new starts: a nonfiction play for five stages. New York, [1974]. pp. 457.

TEXTBOOKS

— Italy.

I LIBRI di testo della scuola elementare; ([by] A. Alberti [and others]). Roma, 1972. pp. 223. *bibliog.*

— United Kingdom.

EDUCATIONAL PUBLISHERS COUNCIL. Books in school: budgeting from need. London, 1972. pp. 12.

TEXTILE INDUSTRY AND FABRICS.

SUDAREV (MIKHAIL SERGEEVICH) Stranitsy istorii: 175 let Mullovskoi sukonnoi fabriki. Ul'ianovsk, 1963. pp. 150. *bibliog.*

SHIRLEY INTERNATIONAL SEMINAR, 5TH, MANCHESTER, 1972. The place of textiles in the economy of a developed country; (papers, etc.). Manchester, [1972]. 1 vol. (various pagings). (*Shirley Institute. Publications. S7*)

— France.

DUBOIS (PIERRE) Recours ouvrier, évolution technique, conjoncture sociale: l'action des délégués du personnel C[onfédération] F[rançaise] D[émocratique du] T[ravail] dans des entreprises textiles du Nord. Paris, [1971]. pp. 142. *bibliog.* (*Paris. Université de Paris XI (Paris-Sud). Centre de Recherches en Sciences Sociales du Travail. Collection "Sciences du Travail". 4*)

BIEGANSKI (M.) L'industrie textile du Nord de la France: structure, emploi, marché du travail. [Lille], Echelon Régional de l'Emploi, 1972. 2 vols.

— Guatemala.

GUATEMALA. Comision Nacional del Salario. 1966. Estudio economico para la determinacion del salario minimo en la industria textil. Guatemala, 1966. pp. 124.

— Mexico.

KEREMITSIS (DAWN) La industria textil mexicana en el siglo XIX. Mexico, 1973. pp. 247.

— Russia.

KUL'BOVSKAIA (NINA KARPOVNA) Ekonomicheskie problemy formirovaniia balansa tekstil'nogo syr'ia. Moskva, 1973. pp. 142. *bibliog.*

— — Russia (RSFSR).

SUDAREV (MIKHAIL SERGEEVICH) Stranitsy istorii: 175 let Mullovskoi sukonnoi fabriki. Ul'ianovsk, 1963. pp. 150. *bibliog.*

— Spain.

ENCISO RECIO (LUIS MIGUEL) Los establecimientos industriales españoles en el siglo XVIII: la manteleria de la Coruña. Madrid, 1963. pp. 265. *bibliog.* (*Universidad de Navarra. Facultad de Filosofia y Letras. Coleccion Historica. 6*)

— United Kingdom.

COTTON AND ALLIED TEXTILES INDUSTRY TRAINING BOARD [U.K.]. Report and statement of accounts. a., 1972/3- Manchester. *Formerly included in the file of British Parliamentary Papers.*

TEXTILE history and economic history: essays in honour of Miss Julia de Lacy Mann; edited by N.B. Harte and K. G. Ponting. Manchester, [1973]. pp. 396. *bibliog.*

KNIGHT (ARTHUR) Private enterprise and public intervention: the Courtaulds experience. London, 1974. pp. 223.

NATIONAL ECONOMIC DEVELOPMENT OFFICE. Industrial review to 1977: textiles. London, 1974. pp. 140.

— United States.

WANSEY (HENRY) Henry Wansey and his American journal, 1794; [reprint of Wansey's Journal based on the first two English editions of 1796 and 1798, with notes and introduction]; edited by David John Jeremy. Philadelphia, 1970. pp. 186. *bibliog.* (*American Philosophical Society. Memoirs. vol.82*)

TEXTILE WORKERS

— France.

BIEGANSKI (M.) L'industrie textile du Nord de la France: structure, emploi, marché du travail. [Lille], Echelon Régional de l'Emploi, 1972. 2 vols.

— India.

SINGH (VIDYA BHUSAN) Wage patterns, mobility and savings of workers in India: a study of Kanpur textile industry. Bombay, 1973. pp. 204.

— United Kingdom.

REACH (ANGUS BETHUNE) Manchester and the textile districts in 1849; edited by C. Aspin. Helmshore, 1972. pp. 122.

THAILAND

— Census.

THAILAND. Census, 1970. 1970 population and housing census: whole kingdom. [Bangkok], 1973. pp. 158.

THAILAND. Census, 1970. 1970 population and housing census: [regional series]. [Bangkok], 1973. 4 pts. (in 1 vol.).

— Economic conditions.

STUDIES of contemporary Thailand: [papers presented at a seminar held at the Australian National University, Canberra, in 1971]; Robert Ho and E.C. Chapman, eds. Canberra, 1973. pp. 416. *bibliogs.* (*Australian National University. Research School of Pacific Studies. Department of Human Geography. Publications. HG/8*)

— Economic policy.

THAILAND. National Economic and Social Development Board. 1973. The third national economic and social development plan, 1972-1976. Bangkok, [1973]. pp. 285,67.

— Industries.

THAILAND. National Statistical Office. 1974. Report of industrial survey in northeast region, 1972. [Bangkok, 1974]. pp. 74. *In English and Thai.*

— Politics and government.

DHIRAVEGIN (LIKHIT) Political attitudes of the bureaucratic elite and modernization in Thailand. Bangkok, 1973. pp. 94. *bibliog.*

INSTITUTE FOR THE STUDY OF CONFLICT. Research Department. Thailand: the dual threat to stability. London, 1974. pp. 16. *bibliog.* (*Institute for the Study of Conflict. Conflict Studies. No. 44*)

— Population.

THAILAND. Manpower Planning Division. 1970. Population of Thailand: adjusted registration data: (estimates of population trends for regions, changwats and amphurs, 1960-68, and population densities, based on adjusted registration data). Bangkok, 1970. 1 pamphlet (various pagings). ([*Publications*]. 5)

STUDIES of contemporary Thailand: [papers presented at a seminar held at the Australian National University, Canberra, in 1971]; Robert Ho and E.C. Chapman, eds. Canberra, 1973. pp. 416. *bibliogs.* (*Australian National University. Research School of Pacific Studies. Department of Human Geography. Publications. HG/8*)

— Social conditions.

NAKAHARA (JOYCE) and WITTON (RONALD A.) Development and conflict in Thailand. Ithaca, N.Y., 1971. pp. 80. *bibliog.* (*Cornell University. Department of Asian Studies. Southeast Asia Program. Data Papers. No. 80*)

STUDIES of contemporary Thailand: [papers presented at a seminar held at the Australian National University, Canberra, in 1971]; Robert Ho and E.C. Chapman, eds. Canberra, 1973. pp. 416. *bibliogs.* (*Australian National University. Research School of Pacific Studies. Department of Human Geography. Publications. HG/8*)

— Social policy.

THAILAND. National Economic and Social Development Board. 1973. The third national economic and social development plan, 1972-1976. Bangkok, [1973]. pp. 285,67.

THALIDOMIDE.

SUNDAY TIMES. The thalidomide children and the law: a report. London, 1973. pp. 156.

THAMESDOWN

— Politics and government.

THAMESDOWN. District Council. Minutes. irreg., 1973/4 (nos.1-5); ceased pbln. [Swindon].

THAMESDOWN. Borough Council. Minutes. irreg., 1974/5 (no.1)- [Swindon].

THEATRE.

BENTLEY (ERIC RUSSELL) Theatre of war: comments on 32 occasions. London, 1972. pp. 428.

— Belgium.

MARTYNOW-REMICHE (ANNE) and WERY (CLAIRE) Vérité théâtrale et aspirations populaires: rapport d'enquête sociologique sur le fait théâtral en milieu ouvrier dans la région liégeoise. Bruxelles, 1971. pp. 77. *bibliog. (Belgium. Direction Générale des Arts et des Lettres. Documentation et Enquêtes. No. 3)*

— Guatemala — Employees.

GUATEMALA. Comision Nacional del Salario. 1966. Monografia para la determinacion del salario minimo en la industria de teatros y cines. Guatemala, 1966. pp. 51.

— United States.

GOLDSTEIN (MALCOLM) The political stage: American drama and theater of the great depression. New York, 1974. pp. 482.

THEATRE AND SOCIETY.

GOLDSTEIN (MALCOLM) The political stage: American drama and theater of the great depression. New York, 1974. pp. 482.

THEISM.

EWING (ALFRED CYRIL) Value and reality: the philosophical case for theism. London, 1973. pp. 292.

THIERRY D'ARGENLIEU (GEORGES LOUIS MARIE).

THIERRY D'ARGENLIEU (GEORGES LOUIS MARIE) Souvenirs de guerre, juin 1940-janvier 1941. [Paris, 1973]. pp. 282.

THOMAS, Earl of Lancaster.

MADDICOTT (J.R.) Thomas of Lancaster 1307-1322: a study in the reign of Edward II. London, 1970. pp. 390. *bibliog.*

THOMAS [BECKET], Saint, Archbishop of Canterbury.

SMALLEY (BERYL) The Becket conflict and the schools: a study of intellectuals in politics. Oxford, 1973. pp. 258.

THOREZ (MAURICE).

CERRETI (GIULIO) Con Togliatti e Thorez: quarant'anni di lotte politiche. Milano, 1973. pp. 387.

THORNE (WILLIAM JAMES).

RADICE (GILES) and RADICE (ELISABETH ANNE) Will Thorne, constructive militant: a study in new unionism and new politics. London, 1974. pp. 134. *bibliog.*

THOUGHT TRANSFERENCE.

HARDY (ALISTER CLAVERING) and others. The challenge of chance: experiments and speculations. London, 1973. pp. 280.

TICINO

— Constitutional history.

BIANCHI (ROBERTO) La fine del regime radicale nel Ticino, 1868-1877. [Fribourg, 1973]. fo. 228. *bibliog.*

MALAGUERRA (PATRIZIO T.) La crisi politica ticinese, 1889-1891, e l'insurrezione del 1890. [Fribourg, 1973]. fo. 197. *bibliog.*

— Economic policy.

PROGRAMMAZIONE economica: rapporto della Commissione consultiva al Consiglio di Stato. Bellinzona, 1968. pp. 364,40.

— Industries.

TICINO (CANTON). Ufficio delle Ricerche Economiche. 1973. Situazioni e tendenze nel settore industriale del cantone Ticino. Bellinzona, 1973. pp. 188. *(Quaderni.8)*

TIERRA DEL FUEGO, ARGENTINE REPUBLIC

— Census.

TIERRA DEL FUEGO [ARGENTINE REPUBLIC]. Direccion General de Estadistica y Census. 1966. Censo territorial de 1966: (poblacion, vivienda, agropecuario); decreto no. 323/65. [Ushuaia?, 1966?]. pp. 141.

— Statistics.

TIERRA DEL FUEGO [ARGENTINE REPUBLIC]. Direccion General de Estadistica y Censos. 1968. Tierra del Fuego en cifras. [Ushuaia?], 1968. 3 vols. (in 1).

TIERRA DEL FUEGO [ARGENTINE REPUBLIC]. Direccion [General] de Estadistica y Censos. 1971. Informaciones de caracter general. [Ushuaia?], 1971. fo. 55. Lacks fo. 18-25.

TILLON (CHARLES).

LE BRAZ (YVES) Les rejetés: l'affaire Marty-Tillon; pour une histoire différente du PCF. Paris, [1974]. pp. 281. *bibliog.*

TIMBER

— Canada.

LOWER (ARTHUR REGINALD MARSDEN) Great Britain's woodyard: British America and the timber trade, 1763-1867. Montreal, 1973. pp. 271.

— United Kingdom.

FURNITURE AND TIMBER INDUSTRY TRAINING BOARD [U.K.]. Report and statement of accounts. a., 1972/3- High Wycombe. *Formerly included in the file of British Parliamentary Papers.*

TIME.

TOULMIN (STEPHEN EDELSTON) and GOODFIELD (JUNE) The discovery of time. London, 1965. pp. 280. *bibliogs.*

TIME ALLOCATION.

OB osnovnykh itogakh izucheniia biudzheta vremeni zhitelei gor. Pskova: doklad o rezul'tatakh issledovaniia, provedennogo v 1964-1967 gg. v sootvetstvii s programmoi sravnitel'nogo mezhdunarodnogo izucheniia biudzhetov vremeni v sotsialisticheskikh i kapitalisticheskikh stranakh. Novosibirsk, 1968. pp. 85.

BOLGOV (VLADIMIR IL'ICH) Biudzhet vremeni pri sotsializme: teoriia i metody issledovaniia. Moskva, 1973. pp. 287.

TIME AND MOTION STUDY.

BUCHAN (IAN CARPENTER) and RICHARDSON (IAN MILNE) Time study of consultations in general practice. [Edinburgh], Scottish Home and Health Department, 1973. pp. 42. *bibliog. (Scottish Health Service Studies. No.27)*

TIME SERIES ANALYSIS.

BARON (RAPHAEL RAYMOND V.) Analysis of seasonality and trends in statistical series: methodology and applications in Israel. Jerusalem, 1973. 3 vols. (in 1). *bibliog. (Israel. Central Bureau of Statistics. Technical Publications. No.39)*

KENDALL (Sir MAURICE GEORGE) Time-series. London, 1973. pp. 197. *bibliog.*

SIMS (CHRISTOPHER A.) Distributed lags. Minneapolis, 1973. 1 vol. (various foliations). *bibliog. (Minnesota University. Center for Economic Research. Discussion Papers. No. 28)*

HÄGG (CLAES) Periodiska betalningsvariationer: en studie i företagsekonomisk tidsserieanalys. Stockholm, [1974]. pp. 143. *bibliog. With English summary.*

TIN.

CONFERENCE ON TIN CONSUMPTION, LONDON, 1972. Conference...(held in London from 13-17 March 1972). London, International Tin Council, 1972. pp. 496.

TIN INDUSTRY.

CONFERENCE ON TIN CONSUMPTION, LONDON, 1972. Conference...(held in London from 13-17 March 1972). London, International Tin Council, 1972. pp. 496.

HATCHER (JOHN) English tin production and trade before 1550. Oxford, 1973. pp. 219. *bibliog.*

TIN MINERS

— Bolivia.

TABOADA TERAN (NESTOR) El precio del estaño: una tragedia boliviana. La Paz, 1960. pp. 271. *A fictionalised account of a true incident.*

TIN MINES AND MINING

— United Kingdom.

HATCHER (JOHN) English tin production and trade before 1550. Oxford, 1973. pp. 219. *bibliog.*

— — Cornwall.

NOALL (CYRIL) The St. Just mining district. Truro, 1973. pp. 179.

TIN ORES

— Zambia.

LEGG (C.A.) The tin belt of the Southern Province. [Lusaka, 1972]. pp. 58. *bibliog. (Zambia. Geological Survey Department. Economic Reports. No.29) 10 maps, plans, etc. in end pocket.*

TITANIUM INDUSTRY

— Russia — Russia (RSFSR).

GOD rozhdeniia 1943-i: istoricheskii ocherk o Bereznikovskom ordena Trudovogo Krasnogo Znameni titano-magnievom kombinate. Perm', 1968. pp. 259.

TITHES

— France.

ASSOCIATION FRANÇAISE DES HISTORIENS ECONOMISTES. Congrès National, 1er, 1969. Les fluctuations du produit de la dîme: conjoncture décimale et domaniale de la fin du moyen âge au XVIIIe siècle; communications et travaux rassemblés et présentés par Joseph Goy et Emmanuel Le Roy Ladurie. Paris, 1972. pp. 397. *(Paris. Ecole Pratique des Hautes Etudes. Section des Sciences Economiques et Sociales. Centre de Recherches Historiques. Cahiers des Etudes Rurales.3)*

TITLES OF HONOUR AND NOBILITY
— Thailand.

JONES (ROBERT BURTON) Thai titles and ranks; including a translation of Traditions of royal lineage in Siam, by King Chulalongkorn. Ithaca, N.Y., 1971. pp. 147. *bibliog. (Cornell University. Department of Asian Studies. Southeast Asia Program. Data Papers. No. 81) Includes original text.*

TITO (JOSIP BROZ).

VEYRIER (MARCEL) Tito et la révolution. Paris, [1974]. pp. 248. *bibliog.*

TLINGIT INDIANS.

OBERG (KALERVO) The social economy of the Tlingit Indians. Seattle, [1973]. pp. 146. *bibliog. (American Ethnological Society. Monographs. 55)*

TOBACCO
— New Zealand.

NEW ZEALAND. Committee of Inquiry into the Tobacco Growing Industry in New Zealand. 1971. Report; [G. Laurence, sole member]. [Wellington, 1971]. pp. 135.

TOBACCO HABIT.
For related heading see SMOKING.

TOBACCO MANUFACTURE AND TRADE
— Colombia.

SIERRA (LUIS F.) El tabaco en la economia colombiana del siglo XIX. [Bogota, 1971]. pp. 174. *bibliog.*

— Reunion Island.

FONTAINE (MAX) and PEYRICHOU (ROGER) La SICA-TABAC. [St. Denis], 1972. fo. 14. *(Réunion. [Secrétariat Général pour les Affaires Economiques. Documentation et Études]. Bulletin de Conjoncture. Supplément. No. 13)*

— United Kingdom.

FOOD, DRINK AND TOBACCO INDUSTRY TRAINING BOARD [U.K.]. Annual report and accounts. a., 1972/3- Croydon. *Formerly included in the file of British Parliamentary Papers.*

TOENNIES (FERDINAND).

MITZMAN (ARTHUR B.) Sociology and estrangement: three sociologists of imperial Germany. New York, 1973. pp. 375, viii.

TOGLIATTI (PALMIRO).

CERRETI (GIULIO) Con Togliatti e Thorez: quarant'anni di lotte politiche. Milano, 1973. pp. 387.

TOGO
— Economic conditions.

FRANCE. Direction de l'Aide au Développement des Etats Francophones d'Afrique au Sud du Sahara et de la République Malgache. Secteur Information Economique et Conjoncture. 1972. Togo 1970-1971: dossier d'information économique. Paris, 1972. pp. 27, [fo. 40].

TOKYO
— Statistics.

TOKYO STATISTICAL YEARBOOK; [pd. by] Tokyo Metropolitan Government. a., 1971. Tokyo. *In Japanese and English.*

TOLL ROADS
— Mathematical models.

WIGAN (M. RAMSAY) and BAMFORD (T.J.G.) An equilibrium model of bus and car travel over a road network. Crowthorne, 1973. pp. 43. *(U.K. Transport and Road Research Laboratory. Reports. LR 559)*

WIGAN (M. RAMSAY) and BAMFORD (T.J.G.) The effects of network structure on the benefits derivable from road pricing. Crowthorne, 1973. pp. 16. *(U.K. Transport and Road Research Laboratory. Reports. LR 557)*

TOLSTOI (DMITRII ALEKSEEVICH).

SINEL (ALLEN) The classroom and the chancellery: state educational reform in Russia under Count Dmitry Tolstoi. Cambridge, Mass., 1973. pp. 335. *bibliog. (Harvard University. Russian Research Center. Studies. 72)*

TONE (THEOBALD WOLFE).

TONE (THEOBALD WOLFE) Freedom the Wolfe Tone way; ([compiled by] Sean Cronin and Richard Roche); with an introduction by Jack Bennett. Tralee, [1973]. pp. 242. *bibliog.*

TONGA
— Constitutional history.

LATUKEFU (SIONE) Church and state in Tonga: the Wesleyan Methodist missionaries and political development, 1822-1875. Canberra, 1974. pp. 302. *bibliog.*

TONNAGE.

INTERNATIONAL CONFERENCE ON TONNAGE MEASUREMENT OF SHIPS, 1969. Final act of the Conference with attachments including the text of the adopted Convention. London, Inter-Governmental Maritime Consultative Organization, [1970]. pp. 83. *In English and French.*

TOOLS.

WILLIAMS (DAVE) and MUNRO (STEPHANIE) Survival scrapbook 3: access to tools. Brighton, [1973]. 1 vol (various pagings). *bibliogs.*

TOPOGRAPHIC MAPS.

CANADA. Program Planning Office for Resource Satellites and Remote Airborne Sensing. Working Group on Cartography and Photogrammetry. 1971. Resource satellites and remote airborne sensing for Canada. Report no.4. Cartography and Photogrammetry; [R.E. Moore, chairman]. Ottawa, 1971. pp. 8. *With French summary.*

TORONTO
— Foreign population.

ZIEGLER (SUZANNE) Characteristics of Italian householders in metropolitan Toronto. Toronto, 1972. fo. 125 . *bibliog. (York University (Toronto). Institute for Behavioural Research. Ethnic Research Programme. Research Reports)*

RESEARCH GROUP FOR EUROPEAN MIGRATION PROBLEMS. Publications. 18. Immigrant integration and urban renewal in Toronto; by Brigitte Neumann [and others]. The Hague, 1973. pp. 101. *bibliog.*

— Politics and government.

CLARKSON (STEPHEN) City lib: parties and reform. Toronto, 1972. pp. 227.

— Population.

BARRETT (FRANK A.) Residential search behavior: a study of intra-urban relocation in Toronto. Toronto, 1973. pp. 257. *bibliog. (York University (Toronto). Department of Geography. Geographical Monographs. No.1)*

TORONTO UNIVERSITY.

BISSELL (CLAUDE T.) Halfway up Parnassus: a personal account of the University of Toronto, 1932-1971. Toronto, [1974]. pp. 197.

TORRES RESTREPO (CAMILO).

TORRES RESTREPO (CAMILO) Obras escogidas. Montevideo, [1968]. pp. 256.

TORRES RESTREPO (CAMILO) Revolutionary writings; [edited with] introduction by Maurice Zeitlin; [amplified and revised version of the 1969 edition, published by Herder and Herder]. rev. ed. New York, 1972. pp. 371.

TORTS
— United Kingdom.

SALMOND (Sir JOHN WILLIAM) On the law of torts; sixteenth edition by R.F.V. Heuston. London, 1973. pp. 647.

WEIR (TONY) A casebook on tort. 3rd ed. London, 1974. pp. 576.

TORTURE.

AMNESTY INTERNATIONAL Report on torture. London, 1973. pp. 224. *bibliog.*

— Turkey.

COUSINS (JANE) Turkey: torture and political persecution. London, 1973. pp. 106.

TOTALITARIANISM.

FAYE (JEAN PIERRE) Langages totalitaires. Paris, [1972]. pp. 771.

TOULON.

FRANCE. Direction de la Documentation. La Documentation Française. Notes et Etudes Documentaires. Nos. 3,976-3, 977. Les villes françaises: Toulon; [par Jacqueline Bouquerel]. [Paris], 1973. pp. 76. *bibliog.*

TOURIST CAMPS, HOSTELS, ETC.

POLAND. Główny Urząd Statystyczny. Statystyka Polski: Materiały Statystyczne. Nr.109(231) Hotele robotnicze, 1971. Warszawa, 1972. pp. 78.

TOURISTS
— America, Latin.

KRAUSE (WALTER) and JUD (G. DONALD) International tourism and Latin American development. Austin, 1973. pp. 74. *bibliog. (Texas Iniversity. Bureau of Business Research. Studies in Latin American Business. No. 15)*

— Austria.

WISCHHAUSEN (HANS) Pfunds: ein Bergdorf wandelt sich zum Fremdenplatz. Innsbruck, 1972. pp. 96. *bibliog.*

— Cyprus.

ILO INTER-REGIONAL MEETING OF EXPERTS IN VOCATIONAL TRAINING FOR THE HOTEL AND TOURIST INDUSTRY, NICOSIA, 1969. Report on meeting... [held in] Nicosia, Cyprus, 24 November-6 December 1969. (ILO/TAP/INT/R.20) Geneva, 1970. pp. 81.

— European Economic Community countries.

EUROPEAN COMMUNITIES. Commission. 1972. Exemption from taxes granted to imports made by travellers. Brussels, 1972. pp. 10. *(Bulletin of the European Communities. Supplements. [1972/7])*

— Germany.

DEUTSCHER FREMDENVERKEHRSVERBAND. 1902-1972, Deutscher Fremdenverkehrsverband, DFV; (verantwortlich für den Inhalt: Ernst Bernhauer). Bonn, [1972]. pp. 144.

— Italy.

ITALY. Ente Nazionale Italiano per il Turismo. Centro di Documentazione. 1966. Il turismo in Italia nel 1965. Roma, 1966. pp. 321. *(Collana di Monografie Turistiche. 6)*

— Kenya.

KENYA. Central Bureau of Statistics. Migration and tourism statistics. irreg., 1968/1971 [1st]- Nairobi.

— **Mediterranean.**

TOURISM, development and economic growth; seminar held under the auspices of the Technical Assistance Programme of the OECD, Estoril, Portugal, 8th-14th May, 1966. Paris, Organisation for Economic Co-operation and Development, 1967. pp. 46.

— **Netherlands Antilles.**

NETHERLANDS ANTILLES. Bureau voor de Statistiek. 1972. De ontwikkeling van het toerisme op de Nederlandse Antillen en een vergelijking van der stay-over toerisme met het Caraibisch gebied. Curacao, 1972. fo. 12.

— **Switzerland — Bern (Canton).**

BERN (CANTON). Statistisches Bureau. 1968. Die Entwicklung des Fremdenverkehrs im Kanton Bern von 1949-1967 in der Sicht der Statistik: Textband. Bern, 1968. fo.68. (*Sonderhefte. 15*)

— **Tunisia.**

NETTEKOVEN (LOTHAR) Massentourismus in Tunesien: soziologische Untersuchungen an Touristen aus hochindustrialisierten Gesellschaften. Starnberg, 1972. pp. 448. *bibliog*.

— **United Kingdom.**

U.K. Parliament. House of Lords. Committee on the Development of Tourism Bill. Official report. d., Jl 14-18 1969 (1st-5th sittings). London. *Photocopies*.

BRITISH TOURIST AUTHORITY. Britain and the Common Market: an assessment of the possible effects on tourism to the UK if Britain joins. [London], 1971. pp. 8.

BRITISH TOURIST AUTHORITY. Tourism and value added tax: a memorandum submitted to H.M. Customs and Excise. London, 1971. pp. 8.

CONFERENCE ON TOURISM AND THE ENVIRONMENT, LONDON, 1971. Tourism and the environment; papers presented at [the] Conference. London, British Tourist Authority, [1972]. pp. 58.

LINDSEY. County Council. Lindsey countryside recreational survey. [Lincoln, 1972]. pp. 86. *Maps in end paper.*

U.K. Department of Industry. Business monitor: Miscellaneous Series. M.6. Overseas travel and tourism. q., 1973- . London.

ARCHER (BRIAN H.) The impact of domestic tourism. [Cardiff], 1973. pp. 128. *bibliog.* (*Wales. University. University College of North Wales. Bangor Occasional Papers in Economics. No. 2*)

DAVIES (E.T.) Tourism on Devon farms: a physical and economic appraisal. Exeter, 1973. pp. 39. (*Exeter. University. Agricultural Economics Unit. Reports. No.188*)

LINDSEY. County Council. The Lindsey coast: a policy for holiday development. [Lincoln], 1973. pp. 21.

P.A. MANAGEMENT CONSULTANTS LTD. Economic Studies Division. The marketing and development of tourism in the English lakes counties; [by] H.F.R. Perrin [and others]. [London], English Tourist Board, 1973. fo. (126).

P.A. MANAGEMENT CONSULTANTS LTD. Economic Studies Division. The marketing and development of tourism in Northumbria; [by] H.F.R. Perrin [and others]. [London], English Tourist Board, 1973. fo. (139).

TOURISM and conservation; report of a one-day conference sponsored by the English Tourist Board and the Countryside Commission in association with the Civic Trust and the Council for the Protection of Rural England..., 6 June, 1974. London, English Tourist Board, [1974]. fo. 42. (*Discussion Papers*)

YOUNG (Sir GEORGE SAMUEL KNATCHBULL) Tourism: blessing or blight?. Harmondsworth, 1973. pp. 191.

— — **Bibliography.**

RECREATION, leisure and tourism: sources of information; proceedings of a...conference held at the Library Association, London...1972; edited by Ken Bradbury. London, 1973. pp. 85. *bibliog.*

— — **Wales.**

DENBIGHSHIRE. County Planning Officer. Tourism and Recreation Research Reports. 4. Farms and tourism in upland Denbighshire; Colin A.J. Jacobs, County Planning Officer. [Ruthin], 1973. pp. 52. *bibliog.*

ARCHER (BRIAN H.) and others. Tourism in Gwynedd: an economic study; (report to Wales Tourist Board by Institute of Economic Research, University College of North Wales). Cardiff, Wales Tourist Board, 1974. pp. 60.

TOYNBEE (ARNOLD JOSEPH).

RABINOWICZ (OSKAR K.) Arnold Toynbee on Judaism and Zionism: a critique. London, 1974. pp. 372.

TRACTOR INDUSTRY

— **Russia.**

VLASOV (BORIS VLADIMIROVICH) and others, eds. Ekonomika avtomobil'noi i traktornoi promyshlennosti. Moskva, 1973. pp. 318.

TRACTORS.

GOTSCH (CARL H.) Tractor mechanization and rural development in Pakistan. Cambridge, Mass., 1972. pp. 65. (*Harvard University. Center for International Affairs. Development Research Group. Economic Development Reports. No. 227*)

NATIONAL COUNCIL OF APPLIED ECONOMIC RESEARCH. Demand for tractors. New Delhi, [1974]. pp. 76.

TRADE AND PROFESSIONAL ASSOCIATIONS

— **France.**

HINKMANN (ULRICH) Die Korporationen des Handels und Handwerks in Frankreich vor der Abschaffung durch die Revolution. Bern, 1972. pp. 117. *bibliog.*

— **Germany.**

HENSEL (RAINER) Der Einfluss der wirtschaftspolitischen Verbände auf die parlamentarische Arbeit. Göttingen, 1973. pp. 190. *bibliog.*

— **United Kingdom.**

COMMISSION OF INQUIRY INTO INDUSTRIAL AND COMMERCIAL REPRESENTATION. Report. London, 1972. pp. 127.

PRIESTLEY (BARBARA) compiler. British qualifications...: a comprehensive guide to educational, technical, professional and academic qualifications in Britain. 5th ed. London, 1974. pp. 986.

TRADE MARKS

— **Benelux.**

MEULENBROEK (BERNARDUS AUGUSTINUS) Het collectieve merk onder de Benelux-merkenwet. Deventer, 1974. pp. 176. *bibliog. With French summary.*

— **Canada.**

CANADA. Bureau of Intellectual Property. Annual report. a., 1972/3 [1st]- Hull, Canada. *In English and French.*

TRADE REGULATION

— **United States.**

GREEN (MARK J.) ed. The monopoly makers: Ralph Nader's study group report on regulation and competition. New York, 1973. pp. 400.

TRADE ROUTES.

LOMBARD (MAURICE) Espaces et réseaux du haut moyen âge. Paris, [1972]. pp. 231. *bibliog.* (*Paris. Ecole Pratique des Hautes Etudes. Section des Sciences Economiques et Sociales. Le Savoir Historique. 2*)

TRADE UNIONS.

KARL (ALBIN) Die deutschen Gewerkschaften und die internationale Gewerkschaftsbewegung. Köln, [1949]. pp. 28. (*Deutscher Gewerkschaftsbund. Gewerkschaftliche Schriftenreihe. Band 1, Heft 6*)

INTERNATIONAL LABOUR ORGANISATION. Labour-Management Relations Series. Geneva, 1957 in progress.

BRUGAROLA (MARTIN) La libertad sindical. Madrid, Organizacion Sindical Española, 1961. pp. 119.

INTERNATIONAL LABOUR CONFERENCE. 54th Session. Reports. 7. Seventh item on the agenda: trade union rights and their relation to civil liberties. Geneva, 1969. pp. 70.

HYMAN (RICHARD) Marxism and the sociology of trade unionism. London, 1971 repr. 1973. pp. 53.

GEWERKSCHAFTEN UND KLASSENKAMPF: kritisches Jahrbuch. a., 1972 [1st]- Frankfurt am Main.

INTERNATIONAL LABOUR CONFERENCE. 59th Session. Reports. 6. Organisations of rural workers and their role in economic and social development: sixth item on the agenda. Geneva, 1973-74. 2 pts.

MULTINATIONAL corporations and labour unions; selected papers from a symposium in Nijmegen [held under the auspices of the Peace Research Centre and the Dutch labour unions] 17th- 19th May 1973; [edited by Kurt P. Tudyka]. [Nijmegen], 1973. pp. 326. *bibliogs.*

STURMTHAL (ADOLF FOX) and SCOVILLE (JAMES G.) eds. The international labour movement in transition: essays on Africa, Asia, Europe and South America. Urbana, Ill., [1973]. pp. 294.

— **Law.**

GIANNOPOULOS (DEMETRIUS C.) La protection internationale de la liberté syndicale: la Commission d'Investigation et de Conciliation en matière de liberté syndicale de l'Organisation Internationale du Travail. Paris, 1973. pp. 274. *bibliog.*

— **Officials and employees.**

INTERNATIONAL LABOUR CONFERENCE. 56th Session. Reports. 5. Fifth item on the agenda: protection and facilities afforded to workers' representatives in the undertaking. Geneva, 1970-71. 2 pts.

— **Political activity.**

ELLIS (JOHN) b. 1930, and JOHNSON (RICHARD WILLIAM) Members from the unions. London, 1974. pp. 31. (*Fabian Society. Research Series. [No.] 316*)

— **America, Latin.**

AMERICAN INSTITUTE FOR MARXIST STUDIES. Bibliographical Series. No. 1 A bibliography of the history of the Latin-American labor and trade union movements. [3rd ed.] New York, 1967. pp. 18.

HAWKINS (CARROLL) Two democratic labor leaders in conflict: the Latin American revolution and the role of the workers. Lexington, Mass., [1973]. pp. 140. *bibliog.*

— **Argentine Republic.**

ONGARO (RAIMUNDO) Solo el pueblo salvara al pueblo. [Buenos Aires], 1970. pp. 143.

ROTONDARO (RUBEN) Realidad y cambio en el sindicalismo. Buenos Aires, [1971]. pp. 429. *bibliog.*

— **Austria.**

[BRUCKNER (WINIFRED)] Karl Maisel: der Mann, der niemals aufgab. [Wien, 1971]. 1 pamphlet (unpaged).

TRADE UNIONS. (Cont.)

FRANTA (KARL) and HORAK (KURT) 70 Jahre Gewerkschaft der Chemiearbeiter: unser Weg. Wien, [1972]. pp. 95. *bibliog.*

VODOPIVEC (ALEXANDER) Die Quadratur des Kreisky: Österreich zwischen parlamentarischer Demokratie und Gewerkschaftsstaat. Wien, [1973]. pp. 368.

HAUTMANN (HANS) and KROPF (RUDOLF) Die österreichische Arbeiterbewegung vom Vormärz bis 1945: sozialökonomische Ursprünge ihrer Ideologie und Politik. Wien, [1974]. pp. 214. *bibliog.* (*Ludwig-Boltzmann-Institut für Geschichte der Arbeiterbewegung. Schriftenreihe. 4*)

— Bolivia.

GARCIA (ANTONIO) Estructura social y desarrollo latinoamericanos. Santiago de Chile, Instituto de Capacitacion e Investigacion en Reforma Agraria, 1969. pp. 134.

— Brazil.

DULLES (JOHN W.F.) Anarchists and communists in Brazil, 1900-1935. Austin, [1973]. pp. 603. *bibliog.*

— — Officials and employees.

MARCONDES (J.V. FREITAS) Radiografia da liderança sindical paulista. São Paulo, 1964. pp. 89. (Instituto Cultural do Trabalho. Série de Monografias Trabalhistas. vol.2)

— Bulgaria — Congresses.

GIAUROV (KOSTADIN) Otcheten doklad na Tsentralniia sŭvet na Bŭlgarskite profesionalni sŭiuzi pred sedmiia kongres. Sofiia, 1972. pp. 96.

— Canada — Quebec.

TREMBLAY (LOUIS MARIE) Le syndicalisme québécois: idéologies de la C.S.N. et de la F.T.Q., 1940-1970. Montréal, 1972. pp. 286. *bibliog.*

DESROSIERS (RICHARD) and HÉROUX (DENIS) Le travailleur québécois et le syndicalisme. 2nd ed. Montréal, 1973. pp. 156.

— Europe, Eastern.

FRANCE. Direction de la Documentation. La Documentation Française. Notes et Etudes Documentaires. Nos. 3,923-3, 924-3,925. Le syndicalisme en Europe de l'Est; [par Thomas Schreiber]. [Paris], 1972. pp. 116. *bibliogs.*

— European Economic Community countries.

STEWART (MARGARET) Trade unions in Europe. Epping, 1974. pp. 220. *bibliog.*

— France.

DUBOIS (PIERRE) Recours ouvrier, évolution technique, conjoncture sociale: l'action des délégués du personnel C[onfédération] F[rançaise] D[émocratique du] T[ravail] dans des entreprises textiles du Nord. Paris, [1971]. pp. 142. *bibliog.* (*Paris. Université de Paris XI (Paris-Sud). Centre de Recherches en Sciences Sociales du Travail. Collection "Sciences du Travail". 4*)

ANDRIEUX (ANDREE) and LIGNON (JEAN) Le militant syndicaliste d'aujourd'hui. Paris, [1973]. pp. 327. *bibliog.*

LEFRANC (GEORGES) Le syndicalisme en France. 8th ed. Paris, 1973. pp. 128. *bibliog.*

MIDOL (LUCIEN) La voie que j'ai suivie: un ingénieur au coeur des batailles sociales, 1900-1970. Paris, [1973]. pp. 221.

OPPENHEIM (JEAN PIERRE) La C.F.D.T. et la planification. Paris, [1973]. pp. 323. *bibliog.*

PIERRE (ROGER) Les origines du syndicalisme et du socialisme dans la Drôme, 1850-1920. Paris, [1973]. pp. 254. *bibliog.*

— Germany.

LEGIEN (CARL) Warum müssen die Gewerkschaftsfunktionäre sich mehr am inneren Parteileben beteiligen?: ein Vortrag... in der Versammlung der Gewerkschaftskommission Berlins und Umgegend am 27.Januar 1915. Berlin, 1915. pp. 47.

DEUTSCHER HOLZARBEITER-VERBAND. Vorstand. Der Deutsche Holzarbeiter-Verband und sein Kampf gegen die Unfallgefahren an den Holzbearbeitungsmaschinen. [Berlin, 1926]. pp. 48.

KARL (ALBIN) Die deutschen Gewerkschaften und die internationale Gewerkschaftsbewegung. Köln, [1949]. pp. 28. (*Deutscher Gewerkschaftsbund. Gewerkschaftliche Schriftenreihe. Band 1, Heft 6*)

FRANCE. Direction de la Documentation. La Documentation Française. Notes et Etudes Documentaires. No. 3,060. Le mouvement syndical dans la République fédérale d'Allemagne; [by] le Centre d'Etudes de Politique Etrangère. Paris, 1964. pp. 36.

RAASE (WERNER) Die freien deutschen Gewerkschaften in den Jahren des ersten Weltkrieges; die Grosse Sozialistische Oktoberrevolution und die freien deutschen Gewerkschaften in der Novemberrevolution, etc. Berlin, [1969]. pp. 182. *bibliog.* (*Bernau. Hochschule der Deutschen Gewerkschaften Fritz Heckert. Beiträge zur Geschichte der Deutschen Gewerkschaftsbewegung. 4*)

GEWERKSCHAFTEN UND KLASSENKAMPF: kritisches Jahrbuch. a., 1972 [1st]- Frankfurt am Main.

BLANK (KARL) Beiträge zum innerdeutschen Gewerkschaftsdialog. (Band 2). Bonn-Bad Godesberg, [1972]. pp. 179. *Band 1 out of print.*

INSTITUT FÜR MARXISTISCHE STUDIEN UND FORSCHUNGEN. Mitbestimmung und Gewerkschaften, 1945 bis 1949: Dokumente und Materialien. Frankfurt/Main, 1972. pp. 128. (*Neudrucke zur Sozialistischen Theorie und Gewerkschaftspraxis. Band 1*)

SCHUSTER (DIETER) 1872-1972, "Schritt für Schritt": ein Jahrhundert Leder- Gewerkschaften. Stuttgart, [1972]. pp. 239. *bibliog.*

BUSS (HANS JOACHIM) Dreimal Stunde Null: Gewerkschaft am Schienenstrang; Aufstieg und Wandlungen 1897-1972. Frankfurt/M., [1973]. pp. 187.

INSTITUT FÜR MARXISTISCHE STUDIEN UND FORSCHUNGEN. Gewerkschaften und Nationalisierung in der BRD: (Dokumente und Materialien). Frankfurt/Main, 1973. pp. 144. (*Neudrucke zur Sozialistischen Theorie und Gewerkschaftspraxis. Band 5*)

SCHUSTER (DIETER) Die deutschen Gewerkschaften seit 1945. Stuttgart, [1973]. pp. 151.

REULECKE (JUERGEN) ed. Arbeiterbewegung an Rhein und Ruhr: Beiträge zur Geschichte der Arbeiterbewegung in Rheinland-Westfalen. Wuppertal, [1974]. pp. 468. *bibliog.*

SCHWENGER (HANNES) Das Ende der Unbescheidenheit: Intellektuelle auf dem Weg zur Gewerkschaft. Frankfurt am Main, [1974]. pp. 103.

SCHWENGER (HANNES) Schriftsteller und Gewerkschaft: Ideologie, Überbau, Organisation. Darmstadt, 1974. pp. 220. *bibliog.*

— — Law.

DAEUBLER (WOLFGANG) and MAYER-MALY (THEO) Negative Koalitionsfreiheit?. Tübingen, 1971. pp. 48.

— Germany, Eastern.

BLANK (KARL) Beiträge zum innerdeutschen Gewerkschaftsdialog. (Band 2). Bonn-Bad Godesberg, [1972]. pp. 179. *Band 1 out of print.*

— Ghana.

DAMACHI (UKANDI GODWIN) The role of trade unions in the development process, with a case study of Ghana. New York, 1974. pp. 175. *bibliog.*

— Guatemala.

SNEE (CAROLE A.) Current types of peasant-agricultural worker coalitions and their historical development in Guatemala. Cuernavaca, 1969. pp. 129. *bibliog.* (*Centro Intercultural de Documentacion. Cidoc Cuadernos. No. 31*)

— Ireland (Republic).

McCARTHY (CHARLES) The decade of upheaval: Irish trade unions in the nineteen sixties. Dublin, [1973]. pp. 263.

MITCHELL (ARTHUR) M.A., Ph.D. Labour in Irish politics, 1890-1930: the Irish labour movement in an age of revolution. Dublin, [1974]. pp. 317. *bibliog.*

— Italy.

TREU (TIZIANO) Sindacato e rappresentanze aziendali: modelli ed esperienze di un sindacato industriale, FIM-CISL, 1954-1970. Bologna, [1971]. pp. 297.

ALLIO (RENATA) L'Organizzazione Internazionale del Lavoro e il sindacalismo fascista. Bologna, [1973]. pp. 149.

ALTIERI (LEONARDO) Sindacato e organizzazione di classe. Milano, 1973. pp. 158. *bibliog.*

BARBADORO (IDOMENEO) Storia del sindacalismo italiano dalla nascita al fascismo. Firenze, 1973. 2 vols. (in 1).

BONZANINI (ANGELO) Appunti per una storia del movimento sindacale in Italia. Roma, 1973. pp. 172.

CONFEDERAZIONE ITALIANA SINDACATI LAVORATORI. Quattro anni CISL, 1969-1973: la presenza, le proposte, l'iniziativa della CISL nella realtà italiana attraverso i fatti e i documenti. [Rome, 1973]. pp. 271.

FORBICE (ALDO) La federazione CGIL, CISL, UIL fra storia e cronaca: inchiesta sul movimento sindacale. Verona, [1973]. pp. 497.

TURONE (SERGIO) Storia del sindacato in Italia, 1943-1969, dalla Resistenza all' "Autunno caldo". Bari, [1973]. pp. 537.

PERONE (GIAN CARLO) Partecipazione del sindacato alle funzioni pubbliche. Padova, 1972. pp. 339. (*Rome. Università. Istituto di Diritto Privato. Pubblicazioni. 14*)

ROMAGNOLI (UMBERTO) Lavoratori e sindacati tra vecchio e nuovo diritto. Bologna, [1974]. pp. 293.

— Japan.

FRANCE. Direction de la Documentation. La Documentation Française. Notes et Etudes Documentaires. No. 2,812. Le syndicalisme japonais; (texte établi par la Maison franco-japonaise, sur la base des documents et des études réunis par Muneya Aoki). Paris, 1961. pp. 39. *bibliog.*

— Netherlands.

MAATSCHAPPIJ KRITISCHE VAKBEWEGING. Baas in eigen bond: (demokratisering van de vakbeweging). Utrecht, 1973. pp. 26.

TE ELFDER URE. Nr.12,14. Vakbeweging. Amsterdam, [1973]. 2 vols.(in 1).

KLAVER (IMKE) Herinneringen van een friese landarbeider: enkele opgetekende zaken uit het jongste verleden tot 1925: inkele oanteikene dingen út de jonge tiid oan 1925; ingeleid door Ger Harmsen. Nijmegen, [1974]. pp. 245. *Parallel Frisian and Dutch texts.*

— Nigeria.

WATERMAN (PETER) Communist theory in the Nigerian trade union movement. The Hague, 1973. pp. 26. (*Hague. Institute of Social Studies. Occasional Papers. No.41*)

COHEN (ROBIN) Labour and politics in Nigeria, 1945-71. London, 1974. pp. 302. *bibliog.*

TRADE UNIONS. (Cont.)

— Norway.

SLEMMESTAD ARBEIDERFORENING. 22. mars 1896-1971: 75 år. [Slemmestad, 1971]. pp. 23.

— Poland.

KLIMEK (JÓZEF) Udział związków zawodowych w procesie karnym. Warszawa, 1973. pp. 159.

TYCH (FELIKS) Związek Robotników Polskich 1889-1892: anatomia wczesnej organizacji robotniczej. Warszawa, 1974. pp. 506. *bibliog.*

— Russia.

TSENTRAL'NYI GOSUDARSTVENNYI ARKHIV OKTIABR'SKOI REVOLIUTSII, VYSSHIKH ORGANOV GOSUDARSTVENNOI VLASTI I ORGANOV GOSUDARSTVENNOGO UPRAVLENIIA SSSR. 1917 God v Dokumentakh i Materialakh. Rabochee dvizhenie v 1917 godu; podgotovili k pechati V.L. Meller i A.M. Pankratova, etc. Moskva, 1926. pp. 371.

SMOLIARCHUK (VASILII IVANOVICH) Prava profsoiuzov v regulirovanii trudovykh otnoshenii rabochikh i sluzhashchikh. Moskva, 1973. pp. 175.

IVANOV (EVGENII AKIMOVICH) Profsoiuzy v politicheskoi sisteme sotsializma. Moskva, 1974. pp. 240.

— — Handbooks, manuals, etc.

SPRAVOCHNIK profsoiuznogo rabotnika, 1972. Moskva, 1972. pp. 527.

— — Law.

PRAVOVYE aspekty deiatel'nosti profsoiuzov SSSR: profsoiuzy - sub"ekty sovetskogo prava. Moskva, 1973. pp. 431.

— Sierra Leone.

SIERRA LEONE. Board of Inquiry into the Docks Dispute. 1967. Report...; by G.S. Panda. Freetown, [1967]. pp. 11,xiv.

— South Africa.

TRADE unionism in South Africa: report of a delegation from the Trades Union congress. London, [1974]. pp. 40.

WORKSHOP ON ORGANISED LABOUR IN SOUTH AFRICAN SOCIETY, CAPE TOWN, 1973. Labour perspectives on South Africa: (proceedings...); edited by Wolfgang H. Thomas. Cape Town, 1974. pp. 259.

— Spain.

ROSSO DE LARRA (ANTONIO) Funcion economico-social del sindicalismo Español. Madrid, Organizacion Sindical Española, 1960. pp. 111.

SPAIN. Consejo Economico Nacional (Organizacion Sindical). 1963. El enlace sindical. [Madrid, 1963]. pp. 32.

GARCIA-NIETO (JUAN N.) and others, eds. La nueva ley sindical: analisis de una protesta; [by a working party of the Instituto de Estudios Laborales]. Barcelona, 1970. pp. 127.

— Sweden.

FRANCE. Direction de la Documentation. La Documentation Française. Notes et Etudes Documentaires. Nos. 4,011-4, 012-4,013. Les syndicats en Suède; [rédigée par Annie Benhamou- Hirtz]. [Paris], 1973. pp. 91. *bibliog.*

— Switzerland — Valais (Canton).

LAUBER (BRUNO) Die Gewerkschaftsbewegung im industrialisierten Agrargebiet des Oberwallis, unter besonderer Berücksichtigung der christlichen Gewerkschaften. Bern, 1974. pp. 204. *bibliog.*

— United Kingdom.

COLE (GEORGE DOUGLAS HOWARD) The working-class movement and the transition to socialism. London, [1934?]. pp. 16. *(Socialist League [1932-39]. Capitalism in Crisis: Forum Series, 1933-4. No.5)*

TURNER (HERBERT ARTHUR) Trade union growth, structure and policy: a comparative study of the cotton unions in England. Toronto, 1962. pp. 413.

SCHMIDMAN (JOHN) British unions and economic planning. University Park, Penn., [1969]. pp. 106. *(Pennsylvania State University. Penn State Studies. No. 27)*

BAIN (GEORGE SAYERS) The growth of white-collar unionism. Oxford, 1970. pp. 233. *bibliog.*

TRADES UNIONS COMMISSION. The Sheffield outrages: report presented to the Trades Unions Commissioners in 1867: with an introduction by Sidney Pollard. Bath, 1971. pp. 452. *(Documents of Social History)* Reprint of 1867 publication. Original also available in British Parliamentary Papers, 1867, vol. xxxii.

UNION OF CONSTRUCTION, ALLIED TRADES AND TECHNICIANS. National Delegate Conference. Report of proceedings. bien., 1972(1st)- London.

BROWN (RAYMOND) M.Sc. (Econ.) Waterfront organisation in Hull 1870-1900. Hull, 1972. pp. 103. *(Hull. University. Occasional Papers in Economic and Social History. No. 5)*

NATIONAL UNION OF SEAMEN. Rules. [London], 1972. pp. 80.

BAIN (GEORGE SAYERS) and others. Social stratification and trade unionism: a critique. London, 1973. pp. 174. *bibliog. (Warwick Studies in Industrial Relations)*

COMMISSION ON INDUSTRIAL RELATIONS [U.K.]. Recognition of white-collar unions in engineering and chemicals. London, H.M.S.O., 1973. pp. 75. *(Studies. 3)*

LARGE (DAVID) and WHITFIELD (ROBERT) The Bristol Trades Council, 1873-1973. Bristol, 1973. pp. 35. *bibliog. (Historical Association. Bristol Branch. Local History Pamphlets. No. 32)*

MACBEATH (INNIS) Cloth cap and after. London, 1973. pp. 228.

UNOFFICIAL REFORM COMMITTEE. The miners' next step: being a suggested scheme for the reorganisation of the Federation; [reprint of work] first published [at Tonypandy] in 1912:...with a new introduction by R. Merfyn Jones. London, 1973. pp. 34. *(International Socialists. History Group. Reprints in Labour History. No. 4)*

AIMS OF INDUSTRY. "Always to be shielded": must we move towards unionocracy?. London, [1974]. pp. 9.

BASNETT (DAVID) Trade union responsibilities. London, 1974. pp. 6. *(Foundation for Business Responsibilities. Seminar Papers)*

ELLIS (JOHN) b. 1930, and JOHNSON (RICHARD WILLIAM) Members from the unions. London, 1974. pp. 31. *(Fabian Society. Research Series. [No.] 316)*

FRASER (WILLIAM HAMISH) Trade unions and society: the struggle for acceptance, 1850-1880. London, 1974. pp. 292. *bibliog.*

HOOBERMAN (BEN) An introduction to British trade unions. Harmondsworth, 1974. pp. 150. *bibliog.*

LANE (ANTHONY D.) The union makes us strong: the British working class, its trade unionism and politics. London, 1974. pp. 320. *bibliog.*

MORAN (MICHAEL) The Union of Post Office Workers: a study in political sociology. London, 1974. pp. 184.

OXFORDSHIRE RECORD SOCIETY. [Oxfordshire Records Series]. vol. 48. Agricultural trade unionism in Oxfordshire, 1872-81; edited by Pamela Horn. [Oxford], 1974. pp. 144.

PANITCH (LEO VICTOR) The Labour Party and the trade unions: a study of incomes policy since 1945 with special reference to 1964-70; [Ph. D. (London) thesis]. 1973[or rather 1974]. fo. 401. *bibliog.* Typescript: unpublished. This thesis is the property of London University and may not be removed from the library. Offprint from "Political Studies: vol. 19, no. 2, in end pocket.

RADICE (GILES) and RADICE (ELISABETH ANNE) Will Thorne, constructive militant: a study in new unionism and new politics. London, 1974. pp. 134. *bibliog.*

TRADES UNION CONGRESS The TUC's initiatives: a record of the TUC's efforts to get Britain back to full-time working. London, 1974. pp. 15.

— — Elections.

INDUSTRIAL RESEARCH AND INFORMATION SERVICES. A.U.E.W.(E.) postal ballots. London, 1973. pp. 32.

— — Ireland, Northern — Directories.

IRELAND, NORTHERN. Ministry of Health and Social Services. Industrial Relations Division. 1972. Directory of principal organisations of employers and workpeople in Northern Ireland. 16th ed. Belfast, 1972. pp. 39.

— — Scotland.

SMITH (J.H.) Historian. Joe Duncan: the Scottish farm servants and British agriculture. [Edinburgh, 1973]. pp. 254.

— United States.

MINTON (BRUCE) and STUART (JOHN) 1912- . Men who lead labor. New York, [1937]. pp. 270. *bibliog.*

FAULKNER (HAROLD UNDERWOOD) and STARR (MARK) Labor in America. [2nd ed.] New York, 1949. pp. 338. *bibliog.*

HASKEL (HARRY) A leader of the garment workers: the biography of Isidore Nagler. New York, 1950. pp. 351. *bibliog.*

PETERSON (FLORENCE) American labour unions: what they are and how they work. 2nd ed. New York, [1952]. pp. 270.

HUTCHINSON (JOHN) of the Institute for Industrial Relations, California University. Hoffa. Los Angeles, 1969. pp. 9. *bibliog. (California University. Institute of Industrial Relations. Reprints. No. 206)* Reprinted from California Management Review, vol. 11, No. 4, 1969.

NATIONAL INDUSTRIAL CONFERENCE BOARD. Conference Board Reports. Studies in Personnel Policy. No.220. White-collar unionization; by Edward R. Curtin. New York, [1970]. pp. 70.

KAUFMAN (STUART BRUCE) Samuel Gompers and the origins of the American Federation of Labor, 1848-1896. Westport, Conn., 1973. pp. 274. *bibliog.*

KUJAWA (DUANE) ed. American labor and the multinational corporation. New York, 1973. pp. 285. *bibliog.*

LYND (ALICE) and LYND (ROBERT STAUGHTON) eds. Rank and file: personal histories by working-class organizers. Boston, [1973]. pp. 297.

PEREZ (JOSÉ G.) Viva la huelga'. the struggle of the farm workers. New York, [1973]. pp. 15.

ROSENBLUM (GERALD W.) Immigrant workers: their impact on American labor radicalism. New York, [1973]. pp. 189.

SCHMIDT (EMERSON PETER) Union power and the public interest. Los Angeles, [1973]. pp. 212.

— — Finance.

SIMLER (NORMAN JAMES) Why don't unions charge high initiation fees?. Minneapolis, 1973. fo. 33. *bibliog. (Minnesota University. Center for Economic Research. Discussion Papers. No. 36)*

— — Negro membership.

FONER (PHILIP SHELDON) Organized labor and the black worker, 1619-1973. New York, 1974. pp. 489. *bibliog.*

— — Political activity.

CADDY (DOUGLAS) The hundred million dollar payoff. New Rochelle, N.Y., [1974]. pp. 448.

TRADE UNIONS. (Cont.)

— — Ohio.

KRUCHKO (JOHN G.) The birth of a union local: the history of U[nited] A[utomobile] W[orkers] Local 674, Norwood, Ohio, 1933 to 1940. Ithaca, N.Y., 1972. pp. 74.

— — Pennsylvania.

DUBINSKY (IRWIN) Reform in trade union discrimination in the construction industry: operation dig and its legacy. New York, 1973. pp. 311. *bibliog.*

TRADE UNIONS, CATHOLIC

— Switzerland.

SCHWEIZERISCHER METALL- UND UHRENARBEITER-VERBAND. Ein Tatsachenbericht über den Christlichen Metallarbeiter- Verband; zur Aufklärung der Funktionäre und der Vertrauensleute des Schweizerischen Metall- und Uhrenarbeiter-Verbandes, SMUV. [Bern], 1950. pp. 69.

LAUBER (BRUNO) Die Gewerkschaftsbewegung im industrialisierten Agrargebiet des Oberwallis, unter besonderer Berücksichtigung der christlichen Gewerkschaften. Bern, 1974. pp. 204. *bibliog.*

TRADE UNIONS AND COMMUNISM

— Italy.

GRAMSCI (ANTONIO) Scritti sul sindacato: [Il Partito Comunista e i sindacati, and articles reprinted mainly from L'Ordine Nuovo for 1921]. Milano, [1972]. pp. 150.

— United Kingdom.

AIMS OF INDUSTRY. Ban: the attack on press freedom. London, [1974]. pp. 5.

IVENS (MICHAEL WILLIAM) Blackshirts under the bed. London, [1974]. pp. 4.

TRAFFIC ASSIGNMENT

— Mathematical models.

WIGAN (M. RAMSAY) and BAMFORD (T.J.G.) An equilibrium model of bus and car travel over a road network. Crowthorne, 1973. pp. 43. *(U.K. Transport and Road Research Laboratory. Reports. LR 559)*

TRAFFIC ENGINEERING.

RADCLIFFE (J.W.) Traffic engineering as an aid to the protection and improvement of the environment. London, 1973. pp. 12. *(Institution of Municipal Engineers. Monographs. no. 18)*

MOEN (ANDERS SIGBJØRN) Trafikk og miljø. [Oslo], Transportøkonomisk Institutt, 1971. pp. 59. *bibliog.* With English summary.

WESTELIUS (ORVAR) The individual's pattern of travel in an urban area. Stockholm, 1972. pp. 202. *bibliog.* *(Sweden. Statens Institut för Byggnadsforskning. Documents. 1972. D2)* With Swedish summary.

BAMFORD (T.J.G.) and WIGAN (M. RAMSAY) The effects on transport benefit evaluation of user misperception of costs. Crowthorne, 1974. pp. 18. *(U.K. Transport and Road Research Laboratory. Supplementary Reports. 23 UC)*

— Mathematical models.

WESTELIUS (ORVAR) The individual's pattern of travel in an urban area. Stockholm, 1972. pp. 202. *bibliog.* *(Sweden. Statens Institut for Byggnadsforskning. Documents. 1972. D2)* With Swedish summary.

— Italy.

CONVEGNO NAZIONALE DEGLI AMMINISTRATORI COMUNALI, PROVINCIALI E REGIONALI, 12, 1973. Traffico, trasporti pubblici, polizia urbana: [proceedings]. Verona, 1973. pp. 111.

— United Kingdom — London.

WEST LONDON STEERING GROUP. West London study; report of the steering group; (with Joint statement and Individual statements by the four participating authorities). [London, Greater London Council], 1973[-74]. pp. (28);5.

PEARCE (KEITH) and STANNARD (CAROL A.) Catford traffic management study. [London, 1973]. 2 vols.(in 1). *bibliog.* *(London. Greater London Council. Intelligence Unit. Greater London Research. Research Reports. No. 17)*

TRAFFIC ESTIMATION

— Underdeveloped areas.

See UNDERDEVELOPED AREAS — Traffic estimation.

— United Kingdom.

TULPULE (A.H.) Forecasts of vehicles and traffic in Great Britain: 1972 revision. Crowthorne, 1973. pp. 18. *(U.K. Transport and Road Research Laboratory. Reports. LR 543)*

— — Mathematical models.

DOWN (D.W.) The national traffic model (1971). [London], 1972. pp. 30. *(U.K. Department of the Environment. Mathematical Advisory Unit. MAU Notes. 239)*

TRAFFIC NOISE.

DIFFEY (JAY) An investigation into the effect of high traffic noise on house prices in a homogenous sub-market. Keele, 1972. pp. 14. *(Keele. University. Statistical Research Unit in Sociology. Occasional Papers. No.1)*

SLADE (G.D.) Motorway noise: characteristics, evaluation, attenuation and a case study. London, 1973. pp. 30. *(Institution of Municipal Engineers. Monographs. No. 19)*

LONDON. Greater London Council. Traffic noise: major urban roads. London, 1970. pp. 20. *bibliog.* *(Urban Design Bulletins. 1.)* 8 charts in end pocket.

TRAFFIC OFFENCES

— Canada.

CANADA. Statistics Canada. Crime and traffic enforcement statistics. a., 1972/1973 [1st issue]- Ottawa. In English and French.

— Finland.

MÄKINEN (TUIJA) Lükennesakot varallisuuteen kohdistuvana rangaistuksena, etc. Helsinki, 1974. fo. 33. *(Kriminologinen Tutkimuslaitos. Sarja M. 35)* With English summary.

TRAFFIC REGULATIONS

— United Kingdom.

MILES (JOHN C.) The Goyt valley traffic experiment, 1970-1971; a report written for the Countryside Commission. London, Countryside Commission, [1972]. pp. 114.

U.K. Department of the Environment. 1973. The highway code. [London, 1973]. pp. 52.

TRAFFIC SURVEYS

— Netherlands.

NETHERLANDS. Central Bureau voor de Statistiek. 1972. Verkeerstellingen 1970. 's-Gravenhage, 1972. 3 vols. (in 1).

— Sweden — Uppsala.

WESTELIUS (ORVAR) The individual's pattern of travel in an urban area. Stockholm, 1972. pp. 202. *bibliog.* *(Sweden. Statens Institut för Byggnadsforskning. Documents. 1972. D2)* With Swedish summary.

— Switzerland — Zürich (Canton).

ZUERICH (CANTON). Tiefbauamt. 1971. Verkehrszählungen 1970. [Zürich, 1971]. pp.27.

— United Kingdom.

FREEMAN FOX AND ASSOCIATES. Speed/flow relationships on suburban main roads; a report on a study carried out for the Road Research Laboratory. London, 1972. pp. 25.

GYENES (L.) 50-point traffic census: the automatic processing of hourly flows. Crowthorne, 1973. pp. 11. *(U.K. Transport and Road Research Laboratory. Reports. LR 558)*

TRAMPS

— United States.

RINGENBACH (PAUL T.) Tramps and reformers 1873-1916: the discovery of unemployment in New York. Westport, 1973. pp. 224. *bibliog.*

TRANSKEIAN TERRITORIES

— Politics and government.

TRANSKEI. Department of the Interior. Report. bien., 1967/1968. Umtata. *No more published.*

— Race question.

REPORTS ON THE STATE OF SOUTH AFRICA. No.25. The Transkei; [and] The case for separate development. London, Department of Information, South African Embassy, 1963. pp. 31.

REPORTS ON THE STATE OF SOUTH AFRICA. No.25. The Transkei: a progress report; [and] Multi-national development in South Africa. rev.ed. London, Department of Information, South African Embassy, 1968. pp. 30.

TRANSPLANTATION OF ORGANS, TISSUES, ETC.

FOX (RENEE CLAIRE) and SWAZEY (JUDITH P.) The courage to fail: a social view of organ transplants and dialysis. Chicago, 1974. pp. 395. *bibliog.*

— Law and legislation

— — Denmark.

BETAENKNING vedrorende lovgivning om transplantation; afgivet af det af Justitsministeriet den 12. oktober 1966 nedsatte udvalg. [Copenhagen], 1967. pp. 33. *(Denmark. Betaenkninger. Nr.454)*

TRANSPORT WORKERS

— Russia — Kazakstan.

VOPROSY sotsial'nogo razvitiia kollektivov transportnykh predpriiatii Kazakhstana. Alma-Ata, 1973. pp. 184.

— United States.

LIEB (ROBERT C.) Labor in the transportation industries. New York, 1974. pp. 125. *bibliog.*

TRANSPORTATION.

BARRELL (DAVID) Cost benefit analysis in transportation planning. [Oxford], 1972. pp. 89. *bibliog.* *(Oxford Polytechnic. Department of Town Planning. Oxford Working Papers in Planning Education and Research. 10)*

GEORGI (HANSPETER) Cost-benefit and public investment in transport: a survey. London, 1973. pp. 204.

HAY (ALAN M.) Transport for the space economy: a geographical study. [London], 1973. pp. 192.

TRANSPORTATION.

HILL (MORRIS) Planning for multiple objectives: an approach to the evaluation of transportation plans. Philadelphia, [1973]. pp. 273. bibliog. (Regional Science Research Institute. Monograph Series. No.5)

WOLKOWITSCH (MAURICE) Géographie des transports. Paris, [1973]. pp. 381. bibliogs.

HARRISON (ANTHONY J.) The economics of transport appraisal. London, 1974. pp. 293. bibliog.

ILLICH (IVAN D.) Energy and equity. London, 1974. pp. 96. bibliog.

STEENBRINK (PETER ANTONIUS) Optimization of transport networks. [Rotterdam, 1974]. pp. 328. bibliogs. With Dutch summary.

— Abstracts.

EUROPEAN CONFERENCE OF MINISTERS OF TRANSPORT. International Co-operation in the field of Transport Economics Documentation. Transdoc. q., Mr 1974(no.1)- Paris. In English, French and German, with abstracts in one of these languages.

— Cost of operation.

SHARP (CLIFFORD H.) Transport economics. London, 1973. pp. 80. bibliog.

— Environmental aspects — United Kingdom.

TRANSPORTATION and environment: policies, plans and practice: proceedings of a symposium held at the University of Southampton, 9-12 April 1973: [organized by the Department of Civil Engineering]; edited by J.H. Earp [and others]. Southampton, [1973]. 1 vol. (various pagings). bibliogs.

— Finance.

ABERLE (GERD) Verkehrsinfrastrukturinvestitionen im Wachstumsprozess entwickelter Volkswirtschaften. Düsseldorf, 1972. pp. 218. bibliog. (Cologne. Universität. Institut für Verkehrswissenschaft. Buchreihe. Nr.27)

BEARE (JOHN BARRINGTON) Stabilization policies: government expenditures on transport in Canada and some lessons from European experience. Toronto, 1974. fo.35. (Toronto. University, and York University (Toronto). Joint Program in Transportation. Research Reports. No.16)

— Mathematical models.

RUITER (EARL R.) A prototype analysis. Cambridge, Mass., 1968. pp. 279. (Massachusetts Institute of Technology. Transportation Systems Division. Search and Choice in Transport Systems Planning. vol. 2)

— Passenger traffic — Bibliography.

NICKEL (BERNHARD E.) compiler. Bibliography: unconventional passenger transportation systems: Bibliographie: unkonventionelle Personentransportsysteme, etc. Bruxelles, International Union of Public Transport, [1973]. pp. 306. In English, French and German.

— Rates.

OORT (COENRAAD JAN) La théorie marginaliste et les prix de transport: une analyse. Rotterdam, 1960. pp. 93. bibliog.

INTERNATIONAL SYMPOSIUM ON TRANSPORTATION PRICING, WASHINGTON, 1969. Criteria for transport pricing: a collection of edited papers presented at the... symposium...; James R. Nelson, editor. Cambridge, M'land, 1973. pp. 327.

— Statistics.

INTERNATIONAL ROAD TRANSPORT UNION. Department of Research and Transport Economics. World transport data: Statistiques mondiales de transport. [Geneva, 1973]. pp. 261. In English and French.

TULPULE (A.H.) An analysis of some world transport statistics. Crowthorne, 1974. pp. 48. (U.K. Transport and Road Research Laboratory. Reports. LR 622)

— America, Latin — Cost of operation.

CHURCHILL (ANTHONY) and others. Road user charges in Central America. [Washington], International Bank for Reconstruction and Development, [1972]. pp. 176. bibliog. (World Bank Staff Occasional Papers. No. 15)

— Belgium — Statistics.

TRANSPORTS EN BELGIQUE, LES: recueil de statistiques; ([pd. by] Service de Promotion et de Coordination des Communications [Belgium]). bien., 1950/1966 (5e éd.), 1972(8e)- Bruxelles.

— Canada.

SCHREINER (JOHN) Transportation: the evolution of Canada's network. Toronto, [1972]. pp. 136. bibliog.

— European Economic Community countries.

COMMITTEE FOR ENVIRONMENTAL CONSERVATION. Transport, the environment and the European Economic Community. London, [1973]. pp. 8.

EUROPEAN COMMUNITIES. Commission. 1973. Communication of the Commission to the Council on the development of the common transport policy: submitted...on 25 October 1973. [Brussels], 1973. pp. 24. (Bulletin of the European Communities. Supplements. [1973/16])

— — Bibliography.

PARTINGTON (LENA) compiler. Transport in the European Community: a preliminary listing of material in the library [of the Department of the Environment] . [London], 1974. pp. 42. (U.K. Department of the Environment. Library. Bibliography Series. No. 169)

— France.

GEOGRAPHIE économique et ferroviaire des pays de la C.E.E. et de la Suisse. Fascicule 6. France, géographie économique et ferroviaire, etc. [Paris. S.N.C.F., 1973]. pp. 335, 48.

— India.

TRIPATHI (P.C.) Rural transport and economic development. Delhi, [1973?]. pp. 200. bibliog.

— Italy.

CONFERENZA SULL'ENTE REGIONALE DEI TRASPORTI, TORINO, 1968. Atti. [Torino], Comitato Regionale per la Programmazione Economica del Piemonte, [1968]. pp. 106.

CONVEGNO NAZIONALE DEGLI AMMINISTRATORI COMUNALI, PROVINCIALI E REGIONALI, 12ᵉ, 1973. Traffico, trasporti pubblici, polizia urbana: [proceedings]. Verona,–1973. pp. 111.

— Norway.

FRØYSADAL (EDVIN) Finnmark: totale godstransporter og persontransporter med offentlige befordringsmidler; transportmønsterets struktur i 1970.[Oslo], Transportøkonomisk Institutt, 1971. 1 vol. (various foliations).

— — Passenger traffic.

BYSVEEN (TOR) Persontransport. Oslo, Norsk Institutt for By- og Regionforskning, [1972] . fo. 147.

— Russia.

FOMIN (VASILII VASIL'EVICH) Lenin i transport. Moskva, 1973. pp. 71.

— — Moldavian Republic.

IAROTSKII (A.S.) ed. Ekonomicheskie problemy transporta Moldavii. Kishinev, 1973. pp. 148.

— Sweden.

NORSTRÖM (GÖRAN) Transportgeografiska studier i svensk utrikeshandel. Stockholm, 1973. pp. 426. bibliog. With English summary.

PRED (ALLAN R.) and TÖRNQVIST (GUNNAR) Systems of cities and information flows: two essays. Lund, 1973. pp. 121. bibliogs. (Lund. Universitet. Geografiska Institution. Lund Studies in Geography. Series B. Human Geography. No. 38)

— Switzerland.

SWITZERLAND. Groupe d'Etude TRANSAS. 1972. Etude préliminaire d'un nouveau système suisse de transport nord-sud: rapport final. [Bern, 1972]. pp. 107.

— United Kingdom.

U.K. Transport Holding Company. Annual report and accounts. a., [N 1971]/Mr 1973; ceased pbln. London. Formerly included in the file of British Parliamentary Papers.

U.K. Central Office of Information. Reference Division. 1971. Inland transport in Britain. rev. ed. London, 1971. pp. 16. bibliog.

CALVERT (ROGER) Transport disintegrated: [with Improving London's rail transport]. London, 1973. pp. 144, 7.

FISHER (H.E.S.) and MINCHINTON (WALTER EDWARD) eds. Transport and shipowning in the Westcountry. Exeter, 1973. pp. 71. (Exeter. University. Department of Economic History. Exeter Papers in Economic History. No.7.)

HAMPSHIRE ARCHIVISTS' GROUP. Publications. No.2. Transport in Hampshire and the Isle of Wight: a guide to the records. [Portsmouth], 1973. pp. 126.

RAMBLERS' ASSOCIATION. Briefs for the Countryside. No.4. Rural transport in crisis. London, [1973]. pp. 23.

SHARP (CLIFFORD H.) Transport economics. London, 1973. pp. 80. bibliog.

SOUTH EAST LANCASHIRE AND NORTH EAST CHESHIRE PASSENGER TRANSPORT EXECUTIVE. Public transport plan for the future. [Manchester], 1973. pp. 107.

U.K. Department of the Environment. 1973. The Maplin project: surface access corridor: a consultation document. [London], 1973. pp. 14, 2 maps.

ALDCROFT (DEREK H.) Studies in British transport history, 1870-1970. Newton Abbot, [1974]. pp. 309.

BAGWELL (PHILIP SIDNEY) The transport revolution from 1770. London, 1974. pp. 460. bibliog.

BRUTON (MICHAEL J.) ed. The spirit and purpose of planning. London, 1974. pp. 233.

COUNCIL FOR THE PROTECTION OF RURAL ENGLAND. Transport - co-ordination or chaos?. London, [1974]. pp. 35.

INDEPENDENT COMMISSION ON TRANSPORT. Changing directions: the report of the Independent Commission on Transport; [Hugh Montefiore, chairman]. London, 1974. pp. 365.

TRADES UNION CONGRESS. Transport Industries Committee. TUC statements on transport: integration of transport, British Rail finance, urban transport. [London, 1974]. pp. 31.

— — Laws and regulations.

BONNER (GEORGE ALAN) British transport law by road and rail. Newton Abbot, [1974]. pp. 406.

— United Kingdom — Passenger traffic.

U.K. Interdepartmental Working Party on Inter-city Transport. 1973. Comparative assessment of new forms of inter-city transport; a report; [W.J. Charnley and subsequently H.G.R. Robinson, chairmen]. [London], 1970-71 [or rather 1973]. 3 vols. (in 1). (U.K. Transport and Road Research Laboratory. Reports. SR1-3)

TRANSPORTATION. (Cont.)

— — Passenger traffic — Mathematical models.

BALCOMBE (R.J.) and others. A parametric model of inter-city passenger transport: an interim report. Crowthorne, 1973. pp. 27. (*U.K. Transport and Road Research Laboratory. Reports. LR 607*)

— — Societies.

CHARTERED INSTITUTE OF TRANSPORT. Handbook. a., current issue only kept. London.

— — Ireland.

NOWLAN (KEVIN B.) ed. Travel and transport in Ireland. Dublin, 1973. pp. 178. *bibliogs.*

— — Scotland.

SCOTTISH TRANSPORT GROUP. Annual report and accounts. a., 1971 [3rd]- Edinburgh. *Formerly included in the file of British Parliamentary Papers.*

WAYNE (FRANCIS) Energy sources for Scottish transport. [Aberdeen, imprint], 1973. pp. 22. *bibliog.*

— — United States.

WINTHER (OSCAR OSBURN) The transportation frontier: trans-Mississippi West, 1865-1890.New York, [1964]. pp. 224. *bibliog.*

— — New York.

NEW YORK (STATE). Department of Transportation. 1973- . Statewide master plan for transportation. [Albany, 1973 in progress].

— — Pennsylvania.

SWETNAM (GEORGE) Pennsylvania transportation. 2nd ed. Gettysburg, 1968. pp. 109. *bibliog. (Pennsylvania History Studies. No. 7)*

TRANSPORTATION, AUTOMOTIVE.

— Cost of operation — Mathematical models.

BAMFORD (T.J.G.) and WIGAN (M. RAMSAY) The effects on transport benefit evaluation of user misperception of costs. Crowthorne, 1974. pp. 18. (*U.K. Transport and Road Research Laboratory. Supplementary Reports. 23 UC*)

— Africa, Subsaharan — Cost of operation.

FEDERWISCH (JACQUES) Etude comparative des côuts et charges de transport par route dans divers pays d'Afrique tropicale. Bruxelles, 1972. pp. 89. (*Académie Royale des Sciences d'Outre-Mer. Classe des Sciences Techniques. [Mémoires in - 8]. Nouvelle Série. tome 17, fasc. 2*)

— Bolivia.

BOLIVIA. Comision Permanente de Racionalizacion del Transporte Automotor. 1966. Informe. La Paz, 1966. 1 vol. (various pagination)

— Canada — Freight.

ARCHAMBAULT (CAMILLE) Theories, objectives and practical problems of road finance: the truckers' viewpoint. [Quebec?, 1956]. fo. 65.

— France.

FRANCE. Délégation à l'Aménagement du Territoire et à l'Action Régionale. 1972. Les grandes liaisons routières: histoire d'un schéma. [Paris], 1972. pp. 103. (*Travaux et Recherches de Prospective. 31*)

— India — Uttar Pradesh — Government ownership.

UNITED PROVINCES OF AGRA AND OUDH. Ad Hoc Committee on Nationalised Road Transport. 1949. Report; [Sir L.P. Misra, chairman]. [Allahabad? 1949?]. pp. 69. *Title page lacking.*

— United Kingdom.

TULPULE (A.H.) Forecasts of vehicles and traffic in Great Britain: 1972 revision. Crowthorne, 1973. pp. 18. (*U.K. Transport and Road Research Laboratory. Reports. LR 543*)

— — Freight.

NATIONAL FREIGHT CORPORATION [U.K.]. Annual report and accounts. a., 1972- London. *Formerly included in the file of British Parliamentary Papers.*

U.K. Department of the Environment. Directorate of Statistics. 1972. The transport of goods by road, 1970-1972. [London], 1972. fo.20,4.

LORRIES and the world we live in; a report to the...Minister for Transport Industries; [D.E.A. Pettit, chairman of the Committee]. London, H.M.S.O., 1973. pp. 72.

U.K. Department of the Environment. Directorate of Statistics. 1974. The transport of goods by road: 1970-1972. rev. ed. London, 1974. pp. 20,4.

— — Mathematical models.

REED (P.W.) A model of inter-urban road haulage operation. [London], 1971. fo. 132. (*U.K. Department of the Environment. Mathematical Advisory Unit. MAU Notes. 242*)

— Zambia.

ZAMBIA. Office of the Road Traffic Commissioner. Annual report. a., 1965/6m, 1969/1970- Lusaka.

TRANSPORTATION AND STATE.

BEARE (JOHN BARRINGTON) Stabilization policies: government expenditures on transport in Canada and some lessons from European experience. Toronto, 1974. fo.35. (*Toronto. University, and York University (Toronto). Joint Program in Transportation. Research Reports. No.16*)

TRANSVAAL

— History.

DENOON (DONALD) A grand illusion: the failure of imperial policy in the Transvaal colony during the period of reconstruction, 1900-1905. London, 1973. pp. 275. *bibliog.*

— Population.

GRICE (DUCHESNE COWLEY) The approaching crisis: land and population in the Transvaal and Natal. Johannesburg, [1973]. pp. 22. (*South African Institute of Race Relations. Presidential Addresses. 1973*)

TRAVEL.

BIT INFORMATION SERVICE. Overland to India - and beyond...... London, 1972. pp. 20.

TRAVEL TIME (TRAFFIC ENGINEERING).

TIME RESEARCH NOTES . [London, Ministry of Transport, 1969 in progress].

TRAVELLERS, ENGLISH.

SWINGLEHURST (EDMUND) The romantic journey: the story of Thomas Cook and Victorian travel. London, 1974. pp. 208. *bibliog.*

TREASON

— Russia.

HOELZLE (ERWIN) Der Geheimnisverrat und der Kriegsausbruch 1914. Göttingen, 1973. pp. 39. (*Ranke-Gesellschaft. Historisch-Politische Hefte. Heft 23*)

KLIAGIN (VASILII SUDOROVICH) Otvetstvennost' za osobo opasnye gosudarstvennye prestupleniia. Minsk, 1973. pp. 268.

TREATIES.

COUNCIL OF EUROPE. European Treaties Series. Strasbourg, 1949 in progress.

BERGSTEN (ERIC E.) Community law in the French courts: the law of treaties in modern attire. The Hague, 1973. pp. 145.

HARASZTI (GYÖRGY) Some fundamental problems of the law of treaties. Budapest, 1973. pp. 439.

ELIAS (TASLIM OLAWALE) The modern law of treaties. Dobbs Ferry, N. Y., 1974. pp. 272. *bibliog.*

GRENVILLE (JOHN ASHLEY SOAMES) The major international treaties, 1914-1973: a history and guide with texts. London, 1974. pp. 575. *bibliog.*

SZTUCKI (JERZY) Jus cogens and the Vienna Convention on the Law of Treaties: a critical appraisal. Wien, 1974. pp. 204. *bibliog. (Österreichische Zeitschrift für Öffentliches Recht. Supplementa. 3*)

TREATY MAKING POWER.

OKEKE (CHRIS N.) Controversial subjects of contemporary international law: an examination of the new entities of international law and their treaty-making capacity. Rotterdam, 1974. pp. 243.

TRENTINO—ALTO ADIGE

— Social life and customs.

COLE (JOHN W.) and WOLF (ERIC ROBERT) The hidden frontier: ecology and ethnicity in an Alpine valley. New York, [1974]. pp. 348. *bibliog.*

TRESSELL (ROBERT) pseud.

BALL (FREDERICK CYRIL) One of the damned: the life and times of Robert Tressell, author of The ragged trousered philanthropists. London, [1973]. pp. 266. *bibliog.*

TRIALS (POLITICAL CRIMES AND OFFENCES)

— Argentine Republic.

VARELA (FELIPE) defendant. Proceso a la montonera de Felipe Varela por la toma de Salta: causas judiciales; estudio preliminar, Felipe Varela y la toma de Salta por Rodolfo Ortega Peña y Eduardo L. Duhalde. [Buenos Aires], 1969. pp. 256.

— Czechoslovakia.

LUND (CAROLINE) The Czechoslovak frame-up trials and the U.S. Communist Party; with Jiri Pelikan's appeal to Angela Davis and statements by the Australian, Dutch and Italian CPs. New York, 1973. pp. 15.

— France.

BETEILLE (PIERRE) and RIMBAUD (CHRISTIANE) Le procès de Riom. [Paris, 1973]. pp. 284. *bibliog.*

CAERLÉON (RONAN) Les Bretons le dos au mur: le F[ront de] L[ibération de la] B[retagne] devant la Cour de Sûreté de l'état. Paris, [1973]. pp. 221.

— Germany.

SOZIALDEMOKRATISCHE Bibliothek: Sammlung von Abhandlungen über Theorie und Geschichte des Sozialismus; (unveränderter fotomechanischer Nachdruck der Originalausgabe 1885-(90), [containing 36 pamphlets]). Leipzig, 1971. 3 vols.

— Italy.

ATTENTATO al Diana: (processo agli anarchici nell'assise di Milano, 9 maggio-1 giugno 1922). Roma, 1973. pp. 213.

— Russia.

BUKOVSKII (VLADIMIR KONSTANTINOVICH) Stories and statements, selected...by Comité international pour la défense des droits de l'homme. Paris, [1971?]. 1 pamphlet (unpaged).

— Spain.

SALABERRI (KEPA) eL PROCESO DE eUSKADI EN bURGOS: EL SUMARISIMO 31/69. pARIS, 1971. PP. 319.

— United States.

BANNAN (JOHN F.) and BANNAN (ROSEMARY S.) Law, morality and Vietnam: the peace militants and the courts. Bloomington, [Ind., 1974]. pp. 241.

TRIALS (RACIAL DEFAMATION)

— France.

LEGAGNEUX (ROBERT) Defendant. Soviet anti-semitism: the Paris trial; edited and with an introduction by Emanuel Litvinoff. London, 1974. pp. 120.

TRIALS (RIOT)

— United States.

BALBUS (ISAAC D.) The dialectics of legal repression: black rebels before the American criminal courts. New York, [1973]. pp. 269.

TRIALS (TREASON)

— South Africa.

The STATE v. the Dean of Johannesburg; prepared for the S.A. Institute of Race Relations by a member of the legal profession. Johannesburg, [1972]. pp. 43.

— Switzerland.

SCHOCH (JUERG) Die Oberstenaffäre: eine innenpolitische Krise, 1915/1916. Bern, 1972. pp. 169. *bibliog.*

TRIBES AND TRIBAL SYSTEM

— India — Bihar.

PRASAD (SAILESHWAR) Where the three tribes meet: a study in tribal interaction. Allahabad, 1974. pp. 232. *bibliog.*

TRIBOLOGY.

U.K. Committee on Tribology. 1973. The introduction of a new technology; Committee on Tribology report. 1966-1972; [H. Peter Jost, chairman]. London, 1973. pp. 150.

TRIER

— Economic history.

LAUFER (WOLFGANG) Die Sozialstruktur der Stadt Trier in der frühen Neuzeit. Bonn, 1973. pp. 369. *bibliog.* (*Bonn. Universität. Institut für Geschichtliche Landeskunde der Rheinlande. Rheinisches Archiv. 86*)

— Social history.

LAUFER (WOLFGANG) Die Sozialstruktur der Stadt Trier in der frühen Neuzeit. Bonn, 1973. pp. 369. *bibliog.* (*Bonn. Universität. Institut für Geschichtliche Landeskunde der Rheinlande. Rheinisches Archiv. 86*)

TRIESTE

— Social history.

MASERATI (ENNIO) Il movimento operaio a Trieste dalle origini alla prima guerra mondiale. [Milan, 1973]. pp. 281.

TRINIDAD AND TOBAGO

— Constitutional history.

MILLETTE (JAMES) The genesis of Crown colony government: Trinidad, 1783-1810. Trinidad, [1970]. pp. 295. *bibliog.*

— History.

MILLETTE (JAMES) The genesis of Crown colony government: Trinidad, 1783-1810. Trinidad, [1970]. pp. 295. *bibliog.*

— Industries.

TRINIDAD AND TOBAGO. Central Statistical Office. Survey of Establishments, 1971. Survey of establishments: preliminary bulletin. [Port-of-Spain], 1972. pp. 12.

TRINIDAD AND TOBAGO. Central Statistical Office. Census of Manufacturing, 1969-70. Census of manufacturing, 1969 and 1970. Port of Spain, 1974. pp. 94.

— Politics and government.

STONE (CARL) Stratification and political change in Trinidad and Jamaica; [revised version of a paper presented at the meeting of the American Political Science Association, Los Angeles, 1970]. Beverly Hills, Calif., [1972]. pp. 39.

— Population.

SIMPSON (JOY M.) A demographic analysis of internal migration in Trinidad and Tobago: a descriptive and theoretical orientation. [Kingston, Jamaica, 1973]. pp. 63.

TRINIDAD AND TOBAGO. Central Statistical Office. 1973. Population abstract 1960-1970, including projections 1970-1985. [Port-of-Spain, 1973]. pp. 58.

TROPICS.

ETUDES de géographie tropicale offertes à Pierre Gourou. Paris, 1972. pp. 599. (*Paris. Ecole Pratique des Hautes Etudes. Section des Sciences Economiques et Sociales. Le Monde d'Outre-Mer Passé et Présent. 1ère Série. Études. 38*)

TRORY (ERNIE).

TRORY (ERNIE) Between the wars: recollections of a communist organiser. Brighton, 1974. pp. 159.

TROTSKII (LEV DAVYDOVICH).

NEDAVA (JOSEPH) Trotsky and the Jews. Philadelphia, 1972. pp. 299. *bibliog.*

WOODS (ALAN) and others. Lenin and Trotsky: what they really stood for. Colombo, 1972. pp. 173. *bibliogs.*

BOR'BA kommunistov protiv ideologii trotskizma. Moskva, 1973. pp. 222.

DZHIBLADZE (D.) Bol'sheviki Zakavkaz'ia v bor'be s trotskistsko- zinov'evskim blokom. Tbilisi, 1973. pp. 69.

FOURTH INTERNATIONAL. International Committee. In defence of Trotskyism. London, 1973. pp. 80.

FRANK (PIERRE) La Quatrième Internationale: contribution à l'histoire du mouvement trotskyste. [2nd ed.]. Paris, 1973. pp. 180. *bibliog.*

The TRANSITIONAL program for socialist revolution; [programme by Leon Trotsky adopted at the Founding Conference of the Fourth International in 1938; with discussions with Trotsky and] introductory essays by Joseph Hansen and George Novack. New York, 1973. pp. 223.

BROSSAT (ALAIN) Aux origines de la révolution permanente: la pensée politique du jeune Trotsky; [with] trois textes de Léon Trotsky, La douma et la révolution, etc. Paris, 1974. pp. 316. *bibliog.*

TRUDEAU (PIERRE ELLIOTT).

WESTELL (ANTHONY) Paradox: Trudeau as prime minister. Scarsborough, Ontario, [1972]. pp. 262.

ZINK (LUBOR J.) Trudeaucracy. Toronto, [1972]. pp. 150.

TRUMAN (HARRY S.) President of the United States.

HAMBY (ALONZO L.) Beyond the New Deal: Harry S. Truman and American liberalism. New York, 1973. pp. 635. *bibliog.*

McCOY (DONALD RICHARD) and RUETTEN (RICHARD T.) Quest and response: minority rights and the Truman administration. Lawrence, Kansas, [1973]. pp. 427. *bibliog.*

MILLER (MERLE) Plain speaking: an oral biography of Harry S. Truman. London, 1974. pp. 448.

SNETSINGER (JOHN) Truman, the Jewish vote, and the creation of Israel. Stanford, [1974]. pp. 208. *bibliog.* (*Stanford University. Hoover Institution on War, Revolution and Peace. Hoover Institution Studies. 39*)

TRUST TERRITORIES

— South West Africa.

HIDAYATULLAH (MOHAMMAD) The South-West Africa case. Bombay, [1967]. pp. 144.

TRUSTS, INDUSTRIAL.

GRIMM (ROBERT) Unternehmerkoalitionen: Kartelle und Trusts. Basel, 1908. pp. 36.

ORGANISATION FOR ECONOMIC CO-OPERATION AND DEVELOPMENT. Committee of Experts on Restrictive Business Practices. 1972. Aggregated rebate cartels: report. Paris, 1972. pp. 59.

— European Economic Community countries — Law.

EEC rules of competition: report of the CBI conference in London on 5 December 1972. London, 1973. pp. 46. *bibliog.*

LEIDEN WORKING GROUP ON CARTEL PROBLEMS. European competition policy: essays...; edited by the Europa Institute of the University of Leiden. Leiden, 1973. pp. 265. *bibliog.* (*Council of Europe. European Aspects. Series E: Law. No.12*)

MACH (OLIVIER) L'entreprise et les groupes de sociétés en droit européen de la concurrence. Genève, 1974. pp. 278. *bibliog.*

SWANN (DENNIS) and LEES (DENNIS SAMUEL) Antitrust policy in Europe: an E[conomists] A[dvisory] G[roup] study. London, [1974]. fo. 106.

— Germany.

BLAICH (FRITZ) Kartell- und Monopolpolitik im kaiserlichen Deutschland: das Problem der Marktmacht im deutschen Reichstag zwischen 1879 und 1914. Düsseldorf, [1973]. pp. 329. *bibliog.* (*Germany (Bundesrepublik). Kommission für Geschichte des Parlamentarismus und der Politischen Parteien. Beiträge zur Geschichte des Parlamentarismus und der Politischen Parteien. Band 50*)

HEYDEN (ALBRECHT VON DER) Das Exportkartell: eine Untersuchung zu den Grundlagen der Beurteilungskriterien für Exportkartelle im deutschen und englischen Recht der Wettbewerbsbeschränkungen und im Vertrag über die Gründung der EWG. Bern, 1972. pp. 298. *bibliog.*

— Russia.

AVDAKOV (IURII KONSTANTINOVICH) and BORODIN (VLADIMIR VASIL'EVICH) Proizvodstvennye ob"edineniia i ikh rol' v organizatsii upravleniia sovetskoi promyshlennost'iu, 1917-1932 gg. Moskva, 1973. pp. 240.

— Sweden.

SWEDEN. Statens Pris-och Kartellnämnd. 1971. Storföretag och koncentrationstendenser: (koncentrationstendenser inom svensk industri under 1960-talet) 1963-1967 (-1970). [Lund, 1971]. pp. 160.

— United Kingdom — Law.

HEYDEN (ALBRECHT VON DER) Das Exportkartell: eine Untersuchung zu den Grundlagen der Beurteilungskriterien für Exportkartelle im deutschen und englischen Recht der Wettbewerbsbeschränkungen und im Vertrag über die Gründung der EWG. Bern, 1972. pp. 298. *bibliog.*

— United States.

MANSFIELD (EDWIN) ed. Monopoly power and economic performance: the problem of industrial concentration. 3rd ed. New York, [1974]. pp. 228. *bibliog.*

TRUSTS, INDUSTRIAL. (Cont.)

RUTTENBERG (STANLEY H.) AND ASSOCIATES, INC. The American oil industry: a failure of anti-trust policy. New York, 1973. pp. 160.

TRUSTS AND TRUSTEES
— United Kingdom.

KEETON (GEORGE WILLIAMS) and SHERIDAN (LIONEL ASTOR) A case-book on equity and trusts. 2nd ed. London, 1974. pp. 369.

TSWANA (BANTU TRIBE).

SEELEY (CAROLINE FRASER) The reaction of the Batswana to the practice of western medicine; [M. Phil.(London) thesis]. 1973. fo. 259. *bibliog. Typescript: unpublished. This thesis is the property of London University and may not be removed from the Library.*

TUCANO INDIANS.

TORRES LABORDE (ALFONSO) Mito y cultura entre los Barasana: un grupo indigena tukano del Vaupes. Bogota, [1971]. pp. 182. *bibliog.*

TUCUMAN (PROVINCE)
— Economic policy.

ARGENTINE REPUBLIC. Consejo Federal de Inversiones. 1973. Analisis y evaluacion del plan de transformacion agro-industrial de la provincia de Tucuman: informe final. Buenos Aires, 1973. pp. 213. *(Serie Tecnica. No. 17)*

TUCUNA INDIANS.

OLIVEIRA (ROBERTO CARDOSO DE) O Indio e o mundo dos brancos: uma interpretação sociologica da situação dos Tukuna. São Paulo, 1972. pp. 139. *bibliog.*

TUNISIA
— Economic history.

PONCET (JEAN) La Tunisie à la recherche de son avenir: indépendance ou néocolonialisme?. Paris, [1974]. pp. 223. *bibliog.*

— Economic policy.

FOOD AND AGRICULTURE ORGANIZATION. 1968. Projet de planification rurale intégrée de la région centrale Tunisie: rapport final. Rome, 1968. pp. 109, map. *English summary. Microfilm: 1 reel.*

WOLFSON (MARGARET) Aid management in developing countries: a case study: the implementation of three aid projects in Tunisia. Paris, Organisation for Economic Co-operation and Development, 1972. pp. 49. *(Development Centre. Technical Papers)*

PONCET (JEAN) La Tunisie à la recherche de son avenir: indépendance ou néocolonialisme?. Paris, [1974]. pp. 223. *bibliog.*

— Rural conditions.

FOOD AND AGRICULTURE ORGANIZATION. 1968. Projet de planification rurale intégrée de la région centrale Tunisie: rapport final. Rome, 1968. pp. 109, map. *English summary. Microfilm: 1 reel.*

— Social conditions.

CAMILLERI (CARMEL) Jeunesse, famille et développement: essai sur le changement socio-culturel dans un pays du tiers-monde, Tunisie. Paris, 1973. pp. 506. *(Centre National de la Recherche Scientifique. Centre de Recherches et d'Etudes sur les Sociétés Méditerranéennes. Collection)*

TUNNELS.

SWITZERLAND. Kommission Eisenbahntunnel durch die Alpen. 1971. Eisenbahntunnel durch die Alpen: Schlussbericht der Kommission, etc.; [with Dokumentationsanhang]. Bern, 1971. 2 pts.

— Europe.

O'REILLY (M.P.) Some examples of underground development in Europe. Crowthorne, 1974. pp. 31. *(U.K. Transport and Road Research Laboratory. Reports. LR 592)*

— United Kingdom.

HALCROW (Sir WILLIAM THOMSON) AND PARTNERS and MOTT, HAY AND ANDERSON. Report on roads in tunnel for the Greater London Council. [London], Greater London Council, 1974. 1 vol. (various pagings).

TURBIO VALLEY.

ARGENTINE REPUBLIC. Consejo Federal de Inversiones. 1963. Programa de desarrollo de la cuenca de Rio Turbio, en función del desarrollo de la explotación del carbón. Tomo 1. Estudio preliminar. [Buenos Aires], 1963. 1 vol. (various pagings).

TURIN
— History.

I COMUNISTI a Torino, 1919-1972: lezioni e testimonianze: (le relazioni e le testimonianze di un corso...organizzato dall'Unione culturale torinese...marzo-aprile 1973); prefazione di Gian Carlo Pajetta. Roma, 1974. pp. 338.

TURKESTAN
— Politics and government.

VOZNIKNOVENIE i razvitie revoliutsionnogo dvizheniia v Kirgizii v kontse XIX - nachale XX vv.; pod redaktsiei K.U. Usenbaeva. Frunze, 1973. pp. 230.

TURKEY
— Economic conditions.

HJARNØ (JAN) Fremmedarbejdere: en etnologisk undersøgelse af arbejdskrafteksportens virkninger i Tyrkiet. København, Nationalmuseet, 1971. pp. 76.

— Economic policy.

TURKEY. Devlet Plânlama Teşkilâti. 1973 A summary of the third five year development plan, 1973-1977. Ankara, 1973. pp. 243.

— Emigration and immigration.

PAINE (SUZANNE) Exporting workers: the Turkish case. London, 1974. pp. 227. *bibliog. (Cambridge. University. Department of Applied Economics. Occasional Papers. 41)*

— Foreign relations — France.

MASSIGLI (RENE) La Turquie devant la guerre: mission à Ankara. [Paris, 1964]. pp. 511.

— — United Kingdom.

SHUKLA (RAM LAKHAN) Britain, India and the Turkish Empire, 1853-1882. New Delhi, [1973]. pp. 262. *bibliog.*

— Politics and government.

KARPAT (KEMAL H.) and others. Social change and politics in Turkey: a structural-historical analysis. Leiden, 1973. pp. 373.

ROEHRBORN (KLAUS) Untersuchungen zur osmanischen Verwaltungsgeschichte. Berlin, 1973. pp. 177. *bibliog. (Islam, Der. Studien zur Sprache, Geschichte und Kultur des Islamischen Orients. Neue Folge. Band 5)*

WEIKER (WALTER F.) Political tutelage and democracy in Turkey: the Free Party and its aftermath. Leiden, 1973. pp. 317. *bibliog.*

MACKENZIE (KENNETH) Turkey: after the storm. London, 1974. pp. 17. *(Institute for the Study of Conflict. Conflict Studies. No. 43)*

— Social conditions.

KARPAT (KEMAL H.) and others. Social change and politics in Turkey: a structural-historical analysis. Leiden, 1973. pp. 373.

— Social history.

KARPAT (KEMAL H.) An inquiry into the social foundations of nationalism in the Ottoman state: from social estates to classes, from millets to nations. Princeton, N.J., 1973. pp. 116. *(Princeton University. Center of International Studies. Research Monographs. No.39)*

— Social life and customs.

MANSUR (FATMA) Bodrum: a town in the Aegean. Leiden, 1972. pp. 264. *pp. 249-264 misplaced before pp. 241-8.*

— Social policy.

TURKEY. Devlet Plânlama Teşkilâti. 1973 A summary of the third five year development plan, 1973-1977. Ankara, 1973. pp. 243.

TURKMENISTAN
— Economic history.

ANNANEPESOV (MURAD) Khoziaistvo turkmen v XVIII-XIX vv.; pod redaktsiei...S.G. Agadzhanova. Ashkhabad, 1972. pp. 283. *bibliog.*

STADELBAUER (JOERG) Bahnbau und kulturgeographischer Wandel in Turkmenien: Einflüsse der Eisenbahn ... in einem Grenzgebiet des russischen Machtbereichs. Berlin, 1973. pp. 520. *bibliog. (Berlin. Freie Universität. Osteuropa-Institut. Wirtschaftswissenschaftliche Veröffentlichungen. Band 34) With summaries in various languages; 11 maps in end pocket.*

— Intellectual life.

DURDYEV (TAGAN) Formirovanie i razvitie turkmenskoi sovetskoi intelligentsii, 1917- 1958 gg.; pod nauchnoi redaktsiei...K. Kerimi i...M. Mosheva. Ashkhabad, 1972. pp. 286.

— Social conditions.

AKMURADOV (KURBANMUKHAMED) Izmenenie sotsial'noi struktury obshchestva v period perekhoda ot sotsializma k kommunizmu; otvetstvennyi redaktor... G.O. Muradova.Ashkhabad, 1972. pp. 216.

TURKS IN DENMARK.

HJARNØ (JAN) Fremmedarbejdere: en etnologisk undersøgelse af arbejdskrafteksportens virkninger i Tyrkiet. København, Nationalmuseet, 1971. pp. 76.

TURKS IN FRANCE.

GARNIER (RAYMOND) L'affaire de Trouhans. Paris, [1973]. pp. 153.

TURNER (FREDERICK JACKSON).

BILLINGTON (RAY ALLEN) Frederick Jackson Turner: historian, scholar, teacher. New York, 1973. pp. 599. *bibliog.*

TUSCANY
— Economic history.

PANE (LUIGI DAL) Industria e commercio nel Granducato di Toscana nell'età del Risorgimento. Bologna, [1971-73]. 2 vols.

— Industries.

CAVALLI (LUCIANO) ed. Classe dirigente e sviluppo regionale: ricerca sulla classe dirigente toscana di Gianfranco Bettin [and others]. Bologna, [1973]. pp. 196.

— Politics and government.

CAVALLI (LUCIANO) ed. Classe dirigente e sviluppo regionale: ricerca sulla classe dirigente toscana di Gianfranco Bettin [and others]. Bologna, [1973]. pp. 196.

TUVA

— Statistics.

TUVA. Statisticheskoe Upravlenie. 1971. Narodnoe khoziaistvo Tuvinskoi ASSR: statisticheskii sbornik. Kyzyl, 1971. pp. 307.

TWENTIETH CENTURY

— Forecasts.

MAGEE (BRYAN EDGAR) and others. Prospects for mankind; [transcript of a discussion with] Herman Kahn and Robert Jungk;...transmitted 31 May 1973. [London, 1973]. fo. 37. *(Thames Television. Something to Say)*

TWENTY—FIRST CENTURY

— Forecasts.

The WORLD in 2000: repo[r]t of a JERC international conference. Tokyo, 1967. pp. 285. *(Japan Economic Research Center. Center Papers. No.8)*

The UNKNOWN urban realm: methodology and results of a content analysis of the papers presented at the congress Citizen and city in the year 2000; by Ulrich Neveling [and others]. The Hague, 1973. pp. 188. *(European Cultural Foundation. Plan Europe 2000. Project 3. vol. 2)*

MULLER (HERBERT JOSEPH) Uses of the future. Bloomington, Ind., [1974]. pp. 264.

THRING (MEREDITH W.) Machines - masters or slaves of man?. Stevenage, Herts, [1974]. pp. 115.

WACHSTUM bis zur Katastrophe?: Pro und Contra zum Weltmodell; ([by] Dennis L. Meadows [and others]); herausgegeben von Horst E. Richter; [based on the proceedings of two meetings in Frankfurt in October, 1973]. Stuttgart, [1974]. pp. 132.

TYNESIDE

— Transit systems.

TYNESIDE PASSENGER TRANSPORT EXECUTIVE. Public transport on Tyneside: a plan for the people. Newcastle upon Tyne, Tyneside Passenger Transport Authority, 1973. pp. 143.

TZOTZIL INDIANS.

CINQ aspects de sociétés latino-américaines; [by Carlos M. Rama and others]. Paris, [1965]. pp. 151. *(Paris. Université. Institut des Hautes Etudes de l'Amérique Latine. Cahiers. No. 7)*

UGANDA

— Commerce.

UGANDA. Customs Department. Trade report. a., 1913/14. Entebbe.

— Politics and government.

GERTZEL (CHERRY) Party and locality in Northern Uganda, 1945-1962. London, 1974. pp. 100. *bibliog.* *(London. University. Institute of Commonwealth Studies. Commonwealth Papers. No. 16)*

— Rural conditions.

TRAPPE (PAUL) Social change and development institutions in a refugee population: development from below as an alternative; the case of the Nakapiripirit settlement scheme in Uganda. (UNRISD Reports. No.71.2) (UNRISD/71.C.87). Geneva, United Nations Research Institute for Social Development, 1971. pp. 102. *bibliog.*

UKRAINE

— Economic conditions.

UKRAINSKAIA SSR: ekonomicheskie raiony. Moskva, 1972. pp. 315. *bibliog. (Akademiia Nauk SSSR. Sovet po Izucheniiu Proizvoditel'nykh Sil. Razvitie i Razmeshchenie Proizvoditel'nykh Sil SSSR)*

— Economic policy.

GOLOBOROD'KO (ALEKSEI NIKONOVICH) Obshchestvennyi kontrol' nad proizvodstvom i raspredeleniem pri sotsializme. Kiev, 1973. pp. 295.

— Executive departments.

GOLOBOROD'KO (ALEKSEI NIKONOVICH) Obshchestvennyi kontrol' nad proizvodstvom i raspredeleniem pri sotsializme. Kiev, 1973. pp. 295.

— Famines.

SVITOVYI KONHRES VIL'NYKH UKRAÏNTSIV. Memorandum...to the general secretary of United Nations, Hon. Dr. Kurt Waldheim. [Munich, 1973]. pp. (4).

— History.

ELWOOD (RALPH CARTER) Russian social democracy in the underground: a study of the RSDRP in the Ukraine, 1907-1914. Assen, 1974. pp. 304. *bibliog. (International Institute of Social History. Publications on Social History. 8)*

— — 1917—1921, Revolution.

RESHETAR (JOHN STEPHEN) The Ukrainian revolution, 1917-1920: a study in nationalism; [reprint of work originally published in 1952]. New York, 1972. pp. 363. *bibliog.*

VELYKYI Zhovten' i hromadians'ka viina na Ukraïni. Kyïv, 1973. pp. 255.

— Industries.

SHEVCHUK (VASYL' PETROVYCH) Na vyrishal'nomu napriami: Komunistychna partiia Ukraïny v borot'bi za naukovo-tekhnichnyi prohres u vazhkii promyslovosti, 1959-1965 rr. Kyïv, 1970. pp. 230.

KOVAL'CHAK (HRYHORII IVANOVYCH) Industrial'nyi rozvytok zakhidnykh oblastei Ukraïny v period komunistychnoho budivnytstva. Kyïv, 1973. pp. 127. *With Russian summary.*

VITRUK (LIUDMYLA DMYTRIVNA) Zhinky-trudivnytsi v period sotsialistychnoï industrializatsiï: na materialakh promyslovosti Ukraïns'koï RSR, 1926-1932 rr. Kyïv, 1973. pp. 120.

— Nationalism.

VOLKONSKII (ALEKSANDR MIKHAILOVICH) Prince. Istoricheskaia pravda i ukrainofil'skaia propaganda. Turin, 1920. pp. 207.

RESHETAR (JOHN STEPHEN) The Ukrainian revolution, 1917-1920: a study in nationalism; [reprint of work originally published in 1952]. New York, 1972. pp. 363. *bibliog.*

KOMUNISTYCHNA partiia - orhanizator zdiisnennia lenins'koï natsional'noï polityky na Ukraïni. Kyïv, 1972. pp. 323.

VASYLEVYCH (BOHDAN PETROVYCH) Lzhemesiï: pamflety i narysy. L'viv, 1973. pp. 187.

— Politics and government.

CHUBAR (VLAS IAKOVYCH) Vybrani statti i promovy. Kyïv, 1972. pp. 628.

KOVALENKO (LEONID ANTONOVYCH) Velyka frantsuz'ka burzhuazna revoliutsiia i hromads'ko-politychni rukhy na Ukraïni v kintsi XVIII st. Kyïv, 1973. pp. 167.

TERESHCHENKO (IURII ILARIONOVYCH) Politychna borot'ba na vyborakh do mis'kykh dum Ukraïny v period pidhotovky Zhovtnevoï revoliutsiï. Kyïv, 1974. pp. 143.

— Population.

ONIKIENKO (VLADIMIR VASIL'EVICH) and POPOVKIN (VALERII ARKADIIOVYCH) Kompleksnoe issledovanie migratsionnykh protsessov: analiz migratsii naseleniia USSR. Moskva, 1973. pp. 159.

— Relations (general) with Communist countries.

VKLAD Ukraïns'koï RSR u naukovo-kul'turne spivrobitnytstvo Radians'koho Soiuza z ievropeis'kymy sotsialistychnymy kraïnamy. Kyïv, 1970. pp. 198.

— Relations (general) with the East (Near East).

CHERNIKOV (IHOR FEDIROVYCH) Druzhnia pidtrymka i spivrobitnytstvo Ukraïns'ka RSR u vidnosynakh Radians'koho Soiuzu z kraïnamy Blyz'koho i Seredn'oho Skhodu, 1922-1939. Kyïv, 1973. pp. 122. *With Russian summary and table of contents.*

UKRAINE, WESTERN

— Politics and government.

OLEKSIUK (MYROSLAV MYRONOVYCH) Prohresyvna presa Zakhidnoï Ukraïny v borot'bi na zakhyst SRSR, 20-30-ti roky. Kyïv, 1973. pp. 228.

UKRAINIANS IN THE UNITED STATES.

SHARON-OLEARCHYK (RENATA MARIA) Types of ethnic identification and generational position: a study of the Ukrainian immigrant group in the U.S.A. [London. 1971?]. pp. 72. *bibliog. (Off print from the Ukrainian Review, Vol.XVIII, Nos. 3 and 4, 1971)*

ULCHI.

BOIKO (VLADIMIR IVANOVICH) Opyt sotsiologicheskogo issledovaniia problem razvitiia narodov Nizhnego Amura; otvetstvennyi redaktor...A.P. Okladnikov. Novosibirsk, 1973. pp. 211.

ULSTER UNIONIST PARTY.

HARBINSON (JOHN F.) The Ulster Unionist Party, 1882-1973: its development and organisation. Belfast, 1973. pp. 252. *bibliog.*

UNDERDEVELOPED AREAS.

WORSLEY (PETER MAURICE) The third world. 2nd ed. Chicago, 1970. pp. 373. *bibliog.*

EUROPEAN COMMUNITIES. Commission. 1972. Memorandum...on a Community policy on development cooperation: programme for initial actions; 2 February 1972. [Brussels], 1972. pp. 23. *(Bulletin of the European Communities. Supplements. [1972/2])*

NORSK SAMBAND FOR DE FORENTE NASJONER. Innføring i u-lands problemer: redaktører: Svein Erik Odden [and] Lilli Tostrup Anderson. Oslo, 1972. pp. 77.

LAUDICINA (PAUL A.) World poverty and development: a survey of American opinion. Washington, D.C., 1973. pp. 126. *bibliog. (Overseas Development Council. Monographs. No 8)*

BALOGH (THOMAS) Baron Balogh. The economics of poverty. 2nd ed. London, 1974. pp. 291.

HOWE (JAMES W.) and others. The U.S. and the developing world: agenda for action 1974; [by] James W. Howe and the staff of the Overseas Development Council. New York, 1974. pp. 211.

HOYLE (BRIAN STEWART) ed. Spatial aspects of development. London, [1974]. pp. 372. *bibliogs.*

— Administration.

BHATTACHARYYA (JNANABROTA) Administrative organisation for development. Brussels, [1972]. pp. 142.

ILCHMAN (WARREN FREDERICK) Administering alternatives and alternatives in administration: labor intensive administration in developmental perspective. Vienna, [1973]. pp. 46,v. *(Wiener Institut für Entwicklungsfragen. Occasional Papers. 73/5)*

INTERREGIONAL SEMINAR ON MAJOR ADMINISTRATIVE REFORMS IN DEVELOPING COUNTRIES, BRIGHTON, 1971. Interregional Seminar...Falmer, Brighton,...25 October - 2 November 1971. (ST/TAO/M/62 and Adds. 1 and 2). New York, United Nations, 1973. 3 vols. (in 1).

UNDERDEVELOPED AREAS. (Cont.)

RIGGS (FRED WARREN) Alternatives, administration and development. Vienna, [1973]. pp. 14. *(Wiener Institut für Entwicklungsfragen. Occasional Papers. 73/4)*

— **Agriculture.**

FOOD AND AGRICULTURE ORGANIZATION. Agriculture Planning Studies. Rome, 1963 in progress. : **AGRICULTURE AND STATE. 1963 in progress.**

BARRETO (ANTONIO) ed. A study of the social and economic implications of the large scale introduction of high-yielding varieties of foodgrain: a selection of readings; an Institute staff study. (UNRISD Reports. No.71.6) (UNRISD/72/C.3). Geneva, United Nations Research Institute for Social Development, 1971. pp. 173. *([Studies on the Green Revolution. No.2])*

GRIFFIN (KEITH) The green revolution: an economic analysis. (UNRISD Reports. No. 72.6). Geneva, United Nations Research Institute for Social Development, 1972. pp. 153. *(Studies on the Green Revolution. No.3)*

PALMER (INGRID) Food and the new agricultural technology. (UNRISD Reports. No.72.9). Geneva, United Nations Research Institute for Social Development, 1972. pp. 85. *(Studies on the Green Revolution. No.5)*

GRIFFIN (KEITH) The political economy of agrarian change: an essay on the green revolution. London, 1974. pp. 264.

INTERNATIONAL ECONOMIC ASSOCIATION. Conference, 1972, Bad Godesberg. Agricultural policy in developing countries: proceedings..., edited by Nurul Islam. London, 1974. pp. 565.

— — **Bibliography.**

U.K. Overseas Development Administration. Land Resources Division. Land Resource Bibliographies. Tolworth, 1971 in progress.

— — **Productivity.**

PALMER (INGRID) Science and agricultural production. (UNRISD Reports. No.72.8). Geneva, United Nations Research Institute for Social Development, 1972. pp. 100. *(Studies on the Green Revolution. No.4)*

— **Armed forces — Political activity.**

KENNEDY (GAVIN) The military in the third world. London, 1974. pp. 368. *bibliog.*

— **Balance of payments.**

MICHALOPOULOS (CONSTANTINE) Payments arrangements for less developed countries: the role of foreign assistance. Princeton, [1973]. pp. 25. *bibliog.* *(Princeton University. Department of Economics and Sociology. International Finance Section. Essays in International Finance. No.102)*

— **Bibliography.**

ORGANISATION FOR ECONOMIC COOPERATION AND DEVELOPMENT. Library. Special Annotated Bibliographies. [Paris], 1964 in progress.

— **Birth control.**

SMITH (THOMAS EDWARD) ed. The politics of family planning in the third world. London, 1973. pp. 352.

— **Book industries and trade.**

PRIORITIES and planning for the provision of books: report of the Commonwealth Asia-Pacific regional seminar held at the India International Centre, New Delhi, India, 21 February to 1 March, 1973. London, Commonwealth Secretariat, 1973. pp. 214.

— **Cities and towns.**

SYMPOSIUM ON URBANIZATION IN DEVELOPING COUNTRIES, NOORDWIJK, 1967. Urbanization in developing countries. The Hague, 1968. pp. 177. *(International Union of Local Authorities. [Publications] .93)*

BERNSTEIN (BEVERLY) A survey of European programmes: education for urbanization in developing countries. [New York, 1972?]. pp. 114. *bibliog.* *(Ford Foundation. International Urbanization Survey. Working Papers. 288)*

INFRASTRUCTURE problems of the cities of developing countries; by Otto H. Koenigsberger [and others]; Beverly Bernstein, editor. [New York, 1972?]. pp. 256. *(Ford Foundation International Urbanization Survey. Working Papers. 287)*

TERZO (FREDERICK C.) Urbanization in the developing countries: the response of international assistance. [New York, 1972?]. pp. 126. *(Ford Foundation. International Urbanization Survey. Working Papers. 286)*

TINKER (HUGH) Race and the Third World city. [New York, 1972?]. pp. 49. *bibliog.* *(Ford Foundation. International Urbanization Survey. Working Papers. 289)*

DWYER (DENIS JOHN) ed. The city in the third world. London, 1974. pp. 253.

GUTKIND (PETER C.W.) Urban anthropology: perspectives on 'third world' urbanisation and urbanism. Assen, 1974. pp. 262. *bibliog.*

— **Civil Service.**

INTERREGIONAL SEMINAR ON MAJOR ADMINISTRATIVE REFORMS IN DEVELOPING COUNTRIES, BRIGHTON, 1971. Interregional Seminar...Falmer, Brighton,...25 October - 2 November 1971. (ST/TAO/M/62 and Adds. 1 and 2). New York, United Nations, 1973. 3 vols. (in 1).

— **Commerce.**

CAMBRIDGE. University. Overseas Studies Committee. [Summer Conference, 1972]. Trade strategies for development; papers of the ninth Cambridge conference on development problems, September 1972...; edited by Paul Streeten. London, 1973. pp. 375.

CARLSSON (BO) and SUNDSTRÖM (ÅKE) Den svenska importen av industrivaror från låglöneländer. Stockholm, 1973. pp.189. *bibliog. With table of contents and summary in English.*

EUROPEAN COMMUNITIES. Commission. 1973. Development of an overall approach to trade in view of the coming multilateral negotiations in GATT: memorandum... to the Council forwarded on 9 April and amended on 22 May 1973. [Brussels], 1973. pp. 12. *(Bulletin of the European Communities. Supplements. [1973/2])*

FUKUDA (HARUKO) Britain in Europe: impact on the third world. London, 1973. pp. 194.

HUGHES (HELEN) ed. Prospects for partnership: industrialization and trade policies in the 1970s; a seminar held at the International Bank for Reconstruction and Development, October 5 and 6, 1972. Baltimore, 1973. pp. 289.

MAHFUZUR RAHMAN (ABUL HASANAT MUHAMMAD) Exports of manufactures from developing countries: a study in comparative advantage. Rotterdam, 1973. pp. 140. *bibliog.*

DORNER (KLAUS) Probleme einer weltwirtschaftlichen Integration der Entwicklungsländer. Tübingen, [1974]. pp. 195. *bibliog. (Bochum. Ruhr-Universität. Institut für Entwicklungsforschung und Entwicklungspolitik. Bochumer Schriften zur Entwicklungsforschung und Entwicklungspolitik. Band 16)*

VEREIN FÜR SOZIALPOLITIK. Schriften. Neue Folge. Band 78. Probleme der weltwirtschaftlichen Arbeitsteilung: (Verhandlungen auf der Arbeitstagung...und des Instituts für Weltwirtschaft in Kiel vom 12.-15. Juli 1973; herausgegeben von Herbert Giersch und Heinz-Dieter Haas. Berlin, [1974]. pp. 651.

— **Communication.**

UNITED NATIONS EDUCATIONAL, SCIENTIFIC AND CULTURAL ORGANIZATION. Department of Mass Communication. Reports and Papers on Mass Communication. Paris, 1953 in progress.

— **Communism.**

TÁBORSKÝ (EDUARD) Communist penetration of the third world. New York, [1973]. pp. 500. *bibliog.*

UL'IANOVSKII (ROSTISLAV ALEKSANDROVICH) Der Sozialismus und die befreiten Länder; (aus dem Russischen übersetzt von einem Übersetzerkollektiv). Berlin, 1973. pp. 452.

— **Community development.**

BHATTACHARYYA (JNANABROTA) Administrative organisation for development. Brussels, [1972]. pp. 142.

— **Crime and criminals.**

CLINARD (MARSHALL BARRON) and ABBOTT (DANIEL J.) Crime in developing countries: a comparative perspective. New York, [1973]. pp. 319.

— **Decentralization in government.**

PRATS (YVES) Décentralisation et développement. [Paris, 1973]. pp. 262. *bibliog. (Institut International d'Administration Publique. Bibliothèque. 2)*

— **Economic conditions.**

KUZ'MIN (STANISLAV ALEKSEEVICH) Sistemnyi analiz ekonomiki razvivaiushchikhsia stran: problemy metodologii. Moskva, 1972. pp. 318. *bibliog.*

SZENTES (TAMÁS) How does the distorted socio-economic structure impede the expansion of accumulation?. Budapest, 1973. pp. 60. *(Magyar Tudományos Akadémia. Afro-Ázsiai Kutató Központ. Studies on Developing Countries. No. 54)*

— **Economic integration.**

DORNER (KLAUS) Probleme einer weltwirtschaftlichen Integration der Entwicklungsländer. Tübingen, [1974]. pp. 195. *bibliog. (Bochum. Ruhr-Universität. Institut für Entwicklungsforschung und Entwicklungspolitik. Bochumer Schriften zur Entwicklungsforschung und Entwicklungspolitik. Band 16)*

— **Economic policy.**

UNITED NATIONS EDUCATIONAL, SCIENTIFIC AND CULTURAL ORGANIZATION. Reports and Papers in the Social Sciences. Paris, 1955 in progress.

SCHIAVO-CAMPO (SALVATORE) and SINGER (HANS WOLFGANG) Perspectives of economic development. Boston, [1970]. pp. 351.

JOHNSON (HARRY GORDON) Controls versus competition in economic development; a public lecture delivered at the University of Ghana,... [in] 1970, and revised subsequently, etc. Accra, 1971. pp. 14.

ADELMAN (IRMA) and MORRIS (CYNTHIA TAFT) Economic growth and social equity in developing countries. Stanford, 1973. pp. 257.

GAITSKELL (Sir ARTHUR) Alternative choices in development strategy and tactics: the Mekong river project in South East Asia as a case study. Vienna, [1973]. pp. 23. *(Wiener Institut für Entwicklungsfragen. Occasional Papers. 73/7)*

BOUMEDIENE (HOUARI) The battle against underdevelopment; being the text of his keynote address to the United Nation's General Assembly, in the Special Session on problems of raw materials and development. Nottingham, [1974]. pp. 19. *(Spokesman, The. Pamphlets. No. 42)*

CAIDEN (NAOMI JOY) and WILDAVSKY (AARON BERNARD) Planning and budgeting in poor countries. New York, [1974]. pp. 369. *bibliog.*

JEFFRIES (IAN) The Stalinist economic system as a model for underdeveloped countries: the development of Soviet thought since 1953; [Ph.D.(London) thesis]. [1974]. fo. 301. *bibliog. Typescript: unpublished. This thesis is the property of London University and may not be removed from the Library.*

LAULAN (YVES) Le Tiers Monde et la crise de l'environnement. [Paris], 1974. pp. 144. *bibliog.*

UNDERDEVELOPED AREAS. (Cont.)

LITTLE (IAN MALCOLM DAVID) and MIRRLEES (JAMES A.) Project appraisal and planning for developing countries. London, 1974. pp. 388. bibliog.

ONYEMELUKWE (CLEMENT CHUKWUKADIBIA) Economic underdevelopment: an inside view. London, 1974. pp. 123.

SCHNEIDER (WINFRIED) Direktinvestitionen und die Politik der Entwicklungsländer. Berlin, [1974]. pp. 198. bibliog. (Institut für Empirische Wirtschaftsforschung. Veröffentlichungen. Band 11)

THIRLWALL (ANTHONY PHILIP) Inflation, saving and growth in developing economies. London, 1974. pp. 256.

VEREIN FÜR SOZIALPOLITIK. Schriften. Neue Folge. Band 77. Beiträge zur Beurteilung von Entwicklungsstrategien; von Reinhard Blum [and others]; herausgegeben von Hermann Priebe. Berlin, [1974]. pp. 150.

VERHULST (MICHEL) An operational approach to planning for industrial development in newly independent countries; [an expanded version of a paper originally appearing in Management sciences in the emerging countries edited by Norman Barish and Michel Verhulst]. Montréal, 1974. fo. 28. (Montréal. Université. Département des Sciences Economiques. Cahiers. No. 7403)

— — Mathematical models.

INTERREGIONAL SEMINAR ON LONG-TERM PROJECTIONS, 2ND, DAKAR, 1971. Long-term projections for development planning: problems and experience: report on the...seminar...[held at] Dakar, Senegal, 16-27 August 1971. (ST/TAO/SER. C/142). New York, United Nations, 1973. pp. 31.

TAYLOR (LANCE) Short-term policy in open developing economies: the narrow limits of the possible. Cambridge, Mass., 1973. pp. 36. bibliog. (Harvard University. Center for International Affairs. Development Research Group. Economic Development Reports. No. 228)

— Education.

INTERNATIONAL INSTITUTE FOR EDUCATIONAL PLANNING. Fundamentals of Educational Planning. Paris, Unesco, 1970 in progress.

UNITED NATIONS EDUCATIONAL, SCIENTIFIC AND CULTURAL ORGANIZATION. Educational Studies and Documents. New Series . Paris, 1971 in progress.

PANITCHPAKDI (SUPACHAI) Educational growth and planning in developing countries. Rotterdam, 1973. pp. 178. bibliog. With Dutch summary.

SELOWSKY (MARCELO) Investment in education in developing countries: a critical review of some issues. Cambridge, Mass., 1973. pp. 68. bibliog. (Harvard University. Centre for International Affairs. Economic Development Reports. No. 232)

— — Bibliography.

ALTBACH (PHILIP G.) and NYSTROM (BRADLEY) compilers. Higher education in developing countries: a select bibliography. Cambridge, Mass., 1970. pp. 113. (Harvard University. Center for International Affairs. Occasional Papers in International Affairs. No. 24)

— Education, Higher.

CONFERENCE TO EVALUATE THE PILOT TEAMS PROJECT, 1967. Pilot teams project: evaluation conference. Paris, ORGANISATION FOR ECONOMIC CO-OPERATION AND DEVELOPMENT, 1968. pp. 260. (Science and Development)

— Farm produce — Marketing — Bibliography.

TORREALBA (PABLO) Agricultural marketing in economic development: an annotated bibliography. [East Lansing, 1971?]. fo. 68. (Michigan State University. Latin American Studies Center. Research Reports. No. 9)

— Fertilizer industry.

DE GUIA (ERIC O.) A comparative study of fertiliser distribution systems in five developing countries. Paris, Organisation for Economic Co-operation and Development, 1972. pp. 137. bibliog. (Development Centre. Studies)

— Finance.

HELLER (PETER S.) An econometric analysis of the fiscal behavior of the public sector in developing countries: aid, investment and taxation. Ann Arbor, 1973. pp. 39. bibliog. (Michigan University. Center for Research on Economic Development. Discussion Papers. No. 30)

HIRSCH (FRED) Reform of the international monetary system with special reference to the interests of developing countries of the Commonwealth; a study. London, Commonwealth Secretariat, 1973. pp. 20. (Commonwealth Economic Papers. No. 3)

PARK (YOON S.) The link between special drawing rights and development finance. Princeton, 1973. pp. 25. bibliog. (Princeton University. Department of Economics and Sociology. International Finance Section. Essays in International Finance. No. 100)

CAIDEN (NAOMI JOY) and WILDAVSKY (AARON BERNARD) Planning and budgeting in poor countries. New York, [1974]. pp. 369. bibliog.

— Foreign economic relations.

CAVADINO (PETER) Get off their backs'.: an account of the way in which aid, trade and private investment are used by the rich countries to maintain their economic and political domination over countries in the Third World. Oxford, 1972 repr. 1973. pp. 24.

DURIEUX (JEAN) The European Community and the developing world; (transcript of... lecture held on 20 March 1972). [London], Civil Service College, [1973?]. fo. 21. (Lectures on the European Community. Series A. No. 11)

FUKUDA (HARUKO) Britain in Europe: impact on the third world. London, 1973. pp. 194.

OVERSEAS DEVELOPMENT COUNCIL. The United States and the developing world: agenda for action, 1973; Robert E. Hunter, project director. Washington, 1973. pp. 162.

PATTISON (KATHERINE JEAN) The European Economic Community and the developing countries: a political analysis with particular reference to association under Part IV of the Rome Treaty; [Ph.D. (London) thesis]. 1973. fo. 379. bibliog. Typescript: unpublished. This thesis is the property of London University and may not be removed from the Library.

— Foreign relations.

McLANE (CHARLES B.) Soviet-Third World relations. London, 1973 in progress. bibliog.

BERTRAND RUSSELL CENTENARY SYMPOSIUM ON SPHERES OF INFLUENCE IN THE AGE OF IMPERIALISM, LINZ, 1972. Spheres of influence and the third world; papers submitted to the Bertrand Russell Centenary Symposium...;[by] Vladimi Dedijer [and others]. Nottingham, 1973. pp. 123.

OVERSEAS DEVELOPMENT COUNCIL. The United States and the developing world: agenda for action, 1973; Robert E. Hunter, project director. Washington, 1973. pp. 162.

KANET (ROGER E.) ed. The Soviet Union and the developing nations. Baltimore, [1974]. pp. 302.

— Illiteracy.

SCHINDELE (HANNO) Alphabetisierungsbetrebungen in der Dritten Welt: Erfolgsvoraussetzungen und Wirkungen in entwicklungssoziologischer Sicht. [Erlangen, imprint, 1973?]. pp. 314,xlvii. bibliog.

— Industrial equipment — Mathematical models.

McCABE (JAMES L.) and MICHALOPOULOS (CONSTANTINE) Tariff policy, equipment production and employment in developing countries. New Haven, Conn., 1973. pp. 45. bibliog. (Yale University. Economic Growth Center. Center Discussion Papers. No. 170)

— Industries.

MAHFUZUR RAHMAN (ABUL HASANAT MUHAMMAD) Exports of manufactures from developing countries: a study in comparative advantage. Rotterdam, 1973. pp. 140. bibliog.

CUKOR (GYÖRGY) Strategies for industrialisation in developing countries; [translated from the Hungarian]. London, [1974]. pp. 265.

TURNER (LOUIS) Multinational companies and the third world. London, 1974. pp. 294. bibliog.

VERHULST (MICHEL) An operational approach to planning for industrial development in newly independent countries; [an expanded version of a paper originally appearing in Management sciences in the emerging countries edited by Norman Barish and Michel Verhulst]. Montréal, 1974. fo. 28. (Montréal. Université. Département des Sciences Economiques. Cahiers. No. 7403)

— Industry and state.

JOHNSON (HARRY GORDON) Controls versus competition in economic development; a public lecture delivered at the University of Ghana,... [in] 1970, and revised subsequently, etc. Accra, 1971. pp. 14.

— Information services.

BRIGHTON. University of Sussex. Institute of Development Studies. Library. Occasional Guides. No. 4. West German, Swiss and Austrian sources of information on Third World countries. Brighton, [1973]. pp. 29.

— Investments, Foreign.

ORGANISATION FOR ECONOMIC CO-OPERATION AND DEVELOPMENT. 1972. Investing in developing countries: facilities for the promotion of foreign private investment in developing countries. rev.ed. Paris, 1972. pp. 110.

REUBER (GRANT LOUIS) and others. Private foreign investment in development; [study sponsored by the O.E.C.D. Development Centre]. Oxford, 1973. pp. 371.

BOS (HENDRICUS CORNELIS) and others. Private foreign investment in developing countries: a quantitative study on the evaluation of the macro-economic effects; (published for the Development Centre of the Organization for Economic Cooperation and Development). Dordrecht, [1974]. pp. 402.

SCHNEIDER (WINFRIED) Direktinvestitionen und die Politik der Entwicklungsländer. Berlin, [1974]. pp. 198. bibliog. (Institut für Empirische Wirtschaftsforschung. Veröffentlichungen. Band 11)

— Labour mobility — Mathematical models.

PORTER (RICHARD C.) Labor migration and urban unemployment in less developed countries: comment. Ann Arbor, 1973. pp. 18. bibliog. (Michigan University. Center for Research on Economic Development. Discussion Papers. No. 29)

— Labour supply.

ILCHMAN (WARREN FREDERICK) Administering alternatives and alternatives in administration: labor intensive administration in developmental perspective. Vienna, [1973]. pp. 46,v. (Wiener Institut für Entwicklungsfragen. Occasional Papers. 73/5)

— Mathematical models.

McCABE (JAMES L.) and MICHALOPOULOS (CONSTANTINE) Tariff policy, equipment production and employment in developing countries. New Haven, Conn., 1973. pp. 45. bibliog. (Yale University. Economic Growth Center. Center Discussion Papers. No. 170)

UNDERDEVELOPED AREAS. (Cont.)

— Land.

INTERNATIONAL GEOGRAPHICAL CONGRESS. 21st Congress, India, 1968. Proceedings of symposium on land use in developing countries, held at the Aligarh Muslim University on 22 to 29 November, 1968. Aligarh, 1972. pp. 299. *bibliogs.*

— — Bibliography.

U.K. Overseas Development Administration. Land Resources Division. Land Resource Bibliographies. Tolworth, 1971 in progress.

— Land reform.

TAI (HUNG-CHAO) Land reform and politics: a comparative analysis. Berkeley, [1974]. pp. 565.

— Medical care.

FOURNIER (ETIENNE) L'action médico-sociale dans les pays en voie de développement. Paris, 1961. pp. 311. *bibliog. (Paris. Université. Institut d'Etude du Développement Economique et Social.Collection Tiers-Monde)*

MAEGRAITH (BRIAN) One world. London, 1973. pp. 246. *bibliog. (London. University. London School of Hygiene and Tropical Medicine. Heath Clark Lectures. 1970)*

— Medicine — Study and teaching.

WHO CONFERENCE ON MEDICAL EDUCATION IN THE EASTERN MEDITERRANEAN REGION, 2ND, TEHERAN, 1970. Aspects of medical education in developing countries: selected papers, etc. Geneva, World Health Organization, 1972. pp. 116. *(Public Health Papers. No. 47).*

— Milk supply.

FAO/WHO EXPERT PANEL ON MILK QUALITY. 1972. Payment for milk on quality. Rome, Food and Agricultural Organization, 1972. pp. 82. *(Agricultural Studies. No. 89)*

— Money.

MAX (HERMANN) El valor de la moneda: la funcion del dinero, la funcion del credito, la funcion de los cambios. Buenos Aires, 1970. pp. 326. *bibliog.*

— Nutrition.

PALMER (INGRID) Food and the new agricultural technology. (UNRISD Reports. No.72.9). Geneva, United Nations Research Institute for Social Development, 1972. pp. 85. *(Studies on the Green Revolution. No.5)*

— Peasantry.

INTERNATIONAL LABOUR CONFERENCE. 59th Session. Reports. 6. Organisations of rural workers and their role in economic and social development: sixth item on the agenda. Geneva, 1973-74. 2 pts.

— Politics.

ADELMAN (IRMA) and MORRIS (CYNTHIA TAFT) Economic growth and social equity in developing countries. Stanford, 1973. pp. 257.

CLARK (ROBERT P.) Development and instability: political change in the non-western world. Hinsdale, Ill., [1974]. pp. 279.

HEEGER (GERALD A.) The politics of underdevelopment. London, 1974. pp. 150.

— Population.

BUTZ (WILLIAM P.) Research and information strategies to improve population policy in less developed countries. Santa Monica, 1972. pp. 82. *bibliog. (Rand Corporation. [Rand Reports]. 952)*

CLINTON (RICHARD L.) ed. Population and politics: new directions in political science research. Lexington, Mass., [1973]. pp. 298.

KOCHER (JAMES E.) Rural development, income distribution, and fertility decline. New York, [1973]. pp. 105. *bibliog. (Population Council. Occasional Papers)*

— — Bibliography.

BRIGHTON. University of Sussex. Institute of Development Studies. Library. Occasional Guides. No. 3. Rural migration in less developed countries: a preliminary bibliography. Brighton, [1973]. pp. 62.

— Produce trade.

POELMANS (JACQUELINE) and LECOMTE (JACQUES) L'agriculture européenne et les pays tiers. Bruxelles, 1972. pp. 180. *bibliog. (Brussels. Université Libre. Institut d'Etudes Européennes. Thèses et Travaux Economiques. 7)*

— Public health.

WORLD HEALTH ORGANIZATION. Technical Report Series. Geneva, 1950 in progress.

WORLD HEALTH ORGANIZATION. Expert Committee on National Health Planning in Developing Countries. 1967. National health planning in developing countries: report. Geneva, 1967. pp. 40. *bibliog. (Technical Report Series. No.350)*

— Race question.

TINKER (HUGH) Race and the Third World city. [New York, 1972?]. pp. 49. *bibliog. (Ford Foundation. International Urbanization Survey. Working Papers. 289)*

— Research.

UNITED NATIONS EDUCATIONAL, SCIENTIFIC AND CULTURAL ORGANIZATION. Science Policy Studies and Documents. Paris, 1965 in progress.

— — Economic aspects.

CONFERENCE TO EVALUATE THE PILOT TEAMS PROJECT, 1967. Pilot teams project: evaluation conference. Paris, ORGANISATION FOR ECONOMIC CO-OPERATION AND DEVELOPMENT, 1968. pp. 260. *(Science and Development)*

— Retail trade.

INTERNATIONAL LABOUR ORGANISATION. Advisory Committee on Salaried Employees and Professional Workers. 6th Session. Reports. 3. The role of non-manual workers in economic and social development, and the need for their training: third item on the agenda. Geneva, 1967. pp. 63.

— Roads — Economic aspects.

HOWE (J.D.G.F.) The sensitivity to traffic estimates of road planning in developing countries. Crowthorne, 1973. pp. 28. *(U.K. Transport and Road Research Laboratory. Reports. LR 516)*

— Rural conditions.

KOCHER (JAMES E.) Rural development, income distribution, and fertility decline. New York, [1973]. pp. 105. *bibliog. (Population Council. Occasional Papers)*

— Salaried employees.

INTERNATIONAL LABOUR ORGANISATION. Advisory Committee on Salaried Employees and Professional Workers. 6th Session. Reports. 3. The role of non-manual workers in economic and social development, and the need for their training: third item on the agenda. Geneva, 1967. pp. 63.

— Saving and investment.

SZENTES (TAMÁS) How does the distorted socio-economic structure impede the expansion of accumulation?. Budapest, 1973. pp. 60. *(Magyar Tudományos Akadémia. Afro-Ázsiai Kutató Központ. Studies on Developing Countries. No. 54)*

— Shipping — Rates.

FASBENDER (KARL) and WAGNER (WOLFGANG) Economist. Shipping conferences, rate policy and developing countries: the argument of rate discrimination. Hamburg, 1973. pp. 357. *bibliog. (Hamburg. Hamburgisches Welt-Wirtschaft-Archiv Studien zur Aussenwirtschaft und Entwicklungspolitik) With German summary.*

— Social conditions.

ADELMAN (IRMA) and MORRIS (CYNTHIA TAFT) Economic growth and social equity in developing countries. Stanford, 1973. pp. 257.

SZENTES (TAMÁS) How does the distorted socio-economic structure impede the expansion of accumulation?. Budapest, 1973. pp. 60. *(Magyar Tudományos Akadémia. Afro-Ázsiai Kutató Központ. Studies on Developing Countries. No. 54)*

WILSON (DES) Minority report: a diary of protest 1970-73. London, 1973. pp. 168.

BIGO (PIERRE) L'eglise et la révolution du tiers monde. Paris, 1974. pp. 284.

— Social policy.

UNITED NATIONS EDUCATIONAL, SCIENTIFIC AND CULTURAL ORGANIZATION. Reports and Papers in the Social Sciences. Paris, 1955 in progress.

NETHERLANDS. Nationale Raad van Advies inzake Hulpverlening aan Minder Ontwikkelde Landen. 1971. Advies sociale aspecten van het ontwikkelingsbeleid. ['s-Gravenhage, 1971]. pp. 36.

— Statistics — Study and Teaching.

ROUND-TABLE discussion on the university teaching of statistics in developing countries;...report containing resolutions arising from the discussion [organized by the International Statistical Institute at The Hague, 1968]. [The Hague, 1969?]. pp. 15.

— Tariffs — Mathematical models.

McCABE (JAMES L.) and MICHALOPOULOS (CONSTANTINE) Tariff policy, equipment production and employment in developing countries. New Haven, Conn., 1973. pp. 45. *bibliog. (Yale University. Economic Growth Center. Center Discussion Papers. No. 170)*

— Taxation.

NGAOSYVATHN (PHEUPHANH) Le role de l'impôt dans les pays en voie de développement: appréciation de l'influence exercée par les structures économiques et socio-politiques sur le prélèvement fiscal. Paris, 1974. pp. 316. *bibliog.*

— Traffic estimation.

HOWE (J.D.G.F.) The sensitivity to traffic estimates of road planning in developing countries. Crowthorne, 1973. pp. 28. *(U.K. Transport and Road Research Laboratory. Reports. LR 516)*

— Unemployed.

COMMONWEALTH SECRETARIAT. Approaches to employment problems in Africa and Asia. London, 1973. pp. 93. *bibliogs. (Youth and Development in the Commonwealth. No.7)*

— Mathematical models.

THIRD world employment: problems and strategy; selected readings; edited by Richard Jolly [and others]. Harmondsworth, 1973. pp. 448. *bibliogs.*

PORTER (RICHARD C.) Labor migration and urban unemployment in less developed countries: comment. Ann Arbor, 1973. pp. 18. *bibliog. (Michigan University. Center for Research on Economic Development. Discussion Papers. No. 29)*

— Vocational education.

INTERNATIONAL LABOUR ORGANISATION. Advisory Committee on Salaried Employees and Professional Workers. 6th Session. Reports. 3. The role of non-manual workers in economic and social development, and the need for their training: third item on the agenda. Geneva, 1967. pp. 63.

INTERNATIONAL LABOUR CONFERENCE. 54th Session. Reports. 6. Sixth item on the agenda: special youth employment and training schemes for development purposes. Geneva, 1969-70. 2 pts.

BUCHWALD (ULRIKE VON) and others. Vocational training in developing countries: a survey of expert experiences: an Institute staff study. (UNRISD Reports. No.73.1) (UNRISD/10/73). Geneva, United Nations Research Institute for Social Development, 1973. pp. 215. bibliog.

— Wages — Minimum wage.

INTERNATIONAL LABOUR CONFERENCE. 54th Session. Reports. 5. Fifth item on the agenda: minimum wage fixing machinery and related problems, with special reference to developing countries. Geneva, 1969-70. 2 pts.

— Women's employment.

YOUSSEF (NADIA HAGGAG) Women and work in developing societies. Berkeley, Calif., [1974]. pp. 137. bibliog. (California University. Institute of International Studies. Population Monograph Series. No. 15)

— Youth — Employment.

INTERNATIONAL LABOUR CONFERENCE. 54th Session. Reports. 6. Sixth item on the agenda: special youth employment and training schemes for development purposes. Geneva, 1969-70. 2 pts.

COMMONWEALTH SECRETARIAT. Approaches to employment problems in Africa and Asia. London, 1973. pp. 93. bibliogs. (Youth and Development in the Commonwealth. No.7)

UNDERGROUND LITERATURE.

INTERNATIONAL DIRECTORY OF LITTLE MAGAZINES AND SMALL PRESSES. a., 1965 [1st]- Paradise, California (formerly El Cerrito, California). Title varies.

— Russia.

"AOÛT Quartorze" jugé par les lecteurs russes; traduit du russe par Lucile Nivat et Alfréda Aucouturier. Paris, [1973]. pp. 190.

UNDERGROUND RAILWAYS

— United Kingdom — London.

EDMONDS (ALEXANDER) History of the Metropolitan District Railway Company to June 1908;... prepared for publication, with preface, notes and an epilogue by Charles E. Lee. London, 1973. pp. 243.

LLEWELYN-DAVIES WEEKS [AND PARTNERS[. SE London and the Fleet Line: a study of land use potential carried out for London Transport Executive. London, 1973. pp. 172.

MAXWELL (W.W.) The contribution of the underground railway to city transport. [London, London Transport Executive, 1973]. fo. 14.

DAY (D.J.) and others. 1971/72 Underground travel survey. [London], London Transport Executive, 1974. 1 pamphlet (various pagings). (Economic and Operational Research Office. Operational Research Reports. 205)

UNEMPLOYED.

INTERNATIONAL LABOUR CONFERENCE. 56th Session. Reports. 4. Fourth item on the agenda: the World Employment Programme. Geneva, 1971. pp. 86.

KALACHEK (EDWARD D.) Labor markets and unemployment. Belmont, Calif., [1973]. pp. 146.

— Mathematical models.

ZAHN (PETER) Economist. Die Phillips-Relation für Deutschland: eine lohn- und inflationstheoretische Untersuchung. Berlin, 1973. pp. 259. bibliog.

MILLER (ROGER LEROY) and WILLIAMS (RABURN M.) Unemployment and inflation: the new economics of the wage-price spiral. St. Paul, [Minn.], 1974. pp. 110. bibliogs.

— Australia.

AUSTRALIA. Department of Labour and National Service. 1970. An analysis of full employment in Australia. Melbourne, 1970. pp. 48. (Labour Market Studies. No.2)

— Canada.

CANADA. Statistics Canada. Consumer Income and Expenditure Division. 1973. Incomes of unemployed individuals and their families; Revenus des chomeurs et de leur famille; 1971. Ottawa, 1973. pp. 90. In English and French.

— — Quebec.

FEDERATION DES TRAVAILLEURS DU QUEBEC. Congrès, 12e, 1971. L'état, rouage de notre exploitation: documents de travail. [Montréal, 1971?]. pp. 143.

— Colombia.

VILLAZON DE ARMAS (CRISPIN) Nueva politica laboral: discursos. Bogota, Ministerio de Trabajo y Seguridad Social, 1972. pp. 34.

— India.

INDIA. Labour Bureau. 1971. Report on survey as to how workers support themselves during retrenchment, lay-off, closure and strikes and collection of data regarding indebtedness. [Delhi, 1971]. pp. 236.

FORUM OF EDUCATION, NEW DELHI. Committee on Education and Total Employment. Educated unemployment in India: challenge and responses: study report of the Committee, etc. Delhi, [1972]. pp. 103.

— Ireland (Republic).

WALSH (BRENDAN M.) The structure of unemployment in Ireland, 1954-1972. Dublin, 1974. pp. 80. bibliog. (Economic and Social Research Institute. Papers. No. 77)

— Italy.

BARBAGLI (MARZIO) Disoccupazione intellettuale e sistema scolastico in Italia, 1859- 1973. Bologna, [1974]. pp. 481.

— Netherlands Antilles.

NETHERLANDS ANTILLES. Bureau voor de Statistiek. 1971. De werkgelegenheidssituatie op Curacao en Aruba in juli 1971 op grond van een gehouden steekproef onderzoek en een vergelijking met 1966. Curacao, 1971. fo. 7.

— Sweden.

BERGLIND (HANS) and LINQUIST (ANNA LENA) Utslagningen på arbetsmarknaden: omfattning och utvecklingstendenser. Lund, 1973. pp. 136. bibliog. With English summary.

— Uganda.

HUTTON (CAROLINE) Reluctant farmers?: a study of unemployment and planned rural development in Uganda. Nairobi, 1973. pp. 331. bibliog. (Makerere Institute of Social Research. East African Studies. No.33)

— Underdeveloped AREAS.

See UNDERDEVELOPED AREAS — Unemployed.

— United Kingdom.

SMITH (BARBARA M.D.) and PARSONS (HELEN K.) The Rugeley study: a report to Rugeley Urban District Council on employment opportunities in Rugeley and district. Birmingham, 1971. fo. 170. (Birmingham. University. Centre for Urban and Regional Studies. Research Memoranda. No.8)

HAYBURN (R.) The national unemployed-worker movement in Eccles 1929-1936; [a] supplement to the 1971-2 lectures [published by the Eccles and District History Society]. [Manchester], 1972. pp. 15.

SALFORD. University. Department of Sociology, Government and Administration. Unemployment and occupational training: [a number of papers delivered for a course at the university, 1971-1972; course organiser, Miss M.P. Reay]. Salford, [1972]. pp. 63.

CHESHIRE (P.C.) Regional unemployment differences in Great Britain; [with] Interregional migration models and their applications to Great Britain; by R. Weeden. Cambridge, [1973]. pp. 105. (National Institute of Economic and Social Research. Regional Papers. 2)

CLARKE (GEORGE) People, technology and unemployment: a brief study of the past, a look at the present, and some thoughts on the future; ... with an appendix by Michael Lee. London, [1973]. pp. 64. bibliog.

EVANS (GRAHAM J.) The change in the 'UV' relationship: some further clues. Coventry, 1973. pp. 21,ii. bibliog. (University of Warwick. Centre for Industrial Economic and Business Research. [Warwick Research in Industrial and Business Studies]. No.33)

SMITH (BARBARA M.D.) Black country employment 1959-1970: an analysis based on employment exchange data and incorporating comparisons between inner and outer exchanges and between the Black country and Birmingham and Great Britain. Birmingham, 1973. fo. 31,89. (Birmingham. University. Centre for Urban and Regional Studies. Research Memoranda. 18) With summary at front.

U.K. [National Register of Archives]. 1973. Labour Party archives: Labour Party Distressed Areas Commission: list of LP/DAC/1-13; compiled by S. Horrocks. London, 1973. fo. 19.

AIMS OF INDUSTRY. Mass unemployment - can it be halted?. London, [1974]. pp. 9.

HILL (MICHAEL J.) Policies for the unemployed: help or coercion?. London, 1974. pp. 16. (Child Poverty Action Group. Poverty Pamphlets. 15)

TAYLOR (JIM) Unemployment and wage inflation: with special reference to Britain and the U.S.A. Harlow, 1974. pp. 120. bibliog.

— — Wales.

WELSH COUNCIL. Unemployment in Wales: a study. [Cardiff?], 1973. pp. 32.

— United States.

FELLNER (WILLIAM JOHN) Employment policy at the crossroads: an interim look at pressures to be resisted. Washington, D.C., 1972. pp. 28. (American Enterprise Institute for Public Policy Research. Domestic Affairs Studies. 9)

VALLEE (ANNIE) and KAWECKI (ANNIE) eds. Le chômage aux Etats-Unis. [Paris, 1972]. pp. 96. bibliog.

KOBRAK (PETER) Private assumption of public responsibilities: the role of American business in urban manpower programs. New York, 1973. pp. 257. bibliog.

MOORE (GEOFFREY H.) How full is full employment?; and others essays on interpreting the unemployment statistics. Washington D.C., 1973. pp. 32. (American Enterprise Institute for Public Policy Research. Domestic Affairs Studies. No. 14)

PALMER (JOHN L.) Inflation, unemployment and poverty. Lexington, Mass., [1973]. pp. 170. bibliog.

SORKIN (ALAN L.) Education, unemployment, and economic growth. Lexington, Mass., [1974]. pp. 186.

TAYLOR (JIM) Unemployment and wage inflation: with special reference to Britain and the U.S.A. Harlow, 1974. pp. 120. bibliog.

— — California.

HUNTINGTON (EMILY H.) Unemployment relief and the unemployed in the San Francisco Bay Region, 1929-34...;issued under the auspices of the Heller Committee for Research in Social Economics of the University of California. Berkeley, 1939. pp. 106.

— — New York (City).

RINGENBACH (PAUL T.) Tramps and reformers 1873-1916: the discovery of unemployment in New York. Westport, 1973. pp. 224. bibliog.

UNEMPLOYED. (Cont.)

— Venezuela — Carabobo.

VENEZUELA. Direccion General de Estadistica. Division de Muestreo. 1973. Investigacion conjunta: encuesta regional de hogares por muestreo, Estado Carabobo, agosto 1968...:empleo, desempleo y analfabetismo. Caracas, 1973. pp. 242.

UNEMPLOYMENT, SEASONAL

— United States.

MURRAY (MERRILL G.) The treatment of seasonal unemployment under unemployment insurance. Kalamazoo, Mich., 1972. pp. 84. *(W.E. Upjohn Institute for Employment Research. Studies in Unemployment Insurance and Related Problems)*

UNEMPLOYMENT, TECHNOLOGICAL.

THOMAS (ROY DARROW) The adjustment of displaced workers in a labour-surplus economy: a case study of Trinidad and Tobago. [Mona, 1972]. pp. 118. *bibliog.*

CLARKE (GEORGE) People, technology and unemployment: a brief study of the past, a look at the present, and some thoughts on the future; ... with an appendix by Michael Lee. London, [1973]. pp. 64. *bibliog.*

STONEMAN (PAUL S.) The effect of computerisation on the demand for labour in the U.K. Coventry, [1974]. pp. 18. *(University of Warwick. Department of Economics. Warwick Economic Research Papers. No. 47)*

UNIATE CHURCH.

DMYTRUK (KLYM IEVHENOVYCH) Svastyka na sutanakh. Kyïv, 1973. pp. 342.

SHYSH (ANATOLII ZAKHAROVYCH) Antyhumannyi kharakter morali uniatstva. Kyïv, 1973. pp. 118.

UNION CIVICA RADICAL.

PINO MONTES DE OCA (O. DEL) ed. La revolucion del 90: Leandro N. Alem, Aristobulo del Valle, etc. Buenos Aires, [1955]. pp. 157.

UNIT TRUSTS.

See INVESTMENT TRUSTS.

UNITED KINGDOM

— Antiquities.

U.K. Ordnance Survey. 1973. Field archaeology in Great Britain. 5th ed. Southampton, 1973. pp. 184. *bibliog.*

CUNLIFFE (BARRINGTON WINDSOR) Iron Age communities in Britain: an account of England, Scotland and Wales from the seventh century B.C. until the Roman conquest. London, 1974. pp. 418. *bibliog.*

— Antiquities, Anglo—Saxon.

MYRES (JOHN NOWELL LINTON) Anglo-Saxon pottery and the settlement of England. Oxford, 1969. pp. 259. *(Rhind Lectures in Archaeology. 1965)*

— Appropriations and expenditures.

CAIRNCROSS (Sir ALEXANDER KIRKLAND) The role and function of the control of public expenditure in economic policy; (transcript of... lecture held on 19 March 1973). [London], Civil Service College, [1973]. fo. 24. *(Lectures on the Control of Public Expenditure. No. 3)*

DU CANN (EDWARD) The Select Committee on Public Expenditure: an assessment of its purpose and early progress; (transcript of... lecture held on 26 February 1973). [London], Civil Service College, [1973]. fo. 20. *(Lectures on the Control of Public Expenditure. No. 2)*

GOLDMAN (Sir SAMUEL) The developing system of public expenditure, management and control; (transcript of... lecture held on 26 March 1973). [London], Civil Service College, [1973]. fo. 34. *(Lectures on the Control of Public Expenditure. No. 4)*

HECLO (HUGH) and WILDAVSKY (AARON BERNARD) The private government of public money: community and policy inside British politics. London, 1974. pp. 399. *bibliog.*

KLEIN (RUDOLF EWALD) and others. Social policy and public expenditure, 1974: an interpretative essay. London, 1974. pp. 94. *bibliog.*

— Armed forces.

The ROLE of the armed forces in peacekeeping in the 1970's; report of a seminar held at the Royal United Services Institute for Defence Studies on Wednesday 4 April 1973. London, 1973. pp. 15.

— — Medical care.

U.K. Defence Medical Services Inquiry Committee. 1973. Report; [Sir Edmund Compton and subsequently Sir Clifford Jarrett, chairmen]. London, 1973. pp. 96.

— Army.

BARZILAY (DAVID) The British army in Ulster. Belfast, 1973. pp. 253.

— — Barracks and quarters.

U.K. Ministry of Public Building and Works. Directorate of Building Development. 1969. Maidstone development project: Invicta Park. London, 1969. pp. 99. *(R and D Papers)*

— Biography.

U.K. Central Office of Information. Reference Division. 1973-. Reference biography service: [notes on British ministers, secretaries of state, etc.]. [London], 1973 in progress. *Current issues only kept.*

— Census — 1971.

LOMAS (G.B. GILLIAN) Census 1971: the coloured population of Great Britain: preliminary report. London, 1973. pp. 117. *bibliog.*

U.K. Census, 1971. Census, 1971: Great Britain: economic activity. London, 1973. pp. 102.

U.K. Census, 1971. Census, 1971: Great Britain: summary tables (1% sample). London, 1973. pp. 176. *Four census forms in end pocket.*

U.K. Census, 1971. Census, 1971: report on the Welsh language in Wales. Cardiff, 1973. pp. 83.

CENSUS atlas of South Yorkshire: computer and laser graphic mapping of 35 selected population characteristics in over 2700 enumeration districts; project director: Bryan E. Coates;...; produced... by the Department of Geography, University of Sheffield. Sheffield, [1974]. pp. 118 (including 37 folding maps).

U.K. Census, 1971. Census, 1971: England and Wales: housing. London, 1974. 4 pts. (in 1 vol.).

U.K. Census, 1971 Census, 1971: England and Wales: usual residence tables. London, 1974. pp. 59.

U.K. Census, 1971. Census, 1971: Great Britain: age, marital condition and general tables. London, 1974. pp. 67.

U.K. Census, 1971. Census, 1971: Great Britain: housing summary tables. London, 1974. pp. 43.

U.K. Census, 1971. Census, 1971: Great Britain: non-private households. London, 1974. pp. 190.

U.K. Census, 1971. Census, 1971: Great Britain: persons of pensionable age. London, 1974. pp. 329.

— Civilization.

VANSITTART (PETER) Worlds and underworlds: Anglo-European history through the centuries. London, 1974. pp. 316. *bibliog.*

— Commerce.

U.K. Public Record Office, Lists and Indexes. Supplementary Series. No. 11. List of Board of Trade records to 1913. New York, Kraus Reprint Corporation, 1964. pp. 266.

[ECONOMIC DEVELOPMENT COMMITTEE FOR PRINTING AND PUBLISHING]. Printing and publishing exports and imports in 1970. [London, National Economic Development Office, 1971?]. 1 pamphlet (unpaged).

HATCHER (JOHN) English tin production and trade before 1550. Oxford, 1973. pp. 219. *bibliog.*

NATIONAL PORTS COUNCIL. Economics Division. United Kingdom international trade, 1980. London, 1973. pp. 80. *bibliog.*

— — Examinations, questions, etc.

SYLVESTER-EVANS (G.) Finance of foreign trade: examination questions answered. London, 1973. pp. 123.

— — Africa, West.

DAVIES (P.N.) The trade makers: Elder Dempster in West Africa, 1852-1972. London, 1973. pp. 526. *bibliog.*

— — Asia.

GHAI (DHARAM P.) The enlargement of the E.E.C. and the Asian Commonwealth countries. London, Commonwealth Secretariat, 1973. pp. 57. *(Commonwealth Economic Papers. No.2)*

— — Burgundy.

MUNRO (JOHN H.A.) Wool, cloth, and gold: the struggle for bullion in Anglo- Burgundian trade, 1340-1478. Brussels, 1972. pp. 241. *bibliog.*

— — Communist countries — Mathematical models.

LOBBAN (P.W.M.) A model for forecasting U.K. exports to the Sino-Soviet bloc. London, 1971. fo. 25. *(London Graduate School of Business Studies. Econometric Forecasting Unit. Discussion Papers. No. 23)*

— Constitution.

HARVEY (JACK) and BATHER (LESLIE) The British constitution. 3rd ed. London, 1972. pp. 585. *bibliogs.*

ASPECTS of constitutional reform; by members of the Political Studies Association. London, 1973. pp. 50. (U.K. Commission on the Constitution, 1969. Research Papers. 6)

THELEN (KLAUS) Die Vereinbarkeit des Vertrages zur Gründung der Europäischen Wirtschaftsgemeinschaft mit der britischen Verfassung. Köln, [1973]. pp. 283. *bibliog.* *(Cologne. Universität. Institut für das Recht der Europäischen Gemeinschaften. Kölner Schriften zum Europarecht. Band 21)*

BROMHEAD (PETER ALEXANDER) Britain's developing constitution. London, 1974. pp. 230. *bibliog.*

— Constitutional history.

ROBERTS (MICHAEL) 1908- , Professor of History. Swedish and English parliamentarism in the eighteenth century. Belfast, 1973. pp. 42. *(Oxford. University. James Ford Special Lectures. 1973)*

— Constitutional law.

DE SMITH (STANLEY ALEXANDER) Constitutional and administrative law. 2nd ed. Harmondsworth, 1973. pp. 750.

PHILLIPS (OWEN HOOD) Leading cases in constitutional and administrative law. 4th ed. London, 1973. pp. 395.

YARDLEY (DAVID CHARLES MILLER) Introduction to British constitutional law. 4th ed. London, 1974. pp. 161.

— Defences.

WILLIAMS (GEOFFREY) Natural alliance for the West: flexibility and global security. London, 1969. pp. 109.

GREENWOOD (DAVID E.) Budgeting for defence. London, 1972. pp. 99.

MONDAY CLUB. Defence Group. Thoughts on defence: [by Anthony Courtney and others]. London, 1974. pp. 9.

UNITED KINGDOM.

— Description and travel.

PROKSHA (LEANID IANUARAVICH) Tuman razveetstsa. Minsk, 1970. pp. 66.

MAISKII (IVAN MIKHAILOVICH) Liudi, sobytiia, fakty. Moskva, 1973. pp. 216.

— Directories.

CIVIC TRUST. Environmental directory: national and regional organisations of interest to those concerned with amenity and the environment. London, 1974. 1 pamphlet (unpaged).

— Economic conditions.

STRACHEY (JOHN ST. LOE) Socialism looks forward. New York, [1945]. pp. 153.

U.K. Central Office of Information. Reference Division. 1971. Britain in brief. 13th ed. London, 1971. pp. 62.

U.K. Central Office of Information. Reference Division. 1972. Britain in brief. 14th ed. London, 1972. pp. 63.

HOUSE (JOHN WILLIAM) ed. The UK space: resources, environment and the future. London, [1973]. pp. 371.

SANT (MORGAN EUGENE CYRIL) The geography of business cycles: a case study of economic fluctuations in East Anglia, 1951-68; [based on the thesis of the same title]. [London, 1973]. pp. 64. (*London. University. London School of Economics and Political Science. Department of Geography. Geographical Papers. No. 5*)

BRITAIN in the Common Market: a new business opportunity: [record of a conference held jointly by the London Graduate School of Business Studies and the Manchester Business School at Peterlee, March 1973]; edited by M.E. Beesley and D.C. Hague. London, 1974. pp. 298.

LIVINGSTONE (JAMES MACCARDLE) The British economy in theory and practice. London, 1974. pp. 230.

PEAKER (ANTONY) Economic growth in modern Britain. London, 1974. pp. 80. *bibliog.*

— — Mathematical models.

BALL (ROBERT JAMES) and others. Preliminary simulations of the London Business School macroeconometric model. London, [1972?]. fo. 16, (21). *bibliog.* (*London Graduate School of Business Studies. Econometric Forecasting Unit. Discussion Papers. No. 24*)

The LONDON business school quarterly econometric model of the U.K. economy; by R.J. Ball [and others]; ([with] appendix: Relationships in the basic model). London, [1972?]. 2 pts. *bibliog.* (*London Graduate School of Business Studies. Econometric Forecasting Unit. Discussion Papers. No.20*)

ASH (J.C.K.) and SMYTH (D.J.) Forecasting the United Kingdom economy. Farnborough, Hants, [1973]. pp. 267.

The MEDIUM term: models of the British economy; edited by G.D.N. Worswick and F.T. Blackaby for the National Institute of Economic and Social Research and the Social Science Research Council; [papers prepared for the conference held in London on 10 and 11 April, 1973]. London, 1974. pp. 246. *bibliogs.*

— Economic history.

BARNSBY (GEORGE) Dictatorship of the bourgeoisie: social control in the nineteenth-century Black Country. London, 1972. 1 vol. (unpaged). *bibliog.* (*Communist Party of Great Britain. Historians' Group. Our History. No.55*)

ARKELL (V.T.J.) Britain transformed: the development of British society since the mid-eighteenth century. Harmondsworth, 1973. pp. 336. *bibliog.*

MILLS (DENNIS R.) ed. English rural communities: the impact of a specialised economy. London, 1973. pp. 259. *bibliog.*

SCOTT (REBECCA JARVIS) Women in the Stuart economy; [M. Phil. (London) thesis] . 1973. fo. 244. *bibliog. Typescript: unpublished. This thesis is the property of London University and may not be removed from the Library.*

ANDERSON (BRUCE LOUIS) ed. Capital accumulation in the industrial revolution. London, 1974. pp. 212. *bibliogs.*

FLOUD (RODERICK) ed. Essays in quantitative economic history. Oxford, 1974. pp. 250. *bibliog.*

PAYNE (PETER LESTER) British entrepreneurship in the 19th century. London, 1974. pp. 80. *bibliog.* (*Economic History Society. Studies in Economic History*)

— — Bibliography.

SEGERS (AGNES) compiler. Het industrieel aspect in het Engels commercialistisch mercantilisme ...: The industrial aspect of English commercial mercantilism, 1660-1727. Brussel, 1973. pp. 176. (*Commission Belge de Bibliographie. Bibliographia Belgica. 119*)

— — Sources.

COBB (HENRY STEPHEN) Sources for economic history amongst the parliamentary records in the House of Lords Record Office. [London, 1973]. pp. 16. (*U.K. Parliament. House of Lords. Record Office. Memoranda. No. 50*)

U.K. [National Register of Archives]. 1973. Labour Party archives: Labour Party Distressed Areas Commission: list of LP/DAC/1-13; compiled by S. Horrocks. London, 1973. fo. 19.

[DOCUMENTS illustrative of English economic history, 1344-1793].34 items (in 2 portfolios).

— Economic policy.

SCHMIDMAN (JOHN) British unions and economic planning. University Park, Penn., [1969]. pp. 106. (*Pennsylvania State University. Penn State Studies. No. 27*)

REGIONAL PLANNING DISCUSSION PAPERS. London, Department of the Environment, [1973? in progress].

CAIRNCROSS (Sir ALEXANDER KIRKLAND) The role and function of the control of public expenditure in economic policy; (transcript of... lecture held on 19 March 1973). [London], Civil Service College, [1973]. fo. 24. (*Lectures on the Control of Public Expenditure. No. 3*)

HOUSE (JOHN WILLIAM) ed. The UK space: resources, environment and the future. London, [1973]. pp. 371.

LIND (HAROLD) Regional policy in Britain and the Six; (transcript of ... lecture held on 13 March 1972). [London], Civil Service College, [1973?]. fo. 28. (*Lectures on the European Community. Series A. No. 10*)

TRADES UNION CONGRESS. General Council. Economic policy and collective bargaining in 1973: (report to a special Trades Union Congress). London, 1973. pp. 46.

U.K. Department of the Environment. Monitoring Group for the Strategic Plan for the South East. 1973. Strategic planning in the South East; a first report. [London], 1973. pp. 106.

WILLIS (KENNETH G.) Economic policy determination and evaluation in the North Pennines. [Newcastle], 1973. pp. 60,vii. *bibliog.* (*Newcastle-upon-Tyne. University. Department of Agricultural Economics. Agricultural Adjustment Unit. Research Monographs. No. 3*)

CAMBRIDGE. University. Department of Applied Economics. Cambridge Economic Policy Group. Prospects for economic management, 1973-77. Cambridge, [1974]. 2 vols. (in 1).

HALFWAY to 1984...1979. London, [1974]. pp. 15.

RURAL resource development; [by] M.C. Whitby [and others] . London, 1974. pp. 244. *bibliog.*

FROST (MARTIN EUGENE) Regional employment change in Great Britain, 1952-68, with special reference to the influence of government policy on the northern region; [Ph.D.(London) thesis]. [1974]. 2 vols. *bibliog. Typescript: unpublished. This thesis is the property of London University and may not be removed from the Library.*

HODGES (MICHAEL) Multinational corporations and national government: a case study of the United Kingdom's experience, 1964-1970. Farnborough, [1974]. pp. 307.

HOPKIN (Sir BRYAN) The control of demand: an inaugural lecture given on 5 March 1974 at University College, Cardiff. Cardiff, [1974]. pp. 15. *bibliog.*

LIVINGSTONE (JAMES MACCARDLE) The British economy in theory and practice. London, 1974. pp. 230.

PEAKER (ANTONY) Economic growth in modern Britain. London, 1974. pp. 80. *bibliog.*

TRADES UNION CONGRESS. General Council. Collective bargaining and the social contract. London, [1974]. pp. 11.

U.K. Central Office of Information. Reference Division. Reference Pamphlets. 80. Regional development in Britain. 2nd ed. London, 1974. pp. 54. *bibliog.*

WOLFF (RICHARD D.) The economics of colonialism: Britain and Kenya, 1870-1930. New Haven, 1974. pp. 203. *bibliog.*

YOUNG (STEPHEN) Intervention in the mixed economy: the evolution of British industrial policy, 1964-72;... with A.V. Lowe. London, 1974. pp. 254. *bibliog.*

— — Mathematical models.

The MEDIUM term: models of the British economy; edited by G.D.N. Worswick and F.T. Blackaby for the National Institute of Economic and Social Research and the Social Science Research Council; [papers prepared for the conference held in London on 10 and 11 April, 1973]. London, 1974. pp. 246. *bibliogs.*

— Emigration and immigration.

COMMUNITY RELATIONS COMMISSION. Facts and figures about Commonwealth immigrants; compiled by Abdul Matin. [London, 1968 repr. 1971]. pp. 20.

JOINT COUNCIL FOR THE WELFARE OF IMMIGRANTS. The unemployed, homeless and destitute: a report on the situation of British Asians in Uganda. Southall, 1970. fo. 14. *Typescript.*

TILBE (DOUGLAS) The Ugandan Asian crisis. London, 1972. pp. 19. (*British Council of Churches. Community and Race Relations Unit. CRRU Booklets*)

PERRY (JANE) The fair housing experiment: community relations councils and the housing of minority groups. London, 1973. pp. 53.

HUMPHRY (DEREK) and WARD (MICHAEL) Passports and politics. Harmondsworth, 1974. pp. 187.

RUNNYMEDE TRUST. Immigration, race and settlement: a reference guide. London pp. 32.

— Executive departments.

WINNIFRITH (Sir ALFRED JOHN DIGBY) The Ministry of Agriculture, Fisheries and Food. London, 1962. pp. 271. (*Royal Institute of Public Administration. New Whitehall Series. No. 11*)

U.K. Civil Service Commission. 1971. The work of government departments. [London], 1971. pp. 64.

U.K. Board of Inland Revenue. 1973. The constitutional development of the Board of Inland Revenue with details of each separate constitution by letters patent from 1849 to 1973. [London, 1973]. fo. (7), 15.

— Foreign economic relations.

FUKUDA (HARUKO) Britain in Europe: impact on the third world. London, 1973. pp. 194.

UNITED KINGDOM. (Cont.)

— — Asia.

FABIAN SOCIETY. Fabian Tracts. [No.] 420. Labour in Asia: a new chapter?; editor, Colin Jackson. London, 1973. pp. 52.

— — Austria.

HELLEINER (KARL F.) Free trade and frustration: Anglo-Austrian negotiations 1860-70. Toronto, [1973]. pp. 152. *bibliog.*

— — East (Near East).

U.K. Central Office of Information. Reference Division. 1956. Britain and Middle East development. London, 1956. pp. 38.

— — Italy.

CUGIS (CARLO DE) ed. Italia e Inghilterra un secolo fa: il nuovo corso nelle relazioni economiche; appendice al Catalogo della mostra tenuta in occasione della settimana brittanica a Milano, 9-17 ottobre 1965.Milano, 1968. pp. 547. *In English, Italian or French.*

— — United States.

CRAPOL (EDWARD P.) America for Americans: economic nationalism and anglophobia in the late nineteenth century. Westport, Conn., 1973. pp. 248. *bibliog.*

— Foreign population.

LOMAS (G.B. GILLIAN) Census 1971: the coloured population of Great Britain: preliminary report. London, 1973. pp. 117. *bibliog.*

KOHLER (DAVID F.) Ethnic minorities in Britain: statistical data. 2nd ed. London, Community Relations Commission, 1974. pp. 19.

PAREKH (BHIKHUBHAI CHHOTALAL) ed. Colour, culture and consciousness: immigrant intellectuals in Britain; edited [on behalf of the Acton Society Trust]. London, 1974. pp. 249.

KOHLER (DAVID F.) Ethnic minorities in Britain: statistical data. 2nd ed. London, Community Relations Commission, 1974. pp. 19.

— Foreign relations.

CARMI (OZER) La Grande-Bretagne et la petite entente. Genève, 1972. pp. 381. *bibliog.*

BUZAN (BARRY GORDON) The British peace movement from 1919 to 1939; [Ph.D. (London) thesis]. 1973. fo. 460. *bibliog. Typescript: unpublished. This thesis is the property of London University and may not be removed from the Library.*

DOHERTY (JULIAN CAMPBELL) Das Ende des Appeasement: die britische Aussenpolitik, die Achsenmächte und Osteuropa nach dem Münchener Abkommen. Berlin, [1973]. pp. 284. *bibliog.*

GILBERT (MARTIN) Sir Horace Rumbold: portrait of a diplomat, 1869-1941. London, 1973. pp. 496.

WATERFIELD (GORDON) Professional diplomat: Sir Percy Loraine of Kirkharle Bt., 1880-1961. London, [1973]. pp. 312.

DOUGLAS-HOME (Sir ALEXANDER FREDERICK) Britain's changing role in world affairs. London, [1974]. pp. 8. *(David Davies Memorial Institute of International Studies. Annual Memorial Lectures. 1974)*

GORE-BOOTH (PAUL HENRY) Baron Gore-Booth. With great truth and respect. London, 1974. pp. 440.

HOWARD (CHRISTOPHER) Britain and the casus belli, 1822-1902: a study of Britain's international position from Canning to Salisbury. London, 1974. pp. 204.

HOWAT (GERALD M.D.) Stuart and Cromwellian foreign policy. London, 1974. pp. 191. *bibliog.*

JONES (ROY ELLIOTT) The changing structure of British foreign policy. London, 1974. pp. 191. *bibliog.*

See also EUROPEAN ECONOMIC COMMUNITY — United Kingdom.

— — Africa.

UZOIGWE (GODFREY N.) Britain and the conquest of Africa: the age of Salisbury. Ann Arbor, [1974]. pp. 403. *bibliog.*

— — Asia.

FABIAN SOCIETY. Fabian Tracts. [No.] 420. Labour in Asia: a new chapter?; editor, Colin Jackson. London, 1973. pp. 52.

— — Bolivia.

QUEREJAZU CALVO (ROBERTO) Bolivia y los ingleses, 1825-1948. La Paz, 1973. pp. 402. *bibliog.*

— — Catholic Church.

WILKIE (WILLIAM E.) The cardinal protectors of England: Rome and the Tudors before the reformation. London, 1974. pp. 262. *bibliog.*

— — East (Near East).

NUTTING (Sir ANTHONY) Britain and Palestine: a legacy of deceit. London, [1972?]. pp. 15.

MANGOLD (PETER) The role of force in British policy towards the Middle East, 1957-1966. [Ph.D. (London) thesis]. 1973. fo. 307. *bibliog. Typescript: unpublished. This thesis is the property of London University and may not be removed from the Library.*

— — France.

BULLEN (ROGER JOHN) Palmerston, Guizot and the collapse of the Entente Cordiale. London, 1974. pp. 352. *bibliog.*

— — Germany.

GILBERT (MARTIN) and GOTT (RICHARD) The appeasers. [2nd ed.] London, 1967. pp. 444. *bibliog.*

BOADLE (DONALD GRAEME) Winston Churchill and the German question in British foreign policy, 1918-1922. The Hague, 1973. pp. 193. *bibliog.*

— — India.

CHAMBERLAIN (M.E.) Britain and India: the interaction of two peoples. Newton Abbot, 1974. pp. 272. *bibliog.*

— — — Sind.

THAIRANI (KALA) British political missions to Sind: a narrative of negotiations from 1799 to 1843 leading up to the state's annexation. New Delhi, 1973. pp. 193. *bibliog.*

— — Italy.

PETRICIOLI (MARTA) L'occupazione italiana del Caucaso: "un ingrato servizio" da rendere a Londra. Milano, 1972. pp. 93. *(Politico, Il. Quaderni. n.10) With English summary.*

— — Malaysia.

SULITSKAIA (TAT'IANA IVANOVNA) Angliia i Malaiziia, 1961-1971. Moskva, 1973. pp. 182. *bibliog.*

— — Persian Gulf.

MEDVEDKO (LEONID IVANOVICH) Vetry peremen v Persidskom zalive. Moskva, 1973. pp. 208.

— — Russia.

RYZHIKOV (VLADIMIR ALEKSANDROVICH) Zigzagi diplomatii Londona: iz istorii sovetsko-angliiskikh otnoshenii. Moskva, 1973. pp. 215.

KAISER (ROBERT G.) Cold winter, cold war. London, 1974. pp. 226. *bibliog.*

— — Spain.

RODRIGUEZ-MOÑINO SORIANO (RAFAEL) La mision diplomatica de Don Jacobo Stuart Fitz James y Falco, XVII Duque de Alba en la Embajada de España en Londres, 1937-1945. [Madrid, 1971]. pp. 144. *bibliog.*

— — Turkey.

SHUKLA (RAM LAKHAN) Britain, India and the Turkish Empire, 1853-1882. New Delhi, [1973]. pp. 262. *bibliog.*

— — United States.

CAMPBELL (CHARLES SOUTTER) From revolution to rapprochement: the United States and Great Britain, 1783-1900. New York, [1974]. pp. 225. *bibliog.*

JONES (WILBUR DEVEREUX) The American problem in British diplomacy, 1841-1861. London, 1974. pp. 260.

KAISER (ROBERT G.) Cold winter, cold war. London, 1974. pp. 226. *bibliog.*

McDONALD (IAN S.) ed. Anglo-American relations since the Second World War. Newton Abbot, [1974]. pp. 264. *bibliog.*

— Government publications.

BAGWELL (PHILIP SIDNEY) Industrial relations. [Dublin, 1974]. pp. 166. *bibliog. (Government and Society in Nineteenth-Century Britain: Commentaries on British Parliamentary Papers)*

CHADWYCK-HEALEY LIMITED and SOMERSET HOUSE INC. A bibliographical guide to major British government publications containing statistics 1801-1965 now republished on microfilm by Chadwyck-Healey/Somerset House. Bishops Stortford, 1974. pp. 45.

— — Bibliography.

COMFORT (A.F.) and LOVELESS (CHRISTINA) compilers. Guide to government data: a survey of unpublished social science material in libraries of government departments in London; compiled for the British Library of Political and Economic Science. London, 1974. pp. 404.

— — Indexes.

IRISH UNIVERSITY PRESS. Index to British parliamentary papers on children's employment. Dublin, [1973]. pp. 443.

— Historical geography.

DARBY (HENRY CLIFFORD) ed. A new historical geography of England. Cambridge, 1973. pp. 767.

RAVENSDALE (J.R.) Liable to floods: village landscape on the edge of the fens, AD 450-1850. London, 1974. pp. 206. *bibliog.*

— History — Sources.

LARKIN (JAMES F.) and HUGHES (PAUL L.) eds. Stuart royal proclamations. Oxford, 1973 in progress.

CAMDEN SOCIETY. [Publications]. 4th Series. vol. 13. Camden miscellany. vol. 25. London, 1974. pp. 278.

— — To 1066.

THOMAS (CHARLES) b. 1928. Britain and Ireland in early Christian times, A.D. 400-800. London, [1971]. pp. 144. *bibliog.*

— — 449—1066, Anglo—Saxon period.

MYRES (JOHN NOWELL LINTON) Anglo-Saxon pottery and the settlement of England. Oxford, 1969. pp. 259. *(Rhind Lectures in Archaeology. 1965)*

FINBERG (HERBERT PATRICK REGINALD) The formation of England, 550-1042. London, 1974. pp. 253. *bibliog.*

UNITED KINGDOM. (Cont.)

— — 1300—1399.

MADDICOTT (J.R.) Thomas of Lancaster 1307-1322: a study in the reign of Edward II. London, 1970. pp. 390. *bibliog.*

— — 1399—1485, Lancaster and York.

KIRBY (JOHN LAVAN) Henry IV of England. London, 1970. pp. 280. *bibliog.*

— — 1485— , Modern period.

McKENDRICK (NEIL) ed. Historical perspectives: studies in English thought and society in honour of J.H. Plumb. London, [1974]. pp. 319. *bibliog.*

— — 1485—1603, Tudors.

CHRIMES (STANLEY BERTRAM) Henry VII. London, 1972. pp. 373. *bibliog.*

— — 1603—1714, Stuarts.

HOWAT (GERALD M.D.) Stuart and Cromwellian foreign policy. London, 1974. pp. 191. *bibliog.*

— — 1642—1660, Puritan Revolution.

MORRILL (J.S.) Cheshire 1630-1660: county government and society during the English revolution. London, 1974. pp. 357. *bibliog.*

— — 1660—1688, Restoration.

MILLER (JOHN) Fellow of Gonville and Caius College, Cambridge. Popery and politics in England, 1660-1668. Cambridge, 1973. pp. 288. *bibliog.*

— History, Local.

IREDALE (DAVID) Local history research and writing: a manual for local history writers. Leeds, [1974]. pp. 225. *bibliog.*

— History, military.

GOOCH (JOHN) The plans of war: the general staff and British military strategy c. 1900-1916. London, 1974. pp. 348. *bibliog.*

— Industries.

COUNCIL FOR SMALL INDUSTRIES IN RURAL AREAS. Report. bien., Ap 1970/Mr 1972 [2nd]- London.

U.K. Central Office of Information. Reference Division. 1971. Industry in Britain: organisation and production. rev. ed. London, 1971. pp. 19. *bibliog.*

COMPETITION in British industry: case studies of the effects of restrictive practices legislation; [by] Dennis Swann [and others]. Loughborough, 1973. pp. 413.

NATIONAL ECONOMIC DEVELOPMENT OFFICE. Industrial review to 1977. London, 1973. pp. 92.

NATIONAL ECONOMIC DEVELOPMENT OFFICE. Process Plant Working Party. Process industries investment forecasts: the eighth report by the...Working Party. London, 1973. pp. 51.

U.K. Business Statistics Office. Census of Production, 1968. Census of production, 1968: analysis of manufacturing industries by employment size of establishment, etc. [London], 1973. pp. 97.

U.K. Central Statistical Office. 1973. Input-output tables for the United Kingdom, 1968. London, 1973. pp. 128. *(Studies in Official Statistics. No.22)*

CHANNON (DEREK F.) Strategy and structure of management in private and state industry. London, 1974. pp. 10.

GEORGE (KENNETH DESMOND) Industrial organization: competition, growth and structural change in Britain. 2nd ed. London, 1974. pp. 225.

HODGES (MICHAEL) Multinational corporations and national government: a case study of the United Kingdom's experience, 1964-1970. Farnborough, [1974]. pp. 307.

JERVIS (FRANK ROBERT JOSEPH) Bosses in British business: managers and management from the industrial revolution to the present day. London, 1974. pp. 184. *bibliog.*

KEETON (GEORGE WILLIAMS) and FROMMEL (S.N.) eds. British industry and European law. London, 1974. pp. 206.

NATIONAL ECONOMIC DEVELOPMENT OFFICE. Process Plant Working Party. Process industries investment forecasts: the ninth report by the...Working Party. London, 1974. pp. 50.

YOUNG (STEPHEN) Intervention in the mixed economy: the evolution of British industrial policy, 1964-72;... with A.V. Lowe. London, 1974. pp. 254. *bibliog.*

— Intellectual life.

ROLPH (C.H.) pseud. [i.e. Cecil Rolph HEWITT] Kingsley: the life, letters and diaries of Kingsley Martin. London, 1973. pp. 413.

STOLLBERG (GUNNAR) Die soziale Stellung der intellektuellen Oberschicht im England des 12. Jahrhunderts. LÜBECK 1973. pp. 184. *bibliog.*

— Kings and rulers.

U.K. Central Office of Information. Reference Division. Reference Pamphlets. 118. The monarchy in Britain. London, 1974. pp. 38. *bibliog.*

— Military history.

MASON (PHILIP) A matter of honour: an account of the Indian army, its officers and men. London, 1974. pp. 580. *bibliog.*

— Military policy.

JOSHUA (WYNFRED) and HAHN (WALTER F.) Nuclear politics: America, France and Britain. Beverly Hills, [1973]. pp. 84. *bibliog. (Georgetown University. Center for Strategic and International Studies. Washington Papers. vol. 1/9)*

GOOCH (JOHN) The plans of war: the general staff and British military strategy c. 1900-1916. London, 1974. pp. 348. *bibliog.*

— Navy.

FRANCE. Direction de la Documentation. La Documentation Française. Notes et Etudes Documentaires. No. 3,727. Les activités maritimes du Royaume-Uni de Grande-Bretagne et d'Irlande du Nord. Paris, 1970. pp. 47.

MACKAY (RUDDOCK FINLAY) Fischer of Kilverstone. Oxford, 1973. pp. 539. *bibliog.*

— — History.

MARDER (ARTHUR JACOB) From the Dardanelles to Oran: studies of the Royal Navy in war and peace, 1915-1940. London, 1974. pp. 301.

— — Pay, allowances, etc.

WINCOTT (LEN) Invergordon mutineer. London, [1974]. pp. 183.

— Occupations — Directories.

UNCAREERS. Directory of alternative work. rev. ed. Birmingham, 1973. pp. 40.

— Officials and employees.

U.K. Civil Service Department. Statistics Division. Statistical Review Series. London, 1969 in progress.

U.K. Civil Service Commission. 1969. Engineers in government service. rev. ed. London, 1969. pp. 54.

U.K. Ministry of Agriculture, Fisheries and Food. 1969. A career in the National Agricultural Advisory Service. [London, 1969]. pp. 20.

U.K. Board of Inland Revenue. 1970. In command at thirty: a career in H.M. Inspectorate of Taxes. [London, 1970]. pp. 13.

U.K. Civil Service Commission. 1970. Architects in government service. London, 1970. pp. 28.

U.K. Civil Service Commission. 1970. Careers for graduates: posts in government service, 1971. [London, 1970]. pp. 109. *bibliog.*

U.K. Civil Service Commission. 1970. Careers for school-leavers: posts in government service, 1971. [London, 1970]. pp. 56.

U.K. Civil Service Commission. 1970. Executive careers: posts in government service. [London], 1970. pp. 24.

U.K. Civil Service Commission. 1970. The scientific civil service. rev. ed. [London], 1970. pp. 91.

U.K. Civil Service Commission. 1970. Today's civil service. [London, 1970]. pp. 22.

U.K. Civil Service Commission. 1971. Accountants in government service. rev. ed. [London], 1971. pp. 20.

U.K. Department of Employment. 1972. Department of Employment staff: annual reports: notes for the guidance of reporting and countersigning officers on the completion of annual reports. [London, 1972]. pp. 24. *(Circulars. 16/18)*

ASSOCIATION OF SCIENTIFIC, TECHNICAL AND MANAGERIAL STAFFS. Civil Service Advisory Committee. The case for middle management in the Civil Service. London, [1973]. pp. 11.

HER MAJESTY'S MINISTERS AND SENIOR STAFF IN PUBLIC DEPARTMENTS. 4 a yr., My 1974 (no.1)- London. *Supersedes HER MAJESTY'S MINISTERS AND HEADS OF PUBLIC DEPARTMENTS .*

SAINTY (JOHN CHRISTOPHER) Officials of the Boards of Trade, 1660-1870. London, 1974. pp. 124. *(London. University. Institute of Historical Research. Office-Holders in Modern Britain. 3)*

— — Yearbooks.

CIVIL SERVICE YEAR BOOK, THE; ([pd. by] Civil Service Department [U.K.]). a., 1974 [1st]- London.

— Parliament.

ASPECTS of parliamentary reform; by members of the Study of Parliament Group. London, 1973. pp. 62. *(U.K. Commission on the Constitution, 1969. Research Papers. 5)*

GRANADA TV NETWORK LIMITED. The state of the nation: Parliament. London, 1973. pp. 272.

WYATT (WOODROW LYLE) Turn again, Westminster. London, 1973. pp. 259.

— — Directories.

WHO DOES WHAT IN PARLIAMENT. a., 1970- London.

— — Elections.

U.K. Central Office of Information. Reference Division. 1973. Parliamentary elections in Britain. rev. ed. London, 1973. pp. 14. *bibliog.*

BUTLER (DAVID HENRY EDGEWORTH) and KAVANAGH (DENNIS A.) The British general election of February 1974. London, 1974. pp. 354. *bibliog.*

CRAIG (FRED W.S.) ed. British parliamentary election results, 1885-1918. London, 1974. pp. 698.

McKIE (DAVID) and COOK (CHRISTOPHER PIERS) The Guardian/Quartet election guide: (the coming election in perspective). London, 1974. pp. 192.

— — History.

BROCK (MICHAEL) The great Reform Act. London, 1973. pp. 411. *bibliog.*

TITE (COLIN G.C.) Impeachment and parliamentary judicature in early Stuart England. London, 1974. pp. 249. *bibliog.*

UNITED KINGDOM. (Cont.)

— — Sources.

COBB (HENRY STEPHEN) Sources for economic history amongst the parliamentary records in the House of Lords Record Office. [London, 1973]. pp. 16. *(U.K. Parliament. House of Lords. Record Office. Memoranda. No. 50)*

— — House of Commons.

BERRINGTON (HUGH) Backbench opinion in the House of Commons, 1945-55. Oxford, 1973. pp. 265.

DU CANN (EDWARD) The Select Committee on Public Expenditure: an assessment of its purpose and early progress; (transcript of... lecture held on 26 February 1973). [London], Civil Service College, [1973]. fo. 20. *(Lectures on the Control of Public Expenditure. No. 2)*

RUSH (MICHAEL) and SHAW (MALCOLM) eds. The House of Commons: services and facilities; edited... for Political and Economic Planning and The Study of Parliament Group. London, 1974. pp. 302. *bibliog.*

WORDEN (BLAIR) The Rump Parliament, 1648-1653. Cambridge, 1974. pp. 427. *bibliog.*

— — Private bills.

ABSE (LEO) Private member. London, 1973. pp. 296. *bibliog.*

— — Rules and practice.

GRIFFITH (JOHN ANEURIN GREY) Parliamentary scrutiny of Government bills. London, 1974. pp. 285.

— Politics and government.

HOGG (QUINTIN McGAREL) Baron Hailsham. The acceptable face of western civilisation. London, 1973. pp. 22. (Conservative Political Centre. [Publications]. No. 535]

NISKANEN (WILLIAM A.) Bureaucracy: servant or master?; lessons from America; with commentaries by Douglas Houghton [and others]. London, 1973. pp. 103. *(Institute of Economic Affairs. Hobart Paperbacks. 5)*

SOCIAL AND COMMUNITY PLANNING RESEARCH. Devolution and other aspects of government: an attitudes survey; prepared for the Office of Population Censuses and Surveys; [by Jean Morton-Williams]. London, 1973. pp. 158. *(U.K. Commission on the Constitution, 1969. Research Papers. 7)*

HEARDER (HARRY) and LOYN (HENRY ROYSTON) eds. British government and administration: studies presented to S.B. Chrimes. Cardiff, 1974. pp. 250. *bibliog.*

LOADES (D.M.) Politics and the nation, 1450-1660: obedience, resistance and public order. Brighton, 1974. pp. 484. *bibliog.*

MACKINTOSH (JOHN PITCAIRN) The government and politics of Britain. 3rd ed. London, 1974. pp. 224. *bibliog.*

PAGE (WILLIAM ROBERTS) Government and politics at work in Britain. Harlow, 1974. pp. 205.

— — Caricatures and cartoons.

CUMMINGS (MICHAEL) These uproarious years: a pictorial post-war history; by Cummings of the Daily Express. London, 1954. pp. 89.

ATHERTON (HERBERT McDONALD) Political prints in the age of Hogarth: a study of the ideographic representation of politics. Oxford, 1974. pp. 294,(64 plates). *bibliog.*

— — 1603—1714.

WORDEN (BLAIR) The Rump Parliament, 1648-1653. Cambridge, 1974. pp. 427. *bibliog.*

— — 1700—1799.

DICKINSON (H.T.) Walpole and the Whig supremacy. London, [1973]. pp. 205. *bibliog.*

— — 1756—1837.

BROCK (MICHAEL) The great Reform Act. London, 1973. pp. 411. *bibliog.*

FURNEAUX (ROBIN) William Wilberforce. London, 1974. pp. 506. *bibliog.*

JARRETT (JOHN DEREK) Pitt the Younger. London, [1974]. pp. 224. *bibliog.*

— — 1800—1899.

MARX (ROLAND) ed. Naissance et triomphe de la démocratie britannique, 1815-1918. [Paris], 1973. pp. 96. *bibliog.*

— — 1837—1901.

COOKE (A.B.) and VINCENT (JOHN RUSSELL) The governing passion: cabinet government and party politics in Britain 1885-86. Brighton, 1974. pp. 516.

RYDER (DUDLEY FRANCIS STUART) 3rd Earl of Harrowby. The Cabinet journal of Dudley Ryder, Viscount Sandon (later third Earl of Harrowby) 11 May - 10 August, 1878. London. *Special supplement, no.10, to BULLETIN OF THE INSTITUTE OF HISTORICAL RESEARCH, November 1974.*

— — 1900— .

FRASER (PETER) Winner of Prince Consort Prize, 1954. Lord Esher: a political biography. London, [1973]. pp. 496. *bibliog.*

WYATT (WOODROW LYLE) Turn again, Westminster. London, 1973. pp. 259.

BOYLE (ANDREW) Poor, dear Brendan: the quest for Brendan Bracken. London, 1974. pp. 377. *bibliog.*

— — 1901—1945.

HYDE (HARFORD MONTGOMERY) Baldwin: the unexpected prime minister. London, 1973. pp. 616. *bibliog.*

— — 1901—1918.

GREGORY (ROY) The miners and British politics, 1906-1914. Oxford, 1968. pp. 207.

MARX (ROLAND) ed. Naissance et triomphe de la démocratie britannique, 1815-1918. [Paris], 1973. pp. 96. *bibliog.*

MORRIS (ANDREW JAMES ANTHONY) ed. Edwardian radicalism 1900-1914: some aspects of British radicalism. London, 1974. pp. 277. *bibliog.*

— — 1945— .

POWELL (JOHN ENOCH) [Speeches and extracts from speeches; consisting mainly of Conservative Central Office News Service press releases]. London, 1969-74. 45 pts. (in 1 vol.) *Mostly duplicated copies, but 3 items are in typescript, 2 are xerograph copies and 1 is printed. Three of the speeches are in French, German, Italian respectively.*

BLONDEL (JEAN) 1929- . Voters, parties, and leaders: the social fabric of British politics. rev. ed. Harmondsworth, 1969 repr. 1972. pp. 272. *bibliog.*

HUGHES (R.J.L.) An ordinary Englishman's politics. Twickenham, 1973. pp. 63.

WILSON (HAROLD) Individual choice in democracy: a speech delivered at an East of Scotland Labour Party meeting at Leith on 20 January, 1973. [London, 1973]. pp. 19. *(Labour Party. Edinburgh Series of Policy Speeches. No. 1)*

BRUCE-GARDYNE (JOCK) Whatever happened to the quiet revolution?: the story of a brave experiment in government. London, 1974. pp. 176.

CONSERVATIVE AND UNIONIST PARTY. Firm action for a fair Britain: the Conservative manifesto, 1974. London, 1974. pp. 32.

CONSERVATIVE AND UNIONIST PARTY. Putting Britain first: a national policy from the Conservatives. London, [1974]. pp. 31.

CONSERVATIVE AND UNIONIST PARTY. The campaign guide, 1974; [edited by Anthony Greenland]. London, 1974. pp. 721.

COUNTER INFORMATION SERVICES. The unacceptable face: special report on the Conservative government, 1970/74. London, [1974]. pp. 15.

GORBIK (VIACHESLAV ALEKSANDROVICH) Antirabochaia politika pravitel'stva konservatorov i polozhenie trudiashchikhsia v poslevoennoi Anglii. Kiev, 1974. pp. 111.

GORODETSKAIA (INNA EFIMOVNA) Velikobritaniia: izbirateli, vybory, partii, 1945-1970. Moskva, 1974. pp. 223.

GRANT (JOHN DOUGLAS) Member of Parliament. London, 1974. pp. 190.

HALFWAY to 1984...1979. London, [1974]. pp. 15.

HECLO (HUGH) and WILDAVSKY (AARON BERNARD) The private government of public money: community and policy inside British politics. London, 1974. pp. 399. *bibliog.*

HODGES (MICHAEL) Multinational corporations and national government: a case study of the United Kingdom's experience, 1964-1970. Farnborough, [1974]. pp. 307.

LABOUR PARTY. Let us work together: Labour's way out of the crisis; the Labour Party manifesto, 1974. London, 1974. pp. 16.

NATIONAL FRONT. For a new Britain: the manifesto of the National Front. Croydon, [1974]. pp. 26.

PROUDFOOT (MARY) British politics and government, 1951-1970: a study of an affluent society. London, 1974. pp. 240. *bibliog.*

ROSE (RICHARD) Politics in England today: an interpretation. London, 1974. pp. 410.

ROSE (RICHARD) The problem of party government. London, 1974. pp. 502. *bibliog.*

— Popular culture.

THOMPSON (DENYS) ed. Discrimination and popular culture. 2nd ed. Harmondsworth, 1973. pp. 237. *bibliogs.*

— Population.

WILLIS (KENNETH G.) Models of population and income: economic planning in rural areas. Newcastle upon Tyne, 1971. pp. 65. *(Newcastle-upon-Tyne. University. Department of Agricultural Economics. Agricultural Adjustment Unit. Research Monographs. No. 1)*

CHESHIRE (P.C.) Regional unemployment differences in Great Britain; [with] Interregional migration models and their applications to Great Britain; by R. Weeden. Cambridge, [1973]. pp. 105. *(National Institute of Economic and Social Research. Regional Papers. 2)*

CORDEY-HAYES (MARTYN) and GLEAVE (D.) Migration movements and the differential growth of city regions in England and Wales:...paper presented at the European Regional Science Association Congress in Vienna, August 1973. London, 1973. pp. 38. *bibliog.* *(Centre for Environmental Studies. Research Papers. 1)*

HOCKLEY (D.) Population projections for the South-East sub-regions. [London], 1973. pp. 30. *bibliog.* *(London. Greater London Council. Department of Planning and Transportation. Research Memoranda. 417)*

HOUSE (JOHN WILLIAM) ed. The UK space: resources, environment and the future. London, [1973]. pp. 371.

HUMAN RIGHTS SOCIETY. Not wanted?: Britain's falling birth rate. London, [1973]. pp. (4).

KLOSS (DIANA M.) and RAISBECK (BERTRAM L.) Law and population growth in the United Kingdom. Medford, Mass., 1973. pp. 47. *(Tufts University. Fletcher School of Law and Diplomacy. Law and Population Monograph Series. No.11)*

SMITH (JOHN) of the Monday Club. When the bough breaks. London, [1973]. pp. 11.

UNITED KINGDOM. (Cont.)

TRANTER (NEIL LIONEL) Population since the industrial revolution: the case of England and Wales. London, 1973. pp. 206. *bibliogs*.

LONDON. University. London School of Economics and Political Science. Department of Geography. Urban change in Britain, 1961-1971...: working reports. London, 1974 in progress.

CRAFTS (N.F.R.) and IRELAND (NORMAN J.) Family limitation and the English demographic revolution: a simulation approach. Coventry, 1974. pp. 42. *(University of Warwick. Department of Economics. Warwick Economic Research Papers. No.43)*

— Race question.

COMMUNITY RELATIONS COMMISSION. Towards a multi-racial society; [by Philip Mason and others]. London, [1967] repr. 1970. pp. 35.

COMMUNITY RELATIONS COMMISSION. Facts and figures about Commonwealth immigrants; compiled by Abdul Matin. [London, 1968 repr. 1971]. pp. 20.

ARROWSMITH (PAT) The colour of six schools. London, 1972. pp. 132. *Not available for consultation.*

BLACK UNITY AND FREEDOM PARTY. Issues. No. 1. Who killed Aseta Simms?: she was murdered. London, 1972. pp. 12.

PULLÉ (STANISLAUS) Police immigrant relations in Ealing: report of an investigation conducted on behalf of the Ealing C[ommunity] R[elations] C[ouncil]. London, [1973]. pp. 88.

TOWNSEND (HERBERT ELLWOOD ROUTLEDGE) and BRITTAN (E.M.) Multiracial education: need and innovation; the preliminary report of the Schools Council Education for a Multiracial Society Project. London, 1973. pp. 104. *(U.K. Department of Education and Science. Schools Council. Working Papers. 50)*

YOUNG SOCIALISTS. Racialism: a threat to all workers. London, [1973]. pp. 7.

DOWNING (JOHN DEREK HALL) Some aspects of the presentation of industrial relations and race relations in some major British news media; [Ph. D. (London) thesis]. [1974]. fo. 287. *Typescript: unpublished. This thesis is the property of London University and may not be removed from the Library.*

HARTMANN (PAUL G.) and HUSBAND (CHARLES H.) Racism and the mass media: a study of the role of the mass media in the formation of white beliefs and attitudes in Britain. London, 1974. pp. 279.

PAREKH (BHIKHUBHAI CHHOTALAL) ed. Colour, culture and consciousness: immigrant intellectuals in Britain; edited [on behalf of the Acton Society Trust]. London, 1974. pp. 249.

RUNNYMEDE TRUST. Immigration, race and settlement: a reference guide. London pp. 32.

SIVANANDAN (A.) Race and resistance: the IRR story. London, 1974. pp. 36.

SLATTER (STUART ST. P.) and others. The employment of non-English speaking workers: what industry must do. [London], Community Relations Commission, 1974. pp. 32.

TAYLOR (FRANCINE) Race, school and community: (a survey of research and literature on education in multi-racial Britain). Windsor, 1974. pp. 200. *bibliog*.

— — Bibliography.

COMMUNITY RELATIONS COMMISSION. Race relations in Britain: a select bibliography with emphasis on Commonwealth immigrants. 3rd ed. [London], 1973. pp. 23.

— Race question — Research grants.

The COMMONWEALTH Foundation Race Relations Bursary Scheme; report of a conference of bursars held in London under the auspices of the Community Relations Commission on 27 September 1972. [London, 1973]. pp. 15. *(Commonwealth Foundation. Occasional Papers. No.16)*

— Relations (general) with Eastern Europe.

SPEAIGHT (RICHARD) Cultural interchange with East Europe. Brighton, [1971]. pp. 105. *(Brighton. University of Sussex. Centre for Contemporary European Studies. Research Papers. No. 2)*

— Relations (general) with India.

MUDFORD (PETER) Birds of a different plumage: a study of British-Indian relations from Akbar to Curzon. London, 1974. pp. 314. *bibliog*.

— Relations (general) with Italy.

INGHILTERRA e Italia nel '900: atti del convegno di Bagni di Lucca, ottobre 1972. Firenze, 1973. pp. 317.

— Relations (military) with Oman.

GULF COMMITTEE. Dhofar: Britain's colonial war in the Gulf; a collection of documents and articles. London, 1972. pp. 72.

— Rural conditions.

WINTER (GORDON) A country camera, 1844-1914: rural life as depicted in photographs from the early days of photography to the outbreak of the First World War; [reprint of work first published in London, 1966]. Harmondsworth, 1973. pp. 120.

COUNCIL FOR SMALL INDUSTRIES IN RURAL AREAS. Report. bien., Ap 1970/Mr 1972 [2nd]- London.

CLOUT (HUGH D.) Rural geography: an introductory survey. Oxford, 1972. pp. 204. *bibliogs*.

KITTERINGHAM (JENNIE) Country girls in 19th century England. Oxford, [1973]. pp. 75. *(History Workshop. Pamphlets. No. 11)*

RURAL resource development; [by] M.C. Whitby [and others]. London, 1974. pp. 244. *bibliog*.

DUNBABIN (J.P.D.) Rural discontent in nineteenth-century Britain. London, 1974. pp. 320.

— Social conditions.

COLE (GEORGE DOUGLAS HOWARD) The crooked world. London, 1933. pp. 135.

BLONDEL (JEAN) 1929- . Voters, parties, and leaders: the social fabric of British politics. rev. ed. Harmondsworth, 1969 repr. 1972. pp. 272. *bibliog*.

U.K. Central Office of Information. Reference Division. 1971. Britain in brief. 13th ed. London, 1971. pp. 62.

JOHNS (EDWARD ALISTAIR) The social structure of modern Britain. 2nd ed. Oxford, 1972. pp. 203. *bibliog*.

U.K. Central Office of Information. Reference Division. 1972. Britain in brief. 14th ed. London, 1972. pp. 63.

FIELD (FRANK) 1942- . Unequal Britain: a report on the cycle of inequality. London, 1974. pp. 64. *bibliog*.

STANWORTH (PHILIP) and GIDDENS (ANTHONY) eds. Elites and power in British society. London, 1974. pp. 261.

SOCIOLOGICAL theory and survey research: institutional change and social policy in Great Britain: [papers of a seminar held in London 1972-73, sponsored by the Survey Unit of the Social Science Research Council]; edited by Timothy Leggatt. London, [1974]. pp. 334. *bibliogs*.

— — Bibliography.

WESTERGAARD (JOHN HARALD) and others, compilers. Modern British society: a bibliography. London, 1974. pp. 131.

— — Statistics.

LOCAL TEST BEDS CONFERENCE, LONDON, 1972. Report. [London, Central Statistical Office, 1972?]. 1 pamphlet (various pagings).

U.K. Social Survey. [Reports. New Series.] 457. The general household survey: introductory report; an inter-departmental survey sponsored by the Central Statistical Office; [by Louis Moss and others]. London, 1973. pp. 371,191.

— Social history.

ARKELL (V.T.J.) Britain transformed: the development of British society since the mid-eighteenth century. Harmondsworth, 1973. pp. 336. *bibliog*.

PLUMB (JOHN HAROLD) The commercialisation of leisure in eighteenth-century England. Reading, 1973. pp. 20. *(Reading. University. Stenton Lectures. 1972)*

BARNIE (JOHN) War in medieval society: social values and the Hundred Years War, 1337-99. London, [1974]. pp. 204. *bibliog*.

DUNBABIN (J.P.D.) Rural discontent in nineteenth-century Britain. London, 1974. pp. 320.

FLINN (MICHAEL W.) and SMOUT (T. CHRISTOPHER) eds. Essays in social history; edited for the Economic History Society. Oxford, 1974. pp. 289. *bibliogs*.

McKENDRICK (NEIL) ed. Historical perspectives: studies in English thought and society in honour of J.H. Plumb. London, [1974]. pp. 319. *bibliog*.

ROGERS (PAT) The Augustan vision. London, [1974]. pp. 318. *bibliog*.

— — Bibliography.

WESTERGAARD (JOHN HARALD) and others, compilers. Modern British society: a bibliography. London, 1974. pp. 131.

— — Sources.

WINTER (GORDON) A country camera, 1844-1914: rural life as depicted in photographs from the early days of photography to the outbreak of the First World War; [reprint of work first published in London, 1966]. Harmondsworth, 1973. pp. 120.

RAZZELL (P.E.) and WAINWRIGHT (R.W.) eds. The Victorian working class: selections from letters to the Morning Chronicle (1849-1851). London, 1973. pp. 338.

BURNETT (JOHN) Ph.D., ed. Useful toil: autobiographies of working people from the 1820s to the 1920s. London, 1974. pp. 364.

PIKE (EDGAR ROYSTON) ed. Human documents of Adam Smith's time. London, 1974. pp. 253.

— Social policy.

COOPER (MICHAEL H.) ed. Social policy: a survey of recent developments. Oxford, [1973]. pp. 278. *bibliogs*.

GLENNERSTER (HOWARD) and HATCH (STEPHEN) eds. Positive discrimination and inequality;... [by] Jack Barnes [and others]. London, 1974. pp. 40. *(Fabian Society. Research Series. [No]. 314)*

HECLO (HUGH) Modern social politics in Britain and Sweden: from relief to income maintenance. New Haven, 1974. pp. 349. *bibliog*. *(Yale University. Yale Studies in Political Science. 25)*

JORDAN (WILLIAM) Poor parents: social policy and the 'cycle of deprivation'. London, 1974. pp. 200.

KLEIN (RUDOLF EWALD) and others. Social policy and public expenditure, 1974: an interpretative essay. London, 1974. pp. 94. *bibliog*.

— Statistics.

SILLITOE (ALAN F.) Britain in figures: a handbook of social statistics. 2nd ed. Harmondsworth, 1973. pp. 187. *bibliog*.

EDWARDS (BERNARD) Sources of social statistics. London, 1974. pp. 276. *bibliogs*.

UNITED KINGDOM. (Cont.)

— — Bibliography.

CHADWYCK-HEALEY LIMITED and SOMERSET HOUSE INC. A bibliographical guide to major British government publications containing statistics 1801-1965 now republished on microfilm by Chadwyck-Healey/Somerset House. Bishops Stortford, 1974. pp. 45.

— British Empire.

U.K. Central Office of Information. Reference Division. 1969. Britain's associated states and dependencies. London, 1969. pp. 46.

GANGAL (S.C.) India and the Commonwealth. Agra, 1970. pp. 152. *bibliog.*

U.K. Central Office of Information. Reference Division. 1970. The Commonwealth in brief. 5th ed. London, 1970. pp. 45.

U.K. Central Office of Information. Reference Division. 1973. Britain and the Commonwealth. London, 1973. pp. 42.

— — Economic conditions.

U.K. British Information Services (New York). Reference Division. 1951. The British colonial territories in 1950: a regional review of progress. New York, 1951. pp. 82.

— — Economic policy.

COMMONWEALTH DEVELOPMENT CORPORATION. Annual report and statement of accounts. a., 1972- London. *Formerly included in the file of British Parliamentary Papers.*

DRUMMOND (IAN MACDONALD) Imperial economic policy, 1917-1939: studies in expansion and protection. London, 1974. pp. 496.

— — History.

HALPERIN (VLADIMIR) Lord Milner and the Empire: the evolution of British imperialism. London, 1952. pp. 256. *bibliog.*

BOWLE (JOHN) The imperial achievement: the rise and transformation of the British Empire. London, 1974. pp. 484.

WOODCOCK (GEORGE) 1912- . Who killed the British empire?: an inquest. London, 1974. pp. 356. *bibliog.*

— — Politics and government.

U.K. British Information Services (New York). Reference Division. 1951. The British colonial territories in 1950: a regional review of progress. New York, 1951. pp. 82.

JOSEY (ALEX) Lee Kuan Yew and the Commonwealth. Singapore, 1969. pp. 112.

MILLER (JOHN DONALD BRUCE) Survey of Commonwealth affairs: problems of expansion and attrition, 1953-1969. London, 1974. pp. 550. *bibliog.*

— — Social conditions.

U.K. British Information Services (New York). Reference Division. 1951. The British colonial territories in 1950: a regional review of progress. New York, 1951. pp. 82.

— — Societies, etc.

U.K. Department of Education and Science. 1973. Sources of information on international and Commonwealth organisations. [London, 1973]. pp. 45.

UNITED NATIONAL INDEPENDENCE PARTY [ZAMBIA]

— Congresses.

UNITED NATIONAL INDEPENDENCE PARTY [ZAMBIA]. Proceedings of the annual general conference... held at Mulungushi, 14th-20th August, 1967. Lusaka, Zambia Information Services, 1967. pp. 56.

UNITED NATIONS.

FRANCE. Direction de la Documentation. La Documentation Française. Notes et Etudes Documentaires. No. 3,734. L'O.N.U. et la décolonisation; [by] Patrick Daillier. Paris, 1970. pp. 48.

RUSSELL (RUTH B.) and CLAUSEN (PETER) The General Assembly: patterns, problems, prospects. New York, 1970. pp. 77.

SAYEGH (FAYEZ A.) and SOUKKARY (SOHAIR A.) Palestine: concordance of United Nations resolutions 1967-1971. New York, 1971. pp. 93.

COMMISSION TO STUDY THE ORGANIZATION OF PEACE. Building peace: reports of the Commission... 1939-1972. Metuchen, N.J., 1973: 2 vols.

HISCOCKS (RICHARD) The Security Council: a study in adolescence. London, 1973. pp. 371. *bibliog.*

HUMANITARIAN intervention and the United Nations: [proceedings of a conference held in Charlottesville, Va. in 1972]; edited by Richard B.Lillich. Charlottesville, Va., 1973. pp. 240. *bibliog. (Virginia University. School of Law. Virginia Legal Studies)*

MISRA (KASHI PRASAD) The role of the United Nations in the Indo-Pakistani conflict, 1971. Delhi, [1973]. pp. 197.

MUSALLAM (SAMI) ed. United Nations resolutions on Palestine, 1947-1972. Beirut, 1973. pp. 225. *(Institute for Palestine Studies. Basic Documentary Series. No. 10)*

GOODRICH (LELAND MATTHEW) The United Nations in a changing world. New York, 1974. pp. 280.

JESSUP (PHILIP CARYL) The birth of nations; [incorporating and amplifying the Barnette Miller Lectures, Wellesley College, 1971]. New York, 1974. pp. 361.

— Armed forces.

WAINHOUSE (DAVID WALTER) and others. International peacekeeping at the crossroads: national support; experience and prospects. Baltimore, [1973]. pp. 634.

EHRLICH (THOMAS) Cyprus, 1958-1967. London, 1974. pp. 164. *(American Society of International Law. International Crises and the Role of Law)*

— Bibliography.

WINTON (HARRY NATHANIEL McQUILLIAN) compiler. Publications of the United Nations system: a reference guide. New York, 1972. pp. 202.

— Economic assistance.

KOHT-NORBYE (OLE DAVID) Foran FN's annet utviklingstiår. [Oslo?], Direktoratet for Utviklingshjelp, 1970. pp. 90.

KOHT-NORBYE (OLE DAVID) Foran FN's annet utviklingstiår. [Oslo?], Direktoratet for Utriklingshjelp, 1970. pp. 90.

— Sanctions.

COMBACAU (JEAN) Le pouvoir de sanction de l'O.N.U.: étude th'eorique de la coercition non militaire. Paris, 1974. pp. 394. *bibliog. (Revue Générale de Droit International Public. Publications. Nouvelle Série. No. 23)*

— Technical assistance.

KOHT-NORBYE (OLE DAVID) Foran FN's annet utviklingstiår. [Oslo?], Direktoratet for Utviklingshjelp, 1970. pp. 90.

— France.

FRANCE. Direction de la Documentation. La Documentation Française. Notes et Etudes Documentaires. No. 3,728. La France et l'O.N.U.; [by] Aleth Manin. Paris, 1970. pp. 32.

WOOD (ROBERT S.) France in the world community: decolonization, peacekeeping, and the United Nations. Leiden, 1973. pp. 226. *bibliog. (John F. Kennedy Institute. Center for International Studies. Publications. Nr.8)*

— Germany.

SCHEUNER (ULRICH) and LINDEMANN (BEATE) eds. Die Vereinten Nationen und die Mitarbeit der Bundesrepublik Deutschland. München, 1973. pp. 339. *(Deutsche Gesellschaft für Auswärtige Politik. Forschungsinstitut. Schriften. Band 32)*

— Mexico.

MEXICO. Secretaria de la Presidencia. 1972. Mexico en las Naciones Unidas: la visita del Presidente Echeverria. Mexico, 1971 [or rather 1972]. pp. 312. *(Cuadernos de Documentacion. Serie Estudios. 2)*

— Norway.

JENSEN (BJØRN) Norway in the United Nations. 3rd ed. Oslo, Royal Ministry of Foreign Affairs, 1971. pp. 35.

— Switzerland.

SWITZERLAND. Conseil Fédéral. 1969. Rapport...à l'Assemblée Fédérale sur les relations de la Suisse avec les Nations Unies, du 16 juin 1969. [Bern?], 1969. pp. 168.

SWITZERLAND. Conseil Fédéral. 1971. Rapport...à l'Assemblée Fédérale sur les relations de la Suisse avec l'Organisation des Nations Unies et ses institutions spécialisées de 1969 à 1971, du 17 novembre 1971. [Bern?], 1971. pp. 71.

UNITED NATIONS CONFERENCE ON TRADE AND DEVELOPMENT.

GHENT. Université. Fakulteit der Rechten. Seminarie voor Hedendaagse Politieke Vraagstukken. UNCTAD-Schriften. 1. UNCTAD; door Toon Colpaert [and others]. Gent, 1973. pp. 336.

UNITED NATIONS EDUCATIONAL, SCIENTIFIC AND CULTURAL ORGANIZATION

— Bibliography.

UNITED NATIONS EDUCATIONAL, SCIENTIFIC AND CULTURAL ORGANIZATION. 1973. Bibliography of publications issued by Unesco or under its auspices: the first twenty-five years, 1946 to 1971. Paris, 1973. pp. 385. *In English and French.*

UNITED NATIONS INDUSTRIAL DEVELOPMENT ORGANIZATION.

UNITED NATIONS INDUSTRIAL DEVELOPMENT ORGANIZATION. Annual report of the Executive Director. a., 1973- Vienna.

UNITED SOUTH AFRICAN NATIONAL PARTY.

UNITED SOUTH AFRICAN NATIONAL PARTY. Statement... as approved by Union Congress of 1957. [Johannesburg], 1957. fo. (18).

GRAAFF (Sir DE VILLIERS) Sir De Villiers Graaff's opening address, Cape Congress, Port Elizabeth, 17.10.1972. Johannesburg, 1972. pp. 29.

UNITED STATES.

CAMPBELL (THOMAS M.) Masquerade peace: America's UN policy, 1944-1945. Tallahassee, [1973]. pp. 226. *bibliog.*

HARGREAVES (ROBERT) Superpower: a portrait of America in the 1970's. New York, [1973]. pp. 628. *bibliog.*

— Appropriations and expenditures.

ADAMS (EARL W.) and SPIRO (MICHAEL H.) The timing of the impact of government expenditures. [Washington, D.C.], United States Arms Control and Disarmament Agency, 1970. fo. 54. *(Publications. 56) Photocopy.*

CAN Congress control spending?: [discussions by] William Proxmire [and others at a meeting sponsored by the American Enterprise Institute, March, 1973]. Washington, D.C., [1973]. pp. 62. *(American Enterprise Institute for Public Policy Research. Town Hall Meetings on Domestic Affairs)*

UNITED STATES.

TAX FOUNDATION. Research Publications. New Series. No. 28. The financial outlook for state and local government to 1980. New York, [1973]. pp. 116.

FEREJOHN (JOHN A.) Pork barrel politics: rivers and harbors legislation, 1947-1968. Stanford, 1974. pp. 288. *bibliog.*

— Armed forces.

AMBROSE (STEPHEN E.) and BARBER (JAMES ALDEN) eds. The military and American society: essays and readings. New York, 1973. pp. 322.

— — Reserves.

BINKIN (MARTIN) U.S. reserve forces: the problem of the weekend warrior. Washington, D.C., [1974]. pp. 63. *(Brookings Institution. Studies in Defense Policy)*

— Army.

BRADFORD (ZEB B.) and BROWN (FREDERIC JOSEPH) The United States army in transition: prepared by Inter- University Seminar on Armed Forces and Society. Beverly Hills, [1973]. pp. 256. *bibliog. (Inter-University Seminar on Armed Forces and Society. [Publications]. vol.4)*

HAUSER (WILLIAM L.) America's army in crisis: a study in civil-military relations. Baltimore, [1973]. pp. 242. *bibliog.*

— — History.

MULLEN (ROBERT W.) Blacks in America's wars: the shift in attitudes from the revolutionary war to Vietnam. New York, 1973. pp. 96. *bibliog.*

— Biography.

MINTON (BRUCE) and STUART (JOHN) 1912- . Men who lead labor. New York. [1937]. pp. 270. *bibliog.*

— Civilization.

DIVERGING parallels: a comparison of American and European thought and action; [papers of study conferences of the European Association for American Studies held in Rome in 1967 and in Brussels in 1970]; edited by A.N.J. den Hollander. Leiden. 1971. pp. 222.

FEINBERG (BARRY) and KASRILS (RONALD) Bertrand Russell's America: his transatlantic travels and writings;... a documented account. London, 1973 in progress. *bibliog.*

PELLS (RICHARD H.) Radical visions and American dreams: culture and social thought in the depression years. New York, [1973]. pp. 424. *bibliog.*

MULLER (HERBERT JOSEPH) Uses of the future. Bloomington, Ind., [1974]. pp. 264.

MUMFORD (LEWIS) Interpretations and forecasts, 1922-1972: studies in literature, history, biography, technics, and contemporary society. [London, 1974]. pp. 522. *First published in New York in 1973.*

PEIRCE (NEAL R.) The deep south states of America: people, politics and power in the seven deep south states. New York, [1974]. pp. 528. *bibliog.*

— Commerce.

NATIONAL FOREIGN TRADE CONVENTION. Declaration; [pd. by] National Foreign Trade Council. a., 1970(57th conv.)- New York.

KNIGHT (RICHARD VICTOR) Employment expansion and metropolitan trade. New York, 1973. pp. 108. *(Columbia University. Graduate School of Business. Conservation of Human Resources Project. Conservation of Human Resources Studies)*

RODGERS (JOHN M.) State estimates of interregional commodity trade, 1963. Lexington, Mass., [1973]. pp. 447. *bibliog.*

U.S. trade in the sixties and seventies: continuity and change; [based on a conference sponsored by the Institute for International Studies of the University of Notre Dame in April 1973]; edited by Kenneth Jameson [and] Roger Skurski. Lexington, Mass., [1974]. pp. 137.

— — China.

NEILAN (EDWARD) and SMITH (CHARLES R.) The future of the China market: prospects for Sino-American trade. Washington, 1974. pp. 94. *bibliog. (American Enterprise Institute for Public Policy Research and Stanford University. Hoover Institution on War, Revolution and Peace. AEI-Hoover Policy Studies. 11)*

WHITSON (WILLIAM W.) ed. Doing business with China: American trade opportunities in the 1970s. New York, 1974. pp. 587.

— Commercial policy.

U.S. trade policy and agricultural exports: [based on papers of a conference organized by the Iowa State University Center for Agricultural and Rural Development]. Ames, Iowa, 1973. pp. 228.

TERRILL (TOM E.) The tariff, politics and American foreign policy, 1874-1901. Westport, Conn., 1973. pp. 306. *bibliog.*

— Congress.

CAN Congress control spending?: [discussions by] William Proxmire [and others at a meeting sponsored by the American Enterprise Institute, March, 1973]. Washington, D.C., [1973]. pp. 62. *(American Enterprise Institute for Public Policy Research. Town Hall Meetings on Domestic Affairs)*

CHAMBERLIN (HOPE) A minority of members: women in the U.S. Congress. New York, 1973. pp. 374.

BARONE (MICHAEL) and others. The almanac of American politics: the senators, the representatives, their records, states and districts, 1974. 2nd ed. London, 1974. pp. 1240.

MAYHEW (DAVID R.) Congress: the electoral connection. New Haven, 1974. pp. 194.

— — Committees.

AMERICAN ACADEMY OF POLITICAL AND SOCIAL SCIENCE. Annals. vol. 411. Changing Congress: the committee system; special editor of this volume Norman J. Ornstein. Philadelphia, 1974. pp. 265.

— — — Bibliography.

BURT (RICHARD) compiler. Congressional hearings on American defense policy: 1947-1971: an annotated bibliography;...edited by Richard Burt and Geoffrey Kemp. Lawrence, Kansas, [1974]. pp. 377. *(New York (City). University. National Security Education Program, and National Strategy Information Center. National Security Studies Series)*

— — House of Representatives.

BELL (RUDOLPH M.) Party and faction in American politics: the House of Representatives, 1789-1801. Westport, Conn., 1973. pp. 311. *bibliog.*

BRADY (DAVID W.) Congressional voting in a partisan era: a study of the McKinley Houses and a comparison to the modern House of Representatives. Lawrence, Kansas, [1973]. pp. 273. *bibliog.*

— Constitution.

BARNETT (WALTER) Sexual freedom and the constitution: an inquiry into the constitutionality of repressive sex laws. Albuquerque, [1973]. pp. 333.

— Constitutional history.

KENT (DONALD H.) and RICHMAN (IRWIN) Pennsylvania and the federal constitution. Harrisburg, Pennsylvania Historical and Museum Commission, 1964. pp. 16. *bibliog.*

STITES (FRANCES N.) Private interest and public gain: the Dartmouth College case, 1819. Amherst, [1972]. pp. 176. *bibliog.*

MARKS (FREDERICK W.) Independence on trial: foreign affairs and the making of the constitution. Baton Rouge, La., [1973]. pp. 256. *bibliog.*

TUGWELL (REXFORD GUY) The emerging constitution. New York, [1974]. pp. 642.

— Defences.

HEAD (RICHARD G.) and ROKKE (ERVIN J.) eds. American defense policy. 3rd ed. Baltimore, 1973. pp. 696. *bibliogs.*

PALMER (JAMES GREGORY) American defense policy and the Vietnam war; [M.Phil. (London) thesis]. 1973. fo. 261. *bibliog. Typescript: unpublished. This thesis is the property of London University and may not be removed from the Library.*

SUTTON (ANTONY C.) National suicide: military aid to the Soviet Union. New Rochelle, N.Y., [1973]. pp. 283. *bibliog.*

PACEM IN TERRIS III, WASHINGTON, D.C., 1973. The military dimensions of foreign policy: volume 2 of...the proceedings of Pacem in Terris III; (edited by Fred Warner Neal and Mary Kersey Harvey). Santa Barbara, Calif., [1974]. pp. 129.

— — Bibliography.

BURT (RICHARD) compiler. Congressional hearings on American defense policy: 1947-1971: an annotated bibliography;...edited by Richard Burt and Geoffrey Kemp. Lawrence, Kansas, [1974]. pp. 377. *(New York (City). University. National Security Education Program, and National Strategy Information Center. National Security Studies Series)*

— Description and travel.

SARTRE (JEAN PAUL) Situations. [Paris, 1947, repr. 1973 in progress].

— Economic conditions.

UNITED STATES. Office of Regional Development Planning. 1967. Guide to economic projections and forecasts. [Washington, 1967 repr. 1968]. pp. 113. *bibliog.*

HOYT (HOMER) According to Hoyt: 53 years of Homer Hoyt: articles on law, real estate cycle, economic base, sector theory, shopping centers, urban growth, 1916-1969. [2nd ed.] [Washington, 1970?]. pp. 855. *bibliog.*

WANSEY (HENRY) Henry Wansey and his American journal, 1794; [reprint of Wansey's Journal based on the first two English editions of 1796 and 1798, with notes and introduction]; edited by David John Jeremy. Philadelphia, 1970. pp. 186. *bibliog. (American Philosophical Society. Memoirs. vol.82)*

ALBAUM (MELVIN) ed. Geography and contemporary issues: studies of relevant problems. New York, [1973]. pp. 590.

FORD (ARTHUR M.) Political economics of rural poverty in the South. Cambridge, Mass., [1973]. pp. 101. *bibliog.*

HANSEN (NILES M.) The future of nonmetropolitan America: studies in the reversal of rural and small town population decline. Lexington, mass [1973]. pp. 187.

LAPP (RALPH EUGENE) The logarithmic century. Englewood Cliffs, [1973]. pp. 263.

LEKACHMAN (ROBERT) Inflation: the permanent problem of boom and bust. New York, [1973]. pp. 121.

MORRISON (RODNEY J.) Expectations and inflation: Nixon, politics and economics. Lexington, 1973. pp. 167.

SCHACHTER (GUSTAV) and DALE (EDWIN L.) The economist looks at society. Lexington, Mass., [1973]. pp. 373. *bibliogs.*

SAMPLE (C. JAMES) Patterns of regional economic change: a quantitative analysis of U.S. regional growth and development. Cambridge, Mass., [1974]. pp. 296. *bibliog.*

— — Mathematical models.

McCALL (JOHN JOSEPH) Earnings mobility and economic growth...: a report prepared for Office of Economic Opportunity. Santa Monica, 1970. pp. 70. *bibliog. (Rand Corporation. [Rand Reports]. 576)*

UNITED STATES. (Cont.)

— Economic history.

FOGEL (ROBERT WILLIAM) Railroads and American economic growth: essays in econometric history. Baltimore, 1964 repr. 1970. pp. 296. *bibliog.*

DEBOUZY (MARIANNE) Le capitalisme "sauvage" aux États-Unis, 1860-1900. Paris, [1972]. pp. 238. *bibliog.*

ERNST (JOSEPH ALBERT) Money and politics in America, 1755-1775: a study in the Currency Act of 1764 and the political economy of revolution. Chapel Hill, N.C., [1973]. pp. 403. *bibliog.*

JOHNSON (EDGAR AUGUSTUS JEROME) The foundations of American economic freedom: government and enterprise in the age of Washington. Minneapolis, [1973]. pp. 335.

CROWLEY (J.E.) This Sheba, self: the conceptualization of economic life in eighteenth-century America. Baltimore, [1974]. pp. 161. *(Johns Hopkins University. Studies in Historical and Political Science. Series 92. No.2)*

DENISON (EDWARD FULTON) Accounting for United States economic growth, 1929-1969. Washington, D.C., [1974]. pp. 355.

ELDER (GLEN H.) Children of the great depression: social change in life experience. Chicago, 1974. pp. 400. *bibliog.*

GORDON (ROBERT AARON) Economic instability and growth: the American record. New York, [1974]. pp. 216.

KIRKENDALL (RICHARD STEWART) The United States 1929-1945: years of crisis and change. New York, [1974]. pp. 308. *bibliogs.*

KROOSS (HERMAN EDWARD) American economic development: the progress of a business civilization. 3rd ed. Englewood Cliffs, [1974]. pp. 564. *bibliogs.*

POTTER (JIM) The American economy between the world wars. London, 1974. pp. 184. *bibliog.*

— Economic policy.

MONETARY CONFERENCE, 1ST, NANTUCKET ISLAND, 1969. Controlling monetary aggregates: proceedings of the...conference...sponsored by the Federal Reserve Bank of Boston. [Boston, 1969]. pp. 174.

OZARKS REGIONAL COMMISSION. Economic development action plan. [Washington, 1972]. pp. 244. *bibliog.*

FOUR CORNERS REGIONAL COMMISSION. Development plan; (with Executive summary and Agricultural addendum). Washington, 1972-73. 3 pts. (in 1 vol). *bibliogs.*

CARSON (ROBERT B.) and others, eds. Government in the American economy: conventional and radical studies on the growth of state economic power. Lexington, Mass., [1973]. pp. 506. *bibliog.*

CUMBERLAND (JOHN HAMMETT) Regional development: experiences and prospects in the United States of America. 2nd ed. Paris, 1973. pp. 170. *bibliog. (United Nations Research Institute for Social Development. Regional Planning. vol. 2)*

MARTIN (ANDREW) The politics of economic policy in the United States: a tentative view from a comparative perspective. Beverly Hills, [1973]. pp. 61. *bibliog.*

MORRISON (RODNEY J.) Expectations and inflation: Nixon, politics and economics. Lexington, 1973. pp. 167.

A NEW look at inflation: economic policy in the early 1970s; [by] Phillip Cagan [and others]. Washington, D.C., [1973]. pp. 172. *(American Enterprise Institute for Public Policy Research. Domestic Affairs Studies. 17)*

GROWTH policy: population, environment and beyond; [by] Kan Chen [and others]. Ann Arbor, [1974]. pp. 237. *bibliog.*

TOBIN (JAMES) The new economics : one decade older. Princeton, N.J., [1974]. pp. 15. *(Princeton University. Woodrow Wilson School of Public and International Affairs. Eliot Janeway Lectures on Historical Economics. 1972)*

WATT (KENNETH E.F.) The Titanic effect: planning for the unthinkable. Stamford, Conn., [1974]. pp. 268.

— Emigration and immigration.

FITZPATRICK (JOSEPH PARNELL) Puerto Rican Americans: the meaning of migration to the mainland. New Jersey, [1971]. pp. 192.

BERNARD (WILLIAM S.) ed. Immigrants and ethnicity: ten years of changing thought; an analysis based on the special [Integration] Seminars of the American Immigration and Citizenship Conference, 1960-1970. New York, [1972]. pp. 73.

LAVOIE (YOLANDE) L'émigration des Canadiens aux États-Unis avant 1930: mesure de phénomène. Montréal, 1972. pp. 89. *bibliog.*

DAVIS (LAWRENCE B.) Immigrants, Baptists and the protestant mind in America. Urbana, [1973]. pp. 230. *bibliog.*

ROSENBLUM (GERALD W.) Immigrant workers: their impact on American labor radicalism. New York, [1973]. pp. 189.

DUCHAC (RENE) La sociologie des migrations aux États-Unis. Paris. [1974]. pp. 566. *bibliog. (Paris. Ecole Pratique des Hautes Etudes. Section des Sciences Economiques et Sociales. Société, Mouvements Sociaux et Idéologies. 1e série. Etudes. 15)*

MILLER (SALLY M.) The radical immigrant. New York, [1974]. pp. 212. *bibliog.*

— Executive departments.

BERKMAN (RICHARD LYLE) and VISCUSI (W. KIP) Damming the West: (Ralph Nader's study group report on the Bureau of Reclamation). New York, 1973. pp. 272.

GROSSMAN (JONATHAN PHILIP) The Department of Labor. New York, 1973. pp. 309. *bibliog.*

MILES (RUFUS E.) The Department of Health, Education and Welfare. New York, 1974. pp. 326. *bibliog.*

— Foreign economic relations.

JAVITS (BENJAMIN A.) Peace by investment. New York, [1950]. pp. 242.

KUJAWA (DUANE) ed. American labor and the multinational corporation. New York, 1973. pp. 285. *bibliog.*

OVERSEAS DEVELOPMENT COUNCIL. The United States and the developing world: agenda for action, 1973; Robert E. Hunter, project director. Washington, 1973. pp. 162.

TERRILL (TOM E.) The tariff, politics and American foreign policy, 1874-1901. Westport, Conn., 1973. pp. 306. *bibliog.*

WEISSKOPF (THOMAS E.) Sources of American imperialism: a contribution to the debate between orthodox and radical theorists. Ann Arbor, 1973. pp. 46. *bibliog. (Michigan University. Center for Research on Economic Development. Discussion Papers. No. 32)*

ARON (RAYMOND) The imperial republic: the United States and the world, 1945- 1973;...translated by Frank Jellinek. Englewood Cliffs, [1974]. pp. 339.

HANDLIN (OSCAR) One world: the origins of an American concept; an inaugural lecture delivered before the University of Oxford on 23 February 1973. Oxford, 1974. pp. 21.

HOWE (JAMES W.) and others. The U.S. and the developing world: agenda for action 1974; [by] James W. Howe and the staff of the Overseas Development Council. New York, 1974. pp. 211.

KUENTZEL (ULRICH) Der nordamerikanische Imperialismus: zur Geschichte der US- Kapitalausfuhr. Darmstadt, 1974. pp. 253. *bibliog.*

NATIONAL PLANNING ASSOCIATION. Reports. No.135. Economic blocs and U.S. foreign policy; by Ernest H. Preeg. Washington, 1974. pp. 198.

— — America, Latin.

IANNI (OCTAVIO) Imperialismo y cultura de la violencia en America Latina; traduccion de Claudio Colombiani y Jose Thiago Cintra. Mexico, 1970. pp. 126.

CONFERENCE ON TRADE POLICIES IN THE AMERICAS, SOUTHERN METHODIST UNIVERSITY, 1972. Trade and investment policies in the Americas; edited by Stephen E. Guisinger. Dallas, [1973]. pp. 101.

— — Canada.

MURPHY (RAE) and STAROWICZ (MARK) eds. Corporate Canada: 14 probes into the workings of a branch-plant economy; a Last Post special; [selected articles]. Toronto, 1972. pp. 156.

PENTLAND (CHARLES CORRIE) The Canadian dilemma. Farnborough, Hants, [1973]. pp. 56. *(Atlantic Institute. Atlantic Papers. 1973.2)*

— — Caribbean Area.

IMPERIALISMO y clases sociales en el Caribe; ([by Mercedes Acosta [and others]). Buenos Aires, [1973]. pp. 235.

— — Europe.

HIERONYMI (OTTO) Economic discrimination against the United States in Western Europe, 1945-1958: dollar shortage and the rise of regionalism. Genève, 1973. pp. 232. *bibliog.*

SCIENCE policy and business: the changing relation of Europe and the United States:...David W. Ewing, editor. Boston, 1973. pp. 110. *(Harvard University. Graduate School of Business Administration. John Diebold Lectures. 1971)*

— — Japan.

UNITED STATES-JAPAN ECONOMIC CONFERENCE, WASHINGTON, D.C., 1973. Perspectives on U.S.-Japan economic relations; [proceedings of the conference sponsored by] United States-Japan Trade Council; edited by Allen Taylor. Cambridge, Mass., [1973]. pp. 274.

— — Philippine Islands.

LICHAUCO (ALEJANDRO) The Lichauco paper: imperialism in the Philippines. New York, 1973. pp. 111.

— — Russia.

SOREVNOVANIE dvukh sistem: ekonomika i trudiashchiesia. Moskva, 1973. pp. 400. *With brief English summaries and table of contents.*

— — United Kingdom.

CRAPOL (EDWARD P.) America for Americans: economic nationalism and anglophobia in the late nineteenth century. Westport, Conn., 1973. pp. 248. *bibliog.*

— Foreign population.

ABRAMSON (HAROLD J.) Ethnic diversity in Catholic America. New York, [1973]. pp. 207. *bibliog.*

— Foreign relations.

ERSHKOWITZ (HERBERT) The attitude of business toward American foreign policy, 1900-1916. University Park, Penn., [1967]. pp. 77. *bibliog. (Pennsylvania State University. Penn State Studies. No. 21)*

KIM (IL-SUNG) Let us intensify the anti-imperialist, anti-U.S. struggle. Pyongyang, 1968. pp. 10. *(Reprinted from Tricontinental, August 12, 1967)*

YOUNG (RAYMOND ARTHUR) La influencia de Godoy en el desarrollo de los Estados Unidos de America, a costa de Nueva España. Mexico, 1968. pp. 146.

IONS (EDMUND SIMON AUBREY) Dissent in America: the constraints on foreign policy. London, 1971. pp. 14. *(Institute for the Study of Conflict. Conflict Studies. No. 18)*

UNITED STATES. (Cont.)

HALL (GUS) Imperialism today: an evaluation of major issues and events of our time. New York, 1972. pp. 382.

HANSEN (JOSEPH) Marxist, and LUND (CAROLINE) Nixon's Moscow and Peking summits: their meaning for Vietnam. New York, [1972]. pp. 31.

LAQUEUR (WALTER ZE'EV) Neo-isolationism and the world of the seventies. New York, 1972. pp. 50. *(Georgetown University. Center for Strategic and International Studies. Washington Papers. vol. [1]/5)*

TATU (MICHEL) Le triangle Washington-Moscou-Pékin et les deux Europe(s). [Paris, 1972]. pp. 149.

AMERICAN ASSOCIATION FOR THE UNITED NATIONS and CARNEGIE ENDOWMENT FOR INTERNATIONAL PEACE. National Policy Panel. Foreign policy decision making: the new dimensions: a report. [New York, 1973]. pp. 103.

GARDNER (LLOYD C.) and others. Creation of the American empire: U.S. diplomatic history. Chicago, [1973]. pp. 540. *bibliogs*.

GARDNER (LLOYD C.) ed. The great Nixon turn-around: America's new foreign policy in the post-liberal era...; essays and articles. New York, 1973. pp. 350.

GRIFFITH (WILLIAM E.) Peking, Moscow, and beyond: the Sino-Soviet-American triangle. Washington, D.C., 1973. pp. 71. *(Georgetown University. Center for Strategic and International Studies. Washington Papers. vol.[1]/6)*

HERO (ALFRED OLIVIER) American religious groups view foreign policy: trends in rank-and-file opinion, 1937-1969. Durham, N.C., 1973. pp. 552.

IVANOVA (INESSA MIKHAILOVNA) Kontseptsiia "atlanticheskogo soobshchestva" vo vneshnei politike SShA. Moskva, 1973. pp. 279.

JONES (ALAN M.) ed. U.S. foreign policy in a changing world: the Nixon administration, 1969-1973. New York, [1973]. pp. 379.

MARKS (FREDERICK W.) Independence on trial: foreign affairs and the making of the constitution. Baton Rouge, La., [1973]. pp. 256. *bibliog*.

MAY (ERNEST RICHARD) "Lessons" of the past: the use and misuse of history in American foreign policy. New York, 1973. pp. 220. *bibliog*.

NATIONAL strategy in a decade of change: an emerging U.S. policy; (a report on a symposium sponsored by the Stanford Research Institute and the Foreign Policy Research Institute, Warrenton, Va., February 1973); edited by William R. Kintner and Richard B. Foster. Lexington, Mass., [1973]. pp. 298.

OVERSEAS DEVELOPMENT COUNCIL. The United States and the developing world: agenda for action, 1973; Robert E. Hunter, project director. Washington, 1973. pp. 162.

PALMER (JAMES GREGORY) American defense policy and the Vietnam war; [M.Phil. (London) thesis]. 1973. fo. 261. *bibliog*. Typescript: unpublished. This thesis is the property of London University and may not be removed from the Library.

PAOLINO (ERNEST N.) The foundations of the American empire: William Henry Seward and the U.S. foreign policy. Ithaca, 1973. pp. 235. *bibliog*.

SIRACUSA (JOSEPH M.) New Left diplomatic histories and historians: the American revisionists. Port Washington, N.Y., 1973. pp. 138. *bibliog*.

SOLBERG (CARL) Riding high: America in the cold war. New York, [1973]. pp. 632. *bibliog*.

SPANIER (JOHN WINSTON) American foreign policy since World War II. 6th ed. New York, 1973. pp. 305. *bibliog*.

THOMAS (JAMES A.) Holy war: the lure of victory and the passing of America as a world power. New Rochelle, [1973]. pp. 272.

WOLPIN (MILES D.) Military indoctrination and United States imperialism. New York, [1973]. pp. 56. *bibliog*. *(American Institute for Marxist Studies. Occasional Papers. No. 13)*

ARON (RAYMOND) The imperial republic: the United States and the world, 1945- 1973;...translated by Frank Jellinek. Englewood Cliffs, [1974]. pp. 339.

BLOOMFIELD (LINCOLN PALMER) In search of American foreign policy: the humane use of power. New York, 1974. pp. 182.

BROWN (SEYOM) New forces in world politics. Washington, D.C., [1974]. pp. 224.

CATLIN (Sir GEORGE EDWARD GORDON) Kissinger's Atlantic charter. Gerrards Cross, 1974. pp. 144.

DEVLIN (PATRICK ARTHUR) Baron Devlin. Too proud to fight: Woodrow Wilson's neutrality. London, 1974. pp. 731. *bibliog*.

ESSAYS on American foreign policy; by David C. DeBoe [and others]; edited by Margaret F. Morris and Sandra L.Myres. Austin, [1974]. pp. 146. *bibliogs*. *(Texas University. Walter Prescott Webb Memorial Lectures. 8)*

HALPERIN (MORTON H.) Bureaucratic politics and foreign policy. Washington, D.C., [1974]. pp. 340. *bibliog*.

KIRKENDALL (RICHARD STEWART) The United States 1929-1945: years of crisis and change. New York, [1974]. pp. 308. *bibliogs*.

KLEBANOFF (SHOSHANA) Middle east oil and U.S. foreign policy, with special reference to the U.S. energy crisis. New York, 1974. pp. 288. *bibliog*.

LAMONT (CORLISS) Voice in the wilderness: collected essays of fifty years. Buffalo, N.Y., [1974]. pp. 327.

LAUTERBACH (ALBERT T.) Psychological challenges to modernization. Amsterdam, 1974. pp. 190.

NATIONAL PLANNING ASSOCIATION. Reports. No.135. Economic blocs and U.S. foreign policy; by Ernest H. Preeg. Washington, 1974. pp. 198.

PACEM IN TERRIS III, WASHINGTON, D.C., 1973. American foreign policy in the age of interdependence: volume 3 of...the proceedings of Pacem in Terris III; (edited by Fred Warner Neal and Mary Kersey Harvey). Santa Barbara, Calif., [1974]. pp. 233.

PACEM IN TERRIS III, WASHINGTON, D.C., 1973. The requirements of democratic foreign policy: ...volume 4 of... the proceedings of Pacem in Terris III; (edited by Fred Warner Neal and Mary Kersey Harvey). Santa Barbara, Calif., [1974]. pp. 125.

PACEM IN TERRIS III, WASHINGTON, D.C., 1973. The Nixon-Kissinger foreign policy: opportunities and contradictions: volume 1 of...the proceedings of Pacem in Terris III; (edited by Fred Warner Neal and Mary Kersey Harvey). Santa Barbara, Calif., [1974]. pp. 167.

POSSONY (STEFAN THOMAS) Waking up the giant: the strategy for American victory and world freedom. New Rochelle, [1974]. pp. 775.

See also EUROPEAN ECONOMIC COMMUNITY — United States.

— — **America, Latin.**

GUILLEN (ABRAHAM) Desafio al Pentagono: la guerrilla latinoamericana. Montevideo, [1969]. pp. 183.

SCHILLING (PAULO R.) El imperio Rockefeller: America Latina documentos; [and] La estrategia norteamericana en America Latina: de la doctrina Monroe al informe Rockefeller; ensayo; [translated from the English by Rosario Lorente]. Montevideo, [1970]. pp. 129.

— — **Asia.**

KIM (IL-SUNG) Let us completely frustrate U.S. imperialist aggression and intervention in Asia: speech... welcoming Samdech Norodom Sihanouk, head of state of Cambodia... April 16, 1973. Pyongyang, 1973. pp. 20.

WILCOX (WAYNE AYRES) The emergence of Bangladesh: problems and opportunities for a redefined American policy in South Asia. Washington, 1973. pp. 79. *(American Enterprise Institute for Public Policy Research. Foreign Affairs Studies. 7)*

— — **Asia, Southeast.**

INDOCHINA handbook 1972: an 'Indochina' special. London, [1972?]. pp. 48. *Articles on the Vietnam conflict previously appearing in the magazine Indo-China.*

— — **Brazil.**

McCANN (FRANK D.) The Brazilian-American alliance, 1937-1945. Princeton, [1973]. pp. 527. *bibliog*.

— — **Canada.**

STANKIEWICZ (WLADYSLAW JOZEF) Canada-U.S. relations and Canadian foreign policy. West Chesterfield, 1973. pp. 47.

LOGAN (R.M.) Canada, the United States and the third Law of the Sea Conference. [Montreal, 1974]. pp. 117. *bibliog*.

— — **Chile.**

URIBE (ARMANDO) Le livre noir de l'intervention américaine au Chili. Paris, [1974]. pp. 224.

— — **China.**

HUNT (MICHAEL H.) Frontier defense and the open door: Manchuria in Chinese-American relations, 1895-1911. New Haven, 1973. pp. 281. *bibliog*.

SERGEICHUK (S.) SShA i Kitai. 2nd ed. Moskva, 1973. pp. 238. *1st ed. has subtitle: politika SShA v otnoshenii Kitaia, 1948-1968.*

THORNTON (RICHARD C.) China, the struggle for power 1917-1972. Bloomington, [1973]. pp. 403.

HSIAO (GENE T.) ed. Sino-American détente and its policy implications. New York, 1974. pp. 319.

— — **Cuba.**

GELLMAN (IRWIN F.) Roosevelt and Batista: good neighbor diplomacy in Cuba, 1933- 1945. Albuquerque, [1973]. pp. 303. *bibliog*.

— — **East (Near East).**

The MIDDLE East: quest for an American policy; [papers of a conference held in 1970 at the 47th session of the Institute of World Affairs, sponsored by the University of Southern California]; edited by Willard A. Beling. Albany, N.Y., 1973. pp. 347.

— — **Europe.**

GASTEYGER (CURT) Europe and America at the crossroads. Paris, [1972]. pp. 50. *(Atlantic Institute. Atlantic Papers. 1971.4)*

BUCHAN (ALASTAIR) Europe and America: from alliance to coalition. Farnborough, Hants, [1973]. pp. 48. *(Atlantic Institute. Atlantic Papers. 1973.4)*

TUTHILL (JOHN W.) The decisive years ahead. Farnborough, Hants, [1973]. pp. 77. *(Atlantic Institute. Atlantic Papers. 1972.4)*

— — **India.**

AZIZ (QUTUBUDDIN) Mission to Washington: an expose of India's intrigues in the United States of America in 1971 to dismember Pakistan. Karachi, 1973. pp. 234.

VENKATARAMANI (M.S.) Bengal famine of 1943: the American response. Delhi, [1973]. pp. 137.

— — **Iran.**

SHEEHAN (MICHAEL KAHL) Iran: the impact of United States interests and policies, 1941-1954. Brooklyn, N.Y., 1968. pp. 88. *bibliog*.

UNITED STATES. (Cont.)

— — Israel.

SNETSINGER (JOHN) Truman, the Jewish vote, and the creation of Israel. Stanford, [1974]. pp. 208. bibliog. (Stanford University. Hoover Institution on War, Revolution and Peace. Hoover Institution Studies. 39)

— — Japan.

DISCORD in the Pacific: challenges to the Japanese-American alliance: [advance reading for the third Japanese- American Assembly, Shimoda, 1972]; edited by Henry Rosovsky. Washington, D.C., 1972. pp. 246.

HERZOG (JAMES H.) Closing the open door: American-Japanese diplomatic negotiations, 1936-1941. Annapolis, Md., [1973]. pp. 295. bibliog.

PEARL Harbor as history: Japanese-American relations, 1931- 1941; (essays... presented at a binational conference held at Lake Kawaguchi, Japan... 1969); edited by Dorothy Borg and Shumpei Okamoto. New York, 1973. pp. 801. (Columbia University. East Asian Institute. Studies)

— — Mexico.

SCHMITT (KARL MICHAEL) Mexico and the United States, 1821-1973: conflict and coexistence. New York, [1974]. pp. 288. bibliog.

— — New Zealand.

LISSINGTON (MARY PATRICIA) New Zealand and the United States, 1840-1944. Wellington, Government Printer, 1972. pp. 114, 1 map. bibliog.

— — Nicaragua.

SELSER (GREGORIO) Sandino; [with texts of political manifestoes, speeches etc.]. Montevideo, [1970]. pp. 125. bibliog.

— — Philippine Islands.

STANLEY (PETER W.) A nation in the making: the Philippines and the United States, 1899-1921. Cambridge, Mass., 1974. pp. 340. bibliog. (Harvard University. Harvard Studies in American- East Asian Relations. 4)

— — Portugal.

CROLLEN (LUC) Portugal, the U.S. and NATO. Leuven, [1973]. pp. 163. bibliog. (Katholieke Universiteit te Leuven. Departement Politieke Wetenschappen. Studies in International Relations. No.1)

— — Puerto Rico.

ESTEFANO (MIGUEL A.D') Puerto Rico: analisis de un plebiscito. La Habana, 1967. pp. 126.

— — Russia.

LIPPMANN (WALTER) The Cold War: a study in U.S. foreign policy: [with The sources of Soviet conduct by George Kennan]. New York, 1972. pp. 81. bibliog.

CLEMENS (WALTER CARL) The superpowers and arms control: from cold war to interdependence.Lexington, Mass., [1973]. pp. 180. bibliog.

PATERSON (THOMAS GRAHAM) Soviet-American confrontation: postwar reconstruction and the origins of the cold war. Baltimore, [1973]. pp. 287. bibliog.

AMERICAN ACADEMY OF POLITICAL AND SOCIAL SCIENCE. Annals. vol. 414. USA - USSR: agenda for communication; special editor of this volume Marvin E. Wolfgang. Philadelphia, [1974]. pp. 239.

CHAYES (ABRAM) The Cuban missile crisis. London, 1974. pp. 157. (American Society of International Law. International Crises and the Role of Law)

KAISER (ROBERT G.) Cold winter, cold war. London, 1974. pp. 226. bibliog.

WILLRICH (MASON) and RHINELANDER (JOHN B.) eds. SALT: the Moscow agreements and beyond. New York, [1974]. pp. 361. bibliog.

— — South Africa.

SEILER (JOHN J.) U.S. foreign policy toward Southern Africa: continuity and change. Johannesburg, 1973. pp. 15, iv.

— — United Kingdom.

CAMPBELL (CHARLES SOUTTER) From revolution to rapprochement: the United States and Great Britain, 1783-1900. New York, [1974]. pp. 225. bibliog.

JONES (WILBUR DEVEREUX) The American problem in British diplomacy, 1841-1861. London, 1974. pp. 260.

KAISER (ROBERT G.) Cold winter, cold war. London, 1974. pp. 226. bibliog.

McDONALD (IAN S.) ed. Anglo-American relations since the Second World War. Newton Abbot, [1974]. pp. 264. bibliog.

— — Vietnam.

TRAN-MINH-TIET. Les relations américano-vietnamiennes de Kennedy à Nixon. Paris, [1971 in progress].

— — Zaire.

WEISSMAN (STEPHEN R.) American foreign policy in the Congo, 1960-1964. Ithaca, 1974. pp. 325. bibliog.

— Full employment policies.

FELLNER (WILLIAM JOHN) Employment policy at the crossroads: an interim look at pressures to be resisted. Washington, D.C., 1972. pp. 28. (American Enterprise Institute for Public Policy Research. Domestic Affairs Studies. 9)

— Government publications — Bibliography.

TOLLEFSON (ALAN M.) and CHANG (HENRY C.) compilers. A bibliography of presidential commissions, committees, councils, panels and task forces, 1961-1972. Minneapolis, 1973. pp. 30.

— — Indexes.

BUCHANAN (WILLIAM W.) and KANELY (EDNA M.) compilers. Cumulative subject index to the Monthly Catalog of United States Government Publications, 1900-1971. Washington, 1973 in progress.

— History.

The NATIONAL experience: a history of the United States; [by] John M. Blum [and others]. 2nd ed. New York, [1968]. pp. 906. bibliogs.

HOLLON (WILLIAM EUGENE) Frontier violence: another look. New York, 1974. pp. 279. bibliog.

OSBORNE (THOMAS J.) and MABBUTT (FRED R.) Paths to the present: thoughts on the contemporary relevance of America's past. New York, [1974]. pp. 164.

— — Sources.

COBEN (STANLEY) ed. Reform, war and reaction: 1912-1932. Columbia, South Ca., 1973. pp. 466.

CONFERENCE ON THE HISTORY OF THE TERRITORIES, WASHINGTON, 1969. The American territorial system; papers and proceedings of the conference...; edited by John Porter Bloom. Athens, Oh., [1973]. pp. 248. (United States. National Archives. National Archives Conferences. vol.5)

— — 1607—1783, Colonial period.

ZIFF (LARZER) Puritanism in America: new culture in a new world. New York, [1973]. pp. 338.

— — 1775—1783, Revolution.

U.K. Public Record Office. 1972. The olive branch petition: facsimile with notes by N.E. Evans. London, 1972. pp. 16. (Museum Pamphlets. No.1)

ERNST (JOSEPH ALBERT) Money and politics in America, 1755-1775: a study in the Currency Act of 1764 and the political economy of revolution. Chapel Hill, N.C., [1973]. pp. 403. bibliog.

MAIN (JACKSON TURNER) The sovereign states, 1775-1783. New York, 1973. pp. 502. bibliog.

SMELSER (MARSHALL) The winning of independence. New York, 1973. pp. 427.

MITCHELL (BROADUS) The price of independence: a realistic view of the American revolution. New York, 1974. pp. 374. bibliog.

— — 1900— .

COBEN (STANLEY) ed. Reform, war and reaction: 1912-1932. Columbia, South Ca., 1973. pp. 466.

KIRKENDALL (RICHARD STEWART) The United States 1929-1945: years of crisis and change. New York, [1974]. pp. 308. bibliogs.

— History, Military.

CUNLIFFE (MARCUS) Soldiers and civilians: the martial spirit in America, 1775-1865.[2nd ed.] New York, 1973. pp. 499.

— Industries.

WHEAT (LEONARD F.) Regional growth and industrial location: an empirical viewpoint. Lexington, [1973]. pp. 223.

— Intellectual life.

DIVERGING parallels: a comparison of American and European thought and action; [papers of study conferences of the European Association for American Studies held in Rome in 1967 and in Brussels in 1970]; edited by A.N.J. den Hollander. Leiden, 1971. pp. 222.

CALHOUN (DANIEL) The intelligence of a people. Princeton, [1973]. pp. 408. bibliog.

PELLS (RICHARD H.) Radical visions and American dreams: culture and social thought in the depression years. New York, [1973]. pp. 424. bibliog.

PURCELL (EDWARD A.) The crisis of democratic theory: scientific naturalism and the problem of value. Lexington, [1973]. pp. 331. bibliog.

— Learned institutions and societies.

BLOLAND (HARLAND G.) and BLOLAND (SUE M.) American learned societies in transition: the impact of dissent and recession...: a report prepared for the Carnegie Commission on Higher Education. New York, [1974]. pp. 130. bibliog.

— Military policy.

AMERICAN arms and a changing Europe: dilemmas of deterrence and disarmament; [by] Warner R. Schilling [and others]. New York, 1973. pp. 218.

HEAD (RICHARD G.) and ROKKE (ERVIN J.) eds. American defense policy. 3rd ed. Baltimore, 1973. pp. 696. bibliogs.

JOSHUA (WYNFRED) and HAHN (WALTER F.) Nuclear politics: America, France and Britain. Beverly Hills, [1973]. pp. 84. bibliog. (Georgetown University. Center for Strategic and International Studies. Washington Papers. vol. 1/9)

MOULTON (HARLAND B.) From superiority to parity: the United States and the strategic arms race, 1961-1971. Westport, Conn., [1973]. pp. 333. bibliog.

TAMMEN (RONALD L.) MIRV and the arms race: an interpretation of defense strategy. New York, 1973. pp. 162. bibliog.

THOMAS (JAMES A.) Holy war: the lure of victory and the passing of America as a world power. New Rochelle, [1973]. pp. 272.

LAWRENCE (RICHARD D.) and RECORD (JEFFREY) U.S. force structure in NATO: an alternative: a staff paper. Washington, [1974]. pp. 136. (Brookings Institution. Studies in Defense Policy)

UNITED STATES. (Cont.)

PACEM IN TERRIS III, WASHINGTON, D.C., 1973. The military dimensions of foreign policy: volume 2 of...the proceedings of Pacem in Terris III; (edited by Fred Warner Neal and Mary Kersey Harvey). Santa Barbara, Calif., [1974]. pp. 129.

— Moral conditions.

LEGMAN (GERSHON) The fake revolt. New York, 1967. pp. 60.

PIVAR (DAVID J.) Purity crusade: sexual morality and social control, 1868-1900. Westport, Conn., 1973. pp. 308. *bibliog.*

— Nationalism.

CRAPOL (EDWARD P.) America for Americans: economic nationalism and anglophobia in the late nineteenth century. Westport, Conn., 1973. pp. 248. *bibliog.*

— Navy.

DENLINGER (HARRY SUTHERLAND) and GARY (CHARLES BINFORD) War in the Pacific: a study of navies, peoples and battle problems; [reprint of work first published in New York in 1936]. New York, 1970. pp. 338.

— — History.

HERZOG (JAMES H.) Closing the open door: American-Japanese diplomatic negotiations, 1936-1941. Annapolis, Md., [1973]. pp. 295. *bibliog.*

— Neutrality.

DEVLIN (PATRICK ARTHUR) Baron Devlin. Too proud to fight: Woodrow Wilson's neutrality. London, 1974. pp. 731. *bibliog.*

— Occupations.

FREEMAN (RICHARD BARRY) The market for college-trained manpower: a study in the economics of career choice. Cambridge, Mass., 1971. pp. 264.

— Officials and employees.

The ROLE of the neutral in public employee disputes; a report on the joint conference of the Association of Labor Mediation Agencies and the National Association of State Labor Relations Agencies...1971; edited by Howard J. Anderson. Washington, D.C., [1972]. pp. 124.

HERSHEY (CARY) Protest in the public service. Lexington, [1973]. pp. 92. *bibliog.*

PUBLIC service professional associations and the public interest; [papers read at a symposium in 1972 in Philadelphia]; editor: Don L. Bowen. Philadelphia, 1973. pp. 308. *(American Academy of Political and Social Science Monographs. [No]. 15)*

SHAFRITZ (JAY M.) Position classification: a behavioral analysis for the public service. New York, 1973. pp. 133. *bibliog.*

— — Appointment, qualifications, tenure, etc.

WEISBERGER (JUNE) Job security and public employees. Ithaca, N.Y., 1973. pp. 88. *(Cornell University. New York State School of Industrial and Labor Relations. Institute of Public Employment. Monographs. No. 2)*

— — Bibliography.

PEZDEK (ROBERT V.) compiler. Public employment: bibliography. Ithaca, 1973. pp. 185. *(Cornell University. New York State School of Industrial and Labor Relations. Bibliography Series. No. 11)*

— Politics and government.

POTTER (DAVID MORRIS) The south and the concurrent majority; edited by Don E. Fehrenbacher and Carl N. Degler. Baton Rouge, [1972]. pp. 89. *(Louisiana State University. Walter Lynwood Fleming Lectures in Southern History. 1968)*

NISKANEN (WILLIAM A.) Bureaucracy: servant or master?; lessons from America; with commentaries by Douglas Houghton [and others]. London, 1973. pp. 103. *(Institute of Economic Affairs. Hobart Paperbacks. 5)*

MABBUTT (FRED R.) and GHELFI (GERALD J.) The troubled republic: American government, its principles and problems. New York, [1974]. pp. 360.

— — Bibliography.

TOMPKINS (DOROTHY LOUISE CAMPBELL) compiler. Research and service: a fifty year record; [publications of the]...Institute of Governmental Studies, University of California, etc. Berkeley, 1971. pp. 154.

— — 1607—1783, Colonial period.

MARTIN (JAMES KIRBY) Men in rebellion: higher governmental leaders and the coming of the American revolution. New Brunswick, [1973]. pp. 263. *bibliog.*

— — 1783—1865.

BELL (RUDOLPH M.) Party and faction in American politics: the House of Representatives, 1789-1801. Westport, Conn., 1973. pp. 311. *bibliog.*

— — 1815—1861.

SILBEY (JOEL HENRY) ed. Political ideology and voting behavior in the age of Jackson. Englewood Cliffs, [1973]. pp. 189. *bibliog.*

— — 1865—1898.

TRELEASE (ALLEN WILLIAM) Reconstruction: the great experiment. New York, [1971]. pp. 224. *bibliog.*

MANTELL (MARTIN E.) Johnson, Grant, and the politics of reconstruction. New York, 1973. pp. 209. *bibliog.*

— — 1898—1945.

GULICK (LUTHER HALSEY) third of the name. Administrative reflections from World War II: [lectures delivered before the fellows of the Southern Regional Training Program in Public Administration at the University of Alabama in 1946]. University, Alabama, [1948]. pp. 139.

ANDERSON (DONALD F.) William Howard Taft: a conservative's conception of the presidency. Ithaca, 1973. pp. 355. *bibliog.*

— — 1900— .

MUCKRAKING: past, present and future; [including papers presented at a conference held at Pennsylvania State University, 1970]; edited by John M. Harrison and Harry H. Stein. University Park, [1973]. pp. 165.

MICHELMAN (IRVING S.) The crisis meeters: business response to social crises. Clifton, N.J., 1973. pp. 418.

REES (DAVID) Harry Dexter White: a study in paradox. London, 1974. pp. 506. *bibliog.*

— — 1945— .

HENNESSY (BERNARD CHARLES) Political internships: theory, practice, evaluation. University Park, Penn., [1970] repr. 1972. pp. 129. *(Pennsylvania State University. Penn State Studies. No. 28)*

COOK (FRED J.) The nightmare decade: the life and times of Senator Joe McCarthy. New York, [1971]. pp. 626.

ANDERSON (JACK) and CLIFFORD (GEORGE) The Anderson papers. New York, [1973]. pp. 275.

CHRISTENSON (REO MILLARD) Challenge and decision: political issues of our time. 4th ed. New York, [1973]. pp. 227. *bibliog.*

CRAWFORD (ANN FEARS) and KEEVER (JACK) John B. Connally: portrait in power. Austin, Texas, 1973. pp. 460. *bibliog.*

GARCIA (F. CHRIS) ed. Chicano politics: readings. New York, [1973]. pp. 225.

GARTNER (ALAN) and others, eds. What Nixon is doing to us. New York, 1973. pp. 258.

HAMBY (ALONZO L.) Beyond the New Deal: Harry S. Truman and American liberalism. New York, 1973. pp. 635. *bibliog.*

HAEFELE (EDWIN T.) Representative government and environmental management. Baltimore, [1973]. pp. 188.

HIKEL (GERALD KENT) Beyond the polls: political ideology and its correlates. Lexington, Mass., [1973]. pp. 150. *bibliog.*

KAMMERMAN (ROY) Poor Richard's Watergate. Los Angeles, 1973. 1 vol. (unpaged).

McCOY (DONALD RICHARD) and RUETTEN (RICHARD T.) Quest and response: minority rights and the Truman administration. Lawrence, Kansas, [1973]. pp. 427. *bibliog.*

MOYNIHAN (DANIEL PATRICK) Coping: essays on the practice of government. New York, [1973]. pp. 430.

ROTHBARD (MURRAY NEWTON) For a new liberty. New York, [1973]. pp. 327.

THOMAS (LATELY) When even angels wept: the Senator Joseph McCarthy affair:a story without a hero. New York, 1973. pp. 654.

WILSON (JAMES Q.) Political organizations. New York, [1973]. pp. 359.

COHEN (RICHARD M.) and WITCOVER (JULES) A heartbeat away: the investigation and resignation of Vice President Spiro T. Agnew. New York, 1974. pp. 373.

DOLBEARE (KENNETH M.) Political change in the United States: a framework for analysis. New York, [1974]. pp. 246. *bibliog.*

EVANS (LES) and MYERS (ALLEN) Watergate and the myth of American democracy. New York, 1974. pp. 206.

GREELEY (ANDREW M.) Building coalitions. New York, 1974. pp. 430.

GRIFFITH (ROBERT) and THEOHARIS (ATHAN G.) eds. The specter: original essays on the cold war and the origins of McCarthyism. New York, 1974. pp. 366.

HALPERIN (MORTON H.) Bureaucratic politics and foreign policy. Washington, D.C., [1974]. pp. 340. *bibliog.*

MILLER (MERLE) Plain speaking: an oral biography of Harry S. Truman. London, 1974. pp. 448.

OSBORNE (THOMAS J.) and MABBUTT (FRED R.) Paths to the present: thoughts on the contemporary relevance of America's past. New York, [1974]. pp. 164.

O'BRIEN (LAWRENCE FRANCIS) No final victories: a life in politics, from John F. Kennedy to Watergate. New York, 1974. pp. 394.

PEIRCE (NEAL R.) The deep south states of America: people, politics and power in the seven deep south states. New York, [1974]. pp. 528. *bibliog.*

PRESTHUS (ROBERT V.) Elites in the policy process. London, 1974. pp. 525.

SAYRE (NORA) Sixties going on seventies. London, 1974. pp. 441.

See also WATERGATE AFFAIR, 1972 .

— Population.

BUTZ (WILLIAM P.) and JORDAN (PAUL L.) Population growth and resource requirements for U.S. education: prepared for the Commission on Population Growth and the American Future. Santa Monica, 1972. pp. 87.

BACHRACH (PETER) and BERGMAN (ELIHU) Power and choice: the formulation of American population policy. Lexington, [1973]. pp. 120.

CLINTON (RICHARD L.) ed. Population and politics: new directions in political science research. Lexington, Mass., [1973]. pp. 298.

POPULATION REFERENCE BUREAU. Options: a study guide to population and the American future. [Washington], 1973. pp. 75. *bibliog.*

UNITED STATES. (Cont.)

TOWARD the end of growth: population in America; [papers originating in a conference held in Buck Hill Fall, Pennsylvania in 1972; by] Charles F. Westoff and others. Englewood Cliffs, N.J., [1973]. pp. 177. *bibliogs.*

The AMERICAN environment: [papers from a seminar held at the Institute of United States Studies in the University of London]; edited by W.R. Mead. London, 1974. pp. 69. *(London. University. Institute of United States Studies. Monographs. 1)*

GROWTH policy: population, environment and beyond; [by] Kan Chen [and others]. Ann Arbor, [1974]. pp. 237. *bibliog.*

KAHN (ELY JACQUES) The American people: the findings of the 1970 census. New York, [1974]. pp. 340.

— Presidents.

POPPER (FRANK) The President's commissions. New York, 1970. pp. 73.

SCHLESINGER (ARTHUR MEIER) the Younger. The imperial presidency. Boston, 1973. pp. 505.

— — Election.

WATERGATE: the full inside story; [by] Lewis Chester [and others]. London, 1973. pp. 280.

BLOOM (MELVYN H.) Public relations and presidential campaigns: a crisis in democracy. New York, [1973]. pp. 349. *bibliog.*

CHASE (JAMES S.) Emergence of the presidential nominating convention, 1789-1832. Urbana, [1973]. pp. 332. *bibliog.*

HART (GARY WARREN) Right from the start: a chronicle of the McGovern campaign. New York, [1973]. pp. 334.

LADD (EVERETT CARLL) and LIPSET (SEYMOUR MARTIN) Academics, politics and the 1972 election. Washington, D.C., [1973]. pp. 99. *(American Enterprise Institute for Public Policy Research. Domestic Affairs Studies. 15)*

SHADE (WILLIAM L.) Social change and the electoral process. Gainesville, 1973. pp. 73. *(Florida University. Monographs. Social Sciences. No. 49)*

WATERGATE: the view from the Left; introduction by Linda Jenness and Andrew Pulley. New York, 1973. pp. 95.

WEIL (GORDON LEE) The long shot: George McGovern runs for president. New York, [1973]. pp. 253.

HESS (STEPHEN) The presidential campaign: the leadership selection process after Watergate. Washington, [1974]. pp. 121. *bibliog.*

MAZMANIAN (DANIEL A.) Third parties in presidential elections. Washington, D.C. [1974]. pp. 163.

RIPON SOCIETY and BROWN (CLIFFORD WATERS) Jaws of victory: the game-plan politics of 1972, the crisis of the Republican Party, and the future of the constitution. Boston, [1974]. pp. 394. *bibliog.*

YARNELL (ALLEN) Democrats and progressives: the 1948 presidential election as a test of postwar liberalism. Berkeley, 1974. pp. 155. *bibliog.*

— — Powers and duties.

ABRAHAM (HENRY JULIAN) Justices and presidents: a political history of appointments to the Supreme Court. New York, 1974. pp. 310. *bibliog.*

HARDIN (CHARLES MEYER) Presidential power and accountability: toward a new constitution. Chicago, 1974. pp. 257.

TUGWELL (REXFORD GUY) and CRONIN (THOMAS E.) eds. The presidency reappraised. New York, 1974. pp. 312. *bibliog.*

— Public lands.

CONFERENCE ON THE PUBLIC LAND LAW REVIEW COMMISSION REPORT, SAN FRANCISCO, 1970. America's public lands: politics, economics and administration; [proceedings of the] conference...; Harriet Nathan, editor. Berkeley, 1972. pp. 395. *bibliog.*

— Race question.

FICKER (VICTOR B.) and GRAVES (HERBERT S.) eds. Deprivation in America. Beverly Hills, [1971]. pp. 149.

KIRBY (JACK TEMPLE) Darkness at the dawning: race and reform in the Progressive South. Philadelphia, [1972]. pp. 210. *bibliog.*

ABERBACH (JOEL D.) and WALKER (JACK L.) Race in the city: political trust and public policy in the new urban system. Boston, [Mass., 1973]. pp. 293.

ANDRESKI (STANISLAV) Prospects of a revolution in the U.S.A. London, 1973. pp. 116.

BROWN (INA CORINNE) Understanding race relations. Englewood Cliffs, [1973]. pp. 275. *bibliog.*

FUSFELD (DANIEL ROLAND) The basic economics of the urban racial crisis. New York, [1973]. pp. 122. *bibliog.*

GREENSTONE (J. DAVID) and PETERSON (PAUL E.) Race and authority in urban politics: community participation and the war on poverty. New York, [1973]. pp. 364.

ELLISON (MARY) The black experience: American blacks since 1865. London, 1974. pp. 334. *bibliog.*

JORDAN (WINTHROP D.) The white man's burden: historical origins of racism in the United States. New York, 1974. pp. 229. *bibliog.*

LINDSEY (PAUL) and LINDSEY (OUIDA) Breaking the bonds of racism. Homewood, Ill., 1974. pp. 242. *bibliog.*

PEIRCE (NEAL R.) The deep south states of America: people, politics and power in the seven deep south states. New York, [1974]. pp. 528. *bibliog.*

WOODWARD (COMER VANN) The strange career of Jim Crow. 3rd ed. New York, 1974. pp. 233. *bibliog.*

— Relations (general) with Africa, Subsaharan.

GOOD (KENNETH) Western domination in Africa. Syracuse, N.Y., 1972. pp. 71. *(Syracuse University. Maxwell Graduate School of Citizenship and Public Affairs. Program of Eastern African Studies. Eastern African Studies. No. 7)*

— Relations (general) with Canada.

LITVAK (ISAIAH ALLAN) and MAULE (CHRISTOPHER JOHN) Cultural sovereignty: the Time and Reader's Digest case in Canada. New York, 1974. pp. 140.

— Relations (general) with China — Bibliography.

McCUTCHEON (JAMES M.) compiler. China and America: a bibliography of interactions, foreign and domestic. Honolulu, [1972]. pp. 75. *(Hawaii University. East-West Bibliographic Series. 1)*

— Relations (general) with Europe.

CONTAGIOUS conflict: the impact of American dissent on European life: [papers of a study conference held by the European Association for American Studies in Geneva in 1972]; edited by A.N.J Den Hollander. Leiden, 1973. pp. 263.

— Relations (general) with Spain.

OLTRA (JOAQUIN) La influencia norteamericana en la Constitucion Española de 1869. Madrid, 1972. pp. 194.

— Rural conditions.

FORD (ARTHUR M.) Political economics of rural poverty in the South. Cambridge, Mass., [1973]. pp. 101. *bibliog.*

GRAHAM (DAVID RALPH) and LUFT (KATHLEEN) The role of business in the economic redevelopment of the rural community. Austin, Tex., 1973. pp. 114. *bibliog.* *(Texas University. Bureau of Business Research. Research Monographs. No. 36)*

NATIONAL PLANNING ASSOCIATION. Reports. No. 134. Toward a rural development policy; by James G. Maddox. Washington, D.C., [1973]. pp. 24. *(National Planning Association. Reports. No. 134)*

— Social conditions.

WANSEY (HENRY) Henry Wansey and his American journal, 1794; [reprint of Wansey's Journal based on the first two English editions of 1796 and 1798, with notes and introduction]; edited by David John Jeremy. Philadelphia, 1970. pp. 186. *bibliog.* *(American Philosophical Society. Memoirs. vol.82)*

NEUHAUS (RICHARD) In defense of people: ecology and the seduction of radicalism. New York, [1971]. pp. 315.

SLOMICH (SIDNEY J.) The American nightmare. New York, [1971]. pp. 285.

EISINGER (PETER K.) The conditions of protest behavior in American cities; [revised version of paper prepared for a seminar panel at the 1971 meeting of the American Political Science Association at Chicago]. Madison, 1972. fo.49. *(Wisconsin University, Madison. Institute for Research on Poverty. Discussion Papers)*

LEARNED (S.S.) An America to love: viewpoints per an immigrant's son. Fontana, Calif., [1972]. pp. 206.

ALBAUM (MELVIN) ed. Geography and contemporary issues: studies of relevant problems. New York, [1973]. pp. 590.

ANDRESKI (STANISLAV) Prospects of a revolution in the U.S.A. London, 1973. pp. 116.

CHRISTENSON (REO MILLARD) Challenge and decision: political issues of our time. 4th ed. New York, [1973]. pp. 227. *bibliog.*

GERSUNY (CARL) and ROSENGREN (WILLIAM RUDOLPH) The service society. Cambridge, Mass., [1973]. pp. 156. *bibliog.*

GLINER (ROBERT) American society as a social problem. New York, [1973]. pp. 393.

LEVITT (THEODORE) The third sector: new tactics for a responsive society. New York, [1973]. pp. 182.

MOYNIHAN (DANIEL PATRICK) Coping: essays on the practice of government. New York, [1973]. pp. 430.

MUCKRAKING: past, present and future; [including papers presented at a conference held at Pennsylvania State University, 1970]; edited by John M. Harrison and Harry H. Stein. University Park, [1973]. pp. 165.

The QUALITY of life in America: pollution, poverty, power and fear; edited by A. David Hill [and others]. New York, [1973]. pp. 549.

REISSMAN (LEONARD) Inequality in American society: social stratification. Glenview, Ill., [1973]. pp. 137.

SCHACHTER (GUSTAV) and DALE (EDWIN L.) The economist looks at society. Lexington, Mass., [1973]. pp. 373. *bibliogs.*

SHADE (WILLIAM L.) Social change and the electoral process. Gainesville, 1973. pp. 73. *(Florida University. Monographs. Social Sciences. No. 49)*

SHOSTAK (ARTHUR B.) and others. Privilege in America: an end to inequality?. Englewood Cliffs, N.J., [1973]. pp. 150. *bibliog.*

DOLBEARE (KENNETH M.) Political change in the United States: a framework for analysis. New York, [1974]. pp. 246. *bibliog.*

KAHN (ELY JACQUES) The American people: the findings of the 1970 census. New York, [1974]. pp. 340.

OSBORNE (THOMAS J.) and MABBUTT (FRED R.) Paths to the present: thoughts on the contemporary relevance of America's past. New York, [1974]. pp. 164.

ROSSI (PETER HENRY) and others. The roots of urban discontent: public policy, municipal institutions and the ghetto. New York, [1974]. pp. 499.

SHOSTAK (ARTHUR B.) Modern social reforms: solving today's social problems. New York, [1974]. pp. 411. *bibliog.*

— Social history.

GREEN (FLETCHER MELVIN) The role of the Yankee in the old South. Athens, Ga., [1972]. pp. 150. *bibliog. (Mercer University. Eugenia Dorothy Blount Lamar Memorial Lectures. No. 11)*

COOK (ANN) and others, eds. City life, 1865-1900: views of urban America. New York, 1973. pp. 292.

PESSEN (EDWARD) Riches, class, and power before the Civil War. Lexington, Mass., [1973]. pp. 378. *bibliog.*

POTTER (DAVID MORRIS) History and American society: essays...; edited by Don E. Fehrenbacher. New York, 1973. pp. 422.

STOTT (WILLIAM) Documentary expression and thirties America. New York, 1973. pp. 361. *bibliog.*

ELDER (GLEN H.) Children of the great depression: social change in life experience.Chicago, 1974. pp. 400. *bibliog.*

— Social policy.

FOUR CORNERS REGIONAL COMMISSION. Development plan; (with Executive summary and Agricultural addendum). Washington, 1972-73. 3 pts. (in 1 vol). *bibliogs.*

MARRIS (PETER) and REIN (MARTIN) Dilemmas of social reform: poverty and community action in the United States. 2nd ed. London, 1972. pp. 309. *bibliog. (Institute of Community Studies. Reports. 15)*

LEVITAN (SAR A.) ed. The federal social dollar in its own back yard. Washington, [1973]. pp. 283.

LEVITT (THEODORE) The third sector: new tactics for a responsive society. New York, [1973]. pp. 182.

ROTHBARD (MURRAY NEWTON) For a new liberty. New York, [1973]. pp. 327.

SOCIAL experiments and social program evaluation; [proceedings of a symposium sponsored by the Washington Operations Research Council held at the National Bureau of Standards, May 1972]; edited by James G. Abert and Murray Kamrass. Cambridge, Mass., [1974]. pp. 199.

TRATTNER (WALTER I.) From poor law to welfare state: a history of social welfare in America. New York, [1974]. pp. 276. *bibliogs.*

— Statistics, Medical.

AMERICAN MEDICAL ASSOCIATION. Center for Health Services Research and Development. Reference data on socioeconomic issues of health;...compiled and edited by Robert J. Walsh. Chicago, 1972. pp. 148.

— Territorial expansion.

CONFERENCE ON THE HISTORY OF THE TERRITORIES, WASHINGTON, 1969. The American territorial system; papers and proceedings of the conference...; edited by John Porter Bloom. Athens, Oh., [1973]. pp. 248. *(United States. National Archives. National Archives Conferences. vol.5)*

GARDNER (LLOYD C.) and others. Creation of the American empire: U.S. diplomatic history. Chicago, [1973]. pp. 540. *bibliogs.*

YOUNG (MARILYN BLATT) ed. American expansionism: the critical issues. Boston, [Mass., 1973]. pp. 184. *bibliog.*

— Territories and possessions.

CONFERENCE ON THE HISTORY OF THE TERRITORIES, WASHINGTON, 1969. The American territorial system; papers and proceedings of the conference...; edited by John Porter Bloom. Athens, Oh., [1973]. pp. 248. *(United States. National Archives. National Archives Conferences. vol.5)*

UNITIZED CARGO SYSTEMS.

RAMCKE (PETER H.) Der Aufbau von Container-Transportsystemen als Planungsproblem der Güterverkehrsbetriebe. Hamburg, 1972. pp. 201. *bibliog.*

ECONOMIC DEVELOPMENT COMMITTEE FOR THE MOVEMENT OF EXPORTS. Port Traffic Working Group. Packing for profit; [R.J.C. Hill, chairman]. London, H.M.S.O., 1973. 2 vols. *bibliog.*

UNIVERSITIES AND COLLEGES.

GOMEZ PEREZ (RAFAEL) Universidad: problema politico. Pamplona, 1971. pp. 139. *bibliog.*

BEREDAY (GEORGE ZYGMUNT FIJALKOWSKI) Universities for all. San Francisco, 1973. pp. 158. *bibliog.*

BUDE (JACQUES) L'obscurantisme libéral et l'investigation sociologique. Paris, [1973]. pp. 223.

The UNIVERSITY on trial: a symposium held on the occasion of the centennial celebrations of the University of Canterbury [at Christchurch in 1973]; [by] Eric Ashby [and others]. Christchurch, N.Z., 1973. pp. 74. *(Christchurch, New Zealand. University of Canterbury. Publications. No.20)*

DAVIN (LOUIS E.) and DETIENNE (J.) Mutations contemporaines; l'université, la C.E.E. et le droit des sociétés. Bruxelles, 1974. pp. 101. *(Liège. Université. Séminaire Interdisciplinaire de Science Economique des Professeurs Harsin et Davin. Documents et Travaux. No. 9)*

EFFICIENCY in universities: the La Paz papers; [revised versions of papers presented at a conference organized by the Esmée Fairbairn Economics Research Centre of Heriot- Watt University at La Paz, Mexico, 1972]; edited by Keith G. Lumsden. Amsterdam, 1974. pp. 278. *bibliog.*

— Administration.

JANNE (HENRI) Les principes généraux de la planification universitaire; (rapport présenté au nom de l'Association Internationale des Universités à la Conférence générale de l'Union des Universités d'Amérique latine, Concepcion, Chili, 1969). Bruxelles, [1971]. pp. 68. *(Brussels. Université Libre. Institut de Sociologie. Etudes des Problèmes de l'Enseignement Supérieur)*

LIVINGSTONE (HUGH) The university: an organizational analysis. Glasgow, [1974]. pp. 122. *bibliog.*

— Entrance requirements.

HEARNDEN (ARTHUR) Paths to university: preparation, assessment, selection. London, 1973. pp. 165. *bibliog. (U.K. Department of Education and Science. Schools Council. Research Studies)*

— Asia, Southeast.

YIP (YAT HOONG) ed. Development of higher education in Southeast Asia: problems and issues. Singapore, 1973. pp. 226.

— Australia — Finance.

AUSTRALIA. Universities Commission. 1969. Fourth report of the... Commission. in AUSTRALIA. Parliament. Parliamentary papers, 1969, vol.2.

UNIVERSITIES AND COLLEGES.

— Chile.

FAGEN (PATRICIA WEISS) Chilean universities: problems of autonomy and dependence. Beverly Hills, [1973]. pp. 52. *bibliog.*

— Denmark.

BETAENKNING om stillingsstrukturen ved universiteterne og de højere laereanstalter; afgivet af det af Undervisningsministeriet den 18. november 1969 nedsatte udvalg. [Copenhagen?], Statens Trykningskontor, 1970. pp. 91.

— France.

CLARK (TERRY NICHOLS) Prophets and patrons: the French university and the emergence of the social sciences. Cambridge, Mass., 1973. pp. 282.

— Germany.

VOGEL (BERNHARD) Demokratie in Not: Universität heute; Chaos oder Reformmodell?. Bonn, [1972]. pp. 51. *(Christlich-Demokratische Union Deutschlands. Wirtschaftsrat. Information. 7)*

— — Admission.

KERN (BAERBEL) Einflüsse sozioökonomischer Faktoren auf die Ausbildungswege von Abiturienten in vier ausgewählten Regionen Niedersachsens: ein Beitrag zur Bildungsmobilität. Göttingen, 1973. 1 vol.(various pagings).

— India — Finance.

INDIA. University Grants Commission. 1968. Schemes of assistance. New Delhi, 1968. pp. 21.

— Italy.

COMITATO NAZIONALE UNIVERSITARIO. Per l'università di domani: atti del congresso del Comitato...[held in Florence in December 1971; with papers by] Giorgio Spini [and others]. Padova, [1972]. pp. 129. *(Documenti)*

— Netherlands.

MARIUS Broekmeyer tussen wetenschap en demagogie: hoe een welbekende slavist op weg naar een betere wereld het spoor bijster raakte. Amsterdam, 1974. pp. 48.

— Nigeria — Curricula.

DADA (PAUL O.A.) Evaluation of local government courses in relation to careers of staff trained in Zaria, 1954-1964. Zaria, 1966. fo. 49. *(Ahmadu Bello University. Institute of Administration. Research Memoranda Series)*

— South Africa.

MARQUARD (LEOPOLD) Academic freedom and responsibility. Johannesburg, 1973. pp. 18. *(Johannesburg. University of the Witwatersrand. Chancellors' Lectures. No. 4)*

— United Kingdom.

JONES (Sir BRYNMOR) Vice-Chancellor of the University of Hull. The British universities: their expanding role;... delivered... in the Guildhall, York on March 31st, 1973 at a presentation ceremony organized by the Yorkshire Executive of the College of Preceptors. London, [1973]. pp. 24. *(College of Preceptors. Sir Philip Magnus Memorial Lectures. 1972/1973)*

STYLER (WILLIAM EDWARD) Post-experience and the universities. Hull, 1973. pp. 19.

NIBLETT (WILLIAM ROY) Universities between two worlds. London, [1974]. pp. 179. *bibliog.*

PRATT (JOHN) and BURGESS (TYRRELL) Polytechnics: a report. London, 1974. pp. 250. *bibliog.*

The UNIVERSITY in an urban environment: a study of activity patterns from a planning viewpoint sponsored by the Centre for Environmental Studies; by Nicholas Abercrombie [and others]. London, 1974. pp. 246. *bibliog.*

UNIVERSITIES AND COLLEGES. (Cont.)

— — Administration.

The CASE for academic freedom and democracy: [by] John Griffith [and others] . London, [1972]. pp. 15.

LIVINGSTONE (HUGH) The university: an organizational analysis. Glasgow, [1974]. pp. 122. *bibliog.*

MOODIE (GRAEME COCHRANE) and EUSTACE (ROWLAND) Power and authority in British universities. London, 1974. pp. 254. *bibliog.*

— — Directories.

CAREERS RESEARCH AND ADVISORY CENTRE. Student life; [edited by J.P. O'Hanlon and Jenny Knight].Cambridge, 1974. pp. 281.

— — Finance.

BEVAN (ERIC GILBERT) An analysis of equipment costs in university science and engineering departments. London, H.M.S.O., 1972. pp. 39. *(Science Policy Studies. No. 5)*

— United States.

CARNEGIE COMMISSION ON HIGHER EDUCATION. Reform on campus: changing students, changing academic programs; a report and recommendations. New York, 1972. pp. 137. *bibliog.*

ACADEMIC transformation: seventeen institutions under pressure; ... a volume of essays sponsored by the Carnegie Commission on Higher Education; [edited by David Riesman and Verne A. Stadtman). New York, [1973]. pp. 489. *bibliogs.*

NASH (GEORGE) The university and the city: eight cases of involvement;... with chapters by Dan Waldorf [and] Robert E. Price; a report prepared for the Carnegie Commission on Higher Education. New York, [1973]. pp. 151. *bibliogs.*

PARSONS (TALCOTT) and PLATT (GERALD M.) The American university. Cambridge, Mass., 1973. pp. 463.

PIFER (ALAN J.) The higher education of blacks in the United States. Johannesburg, 1973. pp. 44. *bibliog. (South African Institute of Race Relations. Hoernlé Memorial Lectures. 1973)*

WHITEHEAD (JOHN S.) The separation of college and state: Columbia, Dartmouth, Harvard, and Yale, 1776-1876. New Haven, 1973. pp. 262. *bibliog. (Yale University. Yale Historical Publications. Miscellany. 97)*

DUBERMAN (MARTIN B.) Black Mountain: an exploration in community. London, 1974. pp. 527.

DUGGER (RONNIE) Our invaded universities: form, reform and new starts: a nonfiction play for five stages. New York, [1974]. pp. 457.

— — Administration.

BLAU (PETER MICHAEL) The organization of academic work. New York, [1973]. pp. 310.

CARNEGIE COMMISSION ON HIGHER EDUCATION. Governance of higher education: six priority problems: a report and recommendations, etc. New York, 1973. pp. 249.

GROSS (EDWARD) and GRAMBSCH (PAUL V.) Changes in university organization, 1964-1971;... a report prepared for the Carnegie Commission on Higher Education. New York, [1974]. pp. 257. *bibliog.*

— — Curricula.

SNYDER (BENSON R.) The hidden curriculum: [paperback edition of work first published in New York in 1971]. Cambridge, Mass., 1973. pp. 200.

— — Employees.

MOORE (WILLIAM) Educationist, and WAGSTAFF (LONNIE H.) Black educators in white colleges. San Francisco, 1974. pp. 226. *bibliog.*

— — Finance.

CARNEGIE COMMISSION ON HIGHER EDUCATION. Higher education: who pays?: who benefits?: who should pay?: a report and recommendations, etc. New York, 1973. pp. 190. *bibliog.*

McMAHON (WALTER W.) Investment in higher education. Lexington, Mass., [1974]. pp. 200. *bibliog.*

UNIVERSITY OF THE WESTERN TERRITORIES (POLAND).

WIKARJAK (JAN) ed. Uniwersytet Ziem Zachodnich i tajne kursy uniwersyteckie 1939- 1945: pokłosie wspomnień. Poznań, 1972. pp. 292. *(Poznań. Uniwersytet. Seria Dzieje UAM. Nr.8). With English and German summaries.*

UNJUST ENRICHMENT

— France.

BAYLE (GABRIEL) L'enrichissement sans cause en droit administratif. Paris, 1973. pp. 227. *bibliog.*

UNMARRIED MOTHERS

— Ireland (Republic).

NATIONAL CONFERENCE ON COMMUNITY SERVICES FOR THE UNMARRIED PARENT, KILKENNY, 1970. The unmarried mother in the Irish community: a report. Kilkenny, 1971. pp. 65.

UPPER ADIGE

— Economic conditions.

ROTHER-HOHENSTEIN (BAERBEL) Bevölkerung und Wirtschaft im Gadertal, Dolomiten. Frankfurt/Main, 1973. pp. 205. *bibliog. (Frankfurt am Main. Universität. Seminar für Wirtschaftsgeographie. Frankfurter Wirtschafts- und Sozialgeographische Schriften. Heft 14)*

— Nationalism.

SPRINGENSCHMID (KARL) Schicksal Südtirol. Graz, [1971]. pp. 269. *bibliog.*

— Politics and government.

SIEGLER (HEINRICH) Die österreichisch-italienische Einigung über die Regelung des Südtirolkonflikts. Bonn, [1970]. pp. 35.

— Population.

ROTHER-HOHENSTEIN (BAERBEL) Bevölkerung und Wirtschaft im Gadertal, Dolomiten. Frankfurt/Main, 1973. pp. 205. *bibliog. (Frankfurt am Main. Universität. Seminar für Wirtschaftsgeographie. Frankfurter Wirtschafts- und Sozialgeographische Schriften. Heft 14)*

TOEPFER (LORE) Die Abwanderung deutschsprachiger Bevölkerung aus Südtirol nach 1955. Innsbruck, 1973. pp. 135. *bibliog.*

UPPER VOLTA.

FRANCE. Direction de la Documentation. La Documentation Française. Notes et Etudes Documentaires. Nos. 3,818-3, 819. La République de Haute-Volta; [by] Gilbert Douté. Paris, 1971. pp. 75. *bibliog.*

— Economic conditions.

UPPER VOLTA. Direction de la Statistique et de la Mécanographie. 1971. Comptes économiques de la Haute Volta 1968. [Paris], 1971. pp. 176. *2 tables in end pocket.*

FRANCE. Direction de l'Aide au Développement des Etats Francophones d'Afrique au Sud du Sahara et de la République Malgache. Secteur Information Economique et Conjoncture. 1973. Haute-Volta 1971-1972: dossier d'information économique. Paris, 1973. pp. 19, fo. 43.

— Emigration and immigration.

UPPER VOLTA. Service de la Statistique et de la Mécanographie. 1972. Enquête démographique par sondage en République de Haute- Volta, 1960-1961: les émigrations; [sous la direction de Rémy Clairin]. [Paris, 1972]. pp. 209.

URAL REGION

— History — 1917—1921, Revolution — Historiography.

OKTIABR' v Povolzh'e i Priural'e: istochniki i voprosy istoriografii. Kazan', 1972. pp. 150.

URBAN ECONOMICS.

DOUGHARTY (L.A.) Forces shaping urban development: the property tax. Santa Monica, 1973. pp. 51. *bibliog. (Rand Corporation. [Papers]. 5022)*

EVANS (ALAN W.) The economics of residential location. London, 1973. pp. 281. *bibliog.*

KOHLER (HEINZ) Economics and urban problems. Lexington, Mass., [1973]. pp. 470. *bibliogs.*

LITHWICK (N. HARVEY) The political economy of urban policy failure. [Ottawa, 1973]. fo. 21. *(Carleton University. Carleton Economic Papers)*

PASHCHENKO (N.E.) and SEGEDINOV (A.A.) Ekonomika gradostroitel'stva: na moskovskom opyte. Moskva, 1973. pp. 264.

RICHARDSON (HARRY W.) The economics of urban size. Farnborough, Hants., [1973]. pp. 243. *bibliog.*

STONE (PETER ALBERT) The structure, size and costs of urban settlements. Cambridge, 1973. pp. 280. *bibliog. (National Institute of Economic and Social Research. Economic and Social Studies. 28)*

BISH (ROBERT L.) and KIRK (ROBERT J.) Economic principles and urban problems. Englewood Cliffs, [1974]. pp. 199.

URBAN EDUCATION.

See EDUCATION, URBAN.

URBAN SOCIOLOGY.

See SOCIOLOGY, URBAN.

URBAN TRANSPORTATION.

SYMPOSIUM ON THE FUTURE OF CONURBATION TRANSPORT, 5TH, MANCHESTER, 1971. Fifth Symposium on the Future of Conurbation Transport, October 19th-21st, 1971: [proceedings of Symposium sponsored by the Department of Extra-Mural Studies, University of Manchester]. Manchester, [1972]. fo. 104.

SYMPOSIUM ON THE FUTURE OF CONURBATION TRANSPORT, 6TH, MANCHESTER, 1972. Sixth symposium on the future of conurbation transport, October 10-12, 1972: [proceedings of Symposium sponsored by the Department of Extra Mural Studies, University of Manchester]. Manchester, [1973]. pp. 110.

BENDIXSON (TERENCE) Instead of cars. London, 1974. pp. 256.

SYMPOSIUM ON THE FUTURE OF CONURBATION TRANSPORT, 7TH, MANCHESTER, 1973. Seventh Symposium on the Future of Conurbation Transport, October 16th-18th 1973: [proceedings of the Symposium sponsored by the Department of Extra-Mural Studies, University of Manchester]. Manchester, [1974]. pp. 100.

— Mathematical models.

DEWEES (DONALD N.) The impact of urban transportation investment on land value. Toronto, 1973. fo. 87. *(Toronto. University, and York University (Toronto). Joint Program in Transportation. Research Reports. No. 11)*

— France — Cost of operation.

FRANCE. Commission d'Etude des Coûts d'Infrastructure de Transport. Groupe des Transports Urbains. 1969. Sur les coûts et la tarification des transports urbains. Arcueil, Institut de Recherche des Transports, 1969. 1 vol. (various pagings). *bibliog.*

— Russia — Azerbaijan.

AKHMEDOV (ALI ISLAMOVICH) and VEZIROV (SHAMSADDIN AGMADOVICH) Gorod i transport. Baku, 1973. pp. 116.

— Spain.

JANE SOLA (JOSE) El transporte colectivo urbano en España; [by] M. Cabre Llistosella [and others]. Barcelona, [1972]. pp. 342.

— United Kingdom.

BRAYBROOKE (DAVID) Traffic congestion goes through the issue-machine: a case-study in issue processing, illustrating a new approach. London, 1974. pp. 62.

URBAN TRANSPORTATION POLICY.

BEESLEY (M.E.) Urban transport: studies in economic policy. London, 1973. pp. 413.

— United Kingdom.

WEST MIDLANDS PASSENGER TRANSPORT EXECUTIVE. A passenger transport development plan for the West Midlands. n.p., [1973?]. pp. 88.

URHOBO.

See SOBO (AFRICAN PEOPLE).

URI (CANTON)

— Economic history.

BIELMANN (JUERG) Die Lebensverhältnisse im Urnerland während des 18. und zu Beginn des 19. Jahrhunderts. Basel, 1972. pp. 229. bibliog.

URUGUAY

— Commerce.

MELGAR (ALICIA) and others. El comercio exportador del Uruguay: periodo 1962-68. Montevideo, [1972]. 2 vols. (in 1). bibliog.

— Constitution.

URUGUAY. Constitution. 1942. Constitucion de la republica, plebiscitada el 29 de noviembre de 1942. Montevideo, 1951. pp. 111.

URUGUAY. Constitution. 1951. Ley constitucional sancionada el 26 de octubre de 1951 que sera sometida a plebiscito de ratificacion el 16 de diciembre de 1951. [Montevideo?], [1951]. pp. 96.

URUGUAY. Constitution. 1952-67. La reforma constitucional de 1966; por Daniel Hugo Martins;...texto de la constitucion de 1967 comparado con el de la constitucion de 1952, etc. Montevideo, 1968. pp. 261.

— Economic policy.

URUGUAY. 1973. Definicion de politicas y estrategias del gobierno uruguayo y analisis de la instrumentacion del plan nacional de desarrollo. [Montevideo], 1973. pp. 77.

— Emigration and immigration.

URUGUAY. Direccion General de Migracion. Memoria. a., 1957. Montevideo.

— Foreign relations.

MARTINEZ MONTERO (HOMERO) Politica exterior de la República, 1961-1962: discursos. Montevideo, 1963. pp. 55. (Uruguay. Ministerio de Relaciones Exteriores. Seccion Artigas. Cuadernos de Politica Exterior. No. 3)

— Industries.

MILLOT (JULIO) and others. El desarrollo industrial del Uruguay: de la crisis de 1929 a la posguerra. [Montevideo, 1973]. pp. 287. bibliog.

— Maps.

URUGUAY. Direccion General de Estadistica y Censos. 1969. Mapas demograficos [elaborados con informacion del IV censo general de poblacion y II de vivienda]. [Montevideo, 1969] 20 maps.

— Politics and government.

FERRANDO (FEDERICO) Articulos politicos; prologo de Jose Pedro Barran. Montevideo, 1969. pp. 47. (Biblioteca Nacional [Uruguay]. Departamento de Investigaciones. Publicaciones)

MAYANS (ERNESTO) ed. Tupamaros: antologia documental. Cuernavaca, 1971. 1 vol. (various pagings). (Centro Intercultural de Documentacion. Cidoc Cuadernos. No.60)

MOSS (ROBERT) Uruguay: terrorism versus democracy. London, 1971. pp. 10. (Institute for the Study of Conflict. Conflict Studies. No. 14)

— Population — Maps.

URUGUAY. Direccion General de Estadistica y Censos. 1969. Mapas demograficos [elaborados con informacion del IV censo general de poblacion y II de vivienda]. [Montevideo, 1969] 20 maps.

— Rural conditions.

CENTRO LATINOAMERICANO DE ECONOMIA HUMANA. Situacion economica y social del Uruguay rural; (estudio realizado...bajo la supervision de George Celestin]. [Montevideo], Ministerio de Ganaderia y Agricultura, [1963?]. pp. 520.

— Social conditions.

MAYANS (ERNESTO) ed. Tupamaros: antologia documental. Cuernavaca, 1971. 1 vol. (various pagings). (Centro Intercultural de Documentacion. Cidoc Cuadernos. No.60)

— Social history.

RAMA (CARLOS M.) Historia social del pueblo uruguayo. Montevideo, 1972. pp. 157.

— Social policy.

URUGUAY. 1973. Definicion de politicas y estrategias del gobierno uruguayo y analisis de la instrumentacion del plan nacional de desarrollo. [Montevideo], 1973. pp. 77.

USPENSKII (GLEB IVANOVICH).

BLANKOFF (JEAN) La société russe de la seconde moitié du XIXe siècle: trois témoignages littéraires: M.E. Saltykov-Ščedrin, Gleb Uspenskij, A.F. Pisemskij. Bruxelles, [1972]. pp. 248. bibliog.

USURY LAWS

— Denmark.

BETAENKNING om åger; afgivet af det af Justitsministeriet den 11. juni 1968 nedsatte udvalg. København, 1971. pp. 46. (Denmark. Betaenkninger. Nr. 604)

UTILITARIANISM.

SMART (JOHN JAMIESON CARSWELL) and WILLIAMS (BERNARD ARTHUR OWEN) Utilitarianism, for and against. Cambridge, 1973. pp. 155. bibliog.

UTOPIAS.

CHAVANNES (ALBERT) The future commonwealth;(or What Samuel Balcom first saw in Socioland); [reprint of work first published in 1892]. New York, 1971. pp. 114.

FELLMAN (MICHAEL) The unbounded frame: freedom and community in nineteenth century American utopianism. Westport, Conn., 1973. pp. 203. bibliog.

PEGUY (CHARLES) Marcel, premier dialogue de la cité harmonieuse; [first published in 1897]; accompagné d'une serie d'articles publiés en 1897 et 1898 dans La Revue socialiste. [Paris, 1973]. pp. 206.

UZBEKISTAN

— Economic history.

EKONOMICHESKIE zakonomernosti i preimushchestva nekapitalisticheskogo puti razvitiia: po materialam Uzbekistana. Tashkent, 1967-73. 2 vols.

— Industries.

EFFEKTIVNOST' kapital'nykh vlozhenii v promyshlennost' Uzbekskoi SSR. Tashkent, 1969. pp. 180.

UZHGOROD.

HRANCHAK (IVAN MYKHAILOVYCH) and PAL'OK (VASYL' VASYL'OVYCH) Misto nad Uzhem: istorychnyi narys. Uzhhorod, 1973. pp. 287. bibliog.

VACATION SCHOOLS

— United Kingdom.

HAWKINS (ERIC) ed. A time for growing: a handbook for organisers of summer projects. London, Community Relations Commission, [1971]. pp. 74. bibliog.

VACIETIS (JUKUMS).

GERMANIS (ULDIS) Oberst Vacietis und die lettischen Schützen im Weltkrieg und in der Oktoberrevolution. Stockholm, 1974. pp. 336. bibliog. (Stockholms Universitet. Acta Universitatis Stockholmiensis. Stockholm Studies in History. 20) With English summary.

VAGRANCY

— United States.

BAHR (HOWARD M.) Skid row: an introduction to disaffiliaton. New York, 1973. pp. 335.

VAL BADIA.

See GADER VALLEY.

VALAIS (CANTON)

— Economic conditions.

ROH (HENRI) Structure de l'économie valaisanne. Sion, 1970. fo. 166. (Valais (Canton). Office Cantonal de Planification. Documents de l'Aménagement du Territoire. 4)

— Economic history.

LAUBER (BRUNO) Die Gewerkschaftsbewegung im industrialisierten Agrargebiet des Oberwallis, unter besonderer Berücksichtigung der christlichen Gewerkschaften. Bern, 1974. pp. 204. bibliog.

VALLE CAUDINA

— History.

DELILLE (GERARD) Croissance d'une sociÉté rurale: Montesarchio et la Vallée Caudine aux XVIIe et XVIIIe siècles. Napoli, 1973 [or rather 1974]. pp. 281. bibliog. (Istituto Italiano per gli Studi Storici. [Publications] 28)

VALLIERES (PIERRE).

REGUSH (NICHOLAS M.) Pierre Vallières: the revolutionary process in Quebec. New York, 1973. pp. 211. bibliog.

VALUE.

Le DEBAT soviétique sur la loi de la valeur; [by] L. Trotsky [and others]. Paris, 1972. pp. 258.

PRAVOTOROV (GEORGII BORISOVICH) Stoimostnye kategorii i sposob proizvodstva: problemy teorii i metodologii. Moskva, 1974. pp. 303.

VALUE ADDED TAX.

SHOUP (CARL SUMNER) The value-added tax. Athens, 1973. pp. 43. (Center of Planning and Economic Research, [Athens]. Lecture Series. 27)

— Bibliography.

EDINBURGH COLLEGE OF COMMERCE. Library. The Common Market: VAT; second select list: periodicals and books; compiler A.J. Macaulay. Edinburgh, 1973. pp. 26. (Reading European)

VALUE ADDED TAX. (Cont.)

— Belgium.

BELGIUM. Administration de la T.V.A., de l'Enregistrement et des Domaines. 1970. Manuel de la T.V.A.. Bruxelles, [1970]. pp. 280.

BELGIUM. Administration de la T.V.A., de l'Enregistrement et des Domaines. 1970. La détaxation des stocks et le régime fiscal des contrats en cours d'exécution au 1er janvier 1971: commentaire de l'arrêté royal no. 21, du 20 juillet 1970. Bruxelles, [1970]. pp. 132.

BELGIUM. Administration de la T.V.A., de l'Enregistrement et des Domaines. 1970. La détaxation des stocks existant au 31 décembre 1970 dans les petites entreprises: commentaire de l'arrêté royal no. 21 du 20 juillet 1970. Bruxelles, [1970]. pp. 39.

BELGIUM. Administration de la T.V.A., de l'Enregistrement et des Domaines. 1971. Les petites et moyennes entreprises et la T.V.A.. Bruxelles, [1971]. pp. 58.

BELGIUM. Administration de la T.V.A., de l'Enregistrement et des Domaines. 1971. Arrêrés d'exécution. Bruxelles, [1971]. pp. 72.

— European Economic Community countries.

DOSSER (DOUGLAS G.M.) Tax harmonisation and the value added tax; (transcript of... lecture held on 6 March 1972). [London], Civil Service College, [1973?]. fo. 18. *(Lectures on the European Community. Series A. No. 9)*

EUROPEAN COMMUNITIES. Commission. 1973. Proposal for a sixth Council directive on the harmonization of member states concerning turnover taxes: common system of value added tax: uniform basis of assessment; submitted to the Council... on 29 June 1973. [Brussels], 1973. pp. 61. *(Bulletin of the European Communities. Supplements. [1973/11])*

SCHIFF (ERIC) Value-added taxation in Europe. Washington, D.C., 1973. pp. 58. *(American Enterprise Institute for Public Policy Research. Foreign Affairs Studies. 8)*

— Germany.

SCHMIDT (ARNOLD) La taxe sur la valeur ajoutée en République Fédérale d'Allemange, à partir du 1er janvier 1968: texte officiel et commentaires. Bruxelles, Office Belge du Commerce Exterieur, 1968. pp. 88.*(Informations du Commerce Extérieur. Suppléments. Série C. No.1)*

— Sweden.

SWEDEN. Finansdepartementet. 1970. The Swedish value added tax: a summary. [Stockholm], 1970. fo. 23.

— United Kingdom.

BRITISH TOURIST AUTHORITY. Tourism and value added tax: a memorandum submitted to H.M. Customs and Excise. London, 1971. pp. 8.

VAT BULLETIN; issued by H M Customs Excise [and the Central Office of Information (U.K.)]. m., Ag 1972 - N 1973 (nos.1-10); ceased pbln. London.

U.K. Customs and Excise Department. 1972. VAT in small shops and businesses. [London, 1972]. pp. (7).

U.K. Customs and Excise Department. 1973. VAT: rebate scheme for stocks which have borne purchase tax (or revenue duty). [London], 1973. pp. 19. *(Notices. No. 748)*

U.K. Customs and Excise Department. 1974. VAT: changes in the rate of tax. [London], 1974. pp. 7. *(Notices. No. 716)*

U.K. Customs and Excise Department. 1974. VAT: special schemes for retailers: application of the standard rate to road fuel etc. and certain food products. [London], 1974. pp. 10. *(Notices. No. 707. Supplement No. 1)*

U.K. Customs and Excise Department. 1974. VAT: special schemes for retailers: application of the zero rate to certain protective boots and helmets. [London], 1974. pp. 4. *(Notices. No. 707. Supplement No. 3)*

U.K. Customs and Excise Department. 1974. VAT: special schemes for retailers: procedures for any change in the standard rate. [London], 1974. pp. 13. *(Notices. No. 707. Supplement No. 2)*

— — Ireland, Northern.

IRELAND, NORTHERN. Ministry of Agriculture. 1973. Value added tax and the farmer: booklet of instructions on VAT. Belfast, 1973. pp. 6.

— United States.

TAX INSTITUTE OF AMERICA. Symposium, 1972. A value-added tax. Princeton, N.J., 1972. pp. 138. *bibliog.*

VANDERVELDE (EMILE).

ABS (ROBERT) Emile Vandervelde. Bruxelles, 1973. pp. 383.

VANN (ROBERT LEE).

BUNI (ANDREW) Robert L. Vann of the Pittsburgh Courier: politics and black journalism. Pittsburgh, [1974]. pp. 410. *bibliog.*

VARELA (FELIPE).

VARELA (FELIPE) defendant. Proceso a la montonera de Felipe Varela por la toma de Salta: causas judiciales; estudio preliminar, Felipe Varela y la toma de Salta por Rodolfo Ortega Peña y Eduardo L. Duhalde. [Buenos Aires], 1969. pp. 256.

VARGAS (GETULIO).

BOURNE (RICHARD) Getulio Vargas of Brazil, 1883-1954: sphinx of the pampas. London, 1974. pp. 236. *bibliog.*

VAUX (CLOTILDE DE).

COMTE (ISIDORE AUGUSTE MARIE FRANÇOIS XAVIER) Confessions and testament of Auguste Comte: and his correspondence with Clotilde de Vaux; edited by Albert Crompton; (translated by several members of the Church of Humanity, Liverpool). Liverpool, 1910. pp. 547.

VEBLEN (THORSTEIN).

VEBLEN (THORSTEIN) Essays, reviews and reports: previously uncollected writings; edited and with an introduction, New light on Veblen, by Joseph Dorfman. Clifton, N.J., 1973. pp. 690.

VEGETABLES

— Canada — Alberta.

PORTER (K.D.) Economics of production and marketing of irrigated fresh vegetables in Alberta: interim [1st] report, 1962, (with [2nd report, 1963] and Final report). Edmonton, Department of Agriculture, [1963-65]. 3 pts. *Library lacks 3rd report.*

— European Economic Community countries.

ECONOMIC DEVELOPMENT COMMITTEE FOR THE AGRICULTURAL INDUSTRY. Common Market Sub-Committee. Horticulture Group. UK farming and the Common Market: outdoor vegetables; a report. London, National Economic Development Office, 1973. pp. 65.

— United Kingdom.

ECONOMIC DEVELOPMENT COMMITTEE FOR THE AGRICULTURAL INDUSTRY. Common Market Sub-Committee. Horticulture Group. UK farming and the Common Market: outdoor vegetables; a report. London, National Economic Development Office, 1973. pp. 65.

VEHICLES.

NASH (CHRISTOPHER A.) The treatment of capital costs of vehicles in evaluating road schemes. [Southampton], 1973. fo. 22. *bibliog. (Southampton. University. Discussion Papers in Economics and Econometrics. No. 7313)*

VENETO

— Economic history.

ZALIN (GIOVANNI) Aspetti e problemi dell'economia veneta dalla caduta della repubblica all'annessione. Vicenza, Comune di Vicenza, 1969. pp. 253.

VENEZUELA

— Boundaries — Guyana.

ROUT (LESLIE B.) Which way out?: a study of the Guyana-Venezuela boundary dispute. East Lansing, [1971]. fo. 130. *bibliog. (Michigan State University. Latin American Studies Center. Monograph Series. No.4)*

— Capitol.

RODRIGUEZ (MANUEL ALFREDO) El capitolio de Caracas: un siglo de historia de Venezuela. Caracas, Ediciones del Congreso de la Republica, 1974. pp. 609. *bibliog.*

— Commerce.

VENEZUELA. Oficina Central de Coordinacion y Planificacion. 1974. Posibilidades de exportacion de la industria venezolana. [Caracas, 1973 or rather 1974]. pp. 165.

— Congress.

RODRIGUEZ (MANUEL ALFREDO) El capitolio de Caracas: un siglo de historia de Venezuela. Caracas, Ediciones del Congreso de la Republica, 1974. pp. 609. *bibliog.*

— Description and travel.

VILA (MARCO AURELIO) Vocabulario geografico de Venezuela. [Caracas], Corporacion Venezolana de Fomento, [1971]. pp. 400.

— Economic conditions.

GURUCEAGA (JUAN DE) ed. Geografia economica de Venezuela. [Caracas, 1959]. pp. 283.

— Economic history.

ARCILA FARIAS (EDUARDO) Economia colonial de Venezuela. 2nd ed. Caracas, 1973. 2 vols. (in 1). *bibliog.*

— Economic policy.

BREWER-CARIAS (ALLAN RANDOLPH) Reforma administrativa y desarrollo economico y social en Venezuela. Caracas, [Comision de Administracion Publica], 1970. pp. 30.*(Cuadernos para la Reforma Administrativa. 2) Reprinted from the International Review of Administrative Sciences, 1970.*

VENEZUELA. Oficina Central de Coordinacion y Planificacion. 1971. IV plan de la nacion, 1970-1974. 2nd ed. [Caracas], 1971. pp. 511.

VENEZUELA. Statutes, etc. 1949-73. La planificacion en Venezuela: normas legales y reglamentarias. Caracas, 1973. pp. 298, 1 map.

OBERTO G. (LUIS ENRIQUE) and CASAS GONZALEZ (ANTONIO) Venezuela y el C[omite] I[nteramericano de la] A[lianza para el] P[rogreso]. [Caracas], Oficina Central de Coordinacion y Planificacion, [1973 or rather 1974]. pp. 137.

— Foreign economic relations.

FORO NACIONAL SOBRE VENEZUELA Y LA INTEGRACION LATINOAMERICANA, CARACAS, 1971. Informe final. Caracas, Oficina Central de Coordinacion y Planificacion, [1972]. pp. 293.

— Industries.

VENEZUELA. Direccion General de Estadistica. Estadisticas industriales: produccion y ventas a nivel nacional (formerly: produccion y ventas). a., 1970- Caracas.

VENEZUELA. Direccion General de Estadistica. Estadisticas industriales: empleo-remuneraciones. a., 1971- Caracas.

VENEZUELA. Direccion General de Estadistica. Estadisticas industriales: energia electrica. a., 1971- Caracas.

VENEZUELA. Direccion General de Estadistica. Estadisticas industriales: operarios u obreros; remuneraciones. a., 1971- Caracas.

VENEZUELA. Direccion General de Estadistica. Estadisticas industriales: productos manufacturados. a., 1971- Caracas.

VENEZUELA. Direccion de Planification Economica. 1974. III encuesta industrial, 1971. [Caracas], 1973 [or rather 1974]. 2 vols. (in 1).

VENEZUELA. Oficina Central de Coordinacion y Planificacion. 1974. Posibilidades de exportacion de la industria venezolana. [Caracas, 1973 or rather 1974]. pp. 165.

— Manufactures.

VENEZUELA. Direccion General de Estadistica. Estadisticas industriales: productos manufacturados. a., 1971- Caracas.

— Maps.

VENEZUELA. Ministerio de Agricultura y Cria. Direccion de Planificacion Agropecuaria. 1960. Atlas agricola de Venezuela. [Caracas, 1960]. unpaged.

— Politics and government.

SADER PEREZ (RUBEN) Temas para un cambio de regimen politico. Caracas, 1971. pp. 220.

TAYLOR (PHILIP BATES) Thoughts on comparative effectiveness: leadership and the democratic left in Colombia and Venezuela. Buffalo, N.Y., 1971. fo. 42,xvi. *(New York State University. Council on International Studies. Special Studies. No. 2)*

— Social policy.

BREWER-CARIAS (ALLAN RANDOLPH) Reforma administrativa y desarrollo economico y social en Venezuela. Caracas, [Comision de Administracion Publica], 1970. pp. 30.*(Cuadernos para la Reforma Administrativa. 2) Reprinted from the International Review of Administrative Sciences, 1970.*

VENEZUELA. Oficina Central de Coordinacion y Planificacion. 1971. IV plan de la nacion, 1970-1974. 2nd ed. [Caracas], 1971. pp. 511.

OBERTO G. (LUIS ENRIQUE) and CASAS GONZALEZ (ANTONIO) Venezuela y el C[omite] I[nteramericano de la] A[lianza para el] P[rogreso]. [Caracas], Oficina Central de Coordinacion y Planificacion, [1973 or rather 1974]. pp. 137.

— Voting registers.

VENEZUELA. Consejo Supremo Electoral. 1969. Datos estadisticos del registro electoral de 1968. Caracas, 1969. pp. 107. *(Serie Estadistica. 1)*

VENICE

— History.

LANE (FREDERIC CHAPIN) Venice: a maritime republic. Baltimore, [1973]. pp. 505. *bibliog.*

— Social history.

BURKE (PETER) Historian. Venice and Amsterdam: a study of seventeenth-century élites. London, 1974. pp. 154. *bibliog.*

VERBAL LEARNING.

KAUSLER (DONALD HARVEY) ed. Readings in verbal learning: contemporary theory and research. New York, [1966]. pp. 578. *bibliog.*

VERBAND DER UNABHÄNGIGEN.

STUEBER (FRITZ) Ich war Abgeordneter: die Entstehung der freiheitlichen Opposition in Österreich. Graz, [1974]. pp. 304.

VERDUN

— Economic history.

MEEH (KUNO) Struktur und Entwicklung des Wirtschaftsraums Verdun: ein Betrachtung und Beurteilung eines französischen Passivraums. Berlin, 1972. pp. 343. *bibliog.*

VERONA

— Economic history.

ZALIN (GIOVANNI) L'economia veronese in età napoleonica: forze di lavoro, dinamica fondiaria e attività agricolo-commerciali. Milano, 1973. pp. 399. *(Economia e Storia. Biblioteca. 2a Serie. 4)*

VERSAILLES, TREATY OF, JUNE 28, 1919 (GERMANY).

WENGST (UDO) Graf Brockdorff-Rantzau und die aussenpolitischen Anfänge der Weimarer Republik. Bern, 1973. pp. 163. *bibliog.*

VERWOERD (HENDRIK FRENSCH).

VERWOERD (HENDRIK FRENSCH) Hoofartikels uit 'Die Transvaler', 1937-1948; saamgestel deur O. Geyser. Kaapstad, 1972. pp. 100.

VIATKA.

See KIROV.

VICTIMS OF CRIME.

SMITH (PETER B.) Groups within organizations: applications of social psychology to organizational behaviour. London, 1973. pp. 134. *bibliog.*

DRAPKIN (ISRAEL) and VIANO (EMILIO) eds. Victimology. Lexington, Mass., [1974]. pp. 262. *bibliogs.*

VIENNA

— Börse.

SCHOEN (EDUARD) Die Liquidation an der Wiener Börse und Vorschläge zur Reform derselben. Wien, 1869. pp. 29.

— Intellectual life.

JANIK (ALLAN) and TOULMIN (STEPHEN EDELSTON) Wittgenstein's Vienna. London, 1973. pp. 314. *bibliog.*

— Population.

GISSER (RICHARD) Die Zuwanderung nach Wien: eine Untersuchung zur Situation der Bundeshauptstadt in der regionalen Bevölkerungsentwicklung. Wien, 1969. 1 vol.(various pagings). *(Österreichisches Institut für Raumplanung. Veröffentlichungen. Nr. 34)*

VIET CONG.

POHLE (VICTORIA) The Viet Cong in Saigon: tactics and objectives during the Tet offensive...; prepared for the Office of the Assistant Secretary of Defense/International Security Affairs, and the Advanced Research Projects Agency. Santa Monica, 1969. pp. 75. *(Rand Corporation. Research Memoranda. 5799)*

VIETNAM

— Commerce.

DEVELOPMENT AND RESOURCES CORPORATION. Export prospects for the Republic of Vietnam; [by Frederick T. Moore, and others]. New York, 1971. pp. 389.

— Foreign relations — Canada.

CULHANE (CLAIRE) Why is Canada in Vietnam?: the truth about our foreign aid. Toronto, 1972. pp. 126.

— — China.

WELCOME the signing of the Paris agreement on Viet Nam. Peking, 1973. pp. 37.

— — Russia.

BOEVAIA solidarnost'', bratskaia pomoshch': sbornik vazhneishikh vneshnepoliticheskikh dokumentov SSSR po v'etnamskomu voprosu, etc. Moskva, 1970. pp. 219.

— — United States.

TRAN-MINH-TIET. Les relations américano-vietnamiennes de Kennedy à Nixon. Paris, [1971 in progress].

— Government publications.

VIETNAM (REPUBLIC). Ministry of Culture, Education and Youth. 1973. Bibliography of Vietnamese official publications, 1960-1971. [2nd ed.] Saigon, 1972 [or rather 1973]. pp. 170.

— History.

MASSON (ANDRÉ) Histoire du Vietnam. 4th ed. Paris, 1972. pp. 128. *bibliog.*

— Industries.

ANOSOVA (LIUDMILA ALEKSANDROVNA) Promyshlennost' Demokraticheskoi Respubliki V'etnam, 1954- 1965. Moskva, 1973. pp. 104. *bibliog.*

— Politics and government.

DUFF (PEGGY) The truth about Thieu: South Vietnam: the facts. London, [1973]. pp. 15. *(Indochina Solidarity Conference. Indochina Information. No.2)*

DUFF(PEGGY) The truth about Thieu: South Vietnam: the facts. London, [1973]. pp. 15. *(Indochina Solidarity Conference. Indochina Information. No. 2)*

— Rural conditions.

NGO VINH LONG Before the revolution: the Vietnamese peasants under the French. Cambridge, Mass., [1973]. pp. 292. *bibliog.*

VIETNAMESE WARS, 1945— .

SHCHEDROV (IVAN MIKHAILOVICH) Groza nad Krasnoi rekoi: reportazhi iz Demokraticheskoi Respubliki V'etnam. Moskva, 1967. pp. 231.

POHLE (VICTORIA) The Viet Cong in Saigon: tactics and objectives during the Tet offensive...; prepared for the Office of the Assistant Secretary of Defense/International Security Affairs, and the Advanced Research Projects Agency. Santa Monica, 1969. pp. 75. *(Rand Corporation. Research Memoranda. 5799)*

BOEVAIA solidarnost'', bratskaia pomoshch': sbornik vazhneishikh vneshnepoliticheskikh dokumentov SSSR po v'etnamskomu voprosu, etc. Moskva, 1970. pp. 219.

BRITISH CAMPAIGN FOR PEACE IN VIETNAM. Trade unions and Vietnam: the story of the first British trade union delegation to Vietnam; an eye-witness account. Manchester, [1970?]. pp. 16.

VASIL'EV (ALEKSEI MIKHAILOVICH) Rakety nad tsvetkom lotosa: V'etnam v dni voiny. Moskva, 1970. pp. 199.

WHITE (RALPH KIRBY) Nobody wanted war: misperception in Vietnam and other wars. rev. ed. Garden City, N.Y., 1970. pp. 386. *bibliog.*

CULHANE (CLAIRE) Why is Canada in Vietnam?: the truth about our foreign aid. Toronto, 1972. pp. 126.

HANSEN (JOSEPH) Marxist, and LUND (CAROLINE) Nixon's Moscow and Peking summits: their meaning for Vietnam. New York, [1972]. pp. 31.

INDOCHINA handbook 1972: an 'Indochina' special. London, [1972?]. pp. 48. *Articles on the Vietnam conflict previously appearing in the magazine Indo-China.*

DUNCANSON (DENNIS J.) Indo-China: the conflict analysed. London, 1973. pp. 19. *(Institute for the Study of Conflict. Conflict Studies. No. 39)*

VIETNAMESE WARS, 1945 —. (Cont.)

PALMER (JAMES GREGORY) American defense policy and the Vietnam war; [M.Phil. (London) thesis]. 1973. fo. 261. *bibliog. Typescript: unpublished. This thesis is the property of London University and may not be removed from the Library.*

THOMAS (JAMES A.) Holy war: the lure of victory and the passing of America as a world power. New Rochelle, [1973]. pp. 272.

GEORGES (ALFRED) pseud. Charles de Gaulle et la guerre d'Indochine. Paris,[1974]. pp. 189.

McCARTHY (MARY THERESE) The seventeenth degree: How it went; Vietnam; Hanoi; Medina; Sons of the morning. New York, [1974]. pp. 451.

SIMON (SHELDON W.) War and politics in Cambodia: a communications analysis. Durham, N.C., 1974. pp. 178. *bibliog.*

THOMPSON (Sir ROBERT GRAINGER KER) Peace is not at hand. London, 1974. pp. 208.

WEST (RICHARD LEAF) Victory in Vietnam;...photographs by Philip Jones Griffiths. London, 1974. pp. 196.

— **Bibliography.**

LEITENBERG (MILTON) and BURNS (RICHARD DEAN) compilers. The Vietnam conflict: its geographical dimensions, political traumas and military developments: [a bibliography]. Santa Barbara, [1973]. pp. 164.

— **Diplomatic history.**

FRANCE. Ministère des Affaires Etrangères. Service d'Information et de Presse. 1973. La France et le Vietnam: recueil des principales déclarations françaises, août 1963-juin 1973: textes et documents. [Paris, 1973?]. pp. 82.

SCHELLHORN (KAI M.) Krisen-Entscheidung: der geheime amerikanische Entscheidungsprozess zur Bombardierung Nord-Vietnams, 1964/65. München, [1974]. pp. 209. *bibliog. (Munich. Universität. Geschwister-Scholl-Institut für Politische Wissenschaft. Münchener Studien zur Politik. 26. Band)*

— **Peace.**

UNITED STATES. 1968. Paris peace talks: statement by the government of the United States of America together with statement by the government of the Republic of Viet-Nam, dated 27 November 1968. in AUSTRALIA. Parliament. Parliamentary papers, 1969, vol.2.

VIETNAM settlement: why 1973, not 1969?; [by] Morton A. Kaplan [and others]. Washington, [1973]. pp. 208. *(American Enterprise Institute for Public Policy Research. Rational Debate Seminars. 7th Series. 1)*

WELCOME the signing of the Paris agreement on Viet Nam. Peking, 1973. pp. 37.

— **Personal narratives, American.**

WILLWERTH (JAMES) Eye in the last storm: a reporter's journal of one year in southeast Asia. New York, 1972. pp. 178.

— **Protest movements — United States.**

BANNAN (JOHN F.) and BANNAN (ROSEMARY S.) Law, morality and Vietnam: the peace militants and the courts. Bloomington, [Ind., 1974]. pp. 241.

— **Public opinion.**

IONS (EDMUND SIMON AUBREY) Dissent in America: the constraints on foreign policy. London, 1971. pp. 14. *(Institute for the Study of Conflict. Conflict Studies. No. 18)*

INDOCHINA SOLIDARITY CONFERENCE. Media Group. The British press and Vietnam. London, 1973. pp. 31. *(Indochina Solidarity Conference. Indochina Information [Series]. No. 3)*

LANG (DANIEL) Patriotism without flags. New York, [1974]. pp. 209. *Articles originally published in The New Yorker.*

VILA

— **Census.**

BROOKFIELD (HAROLD CHILLINGWORTH) and GLICK (PAULA BROWN) The people of Vila: report on a census of a Pacific island town. Canberra, 1969. fo.65. *(Australian National University. Research School of Pacific Studies. Department of Human Geography. Publications. HG/1)*

VILLAGE COMMUNITIES

— **Niger.**

RAYNAUT (CLAUDE) Structures normatives et relations électives: étude d'une communauté villageoise haoussa. Paris, [1973]. pp. 314. *bibliog.*

VILLAGES

— **Asia, Southeast.**

FREESTONE (COLIN S.) The south-east Asian village: (a geographic, social and economic study). London, 1974. pp. 109. *bibliog.*

— **Canada — Quebec.**

VERDON (MICHEL) Anthropologie de la colonisation au Québec: le dilemme d'un village du Lac-Saint-Jean. Montréal, 1973. pp. 283.

— **Egypt.**

FAKHOURI (HANI) Kafr El-Elow: an Egyptian village in transition. New York, 1972. pp. 134. *bibliog.*

HARIK (ILIYA F.) The political mobilization of peasants: a study of an Egyptian community. Bloomington, Ind., [1974]. pp. 309. *bibliog. (Indiana University. International Development Research Center. Studies in Development. No.8)*

— **Germany.**

SPINDLER (GEORGE D.) and others. Burgbach: urbanization and identity in a German village. New York, [1973]. pp. 148. *bibliog.*

— **Guyana.**

RAUF (MOHAMMAD A.) Indian village in Guyana: a study of cultural change and ethnic identity. Leiden, 1974. pp. 120. *bibliog.*

— **India.**

LAKSHMANNA (CHINTAMANI) Caste dynamics in village India. Bombay, [1973]. pp. 144. *bibliog.*

GUPTA (GIRI RAJ) Marriage, religion and society: pattern of change in an Indian village. Delhi, [1974]. pp. 187. *bibliog.*

KESSINGER (TOM G.) Vilyatpur 1848-1968: social and economic change in a north Indian village. Berkeley, [1974]. pp. 227.

— — **Mysore.**

VENKATARAYAPPA (K.N.) Rural society and social change: (a study of some villages in Mysore). Bombay, 1973. pp. 264.

— **Italy — Trentino—Alto Adige.**

COLE (JOHN W.) and WOLF (ERIC ROBERT) The hidden frontier: ecology and ethnicity in an Alpine valley. New York, [1974]. pp. 348. *bibliog.*

— **Mexico.**

ROMANUCCI-ROSS (LOLA) Conflict, violence, and morality in a Mexican village. Palo Alto, Calif., 1973. pp. 202. *bibliog.*

GONZALEZ Y GONZALEZ (LUIS) San José de Gracia: Mexican village in transition;... translated by John Upton. Austin, [1974]. pp. 362. *bibliog.*

— **Norway.**

TVEIT (NORVALD) Eit vegopprør i Bygde-Norge: Fjaerland. Oslo, 1973. pp. 118.

— **Papua New Guinea.**

MORAUTA (LOUISE HELEN MARGARET) Beyond the village: local politics in Madang, Papua New Guinea. London, 1974. pp. 194. *bibliog. (London. University. London School of Economics and Political Science. Monographs on Social Anthropology. No. 49)*

— **Senegal.**

ROCH (JEAN) Eléments d'analyse du système agricole en milieu wolof mouride: l'exemple de Darou Rahmane II. [Dakar], Office de la Recherche Scientifique et Technique Outre-Mer, Centre de Dakar-Hann, 1968. fo. 56. *bibliog.*

— **Spain.**

LUQUE BAENA (ENRIQUE) Estudio antropologico social de un pueblo del sur. Madrid, [1974]. pp. 251. *bibliog.*

— **Turkey.**

TURKEY. Social Planning Department. Social Structure Research Group. 1974. Modernization in Turkish villages; [by] Ahmet Tuğaç [and others]. Ankara, 1973 [or rather 1974]. pp. 386.

— **United Kingdom.**

DEWINDT (EDWIN BREZETTE) Land and people in Holywell-cum-Needingworth: structures of tenure and patterns of social organization in an East Midlands village, 1252-1457. Toronto, 1972. pp. 299. *bibliog. (Pontifical Institute of Mediaeval Studies. Studies and Texts. 22)*

LINDSEY. County Council. Communities in rural Lindsay, present and future. Lincoln, 1973. pp. 52.

AMBROSE (PETER JOHN) The quiet revolution: social change in a Sussex village, 1871-1971. London, 1974. pp. 239.

ASHBY (MABEL K.) The changing English village: a history of Bledington, Gloucestershire, in its setting, 1066-1914. Kineton, 1974. pp. 425.

RAVENSDALE (J.R.) Liable to floods: village landscape on the edge of the fens, AD 450-1850. London, 1974. pp. 206. *bibliog.*

SPUFFORD (MARGARET) Contrasting communities: English villagers in the sixteenth and seventeenth centuries. London, 1974. pp. 374.

— — **Ireland, Northern.**

HENDRY (JOHN) The village study as a live project. Oxford, 1971. pp. 48. *(Oxford Polytechnic. Department of Town Planning. Oxford Working Papers in Planning Education and Research. 7)*

VILLEINAGE

— **Russia.**

ZIMIN (ALEKSANDR ALEKSANDROVICH) Kholopy na Rusi, s drevneishikh vremen do kontsa XV v. Moskva, 1973. pp. 341.

VINNITSA (OBLAST')

— **Politics and government.**

NARYSY istoriï Vinnyts'koï oblasnoï partiinoï orhanizatsiï. Odesa, 1972. pp. 328.

— **Statistics.**

VINNITSA (OBLAST'). Statystychne Upravlinnia. Narodne hospodarstvo Vinnits'koï oblasti: statystychnyi zbirnyk. Kyïv, 1969. pp. 240.

VIOLENCE.

BONDURANT (JOAN VALERIE) ed. Conflict: violence and nonviolence. Chicago, 1971. pp. 206.

PROTEST, violence and social change; [edited by] Richard P. Bowles [and others]. Scarborough, Ont., [1972]. pp. 209. *bibliog.*

ARON (RAYMOND) Histoire et dialectique de la violence. [Paris, 1973]. pp. 273.

HIRSCH (HERBERT) and PERRY (DAVID C.) eds. Violence as politics: a series of original essays. New York, [1973]. pp. 262. *bibliog.*

MICHAUD (YVES ALAIN) ed. La violence. [Paris, 1973]. pp. 96.

FRASER (JOHN) b. 1928. Violence in the arts. London, 1974. pp. 192.

HOLLON (WILLIAM EUGENE) Frontier violence: another look. New York, 1974. pp. 279. *bibliog.*

PRIESTLAND (GERALD) The future of violence. London, 1974. pp. 174. *bibliog.*

— Moral and religious aspects.

EPPSTEIN (JOHN) The cult of revolution in the Church. New Rochelle, [1974]. pp. 160.

— Mexico.

ROMANUCCI-ROSS (LOLA) Conflict, violence, and morality in a Mexican village. Palo Alto, Calif., 1973. pp. 202. *bibliog.*

— United Kingdom.

WILLIAMS (SHIRLEY) Freedom and order in a liberal society. Liverpool, 1973. pp. 17. (*Eleanor Rathbone Memorial Trust. Eleanor Rathbone Memorial Lectures. 20*)

— — Ireland, Northern.

NEW ULSTER MOVEMENT. Publications. 6. Violence and Northern Ireland. Belfast, 1972. pp. (16).

VIRGIN ISLANDS

— Politics and government.

PAIEWONSKY (RALPH M.) Messages of the Governor of the Virgin Islands...from February 2, 1967 to December 24, 1968. [St. Thomas, 1969]. pp. 257.

VIRGINIA

— Emigration and immigration.

CRAVEN (WESLEY FRANK) White, red, and black: the seventeenth-century Virginian. Charlottesville, 1971. pp. 114. (*Virginia University. Richard Lectures. 1970*)

— Population.

CRAVEN (WESLEY FRANK) White, red, and black: the seventeenth-century Virginian. Charlottesville, 1971. pp. 114. (*Virginia University. Richard Lectures. 1970*)

VISUAL PERCEPTION.

HABER (RALPH NORMAN) and HERSHENSON (MAURICE) The psychology of visual perception. New York, [1973]. pp. 398. *bibliogs.*

PYKETT (ANDREW NICHOLAS) The sense of place and the perceived environment : a theory, and its application in the London borough of Camden; [Ph.D. (London) thesis]. [1974]. fo. 299. *bibliog. Typescript: unpublished. This thesis is the property of London University and may not be removed from the library.*

VITAL STATISTICS.

UNITED NATIONS. Statistical Office. Statistical Papers. Series M. No.19. Rev. 1. Principles and recommendations for a vital statistics system. (ST/STAT/SER.M/19/Rev.1) New York, 1973. pp. 220.

VITICULTURE

— France.

FRANCE. Direction de la Documentation. La Documentation Française. Notes et Etudes Documentaires. Nos. 3,956-3, 957. Les productions végétales en France: la vigne et le vin. [Paris], 1973. pp. 82. *bibliog.*

— Germany.

SCHEUTEN (ROLF) Stellung und Bedeutung der Winzergenossenschaften in der Bundesrepublik Deutschland. Köln, [1972]. pp. 356. *bibliog.* (*Institut für Mittelstandsforschung. Schriften zur Mittelstandsforschung. Band 46*)

GERMANY (BUNDESREPUBLIK). Bundesministerium für Ernährung, Landwirtschaft und Forsten. Ertragslage des Garten- und Weinbaues. a., 1973- Bonn.

— Germany, Eastern.

WEINHOLD (RUDOLF) Winzerarbeit an Elbe, Saale und Unstrut: eine historisch- ethnographische Untersuchung der Produktivkräfte des Weinbaus auf dem Gebiete der DDR. Berlin, 1973. pp. 419. *bibliog.* (*Akademie der Wissenschaften der DDR. Zentralinstitut für Geschichte. Veröffentlichungen zur Volkskunde und Kulturgeschichte. Band 55*)

VITTORIO (GIUSEPPE DI).

PISTILLO (MICHELE) Giuseppe Di Vittorio, 1907-1924: dal sindacalismo rivoluzionario al comunismo. Roma, 1973. pp. 340. *With an appendix of articles by Di Vittorio.*

VLADIMIR (OBLAST')

— Statistics.

VLADIMIR (OBLAST'). Statisticheskoe Upravlenie. Narodnoe khoziaistvo Vladimirskoi oblasti v vos'moi piatiletke, 1966-1970 gody; pod obshchei redaktsiei...Egorova N.N. i Kurenkovoi E.I. Vladimir, 1972. pp. 308.

VOCATIONAL EDUCATION

INTERNATIONAL LABOUR CONFERENCE. 59th Session. Reports. 8. Human resources development: vocational guidance and vocational training; eighth item on the agenda. Geneva, 1973-74. 2 pts.

INTERGOVERNMENTAL CONFERENCE ON THE UTILISATION OF HIGHLY QUALIFIED PERSONNEL, 2ND, VENICE, 1971. The utilisation of highly qualified personnel: [report on] Venice Conference 15th-27th October 1971. Paris, Organisation for Economic Co-operation and Development, 1973. pp. 427. *The 1st Conference was entitled and catalogued POLICY CONFERENCE ON HIGHLY QUALIFIED MANPOWER, PARIS, 1966.*

— Africa, Subsaharan.

WOOD (A.W.) Informal education and development in Africa. The Hague, 1974. pp. 312. *bibliog.* (*Hague. Institute of Social Studies. Publications. Paperback Series. 10*)

— Botswana.

VAN RENSBURG (PATRICK) Report from Swaneng Hill: education and employment in an African country. Stockholm, 1974. pp. 235.

— Canada — Statistics.

CANADA. Statistics Canada. Publicly-supported vocational training involving the private sector. a., 1971/2 [1st]- Ottawa. *In English and French.*

— Cyprus.

ILO INTER-REGIONAL MEETING OF EXPERTS IN VOCATIONAL TRAINING FOR THE HOTEL AND TOURIST INDUSTRY, NICOSIA, 1969. Report on meeting... [held in] Nicosia, Cyprus, 24 November-6 December 1969. (ILO/TAP/INT/R.20).. Geneva, 1970. pp. 81.

— Denmark.

KIIL (PER) Adult vocational training. 2nd rev. ed. Copenhagen, 1972. pp. 26. (*Social conditions in Denmark. 8*)

— France.

FRANCE. Secrétariat Général du Comité Interministériel de la Formation Professionnelle et de la Promotion Sociale. 1969. La politique coordonnée de la formation professionnelle et de la promotion sociale. [Paris, 1969]. 1 vol.(various pagings).

FRANCE. Comité du Travail Féminin. 1972. Formation professionnelle: rapport de la Commission. [Paris], 1972. fo. 51.

FRANCE. Direction de la Documentation. La Documentation Française. Notes et Etudes Documentaires. Nos. 3,864-3, 865. La formation professionnelle continue et la promotion sociale en France, par Jean-Michel Belorgey. [Paris], 1972. pp. 56. *bibliog.*

FRANCE. French Embassy, London. Service de Presse et d'Information. 1972. Continuous vocational training and social promotion in France. London, [1972]. pp. 39.

— Italy.

CENTRO STUDI INVESTIMENTI SOCIALI. La formazione professionale in Italia. Bologna, [1972]. 2 vols.(in 1).

— Paraguay.

MAS GARCIA (A.) Promocion profesional de trabajadores en Paraguay: un desafio, una respuesta. Asuncion, 1972. pp. 143. *bibliog.*

— Underdeveloped areas.

See UNDERDEVELOPED AREAS — Vocational education.

— United Kingdom.

U.K. Department of Education and Science. Schools Council. Working Party on the Transition from School to Work. 1972. Careers education in the 1970s; report; [Dame Muriel Stewart and subsequently L.J. Drew, chairmen]. London, 1972. pp. 117. *bibliog.* (*Schools Council. Working Papers. 40*)

STYLER (WILLIAM EDWARD) Post-experience and the universities. Hull, 1973. pp. 19.

U.K. Department of Education and Science. 1973. Careers education in secondary schools. London, 1973. pp. 87. (*Education Surveys. 18*)

— United States.

BOLINO (AUGUST C.) Career education: contributions to economic growth. New York, 1973. pp. 234. *bibliog.*

MINCER (JACOB) Schooling, experience and earnings. New York, 1974. pp. 152. *bibliog.* (*National Bureau of Economic Research. Human Behavior and Social Institutions. 2*)

— Yugoslavia.

BREKIĆ (JOVO) ed. Planiranje kadrova i obrazovanja u organizacijama udruženog rada. Zagreb, 1973. pp. 162. *bibliog.*

VOCATIONAL GUIDANCE.

INTERNATIONAL LABOUR CONFERENCE. 59th Session. Reports. 8. Human resources development: vocational guidance and vocational training; eighth item on the agenda. Geneva, 1973-74. 2 pts.

TIMPERLEY (STUART R.) Personnel planning and occupational choice. London, 1974. pp. 236.

— Belgium.

PASQUASY (RENE) and SIRON (R.) L'orientation scolaire et professionnelle en Belgique. Bruxelles, [1972]. pp. 128. *bibliog.*

VOCATIONAL GUIDANCE. (Cont.)

— Canada.

DODGE (DAVID A.) and SWAN (NEIL M.) Factors influencing career choices of students: an empirical examination of some aspects of the neoclassical theory of choice in labour markets. Kingston, 1971. 1 vol. (various foliations). *(Kingston, Ontario. Queen's University. Institute for Economic Research. Discussion Papers. No. 48)*

CANADA. Department of Manpower and Immigration. Career outlook: university and community college: environmental sciences and studies. a., 1972/3- Ottawa. *In English and French.*

— France.

FRANCE. Centre d'Etudes et de Recherches sur les Conditions d'Emploi et de Travail des Jeunes. 1971. Emplois proposés aux jeunes de 1959 à 1969 (par la Section d'Accueil des Jeunes) [du] B[ureau de la] M[ain d'] O[euvre] spécialisé de Paris. Paris, 1971. pp. 100.

GOURCEAUD (ANNE MARIE) and LARRIEU (ROUMAIN) Premier bilan des stages de préformation dans la région Midi-Pyrénées. Toulouse, Echelon Régional de l'Emploi, 1971. fo.34,2.

— Germany.

GERMANY (BUNDESREPUBLIK). Bundesanstalt für Arbeit. Berufsberatung: Ergebnisse der Berufsberatungsstatistik. a., 1971/2- Nürnberg.

KERN (BAERBEL) Einflüsse sozioökonomischer Faktoren auf die Ausbildungsentscheidungen von Abiturienten in vier ausgewählten Regionen Niedersachsens: ein Beitrag zur Bildungsmobilität. Göttingen, 1973. 1 vol.(various pagings).

— Italy.

MILAN (PROVINCE). Contributi: Problemi Socio-Economici della Circoscrizione Provinciale Milanese. n. 3. 10 anni di esperienze sull'orientamento dei giovani. Milano, 1967. pp. 294.

— United Kingdom.

U.K. Central Youth Employment Executive. Choice of Careers . [London], 1969 in progress.

CAREERS GUIDE: opportunities in the professions, industry, commerce and the public service; [pd. by] Department of Employment [U.K.]. a. (formerly irreg.), 1970(8th)- London. *From 1970 only every 5th yr. kept permanently.*

U.K. Civil Service Commission. 1970. Careers for graduates: posts in government service, 1971. [London, 1970]. pp. 109. *bibliog.*

U.K. Civil Service Commission. 1970. Careers for school-leavers: posts in government service, 1971. [London, 1970]. pp. 56.

ECONOMIC DEVELOPMENT COMMITTEE FOR ELECTRONICS. Subcommittee on Electronics and the Schools. Careers literature: its preparation and distribution. [London, National Economic Development Office, 1972]. pp. (10).

U.K. Department of Education and Science. Schools Council. Working Party on the Transition from School to Work. 1972. Careers education in the 1970s; report; [Dame Muriel Stewart and subsequently L.J. Drew, chairmen]. London, 1972. pp. 117. *bibliog. (Schools Council. Working Papers. 40)*

GRADUATE opportunities, 1975; ([with] GRID '75: GO's recruiters index and directory). London, [1974]. pp. 824. *GRID '75 in end pocket.*

VOCATIONAL REHABILITATION

— Netherlands.

SOCIALE werkvoorziening: rapport van een interdepartementale werkgroep, 22 maart 1973. 's-Gravenhage, 1973. pp. 127. *(Netherlands. Ministerie van Sociale Zaken. Verslagen en Rapporten: Sociale Zaken. 1973. 3)*

— Norway.

HELLE (KARI MARIE) Arbeidstakere i vernede bedrifter. [Oslo], Arbeidsdirektoratet, 1972. fo. 73. *bibliog.*

VOCKE (WILHELM) Bundesbankpräsident.

VOCKE (WILHELM) Bundesbankpräsident. Memoiren. Stuttgart, [1973]. pp. 223.

VOLGA BASIN

— Economic conditions.

PROBLEMY razvitiia i razmeshcheniia proizvoditel'nykh sil Povolzh'ia. Moskva, 1973. pp. 272. *bibliog.*

— History — 1917—1921, Revolution — Historiography.

OKTIABR' v Povolzh'e i Priural'e: istochniki i voprosy istoriografii. Kazan', 1972. pp. 150.

VOLOGDA (OBLAST')

— Statistics.

VOLOGDA (OBLAST'). Statisticheskoe Upravlenie. Narodnoe khoziaistvo Vologodskoi oblasti v vos'moi piatiletke: statisticheskii sbornik. [Vologda], 1971. pp. 188.

VOLTA RIVER.

FOOD AND AGRICULTURE ORGANIZATION. 1963. Final report on survey of the Lower Volta river flood plain. Rome, 1963. 5 vols. Microfilm: 1 reel.

VOLUNTEER WORKERS IN SOCIAL SERVICE.

MORRIS (ROBERT CRANE) Overseas volunteer programs: their evolution and the role of governments in their support. Lexington, Mass., [1973]. pp. 352. *bibliog. (Center for a Voluntary Society. Voluntary Action Research Series)*

— United Kingdom.

COLVILLE (JOHN MARK ALEXANDER) Viscount Colville of Culross. The government and the voluntary movement: with special reference to London. London, [1972]. pp. 6.

CROSSMAN (RICHARD HOWARD STAFFORD) The role of the volunteer in the modern social service. Oxford, [1973]. pp. 32. *(Oxford. University. Sidney Ball Lectures. 1973)*

DAVIES (CAROLYN) and FILSON (DEBORAH) Social services volunteers and the community: a study of the role of 'voluntary services liaison officer' in local authority social services departments. [London], Department of Health and Social Security, 1973. fo. 19.

U.K. Social Work Service. 1973. Voluntary activity and the personal social services. [London], 1973. fo. 9.

VON NEUMANN (JOHN).

AFRIAT (S.N.) Production duality and the von Neumann theory of growth and interest. Meisenheim am Glan, [1974]. pp. 78. *bibliog.*

VORARLBERG

— Economic policy.

WURZER (RUDOLF) Raumordnung Vorarlberg. [Bregenz], Amt der Vorarlberger Landesregierung, 1971. 2 vols.

— History.

WITZIG (DANIEL) Die Vorarlberger Frage: die Vorarlberger Anschlussbewehung an die Schweiz,...1918-1922. Basel, 1974. pp. 527. *bibliog.*

— Population.

WELTI (LUDWIG) Siedlungs- und Sozialgeschichte von Vorarlberg; aus dem Nachlass herausgegeben von Nikolaus Grass. Innsbruck, 1973. pp. 233. *bibliog. (Innsbruck. Universität. Studien zur Rechts-, Wirtschafts- und Kulturgeschichte. 1)*

— Social history.

WELTI (LUDWIG) Siedlungs- und Sozialgeschichte von Vorarlberg; aus dem Nachlass herausgegeben von Nikolaus Grass. Innsbruck, 1973. pp. 233. *bibliog. (Innsbruck. Universität. Studien zur Rechts-, Wirtschafts- und Kulturgeschichte. 1)*

VORONEZH (OBLAST')

— Industries.

POLIVANOV (ALEKSEI SERGEEVICH) and POPOV (P.A.) Razvitie promyshlennosti Voronezhskoi oblasti za 50 let Sovetskoi vlasti, 1917-1967 gg. Voronezh, 1968. pp. 108.

— Statistics.

VORONEZH (OBLAST'). Statisticheskoe Upravlenie. Narodnoe khoziaistvo Voronezhskoi oblasti: statisticheskii sbornik. Voronezh, 1972. pp. 252.

VOTING.

NEWLAND (ROBERT A.) and BRITTON (FRANK S.) How to conduct an election by the single transferable vote. London, 1973. pp. 32. *bibliog. With 4 specimen forms.*

LAKEMAN (ENID) How democracies vote: a study of electoral systems. 4th ed. London, 1974. pp. 317. *bibliog.*

— Australia.

HUGHES (COLIN ANFIELD) and GRAHAM (BRUCE DESMOND) Voting for the Australian House of Representatives, 1901-1964. Canberra, 1974. pp. 544,xii. *Supplement to the same authors' A handbook of Australian government and politics 1890-1964, to which it also contains Corrigenda.*

— Germany.

LAVIES (RALF RAINER) Nichtwählen als Kategorie des Wahlverhaltens: empirische Untersuchung zur Wahlenthaltung in historischer, politischer und statistischer Sicht. Düsseldorf, [1973]. pp. 194. *bibliog. (Germany (Bundesrepublik Deutschland). Kommission für Geschichte des Parlamentarismus und der Politischen Parteien. Beiträge zur Geschichte des Parlamentarismus und der Politischen Parteien. Band 48)*

SAARBRUECKEN. Universität. Annales Universitatis Saraviensis. Rechts- und Wirtschaftswissenschaftliche Abteilung. Band 71. Faktoren der Wahlentscheidung: eine wahlsoziologische Analyse am Beispiel der saarländischen Landtagswahl 1970... ; von Jürgen W. Falter. Köln, 1973. pp. 256. *bibliog.*

— India.

VARMA (SHANTI PRASAD) and NARAIN (IQBAL) Voting behaviour in a changing society: a case study of the fourth general election in Rajasthan. Delhi, 1973. pp. 385.

— Switzerland.

ENGLER (URS) Stimmbeteiligung und Demokratie: Aspekte eines schweizerischen Problems. Bern, 1973. pp. 318. *bibliog.*

— United States.

GABRIEL (RICHARD A.) The ethnic factor in the urban polity. New York, 1973. pp. 149.

PIELE (PHILIP K.) and HALL (JOHN STUART) Budgets, bonds and ballots: voting behavior in school financial elections. Lexington, [1973]. pp. 216. *bibliog.*

SILBEY (JOEL HENRY) ed. Political ideology and voting behavior in the age of Jackson. Englewood Cliffs, [1973]. pp. 189. *bibliog.*

VOTING RESEARCH

— **South Africa.**

SCHLEMMER (LAWRENCE) Privilege, prejudice and parties: a study of political motivation among white voters in Durban. Johannesburg, 1973. pp. 85.

VOZNESENSKII (ALEKSANDR ALEKSEEVICH).

UCHENYI-kommunist: k 75-letiiu so dnia rozhdeniia A.A. Voznesenskogo. Leningrad, 1973. pp. 144. *bibliog.*

VYATKA.

See KIROV.

WACHENHEIM (HEDWIG).

WACHENHEIM (HEDWIG) Vom Grossbürgertum zur Sozialdemokratie: Memoiren einer Reformistin; [edited by Susanne Miller]. Berlin, 1973. pp. 155. *(IWK: internationale wissenschaftliche Korrespondenz zur Geschichte der deutschen Arbeiterbewegung. Beihefte. 1)*

WAGE PAYMENT SYSTEMS.

U.K. National Board for Prices and Incomes. NBPI Guides. [2]. Payment by results. [London, 1968]. pp. 16.

SHARPE (PETER) Payment systems and incentives. London, [1973]. pp. 12.

— **France.**

BUNEL (JEAN) La mensualisation: une réforme tranquille?. Paris, [1973]. pp. 239. *bibliog.*

— **United Kingdom.**

JONES (MEURIG D.) The make-up and payment of wages. London, [1973]. pp. 11. *(Working Together Campaign. Working Together Studies)*

WAGE—PRICE POLICY.

MILLER (ROGER LEROY) and WILLIAMS (RABURN M.) Unemployment and inflation: the new economics of the wage-price spiral. St. Paul, [Minn.], 1974. pp. 110. *bibliogs.*

— **Austria.**

SUPPANZ (HANNES) and ROBINSON (DEREK) Prices and incomes policy: the Austrian experience. Paris, Organisation for Economic Co-operation and Development, 1972. pp. 72.

— **United States — Mathematical models.**

ASKIN (A. BRADLEY) and KRAFT (JOHN) Econometric wage and price models: assessing the impact of the Economic Stabilization Program. Lexington, Mass., [1974]. pp. 152. *bibliog.*

WAGES.

INTERNATIONAL LABOUR ORGANISATION. Labour-Management Relations Series. Geneva, 1957 in progress.

FRANCE. Centre d'Etude des Revenus et des Coûts. 1971. La hiérarchie des salaires: un essai de comparaison internationale. [Paris, 1972]. pp. 47. *(Documents. No. 12)*

— **Dismissal wage — India.**

INDIA. Labour Bureau. 1971. Report on survey as to how workers support themselves during retrenchment, lay-off, closure and strikes and collection of data regarding indebtedness. [Delhi, 1971]. pp. 236.

— **Mathematical models.**

ROWLEY (JOHN CHRISTOPHER ROBIN) and WILTON (D.A.) Quarterly models of wage determination: some new efficient estimates. Kingston, 1971. fo. 22. *bibliog. (Kingston, Ontario. Queen's University. Institute for Economic Research. Discussion Papers. No. 51)*

ZAHN (PETER) Economist. Die Phillips-Relation für Deutschland: eine lohn- und inflationstheoretische Untersuchung. Berlin, 1973. pp. 259. *bibliog.*

PEEL (D.A.) and BRISCOE (GEOFFREY) Another look at the role of excess demand variables in determining money wage inflation. Coventry, 1974. pp. 32. *bibliog. (University of Warwick. Centre for Industrial, Economic and Business Research. [Warwick Research in Industrial and Business Studies]. No.53)*

— **Minimum wage.**

INTERNATIONAL LABOUR CONFERENCE. 54th Session. Reports. 5. Fifth item on the agenda: minimum wage fixing machinery and related problems, with special reference to developing countries. Geneva, 1969-70. 2 pts.

WEST (E.G.) Towards a comprehensive economic theory of minimum wage laws. Ottawa, 1972. fo. 53. *(Carleton University. Carleton Economic Papers)*

— — **Guatemala.**

GUATEMALA. Comision Nacional del Salario. 1966. Estudio económico para la determinacion del salario minimo en la industria de la construccion. Guatemala, 1966. pp. 84.

GUATEMALA. Comision Nacional del Salario. 1966. Estudio economico para la determinacion del salario minimo en la industria de substancias y productos quimicos. Guatemala, 1966. pp. 68.

GUATEMALA. Comision Nacional del Salario. 1966. Estudio economico para la determinacion del salario minimo en la industria textil. Guatemala, 1966. pp. 124.

GUATEMALA. Comision Nacional del Salario. 1966. Monografia para la determinacion del salario minimo en la industria de teatros y cines. Guatemala, 1966. pp. 51.

GUATEMALA. Comision Nacional del Salario. 1966. Monografia para la determinacion del salario minimo en la industria de alcoholes, bebidas alcoholicas, destiladas y fermentadas. Guatemala, 1966. pp. 59.

— **Statistics.**

SVENSKA ARBETSGIVAREFÖRENINGEN. Research Department. Direct and total wage costs for workers: international survey, 1961-1971. [Stockholm], 1973. pp. 78. *In various languages.*

— **Argentine Republic — Statistics.**

ARGENTINE REPUBLIC. Direccion Nacional de Recursos Humanos. Division de Estadisticas Sociales. 1971. Convenciones colectivas de trabajo: analisis de las actualizaciones de convenios colectivos de empresa, 1967, 1968, 1969 y 1970; indice de los salarios basicos de convenios. Buenos Aires, 1971. pp. 120.

— **Australia.**

AUSTRALIA. Commonwealth Bureau of Census and Statistics. Wage rate indexes. irreg., Je 1968/Je 1972- Canberra.

— **Belgium.**

VERLINDEN (CHARLES) and others, eds. Dokumenten voor de geschiedenis van prijzen en lonen in Vlaanderen en Brabant...(XIVe-XIXe eeuw). Brugge, 1959 in progress. *bibliogs. (Ghent. Université. Faculté de Philosophie et Lettres. Recueil de Travaux. Fascicules 125, etc.)*

— **Canada.**

CANADA. Statistics Canada. Accommodation, food and recreational services: employment, earnings and hours of work. irreg., 1972- Ottawa. *In English and French.*

SMITH (DOUGLAS A.) Economic policy and the U.S. impact on manufacturing wages in Canada. [Ottawa], 1973. fo. 38. *bibliog. (Carleton University. Carleton Economic Papers)*

— **Communist countries.**

UCHENYE ZAPISKI KAFEDR OBSHCHESTVENNYKH NAUK VUZOV LENINGRADA. Politicheskaia Ekonomiia. vyp. 14. Raspredelitel'nye otnosheniia sotsializma i ikh razvitie na sovremennom etape. Leningrad, 1973. pp. 208.

— **European Economic Community countries.**

EUROPEAN COMMUNITIES. Statistical Office. Social Statistics. Luxembourg, 1960 in progress.

— **France.**

FRANCE. Institut National de la Statistique et des Etudes Economiques. Collections de l'I.N.S.E.E. SÉRIE M. Ménages . Paris, 1970 in progress.

SILVESTRE (JEAN JACQUES) Les salaires ouvriers dans l'industrie française. Paris, [1973]. pp. 416. *bibliog.*

— **Germany.**

ARNDT (ERICH) Währungsstabilität und Lohnpolitik: über die wirtschaftlichen und sozialen Folgen von Inflationen. Tübingen, 1973. pp. 60. *With summaries in various languages.*

HAUSCHILD (URSULA) Studien zu Löhnen und Preisen in Rostock im Spätmittelalter. Köln, 1973. pp. 229. *bibliog. (Hansischer Geschichtsverein. Quellen und Darstellungen zur Hansischen Geschichte. Neue Folge. Band 19)*

BLECHSCHMIDT (AIKE) Löhne, Preise und Gewinne, 1967-1973: Materialien zur "Lohn-Preis-Spirale" und Inflation. Lampertheim, 1974. pp. 270. *bibliog.*

— **India.**

SINGH (VIDYA BHUSAN) Wage patterns, mobility and savings of workers in India: a study of Kanpur textile industry. Bombay, 1973. pp. 204.

— — **Bengal, West.**

WEST BENGAL. Bureau of Applied Economics and Statistics. 1971. Report on earners' survey, 1962 for Calcutta. [Calcutta], 1970 [or rather 1971]. pp. 71.

WEST BENGAL. Bureau of Applied Economics and Statistics. 1972. Report on earners' survey, 1962 for urban areas of West Bengal excluding Calcutta and its industrial areas. [Calcutta], 1972. pp. 68.

— **Ivory Coast.**

IVORY COAST. Office National de Formation Professionnelle. 1972. Le secteur privé et para-public en Côte d'Ivoire, 1971: résultats de l'enquête main d'oeuvre, 1971. 2e partie: les données individuelles de la main d'oeuvre salariée. [Abidjan], 1972. fo. 245.

— **New Zealand.**

NEW ZEALAND. Royal Commission on Salary and Wage Fixing Procedures in the New Zealand State Services, 1972. Salary and wage fixing procedures in the New Zealand State Services, 1972; report; [Sir Thaddeus McCarthy, chairman]. Wellington, 1972. pp. 112.

— **Norway.**

NORWAY. Statistiske Centralbyrå. 1973. Lønnsstruktur og lønnsutvikling 1960-1971. Oslo, 1973. pp. 96. *(Statistiske Analyser. 6) With English summary.*

— **Pakistan.**

RAHMAN (M. AKHLAQUR) The analysis of relative wage and salary structure in Pakistan. [Karachi, 1970]. fo. 202. *bibliog.*

— **Portugal.**

CORREIA (HERMINIA GALVÃO) Inquerito "remunerações/1969" (Comercio) resultados e análise. Lisboa, 1970. pp. 119. *(Fundo de Desenvolvimento da Mão-de-Obra. Cadernos. 35) With abstracts in English, French and German.*

— **South Africa.**

SOUTH AFRICA. Bureau of Statistics. Gross geographic product by magisterial district. irreg., 1968[1st]- Pretoria.

WAGE determinations current in South Africa at 30 June 1973: a fact paper; compiled by Laura Metter [and others] for the S.A. Institute of Race Relations. Johannesburg, 1973. pp. 380. *bibliog.*

WAGES. (Cont.)

— Underdeveloped areas.

See UNDERDEVELOPED AREAS — Wages.

— United Kingdom.

SMITH (GEORGE WILLIAM QUICK) Lorry drivers' wages and conditions of employment: a practical guide which includes points on the law relating to employment together with a ready reckoner based on the 44-hour week. London, 1948. pp. 74.

U.K. National Board for Prices and Incomes. NBPI Guides. 5. Salary structures. [London, 1970]. pp. 9.

COMMISSION ON INDUSTRIAL RELATIONS [U.K.]. Keg and Drum Wages Council. London, H.M.S.O., 1973. pp. 36. *(Reports. No. 48)*

COMMISSION ON INDUSTRIAL RELATIONS [U.K.]. Boot and Floor Polish Wages Council (Great Britain). London, H.M.S.O., 1973. pp. 17. *(Reports. No. 51)*

COMMISSION ON INDUSTRIAL RELATIONS [U.K.]. Coffin Furniture and Cerement-making Wages Council. London, H.M.S.O., 1973. pp. 32. *(Reports. No. 46)*

FIELD (FRANK) 1942- , ed. Low pay; Acton Society Trust essays. London, 1973. pp. 141.

U.K. Pay Board. 1973. Pay Board: a guide to its work in stage 3. [London, 1973]. pp. 36.

ECONOMIC DEVELOPMENT COMMITTEE FOR BUILDING. Earnings in the building industry: a survey of operatives' earnings and hours in May 1973. [London, National Economic Development Office, 1974]. pp. 30.

PANITCH (LEO VICTOR) The Labour Party and the trade unions: a study of incomes policy since 1945 with special reference to 1964-70; [Ph. D. (London) thesis]. 1973[or rather 1974]. fo. 401. *bibliog. Typescript: unpublished. This thesis is the property of London University and may not be removed from the library. Offprint from "Political Studies: vol. 19, no. 2, in end pocket.*

TAYLOR (JIM) Unemployment and wage inflation: with special reference to Britain and the U.S.A. Harlow, 1974. pp. 120. *bibliog.*

U.K. Pay Board. 1974. Experience of operating a statutory incomes policy. [London], 1974. pp. 49.

— United States.

JOHNSEN (JULIA EMILY) compiler. Wage stabilization and inflation. New York, 1943. pp. 187. *bibliog.*

BLUESTONE (BARRY) and others. Low wages and the working poor. Ann Arbor, 1973. pp. 215. *(Michigan University, and Wayne State University. Institute of Labor and Industrial Relations. Policy Papers in Human Resources and Industrial Relations. 22)*

TAYLOR (JIM) Unemployment and wage inflation: with special reference to Britain and the U.S.A. Harlow, 1974. pp. 120. *bibliog.*

— — Mathematical models.

McCALL (JOHN JOSEPH) Earnings mobility and economic growth...: a report prepared for Office of Economic Opportunity. Santa Monica, 1970. pp. 70. *bibliog. (Rand Corporation. [Rand Reports]. 576)*

BARRETT (NANCY SMITH) and others. Prices and wages in U.S. manufacturing: a factor analysis. Lexington, Mass., [1973]. pp. 212. *bibliog.*

— — New York.

BURSTEIN (ABRAHAM C.) Changes in wage and salary employment, New York City, 1960- 1968, and problems of balance between demand and supply of skills. New York, 1970. fo. various.

NEW YORK (STATE). Department of Labor. Division of Research and Statistics. 1973. Employment statistics. Vol. 10. Civilian work force, New York State, major areas and counties, 1966-1970; employees in nonagricultural establishments, by industry..., by month, 1966-1970...[and] annual averages, 1966-1970; earnings and hours in nonagricultural establishments..., 1966-1970. Albany, 1973. pp. 214.

— Uruguay.

URUGUAY. Instituto Nacional del Trabajo. Departamento Administrativo. 1957. Estadistica de salarios, periodo 1952-1956. [Montevideo], 1957. fo. 178.

— Venezuela.

VENEZUELA. Direccion General de Estadistica. Estadisticas industriales: empleo-remuneraciones. a., 1971- Caracas.

VENEZUELA. Direccion General de Estadistica. Estadisticas industriales: operarios u obreros; remuneraciones. a., 1971- Caracas.

— Zambia.

ZAMBIA. Central Statistical Office. Employment and earnings. irreg., 1966/1968- Lusaka.

WAGES AND PRODUCTIVITY

— Australia.

RIACH (PETER ANDREW) and HOWARD (WILLIAM A.) Productivity agreements and Australian wage determination. Sydney, [1973]. pp. 176.

— Russia.

FEDORENKO (NIKOLAI PROKOF'EVICH) and BUNICH (PAVEL GRIGOR'EVICH) eds. Mekhanizm ekonomicheskogo stimulirovaniia pri sotsializme: opyt i problemy. Moskva, 1973. pp. 255.

— United Kingdom.

The FUTURE of productivity bargaining; papers presented at a conference organised by Brunel University Management Programme, London, 8 November 1973; editor, Peter Seglow. [London, 1973?]. fo. 61.

WALES

— Economic conditions.

REES (GRAHAM L.) and others. Survey of the Welsh economy. London, 1973. pp. 183. *(U.K. Commission on the Constitution, 1969. Research Papers. 8)*

— Economic policy.

LEWIS (T. VIVIAN) and WALTERS (F. DONALD) Wales - a blueprint. London, 1974. pp. 71. *(Conservative Political Centre. [Publications]. No. 552)*

— History.

EVANS (GWYNFOR) Wales can win. Llandybie, 1973. pp. 145.

HEARDER (HARRY) and LOYN (HENRY ROYSTON) eds. British government and administration: studies presented to S.B. Chrimes. Cardiff, 1974. pp. 250. *bibliog.*

— Industries.

TOMKINS (CYRIL R.) and LOVERING (JOHN) Location, size, ownership and control tables for Welsh industry. [Cardiff?], Welsh Council, 1973. pp. 39.

— Nationalism.

EVANS (GWYNFOR) Nonviolent nationalism. New Malden, Surrey, [1973]. pp. 24. *(Fellowship of Reconciliation. Alex Wood Memorial Lectures. 1973)*

EVANS (GWYNFOR) Wales can win. Llandybie, 1973. pp. 145.

MADGWICK (PETER JAMES) and others. The politics of rural Wales: a study of Cardiganshire. London, 1973. pp. 272. *bibliog.*

MORGAN (WILLIAM JOHN) ed. The Welsh dilemma: some essays on nationalism in Wales. Llandybie, 1973. pp. 128.

JONES (ROBERT TUDUR) The desire of nations. Llandybie, 1974. pp. 207.

— Politics and government.

LEWIS (T. VIVIAN) and WALTERS (F. DONALD) Wales - a blueprint. London, 1974. pp. 71. *(Conservative Political Centre. [Publications]. No. 552)*

WELSH COUNCIL. Observation on the Kilbrandon report. [Cardiff?], 1974. pp. 13.

— Social policy.

LEWIS (T. VIVIAN) and WALTERS (F. DONALD) Wales - a blueprint. London, 1974. pp. 71. *(Conservative Political Centre. [Publications]. No. 552)*

WALL STREET.

SUTTON (ANTONY C.) Wall Street and the Bolshevik revolution. New Rochelle, N.Y., [1974]. pp. 228. *bibliog.*

WALLIS (CANTON).

See VALAIS (CANTON).

WALLONIA

— Politics and government.

SEILER (DANIEL) and RAES (JEAN) Idéologie et citoyens: analyse des attitudes politiques d'un échantillon de l'électorat wallon. Bruxelles, [1970]. pp. 219. *bibliog. (Namur. Facultés Universitaires Notre Dame de la Paix. Collection Questions Economiques, Sociales et Politiques)*

WALLOON MOVEMENT.

GROUPE B/Y. Quelle Wallonie? Quel socialisme?: les bases d'un rassemblement des progressistes. Liège, [1971]. pp. 234.

BECQUET (CHARLES FRANÇOIS) Le différend wallo-flamand. [Nalinnes-lez-Charleroi], 1972 in progress. *bibliog. (Institut Jules Destrée pour la Défense et l'Illustration de la Wallonie. Etudes et Documents)*

SEMAINE SOCIALE WALLONNE. 54me Semaine. La Wallonie et la répartition du pouvoir; [by] M. Galderoux [and others]. Bruxelles, 1972. pp. 256.

WALLOONS IN THE UNITED KINGDOM.

MAGEN (BEATE) Die Wallonengemeinde in Canterbury von ihrer Gründung bis zum Jahre 1635. Bern, 1973. pp. 287. *bibliog.*

WALLPAPER.

KRAAY (J.M.A. VAN) An application of the product life cycle concept in international marketing, in particular regarding the wall paper market. Tilburg, 1973. pp. 33. *bibliog. (Tilburg. Katholieke Hogeschool. Tilburg Institute of Economics. Research Memoranda. EIT 41)*

WALPOLE (ROBERT) 1st Earl of Orford.

DICKINSON (H.T.) Walpole and the Whig supremacy. London, [1973]. pp. 205. *bibliog.*

WALRAS (LEON).

MORISHIMA (MICHIO) Short lectures on Leon Walras. Siena, 1973. pp. 72. *(Offprint from Economic Notes, vol.2, no.2) With French and German summaries.*

WALTHAM FOREST

— Population.

WALTHAM FOREST. Chief Planning Officer. Population estimates for Waltham Forest 1971-1991. [London], 1971. 1 vol.(unpaged).

— Social conditions.

WALTHAM FOREST. Planning Department and Social Services Department. Survey of social stress. [London], 1973. pp. 23 with map.

WANDSWORTH

— Civic improvement.

WANDSWORTH. Borough Council. Tomorrow's Putney: a document for public consultation. [London], 1973. fo. 41. *With questionnaire and leaflet in end-pocket.*

WANSEY (HENRY).

WANSEY (HENRY) Henry Wansey and his American journal, 1794; [reprint of Wansey's Journal based on the first two English editions of 1796 and 1798, with notes and introduction]; edited by David John Jeremy. Philadelphia, 1970. pp. 186. *bibliog. (American Philosophical Society. Memoirs. vol.82)*

WANSTEAD

— Orphans and orphan asylums.

GRIST (DONALD HONEY) A Victorian charity: the Infant Orphan Asylum at Wanstead. London, [1974]. pp. 109,xxxviii.

WAR.

KENDE (ISTVÁN) Local wars in Asia, Africa and Latin America, 1945-1969. Budapest, 1972. pp. 110. *bibliog. (Magyar Tudományos Akadémia. Afro-Azsiai Kutató Központ. Studies in Developing Countries. No. 60)*

BEITZ (CHARLES R.) and HERMAN (THEODORE) eds. Peace and war. San Francisco, [1973]. pp. 435. *bibliogs.*

FERRIS (WAYNE H.) The power capabilities of nation-states: international conflict and war. Lexington, [1973]. pp. 191. *bibliog.*

WALLACE (MICHAEL DAVID) War and rank among nations. Lexington, Mass., [1973]. pp. 142. *bibliog.*

BRODIE (BERNARD) War and politics. London, 1974. pp. 514.

NORTHEDGE (FREDERICK SAMUEL) ed. The use of force in international relations. London, 1974. pp. 258.

SYMCOX (GEOFFREY) ed. War, diplomacy and imperialism, 1618-1763: [selected documents]. London, 1974. pp. 338. *bibliog.*

— Economic aspects.

MORSOMME (ALBERT) Anatomie de la guerre totale: ses aspects économiques et financiers. Bruxelles, [1971]. pp. 279. *bibliog.*

BARBERA (HENRY) Rich nations and poor in peace and war: continuity and change in the development hierarchy of seventy nations from 1913 through 1952. Lexington, Mass., [1973]. pp. 213. *bibliog.*

DUBY (GEORGES) Guerriers et paysans, VII-XIIe siècle: premier essor de l'économie européenne. [Paris, 1973]. pp. 308. *bibliog.*

DUBY (GEORGES) The early growth of the European economy: warriors and peasants from the seventh to the twelfth century;... translated by Howard B. Clarke. London, [1974]. pp. 292. *bibliog.*

— Psychological aspects.

WHITE (RALPH KIRBY) Nobody wanted war: misperception in Vietnam and other wars. rev. ed. Garden City, N.Y., 1970. pp. 386. *bibliog.*

INTERNATIONAL INSTITUTE FOR PEACE. Symposium, 1971. Aggressionstrieb und Krieg;...herausgegeben von Walter Hollitscher; (aus dem Englischen übersetzt von Rudolf Hermstein). Stuttgart, [1973]. pp. 164.

WAR (INTERNATIONAL LAW).

KALSHOVEN (FRITS) and RÖLING (BERNARD VICTOR ALOYSIUS) De positie van de niet-bezette burgerbevolking in een gewapend conflict, in het bijzonder met het oog op de massaal werkende strijdmiddelen, NBC-wapens: praeadviezen. [Deventer], 1970. pp. 78. *(Nederlandse Vereniging voor Internationaal Recht. Mededelingen. No. 61)*

CONFERENCE ON CONTEMPORARY PROBLEMS OF THE LAW OF ARMED CONFLICTS, 1969. Report. New York, 1971. pp. 119. *(Carnegie Endowment for International Peace, Conferences on Contemporary Problems of International Law. 1)*

STOCKHOLM INTERNATIONAL PEACE RESEARCH INSTITUTE. Napalm and incendiary weapons: legal and humanitarian aspects; SIPRI interim report [prepared by Malvern Lumsden from the papers of the SIPRI Symposium on Napalm and Incendiary Weapons held in Stockholm in 1972]. Stockholm, [1972]. fo. 125. *bibliog.*

KALSHOVEN (FRITS) The law of warfare: a summary of its recent history and trends in development. Leiden, 1973. pp. 138. *bibliog. (Institut Henry Dunant. "Teneat Lex Gladium". No.2)*

BOND (JAMES EDWARD) The rules of riot: internal conflict and the law of war. Princeton, [1974]. pp. 280. *bibliog.*

ZOUREK (JAROSLAV) L'interdiction de l'emploi de la force en droit international. Leiden, 1974. pp. 128. *bibliog. (Institut Henry Dunant. "Teneat Lex Gladium". No. 3)*

WAR AND EMERGENCY POWERS

— Colombia.

AYERBE MUÑOZ (RODRIGO) El estado de emergencia: comentarios al nuevo articulo 122 de la constitucion nacional. Bogota, 1971. pp. 223. *bibliog.*

WAR AND SOCIALISM.

BOUDIN (LOUIS BOUDIANOFF) Socialism and war: [reprint of the work originally published in 1916]; with a new introduction...by James Weinstein. New York, 1972. pp. 267.

BRINGOLF (WALTHER) Perspektiven der sozialistischen Bewegung der Schweiz. [Schaffhausen, 1940]. pp. 26.

SOZIALISTISCHE JUGEND DER SCHWEIZ. Zeigt der Sozialismus einen Ausweg?: (unsere Antwort an Nationalrat Bringolf'.); Kapitulation vor dem Kapitalismus oder sozialistische Perspektiven?. [Zürich, 1940]. pp. 30.

WAR AND SOCIETY.

HARVIE (CHRISTOPHER) War and society in the nineteenth century: prepared...for the [War and Society] Course Team. Bletchley, 1973. pp. 208. *bibliogs. (Open University. Arts: a third level course: war and society. Block IV, units 10-13)*

OPEN UNIVERSITY. War and Society Course Team. The revolutionary and Napoleonic period; [course material prepared by Clive Emsley and Ian Donnachie]. Bletchley, 1973. pp. 168. *bibliog. (Open University. Arts: a third level course: war and society. Block III, units 6-9)*

MARWICK (ARTHUR J.B.) War and social change in the twentieth century: a comparative study of Britain, France, Germany, Russia and the United States. London, 1974. pp. 258. *bibliog.*

WAR CRIMES.

DAVIDSON (EUGENE) The Nuremberg fallacy: wars and war crimes since world war II. New York, [1973]. pp. 331. *bibliog.*

— Trials — Germany.

HENKYS (REINHARD) Die nationalsozialistischen Gewaltverbrechen: Geschichte und Gericht; mit...einem Beitrag von Jürgen Baumann; herausgegeben von Dietrich Goldschmidt. Stuttgart, [1964]. pp. 392. *bibliog.*

WARRANTS (LAW)

— United Kingdom.

HARRIS (BRIAN) Warrants of search and entry: a handbook for magistrates, police officers and others. Chichester, [1973]. pp. 85.

WARSAW

— History — 1944, Uprising of.

CIECHANOWSKI (JAN MIECZYSLAW) The Warsaw rising of 1944. Cambridge, 1974. pp. 332. *bibliog. (National Association for Soviet and East European Studies. Soviet and East European Studies)*

WARWICKSHIRE

— Economic conditions.

WARWICKSHIRE. County Council. County structure plan, 1973. Warwick, 1973. 8 pts. (in 1 vol.). *Comprises Written statement; Report of survey; Supplementary reports 1-6.*

— History.

SMITH (CHRISTOPHER J.) The civic heraldry of Warwickshire: an account of the armorial bearings of local authorities in Warwickshire prior to the local government reforms of 1974. [Coventry, 1973]. pp. 63. *(Historical Association. Coventry Branch. Coventry and Warwickshire History Pamphlets. No. 9)*

— Social conditions.

WARWICKSHIRE. County Council. County structure plan, 1973. Warwick, 1973. 8 pts. (in 1 vol.). *Comprises Written statement; Report of survey; Supplementary reports 1-6.*

WASHINGTON, D.C.

— Schools.

SILVER (CATHERINE BODARD) Black teachers in urban schools: the case of Washington, D.C.. New York, 1973. pp. 222. *bibliog.*

SMITH (SAM) Captive capital: colonial life in modern Washington. Bloomington, [1974]. pp. 303. *bibliog.*

WASTE LANDS

— United Kingdom.

U.K. Department of the Environment. 1971-72. Derelict land: summary of returns to DOE circular[s] No. 4/71 [and] No. 5/72. [London, 1971-72]. 2 pts.

WASTE PRODUCTS.

A SURVEY of the locations, disposal and prospective uses of the major industrial by-products and waste materials; [by] W. Gutt [and others]. Garston, [1974]. pp. 82,1 map. *(Building Research Establishment [U.K.] Current Papers. 74/19)*

WATER

— Economic aspects — United Kingdom.

U.K. Steering Group on Water Authority Economic and Financial Objectives. 1973. The water services: economic and financial policies; first report to the Secretary of State for the Environment; [J.A. Jukes, chairman]. London, 1973. pp. 63.

— Laws and legislation.

UNITED NATIONS. Economic Commission for Asia and the Far East. Water Resources Series. Nos. 23 onwards. New York, 1963 in progress.

— — Canada.

LA FOREST (GERARD V.) and others. Water law in Canada: the Atlantic provinces. Ottawa, Information Canada, 1973. pp. 550.

WATER. (Cont.)

— — Russia.

KOLBASOV (OLEG STEPANOVICH) Teoreticheskie osnovy prava pol'zovaniia vodami v SSSR. Moskva, 1972. pp. 227.

— — — Ukraine.

UKRAINE. Statutes, etc. 1972. Vodnyi kodeks Ukraïns'koï RSR. Kyïv, 1973. pp. 95.

— Pollution.

HARTOG (H. DEN) The economic impact of pollution abatement: the case of water pollution by degradable organic matter. [The Hague], 1973. 1 vol.(various pagings). *(Netherlands. Centraal Planbureau. Occasional Papers. 1973/No.1)*

— — Canada.

CANADA-QUEBEC ST. LAWRENCE RIVER WORKING GROUP. Report for the fiscal year. a., 1972/3[1st]- Ottawa. *In English and French.*

— — France.

PICARD (JOSEPH) Orientation de la politique de l'eau au VIe Plan; exposé présenté le 21 octobre 1971 au Comité National de l'Eau, etc. [Paris, 1971]. pp. 22.

L'ORIENTATION et la mise en oeuvre de la politique de l'eau en France. Paris, 1973. pp. 131. *(Environnement. 13)*

— — United Kingdom.

U.K. Department of the Environment. 1973. River pollution survey of England and Wales, updated 1972: discharges of sewage and industrial effluents. London, 1973. pp. 20.

WATER, UNDERGROUND.

UNITED NATIONS. Economic Commission for Asia and the Far East. Water Resources Series. Nos. 23 onwards. New York, 1963 in progress.

WATER DISTRICTS

— United Kingdom

The NEW water industry: management and structure; report of the Management Structure Committee appointed by the Secretary of State to consider and advise on forms of management structure in the regional water authorities; [Sir George Ogden, chairman]. London, H.M.S.O., 1973. pp. 83.

WATER QUALITY MANAGEMENT

— United States.

SHERWANI (JABBAR K.) Effect of low-flow hydrologic regimes on water quality management. Raleigh, N.C., 1971. pp. 177. *bibliog.* (North Carolina University. Water Resources Research Institute. Reports. No. 26)

WATER RESOURCES DEVELOPMENT.

URBAN WATER ECONOMICS SYMPOSIUM, UNIVERSITY OF NEWCASTLE, NEW SOUTH WALES, 1973. Proceedings of the...Symposium...; editor Colin Aislabie. Newcastle, N.S.W., 1973. pp. 188.

— Environmental aspects — United States.

GOLDMAN (CHARLES REMINGTON) and others, eds. Environmental quality and water development. San Francisco, [1973]. pp. 510. *bibliogs.*

— Asia.

UNITED NATIONS. Economic Commission for Asia and the Far East. Water Resources Series. Nos. 23 onwards. New York, 1963 in progress.

— Australasia.

UNITED NATIONS. Economic Commission for Asia and the Far East. Water Resources Series. Nos. 23 onwards. New York, 1963 in progress.

— Canada.

The MACKENZIE basin: proceedings of the intergovernmental seminar held at Inuvik, N.W.T., June 24-27, 1972. Ottawa, Information Canada, 1973. pp. 131.

— France.

FRANCE. Mission Déléguée de Bassin Rhône-Méditerranée-Corse. 1971. Les problèmes de l'eau dans le bassin Rhône- Méditerranée-Corse: projet de livre blanc. [Paris], 1971. pp. 60. *(France. Délégation à l'Aménagement du Territoire et à l'Action Régionale. Travaux et Recherches de Prospective. 22)*

PICARD (JOSEPH) Orientation de la politique de l'eau au VIe Plan; exposé présenté le 21 octobre 1971 au Comité National de l'Eau, etc. [Paris, 1971]. pp. 22.

FRANCE. Mission Déléguée de Bassin Loire-Bretagne. 1972. L'eau dans le bassin Loire-Bretagne. [Paris, 1972]. pp. 103. *(France. Délégation à l'Aménagement du Territoire et à l'Action Régionale. Travaux et Recherches de Prospective. 27)*

FRANCE. Secrétariat Permanent pour l'Etude des Problèmes de l'Eau. 1972. The development of water basin agency action during plan VI. Paris, 1972. pp. 43. *(Environnement. 10)*

FRANCE. Ministère de la Protection de la Nature et de l'Environnement. 1973. Bilan d'activité des agences financières de bassin "1969- 1972". [Paris, 1973?]. pp. 15.

L'ORIENTATION et la mise en oeuvre de la politique de l'eau en France. Paris, 1973. pp. 131. *(Environnement. 13)*

— Kenya.

CARRUTHERS (I.D.) Impact and economics of community water supply: a study of rural water investment in Kenya. Ashford, Kent, 1973. pp. 120. *bibliog.* (London. University. Wye College. School of Rural Economics and Related Studies. Agrarian Development Studies. Reports. No.6)

— Russia.

ISPOL'ZOVANIE vodnykh resursov v narodnom khoziaistve. Moskva, 1970. pp. 214. *bibliog.*

DOLGOPOLOV (KONSTANTIN VASIL'EVICH) and FEDOROVA (EVGENIIA FEDOROVNA) Voda - natsional'noe dostoianie: geograficheskie problemy ispol'zovaniia vodnykh resursov. Moskva, 1973. pp. 256. *bibliog.*

— — Azerbaijan.

KASHKAI (RENA M.) Vodnyi balans Bol'shogo Kavkaza: v predelakh Azerbaidzhanskoi SSR. Baku, 1973. pp. 84. *bibliog.*

— South Africa — Natal.

SHAND (NINHAM) AND PARTNERS. Water resources of the Natal South Coast; submitted to the Town and Regional Planning Commission. Natal, 1971. pp. 31. *bibliog.* (Natal. Town and Regional Planning Commission. Natal Town and Regional Planning Reports. vol. 18) *17 maps in end pocket.*

— Spain.

LOPEZ PALOMERO (FELIX V.) El trasvase Tajo-Segura. Madrid, 1969. pp. 166.

— United Kingdom.

EAST SUFFOLK AND NORFOLK RIVER AUTHORITY. Water Resources Act, 1963: first survey of water resources and demands. [NORWICH[/(?/. 2 vols. *9 maps in end pocket.*

MANAGEMENT of national and regional water resources; proceedings of the conference sponsored by the Institution of Civil Engineers [and others], London, 3-4 October 1972; (editor, Barry Cripps). [London], 1973. pp. 98.

MERSEY AND WEAVER RIVER AUTHORITY. Statement of policy for ground-water management in accordance with proposal No. 13 of the first periodical survey. Warrington, 1973. pp. 17.

U.K. Department of the Environment. 1973. A background to water reorganisation in England and Wales. London, 1973. 35, 2 maps.

U.K. Water Resources Board. 1973. Water resources in England and Wales. London, 1973. 2 vols. (in 1). *(Publications. Nos. 22-23) 5 maps and diagram in end pocket.*

— — Scotland.

SCOTLAND. Scottish Developement Department. 1973. A measure of plenty: water resources in Scotland: a general survey Edinburgh, 1973. pp. 100. *Map in end pocket.*

— United States.

SCHRAMM (GUNTER) and BURT (ROBERT E.) An analysis of federal water resource planning and evaluation procedures. Ann Arbor, 1970. pp. 106.

NATIONAL WATER COMMISSION [UNITED STATES]. Review draft: proposed report of the...Commission; [Charles F. Luce, chairman]. Washington, D.C., 1972. 2 vols.

REGIONAL growth and water resource investment; [by] W. Cris Lewis [and others]. Lexington, mass [1973]. pp. 172.

— — California.

WATER, growth and politics in coastal California: the Diablo Canyon desalting facility; by K.N. Lee [and others]. Berkeley, 1972. pp. 145. *bibliog.* (California University. Institute of Governmental Studies. Working Papers. No. 2)

— — North Carolina.

MOREAU (DAVID H.) and others. Regional water resource planning for urban needs. Raleigh, N.C., 1973 in progress. *bibliog.* (North Carolina University. Water Resources Research Institute. Reports. No.77)

WATER SUPPLY.

ORGANISATION FOR ECONOMIC CO-OPERATION AND DEVELOPMENT. Water Management Sector Group. 1972. Water management: basic issues. Paris, 1972. pp. 546. *In English and French.*

CIBA FOUNDATION. Symposia. Human rights in health: Ciba Foundation symposium 23 (new series); [proceedings; edited by Katherine Elliott and Julie Knight]. Amsterdam, 1974. pp. 304. *bibliogs.*

— Australia — New South Wales.

BURLING (J.R.) An examination of urban water supply systems in the Clarence and Richmond river valleys of New South Wales; (a study undertaken...for the Clarence and Richmond-Tweed Regional Development Committees and the N.S.W. Department of Decentralisation). [Armidale, 1969]. fo. 59, 3 maps. *bibliog.* (University of New England, Armidale. Department of Geography. Research Series in Applied Geography. No. 30)

— Bangladesh.

BEM (CHRIS) A well of living waters: letters from Bangladesh. Manchester, 1972. pp. 10.

— United Kingdom.

EAST SUFFOLK AND NORFOLK RIVER AUTHORITY. Water Resources Act, 1963: first survey of water resources and demands. [NORWICH[/(?/. 2 vols. *9 maps in end pocket.*

U.K. Department of the Environment. 1973. A background to water reorganisation in England and Wales. London, 1973. 35, 2 maps.

U.K. Department of the Environment. 1973. Water reorganisation: the National Water Council and the central organisations for planning, research and data collection. [London, 1973]. fo. 15.

U.K. Water Resources Board. 1973. Water resources in England and Wales. London, 1973. 2 vols. (in 1). *(Publications. Nos. 22-23) 5 maps and diagram in end pocket.*

— — Finance.

U.K. Steering Group on Water Authority Economic and Financial Objectives. 1973. The water services: economic and financial policies; first report to the Secretary of State for the Environment; [J.A. Jukes, chairman]. London, 1973. pp. 63.

— — Scotland.

SCOTLAND. Scottish Developement Department. 1973. A measure of plenty: water resources in Scotland: a general survey Edinburgh, 1973. pp. 100. *Map in end pocket.*

— — Wales.

SOUTH WEST WALES RIVER AUTHORITY. Water resources: a study of the resources, demands and future development of water supplies in the area of the South West Wales River Authority. Llanelli, 1970. 2 pts. (in 1).

— United States.

FORECASTING water demands; by Russell G. Thompson [and others]. Arlington, Virginia, National Water Commission, 1971. pp. 337.

— — Arizona.

KELSO (MAURICE M.) and others. Water supplies and economic growth in an arid environment: an Arizona case study. Tucson, [1973]. pp. 327. *bibliog.*

WATERGATE AFFAIR, 1972— .

KAMMERMAN (ROY) Poor Richard's Watergate. Los Angeles, 1973. 1 vol. (unpaged).

MANKIEWICZ (FRANK) Nixon's road to Watergate. London, 1973. pp. 271.

WATERGATE: the full inside story; [by] Lewis Chester [and others]. London, 1973. pp. 280.

WATERGATE: the view from the Left; introduction by Linda Jenness and Andrew Pulley . New York, 1973. pp. 95.

BERNSTEIN (CARL) and WOODWARD (BOB) All the President's men. London, 1974. pp. 349.

McCARTHY (MARY THERESE) The mask of state: Watergate portraits. New York, [1974]. pp. 165.

RIPON SOCIETY and BROWN (CLIFFORD WATERS) Jaws of victory: the game-plan politics of 1972, the crisis of the Republican Party, and the future of the constitution. Boston, [1974]. pp. 394. *bibliog.*

WEALTH.

BARTLETT (RANDALL) Economic foundations of political power. New York, [1973]. pp. 206. *bibliog.*

KISSLING (HANS) Die Umverteilung bestehender Vermögenswerte als Mittel der Vermögenspolitik. [Zürich, imprint], 1973. pp. 191. *bibliog.*

SCHLOTTER (HANS GUENTHER) Systemstabilisation durch Vermögenspolitik. Berlin, [1974]. pp. 104. *bibliog.*

— Mathematical models.

ZERWAS (ARNOLD) Simulationsexperimente zur Einkommens- und Vermögensverteilung. Berlin, [1974]. pp. 149. *bibliog.*

— France.

DAUMARD (ADELINE) and others. Les fortunes français au XIXe siècle: enquête sur la répartition et la composition des capitaux privés à Paris, Lyon, Lille, Bordeaux et Toulouse d'après l'enregistrement des déclarations de succession. Paris, 1973. pp. 603. *bibliog.* *(Paris. Ecole Pratique des Hautes Etudes. Section des Sciences Economiques et Sociales. Centre de Recherches Historiques. Civilisations et Sociétés. 27)*

— Germany.

BOSCH (HEINZ DIETER) Zur Vermögenssituation der privaten Haushalte in der Bundesrepublik Deutschland. Berlin, [1971-73). 2 vols.(in 1). *bibliog.* *(Bonn. Universität. Institut für das Spar-, Giro- und Kreditwesen. Untersuchungen über das Spar-, Giro- und Kreditwesen. Band 60)*

— United Kingdom.

LABOUR RESEARCH DEPARTMENT. The 2 nations: inequality in Britain today. London, 1973. pp. 28.

ATKINSON (A.B.) Unequal shares: wealth in Britain. rev. ed. Harmondsworth, 1974. pp. 277. *bibliog.*

POLANYI (GEORGE) and WOOD (JOHN B.) How much inequality?: an inquiry into the evidence. London, 1974. pp. 85. *(Institute of Economic Affairs. Research Monographs. 31)*

— — Wales.

REVELL (JACK) and TOMKINS (CYRIL R.) Personal wealth and finance in Wales. [Cardiff?], Welsh Council, 1974. pp. 71.

— United States.

HUBER (JOAN) and FORM (WILLIAM HUMBERT) Income and ideology: an analysis of the American political formula. New York, [1973]. pp. 226. *bibliog.*

PESSEN (EDWARD) Riches, class, and power before the Civil War. Lexington, Mass., [1973]. pp. 378. *bibliog.*

WEALTH TAX.

See PROPERTY TAX.

WEAVERS

— United Kingdom.

ELBOURNE (ROGER PHILLIP) Industrialization and popular culture: a case study of Lancashire handloom weavers, 1780-1840; [M. Phil. (London) thesis]. [1974]. fo. 243. *bibliog.* Typscript: unpublished. This thesis is the property of London University and may not be removed from the library.

WEBB (BEATRICE).

MAISKII (IVAN MIKHAILOVICH) Liudi, sobytiia, fakty. Moskva, 1973. pp. 216.

U.K. National Register of Archives. 1973. Labour Party archives: Beatrice Webb newsletters, 1922-6. London, 1973. single sheet.

WEBB (SIDNEY) 1st Baron Passfield.

MAISKII (IVAN MIKHAILOVICH) Liudi, sobytiia, fakty. Moskva, 1973. pp. 216.

WEBER (MAX).

RUNCIMAN (WALTER GARRISON) A critique of Max Weber's philosophy of social science. Cambridge, 1972 repr. 1973. pp. 106.

BEETHAM (DAVID) Max Weber and the theory of modern politics. London, 1974. pp. 287. *bibliog.*

MOMMSEN (WOLFGANG JUSTIN) Max Weber und die deutsche Politik, 1890-1920. 2nd ed. Tübingen, 1974. pp. 586. *bibliog.*

MOMMSEN (WOLFGANG JUSTIN) The age of bureaucracy: perspectives on the political sociology of Max Weber. Oxford, [1974]. pp. 124. *bibliog.*

WEIGHTS AND MEASURES

— United Kingdom.

GRIERSON (PHILIP) English linear measures: an essay in origins. Reading, 1972. pp. 37. *(Reading. University. Stenton Lectures. 1971)*

WEITLING (WILHELM).

Die KOMMUNISTEN in der Schweiz nach den bei Weitling vorgefundenen Papieren: wörtlicher Abdruck des Kommissionalberichtes an die Hohe Regierung des Standes Zürich; ([by] Johann Caspar Bluntschli);...als Anhang, Sebastian Seiler: Der Schriftsteller Wilhelm Weitling und der Kommunistenlärm in Zürich; eine Verteidigungschrift...; [reprint of the original editions of 1843]. Glashütten im Taunus, 1973. pp. 130,26.

WELFARE ECONOMICS.

TINBERGEN (JAN) Meten in de menswetenschappen. Assen, 1971. pp. 50. *bibliog.*

BITSAXIS (EVAN) Welfare versus freedom. Athens, 1972. pp. 383.

CHIPMAN (JOHN SOMERSET) and MOORE (JAMES C.) The end of the new welfare economics. Stanford, 1973. pp. 72. *bibliog.* *(Stanford University. Institute for Mathematical Studies in the Social Sciences. Technical Reports. [New Series]. No. 102)*

NATH (S.K.) A perspective of welfare economics. London, 1973. pp. 73. *bibliog.*

PHELPS (EDMUND S.) ed. Economic justice: selected readings. Harmondsworth, 1973. pp. 479. *bibliogs.*

TAUSSIG (MICHAEL K.) Alternative measures of the distribution of economic welfare. Princeton, 1973. pp. 89. *(Princeton University. Department of Economics and Sociology. Industrial Relations Section. Research Report Series. No. 116)*

ROBBINS (HORACE H.) Fictive capital and fictive profit: the welfare-military state; a political economy based on economic fictions. New York, [1974]. pp. 417.

ROHRLICH (GEORGE F.) Social economics: concepts and perspectives. Patrington, Yorks., 1974. pp. 30. *(International Institute of Social Economics. Monographs. No. 2)*

— Mathematical models.

WILLIG (ROBERT) Consumer's surplus: a rigorous cookbook. Stanford, 1973. pp. 55. *bibliog.* *(Stanford University. Institute for Mathematical Studies in the Social Sciences. Technical reports. [New Series]. No. 98)*

WELFARE WORK IN INDUSTRY

— Norway.

NORWAY. Arbeidstilsynskomitéen. 1971. Innstilling om organisering og effektivisering av Arbeidstilsynet på det lokale plan. Orkanger, 1971. pp. 52.

WELLINGTON, NEW ZEALAND

— Economic conditions.

WELLINGTON REGIONAL PLANNING AUTHORITY. Towards a metropolitan development strategy: a presentation of a metropolitan planning methodology. Wellington, 1971. pp. 115.

— Politics and government.

NEW ZEALAND. Local Government Commission. 1970. Wellington local government area: final scheme. [Wellington], 1970. pp. 10. *Map in end pocket.*

— Social conditions.

WELLINGTON REGIONAL PLANNING AUTHORITY. Towards a metropolitan development strategy: a presentation of a metropolitan planning methodology. Wellington, 1971. pp. 115.

WELSH LANGUAGE.

U.K. Census, 1971. Census, 1971: report on the Welsh language in Wales. Cardiff, 1973. pp. 83.

WENDLAND (HEINZ—DIETRICH).

GRENHOLM (CARL HENRIC) Christian social ethics in a revolutionary age: an analysis of the social ethics of John C. Bennett, Heinz-Dietrich Wendland and Richard Shaull. Uppsala, 1973. pp. 351. *bibliog.*

WEST FLANDERS

— Economic conditions.

DORNBURG (CHRISTIAN) Regionale Struktur und staatliche Entwicklungsplanung im Problemgebiet Westhoek, Provinz Westflandern/Belgien. Bonn, 1971. pp. 65. *bibliog. (Deutscher Verband für Wohnungswesen, Städtebau und Raumplanung. Kleine Schriften. 41)*

WEST INDIANS IN THE UNITED KINGDOM.

COMMUNITY RELATIONS COMMISSION. The background to the educational difficulties of some West Indian children in Britain. [London, 1971]. pp. 4.

LEE (TREVOR ROSS) Concentration and dispersal: a study of West Indian residential patterns in London, 1961-1971; [Ph.D. (London) thesis]. 1973. fo. 351. *bibliog. Typescript: unpublished. This thesis is the property of London University and may not be removed from the Library.*

WEST INDIES.

U.K. Central Office of Information. Reference Division. 1957. The West Indies: a nation in the making. London, 1957. pp. 56. *bibliog.*

— Economic history.

SHERIDAN (RICHARD BERT) Sugar and slavery: an economic history of the British West Indies, 1623-1775. Baltimore, 1974. pp. 529. *bibliog.*

— Foreign economic relations — Canada.

WEST INDIES, UNIVERSITY OF THE. West Indies-Canada economic relations; selected papers prepared by the university...in connection with the Canada- Commonwealth Caribbean conference, July 1966. [Mona], 1967. pp. 137.

— Politics and government.

HOYOS (F.A.) Grantley Adams and the social revolution: the story of the movement that changed the pattern of West Indian society. London, 1974. pp. 280. *bibliog.*

WEST IRIAN.

See IRIAN BARAT.

WEST NEW GUINEA.

See IRIAN BARAT.

WESTHOEK

— Economic conditions.

DORNBURG (CHRISTIAN) Regionale Struktur und staatliche Entwicklungsplanung im Problemgebiet Westhoek, Provinz Westflandern/Belgien. Bonn, 1971. pp. 65. *bibliog. (Deutscher Verband für Wohnungswesen, Städtebau und Raumplanung. Kleine Schriften. 41)*

WESTMINSTER

— Social conditions.

WESTMINSTER. Department of Architecture and Planning. Social and community services. London, [1974]. pp. 109. *(Westminster Development Plan Publications. Topic Papers. T2)*

WHEAT

— Prices — India.

SINGH (VIDYA BHUSAN) An evaluation of fair price shops. New Delhi, [1973]. pp. 132.

WHITE (HARRY DEXTER).

REES (DAVID) Harry Dexter White: a study in paradox. London, 1974. pp. 506. *bibliog.*

WHITE RUSSIA.

SAVETSKAIA Belarus': Sovetskaia Belorussiia. Minsk, 1973. pp. 32. *In White Russian and Russian.*

— Commerce.

MIKHNEVICH (LEONID MIKHAILOVICH) Torgovlia Belorussii, 1900-1970 gg. Minsk, 1973. pp. 223.

— Commercial policy.

PROSKURIN (ANATOLII PETROVICH) Upravlenie torgovlei v Belorusskoi SSR, 1921-1970. Minsk, 1973. pp. 206.

— Constitutional history.

OCHERKI istorii gosudarstva i prava BSSR. vyp.2. Minsk, 1969. pp. 382.

— Economic history.

MARTINKEVICH (F.S.) and DRITS (V.I.) eds. Razvitie ekonomiki Belorussii v 1921-1927 gg. Minsk, 1973. pp. 335.

— Executive departments.

NIKONOVICH (BORIS FEOFILOVICH) KPB v bor'be za osushchestvlenie leninskikh printsipov narodnogo kontrolia. Minsk, 1973. pp. 208.

— History — 1918—1920, Allied intervention.

SELIVANOV (PANTELEIMON ALEKSEEVICH) Voennoe stroitel'stvo v Belorussii v period razgroma pokhodov Antanty. Minsk, 1973. pp. 208.

— Industries.

PROBLEMY formirovaniia i ispol'zovaniia fonda razvitiia proizvodstva. Minsk, 1973. pp. 248.

— Intellectual life.

PROKOSHINA (EKATERINA SERGEEVNA) Ocherk svobodomysliia i ateizma v Belorussii v XIX v. Minsk. 1973. pp. 226.

— Maps.

OSTROWSKI (WIKTOR) ed. The ancient names and early cartography of Byelorussia...material for historical research and study, etc. 2nd ed. London. 1971. pp. 24. 33 plates.

— Nationalism.

BAZHKO (ALES' TSIMAFEEVYCH) Tatal'nae bankrutstva. Minsk, 1973. pp. 119.

— Politics and government.

GERASIMENKO (GEORGII GEORGIEVICH) Deiatel'nost' Kompartii Belorussii po vovlecheniiu trudiashchikhsia mass v upravlenie gosudarstvom, 1925-1937. Minsk, 1973. pp. 230.

— Population.

MONICH (ZINAIDA IVANOVNA) Intelligentsiia v strukture sel'skogo naseleniia: na materialakh BSSR. Minsk, 1971. pp. 166.

— Rural conditions.

MONICH (ZINAIDA IVANOVNA) Intelligentsiia v strukture sel'skogo naseleniia: na materialakh BSSR. Minsk, 1971. pp. 166.

— Statistics.

WHITE RUSSIA. Tsentral'noe Statisticheskoe Upravlenie. 1971. Narodnoe khoziaistvo Belorusskoi SSR v 1970 godu: statisticheskii sbornik. Minsk, 1971. pp. 416.

WHITE RUSSIA. Tsentral'noe Statisticheskoe Upravlenie. 1972. Narodnoe khoziaistvo Belorusskoi SSR v 1971 godu: statisticheskii sbornik. Minsk, 1972. pp. 223.

STATISTICHESKII EZHEGODNIK BELORUSSKOI SSR; ([pd. by] Tsentral'noe Statisticheskoe Upravlenie pri Sovete Ministrov Belorusskoi SSR). a., 1973 [1st]- Minsk.

WHITEHAVEN

— Civic improvement.

NAPPER, ERRINGTON, COLLERTON, BARNETT. Whitehaven: a new structure for a Restoration town; [report prepared for the Municipal Borough of Whitehaven]. [Newcastle upon Tyne, 1971]. pp. 114.

WHITSUNTIDE.

HOWKINS (ALUN) Whitsun in 19th century Oxfordshire. Oxford, [1973]. pp. 68. *(History Workshop. Pamphlets. No. 8)*

WHOLESALE TRADE

— European Economic Community countries.

ECONOMIC DEVELOPMENT COMMITTEE FOR THE DISTRIBUTIVE TRADES. Common Market Working Group. The distributive trades in the Common Market; a report; [J. Jefferys, chairman]. London, H.M.S.O., 1973. pp. 134. *bibliog.*

— Germany.

GERMANY (BUNDESREPUBLIK). Statistisches Bundesamt. Grosshandel. a., 1970/1971 [1st]- Wiesbaden. *In 2 pts., 1. Umsätze und Beschäftigte; 2. Wareneinkauf, Lagerbestand und Rohertrag. (Gross- und Einzelhandel, Gastgewerbe, Fremdenverkehr. Reihe 1)*

— South Africa.

SOUTH AFRICA. Bureau of Statistics. 1973- . Census of wholesale and retail trade, 1966-67. Pretoria, [1973 in progress]. (Reports. No. 04-11-01 and 04-41-01, etc.) *iN eNGLISH AND aFRIKAANS.*

WIDNES

— Civic improvement.

WIDNES. Borough Council. The urban renewal of Widnes: an appraisal at June. 1968. Widnes. [1968]. fo. 43.

WIDOWS

— France.

CARLIER-MACKIEWICZ (NICOLE) Les veuves et leurs familles dans la société d'aujourd'hui: étude sociologique. [Paris, 1971]. pp. 284. *bibliog. (Caisse Nationale des Allocations Familiales. Etudes C.A.F. 13)*

— United States.

LOPATA (HELENA ZNANIECKI) Widowhood in an American city. Cambridge. Mass.. [1973]. pp. 369. *bibliog.*

WIEGEL (HANS).

WERF (HANS VAN DER) Hans Wiegel: profiel van een politicus. Baarn. [1973]. pp. 99.

WIFE BEATING.

PIZZEY (ERIN) Scream quietly or the neighbours will hear. Harmondsworth. 1974. pp. 143.

WILBERFORCE (WILLIAM).

FURNEAUX (ROBIN) William Wilberforce. London. 1974. pp. 506. *bibliog.*

WILD LIFE, CONSERVATION OF.

SPENCE (A. MICHAEL) Blue whales and applied control theory. Stanford. 1973. pp. 52. *bibliog. (Stanford University. Institute for Mathematical Studies in the Social Sciences. Technical Reports. [New Series]. No. 108)*

— Africa.

POLLOCK (NORMAN CHARLES) Animals. environment and man in Africa. Farnborough, Hants.. [1974]. pp. 159.

— **United Kingdom.**

SOUTH HAMPSHIRE PLAN ADVISORY COMMITTEE. Study Reports. Group A. Rural Conservation. No. 4. Natural history. Winchester, [1969]. pp. (27).

— — **Wales.**

MERIONETH. County Planning Office. Merioneth structure plan: (subject report no. 11): wildlife conservation. Dolgellau, [1973]. fo. 32.

WILD LIFE RESEARCH

— **Canada.**

CANADA. Program Planning Office for Resource Satellites and Remote Airborne Sensing. Working Group on Forestry and Wildlands. 1971. Resource satellites and remote airborne sensing for Canada. Report no.5. Forestry and wildlands; [L. Sayn-Wittgenstein, chairman]. Ottawa, 1971. pp. 17. *With French summary.*

WILKES (JOHN).

WILLIAMSON (AUDREY) Wilkes: 'a friend to liberty'. London, 1974. pp. 254. *bibliog.*

WILKINSON (ELLEN CICELY).

U.K. National Register of Archives. 1973. Labour Party archives: Ellen Wilkinson press cuttings, 1924-36. London, 1973. single sheet.

WILLIAM, of Ockham.

McGRADE (ARTHUR STEPHEN) The political thought of William of Ockham: personal and institutional principles. London, 1974. pp. 269. *bibliog.*

WILLS

— **United Kingdom.**

BAILEY (STANLEY JOHN) The law of wills, including intestacy and administration of assets: an introduction to the rules of law, equity and construction relating to testamentary dispositions. 7th ed. London, [1973]. pp. 364.

WILLWERTH (JAMES).

WILLWERTH (JAMES) Eye in the last storm: a reporter's journal of one year in southeast Asia. New York, 1972. pp. 178.

WILMINGTON, DELAWARE

— **History.**

HOFFECKER (CAROL E.) Wilmington, Delaware: portrait of an industrial city, 1830-1910. [Charlottesville], 1974. pp. 187. *bibliog.*

WILSON (THOMAS WOODROW) President of the United States.

DEVLIN (PATRICK ARTHUR) Baron Devlin. Too proud to fight: Woodrow Wilson's neutrality. London, 1974. pp. 731. *bibliog.*

WINCOTT (LEN).

WINCOTT (LEN) Invergordon mutineer. London, [1974]. pp. 183.

WINDWARD ISLANDS

— **Officials and employees — Salaries, allowances, etc.**

U.K. Colonial Office. 1953. Report of an inquiry into the salaries and emoluments of the civil services of the Windward Islands; by C.J. Hodgens. [St. George'S!, 1953. PP. 131.

WINE AND WINE MAKING

— **Law and legislation — Italy.**

FAVARETTI (GIORGIO) and MERLO (MAURIZIO) Effetti economici della legge sulla denominazione d'origine dei vini: il Collio goriziano. [Padova, 1973?]. pp. 128.

— **France.**

FRANCE. Direction de la Documentation. La Documentation Française. Notes et Etudes Documentaires. Nos. 3,956-3, 957. Les productions végétales en France: la vigne et le vin. [Paris], 1973. pp. 82. *bibliog.*

— **Norway.**

LINDEMAN (GUNNAR) Trekk av A.s Vinmonopolets historie 1922-1972; utgitt ved A. s Vinmonopolets 50- års jubileum. [Oslo?], 1972. pp. 308.

WINNIG (AUGUST).

RIBHEGGE (WILHELM) August Winnig: eine historische Persönlichkeitsanalyse. Bonn-Bad Godesberg, [1973]. pp. 315. *bibliog. (Friedrich-Ebert-Stiftung. Forschungsinstitut. Schriftenreihe. Band 99)*

WINNIPEG

— **General strike, 1919.**

REA (J.E.) compiler. The Winnipeg general strike. Toronto, [1973]. pp. 121. *bibliog.*

— **History — Sources.**

REA (J.E.) compiler. The Winnipeg general strike. Toronto, [1973]. pp. 121. *bibliog.*

— **Politics and government.**

MANITOBA. 1971. Proposals for urban reorganization in the Greater Winnipeg area.[Winnipeg, 1971]. pp. 40.

WINSTANLEY (GERARD).

WINSTANLEY (GERARD) The law of freedom and other writings; edited...by Christopher Hill. Harmondsworth, 1973. pp. 395. *bibliog.*

WIRE INDUSTRY

— **United Kingdom.**

SETH-SMITH (MICHAEL) Two hundred years of Richard Johnson and Nephew. Manchester, 1973. pp. 292. *bibliog.*

WIRIYAMU

— **Massacre, 1972.**

HASTINGS (ADRIAN) Wiriyamu. London, 1974. pp. 158.

WIRTH (JOSEPH).

GERMANY . Reichskanzlei. 1921-1922. Die Kabinette Wirth I und II: 10. Mai 1921 bis 26. Oktober 1921, 26. Oktober 1921 bis 22. November 1922; bearbeitet von Ingrid Schulze-Bidlingmaier. Boppard am Rhein, 1973. 2 vols. *(Akten der Reichskanzlei, Weimarer Republik)*

WISCONSIN

— **Economic conditions — Statistics.**

DAVID (MARTIN HEIDENHAIN) and others. Linkage and retrieval of microeconomic data: a strategy for data development and use: a report on the Wisconsin assets and incomes archives. Toronto, [1974]. pp. 296. *bibliog.*

— **Economic history.**

MERK (FREDERICK) Economic history of Wisconsin during the Civil War decade. 2nd ed. Madison, [1971]. pp. 414.

WALSH (MARGARET) The manufacturing frontier: pioneer industry in antebellum Wisconsin, 1830-1860. Madison, Wisc., 1972. pp. 263. *bibliog.*

— **Industries.**

WALSH (MARGARET) The manufacturing frontier: pioneer industry in antebellum Wisconsin, 1830-1860. Madison, Wisc., 1972. pp. 263. *bibliog.*

— **Politics and government.**

THELEN (DAVID P.) The new citizenship: origins of progressivism in Wisconsin, 1885-1900. Columbia, Mo., [1972]. pp. 340. *bibliog.*

WITCHCRAFT.

NEWALL (VENETIA) ed. The witch figure: folklore essays by a group of scholars in England honouring the 75th birthday of Katharine M. Briggs. London, 1973. pp. 239. *bibliog.*

— **Mexico.**

SELBY (HENRY ANDERSON) Zapotec deviance: the convergence of folk and modern sociology. Austin, [Texas, 1974]. pp. 166. *bibliog.*

— **Nigeria.**

HIVES (FRANK) Ju-ju and justice in Nigeria; told by Frank Hives and written down by Gascoigne Lumley. Harmondsworth, 1940. pp. 192. *First published in 1930.*

— **Papua New Guinea.**

HAYES (RITA THERESA) Sorcery and power among the Kwoma of Sepik New Guinea; [M. Phil. (London) thesis]. 1973[or rather 1974]. fo. 304. *bibliog. Typescript: unpublished. This thesis is the property of London University and may not be removed from the library.*

— **United States.**

BOYER (PAUL) Historian, and NISSENBAUM (STEPHEN) Salem possessed: the social origins of witchcraft. Cambridge, Mass., 1974. pp. 231.

WITNESSES

— **Russia.**

SMYSLOV (VIKTOR IVANOVICH) Svidetel' v sovetskom ugolovnom protsesse. Moskva, 1973. pp. 160.

WITTGENSTEIN (LUDWIG).

BINKLEY (TIMOTHY) Wittgenstein's language. The Hague, 1973. pp. 227. *bibliog.*

DILMAN (ILHAM) Induction and deduction: a study in Wittgenstein. Oxford, 1973. pp. 225. *bibliog.*

HUNTER (J.F.M.) Essays after Wittgenstein. London, 1973. pp. 202.

JANIK (ALLAN) and TOULMIN (STEPHEN EDELSTON) Wittgenstein's Vienna. London, 1973. pp. 314. *bibliog.*

WITTGENSTEIN (LUDWIG) Letters to C.K. Ogden, with comments on the English translation of the Tractatus logico-philosophicus; edited with an introduction by G.H. von Wright; and an appendix of letters by Frank Plumpton Ramsey. Oxford, 1973. pp. 90.

WIVES.

MICHEL (ANDREE) Activité professionnelle de la femme et vie conjugale. Paris, 1974. pp. 190. *bibliog.*

WOLLSTONECRAFT (MARY).

See GODWIN (MARY).

WOMAN.

WOMEN in the struggle for liberation. Geneva, 1973. pp. 169. *bibliogs. (World Student Christian Federation. WSCF Books. vol. 3, no. 2/3)*

— **Employment.**

GALENSON (MARJORIE) Women and work: an international comparison. Ithaca, 1973. pp. 120. *bibliog. (Cornell. University. New York State School of Industrial and Labor Relations. ILR Paperbacks. No. 13)*

WOMAN. (Cont.)

— — Argentine Republic.

GUEVARA (RAFAEL EDUARDO) La mujer y la seguridad social en la legislacion argentina...; trabajo encomendado por el Ministerio de Cultura y Educacion para la Conferencia Interamericana Especializada sobre Educacion Integral de la Mujer. Buenos Aires, Centro Nacional de Documentacion e Informacion Educativa, 1972. pp. 45.

— — Belgium.

WAETER (D. VAN DE) Vrouw en arbeid. [Brussels], Rijksinstituut voor Ziekte- en Invaliditeitsverzekering, 1971. pp. 206.

HANQUET (HUBERTE) Travail professionnel des femmes et mutations sociales. Bruxelles, [1972]. pp. 405. bibliog.

SCHOONBROODT (JOSEPH) Les femmes et le travail: mille travailleuses parlent; sur une enquête d'Etienne Rohaert et du service féminin de la C[onféderation des] S[yndicats] C[hrétiens]. Bruxelles, [1973]. pp. 166. bibliog.

— — France.

LANTIER (FRANÇOISE) and others. La structure d'emploi féminin dans trois régions: La Rochelle, Limoges, Montluçon. [Paris], Association Nationale pour la Formation Professionnelle des Adultes, 1971. 2 vols.

CONFERENCE NATIONALE DES FEMMES SALARIEES, 5E, 1973. Les femmes salariées: travaux. Paris, [1973]. pp. 249.

ORANGE (M.) Le travail féminin dans la région Midi-Pyrénées: I: étude statistique. Toulouse, Echelon Régional de l'Emploi, 1973. fo.78.

MICHEL (ANDREE) Activité professionnelle de la femme et vie conjugale. Paris, 1974. pp. 190. bibliog.

ORANGE (M.) and CLEMENT (S.) Le travail féminin dans la région Midi-Pyrénées: 3ͤ étude sociologique. Toulouse, Echelon Régional de l'Emploi, 1974. fo. 161.

— — Germany.

MENSCHIK (JUTTA) Gleichberechtigung oder Emanzipation?: die Frau im Erwerbsleben der Bundesrepublik. new ed. Frankfurt am Main, 1973 repr. 1974. pp. 192. bibliog.

— — Germany, Eastern.

KULKE (CHRISTINE) Die Berufstätigkeit der Frauen in der industriellen Produktion der DDR: zur Theorie und Praxis der Frauenarbeitspolitik der SED. Berlin, 1967. pp. 323. bibliog.

— — Netherlands.

NETHERLANDS. Staatssecretaris van Financiën. 1970. Nota fiscale positie van de werkende gehuwde vrouw. 's-Gravenhage, 1970. pp. 37.

REBELSE meiden blijven strijden. Den Haag, 1974 in progress.

— — Russia — Ukraine.

VITRUK (LIUDMYLA DMYTRIVNA) Zhinky-trudivnytsi v period sotsialistychnoï industrializatsiï: na materialakh promyslovosti Ukraïns'koï RSR, 1926-1932 rr.Kyïv, 1973. pp. 120.

— — South Africa.

WESSELS (DINA M.) The employment potential of graduate housewives in the P[retoria-] W[itwatersrand-] V[ereeniging] region. Pretoria, South African Human Sciences Research Council, 1972 in progress. bibliog.

— — Sweden.

SELLERBERG (ANN MARI) Kvinnorna på den svenska arbetsmarknaden under 1900-talet: en sociologisk analys av kvinnornas underordnade position i arbetslivet. Lund, [1973]. pp. 308. bibliog. With English summary.

— — Thailand.

MAURER (KENNETH) and others. Marriage, fertility, and labor force participation of Thai women: an econometric study;... a report prepared for Agency for International Development. Santa Monica, 1973. pp. 54. bibliog. (Rand Corporation. [Rand Reports]. 829)

— Underdeveloped areas.

See UNDERDEVELOPED AREAS — Women's employment.

— — United Kingdom.

HOLCOMBE (LEE) Victorian ladies at work: middle-class working women in England and Wales, 1850-1914. Hamden, Conn., 1973. pp. 253.

MICHAELS (RUTH) New opportunities for women: a survey of mature women students. Hatfield, 1973. pp. 36. (Hatfield Polytechnic. Occasional Papers. No.1)

SCOTT (REBECCA JARVIS) Women in the Stuart economy; [M. Phil. (London) thesis] . 1973. fo. 244. bibliog. Typescript: unpublished. This thesis is the property of London University and may not be removed from the Library.

SMITH (BARBARA M.D.) Black country employment 1959-1970: an analysis based on employment exchange data and incorporating comparisons between inner and outer exchanges and between the Black country and Birmingham and Great Britain. Birmingham, 1973. fo. 31,89. (Birmingham. University. Centre for Urban and Regional Studies. Research Memoranda. 18) With summary at front.

U.K. Department of Employment. 1973. Equal opportunities for men and women: government proposals for legislation. [London, 1973]. pp. 32.

U.K. National Register of Archives. 1973. Labour Party archives: miscellaneous accessions: Standing Joint Committee of Industrial Women's Organisations: note on first minute book compiled by R.A. Storey. London, 1973. single sheet.

U.K. National Register of Archives. 1973. Women's Labour League records deposited in the Labour Party archives, Transport House; listed by T.W.M. Jaine. London, 1973. fo. 7.

MEPHAM (G.J.) Equal opportunity and equal pay: a review of objectives, problems and progress. London, 1974. pp. 209. bibliog.

— — United States.

LYLE (JEROLYN R.) and ROSS (JANE L.) Women in industry: employment patterns of women in corporate America. Lexington, [1973]. pp. 164. bibliog.

MADDEN (JANICE FANNING) The economics of sex discrimination. Lexington, Mass., [1973]. pp. 140. bibliog.

SWEET (JAMES A.) Women in the labor force. New York, [1973]. pp. 211. bibliog.

— History and condition of women.

A REPLY to John Stuart Mill on the subjection of women. Philadelphia, 1870. pp. 242.

NOVACK (GEORGE) Revolutionary dynamics of women's liberation. New York, 1969 repr. 1973. pp. 22. (Reprinted from The Militant, October 17, 1969)

McCLUNG (NELLIE LETITIA) In times like these; [reprint of work originally published in 1915]; introduction by Veronica Strong-Boag. Toronto, [1972]. pp. 129. bibliog.

BULLOUGH (VERN L.) and BULLOUGH (BONNIE) The subordinate sex: a history of attitudes towards women. Urbana, [1973]. pp. 375. bibliog.

ROSSI (ALICE S.) ed. The feminist papers: from Adams to de Beauvoir. New York, 1973. pp. 716. bibliog.

ROWBOTHAM (SHEILA) Woman's consciousness, man's world. Harmondsworth, 1973 repr. 1974. pp. 136. bibliog.

SCOTT (REBECCA JARVIS) Women in the Stuart economy; [M. Phil. (London) thesis] . 1973. fo. 244. bibliog. Typescript: unpublished. This thesis is the property of London University and may not be removed from the Library.

COMER (LEE) Wedlocked women. Leeds, 1974. pp. 287. bibliog.

HELD (THOMAS) and LEVY (RENE) Die Stellung der Frau in Familie und Gesellschaft: eine soziologische Analyse am Beispiel der Schweiz. Frauenfeld, [1974]. pp. 378. bibliog. (Schweizerische Gesellschaft für Soziologie. Reihe Soziologie in der Schweiz. 1) With summaries in French and English.

THOMPSON (ROGER) Women in Stuart England and America: a comparative study. London, 1974. pp. 276.

— Legal status, laws, etc.

— — Germany.

MEYER-HARTER (RENATE) Die Stellung der Frau in der Sozialversicherung: Lageanalyse und Reformmöglichkeit. Berlin, [1974]. pp. 191. bibliog.

— — Germany, Eastern.

KUHRIG (HERTA) Equal rights for women in the German Democratic Republic. Berlin, 1973. pp. 159. (GDR Committee for Human Rights. Publications. No. 5)

— — Portugal.

PORTUGAL. Secretaria de Estado da Informação e Turismo. Direcçao Geral de Informação. 1971. The legal situation of the Portuguese woman. [Lisbon?], 1971. pp. 29.

— — Switzerland.

HALLER-ZIMMERMANN (MARGARETA) Die UNO- Menschenrechtskonventionen und die rechtliche Stellung der Frau in der Schweiz. Zürich, [1973]. pp. 197. bibliog. (Zuerich. Universität. Rechts- und Staatswissenschaftliche Fakultät. Zuercher Beiträge zur Rechtswissenschaft. [Neue Folge]. Heft 431)

— — United Kingdom.

COOTE (ANNA) and GILL (TESS) Women's rights: a practical guide. Harmondsworth, 1974. pp. 349.

— — United States.

JOHNSEN (JULIA EMILY) compiler. Special legislation for women. New York, 1926. pp. 142. bibliog.

BOYLAN (BRIAN RICHARD) The legal rights of women. New York, [1971]. pp. 156.

— Rights of women.

JOHNSEN (JULIA EMILY) compiler. Special legislation for women. New York, 1926. pp. 142. bibliog.

NOVACK (GEORGE) Revolutionary dynamics of women's liberation. New York, 1969 repr. 1973. pp. 22. (Reprinted from The Militant, October 17, 1969)

HEYMANN (LIDA GUSTAVA) and AUGSPURG (ANITA) Erlebtes-Erschautes: deutsche Frauen kämpfen für Freiheit, Recht und Frieden 1850-1940; herausgegeben von Margrit Twellmann. Meisenheim am Glan, 1972. pp. 311. bibliog.

McCLUNG (NELLIE LETITIA) In times like these; [reprint of work originally published in 1915]; introduction by Veronica Strong-Boag. Toronto, [1972]. pp. 129. bibliog.

DOLMENT (MARCELLE) and BARTHE (MARCEL) La femme au Québec. Montréal, [1973]. pp. 158. bibliog.

MURPHY (IRENE LYONS) Public policy on the status of women: agenda and strategy for the 70s. Lexington, [1973]. pp. 129. bibliog.

REID (ELIZABETH) and ALTMAN (DENNIS) Equality: the new issues; [2 lectures originally delivered at the 1973 Fabian Winter Lecture Series Equality under Labor]. Melbourne, [1973?]. pp. 16. (Victorian Fabian Society. Victorian Fabian Pamphlets. [No]. 28)

ROSSI (ALICE S.) ed. The feminist papers: from Adams to de Beauvoir. New York, 1973. pp. 716. *bibliog.*

ROWBOTHAM (SHEILA) Woman's consciousness, man's world. Harmondsworth, 1973 repr. '1974. pp. 136. *bibliog.*

THOENNESSEN (WERNER) The emancipation of women: the rise and decline of the women's movement in German social democracy, 1863-1933; translated by Joris de Bres. [London], 1973. pp. 185. *bibliog.*

COOTE (ANNA) and GILL (TESS) Women's rights: a practical guide. Harmondsworth, 1974. pp. 349.

— Social and moral questions.

KIM (IL-SUNG) On the work of the Women's Union. Pyongyang, 1971. pp. 67.

COSTA (MARIAROSA DALLA) and JAMES (SELMA) Le pouvoir des femmes et la subversion sociale. [Genève, 1973]. pp. 151.

REID (ELIZABETH) and ALTMAN (DENNIS) Equality: the new issues; [2 lectures originally delivered at the 1973 Fabian Winter Lecture Series Equality under Labor]. Melbourne, [1973?]. pp. 16. *(Victorian Fabian Society. Victorian Fabian Pamphlets. [No]. 28)*

SAFILIOS-ROTHSCHILD (CONSTANTINA) Women and social policy. Englewood Cliffs, [1974]. pp. 197. *bibliog.*

— Suffrage — Switzerland — Bern (Canton).

BERN (CANTON). Statistisches Bureau. 1968. Fakultatives Frauenstimmrecht in den Gemeinden, Abstimmung vom 18. Februar 1968, etc. Bern, 1968. fo.22, 46. *(Sonderhefte. 12) In French and German.*

WOMEN, ALTAI.

TOSHCHAKOVA (EKATERINA MAKAROVNA) Zhenshchina v obshchestve i sem'e u sovremennykh altaitsev; otvetstvennyi redaktor... L.P. Potapov. Novosibirsk, 1973. pp. 58.

WOMEN, MOHAMMEDAN.

MASSELL (GREGORY J.) The surrogate proletariat: Moslem women and revolutionary strategies in Soviet Central Asia, 1919-1929. Princeton, [1974]. pp. 448. *bibliog.*

WOMEN AND SOCIALISM.

OUTSHOORN (JOYCE) Vrouwenemancipatie en socialisme: een onderzoek naar de houding van de SDAP ten opzichte van het vrouwenvraagstuk tussen 1894 en 1919. [Nijmegen], 1973. pp. 111. *bibliog.*

THOENNESSEN (WERNER) The emancipation of women: the rise and decline of the women's movement in German social democracy, 1863-1933; translated by Joris de Bres. [London], 1973. pp. 185. *bibliog.*

U.K. National Register of Archives. 1973. Labour Party archives: miscellaneous accessions: Standing Joint Committee of Industrial Women's Organisations: note on first minute book compiled by R.A. Storey. London, 1973. single sheet.

U.K. National Register of Archives. 1973. Women's Labour League records deposited in the Labour Party archives, Transport House; listed by T.W.M. Jaine. London, 1973. fo. 7.

WOMEN AS BANKERS.

NORWAY. Likelønnsrådet. 1971. Kvinner i bankvirksomhet: en undersøkelse av lønn, stilling og utdanning: 9. melding om lønnsspørsmål. Oslo, 1971. pp. 27.

WOMEN AS TEACHERS.

FULTON (OLIVER) Rewards and fairness: academic women in the United States. Edinburgh, 1973. pp. 94. *bibliog. (Edinburgh. University. Centre for Research in the Educational Sciences. Occasional Papers. No. 15)*

WOMEN in higher education: [including papers presented at the 55th Annual Meeting of the American Council on Education]; edited by W. Todd Furniss [and] Patricia Albjerg Graham. Washington, D.C., [1974]. pp. 336.

WOMEN STUDENTS

— United States.

WOMEN in higher education: [including papers presented at the 55th Annual Meeting of the American Council on Education]; edited by W. Todd Furniss [and] Patricia Albjerg Graham. Washington, D.C., [1974]. pp. 336.

WOMEN IN AFRICA.

LITTLE (KENNETH LINDSAY) African women in towns: an aspect of Africa's social revolution. Cambridge, 1973. pp. 242. *bibliog.*

WOMEN IN AUSTRIA.

PROFT (GABRIELE) Der Weg zu uns'.: die Frauenfrage im neuen Österreich. Wien, [1945]. pp. 24. *(Sozialistische Partei Österreichs. Sozialistische Hefte. Folge 4)*

ROSENMAYR (LEOPOLD) and KREUTZ (HENRIK) Rollenerwartung der weiblichen Jugend: eine empirische Untersuchung über Erwartungen und Dispositionen weiblicher Jugendlicher in Österreich. Wien, 1973. pp. 423. *bibliog. (Österreichisches Institut für Jugendkunde. Beiträge zur Jugendkunde. Band 16) With English summary.*

WOMEN IN CANADA.

McCLUNG (NELLIE LETITIA) In times like these; [reprint of work originally published in 1915]; introduction by Veronica Strong-Boag. Toronto, [1972]. pp. 129. *bibliog.*

STATUS OF WOMEN IN CANADA; [pd. by] Minister of Labour, Minister responsible for the Status of Women. a., 1973- Ottawa. *In English and French.*

DOLMENT (MARCELLE) and BARTHE (MARCEL) La femme au Québec. Montréal, [1973]. pp. 158. *bibliog.*

WOMEN IN CHINA.

YOUNG (MARILYN BLATT) ed. Women in China: studies in social changes and feminism. Ann Arbor, Mich., 1973. pp. 259. *bibliog. (Michigan University. Center for Chinese Studies. Michigan Papers in Chinese Studies. No. 15)*

WOMEN IN CHRISTIANITY.

TAVARD (GEORGE HENRI) Woman in Christian tradition. Notre Dame, Ind., [1973]. pp. 257.

WOMEN IN EASTERN GERMANY.

GAST (GABRIELE) Die politische Rolle der Frau in der DDR. Düsseldorf, [1973]. pp. 306.

WOMEN IN GERMANY.

HEIDEMANN (CLAUS) and STAPF (KURT HERMANN) Die Hausfrau in ihrer städtischen Umwelt: eine empirische Studie zur urbanen Ökologie am Beispiel Braunschweigs. Braunschweig, 1969. pp. 156. *bibliog. (Technische Universität Braunschweig. Institut für Stadtbauwesen. Veröffentlichungen. Heft 4)*

HEYMANN (LIDA GUSTAVA) and AUGSPURG (ANITA) Erlebtes-Erschautes: deutsche Frauen kämpfen für Freiheit, Recht und Frieden 1850-1940; herausgegeben von Margrit Twellmann. Meisenheim am Glan, 1972. pp. 311. *bibliog.*

THOENNESSEN (WERNER) The emancipation of women: the rise and decline of the women's movement in German social democracy, 1863-1933; translated by Joris de Bres. [London], 1973. pp. 185. *bibliog.*

— Bibliography.

GERMANY (BUNDESREPUBLIK). Deutscher Bundestag. Wissenschaftliche Dienste. 1972. Die Situation der Frau in Deutschland: Auswahlbibliographie.3rd ed. Bonn, 1972. pp. 136. *(Bibliographien. 31)*

WOMEN IN ITALY.

REGGIO NELL'EMILIA (PROVINCE). Amministrazione Provinciale. La donna reggiana nella Resistenza: atti del convegno tenuta... 5 aprile 1965. [Reggio Emilia, 1967]. pp. 122.

FRABOTTA (BIANCAMARIA) ed. Femminismo e lotta di classe in Italia, 1970-1973: (analisi, documenti e prospettive). Roma, [1973]. pp. 256. *bibliog.*

WOMEN IN JAPAN.

FRANCE. Direction de la Documentation. La Documentation Française. Notes et Etudes Documentaires. No. 2,764. Aperçu historique sur le mouvement féministe japonais; (texte établi par la Maison franco-japonaise, avec la collaboration de Magara Kondo). Paris, 1961. pp. 21.

WOMEN IN KOREA.

KIM (IL-SUNG) On the work of the Women's Union. Pyongyang, 1971. pp. 67.

KIM (IL-SUNG) On the tasks of the Women's Union: speech addressed to the Women's Union functionaries...who are to attend the first conference of the Democratic Women's Union of North Korea, May 9, 1946. Pyongyang, 1973. pp. 17.

WOMEN IN POLITICS.

CHAMBERLIN (HOPE) A minority of members: women in the U.S. Congress. New York, 1973. pp. 374.

GAST (GABRIELE) Die politische Rolle der Frau in der DDR. Düsseldorf, [1973]. pp. 306.

CURRELL (MELVILLE E.) Political woman. London, 1974. pp. 201. *bibliog.*

JAQUETTE (JANE S.) ed. Women in politics. New York, [1974]. pp. 367. *bibliog.*

WOMEN IN PUBLIC LIFE.

UNITED NATIONS. Commission on the Status of Women. 1972. Participation of women in community development; report of the Secretary-General. (E/CN.6/514/Rev.1) New York, 1972. pp. 68.

FRANCE. Direction de la Documentation. La Documentation Française. Notes et Etudes Documentaires. Nos. 4,056-4, 057. Les femmes dans la fonction publique, par Geneviève M. Bécane-Pascaud. [Paris], 1974. pp. 74. *bibliog.*

WOMEN IN SOVIET CENTRAL ASIA.

MASSELL (GREGORY J.) The surrogate proletariat: Moslem women and revolutionary strategies in Soviet Central Asia, 1919-1929. Princeton, [1974]. pp. 448. *bibliog.*

WOMEN IN SWEDEN.

SWEDEN. Socialdepartementet. 1970. Family planning and the status of women in Sweden: report... to the United Nations. Stockholm, 1970. fo. 63. *(Stencil. 1970. 3)*

WOMEN IN SWITZERLAND.

HELD (THOMAS) and LEVY (RENE) Die Stellung der Frau in Familie und Gesellschaft: eine soziologische Analyse am Beispiel der Schweiz. Frauenfeld, [1974]. pp. 378. *bibliog. (Schweizerische Gesellschaft für Soziologie. Reihe Soziologie in der Schweiz. 1) With summaries in French and English.*

WOMEN IN THE NETHERLANDS.

OUTSHOORN (JOYCE) Vrouwenemancipatie en socialisme: een onderzoek naar de houding van de SDAP ten opzichte van het vrouwenvraagstuk tussen 1894 en 1919. [Nijmegen], 1973. pp. 111. *bibliog.*

WOMEN IN THE UNITED KINGDOM.

CO-OPERATIVE UNION. (Women in the co-operative movement): report of study group on the situation and role of women in the co-operative movement. Manchester, [1973?]. pp. 8.

SCOTT (REBECCA JARVIS) Women in the Stuart economy; [M. Phil. (London) thesis] . 1973. fo. 244. *bibliog. Typescript: unpublished. This thesis is the property of London University and may not be removed from the Library.*

CURRELL (MELVILLE E.) Political woman. London, 1974. pp. 201. *bibliog.*

THOMPSON (ROGER) Women in Stuart England and America: a comparative study. London, 1974. pp. 276.

WOMEN IN THE UNITED STATES.

MURPHY (IRENE LYONS) Public policy on the status of women: agenda and strategy for the 70s. Lexington, [1973]. pp. 129. *bibliog.*

SKLAR (KATHRYN KISH) Catherine Beecher: a study in American domesticity. New Haven, Conn., 1973. pp. 356. *bibliog.*

THOMPSON (ROGER) Women in Stuart England and America: a comparative study. London, 1974. pp. 276.

WOMEN IN TRADE UNIONS

— United Kingdom.

GOLDMAN (HAROLD) Emma Paterson: she led woman into a man's world. London, 1974. pp. 127. *bibliog.*

WOMEN IN UGANDA.

ELAM (YITZCHAK) The social and sexual roles of Hima women: a study of nomadic cattle breeders in Nyabushozi county, Ankole, Uganda. Manchester, [1973]. pp. 243. *bibliog.*

WOMEN'S COLLEGES

— Russia.

VALK (SIGIZMUND NATANOVICH) and others, eds. Sankt-Peterburgskie Vysshie zhenskie (Bestuzhevskie) kursy, 1878- 1918: sbornik statei. 2nd ed. Leningrad, 1973. pp 303 (xxxii).

WOMEN'S INTERNATIONAL LEAGUE FOR PEACE AND FREEDOM.

HEYMANN (LIDA GUSTAVA) and AUGSPURG (ANITA) Erlebtes-Erschautes: deutsche Frauen kämpfen für Freiheit, Recht und Frieden 1850-1940; herausgegeben von Margrit Twellmann. Meisenheim am Glan, 1972. pp. 311. *bibliog.*

WOMEN'S LIBERATION MOVEMENT.

COSTA (MARIAROSA DALLA) and JAMES (SELMA) Le pouvoir des femmes et la subversion sociale. [Genève, 1973]. pp. 151.

ROSSI (ALICE S.) ed. The feminist papers: from Adams to de Beauvoir. New York, 1973. pp. 716. *bibliog.*

COMER (LEE) Wedlocked women. Leeds, 1974. pp. 287. *bibliog.*

WOOD—PULP INDUSTRY.

WAYMAN (MORRIS) and others. Guide for planning pulp and paper enterprises. Rome, Food and Agriculture Organization, 1973. pp. 379. *bibliog. (Forestry and Forest Products Studies. No.18)*

— Norway.

MYHRER (ERIK) The Norwegian pulp and paper industry. Oslo, 1971. pp. 15. *(Norway. Utenriksdepartementet. Presseavdelingen. Reference Papers. 1971. 220)*

WOOD—USING INDUSTRIES

— Information services.

UNITED NATIONS INDUSTRIAL DEVELOPMENT ORGANIZATION. Guides to Information Sources. No. 9. Information sources on building boards from wood and other fibrous materials (UNIDO/LIB/SER.D/9). New York, United Nations, 1974. pp. 82. *bibliog.*

— Finland.

HALMEKOSKI (MATTI) Metsäteollisuuslaitoksen sijaintipaikan valintaan vaikuttavista tekijöistä metsätalouden liiketieteen kannalta. Helsinki, 1971. fo. 75. *(Finland. Valtakunnansuunnittelutoimisto. Julkaisusarja B. 14) With English summary.*

— Russia — Ukraine.

PYLA (VASYL' IVANOVYCH) Rozvytok lisopererobnoï promyslovosti na osnovi kompleksnoho vykorystannia derevyny. Kyïv, 1973. pp. 152. *bibliog.*

— Sweden.

SWEDEN. Inrikesdepartementet. Västsvenska Skogsindustriutredningen. 1969. Skogsindustri i södra Sverige: utvecklingstendenser och lokaliseringsförutsättningar för sågverk och massaindustrier. Stockholm, 1969. pp. 138. *(Sweden. Statens Offentliga Utredningar. 1969. 21)*

WOODWORKERS

— Germany.

DEUTSCHER HOLZARBEITER-VERBAND. Vorstand. Der Deutsche Holzarbeiter-Verband und sein Kampf gegen die Unfallgefahren an den Holzbearbeitungsmaschinen. [Berlin, 1926]. pp. 48.

— United Kingdom.

UNION OF CONSTRUCTION, ALLIED TRADES AND TECHNICIANS. National Delegate Conference. Report of proceedings. bien., 1972(1st)- London.

WOODWORKING INDUSTRIES.

— Germany — Safety measures.

DEUTSCHER HOLZARBEITER-VERBAND. Vorstand. Der Deutsche Holzarbeiter-Verband und sein Kampf gegen die Unfallgefahren an den Holzbearbeitungsmaschinen. [Berlin, 1926]. pp. 48.

WOOL TRADE AND INDUSTRY

— Australia.

AUSTRALIAN WOOL SALE STATISTICS: analysis of Australian wool sold at auction in Australia; ([pd. by] Australian Wool Corporation. a., 1970/71 (no.1)- Melbourne. *In 2 pts., Statistical analyses A and B.*

CAMPBELL (KEITH O.) Whither the wool country?: an economic perspective. Sydney, [1972?]. pp. 75-82. *(Sydney. University. Department of Agricultural Economics. Miscellaneous Papers. No.63) (Offprint from The Australian Quarterly, vol. 44, no. 4)*

AUSTRALIA. Bureau of Agricultural Economics. 1973. Statistical handbook of the sheep and wool industry. 4th ed. Canberra, 1973. 1 vol. (unpaged).

— European Economic Community countries.

ECONOMIC DEVELOPMENT COMMITTEE FOR THE AGRICULTURAL INDUSTRY. Common Market Sub-Committee. Livestock Group. UK farming and the Common Market: sheep and wool; a report. London, National Economic Development Office, 1974. pp. 61.

— United Kingdom.

WOOL, JUTE AND FLAX INDUSTRY TRAINING BOARD [U.K.]. Report and statement of accounts. a., 1972/3- Bradford. *Formerly included in the file of British Parliamentary Papers.*

ECONOMIC DEVELOPMENT COMMITTEE FOR THE AGRICULTURAL INDUSTRY. Common Market Sub-Committee. Livestock Group. UK farming and the Common Market: sheep and wool; a report. London, National Economic Development Office, 1974. pp. 61.

WORCESTERSHIRE

— Surveys.

WORCESTERSHIRE. Planning Department. Worcestershire structure plan; ([with Report of survey [and] Supporting information). [Worcester, 1973]. 5 vols. (in 3).

WORK.

GOLDRING (PATRICK) Multipurpose man. London, 1973. pp. 120.

MILLS (TED) Quality of work: an emerging art and science. [London, 1973]. pp. 18. *(Working Together Campaign. Working Together Studies)*

WORK in America; report of a special task force to the Secretary of Health, Education, and Welfare; prepared under the auspices of the W.E. Upjohn Institute for Employment Research; [James O'Toole, chairman]. Cambridge, Mass., 1973. pp. 262. *bibliog.*

ANDERSON (NELS) Man's work and leisure. Leiden, 1974. pp. 146.

CLAYRE (ALASDAIR) Work and play: ideas and experience of work and leisure. London, [1974]. pp. 261.

CROWLEY (J.E.) This Sheba, self: the conceptualization of economic life in eighteenth-century America. Baltimore, [1974]. pp. 161. *(Johns Hopkins University. Studies in Historical and Political Science. Series 92. No.2)*

SALAMAN (GRAEME) Community and occupation: an exploration of work/leisure relationships. London, 1974. pp. 136. *bibliog. (Cambridge. University. Department of Applied Economics. Cambridge Papers in Sociology. No. 4)*

— Psychological aspects.

BELL (CLIFFORD R.) Men at work. London, 1974. pp. 119. *bibliogs.*

WORK MEASUREMENT.

U.K. Department of Health and Social Security. 1972. Work measurement in radio-diagnostic departments. London, 1972. pp. 42. *(Management Services (NHS) [Reports]. 5)*

SCIENZA e organizzazione del lavoro: [proceedings of two meetings held by the Istituto Gramsci, 1972]. Roma, 1973. pp. 191. *bibliog.*

WORKMEN'S COMPENSATION

— Australia.

GLASBEEK (HARRY JACQUES) and EGGLESTON (E.M.) Cases and materials on industrial law in Australia. Sydney, 1973. pp. 590.

— Belgium.

BELGIUM. Office National de Sécurité Sociale. 1972. Aperçu du régime général de sécurité sociale des travailleurs: commentaire de la loi 27 juin 1969, révisant l'arrêté-loi du 28 décembre 1944 concernant la sécurité sociale des travailleurs et de l'arrêté royal organique du 28 novembre 1969, pris en exécution de la loi du 27 juin 1969. [Brussels], 1972. [fo. 141]

— Denmark.

DENMARK. Statutes, etc. 1933-68. The Industrial Injuries Act, 1933, as amended. [Copenhagen?], 1968. pp. 35.

— New Zealand.

NEW ZEALAND. General Assembly. House of Representatives. Select Committee on Compensation for Personal Injury. 1970. Report...; G.F. Gair, chairman. Wellington, 1970. pp. 84.

CAMPBELL (IAN B.) The Accident Compensation Act 1972. Wellington, 1973. fo. 36. *(Victoria University of Wellington. Industrial Relations Centre. Occasional Papers in Industrial Relations. No. 7)*

— Norway.

ERSTATNING ved yrkesskader; fra et utvalg oppnevnt ...av 6. mai 1970. Oslo, 1972. pp. 35. *(Norway. Norges Offentlige Utredninger. 1972. 2)*

— Russia.

ASTRAKHAN (EVGENII IVANOVICH) Trudovoe uvech'e i izhdivenstvo. Moskva, 1967. pp. 104. *bibliog.*

— Sweden.

SWEDEN. Socialdepartementet. Utredningen angående Yrkesskadeförsäkringens Finansiering. 1970. Yrkesskadeförsäkringens finansiering. Stockholm, 1970. pp. 112. *(Sweden. Statens Offentliga Utredningar. 1970.49)*

— Switzerland.

SWITZERLAND. Caisse Nationale Suisse d'Assurance en Cas d'Accidents. 1969. Guide de l'assurance obligatoire contre les accidents; à l'usage des chefs d'entreprises et des assurés. 17th ed. [Lucerne], 1969. pp. 182.

— United Kingdom.

KINNERSLY (PATRICK) The hazards of work: how to fight them. London, 1973. pp. 394.

DOUGLAS-MANN (BRUCE LESLIE HOME) and others. Accidents at work: compensation for all; [prepared by a subcommittee of the Society of Labour Lawyers and submitted as evidence to the Royal Commission on Civil Liability and Compensation for Personal Injury]. London, 1974. pp. 16.

FABIAN SOCIETY. Fabian Tracts. [No.] 428. Industrial injuries: a new approach; [by] E.A. Webb:... the evidence of the Post Office Engineering Union to the Royal Commission on Civil Liability and Compensation for Personal Injury. London, 1974. pp. 24.

— United States.

LOGAN (JOHN E.) An analysis of workmen's compensation: South Carolina and the United States. [Colombia], 1972. pp. 206. *bibliog. (South Carolina University. Bureau of Business and Economic Research. Essays in Economics. No.26)*

WORKS COUNCILS
— Germany.

FICHTER (TILMAN) Kampf um Bosch: ... die Betriebspolitik der KPD nach 1945, am Beispiel der Firma Robert Bosch GmbH; [and] Eugen Eberle: Sieben Jahre offensiver Kampf gegen das Kapital. Berlin, [1974]. pp. 191. *bibliog.*

— Italy.

ACCORNERO (ARIS) Gli anni '50 in fabbrica, con un diario di Commissione interna. Bari, [1973]. pp. 334.

ALBANESE (L.) and others. I consigli di fabbrica. Roma, [1973]. pp. 140. *bibliog. (Reprinted from Il Contemporaneo, n. 46, 1972)*

SALVARANI (GIANNI) and BONIFAZI (ALBERTO) Le nuove strutture del sindacato: origini, esperienze e prospettive del movimento dei delegati in Italia. Milano, [1973]. pp. 209. *bibliog.*

— Spain.

REGUERA SEVILLA (JOAQUIN) El jurado de empresa: nueva institucion de nuestro derecho social; ([with] Apendice con indice de conceptos). 2nd ed. Madrid, 1961-65. 2 pts. (in 1 vol.).

— Yugoslavia.

FRANCE. Direction de la Documentation. La Documentation Française. Notes et Etudes Documentaires. Nos. 4,008-4, 009-4,010. L'autogestion yougoslave, 1950-1972, par Kruno Meneghello- Dincic. [Paris], 1973. pp. 71.

GORUPIĆ (DRAGO) The enterprise and the development of Yugoslav economic system: articles. Zagreb, 1974. pp. 159. *One article in French.*

WORLD COUNCIL OF CHURCHES.

HUERNI (BETTINA S.) Der Beitrag des Ökumenischen Rates der Kirchen zur Entwicklungshilfe. Bern, [1973]. pp. 360. *bibliog. With English summary.*

WORLD HISTORY.
See HISTORY UNIVERSAL.

WORLD POLITICS.

PONCE (ANIBAL) El viento en el mundo: examen de la España actual en el centenario de Fourier. Buenos Aires, 1963. pp. 188.

ONE WORLD ONLY, 1967. One world only: a forum on international cooperation; (editor: Klaus W. Bender). Tokyo, [1968?]. pp. 84. *(Friedrich-Ebert-Stiftung. Asian Labour Institute. Reports. 1)*

BERG (OLE) Den politiske kultur og stabiliteten i det Euratlantiske Samfunn: nedtrappingen av 'den kalde krig'. Kjeller, Forsvarets Forskningsinstitutt, 1970. fo. 86. *(Norway. Forsvarets Forskningsinstitutt. Notater. S-217)*

WORSLEY (PETER MAURICE) The third world. 2nd ed. Chicago, 1970. pp. 373. *bibliog.*

KEOHANE (ROBERT O.) and NYE (JOSEPH S.) eds. Transnational relations and world politics. Cambridge, Mass., [1971] repr. 1973. pp. 428. *bibliog.*

BERTRAND RUSSELL CENTENARY SYMPOSIUM ON SPHERES OF INFLUENCE IN THE AGE OF IMPERIALISM, LINZ, 1972. Spheres of influence in the age of imperialism; papers submitted to the Bertrand Russell Centenary Symposium...;[by] Noam Chomsky [and others]. Nottingham, 1972. pp. 144.

LAQUEUR (WALTER ZE'EV) Neo-isolationism and the world of the seventies. New York, 1972. pp. 50. *(Georgetown University. Center for Strategic and International Studies. Washington Papers. vol [1]/5)*

STRUYE (PAUL) Problèmes internationaux 1927-1972: [collection of articles originally published in "Libre Belgique"]. Namur, 1972. 2 vols. *(Namur. Facultés Universitaires Notre-Dame de la Paix. Faculté de Droit. Travaux. No.6)*

WORLD politics and the Jewish condition; essays prepared for a task force on the world of the 1970s of the American Jewish Committee; edited...by Louis Henkin. New York, [1972]. pp. 342.

BERTRAND RUSSELL CENTENARY SYMPOSIUM ON SPHERES OF INFLUENCE IN THE AGE OF IMPERIALISM, LINZ, 1972. Spheres of influence and the third world; papers submitted to the Bertrand Russell Centenary Symposium...;[by] Vladimi Dedijer [and others]. Nottingham, 1973. pp. 123.

BRANDES (VOLKHARD) Die Krise des Imperialismus: Grenzen der kapitalistischen Expansion und der Wiederaufbau der Arbeiterbewegung. Frankfurt am Main, [1973]. pp. 106.

[CARRERO BLANCO (LUIS)] Comentarios de un español; las tribulaciones de Don Prudencio; diplomacia subterranea; ([by] "Juan de la Cosa" [pseud.]). Madrid, 1973. pp. 339.

COMMISSION TO STUDY THE ORGANIZATION OF PEACE. Building peace: reports of the Commission... 1939-1972. Metuchen, N.J., 1973. 2 vols.

CONFERENCE OF HEADS OF STATE OR GOVERNMENT OF NON-ALIGNED COUNTRIES. Neither East nor West: the basic documents of non-alignment [selected from the proceedings of the 1st-3rd conferences, 1961, 1964 and 1970]; edited by Henry M. Christman. New York, [1973]. pp. 206.

CONFLITS et coopération entre les états; 1971: prélude à un nouvel ordre international?. Paris, 1973. pp. 270. *(Fondation Nationale des Sciences Politiques. Travaux et Recherches de Science Politique. 25)*

ERA of negotiations: European security and force reductions; [by] Wolfgang Klaiber [and others]. Lexington, Mass., [1973]. pp. 192.

GRIFFITH (WILLIAM E.) Peking, Moscow, and beyond: the Sino-Soviet-American triangle. Washington, D.C., 1973. pp. 71. *(Georgetown University. Center for Strategic and International Studies. Washington Papers. vol.[1]/6)*

HAUSER (OSWALD) ed. Weltpolitik, 1933-1939: 13 Vorträge [given at two meetings of the Ranke-Gesellschaft in 1970 and 1971]. Göttingen, [1973]. pp. 292.

HÄGGLÖF (GUNNAR) Fredens vägar, 1945-1950. Stockholm, [1973]. pp. 213.

SOLBERG (CARL) Riding high: America in the cold war. New York, [1973]. pp. 632. *bibliog.*

SULZBERGER (CYRUS LEO) An age of mediocrity: memoirs and diaries, 1963-1972. New York, 1973. pp. 828.

TROTMAN (DONALD A.B.) Guyana and the world...: commentaries on national and international affairs,1968-1973. [Georgetown], [1973?]. pp. 100.

YIN (CHING-YAO) Negotiations in an era of negotiation. [Taipei], 1973. pp. 69. *(Asian Peoples' Anti-Communist League. Pamphlets. No. 171)*

BROWN (SEYOM) New forces in world politics. Washington, D.C., [1974]. pp. 224.

BUCHAN (ALASTAIR) Change without war: the shifting structures of world power. London, 1974. pp. 112. *(British Broadcasting Corporation. Reith Lectures. 1973)*

BUCHAN (ALASTAIR) The end of the postwar era: a new balance of world power. London, [1974]. pp. 347.

CATLIN (Sir GEORGE EDWARD GORDON) Kissinger's Atlantic charter. Gerrards Cross, 1974. pp. 144.

CAUTE (DAVID) Collisions: essays and reviews. London, 1974. pp. 231.

DOUGLAS-HOME (Sir ALEXANDER FREDERICK) Britain's changing role in world affairs. London, [1974]. pp. 8. *(David Davies Memorial Institute of International Studies. Annual Memorial Lectures. 1974)*

HIGGINS (HUGH) The cold war. London, 1974. pp. 141. *bibliog.*

LUKASHUK (IGOR' IVANOVICH) Otnosheniia mirnogo sosushchestvovaniia i mezhdunarodnoe pravo: problemy mezhdunarodno-pravovogo regulirovaniia. Kiev, 1974. pp. 207.

MADARIAGA (SALVADOR DE) Morning without noon: memoirs. Farnborough, 1974. pp. 441.

NEUBERT (HARALD) Der antiimperialistische Kampf und die Politik der friedlichen Koexistenz: zur Strategie der kommunistischen Weltbewegung in der Auseinandersetzung zwischen Sozialismus und Imperialismus. Berlin,1974. pp. 80.

— Bibliography.

WALES. University. University College of Wales. Library. The Ifor B. Powell pamphlet collection in the Library of University College, Cardiff: a checklist. Cardiff, 1972. pp. 35.

— Dictionaries and encyclopaedias.

GROMYKO (ANDREI ANDREEVICH) and others, eds. Diplomaticheskii slovar'. [3rd ed.]. Moskva, 1971-73. 3 vols.

— Sources.

GRENVILLE (JOHN ASHLEY SOAMES) The major international treaties, 1914-1973: a history and guide with texts. London, 1974. pp. 575. *bibliog.*

WORLD WAR, 1939—1945.

ISTORIIA vtoroi mirovoi voiny, 1939-1945. Moskva, 1973 in progress.

HEIFERMAN (RONALD) World War II; introduced and edited by S.L. Mayer. London, 1973. pp. 256.

WORLD WAR, 1939—1945. (Cont.)

MARWICK (ARTHUR J.B.) War and social change in the twentieth century: a comparative study of Britain, France, Germany, Russia and the United States. London, 1974. pp. 258. *bibliog.*

— Aerial operations.

SALLAGAR (F.M.) Operation "STRANGLE" (Italy, Spring 1944): a case study of tactical air interdiction. Santa Monica, 1972. pp. 95. *bibliog. (Rand Corporation. [Rand Reports]. 851)*

— Aerial operations, German.

STRACHEY (JOHN ST.LOE) Post D: some experiences of an air raid warden. London, 1941. pp. 135.

GALLAND (A.) and others. The Luftwaffe at war, 1939-1945;...English version edited by David Mondey. Chicago, 1973. pp. 247.

— Campaigns.

WALLACH (JEHUDA L.) Das Dogma der Vernichtungsschlacht: die Lehren von Clausewitz und Schlieffen und ihre Wirkungen in zwei Weltkriegen; (aus dem Englischen von Hans Jürgen Baron von Koskull). Frankfurt am Main, 1967. pp. 475. *bibliog.*

FOERSTER (GERHARD) and others. Der zweite Weltkrieg: militärhistorischer Abriss. Berlin, 1974. pp. 482. *bibliog.*

— — Iraq.

WARNER (GEOFFREY) Iraq and Syria, 1941. London, 1974. pp. 180. *bibliog.*

— — Italy.

ITALY. Stato Maggiore Esercito. Ufficio Storico. 1971. Il Corpo italiano di liberazione aprile-settembre 1944: narrazione, documenti. 2nd ed. Roma, 1971. pp. 342.

— — Madagascar.

DOWER (KENNETH CECIL GANDAR) Into Madagascar. Harmondsworth, 1943. pp. 111.

— — Russia.

LENZI (LORIS) Dal Dnieper al Don: la 63a Legione Cc.Nn. Tagliamento nella campagna di Russia; documentazione del Gruppo Reduci della Legione. Roma, [1972]. pp. 479.

— — Syria.

WARNER (GEOFFREY) Iraq and Syria, 1941. London, 1974. pp. 180. *bibliog.*

— Catholic Church.

KOŚCIÓŁ KATOLICKI NA ZIEMIACH POLSKI W CZASIE II WOJNY ŚWIATOWEJ: materiały i studia; [pd. by] Akademia Teologii Katolickiej. irreg., 1973 (zeszyt 1)- Warszawa.

— Causes.

PEARL Harbor as history: Japanese-American relations, 1931- 1941; (essays... presented at a binational conference held at Lake Kawaguchi, Japan... 1969); edited by Dorothy Borg and Shumpei Okamoto. New York, 1973. pp. 801. *(Columbia University. East Asian Institute. Studies)*

DOHERTY (JULIAN CAMPBELL) Das Ende des Appeasement: die britische Aussenpolitik, die Achsenmächte und Osteuropa nach dem Münchener Abkommen. Berlin, [1973]. pp. 284. *bibliog.*

— Censorship.

BENS (ELS DE) De Belgische dagbladpers onder Duitse censuur, 1940-1944. Antwerpen, [1973]. pp. 564. *bibliog.*

— Congresses.

SOSINSKII (SERGEI BRONISLAVOVICH) Aktsiia "Argonavt": Kryms aia konferentsiia i ee Ssha M0skva, 1970. pp. 127 *bibliog.*

— Conscript labour — Belgium.

SELLESLAGH (FRANS) ed. L'emploi de la main d'oeuvre belge sous l'occupation, 1940. Bruxelles, 1970. pp. 127. *(Centre de Recherches et d'Etudes Historiques de la seconde Guerre Mondiale [Belgium]. Documents. 1)*

— Deportations from France.

MOINE (ANDRE) La déportation et la résistance en Afrique du Nord, 1939- 1944. Paris, [1972]. pp. 310. *bibliog.*

— Diplomatic history.

GILBERT (MARTIN) and GOTT (RICHARD) The appeasers. [2nd ed.] London, 1967. pp. 444. *bibliog.*

PROCTOR (RAYMOND) Agonia de un neutral: las relaciones hispanoalemanas durante la segunda guerra mundial y la Division Azul. [Madrid, 1972]. pp. 354. *bibliog.*

VANLANGENHOVE (FERNAND) La Belgique et ses garants, l'été 1940: contribution à l'histoire de la politique extérieure de la Belgique pendant la Seconde Guerre mondiale. Bruxelles, 1972. pp. 228. *bibliog. (Académie Royale de Belgique. Classe des Lettres et des Sciences Morales et Politiques. Mémoires. Collection in-8°. 2ème Série. Tome 61, fasc. 3)*

HABERL (OTHMAR NIKOLA) Die Emanzipation der KP Jugoslawiens von der Kontrolle der Komintern/KPdSU, 1941-1945. München, 1974. pp. 86. *bibliog. (Munich. Südost-Institut München. Untersuchungen zur Gegenwartskunde Südosteuropas. 8)*

JUKIC (ILIJA) The fall of Yugoslavia: translated by Dorian Cooke. New York, [1974]. pp. 315. *bibliog.*

— Economic aspects — Baltic States.

CZOLLEK (ROSWITHA) Faschismus und Okkupation: wirtschaftspolitische Zielsetzung und Praxis des faschistischen deutschen Besatzungsregimes in den baltischen Sowjetrepubliken während des zweiten Weltkrieges. Berlin, 1974. pp. 224. *bibliog. (Akademie der Wissenschaften der DDR. Zentralinstitut für Geschichte. Schriften. Band 39)*

— — Europe.

FREYMOND (JEAN) Le IIIe Reich et la réorganisation économique de l'Europe, 1940-1942: origines et projets. Leiden, 1974. pp. 302. *bibliog. (Geneva. Graduate Institute of International Studies. Collection de Relations Internationales.3)*

— — Germany.

HASS (GERHART) and SCHUMANN (WOLFGANG) eds. Anatomie der Aggression: neue Dokumente zu den Kriegszielen des faschistischen deutschen Imperialismus im zweiten Weltkrieg. Berlin, 1972. pp. 239.

KEHRL (HANS) Krisenmanager im Dritten Reich: 6 Jahre Frieden, 6 Jahre Krieg; Erinnerungen; mit kritischen Anmerkungen und einem Nachwort, von Erwin Viefhaus. Düsseldorf, 1973. pp. 552.

RIEDEL (MATTHIAS) Eisen und Kohle für das Dritte Reich: Paul Pleigers Stellung in der NS-Wirtschaft. Göttingen, [1973]. pp. 375. *bibliog.*

FRITZ (MARTIN) German steel and Swedish iron ore, 1939-1945. Göteborg, 1974. pp. 137. *bibliog. (Göteborgs Universitet. Ekonomisk-Historiska Institutionen. Meddelanden. 29)*

— — Sweden.

FRITZ (MARTIN) German steel and Swedish iron ore, 1939-1945. Göteborg, 1974. pp. 137. *bibliog. (Göteborgs Universitet. Ekonomisk-Historiska Institutionen. Meddelanden. 29)*

— Education and the war.

WIKARJAK (JAN) ed. Uniwersytet Ziem Zachodnich i tajne kursy uniwersyteckie 1939- 1945: pokłosie wspomnień. Poznań, 1972. pp. 292. *(Poznań. Uniwersytet. Seria Dzieje UAM. Nr.8). With English and German summaries.*

— Governments in exile.

[MANNHEIMER (KAJ)] Norge och den norska exilregeringen under andra världskriget: undersökning utförd på uppdrag av Grundlagberedningen. Stockholm, 1972. pp. 165. *(Sweden. Statens Offentliga Utredningar. 1972. 18)*

GILLOIS (ANDRE) Histoire secrète des Français à Londres de 1940 à 1944. [Paris, 1973]. pp. 399. *bibliog.*

— Jews.

STEINBERG (LUCIEN) Le Comité de défense des Juifs en Belgique 1942-1944. [Brussels, 1973]. pp. 198. *bibliog.*

ADLER (HANS GUENTHER) Der verwaltete Mensch: Studien zur Deportation der Juden aus Deutschland. Tübingen, 1974. pp. 1076. *bibliog.*

STEINBERG (LUCIEN) Not as a lamb: the Jews against Hitler;...translated by Marion Hunter. Farnborough, [1974]. pp. 358. *bibliog.*

WAAGENAAR (SAM) The Pope's Jews. London, 1974. pp. 487. *bibliog.*

— Manpower — Russia.

DOKUCHAEV (GEORGII ANTONOVICH) Rabochii klass Sibiri i Dal'nego Vostoka v gody Velikoi Otechestvennoi voiny. Moskva, 1973. pp. 423.

— Naval operations.

THIERRY D'ARGENLIEU (GEORGES LOUIS MARIE) Souvenirs de guerre, juin 1940-janvier 1941. [Paris, 1973]. pp. 282.

— Naval operations, Italian.

ITALY. Marine Militare. Ufficio Storico. 1972- . La Marina italiana nella seconda guerra mondiale. vol. 21. L'organizzazione della Marina durante il conflitto: compilatore: Giuseppe Fioravanzo. Roma, 1972 in progress.

ITALY. Marina Militare. Ufficio Storico. 1972. La marina italiana nella seconda guerra mondiale. Volume I. Dati statistici; [compiled by] Giuseppe Fioravanzo [and] Francesco Manzo. 2nd ed. Roma, 1972. pp. 374.

— Peace.

MARTIN (BERND) Friedensinitiativen und Machtpolitik im Zweiten Weltkrieg, 1939-1942. Düsseldorf, [1974]. pp. 570. *bibliog.*

— Personal narratives, British.

DOWER (KENNETH CECIL GANDAR) Into Madagascar. Harmondsworth, 1943. pp. 111.

— Personal narratives, French.

THIERRY D'ARGENLIEU (GEORGES LOUIS MARIE) Souvenirs de guerre, juin 1940-janvier 1941. [Paris, 1973]. pp. 282.

— Personal narratives, Italian.

MASSOLA (UMBERTO) Memorie, 1939-1941. Roma, 1972. pp. 167.

— Personal narratives, Russian.

SABIK-VOGULOV ( ) V pobezhdennoi Germanii. n.p., 1947. pp. 78.

— Personal narratives, Swedish.

WAHLBÖACK (KRISTER) ed. Regeringen och kriget: ur statsrådens dagböcker, 1939-41. Stockholm, [1972]. pp. 191.

— Pictorial works.

GALLAND (A.) and others. The Luftwaffe at war, 1939-1945;...English version edited by David Mondey. Chicago, 1973. pp. 247.

WORLD WAR, 1939—1945. (Cont.)

— Prisoners and prisons.

BOEHME (KURT WILLI) and WOLFF (HELMUT) eds. Aufzeichnungen über die Kriegsgefangenschaft im Westen. München, 1973. pp. 552. (*Zur Geschichte der deutschen Kriegsgefangenen des zweiten Weltkrieges. Beihefte. 2*) Use restricted. See note at series entry.

— Prisoners and prisons, American.

BOEHME (KURT WILLI) Die deutschen Kriegsgefangenen in amerikanischer Hand: Europa. München, 1973. pp. 340. (*Zur Geschichte der deutschen Kriegsgefangenen des zweiten Weltkrieges. Band 10/2*) Use restricted.

BETHELL (NICHOLAS WILLIAM) 4th Baron Bethell. The last secret: forcible repatriation to Russia, 1944-7. London, 1974. pp. 224.

— Prisoners and prisons, British.

BETHELL (NICHOLAS WILLIAM) 4th Baron Bethell. The last secret: forcible repatriation to Russia, 1944-7. London, 1974. pp. 224.

— Prisoners and prisons, German.

APALSET (JAKOB) Heimsending av norske fangar frå Tyskland 1945: planar og forhandlingar 1944-45. [Oslo, 1970]. pp. 42. *bibliog.*

LEON-JOUHAUX (AUGUSTA) Prison pour hommes d'état. Paris, [1973]. pp. 176.

— Prisoners and prisons, Russian.

RATZA (WERNER) Die deutschen Kriegsgefangenen in der Sowjetunion: der Faktor Arbeit; mit einer Einleitung des Herausgebers. München, 1973. pp. 384. (*Zur Geschichte der deutschen Kriegsgefangenen des zweiten Weltkrieges. Band 4*) Use restricted.

— Propaganda.

VERKIJK (DICK) Radio Hilversum, 1940-1945: de omroep in de oorlog. Amsterdam, [1974]. pp. 832.

— Secret service.

WHALEY (BARTON) Codeword Barbarossa. Cambridge, Mass., [1973]. pp. 376. *bibliog.*

— Sources.

KRYM v period Velikoi Otechestvennoi voiny 1941-1945: sbornik dokumentov i materialov. Simferopol', 1973. pp. 488.

DASHICHEV (VIACHESLAV IVANOVICH) ed. Bankrotstvo strategii germanskogo fashizma: istoricheskie ocherki, dokumenty i materialy. Moskva, 1973. 2 vols.

FOERSTER (GERHARD) and GROEHLER (OLAF) eds. Der zweite Weltkrieg: Dokumente. Berlin, 1974. pp. 587.

— Underground movements — Africa, North.

MOINE (ANDRE) La déportation et la résistance en Afrique du Nord, 1939- 1944. Paris, [1972]. pp. 310. *bibliog.*

— — Austria.

DOKUMENTATIONSARCHIV DES ÖSTERREICHISCHEN WIDERSTANDES. Festschrift: 10 Jahre Dokumentationsarchiv des österreichischen Widerstandes. Wien, [1973]. pp. 28.

— — Belgium.

STEINBERG (LUCIEN) Le Comité de défense des Juifs en Belgique 1942-1944. [Brussels, 1973]. pp. 198. *bibliog.*

— — France.

FOURCADE (MARIE MADELEINE) Noah's ark: (the story of the Alliance intelligence network in occupied France);...translated by Kenneth Morgan. London, 1973. pp. 377.

SCHAUL (DORA) ed. Résistance: Erinnerungen deutscher Antifaschisten; [by] Otto Niebergall [and others]. Frankfurt/ Main, 1973. pp. 477.

— — Italy.

REGGIO NELL'EMILIA (PROVINCE). Amministrazione Provinciale. La donna reggiana nella Resistenza: atti del convegno tenuta... 5 aprile 1965. [Reggio Emilia, 1967]. pp. 122.

MASSA. Amministrazione Comunale. La resistenza continua...... Massa, 1968. 1 vol. (unpaged).

MILAN (PROVINCE). Amministrazione Provinciale. Dalla Resistenza: uomini, eventi, idee della lotta di liberazione in Provincia di Milano; a cura di Gianfranco Bianchi. Milano, [1969]. pp. 247.

JACO (ALDO DE) Le quattro giornate di Napoli: la città insorge. 3rd ed. Roma, 1972. pp. 321.

LAZAGNA (GIOVANNI BATTISTA) Ponte rotto: la lotta al fascismo; dalla cospirazione all'insurrezione armata. Milano, [1972]. pp. 333.

MASSOLA (UMBERTO) Memorie, 1939-1941. Roma, 1972. pp. 167.

SAVANI (PRIMO) Antifascismo e guerra di liberazione a Parma: cronache dei tempi.Parma, 1972. pp. 261.

UNIONE REGIONALE DELLE PROVINCIE TOSCANE. Contro ogni ritorno: dal fascismo alla costituzione repubblicana. [Florence, 1972]. pp. 135.

CURIEL (EUGENIO) Scritti, 1935-1945; a cura di Filippo Frassati. Roma, 1973. 2 vols.

LONGO (LUIGI) I centri dirigenti del PCI nella Resistenza. Roma, 1973. pp. 515.

MASSOLA (UMBERTO) Gli scioperi del '43: marzo-aprile; le fabbriche contro il fascismo. Roma, 1973. pp. 193.

Il 1943: le origini della rivoluzione antifascista. Roma, 1974. pp. 199. (*Critica Marxista. Quaderni. n.7*)

AMENDOLA (GIORGIO) Lettere a Milano: ricordi e documenti, 1939-1945. Roma, 1974. pp. 763. *bibliog.*

SPINELLA (MARIO) Memoria della Resistenza. [Milan], 1974. pp. 268.

— — Poland.

WIKARJAK (JAN) ed. Uniwersytet Ziem Zachodnich i tajne kursy uniwersyteckie 1939- 1945: pokłosie wspomnień. Poznań, 1972. pp. 292. (*Poznań. Uniwersytet. Seria Dzieje UAM. Nr.8*). With English and German summaries.

CIECHANOWSKI (JAN MIECZYSLAW) The Warsaw rising of 1944. Cambridge, 1974. pp. 332. *bibliog.* (*National Association for Soviet and East European Studies. Soviet and East European Studies*)

— — Russia — Russia (RSFSR).

LOGUNOVA (TAT'IANA AFANAS'EVNA) Partiinoe podpol'e i partizanskoe dvizhenie v zapadnykh i tsentral'nykh oblastiakh RSFSR, iiul' 1941-1943 gg. Moskva, 1973. pp. 228.

— — Yugoslavia.

ŽIVANOVIĆ (SERGIJE M.) Treći srpski ustanak, 1941. Čikago, 1962-66. 3 vols(in 1). *Cover has title: Djeneral Mihailović i njegovo delo.*

JUKIC (ILIJA) The fall of Yugoslavia: translated by Dorian Cooke. New York, [1974]. pp. 315. *bibliog.*

— Belgium.

JONGHE (ALBERT DE) Hitler en het politieke lot van België, 1940-1944: de vestiging van een zivilverwaltung in België en Noord- Frankrijk. Antwerpen, 1972 in progress. *bibliog.*

VANLANGENHOVE (FERNAND) La Belgique et ses garants, l'été 1940: contribution à l'histoire de la politique extérieure de la Belgique pendant la Seconde Guerre mondiale. Bruxelles, 1972. pp. 228. *bibliog.* (*Académie Royale de Belgique. Classe des Lettres et des Sciences Morales et Politiques. Mémoires. Collection in-8.° 2ème Série. Tome 61, fasc. 3*)

— France.

CAHIERS FRANÇAIS, LES (formerly Les Documents, previously Documents d'information); [pd. by] Comité Français de la Libération Nationale, Commissariat à l'Information). m. (formerly s-m.), Oc 1 1941 - My 1944 (nos.[3]-55). Londres.

CAHIERS FRANÇAIS D'INFORMATION. [Paris], 1945-48. 12 parts.

AUDIAT (PIERRE) Paris pendant la guerre, juin 1940 - août 1944. [Paris, 1946]. pp. 333.

BETEILLE (PIERRE) and RIMBAUD (CHRISTIANE) Le procès de Riom. [Paris, 1973]. pp. 284. *bibliog.*

MYSYROWICZ (LADISLAS) Autopsie d'une défaite: origines de l'effondrement militaire français de 1940. Lausanne, [1973]. pp. 385. *bibliog.*

— Germany.

WHALEY (BARTON) Codeword Barbarossa. Cambridge, Mass., [1973]. pp. 376. *bibliog.*

— Iraq.

WARNER (GEOFFREY) Iraq and Syria, 1941. London, 1974. pp. 180. *bibliog.*

— Italy.

LENZI (LORIS) Dal Dnieper al Don: la 63a Legione Cc.Nn. Tagliamento nella campagna di Russia; documentazione del Gruppo Reduci della Legione. Roma, [1972]. pp. 479.

SEROVA (OL'GA VASIL'EVNA) Italiia i antigitlerovskaia koalitsiia, 1943-1945. Moskva, 1973. pp. 272. *bibliog.*

— Nigeria.

OLUSANYA (G.O.) The Second World War and politics in Nigeria, 1939-1953. Lagos, 1973. pp. 181. *bibliog.*

— Poland.

KOŚCIÓŁ KATOLICKI NA ZIEMIACH POLSKI W CZASIE II WOJNY ŚWIATOWEJ; materiały i studia; [pd. by] Akademia Teologii Katolickiej. irreg., 1973 (zeszyt 1)- Warszawa.

CIECHANOWSKI (JAN MIECZYSLAW) The Warsaw rising of 1944. Cambridge, 1974. pp. 332. *bibliog.* (*National Association for Soviet and East European Studies. Soviet and East European Studies*)

— Russia.

WHALEY (BARTON) Codeword Barbarossa. Cambridge, Mass., [1973]. pp. 376. *bibliog.*

— — Ukraine.

KRYM v period Velikoi Otechestvennoi voiny 1941-1945: sbornik dokumentov i materialov. Simferopol', 1973. pp. 488.

— Spain.

PROCTOR (RAYMOND) Agonia de un neutral: las relaciones hispanoalemanas durante la segunda guerra mundial y la Division Azul. [Madrid, 1972]. pp. 354. *bibliog.*

— Sweden.

WAHLBÄCK (KRISTER) ed. Regeringen och kriget: ur statsrådens dagböcker, 1939-41. Stockholm, [1972]. pp. 191.

FRIBERG (LENNART) Styre i kristid: studier i krisförvaltningens organisation och struktur, 1939-1945. Stockholm, 1973. pp. 444. *bibliog. With English summary.*

WORLD WAR, 1939—1945. (Cont.)

HIRDMAN (YVONNE) Sverges kommunistiska parti, 1939-1945. Stockholm, 1974. pp. 311. *bibliog.* *With English summary.*

MOLIN (KARL) Försvaret, folkhemmet och demokratin: socialdemokratisk riksdagspolitik, 1939-1945. Stockholm, 1974. pp. 463. *bibliog. With English summary.*

— **Switzerland.**

ALLGOEWER (WALTHER) Nationaler Widerstand, Herbst 1940. Aarau, [1940]. pp. 30. (*Jungliberale Bewegung der Schweiz. Schriften. Heft 6*)

BRINGOLF (WALTHER) Perspektiven der sozialistischen Bewegung der Schweiz. [Schaffhausen, 1940]. pp. 26.

SOZIALISTISCHE JUGEND DER SCHWEIZ. Zeigt der Sozialismus einen Ausweg?: (unsere Antwort an Nationalrat Bringolf'.); Kapitulation vor dem Kapitalismus oder sozialistische Perspektiven?. [Zürich, 1940]. pp. 30.

— **Syria.**

WARNER (GEOFFREY) Iraq and Syria, 1941. London, 1974. pp. 180. *bibliog.*

— **United States.**

GULICK (LUTHER HALSEY) third of the name. Administrative reflections from World War II: [lectures delivered before the fellows of the Southern Regional Training Program in Public Administration at the University of Alabama in 1946]. University, Alabama, [1948]. pp. 139.

CONRAT (MAISIE) and CONRAT (RICHARD) eds. Executive order 9066: the internment of 110,000 Japanese Americans: [photographs taken by Dorothea Lange and others].Cambridge, Mass., 1972. pp. 120.

BARRON (GLORIA J.) Leadership in crisis: FDR and the path to intervention. Port Washington, N.Y., 1973. pp. 145. *bibliog.*

STEELE (RICHARD W.) The first offensive, 1942: Roosevelt, Marshall and the making of American strategy. Bloomington, [1973]. pp. 239. *bibliog.*

WORTH.

SCHEIBE (KARL E.) Beliefs and values. New York, [1970]. pp. 159. *bibliog.*

GUENDLING (JOHN E.) Value systems: the moral and eudaemonic components. Chicago, [1973]. pp. 151.

ROKEACH (MILTON) The nature of human values. New York, [1973]. pp. 438. *bibliog.*

WUPPERTAL

— **Economic history.**

REULECKE (JUERGEN) Die wirtschaftliche Entwicklung der Stadt Barmen von 1910 bis 1925. Neustadt an der Aisch, 1973. pp. 219. *bibliog.* (*Bergischer Geschichtsverein. Bergische Forschungen. Band 10*)

— **History.**

WERNER (GERHART) Aufmachen! Gestapo!: ÜBER DEN Widerstand in Wuppertal, 1933- 1945; mit Beiträgen von Karl Ibach [and others]. Wuppertal, 1974. pp. 62.

WYATT (WOODROW LYLE).

WYATT (WOODROW LYLE) Turn again, Westminster. London, 1973. pp. 259.

WYNDHAM SCHOOL, EGREMONT.

SHARP (JOHN ROBERT INGLE) Open school: the experience of 1964-1970 at Wyndham School, Egremont, Cumberland. London, 1973. pp. 132.

X—RAY MICROSCOPE.

MEDFORD (R.D.) Curiosity oriented research: an experimental study: x-ray holography. Chilton, Programmes Analysis Unit, 1974. pp. 24. ([*Publications*]. *P.A.U. M.21*)

XENOPOL (ALEXANDRU DIMITRIE).

BOICU (L.) and ZUB (AL.) eds. A.D. Xenopol: studii privitoare la viața și opera sa. București, 1972. pp. 443. *With French summaries and table of contents.*

YAKA.

See BAYAKA.

YALE UNIVERSITY.

KELLEY (BROOKS MATHER) Yale:a history. New Haven, 1974. pp. 588.

YALTA CONFERENCE, 1945.

See WORLD WAR, 1939—1945 —
 Congresses.

YEARBOOKS.

UNIVERSALIA: les événements, les hommes, les problèmes en [ ]. a., 1974 (en 1973) [1st issue]- Paris. *Supplements ENCYCLOPAEDIA universalis.*

YEMEN

— **Politics and government.**

BELL (J. BOWYER) Southern Arabia: violence and revolt. London, 1973. pp. 14. (*Institute for the Study of Conflict. Conflict Studies. No.40*)

YEMEN, SOUTHERN

— **Politics and government.**

BELL (J. BOWYER) Southern Arabia: violence and revolt. London, 1973. pp. 14. (*Institute for the Study of Conflict. Conflict Studies. No.40*)

YORKSHIRE

— **Historical geography.**

PORTER (JOHN) Ph.D. The reclamation and settlement of Bowland, with special reference to the period 1500-1650; [Ph.D.(London) thesis]. 1973[or rather 1974]. fo. 267. *Typescript: unpublished. This thesis is the property of London University and may not be removed from the library.*

— **Politics and government.**

YORKSHIRE. North Riding. County Council. A history of the North Riding of Yorkshire County Council, 1889-1974; edited by M.Y. Ashcroft. Northallerton, 1974. pp. 174.

— **Population — Maps.**

CENSUS atlas of South Yorkshire: computer and laser graphic mapping of 35 selected population characteristics in over 2700 enumeration districts; project director: Bryan E. Coates;...; produced... by the Department of Geography, University of Sheffield. Sheffield, [1974]. pp. 118 (including 37 folding maps).

— **Social conditions — Maps.**

CENSUS atlas of South Yorkshire: computer and laser graphic mapping of 35 selected population characteristics in over 2700 enumeration districts; project director: Bryan E. Coates;...; produced... by the Department of Geography, University of Sheffield. Sheffield, [1974]. pp. 118 (including 37 folding maps).

YORUBAS.

LLOYD (PETER CUTT) Power and independence: urban Africans' perception of social inequality. London, 1974. pp. 248. *bibliog.*

YOUNG (ARTHUR) F.R.S.

GAZLEY (JOHN GEROW) The life of Arthur Young, 1741-1820. Philadelphia, 1973. pp. 727. *bibliog.* (*American Philosophical Society. Memoirs. vol. 97*)

YOUNG COMMUNIST INTERNATIONAL.

SCHUELLER (RICHARD) and others. Geschichte der Kommunistischen Jugendinternationale;...zuerst erschienen...Berlin 1929/31. München, [1970]. 3 vols. *bibliog.* *Band 2 is of the original edition.*

YOUNG COMMUNIST LEAGUE

— **Russia.**

VSESOIUZNYI LENINSKII KOMMUNISTICHESKII SOIUZ MOLODEZHI. Tsentral'nyi Komitet. Dokumenty TsK VLKSM, 1972. Moskva, 1973. pp. 304.

— — **Kazakstan.**

LENINSKOMU komsomolu Kazakhstana 50 let. Alma-Ata, 1972. pp. 223.

YOUTH.

BELGIUM. Direction Générale de la Jeunesse et des Loisirs. 1970. La participation civique des jeunes. [Brussels], 1970. pp. 166. (*Cahiers JEB. 14me année. No. 2. Juin 1970*)

UNITED NATIONS EDUCATIONAL, SCIENTIFIC AND CULTURAL ORGANIZATION. Educational Studies and Documents. New Series. Paris, 1971 in progress..

MAY (ANTHONY R.) and others. Mental health of adolescents and young persons: report on a technical conference, Stockholm, 9-13 June, 1969. Geneva, World Health Organization, 1971. pp. 72. (*Public Health Papers. No.41*)

LEECH (KENNETH) Youthquake: the growth of a counter-culture through two decades. London, 1973. pp. 246.

VENEZUELA. Despacho del Ministro de Estado para la Juventud, la Ciencia y la Cultura. 1973. Primer informe sobre la juventud venezolana. [Tomo 1]. Documento de trabajo. Juventud y sociedad. Caracas, 1973. fo. 166. *bibliog.*

HEER (FRIEDRICH) Challenge of youth; (translated from the German by Geoffrey Skelton). London, [1974]. pp. 224. **See also CONFLICT OF GENERATIONS.**

— **Employment — France.**

FRANCE. Centre d'Etudes et de Recherches sur les Conditions d'Emploi et de Travail des Jeunes. 1971. Emplois proposés aux jeunes de 1959 à 1969 (par la Section d'Accueil des Jeunes) [du] B[ureau de la] M[ain d'] O[euvre] spécialisé de Paris. Paris, 1971. pp. 100.

GOURCEAUD (ANNE MARIE) and LARRIEU (ROUMAIN) Premier bilan des stages de préformation dans la région Midi- Pyrénées. Toulouse, Echelon Régional de l'Emploi, 1971. fo.34,2.

CENTRE D'ETUDES ET DE RECHERCHES SUR LES QUALIFICATIONS. Les emplois tenus par les jeunes de 17 ans. Paris, 1972. pp. 126. (*Dossiers. 3*)

CENTRE D'ETUDES ET DE RECHERCHES SUR LES QUALIFICATIONS. Les possibilités d'emploi selon les qualifications acquises dans les formations initiales. [Paris], 1972. pp. 147. (*Dossiers. 4*)

— — **Russia.**

SHEBANOVA (ANNA IVANOVNA) Pravo i trud molodezhi. Moskva, 1973. pp. 223.

VASIL'EVA (EVELINA KARLOVNA) Sotsial'no-professional'nyi uroven' gorodskoi molodezhi: po materialam vyborochnogo obsledovaniia shkol'nikov i molodezhi Leningrada. Leningrad, 1973. pp. 142.

ORLOVSKII (IURII PETROVICH) Trud molodezhi v SSSR: pravovoe issledovanie. Moskva, 1974. pp. 256.

— **Underdeveloped areas.**

See UNDERDEVELOPED AREAS —
 Youth — employment.

— — United Kingdom.

BARBER (C. RENATE) A follow up of school leavers in Oxford City. Oxford, 1968. pp. 11. *bibliog.* (*Oxford Polytechnic. Social Science Research Unit. Occasional Papers. 2*)

U.K. Social Survey. [Reports. New Series.] 427. Looking forward to work: a report on the first stage of a follow-up survey of fifteen and sixteen year old boy school-leavers, carried out...on behalf of the Central Youth Employment Executive; [by] Roger Thomas [and] Diana Wetherell. London, 1974. pp. 436.

— — United States.

CARROLL (STEPHEN J.) Part-time experience and the transition from school to work...: a report prepared for Office of Economic Opportunity. Santa Monica, 1970. pp. 71. *bibliog.* (*Rand Corporation. [Rand Reports]. 575*)

BULLOCK (PAUL) Aspiration vs. opportunity: "careers" in the inner city. Ann Arbor, 1973. pp. 177. (*Michigan University, and Wayne State University. Institute of Labor and Industrial Relations. Policy Papers in Human Resources and Industrial Relations. 20*)

— Information services.

VENEZUELA. Despacho del Ministro de Estado para la Juventud, la Ciencia y la Cultura. 1973. Primer informe sobre la juventud venezolana. [Tomo 2]. Anexo. Centro de informacion para la juventud: anteprogecto. Caracas, 1973. 1 vol.(unpaged).

— Recreation.

VENEZUELA. Despacho del Ministro de Estado para la Juventud, la Ciencia y la Cultura. 1973. Primer informe sobre la juventud venezolana. [Tomo 1]. Documento de trabajo. Situacion del deporte. Caracas, 1973. 1 vol.(various pagings).

— America, Latin.

CURSO REGIONAL INTERAMERICANO SOBRE COLOCACION FAMILIAR, ADOPCION, Y LIBERTAD VIGILADA, MONTEVIDEO, 1970. I curso regional..., Montevideo, Octubre 5 al 25 de 1970. Montevideo, Inter-American Children's Institute, 1972. pp. 313. *bibliog.*

— Asia.

POPULATION, politics, and the future of southern Asia; [papers presented at a conference convened by the Southern Asian Institute of Columbia University, 1971]; edited by W. Howard Wriggins and James F. Guyot. New York, 1973. pp. 402.

— Austria.

ROSENMAYR (LEOPOLD) and KREUTZ (HENRIK) Rollenerwartung der weiblichen Jugend: eine empirische Untersuchung über Erwartungen und Dispositionen weiblicher Jugendlicher in Österreich. Wien, 1973. pp. 423. *bibliog.* (*Österreichisches Institut für Jugendkunde. Beiträge zur Jugendkunde. Band 16*) *With English summary.*

— Colombia.

CONFERENCIA NACIONAL SOBRE FAMILIA, INFANCIA Y JUVENTUD, la, BOGOTA, 1970. Prima conferencia nacional sobre familia, infancia y juventud; celebrada en Bogota del 2 al 7 de marzo de 1970, con el patrocinio del...UNICEF. Bogota, 1970. pp. 576.

— Denmark.

DENMARK. Kontaktudvalgt mellem Ungdomsorganisationerne og Statsadministrationen. 1970. Samfundet og ungdommen. [Copenhagen?], 1970. pp. 167. (*Denmark. Betaenkninger. Nr.559*)

— Europe.

UNITED NATIONS. Department of Economic and Social Affairs. European Social Development Programme. Reports. New York, 1967 in progress.

— France.

FRANCE. Direction de la Documentation. La Documentation Française. Notes et Etudes Documentaires. Nos. 3,876-3, 877. Mouvements et organisations de jeunesse en France, par Elie Ferrier. [Paris], 1972. pp. 59. *bibliog.*

COLIN (HELENE) and PARADELLE (MICHEL) Les jeunes et le mouvement communautaire: approche sociopsychanalytique. Bruxelles, 1974. pp. 192.

— Germany.

STEPHENS (FREDERICK J.) Hitler youth: history, organisation, uniforms and insignia. London, 1973. pp. 88. *bibliog.*

— — Political activity.

ECKERT (RAINER) and SEIDERER (AXEL) Sozialdemokratie und Jungsozialisten: Politik, Programm und Gesellschaftstheorie; eine marxistische Kritik. Frankfurt/Main, 1974. pp. 194.

— Germany, Eastern.

FREIE DEUTSCHE JUGEND. Free German Youth: from the beginning to the present tasks of the socialist youth organization. Dresden, [1973?]. pp. 31.

— Hong Kong.

CHANEY (DAVID C.) and PODMORE (DAVID B.L.) Young adults in Hong Kong: attitudes in a modernizing society. Hong Kong, 1973. pp. 206. *bibliog.* (*Hong Kong. University. Centre for Asian Studies. Occasional Papers and Monographs. No. 10*)

— Italy.

MILAN (PROVINCE). Contributi: Problemi Socio-Economici della Circoscrizione Provinciale Milanese. n. 3. 10 anni di esperienze sull'orientamento dei giovani. Milano, 1967. pp. 294.

SCARPATI (ROSARIO) and others, eds. La condizione giovanile in Italia. Milano, [1973]. pp. 350. (*Istituto per gli Studi sullo Sviluppo Economico e il Progresso Tecnico. Collana Isvet. n. 23*)

— Jamaica.

PHILLIPS (A.S.) Adolescence in Jamaica. Kingston, Jam., [1973]. pp. 148. *bibliog.*

— Netherlands.

LOUW (ANDRE VAN DER) Rood als je hart: 'n geschiedenis van de AJC. Amsterdam, [1974]. pp. 296. *bibliog.*

— Russia.

ELISEEV (GENNADII PAVLOVICH) Molodezh' i sotsialisticheskoe sorevnovanie: istoriia, opyt, problemy. Moskva, 1969. pp. 103. *bibliog.*

BORIAZ (VADIM NIKOLAEVICH) Molodezh': metodologicheskie problemy issledovaniia. Leningrad, 1973. pp. 155.

GOURE (LEON) The military indoctrination of Soviet youth. New York, [1973]. pp. 75. *bibliog.* (*National Strategy Information Center. Strategy Papers. No. 16*)

— Switzerland — Political activity.

NOBS (ERNST) Die bürgerliche Jugendbewegung der Schweiz. Zürich, [1915]. pp. 40.

— United Kingdom.

SCHOFIELD (MICHAEL) The sexual behaviour of young adults: a follow-up study to The sexual behaviour of young people. London, 1973. pp. 251. *bibliog.*

TUC YOUTH CONFERENCE, LONDON, 1974. Trade union youth in conference: report of the first...conference, etc. London, [1974]. pp. 59.

HAIN (PETER) Radical liberalism and youth politics. London, [1973]. pp. 20. (*Liberal Party. Strategy 2,000. 1st Series. No. 3*)

— United States.

CLARK (TED) and JAFFE (DENNIS T.) Toward a radical therapy: alternate services for personal and social change. New York, [1973]. pp. 287. *bibliog.*

— Venezuela.

VENEZUELA. Despacho del Ministro de Estado para la Juventud, la Ciencia y la Cultura. 1973. Primer informe sobre la juventud venezolana. [Tomo 1]. Conclusiones diagnosticas sobre la juventud venezolana. Caracas, 1973. fo. 203.

VENEZUELA. Despacho del Ministro de Estado para la Juventud, la Ciencia y la Cultura. 1973. Primer informe sobre la juventud venezolana. [Tomo 1]. Documento de trabajo. Estudio por areas de la juventud venezolana.Caracas, 1973. 2 vols. *bibliog.*

VENEZUELA. Despacho del Ministro de Estado para la Juventud, la Ciencia y la Cultura. 1973. Primer informe sobre la juventud venezolana. [Tomo 1]. Documento de trabajo. Situacion del deporte. Caracas, 1973. 1 vol.(various pagings).

VENEZUELA. Despacho del Ministro de Estado para la Juventud, la Ciencia y la Cultura. 1973. Primer informe sobre la juventud venezolana. [Tomo 1]. Anexo. Estudio sociodemografico de la juventud venezolana. Caracas, 1973. 1 vol. (various pagings). *bibliog.*

VENEZUELA. Despacho del Ministro de Estado para la Juventud, la Ciencia y la Cultura. 1973. Primer informe sobre la juventud venezolana. [Tomo 1]. Anexo. (Proyecto juventud): expectativas y motivaciones de la juventud de Caracas; Valentin Sosnowsky, director del estudio. Tomo 3. Caracas, [1973]. 1 vol. (various pagings).

VENEZUELA. Despacho del Ministro de Estado para la Juventud, la Ciencia y la Cultura. 1973. Primer informe sobre la juventud venezolana. Tomo 2. Bases preliminares para una politica juvenil. Caracas, 1973. fo. (379).

VENEZUELA. Despacho del Ministro de Estado para la Juventud, la Ciencia y la Cultura. 1973. Primer informe sobre la juventud venezolana. [Tomo 2]. Anexo. Voluntariado juvenil para el desarrollo. Caracas, 1973. 1 vol. (various pagings). *bibliog.*

VENEZUELA. Despacho del Ministro de Estado para la Juventud, la Ciencia y la Cultura. 1973. Primer informe sobre la juventud venezolana. [Tomo 2]. Anexo. Centro de informacion para la juventud: anteprogecto. Caracas, 1973. 1 vol.(unpaged).

— — Public opinion.

VENEZUELA. Despacho del Ministro de Estado para la Juventud, la Ciencia y la Cultura. 1973. Primer informe sobre la juventud venezolana. [Tomo 1]. Anexo. Opiniones de sectores influyentes sobre la juventud venezolana. Analis de prensa. 1. Caracas, 1973. 2 pts.(in 1 vol.). *bibliog.*

YOUTH, RURAL.

See RURAL YOUTH.

YOUTH AND NARCOTICS.

See NARCOTICS AND YOUTH.

YOUTH CONSERVATION CORPS.

SCOTT (JOHN C.) of the University of Michigan, and others. Toward environmental understanding: an evaluation of the 1972 Youth Conservation Corps; a report prepared for the U.S. Forest Service...and the U.S. Department of the Interior. Ann Arbor, Mich., 1973. pp. 319.

YOUTH VOLUNTEER WORKERS IN DEVELOPING COUNTRIES.

MORRIS (ROBERT CRANE) Overseas volunteer programs: their evolution and the role of governments in their support. Lexington, Mass., [1973]. pp. 352. *bibliog.* (*Center for a Voluntary Society. Voluntary Action Research Series*)

VENEZUELA. Despacho del Ministro de Estado para la Juventud, la Ciencia y la Cultura. 1973. Primer informe sobre la juventud venezolana. [Tomo 2]. Anexo. Voluntariado juvenil para el desarrollo. Caracas. 1973. 1 vol. (various pagings). *bibliog*.

YUGOSLAVIA

— Commerce.

PERTOT (VLADIMIR V.) Anketa o tendencijama promjena odnosa vrijednosti u našoj vanjskoj razmjeni 1955-1970; anketu izveo i tekst napisao ... Vladimir Pertot, etc. Zagreb, 1973. pp. 91.

— Constitution.

LANG (RIKARD) and others, eds. Privredni sistem i ustavna reforma: zbornik radova. Zagreb, 1973. pp. 302. *bibliog*.

— Constitutional history.

FRANCE. Direction de la Documentation. La Documentation Française. Notes et Etudes Documentaires. No. 3,070. L'évolution des institutions yougoslaves d'après les constitutions de 1946-1953 et 1963; [by] Kruno Meneghello- Dincic. Paris, 1964. pp. 22.

— Economic conditions.

VOJNIĆ (DRAGOMIR) and others, eds. Aktuelni problemi privrednih kretanja Jugoslavije. Zagreb, 1973. pp. 150.

GORUPIĆ (DRAGO) The enterprise and the development of Yugoslav economic system: articles. Zagreb, 1974. pp. 159. *One article in French*.

— — Statistics.

YUGOSLAVIA. Savezni Zavod za Statistiku. Studije, Analize i Prikazi. 61. Privredni bilansi Jugoslavije, 1966-1971; Economic balances of Yugoslavia, 1966-1971. Beograd, 1973. pp. 257. *With English summary*.

— Economic policy.

LANG (RIKARD) and others, eds. Privredni sistem i ustavna reforma: zbornik radova. Zagreb, 1973. pp. 302. *bibliog*.

SACKS (STEPHEN R.) Entry of new competitors in Yugoslav market socialism. Berkeley, [1973]. pp. 141. *bibliog*. (*California University. Institute of International Studies. Research Series. No. 19*)

HAGEMANN (MICHAEL) and KLEMENČIČ (ALEKKA) Die sozialistische Marktwirtschaft Jugoslawiens. Stuttgart, 1974. pp. 303. *bibliog*.

— Foreign relations.

JUKIC (ILIJA) The fall of Yugoslavia: translated by Dorian Cooke. New York, [1974]. pp. 315. *bibliog*.

— Nationalism.

KULUNDŽIĆ (ZVONIMIR) Atentat na Stjepana Radića i njegova prava pozadina. Zagreb, 1962. unpaged. *Offprints from Slobodni dom*.

— Politics and government.

PETROVIĆ (LAZAR) Versaljska Jugoslavija: nekoliko marksističkih osvrta na njenę političke borbe i borce. Cleveland, 1950. pp. 109. *Clanci iz Radničke Borbe*.

KULUNDŽIĆ (ZVONIMIR) Atentat na Stjepana Radića i njegova prava pozadina. Zagreb, 1962. unpaged. *Offprints from Slobodni dom*.

FRANCE. Direction de la Documentation. La Documentation Française. Notes et Etudes Documentaires. Nos. 3,888-3, 889. Le nouveau fédéralisme yougoslave, par Krudo [sic] Meneghello-Dincic. [Paris], 1972. pp. 71.

LENDVAI (PAUL) National tensions in Yugoslavia. London, 1973. pp. 17. (*Institute for the Study of Conflict. Conflict Studies. No. 25*)

VEYRIER (MARCEL) Tito et la révolution. Paris, [1974]. pp. 248. *bibliog*.

— Relations (general) with France.

FRANCE. Direction de la Documentation. La Documentation Française. Notes et Etudes Documentaires. No. 3,773. Les relations franco-yougoslaves, 1945-1970; [by] Paul Yankovitch. Paris, 1971. pp. 29.

— Skupština — Rules and practice.

YUGOSLAVIA. Savezna Skupština. Secretariat of Information. 1967. Rules of procedure of the Federal Assembly of the Socialist Federal Republic of Yugoslavia. Belgrade, [1967]. pp. 158.

YUGOSLAVS IN THE UNITED STATES.

PETROVIĆ (LAZAR) Versaljska Jugoslavija: nekoliko marksističkih osvrta na njenę političke borbe i borce. Cleveland, 1950. pp. 109. *Clanci iz Radničke Borbe*.

ETEROVICH (ADAM SLAV.) Yugoslavs in Nevada 1859-1900: Croatians, Dalmatians, Montenegrins, Hercegovinians. San Francisco, 1973. pp. 263. *bibliog*.

ZAIRE.

FRANCE. Direction de la Documentation. La Documentation Française. Notes et etudes documentaires. Nos. 3,765-3,766. La République démocratique du Congo; [by] Jacques Leguèbe. Paris, 1971. pp. 63. *bibliog*.

— Economic conditions.

BANQUE DU ZAIRE. Rapport annuel. a., 1971/2- Kinshasa.

FRANCE. Direction de l'Aide au Développement des Etats Francophones d'Afrique au Sud du Sahara et de la République Malgache. Secteur Information Economique et Conjoncture. 1973. Zaire 1970-1971: dossier d'information économique. Paris, 1973. fo. 24,21.

— Foreign relations — United States.

WEISSMAN (STEPHEN R.) American foreign policy in the Congo, 1960-1964. Ithaca, 1974. pp. 325. *bibliog*.

— History.

STORME (MARCEL) La mutinerie militaire au Kasai en 1895: introduction. Bruxelles, 1970. pp. 162. *bibliog*. (*Académie Royale des Sciences d'Outre-Mer. Classe des Sciences Morales et Politiques. [Meémoires in -8?. Nouvelle Série. [Tome] 38. [Fasc.] 4*)

— Officials and employees.

VIEUX (SERGE A.) Le statut de la fonction publique: le décret-loi du 20 mars 1965 et ses mesures d'exécution. Kinshasa, Office National de la Recherche et du Développement, 1970. pp. 628.

— Politics and government.

LUMUMBA (PATRICE) Lumumba speaks: the speeches and writings of Patrice Lumumba, 1958-1961; edited by Jean Van Lierde; translated... by Helen R. Lane; introduction by Jean-Paul Sartre. Boston, [1972]. pp. 433.

VANDERLINDEN (JACQUES) Contribution à l'étude de la crise congolaise de 1960: notes au sujet de quelques documents inédits relatifs aux réactions du secteur privé. Bruxelles, 1972. pp. 93. *bibliog*. (*Académie Royale des Sciences d'Outre-Mer. Classe des Sciences Morales et Politiques. [Mémoires in-80Nouvelle Série. [Tome] 42. [fasc.] 1*)

— Presidents.

CENTRE DE RECHERCHE ET D'INFORMATION SOCIO-POLITIQUES. Etudes Africaines du CRISP. Le régime présidentiel au Zaire. Bruxelles, 1972. fo. 51.

— Yearbooks.

PROFILES OF ZAIRE; (issued by the President of the Republic of Zaire's Office). irreg., [1973? (1st ed.)]- Kinshasa.

ZAMBIA

— Economic policy.

ZAMBIA. Ministry of Development Planning and National Guidance. Annual report. a., 1971(1st)- Lusaka.

— Foreign relations.

UNITED NATIONAL INDEPENDENCE PARTY [ZAMBIA]. Proceedings of the annual general conference... held at Mulungushi, 14th-20th August, 1967. Lusaka, Zambia Information Services, 1967. pp. 56.

— History.

ROBERTS (ANDREW D.) A history of the Bemba: political growth and change in north- eastern Zambia before 1900. London, 1973. pp. 420. *bibliog*.

— Manufactures.

YOUNG (ALISTAIR) Industrial diversification in Zambia. New York, 1973. pp. 328. *bibliog*.

— Politics and government.

UNITED NATIONAL INDEPENDENCE PARTY [ZAMBIA]. Proceedings of the annual general conference... held at Mulungushi, 14th-20th August, 1967. Lusaka, Zambia Information Services, 1967. pp. 56.

FRANKLIN (HENRY) The flag-wagger. London, 1974. pp. 204.

— Public works.

ZAMBIA. Ministry of Power, Transport and Works. Buildings Branch. Report. a., 1965/6, 1968- Lusaka.

— Race question.

MULEMBA (H.) The progress of Zambianisation in the mining industry (December, 1968). Lusaka, Ministry of Labour, 1969. pp. 11.

— Social policy.

ZAMBIA. Ministry of Development Planning and National Guidance. Annual report. a., 1971(1st)- Lusaka.

— Statistics.

ZAMBIA. Central Statistical Office. Statistical year-book. a., 1968- Lusaka.

— Statistics, Vital.

ZAMBIA. Central Statistical Office. Registered births, marriages and deaths (Vital statistics). a., 1966, 1968- Lusaka.

ZANARDELLI (GIUSEPPE).

CHIARINI (ROBERTO) Politica e società nella Brescia zanardelliana: le elezioni politiche a suffragio ristretto, 1876-1880. Milano, 1973. pp. 341. (*Pavia. Università. Instituto di Storia Moderna e Contemporanea. Collana. 5*)

ZANDER (ERNST).

ROEDER (ELMAR) Der konservative Journalist Ernst Zander und die politischen Kämpfe seines "Volksboten". München, 1972. pp. 339. *bibliog*. (*Munich. Stadtarchiv. Neue Schriftenreihe. Band 58*)

ZANDES.

EVANS-PRITCHARD (Sir EDWARD EVAN) ed. Man and woman among the Azande. London, 1974. pp. 197.

ZANZIBAR

— History — Sources.

ITALY. Ministero degli Affari Esteri. Comitato per la Documentazione dell'Opera dell'Italia in Africa. L'Italia in Africa. Serie Storica. Vol. 2. Oceano Indiano. Tomo 2. Documenti relativi a Zanzibar e al Benadir. 1884-1891; a cura di Carlo Giglio. Roma, 1967. pp. 397.

ZAPOTEC INDIANS.

SELBY (HENRY ANDERSON) Zapotec deviance: the convergence of folk and modern sociology. Austin, [Texas, 1974]. pp. 166. *bibliog.*

ZELLE (MARGARETHA GEERTRUIDA).

ALDANOV (MARK ALEKSANDROVICH) pseud. [i.e. LANDAU (MARK ALEKSANDROVICH)] Iunost' Pavla Stroganova i drugie kharakteristiki. Belgrad, [1935?]. pp. 188.

ZETKIN (CLARA).

CLARA Zetkin: Kämpferin für die proletarische Weltrevolution. Moskau, 1933. pp. 56.

ZIMBABWE AFRICAN PEOPLES UNION (RHODESIA).

MOYO (TEMBA) The organizer: story of Temba Moyo; (recorded and edited by Ole Gjerstad). Richmond, B.C., [1974]. pp. 86.

SILUNDIKA (GEORGE) Zimbabwe Zapu '2': Zimbabwe African People's Union; [report of an interview by Ole Gjerstad]. Richmond, B.C., [1974]. pp. 26.

ZIMMERMANN (MARIAN).

STUDIA z zakresu prawa administracyjnego; ku czci Prof. dra Mariana Zimmermanna. Poznań, 1973. pp. 167. *(Poznań. Poznańskie Towarzystwo Przyjaciół Nauk. Wydział Historii i Nauk Społecznych. Komisja Nauk Społecznych. Prace. t.16, z.2)*

ZINI (ZINO).

ZINI (ZINO) La tragedia del proletariato in Italia: diario 1914-1926; [edited by] Giancarlo Bergami. Milano, 1973. pp. 275. *bibliog.*

ZINOV'EV (GRIGORII EVSEEVICH).

DZHIBLADZE (D.) Bol'sheviki Zakavkaz'ia v bor'be s trotskistsko- zinov'evskim blokom. Tbilisi, 1973. pp. 69.

ZIONISM.

See JEWS — Restoration.

ZJEDNOCZONE STRONNICTWO LUDOWE.

ZARYS historii polskiego ruchu ludowego. Warszawa, 1963-70. 2 vols. *bibliog.*

ZOMBA

— Markets.

MALAWI. National Statistical Office. 1971. Zomba town market survey, 1970-1971. Zomba, 1971. pp. 70.

ZONING

— United States.

BABCOCK (RICHARD F.) and BOSSELMAN (FRED P.) Exclusionary zoning: land use regulation and housing in the 1970s. New York, 1973. pp. 210.

LINOWES (R. ROBERT) and ALLENSWORTH (DON TRUDEAU) The politics of land use: planning, zoning, and the private developer. New York, 1973. pp. 166.

ZOSHCHENKO (MIKHAIL MIKHAILOVICH).

ERSHOV (LEONID FEDOROVICH) Iz istorii sovetskoi satiry: M. Zoshchenko i satiricheskaia proza 20-40-kh godov. Leningrad, 1973. pp. 155.

ZUEBLIN—SPILLER (ELSE).

VEREIN FÜR WIRTSCHAFTSHISTORISCHE STUDIEN. Schweizer Pioniere der Wirtschaft und Technik. 26. Zwei Pionierinnen der Volksgesundheit: Susanna Orelli- Rinderknecht, 1845-1939; Else Züblin-Spiller, 1881-1948. Zürich, 1973. pp. 103. *bibliog.*

ZUERICH (CANTON)

— Economic policy.

INITIATIVEN der Gegenwart, Chancen der Zukunft: Bevölkerung und Wirtschaft in der Region Zürich; herausgegeben von der Zürcher Handelskammer anlässlich ihres 100 jährigen Bestehens; [by] Harald Jürgensen [and others]. Zürich, 1973. pp. 265.

— Nationalrat — Elections.

ZUERICH (CANTON). Statistisches Amt. 1968. Die Nationalratswahlen 1967 im Kanton Zürich. Zürich, 1968. pp. 95. *(Statistische Mitteilungen. 3. Folge. Heft 64)*

— Population.

INITIATIVEN der Gegenwart, Chancen der Zukunft: Bevölkerung und Wirtschaft in der Region Zürich; herausgegeben von der Zürcher Handelskammer anlässlich ihres 100 jährigen Bestehens; [by] Harald Jürgensen [and others]. Zürich, 1973. pp. 265.

ZUERICH (CITY)

— Civic improvement.

IBLHER (PETER) and JANSEN (GEORG DIETRICH) Die Bewertung städtischer Entwicklungsalternativen mit Hilfe sozialer Indikatoren, dargestellt am Beispiel der Stadt Zürich. Göttingen, [1972]. pp. 658. *(Hamburg. Hansische Universität. Institut für Europäische Wirtschaftspolitik. Wirtschaftspolitische Studien. 29)*

DORN (KLAUS) Die Altstadt von Zürich: Veränderung der Substanz, Sozialstruktur und Nutzung. Teufen, [1974]. pp. 187. *bibliog.*

— Social conditions.

IBLHER (PETER) and JANSEN (GEORG DIETRICH) Die Bewertung städtischer Entwicklungsalternativen mit Hilfe sozialer Indikatoren, dargestellt am Beispiel der Stadt Zürich. Göttingen, [1972]. pp. 658. *(Hamburg. Hansische Universität. Institut für Europäische Wirtschaftspolitik. Wirtschaftspolitische Studien. 29)*

— Social history.

DORN (KLAUS) Die Altstadt von Zürich: Veränderung der Substanz, Sozialstruktur und Nutzung. Teufen, [1974]. pp. 187. *bibliog.*

ZUIDER ZEE.

THIJSSE (J. TH.) Een halve eeuw Zuiderzeewerken, 1920-1970. Groningen, 1972. pp. 470. *bibliog.*

ŽUJOVIĆ (ŽIVOIN).

KARASEV (VIKTOR GEORGIEVICH) Serbskii demokrat Zhivoin Zhuevich: publitsisticheskaia deiatel'nost' v Rossii v 60-kh godakh XIX v. Moskva, 1974. pp. 334.

ZULUS

— Kings and rulers.

ROBERTS (BRIAN) The Zulu kings. London, 1974. pp. 388. *bibliog.*

ZVEREV (ARSENII GRIGOR'EVICH).

ZVEREV (ARSENII GRIGOR'EVICH) Zapiski ministra. Moskva, 1973. pp. 270.

List of subject headings used
in the Bibliography
arranged under topics

TABLE OF SUBJECT SUB-DIVISIONS

SUBJECT SUB-DIVISIONS UNDER NAMES OF CONTINENTS, COUNTRIES, STATES OR TOWNS

Works on the following subjects, if confined to a particular geographical area, are entered not under subject, but under the name of the country, etc., with the subject sub-division. At the end of the entries under countries are references to the smaller areas comprised therein, e.g. from United Kingdom —Social conditions to the sub-division Social conditions under Banbury, Cumberland, etc. Such references may serve also in a few cases, such as Municipal Government, where the reference from the subject is made to subject sub-divisions 'under the names of towns', without listing the names of towns.

Air force
Annexation
Antiquities
Appropriations and expenditures
Armed forces
Army

Bibliography
Bio-bibliography
Biography
Boundaries

Capital
Census
Centennial celebrations, etc.
Charters, grants, privileges
Church history
Civilization
Claims
Climate
Clubs
Colonies
Colonization
Commerce
Commercial policy
Commercial treaties
Constitution
Constitutional conventions
Constitutional history
Constitutional laws
Courts and courtiers

Defences
Description and travel
Dictionaries and encyclopaedias
Diplomatic and consular service
Directories
Discovery and exploration

Economic conditions
Economic history
Economic integration
Economic policy
Emigration and immigration
Executive departments

Exiles

Fairs
Famines
Foreign economic relations
Foreign opinion
Foreign population
Foreign relations
Foreign relations—Treaties
Foreign relations administration

Gazeteers
Genealogy
Gentry
Government property
Government publications
Government vessels
Governors

Historic houses, etc.
Historical geography
History
History, Local
History, Military
History, Naval

Industries
Intellectual life
International status

Kings and rulers

Languages
Learned institutions and societies

Manufactures
Maps
Military policy
Militia
Minorities
Moral conditions

Nationalism
Native races
Navy

Neutrality
Nobility

Occupations
Officials and employees

Parliament (Congress, Nationalrat, etc.)
Peerage
Politics and government
Population
Presidents
Public buildings
Public lands
Public works

Race question
Registers
Relations (general) with (country)
Relations (military) with (country)
Religion
Religion and mythology
Rural conditions

Sanitary affairs
Seal
Semi-centennial celebrations, etc.
Social conditions
Social history
Social life and customs
Social policy
Statistics
Statistics, Medical
Statistics, Vital
Surveys

Territorial expansion
Territories and possessions
Tornadoes

Vice-Presidents
Voting registers

Year-books

SUBJECT SUB-DIVISIONS USED ONLY UNDER NAMES OF CITIES OR TOWNS

Works on the following matters, if confined to a particular region or country, are entered under the subject, with local sub-division; if confined to a particular city or town, under the name of the city or town, with subject sub-division. References to particular cities or towns are made under the local sub-division of the subject.

Almshouses and workhouses
Ambulance service
Amusements

Benevolent and moral institutions and societies
Bridges
Buildings

Cemeteries
Charities
Civic improvement
Clubs

Description
Docks

Earthquake
Evening and continuation schools
Exhibitions
Fires and fire prevention

Fortifications

Gilds
Growth

Harbour
Hospitals
Hotels, taverns, etc.

Libraries
Lodging-houses

Markets
Massacre
Music-halls (Variety-theatres, cabarets, etc.)

Office buildings

Parks
Police
Poor
Port

Porters
Prisons and reformatories
Public laundries

Rapid transit
Recreation areas
Recreational activities
Riots

Schools
Sewerage
Stock Exchange (Beurs, Bourse, etc.)
Street cleaning
Streets
Suburbs and environs
Synagogues

Theatres
Transit systems

Water-supply

BIOGRAPHY.

AGRICULTURE. (including ANIMAL AND PLANT INDUSTRIES)

General.

AERIAL PHOTOGRAPHY IN AGRICULTURE.
AERIAL PHOTOGRAPHY IN FORESTRY.
AGRICULTURAL ADMINISTRATION
AGRICULTURAL ASSISTANCE, DANISH
AGRICULTURAL ASSISTANCE, SWEDISH
AGRICULTURAL COLONIES
AGRICULTURAL CREDIT
AGRICULTURAL EDUCATION.
AGRICULTURAL EXTENSION WORK
AGRICULTURAL GEOGRAPHY.
AGRICULTURAL INNOVATIONS.
AGRICULTURAL LAWS AND LEGISLATION
AGRICULTURAL MACHINERY
AGRICULTURAL PRICE SUPPORTS
AGRICULTURAL PRICES
AGRICULTURAL SOCIETIES
AGRICULTURAL WAGES
AGRICULTURE.
AGRICULTURE, COOPERATIVE
AGRICULTURE AND STATE.
CONSOLIDATION OF LAND HOLDINGS.
COOPERATIVE MARKETING OF FARM PRODUCE
COTTON GROWING AND MANUFACTURE
CROP YIELDS.
DAIRYING
EGG TRADE
FAMILY FARMS
FARM INCOME
FARM MANAGEMENT.
FARM MECHANIZATION
FARM PRODUCE
FARMERS
FARMS
FARMS, COLLECTIVE
FARMS, SIZE OF
FEEDS
FERTILIZER INDUSTRY.
FERTILIZERS AND MANURES.
FLAX INDUSTRY
FOREST PRODUCTS
FOREST REPRODUCTION
FORESTRY SOCIETIES
FORESTS AND FORESTRY
FRUIT CULTURE
FUR TRADE
GRAIN TRADE.
HILL FARMING
HORTICULTURE
IRRIGATION.
MARKETING OF LIVESTOCK
MEAT INDUSTRY AND TRADE
MILK SUPPLY
MILK TRADE
PART-TIME FARMING
PESTICIDES.
PLANTATIONS.
PRODUCE TRADE
RECLAMATION OF LAND
SMALL HOLDINGS
SOIL SURVEYS
SOILS.
STATE FARMS
STOCK AND STOCK BREEDING
SUGAR GROWING
VITICULTURE
WILD LIFE, CONSERVATION OF.
WILD LIFE RESEARCH

Particular animals and animal products.

BEEF.
BLUE WHALE.
BUTTER.
CATTLE
MILK
POULTRY
SHEEP
SWINE

Particular crops and plant products.

BEETS AND BEET SUGAR
BETEL NUTS.
CARROTS.
COCONUT.
COCONUT OIL.
COFFEE
COPRA.
GRAIN
HOPS.
JUTE
MARIHUANA.
MARINE ALGAE
OATS.
PALM OIL.
PEPPER.
RICE
RUBBER.
SUGAR
TEA.
TIMBER
TOBACCO
VEGETABLES
WHEAT

Fisheries.

FISH TRADE
FISHERIES
FISHING BOATS.
SALMON FISHERIES.

BIBLIOGRAPHY AND GENERAL WORKS.

ABBREVIATIONS.
ABBREVIATIONS, PORTUGUESE.
ABBREVIATIONS, SPANISH.
ABBREVIATIONS, YUGOSLAV.
ACRONYMS.
AUDIO-VISUAL LIBRARY SERVICE.
BIBLIOGRAPHICAL SERVICES.
BIBLIOGRAPHY
BIBLIOGRAPHY, NATIONAL
BOOK CLUBS
BOOKS.
BOOKS AND READING.
BOOKS AND READING FOR CHILDREN.
BOOKSELLERS AND BOOKSELLING
BRITISH MUSEUM.
BUSINESS LIBRARIES.
CATALOGUES, BOOKSELLERS
CATALOGUES, LIBRARY.
CATALOGUING.
CHARTERS
CITATION INDEXES
CLASSIFICATION
CONTENT ANALYSIS (COMMUNICATION)
DATA LIBRARIES.
DOCUMENTATION.
ENCYCLOPAEDIAS AND DICTIONARIES.
FOOD AND AGRICULTURE ORGANIZATION
GOVERNMENT PUBLICATIONS.
HISTORICAL LIBRARIES
ILLUSTRATED BOOKS.
INCUNABULA
INFORMATION SERVICES.
INFORMATION STORAGE AND RETRIEVAL SYSTEMS.
INFORMATION THEORY.
LIBRARIES
LIBRARIES, GOVERNMENTAL, ADMINISTRATIVE, ETC.
LIBRARIES, SPECIAL.
LIBRARIES, UNIVERSITY AND COLLEGE
LIBRARIES AND STATE
LIBRARY ADMINISTRATION.
LIBRARY FINANCE.
LIBRARY OF CONGRESS.
LIBRARY SCHOOLS AND TRAINING.
LITTLE MAGAZINES
LITTLE PRESSES
MANUSCRIPTS
MUSEUMS
NAVAL MUSEUMS.
PERIODICALS
PRINTED EPHEMERA
PRINTING
PRINTING, PRACTICAL
PROHIBITED BOOKS.
PUBLIC LENDING RIGHTS (OF AUTHORS)
PUBLISHERS AND PUBLISHING.
SCIENTIFIC LIBRARIES.
SUBJECT HEADINGS
YEARBOOKS.

BIOGRAPHY.

ABSE (LEO).
ADAMS (Sir GRANTLEY HERBERT).
ADEMOLA (Sir ADETOKUNBO).
ADENAUER (KONRAD).
ADLER (MAX
AGNEW (SPIRO THEODORE).
ALBIZU CAMPOS (PEDRO).
ALINSKY (SAUL DAVID).
ALLEN (RICHARD).
ALLENDE (SALVADOR).
ALTHUSSER (LOUIS).
AMBEDKAR (BHIMARAO RAMJI).
AMENDOLA (GIOVANNI).
AMERY (JULIAN).
AMIN (IDI).
ANNUNZIO (GABRIELE D').
APEL (HANS).
ARBOLEYA MARTINEZ (MAXIMILIANO).
ARCISZEWSKI (FRANCISZEK ADAM).
ARNAL (MOSEN JESUS)
ARTSYBASHEV (MIKHAIL PETROVICH).
AUGSPURG (ANITA).
AVALOV (ZURAB DAVIDOVICH)
AWOLOWO (OBAFEMI).
AZAÑA Y DIAZ (MANUEL).
BAECK (LEO).
BAESCHLIN (HEINRICH THEOPHIL).
BAKUNIN (MIKHAIL ALEKSANDROVICH).
BALDWIN (STANLEY) 1st Earl Baldwin.
BALMACEDA (JOSE MANUEL).
BANCROFT (HUBERT HOWE).
BANDA (HASTINGS KAMAZU).
BARING (EVELYN) 1st Earl of Cromer.
BARNARD (CHESTER IRVING).
BARRY (TOM).
BARTHOU (LOUIS).
BAUER (OTTO).
BAUSSART (ELIE).
BAZILI (NIKOLAI ALEKSANDROVICH)
BEBEL (AUGUST).
BECCARIA BONESANA (CESARE) Marchese.
BECKER (CARL LOTUS).
BECKERATH (ERWIN VON)
BEECHER (CATHERINE ESTHER).
BEN-GURION (DAVID).
BENJAMIN (WALTER).
BENN (ANTHONY NEIL WEDGWOOD).
BENNETT (JOHN COLEMAN).
BENTHAM (JEREMY).
BENTINCK (Lord WILLIAM CAVENDISH).
BERGER (VICTOR L.)
BERKELEY (GEORGE) Bishop of Cloyne.
BERNHEIM (EMILE).

BIOGRAPHY.

BETHMANN-HOLLWEG (THEOBALD VON).
BHUTTO (ZULFIKAR ALI).
BISMARCK-SCHOENHAUSEN (OTTO EDUARD LEOPOLD VON) Prince.
BISSELL (CLAUDE T.)
BLUM (LEON).
BODIN (JEAN).
BOEHM-BAWERK (EUGEN VON)
BOEHNY (FERDINAND).
BOLIVAR (SIMON).
BOLLARDIERE (JACQUES MARIE ROCH ANDRE PARIS DE).
BONHOEFFER (DIETRICH).
BOOT (JESSE) 1st Baron Trent.
BOOTH FAMILY.
BOURBON FAMILY.
BRACKEN (BRENDAN).
BRANDT (WILLY).
BRETT (REGINALD BALIOL) 2nd Viscount Esher
BREZHNEV (LEONID IL'ICH).
BRIAND (ARISTIDE).
BROCKDORFF-RANTZAU (ULRICH EDUARD FERDINAND ALEXANDER VON) Graf.
BROEKMEYER (MARIUS)
BROWN (GEORGE) Communist.
BROWN (JOHN) American abolitionist.
BUCKERIDGE (NICHOLAS).
BUDENNYI (SEMEN MIKHAILOVICH).
BUKHARIN (NIKOLAI IVANOVICH).
BUKOVSKII (VLADIMIR KONSTANTINOVICH).
BUNKE (HAYDEE TAMARA)
BURKE (EDMUND).
BURNEY (HENRY).
CAFIERO (CARLO).
CAIRNES (JOHN ELLIOTT).
CAMARA (HELDER) Archbishop of Olinda and Recife.
CAMPBELL (ALEXANDER).
CANNING (GEORGE).
CARDIJN (JOSEPH).
CARRERO BLANCO (LUIS).
CASAS (BARTOLOME DE LAS) Bishop of Chiapa.
CASTRO RUZ (FIDEL).
CECIL FAMILY.
CHABAN-DELMAS (JACQUES).
CHIANG (CHING).
CHICHERIN (GEORGII VASIL'EVICH).
CHICHESTER (ARTHUR) Baron Chichester of Belfast.
CHUBAR (VLAS IAKOVYCH).
CHURCHILL (Sir WINSTON LEONARD SPENCER).
CLARKE (SAMUEL).
CLARKSON (STEPHEN).
CLAUSEWITZ (CARL VON).
CLAYTON (GEOFFREY HARE) Archbishop of Cape Town.
CLEMENCEAU (GEORGES EUGÈNE BENJAMIN).
CLIVE (ROBERT) Baron Clive.
CODREANU (CORNELIU ZELEA).
COLBERT FAMILY.
COLE (GEORGE DOUGLAS HOWARD).
COLLINS (MICHAEL).
COLWELL (MARIA).
COMTE (ISIDORE AUGUSTE MARIE FRANÇOIS XAVIER).
CONNALLY (JOHN BOWDEN).
CONSTANT DE REBECQUE (HENRI BENJAMIN DE).
COOK (THOMAS).
COOLS (ANDRÉ).
COURTET (VICTOR).
CRISPI (FRANCESCO).
CROSTHWAITE (Sir CHARLES HAUKES TOD).
CURTIS (DOUGLAS).

DAVENPORT (NICHOLAS).
DAVIES (JOHN PATON).
DAVIS (JOHN WILLIAM).
DAVITT (MICHAEL)
DAWES (HENRY LAURENS).
DAY (DOROTHY).
DE VALERA (EAMON).
DEGRELLE (LEON).
DELBOS (YVON).
DEWEY (JOHN).
DIDEROT (DENIS).
DIETZGEN (JOSEPH).
DORR (THOMAS WILSON).
DRAGOMANOV (MIKHAIL PETROVICH).
DULLES (JOHN FOSTER).
DUMBA (CONSTANTIN THEODOR).
DUMONT (LOUIS).
DUNCAN (JOSEPH F.)
DUPLESSIS (MAURICE)
DUPUY (BENOÎT MARIE).
DURKHEIM (EMILE).
ELIZABETH I, Queen of England.
ENGELS (FRIEDRICH).
ERZBERGER (MATTHIAS)
ESCHERICH (GEORG).
FAISAL I, King of Iraq.
FELTRINELLI (GIANGIACOMO).
FERDINAND II, King of the Two Sicilies.
FERREIRA DA SILVA (VIRGOLINO) known as Lampião.
FFRENCH-BEYTAGH (GONVILLE AUBIE) Dean of Johannesburg.
FISCHER (ERNST)
FLETCHER (JOHN WILLIAM).
FORD (GERALD RUDOLPH) President of the United States.
FOSTER FAMILY.
FOURIER (FRANÇOIS CHARLES MARIE)
FRANCIS JOSEPH I, Emperor of Austria.
FRANKLIN (HENRY).
FREGE (GOTTLOB).
FREUD (SIGMUND).
FRONDIZI (ARTURO)
GAMBETTA (LEON MICHEL).
GANDHI (INDIRA).
GANDHI (MOHANDAS KARAMCHAND).
GARIBALDI (GIUSEPPE).
GASPERI (ALCIDE DE).
GAULLE (CHARLES DE).
GENTILE (GIOVANNI).
GEORGE (DAVID LLOYD) 1st Earl Lloyd George.
GEORGE IV, King of Great Britain and Ireland.
GERLACH (HELLMUT VON).
GERTSEN (ALEKSANDR IVANOVICH).
GERTSEN (NATALIIA ALEKSANDROVNA)
GIANNINI (GUGLIELMO)
GIOLITTI (GIOVANNI).
GIRAUD (HENRY).
GODOY Y ALVAREZ DE FABIA (MANUEL DE) Duque de Alcudia.
GODWIN (MARY).
GOEBBELS (JOSEPH).
GOKHALE (GOPAL KRISHNA).
GOMPERS (SAMUEL).
GORE-BOOTH (PAUL HENRY) Baron Gore-Booth.
GOR'KII (MAKSIM) pseud.
GORTER (HERMAN).
GOSCHEN (GEORGE JOACHIM) 1st Viscount Goschen.
GOUBERVILLE (GILLES DE).
GOUGH (RICHARD).
GRABSKI (WŁADYSŁAW).
GRAMSCI (ANTONIO).
GRANT (CLARA ELLEN).
GRANT (JOHN DOUGLAS).
GRANT (ULYSSES SIMPSON) President of the United States.
GRAVE (JEAN).
GRIFFITH (ARTHUR).

GRIPENSTEDT (JOHAN AUGUST).
GROENMAN (SJOERD).
GROOT (PAUL DE).
GROS (JOSE).
GUEVARA (ERNESTO).
GURVICH (GEORGII DAVYDOVICH).
HABERMAS (JUERGEN).
HÄGGLÖF (GUNNAR).
HALL (DANIEL GEORGE EDWARD).
HALLIER (JEAN EDERN).
HAMELIN (JACQUES FELIX EMMANUEL).
HAMILTON (ANNE) Duchess of Hamilton.
HANSSEN (GEORG).
HANUSCH (FERDINAND).
HARDIE (JAMES KEIR).
HASSELMANN (WILHELM).
HAUSHOFER (ALBRECHT).
HAY (JOHN) 2nd Earl of Tweeddale.
HEGEL (GEORG WILHELM FRIEDRICH).
HEIDEGGER (MARTIN).
HEINEMANN (GUSTAV W.)
HENRY IV, King of England.
HENRY VII, King of England.
HEREN (LOUIS).
HERTER (CHRISTIAN ARCHIBALD).
HERZL (THEODOR).
HESS (RUDOLF).
HEUSS (THEODOR).
HEYMANN (LIDA GUSTAVA)
HEYWORTH (LAWRENCE).
HIRSCHVOGEL FAMILY.
HITLER (ADOLF).
HIVES (FRANK)
HOBBES (THOMAS).
HOBBS (MAY).
HOCKING (WILLIAM ERNEST)
HOFFA (JAMES RIDDLE).
HOHOFF (WILHELM).
HOPE FAMILY.
HOWELL (GEORGE).
HSI-LIANG.
HUGENBERG (ALFRED).
HUME (DAVID).
IATSUNSKII (VIKTOR KORNEL'EVICH).
IDEMITSU (SAZO).
JACKSON (ANDREW) President of the United States.
JACKSON (Sir GEOFFREY HOLT SEYMOUR).
JAKSCH (WENZEL).
JAUREGUI (ARTURO)
JENGHIS KHAN, Great Khan of the Moguls.
JOHNSON (ANDREW) President of the United States.
JOHNSON (HARRY GORDON).
JOHNSON (JAMES WELDON).
JOHNSON (LYNDON BAINES) President of the United States.
JUNG (CHARLES GUSTAVE).
KADAR (JANOS).
KANT (IMMANUEL).
KEHRL (HANS).
KENNEDY (JOHN FITZGERALD) President of the United States.
KENYATTA (JOMO).
KEYNES (JOHN MAYNARD) 1st Baron Keynes.
KHRUSHCHEV (NIKITA SERGEEVICH).
KIM (DAE-JUNG)
KIM (HYONG JIK).
KIM (IL-SUNG)
KISSINGER (HENRY ALFRED)
KIROV (SERGEI MIRONOVICH).
KLAVER (IMKE).
KLIUCHEVSKII (VASILII OSIPOVICH).
KOERNER (THEODOR).
KORNILOV (LAVR GEORGIEVICH).
KREISKY (BRUNO).
KRONACKER (PAUL).
KRUGER (STEPHANUS JOHANNES PAULUS).
KRUPP FAMILY.

BIOGRAPHY.

KUCKHOFF (GRETA).
KUECHENHOFF (ERICH).
KUUSINEN (AINO).
LABRIOLA (ANTONIO).
LAING (RONALD DAVID).
LAMBTON (ANTONY CLAUD
 FREDERICK) Viscount Lambton.
LANG (OTTO).
LARSSON FAMILY.
LASSALLE (FERDINAND JOHANN
 GOTTLIEB).
LAWRENCE (THOMAS EDWARD).
LEARY (TIMOTHY).
LEE (ARTHUR HAMILTON) 1st Viscount
 Lee of Fareham.
LEE (KUAN YEW).
LEFEBVRE (GEORGES)
LEHÁR (ANTON).
LENIN (VLADIMIR IL'ICH).
LEOPOLD II, King of the Belgians.
LEVERIDGE (ANNA MARIA).
LÉVI-STRAUSS (CLAUDE).
LEVIN (SHNEER MENDELEVICH).
LEVY-BRUHL (LUCIEN).
LEWIN (HUGH).
LEYH (GEORG).
LIANG (CHI-CHAO).
LIBERMAN (EVSEI GRIGOR'EVICH).
LIEBKNECHT (KARL).
LIEBKNECHT (WILHELM PHILIPP
 MARTIN CHRISTIAN LUDWIG).
LINTON (WILLIAM JAMES).
LIST (GEORG FRIEDRICH).
LO (JUI-CHING).
LOCKE (JOHN).
LOEFFLER (TOBIAS).
LORAINE (Sir PERCY LYHAM).
LOUIS XIV, King of France.
LOUIS XVI, King of France.
LOWE (ROBERT) 1st Viscount Sherbrooke.
LUKÁCS (GEORG).
LUMUMBA (PATRICE).
LUR'E (ALEKSANDR L'VOVICH).
LUTZ (RALPH HASWELL).
LUXEMBURG (ROSA).
MACAULAY (THOMAS BABINGTON)
 Baron Macaulay.
MACAULAY FAMILY.
MACDONALD (Sir JOHN ALEXANDER).
MACEK (VLADKO).
MACLEAN (JOHN).
MADARIAGA (SALVADOR DE).
MAISEL (KARL).
MAISKII (IVAN MIKHAILOVICH).
MAKARIOS III, Archbishop and Ethnarch of
 Cyprus.
MAKAROV (PAVEL VASIL'EVICH).
MALCOLM X, pseud.
MALINOWSKI (BRONISŁAW).
MALRAUX (ANDRE).
MAN (HENRI DE).
MAO (TSE-TUNG).
MARC (ALEXANDRE).
MARIGHELA (CARLOS).
MARTY (ANDRE).
MARX (KARL).
MASSIGLI (RENE).
MASSINGHAM (HENRY WILLIAM).
MATTEOTTI (GIACOMO).
MATVEEV (ANDREI ARTAMONOVICH).
MAUDLING (REGINALD).
MAZZINI (GIUSEPPE).
McCARTHY (JOSEPH RAYMOND).
McGOVERN (GEORGE STANLEY).
MEAD (GEORGE HERBERT).
MEDINA (Sir SOLOMON DE).
MEINBERG (ADOLF).
MELGAREJO (MARIANO).
MELROSE (WILLIAM).
MENDÈS-FRANCE (PIERRE).
MENDIETA Y NUÑEZ (LUCIO).
MICHELS (ROBERT).
MIDOL (LUCIEN).

MIHAILOVIĆ (DRAZA).
MILL (JOHN STUART).
MILNER (ALFRED) 1st Viscount Milner.
MOHAMMED REZA PAHLAVI,
 Shahanshah of Iran.
MONNET (JEAN).
MONTGOMERY (BERNARD LAW) 1st
 Viscount Montgomery of Alamein.
MONTGOMERY FAMILY.
MORE (Sir THOMAS) Saint.
MORGAN (JOHN PIERPONT).
MORRIS (HENRY).
MOSCA (GAETANO).
MOTIER (MARIE JEAN PAUL ROCH
 YVES GILBERT) Marquis de la Fayette.
MOUNTFORD (CHARLES PEARCY).
MOYO (TEMBA).
MUELLER (HERMANN).
MULVANY (WILLIAM THOMAS).
MUSSOLINI (BENITO).
MUTASA,(DIDYMUS NOEL EDWIN)
NABARRO (Sir GERALD DAVID NUNES).
NAGLER (ISIDORE).
NAPOLÉON I, Emperor of the French.
NEALE (EDWARD VANSITTART).
NECHAEV (SERGEI GENNADIEVICH)
NECKER (JACQUES).
NEGRELLI (LUIGI).
NEHRU (JAWAHARLAL).
NEHRU (MOTILAL).
NEURATH (OTTO).
NEWTON (Sir ISAAC).
NICHOLAS II, Emperor of Russia.
NIEKISCH (ERNST).
NIEUWENHUIS (FERDINAND DOMELA).
NIXON (RICHARD MILHOUS) President of
 the United States.
NORTH (JOHN THOMAS).
NOVOSIL'TSEV (NIKOLAI
 NIKOLAEVICH).
NYERERE (JULIUS KAMBARAGE).
O'BRIEN (LAWRENCE FRANCIS).
O'CONNELL (DANIEL).
O'DONOVAN ROSSA (DIARMUID)
ONYEAMA (DILLIBE).
OPPENHEIMER (HARRY FREDERICK).
OPPENHEIMER (Sir ERNEST).
ORELLI-RINDERKNECHT (SUSANNA).
OTTO, Archduke of Austria.
OVANDO CANDIA (ALFREDO)
OWEN (ROBERT).
OZOLIN (KONSTANTIN IVANOVICH).
PAEPE (CESAR DE).
PAGET (WILLIAM) 1st Baron Paget.
PAISLEY (IAN).
PAKENHAM (FRANCIS AUNGIER) 7th
 Earl of Longford.
PARE (WILLIAM).
PAREKH (NAGIN).
PARETO (VILFREDO).
PARKER (PETER).
PARSONS (TALCOTT).
PATERSON (EMMA).
PATON (ALAN).
PEARSON (LESTER BOWLES).
PEIRCE (CHARLES SANTIAGO
 SANDERS).
PELHAM-HOLLES (THOMAS) 1st Duke of
 Newcastle.
PEÑALOZA (ANGEL VICENTE).
PENG (MING-MIN).
PENN (WILLIAM).
PEPPERELL (ELIZABETH).
PERON (JUAN DOMINGO).
PESCH (HEINRICH).
PETAIN (HENRI PHILIPPE BENONI
 OMER JOSEPH)
PETER I, called the Great, Emperor of Russia.
PETERS (RICHARD STANLEY).
PETITOT (EMILE).
PEYER IM HOF (JOHANN FRIEDRICH).
PHILBY (HAROLD ADRIAN RUSSELL)
PHILIP, Duke of Burgundy, called the Good.

PIAGET (JEAN).
PIATNITSKII (OSIP ARONOVICH) pseud.
PILLER (NORMAN).
PINCHOT (GIFFORD) 1970.
PINTO (RUI DE).
PIRANDELLO (LUIGI).
PISEMSKII (ALEKSEI
 FEOFILAKTOVICH).
PITT (Right Hon. william).
PLATO.
PLEIGER (PAUL).
PLEKHANOV (GEORGII
 VALENTINOVICH).
PLUMB (JOHN HAROLD).
PLUNKETT (JOHN HUBERT).
POPPER (Sir KARL RAIMUND).
POSNER (WILLIAM).
POTTER FAMILY.
POUGET (EMILE).
POWELL (JOHN ENOCH).
PRAGIER (ADAM).
PRAT DE LA RIBA (ENRIC).
PRIMAKOV (VITALII MARKOVICH).
PRIMO DE RIVERA Y SAENZ DE
 HEREDIA (JOSE ANTONIO).
PROUDHON (PIERRE JOSEPH).
RABBE (ALPHONSE).
RABINOWICZ (OSKAR K.)
RADIĆ (STJEPAN).
RADISHCHEV (ALEKSANDR
 NIKOLAEVICH).
RATHENAU (WALTHER).
RAVERA (CAMILLA).
RAWLS (JOHN)
REBELO DA SILVA (LUIS AUGUSTO).
REED (ALEXANDER WYCLIF)
REIMANN (MAX).
RENAN (ERNEST).
RENNER (KARL).
RETZLAW (KARL).
RHODES (CECIL JOHN)
RIVAS VICUÑA (MANUEL)
ROBERTSON (Sir JAMES WILSON).
ROCKEFELLER FAMILY.
ROLPH (C H) pseud.
ROMMEL (ERWIN).
ROOSEVELT (FRANKLIN DELANO)
 President of the United States.
ROSA (JOÃO GUIMARÃES).
ROSAS (JUAN MANUEL DE).
ROSENBERG (ALFRED).
ROSSELLI (CARLO).
ROUSSEAU (JEAN JACQUES).
ROY (MANABENDRA NATH).
RUMBOLD (Sir HORACE MONTAGUE).
RUSKIN (JOHN).
RUSSELL (BERTRAND ARTHUR
 WILLIAM) 3rd Earl Russell.
RYDER (DUDLEY FRANCIS STUART) 3rd
 Earl of Harrowby.
RYGG (NICOLAI THEODORIUS NILSSEN)
RYNER (HAN) pseud.
SABATE LLOPART (FRANCISCO).
SAKHAROV (ANDREI DMITRIEVICH).
SALTYKOV-SHCHEDRIN (MIKHAIL
 EVGRAFOVICH).
SANDINO (AUGUSTO CESAR).
SARTRE (JEAN PAUL).
SASTRI (V.S. SRINIVASA)
SAUD 1, King of Saudi Arabia.
SCHEEL (WALTER).
SCHLIEFFEN (ALFRED VON) Graf.
SCHMID (WERNER).
SCHROEDER (GERHARD).
SCHUMACHER (KURT).
SECONDAT (CHARLES LOUIS DE) Baron
 de Montesquieu.
SERRATI (GIACINTO MENOTTI).
SEWARD (WILLIAM HENRY).
SHAULL (RICHARD).
SHCHETKIN (STEPAN PETROVICH).
SIBERCH (JOHN).
SIDIYYA AL-KABIR, Shaikh.

BIOGRAPHY.

SIKORSKI (WŁADYSŁAW).
SMALLEY (GEORGE WASHBURN).
SMALLWOOD (JOSEPH ROBERTS)
SMITH (ADAM).
SOLZHENITSYN (ALEKSANDR ISAEVICH).
SOMBART (WERNER).
SONNINO (SIDNEY) Baron.
SORENSEN (REGINALD WILLIAM) Baron Sorensen.
SPAAK (PAUL HENRI).
SPANN (OTHMAR).
SPERANSKII (MIKHAIL MIKHAILOVICH) Graf
SRAFFA (PIERO).
STÄL-HOLSTEIN (ANNE LOUISE GERMAINE DE) Baronne.
STALIN (IOSIF VISSARIONOVICH).
STEKLOV (IURII MIKHAILOVICH).
STENBOCK (JOHAN GABRIEL)
STEPNIAK (SERGEI) pseud.
STETTINIUS (EDWARD REILLY).
STOCKS (MARY DANVERS) Baroness Stocks.
STRAUSS (FRANZ JOSEF).
STRESEMANN (GUSTAV).
STROGANOV (PAVEL ALEKSANDROVICH) Graf.
STUART FITZ JAMES Y FALCO (JACOBO) 17th Duke of Alba.
STUEBER (FRITZ).
SUKARNO, President of Indonesia.
SULZBERGER (CYRUS LEO).
SVEVO (ITALO) pseud.
SYMES (REGINALD ANTHONY COLMER).
TAFT (WILLIAM HOWARD) President of the United States.
TARDIEU (ANDRÉ PIERRE GABRIEL AMÉDÉE).
TASCA (ANGELO).
TAVERNE (DICK).
TAWNEY (RICHARD HENRY).
TAYLOR (GORDON RATTRAY).
THIERRY D'ARGENLIEU (GEORGES LOUIS MARIE)
THOMAS, Earl of Lancaster.
THOMAS [BECKET], Saint, Archbishop of Canterbury.
THOREZ (MAURICE).
THORNE (WILLIAM JAMES).
TILLON (CHARLES).
TITO (JOSIP BROZ).
TOENNIES (FERDINAND).
TOGLIATTI (PALMIRO).
TOLSTOI (DMITRII ALEKSEEVICH).
TONE (THEOBALD WOLFE).
TORRES RESTREPO (CAMILO).
TOYNBEE (ARNOLD JOSEPH).
TRESSELL (ROBERT) pseud.
TRORY (ERNIE).
TROTSKII (LEV DAVYDOVICH).
TRUDEAU (PIERRE ELLIOTT).
TURNER (FREDERICK JACKSON).
USPENSKII (GLEB IVANOVICH).
VACIETIS (JUKUMS).
VALLIERES (PIERRE).
VANDERVELDE (EMILE).
VANN (ROBERT LEE).
VARELA (FELIPE).
VARGAS (GETULIO).
VAUX (CLOTILDE DE).
VEBLEN (THORSTEIN).
VERWOERD (HENDRIK FRENSCH).
VITTORIO (GIUSEPPE DI).
VOCKE (WILHELM) Bundesbankpräsident.
VON NEUMANN (JOHN).
VOZNESENSKII (ALEKSANDR ALEKSEEVICH).
WACHENHEIM (HEDWIG).
WALPOLE (ROBERT) 1st Earl of Orford.
WALRAS (LEON).
WANSEY (HENRY).
WEBB (BEATRICE).
WEBB (SIDNEY) 1st Baron Passfield.
WEBER (MAX).
WEITLING (WILHELM).
WENDLAND (HEINZ-DIETRICH).
WHITE (HARRY DEXTER).
WIEGEL (HANS).
WILBERFORCE (WILLIAM).
WILKES (JOHN).
WILKINSON (ELLEN CICELY).
WILLIAM, of Ockham.
WILLWERTH (JAMES).
WILSON (THOMAS WOODROW) President of the United States.
WINCOTT (LEN).
WINNIG (AUGUST).
WINSTANLEY (GERARD).
WIRTH (JOSEPH).
WITTGENSTEIN (LUDWIG).
WYATT (WOODROW LYLE).
XENOPOL (ALEXANDRU DIMITRIE).
YOUNG (ARTHUR) F.R.S.
ZANARDELLI (GIUSEPPE).
ZANDER (ERNST).
ZELLE (MARGARETHA GEERTRUIDA).
ZETKIN (CLARA).
ZIMMERMANN (MARIAN).
ZINI (ZINO).
ZINOV'EV (GRIGORII EVSEEVICH).
ZOSHCHENKO (MIKHAIL MIKHAILOVICH).
ZUEBLIN-SPILLER (ELSE).
ZUJOVIĆ (ZIVOIN).
ZVEREV (ARSENII GRIGOR'EVICH).

COMMERCE AND INDUSTRY.

General.

ACCOUNTING.
ADVERTISING.
ADVERTISING, NEWSPAPER
AIMS OF INDUSTRY.
ANDEAN GROUP.
APPRENTICES
ARBITRATION, INDUSTRIAL.
AUDITING.
BIG BUSINESS
BOOKKEEPING.
BOUNTIES
BUSINESS.
BUSINESS AND POLITICS
BUSINESS CYCLES.
BUSINESS EDUCATION
BUSINESS ETHICS.
CANVASSING.
CENTRAL AMERICAN COMMON MARKET.
CENTRAL BUSINESS DISTRICTS
CHAMBERS OF COMMERCE
COMMERCE.
COMMERCIAL ASSOCIATIONS
COMMERCIAL FINANCE COMPANIES
COMMERCIAL LEASES
COMMERCIAL POLICY.
COMMERCIAL PRODUCTS.
COMMERCIAL VEHICLES.
COMMODITY EXCHANGES
COMPETITION.
COMPETITION, INTERNATIONAL.
CONSOLIDATION AND MERGER OF CORPORATIONS
CONSUMER EDUCATION.
CONSUMER PROTECTION
CONSUMERS.
COOPERATION.
COOPERATIVE MARKETING OF FARM PRODUCE
COOPERATIVE SOCIETIES
CORPORATIONS.
CORPORATIONS, AMERICAN.
CORPORATIONS, BRITISH.
CORPORATIONS, FOREIGN
CORPORATIONS, INTERNATIONAL.
CORPORATIONS, NON-PROFIT
CORPORATIONS, PUBLIC.
DANGEROUS GOODS
DEFENCE CONTRACTS
DEPARTMENT STORES
DESIGN, INDUSTRIAL.
DISTRIBUTIVE EDUCATION.
DIVERSIFICATION IN INDUSTRY
DURABLE GOODS, CONSUMER.
EAST-WEST TRADE (1945-).
ECONOMIES OF SCALE.
EFFICIENCY, INDUSTRIAL.
EMPLOYEE MORALE.
EMPLOYEE OWNERSHIP.
EMPLOYEES, DISMISSAL OF
EMPLOYEES, RATING OF.
EMPLOYEES, RELOCATION OF
EMPLOYEES, TRAINING OF.
EMPLOYEES' MAGAZINES, HANDBOOKS, ETC.
EMPLOYEES' REPRESENTATION IN MANAGEMENT.
EMPLOYERS' ASSOCIATIONS
EMPLOYMENT (ECONOMIC THEORY).
EMPLOYMENT AGENCIES
EMPLOYMENT FORECASTING
EMPLOYMENT MANAGEMENT.
EMPLOYMENT STABILIZATION
EXECUTIVES, TRAINING OF.
EXPORT CREDIT
EXPORT MARKETING
FACTORIES
FACTORY AND TRADE WASTE.
FACTORY INSPECTION
FIRMS.
FOOD PRICES
FOOD SUPPLY.
FOREIGN TRADE PROMOTION
FOREIGN TRADE REGULATION.
FRANCHISES (RETAIL TRADE).
GOVERNMENT BUSINESS ENTERPRISES
GOVERNMENT OWNERSHIP.
HANDICRAFT
IMPERIAL PREFERENCE.
IMPORT QUOTAS
INCENTIVES IN INDUSTRY.
INDUSTRIAL ACCIDENTS.
INDUSTRIAL CAPACITY
INDUSTRIAL DISTRICTS.
INDUSTRIAL EQUIPMENT
INDUSTRIAL HYGIENE.
INDUSTRIAL MANAGEMENT
INDUSTRIAL ORGANIZATION.
INDUSTRIAL PROCUREMENT
INDUSTRIAL PROJECT MANAGEMENT
INDUSTRIAL PROMOTION.
INDUSTRIAL RELATIONS.
INDUSTRIAL SAFETY
INDUSTRIAL STATISTICS
INDUSTRIAL SURVEYS.
INDUSTRIALIZATION.
INDUSTRIES, LOCATION OF.
INDUSTRIES, SIZE OF.
INDUSTRY
INDUSTRY AND EDUCATION.
INDUSTRY AND STATE.
INTERNATIONAL BUSINESS ENTERPRISES.
INTERNATIONAL FEDERATION OF COTTON AND ALLIED TEXTILE INDUSTRIES.
INVENTORIES
INVENTORY CONTROL
LATIN AMERICAN FREE TRADE ASSOCIATION COUNTRIES
LIQUIDATION
MANAGEMENT.
MANAGEMENT GAMES.
MARKETING.
MARKETING MANAGEMENT.
MARKETING OF LIVESTOCK

COMMERCE AND INDUSTRY.

MARKETING RESEARCH.
MARKS OF ORIGIN.
MATERIALS
MATERIALS MANAGEMENT.
MEDIATION AND CONCILIATION, INDUSTRIAL
METRIC SYSTEM.
MINORITY BUSINESS ENTERPRISES
NEGROES AS BUSINESSMEN.
OCCUPATIONAL DISEASES.
OCCUPATIONS.
OFFICE BUILDINGS.
OFFICES
ORGANIZATION OF THE PETROLEUM EXPORTING COUNTRIES.
PATENTS
POWER RESOURCES.
PRODUCTION MANAGEMENT.
PRODUCTION PLANNING.
PRODUCTIVITY.
PROFESSIONAL EDUCATION
PROFESSIONS.
PROMOTERS.
PSYCHOLOGY, INDUSTRIAL.
PUBLIC CONTRACTS
PUBLIC UTILITIES.
QUALITY CONTROL.
RADIO ADVERTISING
RAILWAYS, INDUSTRIAL
RAW MATERIALS
RECRUITING OF EMPLOYEES
REPLACEMENT OF INDUSTRIAL EQUIPMENT.
RESEARCH, INDUSTRIAL.
RETAIL TRADE.
SALES FORECASTING
SALES PROMOTION.
SEASONAL INDUSTRIES.
SERVICE INDUSTRIES.
SHOPPING
SHOPPING CENTRES.
SHOPPING MALLS
SMALL BUSINESS.
STANDARDIZATION
STOCK COMPANIES
STORE LOCATION
STORES, TRAVELLING.
SUPERMARKETS
TECHNICIANS IN INDUSTRY.
TELEVISION IN ADVERTISING.
TIME ALLOCATION.
TRADE MARKS
TRADE REGULATION
TRADE ROUTES.
UNITED NATIONS CONFERENCE ON TRADE AND DEVELOPMENT.
UNITED NATIONS INDUSTRIAL DEVELOPMENT ORGANIZATION.
VOCATIONAL GUIDANCE.
WELFARE WORK IN INDUSTRY
WHOLESALE TRADE
WORK MEASUREMENT.
WORKMEN'S COMPENSATION

Occupations and professions.

ACCOUNTING AS A PROFESSION.
AEROPLANE INDUSTRY WORKERS
AGRICULTURAL LABOURERS.
AGRICULTURE AS A PROFESSION.
AGRICULTURISTS
ARCHITECTURE AS A PROFESSION.
ARTISANS
AUTOMOBILE INDUSTRY WORKERS
BANK EMPLOYEES
BANKING AS A PROFESSION.
BUSINESSMEN.
CAPITALISTS AND FINANCIERS
CARTOONISTS
CHEMICAL WORKERS
CHIMNEY SWEEPS.
CITY PLANNERS
CIVIL ENGINEERS

CLERKS.
CLOTHING WORKERS
COAL MINERS
CONSTRUCTION WORKERS
DIPLOMATS, BRITISH
DIPLOMATS, FRENCH
DIPLOMATS, RUSSIAN
DIPLOMATS, SWEDISH
DIRECTORS OF CORPORATIONS
DOCK WORKERS.
ENGINEERING AS A PROFESSION.
ENGINEERS
EXECUTIVES
FIREMEN.
FISHERMEN
FOREMEN
FORESTERS
FOUNDRYMEN
FRONTIER WORKERS.
HEALTH OFFICERS
HOTELS, TAVERNS, ETC.
IRON AND STEEL WORKERS
JUDGES.
LAWYERS
LEATHER WORKERS
LIBRARIANS
LONGSHOREMEN
LUMBERMEN
MANUFACTURERS
MEDICAL AUXILIARIES
MEDICAL PERSONNEL
MEDICAL TECHNOLOGISTS.
MERCHANTS.
MERCHANTS, AMERICAN.
MERCHANTS, BELGIAN.
MERCHANTS, GERMAN.
METAL WORKERS
MILITARY SERVICE AS A PROFESSION.
MINERS
NEGRO TEACHERS.
OCCUPATIONAL THERAPISTS
PHYSICAL THERAPISTS
PHYSICIANS.
PHYSICISTS
PRINTERS
ROAD TRANSPORT WORKERS
SCIENCE AS A PROFESSION.
SCIENTISTS.
SEAMEN.
SHIPBUILDING WORKERS
SHOP ASSISTANTS.
SOCIAL WORK AS A PROFESSION.
STENOGRAPHERS.
SUGAR WORKERS
TEACHERS.
TEXTILE WORKERS
TIN MINERS
TRANSPORT WORKERS
WEAVERS
WOMEN AS BANKERS.
WOODWORKERS

Particular trades and industries.

AEROPLANE INDUSTRY AND TRADE
AEROSPACE INDUSTRIES
AGGREGATES (BUILDING MATERIALS).
ALUMINIUM INDUSTRY AND TRADE.
ART INDUSTRIES AND TRADE
ASTRINGENTS.
ATOMIC ENERGY INDUSTRIES.
ATOMIC POWER-PLANTS
AUTOMOBILE INDUSTRY AND TRADE
BEARINGS (MACHINERY)
BEVERAGES.
BOOK INDUSTRIES AND TRADE.
BOOTS AND SHOES
BRASS INDUSTRY AND TRADE
BREEDER REACTORS.
BREWING INDUSTRIES
BRICK TRADE
BUILDING
BUILDING MATERIALS.

BUILDING MATERIALS INDUSTRY
BUILDINGS
BUILDINGS, PREFABRICATED.
BULB INDUSTRY
CANNING AND PRESERVING
CATERERS AND CATERING
CATTLE TRADE
CEMENT INDUSTRIES
CERAMIC INDUSTRIES
CHEMICAL INDUSTRIES
CHROMIUM
CINEMAS
CIVIL ENGINEERING
CLAY INDUSTRIES
CLOCK AND WATCHMAKING
CLOTHING TRADE
COAL
COAL MINES AND MINING
COFFEE TRADE
COKE INDUSTRY.
COMPUTER INDUSTRY
CONSTRUCTION INDUSTRY.
COPPER INDUSTRY AND TRADE
COPPER MINES AND MINING
COTTAGE INDUSTRIES
COTTON GROWING AND MANUFACTURE
COTTON TRADE
CUTLERY
DIAMONDS.
DRUG TRADE (PHARMACEUTICAL).
DYE INDUSTRY
EGG TRADE
ELECTRIC ENGINEERING
ELECTRIC INDUSTRIES
ELECTRIC POWER PLANTS
ELECTRICITY SUPPLY
ELECTRONIC DATA PROCESSING.
ELECTRONIC INDUSTRIES
ENGINEERING
FERTILIZER INDUSTRY.
FERTILIZERS AND MANURES.
FIBRES, SYNTHETIC.
FLAX INDUSTRY
FLOUR MILLS
FOOD, FROZEN.
FOOD INDUSTRY AND TRADE
FOUNDING.
FUR TRADE
FURNITURE INDUSTRY AND TRADE
GAS, NATURAL.
GAS INDUSTRY.
GLASS INDUSTRY AND TRADE
GRAIN TRADE.
GROCERY TRADE
HOUSEHOLD APPLIANCES.
HYDRAULIC ENGINEERING
INDUSTRIALIZED BUILDING
IRON INDUSTRY AND TRADE
KNIT GOODS.
KNIT GOODS INDUSTRY
LACE AND LACE MAKING
LEAD MINES AND MINING
LEATHER INDUSTRY AND TRADE
LIQUOR TRAFFIC
LOCOMOTIVES
LUMBER TRADE
MACHINE TOOLS.
MACHINERY
MAGNESIUM INDUSTRY AND TRADE
MEAT INDUSTRY AND TRADE
MECHANICAL ENGINEERING
METAL TRADE
MILK SUPPLY
MILK TRADE
MILLS AND MILL WORK.
MINERAL INDUSTRIES
MINES AND MINERAL RESOURCES
MINING CORPORATIONS
MINING INDUSTRY AND FINANCE
MOVING PICTURE INDUSTRY
NAVAL ARCHITECTURE.
NEWS AGENCIES.

COMMERCE AND INDUSTRY.

NEWSPAPER AND PERIODICAL WHOLESALERS
NEWSPAPER PUBLISHING
NITRATES.
NONFERROUS METAL INDUSTRIES
NUCLEAR REACTORS
OIL INDUSTRIES
OILS AND FATS
OILS AND FATS, EDIBLE.
OPIUM TRADE.
PAPER MAKING AND TRADE.
PETROLEUM IN SUBMERGED LANDS
PETROLEUM INDUSTRY AND TRADE.
PETROLEUM PRODUCTS
PETROLEUM REFINERIES
PHOSPHATE INDUSTRY
PLASTICS INDUSTRY AND TRADE
POLISHES.
POTASH INDUSTRY AND TRADE.
POTTERY
PRINTING INDUSTRY
PRODUCE TRADE
PUBLISHERS AND PUBLISHING.
QUARRIES AND QUARRYING
REACTOR FUEL REPROCESSING.
REAL ESTATE BUSINESS
RIBBONS.
RUBBER INDUSTRY AND TRADE
RUG AND CARPET INDUSTRY
SCRAP METAL INDUSTRY
SHIPBUILDING
SILK MANUFACTURE AND TRADE
SKIS AND SKIING
STEAM POWER PLANTS
STEEL INDUSTRY AND TRADE.
SUGAR TRADE.
SWORDS.
TABLE-CLOTHS
TEA TRADE
TEXTILE INDUSTRY AND FABRICS.
TIN.
TIN INDUSTRY.
TIN MINES AND MINING
TITANIUM INDUSTRY
TOBACCO MANUFACTURE AND TRADE
TOOLS.
TOURIST CAMPS, HOSTELS, ETC.
TOURISTS
TRACTOR INDUSTRY
TRACTORS.
WALLPAPER.
WINE AND WINE MAKING
WIRE INDUSTRY
WOOD-PULP INDUSTRY.
WOOD-USING INDUSTRIES
WOOL TRADE AND INDUSTRY

ECONOMICS.

see also AGRICULTURE; COMMERCE AND INDUSTRY; FINANCE; TRANSPORT

AGE AND EMPLOYMENT.
ALIEN LABOUR
BONUS SYSTEM
BRAIN DRAIN
CAPITALISM.
CENSUS.
CHRISTIANITY AND ECONOMICS.
CHURCH AND ECONOMICS.
CHURCH AND LABOUR
CIVIL SERVICE PENSIONS
COLLECTIVE BARGAINING.
COLLECTIVE LABOUR AGREEMENTS.
COLLECTIVISM.
COMMUNES (CHINA).
COMMUNISM.
COMPAGNONNAGES.
CONSUMPTION (ECONOMICS).
COST.
COST AND STANDARD OF LIVING.
COST EFFECTIVENESS.
COSTS, INDUSTRIAL.
COUNCIL FOR MUTUAL ECONOMIC ASSISTANCE.
DENTAL ECONOMICS.
DISABILITY EVALUATION
DISCRIMINATION IN EMPLOYMENT
DIVISION OF LABOUR.
DOMESTIC ECONOMY
DWELLINGS.
ECONOMIC ASSISTANCE.
ECONOMIC ASSISTANCE, AMERICAN.
ECONOMIC ASSISTANCE, BRITISH.
ECONOMIC ASSISTANCE, DANISH.
ECONOMIC ASSISTANCE, DOMESTIC
ECONOMIC ASSISTANCE, DUTCH.
ECONOMIC ASSISTANCE, EUROPEAN.
ECONOMIC ASSISTANCE, GERMAN.
ECONOMIC ASSISTANCE, NORWEGIAN.
ECONOMIC ASSISTANCE, SWEDISH
ECONOMIC ASSISTANCE IN AFGHANISTAN.
ECONOMIC ASSISTANCE IN THE BRITISH EMPIRE.
ECONOMIC ASSISTANCE IN TUNISIA.
ECONOMIC CONDITIONS.
ECONOMIC DEVELOPMENT.
ECONOMIC FORECASTING.
ECONOMIC HISTORY.
ECONOMIC INDICATORS
ECONOMIC LEGISLATION
ECONOMIC POLICY.
ECONOMIC RESEARCH.
ECONOMIC STABILIZATION.
ECONOMIC SURVEYS.
ECONOMIC ZONING
ECONOMICS.
ECONOMICS, COMPARATIVE.
ECONOMICS, MATHEMATICAL.
ECONOMICS, PRIMITIVE.
ECONOMISTS.
ECONOMISTS, ARGENTINIAN.
ECONOMISTS, AUSTRIAN.
ECONOMISTS, GERMAN.
ECONOMISTS, RUSSIAN.
ECONOMISTS, SPANISH.
EIGHT HOUR MOVEMENT.
ENTREPRENEUR.
EQUAL PAY FOR EQUAL WORK
EXCHANGE
EXTERNALITIES (ECONOMICS).
FAMILY ALLOWANCES.
FULL EMPLOYMENT POLICIES
GENERAL AGREEMENT ON TARIFFS AND TRADE.
GENERAL STRIKE, UNITED KINGDOM, 1926.
GEOGRAPHY, ECONOMIC.
GOVERNMENT PURCHASING
GOVERNMENT SPENDING POLICY
GROSS DOMESTIC PRODUCT
GROSS NATIONAL PRODUCT
HOLIDAYS.
HOME LABOUR
HOME OWNERSHIP.
HOURS OF LABOUR.
HOUSE BUYING.
HOUSING.
HOUSING, COOPERATIVE
HOUSING MANAGEMENT.
HOUSING, RURAL
HUMAN CAPITAL.
HUMAN ENGINEERING.
INCLOSURES.
INDENTURED SERVANTS
INDEX NUMBERS (ECONOMICS).
INFORMATION THEORY IN ECONOMICS.
INTEREST AND USURY.
INTERINDUSTRY ECONOMICS.
INTERNATIONAL ECONOMIC INTEGRATION.
INTERNATIONAL ECONOMIC RELATIONS.
INTERNATIONAL LABOUR ORGANISATION.
JOB ANALYSIS.
JOB SATISFACTION.
KUWAIT FUND FOR ARAB ECONOMIC DEVELOPMENT.
LABOUR AND LABOURING CLASSES.
LABOUR CONTRACT
LABOUR COSTS
LABOUR DISCIPLINE
LABOUR ECONOMICS
LABOUR DISPUTES.
LABOUR EXCHANGES
LABOUR MOBILITY.
LABOUR SERVICE
LABOUR SUPPLY.
LAND
LANDLORD AND TENANT
LIQUIDITY (ECONOMICS).
MANPOWER
MAY DAY (LABOUR HOLIDAY).
MEDICAL CARE, COST OF
MEDICAL ECONOMICS.
MERCANTILE SYSTEM
MIGRANT LABOUR.
MONOPOLIES.
MULTIPLIER (ECONOMICS).
NEGOTIATION.
NETWORK ANALYSIS (PLANNING).
NONWAGE PAYMENTS
OLD AGE PENSIONS
OLIGOPOLIES.
OPERATIONS RESEARCH.
ORGANISATION FOR ECONOMIC COOPERATION AND DEVELOPMENT
OVERTIME
PART-TIME EMPLOYMENT
PENSION TRUSTS
PENSIONS
PENSIONS, MILITARY
PHYSIOCRATS.
PICKETING
PLANNING.
POPULATION.
POPULATION RESEARCH.
PRICE INDEXES
PRICE REGULATION
PRICES.
PRIEST WORKERS.
PRIVATE PROPERTY
PRODUCTION (ECONOMIC THEORY).
PROFIT.
PROFIT SHARING.
PROPERTY
PUBLIC HOUSING
PURCHASING POWER
RATIONING, CONSUMER
REAL PROPERTY
RENT
RENT (ECONOMIC THEORY).
RENT SUBSIDIES
RESIDENTIAL MOBILITY
RESTRAINT OF TRADE
RISK.
SALARIED EMPLOYEES.
SEASONAL LABOUR
SEASONAL VARIATIONS (ECONOMICS)
SELF-EMPLOYED
SHARE-CROPPING.
SHIFT SYSTEMS.
SHOP STEWARDS
SIT DOWN STRIKES
SKILLED LABOUR
SOCIALIST COMPETITION.
SPACE IN ECONOMICS.
STRIKES AND LOCKOUTS.
SUBSIDIES.
SUBSTITUTION (ECONOMICS)
SUPPLEMENTARY EMPLOYMENT
SUPPLY AND DEMAND.
SURVIVORS' BENEFITS

FINANCE.

SYNDICALISM
TECHNICAL ASSISTANCE.
TECHNICAL ASSISTANCE, AMERICAN
TECHNICAL ASSISTANCE, BRITISH.
TECHNICAL ASSISTANCE, DANISH.
TECHNICAL ASSISTANCE, EUROPEAN.
TECHNICAL ASSISTANCE, FRENCH
TECHNICAL ASSISTANCE, ISRAELI
TECHNICAL ASSISTANCE, NORWEGIAN.
TECHNICAL ASSISTANCE, RUSSIAN
TECHNICAL ASSISTANCE IN EAST AFRICA.
TECHNICAL ASSISTANCE IN PERU.
TECHNICAL ASSISTANCE IN ZAMBIA.
TECHNOCRACY.
TEMPORARY EMPLOYMENT
TIME AND MOTION STUDY
TRADE AND PROFESSIONAL ASSOCIATIONS
TRADE UNIONS.
TRADE UNIONS, CATHOLIC
TRADE UNIONS AND COMMUNISM
TRUSTS, INDUSTRIAL.
UNDERDEVELOPED AREAS.
UNEMPLOYED.
UNEMPLOYMENT, SEASONAL
UNEMPLOYMENT, TECHNOLOGICAL.
URBAN ECONOMICS.
VALUE.
WAGE PAYMENT SYSTEMS.
WAGE-PRICE POLICY.
WAGES.
WAGES AND PRODUCTIVITY
WEALTH.
WELFARE ECONOMICS.
WOMEN IN TRADE UNIONS
WORK.
WORKS COUNCILS

EDUCATION.

General.

ACADEMIC ACHIEVEMENT.
AFRICAN STUDIES.
AGRICULTURAL EDUCATION.
BUSINESS EDUCATION
CHURCH SCHOOLS
COMMUNISM AND EDUCATION.
COMMUNISM IN EDUCATION
COMMUNIST EDUCATION
COMMUNITY AND COLLEGE.
COMMUNITY AND SCHOOL.
CORRESPONDENCE SCHOOLS AND COURSES.
CREATIVE THINKING (EDUCATION).
DEGREES, ACADEMIC
DISSERTATIONS, ACADEMIC
DISTRIBUTIVE EDUCATION.
DOMESTIC EDUCATION
EDUCATION.
EDUCATION, COMPARATIVE.
EDUCATION, ELEMENTARY.
EDUCATION, HIGHER.
EDUCATION, HUMANISTIC.
EDUCATION, PRESCHOOL.
EDUCATION, SECONDARY.
EDUCATION, URBAN
EDUCATION AND STATE.
EDUCATION OF ADULTS.
EDUCATION OF CHILDREN.
EDUCATION OF PRISONERS.
EDUCATION OF WOMEN.
EDUCATIONAL ACCOUNTABILITY.
EDUCATIONAL ANTHROPOLOGY.
EDUCATIONAL ASSISTANCE.
EDUCATIONAL ASSISTANCE, AUSTRALIAN
EDUCATIONAL EQUALIZATION.
EDUCATIONAL INNOVATIONS.
EDUCATIONAL LAW AND LEGISLATION

EDUCATIONAL PLANNING.
EDUCATIONAL PSYCHOLOGY.
EDUCATIONAL RESEARCH.
EDUCATIONAL SOCIOLOGY.
EDUCATIONAL STATISTICS.
EDUCATIONAL TESTS AND MEASUREMENTS.
EMPLOYEES, TRAINING OF.
EUROPEAN STUDIES.
EXAMINATIONS.
GIFTED CHILDREN.
GRADUATES
HANDICAPPED CHILDREN
HEALTH EDUCATION.
HIGHER EDUCATION AND STATE
HOME AND SCHOOL.
HUMANITIES.
ILLITERACY.
INDUSTRY AND EDUCATION.
INTELLECTUAL LIFE.
INTELLECTUALS.
INTERNATIONAL UNIVERSITY EXCHANGE FUND.
IRANIAN STUDENTS IN FOREIGN COUNTRIES.
LATIN AMERICAN STUDIES.
LEARNING, PSYCHOLOGY OF.
LIBRARY SCHOOLS AND TRAINING.
MORAL EDUCATION.
NEGRO UNIVERSITIES AND COLLEGES.
NORTHERN IRELAND STUDIES.
NURSERY SCHOOLS.
OCCUPATIONAL TRAINING
ORIENTAL STUDIES
PERSONNEL SERVICE IN EDUCATION.
POLITICS AND EDUCATION.
PROFESSIONAL EDUCATION
PROJECT METHOD IN TEACHING.
RADIO IN ADULT EDUCATION.
RADIO IN EDUCATION.
RELIGIOUS EDUCATION
RURAL SCHOOLS
RUSSIAN STUDIES.
SCHOLARSHIPS
SCHOOL BUILDINGS
SCHOOL CHILDREN.
SCHOOL HYGIENE
SCHOOL INTEGRATION
SCHOOL MANAGEMENT AND ORGANIZATION.
SCHOOL SOCIAL WORK
SCHOOLS.
SCIENCE AND THE HUMANITIES.
SEX INSTRUCTION.
SOCIAL WORK EDUCATION
SOCIALISM AND EDUCATION.
STUDENT AID
STUDENT COUNSELLORS, TRAINING OF.
STUDENT HOUSING
STUDENT STRIKES
STUDENT UNIONS.
STUDENTS
STUDENTS, FOREIGN
STUDENTS, INTERCHANGE OF.
STUDENTS, JEWISH
STUDENTS' SOCIETIES
TEACHER-STUDENT RELATIONSHIPS.
TEACHERS, TRAINING OF
TEACHERS' UNIONS
TEACHING.
TEACHING, FREEDOM OF
TECHNICAL EDUCATION
TELEVISION IN ADULT EDUCATION .
TELEVISION IN EDUCATION
TEXTBOOKS
UNITED NATIONS EDUCATIONAL, SCIENTIFIC AND CULTURAL ORGANIZATION
UNIVERSITIES AND COLLEGES.
VACATION SCHOOLS
VERBAL LEARNING.
VOCATIONAL EDUCATION

WOMEN AS TEACHERS.
WOMEN COLLEGE STUDENTS
WOMEN'S COLLEGES

Educational institutions.

DARTMOUTH COLLEGE
FRANKFURT-AM-MAIN UNIVERSITY
FREIBURG IM BREISGAU UNIVERSITY.
GOETTINGEN UNIVERSITY.
GRENOBLE UNIVERSITY.
IBADAN UNIVERSITY.
KENT STATE UNIVERSITY.
MEXICO UNIVERSITY
MOSCOW UNIVERSITY
NIJMEGEN UNIVERSITY.
OPEN UNIVERSITY.
OXFORD UNIVERSITY.
PAVIA UNIVERSITY.
POZNAŃ UNIVERSITY.
ROYAL WANSTEAD SCHOOL.
STANFORD UNIVERSITY.
STIRLING UNIVERSITY.
TEXAS UNIVERSITY.
TORONTO UNIVERSITY.
UNIVERSITY OF THE WESTERN TERRITORIES (POLAND).
WYNDHAM SCHOOL, EGREMONT
YALE UNIVERSITY.

FINANCE.

General.

ACTUARIAL SCIENCE.
AGRICULTURAL CREDIT
ASSESSMENT
BALANCE OF PAYMENTS.
BANK EXAMINATION
BANKS AND BANKING.
BANKS AND BANKING, CENTRAL.
BANKS AND BANKING, INTERNATIONAL.
BUDGET.
BUDGET IN BUSINESS
BUILDING AND LOAN ASSOCIATIONS
CAPITAL.
CAPITAL BUDGET
CAPITAL GAINS TAX
CAPITAL INVESTMENTS.
CAPITAL LEVY
COINAGE
COMMERCIAL FINANCE COMPANIES
COMMONWEALTH DEVELOPMENT CORPORATION.
CONSUMER CREDIT
CONVERTIBILITY (MONEY).
COST ACCOUNTING.
CREDIT
DEBTS, PUBLIC
DECIMAL SYSTEM.
DEFICIT FINANCING
DEVELOPMENT BANKS.
DEVELOPMENT CREDIT CORPORATIONS
DIVIDENDS
DOG RACING
DOLLAR.
EMIGRANT REMITTANCES
ESCALATOR CLAUSE
ESTATE PLANNING
EUROBOND MARKET.
EURODOLLAR MARKET.
EUROPEAN FUND.
EXPENDITURES, PUBLIC.
EXPORT CREDIT
FEDERAL RESERVE BANKS.
FINANCE.
FINANCIAL INSTITUTIONS.
FLOW OF FUNDS
FOREIGN EXCHANGE.
FRIENDLY SOCIETIES

FINANCE.

FUND RAISING.
GIFTS
GOLD.
GOVERNMENT LENDING
GRANTS IN AID.
GUARANTEED ANNUAL INCOME.
INCOME.
INCOME TAX
INDUSTRIAL LOAN ASSOCIATIONS
INFLATION (FINANCE).
INFLATION (FINANCE) AND ACCOUNTING.
INHERITANCE AND TRANSFER TAX.
INSTITUTIONAL INVESTMENTS
INSURANCE
INSURANCE, AGRICULTURAL
INSURANCE, AUTOMOBILE
INSURANCE, CREDIT
INSURANCE, DISABILITY
INSURANCE, FIRE
INSURANCE, HEALTH.
INSURANCE, HOSPITALIZATION
INSURANCE, LIFE
INSURANCE , MATERNITY
INSURANCE, SOCIAL.
INSURANCE, STRIKE
INSURANCE, UNEMPLOYMENT
INSURANCE COMPANIES
INTERGOVERNMENTAL FISCAL RELATIONS
INTERGOVERNMENTAL TAX RELATIONS
INTERNAL REVENUE
INTERNATIONAL FINANCE.
INTERNATIONAL LIQUIDITY.
INTERNATIONAL MONETARY FUND
INVESTMENT ADVISERS.
INVESTMENT BANKING
INVESTMENT CLUBS.
INVESTMENT OF PUBLIC FUNDS
INVESTMENT TRUSTS.
INVESTMENTS.
INVESTMENTS, AMERICAN.
INVESTMENTS, BRITISH
INVESTMENTS, DUTCH.
INVESTMENTS, EUROPEAN
INVESTMENTS, FOREIGN.
INVESTMENTS, FRENCH
INVESTMENTS, GERMAN
INVESTMENTS, SWEDISH
LOANS
LOANS, AMERICAN.
LOCAL FINANCE
MEDICAL FEES
METROPOLITAN FINANCE
MINTS
MONETARY UNIONS.
MONEY.
NATIONAL INCOME.
PAYMENT.
POSTAL SAVINGS BANKS
PRECIOUS METALS.
PROFITS TAX
PROGRAMME BUDGETING.
PROPERTY TAX
REAL ESTATE INVESTMENT.
REAL ESTATE INVESTMENT TRUSTS
REAL PROPERTY TAX
REGISTRATION TAX
REVENUE
SALES TAX
SAVING AND INVESTMENT.
SAVINGS BANKS
SECURITIES
SHIPPING BOUNTIES AND SUBSIDIES.
SINGLE-TAX.
SMALL BUSINESS INVESTMENT COMPANIES.
SOCIAL SECURITY TAXES
SPECIAL DRAWING RIGHTS.
STOCK COMPANIES
STOCK EXCHANGE
STOCKHOLDERS
STOCKS
SUPPORT (DOMESTIC RELATIONS)
TARIFFS.
TAX AUDITING
TAX CREDITS
TAX DEDUCTIONS
TAX EVASION.
TAX PLANNING
TAXATION
TAXATION, DOUBLE.
TAXATION, EXEMPTION FROM
TAXATION, PROGRESSIVE.
TAXATION OF ALIENS
TITHES
VALUE ADDED TAX.
WALL STREET.

Banks, exchanges, etc.

BANCO DE PORTUGAL.
BANK FOR INTERNATIONAL SETTLEMENTS.
BANK OF CANADA.
BANK OF ENGLAND.
BANK OF JAPAN.
BANQUE CENTRALE DES ETATS DE L'AFRIQUE EQUATORIALE ET DU CAMEROUN.
BANQUE DE FRANCE.
BANQUE DU ZAIRE
DEUTSCHE BUNDESBANK.
EUROPEAN INVESTMENT BANK.
GOSUDARSTVENNYI BANK SSSR.
INTERNATIONAL BANK FOR ECONOMIC COOPERATION.
INTERNATIONAL BANK FOR RECONSTRUCTION AND DEVELOPMENT.
INTERNATIONAL INVESTMENT BANK.
RESERVE BANK OF NEW ZEALAND.
SUOMEN PANKKI

GEOGRAPHY, GEOLOGY AND METEOROLOGY.

General.

AERIAL PHOTOGRAPHY IN GEOLOGY.
AERIAL PHOTOGRAPHY IN GLACIOLOGY.
AERIAL PHOTOGRAPHY IN HYDROLOGY.
AGRICULTURAL GEOGRAPHY.
ANTARCTIC REGIONS.
ANTHROPOGEOGRAPHY.
ARCTIC REGIONS.
AREA STUDIES.
ASTRONAUTICS IN EARTH SCIENCES.
ATLANTIC, THE
ATLASES.
BOGS, FENS AND MARSHES
BOUNDARIES (ESTATES)
CENTRAL PLACES.
CITIES AND TOWNS.
CLIMATOLOGY.
COAST CHANGES.
COASTS
CONSERVATION OF NATURAL RESOURCES
CONTINENTAL SHELF.
DESERTS
DIET
DISCOVERIES (IN GEOGRAPHY)
DRAINAGE.
DROUGHTS
EARTH
ECOLOGICAL RESEARCH
ECOLOGY.
ENVIRONMENTAL ENGINEERING.
ENVIRONMENTAL POLICY.
EUROPEAN ECONOMIC COMMUNITY ASSOCIATED COUNTRIES.
EXPLORERS, Portuguese.
FLOOD CONTROL
FLOODS.
GEOGRAPHICAL RESEARCH.
GEOGRAPHY.
GEOGRAPHY, ECONOMIC.
GEOGRAPHY, MATHEMATICAL.
GEOGRAPHY, POLITICAL.
GEOLOGY
GEOTHERMAL RESOURCES
GLACIAL EPOCH.
GLACIERS
GREEN BELTS
HUMAN ECOLOGY.
HYDROLOGY.
ICE
INTERNATIONAL GEOPHYSICAL YEAR, 1957-1958
ISLANDS
ISOSTASY.
LAND
LANDSCAPE.
LANDSCAPE PROTECTION.
MARINE POLLUTION.
MARINE RESOURCES.
MARINE RESOURCES CONSERVATION
METEOROLOGY
METROPOLITAN AREAS
MINERAL RESOURCES IN SUBMERGED LANDS.
MINES AND MINERAL RESOURCES
MONSOONS.
MOUNTAINS
NAMES, GEOGRAPHICAL
NATIONAL PARKS AND RESERVES
NATURAL RESOURCES
NATURE CONSERVATION
OCEAN BOTTOM.
OCEANOGRAPHY.
OIL POLLUTION OF RIVERS, HARBOURS, ETC.
PETROLEUM.
PHYSICAL GEOGRAPHY.
POLLUTION.
PROSPECTING.
RECLAMATION OF LAND
REGIONAL PLANNING.
RESERVOIRS
RIVERS.
SAND
SLOPES.
SMOG
SOIL EROSION
SOIL PHYSICS.
SOIL SURVEYS
SOILS.
STEPPES.
SUBMARINE GEOLOGY.
SURVEYING.
TOPOGRAPHIC MAPS.
TRAVEL.
TRAVELLERS, ENGLISH.
TROPICS.
WASTE LANDS
WASTE PRODUCTS.
WATER
WATER, UNDERGROUND.
WATER QUALITY MANAGEMENT
WATER RESOURCES DEVELOPMENT.
WATER SUPPLY.
YOUTH CONSERVATION CORPS.
ZONING

Rocks, minerals, etc.

GRAVEL
IRON ORES.
SALT
STRONTIUM ORES
TIN ORES

GEOGRAPHY, GEOLOGY AND METEOROLOGY.

Individual countries and places

Africa

ABIDJAN
AFRICA
AFRICA, CENTRAL
AFRICA, EAST
AFRICA, NORTH
AFRICA, SUBSAHARAN.
AFRICA, WEST
ALGERIA
ANGOLA.
ARAB COUNTRIES
BANDAMA RIVER
BENADIR
BOPHUTHATSWANA
BOTSWANA
BURUNDI
CAMEROONS
CAMEROUN.
CAPE OF GOOD HOPE
CAPE TOWN
CAPE VERDE ISLANDS
CASABLANCA.
CENTRAL AFRICAN REPUBLIC.
CHAD
CISKEIAN TERRITORIAL AUTHORITY
CONGO (BRAZZAVILLE)
CUNENE RIVER
DAHOMEY
DURBAN
EAST LONDON
EGYPT
ERITREA
ETHIOPIA
FREETOWN
GABON
GAMBIA
GAZANKULU
GHANA.
IBADAN
IVORY COAST.
JOHANNESBURG
KAFR EL-ELOW
KANO (STATE)
KENYA
KUMBA
KWAZULU (TERRITORY)
LAGOS
LESOTHO
LIBERIA
LIBYA.
LILONGWE
LUANDA.
MADAGASCAR
MADEIRA
MALAWI
MAURITANIA
MAURITIUS.
MBALE
MOROCCO
MOZAMBIQUE.
NATAL
NIGER
NIGERIA
NUBIA
OKPE
OUAGADOUGOU
OVAMBOLAND.
POINTE-NOIRE.
PORT ELIZABETH.
PORT LOUIS, MAURITIUS
PORTUGUESE GUINEA.
REUNION ISLAND
RHODESIA
RHODESIA AND NYASALAND, FEDERATION OF.
RWANDA
SAHARA
SAN PEDRO (IVORY COAST)
SÃO TOMÉ E PRINCIPE
SENEGAL
SHABA
SIERRA LEONE
SOMALILAND
SOUTH AFRICA
SOUTH WEST AFRICA
SUDAN
SWAZILAND
TANZANIA
TOGO
TRANSKEIAN TERRITORIES
TRANSVAAL
TUNISIA
UGANDA
UPPER VOLTA.
VOLTA RIVER
WIRIYAMU
ZAIRE.
ZAMBIA
ZANZIBAR
ZOMBA

America, Latin.

AMAZON VALLEY
AMERICA
AMERICA, LATIN
ANDAHUAYLAS (PROVINCE)
ANTIOQUIA
ARGENTINE REPUBLIC
BAHAMAS
BAHIA
BARBADOS
BELO HORIZONTE
BOGOTA
BOLIVIA
BRASILIA
BRAZIL.
BRITISH VIRGIN ISLANDS
BUENOS AIRES (PROVINCE)
CARABOBO
CARACAS
CARIBBEAN AREA
CARTAGENA, COLOMBIA
CATAMARCA (PROVINCE)
CHILE .
COLOMBIA
CUBA
DOMINICA
DOMINICAN REPUBLIC
DUTCH GUIANA
ECUADOR
ENTRE RIOS
FRENCH WEST INDIES
GRENADA
GUADELOUPE
GUATEMALA.
GUYANA
HAITI
HONDURAS
JAMAICA
LA PAMPA
LIMA
MARTINIQUE.
MENDOZA (PROVINCE)
MEXICO
MEXICO CITY.
NETHERLANDS ANTILLES.
NICARAGUA
PANAMA.
PARAGUAY
PERU
PUANGUE VALLEY
PUERTO RICO
RIO GRANDE DO SUL
SALVADOR
SAN JOSE DE GRACIA.
SAN JUAN, PUERTO RICO
SAN JUAN LA LAGUNA
SANTANDER (COLOMBIA)
SANTIAGO DEL ESTERO (PROVINCE)
TAMBOPATA VALLEY, PERU
TEHUANTEPEC (ISTHMUS)
TIERRA DEL FUEGO, ARGENTINE REPUBLIC
TRINIDAD AND TOBAGO
TUCUMAN (PROVINCE)
TURBIO VALLEY.
URUGUAY
VENEZUELA
VIRGIN ISLANDS
WEST INDIES.
WINDWARD ISLANDS

America, North.

ALABAMA
ALASKA
AMERICA
AMERICA, NORTH
APPALACHIAN MOUNTAINS
ARIZONA
ATLANTA
BOSTON, MASSACHUSETTS
BRITISH COLUMBIA
CALIFORNIA
CANADA
CHICAGO
COLUMBIA, MARYLAND.
COLUMBIA RIVER.
DETROIT
DISTRICT OF COLUMBIA
GEORGIA (UNITED STATES)
GREAT LAKES
GREENLAND
ILLINOIS
INDIANA
LOS ANGELES
MACKENZIE RIVER.
MANITOBA
MARYLAND
MASSACHUSETTS
MINNESOTA
MISSISSIPPI
MONTREAL
NEBRASKA
NEVADA (STATE).
NEW BRUNSWICK
NEW ENGLAND
NEW HAVEN
NEW MEXICO
NEW ORLEANS
NEW YORK (CITY).
NEW YORK (STATE)
NEWARK, NEW JERSEY
NEWFOUNDLAND
NORTH CAROLINA
ONTARIO
PENNSYLVANIA
PHILADELPHIA
PORTLAND, OREGON
QUEBEC (PROVINCE)
RHODE ISLAND
SALEM, MASSACHUSETTS
SAN FRANCISCO
SASKATOON
SOUTH CAROLINA
TEXAS
TORONTO
UNITED STATES.
VIRGINIA
WASHINGTON, D.C.
WILMINGTON, DELAWARE
WINNIPEG
WISCONSIN

Asia.

ADEN.
AFGHANISTAN
ANDHRA PRADESH
ARAB COUNTRIES
ARMENIA
ASIA
ASIA, SOUTHEAST
BAGUIO CITY
BANGALORE
BANGLADESH

GEOGRAPHY, GEOLOGY AND METEOROLOGY.

BENGAL
BENGAL, WEST
BIHAR
BODRUM.
BOMBAY (CITY)
BOMBAY (PRESIDENCY)
BOMBAY (STATE)
BORNEO
BUKHARA (OBLAST')
BURMA.
BURYAT REPUBLIC
CALCUTTA
CAMBODIA
CHELYABINSK (OBLAST')
CHINA
COLOMBO
CYPRUS
DHOFAR
DUSHANBE.
EAST (FAR EAST)
EAST (NEAR EAST)
GAZA STRIP.
GOA, DAMAN AND DIU
GUJARAT
HONG KONG
HORMUZ
HYDERABAD (CITY)
HYDERABAD (STATE)
INDIA
INDIAN OCEAN REGION
INDONESIA.
IRAN
IRAQ
IRKUTSK (OBLAST')
ISRAEL
JAPAN
JAVA
JERUSALEM
KARAKALPAK REPUBLIC
KAZAKSTAN
KIANGSI
KIRGHIZIA
KONKU
KOREA
KRASNOYARSK (KRAI)
KUSTANAI (OBLAST')
LAOS
LEBANON
LUDHIANA
MACAO
MAGNITOGORSK
MALAYA
MALAYSIA
MANCHURIA
MEKONG RIVER
MONGOLIA
MYSORE
NEPAL
NORIL'SK
OMAN
OMSK (OBLAST')
ORISSA
OSAKA
PAKISTAN
PALESTINE
PERSIAN GULF.
PHILIPPINE ISLANDS
PUNJAB
PUNJAB (INDIA)
RED SEA.
RUSSIA
RUSSIA (RSFSR)
SABAH.
SAUDI ARABIA.
SHATT AL ARAB RIVER.
SIBERIA
SIKKIM
SIND
SINGAPORE
SOVIET CENTRAL ASIA
SOVIET NORTH

SRI LANKA
SVERDLOVSK (OBLAST')
SYRIA
SZECHWAN
TAIWAN
TAJIKISTAN
TEL-AVIV
THAILAND
TOKYO
TURKESTAN
TURKEY
TURKMENISTAN
TUVA
UZBEKISTAN
VIETNAM
YEMEN
YEMEN, SOUTHERN

Australia and Oceania.

AUCKLAND
AUSTRALASIA
AUSTRALIA.
CANBERRA
CHATHAM ISLANDS
FIJI ISLANDS
FRENCH POLYNESIA
HAWAIIAN ISLANDS
IRIAN BARAT
MALAITA
MELBOURNE
MICRONESIA
NEW CALEDONIA
NEW GUINEA
NEW HEBRIDES
NEW SOUTH WALES
NEW ZEALAND
NORTHERN TERRITORY
OCEANIA
PACIFIC, THE.
PACIFIC OCEAN
PAPUA NEW GUINEA
QUEENSLAND
SAMOA
SOLOMON ISLANDS
TASMANIA
TONGA
VILA
WELLINGTON, NEW ZEALAND

Europe.

AACHEN
ALBANIA
ALSACE
ALTENA
AMSTERDAM
ANDALUSIA
ANGERS
ANTWERP
APULIA
ARKHANGEL'SK (OBLAST')
ARRAS
AUSTRIA
AUSTRIA-HUNGARY
AZERBAIJAN
AZORES
BADEN-WUERTTEMBERG
BAKU
BALKAN STATES
BALTIC, THE
BALTIC STATES
BANAT
BARCELONA
BASEL (CITY)
BASEL-LAND (CANTON)
BASEL-STADT (CANTON)
BASQUE PROVINCES
BAVARIA
BEIJERLAND
BELGIUM
BENELUX
BERLIN

BERN (CANTON)
BESANÇON.
BESSARABIA
BIELLA
BLENIO VALLEY.
BOLOGNA
BOLOGNA (PROVINCE)
BORDEAUX
BRABANT (DUCHY)
BREMEN
BRESCIA (PROVINCE)
BREST
BRITTANY
BRUNSWICK
BRUSSELS
BUDAPEST.
BUKOVINA
BULGARIA
BURGENLAND
BURGUNDY
CADIZ
CALABRIA
CASSEL
CATALONIA
CAUCASUS
CHARENTE
CHECHEN INGUSH REPUBLIC
CHUVASH REPUBLIC
CLAUSTHAL-ZELLERFELD
COLOGNE
CONSTANCE
CORSICA
CÔTE D'AZUR
COUVIN
CRIMEA
CROATIA
CZECHOSLOVAKIA.
DANUBE VALLEY
DELFT
DENMARK
DNEPROPETROVSK
DONETS BASIN
DORTMUND
DUISBURG
EFERDING
EIRIK RAUDES LAND.
EL BIERZO, SPAIN
EMILIA-ROMAGNA.
EMME VALLEY
ENTLEBUCH
ESSEN
ESSONNE (DEPARTMENT)
ESTONIA.
EUROPE
EUROPE, EASTERN
EUROPEAN ECONOMIC COMMUNITY
  COUNTRIES.
EUROPEAN FREE TRADE ASSOCIATION
  COUNTRIES
FENDELS
FERENBALM
FINLAND.
FINNMARK
FLANDERS
FLORENCE
FOS.
FRANCE
FRANKFURT AM MAIN
FREIBURG (CANTON)
FRIESLAND
FRIULI-VENEZIA GIULIA
GADER VALLEY.
GALICIA (EASTERN EUROPE)
GALICIA (SPAIN)
GDAŃSK
GENEVA (CITY)
GEORGIA
GERMANY
GERMANY, EASTERN.
GIBRALTAR
GOERLITZ
GOR'KII (OBLAST')
GRANADA (PROVINCE)

GEOGRAPHY, GEOLOGY AND METEOROLOGY.

GRAUBUENDEN
GREECE
GROSSETO (PROVINCE)
HAGUE
HAMBURG
HANOVER
HAUTE-LOIRE
HEERHUGOWAARD
HEIDELBERG
HELSINKI
HESSE
HUNGARY
ICELAND
ILLE ET VILAINE (DEPARTMENT)
IRELAND (REPUBLIC)
ISERLOHN
ITALY
IVANO-FRANKOVSK (OBLAST').
IVANOVO (OBLAST')
JURA
KABARDINOBALKARIAN REPUBLIC
KALININGRAD (OBLAST')
KALMYK REPUBLIC.
KARELIA
KHARKOV.
KIROV (OBLAST')
KREFELD
KRONSTADT
KUBAN'
KUIBYSHEV (OBLAST')
LANDSHUT
LANGUEDOC
LATVIA
LAZIO
LE VAUDREUIL.
LEIPZIG
LENINGRAD
LENINGRAD (OBLAST')
LIECHTENSTEIN
LIEGE (PROVINCE)
LIMOUSIN
LITHUANIA
LOIRE (REGION)
LOMBARDY
LUBIN
LUCERNE (CITY)
LUEBECK
LUECHOW-DANNENBERG
LUXEMBOURG
LYONS
MADRID.
MAINZ
MALTA
MANNHEIM
MARI REPUBLIC
MARSEILLES
MASSA
MEDITERRANEAN.
MEUSE (DEPARTMENT)
MILAN (CITY)
MILAN (PROVINCE)
MOLDAVIA.
MOLDAVIAN REPUBLIC
MONTPELLIER.
MOSCOW
NAESTVED
NAMUR (PROVINCE)
NANCY.
NANSA VALLEY.
NANTES
NAPLES
NAVARRE
NETHERLANDS
NORD (DEPARTMENT)
NORMANDY
NORRLAND
NORTH HOLLAND
NORTH OSSETIAN REPUBLIC
NORTH RHINE-WESTPHALIA
NORWAY
NUREMBERG
ODER RIVER.

ODESSA
OLORON-SAINTE-MARIE
OSLO
OUDENAARDE
PARIS.
PARMA (PROVINCE)
PFUNDS
PIEDMONT
PIOMBINO
PISA
POITOU
POLAND.
POLESINE
PORTUGAL
PRUSSIA
PSKOV
PSKOV (OBLAST')
REGGIO NELL'EMILIA (PROVINCE)
REUTLINGEN
RHINE
RHONE RIVER.
RIGA
ROANNE
ROME (CITY).
ROSTOCK
ROUMANIA
ROVERUD
RUHR
RUSSIA
RUSSIA (RSFSR)
SAARLAND
SAINT-ETIENNE.
SARAGOSSA (PROVINCE)
SARDINIA
SARTHE (DEPARTMENT)
SCANDICCI
SCANDINAVIA.
SCHAFFHAUSEN
SEINE-SAINT-DENIS.
SICILY
SLOVAKIA
SOLOTHURN
SPAIN
STAVROPOL' (KRAI)
STOCKHOLM
STRASBOURG.
SWEDEN
SWITZERLAND
TATAR REPUBLIC
TICINO
TOULON.
TRENTINO-ALTO ADIGE
TRIER
TRIESTE
TURIN
TUSCANY
UKRAINE
UKRAINE, WESTERN
UPPER ADIGE
URAL REGION
URI (CANTON)
UZHGOROD.
VALAIS (CANTON)
VALLE CAUDINA
VENETO
VENICE
VERDUN
VERONA
VERONA (PROVINCE)
VIENNA
VINNITSA (OBLAST')
VLADIMIR (OBLAST')
VOLGA BASIN
VOLOGDA (OBLAST')
VORARLBERG
VORONEZH (OBLAST')
WALLONIA
WARSAW
WEST FLANDERS
WESTHOEK
WHITE RUSSIA.
WUPPERTAL
YUGOSLAVIA

ZUERICH (CANTON)
ZUERICH (CITY)
ZUIDER ZEE.

United Kingdom.

ABERDEEN
ANGLESEY
BATTLE
BEDFORDSHIRE
BELFAST
BEXLEY
BIRMINGHAM
BLEDINGTON
BOWLAND FOREST.
BRENTWOOD
BRISTOL
CAMBRIDGE
CAMBRIDGESHIRE
CAMDEN.
CANTERBURY
CARDIGANSHIRE
CHELMSFORD
CHEPSTOW
CHESHIRE
CORNWALL.
COVENTRY
DEE, RIVER.
DEVONSHIRE
DROITWICH
DURHAM (COUNTY)
EDINBURGH
ELY
ESSEX
FLINTSHIRE
GAINSBOROUGH
GATESHEAD
GLENROTHES.
GRIMSBY
HAMPSHIRE
HAMPSTEAD
HILLINGDON
HOXTON
HULL
HUMBERSIDE
IPSWICH
IRELAND.
IRELAND, NORTHERN
IRISH SEA.
KENSINGTON AND CHELSEA
KIRKBY
LAKE DISTRICT, UNITED KINGDOM.
LAMBETH
LANCASHIRE
LEEDS
LEICESTER
LEICESTERSHIRE
LINCOLNSHIRE
LIVERPOOL
LONDON
MAGHULL
MAIN, RIVER (NORTHERN IRELAND).
MALDON
MANCHESTER
MANNINGTREE
MERIONETH
MYDDLE
NEW DURHAM
NEW WINDSOR
NEWCASTLE-UPON-TYNE
NEWRY
NORTHAMPTON
NORTHUMBERLAND
NOTTINGHAM
OLDHAM
OXFORD
OXFORDSHIRE
PEAK NATIONAL PARK.
PENNINE CHAIN.
PETERBOROUGH
PETERLEE
RINGMER
ROTHERHAM

GEOGRAPHY, GEOLOGY AND METEOROLOGY.

RUGELEY
SCOTLAND
SHEFFIELD
SHETLAND ISLANDS
SHROPSHIRE
SKELMERSDALE
SKYE
SOUTH SHIELDS
SOUTHAMPTON
STAFFORDSHIRE
STIRLING
SUNDERLAND
THAMESDOWN
TYNESIDE
UNITED KINGDOM
WALES
WALTHAM FOREST
WANDSWORTH
WANSTEAD
WARWICKSHIRE
WESTMINSTER
WHITEHAVEN
WIDNES
WORCESTERSHIRE
YORKSHIRE

HISTORY.

General.

ARCHAEOLOGY.
ARCHAEOLOGY, INDUSTRIAL
ARCHIVES
CHURCH HISTORY.
CIVILIZATION.
CIVILIZATION, MODERN.
CIVILIZATION, OCCIDENTAL.
COMMUNISTIC SETTLEMENTS
CROWN LANDS
CRUSADES.
ECONOMIC HISTORY.
FEUDALISM.
HISTORIANS, AMERICAN.
HISTORIANS, POLISH
HISTORICAL LIBRARIES
HISTORICAL SOCIETIES
HISTORIOGRAPHY.
HISTORY
HISTORY, LOCAL
HISTORY, MODERN
HISTORY, UNIVERSAL.
LAND SETTLEMENT
LAND TENURE.
LAND TITLES
MANORS
MILITARY HISTORY
MOHAMMEDAN EMPIRE.
NAVAL HISTORY
PALAEOGRAPHY, ITALIAN.
PAPACY
PEASANT UPRISINGS.
SERFDOM
SOCIAL HISTORY.
TITHES
TWENTIETH CENTURY
TWENTY-FIRST CENTURY
VILLEINAGE

International (including wars).

CRIMEAN WAR, 1853-1856.
EUROPEAN WAR, 1914-1918.
HUNDRED YEARS' WAR, 1339-1453.
INDUS WATERS TREATY, 1960.
ISRAEL-ARAB CONFLICT, 1948- .
ISRAEL-ARAB WAR, 1967.
ISRAEL-ARAB WAR, 1973.
ITALO-ETHIOPIAN WAR, 1935-1936.
LITTLE ENTENTE, 1920-1939.
MUNICH FOUR POWER AGREEMENT, 1938.
NORTHERN WAR, 1700-1721.
PEARL HARBOR, ATTACK ON, 1941.
RECONSTRUCTION (1939-1951)
RUSSO-FINNISH WAR, 1939-1940.
RUSSO-JAPANESE WAR, 1904-1905.
SOUTH AFRICAN WAR, 1899-1902
STRAITS QUESTION.
VERSAILLES, TREATY OF, JUNE 28, 1919 (GERMANY).
VIETNAMESE WARS, 1945- .
WORLD WAR, 1939-1945.

American territories.

AMERICAN LOYALISTS.
DORR REBELLION, 1842.
FRONTIER AND PIONEER LIFE
PLANTATION LIFE
RECONSTRUCTION (UNITED STATES).
SECESSION

Asiatic territories.

ARMENIAN QUESTION
EASTERN QUESTION (FAR EAST)
EASTERN QUESTION (NEAR EAST).
INDIA-PAKISTAN CONFLICT, 1971.
KOREAN REUNIFICATION QUESTION (1945-)
TAIPING REBELLION, 1850-1864.

European territories.

ANSCHLUSS MOVEMENT, 1918-1938.
ANTINAZI MOVEMENT.
BERLIN QUESTION (1945-).
BYZANTINE EMPIRE
CONCORDAT OF 1929 (ITALY).
CONCORDAT OF 1933 (GERMANY).
DENAZIFICATION.
EIRIK RAUDES LAND.
FLEMISH MOVEMENT.
GERMAN REUNIFICATION QUESTION (1949-).
GREECE, ANCIENT
HANSA TOWNS.
HANSEATIC LEAGUE.
HOLY ROMAN EMPIRE
JACOBINS.
POLISH QUESTION.
RENAISSANCE
ROME, ANCIENT
SANSCULOTTES.
SCHLESWIG-HOLSTEIN QUESTION.

United Kingdom.

CHARTISM.
FENIANS
GENERAL STRIKE, UNITED KINGDOM, 1926.
HERALDRY
HIDAGE.
INCLOSURES.
INVERGORDON MUTINY, 1931.
IRISH QUESTION.
IRON AGE.
LEVELLERS.
PEWTER, BRITISH.
POTTERY
SWORDS.

Colonial companies.

BRITISH SOUTH AFRICA COMPANY.
DUTCH WEST INDIA COMPANY.
EAST INDIA COMPANY.

LANGUAGE, LITERATURE AND THE ARTS.

Language.

AFRICAN LANGUAGES.
BILINGUALISM.
CHINESE LANGUAGE
CREOLE DIALECTS
ENGLISH LANGUAGE
ENGLISH LANGUAGE IN THE UNITED STATES.
GENERATIVE GRAMMAR.
GERMAN LANGUAGE
GRAMMAR, COMPARATIVE AND GENERAL.
HYPOTHESIS.
ITALIAN LANGUAGE
LANGUAGE AND LANGUAGES.
LANGUAGES
LANGUAGES, MODERN
LINGUISTIC CHANGE.
LINGUISTIC GEOGRAPHY.
LINGUISTICS.
MALAY LANGUAGE
MEANING.
MULTILINGUALISM.
NEGRO-ENGLISH DIALECTS.
PSYCHOLINGUISTICS.
ROMANCE LANGUAGES.
SOCIOLINGUISTICS.
SPEECH
WELSH LANGUAGE

Literature.

AFRICAN LITERATURE
AFRICANS IN LITERATURE.
AMERICAN PERIODICALS.
ARABIC LITERATURE
AUSTRIAN LITERATURE
AUSTRIAN WIT AND HUMOUR.
AUTHORS, DUTCH.
AUTHORS, GERMAN.
AUTHORSHIP.
AUTOGRAPHS
BELGIAN NEWSPAPERS.
CANADIAN PERIODICALS.
CHILDREN'S PERIODICALS, BELGIAN.
CHILDREN'S PERIODICALS, FRENCH.
CHINESE LITERATURE
COMMUNISM AND LITERATURE.
DECADENCE IN LITERATURE.
ENGLISH LITERATURE
ENGLISH NEWSPAPERS.
ENGLISH PERIODICALS.
EUROPEAN NEWSPAPERS
EUROPEAN PERIODICALS
FRENCH FICTION.
FRENCH LITERATURE
FRENCH NEWSPAPERS.
FRENCH PERIODICALS.
GERMAN DRAMA.
GERMAN NEWSPAPERS.
GERMAN PERIODICALS.
ITALIAN NEWSPAPERS.
ITALIAN PERIODICALS.
JOURNALISM.
KOREAN LITERATURE.
LABOUR AND LABOURING CLASSES IN LITERATURE.
LEGENDS
LITERARY SOCIETIES
LITERATURE.
LITERATURE, IMMORAL.
LITERATURE AND SOCIETY.
NEWSPAPERS
POLISH LITERATURE.
POLITICAL POETRY, ENGLISH.
POLITICAL POETRY, PORTUGUESE.
POLITICAL SATIRE, AUSTRIAN.
POLITICAL SATIRE, ITALIAN.
POLITICAL SATIRE, RUSSIAN.

LAW.

POLITICS IN LITERATURE.
PRESS.
ROMANTICISM.
RUSSIAN LITERATURE.
RUSSIAN PERIODICALS.
SATIRE, RUSSIAN.
SPANISH PERIODICALS.
STATE ENCOURAGEMENT OF SCIENCE, LITERATURE AND ART.
UNDERGROUND LITERATURE.

The Arts.

ARCHITECTURE
ART.
ART, PRIMITIVE.
ART AND SOCIETY.
ART AND STATE
ART OBJECTS.
ARTS, THE
CARICATURES AND CARTOONS
COMMUNISM AND THE ARTS.
CULTURAL PROPERTY, PROTECTION OF.
FOLK SONGS, BRITISH.
MINIATURE PAINTINGS, INDIC
MINIATURE PAINTINGS, PERSIAN
MUSIC AND SOCIETY.
MUSIC FESTIVALS.
ORCHESTRA.
PERFORMING ARTS
POLITICAL BALLADS AND SONGS, ITALIAN.
PREUSSISCHE AKADEMIE DER KÜNSTE.
RADIO BROADCASTING.
STATE ENCOURAGEMENT OF SCIENCE, LITERATURE AND ART.
THEATRE.
THEATRE AND SOCIETY.

LAW.(including INTERNATIONAL LAW).

General.

APPELLATE PROCEDURE
BURDEN OF PROOF
CONFIDENTIAL COMMUNICATIONS
CONTEMPT OF COURT
COSTS (LAW)
COURTS
EUROPEAN CONVENTION ON HUMAN RIGHTS.
EVIDENCE (LAW)
EXTRAORDINARY REMEDIES
HONESTY.
JUDGEMADE LAW
JUDICIAL ASSISTANCE
JUDICIAL REVIEW
JUDICIAL STATISTICS
JURISDICTION
JURISPRUDENCE.
JURY
JUSTICE.
JUSTICE, ADMINISTRATION OF
JUSTICE AND POLITICS
JUSTICES OF THE PEACE
LAW.
LAW, COMPARATIVE.
LAW AND FACT
LAW AND POLITICS.
LAW ENFORCEMENT
LAW REFORM
LAW REPORTS, DIGESTS, ETC.
LEGAL AID.
MUNICIPAL COURTS
NOTARIES
OBSCENITY (LAW)
RULE OF LAW
SEX AND LAW
SOCIAL LEGISLATION
SOCIOLOGICAL JURISPRUDENCE.
STATUTES
WARRANTS (LAW)
WITNESSES

Public law.

ABUSE OF ADMINISTRATIVE POWER
ADMINISTATIVE LAW
ADMINISTRATIVE COURTS
ADMINISTRATIVE DISCRETION
ADMINISTRATIVE LAW
ADMINISTRATIVE REMEDIES.
ADMINISTRATIVE RESPONSIBILITY
AGRICULTURAL LAWS AND LEGISLATION
COMPENSATION (LAW)
CONSTITUTIONAL COURTS
CONSTITUTIONAL LAW.
ECONOMIC LEGISLATION
EDUCATIONAL LAW AND LEGISLATION
ELECTION LAW
EMIGRATION AND IMMIGRATION LAW
EMINENT DOMAIN
ENVIRONMENTAL LAW.
IMPEACHMENTS
INITIATIVE, RIGHT OF
LEGISLATION
LEGISLATIVE BODIES.
MEDICAL LAWS AND LEGISLATION
MILITARY LAW
MISCONDUCT IN OFFICE
NARCOTIC LAWS
PHARMACY
POLITICAL CRIMES AND OFFENCES
POOR LAWS
PRESS LAW
PUBLIC POLICY (LAW)
SEDITION
TREASON
UNJUST ENRICHMENT
WATER

Civil law and procedure.

ACCIDENT LAW
CIVIL LAW
CIVIL PROCEDURE.
COMPENSATION (LAW)
CONSENT (LAW)
CONVEYANCING
DAMAGES
DESERTION AND NON-SUPPORT
DILAPIDATIONS.
DOMESTIC RELATIONS
EQUITY
EXECUTIONS (LAW)
HUSBAND AND WIFE
ILLEGITIMACY.
INHERITANCE AND SUCCESSION
LAND TENURE.
LANDLORD AND TENANT
LIBEL AND SLANDER
MARRIAGE LAW
MARRIED WOMEN
MATRIMONIAL ACTIONS
MEDICAL JURISPRUDENCE.
NECESSITY (LAW)
NEGLIGENCE
OBLIGATIONS (LAW)
PARENT AND CHILD (LAW)
PARTIES TO ACTIONS
PERSONAL INJURIES
PERSONAL PROPERTY.
PRIVACY, RIGHT OF.
PROBATE LAW AND PRACTICE
SELF-DEFENCE (LAW)
SELF-INCRIMINATION
SMALL CLAIMS COURTS.
SUPPORT (DOMESTIC RELATIONS)
TORTS
TRUSTS AND TRUSTEES
WILLS

Commercial, industrial and labour laws.

ARBITRATION AND AWARD
BANKING LAW
BANKRUPTCY
BILLS OF LADING.
BUSINESS LAW
COMMERCIAL CRIMES
COMMERCIAL LAW
CONCESSIONS
CONTRACTS
COPYRIGHT
CORPORATION LAW
DESIGN PROTECTION
INDUSTRIAL LAWS AND LEGISLATION.
LABOUR COURTS
LABOUR LAWS AND LEGISLATION
LIQUIDATION
MINING LAW.
PARTNERSHIP
PATENT LAWS AND LEGISLATION
PETROLEUM LAW AND LEGISLATION.
SALES
USURY LAWS

Criminal law and procedure.

BREACH OF THE PEACE
CAPITAL PUNISHMENT
CONSPIRACY
CONVICT LABOUR
CRIMINAL INVESTIGATION
CRIMINAL JUSTICE, ADMINISTRATION OF
CRIMINAL LAW
CRIMINAL LIABILITY
CRIMINAL PROCEDURE
DEFENCE (CRIMINAL PROCEDURE)
EVIDENCE, CRIMINAL
EXECUTIONS AND EXECUTIONERS
FINES (PENALTIES)
FRAUD
LIABILITY FOR ROAD ACCIDENTS.
OFFENCES AGAINST PROPERTY
OFFENCES AGAINST THE PERSON
PUBLIC DEFENDERS
RAPE
SECURITY (LAW).
SENTENCES (CRIMINAL PROCEDURE)
SHOPLIFTING.
TRIALS (POLITICAL CRIMES AND OFFENCES)
TRIALS (RACIAL DEFAMATION)
TRIALS (RIOT)
TRIALS (TREASON)

Ecclesiastical law.

INTERDICT (CANON LAW).

Foreign law.

ADAT LAW
LASTENAUSGLEICH (1949-).
LAW, MOHAMMEDAN

Conflict of laws, civil and criminal.

COPYRIGHT, INTERNATIONAL.
EXTRADITION.
INTERNATIONAL LAW, PRIVATE

International law.

AGGRESSION (INTERNATIONAL LAW).
ARBITRATION, INTERNATIONAL.
CHILDREN (INTERNATIONAL LAW).
CIVIL RIGHTS (INTERNATIONAL LAW).
CIVIL WAR.
CONSULAR LAW.
CONTRACTS (INTERNATIONAL LAW).
COURT OF JUSTICE OF THE EUROPEAN COMMUNITIES.

LAW.

CRIMES ABOARD AIRCRAFT
CRIMINAL JURISDICTION.
DIPLOMATIC NEGOTIATIONS IN INTERNATIONAL DISPUTES.
DUE PROCESS OF LAW.
FREEDOM OF MOVEMENT.
GENEVA CONVENTIONS.
GUERRILLAS (INTERNATIONAL LAW).
HIJACKING OF AIRCRAFT.
INDUS WATERS TREATY, 1960.
INTERNATIONAL AND MUNICIPAL LAW
INTERNATIONAL LAW.
INTERVENTION (INTERNATIONAL LAW).
JURISDICTION (INTERNATIONAL LAW).
JURISDICTION OVER AIRCRAFT
LABOUR LAWS AND LEGISLATION, INTERNATIONAL.
MARITIME LAW.
OCEAN BOTTOM.
PACIFIC SETTLEMENT OF INTERNATIONAL DISPUTES.
PERSONS (INTERNATIONAL LAW).
PROTECTORATES.
RECOGNITION (INTERNATIONAL LAW).
RESTITUTION AND INDEMNIFICATION CLAIMS (1933-)
SANCTIONS (INTERNATIONAL LAW).
SELF-DEFENCE (INTERNATIONAL LAW).
SOVEREIGNTY.
TERRITORIAL WATERS
TREATIES.
TREATY MAKING POWER.
WAR (INTERNATIONAL LAW).

MATHEMATICS AND STATISTICS.

AGGREGATES.
ALGORITHMS.
ARTIFICIAL INTELLIGENCE.
CLUSTER ANALYSIS.
COMPUTER SIMULATION.
COMPUTER STORAGE DEVICES
COMPUTERS.
CONTROL THEORY.
CURVES.
CYBERNETICS.
DEMOGRAPHY.
DIGITAL COMPUTER SIMULATION.
DISTRIBUTION (PROBABILITY THEORY).
DIVORCE
DYNAMIC PROGRAMMING
ECONOMICS, MATHEMATICAL.
EDUCATIONAL STATISTICS.
EQUATIONS.
EQUATIONS, SIMULTANEOUS.
FACTOR ANALYSIS.
FECUNDITY.
FORTRAN (COMPUTER PROGRAMME LANGUAGE).
FUNCTIONS, TRANSCENDENTAL.
GAMES, THEORY OF.
GEOGRAPHY, MATHEMATICAL.
GRAPH THEORY.
GROUPS, THEORY OF.
INDUSTRIAL STATISTICS
INTEGER PROGRAMMING.
JUDICIAL STATISTICS
LEAST SQUARES.
LINEAR PROGRAMMING.
MARKOV PROCESSES.
MATHEMATICAL OPTIMIZATION.
MATHEMATICS.
MEDICAL STATISTICS.
METRIC SYSTEM.
MODEL THEORY.
MONTE CARLO METHOD.
MORTALITY.
POPULATION FORECASTING.
PROBABILITIES.

PROGRAMMING (ELECTRONIC COMPUTERS).
PROGRAMMING (MATHEMATICS).
REGISTERS OF BIRTH, ETC.
REGRESSION ANALYSIS.
SAMPLING (STATISTICS).
SET FUNCTIONS.
SET THEORY.
SIMULATION METHODS.
STATISTICAL DECISION.
STATISTICS
STOCHASTIC PROCESSES.
SYSTEM ANALYSIS.
SYSTEM THEORY.
TIME SERIES ANALYSIS.
VITAL STATISTICS
WEIGHTS AND MEASURES

MILITARY AND NAVAL SCIENCE.

AIR RAID PRECAUTIONS.
AIR WARFARE
ARMAMENTS.
ARMED FORCES.
ARMIES
ATOMIC BOMB
ATOMIC WEAPONS.
BIOLOGICAL WARFARE.
BLOCKADE.
BOMBING, AERIAL.
BORDER PATROLS
CHEMICAL WARFARE.
CIVILIAN DEFENCE.
DEFENCE CONTRACTS
DEFENCES, NATIONAL.
DETERRENCE (STRATEGY).
EXSERVICEMEN
GUERRILLA WARFARE.
INTERCONTINENTAL BALLISTIC MISSILES.
JEWS AS SOLDIERS
MILITARISM
MILITARY ASSISTANCE, AMERICAN
MILITARY ASSISTANCE, BELGIAN
MILITARY BASES, AMERICAN
MILITARY HISTORY
MILITARY LAW
MILITARY SERVICE, COMPULSORY
MUNITIONS.
MUTINY
NAPALM
NAVAL ART AND SCIENCE.
NAVAL HISTORY
NAVAL MUSEUMS.
NAVAL TACTICS.
NEGROES AS SOLDIERS.
PENSIONS, MILITARY
POLITICS AND WAR.
PRISONERS OF WAR, GERMAN.
PRISONERS OF WAR, NORWEGIAN.
PRISONERS OF WAR, RUSSIAN.
PROJECTILES, INCENDIARY
PSYCHOLOGY, MILITARY.
SOCIOLOGY, MILITARY.
SOLDIERS
STRATEGY.
WAR.

PHILOSOPHY AND RELIGION.

Philosophy.

ACT (PHILOSOPHY).
AESTHETICS
ANALYSIS (PHILOSOPHY).
BELIEF AND DOUBT.
BUSINESS ETHICS.
CAUSATION.
CHANCE.
CHRISTIAN ETHICS
COMMUNIST ETHICS.

CONDUCT OF LIFE.
DIALECTIC.
ENLIGHTENMENT.
ETHICAL RELATIVISM.
ETHICS.
EXISTENTIALISM.
FREE THOUGHT.
FREE WILL AND DETERMINISM.
FRIENDSHIP.
GENEROSITY.
HUMANISM
HUMANISTIC ETHICS.
IDEALISM.
IDEOLOGY.
JOY AND SORROW.
JUDGMENT.
KNOWLEDGE, THEORY OF.
LIFE.
LOGIC.
LOGIC, SYMBOLIC AND MATHEMATICAL.
LONELINESS.
LOVE.
MATERIALISM.
MEANING.
METAPHYSICS.
METHODOLOGY.
MIND AND BODY.
MORAL EDUCATION.
NEOSCHOLASTICISM.
NOMINALISM.
OBEDIENCE.
PERSONALISM
PHILOSOPHICAL ANTHROPOLOGY.
PHILOSOPHY.
PHILOSOPHY, AMERICAN.
PHILOSOPHY, ARMENIAN.
PHILOSOPHY, BRITISH.
PHILOSOPHY, CHINESE.
PHILOSOPHY, ITALIAN.
PHILOSOPHY, MODERN.
PHILOSOPHY, ROUMANIAN.
PHILOSOPHY, RUSSIAN.
PHILOSOPHY, URUGUAYAN.
PHILOSOPHY, WHITE RUSSIAN.
POLITICAL ETHICS.
POSITIVISM.
REASONING.
RELATIVITY.
SCHOLASTICISM.
SCIENCE AND ETHICS.
SOCIAL ETHICS.
SPACE AND TIME.
STRUCTURE (PHILOSOPHY).
TIME.
UTILITARIANISM.
WORTH.

Religion.

AFRICAN METHODIST EPISCOPAL CHURCH.
ANTICLERICALISM
ATHEISM.
BAPTISTS
BENEDICTINES IN THE UNITED KINGDOM.
BIBLE, NEW TESTAMENT
BRAHMANS.
BRITISH COUNCIL OF CHURCHES
CALVINISM
CARDINALS
CATHOLIC ACTION
CATHOLIC CHURCH
CATHOLIC CHURCH IN BRAZIL.
CATHOLIC CHURCH IN GERMANY.
CATHOLIC CHURCH IN IRELAND.
CATHOLIC CHURCH IN LATIN AMERICA.
CATHOLIC CHURCH IN MOZAMBIQUE.
CATHOLIC CHURCH IN POLAND.
CATHOLIC CHURCH IN SWITZERLAND

POLITICAL SCIENCE, POLITICS AND GOVERNMENT.

CATHOLIC CHURCH IN THE ARGENTINE REPUBLIC.
CATHOLICS IN ITALY.
CATHOLICS IN MEXICO.
CATHOLICS IN SICILY.
CATHOLICS IN SPAIN.
CATHOLICS IN SWITZERLAND
CATHOLICS IN THE UNITED KINGDOM.
CATHOLICS IN THE UNITED STATES.
CHRISTIAN ETHICS
CHRISTIAN SCIENCE
CHRISTIANITY.
CHRISTIANITY AND ECONOMICS.
CHRISTIANITY AND INTERNATIONAL AFFAIRS.
CHRISTIANITY AND OTHER RELIGIONS.
CHRISTIANITY AND POLITICS.
CHRISTIANITY IN AFRICA.
CHRISTIANS IN CHINA.
CHRISTIANS IN IRELAND.
CHURCH AND ECONOMICS.
CHURCH AND LABOUR
CHURCH AND RACE PROBLEMS
CHURCH AND SOCIAL PROBLEMS.
CHURCH AND STATE
CHURCH AND STATE IN BRAZIL.
CHURCH AND STATE IN COMMUNIST COUNTRIES.
CHURCH AND STATE IN FRANCE.
CHURCH AND STATE IN IRELAND.
CHURCH AND STATE IN ITALY.
CHURCH AND STATE IN LATIN AMERICA.
CHURCH AND STATE IN MALTA.
CHURCH AND STATE IN MEXICO.
CHURCH AND STATE IN RUSSIA.
CHURCH AND STATE IN SARDINIA.
CHURCH AND STATE IN THE ARGENTINE REPUBLIC.
CHURCH AND STATE IN THE UNITED KINGDOM.
CHURCH AND STATE IN TONGA.
CHURCH AND STATE IN ZAIRE.
CHURCH AND UNDERDEVELOPED AREAS.
CHURCH HISTORY.
CHURCH PROPERTY
CHURCH SCHOOLS
CLERGY
COMMUNISM AND CHRISTIANITY
COMMUNISM AND ISLAM.
COMMUNISM AND RELIGION.
CONCORDAT OF 1929 (ITALY).
CONCORDAT OF 1933 (GERMANY).
CONFUCIUS AND CONFUCIANISM.
DUKHOBORS.
FREE CHURCH OF SCOTLAND.
FRIENDS, SOCIETY OF
FRIENDS, SOCIETY OF, AND WORLD POLITICS.
GALLICANISM.
GOD.
JESUITS IN LATVIA.
JUDAISM.
KORAN.
LUTHERAN CHURCH IN DENMARK.
LUTHERAN CHURCH IN FINLAND.
LUTHERAN CHURCH IN RUSSIA.
METHODISM.
METHODIST CHURCH IN THE UNITED KINGDOM.
METHODIST CHURCH IN TONGA.
METHODISTS IN THE UNITED KINGDOM.
MISSIONARIES, AMERICAN.
MISSIONS
MISSIONS, MEDICAL
MOHAMMEDANISM.
MOHAMMEDANISM AND STATE.
MOHAMMEDANS IN INDIA.
MOHAMMEDANS IN NIGERIA.
MOHAMMEDANS IN THE GAMBIA.

MOHAMMEDANS IN THE PHILIPPINE ISLANDS.
MONASTICISM AND RELIGIOUS ORDERS
OPUS DEI.
PAPACY
PASTORAL COUNSELLING.
PASTORAL THEOLOGY.
PENTECOSTAL CHURCHES
PRESS, CATHOLIC.
PURITANS.
QUIETISM.
RADIO IN RELIGION.
RASKOLNIKS.
REFUGEES, RELIGIOUS.
RELIGION
RELIGION AND POLITICS.
RELIGION AND SOCIOLOGY.
RELIGION AND STATE
RELIGIONS.
RELIGIOUS EDUCATION
REVOLUTION (THEOLOGY).
SCIENTOLOGY.
SECTS
SHAKERS.
SHAMANISM.
SOCIALISM, CHRISTIAN.
SOCIALISM AND CATHOLIC CHURCH.
SOCIALISM AND RELIGION.
SOCIOLOGY, CHRISTIAN
SUFISM.
TELEVISION IN RELIGION.
THEISM.
TRADE UNIONS, CATHOLIC
UNIATE CHURCH.
WHITSUNTIDE.
WOMEN IN CHRISTIANITY.
WORLD COUNCIL OF CHURCHES.

POLITICAL SCIENCE, POLITICS AND GOVERNMENT.

General.

ADMINISTRATION.
ADMINISTRATIVE ACTS
ADMINISTRATIVE AGENCIES
ADMINISTRATIVE AND POLITICAL DIVISIONS
ADMINISTRATIVE PROCEDURE.
ALIENS
AMENDMENTS (PARLIAMENTARY PRACTICE).
ANARCHISM AND ANARCHISTS.
ANTICOMMUNIST MOVEMENTS
ANTISEMITISM.
APPANAGE.
ART AND STATE
ASSASSINATION.
ATOMIC WEAPONS AND DISARMAMENT.
ATROCITIES
AUTHORITARIANISM.
AUTHORITY.
BALANCE OF POWER.
BUREAUCRACY.
BUSINESS AND POLITICS
CABINET MINISTERS
CABINET SYSTEM
CAMPAIGN FUNDS.
CENSORSHIP.
CENTRE PARTIES
CHILDREN AND POLITICS.
CHRISTIANITY AND INTERNATIONAL AFFAIRS.
CHRISTIANITY AND POLITICS.
CHURCH AND STATE
CIVICS, AMERICAN.
CIVICS, NORTHERN IRISH.
CIVIL RIGHTS.
CIVIL SERVICE

CIVIL SUPREMACY OVER THE MILITARY
COALITION GOVERNMENTS.
COLONIES.
COLONIES IN AFRICA.
COMMITTEES.
COMMUNISM.
COMMUNISM AND CHRISTIANITY
COMMUNISM AND EDUCATION.
COMMUNISM AND ISLAM.
COMMUNISM AND LITERATURE.
COMMUNISM AND RELIGION.
COMMUNISM AND THE ARTS.
COMMUNISM AND ZIONISM.
COMMUNISM IN EDUCATION
COMMUNIST PARTY PURGES.
COMMUNIST REVISIONISM.
COMMUNIST STATE.
COMMUNIST STRATEGY.
COMMUNISTIC SETTLEMENTS
COMMUNISTS
COMMUNITY POWER.
CONCENTRATION CAMPS
CONFEDERATION OF STATES.
CONFLICT OF INTERESTS (PUBLIC OFFICE)
CONSERVATISM.
CONSTITUTIONS.
CONSTITUTIONS, STATE
CORPORATE STATE.
CORRUPTION (IN POLITICS)
COUNTERREVOLUTIONS
COUPS D'ETAT.
DECENTRALIZATION IN GOVERNMENT.
DEMOCRACY.
DIPLOMACY.
DIPLOMATIC DOCUMENTS.
DISARMAMENT.
ECONOMIES OF SCALE.
EDUCATION AND STATE.
ELECTIONS.
ELITE.
ESPIONAGE, RUSSIAN
EUROPEAN COOPERATION.
EUROPEAN FEDERATION.
EXECUTIVE ADVISORY BODIES
EXECUTIVE POWER
FASCISM.
FEDERAL GOVERNMENT.
FRIENDS, SOCIETY OF, AND WORLD POLITICS.
GENOCIDE
GEOGRAPHY, POLITICAL.
GOVERNMENT, COMPARATIVE.
GOVERNMENT, RESISTANCE TO.
GOVERNMENT AND THE PRESS
GOVERNMENT INFORMATION
GOVERNMENT LIABILITY
GOVERNMENT PUBLICITY
GOVERNMENTAL INVESTIGATIONS
GREAT POWERS.
GUERRILLAS
HIGHER EDUCATION AND STATE
HOME RULE
IMPEACHMENTS
IMPERIALISM.
INDEPENDENT REGULATORY COMMISSIONS
INDIVIDUALISM.
INDUSTRY AND STATE.
INITIATIVE, RIGHT OF
INSURGENCY
INTELLIGENCE SERVICE
INTERNAL SECURITY
INTERNATIONAL AGENCIES.
INTERNATIONAL AGENCIES IN EUROPE
INTERNATIONAL COOPERATION.
INTERNATIONAL OBLIGATIONS.
INTERNATIONAL ORGANIZATION.
INTERNATIONAL POLICE.
INTERNATIONAL RELATIONS.
INTERNATIONALISM.

POLITICAL SCIENCE, POLITICS AND GOVERNMENT.

JUDICIAL REVIEW OF ADMINISTRATIVE ACTS
JUSTICE AND POLITICS
KINGS AND RULERS
LAW AND POLITICS.
LEADERSHIP.
LEGISLATORS.
LIBERALISM.
LIBERTY.
LIBERTY OF INFORMATION
LIBERTY OF SPEECH
LIBERTY OF THE PRESS
LOBBYING.
LOBBYISTS
LOCAL GOVERNMENT.
LOCAL GOVERNMENT OFFICIALS AND EMPLOYEES
MARXISM.
MEDIATION, INTERNATIONAL.
METROPOLITAN GOVERNMENT
MILITARISM
MILITARY SERVICE, COMPULSORY
MINORITIES.
MISCONDUCT IN OFFICE
MOHAMMEDANISM AND STATE.
MONARCHY.
MOVING PICTURES IN PROPAGANDA.
MUNICIPAL GOVERNMENT
MUNICIPAL POWERS AND SERVICES BEYOND CORPORATE LIMITS
MUNICIPAL RESEARCH.
MUNICIPAL SERVICES
NATIONALISM.
NATIONALISM AND SOCIALISM.
NEUTRALITY.
OFFICIAL SECRETS
OMBUDSMAN.
OPPOSITION (POLITICAL SCIENCE).
PACIFIC SETTLEMENT OF INTERNATIONAL DISPUTES.
PACIFISM.
PARLIAMENTARY PRACTICE.
PARTY DISCIPLINE
PASSIVE RESISTANCE.
PATRIOTISM
PATRONAGE, POLITICAL
PEACE.
PEACE TREATIES
PEACE SOCIETIES.
PEACEFUL CHANGE (INTERNATIONAL RELATIONS).
PEASANT UPRISINGS.
PLEBISCITE
POLICE, POLITICAL AND SECRET
POLITICAL CLUBS
POLITICAL CONVENTIONS.
POLITICAL CRIMES AND OFFENCES
POLITICAL ETHICS.
POLITICAL PARTICIPATION.
POLITICAL PARTIES.
POLITICAL PRISONERS
POLITICAL PSYCHOLOGY.
POLITICAL SCIENCE.
POLITICAL SCIENCE RESEARCH.
POLITICAL SOCIALIZATION.
POLITICAL SOCIOLOGY.
POLITICS, PRACTICAL.
POLITICS AND EDUCATION.
POLITICS AND WAR.
POLITICS IN LITERATURE.
POLITICS IN MOVING PICTURES.
POPULAR FRONTS.
POPULATION TRANSFERS
PRECEDENCE
PREFECTS (FRENCH GOVERNMENT).
PREFERENTIAL BALLOT.
PRESIDENTS.
PRESS AND POLITICS
PRESSURE GROUPS
PROGRESS.
PROLETARIAT.
PROPAGANDA.
PROPORTIONAL REPRESENTATION.

PUBLIC RELATIONS AND POLITICS.
PUBLIC SERVICE.
RADICALISM.
RADIO IN POLITICS
RADIO IN PROPAGANDA.
REFERENDUM
REFUGEES, AFRICAN.
REFUGEES, ARAB.
REFUGEES, DUTCH
REFUGEES, AUSTRIAN.
REFUGEES, GERMAN.
REFUGEES, JEWISH.
REFUGEES, RUSSIAN.
REGICIDES.
REGIONALISM.
REGIONALISM (INTERNATIONAL ORGANIZATION).
RELIGION AND POLITICS.
RELIGION AND STATE
REPRESENTATIVE GOVERNMENT AND REPRESENTATION.
REVOLUTIONISTS.
REVOLUTIONS.
RIGHT AND LEFT (POLITICAL SCIENCE).
SALE OF PUBLIC OFFICE
SCIENCE AND STATE.
SECURITY, INTERNATIONAL.
SELF-DETERMINATION, NATIONAL.
SEPARATION OF POWERS
SOCIALISM.
SOCIALISM, CHRISTIAN.
SOCIALISM AND CATHOLIC CHURCH.
SOCIALISM AND EDUCATION.
SOCIALISM AND RELIGION.
SOCIALISM AND YOUTH.
SOCIALISTS.
SOVIETS
SPHERES OF INFLUENCE.
STATE, THE.
STATE GOVERNMENTS
STATE SUCCESSION
STATES, NEW.
STATES, SMALL.
STATESMEN.
SUBVERSIVE ACTIVITIES.
SUFFRAGE
TECHNOLOGY AND STATE.
TELEVISION IN POLITICS
TERRORISM.
TITLES OF HONOUR AND NOBILITY
TOTALITARIANISM.
TRADE UNIONS AND COMMUNISM
TREASON
TREATIES.
TREATY MAKING POWER.
TRUST TERRITORIES
UTOPIAS.
VOTING.
VOTING RESEARCH
WAR.
WAR AND EMERGENCY POWERS
WAR AND SOCIALISM.
WAR CRIMES.
WOMEN AND SOCIALISM.
WOMEN IN POLITICS.
WORLD POLITICS.

Particular countries, nationalities, parties, organizations, etc.

ACCION NACIONAL (MEXICO).
AFRICAN NATIONAL COUNCIL.
AFRO-ASIAN PEOPLE'S SOLIDARITY MOVEMENT.
ALLIANCE FOR PROGRESS.
ATLANTIC COMMUNITY.
BHARATIYA JANA SANGH.
BLACK PANTHER PARTY.
BLACK POWER.
CARLISTS.
CHINESE REVOLUTIONARY PARTY.
CHURCH AND STATE IN BRAZIL.

CHURCH AND STATE IN COMMUNIST COUNTRIES.
CHURCH AND STATE IN FRANCE.
CHURCH AND STATE IN IRELAND.
CHURCH AND STATE IN ITALY.
CHURCH AND STATE IN LATIN AMERICA.
CHURCH AND STATE IN MALTA.
CHURCH AND STATE IN MEXICO.
CHURCH AND STATE IN RUSSIA.
CHURCH AND STATE IN SARDINIA.
CHURCH AND STATE IN THE ARGENTINE REPUBLIC.
CHURCH AND STATE IN THE UNITED KINGDOM.
CHURCH AND STATE IN TONGA.
CHURCH AND STATE IN ZAIRE.
COMMUNIST COUNTRIES
COMMUNIST PARTIES.
COMMUNIST PARTY
COMMUNISTS, FRENCH.
COMMUNISTS, GERMAN.
CONSERVATISM IN FRANCE.
CONSERVATISM IN GERMANY.
CONSERVATISM IN THE UNITED KINGDOM.
CONSERVATIVE PARTY (UNITED KINGDOM).
COUNCIL OF EUROPE.
DEMOCRATIC PARTY (UNITED STATES).
DEMOCRATISCHE SOCIALISTEN '70.
DENAZIFICATION.
DEUTSCHE DEMOKRATISCHE PARTEI.
DEUTSCHE VOLKSPARTEI.
EUROPEAN ATOMIC ENERGY COMMUNITY.
EUROPEAN COAL AND STEEL COMMUNITY.
EUROPEAN COMMUNITIES.
EUROPEAN CONVENTION ON ESTABLISHMENT (INDIVIDUALS).
EUROPEAN ECONOMIC COMMUNITY.
EUROPEAN FREE TRADE ASSOCIATION.
EUROPEAN PARLIAMENT.
EUROPEAN RESETTLEMENT FUND.
EUZKADI TA ASKATASUNA.
FLEMISH MOVEMENT.
FREE PARTY (TURKEY)
FREEMASONS
FREIE DEMOKRATISCHE PARTEI.
FRONT DE LIBERATION DU QUEBEC.
FUERZA DE ORIENTACION RADICAL DE LA JOVEN ARGENTINA.
HRVATSKA SELJACKA STRANKA.
INDIAN NATIONAL CONGRESS.
INSTITUTE OF PACIFIC RELATIONS.
INTERNATIONAL, THE.
IRISH REPUBLICAN ARMY.
IRISH WORKERS' PARTY.
JACOBINS.
JEWISH ARAB RELATIONS.
JEWISH QUESTION.
LABOUR PARTY
LEAGUE OF NATIONS.
LIBERAL PARTY
LIBERALISM IN BELGIUM.
LIBERALISM IN CHINA.
LIBERALISM IN FRANCE.
LIBERALISM IN GERMANY.
LIBERALISM IN MEXICO.
LIBERALISM IN THE UNITED STATES.
LLIGA CATALANA.
LOYALTY-SECURITY PROGRAM, 1947- .
MOVIMIENTO NACIONALISTA REVOLUCIONARIO.
NATIONAL FRONT.
NATIONAL GREENBACK PARTY.
NATIONAL SOCIALISM.
NATIONALDEMOKRATISCHE PARTEI DEUTSCHLANDS [BUNDESREPUBLIK].
NIGERIAN PEOPLE'S UNION.

NORDISK RÅD.
NORTH ATLANTIC TREATY ORGANIZATION.
ORGANIZATION OF AMERICAN STATES.
ORGANIZATION OF CENTRAL AMERICAN STATES.
PANAFRICANISM.
PARTI QUEBECOIS.
PARTI SOCIALISTE UNIFIE.
PARTIDO APRISTA PERUANO.
PARTIDO DEMOCRATA CRISTIANO (CHILE)
PARTIDO NACIONAL DEL URUGUAY.
PARTIDO RADICAL (CHILE).
PARTIJ VAN DE ARBEID.
PARTITO COMUNISTA D'ITALIA (MARXISTA-LENINISTA).
PARTITO OPERAIO ITALIANO
POLITICAL BALLADS AND SONGS, ITALIAN.
POLITICAL POETRY, ENGLISH.
POLITICAL POETRY, PORTUGUESE.
POLITICAL POSTERS, FRENCH.
POLITICAL POSTERS, GERMAN.
POLITICAL SATIRE, AUSTRIAN.
POLITICAL SATIRE, ITALIAN.
POLITICAL SATIRE, RUSSIAN.
POPULISM IN POLAND.
POPULISM IN RUSSIA.
POPULISM IN THE UKRAINE.
POPULISM IN THE UNITED STATES.
PROGRESSIVISM (U.S. POLITICS).
PROPAGANDA, ANTIRUSSIAN.
PROPAGANDA, ARAB.
PROPAGANDA, COMMUNIST.
PROPAGANDA, ISRAELI.
PROPAGANDA, RUSSIAN
RADICALISM IN BANGLADESH.
RADICALISM IN BELGIUM.
RADICALISM IN FRANCE.
RADICALISM IN GERMANY.
RADICALISM IN JAPAN
RADICALISM IN INDIA.
RADICALISM IN RUSSIA.
RADICALISM IN SRI LANKA.
RADICALISM IN SWITZERLAND.
RADICALISM IN THE UNITED KINGDOM.
RADICALISM IN THE UNITED STATES.
RAZA UNIDA PARTY.
REFUGEES IN AFRICA.
REFUGEES IN GERMANY.
REFUGEES IN RUSSIA.
REFUGEES IN SWEDEN.
REFUGEES IN THE CENTRAL AFRICAN REPUBLIC.
REFUGEES IN THE UNITED KINGDOM.
REFUGEES IN UGANDA.
REPUBLICAN PARTY (UNITED STATES).
RESTITUTION AND INDEMNIFICATION CLAIMS (1933-)
REVOLUTIONISTS, FRENCH.
REVOLUTIONISTS, KOREAN.
REVOLUTIONISTS, RUSSIAN.
SECESSION
SINN FEIN.
SITUATIONIST INTERNATIONAL.
SOCIAAL-DEMOKRATISCHE ARBEIDERS PARTIJ.
SOCIAL DEMOCRATIC PARTY (GERMANY).
SOCIAL DEMOCRATIC PARTY (LATVIA).
SOCIAL DEMOCRATIC PARTY (POLAND).
SOCIAL DEMOCRATIC PARTY (RUSSIA).
SOCIAL DEMOCRATIC PARTY (SWEDEN).
SOCIAL DEMOCRATIC PARTY (SWITZERLAND).
SOCIALISM IN AUSTRIA.
SOCIALISM IN BANGLADESH.
SOCIALISM IN BELGIUM.

SOCIALISM IN BOLIVIA.
SOCIALISM IN CANADA.
SOCIALISM IN CHILE.
SOCIALISM IN CUBA.
SOCIALISM IN CZECHOSLOVAKIA.
SOCIALISM IN EUROPE.
SOCIALISM IN FRANCE.
SOCIALISM IN GERMANY.
SOCIALISM IN HUNGARY.
SOCIALISM IN INDIA.
SOCIALISM IN IRELAND (REPUBLIC).
SOCIALISM IN ITALY.
SOCIALISM IN LATIN AMERICA.
SOCIALISM IN NIGERIA.
SOCIALISM IN NORWAY.
SOCIALISM IN POLAND.
SOCIALISM IN ROUMANIA.
SOCIALISM IN RUSSIA.
SOCIALISM IN SICILY.
SOCIALISM IN SPAIN.
SOCIALISM IN SWEDEN.
SOCIALISM IN SWITZERLAND.
SOCIALISM IN TANZANIA.
SOCIALISM IN THE ARGENTINE REPUBLIC
SOCIALISM IN THE NETHERLANDS.
SOCIALISM IN THE UNITED KINGDOM.
SOCIALISM IN THE UNITED STATES.
SOCIALISM IN YUGOSLAVIA.
SOCIALIST PARTY (AUSTRIA).
SOCIALIST PARTY (FRANCE).
SOCIALIST PARTY (ITALY).
SOCIALIST PARTY (POLAND).
SOCIALIST PARTY (UNITED STATES).
SOCIALISTS, GERMAN.
SOCIALISTS, YUGOSLAV.
SOIUZ RUSSKOGO NARODA.
SOIUZ SEMNADTSATOGO OKTIABRIA.
STATESMEN, BRITISH.
STATESMEN, KENYAN.
STATESMEN, RUSSIAN.
SYMBIONESE LIBERATION ARMY.
TANGANYIKA AFRICAN NATIONAL UNION.
ULSTER UNIONIST PARTY.
UNION CIVICA RADICAL.
UNITED NATIONAL INDEPENDENCE PARTY [ZAMBIA]
UNITED NATIONS.
UNITED SOUTH AFRICAN NATIONAL PARTY.
VERBAND DER UNABHÄNGIGEN.
VIET CONG.
WALLOON MOVEMENT.
WATERGATE AFFAIR, 1972- .
WOMEN'S INTERNATIONAL LEAGUE FOR PEACE AND FREEDOM.
YOUNG COMMUNIST INTERNATIONAL.
YOUNG COMMUNIST LEAGUE
ZIMBABWE AFRICAN PEOPLES UNION (RHODESIA).
ZJEDNOCZONE STRONNICTWO LUDOWE.

PSYCHOLOGY.

ACHIEVEMENT MOTIVATION.
ADJUSTMENT (PSYCHOLOGY).
ADOLESCENCE.
AGE (PSYCHOLOGY).
AGGRESSIVENESS (PSYCHOLOGY).
ANTIPATHIES AND PREJUDICES.
ATTENTION
ATTITUDE (PSYCHOLOGY).
ATTITUDE CHANGE.
AUTISM.
CHILD PSYCHIATRY.
CHILD STUDY.
CHOICE (PSYCHOLOGY)
COGNITION.
CONFLICT (PSYCHOLOGY).
DECISION-MAKING.

DEPRESSION, MENTAL.
DREAMS.
EDUCATIONAL PSYCHOLOGY.
EMOTIONS.
ETHNOPSYCHOLOGY.
FEAR.
GENETIC PSYCHOLOGY.
GOAL (PSYCHOLOGY).
HUMAN BEHAVIOUR.
HUMAN INFORMATION PROCESSING.
IDENTIFICATION (PSYCHOLOGY).
INSANE, CRIMINAL AND DANGEROUS
INTELLECT
INTELLIGENCE LEVELS.
INTEREST (PSYCHOLOGY).
INTERPERSONAL RELATIONS.
LEARNING, PSYCHOLOGY OF.
MEMORY.
MOTIVATION (PSYCHOLOGY).
MOTOR ABILITY
OBSESSIVE-COMPULSIVE NEUROSES.
OPTICAL ILLUSIONS.
PAIN.
PERCEPTION.
PERSONALITY.
PHYSIOGNOMY
POLITICAL PSYCHOLOGY.
PSYCHIATRY.
PSYCHOANALYSIS.
PSYCHOBIOLOGY.
PSYCHOLINGUISTICS.
PSYCHOLOGICAL RESEARCH.
PSYCHOLOGY.
PSYCHOLOGY, COMPARATIVE.
PSYCHOLOGY, FORENSIC.
PSYCHOLOGY, INDUSTRIAL.
PSYCHOLOGY, MILITARY.
PSYCHOLOGY, PATHOLOGICAL.
PSYCHOMETRICS.
PSYCHOTHERAPY.
READING, PSYCHOLOGY OF.
SATISFACTION
SCHIZOPHRENIA.
SCHIZOPHRENICS.
SENSES AND SENSATION.
SOCIAL PSYCHOLOGY.
THOUGHT TRANSFERENCE.
VERBAL LEARNING.
VISUAL PERCEPTION.

PUBLIC HEALTH AND MEDICINE.

ABORTION.
ACCIDENTS.
AIR
ALCOHOL
ALCOHOLISM
ANATOMY, HUMAN
APHASIA.
ARTHRITIS.
ARTIFICIAL INSEMINATION, HUMAN.
BENZENE
BIRTH CONTROL.
BLIND
BLOOD
BRAIN.
BRAIN RESEARCH.
CANCER.
CEREBRAL PALSIED CHILDREN
CERVIX UTERI
CHEMICALS
CHEST
CHOLERA.
CITY NOISE.
COMMUNITY HEALTH SERVICES
COMMUNITY MENTAL HEALTH SERVICES
CONCEPTION
CONTRACEPTIVES.
CORONARY HEART DISEASE.
DEAF
DEATH.

PUBLIC HEALTH AND MEDICINE.

DENTAL CARE
DENTAL ECONOMICS.
DENTISTRY
DIAGNOSIS, RADIOSCOPIC.
DIALYSIS.
DISABILITY EVALUATION
DRINKING WATER
DRUGS.
DUST
ENVIRONMENTAL HEALTH.
EPIDEMIOLOGY.
EUTHANASIA.
FOOD.
FOOD ADDITIVES.
FOOD CONSUMPTION
FOOD CONTAMINATION.
FOOD POISONING.
FOOD PRESERVATIVES.
HALLUCINOGENIC DRUGS.
HANDICAPPED
HANDICAPPED CHILDREN
HEALTH ATTITUDES.
HEALTH EDUCATION.
HEROIN
HIP JOINT
HOMOEOPATHY.
HOSPITAL CARE
HOSPITALS
HOSPITALS, GYNAECOLOGIC AND
   OBSTETRIC.
HYGIENE, PUBLIC.
INDUSTRIAL ACCIDENTS.
INDUSTRIAL HYGIENE.
INFANTS
LONG-TERM CARE OF THE SICK.
LONGEVITY.
MALNUTRITION.
MATERNAL AND INFANT WELFARE
MEDICAL CARE.
MEDICAL CARE, COST OF
MEDICAL CENTRES.
MEDICAL ECONOMICS.
MEDICAL FEES
MEDICAL GEOGRAPHY.
MEDICAL JURISPRUDENCE.
MEDICAL LAWS AND LEGISLATION
MEDICAL RESEARCH
MEDICAL STATISTICS.
MEDICINE
MEDICINE, PRIMITIVE.
MEDICINE, STATE.
MENTAL DEFICIENCY.
MENTAL HYGIENE.
MENTAL ILLNESS.
MENTALLY HANDICAPPED.
MENTALLY HANDICAPPED CHILDREN
MENTALLY ILL
MISSIONS , MEDICAL
NARCOTIC HABIT.
NARCOTICS.
NATIONAL ASSOCIATION FOR MENTAL
   HEALTH.
NEUROLOGY.
NOISE.
NURSES AND NURSING.
NUTRITION.
NUTRITION SURVEYS
OBSTETRICS.
OCCUPATIONAL DISEASES.
OLD AGE
ORTHOPAEDIA
PAIN.
PERFUSION PUMP (HEART).
PESTICIDES.
PHYSICALLY HANDICAPPED
PHYSICALLY HANDICAPPED CHILDREN
PHYSICIAN AND PATIENT.
PHYSIOGNOMY
PHYSIOLOGY.
PREGNANCY.
PREVENTIVE DENTISTRY.
PROTEINS.
PSYCHIATRIC CLINICS

PSYCHIATRIC HOSPITALS
PSYCHIATRY.
PSYCHOBIOLOGY.
PSYCHOLOGY, PATHOLOGICAL.
PSYCHOTHERAPY.
PUBLIC HEALTH RESEARCH
RADIOACTIVE WASTE DISPOSAL.
RED CROSS.
REFUSE AND REFUSE DISPOSAL
REHABILITATION
RHEUMATISM.
ROAD ACCIDENTS
SCHOOL HYGIENE
SICK
SICKLE-CELL ANAEMIA.
SLEEP.
SMOKING.
SOCIAL MEDICINE.
SOCIAL PSYCHIATRY.
SPINA BIFIDA
STERILIZATION (BIRTH CONTROL).
STRESS (PHYSIOLOGY).
TERMINAL CARE.
THALIDOMIDE.
TRANSPLANTATION OF ORGANS,
   TISSUES, ETC.

SCIENCE AND TECHNOLOGY.

AGRICULTURAL INNOVATIONS.
ATOMIC ENERGY.
ATOMIC ENERGY RESEARCH
ATOMIC POWER
AUTOMATION
BIOLOGICAL CHEMISTRY.
BIOLOGICAL WARFARE.
CHEMICAL WARFARE.
DIFFUSION OF INNOVATIONS.
EARTH SCIENCE RESEARCH
ENVIRONMENTAL POLICY RESEARCH.
FORECASTING.
GENETIC RESEARCH.
GENETICS.
MAN-MACHINE SYSTEMS.
NUCLEAR PHYSICS
ODOUR CONTROL
PHYSICS
RADIO.
RADIOACTIVE FALLOUT.
RAND CORPORATION.
REMOTE SENSING SYSTEMS.
RESEARCH.
SALINE WATER CONVERSION.
SCIENCE.
SCIENCE AND ETHICS.
SCIENCE AND STATE.
SCIENCE AND THE HUMANITIES.
SCIENTIFIC LIBRARIES.
SPACE FLIGHT.
SPACE SCIENCES.
STATE ENCOURAGEMENT OF SCIENCE,
   LITERATURE AND ART.
SYSTEMS ENGINEERING
TECHNOLOGICAL FORECASTING
TECHNOLOGICAL INNOVATIONS.
TECHNOLOGISTS
TECHNOLOGY
TECHNOLOGY AND STATE.
TECHNOLOGY ASSESSMENT.
TECHNOLOGY TRANSFER.
TRIBOLOGY.
X-RAY MICROSCOPE.

SOCIOLOGY, ANTHROPOLOGY AND ETHNOLOGY.

General.

ABOLITIONISTS.
ACCULTURATION.
ADOPTION
AGING.

ALCOHOLICS
ALCOHOLISM
ALIENATION (SOCIAL PSYCHOLOGY).
ALMSHOUSES AND WORKHOUSES
ANTHROPOLOGISTS.
ANTHROPOLOGISTS, BRITISH.
ANTHROPOLOGY.
APARTMENT HOUSES
AQUATIC SPORTS FACILITIES
ART, PRIMITIVE.
ART AND SOCIETY.
ASSIMILATION (SOCIOLOGY).
ASSOCIATIONS, INSTITUTIONS, ETC.
AUTOMOBILE THIEVES
BEGGING
BOYS
BRIDE PRICE.
BRIGANDS AND ROBBERS
BRITISH BROADCASTING
   CORPORATION.
CASTE
CHARITIES
CHARITY.
CHARITY ORGANIZATION.
CHILD WELFARE.
CHILDREN
CHILDREN IN COLOMBIA.
CHILDREN IN FINLAND.
CHILDREN IN HONG KONG.
CHILDREN IN TAIWAN.
CHILDREN IN THE UNITED KINGDOM.
CHILDREN IN THE UNITED STATES.
CHILDREN OF DIVORCED PARENTS.
CHILDREN OF IMMIGRANTS
CHILDREN OF MILITARY PERSONNEL
CHURCH AND RACE PROBLEMS
CHURCH AND SOCIAL PROBLEMS.
CITIES AND TOWNS.
COMMUNICATION.
COMMUNICATION IN THE SOCIAL
   SCIENCES.
COMMUNICATIONS RESEARCH.
COMMUNISM.
COMMUNITY.
COMMUNITY AND COLLEGE.
COMMUNITY AND SCHOOL.
COMMUNITY CENTRES
COMMUNITY DEVELOPMENT.
COMMUNITY LIFE.
COMMUNITY ORGANIZATION.
COMMUNITY WELFARE COUNCILS
CONFLICT OF GENERATIONS.
CORPORAL PUNISHMENT.
COUNSELLING.
COUNTRY HOMES
CRIME AND CRIMINALS.
CRIME PREVENTION
CRIMINAL ANTHROPOLOGY.
CRIMINAL REGISTERS
CRIMINAL STATISTICS
CRUELTY TO CHILDREN
CULTURAL RELATIONS.
CULTURE.
DAY NURSERIES.
DELINQUENT GIRLS
DELINQUENT WOMEN
DELINQUENTS
DEMONSTRATIONS
DEVIANT BEHAVIOUR.
DISASTER RELIEF.
DISASTERS
DISCRIMINATION
DISSENTERS.
DIVORCEES.
DOWRY
DRINKING AND ROAD ACCIDENTS
DRUGS.
EDUCATIONAL ANTHROPOLOGY.
EDUCATIONAL SOCIOLOGY.
EGOISM.
ELITE.
EMIGRATION AND IMMIGRATION.
ENCOMIENDAS (SPANISH AMERICA).

SOCIOLOGY, ANTHROPOLOGY AND ETHNOLOGY.

ENDOGAMY AND EXOGAMY.
ENDOWMENTS.
EQUALITY.
ESTATES (SOCIAL ORDERS)
ETHNOLOGY.
EVALUATION RESEARCH (SOCIAL ACTION PROGRAMMES)
EXCAVATIONS (ARCHAEOLOGY)
EXSERVICEMEN
FAIRS.
FAMILY.
FAMILY SIZE.
FAMILY SOCIAL WORK
FAMINES.
FASHION.
FATHER SEPARATED CHILDREN.
FATHERS.
FOLK LORE
FOOD HABITS.
FOOD RELIEF.
FOSTER HOME CARE.
FOUNDLINGS
FUND RAISING.
GAMBLING
GAMES
GAUCHOS.
GAY LIBERATION MOVEMENT.
GIFTED CHILDREN.
GIRLS.
HALFWAY HOUSES
HANDICAPPED
HEROIN
HIPPIES
HOLIDAYS.
HOME AND SCHOOL.
HOME HELPS.
HOMICIDE
HOMOSEXUALITY.
HUNTING
ILLEGITIMACY.
INDUSTRIAL SOCIOLOGY.
INTERNATIONAL RELIEF.
INTERPERSONAL RELATIONS.
INTERVIEWING.
ISRAEL INSTITUTE OF APPLIED SOCIAL RESEARCH.
JUVENILE COURTS
JUVENILE DELINQUENCY
KINGS AND RULERS (IN RELIGION, FOLK-LORE, ETC.)
KINSHIP.
KNOWLEDGE, SOCIOLOGY OF.
LABOUR REST HOMES
LEGENDS
LEISURE .
LIQUOR PROBLEM
LITERATURE AND SOCIETY.
LODGING HOUSES
LONG LARTIN PRISON.
MAFIA.
MAN.
MAN, PREHISTORIC
MANA.
MARIHUANA.
MARRIAGE.
MARRIAGE GUIDANCE.
MASS MEDIA.
MASS SOCIETY.
MATRILINEAL KINSHIP.
MEDICINE, PRIMITIVE.
MEN.
MENTALLY HANDICAPPED.
MENTALLY HANDICAPPED CHILDREN
MENTALLY ILL
MIDDLE CLASSES
MISCEGENATION.
MOTHERS.
MOVING PICTURES.
MUSIC AND SOCIETY.
MUSIC FESTIVALS.
MYTHOLOGY.
NARCOTIC HABIT.
NARCOTICS.

NARCOTICS, CONTROL OF.
NARCOTICS AND YOUTH
NATIONAL CHARACTERISTICS, JAPANESE.
NATIONAL URBAN LEAGUE.
NOMADS
OCCUPATIONAL MOBILITY
OLD AGE
OLD AGE HOMES
OLD AGE PENSIONS
OLYMPIC GAMES.
ORGANIZATION.
ORGANIZATIONAL CHANGE.
ORGANIZATIONAL RESEARCH.
OUTDOOR RECREATION
PARENT AND CHILD.
PARKS
PAROLE
PEASANTRY.
PHENOMENOLOGY.
PHILOSOPHICAL ANTHROPOLOGY.
PHYSICALLY HANDICAPPED
PHYSICALLY HANDICAPPED CHILDREN
PLANNING.
PLAY.
PLAY SCHOOLS.
PLAYGROUNDS.
PLURALISM (SOCIAL SCIENCES).
POLICE.
POLITICAL SOCIALIZATION.
POLITICAL SOCIOLOGY.
POLITICS IN MOVING PICTURES.
POLYGAMY
POOR.
POOR LAWS
POVERTY.
POWER (SOCIAL SCIENCES).
PRISONERS
PRISONS.
PROBATION
PROBLEM CHILDREN
PROGRESS.
PROSTITUTION
PSYCHIATRIC SOCIAL WORK.
PUBLIC HOUSING
PUBLIC OPINION
PUBLIC OPINION POLLS.
PUBLIC RELATIONS
PUBLIC RELATIONS AND POLITICS.
PUNISHMENT.
RACE.
RACE DISCRIMINATION
RACE PROBLEMS.
RADIO AUDIENCES
RADIO BROADCASTING.
RECIDIVISTS
RECREATION
RECREATION AREAS
RECREATION RESEARCH.
RED CROSS.
REFORMATORIES
REFORMATORIES FOR WOMEN
REGIONAL PLANNING.
REHABILITATION, RURAL
REHABILITATION OF CRIMINALS.
REHABILITATION OF JUVENILE DELINQUENTS
RELIGION AND SOCIOLOGY.
RELOCATION (HOUSING)
REMAND HOMES
REPARATION.
RETIREMENT.
RIOTS
RITES AND CEREMONIES.
ROYAL NATIONAL LIFE-BOAT INSTITUTION.
ROYAL TOUCH.
RURAL CONDITIONS
RURAL FAMILIES
RURAL URBAN MIGRATION
RURAL YOUTH
SCHOOL SOCIAL WORK
SELF-DEFENCE.

SELF-HELP GROUPS
SEMIOLOGY.
SERFDOM
SEX.
SEX CUSTOMS.
SEX ROLE.
SEXUAL PERVERSION.
SINGLE PARENT FAMILY
SINGLE PEOPLE
SINGLE WOMEN.
SLAVE TRADE
SLAVERY.
SLAVERY IN AMERICA.
SLAVERY IN ANGOLA.
SLAVERY IN CUBA.
SLAVERY IN PEMBA
SLAVERY IN THE BRITISH EMPIRE.
SLAVERY IN THE UNITED KINGDOM.
SLAVERY IN THE UNITED STATES.
SLAVERY IN THE WEST INDIES.
SLAVERY IN ZANZIBAR
SLUMS
SMALL GROUPS
SMOKING.
SOCCER
SOCIAL ACTION.
SOCIAL ADJUSTMENT.
SOCIAL CASE WORK.
SOCIAL CHANGE.
SOCIAL CLASSES.
SOCIAL CONDITIONS.
SOCIAL CONFLICT.
SOCIAL CONTROL.
SOCIAL CREDIT.
SOCIAL ETHICS.
SOCIAL EXCHANGE.
SOCIAL GROUP WORK
SOCIAL GROUPS.
SOCIAL HISTORY.
SOCIAL INDICATORS
SOCIAL INTERACTION.
SOCIAL ISOLATION.
SOCIAL LEGISLATION
SOCIAL MOBILITY.
SOCIAL PARTICIPATION.
SOCIAL POLICY.
SOCIAL PROBLEMS.
SOCIAL PSYCHIATRY.
SOCIAL PSYCHOLOGY.
SOCIAL REFORMERS
SOCIAL ROLE.
SOCIAL SCIENCE RESEARCH.
SOCIAL SCIENCES.
SOCIAL SCIENTISTS.
SOCIAL SERVICE.
SOCIAL SETTLEMENTS.
SOCIAL SURVEYS.
SOCIAL WORK EDUCATION
SOCIAL WORK WITH CHILDREN
SOCIAL WORK WITH DELINQUENTS AND CRIMINALS
SOCIAL WORK WITH SINGLE PEOPLE
SOCIAL WORK WITH THE BLIND
SOCIAL WORK WITH THE PHYSICALLY HANDICAPPED
SOCIAL WORK WITH YOUTH
SOCIAL WORKERS
SOCIALISM AND YOUTH.
SOCIALIZATION.
SOCIALLY HANDICAPPED
SOCIALLY HANDICAPPED CHILDREN.
SOCIETY, PRIMITIVE.
SOCIOLINGUISTICS.
SOCIOLOGICAL JURISPRUDENCE.
SOCIOLOGICAL RESEARCH.
SOCIOLOGY.
SOCIOLOGY, CHRISTIAN
SOCIOLOGY, MILITARY.
SOCIOLOGY, RURAL.
SOCIOLOGY, URBAN.
SPORTS
SQUATTERS

SOCIOLOGY, ANTHROPOLOGY AND ETHNOLOGY

STATICS AND DYNAMICS (SOCIAL SCIENCES).
STEALING.
STRUCTURALISM.
SUBURBAN HOMES.
SUBURBS.
SUICIDE.
SUMMER HOMES
TELEVISION AND CHILDREN.
TELEVISION AUDIENCES
TELEVISION BROADCASTING.
TELEVISION BROADCASTING OF NEWS
TEMPERANCE.
THEATRE AND SOCIETY.
TORTURE.
TRAMPS
TRIBES AND TRIBAL SYSTEM
UNDERDEVELOPED AREAS.
UNITED NATIONS EDUCATIONAL, SCIENTIFIC AND CULTURAL ORGANIZATION
UNMARRIED MOTHERS
VAGRANCY
VICTIMS OF CRIME.
VILLAGE COMMUNITIES
VILLAGES
VILLEINAGE
VIOLENCE.
VOCATIONAL REHABILITATION
VOLUNTEER WORKERS IN SOCIAL SERVICE.
WAR AND SOCIETY.
WELFARE ECONOMICS.
WIDOWS
WIFE BEATING.
WITCHCRAFT.
WIVES.
WOMAN.
WOMEN, ALTAI.
WOMEN, MOHAMMEDAN.
WOMEN AND SOCIALISM.
WOMEN AS BANKERS.
WOMEN AS TEACHERS.
WOMEN IN AFRICA.
WOMEN IN AUSTRIA.
WOMEN IN CANADA.
WOMEN IN CHINA.
WOMEN IN CHRISTIANITY.
WOMEN IN EASTERN GERMANY.
WOMEN IN GERMANY.
WOMEN IN ITALY.
WOMEN IN JAPAN.
WOMEN IN KOREA.
WOMEN IN POLITICS.
WOMEN IN PUBLIC LIFE.
WOMEN IN SOVIET CENTRAL ASIA.
WOMEN IN SWEDEN.
WOMEN IN SWITZERLAND.
WOMEN IN THE NETHERLANDS
WOMEN IN TRADE UNIONS
WOMEN IN THE UNITED KINGDOM.
WOMEN IN THE UNITED STATES.
WOMEN IN UGANDA.
WOMEN'S LIBERATION MOVEMENT.
YOUTH.
YOUTH CONSERVATION CORPS.
YOUTH VOLUNTEER WORKERS IN DEVELOPING COUNTRIES.

Particular races, tribes and nationalities.

AKANS (AFRICAN PEOPLE).
ALGERIANS IN FRANCE.
AMHARAS.
ARABS IN ISRAEL.
ARABS IN PALESTINE.
ARAUCANIAN INDIANS
ARMENIANS IN TURKEY.
ARYANS.
ASIATICS IN THE UNITED KINGDOM.
AUSTRALIAN ABORIGINES.
AUSTRIANS IN ITALY
BAHIMA (AFRICAN PEOPLE).
BANTUS.
BAROLONG BOO RATSHIDI.
BATETELA (AFRICAN TRIBE).
BAYAKA.
BEMBA (AFRICAN TRIBE).
BHILS.
BRITISH IN AUSTRALIA.
BRITISH IN INDIA.
BRITISH IN THE WEST INDIES.
BULGARIANS IN THE UKRAINE.
CHINESE IN AUSTRALASIA.
CHINESE IN NORTH AMERICA.
CHINESE IN THE UNITED STATES
COLOURED PEOPLE (SOUTH AFRICA).
CORNISHMEN IN THE UNITED STATES.
EAST INDIANS IN AFRICA.
EAST INDIANS IN GUYANA.
EAST INDIANS IN NATAL.
EAST INDIANS IN SOUTH AFRICA.
EAST INDIANS IN THE BRITISH EMPIRE.
EAST INDIANS IN THE UNITED KINGDOM.
EAST INDIANS IN TRINIDAD.
EAST INDIANS IN UGANDA.
ESKIMOS.
EUROPEANS IN NIGERIA.
FRENCH CANADIANS.
FRENCH IN FOREIGN COUNTRIES.
GERMANS.
GERMANS IN BRAZIL.
GERMANS IN CZECHOSLOVAKIA.
GERMANS IN FRANCE.
GERMANS IN ITALY.
GERMANS IN POLAND.
GERMANS IN RUSSIA.
GERMANS IN THE BALTIC STATES.
GERMANS IN THE UNITED KINGDOM.
GERMANS IN THE UNITED STATES.
GILYAKS.
GIPSIES
GOLDS.
GOROKANS.
GREEKS IN TURKEY.
HAITIANS IN THE DOMINICAN REPUBLIC.
HAUSAS
IBOS.
IK.
INDIANS OF CENTRAL AMERICA
INDIANS OF MEXICO.
INDIANS OF NORTH AMERICA.
INDIANS OF SOUTH AMERICA
IRISH IN THE UNITED STATES.
IROQUOIS INDIANS.
ISOKO (AFRICAN PEOPLE).
ISRAEL AND THE DIASPORA
ITALIANS IN CANADA.
ITALIANS IN SWITZERLAND.
JAPANESE IN BRAZIL.
JAPANESE IN THE UNITED STATES.
JEWS
JEWS IN AUSTRIA.
JEWS IN BELGIUM.
JEWS IN FRANCE
JEWS IN GERMANY.
JEWS IN ITALY
JEWS IN LATIN AMERICA.
JEWS IN RUSSIA.
JEWS IN SYRIA.
JEWS IN THE NEAR EAST
JEWS IN THE UNITED STATES.
JIVARO INDIANS.
KABYLES.
KAFIRS (AFRICAN PEOPLE).
KAZAKS IN RUSSIA.
KUMAS (NEW GUINEA TRIBE).
LANGOS.
LAPPS.
LATVIANS IN GERMANY.
MANDINGO (AFRICAN PEOPLE).
MAORIS.
MASAI.
MATABELE.
MATAKAM (AFRICAN PEOPLE).
MESKHETIANS.
MEXICANS IN THE UNITED STATES.
MOHAVE INDIANS.
MOLUCCANS IN THE NETHERLANDS.
MONGOLS
MONTAGNARDS (VIETNAMESE TRIBES).
MOSQUITO INDIANS.
MOURIDES.
MURSI.
NAGAS.
NAVAHO INDIANS.
NEGRO RACE
NEGRO YOUTH
NEGROES.
NEGROES IN BRAZIL.
NEGROES IN PORTUGAL.
NEGROES IN SOUTH AFRICA.
NEGROES IN THE UNITED KINGDOM.
OROKAIVAS.
PATIDARS.
POLES IN FRANCE
POLES IN KAZAKSTAN.
POLES IN THE UNITED STATES.
PORTUGUESE IN ANGOLA.
PUERTO RICANS IN THE UNITED STATES.
ROUMANIANS IN AUSTRIA-HUNGARY.
RUSSIANS IN CHINA.
RUSSIANS IN EASTERN EUROPE.
RUSSIANS IN FOREIGN COUNTRIES.
RUSSIANS IN KAZAKSTAN.
RUSSIANS IN SIBERIA.
RUSSIANS IN THE CAUCASUS.
RUSSIANS IN THE TATAR REPUBLIC.
SCOTCH IN IRELAND.
SERBS IN RUSSIA.
SERERS.
SHARANAHUA INDIANS.
SIBERIANS.
SIKHS IN THE UNITED KINGDOM.
SOBO (AFRICAN PEOPLE).
SOGAS
SPANIARDS IN RUSSIA.
SURINAMESE IN THE NETHERLANDS.
TATARS.
TAUSUG.
TLINGIT INDIANS.
TSWANA (BANTU TRIBE).
TUCANO INDIANS.
TUCUNA INDIANS.
TURKS IN DENMARK.
TURKS IN FRANCE.
TZOTZIL INDIANS.
UKRAINIANS IN THE UNITED STATES.
ULCHI.
WALLOONS IN THE UNITED KINGDOM.
WEST INDIANS IN THE UNITED KINGDOM.
YORUBAS.
YUGOSLAVS IN THE UNITED STATES.
ZANDES.
ZAPOTEC INDIANS.
ZULUS

TRANSPORT AND COMMUNICATIONS.

General.

AERONAUTICS
AERONAUTICS, COMMERCIAL.
AERONAUTICS AND STATE
AEROPLANES
AIR LINES
AIR TRAFFIC CONTROL
AIR-SHIPS.
AIRPORT NOISE.
AIRPORTS
ASTRONAUTICS IN EARTH SCIENCES.
AUTOMOBILE DRIVERS

TRANSPORT AND COMMUNICATIONS.

AUTOMOBILE OWNERSHIP.
AUTOMOBILE PARKING
AUTOMOBILE PURCHASING.
AUTOMOBILES.
BRIDGES
CAB AND OMNIBUS SERVICE
CANALS
CANALS, INTEROCEANIC.
CARGO HANDLING.
CARGO PREFERENCE.
CHARTER PARTIES.
CHOICE OF TRANSPORTATION
CITY TRAFFIC.
COASTWISE SHIPPING
COLLISIONS AT SEA
COMMERCIAL VEHICLES.
COMMUNICATION AND TRAFFIC
COMMUNITY ANTENNA TELEVISION
COMMUTING
CONCORDE (JET TRANSPORTS).
CYCLING
DANGEROUS GOODS
DRINKING AND ROAD ACCIDENTS
EARTH STATIONS (SATELLITE TELECOMMUNICATION)
ELECTRICITY IN TRANSPORTATION.
FISHING BOATS.
FLIGHT CREWS
FREE PORTS AND ZONES
FREIGHT AND FREIGHTAGE
FREIGHTERS.
HARBOURS.
INLAND NAVIGATION
INLAND WATER TRANSPORTATION
LIABILITY FOR ROAD ACCIDENTS.
LOAD-LINE.
LOCAL TRANSIT.
LOCOMOTIVES
MARINE ACCIDENTS.
MERCHANT MARINE
MERCHANT SHIPS
MOTOR BUS LINES
MOTOR BUSES.
MOTOR TRUCKS.
MOTOR VEHICLES.
NAVAL ARCHITECTURE.
ORIGIN AND DESTINATION TRAFFIC SURVEYS
PEDESTRIANS
PETROLEUM CONSERVATION.
POSTAL SERVICE
RADIO.
RADIO BROADCASTING.
RAILWAYS
RAILWAYS, ELEVATED.
RAILWAYS, INDUSTRIAL
RAILWAYS AND STATE
ROAD ACCIDENTS
ROAD CONSTRUCTION
ROAD SAFETY
ROADS
SAILING SHIPS.
SEARCH AND RESCUE OPERATIONS.
SHIPPING
SHIPPING BOUNTIES AND SUBSIDIES.
SHIPPING CONFERENCES.
SHIPS
SONIC BOOM.
STABILITY OF SHIPS.
TANK-VESSELS.
TELECOMMUNICATION.
TELEGRAPH
TELEPHONE
TELEPHONE, AUTOMATIC.
TELEVISION
TOLL ROADS
TONNAGE.
TRADE ROUTES.
TRAFFIC ASSIGNMENT
TRAFFIC ENGINEERING.
TRAFFIC ESTIMATION
TRAFFIC NOISE.
TRAFFIC OFFENCES

TRAFFIC REGULATIONS
TRAFFIC SURVEYS
TRANSPORTATION.
TRANSPORTATION, AUTOMOTIVE.
TRANSPORTATION AND STATE.
TRAVEL TIME (TRAFFIC ENGINEERING).
TUNNELS.
UNDERGROUND RAILWAYS
UNITIZED CARGO SYSTEMS.
URBAN TRANSPORTATION.
VEHICLES.

Individual undertakings, etc.

CANADIAN NATIONAL RAILWAYS.
CANADIAN PACIFIC LIMITED.
CHANNEL TUNNEL.
CHEMIN DE FER DU NORD.
ELDER DEMPSTER LINES.
HOLLAND-AMERICA LINE.
ROYAL NATIONAL LIFE-BOAT INSTITUTION.
SUEZ CANAL.

Ref
Z
7161
L84
v.32
1974